DPR Public Record Office, Dublin
DRS Royal Dublin Society
DT Trinity College, Dublin
DU Durham University
DUC Durham Cathedral
DUS Ushaw College, Durham
DWL Worth Library, Dublin

E Edinburgh University
EC Eton College
ECP Royal College of Physicians, Edinburgh
ECS Royal College of Surgeons, Edinburgh
EH Huntly House, Edinburgh
ELY Ely Cathedral (dispersed; many at C)
EN National Library of Scotland (Advocates'),
    Edinburgh
ENC New College, Edinburgh
EO Royal Observatory, Edinburgh
ER Scottish Record Office, H.M. General Register
    House, Edinburgh
ES Signet, Edinburgh (partly dispersed)
ESS Speculative Society, Edinburgh
EU United Free Church College, Edinburgh

FARM Farm Street Church, London (includes
    Gillow Library)
FM University of Miami, Miami, Fla.
FONMON Fonmon Castle, Glamorgan (available through
    University College, Cardiff)
FSF F. S. Ferguson, London (dispersed; most
    at O, EN, IU)
FU University of Florida, Gainesville

GB Baillie's Institution, Glasgow
GC Gloucester Cathedral
GF United Free Church College, Glasgow
GH Hunterian Museum, Glasgow
GK Sir Geoffrey Keynes, London
GM Mitchell Library, Glasgow
GU Glasgow University

HC Cushing Library, Yale Medical School,
    New Haven, Conn.
HEYTHROP Heythrop College, London
HG Gray Library, Haddington (deposited
    at EN)
HH Crawford Library (partly dispersed; broadsides,
    proclamations, and ballads at MR)
HM McMaster University, Hamilton, Ontario
HR Royal Library, The Hague
HUTH Huth Sale Catalogue

I Innerpeffray, Perthshire, Scotland
IAU University of Iowa, Iowa City
IE Earlham College, Richmond, Ind.
IEG Garrett Theological Seminary, Evanston, Ill.
    (Seabury-Western Theological Seminary)

INU Indiana University, Bloomington
IU University of Illinois, Urbana

JF Fulton Library, Yale Medical School,
    New Haven, Conn.

KEW Royal Botanic Gardens, Kew
KIRK Rudolf Kirk, San Marcos, Texas
KQ Queen's University, Kingston, Ontario
KT Transylvania University, Lexington, Ken.
    (law books dispersed)
KU University of Kansas, Lawrence
KYU University of Kentucky, Lexington

L British Library, London
L(lost) British Library – destroyed in war
LAD Admiralty, London
LAI Royal Art Institution, London
LAS Royal Agricultural Society, London
LB Baptist Union, London
LBS British and Foreign Bible Society, London
    (dispersed; many at O)
LC Library of Congress, Washington, D.C.
LCH Chemical Society, London
LCL Congregational Library, London
LCP Royal College of Physicians, London
LCS Royal College of Surgeons, London
LE Leicester Central Library
LF Friends' Library, London
LFEA Lough Fea Library, Ireland (dispersed;
    rebellion tracts at DN)
LG Guildhall, London
LGI Gray's Inn, London
LHO Home Office Library, Queen Anne's Gate, London
LI Inner Temple, London
LIB Royal Institute of British Architects, London
LIC Liverpool Cathedral
LIL Incorporated Law Society, London
LIU Liverpool University
LL Lincoln's Inn, London
LLL London Library
LLP Lambeth Palace, London
LLU Leeds University, Leeds
LM Medical Society, London (dispersed; mostly at
    LWL and TO)
LMT Middle Temple, London
LN National Laboratory of Psychical Research, London
LNC Lincoln Cathedral
LNH British Museum (Natural History), London
LNM National Maritime Museum, Greenwich
LP St. Paul's Cathedral, London
LPC Privy Council Office, London
LPM Peel Meeting, London
LPO Patent Office, London (at L)
LPR Public Record Office, London
LR Royal Society, London
LS Society of Antiquaries, London

SHORT-TITLE CATALOGUE

OF BOOKS PRINTED IN ENGLAND, SCOTLAND, IRELAND,

WALES, AND BRITISH AMERICA

AND OF ENGLISH BOOKS PRINTED IN OTHER COUNTRIES

1641-1700

SHORT-TITLE CATALOGUE

OF BOOKS PRINTED IN ENGLAND, SCOTLAND, IRELAND,

WALES, AND BRITISH AMERICA

AND OF ENGLISH BOOKS PRINTED IN OTHER COUNTRIES

1641-1700

Compiled by Donald Wing of the Yale University Library

Second edition, revised and enlarged

In Three Volumes

VOLUME II

E2927—O1000

Revised and edited by Timothy J. Crist
with the assistance of
Janice M. Hansel, Phebe A. Kirkham, Jeri S. Smith, and others

THE MODERN LANGUAGE ASSOCIATION OF AMERICA

NEW YORK, 1982

The preparation of this volume was made possible
by grants from the Program for Research Tools and
Reference Works of the National Endowment for
the Humanities, an independent federal agency,
and by the John Ben Snow Foundation.

LIBRARY OF CONGRESS CATALOG CARD. NO.: 70-185211

ISBN 0-87352-045-9

PREFACE

The publication of this revised second volume of Donald Wing's *Short-Title Catalogue* marks an important stage in the preparation of a complete listing of all English books printed between the years 1641 and 1700. In the 1930s Donald Wing began collecting notes in order to continue Pollard and Redgrave's *Short-Title Catalogue, 1475-1640* (1926) to the close of the seventeenth century. Despite the interruptions of war, he was able to publish the original three volumes of his *Short-Title Catalogue, 1641-1700* between 1945 and 1951. During the following two decades he continued to locate new titles, identify new editions, and list additional copies of books. At the time of his death in 1972, he had published the first volume of the revision and had started work on a typescript of this second volume.

Since his death, Wing's work has been carried on by the Wing STC Revision Project at the Yale University Library. Using his extensive notes we have added hundreds of new titles and recorded thousands of previously unlisted copies. We have taken special care to reach for greater accuracy in the entries and to eliminate inconsistencies of method. To avoid the unfortunate mistakes that plagued the revised first volume, we have checked the entries through two sets of galleys and page proofs. Nonetheless, while we expect this volume to prove a worthy successor to the original volume, we are fully aware that still more information will be forthcoming.

A word should be added about Donald Wing. After graduating from Yale in 1926, Wing spent a year at Trinity College, Cambridge. He then earned his M.A. at Harvard, before completing his Ph.D. in English at Yale in 1932. Wing worked for over forty years in the Yale Library; he served as Head of Accessions (1939-45), Associate Librarian (1945-65), and Associate Librarian for Collections of the Libraries (1966-70).

Yale's acquisition of Falconer Madan's personal collection of Oxford books, and the need to make sense of Yale's holdings of early English books, provided Wing with reason to begin collecting notes while still in his twenties toward what would become this catalogue. He wrote out a slip for each title; on it he noted author, short-title, imprint, format, edition, and number of pages. He listed the location of copies, giving the British Museum and Yale shelf numbers and noting unusual provenance. He examined the bibliographical reference works and added specific citations for each book. He searched sale catalogues from the nineteenth century for rare titles and noted the appearance of uncommon items at auction or in current booksellers' catalogues. He not only looked at each tract in the Thomason Collection at the British Museum but also examined at least one copy of most of the titles he listed. To fill in details, he corresponded with librarians and scholars. Remarkably, Wing compiled his *Short-Title Catalogue* during his spare time, except for a year in England in 1936 on a Guggenheim Fellowship and a sabbatical leave late in his life from Yale University.

Wing considered his task to be enumerative bibliography, not descriptive bibliography. Keeping in mind Pollard and Redgrave's warning that "when scrupulous care is evident in some entries, it is expected in all," Wing structured his entries on the basics of author, title, imprint, date, format, and locations and did not attempt to go beyond this point. This revised volume remains an effort at enumerative bibliography, and as we can confirm, there remains much work for descriptive bibliographers.

At the time of Wing's death, soon after the publication of the revised first volume, galleys for this second volume were being prepared. The printers were working from a copy of the first edition, supplemented by typescript corrections and alterations prepared under Wing's guidance. Before completion, however, the galleys were recalled from the printer when the serious problems caused by Wing's decision to alter entry numbers in the revised first volume became apparent. In due course, the galleys and typescript were returned with the original numbering restored but with no further revision. The decision not to review carefully the typescript led to a flawed first galley and slowed subsequent work. As a result, much of the revision of this volume took place in galleys. Second galleys were required because of the extent of the corrections and additions made to the first.

In 1975 the Index Committee of the Modern Language Association approached the National Endowment for the Humanities for a grant to complete the revision of the second and third volumes. The NEH awarded a three-year grant, which it has since extended. The

v

Modern Language Association also provided substantial support, and the Yale University Library provided office space and other facilities.

During the course of this revision, the editors undertook an entry-by-entry review of the volume. We read through the 267 volumes of the *National Union Catalog, Pre-1956 Imprints* corresponding to the letters covered in this volume in search of new entries, variants, and additional locations. We compared our galleys with annotated copies of Wing at the Huntington Library, the William Andrews Clark Library, the Folger Library, the University of Illinois at Urbana, Harvard, the University of Toronto, the John Rylands University, Lambeth Palace, the British Library, and Trinity College, Dublin. At Harvard we also read through the Houghton Library card catalogue.

The New York Public Library, Princeton University, McGill University, the University of North Carolina at Chapel Hill, Duke University, Hebrew Union College, the University of California at Davis, Seabury Western Theological Seminary, the University of Rochester, the Newberry Library, and the Essex Institute each provided detailed information about their Wing-period holdings. In England, the Cambridge University Library and the Bodleian Library provided extensive help, and Lincoln Cathedral, Liverpool University, Leeds University, Durham University, the University of Nottingham, and the Birmingham Reference Library sent lists of their holdings. The National Library of Scotland, Glasgow University, and Dunblane Cathedral cooperated generously, and in Northern Ireland Belfast University prepared a list of holdings.

Troves of Wing books, pamphlets, and broadsides were found at the Sutro Library, the National Library of Ireland, and the Public Record Office in London. Smaller collections of rare items were examined at the Yale Center for British Arts, the Zion Research Collection at Boston University, the Pierpont Morgan Library, the India Office Library, Regents Park College in Oxford, and the New College Library (now deposited at Dr. Williams's Library). In addition, various collections became accessible through printed catalogues, including those of Gloucester Cathedral, the Wellcome Library, the Cashel Diocesan Library, and St. David's Library in Lampeter, Wales. (A full listing of the catalogues, articles, and books used in the revision is planned for the third volume.)

We also corresponded with and visited many other libraries in order to identify new acquisitions and confirm old holdings. In each case, librarians responded fully to our requests for information. The improvements in this volume are in large part due to their unstinting cooperation.

SCOPE AND METHOD

Scope

The ground rules of this revised volume remain the same as those used by Donald Wing for his parent volumes of 1945-51. We have tried to list all "English" books printed between 1641 and 1700 inclusive that exist today. By "English" is meant all works printed in England, Scotland, Ireland, Wales, and British America, as well as all works printed anywhere else in English. Works by English authors printed in other languages outside these limits are not included. The major exclusion to these rules is periodical literature.

Method

Except for conventional phrases, such as "By the King," the opening words of every title have been retained. Any abridgment carries ellipsis marks to indicate an omission. London is assumed as the place of publication. Anonymous pieces may provide problems for the casual users of this catalogue; these items may be found under the opening words of the title or under various institutional author headings, such as England Parliament, Scotland Estates, the names of monarchs, Oxford and Cambridge Universities, the Churches of England and Scotland, and almanacs. For the most part, anonymous works within the various categories are listed alphabetically. A major exception is the revised London section in this volume, which has been greatly expanded and arranged chronologically under appropriate subheadings.

SYMBOLS OF LOCATION

At the end of each entry appears a list of symbols denoting libraries that hold a copy of that particular printed item. A semicolon divides libraries in the British Isles from those located elsewhere. The names of these libraries and the symbols used to represent them follow in two lists at the end of this preface; for convenience to users of this catalogue the symbol list is also provided on the endpapers of each volume.

When possible, we have listed copies of a particular book at London, Oxford, Cambridge, Scotland, and Ireland in the British Isles. Provincial English and Welsh libraries take priority in filling a complement of five locations over Oxford and Cambridge colleges if there is a copy in the Bodleian Library or Cambridge University Library. The same rule applies to other London libraries besides the British Library. In Scotland our first choice is the National Library and in Ireland it is Trinity College, Dublin.

In the United States we list, in alphabetical order, the Huntington, Clark, or another California library; the Newberry, Illinois, Chicago, or another midwestern library; the Folger or Library of Congress in Washington; a Texan or southern library; Harvard; and Yale. A New York collection is also usually noted. We top up with Canadian and Australian or New Zealand libraries.

Because a library is listed in some entries, it does not follow that *all* that library's holdings are listed. *This is not a census of copies* but only a guide to inform scholars where a given entry may conveniently be consulted. Occasionally, we give more than five or six North American locations when a book is very rare in the British Isles, or vice versa. *Only when a book is listed with fewer than five locations on either side of the semicolon should one draw even tentative conclusions about its rarity.* All copies reported to the Wing STC Revision Project, however, are listed and available in the Project's manuscript in the Yale University Library. Inquiries may be addressed to the Editor.

ANONYMOUS WORKS AND PSEUDONYMS

All anonymous works should be looked for under the beginning of the title. If not found, a cross-reference to the attributed author will usually be given there. We assume no responsibility for authority of attributions, although we have tried to follow the British Library catalogue and recent scholarship.

Although works are not listed under pseudonyms, a cross-reference from the pseudonym to an author's name is included when the pseudonym was used exclusively by that author.

NUMBERING OF ENTRIES

Wing numbers have become a standard form of identification for books published in England or in English between 1641 and 1700. Scholars use the numbers to guide their readers to their printed sources; booksellers use the numbers to help purchasers; and some libraries use the numbers to shelve their books. Unfortunately, about seven or eight percent of the numbers in the revised first volume were reassigned. Most entries were shifted one or two numbers to fill gaps caused by moving entries elsewhere. Confusingly, some new entries appeared with numbers assigned to an entirely different work in the first edition. A complete list of these number changes, giving a correlation of old and new numbers and providing references for those items moved to places in the second and third volumes, is published in this volume.

Users of this second volume may be assured that no number has been reassigned in this volume, except those designated "Entry cancelled" in the first edition and thus never allocated in print for a specific book. To maintain consistency of style with the first volume, a letter (as opposed to a decimal) system has been used to designate new entries.

In 1968, in hopes of tracking down more entries, Donald Wing published A *Gallery of Ghosts*, a listing not of true ghosts but of books that he believed had once existed and perhaps still survived. He assigned tentative Wing numbers to them, preceded by "0." These tentative numbers have been ignored in assigning new numbers in order to avoid unexplained gaps in the numbering order. Although, for example, "0 K290A" was later located and is now "K290A" in this volume, the number might have been used for some other work had the "ghost" been laid to rest or not found. If an intermediate title had been located, "0 K290A" in *Gallery of Ghosts* would have been designated "K290B" here.

CANCELLED ENTRIES

Some entries have been moved in this volume because of new attribution or correction of title. Other entries have been cancelled entirely because they were recognized to be serials or true ghosts, to have been published abroad in a foreign language, or to have been printed before 1641 or after 1700. In each instance the number designating the moved or cancelled entry has not been reassigned. For those entries that have been moved, there is a full reference with the title, date, and new author or title. For cancelled entries there is a note of explanation, such as "Entry cancelled. Serial."

"ANR. ED."

In the first edition of the catalogue and in the first volume of this revision Wing used the term "another edition" (abbreviated as "anr. ed.") to indicate that an item is related to the preceding entry but is in some way distinct. In many instances, "anr. ed." indicates another setting of type, but it can also refer to another issue or variant state of the same edition, if there are differences on the title page. This terminology is admittedly confusing, but it has been continued in this volume because Wing's notes are not usually sufficient to determine the exact relationship among these entries, and the difficulties involved in obtaining the necessary information to change policy are insurmountable in terms of time and funding.

VARIANTS

Wing generally differentiated one entry from another by means of information on the title page, although occasionally he used other distinctions such as the number of pages. Although we have been able to sort out, for many books, less apparent differences in existing copies and have created new entries to reflect this knowledge, for the most part we have continued Wing's practice and used the title page as the determining factor. In order to ease the effect of this decision, we have used "(var.)" at the end of some entries to indicate that we are aware of variants among the copies. Such variants range in magnitude from the inclusion of an errata list to another setting of type. We realize that this compromise may frustrate those who possess one copy of a book and wish to know exactly how it may vary from another, but we decided to err on the side of providing some indication that a variant exists rather than ignoring it altogether.

SHORT PAMPHLETS AND BROADSIDES

Asterisks have been inserted immediately following the notes of format to indicate pamphlets of fewer than fifty pages. Broadsides, loosely defined as single sheets of any size printed on one or both sides, are described as "brs." Where two broadside ballads are printed on the opposite sides of the leaf, each is given a separate entry. "Cap., 4°.*" designates a work in quarto of fewer than fifty pages without a title page but with a caption title.

MINOR POINTS

The sequence of entries for editions or issues printed in the same year does not necessarily indicate the sequence of printings.

Hebrew and Arabic type have not been used. Works beginning with such titles have "[Hebrew]" or "[Arabic]" and then the subtitle.

When the author's name does not appear on the title page or appears only with initials, it has been placed within brackets.

Parts of books, even with new title pages, have been omitted. Only when both pagination and signatures start again is the title entered. This practice allows entry for items that are called for on other title pages; they are included here because they may also have been issued separately.

Works are entered at the original author, not at the translator.

One aspect of previous policy has been reversed. A number of entries were cancelled in the revised first volume because the only known copy (usually at the Guildhall Library, London, the British Library, or the Dublin Public Record Office) was lost or destroyed in time of war or by fire. Because other copies occasionally turn up, the original entry is now listed in full with the notation "(lost)" after the location symbol.

Hundreds of scholars and librarians have contributed to this volume by pointing out corrections, sending offprints of articles, providing lists of acquisitions, and answering our queries. The National Endowment for the Humanities provided grants to enable the revision to continue, the Yale University Library made office space available, and the Index Fund of the Modern Language Association of America underwrote printing costs. Walter S. Achtert of the MLA has been a continuing source of support and encouragement.

But primary credit for the preparation of this volume is due to those who were part of the revision staff during the last eight years. Jeri Smith, who had assisted Donald Wing, kept the revision project alive until the 1976 NEH grant permitted full-time work. Phebe Kirkham and Janice Hansel, the latter as Assistant Editor, each put in several years of work making the volume more complete. William Mitchell, Kathleen Sommers, Larry Holley, and Matthew Seccombe worked part-time for varying periods for the Wing Project. I am deeply grateful to each of them.

OPE Pembroke College, Oxford
OQ Queen's College, Oxford
OR Radcliffe Camera, Oxford (= O)
ORP Regent's Park, Oxford
OS St. John's College, Oxford
OSA St. Anne's College, Oxford
OSU Ohio State University, Columbus
OU University College, Oxford (deposited at O)
OW Worcester College, Oxford
OWA Wadham College, Oxford
OWC College of Wooster, Wooster, Ohio

P Plume Library, Maldon, Essex
PAP American Philosophical Society, Philadelphia
PAPANTONIO Michael Papantonio, New York (dispersed;
      some to MWA)
PBL Lehigh University, Bethlehem, Pa.
PBM Bryn Mawr College, Bryn Mawr, Pa.
PC Peterborough Cathedral (deposited at C)
PCP College of Physicians, Philadelphia
PFL Philadelphia Free Library
PGN Philip G. Nordell, Philadelphia
PH Haverford College, Haverford, Pa.
PHS Historical Society of Pennsylvania, Philadelphia
PJB P. J. Baldwin, Toronto (now belongs to
      Audrie J. Cossar, Peterborough, Ontario)
PL Library Company of Philadelphia
PMA Allegheny College, Meadville, Pa.
PPT Pittsburgh Theological Seminary
PRF Rosenbach Foundation, Philadelphia
PS Preussische Staats-Bibliothek, Berlin
PSC Swarthmore College, Swarthmore, Pa.
PSCO Pennsylvania State University, University Park
PT Temple University, Philadelphia
PU University of Pennsylvania, Philadelphia
PUL University of Pennsylvania Law School, Philadelphia
      (Biddle Law Library)
PW Westtown School, Westtown, Pa.

R Rothamsted Experimental Station, Harpenden,
      Herts.
RB Northern Baptist College, Manchester (= NM)
RBU Brown University, Providence, R.I.
RE Renishaw, Derbyshire
RHT Robert H. Taylor Collection, Princeton, N.J.
RIPON Ripon Cathedral
RNR Redwood Library, Newport, R.I.
RPJ John Carter Brown Library, Providence, R.I.
RPL Reigate Public Library
RU University of Reading

SA St. Andrews University
SC Salisbury Cathedral
SCU University of South Carolina, Columbia

SE Essex Institute, Salem, Mass.
SHR Shropshire County Library
SP Petyt Library, Skipton, Yorkshire
SR Royal Library, Stockholm
SS William Salt Library, Stafford
SW Washington University, St. Louis, Mo.
SYON Syon Abbey, South Brent, Devon

TO University of Toronto
TNJ Joint University Libraries, Nashville, Tenn.
TSM Southern Methodist University, Dallas, Texas
TU University of Texas, Austin

UCLA University of California, Los Angeles

V University of Virginia, Charlottesville
VC Vassar College, Poughkeepsie, N.Y.
VH Hofbibliothek, Vienna

W Donald G. Wing, Woodbridge, Conn.
WARE Ware College, Armwell End, Ware, Herts.
WC Wellesley College, Wellesley, Mass.
WCA St. George's Chapel, Windsor Castle
WCL Chapin Library, Williams College,
      Williamstown, Mass.
WDA United States Department of Agriculture,
      Washington, D.C.
WES Wesleyan University, Middletown, Conn.
WF Folger Library, Washington, D.C.
WG Georgetown University, Washington, D.C.
WGS United States Geological Survey, Washington, D.C.
WM Wandsworth Meeting
WPO United States Patent Office
WSC Washington State University, Pullman
WSG National Library of Medicine, Bethesda, Md.
WSL Lewis Walpole Library, Farmington, Conn.
WU University of Wisconsin, Madison
WWC Washington Cathedral Library, Washington, D.C.

Y Yale University, New Haven, Conn.
YB Birkbeck Library, York
YBA Yale Center for British Arts, New Haven, Conn.
YD Yale Divinity School, New Haven, Conn.
YL Yale Law School, New Haven, Conn.
YM York Minster
YS York Subscription Library

ZAP Auckland Public Library, New Zealand
ZAS St. John's College, Auckland, New Zealand
ZDU University of Otago, Dunedin, New Zealand
ZWT Turnbull Collection, Wellington, New Zealand

LIBRARIES AND SYMBOLS

Abbotsford, Scotland: A
Aberdeen City Charter Room: AC
Aberdeen University: AU
Admiralty, London: LAD
All Souls College, Oxford: OAS
Allegheny College, Meadville, Pa.: PMA
American Antiquarian Society, Worcester, Mass.: MWA
American Baptist Historical Society, Rochester, N.Y.: NHC
American Philosophical Society, Philadelphia: PAP
Auckland Public Library, New Zealand: ZAP

Baillie's Institution, Glasgow: GB
Bailliol College, Oxford: OB
Baldwin P. J., Toronto: PJB (now belongs to Audrie J. Cossar, Peterborough, Ontario)
Ballien Library, University of Melbourne, Australia: AMB
Bamburgh Castle Library, University of Durham: BAMB
Bangor Cathedral: BANGOR (deposited in the University College of North Wales)
Baptist College, Bristol: BB (mostly dispersed)
Baptist College, Manchester: MAB
Baptist College, Rawdon: RB (at NM)
Baptist Union, London: LB
Barr Smith Library, University of Adelaide, Australia: AAS
Bath Municipal Library: BML
Bedford Public Library: BP
Bevan-Naish Collection, Woodbrooke College, Birmingham: BBN
Bibliothèque de l'Université de Louvain: BL
Bibliothèque Nationale, Paris: BN
Birkbeck Library, York: YB
Birmingham Central Reference Library: BC
Birmingham University: BIU
Blackfriars Priory, Oxford: OBL
Blairs College, Aberdeen: AB
Bodleian Library, Oxford: O
Boston Athenaeum, Boston: MBA
Boston Public Library, Boston: MB
Bowdoin College, Brunswick, Maine: MBC
Brasenose College, Oxford: OBR
Bristol Museum: BM
Bristol Reference Library: BR
British and Foreign Bible Society, London: LBS (dispersed; many at O)
British Library, London: L
British Museum (Natural History), London: LNH
Brown University, Providence, R.I.: RBU
Bryn Mawr College, Bryn Mawr, Pa.: PBM
Buffalo and Erie County Public Library, Buffalo, N.Y.: BBE
Bury St. Edmunds Cathedral Library: BSE
Bute, Marquis of: BUTE

California State Library, Sacramento: CSL
Cambridge University Archives: CA
Cambridge University Library: C
Cardiff Public Library: CPL
Cashel Diocesan Library: CD
Castle Museum, Norwich: NCM
Chapin Library, Williams College, Williamstown, Mass: WCL
Chatsworth House, Derbyshire: DCH
Chemical Society, London: LCH
Chetham's Library, Manchester: MC
Christ Church, Oxford: OC
Christ's College, Cambridge: CCH
Clare College, Cambridge: CCL
Claremont Colleges Library, Claremont, Calif.: CCC
College of Physicians, Philadelphia: PCP
College of Wooster, Wooster, Ohio: OWC
Columbia University, New York: NC
Columbia University Law School, New York: NCL
Commonwealth National Library, Canberra, Australia: ANL
Congregational Library, Boston: MCL
Congregational Library, London: LCL
Connecticut Historical Society, Hartford: CHS
Cornell University, Ithaca, N.Y.: NIC
Corpus Christi College, Cambridge: CCO
Corpus Christi College, Oxford: OCC
Coventry Central Library: CC
Crawford Library: HH (partly dispersed; broadsides, proclamations, and ballads at MR)
Cushing Library, Yale Medical School, New Haven, Conn.: HC

Dr. Williams's Library, London: LW
Downing College, Cambridge: CDC
Downside School, Stratton on the Fosse, Bath, Somerset: DOWNSIDE
Dublin Castle: DCA
Dublin Public Libraries, Pearse St., Dublin: DMC, DML
Duke University, Durham, N.C.: NCD
Dulwich College: DC
Dundee University: D
Durham Cathedral: DUC
Durham University: DU
Dyce Collection, Victoria and Albert Museum, London: LVD

Earlham College, Richmond, Ind.: IE
Edinburgh University: E
Ely Cathedral: ELY (dispersed; many at C)
Emmanuel College, Cambridge: CE
Essex Institute, Salem, Mass.: SE
Eton College: EC
Exeter College, Oxford: OE

Farm Street Church, London: FARM (includes Gillow Library)
Ferguson, F. S., London: FSF (dispersed; most in O, EN, IU)
First Congregational Library, Belfast: BF
Fisher Library, University of Sydney, Australia: ASU
Fitzwilliam Museum, Cambridge: CF
Folger Library, Washington, D.C.: WF
Fonmon Castle, Glamorgan: FONMON (available through University College, Cardiff)
Fordham University, New York: NF
Forster Collection, Victoria and Albert Museum, London: LVF
The Francis A. Countway Library of Medicine (Boston Medical Library), Boston: MBM
Francis Bacon Foundation, Claremont, Calif.: CPB
Friends' Library, London: LF
Fulton Library, Yale Medical School, New Haven, Conn.: JF

Garrett Theological Seminary, Evanston, Ill.: IEG
General Register House, Edinburgh: ER
General Theological Seminary, New York: NGT
Georgetown University, Washington, D.C.: WG
Glasgow University: GU
Gloucester Cathedral: GC
Goldsmiths' Library, University of London: LUG
Gonville and Caius College, Cambridge: CCA
Gray Library, Haddington: HG (deposited at EN)
Gray's Inn, London: LGI
Greyfriars Priory, Oxford: OG
Grolier Club, New York: NG
Guildhall, London: LG
Guilford College, Guilford, N.C.: NGC

Harvard Law School, Cambridge, Mass.: MHL
Harvard University, Cambridge, Mass.: MH
Haverford College, Haverford, Pa.: PH
Hebrew Union College, Ohio: OHU
Henry E. Huntington Library, San Marino, Calif.: CH
Hertford College, Oxford: OH
Heythrop College, London: HEYTHROP
Historical Society of Pennsylvania, Philadelphia: PHS
Hofbibliothek, Vienna: VH
Home Office Library, Queen Anne's Gate, London: LHO
Hunterian Museum, Glasgow: GH
Huntly House, Edinburgh: EH
Huth Sale Catalogue: HUTH

Incorporated Law Society, London: LIL
Indiana University, Bloomington: INU
Inner Temple, London: LI
Innerpeffray, Perthshire, Scotland: I
Institute of Electrical and Electronics Engineers, New York: NA

Jesus College, Cambridge: CJ
Jesus College, Oxford: OJ
John Carter Brown Library, Providence, R.I.: RPJ
John Crerar Library, Chicago: CJC
John Johnson Collection, Bodleian Library, Oxford: OP (= Meade Collection)

John Rylands University Library of Manchester (Deansgate): MR
John Rylands University Library of Manchester (Oxford Road): MAU
Johns Hopkins University, Baltimore, Md.: MBJ
Joint University Libraries, Nashville, Tenn.: TNJ

Kendall Whaling Museum, Sharon, Mass.: MSK
Keynes, Sir Geoffrey, London: GK
King's College, Cambridge: CK
King's Inn, Dublin: DK
Kirk, Rudolf, San Marcos, Texas: KIRK

Lambeth Palace, London: LLP
Lamport Hall, Northampton: NL
Leeds University, Leeds: LLU
Lehigh University, Bethlehem, Pa.: PBL
Leicester Central Library: LE
Leighton Library, Dunblane Cathedral, Dunblane: DL
Lewis Walpole Library, Farmington, Conn.: WSL
Library Company, Burlington, N.J.: NBL
Library Company of Philadelphia: PL
Library of Congress, Washington, D.C.: LC
Lincoln Cathedral: LNC
Lincoln College, Oxford: OL
Lincoln's Inn, London: LL
Linen Hall Library, Belfast: BLH
Liverpool Cathedral: LIC
Liverpool University: LIU
London Library: LLL
London School of Economics: LSE
Los Angeles County Law Library: CLL
Lough Fea Library, Ireland: LFEA (dispersed; rebellion tracts at DN)
Loyola University, Chicago: CL

McMaster University, Hamilton, Ontario: HM
Magdalen College, Oxford: OM
Magdalene College, Cambridge: CM
Manchester Free Public Library: MP
Manchester Free Reference Library: MRL
Marischal College, Aberdeen: AM
Marsh's Library, St. Patrick's, Dublin: DM
Maryland Historical Society, Baltimore: MAH
Massachusetts Archives, Boston: MBS
Massachusetts Historical Society, Boston: MHS
Massachusetts Horticultural Society, Boston: MHO
Medical Society, London: LM (dispersed; most at LWL and TO)
Merton College, Oxford: OME
Metropolitan Museum of Art, New York: NMM
Middle Temple, London: LMT
Mitchell Library, Glasgow: GM
Moore Theological College, Newtown, N.S.W., Australia: MOORE
Muirhead, Arnold, St. Albans: M

Nangle, Benjamin C., Woodbridge, Conn.: BCN (dispersed)
National Laboratory of Psychical Research, London: LN
National Library of Ireland, Dublin: DN
National Library of Medicine, Bethesda, Md.: WSG
National Library of Scotland (Advocates'), Edinburgh: EN
National Library of Wales, Aberystwyth: AN
National Maritime Museum, Greenwich: LNM
New College, Edinburgh: ENC
New College, Oxford: ON
New Jersey Historical Society, Newark: NJH
New York Academy of Medicine, New York: NAM
New York Historical Society, New York: NHS
New York Public Library: NN
New York State Library, Albany: NS
Newberry Library, Chicago: CN
Newcastle Society of Antiquaries: NSA
Newcastle upon Tyne City Libraries: NE
Nordell, Philip G., Philadelphia: PGN
Norfolk and Norwich Literary Institution, Norwich: NO
Northampton, Marquis of: CASTLE ASHBY
Northern Baptist College, Manchester: NM
Northwestern University Medical School, Chicago: CNM
Norwich Central Library: NPL

Ohio State University, Columbus: OSU
Osler Library, McGill University, Montreal: MMO
Oxford University Archives: OA

Papantonio, Michael, New York PAPANTONIO (dispersed;
    some to MWA):
Patent Office, London (at L): LPO
Pathology Laboratory, Cambridge: CPA
Peabody Institute, Baltimore, Md.: MBP
Peel Meeting, London: LPM
Pembroke College, Cambridge: CPE
Pembroke College, Oxford: OPE
Pennsylvania State University, University Park: PSCO
Peterborough Cathedral PC (deposited at C)
Peterhouse, Cambridge: CP
Petyt Library, Skipton, Yorkshire: SP
Philadelphia Free Library: PFL
Pierpont Morgan Library, New York: NNM
Pittsburgh Theological Seminary: PPT
Plume Library, Maldon, Essex: P
Preussische Staats-Bibliothek, Berlin: PS
Princeton Theological Seminary, Princeton, N.J.: NPT
Princeton University, Princeton, N.J.: NP
Privy Council Office, London: LPC
Public Library of South Australia, Adelaide: ASP
Public Record Office, Dublin: DPR
Public Record Office, London: LPR

Queen's College, Cambridge: CQ
Queen's College, Oxford: OQ
Queen's University, Belfast: BQ
Queen's University, Kingston, Ontario: KQ

Radcliffe Camera, Oxford: OR (= O)
Redpath Library, McGill University, Montreal: MM
Redwood Library, Newport, R.I.: RNR
Regent's Park, Oxford: ORP
Reigate Public Library: RPL
Renishaw, Derbyshire: RE
Ripon Cathedral: RIPON
Robert H. Taylor Collection, Princeton, N.J.: RHT
Rosenbach Foundation, Philadelphia: PRF
Rothamsted Experimental Station, Harpenden, Herts.: R
Roy G. Neville Library, Calif.: CRN
Royal Agricultural Society, London: LAS
Royal Art Institution, London: LAI
Royal Botanic Gardens, Kew: KEW
Royal College of Physicians, Edinburgh: ECP
Royal College of Physicians, London: LCP
Royal College of Surgeons, Edinburgh: ECS
Royal College of Surgeons, London: LCS
Royal Dublin Society: DRS
Royal Institute of British Architects, London: LIB
Royal Irish Academy, Dublin: DI
Royal Library, Stockholm: SR
Royal Library, The Hague: HR
Royal Observatory, Edinburgh: EO
Royal Society, London: LR
Royal Society of Literature, London: LSL
Royal Society of Medicine, London: LSM
Royal United Service Institution, London: LUS (dispersed)
Rutgers University, New Brunswick, N.J.: NR

St. Andrews University: SA
St. Anne's College, Oxford: OSA
St. David's University College, Lampeter, Wales: LSD
St. George's Chapel, Windsor Castle: WCA
St. John's College, Auckland, New Zealand: ZAS
St. John's College, Cambridge: CS
St. John's College, Oxford: OS
St. Louis University, St. Louis, Mo.: MSL
St. Mark's Church, Niagara-on-the-Lake, Canada: NIA
St. Mary's Seminary, Birmingham (Oscott College): BSM
St. Paul's Cathedral, London: LP
Salisbury Cathedral: SC
Scottish Record Office, H.M. General Register House,
    Edinburgh: ER
Seabury-Western Theological Seminary, Evanston, Illinois: IEG
Selly Oak Colleges Library, Birmingham: BSO
Selwyn College, Cambridge: CSE
Shropshire County Library: SHR
Sidney Sussex College, Cambridge: CSSX
Signet, Edinburgh: ES (partly dispersed)
Sion College, London: LSC
Society of Antiquaries, London: LS
Society of Genealogists, London: LSG
Southern Methodist University, Dallas, Texas: TSM
Speculative Society, Edinburgh: ESS
Stanford University, Stanford, Calif.: CSU

State University of New York at Buffalo: BU
Sutro Branch, California State Library, San Francisco: CSS
Swarthmore College, Swarthmore, Pa.: PSC
Syon Abbey, South Brent, Devon: SYON

Taylor, Robert H., Princeton, N.J.: RHT
Temple University, Philadelphia: PT
Thomason Collection, British Library, London: LT
Transylvania University, Lexington, Ken.: KT
  (law books dispersed)
Trinity College, Cambridge: CT
Trinity College, Dublin: DT
Turnbull Collection, Wellington, New Zealand: ZWT

Union College, Schenectady, N.Y.: NSU
Union Theological Seminary, New York: NU
United Free Church College, Edinburgh: FU
United Free Church College, Glasgow: GF
United States Department of Agriculture,
  Washington, D.C.: WDA
United States Geological Survey, Washington, D.C.: WGS
United States Patent Office: WPO
University College, Cardiff: CUC
University College, London: LUC
University College, Oxford: OU (deposited at O)
University of California, Berkeley: CB
University of California, Davis: CDA
University of California, Los Angeles: UCLA
University of California, Los Angeles, Biomedical Library: CLM
University of California, Santa Barbara: CSB
University of Chicago: CU
University of Cincinnati, Ohio: OCI
University of Florida, Gainesville: FU
University of Illinois, Urbana: IU
University of Iowa, Iowa City: IAU
University of Kansas, Lawrence: KU
University of Kentucky, Lexington: KYU
University of London: LU
University of Massachusetts, Amherst: MA
University of Miami, Miami, Fla.: FM
University of Michigan, Ann Arbor: MU
University of Minnesota, Minneapolis: MIU
University of North Carolina, Chapel Hill: NCU
University of Nottingham: NOT
University of Otago, Dunedin, New Zealand: ZDU

University of Pennsylvania, Philadelphia: PU
University of Pennsylvania Law School, Philadelphia: PUL
  (Biddle Law Library)
University of Queensland, St. Lucia, Australia: AQU
University of Reading: RU
University of Rochester, Rochester, N.Y.: NRU
University of South Carolina, Columbia: SCU
University of Texas, Austin: TU
University of Toronto: TO
University of Virginia, Charlottesville: V
University of Western Ontario, London, Ontario: OLU
University of Wisconsin, Madison: WU
Ushaw College, Durham: DUS

Vassar College, Poughkeepsie, N.Y.: VC
Victoria and Albert Museum, London: LV
Victoria State Library, Melbourne, Australia: AVP

Wadham College, Oxford: OWA
Wandsworth Meeting: WM
Ware College, Armwell End, Ware, Herts.: WARE
Washington Cathedral Library, Washington, D.C.: WWC
Washington State University, Pullman: WSC
Washington University, St. Louis, Mo.: SW
Watkinson Library, Hartford, Conn.: CHW
Wellcome Institute for the History of Medicine, London: LWL
Wellesley College, Wellesley, Mass.: WC
Wesleyan University, Middletown, Conn.: WES
Westtown School, Westtown, Pa.: PW
William A. Clark Library, Los Angeles: CLC
William Salt Library, Stafford: SS
Wing, Donald G., Woodbridge, Conn.: W
Worcester College, Oxford: OW
Worth Library, Dublin: DWL

Yale Center for British Arts, New Haven, Conn.: YBA
Yale Divinity School, New Haven, Conn.: YD
Yale Law School, New Haven, Conn.: YL
Yale University, New Haven, Conn.: Y
York Minster: YM
York Subscription Library: YS

Zeeland Academy, Middelburg, Netherlands: MZ
Zion Research Library, Boston University, Boston, Mass.: MBZ

SHORT-TITLE CATALOGUE

OF BOOKS PRINTED IN ENGLAND, SCOTLAND, IRELAND, WALES, AND BRITISH AMERICA
AND OF ENGLISH BOOKS PRINTED IN OTHER COUNTRIES

1641-1700

E

2927 England anatomized: her disease discovered. [*London*, 1659.] cap., 4°.* LT, O, BC; MIU, Y.

England and East-India. 1697. *See* Pollexfen, John.

2928 England & Scotland: or, the proceedings of the Parliament. *Oxford, printed*, 1644. 4°.* MADAN 1663. O, C, CT, E, DT; MH, MM, Y.

2929 —[Anr. ed.] *Oxford, by Henry Hall*, 1644. 4°.* MADAN 1664. LT, O, C, CJ; CH, CLC, MBP, NU.

England and Scotland united. 1647. *See* H., I.

2930 England and Scotlands covenant. [*London*], *for Edw. Husbands*, [1643/4]. 8°.* LT, O, LNC; CH.

2931 —[Anr. ed.] [*London*], *for Edw. Husband*, 1645. 12°. O, OC, LSD; NU.

2931A —[Anr. ed.] —, 1646. 12°. L, LNC; CLC.

2931B —[Anr. ed.] —, 1647. 8°. L; NU.

England bought and sold. 1681. *See* Nalson, John.

2931C England, defrauded, by the exportation of boxes, . . . for clocks. [*London?* 1700.] brs. L.

2932 England enslaved under Popish successors. *For Jonathan Wilkins*, 1681. 4°.* O, LIL, SP; CLC, NU.

2933 Angland in a ballance; or, a modifyein for avoydance another . . . warre. [*n.p.*], *printed*, 1648. 4°.* DT.

2934 England know thy drivers. *For J. L.*, 1647. 4°.* LT; CSS, WF.

2935 England must pay the piper. [*London*, 1691.] cap., 4°.* LUG, CT, LSD, MR, E; CH, MBA, PU, TU.

England still freshly lamenting. 1660. *See* P., W.

2936 England undeceived. *For Tim Goodwin*, 1691. 4°.* L, O, LUG, CT; NC, NCD, PU, WF.

2936A England vniting to her soveraign. *For Charls Thomlinson*, 1660. 4°.* O; CSS, NN, WF.

2937 Englands absolute monarchy. *For Thomas Bankes*, 1642. 4°.* LT, O, DT; CH, CN, CU, IU, NU, WF, Y.

England's advocate. 1699. *See* N., A.

England's alarum: being. 1693. *See* Dunton, John.

2938 Englands alarm from the North. *By Robert White*, 1648. 4°.* LT, O, MR, EN, DT; CH, CN, MH, WF, Y.

2939 England's alarm: or, a most humble . . . petition. *For Thomas Pasham*, 1679. fol.* L, O, C, DU, LNC; CH, CN, MH, TU, WF, Y, AVP.

2940 Englands alarum, or endevors for freedom. [*London*], 1648. 4°.* MR.

Englands alarm. The state-maladies. 1659. *See* H., J.

2941 Englands alarm to vvar against the beast. [*London*], *for Thomas Vnderhill*, 1643. 4°.* LT, C, CT, EC, SP, EN; CH, MB, MH, NU, WF.

Englands almanack. 1700. *See* Almanacs. L., T.

Englands anathomy. [1653.] *See* D., T.

2942 Englands apology, for its late change. *By M. S. for Livewel Chapman*, 1651. 4°.* L, O, DT; CSS, MHL, NU, WF, Y.

2943 —[Anr. ed.] *By Matthew Simmons*, 1651. 4°.* LT, O, BC, CD; CLC, CSS, IU, MH, MU.

Englands appeale from. 1673. *See* Lisola, François Paul, baron de.

2943A England's appeal, to her high court at Parliament. [*London?* 1695.] cap., 4°.* L, LSD.

2944 Englands appeale to its ovvn army. [*Oxford, by J. Harris and H. Hills*, 1647.] 4°.* MADAN 1934. O; CH, Y.

2945 Englands appeal to the Parliament at Oxford. colop: *For R. Janeway*, 1681. brs. L, O, C, LNC; CDA, IU, MBA, MH, NN, Y.

Englands birth-right. [*n.p.*, 1645.] *See* Lilburne, John.

2946 England's black tribunall. *For J. Playford*, 1660. 8°. LT, O, OC, CS, RU, EN; CH, CN, MH, WF, Y.

2947 —"Fourth" edition. —, 1660. 8°. CH, CLC, MHL, Y.

2948 —Twelfth edition. *For Simon Neale*, 1674. 8°. L; IU, LC.

2949 —"Third" edition. *For J. Playford*, 1680. 8°. T.C.I 387. L, O; MBP, MH, NCU, TU, WF, Y.

2950 —[Anr. ed.] *For E. M.*, [1700?]. 8°.* L.

2951   England's calamity. *By T. Dawks. Sold by Langley Curtis,* [1680?]. brs. L.

2951A   England's captivity returned. [*London*, 1660?] brs. O.

England's changeling. [n.p.], 1659. *See* Willis, Humphrey.

Englands comfort. 1641. *See* Taylor, John.

Englands complaint or a sharp reproof. 1648. *See* Gatford, Lionel.

2952   Englands complaint, or, the church. [*London*, 1642.] cap., 4°.* LT, LNC, MR, DT; CH, MH, MU.

Englands compleat law-judge. 1656. *See* Paxton, Edward.

2953   Englands concern in the case of His R. H. *For H. R.,* 1680. 4°.* L, O, CS, ESS; CH, IU, MH, MIU, WF, Y.

2954   Englands condition considered, and bewailed. *For Robert White, Jan.* 18, 1648. 4°.* LT, O, BP, LLU, MR; CH, CU, MH, WF, Y.

England's confusion: or, a true. 1659. *See* Anglesey, Arthur Annesley, *earl.*

Englands congratulatorie entertainment. [n.p.], 1641. *See* Cragg, John.

2954A   Englands cordiall physick. [*London*, 1645.] brs. L.

Englands covenant. 1643. *See* Clarke, Samuel.

2954B   Englands crisis: or, the world well mended. [*London,* 1689.] brs. L.

England's danger. [n.p., 1698.] *See* Smith, Thomas.

2955   Englands darling. [*London*], *for J. Wright, J. Clark, W. Thackery, and T. Passenger,* [1681–84]. brs. L, CM, HH, GU; MH, Y.

2955A   Englands day of joy and reioycing. *For W. Gilbertson,* [1660]. brs. MH.

2956   Englands deadly disease. *For George Lindsey,* 1647. 4°.* LT, O, LG, DT; NU, WF.

England's delight in this Parliament. 1680. *See* Sambach, William.

2957   England's delightful new songs. *For John Back,* [1685]. 8°. O.

2957A   England's deliverance from Popery and slavery. *For Eleanor Smith, and are to be sold by John Whitlock,* 1695. brs. MH.

2958   Englands deliverance or, the great and bloody plot discovered. [*London*], *for T. Vere, and W. Gilbertson,* 1661. 8°.* LT.

England's deplorable condition. 1659. *See* F., E. de C. V.

2959   Englands directions for members elections. [*London,* 1660.] brs. LT, O; MH, Y.

2960   Englands discoverer; or the Levellers creed. *For G. Wharton,* 1649. 4°.* LT, LUG, OC, DT; CH, NC, NN, Y.

England's distempers. 1677. *See* Allen, Richard.

Englands diurnall. [n.p., 1643.] *See* H., I.

2961   Englands division, and Irelands distraction. *For Thomas Bates,* 1642. 4°.* LT, DN; Y.

2961A   England's doleful complaint. *Printed,* 1651. brs. L.

2962   Englands dolefull lamentation: or the cry of the oppressed. [*London*], *printed,* 1647.* LT, DT; CLC, NC, NS.

Englands doxologie. 1641. *See* L., J.

2962A   England's dust and ashes. 1648. 4°. NU.

2962B   Englands fair garland. [*London*], *for R. Kell,* 1687. 8°.* CM.

2963   —[Anr. ed.] —, 1688. 8°.* O.

Englands faithful physician. 1666. *See* Hart, John.

England's faithfull reprover. 1653. *See* Samwaies, Richard.

2964   Englands faiths defender vindicated. *For Charles King,* 1660. 4°.* LT, DU, EN; MH.

Englands fortresse. 1648. *See* Calver, Edward.

2964A   England's friendly and seasonable advice. [*London*, 1648?] 4°.* L.

2965   Englands genius pleading. *For J. Jones,* 1660. brs. LT, O.

2966   Entry cancelled. *See following entry.*

2967   England's glory begun. *For Rich. Baldwin,* 1698. 4°.* O, LUG; MH, NC, NS.

2968   Entry cancelled.

Englands glory. By the benefit. 1669. *See* Carter, William.

2969   Englands glory in her royall King. [*London*], *printed in the yeare,* 1641. 4°.* LT, O, C, E, DT; CH, CN, MH, WF, Y.

Englands glory, or, an exact. 1660. *See* Brooke, Nathaniel.

England's glory: or, the great. 1694. *See* Mackworth, *Sir* Humphry.

2970   Englands golden treasury. *For T. Lacy,* 1694. 8°. L, O.

2970A   —Fourth edition. —, 1699. 12°. L.

2970B   —Fifth edition. —, 1700. 8°. CLC.

2970C   England's golden watch-bell. [*London*], *for W. Thackeray,* [1688–89]. 8°.* O.

2971   England's grand memorial. *By Th. Dawks,* 1679. brs. L, O; CH.

2972   Englands gratulation on the landing of Charles the Second. *For VVilliam Gilbertson,* [1660]. 4°.* MH.

Englands great deliverance. 1689. *See* S., T.

England's great happiness. 1677. *See* Houghton, John.

2973   England's great interest, by encouraging the setting up the royal fishery. *Published by allowance of the Company of the Royal Fishery, for H.M. and sold by J. Whitelock,* 1695. 8°.* L; NC, NN, PU.

2974   No entry.

Englands great interest in the choice. [n.p., 1679.] *See* Penn, William.

England's great interest in the well planting. Dublin, 1656. *See* Lawrence, Richard, *colonel.*

2974A   England's great prognosticator. *For Francis Grove,* [1660–61]. brs. EUING 96. GU.

2975   Englands grievances in times of Popery. *For Joseph Collyer and Stephen Foster,* 1679. 4°.* T.C.I 366. L, O, OC, CT; CH, CLC, CN, NP, NU, WF, Y.

2976   Entry cancelled.

England's happiness. 1687. *See* England's happiness or, the only way.

2976A   England's happiness a hundred years hence. [*London?* 1700.] brs. L.

2977   England's happiness improved. *By Roger Clavill,* 1697. 8°. O, CT; CJC, LC, Y.

2977A —Second edition. *For Roger Clavill and sold by D. Mid-winter and T. Leigh,* 1699. 8°. LLU; WF.

2978 England's happiness in a lineal succession. *By H. Clark, for John Taylor,* 1685. 12°. T.C.II 144. L, O, C, MC, MR; CLC, LC, MH, WF, Y.

2978A England's happiness or a health. *By R. M. for James Deane,* 1688. brs. OP.

2978B England's happiness or, the only way to make a nation truly happy. *By J. Astwood for the author,* 1687. 4°.* L, O, LIL, DT; CN.

2979 Englands happiness restored. *By D. M.,* 1679. brs. L, O; CLC, CN, MH, TU, Y.

2980 Englands hazzard. [*London,* 1648.] cap., 4°.* LT, DT.
Englands heroick champion. [1660.] *See* W., J.
Englands honour, and Londons glory. [1660.] *See* W., I.

2981 Englands hvmble remonstrance to their King. *For G. L.,* 1643. 4°.* LT, MR.

2982 England's Ichabod, glory departed. *For Edw. Blackmore,* 1650[1]. 4°.* LT, DT; CH.
Englands Iliads. Oxford, 1645. *See* Wharton, George.

2983 England's imminent danger and only remedy. *For Thomas Dring,* 1671. 8°. T.C.I 57. L, O, LG, EN, CD; CLC, IAU, MM, WF, Y.

2983A Englands improvement, and seasonable advice. *Printed,* 1691. 4°.* L, R; WU.
England's improvements. [n.p., 1680.] *See* Yarranton, Andrew.

2984 Entry cancelled.
England's independency upon the papal power. 1674. *See* Davies, *Sir* John.
England's interest. 1697. *See* Moore, *Sir* Jonas.
Englands interest asserted. 1669. *See* Carter, William.
Englands interest by trade. 1671. *See* Carter, William.

2985 Englands intrest [*sic*] endangered. [*London,* 1689.] cap., 4°.* MH, NC.
Englands interest in securing. 1689. *See* Carter, William.
England's interest; or, a brief. 1696. *See* Puckle, James.
Englands interest; or, the great. 1682. *See* Verney, Robert.
Englands jests. 1687. *See* Crouch, Humphrey.

2986 Englands ioy and sorrow. *For F. Coules,* 1641. 4°.* L, OC, LLU; CH, Y.
Englands joy, expressed. 1660. *See* H., J.

2987 England's joy, for London's loyalty. *For the author,* 1664. brs. MH.

2988 Englands joy for the coming in of . . . Charles the II. *For H. Brome,* 1660. brs. LT, O, OC, MC.

2988aA Englands joy in a lawful triumph. *For F. G.* [1660]. brs.

2988bA —[Anr. ed.] *For John Andrews,* [1660]. brs. EUING 99. GU. EUING 98. GU.

2988A Englands joy or a relation. *By Thomas Creak,* 1660. 4°.* L.

2989 England's joyalty for London's safety. *By R. H. for I.H.,* 1641. 4°. LT, O.

2990 Englands ioyalty, in ioyfull expressions. *For John Harison,* 1641. 4°.* Y.
Englands joyfull holiday. [1661.] *See* G., O.

2990A England's joyfull welcome to the King. [*London*], *for C. Dennisson,* [1688]. brs. O, CM.
Englands jubile. 1660. *See* Chamberlayne, William.
England's jubilee. 1699. *See* G., W.

2991 Englands ivstification for her religion. *Printed at London,* 1641. 8°. L, O; TU.

2991A Entry cancelled.
Englands lamentable slaverie. [n.p.], 1645. *See* Walwyn, William.

2991B Entry cancelled.
Englands lamentation. 1647. *See* Englands doleful lamentation.
Englands lamentation for the duke. 1679. *See* F., J.
England's lamentation, or. [n.p.], 1665. *See* Hubbersty, Stephen.
England's lessons. 1656. *See* Clark, Henry.
Englands looking-glasse. 1641. *See* Calamy, Edmund.

2992 England's losse, and lamentation. *For L. Chapman,* 1642[3]. 4°.* LT, O, CC, CCL, DT; CLC, TU.

2993 Englands mad petition. *Printed at London,* 1647. 4°.* LT; CH, CLC, Y.

2993A Englands memorial, or thankful remembrance . . . Popish plot. *Printed,* 1678. brs. L.
Englands memento. 1646. *See* P., R.

2994 Englands mercies in the midst of miserys. *For J. Deacon,* [1688]. brs. L; MH.

2995 England's mercy explained. colop: *For N. Ponder, and S. Lee,* [1680]. brs. L, O.
England's merry jester. 1693. *See* S., J.
Englands miserie and remedie. [n.p., 1645.] *See* Overton, Richard.

2996 Englands miserie, if not prevented. *By T. P. and M. S. August 18.* 1642. 4°.* LT, O; CH, MH, Y.

2997 Englands monarch, or a conviction. *By Thomas Paine,* 1644. 4°.* C; CSS, CU, IU, MH, WF, Y.
England's monarchs. 1685. *See* Crouch, Nathaniel.
Englands monarchy. 1660. *See* Peirce, *Sir* Edmond.

2998 Englands monument of mercies. [*London*], *for S. W. and I. P.,* 1646. brs. LT.

2999 England's most dreadful calamity by the late floods. [*London*], *for P. Brooksby in West-Smithfield,* 1682. 4°.* L, O, LSD; CH.

3000 England's mournful elegy for the dissolving the Parliament. colop: *For S. N.,* [1681]. brs. L, O, CT; CH, CN, MH, NCD, PU, Y.
Englands murthering monsters. [n.p., 1660.] *See* P., G.

3001 England's new bell-man. [*London*], *for W. O.,* [1690]. brs. L, O. (var.)

3001A —[Anr. ed.] *Printed for F. Coles, T. Vere, and W. Gilbertson,* [1658–64]. brs. O.

3001B —[Anr. ed.] [*London*], *printed for F. Coles, T. Vere, and J. Wright,* [1663–74]. brs. O.

3002 —[Anr. ed.] [*London*], *for A. M. W. D. and Tho. Thackeray,* [1695?]. brs. L, O, CM, HH; MH.
Englands new chains. [n.p., 1649.] *See* Lilburne, John.

3003 Englands new directory: commanded. [*London*], *printed,* 1647. 4°.* LT, O, OC; CH, MH.

England's new remembrancer. 1691. See J., S.

3003A England's new wonders. For J. Blair, and reprinted Aberdeen, by John Forbes, 1697. 12°.* LWL.

3004 England's New-yeares gift, or, a pearle. By Robert Austin, 1648. 4°.* LT, O, MR, DT; CH, CU, MH, WF.

Englands oaths. 1642. See Ingoldsby, William.

3005 England's object; or, good and true newes . . . Hugh Peters. [London], for F. Coles, T. Uere, and W. Gilbertson, [1660]. brs. O.

3006 Englands obligations to Captain William Bedlowe. By Th. Dawks, 1679. brs. L; MH, WCL, AMB.

3007 —Second edition. —, 1679. brs. LG; CH.

Englands old religion. Antwerp, 1658. See Beda, venerabilis.

3008 England's over-joy at the Duke of Monmouth's return. By T. Dawks, 1679. brs. L, O, C; CLC, TU.

England's Palladion. 1666. See Simpson, Thomas.

Englands path. 1700. See Puckle, James.

3009 Englands peace-offering. [n.p.], printed, 1643. 8°.* O.

3010 Englands petition to Gods deare servant, . . . Charles. [London], printed, 1646. 4°.* LT, DT, BLH.

3011 Englands petition, to her gratious king. That he Arminius. [Amsterdam, 1641.] brs. LT, O.

3012 Englands petition to King Charles. Printed, 1648. 4°.* LT, MR, SP; MH, MIU.

Englands petition to the two houses. Oxford, 1643. See R., N.

3013 Englands petition to their King. [London], printed May 5, 1643. 4°.* LT, C, LG, CJ, BR, SP; CH, CN, MH, NU, WF, Y.

3014 —[Anr. ed.] — May 10, 1643. 4°.* O; CH, MH.

3015 —[Anr. ed.] — May 13, 1643. 4°.* L, C, E, DT; CSS, CU, MH, NR.

3016 —[Anr. ed.] — May 20, 1643. 4°.* O; CLC, MH.

3016A —[Anr. ed.] — May 25, 1643. 4°.* O.

3017 Englands petition to their soveraigne King. For Tho. Bates, 1646. 4°.* LT, MR.

3017A Englands pleasant may-flower. [London], for W. Gilbertson, [1660]. brs. EUING 100. GU.

3018 Englands present case stated. [London], printed, 1659. 4°.* L, O, LLU, MR, WCA; CH, MH, MU, WF, Y.

Englands present distractions. 1642. See G., H.

England's present interest. [n.p.], 1675. See Penn, William.

3019 Englands pride. [London], for J. Deacon, [1684–95]. brs. HH.

Englands proper and onely way. 1648. See Hare, John.

3020 Englands prosperity. For Nicholas Iones, [1642]. 4°.* LT, MR; CH, MH, NC, NU, Y.

3021 Englands publick faith. [London, 1655.] brs. LT.

3022 Englands redemption: or, a path way to peace. For Charles King, 1660. 4°.* LT, O; MH.

3022A England's rejoycing at that happy day. For F. G., [1660]. brs. EUING 95. GU.

3023 Englands reioycing at the prelats downfall. England, printed, 1641. 4°.* L, O, C, YM, DT; CH, CU, MH, NU, WF, Y.

3024 Entry cancelled.

England's rejoycing for the Parliaments returne. 1641. See Bond, John, of St. John's, Cambridge.

3025 England's remarques. colop: For W. Jacob, and L. Curtis, 1676. fol.* T.C.1 253. L, O.

3026 England's remarques: giving. For Langley Curtis, 1678. 12°. L, O, C, OC; CH, CLC, CN, NP, WF, Y.

3027 —[Anr. ed.] For Langley Curtis, and sold by Tho. Mercer, 1682. 12°. L, OB, GU; CN, OSU.

3028 Englands remedy of a deadly malady. [London], printed, 1647. 4°.* LT, LG, E; IU, MH.

Englands remembrancer. 1676. See Clarke, Samuel.

3029 England's remembrancer; being a collection of farewell-sermons. Printed, 1663. 8°. L, O, C, AN, BC, DU; MH, NPT, WF, Y.

3029A —[Anr. ed.] Printed, 1666. 8°. CT.

3030 Entry cancelled. See following entry.

3031 England's remembrancer, for the late discovery . . . meal tub. Printed, 1679. brs. L, O; CLC, MH.

3032 Englands remembrancer: in two parts. For Tho: Vnderhill, Febr. 4th 1645[6]. 4°.* LT, O, AN, DT, CD; CH, MH, MIU, WF, Y.

3033 —[Anr. ed.] For Tho: Vnderhill, March 11. 1645[6]. 4°.* LT, O, LLU, DU, DT; MH, NU.

3034 Englands remembrancer: or, a catalogue. For Tho: Vnderhill, 1645. 4°.* LT, O, YM, A, DT; CH, MH, MIU, WF, Y.

3035 Englands remembrancer; or, a warning. By Thomas Paine, for Francis Eglesfield, 1644. 4°.* LT, MR, SP, DT; CH, CLC, NU, WF, Y.

3036 England's remembrancer: setting forth the beginning of Papal tyrannies. For E. Smith, 1682. 8°. NU, PU, WF, Y.

3037 Englands remembrancers: or, a word in season. [London, 1656.] cap., 4°.* LT, O, CS, LSD, MR; CSS, CU, MH, NP, TU, WF, Y.

3038 Englands remembrances. colop: Printed at London the 12. of Iune, 1659. cap. 4°.* O; CH, MH.

3039 Englands remonstrance to their King. [London], for G. Horton, 1648. 4°.* LT; CH, TU.

3040 —[Anr. ed.] [London], printed, 6. March 1648. 4°.* MH.

3041 Englands repentence Englands only remedy. By D. Maxwell, 1659. 4°.* LSD; CH, IU, MH.

3041A Englands royall conquest. For Richard Burton, [1666]. brs. EUING 101. O, GU.

3042 Englands royal renown. [London], for J. Deacon, [1685]. brs. L, O.

Englands sad posture. [1644.] See Calver, Edward.

3043 Englands safety in navie and fortifications. [London], for Io: Ch: and Iohn Bull, 1642. 4°.* LT, O, LG; CH, CN, MM, NN, WF, Y.

3044 Englands safety in the laws supremacy. Printed 1659. 4°.* LT, O, LVF, CT, LSD; CH, IU, LC, NU, WF, Y.

3045 England's safety: or, the two unanimous votes. For A. Brewster, 1679. fol.* L, O, C, LNC, EN; CH, MH, NP, TU, WF.

3046 Englands satisfaction in eight qveries. [London, 1643.] cap., 4°.* LT, O, MR, SP, DT; CH, IU, MH, NU, WF, Y.

3047 Englands second alarm to vvar. For Thomas Vnderhil, 1643. 4°.* LT, C, CT, EC, SP; CH, MH, NU, WF.

[4]

3048   England's second happiness. *For James Dean*, 1685. brs.
MH.

3049   England's second warning-piece. [*London?* 1680.] cap.,
fol.* O, C, LG, LNC, MR; CH, CLC, MH, PU, TU, WF, Y.
Englands selected characters. 1643. *See* Breton, Nicholas.

3050   Englands settlement mistaken. *By D. Maxwell*, 1660.
4°.* O, LG; CSS, MH, MM.

3051   Englands settlement, upon the two solid foundations.
Printed, 1659. 4°.* LT, O, OC, BC, MR; CH, MH, MU, TU,
WF.

3052   Englands sin and shame. 1672. brs. L.
England's solar pill. [1680.] *See* Fletcher, Richard.

3053   Englands sole remedy. [*London*], *printed*, 1648. 4°.* LT,
O, LL, MR; CH, MH, NU.

3053A Entry cancelled.
Englands sorrow. [1685?] *See* Knap, John.

3054   England's standard. *For Livewel Chapman*, 1659. 4°.* L,
O, OC; CH, MH, MU, TU, Y.

3055   Englands summons. 1650. 12°. L, A.

3056   Englands tears and lamentation. *For William Ley*, 1642.
4°.* L, O; CN, Y.
England's teares for. 1644. *See* Howell, James.

3057   Englands thankfvlnesse. *For Michael Sparke, senior*, 1642.
4°. CT, DT; WF.
England's thankes. 1642. *See* R., B.

3058   Englands third alarm to vvarre. *For Thomas Vnderhill*,
1643. 4°. LT, O, SP, EN; CH, MH, MU, WF, Y.
England's threnodie. [n.p., 1648.] *See* Ross, Alexander.

3059   Englands tribute of tears. [*London*], *for J. Millet*, [1690].
brs. L, CM, HH; MH.

3060   Englands triumph. A more exact history. *By J. G. for
Nathaniel Brook*, 1660. 8°. L, O, SS, E, EN; CH, CLC, CN,
MH, WF.

3060A England's tryumph and Holland's downfall. *For F. Coles,
T. Vere, and J. Wright*, [1666?]. brs. EUING 93. GU.

3061   Englands triumph and joy for the meeting of . . . Parliament. colop: *For H. R.*, 1681. brs. L; CH, CN, MBA,
MH, WF, Y.

3062   Englands triumph and Londons glory. *For John Jones*,
1661. brs. L.

3063   England's triumph: or, a poem. colop: *Printed, and are to
be sold by Randall Taylor*, 1686. brs. O; CH, Y.

3064   Englands triumph. Or the Rump routed. *For James Johnson*, [1660?]. brs. L, O; MH.

3065   Englands triumph: or, the subjects joy. [*London*], *for J.
Hose*, [1675?]. brs. L, O, HH, GU; MH.

3065A England's triumphs for the Prince of Wales. *For P. L.*,
1688. brs. L, O; CH, CN.

3066   —[Anr. ed.] *London, for P. L., and reprinted at Edinburgh,
by the heir of Andrew Anderson*, 1688. brs. ALDIS 2758.
O, HH, EN.

3067   England's troublers troubled. [*London*], *printed*, 1648.
4°.* LT, O, MR; CH, Y.
Englands trovbles anatomized. 1644. *See* Cokayne, John.
Englands unanimous sence. 1680. *See* S., J.

3068   England's universal distraction. [*London*], *printed*, 1659.
4°.* C, BC, DU, MR; CH, MH, MU, NU, WF, Y.

3068A Englands valour and Hollands terrour. [*London*], *for F.
Coles, T. Vere, W. Gilbertson, and J. Wright*, [1663–65].
brs. EUING 103. GU.

3069   Englands vanity: or the voice. *For John Dunton*, 1683. 8°.
T.C.II 12. L, O, LLL; CH, CN, LC, MH, WF, Y.

3070   Englands vote for a free election. [*London*, 1660.] brs. LT.
Englands wants. 1667. *See* Chamberlayne, Edward.
England's warning; or. 1664. *See* Swinton, John.

3071   England's warning: or, England's sorrow. *For T. Passinger*, 1667. 12°. LG.

3071A Englands warning-piece; or, a caviat for wicked sinners.
[*London*], *for R. Burton*, [1641–74]. brs. O.
England's warning-peece: or the history. 1659. *See*
Spencer, Thomas.

3072   England's warning-piece. Or, the most strange . . . pre-
dictions. *For Francis Coles*, 1661. 4°.* LT, CS; MH, OHU.
England's warning-piece: or, the unkenneling. 1654. *See*
Corbet, Jeffrey.
Englands way to wealth. 1699. *See* Puckle, James.

3073   No entry.

3074   Entry cancelled.
Englands weeping spectacle. [n.p.], 1648. *See* Lilburne,
John.

3075   Englands wolfe with eagles clawes. *By Matthew Simmons*,
1647. brs. LT, CJ.
England's worthies. 1647. *See* Vicars, John.

3075A **Englefield, Anthony.** Anthony Englefield . . . appellant. Sir Charles Englefield . . . respondent. The appellants case. [*n.p.*, 1687.] brs. L.

3075B **Englefield, *Sir* Charles.** The case of. [*n.p.*, 1687.] brs. L.

3076   **E[nglish], F[rancis].** Propugnaculum pietatis. *Printed*,
1667. 8°. O, LW; MH, NPT.

3077   No entry.

3078   **English, Peter.** The survey of policy. *Leith, printed*,
1653[4]. 4°. ALDIS 1476. LT, BC, EN; CH, MH, Y.
English academy. 1672. *See* L., P.
English acquisitions. 1700. *See* Crouch, Nathaniel.
English adventures. 1676. *See* Orrery, Roger Boyle, *earl
of.*
English and Dutch affaires. 1664. *See* W., W.

3079   Entry cancelled.
English and French cook. 1674. *See* P., T.

3079A The English and Low-Dutch instructer. *Tot Rotterdam,
by Isaak Naeranus*, 1678. 12°. WF.

3079B —[Anr. ed.] *Tot Rotterdam, by Gerard Van der Vluyn*,
1678. 12°. CLC.
English and Scottish Protestants. 1642. *See* Mason,
Robert.
English and Welsh mines. 1699. *See* Stringer, Moses.

3080   Entry cancelled.
English answer to the Scotch speech. 1668. *See* K., W.
English ballad. 1695. *See* Prior, Matthew.
English ballance. [n.p.], 1672. *See* MacWard, Robert.

3081   The English banner of truth displayed. *For Giles Calvert*,
1650. 4°.* LT, O, BC, MR, DT; CH, CLC, MH, NU, WF, Y.

3082   The English Catholike Christian. *By R. Leybourn*, 1649.
4°.* LT, O.

[5]

English chapman's . . . almanack. 1692. *See* Almanacs.

English chronology. Oxford, 1696. *See* Smithurst, Benjamin.

English Cretes. 1695. *See* W., T.

English dancing-master. [n.p.], 1651. *See* Playford, John.

3083   The English devil: or, Cromwel. *By Robert Wood, for George Horton*, 1660. 4°.* LT.

English dictionary. 1642. *See* Cockeram, Henry.

3083A The English donatizing church: or a parallel. [n.p., 1660–1700?] 4°. FARM.

English empire in America. 1685. *See* Crouch, Nathaniel.

English episcopacy. 1660. *See* Peirce, *Sir* Edmond.

English examples. 1676. *See* Leedes, Edward.

English expositor. 1641. *See* Bullokar, John.

3083B The English farrier. *For John Wright*, 1649. 4°. L (t.p.), O.

3084   The English fortune-teller. *For A. R. and C. A.*, 1642. 4°.* L, OW; MH.

3085   —[Anr. ed.] —, 1643. 4°.* LT.

3086   —[Same title.] *For W. Thackerary* [sic], *T. Passenger, and W. Whitwood*, [1686–88]. brs. L, O, CM, HH, GU; CU, MH.

3087   The English guide to the Latin tongue. *For R. Royston*, 1675. 8°. T.C.I 220. L, O, C; WF.

English Gusman. 1652. *See* Fidge, George.

3088   An English herbal. [London], *sold by A. C.*, [1690?]. Sixes. L; MHS, MIU, WF, HC.

3089   The English hermite, or, wonder of this age: . . . life of Roger Crab. *Printed*, 1655. 4°.* LT; CH.

English heroe. 1687. *See* Crouch, Nathaniel.

English house-wife. 1649. *See* Markham, Gervase.

English Iliads. 1674. *See* Warly, John.

3090   Entry cancelled.

English intelligencer. [1642.] *See* H., C.

3090A An English introduction to the Latin tongue. *Roger Daniel*, 1659. 8°. L, C.

3090B —[Anr. ed.] *Dublin, by Benjamin Tooke, and are to be sold by Joseph Wilde*, 1670. 8°. L (t.p.).

3090C —[Anr. ed.] *By John Redmayne*, 1675. 8°. T.C.I 223. OC.

3091   —[Anr. ed.] *By Eliz. Redmayne*, 1683. 8°. T.C.II 57. L, LIU, NOT; PL, WF.

3092   —[Anr. ed.] —, 1699. 8°. L, O, LIU.

3093   The English Irish sovldier. *Printed at London for R. Wood, and A. Coe*, 1642. brs. LT.

3094   The English Jeroboam. *For Walter Davies*, 1683. fol.* L, O, C, DU, EN.

English-law. 1651. *See* Cock, Charles George.

English liberties. [1680.] *See* Care, Henry.

3095   English liberty and property asserted. *For Livewell Chapman*, 1657. 4°.* LT, O, LG, SP; CLC, CN, CSS, IU.

English lovers. 1662. *See* Dauncey, John.

English loyalty; or. [1689.] *See* D., M.

3096   English loyalty vindicated. *For Nath. Thompson*, 1681. 4°.* L, O, C, CS, P, EN; CH, MH, NPT, NU, WF.

3097   The Englishman, or a letter. [London], *printed*, 1670. 4°.* L, O, LF, MR, YM, DT; CLC, MH, NU, PSC, Y.

3098   The English manner of swearing vindicated. *By R. W. for M. Pitt*, 1687. 4°.* LC, MH.

3099   The English-man's allegiance. [London, 1691?] 4°.* L, O, CT, MR, AU; CH, MM, WF.

Englishman's choice. 1694. *See* Defoe, Daniel.

3099A The Englishman's complaint. [London, 1689.] cap., fol.* L, O, OC, HH; CLC.

3099B —[Anr. ed.] [n.p., 1691.] brs. O.

3100   The English-man's happiness under a Protestant-prince. colop: *For T. B.*, 1681. cap., fol.* L, O, C, LG, MR; CH, CN, NN, PU, Y.

3101   The English-man's question. *Printed*, 1673. 4°.* L, MR, SP; CLC.

English-mans right. 1680. *See* Hawles, *Sir* John.

3102   The English manufacture discouraged. [London? 1697.] brs. L.

English martyrologe. [n.p.], 1672. *See* Watson, John.

3103   The English memorial. The 99th edition. *Muscovia, by Passive Obedience and Non-Resistance: and are to be sold by Licurgus Theocratus in Laodicea*, [1688]. 4°. L; Y.

3103A The Englishmen's victory over the Spaniards. *By and for W. O. and to be sold by J. Dea[con]*, [1690?]. brs. L.

3104   The English midwife enlarged. *For Rowland Reynolds*, 1682. 8°. T.C.I 465. LCP, LCS, E, GH; CH, LC, MU, WSG, HC.

3104A —[Anr. ed.] *For Thomas Sawbridge*, 1682. 8°. MAU.

3105   The English military discipline. [London], *sold by John Overton*, 1672. 4°. T.C.I 107. CH, WF, YBA.

3105A —[Anr. ed.] *For Robert Harford*, 1680. 8°. T.C.I 373. L, O, CS, DN; CH, MH, MU, WF, Y.

3105B The English mounsieur, a comical novel. *For W. Cademan*, 1679. 12°. T.C.I 369. O; CH, CLC.

English mounsieur. 1674. *See* Howard, James.

3106   The English mountebank. [London], *printed*, 1647. 4°.* LT, OC, DT; CH, MH, TU, WF, Y.

English nunne. [n.p., 1642.] *See* Anderton, Lawrence.

English oracle. 1679. *See* C., A.

English orator. 1680. *See* Richards, William.

English orthographie. Oxford, 1668. *See* Price, Owen.

3106A English orthography, containing the art of writing. colop: *By Joseph Hindmarsh*, 1686. cap., 8°. CLC.

English orthography or the art of writing and spelling. 1687. *See* Chalmer, John.

3107   Entry cancelled. Date: [1705?]

English part of Bibliotheca generalis. [n.p.], 1691. *See* Bibliotheca generalis.

English pilot. 1671. *See* Seller, John.

3108   The English pilot, The fourth book. *For John Thornton; and Richard Mount*, 1698. fol. LAD; MH, PHS, V, Y.

3109   The English Pope. *For Robert Bostock*, 1643. 4°.* LT, O, C, EN, DT; CH, CN, MH, WF, Y. (var.)

3110   The English post. [London], *printed*, 1641. 4°.* LT, O, C, SP, YM; WF, Y.

3111   The English prelates. [London], *printed*, 1661. 4°.* L, O, BC, DU, DT; CH, MH, WF, Y.

3112   Entry cancelled. *See* E3113B.

3113   The English Presbyterian and Independent reconciled. *Printed*, 1651. 4°. LT, O, CCA, YM, E; NC, NU.

3113A —[Anr. ed.] *For Edward Brewster*, 1656. 4°. O.

3113B —[Anr. ed.] —, 1657. 4°. LT, C; NU.
3114 Entry cancelled.
     English Presbytery. 1680. See Collinges, John.
     English princess. 1667. See Caryl, John.
3115 Entry cancelled.
     English princess, or, the dutchess-queen. 1678. See
       Préchac, Jean sieur de.
     English prosodia. 1685. See Thomas, James.
     English puritanisme. [n.p.], 1641. See Bradshaw, Wil-
       liam.
     English Rechabite. [1681.] See Whitehall, Robert.
     English rogue. 1666. See Head, Richard.
     English rogue a new comedy. 1668. See Thompson,
       Thomas.
3115A The English rogue. Containing a brief discovery of . . .
       cheats. [London], for J. Blare, 1688. 8°.* O.
     English rudiments. 1665. See Du-Gard, William.
3116 English Sampson his strength prov'd. By J. W., 1699.
       brs. L.
3117 The English schole-master. Amsterdam, printed, 1646. 12°.
       L, O, CT; MB, MH.
3118 —[Anr. ed.] Amsterdam, by Iohn Bouman, 1658. 12°. L.
3118A —[Anr. ed.] t'Amsterdam, by Ian Bouman, 1663. 12°. MB,
       MH, NC.
3118B The English seamans resolution. [London], for F. Coles,
       T. Vere, and J. Wright, [1663–74]. brs. EUING 106. GU.
3119 The English souldiers standard. [London], printed, 1649.
       4°.* LT, OC, MR, E, EN; IU, MH, MM, WF, Y, ZAP.
3120 The English Spira. For Tho. Fabian, 1693. 8°. L, LIL, OC;
       IU, MH, MIU, RPJ, WF.
3121 —Second edition. —, 1693, 8°. NU.
3121A The English spy. For Sam. Norris, 1691. 12°. L, O; CLC,
       IU.
     English translation. 1650. See Sydenham, Cuthbert.
3121B The English travellers companion. For Tho. Basset &
       Rich. Chiswell, 1676. 8°. L.
3122 The English tyrants. Printed, 1649. 4°.* LT, O, LG; CH,
       CN, MH, MU, NU, WF, Y.
3123 The English villain: or the grand thief . . . Richard
       Hanam. For Iohn Andrews, [1656]. 8°.* LT, O.
     English villanies. 1648. See Dekker, Thomas.
3124 An English winding-sheet for the East-India manufac-
       tors. [London, 1700.] cap., 4°.* C, INDIA OFFICE; NC.
3124A The English womens chastity. [London], 1695. brs. L.
3125 Ἐνιαυτος: or, a course of catechising. Imprinted at Lon-
       don by James Cottrel, for Hen. Marsh, 1664. 8°. O, LNC,
       BLH; NU.
3126 —Second edition. For Francis Kirkman, 1674. 12°. T.C.I
       166. L, YM, E, DT.
3126A —"Second" edition. By J. C. for Fra. Kirkman, 1674.
       12°. L, O, CS; CH, CLC, NGT, WF, ZWT.
3127 Ενιαυτος τεραστιος. Mirabilis annvs, or the year of pro-
       digies. [London], printed, 1661. 4°. 64p. L, O, C, EN; CH,
       MH.
3127A —[Anr. ed.] —, 1661. 4°. 88pp. L, O, C, MR, EN, DT; CH,
       MH, MIU, NU, WF, Y.

Enigmaticall characters. [n.p.], 1658. See Flecknoe,
  Richard.
Enjoyment. [n.p., 1679.] See Rochester, John Wilmot,
  earl of.
Enlargement of a former catechism. 1641. See V., D.
3128 Enneades arithmeticae: the numbring nines. For J. Mox-
       on, 1684. 8°. T.C.II 84. L; CLC.
3128A Enniskillen, Connor Maguire, baron. The last speech-
       es and confession of. By Iane Coe. [1645.] 4°.* LT, O, C,
       EN, DT; CH, MH, WF, WU, Y.
3129 Enos, Walter. Alexipharmacon, or a soveraigne anti-
       dote. Waterford, by Thomas Bourke, 1644. 4°. DT.
3130 —The second part of the svrvey. Printed at Kilkenny,
       1646. 4°. C, DI; CH.
3131 —A survey of the articles of the late rejected peace con-
       cluded. Printed at Kilkenny, 1646. 4°. L, DN, DT.
     Ενωτικον, sive. Oxonii, 1675. See Smith, Thomas.
     Enquiry. See Inquiry.
     Inrichment of the weald of Kent. 1656. See Markham,
       Gervase.
3132 Entry cancelled.
     Ensuing declaration. Kilkenny, 1648. See Ireland.
3133 Ent, Sir George. Animadversiones in Malachiae
       Thrustoni M. D. diatrabam de respirationis usu
       primario. Typis, prostant vero venales, 1685. 8°. L, LWL;
       CNM, PCP, HC.
3134 —Αντιδιατριβη. Sive animadversiones in Malachiæ.
       Typis J. M. Impensis Guil. Bromwich, 1679. 8°. T.C.I
       343. L, O, C, LCP, GH, CD; MBA, NAM, TO, WSG, Y.
3134A ——[Anr. ed.] —, 1681. 8°. L; CU, PCP.
3135 —Apologia pro circulatione. Excudebat Rob. Young, 1641.
       8°. O, C, LCP, OM, DT; MMO, NCD, HC.
3135A ——[Anr. ed.] —, & venales extant apud Guil. Hope,
       1641. 8°. C, CS.
3136 —— Second edition ["circuitione"]. Typis M. F., im-
       pensis G. Kettilby, 1685. 8°. T.C.II 130. L, O, C, LCP, GH;
       CU, PCP, WSG.
3137 Entry cancelled.
     —Grounds of unity in religion. [n.p.], 1679. See title.
     Enter into thy closet. 1663. See Wetenhall, Edward, bp.
     Entertainment of the Lady Monk. [n.p.], 1660. See Yeok-
       ney, Walter.
3137A The entertainment perform'd at the Theatre-Royal.
       colop: For A. Baldwin, 1698. cap., 4°.* L, O; MH.
     Entertainments for Lent. 1661. See Caussin, Nicolas.
     Enthusiasm of the Church of Rome. 1688. See Wharton,
       Henry.
3137B Enthusiasmus divinus: the guidance of the Spirit of God.
       For the author, 1697. 8°.* Y.
     Enthusiasmus triumphatus, or. 1656. See More, Henry.
3138 An entire vindication of Dr. Sherlock. Printed, and are to
       be sold by Randal Taylor, 1691. 4°.* L, CT, MR, D, DT;
       CH, MH, NN, NRU, WF, Y.
     Entrance of Mazzarini. Oxford, 1657. See Tanner,
       Thomas, of Winchfield.
3138A An entrance of the form of sound words. By A. M. for
       Christopher Meredith, 1653. 8°. PL.

3138B Entretiens sur l'ancien état. *Imprimé à Londres, chez Richard Baldwin,* [1696]. 12°. L, O.

3139 **Entwhistle, Edmund.** A sermon preached . . . June 3, 1697. *By J. H. for Henry Mortlock and John Minshull,* 1698. 4°. L, OC, OM, CT, BAMB, LIU; CH, NS.

Envy and folly. 1695. *See* C., G.

3140 The envy of the Popish prelates. *Printed at London for I. C.,* 1642. 4°.* LT, C; Y.

Ephelia, *pseud. See* Philips, *Mrs.* Joan.

Ephemeris add annum. 1686. *See* Almanacs. Halley, Edmond.

Ephemeris Parliamentaria. 1654. *See* Fuller, Thomas.

3141 An emphemeris or diary. Shewing the interest. *Printed,* 1667. 8°. CT.

Ephesian and Cimmerian matrons. [n.p.], 1668. *See* Charleton, Walter.

3141A Epicedia: or funeral verses upon . . . Mr. Humphrey Colles. [*London?* 1661.] brs. O.

3142 Epicedion in Dorislaüm. [*London,* 1649.] brs. LT.

Epicedium nobilissimi. [n.p., 1646.] *See* Nisbet, John.

3143 An epicædium on the death of Her most serene Majesty Henrietta Maria. [*n.p.,* 1669.] brs. HH.

Epicedium, or, a funeral essay. 1695. *See* Ogden, Samuel.

3144 **Epictetus.** Enchiridion. *Cantabrigiæ, ex academicæ typographeo. Impensis G. Morden,* 1655. 8°. L, O, C, EN, DT; BN, CH, IU, MH, NU, PL, WF, Y.

3145 — —[Anr. ed.] *Typis Tho. Roycroft, impensis Rob. Beaumont,* 1659. 8°. LT, O, C, CT, E; CLC, IU, NC, WSC, Y.

3145A — —[Anr. ed.] *Typis Tho. Roycroft, impensis Joh. Shirley,* 1659. 8°. DUS; IU, PL.

3146 — —Enchiridion: una cum Cebetis tabula. *Typis Jacobi Flesher, prostant apud Guilielmum Morden,* 1670. 8°. L, O, C, EN, DT; BN, CLC, CN, MBP, PBL, PL, WF, WG, Y. (var.)

3147 — ʼΕπικτητου ʼεγχειριδιον. *Oxonii, e theatro Sheldoniano,* 1670. 8°. MADAN 2853. L, O, C, AN, MR, CD; CLC, CN, IU, PL, Y.

3148 — —[Anr. ed.] —, 1680. 12°. MADAN 3264. L, O, C, LCP, CT, YM; CH, CLC, IU, LC, NCU, PL, Y.

3149 —Epicteti Enchiridion made English. *By Ben. Griffin for Sam. Keble,* 1692. 8°. T.C.II 394. L, O, C, EN, DT; CH, CN, LC, MH, MU, WF, Y.

3150 — —[Anr. ed.] *For Sam. Keble, to be sold by Roger Clavel,* 1695. 8°. L, C, LLU; CLC, CN, NCU, NP, WF, Y.

3151 — —[Anr. ed.] —, 1697. 12°. L, O, LLU, DT; CH, CLC, CSU, IU, PU, TU, Y.

3151A — —[Anr. ed.] *Dublin, by Joseph Ray, to be sold by Patrick Campbell, Jacob Milner, and John Gill,* 1699. DN; CLC, OSU.

3152 —The life, and philosophy, of. *By T. R. for John Martyn,* 1670. 8°. T.C.I 31. L, O, LL, CT, AN, DU; CH, CN, OCI, WF, Y.

3153 —Epictetus his morals. *For Richard Sare, and Joseph Hindmarsh,* 1694. 8°. T.C.II 493. L, O, C, E, BQ; CH, CU, MH, TU, WF, Y.

3154 — —Second edition. *For Richard Sare.* 1700. 8°. T.C.III 160. L, O, C, AN, NPL, DT; CH, CU, PL, WF, Y.

Epictetus junior. 1670. *See* La Rochefoucauld, François; *duc de.*

3155 **Epicurus.** Epicvrvs's morals. *By W. Wilson for Henry Herringman,* 1656. 4°. LT, O, C, DU, BQ; CH, CU, MH, WF, Y.

3155A — —[Anr. ed.] *For H. H., and are to be sold by S. Miller,* 1670. 8°. T.C.I 28. L, O, LCP, LI, E; CN, CU, LC, NPT, WF.

3156 — —[Anr. ed.] *For H. Herringman,* 1670. 8°. DM; CH, CLC, IU, NC, WF, Y.

Epigram upon my lord All-pride. [1682.] *See* Rochester, John Wilmot, *earl of.*

Επιγραμματα. 1668. *See* Elys, Edmund.

3157 Entry cancelled.

Epigrammata sacra selecta. 1682. *See* Crashaw, Richard.

Epigrammatum delectus. 1683. *See* Nicole, Pierre.

Epigrams, divine. [n.p.], 1646. *See* Urquhart, *Sir* Thomas.

Epigrams of all sorts. 1669. *See* Flecknoe, Richard.

Epigrams upon the paintings. 1700. *See* Elsum, John.

Epilogue to Mr. Lacy's new play. [n.p., 1684.] *See* Haines, Joseph.

3158 Entry cancelled.

Epilogue to the French midwife's tragedy. 1688. *See* Settle, Elkanah.

Epinicia Carolina, or. 1660. *See* W., S.

3158A Επινιχιον. Sive invictissimi principis. [*London?* 1690.] cap., fol.* L, O; MB, Y.

3159 Epipapresbyter, grand-child to Smectymnuus. *By George Croom,* 1685. brs. L, O, HH; CH, MH, NCD, Y.

Episcopacy and presbytery. Oxford, 1644. *See* Ferne, Henry.

Episcopacie not abivred. [n.p.], 1641. *See* Maxwell, John, *abp.*

Episcopal almanack. 1674. *See* Almanacs. W., W.

3160 Episcopal government and the honour of the present bishops. *For Henry Brome,* 1679. 4°.* L, O, LL, MR, EN; CH, CN, NU, WF, Y.

3161 —[Anr. ed.] *Dublin, reprinted* 1679. 4°.* DIX 175. CD, DT.

Episcopal government instituted. 1641. *See* Rollock, Robert.

Episcopall inheritance. Oxford, 1641. *See* Langbaine, Gerard.

Episcopal jurisdiction. Dublin, [1671]. *See* Stanhope, Arthur.

3162 **Episcopius, Simon.** Opera theologica. Second edition. *Ex officina Mosis Pit.* 1678. fol. T.C.I 306. L, O, C, DUS, EN, CD; IU, MBP, MH, NIC, Y.

3162A — —"Second" edition. *Hagae-Comitis, et vaeneunt Londini,* 1678. fol. LSD.

3163 —The Popish labyrinth. *For Francis Smith,* 1673. 8°. T.C.I 142. L, O, C, LLL, E; CH, WF.

Epistle apologetical. [n.p.], 1674. *See* Cressy, Hugh Paulin.

Epistle by the life. [n.p.], 1665. *See* Greene, Thomas.

3164 An epistle by way of testimony, to Friends. colop: *For Thomas Northcott,* 1690. fol.* LF, OC; PH.

Epistle congratulatory. Oxford, 1684. *See* Corbet, John.

Epistle containing a salutation. [n.p., 1682.] See Penn, William.

Epistle declaratory. [n.p.], 1657. See Leyburn, George.

Epistle directed to all. 1641[2]. See Bernard, Richard.

Epistle for the strengthening. [n.p., 1670.] See Fell, Leonard.

Epistle from our monethly meeting. [n.p., 1692.] See Rigge, Ambrose.

Epistle from the meeting. [n.p., 1696.] See Bealing, Benjamin.

Epistle from the people. [n.p., 1668.] See Fox, George.

Epistle from the spirit. [n.p.], 1663. See Smith, William.

Epistle general containing. [n.p.], 1664. See Bayly, William.

Epistle general to them. 1660. See Fox, George.

Epistle in the love of God. 1696. See Fisher, Abigail.

3164aA An epistle of a Catholique to his friend a Protestant. [n p.], printed in the year, 1659. 4°.* BSM, DUS; CLC, WF.

Epistle of caution. 1681. See Taylor, Christopher.

3164A An epistle of caution to all Friends professing. T. Sowle, 1698. 8°.* L, LF; PH.

Epistle of consolation. [n.p., 1666.] See Whitehead, George.

Epistle of farewell. [n.p., 1699.] See Penn, William.

Epistle of love and good advice. [n.p., 1683.] See Docwra, Anne.

Epistle of love, and of consolation. 1661. See White, Dorothy.

Epistle of love to Friends. [n.p., 1680.] See Townsend, Theophila.

Epistle of the barbarous assault. 1660. See N.

Epistle of the monthly . . . meeting. [n.p., 1693.] See Bealing, Benjamin.

Epistle or letter from a prvdent . . . scholler. [n.p.], 1646. See W., N.

3165 An epistle to a member of Parliament concerning Mr. George Oldner's invention. [n.p.], printed, 1699. brs. L, MC; CH.

Epistle to all Christians. 1682. See Fox, George.

Epistle to all friends. [n.p.], 1674.] See Wollrich, Humphry.

Epistle to all people. 1657. See Fox, George.

Epistle to all that's young. [n.p.], 1672.] See Crook, John.

Epistle to all the Christian magistrates. 1659. See Gould, Ann.

Epistle to all young. 1696. See Love, John.

Epistle to be communicated. [n.p.], 1677.] See Dirrecks, Geertrude Niessen.

Epistle to be read. [n.p.], 1666. See Fox, George.

Epistle to Charles Montague. [n.p.], 1691.] See Stepney, George.

Epistle to Friends. [n.p.], 1665?] See Parker, Alexander.

Epistle to Friends for them. [n.p.], 1679.] See Fox, George.

3165A An epistle to Friends, given forth from Leinster. [London], printed, 1699. 8°.* LF, DN, DT; PH, PSC.

Epistle to Friends, in the truth. [n.p.], 1676.] See Taylor, Christopher.

Epistle to magistrates. [1685.] See T., W.

3166 Entry cancelled.

Epistle to Mr. Dryden. [1688.] See Rymer, Thomas.

3167 An epistle to Sr. Richard Blackmore, occasion'd by the new session of the poets. For A. Baldwin, 1700. fol.* CS; CLC, IAU, MB, MH, TU, Y.

Epistle to the authour. [n.p.], 1663. See Canes, John Vincent.

Epistle to the beloved. 1660. See B., E.

Epistle to the flock. [n.p., 1670.] See Smith, William.

Epistle to the flock. [n.p.], 1674. See Tomlinson, William.

Epistle to the Greeks. 1661. See Perrot, John.

Epistle to the houshold. 1682. See Fox, George.

Epistle to the learned Manasseh Ben Israel. 1650. See S., E.

Epistle to the monthly. [n.p., 1692.] See Crisp, Stephen.

3168 An epistle to the reader. The end of this print. colop: By Henry Hills and John Field, 1654. 4°.* LT; CH, CN, MM, NU, WF.

Epistle to the Right Honourable Charles Earl of Dorset. 1690. See Halifax, Charles Montague, earl of.

3168A An epistle to the right honourable Charles Montagu, . . . upon the general peace. For E. Whitlock, 1698. fol. T.C.III 55. L.

Epistle to the whole flock. [n.p., 1676.] See Willsford, John.

Epistles of Phalaris. 1699. See Whately, Solomon.

Epistles to the King. 1682. See Wycherley, William.

Epistola ad H. Hody. 1691. See Grascombe, Samuel.

3169 Epistola ad regiam societatem Londinensem. Veneunt apud Rand. Taylor, 1693. 4°.* L, O, LLP, DU; CLC, HC.

3170 Entry cancelled.

Epistola medio-Saxonica. 1653. See Wingfield, Augustus.

3170A Epistola studiosi Oxoniensis. [London?] Anno 1643. 4°.* L, O; MH.

Epistola veridica. 1659. See Dury, John.

Epistolæ Ho-Elianæ. 1645. See Howell, James.

3170B Epistolæ obscurorum virorum. Apud editorem, [1680]. 12°. L, EN; NIC, RBU, WF, WG, Y.

3170C —[Anr. ed.] —, 1689. 12°. L, O, GU; CB, CN, MBP, MIU, NSU, Y.

3170D The epitaph of the most renowned . . . Bedloe. [London, 1680.] brs. CN.

Epitaph on Don Quicksot. [n.p., 1694.] See Guidott, Thomas.

3171 An epitaph on Mr. Francis Wolley. [London, 1659/60.] brs. C; MH.

3172 An epitaph on Mr. John Smith. By G. Croom, 1684. brs. L, O; CLC, NCD.

3172A Epitaph on the death of . . . Sr. Rodger Hog. [Edinburgh, 1700.] brs. EN.

3172B An epitaphe on the king. [London, 1649.] brs. Y.

Epitaph on the late deceased. 1655. See Longe, J.

3172C An epitaph. On the worst, and most wicked . . . C. I. By G. L. for the author, 1681. brs. L.

3172D An epitaph upon a late worthy member . . . John Upton. [n.p., 1641.] brs. L.

3173   An epitaph upon His late Majesty, King Charles the II. [*London*], *for P. Brooksby*, 1685. brs. L, O; CLC, MH, WF.

Epitaph upon Sir Kenelm Digby. 1665. *See* F., R.

Epitaph upon the solemn league. 1661. *See* H., E.

Epitaph upon Thomas late Lord Fairfax. [n.p., 1680.] *See* Buckingham, George Villiers, *duke of*.

Epitaph. Within this sacred vault. [n.p., 1649.] *See* B., A.

Epitaphe de Charles Second. 1685. *See* Brevint, Daniel.

3173A   Epitaphia Thomæ Freke. [*London*], 1657. fol.* OC.

3174   Entry cancelled.

Epitaphium Edwardi comitis Sandwich. 1672. *See* Memoriæ sacrum Edvardi.

3174A   Epitaphium herois illustrissimi Roberti Comitis de Warwick. [*London?* 1658.] brs. MH.

3174B   Epitaphium honorabilis . . . Nathanelis Brent. 1652. brs. OC.

3174C   Epitaphium nobilissimi Henrici. [*London*, 1649.] brs. L.

Epitaphium Roberti Blakii. [n.p.], 1658. *See* Fisher, Payne.

Epithalamium and well-wishings. [n.p.], 1686. *See* F., G.

Epithalamium mysticum. Edinburgi, 1677. *See* Fergusson, David.

3174D   Epithalamium on the auspicious match betwixt . . . the Earl of Wigtown. [*Edinburgh?* 1698.] brs. EN.

Epithalamium: or. 1650. *See* Lawrence, Leonard.

3175   Epithalamium. Or, a wedding song. [*n.p.*, 1689.] brs. HH.

Epithalamium upon the auspicious nuptials. [n.p.], 1658. *See* C., J.

3176   An epithalamium upon the happy nuptials of Sᵣ John Busby. [*London*, 1668.] brs. L.

3177   Entry cancelled.

Epithalamium upon the marriage of Capt. William Bedloe. 1679. *See* Duke, Richard.

3178   The epitome of a new man. *For the author*, 1659. 4°. O.

Epitome of all the lives. 1639 [*i.e.*, 1693]. *See* Crouch, Nathaniel.

Epitome of ecclesiastical history. 1683. *See* Shirley, John.

3178A   Epitome of English orthography. *Boston, by B. Green*, 1697. 8°.* EVANS 782. MWA.

3178B   An epitome of gospel mystery. [*London*, 1700.] brs. MH.

Epitome of grammar. Oxford, 1668. *See* Barbour, John.

Epitome of history. 1661. *See* C., H.

Epitome of most experienced. [n.p.], 1651. *See* Wood, Owen.

Epitome of sacred scriptvre. 1644. *See* Belke, Thomas.

Epitome of the art. 1669. *See* Blagrave, Joseph.

3178C   The epitome of the Bible. *For Jonathan Robinson*, 1678. 12°. T.C.I 311. LLL.

Epitome of the whole art. 1692. *See* Moxon, Joseph.

3179   An epitomie of tyranny in the Island of Guernzey. [*n.p.*], *printed*, 1659. 4°.* LT; CSS, WF, Y.

3180   No entry.

Epitome or briefe discoverie. 1646. *See* Leighton, Alexander.

3181   An epode to his worthy friend Mr. John Dryden, to advise him not to answer two malicious pamphlets. colop: *By J. Grantham*, 1683. brs. L, O, LLP, EN; CH, CLC.

3182   Eppellatio supremi concilii confœderatorum Catholicorum. *Kilkeniæ*, 1648. 4°.* DN.

3183   Epulæ Thyesteæ: or, the thanksgiving-dinner. *Printed*, 1648 [*i.e.*, 1649]. 4°.* LT, OC, LNC; CH, MH, MIU, TU, WF.

3184   —[Anr. ed.] —, 1649. 4°.* L, CT, MR; CN, CSS, MH, Y.

Equal ballance. 1659. *See* Wastfield, Robert.

Equallity of the ministery. [n.p.], 1641. *See* F., D.

3185   Equitable and necessary considerations. *For Thomas Underhill*, 1642. 4°.* LT, O, AN, LLU, YM; CLC, MH, MHS, WF, Y.

3186   The eqvity of the solemne leagve. [*London*], *for John Field*, 1644. 4°.* LT, O, CJ; MH, MIU, NU, WF, Y.

3187   **Erasmus, Desiderius.** Adagiorum. *Oxoniæ, typis W. Hall, & venales prostant apud Thomas Bowman & Amos Curteyne*, 1666. 12°. MADAN 2741. L, O, C, DC, ENC; CH, IU, MBC, VC, Y.

3187A   ——[Anr. ed.] *Oxoniæ, typis W. Hall & venales prostant apud Tho. Bowman*, 1666. 12°. O; LC, MM, WF.

3187B   ——[Anr. ed.] *Oxoniæ, typis W. Hall, & venales prostant apud Amos Curteyne*, 1666. 12°. CLC, MH.

3187C   —Colloquia. *Excudebat Rogerus Daniel*, 1655. 12°. MB.

3187D   ——[Anr. ed.] *Dublinii, typis Andreæ Crooke*, [1690]. 12°. L.

3188–89   Entries cancelled. Ghosts.

3190   —The colloquies. *By E. T. and R. H. for H. Brome, B. Tooke, and T. Sawbridge*, 1671. 8°. T.C.I 73. L, O, C, AN, LLU, A; CH, CN, MBP, TU, WF, Y.

3191   —Colloquiorum. *In ædibus Milonis Flesher*, 1643. 8°. L, O, CT.

3191A   ——[Anr. ed.] —, 1649. 8°. L, O.

3191B   ——[Anr. ed.] *In ædibus Iacobi Flesher*, 1653. 8°. O; CH, IU, MH.

3192   ——[Anr. ed.] —, 1657. 8°. DT; IU.

3192A   ——[Anr. ed.] —, 1662. 8°. L, OC; CLC.

3193   ——[Anr. ed.] —, 1666. 8°. O; MH, Y.

3193A   ——[Anr. ed.] —, 1670. 8°. O, CS, AN; CLC, IU, NP.

3193B   ——[Anr. ed.] *In ædibus Eliz. Flesher*, 1672. 8°. LW, BSM; NIC.

3194   ——[Anr. ed.] —, 1676. 8°. L, D, DT; IU, MIU, WC.

3194aA   ——[Anr. ed.] *For John Seymour, sold by Peter Parker and Thomas Guy*, 1678. 12°. O, MR.

3194A   ——[Anr. ed.] *In ædibus Eliz. Flesher*, 1683. 8°. T.C.II 52. L, O, LLL; CN, IU, WF.

3194B   ——[Anr. ed.] —, 1688. 8°. L, O, DC; IU.

3195   ——[Anr. ed.] *Impensis Guil. Freeman*, 1692. 8°. T.C.II 432. L, O, C, LL; IU.

3195A   ——[Anr. ed.] —, 1696. 8°. O, GU; CLC.

3196   ——[Anr. ed.] —, 1697. 8°. L; CH.

3196A   ——[Anr. ed.] —, 1699. 8°. O, NPL.

3196B   ——[Anr. ed.] —, 1700. 8°. O, DL, AN; NIC.

3197   —Des. Erasmi . . . De utraq, verborum. *Impensis Johannes Wright*, [1650?]. 12°. L, O, C, LSC; CH, CLC, CSU, IU.

3197A   ——[Anr. ed.] *Impensis Samuelis Speed*, 1660. 12°. O, CK, LIU; NIC.

3197B   ——[Anr. ed.] *Impensis Johanis Wright*, 1668. 12°. O; IU, WF.

3197C — —[Anr. ed.] *Impensis M. Wotton & G. Conyers*, 1685. 12°. MIU.

3198 —Des. Erasmi Roterodami. Dialogus, cui titulus Ciceronianus. *Oxoniæ, typis L. Lichfield*, 1693. *Prostant venales apud Christoph. Coningsby . . . Londinensem.* 12°. L, O, C, AN, LVD, MAU; CH, CN, MH, MU, TO, WF.

3198A —Dicta sapientum. *Edinburgh, Society of Stationers*, 1665. 8°. ALDIS 1789.7. EH.

3198B —Dicta sapientium e Græcis. *Edinburgi, excudebat Hæres Andreæ Anderson*, 1684. 8°. GU.

3199 — —[Anr. ed.] *Glasguæ, ex typis Roberti Sanders*, 1693. 4°.* ALDIS 3297.5. GU.

3199A — —[Anr. ed.] *Edinburgi, apud Andreæ Anderson hæredes et successores*, 1695. 8°. ALDIS 3460.1. GU.

3200 —Enchiridion militis Christiani. *Cantabrigiæ, ex officina Joh. Hayes, impensis Guil. Graves, jun.*, 1685. 12°. T.C.II 147. L, O, C, CT, AN, MAU, CD; BN, CH, CN, PL, WF, Y.

3201 —Epistolarum. *Excudebant M. Flesher & R. Young*, 1642. *Prostant apud Cornelium Bee.* fol. L, O, C, EN, DT; CH, CU, MH, PL, WF, Y.

3201A — —[Anr. ed.] *Excudebant M. Flesher & R. Young*, 1642. *Sumptibus Adriani Vlacq.* fol. O, C, CM, BR, NE; CLC, CN, NCU, PL, PU, VC.

3201B —Epitome colloquiorum. *Typis Johannis Redmayne*, 1673. 12°. O.

3202 — —[Anr. ed.] *Glascuæ, excudebat Robertus Sanders*, 1674. sixes.* ALDIS 2021.3 GU, HG.

3202A — —[Anr. ed.] —["*Glasguæ*"], 1684. sixes.* WF.

3202B — —[Anr. ed.] *Edinburgh, ex officina Societatis Bibliopolarum*, 1691. 8°. ALDIS 3142.7. EN.

3203 —Familiarum colloqui. 1649. 8°. LW, DC.

3203A — —[Anr. ed., "colloquia."] *Ex officina Rogeri Danielis*, 1652. 12°. L.

3204 Entry cancelled.
 —Familiarum colloqui. 1657. See Colloquiorum.

3204A — —[Anr. ed.] —, 1657. 12°. CM.

3204B — —Eleventh edition. *Typis Johannis Redmayne*, 1673. 12°. AN.

3204C — —Twelfth edition. *Ex officina J. Redmayne*, 1677. 12°. CS.

3204D — —Thirteenth edition. *Excudebat S. R. & venales prostant apud Dorman Newman, & apud Thomam Cockeril*, 1681. 12°. DUS.

3204E — —Fourteenth edition. *Excudebat R. R. & venales prostant apud Dorman Newman, & apud Thomam Cockerill*, 1686. 12°. IU.

3204F — —"Fourteenth" edition. —, 1692. 12°. Y.

3205 Entry cancelled.
 [–] *Jvlivs Secundus. Dialogvs anonymii. Oxonii*, 1680. *See* Julius II, *pope.*

3205A —A manual for a Christian soldier. *For William Rogers*, 1687. 12°. T.C.II 175. L, O, OC, LSC, EN; CH, CLC, IU, OCI, WF, Y.

3206 —Moriæ encomium. *Oxoniæ, typis. W. Hall, impensis F. Oxlad sen. & F. Oxlad jun.*, 1633 [i.e., 1663]. 12°. MADAN 2638. L, O, C, CK, AN, P, DT; CH, CN, MH, TU, WF, Y.

3207 — —[Anr. ed.] *Oxoniæ, typis. W. Hall prostant venales apud S. Bolton*, 1668. 12°. MADAN 2799. L, O, C, AN, DU, ENC; CH, IU, MH, NU, PL, Y.

3208 —Moriæ encomium; or the praise of folly. *For William Leak*, 1668. 8°. L, O, LSC, CCH, LLU; CH, CN, MH, PBL, WF, Y.

3208A —The Pope shut out of Heaven. *Sold by Roger Vaughan, and J. Williams junior*, 1673. 4°.* T.C.I 154. L, LW; CN.

3208B — —[Anr. ed.] *For Roger Vaughan, and are to be sold by the book-sellers*, 1673. 4°.* CT; IU, WF.

3208C —Preparatio ad mortem. *For Samuel Keble*, 1700. 12°. D.

3208D —Select colloquies. *For R. Bentley and R. Sare*, 1689. 8°. O, OC, OM; NCD.

3209 —Seven new colloquies. *For Charles Brome*, 1699. 8°. T.C.III 125. L, O, AN; CLC, MH, NU, Y, ZWT.

3210 —Twenty select colloquies. *By Tho. Newcomb for Henry Brome*, 1680. 8°. T.C.I 374. L, O, C, AN, NE, EN; CH, MH, TU, WF, Y. (var.)

3211 — —[Anr. ed.] *By Tho. Newcomb, for Henry Brome*, 1689. 12°. NP, NU.

3212 — —[Anr. ed.] *For Charles Brome*, 1699. 8°. T.C.III 159. L, O, C; CN, MBP, MH, NCD, NP, WF, Y.

3213 —Twenty two select colloquies. Second edition. *For R. Bentley, and R. Sare*, 1689. 8°. T.C.II 296. L, O, C, LVF, GC; CH, CLC, CU, MIU, Y.

3214 — —Third edition. *For R. Sare and H. Hindmarsh, sold by W. Davis*, 1699. 8°. L, O, C, CT, BLH, DM; CH, CLC, CN, LC, MH, NP, TU, Y.

3215 —Witt against wisdom. *Oxford, by L. Lichfield, for Anthony Stephens*, 1683. 8°. L, O, C, LL, P; CH, CN, LC, MH, TO, WF, Y.

3216 Erasmus redivivus. Wherein. *Printed*, 1699. 4°. DT; INU, OCI, WF.

Erastophil, *pseud.*

Erastus, Thomas. The nullity of church censures. *For G. L.*, 1659. 8°. LT, C, DU, E, DT; CLC, NPT, NU.

3218 —A treatise of excommunication. *For L. Curtis*, 1682. 4°. L, O, C, LLP, BP, EC; CSS, IU, MH, MIU, NAM, WF.

Erastus junior. 1660. See Lewgar, John.

3219 Erastvs: or, the Roman prince. *For Dorman Newman and Benj. Alsop*, 1684. 8°. T.C.II 71. L, O; CH, CLC, CN.

Erastus senior. [n.p.], 1662. See Lewgar, John.

3220 **Eratt, William.** Anabaptism considered. *By W. B. for A. and J. Churchill and for Robert Clark in York*, 1700. 4°.* BAMB; CLC.

3221 **Erbery, William.** The armies defence. *By T. N. for Giles Calvert*, 1648. 4°.* LT, DT; IU, ZAP.

3222 —The babe of glory. *By J. C. for Giles Calvet [sic]*, 1653. 4°. LT, C, ORP, AN; Y.

3223 —The Bishop of London. *Printed at London*, 1652 [3]. 4°.* LT, C, LG, AN, CPL, DU, DT; MH, NU, Y.

3224 —A call to the churches. *Printed at London*, 1653. 4°. LT; MU.

3225 No entry.
 —General epistle to the Hebrews. 1652. *See* —Bishop of London.

3226 —The grand oppressor. *By G. D. for Giles Calvert*, 1652. 4°. LT, AN, MR.

3227 —The great earthquake. *For Giles Calvert*, 1654. 4°. LT, O, OP, AN; NU, WF, Y.

3228 —Jack Pudding: or, a minister made a black-pudding. *Printed at London*, 1654. 4°.* LT.

3229 —The Lord of Hosts. *By Tho. Newcomb for Giles Calvert*, 1648. 4°.* LT, CM, CT, BBN, MR, DT; CH, NU.

3230 —The madman's plea. *Printed*, 1653. 4°.* LT, ORP, AN.

3231 —The man of peace. *Imprinted at London, by James Cottrel*, 1654. 4°.* LT; MH, MWA.

3232 —Ministers for tythes. *By J. C. for Giles Calvet [sic]*, 1653. 4°.* LT, LSC, MR; CH, MH, Y.

3233 —A monstrous dispute. *By J. C. for Giles Calvet [sic]*, [1653]. 4°.* LT, LG; MH, NU, Y.

3234 —Nor truth, nor error. *[London], printed*, 1647. 4°.* MADAN 1953. LT, CT, MR, YM; NU, WF, Y.

3234A — —[Anr. ed.] *For G. Calvert*, 1647. 4°.* CT.

3235 Entry cancelled.
       —North star. 1653. *See* —Babe of glory.

3236 —An olive leaf. *Imprinted at London, by J. Cottrel*, 1654. 4°.* LT, CS, MR; MH, MWA, Y.

3237 Entry cancelled.
       [–] Περιαμμα επιδημιον or, vulgar errours. 1659. *See* Walker, Obadiah.

3238 —The sword doubled. *By G. D. for Giles Calvert*, 1652. 4°. LT, AN, DT.

3239 —The testimony of. *For Giles Calvert*, 1658. 4°. L, O, C, LCL, E, AN; IU, NHC, NU, TO, WF.

       Ercker, Lazarus. Fleta minor. 1683. *See* Pettus, *Sir* John.

3240 Entry cancelled.
       Ερευνολητης. Essay, on infant baptism. 1674. *See* Blinman, Richard.

3240A **Erlam, [John].** Glad tidings of the everlasting gospel. *Printed by J. T. for author*, 1659. 4°. L.

3241 **[Ernulfus.]** The Popes dreadful curse. colop: *Printed and are to be sold by L. C.*, 1681. brs. L, O, OB, HH; CH, CN, PU, Y.

3241A — —[Anr. ed.] *Dublin, reprinted for Joseph Howes*, 1681. brs. DT; MH.
       Eromena: or. 1683. *See* Chamberlayne, William.

3242 Ερωτοπολις. The present state of Betty-land. *For Tho. Fox*, 1684. 12°. T.C.II 103. L, O, OP, DT; CH, CN, MH, WF, Y.

3243 **Erra Pater.** A prognostication for ever. *By Richard Bishop, [after 1648]*. 8°.* O; LC.

3243A — —[Anr. ed.] *For Robert Scot, Thomas Basset, and Richard Chiswel, and the executor of J. Wright*, 1686. 8°.* LC.

3243B — —[Anr. ed.] *For Thomas Basset, Richard Chiswell, Samuel Smith, Benjamin Walford, and George Conyers*, 1695. 8°. PL, WF.

3244 — —[Anr. ed.] *For R. Chiswel, B. Walford, and G. Conyers*, 1700. 8°.* L.

3245 — Erra Pater's prophesy. *[London], for Iames Norris*, [1683]. brs. L, OP; CLC.

3245A —Erra Pater's usefull and necessary observations. *[London], for P. Brooksby, J. Deacon, J. Blare, J. Back, [1691]*. 8°. OC.
       Errata to the Protestant Bible. 1688. *See* Ward, Thomas.

3246 **E[rrington], A[nthony].** Catechistical discovrses. *Paris, by P. Targa*, 1654. 8°. O, C, BSM, DT; CH, CN, MH, TU, WF, WG, Y.

3247 **Errol, John,** *earl of.* Advertisement from. *[Aberdeen, Forbes, younger]*, 1680. brs. ALDIS 2182. AC.
       Errour non-plust. [n.p.], 1673. *See* Sergeant, John.

3248 Errors appearing in the proceedings in the House of Peers. 1661. 4°. L, BC.
       Errors of the Church of Rome. 1687. *See* Whitby, Daniel.
       Errors of the common catechisme. 1645. *See* Hughes, Lewis.

3249 **Erskine, David.** Disputatio juridica. *Edinburgi, ex officina typographica hæredum Andreæ Anderson*, 1698. 4°.* ALDIS 3749. EN.

3249A **Erskine, John.** Disputatio juridica, de transactionibus. *Edinburgi, ex officina typographica hæredum Andreæ Anderson*, 1700. 4°. GU.

3249B **Erskine, William.** Reasons offered to the consideration of his Grace, . . . by several salt-masters. *[Edinburgh, 1696.]* brs. EN.

3250 **Erswicke, John.** A briefe note of the benefits . . . of fish-dayes. *For Tho: Bankes*, 1642. 4°.* LT, O, C, LG, LUG; CH, MH, MM, WF.
       Eruditionis ingenuæ. Oxoniæ, 1657. *See* Zouche, Richard.

3251 Entry cancelled.
       Eschallers de la More, Thomas. *See* Delamore, Thomas de Eschallers.

3252 **Escholt, Michael Peterson.** Geologia Norvegica. Or, a brief instructive remembrancer. *By J. H. for S. Thomson*, 1663. 8°. L, O, C, OR; CLC.

3253 **Espagne, Jean d'.** Abbrege du sermon funebre sur . . . Philippe Comte de Pembroke. *Londres, par Tho. Newcomb*, 1650. 4°.* CH.

3254 —The abridgement of a sermon preached . . . Septemb. 12. 1648. *By Ruth Raworth for Tho. Whitaker*, 1648. 8°. LW, CM, E, EN; CH.

3254A —Advertissment touchant la fraction . . . du pain. *Londres, chez Ruth Raworth pour Tho. Whitaker*, 1648. 4°.* BN, CH.

3255 —Yr arfer o weddi yr arglwydd. *Gan Joa. Streater, tros Philip Chetwinde*, 1658. 12°. L, AN.

3256 —Considerations representée en un sermon. *Par Tho. Newcomb, pour Antoine Williamson*, 1652. 12°. LT, LW; CH.

3257 —The eating of the body of Christ. *By T. N. for Anthony Williamson*, 1652. 8°. LT, C, LSC, LW; MH, NU.

3258 Entry cancelled.
       [–] Enchyridion. 1651. *See* Espagnet, Jean d'.

3259 —Essay des merveilles de Diev. . . . Première partie. *A Londres, chez A. Williamson*, 1657. 8°. L, O; CLC.

3259A — —[Anr. ed.] *Imprima par Guill. Godbid, pour H. Herringman*, 1662. 8°. CASTLE ASHBY; CLC, WF.

3260 —An essay of the wonders of God. *By William Godbid for Henry Herringman*, 1662. 8°. L, O, C, LCL, P; CH, CLC, MH, PAP, Y, AVP.

3261 —Examen de xvii. maximes Judaiques. *A Londres, par A. Williamson*, 1657. 8°. L, O; CLC.

3262 —The harmony of the Old and New Testament. *Printed and are to be sold by Thomas Malthus*, 1682. 8°. T.C.I 503. L, O, CT, EC, EN.

3262A —The joyfull convert. *By I. Leach*, 1658. 12°.* L; WF.

3263 —New observations upon the creed. *By Ruth Raworth, for Thomas Whitaker*, 1647. 8°. L, O, LW, CM, EN.

3263A —New observations upon the decalogue. *By Thomas Newcomb, for Joshua Kirton*, 1652. 8°. LW, CM.

3264 —Novelles observations sur le decalogue. *A Londres, chez Tho. Newcomb pour Tho. Whitaker*, 1649. 8°. O, LNC, DT.

3265 —Novvelles observations sur le symbole de la foy. *A Londres, chez R. R. pour Thomas Whitaker*, 1647. 8°. O, CM, DT; CH.

3266 Entry cancelled.
—Observations on the decalogue. 1652. *See* New observations.

3267 —Popvlar errors. *For Tho. Whittaker*, 1648. 12°. L, O, LW, CS, AN, NE; CH, CLC.

3268 Entry cancelled.
—Sermon on the eclipse. 1652. *See* Considerations.

3269 —Shibbóleth, ou, reformation. *Imprimé à Londres, chez Thomas Maxey, pour Antoine Williamson*, 1653. 8°. L, CM, LLU.

3270 —Shibbóleth or the reformation. *By T. W. for Anthony Williamson*, 1655. 8°. LT, C, LW, P, DT; MH, Y.

3271 — —[Anr. ed.] *Printed*, 1656. 8°. NU.

3272 —L'usage de l'oraison dominicale. *Imprimé à Londres, chez R. R. pour Richard Whitaker*, 1646. 12°. LT; CH.

3273 —The use of the Lords Prayer. *By Ruth Raworth, for Richard Whitaker*, 1646. Sixes. O; CH.

3274 — —[Anr. ed.] *Edinburgh, by the heir of Andrew Anderson*: 1688. 8°.* ALDIS 2759.6. EN.

3275 — —[Anr. ed.] *Edinburgh, printed*, 1689. 12°.* ALDIS 2981. EN; NU.

3276 [–] Use of the Lord's Prayer vindicated. *Edinburgh, J. Reid*, 1680. 8°. ALDIS 2234. EN.

3276A [Espagnet, Jean d'.] Enchyridion physicæ restitutæ; or, the summary. *By W. Bentley, to be sold by W. Sheares, and Robert Tutchein*. 1651. 12°. O, LWL, OC, GU; CLC, MH, PU, TU, WF, WU.

3277 [Esprit, Jacques.] The falshood of human virtue. *For Timothy Child*, 1691. 8°. L, O, C, LSC, MR; CLC, CU, NU, WF, Y.

Esprit du Christianisme. 1694. *See* Abbadie, Jacques.

Esquemelin. *See* Exquemelin.

3277A The esquire's tragedy. *[London], for J. Blare*, [1684?]. brs. CM.

3277B An essay against simony. *For R. Clavell*, 1694. 4°. T.C.II 519. NE.

3277C An essay against the transportation . . . of men to the plantations. *Edinburgh*, 1699. fol.* ALDIS 3846.5. LUG.

3278 Entry cancelled.
Essay concerning a vacuum. 1697. *See* Jackson, Joseph.

3279 An essay concerning adepts. *By J. Mayos, to be sold by J. Nutt*, 1698. 8°. L, O, C, LCP; CLC, CN.

Essay concerning church government. [n.p.], 1689. *See* Cunningham, Alexander.

Essay concerning critical. 1698. *See* Rymer, Thomas.

3280 An essay concerning friendly reproof. *For R. Cumberland*, 1696. 12°. L, C, OC, NE, RPL; CH, CLC, CN, NU, WF, Y.

Essay concerning humane understanding. 1690. *See* Locke, John.

Essay concerning liberty. Dublin, 1699. *See* H., J.

Essay concerning obedience. 1694. *See* Tindal, Matthew.

Essay concerning preaching. 1678. *See* Glanvill, Joseph.

Essay concerning the divine right. 1700. *See* Leslie, Charles.

3280A An essay concerning the obedience to the supreme powers. *For R. Baldwin*, 1694. 4°. T.C.II 482. L.

Essay concerning the power. 1697. *See* Tindal, Matthew.

Essay concerning toleration. 1690. *See* Locke, John.

Essay for advancement. 1651. *See* Dymock, Cressy.

3281 An essay for lowering the gold. *For Timothy Goodwin*, 1696. 4°.* L, O, LUG, CT, DT; CH, INU, MH, NC, WF, Y.

Essay for reformation. [1699.] *See* T., M.

Essay for regulating. 1696. *See* Vickaris, A.

Essay for the conversion. Dublin, 1698. *See* Coxe, Sir Richard.

Essay for the discovery and discouraging of the new spring schism. 1652. *See* Henden, Simon.

Essay for the discovery of some new geometrical problems. 1697. *See* Keith, George.

3282 An essay for the raising a national fishery. *Printed and are to be sold by J. Nut*, 1700. 4°.* L, O; CH, MH, NC, WF, Y.

3283 An essay for the regvlation of the practice of physick. *For Tho. Taylor*, 1673. 4°.* T.C.I 134. L, O, OR, CCA, GU; MIU.

3284 Entry cancelled. Date: [1711?]

3284A An essay how to raise above six hundred thousand pounds. *[London? 1696.]* brs. L.

Essay in defence of the female sex. 1696. *See* Astell, Mary.

Essay in morality. 1682. *See* Bright, George.

Essay (in verse). 1665. *See* Wild, Robert.

3285 An essay in verse on the fourth day of November. *[London? 1690.]* fol.* MR.

3286 Entry cancelled.
Essay of a character. 1700. *See* Tate, Nahum.

Essay of afflictions. [n.p.], 1647. *See* Duncon, John.

Essay of moral rules. 1677. *See* M., J.

3286A An essay of the form and constitution of a particular Christian church. Third edition. *For John Marshall*, 1700. Sixes. T.C.III 204. CH.

Essay of the great effects. 1685. *See* Boyle, Robert.

3286B An essay of the profits incident to the mayoralty of London. *[London? 1695.]* brs. CM; MH.

Essay of transmigration. 1692. *See* Bulstrode, Whitelock. Μετεμψυχωσις.

3287 No entry.

Essay on grief. Oxford, 1695. *See* W., R.

3288 An essay on hypocrisie. *By J. C. and Freeman Collins, for Charles Yeo in Exon,* 1683. 4°.* L, WCA; CLC.

Essay on the certainty. 1698. *See* Sheeres, *Sir* Henry.

3289 Entry cancelled.

Essay on the coin. 1695. *See* Praed, John.

Essay on the East-India trade. 1696. *See* Davenant, Charles.

Essay on the fleet. 1672. *See* D., J.

Essay on the memory. 1695. *See* Burnet, Gilbert, *bp.*

Essay on wool. 1693. *See* Child, *Sir* Josiah.

3290 An essay; or, a narrative of the two great fights. *By E. C. for Henry Brome,* 1666. fol.* MH, TU, Y.

3291 An essay, or, modest proposal, . . . to encrease the number of people. [*London?* 1693.] 4°.* LUG; MH, Y.

Essay, proving. 1698. *See* Dunton, John.

Essay tending to issue. 1674. *See* Blinman, Richard.

Essay to a continuation. 1660. *See* Wild, Robert.

3291A An essay to a further discovery of terra firma. 1665. 4°.* LUG, LNC.

3292 An essay to ecclesiastical reconciliation. *Printed,* 1685. 4°.* LIL, MR; MM.

3293 —[Anr. ed.] —, 1686. 4°.* L, LSD, BLH; CH, MH.

Essay to heraldry. 1684. *See* Blome, Richard.

3294 An essay to raise a present supply. [*London,* 1700?] brs. NC.

3294A An essay to render the Church of England. *For J. Lawrence,* 1690. NP, OCI.

Essay to revive. 1673. *See* Makin, *Mrs.* Bathshua.

3294B An essay to suppress prophaness [*sic*] and immorality . . . humbly submitted to . . . Parliament. *For the author,* 1699. 4°.* LLP, LIU.

3294C An essay to the explaining of the revelation. *By Henry Hills and to be sold by George Sawbridge,* 1661. 4°. L; CLC, IU.

Essay touching the gravitation. 1673. *See* Hale, *Sir* Matthew.

3295 Entry cancelled.

Essay touching the Reformation. 1648. *See* Experimental essay touching.

3295A An essay toward settlement. [*London,* 1659.] brs. L; MH, NC.

3295B —[Anr. ed.] [*London*], *for Giles Calvert,* 1659. brs. LT, OC; MHS.

3295C An essay toward the clearer discovery. [*London*], *printed,* 1700. 4°.* T.C.III 155. O, MR; WF.

3296 An essay toward the composing of present differences. [*London*], *printed,* 1650. 4°.* O, C, OCC, EN; CH, CN, NN, NU, Y.

Essay towards a character. [n.p., 1685.] *See* A., P.

3296A An essay towards a general history of whoring. *For Richard Baldwin,* 1697. 8°. T.C.III 42. L, OC; CLC, WF, WSG, Y.

3297 An essay towards a scheme, or model. *For the author,* 1691. fol.* L, C, LUG, EN; MH, WF.

Essay towards a universal alphabet. [n.p., 1686.] *See* Lodowyck, Francis.

Essay towards the allaying. [n.p., 1695.] *See* Crisp, Thomas.

Essay towards the deciding. 1661. *See* C., D.

Essay towards the present. [n.p.], 1693. *See* Penn, William.

3297A An essay towards the rendring the first thirty Psalms . . . less obnoxious to exceptions. *For the Company of Stationers,* 1697. 12°. LLP.

Essay towards the settlement. 1681. *See* Harley, *Sir* Edward. Humble essay.

Essay towards the theory. [n.p.], 1700. *See* D'Urfey, Thomas.

3298 An essay upon excising several branches . . . brewing trade. [*London,* 1699?] 4°.* L, LSD; MH, NC, WF.

3298A An essaye upon His Royal Highness the Duke of York his adventure against the Dutch. *For W. Gilbert,* 1672. brs. L; CH.

Essay upon poetry. 1682. *See* Buckingham, John Sheffield, *duke of.*

Essay upon projects. 1697. *See* Defoe, Daniel.

3299 An essay upon satyr. *For Tho. Dring,* 1680. 8°. T.C.I 385. LLU; CH, MH, WC.

Essay upon taxes. 1693. *See* Temple, *Sir* William.

Essay upon the action. [1680.] *See* Le Faucheur, Michel.

Essay upon the advancement. [n.p., 1673]. *See* Temple, *Sir* William.

Essay upon the change of manners. 1681. *See* Nalson, John.

Essay upon the inscription. Edinburgh, 1678. *See* Cunningham, James.

Essay upon the late victory. 1665. *See* Wild, Robert.

3300 An essay upon the necessity of raising the value of twenty millions of pounds. *Printed and sold by John Whitlock,* [1696]. 4°.* L; CH, WF.

3301 An essay upon the original and designe of magistracie. [*Edinburgh*], *printed,* 1689. 4°.* ALDIS 2884. L, DU, AU, A, EN; CLC, CN, MH, MIU, WF, Y.

3301A —[Anr. ed.] [n.p.], *printed in the year,* 1695. 4°.* CH.

Essay upon the probable methods. 1699. *See* Davenant, Charles.

Essay upon the third Punique war. 1671. *See* Ross, Thomas.

Essay upon ways. 1695. *See* Davenant, Charles.

Essayes about general. 1659. *See* Horne, John.

Essays and characters. 1661. *See* G., L.

Essays, and maxims. 1698. *See* Halifax, George Savile, *marquess.*

Essayes of anatomy. Edinburgh, 1691. *See* Beddevole, Dominique.

Essays of love and marriage. 1673. *See* H., J.

Essayes of natural experiments. 1684. *See* Accademia del Cimento, Fiorenze.

Essays on several important subjects. [n p.], 1676. *See* Glanvill, Joseph.

Essayes or moral discourses. 1671. *See* Culpeper, Thomas, *younger.*

3302 Entry cancelled.

Essays towards a union. 1689. *See* Freke, William.

3303 Essayes upon several subjects. *By Richard Cotes for Edward Husband,* 1651. 4°.* L, BC, DT; CSS, MH, NN, WF, Y.

Essex. The particular rates of wages. [n.p., 1651]. *See* Particular rates.

3304 **Essex, Arthur Capel, earl of.** The Earl of Essex his speech at the delivering. colop: *For Benj. Harris,* 1681. brs. L, O, C, DU, SP; CH, MH, MIU, NP, PL.

3305 —The Earl of Essex, his speech at the delivery of the petition. colop: *For Francis Smith,* 1681. brs. L, OP, CT, LIU; CH, IU, MH, PU, Y.

3305A ——[Anr. ed., "Essex's speech."] colop: *For Francis Smith,* 1681. brs. L, C, MR; CH, MH, PL, WF, Y.

3306 **Essex, Robert Devereux, 2d earl of.** The Earle of Essex hjs letter to the Earle of Sovthampton. *By Lvke Norton for T. T.,* [1642]. 4°.* LT, DU, SS, DT; CH, MH, WF.

3307 —A precious and most divine letter. *For Iohn Bellamy, and Ralph Smith,* 1643. 4°.* L; WF.

3308 ——[Anr. ed.] [*London*], 1643. 4°.* LT, MR; CB, MH, WF.

3309 Entry cancelled.

[Essex, Robert Devereux], **3d earl.** Camp discipline. 1642. *See* Newark, David Leslie, *baron.*

3310 —A copy of a letter from. *Oxford, by Leonard Lichfield,* 1645. 4°.* MADAN 1769. O, C, SS; CH, MIU, WF.

3311 —The copy of a letter sent from. *By L. N. for E. Husbands and J. Franck,* 1642. 4°.* L, CJ, BR, EC, SS, DN; CLC, CSS, CU, MH, Y.

3312 ——[Anr. ed.] *Sept. 22. for Iohn Wright.* 1642. 4°.* LT, O; MH, WF.

3313 —The copy of a letter written from His Excellency, to the County of Warwick. *For H. Blunden, October 13.* 1642. brs. LT, BC, EC, LNC, LSD, SS; MH.

3313A —The Earl of Essex his declaration. *For Th. Thompson October 18,* 1642. 4°.* Y.

3314 —Lawes and ordinances of warre. *For Iohn Partridge and Iohn Rothwell, September* 1642. 4°.* LT, O, C, DU, DT; CH, MH, MU, WF, Y.

3314A —[Anr. ed., "laws."] *For John Partridge, and John Rothwell, May* 13, 1643. 4°.* CH, MH, MIU, WF.

3315 ——[Anr. ed.] *For John Partridge and John Rothwell,* 1643. 4°.* LT, C, LCL, DT; CH, CDA.

3316 ——[Anr. ed.] *For Luke Fawne,* 1643. 4°.* LT, LSD; CSS, LC.

3316A ——[Anr. ed.] *Printed in the yeer* 1646. 4°. L(t.p.), NL; WF.

3317 —A letter from His Excellencje. *For Edw. Husband, June* 17. 1643. 4°.* LT, O, DU, LNC, A, DT; CH, MH, MU, WF, Y.

3318 —A letter from His Excellency. [*London*], *for Laurence Blaiklock, January* 13. 1644. 4°.* LT, O, MR; CN, MH, WF.

3319 —A letter from the Earl of Essex. *Bristoll, by Robert Barker, and John Bill,* 1645. 4°.* C.

3320 [–] His Excellencies letter of the 30 of Ianuary, 1643. To the Earle of Forth. *Printed at London for Laurence Blaiklocke, Febr.* 10, 1643[4]. brs. LT; CH.

3321 —A letter sent from. *Septemb.* 19, 1642. *London for William Gay.* brs. LT, LG, CT, EC; CH, WF.

3322 —The Earle of Essex his letter to Master Speaker. July 9. 1643. *Oxford, by Henry Hall,* 1643. 4°.* MADAN 1420. LT, O, LSC, CT, BR; CH, CSS, WF.

3322A —The Earle of Essex his letter to the Earle of Southampton. *By Lvke Norton, for T. T.,* [1642]. 4°.* SS.

3323 —A letter written from . . . 19th of June, 1643. *By Richard Bishop for Lawrence Blaiklock,* 1643. 4°.* L, O, DU, MR, SP; CH, CSS, MH, WF, Y.

3324 —Most hapy [*sic*] and wellcome newes, from. *For T. Rider,* 1643. 4°.* LT, O; WF.

3325 —A paper delivered into the Lords House by. *For Thomas Hewer,* 1645. 4°.* LT, O, C, EN, DT; CH, CN, MH, WF, Y.

3326 —A proclamation by . . . 28 February 1643 [4]. *For T. G.,* 1643[4]. brs. STEELE 2534. LT; WF.

3327 —A proclamation by . . . for the defence of the Protestant religion. *For T. G.,* 1644. 4°.* LT, O, MR; MH, WF, Y.

3328 —A proclamation to prevent plundering. 24 April 1643. *For Edw: Husbands,* 1643. brs. STEELE 2413. LT, O, LG; MH.

3329 —The resolution of. *July* 28. [*London*], *for J. Wels,* 1642. 4°.* Y.

3330 —Robert Earle of Essex Captaine Generall . . . to all those . . . 18 May 1643. [*London,* 1643.] brs. STEELE 2424. LT; MH.

3331 —Several propositions propovnded by. [*London*], *for I. White, September* 21, 1642. 4°.* LT; WF.

3332-4 No entries.

3335 —The Earle of Essex his speech in the Artilrie garden. [*n.p.*], *Iuly.* 28. *for Thomas Baley,* 1642. 4°.* LT, O, LLU, SS; CH, Y.

3336 —True and happy newes from Worcester. *For Tho. White. Septem.* 26, [1642]. 4°.* LT.

3337 —Tvvo letters. [*London*], *for Edward Husbands, Sept.* 1. 1643. 4°.* LT, O, BC, DT; IU, MH, MM, WF.

3338 —Tvvo letters from His Excellencie. *By John Field for Edw: Husbands, June* 23. 1643. 4°.* LT; CLC, MH.

3339 —Tvvo proclamations. *March* 8, 1642[3], *London, for Iohn Frank.* 4°.* LT, CT, LNC, LSD, MR; CH, CLC, CN, MH, Y.

3340 —A vvorthy speech spoken by. *For Henry Fowler. Sept.* 29. 1642. 4°.* LT, CJ, BC, YM; CH, CN, MH, WF, Y.

3341 The Essex ballad. *Printed at London,* 1680. brs. L, O, HH; CH, MH, PU, WF, Y.

3342 Entry cancelled.

Essex champion. [1690.] *See* Winstanley, William.

3342A The Essex vvatchmen's vvatchword. *For Ralph Smith,* 1649. 4°.* LT, O, LG, DU, SP; CH, CN, MH, NU, WF, Y.

Essexian triumviri. 1684. *See* D., B.

3343 Essex's excellency. [*London*, 1679.] fol.* L, O, C, BC, SP, EN; CH, IU, MH, TU, WF, Y.

3344 The established test. *By T. N. for Jonathan Edwin*, 1679. 4°. T.C.I 342. L, O, C, EN, DT; CH, CN, TU, WF, Y.
Establishment. 1654. *See Στερεωμα.*

3345 The establishments made by the General Assemblie. *Printed at Kilkenny*, 1647. cap., 4°.* DN, DT.

3346 No entry.
Estate of the poor. 1688. *See Dagget, George.*

3346A **Estcourt, Richard.** As I was walking. [*London*, 1700?] brs. L; CH.

3347 **Estienne, Charles.** Dictionarium historicum. *Oxonii, ex typographeo Guilielmi Hall, impensis ejusdem, & Guilielmi Downing*, 1670. fol. MADAN 2865. L, O, C, OC, CS, BC; CH, PL. (var.)

3347A — —[Anr. ed.] *Oxonii, ex officina Guilielmi Hall; impensis ejusdem, & Guilielmi Downing, prostant venales apud Joh. Williams*, 1670. fol. NE, DN, DT; BBE, CB, IU, NCD, NP, TU, Y.

3348 — —[Anr. ed.] *Oxonii, excudebat G. H. & G. D. Sumptibus Johan. Williams* [*London*], *Georg. VVest, Amos Curteyne, & Johan. Crosley*, 1671. fol. T.C.I 62. MADAN 2909. L, O, C, E, DT; BN, CH, CSU, IU, LC, TU, Y.

3348A — —[Anr. ed.] *Oxonii, tipis, G. H. & G. D. Prostant Londini apud Gul. Wells & Rob. Scott*, 1671. fol. CT, WCA, DL; CN.

3349 — —Second edition. *Impensis B. Tooke, T. Passenger, T. Sawbridge, A. Swalle & A. Churchill*, 1686. fol. L, O, C, E, DT; BN, CH, CN, PL, WF, Y.

3350 **Estienne, Henri.** The art of making devises. *By W. E. and J. G.*, 1646. 4°. LT, O, C, CE, EN; BN.

3350A — —[Anr. ed.] —, *and are to be sold by Richard Royston*, 1646. 4°. O, GU; LC, WF, AVP.

3350B — —[Anr. ed.] *By W. E. and J. G. and are to be sold by Richard Marriot*, 1646. 4°. CH, CN, SW, Y.

3350C — —[Anr. ed.] *By W. E. and J. G. and are to be sold by Humphrey Moseley*, 1646. 4°. O.

3351 — —[Anr. ed.] *For Richard Royston*, 1648. 4°. L, O, EN; CH, CU, LC, MIU, NCU, WCL.

3352 — —[Anr. ed.] *For Iohn Holden*, 1650. 4°. L, O, C, LIU, EN; CH, INU, LC, MH, WF, JF, WSL.

3352A — —Second edition. *For Hen. Herringman*, 1655. 4°. GU; IU.

3353 [**Estienne, Henri**], *1528–1598.* The history of the life of Katharine de Medicis. *For John Wyat*, 1693. 8°. T.C.II 424. L, O, CT, DU, DT; CH, CN, MIU, WF, Y.

3354 [**Estlacke, Francis.**] A Bermudas preacher proved a persecutor. *By John Bringhurst*, 1683. 4°. LF, OC, BBN, BC; LC, MU, RPJ.

3355 No entry.

3356 **Eston, John.** The falling stars. *By Francis Leach*, 1653. 8°.* LT.

Estratto di due trattati. [*London?* 1695.] *See Fitzgerald, Robert.*

3356A **Estrella, Paulino da.** Flores del desierto, cogidas. [*London*], 1667. 12°. CLC.

3357 **Estwick, Francis.** Some errors of the Quakers detected. *For the author, in London*, 1697. 8°. O.

3358 **Estwick, Nicolas.** Christ's submission. *By George Miller*, 1644. 4°.* LT, O, C, EC, YM; CH, CU, NPT, NU, WF, Y.

3359 Entry cancelled.
—Dialogue between a comformist. 1668. *See* E., N. Dialogue betwixt.

3360 —Mr. Bidle's confession of faith. *By Tho. Maxey for Nath. Elkins*, 1656. 4°. LT, O, C, P, CD; MB, MH, MIU, NU, WF.

3360A — —[Anr. ed.] *For Nath. Ekins and for the use and benefit of Tho. Gibbs*, 1657. 4°. NPT.

3361 —Πνευματολογια: or, a treatise. *By William Du-gard, for Ralph Smith*, 1648. 4°. LT, O, C, E, DT; CH, MH, NPT, NU, Y.

3362 **Estwick, Sampson.** A sermon preached . . . January 30. 1697/8. *For Tho. Bennet*, 1698. 4°.* T.C.III 52. L, O, C, LG, LLP, LP, CT, NE; NU.

3363 —The usefulness of church-musick. *For Thomas Bennett*, 1696. 4°.* T.C.II 598. L, O, C, LW, CT; CLC, CN, LC, TSM, WF, Y.

3364 Entry cancelled.
Et à dracone: or, some reflections. 1668. *See Bethel, Slingsby.*

3364A Etablissement de la Societe des enfans de Nismes. [*London*, 1683.] cap., fol.* L.

Etat present de Danemarc. 1694. *See Molesworth, Robert Molesworth, viscount.*

3365 The eternal gospel once more testified unto. *For Allen Banks*, 1681. 8°. L, O, C, LCL, LLP, CM; CN, CU.

Eternal, substantial truths. 1661. *See Fox, George.*

Ethel and Smith. [1681.] *See Bethel and Smith.*

3366 Entry cancelled.

Etherege, Sir George. Account of the rejoycing. 1688. *See title.*

3367 —The comical revenge. *For Henry Herringman*, 1664. 4°. 92pp. L, O; CH, CLC, PRF, TU, WCL.

3368 — —[Anr. ed.] —, 1664. 4°. 71pp. L, O, CM; CLC, MH, TU, WF, Y.

3369 — —[Anr. ed.] —, 1667. 4°. L, O, LLU, LSD; CH, CN, MH, TU, WF, Y.

3370 [–] —[Anr. ed.] —, 1669. 4°. L, O, C, LVD, EN; CH, CN, MH, WF, Y. (var.)

3371 — —[Anr. ed.] *For H. Herringman, sold by Francis Saunders*, 1689. 4°. T.C.II 295. L, O, LLU, DT; BN, CLC, CU, MH, WF, Y.

3372 — —[Anr. ed.] *For Henry Herringman, and are to be sold by Samuel Manship*, 1690. 4°. L, O; CH, CU, MH, WF, Y.

3373 — —[Anr. ed.] *By T. Warren, for Henry Herringman, to be sold by J. Tonson, F. Saunders, T. Bennet, and K.* [*i.e.* R.] *Bentley*, 1697. 4°. L, O, LVF, OW, EN; CLC, CN, MH, MU, WF, Y.

3373A — —[Anr. ed.] *By T. Warren for Henry Herringman*, 1697. 4°. LLU.

3374   —The man of mode. *By J. Macock, for Henry Herringman,*
       1676. 4°. T.C.I 255. L, O, C, LVD, EN, CD; CH, CN, LC,
       MH, TU, WF, Y.

3375   ——[Anr. ed.] *By J. Macock, for Henry Herringman, and*
       are to be sold by Jos. Knight, and Fr. Saunders, 1684. 4°.
       T.C.II 64. L, O, CT; BN, CLC, CU, MH, TU, WF, Y.

3376   ——[Anr. ed.] *By T. Warren, for Henry Herringman, to*
       be sold by R. Bentley, J. Tonson, F. Saunders, and T.
       Bennet, 1693. 4°. L, O, LG; CLC, CU, MH, PBL, WF, Y.

3377   Entry cancelled. Ghost.

3378   —She wou'd if she cou'd. *For H. Herringman, 1668. 4°.*
       T.C.I 3. L, O, OC, CS, LLU; CH, CN, MH, TU, WF, Y.

3379   ——Second edition. *[London], in the Savoy: by T. N. for*
       H. Herringman, 1671. 4°. L, O, LVD, LVF, EN; CLC, IU,
       MH, TU, WF, Y.

3380   ——Third edition. *By T. Warren for Henry Herringman,*
       and are to be sold by R. Bentley, J. Tonson, F. Saunders,
       and T. Bennet, 1693. 4°. L, O, C, LLU; CH, IU, MH, TU,
       WF, WSC, Y.

3380A —A song in the comedy called Sir Fopling Flutter.
       [London? 1698.] brs. CLC.

3381   **E[therington, I[ohn].** The Anabaptists ground-work.
       by M. Simmons, 1644. 4°.* LT, O, C, CT, MR; CH, NHC,
       NU, WF, Y.

3382   [–] A brief discovery of the blasphemous doctrine of
       familisme. *By Matthew Simmons. 1645. 4°.** LT, E, DT;
       MH, NU, RPJ, WF, Y.

3383   —The deeds of Dr Denison. *By F. L. to be sold by Iohn*
       Wright, 1642. 4°.* LT; MH, WF, Y.

3384   —The defence of. *[London], printed, 1641. 4°.* LT, O, LW;
       CH, MH, MHL.

       Etrennes ou conseils. 1682. *See* Halifax, George Savile,
       marquis of.

       Etten, Henry van, *pseud.* *See* Leurochon, Jean.

3384A **Ettmüller, Michael.** Opera omnia. *Prostant venales*
       apud Sam. Smith, 1685. 4°. T.C.II 139. O.

3385   ——[Anr. ed.] *Prostant apud Sam. Smith, 1688. fol.* T.C.II
       254. O, C, OME, MC; MIU, NAM, NIC, TO, WF.

3385aA ——[Anr. ed.] *For F. Hubbard and A Bell, 1700.* WF.

3385A —Ettmullerus abridg'd. *For E. Harris, F. Hubbard and A.*
       Bell, 1699. 8°. L, LWL, MAU; CLM, NAM, WF, WSG, HC.

       Ευαγγελιογραφα, or. 1656. See Lewis, John.

       Ευασμος βασιλικος. 1662. See Ayleway, William.

       Eubulus. Or. *[n.p.], 1660. See* L., G.

3386   *Ευχαριστια;* or a grateful acknowledgement unto
       Heaven. *For Walter Kittilby [sic], 1684. 4°.** L, O, WCA;
       CH, WF.

3386A —Second edition. *By H. C. Sold by W. Davis, 1685. 4°.**
       O, BR, SP, LSD.

3387   Eucharisticon; or, an heroick poem. *[London? 1697.]* cap.,
       4°.* L; CH, IU, MB, MH, Y.

3388   Eucharisticon pro recuperata valetudine Olivari. *[London,*
       1654.] brs. L; CH, WF, Y.

3389   **Euclid.** Compendium Euclidis curiosi. Or, geometrical
       operations. *By J. C. for Joseph Moxon, and sold at his*
       shop, and by James Moxon, 1677. 4°.* T.C.I 274. O, C,
       LR, GU, DT; CSU, MH, MU, WF.

3390   —Euclidis data. *Cantabrigiæ, ex officina Joann. Field. Im-*
       pensis Guilielmi Nealand, 1657. 8°. L, LR, OC, CCO, CT;
       BN, CH, V.

3391   —Euclidis elementa geometrica. *Typis T. R. impensis Joh.*
       Martyn, 1666. 12°. L, O, C, YM, E; CH, MU, NC, PL, WF, Y.

3392   ——[Anr. ed.] *Typis J. M. impensis Joh: Martyn, 1678.*
       12°. T.C.I 320. L, O, C, EN, DT; CLC, IU, NC, PL, WF, Y.

3392A —Euclidis elementorum libri xv. *Cantabrigiæ, ex aca-*
       demiæ typographeo. Impensis Guilielmi Nealand, 1655-
       57. 2 vols. 12°. L, C, OC, CP, E, DN; BN, CSU, IU, MH, NC,
       PL.

3393   ——[Anr. ed.] *Excudebat R. Daniel, impensis Guil. Nea-*
       land, 1659. 8°. L, O, C, DC, NPL; CH, IU, MH, NC, WF, AVP.

3394   ——[Anr. ed.] *Typis J. Redmayne; prostant apud J. Wil-*
       liams, & J. Dunmore, 1678. 8°. T.C.I 377. L, O, C, E, DT;
       CH, CU, MH, NC, PL, WF, Y.

3395   ——[Anr. ed.] *Apud Car. Mearne, 1685. 8°.* L, O, LWL,
       CT; BN, CB, MB, MU, NN.

3395A ——[Anr. ed.] *Apud Abel Swalle, 1687. 8°.* LIU, LNC.

3395B —Elements of arithmetic. *For William & Joseph Marshal,*
       [1690]. 12°. CLC.

3396   —Euclides elements of geometry. *By Robert and William*
       Leybourn for Richard Tomlins and Robert Boydell, 1651.
       4°. L, C, CT, GC, GU, E; CH, IU, MH, MHS, NC, PL, Y.

3397   —Euclide's elements. *By R. Daniel, for William Nealand*
       in Cambridge; 1660. 8°. L, O, C, AN, DC, E; CH, IU, MH,
       NC, PL, WF, Y.

3398   —Euclid's elements of geometry. *By R. & W. Leybourn,*
       for George Sawbridge, 1661. fol. L, O, C, LIU, E, GU; CH,
       MH, MU, NP, PBL.

3398A ——[Anr. ed.] *By R. & W. Leybourn, for Richard Tom-*
       lins, 1661. fol. C, OC, CS, AN; MII, NIC, NC, PL, PU.

3398B ——Second edition. *For Christopher Hussey & E. P.,*
       1686. 12°. L, AN; LC.

3398C ——[Anr. ed.] *By R. and W. Leybourn, 1699. 8°.* V.

3399   —The elements of Euclid. *For Philip Lea, 1685. 12°.* T.C.II
       152. L, CM, DT; CH, CLC, IU, MB, MH, NC, Y.

3400   ——[Anr. ed.] *Oxford, by L. Lichfield for Anthony*
       Stephens, 1685. 8°. L, O, C, LWL, NOT; CLC, MIU, NC.

3401   ——Second edition. *For M. Gillyflower, and W. Free-*
       man, 1696. 8°. L, O, C, LWL, EC, RU; CH, CLC, IU, PL, TO.

3402   ——Third edition. *Oxford, by L. L. for M. Gillyflower,*
       and W. Freeman, 1700. 8°. T.C.III 204. L, O, C, CT, E; BN,
       CLC, NC, NP, PL, WF.

3403   No entry.

3404   —*Ευκλείδου τα σωζομενα.* Euclidis geometræ. *Oxoniæ,*
       e theatro Sheldonio, [1677]. * MADAN 3141. O (specimen).

3405   —Euclidis sex primi elementorum. *Excudebat J. F. impen-*
       sis Edwardi Story, 1654. 12°. L, LR, OC, CJ; CB, CLC, OCI,
       WF, HC.

3406   ——[Anr. ed.] *Cantabrigiæ, excudebat J. Field, impensis*
       Edwardi Story, 1665. 12°. L, O, C, LWL, CT, NPL; CH,
       MIU, NC, NP, WU.

       Euclides metaphysicus. 1658. *See* White, Thomas.

       Eucolpius, *pseud.*

3407   Entry cancelled.

Eudes de Mezeray, François. *See* Mezeray, François Eudes de.

3408 No entry.

3409 **E[uer], S[amson].** Doctrina placitandi ou l'art & science de bon pleading. *By the assigns of R. and E. Atkins, for Robert Powlet, 1677. 4°.* L, O, C, LL, DT; CH, CU, LC, MHL, NCL, PL, PUL, YL.

3410 [–] —[Anr. ed.] *By the assigns of R. and E. Atkins, for Robert Pawlet, to be sold by H. Twyford, T. Basset, S. Heyrick, and T. Dring, 1677. 4°.* T.C.I 282. KT, LC.

3411 [–] Tryals per pais; or, the law concerning juries. *By John Streater, James Flesher, and Henry Twyford; the assigns of Richard Atkyns, and Edward Atkyns, 1665. 8°.* L, O; CH, LC, MHL, MIU, YL.

3411A [–] —[Anr. ed.] *By John Streater, and James Flesher, the assigns of Richard Atkyns, 1665.* PUL, WF.

3412 [–] —[Anr. ed.] *For George Dawes, 1666. 8°.* L, LL, NE; CLC, LC, MIU, PUL.

3413 [–] —Second edition. —, *1682. 8°.* T.C.I 498. L, O, LL, CJ; CLC, MHL, NCL, PU, WF.

3413A [–] —"Second" edition. —, *and are to be sold by Matthew Wotton, 1685. 8°.* L, DU, CD; CH, LC, MH.

3414 [–] —Third edition. *By the assigns of Rich. and Edw. Atkins, for John Walthoe, 1695. 8°.* L, O, LM, OC; LC, MIU, PH, PUL.

3414A [–] —"Third" edition. —, *1700. 8°.* BAMB.

Evgenia's teares. 1642. *See* Reynolds, Edward, *bp.*

Eugenius, *junior, pseud.*

Eugenius Philalethes, *pseud.*

Eugenius Theodidactus, *pseud. See* Heydon, John.

Evphrates. 1655. *See* Vaughan, Thomas.

3415 **Euripides.** Ευριπιδου σωζομενα απαντα ..., Euripidis quæ extant omnia. *Cantabrigiæ, ex officina Johan Hayes. Impensis Richardi Green Cantab. 1694. brs.* OP.

3416 — —[Same title.] *Cantabrigiæ, ex officina Johan Hayes, impensis Richardi Green, Cantab. 1694. fol.* L, O, C, MR, EN, DT; BN, CH, IU, MH, MU, TO, WF, Y, AVP.

Evropa. Cupid crucified. 1649. *See* Theocritus.

3417 Europæ modernæ speculum: or, a view. *By T. Leach, for Tho. Johnson, 1665. 8°.* L, O, CT, EN; CH, NHS, Y.

3417A —[Anr. ed.] *For Peter Parker, 1666. 8°.* L, O, LLU, CS, EC, SP; CLC, WF, Y.

Europe a slave. 1681. *See* Cerdan, Jean Paul, *comte de.*

European mercury. 1641. *See* Wadsworth, James.

3418 Europe's chains broke. *For Richard Baldwin, 1692. 12°.* T.C.II 414. CT.

Europe's tears. Newcastle, [1695]. *See* S., J.

3418A Europes transactions, discovered in a dialogue. *colop: For W. B., 1689. brs.* CH.

3419 **Eusebius Pamphili, *bp.*** An abridgement, or a compendious commemoration of. *[Rotterdam], for the author and are to be enquired for at Tho. Simmons, and Rob. VVilsons in London, and also at Tho. VVillans in Kendall. 1661. 8°.* L, O, C, LF; PH, PSC, SE, WF.

3420 —An abrigment of Eusebius. Second edition. *For Francis Holden, 1698. 8°.* T.C.III 93. L, LCL, LF, AN, MR; CH, IE, MH, PH, Y.

3421 —The ancient ecclesiasticall histories. Fifth edition. *By Abraham Miller, sold by Edw. Dod and Nath. Ekins, 1650. fol.* L, O, C, EN, BLH; CLC, MBA, MH, MIU, PPT, WF.

3421A — —Sixth edition. *By Abraham Miller and are to be sold by George Sawbridge, 1663. fol.* WF.

3422 — —"Sixth" edition. *By Abraham Miller, to be sold by Thomas Williams, 1663. fol.* O; CLC, CN, NP, NU, TU, Y.

3422A — —"Sixth" edition. *By Abraham Miller, and are to be sold by Francis Tyton, 1663. fol.* L, LLU; Y.

3422B — —"Sixth" edition. *By Abraham Miller, to be sold by Luke Fawn, 1663. fol.* O, CK; BBE.

3423 —The history of the church. *Cambridge, by John Hayes, for Han. Sawbridge, 1683. fol.* T.C.II 8. L, O, C, DU, ENC; CLC, FU, IU, NU, TSM, V, AVP.

3424 — —[Anr. ed.] *Cambridge, by John Hayes, for Nathaniel Rolls, 1692. fol.* T.C.II 430. L, C, OC, BAMB, E; CLC, IU, MH, PL, WF.

3424A —Eusebius his life of Constantine. *By Abraham Miller, 1663. fol.* TU.

3425 Entry cancelled.

—Meditation of life. Oxford, 1682. *See* Nieremberg, Juan Eusebio.

Eusebius, Ernestus de. *See* Alexander VII.

3426 **Eustace, *Sir Maurice.*** A copie of a letter from. *By A. N. for Edw. Husbands and Iohn Frank, 1642. 4°.** LT, C, MR, DN.

3427 —A letter from. *By E. G., for I. Wright. May 7. 1642. 4°.** LT, LL, LVF, MR, DN; MH.

3428 —The speech of . . . 8 May 1661. *For Abel Roper, 1661. 4°.** L, C, OC, LSD, BLH; CN, MH, WF.

3429 **Eustachius.** Ethica. *Cantabrigiæ, ex academiæ typographeo, impensis Guilielmi Morden, 1654. 8°.* L, C; CLC, MH, MWA.

3429A — —[Anr. ed.] *Ex officina Rogeri Danielis, 1658. 8°.* O, LLP, BANGOR, BSE, LLU; Y.

3429B — —[Anr. ed.] *Typis J. R. impensis Joh. Williams, 1666. 8°.* L, O, CCO; BBE, CH.

3429C — —[Anr. ed.] *Typis I. R. impensis Ioh. Williams, 1671. 8°.* L, C, CP, BC; CH, CN, NC, PU, WF.

3430 — —[Anr. ed.] *Ex officina J. Redmayne, 1677. 8°.* T.C.I 93. L, O, LIL, OC, CT, DU, YM; CH, CN, IU, PL.

3430A — —[Anr. ed.] *Ex officinâ Elizabethæ Redmayne, 1693. 8°.* WF.

3431 — —[Anr. ed.] —, *1693. Prostant venales apud H. Dickinson, E. Hall, Cantab. 8°.* L, O, C, BR, DC; IU.

3432 —Summa philosophiæ. *Cantabrigiæ, ex officina Rogeri Danielis, 1648. 8°.* L, C, LW; MH, Y.

3433 — —[Anr. ed.] —, *1649. 8°.* L, C, OC, NPL, YM, CD; CH, CU, IU, MH, WF.

Eutactus Philodemius, *pseud. See* Ascham, Antony.

Euterpe revived. 1675. *See* Flecknoe, Richard.

3434 **Eutropius.** A breviary of Roman history. *For Jo. Hindmarsh, 1684. 8°.* T.C.II 60. L, O, C, LLU, SP; CH, LC, MBA, MH, OSU, Y.

3435 —Historiæ Romanæ breviarium. *Prostant apud Benj. Tooke & Tho. Cockeril, 1694. 12°.* T.C.II 502. RPL; CLC, IU.

3436   — —[Anr. ed.] *Oxonii, e theatro Sheldoniano. Impensis Ab. Swall & Tim. Child, Londini,* 1696. 8°. L, O, C, EC, LSD; CH, Y.

3437   **Eutychius.** Eutychii patriarchae Alexandrini annalium. Tomus alter. *Oxoniis, excudebat Hen: Hall,* 1654. 4°. MADAN 2297n. L, O, C, OM, CD; CU, Y.

3438   —[Arabic] Contextio gemmarum. *Oxoniæ, excudebat H. Hall,* 1656. 4°. MADAN 2297. L, O, C, OM, E, CD; CU, Y.

3439   — —[Anr. ed.] *Oxoniæ: impensis Humphredi Robinson [Londinii],* 1658–9. 2v. 4°. MADAN 2385. LT, O, CT, EN, DT; BN, CH, CU, NPT, PL, WF, AVP. (var., 1658–58 or 1659–58.)

3440   —Eutychii Ægyptii patriarchæ orthodoxorum. . . Ecclesiæ suæ origines. *Excudebat Richardus Bishopus,* 1642. 4°. L, O, CP, GC, DT; BN, CH, MH, PU, Y.

3440A   — —[Anr. ed.] —, 1642. *Prostant apud R. & T. Whitakerum.* 4°. C, CM, DUS, EN, DT; BN, CLC, NP, PL, WF, Y.

Evagoras: a romance. 1677. See L., L.

3441   **Evance, Daniel.** A baptismal catechisme. *By E. T. for Nathanael Webb and William Grantham,* 1655. 4°.* NU.

3442   —Justa honoraria. *For Edward Husband,* [1646]. 4°.* LT, O, CT, SS, DT; CN, MIU, TU, WF, Y.

3443   —The noble order. *By T. W. for Abel Roper,* 1646. 4°. LT, O, C, EN, DT; CH, CU, MH, NU, TU, WF, AVP.

Evangelium armatum. 1663. See Assheton, William.

Evangelium regni. 1652. See Niclas, Hendrik.

3444   **Evank, George.** A farewell sermon. *[London],* printed, 1663. 4°.* C, LW; MH, MWA, NU.

Evans, Arise. See Evans, Rhys.

3445   [**Evans, John**]. The case of kneeling . . . Part I. *By J. Redmayne, Jun. for T. Basset, B. Took, and F. Gardiner,* 1683. 4°. L, O, CT, BP, DT; CN, CSB, MBP, NU, WF, Y.

3446   [–] —Second edition. *By J. C. and Freeman Collins, for Fincham Gardiner,* 1683. 4°. L, O, C, OC, LLU; CH, CU, MH, NU, WF, Y.

3447   [–] —[Anr. ed.] *For T. Basset, B. Took, and F. Gardiner,* 1683. 4°. T.C.II 15. L, O, CT, DU, BLH; CN, CSS, PU, TU, WF.

3448   [–] The case of kneeling. Part II. *For T. Basset; B. Took; and F. Gardiner,* 1683. 4°. L, O, CT, BP, E, DT; CH, CN, NU, WF, Y.

3449   [–] —[Anr. ed.] *For T. Basset; and B. Took,* 1685. 4°.* L, C, O, OC, OCC, LIU; CLC, CU, MH, NU, WF.

3450   —Moderation stated. *For Walter Kettilby,* 1682. 4°. T.C.I 504. L, O, CT, LSD, CD; CH, CN, MH, NCD, NU, WF, Y.

3451   —Some thoughts. *For Sam. Crouch,* 1695. 4°.* O; NU.

3452   —The universall medicine. *By Richard Hodgkinsonne,* 1642. 4°. L, C; PCP, PL.

3452A   — —[Anr. ed.] —, 1651. 4°. IU, PCP.

3452B   **Evans, John,** *quack.* John Evans, his hummums . . . where persons may sweat. *[London, after* 1679.] brs. L.

3453   **Evans, Katherine.** A brief discovery of God's eternal truth. *For R. Wilson,* 1663. 4°. LF; NU, PH, WF.

3454   **Evans, Rhys.** The bloudy vision of John Farly. *[London],* printed, 1653. 8°. LT, O, CT, AN, DC; CLC, IU, MB, PHS, Y.

3455   —The declaration of. *For G. Convert,* 1654. 4°.* LT.

3456   —An echo to the book called A voyce from Heaven. *[London], for the authour,* 1653. 8°. L, AN, MR; CH, NGT, WF, JF.

3456A   — —[Anr. ed.] —, 1653. 8°. CM, AN.

3457   —An eccho to The voice from Heaven. *[London], for the authour,* 1652. 8°. LT, O, C, AN, DU, DT; CLC, IU, WF, Y.

3458   —The Euroclydon winde commanded to cease. *[London], for the author,* 1653. *But according to the misapprehension of the vulgar,* 1654. 8°. LT, OC, CT.

3459   —The great & bloody visions. *For G. Convert,* 1654. 4°.* LT, O.

3460   [–] King Charls his starre. *[London], printed,* 1654. 8°.* LT, O.

3461   [–] Light for the Iews. *For the author,* 1656 [1664]. 8°. L, O, DCH, LLU; MH, OHU.

3462   —Mᵣ Evans and Mᵣ Penningtons prophesie. *[London], printed,* 1655. 4°.* LT.

3463   —A rule from Heaven. *For the author,* 1659. 8°. L, O.

3464   —To His Excellencie the Lord General Cromwell, . . . the humble petition of. *[London,* 1653.] brs. LT, LNC.

3465   Entry cancelled.

—To His Excellencie the Lord General Cromwell, . . . the petition of. *[n.p.,* 1653.] *See* —Voice from heaven, 1652.

3466   —To the Jews nation. *[London,* 1655.] 8°. DC.

3467   —To the most high and mighty prince, Charles the II . . . an epistle. *For Richard Lowndes, and Simon Gape,* 1660. 8°. LT.

3468   [–] A voice from Heaven. *[London], printed,* 1652. 8°. LT, C, DC, MR, DT; CH, MH, TO, WF, Y. (var.)

3469   — —[Anr. ed.] —, 1652. 8°.* O, OC, CM, AN, ES.

3470   [–] —[Anr. ed.] —, 1653. 8°. L, O, AN, MR; CH, IU, MM, NGT, WF, JF.

3471   —The voice of King Charls the father. *Printed at London for the author,* 1655. 8°. L, O, C, AN.

3472   —The voice of Michael. *[London], printed,* 1653. *Or as the vulgar think it,* 1654. 8°.* LT, O.

3473   —The voice of the iron rod. *For the author,* 1655. 8°.* LT, C, OC, AN.

3474   —The voice of the people for a King. *For the author,* 1659. 4°.* MH.

3474A   —A winding-sheet for the Presbyterian, or a mite touching the ordination of ministers. *[n.p.], sold by the author at Mr. Cadelth's,* [1652?] 4°.* DT.

3474B   Evan's gamesome frollick, or. *[London], for J. Back,* [1690?]. brs. O.

3475   Eve revived, or The fair one stark-naked. *By William Downing,* 1684. 12°. T.C.II 50. CN.

3476   **Evelyn, George.** The case of. *[n.p.,* 1698.] brs. O.

3477   — —[Anr. ed.] *[n.p., c.* 1698.] brs. L, O, GK.

3477A   —The declaration of. *[London],* 1699. brs. OC (lost).

3478   **Evelyn, Sir John.** The charge delivered at the Lords barre by. *For V. V.,* 1647. 4°.* LT, CT, MR; MH, MIU, MU, Y.

3479   —Sir John Evelyn his report from the committee. *[London], printed,* 1641. 4°.* LT, OH, DU, LLU, DT; CH, MH, MU, WF, Y.

3480 E[velyn], J[ohn]. Acetaria. *For B. Tooke*, 1699. 8°. T.C.III
       158. KEYNES 105. L, O, C, LVF, DU; CH, CU, LC, MH, NAM,
       TU, WCL, WF, Y.

3481 [–] An apologie for the royal party. [*London*], *anno Dom.*
       1659. 4°.* KEYNES 17. O, OC, LVF, DU; MIU, TU.

3482 [–] —[Anr. ed.] [*London*], 1659. 4°.* KEYNES 18. LT, O,
       LVF, OM, MR; CU, MBC, MH, MIU, NN, Y.

3483 [–] —Second edition. [*London*], *anno Dom.* 1659. 4°.*
       KEYNES 19. O; CH.

3484 [–] —[Anr. ed.] —, 1659. 4°.* KEYNES 20. GK.

3485 [–] A character of England. *Londons* [sic] *for Jo. Crooke*,
       1659. 12°. KEYNES 14. OC; CH, MH, Y.

3486 [–] —[Anr. ed.] *For Jo. Crooke*, 1659. 12°. KEYNES 15. L, O,
       CCH, NOT, WCA, GK; MH, Y.

3487 [–] —Third edition. *For John Crooke*, 1659. 12°. KEYNES
       16. LT, O, C, LVF, DU; GH, CLC, CN, MH, RPJ, WF.

       [–] Epigrams upon the paintings. 1700. *See* Elsum, John.

3488 —Fumifugium: or the inconveniencie of the aer. *By W.*
       Godbid for Gabriel Bedel, and Thomas Collins, 1661. 4°.*
       KEYNES 23. L, O, C, LVF, DM; BN, CLC, CN, MH, WCL, WF.

3489 — —[Anr. ed.] —, 1661. 4°.* KEYNES 24. L; CH, MH, Y.

3490 [–] The history of the three late famous impostors. [*Lon-*
       don], *in the Savoy, for Henry Herringman*, 1669. 8°. T.C.I
       9. KEYNES 89. L, O, C, AN, LVF, DT; CH, CN, MH, WF, Y.

3490A [–] A journey to England. *Printed, and sold by A. Baldwin*,
       1700. 8°.* L, OC, CS; CLC, INU, WF, Y.

3491 —Kalendarium hortense: or, the gardners almanac.
       Second edition. *By Jo. Martyn and Ja. Allestry*, 1666.
       8°. KEYNES 58. L, O, RU, WCA, GK; Y.

3492 — —Third edition. —, 1669. 8°. KEYNES 59. L, O, AN, GK;
       BBE, CH, NCD, WF, Y.

3493 — —Third edition. *By John Martyn and James Allestry*,
       1669. fol.* T.C.I 23. KEYNES 60. L, O, C, MR, GK; CH, LC,
       MU, NP, JF.

3494 — —Fourth edition. *By John Martyn*, 1671. 8°. T.C.I 76.
       KEYNES 61. L, OC, CAMB. BOTANY.

3495 — —Fifth edition. —, 1673. 8°. T.C.I 166. KEYNES 62. L,
       O, YM, GK; BN, CLC, MH, MM.

3496 — —Sixth edition. —, 1676. 8°. T.C.I 260. KEYNES 63. L,
       O, C, EN, GK; CLC, MH, MWA, PL.

3497 — —Seventh edition. *For T. Sawbridge, G. Wells, and R.*
       Bently, 1683. 8°. T.C.II 55. KEYNES 65. L, O, BR, SP, GK;
       CH, LC, MH, PL, HC.

3498 — —Eighth edition. *For R. Chiswell, T. Sawbridge, and*
       R. Bently, 1691. 8°. KEYNES 66. L, O, CT, EN, GK; CH, IU,
       MHO, NC, WF, Y.

3499 — —"Eighth" edition. *For Matthew Gillyflower, and*
       James Partridge, 1691. 8°. KEYNES 67. L, LG, OC, GK; Y.

3500 — —Ninth edition. *For Rob. Scott, Ri. Chiswell, Geo.*
       Sawbridge, and Benj. Tooke, 1699. 8°. KEYNES 68. CM,
       CT, GK; CLC, MH, NIC, NP.

3501 — —"Ninth" edition. *For George Huddleston*, 1699. 8°.
       KEYNES 69. L, LWL, SHR; CLC, MH, MU, NP, WDA, WF.

3502 — —"Ninth" edition. *For Francis Fawcet*, 1699. 8°.
       KEYNES 70. L, O, C, AN, GK; CH, Y.

3503 [–] The late news or message from Bruxels unmasked.
       For Richard Lowndes, 1660. 4°.* KEYNES 21. L, O, GK;
       CH, CLC, MH, PL, TU, Y.

3504 —Navigation and commerce. *By T. R. for Benj. Tooke*,
       1674. 8°. T.C.I 171. KEYNES 92. L, O, C, EN, DT; BN, CH,
       CN, LC, MH, NC, WCL, WF, Y.

3505 —Numismata. A discourse of medals. *For Benj. Tooke*,
       1697. fol. T.C.III 52. KEYNES 104. L, O, C, EN, DT; BN,
       CH, CN, LC, MH, NP, WF, Y, AVP.

3506 —A panegyric to Charles the Second . . . xxxiii. [sic] of
       April. *For John Crooke*, [1661]. fol.* KEYNES 22. L, LG,
       GK; CLC, MH, ZWT. ·

3507 —A philosophical discourse of earth. *For John Martyn*,
       1676. 8°. T.C.I 220. KEYNES 93. L, O, C, MR, EN; CH, IU,
       MH, NC, WF, Y, HC.

3508 [–] Pomona, or an appendix. *By John Martyn and James*
       Allestry, 1664. fol. KEYNES 52. L, O, C, E, GK; CH, CU, LC,
       MHO, PL, Y, JF.

3509 [–] —Second edition. —, 1670. fol. KEYNES 53. L, O, C,
       DU, MR, GK; CH, LC, MH, PL, WDA, WF, Y, JF.

3510 —Publick employment and an active life prefer'd. *By*
       J. M. for H. Herringman, 1667. 8°. KEYNES 85. L, CT, OP,
       EC, GK; CLC, CU, MH, OCI, TU, Y.

3511 —Publick employment and an active life with. *By J. M.*
       for H. Herringman, 1667. 8°. KEYNES 86. L, O, LW, EN,
       GK; CH, CN, MH, NP, WF, JF.

3512 — —[Anr. ed.] —, 1667. 8°. KEYNES 87. EN; CH, CLC, WF,
       Y.

3513 —Sculptura: or the history. *By J. C. for G. Beedle, and T.*
       Collins, and J. Crook, 1662. 8°. KEYNES 33. L, O, C, DT,
       GK; BN, CH, CLC, IU, LC, MH, WF, Y.

3514 —The state of France. *By T. M. for M. M. G. Bedell, &*
       T. Collins, 1652. 12°. KEYNES 2. LT, LVF; CN, NP.

3515 — —[Anr. ed.] —, 1652. 12°. KEYNES 3. L, O, CT, LLU, SC,
       GK; CH, IU, MH, PL, WF, Y.

3516 —Sylva, or a discourse of forest-trees. *By Jo. Martyn, and*
       Ja. Allestry, 1664. fol. KEYNES 40. L, O, C, AN, E, DM;
       CH, CU, MH, NC, NP, WDA, WF, Y, JF.

3517 — —Second edition. —, 1670. fol. T.C.I 24. KEYNES 41.
       L, O, C, DU, MR, GK; CLC, IU, LC, MU, NCD, Y, JF.

3518 — —Third edition. *For John Martyn*, 1679. fol. T.C.I 344.
       KEYNES 42. L, O, C, DT, GK; BN, CH, CU, MH, WF, Y, AVP.

3519 [–] Tyrannus or the mode. *For G. Bedel, and T. Collins,*
       and J. Crook, 1661. 8°. KEYNES 32. L, O, OC, GK; CH, MH.

3519A Evelyn, John, *younger*. To the King: a congratulatory
       poem. *For R. Bentley*, 1685. fol.* OC (dispersed).

3520 [Evelyn, Mary.] The ladies dressing-room unlock'd.
       Second edition. *For Joseph Wild*, 1700. 4°.* KEYNES
       102. L.

3521 [–] Mundus muliebris: or, the ladies dressing-room un-
       lock'd. *For R. Bentley, Covent Garden*, 1690. 4°.* T.C.II
       322. KEYNES 99. L, O, CT, DT, GK; CH, CLC, CN, NNM,
       RHT.

3522 [–] —Second issue. *For R. Bentley, Covent-Garden*, 1690.
       4°.* T.C.II 336. KEYNES 100. OC, GK, DU, LLU; CLC, MH.

3523 [–] —Second edition. *For R. Bentley*, 1690. 4°.* KEYNES
       101. T.C.II 388. L, O, CK, CT, GK; CLC, MH, TU, WF, WU, Y.

3523A —The picture of the Princesse Henrietta. [*London*], 1660. brs. oc (lost).

3524 **Evelyn, Robert.** A direction for adventvrers. [*London*], *printed*, 1641. 4°.* CH.

3525 Even in the twinkling of an eye. [*London*], *for F. Coles, T. Vere, I. Wright, J. Clarke, W. Thackeray, and T. Passenger*, [1678–80]. brs. L, O, CM.

3526 Entry cancelled.
Evening sacrifice. [n.p.], 1643. *See* Reading, John.

3526A **Evenkellius, Acatius.** Γυμνασιαρχον, or the schoole of potentates. *By Richard Bishop*, 1648. 8°. L, O; CH, CN, IU.

3527 **Everard, Edmund.** The depositions and examinations of. *For Dorman Newman*, 1679. fol.* L, O, C, EN, DT; CH, CN, MH, NU, WF, Y, AVP.

3528 —Discourses on the present state. *For Dorman Newman*, 1679. fol.* T.C.I 361. L, O, C, EN, DT; BN, CH, CN, LC, MH, NP, NU, TU, WF, Y.

3529 [–] The great pressures and grievances of the Protestants in France. *By E. T. and R. H. for T. Cockeril; and R. Hartford* [sic], 1681. fol. T.C.I 419. L, O, SP; CH, NN, PU, WF, Y.

3530 **Everard, Giles.** Panacea. *For Simon Miller*, 1659. 8°. LT, O, OM, CE, GU; CH, MH, NN, WF, HC.

3531 **Everard, John, 1575?–1650?.** The gospel-treasury opened. *By John Owsley, for Rapha Harford*, 1657. 8°. O, LW; NU, PH.

3532 ——Second edition. *By I. O. for Rapha Harferd* [sic], 1659. 8°. L, O, LSC, MR; CH, FU, WES, Y.

3532A ——"Second" edition. *For Benj. Clarke*, 1679. 8°. T.C.I 362. BSO; CLC, NPT, PH, PSC, WES.

3533 —Some gospel-treasures opened. *By R. W. for Rapha Harford*, 1653. 8°. LT, ORP, CS, DCH, E, DT; CU, MH, NPT, WF, Y.

3534 **Everard, John, *Quaker*.** The universal love of God. *Printed and sold by T. Sowle*, 1697. 8°.* LF; PHS.

3534A [**Everard, John**], *missioner*. A winding-sheet for the schism of England. *Printed at Dublin, permissu superiorum*, 1687. 8°. DUS, NE, WARE, DT; WF, WG.

3535 **Everard, Margaret.** An epistle of. colop: *For Brabazon Aylmer*, 1699. 4°.* LF, LLP, OC, MR; PH, PSC.

3536 **Everard, Robert.** An antidote for the Newcastle priests. [*London*], *for the author, to be sold by W. L.*, 1652. 4°.* MH.

3537 —The creation and fall of Adam. [*n.p.*], 1649. 8°. ORP.

3538 —An epistle to the several congregations. *Paris, printed*, 1664. 4°.* O, OC, DUS, WCA; IU, NHC, WF, Y.

3539 ——Second edition. [*London?*], *printed*, 1664. 8°. L, O, C, LCL, DU; CH, CN, IU, NU, TU.

3540 —Nature's vindication. *For the author; to be sold by W. Larnar*, 1652. 8°. L, ORP.

3541 —Robert Everards three questions. [*London*, 1655.] cap., 4°.* LT.

3542 **Everard, Thomas.** Proposals for the speedy procuring. [*London*, 1695.] brs. NC.

3543 —Stereometry made easie. *By J. Playford, for R. Clavel, and C. Hussey*, 1684. 12°. T.C.II 50. L, BC; CH, WF, WG, HC.

3543A ——Second edition. *For Robert Clavel and Christopher Hussey*, 1689. 8°. T.C.II 264. LIU; CH, TO, VILLANOVA.

3543B ——Third edition. *For R. Clavell*, 1696. 8°. T.C.II 606. L, CAMB. WHIPPLE; CLC, INU, NC.

3544 **Everard, William.** The declaration and standard of the Levellers of England. *Imprinted at London, for G. Laurenson, Aprill 23*, 1649. 4°.* LT, O.

3545 **Everardt, Job.** An epitome of stenographie. [*London*], *by M. S. for Lodowick Lloyd*, 1658. 8°. LT, O, CM, MC, EN; CH, LC, NN, NS, Y.

3545A **Everenden, Humphrey.** Reward of the wicked. Ninth edition. *Glasgow, Robert Sanders*, 1696. 12°. ALDIS 3559. GU.

3546 **Everett, George.** Encouragement for seamen & mariners. *Printed*, 1695. 4°.* L, C, LG, LUG, CM; CH, CN, MH, NC, WF, Y.

3546A [–] A letter to Mr. Miles Prance. colop: *For M. G.*, [1682]. brs. L, O, OC, HH; CH, MH, NU, TU, WF, Y.

3547 —Loyalty and fidelity, rejected. *Printed*, 1698/9. 4°.* L; MH, NN, WF, Y.

3548 —The path-way to peace and profit: . . . royal navy. *For the author; to be sold by Randal Taylor*, 1694. 4°.* L, O, C, LG, GU; CH, CN, NC, WF, Y.

3548A ——[Anr. ed.] *Taylor* 1695. 4°.* LC.

3548B [–] A second letter to Mr. Miles Prance. colop: *For N. Thompson*, 1682. cap., fol.* L, O, OC, MR; CH, NU, PU, TU, WF, Y.

3549 —A word in season. [*London?* 1700.] brs. L.
Everlasting gospel. [n.p.], 1649. *See* Douglas, *Lady* Eleanor.
Everlasting joys. 1656. *See* Hart, John.
Everlasting prognostication. Aberdeen, 1686. *See* Almanacs.

3549A **Every, John.** Speculum mercativum, or The young merchant's glass. *For William Birch*, 1674. fol.* T.C.I 150. Y.

3549B ——[Anr. ed.] —, *sold by Benjamin Billingsley*, 1674. fol. MIU.

3549C Every man and woman their own doctor. *For L. White*, 1676. 4°.* MU.
Every man his own doctor. 1671. *See* Archer, John.

3550 Every mans case: or, a brotherly support to Mr. Larner. [*London, May 2*, 1646.] brs. LT.

3551 —[Anr. ed.] [*London, Larner's last press, May 9*, 1646.] 4°.* LT.

3552 Every man's companion. *For Francis Cossinet*, [1661]. 8°.* O.
Every mans right. [n.p.], 1646. *See* Frese, James.

3553 Every woman her own midwife. *S. Neale*, 1675. 4°. LC.

3554 **Eves, George.** The churches patience. *For G. Bedell, and T. Collins*, 1661. 4°.* LT; MH, MWA.
Evident demonstration. [n.p., 1660.] *See* Fell, Margaret.

3555 The evil eye plucked out. *For Rob. Clavel, and are to be sold by H. Brome*, 1670. 8°. T.C.I 26. L, O, P, EN, DT; CH, MH, MM, NU, Y.

3555A The evil spirit cast-out. *Printed by E. Golding*, 1691. 8°. GU; SE.

3555B The evill spirit conjur'd, and cast out of Parliament. *For R. F.*, 1653[4]. 8°. WF.

3555C **Ewbancke, George.** The pilgrim's port. *For Charles Tyus, and for R. Lambert in York*, 1660. 12°. L.

3555D **Ewel, Edward.** A brief account of the qualifications, vertues and use of . . . panareton. [*London*, 1690?] brs. L.

3556 **Ewen, Thomas.** The church of Christ in Bristol. [*n.p.*], 1657. 4°. LF, BBN.

3557 **Ewer, Isaac.** A full and particular relation of the manner of . . . taking of Chepstow Castle. *By Matthew Simmons, for Henry Overton*, 1648. 4°.* LT, AN.

Ex nihilo omnia, or. 1692. *See* Mogridge, Anthony.

3557A Ex spinosa anonymi sylva folia quædam. [*Edinburgh?* 1649.] 4°. ALDIS 1365.6. L; WF.

3558 Ex ungue leonem: or, a proof (by ten dozen) of . . . epigrams. *Printed at London, by James Cottrel*, 1654. 8°. O.

Exact abridgment of all the trials. 1690. *See* N., P.

Exact abridgement of the general history. 1698. *See* Ferrar, Richard.

3559 The exact account and solemn manner of assembling the Parliament of Scotland. *For Randolph Taylor*, 1681. fol.* L, O, OP, CCA; CH, WF, AVP.

Exact account of a late famous defeat. [1690]. *See* B., W.

3560 An exact account of all who are the present members of the Kings College of physicians. *Londgn* [*sic*]: *for Henry Brome*, 1673. brs. O.

3561 —[Anr. ed.] *Printed*, 1676. brs. L, O.

3562 An exact account of His Majesties progress. colop: *For Langley Curtiss*, 1690. brs. L, C, DN; Y.

3503 An exact account of Major-General Kirke's safe arrival. colop: *For J. Wilson*, 1689. brs. OC, MC, DN; Y.

Exact account of Romish doctrine. 1679. *See* Morton, Thomas, *bp.*

3564 An exact account of the affairs in Ireland. colop: *For H. Jones*, 1689. brs. L; CH, WF, Y.

3564A —[Anr. ed.] colop: *For Richard Baldwin*, 1689. brs. L, C, OC; Y.

3565 An exact account of the ceremonial at the coronation of Their most excellent Majesties. colop: [*London*], *in the Savoy: by Edward Jones*, 1689. fol.* L, O, MC; CH, CN, PL, WF, Y.

3566 An exact account of the daily proceedings of the commissioners of oyer and terminer at York. *Dublin, for Sam. Dancer*, 1663. 4°.* DIX 120. LL, CD.

3567 An exact account of the Duke of Schomberg's happy voyage. *For R. Brown*, 1689. brs. L, C, MC; CH.

3568 —[Anr. ed.] *Reprinted Edinburgh*, 1689. brs. ALDIS 2885. L, EN; CSS.

3569 An exact account of the Elector of Saxony's passing the Rhine. *For R. Bauldwin*, 1691. brs. MH.

3570 —[Anr. ed.] *Reprinted Edinburgh*, 1691. brs. ALDIS 3144. L, EN.

3570A An exact account of the great and solemn rejoycing for . . . Prince of Wales. colop: [*London*], *by E. Jones*, 1688. brs. L.

3571 An exact account of the King of Sweden's dangerous sickness. *For Gabriel Kunholt*, 1679. LNC, EN; CH, MH.

3572 An exact account of the King's march to Ardee. colop: *For R. Baldwin*, [1690]. brs. C, MC; Y.

Exact account of the late action. 1690. *See* W., J.

3573 A [*sic*] exact account of the late bloody fight between Capt. Hastings. 1681. brs. O.

3574 An exact account of the late engagement. [*London*], *in the Savoy, by Tho. Newcomb*, 1669. 4°.* O, MR, P; MH, Y.

3574A —[Anr. ed.] *Edinburgh, A. Anderson*, 1669. 4°.* EN

3574B An exact account of the manner of the execution of Algernon Sidney. colop: *By E. Mallet*, 1683. cap., fol.* L; WF.

3575 An exact account of the most considerable transactions. colop: *For Richard Baldwin*, 1689. brs. L, O, C, OC, MC; CH, Y.

3575A An exact account of the most remarkable fires. *For Richard Head*, 1667[8]. brs. L, LG.

3576 Entry cancelled.

Exact account of the number, names, 1687. *See* Exact and true account of the number, names.

3576A An exact account of the number of Parliament-men. [*London*], *sold by William Berry*, 1679. 8°.* MH, WF.

3577 An exact account of the present posture of affairs in Dublin. colop: *For Roger Smith*, 1689. brs. L, C, OC, MC, DN; MH.

3578 An exact account of the proceedings at Guild-hall. colop: *For Benj. Tooke*, 1682. brs. L, O, LG, HH; CH, CN, MH, WF.

3579 An exact account of the procedings [*sic*] at the Old Bayly [13 July 1683]. colop: *By E. Mallet*, 1683. fol.* L, LLU; CH, MH, MIU, WF, Y.

3579A —[Anr. ed.] *For G. P.*, 1683. brs. L.

3580 —[Anr. ed.] *Edinburgh, re-printed by the heir of Andrew Anderson*, 1683. fol. ALDIS 2378. L, EN; CLC, MIU.

3581 An exact account of the raising the siege of London-Derry. colop: *For R. Wood*, 1689. brs. L, C, MC; MH.

Exact accompt of the receipts. 1660. *See* R., M.

3582 An exact account of the royal army under . . . Schomberg. colop: *For R. Williams*, 1689. brs. L, C, OC, MC, DN; CH, MH.

3582A An exact account of the siege of Namur. *For Tim. Goodwin*, 1695. 4°. L; CH, CLC, CSS, PL, UCLA, WF.

3583 An exact account of the success . . . army in Ireland. *Printed at London, and re-printed at Edinburgh*, 1691. brs. ALDIS 3145. EN; Y.

3584 An exact account of the taking by storm . . . of Athlone. *For R. Baldwin*, 1691. brs. MC; CH.

3585 —[Anr. ed.] *London, reprinted Edinburgh*, 1691. brs. ALDIS 3146. EN.

3585A An exact account of the taking of the pass of Butlers-Bridge. colop: *For G. Goodman*, 1690. brs. L, C, DN; Y.

3586   An exact account of the total defeat of the Irish army. *For R. Baldwin*, 1691. brs. DUS, MC; CN, MH.

3587   An exact account of the trial between Sr. William Pritchard. *Printed and sold by Richard Janeway*, 1689. fol.* T.C.II 250. L, O, CT, RU, SP; CH, CN, MH, NN, TO, WF, Y.

3588   An exact account of the tryal of Algernoon Sidney. colop: *For E. Mallet*, 1683. fol.* L, O, MR; CH, WF.

3589   —[Anr. ed.] *Reprinted Edinburgh*, 1683. fol.* ALDIS 2379. L, EN.

3590   An exact account of the trials of the several persons arraigned. *By G. Hills, to be sold by L. Curtiss*, 1678. 4°.* L, O, LL, BAMB, LSD; CH, MBA, WF, Y.

3591   An exact account of the whole proceedings against the Right Reverend Father in God, Henry [Compton] Lord Bishop of London. *Printed*, 1688. 4°.* L, O, CS, MR, EN, DT; CH, IU, MH, NU, WF, Y.

3592   Exact and certaine newes from the siege at Yorke. *Iuly 3. London, for Mathew Welbanke*, 1644. 4°.* LT; CN, LC, MH, MM, Y.

3593   An exact and compleat diary of the siege of Keyserwaert. *For Richard Baldwin*, 1689. 4°.* L, O, OM, MR; CH, LC, MM, WF.

3594   An exact and compleat journal . . . of the confederate fleets and armys. *For John Whitlock*, 1696. 4°.* C.

3595   An exact and faithful account brought to a person of quality. *For J. C.*, 1689. brs. L, C, DN.

        Exact and faithful account of the late bloody engagement. 1681. *See* Booth, William.

3595A An exact and faithful account of the late bloody fight between Captain Hastings. *John Gain*, 1681. brs. LNM.

3595B An exact and faithful journal of the famous siege of Barcelona. *For Richard Sare, to be sold by E. Whitlock*, 1698. 4°.* L; MB, MIU, WF.

3596   Entry cancelled. Ghost.

3597   An exact and faithful list of those worthy gentlemen & citizens His Majesty has been pleased to commissionate anew. colop: *For Langley Curtiss*, 1690. brs. L, O, C, LG; CH, PL, WF, Y.

        Exact and faithful narrative. 1680. *See* Oates, Titus.

3598   An exact and faithful relation of the process pursued by Dame Margaret Areskine. *Edinburgh, at the society of stationers*, [1690]. 4°. L.

        Exact and full relation of all the proceedings. [n.p.], 1643. *See* R., S.

        Exact and full relation of the great victory. 1647. *See* Rowe, Matthew.

        Exact and full relation of the last fight. 1644. *See* Ellis, Thomas.

3599   An exact and humble remonstrance touching the late conflict of armies. *By J. M.*, 1645. 4°.* LT; WF.

3600   An exact and impartial account from Ireland of the death of . . . Tyrconnel. *For H. Jones*, 1691. brs. MH.

3600A An exact and lively mapp or representation of boothes, . . . upon the ice. [*London*], *printed and sold by William Warter*, [1683/4]. brs. T.C.II 62. L.

        Exact and most impartial accompt. 1660. *See* Nottingham, Heneage Finch, *earl of*.

3600B An exact and necessary catalogue of pentioners in the Long Parliament. colop: *Printed*, 1699. cap., fol.* L, CT; CH, MB.

3601   An exact and particular account of the defeat . . . in the county of Cork. *By W. Bonny*, 1691. brs. MH.

3602   An exact and perfect list of the names of the Knights. *By Tho. Newcomb*, 1664/5. 8°.* L, LG, NE; CH, CLC, CN, WF, Y.

3603   An exact and perfect relation of every particular of the fight at VVorcester. *By Francis Leach*, 1651. 4°.* CH, MH, WF, Y.

3604   An exact and perfect relation of the arrival of the ship the James and Mary. [*n.p.*, 1687.] brs. L, O; CH, LC, MHS, NN.

3605   An exact an[d] perfect relation of the happy proceedings of the Earl of Bedford. *For Henry Seymour, Septem. 30*, 1642. 4°.* L; Y.

3606   An exact and perfect relation of the proceedings of Sr Hugh Cholmly. *For J. Harris, Jan. 28. 1643*. 4°.* LT, YM; WF, Y.

3607   An exact and perfect relation of the proceedings of the army. *For Samuel Gellibrand, July 14, 1645*. 4°.* O, BR; Y.

        Exact and perfect relation of the terrible. 1652. *See* White, Thomas.

3607A An exact and plain threefold table. *For S. Crouch*, 1697. brs. MH.

3608   An exact and true account of the blowing up of the French magazine. colop: *For Langley Curtiss*, 1690. brs. CH, MH.

3608A An exact and true account of the number, names, . . . of all the publick schools in England. *By G. Croom for J. Weld*, 1687. brs. L, LG; CU.

3608B An exact and true account of the proceedings . . . Old-Bayly . . . [17 January 1682]. colop: *By George Croom*, 1682. fol.* O, OC.

3609   An exact and true account of the taking five French ships. colop: *Printed in London, and re-printed at Edinburgh*, 1690. brs. ALDIS 3038. HH, EN, DN; HR.

        Exact and true definition. [*London*, 1663?] *See* Worcester, Edward Somerset, *marquis*.

3610   An exact and true relation how eighteene French and Irish men, . . . were apprehended. *For Iohn Wright*, 1641[2]. 4°.* LT, O, C, DN.

3611   An exact and true relation in relieving the resolute garrison of Lyme. [*London*], *Iune 10. for Mathew Walbancke*, 1644. 4°.* LT, O, CM; CH, WF.

        Exact and true relation of a bloody fight. 1642. *See* Foulis, *Sir* Henry.

3612   An exact and true relation of a most cruell . . . murther. *For E. Husbands and I. Franck, Sept. 17, 1642*. 4°.* LT; CLC.

3613   An exact and trve relation of that tumultuous behaviour of divers citizens. [*London*], *for B. A. & R. D., Decemb. 13. 1642*. 4°.* LT, MR; CN, MH, MU, TU, Y.

3614 A [sic] exact and true relation of the battell fought on Saturday last at Acton. *For Tho: Cook. Novemb.* 14. 1642. 4°.* LT, LNC; MH, MIU.

3615 An exact and true relation of the behaviour of Edmund Kirk. colop: *By Elizabeth Mallet,* [1684]. cap., fol.* L; IU, WF.

3616 An exact and true relation of the birth, and life of Simon Morin. *Printed,* 1663. 4°.* L, O.

3617 An exact and true relation of the dangerous and bloody fight. *By Iohn Field, for Edward Husbands and John Franck, October 28.* 1642. 4°.* LT, O, CCA, BC, DU: CLC, CN, LC, WF, Y.

3618 —[Anr. ed.] *For I. Wright, Octob.* 29. 1642. 4°.* MH, WF.

3618A —[Anr. ed.] *For Francis Wright,* 1642. 4°.* L, MR; IU, MH, Y.

3618B —[Anr. ed.] *For Francis Coles,* 1642. 4°.* D, EN, E; NCD, NU, MIU.

3618C —[Anr. ed.] *For Edward Blackmore, October 28,* 1642. 4°.* L, O, OC; CH, Y.

3619 An exact and true relation of the examination, tryal, and condemnation of the German princesse, . . . Mary Carlton. *For R. O.,* 1672. 4°.* OC, SP; CN, MH, Y.

Exact and true relation of the great. 1653. *See* R., J.

3620 An exact and true relation of the landing of Her Majestie at Portsmouth. *For C. Wildebergh, and John Ruddiard,* 1662. brs. L.

3621 An exact and true relation of the late plots. *For Francis Coules,* 1641. 4°.* LT, O, EC, LNC, MR, DT; MH, WF, Y.

3622 An exact and true relation of the many severall messages. *For Fra. Coles, August 19th* 1646. 4°.* LT, O, AN, MR, DT; WF.

3623 An exact and true relation of the present posture of affairs in Ireland. colop: *For James Partridge,* 1689. brs. L, O, DUS, MC; CH, Y.

3624 An exact and trve relation of the taking of Arvndel Castle. *For George Lindsey,* 1644. fol.* LT.

3625 An exact and true relation of the wonderfull vvhirle-vvind. *By T. F. for Fr. Coles,* 1660. 4°.* LT; CH.

3626 An exact and true relation of two great claps of thunder. [n.p.], 1661. brs. CHRISTIE-MILLER.

3627 An exact and true table of the fees of the . . . head-searcher, and . . . five under searechers [sic] in the port of London. [London, 1679/80.] brs. CH, MH.

3627A —[Anr. ed.] *For the author to be sold by Francis Smith,* [1679–80]. brs. L, MH.

3627B Exact and wonderful history of Mother Shipton. *Published by J. Conyers,* [c. 1675]. 12°.* CM.

3628 An exact book of most approved presidents. *Printed and are to be sold by Rob. Pawley,* 1663. 8°. O.

Exact catalogue of all the comedies. Oxon, 1680. *See* Langbaine, Gerard, *younger.*

3629 Entry cancelled. *See following entry.*

3629A An exact catalogue of the names of several ministers lately ejected. *Printed,* 1663. 4°.* L, LW, NE; MB, MM, NU, WF, Y.

3629B —[Anr. ed.] —, 1669. 4°. NGT.

3630–1 Entries cancelled.

Exact character, or narrative of . . . Oliver Cromwell. 1658. *See* W., T. L.

Exact collection of choice declarations. 1653. *See* Sheppard, William, *comp.*

3632 An exact collection of farevvel sermons. [London], printed, 1662. 8°. L, LW; MH, NU, WES, Y. [=C 241.]

3633 Entry cancelled.

Exact collection of many wonderful prophecies. 1689. *See* C., P.

3634 Entry cancelled.

Exact collection of the choicest poems. [1662.] *See* Brome, Alexander. Rump: or.

Exact collection or catalogue. 1663. *See* Crowe, William.

Exact constable. 1660. *See* Wingate, Edmund.

Exact copy of a letter, sent to William Laud. 1641. *See* A.

3635 An exact copie of the Irish rebels covenant. *Imprinted by Robert Young and Evan Tyler, to be sold by Andro Wilson, in Edinburgh,* 1641. 4°.* ALDIS 1002. L, C, D.

3636 An exact copy of the petition of the Protestants in France. *Printed,* 1680. fol.* BC, MR, SP; CH, MH, NCD, WF, Y.

3637 July 20. 1642. An exact coranto. *By L. N. and I. F. for E. Husbands and I. Franck,* [1642]. 4°.* L, O, EC; Y.

Exact dealer. 1688. *See* Hill, John.

Exact delineation of . . . Bristoll. 1671. *See* M., I.

3638 An exact description of a Roundhead. *For George Thomlinson,* 1642. 4°.* LT, LG, LLU; CN, NU, TU, WF, Y.

3639 An exact description of Prince Ruperts malignant she-monkey. [London], *for E. Johnson,* 1643. 4°.* LT, CS, NE; CH, MH, TU.

3639A An exact description of the government of . . . Geneva. *For L. Chapman.* 1659. 4°.* L; WF.

3640 Entry cancelled.

Exact description of the growth, quality, and vertues of the leaf tee, alias tay. [n.p., 1664.] *See* Garway, Thomas.

3640A An exact description of the roads of Ireland. *By William Downing for Robert Hayhurst,* 1690. brs. OC, DN.

Exact diary of the late expedition. 1689. *See* Whittle, John.

3641 An exact diary of the siege of the city of Ments. *Printed, to be sold by R. Janeway,* 1689. 4°.* L; CH, MIU, WF, Y.

3642–3 No entries.

Exact dyarie or a breife relation of the progresse of Sir William Wallers army. 1644. *See* Coe, Richard.

3644 An exact discovery of the mystery of iniquity. *By Tho. James for Benj. Harris,* 1679. 4°.* L, O, CT, EN, DT; CLC, LC, MH, NU, Y. (var.)

3644aA —[Anr. ed.] *By Tho. James,* 1679. 4°.* LIU; WF.

3644A —[Anr. ed.] *Reprinted at Dublin,* 1679. fol.* DIX 173. L, CD, DK, DM, DN, DT; CN, IU.

Exact diurnall. [n.p.], 1647. *See* Neville, Henry.

3644B The exact effigies of a monstrous Tartar. *For W. Gilbertson and H. Marsh,* 1664. brs. O.

Exact history. 1660. *See* Dauncey, John.

3645 An exact journal of the engagement between the English fleet and the French. colop: *For Richard Baldwin*, 1692. brs. MH.

3646 An exact journal of the siege of Coni. *For Tho. Basset*, 1691. 4°.* L, DT; CH, WF.

3647 An exact journal of the siege of Lymerick. colop: *For Abraham Mason*, 1691. brs. MH.

3648 An exact journal of the siege of Namur. *For J. Whitlock*, 1695. 4°.* L, O, OC, CS; CH, IU, MH, WF, Y.

3649 An exact journal of the siege of Tangier. *Printed at London for Joseph Hindmarsh*, 1680. fol.* T.C.I 417. L, O, C, MR, EN; CH, CLC, MH, PU, WF, Y.

3650 An exact journal of the victorious expedition of the confederate fleet. *For J. Whitlock*, 1695. 4°.* T.C.II 557. L, LLL, LNM; CH, MH, PU, WF, Y.

3651 An exact journal of the victorious progress of Their Majesties forces under . . . Gen. Ginckle. *For Randolph Taylor*, 1691. 4°.* T.C.II 380. L, O, C, MR, DN; HR, CH, CN, MH, WF, Y.

3652 The exact law-giver. *For Thomas Bassett*, 1658. 8°. LT, O, LL, EN; CH, MB, MHL, PUL, WF.

Exact legendary. [n.p.], 1641. *See* H., A.

3653 Entry cancelled.

Exact list of all the men, women and boys that died. 1699. *See* Company of Scotland. Exact history.

3654 An exact list of all Their Majesties forces. *For Richard Baldwin*, 1692. brs. L, OC, DU; WF.

3654A An exact list of the confederate army. *For A. Mason*, 1672. brs. Y.

Exact list of the conspirators discover'd. 1696. *See* Hue and cry after the Duke of Berwick (verso).

3655 An exact list of the French army in Flanders. *For Robert Hayhurst*, 1691. brs. L, LG.

3656 An exact list of the French fleet. [*n.p.*], 1691. brs. L, MC.

3657 An exact list of the Lords spiritual & temporal, who sate. *By T. B., and are to be sold by Randal Taylor*, 1689. 4°.* L, O, C, LUG, LSD, DN; CH, CN, MH, WF, Y.

3658 An exact list of the members of both Houses of Parliament. *By J. Leake for Arthur Jones*, 1685. brs. MH.

3659 An exact list of the names of every commander. *Imprinted at London for Henry Overton*, 1642. brs. LT, O, LNC; Y.

3659A An exact list of the royal confederate army. *For H. Jones*, 1691. brs. L; CN.

3659B —[Anr. ed.] *Edinburgh, by the heir of A. Anderson*, 1691. brs. EN.

3659C An exact list of the whole writers to His Majesty's signet. [*Edinburgh*, 1692.] brs. L.

3660 An exact list of Their Majesties and the Dutch fleet. *For Richard Baldwin*, 1692. brs. O, LG, OC, HH, DU; CH, IU.

3661 —[Anr. ed.] —, 1693. brs. L, C; CH, NNM.

Exact list of Their Majesties forces. 1690. *See* J., W.

Exact narration. 1650. *See* Isaacson, Henry.

3661A An exact narrative and order of the nobility. *By J. B. and are to be sold by Walter Davis*, 1685. brs. O.

3662 An exact narrative and relation of His most sacred Majesties escape from Worcester . . . 1651. *Printed*, 1660. 4°.* LT, AN; CH, WF.

3662A —[Anr. ed.] *For G. Colborn*, 1660. 4°.* L, OC, CM; CLC, WF, Y.

3663 An exact narrative of every dayes proceedings. [*London*], *for Robert Bostock, June 20*, 1648. 4°.* LT; CH, CLC, NU, WF.

3664 An exact narrative of the attempts made upon the Duke of Glocester. *Printed, and are sold by F. Eglesfield*, 1655. 4°.* LT, BC, DU; CH, NU, TO, WF, Y.

3665 An exact narrative of the bloody murder, and robbery committed. By Stephen Eaton. [*London*], *for R. Taylor*, 1669. 4°.* L, LG; CH.

3666 The exact narrative of the conflict at Dunkeld. colop: *Edinburgh, printed*, 1689. cap., 4°.* ALDIS 2886. MR, EN, ES; WF.

3666A —[Anr. ed.] colop: *Edinburgh: printed according to order. And reprinted at London, for Ric. Chiswell*, 1689. brs. CH.

3667 An exact narrative of the resolute attempt. *Edinburgh, by Evan Tyler*, 1666. fol. ALDIS 1814. EN.

3668 An exact narrative of the tryal and condemnation of John Twyn. *By Thomas Mabb for Henry Brome*, 1664. 4°.* L, O, CT, LSD, EN; CH, CN, NU, PUL, WF, Y.

3669 Entry cancelled.

Exact narrative of the tryals of the pyrats. 1675. *See* Grand pyrate, 1676.

3670 An exact plan of Lymerick. *For R. Hayhurst*, 1691. brs. MH.

3671 An exact prospect of His Majesties forces, encamped. *Printed, to be sold by Walter Davis*, [1686]. brs. L, O.

3672 An exact relation, of a battell fought by the Lord Moore. *Printed*, 1641. 4°.* LT, O, LLL, CT, EC, DN; CN, MIU, WF.

3673 An exact relation of a famous battell fought . . . tenth of October. *For Th. Tompson, October 15*, 1642. 4°.* Y.

3674 No entry.

Exact relation of all such occurrences. 1642. *See* Mervyn, Sir Audley.

Exact relation of all the late revolutions. [n.p., 1675.] *See* W., E.

3675 An exact relation of all the transactions and proceedings, between the King of Denmark. *For Simon Miller*, 1659. 4°.* L, O, MR; Y.

3675A An exact relation of an honovrable victory obtained by the Parliaments forces in Yorkshire. *May 27. Printed* [sic] *Iohn Wright*. 1643. 4°.* IU.

3676 An exact relation of foure notable victories. *Febr. 26. London, by Bernard Alsop*, 1644. 4°.* LT.

3677 An exact relation of foureteen dayes passages from Portsmouth. *For Benjamin Allen*, 1642. 4°.* LT, EC.

3678 An exact relation of Prince Rupert his marching out of Bristoll. *For Iohn Wright, 18. Sept.* 1645. 4°.* LT, BR, LIU, DT; CSS, IU, Y.

3679 An exact relation of routing the Irish army. *For J. Smith*, 1691. brs. MC; MH.

3679A An exact relation of several material actions. *For T. Hawkins*, 1691. brs. Y.

3680 An exact relation of that famous and notable victorie obtained at Milford-Haven. *By Moses Bell, 25. Iuly* 1644. 4°.* LT, AN; CSS, WF.

[25]

3681 An exact relation of the apprehension, examination, execution and confession, of Thomas Bullaker. *For Iohn Wright*, 1642. 4°.* LT, LG.

3682 An exact relation of the barbarous murder committed on Lawrence Corddel. *By J. Jones*, 1661. 4°.* L, O, C; MH.

3683 An exact relation of the bloody and barbarous massacre at Bolton. *By R. W. for Christopher Meredith, August 22.* 1644. 4°.* LT, LLU, DT; WF.

3684 An exact relation of the bloody and barbarous murder, committed by Miles Lewis. *For J. C., Novemb*, 30. 1646. 4°.* LT; IU.

3685 An exact relation of the defeat of the rebels at Bothwell-Bridge. *[London], in the Savoy: by Tho. Newcomb*, 1679. fol.* L, O, LL, DU, LNC; CH, IU, MBA, MH, WF, Y.

Exact relation of the delivering. 1643. *See* Stapleton, *Sir* Philip.

3686 An exact relation of the discoverie of a great plot for the surprizall of Yorke. *For G. W.*, 1648. 4°.* LT; CSS, Y.

3687 Entry cancelled.

Exact relation of the engagement. 1673. *See* Exact relation of the several engagements.

3688 An exact relation of the entertainment of . . . William III. *Printed, and are to be sold by Randal Taylor*, 1691. 8°.* T.C.II 359. L, O, LIU, DT; CN, MBP, MH, NS, WF.

3688A —[Anr. ed., "a description of Holland."] *Printed*, 1691. 8°. L.

3689 An exact relation of the glorious victory obtain'd upon the French. colop: *For Richard Baldwin*, 1689. brs. O, OC, HH, MC, DN.

3690 An exact relation of the grand ceremony of the marriage of Charles the II. *For Dorman Newman*, 1679. fol.* L, O, OC, LNC, EN; CH, LC, MH, TU, WF, Y.

3691 Entry cancelled.

Exact relation of the King James's embarking. Edinburgh, 1690. *See* Exact relation of the late King.

Exact relation of the last newes. [n.p.], 1644. *See* R., W.

3692 An exact relation of the late King James's embarking. colop: *For R. Baldwin*, 1690. brs. L; Y.

3692A An exact relation of the [late] King James's embarking. *Reprinted at Edinburgh by the heir of Andrew Anderson*, 1690. brs. ALDIS 3040. L, EN; CSS.

3692B —[Anr. ed.] colop: *Printed at Edinburgh, and re-printed at Glasgow by Robert Sanders*, 1690. brs. L, EN; Y.

3693 Entry cancelled.

Exact relation of the late plots. 1641. *See* Exact and true relation.

Exact relation of the most execrable. 1665. *See* Byam, William.

3694 An exact relation of the most remarkable transactions . . . in Ireland. colop: *For J. Morris*, 1689. brs. L, C, OC, MC, DN; Y.

Exact relation of the persecutions. 1689. *See* Orpen, Richard.

Exact relation of the proceedings and. 1654. *See* D., L.

3695 Entry cancelled.

Exact relation of the proceedings of the Army. 1645. *See* Exact and perfect relation.

3695A An exact relation of the proceedings of the Cavaleers. *For Iohn Damm*, 1643. 4°.* WF.

3695B An exact relation of the progresse of Ioseph VValsh. [*London*], printed, 1650. 4°.* MR.

3696 An exact relation of the several engagements . . . fleet. *For J. B.*, 1673. 4°.* L, O, C, BR, MR; CH, CN, MH, WF, Y. (var.)

3697 An exact relation of the siege before Yorke. *For R. White, June 12.* 1644. 4°.* LT, YM, A, DT; MM, Y.

3698 An exact relation of the surrender of Scarborough Castle. *For Iohn Field*, [1645]. 4°.* LT, O.

3699 An exact relation of the tryall & examination of . . . John Morris. [*London*], printed, 1649. 4°.* LT, CT, AN, BC, MR; CH, ZAP.

3700 An exact relation of the whole proceedings of gallant Col. Mitton. *For Laurence Chapman*, [1646]. 4°.* LT, AN, DT.

3701 An exact relation of two bloudy fights at sea, near Cherbrook. *For J. H. August 26.* 1650. 4°.* LT.

Exact relation of two victorious battels. [1642.] *See* Buller, John.

3702 An exact relation shewing how the governour of Portsmouth Castle delivered it up. [n.p.], *August 5. for Io. Hundgate*, 1642. 4°.* LT.

3703 An exact representation of the late comet. *S. Edman*, 1677. brs. O; CLEVELAND PUB. LIB.

3703A Exact rules of grammar . . . or, the common accidents reformed. *For John Streater*, 1655. 4°. L (t.p.).

3704 —[Anr. ed.] *For J. Streater*, 1656. 8°. L, LG, OP; NC.

Exact summary. 1650. *See* Rivet, *Dr.*

Exact survey of divine soule-saving faith. 1673. *See* E., F. J.

Exact survey of the affaires of the United Netherlands. 1665. *See* H., T.

Exact survey of the grand affairs. 1689. *See* Courtilz, Gatien de.

Exact survey of the United Provinces. 1673. *See* W., T.

3705 An exact table of fees, of all the courts. *By the assigns of Richard and Edward Atkyns; for John Walthoe*, 1694. 8°. T.C.II 478. L, O, CT, DUS, EC; LC, MHL, Y.

3705A —Second edition. —, 1694. 8°. O.

3706 —Third edition. —, 1697. 8°. L, EN; CH, CLC, WF.

Ex-ale-tation of ale. 1646. *See* Mews, Peter, *bp.*

Exaltatio alæ. [n.p.], 1666. *See* Mews, Peter, *bp.*

3706aA The exaltation of Christmas pye. [*London*], printed 1659. 4°.* L, O; Y.

Exalted Diotrephes. 1681. *See* Snead, Richard.

Examen confectionis. 1692. *See* Chauncy, Isaac.

Examen historicum. 1659. *See* Heylyn, Peter.

Examen legum. 1656. *See* Booth, A.

3706A An examen of the pretences and character of Mr. William Russel, *Printed*, 1700. 4°.* O; NPT.

Examen of the sermon. 1645. *See* Tombes, John.

3707 An examen of the way of teaching the Latin tongue. *By T. N. for J. Martyn*, 1669. 8°. T.C.I 14. L, O, LSC, CE, CT, AN, DU; CSS, IU, TU, WF.

Examen poeticum: being. 1693. *See* Dryden, John.

3708   Examen poeticum duplex. *Impensis Ric. Wellington,* 1698. 8°. T.C.III 80, L, O, C, P, EN; CH, CLC, CU, IU, WF, Y.

Examen quotidionum. 1658. *See* Ussher, James.

Examination and confession of Captaine Lilbourne. 1642. *See* Felton, William.

3709   The examination and confession of Colonel John Lambert. *For Nathan Webb,* [1660?]. 4°.* MR; ZWT.

3710   The examination and tryall of Margaret Fell. [*London*], *printed,* 1664. 4°.* L, LF, OC, MR, EN; CH, CN, TU, WF, Y.

3711   The examination, confession, and execution of Ursula Corbet. *For John Andrews,* [1660/1]. brs. HH.

3712   The examination, confession, triall and execution of Joane Williford. *For J. G., October* 2. 1645. 4°.* LT; CH, MH, NIC, OSU, V.

3713   An examination examined. colop: *Printed at London for J. W. J.,* [1645]. cap., 4°.* LT, O, MR; Y.

Examination of a late treatise. 1697. *See* W., S.

Examination of a printed pamphlet. 1465 [*i.e.* 1645]. *See* Innes, James.

3714   Entry cancelled.

Examination of Captain William Bedlow deceased. 1680. *See* Guilford, Francis North, *baron.*

3715   The examination of Colonell Lunsford. [*London*], *for Tho. Cooke, Novemb.* 19. 1642. 4°.* LT; MH, MIU.

3716   The examination of David Alexander. colop: *Octob.* 20., *for John Wright,* [1642]. cap., 4°.* MR.

Examination of Dr. Comber's. 1690. *See* Bolde, Samuel.

Examination of Dr. Woodward's. 1697. *See* Arbuthnot, John.

3717   The examination of Edw. Fitzharris. *For Thomas Fox,* 1681. fol.* L, O, C, AN, DU, MR; CH, CN, TU, WF, Y. (var.)

3717A   The examination of Francisco de Faria. [*Dublin*], *reprinted,* 1680. 4°.* MR, CD, DT.

3718   The examination of George Leddoze. *For Laurence Blaiklock, Septemb.* 1, 1642. 4°.* LT; CH, MH, WF.

Examination of Henry Mayo. [n.p., 1643.] *See* Prynne, William. Romes master-peece.

3719   The examination of Iosvah Hill. *For Edward Husbands and John Franke,* 1642. brs. STEELE 2261. LT.

3719A   The examination of Lily's grammar. *For John Salusbury,* 1688. Y.

3720   The examination of Mr. VVil. Prynne. *For H. Beck,* 1648[9]. 4°.* LT, MR; CH, MH, Y.

3721   Entry cancelled.

Examination of part of Père Simons critical history. 1682. *See* Filleau de la Chaise, Jean. Excellent discourse.

3722   An examination of severall votes. [*London,* 1648.] 4°.* MR; MIU.

3723   —[Anr. ed.] colop: *Printed at Paris, reprinted at London,* 1648. cap., 4°.* O, MR; MH, WF.

3724   The examination of Sir Ralph Hopton. *Printed,* 1642. 4°.* L, LNC, MR; MH, MIU, Y.

Examination of such particulars. Oxford, 1644. *See* Williams, Griffith, *bp.*

Examination of sundry scriptures. 1645. *See* Hollingworth, Richard.

Examination of the arguments. 1691. *See* Downes, Theophilus.

3725   The examination of the bishops. *For H. W.,* 1688. 4°.* L, O, CS, MR, EN, DM; MH, MIU, NU, WF, Y.

3725A   The examination of the captains . . . in Sussex. *For William Tracy,* [1689]. brs. LG; CH.

3726   An examination of the case of the suspended bishops. *For Roger Alwin,* 1690. 4°.* T.C.II 339. L, LW, CT, EC, DM; CH, CU, MH, NU, WF, Y.

3727   An examination of the impartial state of the case of the Earl of Danby. *Printed, and are to be sold by Walter Davis,* 1680. fol.* L, C, OC, DU, EN; CH, CN, MBP, MH, WF, Y.

Examination of the observations. [n.p.], 1643. *See* Jones, John, *gent.*

3728   Entry cancelled.

Examination of the principal texts. 1692. *See* Nye, Stephen. Accurate examination.

Examination of the scruples. 1689. *See* Allix, Pierre.

3729   An examination of the seasonable and necessarie warning concerning present dangers and duties. *By William Du-gard,* 1650. 4°.* LT, CT, MR, EN, DT; HR, CH, MBP, NU, WF, Y. (var.)

Examination of Tilenus. 1658. *See* Womock, Laurence, *bp.*

3730   The examinations and informations upon oath of Sir Thomas Cooke. [*London,* 1695.] cap., 4°.* L, O, C, LG, LUG, LSD, MR; CH, CU, MH, WF, Y.

Examinations, censures. 1650. *See* Lucy, William, *bp.*

3730A   The examinations of Faithful Commins Dominican fryar. [*Dublin*], *printed in the year,* 1679. 4°.* CD (dispersed).

3731   The examinations of Henry Barrow. *For William Marshall,* [c. 1684]. 4°.* LIU, LSD, YM; NHC, NN, NU, WF, Y.

3731A   The examinations of Thomas Heth, a Jesuit. [*Dublin*], *printed,* 1679. 4°.* DIX 142. DI; NIC.

3732   The examiner defended, in a fair and sober answer. *By James Cottrel,* 1652. 4°. LT, O, AN, BC; MH, PL.

Examiner examined: being. 1691. *See* Comber, Thomas.

3733   The examiner examined. Certaine questions. *Printed at London for John Wright,* 1652. 4°.* LT, LW, DT; NU.

3734   Examples for kings. *For Henry Hutton,* 1642. 4°.* LT, OC, CT, EN, DT; CH, IU, MH, MM, WF, Y.

3734A   Examples for London or a parallel. *For Henry Hutton,* 1642. 4°.* WF.

3734B   Exceeding good and joyfull newes from Hull. *Printed for John Cave,* 1642. 4°.* L.

Exceeding good and true newes. 1642. *See* Russell, Thomas.

3735   Exceeding good newes againe from Ireland. *For John Thomas,* [1641/2]. 4°.* O, C, DN.

Exceeding good newes from Beverley. 1642. *See* G., T.

Dublin, Ianuary, 31. 1641. Exceeding good newes from Ireland. 1641. *See* Lancton, Thomas.

3736   No entry.

Exceeding good newes from Ireland. 1646. *See* B., W.

Exceeding good nevves from Ireland. 1647. *See* J., H.

Exceeding good nevves from Ireland. Being. 1647. *See* B., W.

3737 Exceeding good news from Oxford-shire. [*London*], *for Tho. Edwards, Aug.* 24, 1642. 4°.* MADAN 1028. LT, O, LNC; WF.

Exceeding good newes from South-Wales. 1648. *See* S., W.

3738 Exceeding good newes from the Earle of Essex. [*n.p.*], *December* 16. *for Joseph Hutton*, 1642. 4°.* LT; CH, WF.

3739 Exceeding good newes from the Isle of VVight. *For John Thomas*, 1641[2]. 4°.* LT; MH, MIU.

Exceeding good newes from the Neweries. 1642. *See* Johnson, Stephen.

3740 Exceeding happy and joyfull newes from the Kings Majesty. *For H. Blund; Sept.* 27. [1642]. 4°.* LT; CH.

3740A Exceeding happy news from Ireland, declaring. *For T. Rider*, 1642. 4°.* LT, DN.

3741 Exceeding happy newes from Oxford. *Sept.* 17. [*London*], *for John Wighf*[*sic*], [1642]. 4°.* MADAN 1040. LT; MH, MIU, WF, Y.

3742 Exceeding joyfull newes from Coventry. [*London*], *for Richard West, October* 19. 1642. 4°.* LT.

3743 Exceeding ioyfvll nevves from Darby. *For Henry Fowler, Septem.* 20. 1642. 4°.* LT, OC, LNC, EN; Y.

3744 Exceeding joyfull newes from Dover. *ondon* [*sic*], *for Hen. Fowler; August* 12. 1642. 4°.* LT, O, EC, LIU; MIU.

3745 Exceeding joyfull newes from His Excellence the Earle of Essex. *For Thomas Cooke, Sept.* 15. [1642]. 4°.* LT, LE.

Exceeding ioyfull nevvs from His Exelence . . . Essex. 1642. *See* Norcroft, John.

3746 Exceeding joyfull newes from Holland. *For Iohn Raymond*, 1642. 4°.* LT, O, MR; CN, WF.

3746A —[Anr. ed.] *By T.F. for Iohn Raymon.* 1642. 4°.* MH.

3747 Exceeding joyful newes from Holland. *For Richard Seymour, August* 5, 1642. 4°.* LT, O, EN; CH.

3748 Exceeding joyfull nevves from Hvll. *July* 16, *London for Edward Iohnson*, [1642]. 4°.* LT, EC, YM.

3748A Exceeding joyfull nevves from Hull. *For I. Norton*, 1642. 4°. OJ.

3749 Exceeding ioyfull newes from Ireland, or a true discovery. *For T. Rider, Aug.* 27, 1642. 4°.* LT, C, LVF, DN.

Exceeding joyfull newes from Ireland, or a true relation. 1641. *See* Lancton, Thomas.

3750 Exceeding joyfull newes from Lincoln-shire. *For Henry Fowler, Aug.* 17, 1642. 4°.* LT; NU, WF.

3751 Exceeding ioyfull news from Oxford-shire. *For Thomas Watson, Agust* [*sic*] 17. 1642. 4°.* MADAN 1026. LT.

3752 Exceeding joyfull nevves from Plymouth. [*London*], *Decemb.* 10. *for H. Blundoll.* 1642. 4°.* LT, O; CH, MH.

3753 Exceeding joyfull newes from Scotland brought over. [*n.p.*], *August* 20. *for J. Horten*, [1642]. 4°.* LT; MH, MIU, TU, WF, Y, ZWT.

3754 Exceeding joyfull news from Scotland: vvherein is declared. *Sept.* 13. *London, for T. Rider*, 1642. 4°.* LT, MR; Y.

3755 Exceeding joyfnll [*sic*] newes from Sovthampton. *June* 22. *London for I. Green. and A. Coe*, 1642. 4°.* LT, DN; Y.

3756 Exceeding joyfull newes from the Cavaleers at Nottingham. *September* 6. *London, for John Wight*, 1642. 4°.* LT, O; Y.

3757 Exceeding joyfull newes from the Earl of Bedford. *For Thomas Berriman; August* 23. 1642. 4°.* LT.

3758 Exceeding joyfull newes from the Earle of Bedford's army. *September* 7. *London, for John Wight* [*sic*], 1642. 4°.* LT; Y.

3759 Exceeding joyfull nevves from the Earl of Essex. *Decemb.* 9. [*London*], *printed for H. Blundo* [*i.e. Blunden*], 1642. 4°.* MADAN 1113. LT, O, LHO, CD; CH, MH.

3760 Entry cancelled.

Exceeding joyfull newes from . . . the Earl of Essex. [1642]. *See* Exceeding joyfull newes from His Excellence.

3761 Exceeding joyfull newes from the Earl of Stamford. [*London*], *for Richard West, October* 22, [1642]. 4°.* LT; CH.

3762 Exceeding joyfull nevves from the Earle of VVarwick. *For A. Coe. July* 16. 1642. 4°.* LT; CH, MH, Y.

3763 Exceeding joyfull newes from the Earl of Warwick. [*London*], *August* 3, *for Thomas Baley*, 1642. 4°.* LT.

3763A Exceeding joyfull nevvs from the Kings most excellent Majesty. *For J. Rider, Aug.* 7, 1642. 4°.* LC.

3764 Exceeding joyfull newes from the Lord Sey. *For Henry Fowler, Sept.* 23. 1642. 4°.* LT, AN.

3765 Exceeding joyfull newes from the narrow seas. *For Iohn Webb, May* 12. 1642. 4°.* O, LNM, EC.

3766 Exceeding joyfull newes from the Prince. [*n.p.*], *August* 19, *for Iames Ragge*, 1642. 4°.* LT, OC, CD; CH.

3767 Exceeding joyfull nevves from the treaty containing. *Imprinted at London, for P. Lovndel*, 1648. 4°.* LT; MH.

3767A Exceeding joyfull newes from Warwick-Castle. *For Iohn Cave, August* 17. 1642. 4°.* MH.

3767B Exceeding joyful nevves from York. *For T. Rjdore*, 1642. 4°.* O, LLU, YM; IU, WF.

3767C Exceeding joyfull news out of Lancashire. *For Robert Wood*, 1643. 4°.* MRL.

3768 Exceeding ioyfull newes out of Surrey. *For Iohn Iohnson*, 1642. 4°.* LT.

3769 Exceeding true and happy nevves from Pomfret Castle. *For Tho: Rider, Octob.* 11. 1642. 4°.* LT; CH, MH.

3770 Exceeding true and happy newes from the Castle of Windsor. *For T. Franklin, Octob.* 20. 1642. 4°.* LT; Y.

3771 Exceeding true and happy newes from the city of Glovcester. *For T. Franklin, Octob.* 15. 1642. 4°.* L.

3772 Exceeding true and joyfull newes from Worcester. [*n.p.*], *Septemb*, 29. *for James Blake*, [1642]. 4°.* LT; CH.

3773 Exceeding true newes from Boston. *For Henry Fowler: September* 7, 1642. 4°.* MADAN 1035. LT, BR; NU, WF.

3774 Exceeding true nevves from Newcastle. *May* 17. *London for J. Horton*, 1642. 4°.* LT, CD; MH.

Exceeding true relation. 1642. *See* Benningfield, W.

3775 Exceeding welcome nevves from Beverley. *For John Rider, Aug.* 4, 1642. 4°.* LT, O, EC, LIU; OWC.

3776 Exceeding welcome news from Ireland. *For Henry Fowler, Septemb. 2. 1642.* 4°.* O, C, EC; MH.

Excellency and equitableness. 1669. *See* H., G.

3776A The excellency and nature of the true spirit of wormwood. [*London*, 1675?] brs. L.

Excellency and usefulnesse. 1663. *See* Barker, *Sir* Richard.

Excellencie of a free-state. 1656. *See* Nedham, Marchamont.

Excellencie of Jesus. 1646. *See* H., J.

3777 The excellency of monarchy. [*London*, 1685?] brs. L, O; MH, MBA, Y, AMB.

3778 Entry cancelled.

Excellencie of physick and chirurgerie. 1652. *See* Fioravanti, Leonardo. Three exact pieces of.

3779 The excellency of the pen and pencil. *By Thomas Ratcliff and Thomas Daniel, for Dorman Newman and Richard Jones,* 1668. 8°. L, O, C, LG, DT; CH, IU, LC, MH, PL, Y.

3779A —[Anr. ed.] *For Dorman Newman,* 1688. 8°. T.C.II 227. L, O, LV, BC; CN, IU, LC, WF.

Excellency of theology. 1674. *See* Boyle, Robert.

3780 An excellent and most-pleasant new sonnet, . . . Diana. [*London*], *by W. O.* [1695?]. brs. L; MH.

3780A The excellent and renowned history of the famous Sir Richard Whittington. *Published by J.* [*Conyers,* 1690?]. 12°.* CM.

3780B —[Anr. ed.] [*London*], *for F. Coles, T. Vere, and* [*J.*] *Wright,* [1663–74]. brs. L.

3781 An excellent and very pretious exercise of a very devout . . . soule. *Bruges,* 1689. 12°. L.

3781A An excellent ballad, intituled, The constancy of Susanna. *For F. Coles, J. Wright, T. Vere and W. Gilbertson,* [1655–58]. brs. L, O; WF.

3782 —[Anr. ed.] *For W. O.,* [1690?]. brs. L.

3783 —[Anr. ed.] [*London*], *for W. Thackeray, J. Millet, and A. Milbourn,* [1689–92]. brs. L, CM, HH.

3784 An excellen balladt [*sic*] intituled The Gaberlunzie-man. [*London,* 1680–90]. brs. HH.

3784A An excellent ballad intituled, The unfortunate love. [*London*], *for F. Coles, T. Vere, and W. Gilbertson,* [1658–64]. brs. EUING 80. O, GU.

3784B —[Anr. ed.] [*London*], *for F. Coles, T. Vere, J. Wright and J. Clarke,* [1674–9]. brs. O.

3785 —[Anr. ed.] *By and for W. Onley, and A. Milbourn,* [1690–95]. brs. L, O, CM, HH.

3785A An excellent ballad, intituled, The wandring prince of Troy. [*London*], *for F. Coles, T. Vere, and J. Wright,* [1663–74]. brs. EUING 87. GU.

3786 —[Anr. ed., "entituled."] [*London*], *by and for A. M.,* [1680–85]. brs. EUING 88. L, O, CM, HH, GU.

3787 —[Anr. ed.] *By R. Gamble,* [1700]. brs. HH.

3788 —[Anr. ed.] *By and for W. O.,* [1700?]. brs. L, O.

3788A An excellent ballad of a Prince of England's courtship. [*London*], *by and for Alex. Milbourn,* [1685]. brs. L.

3788B —[Anr. ed.] *By & for W. O.,* [1700?]. brs. L.

3788C —[Anr. ed.] [*London*], *by and for A.M.,* [1700?]. brs. NNM.

3788D —[Anr. ed.] *By and for W.O. and sold by C. Bates,* [1700?]. brs. NNM.

3788E An excellent ballad of George Barnwel. [*London*], *for F. Coles, T. Vere, and W. Gilbertson,* [1658–64]. brs. EUING 81. O, GU.

3789 —[Anr. ed.] [*London*], *for F. Coles, T. Vere, J. Wright, and J. Clarke,* [1675?]. brs. L, O; MH.

3790 —[Anr. ed.] *By and for W. O. and A. M.,* [1690–97]. brs. L, HH.

3791 An excellent ballad of noble marquess and patient Grissel. *By and for W. O.,* [1690?]. brs. L, NNM.

3792 —[Anr. ed.] [*London*], *by and for Alex. Milbourn,* [1690?]. brs. L, CM, HH.

3792A An excellent ballad of Patient Grissel. *For F. Coles, T. Vere, and W. Gibertson*[*sic*], [1658–64]. brs. EUING 85. GU.

3792B An excellent ballad of St. George and the dragon. [*n.p.,* 1700?] brs. L.

3793 An excellent ballad of St. George for England. [*London*], *by and for Alex. Milbourn,* [1693]. brs. L, O, CM, HH.

3793A —[Anr. ed.] [*n.p.,* 1695?]. brs. L; NNM.

3793B —[Anr. ed.] [*London*], *by and for W. O.,* [1695?]. fol. L.

3793C An excellent ballad of that most dreadful combate, . . . the dragon of Wantley. *By and for C. Brown, and T. Norris, and sold by J. Walter,* [1700?]. brs. L.

3794 An excellent ballad of the birth and passion. [*London*], *for F. Coles, T. Vere, and J. Wright,* [1663–74]. brs. O.

3795 An excellent ballad of the mercers son. [*London*], *by and for A. M.,* [c. 1690]. brs. HH.

3796 —[Anr. ed.] [*London*], *for and sold by W. Thackeray, J. M. and A. M.,* [1689–92]. brs. EUING 90. L, CM, HH, GU.

Excellent ballad upon a wedding. 1698. *See* F., F.

3797 An excellent collection of books. [*London, sold 2 July* 1694.] 4°. L, LV, OP.

3798 An excellent collection of Greek, Latin, and English books. [*London, sold 12 April* 1692.] 4°. L.

Excellent comedy. 1651. *See* S., J.

Excellent discourse. 1682. *See* Filleau de la Chaise, Jean.

3798A An excellent ditty called The shepherds wooing fair Dulcina. [*London*], *for F. Coles, T. Vere, and W. Gilbertson,* [1658–64]. brs. O.

3799 —[Anr. ed.] [*London*], *for F. Coles, T. Vere, J. Wright, and J. Clarke,* [1674–79]. brs. L, O, CM, HH; MH.

3800 An excellent example to all young-men. *By M. H. and J. M. to be sold by J. Deacon,* 1684. brs. L.

3800A An excellent introduction to architecture. *For Robert Prick,* 1670. 4°. L, CT, DCH.

3801 —[Anr. ed.] 1679. fol. L.

3801A An excellent letter written by a prisoner. [*London?* 1646.] cap., 4°.* NC, NP.

Excellent medley. [1663–74.] *See* Parker, Martin.

Excellent memorables. 1691. *See* Baxter, Richard.

3802 Entry cancelled.

Excellent new ballad. [*London*], 1682. *See* Excellent new ballad, to the tune of.

3803 An excellent new ballad between Tom the Tory. *For R. H.,* 1678. brs. O, C; CH.

3804 An excellent new ballad, intituled King William. [*n.p., c.* 1690–94.] brs. HH.

3804A An excellent new ballad, intituled The constancy of Susanna. colop: [*London*], *by and for A. M.*, [1692]. brs. WF.

3804B An excellent new ballad, intitled, The cripple of Cornwall. [*London*, 1700?] fol. brs. L.

3804C An excellent new ballad of the birth . . . Christ. *For F. Coles, M. Wright, T. Vere, and W. Gilbertson*, [1658]. brs. EUING 83. GU.

3805 An excellent new ballad of the plotting head. [*London*], *for R. Moor*, 1681. brs. L, O, MC.

3805A —[Anr. ed.] *For P. M.*, 1681. brs. CH.

3806 An excellent new ballad, to the tune of, How vnhappy is Phillis. [*London*], *for Benjamin Harris, to be sold by Langley Curtis*, 1681. brs. L, O, C, LLU; CH, CN, MH, PU, WF, Y. (var.)

3806A —[Anr. ed.] —, 1682. brs. HH.

3807 An excellent new hymne to the mobile. *By Nath. Tompson*, 1682. brs. L, O; CH, MH.

3808 Entry cancelled. Date: [1628–29]. STC 17777.7.

3809 An excellent new play-house song, called, Love for money. [*London*], *for J. Conyers*, [1688]. brs. HH; MH.

3809A An excellent new play-house song, call'd, The bonny grey-ey'd morn. *By and for A. M.*, 1697. brs. CM.

3809B —[Anr. ed.] [*n.p.*, 1700?] brs. EN.

3810 An excellent new play-house song, called, The bonny milk-maid. [*London*], *by and for A. M.*, [1695]. brs. L, HH.

3810A —[Anr. ed.] [*London*, 1700?] brs. L.

3811 An excellent new play house song, call'd, The faithful lovers. [*London*], *for Charles Barnet*, 1694. brs. HH.

3812 An excellent new playhouse song call'd, The West-country fairing. *Printed and sold by T. Moore*, 1697. brs. MH.

3813 An excellent new poem upon the happy proceedings. [*London*, 1693.] brs. MH.

3814 An excellent new Scotch song. [*London*], *by and for A. M.*, [1695]. brs. HH.

3814A An excellent new song, call'd, Celemene. *Printed and sold by T. Moore*. 1697. brs. NNM.

3814B An excellent new song, call'd, Nelly's constancy. [*London*], *printed and sold by Charles Barnet*, [1686]. brs. CM.

3814C —[Anr. ed.] [London], *by and for A. M.*, [1695?]. brs. L.

3815 An excellent new song, call'd, The charming regents wish. [*London*], *for Charles Bates*, [1691–2]. brs. HH.

3815A An excellent new song, call'd, The intire lovers; or, Celia's answer to Strephon's complaint. *Printed and sold by T. Moore*, 1696. brs. NNM.

3816 An excellent new song, call'd The fairy queen. Llondon [*sic*], *printed and sold by T. Moore*, [1692–95]. brs. L, CM, HH.

3816A An excellent new song, call'd, The false-hearted young man. *By and for A. M.*, 1697. brs. CM.

3817 An excellent new song, call'd, The father outwitted. *By and for A. M. and sold by E. Brookesby*, [1695–1703]. brs. HH.

3818 An excellent new song, called, The female duel. [*London*], *printed and sold by P. Pelcomb*, [1700]. brs. L, CM, HH.

3819 Entry cancelled.
Excellent new song called. The frighted French. 1695. *See* Excellent song, call'd the frighted French.

3820 An excellent new song, called The gentlemans resolution. [*London*], *for Charles Barnet*, [1700]. brs. L, HH.

3821 An excellent new song, called, The intreagues of love. [*London*], *for Charles Barnet*, [1700?]. brs. L, CM, HH.

3821A An excellent new song, call'd, The lady's policy. *Printed, and sold by T. Moore*, 1693. brs. CM.

3822 An excellent new song, call'd, The languishing swain. [*London*], *for J. Blare*, [1685?]. brs. L, CM, HH.

3823 An excellent new song, called, The politick lady. [*London*], *for J. Conyers*, [1688–91]. brs. HH.

3824 An excellent new song, called, The praise of women. [*London*], *by and for A. M.*, [1690–97]. brs. HH.

3824A —[Anr. ed.] *By Tho. Moore*, 1695. brs. MRL.

3825 An excellent new song, called, The private encounter. [*London*], *for Charles Barnet*, [1697]. brs. L, HH.

3826 An excellent new song called The ruined virgin. [*London*], *printed for, and sold by Charles Barnet*, [1690?]. brs. L, CM, HH.

3827 An excelent new song call'd, The slighted lover. [*London*], *printed and sold by R. Liford*, [1690?]. brs. HH.

3828 An excellent new song, call'd, The unkind parents. [*London*], *for J. Blare*, [1690?]. brs. L, CM, HH.

3828A An excellent new song, intituled, Valiant Jockie. [*n.p.*, 1700?] brs. EN.

3828B An excellent new song lately composed, intituled The new way of Pittcathly well. [*Scotland*, 1700?] brs. EN.

3828C An excellent new song lately composed, intituled, the pearl of the Irish nation. [*n.p.*, 1690?] brs. L.

3829 An excellent new song, much in request. [*London*? 1670.] brs. L.

3830 An excellent new song, of the two happy lovers. [*London*], *printed P. Brooksby* [*sic*], [1685]. brs. CM, HH.

3831 An excellent new song of the unfortunate Whig's. [*London*], *for S. Maurel*, 1682. brs. L, O.

3832 An excellent new song on Lewis le Grand. *By T. M.*, [1689]. brs. O.

3832A An excellent new song on the late victories over the Turks. [*London*], *by Nat. Thompson*, [1684]. brs. O.

3832B An excellent new song; or, A true touch of the times. [*London*], *printed for P. Brooksby*, [1685–88]. brs. EUING 82. GU.

3833 —[Anr. ed.] [*London*], *for P. Brooksby, J. Deacon, J. Blare. J. Back*, [1690?]. brs. L; MH.

3833A An excellent new song: or the loyal Tory's delight. *For J. Dean*, 1683. brs. O.

Excellent observations. 1650. *See* Raleigh, *Sir* Walter.
Excellent piece. 1658. *See* Brathwaite, Richard. Honest ghost.

3833B An excellent receipt to make a compleat commonwealth-oleo. [*London*, 1659?] brs. LT, O; MH, WF, Y.

3834 An excellent receipt to make a compleat Parliament. [*London*, 1659.] brs. LT, O.

3834A Entry cancelled.

Excellent relation of a battell. 1641. *See* Exact relation of a battell.

3834B An excellent song, call'd lullaby. [*London*, 1670?] brs. L; MH.

3835 An excellent song, call'd The frighted French. *Printed and sold by T. Moore*, 1695. brs. L, HH.

3836 An excellent song, called, The shooe-makers travell. [1690?] brs. O.

3837 Entry cancelled. Date: [1628–29]. STC 22918.7.

3837A An excellent song, wherein you shall finde great consolation. *For F. Coles, T. Vere, and J. Wright*, [1663–74]. brs. O.

3837B An excellent sonnet of the unfortunate loves of Hero and Leander. *By and for W. O.*, [1700?]. brs. O.

Excellent virtues. 1674. *See* H., J.

3838–9 Entries cancelled.

Excellent woman described. 1692. *See* DuBosc, Jacques.

Excellent woman discoursed. 1669. *See* Collinges, John.

Exceptions against some passages. 1656. *See* Woodward, Hezekiah.

Exceptions against Will Rogers's cavills. 1682. *See* Penington, John.

Exceptions many. Oxford, 1653. *See* Ley, John.

3840 Entry cancelled.

Exceptions of Mr. Edwards. 1695. *See* Nye, Stephen.

3841 The exceptions of the Presbyterian brethren. [*n.p.*, 1662.] cap., 4°.* O, EN; CN, MBA, PH.

3841A Exceptions to Edward Mosley's bill in Parliament. [*London*, 1671?] brs. LPR.

Exchanges ready computed. [*n.p.*, 1655.] *See* Collins, John.

Excise anatomiz'd. [*n.p.*, 1659.] *See* Crofton, Zachary.

3842 The excise-mens lamentation. *For G. Horton*, 1652. 4°.* LT.

Excise rectify'd. 1695/6. *See* Farthing, John.

3843 Exclamatio pavpervm: The exclamation. [*London*], *printed*, 1648. 4°.* LT; MH, NU, WF, Y.

Exclamation against an apology. 1670. *See* Elys, Edmond.

3844 An exclamation against Julian. [*London*, 1679?] * L, O, LG; CH, CLC, CN, MH, TSM, TU, WF, Y.

Exclamation against Popery. 1678. *See* Wild, Robert.

3845 An exclamation against the whore of Babylon. *For R. G.*, 1679. 4°.* O; MH.

3846 Exclamation from Tunbridge. *For J. How.*, 1684. brs. L, O.

Exclamation to all those. 1670. *See* Elys, Edmond.

Exclames of Rhodophaea. [*n.p.*], 1661. *See* O., J.M.

Excommunicatio excommunicata. 1658. *See* Allen, Isaac.

3847 Excommunication excommunicated. *Printed*, 1680. 4°.* L, O, CT, BR, YM, DT; CH, CN, NU, WF, Y.

3848 The execution and confession with the behaviour & speeches of Capt. Thomas Walcott. colop: *By J. Grantham*. 1683. fol.* L, LPR; CH, CLC, MH.

3849 The execution and confessions of the seven prisoners . . . 19th December; 1679. [*London?* 1679.] cap., fol.* MR; WF.

3850 The execution, last speeches and confessions of the thirteen prisoners . . . 24th October, 1679. [*London?* 1679.] fol.* L, O, MR; WF.

3850A The execution of Ed. Fitz-Harris, and Oliver Plunket. colop: *By D. Mallet*, [1681?]. cap., 4°.* L; CH, TU.

3851 The execution of Henry Bury. *For L. C.*, 1678/9. 4°.* DU; CH, MH.

3851A —[Anr. ed.] *For D.M.* 1679. 4°.* IU.

3852 The execution of James Halloway. colop: *by E. Mallet*, 1684. brs. L, O; CH, IU.

3853 The execution of Mr. Robert Foulks. *For R. G.*, 1678/9. 4°.* MR, EN; CH, MH, NR.

3854 The execution of the Covenant. *For A. Rice*, 1661. brs. L, C(impf.), LNC; NN.

3854A The execution of the 11 prisoners. *D. M.*, 1679. 8°.* L.

3855 The fxecution [*sic*] of the late King, justified. *By M. Simmons*, 1649. 4°.* LT, DT; CH, MH, MM.

3855A The execution of the Popish lord. [*London*], *for P. Brooksby*, [1688]. cap., 4°.* O.

3855B The execution of two persons at Tyburn for the murdering of Sir Edmund-bury Godfrey. *For D. M.*, 1679. 4°.* O.

3855C The execution of William Howard . . . Stafford. colop: [*London*], *for T. Davis*, 1680. cap., fol.* O, OP, MR; WF.

3856 The execution of William Ireland. *For R. G.*, 1678/9. 4°.* EN; CH, MH, Y. (var.)

3856A The execution of William Lord Russel. colop: *By J. Grantham*, 1683. brs. CH, Y, ZWT.

3857 **Exell, Joshua.** Plain and exquisite Scripture-proof. *For the author, to be sold by Thomas Parkhurst; and by William Langford, in Warmister*, 1693. 4°. O, BB, EN; TO, WF.

3858 —A serious enquiry. *For R. Man*, 1693. 4°. T.C.II 436. L, O, AU; NPT, NU, TO.

3859 Entry cancelled.

Exemplar literarum. 1679. *See* To the nobility of England.

3860 The exercise for yong artillery men. *For Michael Sparke Senior*, 1642. 4°.* L, O, LG.

3861 The exercise of musquet and pike. *By Nat. Thompson*, 1684. fol. O.

3862 The exercise of the English. [*London*, 1642.] 4°.* LT, O; CH.

3863 The exercise of the foot. *By Charles Bill and Thomas Newcomb*, 1690. 8°. O, C, GC; CH, CN, PL, SE, WF, Y.

3864 —[Anr. ed.] *By Charles Bill and the executrix of Thomas Newcomb*, 1696. 8°. O.

3864A —[Anr. ed.] 1699. 8°. O.

Exercise of the spirit. [*n.p.*], 1686. *See* Laythes, Thomas.

3864B Exercitatio de religione. *Excudebat B. Griffin*, 1689. 4°.* C.

3864C Exercitatio de vera S. Sti nominis Jesu etymologia. *Prostant venales apud T. Garthwait*, 1652. 12°. L, CT, DUS; CLC.

Exercitatio geometrica. 1658. *See* White, Thomas.

Exercitation about infant-baptisme. 1646. *See* Tombes, John.

3865 The exercitation answered. *For John Wright*, 1650. 4°.
LT, O, C, EN, DT; CH, MH, MU, TU, WF, Y.
Exercitation concerning usurped powers. [n.p.], 1650.
See Gee, Edward, *elder.*
Exercitation on that. 1680. *See* Alsop, Vincent.

3865A An exhortation and admonition of the Friends. [*London,*
1672.] brs. LF; PH.
Exhortation & caution. [n.p., 1693.] *See* Keith, George.
Exhortation by way of epistle. 1696. *See* Field, John.

3866 An exhortation directed to the elders . . . of Lancaster.
By J. M. for Luke Favvn, 1655. 4°.* LT.
Exhortation given forth. 1694. *See* Lombe, Henry.

3866A An exhortation of the Friends. [*London,* 1672.] brs. LF;
PH.

3866AB The exhortation that a father gave to his children.
Printed at London for Francis Cotes, 1648. brs. L.

3866B An exhortation to a free and impartial enquiry. [*London,*
1691.] 4°.* L, DT; CH, Y.
Exhortation to all Dissenters. 1695. *See* Stafford, Richard.
Exhortation to all people. 1685. *See* Fox, George.

3867 An exhortation to catechizing. *By T. R. and E. M. for*
Samuel Gellibrand, 1655. 4°.* LT, O, OC, CT, P; CLC,
NGT, NU, WF, Y.
Exhortation to repentance. Amsterdam, 1688. *See*
Shower, John.

3868 An exhortation to the people of Ireland. *Dublin, by*
Andrew Crook, 1690. 4°.* DIX 240. DN.
Exhortation to the restoring. 1641. *See* Davenport, John.
Exhortation to the taking. [n.p., 1643.] *See* England:
Laws, Statutes. Collection of all the publicke orders,
1646.
Exhortation to youth. 1681. *See* Shower, John.

3869 An exhortation vnto the learned divines. *In Amsterdam,*
for the author, and are tobee [sic] sold by Iohn Crosse, 1643.
4°.* NU.

3870 An exit to the exit tyrannus. [*London,* 1660.] brs. LT, O;
MH.

3871 Entry cancelled.
Expediency of an explicit stipulation. 1674. *See* Cathol-
icon.
Expedient for composing. 1649. *See* Hammond, Henry.
Mysterium.
Expedient for peace. [n.p., 1692.] *See* Bonifield, Abra-
ham.
—[Same title.] 1693. *See* Sandilands, Robert.

3872 An expedient for peace: perswading an agreement.
colop: *For the author*, 1688. cap., 4°.* L, O, LIU, EN, CD;
CH, CN, MH, NU, WF, Y.

3872AA —[Anr. ed.] *By George Larkin*, 1688. 4°.* L, OC, CS,
BANGOR, DU; CH, CN, MH, MIU, PU.

3872A An expedient for peace amongst Christians. Second part.
George Larkin and R. Janeway, 1689. 4°.* L, O, SP, DU;
CH, CLC.

3873 An expedient for the preventing any difference. *For Giles*
Calvert, 1659. 4°.* LT, O, LLU, MR, DT; CSS, MH, MU,
WF, Y.

3874 An expedient, or, a sure & easy way of reducing all
dissenters. [*London,* 1662.] cap., 4°.* L, O, OC, CJ, EN;
CH, CN, NC, NU, TU, WF, Y.

3875 —[Anr. ed.] colop: 1672. cap., 4°.* L, O, LW, CT; MM,
NGT, PL, WF.
Expedient to avoid. [n.p., 1695.] *See* Wood, William.
Expedient to preserve. 1647. *See* Marshall, Stephen.

3876 An expedient which with an easier burden. [*London,*
1695?] brs. L.

3877 Expedients for publique peace. [*London*], *printed*, 1660.
4°.* LT, O; CN, MH, ZWT.

3877A Expedients proposed for the easing and advantaging the
coal-trade. [*n.p.,* 1670.] fol.* L, LPR. (var.)

3877B Expedients proposed . . . an answer. [*London,* 1670.] brs.
O, LPR.

3877C Expedients proposed . . . reply to the answer. [*London,*
1670.] fol.* MB.
Expedition of His Highness. [n.p., 1688.] *See* Burnet,
Gilbert, *bp.*
Experienc'd angler. 1662. *See* Venables, Robert.
Experienc'd farrier. 1691/2. *See* R., E.
Experienc'd fowler. 1697. *See* Smith, John.

3878 The experienced jocky. *For Will. Whitwood*, 1684. 12°.
T.C.II 101. L, C; CH, WF, Y.

3879 The experienced market man and woman. *Edinburgh,*
printed and sold by James Watson, 1699. 8°.* ALDIS 3848.
L.
Experiences and tears. 1652. *See* B., W.

3880 An experimentall essay touching the reformation of the
lawes of England. *By Matthew Simmons*, 1648. 4°.* LT,
O, DT; CH, CSS, MHL, WF, YL.
Experiments and notes. Oxford, 1680. *See* Boyle, Rob-
ert.
Expert doctor's dispensatory. 1657. *See* Morel, Pierre.

3881 The expert gardener. *By William Hunt*, 1654. 4°. LT, O;
CH, IU, WF, Y.
Expiation of a sinner. 1646. *See* Crell, John.

3882 The explanation of a former act. [*London?* 1685.] brs. L,
O; MH.
Explanation of some truths. 1645. *See* Buchanan, David.

3883 An explanation of the agreement of the 21. of Decemb.
last. *Printed at Oxford by Leonard Lichfield, Jan.* 16, 1642.
4°.* MADAN 1187. L, O.

3883A An explanation of the assemblies shorter catechism. 1682.
12°. LCL.

3884 An explanation of the Assembly of Divines shorter
catechism. Second edition. *For J. Robinson*, 1695. 12°.
LW; NU.
Explanation of the Lord Treasurer's. [n.p.], 1679. *See*
Leeds, Thomas Osborne, *earl of.*
Explanation of the Roman Catholicks. [n.p.], 1656. *See*
Davenport, Francis.

3885 An explanation of the Scots Commis[s]ioners, their
declaration. [*Edinburgh,* 1641.] brs. STEELE 1838. ALDIS
1003. ES.

3886 An explanation of the terms, orders, and usefulness of
the liturgy. *For Sam. Keble*, 1692. 8°.* T.C.II 330. O, OC.

3886A —[Anr. ed.] [1700.] 8°.* CT.

3886B The explanation. To the tune of Hey boys up we go. [*London?* 1685.] brs. O, C; MH.

Explanatory notes. 1698. *See* Butler, John.

Explication of the creed. 1679. *See* Rawlet, John.

3887 Entry cancelled.

Explication of the diall. Liege, 1673. *See* Hall, Francis.

Explication of the shorter. 1669. *See* W., S.

Explicatory catechism. 1675. *See* Vincent, Thomas.

Exploits discovered. 1643. *See* R., H.

3887A Exporting unmanufactured goods. [*London?* 1680.] brs. L.

Exposition of Ecclesiastes. 1680. *See* Sykes, George.

3888 An exposition of the Brownists pater-noster. [*London*, 1642.] brs. LT.

3888aA —[Anr. ed.] [*London*], for F. L., [1642]. brs. LT.

3888bA —[Anr. ed.] *For Thomas Underhill*, 1642. brs. LT.

Exposition of the church-catechism. 1695. *See* Seller, Abednego.

Exposition of the doctrine. 1686. *See* Wake, William, *abp*.

3888cA An exposition of the holy ornaments and ceremonies at Mass. *For N. T.*, 1686. 12°. O, LLP.

Exposition of the Protestant rule. 1688. *See* Pulton, Andrew. Full and clear exposition.

Exposition of the whole book. 1689. *See* Knollys, Hanserd.

3888dA An exposition on that most excellent prayer in the liturgy. *For Brabazon Aylmer*, 1698. 8°.* L; WF.

Exposition on the church-catechism. 1685. *See* Ken, Thomas, *bp*.

Exposition on the fourth chapter. 1693. *See* Cross, Walter.

Exposition upon Sir George Ripley's. 1677. *See* Starkey, George.

3888A An exposition upon the second Psalme. *For Livewell Chapman*, 1655. 4°. NPT.

Expostulation with the bishops. [n.p., 1662.] *See* Whitehead, John.

Expostulation with Thomas Lloyd. [n.p., 1692.] *See* Budd, Thomas.

Expostulatory appeal to the professors. [n.p., 1680?] *See* Bathurst, Elizabeth.

3889 An expostulatorie (but friendly) adhortation to that part of the ministry of England. [*n.p., c.* 1655–65.] cap., 4°.* OU.

3890 An expostulatory letter to the author of the late slanderous libel. *Printed*, 1671. 4°.* O, DM; CLC, MH, NU, WF.

3891 An express from the African and Indian Scots. *Edinburgh, by John Reid*, 1699. brs. ALDIS 3849. EN.

3892 An express from the knights and gentlemen now engaged with Sir George Booth. [*London*, 1659.] brs. LT, O, OC; MH, MIU.

3893 An expresse relation of the passages and proceedings of His Majesties armie. [*Oxford, by H. Hall*], printed, 1643. 4°.* MADAN 1407. O; CH, CLC, WF, Y.

3894 **Exquemelin, Alexandre Olivier.** Bucaniers of America. *For William Crooke*, 1684. 4°. T.C.II 60. L, O, C, CT, EN, DN; CH, CN, LC, MH, MU, NN, RPJ, WF, Y.

3895 Entry cancelled. Ghost.

3896 — —Second edition. *For William Crooke*, 1684. 4°. T.C.II 77. L, C, LL, WCA, DT; CH, CLC, LC, RPJ, Y.

3897 — —The second volume. *For William Crooke*, 1685. 4°. T.C.II 112. L, LG, CT, LSD, WCA; CH, IU, MH, PL, RPJ, WF, Y.

3898 —The history of the bucaniers. *For Tho. Malthus*, 1684. 12°. T.C.II 70. L, O, OC, CS; CH, CN, LC, MH, RPJ.

3898A — —Second edition. *For William Whitwood, and sold by Anthony Feltham*, 1695. 4°. T.C.II 573. CH, NN, NS, Y.

3899 [–] — Fifth edition. *For Tho. Newborough, John Nicholson, and Benj. Tooke*, 1699. 8°. T.C.III 78. L, O, C, E, DM; CH, CN, LC, MH, PL.

3900 An extempore sermon preached at the request. [*London*, 1680.] brs. L, O; MH, WF.

3901 An extempore sermon preached upon malt. *Reprinted Edinburgh*, 1691. brs. ALDIS 3147. EN.

Extemporary sermon upon malt. [n.p., 1685.] *See* Dod, John.

Extent of the sword. [n.p., 1653.] *See* L., T.

3902 **Exton, John.** The maritime diceologie. *By Richard Hodgkinson*, 1664. fol. L, O, CCA, EN, CD; CLC, MU, PL, WF, YL.

3903 The extortioners and stock-jobbers, detected. colop: *For E. Whitlock*, 1696. cap., fol.* NC.

3903A An extract from the Dutch printed cargoes. [*London?* 1697.] brs. MH.

Extract of a letter from a person. [n.p.], 1660. *See* R., T.

3904 Entry cancelled.

Extract of a letter from Brussels. 1660. *See* R. T. Extract of a letter from a person.

3905 An extract of a letter from Yorke. *August 5. London for Abel Roper*, 1642. 4°.* LT, OC, CT, DU; WF.

3905A —[Anr. ed.] *August 9. London, for A.R.* 1642. 4°.* LLU, MR; CH, CLC.

3906 An extract of a letter from York. *Printed*, 1659[60]. brs. LT, O, LG, CJ, YM; MH.

3907 An extract of all the passages from Hull. *For Benjamin Allen and Iohn Bull, July 19.* 1642. 4°.* LT, EC, SP, YM; CH, MH, WF.

3908 An extract of certain papers of intelligence, from Cambrjdge. [*London*], printed, 1647. 4°.* LT, O, C, LIU, SP; CSS, MIU, Y, ZAP.

3909 An extract of letters, wherein is related, certaine remarkable passages from Yorke. *By R. O. & G. D. for Benjamin Allen, August 9.* 1642. 4°.* LT, O, EC.

3910 An extract of severall letters from Scotland: concerning the defeat. *For Edward Husbands*, 1645. 4°.* LT, MR, E; CH, MH, MU, WF.

3911 An extract of severall letters from Scotland; sent. [*London*], *for R. Bostock and Samuell Gellibrand, April* 15, 1645. 4°.* LT, O, DT.

3912 Jvne 22. 1642. An extract of severall letters sent from Yorke. [*London*], published, 1642. 4°.* LT, SP, YM; CH, IU, WF, Y.

3913 An extract of severall letters vvhich came. *By Luke Norton*, 1642. 4°.* LT, O, MR.

3914 An extract of so much of the Act of 9 and 10 Gul. III. [*n.p.*, 1698.] fol. O.

3914A An extract of the acts against importing Irish Cattel. [*London*, 1680.] brs. MH.

3915 An extract of the Acts of the Nationall Synod of the Reformed Churches of France. *Printed at London for John Field, Jan.* 28. 1644[5]. 4°.* LT, LW, MR; CSS, MH, NU, Y.

Extract out of a letter. [*n.p.*], 1659. *See* C., H.

3915A An extract out of several libels. [*London*, 1683?] brs. LPR; CN.

Extraction of mans soul. 1655. *See* Woolner, Henry.

3916 Extracts of some letters. [*London*], *for I. B. and R. S., Decemb.* 16. 1642. 4°.* L, MR; MH, MIU, WF.

Extraneus vapulans. 1656. *See* Heylyn, Peter.

3917 Extraordinaire contenant les derniers propos. *Londres, N. Bourne*, 1649. 4°.* HH.

Extraordinary adventures. 1683. *See* Crouch, Nathaniel.

3917A The extraordinary case of several persons . . . Exchequer. [*London?* 1700.] brs. L.

3918 An extraordinary collection of original pictures . . . ninth . . . November, 1691. [*n.p.*], 1691. 4°.* L.

3919 An extraordinary collection of paintings, . . . 20th . . . January, 1690/91. [*n.p.*], 1691. 4°.* L.

3920 An extraordinary collection of paintings, . . . 5th . . . May, 1691. [*n.p.*], 1691. 4°.* L.

3921 An extraordinary collections of pictures, . . . 21st . . . May, 1691. [*n.p.*], 1691. 4°.* L.

3922 An extraordinary collection of pictures, . . . 10th, . . . June, 1691. [*n.p.*], 1691. 4°.* L.

3923 An extraordinary collection of pictures, . . . 21st of October. [*n.p.*, 1691.] brs. L.

3924 An extraordinary collection of pictures, . . . 30th, . . . October. [*n.p.*, 1691.] brs. L.

3925 An extraordinary collection of pictures, . . . 12th. of November. [*n.p.*, 1691.] brs. L.

3926 An extraordinary collection of pictures, . . . 2d of December. [*n.p.*, 1691.] brs. L.

3927 An extraordinary collection of pictures, . . . 7th. of December. [*n.p.*, 1691.] brs. L.

3928 An extraordinary collection of pictures, . . . 3d. of February. [*n.p.*, 1692.] brs. L.

3929 An extraordinary collection of pictures . . . 25th of February. [*n.p.*, 1692.] brs. L.

3930 An extraordinary collection of pictures, . . . 23d . . . March. [*n.p.*, 1692.] brs. L.

3931 An extraordinary collection of pleasant & merry humour's. [*London*], *sold by Iohn Young*, [1700?]. obl. sixes. * HH.

Extraordinary deliverance. 1642. *See* Fiennes, Nathaniel, elder.

3931A An extraordinary express sent from Pasquin at Rome. *For Henry Hills*, 1690. 12°. O, P; NPT.

3932 Extraordinary newes from Col. John Barker. [*London*], *by E. G., for John Rothwell*, 1644. brs. L.

3933 Extraordinary newes from Constantinople, November the 27, 1641. *For Francis Constable and Iohn Thomas*, 1641. 4°.* LT, O, LLU, SP, E; CH, CN, WF.

Extraordinary newes from the court. 1650. *See* B., T.

Extravagant poet. 1681. *See* Oudin, César François, *sieur de Préfontaine.*

Extravagant shepherd. 1653. *See* Sorel, Charles.

3933A The extravagant spend-thrift. [*London*], *for J. Back*, [1665?]. brs. O.

3934 The extravagant youth. [*London*], *for J. Deacon*, [1684–5]. brs. L, CM, HH; MH.

3935 The eye clear'd; or a preservative for the sight. [*London*], *for G. Bishop, June* 25. 1644. 4°.* LT, O, OW; CH, MH, TU, WF, HC.

3936 An eye-salve for the armie. [*London*], *printed*, 1647. 4°.* LT, O; CH, MH, Y, ZAP.

3937 An eye-salve for the city of London. [*London*], *printed*, 1648. 4°.* LT, LG, OC, SC; CH, IU, MH, MIU, NU, Y.

3938 Eye-salve for the English armie. 1660. 4°. O, LG, BC; NN, Y.

3939 Entry cancelled.

Eye-salve for the kingdome. 1647. *See* Little eye-salve.

3940 [**Eyre, *Mrs.* Elizabeth (Packington).**] A letter from a person of quality in the North. *For Awnsham Churchill*, 1689. 4°.* T.C.II 292. O, C, LLP, CT, BR; CH, IU, MH, NU, WF, Y.

3941 **Eyre, John.** The exact surveyor. *For Nath: Brook*, 1654. 8°. L, O, OC, DC; CLC, IAU, MU, NC, WF.

3942 **Eyre, Robert.** A discourse concerning the nature and satisfaction of a good . . . conscience. *For B. Aylmer*, 1693. 4°.* T.C.II 450. O, OU, MR, NPL; CH, IU, NU, WF, Y.

3943 —The sinner a traitor. *By W. Bowyer, for Walt. Kettilby*, 1700. 4°.* T.C.III 209. L, O, C, EC, WCA; CH, IU, MH, WF, Y.

3943A **Eyre, William.** A brief of the case of. [*London*, 1675?] brs. LPR.

3943B —The case of . . . concerning his estate in Ireland. [*London*, 1675.] cap., 4°.* LPR.

—Case of . . . concerning his right. [*n.p.*, 1670?] *See title.*

—Case of William Eyre, gent. bayliffe. [*n.p.*, 1675?] *See title.*

3944 —Christ's scepter. *By G. Dawson, for Livewell Chapman*, 1652. 4°.* L, LW, OH, LSD; CH, NU.

3945 —A particular deduction of the case of William Eyre. [*London?* 1675.] cap., 4°.* L, O, C, LPR, OC; WF.

3945A —The serious representation of Col. William Eyre. [*London*, 1649.] cap., 4°.* CSS.

3946 [–] A vindication of the letter out of the North. *For Awnsham Churchill*, 1690. 4°.* T.C.II 305. L, LLP, OC, CT, EC; CH, CN, NU, WF, Y.

3947 —Vindiciæ justificationis gratuitæ. Justification. *For R. I. to be sold by Tho. Brewster*, 1654. 4°. LT, O, LW, E, ENC; CLC, IU, NPT, NR.

3947A — —[Anr. ed.] *For R. I. to be sold by Edward Forrest, Oxford*, 1654. 4°. MADAN 2255. O; MH, NN, Y.

3948 — —Second edition. *Printed, and sold by John Vousden*, 1695. 8°. T.C.II 561. L, LW; CLC, LC, MH, NPT, NU, WF, Y.

3949 **Eyres, Joseph.** The church-sleeper awakened. *By W. Godbid, for Joseph Cranford,* 1659. 12°. LT.

3949A **[Eyston], Bernard Francis.** The Christian duty composed. *Printed at Aire by Claude François Tulliet,* 1684. 4°. L, O, BSM; CH, CN, NU, TU, WF, WG, Y.

3949B —A clear looking-glass. *Printed at Roane,* 1654. 12°. CN.

3950 Entry cancelled.

Eyzat, *Sir* Edward. *See* Eizat, *Sir* Edward.

Ezekiel cap. 2. [n.p., 164–?] *See* Douglas, *Lady* Eleanor.

Ezekiel's wheels. 1653. *See* Morton, Thomas, *bp.*

F

F. Fida pastora. 1658. *See* Fletcher, John.

1 —A letter sent from a private gentleman to a friend in London. [*Oxford*], *for William Webb,* 1642. 4°.* MADAN 1285. L, O, C, OC, CT, BC; CH, CLC, CN, MIU, WF.

1A [–] —[Anr. ed.] [*London*], *for V. N.,* 1642. 4°.* LT, O, C, DU, LLU, LNC; CSS, CN, MIU, MH, NCD, WF, Y. (var.)

F., A. Few lines in true love. 1694. *See* Fisher, Abigail.

—Liturgical discourse. [n.p.], 1670. *See* Mason, Richard.

—New prognostication. Edinburgh, 1674. *See* Almanacs.

—Scotland's present duty. [n.p.], 1700. *See* Foyer, Archibald.

2 —Strange newes from Yorke. *For Iohn Thomas,* 1642. 4°.* LT, LLU, LNC, YM; Y.

F., B. World's honour detected. 1663. *See* Furly, Benjamin.

F., Br. Manvall of the third order. 1643. *See* Mason, Richard.

F., C. Copy of a letter by a minister. 1665. *See* Flower, Christopher.

—Genealogie of Christianity. 1650. *See* Feake, Christopher.

3 —A letter to His Grace the D. of Monmouth, this 15th. of July, 1680. [*London?* 1680]. cap., fol.* L, O, C, MC, EN; CH, MH, MM, PU, WF, Y.

4 Entry cancelled. *See preceding entry.*

4A Entry cancelled.

—Pluto furens. Amstelodami, 1669. *See* Carr, William.

5 —VVit at a venture. *For Jonathan Edwin,* 1674. 8°. T.C.I 170. L, O; CH, CN, MH, WCL, WF, Y.

6 F., D. The Dutch-mens pedigree. *Printed,* 1653. brs. LT.

7 —The equallity of the ministery plainly described. [*London*], *printed,* 1641. 4°.* LT, O, C, E, DT; CH, CN, MH, TU, WF.

8 —A letter of address to the Protector. [*London,* 1657.] cap., 4°.* LT, O, LIU, NPL; CH, MH, NU, Y.

—Poor man's plea. 1698. *See* Defoe, Daniel.

9 —Reason and judgement. *Oxford: by J. W. for Will. Thorne,* 1663. 4°. MADAN 2648. L, O, C, LW, MR; CH, MBP, NC, NU, Y.

10 — —[Anr. ed.] *By J. C. for H. Marsh,* 1663. 4°. O, LW, OC, CS; CLC, IU, NU, WF.

11 —Statuta vetera & recentiora. A mcthodical collection. *By John Streater, Eliz. Flesher, and H. Twyford, assignes of Rich. Atkyns and Ed. Atkyns. To be sold by G. Sawbridge, J. Place, J. Bellinger, W. Place, T. Basset, R. Pawlet, C. Wilkinson, T. Dring, W. Jacob, C. Harper, J. Leigh, J. Amery, J. Poole,* 1672. 8°. T.C.I 124. L, C, DC; CH, LC, MIU, WF.

F., E. Alarm to trumpets. 1651. *See* Ford, Edward.

—Christian caveat. 1650. *See* Fisher, Edward.

12 —The emblem of a virtuous woman. [*London?* 1650.] 8°. CH.

13 Entry cancelled.

—Fair play in the lottery. [n.p., 1660.] *See* Ford, Edward.

—Faith in five fundamental. 1650. *See* Fisher, Edward.

—Famous and pleasant history. [1680.] *See* Forde, Emanuel.

—History of the life, reign. 1680. *See* Falkland, Henry Cary, *viscount.*

14 —A letter from a gentleman of quality in the country, to his friend. [*London*], *printed,* 1679. fol.* L, O, C, DU, EN; CH, CN, MH, WF, Y. (var.)

—London's gate. 1647. *See* Fisher, Edward.

—Looke not upon me. [n.p.], 1648. *See* Fornis, Edward.

—Madruddyn. 1651. *See* Fisher, Edward.

—Marrow of modern divinity. 1645. *See* Fisher, Edward.

15 —Newes from Heaven both good and true. *By R. O. & G. D.,* 1641. 4°.* L; CH, CU, MH, NU, WF, Y.

—News from Hell. 1680. *See* Panton, Edward.

—Questions preparatory. 1655. *See* Fisher, Edward.

16 —Rome for the Great Tvrke. *By T. F. for F. Coles,* 1664. 4°.* MH.

—Scriptvres harmony. 1643. *See* Fisher, Edward.

—Touch-stone for a communicant. 1647. *See* Fisher, Edward.

17 —A true relation of a great and wonderfull victory obtained by Captain Ashton. *For Edw. Husbands, May* 8. 1643. 4°.* LT; CLC, MH, WF.

18 F., E. deC. V. England's deplorable condition. *For the author, to be sold by Richard Skelton,* 1659. 4°. L; CU.

F., F. Apobaterion vel. 1655. *See* Fisher, Payne.

19 Entry cancelled.

—Excellent ballad upon a wedding. 1698. *See* Fane, *Sir* Francis.

19A —A gratulatory song of peace. [*n.p.*, 1652.] brs. O.

—Panegyrick to the Kings. 1662. *See* Fane, *Sir* Francis.

—Pindarick ode on the sacred memory. 1685. *See title.*

—Socinian controversy. 1693. *See* Fullwood, Francis.

F., G. Answer to a paper which. 1658. *See* Fox, George.

—Answer to Doctor Burgess his book. 1659. *See* Fox, George.

—Ansvver to several new laws. [n.p.], 1678. *See* Fox, George.

—Answer to the arguments. [n.p., 1661.] *See* Fox, George.

—Answer to Thomas Tillams book. 1659. *See* Fox, George.

—Arraignment of popery. 1667. *See* Fox, George.

—Cæsar's due. [n.p.], 1679. *See* Fox, George.

—Catechism for children. 1657. *See* Fox, George.

—Catechismus pro parvulis. 1660. *See* Fox, George.

—Clear discovery. [n.p.], 1662. *See* Fox, George.

20 —The clerks assistant: being a collection. *By S. R. for John Kidgell.* 1683. 8°. T.C.II 61. O; IU, MH, NCL, NR, WF.

20A —The clerks grammar enlarged. Second edition. *By the assigns of R. and E. Atkins; sold by P. Browne,* 1692. 8°. LC.

20B —The clerk's grammar, wherein. *By T. B. for J. Kidgil,* 1683. 12°. T.C.II 61. CH, CLC, MH, NR.

—Concerning Christ. [n.p.], 1677. *See* Fox, George.

—Concerning good-morrow. 1657. *See* Fox, George.

—Concerning meeting. [n.p., 1683.] *See* Fox, George.

—Concerning sons. [n.p., 1660?] *See* Fox, George.

—Concerning the antiquity. 1689. *See* Fox, George.

—Concerning the apostate. 1689. *See* Fox, George.

—Concerning the traditions. [n.p., 1688.] *See* Fox, George.

—Controversie which hath been. [n.p., 1666.] *See* Fox, George.

—Cry for repentance. Lonnon [*sic*], 1656. *See* Fox, George.

—Cunctis Christi. 1660. *See* Fox, George.

—Cunctis viam. 1660. *See* Fox, George.

—Declaration against all profession. 1655. *See* Fox, George.

—Declaration concerning fasting. 1656. *See* Fox, George.

—Declaration of the difference. 1656. *See* Fox, George.

—Declaration of the ground of error. 1657. *See* Fox, George.

—Distinction between the phanatick. 1660. *See* Fox, George.

—Distinction between true liberty. [n.p., 1685.] *See* Fox, George.

—Distinction betwixt the two suppers. [n.p.], 1685. *See* Fox, George.

—English Gusman. 1652. *See* Fidge, George.

—Epistle general to them. 1660. *See* Fox, George.

—Epistle to all Christians. 1682. *See* Fox, George.

—Epistle to all people. 1657. *See* Fox, George.

—Epistle to be read. [n.p.], 1666. *See* Fox, George.

—Epistle to friends for them. [n.p., 1679.] *See* Fox, George.

21 —An epithalamium and well-wishings for . . . Mr. Henry Sheibel. [*n.p.*], 1686. fol.* L.

—Eternal, substantial truths. 1661. *See* Fox, George.

—Exhortation to all people. 1685. *See* Fox, George.

—Fevv vvords to all such. 1669. *See* Fox, George.

—For the holy women. [n.p.], 1686. *See* Fox, George.

—For the King and his council. [n.p., 1660.] *See* Fox, George.

—General epistle to all friends. [n.p., 1664.] *See* Fox, George.

—General epistle to be read. [n.p.], 1662. *See* Fox, George.

—General epistle to friends. [n.p.], 1667. *See* Fox, George.

—Gospel family-order. [n.p.], 1676. *See* Fox, George.

—Gospel liberty, and. [n.p.], 1668. *See* Fox, George.

—Great eater. 1652. *See* Fidge, George.

—Ground of desperation. [n.p., 1656.] *See* Fox, George.

—Ground of high places. 1657. *See* Fox, George.

—Heathens divinity. [n.p.], 1671. *See* Fox, George.

—Here all may see a clear. [n.p.], 1680. *See* Fox, George.

—Here all may see that. 1656. *See* Fox, George.

—Here are several queries. 1657. *See* Fox, George.

—Here is declared. 1658. *See* Fox, George.

—Here you may see. 1660. *See* Fox, George.

—Hind's ramble. 1651. *See* Fidge, George.

—Honest, plain, down-right dealing. [n.p., 1660.] *See* Fox, George, *younger.*

—How God's people. 1687. *See* Fox, George.

—Institutiones pietatis. [n.p.], 1676. *See* Fox, George.

—Instruction to judges. [1657.] *See* Fox, George.

—Instructions for right spelling. [n.p.], 1680. *See* Fox, George.

—Instructions of godliness. [n.p.], 1676. *See* Fox, George.

—Inward and spiritual warfare. [n.p.], 1690. *See* Fox, George.

—Lamb's officer. 1659. *See* Fox, George.

—Line of righteousness. 1661. *See* Fox, George.

—Litvrgical considerator. 1661. *See* Firmin, Giles.

—Looking-glass for the Jews. [n.p.], 1674. *See* Fox, George.

—Margarita in Anglia. [n.p.], 1660. *See* Fox, George.

—Measuring-rule concerning liberty. [n.p., 1661.] *See* Fox, George.

—Oh people! [n.p.], 1670. *See* Fox, George, *younger.*

—Old Simon. 1663. *See* Fox, George.

—Pearle found. 1658. *See* Fox, George.

—Possession above. [n.p., 1675.] *See* Fox, George.

—Presbyterial ordination. 1660. *See* Firmin, Giles.

—Priests and professors. 1657. *See* Fox, George.

—Priests fruits. 1657. *See* Fox, George.

—Primitive ordination. [n.p.], 1675. *See* Fox, George.

—Pro imperatore. 1660. *See* Fox, George.

—Queries concerning tythes. [n.p., 1663.] *See* Fox, George.

—Questions between the conformist. 1681. *See* Firmin, Giles.

—Reply to the pretended. 1658. *See* Fox, George.

—Responsio ad chartam. 1660. *See* Fox, George.

—Royal law of God. [n.p.], 1671/2. *See* Fox, George.

—Scripture testimony. [n.p., 1688.] *See* Fox, George.

—Second covenant. 1657. *See* Fox, George.

—Serious peoples reasoning. 1659. *See* Fox, George.

—Several papers given forth. [n.p.], 1671. *See* Fox, George.

—Several plain truths. 1684. *See* Fox, George.

—Several treaties worthy. 1691. *See* Fox, George.

—Something in answer. [n.p.], 1660. *See* Fox, George.

—Something in answer to Lodowick. 1667. *See* Fox, George.

—Spirit of envy. 1663. *See* Fox, George.

—Teachers of the world. 1656. *See* Fox, George.

—That all might see. 1657. *See* Fox, George.

—These queries. [n.p., 1685.] *See* Fox, George.

—This is an encouragement. [n.p.], 1676. *See* Fox, George.

—This is to all. 1657. *See* Fox, George.

—Three general epistles. [n.p.], 1664. *See* Fox, George.

—To all kings. 1685. *See* Fox, George.

—To all people in all Christendom. [n.p., 1663.] *See* Fox, George.

—To all that professe. 1661. *See* Fox, George.

—To all that would know. 1655. *See* Fox, George.

—To all the nations. 1660. *See* Fox, George.

—To both houses of Parliament. 1660. *See* Fox, George.

—To friends in Barbadoes. [n.p., 1666.] *See* Fox, George.

—To the chief magistrate. [n.p., 1684.] *See* Fox, George.

—To the high and lofty ones. [n.p., 1655.] *See* Fox, George.

—To the Parliament. 1659. *See* Fox, George.

—To the people of Uxbridge. 1659. *See* Fox, George.

—To those that have been. [1660.] *See* Fox, George.

—To you that are crying. [n.p., 1657.] *See* Fox, George.

22 —The touchstone of precedents. *For Awnsham Churchill*, 1682. 8°. T.C.I 460. O, LI, LL, LMT; LC, MIU, PL, WF.

—True account of the sensible, thankful. [n.p.], 1686. *See* Fox, George.

—True Christians distinguished. 1689. *See* Fox, George.

—True marriage. [n.p., 1679.] *See* Fox, George.

—True relation of the unlawful. [n.p., 1660.] *See* Fox, George, *younger.*

—Truth's triumph. 1661. *See* Fox, George.

—Turcæ et omnibus. 1660. *See* Fox, George.

—Visitation to the Iewes. 1656. *See* Fox, George.

—Warning from the Lord. 1654. *See* Fox, George.

—Warning to all teachers. 1657. *See* Fox, George.

—Warning to all the merchants. 1658. *See* Fox, George.

—Warning to England. 1674. *See* Fox, George.

—What election. [n.p.], 1679. *See* Fox, George.

—Word in the behalf. 1660. *See* Fox, George.

F., H. Answer to Mr. Spencer's book. 1660. *See* Ferne, Henry, *bp.*

—Camp at Gilgal. Oxford, 1643. *See* Ferne, Henry, *bp.*

—Of the division. 1652. *See* Ferne, Henry, *bp.*

—Plain record. 1661. *See* Fell, Henry.

23 —A true and exact relation of the severall informations . . . of . . . witches. *By M. S. for Henry Overton, and Benj. Allen*, 1645. 4°.* LT, O, MR, YM, GU; CH, CN, CU, WF, Y.

24 Entry cancelled.

—The unlavvfulnesse of the new covenant. Oxford, 1643. *See* Ferne, Henry.

25 **F., I.** A new proclamation: or a warning peece against all blasphemers. *For M. S.* 1653. 4°.* LT; MH, Y.

26 —A sober inquiry, or, Christs reign. *Printed*, 1660. 8°. L; IU, NU, WF.

27 —Two epistles of Paul to Timothy opened. [*London*], printed, 1677. 4°. NU.

F., J. 1678. An almanack. Boston, 1678. *See* Almanacs: Foster, John.

—Apology for the people. 1699. *See* Field, John.

28 —A brief historical relation of the empire of Russia. *By J. C. for William Larnar*, 1654. 8°. LT.

—Carmen pastorale lugubre. A pastoral elegy. 1700. *See* Fowler, John.

29 —A compendiovs chatechisme. *By Tho: Paine, to be sold by Andrew Kembe*. 1645. 8°.* LT; PL.

30 Entry cancelled.

—Correct tide table. [1684.] *See* Flamsteed, John.

—Cryptomenysis patefacta. 1685. *See* Falconer, John.

—Dead saint speaking. 1679. *See* Fairfax, John.

31 No entry.

—Declaration of the reasons. 1689. *See* Protestant association.

—Didascaliæ: discourses. [n.p.], 1643. *See* Ferret, John.

—Dr. Pierce his preaching exemplified. 1663. *See* G., N.

32 —An elegy on the death of His Grace the Duke of Grafton. *By Richard Cheese, Jun.*, 1690. brs. L.

33 — —[Anr. ed.] *By Richard Cotes, Jun.*, 1690. brs. L.

34 —Englands lamentation for the Duke of Monmouth's departure. *Printed*, 1679. brs. L, O, LNC; CH, MBA, MH, MU, TU.

35 Entry cancelled.

—Falacies of Mr. VVilliam Prynne, discovered. Oxford, 1644. *See title.*

—Friendly advice, in the spirit. 1688. *See* Field, John.

36 —A friendly letter of advice to the souldiers. [*London*], printed, 1659. 4°.* LT, O, MR; IIR, CII, CN, MH, MU, WF.

36A —A further account of the state of Ireland. *For J. C.*, 1689. brs. C, DN; Y.

—God's goodness to his Israel. 1700. *See* Forbes, James.

37 —The golden fleece: or, old England restored. *For Langley Curtis*, 1679. 4°.* L, LUG, OB, OC, DT; CLC, CU, MH, NC, WF, Y.

38 —The golden fleece revived. *Printed*, 1689. 4°.* SP; NC, Y.

38A —The humble and just outcry and appeale of all the inslaved. [*London*, 1649.] brs. MIU.

39 —John the Divine's divinity. *For Giles Calvert*, 1649. 8°. O.

40 —The laws discovery. *By R. I. for G. B.*, 1653. 4°.* LT, O, MR; CH, LC, MIU, WF.

41 —A letter out of France. *For Robert Cutler*, 1672. fol. * O, OC, MR; CH, WF.

42 —The merchant's ware-house laid open. *For John Sprint, and Geo. Conyers*. 1696. 4°.* T.C.II 605. L; WF, Y.

—Movnt Pisgah. 1689. *See* Flavell, John.

—Nehushtan: or, John Elliot's. 1694. *See* Forbes, James.

42A —A new letter to all drunkards. *By J. Bradford*, 1696. 8°. OC.

—New light of alchemy. 1674. *See* Sendivogius, Michael.

—A new prognostication. Edinburgh, 1685. *See* Almanacs.

—Proof of a good preacher. 1661. *See* Younge, Richard.

—Reasonableness of personal. 1691. *See* Flavell, John.

—Reply unto Thomas Crisp. [n.p., 1682.] *See* Field, John.

—Rewards of vertue. 1661. *See* Fountain, John.

—Rules for explaining. 1692. *See* Falconer, John.

43 —Strange and wonderful news from sea. *For Philip Brooksby*, 1672. 4°.* HUTH.

—Thomas Crisp's envy. 1682. *See* Field, John.

—To our valiant English nation. 1671. *See* Favel, John.

44 —To the Right Honorable (his Excellency) Oliver Cromwel. [*London*, 1653.] cap., 4°.* LT; CH.

—Token for mourners. 1680. *See* Flavell, John.

—Turtle-dove. Edinburgh, 1664. *See* Fullarton, John.

—Zealous beleevers. [n.p.], 1643. *See* Ferret, John.

45 **F., J. M.** An appeale to Heaven. colop: *Printed*, 1644. cap., 4°.* LT, MR; MH, MU, NU, WF.

46 **F., L.** An answer returned to the letter from Legorn. [*London*, 1680.] cap., fol.* L, O, C, MR, EN; CH, CN, MH, TU, WF, Y.

46A —A speedy remedie against spirituall incontinencie. [*London*], *printed* 1646. 4°. L (t.p.), LW.

F., M. Call unto the seed. [1668.] *See* Fell, Margaret.

—Daughter of Sion. [n.p.], 1677. *See* Fell, Margaret.

—Declaration and an information. 1660. *See* Fell, Margaret.

—Letter sent to the king. [n.p., 1666.] *See* Fell, Margaret.

—Loving salutation to the seed. 1657. *See* Fell, Margaret.

—Standard of the Lord. [n.p.], 1667. *See* Fell, Margaret.

—This is to the clergy. 1660. *See* Fell, Margaret.

—Touch-stone, or. 1667. *See* Fell, Margaret.

—True testimony. 1660. *See* Fell, Margaret.

—Two general epistles. 1664. *See* Fell, Margaret.

—Women's speaking. 1666. *See* Fell, Margaret.

47 **F., N.** A great plot discovered against the whole kingdome. *For G. Cotton*, Feb. 8, 1647. 4°.* LT, EN.

—Vnparallel'd reasons. 1642. *See* Fiennes, Nathaniel.

47A **F., O.** Panegyris Jacobo II. *Anno* 1685. fol. * CCO; MH.

48 Entry cancelled.

F., P. Chronosticon. 1662. *See* Fisher, Payne.

—Deus, et rex. [1675.] *See* Fisher, Payne.

—Impressio novissima. [n.p., 1677.] *See* Fisher, Payne.

—Impressio secunda. [n.p., 1675.] *See* Fisher, Payne.

49 —Obsequies offer'd up to the dear . . . Sr Paul Pindar. [*London*, 1650.] brs. LT.

—Tombes, monuments. [1684.] *See* Fisher, Payne.

F., R. Advertisements to avoid. [n.p., 1680.] *See* Fletcher, Richard.

—Animadversions on a petition. [n.p.], 1653. *See* Flecknoe, Richard.

—Antichrists man of war. 1655. *See* Farnworth, Richard.

50 —The army's martyr. *Printed at London*, 1649. 4°.* LT, O, LP, MR, DT; CH, CU, NU, PT, WF.

—Brazen serpent. 1655. *See* Farnworth, Richard.

—Bunch of grapes. [n.p., 1654-55.] *See* Farnworth, Richard.

—Christian religious meetings. [n.p., 1664.] *See* Farnworth, Richard.

—Death in triumph. 1683. *See* Franklin, Robert.

—Εἰκων Βασιλικη, or, the true pourtraiture. 1660. *See* Lloyd, David.

—Enigmaticall characters. [n.p.], 1658. *See* Flecknoe, Richard.

—Epigrams of all sorts. [n.p.], 1670. *See* Flecknoe, Richard.

51 —Epitaph upon . . . Sir Kenelm Digby. *For H. Herringman*, 1665. brs. O.

—Fifty five enigmatical characters. 1665. *See* Flecknoe, Richard.

—First part of The young clerks guide. 1649. *See* Hutton, *Sir* Richard.

—Gospel liberty sent. [n.p., 1664.] *See* Farnworth, Richard.

—Heart opened. [n.p., 1654.] *See* Farnworth, Richard.

—Holy Scriptures. 1655. *See* Farnworth, Richard.

52 —A letter from a gentleman to the honourable Ed. Howard. [*London*], *by Thomas Newcomb*, 1668. 4°.* LVD; CH, CLC, MU, TU, WF.

—Loving salutation with several seasonable exhortations. [n.p.], 1665. *See* Farnworth, Richard.

—Missale Romanvm. [n.p.], 1674. *See* Fuller, Robert.

—Ορθοτονια, seu. 1650. *See* Franklin, Richard.

52A —The present state of Carolina. *By John Bringhurst*, 1682. 4°.* L; CH, NHS, NN, RPJ.

—Publique worship. [n.p.], 1664. *See* Farnworth, Richard.

—Quæstio quodlibetica, or. 1653. *See* Filmer, *Sir* Robert.

—St. Leonard's Hill. A poem. 1666. *See* Fage, Robert.

53 —The Scot arraigned. *By James Moxon*, 1651. 4°.* LT, EN; Y.

—Sixty nine enigmatical characters. 1665. *See* Flecknoe, Richard.

—Sober enquiry into the nature. 1673. *See* Ferguson, Robert.

—Syzygiasticon instauratum. 1654. *See* Almanacs. Fitzsmith, Richard.

—Tolleration sent down. [n.p.], 1665. *See* Farnworth, Richard.

—True and faithful account. 1665. *See* Flecknoe, Richard.

53A —A true relation of the bloody attempt by James Salowayes. *By Dickinson*, 1663. 4°.* LG.

—VVitchcraft cast out. 1655. *See* Farnworth, Richard.

F., S. Baptism before. 1669. *See* Fisher, Samuel.

54 —Death in a new dress. *For Isaac Pridmore*, 1656. 4°.* LT.

55 —A designe to save the kingdome. *By T. F. for John Rothwell*, 1648. 8°.* LT.

56-56A Entries cancelled.

—Female advocate. 1686. *See* Egerton, Sarah Fyge.

57 —A letter to a friend concerning the late answers. [*London*, 1687.] brs. L, LLP.

58 — —[Anr. ed.] [*London*], *printed*, 1687. 4°.* L, C, LCL, OC, DU, MR; MB, MM, NC, NU, Y.

59 Entry cancelled.

—Longitudinis inventæ explicatio non longa, or. 1699. *See* Fyler, Samuel.

60 —Mr. Toland's Clito dissected. *Printed* 1700. 4°.* L, LG, CT, LSD, AU; CH, CLC, CN, NP, VC, WF, Y.

—Novelty of the modern. 1682. *See* Felgate, Samuel.

60A —Youths sure guide to heaven. *Printed*, 1668. 12°. WF.

F., T. Annals of King James. 1681. *See* Frankland, Thomas.

—Αυτοκατακριτος. Or. 1668. *See* Ford, Thomas.

—Citizens sacred entertainment. 1666. *See* Fydge, Thomas.

—Comment upon Ruth. 1654. *See* Fuller, Thomas.

—Eclectical chiliasm. 1700. *See title.*

61 —The fanatick in his colours. *For H. Marsh,* 1661. 12°. CLC, NU.

—Guide to the blind. 1659. *See* Forster, Thomas.

—Hunting of the fox: or flattery displayed. 1657. *See* Harflete, Henry.

62 —A letter from a person of quality on board the William and Mary. 1676. 4°. L, O, EN, DT.

—Lusus fortunæ: the play. [n.p.], 1649. *See* Forde, Thomas.

—Panegyrick to his renowned. 1660. *See* Flatman, Thomas.

63 —The Parliament of the third and fourth years. *For John Williams and Francis Eglesfield,* 1660. fol. O, CM.

63A —Φιλανθρωπια, or, a holding forth. [*London?* 1659.] cap., 4°.* CT; MH, Y.

—Practice of the exchequer. 1658. *See* Osborne, Peter.

—Proposals for the imployment. 1681. *See* Firmin, Thomas.

—Proposals humbly offered. [n.p., 1685?] *See* Firmin, Thomas.

—Reformation sure. 1641. *See* Ford, Thomas.

—Sermon of contentment. 1648. *See* Fuller, Thomas.

—Singing of psalms. 1653. *See* Ford, Thomas.

—Some proposals for the imploying. 1678. *See* Firmin, Thomas.

—Times anatomiz'd. 1647. *See* Ford, Thomas.

—Virtus rediviva. 1661. *See* Forde, Thomas.

—Warlike directions. 1643. *See* Fisher, Thomas.

64 —The way to peace, by the proposal. *For A. Strange,* 1682. fol.* L, O, DU, DT; CH, NU, PU, WF, Y.

65 **F., W.** An elegy, in memory of that famous, learned, reverend, and religious Doctor Oldsworth. [*n.p.,* 1649.] brs. LT, O; MH.

—Meteors: or. [n.p.], 1654. *See* Fulke, William.

66 **Faber, Albertus Otto.** De auro potabili medicinali. [*London*], *for the author,* 1677. 4°. L, O, LCP, LF, CT; CLC.

67 —Paradoxon de morbo gallico, Libr. II. or, A paradox. *Printed,* 1662. 12°. L, OB.

68 —A relation of some notable cures. [*London,* 1663.] 4°. L.

69 —A remonstrance in reference to the act. *Printed,* 1664. 4°.* L, LF, LPR, BBN; CH, PH, PSC.

70 —Some kindling sparks. *Printed,* 1668. 4°. L.

70A The fable of the sun and frogs, . . . applyed to . . . the French and Dutch. *For William Gilbert,* 1672. 4°.* MH, WF.

Fables of young Æsop. 1700. *See* H., B.

71 **Fabrice, Guillaume.** Cista militaris, or a military chest. *By W. Godbid, to be sold by Moses Pitt,* 1674. 8°.* L, O, C, LWL, MAU; PCP, UCLA, WF, HC.

72 —His experiments in chyrurgerie. *By Barnard Alsop,* 1642. 4°. DT; CH, NC.

72A ——[Anr. ed.] —, 1643. 4°. LT, O, C, LCS, LW; MHS, NAM, WSG.

72B —The surgeon's military chest. *For C. Shortgrave,* 1686. LSC.

73 **Fabricius, Joannes Ludovicus.** Janus Alexandrus Ferrarius . . . his epistles. *By Thomas Ratcliffe and Nathaniel Thompson,* 1673. T.C.I 136. O, NE, P; NU, WF, Y.

74 —Jani Alexandri Ferrarii Cœnobitæ Augustiniani Euclides. *Prostant venales apud Guliel. Gilbert,* 1673. 4°.* T.C.I 129. L, O, LLP, CT, DU, MR; CH, NU, WF.

74A ——[Anr. ed.] *Oxonii,* 1680. 8°. MADAN 3265n. L, O; LC, MB, NU, Y.

75 **Fabricius, Johannes Seobaldus.** C. Julius Cæsar numismaticus. *Typis Benneti Griffin, impensis Jonathanis Edwin,* 1678. 8°. L, O, C, OM, CT, EC; BN, CLC, IU, MWA.

76 —De vnitate ecclesiæ. *Oxoniæ, excudebat Hen. Hall impensis Ric. Davis,* 1676. 8°. T.C.I 229. MADAN 3105. L, O, C, YM, EN; BN, CH, WF.

76A ——[Anr. ed.] —, 1677. 4°. BC.

77 —Epistola Irenica. *Typis Thomæ Newcombii, impensis Jonathanis Edwin,* 1677. 8°. T.C.I 276. L, O, LW, OC, OCC, CT, DT; CLC.

Faces about. 1644. *See* Prynne, William.

Faction supplanted. 1663. *See* Harvey, Christopher.

78 The factious citizen. *For Thomas Maddocks,* 1685. 4°. L, O; CH, CN, LC, MB, MU, NC, TU, WF.

79 Entry cancelled. Ghost.

80 Factum comitis Argatheliæ seu de Argyll. [*Edinburgh?*], 1684. 4°. ALDIS 2451.5. L, O, P.

80A Factum, for the English merchants. [*London,* 1645.] cap., fol.* L.

80B Factum of the French, and other Protestants in the Saxony. [*London?* 1681.] cap., fol.* LPR; MH.

80C **Facy, William.** The complement of stenography. *For the author,* 1672. LC.

81 Entry cancelled.

Faerie leveller. [n.p.], 1648. *See* Spenser, Edmund.

81A **Færno, Gabrieldo.** Centum fabulæ. *By S. Griffin for John Overton,* 1666. 8°. O.

82 ——[Anr. ed.] *Impensis H. Brome,* 1672. 8°. T.C.I 99. L, O, LW, AN, LLU, P; BN, IU, MH, Y. (var.)

82aA **Fage, Robert.** Cosmography or A description of the whole world. *By W.G. for Peter Stent,* 1663. 8°. L.

82bA ——[Anr. ed.] *By S. Griffin for John Overton,* 1666. 8°. O.

82A ——[Anr. ed.] —, 1667. 8°. CLC, WCL, WF.

82B ——[Anr. ed.] *By H. B. for Iohn Overton,* 1671. 8°. T.C.I 91. CH, MU.

83 —A description of the whole world. *By J. Owsley, and sold by Peter Stent,* 1658. 8°. LT, O, LSC, BC; CH, IU, RPJ, WF, Y.

84 Entry cancelled.

—Lawfulnesse. 1645. *See* Fage, Robert, *jr.*

85 [–] St. Leonard's hill. A poem. *For John Simms,* 1666. 4°.* L, O; WF, Y.

85A **Fage, Robert, *jr.*** The lawfulnesse of infants baptisme. *By W. Wilson,* 1645. 8°.* LT; CH.

85B —A protestation attested. [*London,* 1644.] brs. OC; MH.

86 **Fagel, Gaspar.** Bibliotheca instructissima, sive catalogus librorum. [*London, 3 Feb.* 1690.] 4°.* L, O, C, OC; MH, JF.

87 —A letter, writ by Mijn Heer Fagel . . . to Mr. James Stewart. colop: *Amsterdam printed*, 1688. fol.* L, O, C, LL, OM, MR, GU; CH, CN, MH, NU, WF.

88 — —[Anr. ed.] colop: *Amsterdam printed*, 1688. cap., 4°.* L, O, C, EN, DT; CH, CN, MH, NU, WF, Y. (var.)

89 — —[Anr. ed.] colop: *Printed*, 1688. 4°.* L, O, OM, CT, AU, DT; HR, CH, IU, MH, NC, NP, WF, Y.

90 —A letter writ by Mijn Heer Fagel, . . . to the Marquiss of Albeville. *Printed at the Hague by James Scheltus*, [1688]. cap., 4°.* L, O, OC, CCA, DU, LIU; CH, CN, MH, WF, Y.

91 —Lettre ecrite par . . . a Monsieur Jacques Stewart. colop: *Imprimé à Londres*, 1688. cap., 4°.* L, O, C; BN, NN, WF.

92 —Literæ illustr: Domini Fagel, . . . ad Dominum Jacobum Steuart. colop: *Printed*, 1688. cap., 4°.* L, O, EN.

92A —Some remarkable passages. [*London?* 1689.] brs. HH; CH.

93 Entry cancelled.
—Their Highness the Prince and Princess of Orange's opinion. 1689. *See* Burnet, Gilbert.

93A The failing & perishing of good men. [*London*], *printed* 1663. 4°.* L, LW; NU, WF, Y.

94 The fair and loyal maid of Bristow. [*London*], *for P. Brooksby*, [*c.* 1675]. brs. L.
Fair and methodical discussion. 1689. *See* Hooper, George.

94A A fair character of the Presbyterian reformling's just and sober vindication. *Printed* 1695. 4°.* L.

95 Fair Cynthia's sorrowful sighs. [1688.] brs. O.
Fair dealer. 1659. *See* Trevanion, John.

95A Fair Flora's departure. [*London*, 1670–90.] brs. L.
Faire in Spittlefields. [*n.p.*], 1652. *See* B., J.

96 The fair lady of the west. *For W. Thackeray, T. Passenger, and W. Whitwood*, [1678]. brs. L, CM, HH; MH, WCL.

97 Fair Lucina conquerd. [*London*], *for Josh. Coniers*, [1683–88]. brs. L, CM, HH; MH, Y.

97A —[Anr. ed.] [*London*], *for P. Brooksby*, [1690?]. brs. L.

98 The fair maid of Dunsmore's lamentation. *By and for W. O. sold by J. Deacon*, [1690?]. brs. L, O.

99 —[Anr. ed.][*London*], *for J. Wright, J. Clarke, W. Thackeray, and T. Passinger*, [1681–84]. brs. EUING 117. L, HH, GU.

100 —[Anr. ed.] [*London*], *for P. Brooksby, J. Deacon, J. Blare, J. Back*, [1691–92]. brs. L, O, CM.

100A —[Anr. ed., "Dunsore's."] [*London*], *for E. Oliver*, [1700?]. brs. O.

101 The fair maid of Islington. *By and for W. O. and sold by C. Bates*, [1698?]. brs. L, O, HH.

101A —[Anr. ed.] [*n.p.*, 1700?] brs. L.
Fair maids choice. [*n.p.*, 1670.] *See* Lanfiere, Thomas.

102 The fair one of Tunis. *For Henry Brome*, 1674. 8°. T.C.I 148. L, O; CH, CN, Y.

102AA Fair play for one's life. *M. Wotton*, [1700?]. 8°.* L.
Fair play in the lottery. [*n.p.*, 1660.] *See* Ford, Edward.
Fair-play on both sides, 1666. *See* Heiron, Samuel.

102BA Fair trade, besides the heavy duties. [*London?* 1700.] cap., fol. * MH, MIU.

102A The fair traders objections against the bill, entituled, A bill for preventing clandestine trading . . . Virginia. [*London?* 1700.] brs. L; NN, V.

103 Fair warning from Tyburn. [*London*, 1680.] fol. O; WF.
Fair warning, or, the burnt child. [*n.p.*, 1649.] *See* Bramhall, John, *abp.*
Fair warning: or, xxv, reasons. 1663. *See* Baxter, Richard.

104 Fair warning: The second part. Or xx. prophesies. *For H. Marsh*, 1663. 4°. L, O, LIL, CT, YM; CH, NU, TU, WF, Y.

104A Fair warning to all English-men. [*London*, 1688?] brs. Y.

105 Fair warning to murderers of infants: being an account of the tryal, . . . of Mary Goodenough. *For Jonathan Robinson*, 1692. 4°.* L; CH, Y.
Fair warning, to take heed. [*n.p.*], 1649. *See* Bramhall, John, *abp.*
Fair warnings to a careless world. 1665. *See* Lloyd, David.

106 [**Fairclough, Richard.**] A pastors legacy. *Printed* 1663. 12°. LW, SP.

107 **Fairclough, Samuel.** Αγιοι αξιοι, or the saints worthinesse. *By R. D. for Tho. Newberry*, 1653. 4°.* L, O, C, LW, ENC; CH, IU, WF, Y.

108 —The prisoners praises. *By John Macock, for Lodowick Lloyd, and Henry Cripps*, 1650. 4°.* LT, LW; RBU, Y.

109 —The trovblers trovbled. *By R. Cotes, for Henry Overton*, 1641. 4°.* LT, O, C, EN, DT; CH, CN, MH, NU, WF, Y.

109A Entry cancelled.
[**Fairclough, Samuel,** *younger.*] Suffolks tears. 1653. *See* title.

110 **Fairebrother, William.** An essay of a loyal brest. *By John Field*, 1660. 4°.* L, O, CT; MH, NN, Y.

110A **Fairfax, Brian.** A copy of a letter. [*London*, 1696?] brs. L.

111 **Fairfax,** *Sir* **Ferdinando.** The answer of . . to a declaration. *For Iohn Franke, March* 3. 1642. 4°.* LT, C, LSD, MR, DT; CH, MH, NC, WF, Y.

112 —A copy of a letter sent from. *For Edward Husbands, Iuly* 6. 1644. 4°.* O, LHO, CT, BC, LLU, YM, CD; MM, WF.

113 —The good and prosperous successe. [*London*], *Ian.* 31. *for Iohn Wright*, 1642. 4°.* L, O, LLU, LNC, YM; CLC, IU, OWC, TU, Y.

114 — —[Anr. ed.] *For J. Wright, January*, 31. 1642. 4°.* LT, CT; CH, CSS, IU, NN, Y.

115 —A happy victory. [*London*], *Decemb.* 17. *for John Wright*, 1642. 4°.* L, O, LLU, MR, YM; CH.

116 —A letter from. *By A. Norton for Iohn Franke*, 1642. 4°.* LT, O, OC, EC, DT; CH, LC, MH, MU, WF, Y.

117 — —[Anr. ed.] *For Iohn Wright*, 1642. 4°.* O, OC; CSS, WF.

118 —A letter from. *For Richard Lownes*, 1642. 4°.* O, CT, LLU, MR; CLC, WF, Y.

119 —A letter from . . . to . . . Robert Earle of Essex. *For I. Wright, Octob.* 18, 1643. 4°.* LT, O, LLU, YM; CN, LC, NIC, PU, WF.

120 —A letter from the . . . committees of the Commons. *By B. Alsop for Robert Wood, May* 18. 1642. 4°.* MR; MH.

120A — —[Anr. ed.] —, *May* 19. 1642. 4°.* C, DT; Y.

120B —A letter or declaration from. *By T. F. for T. Bankes*. 1642. 4°.* MH.

121   —A letter sent from. [*London*], *for Edw. Husbands, April 19,* 1644. 4°.* LT, O, C, CT, YM, DT; MM, NU, WF, Y.

121A   — —[Anr. ed.] —, *May 29.* 1644. 4°.* MH.

121B   [—] A miraculous victory obtained. [*London*], *May 29. for Edw. Husbands,* 1643. 4°.* LT, O, LLU, YM, EN; CSS, CN, MBP, MH, MIU, Y.

121C   [—] — [Anr. ed.] [*London*], *for Iohn Wright, May 29.* 1643. 4°.* WF.

122   [–] A reall protestation of many, and very eminent persons in the county of Yorke. *For H. Blunden,* 1642. 4°.* LT, LLU MR, YM,; CH, IU, MM, Y.

122A   [–] —[Anr. ed., "manie."] *For Joseph Hundgate,* 1642. 4°.* LLU.

123   —A second letter from. *For Iohn Wright, January 5.* 1642. 4°.* LT, O, OC, LLU, SP, YM; CH, IU, LC, MB, WF, Y.

124   [**Fairfax, Henry.**] An impartial relation of the whole proceedings against . . . Magdalen Colledge. [*London*], *printed,* 1688. 40 pp. 4°.* L, O, CT, EN, DT; CLC, MH, MU, WF, Y.

125   [–] —[Anr. ed.] [*London*], *printed,* 1688. 36 pp. 4°.* T.C.II 250. L, O, C, DC, MR, DT; CH, CN, CSU, LC, MH, NU, Y.

126   [–] —Second edition ["illegal proceedings"]. *Printed and are to be sold by Richard Baldwin,* 1689. 4°. L, OC, MR, DU, DT; CH, CU, MH, NU, WF, Y.

127   **F[airfax], J[ohn].** The dead saint speaking. *By A. M. and R. R. for Edward Giles,* 1679. 4°. L, LW; CU, NU.

128   Entry cancelled. *Part of —*Πρεσβυτερος.

129   —Πρεσβυτερος διπλης τιμης αξιος; or the true dignity. *By H. H. for Tho. Parkhurst,* 1681. 8°. L, LCL, OC, CS, P; CH, CLC, MII, NPT, NU, WF.

130   —Primitiæ synagogæ. A sermon. *For Tho. Parkhurst.* 1700. 4°. T.C.III 197. L, EN; CLC, MHS.

131   **Fairfax, Nathaniel.** A treatise of the bvlk and selvedge of the vvorld. *For Robert Boulter.* 1674. 8°. T.C.I 154. L, O, C, LIU, GU; CLC, CU, MU, NP, NU, Y.

132   No entry.

133   Entry cancelled.
     Fairfax, *Sir* Thomas. Agreement prepared. 1649. *See title.*

134   —Another letter from . . . June 8. 1647. *For Lawrence Chapman,* 1647. 4°.* LT, O, C, LIU, DT; CH, MH, NN, Y, ZAP.

135   Entry cancelled.
     —Answer of. 1642. *See* Fairfax, *Sir* Ferdinando.

136   No entry.
     — —[Same title.] 1647. *See* Linfield, E.

137   —The articles of agreement between the Lord Generall, and the Kentish-men. *By B. A.,* 1648. 4°.* LT, O, LG, AN; MIU, Y.

138   —Articles of agreement concluded and agreed on by His Excellency Sir Thomas Fairfax. *For John Wright, 25 July* 1646. 4°.* LT, O, BC; CH, MH, Y.

139   —A declaration from . . . and his councell of warre: concerning their proceedings in the proposalls . . . [2 August 1647]. *Printed at Cambridge [by R.D.],* 1647. 4°.* C, CT; IU, WF.

139A   — —[Anr. ed.] *By Matthew Simmons.* 1647. 4°.* MR, CD.

140   Entry cancelled.
     — —[Anr. ed.] —, *for George Whittington,* 1647. *See title.*
     — —[Anr. ed.] *Oxford,* 1647. *See title.*
     —Declaration from . . . concerning the delaies. 1647. *See title.*
     —Declaration from . . . of their resolutions. 1647[8]. *See title.*

141   —A declaration of . . . and his councell of warre . . . shewing the grounds of their present advance towards . . . London. *For George Whittington,* 1647. 4°.* LT, O, C, LLU, CD; CH, IU, MH, NU, TU, WF.

141A   — —[Anr. ed.] *Oxford, by J. Harris and H. Hills,* 1647. 4°.* MADAN 1951. O, GH; CSS.

142   —A declaration of . . . against a printed pamphlet . . . [12 August 1647]. *For John Rothwell,* 1647. brs. STEELE 2725. LT.

143   —A declaration of . . . disclaiming a pamphlet . . . [19 June 1647]. *By Richard Cotes,* 1647. 4°.* LT, MR; PU.

143A   —A declaration of . . . and his councel of war, in obedience to several ordinances of Parliament, for disbanding. *For Edward Husband, Jan. 4.* 1647[8]. 4°.* WF.

144   — —[Anr. ed.] —, *Jan. 5.* 1647[8]. 4°.* LT, O, LG, CCA, MR, DT; CB, CH, CU, MH, WF.

145–5B Entries cancelled.
     —Declaration of . . . and his generall council of officers, shewing the grounds. 1648. *See title.*

146   Entry cancelled. *See below,* F 150.

147   Entry cancelled.
     —Declaration of . . . Nov. 30, 1648. *See* Declaration of His Excellency. [D 610B.]

148   Entry cancelled.
     —Declaration of . . . Dec. 8, 1648. 1648. *See* —A letter of.

149   —A declaration of His Excellencie the Lord Generall Fairfax: to the Lord Major. *For C.W.* 1648. 4°.* LT, CJ, MR; CH.

150   —A declaration of . . . . Concerning the supply of bedding . . . [8 December 1648]. *By John Macock, for John Partridge.* 1648. 4°.* LT, LG, CT, ESS, CD; CH, CU, MH, MU, WF, Y.

151   —A declaration of . . . concerning their resolution to preserve . . . trade . . . [15 December 1648]. *For John Partridge and George Whittington.* 1648. brs. STEELE 2808. LT, O, LG, LUG; MH.

151A   — —[Anr. ed.] *For John Partridge,* 1648. brs. MIU.

152   [–] A declaration of the engagements, remonstrances, representations . . . [27 September 1647]. *By Matthew Simmons,* 1647. *See title* [D 664].

152A   [–] —[Anr. ed.] *By Math: Simmons for George Whittington,* 1647. 4°. L, DU; NPT.

153   Entry cancelled.
     [–] —[Anr. ed.] *Oxford,* 1647. *See* Declaration of . . . and his councell of warre . . . shewing the grounds.
     [–] Declaration of Thomas Lord Fairfax, and the chief of the gentlemen . . . York. 1659. *See title.*
     [–] Declaration of Thomas Lord Fairfax and the knights, 1659. *See title.*

154 —The declaration of . . . and the rest of the Lords, . . . of York. [13 February 1659.] *For James Williamson,* [1660]. brs. LT, O, LG, CJ; MH.

154A —The declaration of the Lord Fairfax, and others of the nobility and gentry of the North parts . . . [13 February 1659]. [*n.p.,* 1660.] brs. CD; MH.

155 —A declaration of the last demands . . . [18 August 1647]. [*London,* 1647.] cap., 4°.* LT; CSS, Y.

156 —A declaration: or, representation from . . . concerning the just and fundamental rights . . . [14 June 1647]. *For George Whittington,* 1647. 4°.* LT, O, C, MR, EN, DT; BN, CH, CN, MH, TU, WF, Y. (var.)

156A ——[Anr. ed.] *Printed* 1647. 4°.* C; WF.

157 Entry cancelled.
——[Anr. ed.] 1647. *See* Declaration from Sir Thomas Fairfax and the army.

158–9 No entries.

160 —The desires of . . . 28. October, 1647. *By T. H. for John Playford,* 1647. 4°.* LT, O, C, OC, LIU; CH, MH, MU, WF, ZAP.

161 Entry cancelled.
—Exact and true relation of the many severall messages. 1646. *See title.*

162 —A further proposal from . . . Desiring the discharge. *For George Whittington,* 1647. 4°.* LT, O, CS, BC, DT; CH, MH, MU, WF, Y.

163 [–] His Majesties whole army in the west conquered. *For Matthew Walbancke,* 16 March 1645[6]. 4°.* LT, O, OC, DT; IU, MH, WF, Y.

163A —The humble petition of His Excellency . . . , and the general council of officers . . . 20 Januarii, 1648. *For Edward Husband,* 1648[9]. 4°.* O, LG, LLU, MR.

164 —The humble proposals and desires of. *By John Field for John Partridge,* Decemb. 7. 1648. 4°.* LT, O, C, OC, CT, CD; BN, CH, CN, MH, WF, Y. (var.)

165 —An humble remonstrance from His Excellency. *For Francis Coles,* June 25. 1647. 4°.* L, O, C, MR, DT; CH, CU, MH, WF, Y.

166 —An humble remonstrance from . . . . Concerning the present state of affairs. *For George Whittington,* 1647. 4°.* LT, O, C, LLU, CD; BN, CH, CN, LC, MH, TU, WF, Y.

166A ——[Anr. ed., "humblf."] —, 1647. 4°.* L, DU, LIU, LLU, MR; CH, CLC, MM, WF.

167 —An humble remonstrance from . . . 14. day of September 1647. *Printed at London, by Robert Ibbitson,* 1647. 4°.* LT, O, C, MR, YM; CH, IU, MH, WF, Y.

168 —An humble representation from . . . Decemb. 7. 1647. *Imprinted at London for George Whittington,* 1647. 4°.* LT, O, C, DC, LLU, MR; CH, MH, NU, TU, WF.

169 ——[Anr. ed.] *Printed at London, by John Clowes, for George Whittington,* 1647. 4°.* L, O, C, BC, LSD; CH, CN, MH, WF, Y.

170 —Sir Thomas Fairfaxs last letter of the treaty with Sir Ralph Hopton. *For Matthew Walbancke,* 18 *March,* 1645. 4°.* LT, O, DT; WF, Y.

171 —Sir Thomas Fairfax's letter from Cornwall. *For John Wright, March* 24. 1645 [6]. 4°.* L, O, OC, SP; CLC, MH, MU, Y.

172 —A letter from . . . June the 6. *For George Whittington,* [1647]. 4°.* LT, O, CT, DC, AU; CH, CLC, MH, WF, Y, ZAP.

173 —A letter from . . . June 29, 1647. *For Laurence Chapman, Iuly* 1. 1647. 4°.* LT, O, LG, MR, CD; CH, CU, MBP, MIU, PT, WF.

174 —A letter from His Excellency . . . July 1. 1647. *For Laurence Chapman, July* 5. 1547 [1647]. 4°.* LT, O, CT, LLU, CD; IAU, MH, MU, NU, WF, Y.

175 —A letter from . . . [16 July 1647]. *Imprinted at London, for George Whittington,* 1647. 4°.* LT, O, ESS; CH, MH, MU, NN, WF, Y.

176 —A letter from . . . 21 August 1647. *For Edward Husband, August.* 24. 1647. brs. STEELE 2726. LT.

177 —A letter from . . . [19 August 1647]. *For Edward Husband, Aug.* 26, 1647. 4°.* LT, O, LLU, MR; CH, WF.

178 —A letter from . . . 8 Novem. *For George Whittington,* 1647. 4°.* LT, MR, YM, DT; MH, MU, ZAP.

179 —A letter from . . . Novemb. 19. 1647. *For Laurence Chapman, November* 22. 1647. 4°.* LT, C, OB, YM, CD; CH, CN, MH, WF, Y.

180 —A letter from . . . fifth of June, 1648. *Imprinted at London for Iohn Wright,* 1648. 4°.* LT, LG, LLL, DT; CH, CLC, IU, MIU.

181 —A letter from . . . [28 August 1648]. *Imprinted at London, for John Wright,* 2 *Septemb.* 1648. 4°.* LT, O, DU, YM; BN, CH, MH, WF, Y.

182 —The Lord Generals letter in answer to the message. *For Laurence Chapman, June* 2. 1648. 4°.* LT, O, LG, LLL; CH, MH, MIU.

183 Entry cancelled.
—Letter in answer. 1647. *See* —Letter from . . . July 1. 1647.

184 —A letter of . . . [8 December 1648]. *By John Field for John Partridge and George Whittington, Decemb.* 9. 1648. 4°.* LT, C, OB, ESS, CD; CH, CU, MH, MU, TU, WF.

185 —Sir Thomas Fairfaxes letter or summons sent to Sir John Berkley. *Imprinted at London for Matthew Walbancke* 6 *April* 1646. 4°.* MADAN 1856. LT, O, OB, DT; CSS.

186 —A letter sent from His Excellency . . . [10 June 1647]. *By Richard Cotes,* 1647. 4°.* LT, O, C, SP, DT; CH, CN, MH, WF, Y.

187 Entry cancelled.
—Letter sent from the Right Honorable the Lord Fairfax. [*n.p.*], 1644. *See* Fairfax, *Sir* Ferdinando.

188 —A letter sent from . . . January 1. 1659. *By John Streater, and John Macock,* 1659[60]. 4°.* LT, O, MR; CLC, MH.

189–190 No entries.

191 —Sir Thomas Fairfax letter to both Houses of Parliament . . . taking of Dartmouth. *Printed at London for John Wright, Ian.* 24. 1645[6.] 4°.* LT, O, MR, SP, CD, DT; IU, MH, MU, Y.

192 Entry cancelled. *See following entry.*

193 —Sir Thomas Fairfax's letter to the Honorable, William Lenthall. *For Edw. Husband, Iuly* 28. 1645. 4°.* LT, O, BR, LSD, SP; MH, NN, Y.

194   —Sir Thomas Fairfax's letter to the Honorable, William Lenthall . . . Sherborn Castle. *For Edward Husband, Aug.* 19. 1645. 4°.* LT, O, EN; MH, MU, NU, TU.

195   —Sir Thomas Fairfax letter to the Honoble William Lenthal . . . Concerning all the passages . . . from Exeter. *For Edw. Husband, Feb. 24, 1645[6]. 4°.* LT, O, C, OC, CT, SP; CJC, CLC, MH, MM, MU.

196   —Sir Thomas Fairfax's letter to the Honoble William Lenthal. *For Edw. Husband, March 23. 1645[6].* 4°.* LT, O, CT, LSD, DT; CLC, CN, MH, WF, Y.

197   —Generall Fairfax's letter to the Honorable William Lenthall . . . . Concerning the storming and taking of Tiverton Castle. *For Edward Husband, Octob. 25. 1645.* 4°.* LT, O, CT, DT; MH, MU, WF.

198   —The Lord General's letter to to [*sic*] the Honorable William Lenthal. *For Edward Husband, June 6. 1648.* 4°.* LT, O, LG, LIU; CH, CLC, IU, MH, PT, WF, Y.

199   Entry cancelled.
      —Letter to the House of Peeres. 1648. *See* —Letter from . . . fifth of June, 1648.

200   Entry cancelled. *See following entry.*

201   —The Lord General's letter to the Lord Major. *For Laurence Blaiklocke,* 1648. brs. LT, LG, LLL, LUG.

202   —A manifesto from . . . June, 27. 1647. *Cambridge, for Benjamin Ridley,* 1647. 4°.* LT, O, C, DC, LIU; MH, MU, NU, WF, Y.

203   Entry cancelled.
      —Master Peter's messuage. 1645. *See* Peters, Hugh.

204   —A message from . . . to the Parliament. *Printed at London, by Robert Ibbitson,* 1647. 4°.* LT, O, C, SP, CD; CSS, MBP, MH, MHS, WF, Y.

205   —New propositions from . . . why he did not conduct His Majesty. *Printed at Oxford by Leonard Brown, and reprinted at London for Robert Williams,* 1647. 4°.* MADAN 1952. LT, O, CT, LIU, LLU; CH, WF.

206   —New propositions from . . . concerning the brotherly meetings of Independents. *Imprinted at London for T. Deane,* 1647. 4°. LT, O, OP, LIU, LLU, YM, DT; CLC, CU.

207   —New propositions from . . . concerning the Kings Majesty. *Printed at London, for Robert Williamson,* 1647. 4°.* LT, CS, LIU, SP; CH, CU, MH.

208   —New propositions sent from. *Printed at London for Adam Marshe,* 1647. 4°.* LT, OC, LIU, DT.

209   —A New-Years gift: presented by Tho. Lord Fairfax. *For R. Smithurst,* 1648. 4°.* LT, CS, MR, DT; KQ, MH, NU, WF.

210   —Orders and rvles, set forth by. *For George Roberts,* [1649]. 4°.* LT, LVF, OB; LC, ZAP.
      —Orders established . . . [14 January 1647/8] . . . for regulating the army. 1646[7]. *See* England: Army Council.
      —Particular charge. 1647. *See* England: Army Council.

211–2 No entries.

213   —A petition from . . . concerning the draught of an agreement of the people. *For John Partridge, R. Harford, G. Calvert, and G. Whittington,* 1649. 4°.* LT, O, C, MR, DT; CH, CN, MH, NU, WF, Y.

214   —The petition of . . . August 16, 1649. *For John Playford,* 1649. 4°.* LT, MR, DT.

215   —A proclamation by . . . 12 February 1648. *For John Playford,* 13 Feb. 1648[9]. brs. STEELE 2828. LT, O, LG, ES; MH.

216   —A proclamation by . . . [20 February 1648/9]. *For John Playford,* 1649. brs. STEELE 2830. LT, O; MH, MHS.

217   —A proclamation by . . . concerning the proceedings of some ministers. *Cambridge, for Nathaniel Smith,* 1647. 4°.* LT, C, MR, DT; PU, Y.

218   —A proclamation by . . . for the regulating of souldiers. *For John Playford,* 1649. brs. STEELE 2836. LT; CH.

219   —A proclamation by . . . forbidding all souldiers to forbear. *For John Playford.* 1649. brs. STEELE 2858. LT; MH.

220   —A proclamation of . . . requiring all persons. *For Thomas Turner.* 1649. 4°.* LT, O, C, LG, BC; CH, CLC, MB, MH, V.

221   —A proclamation to prevent abuses by the souldiers . . . 1 July, 1647. *For Humphrey Haward,* 1647. brs. STEELE 2710. LT, O, OP; CLC.

221A   Entry cancelled.
      —Proposals delivered to the Earl of Nottingham. 1647. *See title.*

222   —Proposalls from . . . October 17. 1647. *Printed at London, by Robert Ibbitson,* 1647. 4°.* LT, LUG, OC, CS, LIU, MR; BN, CH, CU, NP, WF, Y.

222A —Proposalls of . . . Decemb. 23. 1647. *By Robert Austin.* 1646[7]. 4°.* O, SP; Y.

223   ——[Anr. ed.] —, 1647. 4°.* LT, BC, LIU, LLU, DT; CH, CU, MH, NP, WF.

224   —The propositions of . . . [27 June 1647]. *By Richard Cotes,* 1647. 4°.* LT, CT, LIU, LLU, MR; CH, CU, MH, MU, WF, Y.

225   —His Excellency Sir Thomas Fairfaxes protestation, in the name of himselfe. *By B. A.,* 1647. 4°.* LT, O, DT.

226   —A remonstrance from . . . concerning their just . . . proceedings. *For George Whittington,* 1647. 4°.* LT, O, C, SP, ENC; CH, IU, MIU, MM, WF.

227   ——[Anr. ed.] *By M. S. for George Whittington,* 1647. 4°.* L, O, C, MR, CD; CH, MH, MU, WF, Y.

227A ——[Anr. ed.] *For J. Harris,* 1647. 4°.* O, KEBLE, CD; CSS, NN, RBU.

228   —A remonstrance from . . . concerning the late discontent and distraction . . . Novemb. 15. 1647. *For George Whittington,* 1647. 4°.* LT, O, C, BC, YM; CH, CN, MH, MU, WF.

229   —A remonstrance of . . . [16 November 1648]. *For John Partridge and George Whittington,* 1648. 4°. LT, O, C, MR, EN, DT; BN, CH, CN, LC, MH, MU, NU, WF, Y.

230   —A representation from . . . expressing the desires of the army . . . [21 September 1647]. *For John Partridge,* 1647. 4°.* LT, O, OC, LLU, YM; CH, MH, PT, WF, Y.

231   —A representation . . . concerning the just and fundamental rights . . . [14 June 1647]. *Cambridge: by Roger Daniel,* 1647. 4°.* L, O, C, CT, LLU; CH, IU, MH, PT.

232   Entry cancelled.
      —Second letter from. 1642. *See* Fairfax, *Sir* Ferdinando.

233 —Severall letters sent from. *By Richard Cotes, London*, 1647. 4°.* L, C, DC, LLU, MR; CH, CN, MIU, WF.

234 —Severall papers from. *For George Whittington*, 1647. 4°.* LT, C, LLU, MR, YM; CH, CLC, MH, PT, WF, Y.

234A —Severall proposals from . . . and the general councel of the armie . . . [22 September 1647]. *By James and Joseph Moxon, for John Pounset*, 1647. 4°.* WF.

235 —Short memorials of Thomas Lord Fairfax. *Printed for Ri. Chiswell*, 1699. 8°. T.C.III 154. L, O, LW, CT, ES, DT; BN, CH, CN, LC, MH, NU, WF, WSL.

236 —Sir Thomas Fairfax Knight Generall of the forces raised by Parliament. [*Oxford, by L. Lichfield*], 1646. brs. MADAN 1881. O, LPR.

237 —Sir Thomas Fairfax . . . suffer the bearer here of [blank]. [*n.p.*], 1646. brs. O, OP.

238 —A svmmons from His Excellency. *For Edward Husband, March* 11. 1645[6]. 4°.* LT, O, CT, SP, DT; CSS, IU, MH, MIU, WF, Y.

239 —Sir Thomas Fairfax his summons sent into Oxford. *By Elizabeth Purslow, May* 14. 1646. 4°.* MADAN 1864. LT, O, OC, DT; IU, PT, WF, Y.

239A —His Excellency Sir Thomas Fairfax taking [notice] of the manifold abuses. [*n.p.*, 164-] brs. WF.

240 —Three letters from. *For Iohn Wright*, 1645. 4°.* LT, O, C, LIU, DT; CH, CLC, CU, NN, WF.

241 —Three letters from. *For Laurence Chapman, Iune* 28. 1647. 4°.* LT, O, C, MR, CD; CH, CN, MH, NU, WF, Y.

242 —Three proclamations by. *For John Partridge and George Whittington*, 1648. 4°.* LT, O, OC, MR, SP; CH, CU, MH, MU, PT, Y.

243 —Two declarations from. *For R. G.*, 1647. 4°.* LT, O, LLU, MR; CH, ZAP.

244 —Two letters from. *For Laurence Chapman, Iuly* 9. 1647. 4°.* LT, C, OC; CU, INU, MH, NCD, ZAP.

245 — —[Anr. ed.] *For Laurence Chapman, Ivly* 10. 1647. 4°.* L, O, C, DC, YM; CH, IU, MH, NU, WF, Y.

246 —Two letters from . . . 20 Aug. 1647. *For J. Wright*, 1647. 4°.* LT, OC, CS, LLU, DT; CH, CN, MH, MU, WF, Y.

247 —Two letters from . . . one to the commissioners. [*London*, 1647.] cap., 4°.* LT, C, OC, MR, CD; CH, CN, MH, WF, Y.

248 —Two letters of His Excellencie . . . [30 May 1647]. *For George Whittington*, 1647. 4°.* LT, O, C, DC, LLU, LSD; CH, MH, MU, WF, Y.

249–50 No entries.

251 —Two letters, the one from the Right Honourable. *For John Wright*, 1645. 4°.* LT; CH, IU, MH, NN, Y.

252 —Two letters: the one, sent to. *For Edward Husband. Aug.* 9. 1645. 4°.* LT, O, CT, BR, CD; CH, MH, NN, Y.

253 —A warrant of. *By John Macock, for John Partridge*, 1649. 4°.* LT, LVF, MR, YM; CN.

254 —By His Excellency the Lord General. Whereas complaints . . . 24 July 1649. [*London*, 1649.] brs. STEELE 2864. LT, C; V.

255 —By His Excellency the Lord Generall. Whereas daily complaints. *For Laurence Chapman*, 1649. brs. STEELE 2871. LT, C; MH.

255A [**Fairfax, Thomas Fairfax**], **4th baron**. Advice to a young lord. *Printed for, and to be sold by R. Baldwin*, 1691. 12°. T.C.II 385. L, O, LV, OCC; CLC, MH, OCI.

255B **Fairfax, Thomas Fairfax, 5th baron**. The case of Thomas Lord Fairfax. [*London*, 1698.] fol. O.

Fairing for maids. [1665.] *See* P., J.

256 Entry cancelled.

Fairing for young-men and maids. [*n.p.*, 1680?] *See* Bowne, Tobias.

Fairing for young-men. [*n.p.*, 1656.] *See* C., H.

257 **Fairman, Lydia**. A few lines given forth. *For Thomas Simmons*, 1659. fol.* L, LF.

Fairy-queen: an opera. 1692. *See* Settle, Elkanah.

Faith & experience . . . Mary Simpson. 1649. *See* Collinges, John.

258 Entry cancelled.

Faith and order of Congregational churches. 1688. *See* Nye, Philip. Declaration of the faith and order owned.

Faith and practice of a church. 1688. *See* Stanley, William.

258A The faith and practice of thirty congregations. *By J.M. for Will. Larnar*, 1651. 8°.* ORP.

Faith by which. 1695. *See* Bright, George.

Faith, doctrine, and religion. 1661. *See* Rogers, Thomas.

Faith in five fundamental. 1650. *See* Fisher, Edward.

258B The faith of one God. *Printed* 1691. 4°. L, C, OC, ENC, DT; CH, CN, MH, NU, WF, Y.

259 The faith of the army reviving. [*London*, 1649.] cap., 4°.* MR.

260 Entry cancelled.

Faith of the Catholick church. [*n.p.*], 1687. *See* Bruzeau, Paul.

Faith vindicated. Lovain, 1667. *See* Sergeant, John.

Faithful account of a great engagement . . . the Pembrooke. 1690. *See* M., C.

260A A faithful account of a great engagement which happened on Good-Friday. colop: *For R. Hayhurst*, 1690. brs. MH.

261 A faithful account of the cruelties done to the Protestants. *For J. Nutt*, 1700. 8°. T.C.III 233. L, O, LLP, BAMB; CLC, NPT.

262 A faithfull account of the late dreadful fire. [*London*], *for Thomas Pierce*, [1676.] 4°.* MR; WF.

Faithful account of the manner. 1681. *See* S., L.

262A A faithful account of the present condition of Lymerick . . . with Tyrconnel's declaration. *For T. Hawkins*, 1691. brs. DUS.

Faithful account of the present state. 1690. *See* C., E.

263 A faithful account of the renewed persecution of the churches of Lower Aquitaine. *For Richard Baldwin*, 1692. 4°.* L, LIL, LPR, CT, SP; CH, MBA, WF.

Faithful account of the sickness. [*n.p.*, 1680.] *See* S., T.

263A A faithful account of the taking the bridge. colop: *For Robert Hayhurst*, 1691. brs. MH.

264 A faithful advertisement to all good patriots. *Printed at Leyden*, 1650. Reprinted [*London*] by W. D., 1650. 4°.* LT, DT; HR, CN, MIU, NN, WF, Y.

Faithful analist. [1660.] *See* G., W.

265   Entry cancelled.
Faithful and conscientious account. 1650. *See* Paget, Thomas.

266   A faithful and impartial account of the behaviour of a party of the Essex free-holders. *For W. K.,* 1679. fol.* T.C.I 369. L, O, C, DU, EC, LNC; CH, IU, MH, PU, WF, Y.

267   A faithful and impartial account of the proceedings in the case of James Duke of Monmouth. *For J. Hayther,* 1682. brs. LW; CH, Y.

268   A faithfull and impartiall relation of what passed betweene His Majesty, and the commissioners. [*London,* 1648.] brs. LT, O, LG, LS, YM, DT; CH, MH.
Faithfull and seasonable advice. [n.p.], 1643. *See* Hartlib, Samuel.
Faithful annalist. 1666. *See* G., W.

268A A faithful compendium of the birth, . . . James Duke of York. [*London,* 1679.] cap., fol.* L; CDA, AMB.

268B Faithful Coridon. [*London*], *for I. Deacon,* [1675]. brs. O.

269   Faithful Damon. [*London*], *for J. Deacon,* [1681]. brs. L, O, HH; MH, WCL, Y. (var.)
Faithfull depository. Newcastle, 1649. *See* Jenison, Robert.

269A Entry cancelled.
Faithfvl discovery of a treacherous design. 1653. *See* Feake, Christopher.

270   The faithful farmer. [*London*], *for J. Blare,* [1685–88]. brs. L, O, HH; MH, Y.

271   A faithful history of the northern affairs of Ireland. *Printed, and are to be sold by Randall Taylor,* 1690. 4°.* L, O, C, EN, AU, DT; CH, CN, MIU, WF, Y.

272   The faithful inflamed lover. [*London*], *for J. Deacon,* [1685–88]. brs. L, O, CM, HH.

273   Faithful Jemmy. [*London*], *for J. Deacon,* [1684–95]. brs. L, CM, HH.

274   The faithful lovers. *London*], *for P. Brooksby,* [1672–96]. brs. O, HH.

274A The faithfull lover's downfall. *For T. Vere,* [1650–80?]. brs. O.

275   The faithful lovers farvvell. *For Sarah Tyus,* [1664?]. brs. EUING 118. L, GU.

276   Entry cancelled.
Faithful lovers of the West. [1680–85.] *See* Blunden, William.

277   The faithful marriner. *For J. Blare,* [1684–90]. brs. L, CM, HH.
Faithfull messenger. 1644. *See* Bakewell, Thomas.

278   Faithfull narrative of the late testimony. [*London*], *printed,* 1654. 4°. LT, DUS, LIU, DT; NU, WF.
Faithful narrative of the life. 1671. *See* Newcome, Henry.

279   The faithfull pastor his sad lamentation. [*London?*], *printed,* 1687. 4°. L, O, DU, E, EN; LC, MH, NC, PU, WF.

279A The faithful protestations and humble remonstrance of the Roman Catholic nobility . . . of Ireland. [*Dublin,* 1666?] brs. DIX. 110. L, LPR.
Faithful rebuke. 1697. *See* Alsop, Vincent.

280   A faithfull relation, of the late occurrences and proceedings of the Scottish army. *For Robert Bostock and Samuel Gellibrand,* 1644. 4°.* LT, O, SP; IU, MH, WF, Y.

281   A faithful relation of the most remarkable transactions . . . at Tangjer. [n.p., 1680.] cap., fol.* L, O; CH, MH, WF, Y.

282   A faithful remembrance and advice to the general council. *For L. Chapman,* 1659. 4°.* LT, O, BC; CLC, CSS, MH, WF.

283   A faithfull remonstrance, of all the chiefe matters. *For J. Wright,* 1642. 4°.* L, O, EC, DN; IU, Y.

284   A faithfull representation of the state of Ireland. *For Giles Calvert,* 1660. 4°.* O, DN; CSS, MH, WF, WU, Y.

285   A faithfull searching home vvord. [*London*], *printed,* 1659. 4°.* LT, MR; CN, MH, Y.

286   The faithful shepherd. [*London*], *for P. Brooksby,* [1685–90]. brs. L, O, HH; WCL.

286A The faithful shepherdess. [*London*], *for Phillip Brooksby,* [1675?]. brs. O.

287   The faithfull souldier. [n.p.], *printed,* 1649. 4°.* L, O; CLC, CN, MH, Y.

288   —[Anr. ed.] colop: *Printed,* 1680/1. cap., fol.* L, O; CH, CN, MH, NC, NP, WF.

289   The faithful squire. [*London*], *for J. Deacon,* [1685–88]. brs. L, O, HH; MH.

290   A faithful subject's sigh. [*London*], *printed,* 1649. 4°.* LT, YM, DT; CH, IU, MH.

290A A faithful testimony against the teachers. [*London?* 1662.] 4°.* MR.
Faithful testimony concerning. 1659. *See* Burrough, Edward.
Faithful testimony for God. 1664. *See* Billing, Edward.
Faithful testimony of High-hall. 1700. *See* Gale, Nathaniel.
Faithful warning once more. [n.p.], 1690. *See* Bingley, William.
Faithful warning to all. [n.p., 1668.] *See* Tomkins, Anthony.
Faithful vvarning to out-side. [n.p., 1661.] *See* Taylor, Thomas.

290B Entry cancelled.
Faithful warning with good advice. [1660?] *See* Mason, Martin.
Faithfull woings. [1655–70.] *See* Wade, John.

291   The faithful, yet imperfect, character of a glorious king, King Charles I. *For Richard Royston,* 1660. 8°. LT, O, C, DU, YM; CH, MH, TU, WF, Y.

292   The faithful young man. [*London*], *for J. Back,* [1685–88]. brs. L, O, HH; MH.

293   The faithful young mans answer. [*London*], *for J. Clarke,* [1674]. brs. EUING 114. L, GU.
Faithfulness of God. 1674. *See* Fleming, Robert.
Faithfvlnesse of the upright. [n.p., 1663.] *See* Complin, Nicholas.
Faithless lover. [1655–80.] *See* Diseased maiden lover.

294   **Faithorne, William.** The art of graveing and etching. [*London*], *pvblished by Willm. Faithorne,* 1662. 8°. L, O, LG, LLL, GK; CH, CN, LC, MH, TU, Y.

[45]

295 **Falconer, David.** Information for My Lord and Lady Nairn. [*n.p.*], 1690. 4°.* EN.

296 **F[alconer], J[ohn].** Cryptomenysis patefacta: or the art of secret information. *For Daniel Brown,* 1685. 8°. T.C.II 137. L, O, C, EN, ES, DT; CH, IU, LC, MH, PL, Y.

297 —Disputatio juridica. *Edinburgh, Watson,* 1699. 4°. ALDIS 3850. EN.

297A —Disputatio juridica, de donationibus. *Edinburgi, ex officina typographica hæredum A. Anderson,* 1700. 4°. ALDIS 3963.5. EN.

298 —Rules for explaining and decyphering all manner of secret writing. *For Dan. Brown; and Sam. Manship,* 1692. 8°. T.C.II 413. L, O, LL, MP, EN; LC, Y.

299 Entry cancelled.
Falconer, Patrick. Anatomie of the messe. 1641. *See* DuMoulin, Pierre.

300 **Faldo, John.** A discourse of the gospel of peace. *For Tho. Cockerill,* 1687. 8°. T.C.II 205. L, LCL; CH, NPT, NU, WF, Y.

301 —Quakerism no Christianity. 1672. 8°. L, ORP, RPL; PH, PL.

302 — —[Anr. ed.] *By Ben. Griffin and are to be sold by Jo. Robinson, and Rob. Boulter,* 1673. 8°. T.C.I 126. L, O, LF, CT, E; BN, CH, KQ, MH, NP, PH, PSC.

303 — —[Anr. ed.] *By B. G. for Jonanthan [sic] Robinson,* 1675. 8°. T.C.I 200. L, O, LF, CE, GU; CH, MH, NU, PH, WF, Y.

304 Entry cancelled.
—Reasonableness of personal reformation, 1691. *See* Flavell, John.

305 [-] The snake in the grass further discovered. *By J. F. and are to be sold by A. Baldwin,* 1698. 8°. T.C.III 84. L, O, LF, CE, CS, NPL; CLC, MH, NU, WF, Y.

306 —XXI. divines . . . cleared. *By J. D. for Dorman Newman, and Jonathan Robinson,* 1675. 8°. T.C.I 195. L, O, LF, OC, CT; CLC, MH, NCD, NU, PH, PL.

307 —A vindication of Quakerism no Christianity. *By B. Griffin for J. Robinson, and Rob. Boulter,* 1673. 8°. T.C.I 154. L, LF, CT, E; CH, MH, MWA, PSC, WF.

308 **Faldo, Thomas.** Reformation of proceedings at law. [*London*], *by Hen: Hils, in Southwarke.* 1649. 4°.* LT, O, C, LL, AN; BN, CSS, MH, MHL, NCL, WF, Y.

309 **Faldo, W.** In diem natalem Regis Augustissimi Caroli. [*London,* 1674.] brs. L, O.

310 **Fale, Thomas.** Horologiographia. The art of dialling. *By Felix Kingstone,* 1652. 4°. L, O, C, AN, DC, E; CH, MH, MU, NC, NPT, WF, Y.

311 **Falgate, Israel.** Interest in epitome. *For George Sawbridge,* 1699. 4°. T.C.III 96. L; IU.

312 —Tables of interest. [*London,* 1700?] 12°. L.
Faliscus, Gratius. *See* Gratius, Faliscus.

313 **F[alkland], H[enry Cary], 1st viscount.** The history of the life, reign and death of Edward II. *By J. C., for Charles Harper, Samuel Crouch, and Thomas Fox,* 1680. fol. T.C.I 368. L, O, CT, EN, DT; CH, MH, MU, WF, Y.

314 —The history of the most unfortunate prince King Edward II. *By A. G. and J. P., and sold by John Playford,* 1680. 8°. T.C.I 382. L, O, C, EN, DT; CH, MBP, MH, MIU, NC, WSL.

314A —The parallel: or The history of . . . Edward the Second. *Printed and are to be sold by R. Baldwin,* 1689. fol. O, OC, CS.

315 **Falkland, Henry Cary, 4th viscount.** The mariage night. *By W. G. for R. Crofts,* 1664. 4°. L, O, LVD, CK, EN; CH, CN, MH, WF, Y.

316 **Falkland, Lucius Cary, viscount.** Discourse of infallibility. 1646. 4°. LCL.

317 —Sir Lucius Cary, . . . his discourse of infallibility. *By Gartrude Dawson, for Iohn Hardesty,* 1651. 4°. LT, O, C, ENC, DT; CH, IU, NU, PL, TU, WF.

318 —A discourse of infallibility. Second edition. *For William Nealand, Cambridge,* 1660. 4°. L, O, C, NPL, EN; CH, CU, MH, PL, WF, Y.

319 —A dravght of a speech. *Oxford, by Leonard Lichfield,* 1644. 4°.* MADAN 1747. O, C, LCL, MR, DT; CLC, CN, IU, OWC, WF.

320 —The Lord Favlkland his learned speech. [*London*], *prtntee [sic]* 1641. 4°.* LT, C, LVF, EC, LLU; CH, CN, MH, TU, WF, Y. (var., "*printed*").

320A —A letter sent from . . . Septemb. 30. *Printed at York by Stephen Bulkley,* 1642. 4°.* C; Y.

321 — —[Anr. ed.] *Printed at York, Octob. 1. and now re-printed at London for J. T., Octob. 7.* 1642. 4°.* LT, C, OC, EC, DT; MH.

322 —Of the infallibilitie of the Chvrch of Rome. *Oxford, by H Hall,* 1645. 4°.* MADAN 1844. O, C, LSC, MR, DT; CH, CN, MH, NU, WF.

323 Entry cancelled. *See following entry.*

324 —A speech made to the Hovse of Commons concerning Episcopacy. *For Thomas Walkely,* 1641. 4°.* LT, O, C, E, DT; CH, CN, MH, WF, Y. (var.)

325 —The speech or declaration of. *Printed,* 1641. 4°.* L, O, LG, CS, BC, LNC; CH, CU, MH, WF, Y.

326 — —[Anr. ed.] *For John Bartlet,* 1641. 4°.* LT, O, C, E, DT; CH, IU, MH, NU, TU, WF, Y.

327 —Two discourses. *For W. Nealand, Cambridge,* 1660. 4°.* C, OB.

328 **Falkner, Robert.** A voice, out of Sion. *Printed,* 1663. 4°.* L, LF, BBN, BP; CLC, PH.

329 **Falkner, William.** Christian loyalty. *By J. M. for Walter Kettilby,* 1679. 8°. T.C.I 326. L, O, C, E, DT; CLC, IU, LC, NPT, NU, TO, Y.

330 — —Second edition. —, 1684. 8°. T.C.II 103. L, OC, WCA, EN, DT; BN, CH, CLC.

331 —Libertas ecclesiastica, or, a discourse. *By J. M. for Walter Kettilby,* 1674. 8°. T.C.I 148. L, O, C, ES, DT; CH, CLC, IU, NU, PBL.

332 — —Second edition. —, 1674. 8°. T.C.I 192. L, O, C, E, DT; CDA, CN, IAU, MBA, NU, Y.

333 — —Third edition. —, 1677. 8°. T.C.I 278. L, O, C, NE, ENC; CH, CLC, CN, IU, NU.

334 — —Fourth edition. —, 1683. 8°. T.C.II 9. L, OC, NPL, YM, DT; BN, CLC, IU, NU, PL, TU, WF.

335 —Two treatises. *For Richard Chiswell, and are to be sold by John Southby, and Luke Meredith,* 1684. 4°. T.C.II 80. L, O, C, D, DT; CH, IAU, MB, MH, NU.

335A ——[Anr. ed.] *For Richard Chiswell*, 1684. 4°. OC, WCA, CD; CLC, MH, NU, TO.

335B ——[Anr. ed.] —, *and sold by William Oliver in Norwich*, 1684. 4°. LSD; WF.

336 —A vindication of liturgies. *For Walter Kettilby*, 1680. 8°. T.C.I 403. L, O, C, EN, DT; BN, CN, CSU, MH, NU, WF.

Fall of Babylon. 1690. *See* Woodroffe, Benjamin.

336A The fall of Babylon or. *For James Watts*, 1688. brs. MH.

Fall of man declared. 1661. *See* Kent, Thomas.

337 The fallacies of Mr. VVilliam Prynne, discovered. *Oxford, by Leonard Lichfield*, 1644. 4°.* MADAN 1544. LT, O, OC, CT, MR, DT; CH, CU, MH, NU, WF, Y.

Fallacy of infants baptisme. 1645. *See* Hobson, Paul.

Fallall, Fardinando, *pseud.*

338 **Falle, Philip.** An account of the Isle of Jersey. *For John Newton*, 1694. 8°. T.C.II 492. L, O, C, EN, DT; BN, CH, IU, LC, MH, NC, WF.

339 —Of the descent of the Paraclet. *For John Newton*, 1695. 4°.* T.C.II 548. L, C, LLP, NPL, DT; CH, NC, NU, TSM, WF, Y.

340 —Of the impunity of bad men. *For John Newton*, 1695. 4°.* T.C.II 536. L, O, C; CH, NC, NU, WF, Y.

341 —A sermon preached . . . April 10th. 1692. *For John Newton*, 1692. 4°.* T.C.II 418. L, O, C, LLP; MIU, NC, NU, Y.

342 —A sermon preached . . . June 12. 1700. *By W. Bowyer, for John Newton*, 1700. 4°. L, O, C, BAMB, EN; CH, NU, PL, WF.

Fallibility and falsehood. 1676. *See* Whitby, Daniel.

Fallibility of the Roman church. 1687. *See* Whitby, Daniel.

False alarum. 1646. *See* Sheppard, Samuel.

343 The false and scandalous remonstrance of the . . . rebells of Ireland. *For Edw. Husbands*, 1644. 4°. LT, O, C, LVF, EN, DT; CH, CN, MH, MU, Y.

False brother. 1650. *See* Sydenham, Cuthbert.

False favourit. 1657. *See* Gerbier, George.

344 The false-hearted glover. [*London*], *for P. Brooksby, J. Deacon, J. Blare, J. Back*, [1688–92]. brs. L, O, HH.

False Jew. Newcastle, 1653. *See* Weld, Thomas.

False judgments. [n.p., 1692.] *See* Keith, George.

False prophets and the false. [n.p., 1652.] *See* Aldam, Thomas.

345 False prophets discovered. *For I. Wright*, 1642. 4°.* OW, CT, LNC; CH, NP, NU.

346 —[Anr. ed.] *For I. W.*, 1642. 4°.* LT.

347 Entry cancelled.

False remonstrance. 1644. *See* False and scandalous remonstrance.

348 Falshood chastized. *For S. Veridicus*, 1665. brs. L.

349 No entry.

Falshood detected. 1690. *See* Maurice, Henry.

Falshood of human virtue. 1691. *See* Esprit, Jacques.

Falsehood of Mr. VVilliam Pryn's. 1645. *See* Robinson, Henry.

Falshood unmaskt. 1676. *See* Patrick, Symon.

350 Famæ posthumæ. 1646. 4°.* SS.

350A The fame and confession of the fraternity . . . Rosie Cross. *By J. M. for Giles Calvert*, 1652. LT, C, RPL, A, GU; CH, CLC, MH, MU, WF, Y.

350B The fame, wit, and glory of the VVest. *For R. Burton*, 164[9]. brs. MAU.

351 A familiar discourse, between George. *By T. N. for Samuel Lowndes*, 1672. 4°.* T.C.I 119. L, O, C, CT; CH, CU, INU, NC, TU, WF, Y.

Familiar discourse or. 1700. *See* Shires, William.

352 Familiar forms of speaking compos'd for the use of schools. Second edition. [*London*], *by J. R. for T. Helder*, 1678. 12°. T.C.I 292. CLC, WCL.

352A —Third edition. *By J. Grover for T. Helder*, 1680. 12°. L; CH, IU.

352B —Fourth edition. *By Tho. James for Tho. Helder*, 1683. 12°. CU, IU, MB.

352C —Sixth edition. *By A. Grover for Tho. Helder*, 1685. 12°. T.C.II 139. L, O; CH, MU, NP, WF.

352D —Seventh edition. *Sold by Thomas Guy*, 1687. 12°. T.C.II 221. IU.

352E —Eighth edition. *By T. J. for Tho. Helder*, 1691. 12°. T.C.II 352. O; TO.

352F —Eleventh edition. *By J. W. for Tho. Helder*, 1695. 12°. GU.

353 Entry cancelled.

Familiares colloquendi formulae. Sixth edition. 1685. *See* Familiar forms.

354 The families best guide. [n.p., c. 1660.] brs. MAGGS.

Family-altar. 1693. *See* Heywood, Oliver.

Family-dictionary. 1695. *See* H., J.

354A Family exercise. *Edinburgh, R. Bryson*, 1641. 8°. ALDIS 1003. 7. EN.

Family-herbal. 1689. *See* Durante, Castore.

Family-hymns. 1695. *See* Henry, Matthew.

355 The family prayers of those poor Christians. *By A. M. for R. Royston*, 1675. 8°.* T.C.I 215. LLP; CH, WF.

Famous and delectable history of Cleocriton. [166–?] *See* C., S.

Famous and delectable history of Don Bellianis. 1673. *See* Fernandez, Geronimo.

355A The famous and delightful history of Fortunatus. Seventh edition. *Printed by and for T. Norris*, [1700?]. 12°. L.

355B The famous and delightful history of the golden eagle. *By and for W. O.*, [c. 1700]. 4°.* O.

356 Famous and effectual medicine. [*London*, 1670?] brs. L.

356A A famous and joyfull victory obtained by Sir Iohn Merricks regiment. [*London*], *Aug. 26. For I. Williams*, 1642. 4°.* MH, PL.

Famous and joyfull victory obtained by the Earl. [n.p., 1642.] *See* Hamblet, John.

357 The famous and notable sayings of an eminent holder-forth. *For T. Lightfoot*, 1691. 8°.* L.

Famous and pleasant history. [1680.] *See* Forde, Emanuel.

Famous and remarkable history. 1656. *See* Heywood, Thomas.

358 Entry cancelled.

Famous and renowned history of Amadis de Gaule. 1652. *See* Lobeira, Vasco.

358A The famous and renowned history of Hector, Prince of Troy. [*n.p.*, 1700?] 4°.* L.

359 The famous and renowned history of Sir Bevis of Southampton. *For W. Thackeray and J. Deacon*, 1689. 4°. L; CH, IU, WF.

359A The famous and renowned history of the memorable . . . hunting on Chevy-Chase. *By and for C. Brown*, [*c.* 1690]. 4°.* CLC.

360 —[Anr. ed.] *By and for W. O.*, [1700?]. brs. L, O.

Famous and renowned history of the nine worthies. [1700.] *See* Crouch, Nathaniel.

361 Entry cancelled. Date: after 1708.

361A The famous and renowned history of the two unfortunate . . . lovers. Hero. *By A. Milbourn, for J. Blare*, [1690?]. 4°.* CH, IU.

361B The famous and renowned history of Valentine and Orson. [*London*], *by W. O. for C. Bates*, [1690–1700]. 4°.* L.

Famous battle between Robin Hood and Maid Marion. [1653.] *See* Sheppard, Samuel.

362 The famous battel between Robin Hood, and the Curtal fryar. [*London*], *for W. Thackeray, J. Millet, and A. Milbourn*, [1689–92]. brs. L, O, HH; MH.

363 —[Anr. ed.] *For F. Coles, T. Vere, and J. Wright*, [1672?]. brs. L.

363A A famous battel fought by the Earle of Bedford. *By I. Williams*, [Octob. 1. 1642]. 4°.* L.

364 A famous battel fought by the Earle of Corke. *For John Greensmith*, 1642. 4°.* LT, DN; WF, Y.

Famous battel of the catts. 1668. *See* Denham, *Sir* John.

365 The famous bull in Cœna Domini. [*London*], *printed*, 1688. 4°.* L, OC, OCC, CS, LIU, DT; CH, MH, TU, WF, Y.

366 —[Anr. ed.] *For Ric. Chiswel*, 1689. 4°.* OB, MR; CLC, NU.

Famous Chinois. 1669. *See* Du Bail, Louis Moreau, *le sieur*.

Famous collection of papers. [*n.p.*, 1695?] *See* Miller, William.

367 The famous conclave wherein Clement VIII was elected Pope. *By E. C. and A. C. for Samuel Lowndes*, 1670. 4°.* T.C.I 37. L, LLP, OC, CT, BP, DU, SP, BLH; CH, CN, IU, Y.

368 A famous conference between Pope Clement the Xth. and Cardinal de Monte Alto. *By T. R. and N. T. for Moses Pitt*, 1674. 4°.* L, O, LIL, OC, CT, WCA; CH, IU, NU, TU.

368A The famous fight at Malago. *By and for W. O., sold by J. Deacon*, [1690?]. brs. L.

369 —[Anr. ed.] *By and for W. O. for A. M. and sold by C. Bats* [*sic*], [1700?]. brs. L, O, CM, HH; MH. (var.)

369A The famous flower of serving-men. *For John Andrews*, [1663?]. brs. EUING 111. LG, GU.

369B —[Anr. ed.] *For Eliz. Andrews*, [1664?]. brs. O.

369C —[Anr. ed.] *Printed* [1670?]. brs. L, O, CM, HH.

370 —[Anr. ed.] [*London*], *for J. Hose*, [1680?]. brs. O.

370A —[Anr. ed.] *By and for W. O. for A. M. and are to be sold by J. Bissel*, [1700?]. brs. NNM.

Famous game of chesse-play. 1672. *See* Saul, Arthur.

Famous history of Aurelius. [1685?] *See* Shirley, John.

371 The famous historie of Fryer Bacon. *By E. Cotes, for F. Grove*, 1661. 4°. L.

372 —[Anr. ed.] *By E. Cotes, and are to be sold by Thomas Passinger*, 1666. 4°. L, OC.

373 —[Anr. ed.] *By M. Clark, and are to be sold by T. Passinger*, 1679. 4°. CM; CH.

374 Entry cancelled.

374 —[Anr. ed.] 1683. *See* History of Fryer Bacon.

374A —[Anr. ed.] *For W. Thackeray and C. Bates*, [1698?]. 4°.* L, O, LN.

375 The famous history of Guy Earl of Warwick. [*London*], *for F. Coles, T. Vere, J. Wright, and J. Clark*, [1674–79]. 8°. O.

376 —[Anr. ed.] [*London*], *for J. Clark, W. Thackeray, and T. Passinger*, 1686. 8°. CM.

Famous history of Montelion. 1661. *See* Forde, Emanuel.

377 The famous history of Palmendos. *By E. Alsop*, 1653. 4°. L, O, CCH; CH, CLC.

378 —[Anr. ed.] *By T. Fawcet, to be sold by F. Coles*, 1663. 4°. L; CH, CN.

Famous history of Pheander. 1661. *See* Roberts, Henry.

378A The famous history of Stout Stukley. *By R. I. for F. Grove*, [*c.* 1650]. 8°. O.

Famous history of that most renowned . . . Arthvr. 1660. *See* Parker, Martin.

Famous history of the noble . . . Palmerin. 1664. *See* Moraes, Francisco de.

Famous history of the seven champions. [1660.] *See* Johnson, Richard.

Famous history of the valiant. 1692. *See* S., J.

379–81 No entries.

The famous history of Valentine and Orson. 1673. *See* Price, Laurence.

382 The famous overthrow: or, the routing of the run-away Dutch. [*n.p.*, 1666]. brs. LPR.

Famous pleasant and delightful history of Ornatus. [1700?] *See* Forde, Emmanuel.

The famous, pleasant, and delightful history of Palladine of England. 1664. *See* Colet, Claude.

Famous romance of Tarsis. 1685. *See* LeVayer de Boutigny, Roland.

383 The famous sea-fight between Captain Ward. *For Fr. Coles*, [1650?]. brs. EUING 108. L, GU; Y.

383A —[Anr. ed.] *By and for W. Onley*, [1700?]. brs. L, O, CM, HH.

384 The famous tragedie of King Charles I. basely butchered. [*London?*], *printed*, 1649. 4°.* L, O, C, LVD, DT; CH, CN, LC, MH, WF, Y.

385 Entry cancelled. Date: 1709.

385A The famous tragedie of the life and death of Mris. Rump. *For Theodorus Microcosmus*, 1660. 4°.* L, EN; CH, CU, MB, MH, PL.

385B —[Anr. ed.] *Printed*, 1660. 4°.* Y.

386 The famous tryal in B. R. between Thomas Neale. [*n.p.*], *printed*, 1696. fol. L, LG, EN; CH, TU, WF.

387 A famous victorie obtained against the Cavaliers in the county of Gloucester. *Feb. 25 for R. Wood*, 1643. 4°.* LT, O, DT; WF.

388 A famovs victorie obtained by Sir Thomas Fairfax, against the Lord Hopton. *By B. A. February 20*, 1646. 4°.* LT, CS.

Famous victory obtained by{ Sir William Brewerton. 1644. *See* Isack, I.

389 A famous victorie obtained by Sir William Waller. *March 31, for Robert Wood*, 1643. 4°.* L, C.

390 A famous victory obtained by the Brittish forces. *For E. Horton, March 1*. 1647. 4°.* LT, C.

390A A famous victory obtained by the citisens [sic] of Coventry. *For R. Wood*, 1642, *August 25*. 4°.* LW, LNC.

390B —[Anr. ed.] *For R. Wood*, 1642, *August 26*. 4°.* LNC.

391 A famous victory obtained by the Right Honorable the Lord Brooks, against [sic]. *For Henry Fowler, the sixt of August*. 1642. 4°.* LT, EC.

391A The famous water of talk and pearl. [*London*, 1670?] brs. L.

Famous woman-drummer. [1660.] *See* Price, Laurence.

392 The phanatick anatomized. *Printed*, 1672. brs. L.

393 Entry cancelled.

Fanatick barber. [n.p., 1655?] *See* Fanaticks barber.

Fanatick history: or. 1660. *See* Blome, Richard.

Fanatick in his colours. 1661. *See* F., T.

394 The phanatick in his colours. colop: *For N. Thompson*, 1681. cap., fol.* L, O, CT, LL, LV; CH, CN, LC, MH, Y.

395 A phanatique league. [*London?*] *for G. H.*, [1660]. brs. LT, O, LG; MH, MIU, Y.

396 Entry cancelled.

Fanatick moderation. [1647.] *See* Hall, Joseph, *bp*.

397 A phanatick play. *Printed*, 1660. 4°.* LT, O, MR; MB, MH, WF.

398 Entry cancelled.

Fanatique powder-plot. [1660.] *See* L'Estrange, *Sir* Roger.

398A A phanatique prayer. [*London*, 1660.] brs. LT, O; CH, MH, Y.

399 Fanatique queries. *For Praise-God-Barebones*, [1660]. 4°.* LT, O, BC, LSD, MR; CH, MH, MIU, NN, OWC, Y.

400 The fanatick rampant or an election at Cambridge. [n.p., 1679.] brs. O, HH; CH, CN, MH, TU, Y.

Phanatical-tenderness. 1684. *See* Godwyn, Thomas.

Fanaticism fanatically imputed. [n.p.], 1672. *See* Cressy, Hugh Paulin.

401 The fanaticks barber. [*London*, 1655?] brs. L, O.

402 The phanatiques creed. *For Henry Brome*, 1661. 4°.* LT, O, OB, MR; CN, LC, NN.

403 The fanatick's dream. [*London?* 1680.] brs. L, O; CH, CLC.

404 The phanaticks plot discovered. [*London*], *for Samuel Burdet*, 1660. brs. LT.

Fancies favourite. [1655-82.] *See* H., C.

405 Fancy's freedom. [*London*], *for W. Whitwood*, [1668?]. brs. L.

406 Phancies phoenix. *For F. Coles, T. Vere, and J. Wright*, [1674?]. brs. L, O, GU.

406A **Fancy, P[eter].** The age & life of man. [*London*], *for J. Williamson*, [1675?]. brs. O.

406B —Joyfull news to the nation. *For Richard Burton*, [1661]. brs. EUING 147. GU.

407 —This is call'd, Maids looke well about you? [1655?] brs. L.

407A **F[ane], Sir F[rancis].** An excellent ballad upon a wedding. *For H. Playford and sold by E. Whitlock*, 1698. fol. O.

408 —Love in the dark. [*London*], *in the Savoy, by T. N. for Henry Herringman*, 1675. 4°. T.C.I 227. L, O, OW, LLU, EN; CH, CN, LC, MH, TU, Y.

408A ——[Anr. ed.] *In the Savoy*, 1671 [i.e. 1675]. 4°. CH.

409 [–] A panegyrick to the Kings most excellent majesty. *By W. Wilson, for Henry Herringman*, 1662. fol.* CH, TU, Y.

410-410A Entries cancelled.

[–] Pindarick ode on the sacred memory. 1685. *See title*.

411 —The sacrifice. *By J. R. for John Weld*, 1686. 4°. T.C.II 168. L, O, EN; CH, CU, LC, NC, WF, Y.

412 ——Second edition. —, 1687. 4°. T.C.II 189. L, O, LVF, OW; BN, CN, LC, MH, TU, Y.

413 ——Third edition. —, 1687. 4°. L, OW, CT, LIU, LLU; CLC, CN, MH, MU, WF, Y.

Fane, Mildmay. *See* Westmorland, Mildmay Fane, *2nd earl of*.

[**Fannant, Edward.**] History of the life, reign. 1680. *See* Falkland, Henry Cary, *1st viscount*.

414 Entry cancelled.

[–] History of the most unfortunate prince. 1680. *See* Falkland, Henry Cary, *1st viscount*.

415 **Fannant, Thomas.** An historical narration of the manner and form of . . . Parliament. [*London*], *printed*, 1641. 4°.* L, O, CT, MR, DT; BN, CH, CN, MH, WF, Y. (var.)

416 [–] A true relation of that memorable Parliament. [*London*], *printed*, 1641. 4°.* LT, O, C, LW, CDC; CH, CLC, CSS, MH, MIU, WF, Y.

416A [–] A true declaration of that memorable Parliament. [*London*], *printed in the yeare of much feare*, 1643. 4°.* SP; CLC.

Fanner, John. Angelus Britannicus. 1664. *See* Almanacs: Tanner.

417 Entry cancelled.

Fanshaw, Mrs. True and wonderful account of a cure. 1681. *See title*.

418 **Fanshawe, Sir Richard.** A proclamation for all persons within our quarters in . . . Devon. *Imprinted at Exeter by Robert Barker, and John Bill*, 1645. brs. LT.

419 **Fanshaw, Sir Thomas.** A declaration of the knights, and gentry of the county of Hertford. *For Daniel Pakeman*, 1660. brs. LT, LG.

420 Entry cancelled.

—Practice of the exchequer court. 1658. *See* Osborne, Peter.

Fanum Sti Albani, poema. 1683. *See* Jones, John.

421 **Farbrother, Roger.** The magistrates concern. *For William Keblewhite*, 1698. 4°.* T.C.III 102. L, O; NGT, NU.

422 [**Farewell, James.**] The Irish Hudibras. *Printed, and are to be sold by Richard Baldwin*, 1689. 4°. T.C.II 276. L, O, C, OW, BQ, DT; CH, CN, MH, NP, TU, WF, Y.

422A The farewell. [*London*, 1688.] brs. C.

422B Farewel proud woman. [*London?* 1700.] brs. L.

Farewell sermons of the late London ministers. 1662. *See* Calamy, Edmund.

423 A farewel to Graves-end. [*London*], for *J. Deacon*, [1683?]. brs. L.

423A A farevvel to hacknay lades. [*London*,] for *F. Coles, T. Vere, J. Wright, and I. Clark*, [1674–79]. brs. O.

424 A farewel to his Royal Highness James. [*n.p.*, 1680.] brs. O, LLU; CN, MH.

Farewel to popery. 1679. *See* Harris, Walter.

425 **Faria, Francisco de.** The information of. *By the assigns of John Bill, Thomas Newcomb, and Henry Hills*, 1680. fol.* L, O, C, EN, DT; BN, CH, CN, MH, WF, Y, AVP.

426 —The narrative of. *By John Gain for Randal Taylor*, 1680. fol.* L, O, C, MR, EN, DN; CH, MBP, MH, WF, Y, AVP. (var.)

427 **Faria e Sousa, Manuel de.** The history of Portugal. *For W. Rogers and Abel Roper*, 1698. 8°. L, CE, E, EN, DT; BN, CH, CN, LC, NC, SW, WF, Y.

427A — —[Anr. ed.] —, *J. Harris and J. Nicholson, T. Newborough and T. Cockerill*, 1698. 8°. OC, NE; PL, RPJ.

427B — —[Anr. ed.] *By W. G. for Peter Dring, J. Harris and J. Harrison; T. Newborough; and T. Cockerill*, 1698. 8°. DUS.

428 —The Portugues Asia. *For C. Brome*, 1695. 8°. T.C.II 522. L, O, C, EN, DT; LC, MIU, NN, WF, Y.

429 **Farindon, Anthony.** LXXX sermons . . . in two volumes. *By Tho. Roycroft for Richard Marriott*, 1672. fol. O, C, LW, OME, DM; CH, MH, NU, TSM, WF.

429A — —Second edition. —, 1672. fol. L, OW, CK, CT, D, DT; CB, CN, MH, MU, NGT, NPT, PL.

430 — —"Second" edition. —, 1673. fol. T.C.I 107. BN.

431 Entry cancelled. Ghost.

432 —Fifty sermons . . . Third and last volume. *By Tho. Roycroft for Richard Marriott*, 1674. fol. T.C.I 162. L, O, C, EN, DT; BN, CH, CN, MH, NPT, TSM.

432A —Forty sermons . . . Second volume. *By J. G. for Richard Marriott*, 1663. fol. L, C, LG, P, SHR; NGT, PPT.

433 Entry cancelled.

—XLVII sermons. 1672. *See* —LXXX sermons. Volume two.

434 —XXX. sermons. *For Richard Marriot*, 1647 [*i.e.* 1657]. fol. L, C, LW, OM, DU, SA; CH, CU, MH, NGT, WF, Y, AVP.

435 —XXX. sermons lately preached. *For Richard Marriot*, 1657. fol. L, C, LCL, LG, NPL, DT; CLC, NU, WF, WSC, Y.

436 —XXXII sermons. *By Tho. Roycroft for Richard Marriott*, 1672. fol. O, CE; CN, IU, OLU, WF.

437 —XXXII sermons. . . . The first volume. Second edition. *By Tho. Roycroft for Richard Marriott*, 1672. fol. L, O, DT; CN, NPT.

438 **Farisol, Abraham ben Mordecai.** [Hebrew] id est, Itinera mundi. *Oxonii, e theatro Sheldoniano, impensis Henrici Bonwick*, 1691. 4°. T.C.II 337. L, O, C, E, DT; CH, LC, NC, PL, RPJ, Y.

439 Entry cancelled. *Part of preceding entry.*

439A **Farmborow, Nicholas.** Fundamenta grammatices, or the foundation. *By M. C. for Robert Clavell*, 1690. 12°. T.C.II 325. CLC.

440 [**Farmer, Jacob.**] A letter sent ovt of Ireland, to one Mr. Bell. *For Iohn Smith*, 1642. 4°.* LT, O, CT, DN; MH, Y.

441 **Farmer, Ralph.** The great mysteries. *By S. G. for William Ballard, in Bristoll; and Joshua Kirton*, 1655. 4°. LT, O, C, LF, BC, E; NU, PH, TO.

441A —The imposter dethron'd. *By R. I. for Edw. Thomas*, 1658. 4°. BR; CN, PH.

442 —The Lord Cravens case stated. *By R. I. for Edward Thomas*, 1660. 4°. LF.

443 [–] A plain-dealing, and plain-meaning sermon, preach't . . . April 6, 1660. *By S. Griffin, to be sold by Thomas Wall, Bristol*, 1660. 4°.* LT, EN; NU.

444 —Sathan inthron'd. *For Edward Thomas*, 1657. 4°. LT, O, CT, BBN, BR, WCA; CH, CLC, NU, PH.

445 **Farmer, Thomas.** A consort of musick. *Sold by H. Playford; and at the author's house*, 1686. obl. 4°. T.C.II 178. L.

445A **Farmer, William.** Art thou a ruler in Israel. *For John Hancock*, 1648. 4°.* D; CLC, Y.

445B The farmers heir. [*London?* 1670.] brs. L.

446 The farmers reformation. *For R. Kell*, [1687–8]. brs. L, HH; MH, Y.

447 The farmers son of Devonshire. [*London*], for *J. Deacon*, [1689–95]. brs. L, O, HH; MH.

448 No entry.

449 **Farnaby, Thomas.** ᵉΗ τῆς ανθολογιας . . . Florilegium. *Apud A. M. pro Christophero Meredith*, 1650. 8°. O, C, LLL, LW, DCH; CU, IU, PL, Y.

450 — —[Anr. ed.] *Apud E. T. & R. H. pro T. Passenger, & T. Sawbridge*, 1671. 8°. T.C.I 76. L; CH, CPB, MB, WF.

451 [–] Index poeticus. *Impensis, & prostant venales per Philemonem Stephens*, 1658. 12°. O; WF, Y.

451A [–] — [Anr. ed.] —, 1663. 12°. L.

452 [–] — [Anr. ed.] *Impensis Philemonis & Johan: Stephani*, 1667. 12°.* C; CLC, IU.

453 [–] — [Anr. ed.] *Typis Andr. Clark, impensis Joh. Wright*, 1672. 12°. O; CN, CU, IU.

453A [–] — [Anr. ed.] *Impensis Joh. Wright*, 1676. 12°.* Y.

453B [–] —[Anr. ed.] *Typis M. White, impensis Joh. Wright*, 1682. 12°. U. OREGON.

453C [–] — [Anr. ed.] [*London*], *typis J. Richardson, impensis G. Conyers & M. Wotton*, 1689. 12°.* L.

453D [–] —[Anr. ed.] *Typis J. Richardson, impensis G. Conyers & M. Wotton*, 1696. 12°. Y.

454 —Index rhetoricus et oratorius. Fourth edition. *Impensis Philemonis Stephani*, 1646. 12°. L, O, LW; CN, IU, MB, MHL, Y.

455 — —Fifth edition. —, 1654. 12°. L; CU, NC, WF.

456 — —[Anr. ed.] —, 1659. 12°. L, O, LI, OC; Y.

456A — —[Anr. ed.] —, 1664. 12°. SW, WF.

456B — —[Anr. ed.] *Impensis Philemonis & Johan. Stephani*, 1667. 12°. CM; CLC, IU.

457 — —[Anr. ed.] *Typis Andr. Clark, impensis Joh. Wright*, 1672. 12°. O, EC; CN, CSU, CU, PL, RBU.

457A — —[Anr. ed.] *Impensis Joh. Wright,* 1676. 12°. L, DUS; Y.

458 — —[Anr. ed.] *Impensis J. Wright; prostat autem vænalis apud S. Crowch,* 1682. 12°. T.C.I 498. L; U. OREGON.

459 — —[Anr. ed.] *Typis Richardsonianis, impensis M. Wotton, & G. Coniers,* 1689. 12°. T.C.II 263. AN; CH, CN, CU, IU, NIA.

460 — —[Anr. ed.] *Typis excuduntur pro Mat. Wotton, & G. Conyers.* 1696. 12°. L, O, E; IU, MBC, Y.

461 —Phrases oratoriae. Eighth edition. *Excudebat T. W. pro C. Meridith,* 1647. 12°. CU.

461A — —"Eighth" edition. *Excudebat T. W. pro Christoph. Meredith,* 1648. 12°. MB.

462 — —Ninth edition. *Typis J. B. & prostant venales apud Andr. Kembe,* 1658. 12°. CM, DC; IU.

462A — —"Ninth" edition. *Typis Andr. Kembe, prostant venales per Eduardum Thomas,* 1661. 12°. DU.

463 — — Tenth edition. *Excudebat Gulielmus Leybourn pro Andræa Kemb, venales apud Edvardum Brewster,* 1664. 12°. O, C, LLU, WCA; PL.

464 —Systema grammaticvm. *Excudebat T. & R. C., impensis Andreæ Crooke,* 1641. 8°. L, O, CT, P, YM; BN, CB, CH, IU, MH, WF.

464A [–] Troposchematologia. *[London], prostant apud Ri. Royston,* 1648. 8°.* L; IU.

464B [–] Τροποσχηματολογια Maximam partem. *[n.p.], prostant apud Samuelem Womack biblio Buriensem.* 1652, [sic] 8°.* CH.

465 [–] —[Anr. ed.]. *Prostant apud R. Royston,* 1660. 8°.* L, NPL; IU, WF, AUCKLAND U.

465A — —Third edition. *Prostant apud Richardum Royston,* 1668. 8°. OC.

465B — —Fifth edition. —, 1677. 8°.* L.

466 [–] —Seventh edition. *[London], prostant apud Richardum Royston,* 1683. 8°. L, O; WF.

467 [–] —Eighth edition. *Apud Lucam Meredith,* 1689. 8°.* T.C.II 293. Y.

467A [–] —Ninth edition. —, 1697. 8°.* L; CH.

468–9 Entries cancelled.

Farnham, R. Curb. 1641. *See* Curb for sectaries.

—False prophets. 1642. *See* False prophets discovered.

470 **F[arnworth], R[ichard].** Antichrists man of vvar apprehended. *For Giles Calvert,* 1655. 4°. LT, O, C, BBN, MR; CH, MH, NU, PH, Y.

471 [–] The brazen serpent lifted up. *For Giles Calvert,* 1655. 4°. LT, O, LF, OC, CT, MR, WCA; PH, PSC, WF.

472 [–] —[Anr. ed.] —, 1658. 4°.* L, LF, MR; CLC, IE, MH, PSC, Y.

472A [–] A brief discovery of the Kingdome of Antichrist. *[London,* 1653.] 8°.* LF.

472B [–] A bunch of grapes, and an iron rod. *[London?], printed,* 1653. 12°.* LF; WF.

473 [–] Cesars penny to be paid. *[London?* 1660.] cap., 4°.* L, C, LF, OC, MR; IE, MH, NU, PH, WF, Y.

474 [–] A call out of Egypt and Babylon. 1653. 4°.* LT, MR, DT; PH.

474A —A call out of false worships. *[London,* 1653.] cap., 8°.* LF; WF.

475 —A character whereby the false Christs. *Printed and are to be sold by Giles Calvert,* 1654. 4°.* LT, LF, BBN, OC, BC; MH, PH.

476 [–] Christian religious meetings allowed. *[London,* 1664.] 4°.* L, O, LF, CS, BBN; CH, MH, NU, PH, Y. (var.)

477 [–] Christian tolleration. *[London],* 1664. 4°.* L, O, C, LF, BBN, DU; CH, IE, MH, PH, WF, Y.

478 —A confession and profession of faith in God. *For Giles Calvert,* 1958 [*i.e.,* 1659]. 4°.* LT, LF; CH, CLC, MH, PH.

479 [–] A discovery of faith; wherein is laid down. *For Giles Calvert,* 1653. 4°.* LT, LF, MR, YM; CH, MH, MU, PH.

479A [–] A discovery of truth and falsehood. *For Giles Calvert,* 1653. 4°. LT, LF, MR; PH.

480 [–] An Easter-reckoning, or, a free-vvill offering. *[London,* 1653.] 4°.* LT, LF, MR; CH, MU, PH, PSC.

481 [–] — [Anr. ed.] *For Giles Calvert,* 1656. 4°.* O, C, LF, OC, CT, YM; CH, MH, NCD, PH, WF, Y.

482 —England's vvarning-peece. *For Tho. Wayte,* 1653. 4°.* LT, LF, BBN, YM; PH, PSC.

483 —The generall-good to all people. *For Giles Calvert,* 1653. 4°. LT, LF, BBN, YM; CH, MH, PH, PSC, WF.

484 [–] Gospel liberty sent down from Heaven. *[London,* 1664.] 4°.* L, LF, OC, BBN; CH, MH, PH, PSC, Y.

485 [–] The heart opened by Christ. *[London],* 1654. 4°.* LT, O, LF, OC; PH.

486 — —[Anr. ed.] *For Giles Calvert,* 1655. 4°. L, LF; PH, WF.

487 [–] The Holy Scriptures from scandals are cleared. *For Giles Calvert,* 1655. 4°. LT, O, LF, BBN, MR; CH, IE, PH, PSC, Y.

488 —The last testimony of . . . Richard Farnworth. *Printed* 1667. 4°.* L, C, LF, BBN, MR; CH, MH, PH, WF, Y.

489 [–] The liberty of the subject by Magna Charta. *[London],* 1664. 4°.* L, O, LF, BBN, YM; CH, IE, MH, PSC, TU, WF, Y.

490 [–] Light risen out of darkness. *For Giles Calvert,* 1654. 4°. LT, LF, BBN, MR; PH, WF.

491 [–] A loving salutation with several seasonable exhortations. *[London], printed,* 1665. 4°.* L, O, LF, OC, BBN; CH, IE, MH, PH, WF, Y.

491A [–] A message from the Lord, to all. *[London], printed,* 1653. 8°.* LF; WF.

491B [–] Moses message to Pharaoh. *[London,* 1653.] cap., 8°.* LF; WF.

492 [–] The priests ignorance. *[London,* 1655.] cap., 4°.* LT, C, LF, BBN; WF, Y.

492A [–] — [Anr. ed.] *For Giles Calvert,* 1656. 4°.* LF, OC; PH, PSC, WF.

493 [–] The publique worship. *[London], printed,* 1664. 4°.* L, C, LF, BBN, MR; MH, PH, PSC.

494 —The pure language of the spirit of truth. colop: *[London], for Giles Calvert,* 1655. cap., 4°.* 7 pp. LT, O, LF, MR; MH, PH, PSC, Y.

495 [–] —[Anr. ed.] colop: —, 1655. cap., 4°.* 8 pp. LT, LF, OC, EN; Y.

496 [–] —[Anr. ed.] colop: —, 1656. cap., 4°.* L, LF, LG, CT, DT; CH, IE, PSC, WF, Y.

497 — —[Anr. ed.] *[London,* 1657?] cap., 4°.* L, O, C, LF; CH, MH, MIU, NU, PH, PSC. (var.)

498 Entry cancelled. Ghost.

499 —The Quakers plea with the bishops. *Printed*, 1663. 4°.* L, O, LF, OC, BP, MR; CDA, MH, PSC, WF, Y. (var.)

500 [–] —[Anr. ed.] *Printed*, 1663. 4°.* LF, SP; CH, MH, PH, WF, Y.

501 [–] The Ranters principles & deceits. *For Giles Calvert*, 1655. 4°.* LT, LF, OC, BBN, MR; MH, PH, PSC, Y.

502 —A rod to drive out the wilde bores. *Printed and are to be sold by Giles Calvert*, 1655. 4°.* LT, LF, OC, BBN, MR; MH, PH, PSC.

502A [–] The saints duty. *Printed*, 1664. 4°.* L, LF; PH.

503 —The Scriptures vindication. *For Giles Calvert*, 1655. 4°.* LT, O, LF, CT; CH, NU, PH, WF, Y.

504 —The spirit of God speaking. *Printed*, 1663. 4°.* L, O, LF, LG, BBN, MR; IE, MH, PSC, WF, Y.

505 [–] The spirituall man iudgeth all things. *For Giles Calvert*, 1655. 4°.* LT, LF, OC, BBN, MR; MH, NU, PH, PSC, Y.

506-7 No entries.

—A tender visitation of heavenly love. 1664. *See title.*

508 [–] A tolleration sent down from Heaven to preach. [*London?*], printed, 1665. 4°.* L, LF, BBN, LIU, MR; CH, MH, PH, WF, Y.

509 [–] A true testimony against the Popes wayes. *For Giles Calvert*, 1656. 4°. LT, O, C, LF, BBN, D; CH, CU, MH, PH.

510 Entry cancelled.

[–] Trumpet of the Lord sounded. 1654. *See* Fox, George.

511 [–] Truth ascended. *Printed*, 1663. 4°.* L, LF, BBN; CLC, IE, PH, PSC.

512 —Truth cleared of scandals. *Printed*, 1654. 4°.* LT, LF, BBN, MR, SS; PH, NHC.

512A [–] Truth exalted and deceit abased. *For Giles Calvert*, 1658. 4°.* O, LF; CH, NGT, PH.

512AB —Vindication against the Scotish contradictors. *For Giles Calvert*, 1655. 4°. OC.

512B —A voice of the first trumpet. *Printed*, 1653. 8°.* LF; WF.

513 [–] VVitchcraft cast out from the religious seed and Israel of God. *For Giles Calvert*, 1655. 4°.* LT, O, LF, BBN, GU; CH, CU, MH, PH, Y.

514 —A vvoman forbidden to speak in the church. *For Giles Calvert*, 1654. 4°.* LT, O, LF, MR; CH, MH, PH, PSC, Y.

515 ——Second edition. —, 1655. 4°.* L, LF, OC; PH.

[–] Written by one. [n.p.], 1653. *See* —Bunch of grapes.

516 **Farquhar, George.** The constant couple. *For Ralph Smith and Bennet Banbury*, 1700. 4°. L, O, DT; CH, LC, MH, NC, TU, WCL, WF, Y.

517 ——Second edition. —, 1700. 4°. CH, NC, NN, PU, WF, Y.

518 —Love and a bottle. *For Richard Standfast and Francis Coggen*, 1699. 4°. L, O, LLU, DT; CH, CN, LC, MH, TU, WCL, WF, Y.

518A —The serenading song in The constant couple. [*London*, 1700.] brs. L.

518B [–] Songs in the new comedy call'd Love and a bottle. [*London*, 1699.] brs. L.

519 [**Farrah, Benjamin.**] Miscellanea sacra, containing. *For John Lawrence; and Joseph Wats*, 1692. 12°. T.C.II 379. O.

520 **Farrar, Richard.** An expedient for the king. [*London*], printed, 1648. 4°.* LT, O, LIU, MR, DT; BN, CH, CN, MH, WF, Y.

521 —A panegyrick to His Excellency, . . . Monck. *By John Macock*, May 22, 1660. brs. LT, HH.

522 —Peace and safety for the whole kingdom. *Printed*, 1648. 4°.* LT, O, C, OC, MR; BN, CH, CN, MH, WF, Y.

523 **Farres, Capt.** A speech spoken. *For Tho. VVatson and Iohn Fares*, 1642. 4°.* LT; BN, MH, MU.

524 No entry.

525 [**Farrington, John.**] Joannis Bidelli (Angli) . . . vita. *Typis Darbianis*, 1682. 8°. L, O, C, LW, EC, MR; MH, WF.

526 A farther account from several letters . . . Quakers in Bristol. colop: *For John Pringhurst* [*sic*], 1682. fol.* L, O, LF; NHC, WF.

Farther account of the Baroccian manuscript. [n.p., 1691.] *See* Grascomb, Samuel.

Farther account of the great divisions. 1693. *See* Keith, George.

526A A farther account of the siege of Lymerick. *For P. Smart*, 1691. brs. OC.

526B A farther account of the victory obtained by the English . . . fleet . . . [26 May 1692]. *By Edw. Jones in the Savoy*, 1692. brs. L, OC, HH; MIU, MWA, WF.

527 —[Anr. ed.] *Edinburgh, reprinted* 1692. brs. ALDIS 3220.9. L, E.

527A A farther account of the victory obtained by Their Majesties . . . fleet . . . [24 May 1692]. [*London*], *by Edw. Jones in the Savoy*, 1692. brs. L, OC, HH; WF. (var.)

528 A farther and full account of the great and entire victory. *London, reprinted Edinburgh*, 1691. brs. ALDIS 3150. L, E, EN; CH.

Farther arguments for passing. [n.p., 1697.] *See* Whiston, James.

529 A farther brief and true narration of the late vvars risen in New-England. *By J. D. for M. K.*, 1676. 4°.* O, LW, WCA; CU, RPJ.

Farther defence. 1698. *See* Settle, Elkanah.

Farther essay. 1696. *See* Astell, *Mrs.* Mary.

530 Farther reasons humbly offered . . . by the artificers working in leather. [*n.p.*, 1690?] brs. Y.

Farther search. 1691. *See* Ames, Richard.

Farther vindication of the present. [n.p.], 1691. *See* Rule, Gilbert.

530A A farther vindication of the Quakers. colop: *For T. Newborough*, Oct. 4, 1690. brs. CT; INU, NN.

531 [**Farthing, John.**] The excise rectify'd. *Printed*, 1695/6. 4°.* L, LG, LUG, EN; CH, MBJ, MH, NC, WF, Y.

532 —Short-writing shortned. *For Tho. Underhill*, 1654. 16°.* MC; LC, NN.

533 ——[Anr. ed.] *For Tho. Parkhurst*, 1684. 8°.* L, O, LU, CM, EN.

534 —To the honourable the knights . . . It is now almost seven years. [*London*, 1695/6.] brs. L, LU, EN; MH, NC, WF, Y.

535 **Farthing, William.** The old mans complaint. [*London*], *by T. H. for J. Clarke*, 1680. brs. L; MH, Y.

536 Farway Bell. A Christmas truth. [*London*], printed, 1646. 4°.* L.

537 Entry cancelled.

[**Farwell, John.**] Letter to Mr. Miles Prance. [1682.] *See* Everett, George.

538   **Fary, John.** God's severity on man's sterility. *By J. D. for Andrew Crook,* 1645. 4°.* LT, LSD, EN; IU, WF.

Fasciculus chemicus: or. 1650. *See* Dee, Arthur.

Fasciculus præceptorum. Oxoniæ, 1660. *See* Airay, Christopher.

539   Fast and loose. Or, the armies figgaries. [*London*], *printed,* 1659. 4°.* O, MR; CH, CU, MH, MIU, MU, NN, Y.

Fast sermon lately preached. 1694. *See* Shank, John.

539A   Fasti Gulielmi Tertii: or, an account. *For John Barnes, and sold by Richard Baldwin,* 1697. sixes. L, C; CH, Y.

540   Entry cancelled.

Fatal beauty of Agnes de Castro. 1688. *See* Brilhac, J. B. de.

541   The fatall blow: or. *Printed,* 1648. 4°.* LT, O, C, LVF, CD, DT; CSS, MH, WF.

542   The fatal discovery. *By J. Orme, for R. Wellington, and sold by Percivil Gilborne, and Bernard Lintott,* 1698. 4°. L, O, LVD, OW, BC, EN; CH, CN, MH, TU, WF, Y. (var.)

Fatall doom. 1655. *See* Hooke, Richard.

542A   The fatall fall of five gentlemen. *For Fra. Grove,* [1649]. brs. MAU.

543   The fatall feasts. *Printed,* 1649. 4°. LG, MR; CSS.

Fatal friendship; a tragedy. 1698. *See* Cockburn, *Mrs.* Catherine Trotter.

Fatal friendship; or the drunkards. 1693. *See* Ames, Richard.

Fatal jealousie. 1673. *See* Payne, Henry Neville.

543A   The fatal junto; containing . . . popish plot. *Printed* 1683. 4°. DU.

544   Fatall prudence, or Democrates. *By J. Bennet for R. Bentley and M. Magnes,* 1679. 12°. T.C.I 349. L, O; CLC, CN, WF.

545   The fate of France. *For Rich. Baldwin,* 1690. 4°. T.C.II 315. L, O, C, AU, DT; CH, NU, WF, Y, MONASH.

545AA   Father a child that's none my own, being the seaman's complaint. [*London*], *for P. Brooksby,* [1680?]. brs. O.

545A   Father Peters's apology to the Pope. colop: *For W. D.,* 1688. brs. L; CH.

546   Father Peters's farewell-sermon. [*London,* 1688.] brs. L, LG; CH, CSS, MH, WF.

547   Father Petre's lamentation. *Printed,* 1689. brs. L; MH, Y.

547A   Father Peters his new-years-gift. [*London,* 1689.] brs. L.

548   Father Peter's policy discovered. *For R. M.,* [1688-9]. brs. L, O, HH; MH, WF.

549   —[Anr. ed.] *Printed,* 1689. brs. CT, MC.

549A   —[Anr. ed.] *For R. M.,* 1689. brs. L, MH.

550   Father Whitebreads walking ghost. [*London,* 1679.] cap., fol.* L, O; CLC, CN, MH, TSM, TU.

551   Fatherly instructions. *Printed,* 1686. 8°. L, O, AN.

552   **F[athers], J[ohn].** The content of a way-faring man; and the accompt of a minister's removal. Two sermons. *By Matthew Simmons,* 1648. 4°.* L, O, LCL, LW, E; NU.

553   —The strife of brethren. *By Matthew Simmons, and are to be sold by Christopher Meredith,* 1648. 4°. L, O, LCL, LW, E; CH.

553A   A fathers advice to his son. [*Edinburgh*], *by the heir of A. Anderson,* 1693. 12°. ALDIS 3298.5. EN.

Fathers covnsell. 1644. *See* Typing, William.

554   The fathers good counsel to his lascivious son. [*London,* 1670?] brs. L.

555   The fathers legacy. *For Henry Brome,* 1678. 8°. T.C.I 299. L, O, CT, NPL, M; CN, PL.

555A   Father's nown child [satire on John Somers]. [*n.p.,* 1694.] brs. O.

Fathers vindicated. 1697. *See* Deacon, John.

556   The father's wholsome admonition. [*London*], *for P. Brooksby, J. Deacon, J. Blare, J. Back,* [1685-91]. brs. L, O, CM, HH; MH.

557   [**Fatio de Duillier, Nicolas.**] Fruit-walls improved. *By R. Everingham; and are to be sold by John Taylor,* 1699. 4°. T.C.III 111. L, O, C, MR, EN, DT; BN, CLC, MBA, MH, WF, Y.

558   —Lineæ brevissimi descensus investigatio geometrica duplex. *Typis R. Everingham prostant apud Johannem Taylor,* 1699. 4°.* L, O, C, LWL, MR; BN, CB, CH, CLC, LC, MB.

558A   **Faulconer, Gervase.** Gratis dictum, or an occasionall discourse. *By T. F. for Henry Seile,* 1655. 4°.* Y.

558B   **Faulconer, Henry.** Verses set forth by. [*London,* 1670?] brs. L.

559   [**Fauntleroy, Thomas.**] Lux in tenebris, or, a clavis to the treasury. *For Francis Tyton,* 1654. 4°.* LT, OC, LUG; CH, Y.

560   **Faustinus.** Faustini presbyteri, Scriptoris seculi quarti. *Oxon: e theatro Sheldoniano,* 1678. 8°. MADAN 3174. L, O, C, OM, CT, DU, DT; CH, MH, NU, WF, Y.

561   Faux's ghost: or, advice to Papists. colop: *For Mr. Benskin,* [1680]. fol.* L, O; CH, MH, NU, WF, Y.

561A   **F[avel], J[ohn].** To our valiant English nation, an encomium. [*London*], *sold by John Favel,* 1671. brs. HH.

562   **Fawcet, Samuel.** A seasonable sermon. *By R. Cotes, for Joh. Sweeting,* 1641. 4°.* LT, O, LG, DT; CH, IU, WF, Y.

563   **Fawket, James.** An account of the late reverend . . . Dr George Seignior. *For Richard Janeway,* 1681. 12°. T.C.I 440. L, O, C, LCL, CT; CLC.

[**Fawne, Luke.**] Beacon flameing. 1652. *See* Cheynell. Francis.

564   [–] A beacon set on fire. *For the subscribers hereof,* 1652. 4°.* LT, O, CT, DU, E, EN, DT; CSS, MH, MIU, NU, TU, WF, Y.

565   [–] A second beacon fired. *For the subscribers,* 1654. 4°.* LT, O, LF, BC, MR, DT; CH, MH, MIU, NS, NU.

566   **Feak, John.** A funeral sermon thundered forth. *For I. P.,* 1660. 4°.* LT, O; Y.

567   **Feake, Christopher.** A beam of light. *By J. C. for Livewell Chapman,* 1659. 4°. LT, O, LIU, LSD; MH, NU, TO, TU, WF, Y.

568   [–] A faithfvl discovery of a treacherous design. *By H. Hills for Thomas Brewster,* 1653. 4°. LT, O, DC, MR, ENC; CH, INU, NU, PH, Y.

569   [–] —Second edition. *For Thomas Brewster,* 1655. 4°. LT, O, CT, LF, ENC; PSC, TO, Y.

570 [–] The genealogie of Christianity. *For Peter Cole*, 1650. 4°.* L, LSC, LW; CH, MM.

571 [–] The new Non-conformist. *Printed at London, for Livewel Chapman*, 1654. 4°.* LT, O, OC; CH, NHC, NU, TO.

572 —The oppressed close prisoner in Windsor-castle, his defiance. *For L. Chapman*, 1655. 4°.* LT, O; CH, NHC, Y.

573 Entry cancelled.
—Word for all. [n.p.], 1660. *See title*.

574 Fear God, honour the king. 1660. 4°. O, C.

574A —[Anr. ed.] *For T. Parker*, 1663. 4°. C.

575 Fearful and lamentable news from Worcestershire. *Printed*, 1674. 4°.* O.

576 Fearefull apparitions or the strangest visions. *For John Hammond*, 1647. 4°.* LT, O, LG; MH.
Fearfull prodigies. 1643. *See* Sofi, Antonio di.

576A **Fearon, Mrs. Jane.** Universal redemption. [*London*], *printed*, 1698. 8°. LF.
Fears and jealousies. [n.p., 1688.] *See* Doolittle, Thomas.
Feast of fat things. 1696. *See* Keach, Benjamin.
Feast of feasts. Oxford, 1644. *See* Fisher, Edward.

576B **Featherstone, Sarah.** Living testimonies. *By Andrew Sowle*, 1689. 8°.* L, LF.

577 **Featley, Daniel.** Ancilla pietatis: or, the hand-maid. Seventh edition. *By James Young, for Nicholas Bourne*, 1647. 12°. L, LIU, P; BN, CLC, MU, NU, WF, Y.

578 ——Eighth edition. *By Will: Hunt for Nicolas Bourne, to be sold by Tho: Eglesfield*, 1656. 12°. L, C, LLP, DU; CH, CLC, IU, LC, NU.

579 ——Ninth edition. *For Thomas Dring*, 1675. 8°. T.C.I 213. L, C, LW, EN, DT; CH, CLC, IU, MHS, NS, NU, TO.

580 —Doctor Daniel Featley revived. *Printed*, 1661. 4°.* L, O, C, MR; CH, NU, Y.

581 —Faetlæi παλιγζενεσια: or Doctor Daniel Featley revived. *For Nath. Brook*, 1660. 12°. LT, O, LW, OB, CS; CLC, NU, WF.

582 —The gentle lash. [*London*], *imprinted*, 1644. 4°.* LT, O, C, LG, MR, P; CH, MH, MU, NU, WF, Y.

583 [–] —[Anr. ed.] *Imprinted at Oxford*, 1644. 4°.* MADAN 1527. O, LW, CJ, NE; CN, CSS, NU, Y.

584 ——[Anr. ed.] —, 1644. 4°.* MADAN 1669. L, O, C, DC, DT; WF.

585 —Καταβαπτισται καταπτυστοι. The Dippers dipt. *For Nicholas Bourne, and Richard Royston*, 1645. 4°. LT, O, C, SP, DT; BN, CH, CN, MU, WF, Y.

585A ——Second edition. —, 1645. 4°. O.

586 ——Third edition. —, 1645. 4°. L, OC, CK, DC, EN; CLC, MH, NHC, NU, Y.

587 ——Fourth edition. —, 1646. 4°. L, O, C, YM, ENC; CH, CN, MH, PL, Y.

588 ——Fifth edition. *For N. B. and Richard Royston*, 1647. 4°. L, O, LW, DU, EC, A; CLC, CU, MB, MU, NHC, RPJ.

589 ——Sixth edition. *By Richard Cotes for N. B. and Richard Royston*, 1651. 4°. L, O, C, E, DT; CLC, CN, MH, NU, WF, Y.

590 ——Seventh edition. *By E. C. for N. Bourne, and R. Royston*, 1660. 4°. LT, OC, CK, SC, YM; CLC, CN, MH, NHC, NU, WF, ZWT.

590A ——"Seventh" edition. *By E. C. for N. B. and Richard Royston*, 1660. 4°.* L, C, CK, SHR, CD; CDA, CLC, NN, ZWT.

591 —The league illegal. *For R. Royston*, 1660. 4°. LT, O, C, EN, DT; CH, CN, MH, WF, Y.

592 —Roma ruens, Romes ruine. *By Thomas Purslow, for Nicholas Bourne*, 1644. 4°. LT, O, C, ENC, DT; CH, CN, NU, WF, Y.

593 [–] Sacra nemesis, the Levites scourge. *Oxford, by Leonard Lichfield*, 1644. 4°. MADAN 1665-7. LT, O, C, E, DT; CH, IU, MH, NU, WF, Y. (var.)

594 —Sacra nemesis, . . . whereunto is added the gentle lash. Second edition. —, 1644. 4°. MADAN 1668. O.

595 —Θρηνοικος. The house of mourning. *By G. Dawson, to be sold by John Williams*, 1660. fol. L, O, P, SC, E; CH, NRU, NU, Y.

596 ——[Anr. ed.] *For John Williams*, 1672. fol. T.C.I 99. L, O, LSC, AN, E, GU, DM; CLC, CN, MIU, TSM, WF.

597 —Vertumnus Romanus, or, a discovrse. *By I. L. for Nicholas Bourne, and Iohn Bartlet*, 1642. 4°. LT, O, C, DC, E; CH, CN, MH, NU, WF, Y. (var.)

597A **Featley, John.** A divine antidote against the plague: or mourning teares. *By Thomas Mabb and are to be sold by Margaret Shears*, 1665. 12°. LWL.

598 —A fountaine of teares. *Amsterdam, for Iohn Crosse*, 1646. 12°. L, O; CH, IU, RPJ, WF, Y.

599 ——[Anr. ed.] *Hen. Twiford and Tho. Brewster*, 1655. 12°. DC.

600 ——[Anr. ed.] *For Obadiah Blagrave, and Richard Northcot*, 1683. 12°. T.C.II 56. L, O, LW, LSD; CH, CU, NU, V, Y.

600A —Tears in time of pestilence. *By W. Godbid*, 1665. 8°. LG; MH.
Febris anomala or. 1659. *See* Whitmore, H.

600B **[Feddeman, John.]** A demonstration, that, Hen. Meriton. [*London?* 1699.] fol.* LF.
Feed my lambs. 1686. *See* D., J.
Feign'd astrologer. 1668. *See* Corneille, Thomas.

601 Feign'd friendship. *For Daniel Brown, F. Coggan; E. Rumballd, and Rob. Gibson*, [1699?]. 4°. T.C.III 141. L, O, OW, LLU, EN; CH, CU, LC, MH, Y.
Feild. *See* Field.

602 **F[elgate], S[amuel].** The novelty of the modern Romish religion. *For Tho. Simmons*, 1682. 8°. O, CE, SP, YM; WF.
Felghenore, Paul. Postilion, or. 1655. *See* Almanacs.
Felgenhauer, Paul.

603 **Fell, Henry.** An alarum of truth. *For Robert Wilson*, 1660. 4°. L, LF, BBN; CH, IE, LC, MH, PH, WF, Y.

604 —For Presbyter John. *For Robert Wilson*, 1660. 4°.* C, LF; WF.

605 [–] A plain record or declaration. *For Robert Wilson*, 1661. 4°.* L, O, LF, BBN, MR; LC, MH, NGT, PH, WF, Y.

606 **Fell, John, bp.** Articles of visitation & enquiry. [*Oxford? at the theater?*], 1679. 4°.* MADAN 3106. O, OB, OC.

607 —The character of the last daies. *At the theater in Oxford*, 1675. 4°.* MADAN 3056. L, O, CS, DU, P; CH, IU, MH, NU, WF, Y.

607A —Cum per nuperam dispensandi. [*Oxford*], 1666. brs. MADAN 2752. O.

608 [–] Grammatica rationis. *Oxonii, e theatro Sheldoniano,* 1673. 12°. MADAN 2974. L, O, LLL, OC, YM; CCC, CLC, IU, Y.

609 [–] —[Anr. ed.] —, 1675. 12°. MADAN 3057. O, CT, BC, NE; CLC, MH, TO, Y.

610 [–] —[Anr. ed.] *Oxonii, e theatro Sheldoniano, prostant apud Joh. Howell,* 1685. sixes. L, O, C, LIU; CH, CU, MH, NP, V, WF, Y.

611 [–] —[Anr. ed.] *Oxonii, e theatro Sheldoniano,* 1697. 12°. O, OME, CM, DU; CH, CLC, IU, Y.

612 [–] In laudem musices carmen sapphicum. [*Oxford, Sheldonian press,* 1672.] brs. MADAN 2927. O.

613 [–] The interest of England stated. [*London*], printed, 1659. 4°.* LT, O, C, LSD, YM, DT; CH, CN, LC, MH, WF, Y.

614 [–] The life and death of that reverend divine, . . . Doctor Thomas Fuller. *Oxford, for R. Hopton,* 1662. 8°. MADAN 2594. L, LW, DU, GK; CN, WCL, Y.

615 [–] —[Anr. ed.] *Oxford: printed,* 1662. 8°. L, O; CN.

616 [–] —[First edition, "The life of that reverend."] *For J. W. H. B. and H. M.,* 1661. 8°. L, O, CT, LSC, GK; CH, CN, MH, WF, Y.

617 —The life of the most learned, reverend and pious Dr. Hammond. *By J. Flesher. for Jo. Martin, Ja. Allestry and Tho. Dicas,* 1661. 8°. L, O, C, LNC, DU; BN, CH, CN, MH, NP, NU, WCL, WF, Y.

618 —Second edition. —, 1662. 8°. L, O, C, DU, LIU; BN, CDA, CLC, CU, MIU, NU.

619 [–] The privileges of the University of Oxford. [*London*], *for Richard Royston,* 1647. 4°.* MADAN 1955. LT, O, C, MR, CD; BN, CH, MH, WF, Y.

619A [–] —[Anr. ed.] [*London*], *Anno* 1647. 4°.* MADAN 1956. O, LLP, OC, CS, MR, DT; CLC, CSS, MH, WF, Y.

620 Entry cancelled.
[–] Seasonable advice to Protestants. 1688. *See* Lloyd, William, *bp.*

621 —A sermon preached . . . December 22. 1680. *At the theater in Oxford,* 1680. 4°.* MADAN 3266. L, O, C, DU, EN; CH, IU, MH, NU, TU, WF, Y.

621A —[Specimen of type.] [*Oxford?* 1687.] 8°.* OC.

622 —A specimen of the several sorts of letter given to the University by. *Oxford, at the theater,* 1693. 8°. O, C, CM, CT, LSD; CLC, NC.

623 — —[Anr. ed.] —, 1695. 4°.* 22 leaves. O, C; CH, MBA, Y.

623A — —[Anr. ed.] —, 1695. 8° in 4s.* 24 leaves. L, O, OAS, CT; BN, CN, PROVIDENCE PUB. LIB.

624 [**Fell, Leonard.**] An epistle for the strengthening and confirming of Friends. [*London,* 1670.] 4°.* L, C, LF, BBN, MR; IU, MH, NC, PH, PSC, Y.

624A [–] A warning to England in general. *By T. Sowle,* 1693. brs. LF; LC, PSC.

625 [**Fell, Lydia.**] A testimony and warning given forth in the love of truth. [*London?* 1676.] cap., 4°.* L, LF, BBN, MR; MU, PH, RPJ, WF, Y.

625A **Fell, Margaret.** A call to the universall seed of God. [*London*], *printed,* 1665. 4°.* L, O, C, LF, BBN; MH, NN, PH, PL, PSC, Y.

626 [–] A call unto the seed of Israel. *For Robert Wilson,* [1668?]. 4°.* L, LF, BBN, MR; CH, IU, MH, PH, PL.

626A [–] The citie of London reprov'd. *For Robert Wilson,* [1660]. brs. LF.

626B —Concerning ministers made by the will of man. *Printed in the 4th month 8th day for M. W.* 1659. brs. CH.

627 [–] The daughter of Sion awakened. [*London*], *printed,* 1677. 4°.* L, LF, CS, BBN; CH, MH, PH, PL, PSC.

628 [–] A declaration and an information from us. *For Thomas Simmons, and Robert Wilson,* 1660. 4°.* L, O, C, BBN, DU; CH, IU, MH, NU, PH, WF, Y.

629 [–] An evident demonstration to Gods elect. colop: *For Thomas Simmons,* 1660. cap., 4°.* L, O, C, LF, MR; CH, MH, PH, WF, Y.

630 — —[Anr. ed.] —, 1660. 4°.* L, LF; IU, Y.

631 —False prophets, anticrists [*sic*]. *For Giles Calvert,* 1655. 4°.* L, LF, BBN; MH, MU, PH.

632 [–] For Manasseth Ben Israel. The call of the Jewes. *For Giles Calvert,* 1656. 4°.* LT, C, LF, BBN; MH, NN, PH.

633 [–] A letter sent to the King from M. F. [*London,* 1666.] 4°.* L, O, C, LF, BBN; PH, PL, PSC, Y.

634 [–] A loving salutation to the seed of Abraham. *For Tho. Simmons,* 1656. 4°.* L, O, LF, OC, BBN; CH, MH, PH, WF, Y.

634AA — —[Anr. ed.] *For Robert Wilson,* 1660. 4°. MH.

634A [–] A paper concerning such as are made ministers. colop: *Printed in the 4th. month, 8th. day for H. W.,* 1659. cap., 4°.* L; MH, PSC.

635 [–] The standard of the Lord revealed. [*London?*], *printed,* 1667. 4°. L, LF, ORP, BBN, YM; CH, MH, MU, PH, PSC.

636 —A testimonie of the touchstone. *For Thomas Simmons,* 1656. 4°. L, LF, CT, MR; CH, MH, PH.

637 [–] This is to the clergy. colop: *For Robert Wilson,* 1660. 4°.* L, LF, BBN, MR; MH, PSC.

638 [–] This was given to Major Generall Harrison. colop: *For Thomas Simmons,* 1660. cap., 4°.* L, LF, BBN, MR; CH, MU, PH, PSC, WF, Y.

638A [–] To the generall councill of officers of the English army. [*London,* 1659.] 4°.* LF; PSC.

638B [–] To the general council of officers. The representation. *By John Clowes,* 1659. brs. LT, O, LG; Y.

638C [–] To the general councel. *For Thomas Simmons,* 1659. 4°.* L, LF; PH, PL.

638D [–] To the magistrats and people of England. [*London*], 1664. brs. LF.

639 [–] A touch-stone, or, a perfect tryal. *Printed,* 1667. 4°. L, O, LF, BBN, DU; BN, CH, MH, NPT, NU, PH, Y.

640 [–] A true testimony from the people of God. *For Robert Wilson,* 1660. 4°.* L, O, LF, CS, BBN; MH, MU, PH, PSC.

641 [–] Two general epistles to the flock of God. *Printed at London,* 1664. 4°.* L, LF, OC; CH, MH, PH, PSC, WF, Y.

642 [–] Women's speaking justified. *Printed,* 1666. 4°.* L, O, LF, OC, MR; CH, IE, PH, RPJ, WF, Y.

643 [–] —Second edition. —, 1667. 4°.* L, LF, DU; CH, IU, MH, PH, PL, Y.

644 [**Fell, Philip.**] Lex talionis: or, the author of Naked truth. *For Henry Brome*, 1676. 4°.* L, O, C, EN, DT; CH, CU, MH, WF, Y, AVP.

645 **Felle, Guillaume.** Juxta solam Scripturam. *Printed*, 1688. 12°. DC; CLC, NU.

646 —La sage folie. [*London*], *imprimé*, 1679. 8°. L, O; BN, CLC, CN, NPT.

646A —Lapis theologorum. 1688. 8°. WARE.
Fellow-traveller through city. [n.p.], 1658. *See* Edmundson, Henry.
Felo de se, or. [n.p.], 1668. *See* Ford, Thomas.

647 [**Feltham, Owen.**] Batavia: or the Hollander displayed. *For G. Widdowes*, 1672. 12°. MH.

647A [–] —[Anr. ed.] *Amsterdam, by Steven Swart*, 1675. 12°. O; CH.

647AB [–] —[Anr. ed.] —, 1677. 12°. CLC.

647B [–] —[Anr. ed.] —, 1680. 12°. L, EN.

647C [–] —[Anr. ed.] *Printed*, 1697. 12°. EN, WF.

648 [–] A brief character of the Low-countries. *For Henry Seile*, 1652. 12°. L, C.

648A [–] —[Anr. ed.] *For R. Lownes and H. Seile, jun.*, 1652. 12°. CT, GK.

649 [–] —[Anr. ed.] *For H. S. and are to be sold by Rich. Lowndes*, 1659. 12°. O, OB, OC, WCA, GK; CH, NR, WF, Y.

650 [–] —[Anr. ed.] —, 1660. 12°. LT, C, DU, E, GK; CLC, CN, MH, MIU, RPJ.

651 — —[Anr. ed.] *For R. Lowndes*, 1662. 12°. L.

652 — —[Anr. ed.] —, 1671. 12°. L, CS; LC, MU.
[–] Lusoria: or occasional pieces. *See* — Resolves.
[–] Poems annent the keeping of Yule. [n.p., 1661.] *See* title.

653 Entry cancelled. Date: 1636.

654 —Resolues. Seventh edition. *For Henry Seile*, 1647. 4°. L, OB, DC, MR; CLC, CN, NP, NU, TO, WF, Y.

654A — —"Seventh" edition. *By R. L. for Henry Seile*, 1647. 4°. LIU.

655 — —Eighth edition. *For Peter Dring*, 1661. fol. L, O, CT, DC, E; CLC, CU, MH, TU, WCL, WF, Y.

655A — —"Eighth" edition. *For A. Seile*, 1661. fol. L, O, CP, BC, BQ; CH, CPB, IU, PU, ASU.

655B — —"Eighth" edition. *By E. Cotes for A. Seile*, 1661. fol. L; Y.

656 — —Ninth edition. *For A. Seile, and are to be sold by Allen Bancks and Charles Harper*, 1670. fol. T.C.I 40. L, C, OME, DU, EN, ENC; CLC, CN, MH, NR, TU, WF, Y.

657 — —Tenth edition. *For Andrew Clark and Charles Harper*, 1677. fol. T.C.I 276. L, O, C, LVD, LLU; CH, CN, IU, LC, TO, WF, Y.

657A — —"Tenth" edition. —, *and are to be sold by Benjamin Billingsley and Samuel Crouch*, 1677. fol. LIU; IU, MH, NRU, PL, PU, Y.

658 — —Eleventh edition. *By M. Clark, for Charles Harper*, 1696. fol. T.C.II 592. L, O, C, LLU, DT; CLC, CU, LC, MH, MU, WSC, Y.

658A [–] Three moneths observations of the Low-Countries. [*London*], *printed anno* 1648. 12°.* L.

658B [–] —[Anr. ed.] *For William Ley*, 1652. 12°.* L.

659 [–] A trip to Holland. [*London*], *printed*, 1699. fol.* T.C.III 98. L, MR; HR, CH, CLC, MH, NC, TU, WF, Y.

659A [–] —[n.p.], 1699. 4°.* UNIV. LIB., AMSTERDAM.

659B —A true and exact character of the Low Countreyes. *For William Ley*, 1652. 12°.* LT, O, LW.
Felton, Daniel. Examination and confession of Captaine Lilbourne. 1642. *See* Felton, William.

660 **Felton, Edmund.** Engins invented to save much blood. [*London*], *for T. Underhill*, 1644. 4°.* LT, O, DT; CH, WF.

661 —An out-cry for justice. [*London*, 1653]. 4°.* OC; NC, Y.

662 —To the right honorable the knights, the humble petition of. *Printed*, 1642. 4°.* C, DT.

663 —To the supreme authority the Parliament . . . the humble proposals of. 1653. brs. L.

664 **Felton, Henry.** The eternal joys of God's presence. *For Tim Goodwin*, 1699. 4°.* T.C.III 151. L, O, LLP; NGT, NU, TSM, Y.

665 [**Felton, William.**] The examination and confession of Captaine Lilbourne and Captaine Viviers. *For T. Wright*, 1642. 4°.* MADAN 1127. LT, O, LVF, MR, DT; MH.

666 **Feltwell, R.** Davids recognition. *For the author, to be sold by Thomas Parkhurst*, 1660. 4°.* LT, O; Y.
Female advocate. 1686. *See* Egerton, Sarah Fyge.
—[Same title.] 1700. *See* Chudleigh, *Lady* Mary.
Female duel. 1661. *See* Toll, Thomas, *ed.*

666A A female elephant. [*London?* 1700.] brs. HUTH.
Female excellence. 1679. *See* Rochester, John Wilmot, *earl of.*
Female excellency. 1688. *See* Crouch, Nathaniel.
Female falsehood. 1697. *See* Villiers, Pierre de.
Female fire-ships. 1691. *See* Ames, Richard.
Female gallant. 1692. *See* Oldys, Alexander.

667 The female Hector. *For N. Dorrington*, 1663. 4°.* Y.

668 The female highway Hector. [*London*], *for C. Bates*, [c. 1690]. brs. HH; MH, Y.
Female poems. 1679. *See* Philips, *Mrs.* Joan.
Female policy. 1695. *See* Ward, Edward.
Female preacher. [1699.] *See* Chudleigh, *Lady* Mary.
Female pre-eminence. 1670. *See* Agrippa, Henricus Cornelius.
Female prelate. 1689. *See* Settle, Elkanah.
Female prince. 1682. *See* Bernard, Catherine.

669 The female ramblers. [*London*], *for P. Brooksby, J. Deacon, J. Blare, J. Back*, [1688–92]. brs. L, HH, GU; MH, Y.

669A —[Anr. ed.] *For J. Wright, J. Clarke, W. Thackeray, and T. Passinger*, 1683. 8°.* CM.

670 The female-triumph: or Mistris White asserted. [*n.p.*], 1647. 4°. CHRISTIE-MILLER.

671 The female warrior. [*London*], *for C. Passinger*, [1681–93]. brs. L, O.

671A Entry cancelled. Date: 1704.

672 The female's frolick. *By and for W. O. for T. Norris*, [1680–90]. brs. HH.
Femmes illustres or. Edinburgh, 1681. *See* Scudéry, Madeleine de.

673   **Fen, James.** A sermon preach'd . . . July the 18th, 1686. *By J. Darby, for Jonathan Robinson,* 1686. 4°.* T.C.II 175. L, C; CH, MH, UCLA, WF, Y.

      Fencer, James, *pseud.* Fencing-master's advice. Edinburgh, 1692. *See* Hope, William.

674   [**Fenelon, François de Salignac de la Mothe.**] The adventures of Telemachus. *For Awnsham and John Churchil,* 1699. 12°. T.C.III 170. L, OC, CS; CH, MH, NC, WF, Y.

674A — —Second edition. *For A. and J. Churchil,* 1700. 12°. T.C.III 201. FONMON, DT; CN.

674B — —Third edition. —, 1700. 16°. MH (imperf.).

674C —The education of young gentlewomen. *For N. R. and sold by T. Leigh and D. Midwinter,* 1699. 12°. T.C.III 96. CM; WF.

675 —The maxims of the saints explained. *For H. Rhodes,* 1698. 12°. L, O, CS, BR, E, BLH; CH, IU, MB, MH, TU, WF, Y.

676   **Fenn, Humphrey.** The last vvill and testament. [*London*], printed, 1641. 4°.* L, LLP, DT; CH, CU, NU, WF, Y. (var.)

677   **Fenn, Matthew.** A few lines touching baptism. *For Matthew Fenn, at Coggshall,* 1697. 8°.* L, MAB.

      [**Fenner, Dudley.**] Assertion for true. 1642. *See* Stoughton, William.

678   **Fenner, William.** The vvorks of. *By T. Maxey, for John Rothwell,* 1651. 4°. L, O, C, CE, P; CLC, CU, IU, NU, WF.

679 — —[Anr. ed.] [*London*], *for W. Gilbertson,* 1657. fol. L, O, LLP, E, ENC, DT; NCU, NU, PJB, PPT, TO, WF.

680 — —[Anr. ed.] [*London*], *by E. Tyler for I. Stafford,* 1657. fol. L, O; CH, CN, MB, TSM, Y.

681 — —[Anr. ed.] *By E. Tyler for E. Stafford,* 1658. fol. O, LW; NPT.

682 —Christs alarm to drowsie saints. *By J. D. & R. L. for John Rothwell,* 1646. 4°. L, O, LCL, P, ENC; CU, IU, NU, WF, Y.

682A — —[Anr. ed.] —, 1648. 4°. PJB.

683 — —[Anr. ed.] *For John Rothwell,* 1650. 4°. L, O, LCL, LW, CS, BLH; CH, CU, MH, NU, WF.

683A —The continuation of Christ's alarm. *For John Rothwell, and Tho. Parkhurst,* 1657. fol. L, O, CD; CH, NU, Y.

684 —The danger of deferring repentance, discovered. *For Jo. Stafford to be sold by Richard Burton,* 1654. 8°.* L.

684A — —[Anr. ed.] *Printed by W. L. and T. J. for William Thackery,* 1676. 8°. GU.

684B — —[Anr. ed.] *By H. B. for W. Thackeray,* 1684. 8°.* LW.

685 —A divine message to the elect soule. *Printed at London by T. R. and E. M. for John Stafford,* 1645. 8°. CH, NGT.

685A — —[Anr. ed.] *By M. S. for John Stafford,* 1645. 8°. CLC, MBC, UCLA.

686 — —Second edition. *Printed at London by T. R. and E. M. for John Stafford,* 1647. 8°. L, C, LCL; NGT, NU.

687 — —"Second" edition. —, 1649. 8°. NPT.

688 — —Third edition. *Printed at London for John Stafford,* 1651. 8°. L; WF.

688A — —"Third" edition —, 1652. 8°. CLC.

689 — —"Third" edition. —, 1653. 8°. MH.

689AA — —Fourth edition. —, 1656. 8°. VC.

689BA — —[Anr. ed.] —. *And part . . . for the use . . . of Edw. Minshew gent.* 1657. 8°. L, P.

689A — —"Fourth" edition. *For John Stafford,* 1664. 8°. NPT.

689B — —"Fourth" edition. *For W. Thackeray,* 1676. 8°. T.C.I 285. L.

690 —Four profitable treatises. *By A. Maxey for J. Rothwel, and Tho. Parkhurst,* 1657. 8°. L, O; CLC, MH.

691 —Four select sermons. *Printed,* 1668. 12°. L; CLC, NPT.

692 —Hidden manna. *Printed at London by R. I. for S. Bowtell,* 1652. 12°. LT, LW, YM; NU, Y.

693 —Practicall divinitie. 1647. 8°. LCL.

694 — —[Anr. ed.] *By T. R. and E. M. for John Stafford,* 1649. 8°. C; NU.

695 — —[Anr. ed.] —, 1650. 8°. L, LW; WF.

696 —Remains of. *For Joseph Cranford,* 1657. fol. LCL, DL; CLC, MB, NU, UCLA, WF.

697 —The riches of grace. *By R. Cotes, for I. Sweeting,* 1641. 8°. O, LW; CLC.

698 —The sacrifice of the faithful. *For John Stafford,* 1648. 8°. C, LCL; CLC, UCLA, WF, Y.

699 — —[Anr. ed.] *For John Stafford,* 1649. 8°. LT.

700 —The souls looking-glasse. *Cambridge, by Roger Daniel; for John Rothwell,* 1643. L, O, C, P, ENC; IAU, IU, NCU, RBU, TU, UCLA.

701 — —[Anr. ed.] *By T. R. & E. M. for John Rothwell,* 1651. 4°. L, O, C, BLH; CB, CU, NU, WF, Y.

702 —The spiritvall man's directorie. *By T. F. for Iohn Rothwell,* 1648. 8°. L, O; Y.

703 — —[Anr. ed.] *For John Rothwell,* 1649. 8°. L; NU.

704 — —[Anr. ed.] —, 1651. 4°. L, O, CP, CS, BLH; CB, CDA, CH, NU, WF.

705 Entry cancelled. — —[Anr. ed.] 1656. *See* — Works.

706 —A treatise of the affections. *By E. G. for I. Rothwell,* 1641. 12°. L, O; CLC, NCU, NU, PJB, WF.

707 — —[Anr. ed.] *By R. H. for I. Rothwell,* 1642. 12°. L, O, LW, MR, EN, ENC; CLC, IU, LC, NF, NU, TO, TU, Y.

708 — —[Anr. ed.] *By A. M. for J. Rothwell,* 1650. 4°. L, O, CS, ES, BLH; CH, CSU, MH, NU, WF, Y.

709 — —[Anr. ed.] *By E. Tyler, for William Gilbertson,* 1657. fol. L, O; CH, NU, TO, Y.

710 —XXIX choice sermons. *By E. T. for John Stafford,* 1657. 4°. CD; NU, TO, Y.

711 Entry cancelled. —Use and benefit. 1657. *See* — Works.

712 —Wilfull impenitency. *By E. G. for Iohn Rothwell,* 1648. 8°. L, O, CT; CLC, NU, Y.

712A — —[Anr. ed.] *For John Rothwell,* 1650. 4°. WF.

713 — —[Anr. ed.] *By T. M. for John Rothwell,* 1651. 4°. L, O, C, LSC, OW, BQ; CH, NU, WF.

714 — —Second edition. *For J. Rothwell,* 1655. 8°. LW, OC, P; MM.

715 Entry cancelled. — —[Anr. ed.] 1656. *See* — Works.

716 — —Fifth edition. *For J. Rothwell,* 1658. 8°. L, LCL, EN.

717 The fennes and meadow grounds in the county of Lincolne. [*London?* 1661.] brs. LUG.

718   **Fenton, Edward.** So short a catechisme. *Imprinted at London by Iohn Dawson*, 1641. 8°.* MH.

718A   — —[Anr. ed.] —, 1643. 8°.* L.

718B   —[Anr. ed.] *For R. Ecles*, 1662. 8°.* MH.

718C   **Fenwick, John,** *1618–1683.* Friends, these are to satisfie you, . . . New Jersey. [*London*], 1675. brs. PHS, PL.

719   **Fenwicke, John,** *of Newcastle.* Christ ruling. *For Benjamin Allen*, 1643. 4°.* L, O, ORP, EN; CH, NPT, NU, Y.

720   Entry cancelled.
—Contemplations upon life and death. 1697. *See* Mornay, Philippe de.

720A   [–] The down fall of the pretended divine authoritie. 1641. 4°.* LT, C, BP, YM, EN; CH, CU, MH, NU, WF.

721   —Englands deliverer. *Newcastle, by S.B.*, 1651. 4°.* E; CH, Y.

721A   [–] A great victorie against the rebels in Ireland. *By B. A.*, *June* 3, 1647. 4°.* LT, DN; CH.

722   Entry cancelled.
[–] Zions joy in her King. 1643. *See* title.

723   **Fenwick, Sir John,** *1645?–1697.* A true copy of the paper deliver'd by. colop: *By J. Orme, for R. Bentley, and A. Bosvile*, [1696/7]. brs. L, O, OC, OM, EN; CLC, MH, PL, WF, Y.

723A   — —[Anr. ed.] —, 1697. brs. BSM; Y.

724   **Fenwick, William.** An exact enqviry. *For Edw: Husbands and Lawrence Blaiklock*, [1643]. 4°. L, EN; CH, IAU, NU, WF.

725   —Zions rjghts and Babels rvine. *By A. N. for Lawrence Blacklocke and Edw Husbands*, 1642. 4°. LT, LCL, OM, DT; CH, WF, Y.

726   [**Fer, Nicolas de.**] Historical voyages and travels over Europe. *For H. Rhodes, and J. Harris*, 1693. 3v. 12°. T.C.II 452. L, O, C.

727   **Ferdinand III,** *emperor.* The answer of the Emperour of Germany. *For George Horton*, 1653. 4°.* LT.

728   —A declaration or manifesto, . . . reasons for warre against . . . Transylvania. [*London*], *for E. Blackmore*, 1644. 4°.* LT, MR; CH, LC, WF, Y.
—Instrumentum pacis. 1648. *See* title.
Ferg, Rob. Dialogue between Sir Roger. Edinburgh, 1696. *See* Ferguson, Robert.

728A   Entry cancelled.
[**Ferguson.**] Late proceedings. Glasgow, 1689. *See* Ferguson, Robert.

728B   **Ferguson, James.** Disputatio juridica. *Edinburgi, ex officina Hæredum Andreæ Anderson*, 1697. 4°. ALDIS 3663.5. GU.

729   Entry cancelled.
Ferguson, Robert. Account of Mr. Ferguson his common-place book. 1675. *See* Glanvill, Joseph.

729A   —R. Fergusson's apology. *For Richard Wier*, 1689. brs. HH.

729B   — —[Anr. ed.] *For John Cox*, 1689. brs. CH, IU.

730   — —[Anr. ed.] colop: *London, for John Cox, and reprinted in Edinburgh*, 1689. brs. ALDIS 2887. L, HH, EN; CN.
[–] An appeal from the country to the city. 1679. *See* Blount, Charles.

731   [–] A brief account of some of the late incroachments. [*London?* 1695.] cap., 4°. L, O, C, MR, EN; CH, CN, MH, NU, WF, Y.

732   [–] A brief justification. *For J. S. and sould by Richard Baldwin*, 1689. 4°.* L, O, C, MR, DT; HR, CLC, CN, LC, MH, MU, NP, Y.

733   [–] —[Anr. ed.] *For J. S. and are to be sold by R. Baldwin*, 1689. 4°.* L, O, C, OC, CT, LSD; CH, CU, LC, MH, NU, Y.

733A   [–] —[Anr. ed.] [*London?* 1689.] 4°.* L, LIU; CLC, CSB, IAU, LC, MH, MM.

734   [–] The design of enslaving England discovered. *For Richard Baldwin*, 1689. 4°. L, O, C, YM, EN; CH, MH, NU, WF, Y.

735   —A dialogue between Sir Roger — and Mr. Rob. Ferg—. colop: *For E. Whitlock*, [1696.] 4°.* CT; WF, Y.

735A   — —[Anr. ed.] *Edinburgh, reprinted, by the heirs and successors of Andrew Anderson*, 1696. 4°.* ALDIS 3552. AU, EN.

736   Entry cancelled.
—Discourse of moral virtue, 1673. *See* — Sober enquiry.

736A   [–] The East-India-Trade a most profitable trade. *Printed*, 1677. 4°.* L, O, C, LUG, LSD, DT; CH, CU, MH, NC, WF, Y.

736B   [–] —[Anr. ed.] *Printed*, 1680. 4°.* L, LG, LUG, OC; CINCINNATI PUB. LIB., MIU, NC, PL.
[–] Great Britain's just complaint. [n.p.], 1692. *See* Montgomery, James.

737   [–] An enquiry into, and detection of the barbarous murther of . . . Essex. [*London*], *anno* 1684. 4°. L, O, C, EN, GU, DT; CLC, IU, MH, NU, WF, Y.

737A   [–] —[Anr. ed. "enquirie"] —, 1684. 4°. L, CS; CH, CLC, MBA, MH.

738   [–] —[Anr. ed.] [*London*], *anno.* 1689. 4°. L, C, BR, MR; CH, CN, LC, TU, Y.

739   [–] —[Anr. ed.] [*London*], *printed*, 1689. 4°. L, OC, CS, RU, DT; CH, IU, MH, PL, WF, Y. (var.)

740   —The interest of reason in religion. *For Dorman Newman*, 1675. 8°. T.C.I 194. L, O, C, AN, E, GU; BN, CH, CU, MH, Y.

741   [–] A just and modest vindication of the proceedings of the two last Parliaments. [*London*, 1681.] cap., 4°.* L, O, C, MR, YM, DT; CH, CN, NU, WF, Y.

742   [–] A just and modest vindication of the Scots design. [*Edinburgh?*], *printed*, 1699. 8°. ALDIS 3859. L, O, C, E, EN, DT; BN, CH, CN, LC, MH, MU, NU, RPJ, WF, Y.

743   —Jvstification only upon a satisfaction. *For D. Newman*, 1668. 8°. L, O, C, DC, SP, AU, E, GU; MH, NU, Y.

744   [–] The knot unty'd. *For Walter Davis*, 1682. 4°.* T.C.I 487. L, O, C, CT, WCA; CH, CU, MH, NU, WF, Y.

745   Entry cancelled.
[–] Mr. Ferguson's lamentation. 1683. *See* title.

746   [–] The late proceedings and votes of the Parliament of Scotland. *Glasgow, by Andrew Hepburn*, 1689. 4°. 63 pp. ALDIS 2902. C, LW, OB, MR, EN; CH, CN, MH, TU, WF, Y.

747   [–] —[Anr. ed., "Parliamemt."] —, 1689. 4°. 63 pp. ALDIS 2902. O, C, MR, SP, WCA; CN, MH, TO.

747A   [–] —[Anr. ed.] —, 1689. 4°.* 39 pp. ALDIS 2903. L, LIU, EN, GU; INU, NU, TU, WF.

747B [–] —[Anr. ed.] —, 1689. 4°.* 42 pp. ALDIS 2903.5. MR, EN, GU; CDA, CH, CSS, CN, MH, TU, Y.

747C [–] —[Anr. ed.] —, 1689. 4°.* 46 pp. L, O, MR; CB, CLC, NC, NCD, NN.

748 Entry cancelled.
[–] Letter to a friend containing certain observations. Dublin, 1682. *See title.*

749 [–] A letter to a person of honour, . . . concerning the black box. [*London*, 1680.] cap., 4°.* L, C, OC, MR, EN; CH, MH, MIU, NU, Y.

750 [–] A letter to a person of honour, concerning the kings disavovving. [*London*, 1680.] cap., 4°.* L, O, C, OC, DU; CH, CN, MH, WF, Y, AVP.

751 —Mr. Fergusons letter to his friends. colop: *For Charles Corbet*, 1683. brs. L, O, LG, OC; CH, CN, WF, Y.

752 [–] A letter to Mr. Secretary Trenchard. [*London*, 1694.] cap., 4°.* L, O, CT, MR, AU, DT; CH, CN, MM, WF, Y.

753 Entry cancelled.
[–] Letter to my Lord . . . Holt. 1694. *See* [–] Letter to the right. Second edition.

754 [–] A letter to the right hononrable [*sic*], my Lord Chief Justice Holt. [*n.p.*, 1694.] cap., 4°.* L, O, DT; MM, NN, Y.

754A [–] —Second edition. *Printed*, 1694. 4°.* O, OC, CT, BSM, DUS, EN; CLC, INU, LC, MB, WF.

754B —Memoire pour servir a l'histoire dangleterre, . . . d'Essex. *Chez Henri Cadman*, 1685. 12°. LLU.

755 Entry cancelled.
[–] The narrative of Mr. John Smith. 1679. *See* Smith, John, *of Walworth.*

756 [–] No Protestant-plot. *For R. Lett*, 1681. 4°.* L, O, C, EN, DT; CH, CN, MH, TU, WF, Y. (var.)

756A [–] A representation of the threatning dangers. [*Edinburgh*, 1687.] 4°. MH, MIU, WF.

757 [–] —[Anr. ed.] [*London*], *printed*, 1689. 4°. T.C.II 260. L, O, C, MR, AU, DT; HR, CH, CN, LC, MH, WF, Y.

758 Entry cancelled.
[–] Second dialogue between the Pope. 1681. *See title.*

759 [–] The second part of No Protestant plot. *For R. Smith*, 1682. 4°.* L, O, C, EN, DT; CH, CN, MH, TU, WF, Y.

760 [–] A sober enquiry into the nature, measure, and principle of moral virtue. *For D. Newman*, 1673. 8°. T.C.I 147. L, O, C, EN, DT; CLC, CN, MH, NU, WF, Y.

761 No entry.

762 [–] The third part of No Protestant plot. *For Richard Baldwin*, 1682. 4°. L, O, C, EN, DT; CH, CN, MH, NU, WF, Y.

762A [–] A treatise concerning the East-India-Trade. *Printed*, 1696. 4°.* L, LG, LUG, EN, ES; CH, LC, MH, MIU, NC, NCD, WF, Y.

763 Entry cancelled.
[–] True settlement of a Christian's faith. [*n.p.*], 1692. *See* Fleming, Robert, *elder.*

764 [–] A view of an ecclesiastick. *For John Marshall*, 1698. 4°. T.C.III 80. L, O, C, CT, EN; CH, IAU, MH, NU.

765 [–] Whether the Parliament be not in law dissolved. [*London*, 1695.] 4°. L, O, CT, MR, EN, DT; CH, IU, NP, TU, WF, Y.

766 [–] Whether the preserving the Protestant religion. [*London*, 1695.] cap., 4°.* L, C, OC, BP, MR; CH, IU, NU, TU, WF, Y.

Ferguson's remonstrance. 1684. *See* R., W.

767 **Fergusson, David.** Epithalamium mysticum. *Edimburgi, typis Thomæ Brown prostat vero venalis ibidem, apud Ioannem Cairns*, 1677. 8°. ALDIS 2100. L, E, EN, GU; MH, OHU, Y.

768 —Nine hundred and forty Scottish proverbs. [*Edinburgh, C. Higgins*], 1659. 8°. ALDIS 1596.7. CHRISTIE-MILLER.

769 ——[Anr. ed.] [*Glasgow?*], *printed*, 1667. 8°.* ALDIS 1836.7. L.

769A ——[Anr. ed.] [*n.p.*], *printed*, 1675. 8°. LLL.

770 —Scottish proverbs. *Edinburgh, by Robert Bryson*, 1641. 4°. ALDIS 1004. EN, ES, AU.

771 **Fergusson, James.** A brief exposition of the Epistles of Paul to the Galatians and Ephesians. *For the company of stationers*, 1656. 8°. LT, O.

772 ——[Anr. ed.] —, 1659. 8°. O, C, LW, EN; CLC, IU, MH, NU, Y.

773 ——[Anr. ed.] *Edinburgh, by Christopher Higgins*, 1659. 8°. ALDIS 1597. O, LW, EN, GU; CLC, NPT, PPT, WF.

774 —A brief exposition of the Epistles of Paul to the Philippians. *Edinburgh: by Christopher Higgins*, 1656. 8°. ALDIS 1540. DL, E, EN; MH, NU.

774A ——[Anr. ed.] *For the company of stationers*, 1656. 8°. WF.

775 —A brief exposition of the first and second Epistles of Paul to the Thessalonians. *By R. W. for Ralph Smith*, 1674. 8°. T.C.I 185. SA, EN; CH, CLC, MH, NU.

776 ——[Anr. ed.] *Glasgow, by Robert Sanders*, 1675. 8°. ALDIS 2052. L, O, C, E, GM; Y.

777 —A brief refutation of the errors. *Edinbvrgh, by George Mosman*, 1692. 8°. ALDIS 3221. O, LW, E, EN, ENC; CH, FU, IU, MBA, NU, WF, AVP.

778 **Ferme, Charles.** Caroli Fermæi . . . analysis logica. *Edinburgi, excudebant hæredes Georgii Andersoni*, 1651. ALDIS 1440. C, E, EN, AU, GU; CH, NU, WF.

779–80 Entries cancelled.

[**Fernandez, Geronimo.**] Famous and delectable history of Don Bellianis. 1673. *See* Kirkman, Francis.

[–] —[Anr. ed.] 1683. *See* [–] Honour of chivalry.

781 [–] The honour of chivalry. *By Bernard Alsop*, 1650. 4°. L, O; CLC, CN, CU, NP, WF, Y.

782 [–] —[Anr. ed.] *By E. A. and T. F. for F. Coles, W. Gilbertson, and C. Tyus*, 1663. 4°. IU.

782A [–] —[Anr. ed.] *By E. Tyler and R. Holt, for Thomas Passinger*, 1672. CLC, INU (imperf.).

783 [–] —[Anr. ed.] *For T. Passenger*, 1678. 4°. T.C.I 316. CLC, CN, WF.

784 [–] —[Anr. ed.] *For Tho. Passinger*, 1683. 4°. T.C.II 21. L, O, CM; CLC, KU, MBP, WF.

785 [–] —[Anr. ed.] *By W. O.*, [1700?]. 4°.* O; IU.

[–] The honour of chivalry . . . the second and third part. 1664. *See* Kirkman, Francis.

786 **F[erne], H[enry].** An answer to Mr. Spencer's book intituled Scripture mistaken. *By R. Norton, for Richard Royston*, 1660. 12°. L, CT, EC, P, SP; BN, CH, CLC.

787 —An appeal to Scripture. *For R. Royston*, 1665. 12°. O, SHR, DT; NU.

788 [–] The camp at Gilgal. *Oxford, by Leonard Lichfield*, 1643. 8°. MADAN 1386. LT, O.

789 —Certain considerations of present concernment. *By J. G. for R. Royston*, 1653. 12°. LT, O, C, NE, DT; BN, CH, CLC, IU, NU, WF, Y.

790 —A compendious discourse. *By J. G. for Richard Royston*, 1655. 12°. L, O, C, OC, P, DT; CDA, CU, MH, NU, WF, Y.

791 —Conscience satisfied. *Oxford, by Leonard Lichfield*, 1643. 4°. MADAN 1307–8. LT, O, C, MR, DT; CH, CU, MH, NU, WF, Y.

792 Entry cancelled.
—Discourse upon the case. 1655. *See* – Compendious discourse.

793 [–] Episcopacy and Presbytery considered. *Oxford, by Leonard Lichfield*, 1644. 4°.* MADAN 1715. O, C, OC, OCC, E, DT; CH, CLC, IU, MM, NU, WF.

794 — —[Anr. ed.] *For Richard Royston*, 1647. 4°.* LT, O, C, EN, DT; CH, CN, MH, NU, WF, Y.

795 [–] Of the division between the English and Romish church. *For R. Royston*, 1652. 12°. LT, C, OM, SHR, E; BN.

796 — —[Anr. ed.] *By J. G. for Richard Royston*, 1655. 12°. L, O, C, OC, NPL, DU; MH, NU, WF, Y.

797 Entry cancelled.
[–] Pian piano. 1656. *See* Harrington, James, *elder*.

798 [–] A plaine favlt in plain-English. *For T. Underhill*, 1643. 4°.* LT, C, EC, YM; CH, TU, WF.

799 —A reply unto severall treatises pleading for the armes. *Oxford, by Leonard Lichfield*, 1643. 4°. MADAN 1473–4. LT, O, CT, EN, DT; CH, CN, MH, WF, Y. (var.)

800 —The resolving of conscience. *Cambridge, by Roger Daniel*, 1642. 4°. L, O, C, CT, LNC, DT; CSS, IU, MH, NU, TU, WF, Y. (var.)

801 — —[Anr. ed.] *Cambridge, for E. Freeman and T. Dunster*, 1642. 4°. L, OH, C, CT, NE; IU, MH, NPT, WF.

802 — —[Anr. ed.] *Printed at York by Stephen Bulkley*, 1642. 4°. L, YM, GH; IU.

803 — —[Anr. ed.] *Printed at Cambridge, and re-printed at London*, 2642 [1642]. 4°.* L, O, C, EN, DT; CH, CN, CSS, LC, MH, NU, TU, WF, Y.

804 — —"Second" edition. *Oxford, for VV. VVebb*, 1643. 4°.* MADAN 1572. O, OCC, MR, YM, EN, CD; MM, TU, Y.

805 [–] A sermon preached . . . the twelfth day of April· *Oxford, by Leonard Lichfield*, 1644. 4°.* MADAN 1618–9. LT, O, C, OM, CT, DT; CH, CU, NU, WF, Y. (var.)

806 —A sermon preached . . . November the 29. 1648. *For R. Royston*, 1649. 4°.* LT, O, C, DU, DT; CLC, IU, MH, TU, WF, Y.

806A [–] The unlavvfulnesse of the new covenant. *Oxford, by Leonard Lichfield*, 1. *March*, 1643. 4°.* L, CS, EC, DT; CN, NU, WF.

807–8E Entries cancelled.
Fernel, Jean. Select medicinal counsels. 1657. *See* Rivière, Lazare. Practice of physick.

808F —Two treatises; the first of pulses. *By Peter Cole*, 1662. 8°. NAM.

808G **Ferrand, Jacques.** Ερωτομανια, or, a treatise discoursing of . . . love. Second edition. *Oxford, for Edward Forrest.* 1645. 8°. MH.

808H [**Ferrar, Richard.**] An exact abridgement of the general history of the world. *By James Moxon, for Samuel Heyrick*, 1698. 8°. L; CLC, MH, MIU, WF, Y.

809 **Ferrarius, Gulielmus.** De bello Batavico. *Prostant apud Gulielmum Cademannum*, 1672. 8°. T.C.I 113. L, O, C, P, WCA; PL.

810 [–] In Britanniarum reges a Samothe . . . disticha. *Prostant apud Gulielmum Cademannum*, 1672. 8°. L, O, CS; CH, PL, WF.

Ferrarius, Jani Alex. *See* Fabricius, Johann Ludwig.

811 Entry cancelled. Published on the Continent.

812 **Ferrarius, Johannes Baptista.** Orationes. *Ex officina Rogeri Danielis*, 1657. 12°. L, O, NPL, YM; CLC, IU, NC, WF, ASU.

813 — [Anr. ed.] *Ex officina Johannis Redmayne*, 1668. 12°. L, O, C, CT, DT; CH, IU, MH, PL, TO, UCLA, WF.

814 **Ferrarius, Philippus.** Lexicon geographicum. *Ex officina Rogeri Danielis*, 1657. fol. L, O, C, NPL, DT; CLC, MU, NN, PU, TO, TU.

815 — —[Anr. ed.] *Et veneunt Parisiis, apud Fredericvm Leonard*, 1665. fol. L.

816 —Tabula longitudinis. *Ex officina Rogeri Danielis*, 1657. fol.* L, CK.

817 **F[erret], J[ohn].** J. F. Didascaliæ; discourses . . . first part. [*Amsterdam*], *imprinted*, 1643. 8°. LT, C.

818 [–] Zealous beleevers are the best subjects. [*Amsterdam*], *imprinted*, 1643. 8°. LT.

819 **Ferriby, John.** The lawfull preacher. *For William Roybould*, 1652. 4°. LT, O, C, YM, E; CLC, NHC, NPT, NU.

819A — —[Anr. ed.] —, 1653. 4°. L, O, LW, CT, SP; CH, MWA, WF.

820 **Ferrier, Auger.** A learned astronomicall discovrse. *By R. Cotes, and are to be sold by Lourence Chapman and Richard Minn*, 1642. 4°.* L, LWL, OC, E; CLC, WF, Y.

820A — —[Anr. ed.]—["*Mynne*"], 1642. 4°.* O; MH, NC.

820B **Ferrier, John.** Thesis theologica. [*London?* 1660.] 12°. L.

820C **Ferus, John.** Σταυροδιδαχη και σταυρονικη the doctrine . . . of the cross. *By Robert White*, 1659. 4°. DC.

821 Festa Anglo-Romana: or, the feasts. *For William Jacob, and John Place*, 1678. 12°. T.C.I 302. O, C, OC, NE, BLH; CH, CLC, MH, WF, Y, ASU.

822 Festa Georgiana, or the gentries & countries joy. *Printed*, 1661. fol.* LT, C; CLC, MH.

823 Entry cancelled.
Festeau, Paul. French grammar. 1667. *See* —New and easie French grammar.

823A — —Second edition. *In the Savoy, by T. N. for Thomas Thornicroft, and are to be sold by Samuel Lowndes*, 1671. 8°. T.C.I 91. LLP; IU.

823B — —"Second" edition. —, 1672. 8°. BN.

823C — —[Anr. ed.] *By W. G. for William Cooper*, 1674. 8°. T.C.I 164. L, O, CQ, BC, LNC; CH.

823D — —Third edition. *By A. C. for Samuel Lowndes*, 1675. 8°. T.C.I 207. L, O, C, CCA, LLU; IU, RBU.

823E — —Fourth edition. *By T. N. for Samuel Lowndes,* 1679. 8°. T.C.I 354. L, O, CS, CT, NOT; WF.

823F — —Fifth edition. *By E. H. for Samuel Lowndes,* 1685. 8°. T.C.II 131. L, CS; CLC, PU.

824 — —Sixth edition. *By E. J. for Samuel Lowndes,* 1693. 8°. C; MH.

824A —A new and easie French grammar. *For Thomas Thorny-croft,* 1667. 8°. L, CE; IU.

825 —New double grammar. *Bruxelles, by Eugenius Henricus Frix,* 1696. 12°. C.

825A —Nouvelle grammaire angloise. *Chez Thomas Thorni-croft,* 1671/2. 8°. T.C.I 98. BN.

825B — —Second edition. *Chez George Wells,* 1675. 8°. LG, CCA, LLU; CLC.

826–7 Entries cancelled.

—Nouvelle grammaire françoise. *See* —French grammar.

828 Festered consciences new-launced. *W. Weekley,* 1650. 4°. L, O, YM; CN.

Festorum metropolis. 1652. *See* Blayney, Allan.

828A The fetching home of May. *For J. Wright, jun.,* [*c.* 1650]. brs. L.

828B The Fetter Lane loyalist. *Engraven printed and sold by Abra: Goulding,* [1681]. brs. L, O.

828C **Fettiplace, Thomas.** The Christian monitor. *By E. Tyler and R. Holt for Will. Miller,* 1672. 12°. T.C.I 101. L, LSC; CLC, WF.

828D —The holy exercises of the heavenly graces. *By J. Cottrel, for S. Speed,* 1662. 12°. LSC.

829 —Scrinia sacra: or. *By W. G. for Peter Dring,* 1666. 8°. CP, DUS.

829A — —[Anr. ed., "Scrutina."] 1670. 8°. P.

830 —The sinner's tears. *For Humphrey Moseley,* 1653. 12°. LT, O; TO, Y.

831 — —[Anr. ed.] *For Anne Moseley,* 1671. 12°. T.C.I 90. O, C, CP.

831A — —[Anr. ed.] *By J. R. for Peter Parker,* 1680. 12°. L; CH, CLC, WF.

832 — —[Anr. ed.] *For Peter Parker,* 1688. 12°. L, O, LSC; NPT, WF.

832A — —[Anr. ed.] —, 1692. 12°. NPT, TU.

832B **Feversham, George Sondes, *earl of.*** Sir George Sondes his plaine narrative to the world. *Printed,* 1655. fol.* L, CT, LNC; CH, CSU, IU, MH, WF.

Few collections. 1646. *See* Haward, Lazarus.

833 A few considerations humbly offered to . . . Parliament, . . . Quakers. [*London?* 1689.] brs. L; PSC.

833A A few gentlemen in the western parts of Derbyshire that get lead. [*London,* 1675?] brs. LPR.

Few ingredients [n.p., 1681.] *See* Richardson, Richard.

Few lines in true love. 1694. *See* Fisher, Abigail.

834 A few lines more. [*n.p.*], 1662. 4°. O.

Few plain reasons. 1688. *See* Barlow, Thomas, *bp.*

Few plain words concerning. [n.p., 1664.] *See* Smith, William, *of Besthorp.*

Few plain words to. [n.p., 1662.] *See* Greene, Thomas.

835 A few proposals offered in humility . . . to the . . . Parliament . . . holding forth a medium. *For L. Chapman,* 1659. 4°.* LT, BQ; MH, MU.

836 A fevv propositions shewing the lawfullnesse of defence. *For Samuel Gellibrand,* 1643. 4°.* LT, O, CT, MR; CH, CN, MH, WF, Y.

Few queries for Thomas Moor. [n.p., 1660.] *See* Fox, George, *elder.*

837 A few short arguments proving that 'tis every Englishman's interest. colop: *By Henry Hills,* 1687. brs. L, O; CH, CN, MM.

838 A few sober queries upon the late proclamation. *Printed,* 1668. 4°.* L, O, C, LPR, NOT, P; CH, CU, MH, NU, WF, Y.

838A —[Anr. ed.] *Printed,* 1685. 4°.* MWA.

838AB A few words among many, about . . . succession. [*n.p.,* 1679/80.] 4°.* O, OC, CT, LIU; CN, WF.

838B —[Anr. ed.] colop: *For R. Janeway,* 1681. cap., 4°.* O, LNC; CH, CLC, INU, MIU, MM, TU.

838C Few words are best. *For W. Gilbertson,* [1640–1655]. brs. EUING 123. GU.

839 A few words concerning the trial of spirits. [*London,* 1673?] 4°.* LF, CT; PH, WF.

Few words in season. 1660. *See* Fletcher, Elizabeth.

Few words of counsel. 1687. *See* Tomkins, Anthony.

Few words to all such. 1669. *See* Fox, George.

Few words to all who. [n.p.], 1665. *See* Ellington, Francis.

Few words to the King. [n.p.], 1675. *See* Milner, Richard.

840 A few words to the people of England. [*London?* 1655.] cap., 4°.* LT, O, LF, CT, BBN; MH, PH, PL, PSC.

Few words unto a particular people. [n.p.], 1669. *See* Smith, William, *of Besthorp.*

841 **Feyens, Joannes.** A new and needful treatise of spirits and wind. *By J. M. for B. Billingsley and O. Blagrave,* 1668. 8°. L, LCS, LSC, MAU; CLC, MMO, NAM, WSG.

841A — —[Anr. ed.] *For Benjamin Billingsley,* 1676. 8°. T.C.I 223. L, LWL; NCD, WSG, HC.

841B — —[Anr. ed.] *By J. M. for Benjamin Billingsley and Obadiah Blagrave.* 1688. 8°. O.

842 **Feyens, Thomas.** De cometa. *Excudebat E. Tyler, impensis Edvar. Story,* 1655. 8°. L, O, CT, EC, SC; CLC, MH.

843 —De viribus imaginationis tractatus. *Ex officina Rogeri Danielis,* 1657. 12°. L, O, CCA, EN, BQ; CU, LC, MMO, MWA, WG.

843A Ffordd y gwr cyffredin. *Printiedig yn Rhydychen,* 1683. 8°. O.

843B Ffurf gweddi i'w harfer. colop: *Charles Bill, ac executris Thomas Newcomb,* 1699. 4°.* AN.

844 **Fialetti, Odoardo.** The whole art of drawing. *For Peter Stint, and Simon Miller,* 1660. obl. 4°. L.

845 Fiat justitia, & ruat cœlum. Or, somewhat offer'd in defence. [*London,* 1679?] cap., fol.* L, O, C, CT, MR, DM; CH, IU, MH, NP, WF, Y.

Fiat lux, or. [n.p.], 1661. *See* Canes, John Vincent.

846 The fickle northern lass. [*London*], *for F. Coles, T. Vere, J. Wright, and J. Clarke,* [1674–79]. brs. L, O, HH; MH.

Fiction found out. [n.p., 1685.] *See* Penn, William.

Fida pastora. 1658. *See* Fletcher, John.

847 Fidelis Achates: or, an historical account. *For John Sprint*, 1699. 8°. T.C.III 124. L, O, C, LLU, AU, EN; CLC, INU, IU, MH, PL.

848 The fidelity of a loyall subject. [*n.p.*, 1698.] 4°. O.

849 **Fidell, Thomas.** A perfect guide for a studious young lawyer. *By Tho. Roycroft, for the author, and are to be sold by John Place*, 1654. 4°. L, C, LI, LL, AN; CH, CN, MHL, NCL, WF, YL.

850 — —[Anr. ed.] *By Tho. Roycroft, for John Place*, 1658. 8°. LT, O, LL, LIU; CLC, LC, MHL, PU.

Fides divina: the ground. 1657. See Writer, Clement.

851 No entry.

852 **F[idge], G[eorge].** The English Gusman. *By T. N. for George Latham, junior*, 1652. 4°. LT.

853 [–] The great eater of Grayes-Inne. *For the author, to be sold by William Reybould*, 1652. 4°.* LT, O, OC; CH.

854 [–] Hind's ramble. *For George Latham*, 1651. 8°.* LT.

855 [–] Wit for money, being a full relation. *For T. Vere and W. Gilbertson*, [1652]. 4°.* L.

856 Entry cancelled.
[–] Wit for money, or poet stutter. 1691. See title.

857 **Fido, George.** Two affadavits. [*London*, 1695.] brs. L.

858 Fye Amaryllis, cease to grieve. [*London*], *T. Cross, junr.*, [1700?]. brs. L.

858A Fy on the wars that hurri'd Willie from me. [*n.p.*, 1700?] brs. EN.

858B **[Field, John]**, *d. 1588*. An advertisement to the Parliament of England. *For Mathew Walbancke*, 1644. 4°.* LT, O, CT, DT; CH, NU, PHS, WCL, Y.

859 **[Field, John]**, **Quaker.** The absurdity & falsness of Thomas Trion's doctrine. *For Tho. Howkins*, 1685. 4°.* O, LF, BBN; IE, NPT, PSC.

860 Entry cancelled.
[–] Advertisement to the Parliament. 1644. See Field, John, *d. 1588*.

860A [–] An answer to a catechism against Quakerism. *For Tho. Northcott*, 1693. 12°.* LF.

861 [–] An apology for the people called Qvakers. *Printed and sold by T. Sowle*, 1699. 4°.* L, O, LF, LLP, MR; CH, MH, PH, WF, Y.

861A [–] A Christian testimony born by the people . . . called Quakers. *By Andrew Sowle*, 1681. 4°.* L, O, LF, OC; MH, PL, PSC, WF.

861B [–] The Christianity of the people, called Quakers. *Printed and sold by T. Sowle*, 1700. brs. LF; PH, MWA, NN, WF.

861C [–] —[Anr. ed.] [*Reprinted at Philadelphia by Reynier Jansen*, 1700.] 4°.* EVANS 910. MWA.

862 [–] The creed-forgers detected. *Printed and sold by T. Sowle*, 1700. 4°.* LF, LLP, BBN; MH, PH, PSC, Y.

863 —A defence of An apology for the people called Quakers. *Printed and sold by T. Sowle*, 1699. 4°.* L, LF, OC, BBN, DT; CH, MH, PH, WF, Y.

863A [–] An exhortation by way of epistle. *For T. Northcot*, 1696. 12°.* LF; PL.

863B —A few words to Nath. Coleman's late epistle. [*London*, 1683.] cap., 4°.* C.

864 [–] Friendly advice, in the spirit of love. *Printed*, 1688. 8°.* LF; PH, PSC.

864A [–] —[Anr. ed.] *For T. Northcott*, 1695. 12°. LF; NU, Y.

864AB —Invitation to all sinners to repent. *By J. Bringhurst*, 1683. 4°. LSC.

864AC [–] A letter to the clergy of the diocess [*sic*] of Norfolk and Suffolk. [*London*, 1699.] cap., 4°.* NPL, DT; MH, PH, PSC, WF.

864B [–] A reply to Benjamin Bird's ignorance. [*London?* 1695.] 8°.* LF.

864C [–] J.F.'s reply unto Thomas Crisp's rapsody. [*London?* 1682.] 4°.* LF; PH, PSC.

864D [–] The scorner rebuked, or a reply. [*London?* 1693.] 8°.* LF.

864E [–] A second letter to the clergy and people of Norfolk and Suffolk. [*London*, 1699.] 4°.* MH.

865 [–] Some observations on the Remarks upon the Quakers. *Printed and sold by T. Sowle*, 1700. 4°.* L, LF, BBN, DU; MH, MU, PH, PSC.

866 [–] A testimony to Christ. *Printed and sold by T. Sowle*, 1697. 4°.* L, LF, CT, BBN; MH, NU, PH, PSC.

867 [–] Thomas Crisp's envy detected. *For Benjamin Clark*, 1682. 4°.* L, LF, BBN; PH.

867A [–] The wandring bird's wings clipt. [*London?* 1695.] 8°.* LF; PH.

868 —The weakness of George Keith's reasons. *Printed and sold by T. Sowle*, 1700. 4°.* LF, BBN; MH, PH, PHS, PSC, RPJ.

869 [–] Wing-clipping no crime. *For Thomas Northcott*, 1696. 8°.* LF.

870 Entry cancelled.
Field of blood. 1681. See Cotton, Sir Robert Bruce.

871 **Fielder, John.** The humble petition and appeal of. *Printed*, 1651. 4°.* LT.

872 **Fielder, Richard.** The case of. [*London*, 1696.] brs. L; MH.

873 **Fiennes, Nathaniel.** An extraordinary deliverance, from a cruell plot, and bloudy massacre. *For I. Wright, March 15. 1642* [3]. 4°.* LT, O, C, EC, DT; CH, CN, MH, MU, Y.

874 —Colonell Fiennes letter to My Lord General. *By T. P. and M. S. for Thomas Vnderhill*, 1643. 4°.* LT, O, C, BR; CSS, NN.

875 —A most true and exact relation of both the battels. *For Joseph Hunscott, Novem. 9, 1642.* 4°.* LT, O, CT, BC, DU; CH, IU, WF, Y.

876 —A relation made in the House of Commons, by. *For R. D.*, [1643]. 4°.* LT, O, CT, BR, DT; CH, CN, MH, WF, Y.

877 —Colonell Fiennes his reply to a pamphlet. *For Thomas Vnderhill*, 1643. 4°.* LT, O, CT, BR, DT; CH, CLC, MM, NN, NU.

878 —A second speech of. [*London*], *printed*, 1641. 4°.* LT, O, C, EN, DT; BN, CH, CN, LC, MH, MU, NU, TU, Y. (var.)

879 —Master Fynes his speech in Parliament: touching. *For F. C. and T. B.*, 1641. 4°.* LT, O, C, BC, SP; CH, CN, MH, WF, Y.

880 —A speech of . . . 9th of Feb. 1640. [*London*], *printed*, 1641. 4°.* LT, O, C, DU, DT; CH, CN, LC, MH, MU, TU, Y. (var.)

881   —The speech of . . . 20th of January, 1657. *By Henry Hills,
       and John Field*, 1657 [8]. 4°.* LT, O, CT, MR, E; CH, CN, LC,
       MH, WF, Y.

882   —The speech of . . . 27th. of January, 1658. *For Henry
       Twyford*, 1659. 4°.* LT, O, CCA, EN, DT; CH, CN, MH, TU,
       WF, Y.

882A   —The true copies of a certificate . . . dated July 17, 1643.
       [*London*, 1643.] cap. LG; NN.

883   [–] Vnparallel'd reasons for abollishing episcopacy. *Printed
       at London for S. S.*, 1642. 4°.* LT, O, C, YM, DT; CH, IU,
       MH, NU, TU, Y.

884   [–] Vindiciæ veritatis, or an answer. [*London*], *printed*,
       1654. 4°. LT, DT; CSS, NU.

       Fiennes, William. *See* Saye and Sele, William Fiennes,
       viscount.

       Fienus, *see* Feyens.

884A   A fiery looking-glass for London. [*London?* 166–?] brs. LG.
       Fiery pillar. 1641. *See* Grosse, Alexander.

885   Entry cancelled.
       [**Fieux, Charles de.**] French rogue. 1672. *See* title.

885A   **Fifield, William.** To my neighbours and Friends of the
       New-River. [*London?* 1675.] brs. LF.

885AB The XV comforts of rash and inconsiderate marriage. *For
       Walter Davis*, 1682. 12°. T.C.I 463. O; CH, WF.

885B   —Third edition. *For S. Heyrick, W. Crooke, and M.
       Gillyflower*, 1683. 12°. T.C.I 515. L, O; MH.

886   —Fourth edition. *For William Crooke, and Matth. Gilly-
       flower*, 1694. 12°. T.C.II 503. L; CLC.

887   Fifteen real comforts of matrimony. *For Benjamin Alsop
       and Thomas Malthus*, 1683. 12°. T.C.II 7. L; CH, WF.

888   Entry cancelled. Serial.
       Fifth book of the most pleasant and delectable history of
       Amadis de Gaule. 1664. *See* Lobeira, Vasco.

889   A fifth collection of papers relating to the present junc-
       ture. *Printed, to be sold by Rich. Janeway*, 1688. 4°.*
       L, O, C, BR, DT; CH, IU, MH, NU, WF, Y. (var.)
       Fifth essay of D. M. 1700. *See* Hill, Oliver.

890   The fifth monarchy, or. *For Livewel Chapman*, 1659. 4°.
       LT, BC; CLC, MH, MU, NN, NU, WF.

891   The fifth of November. *Oxford, for H. Hall and W. Webb*,
       1644. 4°.* MADAN 1605. LT, O, CT, DU, EN, DT; CN, WF,
       Y.

891A   —[Anr. ed.] —, 1644. 4°.* MADAN 1607. LT; CH.

892   —[Anr. ed.] *Oxford, printed*, 1644. 4°.* MADAN 1606. O, C;
       NU, Y.
       Fifty five enigmatical characters. 1665. *See* Flecknoe,
       Richard.

893   LIX. exceptions against the Booke of common prayer.
       colop: *For R. B.*, 1644. 4°.* LT, MR, DT; NNM, NU.
       Fifty queries. 1675. *See* Brandon, John.
       Fifty questions. 1647. *See* Richardson, Samuel.

894   A fight at Dunin at Scotland. *Edinburgh*, 1652. 4°.* ALDIS
       1462.3. LT.

895   A fight at sea between the Parliament ships. *For H. Becke*,
       1648. 4°.* LT, DN; CSS.

896   A fight at sea two ships taken by Prince Charles his
       officers. *For H. Becke*, 1648. 4°.* LT; MH.

897   Entry cancelled.
       Fight at sea upon the coast of Cornwall. 1652. *See* Another
       bloudy fight.

898   A fight between an English fire-ship. [*London*], *for J.
       Bissel*, [1689–90]. brs. HH.

899   Entry cancelled.
       Fight in France between the king's army. 1652. *See* Great
       and bloudy fight.
       Fight in Ireland. [n.p., 1649.] *See* L., R.

900   The fight in Kent betweene the army. *For H. Becke*, 1648.
       4°.* LT, LG, SP; MH, MIU, WF, Y.

901   A fight in the North at the Dales in Richmondshire. *For
       R. Woodas*, 1647. 4°.* LT, LLU, DT.

902   Entry cancelled.
       Fight neer Newark. 1648. *See* Bloudy fight.

903   A fight: the Lord Goring beaten. *For Richard Smithurst*,
       1648. 4°.* LT, O, AN; CLC, WF, Y.
       Figure of five. [n.p., 1645?] *See* Parker, Martin.
       Figure of foure. 1654. *See* Breton, Nicholas.
       Figure of nine. 1662. *See* Smithson, Samuel.
       Figure of seven. 1647. *See* Parker, Martin.
       Figure of six. 1652. *See* N., D.
       Figure of the true. 1655. *See* Niclas, Hendrik.
       Filacers office. [1657.] *See* B., J.

904   [**Filleau de la Chaise, Jean.**] An excellent discourse
       proving the divine original. *For Tho. Parkhurst*, 1682.
       8°. T.C.I 504. L, O, LW, CT, E; NPT, NRU, UCLA, WF, Y.

905   Entry cancelled.
       [**Filmer, Edward.**] Defence of dramatick poetry. 1698.
       See Settle, Elkanah.

906   Entry cancelled.
       [–] Farther defence of dramatick poetry. 1698. *See* Settle,
       Elkanah.

907   [–] The unnatural brother. *By J. Orme, for Richard Wilkin*,
       1697. 4°. T.C.III 15. L, O, C, LVF, EN; CH, CN, LC, MH, TU,
       WF, Y.

908   Entry cancelled. Ghost.

909   [**Filmer, Sir Robert.**] An advertisement to the jury-men
       of England. *By I. G. for Richard Royston*, 1653. 4°.* LT,
       O, C, GU, DM; CH, MH, NU, WF, Y.

910   [–] The anarchy of a limited or mixed monarchy.
       [*London*], *printed*, 1648. 4°.* LT, O, C, OM, MR; BN, CH,
       CN, LC, MH, NU, Y.

911   [–] A discourse whether it may be lawful to take use for
       money. *For Will. Crook*, 1678. 12°. T.C.I 293. L, O, C,
       LL, E; CH, CU, MH, WF, Y.

912   [–] The free-holders grand inqvest. [*London*], *printed*,
       [1648]. 4°. LT, O, C, MR, DT; BN, CH, CN, MH, WF, Y. (var.)

913   [–] —[Anr. ed.] *Printed*, 1679. 8°. 372 pp. LCL, LI, LNC, GU,
       DT; CH, CN, NU, PL, WF.

914   — —[Anr. ed.] —, 1679. 8°. 346 pp. L, C, OM, EN, DT; CLC,
       CN, MH, NC, TSM, Y.

915   — —[Anr. ed.] —, 1680. 8°. L, O, C, CT, ENC; CSU, CU,
       LC, MH, MHL, TO.

916   — —Fourth edition. *For Rich. Royston*, 1684. 8°. T.C.II
       106. L, LVF, LW, DU, P, DT; BN, CH, MH, MU, NC, TU.

917 [–] The necessity of the absolute power. *At London, printed,* 1648. 4°.* LT, O, C, YM, DT; BN, CH, CN, MH, NU, WF.

918 [–] Observations concerning the originall of government. *For R. Royston,* 1652. 4°. LT, O, C, EN, DT; BN, CH, CN, MH, WF, Y, ZWT. (var.)

919 —Observations concerning the original . . . forms of government. *For R. R. C. and are to be sold by Samuel Keble and Daniel Brown,* 1696. 4°. L, CS, P, EN, BLH; CU, MBC, MHL, NP, Y.

920 — —[Anr. ed.] *For R. R. C., sold by T. Axe,* 1696. 4°. LLU, BLH, DT; CH, IAU, LC, MHL, MU, NP, NRU.

921 [–] Observations upon Aristotles politiques. *For R. Royston,* 1652. 4°. LT, O, C, NE, E; BN, CH, CN, LC, MH, Y.

922 —Patriarcha: or, the natural power of kings. *Printed and are to be sold by Walter Davis,* 1680. 8°. L, O, C, EN, DT; CH, CN, MH, NU, TU, WF, WSC, Y.

923 — —[Anr. ed.] *For Ric. Chiswell, Matthew Gillyflower and William Henchman,* 1680. 8°. L, O, LVF, CS, BLH, DT; BN, CH, CU, LC, MH, Y.

924 — —Second edition. *For R. Chiswell, W. Hensman, M. Gilliflower, and G. Wells,* 1685. 8°. T.C.II 140. L, O, LG, CT, DU, SA, DT; CH, MH, MHL, NC, NPT, YL.

925 —Political discourses of. *Printed* 1680. 8°. L, MR, P, ES; CLC, NP.

926 —The power of kings. *For W. H. & T. F. and are to be sold by Walter Davis,* 1680. fol.* L, O, C, OC, SP; CH, CN, MH, WF, Y.

927 [–] Quæstio quodlibetica, or a discourse, whether it may bee lawfull to take vse for money. *For Humphrey Moseley,* 1653. 12°. LT, O, C, CT, DC; CH, IU, LC, MH, NC, Y.

928–9 Entries cancelled.
     [–] Reflections. 1679. *See* —Free-holders.
     Final protest. [n.p., 1659.] *See* L'Estrange, *Sir* Roger.

930 **Finch, Edward.** An ansvver to the articles preferred against. *[London], printed,* 1641. 4°.* LT, O, C, LLU, LNC; CH, CN, WF, Y.

930A [**Finch, Francis.**] Friendship. *[London,* 1654.] 4°. OC; Y.

     Finch, Heneage. *See* Nottingham, Heneage Finch, *1st earl.*

     Finch, Heneage. *See* Winchelsea, Heneage Finch, *2d earl.*

931 **Finch, *Sir* Henry.** Law, or a discourse thereof. *(By permission of the company of stationers) for C. Adams, J. Starkey, & T. Basset,* 1661. 8°. L, OC, CS, DUS, CD; CLC, CU, LC, MHL, YL.

931A — —[Anr. ed.] 1671. 8°. LLL.

932 — —[Anr. ed.] *By the assigns of Richard and Edward Atkins; for H. Twyford, F. Tyton, J. Bellinger, M. Place, T. Basset, R. Pawlet, S. Heyrick, C. Wilkinson, T. Dring, W. Jacob, C. Harper, J. Leigh, J. Ammery [sic], J. Place, and J. Poole,* 1678. 8°. L, O, LIL, CS, SA; CH, IU, LC, MHL, TU, YL.

933 —A summary of the common-law. *Printed,* 1654. 8°.* CE; MH.

934 — —[Anr. ed.] —, 1673. 8°. L, DU.

935 **Finch, Henry, *Capt.*** A true relation of the twenty-weeks siege of Londonderry. *By R. I. for S. G. & A. W.,* 1649. 4°.* LT, O, C, DN; NN.

936–9 No entries.

     Finch, John, *baron.* *See* Fordwich, John Finch, *baron.*

940 [**Finch, Leopold William.**] The case of Mr. Jonas Proast. *[Oxford,* 1693.] cap., fol.* O, OC; MH.

941 **Finch, Martin.** Animadversions upon Sir Henry Vanes book, entituled The retired mans meditations. *For Joseph Barber,* 1656. 8°. LT, LW, CE; MB.

942 —An answer to Mr. Thomas Grantham's book. *By T. S. for Edward Giles in Norwich,* 1691. 8°. T.C.II 378. L, O, C, LCL, ORP; NPT, RBU.

943 —A manuall of practical divinity. *By R. W. for Thomas Brewster,* 1658. 8°. L, O, LCL.

944 —Milk for babes in Christ. *For Tho. Brewster,* 1653. 8°. LT.

944AA — —Second edition. —, 16[55]. 8°. CLC.

944A — —Third edition. *By R. W. for Thomas Brewster,* 1658. 8°. NPT.

944B —Of the conversion. *For Henry Mortlock,* 1680. 8°. T.C.I 368. NPL; TO.

945 —A sermon preach'd . . . 25th day of January, 1690. *For Edward Giles, in Norwich,* 1695. 4°.* O, LW, NPL.

946 **Finch, William.** Several goods and merchandizes belonging to . . . 4th of June, 1674. [n.p., 1674.] brs. OP.

947 **Finett, *Sir* John.** Finetti Philoxenis: som choice observations. *By T. R. for H. Twyford, and G. Bedell,* 1656. 8°. LT, O, C, MR, ES, DT; BN, CH, CN, LC, MH, MU, NCL, WF, Y.

948 —Some choice observations. 1658. 8°. EN.

948A **Finger, Gottfried.** A collection of musick in two parts. *By Tho. Moore, for John Banister,* 1691. fol.* NN (film).

949 —Sonatæ XII. *Londoni [sic],* 1688. 4°. L; CLC, NN.

950 **Finglas, John.** A sermon preached . . . on 5th of November, 1690. *Dublin, by Joseph Ray,* 1690. 4°.* DIX 239. C, DN.

951 —A sermon preached at Deptford . . . on Trinity Monday. *Printed,* 1695. 4°.* L, O; WF.

951A —A sermon preached at the Chappel Royal . . . [6 January 1694/5]. *For the author,* 1695. 4°. LLP.

951B **Fioravanti, Leonardo.** An exact collection of the choicest . . . experiments. *By G. Dawson, and are to be sold by John Saywell,* 1653. 4. WU.

952 — —[Anr. ed.] *For William Shears,* 1659. 4°. C, LCP.

953 —Three exact pieces of. *By G. Dawson, and are to be sold by William Nealand,* 1652. 4°. LT, O, C, LW, E, GU; BN, CLC, CNM, LC, MH, MMO, NAM, HC.

954 Fire from Heaven. *Printed,* 1649. 4°.* LT, BC; CH, MBP.
     Firebrand taken out. 1654. *See* Hart, John.
     Fire's continued. [n.p., 1690.] *See* Parkinson, James.

954A **Firmin, Giles.** The answer of. *For John Lawrence,* 1689. 4°.* LCL, LW, CK; CH, Y.

955 [–] The litvrgical considerator considered. *For Ralph Smith,* 1661. 4°. LT, O, DC, EN, DT; MIU, NNM, NU, PSC, WF.

956 [–] —Second edition. —, 1661. 4°. L, CS, EC, EN, DT; CH, MH, MIU, NGT, NU, Y.

957 —Meditations upon Mr Baxter's review. *[London], printed,* 1672. 4°.* T.C.I 115. O, LCL; MB.

958 —Of schism. *By T. C. for Nathanael Webb, and William Grantham*, 1658. 8°. LT, O, LCL, LW, OCC; LC, MBA, MH, NN, RPJ, Y.

959 —Πανουργια. A brief review. *For John Lawrence*, 1693. 4°.* L, O, LCL, LW, ENC; CH, MB, MH, NN, WF, Y.

960 —The plea of the children. *For Tho. Simmons*, 1683. 8°. T.C.II 25. LW.

961 [–] Presbyterial ordination vindicated. *For Nathanael Webb*, 1660. 4°. LT, O, C, EN, DT; CH, IU, MH, NU, WF, Y.

962 [–] The questions between the Conformist. *For Tho. Cockerill*, 1681. 4°. L, O, CPE, EN, DT; CH, CU, NU, WF, Y.

963 —The real Christian. *For Dorman Newman*, 1670. 4°. T.C.I 42. L, O, C, LW, E; CH, IU, MH, TU, WF, Y.

963A —Scripture-warrant sufficient proof. *For Tho. Parkhurst*, 1688. 8°. LW; MB.

964 —Separation examined. *By R. I. for Stephen Bowtell*, 1652. 4°. LT, O, OC, E, BLH; CH, MH, NU, RPJ, WF, Y.

965 —A serious question stated. *By R: I: for Stephen Bowtell*, 1651. 4°. L, LW, CM, P, EN; MH, NCD, NHC, NU, WF, Y.

966 —A sober reply to the sober answer. *By J. G. to be sold by Robert Littlebury*, 1653. 4°. L, O, LW, OB, EN; MB, NN, NPT, NU, TO, WF.

966A [–] Some remarks upon the Anabaptist answer. *For John Lawrence*, 1692. 4°.* TO.

967 —Stablishing against shaking. *By J. G. for Nathanael Webb and William Grantham*, 1656. 4°. LT, O, C, LF, DT; CH, IU, MB, NU, PH, PSC, WF.

968 —Tythes vindicated. *For Nath. Webb and William Grantham*, 1659. 4°.* LT, LSC, E; NU.

969 —Weighty questions discussed. *For the author*, 1692. 4°.* L, O, C, LCL; NU.

970 Entry cancelled.

F[irmin], T[homas]. Proposals for the imployment. 1681. *See* —Some proposals.

970A [–] Proposals humbly offered to the . . . Commons, for the advancing . . . revenue. [*London, c. 1685.*] cap., fol.* O; Y.

971 [–] Some proposals for the imploying of the poor. *For Brabazon Aylmer*, 1678. 4°.* L, LG, LUG, CS, DT; CH, CU, MH, NU, Y.

972 [–] —[Anr. ed., "imployment."] *By J. Grover, and are to be sold by Francis Smith, and Brab. Aylmer*, 1681. 4°. L, O, C, LUG, OM; CLC, CN, MH, WF, Y.

973 The first and large petition of the citie of London. [*London*], *printed* 1641. 4°.* LT, O, C, EN, DT; CH, IU, MH, TU, WF, Y.

973A —[Anr. ed., "city."] —, 1641. 4°.* L, O, DU; MH, NGT, NU, Y.

First and second parts of Invisible John. 1659. *See* Barkstead, John.

First and second priesthood. [n.p., 1657.] *See* Smith, Humphrey.

First and second volume of letters. 1691. *See* Marana, Giovanni Paolo.

First anniversary. 1655. *See* Marvell, Andrew.

974 Entry cancelled.

First apparition of Bishop Goodman's ghost. [n.p.], 1681. *See* Goodman, Godfrey, *bp.*

First century. 1643. *See* White, John.

First days entertainment. 1657. *See* Davenant, *Sir* William.

975 The first dayes proceedings, at the tryal of Lieut. Col. John Lilburne. [*n.p.*, 1649.] cap., 4°.* DT; CH, MIU, NU.

First epistle. [n.p.], 1648. *See* Niclas, Hendrik.

First exhortation. 1656. *See* Niclas, Hendrik.

First-fruits. 1657. *See* Vaughan, Rice.

976 First, Great Britaines confession. [*London*, 1643.] brs. LT, O.

First last. 1666. *See* Oldfield, John.

First man. 1643. *See* Greene, John.

977 The first new persecution. *For G. Calvert*, 1654. 4°.* LT, MR, LF; CH, CLC.

977A The first part of Dr. Faustus, abreviated [sic]. [*London*], *by I. M[illet], for I. Deacon & C. Dennisson*, [c. 1690]. 12°.* CM.

978 First part of the history of England. *For J. C. and are to be sold by William Grantham, Henry Brome, Thomas Basset, Robert Horne*, 1668. fol. O, CT, LIU, DT; CH, IU, WF.

978A The first part of the last wil and testament. [*London*], *printed*, 1649. 4°.* LT, O, OC; CH, LC, MH.

979 Entry cancelled.

First part of the no lesse rare, then excellent and stately historie, of . . . Palmerin of England. 1664. *See* Hurtado, Luis.

First part of the pleasant and princely. 1678. *See* Deloney, Thomas.

First part of the renowned historie. [n.p.], 1646. *See* C., W.

980 The first part of the Widdow of Watling Street. [*London*], *for Fr. Cowles*, [1650?]. brs. L, CM.

First principles. 1677. *See* Downe, Thomas.

980A The first rule of the glorious virgin S. Clare. *Printed at Rouen*, 1658. 12°. L, O.

980B —[Anr. ed.] *Audomari* [St. Omers], *typis Thomae Geubels*, 1665. 12°. BSM; CN.

981 The first search: after one grand cause. *By Robert White*, [1644]. 4°.* LT, O, C, MR, DT; CH, MB, MH, NNM, NU.

First sermon. 1686. *See* Ellis, Philip.

First state of Mahumedism. 1679. *See* Addison, Lancelot.

981A The first steps, . . . popish pomp. *By T. Dawks*, [1681?]. 4°.* LSD.

First table. 1674. *See* Heylyn, Peter.

982 **Firth, William.** A saints monument. *For Ed. Brewster*, 1662. 8°. L, LSC; IU.

983 [**Fish, Simon.**] The very beggars petition. [*London*], 1680. fol.* O, LG, LVF, MR; CH, MH, NU, WF, Y.

Fish, Thomas. A sermon preached . . . 29th of May. 1685. *See* Fysh, Thomas.

984 [**Fishburn, C.**] A musical entertainment perform'd on November xxii. 1683. *By J. Playford junior*, 1684. 4°.* L; MH, WF.

984A [**Fisher, Abigail.**] An epistle in the love of God. *Printed and sold by T. Sowle*, 1696. 8°.* LF; PHS.

984B [–] A few lines in true love. *By T. Sowle*, 1694. 4°.* L, LF; PSC.

984C [–] —Second edition. —, 1694. 4°.* LF; LC, PH, PSC.

985 [–] —[Anr. ed.] *Printed and sold by T. Sowle*, 1696. fol.* LF, BBN.

986 [–] A salutation of true love. *For Thomas Northcott*, 1690. 4°.* L, LF; PH.

[Fisher, Edward.] An answer to [J. Henry's] sixteen quaeries. 1650. *See* —Christian caveat.

987 [–] An appeale to thy conscience. [*London*], *printed in the nineteenth yeare*, [1643]. 4°.* MADAN 1749. LT, O, C, MR, DT; CH, IU, MH, NU, WF, Y.

988 [–] —Third edition. *Oxford, reprinted by H. Hall*, 1644. 4°. MADAN 1749. L, MR, YM; CH, CLC, OWC, Y.

989 [–] A Christian caveat. *For E. Blackmore*, 1650. 4°. LT, O, CT, MR, DT; MH, NU, WF, Y.

989A [–] —[Anr. ed.] *For R. Lowndes*, 1650. 4°. CS.

989B — —Fourth edition. *For E. Blackmore, and R. Lowndes*, 1651. 4°. O; NCU.

990 — —"Fourth" edition. *For E. Blackmore, and R. Lowndes*, 1652. 4°. L, C, CE, DU, EN; CH, IU, OWC, PU, Y.

991 — —Fifth edition. —, 1653. 4°. L, O, C, CT, ENC; BBE, CLC, MBP, NPT, WF.

992 — —[Anr. ed.] *For Edw: Blackmore, and R. Lowndes*, 1655. 4°. L, LSD; CLC, MH, NU.

993 [–] Faith in five fundamentall principles. *For John Wright*, 1650. 8°. LT, O, OC.

994 [–] The feast of feasts. *Oxford, by Leonard Lichfield*, 1644. 4°.* MADAN 1598. LT, O, C, DC, DT; CH, CN, NU, WF, Y.

995 [–] London's gate to the Lord's table. *For Iohn Wright*, 1647. 12°. LT, O, LCL.

995A [–] Madruddyn y difinyddiaeth diweddaraf. *Gan T. Mabb a A. Coles, dros William Ballard, Bristol*, 1651. 8°: L, AN, CPL.

[–] Manifest and breife discovery. 1646. *See* A., I.

996 [–] The marrow of modern divinity. *By R. W. for G. Calvert*, 1645. 8°. LT, CT, P, DT; CLC.

997 [–] —Second edition. *By R. Leybourn, for Giles Calvert*, 1646. 8°. L, O, LW, AN, SHR, EN; MH, MU, NGT, NU, WF.

997A [–] —Third edition. *For Giles Calvert*, 1646. 8°. L; MU, TO.

997AB [–] —Fourth edition. *By John Dever & Robert Ibbitson for Giles Calvert*, 1646. 8°. LW; TO.

997B [–] —Fifth edition. *By R. Ibbitson for G. Calvert*, 1647. 8°. L; CLC, MH.

998 [–] —Seventh edition. *Printed at London by G. Dawson, for Giles Calvert*, 1650. 8°. L, C, CD.

998A [–] —"Seventh" edition. —, 1651. 8°. MH.

998AB [–] —Eighth edition. *By J. S. for J. Wright*, 1658. 8°. O, LSC, LW, CT; CLC, MB, Y.

998B [–] —Ninth edition. *For Nath. Hillar*, 1699. 12°. AN, GU; CU, MH, Y.

999 [–] The marrow of moderne divinity. The second part. *For John Wright*, 1649. 8°. LT, CM, AN; MH, TO, WF.

999A [–] —Second edition. *By J. S. for John Wright*, 1658. 8°. LW, O; MB, Y.

1000 [–] Questions preparatory to the better, free, . . . Lords Supper. *For Edw: Blackmore, and R. Lowndes*, 1655. 4°.* ORP, MR, NPL, YM; NU.

1001 [–] The Scriptvres harmony. *By Richard Cotes, for William Hope*, 1643. 4°. LT, O, C, EN, DT; CH, IAU, IU, NU.

1002 [–] A touch-stone for a communicant. *For Iohn Wright*, 1647. 12°. LT; CH.

Fisher, Fitzpayne. *See* Fisher, Payne.

1003 **Fisher, George.** Fisher's new spelling book. *For G. Conyers*, 1700. 16°. T.C.III 175. CLC, NC.

1004 **Fisher, James.** The wise virgin. *For John Rothwell*, 1653. 8°. L, C, LCL, LW; CLC, IAU.

1005 — —Second edition. —, 1654. 8°. LT; NPT.

1006 — —Third edition. —, 1656. 8°. O, OB; Y.

1007 — —Fourth edition. —, 1658. 8°. O, LCL.

1008 — —Fifth edition. *For Charles Tyus*, 1664. 8°. L, C; CLC, NPT.

1008A **F[isher], Jo.** Cardologie. *For Nath. Webb*, 1662. 8°. DU.

1009 **[Fisher, John.]** A position and testimony against all swearing. *Printed*, 1692. 8°. L, LF.

1010 **Fisher, Joseph.** The honour of marriage. *For Brabazon Aylmer*, 1695. 4°.* L, O, C, CT, BAMB, BLH; CH, IU, MH, NU, WF, Y.

1011 **Fisher, Payne.** Armachanus redivivus. *Typis Gulielmi Godbid*, 1658. fol.* L, O, C.

1012 [–] Αποβατεριον. Vel in adventum legati. *Typis New-combianis*, 1655. fol.* LT, CCO.

1013 [–] The atchievements of the kings of England since King Egbert. *For L. Curtis, and Tho. Simmons*, 1682. 8°. L; CH, CLC, CN, MH, WF.

1013A —Carmen heroicum in laudes D. Josephi Williamson. 1677. fol. O.

1014 —The catalogue of most of the memorable tombes. *Printed*, 1668. 4°. L, O, LG; CU, IU.

1014A [–] Chronosticon in decollationem Caroli regis. [*London*, 1661.] brs. LT; MH.

1014B [–] —[Anr. ed.] *By Thomas Childe and Leonard Parry*, 1662. brs. L; CH.

1014C [–] D. M. Johannis Freke amigeri, primogeniti Thomae Freke equitis aurati. [*n.p.*, 1656?] fol.* L.

1014D —Deus & rex. *Anno Gratiae*, 1657. fol.* CS.

1015 [–] Deus, et rex. *Lond. è Fleet*, [1675]. 4°. L, O, C, CK, EN; CH, CLC, CN, MH, TU, Y. (var.)

1015A — —[Anr. ed.] [*London*, 1678.] 4°. BBE.

1015B —Elogia sepulchralia. 1675. 4°. O.

1016 —Elogium sepulchrale pro victoriosissimo Georgio Monacho. [*Londini*, 1670.] brs. O.

1017 —Epinicion: vel elogium Lodovici XIV. [*London*, 1658.] fol. L, O, OB, MR; CN.

1018 [–] Epitaphium Roberti Blakii. [*n.p.*], 1658. brs. O.

1019 —Heic jacet bellicosissimus ille Robertus Bartu. [*n.p.*], *Jan.* 1, 1668. brs. O; CH.

1020 [–] Impressio novissima carminis heroici . . . Josephi Williamson. [*Londini, typis Gulielmi Downing*, 1677.] 4°.* L; TU.

1021 [–] Impressio secunda carminis heroici. *Typis T. B.*, 1675. 4°.* L, O, C, CS.

1022 —In celeberrimam naumachiam. *Typis Tho. Newcomb,* 1650. fol.* L, CT, FONMON; CH, CLC, IU, MH, WF.

1022A [–] In obitum serenissimi . . . Olivari. *Excudebat Joannes Field,* 1658. brs. MH.

1022B —In secundam inauguralis . . . Olivari. 1657. fol.* LLL.

1023 [–] Inavgvratio Olivariana. *Typis Newcombianis,* 1654. 4°. L, O, CK, EN, ES; BN, CH, CN, MH, WF, Y.

1024 ——Second edition. *Impensis Edoardi Blackmore,* 1656. fol. O, CT; IU, MH, Y.

1025 No entry.

1026 —Integerrimo vere viro, . . . Gulielmus Freke. [*n.p.*], 1657. brs. O.

1027 [–] Irenodia gratulatoria, sive . . . Oliveri Cromwelli. [*London*], *typis T. Newcomb, prostant à Johanne Holden,* 1652. 4°. LT, O, C, EN, BQ; CH, CN, PL, WF, Y.

1028 [–] Juxta suorum cineres . . . Coll. Henricus Norwood. [*London*], *typis Gulielmi Downing,* 1690. brs. O.

1029 —Marston-Moor: sive de obsidione prælioque. *Typis Thomæ Newcomb,* 1650. 4°. LT, O, C, CT, EN; CH, CN, PL, WF, Y.

1030 [–] Miscellania quædam eiusdem authoris. [*London,* 1655.] fol.* IU.

1031 —Oratio anniversaria. *Typis Rogeri Danielis, & væno extant per Edoardum Blackmoore,* 1655. fol.* L, C, LMT, CT; CH, CN, MH, TU, WF, Y.

1032 [–] Oratio secunda anniversaria. *Typis J. G. & væn. per Edoardum Blackmore,* 1657. fol.* L, C, LMT, NE; IU, MH, TU, WF, Y.

1033 [–] Pæan triumphalis. *Typis Rogeris Danielis, & venum prostant per Edoardum Blackmoore,* 1657. fol.* L, C, LMT; CATHOLIC UNIV., CH, IU.

1034 —Piscatoris poemata. *Typis Thomæ Newcombii,* 1656. fol. L, O, LMT, CT; CH, IU, MH, PU, TU, WF, Y. (var.)

1035 [–] Poems on several choice and various subjects. *By Ja: Cottrel; to be sold by S. Speed,* 1663. 8°. L.

1036 [–] Pro navali Anglorum. 1653. fol.* L, MR; MH.

1037 [–] Rex & episcopus; vel panegyricum pro hierarchia restaurata. *Typis Rogeri Danielis & J. de Rubrâ-Manu,* 1662. fol.* CT, DU; MH.

1038 [–] Solis septentrionalis. *Londoni [sic], typis R. H. væn per Ed. Blackmore,* 1656. fol.* L, LMT, OB, CT; CH, IU, MH, TU, WF, Y.

1039 [–] A synopsis of heraldry. *For L. Curtis, and T. Simmons,* 1682. 8°. L, O, CT, MAU, BLH; CH, CN, MH, WF, Y.

1040 —Threnodia triumphalis in obitum . . . Olivari. *Excudebat Ja: Cottrel,* 1658. fol.* L, O, CCO, MR, NE; CATHOLIC UNIV.

1040A ——[Anr. ed.] *By James Cottrel,* 1659. fol.* GU; CATHOLIC UNIV., MH, WF.

1041 [–] The tombes, monuments, and sepulchral inscriptions. *For the author,* [1684]. 4°. L, O, LL, MR, EN; CH, CLC, CN, MH.

1042 [–] —[Anr. ed.] [*London*], *from the fleet* [1684]. 4°. L, O, C; CLC, WF, Y.

1043 [–] —[Anr. ed.] *For the author,* [1688]. 4°. O, C.

1043A [–] Unio beatissima mitræ & coronæ. [*London,* 1662?] fol.* Y.

1043B [–] Vtriusque primariis. [*London*], *typis Gulielmi Downing,* 1677. 4°. * O.

1044 —Veni: vidi: vici: the triumphs. *For Iohn Tey,* 1652. 8°. LT, O, C, CT, LLU, ES; CH, CN, MH, WF, Y.

1045 **Fisher, Peter.** For the right worshipful the knights . . . of Suffolke. *For Christopher Meredith,* 1648. 4°.* LT.

1046 **Fisher, Samuel,** *d. 1665.* An additionall appendix to the book entituled Rusticus. *For Robert Wilson,* 1660. 4°.* L, O, LF, BBN, DU; CH, MH, NCU, PL, WF, Y.

1047 —Αποκρυπτα αποκαλυπτα. Velata. *For Robert Wilson,* 1661. 4°.* L, O, CT, BBN, GU; CH, MH, PH, WF, Y.

1048 [–] Baptism before, or after. *By J. D. to be sold by Francis Smith,* 1669. fol. L.

1049 —Christianismus redivivus, Christndom both unchrist'ned. *By Henry Hills, to be sold by Francis Smith,* 1655. fol. O, LF, LLL, ORP; PH, RPJ, SE, WF.

1050 [–] Christ's light springing. [*n.p.,* 1660.] cap., 4°.* DU; CH, MH, PH, PSC, WF, Y.

1051 —Επισκοπος αποσκοπος. The bishop busied. [*London*], *printed, August* 1662. 4°. L, LCL, LF, BBN; CH, MH, NCD, PH, PSC, WF.

1052 Entry cancelled.
——[Anr. ed.] [*n.p.,* 1662?] *See* —Testimony.

1052A–3 Entries cancelled.
—Honour the King. 1673. *See* Fisher, Samuel, *d. 1681.*
—Love-token. 1655. *See* Fisher, Samuel, *d. 1681.*

1054 —One antidote more. *For Robert Wilson,* [1660?]. 4°. L, O, C, LF, BBN; CH, MH, PH, PSC, WF, Y.

1055 —Παιδοβαπτιζοντες παιδιζοντες. Baby-baptism. *By Henry Hills, to be sold by Will. Larnar, and Richard Moon,* 1653. fol. C, LF, ORP, AN, BAMB, SA, CD; IU, NPT, NU, PH, WF, Y.

1056 —Rusticus ad academicos. *For Robert Wilson,* 1660. 4°. L, O, C, LF, E, DT; CH, CN, MH, PH, WF, Y.

1057 —The scorned Quakers true and honest account. [*London,* 1656.] cap., 4°.* LT, O, LF, CT, BBN, EN; CH, MH, PH, WF.

1058 —The testimony of truth exalted. [*London*], *printed,* 1679. fol. L, O, C, LF, OC; BN, CH, MH, PH, WF, Y.

1059 —To the Parliament of England, and the several members. [*London,* 1659.] cap., 4°.* L, O, C, LF, BBN; CLC, MH, PH, PSC, Y.

1059A **Fisher, Samuel,** *d. 1681.* Honour the King. A sermon. *For George Calvert, and Hierom Gregory, in Birmingham,* 1673. 4°.* BC; IU, Y.

1059B —A love-token for mourners. *By A.M. for T. Underhill,* 1655. 12°. O, LCL, LW, CS; NPT.

1060 **F[isher], T[homas].** Warlike directions. Second edition. *By Thomas Harper,* 1643. 8°. L, C.

1061 [–] —Third edition. —, 1644. 8°. O.

1061A **Fishing Company [Scotland].** Act by the general meeting . . . licensing the exportation of herring . . . [12 July 1678]. *Edinburgh, by the heir of Andrew Anderson,* 1678. brs. ALDIS 2110.7. EN.

—Names of the members. [*n.p.,* 1672.] *See* title.

1062 **Fiske, John.** The watering of the olive plant. *By Samuel Green at Cambridg in New-England.* 1657. 8°. EVANS 45. MB, MHS, NN.

1063 **Fitch, James.** An explanation of the solemn advice. *Boston in New-England: by S. Green for I. Vsher,* 1683. 8°. EVANS 341. CHS, MB, MBA, MHS, Y.

1064 —The first pinciples [*sic*] of the doctrine of Christ. *Boston, by John Foster,* 1679. 8°. EVANS 267. CHW, MH, NN, V.

1065 —An holy connexion. *Cambridge [Mass.], by Samuel Green,* 1674. 12°.* EVANS 187. CH, MB, MH, MWA, Y.

1066 —Peace the end of the perfect and upright. *Cambridge [Mass.]: by Samuel Green,* 1672. 4°.* EVANS 167. CH, MH, MWA, NN, RPJ.

1066A **Fitch, John.** John Fitch, esq; appellant . . . hardships. [*n.p.,* 1698?] brs. L.

1067 **Fitton, Alexander.** A reply to a paper, intituled, A true account. [*London,* 1685.] fol. L.

1068 **Fitz–Brian, R.** The good old cause dress'd. *For G. C.* 1659. 4°.* LT, O, C, MR; HR, CLC, CN, NN, NU, PL, WF.

1069–70 Entries cancelled.

Fitz–Geoffry, Charles. *See* Fitzjeffrey, Charles.

1071 **Fitzgerald, Edward.** The copie of the Lord Fitzgeralds letter intercepted. *By Jane Coe,* 1647. 4°.* LT, LVF, DN; WF.

1072 **Fitzgerald, David.** A narrative of the Irish Popish plot. *For Tho. Cockerill,* 1680. fol.* L, O, C, EN, DT; CH, CU, LC, MH, WF, Y.

1073 **Fitzgerald, Gerald.** A letter, or paper, signed by. *Printed at Dublin, by W. Bladen,* 1651. 4°.* DIX 89. L, CD, DK.

1074 **Fitz–Gerald, John.** The narrative of. *For Richard Janeway,* 1681. fol.* L, O, CM, MR, DN; CH, MBA, TU, WF, Y.

1075 **Fitzgerald, Maurice.** A short narrative of. [*London?*], 1680. fol.* O, CM, LNC, MR, BLH; CH, CU, MU, PU.

1076 [–] A true discovery of the Irish Popish plot. colop: *By N. Thompson for the author,* 1681. brs. L, O, OP, HH; CH, MH, PU, WF, Y.

1077 [**Fitzgerald, Robert.**] Additions au traité de l'eau de mer douce. *A Londres,* 1684. 8°.* L.

1078 [–] Aqua salsa dulcorata. *Impensis Edvardi Brewster,* 1683. 4°.* L, OC, EC, GU; CH, CLC, WF, Y, HC.

1079 [–] —Second edition. *Excudebat J. Gain, pro Gulielmo Cademan,* 1684. 8°.* I, O, LWL, OC, GK; BN.

1080 [–] A brief of two treatises. [*London,* 1684?] brs. L, OC.

1080A [–] —[Anr. ed., mentions "the late King."] [*London,* 1685?] brs. L.

[–] Certificates of several captains. [*n.p.*], 1685. *See* title.

1081 [–] L'eau de mer douce. 1683. 4°.* BN.

1081A [–] —Troisieme edition. *A Londres* 1684. 4°.* MR.

1081B [–] Estratto di due trattati. [*London?* 1695.] fol.* L.

1082 [–] Farther additions to a small treatise called Salt-water sweetned. Ninth edition. *By John Harefinch,* 1684. 8°.* L, O, LG; CH, NC.

1083 No entry.

1084 [–] —Tenth edition. [*London*], —, 1685. 8°.* L, GK; NN.

1085 —Hasser de aqua salada dulce. [*London?* 1683.] 4°. L, C.

1086 —Nouvelles experiences. *A Londres,* 1684. 4°.* L, MR.

1087 [–] Salt-water sweetned. *For Will. Cademan,* 1683. 4°.* T.C.I 49. L, O, C, EN, DT; CH, CLC, MH, WF, Y.

1087A [–] —Second edition. *For William Cademan,* 1683. 4°.* LWL, CS.

1088 ——[Anr. ed.] *Dublin, Joseph Ray,* 1683. 4°.* DIX 200. DT, CD.

1088A ——Third edition. *For William Cadman,* 1683. 4°.* LSD; MH.

1089 ——Fourth edition. *For John Harefinch,* 1684. 4°.* L, O, C, LWL, NE; NAM, PL, WU.

1089A ——Fifth edition. *By John Harefinch,* 1684. 8°. PL.

1090 [–] The supplement to a small treatise called Salt-water sweetned. Eighth edition. *By John Harefinch,* 1684. 8°.* L; BN, LC, Y.

1091 **Fitz–Harris, Edward.** The confession of. colop: *For S. Carr,* 1681. brs. L, O, C, LG, DT; CH, LC, MH, MU, WF, Y.

1092 ——[Anr. ed.] —, 1681. fol.* L, O, C, BC, LSD; CH, CN, LC, MH, PU, TU, Y.

1093 ——[Anr. ed.] colop: *Edinburgh, re-printed by the heir of Andrew Anderson,* 1681. cap., fol.* ALDIS 2266. AU, EN; MH, NC, Y.

1093A ——[Anr. ed.] [*Dublin,* 1681.] cap., fol.* DI.

—Some short but necessary animadversions. 1681. *See* title.

1094 —The last speech of. colop: *For R. Harbottle, and sold by R. Janeway,* 1681. brs. L, O, C, HH, LSD; CH, CN, MH, WF, Y.

Fitz-Harris his farewel. [*n.p.,* 1681.] *See* Gibbs, Richard.

1095 Fitz-Harys's last sham detected. colop: *For R. Baldwin,* 1681. cap., fol.* L, O, LG, DU, MR; CH, MH, TU, WF, Y.

1096 **Fitzherbert, Sir Anthony.** The new natura brevium. *For W. Lee, M. Walbank, D. Pakeman, and G. Bedell,* 1652. 8°. L, O, C, LIL, BAMB; CH, CN, LC, MHL, NCL, WF.

1097 ——[Anr. ed.] *By John Streater, James Flesher, and Henry Twyford, assigns of Richard Atkins and Edward Atkins,* 1666. 8°. L, OJ, CT, RU, DT; CLC, CN, LC, MHL, MU.

1098 ——[Anr. ed.] *By George Sawbridge, Thomas Roycroft, and William Rawlins, assigns of Richard Atkins and Edward Atkins,* 1677. 8°. T.C.I 263. L, C, SA, DT; CH, LC, MB, MHL, NCL, PUL.

1099 ——[Anr. ed.] *By W. Rawlins, S. Roycroft, and M. Flesher, assigns of Richard and Edward Atkins,* 1686. 8°. L, OC, LLU; LC, MHL, Y.

1100 ——[Anr. ed.] *By W. Rawlins, S. Roycroft, and M. Flesher, assigns of Richard and Edward Atkins, to be sold by Charles Harper, William Crooke, and Richard Tonson,* 1687. 8°. T.C.II 195. O, CT, LIL, NPL; CH, MHL, NS, PUL, Y.

1101 Entry cancelled. Ghost.

1102 **Fitzherbert, Thomas.** A treatise concerning policy. *For Abel Roper,* 1652. 4°. L, O, C, LW, SP; BN, CH, CU, NU, WF, Y.

1103 —A treatise of policy. . . . Part I. Third edition. *London [St. Omer], by Thomas Hales,* 1695. 8°. L, RU, WARE; CL, CLC, CN, CU, WF, WU.

1103A —A treatise of policy . . . Part II. Third edition. *London [St. Omer], by Thomas Hales,* 1695. 8°. DU; CN.

1104 —Third edition. *London [Saint Omer], by Thomas Hales,* 1696. 8°. L; CN, WU.

1104A ——[Anr. ed.] —, 1697. 8°. CN, CU, MH, MSL, WF, WU.

1104B **Fitzjeffrey, Charles.** The blessed birth-day. Third edition. *By T. M. for Stephen Chatfield,* 1654. 8°.* LT, O; WF.

1104C [–] God's blessing upon the providers of corne. *For M. S.,* 1648. 4°. LT, LUG; CH, CU, NC.

Fitzroy, James. *See* Monmouth, James Fitzroy, *duke.*

Fitz–Simon, Thomas. Primer more ample. Rouen, 1669. *See title.*

Fitzsmith, Richard. Syzygiasticon. 1654. *See* Almanacs.

1105 **Fitz–Waters.** Colonell Fitz-Waters, his petition to . . . Commons. *Printed,* 1642. 4°.* LT, DN; Y.

1106 **Fitz–William, John.** A sermon preach'd . . . 9th of September, 1683. *For Will. Nott,* 1683. 4°.* T.C.II 38. L, O, C, LSD, WCA; CH, MH, NU, WF, Y.

Five captious questions. 1673. *See* Gataker, Charles.

Five cases of conscience. 1666. *See* Sanderson, Robert, *bp.*

Five discourses. 1700. *See* Leslie, Charles.

Five faithfull brothers. 1660. *See* H., T.

1107 Five important queries humbly propounded. *By Nathaniel Thompson,* 1681. 4°.* L, O, LF, CS, LSD; CH, CN, CU, MH, PU, Y.

Five letters concerning. [n.p.], 1690. *See* LeClerc, Jean.

1108 Five letters from a gentleman in Scotland. *[London,* 1689.] cap., fol.* LL, EN; CH, CN, Y.

1109 Entry cancelled.

Five lookes over the professors of the English Bible. 1642. *See* Walker, Henry.

Five love-letters from. 1678. *See* Alcoforado, Marianna d'.

1110 Five love-letters written by a Cavalier. *For R. Bentley, and M. Magnes,* 1683. 12°. T.C.I 512. L; MH, WF.

1111 —[Anr. ed.] *For R. Bentley,* 1694. 12°. L; TSM, WF, Y.

1112 Five matters of state. *For F. Coules, and T. Bates,* 1642. 4°.* O, OB, YM; MB, WF, Y.

1113 Five merry wives of Lambeth. [1680?] brs. O.

1114 Five most noble speeches spoken to His Majestie. *For John Greensmith,* 1641. 4°.* LT, LG, CCA, LNC, YM; CH, LC, MH, NU, WF, Y.

1115 Five new letters from Ostend. *For D. M.,* 1678. 8°.* O, EN.

1116 Five orthodox sermons. *By W. Godbid, and are to be sold by several stationers,* 1659. 8°. C.

1117 Five philosophical questions. *For George Badger,* 1650. 4°.* LT, C, GK, DT; CN, CSS, IU, NU, WF.

1117A —[Anr. ed.] *For G. B.,* 1653. 4°.* BC.

1118 Five proposals presented to the General Council of the officers. *By J. C. for Livewel Chapman,* 1659. brs. LT, O, LG.

1118A Five queries humbly tender'd . . . East India silks. *[London?* 1696.] brs. L; MH, Y.

1119 Five questions propounded to the people of England. [n.p., 1690.] brs. L, O, OC; WF.

1120 Five remarkable passages, which have very lately happened. *For F. Cowles, and T. Bates,* [1642]. 4°.* LT, O, C, BR, YM; CSS, MH, MU, NU, WF, Y.

1120A Five romances in one volume. *For Francis Saunders,* 1696. 8°. L (t.p.).

1121 Five severall papers, delivered by the king. *By Robert Ibbitson,* [1648]. 4°.* LT; MH, TU, WF.

Five short treatises. [n.p., 1688.] *See* Walker, Obadiah.

1122 Five speciall passages. *For Edward Blackmore, Iune 8.* 1642. 4°.* O, OC, CJ, BAMB, LIU, YM; CN, CSS, LC, MH, Y.

1122A —[Anr. ed.] —, 1642. *May 8 [sic].* 4°.* WF.

1123 Five strange and wonderfull prophesies. *[London,* 1651.] cap., 4°.* LT, DM; MH, WF.

1124 Five strange wonders, in the North and West of England. *By W. Thomas,* 1659. 4°.* O; CH, CSS, WF.

Five strange wonders of the world. [n.p.], 1674. *See* Price, Laurence.

Five treatises of the philosophers stone. 1652. *See* Alphonso, *King of Portugal.*

1125 Five wonders in the month of July. *H. Jones,* 1691. 8°.* L, O.

1126 Five vvonders seene in England. Second edition. *By J. C.,* 1646. 4°.* LT; WSG, Y.

1126A Entry cancelled.

Five years of King Iames. 1643. *See* Wilson, Arthur.

1127 Flagellum Dei: or, a collection. *For C. VV.,* 1668. 4°.* L, O; WF, WSL.

Flagellum flagelli: or. 1645. *See* Sadler, John.

Flagellum Mercurii anti-ducalis: or, the author. [n.p., 1679.] *See* Gibbon, John.

1127A Flagellum muliebre or a satyr. *Printed,* 1695. 4°.* LIU; Y.

Flagellum: or. 1663. *See* Heath, James.

1128 Flagellvm poeticvm: or, a scourge for a wilde poet. *For J. L.,* 1672. 4°.* L, LG, OC, OW, DT; CH, INU.

Flagitiosus Mercurius flagellatus. [n.p., 1697.] *See* Partridge, John.

1129 **Flamand.** The art of preserving and restoring health. *For R. Bently; H. Bonwick; and S. Manship,* 1697. 12°. T.C.III 14. L, C, LCS, LWL, OC, MAU; CH, NN, WF.

1130 Flaming islands: or, a full description . . . Fyal. *[London],* for Phillip Brooksby, 1672. 4°.* L, LWL; WF.

1131 —[Anr. ed.] *Reprinted Edinburgh,* 1672. 4°. ALDIS 1944. EN.

1132 A flaming whip for lechery. *For Eliz. Harris,* 1700. 8°. L; CH, Y.

1132A **Flaminius, Marcus Antonius.** The scholars vade mecum. *By T. Sawbridge; to be sold by Rowland Reynolds,* 1674. 8°. L, O; IU.

1133 ——[Anr. ed.] *For Rowland Reynolds,* [1675?]. 8°. T.C.I 212. C; MB.

Flamma sine fumo. 1662. *See* Watkyns, Rowland.

1134 **Flamsteed, John.** A correct tide table. *For J. Baker,* [1683]. brs. O.

1134A [–] ——[Anr. ed.] —, [1684]. brs. O.

1134B ——[Anr. ed.] *For J. Stafford, and are to be had at Captain Bakers. And at Mr. Mordents,* [1687?]. brs. L.

1135 ——[Anr. ed.] *For William Court,* [1692]. brs. O.

1136 Entry cancelled.
—De inaequalitate. 1672. *See* Horrocks, Jeremiah. Opera posthuma.

1137 [–] The doctrine of the sphere. *By A. Godbid and J. Play-ford*, 1680. 4°. L, O, CJ, LIU, CD; CLC, PL, RBU, WF, Y.

1138 —Flemstadts most strange and wonderful prophecy. [*London*, 1695.] 4°.* L.

1139 ——[Anr. ed.] *For E. Golding*, 1695. 4°.* L.
Flanders or, an exact. 1658. *See* Lupton, Donald.
Flanders: or, the Spanish. 1691. *See* Echard, Laurence.
[**Flatman, Thomas.**] Introduction to astrology. 1661. *See* Phillips, John.
[–] Montelion, 1660. [n.p., 1659.] *See* Almanacs: Phillips, John.

1140 [–] Naps upon Parnassus. *By express order from the wits, for N. Brook*, 1658. 8°. MADAN 2363. LT, O, OB, OW, LLU; CH, CLC, CN, MH, WCL, WF, Y.

1141 —On the death of our late sovereign lord King Charles II. *For Benj. Tooke*, 1685. fol.* T.C.II 126. L, O, LLP, CT, MR; CH, CN, MH, TU, WF, Y, AVP.

1142 ——[Anr. ed.] *Edinburgh, re-printed by the heir of Andrew Anderson*, 1685. 4°.* ALDIS 2547. EN, AU; CH.

1143 —On the death of the illustrious Prince Rupert. *For Benj. Tooke*, 1683. fol.* L, O, LLP, LLU, EN; CH, MH, TU, WF, Y.

1144 —On the death of the Right Honorable the Duke of Ormond. *For Benj. Tooke*, 1688. fol.* L, MR; CH, MH, TU, Y.

1145 Entry cancelled. Ghost.

1146 —On the death of the Right Honorable Thomas Earl of Ossory. colop: *Printed at Dublin by Benjamin Tooke and John Crooke. Sold by Mary Crooke*, 1680. cap., fol.* DIX 176. L.

1147 —On the death of the truly valiant and loyal George, duke of Albemarle. *For Henry Brome*, 1670. fol.* L, O, CS, EC, LNC; BN, CH, IU, MH, TU, WF, Y.

1148 ——[Anr. ed.] *Dublin, reprinted by Benjamin Tooke to be sold by Samuel Dancer*, [1670?]. 4°.* DIX 361. L, DT.

1149 [–] A panegyrick to his renowed [*sic*] Majestie, Charles the Second. *For Henry Marsh*, 1660. brs. LT, O; MH, WF, Y.

1150 —A pindarique ode on the death of . . . earl of Ossory. *By J. G. for Benjamin Tooke*, 1681. fol.* T.C.I 418. L, O, LG, CT, LSD; CH, CN, MH, TU, WF, Y.

1151 —Poems and songs. *By S. and B. G. for Benjamin Took, and Jonathan Edwin*, 1674. 8°. T.C.I 170. L, O, LW, CT, DU, LNC; CH, CN, LC, MH, NC, NNM, Y.

1152 ——Second edition. —, 1676. 8°. T.C.I 261. L, O, LLL, CT; BN, CH, IU, LC, MH, TU, Y.

1153 ——Third edition. *For Benjamin Tooke*, 1682. 8°. T.C.I 466. L, O, LVD, BC, LLU, EN; CH, CU, MH, TU, WF, Y. (var.)

1154 ——Fourth edition. —, 1686. 8°. T.C.II 172. L, O, LVD, CT, LIU, GK; CH, CN, LC, MH, MU, NP, WF, Y, AVP.

1155 —A song for St. Cæcilia's day. *For John Carr*, 1686. brs. MH, TU.

1155A The flattering damsel. [*London*], *for John Andrews*, [1650–56]. brs. L.

1156 A flattering elegie, vpon the death of King Charles. [*n.p.*], *printed*, 1649. 4°.* O, LVF; CH, MH.

1156A The flattering young man and the modest maid. [*n.p.*, 1700?] brs. EN.

1157 **Flavell, John.** The balm of the Covenant. *For J. Har-ris*, 1688. 12°. T.C.II 215. L, LCL, EN; CLC, MIU, Y.

1158 —Divine conduct. *By R. W. for Francis Tyton*, 1678. 8°. T.C.I 328. L, O, C, LCL, LSC; CH, IU, NCU, NU, Y.

1158A ——[Anr. ed.] *Edinburgh, by John Cairns*, 1681. 8°. ALDIS 2267.I. CLC.

1158B ——[Anr. ed.] *Edinburgh, by the heir of Andrew Anderson*, 1682. 8°. CDA.

1159 ——[Anr. ed.] *By S. Bridge, for Tho. Parkhurst*, 1698. 8°. T.C.III 85. L, E; MH, Y.

1159A —England's duty. *For Matthew Wotton*, 1689. 8°. T.C.II 269. LW; MH, MHS, NU, V, Y.

1160 —An exposition of the Assemblies catechism. *For Tho. Cockerill*, 1692. 8°. T.C.II 451. L, O, C, LCL; MB, PL.

1160A ——Second edition. —, 1695. 8°. ENC; NN, V.

1161 ——[Anr. ed.] *Edinburgh, re-printed by the heirs and successors of Andrew Anderson*, 1695. 12°. ALDIS 3460.5. C, EN; CLC.

1162 —The fountain of life opened. *By Rob. White, for Francis Tyton*, 1673. 4°. T.C.I 116. L, O; CH, FU, MH, NU, TSM, Y.

1163 ——Second edition. *For Thomas Parkhurst*, 1698. 4°. T.C.III 85. L, LSC, SHR, E; CH, CLC, MH, NN, PU, RBU, TSM, WF.

1164 ——Third edition. —, 1700. 4°. T.C.III 205. L, LCL, LW, MR; NGT, SE, TSM, AVP.

1165 —Husbandry spiritualized. *Printed and are to be sold by Robert Boulter*, 1669. 4°. T.C.I 8. L, O, C, BLH; CH, IU, MH, NU, PU, WF.

1165A ——[Anr. ed.] 1671. 4°. GU (impf.).

1166 ——Third edition. *Printed, to be sold by Robert Boulter*, 1674. 4°. L, LCL, LSC, OB, LLU; IU, MB, WU, Y.

1167 ——Fourth edition. —, 1678. 4°. L, LWL, AN; CLC, CN, MH, NCD, WU.

1167A ——[Anr. ed.] *For T. Parkhurst and D. Newman*, 1693. 8°. T.C.II 521. L; CLC.

1168 ——Sixth edition. *For T. Parkhurst: and H. Newman*, 1700. 12°. T.C.III 164. O; MH.

1169 —The method of grace. *By M. White, for Francis Tyton*, 1681. 4°. T.C.I 414. L, LSC; CLC, IU, NCD, NU, TSM, WF, Y.

1170 ——Second edition. *For Tho. Parkhurst*, 1699. 4°. T.C.III 146. L, LCL, LW, AN, E; CDA, CH, NR, Y.

1171 [–] Movnt Pisgah. *By J. R. for Matthew Wotton*, 1689. 4°. T.C.II 269. L, LW, DT; MH, NU.

1171A —Navigation spiritualized. *By J. C. for Thomas Fabian*, 1677. 8°. T.C.I 296. CLC, Y.

1172 ——[Anr. ed.] —, 1682. 8°. L; Y.

1172A ——[Anr. ed.] *By F. Collins for Thomas Fabian*, 1690. 8°. CLC.

1173 ——Fourth edition. *For M. Fabian*, 1698. 8°. T.C.III 85. L, E.

1173A — —"Fourth" edition. *For Thomas Parkhurst, 1698. 8°.* WF.

1174 —A new compass. *For the author, sold by R. Tomlins, 1664.* CLC, CN.

1175 —Πλανηλογια. A succinct. *By R. Roberts, for Tho. Cockerill, 1691. 8°.* T.C.II 331. LCL, LW, AN, DU, SHR; CH, MBA, MH, NU, WF.

1176 —Πνευματολογια. A treatise. *For Francis Tyton, 1685. 4°.* L, O, LSC, SHR; CLC, NU, VC, WF, Y.

1177 — —Second edition. *By J. D. for Tho. Parkhurst, 1698. 4°.* T.C.III 85. L, O, LSD, EC, E; CH, FU, IU, NF, NPT, NU, WF.

1177A — A practical treatise of fear. *By H. H. for Robert Boulter, 1681. 8°.* NAM.

1178 — —[Anr. ed.] —, 1682. 8°. L.

1179 — —[Anr. ed.] *[Edinburgh], printed [by John Reid], 1684. 12°.* Y.

1180 —Preparations for sufferings. *For R. Boulter, 1681. 8°.* T.C.I 471. LCL, LW; OLU.

1180A [–] Proposals for printing the whole works of. *[For Thomas Parkhurst, Andrew Bell, and Thomas Cockerill], 1700. fol.** DL.

1180B —The reasonableness of personal reformation. *For Thomas Cockerill, 1691. 12°.* T.C.II 355. GU; CU, MH, MHS, MIU, MWA, WF.

1181 —Mr. John Flavell's remains. *For Tho. Cockerill, 1691. 8°.* L, O, LCL.

1182 — —[Anr. ed.] *Belfast, by Patrick Neill and Company, 1700. 12°.* YOUNG (dispersed?).

1183 —Sacramental meditations. *For Jacob Sampson, 1679. 12°.* T.C.I 381. LCL; CH, NU, WF.

1184 — —[Anr. ed.] *Glasgow. By Robert Sanders, 1680. 12°.* ALDIS 2197.5. I.

1185 — —[Anr. ed.] *For Nath. Crouch. 1690. Sixes.* T.C.II 283. L, C, LLU; CLC.

1186 — —Fourth edition. —, 1700. 12°. L; MBA.

1187 —A saint indeed. *By W. R. and are to be sold by Robert Boulter, 1668. 8°.* O, LCL.

1187A — —[Anr. ed.] *By A. I. and to be sold by Robert Boulter, 1668. 8°.* PL.

1187B — —[Anr. ed.] *By W. R. to be sold by Robert Boulter, 1670. 8°.* BSO; CLC, WF.

1188 — —[Anr. ed.] —, 1671. 8°. L; CH, CLC, NCD.

1189 — —[Anr. ed.] *By T. N. to be sold by Robert Boulter, 1673. 8°.* L, O, C.

1190 — —[Anr. ed.] *By W. R. to be sold by Robert Boulter, 1675. 8°.* T.C.I 214. MR; NU.

1191 — —[Anr. ed.] —, 1677. 8°. C; IU, NGT.

1191aA — —[Anr. ed.] —, 1680. 8°. CDA.

1191A — —[Anr. ed.] *For T. Parkhurst, and D. Newman, 1684. 12°.* T.C.II 119. O; Y.

1192 — —[Anr. ed.] —, 1689. 12°. LCL; CH.

1193 — —[Anr. ed.] *Edinburgh, by the heirs and successors of Andrew Anderson, 1696. 12°.* ALDIS 3560.5. EN.

1194 — —[Anr. ed.] *For Tho. Parkhurst, and H. Newman, 1698. 12°.* T.C.II 521. L, LSC.

1195 —The seamans companion. *For Francis Titon, 1676. 8°.* T.C.I 251. L.

1196 — —[Anr. ed.] *Glasgow, by Robert Sanders, 1681. 12°.* ALDIS 2267.5. I.

1197 —A token for mourners. *For Robert Boulter, 1674. 8°.* T.C.I 176. L, O, C, LCL, OC; CH, CLC, WF.

1198 [–] —[Anr. ed.] —, 1680. 12°. L, O; CLC, Y.

1198A — —[Anr. ed.] *For T. Parkhurst, and D. Newman, 1690. 12°.* T.C.II 326. EN.

1199 — —[Anr. ed.] *For Tho. Parkhurst, 1694. 12°.* T.C.II 521. NU.

1200 —The touchstone of sincerity. *By M. White, for F. Tyton, 1679. 12°.* T.C.I 328. L, O, LCL; PMA, Y.

1201 —- —[Anr. ed.] *Edinburgh, by the heir of A. Anderson, 1684. 12°.* ALDIS 2452. I.

1202 — —[Anr. ed.] *For Tho. Parkhurst, 1698. 12°.* T.C.III 85. L; MB.

1203 Entry cancelled.
—Tractatus. Oxonii, 1651. *See* Flavell, John, *of Wadham College.*

1204 —Two treatises. *By H. H., for Robert Boulter, 1682. 8°.* T.C.I 471. LCL; CLC, IU, LC, TU, WF, Y.

1205 — —[Anr. ed.] *Glasgow, by Robert Sanders, 1684. 12°.* ALDIS 2453. GM; TO.

1205A —Vindiciæ legis & foederis; or, a reply. *For M. Wotton, 1690. 12°.* LW; NPT.

1205B **Flavell, John,** *of Wadham College.* Tractatus de demonstratione methodicus. *Oxonii, excudebat H. Hall impensis Guil. Webb, 1651. 8°.* MADAN 2167. O, LW, BC; CLC, Y.

1206 **Flavell, Phineas.** The grand evil discovered. *For Samuel Crouch, 1676. 8°.* T.C.I 244. O, C.

1207 **Fléchier, Valentin Esprit,** *bp.* The life of the Emperour Theodosius. *By F. L. for F. Saunders; and T. Bennet and J. Knapton, 1693. 8°.* T.C.II 452. L, O, C, E, DT; CH, CU, NC, TU, WF, Y.

1208 **F[lecknoe], R[ichard].** Animadversions on a petition delivered to the honourable House of Parliament. *[London], printed, 1653. 8°.* OB; CH, NR.

1209 —Ariadne deserted by Theseus. *[London], printed, 1654. 8°.** LLP; CH.

—Characters made at several times. 1673. *See* —Collection of the choicest.

1210 —A collection of the choicest epigrams and characters of. *[London], for the author, 1673. 8°.* L, C; CH, CLC, CN, MH, TU, WF.

1211 —The damoiselles à la mode. A comedy. *For the author, 1667. 8°.* L, O, OW, EN; CH, CN, MH, WF, Y.

1212 [–] The diarium, or journall. *For Henry Herringman, 1656. 8°.* LT, O; CH, CN, MH, NC, WF, Y.

1213 —Enigmaticall characters. *[London], anno Dom. 1658. 8°.* L, O; CH, CLC, IU, LC, MH, RHT, WF, Y.

1214 —Rich. Flecknoe's Ænigmatical characters. Second edition. *By R. Wood, for the author, 1665. 8°.* L, O, LVD; CH, CLC, MBP, MH, RHT, WF.

1215 Entry cancelled.
— —[Anr. ed.] 1669. *See* —Sixty-nine.

1216 —Epigrams made at several times. *For the author,* 1673. 8°. CLC, IU, WF.

1217 —Epigrams of all sorts, I book. *For the author,* 1669. 8°.* L, O, CASTLE ASHBY; CH, WF.

1218 — —Second edition. *For the author and Will. Crook,* 1670. 12°. T.C.I 39. L, O, C, LVD, EN; CH, CN, LC, MH, WF, Y.

1219 — —[Anr. ed.] *For the author,* 1671. 8°. L, O, LLU; CH, CN, NP, OSU, WF, Y.

1220 —Erminia. *For the author,* 1661. 8°. L, LVD, EN; CH.

1221 — —[Anr. ed.] *For William Crook,* 1665. 8°. O; WF.

1222 [–] Euterpe revived. *Printed at London, and are to be sold by the booksellers of London and Westminster,* 1675. 8°. T.C.I 197. L, O; CH, MH.

1223 —A farrago of several pieces. *For the author,* 1666. 8°. O, LLU; CH, CLC, IU, NR, WF.

1224 [–] Fifty five enigmatical characters. *For William Crook,* 1665. 8°. O; CN, NPT.

1225 —Heroick portraits. *By Ralph Wood, for the author,* 1660. 8°. L, O, LIU; BN, CH, CLC, IU, MH.

1226 —The idea of His Highness Oliver. *Printed,* 1659. 8°. L, O; CH, IU.

1227 [–] The life of Tomaso. [*n.p.*], *for the author,* 1667. 8°. O.

1228 [–] Love's dominion. *Printed,* 1654. 8°. L; CH, CLC, MH, TU.

1229 —Love's kingdom. *By R. Wood for the author,* 1664. 8°. L, O, LVD; CH, LC, MH, MU, WF, Y.

1230 — —[Anr. ed.] *For Simon Neale,* 1674. 8°. L; CH, WF.

1230A —The marriage of Oceanus and Britiania. [*London*], *printed,* 1659. 8°.* CH.

1231 —Miscellania. Or, poems. *By T. R. for the author,* 1653. 8°. LT, O, LVD, CE; CH, CLC, MH, WF, Y.

1231aA —[Anr. ed.] *By Tho. Roycroft, for J. Martin, and J. Allestrye,* 1653. 8°. WCL.

1231A [–] The portrait of William Marquis of New-Castle. *By Thomas Creake,* 1660. 4°.* CH.

1232 —A relation of ten years travells. *For the author,* [1656?]. 8°. L, O, C, SP; CH, CN, MH, RPJ, WCL.

1233 No entry.

1234 [–] Seventy eight characters. *Printed,* 1677. 8°. O, OW.

1235 [–] Sr William D'avenant's voyage to the other world. *For the author,* 1668. 8°.* L, O; CH, WF.

1236 [–] Sixty nine enigmatical characters. *For William Crook,* 1665. 12°. L, LW; LC, MU, WF.

1237 [–] A treatise of the sports of wit. [*London*], *for the author,* 1675. *Inquire for them at Simon Neals.* 8°. T.C.I 196. CH, CN.

1238 [–] A true and faithful account of what was observed in ten years travells. *For William Crook,* 1665. 8°. L; CH, Y.

1238A The Fleetstreet dialogue. colop: [*London*], *for John Carr,* 1693. cap., fol.* CH, MH.

1239 **Fleetwood, Charles.** The Lord General Fleetwoods answer to the humble representation of Collonel Morley. [*London,* 1659.] 4°.* LT, O, C, MR, DT; CH, CU, MH, WF, Y.

1240 Entry cancelled.

1241 [–] Letter from the officers at Whitehall. 1659. *See title.*

1241 —To the supream authority, the Parliament . . . the humble petition of. [*London,* 1659.] brs. LT, O, OC; CH, MH.

1241A —Whereas several officers . . . 13 February 1653. *Dublin, by VVilliam Bladen,* 1653. brs. PL.

1241B —Whereas the lord in mercies . . . 21 December 1652. *Dublin, by VVill. Bladen,* 1652. brs. STEELE 2p 508. PL.

1242 Entry cancelled.

  Fleetwood, E. Sermon preach'd Augt. the 4th 1700. Dublin, 1700. *See* Fleetwood, William.

1242A **Fleetwood, James.** The Bishop of Worcester's letter. [*London,* 1679.] cap., 4°.* MR; CH.

1243 [**Fleetwood, William**], *bp.* An account of the life and death of the Blessed Virgin. *By H. Clark, for Thomas Newborough,* 1687. 4°. L, O, CT, AN, EN, DT; CH, IU, LC, MH, NU, TU, Y.

1244 [–] —[Anr. ed.] —, 1688. 4°. L, O.

1245 Entry cancelled. Ghost.

1246 Entry cancelled.

  Annalium tam regum Edwardi V. 1679. *See* Fleetwood, William, *recorder.*

1246A —A funeral sermon on . . . Duke of Glocester . . . Aug. the 4th, 1700. *London, printed; and re-printed in Dublin, sold by Matthew Gunn,* 1700. 4°.* C, BR, BLH, DM.

1247 —Inscriptionum antiquarum sylloge. *Impensis Guil. Graves, Cantabrigiensis, & prostant apud Tim. Childe,* 1691. 8°. T.C.II 348. L, O, C, AN, EN, DT; BN, CH, CU, NU, TO, Y.

1247aA — —[Anr. ed.] *Impensis Guil. Graves, Cantabrigiensis,* 1691. 8°. CS, DU; LC, U. ALBERTA.

1247A [–] The life and death of the B. Virgin. *Printed and are to be sold by Randal Taylor,* 1688. 4°.* L, O, LW, CS, DU; CLC, MH, MB, NU, PL, Y.

1248 —A sermon against clipping. *By Tho. Hodgkin, to be sold by John Whitlock,* 1694. 4°.* L, O, C, NE, GH; CH, CU, LC, MH, NP, NU, WF, Y.

1249 —A sermon of the education of children, . . . Nov. 1, 1696. *For Thomas Newborough,* 1696. 4°.* T.C.II 598. L, O, C, EC, DT; CH, CN, MBA, NU, WF, Y.

1250 —A sermon preached at Christ-Church, . . . St. Stephen's day. *For Edw. Brewster, and Ric. Chiswell,* 1691. 4°.* T.C.II 357. L, O, C, SHR, DT; CLC, MH, NU, WF, Y.

1251 —A sermon preached before the university . . . 25th of March, 1689. *Cambridge, by John Hayes; for William Graves there,* 1689. 4°.* T.C.II 246. L, O, C, NE, DT; CH, CN, NU, TU, WF, Y.

1252 —A sermon preached . . . 5th of November, 1691. *For Tho. Bassett, and Tho. Dring;* 1691. 4°.* T.C.II 376. L, O, C, SHR, DT; CH, IU, NP, NU, WF, Y. (var.)

1253 —A sermon preach'd . . . 11th of April, 1692. *For Thomas Newborough,* 1692. 4°.* T.C.II 438. L, O, C, OC, EC, LSD; CH, LC, NU, TU, WF.

1254 —A sermon preached . . . December the xi. 1692. *For Thomas Newborough,* 1693. 4°.* T.C.II 438. L, O, C, EC, BR, DT; CH, CLC, IU, MBA, WF, Y.

1255 —A sermon preach'd . . . February the 12th. 1692/3. *For Thomas Newborough*, 1693. 4°.* T.C.II 438. L, O, C, BR, DT; CH, CN, MH, WF, Y.

1256 —A sermon preach'd . . . January 30, 1698/9. *For Thomas Newborough*, 1698/9. 4°.* L, O, C, BC, EC; CH, IU, MBA, TU, WF, Y.

1257 —A sermon preach'd August the 4th 1700. *For C. Harper*, 1700. 4°.* T.C.III 207. L, O, C, GU, DT; CH, CN, MBA, NU, WF, Y.

1257A ——[Anr. ed.] [1700?] 8°.* EN.

——[Anr. ed.] *Dublin*, 1700. *See* —Funeral sermon.

1258 —A sermon preach'd . . . November the 5th. 1700. *For Charles Harper*, 1700. 4°.* T.C.III 207. L, O, CS, OC, MR; CH, CN, MBA, WF, Y.

1259 **Fleetwood, William,** *Col.* An unhappy vievv of the vvhole behaviour of . . . Buckingham. *For R. Smith*, 1648. 4°.* LT, LLL, MR, DU; CH, CN, MH, MIU, RPJ, Y.

1259A **Fleetwood, William,** *recorder.* Annalium tam regum Edwardi V. *By George Sawbridge, William Rawlins, and Samuel Roycroft, assigns of Richard and Edward Atkins. To be sold by H. Twyford, F. Tyton, J. Bellinger, T. Basset, R. Pawlet, S. Heyrick, C. Wilkinson, T. Dring, W. Jacob, C. Harper, J. Leigh, J. Amery, J. Place, and J. Poole*, 1679. fol. L, LGI, LMT, CJ, NOT, DT; CU, OSU, TO.

1260 —The office of a justice of peace. *By Ralph Wood for W. Lee, D. Pakeman, and G. Bedell*, 1658. 8°. LT, O, LSC, CT; CH, CLC, CLL, WF.

1260A **Fleming, Giles.** His majesty's pedigree. *For Tho. Rooks*, 1664. 8°. O.

1261 —Stemma sacrvm, the royal progeny delineated. *For Robert Gibbs*, 1660. 8°. LT, O, C, MR, ES; CH, CU, MH, NU, WF, Y.

1261A **Fleming, John.** Disputatio juridica. *Edinburgh, G. Mosman*, 1694. 4°.* ALDIS 3369.5. EN, GU.

1262 **[Fleming, Robert],** *elder.* Britain's jubilee. colop: *By Randal Taylor*, 1689. 4°.* L, O; MH.

1263 [–] The church wounded and rent. [*Edinburgh?*], *printed* 1681. 4°. ALDIS 2257.5. L, O, E, EN; NPT, NU, TO, Y.

1263A —The confirming worke of religion. *At Rotterdam, by Reinier Leers*, 1685. 8°. L, O, LW; CH, UCLA, WF.

1263B ——[Anr. ed.] *For Tho. Parkhurst*, 1693. 8°. T.C.II 463. L, O, C, LG, NE, ENC; CLC, MH, MIU, NU, WF.

1264 —A discourse of earthquakes. *For Thomas Parkhust* [sic], *and Jonathan Robinson*, 1693. 8°. T.C.II 451. L, O, C, LLP, LW; CH, MH, RPJ, TO, WF, Y.

1264A —An epistolary discourse on the great assistance to a Christian's faith. *For Tho. Parkhurst*, 1692. 12°. T.C.II 419. O, LCL, LLP, LW, ENC; CLC, MH, NU, Y.

1264B —The faithfulness of God. *For Thomas Parkhurst*, 1674. 8°. L, LCL, CE, E, ENC; CH, IU, MH, MWA, NU, TO, Y.

1265 [–] The fulfilling of the Scripture. [*Rotterdam*], *printed*, 1669. 12°. LCL, E; CLC, IU, MBP, Y.

1266 [–] —Second edition. [*Amsterdam*], *printed*, 1671. 12°. L, LSC, DU, EN, DT; CH, CLC, MBA, MH, MWA, NCD, WF.

1267 [–] —Third edition. [*Rotterdam?*], *printed*, 1681. 8°. L; MH, NU.

1268 [–] —"Third" edition. [*London*], *printed*, 1681. 8°. L, C, LG, LW, LSD, RPL; CH, MH, Y.

1269 ——"Third" edition. [*n.p.*], *sold by Andrew Bell and Jonas Luntley*, [1693]. 8°. LCL, LW; MBA, MH, NU, WF.

1269A ——"Third" edition. *D. Burgess*, [1693]. 8°. EN.

1269B [–] The one necessary thing to be sought. [*n.p.*], *printed*, 1679. 12°. O, LCL; NU.

1269C [–] —[Anr. ed.] 1681. 4°. LCL.

1270 [–] The present aspect of our times. *For Thomas Parkhurst*, 1694. 4°.* L, BLH; CH, CLC, MH, NU, WF, Y.

1271 Entry cancelled.

[–] Rod, or the sword. 1695. *See* Fleming, Robert, *younger.*

1272 [–] Scripture truth confirmed. [*Rotterdam*], *printed*, 1678. 8°. L, LCL, LLP, EN; CH, CLC, MH, NU, TO, WF, Y.

1272A [–] —[Anr. ed.] *Edinburgh, for G. Mosman*, [1691]. ALDIS 3093. EN.

1273 [–] A short and plain account of the doctrine of the Romish church. *For Tho. Parkhurst*, 1675. 8°. T.C.I 204. O; CH, CN, WF.

1274 [–] A survey of Quakerism. *For Tho. Parkhurst*, 1677. 8°. T.C.I 271. L, O, C, LF, EN; PL, PSC.

1275–6 Entries cancelled.

—Θεοκρατια. 1699. *See* Fleming, Robert, *younger.*

1277 —Three elegies. *Edinburgh, printed*, 1692. 4°.* ALDIS 3222. L, O, E, EN; IU.

1277A [–] The true settlement of a Christian faith. [*Edinburgh?*], *printed*, 1692. 8°. O, LW, AN.

1277B [–] The truth and certainty of the Protestant faith. [*Rotterdam*], *printed* 1678. 8°. L, LCL, EN; MH, NU, TO, Y.

1278–81 Entries cancelled.

Fleming, Robert, *younger. See also* Fleming, Robert, *elder.*

1282 —The mirrour of divine love unvail'd. *By J. A. for John Salusbury*, 1691. 8°. T.C.II 370. L, O, LCL, CT, EN; CH, CN, LC, MH, WF, Y.

1283–4 Entries cancelled.

[–] One necessary thing. [*n.p.*], 1679. *See* Fleming, Robert, *elder.*

1285 [–] The rod, or the sword. *For Tho. Parkhurst*, 1694. 8°. O, LCL, LW, AU, GU; LC, NU, Y.

1285A —Θεοκρατια, or the divine government. *For Andrew Bell*, 1699. 8°. L, O, LCL, DC, EN; CH, CLC, NU, Y.

1285B ——Second edition. —, 1700. 8°. O, EN; MH, NC, NGT, WF.

1286–7 Entries cancelled.

[–] True settlement. [*n.p.*], 1692. *See* Fleming, Robert, *elder.*

[–] Truth and certainty. [*n.p.*], 1678. *See* Fleming, Robert, *elder.*

1288 **Flemming, Oliver.** Humble narrative of. [*London?* 1655.] cap., 4°.* L, O; CLC, MIU, Y.

1289 —To the honourable the knights, citizens and burgesses in Parliament assembled. The humble petition. [*London*, 1655.] cap., 4°.* L, O; CLC, MM, Y.

1290 **Fleta.** Fleta seu commentarius. *Typis M. F. prostant apud Guilielmum Lee, Mathæum Walbancke, & Danielem Pakeman,* 1647. 4°. L, O, C, EN, DT; CLC, IU, LC, NCL, NF, Y.

1290A ——[Anr. ed.] *Typis M. F. prostant apud Guil. Lee & Dan. Pakeman,* 1647. fol. L, O, LSD; CH, LC, PUL, WF, AVP.

1291 ——Second edition. *Typis S. R. prostant apud H. Twyford, T. Bassett, J. Place, & S. Keble,* 1685. 4°. L, LL, CT, AN, E, DT; CH, IU, LC, MH, MHL, NCI, NP.

1292 Entry cancelled.

[Fletcher, Andrew.] Defence of the Scots settlement. Edinburgh, 1699. *See* Foyer, Archibald.

1293 [–] Discorso delle cose di Spagna. *Napoli* [*Edinburgh, Geo. Mosman?*], 1698. 8°. ALDIS 3746. L, O, C, EN, DT; CLC, IU, MH, WF, Y.

1294 [–] A discourse concerning militia's. *Printed,* 1697. 4°.* L, O, C, CT, MR; CH, CN, LC, MH, PU, WF, Y.

1295 [–] A discourse of government with relation to militia's. *Edinburgh; printed,* 1698. 8°. ALDIS 3747. L, O, C, EN, DT; CH, CN, MH, WF, Y.

1296 [–] Overtures offered to the Parliament. *Edinburgh, by John Reid,* 1700. 4°.* ALDIS 3994. L, LUG, EN; MIU, RPJ, Y.

1297 [–] A short and impartial view of the manner and occasion of the Scots colony's coming away from Darien. [*Edinburgh*], printed, 1699. 4°.* ALDIS 3831.5. L, O, MR, EN, ES; CH, CN, LC, MH, NU, RPJ, WF, Y.

1297A [–] Some thought concerning the affairs of this session of Parliament. [*Edinburgh?*], printed, 1700. 4°.* CLC, NN, RPJ, WF, Y.

1298 [–] Two discourses concerning the affairs of Scotland. *Edinburgh,* 1698. 8°. ALDIS 3810. L, O, C, EN, DT; CLC, CU, MH, NU, WF, Y.

1299 **Fletcher, Benjamin.** An account of several passages and letters. colop: *Printed and sold by William Bradford, in New-York,* 1693. fol.* EVANS 674. RPJ.

1300 —Benjamin Fletcher, Capiteyn Generael, . . . Aen alle officieren ende bedienaers. *Gedruckt tot Nieuw-Yorke, by William Bradfordt,* 1693. brs. EVANS 670. COLLEGIATE CHURCH, NEW YORK.

1301 —By His Excellency. . . . A proclamation . . . 29th day of April, 1693. [*Philadelphia, by William Bradford,* 1693.] brs. EVANS 668. LC, NHS.

1302 —By His Excellency. . . . A proclamation . . . 27th day of July. 1693. *By William Bradford, of New York,* 1693. brs. EVANS 671. LPR.

1302A —By His Excellency . . . A proclamation . . . 19th day of August. 1693. *New York, printed and sold by William Bradford,* 1693. brs. NHS.

1303 —By His Excellency. . . . A proclamation . . . thirteenth day of November. 1693. *Printed and sold by William Bradford, of New York,* 1693. brs. EVANS 676. NN, NS.

1303A —By His Excellency. . . . A proclamation . . . April 22, 1695. *Printed and sold by William Bradford in New York,* 1695. brs. EVANS 733. NS.

1304 —By His Excellency. . . . A proclamation . . . sixth day of June, 1695. *Printed and sold by William Bradford* [*New York*], 1695. brs. EVANS 734. NS.

1305 —By His Excellency. A proclamation . . . ninth day of January, 1695/6. [*New York, by William Bradford,* 1696.] brs. EVANS 759. COLLEGIATE CHURCH, NEW YORK.

1306 —By His Excellency. . . . A proclamation . . . 27th day of February, 1695/6. *Printed and sold by William Bradford of New York,* 1695[6]. brs. EVANS 760. NS.

1306A —By his Excellency . . . A proclamation . . . 27th day of February 1695/6. [*New York, by William Bradford,* 1696.] brs. EVANS 761. NS.

1307 —By his Excellency. . . . A proclamation . . . one and twentieth day of April, 1696. *By William Bradford, New-York,* 1696. brs. EVANS 762. NS.

1308 —By His Excellency. . . . A proclamation . . . eleventh day of May, 1696. *By William Bradford, of New York,* 1696. brs. EVANS 763. NS.

1309 —By His Excellency. . . . A proclamation . . . 21st day of May, 1696. *Printed and sold by William Bradford,* [*New York*], 1696. brs. EVANS 764. NS.

1310 —By His Excellency. . . . A proclamation . . . 11th day of June, 1696. *Printed and sold by William Bradford, in New York,* 1696. brs. EVANS 765. NS.

1311 —By His Excellency. . . . A proclamation . . . 2d day of July, 1696. *Printed and sold by William Bradford, in New York,* 1696. brs. EVANS 766. NS.

1312 —By His Excellency. . . . A proclamation . . . first day of August, 1696. *By William Bradford, in New York,* 1696. brs. EVANS 767. NS.

1313 —By His Excellency. . . . A proclamation . . . second day of August, 1696. *By William Bradford, in New York,* 1696. brs. EVANS 768. NS.

1314 —By His Excellency. . . . A proclamation . . . twelfth day of September, 1696. *By William Bradford, of New-York,* 1696. brs. EVANS 769. NS.

1315 —By His Excellency. . . . A proclamation . . . twelfth day of September, 1696. *By William Bradford, of New York,* 1696. brs. EVANS 770. NS.

1316 —By His Excellency. . . . A proclamation . . . twelfth day of September, 1696. *By William Bradford, of New-York,* 1696. brs. EVANS 771. NN.

1317 —By His Excellency. . . . A proclamation . . . 25th day of March 1697. *By William Bradford of New-York,* 1697. brs. EVANS 804. NS.

1318 —By His Excellency. . . . A proclamation . . . 15th day of April, 1697. *By William Bradford of New-York,* 1697. brs. EVANS 805. NS.

1319 —By His Excellency. . . . A proclamation . . . 31th [*sic*] day of May, 1697. *By William Bradford, of New-York,* 1697. brs. EVANS 806. NS.

1320 —By His Excellency. . . . A proclamation . . . 4th day of June, 1697. *By William Bradford of New-York,* 1697. brs. EVANS 807. NS.

1321 —By His Excellency. . . . A proclamation . . . 21th [*sic*] day of October, 1697. *By William Bradford, of New-York,* 1697. brs. EVANS 808. NS.

1322 —By His Excellency. . . . A proclamation . . . 4th day of November, 1697. *By William Bradford, of New-York,* 1697. brs. EVANS 809. NS.

1323 —By His Excellency. . . . A proclamation . . . 26th day of February 1697/8. *By William Bradford, of New-York,* 1697/8. brs. EVANS 835. NS.

1324 —By His Excellency. . . . A proclamation . . . 26th day of February, 1697/8. *By William Bradford, of New-York,* 1697/8. brs. EVANS 836. NS.

1325–6 Entries cancelled.
[–] By His Excellency . . . A proclamation. Whereas I have found. [n.p.], 1695. *See* —Proclamation . . . April 22, 1695.
[–] By His Excellency . . . A proclamation. Whereas sundry. [n.p.], 1695[6]. *See* —Proclamation . . . 27th day of February 1695/6.

1326A —A speech made by . . . [24 October 1692]. [*New York*], *by William Bradford,* 1693. brs. NHS.

1326B —A speech of . . . [12 September 1693]. [*New York, by William Bradford,* 1693.] fol. * NHS.

1326C —The speech of . . . [7 April 1696]. [*New York, W. Bradford*], 1696. cap., fol.* LPR; LC.

1327 —Benjamin Fletcher, Captain General. . . . To all officers and ministers . . . [8 June 1693]. *Printed by William Bradford, of New-York,* 1693. brs. EVANS 669. NHS, NS.

1328 [**Fletcher, Elizabeth.**] A few words in season to all the inhabitants of the earth. *Printed, and are to be sold by Robert Wilson,* 1660. 4°.* L, LF, BBN, MR; CH, MH, MU, NU, PH, Y.

1329 Entry cancelled.
Fletcher, Francis. World encompassed by Sir Francis Drake. 1652. *See* D., R. Sir Francis Drake revived. Vol. II.

1330 **Fletcher, Giles.** The history of Russia. [*London*], 1643. 12°. LT, O, CK, CS, DC; BN, CH, CLC, MIU, WF, Y.

1331 ——[Anr. ed.][*London,* 1656.] 12°. LT, OC.

1332 ——[Anr. ed.] *By Roger Daniel for William Hope and Edward Farnham,* 1657. 8°. O, C, CK; CLC, IU.

1333 —Israel redux: or the restauration of Israel. *By S. Streater, for John Hancock,* 1677. 12°. T.C.I 342. L, O, C, LCL, CK; CH, MH, NC, WF, Y.

1334 [**Fletcher, Henry.**] The perfect politician. *By I. Cottrel, for William Roybould, and Henry Fletcher,* 1660. 8°. LT, O, NE; CH, CU, LC, MH, WF, Y.

1335 [–]—Second edition. *Printed,* 1680. 8°. T.C.I 376. L, LG, OC, CS, DU, E; CH, IU, MH, NN, WF, Y.

1335A [–]—"Second" edition. *For John Crump,* 1680. 8°. NCD.

1336 [–]—Third edition. *For J. Crumpe,* 1681. 8°. L, LLL, LW, CS, BC, MR; CH, IU, NU, TU, WF, Y.

1337 **Fletcher, John, *d. 1613.*** The differences, causes, and judgements of urine. *By John Legatt,* 1641. 8°. L, C, LWL, E, GU, AU; BN, CJC, CLM, WF, WSG.

Fletcher, John, *dramatist.* Beggars bush. 1661. *See* Beaumont, Francis.
—Bonduca. 1696. *See* Beaumont, Francis.

1338 [–] The chances. *For A. B. and S. M. and sold by Langley Curtis,* 1682. 4°. L, O, LLU, EN; CH, LC, MH, NP, TU, WF, Y.

1339 ——Second edition. *For R. Bently,* 1692. 4°. L, LG, LVF, OW, DT; CH, MH, MU, TU, WF, Y.

[–] The common-wealth of women. 1686. *See* D'Urfey, Thomas.
—Elder brother. 1650. *See* Beaumont, Francis.

1340 —The faithful shepherdesse. Fourth edition. *For Ga. Bedell and Tho. Collins,* 1656. 4°. L, LIU, NOT; CH, LC, MB, MH, RHT, WF, Y.

1341 ——Fifth edition. *For G. Bedell and T. Collins,* 1665. 4°. L, O; CH, CLC, IU, MH, PU, WF, Y.

1342 —Fathers own son. *For Robert Crofts,* [1660?]. 4°. O; CH, Y.

1343 —La fida pastora. Comœdia pastoralis. *Typis R. Danielis, impensis G. Bedell & T. Collins,* 1658. 8°. LT, O, CM, P, E; CH, CU, MH, WF, Y.

1344 [–] The humorous lieutenant. *For H. N. and sold by William Chandler, and Ralph Smith,* 1697. 4°. T.C.III 55. L, O, LG, LLU, DT; CH, CN, MH, TU, WF, Y.

1345 [–] The island princess. *For H. R. and A. M., and are to be sold by William Cademan and Robert Pask,* 1669. 4°. T.C.I20. L, O, LGI, OC, A; CH, CN, LC, MH, TU, WF, Y.

1346 No entry.
[–] —[Same title.] 1687. *See* Tate, Nahum.

1347 —The night-walker. *For Andrew Crook,* 1661. 4°. L, O, OW, EN; CH, CU, LC, MH, NP, Y.

1348 —The pilgrim. *For Benjamin Tooke,* 1700. 4°. T.C.III 199. A–G⁴, H². L, O, OC, EN; CH, CN, LC, MH, TU, Y.

1349 ——[Anr. ed.] —, 1700. 4°. T.C.III 231. A–F⁴, X¹, B–D². L; CLC, PU, TU, WCL, WF, Y.

—Prophetess. 1690. *See* Beaumont, Francis.

1350 —Rollo, Duke of Normandy. *By R. Holt for Dorman Newman,* 1686. 4°. T.C.II 171. L, BC, EN; CH, CU, MH, WF, Y.

—Rule a wife. 1697. *See* Beaumont, Francis.

1351 Entry cancelled.
—Thierry and Theodoret. 1649. *See* —Tragedy of Thierry.

1352 —The tragedy of Thierry. [Second edition.] *For Humphrey Mosely,* 1648. 4°.* L, O, C, LG, OW; CH, MH, WF, Y.

1353 ——[Anr. ed.] —, 1649. 4°.* L, O, OC, CT; CH, CN, MH, TU, WF, Y.

1354 [–] Valentinian: a tragedy. *For Timothy Goodwin,* 1685. 4°. T.C.II 99. L, O, C, MR, EN; CH, CN, LC, MH, TU, WF, Y, AVP.

1354A [–] —[Anr. ed.] *For Henry Herringman, sold by Jos. Knight & Fr. Saunders,* 1685. 4°. Y.

—Wild-goose chase. 1652. *See* Beaumont, Francis.
—Wit without money. 1661. *See* Beaumont, Francis.

1355 **Fletcher, Phineas.** A father's testament. *By R. White, for Henry Mortlock,* 1670. 8°. T.C.I 29. L, O, C, LVD, LW; CH, CLC, CN, NP, WF.

1356 **Fletcher, R.** Radius Heliconicus: or, the resolution. [*London,* 1651]. brs. LT; MH.

1356A [**Fletcher, Richard.**] Advertisements to avoid being deceived. [*London,* 1680.] brs. L.

1357 —A character of a true physician. *For the author*, 1676. 8°.* L; WSG. (var.)

1357A [–] England's solar pill. *For the author, by Tho. James*, [1680?]. brs. L.

1357B ——[Anr. ed.] *For R. Fletcher by Tho. James*, [1680–90]. brs. L.

1358 —Good tydings to the sick and lame. *For the authors*, 1674. 4°.* L.

1359 —Starkey revived; . . . Part I. [*London*], *for the author*, 1676. 8°.* L; MH.

1359A —A vindication of chymistry. [*London*, 1676.] cap., 8°. L.

1359B —The vertues of that well-known . . . medicine Fletcher's powder. *By Thomas James for the author*, 1677. brs. MH.

1360 ——[Same title.] colop: *By Tho. James for the author*, 1679. cap., 8°.* L; WF.

1361 **Fletcher, Robert.** True newes from Ireland. *For I. Bull*, 1642. brs. LT, EC, HH.

1362 **Fletcher, Thomas.** Poems on several occasions. *For Charles Harper*, 1692. 8°. T.C.II 393. L, O, C, LVD, DT; CH, CN, MH, WF, Y.

1363 **Fleury, Claude.** An historical account of the manners. *For Thomas Leigh*, 1698. 8°. T.C.III 81. L, O, CT, MR, GU; CH, CN, NU, TU, WF, Y.

1364 —The history, choice, and method of studies. *For S. Keble; John Hindmarsh; D. Brown; and R. Sare*, 1695. 8°. T.C.II 526. L, O, C, DU, E, DT; CH, CN, CU, MU, WF, Y.

1364A [–] The manners of the Israelites. *For William Freeman*, 1683. 12°. T.C.I 510. L, LLP, CM, CS, CT; CLC, OHU, UCLA, WF.

1364B **Fleury, Pierre.** Discours. *Pour W. Redmayne, et se vend par tous les libraires françois*, 1697. 4°. OC.

1364C The flight of Popedom out of England. [*Holland?* 1689?] brs. L.

Flint, Josiah. Almanack. Cambridge [Mass.], 1666. *See* Almanacs.

Floating island. [n.p.], 1673. *See* Head, Richard.

1365 Floddan Field in nine fits. *By P. L. for H. B. VV. P. and S. H.*, 1664. 8°. L, O; CH, CLC, IU, MH, TU, Y.

1365A Flora, flowers, fruicts, beastes, birds. [*London*], *printed and sould by Peter Stent*, [1660–65?]. fol. L.

1366 Flora's departure. [*London*], *for J. Deacon*, [1680?]. brs. L; Y.

1366A Flora's fair garland. [*London*], *by J. M. for P. Brooksby*, 1688. 8°.* O; NNM.

Flora's farewel. [n.p., 1656.] *See* Price, Laurence.

1367 Flora's lamentable passion. [*London*], *for J. Deacon*, [1685?]. brs. L, CM; MH.

Flora's vagaries. 1670. *See* Rhodes, Richard.

Floriana. A pastoral. 1681. *See* Duke, Richard.

1368 **Florio, Giovanni.** Vocabulario Italiano e Inglese. *By T. Warren for Jo. Martin, Ja. Allestry and Tho. Dicas*, 1659. fol. L, O, C, E, DT; BN, CH, MU, PL, TU, WF, Y.

1369 ——Second edition. *By R. Holt, and W. Horton, for R. Chiswell, T. Sawbridge, G. Wells, and R. Bentley; to be sold by Sam. Crouch*, 1688. fol. T.C.II 213. L, O, AN, BAMB, MR, DT; CH, CN, MH, WF, Y, AVP.

1369A ——[Anr. ed.] *By R. H. and W. H. for R. C. T. S. G. W. and R. B. and are to be sold by Thomas Sawbridge, Samuel Crouch, and Thomas Horne, and Matthew Gilliflower*, 1690. fol. L; NN.

1370 **Florus, Lucius Annæus.** The history of the Romans. *By R. B. to be sold by Daniel Pakeman*, 1658. 8°. LT, CS, LLU; CLC.

1371 —L. Julii Flori Rerum à Romanis gestarvm. *Oxoniæ, excudebat Henricus Hall, impensis Tho: Robinson*, 1650. 12°. MADAN 2035**. O, CT, BC, RPL, DT; IU, MB, Y.

1372 ——[Anr. ed.] —, 1661. 8°. MADAN 2556. L, O, C, CT, EC; CLC, IU, NC.

1373 ——[Anr. ed.] *Cantabrigiæ, ex officina Ioannis Field*, 1664. 12°. O, C, CT.

1374 ——[Anr. ed.] *Cantabrigiæ, ex officina Ioann. Field*, 1667. 12°. L, CT; CH, IU, MH.

1375 ——[Anr. ed.] *Oxoniæ, excudebat Henricus Hall impensis Geo: West*, 1669. 12°. MADAN 2828. L, O, C, YM; CLC, CN, MH, PU, Y.

1376 ——[Anr. ed.] *Cantabrigiæ, ex officina Ioannis Hayes*, 1680. 12°. L, O, C, CS, BQ; CLC, IU, MIU.

1377 ——[Anr. ed.] *Apud Johannem Gellibrand*, 1683. 12°. T.C.II 52. L, O, C, OC, BSE; CH, CLC, IU, PL, TU, WF.

1378 ——[Anr. ed.] *Impensis R. Clavell, H. Mortlock, & S. Smith*, 1692. 8°. T.C.II 411. L, O, C, BAMB, SHR; CH, IU, MH, NC, WF, Y.

1379 —The Roman history of. *By T. J. for Samuel Speed*, 1669. 8°. T.C.I 7. L, BSO; CH, CLC, IU, MH, MU, PU.

1380 ——[Anr. ed.] *By J. C. for Samuel Speed*, 1672. 8°. L, O, AN; CLC, CN, SW, WF, Y.

1381 ——[Anr. ed.] *By John Redmayne*, 1676. 8°. L, O, OC, LLU; CLC, CU, MH, NN, Y.

1381A —The imperfection of most governments. colop: *For Langley Curtiss*, [1680]. cap., fol.* L, C, OC; CH, CLC, MH, PU.

Florus Anglicus; or. 1656. *See* Bos, Lambert van den.

Florus Hungaricus: or. 1664. *See* Howell, James.

1382 Flos ingenii vel evacuatio discriptionis. Being. *Printed*, 1674. brs. L.

Flosculi historici. Oxoniæ, 1663. *See* Bussieres, Jean de.

Flosculum poeticum. Poems. 1684. *See* Ker, Patrick.

1382A La flote triomphante. What can resist. [*London?* 1694.] brs. HH.

1382B [**Flower, Christopher.**] The copy of a letter, by a minister. *By T. R.*, 1665. 4°.* MR.

1383 —Mercy in the midst of judgment. *For Nath. Brooke*, 1669. 4°.* L, O, C, GH.

1384 —The passion-flower: a sermon. *For Nathaniel Brook*, 1666. 4°. C.

1384A [–] The penitent prisoner. *For John Williams*, 1675. 8°.* L, O, C; Y.

1385 **Flower, John.** Englands late miseries. *For Giles Calvert*, 1651. 4°.* O, LMT, BC; CU, PAP, WF.

1386 —Several queries concerning the church. *By T. Mabb for Edward Thomas*, 1658. 8°. LT, O, LW.

Flower-garden. 1671. *See* Hughes, William.

1387   **Floyer**, *Sir* **John**. An enquiry into the right use and abuses of the . . . baths. *For R. Clavel*, 1697. 8°. T.C.III 14. L, O, LCP, BR, MAU, AM; CH, MIU, MMO, WF, HC.

1388   —Φαρμακο-βασανος: or, the touch-stone of medicines. *For Michael Johnson in Litchfield: to be sold by Robert Clavel*, 1687. 2v. 8°. T.C.II 199. L, O, C, MAU, E; MMO, NAM, PL, HC, JF.

1388A — —[Anr. ed.] *Printed for Michael Johnson, Bookseller; and are to be sold at his shops.* 1687. LIU; PU, WF, WSG.

1389   —The preternatural state of animal humours described. *By W. Downing, for Michael Johnson. To be sold by Robert Clavel, Sam. Smith, and Benjamin Walford*, 1696. 8°. L, C, LCS, LWL, AM, E; CH, MWA, NAM, TO, WSG.

1390   [–] A treatise of the asthma. *For Richard Wilkin*, 1698. 8°. T.C.III 94. L, O, C, LCS, AM; CH, CJC, MMO, WSG, HC.

1391   **Fludd**, **Robert**. Mosaicall philosophy. *For Humphrey Moseley*, 1659. fol. L, O, WCA, E, ES; CH, CU, MH, WF, HC.

Fly 1658. An almanack. 1658. *See* Almanacs.
Flying post with a packet. 1678. *See* P., W.

1392   The flying serpent, . . . *Saffron Walden. Printed and sold by Peter Lillicrap*, [1669?]. 4°. L.

Flyting betwixt Polwart. [n.p.], 1688. *See* Hume, Alexander.

1393   Foedvs pactumq. *Impensis Radulphi Smith*, 1644. 4°.* LT, O, MR, YM, EN; NC, NU, TU, WF, Y.

1394   Foedus sacro-sanctum. *Edinburgi, excudebat Evan Tyler*, 1643. 4°.* ALDIS 1082. E, EN; CH, NU, WF, Y.

1395   [**Foigny**, **Gabriel de**.] A new discovery of terra incognita Australis. *For John Dunton*, 1693. 12°. T.C.II 464. L, O, CAMB. ZOOLOGY, E; CLC, CN, MH, LC, NN, WF.

1396   Foirceadul aithghearr. Second edition. *Nglasgo, le Aindra Ainderson*, 1659. 12°. ALDIS 1598. L, GU; Y.

1396A —[Anr. ed.] *Ar nar chur a ngclo a Nduneduin le Oighreachaibh Aindra Ainderson*, 1694. 12°. EN.

1397   Entry cancelled.
Fole, William. Comfortable words. 1671. *See* Jole, William.

1397A **Foley**, **Philip**. The case of . . . concerning his election . . . as burgess for . . . Bewdley. [*London*, 1679.] brs. LPR.

1397B [**Foley**, **Samuel**], *bp.* A catalogue of books . . . sold . . . [9 September 1695]. *Dublin, by Jos. Ray*, 1695. 4°. C; NG.

1398   —An exhortation to the inhabitants of Down & Connor. *Dublin, by Joseph Ray*, 1695. 4°. DIX 266. L, DT, BLH, CD; CH, CLC.

1399   —A sermon preached at the primary visitation. *For Moses Pitt*, 1683. 4°.* L, O, C, OM, DT; CH, CLC, WF.

1399A [–] This is to give notice, that the books of . . . which remain unsold. colop: *Dublin, by Joseph Ray*, 1695. cap., 4°.* NG.

1400   —Two sermons. *For Moses Pitt*, 1683. 4°. L, O, C, BANGOR, DT; CLC, WF.

1400A **Foley**, **Thomas**. The case of . . . concerning his election for . . . Bewdley. [*London*, 1677.] brs. LPR.

1400B **Folger**, **Peter**. A looking glass for the times. [*Boston, by John Foster*, 1676.] EVANS 211. MWA.

1401   The follies of France. colop: *For Timothy Goodwin*, 1690. cap., 4°.* L, O, EN; CH, MH.

Follower of the Lamb, [n.p., 1660.] *See* Perrot, John.

1401A The following collections or pious little treatises. *Printed at Douay, by Mi. Mairesse*, 1684. 8°. BUTE; CN.

1402   The following lines are engraven in the Roman language. *By J. M. for W. Davis*, 1684. brs. L, O; CH, MH, Y.

1402A The following proposals are humbly offered the . . . Commons . . . relief of the French refugees. [*London?* 1696.] brs. L; MH, Y.

Following proposals for. Edinburgh, 1695. *See* Briscoe, John.

Following speech being spoke. [n.p., 1694.] *See* Knight, Sir John.

Folly and envy. 1694. *See* Bridgman, Robert.

Folly and madnesse. [n.p.], 1659. *See* Say and Sele, William Fiennes, *viscount*.

Folly in print. 1667. *See* Raymund, John.
Folly of love. 1691. *See* Ames, Richard.

1403   The folly of priest-craft. *For Richard Baldwin*, 1690. 4°. T.C.II 326. L, O, OW, CT; CII, CN, LC, MII, TU, WT, Y.

1403A The folly of the late dispersed declaration. [*London?* 1693.] cap., fol.* LUG.

1404   Folly plainly made manifest. [*London*], *for I. Deacon*, [1684–95]. brs. HH; MH.

Fond lady. 1684. *See* Duffet, Thomas.

Fons Moffetensis. Edinburgi, 1659. *See* Mackaile, Matthew.

1405   Entry cancelled.
Fonseca, **Christoval de**. Discourse. 1652. *See* – Θειον.

1405A —Relaçam das festas de palacio. *Na officina de J. Martin, Ja. Allestry, & Tho. Dicas*, 1663. 4°.* L; MH, WF.

1405B —Θειον ενωτικον. A discourse of holy love. *By J. Flesher, for Richard Royston*, 1652. 12°. LT, O, C, BC, P; CH, CN, NU, WF, Y.

Font guarded. 1652. *See* Hall, Thomas.

1406   **Fontaine**, **Nicolas**. History of the New Testament. *By Samuel Roycroft for Richard Blome*, 1688. fol. L, C, CM, MR, DT; LC, MIU, NU, WF, YBA.

1406A —The history of the Old and New Testament. *Printed for and sold by Richard Blome, Mr. Saunders, Mr. Wilkinson and Mr. Freeman, Mr. Clavel and Mr. Brome, Mr. Horn, and Mr. Southby, Mr. Richards, and by other booksellers*, 1691. 8°. BLH; NIC, NN, TSM, PUB. LIB., NEW SOUTH WALES.

1406B — —[Anr. ed.] *Printed and sold by S. Sprint, J. Nicholson, J. Pero, and R. Clavel*, 1697. 8°. CS; CPB, TU, AMB.

1407   [–] —Second edition. *For S. and J. Sprint, C. Brome, J. Nicholson, J. Pero, and Benj. Tooke*, 1699. 4°. T.C.III 162. L, O, DUS, NPL, YM, DT; CH, CLC, FU, IEG, Y.

1408   [–] The history of the Old Testament. *By Samvel Roycroft, for Richard Blome: as also by Mr. Nott; Mr. Lownes; Mr. Southby; and by Mr. Richards*, 1690. fol. L, C, CM, MR; LC, MIU, NU, PU, WF, YBA.

1409   Entry cancelled.

      Fontaine, Nicolaus. Womans doctour. 1652. *See* Fonteyn, Nicholaas.

1410   **Fontaines, Louis.** A relation of the country of Jansenia. *For the author, and sold by A. Banks, and C. Harper,* 1668. 12°. T.C.I 2. L, C, DC, DCH, DU; CH, CN, IU, WF, Y.

1410A   [**Fontenelle, Bernard Le Bovyer.**] Dialogues of the dead . . . The second part. *For R. B.,* 1685. 12°. T.C.II 116. L, O; CSU, MH, WG, Y.

1411   —A discourse of the plurality of worlds. *Dublin, by Andr. Crook and Sam. Helsham, for William Norman,* 1687. 4°. DIX 224. L, DT, DK; CH, CLC, MH, Y.

1412   [–] A discovery of new worlds. *For William Canning,* 1688. 8°. T.C.II 233. L, C; CH, CN, LC, NP, Y.

1412A   [–] —[Anr. ed.] *For Will. Canning,* 1688. 8°. CB, LC, Y.

1412B   [–] Entretiens sur le pluralité des mondes. *Chez Abel Swalle,* 1687. 12°. Y.

1412C   [–] The French Lucian. *For R. Bentley,* 1693. 12°. CLC, WF.

1413   [–] The history of oracles. *Printed,* 1688. 8°. T.C.II 230. L, O, C, LL, SP; CH, CN, LC, MH, TU, Y.

1413A   [–] —[Anr. ed.] *By W. O. for S. Briscoe,* 1699. 8°. IU, MH, MU.

1413B   [–] Lucian's ghost. *For James Norris,* 1684. 12°. T.C.II 50. O, CS; CN, IU.

1414   [–] New dialogues of the dead. *For D. Y.,* 1683. 12°. L, O; CLC, WF, Y.

1415   [–] —[Anr. ed.] *For D. Y.,* 1684. 12°. O; CH, CLC, MH, WG, Y.

1416   [–] A plurality of worlds. *For R. Bentley and S. Magnes,* 1688. 8°. T.C.II 219. L, C, LVD, LLU, GU, DT; CLC, MH, NC, OCI, Y.

1417   [–] —Second edition. *For R. Bentley,* 1695. 8°. T.C.II 591. L, O, CK, RPL, GK; CLC, CN, MBJ, TU, WF, Y.

1418   —The theory or system of several new inhabited worlds. *By W. O. for Sam. Briscoe,* 1700. 8°. CH, IU, NP, TU.

1418A   **Fonteyn, Nicolaas.** The womans doctour. *For John Blague and Samuel Howes,* 1652. 12°. LT, LSC, LWL; WF.

      Food and physick. 1665. *See* D., T.

      Foole that I was. [n.p., 1642.] *See* Killigrew, Thomas, elder.

      Fool turn'd critick. 1678. *See* D'Urfey, Thomas.

1419   The fooles complaint to Gotham Colledge. *Printed by Ridibundus,* 1643. 4°.* LT, O; NCD, Y.

1420   Fools in earnest. [*n.p.,* 1683.] brs. O; CLC, MH, Y.

      Fooles of fate. [n.p.], 1648. *See* Taylor, John.

1421   **Foord, John.** Johannis Foord. Expositio libri Paslmorum. *Extant Londini apud Edwardum Brewster,* 1646[7]. 4°. LT, LW, CS, MC, P, DT; BN, MWA, NPT, TO, WF.

1422–3   Entries cancelled.

      Foot, Thomas. By the Major. We charge. [1649.] *See* London. Lord Mayor. [Foote, Thomas.]

1424   Entry cancelled.

      Forasmuch as notwithstanding. [n.p., 1656.] *See* London. Lord Mayor. [Tichborne, *Sir* Robert.]

1425   London, Anno. Dom. 1647. Forasmuch as the right worshipful Sir John Wollaston Kt. [*London,* 1648.] brs. LT.

1426   Entry cancelled.

      Forasmuch as to the Court. [n.p.], 1648. *See* London. Lord Mayor. [Warner, *Sir* John.]

1427   For encouraging the coining of silver. [*London*], 1692/3. brs. NC, PU.

      For England's information. 1679. *See* Varney, John.

      For every individuall member. [n.p., 1647.] *See* Lilburne, John.

      For every individuall member. [n.p., 1649.] *See* Burt, Nathaniel.

1427A   For God's worship. [1683?] 8°. L.

1428   Entry cancelled.

      For His Excellency Gen. Monck. Oxford, 1660. *See* L'Estrange, *Sir* Roger.

1429   For information to all people where to deliver their letters by the penny post. [*London,* 1680.] brs. MH.

      For Manasseth Ben Israel. 1656. *See* Fell, Margaret.

      For our faithful. [n.p., 1647.] *See* Sexby, Edward.

1430   For paying the Irish transport-ships. [*n.p.,* 1690?] brs. Y.

      For prevention. 1655. *See* Baxter, Richard.

      For supplying. [n.p., 1696.] *See* N., T.

1430A   For that the taking of impositions post mortem is not now in use . . . [scheme of bill proposed by Heralds]. [*London,* 1667?] brs. LPR.

1430B   For the benefit of the new hospital . . . in Dublin. [*London,* 1700?] brs. L.

1430C   For the creditors of Sir Robert Vyner. [*London,* 1684.] cap., fol.* L.

1430D   For the Earl of Cleveland. [*London?* 1666.] brs. L.

1430E   For the encouragement of the consumption of the woollen manufacture. [*London?* 1680?] brs. L; MH.

1430F   For the encouragement of the woollen manufacture. [*London?* 1680?] brs. L; MH.

      For the holy women. [n.p.], 1686. *See* Fox, George.

      For the King, and both Houses. 1661. *See* Fox, George.

      For the King and both Houses. [n.p., 1670.] *See* Whitehead, Anne.

      For the King and both Houses. [n.p.], 1675. *See* Hookes, Ellis.

1431   For the King and both Houses of Parliament being a brief . . . relation. [*London?* 1663.] brs. L, LF; CH.

1432   For the King and both Houses of Parliament: being a declaration of the present suffering. *Printed,* 1664. 4°.* L, LF, LW, OC, DU; MH, NU, PSC, Y.

1433   For the King and both Houses of Parliament: being a further relation . . . Quakers. [*London,* 1670.] brs. LF.

1434   For the King and both Houses of Parliament. Being a short declaration. [*London?* 1660.] cap., 4°.* L, OC.

1435   For the King and both Houses of Parliament. Being a short relation. *Printed,* 1661. fol.* LC, MB, MH, PH, RPJ.

1436   For the King and both Houses of Parliament. For you (who have known . . .) . *For Thomas Simmons,* 1660. fol.* L, LF, DU; MB, NU, RPJ.

1436A   For the King, and his councill at White hall. Being a breif relation. *For Robert Wilson,* [1661]. brs. MH, PH.

For the King and his council, these. [n.p., 1660.] *See* Fox, George.

For the King and Parliament. [n.p.], 1664. *See* Bayly, William.

For the Parliament sitting. [1659.] *See* Lynam, Margaret.

1437 For the right honourable Captaine General Cromwel. [*London*, 1653.] cap., 4°.* LT, O; CSS.

1438 For the right honourable the Lords and Commons. . . . Right Honourable, as we are very sensible. *For John Wright*, 1648. brs. LT; MH, PU.

1438A For the right noble . . . Monmouth . . . the humble supplication of the nonconformists. [*n.p.*, 1679?] brs. L.

1438B For the scurvy, pox, and dropsie . . . effectual pills. [*London*, 1700?] brs. L.

1438C For the selling of herrings in . . . Yarmouth. [*London*, 1700?] brs. LG.

1438D For the under-officers and souldiers. [*Edinburgh*], *by Evan Tyler*, 1656. brs. ALDIS 1412. 3. WF.

For Whitson tyds. [*n.p.*], 1645. *See* Douglas, *Lady* Eleanor.

For your whoredoms. [*n.p.*, 1660.] *See* Fox, George.

1439 [**Forbes, Alexander Forbes**], *baron*. An anatomy of independency. *For Robert Bostock*, 1644. 4°. LT, O, CT, BC, DT; CH, CU, MH, NU, WCL, WF, Y.

1440 —A trve copie of two letters. *By L. N. for Henry Overton*, 1642. 4°.* LT, O, EC, EN, DT; CH, CLC, WF, WU, Y.

1441 —The whole body of arithmetick. *By J. B. for Dorman Newman*, 1676. 8°. T.C.I 255. L, O, C, LLP, LU.

1442 **Forbes, James.** The Christian directed. *By J. Brudenell, for Tho. Parkhurst*, 1700. 8°. T.C.III 197. LCL; MH, MWA.

1443 [–] God's goodness to His Israel. *For Tho. Parkhurst*, 1700. 8°. L, LW; CH, MH, MWA, WF.

1444 [–] Nehvshtan: or, John Elliot's saving grace. *For Thomas Cockeril*, 1694. 4°.* LF, BBN, DT; MH, MU, Y.

[**Forbes, John.**] Cantus, songs. Aberdene, 1662. *See* Davidson, Thomas.

1445 —Festival songs. [*Aberdeen*], *Bon-Accord, by the author*, 1681. 8°.* ALDIS 2268. HH.

1445A —Long Lent, 1685. [*Edinburgh?* 1685.] brs. ALDIS 2547. 5. EN.

—Mariner's everlasting almanack. Aberdeen, 1683. *See* Almanacs.

1446 —Psalm tunes to four voices. colop: *Aberdene, by Iohn Forbes*, 1666. 4°. ALDIS 1822. CH.

1447 [–] [Psalm tunes harmonised.] colop: *Aberdene, by Iohn Forbes younger*, 1671. 4°. ALDIS 1928. EN.

1448 [–] The whole yearly faires. *Aberdeen, by Iohn Forbes, August 22*, 1684. 12°.* ALDIS 2498. ES.

1449 **Forbes, John**, *minister*. Seasonable and vsefull directions. *Printed at London, by R. C. for J. Bellamie*, 1643. 8°.* LT.

1450 **Forbes, Robert.** Reverendissimo in Christo Patri . . . Ioanni Paterson. *Aberdoniæ, excudebat Ioannes Forbes*, 1680. 4°.* ALDIS 2229. L.

1451 —Theses philsopohicæ. *Abredoniis, e typographeo Jacobi Broun*, 1656. 4°.* ALDIS 1557. O, AU.

1452 — —[Anr. ed.] —, 1660. 4°.* ALDIS 1678. O, AU.

1453 — —[Anr. ed.] *Aberdoniæ, excudebat Joannis Forbes*, 1684. 4°.* ALDIS 2494. EN.

1454 **Forbes, William**, *bp.* Considerationes modestæ et pacificæ. *Typis Thomæ Roycroft, impensis Jo. Martin, Jacobi Allestrye, & Tho. Dicas*, 1658. 8°. LT, O, C, EN, DT; CH, IU, NR, NU, WF, Y.

1455 —Disputatio juridica. *Edinburgi, ex officinâ typographicâ hæredum Andreæ Anderson*, 1696. 4°.* ALDIS 3561. EN.

1456 —Poemata miscellanea. *Imprimebat S. B. pro W. C.*, 1642. O, EN, E; CH.

Forbidden fruit. 1642. *See* Franck, Sebastian.

1457 Entry cancelled.

[**Force, Peter.**] Virginia and Maryland. 1655. *See* title.

1458 Forced divinity, or two sermons. *For F. C.*, [1650?] 8°. L.

Forc'd marriage. [n.p., 1676–85.] *See* Pope, Walter.

Forced uniformity. [n.p., 1675.] *See* Hutchinson, Thomas.

1458A **F[ord], E[dward].** An alarm to trumpets. *By R. I. for E. F.*, 1651. 8°.* LT.

1459 —The despairing lover. *Printed at London for F. Coules.* [1650?]. fol.* L.

1460 —An echo, or the trumpeter's triumph. *For Francis Coles*, 1644. 8°.* CH.

1461 [–] Fair play in the lottery. [*London*, 1660.] 12°. LT.

1462 [–] VVine and women. *By John Hammond*, 1647. 8°.* LT; CH.

1463 Entry cancelled.

Ford, Emanuel. Alarm to trumpets. 1651. *See* Ford, Edward.

1464 **Ford, John.** An essay of original righteousness. [n.p.], *printed*, 1657. 12°. O.

1465 —A narrative of the manner of celebrating . . . coronation in . . . Bath. *For Edward Thomas*, 1661. brs. LT.

1466 —The reasonableness of personal reformation. 1691. 12°. LCL.

1466A **Ford, John**, *dramatist*. Comedies, tragi-comedies; and tragidies. 1652. 4°. EN.

1467 —The sun's-darling. *By I. Bell, for Andrew Penneycuicke*, 1656. 4°.* L, O, LVD, CT, EN; CH, LC, MH, WF, Y. (var.)

1468 — —Second edition. —, 1657. 4°. L, O, LVF, DC, EN; CH, IU, LC, MH, WF, Y. (var.)

1469 [**Ford, Philip.**] Certaine intelligence from Yorke. *For H. Blunden*, 1642. 4°.* LT, LHO, EC; CH, MM, Y.

1470 —A vindication of William Penn. colop: *For Benjamin Clark*, 1683. brs. L, O, LF; CH, LC, MH, PHS, RPJ.

1471 **Ford, R.** A further attempt towards the reformation of the coin. *For Thomas Cockerill, Sen*ʳ*. & Jun*ʳ*.* 1696. 4°.* L, O, LUG; INU, MH, NC, PL, PU, WF, Y, ANL.

Ford, Sir Richard. By the maior. 1671. *See* London. Lord Mayor. [Ford, *Sir* Richard.]

1472 —The speech of . . . made at Guild-hall. *For N. B.*, 1670. 4°.* LG, LL, DU, LSD, SP; CH, CSS, MM, AVP.

1473 —To the High Court of Parliament . . . the humble petition of. [London, 1654.] brs. LT.

1474 [**Ford, Robert.**] A testimony concerning George Russell. [London, 1680.] 4°.* L, LF.

1475 [**Ford, Simon.**] Ambitio sacra. Oxonii, excudebat H. Hall. Impensis Aliciæ Curteyne, 1650. 4°.* MADAN 2029. L, O, C, CT, DT; CLC, MH, WF, Y.

1476 —Baptism for the dead. For A. and J. Churchill, 1692. 4°.* T.C.II 409. L, O, C, SC, DT; CH, CN, MH, NU, WF, Y.

1477 —The blessedness of being bountifull. For James Collins, 1674. 8°. T.C.I 162. L, O, LW, OC, CS; CH, CLC, NU, WF.

1478 —Carmen funebre; ex occasione Northamtonæ conflagratæ. Apud H. Brome, 1676. 4°.* T.C.I 258. L, O, OB, CT, DU; CLC, IU, NC, TU, WF, Y.

1478A —The catechism of the Church of England. Printed 1694. NGT.

1479 [–] Conflagratio Londinensis poetice depicta. The conflagration of London. Second edition. For Sa: Gellibrand, 1667. 4°.* L, O, C, LG, GH; CH, CN, MH, TU, WF, Y.

1480 [–] The conflagation of London. For Sa. Gellibrand, 1667. 4°.* L, O, LG, CT, EN; CH, CN, MH, TU, WF, Y.

1481 —A dialogue, concerning the practicall use. By S. G. for John Rothwel, 1654. 8°. LT, O, C, SS; CH, MH, NHC, NPT, NU, WF.

1481A — —[Anr. ed.] By S. G. for John Rothwel, sold by Richard Jones, in Reading, 1655. 8°. O, ORP.

1482 — —[Anr. ed.] By T. M. for John Rothwel, 1657. 8°. LCL, LW, OC, CS, NE, DT; CH, NPT, NU, TO, WF, Y.

1483 Entry cancelled. Ghost.

1484 —A discourse concerning Gods judgements. By A. C. for Hen. Brome, 1678. 8°. T.C.I 287. L, O, C, LCL, GH; CH, IU, MH, NU, WF, Y.

1484A — —[Anr. ed.] For Hen. Brome, 1678. 12°. O, CT, BC; MH.

1485 —‛Ησυχια Χριστιανου, or, a Christian's acquiescence. By R. D. for John Baker, 1665. 8°. L, O, LW, CT, MR; CLC, IU, NPT, WF.

1486 —The fall and funeral of Northampton. For John Wright, and are to be sold by William Cocktain, in Northampton, 1677. 4°.* T.C.I 266. L, O, OB, OC, LLU; CDA, MH, WF.

1487 —The great interest of states . . . The second part. By W. Wilson, for Francis Eglesfield, 1646. 4°.* LT, O, C, OC, DT; CH, CLC, IU, NU, WF.

1487A — —[Anr. ed.] —, and are to be sold by John Long, in Dorchester, 1646. 4°.* C, ORP.

1488 [–] Londini quod reliqvvm. Or, Londons remains. For Sa: Gellibrand, 1667. 4°. L, O, C, EN, CD; CH, CN, MH, WF, Y.

1489 [–] Londini renascentis imago poetica. Excudebat A. M. pro Sa: Gellibrand, 1668. 4°.* L, O, LG, CT, GH; CH, CN, MH, WF, Y.

1490 [–] Londons resurrection. By A. M. for Sa: Gellibrand, 1669. 4°.* T.C.I 89. L, O, LG, CT, SP; CH, CN, MH, NC, WF, Y.

1491 —Παραλληλα δυσταραλληλα, or, the loyal subjects indignation. By J. H. for Samuel Gellibrand, 1661. 4°. L, O, LW, MR, EN; CH, CLC, NN, NU, Y.

1492 —Παραλληλα; or the loyal subjects exaltation. By Abraham Miller for Samuel Gellibrand, 1660. 4°. LT, O, C, LW, OC; CH, MH, NC, TU.

1492A — —[Anr. ed.] By A. M. for Samuel Gellibrand, 1660. 4°. BP, WCA, D; CLC, CSS, MH, NU, WF.

1493 —A plain and profitable exposition. By T. B. for John Gellibrand, 1684. 8°. T.C.II 94. L, O, C, LLP, CD; CLC, NU.

1493A — —[Anr. ed.] For J. Gellibrand and for Samp. Evans, in Worcester, 1684. 8°. LW, CS, NE; Y.

1494 — —Second edition. By T. B. for T. Sawbridge, 1686. 8°. T.C.II 172. OC; IU, PL, WF.

1495 —Poemata Londinensia. By A. M. for Sa: Gellibrand, 1668. 4°.* LP, EC; CH.

1496 —Primitiæ regiminis Davidici. Or, the first-fruits of Davids government. By S. G. for John Rothwel, 1654. 4°.* L, O, OC, CT, BC, LLU; CH, MIU, NPT, NU, TU, WF.

1496A — —[Anr. ed.] —, 1656. 8°.* O.

1497 Entry cancelled.

  — —Third edition, 1656. See —Dialogue. 1657.

1498 —The restoring of fallen brethren. For Henry Mortlock. 1697. 4°.* T.C.III 19. L, O, C, CT, LIU; CH, MH, TSM, WF, Y.

1499 [–] The second part of the dialogue concerning the practical use. By T. Maxey, for John Rothwel, 1656. 8°. LLP, OC, NE, DT; CH, NU, TO, Y.

1500 No entry.

1501 Entry cancelled.

  [–] Sermon of catechizing. 1656. See —Dialogue. 1657.

1502 —A short catechism. By S. G. for John Rothwell, 1657. 8°.* L, O, LCL, LLP, LW, CM; IU, NU, TO. (var.)

1503 —The spirit of bondage. By T. Maxey, for Sa: Gellibrand, 1655. 8°. LT, O, CS, BC, GU; CLC, CN, NPT, NU, WF.

1504 —Θαυμασια κυριου ἐν βυθω. Or the Lords wonders in the deep. Oxford, by W. Hall for Samuel Pocock, 1665. 4°.* MADAN 2699. L, O, C, LSD, YM, BLH; CH.

1505 [–] Three poems relating to the late dreadful destruction of . . . London by fire. For Sa: Gellibrand, Nov. 20. 1667. 4°. L, LNC; CH.

1506 Entry cancelled. See following entry.

1507 **Ford, Stephen.** An epistle to the Church of Christ. Oxford, by A. Lichfield, for T. Robinson, 1657. 4°.* MADAN 2336. O, C, LG, LW, MR; MH, NU, Y.

1508 —Eternal glorification begun. For Nath. Crouch, 1675. 8°. O, C, LCL; CLC.

1509 —The evil tongue tryed. For Nath. Crouch, 1672. 12°. T.C.I 109. O, LSC; CLC.

1510 —A gospel-church. Printed, 1675. 8°. L, LCL, LW, ORP; CH, IU, NHC, NPT, NU, WF.

1511 **F[ord], T[homas].** Αυτοκατακριτος. Or, the sinner condemned. For Edward Brewster, and are to be sold by Anne Dight, in Exon, 1668. 8°. L, LW; NPT.

1511A [–] —[Anr. ed.] For Edward Brewster, 1668. 8°. O; NU.

1511B [–] —[Anr. ed.] —, and are to be sold by Giles Widowes, 1668. 8°. CLC.

1512 [–] Felo de se, or the bishops condemned. [London], printed, 1668. 4°.* LCL, OB, BC, SP, DT; CH, MH, NU, WF, Y.

[80]

1513 —Grace and mercy to a sinner. *By Joseph Moxon, for Francis Cossinett,* 1657. 8°. L.

1514 —Λογος αυτοπιστος, or, scripture's self-evidence. *For Edward Brewster, and are to be sold at Mr. Marriotts,* 1667. 12°. LCL, LW; MH.

1515 [–] Reformation sure and stedfast. *By J. D. for Henry Overton,* 1641. 4°.* LT, O, C, MR, EN; CH, IU, MH, NU, WF, Y.

1516 [–] Singing of psalmes the duty of Christians. *By A. M. for Christopher Meredith,* 1653. 8°. LT, LCL, LW, CT; LC, MU, NPT.

1517 ——Second edition. *By W. B. for F. Eglesfield,* 1659. 12°. L, LSC, ORP; LC, MWA, NPT, NU.

1518 [–] The times anatomiz'd. *For W. L.,* 1647. 12°. LT; CU, MH.

1519 **[Forde, *Sir* Edward.]** A designe for bringing a navigable river from Rickmansworth. *For John Clarke,* 1641. 4°.* L, O, C, LG, LUG; CSU, MH, Y. (var.)

1520 —Experimented proposals how the King may have money. *By William Godbid,* 1666. 4°.* L, O, LSD, LG, NE; CU, MH, NC, WCL, Y.

1521 **F[orde], E[manuel].** The famous and pleasant history of Parismus. *By W. Onley, for J. Blare,* [1690?]. 8°. L, LIU; CN, FU, NNM, PU.

1522 [–] —[Anr. ed.] *By W. O. and sold by J. Blare and G. Conyers,* 1699. 4°. L.

1523 [–] The famous history of Montelion. *By E. Alsop, and Robert Wood, to be sold by Francis Grove, William Gilbertson, and Charles Tyus,* 1661. 4°. L.

1524 ——[Anr. ed.] *By E. Alsop and Robert Wood for S. S., to be sold by Francis Coles and Charles Tyus,* 1663. 4°. L, OC; NC.

1525 [–] —[Anr. ed.] *By T. F. for S. S. and are to be sold by William Thackeray,* 1668. 4°. CH, Y.

1525A [–] —[Anr. ed.] —, 1671. 4°. CCH.

1526 ——[Anr. ed.] *By A. P. for W. Thackeray and T. Passenger,* 1673. 4°. T.C.I 295. L; CN, WCL.

1527 ——[Anr. ed.] *Sold by W. Thackeray and T. Passenger,* 1677. 4°. HARMSWORTH.

1528 [–] —[Anr. ed.] *By T. Haly, for W. Thackeray, and T. Passenger,* 1680. 4°. L, C; CN.

1528A [–] —[Anr. ed.] —, 1682. 4°. SE.

1529 ——[Anr. ed.] *By J. R. and W. W. for W. Thackeray and T. Passenger,* 1687. 4°. O, CM, EN; CN, CU.

1530 [–] —[Anr. ed.] *By W. O. for E. Tracy and C. Bates,* [c. 1690]. 4°. L, EN; CN, MIU, NP, WF.

1531 ——[Anr. ed.] *For W. Thackeray, and E. Tracey,* 1695. 4°. T.C.III 31. L, CK, EN; CH, CLC, CN, Y.

1531A —The famous, pleasant and delightful history of Ornatus. *[London], for B. Deacon,* [1700?]. 4°. O; CN, Y.

1532 [–] The most famous, delectable, and pleasant history of Parismus. *By J. Millit, for W. Thackeray,* 1649. 4°. L.

1533 [–] —[Anr. ed.] *By B. Alsop,* 1649. 4°. L; CH, CN, NP.

1533AA ——Fifth edition. *By E. Alsop for John Andrews,* 1657. 4°. L; WF.

[–] —[Anr. ed.] [c. 1660.] *See* —Pleasant history.

1533A ——Sixth edition. *By E. Alsop, for Francis Grove, and William Gilbertson,* 1661. 4°. CH, CN, MH.

1533B ——Seventh edition. *By G. Purslow, for F. Coles, T. Vere, W. Gilbertson, and J. Wright,* 1664. 4°. O; CN, NCU, NP.

1533C [–] —Eighth edition. *For Eldes, T. Vere and J. Wright,* 1669. 4°. O.

1534 ——Ninth edition. *By A. P. for F. Coles, T. Vere, and J. Wright,* 1671-2. 4°. L, O, CM, LSD; CH, CN, NP, WF, Y.

1535 No entry.

1536 ——Eleventh edition. *By T. H. for F. Coles, T. Vere, J. Wright, J. Clarke, W. Thaceray [sic] and T. Passenger,* 1681. 2 pts. 4°. T.C.I 480. CLC, CN, IU, MIU, NP, WF.

1537 ——Twelfth edition. *By M. H. and J. M. for J. Wright, J. Clarke, W. Thackeray, and T. Passinger,* 1684. 4°. L, LLL; CN, LC, MH, NCU, NP, Y.

1538 ——Thirteenth edition. *By J. Millet for W. Thackeray,* 1689. 4°. L, O, CS, BC; CH, CLC, CN, NP, WF, Y.

1539 [–] —The first part. Fourteenth edition. *By W. Wilde,* 1696. 4°. T.C.II 572. L, O, C; CN, CSU, NP, TU, WF.

1540 [–] —The second part. *By W. Wilde,* 1696. 4°. O; CN, CSU, NP, TU, WF.

1541 —The most pleasant historie of Ornatus and Artesia. *By B. A.,* 1650. 4°. L.

1541A ——[Anr. ed.] *By E. Alsop and R. Wood, for Thomas Vere and William Gilbertson,* 1662. 4°. MH.

1542 ——Seventh edition. *By J. W. for Thomas Vere, and William Whitwood,* 1669. 4°. BP; NP.

1543 [–] —Eighth edition. *By M. White, for J. Wright, J. Clark, W. Thackeray, and Tho. Passenger,* 1683. 4°. L, CM; CN, NP, Y, U. ALBERTA.

1544 [–] The most renowned and pleasant history of Parismus. *By A. P. and T. H. for F. Coles, T. Vere, J. Wright, and J. Clarke,* 1677. 4°.* CCH; Y.

1544A [–] —[Anr. ed.] *By H. B. for J. Wright, J. Clark, W. Thackeray, and T. Passenger,* 1683. 4°. LC.

1545 [–] Of the famous and pleasant history of Parismus. *By W. Onley, for Josiah Blare; and for George Conyers,* [1690?]. 4°. L; CU.

1545A —The pleasant history of Parismus. *By J. B. for Charles Tyus,* [c. 1660]. 4°.* CN.

Forde, Thomas. Fænestra in pectore. 1660. *See* —Virtus rediviva.

—Fragmenta poetica. 1660. *See* —Virtus rediviva.

1546 Entry cancelled.

—Love's labyrinth. 1660. *See* —Virtus rediviva.

1547 [–] Lusus fortunæ; the play of fortune. *[London], for R. L.,* 1649. 8°. LT, LLL, DT; CH, Y.

1548 Entry cancelled.

—Theatre of wits. 1660. *See* —Virtus rediviva.

1548A ——[Anr. ed.] *By R. & W. Leybourn, for Thomas Basset,* 1661. 8°. O; MH.

1549 —Virtus rediviva: or, a panegyrick. *By R. & W. Leybourn, for William Grantham,* 1660. 8°. LT, O, C, OW, EN; CH, CN, LC, MH, WF. (var.)

1550 [–] Virtus rediviva a panegyrick. *By R. & W. Leybourn, for William Grantham; and Thomas Basset,* 1661. 8°. LT, OW; CH, CN, CU, MH, WCL, WF, Y, AVP.

1550A [–] —[Anr. ed., "panegyricke."] *By R. and W. Leybourn, for William Grantham,* 1661. 8°. L.

1551 Entry cancelled.

Fordun, John. Historiæ Brittanicæ. Oxoniæ, 1691. *See* Gale, Thomas.

1551A **Fordwich, John Finch,** *baron.* The coppy of a letter sent from. [*London*], *printed,* 1641. 4°.* LT, OC, DU, SC, WCA; CH, MH, NN, Y.

1551B —A letter sent to the Right Honourable the Lord Chamberlaine. [*London?* 1641.] brs. LT; CH, MH, Y.

1551C —L. F. Lord Keeper his speech before the Kings Majesty. [*London*], *printed, and are to be sold by Richard Cotton,* 1641. 4°.* LT, CT, BC, MR; CLC, MH, NU, WF, Y.

1551D —The Lord Finch his speech in . . . Commons. [*London*], *printed,* 1641. 4°.* LT, O, CT, BC, EC; CH, IU, MH, WF, Y.

1551E Entry cancelled.

—Lord Keepers speech. 1641[2]. *See* Littleton, Edward, *baron.*

1551F Foreign advices. *By Edw. Jones in the Savoy,* 1695. brs. HH.

1552 Forraign and domestick prophesies. *Printed, and are to be sold by Lodowick Lloyd,* 1659. 4°. LT.

Forreign excise considered. 1663. *See* S., W.

1553 Forraigne intelligence. By letters from a gentleman in London. [*Kilkenny,* 1648.] 4°.* CH.

Foreigners. A poem. 1700. *See* Tutchin, John.

1554 **Foreness, E.** A sermon preached . . . 9th of September. *By Miles Flesher, for William Abbington,* 1683. 4°.* T.C.II 60. L, O, OC, MP, BLH; CH, CLC, NU, WF, Y.

1555 —A sermon preached . . . July 11. 1684. *For Peter Swinton, at Knutsford,* 1684. 4°.* L, O, MR, D, BLH; CH, CU, WF, Y.

Forerunner of Christ's peaceable kingdom. 1665. *See* Sherwin, William. Προδρομος.

1555A The forerunners work. *Printed,* 1652. 4°.* WF.

Forest of varieties. 1645. *See* North, Dudley North, *3rd baron.*

Forest promiscuous. 1659. *See* North, Dudley North, *3rd baron.*

1556 Fore-warn'd, fore-arm'd: or, a caveat to batchelors. *By T. Snowden,* 1684. brs. L, O; CLC, MH.

1556aA —[Anr. ed.] *Edinburgh, J. van Solingen & J. Colmar,* 1685. brs. ALDIS 2548.7. EN.

1556A Fore-warn'd, fore-arm'd: or, England's timely warning. *For John Powel,* 1682. 4°.* L, LSD, BLH; CH, WF.

Fore-warning and a word. 1660. *See* Crane, Richard.

1557 The forfeitures of Londons charter. [*London*], *for the author, and are to be sold by Daniel Brown, and Thomas Benskin,* 1682. 4°.* T.C.I 487. L, O, LVF, CT, LSD; CH, CN, MH, NU, WF, Y.

1558 Forgery detected. *By J. D. for Fr. Smith,* 1673. 4°.* L, O, OC, LIU, EN; MH, NN, PL, RPJ, Y.

Forgetfulness of God. 1683. *See* Disney, William.

1559 The forlorn damsel. [*London*], *for P. Brooksby,* [1674-95]. brs. L, O, HH, GU.

1559A The forlorn hope of Irelands bleeding list. *By F. Neile,* 1653. 4°.* DN.

1559B The forlorn lover: declaring how a lass. *For F. Coles, T. Vere, and J. Wright,* [1663-74]. brs. O.

1560 —[Anr. ed.] *By W. O.,* [1675?]. brs. L, CM; MH.

1561 The forlorn lover's lament. [*London,* 1670?] brs. L.

1561A Form and overture for an additional Act. [*Edinburgh,* 1698.] brs. ALDIS 3750. 5. EN.

Form and order of the coronation. Aberdeen, 1651. *See* Douglas, Robert.

Form for church government. 1647. *See* Gillespie, George.

1562 The form of a certificate to be used by Justices of Peace. [*London,* 1655.] brs. LT.

1563 The form of an address. *By Th. Dawks, for Edw. Powel,* 1682. fol.* L, O, C, EN; CH, CLC, PL, WF.

1563A The form of an agreement to be made between the Lords Commissioners of His Majesties treasury. colop: *By Charles Bill and the executrix of Thomas Newcomb,* 1697. cap., fol.* LPR; MH.

1564 Form of an indenture between the sheriff and the burgesses. [*London*], 1654. brs. LG; V, Y.

1565 Form of an indenture between the sheriff and the electors. [*London,* 1654.] brs. LG; MH, V, Y.

1565A A form of church matters. *For H. C.,* 1660. 4°.* MIU.

1566 A form of consecration or dedication of churches. *Dublin, by John Crook, and sold by Sam. Dancer,* 1666. 4°.* DIX 130. C, OM, CD, DM, DT; CH.

1566A —[Anr. ed.] *Dublin, by J. Crook,* 1666. 4°.* LW.

1567 A forme of ecclesiasticall government: fitted. *For John Hancock,* [1642]. 4°. LT, LIU, DT; MH, Y.

Form of government. 1642. *See* Cotton, *Sir* Richard Bruce.

1568 The form of His Majestie's coronation-feast. *For R. Crofts,* 1661. brs. LT, LL.

Form of instrument subscribed. [n.p., 1699?] *See* Oldner, George.

Form of prayer and humiliation. 1690. *See* Seller, Abednego.

1569 A form of prayer, &c. translated from the Dutch. [*London,* 1688.] brs. L, O, C, OC, LSD; CH, NP.

1570 —[Anr. ed.] colop: *Exeter, by J. B.,* 1688. cap., 4°.* L, O, OC.

1571 Entry cancelled.

Form of prayer for the signal victory. 1692. *See* Church of England. A form of prayer and thanksgiving . . . 27th day of . . . October.

1572 The forme of prayers and administration. *Printed first at Geneva 1558. Now re-printed at London,* 1643. 4°.* LT, O, LLP, OC, SP, EN, DT; CH, NU.

Form of sound words. 1682. *See* Brandon, John.

1572A A form of thanksgiving for the great mercy . . . Monch. *By T. Mabb for William Shears,* 1660. brs. L.

Form of thanksgiving to be used thorowout. . . . Lincoln. 1641. *See* Church of England.

1573   The forme of the commission for a new valuation. *Edinburgh, by Evan Tyler,* 1649. 4°.* ALDIS 1365. 7. EN; WF.

1574   The form of the insurance proposed in the mine-adventure. [*London,* 1698?] brs. MH.

1575   The form of the intended coronation oath. *For J. Lyford,* 1689. brs. O, DU, LIU, MC.

1576   —[Anr. ed.] *Edinburgh, re-printed,* 1689. brs. ALDIS 2888. EN; CH, CN.

1577   The form of the new commissions. *Printed at Loydon* [*sic*], 1659. brs. LT, O; MH, MIU.

1578   The form of the oaths. [*London,* 1692?] fol. L.

1579   The form of the proceeding to the coronation of . . . King James the Second. *By Thomas Newcomb in the Savoy,* 1685. brs. L, O, LVF, DU, MC; CH, IEG, IU, MIU.

1579A   —[Anr. ed.] —*and re-printed at Edinburgh, by the heir of Andrew Anderson,* 1685. brs. ALDIS 2549. EN; CH, Y.

1580   The form of the proceeding to the coronation of Their Majesties. colop: [*London*], *in the Savoy: by Edward Jones.* 1689. cap., fol.* L, O, LG, MC, DT; CH, CN, PL, TU, WF, Y.

1581   —[Anr. ed.] colop: *Edinburgh, re-printed,* 1689. fol.* ALDIS 2889. EN; CH.

1582   The form of the proceeding to the funeral of . . . Queen Mary II. colop: [*London*], *in the Savoy: by Edw. Jones* 1694/5. cap., fol.* L, O, C, LG, MC, SP; CLC, IU, MH, PL, Y.

1582A   —[Anr. ed.] *Edinburgh, by the heir of A. Anderson,* 1694/5. fol.* EN.

1582B   —[Anr. ed.] *Edinburgh, by the heirs and successors of A. Anderson,* 1695. fol.* ALDIS 3461. 3. EN.

1582C   —[Anr. ed.] *Dublin, Andrew Crook,* 1695. brs. DIX 380. L.

1583   The form of writs to be issued. *By Iohn Redmayne,* 1660. brs. STEELE 3171. LT; CH, IU, MH, Y.

Formatives of the four conjugations. 1686. *See* Thomas, James.

Former ages never heard of. 1654. *See* Vicars, John.

1584   The former rates being printed by a false copy. [*London,* 1641.] brs. L, O, LG, LUG, NOT; MH, WF, Y.

1584A   Forms of prayer, collected for the private use of a soldier. *For H. Bonwicke,* 1687. 12°. T.C.II 205. LLP.

1584B   Forms of prayer used in the Reformed Churches in France. *By E. Tracy, and are to be sold by M. Baldwin,* 1699. 8°. LLP.

1585   Forms of private devotion. *For Robert Clavell,* 1691. 8°. T.C.II 345. O, CS; WF.

1585A   Formulæ adorandi. Or a religious and devout poem. *For Rich. Royston,* 1676. brs. O; CH.

Formulæ bene placitandi. A book. 1671. *See* Brown, William.

Formulæ oratoriæ. 1670. *See* Clark, John.

1586   [**Fornace, W.**] The King's Majesties propositions to the Lords and Commons. [*London*], *Febr.* 22, 1647. 4°.* LT.

1587   **Forneret, André Frédéric.** Dissertatio theologica. *Oxoniae, excudebat Hen. Hall impensis authoris,* 1673. 4°.* MADAN 2975. L, O, LLP, OCC, CT, BC; CN, Y.

1588   **F[ornis], E[dward].** Looke not upon me. [*London*], *printed,* 1648. 4°.* L, LSC, MR; MH, MM, MWA, NU, ZWT.

1588A   **Forrest, James.** A brief defence of the old . . . method of curing . . . fevers. *Edinburgh, by George Mosman,* 1694. 24°. ALDIS 3370. E.

1588B   Forresta de Windsor, in Com. Surrey. The meers, meets, limits. *For Matthew Walbancke,* 1646. 4°.* L; MH.

1588C   **Forrester, Alexander.** Disputatio juridica. *Edinburgh, ex officinâ typographicâ Georgii Mosmen,* 1694. 4°.* ALDIS 3370.5. EN, GU.

1589   [**Forrester, David.**] The differences of the time. *Edinbvrgh, by the heir of Andrew Anderson,* 1679. 12°. ALDIS 2152. L, LW, NE, E, EN, ES; CH, CLC, IU, NPT, NU, WF, Y.

1590   **Forrester, Duncan.** Magnificis . . . dominis J. Smith de Grottall. *Edinburgi, J. Lindesay,* 1645. brs. ALDIS 1203. E.

1591   —Nobilissimo . . . a Cambello. *Edinburgi, J. Bryson,* 1641. brs. ALDIS 1022. E.

1592   — —[Same title]. *Edinburgi, Lithgow,* 1649. brs. ALDIS 1392. E.

1593   Entry cancelled. *See preceding entry.*

1594   [**Forrester, Thomas.**] A counter-essay. *Edinburgh, by the heir of Andrew Anderson,* 1692. 4°. ALDIS 3216. L, EN, ENC, BLH; CLC, NU, Y.

1595   [–] —[Anr. ed.] *Edinburgh,* 1693. 4°. ALDIS 3295. 5. L.

1596   —The hierarchical bishops claim. *Edinburgh, by James Watson,* 1699. 4°. ALDIS 3851. L, O, C, E, AU; CH, IU, MH, NPT, NU, WF, Y.

1597   [–] Rectius instruendum; or, a review. [*Edinburgh*], *printed,* 1684. 8°. L, A, EN, ENC, GU; CH, MH, NU, WF, Y.

1597A   **Forrestus, Phil.** In honorem ecclesiæ Gallo-Londinensis . . . Carmen panegyricum. 1666. 4°.* L, O.

1597B   The forsaken damosel. [*London*], *for F. Hose,* [1675?]. brs. O.

1598   The forsaken lover. [*London*], *for H. Green,*]1690?]. brs. HH.

1599   The forsaken maids frollick. [*London*], *for W. Whitwood,* [1660–77]. brs. L, OP, HH; MH.

1600   Forsomickle as [blank] collector of the excise. [*Aberdeen, Forbes, younger*], 1670. brs. ALDIS 1901. AC.

1601   **Forster, John.** Englands happiness increased. *For A. Seile,* 1664. 4°.* L, O, LUG, R; NN, WDA.

1602   **Forster, Mark.** Arithmetical trigonometry. *By J. Richardson for William Court,* 1690. 8°. C, LW; PL, WU.

1602A   — —[Anr. ed.] *For R. Mount,* 1700. 8°. L, O; CLC, MU.

1603   [**Forster, Mary.**] A declaration of the bountifull loving-kindness. [*London*], *printed,* 1669. 4°.* L, C, LF, BBN, MR; IE, MU, NR, PH, PL, PSC.

1603A   — —[Anr. ed.] *Printed and sold by T. Sowle,* 1693. 4°.* L, LF; IU, PHS, Y.

1604   —Some seasonable considerations. *Printed and sold by Andrew Sowle,* 1684. 4°.* L, O, LF, BBN, MR; CH, MH, MU, PH, PSC, Y.

1605   [–] These several papers was sent to the Parliament. *For Mary Westwood,* 1659. 4°. L, LF, BBN, MR, EN; CH, MH, NU, PL, PSC, WF.

1606   **Forster, Richard.** Prerogative and privilege. *For B. Tooke and W. Kettilby,* 1684. 4°.* T.C.II 69. L, C, WCA, D; CH, CN, NU, WF, Y.

1607 **F[orster], T[homas].** A guide to the blind pointed to. *For the author, to be sold by G. Calvert, & N. Brooks,* 1659. 8°. L, LF; MU.

1608 ——[Anr. ed.] [*London*], *printed,* 1671. 8°. L; PH, PSC.

1609 ——[Anr. ed.] —, 1676. 8°. LF; BN, PH.

1610 [–] The lay-man's lawyer. *By T. R. for H. Twyford, and J. Place,* 1654. 8°. L, EN; CH, MHL, PUL, WF.

1611 ——[Anr. ed.] *For H. Twyford and J. Place,* 1656. 8°. L, O, LGI, NPL; CLL, LC, MHL, MU, PU, WF.

1611A **Forster, William.** Forster's arithmetick. *For George Sawbridge,* 1667. 12°. O.

1611B ——[Anr. ed.] *By John Streater; sold by George Sawbridge,* 1673. 12°. T.C.I 130. L.

1611C ——[Anr. ed.] *For Thomas Sawbridge,* 1686. 12°. T.C.II 172. L, O; WF.

Fort-royal. 1649. *See* Hart, John.

1611D [**Fortescue, Anthony.**] A letter sent to the right honourable Edward, Earle of Manchester. [*London*], *printed,* 1648. 4°.* IU, MH, MIU.

1612 **Fortescue, Sir John.** De laudibus legum Angliæ; written by. (*By permission of the Company of Stationers*), *for Abel Roper,* 1660. 8°. L, O, CM, SC, EC; CH, CN, MBP, MHL, NCL, WF, YL.

1613 ——[Anr. ed.] *By John Streater, Eliz. Flesher and H. Twyford, assignes of Rich. Atkyns and Edward Atkyns, to be sold by G. Sawbridge, J. Place, J. Bellinger, Wil. Place, T. Basset, Rob. Paulet, Christ. Wilkinson, Tho. Dring, Wil. Jacob, Ch. Harper, J. Leigh, J. Amery, J. Poole,* 1672. 8°. T.C.I 124. L, O, C, EN, DT; CLC, IU, MH, NCL, WF, YL.

1614 **Forth, Patrick Ruthven,** *earl of.* The copy of His Excellency the Earle of Forth's letter. *Oxford, March 7, by Leonard Lichfield,* 1643. 4°.* MADAN 1554. O, C, LSC; BN, CH, MH, Y.

1615 —A letter from . . . 15 Feb. 1643. *For J. C. and T. G.,* 1643. 4°.* LT, C, LSD, BLH, DN; MH, MU, PRF, WF, Y.

Fortification and military discipline. [n.p.], 1688. *See* S., J.

1616 **Fortrey, Samuel.** Englands interest. *Cambridge, by John Field,* 1663. 8°. L, O, C, LUG, EN, DT; MHS, MU, NC, NN, Y.

1617 ——[Anr. ed.] *For Nathanael Brook,* 1673. 8°. T.C.I 164. L, C, OC, LIU, LSD; BN, LC, MH, MIU, NC, WF.

1617A The fortunate lawyer. *For J. Sharp,* 1695. brs. MH.

1618 Fortunate rising, or the Rump upward. *For Henry James,* [1660]. brs. LT, O.

1619 The fortune of France. *For Jonathan Edwin,* 1678. 4°.* T.C.I 302. L, O, C, LUG, CT, DU; CH, CN, MBA, WF, Y.

1620 Fortune's bounty. *Printed; to be sold by B. Bragge,* [1700?]. 4°.* L, OC, DT; CH, WF.

Fortunes tennis-ball. 1672. *See* Sheppard, Samuel.

Fortune's uncertainty. 1667. *See* Croke, Charles.

1621 Fovrtie articles in the High Covrt of Parliament, against William Lang. *For Tho. Bates,* [1642]. 4°.* LT, O, LLU, LNC, MR; CH, CLC.

1621A —[Anr. ed.] —, 1641[2]. 4°.* CH, MH, WF, Y.

1622 Fourty four qveries to the life of Queen Dick. [*London*], *printed,* 1659. 4°.* LT, O, OC, LSD, MR; CH, CN, MH, WF, Y.

1623 **Foster, George.** The pouring forth of the seventh and last viall. [*London*], *printed,* 1650. 4°. LT, O; CU.

1624 —The sounding of the last trumpet. [*London*], *printed,* 1650. 4°. LT, BP, LIU, E, DT; CN, CU, MIU, NU, PH.

1625 **Foster, Henry.** A true and exact relation of the marchings of the two regiments. *For Benjamin Allen, Octob. 2.* 1643. 4°.* LT, LG; MH, WF, Y.

1625A ——[Anr. ed.] *For Ben. Allen, Octo. 2.* 1643. 4°.* O, LG, LSD; CLC, MH.

Foster, John. Almanack. Cambridge [Mass.], 1675. *See* Almanacs.

1626 No entry.

1627 **Foster, Nicholas.** A briefe relation of the late horrid rebellion. *By I. G. for Richard Lowndes, and Robert Boydell,* 1650. 8°. LT, O, C, DT; CH, LC, MH, MU, MWA, NN, RPJ, Y.

1628 **Foster, Richard.** An appeal to the present rulers in Englands Israel. *For Charles Sumptner,* 1650. 4°.* LT, O, DT; INU.

1629 **Foster, Samuel.** The art of dialling. *By J. R. for Francis Eglesfield,* 1675. 4°. T.C.I 122. LR, EN.

1629A ——Second edition. —, 1675. 4°. OC.

1629B —The art of measuring. *For John Williamson,* 1677. 8°. T.C.I 279. L; PMA, WF.

1630 —De instrumentis planetariis. *Ex officina Leybourniana,* 1659. fol. L, O, C, LWL, E, DT; BN, CLC, MU, NC, PL, Y.

1631 —The description and use of the nocturnal. [*London,* 1685?] cap., 4°.* L, C, LR, CT; CLC, MU.

1632 —Elliptical, or azimuthal horologiography. *By R. & W. Leybourn, for Nicholas Bourn,* 1654. 4°. LT, O, C, LG, SA; CH, MH, NN, WF, Y.

1633 —The geometrical square. *By R. & W. Leybourn,* 1659. fol. L, O, C, LWL, E, DT; BN, CLC, MU, NC, PL, Y.

1634 —Miscellanea. *Ex officina Leybourniana,* 1659. fol. L, O, C, LWL, E, DT; BN, CLC, IU, MH, MU, NC, WF, Y.

1635 —Posthuma Fosteri: the description of a ruler. *By Robert and William Leybourn, for Nicholas Bourn,* 1652. 4°. LT, O, C, LG, SA; CH, LC, NN, WF, Y.

1635A ——[Anr. ed.] *By Robert & William Leybourn,* 1654. 4°. L.

1636 —The uses of a quadrant. *For Francis Eglesfeild, to be sold at the Marygold; and by A: Thompson,* 1652. 8°. LT.

1637 [**Foster, T.**] A winding-sheet for England's ministry. [*London,* 1658?] 4°. O, LF; CH, PH, PSC, WF, Y.

Foster, William. Ephemeris. 1662. *See* Almanacs.

1638 [**Fothergill, Thomas.**] The deep sighes and sad complaints of some late souldiers. [*London,* 1653.] cap., 4°.* LT.

1639 **Fouler, William.** Truths vindication. *For the author, to be sold by Thomas Mathews,* 1652. 8°.* LT; WF.

1639A **Foulis, Sir Henry.** An exact and true relation of a bloody fight. *For John Frank, Decem. 21.* 1642. 4°.* L, YM; CH, WF.

1640   **Foulis, Henry.** The history of Romish treasons. *By J. C. for Tho. Basset,* 1671. fol. T.C.I 72. L, O, C, LW, SHR, EN; CH, CLC, LC, MIU, NU, TU, Y.

1640A   —[Anr. ed.] *By J. C. for Richard Chiswell,* 1671. fol. OC, CT; MH, WF.

1640B   ——[Anr. ed.] *By J. C. for Thomas Dring,* 1671. fol. GC; TSM.

1641   ——Second edition. *For Thomas Basset, Richard Chiswell, Christopher Wilkinson, and Thomas Dring,* 1681. fol. T.C.I 446. L, O, C, EN, DT; BN, CH, CN, MH, NU, WF, WSC, Y.

1642   —The history of the wicked plots. *By E. Cotes, for A. Seile,* 1662. fol. L, O, DU, EN, ES; CH, IU, NU, WF, Y.

1643   ——Second edition. *Oxford, by Hen. Hall for Ric. Davis,* 1674. fol. T.C.I 173. MADAN 3009. L, O, C, AN, EN, DT; BN, CLC, IU, LC, MBP, NU, WF, WSC, Y.

1643A   **Foulis, Sir James.** Answers for Sir James Fowlis . . . to the petition . . . by Dame Margare Areskin. [*Edinburgh,* 1691?] fol. EN.

        Foulis, Oliver, *pseud.* See Lloyd, David.

1643B   **Foulis, William.** Disputatio juridica. *Edinburghi, J. Watson,* 1700. 4°.* ALDIS 3964. 5. EN.

1644   **Foulkes, Robert.** An alarme for sinners. *For Langley Curtis,* 1679. 4°.* T.C.I 340. L, O, C, AN, DU, EN; CH, CU, LC, MH, NU, WF, Y.

        Foundation of Christian religion. 1641. *See* Perkins, William.

1645   The foundation of faith, and the substance of the Bible. *For T. Crosse,* 1660. brs. L.

1645A   —[Anr. ed.] *Printed and sold, by T. Bickerton,* [1690]. 4°. L.

1646   Entry cancelled.

        Foundation of the universitie of Cambridge. 1651. *See* Langbaine, Gerard, *elder.*

        Foundation of the universitie of Oxford, 1651. *See* Langbaine, Gerard, *elder.*

        Foundation of true preaching. 1687. *See* Smith, Richard.

        Foundations of freedom. 1648. *See* Lilburne, John.

1647   **F[ountain], J[ohn].** The rewards of vertue; a comedie. *By Ja. Cottrel for Hen. Fletcher,* 1661. 4°. O; CH, CLC, CU, MH, MU, WF.

1648   **Fountaine, Edward.** A brief collection of many rare secrets. *Printed,* 1650. 4°.* L.

1648A   —The experimentall receipts of. 1661. 4°.* LG.

1648B   ——[Anr. ed.] 1665. 4°.* LP; HC.

1648C   —Melancholy's bane. *For the author,* 1654. 8°. L.

1649   —A precious treasury of tvventy rare secrets. *Printed,* 1649. 4°.* L; MM.

        Fountaine, Lewis. See Fontaines, Louis.

        Fountaine of free grace. 1645. *See* Saltmarsh, John.

        [Fouquet, Nicolas.] The counsels of wisdom. 1680. *See* Boutauld, Michel.

1650   —Essays. *For Thomas Metcalfe; sold by William Freeman,* 1694. 8°. T.C.II 512. BSM, DUS; CH, MIU, Y.

        Foure ages of England. 1675. *See* Cowley, Abraham.

1650A   Four and twenty queries relating to the East-India trade. *Printed, and are to be sold by A. Baldwin,* 1699. brs. HH; MIU.

1651   The four bloody murders lately committed. *For Jonathan Edwin,* 1673. 4°.* MR; CH, CLC.

        Four centuries of select hymns. 1668. *See* Barton, William.

1652   Four choice carols. [*n.p.,* 1700?]. brs. L.

        Four conferences. Oxford, 1688. *See* Coles, Gilbert.

1653   Fovre deliberate, and solid qveries. *Printed,* 1647. 4°.* LT, DT; NU.

        Four for a penny. 1678. *See* Winstanley, William.

1654   Foure fugitives meeting. [*London*], *printed,* 1641. 4°.* L, LG, LVF, OC; CN, WCL, WF, Y.

        Four grand enquiries. 1656. *See* Woodward, Hezekiah.

1655   Four grand questions proposed. *Printed,* 1689. 4°.* L, OC, LIU, EN, DT; CH, CLC, CN, NU, WF, Y.

1656   Four great and horrible murders. *Printed,* 1674. 4°.* O; CH.

1657   Fovr great victories: obtained by Major Generall Poyntz. *By Jane Coe,* 1645. 4°.* LT; CLC.

1658   The four great years of the plague. *For Peter Cole,* 1665. brs. O.

1658A   June the 7. The foure last remarkable matters. *Printed,* 1642. 4°.* LNC; Y.

1659–60 Entries cancelled.

        Four-legg'd elder. [*n.p.,* 1647.] *See* Birkenhead, Sir John.

1661   The four-legged Quaker. [*n.p.,* 1664.] brs. O; MH.

1661A   Four letters from the Queen in France. [*London,* 1651.] 4°.* DU.

1662   Foure matters of high concernment. *By R. Oulton & G. Dexter, for F. Coules & T. Banks,* 1641. 4°.* LT, O, CJ, DT; CH, IU, NN, WF, Y.

1663   Four novels in one vol. viz. The gallants. *For Fr. Saunders,* 1697. L (t.p.).

1664   The fovre petitions of Hvntington shire. *For Iohn Hammond,* 1642. 4°.* LT, LNC, NPL, DT; MH, WF.

1665   Four petitions to His Excellency Sir Thomas Fairfax: viz. *For Laurence Chapman, June* 18, 1647. 4°.* LT, O, MR, ESS, CD; CH, NC, NCD, WF, Y.

1665A   Foure pious, godly and learned treatises. *For Thomas Slater,* 1652. 4°. NU.

        Foure propositions propounded. 1647. *See* Neale, R.

1666   Four qveries resolved for the satisfaction. *For John Hancock,* 1645. 4°.* LT, O, YM, DT; MH, NU, PL, TU, Y.

1667   IV. queries resolved. I. Whether it be lawful. [*London,* 1688.] 4°.* L, MR, EN, DT, CD; CH, MH, TO, WF, Y.

1668   Four questions debated. *Printed,* 1689. 4°.* L, O, C, BC, DU, AU; CH, CN, MBA, NP, PU, WF, Y.

1669   —[Anr. ed.] [*Edinburgh*], *re-printed,* 1689. 4°.* ALDIS 2889. 5. L, O, EN, A; CLC, MIU, Y.

1670   —[Anr. ed.] [*Edinburgh?*], 1695. 4°.* ALDIS 3461. 5. EN.

        Foure serious questions. [1645.] *See* Prynne, William.

        Four small copies. Oxford, 1667. *See* Peers, Richard.

1671   Fovre speeches delivered in Gvild-Hall . . . sixth of October, 1643. *By R. Cotes, for Jo. Bellamie,* 1646. 4°.* LT, O, C, EN, DT; CH, MH, MU, WF, Y.

1672   Foure strong castles taken by the Parliaments forces. *For Matthew Walbancke, April* 27. 1646. 4°.* LT, C, OC, AN, BR, DT.

1673 Foure true and considerable positions. [*London*, 1649.] brs. LT, O.

1674 Foure wonderfull, bloudy, and dangerous plots discovered. *For Iohn Gilbert*, 1642. 4°.* LT, NPL.

1675 The four wonders of this land. [*London*], *for P. Brooksby*, [1690?]. brs. L.

1676 [**Fourcroy**], *abbé*. A new and easy method. *For Ri. Baldwin and Wi. Lindsey*. 1695. 12°. T.C.II 527. L, CS, CT, NE; IU, PU, Y.

1677 [–] — [Anr. ed.] *For R. Wellington*, 1695. 12°. L.

1678 [–] —[Anr. ed.] —, MDCXVII [1697]. 12°. T.C.III 13. O, C, NOT.

1679 [–] — Second edition. *Dublin*, re-printed 1700. 12°. DIX 324. DN.

1680 Fourteen articles of peace. Propounded . . . Tork [*sic*]. *For E. Blackmore, Octo. 4*. 1642. 4°.* LT, O, CJ, SC, YM; CLC, MH, MM, TU, WF.

Fourteen articles of treason. Oxford, 1643. *See* Dobson, Edward.

1681 XIV considerations. [*London*], *for W. Larnar*, 1642. 4°. O.

1682 Entry cancelled.

Fourteen papers. Viz. 1689. *See* Burnet, Gilbert.

1683 Fourteen queries offered. *Printed*, 1659. 4°.* C, LLU, DT; CH, MH, WF.

Fourteene strange prophesies. [n.p.], 1648. *See* Shipton, Ursula.

1684 The fourth (and last) collection of poems, satyrs. *Printed*, 1689. 4°.* L, O, OC, LLU, MR; CH, IU, MH, NU, TU, WF, Y.

1685 The fourth (and last) collection of the newest and most ingenious poems. *Printed*, 1689. 4°.* L, O, BR; CN, CSB, Y, AVP.

1686 A fourth collection of papers. *Printed, and are to be sold by Rich. Janeway*, 1688. 4°.* L, O, C, BR, DT; CH, CN, MH, TU, WF.

1687 —[Anr. ed.] —, 1689. 4°.* L, OB, DUS, LIU, NPL; CLC, MB, MIU, RPJ, WF, Y.

Fourth letter. 1688. *See* Pelling, Edward.

1688 A fourth paper presented by divers citizens . . . Sept. 12, 1682. colop: *For E. Smith*, 1682. brs. O, C, LG; CH, CN, MH, SE, WF.

Fourth paper, presented by Maior Butler. 1652. *See* Williams, Roger.

Fourth part of Naked truth. 1682. *See* Hickeringill, Edmund.

Fourth part of The present state. 1683. *See* Chamberlayne, Edward. Present state.

Fourth word to the wise. [n.p., 1647.] *See* Musgrave, John.

1689 Entry cancelled.

Fowke, Sir John. Whereas the Lord Generall hath received a message. [n.p., 1653.] *See* London. Lord Mayor. [Fowke, Sir John.]

1690 —Alderman Fowke's speech. colop: *By Iohn Redmayne*, 1659. cap., 4°.* CH, MH, MM, MU, TU.

Fowle, Thomas. Speculum uranicum. 1680. *See* Almanacs.

1691 **Fowler.** A discourse against transubstantiation. *Dublin, for Jacob Milner, and Samuel Adey*, 1699. 4°.* DIX 309. DT, DI, DN, BLH.

1692 **Fowler, Christopher.** Dæmonium meridianum. Satan at noon. *For Francis Eglesfield*, 1655. 4°. LT, O, C, LCL, E; CLC, NHC, NU, WF, Y.

1693 — —The second part. *For Fra: Eglesfield*, 1656. 4°. LT, O, RU; MH, NHC, NU.

1694 —A sober answer to an angry epistle. *For Samuel Gellibrand*, 1656. 4°. LT, O, C, LF, OC, BR; CLC, NU, PH.

1695 [**Fowler, Edward**], *bp*. An ansvver to the paper delivered by Mr. Ashton at his execution. *For Robert Clavell*, 1690. 4°.* T.C.II 361. L, OB, CT, BP, MR, EN, DT; HR, CH, CN, MH, WF, Y.

1696 [–] Certain propositions, by which the doctrin. *For Brabazon Aylmer*, 1694. 4°.* T.C.II 517. L, O, C, BAMB, EN; CH, MH, MU, NPT, NU, WF.

1696A [–] —[Anr. ed.] [*London*, 1694?] cap., 4°.* WCA.

1697 [–] A defence of The resolution of this case. *By J. H. for B. Aylmer*, 1684. 4°. T.C.II 39. L, O, CS, LSD, YM; CH, CN, MH, WF, Y.

1697A [–] —[Anr. ed.] *For B. Aylmer*, 1684. 4°.* LW, OC, CJ, DUS; CH.

1698 —The design of Christianity. *By E. Tyler and R. Holt for R. Royston, and Lodowick Lloyd*, 1671. 8°. T.C.I 84. L, O, C, EN, DT; CLC, IU, NPT, PL, TU, WF, Y.

1699 — —Second edition. *For R. Royston*, 1676. 8°. T.C.I 259. L, C, ORP, CT, BP, SP; CLC, MBA, MBZ, MH, MHS, NU.

1700 — —Third edition. *By J. H. for Luke Meredith*, 1699. 8°. T.C.III 116. L, O, C, GC, BQ, DT; CLC, NC, NN, PBL, WF.

1701 [–] Dirt wip't off; or a manifest. *By R. N. for Richard Royston*, 1672. 4°. T.C.I 116. L, O, C, LCL, BP; CH, CLC, CU, NN, WF, Y.

1702 —A discourse of offences. *By J. Heptinstall, for Brabazon Aylmer*, 1683. 4°.* T.C.II 39. L, O, C, GC, DT; CH, IU, MH, NU, TU, WF, Y.

1703 [–] A discourse of the great disingenuity. *For Brabazon Aylmer*, 1695. 8°. L, O, C, LW, DC; CLC, INU, NU, PL, Y.

1704 Entry cancelled. Ghost.

1705 Entry cancelled.

[–] Fourth note. 1687. *See* Notes of the church.

1706 [–] A friendly conference between a minister and a parishioner of his. *By T. R. for Robert Clavell*, 1676. 8°. T.C.I 215. L, O, C, LF, YM; CH, MH, NU, PH, PSC, WF, Y.

1707 —The great wickedness. *For Brabazon Aylmer*, 1685. 4°.* T.C.II 143. L, O, C, BAMB, EN; CH, CU, MH, TU, WF, Y.

1708 — —Second edition. —, 1685. 4°.* L, LL, CS, MR, WCA; WF, Y.

1709 —Libertas evangelica. *By R. Norton, for Richard Royston, and Walter Kettilby*, 1680. 8°. T.C.I 401. L, O, LW, CS, DU, DT; BN, CLC, LC, MH, NU, PL, Y.

1710 Entry cancelled.

[–] Loyal martyr vindicated. [n.p., 1691.] *See* title.

1711 [–] The principles and practices. of certain moderate divines. *For Lodowick Lloyd*, 1670. 8°. T.C.I 29. L, O, C, P, E; CH, CLC, CN, NCU, NU, WF.

1712 [–]—Second edition. —, 1671. 8°. T.C.I 62. L, O, C, AN, EC, EN, DT; BN, CLC, CU, MH, MIU, Y.

1713 [–] The resolution of this case of conscience, whether. *By Henry Hills, jun. for Fincham Gardiner*, 1683. 4°. T.C.II 14. L, O, C, EN, DT; CH, CN, MH, NU, WF, Y.

1714 [–]—Second edition. *For Fincham Gardiner*, 1683. 4°. L, O, CT, YM, DT; CH, MH, NU, TU, WF.

1714A Entry cancelled.
[–] Resolution of this case, viz. 1683. *See* Franklin, John.

1714B —A scriptural catechism. *For Richard Cumberland*, 1696. 8°. O, EC.

1715 [–] A second defence of the propositions. *For B. Aylmer*, 1695. 4°. T.C.II 556. L, O, C, SHR, EN; CH, MH, MU, NU, WF, Y.

1716 —A sermon preached . . . Aug. 7. 1681. *For R. Royston, and Walter Kettilby*, 1681. 4°.* T.C.I 458. L, O, C, E, DT; CLC, CN, MH, NU, TU, WF, Y.

1717 — —Second edition. —, 1681. 4°.* L, C, LW, CT; CH, MH, NP, V, WF, Y.

1718 —A sermon preached . . . December the 9th, 1684. *By T. B. for Braybazon Aylmer* [*sic*], 1685. 4°.* T.C.II 110. L, O, C, MR, DT; CH, IU, NU, TU, WF, Y.

1719 —A sermon preached before the . . . Lord Maior of London, . . . Wednesday in Easter week. *By T. M. For Brabazon Aylmer*, 1688. 4°.* L, O, C, LIU, LSD; CLC, NU, TU, WF, Y.

1720 —A sermon preached . . . April the xvith. 1690. *By T. M. for Brabazon Aylmer; and Awnsham Churchill*, 1690. 4°.* T.C.II 310. L, O, C, GC, DT; CH, NU, TU, WF, Y.

1720A — —[Anr. ed.] *By T. M. for Awnsham Churchill*, 1690. 4°.* CD.

1721 —A sermon preached . . . March 22. 1690/1. *By T. M. for Ric. Chiswel*, 1691. 4°.* T.C.II 357. L, O, C, CT, BAMB, CD; CH, IU, NPT, TSM, WF, Y.

1722 —A sermon preach'd . . . sixth of December, 1692. *By T. M. for B. Aylmer, and A. and J. Churchil*, 1692. 4°.* T.C.II 437. L, O, C, LG, LLP; CLC, NU, PL, TSM, WF, Y.

1723 —A sermon preached . . . Easter-Monday, 1692. *For Ric. Chiswel*, 1692. 4°.* T.C.II 401. L, OC, CT, NE, WCA; CH, IU, NGT, PL, WF, Y.

1724 —A sermon preached . . . sixteenth of April, 1696. *For B. Aylmer*, 1696. 4°.* T.C.II 576. L, O, C, BAMB, SHR; CH, CN, NU, WF, Y.

1725 —A sermon preach'd . . . June 26. 1699. *For B. Aylmer*, 1699. 8°. L, LLP, OC, BAMB, DC, EC; MH, WF.

1725A [–] Twenty eight propositions, by which. 1693. 4°. MU (imperf.).

1726 [–] A vindication of a late undertaking. *Printed*, 1692. 4°.* L, OC, BC; MH, MWA, NR, PU, WF.

1727 [–] A vindication of an undertaking of certain gentlemen. *Printed*, 1692. 4°.* L, O, OCC, SP, DT; CLC, MH, MWA, NC, WF, Y.

1728 [–] A vindication of the divines of the Church of England. *For Brabazon Aylmer*, 1689. 4°.* L, C, OC, YM, DT; CH, CN, MH, NU, WF, Y.

1729 [–] A vindication of The friendly conference. *By Sam. Roycroft, for R. Clavel*, 1678. 8°. T.C.I 293. I, C, LF, OC, BC; CH, MH, MU, PH, WF, Y.

1729A **Fowler, James.** The catechism of the Church of England, poetically paraphrased. *By Tho. Hodgkin*, 1678. 8°. I.

1730 **Fowler, John.** Carmen pastorale lugubre. A pastoral elegy. *By W. O. for the author, and sold by Bennet Banbury; and J. Nutt*, 1700. fol.* T.C.III 215. LLP, MR; CLC, IU, MH, TU, Y.

1731 —The history of the troubles of Suethland and Poland. *By Thomas Roycroft for Thomas Dring*, 1656. fol. L, O, CT, EN, DT; BN, CH, CLC, NC, WF, Y.

1732 — —[Anr. ed.] *By Thomas Roycroft for Henry Twyford*, 1656. fol. L, OC; LC, MH, MU, PHS, TO, WF, AMB.

1732A **Fowler, Matthew.** Gods esteem of the death of his saints. *By William Godbid*, 1656. 4°.* BLH; MH, MWA.

1733 —Ἡ ἀνωθεν σοφια, or the properties of heavenly wisdom. *For Benj. Tooke*, 1682. 4°. T.C.I 469. CT, SHR; CH, TSM, V, WF.

1734 Entry cancelled.
—Sermon preached. 1656. *See* —Gods esteem.

1735 —Totum hominis, being a sermon . . . November 26. 1661. *By H. L. to be sold by Henry Eversden*, 1662. 4°.* L, C.

1736 **Fowler, Robert.** A Quaker's sea-journal. *For Francis Cossinet*, 1659. 4°.* L.

1737 Entry cancelled. Date: 1709.

1738 **Fox, Francis.** A sermon preached . . . July 3, 1683. *For Walter Kettilby*, 1683. 4°.* T.C.II 37. L, O, C, CT, BAMB; CH, MBA, NU, WF, Y.

1739 **[Fox, George], elder.** A tous ceulx, qui vouldroyent cognoistre la voye au royaume. *Imprimé à Londres povr Giles Calvert*, 1655. 4°.* LT, O.

1740 [–] A tous ceulx qui voudront cognoistre. *Re-imprimé à Londres pour M. W. Lané*, 1661. 4°.* L, LF; PH.

1740A [–] A tous governeurs, peuples. [*London?* 1661.] 4°.* LF.

1740B [–] All Friends everywhere. [*London, by John Bringhurst*, 1683.] cap., 4°.* L, LF, OC, MR; MH, PSC.

1740C [–] All you people that have had a tenderness formerly. [*n.p.*, 1660?] brs. L.

1741 —The ancient simplicity. [*London*, 1661.] brs. L.

1742 [–] An answer to a paper which came from the Papists. *For Thomas Simmons*, 1658. 4°. L, O, LF, CT, BBN; IE, MH, PH, RPJ, Y.

1743 [–] An answer to Doctor Burgess his book. *For Tho. Simmons*, 1659. 4°.* L, LF, OC, CT, BP; MH, PH, PL, PSC, Y.

1744 [–] An ansvver to several new laws and orders. [*London*], *printed*, 1678. 4°.* L, O, LF, BBN, MR; CH, MH, MU, NN, RPJ, WF, Y.

1745 [–] An answer to the arguments of the Iewes. colop: *For M. W.*, [1661]. 4°. L, LF, BBN, MR; CH, MH, NN, PH, PSC, RPJ.

1746 —An answer to the speech or declarlation [*sic*] of the Great Turk. [*London*], *printed, and sold, by A. Sowle*, 1688. 4°.* L, O, LF, MR; MH, NNM, PH, PSC, RPJ, Y.

1747 [–] An answer to Thomas Tillams book. *For Thomas Simmons*, 1659. 4°.* L, O, LF, CT, BBN; MH, MU, NNM, NU, PH, RPJ, Y.

1748 [–] The arraignment and condemnation of Popery. [*London*], *printed*, 1675. 8°. L, C, LF, LLP, CT; CH, MIU.

1749 [–] —[Anr. ed., "arraignment of Popery."] —, 1679. 8°. LF, CT; PH.

1750 [–] —[Anr. ed.] *Printed and sold by T. Sowle*, [1684?]. 4°. LF, LIU; IE, NU, PH, PSC.

1750A [–] The arraignment of Popery. *Printed*, 1667. 4°. L, O, LF, MR, BLH; CLC, LC, MH, PH, PSC, Y. (var.)

1750B [–] —[Anr. ed.] [*London*], *printed*, 1669. 4°. L, O, C, LF, BBN, DT; CH, CN, PH, RPJ, WF, Y. (var.)

1751 —A battle-door for teachers. *For Robert Wilson*, 1660. fol. L, O, C, LF, AN, EN; CH, CN, IC, MU, NU, PH, WCL, WF, Y.

1752 —The beginning of tythes. [*London*], *printed*, 1676. 4°.* L, LF, BBN; IE, MH, PH, PHS.

1753 [–] Cæsar's due rendred unto him. [*London*], *printed*, 1679. 4°.* LF, BBN; CH, MB, PH, PL, RPJ, WCL, WF.

1754 —Cain against Abel. [*London?*], *printed*, 1675. 4°.* O, LF, BBN, MR; CLC, LC, MH, MU, NC, PH, RPJ, Y.

1755 [–] Canons and institutions. *Printed*, 1669. 8°.* L, O, C, LF, EN; CH, PH, PSC, WF.

1756 [–] A catechisme for children. *For Giles Calvert*, 1657. 8°. L, LF, MR.

1756A [–] —Second edition. —, 1657. 8°. LT, O, LF.

1756B [–] —[Anr. ed.] *For Thomas Simmons*, 1658. 8°. LF.

1756C [–] —[Anr. ed.] —, 1660. 8°. LF; PH.

1757 [–] Cathechismus pro parvulis. *Pro Roberto Wilson*, 1660. 8°. LF; BN.

1758 —The cause why Adam & Eve were driven out. *For Benjamin Clark*, 1683. 4°.* L, LF, OC, BBN, MR; CH, MH, NN, PH, PSC, WF, Y.

1759 —The Christian judges, so called. [*London?*], *printed*, 1676. 4°.* L, O, LF, BBN; CH, MH, NN, PH, PSC, WF, Y.

1760 —Christian liberty commended. [*London?*], *printed*, 1675. 4°.* L, O, C, LF, BBN; CH, IU, PH, PSC, RPJ, Y.

1761 [–] Christ's light the only antidote. [*London?*], *printed*, 1662. 4°.* L, LF, BBN, MR; CLC, MH, NNM, PH, PSC, WF, Y.

1762 —Christ's parable of Dives and Lazarus. [*London*], *printed*, 1677. 4°.* L, C, LF, OC, BBN; CH, CSB, PH, WF, Y.

1763 [–] A clear discovery wherein. [*London*], *printed*, 1662. 4°.* L, LF; CH, NP, PH, RPJ.

1764 —A collection of many select and Christian epistles. Second volume. *Printed and sold by T. Sowle*, 1698. fol. L, O, LF, CT, LLU; CH, CN, LC, MH, NU, PL, Y.

1765 [–] Concerning Christ the spiritual and holy head. [*n.p.*], *printed*, 1677. 4°.* L, O, LF; CH, MH, PH, PSC.

1765A [–] Concerning daily sacrifices and offerings. [*London*, 1688.] brs. LF.

1766 [–] Concerning good-morrow, and good-even. *For Thomas Simmons*, 1657. 4°.* LT, O, LF, BBN; PH, PSC, RPJ, Y.

1767 [–] Concerning marriage. colop: *For Thomas Simmons*, 1661. cap., 4°.* L, O, LF, BBN, DT; CH, CN, MH, PH, PSC, RPJ, Y.

1768 [–] Concerning meeting in houses. [*London*, 1683.] 4°.* L, LF, BBN, MR; PH, WF.

1769 —Concerning persecution in all ages to this day. *By John Bringhvrst*, 1682. 4°.* L, O, LF, BBN, MR; CH, CN, MH, PH, PSC, WF, Y.

1770 —Concerning revelation, prophecy. [*London*], *printed*, 1676. 4°. L, O, LF, BBN, MR; CH, MH, NU, PH, PSC, Y.

1771 [–] Concerning sons and daughters. colop: *By M. W.*, 1660. cap., 4°.* PSC.

1772 [–] —Second edition. colop: *For M. W.*, [1661]. 4°.* L, LF, OC, BBN; NNM, PH, PSC, RPJ, Y.

1772A [–] Concerning such as have forbidden preaching. *For Thomas Howkins*, 1684. fol.* LF; PH.

1772B [–] Concerning such as shall enter. [*London?* 1684.] 4°.* LF.

1773 [–] Concerning the antiquity of the people of God. *Printed*, 1689. 4°. C, LF, OC, BBN; PSC.

1774 [–] Concerning the apostate Christians. *By Andrew Sowle*, 1688. 4°. L, O, LF, BBN, ENC, DT; NNM, NU, PH, PSC, Y.

1775 —Concerning the living God of truth. *For Benjamin Clark*, 1680. 4°.* L, O, LF, OC, BBN; CH, MH, PH, RPJ, WF.

1775A [–] Concerning the pure and undefiled religion. *By John Bringhurst*, 1685. fol.* LF.

1775B [–] Concerning the traditions. [*London*, 1688.] cap., 4°.* L, O, LF, ENC, DT; CLC, LC, NNM, PH, WF, Y.

1776 —Concerning the true baptism and the false. [*London*, 1676.] 4°.* L, O, LF, OC, BBN; PH, PSC, Y.

1776A [–] Concerning the upright and good conversation. *By John Bringhurst*, 1682. fol.* LF.

1777 [–] A controversie which hath been. [*London?* 1666.] cap., 4°.* L, C, LF, OC, BBN, MR; CN, MH, PH, PSC, RPJ, Y.

1778 [–] The copies of several letters. *For Thomas Simmons*, 1660. 4°. L, OC, MR, YM; CH, MH, PH, PSC, RPJ, WF, Y.

1779 [–] A cry for repentance. *Lonnon* [*sic*], *for Thomas Simmons*, 1656. 4°.* LT, LF, BBN; CH, IE, MH, PH, PSC, Y.

1780 [–] The cry of the oppressed. *For Giles Calvert*, 1656. 4°.* LT; MBZ, Y.

1781 [–] Cunctis Christi apostolorum sanctorumque. To all the professors. *For Robert Wilson*, 1660. 4°.* L, O, LF, BBN; BN, PH, Y.

1782 [–] Cunctis viam in regnum. *Pro Roberto Wilson*, 1660. 4°.* L, MR; BN, WF.

1782A [–] Dear friends, keep your meetings. [*n.p.*, 1664.] brs. L; PH.

1783 [–] A declaration against all Poperie. [*London*, 1655.] cap., 4°.* LT, LF, OC, CT, BBN, DT; CH, PH, PSC, Y. (var.)

1784 [–] A declaration against all profession. *For Giles Calvert*, 1655. 4°.* LT, LF; PH.

1785 [–] A declaration concerning fasting, and prayer. *For Thomas Simmons*, 1656. 4°.* LT, O, C, LF, BBN; CH, IE, MH, PH, PSC, WF, Y.

1786 [–] A declaration from the harmless & innocent people of God, called, Quakers. "Second" edition. [*London*, 1660.] cap., 4°. C, LF, LPR, OC; CH, MU, PH, PSC, RPJ, WF, Y.

1787 [–] —"Third" edition. colop: *For Robert Wilson*, 1660. 4°.* L, O, LF, MR; CH, IE, PH, PSC, RPJ, WF.

1788 [–] —[Anr. ed.] [*London*, 1684?] 4°.* L, LF, LG; CH, IE, LC, MH, PH, PSC, RPJ.

1789 [–] —[Anr. ed.] colop: *Reprinted by John Bringhurst,* 1684. cap., 4°.* LF, BP; NU, PSC, RPJ, VC, Y.

1790 [–] A declaration of the difference of the ministers of the word. *For Giles Calvert,* 1656. 4°.* LT, O, LF, OC, BBN; IE, MH, NNM, PH, PSC, WF, Y.

1791 [–] A declaration of the ground of error. *For Giles Calvert,* 1657. 4°.* LT, O, LF, BBN, MR; MH, MU, NU, PH, Y. (var.)

1792 —A declaration to the Iews. *For John White,* 1661. 4°.* L, O, LF, BBN; CH, MBZ, MH, PSC, WF.

1793 [–] A demonstration to the Christians. [*London*], *printed,* 1679. 4°.* L, LF, BBN, MR; MH, MU, NNM, PH, PSC, RPJ, Y.

1794 [–] The devil was and is the old informer. *By John Bringhurst,* 1682. 4°.* L, LF; CH, MH, PH, PSC, SYRACUSE.

1795 [–] —[Anr. ed.] colop: *By John Bringhvrst,* 1682/3. cap., 4°.* L, O, LF, BBN, MR; CH, CN, MH, NU, PH, RPJ, WF, Y.
—A dialogue between. 1700. *See* Young, Samuel.

1795AA [–] A discovery of some fruits. colop: *For T. Simmons,* 1656. cap., 4°.* LT, LF, OC; CH, MH, MU, PH.

1795A [–] A distinction between the new covenant and the old. [*London*], 1679. brs. LF; PII.

1796 [–] A distinction between the phanatick spirit. *For Robert Wilson,* 1660. brs. LF, BBN, EN; PH, PSC.

1797 [–] A distinction between true liberty. [*London*, 1685.] cap., 4°.* L, LF, BBN, BC, MR; IE, MH, NNM, PH, PSC, WF, Y.

1798 [–] A distinction betwixt the two suppers of Christ. [*London*], *printed,* 1685. 4°.* LF, BBN; PH, PSC, Y.

1799 —An encouragement for all to trust in the Lord. *For John Bringhurst,* 1682. 4°.* L, LF, OC; PH, PSC, WF, Y.

1800 —An epistle concerning the government of Christ. *For Benjamin Clark,* 1681. 4°. L, C, LF, OC, BBN; CH, NNM, PH, PHS, PSC.

1801 [–] An epistle from the people. [*London*], *printed,* 1668. 4°.* L, C, LF; CH, PH, PSC, RPJ.

1802 [–] An epistle general to them who are. *For Thomas Simmons,* 1660. 4°.* L, LF, CT, MR, GU; CH, IU, LC, MH, PH, RPJ, Y.

1803 [–] —[Anr. ed.] *For Tho: Simmons,* 1660. 4°.* LF, CT.

1803A [–] An epistle to all Christians, Jews, and Gentiles. *For John Bringhurst,* 1682. brs. LF.

1804 [–] An epistle to all Christians to keep to yea, yea, and nay, nay. *For Benjamin Clark,* 1682. 4°.* C, LF, BBN; PH, PHS, PSC, RPJ, WF.

1804A —An epistle to all my dear friends . . . in America. *Swarthmore, Eng.,* 1675. brs. PH, PSC.

1805 [–] An epistle to all people on the earth. *For Giles Calvert,* 1657. 4°.* LT, LF; MH, PH, PSC, Y.

1805A —An epistle to all planters. *For Ben. Clark,* 1682. brs. L, LF, OC; MH, PHS.

1806 —An epistle to all professors in New-England. [*London?*], *printed,* 1673. 4°.* L, O, LF, BBN, MR; CH, LC, MH, MU, NC, PH, RPJ, WF.

1807 [–] An epistle to be read in all the assemblies of the righteous. [*London*], *printed,* 1666. 4°.* L, LF, OC, CT, BBN, EN; CH, CN, MH, PH, PSC, WF, Y.

1808 Entry cancelled.
—Epistle to be read in all the Christian meetings. [*London*], 1662. *See* —General epistle.

1809 [–] An epistle to be read in the men and womens meetings. [*London*, 1677.] cap., 4°.* L, LF, BBN, MR; MH, NU, PH, PHS, PSC.

1810 [–] An epistle to Friends, by G. F. [*London*, 1678.] cap., 4°.* L, LF, MR; CH, MH, PSC, RPJ, Y.

1811 [–] An epistle to Friends for them to read. [*London*, 1679.] cap., 4°.* L, O, LF, OC, BBN, MR; NNM, PH, PSC, Y.

1812 [–] An epistle to the houshold of the seed of Abraham. *Printed and sold by John Bringhurst,* 1682. 4°. C, LF, BBN; PH, PSC.

1813 — —[Anr. ed.] [*London*], *re-printed,* 1698. 4°.* MH, PH, PSC, RPJ, Y.

1814 [–] The eternal, substantial truths. *For Robert Wilson,* 1661. 4°.* L, LF, ORP, BBN, MR; CH, NP, PH, PSC, Y.

1815 [–] An exhortation to all people, to pureness. *By John Bringhurst,* 1685. 4°.* L, O, LF; MH, NNM, PH, PSC, WF, Y.

1816 —An exhortation to all them that profess themselves Christians. [*London*], *printed,* 1680. 4°.* LF, BBN; MH, PH, RPJ, WF.

1816A [–] An exhortation to faith. 1656. brs. LT.

1817 [–] A few plain vvords by vvay of querie. *For Robert Wilson,* 1660. brs. L, LF; CH.

1817A [–] A few queries for Thomas Moor. [*London?* 1660.] 4°.* L, LF, CT; PH, PSC.

1818 [–] A few vvords to all such (whether Papists or Protestants). *Printed,* 1669. 4°.* L, O, C, LF, MR; CH, CN, LC, MH, PH, Y.

1819 —For all the bishops and priests. [*London*, 1674.] 4°. L, O, LF, CT; BN, CH, MH, PH, RPJ, Y.

1820 [–] For the holy women that trust in God. [*London*, 1686.] 4°.* L, LF, BBN; U. MISSOURI.

1821 [–] For the King, and both Houses. *For Robert Wilson,* 1661. 4°.* L, LF, BBN, LIU, MR; CH, MH, MU, PH, PSC, WF.

1822 [–] For the king and his Council, these. [*London*, 1660.] cap., 4°.* L, LF, LG, BBN, MR; CH, MH, PH, PSC, RPJ, WF, Y.

1823 —For the Pope, cardinals and Jesuites. *For John White,* 1661. 4°. L, O, LF, BBN; LC, MBZ, PL, PSC.

1823A [–] For your whoredoms in the city of London. [*London?* 1660.] cap., fol.* L, LF.

1823B [–] Friend! Who art called a teacher. *For Robert Wilson,* 1660. brs. L.

1824 [–] A general epistle to all Friends. All my dear friends. colop: [*London*], *for M. W.,* [1664]. cap., 4°.* L, LF, OC, BBN; MH, PH, PSC, RPJ, Y.

1825 [–] A general epistle to be read in all the Christian meetings. [*London*], *printed,* 1662. 4°.* L, O, LF, BBN, MR; CH, CN, MH, PH, PSC, WF, Y.

1826 [–] A generall epistle to Friends. *Printed,* 1667. 4°.* L, LF, OC, CT, BBN, MR; MH, PH, PSC, RPJ, WF.

1827 [–] —[Anr. ed.] —, 1668. 4°.* L, LF; CN.

1828 [–] A general epistle to Freinds [*sic*] by G. F. 1670. [*London?* 1670.] cap., 4°.* L, OC, MR; CH, MH, NNM, PH, RPJ, Y.

1829 [–] Gospel family-order. [*London*], *printed,* 1676. 4°.* L, LF, BBN; CH, LC, MH, MU, PH, PSC.

1830 No entry.

1831 [–] Gospel-liberty, and the royal-law of love. [*London*], *printed*, 1668. 4°. L, C, LF, OC, BBN; CH, MH, PH, PSC, RPJ, WF, Y.

1832 —The great mistery of the great whore unfolded. *For Tho: Simmons*, 1659. fol. L, O, C, LF, LW, E; CDA, MH, NU, PH, RPJ, WF, Y.

1833 [–] The ground of desperation. [*London*, 1656.] brs. LT, LF, OC; PH, PSC.

1834 [–] The ground of high places. *For Thomas Simmons*, 1657. 4°.* LT, LF; CH, IE, PH, PSC, WF, Y.

1835 [–] The heathens divinity. [*London*], *printed*, 1671. 4°.* L, O, LF, CS, BBN; CH, CN, MH, PH, WF, Y.

1836 [–] —Second edition. —, 1672/3. 4°.* L, O, LF; CH, MH, NC, NU, PH, PSC, Y.

1837 [–] Here all may see a clear distinction. [*London*], *printed*, 1680. 4°. L, LF, MR; CH, IE, NU, PH, WF.

1838 [–] [Here all may see, that] [*sic*] justice and judgement is to rule. *For Thomas Simmons*, 1656. 4°.* LT, LF, CT; CH, IE, PH, PSC, RPJ, WF.

1839 [–] Here are several queries. *For Giles Calvert*, 1657. 4°.* LT, LF, CT, BBN; CH, MH, NU, PH, RPJ, WF.

1840 [–] Here is declared the manner of the naming of children. *For Thomas Simmons*, 1658. 4°.* L, O, LF, BBN, MR; CH, CN, PH, RPJ.

1841 [–] Here you may see what was the true honour. *For Robert Wilson*, 1660. 4°.* L, LF, CT, BBN, MR; MH, NU, PH, PSC, Y. (var.)

1842 Entry cancelled.

1843 No entry.
    —Hidden things brought to light. [n.p.], 1678. *See* Rich, Robert.
    —Honest, upright. 1659. *See* Fox, George, *younger*.

1844 [–] How God's people are not to take the names. *Printed*, 1687. brs. L, LF, BBN; PH.

1845 —The hypocrites fast. [*London*], *printed*, 1677. 4°.* L, LF, CS, BBN; CDA, CLC, PH, PSC, WF.

1846 [–] Iconoclastes: or a hammer. [*London?*], *printed*, 1671. 4°.* L, O, LF, OC, CT, BBN; CH, MH, NNM, PH, Y.

1847 [–] Institutiones pietatis. [*London*], *printed*, 1676. 8°. C; BN, PHS, PL.

1848 [–] An instruction to judges & lawyers. *For Thomas Simmons*, [1657]. 4°.* L, O, LF, CT, BBN; IE, MH, PH, WF, Y.

1849 [–] Instructions for right spelling. [*London?*], *printed*, 1673. 12°. L, LF.

1850 [–] —[Anr. ed.] [*London*], 1680. 12°. BN.

1851 — —[Anr. ed.] *For Benjamin Clark*, 1683. 12°. LF; CB, IU, PSC.

1851A [–] —[Anr. ed.] *Printed and sold by T. S.*, 1691. 12°. LF; CH.

1851B [–] —[Anr. ed.] *Printed and sold by T. Sowle*, 1694. 12°. MH.

1852 — —[Anr. ed.] [*London*], *printed and sold by T. Saule*, 1697. 12°. LF; PSC, WF.

1852A — —[Anr. ed.] —, 1700. 12°. LF, LLL.

1853 Entry cancelled.

[–] Instructions of godliness. [n.p.], 1676. *See* —Institutiones pietatis.

1853A [–] The inward and spiritual warfare. [*London*], *printed*, 1690. 4°.* LF, OC; PSC.

1853B —John James, I hearing that thou doest make a noise. *For M. W.*, [1658]. 4°.* L, LF.

1854 —A journal. *For Thomas Northcott*, 1694. fol. L, O, C, LF, DT; CLC, CN, MH, PSC, RPJ, WF, Y, AVP.

1855 [–] The Lambs officer is gone forth. *For Thomas Simmons*, 1659. 4°.* L, O, C, LF, BBN; MH, PH, PSC, RPJ, Y.

1856 —The law of God, the rule for law-makers. *For Giles Calvert*, 1658. 4°.* LT, LF, OC, BBN, DUS; IE, PH, RPJ, Y.

1857 [–] The line of righteousness. *For Robert Wilson*, 1661. 4°.* L, LF, LUG, BBN, MR; CH, IU, MH, PH, WF, Y.

1858 — —[Anr. ed.] [*London*], *printed*, 1674. 4°.* L, C, LF, BBN, MR; CH, MH, PSC, WF, Y. (var.)

1859 [–] A looking-glass for the Jews. [*London*], *printed*, 1674. 8°. L, O, LF, OC; PH.

1860 —The man Christ Jesus the head of the church. [*London*], *printed*, 1679. 4°.* L, LF, BBN, MR; CH, MH, NU, PH, WF, Y.

1861 [–] Margarita in Anglia. [*London*], *pro Roberto Wilson*, 1660. 4°.* LSD; BN, PH, WF, Y.

1862 [–] A measuring-rule concerning liberty. [*London*, 1661.] 4°.* L, LF, BBN, MR; CH, MH, NNM, NP, PH, PSC, Y.

1863 —A message from the Lord. *Printed*, 1654. 4°.* LT, O, C, LF, BBN; CH, MH, PH, PSC, RPJ.

1864 —A New-England fire-brand quenched. [*London*], *printed*, 1678. 4°. ORP; CH, MB, MH, NN, PH, RPJ, Y.

1865 — —[Anr. ed.] — 1679. 4°. L, LF, CT; PHS, PL, RPJ, WF, Y.

1866 — —The second part. [*London*], *in the year*, 1678. 4°. L, LF, OC, ORP, MR; MU, PL, RPJ, WF, Y.

1867 [–] Newes coming up out of the North. *For Giles Calvert*, 1654. 4°.* LT, O, LF, CT, BBN; LC, MH, NNM, PH.

1868 [–] —[Anr. ed., "nevves".] —, 1655. 4°.* L, C, LF, CT, DU; CH, IU, MH, PH, WF, Y.

1869 —Of bowings. *For Thomas Simmons*, 1657. 4°.* LT, O, LF, CT, BBN; NU, PH, PL, RPJ, Y.

1870 [–] Old Simon the sorcerer. *Printed*, 1663. 4°.* L, O, LF, BBN; CH, PH, RPJ, WF, Y.

1871 —Omnibus magistratibus. [*London*, 1656.] 4°.* LT, O, LF; PH.

1871A [–] Omnibus, vel ullis illorum in mundo Regibus. To all Kings. [*London*, 1660.] 4°.* LT, LF.

1871B [–] Our covenant with God. *For Thomas Simmons*, 1660. brs. L, O; CH, PH, PSC.

1872 [–] A paper sent forth into the world from them that are scornfully called Quakers. colop: *Printed, and are to be sold by Giles Calvert*, 1654. cap., 4°.* LT, O, LF, BC, MR; CH, MH, NU, PH, PSC, RPJ, Y.

1873 [–] —[Anr. ed.] —, 1655. cap., 4°.* L, LF; CH.

1874 [–] —[Anr. ed.] —, 1656. cap., 4°.* C, LF, OC; PSC.

1875 [–] —[Anr. ed.] —, 1657. cap., 4°.* LF; CH, PL, PSC.

1875A [–] —[Anr. ed.] [n.p., 1658?] cap., 4°.* CH, LC, MH.

1876 [–] —[Anr. ed.] colop: *For Thomas Simmons*, 1659. cap., 4°.* L, C, LF; CH, MH, PH, PSC, Y.

1876aA [–] —[Anr. ed.] colop: *For Thomas Simmons*, [1659]. cap., 4°.* OC.

1876A [–] A paper to Friends, and others. *By John Bringhurst*, 1682/3. brs. LF.

1877 —The Papists strength. *For Thomas Simmons*, 1658. 4°. L, O, LF, BBN; CH, NPT, PH, RPJ, WF, Y.

1878 [–] The pearle found in England. *For Thomas Simmons*, 1658. 4°.* L, LF, CT, BBN, EN; CN, MH, PH, PSC, Y. (var.)

1879 [–] —Second edition. —, 1658. 4°.* LF; Y.

1880 [–] —[Anr. ed.] *For Robert Wilson*, 1660. 4°.* LF, CT, LSD, YM; BN, PH, WF.

1880A —The people of God in scorn called Quakers their love. [*London*], *printed*, 1676. 4°.* C, MR; CH, MH, NNM, PH, PSC.

1881 —Possession above profession. [*London*], *printed*, 1675. 4°.* L, O, LF, OC, BBN, MR; CH, MH, MU, PH, Y.

1882 [–] The priests and professors catechisme. *For Giles Calvert*, 1657. 4°.* LT, LF, BBN; CH, MH, NPT, NU, PH, RPJ, Y.

1883 [–] The priests fruits made manifest. And the fashions. *For Thomas Simmons*, 1657. 4°.* LT, LF; CH, MH, PH, PSC, RPJ, WF.

1883A [–] The priests fruits made manifest, and the vanity. *For Thomas Simmons*, 1657. 4°.* LF, MR; IE, MH, PH.

1883B [–] A primmer and catechism for children. [*London*], *printed*, 1670. 12°. L, LF.

1884 —A primer for the schollers. *For Thomas Simmons*, 1659. 4°. MADAN 2424. L, O, LF, CT, BBN; MH, NC, NU, PH, WCL, Y.

1885 —Primitive ordination and succession, of bishops. [*London?*], *printed*, 1675. 4°. L, O, LF, CT, BBN; CH, CN, MH, PH, RPJ, WF, Y.

1886 [–] La primitiue ordination et succcssion dcs cveques. [*London?*], *imprimée*, 1686. 4°. L, LF, BBN; PH, PSC, V.

1887 —Principia quædam illius electi a Deo populi. *Pro Roberto Wilson*, 1662. 4°.* LF; BN, PH.

1888 [–] Pro imperatore Chinensi. *Pro Roberto Wilson*, 1660. 4°.* LF; BN, PH, Y.

1888A [–] The promise of God proclaimed. *For Thomas Simmons*, 1660. brs. O; MB, PH.

1889 —The Protestant Christian-Quaker. *For Benjamin Clark*, 1680. 4°.* L, C, LF, OC, BBN; CH, MH, NNM, PH, WF.

1889A [–] Queries concerning tythes. [*London?* 1663.] brs. L, LW.

1890 [–] A reply to the pretended vindication of the answer. *For Thomas Simmons*, 1658. 4°.* L, CT, LF, BBN; CH, MH, PH, RPJ, WF.

1891 [–] Responsio ad chartam. *Pro Roberto Wilson*, 1660. 4°.* LF; BN.

1892 [–] The royal law of God revived. [*London*], *printed*, 1671/2. 4°.* L, LF, OC, CT, BBN; CH, MH, NNM, PH, PSC, Y.

1893 [–] The saints (or they that are born of the spirit). *By John Bringhurst*, 1683. 4°.* C, LF, OC, BBN; CLC, PH, PHS, WF.

1894 [–] Saul's errand to Damascus. *For Giles Calvert*, 1653. 8°.* LT, LF, BP; NNM, PSC, WF.

1895 [–] —[Anr. ed.] —, 1654. 4°.* L, O, LF, CT, AN, MR; CH, CU, MH, PH, PSC, Y.

1895A [–] —[Anr. ed.] —, 1655. 4°.* LF.

1896 —Scriptunculæ quædam Anglico-Latinæ, . . . some papers. *Pro Roberto Wilson*, 1660. 4°. LF, LLP, CT, DC; BN, LC.

1897 [–] A Scripture testimony against persecution. [*London*, 1688.] cap., 4°.* L, C, LF, BBN; NNM, Y.

1897A [–] A Scripture testimony to the saint's practices. [*London?* 1672.] 4°.* LF; MH, NR, PH, PSC.

1898 [–] The second covenant, which doth manifestly make known. *For Thomas Simmons*, 1657. 4°.* L, LF, BBN, MR; IE, PH, PSC, WF.

1899 [–] The secret workes of a cruel people. *Printed*, 1659. 4°.* LF; CH, CN, MH, PL, RPJ, Y.

1900 [–] The serious peoples reasoning. *For Thomas Simmons*, 1659. 4°.* L, O, C, LF, BBN; MH, NNM, PH, PSC, Y.

1901 —Several papers given forth: the heads of which. *For Thomas Simmons*, 1660. 4°. L, O, LF, BBN, MR; NP, PH, PSC, Y.

1902 [–] Several papers given forth for the spreading of truth. [*London*], *printed*, 1671. 4°. L, O, LF, CT, BBN; BN, CH, MH, MU, PH, RPJ, WF, Y.

1903 —Severall papers: some of them given forth by. [*London*], *printed*, 1653. 4°.* LT, LF, OC, MR; CH, MH, NN, PH, PSC.

1904 ——[Anr. ed.] —, 1654. 4°.* L, O, LF, OC, MR; PH, PSC.

—Several petitions answered. 1653. *See* Nayler, James.

1904A [–] Several plain truths manifested and declared. *Printed and sold by Andrew Sowle*, 1684. 4°.* L, LF; PH, PHS, PSC.

1905 [–] Several treatises worthy of every true Christian's serious consideration. *For Thomas Northcott*, 1691. 4°. C, LF; CH, PH, PHS.

1905A [–] A short epistle to Friends. 1678. brs. LF.

[–] Silent meeting. [n.p.], 1671. *See* Britten, William.

1906 —A small treatise concerning swearing. *Printed*, 1675. 8°. LF, OC, BBN; PSC, PU.

1907 —Some principles of the elect people of God. *For Robert Wilson*, 1661. 4°.* L, LF, BBN, DT; MH, PH, PL, PSC, RPJ.

1908 Entry cancelled.

[–] —[Anr. ed.] [n.p.], 1671. *See* Penington, Isaac, *jr.*

1908A [–] Some queries to all the teachers. [*London?* 1666.] brs. L; PSC.

1909 [–] Something by way of query to the Bishop's courts. [*London*], *printed*, 1671. brs. L, LF, CT; PSC.

1909A [–] Something concerning silent meetings. [*London?* 1657.] brs. L, LF, MR; CH, PH, PSC.

1910 [–] Something in answer to a book called, Fiat lux. *Printed*, 1667. 4°.* O, LF, BBN; CH, IE, NU, PH.

1911 —Something in answer to a law. [*London*, 1679.] 4°.* LF; CH, PH, PHS, RPJ.

1912 [–] Something in ansvver to a letter (which I have seen). [*London*, 1678?] cap., 4°.* L, LF, BBN; CH, MH, PH, RPJ, WF.

1913 —Something in ansvver to all such as falsly say, The Quakers are no Christians. *Printed and sold by Andrew Sowle*, 1682. 4°.* L, C, LF, OC; MH, PH, PSC, RPJ, WF.

1914 [–] Something in answer to Lodowick Muggleton's book. *Printed*, 1667. 4°.* L, LF, BBN; CH, MH, PH, RPJ, WF.

1915 [–] Something in answer to that book. *For Robert Wilson,* 1660. 4°.* L, LF, CT, BBN, MR; CN, PH, PSC, WF, Y.

1916 [–] Something in ansvver to the old Common-Prayer-Book. *For Robert Wilson,* 1660. 4°.* L, LF, CT, BBN, DU; CH, CN, MH, NU, PH, RPJ, Y.

1916A [–] The spirit of envy, lying and persecution. *Printed,* 1663. 4°.* L, LF; MH, PH, PSC.

1917 —The spirit of man. [*London*], *printed,* 1677. 4°.* L, C, LF, OC, BBN; CH, MH, PH, PSC, WF, Y.

1918 —The spiritual man Christ Jesus. [*London*], *printed,* 1677. 4°.* L, O, LF, BBN, MR; CH, MH, NNM, PH, Y.

1919 —A spiritual or Heavenly salutation. *For Thomas Northcott,* 1690. 4°.* L, LF, BBN; CH, NNM, PH.

1920 —Spiritualis necnon divina salutatio. *Impensis Thomæ Northcott,* 1690. 4°.* L, O, LF, BBN; CH, CN, LC, MH, PH, PSC, RPJ, Y.

1921 —The state of the birth. [*London*], *printed,* 1683. 4°.* NU.

1922 ——[Anr. ed.] *Printed and sold by Andrew Sowle,* 1683. 4°.* C, LF, BBN; MH, NU, PH, PSC.

1923 —The summ of such particulars as are charged against George Fox . . . with . . . his answer. colop: *For Thomas Simmons,* 1660. cap., 4°.* L, O, CT, BBN, EN; CH, MH, PH, PSC, RPJ, Y.

1923A [–] Surely the Magistrates of Nottingham are blinde. colop: *For Thomas Simmons,* 1659. brs. L, LF.

1924 [–] The teachers of the world unvailed. *For Thomas Simmons,* 1655. 4°.* CH, PH.

1924A [–] —[Anr. ed.] —, 1656, 4°.* LT, O, C, OC, BBN; CH, PH, PSC, WF.

1925 —A testimony concerning justification. [*London*], *printed,* 1677. 4°.* L, LF, CS, BBN, MR; CH, MH, NU, PH, PSC.

1926 ——[Anr. ed.] —, 1680. 4°.* L, LF; WF.

1926A [–] A testimony concerning our dear Friend . . . George Watt. [*London,* 1688.] 4°.* LF; PH, PSC.

1926B [–] A testimony concerning the blood. [*London?* 1678.] 4°.* LF, LLL, MR; PH, PSC.

1927 —A testimony for all the masters of ships. [*London*], *printed,* 1677. 4°.* L, LF, BBN; CN, PH, PHS, WF.

1927A ——Second edition. —, 1677. 4°.* LF; PH.

1928 —A testimony for God's truth. [*London*], *by A. Sowle,* 1688. 4°.* L, LF, BBN; NNM, PSC.

1929 —A testimony of the trve light. *For Giles Calvert,* 1657. 4°. LT, O, LF, CT, BBN; CH, CN, MH, NU, PH, RPJ, Y.

1930 —A testimony, of what we believe of Christ. [*London*], *printed,* 1677. 4°. L, LF, BBN, MR; CH, MH, PH, PSC, WF, Y.

1931 [–] That all might see who they were. *For Thomas Simmons,* 1657. 4°.* L, LF, BBN, MR; CH, IE, MH, NU, PH, Y.

1932 [–] These queries are given forth. colop: [*London*], *for M. W.,* [1665?]. cap., 4°.* L, LF, OC, BBN; NCD, PH, PSC.

1932aA [–] —[Anr. ed.] colop: [*London*], *for E. L.,* [167p?]. cap., 4°. PL.

1932A [–] Thirty of the priests errours published. *For Robert Wilson,* 1660. brs. L, LF; PH.

1933 —This for each Parliament-man. *For Thomas Simmons,* 1656. 4°.* L, O, LF, MR; IE, PH, PSC, RPJ, WF.

1933A [–] This is a controversy. [*London*], *printed,* 1664. 4°.* LF, DT; PH, WF, Y.

1933B —This is a warning to all that profess Christianity. [*London?* 1679.] 4°.* L, LF; MH, PH.

1934 [–] This is an encouragement to all the womens-meetings. [*London*], *printed,* 1676. 8°. LF, CT; IE, MM, NU, PH, PSC.

1935 [–] This is to all officers. *For Thomas Simmons,* 1657. 4°.* LT, O, LF, MR; CH, IE, PH, RPJ, Y.

1936 [–] This is to all people who stumble. [*London*], *for Mary Westwood,* 1660. brs. L, LF, BBN; PH, PSC.

1936A [–] This is to all the prisoners. colop: *By J. B.,* 1684. 4°.* LF, OC; PH, PSC.

1937 [–] Three general epistles to be read. [*London*], *printed,* 1664. 4°.* L, O, LF, BBN; CH, MH, NN, PH, PSC, RPJ, Y.

1938 [–] To all kings, princes. *By John Bringhurst,* 1685. 4°.* L, C, LF, MR; CH, CN, LC, MH, NR, NU, PH, RPJ.

1939 —To all magistrates and people in Christendom. [*London*], *printed,* 1676. 4°.* L, O, C, LF, BBN; CH, MH, NU, PH, WF, Y.

1939A [–] To all magistrates in Christendom. *Printed,* 1686. brs. L, LF, DL.

1940 [–] To all people in Christendom. colop: [*London*], *for M. W.,* 1663. cap., 4°.* L, LF, OC, BBN; MH, NNM, NP, PH, Y.

1941 —To all rulers and magistrates. *By John Bringhvrst,* 1683. 4°.* L, LF, BBN; CH, MH, MU, NNM, PH, Y.

1941A [–] To all that professe Christianity. *For Thomas Simmons,* 1661. 4°.* L, LF, BBN, MR; CH, IE, MH, NU, PH, WF, Y.

1942 [–] To all that would know. [*London*], 1653. 4°.* LF, MR.

1942A ——[Anr. ed.] [*London,* 1654.] 4°.* LT, C, LF; PH, PU.

1943 [–] —[Anr. ed.] *Printed at London,* 1655. 4°.* L, O, C, LF, CT, MR; CB, CH, PH, PSC, Y.

1944 Entry cancelled. Ghost.

1944A [–] —Fourth edition. *For Giles Calvert,* 1658. 4°.* L, LF, MR; CH, PH, PSC.

1945 [–] —"Fourth" edition. *For Robert Wilson,* 1660. 4°.* L, LF, CT, MR, YM; BN, CH, MH, PH, WF, Y.

1946 ——[Anr. ed.] [*London?*], *printed,* 1671. 4°.* L, LF, OC, CT, AN; CH, MH, NU, PH, WF, Y.

1947 ——[Anr. ed.] —, 1675. 4°.* L, LF; NC, PH, RPJ.

1947A ——"Fifth" edition. *For Thomas Northcott,* 1691. 4°.* LF.

1948 [–] To all the ignorant people. [*London,* 1655.] cap., 4°.* LT, LF, OC, CT, MR; PH, PSC.

1949 —To all the Kings, princes, and governours. [*London*], *printed,* 1677. 4°.* LF, BBN, MR; CH, MH, PH, V, WF, Y.

1949A [–] To all the magistrates in London, &c. [*n.p.,* 1657?] brs. L.

1950 [–] To all the nations under the whole heavens. *For Robert Wilson,* 1660. 4°.* L, LF, CT, BBN; CH, MH, PH, PSC, WF, Y.

1951 [–] To all the people who meet. colop: *For Thomas Simmons,* 1657. cap., 4°.* L, LF, OC, CT, MR; CH, IE, PH, PSC, RPJ, WF.

1952 [–] To both Houses of Parliament. Friends, here is a few things. *For Thomas Simmons,* 1660. brs. L, LF, BBN; CH, PH, PL, Y.

1953   [–] To Friends in Barbadoes. [*London?* 1666.] cap., 4°.* L, LF, CT, BBN, MR; LC, PH, V.

1954   [–] To the chief magistrate. [*London,* 1684.] brs. L, LF, LPR, BBN; CH, PH, Y.

1955   [–] To the Councill of officers. [*London,* 1659.] cap., 4°.* L, C, LF, OC, BBN; CH, CN, MH, PH, RPJ, WF, Y.

1955A   [–] To the flock of Christ. *For Benjamin Clark,* 1681. brs. L, LF.

1956   [–] To the Great Turk. *For Ben. Clark,* 1680. 4°.* L, LF, BBN, LLU, MR; CH, MH, NNM, PH, WF, Y.

1956A   [–] To the high and lofty ones. [*London?* 1655.] cap., 4°.* L; PH.

1957   —To the ministers, teachers, and priests . . . in Barbadoes. [*London*], *printed,* 1672. 4°. L, LF; CH, PH, RPJ, V.

1957A   [–] To the Parliament of the Commonwealth of England. A declaration of the sufferings . . . in New England. [*n.p.,* 1659?] cap., 4°.* L; CLC.

1958   [–] To the Parliament of the Comon-wealth [*sic*] of England. Fifty nine particulars. *For Thomas Simmons,* 1659. 4°.* L, O, LF, CT, BBN; CLC, MH, MU, PL, RPJ, Y.

1959   [–] To the people of Uxbridge. *For Thomas Simmons,* 1659. brs. L, LF, BBN.

1960   [–] To the Pope and all his magistrates. *For Thomas Simmons,* 1661. 4°.* L, LF, BBN, MR; CH, MH, NU, PH, WF, Y.

1961   [–] To the Protector and Parliament. *For Giles Calvert,* 1658. 4°. LT, LF, OC, MR; CH, NU, PH, RPJ, Y.

1962   [–] To thee, Oliver Cromwell. colop: *For Giles Calvert,* 1655. 4°.* O, C, LF, MR; NHS, PH.

1963   [–] To those that have been formerly in authority. *For Robert Wilson,* [1660]. 4°.* L, LF, CT, BBN, MR; CH, MH, NP, PH, PSC, Y.

1964   [–] To you that are crying. colop: *For Thomas Simmons,* [1657]. cap.,4°.* L, LF, OC, CT, BBN; CH, IE, LC, PH, PSC, WF, Y.

1965   [–] A true account of the sensible, thankful and holy state of God's people. [*London*], *printed,* 1686. 4°.* LF, BBN; CH, MH, PH, WF.

1966   [–] The true Christians distinguished. *For Thomas Northcott,* 1689. 4°.* L, LF, BBN; RPJ.

1967   [–] True ivdgement, or, the spiritual-man. *For Giles Calvert,* 1654. 4°.* LT, LF, BBN; CH, MH, PH, PSC, Y.

1968   [–] The true marriage declared. [*London,* 1679.] 4°.* L, LF; PH.

1969   [–] The trumpet of the Lord sounded. *For Giles Calvert,* 1654. 4°.* LT, LF, BBN, DT; PH, PSC.

1970   —Truth's defence. [*n.p.*], *for Tho: Wayt, in York,* 1653. 4°. LT, LF, OC, BBN, YM; MH, PSC.

1971   [–] Truth's triumph in the eternal power. *For Thomas Simmons,* 1661. 4°.* L, LF, CT, BBN, DT; MBZ, NU, PH, PL, WF, Y.

1971A   [–] Trying of spirits in our age now. *For Benjamin Clark,* 1683. 4°.* L, LF, OC; CN, PH, PSC, WF.

1972   [–] Turcæ et omnibus sub ejus ditione, to the Turk. *For Robert Wilson,* 1660. 4°.* L, O, LF, BBN; PH, WF.

1973   —Tythes, offerings, and first-fruits. *For Benjamin Clark,* 1683. 4°.* L, O, C, LF, BBN; MH, PH, PSC, RPJ, Y.

1974   —The unmasking and discovering of anti-Christ. colop: *For Giles Calvert,* 1653. cap., 4°.* L, LF, OC, BBN, MR; MH, NNM, PH, PSC, RPJ, Y.

1975   —The vialls of the wrath of God. *For Giles Calvert,* 1654. 4°.* L, LF; Y.

1976   — —[Anr. ed.] —, 1655. 4°.* L, O, LF, OC, MR; CH, IE, MH, PH, WF, Y.

1977   —Vires pontificorum fractæ. *Apud Thomam Simmons,* 1659. 4°. LF; BN.

1978   [–] A visitation to the Iewes, *For Giles Calvert,* 1656. 4°.* LT, C, LF, CT, BBN, MR; CH, MH, PH, RPJ, WF, Y.

1979   [–] A voice of the Lord to the heathen. colop: *For Thomas Simmons,* 1656. 4°.* L, LF, OC, CT, BBN; CH, PH, PSC, RPJ.

1980   [–] A warning from the Lord, to all such as hang down the head. *For Giles Calvert,* 1654. 4°.* LT, LF, OC, BBN, MR; CH, MH, PH.

1980A   [–] —[Anr. ed.] *Printed at London,* 1654. 4°.* CII, MII, PII, PSC.

1981   [–] A vvarning from the Lord to the Pope. *For Giles Calvert,* 1656. 4°.* LT, LF, CT, BBN, DT; CN, MH, PH, PSC, RPJ, WF, Y.

1982   —A warning to all in this proud city, called London. [*London,* 1655.] brs. LT, LF.

1983   —A warning to all teachers of children. colop: *For Thomas Simmons,* 1657. cap., 4°.* LT, LF, BBN; CH, IE, PH, RPJ.

1984   [–] —[Anr. ed.] *For Thomas Simmons,* 1657. 4°.* MR; CH, MH, NPT, RPJ, WF, Y.

1985   [–] A warning to all the merchants in London. *For Thomas Simmons,* 1658. 4°.* L, LF, BBN; CH, IE, MH, NC, PH.

1986   [–] A warning to England and to all . . . Christians. [*London*], *printed,* 1674. 12°.* L, LF, OC, BBN, MR; PH.

1987   —A warning to the world. *For Giles Calvert,* 1655. 4°.* LT, O, LF, BBN; CH, NNM, NU, PH, PSC, Y.

1987A   [–] A way to prevent the indignation. *For John Bringhurst,* 1682. brs. LF.

1987B   — —[Anr. ed.] —, 1683. brs. LF.

1988   [–] The West answering to the North. *For Giles Calvert,* 1657. 4°. LT, MR; CH, CU, PH, PSC, WF.

1989   [–] What election and reprobation is. [*London*], *printed,* 1679. 4°. L, LF, BBN, MR; BN, CH, MH, NNM, PH, Y.

1989A   [–] What the unchangable God is. [*London?* 1685.] cap., 4°.* L, LF, MR; CH, IAU, PH, PSC, Y.

1990   [–] Why we deny the teachers. 1656. PSC.

1991   —The vvoman learning in silence. *For Thomas Simonds,* 1656. 4°.* LT, O, C, LF, BBN; CH, NNM, PH.

1991A   [–] A word from the Lord, to all the world. *For Giles Calvert,* 1654. 4°.* LT, O, OC, DC; PH, PL, PSC.

1992   —A word from the Lord, vnto all the faithlesse. [*London*], *printed,* 1654. 4°.* L, O, C, LF, BBN; NHC, PH, PSC.

1993   [–] A word in the behalf of the King. *For Robert Wilson,* 1660. 4°.* L, LF, CT, BBN, MR; CH, MH, PH, PSC, WF, Y.

1994   —A word of admonition to such as wander. *For Thomas Howkins,* 1684. 4°.* L, LF, OC, BBN; CLC, MH, PH, PSC, WF.

1995   [**Fox, George**], *younger*. The breathings of true love. colop: *For Robert Wilson*, 1660. cap., 4°.* L, LF, BBN, MR; CH, MH, PH, PSC, WF, Y.

1996   —A collection of the several books and writings. *For Robert Wilson*, 1662. 8°. L, O, C, LF, DU; CH, NU, PH, PSC, SW.

1997   — —Second edition. *Printed*, 1665. 8°. L, O, LF, OC, CT; BN, CH, CN, PH, WF, Y.

1998   —Compassion to the captives. *For Thomas Simmons*, 1656. 4°.* LT, LF, BBN, MR; CH, MH, PH, PSC, Y.

1998A   — —[Anr. ed.] *For Robert VVilson*, 1662. 4°. IU.

1999   —The dread of Gods power. *For Robert Wilson*, [1660]. 4°.* L, O, C, LF, BBN; CH, MH, PH, PSC, WF, Y. (var.)

2000   —Englands sad estate. *For Robert Wilson*, 1661. 4°.* L, O, C, LF, BBN; CH, CU, MH, PH, WF, Y. (var.)

2001   —An exhortation to families. [*London*, 1659.] brs. L, O, LF, CT, BBN; CH, PH, WF, Y.

2002   —A few plain words. *For Thomas Simmons*, 1659. 4°.* L, O, LF, BBN, MR; PL.

2002A   —A few queries to the teachers. *For Robert Wilson*, 1660. brs. L, LF; CH, WF.

2003   —For the Parliament of England and their army. colop: *For M. W.*, 1659. brs. LF.

2003A   — —[Anr. ed.] [*London*, 1660.] brs. L, LF; PL, WF.

2004   [–] A general epistle and a tender greeting. colop: *For Robert Wilson*, 1660. cap., 4°.* L, LF, CT, MR; CH, IU, MH, PH, PSC, WF, Y. (var.)

2005   [–] Honest, plain, down-right-dealing. colop: *For Robert Wilson*, 1660. cap., 4°.* LT, O, C, LF, BBN; CH, CN, MH, NGC, PH, PSC, WF, Y. (var.)

2005A   —Honest, vpright, faithful, and plain dealing. *For Thomas Simmons*, 1659. 4°.* L, LF; CH, PH.

2006   —A message of tender love. *For Thomas Simmons*, 1660. 4°.* L, LF, CT, BBN, MR; CH, MH, PH, PSC, WF, Y.

2006A   —Vn mot au people du monde. *Imprimé à Londre pour M. W.*, [1659?]. 4°.* LF.

2007   —A noble salutation, and a faithful greeting. *For Giles Calvert*, 1660. 4°.* L, C, LF, OC, BP, EN; CH, CN, LC, MH, PH, Y. (var.)

2008   — —[Anr. ed.] *For S. D. and are to be sold by Robert Wilson*, 1660. 4°.* LF, CT, LIU, EN; CH, IU, MH, PH, WF, Y.

2009   — —[Anr. ed.] *For Robert Wilson*, 1660. 4°.* LT, O, LF, CT, MR, CD; NU, PH, PSC, WF, Y. (var.)

2009A   [–] Oh people! my bowels yearn. [*London?* 1670.] brs. L, OC.

2010   —The testimony of God. colop: *For Thomas Simmons*, 1660. cap., 4°.* L, O, LF, BBN; CH, MH, PH, PSC, WF, Y.

2011   —This is for you. *For Thomas Simmons*, 1659. 4°.* L, LF, BBN.

2012   Entry cancelled. —To all that professe Christianity. 1661. *See* Fox, George, *elder*.

2013   [–] To the called of God. colop: *For Thomas Simmons*, 1660. cap., 4°.* L, O, C, LF, BBN; CH, LC, MH, PH, Y.

2014   —A true relation of the unlawful and unreasonable proceedings. colop: *For Robert Wilson*, 1660. cap., 4°.* L, LF, BBN; CH, IU, MH, PH, PSC, WF, Y.

2015   —Two epistles. *For William Warwick*, 1663. 4°.* L, O, LF, OC, MR; MH, PSC.

2016   —Two general epistles. *For William Warwick*, 1663. 4°.* L, O, C, LF, BBN; IE, PH, PSC, WF, Y.

2017   —A visition [*sic*] of love. *For Thomas Simmons*, 1659. 4°.* L, MR; CH, MH, PH, PHS, PL, Y.

2018   —A visitation of love. —, 1659. 4°.* L, O, C, LF; PH, PL, PSC, Y.

2019   Entry cancelled. [–] What the unchangable God is. [n.p., 1685.] *See* Fox, George, *elder*.

2020   [–] A word to the people of the world. colop: *For Thomas Simmons*, 1659. 4°.* L, O, LF, CT, BBN; PH, PSC, Y.

2020A   — —[Anr. ed.] —, 1660. 4°.* L, LF, GU; CH, MH.

2021   —The words of the everlasting and true light. *For Thomas Simmons*, 1659. 4°.* L, O, C, LF, BBN; CH, MH, PH, PSC, WF, Y. (var.)

Fox, John, *pseud. See* Bayle, Pierre.

2022   **Fox, John.** The door of Heaven opened. *For Sam. Sprint*, 1676. 12°. T.C.I 250. L, LCL, LSC; CLC, NU, NPT.

2022A   — —[Anr. ed.] *For Samuel Sprint*, 1689. 12°. TO.

2022B   [–] Time and the end of time. [*London?* 1664?] CLC.

2022C   [–] —[Anr. ed.] *Printed*, 1669. 12°. CLC.

2023   — —[Anr. ed.] *For Tho. Passinger, and Tho. Sawbridge*, 1670. 12°. Y.

2024   — —[Anr. ed.] *For George Calvert and Sam. Sprint*, 1670. 12°. T.C.I 13. L; IU.

2025   — —[Anr. ed.] *For William Rawlins*, 1671. 12°. L, LLL, LW, DC.

2026   — —[Anr. ed.] *Printed and are to be sold by G. Calvert*, 1674. 8°. O, DT.

2026A   — —[Anr. ed.] *By William Rawlins, and are to be sold by George Calvert, and Samuel Spring*, 1679. 12°. CH.

2027   — —[Anr. ed.] *For John Pickard*, [1680?]. 12°. L, LLL.

2027A   — —[Anr. ed.] *For William Rawlins, to be sold by Samuel Sprint and Ralph Sympson*, [1680?]. 12°. L, LW, DU; CLC, MH, NGT, U. ALBERTA, WF.

2027B   — —[Anr. ed.] *By William Rawlins, and are to be sold by George Calvert, and Samuel Sprint*, 1681. 12°. P, BLH; MH.

2027C   — —[Anr. ed.] —, 1683. 12°. L, LSC, AN; CLC, IU, WF, Y.

2028   — —[Anr. ed.] *Belfast, by Patrick Neill and company*, 1700. 12°. BLH.

2028A   **Fox, John**, *gent*. John Fox gent. plaintiff: and Simon Harcourt esq. defendant. [n.p., 1694.] brs. L.

Fox, Margaret. *See* Fell, Margaret.

2029   The fox-chace. *By and for W. O.*, [1690?]. brs. L. (var.)

2029A   —[Anr. ed.] —*and sold by C. Bates*, [1700?]. brs. NNM.

2030   The fox-hunting. [1680?] brs. L, LADY MARGARET HALL.

2031   The fox too cunning for the lyon. *For Charles Tyus*. [1659–63]. brs. L, HH; MH, Y.

2032   The fox unkennel'd. *By J. Benson*, [1672]. brs. L, O.

2032A   **Foxcroft, John.** The altogether-Christian. *By J. Darby for J. Robinson*, 1695. 4°. T.C.II 537. C.

2033   —The beauty of magistracy. *By J. D. for Jonathan Robinson*, 1697. 4°.* T.C.III 12. L, LLP, LW, SC; CH, IEG, Y.

2034   —The good of a good government. *For Tho. Badger, and are to be sold by G. Badger,* 1645. 4°.* LT, C, LCL, OM, EN, DT; CH, MH, MU, WF, Y.

2035   **Foxe, John.** Acts and monuments of matters most speciall . . . in the church. Eighth edition. *For the company of stationers,* 1641. 3v. fol. L, O, C, ENC, DT; CH, CN, NNM, NU, WF, Y.

2036   ——Ninth edition. —, 1684. 3v. fol. L, O, C, MR, ES, CD; BN, CH, IU, MH, NU, WF, Y.

2037   —A brief historical relation. *For William Redmayne,* 1676. 8°. T.C.I 217. L, O, C, DU; WF.

2037A   [–] A brief history of the most material passages and persecutions. *For William Redmayne,* 1686. 8°. IU.

2038   —Christus triumphans. Comœdia apocalyptica. *Impensis Rob. Clavel,* 1672. 8°. T.C.I 104. L, O, C, CK, ENC; CH, CU, RHT, WF.

2039   ——[Anr. ed.] —, 1676. 8°. CN, RBU.
       [–] Continuation of the histories. 1641. *See title.*

2040   Entry cancelled.
       —Idem iterum. [n.p., 1686.] *See title.*

2041   —King Jesvs is the beleevers prince. *By J. Dawson,* 1645. 8°.* LT, ORP; MB, NHC, Y.

2042   [–] Μαρτυρολογια αλφαβετικη, or, an alphabetical martyrology. *For R. Butler,* 1677. 8°. L, O; IAU, IU.

2043   —Of free justification by Christ. *For Tho. Parkhurst,* 1694. 8°. T.C.II 520. LCL, LLP, LW, RPL, ENC; CH, IU, MU, NU, WF, Y.

2044   [–] Proposals for printing the Book of Martyrs. [London, 1683.] brs. LG (lost).
       Foxes and firebrands. 1680. *See Nalson, John.*

2044A   The foxes craft discouered. [London], printed, 1649. 4°.* LT; CLC, MH.

2044B   [**Foxle, George.**] The groans of the spirit. Third edition. *For Michael Spark,* 1652. 12°. L; CLC.

2045   **Foxon, William.** A brief discovery of the particular. *By James and Joseph Moxon, for William Larnar,* 1649. 8°. LT.
       Foxonian Quakers. 1697. *See Young, Samuel.*

2046   **Foy, Nathaniel,** *bp.* A sermon preached . . . the 23d. of Octr., 1698. *Dublin, by Andrew Crook, for Samuel Adey,* 1698. 4°.* DIX 300. L, O, C, DT, DM; WF, Y.

2046A   **Foy de la Neuville.** An account of Muscovy. *For Edward Castle,* 1699. 8°. T.C.III 123. L, O, C, LLL; CH, CLC, MH, RPJ, WF.

2047   [**Foyer, Archibald.**] A defence of the Scots settlement at Darien. With an answer. [n.p.], printed, 1699. 4°. 60pp. LIU; CN, CSU, NN, RPJ, WF, Y.

2047A   [–] —[Anr. ed.] *Edinburgh,* printed, 1699. 8°. 86pp. A–F⁸. L, O, DU, EN, GU, DT; CH, CLC, CN, MH, MU, RPJ.

2047B   [–] —[Anr. ed.] —, 1699. 8°. 86pp. A–M⁴. O, C, LLP, EN, DT; CN, IU, MB, RPJ, Y.

2047C   [–] —[Anr. ed.] *Edenburgh,* printed, 1699. 8°. 57pp. L, DT; NC, NN.

2048   [–] Scotland's present duty. [Edinburgh], printed, 1700. 4°.* ALDIS 3965. L, O, MR, EN, GU; CH, CN, NU, WF, Y.

2049   **Fracastoro, Girolamo.** Syphilis: or, a poetical history. *For Jacob Tonson,* 1686. 8°. L, O, C, MAU, E; BN, IU, KU, MMO, NAM, JF.

2050   A fraction in the assembly. *Printed,* 1648. 4°.* LT, O; WF.
       Fragmenta antiquitatis. 1679. *See Blount, Thomas.*
       Fragmenta aulica or. [n.p.], 1662. *See S., T.*

2051   Entry cancelled.
       Fragmenta regalia. 1641. *See Naunton, Sir Robert.*

2052   **Frame, Richard.** A short description of Pennsilvania. *Printed and sold by William Bradford in Philadelphia,* 1692. 4°.* EVANS 594. NC, PL.
       Frame of the government. [n.p.], 1682. *See Penn, William.*

2052AA   **Frampton, Robert.** Glouces'. Dioces. Nov. 15. 1682 . . . Whereas we are credibly informed. [London, 1682.] brs. WCL.

2052BA   ——Whereas in pursuance. [London], 1682. brs. WCL.

2052A   **France.** The treaty and alliance between the Commissioners . . . States General. *Printed,* 1662. 4°.* MH, WF.

2052B–3   Entries cancelled.
       —Censure and declaration. 1700. *See title.*
       —Treaty of peace between the crowns. 1660. *See Louis XIV, King of France.*

2053A   **France. Parliament.** The proceedings of the Parliament of Paris, upon the Pope's Bull. *For R. Bentley, and are to be sold by Randal Taylor,* 1688. 4°.* T.C.II 216. L, O, CT, GU, CD; CH, CU, LC, MH, NP, NU, TU, Y.

2053B   La France n'ayant pas cessé. *Re-printed in London, by A. Churchill,* 1683. brs. OC.
       France no friend. 1659. *See Retz, Jean François Paul, cardinal.*
       France painted. 1656. *See Heylyn, Peter.*

2054   **Frances, Robert.** The dying speech of. colop: *By George Croom,* 1685. cap., fol.* L, O, OC, MR, SP; CH, CU, MH, PU, TU, WF, Y.

2055   **Francesse, Peter.** All gentlemen and others, may be pleased to take notice. [London, 1656.] brs. LT.

2056   **Francine, Alessandro.** A new book of architecture. *By J. Darby for Robert Pricke,* 1669. fol. T.C.I 19. L, C, DCH; CLC, LC, NC, WF, YBA.
       Francis, *abp. of Paris.* *See* Harlay de Chanvallon, François de, *abp.*
       Francis, Angelus. *See* Mason, Richard Angelus.

2057   **Francis, Benjamin.** Poems. *By T. R. for the author,* 1660. 8°. L; CH, MH.
       Francis, Claude. *See* François, Claude.

2058   **Francis, Philip.** The answer of. [n.p., 1644.] cap., 4°.* C.

2059   —The misdemeanors of a traytor. *By Jane Coe.* 1644. 4°.* LT, MR.

2060   **Francis, William.** A discourse concerning the holy fast of Lent. colop: [London], *for the author, William Francis,* 1686. 4°.* OC, CS, LSD; Y.

2061   **Francisco de los Santos.** The Escurial. *For T. Collins and J. Ford,* 1671. 4°.* L, O, CS, P, MR; CLC, MBA, MH, WF, Y.

2062   Entry cancelled.

Francisco Manoel [de Mello]. Government of a wife. 1697. *See* Mello, Francisco Manuel de.

Franciscus, Ignatius, *pseud.*

2063 Entry cancelled.

Franck, Johann Wolfgang. Remedium melancholiæ. 1690. See title.

2064 Franck, Richard. Northern memoirs. *For the author, to be sold by Henry Mortclock [sic], 1694.* 8°. L, O, MR, EN, AU; CN, LC, MH, NN, Y.

2065 —A philosophical treatise of the original and production of things. *By John Gain, and are to be sold by S. Tidmarsh, and S. Smith, 1687.* 8°. L, O, ES, GU; CH, CN, LC, MH, NP, WCL, Y.

2066 [Franck, Sebastian.] The forbidden fruit. *By T. P. and M. S. for Benjamine Allen, 1642.* 12°. CU, IU, WF, Y.

2066A Franco, Solomon. Truth springing out of the earth. *By J. Flesher, for the authour, 1668.* 4°. L, O, C, LSD, SHR; NU, OHU, WF, Y.

2066B ——[Anr. ed.] *By J. Flesher, for John Williams, 1670.* 4°. L.

2067 François, I. A looking-glasse for princes. *By W. Jones, 1642.* 4°.* O.

2068 François de Sales, *Saint.* Conduite de la confession. *A Londres, imprime chez Henry Hills, 1686.* 16°. L; NU, WF.

2068A —An introduction to a devout life. *Printed at Paris, 1662.* 12°. WF, Y.

2069 ——[Anr. ed.] *Dublin, printed and are to be sold by Joseph Wilde, 1673.* 12°. DIX 149. C, DN, E; CLC.

2069A ——[Anr. ed.] *Dublin: by Benjamin Tooke, and are to be sold by Joseph Wilde, 1673.* 12°. CS, CD.

2070 ——[Anr. ed.] *[London], for T. D., 1675.* 12°. L, O, BSM, DUS; CN, IU, MB, TU.

2070A ——[Anr. ed.] *[n.p., 1675?]* 12°. O.

2071 ——[Anr. ed.] *By Henry Hills, for Mat. Turner, 1686.* 12°. L, OC, BSM; CLC, CN, LC, NU, TU, WF.

2072 —A new edition of the introdvction to a devovt life. *At Paris, by Gilles Blaizot, 1648.* 8°. L, OC, DUS; TU, WF.

2072A — —[Anr. ed.] *[London], printed, 1669.* 12°. LSC; CLC, MH, NPT.

2072B —Vive Jesus. The rule of St. Austin. *Paris, for Rene Guignard, 1678.* 8°. L.

2073 François, Claude. A sermon at the funeral of . . . Turenne, . . . December 15, 1675. *By W. G. to be sold by Moses Pitt, 1677.* 4°.* L, O, CT, BR, EN; CH, MB, NU, WF, Y.

2074 Frank, Mark. A course of sermons. *For J. Martyn, H. Brome, and R. Chiswell; to be sold by Dorman Newman, and Jonathan Edwin, 1672.* fol. LCL, LW, SA.

2074A —LI sermons, preached by. *By Andrew Clark for John Martyn, Henry Brome, and Richard Chiswell, 1672.* fol. T.C.I 84. L, O, CJ, P, YM; WF, Y, MOORE.

2074B — —[Anr. ed.] —, *sold by Jonathan Edwin, 1672.* fol. NE; LC.

2075 Franke, Walter. The epitome of divinity. *By J. G. for Francis Eaglesfield, 1655.* 8°. L, C, LW, EN; CLC, IU, MH, UCLA, WF.

2076 [Frankenburgh, Abraham van.] A warning against the deceit. *[London], printed, 1677.* 8°. O, LF, BBN, MR; MH, MU, PH, PSC, Y.

2076A [Frankenstein, Christian Gottfried.] The history of the intrigues . . . of Christina. *For Richard Baldwin, 1697.* 12°. O; Y.

2077 Frankland, Richard. Reflections on a letter writ by a nameless author. *For A. & J. Churchill, and sold by F. Bently, in Halifax, 1697.* 4°. T.C.III 23. L, LCL, CT, BAMB; CH, MH, TO, Y.

2078 [Frankland, Thomas.] The annals of King James and King Charles the First. *By Tho. Braddyll, for Robert Clavel, 1681.* fol. T.C.I 428. L, O, CT, EN, DT; CH, CN, LC, MH, MU, NU, WF, Y.

2079 Franklin, Gracious. A soft ansvver to Captain Freeman's passionate book. *Printed and sold by Ruth Raworth, 1648.* 4°.* LT; CH, NHC.

2080 Franklin, Jacob. A bloody plot, practiced by some Papists. *For John Thomas, 1641.* 4°.* LT, O, CT, EC; CLC.

2081 [Franklin, John.] A resolution of this case, viz. whether it be lawful. *By A. Grover, for Walter Kettilby, 1683.* 4°. L, O, C, OC, DT; CH, IU, MH, NU, WF, Y.

2082 [–] A resolution of two cases of conscience. *For Walter Kettilby, 1683.* 4°.* L, O, C, GU, DT; CH, IU, MH, NU, WF, Y.

2083 Franklin, Richard, *fl. 1675.* A discourse on Antichrist. *For the author, 1675.* 4°.* L, O, LCL, LLP, LNC; CH, CLC, CU, NU, WF.

2083A ——[Anr. ed.] *For Benjamin Billingsley, 1675.* 4°.* T.C.I 210. CT, BAMB, NE; CH, CU, Y.

2084 F[ranklin], R[ichard], *d. 1632.* Ὀρθοτονια, seu tractatus de tonis. Third edition. *Excudebat Guil. Du-Gard, pro Guil. Sheres, 1650.* 12°. L, CCA, SC; IU, WF.

2085 [–] —Fourth edition. *Impensis Tho. Helder, 1673.* 12°. T.C.I 130. O, C, CS, CT; CH, CLC, IU, PL, TO.

2086 F[ranklin], R[obert]. Death in triumph. *For the author, 1683.* 4°.* L, CT; CH, Y.

2087-8 Entries cancelled.

—Murderer punished. 1668. *See* Alleine, Richard.

2089 Franklin, Thomas. An epistle written from Lucifer. *Printed, 1642.* 4°.* LT.

2090 [Franklin, William.] A letter from Tangier concerning. colop: *For J. S., 1682.* brs. L, O; CH, MH, Y.

2091 The frantick lover. *[London], for J. Deacon, [1685–88].* brs. L, O, CM, HH; MH.

2092 The frantick mother. *[London], for B. Deacon, [1670].* brs. L.

2093 The frantick 'squire. *[London], for P. Brooksby, Deacon, J. Blare, J. Black, [c. 1690].* brs. L, CM, HH; MH.

2094 Frantze, Wolfgang. The history of brutes. *By E. Okes, for Francis Haley, 1670.* 8°. T.C.I 43. L, LNH, LLU, CD; CH, CLC, WF, Y.

2095 Fraser, Alexander. Determinationes philosophicæ. *Abredeis, excudebat Ioannes Forbesius, 1693.* 4°.* ALDIS 3297. AU.

2096 —Theses philosophicæ. *Abredeis, excudebat Ioannes Forbesius, 1697.* 4°.* ALDIS 3712. AU.

2097 **Fraser, Andrew.** By Andrew Fraser . . . Advertisement for collecting . . . excyse. [*Aberdeen, John Forbes*], 1685. brs. ALDIS 2532. AC.

2098 —Advertisement . . . For the suppression of vagabonds. *Aberdeen,* [*John Forbes*], 1693. brs. ALDIS 3288. AC.

2098A **Fraser, George.** Positiones aliquot philosophicæ. *Abredeis, Ioannes Forbesius,* 1691. 4°.* ALDIS 3167. GU.

2099 —Theses philosophicæ. *Abredeis, excudebat Ioannes Forbesius,* 1695. 4°.* ALDIS 3510. AU.

Fraterna correptio: or. 1655. *See* Crofton, Zachary.

Fratres in malo, or. [n.p.], 1660. *See* Ogilvy, Michael.

Fraud and oppression. [n.p.], 1676. *See* Carew, George.

Frauds of Romish monks. 1691. *See* Gavin, Antonio.

2099A **F[reake], W[illiam].** The happinesse of a good old age. *For R. H.,* 1641. 8°.* MH.

Fréart, Roland. *See* Chambray, Roland Fréart, *sieur de.*

2100 **Frederick III of Denmark.** The King of Denmark, his declaration . . . May 17. 1653. *Printed at Copenhagen, 1653, and reprinted, at London for Henry Cripps and Lodowick Lloyd,* 1653. 4°.* LT, CCA, MR; CH, CSS, MIU, WF.

2101 —A declaration of . . . [24 June 1659]. *By E. C. for Henry Eversden,* 1659. 4°.* LT, OC, CCA; CSS, WF.

2101A —Extract of the treatie of peace between. [*Edinburgh? 1700.*] brs. HH.

2102 —Jus feciale armatæ Daniæ; with a short demonstration. *Printed,* 1657. 4°.* MR; CSS.

2103 —The King of Denmark's message to the States of Holland. *For James Williams,* 1652. 4°.* LT.

2104 **Frederick Henry, *prince of Orange.*** An ordinance or proclamation by. *For Andrew C. and Marmaduke B.,* 1641. 4°.* LT, EC, DT; CSS, MHL, WF, Y.

2105 Entry cancelled.
—Royal embassage. [n.p.], 1641. *See title.*

2106 —The royal message from the Prince of Orange. [*London*], *for Tho. Powel,* 1641. 4°.* LT, BAMB; CLC, MH, Y.

2107 **Frederick William, *elector of Brandenburg.*** The declaration of . . . [17/27 September 1658]. *For Simon Miller,* 1658. 4°.* O; CH, CSS, MM, WF.

2107A ——[Anr. ed.] *Printed,* 1658. 4°.* SP.

2108 Entry cancelled.
—Declaration of. 1689. *See* Frederick III, *elector of Brandenburg.*

2108A —A letter from the Duke of Brandenburg. colop: *For T. Davis,* 1680. brs. O, EN; CH, MH.

2109 —A letter written by. [*London*], 1659. 4°.* LT; CSS, WF.

2110 ——[Anr. ed.] *By J. C. for John Crooke,* 1659. 4°.* LT; CSS.

2110A ——[Anr. ed.] [*London*], 1669 [*i.e.* 1659]. 4°.* MH.

2110B **Frederick III, *elector of Brandenburg.*** Declaration of . . . concerning the present war with France . . . [3/13 April 1689]. *For Richard Chiswell,* 1689. 4°.* O, CT, EN, CD; CH, CN, MH, MIU, WF, Y.

2110C A free and full Parliament or General Monks. *For W. Gilbertson,* [1660]. brs. MH.

Free and impartial inquiry. 1673. *See* Eachard, John.

Free-born subject. 1679. *See* L'Estrange, *Sir* Roger.

Free but modest censure. 1698. *See* B., F.

2111 A free conference concerning the present revolution of affairs in England. *Printed: and are to be sold by R. Baldwyn,* 1689. 4°.* L, O, CT, DU, LSD; CLC, CN, NU, WF, Y.

2112 A free conference touching the present state of Enland [*sic*]. *By E. T. for R. Royston,* 1668. 8°. L, O, CT, DU, DT; CLC, CN, NC, WF, Y. (var.)

2113 —[Anr. ed.] *For Richard Royston, to be sold by Richard Chiswell,* 1673. 8°. O, SP, DT; CN, MH, Y.

2113A —[Anr. ed.] 1678. 8°. DT.

2113B The free customs, benefits and priviledges . . . of Stepney. *For Edward Husband,* 1651. 4°. L, O, DT.

2113C —[Anr. ed.] *For Henry Twyford,* 1675. 4°. L; WF, Y.

Free discourse. 1697. *See* Howard, *Sir* Robert.

Free grace exalted. 1670. *See* Sterry, Peter.

2113D The free holder's answer to Mr. John Briscoe's proposals. [*London,* 1695.] brs. LG.

2114 The freeholders choice. [*London,* 1679.] cap., fol.* L, O, C, OC, LNC, EN; CH, IU, MH, TU, WF, Y.

Free-holders grand inqvest. [*n.p.,* 1648.] *See* Filmer, *Sir* Robert.

2115 Entry cancelled.

Free inquiry into the causes. 1675. *See* Eachard, John.

Free and impartial. 1673.

Free enquiry into. 1685/6. *See* Boyle, Robert.

Free mans plea. 1648. *See* L., R.

2116 Free-men inslaved: or, reasons humbly offered to . . . Commons . . . for the taking off the excise upon beer. [*London?* 1660?] brs. L, LG; MH, NC.

2117 A free-Parliament-letany. [*London,* 1660.] brs. LT, O; MH, WF, Y.

2118 —[Anr. ed.] [*n.p.,* 1680.] brs. L.

Free Parliament proposed. [*n.p.,* 1660.] *See* L'Estrange, *Sir* Roger.

2119 No entry.

Free-Parliament quæres. [*n.p.*], 1660. *See* More, Henry.

Free ports. 1651. *See* Whitelocke, *Sir* Bulstrode.

2119A Free, regulated trade, particularly to India. [*London?* 1691.] cap., fol.* LUG, DU; MH, NC, Y.

2120 The free state of Noland. *For J. Whitlock,* 1696. 4°. T.C.II 571. L, O, CAMB. SCOTT POLAR, LSD, DT; CH, CN, INU, MB, MH, TO, ZWT.

Free thoughts concerning officers. [*n.p.,* 1698.] *See* Trenchard, John.

Free thoughts in defence. 1700. *See* Day, Robert.

2121 Free thoughts occasioned by the heads of agreement. *For Tim. Goodwin,* 1691. 4°.* T.C.II 395. O, C, LG, BAMB, AU; CLC, CN, LC, MH, NU, WF, Y.

2122 —Second edition. —, 1691. 4°.* L, O, C; CH, WF.

2123 Entry cancelled. Free thoughts of the penal laws. 1688. *See* Wetenhall, Edward.

Free trade. 1651. *See* Misselden, Edward.

2123A **Freebairn, David.** A catalogue of books to be sold . . . the sixth of May, 1700. *Edinburgh,* 1700. 8°. EN.

2124 Entry cancelled. *See following entry.*

2125 Freedom of elections to Parliament. *For Dan. Brown and Tim. Goodwin*, 1690. 4°.* T.C.II 323. L, O, CT, BC, SP; CLC, CN, LC, MH, WF, Y.

2125A Freedom of religious worship. [*London*], *printed*, 1654. 4°. O, SP, EN; NU.

2125B The freedom of the fair sex asserted. *Printed and are to be sold by J. Nutt*, 1700. 4°.* L; MB, WF.

2125C The freeholders of the county of Leicester . . . [contested election for M.P.]. [*London*, 1679?] brs. MR.

2126 **Freeman, Edward.** To the Parliament of the Commonwealth . . . the humble petition of the subscribers. [*London*, 1654.] brs. LT.

2127 **Freeman, Francis.** A brief description of a conference betwixt a nationall Presbyterian. *For Giles Calvert*, 1647. 4°.* L, LCL, SC; NU.

2128 —VIII problems propounded. *By Barnard Alsop*, 1646. 4°.* LT, O, OJ, MR, DT.

2129 —Light vanquishing darknesse. *Printed*, 1650. 4°. LT.

2130 —To the honourable the House of Commons . . . the humble petition and remonstrance of. [*London*, 1649?] brs. L.

2131–2 Entries cancelled.

Freeman, *Sir* George. *See* Freman, *Sir* George.

Freeman, Goodlove, *pseud.*

Freeman, Ireneus, *pseud.*

2133 [**Freeman, John.**] A new letter from Windsor. colop: *Printed*, 1681. brs. O; CH, CN, AVP.

2134 —A sermon preached . . . March the 12. Anno. Dom. 1643. *Printed*, 1643. 4°.* LT, O, C, MR, DT; CH, NP, NU, WF, Y.

2135 **Freeman, Lyon.** The Common-wealths catechism. *By John Clowes*, 1659. 8°.* LT, O; WF.

2136 [**Freeman, *Sir* Ralph.**] Imperiale, a tragedy. *By Thomas Harper, and are to be sold by Robert Pollard*, 1655. 4°. L, O, LVD, OW, DC, EN; CH, CN, MH, NC, TU, WF, Y.

2137 No entry.

2138 [**Freeman, Samuel.**] The case of mixt communion. *For T. Basset, B. Tooke, and F. Gardiner*, 1683. 4°.* T.C.II 15. L, O, C, GU, DT; CH, CN, MH, WF, Y.

2139 [–] —Second edition. —, 1684. 4°.* L, O, C, OC, DT; CH, CN, CSB, MH, TU, Y.

2140 [–] A discourse concerning invocation of saints. *For Ben. Tooke, and F. Gardiner*, 1684. 4°. T.C.II 59. L, O, C, EN, DT; BN, CH, CU, MH, WF, Y.

2141 —The Israelite indeed. *For Edward Gellibrand*, 1682. 4°.* T.C.I 492. L, O, C, OCC, LSD; CLC, MBA, NU, WF, Y.

2142 [–] A plain and familiar discourse by way of dialogue. *For R. Clavel, and B. Tooke*, 1687. 4°. L, O, C, EN, DT; CH, CU, MH, MU, NU, TU, Y.

2143 —A sermon preach'd . . . May 24th 1682. *For Edward Gellibrand*, 1682. 4°.* T.C.I 492. L, O, C, NE, SHR; CH, MBA, TSM, WF, Y.

2144 —A sermon preached . . . 8th of October, 1682. *By Tho. Moore for Edward Gellibrand*, [1682], 4°.* L, O, BAMB, SC, DT; CH, CLC, NU, PU, WF, Y.

2145 —A sermon preach'd . . . August the 26th. 1690. *For Richard Chiswell*, 1690. 4°.* T.C.II 333. L, O, C, CT, BAMB, LIU; CH, CLC, NCD, TU, WF.

2146 —A sermon preached . . . fifth of November, 1690. *For Ric. Chiswell*, 1690. 4°.* T.C.II 333. L, O, C, BAMB, DT; CH, NP, NU, WF, Y.

2147 —A sermon preach'd . . . December the 10th. 1693. *For Ric. Chiswell*, 1694. 4°.* T.C.II 499. L, O, C, CT, BAMB; CH, MIU, NU, TO, WF.

2148 —A sermon preached . . . Tuesday in Easter-Week, 1694. *For Ric. Chiswell*, 1694. 4°.* T.C.II 499. L, OC, CT, SHR, WCA; CB, CLC, NU, WF, Y.

2149 —A sermon preach'd . . . on Easter-Tuesday, 1698. *By Tho. Warren for Thomas Bennet*, 1698. 4°.* L, O, LLP, OC, BAMB; MH, TSM.

2150 —A sermon preach'd at the funeral of . . . Duke of Bedford. *For E. Rumball*, 1700. 4°.* L, O, OC, CS, BLH; CH, MBZ, MH, WF.

2151 **Freeman, Thornburgh.** An elegie on the death of George Monck. *By and for Thomas Ratcliffe, and Thomas Daniel*. 1670. brs. MH.

2151A The freeman's oath of the Hamborough-company. [*London?* 1680.] brs. L; MH.

2152 The free-mens petition. [*London*, 1659.] brs. L, O, LG, LS; MH.

Freeness of Gods grace. 1668. *See* W., H.

2153 Freezland-Fair. [*London*], *for Charles Corbet*, 1684. brs. L, O, LLP; CLC, MH.

2154 [**Freher, Philip.**] A treatise touching the peace of the church. *For George Thomason*, 1646. 4°. LT, O, CS, MR, EN; BN, MM, NU.

2155 **Freire de Andrade, Jacinto.** The life of Dom John de Castro. *For Henry Herringman*, 1664. fol. L, O, C, MR, E, DM; CH, CU, MH, RPJ, WF, Y. (var.)

2156 — —Second edition. *For H. Herringman, sold by R. Bentley, and D. Brown*, 1693. fol. T.C.II 467. L; CLC, LC.

2157–60 No entires.

Freize, James. *See* Frese, James.

[**Frejus, Roland de**], *sieur.* Letter, in answer. 1671. *See* Charant, Antoine.

2161 —The relation of a voyage made into Mauritania, in Africk. *By W. Godbid, and are to be sold by Moses Pitt*, 1671. 8°. T.C.I 73. L, O, CT, EN, DT; CH, CN, LC, MH, Y.

[**Freke, William.**] Account of the growth of deism. 1696. *See* Stephens, William.

2162 [–] The Arrian's vindication of himself. [*London*, 1691.] cap., 4°.* O, LW, OC, LLP, MR, E; IU, MU, NU, Y.

2163 [–] A dialogue by way of question. [*London*, 1693.] cap., 4°.* O, C, LW, LSD, WCA, DT; CN, MH, NGT, WF, Y.

2163A [–] Essays towards a union. *Printed* 1689. 8°. O, LLP, OC.

2164 [–] A full enquiry into the power of faith. *Printed*, 1693. 4°. L, O, LLP, LW, OC; MH, MIU, NGT, NU, WF.

[–] Remarks on some late sermons. 1695. *See* Leslie, Charles.

2165 —Select essays. *For Tho. Minors*, 1693. 8°. L, O, C; CH, CN, MH, WF, Y.

2166   [–] A vindication of the Unitarians. [*London*, 1687.] 4°.*
        L, O, CT, DU, EN; CH, IU, NPT.

2167   [–] —Second edition. *Printed*, 1690. 4°.* L, O, BAMB, E,
        DT; CLC, IU, NPT, NU, WF, Y.

2167A   **Freman, *Sir* George.** A dehortation from all sinne. *By
        A. M.*, 1663. 4°.* L; BROOKLYN PUB. LIB.

2167B   —Golden remains of. *By J. M. to be sold by Henry
        Bonwicke*, 1682. 8°. T.C.I 464. L, CT; IU, Y.

2167C   [–] Physiologia: or the nature of externals. *By Abraham
        Miller*, 1665. 12°. CLC.

2168   **[Frèmont d'Ablancourt, Nicolas.]** The doctor's
        physician. *For Joseph Hindmarsh*, 1685. 12°. T.C.II 97.
        L; CH, CLC, NAM, NN, WF.

2169   **French, John.** The art of distillation. *By Richard Cotes,
        and are to be sold by Thomas Williams*, 1651. 4°. LT, O,
        LWL, CT, DC, GU; CH, LC, MH, MU, Y, HC.

2170   ——Second edition. *By E. Cotes, for Thomas Williams*,
        1653. 4°. L, C, LWL, CT, GU; BN, CH, NN, PBL, WU, Y.

2171   ——Third edition —, 1664. 4°. L, C, LCP, LWL; CLC,
        MBA, WSG, WU.

2172   —Fourth edition. — ["*T. Williams*"], 1667. 4°. L, C,
        LCS, LWL, CT, GU; CH, MH, WF, WU, Y.

2173-4 Entries cancelled.
        [–] Chymicall dictionary. 1650. *See* Sendivogius,
        Michael. New light.
        —New light of alchemie. 1650. *See* Sendivogius,
        Michael.

2175   —The York-shire spaw. *For E. Dod, and N. Ekins*, 1652.
        8°. LT, O, LWL, CT, GH; CH, CLM, MH, MIU, PL, WU.

2176   ——[Anr. ed.] *For Nath: Brook*, 1654. 4°. L, O, CS, YM,
        EN; NAM.

2176A   ——[Anr. ed.] *For Richard Lambert*, 1654. 4°. WF.

2177   **[French, Nicholas.]** The bleeding Iphigenia. [*London*,
        1675.] cap., 12°. L, DT.

2178   [–] The dolefull fall of Andrew Sall. [*Louvain?*], *superi-
        orum permissu*, 1674. 8°. L, C, BQ, CD, DT; CH, NU.

2179   [–] A narrative of the Earl of Clarendon's settlement.
        Lovain, printed, 1668. 8°.* L, O, DN; MH.

2180   [–] A narrative of the settlement and sale of Ireland.
        Lovain, printed, 1668. 4°.* C, P, DT; CH, MH, WF.

2181   Entry cancelled.
        [–] Polititians cathechisme. Antworp, 1658. *See* Talbot,
        Peter.

2182   [–] Querees, propounded by the Protestant partie. *Paris,
        by Iohn Belier*, 1644. 4°.* L, C, DN; CH.

2183   [–] The vnkinde desertor of loyall men and true frinds.
        [*Paris*], *superiorum permissu*, 1676. 8°. L, O, C, DN, DT;
        CH, MH, NP, WF.

        French ambassador's speech. Dublin, 1700. *See* Briord,
        Gabriel, *comte de*.

2183A   A French and English grammar. *Deepe* [*sic*], *by Steeven
        Acher*, 1657. L(t.p.).

        French charity. 1655. *See* Cotton, *Sir* Robert Bruce.
        Answer.
        French conjurer. 1678. *See* Porter, Thomas.
        French conquest. 1693. *See* Lawton, Charlwood.

2183B   The French convert. *For John Guuillim*, 1696. 8°. CT; Y.

2183C   —Second edition. —, 1699. 8°. L; WF.

2184   The French dancing-master. *Printed*, 1666. brs. L.

        French gardiner. 1658. *See* Bonnefons, Nicholas de.
        French grammar. *See* Festeau, Paul.

2185   The French intrigues discovered. *For R. Baldwin*, 1681.
        fol.* T.C.I 453. L, O, C, MR, EN; CH, CN, MH, WF, Y, AVP.

        French intrigues; or. 1685. *See* Courtilz de Sandras,
        Gatien de.

2185A   The French King conquered. *For William Birch*, 1678.
        4°. SP.

2185B   The French King proved a bastard. Second edition.
        Abel Roper, 1691. 12°. L.

2185C   The French Kings lamentation for the death of so many
        of his generals. colop: *For T. Tillier*, 1691. brs. CN.

2185D   The French King's lamentation for the loss of his fleet.
        colop: *For R. Stafford*, 1692. brs. CN.

2186   The French King's lamentation, for the loss of his great
        general the duke of Luxemburg. colop: *For J. Whit-
        lock*, 1695. brs. MH.

        French Lucian. 1693. *See* Fontenelle, Bernard Le Bovier.
        French-man and the Spaniard. 1642. *See* Garcia, Carlos.

2187   The French man gull'd of his gold. *For John Clarke*,
        [1680?]. brs. O.

2188   The French-man's lamentation. [*London*], *for W.
        Thackery, and I. Hose*, [1675]. brs. L, HH, GU; MH, Y.

2189   The Frenchmens wonder. *For F. Coles, T. Vere, J.
        Wright, and J. Clarke*, [1674-79]. brs. O.

2190   The French mountebank. *For R. Austin and A. Coe*, 1643.
        4°.* LT, OW.

2191   The French pastry-cooke. [*London*], *N. Brooke*, 1656.
        12°. L.

2192   Entry cancelled.
        French perfumer. 1696. *See* Barbe, Simon.

2193   The French plot detected. colop: *For J. Wright*, 1693.
        brs. L, HH; MH.

2194   The French politician found out. *For Robert Harford*,
        1680. 4°. L, O, CT, LSD, DT; CH, CN, MH, WF, Y.

2195   A French prophecy. *For J. Harris*, 1690. 8°.* ENC; CU,
        INU, LC, NN, TO.

2196   —[Anr. ed.] colop: *For J. Harris*, 1691. cap., 4°. L, O, CT,
        BR, EN; CH, PL, WF.

2196A   The French prophet: being the famous predictions fore-
        telling the fate of France. *For H. Marston*, 1692. 4°. O.

2196B   The French rogue. *By T. N. for Samuel Lowndes*, 1672.
        8°. O; CLC, CN, MH, Y.

2196C   —[Anr. ed.] *For No. Boddington*, 1694. 12°. T.C.II 522.
        WF.

        French schoole-master. 1641. *See* Sainliens, Claude de.
        French spy. 1700. *See* Courtilz de Sandras, Gatien.

2196D   The French way of exercising the infantry. *For Dorman
        Newman and Jonathan Edwin*, 1672. fol.* T.C.I 120. L,
        OC, CASTLE ASHBY; Y.

2197   Entry cancelled.
        Frenus, T. De viribus imaginationis. 1657. *See* Feyens,
        Thomas.

2197aA **[Frese, James.]** Another why not. [*London*], *by I. B. and
        I. F.*, 1649. * LSE.

2197bA [–] A declaration and appeale. [*London*, 1645.] brs. LT.

2197A [–] Every mans right: or, Englands perspective-glasse. [*London*], printed, 1646. 4°.* LT, MR, EN, DT; CLC, IU, MH, WF.

2197B —The Levellers vindication. *For George Lindsey*, [1649]. 4°.* LT, O, MR; CN, MH, WF.

2197C —A moderate inspection. [*London*, 1656.] cap., 4°.* LT, OC, MR; CH, CSS.

2197D —The ovtcry! and just appeale. colop: *By T. Fawcet*, 1659. cap., 4°.* LT, OC, LSD, MR; CSS, MH, NN, WF, Y.

2197DA —A packet of newes. *Printed for Matthew Simmons*, 1651. 4°. LG, GU.

2197E —A second why not. [*London*], *by I. G. for I. B. and I. F. to be sold by G. Lindsey*, 1649. brs. LT; CSS.

2197EA —Sions approaching glory. *For W. Larnar*, 1652. 4°. NN.

2197F [–] Times present mercy. [*London*], printed, 1647. 4°.* CN, CSS, WF.

2197G [–] Why not eight queries. [*London*, 1649.] brs. LT.

Fresh bit of mutton. [n.p.], 1462 [i.e. 1642]. *See* Calfine, Giles.

2198 Fresh intelligence of another nevv and great victory. *For A. N.*, 1643. 4°.* LT; CH, CLC, WF.

Fresh memorial. 1693. *See* Beverley, Thomas.

2198A Fresh news from Cockery. colop: *Printed at Dumpenderlaw, for the Company of Stationers in Glads-moor*, [c. 1690]. cap., 4°.* ALDIS 3040.5. MH.

Fresh relation. [n.p., 1679.] *See* W., T.

Fresh suit. 1677. *See* Lamb, Thomas.

2199 A fresh whip for all scandalous lyers. *Printed*, 1647. 4°.* LT, DT; CH, MH, MIU, MM, TU, WF, Y.

2200 [**Frewen, Henry.**] An admirable speech made by the Maior of Reading. *Printed at London*, 1654. 4°.* LT, RU.

2201 Entry cancelled.

Frewen, Accepted, *bp.* Articles of visitation. York, 1662. *See* Church of England. York.

2202 **Frezer, Augustine.** The divine original. *At Rotterdam, by Reinier Leers*, 1685. 4°.* L, O, C, DU, WCA; CLC.

2202A ——[Anr. ed.] —, *and are to be sold by Nicholas Cox*, 1685. 4°.* BC.

2203 —The divine original and the supreme dignity of kings. *Oxford, by L. Lichfield, and are to be sold by Nicholas Cox*, 1685. 4°.* T.C.II 143. L, O, C, CT, LSD, WCA; CB, CLC, CN, WF, Y.

2204 —The wickedness and punishment of rebellion. *At Rotterdam, by Reinier Leers*, 1686. 4°.* L, O; CLC.

2205 The frier and the boy. *Glasgow, printed*, 1668. 8°.* ALDIS 1841.5. L.

2205A —[Anr. ed.] [*London?* 1690.] 12°.* CM.

2206 —[Anr. ed.] [*Glasgow*], printed, 1698. 8°.* ALDIS 3751. MH.

2207 Entry cancelled.

Frier Bacon his discovery of the miracles. 1659. *See* Bacon, Roger.

Friar disciplined. Gant, 1674. *See* Talbot, Peter, *abp.*

2207A The fryer well fitted. *For F. Coles, T. Vere, and J. Wright*, [1663–74]. brs. O.

2208 —[Anr. ed.] [*London*], *for W. Thackeray and T. Passinger*, [1670–82]. brs. L, O, CM, HH; MH, Y.

2208A —[Anr. ed.] *Printed by and for W. O., and sold by J. Walter*, [1690]. fol. L.

2209 The friers lamenting. *Printed at London*, 1641. 4°.* LT, WCA; CH, MH, MIU, TU, WF, Y.

2210 The friers last fare-well. *By Iohn Hammond*, 1642. 4°.* LT; WF.

2211 **Frick, Christoph.** A relation of two several voyages. *For Printed* [*sic*] *D. Brown, S. Crouch, J. Knapton, R. Knaplock, J. Wyate, B. Took, and S. Buckley*, 1700. 8°. T.C.III 154. L, O, C, DCH, DT; CH, CN, MH, MU, WF, Y.

2212 **Friend,** *Sir John.* A true copy of the papers delivered by. colop: *For William Rogers*, 1696. brs. L, LG, CCA, DU, EN; CH, CLC, IU, MH, PU, WF, Y.

2212A ——[Anr. ed.] colop: *London printed, and reprinted in Dublin*, [1696]. brs. LIU; WF.

2213 A friend to Cæsar. *For Robert Harford*, 1681. fol.* L, O, LUG, OC, SP, DU; CH, INU, MH, WF, Y, AVP.

Friendly advice, in the spirit. 1688. *See* Field, John.

2214 Friendly advice to extravagants. [*London*], *for F. Cole, T. Vere, J. Wright, J. Carlk* [*sic*], *W. Thackery, & T. Passenger*, [1678–80]. brs. HH; MH, Y.

Friendly advice to Protestants. 1680. *See* D., M.

2215 Friendly advice to the correctour of the English press at Oxford. *For Robert Clavell*, 1682. fol.* T.C.I 486. L, O, C, AN, MR; CH, NN, Y.

Friendly advice to the gentlemen-planters. [n.p.], 1684. *See* Tryon, Thomas.

Friendly and seasonable advice. 1674. *See* Comber, Thomas.

Friendly call; or. 1679. *See* Allen, William.

2216 A friendly caveat to all true Christians. *For VV. Thackeray, T. Passenger, and VV. Whitwood*, [1670–77]. brs. L, HH; MH.

Friendly check. 1645. *See* E., S.

Friendly conference between. 1676. *See* Fowler, Edward, *bp.*

Friendly conference between the suffering saints. 1699. *See* Young, Samuel.

Friendly conference concerning. 1689. *See* C.

2217 The friendly conference: or, an hue and cry after the Popes Holiness. [*London*], *for M. B.*, 1673. 4°.* L; MIU, TU.

Friendly debate between a conformist. 1666. *See* Patrick, Symon, *bp.*

Friendly debate, between a Roman Catholick. 1688. *See* Tenison, Thomas.

2218 A friendly debate between Dr. Kingsman. *For Jonathan Robinson*, 1689. 4°. T.C.II 260. L, O, C, EN, BLH; CH, CN, LC, MH, WF, Y.

Friendly debate between Satan. [n.p.], 1676. *See* Danson, Thomas.

Friendly debate betwixt two neighbours. [n.p., 1668.] *See* Patrick, Symon, *bp.*

2218A Numb. 1 A friendly debate upon the next elections of Parliament. [*London*, 1688.] cap., fol.* O; CH, IU, LC, WF.

2218B   —[Anr. ed., without "Numb. 1."] [*London*, 1688.] brs. L.

2218C   —[Same title, "Numb. 2."] [*London*, 1688.] cap., fol.* O; INU.

2219   A friendly dialogue between a livery-man. *Printed, and are to be sold by Richard Baldwin*, 1695. 4°.* L, O, LG; Y.

2219A   —Second edition. *Printed, and to be sold by John Whitlock*, 1695. 4°.* MIU, WF.

2219B   A friendly dialogue between two country-men. *For the author*, 1699. brs. CN.

2220   A friendly dialogue between two London-apprentices, the one a Whigg. colop: *For Richard Janeway*, 1681. cap., fol.* L, CT; CN, PU, WF, Y, AVP.

2221   Entry cancelled.

    Friendly discourse between an English dissenter. 1697. *See* LaFite, Daniel.

    Friendly discourse concerning profane cursing. 1697. *See* S., H.

    Friendly epistle. 1698. *See* Young, Samuel.

    Friendly letter of advice. [n.p.], 1659. *See* F., J.

2222   A friendly letter to all young men . . . of the Church of England. colop: *For Dan. Brown*, 1688. cap., 4°.* O; WF, Y.

2223   —[Anr. ed.] *Dublin, re-printed for Jacob Milner*, 1695. 24°.* DIX 265. DN.

2223A   A friendly letter to all young men, shewing the benefit. Fifth edition. *Printed and are to be sold by W. Downing*, 1699. 12°. LIU; MH.

2224   A friendly letter to Father Petre. *For Richard Baldwin*, 1690. 4°.* L, O, LLL, CT, DU, WCA; CH, MH, TU, WF, Y.

2224A   A friendly letter to such as have voices in election of members. *Printed and sold by John Whitlock*, 1695. brs. L, O, GU; CN.

    Friendly letter to the flying clergy. 1665. *See* W., J.

2225   The friendly monitor. *For Sam. Crouch*, 1692. 8°. T.C.II 409. L, O, C, OC; WF, Y.

    Friendly society. A proposal for insuring houses. [n.p., 1691?] *See* Proposal for insuring.

2226   The friendly society for widows. colop: *By F. C.*, 1696. brs. L; MH.

2227   The friendly society, or, a proposal . . . [fire insurance]. [*London*, 1684.] brs. L, LG; CH, NP.

2228   The friendly society settled. *By William Horton, October* 1684. brs. L.

2229   The friendly vindication of Mr. Dryden. *Cambridge, printed*, 1673. 4°.* L, O, LVD, LSD, A; CLC, CU, MH, TU, WF, Y.

    Friends advice. [1658–60.] *See* Campion, Thomas.

    Friends, and all people. 1660. *See* Stodart, Amos.

    Friendship. [1654.] *See* Finch, Francis.

2230   **Frierson, Henry.** A letter of a great victory. *By Robert Ibbitson*, [1648]. brs. LT.

2230A   Entry cancelled.

    Frikius, Christopher. *See* Frick, Christoph.

2231   A frivolous paper, in form of a petition. *For W: Ley and F. I:*, 1642. 4°.* L, O, DT; CLC, CN, LC, PU, Y.

2232   —[Anr. ed.] *For Stephen Bowtell*, 1642. 4°.* LT, LG, OC, CS, MR, CD; CLC, CU, MH, NU, WF.

2232A   —[Anr. ed., enlarged.] —, 1642. 4°.* O, LG; MH.

    Frog. [167–?] *See* Ogilby, John.

2233   **Froger, François.** A relation of a voyage, made in the years 1695, 1696, 1697. *For M. Gillyflower; W. Freeman, M. Wotton; J. Walthoe; and R. Parker*, 1698. 8°. L, O, CS, DU, EN; CH, CN, LC, MH, RPJ, WF, Y.

2234   The frogges of Egypt. [*London*], *printed*, 1641. 4°.* LT, LVF, EN; CH.

2235   **Froidmont, Libert.** Meteorologicorvm libri sex. *Typis E. Tyler, impensis Ed. Story, apud quem væneunt Cantabrigiæ*, 1656. 8°. O, C, LWL, SC, EC; CJC, CLC, MH, MU, NIC.

2236   ——[Anr. ed.] *Typis & impensis J. Redmayne, pro Georgio West, apud quem prostant Oxonii*, 1670. 8°. MADAN 2853*. L, O, LWL, CS, LLU; CH, LC, MB, MU, PL, WF, Y.

    Frolick to Horn Fair. 1700. *See* Ward, Edward.

    From a gentleman of Boston. [n.p., 1689.] *See* N., N.

2237   From a person of quality in Scotland, to a person of honor in London, concerning . . . James. colop: *For Joseph Heath-coat*, 1681. brs. CH.

2238   From aboard the Van-herring. A letter from Legorn, Decem. 1. 1679. [*London*, 1679.] cap., fol.* L, O, C, MR, EN; CH, CN, LC, MH, WF, Y.

    From aboard the Van-herring. Another letter from Legorn. [n.p.], 1680. *See* B., J.

2239   From aboard the Van-Herring, being a full relation. colop: *Printed*, 1680. brs. L, O, LG, OP, HH; CH, CN, MBA, WF, Y.

    From aboard the Van Herring. The answer. [n.p., 1681.] *See* B., J.

2239A   From our half-years meeting in Dublin. [*London*, 1691.] 8°.* L, LF; PH.

2239B   From our women's meeting held at York. [*London*, 1692.] cap., 4°.* L, LF; PH.

2239C   From our womens yearly meeting held at York. [*London*, 1698.] cap., 4°.* LF.

2240   —[Same title.] [*London*, 1700.] cap., 4°.* L, LF; Y.

2240A   From our yearly meeting at York. [*London*, 1690.] cap., 4°.* LF.

2240B   From the committee at sequestrations. *J. Hammond*, 1643. brs. LT; MH.

2241   From the insurance-office for houses. [*London*, 1681.] brs. L.

2242   6. Julii, 1648. From the Leaguer at Colchester, more certain news. *For Edward Husband, July* 8. 1648. 4°.* LT; CH, Y.

    From the rendezvous. York, 1647. *See* H., R.

2242aA   From the society for improving of money. [*London?* 1680.] brs. L.

2242bA   From the undertakers of the Royal Academy. [*London?* 1695.] brs. LG.

2242A   From the women's meeting dated York. [*London*, 1696.] cap., 4°.* LF.

2242B   From the yearly meeting at Burlington. [*Philadelphia, by W. Bradford*, 1692.] brs. MHS, PRF.

2243 **Fromman, Andreas.** Synopsis metaphysica. *Oxoniæ, typis H. Hall, impensis Th. Gilbert,* 1669. 8°. MADAN 2829. O, C, LW; AUSTRALIAN NAT. UNIV.

2244 ——[Anr. ed.] *Oxoniæ, typis L. Lichfield, impensis Tho. Gilbert, et Elis. Gilbert,* 1691. 12°. L, C, LL, OC, BC; CU, PL, TO, WF, Y.

Fromondus, Libertus. *See* Froidmont, Libert.

2244aA **Frontinus, Sextus Julius.** The stratagems of war. *For S. Heyrick, and R. Sare,* 1685. 12°. CLC.

2244A ——[Anr. ed.] *For S. Heyrick, J. Place, and R. Sare,* 1686. 12°. T.C.II 170. L, O, CM; MH, MIU, PU, TO, WF.

Frontispice [*sic*] of the King's book. [n.p., 1650.] *See* Somner, William.

2245 **Frost, John.** Fides justificat. [*n.p.*, 1656.] brs. O.

2246 —Select sermons. *Cambridge, by John Field,* 1657. fol. L, O, C, LCL, LW; WF.

2247 ——[Anr. ed.] *Cambridge: by John Field, to be sold by Thomas Pierrepont, London,* 1658. fol. L, O, C, CT, GU; CH, NPT, NU.

2247A **Frotte, Pierre.** Some particular motives. colop: *By James Langford,* 1691. cap., 4°.* L, LLP; MBA.

2247B ——[Anr. ed.] *For Richard Baldwin,* 1691. 4°.* L, LLP, OC.

2248 The frowns of fate. [*London*], *for J. Deacon,* [1684–95]. brs. L, CM, HH.

2249 **Froysell, Thomas.** [Hebrew], or, the beloved disciple. *By M. S. for Thomas Parkhurst,* 1658. 8°. L, C, LCL, LSC, LW, DU; CH, CLC, CU, WF, Y.

2249A —The gale of opportunity. *By M. S. and are to be sold by H. B.,* 1652. 4°.* LW; TO.

2250 ——[Anr. ed.] *By M. S. for Thomas Parkhurst,* 1658. 8°. L, C, LW; CH, CLC, CU, Y.

2251 —Sermons concerning grace. *For Tho. Parkhurst,* 1678. 4°. T.C.I 289. L, O, C, LCL, AN; CLC, IU, MH, NP, Y.

Fructifera, Lapis, *pseud.*

Fruit-walls improved. 1699. *See* Fatio de Duiller, Nicolas.

2251A [A fruteful?] and learned sermon preached in London. [*London*], *printed,* 1670. 8°.* MH.

2252 Fruitfull England like to become a barren wilderness. *Printed,* 1648. 4°.* LT, LIU, MR; CH, CLC, MH, WF, Y.

Fruitful wonder. 1674. *See* P., J.

2253 The fruits of faith. [*London*], *sould by Rich. Tompson,* [1656]. brs. LT.

Fruits of unrighteousnes and injustice. 1658. *See* Smith, Humphry.

2254 **Fry, John.** The accuser sham'd. *For John Harris, Febr.* 1648. 4°.* LT, O, C, OC, MR; CH, CSS, CU, MM.

2255 —The clergy in their colovrs. *For Giles Calvert,* 1650. 8°. LT, O, YM; CLC, NU. (var.)

2256 [–] Θειος. Divine beames of glorious light. *By Robert Ibbitson,* 1651. 4°.* LT, LG, DT; CLC.

2257 **Fryer, John.** A new account of East-India. *By R. R. for Ri. Chiswell,* 1698. fol. L, O, C, MR, EN, DT; BN, CLC, CU, LC, MH, NC, NN, WF, Y.

Fryke, Christopher. *See* Frick, Christoph.

2257aA **Fryth, Richard.** A probable calculation of the moneys. [*London,* 1700?] brs. L; NC.

2257A **Fuce, Joseph.** The fall of a great visible idol. *For Thomas Simmons,* 1659. 4°. L, LF, MR.

2258 —A special warrant given forth. *Printed,* 1663. 4°.* L, LF, CT, BBN, MR; CSS, IE, MH, PH, WF, Y.

2258A —A visitation by way of declaration. *For Thomas Simmons,* 1659. 4°. LF; PL.

Fuga peccati. 1677. *See* DuBois, Nicholas.

2259 The fugitive statesman. *By A. Grover,* 1683. 12°. T.C.II 3. L, O, CT, A; CLC, CN, PU, TU, Y.

2259A Fulfilling of prophecies: or the prophecies . . . of . . . James Ussher. colop: *Printed, and are to be sold by R. Baldwin,* 1689. brs. DN; CH.

Fulfilling of the Scripture. [*n.p.*], 1669. *See* Fleming, Robert.

2260 **F[ulke], W[illiam].** Meteors. *For William Leake,* 1654. 8°. L, LLU; CH, CLC, MH, WF, WU.

2260A [–] ——[Anr. ed.] —, 1655. 8°. L, O, LCL, CS; MB, MH, WF, Y.

2261 [–] ——[Anr. ed.] —, 1670. 8°. T.C.I 32. L, C, OC, LLU, NE; CLC, LC, MH, MU, Y.

Full account from Ireland. [1700?] *See* Mount, *Mr.*

2261A A full account of a bold and barbarous murther . . . William Culliford. *By George Croom,* 1684. brs. O.

2262 Full account of a conspiracie of Papists. 1689. brs. LG (lost).

2262A A full account of a most tragycal . . . murther. *By D. Edwards,* 1699. brs. CN.

2263 A full account of a terrible and bloody fight. *By George Croom,* 1689. brs. O, HH.

2263A A full account of King Williams royal voyage. colop: *For Tho. Benson,* 1690. brs. L; Y.

2264 A full account of the apprehending of the Lord Chancellor. [*London*], 1688. brs. L, O, C; Y.

Full account of the apprehending. [n.p.], 1684. *See* T., M.

2265 A full account of the barbarous and unhumane usages. [*n.p.*, 1650–97.] fol. CN.

2266 Entry cancelled.

Full account of the damages. 1689. *See* Full and true account.

Full account of the great victory. 1689. *See* Wolseley, William.

2267 A full account of the late dreadful earthquake at Port Royal in Jamaica. colop: *For Jacob Tonson, and sold by R. Baldwyn.* 1692. brs. L, LG, LL, OC, DT; MH, MU, RPJ.

2268 —[Anr. ed.] *Edinburgh, re-printed by John Reid,* 1692. brs. ALDIS 3223. HH.

2269 —[Anr. ed.] *Printed at Edinburgh, and re-printed at Glasgow,* 1692. brs. ALDIS 3224. EN.

2269A A full account of the late siege and surrender of the city of Mons. *For Robert Hayhurst* [1691]. fol.* CT; CH.

2270 Entry cancelled.

Full account of the murther of William Culliford. 1684. *See* Full account of a bold.

2270A A full account of the rise, progress, and advantages of Dr. Assheton's proposal. *By B. Aylmer.* 1699. 12°. L, LSD.

2271 —[Anr. ed.] *For B. Aylmer,* 1700. 12°. L, OC.

2272   A full account of the situation, former state, and late siege of Stetin. *For Dan. Brown*, 1678. 12°. T.C.I 300. L, O, OC, LLU, GU, CD; CH, CLC, INU, WF, Y.

2273   A full account of the tryal of Godfrey Cross. colop: *For Langley Curtiss*, 1690. brs. L; CH, CN.

2274   —[Anr. ed.] *Edinburgh, by the heir of A. Anderson*, 1690. brs. ALDIS 3041. C, EN; MH.

2275   A full and certain account of the last great wind. *By J. B. for Dorman Newman*, [1662]. 4°.* L; CLC, MH, WU.

2275A A full and certain relation concerning the horrid plot of the Papists. *For Lawrence White*, 1678. 4°.* MH.

       Full and clear answer to a book. [n.p.], 1681. *See* Brady, Robert.

2276   A full and cleare answer to a false and scandalous paper. [*London*, 1642?] cap., 4°.* DT; Y.

       Full and clear exposition. [n.p., 1687.] *See* Pulton, Andrew.

       Full and compleat answer. 1642. *See* Taylor, John.

2277   A full and exact relation of the affairs in Ireland. *For A. R.*, 1689. brs. O; Y.

2277AA The full and exact relation of the apprehension . . . regicides. *For Nath. Brooke and Edw. Thomas*, 1662. brs. L.

2277A A full and exact relation of the fight betwixt the Henry, . . . and the Marine. colop: *By R. E., and are to be sold by J. Whitlock*, 1695. brs. MH.

2278   A full an [sic] exact relation of the horrid murder committed upon . . . Col. Rainsborough. *For R. A.*, 1648. 4°.* LT.

2279   A full and exact relation of the storming and taking of Dartmouth. *For Edw. Husband, January 23, 1645.* 4°.* LT, O, DT; CSS, MH, WF, Y.

2280   A full and exact relation of two old men. *For N. Thompson*, 1680. fol.* L, LWL; MH.

2280A —[Anr. ed.] *For N. T.*, 1680. fol.* O; CH, WF.

2281   A fvll and faithfvll accompt of the passages . . . Feb 1. 1646. *By Rich. Cotes*, 1646. 4°.* MR; NU.

       Full and final proof. 1680. *See* C., E.

2282   A full and impartial account of all the secret consults. *For Richard Chiswell*, 1689. 4°. T.C.II 306. L, O, C, OC, AN, LIU, BLH, DT; MH, MIU, NU.

2283   —[Anr. ed.] *For Richard Baldwin*, 1690. 4°. L, OC, MR, BQ, DT; CH, CN, MH, WF, Y.

2284   A full and impartial account of the late besieging . . . of the famous castle of Killishandra, . . . Ulster. colop: *For R. H.*, 1690. brs. C, MC; Y.

2285   A full and impartial relation of the late brave & great actions. colop: *For John Tattenham*, 1689. brs. MC, HH, DN.

2286   A full and particular account of the seizing and imprisonment of the Duke of Tyrconnel. colop: *For R. Hayhurst*, 1690. brs. L, C; CH.

2286A A full and particular account of the seizing the famous Captain Wither. [*London*], *for T. Taverner*, 1692/3. brs. C.

2286B A full and perticular [sic] relation of that strange, horrible . . . murther . . . Dr. Clench. *For Alex. Milbourn*, 1682 [i.e., 1692]. brs. CN.

2287   A full and particular relation of the taking the town . . . of Kinsale. *For Langley Curtiss*, [1690]. brs. MC; MH, NP.

2288   A full and perfect account of the particulars of the terrible and bloody fight . . . Esseck. colop: *By N. T.*, 1687. brs. L, O, C; MH.

2289   —[Anr. ed.] colop: *Holy-Rood-House, by James Watson*, 1687. brs. ALDIS 2689. L, HH, EN.

2289A A full and perfect account of the seizing seven of K. James's officers. *For R. H. and H. Jones*, 1690. brs. OC; CH.

2289B A full and perfect account of the state and condition of . . . Ulster. colop: *For H. Younge*, 1690. brs. OC; CH, PL, Y.

2290   A full and perfect relation of a great and signal victory. colop: *For S. Crouch*, 1689. fol. O, C, OC; CH, MH.

2291   A full and perfect relation of the great plot and terrible conspiracy. *For G. Horton*, 1654. 4°.* LT; CH, CSS.

       Full and satisfactorie ansvvere. 1645. *See* Burton, Henry.

2292   A full and the truest narrative of the most horrid, barbarous and unparalled murder. *By T. Mabb for J. Saywell*, 1657. 4°.* LT, O, FONMON.

2292A A full and true account both of the life: . . . of Susan Fowls. *Printed for J. Read*, 1698. 8°.* L.

2292B A full and true account of a bloody and barbarous murther . . . Southwark. colop: [*London*], *sold by R. Janeway*, 1690. brs. CN.

       Full and true account of a bloody and dismal fight. [1690]. *See* L., J.

2293   A full and true account of a bloody fight between the late King James. *By G. C. for J. Watson*, 1690. brs. MC.

2293A A full and true account of a great and signal victory. colop: *For Richard Chiswell*, 1689. brs. CH.

2293B —[Anr. ed.] [*Edinburgh*], re-printed 1689. brs. ALDIS 2889.7. L, EN.

2293C A full and true account of a great rencounter. *By W. Downing*, 2689 [i.e. 1689]. brs. L, DUS, DN.

2293D A full and true account of a most barbarous and bloody murther . . . by Esther Ives. *For P. Brooksby*, [1686]. 4°.* O.

2293E A full and true account of a most barbarous and bloody murther . . . by Edward Williams. *For William Alkin*, 1700. brs. CN.

2293F A full and true account of a most barbarous murther . . . by John Davis. *For A. H.*, 1699. brs. CN.

2293G A full and true account of a most barbarous murther . . . on . . . Mrs. Johannah Williams. *For T. Lightbody*, 1699. brs. CN.

2294   A full and true account of a most bloody and horrid conspiracy. *For Clem. Knell*, 1696. brs. L.

2294AA A full and true account of a most horrid and barbarous design . . . Mr. J. Frampton. colop: *Printed for the author, and sold by E. Baldwin*, 1698. 4°.* L.

2294bA A full and true account of a most vile . . . murder . . . Justice Parry. *For H. Smith*, 1700. brs. OP.

2294CA A full and true account of a new & horrid conspiracy against His Majesty. colop: *For G. Harris*, 1698. brs. LIU.

2294A A full and true account of a notorious and bold robbery. colop: *By J. W.*, 1700. brs. CH.

2294B A full and true account of a sad . . . accident. *By H. Hills*, [1700]. brs. L.

2295 A full and true account of a strange apparition. *By G. C. for J. Cox*, 1685. 4°.* O, HH.

Full and true account of a terrible and bloody engagement at sea. [1690]. *See* H., J.

2296 A full and true account of a terrible . . . fight between Tom Brown, the poet, and a bookseller. [*London*, 1700?] brs. L.

2296A A full and true account of a total victory over the Turks. [*London*, 1697.] brs. EN; CSS.

2297 A full and true account of all the proceedings in Ireland. colop: *For H. Jones*, [1690]. brs. MH, Y.

2297A The full and true account of all the proceedings in Scotland since the Rebellion. *Printed*, 1679. 4°.* EN.

2298 A full and true account of all the remarkable actions. colop: *For Richard Baldwin*, 1689. brs. L, C, OC, MC, DN; CH.

2299 A full and true account of his Grace Duke Schomberg's marching. colop: *For J. Green*, 4689 [*i.e.* 1689]. brs. C, OC, MC, DN; CH.

2300 A full and true account of the apprehending James Whitney. *For Randal Taylor*, [1692]. brs. L.

2300A A full and true account of the apprehending Sir Adam Blaire. colop: *For R. Baldwin*, 1689. brs. CH, CLC, UCLA, WF.

2301 A full and true account of the barbarous rebellion . . . at Ipswich. *By W. Downing*, 1689. brs. L, O, C, HH; CH, CSS, MIU, Y.

2302 A full and true account of the barbarous . . . usage of Mr. George Willington. *Printed and sold* [*torn*], [1700]. 8°.* L.

2302AA A full and true account of the behaviour . . . Mr. Richard Buttler. *For J. Williams*, 1695. brs. MR; CLC.

2302bA A full and true account of the behaviour of Sir John Fenwick. *By D.E.*, 1696/7. brs. BSM.

2302A A full and true account of the besieging . . . Carrickfergus. colop: *For Richard Baldwin*, 1689. brs. L, C, OC, DN; CH, Y.

2302B A full and true account of the confession, behaviour, . . . of Greenway Feild. colop: *For J. C.*, 1689. brs. MR.

2302C A full and true account of the damages . . . in Ireland. *For W. Cadman*, 1683. brs. O.

2303 A full and true account of the death of George Lord Jeffries. *For R. Gifford*, 1689. brs. L, O, HH; CN.

2303A A full and true account of the discovery of the late treasonable plot in Scotland. *For Rich. Baldwin*, 1690. brs. L, C, EN.

2304 A full and true account of the great battel . . . Presburg. *For Edw. Brewster*, 1683. fol.* T.C.II 43. L, O, OC; CH, LC, NCD, WF, Y.

2304A A full and true account of the inhumane and bloody cruelties of the Papists. *For Peter Richman*, 1689. 4°.* CH.

2305 A full and true account of the lamentable and dreadful fire. *For Langley Curtis*, 1682. fol.* O, LG, HH.

2306 A full and true account of the landing and reception of the late King James at Kinsale. colop: *By D. M.*, 1689. brs. L, O, C, DN; CH, Y.

2307 A full and true account of the landing of the late King James II. in Ireland. colop: *For R. Baldwin*, 1689. brs. L, O, C, OC; CH, CN, Y.

Full and true account of the late blazing star. [n.p., 1680.] *See* Nesse, Christopher.

Full and true account of the late brave action. 1690. *See* W., L.

2307A Full and true account of the late horrid . . . massacre of the . . . Bishop, and Dean of Waterford. *Nondon* [*sic*], *for R. Jones*, 1689. brs. DN.

2307B A full and true account of the late revolution in Dublin. colop: *By D. M.*, [1690]. cap., fol* DN; Y.

2307C A full and true account of the late revolution in Savoy. colop: *For Richard Baldwin*, 1690. brs. HH; CN.

2307D A full and true account of the loss of their Majesties ship. *Printed*, 1695. 4°.* O.

2308 A full and true account of the notorious wicked life of . . . John Taylor. *For Benj. Harris*, 1678. 4°.* L, BR, DU.

2308A A full and true account of the penitence of John Marketman. *For Samuel Walsall*, 1680. 4°.* T.C.I 396. L, O, C, LW, LSD; CLC, CSS, WF, Y.

2308B A full and true account of the penitent behaviour . . . Mr. Edmund Allen. *For J. Williams*, 1695. brs. MR; CLC.

2309 A full and true account of the proceedings at the sessions . . . April 26. colop: [*London*], *for T. Benskin*, 1682. fol.* O, LIU, MR.

2310 A full and true account of the proceedings at the sessions . . . in the Old Bayley, June 1 and 2, 1682. colop: [*London*], *for T. Benskin*, 1682. fol.* LL, LIU.

2310aA —[Same title.] Septemb. 6. colop: [*London*], *For T. Benskin*, 1682. fol.* O; Y.

2310bA A full and true account of the proceedings of Tho. Harris. *By Randal Taylor*, 1688. brs. O.

2310A A full and true account of the sad and dreadful fire . . . in . . . Southwark. colop: *For T. R.*, 1689. brs. LG; MH, Y.

2310B A full and true account of the sad and dreadful storm . . . [12 January 1689/90]. *For P. Brooksby, J. Deacon, J. Blare, J. Back*, [1690.] 4°.* CSS.

2310C A full and true account of the several skirmishes . . . Kingsale, Cork, and Dublin. colop: *For H. Jones*, 1690. brs. DN.

2311 A full and true account of the strange and wonderful apparation. colop: *For W. Trimmel*, 1700. 8°.* O.

2311aA A full and true account of the strange discovery of the supposed murther of Mr. Thomas Tedder. *For B. H.*, 1699. brs. CN.

2311A A full and true account of the surrendring of Charlemont. *For Richard Baldwin*, 1690. brs. CH.

2311AB A full and true account of the taking of Count . . . Coningsmark. *For E. Brooks*, 1681[2]. brs. O, DCH.

2311B A full and true account of the taking the city of Mentz. colop: *For Richard Chiswell*, 1689. brs. L, HH; CH, CLC.

2311BA —[Anr. ed.] *For Ric. Chiswell*, 1689. brs. L.

2311BB A full and true account of the taking the late Duke of Monmouth. *Dublin, for John Bentley*, 1685. brs. DMC.

2311BC A full and true account of the tryal, condemnation . . . of Augustin King. colop: *By George Croom*, [1688]. cap., fol.* O; CLC.

2311BD A full and true account of the tryal . . . of the Scotch rebels. *For J. Pardo*, 1689. brs. C; CLC, CN.

Full and true account of the two great victories. [n.p.], 1690. *See* W., P.

2311BE A full and true account of the wonderful eruptions. *Printed* 1687. 4°.* OC.

2311BF —[Same title.] *Printed*, 1689. 4°.* L.

2311C A full and true account of two famous and signal victories. colop: *For T. Cooper*, 1690. brs. CH, Y.

2312 A full and true discovery of all the robberies, pyracies, . . . of . . . Capt. James Kelly. colop: [*London*], *by J. Johnson*, 1700. brs. L, MR.

2312A A full and true narrative of one Elizabeth Middleton. [*London*], *printed for F. T.*, 1679. 8°.* O; IU.

2313 A full and true relation as well of the blowing-up of the Ann frigat. [*London*], *by A. Purslow*, 1673. 4°.* OC, MR; LC, NN.

2313A A full and true relation of a bloody and dismal fight. *For J. Bishop*, 1659. brs. C.

2314 A full and true relation of a comet. [*London*, 1679.] cap., fol.* L, O; CLC, MH, TU. (var.)

2314AA A full and true relation of a dreadful and terrible storm, . . . at Forte St. George. *By George Croom*, 1685. brs. O, HH.

2314A The full and true relation of a dreadful storm . . . in the city of Millain. colop: *For T. Davies*, 1680. cap., fol.* L; CH, MH, WF.

2315 A full and true relation of a horrid and bloody murther committed between Ravensden and Bedford. *Printed*, 1679. 4°.* Y.

2315A Entry cancelled. Date: 1701.

2315B A full and true relation of a maid living in Newgate-street. [*London*, 1680.] brs. MH, Y.

2315BA A full and true relation of a most barbarous and cruel robbery. *For D. M.*, 1677. 4°.* Y.

2315C A full and true relation of a most barbarous and dreadful murder; . . . Mrs. Kirk. *By Elizabeth Mallet*, 1684. brs. O, LG; CH, IU.

Full and true relation of a new hellish. 1679. *See* S., W.

2316 The full and true relation of all the proceedings at the Assizes holden at Chelmsford. [*Chelmsford?*, 1680.] cap., fol.* L, O, LL; MH, PU.

2316A A full and true relation of all the proceedings at the assizes holden at Maidstone. [*London*, 1680]. cap., fol.* O; MH.

2317 Full and true relation of an English vessel. *For W. Harris*, 1677. CHRISTIE-MILLER.

2318 —[Anr. ed.] *For W. Harris*, [c. 1690]. 4°.* L; CH.

2318A A full and true relation of an horrid and bloody murther. *Printed*, 1679. 4°.* Y.

2318B A full and true relation of his excellency the Pope's Nuncio making his public entry. *Printed*, 1687. brs. O, C, DC, DU; MH, WF.

2318C A full and true relation of the appearing of a dreadful ghost. colop: *For Richard Cheese*, 1690. brs. LG.

2318D A full and true relation of the apprehension of five . . . persons. [*London*], *for E. O.*, [1677]. 4°.* OC, Y.

2319 A full and true relation of the death and slaughter of a man and his son . . . lightning. *For John Harding*, 1680. fol.* L, O, OB; CH, MH.

2320 A full and true relation of the death of K. James. colop: *For Rob. Hayhurst*, 1689. cap., 4°.* L, O, LLP; CH, MH.

2321 Entry cancelled.

Full and true relation of the defeat. 1644. *See* Full and true relation of the great defeat.

2321A A full and true relation of the elephant that is brought over. [*London*], *for William Sutten*, 1675. brs. MH.

2322 A full and true relation of the examination and confession of W. Barwick. colop: *For Isaac Cleave*, [1690]. cap., fol.* L, MR; CN.

2322A A full and true relation of the execution of two persons . . . for murdering Sir Edmundbury-Godfrey. [*London*], *for W. C.*, 1679. 4°.* OB.

2322B A full and true relation, of the fortunate victory over the Moors. [*n.p.*, 1680.] fol. EN.

2323 A full and true relation of the glorious victory of the Christians. [*London*, 1687.] cap., 4°. L, O; WF.

2324 A full and true relation of the great and wonderful revolution . . . of Siam. *For Randal Taylor*, 1690. 4°.* L, O, CS, BR, DT; CH, CU, MH, MU, WF, Y.

2325 Entry cancelled.

Full and true relation of the great battle. 1642. *See* Kightley, Edward.

2325A A full and true relation of the great defeat given to Sir Ralph Hopton. *By Bernard Alsop and Andrew Coe*, 1644. 4°.* O; MIU.

2326 A fvll and trve relation of the late great victory. *For Hen: Overton, and Edward Blackmore, Aprill the* 12. 1643. 4°.* LT; CH, WF, Y.

2327 A full and true relation of the murther of Doctor Urthwait. [*London*, 1689.] brs. L, HH.

2328 Entry cancelled.

Full and true relation of the Pope's nuncio. 1687. *See* Full and true relation of his excellency.

2329 A full and true relation of the remarkable fight betwixt Capt. Hamilton. colop: *For Rich. Chiswell*, 1689. brs. C, OC, OP, MC; MH.

2330 A full and true relation of the several actions and particulars. *For Edward Husband, July* 1. 1646. 4°.* MADAN 1892. LT, O, DT; CH, IU, WF, Y.

2331 A full and true relation of the taking Cork. *For Langley Curtiss*, [1690]. brs. L, DUS, MC; CH, MH.

2332 Entry cancelled. *See following entry.*

2333 —[Anr. ed., "of Cork."] *Edinburgh, re-printed by the heir of A. Anderson,* 1690. brs. ALDIS 3042. L, EN, DN; WF.

2334 A full and true relation of the tryal and condemnation of twelve notorious highway-men. *[London,* 1679.] cap., fol.* L, O, LNC; CLC, MH, WF.

2335 A full and true relation of the tryal, condemnation, and execution of Anne Foster. *For D. M.,* 1674. 4°.* L.

2336 A full and true relation of the whole transactions of the Company of Vintners. *[London,* 1654.] cap., 4°.* NC.

2337 A full and true relation of two very remarkable tryals . . . third of October. colop: *For W. H. and T. F.,* 1680. fol.* O, IG, MR; CH, MH, WF, Y.

2338 Entry cancelled. *See* F2292.

2338A The full and whole proceedings of the new High-Court. colop: *For Ed. Golding,* 1691. cap., 4°.* L, LLP; WF.

Full answer and confutation. [n.p.], 1673. *See* Castlemaine, Roger Palmer, *earl.*

2339 A full answer paragraph by paragraph, to Sir John Fenwick's paper. *For Richard Baldwin,* 1697. 4°.* L, OC, DT; CH, INU, MB, WF, Y.

Full ansvver to a printed paper. 1645. *See* Palmer, Herbert.

2340 A full answer to a scandalous pamphlet, intituled, A character of a London diurnall. *By E. P. for Francis Coles and Lawrence Blaikeloke,* 1645. 4°.* MADAN 1765. LT, O, YM, DT; MH, WF, Y.

Full answer to all the particulars. [n.p.], 1684. *See* Brady, Robert.

Full answer to all the popular. 1689. *See* Long, Thomas.

Full answer to an infamous. [n.p.], 1648. *See* Clarendon, Edward Hyde, *earl of.*

2341 A full answer to Dr. Tenisons conferences. colop: *By Henry Hills,* 1687. brs. L, HH; CH, MIU, NU, WF, Y.

Full answer to that question. 1680. *See* Cheyney, John.

2342 A full answer to the depositions. *For Simon Burgis,* 1689. fol.* T.C.II 256. L, O, C, EN, CD; CH, CN, MH, WF, Y, AVP.

2343 A full answer to the Levellers petition. *[London],* printed, 1648. 4°.* O, OC, MR; CH, MH, NC, NU.

Full answer to the second defence. [n.p., 1687.] *See* Johnston, Joseph.

2343A A fvll declaration of all particulers. *Aprill.* 18, *for R. D.,* 1643. 4°.* LT, CT, BR, DT; CH, CSS, MH, NU, Y, ASU.

Full declaration of the true state. 1660. *See* Prynne, William.

2344 A full description of the manner of executing the sentence upon Titus Oats. *For Tho. Graves,* 1685. brs. HH; MH.

2344A A full description of these times. *[London],* printed for *A. B.,* [1688]. brs. L, O.

2345 Entry cancelled.

Full discovery of a foul concealment. 1652. *See* Bagwell, William.

2346 Entry cancelled.

Full discovery of the false evidence. 1688. *See* Lamb, Catharine.

2347 A full discovery of the late fanatical plot in Scotland. *Edinburgh, by the heire of Andrew Anderson, reprinted at London for Walter Davis,* 1685. brs. O, LL, OB, HH; PL, Y.

2348 The full discovery of the late horrid murther . . in Holbourn. *[London], for John Millet,* 1674. 4°.* LG.

2348A The full examination of six suspected Catholick gentlemen. *For W. Downing,* 1689. brs. CH.

Full inquiry. 1693. *See* Freke, William.

2349 A full narration of the late riotous tumult. *Imprinted at London for John Wright,* 1648. 4°.* LT, O, LG, MR, DT; CH, CN, MH, MIU, WF, Y.

2350 A full narative [*sic*] of all the proceedings betweene His Excellency the Lord Fairfax and the mutineers. *For George Roberts,* 1649. 4°.* MADAN 2014. LT, EN; CH, MH, Y.

2351 A full narrative of the Pope's death. colop: *For S. Crouch,* 1689. cap., 4°.* L, O; CH, CN.

2351A —[Anr. ed.] colop: *Re-printed* 1689. cap., 4°.* L.

2352 A full narrative, or, a discovery of the priests and Jesuites. *[London?], printed,* 1679. fol.* T.C.I 373. L, O, C, MR, DU; CH, MH, PL, WF, Y.

Full particulars. [1653.] *See* Smith, Jacob.

2353 Full proceedings of the High Court of Justice against King Charles. *For William Shears,* 1654. 8°. LT, DU; CH, CN, CU.

2354 —[Anr. ed.] —, 1655. 8°. LT; CH, CLC, NRU, YL.

2355 A fvll relation concerning the wonderfull and wholsome fountain . . . Halberstadt. *By T. W. for Joshua Kirton,* 1646. 4°.* LT, O, C, MR, DT; CH, CJC, CU, WF, WSG, Y.

2356 A fvll relation, not only of our good successe. *By G. Miller for W. Bladen,* 1642. 4°.* LT, O, LG, EC, MR; CH, CSS, MH, WF, Y.

2356A —[Anr. ed.] *For William Bladen,* 1642. 4°.* CD; NN.

2357 A full relation of a barbarous murther, committed upon . . . Esq; Beddingfield. colop: *By George Croom,* 1684. brs. L, O; CH, IU, PU.

2358 A full relation of all the late proceedings of His Majesties army in the county of Yorke: . . . August 19, 1642. *August 20, for Iohn Wright,* 1642. 4°.* LT, O, LNC, YM, EC; CH, MH.

2358A —[Anr. ed.] *For Iohn Wright,* 1642. 4°.* YM; MH, WF, Y.

2359 A full relation of His Majesties proceedings at Newcastle. *For William Iohnson,* 1646. 4°.* LT, MR, DT; CH, MH, Y.

2360 A full relation of the behaviour and confessions of the six prisoners. *[London], printed,* 1675. 4°.* LG.

2360A A full relation of the birth, parentage, education . . . of Mrs. Margaret Martel. *Printed and sold by J. Bradford,* 1697. 8°. L.

2361 A full relation of the contents of the black box. *[n.p.], printed,* 1680. 4°.* L, O, C. LSD, DT; CH, IU, MH, WF, Y.

Full relation of the desperate designe. 1645. *See* W., C.

Full relation of the great defeat. 1643. *See* N., W.

2362 A full relation of the great victory obtained by the Parliaments forces. *Imprinted at London, for Iohn Wright,* 1648. 4°.* LT, O, OC, MR; CH, CN, MH, WF, Y.

2363 A full relation of the late expedition of the right honourable, the Lord Monroe. *For J. Wright, August 27.* 1644. 4°.* LT, O, C, CT, DN; CH, CSU, MH, WF, Y.

2364 A full relation of the late proceedings, victory. [*London*], *by John Field, Jan.* 8. 1644. 4°.* LT, O, CT; CN, WF.

2365 No entry.
Full relation of the late victory. 1644. *See* Stewart, *Capt.*
Full relation of the murder. 1648. *See* Barnard, J.

2366 A full relation of the particulars and manner of the late great victory. *Printed at Edenburgh, reprinted at London by E. G., May* 14, 1650. 4°.* LT; CSS.

2367-8 Entries cancelled.
Full relation of the passages. Oxford, 1645. *See* Dugdale, *Sir* William.

2368A A full relation of the proceedings. *For Laurence Chapman, November* 16. 1647. 4°.* LT, O, CT, DC, MR; MH, MIU, WF, Y.

2369 A full relation of the Scots besiedging Newcastle. *By Bernard Alsop*, 1644. 4°.* LT, YM; Y.

2370 A full relation of the Scots martch. *By Andrew Coe.* 1644. 4°.* L; CH, CLC, MIU, WF, Y.

2370A A full relation of the siege of Banbury-castle. 1644. 4°.* O.

2371 A full relation of the surrendring of Kulmore. colop: *For Richard Baldwin*, 1689. brs. L, O, C, MC, DN; CH, WF, Y.

2372 A full relaton [*sic*] of the takinng [*sic*] of Bath. *By Barnard Alsop, and Iane Coe.* 1645. 4°.* LT; MH.

2373 A full relation of the victory obtained against Iames Marquesse of Montrose. *E. G.*, 1650. 4°.* CHRISTIE-MILLER.

2374 A full relation of the whole proceedings of the late rising. *For Francis Leech, July* 2, 1647. 4°.* LT, O, AN, DC, LLU, DT; WF.

2375 A full relation or dialogue between a Loyallist. [*London*], *for Fr. Coles.* 1661. 8°.* LT.
Full reply to certaine. 1644. *See* Prynne, William.

2376 Entry cancelled. Ghost.

2377 Full satisfaction concerning the affaires of Ireland. [*London*], *printed*, 1648. 4°.* LT, O, C, DN; MH.

2377A The full trial between Henry Duke of Norfolk, plaintiff, and John Germaine. *Printed*, 1693. fol.* LLP, LLU; CH, LC, WF.

2378 The full tryals, examination and condemnation of four notorious witches. *By I. W.*, [1690?]. 8°.* L, O.

2378A A full, true and particular account of the ghost. [*n.p.*], *printed by F. C.*, [1700?]. 4°.* L.

2379 The full trvth of the Welsh-affaires. [*London*], *printed*, 1648. 4°.* LT, AN; WF.

2380 The full view of Canterburies fall. [*London*, 1644/5.] brs. LT.
Full view of the doctrines. 1688. *See* Patrick, John.
Full vindication and ansvver. 1647. *See* Prynne, William.

2381 F[ullarton], J[ohn]. The turtle-dove. *Edinburgh, by Andrew Anderson*, 1664. 12°. ALDIS 1784. L, O, EN; CH, IU, Y.

2381aA Fullarton, Patrick. Disputatio juridica, de mutuo. *Edinburgi, ex officina hæredum Andreæ Anderson*, 1700, 4°. ALDIS 3966.5. EN, GU.

2381bA Fuller, Abraham, *of Bishopgate.* The humble confession of. [*London*, 1657.] brs. MH.

2381A Fuller, Abraham, *of Ireland.* The testimony of. [*London*], *printed*, 1687. 8°.* LF; PSC.

2382 Fuller, Francis. Of the shortness of time. *For Tho. Parkhurst. And John Barnes*, 1700. 8°.* T.C.III 161. L, LCL, LW; CH.

2383 —Peace in war by Christ. *For Tho. Parkhurst*, 1696. 4°.* L, LW; MH, NPT, WF.

2384 —Some rules how to use the world. *By John Richardson for Thomas Parkhurst*, 1688. 8°.* T.C.II 229. L, O, LCL, LW; CH, CLC, NPT, NU, TO, WF.

2384A ——[Anr. ed.] — *and Obadiah Smith in Daventree*, 1688. 8°. M; FU.

2385 —A treatise of faith. *For J. Robinson, and O. Smith, in Daventry*, 1684. 8°. T.C.II 92. LCL.

2385A —A treatise of faith and repentance. *By J. D. for Obed. Smith in Daventry*, 1684. 8°. O; CLC, MM, WF.

2386 ——[Anr. ed.] *By J. D. to be sold by Jonathan Robinson. And by Obed Smith in Daventry*, 1685. 8°. L, LCL, LW, CT, DU, NU, TO.

2387 —A treatise of grace and duty. *By John Richardson for Thomas Parkhurst*, 1688. 12°. L, O, LCL, LSC; CLC, NPT, TO.

2388 ——[Anr. ed.] *By J. Richardson, for Obed Smith, in Daventry*, 1689. 8°. L; WF.

2389 —[Hebrew] Words to give to the young-man knowledg. *By J. P. for Obed Smith, in Daventry*, 1685. 8°. T.C.II 135. L, O, LCL, LW; CH, CLC, NPT, TO, WF.

2390 Fuller, Ignatius. Peace and holiness. *By Evan Tyler, and Ralph Holt, for R. Royston*, 1672. 8°. T.C.I 95. L, O, C, YM, CD; CH, IU, TU, WF, Y.

2391 —A sermon at the funerals of Mrs. Anne Norton, . . . July 12. 1671. *By E. T. and R. H. for R. Royston*, 1672. 8°. L, LLP, CD; CH, TU, WF, Y.

2392 —A sermon to the clergie. *By Evan Tyler, and Ralph Holt, for R. Royston*, 1672. 8°. L; CH, WF, Y.

2393 Fuller, John. Γαμαλιηλ παλιψυχος or seasonable advice. *For the author, by John Gain*, 1681. 4°.* L, O; NU.

2394 Fuller, Nicholas. The argument of. *For N. Vavasour*, 1641. 4°.* LT, O, C, SC, DT; CH, IU, MH, NU, TU, WF, Y.

2395 F[uller], R[obert]. Missale Romanvm vindicatvm. Or, the mass vindicated. [*n.p.*], *printed*, 1674. 12°. L, O, CS, DU, MR; CH, CLC, CN, NU, WF, Y.

2396 Fuller, Samuel. Canonica svccessio. *Cantabrigiæ, ex officina J. Hayes*, 1690. *Impensis H. Dickinson, Cantab. Et prostant venales apud S. Smith*, 4°. L, O, C, MC, DT; CH, MH, NPT, NU, WF, Y.

2397 —Ministerium ecclesiæ Anglicanæ. [*n.p.*], 1679. brs. L, O, LNC.

2398 —A sermon preached . . . June the 25th, 1682. *By M. Flesher, for Jacob Tonson*, 1682. 4°. L, C, OC, CT, SP; CH, IU, MH, NU, WF, Y.

2399 ——June 25. 1693. *For Jacob Tonson:* 1693. 4°.* L, C, OC, OM, LNC; CH, NPT, WF, Y.

2400 **[Fuller, Thomas.]** Abel redevivus. *By Tho. Brudenell for John Stafford,* 1651. 4°. L, O, C, MP, ENC; CH, CU, NU, TU, WCL, WF, Y. (var.)

2401 [–] ——[Anr. ed.] *Sould by Iohn Stafford,* 1652. 4°. L, OC, MR, ES, GK; MH, RBU.

2402 [–] An alarum to the counties of England. [*London*], *printed,* 1660. 4°.* L, O, MR, E; CH, CLC, NN, WF, Y.

2403 —Andronicvs. *By W. Wilson, for John Williams,* 1646. 8°. O, C, OS, CT, ES; CLC, IAU, IU, NU, WF.

2404 Entry cancelled.

2405 ——[Anr. ed.] *By W. W. for John Williams,* 1646. 8°. LT, O, CE, MP, EN; CH, CN, MH, MU, WF, Y. (var.)

2406 ——"Second" edition. —, 1646. 8°. O, C, CK, MP, GK; CLC, CN, TO, TSM, Y.

2407 ——Third edition. *By G. D. for John Williams,* 1649. 8°. L, O, MP, GK; CH, TSM, Y.

2408 [–] ——[Anr. ed.] *For Richard Hall,* 1661. 8°. L, O; CH.
—Anglorum speculum, or. 1684. See S., G.

2409 [–] Antheologia, or the speech of flowers. *Lonon [sic], for John Stafford,* 1655. 8°. LT, C, LLU, MR; CH, WCL, WU.

2410 —The appeal of iniured innocence: unto the . . . reader. *By W. Godbid, and are to be sold by John Williams,* 1659. fol. L, O, C, EN, DT; BN, CH, CN, MH, WF, Y.

2411 —The best name on earth. *By R. D. for John Stafford,* 1657. 8°. LT, O, C, MP, BQ, GK; CH.

2412 —The best name on earth. Together with severall other sermons lately preached. *For John Stafford,* 1659. 8°. L, MP, GK.

2413 ——[Anr. ed.] *For the use and benefit of William Byron,* 1659. 8°. LW, CE; WF, Y.

2414 —The cause and cure of a vvounded conscience. *For John Williams,* 1647. 8°. L, O, C, LSC, MP; CH, CU, NU, WF, Y.

2415 ——Second edition. *By G. D. for John Williams,* 1649. 8°. L, C, MP, P, GK; CDA, CH, MH, Y.

2416 —The church-history of Britain. *For Iohn Williams,* 1655. fol. L, O, C, EN, DT; BN, CLC, MH, MU, WF, Y.

2417 ——[Anr. ed.] —, 1656. fol. L, O, CT, MP, DT; BN, MH, PL, TSM, WF.

2418 —A collection of sermons. *For John Stafford,* 1656. 8°. L, O, MP, GK; CB, CLC, MH, NR, WF.

2419 ——[Anr. ed.] —, 1657. 8°. C, GK; IU, MH, TSM, Y.

2420 [–] A comment on Ruth. *For G. and H. Eversden,* 1654. 8°. LT, O, C, GK, A; CLC, CU, MH, NU, WF, Y. (var.)

2421 —A comment on the eleven first verses of the fourth chapter of S. Matthew's gospel. *By Ja: Cottrel, for George Eversden,* 1652. 8°. L, O, CT, MP, GK; CH, IU, MH, NU, WF, Y.

2422 [–] Ephemeris Parliamentaria. *For John Williams and Francis Eglesfield,* 1654. fol. L, O, C, ES, DT; BN, CH, CN, LC, MH, NU, WF, Y.

2423 —A fast sermon preached on Innocents day. *By L. N. and R. C. for John Williams.* 1642. 4°.* LT, O, C, MP, DT; CH, CLC, MH, WF, Y.

2424 —Feare of losing the old light. *By T. H. for Iohn Williams,* 1646. 4°.* LT, O, CT, MP, DT; CH, MH, MIU, WF, Y.

2425 —Good thoughts in bad times. *Exeter, for Thomas Hunt,* 1645. 12°. LT, O, MP; CH, MH.

2426 ——[Anr. ed.] *By R. C. for Andrew Cook [sic] and John Williams,* 1645. 12°. O; Y.

2427 ——[Anr. ed.] *By I. D. for John Williams,* 1646. 12°. O, GK; Y.

2428 ——[Anr. ed.] *For John Williams.* 1647. 12°. LW, GK.

2429 ——[Anr. ed.] *By W. B. for J. Williams,* 1649. 12°. L, O, CT, MP, GK; CLC, LC, MH, NU, TO.

2430 ——[Anr. ed.] —, 1652. 12°. L, CK, MP; CH, MH, SW.

2431 ——[Anr. ed.] *By R. D. for J. VVilliams,* 1657. 12°. L, CT, GK, M; MHS, NPT, TO, Y.

2432 ——[Anr. ed.] *By I. R. for I. Williams.* 1659. 12°. L, OC, OCC, EC, WCA, GK; CH, NC, NPT, WF.

2433 ——[Anr. ed.] *By S. G. for John Williams.* 1665. 12°. O; MH.

2434 ——[Anr. ed.] *By J. R. for John Williams.* 1669. 12°. T.C.I 28. L, O, DC, GK; MH, NN, NU, Y.

2435 ——[Anr. ed.] *For John Williams,* 1680. 12°. LSC, LIC, MP, ES, GK; CH, CN, MH, Y.

2436 —Good thoughts in worse times. *By W. W. for John Williams,* 1647. 12°. LT, O, CE, MP, GK; MH, NU, RHT, Y.
——[Other eds.] 1649, 1652, 1657, 1659, 1665, 1669, and 1680. See —Good thoughts in bad times.

2437 [–] A happy handfull. *For John Williams,* 1660. 4°. LT, O, LW, CS; CN, MH, MU.

2438 —The historie of the holy warre. Third edition. *Cambridge, by Roger Daniel, and are to be sold by John VVilliams,* 1647. fol. L, O, C, E, DT; CH, CU, MH, NU, WF, Y, ZWT. (var.)

2439 — —Fourth edition. [*Cambridge*], *by Thomas Buck: and are to be sold by Philemon Stephens,* 1651. fol. L, O, C, MP, DN, CH, IU, MH, NU, WF, Y, AVP.

2440 —The history of the worthies of England. *By J. G. W. L. and W. G.,* 1662. fol. L, O, C, EN, DT; CH, CN, LC, MU, NP, WF, Y.

2441 ——[Anr. ed.] *By J. G. W. L. and W. G. for Thomas Williams,* 1662. fol. O, OW, CT, LLU; CPB, CH, MIU, RHT, WCL.

2442 Entry cancelled.
—History of Waltham-Abby. 1655. See —Church-history.

2443 —The holy state. *Cambridge: by Roger Daniel for John Williams,* 1642. fol. L, O, C, AN, E, DT; BN, CH, CN, MH, MU, NP, WF, Y, AVP.

2444 ——Second edition. *Cambridge: by R. D. for John Williams,* 1648. fol. L, O, C, MR, EN; CH, CN, MH, NU, Y.

2445 ——Third edition. *By R. D. for John Williams,* 1652. fol. L, O, C, MP, EN; CH, MH, NPT, NU, Y.

2446 ——Fourth edition. *By John Redmayne for John Williams,* 1663. fol. L, O, CT, MP, E; CH, CLC, MIU, NCU, TSM, Y, AVP.

2447 —The infants advocate. *By R. Norton, for J. Williams,* 1653. 8°. LT, O, C, LSC, MP; CH, IU, MH, NU, WF, Y.

2448 —Jacobs vow. A sermon. *Oxford, by Leonard Lichfield,* 1644. 4°.* MADAN 1640. O, DC, DT; CH.

2449 —The just mans funeral. [*London*], *by William Bentley, for John Williams,* 1649. 4°.* LT, O, C, EN, DT; CH, MH, NPT, NU, WF, Y.

2450 —Life out of death. A sermon. [*London*], *for John Williams,* 1655. 8°.* LT, O, C, MP, GK; CH, CLC, LC, MH, NU, WF, Y.

2451 —Mixt contemplations in better times. *By R. D. for Iohn Williams,* 1660. 8°. LT, O, C, MP, ES; CH, CN, MH, MU, WF, Y.

2452 —A panegyrick to His Majesty. *For John Playford,* 1660. 4°.* L, O, C, LLU, GK; CH, MH, NP, WF.

2453 —Perfection and peace: delivered in a sermon by. *By Roger Norton for Iohn Williams,* 1653. 8°.* O, C, LW, OC, MP, GK; CDA, CH, MH, NPT, Y.

2454 —Perfection and peace: delivered in a sermon preached. *By Roger Norton for Iohn Williams,* 1653. 8°.* LT, O, C, EN, GK; CLC, IU, MH, NHC, WF, Y.

2455 —A Pisgah-sight of Palestine. *By J. F. for John Williams.* 1650. fol. L, O, C, EN, DT; CH, CN, MH, TU, WF, Y, AVP.

2456 Entry cancelled. Ghost.

2457 ——[*Anr. ed.*] *By R. Davenport for John Williams,* 1662. fol. L, C, OM, MP, E, DT; BN, CLC, MH, MU, NC, WCL, Y.

2458 —A sermon of assvrance. *By J. D. for John Williams,* 1647. 4°.* L, O, LSC, MP, GK; CN, WF, Y.

2459 ——[*Anr. ed.*] —, 1648. 4°.* O, LL, CT, YM, GK; CLC, CN, NU, WF, Y.

2460 [–] A sermon of contentment. *By J. D. for John Williams.* 1648. 8°. L, O, CE, GK; MH.

2461 —A sermon of reformation. *Printed,* 1643. 4°.* L, O, C, MP, GK; CH, MH, NU, WF, Y.

2462 ——[*Anr. ed.*] *By T. B. for John Williams,* 1643. 28 pp. 4°.* LT, O, C, MP, DT; CH, CU, MH, NU, WF, Y.

2463 ——[*Anr. ed.*] —, 1643. 31 pp. 4°.* LT; CH.

2464 —A sermon preached at St. Clemens Danes . . . at the funeral of Mr. George Heycock. *By R. W.,* 1657. 4°.* L, C, MP.

2465 —A sermon preached at the Collegiat Church of S. Peter . . . 27. of March. *For John Williams,* 1643. 4°.* LT, O, C, MR, DT; CLC, IU, MH, NU, WF, Y.

2466 ——[*Anr. ed.*] *By Will. Bently, for John Williams,* 1654. 8°. LT, O, C, MP, GK; CH, CLC, MH, NU, TO, WF, Y.

2467 [–] The sovereigns prerogative. *For Martha Harrison,* 1657. fol. L, O, OME, AN, MR; CLC, CN, MH, MIU.

2468 [–] —[*Anr. ed.*] *For Henry Marsh,* 1658. fol. L, C, LW, LIU, BLH; CDA, WF, Y.

2469 ——"Second" edition. —, 1660. fol. L, C; BN, CLC, NC, NRU.

2470 [–] Triana. *For John Stafford,* 1654. 12°. L.

2470A [–] —[*Anr. ed.*] —, 1655. 12°. O.

2470B ——[*Anr. ed.*] *For J. Stafford,* 1658. NPL (t.p.).

2470C ——[*Anr. ed.*] *For Iohn Stafford,* 1660. 12°. LLU.

2471 ——[*Anr. ed.*] *For John Stafford,* 1664. 12°. L; CN.

2472 —A triple reconciler. *By Will. Bently, for John Williams,* 1654. 8°. LT, O, MR, P, GK; CH, IU, MWA, NU, WF, Y.

2473 ——[*Anr. ed.*] *By Will. Bentley, for Will. Shears,* 1654. 8°. O, C, LW, DU, GK; CH, CLC, MH, WF, Y.

2473A ———[*Anr. ed.*] *Printed and to be sold by Peter Parker,* 1679. 8°. EC, SP.

2474 —Truth maintained. *Printed at Oxford,* 1643. 4°. MADAN 1545. LT, O, C, CT, MP, DT; CH, CN, MH, NPT, WF, Y.

2475 ——[*Anr. ed.*] *Printed at London,* 1643. 4°. LW; NU.

2476 —Two sermons. *For G. and H Eversden,* 1654. 8°. L, O, C, LSC, GK; CLC, CN, MH, NU, WF, Y.

2476A [**Fuller, William.**] An abstract of a brief discovery. *Printed and sold by Jer. Wilkins,* 1696. 4°.* Y.

2477 —Mr. Fuller's answer to the Jacobites. *For the author; and to be sold by Eliz. Harris,* 1700. 8°.* L, O, BSM, AU; CU, IU, KU, MH, TO, WF, Y.

2478 —Mr. Fuller's appeal to both Houses. *For the author,* 1697. 4°.* L, O, LLL, CT; CH, IU, MH, WF, Y.

2479 —A brief discovery of the true mother of the pretended Prince of Wales, . . . Mary Grey. *For the author,* 1696. 8°. L, O, C, EN, DT; BN, CH, CN, LC, MH, NU, Y. (var.)

2480 ——[*Anr. ed.*] *Printed at London and reprinted at Edinburgh,* 1696. 4°.* ALDIS 3562. L, O, LLL, EN, AU; MH, TSM, WF.

2481 [–] The cheaters speculum. [*c.* 1700.] 8°. O.

2481A —La decouverte de la veritable mere du pretendu. *A Londres, pour J. Delage,* 1696. 8°.* EN.

2482 —A further confirmation that Mary Grey was the true mother of the pretended Prince of Wales. *For the author,* 1696. 4°.* L, O, C, AU, EN; CH, CN, LC, MH, Y.

2483 Entry cancelled. Ghost.

2484 —Mr. Fuller's letter to the right honourable the Lord Mayor. *For the author; and to be sold by Eliz. Harris,* 1700. 8°.* L, O, LG, CT, AN, AU; CH, CU, IU, MH, TO, Y.

2485 —A plain proof of the true father and mother of the pretended Prince of Wales. *For the author,* 1700. 8°. L, O, CT, LVF, EN; CLC, CN, MH, WF, Y.

2486 —Mr. William Fuller's third narrative, containing. *Printed,* 1696. 4°. L, O, C, AU, EN; CH, IU, LC, MH, NU, Y.

2486A —To the honble the Commons . . . the humble petition of. [*London,* 1692.] brs. L, LPR.

2486B **Fuller, William,** *bp.* A copy of the letter and annexed postscript of . . . the Lord Bishop of Lincoln. [*n.p.,* 1672?] brs. LNC.

A fvller ansvver to a treatise. 1642. *See* Herle, Charles.

2487 A fvller answer to the moderatovr. colop: [*London*], *printed,* 1643. cap., 4°.* LT, O, C, MR, DT; CH, MH, MU, WF, Y.

2488 A fvller narrative of the late victory obtained by Col: Generall Poyntz. *For Iohn Field, Sept.* 30. 1645. 4°.* LT; WF.

2489 A fuller relation from Bridgewater. *For Edw. Husband, Iuly* 26. 1645. 4°.* LT, O, BR, DT; MH.

2490 A fuller relation of a great victory obtained against the Welsh forces. *For Edward Husband, May* 11. 1648. brs. STEELE 2759. LT, C, AN.

2491 A fuller relation of Sir Thomas Fairfax's rovting all the kings armies in the VVest. *For Mathew Walbanck, Feb.* 21. 1645. 4°.* LT, O, YM, DT; MH, OWC, Y.

2491A A fuller relation of that miraculous victory . . . Wake-field. *For Iohn Wright*, 1643. 4°.* L, O, LLU, SP, A, DT; CH, CLC, IU, WF.

A fuller relation of the great victory obtained. 1644. *See* A., E.

2492 A fuller relation of the taking of Bath. *For Thomas Bates*, 1645. 4°.* LT, O, LSD; CH, MH, WF.

2493 **Fullerton, Isaac.** Disputatio juridica. *Edinburgi, ex officinâ typographicâ Hæredvm Andreæ Anderson*, 1696. 4°.* ALDIS 3563. EN.

2494 **Fullertoune, John.** A short testimony. [*Aberdeen, John Forbes younger*], 1671. 4°.* ALDIS 1923.2. EN; PL.

2495 [**Fullwood, Francis.**] Agreement betwixt the present and the former government. *For A. C. and are to be sold by Charles Yeo, in Exon*, 1689. 4°. L, O, CCA, EN; CLC, CN, NRU, WF, Y.

2496 [–] —[Anr. ed.] *For Awnsham Churchill*, 1689. 4°. L, O, CS, SP, ESS, DT; CH, CN, LC, MH, NU, Y.

2497 —The case of the times discuss'd. *For Jonathan Wilkins*, 1683. 8°. O, LL, LLP, CS, P; WF.

2498 —The churches and ministery of England. *By A. M. for George Treagle at Taunton, and are to be sold at London by William Roybould*, 1652. 4°. LT, O, LCL, CT, BR, BLH; CLC, MH, NU, WF, Y.

2499 [–] A dialogue betwixt Philautus and Timotheus. *For Rich. Royston*, 1681. 4°.* L, O, BR; CH, MIU, NU, PU, WF, Y.

2500 —A discourse of the visible church. *By Tho. Ratcliffe, for Abel Roper*, 1658. 4°. LT, O, CS, BR, NE; NP.

2501 [–] The doctrine of schism fully opened. *By S. G.' and B. G. for James Collins, and John Wright*, 1672. 8°. T.C.I 115. O, LSC, LW, DU; NPT, NSU, NU, WF.

2501A [–] —[Anr. ed.] *By S.G. and B.G. for James Collins, and sold by Abisha Brocas in Exon*, 1672. 8°. OC.

2502 —The establish'd church. *For R. Royston*, 1681. 8°. T.C.I 444. L, O, NE, DT; CB, MIU.

2503 —The General Assembly. *By E. Cotes for James Collins, and are to be sold by Abisha Brocas in Exon.*, 1667. 4°.* O, LL, LW; WF.

2504 ——[Anr. ed.] *By E. Cotes, for James Collins*, 1667. 4°.* L, C, OC, WCA, BAMB; CH, NGT, NU.

2505 [–] The grand case of the present ministry. *By J. Macock for T. Dring, and are to be sold . . . by M. Mitchel*, 1662. 8°. L, O, C, EN, CD; CH, IU, WF, Y.

2506 [–] —[Anr. ed.] *By J. Macock, for T. Dring, sold by M. Mitchel*, 1663. 8°. L, O, LW, OB, CT; CLC, IU, NU.

2507 [–] Humble advice to the conforming and non-conforming ministers. *For James Collins*, 1672. 8°. T.C.I 116. L.

2508 [–] —[Anr. ed.] —, 1673. 8°. L, C, OC; WF, Y.

2508A [–] —[Anr. ed.] *For J. Collins and are to be sold by Abisha Brocas in Exon*, 1673. 8°. SP.

2509 —Leges Angliæ. The lawfulness. *For R. Royston*, 1681. 8°. T.C.I 429. L, O, CT, YM, DT; IU, MHL, NU, NN, YL.

2509A — —[Anr. ed.] *For R. Royston, and are to be sold by George May, in Exon*, 1681. 8°. C, SP; WF.

2510 —The necessity of keeping our parish-churches. *By E. T. and R. H. for James Collins*, 1672. 4°.* L, O, C, MR, DT; CH, CN, NU, TU, WF, Y.

2511 [–] Obedience due to the present king. *For Awnsham Churchill*, 1689. 4°.* T.C.II 256. L, O, CT, EN, DT; CH, CN, MH, NU, WF, Y.

2512 [–] —[Anr. ed.] [*Edinburgh?*], 1689. 4°.* ALDIS 2924. L, EN.

2513 —A parallel: wherein it appears. *For A. and J. Churchill*, 1693. 4°.* T.C.II 463. L, C, CT, MR, E; NU.

2514 [–] A review of the grand case. *For T. Dring, sold by M. Mitchel*, 1663. 8°. L, O, CJ, SHR, EN; NCD, NU, WF.

2515 —Roma ruit. The pillars of Rome broken. *For Richard Royston*, 1679. 8°. T.C.I 375. L, LCL, OM, CT, MC, DT; CH, MH, MU, NU, WF, Y.

2516 [–] The Socinian controversie. *For A. and J. Churchil*, 1693. 4°.* T.C.II 463. L, O, C, CT, EN; CLC, CN, IU, NU, Y.

2517 [–] Some necessary & seasonable cases of conscience. *Printed*, 1661. 12°. LT, O, LW, OC, CS, NPL; IU, NU, Y.

2517A [–] —[Anr. ed.] *For Thomas Dring*, 1662. 12°. C, SP; CH, IU, WF.

2517B [–] —[Anr. ed.] *For T. Dring and M. Mitchell*, 1662. 12°. L, CT, NPL; CLC, PL.

2518 Entry cancelled.

[–] Toleration not to be abused by the Independents. 1672. *See* title.

2519 [–] Toleration not to be abused or, a serious question. *By S. and B. Griffin, for James Collins*, 1672. 4°.* O, C, LW, P, EN; CH, CN, NU, WF, Y.

2520 —A true relation of a dispute. *By A. M. for Abel Roper*, 1656. 4°.* LT, LF, LLP, E; Y.

2521 —Vindiciæ mediorum & mediatoris. Or, the present reigning errour. *By Tho: Roycroft, to be sold by Jo: Ridley*, 1651. 12°. LT, O, LCL, LW, DC; CH, Y.

2522 **Fullwood, Peter.** Concio ad magistratum a nation's honour. *By John Lock for E. Calvert*, 1673. 4°.* L, O.

2523 [**Fulman, William.**] Academiæ Oxoniensis notitia. *Oxoniæ, typis W. H. impensis R. Davis*, 1665. 4°. MADAN 2689–90. L, O, CT, SC, DT; CH, CN, MH, WF, Y. (var.)

2524 [–] Notitia Oxoniensis academiæ. *Typis T. R., impensis Ric. Davis* [*Oxon.*], 1675. 4°. T.C.I 221; MADAN 3036. L, O, CS, EN, DT; CLC, IU, MH, NC, TU, WF, Y.

2525 [–] Rerum Anglicarum Scriptorum veterum. *Oxoniæ, e theatro Sheldoniano*, 1684–91. 3v. fol. L, O, CT, EN, DT; CH, CN, LC, NC, WF, Y, AVP.

2526 [–] A short appendix to the life of Edmund Stanton. *Printed*, 1673. 12°.* O.

Fulnesse of God's love. [n.p.], 1643. *See* S., L.

Fulness of the times. [n.p., 1680.] *See* T., E.

2527 **Fulwar, Thomas, bp.** A sermon preached . . . October 2. 1642. *Printed*, 1642. 4°.* LT, O, C, LSC, YM; NU, WF.

2527A Fumblers Hall, kept and holden. *For J. Clarke, W. Thackeray, and T. Passinger*, [1675]. 12°. CM.

Fumifugium. 1661. *See* Evelyn, John.

A fund for supplying and preserving our coin. [1695?] *See* Chamberlen, Hugh.

Fundamenta chymica: or. 1658. *See* Combach, Ludovicus.

Fundamenta grammatica. 1690. *See* Farmborow, Nicholas.

Fundamental charter. 1695. *See* Sage, John, *bp.*

Fundamental constitution of the English. 1690. *See* Atwood, William.

Fundamental constitutions of Carolina. [n.p., 1670.] *See* Locke, John.

2528   Fundamental law the true security. *For John Kidgell and Thomas Malthus,* 1683. 8°. T.C.II 33. L, O, LW, OB, CT, EN; LC, MH, NC, NP, WF.

2529   The fundamental lawes and liberties. [*London,* 1653.] cap., 4°.* LT, BC; CSS, MH, Y.

2529A Fundamental positions and queries thereupon. [*London?* 168–?] cap., fol.* OC, BSM; CH, MH, WF.

2530   Fundamentals of the Protestant religion. *For Randal Taylor,* 1689. 8°. O, CT.

2531   A funeral eclogue sacred to . . . Queen Mary. *For John Whitlock,* 1695. fol.* L, LSD, EN; CH, IU, MH, TU, WF.

Funeral eclogue to the pious memory of . . . Mrs. Wharton. 1685. *See* Gould, Robert.

Funeral elegies. Or. [1655.] *See* H., S.

2531A A funeral elegy in commemoration of . . . Sir John Johnston. *For J. Millet,* [1690]. brs. CN.

Funeral elegy on the right honourable . . . Castleton. [1670.] *See* Sh., Jo.

Funerall elegie on the unfortunate death. 1644. *See* A., J.

2532   A funeral elegy vpon the death of . . . John Winthrop. [*Boston, John Foster?*], 1676. brs. MHS.

2533   A funerall ellegie, upon the death of Mr. John Pim. [*London*], by *Iohn Hammond,* [1643]. brs. LT, O; MH.

Funeral elegy upon the death of the Queen. 1695. *See* Walsh, William.

2534   A funerall elegie upon the deplorable and much lamented death of the . . . Earle of Essex. *By Iohn Hammond,* 1646. brs. LT.

2535   A funerall elegy upon the most honored upon earth, . . . Earl of Essex. *London,* 1646. *To be sold by Iohn Hancock.* brs. L.

2536   A funeral elegy upon the most honored upon earth, . . . Earl of Essex. *By John Macock for William Ley,* 1646. brs. L.

2536A A funeral elegy, upon the much lamented death of . . . Mary, Lady Dowager, Countess of Warwick. *For Tho. Parkhurst,* 1678. brs. MH.

Funeral gift. 1690. *See* Seller, Abednego.

2537   A funerall monument: or the manner of the herse of . . . Essex. [*London*], *for J. Hancock,* 1646. brs. LT; MH.

2538   The funeral of the good old cause. *For R. Royston,* 1661. 4°.* L, O, LIU, SP; CH, IU, MH, NU, WF, Y.

Funeral of the mass. 1673. *See* Derodan, David.

2539   A funeral-oration upon Favorite, my lady * * * lapdog. *Printed,* 1699. fol.* IU, TU, WF, Y.

Funeral sermon at the interrment. Edinburgh, 1699. *See* Scott, Robert.

Funeral sermon, occasioned. 1674. *See* Ryther, John.

Funeral sermon of Mr. Miles Pinckeney. Paris, 1675. *See* Lutton, Edward.

2539A A funeral sermon on the occasion of the death of Algernon Sidney, Esq. *For J. Smith,* 1683. 4°.* L, LSD.

Funeral sermon preached at Newport-Pagnell. 1697. *See* Gibbs, John.

Funeral sermon preached on the occasion. 1683. *See* B., W.

Funeral sermon preached upon the death of . . . Francis Holcroft. 1692. *See* Milway, Thomas.

Funeral tears upon the death of Captain William Bedloe. [1680.] *See* Duke, Richard.

Funus corporis. 1646. *See* Hatcher, Robert.

Fur prædestinatus. 1651. *See* Slatius, Henricus.

2540   [**Furetiere, Antoine.**] Scarron's city romance. *In the Savoy, by T. N. for H. Herringman,* 1671. 8°. T.C.I 73. L, O, OP; CH, IU, MH, NP, WF, Y.

2541   **F[urly], B[enjamin].** The world's honour detected. *For Robert Wilson,* 1663. 4°. L, LF, LW; CLC, IE, MH, PH, WF.

2541A **Furly, John.** A testimony to the true light. [*London*], *printed,* 1670. 4°.* CH.

2542   — —Second edition. [*London*], *printed,* 1670. 4°.* L, O, C, LCL, LF, BBN; CU, MII, NU, PII, WF. (var.)

Furmetary. 1699. *See* King, William.

Furor poeticus. 1660. *See* Wither, George.

2543   Entry cancelled.

Further account of East-New-Jersey. Edinburgh, 1683. *See* Lockhart, George.

Further account of New Jersey. [n.p.], 1676. *See* Hartshorne, Richard.

2543A A further account of the actions done . . . Mons. colop: *Edinburgh, re-printed,* 1691. brs. ALDIS 3148.5. L; CN.

2544   A further account of the proceedings against the rebels in Scotland. [*n.p.,* 1679.] cap., fol.* L, O, LG, EN, DT; CH, CN, MH, WF, Y.

2544A —[Anr. ed.] [*Dublin*], *reprinted* 1679. 4°.* L, CD, DT.

2545   A further account of the proceedings against the rebels in the West. colop: *By E. Mallet,* 1685. cap., fol.* L, O, LIU, MR; CH, MH, MIU, WF, Y.

Further accompt of the progresse. 1659. *See* Eliot, John.

Further account of the province. [n.p., 1685.] *See* Penn, William.

Further account of the state of Ireland. 1689. *See* F., J.

2546   A further account of the tryals of the New-England witches. *For J. Dunton,* 1693. 4°. L, O, C, LSC, EN; CH, LC, MH, NN, RPJ, Y.

2547   A further account of the victory obtained by the English and Dutch fleet. [*London*], *by Edw. Jones,* 1692. brs. LPR, MC; MH, MIU, Y.

2548   —[Anr. ed.] London, *Edinburgh reprinted,* 1692. brs. ALDIS 3042.3. L, E.

Further additions. 1684. *See* Fitzgerald, Robert.

Further advice to a painter. 1673. *See* Denham, *Sir* John.

2549   A further and full account of the surrender of Galway. *Reprinted Edinburgh,* 1691. brs. ALDIS 3149. EN.

2549A A further and full account of the . . . victory . . . in Ireland. *Printed at London, and re-printed at Edinburgh,* 1692. brs. ALDIS 3150. EN.

2550 A further and more particular account of the barbarous murther, of Philip Parry. *By J. W.,* 1700. brs. L.

2550A A further and more perticular account of the cruel desperate and bloody fight . . . in Ireland. *For W. J.,* 1700. brs. CH.

2551 A further and more particular account of the total defeat. [*n.p.,* 1679.] cap., fol.* L, O, BC, LNC, EN; CH, IU, MH, ZWT.

2551A A further and more true account of the apprehending and taking, of Gerhard Denelius. *By J. W.,* 1700. brs. O.

2551B A further answer of the governour and company of white-paper-makers to the paper-sellers. [*London,* 1690.] brs. MH.

2552–3 Entries cancelled.

Further collection. 1692. *See* State tracts.

Further considerations about a standing army. 1699. *See* Some further.

2554 Further considerations against laying new duties on paper. [*n.p.,* 1698.] brs. LG (lost).

Further considerations concerning raising. 1695. *See* Locke, John.

2554A Further considerations, for the putting the laws . . . wooll. [*London?* 1696.] brs. MH.

Further continuation and defence. 1670. *See* Patrick, Symon, *bp.*

2555 A further continuation of the curious collection of paintings, . . . 14th . . . November, 1690. [*London*], 1690. 4°.* L.

Further defence of the report. 1698. *See* Lobb, Stephen.

2556 The further depositions and proceedings in the House of Lords. *Printed,* 1692. 8°.* O; Y.

Further discovery of M. Stubbe. 1671. *See* Glanvill, Joseph.

Further discovery of that generation. Gateside, 1654. *See* Weld, Thomas.

Further discovery of the mystery of Jesuitism. 1658. *See* Jarrige, Pierre.

Further discovery of the mystery of the last times. 1651. *See* Mercer, Richard.

Further discovery of the office. 1648. *See* Hartlib, Samuel.

Further discovery of the plot. 1680. *See* L'Estrange, *Sir* Roger.

Further discovery of the spirit. [*n.p.,* 1694.] *See* Keith, George.

Further essay. 1695. *See* Lowndes, William.

Further evidence. 1659. *See* K., I.

2557 A further explication of the proposal relating to the coyne. [*Edinburgh,* 1697.] 4°.* ALDIS 3664. L, LUG; RPJ, WF, Y.

2557A A further full and plain discovery of the Irish forfeitures. [*London?* 169–?] brs. L.

2558 A further inquiry for truth. *Printed,* 1642. 4°.* O, MR, DT; MH, Y.

2559 —[Anr. ed.] —, 1643. 4°.* LT.

Further instructions for Cap: Thomas Allen. 1649. *See* Rupert, *prince.*

2560 Further instructions unto Charles Fleetwood. *Dublin, by William Bladen,* 1653. 4°.* DIX 351. CD.

Further justification. 1673. *See* Stubbe, Henry.

2560A A further narrative of the passages of these times. [*London*], *by M. S. for Thomas Jenner,* [1658]. 4°. L, LG, LLL, MR; CH, CLC, MBP, MH, WF.

2561 The further proceedings of the countie of Kent. *By B. A.,* 1648. 4°.* L.

2562 Further proofs of the personality. [*n.p.,* 1675.] brs. O.

2563 Further proposals for amending and settling the coyn. *Printed and sold by M. Whitlock,* 1696. 4°.* LUG, LSD, GH; MH, NC, PU, Y, ANL.

Further quæries upon the present state. [1690.] *See* E., S.

2564 Further reasons against increasing the number of hackney-coaches. [*London,* 1690?] brs. CH.

2565 Further reasons for inlarging the trade to Russia. [*London?* 1695.] brs. L, O, LG; MH.

2566 Entry cancelled.

Further supplement to the Cabala. 1663. *See* Cabala. sive scrinia.

2566A A further testimony to truth; . . . by some baptized congregations. *For Livewell Chapman,* 1659. brs. MHS.

Further vindication. [*n.p.,* 1689.] *See* Mather, Increase.

Further vindication of Mr. Owen. 1699. *See* Gipps, Thomas.

Future state. 1653. *See* Jones, George.

2567 **F[ydge], T[homas].** The citizens sacred entertainment. *By E. C. to be sold by H. Eversden, W. Flindel, and W. Fairfax,* 1666. 8°. L, LW, BC; CN.

2567A **F[yler], S[amuel].** Longitudinis inventæ explicatio. *For the author,* 1699. 4°.* L; MH, WF.

2567B —[Anr. ed.] —, 1700. 4°.* O.

2568 —A sermon preach'd in the cathedral church. *By E. T. and R. H. for Thomas Flesher,* 1682. 4°.* L, O, C, LSD, WCA; CH, CLC, NGT, WF, Y.

2569 **Fysh, Thomas.** A sermon preached upon the 29th of May. *By T. Snowden for Sam. Smith,* 1685. 4°.* LSD; NU.

2569A ——[Anr. ed.] *For Sam. Smith,* 1685. 4°.* T.C.II 123. L, O, C, CK, DU; CH, WF, Y.

G

1   **G.** The tryal of skill, performed in Essex. [*n.p.*, 1689.] brs. L, C; PL, Y.

2   **G., A.** Legis fluvius: or, the fountain of the law opened. *By J. C. for T. Rooks*, 1658. 8°. LT, LL; WF, YL.

—Some few questions. 1661. *See* Walsh, Peter.

2A   —The speech which was to have been delivered. *Edinburgh, by Robert Bryson*, 1641. 4°.* ALDIS 1021. EN; WF.

—True and perfect relation. 1654. *See* Griffith, Alexander.

G., A. C. E. Anti-Fimbria. 1679. *See* Warner, John.

G., B. Proposal humbly offered. [*n.p.*], 1662. *See* Butler, Samuel.

2B   —The relation of a strange apparition in the air . . . [19 August 1653] . . . on the borders. [*Edinburgh?*], *printed*, 1654. 8°.* WF.

3   **G., C.** An elegie upon the most lamented death of the . . . Earle of Essex. [*London*, 1646.] cap., 4°.* LT, O, LG, CT, LLU, EN; CH, MH, TU, WF, Y.

— Elogium heroinum: or. 1651. *See* Gerbier, Charles.

4–5   Entries cancelled.

—Second volume of The post-boy robb'd. 1693. *See* Gildon, Charles.

—True manner and forme. 1676. *See title.*

G., C. F. God's blessing. 1648. *See* Fitzjeffrey, Charles.

6   Entry cancelled.

G., Charles. Modest cavallieres advice. [*n.p.*], 1647. *See* Gerbier, Charles.

7   Entry cancelled. Date: 1726.

8   **G., D.** A letter from St Omars [*sic*]. *Printed*, 1679. fol.* L, O, C, DU, EN; CH, CN, MH, WF, Y.

—Sermon preached in the cathedral. 1686. *See* Grenville, Denis.

9   —A Sunday's adventure, or, walk to Hackney. *For John Kidgel*, 1683. 12°. T.C.II 29. L; Y.

G., E. Civil wars of Bantam. 1683. *See title.*

10   —A description of the island and city of Candia. *Sold by John Overton*, 1668. brs. O.

—Diegerticon ad Britanniam. [*n.p.*, 1666] *See* Gayton, Edmund.

11   —A discourse of friendship. *Sold by George Calvert*, 1675. 8°. T.C.I 220. MH.

11A   — —[Anr. ed.] *By J. B. for the author, to be sold by T. Fabian*, 1676. 8°. L; CU.

11B   —Four of the choicest new songs. *Printed, and sold by A. Chamberlain*, [1684?]. brs. L.

12   —The horrid, direful, prodigious, and diabolical practice of the Jesuits discovered. *For A. C.*, 1679. 4°. L; NIC, NU, Y.

12A   — —[Anr. ed.] [*Dublin?*], *reprinted*, 1679[80]. 4°.* CD.

—Letter to the superiors. 1688. *See* Gee, Edward, *younger.*

—Librorum manuscriptorum. Oxonii, 1692. *See* Tenison, Thomas, *abp.*

—Lord Maior of Londons letter. [*n.p.*, 1642.] *See* Gurney, *Sir* Richard.

—Pax vobis, or. [n.p.], 1679. *See* Griffith, Evan.

13   —A prodigious & tragicall history of the arraignment, tryall, confession, . . . of six witches. *For Richard Harper*, 1652. 4°.* LT, O; CH, MH.

—Sermon preached at Alderly. 1677. *See* Griffith, Evan.

14   —Strephons complaint for the death of his Daphne. *For Absalon Chamberlain*, 1684. brs. L, O; CLC, WF.

15   —The suspence upon Sixty Six. *Printed*, 1666. brs. L.

—To Mr. Robert Whitehall. [n.p., 1666.] *See* Gayton, Edmund.

16   No entry.

—Upon the meeting of the sons of the clergy. 1655. *See* Gayton, Edmund.

17   —Wast land's improvement. [*London*, 1653.] cap., 4°.* LT, LIU.

18   **G., F.** Advise to a friend discontented. *By Thomas Creake*, 1660. 4°.* LT; MH, PL, WF, Y.

—Arraignment of popery. [n.p.], 1669. *See* Fox, George.

19   —The dying man's last legacy. *By George Croom*, 1685. brs. O, HH.

—Loyalists reasons. Edinburgh, 1689. *See* Cullen, Francis Grant, *lord.*

—Man in the moone. 1657. *See* Godwin, Francis.

—'Ονομαστικον βραχυ, sive. 1652. *See* Gregory, Francis.

—Short discourse. 1694. *See* Gallimore, Francis.

19A   **G., G.** An account of Lieut. Gen. Douglas's late expedition. colop: *For Richard Baldwin*, 1690. brs. L.

—Bold challenge. [n.p.], 1652. *See* Griffith, George, *bp.*

20   Entry cancelled.

—Ecclesiastical history of France. 1676. *See* Gearing, William.

—History of the church of Great Britain. 1674. *See* Gearing, William.

21   —A reply, to a namelesse pamphlet, intituled, An answer to a speech without doors. *For R. Leybourn*, 1646. 4°.* LT, LW, OC, EN, DT; CLC, LC, MH, MU, NU, WF, Y.

G., G. G. Two great mysteries. 1653. *See* Goodman, Godfrey, *bp.*

G., H. Antiquity of common-wealths. 1652. *See* Grotius, Hugo.

—Baptist not Babylonish. 1672. *See* Grigg, Henry.

22   —Cur percussisti: or Balaam reproved. *For the author*, 1661. brs. L.

—Curiosities in chymistry. 1691. *See* Gregg, Hugh.

23   —Divrnall occvrrences, truly relating. *By Richard Herne*, [1642.] 4°.* LT; ASU.

24   —Englands present distractions. *For Francis Wright*, 1642. 4°.* LT, DT; CH, IU, MH, NU, WF, Y.

—Late libeller's folly. 1694. *See* Gouldney, Henry.

—Light from the sun. [n.p.], 1672. *See* Grigg, Henry.

24A   —A narrative of the proceedings of the northern armies. *For G. Horton*, 1659. 4°.* LT, MR; Y.

24B —A prudent and secure choyce. [*London*], *printed*, 1650. 8°. LLP; CN.

25 —Reflections upon the animadversions. *By A. W. for John Martyn, James Allestry, and Thomas Dicas*, 1662. 4°.* L, O, LW, CJ, EN; Y.

26 [–] Scanderbeg redivivus. *By H. C. for Tho. Malthus*, 1684. 12°. T.C.II 70. L, O, OC, EN; CH, CLC, CSU, MH, WF.

27 —A trve relation of the proceedings of His Excellence the Earle of Essex. *For Iohn Matthewes*, [1642]. 4°.* LT, SS.

G., I. Gods deliverance. 1642. *See* Grant, John.

28 —Little-vvits protestation. *For F. Coules*, 1642. 4°.* LT, O, OW; WF, Y.

29 —The wonder of our times: being a true and exact relation of the body of a mighty giant. *By R. Austin, for W. Ley*, 1651. 4°.* LT.

30 Entry cancelled.
    —Worlds riddle. [n.p.], 1641. *See* Greene, John.

31 **G., J.** Ἀκαματον πυρ. Or, the dreadful burning of London. *For Henry Herringman*, 1667. 4°.* L, O, LG, GH, DT; CLC, MH, TU, WF, Y.

32 Entry cancelled.
    —Ancient of dayes. 1657. *See* Gibson, John.
    —Astrological predictions. 1679. *See* Gadbury, John.
    —Brief relation of the life . . . Vincent Wing. 1670. *See* Gadbury, John.
    —Butchers blessing. 1642. *See* Goodwin, John.
    —Cata-baptism. 1655. *See* Goodwin, John.
    —Christians liberty. 1645. *See* Graunt, John.

33 —The chvrches pvblick order. *For W. W.*, 1643. 4°. O, LNC.
    —Clarior e tenebris: or. 1683. *See* Garbrand, John.
    —Cure of deadly doctrine. [n.p., 1649.] *See* Graunt, John.

34 —Damon: a pastoral, lamenting . . . Purcell. *By J. Heptinstall for Henry Playford*, 1696. fol.* T.C.II 590. L; CLC, MH.
    —Discourse about ceremonies. 1696. *See* Gailhard, Jean.

35 Entry cancelled.
    —Dis-satisfaction satisfied. 1654. *See* Goodwin, John. Συγκρητισμος.
    —Ειρηνομαχια. The agreement. 1652. *See* Goodwin, John.
    —First man. 1643. *See* Greene, John.
    —Holy and profitable sayings. 1678. *See* Gosnold, John.
    —Independencie Gods veritie. 1647. *See* Goodwin, John.

35A —A letter from an honourable person in London. [*London*, 1660]. brs. MH.

35B —The memoires of Mary Carleton. *For Nath. Brooke and Dorman Newman*, 1673. T.C.I 126. 8°. L; CH, CLC, LC, WF.
    —Νεοφυτοπρεσβυτερος, or. [n.p.], 1648. *See* Goodwin, John.

36 —New discovery of the horrid association and conspiracy. *For Jonathan Greenwood*, 1690. 4°. LIL, SP.
    —Notes and observations vpon some passages. Oxford, 1646. *See* Gregory, John.
    —Παντα δοκιμαζετε. 1664. *See* Goad, John.
    —Petitionary remonstrance. 1659. *See* Gauden, John, bp.
    —Philadelphia: or, xl queries. 1653. *See* Goodwin, John.
    —Philastrogus knavery. 1652. *See* Gadbury, John.

37 —A play-book for children. *For John Harris*, 1694. 12°. T.C.II 513. O.
    —Ψευδο-αστρολογος: or. 1660. *See* Gadbury, John.
    —Qvære, concerning the church-covenant. 1643. *See* Goodwin, John.
    —Royal favourite. 1682. *See* Garbrand, John.
    —Sage senator. 1660. *See* Grimefield, John.

38 —Satisfaction in religion. *Matthew Turner*, 1687. 12°. DUS.
    —Seasonable discourse. 1689. *See* title.

39 Entry cancelled.
    —Seasonable sermon. 1690. *See* Goodman, John.
    —Serious advice to a preservative. 1695. *See* Gailhard, Jean.

40 —A sermon of the passion. *For Matthew Turner*, 1686. 4°.* L, O, BSM, MC, WCA, BLH; CH, CLC, MH, NU, WF.
    —Shepheards farewell. [n.p.], 1645. *See* Grant, John.
    —Six book-sellers proctor. 1655. *See* Goodwin, John.
    —Some observations upon the keeping. 1694. *See* Gailhard, Jean.
    —Some philosophical considerations. 1667. *See* Glanvill, Joseph.

41 —Strange news from Plymouth. *For J. Conyers*, 1684. 4°. L, O; CN, WF, Y, ZWT.
    —Συγκρυτισμος. Or. 1654. *See* Goodwin, John.
    —True reformation. 1643. *See* Graunt, John.
    —Truths defender. 1651. *See* Graunt, John.
    —Truths victory. 1645. *See* Graunt, John.
    —Vindication of James Magrath. [n.p.], 1682. *See* Magrath, James.

42 Entry cancelled.
    —Word from the Lord to all the world. 1654. *See* Fox, George, *elder*.

G., J. G. Just and sober vindication. 1694. *See* Gailhard, Jean.

42A —The trumpet in Sion. *Printed and are to be sold by Dan. Browne*, 1700. 4°. T.C.III 182. OC.

43 **G., L.** The court's apology. *Printed*, 1663. 8°.* L, O; NU.

44 Entry cancelled.
    —Essayes and characters. [n.p.], 1661. *See* Griffin, Lewis.

44A —Overbury revived. *Sold by Henry Marsh*, 1661. 12°. OB.

45 —The Presbyterian bramble. *Printed*, 1661. 4°.* O, E; CLC.

45A —A project humbly offered to both Houses for . . . raising of a million. *For the authors*, 1693. brs. L, MC.
    —Publick good. 1657. *See* Gatford, Lionel.

G., M. Account of the Jesuites. [n.p.], 1661. *See* Greene, Martin.
    —Αυτοκατακριτοι. Or. 1679. *See* Greene, Martin.

46 Entry cancelled.
    —Defence of a treatise. 1643. *See* Giles, Mascall.

47 —The glorious excellencie of the spirit of adoption. *By Jane Coe, for Henry Ouerton*, 1645. 8°. LT; CH.
    —King's life-guard. 1665. *See* Griffith, Matthew.

47A —A plain discourse on the mercy of having good parents. [*London?*], *printed*, 1668. 12°. L.
    —Supplement to the Negro's. 1681. *See* Godwin, Morgan.
    —Voyce of truth. 1676. *See* Greene, Martin.

G., N. Dr. Pierce his preaching confuted. [n.p., 1663.] *See* Dobson, John.

48 —Dr. Pierce his preaching exemplified. [*London?*], 1663. 4°.* MADAN 2625. O, DU.

49 **G., O.** Englands joyfull holiday. [1661.] brs. O.

G., P. Poem occasioned by the magnificent proceeding. 1695. *See* Gleane, *Sir* Peter.

G., R. Ars clericalis. 1690. *See* Gardiner, Robert.

50 Entry cancelled. Ghost.

51 Entry cancelled.

—Censure upon Lilly's grammar. 1684. *See* Garthwaite, Richard.

52–3 Entries cancelled.

—Compleat constable. 1692. *See* Gardiner, Robert.

53A A copy of a letter from an officer of the army in Ireland. [*London*, 1656.] cap., 4°. LT, O, C, BC, DT; CH, CN, MH, TU, WF, Y.

—French-man and the Spaniard. 1642. *See* Garcia, Carlos.

—Instructor clericalis. 1693. *See* Gardiner, Robert.

54 —Interrogatories on the part and behalf of the people of England. [*London?* 1689.] brs. L, O, C, OC, HH; CH, MH, PL, WF.

55 —A letter sent from a gentleman in the Hague. [*London*, 1649.] 4°.* LT, O, MR; CH, MH, WF.

—Ludus scacchiæ; a satyr. 1675. *See title.*

—Prognosticon. 1666. *See* Almanacs.

—Satyr against wooing. 1698. *See* Gould, Robert.

56 —A sermon of mortalitie. *By R. Constable*, 1650. 4°.* O, LW.

—Short sentences. [n.p., 1679.] *See* Greenway, Richard.

—Spiritual order. [n.p., 1675.] *See* Gordon, Robert.

—Testimony to the true Saviour. 1669. *See* Gordon, Robert.

56A —To the right worshipful John Hubland. [*London*, 1689.] brs. Y.

57 —A treatise of tithes. *By J. F. for W. Lee*, 1653. 4°.* LT, O, C, LLP, LUG, OC, BC; CH, MHL, NC, NU, WF.

58 —The true relation of the arrivall of thirty Flemish ships. [*London*], *printed*, 1648. 4°.* LT, LG; CSS.

—Virginia's cure. 1662. *See* Gray, Robert.

58A **G., S.** A discourse concerning bodily worship. *For G. Bedell*, 1650. 4°. O, LSC.

—Glass for the people. [n.p.], 1676. *See* Groome, Samuel,

—Historical account of the antiquity. 1692. *See* Grascombe, Samuel.

—Ορθολατρεια: or. 1650. *See* Gunton, Simon.

59 Entry cancelled.

—Separation of the Church of Rome. 1691. *See* Grascombe, Samuel.

60 Entry cancelled.

G., T. Ars sciendi. 1681. *See* Gowan, Thomas.

—Careless shepherdess. 1656. *See* Goffe, Thomas.

—Century of observations. 1686. *See* Guidott, Thomas.

—Charity and integrity. 1696. *See* Gregory, Thomas.

—Christian directions. 1674. *See* Gouge, Thomas.

—Covrt of the gentiles. Oxon, 1669. *See* Gale, Theophilus.

60A —The danger is over. *Printed*, 1696. 4°.* Y.

61 —Ελεοθριαμβος: being England's triumphs. *For F. Blithe, to be sold by Richard Baldwin*, 1698. fol.* L, AU.

62 —An encomium, or congratulatory poem. *By H. Bruges*, 1674. brs. L, HH; CH.

63 —Exceeding good newes from Beverley. *For I. T., Iuly* 20. 1642. 4°.* LT, O, OC, EC, YM; IU.

—Further vindication. [n.p., 1699.] *See* Gipps, Thomas.

—Law against bankrupts. 1694. *See* Goodinge, Thomas.

64 —A letter in answer to two main questions. *For M. T.*, 1687. 4°.* L, O, OC, DU, MR; CH, CN, MIU, WF, Y.

65 —A plain discovery how the enemy and Popish faction. [*London*], *printed*, 1649. 4°.* LT, DT; WF.

65A —The plain mathematician. *For A. C. to be sold by William Crook*, 1664. 8°. WF.

—Plain testimony. [n.p.], 1691. *See* Goodaire, Thomas.

—Principlau neu bennau. 1676. *See* Gouge, Thomas.

—Principles of Christian religion. 1668. *See* Gouge, Thomas.

—Quæries examined. 1676. *See* Grantham, Thomas.

66 —The saints comfort. *For John Harris*, 1685. 8°. CH, NU.

—Tentamen novum. 1696. *See* Gipps, Thomas.

—True and exact account of Sadler's well. 1684. *See* Guidott, Thomas.

—True idea. 1669. *See* Gale, Theophilus.

—Word to sinners. 1672. *See* Gouge, Thomas.

66A **G., W.** An abridgment of the English history. *For W. Gilbertson*, 1660. 12°. L; Y.

—Ανθολογια. The life. 1651. *See* Garret, William.

—Arraignment of ignorance. 1659. *See* Gearing, William.

67 —The case of succession to the crown. [n.p.], *printed*, 1679. 4°.* L, O, C, LSD, EN; CH, CLC, IU, MM, NU, WF, Y.

—Defence of Dr. Sherlock's preservative. 1688. *See* Giles, William.

68 —England's jubilee and Rome's downfall. *Printed*, 1699. brs. O.

69 —The faithful analist. *For W. Gilbertson*, [1660]. 12°. O; CH, MB, NC.

69A — —[Anr. ed.] *For R. Gilbertson*, [1660]. 12°. Y.

70 — —[Anr. ed.] *For Will. Whitwood*, 1666. 12°. EN; WF, Y.

—In memorie of that. [n.p., 1649.] *See* Wharton, George.

71 —A just apologie for an abvsed armie. *For H. Overton*, 1646. 4°.* LT, C, MR, YM; CH, CN, IU, LC, Y.

—Memento's to the world. [n.p.], 1680. *See* Green, William.

72 —Proposals by . . . shewing how to raise two millions. [n.p., 1695.] fol. L, O.

—Resolution of three important questions. [1688.] *See* Garret, Walter.

—Sabbaths sanctification. 1641. *See* Gouge, William.

—Sound-hearted Christian. 1670. *See* Greenhill, William.

—Status ecclesiæ. 1676. *See* Gearing, William.

73 No entry.

G., Z. Excise anotomiz'd [*sic*]. [*London*, 1659.] *See* Crofton, Zachary.

73A **Gabay, Jonas.** To all Christian readers. [*London?* 1676.] brs. L, LPR.

74 **Gadbury, John.** Animal cornutum, or the horn'd beast. *For William Larnar*, 1654. 8°. LT.

74A [–] Astrological predictions for the year 1679. *For R. G.*, 1679. 4°.* L; IU.

74B —Αστρολογοναυτης or, the astrological seaman. *By Matthew Street*, 1697. 8°. WF.

74C [–] A ballad. The third part. [*London*, 1679?] brs. L; MH, AMB. (var.)

75 [–] A ballad upon the Popish plot. [*London?* 1679.] brs. L, O, LG, LL, HH, LLU; CH, MBA, MH, TU, Y.

75A —A brief relation of the life and death of . . . Vincent Wing. *Printed by T. Milbourn*, 1669. 4°.* L.

76 [–] —[Anr. ed.] *By T. M.*, 1670. 4°.* L, O, CD; CLC.

76A — —[Anr. ed.] *By T. Milbourn for John Stephens*, 1670. 4°.* L, O, LSD; WF.

77 —Britains royal star. *For Sam. Speed*, 1661. 4°. LT, O; MH, NHC, NN.

78 —Cardines cœli, or an appeal. *Printed*, 1684. 4°. T.C.II 102. L, CM, E, DT; SYRACUSE, WU.

78A — —[Anr. ed.] *For M. G. and sold by Daniel Brown, Sam. Sprint, & John Guillim*, 1685. 4°. O, LSD; MH, NN.

79 —Cœlestis legatus: or, the coelestial ambassadour. *By E. B. to be sold by John Allen*, 1656. 4°. LT, O, LWL, P; CH, TU.

80 —Collectio genitvrarvm: or, a collection. *By James Cottrel*, 1662. fol. L, O, LN, LWL, OC, E; CLC, CN, MH, TU, WF, Y.

81 —De cometis; or, a discourse. *For L. Chapman*, 1665. 4°. L, O, LG, LWL, EO; CJC, CLC, LC, MH, WU, Y.

    —Diarium astronomicum. 1675. *See* Almanacs.

    —Diary astronomical. 1666. *See* Almanacs.

82 —Dies novissimvs: or, Dooms-day. *By James Cottrel*, 1664. 4°. L, O, C, P, GU; CH, MH, MM, NU, WF.

    —Ephemerides. 1672. *See* Almanacs.

    —Εφημερις. 1659. *See* Almanacs.

83 —Festum festorum: or, a discourse. *By N. Thompson, for the company of stationers*, 1687. 8°. L, O, LLP, CM, GK; CH, WF, Y.

84 —Γενεθλιαλογια, or, the doctrine of nativities. *By Ja: Cottrel, for Giles Calvert, William Larnar, and Daniel White*, 1658. fol. L, O, C, E, DT; IU, LC, MH, PL, Y.

84A —Second edition. *For William Miller*, 1661. fol. A; CH, CLC.

    —Jamaica almanack. 1672. *See* Almanacs.

85 —The just and pious scorpionist. *By J. D. for Robert Boulter*, 1677. 4°.* T.C.I 276. L, O, LR, LWL, GU; CH, MH, NPT, WF, Y.

86 —London's deliverance predicted. *By J. C. for E. Calvert*, 1665. 4°.* L, O, C, MR, E; MBP, MHM.

86A — —[Anr. ed.] —, 1666. 4°.* LG.

87 —Magna veritas: or, John Gadbury, . . . not a Papist. *By A. M. and R. R.*, 1680. fol.* O, C, LWL, LLU, DU; CH, IU, MH, TU, WF, Y.

88 Entry cancelled.

    [–] Mene tekel. [1688.] *See* Partridge, John.

88A [–] The nativity of that most illustrious . . . Carolus Gustavus. *Printed*, 1659. 4°.* LT, O, LLL, LWL; MH, MIU.

89 —The nativity of the late King Charls. *By James Cottrel*, 1659. 8°. LT, O, C, EN, ES; BN, CH, CLC, IU, LC, MH, WF, Y.

90 [–] The nativity of the most valiant and puissant monarch Lewis the Fourteenth. *Printed*, 1680. 4°.* T.C.I 385. L, O, OH, CT; CLC, MBA, MH.

91 —Natura prodigiorum: or, a discourse. *By J. C. for Fr. Cossinet, and Tho. Basset*, 1660. 8°. LT, O, LN, LWL, SP; CLC, MH, WF, WU, Y.

92 — —Second edition. *For Fr. Cossinet*, 1665. 8°. L, LN; MH, NIC, PU.

92A —Nauticum astrologium. *For Matthew Street*, 1691. 8°. L.

92B — —[Anr. ed.] —, 1696. 8°. L.

93 [–] Νεοφυτο-'αστρολογος: the novice-astrologer instucted. *For E. C.*, 1660. 8°. LT.

93A [–] A new narrative of the popish plot. [*London*, 1680?] cap., 4°.* L, O, CT, DU, SP; CH, MH, MIU, WF, Y.

94 —Nuncius astrologicus: or, the astrological legate. *By J. Cottrel, for F. Cossinet*, 1660. 8°. LT; CLC, NIC.

95 —Obsequium rationabile, or a reasonable service. *For William Berry*, 1675. 8°. T.C.I 211. L, O, LR, EN; MH.

95A —Observations on the proceedings of the Dutch, shewing the total destruction . . of the Prince of Orange. [*Dublin*, 1688.] brs. SOUTHAMPTON PUB. LIB.

96 —His past and present opinion of the Ottoman . . . power. [*London*], *by Nathaniel Thompson*, 1683. 4°.* L, O, OC, EN.

97 [–] Philastrogus knavery epitomized. *Printed*, 1652. 4°.* LT; CSS, MH, WSG, HC.

    —Προγνοστκιον. [1658.] *See* Almanacs.

97A Entry cancelled.

    —Gadburies prophetical sayings. 1690. *See* title.

97B [–] Ψευδο-αστρολογος. Or, the spurious prognosticator. *Printed*, 1660. 4°.* L, O, LWL; MH, MIU.

97C —The scurrilous scribler. [*London*, 1693.] brs. O.

    —Speculum astrologicum. 1656. *See* Almanacs.

98 —Thesaurus astrologiæ: or, an astrological treasury. *For Thomas Passenger*, 1674. 8°. T.C.I 179. L, O, C, LN, E; CH, CLC, MH, NN, WF, WSG, Y.

99 [–] A true narrative of the horrid hellish Popish-plot. First part. [*n.p.*, 1682.] brs. L, O, EC; CH, MH, MIU.

100 [–] —Second [third] part. [*n.p.*, 1682.] brs. L, LS, EC; CH, MH.

100A —Vox solis; or, an astrological discourse. *By James Cotterel, for Eliz. Calvert*, 1667. 4°.* L.

    —West-India . . . almanack. [*n.p.*, 1673.] *See* Almanacs.

101 **Gadbury, Timothy.** A health to the king. *For W. Gilbertson*, 1660. 4°.* O.

102–3 Entries cancelled.

    —Young seamans guide. 1659. *See* Almanacs.

103A Gadburies prophetical sayings; or, the fool, colop: *For Richard Baldwin*, 1690. brs. L; CH, MH.

104 **Gaderus, C. D. L. H.** Doctrinæ antiquæ de natura. *Apud J. Martin et J. Alestrey*, 1654. 12°. O, E; BN.

104A [**Gaetani, Enrico**], *cardinal.* Instructions for young gentlemen. *By T.N. for Fr. Bowman*, 1650. 12°. CSS.

105 **Gaffarel, Jacques.** Vnheard-of curiosities. *By G. D. for Humphrey Moseley*, 1650. 8°. LT, O, C, E, DT; CLC, CU, LC, MH, WF, Y.

106 A gagge for lay-preachers. [*London*, 1652.] brs. LT.

    Gagg for the Quakers. 1659. *See* Smith, Thomas.

Gagg to love's advocate. 1651. *See* Hinde, John.

107 [**Gage, John.**] The Christian sodality. First tome. [*Paris?*], *printed*, 1652. 8°. L, O, BSM, DUS, DT; CLC, CN, MH, NU, TU, WF, Y.

108 **Gage, Thomas.** A duell between a Iesuite and a Dominican. colop: *Printed at London for Tho. Williams, 1651.* cap., 4°.* LT, O, YM; MH.

109 —The English-American. *By R. Cotes, and are to be sold by Humphrey Blunden, and Thomas Williams,* 1648. fol. L, O, CT, E, DT; CH, CN, LC, MH, MU, NU, RPJ, Y.

110 Entry cancelled.
    — —Second edition. 1655. *See* —A new survey. Second edition.

111 —A full survey of Sion and Babylon. *By W. Bentley, to be sold by Joshuah Kirton,* 1654. 4°. O, C, LW, BC, MR; CLC, IU, Y.

112 No entry.

113 A new survey of the West India's. Second edition. *By E. Cotes, and sold by John Sweeting,* 1655. fol. L, O, C, CK, SHR, ES; BN, CH, CN, LC, MH, RPJ, Y, AVP.

114 — —Third edition. *By A. Clark and are to be sold by John Martyn, Robert Horn, and Walter Kettilby,* 1677. 8°. T.C.I 258. L, O, C, LAD, DUS; BN, CH, CN, LC, NC, RPJ, Y.

115 — —Fourth edition. *By M. Clark, for J. Nicolson and T. Newborough,* 1699. 8°. T.C.III 130. L, C, LL, EN, DM; CLC, CN, LC, MH, MU, RPJ, Y.

116 —The tyranny of Satan. *By Tho. Badger, for Humphrey Mosley,* 1642. 4°.* LT, O, C, WCA; LC, MBP, MWA, NU, TO, Y.

117 **Gailhard, Jean.** The blasphemous Socinian heresie disproved. *For R. Wellington, and J. Hartley,* 1697. 8°. T.C.III 12. L, O, CT, E, ENC; CLC, NU.

118 —The compleat gentleman. [*London*], *in the Savoy: by Tho. Newcomb, for John Starkey,* 1678. 8°. T.C.I 302. L, O, LW, CT, BLH; CH, CN, MH, WF, Y.

119 —The controversie between Episcopacie. [*London*], *for the author,* 1660. 4°. LT, DU; CH, MBA.

120 [–] A discourse about ceremonies. *Printed, and are to be sold by Richard Baldwin,* 1696. 4°. ON; NU.

121 —The epistle and preface to the book against the . . . Socinian heresie vindicated. *For J. Hartley,* 1698. 8°. T.C.III 52. L, O, CT, OC, BAMB; CLC.

121A —Four tracts. *For D. Brown and R. Smith,* 1699. 4°. T.C.III 135. OC.

122 [–] A just and sober vindication of the observations. *Printed, and are to be sold by Ric. Baldwin,* 1694. 4°. L, C, OB, ON, CCA; MM.

123 —A plea for free-grace. *For George Grafton,* 1696. 8°. NU.

124 —The present state of the princes . . . of Italy. *For John Starkey,* 1668. 12°. T.C.I 2. L, O, C, LLU, DU; CH, CN, UCLA, WU, Y.

124A — —Second edition. —, 1669. 12°. MBA.

125 — —"Second" edition. —, 1671. 12°. T.C.I 76. L, O, OC, CM, CT; CH, CLC, LC, MBA, WF.

126 —The present state of the republick of Venice. *For John Starkey,* 1669. 12°. T.C.I 5. L, O, C, E, DT; CH, CU, PL, WF, Y.

127 —The right of the church asserted. *For J. Rothwell,* 1660. 4°.* LT, O, BC, DU, GU; MH, NU, WF.

128 [–] Serious advice to a preservative. *For Geo. Grafton, to be sold by Ric. Baldwin,* 1695. 4°.* ON, CT; NU.

129 [–] Some observations upon the keeping the thirtieth of January. *Printed, and are to be sold by Ric. Baldwin,* 1694. 4°. O, C, LCL, OB, BC; CLC, CN, NU, PL, WF, Y.

130 —The true character of the spirit and principles of Socinianism. *For J. Hartley,* 1699. 8°. L, O, CS; CLC.

131 —Two discourses. *For Walter Davis,* 1682. 8°. L, O, CT, P, CD; CH, LC, NCU, PL, WF, Y.

Gainsayer convinced. 1649. *See* Thache, Thomas.

131A **Gainsborough, Katherine,** *countess*. Baptist, earl of Gainsborough . . . appellants. Katherine countess dowager of Gainsborough, respondent. The respondents case. [*n.p.*, 1693.] brs. L.

    Gaire, *lord mayor*. *See* Gayer, Sir John.

132 [**Gale, Nathaniel.**] The faithful testimony of High-hall detected . . . Part. I. *Printed,* 1700. 4°.* O; NPT.

133 **Gale, Theophilus.** The anatomie of infidelitie. *By J. D. for Jonathan Robinson,* 1672. 8°. O, LCL, BC, P, EN; IU, MH, MWA, NF, NU.

134 — —[Anr. ed.] *By J. D. for Giles Widdows,* 1672. 8°. T.C.I 110. L, CS; MH, NU, TO, WF.

134A — —[Anr. ed.] *By J. Darby, for Jonathan Robinson and Giles Widdows,* 1672. 8°. EN; CH, CLC, MBZ.

135 —Christ's tears for Jerusalem's unbelief. *For M. Widdowes,* 1679. 8°. LCL; NPT.

136 [–] The covrt of the Gentiles: . . . Part I. *Oxon: by Hen: Hall for Tho: Gilbert,* 1669. 4°. T.C.I 14. MADAN 2830. L, O, CS, EN, DT; CH, CU, MH, NU, WSC, Y.

137 — —Second edition. *Oxon by H. Hall for Tho. Gilbert,* 1672. 4°. T.C.I 105. MADAN 2928. L, O, C, E, DT; BN, CH, CN, MH, WF, Y.

138 — —Part II. *Oxford, by Will: Hall for Tho: Gilbert,* 1670. 4°. T.C.I 56. MADAN 2854. L, O, C, MR, BQ; CLC, MH, MU, NF, TO, WF.

139 — — —[Anr. ed.] —, 1671. 4°. MADAN 2887. L, O, CT, EN, DT; CH, CU, MBP, NU, Y.

140 — — —Second edition. *By J. Macock for Thomas Gilbert,* 1676. 4°. O, C, OM, DU, DT; BN, CLC, CN, MH, MU, WF.

141 — —Part III. *By A. Maxwell and R. Roberts, for T. Cockeril,* 1677. 4°. L, O, C, EN, DT; BN, CH, CN, MH, WF, Y.

142 — —Part IV. *By J. Macock, for Thomas Cockeril,* 1677. 4°. T.C.I 283. L, O, CT, EN, DT; BN, CLC, CN, MH, WF, Y.

142A — — —[Anr. ed.] *For William Freeman,* 1682. 4°. T.C.I 497. CLC.

143 — —Part IV . . . Book III. *For John Hill, and Samuel Tidmarsh,* 1678. 4°. T.C.I 322. L, O, C, CK, DC; CH, MH, MU, NU, WF.

144 —A discourse of Christ's coming. *For John Hancock senior and junior,* 1673. 8°. T.C.I 140. L, O, C, LCL; MH, NF, NPT, NU, Y.

145 —Idea theologiæ. *Impensis J. Robinson, & R. Boulter,* 1673. 12°. T.C.I 142. L, O, CT, E, GU; BN, CH, CLC, MH, NU, Y.

146   [–] The life and death of Mr. John Rowe. *For Francis Tyton*, 1673. 12°. T.C.I 132. L, O, LW, DU, P; CH, CLC, CU, NU, TO, WF.

147   [–] The life and death of Thomas Tregosse. *Printed*, 1671. 8°. T.C.I 116. L, O, C, LCL, DU, SP.

148   —Philosophia generalis. *Typis J. M. pro J. Robinson, & J. Hancock*, 1676. 8°. T.C.I 258. L, O, C, E, DT; BN, CH, IU, MH, NPT, PL, WF, Y.

149   —Theophilie: or a discourse. *By R. W. for Francis Tyton*, 1671. 8°. L, O, C, LCL, AN, ENC; CH, MH, NF, NU, Y.

150   — —[Anr. ed.] *By R. W. for Giles Widdows*, 1671. 8°. T.C.I 63. L, BC, DL; NC, PPT, TO, TU, WF, Y.

151   [–] The true idea of Jansenisme. *For Th. Gilbert in Oxon.* 1669. 8°. T.C.I 21; MADAN 2831. L, O, C, LCL, DT; CLC, CU, MH, NU, WF, Y.

152   [–] —[Anr. ed.] *For E. Calvert, and G. Widdows*, 1669. 8°. L, CT, SHR, WCA, EN; CH, CU, MH, MU, NU, WF.

153   No entry.

154   **Gale, Thomas.** Historiæ Britannicæ. *Oxoniæ, e theatro Sheldoniano*, 1691. 2v. fol. T.C.II 360. L, O, C, EN, DT; BN, CH, CU, MH, WF, Y, AVP (V.I).

155   [–] Historiæ poeticæ scriptores antiqui. *Parisiis, typis F. Muguet, prostant apud R. Scott, Londinensem*, 1675. 8°. T.C.I 221. L, O, CCA, MR, EN, DT; CH, IU, MBA, PL, WF, Y.

155A [–] —[Anr. ed.] *Prostant apud R. Scott*, 1676. 8°. NORTH-WESTERN.

156   [–] Opuscula mythologica. *Cantabrigiæ, ex officina J. Hayes, impensis Joann. Creed*, 1671. 8°. T.C.I 68. L, O, C, E, BQ; BN, CH, CU, MH, WF, Y.

157   —Rhetores selecti. *Oxonii, e theatro Sheldoniano*, 1676. 8°. T.C.I 258. MADAN 3118. L, O, C, EN, DT; CLC, CU, MH, PL, WF, Y.

158   No entry.

159   **Galenus, Claudius.** Galens art of physick. *By Peter Cole*, 1652. 8°. LT, LSC, LWL, CE; MH, NN, WSG, HC.

159A — —[Anr. ed.] —, 1657. 8°. O; CLC.

159B — —[Anr. ed.] —, 1662. 8°. LWL; NCU, HC.

160   — —[Anr. ed.] *By J. Streater, sold by J. Wright*, 1671. 8°. T.C.I 93. C, CT; MIU, MMO, PBL, WF, HC.

161   —Galen's method of physick. *Edinburgh, by A. A. for George Swintoun, and James Glen*, 1656. 12°. ALDIS 1541. LT; WSG, HC.

162   **Galen, Christopher Bernard Matthew van.** A letter to the bishop of Munster. *Printed*, 1666. 4°.* L.

163   —Letter sent by . . . to the Lords the States-General. *Oxford, by William Hall to be sold by Thomas Bowman*, 1665. 4°.* MADAN 2693. L, O, CT, DT; CH, CLC, LC, Y.

164   [–] A letter sent by. *[London], by the original, printed by command for F. B. esquire*, 1655. 4°.* LNC; NN.

165   Entry cancelled.

      Galilei, Galileo. Dialogusde systema mundi. 1663. *See —* Systema cosmicvm.

166   Entry cancelled.

      —Mathematical discourses. 1665. *See* Salusbury, Thomas. Mathematical Collections. 1661–65.

167   —Sidereus nuncius. *Typis Jacobi Flesher; prostat apud Cornelium Bee*, 1653. 8°. L, O, C, LCP, EN; CH, IU, MBA, PL, TO, Y, HC. (var.)

167A — —[Anr. ed.] *Typis Jacobi Flesher*. 1653. 8°. IU, MH. (var.)
      — —[Anr. ed.] *[n.p.]*, 1682. *See* Gassendi, Pierre. Institutio astronomica. 1683.

168   —Systema cosmicvm. *Prostat vænale apud Thomam Dicas*, 1663. 8°. L, O, C, DC, ENC, DM; CH, CJC, MH, WF, Y.

169   **Galland, Antoine.** The remarkable sayings, apothegms, . . . of the Eastern nations. *For Richard Baldwin; and William Lindsey*, 1695. 12°. L, O, C, EN, DT; CH, CN, NC, WF, Y.

170   The gallant history of the life and death of that most noble knight, Sir Bevis. *[London], by A. M. for J. Deacon*, [1691?]. 4°.* T.C.II 397. L, O, CM.

171   —[Anr. ed.] *[London], by A.M. for B. Deacon*, [1700?]. 4°. L, CM; WF.

      Gallant ladies. 1685. *See* Poisson, Raymond.
      Gallant news. 1646. *See* H., F.

172   Gallant newes for London. *[London?], printed*, 1647. 4°.* LT, MR, DT.

172A Gallant newes from Ireland. *[London], for Edward Wright*, [1649.] brs. MAU.

172B Gallant news of late I bring. *Printed for Francis Grove*, [1660]. brs. EUING 130. GU.

173   The gallant rights, Christian priviledges, solemn institutions of the sea-green order. *[London, 1648.]* brs. LT, LS; MH.

173A The gallant sea-fight. *[London? 1692.]* brs. L.

174   The gallant seaman's resolution. *[London], by and for A. Milbourn*, [1670–97]. brs. CM, HH; MH.

174A —[Anr. ed.] *By and for W. O. for A. M. and sold by the booksellers*, [1700?]. brs. O.

      Gallant seamans return. *[n.p., 1678–80.] See* Lanfiere, Thomas.

174B The gallant she-souldier. *For Richard Burton*, [1655]. brs. L.
      Gallant siege. 1646. *See* P., M.
      Gallant victory. 1647. *See* Moore, Francis.

175   Gallantry all-a-mode. *[London], for F. Coles, T. Vere, J. Wright and J. Clark*, [1674–79]. brs. L.

176   Gallantry a-la-mode. *By T. R. & N. T. for the author*, 1674. 8°. T.C.I 163. L, LG; CH, CU, MH, OCI, Y.

176A–7 Entries cancelled.
      Gallantry unmasked. 1690. *See* Modern novels, vol. II.
      Galants. 1685. *See* Poisson, Raymond.

178   **Gallaway, William.** Reflections upon Mr. Johnson's notes on the pastoral letter. *For the author, and are to be sold by Randal Taylor*, 1614 [*i.e.*, 1694]. 4°. T.C.II 528. L, O, C, LCL, DU; CH, CN, TU, WF, Y.

179   —A sermon preached . . . July 24. 1692. *For Rich. Baldwin*, 1692. 4°.* L, CT; MBA, MM.

180   —A thanksgiving-sermon. *For Hugh Newman*, 1697. 4°.* T.C.III 64. L, O, C, LLP; MH.

      Gallen, Thomas. Almanack. [1642.] *See* Almanacs.
      —Complete pocket almanack. 1686. *See* Almanacs.
      Gallen, William.
      —New almanack. [1658.] *See* Almanacs.

Galliæ flagellum, or. 1696. *See* Perron, W.

Galliæ notitia; or. 1691. *See* Besogne, Nicolas.

Galliæ speculum, or. 1673. *See* Care, Henry.

Gallienus redivivius, or. Edinbvrgh, 1695. *See* Leslie, Charles.

180A **G[allimore], F[rancis].** A short discourse. *For Hen. Hammond at Bath and at the Devizes, 1694.* 4°. L.

Gallobelgicus, *pseud.*

181 **[Gallonio, Antonio.]** The holy life of Philip Nerius. *At Paris, 1659.* 8°. LT, O, LW, OM, DU, P; CH, CLC, WF.

181A **Gallus, Cornelius.** Elegies of old age. *For B. Crayle, 1688.* 8°. T.C.II 217. L; CLC, MH.

181B —The impotent lover. *For B. Crayle, 1689.* 8°. T.C.II 253. L, O, LG, DT; CH, MH, WF.

182 **Gallus, Ewaldus.** Παιδολογιαι. η παιδολογιδια. Pueriles confabulatiunculæ. *Oxoniæ, typis Lichfieldianis, veneunt apud Ric. Davis, 1666.* 8°. MADAN 2742. L, O.

182A ——[Anr. ed.] *Oxoniæ, typis Lichfieldianis, impensis Ric. Davis, 1666.* WF.

183 — —[Anr. ed.] *Oxonii, e theatro Sheldoniano, 1672.* 8°. MADAN 2742n. L; CCC.

183A — —[Anr. ed.] *Cantabrigiæ, ex officina Joann. Hayes, 1677.* 8°. L (t.p.).

184 — —[Anr. ed.] *Dublinii, excudebat B. Took, prostant venales per A. Crook, & ab. S. Helsham, 1686.* 8°. DIX 222. DN.

Galtruchius. *See* Gautruche.

Gamaches, Cyprien de. *See* Cyprien de Gamaches.

185 **Gamble, John.** Ayres and dialogues for one. Second book. *By W. Godbid for Nathaniel Ekin, 1659.* fol. L; CH, WF.

186 —Ayres and dialogues (to be sung to the theorbo-lvte . . .). *By William Godbid, for the author, 1656.* fol. L, CT, GU; IU, LC, MH, WF.

187 — —[Anr. ed.] *By W. Godbid for Humphry Mosley, 1657.* fol. O, CCH; CH, WF.

187A — —[Anr. ed.] *By W. Godbid for the author, 1658.* fol. MH.

188 The game at chesse. *For Thomas Iohnson, Febr. 2. 1643.* 4°.* LT; CN, MH, NS, PL, TU, Y.

189 The game is up: or, xxxi new qværies. *[London], printed, 1659.* 4°.* LT, O, LG, LSD, RU; CH, CLC, MIU, WF.

Gaming-humour considered. 1684. *See* Morton, Charles.

190 **Gammon, John.** Christ a Christian's life. *By J. R. for W. Marshall, 1691.* 8°. T.C.II 367. L, LCL.

191 **Gand, Louis de.** Apologeticon . . . proseipso. 1659. 4°. L.

192 —Lettre du Sieur. *[London, 1656.]* cap., 4°.* LT.

193 —Parallelum Olivæ. *Ex typographiâ R. I., 1656.* fol. L, O, C, EN, DT; BN, CH, IU, MH, WCL, WF, Y.

193A —Le Sr. DeGand, . . . ent audience, . . . Protecteur. *[n.p., 1654.]* 4°. CH.

194 —Sol Britannicus. *Excudebat J. Beale & S. Buckley, 1641.* 8° in 4s. L, O, C, EN, DL, DT; CH, CLC, CU, MM, WF.

195 —To the right honourable the knights, . . . the humble petition of. *[London, 1641.]* brs. LT.

196 **Gander, Joseph.** A vindication of a national-fishery. *For F. Coggan, 1699.* 8°. L, CT, LUG, EN; CH, MH, WF.

197 **[Gandy, Henry.]** An answer to some queries, concerning schism. *Printed, 1700.* 4°. L, O, CT, MR, EN; CLC, INU, LC, NU, Y, AVP.

198 The gang or the nine worthies. *For Charls Gustavus,* [1660]. brs. LT, O, EN.

199 **Gannacliff, John.** Gospel truths scripturally asserted. *Printed, and sold by T. Sowle, 1692.* 4°.* O, C, LF, BBN; IE, PSC, WF.

199A — —[Anr. ed.] 1698. 8°.* PH.

200–1 Entries cancelled.

Ganning, Nicholas. Exhortation to the late-ordained ministers. 1656. *See* Brinsley, John, *younger.* The sacred ordinance.

202 **G[arbrand], J[ohn].** Clarior e tenebris: or, a justification of two books. *For Thomas Dring, 1683.* 4°.* T.C.II 19. O, LL, LIU, DT; CH, CLC, MIU, MM, NC, WF.

203 [–] The grand inquest. *For James Vade, 1680.* 4°.* T.C.I 441. L, O, CT, EN, DT; CH, IU, MH, NP, NU.

204 [–] —Second edition. —, 1680. 4°.* L, O, DUS, LNC, MR, BLH; WF, Y.

205 [–] —Third edition. —, 1681. 4°.* DU, BC, SP, DN; LC, MH, AVP.

206 [–] The royal favourite clear'd. *For James Vade, 1682.* 4°. L, O, LVF, BC, LSD, EN, DT; MM, PU, WF.

207 **Garbutt, Richard.** A demonstration of the resurrection. *For Samuel Gellibrand, 1657.* 12°. LT, O, C, SP, YM; CH, CLC, IU.

207A ——[Anr. ed.] —, 1669. 12°. T.C.I II. L, LLP, LSC, LW, CE, MR, YM, EN; WF, Y.

208 —One come from the dead. *For Francis Smith,* [1675?]. 8°. T.C.I 233. O, C, OC, YM; CLC, NPT, TO.

209 Entry cancelled.

—Resurrection. 1669. *See* —Demonstration of the resurrection.

209A **Garcia, Carlos.** The antipathy betweene the French and Spaniard. *[London], sold by R. Martine, 1641.* 12°. NN, WF.

210 [–] The French-man and the Spaniard. *For Humphrey Mosley, 1642.* 12°. L, DC, SP; CH, CN, MH, MU, Y.

211 [–] Guzman, Hinde and Hannam outstript. *Printed, 1657.* 12°. CH, LC, WCL.

212 —Lavernæ, or the Spanish gipsy. *London, not in Newgate, 1650.* 12°. L; CLC.

213 **Garcia, Petrus.** Caram vel ridicvlvs caramveli convicto. *[Londini], 1643.* 12°. LT.

214 **Garcilaso de la Vega.** The royal commentaries of Peru. *By Miles Flesher for Richard Tonson, 1688.* fol. O, CS, OME; MWA, NC, PL, V, WF.

215 — —[Anr. ed.] *By Miles Flesher, for Samuel Heyrick, 1688.* fol. C, CT; CDA, MU, NC, PL, V, Y.

216 — —[Anr. ed.] *By Miles Flesher for Christopher Wilkinson, 1688.* fol. L, CK, WCA, E, DT; CH, CU, MH, NP, Y.

217 — —[Anr. ed.] *By Miles Flesher, for Jacob Tonson, 1688.* fol. L, O, OC, BC, LSD, MR; CH, CN, LC, MH, RPJ, Y.

218 **[Garden, George.]** An apology for M. Antonia Bourignon. *For D. Brown; S. Manship; R. Parker; and H. Newman, 1699.* 8°. T.C.III 153. L, O, CPE, BAMB, EU; CLC, NPT, NU, WF, Y.

[–] Case of the present. 1690. *See* Sage, John.

[–] Queries and protestation. 1694. *See* Ridpath, George.

219 **[Garden, James.]** Comparative theology. [*London*], 1700. 8°. L, RPL, BC, AU; CH, CLC, WF.

219A [–] Discursus academicus de theologia comparativa. *Impensis Dan. Brown, et H. Newman*, 1699. L, O, LSC, LW; NU, WF, Y.

220 —Theses theologicæ. *Aberdoniæ, typis Ioannis Forbesii*, 1691 [*i.e.*, 1681]. 4°.* ALDIS 2269. E.

Garden of delight. 1658. *See* Tompson, John.

Garden of spirituall flowers. 1643. *See* Rogers, Richard.

Garden of Zion. Glasgow, 1644. *See* Boyd, Zachary.

Gardeners labyrinth. [n.p.], 1652. *See* Hill, Thomas.

221 Entry cancelled.

Gardiner, George. *See* Gardyner, George.

222 **Gardiner, Henry.** New-Englands vindidation. *For the autheur*, 1660. 4°.* RPJ.

223 **Gardiner, James,** *bp.* Advice to the clergy of the diocese of Lincoln. *For John Everingham*, 1697. 4°.* O, CM, BP, EC, SC; CH, CLC, NU, Y.

223A — —Second edition. —, 1697. 4°.* L, C, LW, OC, BAMB; CDA, CLC, IU, WF.

224 —Articles concerning matters ecclesiastical. *For Brab. Aylmer*, 1700. 4°.* EC, SP; Y.

225 —Letter to the clergy. 1699. brs. LG (lost).

226 [–] A new declaration presented to the Commons of England. *Oxford, for Leonard Williamson*, 1647. 4°.* MADAN 1939. L, OW.

227 —A sermon preach'd . . . 11th of December, 1695. *For John Everingham*, 1695. 4°.* L, O, C, DU, EN, DT; CH, MH, TU, WF, Y.

227A —A sermon preached . . . September the 8th 1700. *By Hugh Newman*, 1700. 4°.* L, LLP, BC.

228 —A thanksgiving-sermon. *For B. Aylmer*, 1696. 4°.* T.C.II 576. L, O, C, LLP; NU, Y.

228A — —[Anr. ed.] —, 1697. 4°.* L, NE.

229 [–] To the Reverend the clergy of the dioecese of Lincoln. colop: *By Charles Bill, and the executrix of Thomas Newcomb*, 1699. cap., fol.* Y.

230 **Gardiner, Ralph.** Englands grievance discovered. *By R. Ibbitson, and P. Stent*, 1655. 8°. L, O, C, DU, EN; BN, CH, MH, MU, NC, WF.

231 **Gardiner, Richard.** A sermon appointed . . . March 27. 1642. *For R. Royston*, 1642. 4°.* LT, O, C, DC, YM; CH, IU, MH, NPT, NU, WF, Y.

232 —XVI sermons preached. *By James Cottrel, for Joseph Barber, and Samuel Speed*, 1659. 8°. LT, O, LW, OM, LLU, P; CLC, IU, NU.

232A —Richardi Gardiner ex Æde Christi Oxon. Specimen oratorium. *Impensis Humfredi Moseley*, 1653. 8°. L.

233 —Richardi Gardiner Herefordensis, Ædis Christi Oxon . . . specimen. *Oxoniæ, excudebat H. Hall, impensis Richardi Davis*, 1657. 8°. MADAN 2337. L, O, OC; IU, WF, Y.

234 — —Third edition. *Oxoniæ, excudebat H. Hall, impensis Ric: Davis*, 1662. 8°. MADAN 2595. L, O, OC, P, YM; Y.

235 — —Fourth edition. *Oxoniæ, excudebat H.H., impensis Ric. Davis*, 1668. 8°. MADAN 2800. L, O, OC, CS; CLC, NU, Y.

236 — —Fifth edition. *Oxoniæ, excudebat Hen. Hall, impensis Ric. Davis*, 1675. 12°. MADAN 3058. L, O, C, DU, EC, DT; CH, CU, MH, WF, Y.

237 **G[ardiner], R[obert].** Ars clericalis: the art of conveyancing. *By the assigns of Richard and Edward Atkins, for Thomas Basset*, 1690. 12°. T.C.II 335. L, ES, DT; CLC, LC, MHL, NCL, MIU.

238 — —Second edition. *By the assigns of R. and E. Atkins, for W. B. and T. B. and are to be sold by T. Bever, R. Battersby; and T. Cater*, 1692. 8°. L, LI, NOT; CLC, IU, MHL, TU, YL.

238A [–] —"Second" edition. *By the assigns of R. and E. Atkyns, for W. B. and T. B. and are to be sold by T. Bever, K. Battersby, and T. Cater*, 1698. 8°. LIL; LC, MH, PU, WF.

238B [–] The compleat constable. *By the assigns of Richard and Edward Atkins, to be sold by Abel Roper and Tho. Beaver*, 1692. 12°. O, CT.

238C [–] —Second edition. *Printed, and are to be sold by Tho. Beaver*, 1700. 12°. L, LG; CH, MHL, WF, Y.

239 [–] Instructor clericalis. *For Tho. Bever*, 1693. 8°. T.C.II 454. L, O, OP; NCL.

240 — —Second edition. *By the assigns of Richard and Edw. Atkyns, for Thomas Bever*, 1697. 8°. LI; MHL, WF.

240A [–] —Third edition. —, 1700. 8°. L, C, BAMB.

241 [–] —Second part. *For T. Bever*, 1695. 8°. LL; NCL, YL.

241A — — —Second edition. —, 1700. 8°. BAMB.

242 [–] A method of pleading by rule. *By the assigns of R. and E. Atkyns; for J. Walthoe*, 1697. 8°. T.C.II 601. L, O, LL, EN; LC, MHL, YL.

243 **[Gardiner, Robert],** *royalist.* A progenie, of prodiges. [*n.p.*], *printed*, 1649. 4°. L, LNC, EN, DT; CLC, MM.

244 **[Gardiner, Samuel.]** A brief examination of the present Roman Catholick faith. *For James Adamson*, 1689. 4°. T.C.II 244. L, O, C, CT, MC, DT; CH, NU, TU, WF, Y.

245 —De efficacia gratiæ. *Cantabrigiæ, per Johannem Field*, 1660. 4°. LT, O, C, EN, DT; CH, MBA, MH, WF, Y.

246 —'Υποτυπωσις, sive Catholicæ circa SS. Trinitatem. *Impensis Benj. Tooke*, 1677. 8°. T.C.I 276. L, O, C, DU, E; BN, MBA, WF, Y, ASU.

247 —Moses and Aaron brethren. *For John Rothwell*, 1653. 4°.* C, LSC, LLU; CH, CLC, MH, NU, WF, Y.

248 —Responsio valedictoria. *Apud G. Crooke*, 1681. 4°. T.C.I 444. L, O, LLP, OM, SC, P.

248A —A sermon preached. *By T. Ratcliff and N. Thompson, for Nath. Ranew*, 1672. 4°.* T.C.I 102. L, O, OCC; CH, WF.

249 —Supremus magistratus. [*n.p.*, 1657.] brs. O.

250 **Gardiner, Thomas.** The path-way to peace. *By J. R. for Johne Browne*, 1643. 4°.* LT, O, LW, DT; CH, MBZ, NPT, TO, WF, Y.

250A **Gardner, John.** The appellants case. [*London?* 169–?] brs. MH.

251 [–] Some reflections on a pamphlet, intituled, England and East-India. *Printed*, 1696. 8°.* L, INDIA OFFICE, LIU, LSD; CU, MH, NC, WF, Y.

252 The gardner at the gallows. 1667. 4°. LG.

252aA **Gardyner, George.** A description of the new world. *For Robert Leybourn, to be sold by Thomas Pirrepoint*, 1651. 8°. LT, LAD; CH, LC, MH, MU, NN, WF, Y.

252A **Garencières, Dudley.** The history of Christ's sufferings. *For S. Lowndes*, 1697. 8°. T.C.III 3. L, OC, CT; CLC, NPT.

253 **Garencières, Théophile.** The admirable virtues, . . . of coral, in physick. *By W. R. for Samuel Sprint*, 1676. 8°. T.C.I 246. L, O, CS; CLC, MBM, NAM, WSG.

254 —Angliæ flagellum. [*London*], *excudit, T. W. pro Richardo Whitaker*, 1647. 12°. L, O, C, LCP, LWL, MAU, DT; BN, CH, NAM, WF, WSG, HC.

255 —A mite cast into the treasury. *By Thomas Ratcliffe*, 1665. 4°.* L, LG, LWL, E; WSG.

256 — —Second edition. —, 1665. 4°.* L, O, LCP, LG; CNM, IU, MBM, MH, WSG.

257 — —Third edition. *By Tho. Ratcliffe*, 1666. 4°.* L, O, C, LUG; WF.

258 **Gargill, Ann.** A brief discovery of that which is called the Popish religion. *For Giles Calvert*, 1656. 4°.* LT, LF, BBN; CH, MH, PH, PSC.

259 —A warning to all the vvorld. *For Giles Calvert*, 1656. 4°.* LT, O, LF, OC, BBN; MH, PH, PSC.
Gargill, Donald. *See* Cargill, Donald.

259A **Garland, Edward.** An answer to a printed book. *For Philemon Stephens*, 1657. 4°. L, O, SP; WF.
Garland of good-will. 1678. *See* Deloney, Thomas.

260 The garland of mirth. *For J. Conyers*, 1688. 4°.* CHRISTIE-MILLER.
Garland of pious and godly songs. Gant, 1684. *See* Wadding, Luke.

261 **Garment, Joshua.** The Hebrews deliverance. *Printed, June 23. 1651.* 4°.* LT.

262 **Garner, Robert.** Mysteries unvailed. [*London*], *for G. Calvert*, 1646. 8°. LW, DT.

262A — —[Anr. ed.] [*London*], *printed*, 1646. 8°. MH.

263 —A treatise of baptisme. [*London*], *printed*, 1645. 4°.* LT, C, ORP, GU, DT; NHC, Y.

264 [**Garnet, Richard.**] The book of oaths. *Printed at London, for W. Lee, M. Walbancke, D. Pakeman, and G. Bedle*, 1649. 12°. LT, O, LG, CM, NOT, DT; CH, CLC, LC, NCL, YL.

265 [–] —[Anr. ed.] *For H. Twyford, T. Basset, B. Griffin, C. Harper, T. Sawbridge, S. Keble, G. Collins, J. Place, and M. Wotton*, 1689. 8°. T.C.II 341. L, O, C, LGL, BC; CH, CLC, LC, NCL, WF, YL.
Garnets ghost. [n.p., 1679.] *See* Oldham, John.

265A [**Garret, Walter.**] De vera ecclesia. *Impensis Rob. Clavell, prostant apud J. Nutt*, 1698. 8°. T.C.III 95. L, O, LLP, BAMB, LSD; WF.

266 —Decimum caput apocalypseos. 1698. 8°.* L, O, LLP, OM, BAMB, P; WF.

267 —Demonstratio luculenta, nova: or, a new method. colop: [*n.p.*], *printed in June* 1700. cap., 4°.* O, LLP.

268 —A discourse concerning Antichrist. *For the author, to be sold by I. Harrison*, 1680. 8°. T.C.I 381. O, LW, OM, CT, DU, P; NPT.

269 —An essay upon the fourth and fifth chapters of the Revelation. *For the author, and sold by Israel Harrison*, 1690. 4°.* O, P.

270 [–] Numb. 2. A paraphrase upon Rev. 1. colop: *Printed, June, 1699. To be had at Mr. Ball's.* cap., 4°.* O, OC.

270A [–]Οιδα σου τα εργα, or the divine fore-knowledge. colop: *Oxford*, 1699/1700. 4°. O, OC.

271 —A persuasive to the study of the Revelation. *Printed, March, 1698/9. To be had at W. Dotchen's; and at Mr. Ball's.* 4°.* O, OC, P.

271A [–] A resolution of three important questions. [*London*], *printed*, 1688. 4°. OC, CS, BAMB.

271B —Theorems. 1690. 4°. P.

271C — —[Anr. ed.] *Printed and are to be sold by the booksellers of London and Westminster*, [1700?]. cap., 4°.* LSD.

271D —The three first chapters of Revelation. 1698. 4°. P.

272 **G[arret], W[illiam].** Ανθολογια. The life & death of Mr. Samuel Crook. *By James Flesher, for Philemon Stephens*, 1651. 8°. LT, O, LW; MH, NU, TU.

272A **Garretson, J[ohn].** English exercises for school-boys. Third edition. *For Tho. Cockerill*, 1691. 12°. IU.

272B — —Seventh edition. —, 1698. 12°. T.C.III 68. CH, IU, MB.

272C [–] The school of manners. [*London*], *for Tho. Cockerill*, [1685]. 12°. T.C.II 116. L (t.p.).
Garroway, Sir Henry. *See* Garway, Sir Henry.

273 [**Garth, Sir Samuel.**] The dispensary; a poem. *Printed, and sold by John Nutt*, 1699. 4°. L, O, LCP, CT, GK; CH, IU, LC, MH, NU, TU, WF, Y, AVP.

274 [–] —Second edition. —, 1699. 8°. L, O, CT, MAU, NE; CH, CU, MH, NP, WSG, Y, HC.

275 [–] —Third edition. —, 1699. 8°. L, O, LCP, CP, DT; BN, CLC, MH, MU, WF, Y, HC.

276 [–] —Fourth edition. —, 1700. 8°. L, O, C, LCS, DT; CH, MH, NC, WF, Y, HC.

277 —Oratio laudatoria, in ædibus collegii Regalis Med. Lond. *Impensis Abelis Roper*, 1697. 4°.* L, O, C, LCP, DT; WF, HC.

277A **G[arthwaite], R[ichard].** A censure upon Lilly's grammar. *By B. W. for George Downs*, 1684. 8°. T.C.II 63. L, OB, CK, CS, DUS; IU, WF, Y.

278 **Garvey, John.** The conversion of Philip Corwine. *Dublin, by Jos. Ray for a society of stationers*, 1681. 4°.* T.C.I 464. DIX 182. L, O, C, EN, DT; CH, MH, PL, WF.

278A **Garway, Mrs.** The incomparable neck-laces of Major Choke . . . sold only by Mrs. Garway. [*London, 1690-1700.*] brs. L.

278B —A most excellent cephalick-water . . . sold only by. [*London, 1695-1700.*] brs. L.

279 **Garway, Sir Henry.** The loyal citizen revived. [*London, 1679.*] cap., fol.* LT, OC, CT, MR, EN; CLC, CN, MH, TU, WF, Y.

280 —A speech made by Alderman Garrovvay, . . . 17. of Ianuary. [*Oxford, by L. Lichfield*], 1642. 4°.* MADAN 1201. L, O, CJ, BR, EN, DT; CH, CLC, CN, MBP, WF, Y.

281 — —[Anr. ed.] [*London*], *printed*, 1643. 4°.* LT, O, C, LG, EN; CH, IU, MH, NU, WF, Y.

282 **Garway, Thomas.** An exact description of . . . tee. [*London, 1660?*] brs. L, O.

283 **Gascoyne, Joel.** Map of the county of Cornwall. [*n.p.*], *sold by J. Thorn, by Charles Blith, in Launceston*, 1700. fol. L.

284   [–] A true description of Carolina. colop: *For Joel Gascoin and R. Greene*, 1682. 4°.* MHS, NN, RPJ.

285   **Gaselee, Robert.** To the honourable the Commons . . . Captain George Stilo his proceedings against me. [*n.p.*, 1698.] cap., fol.* L.

286   **Gaskarth, John.** A description of the unregenerate. *Cambridge, at the University Press, for Edmund Jeffery*, 1700. 4°.* T.C.III 209. L, O, C, CT, WCA; CH, CLC, LC, MBA, NPT, WF, Y.

287   —Insanientis sapientiæ. *Cantabrigiæ, typis academicis, impensis Edmundi Jeffery*, 1700. 4°.* T.C.III 216. L, O, C, NE, EN; CH, CLC, WF, Y.

288   —A sermon preached . . . October 30. *For Walter Kettilby*, 1685. 4°.* T.C.II 111. L, O, C, BR, SHR; CH, NU, TU, WF, Y.

289   —A sermon preached upon the first occasion after the death . . . Duke of Lavderdale. *For Walter Kettilby*, 1683. 4°. T.C.II 14. L, O, C, EN, BLH; CLC, MH, NU, WF, Y.

290   [**Gaskin, John.**] A just defence and vindication of gospel ministers. *By W. G. for the author, and are to be sold by Isaac Pridmore*, 1660. 4°. O, LF, BLH.

290A **Gassendi, Pierre.** Institutio astronomica. *Typis Jacobi Flesher.* 1653. 8°. WF.

291   ——Second edition. —. *Prostant apud Cornelium Bee*, 1653. 8°. L, O, C, ENC, DT; BN, CSB, CU, LC, MBC, MH, MU, NC, Y, HC.

291A ——"Second" edition. *Typis Jacobi Flesher. Prostant apud Gulielmum Morden, Cantabrigiensem*, 1653. 8°. L, O, C, BC, EC; CH, CLC, MBA, MH, MIU, PL, RPJ. (var.)

292   — —Fifth edition. *Typis Eliz. Flesher. Prostant apud Gulielmum Morden, Cantabrigiensem*, 1675. 8°. L, O, C, LLL; CLC, MH, NC, NCD, PL, Y.

293   — —"Third" edition. *Impensis Hen. Dickinson*, 1683. 8°. L, O, C, ENC, EO; BN, CH, CJC, LC, MH, WF, HC.

293A —Institutio logica. *Ex officina Rogeri Danielis*, 1660. 12°. L, O, CS, BIU, SHR; CLC, CU, PAP, PL. (var.)

294   ——[Anr. ed.] *Ex officina Johannis Redmayne*, 1668. 12°. L, O, C, E, DT; MB, MH, PU, WF, Y.

295   —The mirrour of true nobility . . . Peiresk. *By J. Streater for Humphrey Moseley*, 1657. 8°. L, O, C, EN, DT, GK; CH, CN, LC, MU, NP, WF, Y.

296   —Philosophiæ Epicuri syntagma. *Ex officina R. Danielis*, 1660. 12°. L, O, C, P, SHR; BN, CH, CLC, MWA, PL.

296A ——[Anr. ed.] *Ex officina Johannis Redmayne*, 1668. 12°. NE; IU, MH, WF.

297   —Three discourses of happiness, virtue, and liberty. *For Awnsham and John Churchil*, 1699. 8°. T.C.III 174. L, O, DU, E, DT, BQ; CH, CN, LC, MH, PL, Y.

298   —The vanity of judiciary astrology. *For Humphrey Moseley*, 1659. 8°. LT, O, C, BAMB, E; CH, LC, MH, NU, JF.

299   — —[Anr. ed.] *For Giles Calvert*, 1659. 8°. OC; MH.

300   **Gastrell, Francis,** *bp.* The certainty and necessity of religion in general. *For Tho. Bennet*, 1697. 8°. T.C.III 12. L, C, LL, NPL, DT; CH, IU, MH, NC, PL, WF, Y.

301   —The certainty of the Christian revelation. *For Thomas Bennet*, 1699. 8°. T.C.III 133. L, O, C, NPL, EN; CH, MH, NU, WF, Y.

302   [–] A defence of some considerations. *For Tho. Bennet*, 1698. 8°. O, LW, DT; CH, MH, PL, WF.

303   [–] Some considerations concerning the Trinity. *Printed; and sold by E. Whitlock*, 1696. 4°. T.C.II 567. L, O, OC, CS, DU; CLC, MH, NPT, NU, Y.

304   [–] —Second edition. *For T. Bennet*. 1698. 8°. T.C.III 83. L, O, C, SHR, DT; CH, IU, MH, NPT, PL, WF.

304A [**Gataker, Charles.**] The apostles Paul and James reconciled. [*London?* 1670.] cap., 4°.* O, LW; CLC.

305   —An examination of the case of the Quakers. *By T. N. for Thomas Collins*, 1675. 4°.* T.C.I 205. L, O, LF, CT, MR; CH, PH, PSC, WF, Y.

306   [–] Five captious questions. *By T. R. for Hen. Brome*, 1673. 4°. O, CT, MR, P, SC, CD; CLC, MIU, NC, NU, WF, Y.

307   —Ichnographia doctrinæ. *Typis J. C. prostantqe* [*sic*] *venales apud H. Brome*, 1681. 4°. T.C.I 432. O, CS, EC, P, SC.

307A [–] Justificatio gratuita, sive, doctrina justicationis. *Impensis Caroli Brome*, 1685. 4°. WF.

308   —The Papists bait. *By T. R. for Hen. Brome*, 1674. 4°. O, C, OM, GC, SC; CH, LC, NU.

      [**Gataker, John.**] City-ministers. 1649. *See* Dell, William.

309   **Gataker, Thomas.** Adversaria miscellanea. *Apud Sa. Gellibrand*, 1659. fol. L, O, C, E, DT; BN, CH, IU, NU, WF, WSC, Y.

310   [–] An answer to Mr. George Walkers vindication. *By E. G. for F. Clifton*, 1642. 4°. CD; NU, Y.

311   —An antidote against errour. *By J. C. for Henry Brome*, 1670. 4°. T.C.I 29. L, O, C, EN, DT; CH, NU, TU, WF, Y.

312   —Antinomianism discovered. *By T. R. and E. M. to be sold by J. B.*, 1652. 4°.* LT, O, LCL, CT, GU; MH, MWA, NPT, NU, WF.

313   —Thomæ Gatakeri Londinatis Cinnus. *Typis J. Flesheri, impensis L. Sadleri*, 1651. 4°. L, O, C, E, DT; CLC, CU, MH, NU, WF, Y.

314   [–] The Covenanters plea against absolvers. *For T. B.*, 1661. 4°. L, O, C, EN, CD; CLC, CN, MH, NU, TU, WF, Y.

315   Entry cancelled.

      —De baptismatis infantilis. 1652. *See* Ward, Samuel.

316   —De diphthongis. *Typis E. G. sumptibus F. Clifton*, 1646. 12°. L, O, OME, CT, DT; MH.

317   —Thomæ Gatakeri . . . De nomine tetragrammato dissertatio. *Excudebat R. Cotes, impensis Phil. Stephani*, 1645. 12°. O, OME, CT, BAMB, LNC, E; MH, WF.

318   —Thomæ Gatakeri. . . . De novi instrumenti. *Typis T. Harperii, impensis L. Sadleri*, 1648. 4°. L, O, C, E, DT; BN, CH, CU, MH, WF, Y. (var.)

319   —A discours apologetical. *By R. Ibbitson for Thomas Newberry*, 1654. 4°. LT, O, CE, E, DT; CH, CU, MH, NU, WF, Y.

320   —Dissertationis de tetragrammato suæ. *Ex officina Rogeri Danielis, impensis Roberti Beaumont*, 1652. 12°. L, O, C, P, DT; MH, NU, WF.

321   —Gods eye on His Israel. *By E. G. for Foulke Clifton*, 1645. 4°. LT, O, C, LW, GU, DT; CH, IU, NPT, NU, WF, Y.

322   [–] The last will and testament of. [*n.p.*], *printed*, 1654. 4°.* O.

323   —A mistake. *By E. G. for F. Clifton*, 1646. 4°.* LT, O, C, EN, DT; CH, IU, NPT, NU, WF.

324   —Mysterious cloudes and mistes. *By E. Griffin, to be sold by Fulke Clifton,* 1648. 4°.* C, OME, CS.

325   —Reverendi viri Dom. Joannis Davenantii. *Typis J. G. venalisqe habetur apud R. Royston,* 1654. 8°. LW, OC, ORP, CT, WCA; NU, WF.

326   —Shadowes without substance. *For Robert Bostock,* 1646. 4°. LT, O, C, LNC, DT; CH, IU, MH, NU, WF, Y.

326A   — —[Anr. ed.] —, 1647. 4°. V.

327   Entry cancelled.

    —Vindicationis dissertationis. 1652. *See* —Dissertationis.

328   —Thomas Gataker B. D. his vindication of the annotations. *By J. L. for Christopher Meredith,* 1653. 4°. O, C, LW, E, DT; NGT, NU, Y.

329   — —[Anr. ed.] *By J. L. for the partners,* 1653. 4°. CK; NU.

330   — —[Anr. ed.] *By J. L. for Richard Thrayle,* 1653. 4°. LW; CH, NU.

331   — —[Anr. ed.] *By J. L. for Philemon Stephens,* 1653. 4°. LT, O, CT, BC, EC; CN, MIU, NPT.

331A   — —[Anr. ed.] *By J. C. for Nicholas Bourn,* 1653. 4°. L, LWL; VC.

331B   — —[Anr. ed.] *By J. L. for Humphey [sic] Robinson and Joshua Kirton,* 1653. BAMB, GU.

331C   — —[Anr. ed.] *By J. L. for Thomas Downes,* 1653. 4°. TO.

    Gate to sciences. 1641. *See* Woodward, Hezekiah.

    Gatehouse salutation. [*London*], 1646. *See* Douglas, *Lady* Eleanor.

332   **Gatford, Lionel.** Englands complaint: or, a sharp reproof. *Printed,* 1648. 4°. LT, O, C, CT, DT; BN, CH, MH, MIU, MM, NU.

333   —An exhortation to peace. *Printed,* 1643. 4°.* LT, O, C, DC, DT; CH, MH, MIU, NU, WF.

333A   —A faithfull and faire warning. *For John Gyles,* 1648. 4°. MH.

333B   —An harmonie of the doctrine of the Reformed Churches. *Cambridge, by Roger Daniel for Richard Ireland and John Milleson,* 1643. C.

334   Entry cancelled.

    —Impartial disquisition. [n.p., 1689?] *See* Ghest, Edmund.

335   —Λογοϲαλεξιφαρμακοϲ, or, hyperphysicall directions. *Oxford, by H. Hall,* 1644. 4°.* MADAN 1710. LT, O, LLP, EN; WSG.

336   —A petition for the vindication of the publique use. *For John Williams,* 1655. 4°. LT, O, C, MR, DT; CLC, IU, MH, NU, WF, Y.

337   [–] Publick good without private interest. *For Henry Marsh,* 1657. 4°.* BBE, CN, LC, MWA, NN, RPJ.

338   —To the most reverend, the arch-bishops, and bishops, . . . the humble remonstrance. [*n.p.,* 1661.] cap., 4°.* LL, CS, MR, NE; CH.

339   —A true and faithfull narrative of the much to be lamented death of Mr. William Tyrrell. *For Iames Lawson,* 1661. 4°.* L, MR; CN.

340   **Gauden, John,** *bp.* Ἀναλυϲιϲ. The loosing of St. Peters bands. *By J. Best, for Andrew Crook,* 1660. 4°.* LT, O, C, EN, CD; CH, IU, MH, NU, TU, WF, Y. (var.)

341   — —[Anr. ed.] *By J. Macock, for Andrew Crook,* 1660. 4°.* L, O, CT, BP, LSD, DT; CH, CLC, FU, MHS, NPT, WF.

342   [–] Anti Baal-berith. *By John Best, for Andrew Crook,* 1661. 4°. LT, O, C, DU, BLH; CH, CN, MWA, NU, TO.

343   —Antisacrilegus. *By J. B. for Andrew Crook,* 1660. 4°.* LT, O, CCH, BR, P; CH, CN, MH, NU, WF, Y.

343A   [–] The bloody court. [*London?*], *for G. Horton,* [1660]. 4°.* LT, O; MH, MM, V.

344   —The case of ministers maintenance. *By Thomas Maxey, for Andrew Crook,* 1653. 4°.* LT, O, C, EN, DT; CH, LC, MIU, NU, V, WF.

344A   —Causa Dei: Gods pleading. *By John Best for Andrew Crook,* 1661. 8°. O, OU, RPL; CLC, NGT.

345   [–] Certaine scrvples and doubts of conscience. [*London,* 1645.] cap., 4°.* LT, O, BC, LNC; CLC, NU, U. OHIO.

346   [–] —[Anr. ed.] *Printed,* 1660. 4°.* LT, O, LSD, AU; CH, CLC, MIU, WF, Y.

347   [–] Χαριϲ και ειρηνη: or some considerations. *For Edward Thomas, and Henry Marsh,* 1662. 4°. O, C, LL, SP, DT; MH, NU, TO, WF, Y.

348   —Considerations touching the liturgy. *By J. G. for John Playford,* 1661. 4°.* LT, C, MR, EN, DT; CH, IU, MH, NU, TU, WF, Y.

349   — —Second edition. —, 1661. 4°.* CS, MR, WCA, DT; CLC, WF.

350   —Consilia. *Typis J. Flesher, & prostant apud Andr. Crook,* 1661. fol.* LT, C, SC.

350A   — —[Anr. ed.] *Typis J. Flesher & prostant apud R. Royston,* 1661. fol.* BC, EC.

351   [–] Cromwell's bloody slaughter-house; . . . discovered. *For James Davis,* 1660. 12°. LT, O; CH, CN, LC, MH, NRU, WF, Y.

    [–] Devilish conspiracy. 1648. *See* Warner, John.

352   —A discourse concerning publick oaths. *For R. Royston,* 1662. 4°. L, LF, CS, DU, P; CH, CN, MH, NU, PH, WF, Y.

353   [–] A discourse of artificial beauty. *For R. Royston,* 1662. 8°. L, O, OC, CK, GU; CH, CN, NU, WF, Y.

354   [–] —[Anr. ed.] *By J. L. for Luke Meredith,* 1692. 12°. T.C.II 435. L, O, GU; MBA, MIU, NU, WF.

355   [–] A discourse of auxiliary beauty. [*London*], *for R: Royston,* 1656. 8°. LT, O, C, GU, DM; CH, CU, MH, WF, Y.

356   —Funerals made cordials. *By T. C. for Andrew Crook,* 1658. 4°. LT, O, C, LI, BC, DCH; CH, CN, MH, NU, WF, Y.

357   —Hieraspistes: a defence. [*London*], *for Andrew Crooke,* 1653. 4°. LT, O, CT, EN, DT; CH, CN, MH, NU, WF, Y.

358   [–] Hinc illæ lachrymæ or the impietie of impunitie. *Printed,* 1648. 4°.* LT; CSS, CU, MB, NU, RPJ, WF.

359   —Ἱερα δακρυα. Ecclesiæ Anglicanæ suspiria. The tears. *By J. G. for R. Royston,* 1659. fol. L, O, C, EN, DT; BN, CH, CN, MH, WF, Y.

359A   — —[Anr. ed.] —, 1660. fol. DU.

360   —Ἱεροτελεϲτια γαμικη. Christ at the wedding. *By E. Cotes, for Andrew Crook,* 1654. 4°.* LT, O, OB, CT, DT; CH, NU, WF.

361   —Κακουργοι sive medicastri: slight healers. *For Andrew Crook,* 1660. 4°. LT, O, C, DU, DT; CH, CU, LC, MH, Y.

361A   — —[Anr. ed., "healings."] —, 1660. L, OB; NU, WF.

362 —The love of trvth and peace. *By T. C. for Andrew Crooke*, 1641. 4°. LT, O, C, DU, DT; CH, IU, MH, NPT, TU, WF, Y, AVP.

363 ——[Anr. ed.] *By G. M. for Andrew Crooke*, 1641. 4°. L, O, CM, PC, EN, DT; CH, CN, CU, MH, NU, TU. (var.)

364 —Μεγαλεια Θεου, Gods great demonstrations. *By J. Best, for Andrew Crook*, 1660. 4°. LT, O, C, DU, EN; CH, MH, NU, WF, Y.

365 [–] A petitionary remonstrance, presented to O. P. *By Thomas Milbourn, for Andrew Crook*, 1659. 4°.* LT, O, LSD, BLH, DT; NU, Y.

366 [–] A pillar of gratitude. *By J. M. for Andrew Crook*, 1661. fol. L, O, C, LL, LIU, E; CH, CLC, FU, MBC, WF.

[–] Plaine English; or, a discourse. [n.p.], 1643. *See* Bowles, Edward.

367 —The religious & loyal protestation. *For Richard Royston*, 1648[9]. 4°.* L, O, C, E, DT; BN, CH, CN, MH, WF, Y.

368 ——[Anr. ed.] *Printed*, 1648[9]. 4°.* LT, O, C, DU, DT; CH, IU, MH, MM.

369 ——[Anr. ed.] *For Richard Royston*, 1660. 4°.* CS, DU, LSD, NE; NU, Y.

370 —A sermon preached . . . Febr. 28, 1659. *For Andrew Crook*, 1660. 4°. L, O, C, LCL, EN; CH, CU, NU, WF, Y. (var.)

371 —A sermon preached . . . Decemb. 17. *By J. Best for Andrew Crook*, 1660. 8°. LT, O, C, LW, DT; BN, CH, IU, MH, TO, WF, Y.

372 —Στρατοσστη λιτέυτικον. A iust invective. *By T. L. for James Davies, and are to be sold by Phil. Stephens*, 1662. 4°. L, C, LSD, NE, E; CN, MH, MIU, TU, Y.

372A ——[Anr. ed.] *For Henry Eversden*, 1662. 12°. CH.

373 —Three sermons. *By R. Bishop, for Andrew Crook*, 1642. 4°. L, O, C, DU, EN; CH, CN, MH, NU, WF, Y.

373A —The whole duty of a communicant. Second edition. *By E. R. for L. C. and Hen. Rodes*, 1685. 12°. T.C.II 106. L, P; NGT.

373B ——Third edition. *By D. M. for Hen. Rodes*, 1687. 12°. WF.

373C ——Fourth edition. *By D. M. for Hen. Rhodes*, 1688. 12°. T.C.II 220. Y.

373D ——Seventh edition. *For N. Boddington*, 16[9]8. 12°. SHR.

373E [**Gaujac**], P[ierre] G[ally] d[e]. The bloudy Babylon. *For George Huddleston*, 1698. 4°.* L, LIU; CH, CLC, NU.

374 [–]True relation of what hath been transacted. *For Sam. Lowndes to be sold by E. Whitlock*, 1698. 4°. LIL; MIU, WF.

375 **Gaule, John.** An admonition moving to moderation. *By Henry Lloyd and Roger Vaughan, for Henry Brome*, 1660. 8°. LT, O; WF, Y.

375A —The Christian conjuring of the quaking spirit. *By R. Vaughan, sold by I. Williams, Francis Eglesfield and Tho. Rookes*, [1662?]. 4°. CT.

376 [–] A collection out of the best approved authors. *For Joshua Kirton*, 1657. 4°. L, O, LN, LWL; CH, CN, CPB, MH, NIC, WF.

377 —Πυϛ-μαντια the mag-astromancer. *For Joshua Kirton*, 1652. 4°. L, O, C, GU, E; CH, IU, MH, NU, WF, Y.

378 —Sapientia justificata, or, a vindication. *For N. Paris, and Tho. Dring*, 1657. 12°. O, C; NU, TO, WF.

379 ——Select cases of conscience touching vvitches. *By W Wilson for Richard Clutterbuck*, 1646. 12°. LT, O, C, DC' GU; CH, CN, MH, NN, WF.

380 —A sermon of the saints. *For Thomas Dring*, 1649. 4°.* LT, C, P, DU, DT; CSS, IU, NN, NU, WF, Y.

381 [**Gaultier, Jacques.**] Al-man-sir or Rhodomontados. *By Peter Lillicrap, for Philip Briggs*, 1672. 8°. T.C.I 97. L, O; CH.

381A **Gaunt, Mrs. Elizabeth.** Last speech. [*London*, 1685.] cap., 4°.* L, BANGOR.

382 **Gautruche, Pierre.** Mathematicæ totius. *Cantabrigiæ, excudebat Joan. Field. Impensis Edwardi Story*, 1668. 8°. L, C, OC, YM, GU; CH, CJC, MH, NC, PL, WF. (var.)

383 ——[Anr. ed.] *Typis M. Clarke, impensis Richardi Green, Cantabrigiensis*, 1683. 8°. L, O, C, CT, P; CH, IU, MH, NPT, PL, WF, Y.

384 —The poetical histories. *By B. G. and are to be sold by Moses Pitt*, 1671. 8°. L, O, C, WCA, E; CH, CN, CU, LC, MH, NCD, WF.

385 ——Second edition. *Printed and are to be sold by Moses Pitt*, 1672. 8°. T.C.I 72. L, O, C, EN; CLC, IU, MSL, U.OHIO, Y.

386 ——Third edition. *By W. G. and are to be sold by M. Pitt*, 1674. 8°. L, O, CT, EC, LLU, ENC; CLC, MU, NC, TU, WF.

387 Entry cancelled. Ghost.

387A —The poetical history. Fourth edition. *By W. G. and are to be sold by M. Pitt*, 1678. 8°. T.C.I 324. L, O, CM, SP; CH, CLC, MH, MU, WF, Y.

388 ——Fifth edition. *For M. Pitt*, 1683. 8°. T.C.I 513. L, O, LSD; CH, CLC, IU, MB, NRU, SW, Y.

389 ——Sixth edition. —, 1685. 8°. L, O, EN, DT; CLC, IEG, IU, WF.

389aA ——"Sixth" edition. *For M. P.*, 1686. 8°. BANGOR.

389bA ——"Fifth" edition. *By F. Collins for Thomas Guy*, 1691. 8°. L; CB, CLC, IU, Y.

389A ——"Sixth" edition. —, 1693. 8°. L, CD; CLC, CN, IU, MIU, NP.

389B ——Seventh edition. —, 1699. 8°. T.C.III 91. L, GU; CH, CLC, IU, PL.

390 [**Gavin, Antonio.**] The frauds of Romish monks. *By Samuel Roycroft, for Robert Clavell*, 1691. 8°. T.C.II 339. O, OC, CE, LLU, WCA; CH, CU, NP, NU, SW.

391 [–] ——Second edition. —, 1691. 8°. L, O, C, BR, P; CH, MU, NU, PBM, Y.

392 [–] ——Third edition. —, 1691. 8°. T.C.II 386. L, O, C, E, DT; CH, INU, PAP, TU, WF.

393 [–] Observations on a journy [*sic*] to Naples. *By Samuel Roycroft, for Robert Clavell*, 1691. 8°. T.C.II 379. L, O, CT, E, DT; CH, CU, LC, MH, NU, TU, WF, Y.

394 —A short history of monastical orders. *By S. Roycroft, for W. Bentley*, 1693. 8°. T.C.II 439. L, O, CE, E, DT; CH, CN, NU, WF, Y.

394A ——[Anr. ed.] *By S. Roycroft, for Rob. Clavell*, 1693. 8°. OC, CT, DU, BLH; CDA, MIU, NN, TSM, TU, WF.

394B ——[Anr. ed.] *For Nath. Sackett*, 1699. 8°. HAMILTON COLL., N.Y.

395   **Gawen, Nicholas.** Ἐξοχη του Χριστου. Christ's pre-eminence. *Oxford, by H. Hall,* 1668. 4°. MADAN 2801. O, C.

395AA   **Gawen, Thomas.** A brief explanation of the . . . holy mass. 1686. 8°. ON.

395A   **Gawler, Francis.** The children of Abraham's faith. [*London*], *printed,* 1663. 4°.* L, C, LF; PH, PL, PSC, WF, Y.

396   —A record of some persecutions. *For Thomas Simmons,* 1659. 4°.* L, LF, LNC; PH, PL, PSC.

397   **Gay, William.** XI choice sermons. *For Humphrey Moseley,* 1655. 8°. LT, O.

398   **Gaya, Louis de.** The art of war. *For Robert Harford,* 1678. 8°. T.C.I 313. L, C, OM; CH, CU, MH, WF, Y.

399   —Marriage ceremonies. *For Abel Roper,* 1697. 12°. L; CH, CN, MIU, WF, Y.

400   — —Second edition. —, 1698. 12°. L, EN; CH, CLC, Y.

401   [–] Matrimonial customs. *For A. S.,* 1687. 8°. O; CLC.

402   [–] Nuptial rites or the several marriage ceremonies. *By T. S. for the author,* 1685. 8°. L.

402A   —A treatise of the arms and engines of war. *For Robert Harford,* 1678. 8°. T.C.I 321. L, OC; NN, PL, WF, Y.

403   **Gayer, Sir John.** A declaration of. [*London*], *printed,* 1647. 4°.* LT, O, LG, OC, MR; CH, CLC, MH, MM, MU, NC.

404   —A salva libertate sent. [*London,* 1648.] brs. LT.

405   —To the right honorable the Lords . . . the humble petition of. [*London,* 1648.] brs. LT, C.

406   **Gayton, Edmund.** The art of longevity. *For the author,* 1659. 4°. L, O, LG, LWL, DC; CH, CU, LC, MH, MMO, WF.

406A   [–] A ballad on the gyants. [*Oxford, by William Hall,* 1662.] brs. MADAN 2579. O.

407   [–] Charity triumphant, or the virgin-shew. *For Nath. Brooks,* 1655. 4°.* LT, LG.

408   [–] Chartæ scriptæ: or a new game at cards. [*Oxford, by L. Lichfield*], 1645. 4°.* MADAN 1824. LT, LLU, DT; CH, CLC, MH, WF, Y.

409   Entry cancelled. [–] Civil wars of Bantam. 1683. *See title.*

410   [–] Diegerticon ad Britanniam. [*Oxford?* 1666.] brs. MADAN 2743. O.

411   —Epulæ Oxonienses. Or a jocular relation. [*Oxford, by W. Hall,* c. 1661.] fol.* MADAN 2544. O.

412   —The glorious and living cinque-ports. *Oxon., by H. H.,* 1666. 4°.* MADAN 2744. L, O; CH, Y.

413   —Hymnus de febribus. Â *Thomâ Warreno,* [1655]. 4°. L, O, LWL, DC, P, SHR; CH, MH, MMO, NAM, WSG, HC.

414   —The lawyer's duel. [*London?* 1655.] fol.* L.

415   —Pleasant notes upon Don Quixot. *By William Hunt,* 1654. fol. L, O, C, LIU, EN; CH, CN, LC, MH, MMO, MU, NC, WF, Y, AVP.

416   —The religion of a physician. *By J. G. for the author,* 1663. 4°. L, GK; CH, CN, MH, NAM.

417   [–] To Mr. Robert Whitehall at the Wels at Astrop. [*Oxford? by Henry Hall?* 1666.] brs. MADAN 2745. O.

418   —To the most illustrious Prince his Highnesse James Duke of York, . . . a votive song. *By Peter Lillicrop* [sic], *to be sold by Peter Kent,* [1645]. brs. L.

419   [–] Upon Mr Bobard's yew-men. [*Oxford,* 1662.] brs. MADAN 2580. O.

420   [–] Upon the meeting of the sons of the clergy. *By T. R.,* 1655. 4°.* LP; CH.

421   [–] Walk knaves, walk . . . By Hodg Turbervil. *Printed,* 1659. 4°.* LT, O, OC, MR, EN; CH, CLC, CN, CU, NN, WF, Y.

422   —Wil: Bagnal's ghost. *By W. Wilson for Thomas Johnson,* 1655. 4°. LT, O, LG; CH, NN.

423   [–] VVit revived: or, a new and excellent way. *For the author,* 1656. 12°. LT.

424   [–] —[Anr. ed.] *For T. E.,* 1674. 12°. CH.

  Gazæus, Angelinus. *See* Gazet, Angelin.

425   **Gazet, Angelin.** Pia hilaria. *Impensis Guil: Morden,* 1657. 12°. L, O, C, BSE, EN, CD; BN, CH, CU, NC, WF, Y.

426   Gazophylacium Anglicanum; containing. *By E. H. and W. H. and are to be sold by Randall Taylor,* 1689. 8°. T.C.II 290. L, O, C, LCL, AN, GU; CH, CN, LC, MH, TU, WF, Y.

  — [Anr. ed.] 1691. *See* New English dictionary.

427   No entry.

428   Entry cancelled.

  Gearing, Henry. Character and trial. 1694. *See* Shower, John. Some account.

429   **G[earing], Will[iam].** The arraignment of ignorance. *For Luke Fawn,* 1659. 8°. LT, O, LW; NPT.

430   —The arraignment of pride. *By R. White, for Francis Tyton,* 1660. 8°. LT, BC; IU, WF.

431   —The beauty and order of the creation. 1668. 12°. LCL.

432   —A bridle for the tongue. *By R. H. for Tho. Parkhurst,* 1663. 8°. L; CLC, WF.

433   —A caveat to the standing Christian. *For John Crook,* 1666. 4°. L.

434   —Clavis cœli; or, a treatise. *By A. M. for F. Tyton,* 1663. 12°. LW; CLC.

435   —The eye and wheel of Providence. *For Francis Tyton,* 1662. 8°. L, LSC; MH, NPT, NU.

435A   —God's soveraignty displayed. *By R. I. for Thomas Parkhurst,* 1667. 12°. LSC; IU, MH, NPT.

435B   [–] The history of the church of Great Britain. *For Philip Chetwin,* 1674. 4°. T.C.I 177. L, O, C, EN, BLH; CH, CN, TU, WF, Y.

435C   [–] —[Anr. ed.] *For Philip Chetwind,* 1675. 4°. L, O, P, E; IU.

435D   [–] —[Anr. ed.] *For P. Chetwin and T. Passinger, and to be sold by Thomas Taylor,* 1675. 4°. C, DU; WF.

435E   —London's remembrancer. *By J. Richardson for Tho. Parkhurst,* 1688. 4°.* L; IU, Y.

436   —The love-sick spouse. *For Nevill Simmons, in Kederminster,* 1665. 4°. O; WF.

436A   —The mischiefs and dangers of the sin of ignorance. *For Luke Fawn,* 1659. 8°. L, LSC.

436B   —The mount of holy meditation. *For Francis Tyton,* 1662. 8°. CLC.

436C   —Philadelphia, or, a treatise. *For Tho. Parkhurst,* 1670. 8°. L; CLC, WF.

437   —A prospect of Heaven. *For Tho. Passenger, and Benj. Hurlock,* 1673. 8°. T.C.I 133. L, O, AN; CLC, IEG, NU, WF, Y.

438   [–] The sacred diary. *By J. D. for Jonathan Robinson,* 1679. 12°. T.C.I 327. L, LSD.

438A [–] Status ecclesiæ Gallicanæ: Or. *For Thomas Passenger; and Ralph Smith*, 1676. 4°. T.C.I 235. L, O, C, NE, EN; CH, NPT, NU, WF, Y.

439 —Wisdom justified of her children. *For Henry Eversden*, 1668. 4°. O; IU.

439A **Gearnon, Anthony.** Parrthas an anma, or paradise of the soul. *Lobhain*, 1645. 12°. L, C, DN; CN.

440–2 Entries cancelled.

Geaves, William. *See* Gearing, William.

Geber. *See* Jabir ibn Haryãn.

443 **Gedde, John.** A new discovery of an excellent method of bee-houses. *For the author, and sold by D. Newman*, 1675. 8°. T.C.I 212. L, O; CH, CLC.

443A — —Third edition. *For the author*, 1677. 8°. O.

444 **Geddes, Michael.** The church-history of Ethiopia. *For Ri. Chiswell*, 1696. 8°. T.C.II 584. L, O, C, EN, DT; CH, CU, MH, NU, WF, Y, AVP.

445 —The Council of Trent no free assembly. *For Brabazon Aylmer*, 1697. 8°. L, O, C, EN, DT; CH, IU, NU, TSM, WF, Y.

446 Entry cancelled.

—History of the church of Malabar. 1694. *See title.*

446A **Geddes, William.** An encomiastick epigram upon the . . . trade of masons. [*Edinburgh, c.* 1682.] brs. EN.

447 —The saints recreation, third part. *Edinbvrgh, by David Lindsay, Mr. James Kniblo, Josua van Solingen and John Colmar*, 1683. ALDIS 2381. L, O, C, EN, AU; CH, CN, MH, WF, Y.

447A [**Gedney, James.**] To the right honourable the Parliment . . . the humble petition of the company of worsted-weavers of . . . Norwich. [*London?* 165–.] brs. LG.

448 **Gee, Edward,** *elder.* The divine right and original. *For George Eversden*, 1658. 8°. LT, O, C, E, DT; CH, IU, MH, NU, VC, WF, Y.

449 [–] An exercitation concerning vsvrped powers. [*London*], *printed*, 1650. 4°. LT, O, C, EN, DT; CH, CN, MH, TU, WF, Y. (var.)

450 [–] A plea for non-subscribers. [*London?*], *printed*, 1650. 4°. LT, O, CT, EN, DT; CLC, CN, MH, NU, TU, WF, Y. (var.)

450A [–] Steps of ascension unto God. Ninth edition. [*London*], *for G. Bedell & T: Collins*, 1656. 24°. O.

451 —A treatise of prayer. *By J. M. for Luke Fawn*, 1653. 8°. LT, LCL, LLL, E, ENC; CLC, MH, NU.

452 [–] A vindication of the oath of allegiance. [*London*], *printed*, 1650[1]. 4°.* LT, O, CT, E, DT; CH, CN, MH, NU, WF, Y.

453 [**Gee, Edward**], *younger.* An answer to the compiler of the Nubes testium. *For Henry Mortlock*, 1688. 4°. L, O, C, EN, DT; CH, CN, MH, TU, WF, Y.

454 [–] The catalogue of all the discourses published against Popery. *Printed, to be sold by R. Baldwin*, 1689. 4°.* T.C.II 291. L, O, C, EN, DT; CH, CN, LC, MH, NU, TU, WF, Y.

455 [–] A letter to Father Lewis Sabran. *For Henry Mortlock*, 1688. cap., 4°.* L, O, C, EN, DT; CH, CN, MH, NU, WF, Y.

456 [–] —[Anr. ed.] *For Henry Motlock* [*sic*], 1688. 4°.* L, O, OC, CT, EC, LLU; CLC, MH, NP, PL, TU, Y.

457 [–] A letter to the superiours, (whether bishops . . .). *For William Rogers*, 1688. 4°.* T.C.II 285. L, O, C, EN, DT; CLC, CN, MH, NU, Y.

458 —Of the improvement of time. *For Brab. Aylmer, and Sam. Smith*, 1692. 4°.* T.C.II 420. L, O, C, EC, WCA; CH, MH, TO, WF, Y.

459 [–] The primitive fathers no Papists. *For Ric. Chiswell*, 1688. 4°. T.C.II 270. L, O, C, EN, DT; CH, IU, MH, NU, TU, WF, Y.

460 [–] A second letter to Father Lewis Sabran. *For Henry Mortlock*, 1688. 4°.* L, O, C, EN, DT; CH, CN, MH, TU, WF, Y.

461 [–] A third letter to F. Lewis Sabran. *For Ric. Chiswell*, 1688. 4°.* T.C.II 270. L, O, C, EN, DT; CH, CN, MH, TU, WF, Y.

462 [–] Veteres vindicati, in an expostulatory letter. *For Henry Mortlock*, 1687. 4°. L, O, C, E, DT; CLC, CN, MH, NU, TU, Y.

463 [–] —Second edition. —, 1687. 4°. L, C, OME, MR, EN; CH, MH, NU, TU, WF, Y.

464 [–] A vindication of the principles of the author of the answer. *For Henry Mortlock*, 1688. 4°.* L, O, C, EN, DT; CH, IU, MH, NU, TU, WF, Y.

465 The gelding of the devil. [*London*, 1670?] brs. L, CM. (var.)

465A —[Anr. ed.] *By E. C. for F. Coles, T. Vere, and J. Wright*, [1663–74]. brs. LG.

466 Entry cancelled.

Gell, Alexander. Gratulatoria dicata . . . Carolo regi. [*n.p.*], 1641. *See* Gil, Alexander.

467 **Gell, John.** The true case of the state of. [*London*, 1650.] cap., 4°.* LT.

468 **Gell, Robert.** Αγγελοκρατια Θεου: or, a sermon. *By John Legatt, to be sold by Nath. Webb, and William Grantham*, 1650. 4°. LT, O, CJ, EN, DT; CN, NR, NU, WF, Y.

468A — —[Anr. ed.] *By John Legatt, to be sold by Nathaniel Brooks*, 1650. 4°. C, CT; IU, MH.

469 [–?] Ειρηνικον: or, a treatise of peace. *By T. J. for Nath. Brooks*, 1660. 4°. L, CT, SP, DU, BLH; MM, NU.

470 —An essay toward the amendment . . . The first part. *By R. Norton for Andrew Crook*, 1659. fol. L, O, C, E, DT; CLC, CU, MH, NU, WF, Y.

471 —Noah's flood returning. *By J. L. to be sold by Giles Calvert*, 1655. 4°.* LT, O, LG, LW, CT; NU, WF, Y.

472 —Gell's remaines. *For Nath. Brooke*, 1676. fol. T.C.I 225. L, O, CK, NPL, E, DM; NP, NR, NU, PPT, Y.

473 —Stella nova. A new starre. *For Samuel Satterthwaite*, 1649. 4°.* LT, O, LCL, CT, DT; CH, CN, MH, TU, WF, Y.

474 **Gellibrand, Henry.** An epitome of navigation. *By Andr. Clark for William Fisher*, 1674. 8°. T.C.I 178. O.

475 — —[Anr. ed.] *For W. Fisher, R. Boulter, T. Passenger, and R. Smith*, 1680. 8°. T.C.I 410. Y.

476 — —Fourth edition. *By B. M. for R. Mount*, 1695. 8°. OH, C, DCH; MU.

477 — —[Anr. ed.] *For Richard Mount*, 1698. 8°. L, EN; MU, SE.

478 —An institution trigonometricall. Second edition. *By R. and W. Leybourn, for William Lugger*, 1652. 8°. LT, C; CH, PL, WF.

479   Entry cancelled.
       —Trigonometria Britanica. 1658. *See* Newton, John.
480   [**Gellibrand, John.**] A catalogue of the libraries of two
       eminent persons. [*Tunbridge Wells*], 8 *Aug.* 1684. fol.*
       L, O.
481   —Catalogus librorum in omni facultate. 1682. Sixes.* O.
482   Gemitus de carcere Nantes. Or, prison-sighs. *Printed,*
       1684. 4°.* L, O, DU, MR; MH, NC, WF.
483   Gemitus ecclesiæ Cambro-Britannicæ; or, the candle-
       sticks. *Printed,* 1654. 4°.* L, C, OB, AN, YM, DT; CH, WF.
       Gemmarius fidelis; or. 1659. *See* Nicols, Thomas.
       Genealogicon Latinum. 1676. *See* Goad, John.
       Genealogies of the high-born prince. [n.p.], 1684. *See*
       Keepe, Henry.
       Genealogies recorded. [n.p.], 1642. *See* Speed, John.
       Genealogie of Christianity. 1650. *See* Feake, Christopher.
484   Genealogy of King Alexander the third. [*n.p.,* 1685.] brs.
       OP.
484A   The genealogy of the lairds of Ednem. *Glasgow, by R.
       Sanders,* 1699. 8°.* ALDIS 3852. EN; LC.
485–6 Entries cancelled.
       Generall accomodations. [n.p., 1650.] *See* Speed, Adol-
       phus.
       Generall advertisement. 1642. *See* England, Parliament.
487   A general and compleat list military. *By J. Gain, for
       Nathan Brooks, at Thomas Knapton's,* 1684. fol.* L, O,
       MR, SP; CH, CN, MIU, WF.
488   The generall and particular acts and articles of the late
       national synod . . . of France. *By T. W. for G. Emerson,*
       1646. 4°.* LT, O, CT, P, EN, DT; CH, IU, MII, NU, WF, Y.
488A   A general and true memorial of what has been done in . . .
       Orange. [*London,* 1687.] fol.* LLP, EN; MH.
       General assembly. 1700. *See* Heywood, Oliver.
488B   The general association, of the gentlemen of Devon, to
       . . . Prince of Orange. *Exon, printed,* 1688. brs. L, LG,
       OC, DU, HH; Y.
489   —[Anr. ed.] —, 1689 [but 1688]. brs. STEELE 3897. L, O, LG,
       LPR, CK, DU, HH, MC, EN; CH, CN, MIU, NC.
490   —[Anr. ed.] *Exon: printed,* 1689. brs. L, O, MC; CN, NC,
       PU, WF.
491   A general bill for this present year. [*London,* 1665.] brs.
       LU, LWL, OP, CM, HH; WF.
491A   —[Same title.] [*London,* 1666.] brs. LWL.
491B   A general bill of all the christnings and burials. [*London,*
       1669.] brs. LPR.
491C   —[Same title.] [*London,* 1670.] brs. LPR.
491D   —[Same title.] [*London,* 1673.] brs. L.
491E   —[Same title.] [*London,* 1674.] brs. L, LPR.
491F   —[Same title.] [*London,* 1675.] brs. L.
491G   —[Same title.] [*London,* 1676.] brs. L.
491H   —[Same title.] [*London,* 1677.] brs. L.
492   —[Same title.] [*London,* 1679.] brs. O, HH; INU.
493   —[Same title.] [*London,* 1680.] brs. O, HH.
493A   —[Same title.] [*London,* 1682.] brs. MH.
494   —[Same title.] [*London,* 1683.] brs. O; CLC, MH.
494A   —[Same title.] [*London,* 1684.] brs. MH.
494B   —[Same title.] [*London,* 1685.] brs. WF.

494C   —[Same title.] [*London,* 1687/8.] brs. PL.
494CA —[Same title.] [*London,* 1688/9.] brs. C.
494D   —[Same title.] [*London,* 1690/1.] brs. OC.
494E   —[Same title.] [*London,* 1691/2.] brs. OC.
494F   —[Same title.] [*London,* 1692/3.] brs. OC.
494G   —[Same title.] [*London,* 1693/4.] brs. OC.
       General bill of mortality. [1646.] *See* Griffith, Matthew.
495   Generall bill of the mortality of the clergy . . . who have
       been imprisoned . . . by the Presbyterians. *Printed,* 1662.
       4°.* O, LG, OC, CJ; CLC, CSU.
495A   The general bills of mortality . . . relation of seven mod-
       ern plagues. *For Francis Coles, Thomas Vere, and John
       Wright,* [1666]. brs. LG; MH.
496   General catalogue of all the stitch'd books. *By J. R.,* 1680.
       L, LIL; LC, NU, Y.
497   Entry cancelled.
       General catalogue of books. 1680. *See* Clavell, Robert.
       General cause of the clothiers. 1648. *See* Talbott, William.
       General charge. 1647. *See* C., L.
       General collection. 1664. *See* Renaudot, Eusebe.
       Generall complaint. [n.p., 1645.] *See* Taylor, John.
497AA A general confession of the true Christian faith. [*London,*
       1656.] 8°.* MB.
497BA General considerations relating to a bill . . . prisons.
       [*London,* 1697.] brs. L; Y.
497CA A general court of the Royal Affrican Company . . . [14
       January 1675]. [*London,* 1675/6.] brs. LPR.
497DA —[11 January 1677.] [*London,* 1677.] brs. LPR.
497EA General courts of elections to be holden. [*London,* 1691.]
       brs. MH.
497FA A generall cry: for the King to come sit with his Par-
       liament. [*London*], *printed,* 1648. 4°.* WF.
       General demands. Aberdene, 1662. *See* Church of Scot-
       land.
       General draught. 1681. *See* Rymer, Thomas.
       General epistle, and a tender. 1660. *See* Fox, George,
       younger.
       Generall epistle, and greeting. 1657. *See* Burrough, Ed-
       ward.
497A   A general epistle given forth by the people . . . called
       Quakers. *Printed and sold by William Bradford at Phila-
       delphia in Pennsilvania,* 1686. 8°.* EVANS 405. LF; NN.
       General epistle given forth from. [n.p.], 1668. *See* Dews-
       bury, William.
       General epistle of love. 1693. *See* Pennyman, John.
       General epistle of universal love. [1698.] *See* Rigge, Am-
       brose.
       General epistle to all Friends, who. [n.p., 1662]. *See* Bayly,
       William.
       General epistle to all Friends. [n.p., 1664.] *See* Fox, George.
       General epistle to all who. [n.p., 1665.] *See* Howgill,
       Francis.
       General epistle to be read. [n.p.], 1662. *See* Fox, George.
       Generall epistle to Friends. [n.p., 1667.] *See* Fox, George.
       General epistle to Friends. [n.p.], 1671. *See* Keith, George.
       General epistle to Friends every where. [n.p., 1682.] *See*
       Parke, James.

General epistle to the dispersed. [n.p.], 1665. *See* Howgill, Francis.

General epistle to the flock. [n.p., 1698.] *See* Banks, John.

General epistle to the people. [n.p., 1693.] *See* Rigge, Ambrose.

General examination. 1689. *See* Sutton, R.

498 The general-excise consider'd. [*London*, 1692.] 4°. L, CT, LSD, MR; CLC, NP, TO, WF, Y.

499 Entry cancelled.

General exercise ordered. [n.p.], 1689. *See* Netherlands.

499A The general greevance of all England. [*London?* 1650.] brs. OP; WF.

General history of earthquakes. 1692. *See* Crouch, Nathaniel.

Generall history of women. 1657. *See* Heywood, Thomas.

500 A general index or alphabetical table to all the philosophical transactions. *By J. M. for John Martyn*, 1678. 4°.* L, C, CM; WF.

General inefficacy. 1670. *See* Beverley, Thomas.

501 General instructions to be observed by the gagers. [*London*, 169–?] brs. NC.

Generall junto. [n.p.], 1642. *See* Parker, Henry.

501A A generall list of the sufring subjects of His Majesty . . . in Barbary. [*London*, 1697.] brs. LNM.

502 General Massey's Bartholomew-fairings. [*London*], *printed*, 1647. 4°.* LT, OC, CT; TU, Y.

General mistake. 1690. *See* W., T.

503 General Monck's resolution. *For John Johnson*, 1659. brs. L, O; MH, WF.

504 A generall note of the prises for binding all sortes of bookes. *Printed at London*, 1646. brs. LT.

504A —[Same title, "prices of."] [*London*, 1669.] brs. MH.

504B —[Same title.] *Printed and sold by John Whitlock*, 1695. brs. L.

505 A general, or no general. [*London*], *printed*, 1659. 4°.* LT, OC, BC, LSD, BQ; CH, CN, MH, MU, WF, Y.

General proposal for the building. [1696.] *See* Johnson, Thomas.

506 The generall remonstrance or declaration of the Catholikes of Ireland. [n.p., 1641.] brs. L.

507 —[Anr. ed.] *For Joseph Hunscott.* 1641. brs. LT, O, LG, CT, EC, LNC, DN; MH.

508 The generall remonstrance or declaration of the seamen. [*London*, 1642.] brs. STEELE 1975. LT, DT.

509 The general resolvtion of the two kingdoms of England and Scotland. [*London*], *Iune 24. for I. Tompson and A. Coe*, 1642. 4°.* LT, LHO; MBP, MH, WF, Y.

509A Generall sailing-orders. *Rotterdam, by Isaac van Lochem*, [1692?]. 4°. GU.

510 A general sale of rebellious household-stuff. *For Allen Banks.* 1682. brs. L, O; CH, MH.

510A —[Anr. ed.] —, 1685. brs. O, OC.

511 A general summons for those belonging to the hen-peck'd frigate. [*London*], *for J. Deacon*, [1688–95]. brs. L, O, HH.

Generall table of Europe. [n.p.], 1670. *See* Comenius, Johann Amos.

General testimony. [n.p.], 1677. *See* Willsford, John.

511A A general testimony from the people of God, called, Quakers. [*Philadelphia, William Bradford*, 1691.] brs. PHS.

511B The generall tutor, or the exact clerk. *T. Lock*, 1659. 8°. L; CLL.

512 The generals dinner at the Lady Crispes. [*London*], *printed*, 1647. 4°.* LT, CT; INU, NP, WF.

Generation of seekers. 1671. *See* Oldfield, John.

512A Generosissimo amplissimoque viro . . . Roberto Vinaro. [*London*, 1674.] brs. L.

513 The generous usurer Mr. Nevell in Thames Street. *For Salomon Johnson*, 1641. 4°.* L, DU; CH, CLC, WF.

Γενεσις και τελος. 1649. *See* Ascham, Antony.

514 Geneva & Rome. *Printed*, 1679. brs. L, O, HH; CLC, MBA, MH, PU.

515–7 Entries cancelled.

Geneva ballad. 1674. *See* Butler, Samuel.

518 The genius of true English-men. *For Francis Smith*, 1680. brs. O; CH.

519 —[Anr. ed.] —, [1681]. brs. L, O; MH, PU, TU, Y.

520 The genius, or expressions of. *For the author*, 1663. 4°.* L.

521 The genteel house-keeper's pastime. *For J. Moxon*, 1693. 8°. L, O; Y.

Gentile sinner. Oxford, 1660. *See* Ellis, Clement.

Gentle craft. 1648. *See* Deloney, Thomas.

Gentle lash. Oxford, 1644. *See* Featley, Daniel.

Gentle reflection. 1682. *See* Andrewes, John.

522 **Gentleman, Tobias.** The best way to make England the richest. *Printed*, [1660]. fol.* LT, OC, LUG; NC, PU, WF.

Gentleman apothecary. 1670. *See* Villiers, Jacob.

Gentleman's calling. 1660. *See* Allestree, Richard.

Gentlemans companion. 1672. *See* Ramesay, William.

Gentleman's compleat jockey. 1696. *See* S., A.

Gentlemans exercise. 1662. *See* Hammond, Anthony.

Gentleman's jocky. 1671. *See* Halfpenny, John.

Gentleman's new jockey. 1687. *See* L., G.

Gentleman's recreation. 1674. *See* Cox, Nicholas.

Gentlemans recreation. 1686. *See* Blome, Richard.

Gentleman's religion. 1693. *See* Synge, Edward, *abp.*

522A The gentlemans resolution. [*London?* 1700.] brs. L.

523 The gentlemen wool merchants and serge-makers case. [n.p., c. 1698.] brs. LL.

523AA The gentlewoman who lived in Red-Lyon-Court . . . hath a most excellent wash to beautifie the face. [*London*, 1690?] brs. L. (var.)

523BA The gentlewoman's cabinet unlocked. Eighth edition. 1673. 12°. L (lost).

523CA —Seventh edition. *By E. C. and are to be sold by John Williamson*, 1675. 8°. L.

523DA —[Anr. ed.] [*London*], *for W. Thackeray and T. Passenger*, [1686–88]. 8°.* CM.

523EA The gentlewoman's delight in cookery. *For J. Back*, [1690?]. 8°.* CM.

523A The genuine epistles of the apostolical fathers, S. Barnabas. *For Ric. Sare*, 1693. 8°. L, O, CP, AN, EC, AU, DT; CH, CN, NU, WF, Y.

Genuine use and necessity. 1697. *See* Addison, Lancelot.

524 **Geoghegan, James.** The last speech and confession of. *Dublin, by Samuel Lee,* 1694. brs. DIX 259. L, DN.

Geographiæ veteris scriptores. Oxoniæ, 1698. *See* Hudson, John, *ed.*

Geographical and historical description. 1696. *See* Boyer, Abel.

524A Geographical cards. *For Henry Brome,* 1676. 16°. T.C.I 231. CT.

Geographicall description of the kingdom of Ireland. 1642. *See* N., G.

Geographical description of the world. 1671. *See* Meriton, George.

525–7 Entries cancelled.
Geographical dictionary. 1662. *See* Du Val, Pierre.

528 The geometry of landskips. *For Richard Baldwin,* 1690. 4°.* T.C.II 315. L, O, LCP, LLP, CS, DT; NN, WF, Y, YBA.

529 **George I,** *prince of Transylvania.* The declaration or, manifesto of . . . to the states and peeres of Hvngarie. *For Edward Blackmore, May 28.* 1644. 4°.* L, MR; CH, WF.

530 **George,** *prince of Denmark.* Prince George his letter to the King. [*n.p.,* 1688.] brs. L, O, C, HH, EN; CH, CN, MH, PL, WF, Y. (var.)

531 **George Frederick,** *prince of Waldeck.* A letter to the States General . . . [15/25 August 1689]. [*London*], *by Edw: Jones in the Savoy,* 1689. brs. CN.

531A ——[Anr. ed.] *For R. Baldwin,* [1689]. brs. C.

532 ——[Anr. ed.] *Edinburgh, re-printed,* 1689. brs. ALDIS 2914. EN; CN.

532A —A more full and impartial account of the fight. *For Abel Roper & Tho. Jones,* [1690]. brs. C; CN.

George Fox digg'd out. Boston, 1676. *See* Williams, Roger.

533 **Georgeson,** *Sir* **P.** The defence of the Parliament of England. *For Timothy Goodwin,* 1692. 4°.* T.C.II 396. L, O, CT, BR, LIU; CH, CN, MH, NU, WF, Y.

534 Georgio Monck Duci de Albemarle, . . . epitaphium. [*London*], *typis Th. Newcomb in ædibus Savoyensibus venales prostant a Gulielmo Nott,* 1670. brs. L, O, DU; CH.

535 —[Anr. ed.] [*London*], *in the Savoy, by Tho: Newcomb, for William Nott, and James Collins,* 1670. brs. L; CH, MH.

536 **Georgirenes, Joseph,** *abp.* A description of the present state of Samos. *By W. G. and sold by Moses Pitt,* 1678. 8°. T.C.I 300. L, O, C, GH, DT; BN, CH, MU, NP, WF, Y.

537 —From the Archbishop of . . . Samos . . . an account. *For A. F.,* 1682. brs. L, O; CH.

Gerard, Charles. *See* Macclesfield, Charles Gerard, *earl of.*

537A **Gerard, Henry.** A strict reckoning. *For the authour,* 1666. 4°.* WCA; Y.

Gerardo, the vnfortunate Spaniard. 1653. *See* Cespedes y Meneses, Gonzalo de.

537B [**Gerardts, Gonsale.**] Doet niet sonder Godt . . . That most renowned doctor. [*London,* 1695?] brs. L.

537C [–] Doet nier sonder Godt . . . that most renowned operator. [*London,* 1695?] brs. L.

537D [–] Niemant mijns gelijck . . . That most renowned Dutch operator. [*London,* 1695?] brs. L.

537E —Nothing without God. These are to give notice. [*London,* 1695?] brs. L.

537F [–] Si de Cupid' ô Venus . . . That most renowned. [*London,* 1695?] brs. L.

538 **Gerbier,** *Sir* **Balthazar.** The academies lecture concerning justice. *For Gabriel Bedel,* 1650. 4°.* LT, CS, MR; CLC, MH, MM.

[–] Advertissement for men. Rotterdam, 1660. *See* —Sommary description.

539 —The art of well speaking. *Printed at London for Robert Ibbitson,* 1650. 4°.* L, O; CH, CN, WF, Y.

540 —A brief discourse concerning the three chief principles. *Printed,* 1662. 8°. L, O, C; CH, CLC, CU, MU, YBA.

541–50 No entries.

551 ——[Anr. ed.] *By Tho. Mabb, for Tho. Heath,* 1664. 8°. O, C; CH, LC, MU, WF, Y.

551A ——[Anr. ed.] *By A. M. for Thomas Heath,* 1665. 8°. EN.

552 —Counsel and advise to all builders. *By Thomas Mabb,* 1663. 8°. L, O, LCP, CCA, BC; CH, IU, MH, NC, WF, YBA.

553 —A discovery of certain notorious stumbling-blocks. *By T. M.,* 1652. 4°.* LT.

554 —The first and second part of counsel and advice to all builders. *By Tho. Mabb, for Tho. Heath,* 1664. 8°. L, O, LUG, LNC; WF, Y.

555 —The first lecture being an introduction to the military architecture. *Printed at London for Robert Ibbitson,* 1650. 4°.* L, O; MB, MH.

556 —The first lectvre, concerning navigation. *By Gartrude Dawson,* 1649. 4°.* LT, DT; LC.

557 —The first lectvre, of an introduction to cosmographie. *By Gartrude Dawson, to be sold by Hanna Allen,* 1649. 4°.* LT, O, CASTLE ASHBY; Y.

558 ——[Anr. ed.] *Printed at London for Robert Ibbitson,* 1649. 4°.* LT, O, P, DT.

559 —The first lectvre of geographie. *By Gartrude Dawson, to be sold by Hanna Allen,* 1649. 4°.* LT; CLC.

560 —The first lecture touching navigation. *Printed at London, for Robert Ibbitson,* 1649. 4°.* LT, O; LC, Y.

561 —The first pvbliqve lectvre. *By Gartrude Dawson,* 1469 [i.e. 1649]. 4°.* LT, DT.

562 ——[Anr. ed.] *By Gartrude Dawson, to be sold by Hanna Allen,* 1469 [i.e., 1649]. 4°.* L.

563 —The interpreter of the academie for forrain langvages. 1648. 4°. LT, O, C, DCH; BN, CLC, CN, LC, MIU, NN, W. (var.)

564 —A letter from . . . [4 May 1646]. [*London,* 1646.] 4°.* LT; CH.

565 —A manifestation. *For the authour,* 1651. 8°.* L; VC, VILLANOVA.

566 —A New-Years resvlt. *By T. M.,* 1652. 4°.* LT.

567 Entry cancelled.
[–] None-such Charles. 1651. *See* title.

568 —A publique lecture on all the languages. *Printed at London, for Robert Ibbitson,* 1650. 4°.* LT, O; CH, MH, Y.

569 —The second lecture being an introduction to cosmo-graphie. *For Robert Ibbitson, 1649.* 4°.* LT, O; CH, RPJ, Y.

570 —Some considerations on the two grand staple-commo-dities. *By T. Mab and A. Coles, 1651.* 4°.* L; CH.

571 —A sommary description, manifesting. *[Rotterdam], for Sir Balthazar Gerbier Kyt Douvilly. 1660.* 4°.* L, O, DCH; CH, NN, PHS, RPJ, Y.

572 —Subsidium peregrinantibus. *Oxford, for Robert Gas-coigne, 1665.* 8°. MADAN 2700. L, O, C; CLC, CN, LC, MH, WF, Y.

573 —To all fathers of noble families. *[London, 1648.]* brs. LT.

574 ——[Anr. ed.] *[London, 1649.]* cap., 8°.* LT.

575 ——[Anr. ed.] *By Robert Ibbitson, 1649.* brs. LT, LS; CH.

576 ——[Anr. ed.] *[London, 1651.]* brs. LT.

577 —Balthazar Gerbier knight to all men that loves trvth. *[Paris, 1646.]* 4°.* LT.

578 —To the honorable the Commons . . . explanation. *[n.p.], 1646.* 4°.* O.

579 —To the Parliament. The humble proposal of. *[n.p., 1650?]* brs. L.

580 —To the Parliament, the most humble remonstrance of. *[London, 1650?]* cap., 4°.* L, O, LUG; W.

581 —To the right honourable the Parliament, and the Coun-cell of State, . . . the most humble expression of. *[n.p., 1649.]* cap., 4°.* L, DU; CSS, NC, W.

582 —To the svpreme avthority, the Parliament . . . The humble remonstrance. *[London, 1651.]* 4°.* L, LUG; CSS, NC.

583 **G[erbier], C[harles].** Elogivm heroinum: or, the praise of worthy women. *By T. M. & A. C. and are to be sold by William Nott, 1651.* 12°. LT; CLC, CN, MH, WF, Y.

583A ——[Anr. ed.] *By T. M. & A. C. and are sold by William Raybould, 1651.* 12°. CH, MB.

583B —The modest cavallieres advice. *[London], printed, 1647.* 4°.* LT, LG; CH, IU, Y.

584 **[Gerbier, George.]** The false favourit disgrac'd. *By Wil. Wilson for Robert Crofts, 1657.* 8°. L, O, CCA; CH, IU, MH, NC, WF, Y.

585 [–] —[Anr. ed.] *For Robert Crofts, 1657.* 8°. L, O, OW; CH, LC, MB, NN, WF.

586 **Geree, John.** Astrologo-mastix, or a discovery. *By Mat-thew Simmons for John Bartlet, 1646.* 4°.* LT, O, C, GU, DT; CH, CN, NU, PL, WF, Y.

587 —A case of conscience resolved. *By Matthew Simmons, for John Bartlet, 1646.* 4°.* LT, O, C, E, DT; CH, CN, NU, WF, Y.

588 —A catechisme in briefe questions. *By R. C. for F. Grove and are to bee sold by Christopher Meredith, 1647.* O; PL.

588A [–] The character of an old English Protestant. *[London, 1670.]* brs. O.

589 —The character of an old English Pvritane. *By W. Wilson for Christopher Meredith, 1646.* 4°.* LT, O, C, EN, DT; CH, CN, NU, WF, Y. (var.)

590 ——[Anr. ed.] *By A. Miller for Christopher Meredith, 1646.* 4°.* O, CE.

591 ——[Anr. ed.] —, *1649.* 4°.* L; MWA.

592 ——[Anr. ed.] *Printed, 1659.* 4°.* OP, MR; CH, MH.

592A ——[Anr. ed.] —, *1666.* 4°.* O.

593 ——[Anr. ed.] —, *1672.* 4°.* L, O, CT, MR.

594 —The character of the sober Non-conformist. *Printed, 1673.* 4°. O.

595 —The down-fall of Anti-Christ. *For Thomas Vnderhill, 1641.* 4°.* LT, O, MR, EN, DT; IU, MBA, MH, NU, WF, Y.

596 —Ιππος πυρρος. The red horse. *For George Latham, 1648.* 4°.* LT, O, LP, DT; CB, CH, CU, IU, NU, WF, Y.

596A —Ireland's advocate. *Printed at Dublin, and re-printed at London for William Bladen, 1642.* 4°.* L.

597 —Iudahs ioy. *By R. Oulton for Iohn Bartlet, 1641.* 4°.* LT, O, C, EN, DT; CLC, MBP, NU, WF, Y.

598 —Καταδυναστης: might overcoming right. *For Robert Bostock, 1649.* 4°.* LT, O, CT, EN, DT; BN, CH, CU, MH, WF, Y.

599 —Σινιορραγια, the sifters sieve broken. *For Christopher Meredith, 1648.* 4°. L, O, LSC, MR; MM, NU, WF.

599A ——[Anr. ed.] *Printed at London, and are to be sold at the Crane, 1660.* 4°. LIU, LSD.

600 —Θειοφαρμακον. A divine potion. *For George Lathum, 1648.* 4°.* LT, O, MR; MM, Y.

601 [–] Touching the subject of svpremacy. *[London], by J. F. for Philemon Stephens, 1647.* 4°.* LT, O, BC, MR, DT; CH, NU, OWC, WF, Y.

602 —Vindiciæ ecclesiæ Anglicanæ. *By Richard Cotes, for Ralph Smith, 1644.* 4°. LT, O, C, EN, DT; CLC, NPT, NU, TO, Y.

603 —Vindiciæ pædo-baptismi: or, a vindication. *By John Field for Christopher Meredith, 1646.* 4°. LT, O, C, ENC, DT; CH, IU, MH, NU, WF, Y, AVP.

604 —Vindiciæ vindiciarvm: or, a vindication. *By A. M. for Christopher Meredith, 1647.* 4°.* LT, O, SP, DT; CH (impf.), MH, MIU, NPT, NU.

605 —Vindiciæ voti. Or a vindication. *By R. Oulton for Iohn Bartlet, 1641.* 4°.* LT, O, CT, BC, DT; CLC, IU, MH, NU, WF, Y.

606 **Geree, Stephen.** The doctrine of the Antinomians. *By R. C. for H. Blunden, 1644.* 4°. LT, O, C, NE, ENC; CH, MH, NPT, NU, WF, Y.

607 —The golden mean. *For Joseph Cranford, 1656.* 8°. LT, LW; NPT.

608 **Gerhard, Johann.** Divine consolations. *For Nath. Crouch, 1680.* 12°. L, LSC, OC; NU.

609 —Meditationes sacrae. *[n.p.], excudebat Rogerus Daniel, 1655.* 24°. CT; IU.

609A ——[Anr. ed.] *Oxoniæ, apud Henricum Hall impensis Roberti Blagrave, 1656.* 12°. MADAN 2298. CS, P, CASTLE ASHBY; CLC.

609B ——[Anr. ed.] *Excudebat R. Daniel, veneunt apud Edm. Bechino bibliopolam Cantabrigiensem, 1657.* 12°. O.

609C ——[Anr. ed.] *Ex officina Roberti Battersby, 1672.* 12°. L, O, CS, DU, NE; IU, MB, MBJ, PU, WF, Y.

609D —Gerards meditations. Seventh edition. *By the printers to the Universitie at Cambridge, 1644.* 8°. L, C, CS, LW, YM; Y.

609E ——Eighth edition. *Cambridge, by Thomas Buck, 1651.* 12°. CLC.

610 ——[Anr. ed.] *Cambridge, by John Hayes, 1670.* 12°. T.C.I 32. L, YM.

611 ——[Anr. ed.] —, *1679.* 12°. T.C.I 378. L, CT; WF.

611A   ——[Anr. ed.] *Edinburgh, by the heir of A. Anderson,* 1681. 12°. ALDIS 2269.5. EN.

611B   ——[Anr. ed.] *Cambridge, by John Hayes,* 1683. 12°. O; NPT.

612   ——[Anr. ed.] *For A. and J. Churchil,* 1695. 12°. T.C.II 541. L; CH.

Gerhard, John. *See* Gerrard, John.

613   The German princess revived. colop: *By George Croom,* 1684. cap., 4°.* O, MR; CN, MH, NN.

614   The Germane spie. *For Randal Taylor,* 1691. 4°. L, O; CH, CN, MM, Y.

615   **Gerrard, John.** The true and perfect speeches of. *Imprinted at London for C. Horton,* 1654. 4°.* LT, LSD; CSS, MH.

Gertrux, Valentine. *See* Greatrakes, Valentine.

616   **Gery, Peter.** Gerii, viri in arte scriptoria . . . or a copie book. *[London], engraven by Wm: Faithorne and are to be sold by him,* [1670]. 4°. L, CM, LIU; CN.

616A   —A copy book containing forty-two copies. *Sold by J. Garret,* 1680. 4°. T.C.I 417. CM.

617   **Gery, Thomas.** An antidote against some erroneous pamphlets. *By T. W. for the author,* 1656. 4°. L, C, YM; CLC, NPT, WF.

618   —The fort-royal of Christianity defended. *By T. C. for Nathanael Web, and William Grantham,* 1657. 12°. LT, O, CE, BC; CLC, NGT, NU, WF.

619   —Holy meditations upon God. *By T. C. for Nathanael Webb and William Grantham,* 1658. 12°. LT.

619A   —A mirrour for Anabaptists. *For Nath. Webb, and W. Grantham,* 1660. 12°. LT, ORP, NU.

620   **G[ery], W[illiam].** Abuses discovered, whereby the creditors. *[London,* 1649.] brs. LT, DT; MII.

620A   — The case of . . . [estate settlement]. *[London,* 1672?] brs. LPR.

621   Entry cancelled.
—Mirrour for Anabaptists. 1660. *See* Gery, Thomas.

622   —Proposals for reformation of abuses. *For William Shears,* 1659. 4°.* LT, O, LL, LUG, BC, LSD; CSS, LC, MHL, WF, Y.

623   **Gesling, Richard.** Artificial fire. *By Richard Cotes for Michael Spark senior,* 1644. brs. LT, LS.

624   **Gesner, Konrad.** The history of four-footed beasts. *By E. Cotes, for G. Sawbridge, T. Williams, and T. Johnson,* 1658. fol. L, O, CT, A, DT; CH, IU, LC, MB, NN, TU, WF, Y.

Gesta Grayorum. 1688. *See* Canning, W.

625   **Gethin, Grace Norton,** *Lady.* Misery's virtues whetstone. Reliquiae Gethinianae. *[London], by D. Edwards for the author,* 1699. 4°. L, C, LLP; CN, NPT, WF.

626   — —Second edition ["misery is"]. —, 1700. 4°. L, O, OB.

627   Entry cancelled. *See previous entry.*

628   **Gething, Richard.** Calligraphotechnia; or. *And are to bee soulde by William Humble,* 1642. fol. CN, NC, Y.

629   ——[Anr. ed.] —, 1652. 4°. L, O, LV; CH, LC.

629A   —Chiro-graphia. *Sold by John Dowle,* [1645]. 8°. CLC, CN, NP.

630   —Digitus Dei, or, a miraculous victory. *For Thomas Bates,* 1642. 4°.* LT, C, EC, DN; MH.

631   —Gething redivivus: or the pens master-piece restored. *By John Best, for John Cade, and for John Dowse,* 1664. 4°. L; CN, NN.

632   **Getsius, Johann Daniel.** Tears shed. *Oxford, by A. L. for Tho. Robinson,* 1658. 8°. MADAN 2386. O, LSC; NU.

633   Des gewesenen Englischen gross-Lantzlers George Lord Jeffries. *London and Amsterdam,* [1689?]. 4°.* LL.

634   **Ghest, [Edmund].** An impartial disquisition. *[London,* 1689?] cap., 4°.* L, O, OC, CT, MR; CLC, MH, NU, WF, Y.

635   The ghost of Charles the Great. *[London,* 1649?] 4°.* MR.

636   The ghost of K. Charls and Seriant Bradsha. *Printed,* 1649. 4°.* TU.

637   The ghost of Sr. John Presbjter. *[London], printed,* 1647. 4°.* LT; CSS, TU, Y.

638   The ghost of the Emperor Charles the Fifth. *For John Newton,* 1690. 4°.* T.C.II 324. C, CT, MR, EN, DT; CH, CLC, CN, MH, WF, Y.

639   The ghost of the late House of Commons. colop: *[n.p.], printed,* 1681. brs. L, O; MH.

640   —[Anr. ed.] *[London], for Benjamin Harris, to be sold by Langley Curtis,* 1681. brs. L, O, MC; CN, MH, NCD, WF, Y.

640A   Ghost of the late lord Viscount–Stafford. *For [R.] M.* 168[2?]. brs. MH.

Ghost of the old House of Commons. [1681.] *See* Roscommon, Wentworth Dillon, *earl of.*

640B   The ghost of Tom Ross to his pupil the D. of Monmouth. *[London?* 1683.] brs. MH.

641   The ghost; or, the woman wears the breeches. A comedy. *By William Bentley for Thomas Heath,* 1653. 4°. LT, O, LVD, OW, EN; CH, CU, LC, MH, TU, Y.

642   The ghosts of Edward Fits Harris and Oliver Plunket. *For Richard Knowles,* 1681. fol.* O; CH, MH, WF, Y.

642A   **Ghyles, Thomas.** A brief and plain description of the joynt-sickness: . . . gout. *For the author,* 1684. 8°.* L.

643   The gyant: or, the miracle of nature. Being that so much admired young-man. *[London,* 1684.] brs. L.

Gyant whipt. [1681.] *See* C., I.

644   **Gibbes, Charles.** XXXI sermons. *By E. Flesher, for R. Royston,* 1677. 4°. T.C.I 272. L, O, CS, YM, ENC; NGT, NU, Y.

645   **[Gibbes, James.]** Good and bad newes from Ireland. *For Nath: Butter, March* 14, 1641. 4°.* LT, C; MIU, MU, WU, Y.

646   **[Gibbon, James.]** Reflections on a book . . . by Mr. Ammonet. *Dublin, printed and sold by Matthew Gunn,* 1696. 4°.* DIX 283. DI.

647   **[Gibbon, John.]** Day-fatality. *[London,* 1679.] cap., fol.* L, O, LG, LNC, EN; CH, MH, MIU, WF, Y.

648   [–]—Second edition. *By Alexander Milbourn, for the author,* 1686. fol. L, MR, SP; CH, CN, MU, PU, U.OREGON.

649   [–] Edovardus confessor redivivus. *By W. D. and sold by Randal Taylor,* 1688. 4°.* LT, O, OBL; CLC, LC, MBP, TU, WF, Y.

649A   [–] Flagellum Mercurii anti-ducalis: or, the author of the dis-ingenuous touch of the times brought to the whipping-post. *[London,* 1679.] cap., fol.* L, C, LNC; CH, MH, Y.

649B   —A funeral elegy, dedicated. *[London?* 1659.] cap., 4°.* CT.

650 —Introductio ad Latinam blasoniam. An essay to. *By J. M. for the author, and sold by J. Crump, by B. Billingsley, and by A. Churchill*, 1682. 8°. T.C.I 497. L, O, C, AN, LIU, DT; CLC, CN, LC, NC, WF, Y.

651 —The nature of justification opened. *For Tho. Parkhurst*, 1695. 4°.* L, LCL, LW, MR, DT; CN, WF.

651A ——[Anr. ed.] *For John Lawrence*, 1695. 4°.* LW; CH, CLC, Y.

652 [–] Prince-protecting providences. colop: *By John Shadd, and Robert Hayhurst, for Walter Davis*, 1682. cap., fol.* L, O, LLP, MR; CH, LC, MH, MIU, NP, WF, Y.

652A [–] Some memorable remarques upon the fourteenth of October. *By A. R., sold by Randal Taylor*, 1687. fol.* NN.

653 [–] A touch of the times, or two letters casually intercepted. [*London*, 1679.] brs. L, O; CH, CLC, MH, PU, WF, Y.

653A [–] Unio dissidentium. Heir apparent. [*London?* 1680.] cap., fol.* L, O, SP; CH, WF.

654 [**Gibbon, Nicholas.**] The reconciler. Earnestly endeavouring. *By Thomas Paine, and are to be sold by Francis Coles*, 1646. 4°.* LT, O, DT; CH, CLC, NPT, NU, Y.

655 —The scheme or diagramme adjusted. [*London*], printed for private hands, [1680?]. fol.* L, OC, WCA.

656 [–] A summe or body of divinitie real. [*n.p.*], 1651. brs. L, O; MH.

657 [–] ——[Anr. ed.] [*n.p.*, 1653.] brs. O.

657A —The tender of. [*London?* 1645.] brs. L.

658 —Theology real and truly scientifical. [*London*, 1687?] fol. L, O, OC.

659 **Gibbons, John.** The perfect speech of. *Printed*, 1651. 4°.* LT, O, LG, LNC; CH, CU, MH, MM, MU, WF.

660 ——[Anr. ed.] *For T. Cook*, 1651. 4°.* O, SP; CSS, Y.

661 —A true and exact copie of Mr. Gibbon's speech. [*London*, 1651.] cap., 4°.* LT; CN, NU, AVP.

661A **Gibbs, J.** A full and particular relation, of Mondays sea engagement. colop: *For H. Jones*, 1690. brs. NP, PL.

662 **Gibbs, [James].** A consolatory poem. *For John Hartley, and sold by John Nutt*, 1700. fol.* T.C.III 215. O; MH, NAM, Y.

662A [**Gibbs, John.**] A funeral sermon preached at Newport-pagnell, April 11. 1697. *For H. Nelme*, 1697. 8°.* MH.

663 —A funeral sermon preached March 13, 1697/8. For Mr. William Hartley. *For Mark Conyers, at Newport-Pagnel: and sold by A. Roper, and G. Conyers*, 1698. In twos.* T.C.III 74. L, C.

664 [**Gibbs, Richard.**] Fitz-Harris his farwel to the world. [*n.p.*, 1681.] brs. L, O, CT; CH, MH, NCD, NNM, TU, Y.

665 [–] An invitation to Mr. John Garlick's house. colop: *By J. R. for the author*, 1683. brs. O.

666 —The new disorders of love. *For R. Bentley and S. Magnes*, 1687. 12°. T.C.II 187. L, O; CLC, CN, MH, Y.

667 **Gibbs, Thomas.** Practical discourses. *By W. Onley, for J. Blare*, 1700. 12°. T.C.III 182. L.

668 **Gibbs, William.** A sermon preached at the funeral of . . . Edward Reynolds. *By John Astwood, for Thomas Cockeril, and Herbert Walwyn*, 1699. 4°.* T.C.III 93. L, O, CT, BC, BLH; CB, CLC, TU, WF, Y.

669 **Gibson, Sir Alexander.** The decisions of the Lords. *Edinburgh, by the heir of Andrew Anderson: and sold by George Mosman*, 1690. fol. ALDIS 3043. L, O, LI, LL, EN; CH, CLC, IU, MBP, AMB.

669A ——[Anr. ed.] *Edinburgh, printed*, 1690. *Sold by Mr. John Tennent and George Stewart*. fol. ALDIS 3043.5. D, E; WF.

669B ——[Anr. ed.] *Edinburgh, sold by George Stewart and John Tennant*, 1690. fol. DL.

669C **G[ibson], J[ohn].** The ancient of dayes is come. colop: *For Giles Calvert*, 1657. cap., 4°.* LT, LF, CT, BBN; PH, PL.

670 —A faithfull testimony for the Lord. *Printed*, 1663. 4°.* L, LF, BBN; PH, PSC, Y.

671 **Gibson, Samuel.** The ruine of the authors. *By M. S. for John Hancock*, 1645. 4°.* LT, O, C, EN, DT; CH, IU, MH, NU, WF, Y.

672 [**Gibson, Thomas.**] The anatomy of humane bodies epitomized. *By M. Flesher for T. Flesher*, 1682. 8°. T.C.I 459. L, C, LCP, LWL, GH, AU; CNM, MH, PU, WSG, HC.

673 ——Second edition. *By J. Heptinstall, for Tho. Flesher*, 1684. 8°. T.C.II 63. L, O, CT, GH, AU; BN, CJC, CU, NAM, PL, HC.

674 ——Third edition. *For Awnsham Churchil*, 1688. 8°. T.C.II 234. L, LCS, OC, CM, MAU, E; CH, CNM, NC, PHS, WF, HC.

675 ——Fourth edition. *By T. W. for Awnsham and John Churchill*, 1694. 8°. T.C.II 495. L, C, LCP, OM, DT; CLM, CU, NAM, TU, Y.

675A ——Fifth edition. —, 1697. 8°. EC, D; CLC, WSG.

676 ——Fifth edition. —, *and sold by Timothy Childe*, 1697. 8°. T.C.III 39. L, LW, MAU, RU, GU, DT; CH, CLM, NAM, NRU.

677 —Syntaxis mathematica: or, a constrvction of the harder problems of geometry. *By R. and W. Leybourn, for Andrew Crook*, 1655. 8°. L, O, LW, OC, CE; MU, PL, RPJ, WF.

678 **Gibson, Thomas, Quaker.** Something offered to the consideration. [*London*, 1665.] cap., 4°.* L, LF, MR, SP; CDA, PH, PL, PSC.

679 **Gibson, Walter.** Proposals . . . to such persons as are desirous to transport themselves to America. [*Glasgow?* 1684.] brs. ALDIS 2453.5. EN; NN.

680 [**Gibson, William.**] A Christian-testimony born by the people. [*London?*] printed, 1679. 4°.* L, O, C, LF, MR; CH, CLC, MH, NCD, PL, WF, Y.

[–] ——[Same title.] 1681. See Field, John.

680A [–] A Christian testimony born by some of the people. *By Andrew Sowle*, 1681/2. 4°. L, O; WF.

681 —Election and reprobation. [*London*], printed, 1678. 4°. L, LF, OC, BBN; BN, MH, PH, PSC, WF.

682 —The everlasting rule born witness unto. [*London*], printed, 1667. 4°.* L, O, C, LF, BBN; IE, MH, PH, PSC.

683 —A false witness examin'd and rebuk'd. [*London*], printed, 1674. 4°.* L, O, LF, BBN, MR; CH, MH, MIU, NCD, PH, Y.

684 —A general epistle. *Printed and sold by John Bringhurst*, 1682. 8°.* O, LF, OC, MR; BN, PH, PL, WF.

685 —Good counsel and advice unto the magistrates . . . of Norwich. [*London*], printed, 1676. 4°.* L; PHS, PL, PSC.

686 —The life of God. [*London*], printed, 1677. 4°. L, LF, OC, BBN; CH, MH, NCD, PH, Y.

687 —A salutation of the Father's love. *Printed*, 1663.* LF, BBN.
—Tythes ended by Christ. [n.p.], 1673. *See* Rudyard, Thomas.

688 —Universal love. [*London*], *printed*, 1671. 4°.* L, O, C, LF, BBN; IE, MH, PH, PSC, WF.
Gideon's fleece. 1684. *See* Guidott, Thomas.

688A **Giffard, Bonaventure.** A sermon preached before the King and Queen. *n.p.*, [1687]. 4°.* BSM, WARE.

689 —A sermon of the nativity. *By Henry Hills; to be sold by him*, 1688. 4°.* L, O, EC, MC, DU; CH, CLC, CN, TU.

690 **Giffard, Francis.** The wicked petition. *For Tho. Dring*, 1681. 4°.* T.C.I 438. L, C, LL, LW, OM; IU, MIU, WF, Y.

691 [**Giffard, John.**] A letter sent to a worthy member of the House of Commons. *By L. N. and I. F. for Edward Husbands and John Franck, August 22.* 1642. 4°.* LT, EC, LNC, MR; CN, MH.

692 —A modest vindication of the case of. [*London*, 1646.] 4°.* NC.

693 **Gifford, A.** Exceeding good nevvs from Nottingham. *For I. T., September 5.* 1642. 4°.* LT.

694 **Gifford, George.** The great mystery of providence. *For S. Crouch*, 1695. 4°.* T.C.II 520. L, O, C, LW, EC; NU.

695 [**Gifford, Humphrey.**] A second accompt of what progress. *By W. Godbid*, 1670. 4°.* L, LG, LUG; CN, MM.

696 **Gifftheyl, Lodowick Frederick.** Two letters directed. *For Rob. Wood*, 1643. 4°.* LT, O, SP, DT; CH, CSS, LC, Y, ZWT.

697 —Two letters directed to the mighty ones. *For T. G.*, 1649. 4°.* LT, CT; MM, Y.

698 Γιγαντομαχια. Or a full, and true relation of the . . . fight. *For Richard Janeway*, 1682. 4°.* L, O, LLU, MR; CH, CN, MH, TU, WF, Y.

698A —[Anr. ed.] *Printed and sold by Richard Janeway*, 168[2?]. 4°.* PU.

699 **Gigas, Johann Michael.** Enchiridion sphæricum. *Oxoniæ sumptibus W. Hall & venales prostant apud F. Oxlad sen. & F. Oxlad jun.*, 1664. 8°. MADAN 2660. O, C, CS, DC; WF, Y.

699A [**Gil, Alexander.**] Decollato Comite Stratfordio. [*London*, 1641.] cap., 4°.* O, CT; WF.

699B —Gratvlatoria dicata sereniss. ac potentiss Carolo Regi. *Sumptibus Ioh: Waterson*, 1641. 4°.* L, O, LLP, OB, CT; CH, WF, Y.

700 [–] The trvth of the Christian religion. *For for* [*sic*] *Joshua Kirton*, 1651. fol. L, E.

701 **Gilbert, Claudius.** The blessed peace-maker. *For Francis Titon*, 1658. 4°. LT, O, CS, CD, BLH, DT; CH, CLC, MH, NCD.

702 —The libertine school'd. *For Francis Tyton*, 1657. 4°. LT, O, CS, YM, DT; CH, CLC, MWA, NCD, NU, WF.

703 —A pleasant walk to Heaven. *For Francis Titon*, 1658. 4°. LT, O, CS, BLH, DT; CH, CLC, MH, NCD, WSC, Y.

704 —A soveraign antidote. *By R. W. for Francis Titon*, 1658. 4°. LT, O, C, CS, DT; CH, CLC, MH, NCD, NU, Y.

705 **Gilbert, Eleazer.** Newes from Poland. *By E. P. for Nathanael Butter*, 1641. 4°.* L, C, LW; WF, Y.

706 —The prelatical cavalier catechized. *For Robert Leyburn, and Richard Wodenothe*, 1645. 4°.* LT, O, YM, A, DT; CH, MM, NU, WF, Y.

707 Entry cancelled.
[**Gilbert, J.**] The Parliamentary censure of the Jesuites. 1642. *See* Parliaments censvre.

708 [**Gilbert, John.**] An ansvver to the bishop of Condom (now of Meavx). *By H. C. for R. Kettlewel and R. Wells*, 1686. 4°. T.C.II 166. L, O, C, EN, DT; CH, IU, MH, NU, TU, WF, Y.

709 —A sermon on the sin of stealing custom. *Exon: by Sam. Darker, and Sam. Farley, for Charles Yeo*, 1699. 4°.* L, O, LLP, OCC; NU, TU.

710 —A sermon preached . . . January 30th, 1698/9. *Exon: by Sam. Darker, and Sam. Farley, for Charles Yeo*, 1699. 4°. L; TU, WF.

711 — —[Anr. ed.] *By Sam. Darker, for Tho. Bennet*, 1699. 4°. T.C.III 134. L, OM, CS, NE; CH, IU, NU, Y.

711A **Gilbert, Michael.** Schematologia grammatica exemplis. *Excudebat S. Roycroft: impensis Roberti Clavell*, 1681. 8°. T.C.I 453. LIU.

712 **Gilbert, Samuel.** The florists vade-mecum. *For Thomas Simmons*, 1682. 12°. T.C.I 487. L, O, CT; MH, WDA, WF.

713 — —Second edition. *For Thomas Simmons*, 1683. 12°. T.C.II 32. L; CLC, WU, Y.

714 — —"Second" edition. *For T. S. and B. Cox*, 1690. 12°. L.

714A — —"Second" edition. *For J. Taylor and J. Wyatt*, 1693. 12°. T.C.II 430. L; CH, CLC, WU, Y.

715 —Fons sanitatis; or the healing-spring at Willowbridge. *For the author*, 1676. 8°.* L, O.

716 — —[Anr. ed.] —, 1677. 8°.* L.

717 Entry cancelled.
—Gardeners almanack. 1682. *See*—Florists vade-mecum.

718 —The right honourable, pourtraid. *For T. Simmons*, 1682. 12°. T.C.I 512. O.

718A [–] The sweet savour of good actions. *For Giles Widdowes*, 1669. 4°.* WCA.

719 **Gilbert, Thomas.** An assize sermon, preached . . . July the 2d 1657. *By A. M. for Francis Tyton*, 1657. 4°.* L, O, LW; CH, NU, WF, Y.

720 —Illustrissimo Guilielmo Henrico Nassavio. [*n.p.*, 1689.] cap., 4°.* O, LW, OB, CT, DU.

721 —A learned and accurate discourse. *For Nath. Hiller*, 1695. 8°.* L, O, LW, EN; CH, MWA, TO, Y.

721A — —[Anr. ed.] *Published by Richard Baldwin*, 1695. 8°.* EC, EN.

722 —Super auspicatissimo regis Guilielmi. [*n.p.*, 1690.] 4°.* O, C, LG, LW, DU, MR.

723 [–] Θρηνωδη: or, Englands passing-bell. *Printed* 1679. 4°.* L, O, DU, EN; CH, IU, MH, NN, TO, TU, Y.

724 —Vindiciæ supremi Dei Dominii. *Apud J. Martin & Ja. Allestrye*, 1655. 8°.* L, C, LW, OC, SC; Y.

725 **Gilbert, William.** The anglers delight. *By H. B. for Christopher Hussey*, 1676. 12°. MH.

725A — —[Anr. ed.] *For W. Birch*, 1676. 8°. T.C.I 247. L; WF.

726 —The young angler's companion. Second edition. *By H. B. for C. Hussey*, 1682. 8°. T.C.I 510. CB, NN, WU, Y.

726A **[Gilby, Anthony.]** A dialogue between a sovldier of Barvvick. [*London*], *printed* 1642. 4°.* L, EC; MWA.

727   **Gildas.** A description of the state of Great Brittain. *Printed and are to be sold by John Hancock*, 1652. 12°. L, LL, CPL, DT; CH, IU, MH, NP, WF, Y.

728   A gilded pill, for a new moulded presbyter. [*London*], *printed*, 1647. 4°.* LT, O; CSS, MB, MH.

729   Gilderoy. [*London?* 1696.] brs. L, HH.

730   **[Gildon, Charles.]** The history of the Athenian society. *For James Dowley*, [1692]. fol.* L, O, C, EN, DT; CH, MH, MU, WF, Y.

730A [–] Letters and essays. *Printed and are to be sold by Daniel Browne*, 1696. 8°. CN, IU, NC.

731   [–] —[Anr. ed.] —*and Tho. Axe*, 1697. 8°. T.C.II 592. MH.

732   [–] Miscellaneous letters and essays. *For Benjamin Bragg*, 1694. 8°. T.C.II 512. L, O, LSC, LLU, E; BN, CH, CN, MH, WF, Y, AVP.

733   [–] —[Anr. ed.] *By D. Brown and T. Axe*, 1696. 8°. T.C.II 592. CN, RPJ, Y.

733A [–] Miscellany poems upon several occasions. *For Peter Buck*, 1692. 8°. L, O, LW, DU, LLU; CH, CN, MH, TU, WF, Y.

734   —Nuncius infernalis: or, a new account from below. *For Thomas Jones*, 1692. 4°.* L; CN, IU, LC, WF.

735   [–] Phaeton: or, the fatal divorce. *For Abel Roper*, 1698. 4°. L, O, OW, LLU, EN; CH, CN, LC, MH, NC, WF, Y.

735A [–] The post-boy rob'd of his mail. *For John Dunton*, 1692. 12°. L, LV; CLC, CN, MH, MU.

736   [–] The Roman brides revenge. *For John Sturton*, 1697. 4°. L, O, LLU; CH, CN, LC, MH, NC, WF, Y.

736A [–] The second volume of The post-boy. *By J. Wilde, for John Dunton*, 1693. 8°. L, O; CN, IU.

737   [–] The songs in Phaeton. *By J. Heptinstall, for Samuel Scott*, 1698. fol.* L; LC, WF.

737A **G[iles], M[ascall].** A defence of treatise against svperstitious Iesu-worship. *Printed at London for Daniel Frere*, 1643. 4°. LT, O, OC, CT, SC; SE.

738   —A treatise against svperstitiovs Jesv-worship. *By T. P. and M. S. for Andrew Kembe*, 1642. 4°. L, EN, DT; IU, NU.

739   **G[iles], W[illiam].** A defence of Dr. Sherlock's preservative against Popery. *For Brab. Aylmer*, 1688. 4°.* L, O, C, EN, DT; CH, CN, PL, TU, WF, Y.

740   — —Second edition. *For B. Aylmer*, 1688. 4°.* L, O, OC, CT, LSD, DT; CH, CLC, LC, NCD, NP, WF, Y.

741   — —Third edition. —, 1688. 4°.* L, O, C, EN, DT; BN, CLC, IU, MH, NU, WF, Y.

741A — —Fourth edition. —, 1688. 4°.* D, DU, BLH.

741B **Gill, Mrs.** Advertisement. At the sign of the Blew-Ball . . . liveth. [*London*, 1690?] brs. L.

742   **Gill, George.** Col. George Gills case. [*London*, 1649.] brs. MH.

742A **Gill, Henry.** A warning and visitation to the inhabitants of Godalming. *For Thomas Simmons*, 1658. 4°.* LF.

      Gillam, Benjamin. Boston ephemeris. Boston [Mass.], 1684. *See* Almanacs.

743   **Gillespie, George.** Aarons rod blossoming. *By E. G. for Richard Whitaker*, 1646. 4°. LT, O, C, EN, DT; BN, CH, CU, MH, WF, Y.

744   —Second edition. —, 1646. 4°. CU, MU, NU.

744A [–] The ark of the covenant opened. The second part. *For Tho. Parkhurst*, 1677. L, O, C, LCL, BLH; CLC, MH, NPT, NU, WF, Y.

744B [–] The ark of the testament opened. Part I. *By R. C.*, 1661. 4°. L, LW, ON, E, ENC, GU; MH, MWA, NU, PCP.

745   [–] An assertion of the government of the Church of Scotland. *Edinburgh, for Iames Bryson*, 1641. 4°. ALDIS 989. LT, C, LW, E, BLH; CLC, IU, MH, NU, WF, Y.

746   [–] —[Anr. ed.] [*Edinburgh*], *printed*, 1641. 4°. ALDIS 989.5. O, C, CJ, BC; MH, PPT.

      [–] Causes of the Lord's vvrath. [n.p.], 1653. *See* Warriston, Archibald Johnston, *lord*.

      [–] Certain briefe observations. [n.p.], 1644. *See* Robinson, Henry.

747   No entry.

748   [–] A dispute against the English-Popish ceremonies. [*Edinburgh*], *printed*, 1660. 4°. ALDIS 1640.5. LT, O, LMT, AN, CT, ENC; CH, MH, NU, WF, Y.

749   [–] A form for church government and ordination. *For Robert Bostock*, 1647. 4°. LT, O, MR, EN, DT; CH, IU, MBP, MH, NU, Y.

750   [–] The humble representation of the commission . . . 28. Aprile 1648. *Printed at London by Edward Griffin for I. R.*, 1648. 4°.* O, C, OW, GM, AU, BLH; CH, CN, MH, NU, WF, Y.

751   Entry cancelled.

      [–] Edinb. 28. April 1648. post meridiem. The humble representation of the commissioners. 1648. *See* Church of Scotland.

752   [–] CXI propositions concerning the ministerie. *Edinburgh: by Evan Tyler*, 1647. 4°.* ALDIS 1266. L, O, E, EN, ENC; CH, CLC, IU, NPT, NU, Y.

753   [–] A late dialogue betwixt a civilian and a divine. *For Robert Bostock*, 1644. 4°.* LT, O, C, EN, DT; CH, MB, NC, VC, WF.

754   —Malè avdis or an answer. *For Robert Bostocke*, 1646. 4°. LT, O, LCL, CS, EN, DT; CH, MH, MIU, NU, WF, Y.

755   —Nihil respondes: or, a discovery of the extream unsatisfactorinesse. *Printed at London for Robert Bostock*, 1645. 4°.* LT, O, C, EN, GU, DT; CH, IU, MH, NPT, NU, WF, Y.

756   —A sermon preached . . . March 27. 1644. *For Robert Bostock*, 1644. 4°.* LT, O, C, E, BLH; CU, MH, TU, WF, Y. (var.)

756A — —[Anr. ed.] *Edinburgh, Evan Tyler*, 1644. 8°.* ALDIS 1136. O, LW, GU, EN; CH.

757   — —Second edition. *For Robert Bostock*, 1644. 4°.* EN; NU.

758   —A sermon preached . . . 27th. of August. 1645. *By F. Neile for Robert Bostock*, 1645. 4°. LT, O, C, EN, BLH; CH, CU, MH, NU, WF, Y.

759   — —[Anr. ed.] —, 1646. 4°.* O, E, GU; BBE, CH, CU, MH, Y.

760   [–] Theoremata CXI de ministerio. *Edinburgi: excudebat Evanus Tyler*, 1647. 4°.* ALDIS 1287. O, MR, E, EN; IU, NU.

760A [–] —[Anr. ed.] *Juxta exemplar quod* —, 1648. 8°. ALDIS 1345.5. EN.

761 —A treatise of miscellany questions. *Edinburgh, by Gedeon Lithgovv, for George Svvintoun,* 1649. 4°. ALDIS 1367. O, C, LW, E, EN, BLH; CH, CU, MH, MU, NU.

762 — —[Anr. ed.] *Printed at Edinburgh, to be sold at London, by Thomas Whitaker,* 1649. 4°. ALDIS 1367.5. LT, O.

762A —An usefull case of conscience discvssed. *Printed at Edinburgh, by the heires of George Anderson, for Andro Wilson,* 1649. 4°.* ALDIS 1368. 34pp. AU, EN; CH, CU, MH, NU.

763 — —[Anr. ed.] —, 1649. 4°.* ALDIS 1368.5. 28pp. L, O, C, E, EN, DT; CH, CLC, CU, MH, NU, WF, Y.

764 — —[Anr. ed.] *By T. R. and E. M. for Ralph Smith,* 1649. 4°.* LT, ORP, MR, E, EN; CH, MH, MIU, NU.

765 [–] VVholsome severity reconciled. *For Christopher Meredith,* 1645. 4°.* LT, O, CT, YM, EN, DT; CH, MH, NU, WF, Y.

766–7 Entries cancelled.

[**Gillespie, Patrick.**] Ark. 1661. *See* Gillespie, George.

768 **Gilman, Anne.** An epistle to Friends. *Printed,* 1662. 4°.* L, O, LF, BBN; IE, MH, PH, PSC.

768A —To the inhabitants of the earth. [*London*], 1669. brs. LF.

769 [**Gilpin, John.**] The Qvakers shaken: or, a fire brand. *Gateside, by S. B. to [be] sould by Will. London, in Newcastle,* 1653. 4°.* L, LF, NE.

770 — —[Anr. ed.] *For Simon Waterson,* 1653. 4°.* LT, O, CM, LF, MR; CII, IU, PH, PL, PSC.

771 [–] —[Anr. ed., "The Quakers shaken: or, a warning."] *By S. G. for Simon Waterson,* 1655. 4°.* LT, O, C, LSD, EN; CLC, PSC, TO, Y.

772 — —[Anr. ed., "The Quakers shaken: or, a discovery."] *Printed at London, and re-printed in Edinburgh,* 1655. 4°.* ALDIS 1517. EN; CLC.

773 **Gilpin, Randolph.** Liturgica sacra. [*London?*] anno Dom., 1657. 8°. L, O, LLP, CM, EC, P, EN; CII, NU.

774 [**Gilpin, Richard.**] The agreement of the associated ministers . . . Cumberland. *By T. L. for Simon VVaterson, & are sold by Richard Scot in Carlisle,* 1656. 4°. LT, O, CT, BC, LSD; CLC, MH, NU, WF, Y, AVP.

775 —An assize-sermon preach'd . . . September the 10th ann. 1660. *For Tho. Parkhurst; and Sarah Burton, at Newcastle,* 1700. 4°.* T.C.III 160. L, O, LW, EN; IU, MB, NC.

776 [–] The comforts of divine love. *For Tho. Parkhurst. And Sarah Button at Newcastle upon Tyne,* 1700. 8°. T.C.III 160. I, LW; WSG.

777 —Dæmonologia sacra. Or, a treatise. *By J. D. for Richard Randel, and Peter Maplisden, in New-Castle upon Tine,* 1677. 4°. L, O, C, LNC, E; CLC, CU, MH, NU, WF, Y.

778 —The temple re-built. *By E. T. for Luke Fawne, to be sold by Richard Scott, in Carlisle,* 1658. 4°.* O, LW, BC, LSD, ENC; CLC.

Ginckell, Godert de. *See* Athlone, Godert de Ginkell, *earl.*

Ginnor, Sarah. *See* Almanacs: Jinner, Sarah.

779 **Gipps, George.** A sermon preached . . . Novemb. 27. *For Christopher Meredith,* 1645. 4°.* LT, O, C, YM, EN, DT; CH, CU, MH, TU, WF, Y.

779A **G[ipps], T[homas].** The further vindication &c of Mr. Owen. [*London,* 1699.] cap., 4°.* OC; MH.

779B [–] The rector of Bury's reply. [*London,* 1699.] cap., 4°.* MH.

780 —Remarks on remarks. *For Ephraim Johnston, in Manchester,* 1698. 4°. L, O, MC, MP, GU, BLH; CH, MH, NPT, WF.

781 —A sermon against corrupting the word. *For Ephraim Johnston in Manchester,* 1697. 4°.* L, O, C, MC, EN; WF, Y.

781A [–] Tentamen novum: proving. *For E. Johnson, in Manchester, and sold by Hen. Mortlock,* 1696. 8°. L, O, OC, CT, LW; CH, NGT, NU, WF.

782 —Tentamen novum continuatum. Or, an answer to Mr. Owen's plea. *By Tho. Warren, for Ephraim Johnson in Manchester,* 1699. 4°. O, LW, CS, MC, MP, BLH; CLC, NU.

783 —Three sermons. *By H. H. for Walter Kettilby,* 1683. 4°. T.C.II I. L, O, CT, MC, EN; CLC, CN, NGT, NU, WF, Y.

784 **Giraffi, Alessandro.** An exact historie of the late revolutions in Naples. *By R. A. for R. Lowndes,* 1650. 8°. LT, O, CT, MR, EN, BQ; CH, IU, MH, NP, HC.

784A — —[Anr. ed.] *By J. G. for John Williams,* 1650. 8°. CK; CLC, FU, LC, MBA, PU, Y.

785 — —Second edition. *By R. A. for Richard Lowndes,* 1650. 8°. L, C; NIC.

785A — —[Anr. ed.] *For R. Lowndes,* 1650. 8°. CT, LNC; CLC, IU, MH, PL, WF, Y.

786 — —[Anr. ed.] —, 1664. 8°. L, O, C, AN, MR, ENC; CH, IU, MH, NC, WF, Y.

787 — —Fourth edition. *Printed, and are to be sold by Peter Parker,* 1679. 8°. L; CLC, PL, TU.

788 [**Girard, Guillaume.**] The history of the life of the Duke of Espernon. *By E. Cotes, and A. Clark, for Henry Brome,* 1670. fol. T.C.I 20. L, O, C, E, DT; CII, CN, LC, MH, MU, NC, Y.

789 Entry cancelled. Continental printing.

789A **Girnigo, Gilpine.** The remarkable prophesies. *Amsterdam* [*Edinburgh*], *J. Nosche,* 1665. 4°. EN.

790 **Gittos, George.** An elegy on the famous Thomas Thin. *Printed,* 1681/2. brs. L; MH.

Give ear you. [n.p., 1660.] *See* Nayler, James.

791 Entry cancelled.

Give me the willow-garland. [1674–79.] *See* Price, Laurence.

Given to the Elector. *Amsterdam,* 1633 [*i.e.,* 1651]. *See* Douglas, *Lady* Eleanor.

Glad tydings, Christ. 1643. *See* B., J.

Glad tydings of joy. [n.p.], 1643. *See* B., J.

Glad-tydings proclaimed. 1662. *See* Crook, John.

791A Glad-tidings to unfortunate venerial patients. [*London,* 1690?] brs. L.

Gladius justitiæ. 1668. *See* Hascard, Gregory.

Glamorgan, Edward Somerset, *earl. See* Worcester, Edward Somerset, *marquis.*

Glance at the glories. 1657. *See* B., E.

792 A glance on the ecclesiastical commission. *For W. Alchorne,* 1690. 4°.* L, O, CS, SP, CD; CB, CN, MH, NU, WF, Y.

792A **Glanius, W.** A new voyage to the East-Indies. *For H. Rodes,* 1682. 12°. T.C.I 494. CB, IU, LC, MH, WF.

793 — —Second edition. —, 1682. 12°. T.C.I 514. L, O, CT, LLL, DCH; CN, MH, NN, WF, Y, AVP.

794 —A relation of an unfortunate voyage to . . . Bengala. *For Henry Bonwick*, 1682. 8°. T.C.I 485. L, O, OB; CH, LC, MIU, WF, Y.

795 **Glanvill, John.** A panegyrick to the king. *For John Newton*, 1967 [i.e. 1697]. fol.* T.C.III 40. L, O; CLC, NP.

796 —A poem: dedicated to the memory, . . . of Her late sacred Majesty. *For John Newton*, 1695. fol.* T.C.II 550. O, C, LLU; CH, IU, MH, TU, WF, Y.

796A —Some odes of Horace imitated. *For John Newton*, 1690. 4°.* T.C.II 336. L; MH, Y.

796B —A song. [*London*, 1695.] fol.* L.

797 **Glanvill, *Sir* John.** The speech of Sergeant Glanvill, in the vpper Hovse. *Printed*, 1641. 4°.* LT, O, C, MR, DT; CH, CN, MH, TU, WF, Y.

798 [**Glanvill, Joseph.**] An account of Mr. Fergvson his common-place-book. *By Andrew Clark, for Walter Kettilby*, 1675. 4°.* T.C.I 220. L, O, C, WCA, EN, DT; CN, NU, WF, Y.

799 [–] A blow at modern Sadducism. *By E. C. for James Collins*, 1668. 8°. L, CT, DU, EN, GK; CH, CLC, CU, LC, MH, NU, WF, Y.

800 — —Fourth edition. *By E. Cotes for James Collins*, 1668. 8°. T.C.I 7. L, C, E, DT, GK; CH, CN, LC, MH, MU, NU, Y.

801 —Catholick charity recommended. *For H. Eversden, and J. Collins*, 1669. 4°. L, O, CT, EN, DT; CH, MH, NU, OCI, WF, Y.

801A —A discourse concerning the difficulties. *For J. Collins*, 1670. 8°. T.C.I 48. GK.

802 —An earnest invitation. *For John Baker*, 1673. 12°. T.C.I 116. C, OC, CT, BC, WCA, GK; CLC.

803 — —Second edition. —, 1674. 12°. T.C.I 157. O, LW, BR, E; NPT.

804 — —Third edition. —, 1677. 12°. T.C.I 276. O, OC, GK; Y.

804A — —Fourth edition. —, 1680. 12°. C; CH, WF.

805 — —"Fourth" edition. *For John Norton*, 1681. 12°. T.C.I 409. L, GK; MH.

805A — —Sixth edition. *For John Baker*, 1684. 12°. T.C.II 105. L, OC, BR; CLC, IU, NU.

806 — —Seventh edition. *For J. Phillips, and J. Watts*, 1688. 12°. T.C.II 263. L, O; CLC, LC, WSC.

806A — —"Seventh" edition. *For J. Baker*, 1688. 12°. EN.

806B — —"Seventh" edition. *For J. Philips*, 1695. 12°. O, GK; CLC, FU, LC.

807 — —Eighth edition. *For J. Phillips and M. Wotton*, 1700. 12°. T.C.III 222. L, O, LW, BR, GK; CLC, NGT, WF, Y.

808 [–] An essay concerning preaching. *By A. C. for H. Brome*, 1678. 8°. T.C.I 309. L, O, CT, NPL, DT; CH, IU, MH, NU, WF, Y.

809 —Essays on several important subjects. *By J. D. for John Baker, and Henry Mortlock*, 1676. 4°. T.C.I 246. L, O, C, EN, DT; BN, CH, CN, LC, MH, MU, NU, WF, Y.

810 —Mr Joseph Glanvill's full vindication. *For John Salusbury*, 1691. brs. L; TU.

811 [–] A further discovery of M. Stubbe. *For H. Eversden*, 1671. 4°.* T.C.I 73. L, C, OC, DU, GK; CH, MIU, MMO, NU, Y.

812 [–] Λογου θρησκεια: or, a seasonable recommendation. *By E. C. and A. C. for James Collins*, 1670. 4°. T.C.I 34. L, O, OC, CT, DU, EN; CH, CU, NU, WF, Y.

813 [–] A loyal tear dropt. *By E. Cotes, to be sold by James Collins*, 1667. 4°.* L, O, C, BR, GK; CH, IU, MH, NP, TU, WF, Y.

813A [–] —[Anr. ed.] *For James Collins, to be sold by Abisha Broccas, in Exon*, 1667. 4°.* NP, WF.

814 [–] Lux orientalis, or an enquiry. *Printed, and are to be sold at Cambridge, and Oxford*, 1662. 8°. L, O, C, ENC, CD; CLC, CU, LC, MH, MU, WF, Y.

815 [–] —[Anr. ed.] *For J. Collins, and S. Lowndes*, 1682. 8°. O, LCL, CS, OME, ES; CLC, IU, MBA, NU, PL, WF, Y.

816 Entry cancelled. Ghost.

817 —Philosophia pia; or, a discourse. *By J. Macock for James Collins*, 1671. 8°. T.C.I 57. L, O, C, E, DT; CLC, CN, MH, WF, HC.

817A [–] A philosophical endeavour towards the defence of the being of witches. *By J. Grismond for James Collins*, 1666. 4°. L, DM.

818 [–] —[Anr. ed.] *Printed*, 1668. 8°. L, O, LN, A; CLC, MH, MIU, MMO, NU.

819 [–] —[Anr. ed.] *By E. Cotes for James Collins*, 1668. 8°. O, GU; CN, NU.

820 —Plus ultra. *For James Collins*, 1668. 8°. L, O, C, AN, EN, DT; CH, CU, LC, MH, MMO, NU, WF, Y.

821 —A præfatory answer to Mr. Henry Stubbe. *By A. Clark, for J. Collins*, 1671. 8°. T.C.I 57. L, O, CT, ENC, ES; CLC, MH, NU, WF, HC.

822 —Saducismus triumphatus. *For J. Collins, and S. Lownds*, 1681. 8°. T.C.I 440. L, O, C, CT, E; CH, CN, MH, TU, WF, Y.

822A [–] —[Anr. ed.] *Printed*, 1682. 8°. NCU.

823 — —Second edition. *By Tho. Newcomb, for S. Lownds*, 1682. 8°. T.C.I 488. L, O, C, BQ, E; CH, CU, LC, MH, V, JF.

824 — —"Second" edition. *For S. Lownds*, 1688. 8°. LMT; IAU, NU, SW, TO.

824A — —Third edition. —, 1688. 8°. NIC.

824B — —"Third" edition. —, 1689. 8°. OC; TU.

825 — —"Third" edition. *For S. L. to be sold by Anth. Baskervile*, 1689. 8°. L, O, AN, BR, ELY, NE; CH, MH, MMO, NCU, VC, Y.

826 — —"Third" edition. *For A. L. and sold by Roger Tuckyr*, 1700. 8°. L, O, EN, GU, DT, GK; CLC, MBP, PU, V, WF, Y.

826A [–] —[Anr. ed.] *Printed*, 1700. 8°. CH.

827 —Scepsis scientifica: or, confest ignorance, the way to science. *By E. Cotes for Henry Eversden*, 1665. 4°. L, O, C, EN, DT; BN, CH, CN, LC, MBP, MH, MMO, MU, WF, Y.

828 —Scire/i tuum nihil est: or, the authors defence of the vanity of dogmatizing. *By E. C. for Henry Eversden*, 1665. 4°. L, O, CS, GU, BQ; CH, CLC, MBP, NA, PL, WF, Y.

829 [–] A seasonable defence of preaching. *By M. Clark, for H. Brome*, 1678. 12°. L, O, LW, DT, GK; CH, IU, NC, NU, Y.

830 —Seasonable reflections and discourses. *By R. W. for H. Mortlock*, 1676. 8°. T.C.I 227. L, O, C, EN, DT; CLC, CU, NU, WF, Y.

831 —Some discourses, sermons. *For Henry Mortlock, and James Collins*, 1681. 4°. T.C.I 448. L, O, LCL, E, DT; CLC, CU, MH, NU, WF, Y.

832   [–] Some philosophical considerations touching the being of witches. *By E. C. for James Collins,* 1667. 4°. L, O, C, YM, GU, DM; CH, CN, MH, WF, Y, JF.

832A   [–] ——Second edition. —, 1667. 4°. CLC.

833   [–] Two choice and vsefvl treatises. *For James Collins, and Sam. Lowndes,* 1682. 8°. T.C.I 515. L, O, CT, EN, DT; CLC, CU, MH, NU, WF, Y.

834   —The vanity of dogmatizing. *By E. C. for Henry Eversden,* 1661. 8°. LT, O, C, ES, DT; CH, CN, LC, MH, MU, NU, WF, Y.

835   —The way of happiness. *By E. C. & A. C. for James Collins,* 1670. 8°. L, O, CE, BC, CD; CLC, CU, LC, MH, NU, Y.

836   ——[Anr. ed.] *For James Collins,* 1677. 12°. L, O, CS; CH, NN.

836A   ——[Anr. ed.] *For Gedeon Schaw in Edinburgh,* 1671. 12°. CN.

837   [–] The zealous, and impartial Protestant. *By M. C. for Henry Brome,* 1681. 4°. T.C.I 420. L, O, C, AN, EN, DT; CH, CU, MH, NU, WF, Y.

838   ——[Anr. ed.] —, 1681. 4°. O, C, LCL, E, EN; TU, WF, Y.

839   **Glanville, Ranulphe *de*.** Tractatvs de legibus. *By J. Streater, H. Twyford, and E. Flesher, the assigns of R. Atkins and E. Atkins, and are to be sold by G. Sawbridge, J. Place, J. Bellinger, W. Place, T. Basset, R. Pawlet, C. Wilkinson, T. Dring, W. Jacob, C. Harper, J. Aymery, J. Pool, J. Leigh,* 1673. 8°. T.C.I 144. O, CS, LL, DU, EN, DT; BN, LC, MHL, NCL, NRU, WF, Y, YL.

    [Glapthorne, Henry.] His Majesties gracious answer to the message. 1643. *See* Charles I.

    [–] Revenge for honour. 1654. *See* Chapman, George.

840   —White-Hall. A poem. *For Francis Constable,* 1643. 4°.* LT, O; CH, Y.

841   No entry.

842   **Glascock, John.** Mary's choice. *By J. H. for Samuel Gellibrand,* 1659. 4°. O, LW, DU; CH, IU, MWA, NU, WF, Y.

843   **Glaser, Christophe.** The compleat chymist. *For John Starkey,* 1677. 8°. T.C.I 273. L, O, C, LCS, GU; CLC, MH, WF, WU, Y.

843A   **Glasgow. Faculty of Surgeons.** Act . . . in favours of poor diseased people. [7 March 1698.] [*Glasgow,* 1698.] brs. ALDIS 3721.3. EN.

    Glass for the people. [n.p.], 1676. *See* Groome, Samuel.

    Glasse for the times. 1648. *See* C., T.

844   A glasse for vveak ey'd citizens. *For Tho: Underhil, Iune* 19. 1646. 4°.* LT; CU, MH, NU, WF, Y.

845   **Glauber, John Rudolph.** The works of. *By Thomas Milbourn, for the author, to be sold at his house; by D. Newman, and W. Cooper,* 1689. fol. T.C.II 275. L, O, LCS, CT, EN; CH, CNM, LC, NN, Y.

845A   ——Second edition. *For the author, to be sold at his house, and by S. Manship,* 1694. fol. PU.

846   —A description of new philosophical furnaces. *By Richard Coats, for Tho: Williams,* 1651. 4°. LT, CT, BR, GU, DT; BN, CH, CJC, LC, MH, WF, Y.

847   [–] Proposals for printing all the works of. 1687. fol.* LG (lost).

848   **Gleane, *Sir* Peter.** An elegy on the death of the Queen. *For Sam. Heyrick,* 1695. fol.* O, LSD; CH, CLC, IU, MH, TU, WF, Y.

848AA   —Gemitus & triumphus. A dream. [*London?* 1693.] brs. EN.

848A   [–] A poem, occasioned by the . . . funeral of . . . Queen Mary II. *For Tho. Chapman, and John Graves, and are to be sold by John Whitlock,* 1695. fol.* L; CH, IU, MH, TU, WF, Y.

848B   Gleanings of refreshment. *By James Young for Thomas Slater,* 1651. 12°. OC.

    Gleanings; or, a collection. 1651. *See* Grove, Robert.

849   **Glemham, *Sir* Thomas.** The declaration of. *For R. W.,* 1648. 4°.* LT, BLH; CH, CSS.

850   —By the governour. I desire that present notice. *Printed at Oxford by Leonard Lichfield,* 1645. brs. MADAN 1834; STEELE 2640. O.

850A   **Glencairn, William Conningham, *earl of*.** A letter from . . . to the governour of Badgenoth. [*Leith*], printed, 1654. 8°.* ALDIS 1491.7. EN; CH, WF.

    Glimpse of eternity. 1667. *See* Caley, Abraham.

851   A glimpse of glory. 1657. 8°. E.

852   A glimpse of joy for the happy restoring. *For John Andrews,* [1660]. brs. LT.

    Glimpse of Sions glory. 1641. *See* Goodwin, Thomas.

    Glimps of the King of glory. 1672. *See* J., T.

853   **Glisson, Francis. . . .** Anatomia hepatis. *Typis Du-Gardianis, impensis Octaviani Pullein,* 1654. 8°. L, O, C, E, DT; BN, CLC, CNM, NAM, WSG, HC.

854   —De rachitide. *Typis Guil. Du-gardi, impensis Laurenti Sadler & Roberti Beaumont,* 1650. 8°. L, O, CT, GH, DT; BN, MMO, PL, TO, WSG, HC.

855   ——[Anr. ed.] *Impensis Joonnis Williams,* 1655. 8°. Y.

856   ——Second cdition. *Typis Th. Roycroft; impensis Laurentii Sadler,* 1660. 12°. L, LCS, CT, E, DT; BN, CH, LC, WSG.

857   Entry cancelled. Continental printing.

858   —Tractatus de natura. *Typis E. Flesher, prostat venalis apud H. Brome & N. Hooke,* 1672. 4°. T.C.I 120. L, O, C, E, DT; BN, CJC, CLC, NP, PU, TO, HC.

859   —Tractatus de ventriculo et intestinis. *Typis E. F. prostat venalis apud Henricum Brome,* 1677. 4°. T.C.I 257. L, O, C, GH, DM; BH, MH, MIU, MMO, WSG, HC.

860   —A treatise of the 'rickets.' *By Peter Cole,* 1651. 12°. LT, LCS, LWL, DC, MAU, GH; BN, HC.

861   ——[Anr. ed.] *By J. Streater,* 1668. 8°. O, LCP; BN, MIU, MMO, NAM, WSG.

862   **Glisson, William.** The common law epitomiz'd. *For Henry Brome,* 1661. 8°. LT, DC; CLC.

863   ——Second edition. *By the assigns of Rich. and Edw. Atkins, for Hen. Brome and Tho. Basset, to be sold by Tho. Burrel, and George Downes,* 1679. 8°. T.C.I 338. C, LI, LIL, OC, NOT; CH, LC, MIU, NC, WF.

864   ——Third edition. *By the assigns of Rich. and Edw. Atkins; to be sold by Tho. Burrel, and Geo. Downes,* 1679. 8°. O, C, LIL, LL, EN; MH, NCL.

865   ——"Third" edition. *By the assigns of Rich. and Edw. Atkins; for Hen. Brome and Tho. Basset,* 1679. 8°. L, O; MHL.

866   —A survey of the law. *For Henry Brome, and Thomas Basset,* 1659. 8°. LT, CD, DT; CH, PUL, WF, YL.

    Globe notes. 1666. *See* H., R.

867 Gloria Britanica [sic]: or, a panegyrick. *By J. B. for Andrew Crook*, 1661. 4°.* LT; CH, MH.

Gloria Britannica, or, the boast. 1689. *See* B., A.

Gloria Deo. [n.p., 1696.] *See* C., G.

Glories of Heaven. 1699. *See* Larkin, George. World to come.

867A Glorifying of God. *For J. Robinson*, 1698. T.C.III 51. LW, CT; CLC, MWA.

868 A glorious and happy victory obtained by the volluntiers of Buckingham. *For I. H. and J. Wright, December 8.* 1642. 4°.* LT.

868A Glorious and miraculuos [sic] battell at York. *Edinburgh, J. Lindesay*, 1644. brs. ALDIS 1136. 5. EN.

Glorious excellencie. 1645. *See* G., M.

Glorious glimmerings. 1663. *See* Perrot, John.

Glorious lover. 1679. *See* Keach, Benjamin.

Glorious name of God. 1643. *See* Burroughes, Jeremiah.

Glorious truth. 1653. *See* Levitt, William.

868B The glorious conquest: or, the repeated victory of . . . the Earl of Marlborough. *[London], for P. Brooksby, J. Deacon, J. Blare, and J. Back*, [1690]. brs. O.

869 Aprill the 15. 1642. A glorious victory, obtained by S. Henry Tichbourne. *Printed at London for John Wright*, 1642. 4°.* LT, O, EC; MH.

870 A glorious victory obtained by Sᵣ. Thomas Fairfax, Jvne, the 14. 1645. *For Robert Wood*, 1645. 4°.* LT, O.

871 A glorious victorie, obtained by Sir VVilliam VValler. *[London], April 1. for Thomas Bates*, 1644. 4°.* E; MBP, MH, NU.

871A A gloriovs victory obtained by the Scots. *For Iohn Thomas*, 1641[2]. 4°.* L, O, LNC; Y.

872 Entry cancelled.

Glorious victory obtained over the rebels at Dundalke. 1642. *See* . . . Glorious victory obtained by S. Henry Tichbourne.

Glory and happiness of the saints. 1692. *See* Ranew, Nathaniel.

Glory be to God. 1652. *See* Hartlib, Samuel.

873 The glory of a true church. *For Tho. Banks*, 1647. 4°.* LT, CT, DT; CH, LC, NU.

Glory of Christ. 1647. *See* Collier, Thomas.

873A The glory of Christ's light vvithin. *[London], printed*, 1669. 4°.* L, O, C, LF, BBN; IE, MU, NU, PH, PSC, Y.

874 The glory of dying in war. *By J. C.*, 1672. brs. L, MC; CH.

875 Entry cancelled.

Glory of free grace display'd. 1680. *See* Lobb, Stephen.

Glory of God's revenge. [n.p.], 1685. *See* Reynolds, John.

Glory of our English fleet. 1673. *See* I., D.

876 The glory of the British seas. *By George Croom*, 1697. brs. L, MC; MH.

877 The glory of the English nation. *For W. Bucknel*, 1681. brs. L, O; MH.

877A —[Anr. ed.] *By George Croom*, 1689. brs. MH.

878 The glorie of the Lord arising. *For Giles Calvert*, 1654. 4°.* LT, O, LF.

879 —[Anr. ed.] —, 1655. 4°.* L, LF, BBN; MH, NCD, PSC.

Glory of the new covenant. [n.p., 1664.] *See* Smith, William.

880 The glory of the Sun-Tavern. *For J. Lutton*, 1672. brs. L.

881 The glory of the West. *For Charles Gustavus*, [1660]. brs. L, O; MH.

882 —[Same title.] *For James Dean*, 1685. brs. O, LG, HH.

883 The glory of these nations. *For Charles Tyus*, [1660]. brs. L.

884 The glory of this kingdome. *For R. R.*, 1643. 4°.* LT, DT; CLC, IU, MH, MU, Y.

Glory of women. 1652. *See* Agrippa, Henricus Cornelius.

Glory sometimes afar off. 1653. *See* Higgenson, Thomas.

Glory to God. [1659.] *See* Nayler, James.

Glory's resurrection. 1698. *See* Settle, Elkanah.

Glossographia: or. 1656. *See* Blount, Thomas.

884A **Gloucester.** At a common councell there held . . . [22 August 1656.] *[London, 1656.]* brs. LT.

884B Gloucester's triumph. *By J.C. for H. Fletcher*, 1660. 4°.* CH.

885 The Gloucester-shire ministers testimony. *By John Clowes*, 1648. 4°.* LT, O, BC, YM; CLC, MIU, Y.

886 —[Anr. ed.] *Re-printed at Edinburgh by Evan Tyler*, 1648. 4°.* ALDIS 1324. EN; CH, MIU, NU, WF, Y.

887 The Gloucestershire tragedy. *[London, 1700?]* brs. L, HH.

888 **Glover, Habakkuk.** An essay, to discover the principal causes. *[London? 1665.]* cap., 4°.* CN, RPJ.

889 **Glover, Henry.** Cain and Abel parallel'd. *By E. Cotes for Henry Brome*, 1664. 4°.* L, O, C; IU, WF.

889A ——[Anr. ed.] *For Henry Brome, to be sold by William Churchill in Dorchester*, 1664. 4°.* Y.

889B —Ἐκδίκησις or a discourse of vengeance. *For Henry Brome, to be sold by William Churchill in Dorchester*, 1664. 4°.* O, OC.

890 —An exhortation to prayer for Jerusalems peace. *By E. Cotes for William Church-hill, in Dorchester*, 1663. 4°.* L, O, C, CJ; NU, WF, ZWT.

[Glyn, *Sir* John.] Monarchy asserted. 1660. *See* Whitelock, Bulstrode.

891 —The replication of Master Glyn. *Printed*, 1641. 4°.* LT, O, C, LIU, MR; CH, CU, LC, MH, NU, WF, Y. (var.)

891A —The replication of Mᵣ Glyn. *Printed*, 1641. 4°.* LT, O, C, CT, AN, MR; CH, CLC, MH, NP, WF.

892 —Master Glyn's reply to the Earle of Straffords defence. *For Lawrence Chapman*, 1641. 4°.* L, O, OC.

893 —Die Mercurii, 21. July 1641, Master Glyns report: The case of the vintners. *[London], printed*, 1641. brs. STEELE 1872. LT.

893A —Master Glyn his speech in Parliament, on Wednesday, the fifth of Ianuary. *Loudon [sic], printed* 1642. 4°.* CCA; CN, MIU.

894 —Mr. Glyn, his speech in Parliament, vpon the reading of the accusation . . . February 19 . . . 1641. *For Iohn Hammond*, 1642. 4°.* LT, O, C, BC, MR; CH, CN, LC, MH, MU, WF, Y.

895 —A speech made in Parliament . . . 5 of January 1641. *For B.W.*, 1641. 4°.* LT, O, LVF, BC, DU; CH, CN, MH, NU, WF, Y.

895A ——[Anr. ed.] —, 1642. 4°.* CCA.

Γνωθι σεαυτον. Nosce teipsum. 1688. *See* Davies, *Sir John.*

Go in peace. 1674. *See* Martin, John.

896 **Goad, Christopher.** Refreshing drops. *By R. W. for Giles Calvert,* 1653. 4°. LT, O, CK, P; CLC, MH, NU, WF, Y.

896A **Goad, John.** Aphorismi astro-meteorologici collecti. *O. Blagrave,* 1686. UNIVERSITY OF OKLAHOMA.

897 —Astro-meteorologica, or aphorism's and discourses. *By J. Rawlins, for Obadiah Blagrave,* 1686. fol. T.C.II 167. L, OB, CT, BAMB, EN; CH, CU, LC, MH, PL, WF.

898 —Astro-meteorologia sana. *Prostant venales apud Samuelem Tidmarsh,* 1690. 4°. T.C.II 337. L,O, C, EN, DT; WF.

899 Entry cancelled. *See following entry.*

900 [–] Autodidactice. A plain & pleasant rode for the Latin scholar. *By J. Rawlins, for H. Bonwicke,* 1687. 8°. T.C.II 201. O, DU; Y.

900A —Genealogicon latinum: a small dictionary. Second edition. *For N. Brook,* 1676. 8°. SP; MH.

901 —'Η ημερα εκεινη. An Advent sermon. *By Tho. Ratcliff, for Humphry Robinson,* 1663. 4°.* L, O, LLP, LP; MH, MWA.

902 [–] Παντα δοκιμαζετε. A sermon. *By J. R. for Humphrey Robinson,* 1664. 4°.* L, O, LP, OCC, EN; CLC, MH, NU.

903 [–] The rudiments of the Latine tongue. *For O. Blagrave,* 1681. 8°. T.C.I 445. C.

904 **Goad, Thomas.** Stimlvvs [*sic*] orthodoxvs. *For William Leak,* 1661. 4°.* L, O, OC, DU, SP, DT; CLC, NU.

904A The goaler's extortion exposed. colop: *Printed aud* [*sic*] *published by Randal Taylor,* [1690]. fol.* O; CN, MH.

904B **Gobert, John.** A true and lively character of a . . . church-member. *By Charles Sumptner for Tho: Brewster, and Greg: Moule,* 1650. 4°.* L, O; Y.

904C **Gobinet, Charles.** Instruction concerning penance. *By J. B. and are to be sold by Mathew Turner and John Tootell,* 1689. 8°. L, BSM; CLC, CN, MSL, WF, WG.

904D —The instruction of youth. *By Henry Hills,* 1687. 8°. L, O; CLC, CN, MSL, WF.

Goblins. 1646. *See* Suckling, *Sir* John.

905 God Almighty call to the healthy. *By George Larkin,* 1687. brs. L.

God and his cloud. 1652. *See* M., J.

God and Mammon. 1646. *See* Sheppard, Samuel.

God and the king: or. [n.p.], 1649. *See* Jenkins, David.

905A God and the King, or monarchy proved. [*London*], 1680. brs. HH.

God and the king. 1663. *See* Mocket, Richard.

906 God appearing for the Parliament. *Printed at London for Edward Husbands.* March 10. 1644[5]. 4°.* LT, O, CT, BP, YM, DT; CH, INU, MH, WF, Y.

God fighting for vs. [n.p.], 1642. *See* B., W.

906A God give you joy . . . a marriage-present. [*London*], *printed,* 1691. 8°. T.C.II 418. O.

God glorified. 1696. *See* S., A.

God made man. 1675. *See* Butler, John.

God save the king. Edinburgh, 1660. *See* Lawrie, Robert.

907 Entry cancelled.

God save the king. At Edjnbvrgh the fifth day of February. Edinburgh, 1649. *See* Scotland. Estates. Estates of Parliament presently.

907A God speed the plow. [*London*], *for W. Gilbertson,* [1640–65.] brs. EUING 127. GU.

908 —[Anr. ed.] *For W. Thackeray, T. Passenger, and W. Whitwood,* [1670–77]. brs. L, CM, HH.

909 —[Anr. ed.] [*London*], *for J. Clarke, W. Thackeray, and T. Passinger,* [1684–86]. brs. HH.

910 **Godard, Thomas.** The deemon of Marleborough. [*London*], *printed,* 1675. 4°.* L.

Godart, [Jean]. *See* Goedaert, Johannes.

911 **Godbolt, John.** Reports of certain cases. *By T. N. for W. Lee, D. Pakeman, and Gabriel Bedell,* 1652. 4°. L, O, LL, CT, DT; CH, LC, MHL, NCL, WF, AVP.

912 ——[Anr. ed.] *By T. N. for W. Lee, D. Pakeman, and G. Bedell,* 1653. 4°. L, OC, CS, EN, DT; CH, CLC, KYU, LC, V.

913 **Goddard, Ezekiel.** To the King's most excellent majesty, . . . the humble petition of. [*London?* 1700.] cap., 4°.* L, DT; MH.

914 **Goddard, Jonathan.** A discourse setting forth the unhappy condition. *By John Martyn and James Allestry,* 1670. 4°. T.C.I 26. L, O, C, GU, DT; BN, CH, CN, LC, MH, NU, WF, Y.

915 — . . . Medicamenta Goddardiana. [*London*], *in the Savoy: by Edw. Jones, and sold by Porter Holme, apothecary,* 1688. brs. L.

916 **Goddard, Thomas.** Miscellanea. *By E. C. for Tho. William, and Will. Thompson, at Harborough,* 1661. 4°. L, O, LCL; IU, NC, NU.

916A ——[Anr. ed.] *By E. C. and are to be sold by Richard Gammon,* 1661. 4°. CLC.

917 —Plato's demon. *By H. Hills, jun., for Walter Kettilby,* 1684. 8°. T.C.II 50. L, O, C, BAMB, DT; BN, CH, CN, LC, MH, WF, Y.

918 [**Godden, Thomas.**] Catholicks no idolaters. [*London*], *printed,* 1672. 8°. L, O, C, MC, DT; BN, CH, CN, MH, WF, Y.

919 [–] A iust discharge to Dr. Stillingfleet's unjvst charge. *Paris, for René Guignard,* 1677. 12°. L, O, C, EN, DT; CH, CN, NU, WF, Y.

920 —A sermon of St. Peter, . . . twenty ninth of June, 1686. *By Henry Hills,* 1686. 4°.* L, O, C, EN, DT; CH, IU, MH, MIU, NU, WF, Y.

920A —[Anr. ed.] —, 1688. 4°.* MH, NN.

921 —A sermon of the nativity. *By Henry Hills,* 1686. 4°.* L, DUS; NU, RBU, WF.

922 —A sermon of the transfiguration. *By Henry Hills,* 1688. 4°.* L, O, LLP, EC; IU, TU.

922A The goddesses glory. [*London*], *for J. Deacon,* [1655]. brs. O.

923 **Godeau, Antoine, bp.** The life of the apostle St. Paul. *By James Young for Henry Twyford,* 1653. 12°. LT, O, C, P; CLC, WF.

924 **Godefroy, Jacques.** The history of the United Provinces of Achaia. *By Andrew Clark for Jonathan Edwin,* 1673. 4°. T.C.I 149. L, OC, C, DU, DT; CH, IU, MH, NC, WF, Y.

God-father's advice. 1699. See R., J.

[**Godfrey, Michael.**] Brief account of the intended. 1694. See Paterson, William.

925 [–] A short account of the Bank of England. colop: *For John Whitlock*, 1695. cap. 4°.* L, O, LG, LUG; INU, MH, NC, Y.

925A [–] —[Anr. ed., "reprinted."][*London*, 1695?] 4°.* LUG; MH.

926 [**Godfrey, N.**] A joyfull message for all loyall subjects. *For Iohn Terrie*, 1647. 4°.* LT, DT; INU.

927 **Godfrey, Robert.** Various injuries & abuses in . . . physick. *By John Darby, for Richard Jones*, 1674. 8°. T.C.I 163. L, O, LCS, LWL, CCA; CH, NN, WSG.

927A Godfrey earle of Augy or Ewe in Normandy . . . had issue [genealogical table]. [*London*, 1647?] brs. LPR. (var.)

Godfrey of Bulloigne. 1687. See Tasso, Torquato.

927B **Godfridus.** The knowledge of things unknowne. *By A.N. for Iohn Stafford*, 1641. 8°. O.

928 — —[Anr. ed.] *By T. B. for John Stafford*, 1649. 8°. L, O.

929 — —[Anr. ed.] *By T. W. for John Stafford*, 1658. 8°. C.

929A — —[Anr. ed.] [*London*], *For John Stafford, to be sold by Charles Tyus*, [1660?]. 8°. L; CLC.

929B — —[Anr. ed.] *For Iohn Stafford, to be sold by Francis Coles*, 166[3?]. 8°. WF.

930 — —[Anr. ed.] *By G. P. for George Sawbridge*, 1668. 8°. C, LWL; CH.

930A — —[Anr. ed.] *By R. W. for Will. Thackeray*, 1673. 8°. L(imp.); Y.

931 — —[Anr. ed.] *For W. T. to be sold by J. Hose*, 1676. 8°. L.

931AA — —[Anr. ed.] *For W. Thackeray*, 1679. 8°. CN.

931A — —[Anr. ed.] [*London*], *by M. H. & are to be sold by W. Thackeray*, 1683. 8°. T.C.II 52. L; CLC, MH.

931B — —[Anr. ed.] [*London*], *for W. Thackeray*, 1685. 8°. LWL; MH.

932 — —[Anr. ed.] [*London*], *by J. M. for W. Thackeray*, [1688]. 8°. L, O.

933 — —[Anr. ed.] *By J. M. for W. Thackeray*, 1691. 8°. L; IU.

933A — —[Anr. ed.] [*London*], *by W. O. for T. Thackeray*, [1693]. 8°. CLC, MH, WF, Y.

933B — —[Anr. ed.] [*London*], *by W. W. for W. Thackeray* [1697]. 8°. CJC, MH.

933C — —[Anr. ed.] [*London*], *by W. Wilde for H. Rhodes*, [1697]. 8°. T.C.III 58. L, LWL.

933D — —[Anr. ed.] [*London*], *for H. Rhodes*, [1700?] 8°. MR; IU.

933E **Godley, Ar.** Grounds of grammar. *For M. Turner*, 1673. 8°. T.C.I 135. L (t.p.).

933F Godliness no friend to rebellion. *For George Palmer*, 1674. 4°.* O, WCA.

Godly and wholsome doctrine. [n.p., 1685.] See Johnson, Samuel.

933G A godly ballad of the creation. [*n.p.*, 1670?] brs. LNC.

933H A godly ballad of the just man Job. *For F. Coles, J. Wright, T. Vere, and W. Gilbertson*, [1655–58]. brs. L.

933I —[Anr. ed.] [*London*], *for F. Coles, T. Vere, I. Wright, J. Clarke, W. Thackeray, and T. Passenger*, [1678–80]. brs. L, CM, HH; MH.

933J A godly ballad of the just mandate. [*London*], *for F. Coles, T. Vere, and J. Wright*, [1663–74]. brs. O.

Godly-fear. 1674. See Alleine, Richard.

934 Entry cancelled.

Godly guide of directions. [167–?] See Tipping, Robert.

935 The godly maid of Leicester. [*London*], *by E. C. for F. Coles, T. Vere, and J. Wright*, [1675]. brs. EUING 129. L, O, GU.

935A —[Anr. ed.] [*London*], *for F. Coles, T. Vere, J. Wright, J. Clarke, W. Thackery, and T. Passinger*, [1678–1680]. brs. MH.

935B —[Anr. ed.] [*London*], *for J. Clark, W. Thackeray, and Thomas Passenger*, [1684–86]. brs. L, CM.

Godly man's delight. [n.p., 1679.] See W., T.

Godly man's enquiry. 1688. See H., S.

936 The godly mans instructions. [*London*], *for Philip Brooksby*, [1672]. brs. HH.

937 The godly man's legacy to the saints. *Printed*, 1680. 4°.* T.C.I 393. L, O, LW, CCH, CS, CT; CLC, CU, MBA, NU, WF, Y.

Godly mans portion. [n.p.], 1663. See Alleine, Richard.

937A A godly new ballad intituled, A dozen of points. [*London*], *for F. Coles, T. Vere, and W. Gilbertson*, [1658–64]. brs. EUING 126. O, GU.

937B —[Anr. ed.] [*London*], *for T. Coles, T. Vere, J. Wright, and J. Clark*, [1674–79]. brs. O, CM.

937C —[Anr. ed.] [*London*], *for W. Thackeray and T. Passinger*, [1686–88]. brs. MH.

Godly sermon. 1680. See Hart, John.

938 A godly song, intitul'd, The earnest petition of a faithful Christian clark of Bodnam. *By and for W. W.*, [1670]. brs. L.

938A A godly warning for all maidens. *For [F. Coles, T. Vere . . ., 1670?]*. brs. O (impf.).

939 A godly warning for all maidens. *For A. M. W. O. and T. Thackeray*, [1680–85]. brs. EUING 128. L, O, CM, HH, GU.

940 —[Anr. ed.] *By and for W. O. and to be sold by C. Bates*, [1700?]. brs. HH.

940A **Godman, Henry.** A funeral sermon preached . . . June 3. 1688. *For Nath. Crouch*, 1688. 4°.* LW; Y.

941 **Godman, William.** [Hebrew] Filius heröum, the son of nobles. *By J. Flesher, for W. Morden in Cambridge*, 1660. 4°.* L, O, C NE, DT; CLC, CN, MH, NU, WF, Y.

941A **Godolphin, Francis.** The case of. [*London? 1698.*] brs. L, O; CH.

942 **Godolphin, John.** Catalogus variorum & insignium librorum. [*Londini*], 11 *Nov.* 1678. 4°. L, O, C, OP, CE; CH, NG.

943 —The holy arbor. *By John Field for Edmund Paxton, and William Roybould*, 1651. fol. L, O, C, BC, LCL; CH, IU, LC, MBC, NC, NPT, NU, Y.

944 —The holy limbeck. *By John Field for Edmund Paxton*, 1650. 12°. LSC, DT; CH, NU.

945 Entry cancelled. *See preceding entry.*

946 —The orphans legacy. *By E. T. and R. H. and are to be sold by Joseph Nevill, and Christopher Wilkinson*, 1674. 4°. T.C.I 155. L, O, C, OM, DT; BN, CH, CN, MHL, NCL, WG.

947 — —Second edition. *For Chr. Wilkinson*, 1677. 4°. T.C.I 263. L, O, C, LMT, LNC, DT; BN, CH, FU, LC, MHL, NC.

948 — —Third edition. *By the assigns of Richard and Edward Atkins, for Christopher Wilkinson,* 1685. 4°. T.C.II 150. L, O, C, LGI, LL; CH, LC, MHL, NC, WF, YL.

949 —Repertorium canonicum. *By S. Roycroft, for Christopher Wilkinson,* 1678. 4°. T.C.I 303. L, C, LL, LNC, DT; CLC, LC, MHL, NCL, NU.

949A — —Second edition. *By the assigns of R. and E. Atkins for C. Wilkinson,* 1680. 4°. CT, PC; NU.

950 — —"Second" edition. *By S. Roycroft, for Christopher Wilkinson,* 1680. 4°. T.C.I 376. L, O, C, DU, DT; BN, CLC, IU, LC, MHL, NCL, WF, YL.

951 — —Third edition. *By the assigns of R. and E. Atkins, for Christopher Wilkinson,* 1687. 4°. T.C.II 213. L, LMT, OC, OM, BR, CD; CLC, CU, MHL, NCL, WF, YL.

952 —Συνηγορος θαλασσιος. A vievv of the admiral iurisdiction. *By W. Godbid for Edmund Paxton, and John Sherley,* 1661. 8°. L, O, C, NE, DT; BN, CLC, CN, MHL, NCL, WF, YL.

953 — —Second edition. *For and sold by George Dawes,* 1685. 8°. L, O, LI, LNM, CP; CH, MB, MHL, NCL, WF.

God's blessing. 1648. *See* Fitzjeffrey, Charles.
God's call. 1663. *See* P., T.
Gods deliverance. 1642. *See* Grant, John.

954 God's glory vindicated. *For William Ley,* 1647. 4°.* LT, O, LSC, DC; CH, NU, VC. [— B2883.]

955 Gods good servant, . . . May 17, 1639. *By A. N. for Richard Lownds,* 1642. 4°.* LT, C, YM; CH, NU, WF, Y.

956 God's goodnesse, and mans ingratitude. *Printed,* 1641. 4°.* LT, O, MR, DT.

God's goodness to His Israel. 1700. *See* Forbes, James.

957 Entry cancelled.
God's goodness vindicated. 1668. *See* Hallywell, Henry. Deus justifacatus.

958 Gods government of His church. [*London*], *printed* 1641. 4°. O, C, BP, MR, EN; CLC, IU, MBP, NU, TU, Y.

Gods gracious presence. 1658. *See* Kaye, William.
Gods gracious thoughts. 1647. *See* Homes, Nathaniel.
God's great and wonderful work. 1676. *See* W., L.

958A Entry cancelled.
Gods great and wonderful work in Somerset-shire. 1674. *See* W., L.

God's holy name magnified. [n.p.], 1665. *See* Crane, Richard.
God's holy order. 1690. *See* Wall, Thomas.
Gods interest. 1687. *See* MacQueen, John.

959 God's judgments against whoring. *For Richard Baldwin,* 1697. 8°. T.C.III 74. L, DT; CH, NAM, WF.

Gods judgements upon drunkards. 1659. *See* Hammond, Samuel.

959A Gods justice against murther. *Printed for John Clarke,* [1668]. 12°.* L.

959B Gods late mercy to England. *For F. Coules and T. Bates,* 1641. 4°.* O, AN; WF, Y.

959C Gods love to his people Israel. *By A. Maxwell,* 1666. 4°. LUC.

960 Gods love to London. *Printed,* 1665. brs. L.
God's love to mankind. 1656. *See* Hoard, Samuel.

960A God's marvelous wonders in England. [*London*], *P. Brooksby,* [1694]. 8°.* L.

960B Gods mercy and justice displayed. *By J. Bennet for R. Miller,* 1679. 4°.* L.

God's revenge against murther. 1680. *See* Tonge, John.
God's revenge against the enemies. 1658. *See* Wall, Thomas.

961 Gods revenge vpon his Parliaments and peoples enemies. *For R. Johnson,* 1643. 4°.* MADAN 1257. LT, LG, DT.

God's sovereignty. 1688. *See* Kingston, Richard.

962 God's strange and terrible judgment in Oxfordshire. *For D. M.,* 1677. 4°.* O, DU, EN.

Gods terrible voice. Cambridge [Mass.], 1667. *See* Vincent, Thomas.

963 Gods voice from Heaven. *By T. P. and M. S.,* 1644. 8°.* LT.

964 God's voice to Christendom. *Edinburgh reprinted,* 1693. 8°. ALDIS 3299. EN.

964A God's wonderful judgment in Lincoln-shire. *For L. C.,* 1679. 4°.* LSD; Y.

964B **Godson, John.** The Bedford-shire prophet risen. colop: *For T. Johnson,* 1690. brs. Y.

965 **Godson, Robert.** Astrologia reformata: a reformation. *For George Sawbridge,* 1696. 8°. O.

966 — —[Anr. ed.] *For G. Sawbridge, to be sold by R. Baldwin,* 1697. 8°. L.

967 **Godwin.** July 18. 1642. A perfect diurnall of all the proceedings. *For Jo. Raworth,* 1642. 4°.* LT, O, EC; CH.

967A **Godwin, Edmond.** God, the believer's best stronghold. *For J. Robinson,* 1698. 8°.* T.C.II 600. LLP.

968 Entry cancelled.
Godwin, Francis, bp . Annals of England. 1675. *See* Bacon, *Sir* Francis. History of the reigns of Henry the Seventh.

969 —The character of Thomas Merkes. [*London,* 1689?] 4°.* CT, MR, CD; CH, MH.

970 [–] The man in the moone. Second edition. *For Joshua Kirton,* 1657. 8°. L, O, EN; CH.

971 **Godwin, Morgan.** The Negro's & Indians advocate. *For the author, by J. D.,* 1680. 8°. T.C.I 366. L, O, C, OM, E, DT; CH, CN, LC, MH, MU, NN, RPJ, WF, Y.

972 [–] The revival: or directions for a sculpture. *By J. Darby,* 1682. brs. O, CS; CH, CLC, RPJ, Y.

973 [–] A supplement to The Negro's & Indian's advocate. *By J. D.,* 1681. 4°.* L, LUG, P, LSD; CH, LC, MH, NU, RPJ.

974 [–] Trade preferr'd. *For B. Took and Isaac Cleave,* 1685. 4°. T.C.II 135. L, O, OCC, CT, LSD; CH, LC, MH, NN, WF, Y.

975 [**Godwyn, Thomas.**] The demeanour of a good subject. *By William Downing, for the author,* 1681. 4°.* O, C, DU; CH, WF, Y.

976 —Moses and Aaron. Sixth edition. *By E. G. and are to be sold by John Williams,* 1641. 4°. L, O, C, AN, NPL, EN; BN, CH, CN, MH, NU, Y.

977 — —Seventh edition. *By S. G. for Andrew Crook and John Williams,* 1655. 4°. L, O, CS, LSD, BQ; CLC, CN, LC, NC, TU, Y.

978 ——Eighth edition. *By S. Griffin, for Andrew Crook, and John Wiillams* [sic], 1662. 4°. L, O, C, LI, A, BQ; CH, IU, NP, TO, WF, Y.

979 ——Ninth edition. *By S. Griffin for Andrew Crook,* 1667. 4°. L, O, C, YM, DT; CLC, CU, LC, NC, PL, Y.

980 ——Tenth edition. —, 1671. 4°. L, O, CM, BR, ES, DT; BN, CH, IU, NU, SE, TU, V, Y.

981 ——"Eighth" edition. *By Richard Hodgkinson, to be sold by William Jacob,* 1672. 4°. L, O, OM, MR; CH, CLC, MIU, NP.

982 ——"Twelfth" edition. —, 1672. 4°. L, O, CT, E, DT; CLC, IU, MB, PL, TO.

983 ——Eleventh edition. *For S. Griffin, R. Scot, T. Basset, J. Wright, and R. Chiswel,* 1678. 4°. L, O, C, BC, DT; BN, MH, MU, NU, PU, Y, AVP.

984 ——Twelfth edition. *For R. Scot, T. Basset, T. Dring, R. Chiswel, B. Griffin, G. Connyers, and M. Wotton,* 1685. 4°. L, O, C, EN, DT; CSU, CU, LC, MH, NC, NPT, Y.

984A ——[Anr. ed.] *For R. Scot, T. Basset, J. Wright, R. Chiswel, B. Griffin, G. Connyers, and M. Wotton,* 1685. 4°. BAMB; CH, IU.

984B ——[Anr. ed.] *By A. Churchill,* 1686. 4°. IAU, PL.

985 [–] Romanæ historiæ anthologia. *Oxford, by Leonard Lichfield for Henry Cripps,* 1642. 4°. MADAN 1286. L, O, C, LIU, SHR; CH, IU, MH, NPT, WF, Y, AVP.

986 ——[Anr. ed.] *By Robert White, for Henry Cripps,* 1648. 4°. L, O, CS, AN, NPL, EN; BN, CLC, CN, NC, PL, V.

987 ——[Anr. ed.] *By J. M. for Henry Cripps of Oxford,* 1655. 4°. MADAN 2275. L, O, C, BC, EC, BQ; CPB, IU, NC, NR, PL, TU, Y.

988 [–] ——Thirteenth edition. *For Henry Cripps of Oxford,* 1658. 4°. MADAN 2387. L, O, CCH, WCA, RU; CLC, CU, TO, WF, Y.

989 [–] ——[Anr. ed.] *By R. W. for Peter Parker,* 1661. 4°. L, O, C, LL, LLL; CDA, IU, NU, PL, TU, Y.

990 [–] ——[Anr. ed.] *By R. W. for Henry Cripps,* 1661. 4°. L, O, CT, BC, EN, BLH; CLC, IU, MH, NP, WF, Y.

990A [–] ——[Anr. ed.] *By R. W. for Peter Parker,* 1666. 4°. NU.

991 ——[Anr. ed.] *By T. J. for Peter Parker,* 1668. 4°. L, O, C, LIU, YM; IU, MBP, NCD, NR, TO, Y.

992 ——[Anr. ed.] *Oxford,* 1671. 4°. LL.

993 ——[Anr. ed.] *By J. C. for Peter Parker,* 1671. 4°. L, CT, BR, LSD, DT; CH, CU, LC, NC, SE, V, Y.

994 ——[Anr. ed.] *By R. W. for Peter Parker,* 1674. 4°. L, O, CM, E, DT; CH, IU, NP, PL, TO, WF, AVP.

995 [–] ——[Anr. ed.] *By M. White, for R. Chiswel, and J. Wright,* 1680. 4°. L, O, BR; BN, CLC, IU, MU, NU, Y, AVP.

996 ——Fourteenth edition. *By J. Darby, for Richard Chiswell,* 1685. 4°. L, O, C, BAMB, BC, EN; CLC, CU, LC, MBP, MH.

996A ——"Fourteenth" edition. *By J. D. for Richard Chiswell, M. Wotton, and G. Connyers,* 1685. 4°. BC; IU.

997 ——[Anr. ed.] *Printed, and sold by Awnsham Churchill,* 1686. 4°. T.C.II 159. L, CM; IAU, IU, NP, PL.

998 ——Fifteenth edition. *For R. Chiswell, M. Wotton, and G. Conyers,* 1689. 4°. T.C.II 325. L, O, CT, BAMB, DT; BN, CLC, IU, LC, MH, PBL, TU.

999 ——[Anr. ed.] *By J. D. for Richard Chiswell, M. Wotton, and G. Connyers,* 1695. 4°. MH.

1000 ——Sixteenth edition. *By J. Dawks, for R. Chiswell, M. Wotton, and G. Conyers,* 1696. 4°. L, O, C, CT; BN, CH, CLC, NC, Y.

1001 **Godwyn, Thomas.** Phanatical tenderness. *Printed and are to be sold by Randall Taylor,* 1684. fol.* L, O, C, OC, BR, MR; CH, WF.

1002 **Goedaert, Johannes.** Johannes Goedartivs de insectis. *Excudebat R. E. sumptibus S. Smith,* 1685. 8°. T.C.II 100. L, O, C, GH, DT; BN, CH, IU, MH, PL, WDA, WF, HC, AVP.

1003 —Johannes Godartius of insects. *York, by John White for M. L.,* 1682. 4°. T.C.I 508. L, O, C, GH, DT; BN, CH, IU, MH, MMO, PL, WF, Y.

1004 **Goeree, Willem.** An introduction to the general art of drawing. *For Rob. Pricke,* 1674. 4°. T.C.I 180. MR; LC, WPO, YBA.

1005 **G[offe], T[homas].** The careles shepherdess. A tragi-comedy. *For Richard Rogers and William Ley,* 1656. 4°. L, O, CT, DC, EN; CH, CN, LC, MH, WF, Y.

—Raging turk. 1656. *See*—Three excellent tragædies.

1006 —Three excellent tragædies. Second edition. *For G. Bedell and T. Collins,* 1656. 8°. MADAN 2290. LT, O, C, OW, EN; CH, CN, LC, MH, WF, Y.

1006A **Gogor, William.** The last speech and testimony of. *[Edinburgh,* 1681.] brs. EN.

1007 —The late speech. colop: *For R. B. and sold by W. Davies,* 1681. brs. L, O, HH; CLC, PU.

1007A ——[Anr. ed.] *For J. Smith,* [1681]. brs. EN.

1007B ——[Anr. ed.] *[Edinburgh,* 1681?] brs. EN; MH.

1008 **[Golbee, John.]** A true and exact relation of the most remarkable passages which have happened at Warwicke. *By T. P. and M. S. for Iohn Hancocke, August the 20.* 1642. 4°.* LT, O.

1009 **Golborne, John.** A friendly apology. *For Henry Mortlock,* 1674. 12°. T.C.I 179. L; CH, CJC, CU, MH, Y.

Gold, Robert. *See* Gould, Robert.

1010 Gold tried in the fire. colop: *[London], printed,* 1647. cap., 4°.* LT, C, LL, LW, MR; CSS, RBU, WF.

1011 The golden age. *By J. Mayos for Rich. Harrison,* 1698. 8°. L, GU; CLC, LC, MH, NAM, WU, Y.

1012 The golden apophthegms. *By John Clowes,* 1660. 4°.* LT; CLC, WF.

1013 No entry.

1014 The golden coast, or a description of Guinney. *For S. Speed,* 1665. 4°. L, OR, DCH; CH, CU, IU, LC, RPJ.

Golden drops of Christian comfort. 1687. *See* M., S.

1015 The golden farmer's last farevveel [sic]. *[London], for P. Brooksby, J. Deacon, J. Blare, and J. Back,* [1691?]. brs. L.

Golden fleece. 1656. *See* S., W.

1016 The golden fleece defended. *[London,* 1647.] cap., 4°.* LT.

Golden fleece: or. 1679. *See* F., J.

1017 The golden garland of most delightful mirth. *[London], for J. Blare,* [1690]. 8°. O, CM.

Golden garland of princely delight. [1690?] *See* Johnson, Richard.

Golden grove. 1655. *See* Taylor, Jeremy, bp.

1018 The golden island. *Edinburgh, by John Reid,* 1699. 8°.* ALDIS 3853. L, EN; MH.

Golden law. 1656. *See* H., S.

Golden rule made plain. 1675. *See* H., C.

Golden rule; or. 1688. *See* Goodman, John.

Golden treasury. 1699. *See* Houghton, Thomas.

Goldesborough. *See* Gouldesborough.

1019   **Goldham, Nathanael.** A reasonable word to the doctors of reason. *By K. Astwood for the author,* 1699. 8°. T.C.III 194. O, LCL, LLP, CT; MBJ, PL, WF.

1020   **Golding, William.** Servants on horse-back. [*London*], *printed,* 1648. 4°.* L; MU, RPJ.

Goldisborough, John. Almanack. 1662. *See* Almanacs.

Goldsmith, John. Almanack. 1674. *See* Almanacs.

1020A   Goldsmiths-hall, the [blank] day of 167[blank]. Whereas complaint. [*London,* 1678.] brs. LG.

Golgotha, or a looking-glass. 1665. *See* V., J.

Goliahs head cut off. 1655. *See* Parnell, James.

1021   **Golius, Theophilus.** Epitome doctrinae . . . Ethicorum Aristotelis. *Ex officina Rogeri Danielis, pro Edvardo Story, Cantabrigiensi,* 1662. 8°. L, CT, BAMB, BC, DT; TO, Y.

1022   **Golty, Richard.** The state of the church. *Printed and published by Randall Taylor,* 1688. 4°.* L, O, OC; CDA, CH, CLC, Y.

1023   **Gombauld, Jean Ogier de.** A discourse of Christianity. *For S. Lowndes,* 1693. 8°. T.C.II 438. L, O, C, LLP, CM.

1024   —The fundamentals of the Protestant religion. *For W. C.,* 1682. 12°. T.C.I 471. C, LW, CT.

1025   [**Gomberville, Marin LeRoy**], *sieur de.* The history of Polexader [sic]. *By Tho. Harper, for Thomas Walkley,* 1647. fol. L, O; CH, CN, MH, NP, PU, Y.

1026   [–] —[Anr. ed.] —, 1648. fol. C, LLP, MR; CN, CU, IAU, PL, V, WF.

1027   No entry.

Gomez de Quevedo Villegas, Francisco. *See* Quevedo y Villegas, Francisco Gomez de.

1028   [**Good, Thomas.**] A brief English tract of logick. [*Oxford, by L. Lichfield*], 1677. 8°.* MADAN 3142. O.

1029   —Firmianus and Dubitantius. *Oxford, by L. Lichfield, for Tho. Hancox, in Hereford,* 1674. 8°. T.C.I 163. MADAN 3010. L, O, CT, EC, LIU; CH, IEG, TSM, WF, Y.

1030   —To the right honorable, the right worshipful, and the reverend, the lords, knights, gentlemen, . . . of Worcester; the humble proposal of. [*n.p.,* 1674.] brs. O.

1031   — —[Anr. ed.] [*Oxford, by Leonard Lichfield,* 1675.] brs. MADAN 3059. O.

1031A   Good admonition, or, keep thy head. [1642.] brs. O.

Good admonitions or wholesome counsel. [1680.] *See* P., I.

Good advice before. [*n.p.*], 1689. *See* Wildman, Sir John.

1032   Good advice to all the free-holders. colop: *For Richard Baldwin,* 1690. cap., 4°.* L, O, SP, DU, LIU; CH, CN, LC, MH, WF, Y.

Good advice to the church. 1687. *See* Penn, William.

1033   Good advice to the creditors. *For S. L.,* 1681. 4°.* NC.

1033A   Good advice to the free-holders of Middlesex. [*London,* 1690.] brs. LG.

Good advice to the pulpits. 1687. *See* Gother, John.

Good-ale monopolized. [n.p.], 1654. *See* Sheppard, Samuel.

Good and bad newes from Ireland. 1641. *See* Gibbes, James.

1034   Good and bad newes from Ireland. Containing. 13*th of Iuly,* 1642 *for Francis Coles.* 4°.* LT, O, EC, MR, DN.

Good and joyful news for England. 1681. *See* Notredame, Michel de.

1034A   Good and joyfull nevves from York. *June 6. For I. Tompson, and A. Coe,* 1642. 4°.* O, CT; Y.

1035   Good and joyfull nevves ovt of Bvckinghamshire. *For Francis Wright,* 1642. 4°.* LT, O, LNC.

Good and prosperous successe. 1642. *See* Fairfax, Sir Ferdinando.

1035A   Good and seasonable advice to the male-contents in England. colop: *Printed and are to be sold by Randal Taylor,* 1689. cap., 4°.* L; CH.

Good and solid reasons. 1688. *See* Boyle, Robert.

1036   Good and true, fresh and new Christmas carols. *Printed at London by E. P. for Francis Coles,* 1642. 4°.* O.

Good and true intelligence from Reading. 1643. *See* Bennet, Isaac.

1036A   Good & true newes from Bedford. *For R. Astine and A. Coe,* 1643. 4°.* L, BP, YM.

Good and true nevves from Ireland. 1642. *See* Johnson, Richard.

1037   Good and true newes from Redding. *For J. G.,* 1643. 4°.* LT, O, DU, RU; MH, WF.

Good angel of Stamford. 1659. *See* Wallas, Samuel.

1038   The good Catholick no bad subject. *Printed,* 1660. 4°.* LT, C, BC, LIU; CH, CLC, NC, NP, NU.

1039   —[Anr. ed.] *For John Dakins,* 1660. 4°.* NU, TU, WF.

1040   The good Christians complaint. *For P. Brooksby, J. Deacon, J. Blare, and J. Back,* 1692. brs. L.

Good Christian's heaven. [1660.] *See* Hooke, Richard.

Good counsel and advice. 1659. *See* Burrough, Edward.

1040A   Good counsel and advice unto the magistrates and people of Norwich. [*London*], *printed,* 1676. 4°.* WF.

1041   Entry cancelled.

Good counsell come from Scotland. Edinburgh, 1646. *See* Church of Scotland.

1041A   Good covnsell in bad times. *For Thomas Watson,* 1647. 4°.* LT, DT; CH, WF.

1041B   Good counsel to be had at a cheap rate. [*London*], *W. Gilbertson,* 1663. 8°.* L.

Good counsell, to the petitioners. [n.p. 1645.] *See* Chidley, Katherine.

Good counsells for the peace. Oxford, 1641. *See* Davenant, John.

1042   Good deeds ill requited. [*London,* 1679?] brs. L, O, OC; CH, IU, MH, TU, WF, Y.

1043   Good English. Or, certain reasons. [*London*], *printed,* 1648. 4°.* LT, O, C, MR, DT; CH, CU, MH, WF, Y. (var.)

1044   The good fellow. A new song. [*London?* 1695.] fol. L.

1045   The good-fellowes advice. *For J. Wright junior*, [1641?]. brs. L.

1046   The good fellowes best beloved. *For Iohn Wright, iunior*, [1641]. brs. L.

1046A   The good fellowes complaint. *By Iohn Hammond*, [1647?]. brs. MAU.

1047   The good fellows consideration. [*London*], *for P. Brooksby*, [1677]. brs. EUING 133. L, HH, GU; MH.

1048   The good-fellows counsel. [*London*], *for P. Brooksby*, [1680–85]. brs. L, O, HH; MH.

1049   The good fellows frolick. [*London*, 1680?] brs. L.

1050   —[Anr. ed.] [*London*], *for J. Coniers*, [1680?]. brs. MH.

1050A   —[Anr. ed.] *By H. B. for J. Seal and sold by J. Conyers*, 1682. brs. L.

1050B   —[Anr. ed.] [*London*], *for P. Brooksby*, [1690?]. brs. O.

    Good help for weak memories. 1671. *See* Lloyd, John.

    Good housewife. [1685?] *See* Tryon, Thomas.

    Good-husbands jewel. 1651. *See* Crowshey, John.

1051   Good luck at last. *For P. Brooksby*, [1672–95]. brs. L, O, HH; MH.

1051A   Good luck to the fortunate. [*London*, 1695.] brs. Y.

    Good manners. [*n.p.*], 1700. *See* Dykes, O.

1052   A good motion. If the rich will deale their bread. [*London*, 1647.] brs. LT.

    Good newes for all parties. [*n.p.*], 1660. *See* B., M.

    Good newes for all true. [*n.p.*], 1641. *See* Mussell, Francis.

    Good news for England. 1689. *See* K., W.

1052A   A good news for England: or a speedy, safe, and easy way. *Printed*, 1689. 4°. L.

    Good news for England; or comfortable tydings. 1641. *See* Guy, William.

1052B   Good news for England, or the heads of a peace. *For the author*, 1695. brs. CN.

1052C   Good news for England, or the peoples triumph. *For M. Wright*, [1660]. brs. EUING 131. GU.

1052D   Good news for the nation. *For P. Brooksby*, [1680?]. brs. MH.

1053   Good news for the poor. *Printed*, 1674. fol.* L, MC.

1054   Good newes from all quarters of the kingdome. *By T. Paine and M. Simmons, September.* 13. 1643. 4°.* LT, O, MR, DT; CN.

    Good news from Banbury. 1642. *See* R., S.

1055   Good newes from Colonel Hollis his regiment. *For Io. Iohnson, August 20*, 1642. 4°.* LG, CD; OWC.

1055A   Good newes from Colchester. *For W. Thomas*, 1659. 4°.* SP.

1056   Good nevves from General Blakes fleet. *For Robert Ibbitson*, 1652. 4°.* LT; CH, WF.

1057   Good nevves from Hvll. *For J. Tompson, and Andrew Coe, June* 15, 1642. 4°.* LT; WF.

    Good newes from Ireland, a true relation. 1642. *See* Courtney, Thomas.

1058   Good newes from Ireland, and from the Irish seas. *For Iohn Thomas*, 1641. 4°.* EC, DN; Y.

1059   Good newes from Ireland, and from the Irish seas. [*London*, 1642.] 4°.* MR; INU.

1060   Good news from Ireland being. *For Iohn Wright*, 15 *Jan.* 1645. 4°.* LT, C, DN; CH, MH, WU.

    Good news from Ireland, being a true. [*n.p.*, 1690.] *See* Crysly, James.

    Good news from Ireland, or a true . . . account. [*n.p.*], 1690. *See* S., W.

1060A   Good newes from Kent. [*London*], *for Jo. Johnson, August 22*, 1642. 4°.* LG, EC, CD; MH.

1061   Good newes from Lincolne-shire. [*London*], *for William Gifford, Septemb.* 5. 1642. 4°.* LT; NU.

1061A   Good news from London-derry. colop: *For J. Williams*, 1689. brs. CH.

1061B   Good newes from Milford-Haven. *J. Coe*, 1644. 4°.* AN.

1062   Good news from Nevv-England. *By Matthew Simmons*, 1648. 4°.* LT, O, DT; CH, CN, MWA, NN, RPJ.

1063   Good newes from Oxford (of the treaty). *By Jane Coe*, 1646. 4°.* MADAN 1872. LT, O, LG; CCC, Y.

1064   Good nevves from Plymouth. *For Francis Wright, Frebr.* [*sic*], 20, 1643. brs. LT; MH.

1065   Entry cancelled.

    Good newes from Portsmouth. 1643. *See* Norton, Richard, *colonel*.

1066   Good news from Redding. [*n.p.*], 1643. 4°. LVF.

    Good news from Scotland. 1648. *See* L., J.

    Good newes from sea. 1643. *See* Thomas, William.

1067   Good news from Somerset-shire. [*London*], *for Richard Thomson, Aug.* 12, 1642. 4°.* CD.

1068   Good newes from Sovth-Hampton. *For Tho. Bates*, 1642. 4°.* LT; CH, CLC, WF.

1069   Good news from the Assembly in Scotland. *For J. W.*, 1642. 4°.* LT, O, EC, EN; CU, MH, NU, WF, Y.

1070   Good news from the English fleet. *David Edwards*, 1690. brs. L.

1070A   —[Anr. ed.] colop: *For T. Clarke*, 1690. brs. MH.

    Good newes from the narrow seas. [1642.] *See* D., Em.

    Good newes from the Netherlands. [*London*, 1660.] *See* L., W.

1070B   Good newes from the Scottish army. *For John Raymond*, 1642. 4°.* DN; INU.

1070C   Good newes from the sea, being a true relation of the late sea-fight. *Laurence Blaiklock, June 26*, 1643. 4°.* LNM.

    Good news from the trained bands. 1643. *See* Walby, Anthony.

1071   Good newes from Westchester. [*London*], *for Iohn Iackson, August* 18, 1642. 4°.* LT, EC.

1072   Good news in bad times. [*London*], *for P. Brooksby*, [1683]. brs. L; CLC, MH.

1073   Good news of Englands approving. *For John Bellamy, and Ralph Smith*, 1643. 4°.* CT, AU; CH, NU, Y.

1074   Good newes ovt of Cheshire. *For Iohn Davis*, [1642]. 4°.* LT, O, CCL, AN; MH.

1075   Good nevves ovt of Flanders. *By T. Badger*, 1644. 4°.* LT; WF.

1076   Good news: proving King William to be the man. *For the author*, 1696. 4°.* Y.

Good news to the good women. 1700. *See* M., M.

Good old cause briefly. 1659. *See* Hubberthorn, Richard.

1077 Entry cancelled.

Good old cause dress'd. 1659. *See* Fitz-Brian, R.

1078 The good old cause explained. [*London*, 1659.] cap., 4°.* O, LG, MR; CH, CN, MH, WF, Y.

Good old cause of England. 1658. *See* P., G.

1079 The good old cause revived. [*London*, 1680?] brs. L, O, LS; MH, Y.

1080 The good old test reviv'd. colop: *Printed and are to be sold by Randal Taylor*, 1687. 4°.* L, O, LSD, MR; CLC, NS, Y.

1080A A good pook, and fit for every Inglish and Irish-man. colop: *For the author*, 1682. cap., fol.* CH.

Good report. [n.p., 1660.] *See* Younge, Richard.

1081 Good Sir W— Knock. The whores lamentation. colop: *For the assigns of Posture-Moll*, 1693. brs. L.

Good sovldier. 1644. *See* Woodward, Hezekiah.

1082 Good thoughts for every day of the month. *For Thomas Dring*, 1656. 12°. LT.

1082A A good warning for all maidens. [*London*], *for F. Coles, T. Vere, and W. Gilbetson [sic]*, [1658–64]. brs. EUING 128. GU.

1082B A good wife is worth gold. [*London*], *for J. Deacon*, [1695?]. O.

1082C A good wife or none. *For F. Coles, T. Vere, and J. Wright*, [1663–74]. brs. O.

Good will towards men. 1675. *See* Barrett, John.

1083 A good wish for England. *Printed at London*, 1641. brs. LT.

1084 The good wives fore-cast. [*London*], *for J. Deacon*, [1685–88]. brs. EUING 132. L, O, HH, GU; MH, WF, Y.

1085 The good-wives lamentation. *For L. C.*, 1678. 4°.* O; MH, Y.

1086 The good-wives vindication. *For L. C.*, 1678. 4°.* O; CH, MH.

Good womans champion. [1650?] *See* A., I.

Good work. 1651. *See* Peters, Hugh.

Good workes. 1641. *See* Udall, Ephraim.

1087 [**Goodaire, Thomas.**] A cry of the just against oppression. colop: *For Thomas Simmons*, 1660. cap., 4°.* MADAN 2470. L, LF, BBN; MH, MU, PH, PSC, Y.

1088 [–] A plain testimony to the antient truth. *Printed, and sold by T. Sowle*, 1691. 4°.* LF, BBN, MR; MU, PH.

1089 [–] A true relation what sentence was passed. colop: *For Thomas Simmons*, 1660. cap., 4°.* MADAN 2471. L, O, LF, BBN; CH, CU, MH, MU, NU, PH, Y.

1090 **Goodall, Charles.** The colledge of physicians vindicated. *By R. N. for Walter Kettilby*, 1676. 8°. T.C.I 226. L, O, C, LCP, MAU, EN; CNM, MH, NAM, WF, WSG.

1091 —The royal college of physicians of London founded. *By M. Flesher, for Walter Kettilby*, 1684. 4°. T.C.II 62. L, O, C, EN, DT; CH, CU, MH, NAM, WF, HC.

1091A —Whereas it hath of late been the endeavour of several members of the physicians colledg . . . Jesuits bark. [*London*, 1676–84.] brs. L.

1092 [**Goodall, Charles**], *younger.* Poems and translations . . . by a late scholar of Eaton. *For Henry Bonwicke*, 1689. 8°. T.C.II 253. L, O, C, LVD, MAU; CH, CN, MH, WF, Y.

1093 **Goode, William.** The discoverie of a pvbliqve spirit. *By I. L. for Christopher Meredith*, 1645. 4°.* LT, O, C, EN, DT; CH, CN, MH, NU, WF, Y.

1094 —Jacob raised. *By T. R. and E. M. for Nath. Webb and Will. Grantham*, 1647. 4°.* LT, O, C, EN, DT; CH, IU, MH, NU, WF, Y.

1095 [–] The new catechisme: according to the forme of the Kirk of Scotland. [*London*], *for H. Perry, and are sold by F. Coules*, 1644. 8°.* LT.

1096 —A new catechisme commanded. *By Bernard Alsop*, 1645. 8°.* LT.

1097 ——[Anr. ed.] —, 1645. 12°.* LT.

1098 Entry cancelled. Serial.

[**Gooden, James.**] Controversial letters. 1673. *See* Walsh, Peter.

1099 [**Gooden, Peter.**] The sum of a conference had between tvvo divines. *By Henry Hills, for him and Matthew Turner*, 1687. 4°.* L, CT, LIL, MC, DT; CH, CN, MIU, NC, WF, Y.

G[oodgroom], R[ichard]. Copy of a letter. [n.p., 1656.] *See title.*

1099A **Goodin, Madam.** By His Majesty's authority . . . is to be seen two monsters. [*London*, 1696.] brs. L.

1099B G[oodinge], T[homas]. The law against bankrupts. *For Richard Southby*, 1694. 8°. T.C.II 478. CLL, LC, MH, PFL, PUL.

1099C [–] —[Anr. ed.] *For S. Heyrick, C. Harper, J. Place, I. Harrison, S. Keble, D. Brown, I. Cleave, W. Rogers, R. Sare, W. Freeman, T. Goodwin, M. Wotton, R. Vincent, A. Roper, & J. Brixey*, 1695. 8°. T.C.II 549. MHL, PFL.

1099D **Goodman, Godfrey, bp.** The first apparition of Bishop Goodman's ghost. [*London*], *by H. B.*, 1681. brs. O; CN, MH, WF.

1099E —Bishop Goodman his proposition. [*London, c. 1650*.] cap., 4°.* CT; MHS.

1100 —Reverendis in Christo patribus. [n.p., 1650.] brs. O.

1101 —To His Highness my Lord Protector. The humble petition and information of. [*London*, 1655.] brs. LT, O, LG, MR; Y.

1102 —To the supreme authority the . . . Commons . . . petition. [*London*, 1649.] brs. L, O.

1103 [–] The two great mysteries of Christian religion. *By J. Flesher*, 1653. 4°. LT, O, C, CT, DU, MR; CH, IU, NGT, NR, NU, WF.

1104 [**Goodman, John.**] A discourse concerning auricular confession. *By H. Hills jun. for Benj. Tooke, and Fincham Gardiner*, 1648 [i.e. 1684.] 4°. L, O, C, E, DT; BN, CH, IU, MH, TU, WF, Y.

1105 [–] —Second edition. —, 1684. 4°. T.C.II 67. L, OH, CT, SC, EN; CLC, CU, MIU, NU, PL.

1106 ——[Anr. ed.] *Dublin, re-printed by Andrew Crook and Samuel Helsham, for Joseph Howes, Samuel Helsham, and Eliphal Dobson*, 1686. 4°.* DIX 219. E, BLH, DI, DM, DT; MH.

1107 [–] The golden rule; or, the royal law. *By Samuel Roycroft, for Robert Clavell*, 1688. 8°. T.C.II 225. L, O, C, EC, SHR; CLC, LC, MU, NU, Y.

1108   Entry cancelled.
        [–] [Anr. ed.] 1697. *See* —Seven sermons.
1109   —The interest of divine providence. *For Rich. Royston,* 1683. 4°.* L, O, C, OM, CT; CH, IU, MH, NU, TSM, WF, Y.
1110   —The leaven of Pharisaism. *By S. Roycroft, for Robert Clavel,* 1688/9. 4°.* T.C.II 244. L, O, C, LG, CD; CH, MH, NU, TU, WF, Y.
1111   [–] The old religion demonstrated. *By J. M. for R. Royston.* 1684. 12°. T.C.II 91. L, O, C, LSC, P; CH, CN, NU, NGT, TU, Y.
1112   [–] —Second edition. —, 1686. 12°. L, O, CE, DU, NE; CDA, CN, NPT, TSM, WF.
1113   — —"Second" edition. *For L. Meredith and sold by R. Wilkin,* 1693. 8°. C, LW, DT; UCLA, WF.
1114   — —Third edition. *By J. L. for Luke Meredith,* 1698. 8°. L, O, C, EC; CLC, FU.
1115   —The penitent pardoned. *By E. Flesher, for R. Royston,* 1679. 4°. T.C.I 327. L, O, C, MC, ENC; CH, CN, LC, TU, Y.
1116   — —Second edition. *By J. Macock, for R. Royston,* 1683. 4°. L, O, C, DC, YM, DM; CH, CLC, IU, NU, WF, Y.
1117   — —Third edition. *By R. Norton for Luke Meredith,* 1689. 4°. T.C.II 293. L, O, LW, DU, E, EN; CH, IU, TU, WF, Y.
1118   — —Fourth edition. *By J. Heptinstall, for L. Meredith,* 1694. 8°. T.C.II 484. L, O, DUS, YM, DT; MBA, NPT, NU, PL.
1119   — —Fifth edition. *By W. Horton, for L. Meredith,* 1700. 8°. L, O, RPL, DT; FU, MH, NGT, SYRACUSE.
1119A   [–] A seasonable sermon preach'd January 26, 1689. *By S. Roycroft, for R. Clavell,* 1690. 4°.* L, LG, LSD, WCA, BLH; CH, RBU, WF, Y.
1119B   [–] —Second edition. *For R. Clavell,* 1690. 12°. O, LLP, OC.
1120   [–] A serious and compassionate inquiry. *By Robert White for Richard Royston,* 1674. 8°. T.C.I 186. L, O, CT, E, CD; CH, CLC, IU, MH, NU, WF.
1121   [–] —Second edition. —, 1675. 8°. L, O, CT, EC, YM; CH, PL, TSM, Y.
1122   [–] —Third edition. —, 1675. 8°. T.C.I 207. O, C, LW, ENC, SC; CB, CH, MH, TU, MOORE.
1122A   [–] —"Third" edition. *By M. Flesher for Richard Royston,* [1684?]. 8°. L, C, NE; FU, MH, PL.
1122B   [–] —Fourth edition. *For Luke Meredith,* 1693. 8°. L, CASTLE ASHBY; CLC, IEG.
1123   —A sermon preached . . . August 29. 1677. *For R. Royston,* 1677. 4°.* L, O, CT, YM, BLH; CLC, IU, NU, TU, WF, Y.
1124   — —[Anr. ed.] —, 1678. 4°.* L, C, OC, EC, MR; CH, CLC, IE, LC, Y, AVP.
1125   —A sermon preached . . . January xxv. 1679. *For R. Royston,* 1680. 4°.* T.C.I 341. L, O, C, MR, CD; CH, NR, NU, TU, WF.
1126   —A sermon preached . . . Decemb. 18th 1681. *For R. Royston,* 1681. 4°.* L, O, C, EC, E; CH, IU, MH, NU, WF, Y.
1127   —A sermon preached . . . xxv. of January, 1684. *By J. Richardson, for R. Royston,* 1685. 4°.* L, O, C, OM; CH, CLC, NU, WF.

1128   —Seven sermons. *For Robert Clavel; and Luke Meredith,* 1697. 8°. T.C.III 43. L, O, C, EN, DT; CH, IU, NU, PL, WF, Y.
1128A   — —[Anr. ed.] *For Luke Meredith,* 1697. 8°. CT, NE.
1129   [–] A winter-evening conference. *By J. M. for R. Royston,* 1684. 8°. T.C.II 59. L, O, OCC, CS, GU; CH, CLC, IU, PL, WF, Y.
1130   [–] —[Anr. ed.] *Edinburgh, by the heir of Andrew Anderson,* 1684. 12°. ALDIS 2499. L, O, I.
1131   [–] —Second edition. *By J. M. for R. Royston,* 1684. 8°. T.C.II 106. L, C, OC, CK, DU; CLC, CU, FU, IU, WF.
1132   [–] —Third edition. *By J. M. for R. Royston,* 1686. 8°. L, O, C, DC, YM; CLC, IU, NC, V, WF.
1133   [–] —Fourth edition. *By J. Leake, for Luke Meredith,* 1689. 8°. T.C.II 293. L, OC, CE, EC; CH, CN, MBP, NGT, TU.
1134   — —Fifth edition. *By J. H. for Luke Meredith,* 1692. 8°. T.C.II 433. L, O, OME, AN, NE, EN; CH, CLC, NCD.
1135   — —Sixth edition. *By J. L. for Luke Meredith,* 1694. 8°. T.C.II 533. L, LW, DT; CLC, LC, MH, NBL.
1136   — —Seventh edition. —, 1698. 8°. T.C.III 85. L, CT, DT; CSB, MH, NU, PL, Y.
1137   — —Eighth edition. —, 1700. 8°. L, O, AN, FONMON, RPL; CDA, CH, CLC, NU, PL, ASU.
1138   [–] —Part III. *By J. M. for R. Royston,* 1686. 8°. T.C.II 165. L, OC, CS; CH, IU, NC, V, WF.
1139   [–] —Part III [Anr. ed.]. *By J. H. for L. Meredith,* 1690. 8°. L, O, EC; CH, CN, NGT, RBU, TU, Y.
1140   — —Part III [Anr. ed.] *By J. L. for L. Meredith,* 1692. 8°. L, O; CH.
1141   — —Part III [Anr. ed.] *By J. H. for L. Meredith,* 1694. 8°. L; CLC, LC, MH, NBL.
1141A   — —Part III [Anr. ed.] —, 1698. 8°. MH, NU, PL, Y.
1141B   — —Part III [Anr. ed.] *By W. B. for L. Meredith,* 1700. 8°. L; CH, CLC, NU, ASU.
1141C   **Goodman, Peter.** Crueltie unvailed. *Printed,* 1661. brs. L.
1142   —The vindication of several persons. 1661. brs. L, O.
1143   **Goodman, Thomas.** The experienc'd secretary. *For N. Boddington,* 1699. 4°. T.C.III 143. CH.
        Goodman Country: to His Worship the City of London. [n.p., 1680.] *See* L'Estrange, *Sir* Roger.
1144   **Goodrick, John.** A sermon preached . . . 26th of July, 1685. *By J. D. to be sold by Israel Harrison,* 1685. 4°.* L, O, LSD; CH, NPT, WF, Y.
1144A   **Goodridge, William.** A breviate of the distressed suffering case of. [*London?* 1687.] brs. LF; PH, WF.
1144AB —Somerset. A breviate of the suffering case of. [*London?* 1687.] brs. MH.
1144B   **Goodwin, Arthur.** Two letters of great consequence. *For Edw. Husbands, March 24.* 1642. 4°.* LT, OJ, MR, SP, DT; CH, MBP, MH, MU, Y.
1144C   **Goodwin, Jacob.** Catalogus medicinarum. [1700?] 12°. L.
1145   [**Goodwin, John.**] Anapologesiates antapologias. Or, the inexcusablenesse. *By Matthew Simmons for Henry Overton,* 1646. 4°. LT, LCL, LW, P, DT; CH, MH, NU.
1146   —Anti-Cavalierisme. *By G. B. and R. W. for Henry Overton,* [1642]. 4°. LT, O, C, MR, DT; CH, CU, MH, WF, Y.

1146A ——[Anr. ed.] —, 1642. 4°.* L, C, LCL, CT, MR, E; CLC,
MH, NGT, WF, Y.

1147 ——[Anr. ed.] *By G. B. and G. W. for Henry Overton,*
1643. 4°.* L, OC, CS, SP, E, EN; CH, MH, MIU, PL, Y.

1148 [–] The apologist condemned. *By J. M. for Henry Cripps
and Lodowick Lloyd,* 1653. 4°.* LT, O, LSC, LIU, P; CH,
CU, MH, NU, PL, WF.

1149 —Απολυτρωσις απολυτρωσεως or redemption re-
deemed. *By John Macock, for Lodowick Lloyd and Henry
Cripps,* 1651. fol. L, O, C, NPL, E; BN, IU, MH, NU, TSM,
WF, Y.

1150 [–] The army, harmelesse. *For John Pounset,* 1647. 4°.*
LT, O, MR, YM, CD; CH, CN, MBP, MH, NU, Y.

1150A [–] The banner of justification displayed. *By E. C. to be
sold by H. Eversden,* 1659. 4°. LSC, CD; TO.

1151 —Βασανισται. Or the triers. *For Henry Eversden,* 1657.
4°.* LT, O, C, YM, DT; CH, CLC, MH, NU, Y.

1152 —The butchers blessing. *For Henry Overton,* 1642. 4°.*
LT, O, C, LIU, LLU; IU, MH, NU, WF, Y.

1153 —Calumny arraign'd and cast. *By M. Simmons for Henry
Overton,* 1645. 4°. LT, O, CS, A, DT; CH, CU, MH, WF, Y.

1154 [–] A candle to see the sunne. colop: [*London*], *by M. S.
for H. Overton.* 1647. cap., 4°.* LT, LW, BC, MR, DT; CN,
MH, NU, WF.

1155 [–] Cata-baptism. *For H. Cripps, and L. Lloyd,* 1655. 4°.
LT, O, CT, NPL, ENC; IU, NHC, NPT, NU, WF.

[–] Certain briefe observations. [n.p.], 1644. *See* Robinson, Henry.

1156 Entry cancelled.
—Certaine select cases resolved. 1651. *See* Goodwin,
Thomas.

1157 —Christ lifted up. [*London?*] *printed,* 1641. 8°.* L; WF.

1158 Entry cancelled.
—Christ set forth. 1642. *See* Goodwin, Thomas.

1159 —The Christians engagement. *By T. Cotes for P. Cole,*
1641. 12°. LW, DC, NPL, P; NPT, TO.

1160 —Confidence dismounted. *By John Macock, for Henry
Cripps, and Lodovick Lloyd,* 1651. 4°.* LT, CS, LIU, LSC,
NPL, P, DT; NU.

1161 —Cretensis: or a briefe answer. *By M. S. for Henry
Overton,* 1646. 4°. LT, O, C, EN, DT; CH, CN, MH, NU,
WF, Y.

1162 ——Second edition. [*London*], *for Henry Overton,* 1646.
4°. L, LW, OC, LLU; CSS, CN, MB, NU, Y.

1163 —The divine authority of the Scriptvres asserted. *By
A. M. for Henry Overton,* 1648. 4°. LT, O, C, E, DT; CLC,
CN, MH, WF, Y.

1164 [–] Ειρηνομαχια. The agreement & distance. *By J.
Macock, for H. Cripps, and L. Lloyd,* 1652. 4°. LT, O, C,
LCL, CT, LIU; CH, CU, NPT, NU, WF.

1165 [–] —[Anr. ed.] *For Peter Parker,* 1671. 8°. LCL, LW, OCC,
MR, SP; CH, CLC, IU, NPT, NU, TO, Y.

1166 —An exposition of the nineth chapter of the Epistle to
the Romans. *By John Macock, for Henry Cripps, and
Lodowick Lloyd,* 1653. 4°. LT, O, C, MR, ENC; CH, CLC,
NPT, NU, WF.

1167 —A fresh discovery. *For the author, to be sold by H. Cripps,
and L.Ll.,* 1654. 4°. LT, LW, LLU, NPL, DT; CH, CLC, NU.

1168 —God a good master. *By T. Cotes, to be sold by W.
Harris,* 1641. 12°. LSC, LW, CE; IU, NPT, U.ALBERTA.

1169 —Hagiomastix, or the scourge. *By Matthew Simmons,
for Henry Overton,* 1646. 4°. LT, C, LCL, MR, DT; CH, CN,
MWA, NHC, NU.

1170 —ʿΥβριστοδικαι. The obstvctovrs of justice. *For
Henry Cripps, and Lodowick Lloyd,* 1649. 4°. LT, O, C,
EN, DT; CH, CN, MH, WF, Y, AVP. (var.)

1171 —Impedit ira animum, or animadversions. [*London*],
printed, 1641. 4°. C, LSC, LW, NPL, P, SP; CLC, CSS, NU, WF.

1172 —Impvtatio fidei. Or a treatise. *By R. O. and G. D. and
are to be sold by Andrew Crooke,* 1642. 4°. LT, O, C, E, DT;
CH, NPT, NU, WF, Y.

1173 [–] Independencie Gods veritie. *For William Ley,* 1647.
8°.* LT; CB, MIU, MM, NU.

1174 —Innocencies triumph. *For Henry Overton,* 1644. 4°.*
LT, O, C, MR, DT; CH, IU, MH, NU, TU, WF, Y.

1175 ——Second edition.—, 1644. 4°.* CJ, CT, BC, P, A;
CDA, MWA, NGT, NU, WF, Y.

1176 [–] Innocency and truth triumphing together. *By Matthew Simmons, for Henry Overton,* 1645. 4°. LT, O, CT,
MR, DT; CH, MH, NU, WF, Y.

1177 No entry.

1178 [–] Irelands advocate: or, a sermon. *For William Larnar,*
1641. 4°.* LT, O, C, LW, DT; IU, NU, WF, WU, Y.

1179 —ʿΟ κριτης της αδικιας Luke 18. *By G. Dawson for
Henry Cripps,* 1649. 4°.* LT, LW, LIU, LLU, EN; CN, MIU,
NU.

1180 Entry cancelled.
[–] M. S. to A. S. with a plea. 1644. *See* S., M.

1181 [–] Mercy in her exaltation. *By J. Macock for H. Eversden,*
1655. 4°. LT, O, LW, ENC; CH, NHC, NU, TO, WF, Y.

[–] Moderate answer to Mr. Prins. 1645. *See* Robinson,
Henry.

1182 —Moses made angry. *By J. M. for Henry Cripps and
Lodowick Lloyd,* 1651. 4°.* LSC, CT, MR, NPL, DT; IU, NU.

1183 [—] Νεοφυτοπρεσβυτερος, or, the yongling elder. [*London*], *for Henry Overton,* 1648. 4°. LT, O, LG, NPL, DT;
CH, IU, MH, NC, NU, WF.

1184 —Os ossis & oris. Or a collection. [*London?*], *printed,*
1643. 4°.* IT, C, OC, MR, DT; CH, IAU, MH, MIU, NU.

1185 [–] Os ossorianvm, or a bone for a bishop to pick. *For
Henry Overton,* 1643. 4°. LT, O, C, AN, MR; CH, CU, LC,
MH, NU, WF.

1186 —The pagans debt, and dowry. *By J. Macock, for H.
Cripps; and L. Lloyd,* 1651. 4°. O, C, CT, MR, SP; CSS,
MH, NPT, NU, WF, WSC.

1187 ——[Anr. ed.] *By T. J. for Peter Parker,* 1671. 8°. T.C.I
75. LCL, LW, OCC, MR, SP; CH, CLC, IU, NPT, NU, TO, Y.

1188 [–] Peace protected, and discontent dis-armed. *By I.
Macock, for H. Cripps, and L. Lloyd,* 1654. 4°. LT, C,
LW, LIU, EN; CH, CU, MH, NU.

1189 [–] Philadelphia; or, XL. queries. *By J. M. for Henry
Cripps and Lodowick Lloyd,* 1653. 8°.* LT, O, LCL, MR,
GU; NHC, NPT.

1190 —Πληρωμα το πνευματικον. Or, a being filled with the spirit. *By E. C. for Henry Eversden*, 1670. 4°. T.C.I 17. L, O, C, NPL, E; CN, NBL, NU, TO, WF, Y.

1191 —A post-script, or appendix. *For H: Overton*, [1646]. 4°.* LT, O, C, P, DT; CN, MH, MWA, NU.

1192 [–?] Prelatique preachers none of Christ's teachers. *Printed*, 1663. 4°. O, CCA, P, YM, EN; CH, MH, NU, PL, Y.

1193–4 Entries cancelled.
—Proposals. [n.p., 1696.] *See* Goodwin, John, *gent*.

1195 [–] A qvære, concerning the church-covenant. *Printed at London for John Bellamie and Ralph Smith*, 1643. 4°.* O, C, MR, E, DT; CLC, IU, NHC, NU, WF, Y.

1196 Entry cancelled.
—Redemption redeemed. 1651. *See* —Απολυτρωσις.

1197 —The remedie of vnreasonableness. *By John Macock, for Lodowick Lloyd, and Henry Cripps*, 1650. 4°.* LT, MR; CH, NU.

1198 Entry cancelled.
—Reply of two of the brethren. 1644. *See title.*

1199 —The retvrne of mercies. *By M. F. for R. D. and H. Overton*, 1641. 12°. C, LW; IU, MHS, NU, WF.

1200 —Right and might well met. *By Matthew Simmons, for Henry Crips*, 1648. 4°. LT, O, C, LIU, EN; CH, CU, NU, WF, Y. (var.)

1201 [–] A short ansvver to A. S. [*London*], *printed*, 1644. 4°.* LT, O, CS, EC, DT; NU, WF.

1202 —Sion-Colledg visited. *By M. S. for Henry Overton*, 1648. 4°.* LT, O, CT, E, DT; CH, CU, NU, WF, Y.

1203 [–] The six book-sellers proctor non-suited. *For H. Cripps, and L. Lloyd*, 1655. 4°.* LW, MR; CSS, NU, PL, WF.

1204 [–] Some modest and humble qveries concerning a printed paper. *By Matthew Simmons for Henry Overton*, 1646. 4°.* LT, C, OJ, BC, DT; CU, MH, NHC, NU, Y.

1205 [–] Συγκρητισμος. Or dis-satisfaction satisfied. *By J. Macock, for H. Cripps, and L. Lloyd*, 1654. 4°.* LT, O, C, LG, EN, DT; CH, IU, MB, PL, NU, Y.

1206 —Θεομαχια; or the grand imprudence. *For Henry Overton*, 1644. 4°. LT, O, CT, NPL, DT; CH, MH, MU, NU, WF.

1207 — —Second edition. —, 1644. 4°. O, CT, MR, SP, A; MH, NU, Y.

1208 —Thirty queries. *By J. M. for Henry Cripps and Lodowick Lloyd*, 1653. 4°.* LT, O, CT, LIU, MR; MH, NPT, NU, PL, WF.

1209 Entry cancelled.
—To the . . . Houses. [n.p., 1698.] *See* Goodwin, John, *gent*.

1210 —Triumviri. *For Henry Eversden*. 1658. 4°. O, C, LCL, LW, NPL; NHC, NPT, NU, WF.

1211 —Twelve considerable serious cautions. *By M. S. for Henry Overton*, 1646. 4°.* LT, O, C, DU, A; CH, CN, MH, NU, WF, Y.

1212 [–] Tvvo hyms, or spiritvall songs; sung in Mr. Goodwins congregation. *By F: N:*, 1651. 8°.* LT; CH.
—Vindication of free-grace. 1644. *See* Lane, Samuel.

1213 —VVater-dipping no firm footing. *By J. M. for Henry Cripps and Lodowick Lloyd*, 1653. 4°. LT, ORP, CT, NPL, E; CH, NPT, NU, WF, Y.

1213A **Goodwin, John, *gent*.** Proposals humbly offered to the . . . House of Commons [for duty on woolen manufacture]. [*London*, 1696.] brs. L, LPR.

1213B —Proposals to the honourable House of Commons . . . to raise four millions. [*London*, 1696?] brs. L; BN.

1213C —To the . . . Houses of Lords and Commons. An abstract. [*London*, 1698?] brs. L.

1214 **Goodwin, Philip.** Dies Dominicus redivivus; or, the Lords Day enlivened. *By J. L. for Andrew Kembe*, 1654. 8°. LT, LCL, LW, P; NU.

1215 —The evangelicall communicant. *By A. M. for Christopher Meredith*, 1649. 8°. L, O, LCL, LW, CS; CH, CLC, NCD, NU, WWC.

1216 — —Second edition. *By R. and W. Leybourn for Andrew Kembe, and are to be sold by Tho. Pierripont [sic], and Edward Brewster*, 1657. 8°. L, LCL, LLP, LSC, EN; CLC, MH, WF.

1217 —The mystery of dreames. *By A. M. for Francis Tyton*, 1658. 8°. LT, O, LCL, LW, E; CLC, CU, LC, MH, NPT, WF, Y.

1218 —Religio domestica rediviva. *By R. & W. Leybourn, for Andrew Kemb; and Edward Brewster*, 1655. 8°. LT, O, LCL, OC, CS; IU, MB, NU.

1219 **Goodwin, Thomas.** The works of. The first volume. *By J. D. and S. R. for T. G. to be sold by Jonathan Robinson*, 1681. fol. T.C.I 437. L, O, C, LCL, ENC; CB, CU, MB, NU, WF, Y, AVP.

1220 — —Second volume. *By J. Darby, and S. Roycroft, for T. G. to be sold by Jonathan Robinson*, 1683. fol. T.C.II 11. L, O, LCL, LW, LSD; CB, CU, MB, NP, NU, Y, AVP.

1221 — —Third volume. *By J. Darby, J. Richardson, and T. Snowden, for T. G. to be sold by Jonathan Robinson*, 1692. fol. T.C.II 449. L, O, LCL, LW, LSD; CB, CU, KT, NP, NU, Y, AVP.

1222 — —Fourth volume. *By J. Darby, T. Snowden, and J. Astwood, for T. G. to be sold by Jonathan Robinson*, 1697. fol. L, O, LCL, LW; CB, CU, MB, NP, NU, Y, AVP.

1223 —Aggravation of sinne. *By T. P. and M. S. for John Rothwell*, 1643. 4°. LT, O, OC, DU, ENC; CH, CU, MU, NU, WF, Y.

1224 —Aggravation of { sinne: and / sinning against } knowledge. *By J. G. for R. Dawlman*, 1650. 4°. L, O, LW, BLH, DT; CH, CU, NPT, NU, WF, Y.

1225 —An apologeticall narration. *For Robert Dawlman*, 1643. 4°.* LT, O, C, MR, EN, ENC; BN, CH, CU, LC, MH, WF, Y.

1226 — —[Anr. ed.] *For Christopher Meredith*, 1644. 4°. L.

1226A —Certaine select cases. *For R. Dawlman*, 1644. 4°. IU, MIU, Y.

1227 — —[Anr. ed.] —, 1645. 4°. C, EN; TSM.

1228 Entry cancelled. *See following entry.*

1229 — —[Anr. ed.] *By M. F. for R. Dawlman*, 1647 [i.e. 1651]. 4°. L, O, CCH, ENC, DT; CH, CN, MH, NF, NU, Y. (var.)

1229A — —[Anr. ed.] *For R. D., to be sold by Thomas Eglesfield*, 1651. 4°. L, O, ORP, CS; IU, MH, WF, Y.

1230 —A childe of light. *By M. F. for R. Dawlman*, 1643. 4°, LT, LCL, LW; CLC, CU, NU, WF, Y.

1231 — —[Anr. ed.] [*London*, 1647.] 4°. L; CH, CN, CU, NF, WF, Y.

1231A   ——[Anr. ed.] *By J. G. for R. Dawlman, to be sold by Hen. Cripps,* 1659. 12°. L; NPT.

1232   —Christ set forth. *By W. E. and J. G. for Robert Dawlman,* 1642. 4°. LT, O, C, SHR, ENC; CH, CU, MU, NU, WF, Y.

1232A   ——[Anr. ed.] *For Charles Greene,* 1642. 12°. L, C, LCL, LW, SP; LC, MH, MU.

1232B   ——Second edition. *For Robert Dawlman,* 1642. 12°. WF.

1232C   ——[Anr. ed.] *Printed,* 1642. 12°. IU.

1233   ——[Anr. ed.] *Printed,* 1643. 12°. L.

1234   ——Fourth edition. *For Robert Dawlman,* 1645. 12°. L; CLC, NR.

1235   ——[Anr. ed.] *By J. G. for R. Dawlman,* 1651. 4°. L, O, LCL, BLH, DT; CH, IU, MH, NC, NU, TU, WF, Y.

1236   ——"Third" edition. *For Robert Dawlman,* 1653. 12°. L, LW; NGT.

1237   —Christ the universall peace-maker. *By J. G. for R. Dawlman,* 1651. 4°. LT, O, C, EN, DT; CH, CN, NU, WF, Y.

1238   —A copy of a remonstrance. *Printed,* 1645. 4°.* LT, O, CT, EC, MR; CH, MH, MWA, MU, NU, WF, Y.

1239   —A discourse of the punishment of sin in Hell. *For Jonathan Robinson,* 1680. 8°. L, O, CP, DU, EN; CH, CU, IU, MB, MH, NU.

1240   Entry cancelled.
      —Discourse of the true nature. 1695. *See* Goodwin, Thomas, *of Pinner.*

1241   —Encouragements to faith. *For R. Dawlman,* 1642. 12°. L; CLC, NR, WF.

1241A   ——[Anr. ed.] —, 1643. 4°.* EN.

1242   ——[Anr. ed.] —, 1645. 4°.* LT, O, CT, DU, ENC; CH, CU, NU, WF, Y.

1243   ——[Anr. ed.] —, 1647. 4°. L, LW; CH, NGT.

1244   ——[Anr. ed.] *By J. G. for R. Dawlman,* 1650. 4°.* L, O, LCL, LLP, DT; CLC, IU, NC, NPT, NU, WF, Y.

1245   Entry cancelled.
      —Fair prospect. 1658. *See* Goodwin, Thomas, *minister at Southweal.*

1245A   [–] A glimpse of Sions glory. *For William Larnar,* 1641. 4°.* LT, O; CU, MH, MM, NU, WF, Y.

1246   —The great interest of states & kingdomes. *For R. Dawlman, and are to be sold by Nath: Webb, and Will: Grantham,* 1646. 4°. LT, O, C, EN, DT; BN, IU, LC, MH, NPT, NU, WF, Y.

1246A   ——[Anr. ed.] *For R. Dawlman,* 1646. 4°. C, SHR, SP, WCA; CH, TU, AVP.

1247   Entry cancelled.
      —Heart of Christ in Heaven. 1642. *See* —Christ set forth.

1248   Entry cancelled.
      —Keyes of the kingdom. 1644. *See* Cotton, John.

1249   —Most holy and profitable sayings. [*London,* 1680.] brs. L; CN.

1250   Entry cancelled.
      —Of the constitution. 1696. *See*—Works. Fourth volume. 1697.

1251   [–] Patience and its perfect work. *By S. Simmons, for Rob. Duncomb,* 1666. 8°. L, O, LW; CLC, NPT, NU, WF.

1252   [–] —[Anr. ed.] *Printed,* 1667. 12°. L, LCL; MH.

1253   Entry cancelled.
      —Punishment of sin. 1680. *See* —Discourse of the punishment.

1253A   —The returne of prayers. *By J. Raworth, for R. Dawlman, to be sold by Luke Fawne,* 1641. 12°. L, O, DU; CLC, CSB, NF.

1254   ——[Anr. ed.] *By M. F. for R. Dawlman,* 1643. 4°. LT, O, LCL, LW; CH, CU, MH, NU, WF, Y.

1255   ——[Anr. ed.] *By J. G. for R. Dawlman,* 1651. 4°. L, O, LW, ORP, BLH; IU, NC, NF, NU, TU, WF, Y.

1255A   ——[Anr. ed.] *By R. H. for R. Dawlman, and are to be sold by W. Gilbertson,* 1659. 12°. L.

1256   —A sermon of the fifth monarchy. *Printed at London, for Livewel Chapman,* 1654. 4°.* LT, O, C, EN, DT; CSS, MWA, NN, NU, TO, WF.

1257   —A state of glory. *By J. G. for Robert Dawlman,* 1657. 4°. LT, O, C, DU, ENC; CH, MH, NU, WF, Y.

1258   [–] Transubstantiation a peculiar article. *Printed,* 1688. 4°. T.C.II 244. L, O, C, E, DT; CH, IU, MWA, NU, WF, Y.

1259   [–] —[Anr. ed.] *Printed,* 1688. 4°.* L; CSS, MH, NCD, NPT, NU.

1260   —The tryal of a Christians growth. *By M. Flesher, to be sold by Henry Overton,* 1641. 8°. L, LSC, OW, NPL, DC; CH, NR.

1260A   ——[Anr. ed.] *By M. Flesher, for R. Dawlman, and L. Fawne,* 1641. 8°. L, OC; MM, NU.

1261   ——[Anr. ed.] *For R. Dawlman,* 1643. 4°. LT, O, LCL, LW; CH, CLC, CU, MH, NU, WF, Y.

1262   ——[Anr. ed.] *By J. G. for R. Dawlman,* 1650. 4°. L, O, LLP, ORP, BLH; CH, IU, NC, NU, TU, Y.

1263   —Two discourses. *By J. D. for Jonathan Robinson,* 1693. 8°. T.C.II 462. L, C, NE; CN, NPT.

1264   —The vanity of thoughts discovered. *For R. Dawlman,* 1643. 4°. LT, O, C, LCL, DU, ENC; CH, CU, MH, NU, WF, Y.

1265   ——[Anr. ed.] *By J. G. for R. Dawlman,* 1650. 4°.* L, O, LCL, BLH, DT; CB, CH, IU, LC, NPT, NU, TU, WF, Y.

1266   —The vvorld to come. *Printed,* 1655. 4°.* LT, LCL, OCC, BSO, MF, NU, TO, TU, WF, Y.

1267   —Zervbbabels encovragement to finish the temple. *For R. D. and are to be sold by Francis Eglesfield,* 1642. 4°. L, O, C, CCH, BC, SHR; BN, CH, CSS, CU, MH, WF, Y.

1268   ——[Anr. ed.] *For R. Dawlman,* 1642. 4°. LT, C, OU, EN, DT; CH, IU, MH, NPT, NU, WF, Y.

1268A   **Goodwin, Thomas,** *of Pinner.* A discourse of the true nature of the gospel. *By J. Darby,* 1695. 4°. L, O, C, SP, EN; NU, WF.

1269   —Of the happiness of princes. *By J. D. for Jonathan Robinson,* 1695. 4°.* L, O, C, LW; CH, NGT, NU, WF, Y.

1270   —A sermon on occasion of the death of . . . Stephen Lobb. *For John Marshall,* [1699]. 4°.* T.C.III 132. L, LW; CLC, Y.

1270A   — —Second edition. —, [1700]. 4°. L; MH.

1270B   **Goodwin, Thomas,** *minister at Southweal.* A fair prospect. *By A. Maxey, for John Rothwell,* 1658. 8°. L, CS, SP; CLC.

1271   **Googe, Barnaby.** A prophecie lately transcribed. *By J. C. for R. Robinson,* 1672. 4°.* L, LSD, MC; HR, CH, RPJ.

1271A   **Gookin, Daniel.** To all persons whom these may concern. [*Boston* [*Mass.*], 1656.] brs. O.

1272   **Gookin, Vincent.** The author and case of transplanting the Irish into Connaught. *By A. M. for Simon Miller,* 1655. 4°. LT, O, C, DN, DT; CH, WF.

1273   [–] The great case of transplantation in Ireland discussed. *For I. C.,* 1655. 4°.* LT, C, OC, BLH, DT; CH, CN, CU, MH, Y.

1274   [–] —[Anr. ed.] *For John Crook,* 1655. 4°.* L, O, C, DN, DT; CH, CN, MH, WF, Y.

1274A   **Goos, Pieter.** The sea-atlas. *By Peter Goos, at Amsterdam,* 1668. fol. WF.

1274B   — —[Anr. ed.] —, 1670. fol. LAD; LC.

1275   **Goosey, Nathaniel.** A resolution of several cases in religion. [*London*], sold by *Jonathan Robinson,* 1692. 8°. NPT.

1276   **Gordon, Alexander.** Tyrocinium linguæ Latinæ, or. *By T. M. for Mathias Walker,* 1664. 8°. L, C; IU, TO, WF, ASU.

        Gordon, George. *See also* Sutherland, George Gordon, *earl of.*

1277   **Gordon, George,** *1st Duke of.* An account of the besieging. colop: *By George Croom,* 1689. brs. L.

1278   —Pædomathes. *Excudebat T. M. impensis authoris, prostat autem venalis apud R. Northcott,* 1689. sixes. L, E; CH, NC.

1279   [**Gordon, James**], *bp.* The reformed bishop. [*London*], *for the author,* 1679. 8°. O, C, AU, E, EN; CH, NGT, WF, Y.

1280   [–] —[Anr. ed.] *For the author, to be sold by Robert Harford,* 1680. 8°. T.C.I 373. L, LLL, LW, D, E, GU; CH, NU.

1281   [–] —[Anr. ed.] *For Edward Poole,* 1689. 8°. T.C.II 264. LCL, CE, EN, SA, BQ, DM.

1282   [–] A request to Roman Catholicks. *For Brab. Aylmer,* 1687. 4°.* L, O, C, EN, DT; CH, CN, MH, NU, WF, Y. (var.)

1283   [–] —Fourth edition. —, 1687. 4°.* L, O, C, DU, A, DT; IU, MH, NU, TU, WF, Y.

1283A   — —Fifth edition. —, 1687. 4°.* L, O, DU, LIU; CLC, IU, MH, NPT, WF.

1284   [–] Some observations on the Fables of Æsop. *Edinburgh, for Mr. Andrew Symson and are to be sold by him and by Mr. Henry Knox,* 1700. 4°. ALDIS 3924. L, E, EN, DT.

        [**Gordon, John.**] Pax vobis, or. [*n.p.*], 1679. *See* Griffith, Evan.

1285   [–] Plain dealing; being a moderate. *Printed, and are to be sold by Richard Baldwin,* 1689. 4°.* T.C.II 314. L, O, LLP, OC, LIU, EU; CU, MH, NU.

        Gordon, Lewis. *See* Huntly, Lewis Gordon, *marquis.*

1286   Entry cancelled.

        Gordon, Nathaniel. Treason and rebellion. 1646. *See* title.

1287   **Gordon, Patrick.** Geography anatomized. *By J. R. for Robert Morden and Thomas Cockerill,* 1693. 12°. T.C.II 457. L, O, LR, E; CH, LC, SYRACUSE, Y, YBA, AMB.

1288   — —Second edition. *For Robert Morden and Thomas Cockerill,* 1699. 4°. T.C.III 127. L, OC; IU, WF, Y, MOORE.

1289   —Theses philosophicæ. *Aberdoniis, imprimebat Edvardus Rabanus,* [1643]. 4°.* ALDIS 1111. AU.

1290   **Gordon, Robert.** Christianity vindicated. *For Robert Boulter,* 1671. 4°. L, O, LF, NE; PHS.

1291   [–] Spiritual order and Christian liberty. [*n.p.,* 1675.] 4°.* L, LF, BP; CH, NU, Y.

1292   [–] A testimony to the true Saviour. *For Robert Boulter,* 1669. 4°.* O.

1293   [–] —[Anr. ed.] *For Robert Boulter,* 1670. 4°.* O, LF, YM; MU, PHS, WF.

1293A   **Gordon,** *Sir* **Robert.** Unto the right honourable, the Lords of Council and Session, the petition of. [*Edinburgh,* 1700?] cap., fol.* CSS.

1294   **Gore, John.** The oracle of God. *For J. P. and are to be sold by Andrew Crooke and Charles Greene,* 1646. 4°.* LSC, BLH; CN, Y.

1295   —The poore mans hope. A sermon. *By T. H. to be sold by Andrew Crooke and Charles Greene,* 1646. 4°.* LSC, BLH; CLC, CN, Y.

1295A   —Ten godly and fruitfull sermons. *For J. P. and are to be sold by Andrew Crooke and Charles Greene,* 1646. 4°. CU, Y.

1296   —The way to prosper. A sermon. *For John Parker,* 1646. 4°. LSC, BLH; CN, Y.

1297   **Gore, Thomas.** Catalogus alphabeticè digestus. *Oxon., excudebat H. H.,* 1668. 4°.* MADAN 2802. L, O, MC; CH, IU.

1298   —Catalogus in certa capita, seu classes, alphabetico ordine. *Oxon. typis Leon. Lichfield, et prostant venales apud Ric. Davis,* 1674. 4°. T.C.I 189; MADAN 3011. L, O, C, AN, DU, EN; BN, CH, CN, MH, WF, Y.

1299   —Nomenclator geographicus. *Oxoniæ, typis Gulielmi Hall,* 1667. 8°. MADAN 2768. L, O, C, AN, LL, EN; BN, CH, IU, MH, WF, Y, HC.

        Gore, William. *See* Goeree, Willem.

1300   **Gorges,** *Sir* **Ferdinando.** America painted to the life. A true history. *By E. Brudenell, for Nathaniel Brook,* 1658. 4°. LT; CH, LC, MB, MH, NP, Y.

1301   —America painted to the life. The history. *By T. J. for Nath. Brook,* 1659. 4°. LT, C; CH, LC, MH, NS, Y.

1302   —America painted to the life. The true history. *For Nath. Brook,* 1659. 4°. LT, O, LW, E, DT; CH, CN, LC, MH, MU, Y.

1303   —A briefe narration of the originall undertakings. *By E. Brudenell, for N. Brook,* 1658. 4°. CH, CN, LC, MH, Y.

1303A   Gorgon's head or the monster of Munster. [*London?* 1660.] 4°.* CT.

        Goring, George. *See also* Norwich, George Goring, *earl of.*

1303B   **Goring, George,** *baron,* *1608—1657.* The declaration of Colonel Goring to the house of Commons, together. [*London*], *printed,* 1641. 4°.* LT, O, C, LNC, SP; CSS, LC, NU, WF, Y. (var.)

1303C   —The declaration of Colonell Goring vpon his examination. [*London*], *printed,* 1641. 4°.* L, O, EC; CH, CLC, IU, MHL, PL, TU, WF, Y.

1303D   [–] The discovery of a great and wicked conspiracie. *For Iohn Wright, Novemb. 28,* 1642. 4°.* LT, O, C, BR, EC, EN; CSS, IU, MH, NU, WF, Y. (var.)

1303E   [–] —[Anr. ed.] Ed. Blackmore, 1642. 4°.* O, LG, OC, MR, CD, DT.

1303F   —True newes from Portsmouth. Being Colonell Goring his speech. For Iohn Cave, August 13. 1642. 4°. LT; MH.

1303G   —George Lord Goring, Generall . . . whereas divers inhabitants. [London, 1645.] brs. STEELE 2631. LT.

1303H   **Gorion ben Syrach.** News from the Jews. For A. G., 1671. 4°. L.

1303I   **Gormanston, Jenico Preston, viscount.** The copy of a letter written from. Dvblin, by VVilliam Bladen, 1642. 4°.* DIX 341. LVF.

1304   ——[Anr. ed.] Imprinted at Dublin, reprinted at London for Benjamin Allen, July 15. 1642. 4°.* LT, O, EC, DN; WF.

1305   [**Gorton, Samuel.**] An antidote against the common plague. By J. M. for A. Crook, 1657. 4°. L; MB.

1305A   [–] —[Anr. ed.] By J. M. for A. C. 1657. 12°. O; IU, LC, RPJ, SE.

1306   —An incorruptible key. [London], printed, 1647. 4°. L; CN, MB, MH, MWA, NN, RPJ, Y.

1307   [–] Saltmarsh returned from the dead. For Giles Calvert, 1655. 4°. LT, O; MB, MH, NU, RPJ, WF.

1308   [–] Simplicities defence. By John Macock, to be sold by Luke Favvne, 1646. 4°. LT, LW, DT; CH, CN, MH, MU, NN.

1309   **Gosling, William.** Seasonable advice for preventing the mischiefe of fire. [London], for H. B., 1643. brs. LT, LG, EC.

1310   **Gosnold, John.** Βαπτισμων διδαχης. Of the doctrine of baptisms. By J. S. for the author, 1657. 4°.* L, O, EN; NU.

1311   ——[Anr. ed.] Reprinted, 1680. 8°. O; NHC.

1311A   [–] Holy and profitable sayings of Mr. J. G. For D. M., 1678. brs. O; MH.

1311B   [–] Of laying on of hands. By John Streater, 1656. 4°.* L; PL.

1312   **Gosnold, Paul.** A sermon preached . . . the ninth day of Aug. 1644. Oxford, by Henry Hall, [1644]. 4°.* MADAN 1674. O, CT, BC, OM, NE; WF.

1312A   Gospel-baptism or, plain proof. 1700. 12°. L; NHC.

        Gospel-call. 1688. See V., W.

        Gospel-commvnion. 1654. See Dury, John.

        Gospel-engine. 1649. See Harford, Rapha.

        Gospel family-order. [n.p.], 1676. See Fox, George.

        Gospel-glasse. 1667. See Stuckley, Lewis.

        Gospel grace. 1695. See Beverley, Thomas. Great gospel grace.

1313   Gospel grovnds; or, Christ declared. Printed at London, [1644]. 8°.* LT, OC; WF.

1313A   ——[Anr. ed.] [London, 1650?] 12°.* L.

        Gospel-liberty, and. [n.p.], 1668. See Fox, George.

        Gospel liberty sent. [n.p., 1664.] See Farnworth, Richard.

        Gospel musick. 1644. See Homes, Nathaniel.

        Gospel net. [n.p.], 1670. See H., T.

        Gospel order. [n.p.], 1700. See Woodbridge, Timothy.

1314   Gospel ordinance revis'd. Printed 1697, to be had at the Baptist Meeting-house in Glasshouse-Yard in Goswel Street. 8°. ORP, CT.

        Gospell-physitian. 1655. See Anthony, John.

        Gospel-separation. 1657. See Lawrence, Richard.

1314A   Gospel-truths held. [1698.] fol.* LF.

        Gospel-tydings. 1663. See Smith, William, of Besthorp.

1315   The gossips braule. Printed, 1655. 4°.* LT.

1316   The gossips feast or, morrall tales. Printed, 1647. 4°.* LT, O, LLU; CN, LC, WF.

1317   The gossips meeting. For F. Coles, T. Vere, J. Wright, and J. Clarke, [1674–79]. brs. O.

1318   **Gostelo, Walter.** Charls Stuart and Oliver Cromvvel united. [London], for the author, 1655. 8°. LT, O, C, LG, EN; CH, CLC, IU, NC, NN, WF, Y.

1319   —The coming of God in mercy, in vengeance. For the authour, Walter Gostelo, London, 1658. 8°. LT, O, LG; CH, NN, PPT, Y.

1320   —For the Lord Protector. [London, 1655.] brs. LT.

1320A   **Gostlin, Edmund.** Aurifodina lingvæ Gallicæ or the gold mine of the French language opened. For Iohn Streater, 1646. 8°. L (t.p.); WF.

1320B   **Gostwicke, Sir William.** The case of . . . [estate settlement]. [London, 1670.] brs. LPR.

1321   **Gostwyke, William.** The Christian merchant describ'd. For B. Aylmer, 1696. 4°.* T.C.II 587. O.

1322   —Pray for the peace. For Randal Taylor, 1692. 4°.* L, O, LSD; CH, CLC, MIU, NU.

1323   —A sermon preached . . . 26th of July 1685. Cambridge, by John Hayes. To be sold by H. Dickinson, and by Walter Davis, London, 1685. 4°.* L, O, C, CT, LSD; MH.

1323A   [**Gother, John.**] Afternoon instructions for the whole year. [London], printed, 1699. 2 vols. 12°. L, BSM, DUS; CN, MSL, TU, WF.

1324   [–] An agreement between the Church of England and Church of Rome. By Henry Hills, 1687. 4°. L, O, CCH, EN, DT; CH, CU, MH, NU, WF, Y.

1325   [–] An amicable accomodation. By H. Hills, 1686. 4°.* L, O, C, E, DT; CH, CN, MH, NU, WF, Y. (var.)

1326   [–] An answer to a discourse against transubstantiation. By Henry Hills, 1687. 4°. L, O, CT, MC, DT; CLC, CN, MH, MIU, WF, Y.

1327   [–] The Catholic represener, or the Papist misrepresented. Second part. By Henry Hills, 1687. 4°. L, O, OC, LSD, DT; CH, CN, MH, NU, WF, Y.

1328   [–] A discourse of the use of images. By Henry Hills, 1687. 4°.* L, O, C, LIL, DUS, DT; CH, MH, MIU, NU, WF, Y.

1328A   [–] Good advice to the papists. By Henry Hills, 1687. 4°.* 48 pp. O, OB, CT, EN; CH, CLC, NU, TU.

1329   [–] —[Anr. ed.] By Henry Hills, 1687. 4°. 70 pp. L, O, C, EN, DT; CH, CN, MH, TU, WF, Y.

1329AA [–] Instructions and devotions for hearing mass. [n.p.], 1694. 12°. D. M. ROGERS.

1329BA [–] —[Anr. ed.] Printed, 1696. 12°. DUS.

1329CA [–] —[Anr. ed.] Printed, 1699. 12°. L; WF.

1329DA [–] Instuctions [sic] and devotions for the afflicted and sick. [London], printed, 1697. 12°. L, O, FARM; CN.

1329EA [–] Instructions for apprentices. [London], printed, 1699. 12°. L, O; WF, Y.

1329FA [–] Instructions for children. [n.p.], 1698. 12°.* O; CLC.

1329gA [–] Instructions for confession and communion. *Printed,* 1696. 12°. DUS.

1329hA [–] —[Anr. ed.] [*n.p.*], 1700. 12°. L, DOWNSIDE.

1329iA [–] Instructions for masters, traders. [*London*], *printed* 1699. 8°. L, O; WF, Y.

1329A [–] Instructions for particular states. [*London*], *printed,* 1689. 12°. L, O, DUS; CH, CLC, CN, CU, MIU, TU, WF.

1329B [–] Instructions for the whole year. Part I. For Lent. [*London*], *printed,* 1695. 12°. L; CLC, CN, TU. (var.)

1329C [–] —[Anr. ed.] —, 1698. 12°. L.

1329D [–] Instructions for the whole year. Part II. For Sundays. [*London*], *printed,* 1695. 12°. BSM; CLC, MSL, TU.

1329E [–] —[Anr. ed.] —, 1698. L, BSM, DUS.

1329F [–] Instructions for the whole year. Part III. For Festivals. [*n.p.*], 1696. 8°. BSM; WF.

1329G [–] —[Anr. ed.] —, 1699. 12°. L, DUS; TU.

1329H [–] Instructions for the whole year. Part IV for Sundays. [*n.p.*], 1698. 12°. FARM; WF.

1329I [–] Instructions for youth. [*London*], *printed,* 1698. 12°. L, O; CLC, WF, Y.

1330 [–] A letter from a Dissenter to the divines. colop: *Printed, and are to be sold by Randal Taylor,* 1687. cap., 4°.* L, O, CS, E, DT; CH, CN, MIU, WF, Y.

1331 [–] —[Anr. ed.] *Re-printed at Holy-Rood-House,* 1687. 4°.* ALDIS 2696. MR, EN, AU; CLC.

1332 [–] Nubes testium: or a collection. *By H. Hills,* 1686. 4°. L, O, C, BSE, EN, DT; CH, CN, MH, NU, WF, Y.

1333 [–] A Papist mis-represented. [*London*], *printed,* 1665 [i.e. 1685]. 4°.* L, O, C, DU, LSD; CH, CLC, CN, NP, NU, WF, Y.

1334 [–] —[Anr. ed.] —, 1685. 4°. 79 pp. L, O, C, EN, DT; CH, CN, MH, NU, WF, Y. (var.)

1334A [–] —[Anr. ed.] —, 1685. 4°. 120 pp. L, OB, CS, CT, BAMB, DUS; CLC, CU, LC, MH, NC, NPT.

1334B [–] —[Anr. ed.] [*London*], *printed,* 1685. 80 pp. 4°. O, BANGOR; MH.

1335 [–] —[Anr. ed.] —, 1685. 63 pp. 4°. L, O, C, DC, DU; CH, CN, MH, WF, Y.

1335A [–] —[Anr. ed.] —, 1685. 127 pp. 4°. L, O, C, LLU, LSD; CLC, CN, MH, NU, WF, Y.

1335B [–] —[Anr. ed., "mispresented."] [*London*], *printed,* 1685. 4°. D.

1335C [–] —[Anr. ed.] —, 1686. 4°. C, LSC.

1336 [–] —[Anr. ed.] *Dublin, by A. C. & S. H. for the society of stationers,* 1686. 4°. DIX 219. L, O, C, EN, DT; CLC, INU, WG, Y.

1337 [–] —Second part. colop: *By Henry Hills,* 1686. 4°. L, O, LIL, MR, E; CLC, CN, MIU, NGT, WF. (var.)

1338 [–] — Part two. —, 1687. 4°. O, DT; MH, Y.

1339 [–] —Third part. *By Henry Hills,* 1687. 4°. L, O, BR, LSD, DT; CH, CN, MH, NU, WF, Y.

1340 [–] Papists protesting. *By Hen. Hills,* 1686. 39 pp. 4°.* L, C, E, EN, DT; CLC, CN, MH, NU, WF.

1341 [–] —[Anr. ed.] —, 1686. 38 pp. 4°.* L, O, CT, MC, CD; CH, CN, NU, PL, WF, Y.

1342 [–] —[Anr. ed.] —, 1687. 4°.* L, OC, OCC, BSE, DT; CH, CN, NPT, WF, Y.

[–] Pax vobis, or. [n.p.], 1679. *See* Griffith, Evan.

1343 [–] Pope Pius his profession of faith vindicated. *By Henry Hills,* 1687. 4°.* L, O, C, BR, DT; CH, CN, MIU, TU, WF, Y.

1344 [–] The Pope's supremacy asserted. *By Henry Hills,* 1688. 4°. L, O, LIL, MR, DT; CH, CN, MH, MIU, WF, Y.

1345 [–] The primitive fathers no Protestants. *By Henry Hills,* 1687. 4°.* L, LIL, OC, BR, DT; CH, IU, MH, TU, WF, Y.

1346 [–] Principles and rules of the gospel. [*London?*], *printed,* 1700. 12°. L, O; CLC, MSL, TU, WF, Y.

1347 [–] Pulpit-sayings, or, the characters of the pulpit-Papist examined. *By Henry Hills,* 1688. 4°. L, O, CT, MC, DT; CH, CN, MH, NU, WF, Y.

1348 [–] Reflections upon the answer to the Papist mis-represented. [*London,* 1686.] cap., 4°.* L, O, C, EN, DT; CH, CN, LC, MH, WF, Y.

1349 [–] A reply to the answer of the amicable accomoda-tion. *By Henry Hills,* 1686. 4°.* L, O, C, EN, DT; CH, CN, MH, NU, WF, Y.

[–] Seasonable discourse about religion. 1689. *See* title.

1349A [–] A short instruction for such as accuse their memory. [*n.p.*], 1698. 12°. O.

1350 [–] Transubstantiation defended. The first part. *By Henry Hills,* 1687. 4°. L, O, C, EN, DT; CH, CN, MH, MIU, WF, Y.

1351 **Gotherson, Daniel.** An alarm to all priests. *By James Cottrel,* 1660. 4°.* LF, BBN, MR; Y.

1352 **Gotherson, Dorothea.** To all that are unregenerated. *Printed,* 1661. 12°.* LF; PSC.

Gothofredus, Jacobus. *See* Godefroy, Jacques.

1353 [**Gott, Samuel.**] The divine history of the genesis of the world. *By E. C. & A. C. for Henry Eversden,* 1670. 4°. T.C.I 27. L, C, LCL, OH, SC; BN, CH, IU, MH, NU, WF, Y.

1354 — An essay of the true happiness. *By Rob. White, for Thomas Vnderhill,* 1650. 12°. LT, O, LW, CT; CLC, NU.

1355 [–] Novæ solymæ libri sex. *Typis Joannis Legati,* 1648. 8°. L, O, LW, LNC, P, EN; ZWT.

1356 [–] — [Anr. ed.] *Typis J. Legati, et venundantur per T. Underhill,* 1649. 8°. E.

1357 Gottlose kunstgriffe Konige. 1697. 4°. C, LL.

1358 **Gouge, Robert.** The faith of dying Jacob. *For Tho. Parkhurst, and Tho. Cockerill,* 1688. 12°. L, C, LCL, BC; CH, CLC, CN, WF, Y.

1358A [**Gouge, Thomas**?] Catecism byrr sy'n cynnwys. 1657. CE.

1359 — Christian directions. *By R. Ibbitson, and M. Wright,* 1661. 4°. LCL, OM, LSD, SP, WCA; MH, NU.

1359A ——Second edition. *By R. I. and are to bee sold by M. Wright.* 1661. 4°. C.

1360 ——[Anr. ed.] *By R. Ibbitson, to bee sold by J. Wright,* 1664. 8°. L, O, LCL, LW, OC; WF.

1360A ——[Anr. ed.] *By A. Maxwell for S. Parker,* 1672. 8°. AN.

1361 [–] —[Anr. ed.] *By A. Maxwell for George Sawbridg, and John Wright,* 1674. 8°. T.C.I 130. L, BLH; NU.

1362 ——[Anr. ed.] *For John Hancock,* 1675. 8°. L, BANGOR.

1363 ——[Anr. ed.] —, 1679. 8°. T.C.I 378. CE; LC, NF, Y.

1364 ——[Anr. ed.] *For Thomas Parkhurst, Benjamin Tooke, Samuel Lee, Samuel Crouch, and Thomas Cockeril,* 1680. 8°. L, LCL, AN; CH, CLC.

1365   ——[Anr. ed.] *By E. Mallet, for Samuel Lee,* 1684. 8°. LG, OME, DU.

1366   ——[Anr. ed.] *For Thomas Parkhurst,* 1690. 8°. T.C.II 343. NU.

1366A ——[Anr. ed.] *For the assigns of Tho. Gouge and sold by the booksellers of London & Westminster,* 1700. 8°. L; MWA.

1367   —Gair i bechaduriaid, a gair i'r sainct. *Printiedig yn Llundain gan A. Maxwell,* 1676. 8°. L, O, AN, CPL; CN, MH, WF.

1368   —God's call to England. *For John Hancock,* 1680. 12°. T.C.I 381. C, LCL, P; Y.

1368A —Gwyddorion y grefydd Gristianogol. *Printiedic yn Llundain gan Tho. Dawks,* 1679. 12°. AN, CPL.

1368B —Hyfforddiadau Christianogol. *Printiedig yn Llundain gan A. Maxwell,* 1675. CPL; CN. [part of D1367.]

1369   [–] Joshua's resolution. *Printed,* 1663. 4°.* L; NU.

1369A [–] Principlau neu bennau y grefydd Ghristianogol. *Printiedig yn Llundain gan A. Maxwell,* 1676. 8°.* L, AN, CPL, LSD; CN, MH, WF. [part of D1367.]

1370   [–] The principles of Christian religion. *By R. L. for Samuel Man,* 1645. 8°.* O; CH.

1371   [–] —[Anr. ed.] *For John Wright,* 1668. 8°.* O.

1371A — —[Anr. ed.] *For J. Wright,* 1670. 8°.* MH.

1372   [–] —[Anr. ed.] *By E. T. and R. H. to be sold by Robert Boulter,* 1672. 8°.* L, C, LCL, DC.

1372A [–] —[Anr. ed.] *By A. M. to be sold by Robert Boulter,* 1673. 8°. L.

1373   ——[Anr. ed.] *By T. Dawks, to be sold by Robert Boulter,* 1675. 8°.* L.

1373A ——[Anr. ed.] *For Robert Boulter,* 1675. 8°. BANGOR; CLC, NU.

1374   ——[Anr. ed.] *By Tho. James for Thomas Parkhurst,* 1679. 8°. T.C.I 348. L, O, LW, ENC; CH, MBA, NU, WF, Y.

1375   ——[Anr. ed.] *For Tho. Parkhurst,* 1680. 8°. AU; CLC, NF, TSM.

1376   ——[Anr. ed.] *By J. and J. How for Samuel Lee,* 1684. 8°. L; NU, Y.

1376A —Rhesswmmau yscrythurawl. *Printiedig yn Llundain gan Tho. Whitledge, a W. Everingham,* 1693. 12°.* AN, CPL; MH.

1376B —The sayings of. *For J. Deacon,* 1681. brs. DCH.

1377   — The surest & safest way of thriving. *For William Rawlins,* 1673. 4°. O, OC, CT, LCL, SP; CH, CU, NC, NU, Y.

1378   ——[Anr. ed.] *By S. and B. G. for Nevil Simmons,* 1676. 12°. L, LUG, LW; CLC, NU, TO, WF, Y.

1378A [–] Traethawd byrr yn erbyn meddwdod. *Gan A. Maxwell,* 1675. 8°.* CPL, LSD; CN. [part of D1367.]

1379   —A word to sinners. 1668. 8°. T.C.I 1. LCL.

1379A [–] —[Anr. ed.] *For John Wright,* 1670. 8°. C; NU, Y.

1380   [–] —[Anr. ed.] *By E. T. and R. H. to be sold by Robert Boulter,* 1672. 8°. T.C.I 123. L, LW; WF.

1381   ——[Anr. ed.] *For Tho. Parkhurst,* 1674. 8°. L, C, BANGOR, BLH; NU.

1381A ——[Anr. ed.] *By S. and B. Griffin for Tho. Parkhurst,* 1677. 8°. IU, MH.

1382   ——[Anr. ed.] *By Tho. Snowden, for Will. Miller, Edw. Thomas, William Bromwich, Robert Clavell, John Wright, Benjamin Allen,* 1680. 8°. L, CE; NU.

1383   ——[Anr. ed.] *By E. Mallet, for Samuel Lee,* 1683. 8°. T.C.II 65. DC; NU, Y.

1384   ——[Anr. ed.] *For the assigns of Thomas Gouge,* 1691. 8°. L; NU.

1385   [–] The young man's guide through the wilderness. *For P. Parker,* 1670. 8°. T.C.I 48. L, BC; MH, NU.

1386   [–] —[Anr. ed.] *By E. T. and R. H. to be sold by Robert Boulter,* 1672. 8°. L.

1387   ——[Anr. ed.] *By S. and B. G. for Nevil Simmons,* 1676. 8°. CLC, NU.

1388   ——[Anr. ed.] *By T. S. and are to be sold by Edward Thomas, Nath. Ponder, Dorman Newman, Sam. Crouch, Ben. Billingsley, Thomas Simmons, Samuel Tidmarsh,* 1680. 8°. CT; NU, Y.

1388A ——[Anr. ed.] *By T. B.,* 1696. 12°. LW; TO.

1389   **Gouge, William.** Briefe answers to the chiefe articles. Fourth edition. *By G. M. for Edward Brewster,* 1642. 8°.* LT.

1390   —A fvnerall sermon preached . . . August 24, 1646. *By A. M. for Joshua Kirton,* 1646. 4°.* LT, O, C, BR, DT; CII, CU, MII, NU, WT, AVP.

1391   —A learned and very vsefvl commentary on the whole epistle to the Hebrewes. *By A.M. T.W. and S.G. for Joshua Kirton,* 1655. fol. L, O, C, SHR, ENC; CH, CN, NU, WF, Y.

1392   —Mercies memoriall. *By George Miller for Joshua Kirton,* 1645. 4°.* LT, O, CK, BC, E, DT; CH, NU, WF, Y.

1393   —The progresse of divine providence. *By G. M. for Ioshua Kirton,* 1645. 4°.* LT, O, C, E, CD; CH, CU, MH, WF, Y.

1394   —The right way. *By A. Miller for Ioshua Kirton,* 1648. 4°.* LT, O, C, OCC, DT; CH, MA, MH, NU, WF.

1395   [–] The Sabbaths sanctification. *By G. M. for Joshua Kirton, and Thomas Warren,* 1641. 4°. O, LSC, OC; NU.

1396   ——[Anr. ed.] —, 1641. 4°.* L, C, LCL, SP, WCA, DT; NF, NU, Y.

1397   —The saints svpport. *By G. M. for Joshua Kirton,* 1642. 4°.* LT, O, C, ENC, DT; CH, CN, MH, WF, Y, AVP.

1398   ——[Anr. ed.] *By George Miller for Joshua Kirton,* 1645. 4°.* O, LLP, OCC, BC, DT; BBE, NN, NU, TU, WF, Y.

1399   —A treatise of apostasy. *By G. M. for John Kirton & T. Warren,* 1641. 4°. NU.

1400   —The whole armour of God. Sixth edition. *For Humphrey Robinson,* 1647. 12°. LNC; CLC, NU.

1401   **[Gough, John.]** The academy of complements. Fourth edition. *By T. Badger for H. Mosley,* 1641. 12°. CLC, IU.

1401A [–] —Sixth edition. —, 1645. 12°. MH, Y.

1401B [–] —Seventh edition. *By M. Bell, for Hum. Moseley,* 1646. 12°. O.

1401C [–] —Ninth edition. *For Humphrey Mosely,* 1650. 12°. IU.

1402   [–] —"Last" edition. *For Humphrey Moseley,* 1650. 12°. L, O; WF, Y.

1403   [–] —[Anr. ed.] —, 1654. 12°. CT.

1404   [–] —[Anr. ed.] —, 1658. 12°. WF.

1405   [–]—[Anr. ed.] *By Tho. Leach, and Tho. Child,* 1663.
       12°. O; MH.
1405A [–]—[Anr. ed.] *For A. Mosley,* 1664. 12°. O.
1405B [–]—[Anr. ed.] *For A. M.,* 1670. 12°. T.C.I 51. L; Y.
1406   [–]—[Anr. ed.] *For P. Parker,* 1684. 12°. O; IU, WF. (var.)
1407   [–]—"Fifth" edition. *For Thomas Passinger,* 1685. 8°.* L.
1408   —Ecclesiæ Anglicanæ θρηνωδια. 1661. *Typis W. G. &
       prostant venales apud Rich. Thrale.* 8°. LT, O, CJ, DU, P,
       EN; BN, NHC.
1409–10 Entries cancelled.
       Gough, Thomas. *See* Gowan, Thomas.
1411   **[Gough, William.]** Londinum triumphans. *For the
       author and are to be sold by L. Curtis,* 1682. 8°. T.C.I 507.
       L, C, LG, EN; CH, Y.
1412   [–]—[Anr. ed.] *For the author and are to be sold by Thomas
       Simmons,* 1682. 8°. L, O, CS, BC, EN; BN, CLC, CN, LC,
       MBP, MH, WF.
1413   —Four sermons. *J. & H. Hammond,* 1695. 12°. L, LCL.
       Goughe, Alexander. The Queen. 1653. *See title.*
1414   **[Gould, Anne.]** An epistle to all the Christian magis-
       trates. *For Thomas Simmons,* 1659. 4°.* L, LF, BBN;
       CH, IU, MBZ, PH, RPJ, Y.
1415   **[Gould, Daniel.]** A brief narration of the sufferings of
       the people called Quakers. [*New York, by William
       Bradford?* 1700.] 12°.* EVANS 911. LF; MHS, PH, PSC, RPJ.
1416   **Gould, John.** A call and a warning. *For Thomas Sim-
       mons,* 1657. 4°.* LT, O, LF, OC, MR; CH, PH.
1417   **Gould, Robert.** The corruption of the times by
       money. A satyr. *For Matthew Wotton,* 1693. 4°.* L, O,
       C, LG, LUG; CH, CN, MH, NP, Y.
1418   —The dream. To Sʳ. Charles Duncomb. *For A. Baldwin,*
       1700. fol.* CS, MR, CD; MH, MIU, WF, Y.
1419   [–] A funeral eclogue to the pious memory of . . . Mrs.
       Wharton. [*London*], *for Joseph Knight, and Francis
       Saunders,* 1685. fol.* LLU, MR; CU, MH, Y.
1420   [–] The laureat. Jack Squabbs history. [*London?* 1687.]
       cap., fol.* L, O, MR; CH, IU, MH, MU, NCD, NRU, WF.
1421   Entry cancelled. *See previous entry.*
       [–] The laurel. 1685. *See title.*
1422   —Love given o're. *For Andrew Green,* 1682. 4°.* MH,
       NP, PL, WF, Y.
1423   [–]—[Anr. ed.]—, 1683. 4°.* L, O; CLC, MH, TU, Y.
1424   [–]—[Anr. ed.] *For R. Bentley, and J. Tonson,* 1685.
       4°. O; TU, Y.
1425   [–]—[Anr. ed.]—, 1686. 4°.* O, C, CT, MR; CLC, CN, MH,
       NP, TU, Y.
1426   [–]—[Anr. ed.]—, 1690. 4°.* T.C.II 342. L, O, LIU, DT;
       CH, MB, MH, AVP.
       —Ludus scacchiæ: a satyr. 1675. *See title.*
1427   [–] Mirana. A funeral eclogue: sacred to the memory of
       . . . Eleanora, late Countess of Abingdon. *For Francis
       Saunders,* 1691. fol.* CLC, MH, Y.
1428   —The mourning swain. *For the author, and sold by John
       Nutt,* 1700. fol.* O, MR; CH, MH, NP, Y.
1429   —A poem most humbly offered . . . Queen Mary. *For
       Jacob Tonson and Francis Saunders,* 1695. fol.* T.C.II
       539. L, O, C, LLU, AU; CH, CN, MH, TU, WF, Y.

1430   ——Second edition. —, 1695. fol.* L, O, C, E; MH, MIU,
       NP, TU, Y.
1431   —Poems. *Printed,* 1689. 8°. L, O, C, LLU, EN; CH, CN, MH,
       WF, Y.
1432   ——Second edition. *For J. K. and sold by R. Baldwin,*
       1697. 8°. L.
1433   [–] Presbytery rough-drawn. *For Joanna Brome,* 1683.
       4°.* L, O, CS, MR, EN; CH, IU, MH, TU, WF, Y.
1434   —The rival sisters. *For Richard Bently, Francis Saunders,
       and James Knapton,* 1696. 4°. L, O, OW, LLU, EN; CH, CN,
       LC, MH, MU, NC, TU, WF, Y.
1435   [–] A satyr against wooing. *Printed,* 1698. 4°.* L, O, DT;
       MH, Y.
1436   [–] A satyrical epistle to the female author of a poem,
       call'd Silvia's revenge. *For R. Bentley,* 1691. fol.* L;
       CH, CU, MH, Y.
1436A [–] A song in the last new tragedy of the rivall-sisters.
       [*London,* 1696.] brs. L.
1436B [–] A song in the play call'd The rival sisters. [*London,*
       1696.] brs. L.
       [–] Sylvia's revenge. 1688. *See* Ames, Richard.
1437   [–] To the society of the beaux-esprits. *For Joseph Knight
       and Francis Saunders,* 1687. 4°.* T.C.II 193. L, O, C, LL,
       OC; CH, IU, MH, TU, WF, Y.
1438   **Gould, William.** Conformity according to canon just-
       ified. *By A. Maxwell, for R. Royston, and are to be sold
       by Abisha Brocas, in Exon,* 1674. 4°. L, O, C, LSD, WCA;
       NCD, NPT, NU, WF, Y.
1439   —Domus mea, domus orationis, a sermon. *For R. Roys-
       ton, and are to be sold by Abisha Brocas, in Exeter,* 1672.
       4°.* T.C.I 110. L, O, DU, LSD, WCA; CLC, MH, NGT, NU,
       WF.
1440   —The generosity of Christian love. *By J. Grover for
       R. Royston,* 1676. 4°.* T.C.I 234. L, O, C, LSD, NE; CLC,
       NU, WF.
1441   —The primitive Christian justified. *For R. Royston,*
       1682. 4°.* T.C.I 459. L, O, C, BR, EN, DT; CH, CN, MH,
       NU, V, WF, Y. (var.)
1442   —Religio Christiana est. [*n.p.,* 1671.] brs. O.
1443   **Gouldman, Francis.** A copious dictionary. *By John
       Field,* 1664. 4°. L, C, OME, DU, E; BN, CH, CN, MB, MU,
       NCU, Y.
1444   ——Second edition. *Cambridge, by John Field, to be sold
       by George Sawbridge,* 1669. 4°. T.C.I 23. L, O, C, BC, SC;
       IU, PL, TU, WF, Y.
1445   ——Third edition. *Cambridge, by John Hayes, to be
       sold by George Sawbridge, John Place, William Place,
       Thomas Bassett, Thomas Dring, and John Leigh, London,*
       1674. 4°. T.C.I 158. L, O, LW, NOT; CH, CU, IU, TU, Y.
1445A ——"Third" edition. *Cambridge, by John Hayes,* 1674.
       4°. L, CCA; LC, TO.
1446   ——Fourth edition. —, 1678. 4°. T.C.I 306. L, O, C, NE,
       ENC; CLC, CN, LC, MH, NC.
1446A [–] Dictionarium etymologicum. *Excudebat Joannes Field,*
       1664. 4°. OC.
1447   Entry cancelled. Ghost.

1447A [–] —[Anr. ed.] *Excudebat Guliemvs Rawlins*, 1673. 4°.
NRU, RPJ.

1447B [–] Dictionarium historio-geographico-poeticum. *Can-tabrigiæ, J. Field*, 1669. CU.

1448 **G[ouldney], H[enry].** A late libeller's folly manifested. *Printed and sold by T. Sowle*, 1694. 8°.* LF, BBN; PH, WF.

1449 [–] A new way of reading the Bible. [*London*, 1699.] 4°.*
LF, BBN; IE, PH.

1450 **Gouldsborough, John.** Reports of . . . in all the courts at Westminster. *By W. W. for Charles Adams*, 1653. 4°. LT, O, C, EN, DT; CH, LC, MHL, NCL, WF, YL, AVP.

1451 — —Second edition. *For Awnsham Churchill*, 1682. 4°. T.C.I 479. O, LL; LC, PUL.

Gourdon. *See* Gordon.

1451A **Goussault, Jacques.** Advice to young gentlemen. *For Tho. Leigh*, 1698. 8°. L, NE, NL, M, EN; WF, Y.

1452 **Gove, Richard.** The communicants guide. *By J. G. for Richard Royston*, 1654. 8°. O, C.

1453 —Pious thoughts vented. *By J. G. for R. Royston*, 1658. 8°. LT, LCL; CLC.

1454 —The saints hony-comb. *For Richard Royston*, 1652. 12°. LT, O, BR; CH, Y.

1454A — —[Anr. ed.] [*London*], —, *and are to be sold by Thomas Miller, in Sherburn*, 1652. 8°. WF.

1454B [–] A soveraigne salve to cure vvounded spirits. *By J. G. for R: Royston*, 1650. 8°. BR; CLC, WF.

1455 [–] —[Anr. ed.] —, *to be sold by Thomas Miller in Sherburne*, 1650. 8°. C, LCL, DC; CLC.

Goveanus, Thomas. *See* Gowan, Thomas.

Government and order. [n.p.], 1641. *See* Henderson, Alexander.

Government described. 1659. *See* S., J.

Government of monarchie, 1659. *See* S., J.

1456 The government of the Church of Scotland fully declared. *Printed at London. To be sold by John Sweeting*, 1647. 4°. L, OC, LIU, SP, EN, DT; NU.

1457 The government op [*sic*] the common-wealth of England. *Printed at London and re-printed at Leith*, 1654. 4°. ALDIS 1491. BC, YM, E, EN; WF.

Government of the people. 1650. *See* Parker, John.

Government of the thoughts. 1694. *See* Allestree, Richard.

Government of the tongue. Oxford, 1674. *See* Allestree, Richard.

1457A **G[owan], T[homas].** Ars sciendi sive logica. *Excudebat per Johannem Richardson, prostant vero apud Thomæ Parkhurst*, 1681. 8°. T.C.I 513. C, CJ, GU, DM; CH, MWA, WF.

1457B [–] —[Anr. ed.] *Prostant venum apud Guilielmum Robinson, Oxonia*, 1682. 8°. L, OC.

1457C [–] —[Anr. ed.] *Prostant venum apud Franciscum Hicks, Cantabridgiæ*, 1682. 8°. CT, CS, EC, DM; CLC, PL.

—Elementa logicae. Dublin, 1683. *See* —Logica.

1457D —Logica elenctica. *Dublinii, excudebat Jos. Ray, sumptibus ejusdem; prostant venales apud Eliph. Dobson*, 1683. 8°. DIX 203. L, LW, OC, CE, GU, DM; CH, TO, WF.

1457E — —[Anr. ed.] *Dublinii, excudebat Jos. Ray, pro Eliphal Dobson*, 1683. 8°. CD; IU.

1457F — —[Anr. ed.] *Dublin, for E. Dobson, sold by A. Churchill in London*, 1683. 8°. L.

1458 **Gower, Humfrey.** A discourse, deliver'd . . . September 1684. *Cambridge, by John Hayes. For John Creed*, 1685. 4°. T.C.II 142. L, O, C, YM, DT; CH, CLC, IEG, NU, WF, Y.

1459 —A sermon preached . . . on Christmas Day, 1684. *By S. Roycroft, for Robert Clavell*, 1685. 4°.* T.C.II 111. L, O, CT, LSD, YM; CH, CU, MBA, NN, WF, Y.

1459A —The speech of Doctor Gower. *Edinburgh, re-printed*, 1681. brs. ALDIS 2269. 7. EN, MH.

1460 **[Gower, John.]** The cow-ragious castle-combat. *For R. M.*, 1645. 4°.* LT; CH.

1461 **Gower, John, Capt.** A trve relation out of Ireland. *For Richard Best*, 1642. 4°.* LT, O, C, EC, BLH, DN; CH, Y.

1462 **Gower, Stanley.** Things now-a-doing. *By G. M. for Philemon Stephens*, 1644. 4°.* LT, O, C, E, DT; CH, CN, MH, NU, WF, Y.

Gowlin: or. [n.p., 1678–82.] *See* D'Urfey, Thomas.

1463 **Graaf, Reinier de.** De succo pancreatico: or, a physical and anatomical treatise. *For N. Brook*, 1676. 8°. T.C.I 236. O, C, LCP, GH, GK; CLM, NAM, RBU, WSG, HC.

1464 **Grabe, Johann Ernst.** Spicilegium SS. patrum. *Oxoniæ, e theatro Sheldoniano*, 1698–9. 2v. 8°. T.C.III 158. L, O, C, ENC, DT; BN, CH, CN, MH, NC, WF, Y.

1465 — —Second edition. *Oxoniæ, e theatro Sheldoniano*, 1700. *Impensis Joannis Oweni*, 2v. 8°. L, O, CCH, EC, DT; BN, CLC, CU, MB, MH, NU.

1466 **Grabu, Louis.** Pastoralle. A pastoral in French. [*London*, 1684.] fol. CM.

1467 Grace imprisoned and vertue despised. [*London*, 1648.] brs. LT.

Grace leading. 1651. *See* Hall, John.

Grace triumphant. 1700. *See* Mather, Cotton.

1467A Graces to be said at the table. *By J. Bell*, 1655. 8°.* C.

1468 **Gracian y Morales, Baltasar.** The courtiers manual oracle. *By M. Flesher, for Abel Swalle*, 1685. 8°. T.C.II 138. L, O, LW, CT, LLU; CH, IU, MH, NC, TU, WF, Y.

1469 —The courtier's oracle. *For Abel Swalle, and Tim. Childe*, 1694. 8°. T.C.II 515. L, O, CT, LLU, M; CLC, CN, FU, MU, NN, WF, Y.

1470 —The critick. *By T. N. for Henry Brome*, 1681. 8°. T.C.I 443. I, O, C, ES, DT; CH, CLC, CU, MH, WF, Y.

1471 [–] The heroe of Lorenzo. *For John Martin and James Allestrye*, 1652. 12°. L, O, C, OC, LLU; CH, CN, MH, WF, Y.

1472 The gracious answer of the most illustrious lady of pleasure. [*London*, 1668.] brs. L; MH.

1472A Gradus ad Parnassum. *Prostant venales apud Abel Swalle*, 1680. 8°. CM.

1472B —[Anr. ed.] *For Benjamin Tooke; and Thomas Cockerill*, 1687. 8°. T.C.II 193. RPL.

1472C —[Anr. ed.] *Impensis Benj. Tooke & Tho. Cockerill*, 1691. 12°. T.C.II 348. C; CH, WF.

1472D —[Anr. ed.] —, 1694. 12°. MB.

1472E —[Anr. ed.] *Impensis Benj. Took, & Tho. Cockerill*, 1698. 12°. BC; Y.

1473   Gradus Simeonis: or, the first-frvits of Philip, Earle of Pembroke. [*London*, 1649.] 4°.* LT, EN; CH, CSS, MH, MIU.

Græcæ grammatices. *Cantabrigiæ*, 1647. *See* Busby, Richard.

1474   Entry cancelled.

Græcorum epigrammatum florilegium novum. 1684. *See* Ανθολογια δευτερα.

1475   **Grævius, Johannes Georgius.** Oratio de auspicatissima expeditione Britannica. *Impensis D. Newman*, 1689. 4°.* T.C.II 288. L, O, C, CT, DT; WF.

Graham, James. *See* Montrose, James Graham, *marquis of.*

Graham, Sir Richard. *See* Preston, Richard Graham, *viscount.*

1476   **Graham, Richard.** Poems. Upon the death of the most honorable, the Lady Marchioness of Winchester. *York. by Alice Broad, and John White*, 1680. fol.* L.

1476A [**Graile, Edmond.**] Timothy's lesson. *Printed* 1699. 12°. EN, AU; WF.

1477   **Graile, John.** A modest vindication of the doctrine. *For Mat. Keinton*, 1655. 4°. LT, O, CT, P, DT; MH, MIU, NU, WF, Y.

1478   —Sacra privata. *Typis J. L. impensis Gualteri Kettilby*, 1699. 8°. L, O, C, LNC, NPL, DT; NGT, WF.

1479   —Three sermons. *For W. Kettilby*, 1685. 8°. T.C.II 95. L, C, NPL; CH, CLC, WF.

1480   [–] The true and real violations. *By J. D. for Brabazon, Aylmer*, 1683. 8°. T.C.II 7. O, CT, P; NC.

Grain of incense. 1643. *See* Reading, John.

Grammaire Françoise. 1674. *See* Festeau, Paul. French grammar.

1481   Grammatica exemplaris. *Anno Dom.* 1661. 8°.* L.

Grammatica rationis. *Oxonii*, 1673. *See* Fell, John, *bp.*

1481A Grammaticæ Græcæ . . . Westmonasteriensis. *Cantabrigiæ*, 1647. 8°. CCA.

Grammaticæ Latinæ institutiones. 1654. *See* Shirley, James.

1481B Grammatical cards. *For S. Mearn, and A. Clark, and are to be sold by J. Seller and J. Hill*, 1677. 12°. L; Y.

Grammatical drollery. 1682. *See* Hickes, William.

Grammaticall miscellanies. *Oxford*, 1660. *See* Merriott, Thomas.

Grammaticarum in Dionysii. 1658. *See* Hill, William.

1481C Grammatices græcæ enchiridion. *Typis Jac. Flesher & voeneunt apud R. Royston*, 1650. 8°.* Y.

Grammaticus analyticus. 1670. *See* E., J.

1482   Grampius congratulation. [*n.p.*], *printed*, 1660. 4°.* F; Y.

1483   **Grana, Otho Henry de, Marquis.** . . . His mandatory letter . . . [12 October 1683]. colop: *For R. Baldwin*, 1683. brs. L, O, HH; CH, WF, Y.

1484   —Otton Henry Marquis Dal Caretto, . . . la France . . . [11 December 1683]. *Re-printed at London by A. Churchill*, 1683. brs. O; CH.

1485   Entry cancelled.

Granadiers loyal health. [*n.p.*], 1683. *See* Grenadiers.

1485A The grand abuses stript and whipt. *By Edward Crowch*, 1672. brs. L.

1486   The grand account. Or, a remonstrance. *Oxford* [*London?*], *printed*, 1647. MADAN 1946-7. LT, O, LUG, CCA, DT; CLC, CN, MH, WF, Y. (var.)

Grand apocalyptical vision. [*n.p.*, 1690.] *See* Beverley, Thomas.

1486A The grand case of conscience concerning. *By John Macock for Francis Tyton*, 1650. 4°.* LT, O, CS, YM, DT; CH, MH, NU, WF, Y.

1486B A grand case of conscience resolved. *For James Collins*, 1672. 4°. OC.

1486C The grand case of conscience stated. [*London*, 1649.] cap., 4°.* LT, O, C; CSS, MH, NHC, NU, Y.

1487   The grand case of England, so fiercely. *For J. Partridge*, 1642. 4°.* LT, O, LG, CT, LIU, DT; IU, MH, NC, NN, WF, Y.

Grand case of the present. 1662. *See* Fullwood, Francis.

1488   The grand catastrophe, or the change of government. *By R. I.*, 1654. 4°.* LT, BC, MR, DT; CLC, CN, NU, WF, Y.

1489   The grand cheat cryed up. [*London*, 1659.] brs. LT, O; CH, Y.

1490   The grand committee for Greenwich hospital. [*n.p.*, 1695.] brs. O.

1491   The grand concern of England. *Printed*, 1673. 4°. L, O, LVF, CT, LLU, DT; CH, IU, LC, MH, NC, Y.

1492   The grand concernments of England ensured. *Printed*, 1659. 4°. LT, OC, CT, BC, DT; CH, IU, MBA, MH, WF, Y.

1493   —[*Anr. ed.*] *Edinburgh, reprinted*, 1659. 4°. ALDIS 1599. L, SP, E, A; NCD.

Grand conspiracy. 1655. *See* Allington, John.

Grand debate between the most reverend . . . bishops. 1661. *See* Baxter, Richard.

1494   Entry cancelled.

Grand debate concerning presbitery. 1648. *See* Reasons presented by the dissenting brethren.

1495   —[*Anr. ed.*] [*London*], *for Anthony Williamson*, 1652. 4°. L, O, YM, E, DT; BBE, CN, NU, WF.

Grand designe: or. [*n.p.*], 1647. *See* Harris, John.

Grand designs of. 1678. *See* Prynne, William.

1496   The grand differences between France, Spain, and the Empire. *For Henry Herringman*, 1657. 8°. O, DC, SP; CH, CLC, NN, RPJ, Y.

Grand errour. 1680. *See* Allen, William.

Grand imposter discovered. 1675. *See* Keach, Benjamin.

Grand impostor examined. 1656. *See* Deacon, John.

1497   The grand imposture: or the mystery of iniquity: a satyr. *Printed*, 1679. fol.* L, O, LLU; CLC, CN, MH, NP, TU, WF.

1498   The grand indictment of high treason . . . Argyle. [*London*], *printed*, 1661. 4°.* LT, O, C, P, EN; CLC, MH, NU, WF, Y.

1498A —[*Anr. ed.*] [*Edinburgh?*], *for the author*, 1661. fol.* CH.

1499   The grand informer, or the prerogative of princes. *Oxford, by I. H. and H. H.*, 1647. 4°.* MADAN 1940. LT, O, OB, CJ; CH, CN, CU, TO, WF, Y.

Grand inquest. 1680. *See* Garbrand, John.

1500   The grand juries address and presentments . . . Bristol.
       colop: *For Joseph Hindmarsh,* 1681. brs. L, O, LG, BR,
       HH; CH, MH, ANL, AVP.

1500A Grand juries address to the mayor . . . of Bristol. *Edin-
       burgh, by the heir of A. Anderson,* 1681. fol. ALDIS 2270.
       AU.

1501   Grand-jurors of the city of Bristoll, their address. [*n.p.*],
       printed with allowance, 1675. 4°.* LL, LSD.

       Grand-jury-man's oath. 1680. *See* Hawles, *Sir* John.

1502   The grand kidnapper at last taken. colop: *For James Read,*
       [1690?]. brs. L.

1503   The grand memorandum. *For Edward Husbands,* 1660.
       brs. LT, LS, HH; CH, MH, WF, Y.

       Grand mistake. [*n.p.,* 1700.] *See* Ward, Edward.

1504   The grand plunderer. [*London*], *printed,* 1643. 4°.* LT, C,
       OW, EC, YM; MH, MIU.

1505   The grand pyrate. *For Jonathan Edwin,* 1676. 4°.* T.C.I
       220. L, LNM, EC, SP, EN; CH, CN, MB, NN, RPJ.

       Grand Pluto's progresse. [*n.p.*], 1647. *See* Wharton, *Sir*
       George.

       Grand Plvtoes remonstrancer. [*n.p.*], 1642. *See* Taylor,
       John.

       Grand politician. 1690. *See* Reinking, Conrad.

       Grand prerogative. 1653. *See* Holland, Guy.

1506   The grand problem briefly discussed. *For Tho. Mercer,
       and sold by Randal Taylor,* 1690. 4°.* C, OC, MR, AU; CN,
       MH, NU, TU, Y.

1507   The grand qvestion concerning taking up armes. [*Ox-
       ford, by L. Lichfield*], *printed,* 1643. 4°.* MADAN 1463.
       O, SP, DT; CH, IU, MH, WF, Y.

1508   —[Anr. ed.] [*London*], *printed,* [1643]. 4°.* LT; MH, Y.

       Grand question, concerning the bishops. 1680. *See*
       Stillingfleet, Edward, *bp.*

       Grand question concerning the judicature. 1669. *See*
       Holles, Denzil Holles, *baron.*

1508A The grand question concerning the prorogation of this
       parliament. [*London,* 1676.] HOUSE OF LORDS (proof
       sheet).

1509   The grand question resolved. *For R. Baldwin,* 1681. fol.*
       T.C.I 475. L, O, LSD; CH, CN, LC, MH, WF.

1509A —[Anr. ed.] *For B. Pratt,* 1681. fol.* L, DCH; PU, WF.

1510   Entry cancelled.

       Grand question resolved, what. 1692. *See* Baxter,
       Richard.

1511   The grand rebels detected. *Printed,* 1660. 4°.* LT, O, LW;
       CH, MH, NU, TU, WF.

1512   The grand seigniors speech to the Ottoman forces.
       colop: *For John Smith.* 1683. brs. L, O, MC, EN; CH,
       CLC, TU.

1512A The grand spie discovered. *By W. Godbid,* 1659. 4°.*
       CSS, MH.

1513   Grand tryal in Westminster Hall. *For G. Horton,* 1654.
       4°. LG; CH, CSS, MH.

       Grand vizier. 1685. *See* Préchac, Jean, *sieur de.*

       Grandeur and glory of France. 1673. *See* Care, Henry.

       Grandeur of the law. 1684. *See* Philips, Henry.

1514   [**Granger, William.**] A diall, wherein is contained a
       remembrance of death. *Printed,* 1648. 4°.* LT, DT; CH,
       TU.

1515   **Grant, Alexander.** Clarissimis, generosis . . . Davidi
       Haliburton . . . theses. colop: *Edinburgi, excudebat
       Georgius Swintoun, & Jacobus Glen,* 1676. cap., 4°.*
       ALDIS 2087. 7. E.

1516–19 No entries.

       Grant, Sir Francis. *See* Cullen, Francis Grant, *lord.*

1520   **G[rant, I[ohn].** Gods deliverance. *For Thomas Paybody,*
       1642. 4°.* LT, O, CT; CH, MBA, MM, RBU, Y.

1521   [–] The shepheards farewell to his beloved flocke. [*Lon-
       don*], *printed,* 1645. 4°.* LT, DT; CH.

1522   [**Grant, Patrick.**] The Nonconformists vindication.
       [*Edinburgh?*], *printed,* 1700. 4°. ALDIS 3990. L, NPL, EN;
       NU, WF.

1523   [**Grant, Thomas.**] The plott and progress of the Irish
       rebellion. *By I. N. for Henry Twyford,* 1644. 4°.*
       LT, O, C, LVF, LNC, DN, DT; CH, MH, MIU, WF, Y.

1524   [**Grant, W. ?**] The antiquity & excellency of globes.
       By M.S. to be sold by Tho. Jenner, 1652. 4°.* LT, O, SC;
       PUB. LIB., NEW SOUTH WALES.

1524A [–] —[Anr. ed.] —, 1657. 4°.* CLC, MB.

1525   **Grant, William.** The vindication of the vicar of Istle-
       worth. [*London*], *printed,* 1641. 4°.* LT, O, LG, LLU, CD;
       CH, NU, TU, WF, Y.

1526   A grant of certain impositions upon beer. *By John Bill,*
       1660. fol.* LT; PU, V, WF.

1526A **Grantham, Caleb.** The godly man's choice. *By Matthew
       Simmons for Henry Overton,* 1644. 12°. L, LSC, M; MH.

1527   **Grantham, Thomas,** *Baptist.* The Baptist against the
       Papist. *Printed,* 1663. 4°. O, C; NU.

1528   —Christianismvs primitivus: or, the ancient Christian
       religion. *For Francis Smith,* 1678. fol. T.C.I 308. L,
       O, LCL, LW, AN, EN; IU, LC, NHC, NRU, NU, RBU.

1529   —The controversie about infants. *Printed,* 1680. 4°. L;
       MHS.

1530   —A dialogue between the Baptist and the Presbyterian.
       Printed, 1691. 4°. L, CCA; CH, IU, NHC, NPT, NU, WF.

1531   —The dying words of. [*London?* 1692.] brs. L, O; CLC.

1532   —The forerunner to a further answer. [*London?* 1691.]
       cap., 4°.* L; NHC, NPT.

1533   —The fourth principle of Christs doctrine vindicated.
       Printed, 1674. 4°. L, O; NHC.

1534   —A friendly epistle to the bishops. *Printed,* 1680. 8°.* O;
       RBU, WF.

1535   —The grand impostor caught. [*London?*], *for the author,*
       1691. 4°.* L, O, NPL; MHS.

1536   —Hear the church. *Printed,* 1687. 4°. L, O, MR; CH, IU,
       NPT, NU, WF.

1537   — —Second edition. —, 1688. 4°. L.

1538   —The infants advocate. *By J. D. for the author,* 1688–90.
       4°. L, O, CK; NPT, NU, WF.

1539   —The loyal Baptist. *For the author, to be sold by Tho.
       Fabian,* 1674. 4°.* L, O; NU.

1540   — —[Anr. ed.] —, 1684. 4°. T.C.II 58. L, O, MRL; NHC,
       NPT.

1541 —The pædo-baptists apology. [*London*], *printed*, 1671. 12°. L, C.

1542 —Presumption no proof. *Printed*, 1687. 4°.* L, O; NHC, NPT, NU.

1543 [–] The prisoner against the prelate. [*n.p., c.* 1662]. 8°. L, O, LCL, ORP, LLU, NOT; CH, CU, IU, MH, NHC.

1543A [–] The quaeries examined. 1676. 4°. L; MHS, NPT.

1544 —A religious contest. *Printed*, 1674. 4°.* L, EN.

1545 —St. Paul's catechism. *Printed*, 1687. 8°. L.

1545A ——Second edition. *By John Darby*, 1693. 8°. ORP.

1546 —The second part of the apology for the baptized believers. *For the author*, 1684. 4°. L, O; NHC.

1547 —The seventh-day-sabbath ceased. *For the author*, 1667. 4°.* LW; MBA, NU.

1548 —A sigh for peace. [*London*], *for the author*, 1671. 8°. L, LCL, LW; NBL.

1549 [–] The slanderer rebuked. [*London?* 1691.] cap., 4°.* L.

1549A —The successors of the Apostles. *Printed*, 1674. 4°.* NHC.

1550 —Truth and peace. *For the author*, 1689. 4°. L, O, LW, DT; NHC, NP, NPT, NU.

1551 **Grantham, Thomas, *M. A.*** A complaint to the Lord Protector. "To be distributed by the author." [*London*, 1656.] 8°.* LT.

1552 [–] A discovrse in derision of the teaching in free-schooles. [*London*, 1644.] cap., 4°.* LT; CLC, IU.

1553 —A marriage sermon. *Printed*, 1641. 8°.* LT, CP, DT; CH, IU, MH.

1554 ——[Anr. ed.] *Printed*, 1641. 4°.* LT, O, CT; CH, MH, WF.

1555 ——[Anr. ed.] *For T. P.*, 1643. 4°. O, SP; CH, Y.

1556 ——Fourth edition. —, 1656. 4°. C, OC, LNC.

1557 ——[Anr. ed.] *Reprinted at London*, 1681. 4°.* NU, PL, Y.

1558 —Μνημοφθοροπαικτης: the brainbreakers-breaker. 1644. 4°.* L, LU, DT; IU.

1559 —A motion against imprisonment. *Printed at London, for Francis Coules*, 1642. 4°.* LT, OC; MH.

1560 —October the 22. 1649. The three-penny cooks. [*London*], *for Thomas Paybody*, 1650. cap., 4°.* LT, OC, DT; IU.

1561–2 Entries cancelled.

Granville, Denis. *See* Grenville, Denis.

Granville, George. *See* Lansdowne, George Granville, baron.

Grapes from Canaan. 1658. *See* Taylor, Francis.

Grapes in the wilderness. 1680. *See* Bell, Thomas.

1563–4 Entries cancelled.

Γραφαυταρκεια, or, the Scriptures sufficiency. 1676. *See* Locke, John.

1565 **[Grascombe, Samuel.]** An admonition for the fifth of November. [*London*, 1690?] cap., 8°.* L, O, OM, CS, LSD; IU, MIU.

1566 [–] An appeal of murther. [*London*, 1693.] cap., 4°.* L, OC, CT, LSD, EN; CH, LC, NC, TU, Y.

1567 [–] An appeal to all true Englishmen. [*London*, 1699.] cap., 4°. L, O, OC, CT, LSD, EN; CU, NC, PU, WF, Y.

1567A [–] An appendix to the foregoing letter, being an answer to Mr. Humphrey Hody's letter. [*London*, 1691.] cap., 4°.* L, DU.

1568 [–] A brief answer to a late discourse. [*London*, 1691.] cap., 4°.* L, O, CT, MR, EN; CH, MH, MIU.

[–] Brief examination of some. [1700.] *See* Milner, John.

1569 [–] Considerations upon the second canon. 1693. 4°.* L, O, C, EN, DT; CH, MIU, NC, WF, Y.

1570 [–] Epistola ad Humtriaum Hody. 1691. 4°. O, CT, LSD; CLC.

1571 [–] A farther account of the Baroccian manuscript. [*Oxford?* 1691.] cap., 4°.* L, O, CT, LSD, MR; CH, MH, MM, WF, Y.

1572 [–] An historical account of the antiquity. *For W. Whitwood*, 1692. 4°. T.C.I 393. L, O, CT, DU, E; LC, MM.

1573 [–] A letter to a friend, in answer to a letter written. *Printed, and are to be sold by Randal Taylor*, 1688. 4°.* L, O, C, BAMB, LSD; MH, NC, NU, WF, Y, AVP.

1574 [–] A letter to Dr. W. Payne. [*London*, 1689.] cap., 4°.* CS, LSD, MR, CD; MBA, TU, Y.

[–] Loyal martyr vindicated. [*n.p.*, 1691.] *See* title.

1575 [–] New court-contrivances. colop: *Printed*, 1693. 4°.* O, C, LLP, CT, MR, AU; CH, WF.

1576 [–] A reply to a vindication of a discourse. *Printed*, 1691. 4°.* L, O, CT, MR, EN, BQ; CH, MH, NU, TU, WF, Y.

1577 [–] The resolution of a case of conscience. [*Oxford*, 1688.] cap., 4°.* L, O, CT, LSD, YM, EN; MB, MM, WF, Y.

1578 —The Scripture-history of the Sabbath. *By W. Bowyer, for Geo. Strahan*, 1700. 12°. T.C.III 168. L, O, LW, CS, DU, EN; CH, CLC.

1578A [–] Separation of the Church of Rome from the Church of England. *For Richard Northcott*, 1691. 4°. LIL, DUS, LSD; MB.

1579 [–] Tvvo letters written to the author of a pamphlet. *Printed*, 1692. 4°.* T.C.II 378. L, O, C, MR, EN; CH, MH, NU, WF, Y.

1579A The grateful acknowledgment of a late trimming regulator. *Printed*, 1688. 4°.* CH, CU, MH, MWA, Y.

Grateful non-conformist. 1665. *See* Wild, Robert.

1580 Gratiæ theatrales, or a choice ternary of English plays. *By R. D.*, 1662. 12°. L, O, LVD; CH, CN, MB, MH, WF, Y.

1581 **Gratius, *Faliscus*.** Grati Falisci cynegeticon. *For Charles Adams*, 1654. 12°. LT, O, C, EN, BQ; CH, CN, MH, NC, WF, Y.

1582 ——[Anr. ed.] *Impensis Car. Harper*, 1699. 8°. T.C.III 142. L, O, MR, EN, DT; CH, IU, NP, PL, WF, Y.

[Gratius, Ortwinus.] Epistolæ obscurorum virorum. [1680.] *See* title.

1583 —Fasciculus rerum expetendarum. *Impensis Richardi Chiswell*, 1690. 2v. fol. L, O, C, EN, DT; CH, CU, MH, WF, Y.

1583A [–] Lamentationes obscurorum virorum. *Apud editorem*, 1689. 8°. L, DT; CH, CLC, CN, MIU, NU.

1584 —Whereas there was printed at Colen by . . . Fasciculus. [*London*, 1688.] cap., fol.* O.

1585 **Gratton, John.** John Baptist's decreasing. [*London*], *printed*, 1674. 8°. L, LF, OC; PH, PL.

1585A ——Second edition. *Printed for and sold by T. Sowle*, 1696. 12°. C, LF; NHC.

1585B —The prisoners vindication. *Printed and sold by Andrew Sowle, 1683. 4°.** LF; MH, PH, PSC, Y.

1585C —To all persecutors. [*London*, 1682.] cap., 4°.* PSC.

1586 [–] A treatise concerning baptism. *Printed for and sold by T. Sowle*, 1695. 12°. L, C, LCL, LF; NBL.

1587 [–] —[Anr. ed.] *Printed and sold by T. Sowle*, 1695. 12°. L, LF; Y.

1588 A gratulatory poem. *Printed*, 1674. brs. L.
Gratulatory verse. 1665. *See* Wild, Robert.

1589 **G[raunt], J[ohn],** *of Bucklersbury.* Christians liberty to the Lords table. *For Humphrey Robinson*, 1645. 4°.* LT, DT; CH, MH, MU, NU, RPJ.

1590 [–] A cure of deadly doctrine. colop: *By M. S. for John Handcock*, 1649. cap., 4°.* LT, LW; NU.

1591 —A defence of Christian liberty. *For Humphrey Robinson*, 1646. 4°.* LT, DT; NU.

1592 ——[Anr. ed.] *For Iohn Hancock*, 1646. 4°.* MH, NU.

1593 —A holy lamp of light. [*London*, 1650.] cap., 4°.* LT, DT; NU.

1593A [–] London's dreadful visitation. *Printed and are to be sold by E. Cotes*, 1665. 4°. L, O, C, LWL, DU, GH; CH, CN, MH, WF, HC, AVP. (var.)

1593B [–] A right use made by a stander by. colop: *By M. Simmons for John Hancock*, 1649[50]. cap., 4°.* LT, SP; CH.

1594 [–] The shipwrack of all false churches. *Printed and are to be sold by G. Calvert*, 1652. 4°.* LT, LNC.

1595 [–] A trve reformation, and perfect restitvtion. *By T. B. to be sold by S. B.*, 1643. 4°.* LT, LLP; CH, CSS, NU, Y.

1596 [–] Truths defender. *By Matthew Simmons*, 1651. 4°.* LT, DT; MH.

1597 [–] Truths victory against heresie. *For H. R.*, 1645. 4°. LT, O, MR; CH, IU, NHC, NU, RPJ, WF, Y.

1598 Entry cancelled.
[–] Use made by. 1649[50]. *See* [–] Right use.

1599 **Graunt, John,** *F.R.S.* Natural and political observations. *By Tho: Roycroft, for John Martin, James Allestry, and Tho: Dicas*, 1662. 4°. L, O, C, DU, DT; CH, CU, MH, PL, PU.

1599A ——Second edition. —, 1662. 4°. L, C, LG, OB, CT; BN, CH, MH, NU, PL, WF, Y.

1600 ——Third edition. *By John Martyn, and James Allestry*, 1665. 8°. MADAN 2701. L, O, C, E, DT; BN, CH, MH, NC, PL, Y.

1601 ——Fourth edition. *Oxford, by William Hall for John Martyn and James Allestry*, [*London*], 1665. 8°. MADAN 2701. O, LW, LWL, MR, SC; CH, LC, NC, WSG, Y, JF.

1602 ——Fifth edition. *By John Martyn*, 1676. 8°. T.C.I 260. L, O, C, LCS, AU, DT; BN, CH, LC, MH, NC, WF, Y.

1603 [–] Reflections on the weekly bills of mortality. *For Samuel Speed*, 1665. 4°.* L, O, LUG, LIU, LNC; CH, MH, NN, WF. (var.)

1604 **[Grave, John.]** Song of Sion. [*London*], *printed* [*for Robert Wilson*], 1662. 4°.* L, O, LF, BBN; CH, LC, PL, RPJ, V, Y.

1604A A grave advise for the suppressing of seminary priests. *Printed, July 19*, 1644. 4°. DT; CLC.

1605 **[Graves, Edward.]** A brief narrative and deduction of the several remarkable cases of Sir William Courten. *Printed*, 1679. fol.* L; RPJ.

1606 The Graves-end tilt-boat. *Printed*, 1699. 8°. L, O; CH, WCL, WF.

Gravius, John. *See* Greaves, John.

1607 **Gray, Andrew.** Directions and instigations to the duty of prayer. *Glasgow, by Robert Sanders*, 1669. 12°. ALDIS 1861. EN, GM, GU.

1607A ——[Anr. ed.] *Edinburgh, by George Swintoun and James Glen*, 1669. 12°. EN; CH, Y.

1607B ——Second edition. *Edinburgh, by Andrew Anderson*, 1670. 16°. MB.

1607C ——[Anr. ed.] *Edinburgh, G. Swintoun, & J. Glen, sold by D. Trench & T. Brown*, 1670. 12°. ALDIS 1902. EN.

1607D ——"Second" edition. —, 1671. ALDIS 1923.5. EN.

1607E ——[Anr. ed.] *Edinburgh, by the heir of Andrew Anderson*, 1679. 12°. ALDIS 2153.2. EN; TO.

1607F ——[Anr. ed.] *Edinburgh*, 1680. 12°. ALDIS 2199.1. YM.

1608 ——Third edition. *Edinburgh, by the heirs and successors of Andrew Anderson*, 1698. 12°. ALDIS 3753. EN; NU, WF.

1608A —Great and precious promises. Third edition. *Edinburgh, by a Society of Stationers*, 1663. 12°. ALDIS 1753.5. EN.

1609 ——[Anr. ed.] *Edinburgh, by George Swintoun and James Glen*, 1669. 12°. ALDIS 1862. L, LW; Y.

1610 ——[Anr. ed.] *Glasgow, by Robert Sanders*, 1669. 12°. ALDIS 1863. EN, GM, GU.

1610A ——[Anr. ed.] *Edinburgh, printed by Andrew Anderson*, 1670. ALDIS 1903. GU.

1610B ——[Anr. ed.] *Edinburgh, G. Swintoun and J. Glen*, 1671. 8°. ALDIS 1923.7. EN.

1611 ——[Anr. ed.] *Edinburgh, by the heir of Andrew Anderson*, 1678. 12°. ALDIS 2128.1. YM, EN, ENC; TO.

1612 ——[Anr. ed.] *Glasgow, by Robert Sanders*, 1686. 12°. ALDIS 2641. GM.

1613 ——[Anr. ed.] *Edinbvrgh, by the heirs and successors of Andrew Anderson*, 1697. 12°. ALDIS 3665. EN; NU, WF.

1614 —The great salvation. *For H. Barnard*, 1694. 8°.* L; CH.

1615 —The mystery of faith. *For Thomas Johnson*, 1660. 8°. LT.

1616 ——[Anr. ed.] *Glasgow, by Robert Sanders*, 1668. 12°. ALDIS 1842. EN, GM, GU.

1617 ——[Anr. ed.] *Edinburgh, by George Swinton and James Glen*, 1669. 12°. ALDIS 1864. L.

1617A ——[Anr. ed.] *Edinburgh, G. Swintoun & J. Glen, sold by D. Trench & T. Brown*, 1670. 12°. ALDIS 1901.5. EN.

1618 ——[Anr. ed.] *Edinburgh, by George Swintoun and James Glen, to be sold by them, and by David Trench and Thomas Brown*, 1671. 12°. ALDIS 1923.9. O, EN.

1618A ——[Anr. ed.] *Edinburgh, by the heir of Andrew Anderson*, 1678. 8°. ALDIS 2128.2. EN; TO.

1618B ——[Anr. ed.] *Edinburgh*, 1684. 12°. ALDIS 2453.7. YM.

1619 ——[Anr. ed.] *Edinburgh, by the heirs and successors of Andrew Anderson*, 1697. 12°. ALDIS 3666. EN; NU, WF.

1619aA —The spiritual warfare. *Edinburgh, by the heir of A. Anderson*, 1670. 8°. EN.

1619A ——[Anr. ed.] *Edinburgh, by George Swinton, James Glen and Thomas Brown, 1672.* 12°. ALDIS 1945. CLC, MH.

1620 ——[Anr. ed.] *By J. D. and sold by Nathaniel Ranew, 1673.* 8°. L, O, ORP, EN.

1620A ——[Anr. ed.] *For W. Marshall, 1679.* 8°. T.C.I 430. O.

1620B ——[Anr. ed.] *Edinburgh, by the heir of Andrew Anderson, 1679.* 12°. ALDIS 2153.4. EN; TO.

1621 ——[Anr. ed.] *Edinburgh, by the heir of Andrew Anderson, 1693.* 12°. ALDIS 3300. L, SA.

1622 ——[Anr. ed.] *Edinbvrgh, by the heirs and successors of Andrew Anderson, 1697.* 12°. ALDIS 3665.5. EN, ENC; NU, WF.

1622A **Gray, E[dmund].** A caution to the unwary. [*London,* 1675.] brs. L.

1622B ——[Anr. ed.] [*London,* 1685?] brs. L.

1622C [–] A doctor in physick . . . attained . . . ways of cure. [*London,* 1675.] brs. L.

1623 **Gray, George.** A short account. *Printed, and sold by T. Sowle, 1692.* 16°.* L, LF, AU; MU, PH, PSC.

1623A **Gray, Patrick Gray, *8th baron.*** Additional information for . . . against the Laird of Pourie. [*Edinburgh,* 1695?] brs. EN.

1623B —Information for . . . against the Laird of Pourie. [*Edinburgh,* 1695?] brs. EN.

1624 **G[ray], R[obert].** Virginia's cure. *By W. Godbid for Henry Brome, 1662.* 4°.* L, LLL; CH, MH, NN, PL, RPJ.

1625 **Gray, Thomas.** Theses hasce philosophicas. [*Aberdeen*], *e typographœo Ioannis Forbesii junioris, 1673.* brs. ALDIS 2004. AU.

[**Gray, William.**] Chorographia, or a svrvey. Newcastle, 1649. *See* Grey, William.

Gray hayres crowned. 1655. *See* Ashe, Simeon.

1626 **Grayes, Isaac.** One out-cry more. *For the author, 1657.* 4°. LF, BP, MR.

1627 —Tithes a curse. *For the author, to be sold by William Larner, and Richard Moon, 1654.* 4°.* LT, LG, OJ.

1628 **Graziani, Antonio Maria.** The history of the war of Cyprus. *By J. Rawlins and sold by Randal Taylor, 1687.* 8°. L, C, LL, LLU, EN; CH, CN, LC, MIU, NP, WF, Y.

1629–30 No entries.

1631 Entry cancelled.

Great advocate. 1682. *See* Heale, William.

1632 The great and ancient charter of the Cinque-Ports. *By T. N. for the mayor and jurats of Hasting, 1682.* 12°. L, LG, LL; CLC, LC, MIU, PU, WF.

1633 A great and bloudy fight at Colchester, and the storming of the town. *For G. Beal, 1648.* 4°.* LT; CH, MIU.

1634 A great and bloudy fight at Colchester upon Sunday last. *For G. Holton, 1648.* 4°.* LT, DT; MIU.

1635 A great and blovdy fight at Dublin in Ireland. *For R. W., 1649.* 4°.* LT, C.

1636 A great and blovdy fight at Dublin between the King of Scots army. *For G. W., 1649.* 4°.* LT, C.

1637 A great and bloudy fight at Penbrook [*sic*] Castle. *Printed at London, 1648.* 4°.* LT, O, AN; CH.

1638 A great and bloudy fight at Scarborough-Castle. *For G.W., 1648.* 4°.* LT; CLC.

1639 A great and blovdy fight at sea: between five men of war. [*London,* 1649.] 4°.* LT, LNM; MH.

1640 A great and bloudy fight at sea, between the Parliaments fleet. *For G. Wharton, 1649.* 4°.* LT; MH.

1641 Entry cancelled.

Great and bloody fight at sea between the Parliaments navy. 1652. *See* Lawson, *Sir* John.

1642 A great and bloudy fight at sea on Monday 16 August. *For Robert Ibbitson, 1652.* 4°.* LT; WF.

1642A A great and bloudy fight in France. *For Geo. Horton, 1652.* 4°.* O.

1643 A great and bloudy fight in France between the Kings army. *By B. A., 1652.* 4°.* LT, MR.

1644 A great and bloody fight in Ireland. *By F: N:, 1652.* 4°.* LT.

Great and bloody fight in Shropshire. 1648. *See* Jones, Robert.

1645 A great and blovdy fight neer Droghedah. *For Robert Williamson, the 12. of September, 1649.* 4°.* LT, C, DN.

1645A Great and bloody news, from Farthing-Ally. [*London,* 1680.] cap., fol.* MH.

1646 Great and bloody news from Tangier. colop: *By D. Mallet, 1680.* cap., fol.* O; Y.

1647 Great and bloody news, from Turnham-Green. colop: [*London*], *by D. M., 1680.* cap., fol.* L, O, CM; CH, MH, Y.

1648 A great and bloody plot against the Protestants. *Printed at London by Robert Ibbitson, 1647.* 4°.* LT, O, C, DT; Y.

1649 A great and bloody plot discovered against his royal majesty, Charles. *For Samuel Chamberlain, 1660.* 4°.* LT, O; NN.

1649A A great and bloody sea-fight between the Parliaments fleet. *By R. W., 1652.* 4°.* SP.

Great & dreadful day. [n.p., 1664.] *See* Bayly, William.

1650 A great and famous sea-fight between the English and the Dutch. *For C. Hancock. 1652.* 4°.* LT.

1651 A great and famous victory obtained by the Parliament's navy. *For Georg Horton, 1652.* 4°.* LT.

1651A Great and glorious news from Ireland. *For William Brown, 1690.* brs. CH.

1652 A great and glorious victory obtained by the English against the French. *Imprinted at London for G. Wharton, 1654.* 4°.* LT.

1653 A great and glorious victory obtained by the Lord Inchequin. [*London*], *for V. V., 1647.* 4°.* LT, O, C, DN.

1653A Great and good news both from Scotland and Ireland. *For W. Partridge,* [1690]. brs. C.

1653B Great and good news for England. [*London*], *for P. Brooksby,* [169–?]. fol.* V.

1654 Great and good news for the Church of England. [*London*], *by I. K. and T. S., 1688.* 4°.* L; CLC, Y.

1654A —[Anr. ed.] *By H. L. and I. K., 1688.* 4°.* L, O; CU, MIU, WF.

1655 Great and good news from his Grace the Duke of Schombergs camp. colop: *For Richard Baldwin, 1689.* brs. L, OC, MC, HH; CH, Y.

1655A Great and good news from Ireland: being . . . Droghedah. colop: *For T. Rogers, 1690.* brs. DN; MH.

1655B   Great and good news from Ireland, giving a true ac-
        count. colop: *For John Southcott*, 1690. brs. L, DN.

1656   Great and good news to the Church of England. *By
        David Edwards*, 1700. brs. L, O, LLP; MH.

1656A   Great and horrible news from Little-Britain. *For D. M.*,
        1679. 4°.* Y.

1656B   Great and horrible news from the city of York. *For
        A. R.*, 1689. brs. MH.

1657   Great and horrible nevvs from the West of England.
        For D. M., 1679. 4°.* L; Y.

1657A   Great and joyful news for England. colop: *By Tho.
        Moore*, 1690. brs. CH, MH.

        Great and new art. Glasgow, 1672. *See* Gregory, James.

        Great and popular objection. 1688. *See* Penn, William.

        Great and sole troubler. 1649. *See* Penington, Isaac, *jr.*

1658   A great & terrible fight at sea neer the coast of Hol-
        land. *For Robert Eeles*, 1653. 4°.* LT.

1659   A great and terrible fight in France. *For George Horton*,
        1652. 4°.* LT, MR.

        Great and weighty considerations, relating to the Duke
        of York. 1680. *See also* Hunt, Thomas.

1660   Great and weighty considerations relating to the D.
        [*London*, 1679.] cap., fol.* L, O, C, LIU, LSD; CH, LC,
        MBP, TU, WF, Y.

1660A   A great and wonderful discovery . . . since that great fire.
        For J. Johnson, 1663. 4°.* CT.

1660B   The great and wonderful miracle wrought. *For G. Eger-
        ton*, 1663. 4°. L, SP.

        Great and wonderful news. [n.p., 1682.] *See* P., J.

1660C   Great and wonderful news from Silverdale. colop: *For
        J. Harris and to be sold by Randal Taylor*, 1693. brs. Y.

1660D   Great and wonderful prophecies. [*London*], *for J. C.*,
        [1689.] 4°.* LG, GU.

1660E   Great and wonderful success. [*London?* 1695.] brs. L.

1660F   A great & wonderfull victory obtained by the Danes.
        By T. M. for Livewel Chapman, 1659. 4°.* LIU; Y.

1661   A great and wonderful victory obtained by the English
        forces. *For Humphrey Hutchinson*, 1655. 4°.* LT.

        Great antiChrist. 1643. *See* Vicars, John.

1662   Entry cancelled.

        Great assize; or. [1680?] *See* Stevens, *Mr.*

        Great assises. 1645. *See* Wither, George.

1663   The great bastard [Louis XIV]. *Printed at Cologne* [*Lon-
        don*], 1689. 4°.* T.C.II 315. L, O, C, MR, DT; CH, CN,
        MH, WF, Y. (var.)

1663A   —[Anr. ed.] *Reprinted at Cologne* [*London*], 1691. 4°. L;
        CH, IU.

        Great benefit. [1663.] *See* B., E.

        Great birth of man. 1686. *See* S., M.

1664   The great boobee. [*London*], *for F. Coles*, [1663]. brs. L, O,
        CM.

1664A   —[Anr. ed.] *For R. I.*, [1656]. brs. EUING 124. L, GU.

1665   Great Brittains arlarm [*sic*]. [*London*], *for P. Brooksby*,
        [1667?]. brs. L, O.

        Great Britain's bitter lamentation. 1670. *See* Rowland,
        John.

1665A   Great Britain's call to repentance . . . Jamaco. [*By E.
        Millet*] *for P. Brooksby, J. Deacon, J. Blare, and J. Back*,
        [1693]. 8°.* L.

1666   Great Brjttajnes distractions. *Printed*, 1642. 4°.* L; CLC,
        MH.

1667   Great Britains glory, or a brief description. *By Tho. Rat-
        cliffe & Nat. Thompson for Jonathan Edwin*, 1672. 4°.*
        T.C.I 111. L, O, LG; CH, WCL, WF, Y.

        Great Britain's glory. [1680.] *See* S., J.

        Great Britain's groans. [n.p.], 1695. *See* Hodges,
        William.

1667AA Great Bittains [*sic*] ioy. [*London*], *for F. Coles, T. Vere, and
        J. Wright*, [1663–74]. brs. O.

        Great Britain's just complaint. [n.p.], 1692. *See* Mont-
        gomery, James.

1667A   Great-Britain's lamentation for her deceased Princess.
        For John Whitlock, 1695. brs. L; MH.

1668   Great Britains lamentation: or, the funeral obsequies.
        By J. Whitlock, 1694/5. brs. L.

1668A   Great Britain's miseries. [*London*], *printed*, 1697. 8°. LIU;
        MM, ANL.

        Great Britains misery. 1643. *See* Smith, George.

1669   Great Brittans rvine plotted. *For Thomas Vnderhill*, 1641.
        4°.* LT.

        Great Britain's tears. 1695. *See* Crosfeild, Robert.

1670   Great Britans vote. *For G. M. and W. H.*, 1648. 4°.
        LT, O, CT, MR, DT; CH, CU, MH, NU, WF.

1670A   Great Britain's warning-piece. [*London*], *for W. Thack-
        eray*, [1688–89]. 8°.* O.

1671   Great Britains wonder: or, Londons admiration . . .
        frost. [*London*], *by M. Haly and J. Millet and sold by
        Robert Walton. And by John Seller*, 1684. brs. T.C.II 72.
        L.

1671A   —[Anr. ed.] *Printed for, and sold by Robert Walton; and by
        John Seller*, 1684. brs. RHT.

        Great calumny. 1700. *See* Robinson, William.

        Great case of liberty. [n.p.], 1670. *See* Penn, William.

1672   The great case of the justices. *By W. D. and are to be sold
        by Randal Taylor*, 1688. 8°. O, OC; NIC.

1673   The great case of toleration stated. *Printed, and sold, by
        Andrew Swole* [*sic*], 1688. 4°.* O, OC, MR; NU, WF, Y.

        Great case of transplantation. 1655. *See* Gookin, Vincent.

        Great case of tythes and. [n.p.], 1665. *See* Howgill,
        Francis.

        Great case of tythes freely. 1657. *See* Pearson, Anthony.

1674   The great case put home. *Oxford, for R. Davis, and are
        to be sold by R. Taylor, London*, 1681. 4°.* O, CT, SP,
        LSD, MR; CH, CN, MH, MU, Y.

1675   —[Anr. ed.] [*London*], *printed*, 1681. 4°.* L, O, OC, OU, DU,
        MR; NU, TSM, WF.

1676   The great champions of England: being a perfect list.
        For Francis Leach, 1646. brs. LT, O.

        Great charter for. 1694. *See* Beverley, Thomas.

1677   The great charter of the forest. *By the assignees of Richard
        and Edward Atkins, for John Kidgell*, 1680. 4°.* T.C.I 394.
        L, LUG, OB, CS, MR, DT; CH, CN, LC, NC, Y.

1677A   —[Anr. ed.] *For John Kidgell*, 1680. 4°.* OC, BC; WF.

1678   At the vendue. The great collection of paintings . . . 8th . . . [February 1692]. [London, 1692.] brs. L.

Great commandment. 1678. See Shaw, Samuel.

1679   The great concern and zeal of a loyal people. For Jonathan Robinson, 1691. 4°. T.C.II 377. L, O; CLC, NP, WF, Y.

1680   A great conspiracy by the Papists. For John Thomas, 1461 [i.e. 1641]. 4°.* L, C, OC, EC, DN; MH, Y.

1681   A great conspiracy of the Papists. For Iohn Thomas, 1641. 4°.* LT, O, C; CH, MM, WF, WU, Y.

1682   A great cry and little wool. [London, 1670.] brs. L, O; MH, WF, Y.

Great cry of oppression. [n.p.], 1683. See Stockdale, William.

Great cures and strange miracles of . . . Valentine Gertrux. 1666. See Greatrakes, Valentine.

Great danger and uncertainty. 1693. See Ellesby, James.

Great day. 1648. See Eachard, John.

1683   No entry.

The great deliverance of . . . Israel. 1652. See E., J.

Great designs. [n.p., 1695.] See C., W.

1684   A great discovery of a damnable plot at Rvgland Castle. By Barnard Alsop, 1641. 4°.* L, O, AN.

1685   A great discoverie of a plot in Scotland. By Bernard Alsop, 1641. 4°.* LT, CT, BC; CN, IU, MBP, WF, Y.

1685A   —[Anr. ed.] [London, 1641.] 4°.* GU; CH.

1686   A great discovery of the Queens preparation. For J. Wright, Decemb. 19, 1642. 4°.* O, EC, LNC, YM, DT; MH, NC, V, WF, Y.

Great doctrines. 1694. See Budd, Thomas.

Great duty of Christians. 1682. See Tomlyns, Samuel.

Great duty of conformity. 1684. See Jones, John.

1687   The great earthquake at Quito in Peru. [London? 1698.] brs. RPJ.

Great eater. 1652. See Fidge, George.

1688   The great eclipse of the sun. [London], by G. B. August, 30. 1644. 4°.* LT, O, CT; CLC, CSS, MH, TU, Y.

1689   The great evil of health-drinking. For Jonathan Robinson, 1684. 12°. L, LW, P, SP; CH, CN, PL, WF, Y.

1690   The great evil of naturalizing aliens discovered. [London, 1670?] cap., 4°. L; NC.

1691   The great feast, at the inthronization of George Neavill. For Edward Husbands, Aprill the first, 1645. 4°.* LT, O, LLU; MH, WF.

1692   The great feast at the sheep-shearing of the city and citizens. [London], printed, 1649. 4°.* TU.

1692A   The great feast of the Gospel-Passover. For the author by James Astwood, and sold by Peter Parker, and John Salusbury, John Laurence, and John Harris, 1694. 8°.* LW; MH.

Great fight at Chepstow. 1648. See W., R.

1693   A great fight at Colchester upon Tuesday. For R. Woodus, 1648. 4°.* LT; CH, MIU.

1694   A great fight at Kingston. For J. G., 1648. 4°.* CU.

Great fight at Market-Harborough. 1646. See Blague, Thomas.

1695   A great fight at Newarke. For Matthew Walbancke, 10 March 1645. 4°.* LT, NOT; MH, Y.

1696   A great fight at sea, between the English, French, Dutch, and Portugals, neer Gibralterre. Imprinted at London, for G. Samuel, 1651. 4°.* LT; WF.

Great fight at Walmer Castle. [n.p.], 1648. See Rogers, Daniel.

A great fight between the Kings forces. Yondon [sic], 1648. See Charles II.

1697   A great fight in Ireland between the Lord Lievt. Cromwels forces. [London], by B. A., 1649. 4°.* LT.

1698   A great fight in Scotland between His Excellency. For G. Horton, 1651. 4°.* LT; CH, Y.

1699   A great fight in Scotland, between the English forces. For G. Horton, 1654. 4°.* LT.

1700   A great fight in the church at Thaxted. For Henry Becke, 1647. 4°.* LT, DT; WF.

Great fight in the kingdome of Ireland. 1647. See Smith, George.

1701   A great fight in VVales between Collonell Horton. Printed at London by Robert Ibbitson, 1648. 4°.* LT, O, AN; Y.

1702   A great fight in Wales sixteen colours taken. By B. A., 1648. 4°.* LT, O, AN; CLC, IU, Y.

1703   A great fight near Pendennis castle. Imprinted at London for R. W. 2. Aprill, 1649. 4°.* LT; MH.

1704   A great fight neer the city of Dublin. Imprinted at London, for R. W., May 2. 1649. 4°.* LT, DN; CSS, MH.

Great gospel-grace. 1695. See Beverley, Thomas.

1704A   The great grievance and oppression of William Edwards. [London? 168-.] brs. CH.

1705   The great grievance of Scotland. Edenburgh, printed, 1689. 8°.* ALDIS 2891. L, O, E, EN; CH, WF, Y.

1705A   The great grievance of traders. [London? 1700.] brs. L.

Great honour. 1697. See Child, Sir Josiah.

1706   The great idol of the masse. For Enoch Prosser, 1680. 4°.* L; CH, MH, PU, WF.

1707   The great inequality of charging publick assessments. [London, 1665?] brs. L.

Great is Diana. 1680. See Blount, Charles.

Great law. 1673. See Shafte, J.

1708   The great loss and damage to England. [London? 1662.] cap., 4°.* L, MR.

1709   The great memorial: or, a list. For Edward Thomas, 1660. brs. LT, HH, CD; CH.

1710   —[Anr. ed.] Edinburgh reprinted by a society of stationers, 1660. brs. ALDIS 1644. EN.

1711   The great messenger of mortality. Printed and sold at the Printing Office, [1660–1700]. brs. L, O, LW; MH, Y.

1712   A great miracle at sea. [n.p., 1645]. 4°.* O.

1712A   Great mischiefs daily arising. [London? 1680.] brs. L.

1713   The great mysterie of God. For John Wright, 1645. 4°. LT, O, CT, MR, DT; CH, LC, MH, Y.

Great necessity. 1697. See C., N.

1714   Great news from a Parliament of women. For A. Chamberlain, 1684. brs. L.

1714A   Great news from Athlone. colop: For W. Brown, [1690]. brs. L; Y.

1715   Entry cancelled.

Great news from Bristol. 1689. *See* W., T.

Great news from Charlemont. [1690.] *See* Wood, P.

1715A Great news from Chester, of the seizing a ship. [*London*], *for J. Norton*, 1689. brs. DN.

1715B Great news from Colonel Kirck. *For John Lyford*, 1689. brs. L.

1716 Great news from Count Teckely. *By George Croom*, 1684. brs. O; CH, CN.

1716A Great news from Dartmouth. *For Richard Baldwin*, 1692. brs. CN.

1717 Great news from Derbyshire. *For Richard Janeway*, 1681. brs. L, O; CH, IU, WF.

1718 Entry cancelled.

Great news from Dublin. 1689. *See* M., J.

Great news from Dublin giving. 1690. *See* Nichols, William.

Great news from Dublin in a letter. 1690. *See* C., T.

1718A Great news from Dundalk. colop: *For R: Hayhurst*, 1690. brs. CH, Y.

Great news from Falmouth. 1690. *See* C., T.

1719 Great news from France giving an account. *For R. Taylor*, [1688]. brs. L, O, C; CH, CU.

1719A Great news from Germany. *For Richard Baldwin*, 1691. brs. CN.

1720 —[Anr. ed.] *Edinburgh, heir of A. Anderson*, 1691. brs. ALDIS 3152. EN.

1721 Great news from Gravesend. *By Alex. Milbourn*, 1689. brs. O.

1722 Great news from Guild-Hall. *Printed*, 1695. brs. L.

1722AA Great news from Hertford-shire. *For Ed. Golding*, 1691. brs. CH.

Great news from Highlake. [1690.] *See* Wood, P.

1722A Great news from His Majesty's camp. colop: *For T. Hawkins*, 1693. brs. MH.

1723 Great news from Ireland. Giving a true account of. I. The motions of the late King James. *By W. Downing*, 1689. brs. L, O, C, DN; CH.

1724 Entry cancelled. *See below*, G1724EB.

1724A Great news from Ireland; an account of the Kings royal camp. colop: [*London*], *for D. Smith*, 1690. brs. MH.

1724B Great news from Ireland, being a full and true relation. colop: *For R. H. and W. Faulkner*, 1690. brs. OC, DN; CH.

1724C Great news from Ireland, being a true account of the late King James's quitting that kingdom. colop: *For Richard Balding*, [1690]. brs. MH.

1724CA Great news from Ireland: being a true relation of the killing. *For R. Hayhurst*, 1691. brs. INU.

1724D Great news from Ireland; being an account of the famous town of Galway. colop: *For Ed. Golding*, 1691. brs. MH.

1724E Great news from Ireland, being motives of encouragement for the officers. colop: *For S. Bourn*, 1689. cap., fol.* L, DN; MH.

1724EA —[Anr. ed.] *By T. Moore*, 1689. fol.* O.

1724EB —[Anr. ed.] *Edinburgh, reprinted in the year*, 1689. fol.* ALDIS 2892. L, LUG, EN; WF.

Great news from Ireland, giving an account of the present state of affairs. [1690.] *See* Crumby, Alexander.

1724F Great news from Kensington. [*London*, 1691.] brs. MH.

1725 Great news from Limerick. colop: *By Tho. Moore*, 1690. brs. L; CH, MH.

1726 —[Anr. ed.] *Printed at London, and re-printed at Edinburgh*, 1690. brs. ALDIS 3045. EN, DN.

1726AA Great news from Lymerick. An account. *For N. Kettlewel*, 1691. brs. OC.

1726A Great news from Lymerick in Ireland. colop: *For Edmund Thorn*, 1690. brs. MH.

1727 Great news from Middle-row in Holbourn. [*London*, 1679/80.] cap., fol.* O; MH, TU.

1728 Great news from Nottingham. [*London*, 1688.] brs. L, O, C; CH, Y.

Great news from Oxford. 1688. *See* T., H.

1729 Great news from Poland. colop: *For the assigns of F. S.* 1683. brs. L; PU, WF.

1729A Great news from Salisbury. [*London*, 1688.] brs. L, C, HH; CH, Y.

Great news from Saxony. [n.p., 1680.] *See* R., B.

1729B Great news from Scotland and Ireland. colop: *For Tho. Salusbury*, 1690. brs. CH, Y.

1729C Great news from Scotland, and London-derry. colop: *For William Thomas*, 1684. brs. MH.

1730 Great news from sea. [*n.p.*], 1680. fol.* O.

1731 Great news from Southwark. *For James Read*, 1695. brs. L.

Great news from the army in Ireland. 1690. *See* Thorowgood, John.

1732 Great news from the army, that went for Scotland. [*London*, 1689.] brs. CH.

1733 Great newes from the Barbadoes. *For L. Curtis*, 1676. 4°.* L, MR; CH, RPJ.

1733A Numb. 1. Great news from the camp at Chester. *By R. Janeway*, 1689. brs. C, DN; Y.

1734 Great news from the Duke of Schomberge's army. *For John Dunton*, 1689. brs. C, DN.

1735 Great news from the English fleet. *For T. P.*, 1688. brs. OC, OP.

1735AA Great news from the French fleet. *By W. D.*, 1693. brs. CN.

1735A Great news from the Isle of Wight. *For J. Gregory.* 1690. brs. L, MH.

1735B Great news from the King in Flanders. *For T. Bunce*, 1691. brs. CN.

1735C Great news from the King of Poland. *For A. G.*, 1682. brs. O, EN; ZWT.

1735D Great news from the King's camp at Namurre, &c. *For J. Salusbury*, 1695. brs. CN.

1735E —[Same title, July 19.] *For John Salusbury*, 1695. brs. CN.

1735F Great news from the North. colop: *For Thomas Rogers*, 1689. brs. L, C.

1735G Great news from the North of England. *For W. Sturt*, 1690. brs. CN.

1736 Great news from the Old-Bayly, Mr. Car's recantation. colop: *By G. Croom*, 1683. brs. L, O; CH, MH, Y.

1737   Great news from the Polish camp. colop: *By E. Mallet*, 1684. brs. L, O.

1737A   Great news from the port of Kingsale in Ireland. [*London*], *for John Ashburne*, 1689. brs. C, DN; MH.

1738   Great news from the Tower. colop: *By George Croom*, 1683. brs. O; CH, MH, Y.

       Great news from the West-Indies. Lodon [*sic*], 1687. *See* H., F.

1738A   Great news from the West of England. colop: *By T. M.*, 1689. brs. CH.

1739   Great news from Tingmouth. colop: *For W. Brown*, 1690. brs. L.

1740   Great news from Westminster. *By D. M.*, 1679. brs. L, O; MBA, MH.

1741   A great over-throw. *For Iohn Hammon*, 1643. 4°.* LT; MIU.

1742   A great overthrow given to the kings forces in Wales. *For Matthew Walbancke*, 26 Feb. 1645[6]. 4°.* LT, O, DT, AN; CH, Y.

       Great physician. Boston, 1700. *See* Mather, Cotton.

1743   A great plot against the Parliament of England. *Imprinted at London for V. V.*, 1647. 4°.* LT; MH.

       Great plot discovered against. 1647. *See* F., N.

1744   A great plot discovered in the North. *For William Iones*, 1646. 4°.* LT, DT.

1744A   A great plot discovered, or the notorious and wicked design. *For G. Horton*, 1661. 4°.* MH.

       Great point. 1681. *See* Brady, Robert.

       Great preparation. 1650. *See* S., T.

       Great preservative. 1662. *See* Barker, *Sir* Richard.

       Great pressures. 1681. *See* Everard, Edmond.

1744B   The great prophecy of King William's success in Flanders. *For C. C. and A. R. and sold by Randal Taylor*, 1692. 4°.* CN, Y.

1745   —[Anr. ed.] *Printed at London and re-printed at Edinburgh*, 1692. 4°.* ALDIS 3225. L, O, MR, E, EN; CN, WF.

       Great propitiation. 1669. *See* Truman, Joseph.

       Great question concerning. 1660. *See* Bagshaw, Edward, *younger*.

1745A   The great question of the authority of the arch-bishops. [*London?* 1690.] cap., 4°.* L, BAMB.

       Great question: or, how. 1690. *See* E., N.

       Great question. [n.p., 1679.] *See* Penn, William.

1746   The great questions concerning the succession. 1680. 4°. L.

       Great questions in the case. [1696.] *See* Collier, Jeremy.

1746A   The great restorer of decay'd nature. [*London*, 1670?] brs. L.

1747   The great robbery in Hatton-Garden. *For L. C.*, 1679. 4°.* NU.

1748   A great robbery in the North. *For George Tomlinson*, *July 28.* 1642. 4°.* LT.

1749   The great robbery in the West. *For L. C.* 1678. 4°.* O.

       Great sacrifice. [n.p.], 1676. *See* Dymock, James.

1750   The great sale of original paintings, . . . Friday [*April*, 1691]. [*London*, 1691.] 4°.* L.

1751   Great satisfaction concerning the death of the Earle of Strafford. [*London*, 1641?] cap., 4°.* L, SP, YM; CH, INU, IU, LC, NP, Y.

       Great Scanderbeg. 1690. *See* Chevreau, Urbain.

1752   The great signs of the times. *For the author, to be sold by J. Nutt*, 1699. 4°.* T.C.III 152. O.

1753–54   Entries cancelled.

       Great sin. 1654. *See* Church of Scotland.

1755   The great sins of drunkenness. *By T. C. to be sold by T. Crosse*, 1656. brs. LT.

1756   Great Straffords farewell to the world. [*London*], *printed*, 1641. 4°.* LLU; CH, CSS, TU.

1756A   The great trap of George Booth. 1659. 4°. L (lost).

1757   The great trappaner of England . . . Thomas Violet. [*London*], *printed*, 1660. 4°.* L, LPR.

       Great treaty of peace. 1677. *See* S., H. L.

1758   The great tryall and arraignment of the . . . late distressed lady. *For W. Gilbertson*, 1663. 4°.* L.

1758A   The great tribunal; or, Christ's glorious appearing in judgment. [n.p., 1700?] brs. L.

       Great trumpet of the Lord. [n.p., 1660]. *See* Moon, John.

1759   Entry cancelled.

       Great Turkes letter. 1645. *See* Mahomet IV.

       Great Turks declaration. 1683. *See* Mahomet IV.

       Great venture. [n.p.], 1668. *See* A., E.

1760   Great victories obtained by the Earle of Denbigh. *By J. Coe*, 1644. 4°.* LT; MH.

1761   Entry cancelled.

       Great victorie against the rebels. 1647. *See* Fenwicke, John.

1762   Entry cancelled.

       Great victory at Appleby. 1648. *See* Ashton, Ralph.

1763   Entry cancelled.

       Great victory at Malpas. 1644. *See* Letters from the Lord Generall his quarters.

1764   A great victory at sea against the Irish rebels. *Printed at London, by Robert Ibbitson*, 1648. 4°.* LT, DN; CH, MH.

1765   A great victory by the blessing of God. *For Robert Ibbitson*, 1651. 4°.* LT; CLC, MIU, Y.

1766   A great victory God hath vouchsafed. *By Robert Ibbitson*, 1651. 4°.* LT, DU, GC, MR, SP; CDA, CH, CN, MH, Y.

1767   A great victorie in the North, obtained by . . . Cromwel. *Printed*, 1648. 4°.* LT.

1768   A great victorie obtained against the enemy, at . . . Taunton. *For R. Austin*, 1645. 4°.* LT; MH, Y.

1768A   A great victorie obtained at Saffron Walden. *By B. A.*, 1648. 4°.* CDC; Y.

1769   A great victory obtained at sea. *For G. Wharton*, 1649. 4°.* LT, DT; MH.

1770   A great victory obtained by Colonell Jones. *For G. Oreton*, 1649. 4°.* LT; MH.

1771   A great victory obtained by Colonel Norton. *By Andrew Coe*, 1644. 4°.* LT, LVF; CSS.

1772   A great victory obtained by Collonell Scroope. *Printed*, 1648. 4°.* LT; Y.

1773 A great victory obtained by Generall Poyntz. *For Edward Husband, Octob.* 21. 1645. 4°.* LT, O, LLU, YM, DT; CB, CLC, MH, MU, NU, WF, Y.

1774 A great victory obtained by his excellency the Lord Gen: Blake. *For George Horton,* 1652. 4°.* LT.

1775 A great victory obtained by His Excellencie . . . Fairfax. *For R. W.,* 1648. 4°.* LT.

1776 A great victory obtained by His Highnesse the Prince of Wales neer the Downs. [*London*], *August* 31. *for R. VV.* 1648. 4°.* LT; MIU.

1777 The great victory obtained by His Maiesties army. [*London?* 1679.] fol.* L, LL, EN; CLC, MH.

1778 The great victory obtain'd by His Majesties army, under . . . Monmouth. *Edinburgh,* 1679. brs. ALDIS 2153.6. BC, MC; CH.

1779 A great victory obtained by Prince Charles his ships. *Imprinted at London, for R. Williamson,* 1649. 4°.* LT, O, LIU.

Great victory obtained by the English against the Dutch. 1652. *See* Stoaks, *capt.*

1780 A great victory obtained by the English against the Hollanders. 1653. 4°. L.

1781 A great victory obtained by the King of France against the Prince of Conde. *Imprinted at London, for George Horton.* 1652. 4°.* LT.

1782 A great victory obtained by the King of France against The Prince of Conde near . . . Estamps. *For G: Horton,* 1652. 4°.* LT; WF.

1783 A great victory obtained by the Kings forces in the West. [*London*], *printed,* 1648. 4°.* LT.

1784 A great victory obtained by the Marquesse of Ormond. *Imprinted at London for R. Williamson, August* 9. 1649. 4°.* LT, C; MH.

1785 A great victory obtained by the Royalists near Huntington shire. *For R. VV.,* 1648. 4°.* LT.

1786 A great victorie obtained in the kingdom of Scotland by the Marquis of Argyle. *Imprinted at London, for G. H.,* 1648. 4°.* LT, MR, DT; CSS, WF, Y.

1787 A great vvonder in heaven. *For Tho. Iackson, Ian.* 23, 1642. 4°.* LT, LNC, DT; WF, Y.

1787A The great work of redemption. *For J. Playford,* 1660. 8°. CLC.

1788 Great York and Albany. *By Nat. Thompson,* 1682. brs. O; CH, MH.

Greatest light. [n.p.], 1674. *See* Wallis, John.

Greatness of mind. 1691. *See* Boyle, Robert.

1789 **Greatrakes, Valentine.** A brief account of Mʳ. Valentine Greatrak's. *For J. Starkey,* 1666. 4°. L, O, C, EN, AU; CH, CNM, MH, MMO, WF, HC.

1790 — —[Anr. ed.] *Dublin, for Samuel Dancer,* 1668. 4°. DIX 136. L, DN.

1791 —The great cures, and strange miracles, . . . by Mr. Valentine Gertrux [sic]. *For John Thomas,* 1666. 4°. CH, MMO.

1792 [**Greaves, Sir Edward.**] Morbvs epidemius anni 1643. Or, the new disease. *Oxford, by Leonard Lichfield,* 1643. 4°.* MADAN 1502. L, O, LCS, OB, DT; CH, HC.

1793 [–] —[Anr. ed.] *Oxford, by Leonard Lichfield,* [1643]. 4°.* MADAN 1503. LT, OR, CM; WF, Y.

1794 —Oratio habita . . . 25 Jul. 1661. *Excudebat Jacobus Cotterel, pro Samuele Speed,* 1667. 4°.* O, LCP, LWL, GH, CD; MBA.

1795 **Greaves, John.** Anonymus Persa de siglis Arabum. *Typis Milonis Flesher,* 1648. 4°. L, O, OC, CT, DT; CH, CLC, IU, MIU, PL, PU, WF.

1796–99 Entries cancelled.

—Astronomica quædam. 1650. *See* Cholgius, *shah.*

—Binæ tabulæ geographicæ. 1652. *See* Nasir Al-Din.

—Chorasmiæ. 1650. *See* Isma'il Ibn'Ali.

1800 —A discovrse of the Romane foot. *By M. F. for William Lee,* 1647. 8°. L, O, C, EN, DT; BN, CH, CN, MH, NC, WF, Y.

1801 Entry cancelled. Ghost.

1802 —Elementa linguæ Persicæ. *Typis Jacobi Flesher: et prostant Cornelium Bee,* 1649. 4°. L, OB, C, E, EN, CD; BN, CLC, IU, MII, WF, Y.

1803 — —[Anr. ed.] *Typis Jacobi Flesher,* 1649. 4°. O, LW, CJ, CT, DT; CH, CLC.

1804 —Pyramidographia; or, a description. *For George Badger,* 1646. 8°. L, O, C, MR, GH; BN, CH, CN, MH, WF, Y.

1805 **Greaves, Thomas.** A brief summe of Christian religion. *Printed at London,* 1656. 8°.* L, CE.

Grebner, Ezekiel, *pseud. See* Cowley, Abraham.

1806 Entry cancelled.

Grebner, Paul. Brief description of the future history of Europe. 1650. *See title.*

1807 —Europes wonder. *Hagve. By John Brown,* 1661. 4°.* CH.

1808 —The prophecie of Paulus Grebnerus. [*London,* 1649.] brs. LT, O, CT; MH.

1808A —The prophecy of Gretnerus. [*London,* 1660?] brs. MH.

1809 —Paul Grebners prophecy concerning these times. colop: *For Thomas Burrel,* 1680. brs. L, LSD; CH, MH, NC, WF, Y.

1809A —The prophecy of Paul Grebner. [*London,* 1688?] brs. O; CH, Y.

Grecian story. 1684. *See* Harington, John.

1810 **Greco, Gioachino.** The royall game of chesse-play. *For Henry Herringman,* 1656. 8°. LT, O, C, LW, E; CH, IU, LC, MH, PL, WF, Y, AVP.

Greek and Roman history. 1692. *See* Walker, Obadiah.

Greek English lexicon. 1658. *See* Cockaine, Thomas.

1810AA The Greeks and Trojans wars. [*London*], *for F. Coles, T. Ve Wright* [sic], *and I. Clarke,* [1674–9]. brs. O.

Greeks' opinion. [n.p.], 1686. *See* Woodhead, Abraham.

1810A [**Green, Bartholomew.**] The printers advertisement. colop: *Boston, by John Allen,* 1700. 12°.* MHS, MWA, RPJ.

Green, Christopher. A new perpetual almanack. [1691.] *See* Almanacs.

1811 **Green, Mary.** Mrs. Mary Green, living at a haberdasher of hats. [*London,* 1693.] brs. L.

1811A [**Green, Robert.**] A message sent from His Highnesse the Prince of Wales. [*London*], *printed* 1648. 4°.* LT, DT; MH, MIU, Y.

Green, Thomas. *See* Greene, Thomas.

1812 G[reen], W[illiam]. Abyssus mali: or, the corruption. *For Tho. Parkhurst*, 1676. 8°. L, O, C, LCL, LW; CLC, IU, MH, Y, PJB.

1812A —Good counsel and advice. *For Robert Wilson*, 1661. brs. LF.

1813 [–] Memento's to the world. *By T. Haly for T. Passinger*, 1680. 4°.* T.C.I 429. L, O, LN, CT; CH, MB, MH, MU, Y.

1814 —The sound of a voyce uttered forth. *Printed*, 1663. 4°.* L, LF, BBN, MR, GU; CH, MH, PH, PSC, Y.

1814A —Unto all that wait in Sion. [*London*, 1665.] cap., 4°.* L, O; CH.

1814B [–] A visitation of love. [*London*], *for M. W.*, 1662. brs. L.

1815 The green-sickness grief. *By E. C. for F. Coles, T. Vere, and J. Wright*, [1685]. brs. EUING 125. O, GU.

1816 Greene, Alexander. The polititian cheated. *For Robert Crofts*, 1663. 4°. L, O, LVD, OW; CH, CU, LC, MH, WCL, WF, Y.

1817 Greene, Giles. A declaration in vindication of the honour of the Parliament. *For Laurence Blaiklock*, 1647. 4°.* LT, C, OC, LSD, MR, DT; CH, MH, NU, WF, Y.

1818 Greene, John. A briefe vnvailing of God and mans glory. *Sold by Thomas Faucet*, 1641. 4°.* L; CH.

1819 Entry cancelled.
—Brownists conventicle. 1641. *See* Taylor, John.

1820 —The chvrches duty. *By F. B. for Philemon Stephens*, 1647. 4°.* LT, O, C, YM, GU, BLH; CH, MH, NU, WF, Y.

1821 [–] The first man, or, a short discourse. *For Benjamin Allen*, 1643. 4°.* LT, C; CH, MH.

1822 —Nehemiah's teares and prayers. *By G. M. for Philemon Stephens*, 1644. 4°.* LT, O, C, GU, DT; CH, IU, MH, NU, WF, Y.

1823 Entry cancelled. *See* Taylor, John.

1824 Entry cancelled. Date: 1615.

1824A [–] The worlds riddle and the saints blisse. [*London*], *sold by Thomas Faucet*, 1641. 4°.* L.

1825 G[reene], M[artin]. An account of the Jesuites life. [*London?*], *printed*, 1661. 8°. L, O, C, LW, OC, BSM; CN, IU, MM, TU, WF.

1826 [–] Αυτοκατακριτοι. Or the Jesuits condemned. *For Charles Harper*, 1679. fol.* T.C.I 373. L, O, C, OB, OC; CH, MB, MH, WF, Y.

1826A [–] The voyce of truth. *At Gant, by Robert Walker*, 1676. 12°. L.

1827 Greene, Richard. The Popish massacre. *By T. D. for John Smith*, 1679. fol.* L, O, C, DU, EN; CH, IU, MBP, TU, WF, Y.

1827AA Greene, Robert. Greens Arcadia. *By G. Purslow, to be sold by Francis Coles*, 1657. 4°. EC.

1827BA [–] The delightful history of Dorastus and Fawnia. [*London*], *for C. Dennison*, [1680?]. 12°.* CM.

1827A [–] The history of Dorastus and Fawnia. *For J. Blare*, [*c.* 1700]. 8°.* WF.

1828 —The honorable history of Frier Bacon. *By Jean Bell*, 1655. 4°. L, LVD, OW, EC, EN; CH, PU, WF, Y.

1829 [–] A most pleasant comedy of Mucedorus. *For Francis Coles*, [*c.* 1656]. 4°. L, CT, OW; CH, WF.

1830 [–] —[Anr. ed.] —, 1663. 4°.* O; MB.

1831 [–] —[Anr. ed.] *By E. O. for Francis Coles*, 1668. 4°.* L, O, OW, CT; CH, MB, NN, WF, Y.

1832 —The pleasant and delightful history of Dorastus. *For G. Conyers*, [1696?]. 8°. L; MB, WF.

1832A ——[Anr. ed.] *By W. O.*, [1700?]. 8°. CN.

1833 —The pleasant history of Dorastus and Fawnia. *For F. Faulkner*, 1648. 4°. L; WF.

1834 ——[Anr. ed.] *For Edward Blackmore*, 1655. 4°. CT.

1835 ——[Anr. ed.] *By R. Ibbitson for I. Wright, to be sold by W. Thackery*, 1664. 4°. CT.

1836 ——[Anr. ed.] *For J. Wright, to be sold by J. Clarke*, 1677. 4°. L.

1836A ——[Anr. ed.] *By H. Brugis for J. Clark, W. Thackeray, and T. Passinger*, 1684. 4°. WF.

1837 ——[Anr. ed.] *For Geo. Conyers*, 1688. 4°. L, CM.

1838 ——[Anr. ed.] *By J. W. for George Conyers.* [1690] 4°.* O.

1839 Greene, Thomas. An alarm to the false shepheards. *For Robert Wilson*, 1660. 4°.* L, LF; MH, MU, PH.

1839A —The cause of an innocent upright-hearted people vindicated. *Printed*, 1663. brs. LF; CH.

1840 —A declaration to the world of my travel. *For Thomas Simmons*, 1659. 4°.* MR; CH, MU, PH, PSC.

1841 [–] An epistle by the life of truth. [*London*], *printed*, 1665. 4°.* L, LF, BBN, MR; MH, MU, PH, PSC.

1841A —An epistle of tender love. [*London*, 1664.] brs. LF; PH.

1842 [–] A few plain words to the inhabitant of England. colop: [*London*], *for W. M.*, 1662. cap., 4°.* L, LF, BBN; PH, PSC.

1843 —A general epistle. [*London*], *printed*, 1665. 4°.* L, LF, BBN; IE, MH, MU, PH, PSC, Y.

1844 —A lamentation taken up for London. [*London*], *printed*, 1665. 4°. L, LF, BBN, MR; PH.

1844A —To both Houses of Parliament. [*London*, 1662]. fol.* LF; CH, PH.

1845 —To both Houses of Parliament, sitting. [*London*, 1662.] fol.* LF; CH.

1846 [–] A trumpet sounded out of Zion. [*London*, 1662.] cap., 4°.* L, LF, OJ, BBN, MR; CH, CLC, IU, MHS, PH.

1847 —A voice of comfort sounded forth. *Printed*, 1665. 4°.* LF, BBN; MH, MU, PH.

1848 Greenhill, William. Ἀξινη προς την ῥιζαν. The axe at the root. *By R. O. & G. D. for Benjamin Allen*, 1643. 4°. LT, O, C, SHR, DT; CH, CN, MH, TU, WF, Y, AVP.

1849 —Catalogus librorum . . . Catalogue of the library. [*London*], 18 Feb. 1678. 4°. L, CS.

1850 [–] A declaration of divers elders and brethren of Congregationall societies. colop: *By M. Simmons for L. Chapman*, 1651. cap., 4°.* LT, DU; WF.

1851 —An exposition of the five first chapters of . . . Ezekiel. *By Matthew Simmons for Benjamin Allen*, 1645. 4°. LT, O, CCA, BR, ENC, BQ; CLC, IU, MH, NC, WF, Y.

1852 ——Second edition. *By M. Simmons for Hanna Allen*, 1649. 4°. LCL, LLP, AN, P, E, GU; MB, MH, MWA.

1853 ——[Anr. ed.] *By M. S. for Hanna Allen, to be sold by John Walker*, 1650. LSC; IU, NU, Y.

1854 —An exposition continued upon the sixt, . . . thirteenth chapters of . . . Ezekiel. *By M. S. for Hanna Allen.* 1649. 4°. LT, O, LCL, BC, ENC, DM; CLC, IU, MB, MH, MWA, WF, Y.

1855 —An exposition continued . . . fourteenth, . . . nineteenth chapters of . . . Ezekiel. *By M. S. for Livewell Chapman,* 1651. 4°. L, O, C, BR, ENC; BN, CH, IU, MH, NU, WF, Y.

1856 —An exposition continued upon the xx, . . . xxix. chapters of . . . Ezekiel. *For Livewell Chapman, to be sold by Henry Mortlock,* 1658. 4°. LT, O, LG, P, ENC; MB, MH, NU, TO, Y.

1857 —The exposition continued upon the nineteen last chapters of . . . Ezekiel. *For Thomas Parkhurst,* 1662. 4°. L, LLP, LW, GU; MH, MWA, TO, Y.

1858 —Sermons of Christ. *By R. I. for Livewell Chapman,* 1656. 8°. LW; CH, NU, Y.

1859 [–] The sound-hearted Christian. *For Nath. Crouch,* 1670. 12°. T.C.I 29. L, C, LCL; CLC, NU, WCL, WF, Y.

1860 — —[Anr. ed.] —, 1671. 8°. O, C, LW; MH, AVP.

1861 **Greenway, Margret.** A lamentation against the professing priest. [*London, c.* 1657.] brs. MADAN 2322. O.

1862 **Greenway, Richard.** An alarm from the holy mountain. colop: *For the author,* 1662. cap., 4°.* L, O, LF, BBN; MU, PH, PSC.

1863 —A call out of gross darkness. *For the author,* 1662. 4°.* L, LF; CH, MU, PSC, Y.

1863A [–] Short sentences. [*London,* 1679.] brs. LF.

1864 Entry cancelled.
—Three general epistles. 1662. *See title.*

1865 **Greenwood, Daniel.** Two sermons. *Oxford, printed,* 1680. 4°.* MADAN 3267–8. O; NU.

1866 Entry cancelled.
—Whereas the right honourable the Councell of State. Oxford, 1651. *See* Oxford University. Jan. 9. 1651. By the Vicechancellour.

1867 **Greenwood, Henry.** Greenvvoods workes. Thirteenth edition. *By Robert Ibbitson,* 1650. 12°. L, LCL; LC, WF.

1868 **Greenwood, Nicholas.** Astronomia Anglicana: containing. *By John Harefinch, for William Hensman,* 1689. fol. T.C.II 302. L, O, C, LW, OM, DU; CH, IU, LC, MH, MU.

1868aA — —[Anr. ed.] —, *and are to be sold by Rest Fenner, in Canterbury.* 1689. fol. PL, WF.

1868A — —[Anr. ed.] *For Richard Mount,* 1699. fol. MU.
—Diarium planetarum. 1690. *See* Almanacs.

1869 **Greenwood, William.** Ἀπογραφη στοργης. Or, a description of . . . love. *For William Place,* 1657. 8°. L, O, DC; NP, WF.

1870 —Βουλευτηριον, or a practical demonstration. *By T. R. for John Place, and William Place,* 1659. 8°. LT, LLP; CLC, MH, MHL.

1871 — —Third edition. *For J. Place,* 1664. 8°. L, C; CB, LC, MH.

1872 — —"Third" edition. *For John Place; and Will: Place,* 1668. 8°. T.C.I 11. DC, LSC; CH, PUL.

1873 — —Fifth edition. *For William Place, and John Place,* 1675. 8°. O, CCA, CP, LIL; CLL, NCD, WF.

1874 — —Sixth edition. *For John Place,* 1685. 8°. T.C.II 171. L, O, BAMB, BQ; CLL, PUL, WF, YL.

1874A —Curia comitatus rediviva. Or, the pratique part. *For John Place and William Place,* 1657. 8°. L, CCA, EN; CU, PU, YL.

1874B **Greeting, Thomas.** The pleasant companion. *For John Playford,* 1675. 4°. L, O; LC, CASE WESTERN. (var.)

1874C — —[Anr. ed.] —, 1676. obl. 8°. DUS.

1874D — —[Anr. ed.] *For J. Playford,* 1680. 4°. LC, MU, WF.

1875 — —[Anr. ed.] —, 1682. 4°. L.

1875A — —[Anr. ed.] —, 1683. 4°. LC.

1876 **Greg, Mother.** The burgess ticket of Buckhaven. *Edinburgh, printed,* 1682. fol.* ALDIS 2332.5. EN.

1876A — —[Anr. ed.] —, 1689. 4°.* ALDIS 2892.5. EN.

1876B — —[Anr. ed.] [*Edinburgh*], *printed,* 1695. 4°.* ALDIS 3463.5. EN.

1877 **G[regg], H[ugh].** Curiosities in chymistry. *By H. C. for Stafford Anson,* 1691. 8°. T.C.II 381. L, O, C, LCS, AU; CLC, MH, MMO, PL, JF. (var.)

1878 [–] —[Anr. ed.] 1692. 4°. LCP.

1879 [–] —[Anr. ed.] *By H. C. for Stafford Anson,* 1696. 8°. T.C.II 608. L.

1879aA **Gregorio, F. di.** Il discepulo instrutto. *For the author,* 1643. 8°. CCA.

1879A **Gregorius Nazianzenus, saint.** A most excellent and pathetical oration. *By W. Godbid for H. Herringman,* 1662. 12°. Y.

1880 **Gregory XV, pope.** Behold! Two letters. [*London*], *printed,* 1642. 4°.* LT, O, C, EC, LNC; CSS, MH, NU, WF, Y.

1881 — [Anr. ed.] [*London,* 1649.] cap., 4°.* LT; MII.

1882 **Gregory, Arthur.** Gregories moot-book. Fourth edition. *For H. Twyford, T. Dring, and J. Place,* 1663. 4°. L, LGI, LIL, LL; CU, MHL, PUL.

1883 **Gregory, David.** Catoptricæ et dioptricæ. *Oxonii, e theatro Sheldoniano,* 1695. 8°. T.C.II 559. L, O, C, EN, DT; BN, CLC, CN, PL, WF, Y.

1883A —De curva catenaria. *Oxoniæ, e theatro Sheldoniano,* 1697. 4°.* O, OC, CT; NN.

1884 —Exercitatio geometrica. *Edinburgi, ex officina typographicâ Jacobi Kniblo, Josuæ Solingensis & Johannis Colmarii,* 1684. 4°. ALDIS 2454. L, O, C, E, EN; LC, PL, Y.

1885 **Gregory, Edmund.** An historical anatomy of Christian melancholy. *For Humphrey Moseley,* 1646. 8°. LT, O, C; MH, CLC, MH.

1886 **Gregory, Francis.** Ἀγαπη, or the feast of love. *By J. Macock, for Richard Royston,* 1675. 4°. T.C.I 234. L, O, LG, EN; CH, CLC, NU, WF, Y.

1887 —Concio ad clervm. *By R. N. for Richard Royston,* 1673. 4°.* L, O, C, LLP, DT; CB, LC, NGT, NU, WF, Y.

1888 —David's returne. *Oxford, by Henry Hall,* 1660. 4°.* MADAN 2495. L, O, SP, BLH; CH, CLC, IU, MH, NU, TU, WF, Y.

1889 —A divine antidote. *For Rich. Sare, and Jos. Hindmarsh,* 1696. 8°. T.C.II 567. O, LW, OC, CS; CLC, NU.

1890 —The doctrine of the glorious Trinity. *For Walter Kettilby,* 1695. 8°. T.C.II 538. L, O, C, OC, NE; CH, CLC, IU, NPT, WF, Y.

1890A   [–] An elegie upon the death of our dread sovereign lord. [*London*, 1649.] brs. LT; MH.

1891   —Ἐπιφανια, or a discourse. [*Oxford, by L. Lichfield*], for *Tho. Bowman*, 1678. 4°. MADAN 3176. L, O; MB, WF.

1891A   ——[Anr. ed.] *Oxford, by L. L. for Thomas Bowman*, 1680. 4°. Y.

1892   —Ἐτυμολογικον μικρον, sive, etymologicum parvum. *Typis J. Flesher, impensis Richardi Royston*, 1654. 8°. L, O, C, LL, DC, DU; BN, CLC, IU, MWA, WF, Y.

1893   ——[Anr. ed.] *Typis E. Tyler & R. Holt pro R. Royston, prostant apud Thomas Passinger*, 1670. T.C.I 51. LW, CM, LLU; CH.

1894   —The grand presumption of the Roman church. *By E. Flesher for R. Royston*, 1675. 4°. T.C.I 215. L, O, LIL, EN, DT; CB, CH, Y.

1895   —The Gregorian account. *By E. Flesher, for Richard Royston*, 1673. 4°.* L, O, SP, WCA, DT; CLC, NGT, NU, Y.

1895A   [–] The last counsel of a martyred King. *For J. Jones*, 1660. 4°.* LT, O.

1896   —A modest plea for the due regulation of the press. *For R. Sare*, 1698. 4°.* T.C.III 81. L, OC, CT, LSD, EN; NR, VC, ZWT.

1897   —Ὁμιλια ἐιρηνικη. Or, a thanksgiving sermon. *For Richard Sare; and sold by E. Whitlock*, 1697. 4°.* L, OC, CK, CS; CH, CN, Y.

1897A   —Ὀνομαστικον βραχυ, sive nomenclatura. *Londini, excudebat J.D.*, [1651]. 8°. O.

1898   [–] —Third edition. *By William Du-Gard, to be sold by Richard Royston*, 1652. 8°. E.

1899   [–] —Fourth edition. *By William Du-Gard; to bee sold by Richard Royston*, 1654. 8°. C.

1899A   [–] —Seventh edition. *By H. L. and R. V. for W. Du-Gard, sold by Richard Royston*, [166–?]. 8°. TO (impf.).

1899B   [–] —Eighth edition. *By H. L. for William Du-Gard; sold by Richard Royston*, 1662. 8°. IU.

1899C   ——[Anr. ed.] *Ex officina R. Danielis*, 1663. 8°. O, OC, BR.

1899D   [–] —[Anr. ed.] *Typis J. Redmayne voeneunt apud Jacobus Allestry*, 1668. 8°. CASTLE ASHBY; WF.

1899E   [–] —[Anr. ed.] *Typis J. Redmayne*, 1672. 8°. CLC, Y.

1899F   ——[Anr. ed.] *Impensis Nathaniel Ranew*, 1674. 8°. T.C.I 182. OC.

1900   [–] —Thirteenth edition. *By J. Macock, for Richard Royston*, 1675. 8°. L, LLP, CCA.

1901   [–] —[Anr. ed.] *Ex officina Elizabethæ Redmayne*, 1684. 8°. T.C.II 77. LL; IU.

1902   [–] —Seventeenth edition. 1685. 8°. MBC.

1902A   ——[Anr. ed.] *Ex officina Elizabethæ Redmayne*, 1693. 8°. EC.

1902B   [–] —Twentieth edition. *By J. L. for Luke Meredith*, 1694. 8°. T.C.II 533. PL.

1903   —The religious villain. *For Sam. Lee and Dan. Major*, 1679. 4°.* T.C.I 367. L, O, CS, BC, SHR; CH, IU, NU, PL, WF, Y.

1904   —The right way to victory. *By E. Flesher, for Richard Royston*, 1673. 4°.* L, O, C, CT, DT; CH, MBA, TU, WF, Y.

1905   —Teares and bloud. *Oxford, by A. and L. Lichfield*, 1660. 4°. MADAN 2496. L, O, OM, DU, DT; CH, MH, NU, TU, WF, Y.

1906   —A thanksgiving sermon. *For R. Sare*, 1696. 4°.* OC, CT; CLC, NU, Y.

1907   —The triall of religions. *By E. Flesher for R. Royston*, 1674. 4°. T.C.I 194. L, O, C, GC, EN; CLC, IEG, NIC, NU, Y.

1908   **Gregory, George.** A bakers-dozen of plain down-right queries. *Printed*, 1659. 4°.* LT, OB; CH, CN, CSS.

1909   **Gregory, James.** Exercitationes geometricæ. *Typis Guilielmi Godbid, & impensis Mosis Pitt*, 1668. 4°.* L, O, C, E, DT; BN, CB, MU, NIC, NN, PL, RBU.

1910   [–] The great and new art of weighing vanity. *Glasgow, by Robert Sanders*, 1672. 8°. ALDIS 1950. L, O, EN, GU, SA; CH, CLC, MH, RBU, WF.

1911   —Nobilissimo viro Georgio. *Edinburgi, ex officina typographica societatis bibliopolarum*, 1690. brs. ALDIS 3097.5. O, CCL, EN.

1912   —Optica promota. *Excudebat J. Hayes, pro S. Thomson*, 1663. 4°. L, O, C, EN, ES; BN, CJC, MH, NN, WF, HC.

1913   **Gregory, John.** The works of. *For R. Royston, and N. Brooks*, 1665. 4°. L, O, CT, LSD, MR; CB, CH, IU, MIU, WF.

1914   ——[Anr. ed.] *For Richard Royston, and Thomas Williams*, 1671. 4°. L, O, C, EN, DT; CH, MH, MIU, MU, NU, Y.

1915   —Fourth edition. *By M. Clark, for Rich. Royston, Benj. Tooke, and Tho. Sawbridge*, 1684. 4°. T.C.II 51. L, O, C, CT, DU, EN; CH, CN, PL, WF, Y.

1916   Entry cancelled.
       [–] Copy of a letter written from Northampton. 1646. *See title.*

1917   No entry.

1918   —Ἡμερα ἀναπανσεως or a discourse. *For Richard Royston*, 1681. 8°. T.C.I 439. L, O, LW, P, E; NPT, UCLA, WF, Y.

1919   ——Second edition. *For L. Meredith*, 1693. 8°. T.C.II 433. O, OC, OM, BANGOR; NGT.

1920   —Notes and observations vpon some passages of Scriptvre. *Oxford, by H. Hall, for Ed. Forrest, junior*; 1646. 4°. MADAN 1879. LT, O, C, GU, DT; CH, IU, NU, WF, Y.

1921   [–] —Second edition. *By R. C. for Richard Roiston*, 1650. 4°. L, O, C, AN, EN, DT; CH, CN, NGT, NP, WF, Y.

1922   ——[Anr. ed.] *By J. Flesher for R. Royston*, 1665. 4°. L, O; CLC, IU, NU, WF.

1923   ——[Anr. ed.] *By R. Norton for R. Royston*, 1671. 4°. L, O, C, LIU; CH, FU, IU, NU, Y.

1924   ——[Anr. ed.] *By M. Clark, for R. Royston*, 1684. 4°. L, O, C, LSC, NE; CB, IU, PL, TU, Y.

1925   —Gregorii opuscula. *For R. Royston*, 1650. 4°. L, O, C, P; CJC, CLC, CN, NU, WF, Y.

1926   —Gregorii posthuma. *By William Du-gard for Laurence Sadler*, 1649. 4°. L, O, CJ, MR, CD; CH, MU, PL.

1927   ——[Anr. ed.] —, 1650. 4°. L, O, C, AN, E, DT; CH, CU, NU, WF, Y.

1928   ——[Anr. ed.] *By J. Grismond for Laurence Sadler*, 1664. 4°. L, O, CE; IU, LC, MU, NU, WF.

1929   ——[Anr. ed.] *By Andrew Clark, for Thomas Williams*, 1671. 4°. L, O, C, OM, DUS, LIU; CH, IU, MB, NU, Y.

1930 ——[Anr. ed.] *By M. Clark, for Benj. Tooke, and Tho. Sawbridge,* 1683. 4°. L, O, OC, CM, NE; CH, IU, PL, TU, WF, Y.

1930A **Gregory, Robert.** To the honourable the knights. [*Dublin,* 1695.] brs. DI.

1931 **G[regory], T[homas].** Charity and integrity of life. *By J. Bradford, for the author,* 1696. 4°.* L, LLP.

1932 —Discourses upon several divine subjects. *For R. Sare,* 1696. 8°. L, C, OC, NE, SHR; CH, PL, WF, Y.

1933 —Μεθ' 'ημων 'ο Θεος. Or the doctrine of a god. *For J. Hindmarsh, and R. Sare,* 1694. 8°. T.C.II 520. L, C, OC; FU, NGT, WF.

Gregory, Father-Greybeard. 1673. *See* Hickeringill, Edmund.

1934 **Grelot, Guillaume Joseph.** A late voyage to Constantinople. *By John Playford, and are to be sold by Henry Bonwicke,* 1683. 8°. T.C.II 43. L, O, C, DU, LLU; CH, IU, LC, MBA, MH, PL, WF, Y.

1934A The granadiers loyal health. [*London*], *for J. Dean,* 1683. brs. MH, Y.

1934B The granadiers [*sic*] loyal health to the King and royal family. [*London*], *for J. Conyers,* [1686]. brs. NNM.

1935 **Grenadine, Sebastian.** Homais Queen of Tunis. *Amsterdam* [*London*], *for Simon the Afrikan* [*R. Bentley?*], 1681. 12°. T.C.I 461. L, O; CLC, NP, WF, Y.

1936 **Grenfield, Henry.** God in the creature. *For George May,* 1686. 8°. T.C.II 158. L, O, C, LCL, SP; MH.

1937 **Grenfield, Thomas.** The fast. *For Henry Brome,* 1661. 4°.* L, O, LL, CT, DT; CN, MM, RBU.

1937A ——Second edition. —, 1661. 4°.* CH, CLC, MH, WF, Y.

1937B **Grenville, Denis.** Articles of enquirie for surveying the bishops lands. *By R. Cotes for John Bellamy,* 1647. 4°.* MIU.

1938 —The compleat Conformist. *For Robert Clavell,* 1684. 4°.* T.C.II 92. L, O, C, DU, DT; CH, CN, NU, WF, Y.

1938aA ——[Anr. ed.] *For Robert Clavell, sold by Hugh Hutchinson in Durham,* 1684. 4°.* OCC.

1938A [–] Counsel and directions. *For Robt. Clavell,* 1685. 8°. T.C.II 149. L, O, LW, CS, DU; CLC, CN, MB, WF, Y.

1939 Entry cancelled.

[–] Declaration made. [1672.] *See* Bath, Henry Bourchier, *earl of.*

1940 —The resigned and resolved Christian. *Printed at Roüen, by William Machuel, for John Baptiste Besongue, and are to be sold by Augustin Besongue, at Paris,* 1689. 4°. L, O; VC.

1941 [–] A sermon preached in the Cathedral Church of Durham. *For Robert Clavel,* 1686. 4°.* T.C.II 155. L, O, OM, BAMB, LSD, WCA, DT; CH, IEG, WF, Y.

1942 **Grenville, Sir Richard.** A letter written by. *For Edward Husband, April* 17, 1646. 4°.* LT, DT; MM, Y.

1943 Entry cancelled. *See preceding entry.*

1943A [–] A narrative of affares [*sic*] of the west, since . . . 1644. [*n.p.*], *printed,* 1647. 4°.* LNC.

Gretnerus. *See* Grebner, Paul.

1944 **Gretser, Jacob.** Rudimenta linguæ Græcæ. *Typis Henrici Hills,* 1687. 12° in sixes. L, O, E, DM; IU, NN, WG.

1944A —The rudiments of the Greek tongue. *By Henry Hills for himself and Matthew Turner,* 1687. 12°. L; WG.

1944B **Gretton, Nicholias.** Divine philosophie. *By 'Jam. Moxon for W. Larnar,* 1651. 8°. Y.

Greville, Fulke. *See* Brooke, Fulke Greville, *baron.*

Greville, Robert. *See* Brooke, Robert Greville, *baron.*

1945 **Grew, Nehemiah.** The anatomy of plants. [*London*], *by W. Rawlins, for the author,* 1682. fol. L, O, C, EN, DT; BN, CH, CNM, LC, MH, MMO, MU, NAM, WSC, WF, Y.

1946 —The anatomy of vegetables begun. *For Spencer Hickman,* 1672. 8°. T.C.I 96. L, O, C, AU, DT; BN, CH, IU, LC, MH, MMO, WF, Y.

1946A [–] At a meeting of the Royal Society . . . proposals made . . . for printing The anatomy of plants. 1681/2. cap., fol.* L.

[–] A brief of two treatises. [*n.p.,* 1687?] *See* Fitzgerald, Robert.

1947 —The comparative anatomy of trunks. *By J. M. for Walter Kettilby,* 1675. 8°. T.C.I 220. L, O, C, E, DT; BN, CH, LC, MH, NAM, WF, WU, Y.

1948 —A discourse made before the Royal Society, Decemb. 10. 1674. *For John Martyn,* 1675. 12°. T.C.I 205. L, O, CM, NE, YM; BN, CH, CLC, LC, MH, WU, JF.

1949 —Dissertatio, quæ complectitur nova experimenta. *Excudebat J. Gain,* [1684?]. 8°.* L, O, C, OC; BN, WU.

1949A —Estratto di due trattati . . . Il primo . . . Il trattato secundo scrite dal. [*London,* 1684?] brs. L.

1950 —Experiments in consort. *For John Martyn,* 1678. 12°. T.C.I 292. L, O, C, AU; BN, CH, CLC, MH, MHS, Y.

1950A —Experiments in consort . . . To which is added. *For John Martyn,* 1678. 12°. LCP, LCS, LWL; JF.

1951 —An idea of a phytological history. *By J. M. for Richard Chiswell,* 1673. 8°. T.C.I 140. L, O, C, E, DT; BN, CH, CLC, LC, MH, MMO, MU, WF, JF.

1952 —Mvsævm regalis societatis. Or a catalogue & description of the natural and artificial rarities. *By W. Rawlins, for the author,* 1681. fol. L, O, C, E, DT; BN, CH, CJC, MBP, MH, WF, Y.

1952A ——[Anr. ed.] *For Tho. Malthous,* 1685. fol. EN; CLC, MH.

1953 Entry cancelled. Ghost.

1954 ——[Anr. ed.] *For S. Holford,* 1686. fol. T.C.II 150. C, LWL, SA, E; CRN, MH, NC.

1954A ——[Anr. ed.] *For Tho. Malthus,* 1686. fol. LLU.

1955 ——[Anr. ed.] *For H. Newman,* 1694. fol. T.C.II 530. L, LWL, RU, E, GU, DT; Y, ZWT.

1956 [–] New experiments, and useful observations. [*n.p.*], *printed,* 1683. 8°.* O, C, LLP, LWL.

1956A [–] —[Anr. ed.] *By John Harefinch,* 1684. 4°.* LG; MH.

1957 [–] —Fourth edition. *February the* 14th. *By John Harefinch,* 1684. 4°.* L, O, C, LWL, NE; CLC, Y.

1957A ——Fifth edition. —, 1684. 8°. PL (impf.).

1957B ——Eighth edition. *May the* 22th. *By John Harefinch,* 1684. 4°.* Y.

1958 ——Eighth edition. *August the* 12th. *By John Harefinch,* 1684. 4°.* BN, LC.

1958A —Ninth edition. *Septemb.* 29. *By John Harefinch,* 1684. 8°.* L, O; CH, NC.

[169]

— —"Ninth" edition. 1684. *See also* Fitzgerald, Robert. Further additions. 1684.

1958B — —"Ninth" edition. *Octob. 13. By John Harefinch*, 1684. 12°.* L.

1958C — —Tenth edition. —, 1685. 12°.* L.

— —"Tenth" edition. 1685. *See also* Fitzgerald, Robert. Further additions. 1685.

1958D [–] Nouvelles experiences. *A Londres* 1684. 4°.* L.

1959 —Tractatus de salis cathartici. amari. *Impensis S. Smith & B. Walford*, 1695. 12°. T.C.II 559. L, O, C, LCS, DT; BN, CLC, IU, NAM, TU, WSG, JF.

1959A — —Second edition. *Typis Johannis Darbei*, 1698. 12°. ECP.

1960 —A treatise of the nature and use. *Printed*, 1697. 12°. L, C, MAU; WF, JF.

1960A — —[Anr. ed.] *By John Darby for Walter Kettilby*, 1697. 8°. T.C.III 40. O, LCS, OC, OM; PL.

1961 — —[Anr. ed.] *Printed*, 1700. 8°. LWL.

1962 —Whereas a book, entituled, Musæum regalis societatis. *[London]*, 1679/80. cap., fol.* L, O.

1963 **Grew, Obadiah.** The Lord Jesus Christ. *For John Brooke in Coventry*, 1669. 12°. CLC, NU.

1964 —Meditations upon Our Saviour's parable. Part I. *By S. Roycroft for Nevill Simmons*, 1678. 4°. T.C.I 318. L, O, C, LCL, AN, DU, ENC; CH, IU, MB, MH, NR, NU, WF.

1965 —Meditations upon the parable. Second part. *For Tho. Parkhurst*, 1684. 4°. T.C.II 93. L, O, C, LCL, LW, DU; MH, NR, NU, WF, AVP.

1966 —A sinners justification. *For N. Simmons*, 1670. 8°. T.C.I 18. LSC, LW, SA, ENC; CH, TO, V, Y.

1967 — —Second edition. *By S. Bridge, for Nath. Hiller*, 1698. 12°. L, C, BC, LCL, LW; CH, NU, WF.

Grey, Elizabeth. *See* Kent, Elizabeth Grey, *countess.*

1968 **Grey, Enoch.** Vox cœli, containing maxims. *For Tho: Williams*, 1649. 4°. LT, LCL, OC, EN, DT; CH, CN, MH, NU, WF, Y.

Grey, Henry. *See also* Stamford, Henry Grey, *earl of.*

1969 [–] A letter to the Lord Grey of Grooby. *[London]*, *for Andrew Coe*, 1644. 4°.* LT; CN, IU, WF, Y.

1969A **[Grey, Nicholas.]** Parabulæ evangelicæ. *Typis J. S. impensis Thomæ Vnderhill*, [1650]. 8°. WF.

1969B **Grey, Thomas,** *Baron Grey of Groby.* Old English blood boyling afresh. *By H. for Giles Calvert*, 1648. 4°.* LT; IU, MH.

Grey, Thomas. *See also* Stamford, Thomas Grey, *2nd earl.*

1970 —Catalogue of the library. *[London]*, 8 Feb. 1694. 4°. L, ST. EDMUND HALL, OXFORD.

1971 **Grey, Thomas,** *M. A.* Loyalty essential. *By Henry Clark, and sold by Walter Davis*, 1685. 4°.* L, O, LSD, DT; CH.

1972–4 No entries.

Grey, Thomas de la. *See* DeGrey, Thomas.

1975 **[Grey, William.]** Chorographia, or a svrvey of Newcastle-upon-Tyne. *Newcastle, by S. B.*, 1649. 4°.* L, O, C, OB, NE, NSA; CH, MH, WF.

1975A [–] —[Anr. ed.] *By J. B.*, 1649. 4°.* O, NE.

1976 **Grice, Thomas.** A short vindication. *For R. C. and to be sold by Randal Taylor*, 1689. 4°.* L, O, OC, MR, EN; CH, NU.

Grief allayed. 1682. *See* Laxton, Thomas.

1977 Grievances desired to be examined. *[n.p., 166–?]*. brs. O.

1977A The grievances of His Majesties subjects residing within . . . Wales. *[London?* 1669.] brs. L.

1978 The grievances of the Church of England. colop: *For R. Baldwin*, 1689. brs. L, O, LG, DU, EC; CH, CN, MB, NU, Y.

1979 The grievances represented by the Estates. *By Edward Jones*, 1689. fol.* L, C, LLP, LUG, MR; CH, TO, WF, Y.

1980 —[Anr. ed.] colop: *Printed at London, and re-printed at Edinburgh*, 1689. cap., fol.* ALDIS 2893. L, OP, MR, EN; MH.

1980A The grieved country-mans complaint. *[London?* 1660.] brs. Y.

1981 **Griffin, Anthony.** An astrological judgement touching theft. *By Peter Lillicrap*, 1665. 8°. L, O.

1981A **[Griffin, Lewis.]** The asses complaint against Balaam. *For the author*, 1661. brs. L; MH.

1981B — —[Anr. ed.] *[London, 1661.]* brs. MH.

1982 —The doctrine of the asse. *For Henry Marsh*, 1661. 4°.* L, C, LCI, EN; CLC, MH, MIU, WF, Y.

1982A [–] Essayes and characters. *[London]*, *printed*, 1661. 4°. O, NE.

1983 —Rules of life. *For Henry Marsh*, 1663. 4°.* L, O, LNC; TU, Y.

1984 —A supplement to the asses complaint. *[London, 1661?]* brs. L, SP.

1985 **Griffin, William.** Newes from London-Derry. *For William Ley*, 1642. 4°.* LT, LNC; IAU.

1986 No entry.

1987 **[Griffith, Alexander.]** Mercurius Cambro-Britannicus; or, news from Wales. *Printed*, 1652. 4°.* LT, O, AN, E; CH, CLC, IU, WF.

1988 [–] Strena Vavasoriensis, a New-Years-Gift. *By F. L.*, 1654. 4°.* LT, O, LCL, LW, AN, DU; CH, CN, MH, WF, Y.

1989 [–] A true and perfect relation of the whole transaction. *By J. G. for Nath. Ekins*, 1654. 4°. L, C, AN, LSD; WF.

1989A [–] —[Anr. ed.] *By J. G. for Math. Ekins*, 1654. 4°. O.

1990 **G[riffith], E[van].** Pax vobis, or ghospell and libertie. *[n.p.]*, 1679. 12°. L, O, EN; BN, CLC.

1991 [–] —[Anr. ed.] *[n.p.]*, *printed*, 1685. 12°. L, CCA, RU, EN, ENC; CB, CLC, NU, WF, (var.)

1992 [–] —Second edition. *[n.p.]*, 1687. 8°. L, O, OC, CS, DT; CLC, MM, WSC.

1992A [–] —Second edition. *[n.p.]*, *for William Grantham*, 1687. 8°. BSM; Y.

1993 [–] —Fourth edition. *[n.p.]*, *printed*, 1687. 8°. O, C, OC, OCC, OM, LSD; CN, MIU, TU.

1994 [–] —Fifth edition. —, 1687. 12°. O, C, BSM; PL.

1995 [–] A sermon preached at Alderly . . . January IV. 1676/7. *By W. G. for William Shrowsbury*, 1677. 4°.* L, O, C, OCC, LIU, EN; CH, CN, NU, WF, Y.

1996 **G[riffith], G[eorge],** *bp.* A bold challenge of an itinerant preacher . . . answered. *[London]*, *printed*, 1652. 4°.* LT, O, AN; CLC, Y.

1997 —Gueddi 'r-arglwydd wedi ei hegluro. *Printiedig yn y theater yn Rhydychen.* 1685. 4°. O, AN, CPL; CH, CLC.

1998 [–] A relation of a disputation between D[r] Griffith. *By M. S., to be sold by Livewell Chapman,* 1653. 4°.* LT; MH.

1999 —A Welsh narrative, corrected. *By A. M. for John Browne,* 1653. 4°.* LT, O, CS, AN, P, YM, E; MH.

2000 **Griffith, John.** The case of Mr. John Griffith. colop: *By George Larkin for the author,* 1683. brs. L, O, LL, EN; CN, WF, Y.

2001 —A declaration of some of those people in or near London, called Anabaptists. *By Thomas Milbourn for Samuel Cleaver,* [1660]. brs. LT, LG.

2002 —God's oracle. *Printed, and are to be sold by Richard Moon and Samuel Clever; and by W. Burden,* 1655. 4°. O, LSC, LSD, MAB; TO, Y.

2002A —Laying on of hands on baptized believers. *For the author and Francis Smith,* 1654. 8°.* ORP.

2003 [–] The searchers for schism search'd. [*n.p.*], *for the author,* 1669. 8°. O.

2003A Entry cancelled.
[–] Some observations made upon the Brasillian root, called ipepocoanha. 1682. *See* Griffith, Richard.

2004 —Some prison-meditations and experiences. [*London*], *printed,* 1663. 8°. L, C, ORP; CH, IU, MH.

2005 —This is a true copy of a letter. [*n.p.,* 1650.] cap., 4°.* LT; BN.

2006 —A treatise touching falling from grace. *By Hen. Hills, to be sold by Richard Moon,* 1653. 4°. LT, O, LSD; CH, TO, WF, Y.

2007 —The unlawfulnesse of mixt-marriages. *For the authour, to be sold by him, and by Enoch Prosser,* 1681. 4°. L; WF.

2008 —A vindication or ivstification of. [*London*], *printed,* 1648. 4°.* LT, AN; BN, CH, MH, MM.

2009 —A voice from the word of the Lord. *For Francis Smith,* 1654. 8°. LT, OC.

2010 **Griffith, Matthew.** The Catholique doctor. *By W. Godbid for John Playford,* 1661. 4°.* L, CS, WCA, DT; CH.

2011 —Christian concord. *By W. G. for T. Firby,* 1661. 4°. LT, C, LLP, LP; NU.

2012 —The fear of God and the King. *For Tho: Johnson,* 1660. 8°. LT, O, C; CH, IAU, MH, NU, WF, Y.

2013 [–] London. { A generall bill of mortality, of the clergie of London . . . 1641 . . . to . . . 1647. [*London,* 1646.] brs. LT, O, LG, CJ, LNC; MH, Y.

2014 Entry cancelled.
[–] General bill of mortality. 1662. *See* title.

2015 [–] The king's life-guard. *By William Godbid for Zachary Watkins,* 1665. 4°. L, O, C, WCA, YM; CLC, NU, WF.

2016 —A patheticall persvvsion to pray for publick peace. *For Richard Royston,* 1642. 4°. LT, O, C, AN, DT; CH, CN, MH, WF, Y.

2016A —The Samaritan revived. *For Tho: Johnson,* 1660. 8°. CLC, MH.

2017 [–] A sermon preached in the citie of London. *Printed,* 1643. 4°.* LT, O, C, CT, BC, DT; CH, CN, MH, WF, Y.

2018 —The spiritual antidote. *By W. G. for John Playford,* 1662. 4°.* L.

2018A **Griffith, Owen.** Abraham's prospect. *For R. Hunt in Hereford,* 1681. 4°.* CPL.

2018B ——[Anr. ed.] *For H. Brome,* 1681. 4°.* LW.

2019 **Griffith, Richard.** A-la-mode phlebotomy. *By T. B., for J. Hindmarsh,* 1681. 8°. T.C.I 417. L, LCS, LWL, OB; MBM, NP, WSG.

2019A [–] Some observations made upon the Brasillian root, called ipepocoanha. *London, printed &c.* [*sic*], 1682. 4°.* L; CH, NN, WSG.

2020 **Griffyth, John.** A sermon preached . . . 3d of October 1692. *For William Rogers,* 1693. 4°.* T.C.II 436. L, O, C, LW, MR; NU.

2021 **Griffyth, W.** Villare Hibernicum; being. *Printed and are to be sold by Richard Janeway,* 1690. 4°.* L, O, LVF, DT, BLH; CH.

2021A **G[rigg], H[enry].** The Baptist not Babylonish. 1672. 16°. L.

2022 [–] Light from the sun of righteousness. [*London*], *printed,* 1672. 8°. L, O, LF.

2023 **Grigge, William.** The Quaker's Jesus. *By M. Simmons, and are to be sold by Joseph Cranford,* 1658. 4°. LT, O, LF, OC, CT, BC.

2024 **Grighor, Abu al-Faraj.** [Arabic] historia compendiosa dynastarvm. *Oxoniæ, excudebat H. Hall impensis Ric. Davis,* 1663. 4°. MADAN 2629. L, O, CS, EN, DT; CH, CN, PL, WF, Y, AVP.

2025 —[Arabic] specimen historiæ arabvm. *Oxoniæ, excudebat H. Hall, impensis Humph: Robinson,* 1650. 4°. MADAN 2034. L, O, C, CT, EN, DT; CH, CN, PL, WF, Y.

2026 Grimalkin, or, the rebel-cat. *For the author,* 1681. fol.* L, O, CT, MR, EN; CH, CU, MH, WF, Y, AVP.

2027 **G[rimefield], J[ohn].** The sage senator delineated. *By Ja: Cottrel, for Sam. Speed,* 1660. 8°. LT, OC, CCA, DC; CH, CN, MIU, WF, Y.

2027A [–] The sage senator: or. *For J. Daniel,* [1660]. 8°. CH, CLC, CN, PT.

Grimes, Ethog. *See* Smith, George.

2028 **Grimston, Sir Harbottle.** Master Grimstons argvment concerning bishops. [*London*], *printed,* 1641. 4°.* LT, O, C, EN, DT; CLC, CN, MH, WF, Y. (var.)

2029 —A Christian New-Years gift. *By R. Daniel, Cambridge,* 1644. 16°.* LT.

2030 No entry.

2031 —M[r]. Grimston his learned speech in the High Court. *Novemb.* 25. *For T. Wright.* 1642. 4°.* LT, O, MR; CLC, CSS, MH, MU, Y.

2032 —Master Grimston his speech, at the Committee . . . the 5. of Ianuary. *Printed,* 1642. 4°.* O, LL, LNC, MR; CLC, CN, MH, RBU, TU.

2033 —M[r]. Grimston his speech, at the Committee sitting in Guild-hall . . . 6. of Ianuary 1641. *Printed at London, for B. W.,* 1642. 4°.* LT, LVF, OH, BC, DU; CLC, CN, MH, WF, Y.

2034-5 No entries.

2036 —Mr. Grimstone, his speech in Parliament: on VVed-
nesday the 19th of Ianuary. *For Iohn Hammond*, 1642.
4°.* LT, O, LVF, EN; MH, NU, WF.

2037 —Mr. Grymstons speech in Parliament upon the accusation. [*London*], *printed*, 1641. 4°.* LT, O, C, MR,
EN; CH, IU, MH, NU, WF, Y. (var.)

2038 —Mr. Grimstons speech, in the High Court. *For Thomas
Walkely*, 1641. 4°.* LT, O, C, EN, DT; CH, CU, MH, WF, Y.

2039 —Master Grimston his speech in the House of Commons. *Iuly 5. for M. T.* 1642. 4°.* LT, O, LNC, YM; CLC,
CN, MH, WF, Y.

2039A —The speech made to Sir John Greenvile, by. *By H. B.*,
[1660]. brs. L; CH, MH.

2040 —The speech of . . . May 29, 1660. *By Edward Husbands
and Thomas Newcomb*, 1660. 4°.* LT, O, C, LIU, DT;
CH, IU, MH, TU, WF, Y. (var.)

2041 — —[Anr. ed.] *Edinburgh, by a society of stationers*, 1660.
brs. STEELE 3p 2175. ALDIS 1645. L, EN, ES; Y.

2042 Entry cancelled. Ghost.

2043 —The speech which the speaker of the House . . . made
. . . 29. of August. *By Edward Husband and Tho. Newcomb*, 1660. 4°.* LT, O, C, MR, DT; CH, CN, MH, WF, Y.

2044 —The speech which the speaker of the House of Commons made unto the king . . . thirteenth day of September, . . . 1660. *By Edward Husbands and Tho. Newcomb*, 1660. 4°.* LT, O, C, LL, DT; CH, CN, MH, WF, Y.

2045 —The speech which the speaker of the House of Commons made . . . November 9. 1660. *By John Bill*, 1660.
fol.* LT, O, C, LL, DT; CH, CLC, WF.

2046 Entry cancelled.
[–] Mr. Speakers speech . . . 22. June 1641. [n.p.], 1641.
See Lenthall, William.

2047 [–] Strena Christiana. *Sumptibus Iohan Wright*, 1644.
12°. LT, O; CLC.

2048 — —Second edition. *Sumptibus Joh. Wright*, 1645.
12°. L.

2049 — —"Second" edition. *Sumptibus A. Crook & Joh.
Wright*, 1674. 12°. L; CLC, IU, WF.

2050 —Two speeches, spoken. *For H. Hutton*, 1643. 4°.* LT,
O, DU, SP, DT; CH, MH, MU, WF, L.

2051 —Master Grimston his worthy and learned speech. *For
W. H.*, 1641. 4°.* LT, BC; CLC, CN, MH, NU, WF, Y.

2052 Entry cancelled.
G[ripps], T[homas]. Tentamen novum. 1696. *See*
Gipps, Thomas.

2053 Grist ground at last. [*London*], *for J. Clark, W. Thackeray,
and T. Passinger*, [1684–86]. brs. L, O, CM, HH; MH, Y.
Groane fetch'd. [n.p.], 1649. *See* King, Henry, *bp.*

2054 The groanes and pangues of Tibvrne. [*London*], *printed
near Tyburne*, 1648. 4°.* LG; TU, Y.

2055 Groanes from Newgate, or, an elegy upon Edward Dun.
By Edward Crowch, 1663. 4°. C; CH.

2056 Groans from New-Gate or an elegy on . . . Thomas Sadler. *For T. M.*, 1677. brs. L.

2056A The groans of France in slavery. [*London?* 1698.] cap.,
4°.* WF.

2057 The groans of Kent. *For G. W.*, [1648]. 4°.* LT, O, LG,
LIU, ESS; CSS, PL, Y.
Groans of the plantations. 1689. *See* Littleton, Edward.
Groans of the spirit. 1652. *See* Foxle, George.

2058 A groatsworth of good counsel for a penny. [*London*],
for P. Brooksby, [1672–95]. brs. L, O, CM, HH; MH.
Groat's worth of wit. [1670.] *See* Lilly, William.

2059 **Groeneveldt, Jan.** Arthritology: or, a discourse of the
gout. *For the author*, 1691. 8°.* L, O, LCP, E.

2060 —De tuto cantharidum. *Typis J. H. prostant venales
apud Johannem Taylor*, 1698. 8°. T.C.III 55. L, O, C, E,
GH; CLC, CLM, PL, TO, WF, HC.

2061 —Dissertatio lithologica. *Typis Joannis Bringhurst*, 1684.
8°. T.C.II 86. L, LCP, LWL, MC, AU, GH; CLC, CLM,
TORONTO ACAD. OF MED., PL.

2062 — —Second edition. *Typis M. Flesher, impensis Abeli
Swalle*, 1687. 8°. L, C, CM, E, GH; BN, CLC, CLM, PL, WSG.

2062A [–] The late censors deservedly censured. *London, for the
author, to be sold by B. Billingsley*, 1689. 4°.* CLM.

2062B [–] —[Anr. ed.] 1698. 4°. L.

2063 —Λιθολογια. A treatise of the stone. *By H. C. for J. T.
to be sold by Rob. Clavel*, 1677. 8°. O, C, LWL, CM, P;
CLM, WSG.

2063A [–] The oracle for the sick. [*London*, 1685?] 8°. L, LWL.

2064 Grondige verklaringe van 't huys der Ghemeenbe in 't
Parlement van Engelandt. *Gedrukt tot Londen by
Edvard Husband*, 1649. 4°.* L; NN.

2065 **G[roome], S[amuel].** A glass for the people of New-
England. [*London*], *printed*, 1676. 4°.* C, LF, LW, BBN;
MB, MBZ, MH, MU, MWA, NN, RPJ.

Groot, Hugo de. *See* Grotius, Hugo.

2066 **Groot, Pieter de.** Two letters from. *Printed, and are to
be sold by Jonathan Edwin*, 1672. fol.* L, LPR, MR; HR,
CH, Y.

2067 **Groot, William.** De principiis juris naturalis enchir-
idion. Second edition. *Cantabridgiæ, ex officina Joann.
Hayes impensis Joann. Creed*, 1673. 8°. T.C.I 130. OC, CT,
DU, P, GU; CH, MH, NCL, WF, Y.

2067A Den grooten vocabulær. *Tot Rotterdam, by Pieter van
Waesbergher*, 1644. 8°. L.

2068 **Grosse, Alexander.** The buddings and blossomings of
old truths. *By W. Bentley for Andrew Crook*, 1656. 8°.
LT, O, LCL, LW, ORP; CLC, MH.

2069 —Christ the Christians choice. *By R. B. for Iohn Bartlet*, 1645. 4°.* LT, O; MH, NU.

2070 —A fiery pillar of heavenly truth. *For John Bartlett*, 1641.
8°. L; Y.

2071 — —Second edition. —, 1644. 12°. L, O, LCL; NU, AVP.

2072 — — Third edition. —, 1645. 12°. L, BQ.

2072A — —[Anr. ed.] *Edinburgh, by James Lindesay to be sold by
Andrew Wilson*, 1645. 16°. ALDIS 1188. E.

2073 — —Fourth edition. *For John Bartlett*, 1646. 12°. L, CT.

2073A — —Fifth edition. *For John Bar[t]let*, 1647. 12°. CH.

2074 — —Sixth edition. —, 1649. 12°. LW; CLC.

2074A — —Seventh edition. —, 1652. 12°. LIU; WF.

2075 — —Tenth edition. —, 1663. 12°. L, O, LCL, GU.

2076 —The happines of enjoying. *By Tho: Brudenell, for John Bartlet,* 1647. 4°. L, LW, BC, YM, DT; CH, NU, WCL, WF, Y.

2077 ——Svveet and soule-perswading indvcements. *By G. M. for Iohn Bartlet,* 1632 [*i.e.* 1642]. 4°. LT, O, LW, BC, AU, EN; CH, CU, MH, WF, Y.

2078 **Grosse, Robert.** Royalty and loyalty. [*London*], 1647. 4°. LT, O, C, ES, DT; CH, CLC, IU, NU, WF, Y.

2079 **Grosseteste, Robert, bp.** Tov 'εν 'αγιοιε . . . de cessatione legalium. *Typis Thomæ Roycroft, prostat autem venale apud Joan. Martin, Ja. Allestrye, & Tho. Dicas,* 1658. 8°. LT, O, C, OM, CT, DU; BN, MH, NU, PU, TO.

2079A ——[Anr. ed.] *Typis Thomæ Roycroft,* 1658. 8°. OC; CU, WF, Y.

2080 **Grosvenour, Samuel.** Hosanna to the Son of David. *For L. Chapman.* 1659. 4°.* NU.

2081 **Grotius, Hugo.** Opera omnia theologica. *Prostant venalia apud Mosem Pitt,* 1679. 3v. fol. T.C.I 352. L, C, YM, ES, DT; CLC, MBA, NC, NP, Y.

2082 —. . . Against paganism. *For the author, to be sold by John Barksdale,* 1676. 8°. L; IU.

2082A —Annotationum selectarum. *Oxoniæ, pro Joh. Barksdale, London,* 1675. 12°.* MADAN 3061. L, LW.

2083 —Anti-Dodwellisme. *For Thomas Simmons,* 1683. 4°.* T.C.II 25. L, O, C, LVF, EN; CH, MBA, PL, WF, Y.

2084 Entry cancelled.
 [–] Antiquity of common-wealths. 1652. *See* —Treatise of the antiquity.

2085 —Grotius his arguments for the truth. *For Jonathan Robinson,* 1686. 8°. T.C.II 239. L, O, C, LW, LLU; CH, MH, NC, PBL, WF.

2086 —H. Grotii baptizatorum puerorum institutio. *Excudebat Johannes Dawson, & vænum dantur apud Johannem Hardestie,* 1647. 8°. LT, EC, LNC; CH, WF, Y.

2086A ——[Anr. ed.] *Typis et sumptibus Gartredæ Dawson,* 1650. 8°. CS.

2087 ——Second edition. *Excudebat Gartreda Dawson, impensis Johannis Hardesti,* 1650. 8°. L, C, LLP, LNC; MH, NU.

2088 ——Fourth edition. *Typis Gartredæ Dawson, & prostant venales apud Johannem Hardesty,* 1655. 8°. O, CCH, OM, LNC, GU.

2088A ——"Fourth" edition. —, 1657. 8°. IU.

2089 ——[Anr. ed.] *Excudebat Gartreda Dawson,* 1657. 8°. LW, LNC; NU.

2090 ——Fifth edition. *Excudebat Gartreda Dawson, & venalis prostant apud Guilielmum Crook,* 1665. 8°. L, LNC.

2091 ——[Anr. ed.] *Typis J. Macock, & prostant venales apud Gulielm. Crook,* 1668. 8°. L, O, C, LNC, E; CLC, LC, MB, NU, RPJ, WF, AVP.

2092 ——[Anr. ed.] *Typis J. Redmayne, jun. & prostant venales apud Gulielm. Crook,* 1682. 8°. T.C.I 515. L, C, LNC, DT; CN, IU, MBP.

2092A ——[Anr. ed.] *Prostant venales apud H. Bonwicke,* 1695. 8°. T.C.II 562. ORP; NPT.

2093 [–] Christ's passion. Second edition. *By J. R. for T. Basset,* 1687. 8°. T.C.II 195. L, O, C, LVF, EN; CH, CU, LC, MH, WF, Y.

2094 [–] —[Anr. ed.] *Printed, to be sold by Jos. Blare,* 1698. 8°. L; NC, NN, TO.

2095 Entry cancelled.
 —Hvgo Grotivs, his consolatory oration. [1652.] *See* — Sophompaneas.

2096 —De coenæ administartione [*sic*]. *Impensis B. Tooke,* 1685. 8°. T.C.II 158. L, O, C, AN, E, DT; CLC, CU, MWA, NC, Y.

2097 Entry cancelled. Ghost.

2098 —Hugo Grotius, de rebus Belgicis. *For Henry Twyford; and Robert Paulet,* 1665. 8°. L, O, C, E, EN; CH, CLC, IU, LC, MH, PL, WF, Y, AVP.

2099 Entry cancelled.
 —De satisfactione Christi. 1661. *See*—Defensio fidei Catholicæ.

2100 —Hugo Grotius de veritate religionis Christianæ. *Oxonii, impensis Gulielmi Webb,* 1650. 4°. MADAN 2032. L, O, OC; IU, MB, NU.

2101 ——"Tenth" edition. *Oxonii, per J. Web & Ed. Forrest,* 1660. 8°. MADAN 2497. O, MR, YM, EN.

2102 ——[Anr. ed.] *Oxonii, excudebat Gulielm. Hall,* 1660. 8°. MADAN 2498. L, O, OC, CT, E; CLC, IU, NU, PL, Y.

2103 ——[Anr. ed.] *Oxonii, typis W. H., impensis Ric. Davis, assign. J. Webb,* 1662. 8°. MADAN 2596. L, O, CM, DU; CLC, IU, MH, NS, WF, Y.

2103A ——[Anr. ed.] *Oxonii, typis W. F. Impensis Ric. Davis.* 1662. 8°. CS; WF.

2104 ——[Anr. ed.] *Oxonii, e theatro Sheldoniano,* 1675. 12°. MADAN 3060. L, O, OC, BAMB, RU; CLC, CN, MBA, NC, Y.

2105 ——[Anr. ed.] *Oxoniæ, e theatro Sheldoniano, impensis Ant. Peisley,* 1700. 8°. L, C, KEBLE, CK, CT; CH, CN, MBP, MH, WF, Y.

2106 —Hvgo Grotivs's defence of Christian religion. *For John Barksdale,* 1678. 8°. T.C.I 318. L, O, C, OB; NU, WF.

2107 —A defence of the Catholick faith. *For Thomas Parkhurst, and Jonathan Robinson,* 1692. 8°. T.C.II 377. L, O, C, LCL, SA, DT; CH, IEG, NCD, WF, Y.

2108 —Defensio fidei Catholicæ. *Excudebat R. Daniel,* 1661. 12°. L, O, C, CT, DC, ENC, DT; NC, NU, PBL, WF.

2109 —His discourses, I. of God. Second edition. *By A. Miller for William Lee,* 1652. 12°. O, CT, EN, DT; IU, WF, Y.

2109A ——"Second" edition. *By A. Miller for William Lee,* 1653. 12°. CS, BLH; CLC, PBL, WU.

2110 —The English version of Hvgo Grotivs his catechisme, *By J. Macock, for William Crooke,* 1668. 8°.* L, O, C, OB, ORP; CLC, LC, MB, NU, WF, Y.

2111 ——[Anr. ed.] *Londini* [*sic*], *by J. Redmayne jun. for William Crooke,* 1682. 8°.* C, DT; IU, MBP, NPT.

2111A —The magistrates authority. *For Joshua Kirton,* 1655. 8°. LCL, SP.

2111B —Hvgo Grotivs, his most choice discourses. Third edition. *For W. Lee,* 1657. 12°. DUS.

2112 ——"Third" edition. *For W. Lee, junior,* 1658. 12°. L, O, BSM, DC, BQ; CLC, CPB, MU, NIC, NU.

2113 ——Fourth edition. *By S. G. and B. G. for William Lee,* 1669. 12°. T.C.I 7. L, O, C, LW, OC; CH, IU, NN, WF, WU, Y, AVP.

2114　—The mourner comforted. *By A. M. for Edward Lee*, 1652. 12°.* L, O, C, CT, EN, BLH; CH, CN, PBL, WF, Y.

2115　——[Anr. ed.] *For William Lee*, 1658. 12°.* L, O, DUS; NU.

2116　——[Anr. ed.] *For Sam Keble*, 1694. 12°. T.C.II 506. L, O, CT, EN; CH.

2117　—Hugo Grotius of the authority of the highest powers. *By T. W. for Joshua Kirton*, 1651. 8°. LT, GC, SC; CLC, IU, MHL, NU, WF, Y.

2118　—Hugo Grotius of the government and rites. *For the translator*, 1675. 4°. L, O, CT; IU, LC, MH, WF.

2119　—The illustrious Hvgo Grotius of the law of warre. *By T. Warren, for William Lee*, 1654. 8°. LT, O, BSM, LIU, LLU; CB, IU, LC, MHL, NC, WCL, Y.

2120　——[Anr. ed.] *By T. Warren, for William Lee*, 1655. 8°. L, CK, CASTLE ASHBY; CH, MHL, NC, WF, Y.

2121　Entry cancelled.
　　　—On the satisfaction. 1692. *See* —Defence.

2122　—On the truth of the Christian religion. 1669. 12°. LW.

2123　—Politick maxims. *For Humphrey Moseley*, 1654. 12°. LT, O, C, CT; CH, CN, MH, MU, Y.

2123A　——[Anr. ed.] —, 1655. 12°. CLC.

2124　—The proceedings of the present Parliament justified. *Printed, and are to be sold by Randal Taylor*, 1689. 4°.* T.C.II 256. L, OC, CT, EN, DT; CH, CN, MIU, WF, Y.

2124A　[–]—[Anr. ed.] *Edinbvrgh, re-printed* 1689. 4°.* ALDIS 2929. L, BP, DL, EN, GU; CLC, IU, MM, NU, TU. (var.)

2125　—Hvgo Grotivs his Sophompaneas, or Ioseph. *By W. H. and are to be sold by Iohn Hardesty*, [1652]. 8°. L, O, C, OW, EN; CH, CN, LC, MH, WF, Y.

2126　—The most excellent Hugo Grotius his three books treating of the rights of war. *By M. W. for Thomas Basset, and Ralph Smith*, 1682. fol. T.C.I 476. LG, CM, LIU, LLU, D; CH, CJC, LC, MH, WF, Y.

2127　—A treatise of the antiquity of the commonwealth of the Batavers. *For Iohn Walker*, 1649. 8°. LT, LI, CT, SP, EN; CH, CN, MBA, NIC, NS, Y.

2128　—The truth of Christian religion. *For Rich. Royston*, 1680. 8°. T.C.I 391. L, O, C, LSD, SHR; CH, CLC, CU, FU, MH, NC.

2129　——Second edition. —, 1683. 8°. L, O, C, CT, NPL; CH, CLC, CN, PBM, PU, WF.

2130　——Third edition. *For Luke Meredith*, 1689. 8°. T.C.II 293. L, CCA, BSE, CODDENHAM PARISH, SUFFOLK; CH, NP, NU, TSM, WCL.

2131　——Fourth edition. *By J. L. for Luke Meredith*, 1694. 8°. T.C.II 533. L, O, C, GC, DT; CLC, LC, NU, WF, Y.

2131A　——Fifth edition. —, 1700. 8°. L, BR; CH, IU, MH, NC, Y.

2131B　——Two discourses, I. Of God . . . II. Of Christ. *By James Flesher for William Lee*, 1652. 12°. L, C; CH, PBL, WF, Y.

2132　Entry cancelled.
　　　——"Second" edition. 1653. *See* —His discourses.
　　　Grotius, W. *See* Groot, William.
　　　Ground of desperation. [n.p., 1656.] *See* Fox, George.
　　　Ground of high places. 1657. *See* Fox, George.
　　　Ground-rules of architecture. 1686. *See* Wotton, *Sir* Henry.

2133　A ground voice, or some discoveries. [*London*, 1655.] cap., 4°.* LT, O; CDA, WF.
　　　Ground-work, or. [n.p.], 1652. *See* Lodowyck, Francis.
　　　Grovnds and cavses. 1656. *See* Whitehead, George.
　　　Grounds and ends. 1647. *See* Cotton, John.

2134　The grovnds and motives inducing His Maiesty to agree to a cessation of armes. *Printed at Oxford, Octob. 19. By Leonard Lichfield*, 1643. 4°.* MADAN 1475. LT, O, C, LVF, EN; CH, CU, MH, WF, Y. (var.)
　　　Grounds & occasions of the contempt. 1670. *See* Eachard, John.

2135　The grounds and occasions of the controversy concerning the unity of God. *Printed and sold by E. Whitlock*, 1698. 4°. L, LLP, LW, EC, WCA; CH, CLC, MH, WF, ZWT.

2135aA　The grounds and principles of religion. 1646. 8°. OC.

2135A　—[Anr. ed.] *By J. L. for.the company of stationers*, 1648. 8°.* E (lost).

2135B　—[Anr. ed.] —, 1649. 8°.* BR.

2135C　—[Anr. ed.] *By R. D.*, 1656. 8°.* O, CE.

2135D　—[Anr. ed.] *By J. H. for the company of stationers*, 1662. 8°. SP.

2135E　—[Anr. ed.] *Printed*, 1667. 8°.* IU.

2136　—[Anr. ed.] *Printed*, 1678. 8°.* L.

2137　—[Anr. ed.] —, 1682. 8°.* L.

2138　—[Anr. ed.] —, 1687. 8°.* NPT, NU.

2138aA　—[Anr. ed.] *Printed and are to be sold by John Whitlock*, 1692. 12°.* MBZ.

2138bA　—[Anr. ed.] *Printed*, 1699. 12°.* L.
　　　Grounds & reasons. [n.p.], 1650. *See* Hall, John.

2138A　The grounds and reasons of the laws against Popery. [*London?* 1688.] brs. INU, MH, PL, TU.

2138B　The grounds of complaint of several merchants. [*London?* 1690.] brs. L, INDIA OFFICE.

2138C　The grounds of infant-baptism. colop: *For J. Lawrence*, 1693. cap., 4°.* LW.

2139　The grounds of military discipline. *For George Lindsey*, 1642. brs. LT.

2140　—[Anr. ed.] [*London*, 1642.] brs. LT.

2141　The grounds of soveraignty and greatness. *By T. R. & N. T. to be sold by Will. Crooke, and Will. Cademan*, 1675. 4°.* T.C.I 219. L, O, LL, CS; CH, NC, Y.

2141A　—[Anr. ed.] *By T. R. & N. T. and are to be sold by Anthony Lawrence and James Thompson*, 1675. 4°.* MIU, WF.

2142　—Second edition. *For W. Davis*, 1685. 4°.* T.C.II 129. L, O; CH, Y.
　　　Grounds of the lawes. 1657. *See* Hawke, Michael.

2143　The grounds of the present war. *For J. S.*, 1669. 4°. LPR, DT; CH.

2144　The grounds of unity in religion. [*London*], *printed*, 1672. 4°.* O, SP, CD; CLC, CSS, IAU, NU.

2145　—[Anr. ed.] —, 1679. 4°.* L, O, BC, DU, SC; CLC, IU, MH, NU, WF, Y.

2146　**Grove, Hugh.** The speech of. *For Sam Burdet*, 1655. 4°.* LT, O; MH, Y.

2147 [Grove, Robert], *bp*. An answer to Mr. Lowth's letter. *For Randal Taylor*, 1687. 4°.* T.C.II 194. L, O, C, BAMB, E, DT; CH, CN, NU, WF, Y.

2148 —Carmen de sanguinis circuitu. *Typis R. E., impensis Gualteri Kettilby*, 1685. 4°.* T.C.II 138. L, O, C, CT, GK; CH, MB, MH, MMO, MU, HC.

2149 Entry cancelled.
      —Catalogue. [n.p., 1697.] *See* —Library.

2150 —Defensio suæ responsionis. *Typis J. M. impensis G. Kettilby*, 1682. 4°. T.C.I 496. L, O, C, MR, DT; MH, NGT, TO, WF, Y.
      [–] Falshood unmaskt. 1676. *See* Patrick, Symon.

2150A Entry cancelled.
      [–] Gleanings. 1651. *See* Groves, Richard.

2150B [–] The library of . . . will be sold . . . [27 April 1697]. [*London*], *catalogues may be had gratis at Mr. Notts, Mr. Bucks, Mr. R. Parkers*, [1697]. 4°.* L, OP; MH.

2151 —Nullus est satisfactionum. [*n.p.*], 1681. brs. O, C; MH.

2152 [–] A perswasive to communion. *By J. Redmayne, jun. for Fincham Gardiner*, 1682/3. 4°.* T.C.II 2. L, O, C, MR, DT; CH, CN, NU, WF, Y.

2153 [–] —Second edition. *By J. Radmayne, for T. Basset, and B. Took*, 1683. 4°.* T.C.II 34. O, C, OC, CT, DT; CLC, MIU, NU, WF, Y.

2153A [–] —"Second" edition. *By J. Redmayne, for Fincham Gardiner*, 1683. 4°.* L, O, C, BSM, SHR; CH, MH, MM, TU, WF.

2154 —Profitable charity. *For Walter Kettilby*, 1695. 4°.* T.C.II 547. L, O, C, BR, EN; CH, NU, PL, WF, Y.

2155 [–] The Protestant and Popish way. *For Walter Kettilby*, 1689. 4°. T.C.II 268. L, O, C, EN, DT; CLC, IU, MH, NU, TU, WF, Y.

2156 Entry cancelled.
      —Refutatio cojusdam scripti. [n.p.], 1681. *See* Jenkyn, William.

2157 —Responsio ad nuperum libellum. *Typis J. M. pro Gualt. Kettilby*, 1680. 4°. T.C.I 395. L, O, C, MR, DT; BN, CH, IU, MH, NU, WF, Y.

2158 [–] Seasonable advice to the citizens. *For Walter Kettilby*, 1685. 4°.* T.C.II 128. L, O, C, SHR, EN; CH, CN, V, WF, Y.

2159 —A sermon preached . . . June the 1st. 1690. *For W. Kettilby*, 1690. 4°.* T.C.II 329. L, O, C, LIU, DT; CH, MH, NU, WF, Y.

2160 [–] A short defence of the Church and clergy of England. *By J. Macock for Walter Kettilby*, 1681. 4°. T.C.I 439. L, O, CT, YM, EN, DT; CH, CN, MH, WF, Y.

2161 [–] A vindication of the Conforming clergy. *For Walter Kettilby*, 1676. 4°. T.C.I 228. L, O, C, YM, CD; CH, CU, NU, WF, Y.

2162 [–] —Second edition. —, 1680. 4°. T.C.I 389. L, O, LG, CS, BP, CD; CLC, CU, MIU, NU, WF.

2162A [Groves, Robert.] Gleanings; or, a collection. *By R. I. and to bee sold by William Raybould*, 1651. 8°. L, O, LCL; CH, CN, WF.

2162B [–] —Second edition. *By R. Ibbitson, and are to be sold by Anthony Williamson*, [1651]. 8°. MB.
      Growth of error. 1697. *See* Lobb, Stephen.

Growth of knavery. 1678. *See* L'Estrange, *Sir* Roger.

2163 [Grueber, Johann.] China and France, or two treatises. *By T. N. for Samuel Lowndes*, 1676. 12°. T.C.I 217. L, O, CS; CLC, IU, Y.

2164 The Grumbletonian crew reprehended. *For Richard Janeway*, 1689. 4°.* L, O, DT; MB, MM.

2164A [Grummet, Christoph.] Sanguis naturæ, or, a manifest declaration. *For A. R. and sold by T. Sowle*, 1696. 8°. L, O, LLU, GU; CJC, CLC, MH, WF, WU, Y.

2164B [Grybius, Johannes.] The lyon disturbed. colop: *Amsterdam, by Steven Swart, Novemb.* 30, 1672. 4°.* L.

      Gualdi, *abbot*. *See* Leti, Gregorio.

2165 Entry cancelled.
      Gualdo, Castor Durante da. *See* Durante, Castore da Gualdo.

2166 Gualdo Priorato, Galeazzo. The history of France. *For William Place; Thomas Basset, Thomas Dring, and John Leigh*, 1676. fol. T.C.I 252. L, O, C, GU, DT; CH, CN, MIU, WF, Y.

2167 —An history of the late warres. *By W. Wilson, to bee sold by Iohn Hardesty, Thomas Huntington, and Thomas Iackson*, 1648. fol. L, O, C, LMT, E; CLC, LC, MH, MU, Y.

2168 —The history of the managements of Cardinal Julio Mazarine, . . . Tom. I. Part I. *By H. L. and R. B.*, 1671. 12°. L, C, OC, P, DT; CH, CU, MIU, WF, Y.

2168A ——[Anr. ed.] —, *and are to be sold by Geo. Calvert, Sam. Sprint, James Magnus, and John Hancock*, 1671. 12°. WF.

2169 ——Tom. I. Part II. *By H. Lloyd for George Calvert and Sam. Sprint, and Christopher Wilkinson*, 1672. 12°. T.C.I 86. L, C, LLU, WCA, DT; CH, CLC, MIU, WF, Y.

2169A ——Tom. I. Part III. —, 1673. 12°. T.C.I 117. OC, LLU, RPL; CH, CLC, PL, ANL.

2169B ———[Anr. ed.] *By H. L. and to be sold by George Calvert and Christopher Wilkinson*, 1673 12°. WF.

2170 [–] —[Anr. ed.] *Printed and are to be sold by S. Keble, and Daniel Brown*, 1691. T.C.II 353. 12°. L; IU.

2171 [–] The history of the sacred and royal majesty of Christina. *For T. W.*, 1658. 8°. LT, O, C, DU, E; CH, CLC, LC, MIU, Y.

2172 —History of . . . Christina . . . the queen of Swedeland. *For A. W.* 1660. 8°. LW, OB, WARE; NN, WF.

2173 Entry cancelled.
      Gualter, Rudolph. *See* Walther, Rudolph.

2173A A guard muster at Guild-hall. [*London?* 1683.] brs. LG.
      Guardian's instruction. 1688. *See* Penton, Stephen.

2174 Guarini, Giovanni Battista. Il pastor Fido, the faithfull shepherd. *By R. Raworth*, 1647. 4°. LT, O, LVD, DC, ES; CH, IU, LC, MH, TU, WF, Y.

2175 [–] —[Anr. ed.] *For Humphrey Moseley*, 1648. 4°. L, O, C, E, BLH; BN, CH, CN, MH, TU, WF, Y.

2176 [–] —[Anr. ed.] *For A. Moseley*, 1664. 8°. L, O, C, LVD, ENC; CH, IU, MH, WC, WF, Y.

2177 ——[Anr. ed.] *For Henry Herringman*, 1676. 8°. T.C.I 259. L, O, LVF, EN, GK; CH, CU, MH, WF, Y, AVP.

2177A ——[Anr. ed.] *For W. Cademan*, 1689. 4°. CT.

2177B ——[Anr. ed.] *For William Cademan, and sold by R. Bently*, 1689. 4°. NCU.

2178 — —[Anr. ed.] *For R. Bentley, J. Tonson, F. Saunders, and T. Bennet,* 1692. 8°. L, O, DT; MSL, WF.

2178A Entry cancelled.
— —[Anr. ed.] 1694. *See* Settle, Elkanah.

2179 **Guarna, Andreas.** Bellum grammaticale. *Edinburgi,* 1652. 8°. ALDIS 1462.6. E.

2180 [–] —[Anr. ed.] *Edinburgh, excudebat, Gideon Lithgo,* 1658. 8°. ALDIS 1576. L, EN; CLC.

2180A [–] —[Anr. ed.] *Glasguæ, excudebat Robertus Sanders,* 1674. 12°. ALDIS 2021.95. GU.

2181 [–] —[Anr. ed.] *Edinbvrgi, ex officina Georgii Mosman,* 1698. 8°. ALDIS 3732. O, E, EN; CLC, CN, IU, WF.

Guerdon, Aaron, *pseud.*

2182 **Guevara, Antonio de.** Spanish letters. *For F. Saunders, and A. Roper,* 1697. 8°. L, CM, LLU, DT; CN, LC, MB, TU, Y.

2182A — —[Anr. ed.] *For A. Roper and F. Saunders,* 1697. 8°. O, DU; CH, CLC, Y.

Guglielmo Augusto, Britanniarum. [1696.] *See* M., M.

2183 **Guide, Philippe.** Numb. 1. An essay concerning nutrition in animals. *For the author, to be sold by H. Rhodes,* 1699. 4°.* L, O, LSD, GH; WF.

2183A —Experience de la vertu singuliere du vin rouge. *A Londre, by M. F.,* 1684. 8°.* L, LCS; NAM.

2184 Entry cancelled.
Guide for strangers. 1647. *See* Woodhouse, John, *surveyor.*
Guide for the penitent. 1660. *See* Duppa, Brian, *bp.*
Guide in controversies. [n.p.], 1667. *See* Woodhead, Abraham.
Guide mistaken. 1668. *See* Penn, William.

2184A The guide of a Christian. *For John Everingham,* 1696. 12°. T.C.III 17. OC.

2184B —Second edition. —, 1697. 12°. L.

2184C A guide to devotion. *For J. Back,* [1682–1703]. 8°. OC.

2184D A guide to English juries. *For Thomas Cockerill,* 1682. 12°. L, LL, CCA, LIU, EN, DM; CH, CLC, NCL, WF, YL, AVP.
Guide to eternal glory. 1676. *See* Wilcox, Thomas.

2185 Entry cancelled.
Guide to heaven from the word. 1664. *See* Hardy, Samuel.

2186 A guide to juries. *For Tho. Cockerill,* 1699. 12°. L, O; CH, CN, MHL, NC, WF.

2187 A guide to knowledge. *For the author, and sold by Tho. Fabian,* 1689. 12°. T.C.II 310. NU.
Guide to scattered flocks. 1684. *See* Hardy, Samuel.
Guide to the altar. 1688. *See* P., T.
Guide to the blind. 1659. *See* Forster, Thomas.
Guide to the customers. 1699. *See* Score, Richard.

2187A A guide to the temple. *By J. L. for A. Jones,* 1685. 12°. T.C.II 111. OC.
Guide to the true religion. 1668. *See* C., J.

2187B A guide to young communicants. Fourth edition. *For G. C.,* [c. 1695]. 12°. T.C.II 552. L.

2188 Guido Faux reviv'd: or, the monks late hellish contrivances expos'd. colop: *For W. Beale,* 1688. cap., 4°.* O; MH, MIU, WF, Y.

2189 **Guidott, Thomas.** Antiquities of the city of Bathe. 1669. 8°. OR, AU; WF.
—An appendix concerning Bathe. 1669. *See* Jorden, Edward. Discourse.

2190 [–] A century of observations. *For Henry Brome,* 1686. 8°. L.

2191 —Thomæ Gvidotti Anglo-Britanni, de thermis. *Excudebat Franciscus Leach, sumptibus authoris. Veneunt apud S. Smith,* 1691. 4°. L, O, CCA, E, DT; BN, CH, IU, NC, WF, HC.

2191A — —[Anr. ed.] *Excudebat Franciscus Leach, sumptibus authoris,* 1691. 4°. L, LWL, CK, CS; CLC, PL.

2192 —A discourse of Bathe. *For Henry Brome,* 1676. 8°. T.C.I 247. L, O, C, LCS, EN; BN, CLC, IU, LC, MH, PL, WF, HC.

2193 [–] An epitaph on Don Quicksot. [*Bath,* 1694.] brs. O.

2194 [–] Gideon's fleece. *For Sam. Smith,* 1684. 4°. T.C.II 47. L, O, LCP, LVF, LSD, DT; CH, MH, MU, TU, WF, Y.

2195 —A letter concerning some observations . . . at Bathe. *By A. C. for Henry Brome,* 1674. 4°.* T.C.I 172. L, O, LWL, OB, BR; CH, CLC, NAM, WF.

2196 Entry cancelled.
—Lives and characters. 1677. *See* —Discourse of Bathe.

2197 —Propositions touching printing a book, entituled, de thermis Britannicis. [*London,* 1686.] cap., fol.* O.

2198 [–] A quære concerning drinking Bath-water. *For George Sawbridge,* 1673. 8°.* L, O, C, BR, DU; CLC, IU, OCI, WF.

2199 —The register of Bath. *For Hen. Hamond,* 1694. 8°. L, O, BR.

2199A — —[Anr. ed.] *By F. Leach, for the author, to be sold by Randal Taylor,* 1694. 8°. CT; CH, CNM, PL.

2200 [–] A true and exact account of Sadler's well. *For Thomas Malthus,* 1684. 4°.* L, LG, OP.

2201 [**Guifthaile, Henry.**] Concerning this present Cain. *By I. L.,* 1648. 4°.* LT.

2202 **Guild, William.** An answer to a Popish pamphlet. *Aberdene, by Iames Brown,* 1656. 12°. ALDIS 1542. E, EN, AU, GU, SA.

2203 —Anti-Christ pointed. *Printed in Aberdene, by Iames Brown,* 1655. 8°. ALDIS 1519. L, AU, GU, SA.

2203A —An antidote agaynst Poperie. *Aberdene, by James Brown,* 1656. 12°. GU.

2204 [–] The humble address both of church and poore. [*London*], *printed,* 1641. 4°.* LT, O, C, EN, DT; CH, MH, NU, WF, Y.

2205 —Isagoge catechetica. *Aberdoniæ, imprimebat Edvardus Rabanus,* 1649. 8°. ALDIS 1369. E, AU, SA; CH.

2206 —Loves entercovrs. *By W. Wilson for Ralph Smith,* 1658. 8°. LT, LCL, LW, BC, E, AU; CH, CLC, MH, NU, WF, Y.

2207 —Moses unveiled. *For Thomas Parkhurst,* 2658 [*sic*]. 8°. LT, C, SA; NU, TO.

2207A — —[Anr. ed.] —, 1658. 8°. AN; CLC.

2207B — —[Anr. ed.] *By F. L. for P. C.,* 1658. 8°. O.

2208 — —[Anr. ed.] *Edinburgh, by the heir of Andrew Anderson,* 1684. 8°. ALDIS 2455. AU.

2209 —The noveltie of Poperie. *Aberdene, by Iames Brown,* 1656. 12°. ALDIS 1544. L, E, AU, GU.

2210 —The old Roman Catholik. *Printed in Aberdene, by E. Raban*, 1649. 8°. ALDIS 1370. L, E, EN, AU, GU; CLC, NU.

2210A [–] A remonstrance to the Kings most excellent majesty. [*London*], *printed* 1643. 4°.* WF, Y.

2211 —The sealed book opened. *By T. R. & E. M. for Anthony Williamson*, 1656. 8°. LT, O, P, E, SA; MB, MH, WF.

2212 —The throne of David. *Oxford, by W. Hall for Rob. Blagrave*, 1659. 4°. MADAN 2442. LT, O, C, E, AU, DT; CHW, CLC, NU, PL, Y.

Guild-hall elegie. [n.p., 1660.] *See* P., O.

2213 **Guilelmus Arvernus, bp. of Paris.** Opera omnia. *F. Hotot: Aurelia, et vaeunt Londini apud R. Scott*, 1674. fol. EN.

2214 **Guilford, Francis North, baron.** The late Lord Chief Justice North's argument. *Printed and are to be sold by Randal Taylor*, 1689. fol.* T.C.II 252. L, LGI, CT, DU, EN; CH, MBA, NU, WF, Y.

2215 —The examination of Captain William Bedlow. *By the assigns of John Bill, Thomas Newcomb, and Henry Hills*, 1680. fol.* L, O, C, MR, DT; CH, CN, MH, MU, WF, Y.

2215A ——[Anr. ed.] [*Dublin*], *reprinted* 1680. 4°.* C, DU, CD.

2216 [–] A philosophical essay of musick. *For John Martyn*, 1677. 4°.* T.C.I 274. L, O, C, OC, ES; CN, LC, MH, PL, WCL, WF.

2217 —The Lord Keeper's speech to Mr. Serjeant Savnders, . . . the 23rd. January, 1682. *For Robert Pawlet*, 1682[3]. fol.* L, O, C, EN, DT; CH, CN, MH, NP, WF, Y.

2217A ——[Anr. ed.] *Dublin, reprinted by Benjamin Took and John Crook, sold by Mary Crook and Andrew Crook*, 1682[3]. 4°.* CD.

2218 **Guillet de Saint-George, Georges.** An account of a late voyage to Athens. *By J. M. for H. Herringman*, 1676. 8°. T.C.I 235. L, O, C, EN, DT; CH, IU, MH, TU, WF, Y.

2219 **Guillim, John.** A display of heraldrie. Fourth edition. *By T. R. for Richard Blome*, 1660. fol. L, O, C, LCP, DC; CLC, CN, MH, NCU, PBL, WF.

2219A ——[Anr. ed.] *By T. R. for Jacob Blome*, 1660. fol. CK, BC, DUS; CSU, LC.

2220 ——Fifth edition. *By T. R. for Jacob Blome, to be sold by John Williams, and Joshua Kirton; Humphrey Tuckey, and Francis Tyton*, 1664. fol. L, C, CK, AN; CLC, Y.

2221 ——Sixth edition. *By J. B. For John Williams and Joshua Kirton; Humphrey Tuckey*, 1666. fol. L.

2222 ——"Fifth" edition. *By S. Roycroft for R. Blome, sold by Francis Tyton, Henry Brome, Thomas Basset, Richard Chiswell, John Wright, and Thomas Sawbridge*, 1679. fol. T.C.I 353. L, O, C, LL, EN, DT; BN, CH, IU, LC, NC, PL, Y, AVP.

2223 —Proposals for the printing of Guillim's Heraldry. [*London*, 1674.] brs. O.

2224 **Guillims, George.** The true copy of a letter sent from Portsmouth. *Printed August* 20, 1642. brs. AN, EC.

2225 Guineas at 21s 6d. will make money plenty. [*London*, 1695/6.] brs. L, LUG, C; MH.

2226 **Guise, Henri, duc de.** Memoires of . . . relating his passage to Naples. *By T. N. for H. Herringman*, 1669. 8°. T.C.I 19. O, OC, CT, LLU, ENC, DT; CH, CN, MH, WF, Y.

Gulielmi Phalerii ad grammaticen. 1652. *See* White, William.

2227 **Gulston, William.** Bibliotheca Gulstoniana. 1688. 4°. L, O, LR, LV.

2228 —Bibliotheca Gulstoniana rediviva. [*London*], 3 *April*, 1689. 4°. OP.

2229 **Gulter, Giles.** The archbishops crveltie. [*London*], *printed*, 1641. 4°.* LT, O, CT, DUS; CH, MH, NC, WF, Y.

2230 **Gumble, Thomas.** The life of General Monck. *By J. S. for Thomas Basset*, 1671. 8°. T.C.I 56. L, O, C, EN, DT; BN, CH, CN, MH, WF, Y.

2231 —La vie du General Monk. *Chez Robert Scot*, 1672. 12°. L, O, C, LLU, DT; BN, CH, CLC, CN, NP, WF, Y.

2232 **Gumbleden, John.** Christ tempted. *For Simon Miller*, 1657. 4°. LT, LCL, CT, SP; MH, NU, WF.

2233 —Two sermons. *For Simon Miller*, 1657. 4°. LT, SP, EN; MH, WF.

Gundomar, count. *See* Sarmiento de Acuna, Diego.

2234 **Gunning, Peter, bp.** A contention for truth. *By J. Moxon, for Francis Smith, sold at his shop, and by John Sweeting*, 1658. 4°. LT, O, CS, P, EN; CH, NP, NU, PL, WF.

2234A [–] —[Anr. ed.] [*London*], 1672. 4°. NPT.

2235 —An extract out of. *Printed, to be sold by R. Taylor*, 1689/90. 8°. T.C.II 346. L, O, LLP, CS.

[–] Lex talionis: or, the. 1676. *See* Fell, Philip.

2236 —The Paschal or Lent-fast. *By R. Norton for Timothy Garthwait*, 1662. 4°. L, O, C, DC, SC; BN, CLC, IU, NU, TU, WF, Y.

2236A [–] Reasons why all good Christians should observe . . . Lent. colop: *For Joseph Hindmarsh*, 1681. cap., 4°.* O, C, LLP, LSD; CH, WF.

2236B —January 26. 1683/4. Reverend brethren in Christ . . . [pastoral letter]. [*n.p.*, 1684.] brs. CT.

2237 Entry cancelled.

—Scisme unmask't. Paris, 1658. *See* Spencer, John.

2238 A gun-powder-plot in Ireland. *For John Thomas*. 1641. 4°.* LT, O, C, MR, BLH; MH, WF, Y. [=C6868.]

Gunpowder-treason. 1679. *See* Barlow, Thomas, bp.

2239 **Gunter, Edmund.** The workes of. Third edition. *By F. N. for Francis Eglesfield*, 1653. 4°. L, O, CT, ES, GU; CLC, MBP, MH, NC, WF, HC.

2240 ——Fourth edition. *By W. L. for Francis Eglesfield*, 1662. 4°. L, O, C, E, DT; CH, LC, NN, PMA, WCL.

2241 ——Fifth edition. *By A. C. for Francis Eglesfield*, 1673. 4°. T.C.I 137. L, O, C, BC, DT; CH, LC, MH, MU, WF, Y.

2242 ——Sixth edition. *For Francis Eglesfield*, 1680. 4°. L, LR, O, EN, DT; BBE, CSU, NC.

—Canon triangulorum. 1652. *See* —Workes. 1653.

2243 [–] The description and use of a portable instrument. *By T. B. for H. Sawbridge*, 1685. 8°. L, C, BC, AU; CH, MH, MB, PL, WF.

2243A —A description of Gunter's quadrant. [*Oxford?* 1690.] brs. L.

2244 **Gunter, Jasper.** Catalogus librorum . . . 20 Martii, 1683/4. [*London*], 20 *Mar*. 1683/4. 4°.* L, O, CS; NG, WSG.

2245   **Gunton, Simon.** Gods house. *For Thomas Dring, 1657.* 12°. LT, O, C, CE, P; NU, Y.

2246   —The history of the church of Peterburgh. *For Richard Chiswell, 1686.* fol. T.C.II 145. L, O, C, EN, DT; BN, CH, CN, MH, WF, Y.

2247   [–] Ορθολατρεια: or, a brief discourse. *For Gabriel Bedell, M. M. and T. C.,* 1650. 4°. LT, O, DU, LSC, DT; CH, CLC, IU, NU, WF, Y.

2248   — —[Anr. ed.] *For G. Bedell, and T. Collins,* 1661. 12°. LT, O, CE; NU.

2249   **Gunton, Timothy.** An extemporary answer. [*London,* 1648.] brs. LT; CH.

2249A Il guoco di Genova, or the most delightful . . . chance of fortune. [*London,* 1662.] brs. MH.

2250   **Gurdon, Brampton.** Probabile est animam. [*Cambridge,* 1696. brs. L, O.

2251   **Gurnall, William.** The Christian in compleat armour. First part. *For Ralph Smith,* 1655. 4°. LT, O, P; CLC, IU, MH, TU, WF, Y.

2252   — —Second edition. —, 1656. 4°. L, O, C, LSD, MR; CH, MH, MU, NU, WF.

2252A — —Third edition. —, 1658. 4°. L, O, LW; CH, NGT, NPT, NU, PPT.

2252B — —Fourth edition. —, 1661. 4°. L, OU, BR.

2252C — —"Fourth" edition. —, 1662. 4°. LCL, LSC, ENC, SA; NGT.

2252D — —"Fourth" edition. —, 1664. 4°. LCL.

2253   — —Second part. —, 1658. 4°. LT, O, LLP, MR; CH, IU, MH, NU, PPT, WF.

2254   — — —Second edition. —, 1659. 4°. L, BR; NGT, NPT, NU.

2254A — — —Third edition. —, 1663. 4°. L, OU.

2254B — — —"Third" edition. —, 1664. 4°. ENC, SA.

2255   — —Third and last part. —, 1662. 4°. L, O, C, LCL, LLP; CLC, KYU, MH, NGT, NU, PPT.

2256   — —[Anr. ed.] —, 1664. 4°. LCL, GU.

2257   — —Fifth edition. —, 1669. fol. T.C.I 22. L, LW, CS, NE, RPL; CDA, CU, MH, TSM, ASU.

2257A — —Sixth edition. *By M. White, for Ralph Smith,* 1679. fol. T.C.I 344. L, DU, NPL, SHR, GU; CH, MB, PPT, WF, Y.

2258   —The Christians labour and reward. *By J. M. for Ralph Smith,* 1672. 8°. T.C.I 101. L, O, C, LCL, LW; CLC, IU, MH, NU, PH, WF, Y.

2259   —The magistrates pourtraiture. *For Ralph Smith,* 1656. 4°.* LT, O, C, LSD, E; CH, IU, MH, NU, WF, Y.

2259A **Gurnay, Edmund.** An appendix unto the homily. *By A. N. for J. Rothwel,* 1641. 12°. CM; IE.

2260   —Gurnay redivivus, or an appendix. [*London*], *republished,* 1660. *Sold by J. Rothwel.* 24°. L, O, LCL, CE, P; CH, NU, TO.

2260A — —Second edition. *For J. Rothwel,* 1660. 24°. CS, SP; IU, WF.

2260B —Toward the vindication of the second commandment. *By E. M. for J. Rothwell,* 1661. 12°. CS; IU, NU, WF.

2261   [**Gurney, Sir Richard.**] The Lord Maior of Londons letter to the King. [*London,* 1642.] brs. STEELE 2200. LT, O, EC, LNC; MH.

[**Guthrie, James.**] Causes of the Lords vvrath. [n.p.] 1653. *See* Warriston, Archibald Johnston, *lord.*

2262   Entry cancelled.

[–] Humble acknowledgement of the sins. 1653. *See* Warriston, Archibald Johnston, *lord.* Causes of the Lords wrath.

2263   [–] The nullity of the pretended-assembly. [*Leith*], *printed,* 1652. 4°.* ALDIS 1463. LT, O, E, EN, ENC; CH, NU, TU, WF, Y.

2264   [–] Protesters no subverters. *Edinburgh, printed,* 1658. 8°. ALDIS 1581. LW, ON, D, EN, GU; CSS, Y.

2265   [–] A treatise of ruling elders. [*Edinburgh*], *printed,* 1652. 12°. ALDIS 1468.5. LT, E.

2265A [–] —[Anr. ed.] *Edinburgh, re-printed by the heir of Andrew Anderson,* 1690. 12°. ALDIS 3102. O, EN.

2265B [–] —[Anr. ed.] —, [1690]. 12°. ALDIS 3102.5. EN.

2266   [–] —[Anr. ed.] *Edinburgh, by George Mosman,* 1699. 16°. ALDIS 3915. L, C, EN; CH, MH, NU, WF, Y.

2267   —The true and perfect speech of. [*London*], *sent from Edenburgh, and printed,* 1661. 4°.* L, O, CT, EN, DT; CH, MH, TU, WF, Y.

2267A —Two speeches of. [*London*], *printed,* 1661. 4°.* LW, BC; CH, WF, Y.

2268   **Guthrie, John.** A sermon preach'd upon breach of covenant. [n.p., 1663?] 4°.* EN, ENC; NU.

2269   —To the suffering Protestants. *Edinburgh* [*London?*], *for A. Kennedy,* 1681. 4°. ALDIS 2271. EN.

2269A —Urim and Thummin. [*London?* 1669]. 4°.* EN.

2269B **Guthrie, William.** The Christian's great interest. *Edinburgh, Higgins, for Paterson, Morison & Falconer, Glasgow,* 1659. 12°. ALDIS 1600. I.

2270   —Fourth edition. *For Dorman Newman,* 1667. 8°. L.

2271   — —[Anr. ed.] *At Glasgow, by Robert Sanders,* 1669. 8°. ALDIS 1864.3. JOHNSTONE.

2272   —Fifth edition. *For Dorman Newman,* 1673. 8°. T.C.I 138. L.

2272A — —[Anr. ed.] *Edinburgh, by the heir of Andrew Anderson,* 1679. 12°. D.

2273   —Seventh edition. *For Dorman Newman,* 1681. 8°. T.C.I 424. LW, YM.

2274   — —[Anr. ed.] *Glasgow, by Robert Sanders,* 1695. 12°. ALDIS 3464. EN, GM.

2275   — —[Anr. ed.] *Belfast, by Patrick Neill and Company,* 1699. 12°. BLH.

2275A —Crumbs of comfort. [*Edinburgh*], *for A. Kennedy,* 1681. 4°.* ALDIS 2272. EN.

2275B —The heads of some sermons preached at Finnick. [n.p.], *printed,* 1680. 8°. A; WF.

2275C —A sermon of Mr. William Guthrey . . . Hosea xiii, ver. ix. [n.p., 1664?] cap., 8°.* EN; WF.

2275D —Two sermons preached . . . at Finnick, the 17 day of August 1662. [*Glasgow*], 1680. 12°.* EN.

2275E — —[Anr. ed.] [n.p.], *printed,* 1689. 4°.* Y.

2276   — —[Anr. ed.] *Glasgow, printed* 1693. 8°.* ALDIS 3300.5. GU.

2277   **Guy, John.** On the happy accession. *By J. Mayos, for R. Harrison,* 1699. fol.* L, AU; CLC, MH, Y.

2277A [**Guy, Robert.**] The longing shepherdess. [*London*], *for F. Coles, T. Vere, and J. Wright*, [1663–74]. brs. O, CM.

2278 [**Guy, William.**] Good newes for England. *For Robert Wood*, 1641. 4°.* C, MR, DN; INU, MIU, Y.

2279 Entry cancelled. *See preceding entry.*

2279A [–] The Protestants last victory over the rebels in Ireland. [*London?* 1641.] brs. INU.

2280 Entry cancelled.
Guy Earl of Warwick. 1661. *See* J., B. Tragical history.

Guzman, Hinde and Hannam. 1657. *See* Garcia, Carlos.

2280A Gweddiau yn yr ystafell. *Rhydychain, L. Lichfield*, 1693. 8°.* AN.

2281 **Gwin, John.** Articles ministred. *For U. U.*, 1641. 4°.* LT, O, C, LLU; CLC, MIU, WF, Y.

2282 **Gwin, Thomas.** To the children of Friends. [*London*, 1690.] brs. LF; PHS.

2282A Y gwir er gwaethed yw. *Thomas Jones*, 1684. 8°. AN.

2283 Gipsies song. *For J. Aliffe*, 1684. LIU; CLC.

H

1 **H., A.** A bitte to stay the stomacks. [*n.p.*], *printed* 1647. 4°. L, O, OC, EN; MH.

2 —The declaration of Duke Hambleton. [*London*], *printed*, 1648. 4°.* LT, O, OCC, MR, EN; NC.

2A Entry cancelled.
—Declaration of. Edinburgh, 1648. *See* Hamilton, James, *duke.*
—Discovery of two unclean spirits. 1657. *See* Holder, Anthony.

3 —An exact legendary compendiously containing the whole life of Alderman Abel. [*London*], *imprinted*, 1641. brs. LT, O, LG; MH.

3A —The Jesuits' catechism. *For Robert Harford*, 1679. 4°. L, O, C, P, EN; CDA, CH, CN, NP, Y.

3B ——[Anr. ed.] [*Dublin?*], *reprinted* 1679. 4°.* DT; WG.

3C ——Second edition. *For Robert Harford*, 1681. 4°. T.C.I 423. L, C, LSD; NU, PU, WF, Y.

3D ——Third edition. *For John Lawrence*, 1685. 4°. O; NN, NU.
—Priscianus embryo. 1670. *See* Huish, Anthony.

4 —A speedy post from heaven. *Printed*, 1642. 4°.* LT, LNC; CH, MH, Y.

5 **H., B.** The fables of AEsop. [*London*], *sold by A. Baldwin*, [1700]. 4°. Y.

6 —The fables of young AEsop. Fourth edition. *Printed and sold by Benj. Harris*, 1700. 12°. L.

7 —Hic, & ubique Venus: sive. *Impensis authoris*, 1667. 12°. L; CH, CLC.

8 —An ode on the anniversary of the coronation. *Dublin, by Jo. Ray*, 1693. fol.* DIX 256. DN.

8A [–] The parliament of bees. A fable. *Printed and sold by Benj. Harris*, 1697. brs. CN.

9 —True, but sad and dolefull newes from Shrevvsbvry. *Imprinted at Yorke, re-printed in London*, 1642. 4°.* LT, OC; CH.

H., C. Art of love. 1700. *See* Hopkins, Charles.

10 —Astrological observations. 1672. 4°.* MR.

10A —The birds noats on May day last. 1655. brs. L.
—Cry of innocent blood. [*n.p.*], 1670. *See* Allen, Robert.
—Divils cruelty. [1663.] *See* Hammond, Charles.

11 —The English intelligencer. *For Iohn Iohnson*, [1642]. 4°.* LT.

12 —Fancies favourite. *For F. Coles, T. Veres* [sic], *J. Wright, and J. Clarke*, [1675]. brs. L, CM, HH; MH, Y.

12A [–]—[Anr. ed.] [*n.p., n.d.*] L, GU.

13 —The Golden Rule made plain. Second edition. *First printed 1660, and now reprinted by J. C. for William Crook*, 1675. 8°.* T.C.I 212. L, LLP, LSD; CH.

14 —A merry new song wherein you may view. *For William Gilbertson*, [1658–60]. brs. L, HH; MH.

15 —A perfect narrative of a sea-fight near the coast of Portugal. *For R. W.*, 1650. 4°.* LT, MR; MH.
—Petty-schoole. 1659. *See* Hoole, Charles.

16 —A philosophical discourse of carthquakes. *For Walter Kettilby*, 1693. 4°.* L, O, OR, CS; CH, MH, NS, WF, Y.

16A —A pleasant discourse betweene conscience and plain-dealing. [*London*], *for Richard Burton*, [1650?]. 12°.* L.

16B ——[Anr. ed.] *For John Wright, John Clarke, William Thackeray and Thomas Passinger*, [1681–84]. 12°.* CM.

17 —A true narrative (in a letter . . .) of the apprehension of . . . Thomas Scot. *By Matthew Inman, to be sold by James Magnes*, 1660. 4°.* LT, O, LNC, MR; MH, MIU, WF, Y.

18 **H., D.** An antidote against Antinomianisme. *For G. B. and R. W.*, [1643]. 4°.* LT, O, C, MR, YM; CH, IU, MH, TU, WF.
—Life of one Jacob Behmen. 1654. *See* Hotham, Durand.

18A —O hone! O hone! A magpye-lecture. *For J. F.*, [1692]. 4°.* CN.

18B **H., D. N.** Miscellanea: consisting of three treatises. *For the author, to be sold by Giles Widdowes*, 1670. fol. Y.

H., E. Apology for distressed innocence. 1663. *See* Hickeringill, Edmund.
—Αποστασια. [*n.p.*], 1653. *See* Hall, Edmund.
—Caroloiades, or. 1689. *See* Howard, Edward.
—Character of a sham-plotter. [*n.p.*, 1681.] *See* Hickeringill, Edmund.

19 —Decus & tutamen: or, our new money. *Printed*, 1696. 8°. L, LUG, RU; MH, NC, WF, Y.

19A —An epitaph upon the solemn league and covenant. *For Philemon Stephens the younger*, 1661. brs. MH.

—Gregory, Father-greybeard. 1673. *See* Hickeringill, Edmund.

—Jamaica viewed. 1661. *See* Hickeringill, Edmund.

19B —The mock-elogie on the funeral of Mr. Caryl. [*London*, 1673.] brs. MH, PU.

20 —A plain and true relation of a very extraordinary cure of Mariane Maillard. *For Randal Taylor*, 1693. 4°.* L, LLP; CH.

—Presentation to London. [n.p., 1659]. *See* Hookes, Ellis.

—Primmer and catechism. 1670. *See* Fox, George, *elder*.

21 —Reasons for the abatement of interest. *For Daniel Brown, and Matt. Gillyflower*, 1692. 8°. T.C.II 385. L, O, OM, CT, EN; CH, CLC, MH, NC, WF.

21A — —[Anr. ed.] *For D. Brown*, 1698. 8°. T.C.III 56. CT.

—Remarks on the new philosophy. 1700. *See* Howard, Edward.

22 —Ρυθμος Βασιλικος: being an heroick poem. *For Richard Baldwin*, 1696. fol.* MIU, TU.

23 —Scripture proof for singing. *By John Astwood, and sold by Nath. Hiller*, 1696. 8°. L, O.

—Sermon preach'd on the 30th of January. 1700. *See* Hickeringill, Edmund.

—Spirit of the martyrs. [1665.] *See* Hookes, Ellis.

24 —Strafford's plot discovered. *By Ruth Raworth, for John Dallam*, 1646. 4°.* LT, O, OC, LLU, YM, DT; CH, NU, WF, Y.

24A —A true copy of a petition. *For the author, and are to be sold by Livewell Chapman*, 1657. 4°.* LT, O, LG, MR, E; CH, CSS, MH, Y.

—Vanity of self-boasters. 1643. *See* Hinton, Edward.

—Woman's conquest. 1671. *See* Howard, Edward.

H., F. Darknesse and ignorance. 1659. *See* Howgill, Francis.

25 —An elogie, and epitaph, consecrated. [*London?*], printed, 1649. 4°.* LT, FONMON; CH, MH, Y.

—General epistle to all who. [n.p., 1665.] *See* Howgill, Francis.

—General epistle to the dispersed. [n.p.], 1665. *See* Howgill, Francis.

—Great case of tythes and. [n.p.], 1665. *See* Howgill, Francis.

25A —Great news from the West-Indies. *Lodon* [*sic*], *for H. Wallis*, 1687. 4°.* O; CH.

—Mistery Babylon. 1659. *See* Howgill, Francis.

—Oaths no gospel ordinance. [n.p.], 1666. *See* Howgill, Francis.

—One of Anti-Christ's. 1660. *See* Howgill, Francis.

—One warning more. 1660. *See* Howgill, Francis.

—Visitation of love, peace. 1664. *See* Howgill, Francis.

—Visitation of the rebellious nation. 1656. *See* Howgill, Francis.

—Woe against the magistrates. 1654. *See* Howgill, Francis.

—VVord to the saints. 1668. *See* Holcroft, Francis.

—Works of darknesse. 1659. *See* Howgill, Francis.

26 **H., G.** Abingtons and Alisbvries present miseries. *By Rich. Herne*, [1642]. 4°.* LT, OC, LIU, LNC; CH, WF.

26A —Ad augustissimum invictissimumque Magnæ Britanniæ regem. [*London*, 1692.] brs. L; MH.

27 —An ansvver to a scandalous lying pamphlet, intitvled Prince Rvpert his declaration. *For Iohn Matthewes*, [1642]. 4°.* LT, CM, MR, GK; CLC, MBP, MH, WF, Y.

27A —A continuation of the most remarkable passages in both Houses. 26 of November, till . . . 3 of December, 1642. *By Richard Herne*, 1642. 4°.* O.

28 —The declaration of John Robins. *By R. Wood*, 1651. 4°.* LT, LG, CM.

29 —Deploratio mortis . . . Caroli II. [*London?* 168–?] brs. CH.

—Discourse about edification. 1683. *See* Hascard, Gregory.

30 —The excellency and equitableness of God's law. *For W. Birch*, 1669. 8°. T.C.I 18. O, C, LW; IU.

—Gladius justitiae. 1668. *See* Hascard, Gregory.

—Grand prerogative. 1653. *See* Holland, Guy.

—A letter from. [n.p., 1697.] *See* Heathcote, *Sir* Gilbert.

30A —A letter from a gentleman in answer to Mr. Mayor. [*London*, 1648.] brs. LPR.

31 —A letter to a member of Parliament for settling guineas. [*London?* 1696.] brs. L, LUG; NC, Y.

32 —Londons triumph, or, His Majesties welcom. *Printed*, 1673. brs. L.

—Memorbilia mundi. 1670. *See* Hooker, G.

32A —Merlinus Anglicus. 1653. 4°. LT.

33 —Nevves from Dvnkirke. *For Iohn Iohnson*, [1642]. 4°.* LT, EC, LNC; WF.

34 —The power of Parliaments asserted. [*London*], printed, 1679. fol.* DT; Y.

35 — —[Anr. ed.] *For T. Davis*, 1681. fol.* L, O, OC, LLU; CH, CN, MH, PU, WF.

36 —The speech and confession of Capt. Brown-Bushel. *Imprinted at London by R. W.*, 1651. 4°.* LT; CH, CSS.

—Sure-footing . . . examined. 1668. *See* Hughes, George.

37 —Two speeches delivered on the scaffold. *For William Loe* [*sic*], 1651. 4°.* LT, LG; MM.

38 —The worlds wonder. *By John Clowes*, 1651. 4°.* LT; CLC, WF.

H., H. Beast that was. 1659. *See* Howet, Henoch.

—Considerations of present use. [n.p., 1646.] *See* Hammond, Henry.

—Daily practice. 1684. *See* Hammond, Henry.

—Hunting of the fox. 1657. *See* Harflete, Henry.

39 —A journal of all proceedings between the Jansenists, and the Jesuits. *By W. W. to be sold by William Place*, 1659. 4°. LT, O, MR; CH, IU, NU, TU, WF, WG.

40 —A letter to a member of Parliament written upon the rumour. *Printed*, 1699. 4°.* L, O; CH, WF.

41 —News from the North; or, a trve relation. *By R. Cotes*, 1648. 4°.* LT, LVF, MR.

—Of the reasonableness. 1650. *See* Hammond, Henry.

—Sermon preached at Worcester. 1686. *See* Humberston, Henry.

—Weary traveller. 1681. *See* Harrison, Henry.

H., I. Allwydd neu agoriad. Lvyck, 1670. *See* Hughes, John.

42 —The Antipodes, or reformation with the heeles upward. *Oxford, printed,* 1647. 4°.* MADAN 1944. LT, O, LW, EN, DT; CH, CN, MH, TU, WF, Y.

—Authority of the magistrate. 1672. *See* Humfrey, John.

—Brief receipt. 1658. *See* Humfrey, John.

43–4 Entries cancelled.

—Complete clerk. 1677. *See* title.

45 —England and Scotland united. *For J. H.,* 1647. 4°. EN.

45A —Englands diurnall. [*London*], *printed,* [1643]. 4°.* LT, DT; CLC, CN, MIU, PUL, Y.

—Fort-royal. 1649. *See* Hart, John.

46 —A list of King James's Irish . . . forces. *By Edw. Jones in the Savoy,* 1697. fol.* L, O, C, LSD; CH, WF, Y.

46A ——[Anr. ed.] *By Ed. Jones, and reprinted in Edinburgh by Jo. Reid,* 1698. brs. ALDIS 3758.5. OP.

47 —Londons remonstrance to the Parliament. *For Iohn Harrison, Iune* 23, 1642. 4°.* LT, O, LG, CCO, LNC; CSS, Y.

48 —Paradise transplanted. *Printed,* 1661. 4°.* L, O; MH.

[–] Petition and articles, or severall charge. 1641. *See* England: Parliament.

—Satans fiery darts. 1647. *See* Hall, Joseph, *bp.*

49 —The souldiers sad complaint. [*London,* 1647.] brs. LT, HH, LLU; Y.

50 —A strange vvonder or a vvonder in a vvoman. *For I. T.,* 1642. 4°.* LT, OC; CH, MH, Y.

—Stumbling-block of disobedience . . . removed. 1658. *See* Harrington, James, *elder.*

51 —A true relation of the late great fight at sea. *Leith, by Evan Tyler,* 1652. 4°.* ALDIS 1469. EN; MH, Y.

52 —Virtue and valour vindicated. *For T. W.,* 1647. 4°.* LT, DT; TU.

H., J. Account of the transactions in the North. 1692. *See* Michelborne, John.

—Admonition to my Lord Protector. 1654. *See* Heath, James.

—Ah, ha; tumulus. 1653. *See* Howell, James.

—Answer to a small treatise. [n.p.], 1693. *See* Hogg, John.

—Answer to several material passages. 1691. *See* Hogg, John.

—Αρχαιοσκοπια: or. 1677. *See* Hanmer, Jonathan.

53 —Astronomia crystallina. *For the author,* 1670. 8°.* L, O; CLC, WF, Y.

54 ——Second edition. —, *sold by N. Brooke, and J. Hancock,* 1676. 8°.* L; CH.

—Best exercise. 1671. *See* Horne, John.

—Brief account of the royal. 1662. *See* Howell, James.

—Brief admonition of some. 1659. *See* Howell, James.

—Brief chronicle of the late. 1663. *See* Heath, James.

55 —A brief narrative of the state of the Protestants in Hungary. *For T. Parkhurst and N. Simmons,* 1677. 4°. L, O, P, WCA, EN; CH, LC, MH, NU, WF.

56 —A choice compendium. *By T. H. for P. Brooksby,* 1681. 8°. T.C.I 432. CH, MH.

—Christ mysticall. 1647. *See* Hall, Joseph, *bp.*

—Christian's blessed choice. 1668. *See* Hart, John.

—Christ's last sermon. 1663. *See* Hart, John.

56AA —A concordance of the chief heads. 1656. LSC.

56A Entry cancelled.

—Cordial for the Cavaliers. 1661. *See* Howell, James.

57 Entry cancelled.

—Daily thoughts. 1651. *See* Henshaw, Joseph.

—Decisions of divers. 1649. *See* Hall, Joseph, *bp.*

58 —The declaration and speech of Colonel Massey. *For G. Horton,* 1650. 4°.* LT; INU.

—Δενδρολογια Dodona's grove. [n.p.], 1644. *See* Howell, James.

—Description and use of a quadrant. 1665. *See* Hewlett, J.

—Description of the last voyage. 1671. *See* Hardy, John.

—Διατριβη περι παιδο-βαπτισμου, or. 1654. *See* Horne, John.

—Discourse of an unconverted man's enmity. 1700. *See* Howe, John.

—Discourse of the empire. 1658. *See* Howell, James.

—Divine considerations. 1676. *See* Halsey, James.

—Divine physician. [n.p.], 1676. *See* Harris, John.

—Divine wooer. 1673. *See* Horne, John.

—Dovvn-right dealing. [n.p.], 1647. *See* Howell, James.

59 —Dreadful news from Limerick. *Printed, and sold by R. Taylor,* 1694. brs. O; MH.

60 —An elegy on the death of Dr. Sanderson. *For W. Gilbertson,* 1663. brs. O.

—Emblems. 1658. *See* Hall, John.

61 —Englands alarm, the state-maladies. *By Tho. Johnson,* 1659. 4°.* LT, O; CN, MH.

62 Entry cancelled.

—Englands diurnall. [n.p., 1643.] *See* H., I.

63 —Englands joy, expressed. *For M. B.,* 1660. brs. LT.

—Epilogue to Mr. Lacy's new play. 1684. *See* Haines, Joseph.

64 —An essay concerning liberty of conscience. *Dublin, printed; to be sold by John Foster,* 1699. 4°. L.

—Essayes about general. 1659. *See* Horne, John.

64A —Essays of love and marriage. *For H. Brome,* 1673. 8°. T.C.I 142. O; CH.

—Everlasting joys. 1656. *See* Hart, John.

—Exact dealer. 1688. *See* Hill, John.

65 —The excellencie of Jesus Christ. *By Barnard Alsop, for Richard Tomlins,* 1646. 8°. LT; CH.

65A —The excellent virtues and uses of the great antidote. 1674. 4°. GU.

65B ——[Anr. ed.] *Printed,* 1679. 4°. PL.

66 —The family-dictionary. *For H. Rhodes,* 1695. 8°. T.C.II 560. L, CS, BC; LC, MH, TSM, WF, Y, AMB.

66AA ——Second edition. —, *and sold by R. Clavel,* 1696. 8°. T.C.II 593. L, O, CE, LLU; NN.

—Florus Hungaricus: or. 1664. *See* Howell, James.

—Fort-royal. 1649. *See* Hart, John.

66A —A full and true account of a terrible and bloody engagement at sea. colop: *For W. Brown,* [1690]. brs. MH.

—Gagg to love's advocate. 1651. *See* Hinde, John.

67–70 Entries cancelled.

—Gentleman's jocky. 1671. *See* Halfpenny, John.

—Grace leading. 1651. *See* Hall, John.

—Grecian story. 1684. *See* Harington, John.

—Grounds & reasons. [n.p.], 1650. *See* Hall, John.
—Heavens glory. 1662. *See* Hart, John.

71 Entry cancelled.
—Historical discourses. 1661. *See* Howell, James. Divers historical discourses.
—History of Polinder. 1651. *See* Harington, John.

72 Entry cancelled.
—History of the life & death of Oliver Cromwell. 1663. *See* Heath, James.
—History of the life and death of Sr. Thomas More. 1662. *See* Hoddesdon, John.

73 Entry cancelled.
—Holy lives. 1654. *See* Hoddesdon, John.
—Holy oyl. [n.p.], 1669. *See* Harrington, James, *elder*.
—Holy order. 1654. *See* Hall, Joseph, *bp*.
—Humble motion to the Parliament. 1649. *See* Hall, John.
—Instructions for forreine travell. 1642. *See* Howell, James.
—Interest of these United Provinces. Middleburg, 1673. *See* Hill, Joseph.
—Jehojadahs iustice. 1645. *See* Hoyle, Joshua.

73A —King Charles his entertainment. *For John Greensmith*, 1641. 4°.* LT, O, LG; CH, CLC, MH, WF, Y.

73B —Lancasters massacre. *For Tho. Vnderhill*, April 1, 1643. 4°.* LT, DT; IU, MH, MIU, Y.

74 —The last newes from the North. *By E. Purslow*, 1646. 4°.* LT, DU, DT.

74A —A letter from a person of quality, to a principal peer. *Printed* 1611 [i.e. 1661]. 4°.* L, O, LUG, EC, LNC, DT; MH, NP, NU, Y.
—Letter to George Keith. 1700. *See* Humfrey, John.
—Loves companion. 1656. *See* Hunter, Josiah.
—Meditations miscellaneous. 1686. *See* Henshaw, Joseph, *bp*.
—Middle-way. 1672. *See* Humfrey, John.
—Miscellanea; or, a mixture. 1669. *See* Henshaw, Joseph, *bp*.

74B —A modell of a Christian society. *Cambridge, by Roger Daniel*, 1647. 8°. O.
—Modern assurancer. 1658. *See* Herne, John.
—Modest representation. 1672. *See* Hely, James.

75 —A most excellent and rare drink. [*London*, 1650.] brs. LT, MH.
—New prognostication. Glasgow, 1667. *See* Almanacs.
—Obligation of human laws. 1671. *See* Humfrey, John.

75A —The original of infant-baptism. *Printed*, 1674. 4°. PL.
—Παροιμιογραφια. Proverbs. 1659. *See* Howell, James.
—Philanglvs; some sober. 1658. *See* Howell, James.

76 —A Pindarick ode on the death of His late sacred Majesty King Charles II. colop: *For S. T. and are to be sold by Randal Tailor*, 1685. cap., fol.* L, O, OP, MC, NE; CH, CLC, CN, MH, PU, AVP.
—Plea for the non-conformists. 1674. *See* Humfrey, John.

76A —A plea for the sequestred. [*London?* 1660?] cap., 4°.* LT, CT, LUG.
—Pleasant and compendious history. 1685. *See* Virgil, Polydore.
—Politicaster: or. 1659. *See* Harrington, James, *elder*.

—Pre-eminence and pedigree. 1645. *See* Howell, James.
—Present state of England, as. 1697. *See* Hodges, James.

77 —The princes first fruits. [*London*], printed, 1648. 4°.* LT; CH, MH, MIU.

77A —The principles of Christian proved. *By R. L. for Samuel Man*, 1645. 8°.* O.
—Prologue to the Northern lass. [n.p.], 1684. *See* Haines, Joseph.

77B —A proposal of one tax. [*London?* 169–?] brs. MH, Y.

77C —A proposition for the safety & happiness of the King. *Printed* 1667. 12°. L, O, C, SC; TO.

77D ——Second edition. —, 1667. 12°. O, C; NU.
—Redeemer's tears. 1684. *See* Howe, John.

77E —Religion justified. *For J. Roberts in Bridgwater*, 1699. 8°. BR, NE.

78 —A remonstrance of the present estate of the Kings armie. *By Tho: Fawcet*, Octob. 12. 1642. 4°.* LT; CLC, WF.

79 —A remonstrance of the present state of things in and about the city. *For Iohn YYright*, [1642.] 4°.* LT, MR; CLC, CN, NU, WF, Y.

79A [–] —[Anr. ed.] [1642.] 4°.* CH.

80 —A remonstrance to the Kingdome, or an appeale. *For Thomas Watson*, 1643. 4°.* O; CH, MH, WF.
—Resolutions and decisions. 1649. *See* Hall, Joseph, *bp*.
—Review of Mr. Horn's. Cambridge, 1660. *See* Hacon, Joseph.
—Satans fiery darts. 1647. *See* Hall, Joseph, *bp*.
—Second part of Massaniello. 1652. *See* Howell, James.
—Select thoughts. 1648. *See* Hall, Joseph, *bp*.
—Self-dedication. 1682. *See* Howe, John.
—Short discourse on the present temper. Edinburgh, 1696. *See* Holland, John.

81 Entry cancelled.
—Some historical remarques. 1663. *See* Howell, James. Last will and testament.
—Supplement to the present state. 1697. *See* Hodges, James.
—Tho. Mori vita. 1652. *See* Hoddesdon, John.

81A —A treatise of the great antidote of Paracelsus. *For the authour*, 1666. 4°.* LG, SP; MB.

82 —A treatise of the great antidote of Van Helmont. *For the author*, 1667. 4°.* L; PL.

82A ——[Anr. ed.] —, 1668. 4°.* C, OB.

82B ——[Anr. ed.] 1671. 4°. LG, MC.
—True and onely causes. 1666. *See* Hodges, John.

82C —A true and perfect relation of that most horrid and hellish conspiracy . . . gunpowder treason. *For Fr. Coles*, 1662. 4°. L, O.

83 ——[Anr. ed.] 1663. 4°. L, C, LIL.
—Two discourses. 1645. *See* Howell, James.

84 —Two essays of love and marriage. *For Henry Brome*, 1657. 12°. L, O, C; CH, Y.
—Two points. [n.p.], 1672. *See* Humfrey, John.
—Two sermons. 1688. *See* Howe, John.

85 —Vain worship and worshipers detected. *For the author*, 1675. 8°. L.
—Vanity of honour. 1678. *See* Halsey, James.

86 Entry cancelled. Ghost.
    —View of that part. 1695. *See* Howe, John.
    —Vindication of the review. Cambridge, 1662. *See* Hacon, Joseph.
    —Way to salvation. 1668. *See* Hieron, John.
87 —A wonderfull and terrible plot of the Papists. *For I. H. and T. H., June* 15, 1642. 4°.* EC.
88–9 No entries.
    —Young clerks tutor. 1662. *See* Cocker, Edward.
    H., Jos. Devout soul. 1644. *See* Hall, Joseph, *bp*.
    H., L. Index Biblicus: or. 1668. *See* Hoar, Leonard.
90 —A perfect divrnall of all the passages and proceedings. *For R. W*., 1648. 4°.* LT.
    H., M. Advice to a daughter. [n.p.], 1699. *See* Halifax, George Savile, *marquis*.
91 —An answer to lame Giles Calfines messe of pottage. [*London*], *printed*, 1642. 4°.* LT, O, C, OC, MR; NC, NU.
    —Brief enquiry into the true nature. 1690. *See* Henry, Matthew.
91A —A copy of verses of the late earthquake. *For John Pike*, 1692. brs. MH.
    —Grounds of the lawes. 1657. *See* Hawke, Michael.
91B —The history of the union of the four famous kingdoms of England, Wales, Scotland and Ireland. *For Thomas Brewster*, 1649 [*i.e.* 1659]. 8°. MH.
92 — —[Anr. ed.] —, 1660. 8°. L, EN; CH, MIU, WF, Y.
93 Entry cancelled.
    —Narrative of the proceedings of the fleet. 1659. *See* Harrison, Mark.
94 Entry cancelled.
    —Nature of schism. 1690. *See* Henry, Matthew. Brief enquiry.
    —Right of dominion. 1655. *See* Hawke, Michael.
    —Vision of the Lord. [n.p.], 1662. *See* Howgill, Mary.
95 —The young cook's monitor. *By William Downing*, 1683. 8°. L.
96 — —Second edition. *For the author*, 1690. 8°. L, O; WF.
    H., N. Amanda. 1653. *See* Hookes, Nicholas.
96A —The compleat tradesman. *For John Dunton*, 1684. L, O, LUG, EN.
97 — —Second edition. —, 1684. 12°. OC, EN; CN, MH, WF.
97A — —Third edition. —, 1684. 12°. T.C.II 48. L, O, LG.
    —Conference betwixt a Papist. 1678. *See* Mayo, Richard.
    —Conference betwixt a Protestant. 1678. *See* Mayo, Richard.
    —Ecclesiastica methermeneutica. 1652. *See* Homes, Nathaniel.
98 —An elegy on Sir George Jeffereys. *Printed*, 1689. brs. HH.
    —Gospel musick. 1644. *See* Homes, Nathaniel.
99 —The ladies dictionary. *For John Dunton*, 1694. 8°. L, O, C, LG, LLU, A, BLH; CH, CN, LC, MH, TU, Y.
100 —The pleasant art of money-catching. *For J. Dunton*, 1684. 12°. T.C.II 48. L; MH, NC, NN, PU.
100A —A short treatise, shewing the causes . . . plague. *For R. Ibbitson*, 1658. 8°.* L.
    —Two conferences. 1678. *See* Mayo, Richard.

—Yea and nay almanack. 1678. *See* Almanacs.
H., O. Advice to an only child. 1693. *See* Heywood, Oliver.
—Baptismal bonds. 1687. *See* Heywood, Oliver.
—General assembly. 1700. *See* Heywood, Oliver.
—Heart treasure. 1667. *See* Heywood, Oliver.
—Israel's lamentation. 1683. *See* Heywood, Oliver.
—Meetness for Heaven. 1679. *See* Heywood, Oliver.
H., P. Annotations on Milton's. 1695. *See* Hume, Patrick.
101 —The Bank of England, and their present method. *For Thomas Speed*, 1697. 8°.* T.C.II 605. L, LUG, LSD; CH, MH.
102 — —Second edition. —, 1697. 8°.* T.C.III 10. CH, CSS, NC, Y.
    —Detection or, discovery. 1641. *See* Harlowe, Pedaell.
103 —A discoverie of truth. [*London*], *printed*, 1645. 8°. LT; CH.
    —Innocency, though under a cloud. 1664. *See* Hobson, Paul.
    —Politicks of France. 1680. *See* Hay, Paul, *marquis of Chastelet*.
    —Πрσσω. [n.p.], 1647. *See* Hardres, Peter.
    —Quakers plea. 1661. *See* Hardcastle, Peter.
    —Stumbling-block of disobedience. 1658. *See* Heylyn, Peter.
104 —Terrible and trve nevves from Beverley. *For M. T*., 1642. 4°.* LT, O, LLU, YM; Y.
    —Undeceiving of the people. 1648. *See* Heylyn, Peter.
    —Voyage of France. 1673. *See* Heylyn, Peter.
H., R. Attempt for the explication. 1661. *See* Hooke, Robert.
    —Catalogue of part of those rarities. [n.p.], 166–? *See* Hubert, Robert.
    —Character of a Quaker. 1671. *See* Austin, Samuel.
    —Christians dayly solace. 1659. *See* Head, Richard.
    —Considerations on the Council. [n.p.], 1671. *See* Woodhead, Abraham.
105 —A dialogue between a Protestant and an [Ana]baptist. *For D. M*., 1678. 4°.* O, EN.
    —Differences about pre-determination. [n.p., 1700.] *See* Hall, Robert.
    —Discourse of the nationall excellencies. 1658. *See* Hawkins, Richard.
    —Discourse of the necessity of church-guides. [n.p.], 1675. *See* Woodhead, Abraham.
    —Examination of sundry scriptures. 1645. *See* Hollingworth, Richard.
    —Fatall doom. 1655. *See* Hooke, Richard.
106 —From the rendezvous of the whole army. *Printed at York by Tho. Broad*, 7 *August*, 1647. 4°. YM.
107 Entry cancelled.
    —Funus corporis et animæ. 1646. *See* Hatcher, Robert.
    —Globe notes. [n.p.], 1666. *See* Holland, Richard.
    —Good Christian's Heaven. [1660.] *See* Hooke, Richard.
    —The good old cause briefly demonstrated. 1659. *See* Hubberthorn, Richard.
108 No entry.
    —History of Genesis. 1690. *See* Herne, R.

—Institutio epithalamium. 1645. *See* Hatcher, Robert.

108A —A letter to a livery-man of London. [*London?* 1695.] brs. L, LG; NN.

109 —A letter written to a friend, a member in the House of Commons. *For J. Crooke*, 1661. 4°.* O, LL; CN, MH.

—Life and death of Mother Shipton. 1684. *See* Head, Richard.

—Life and death of the English rogue. 1679. *See* Head, Richard.

—Loyall subiects retiring-roome. Oxford, 1645. *See* Harwood, Richard.

109A —The maidens nay. [*London*], *for F. Coles, T. Vere, and J. Wright*, [1663–74]. brs. L, O, HH; MH.

—Miss display'd. 1675. *See* Head, Richard.

—Paideutica. 1646. *See* Hatcher, Robert.

—Paradoxical assertions. 1659. *See* Heath, Robert.

—Parallels; or. 1675. *See* Hames, Robert.

110 —Plus ultra or the second part of the character of a Quaker. *Printed*, 1672. 4°.* I, O, C, LF, EN; CH, CN, MH, WF, Y.

—Prevention of poverty. 1674. *See* Haines, Richard.

—Profitable method. [n.p., 1679.] *See* Haines, Richard.

—Proposals for building. 1677. *See* Haines, Richard.

—Proteus redivivus: or. 1675. *See* Head, Richard.

—Rational account of the doctrine. [n.p.], 1673. *See* Woodhead, Abraham.

—Rebukes of a reviler. 1657. *See* Hubberthorn, Richard.

—Red sea. 1666. *See* Head, Richard.

111 —Remarks on some eminent passages in the life of the famed Mr. Blood. *For John Norris*, 1680. fol.* T.C.I 417. L, O, C, MR, DT; CH, CLC, CN, MIU, WF, Y.

112 Entry cancelled. = H 114.

113 —Remarks on the life and death of the fam'd Mr. Blood. *For R. Janeway*, 1680. fol.* O; LC.

114 ——Second edition. *For Richard Janeway*, 1680. fol.* L, O, C, AN, BAMB; CH, CN, MH, WF, Y.

—School of recreation. 1684. *See* Howlet, Robert.

—Second part of the young clerks gvide. 1653. *See* Hutton, *Sir* Richard.

114A —Shimei's curses on King David. *For H. Marsh*, 1660. 8°. LSC.

—Some arguments. 1699. *See* Hall, Robert.

—Something that lately passed. 1660. *See* Hubberthorn, Richard.

—Third part of the young clerks guide. 1659. *See* Hutton, *Sir* Richard.

115 —A touch-stone, or, triall and examination. *For Giles Calvert*, 1647. 4°.* LT, MR, DT; IU.

—True guide. 1646. *See* Hollingworth, Richard.

—Young clerk's guide. 1650. *See* Hutton, *Sir* Richard.

115A **H., R. B.** An alarum to pamphleteers. *Printed*, 1659. 4°.* CH, MIU, Y.

H., S. Ανθρωπωλογια or. 1680. *See* Haworth, Samuel.

116 —The arch-cheate, or. *For M. W. Oct.* 4, 1644. 4°.* LT, O; CSS, NU, UCLA, V, WF.

—Army-armed. 1653. *See* Hunton, Samuel.

—D. E. defeated. 1662. *See* Holden, Samuel.

—Declaration. 1667. *See* Hutchinson, Samuel.

—Designe for plentie. [1652.] *See* Hartlib, Samuel.

—England's lamentation, or. [n.p.], 1665. *See* Hubbersty, Stephen.

117 —Funerall elegies. Or the sad muses in sables. *By Tho. Wilson*, [1655]. 4°.* LT, O.

118 —The godly man's enquiry. *For W. Churchill, in Dorset*, 1688. 8°. C.

119 Entry cancelled.

—Golden law. 1656. *See* Hunton, Samuel.

—His Highnesse the Lord-Protector protected. 1654. *See* Hunton, Samuel.

—Iter Lvsitanicvm. 1662. *See* Hinde, Samuel.

120 Entry cancelled.

—King of kings. 1655. *See* Hunton, Samuel.

121 —Knaves and fooles in folio. *By M. Simmons for R. H.*, 1648. 4°.* LT, O, LIU, DT; CH, MB, MBJ, MH, WF, Y.

—Londons charitie. 1649. *See* Hartlib, Samuel.

—Parliaments reformation. 1646. *See* Hartlib, Samuel.

122 —Prosopopeia, or, the states and their steward. *For R. Harford*, 1650. 8°.* LT.

123 —Rectifying principles. *For R. H.*, 1648. 4°.* LT, LLL.

124 Entry cancelled.

—Second guide to heaven. 1687. *See* Hardy, Samuel.

124A —The subjects joy. 1643. YM.

125 —This last ages looking-glasse. *Printed at York by Stephen Bulkley*, 1642. 4°.* LT.

126 —The Trap-Pannians alias Trap-Pallians alias Trap-Tonians. [*London*, 1653.] cap., 4°.* LT.

127 —A triumphant panegyrick in honour and memory of King Charles. *By Thomas Ratcliffe*, 1661. brs. LT.

127A —Yorkshire's triumph. 1643. 4°. YM.

128 **H., T.** A Ha! Christmas. *For R. L.*, 1647. 4°.* LT, O, LLL, LLP, DT; CLC.

129 —An accompt of both the fleets. *By A. P.*, 1673. fol.* L, O; CH.

—An account of several new inventions. 1691. *See* Hale, Thomas.

129A —Articles proposed to the Catholiques of England. [*Paris*, 1648.] L (impf.).

—Brief relation of some part. [n.p.], 1672. *See* Holme, Thomas.

130 —The Cavaliers thanks-giving. *By I. C. for the author*, 1661. 4°.* LT; MH.

131 —Compulsion of conscience condemned. *For John How, and Thomas Knowles*, 1683. 4°.* O, SP, BLH; CH, MH, NU, WF, Y.

—Conjugall counsell. 1653. *See* Hilder, Thomas.

—Dialogue between a Christian. 1673. *See* Hicks, Thomas.

132 —An earnest exhortation for the publike reading of Common-Prayer. *For H. T.*, 1647. 4°.* LT, OC, BAMB, DT; CSS, MH, NU.

132A ——[Anr. ed.] *By R. L. for T. H.*, 1647. 4°.* MH.

132B —An exact survey of the affaires of the United Netherlands. *By Thomas Mabb for Thomas Johnson*, 1665. 12°. L, LUG, CT; WF, ANL.

133   — —[Anr. ed.] *For Peter Parker,* 1672. 12°. L.
    —Famous and remarkable history. 1656. *See* Heywood, Thomas.

134   —The five faithfull brothers. *For W. Gilbertson,* 1660. 8°.* L.
    —Generall history of women. 1657. *See* Heywood, Thomas.

135   [–] The gospel net. [*n.p.*], *printed,* 1670. 4°.* O.

135A   —A guide for the childe and youth, in two parts. *By T. J. for Dixy Page,* 1667. 16°. KEELE.

136   —Haslerig & Vain or, a dialogue. *For William Gilbertson,* [1660.] 8°.* LT.
    —History of the civil wars. [*n.p.*], 1679. *See* Hobbes, Thomas.
    —Immortality of the soule. 1645. *See* Hooker, Thomas.

136A   —Iter boreale. The second part. *For Henry Brome,* 1660. brs. L; MH.

137   —The lamentable complaint of the North-west countrey-man. *Printed,* 1645. 4°.* LT; Y.

138   —The last nevves from Yorke. *Fo* [sic] *M. T., Iuly* 7. 1642. 4°.* LT, O, OC, LLU; CLC, MH, Y.
    —Letter to a member of Parliament: shewing. 1697. *See* Houghton, Thomas.

139   —A looking-glasse for vvomen. *For R. W.,* 1644. 4°.* LT; MH, Y.

140–2   Entries cancelled.
    —Political aphorisms. 1690. *See* Harrison, Thomas.
    —Principia et problemata. 1674. *See* Hobbes, Thomas.

143   —A proposal for the raising the summe. [*London,* 1690.] brs. L; MH.

144   —A proposal to make good the coyn. [*London?* 1695.] brs. L, O, LUG; MH.

145   Entry cancelled. Date: 1638.
    —Topica sacra: spiritual logick. 1658. *See* Harrison, Thomas.
    —Treatise of marriage. 1673. *See* Hodges, Thomas.
    —Tythes no maintenance. 1652. *See* Heath, Thomas.
    —Vanity of man. 1676. *See* Hodges, Thomas.

146   —A vindication of kings and nobles. *For R. L. Nov.* 15. 1647. 4°.* L; CH, MH, NU, WF, Y.

147   Entry cancelled.
    H.,V. London drollery. 1673. *See* Hickes, William.

148   **H., W.** Ancilla divinitatis, or, the hand-maid. *Printed,* 1659. 4°.* L.
    —Anglo-Jvdævs, or. 1656. *See* Hughes, William, *of Gray's Inn.*
    —Antidote against that poysonous. 1676. *See* Haworth, William.

149   —Arguments proving, the iurisdiction. *For Thomas Wakley,* 1641. 4°.* L, O, BC, AN.
    —Balaams reply to the asse. 1661. *See* W., H.
    —Catholick naked truth. 1676. *See* Hubert, William. Puritan convert.

150   —A changling no company. *By M. Simmons, for Thomas Parkhurst,* 1660. 4°. LT, LLL.
    —Compleat fencing-master. 1692. *See* Hope, *Sir* William.

    —Conduct and conveyance. [*n.p.*], 1690. *See* Houschone, William.

151   —A congratulation to our newly restored Parliament. *By J. T.,* 1659. brs. LT, LUG; MH.

152   [–] A discourse concerning the queries proposed. *For Richard Wodenothe,* 1648. 4°.* LT, O, LSC, SP, DT; CLC, MH, NU, WF, Y.

153   — —[Anr. ed.] 1649. 4°.* E.

154   —A diurnall of sea designes. *For W. S.,* 1642. 4°.* LT, OW, EC, LIU, LNC; MH, NU.
    —Farewel to Popery. 1679. *See* Harris, Walter.
    —Fencing-master's advice. Edinburgh, 1692. *See* Hope, *Sir* William.
    —Grammatical drollery. 1682. *See* Hickes, William.

155   —The infallible guide to travellers. *For T. B.,* 1682. 8°.* L, OQ.

156   —A letter concerning the test, and persecution for conscience. *For Matthew Turner,* 1687. 4°.* L, O, C, DU, LSD; CH, CN, MH, WF, Y.

157   —A more perfect and particular relation of the late great victorie in Scotland. *By M. B. for Robert Bostock,* 25 *Sep.* 1645. 4°.* LT, O, C, MR, EN; CN, MH, WF, Y.
    —Observations vpon historie. 1641. *See* Habington, William.
    —Oxford drollery. Oxford, 1671. *See* Hickes, William.

158   —A perfect and most usefull table to compute the year. *For the use of W. H. the author, to be sold by Master Michell, and by Tobias Jorden in Gloucester,* 1656. brs. LT.
    —Poems. 1655. *See* Hammond, William.

159   —The practice of the sheriff's court, London. *By John Redmayne,* 1662. 8°. L (lost).

160   Entry cancelled.
    —Puritan convert. [*n.p.*], 1676. *See* Hubert, William.

161   —A relation of the good successe of the Parliaments forces. [*Cambridge*], *by W. F.,* 1644. 4°.* LT.
    —Remarks on the affairs. 1691. *See* Harris, *Sir* Walter.
    —Scots fencing-master. Edinbvrgh, 1687. *See* Hope, *Sir* William.
    —Spirit of prophecy. 1679. *See* Hughes, William, *hospitaller.*
    —Sword-man's vade-mecum. Edinburgh, 1691. *See* Hope, *Sir* William.
    Ha, Jo. Nahash redivivus. 1649. *See* Harrison, John.

162   **Haak, Theodore,** *ed.* The Dutch annotations. *By Henry Hills, for John Rothwell, Joshua Kirton, and Richard Tomlins,* 1657. 2v. fol. L, O, C, LBS, E, DT; CH, IU, NU, WF, Y, AVP.

163   Entry cancelled.
    [**Habernfeld, Andreas**], *ab.* Grand designs of the Papists. 1678. *See* Prynne, William.

164   —A true narrative of the Popish-plot. *For Robert Harford,* 1680. fol.* L, O, C, CT, LSD, MR; CH, CLC, CN, MH, WF, Y.
    [**Habert, Philippe.**] Temple of death. 1695. *See title.*

164A   **Habington, William.** The history of Edward IV. 1642. fol. DCH.

165   — —[Anr. ed.] *For F. Tyton,* 1648. fol. BN, U.WASHINGTON, SEATTLE.

166 [–] Observations vpon historie. *By T. Cotes, for Will. Cooke,* 1641. 8°. L. LW, BC, SP, DU; CH, CN, IU, MU, PL.

167 —Præces principum. *For John Place,* 1659. fol. L, OC, MR; CH, CLC, CN, NCD, WF.

168 **Hacke, William.** A collection of original voyages. *For James Knapton,* 1699. 8°. T.C.III 138. L, O, C, EN, DT; CH, CN, LC, MH, WF, Y, AVP.

169 **Hacket, John, *bp.*** A century of sermons. *By Andrew Clark for Robert Scott,* 1675. fol. T.C.I 203. L, O, C, DU, E; BN, CH, CLC, CU, IU, NU, WF, Y.

     [–] Christian consolations. 1671. *See title.*

170 [–] Loiola. *Typis R. C. sumptibus Andr. Crooke,* 1648. 12°. L, O, C, LVD, EN; CH, CN, MH, WF, Y.

171 —Scrinia reserata: a memorial. [*London*], *in the Savoy: by Edw. Jones, for Samuel Lowndes,* 1693. fol. T.C.II 452. L, O, C, NOT, EN, DT; BN, CH,CN,LC, MH,NU, WF,Y,AVP.

172 —A sermon preached . . . 22 of March anno 1660. *By W. Wilson, for John Place,* 1660. 4°.* LT, O, C, DU, BLH; CH, CN, MH, NU, WF, Y. (var.)

173 **Hackett, Thomas.** A sermon preached . . . May 9. anno 1661. *By D. Maxwell, for Tho. Davies and Th. Sadler,* 1662. 4°.* O, CS, DT; CH, WF.

174 —A sermon preached . . . Tvesday in Easter-week, anno Dom. 1672. *For Benjamin Tooke,* 1672. 4°. T.C.I 101. L, O, CS, DT; CH, NU, WF, Y.

175 **Hackluyt, John.** An alarm for London. *By I. Coe,* 1647. 4°.* LT, C, MR, DT; MH, TU.

175A The hackney coachmens case. [*London?* 1692.] brs. L.

176 The hackney damsells' pastime. [*London*], *for Charles Bates,* [1685?]. brs. L, CM, HH.

176A **Hacon, Joseph.** A review of a late heterodox catechism. *Cambridge, by J. F. and are to be sold by J. H.,* [1644]. 4°. C, LLP.

177 [–] A review of Mʳ Horn's catechisme. *Cambridge, by John Field,* 1660. 8°. O, C, CM.

178 [–] A vindication of the review, or, . . . Mr. Horn's catechisme. *Cambridge: by John Field,* 1662. 8°. O, C, CM; WF.

179 Fryday May 17, 1661. Hactenus Anglorvm nvlli, an ode on the fair weather. *By Iohn Clowes, for the author,* 1661. brs. LT.

180 Hactenus inaudita: or, animadversions. *By J. M. for Jo. Martin & Jo. Allestry,* 1663. 8°. L, CS.

181 **Haddock, Thomas.** How all the inhabitants of London . . . may be furnish'd with coles. colop: [*n.p.*], *for Thomas Haddock,* 1690. brs. Y.

     [**Haddon, Walter.**] Reformatio legum. 1641. *See Cranmer, Thomas.*

182 [**Hadfred, John.**] A wonderfull and strange miracle or Gods just vengeance. *For Henry Hvtton,* 1642. 4°.* LT; MH.

     Haec and hic: or, the feminine gender. 1683. *See Norris, James.*

183 [**Haeften, Benedict von.**] Schola cordis or the heart of it selfe. *For H. Blunden,* 1647. 12°. L; NN.

184 [–] The school of the heart. *For Lodowick Lloyd,* 1664. 12°. L; WF.

184A [–] —[Anr. ed.] *For L. Ll., to be sould by Samuel Snignel,* 1674. 12°. WF.

185 [–] —Third edition. *For Lodowick Lloyd,* 1675. 12°. T.C.I 165. L, C; CH.

185A [–] —"Third" edition. —, 1676. 12°. CH, CLC, IU, NCD, WCL.

     Haemmerlein, Thomas. *See Thomas à Kempis.*

186 **Haggar, Henry.** The foundation of the font. *For Giles Calvert,* 1653. 4°. LT, MAB, MC; NHC.

187 —No king but Jesus. *For Giles Calvert,* 1652. 4°. CD; NU, WF.

188 —The order of causes. *By James Cottrel, for Richard Moone.* 1654. 4°.* LT, O, C, LCL, GU.

188A — —Third edition. —, 1655. 4°.* CS.

189 — —Fourth edition. —, 1655. 4°.* LT, O; TO.

190 — —Fifth edition. *For Francis Smith,* 1659. 4°.* LT, O; NU, Y.

     — —"Fifth" edition. 1691. *See Grantham, Thomas.* Dialogue.

190A Hagnelion jechidatho . . . or, eye-salve. *Printed,* 1696. 4°.* LW.

191 **Hailes, John.** A word of advice. *By T. Sowle,* 1693. brs. LF.

192 **H[aines], J[oseph].** The epilogue to Mr Lacy's new play, Sir Hercules Buffoon. colop: *For Joseph Hindmarsh,* 1684. brs. L, O, CT; CLC.

193 —A fatal mistake. *By T. H., sold by Randal Taylor,* 1692. 4°. L, EN; MH, Y.

194 —The fatal mistake. *For Sam. Briscoe, sold by Eliz. Whitlock,* 1696. 4°. L, O, OW, ES; CH, CN, NC, TU, WF.

195 [–] Prologue to the Northern lass. colop: [*London*], *for C. Corbet,* 1684. brs. L, O, LLP, MC; CH, CLC, CN, MH, NP.

     —Mr Haynes his recantation. 1689. *See Brown, Thomas.*

196 —Haynes his Reformation prologue. colop: *For R. Bentley,* 1692. brs. CN, IU, MH.

197 —A satyr against brandy. colop: [*London*], *for Jos. Hindmarsh,* 1683. brs. L, O, LLP, HH, MC; CH, MBP, MH, TU, WF, Y.

197A [–] —[Anr. ed.] colop: *For P. W.,* 1689. brs. MH, Y.

198 **Haines, Richard.** Aphorisms upon the new way of improving cyder. *By George Larkin, for the author,* 1684. fol.* L, O, MR, EN; CLC, IU, NC, WF, Y.

199 —Haines his appeal to the General Assembly of dependent Baptists. [*London?* 1680.] fol. L.

200 —A breviat of some proposals. *For Langley Curtis,* 1679. 4°.* L, LUG, OC, CT, MP; CH, IU, LC, MH, NC, PU, WF, Y.

200A —England's weal. [*London*], 1680. 4°. L, O, MP; IU.

201 — —[Anr. ed.] *For Langley Curtis,* 1681. 4°.* T.C.I 422. L, O, LCL, CS, MP; CH, IU, LC, MH, NC, WF, Y.

201AA —A method of government. *For Langley Curtis,* 1670. 4°.* O, LCL, LPR.

201A — —[Anr. ed.] *For Langley Curtis,* 1679. 4°.* L, LUG, CS, MP; CH, CN, MH, WF, Y.

202 —A model of government. *For D. M.,* 1678. 4°.* L, LNC, MP; CH, IU, NC, PL, WF, Y.

202A — —[Anr. ed.] 1681. 4°.* NC.

202B —New lords, new laws. *Printed* 1674. 4°. O, OC.

203   [–] The prevention of poverty. *For Nathaniel Brooke*, 1674. 4°.* T.C.I 188. L, O, C, EN, DT; CH, IU, LC, MH, NC, WF, Y.

204   [–] —[Anr. ed.] *For H. H.*, 1677. 4°.* LUG; NC, WF.

204A [–] A profitable method . . . linnen manufacture. colop: *For D. M.*, 1679. fol.* MR; MH, PU, AMB.

205   [–] Proposals for building in every county a working-alms-house. *By W. G. for R. Harford*, 1677. 4°.* T.C.I 302. L, LUG, CS, LLU, DT; CH, CN, MH, WF, Y.

205A —The proposals for promoting the woollen manufactory. 1679. 4°. L.

206   [–] Provision for the poor. *For D. M.*, 1678. 4°.* L, O, LVF, MP; MH.

206A —A supplement to the treatise entituled Aphorisms. *By Tho. James for the author*, 1684. brs. LG.

207   The hainousness of injustice. 1698. 4°. O.

Hains, Joseph. *See* Haines, Joseph.

208   **Hakewill, George.** A dissertation with Dr. Heylyn. *By J. R. for George Thomason, and Octavian Pullen*, 1641. 4°. LT, O, C, EN, DT; CLC, IU, MH, NU, WF.

209   —A short, but cleare, discovrse. *By Iohn Raworth, for George Thomason and Octavian Pullen*, 1641. 4°.* LT, O, CT, E, DT; CH, NU, WF, WSC, Y.

    [Hakewill, William.] Learned and necessary argument. 1641. *See* Whitelocke, *Sir* James.

210   —The libertie of the subject. *By R. H.* 1641. 4°. LT, O, C, YM, DT; BN, CH, CN, LC, MBP, MHL, NC, WF, Y.

211   —The manner how statvtes are enacted. *By T. H. for Iohn Benson*, 1641. 12°. L, C, DU; CLC, IU, MHL, MIU, NC, WF.

212–3 Entries cancelled.

    —[Anr. ed.] 1659. *See* —Modus tenendi.

214   [–] The manner of holding Parliaments in England. *[London], printed*, 1641. 4°. LT, O, C, MR, DT; CH, IU, LC, MHL, NCL, WF, Y.

215   —Modus tenendi Parliamentum: or, the old manner. *By J. G., to be sold by Abel Roper*, 1659. 12°. LT, O, SC; BN, CH, MHL, MU, PBM, V, AVP.

215A ——[Anr. ed.] *For Iohn Benson*, 1659. 12°. LGI, LL, SC; CLC, CN, IU, MH, MU, V.

216   ——[Anr. ed.] *For Abel Roper*, 1660. 8°. L, LL, LIU, RU, SC; BN, CH, CN, MHL, WF, Y.

217   ——[Anr. ed.] —, 1671. 12°. T.C.I 69. L, O, C, E, EN; BN, CH, CN, LC, MHL, Y.

218   [–] The order and course of passing bills in Parliament. *[London], for I. Benson*, 1641. 4°. LT, O, C, MR, DT; CSS, IU, MHL, NCL, WF, Y.

219   **[Hale, Charles.]** An advertisement shewing that all former objections. colop: *Printed May*, 1696. cap., fol.* L, EN; Y.

220   [–] The antelope's evidence. Third edition. colop: *Printed 16 May*, 1698. cap., fol.* L.

220A [–] Mill'd lead sheathing for ships. colop: *Printed February*, 1695/6. cap., fol.* WF, Y.

221   [–] A proposition demonstrated that mill'd-lead is a better covering. *Printed March 26th*, 1694. brs. L; Y.

222   [–] A second advertisement relating to the mill'd-lead-sheathing. *Printed April 5*, 1700. brs. L.

223   — Short accompt of the first motives. [*London*, 1700?] brs. L, EN.

224   **[Hale, *Sir* Matthew.]** A collection of modern relations . . . concerning witches. Part I. *For John Harris*, 1693. T.C.II 456. L, O, C, E, GU; CLC, CN, LC, MH, NN, Y.

225   [–] Contemplations moral and divine. *By William Godbid, for William Shrowsbury, and John Leigh*, 1676. 8°. T.C.I 233. L, O, C, E, DT; BN, CLC, CN, NU, WF, Y. (var.)

225A [–] —[Anr. ed.] —, 1677. 8°. L, LLP, OH, LNC, LSD; CDA, CH, CLC, CU, IU, NP.

226   ——[Anr. ed.] *For William Shrowsbury, and John Leigh*, 1679. 2 pts. 8°. T.C.I 346. I, O, LL, CK, EN; BN, CLC, MIU, PL, TU, WF, Y.

227   ——[Anr. ed.] *For William Shrowsberey, and J. Leigh, sold by J. Phillips and H. Rodes*, 1682. 2 pts. 8°. T.C.I 488. L, LLP, OM, CT, RU; CLC, CU, IU, PU, Y.

227A ——[Anr. ed.] *For William Shrowsbury, and John Leigh*, 1682. 8°. L (t.p.); NU, WCL.

228   ——[Anr. ed.] *For William Shrowsbery, and John Leigh*, 1685. 2 pts. 8°. L, O, C, KEBLE, BLH; BBE, MU, NU, TU, WF.

228A ——[Anr. ed.] *For W. Shrowbury and S. Leigh*, 1688. 8°. CLC, CN, MIU, NU.

229   ——[Anr. ed.] *For W. Shrowsbery, and S. Leigh, to be sold by J. Phillips, and H. Rodes*, 1689. 2 pts. 8°. T.C.II 281. L, O, C, LIU, DT; CH, CSB, NCD, NCU, TO, TU.

230   ——[Anr. ed.] *For William Shrowsbery; and Charles Harper*, 1695. 2 pts. 8°. T.C.II 562. L, BC, LNC; CLC, IU, MH, PL, WF, Y.

230A ——[Anr. ed.] *For William Shrowsbury, sold by Richard Wellington*, 1696. 8°. L, EN.

231   ——[Anr. ed.] *For William Shrowsbury; Dan. Midwinter and Tho. Leigh*, 1699. 8°. T.C.III 165. L, O; CLC, IU, NP, NU, PPT, TU.

231A [–] —[Anr. ed.] *For W. Shrowsbury*, 1700. 8°. KEBLE, AN, BANGOR; CN, TO, AUSTRALIAN NATIONAL U.

232   [–] —Second part. *For William Shrowsbury, and John Leigh*, 1676. 8°. L, O, LCL, OC, NPL, DT; CLC, CN, SW, Y. (var.)

232A [–] ——[Anr. ed.] —, 1677. 8°. T.C.I 233. O, C, LL, LIU, E; BN, CLC, MIU, Y.

232B [–] ——[Anr. ed.] —, 1679. 8°. MM.

232C ——[Anr. ed.] —, 1682. 8°. CT.

233   ——[Anr. ed.] —, 1685. 8°. L, BR; MM, NU, WF.

234   ——[Anr. ed.] *For William Shrewsbury and Susanah Leigh*, 1688. 8°. L, C; CH, CSB, NCD, TU.

235   ——Third part. *For William Shrowsbury and are to be sold by R. Wellington*, 1696. 8°. L, DC, NPL, CD; CH, CN, CSB, IU, MH, TU, Y.

235A ———Second edition. *For William Shrowsbury*, 1700. 8°. KEBLE, LIU; CLC, CN, MIU, NU, TO, WF.

236   [–] De successionibus apud Anglos; or a treatise. *Printed and are to be sold by A. Baldwin*, 1699. 8°. L, C, LGI, DU, EN; CH, IU, MU, TU, Y.

236A ——[Anr. ed.] *By R. Battersby*, 1700. 8°. L, O, LLP, MAU; CH, CU, TO, WF, YL.

237   ——[Anr. ed.] *For S. S.*, 1700. 8°. LL, DC, EN, GK; CU, MHL.

238   [–] Difficiles nugæ, or. *By W. Godbid for William Shrows-bury*, 1674. 8°. T.C.I 171. L, OC, C, E, DT; BN, CH, CLC, MH, MM.

239   [–] —Second edition. —, 1675. 8°. L, O, C, LL, DC; CLC, LC, MB, MH, WF, Y.

240   —A discourse of the knowledge of God. *By B. W. for William Shrowsbery*, 1688. 8°. L, O, C, MR, DT; CH, CU, MU, NU, WF, Y.

240A ——[Anr. ed.] *For William Shrowsbury, and are to be sold by Richard Chiswell*, 1688. 8°. CT; IU.

241   —A discourse touching provision for the poor. *By H. Hills for John Leigh*, 1683. 12°. L, O, C, CT, GU; BN, CH, MH, NC, PL, WF, Y.

242   ——[Anr. ed.] *For William Shrowsbery*, 1683. 8°.* L, O, LUG, OC, DU; CLC, CU, IU, NAM, PL, WF.

243   ——[Anr. ed.] *For Mat. Gillyflower; and Tim Goodwin*, 1695. 12°. L, LUG, OB, CS, SHR; CLC, MH, NCD, WF.

244   [–] An essay touching the gravitation. *By W. Godbid, for William Shrewsbury*, 1673. 8°. T.C.I 154. L, O, C, LNC, DM; MH, NN, WU, Y.

245   [–] —Second edition. —, 1675. 8°. L, O, CS, LLU, DT; CH, CLC, WSG, HC.

246   —The father's New-Yeare-gift. *For W. Booker*, 1685. 12°. MH.

247   —The judgment of the late . . . Sir Matthew Hale. *For B. Simmons*, 1684. 4°. T.C.II 38. L, O, C, EN, DT; CLC, CU, MH, NU, WF, Y.

      [–] Jura coronæ. 1680. *See* Brydall, John.

247A —A letter from. *By J. Playford for W. Shrowsbery*, 1684. 4°.* LC, NC.

248-9 Entries cancelled.

      [–] London's liberties. 1651. *See* title.

250   —Magnetismus magnus: or. *For William Shrowsbury*, 1695. 8°. L, O, C, E, DT; CH, IU, MH, PU, WF, HC.

251   Entry cancelled. Ghost.

252   [–] Observations touching the principles of natural motions. *By W. Godbid, for W. Shrowsbery*, 1677. 8°. T.C.I 267. L, O, C, E, DT; CH, MU, PL, WF, Y.

253   [–] Pleas of the crown. *For Richard Tonson, and Jacob Tonson*, 1678. 4°. T.C.I 303. L, CT; CN, LC, MH, WF, YL.

254   ——[Anr. ed.] *By the assigns of Richard Atkyns and Edward Atkyns, for William Shrewsbury, and John Leigh*, 1678. 8°. T.C.I 312. L, O, LGI, CT, DC; CH.

255   ——[Anr. ed.] *By the assigns of Richard Atkyns and Edward Atkyns, for William Shrewsbury, and John Leigh; to be sold by Robert Clavel*, 1682. 8°. T.C.I 467. L, O, C, LLP, EN; CLC, LC, MHL, MIU, NCL.

255A ——[Anr. ed.] *By the assigns of Richard Atkyns and Edward Atkyns, for William Shrewsbury, and John Leigh*, 1682. 8°. TU, WF.

256   ——[Anr. ed.] *By the assigns of Richard Atkins and Edward Atkins; for William Shrewsbury, and John Leigh*, 1685. 8°. T.C.II 119. L, O, C, LMT, OC, AN; IU, MHL, MIU, NCL, PUL.

256A ——[Anr. ed.] *By the assigns of Rich. Atkins and Edw. Atkins, for W. S. and J. L. to be sold by J. Walthoe*, 1685. 8°. WCA.

257   ——[Anr. ed.] *By the assigns of Richard and Edward Atkyns, for W. Shrewsbury*, 1694. 8°. L, O, C, AU, DT; CLC, LC, MHL, TU, YL.

258   —The primitive origination of mankind. *By William Godbid, for William Shrowsbery*, 1677. fol. T.C.I 271. L, O, C, EN, DT; BN, CH, IU, LC, MH, NP, TU, WSC, Y.

259   —Several tracts. *By J. P. for W. Shrowsbery:* 1684. 8°. T.C.II 75. L, O, C, ENC, DT; CH, CN, LC, MHL, NU, WF, Y.

260   —A short treatise touching sheriffs accompts. *Printed, and are to be sold by Will. Shrowsbery*, 1683. 8°. T.C.I 507. L, O, C, DU, GU; CH, CN, LC, MH, Y.

260A —Some necessary and important considerations. Sixth edition. *By John How*, 1697. *And are freely given away by J. P[ennyman]*. 8°.* SP.

260B ——Ninth edition. *By John How*, 1697. *And are freely given away by J. P.* 8°.* OC, CT.

261   ——Tenth edition. *Printed* 1697. *And are freely given away by me . . . John Pennyman*. 8°.* L, O, LL, OB, M; VC.

262   — —Second edition. *By John How*, [1700?]. 8°.* L; WF.

263   [–] A treatise, shewing how usefull, . . . the inrolling . . . of all conveyances of lands. *For Mat. Wotton*, 1694. 4°.* L, O, C, LUG, LSD; CH, MH, NC, WF.

264   [–] —Second edition. —, 1695. 4°.* L, LUG; NC, Y.

265   **H[ale], T[homas].** An account of several new inventions. *For James Astwood, and sold by Ralph Simpson*, 1691. 12°. L, O, LG, LUG, LIU, EN; BN, CH, CJC, MH, LC, WCL, WF, Y.

265A [–] A detection of the shipwrights. 1699. brs. EN.

265B [–] Mill'd lead demonstrated to be a better . . . covering. colop: *Printed November 20*, 1693. fol.* C, LUG.

266   —Mr. Hale's reflections upon a paper lately . . . printed and published by John Fincher. *Printed August* 1699. brs. Y.

266A —That the bringing on boards above. [*London*], 1697. brs. EN.

266B **Hales, Edward,** *University College, Oxford.* A speech spoken by. colop: *For A. M.*, 1687. brs. L, O, OC; CN, WF, Y.

267   **Hales, Sir Edward.** Two speeches spoken in Parliament, . . . twentieth day of Januarie, 1641. *For F. C. and T. B.*, 1641. 4°.* LT, O, C, LVF, AN; CH, CN, IU, MH, WF, Y.

      [Hales, John.] Ἀυτομαχια: or. 1643. *See* Du Moulin, Louis.

      [–] Brevis disquisitio. 1653. *See* Biddle, John.

268   [–] Disputatio de pace, &c.; or, a discourse. 1653. 8°. O, BAMB; CH.

268A —Four tracts. 1677. 8°. L, LLP.

269   —Golden remains. *For Tim: Garthwait*, 1659. 4°. LT, O, C, AN, AU, DT; BN, CH, CN, MH, NU, WF, Y.

270   ——[Anr. ed.] *For R. Pawlet*, [1659]. 4°. L, EN.

271   ——Second edition. *By Tho. Newcomb, for Robert Pawlet*, 1673. 4°. T.C.I 143. L, O, C, EN, DT; CLC, CU, MH, NP, NU, WF, Y.

272   ——Third edition. *By T. B. for George Pawlet*, 1688. 8°. L, O, CM, SHR, EN; CLC, MH, MU, NR, TU, WF, Y.

273   [–] Of the blasphemie against the Holy-ghost. [*London*], *printed*, 1646. 4°.* LT, OC, MR, EN, DT; CH.

274 —Sermons preach'd at Eton. *By J. G. for Richard Marriot,* 1660. fol. L, C, LI, LW, EC; PL, WF.

275 ——Second edition. *By T. Newcomb, for Richard Marriot,* 1673. 4°. T.C.I 137. L, O, C, EN, CD; CB, CH, CLC, MIU, NGT, TO.

276 —Several tracts. *For John Blyth,* 1677. 8°. L, LCL, LW, SHR, DT; BN, CLC, CN, LC, MU, WF, Y.

276A ——[Anr. ed.] *Printed* 1677. 8°. O, CK, CT, DU, NE; CLC, NCU, WF.

277 [–] A tract concerning schisme. *For R. B.* 1642. 4°.* L, O, C, EN, DT; CH, CLC, CN, MB, NU, TU, WF, Y.

278 [–] —[Anr. ed.] *Oxford, by Leonard Lichfield for Edward Forrest,* 1642. 4°.* MADAN 1287. LT, O, C, LIU, DT; CH, OCI, WF.

279 ——[Anr. ed.] *Printed,* 1700. 4°.* L, O, C, MR, EN; CH, CN, NN, Y.

280 —A tract concerning the sin against the Holy Ghost. *For John Blyth, at Mr. Playfords shop,* 1677. 8°. L, O, C, DL, DT; CH, IU, LC, NU, TU, WF.

281 [–] The vvay tovvards the finding of a decision of the chiefe controversie. *Printed,* 1641. 4°.* LT, O, C, OME, DT; CLC, MH, NU, WF, Y.

282 **Halesiados.** A message from the Normans. [*London*], *printed,* 1648. 4°.* L, O; CLC.

283 **H[alfpenny], J[ohn].** The gentleman's jocky. *For Hen. Twyford and Nath. Brook,* 1671. 8°. T.C.I 88. L, LCS, R; CH, Y.

283A [–] —Second edition. —, 1672. 8°. L, CT; Y.

283B [–] —Third edition. —, 1674. 8°. L, O; WF, Y.

283C [–] —Fourth edition. —, 1676. 8°. T.C.I 240. O, C; CLC, WSG, Y.

283D [–] —Fifth edition. *For Hen. Twyford, Obadiah Blagrave, R. Harford; to be sold by William Rogers,* 1679. 8°. T.C.I 354. L, CS, MR; Y.

283E [–] —Sixth edition. *For H. Twyford, O. Blagrave, R. Harford and are to be sold by William Rogers,* 1681. 8°. T.C.I 447. L; Y.

283F [–] —Seventh edition. *For Marcy Browning,* 1681. 12°. CT; CLC.

283G [–] —"Seventh" edition. *For H. Twyford, and O. Blagrave, and are to be sold by W. Rogers,* 1683. 8°. T.C.II 8. LWL; MH, WF, Y.

283H [–] —Eighth edition. *For H. T. and O. B. and sold by Timothy Goodwin,* 1687. 8°. T.C.II 189. L; CSU, Y.

284 **Halhead, Henry.** Inclosure thrown open. *By Ja. Cottrel, for Giles Calvert,* 1650. 4°.* LT, O, C, MR, DT.

285 **Halhead, Myles.** A book of some of the sufferings. [*London*], *printed and sold by A. Sowle,* 1690. 4°.* LF, BBN; CH, IE, MH, NU, PH, Y.

286 **Haliburton, Th.** Disputatio juridica, de sepulchro violato. *Edinburgh, by the heirs of A. Anderson,* 1698. 4°. ALDIS 3754. EN.

287 **[Halifax, Charles Montagu],** *earl of.* An epistle to the right honourable Charles Earl of Dorset. *For Francis Saunders,* 1690. fol.* T.C.II 336. L, O, CS, LLU, AU, DN; CH, CU, MH, TU, WF, Y.

288 [–] —Second edition. —, 1690. fol.* L, OC, LIU, GK; CLC, CN, MH, TU, WF, Y.

288A —Epistola nobilissimi Caroli Mountague. *Typis Jacobi Doveri,* 1696. 4°.* CN, MH.

288B [–] The man of honour. [*London,* 1689.] cap., 4°.* L, OC, CT, LLU, EN; CH, CLC, MH, MIU, PSC, WF, Y.

289 Entry cancelled.

[Halifax, George Savile], *marquis of.* Address to both houses. 1681. *See* [–] Seasonable address.

290 [–] Advice to a daughter. Sixth edition. [*London*], *for M. Gillyflower and B. Tooke,* 1699. 12°. L, LIU; WF.

291 [–] The anatomy of an equivalent. [*London,* 1688.] cap., 4°.* L, O, C, MR, EN, DT; CH, CN, IU, LC, NU, WF, Y.

292–5 Entries cancelled.

[–] Answer to the letter to a Dissenter. 1687. *See title.*

[–] Character of a trimmer. 1682. *See title.*

296 [–] The character of a trimmer. His opinion. *Printed* 1688. 4°.* L, O, C, MR, EN; CLC, CN, MH, TU, WF, Y.

297 [–] —Second edition. *For Richard Baldwin,* 1689. 4°.* L, O, C, EN, DT; CH, CU, MH, NU, WF, Y.

298 [–] —Third edition. —, 1689. 4°.* L, OC, BC, DUS, MR; CLC, CN, IU, WF, Y.

299 [–] —[Anr. ed.] *Printed,* 1689. 4°.* L, O, MR; CH, WF, Y.

300 [–] —"Third" edition. *For Rich. Baldwin,* 1697. 4°. L; CLC, NU.

301 [–] The character of the Protestants of Ireland. *For Dorman Newman,* 1689. 4°.* T.C.II 291. L, C, LUG, SP, DT; CH, MH, MIU, NU, WF, Y.

302 —Conseil d'un homme de qualité. *M. Gillyflower,* 1697. 8°. BN.

303 Entry cancelled.

[–] Essays, and maxims. 1698. *See* Quarles, Francis. Institutions, essays.

303A [–] Etrennes ou conseils. *Chez Jaques Partridge & Matieu Gilliflower,* 1692. 8°. L, M; MHS, Y.

[–] Following maxims. [n.p.], 1693. *See* Almanzor.

[–] Historical observations. 1689. *See* Howard, *Sir Robert.*

[–] Institutions, essays. 1695. *See* Quarles, Francis.

304 [–] The lady's New-Years gift. *Printed, and are to be sold by Randal Taylor,* 1688. 12°. T.C.II 219. L, O, OC, OCC, CS; CN, MH, WF, Y.

305 [–] —Second edition. *For Matt. Gillyflower, and James Partridge,* 1688. 12°. L, O; CH, CLC, CN, MIU, NP, PT.

305A [–] —Third edition. —, 1688. 12°. L, O, C, OC, M; CLC, MB, PU, WF, Y.

306 [–] —"Third" edition. *Edinburgh, by John Reid, for James Glen, and Walter Cunningham,* 1688. 8°. T.C.II 235. ALDIS 2765.7. L, EN.

306A [–] —Fourth edition. *For Matth. Gilliflower and James Partridge,* 1692. 8°. LIU, M; Y.

306B [–] —"Fourth" edition. *For M. G. and J. P., to be sold by Thomas Chapman,* 1692. 12°. MH.

307 [–] —Fifth edition. *For M. Gillyflower, to be sold by Francis Wright,* 1696. 12°. L.

307A [–] —Sixth edition. *Dublin, by J. B. & S. P. for Jacob Milner, and Thomas Shepherd,* 1699. 12°. L, DT.

307B [–] —"Sixth" edition. *By W. H. for M. Gillyflower,* 1699. 8°. CLC.

308–8A Entries cancelled.
[–] Letter from a clergy-man. [n.p., 1688.] *See* Sherlock, William.

309 [–] A letter from a nobleman in London. [*London?* 1689/90.] 4°.* LL, MR; BN, MH, TU.

310 [–] A letter of friendly admonition. [*London*], printed, 1647. 4°. L, O, CCO, P, DT; CH, CLC, IU, MH, TU.

311 [–] A letter to a Dissenter. [*London*, 1687.] cap., 4°.* 7 pp. L, O, C, MC, AU, DT; CH, CN, MH, NU, WF, Y.

312 [–] —[Anr. ed.] *For G. H.*, 1687. 4°.* 10 pp. L, O, C, MR, EN; CH, CN, MH, NU, WF, Y.

313 [–] —[Anr. ed.] —, 1687. 4°.* 17 pp. L, O, LIU, WCA; CH, CN, MH, NU, WF.

314 [–] Lettre écrite à un nonconformiste. *A Londres, pour G. H.*, 1687. 12°. O, C, LLU; UCLA.

315 —Miscellanies by. *For Matt. Gillyflower*, 1700. 8°. T.C.III 174. L, O, C, DC, EN; BN, CH, CN, TU, WF, Y. (var.)

316 [–] Observations upon a late libel, called A letter from a person of quality. colop: [*London*], *for C. M.*, 1681. cap., fol.* L, O, LG, CT, DM; CH, CU, MH, WF, Y, AVP.

317 [–] —[Anr. ed.] colop: [*London*], *for C. Mason*, 1681. fol.* CK; CH, MH, MH.

317A [–] —[Anr. ed.] *Printed* 1681. 8°.* OC.

317B [–] —[Anr. ed.] [*Dublin*, 1681.] cap., 4°.* DIX 181, O, DI, DU.

318 Entry cancelled.
[–] Remarkes upon a pamphlet. [n.p., 1687.] *See* W., T.

319 [–] A rough draught of a new model at sea. *For A. Banks*, 1694. 4°.* L, O, C, CT, LSD, DT; CN, MH, NN, WF, Y.

320 [–] A seasonable address to both Houses of Parliament concerning the succession. *Printed*, 1681. 4°.* L, O, C, LSD, EN, DT; CH, CN, MH, NU, WF, Y. (var.)

320A [–] —[Anr. ed.] *Edinburgh, re-printed*, 1681. 4°.* ALDIS 2306. L, EN, GU.

321 Entry cancelled.
[–] Second letter to a Dissenter. 1687. *See* Lobb, Stephen.

322 [–] Some cautions offered to the consideration of those who are to chuse members. *Printed*, 1695. 4°.* L, O, C, MR, EN, DT; CH, CN, MH, NU, WF, Y.

323 Halifax law translated to Oxon. [*London*], *printed*, 1648. 4°.* MADAN 1985. LT, O; IU, MIU, WF, Y.

324 **Hall, Anne.** A brief representation and discovery. *By J. L. for Philemon Stephens*, 1649. 4°.* LT, O.

325 **H[all], E[dmund].** Ἡ αποστασια ο αντιχριστος: or, a Scriptural discourse. [*London*], *printed*, 1653. 4°. LT, O, E, DT; CLC, CN, MH, NU, WF.

326 [–] Lazarus's sores licked. *Printed at London*, 1650. 4°.* LT, LSC, LW, LIU, DT; CH, NU, Y.

327 [–] Lingva testivm. [*London*], 1651. 4°. LT, O, CT; CH, CN, MH, NU, WF, Y.

328 [–] Manus testium movens: or. [*London*], *printed*, 1651. 4°. LT, O, LW, CS; MH, NU, WF.

329 [–] A sermon preached at Stanton-Harcourt Church. *Oxford, by A. & L. Lichfield*, 1664. 8°. MADAN 2661. O, OE.

330 No entry.
[–] A true copy of a petition. 1657. *See* H., E.

331 **Hall, Francis.** An appendix to Clavis horologiæ. *Printed at Liege, by Guillaume Street*, 1673. *Reprinted at London*, 1685. 4°. L, C; CH, CN, MB, MH, NC.

332 —An explication of the diall. *Liege, by Guillaume Henry Streel*, 1673. 4°. L, O, C, LG, MR, E; CLC, CN, MH, WF.

333 —A sharp but short noise of warr. *By Matthew Simmons*, 1650. 4°.* LT, DT.

334 —Tractatus de corporum inseparabilitate. *Typis Thomæ Roycroft, impensis Joan. Martin, Ja. Allestry & Tho. Dicas* 1661. 8°. L, O, LCP, CCA, E; CH, IU, MH, WF, HC. (var.)

335 **Hall, George, bp.** A fast-sermon, preached . . . Octob. 3. 1666. *For Timothy Garthwait*, 1666. 4°.* L, O, C, DC, DT; CH, CLC, IU, MIU, WF, WSG, Y.

336 —Gods appearing for the tribe of Levi. *By Tho: Roycroft, for Philemon Stephens*, 1655. 4°.* LT, O, C, LVF, MR; CH, IU, MH, NU, WF, Y.

337 [–] The triumphs of Rome. *Printed*, 1655. 4°. L, O, C, CT, DC, SP, SA; IU, MH, TSM.

338 [–] —[Anr. ed.] *For Henry Mortlack and James Collins*, 1667. 8°. L, O, LIL, CT, DU; CH, IU, RPJ, WF, Y.

339 —Two sermons. *By J. O. for Anth. Hall*, 1641. 4°.* L, O, C; IU, MH.

339A **[Hall, Henry.]** Digitus testium, or a dreadful alarm. *Printed* 1650. 4°.* LT, O, C; CH, MH, NU, NC, Y.

340 **Hall, Henry.** Heaven ravished. [*London*], *by J. Raworth, for Samuel Gellibrand*, 1644. 4°. LT, O, C, EN, DT; CH, IU, MH, TU, WF, Y.

341 Entry cancelled.
Hall, J. Gagg. 1651. *See* Hinde, John.

342 No entry.

343 **[Hall, John], poet.** An answer to some queries propos'd by W. C. *Oxford, by Leon. Lichfield, for John Buckeridge in Marlebrough*, 1694. 4°.* O, C, LUG; IU, WF.

343A [–] Confusion confounded. *By Henry Hills*, 1654. 4°.* LT, O, C, OC, CT; CH, CU, MH, NU, WF, Y.

344 [–] Emblems. [*Cambridge*], *By R. Daniel*, 1658 [second title dated 1648]. 8°. L.

344A — —[Anr. ed.] —, [1658]. 8°. CH, MH.
[–] A gagg to love's advocate. *See* Hinde, John.

345 Entry cancelled.
[–] Grace leading. 1651. *See* Hall, John, *divine*.

346 [–] The grounds & reasons of monarchy considered. [n.p.], *corrected and reprinted according to the Edenburgh copy*, 1650. 12°. L, O, C, NPL; CN, CSS, CU, NU.

347 [–] —[Anr. ed.] *Edinburgh, Evan Tyler*, 1651. 4°. ALDIS 1445. LVF, AU, EN; MM, WF, Y.

348 [–] —[Anr. ed.] [*London*], *corrected and reprinted according to the Edenburgh copy*, 1651. 12°. C, LGI; CH, CU.

349 —Horæ vacivæ, or, essays. *By E. G. for J. Rothwell*, 1646. 12°. LT, O, CS, EC, YM; CH, CN, LC, MH, WF, Y.

350 [–] An humble motion to the Parliament. *For John Walker*, 1649. 4°.* MADAN 2023. L, O, C, LUG, DT; CLC, CU, MH, NU, Y.

351 Entry cancelled.
—Jacob's ladder. 1672. *See* Hall, Joseph, *bp*.

352   [–] A letter written to a gentleman in the country, touch-
       ing the dissolvtion. *By F. Leach, for Richard Baddeley,*
       1653. 4°.* LT, AN, BC, MR, E, DT; CH, CLC, CN, NU, TU,
       WF, Y.

353   —Paradoxes. *For John Walker,* 1650. 12°. L; CLC.

354   [–] —[Anr. ed.]. *For Francis Eaglesfield,* 1653. 12°. LT, MR;
       CN, IU, MH.

355   —Poems. *Cambridge, by Roger Daniel,* 1646. *For J. Roth-
       well* [*London*]. LT, O, C, CT, DU, EN; CH, IU, LC, MH, WC, Y.

355A   — —[Anr. ed.] *For Francis Eaglesfield,* 1656. 12°. O.

355B   [–] A true account and character of the times. [*London,*
       1647.] cap., 4°.* LT, O, OC, DU, DT; CH, MH.

355C   **H[all], J[ohn],** *divine.* Grace leading unto glory. *By B.
       Alsop,* 1651. 8°. L.

356   **Hall, John,** *physician.* Select observations on English
       bodies. *For John Sherley,* 1657. 12°. L, O, LCS, CT, BC; CH,
       MH, NN, WF, Y, HC.

357   — —Second edition. *By J. D. for Benjamin Shirley,* 1679.
       8°. T.C.I 363. L, C, OR, CT; CH, MB, MH, PU, WF, HC.

358   — —[Anr. ed.] *For William Marshall,* 1683. 8°. T.C.I 514.
       L, O, LWL, E; CH, MMO, NRU, WSG, AVP.

359   — —[Anr. ed.] *By H. H. and are to be sold by Samuel
       Eddowes,* 1683. 8°. LCS, LWL; CH.

359A   **Hall, John,** *of Gray's Inn.* A serious epistle to Mr. W.
       Prynne. *For John Place,* 1649. 4°.* O, CCA; CSS.

359B   [–] —[Anr. ed.] *Printed,* 1649. 4°.* LT, O, CT, BC; CH, CN,
       CSS, MH, NU, WF, Y.

360   **Hall, John,** *of Richmond.* Of government and obedience.
       *By T. Newcomb, for J. Kirton, A. Roper, G. Bedell, and
       G. Sawbridge,* 1654. fol. L, O, C, CT, EN; BBE, CH, CN, NU,
       WF, Y.

361   [–] The true Cavalier examined. *By Tho. Newcomb,* 1656.
       4°. LT, O, LCL, CT, DT; MIU, NU, WF, Y.

361A   **Hall, John,** *fl.* 1695. The case of. [*London,* 1695.] brs. Y.

361B   **Hall, Joseph,** *bp.* The works of. *By Miles Flesher,* 1647.
       fol. C, CK, LSD, CD; BN, NCU.

362   — —[Anr. ed.] *By M. Flesher, and are to be sold by Andr:
       Crooke,* 1647. fol. L, O, CE, NPL, DT; CH, CU, MH, NF, AVP.

362AA — —[Anr. ed.] *By M. Flesher for Ch. Meredith,* 1647. fol.
       CPE, LLU.

362BA — —[Anr. ed.] *By M. Flesher for Ed. Brewster,* 1647. fol. O;
       IU.

362A   — —[Anr. ed.] *By M. Flesher, and are to be sold by Rich.
       Tomlins,* 1648. fol. L, LG, BC; IU, NCD, SW, WF.

363   Entry cancelled.
       —Answer to the tedious vindication. 1641. *See* —Short
       answer.

364   —An apologeticall letter to a person of qvality. *For N. B.,*
       1655. 4°.* LT, O, DU, P; MH.

365   —The balme of Gilead. *By M. Flesher, for Nat: Butter,*
       1646. 12°. L, C; CH, CU, IU, NCU, NU, Y.

366   — —[Anr. ed.] *By Thomas Newcomb; to be sold by John
       Holden,* 1650. 12°. L, O, C, NOT; CH, CLC, IU, MH, WF, Y.

367   — —[Anr. ed.] *By Will: Hunt,* 1652. 12°. O, LIU, AN; CN,
       IU, MBJ, MH.

368   — —[Anr. ed.] *For Will. Hope,* 1655. 12°. L, C; CH, IU.

369   — —[Anr. ed.] *By William Hunt,* 1660. 12°. L, NPL, BLH;
       IU, MH, NPT.

370   [–] The breathings of the devout soul. *Printed,* 1648. 12ᵛ.
       L, O, NPL; CH, IU.

371   —Cases of conscience. Third edition. *By R. H. and J. G.,
       to be sold by Fr. Eglesfield,* 1654. 12°. L, O, CS, P, EN;
       FU, MH, MIU, WF, Y.

372   —Characters of vertue and vice. *For Francis Saunders,*
       1691. 4°.* T.C.II 370. L, O, C, DU, DT; CH, CN, MH, TU,
       WF, Y.

372A   —Χειροθεσια: or a confirmation. *For John Place,* 1651. CS
       IU.

373   [–]Χειροθεσια. Or, the apostolique institvtion. *By J. G.
       for Nathanael Butter,* 1649 [i.e. 1659]. 12°. LT, C, LW, CT,
       P; CH, MB, NR, NU, Y.

374   [–] Christ mysticall. *By M. Flesher, and are to be sold by
       William Hope, Gabriel Beadle, and Nathaniel Webbe,*
       1647. 12°. L, P, DT, GK; CH, IU, MH, NU, WF, Y.

375   —The contemplations. The second tome. *By James
       Flesher,* 1661. fol. C, LLP, CK, LNC, MR; IEG, MH, TO.

376   —Contemplations upon the remarkable passages. *By E.
       Flesher, and are to be sold by Jacob Tonson,* 1679. 4°. T.C.I
       347. L, CK, LIU, LSD, YM; CLC, IU, MH, NU, WF, Y.

377   Entry cancelled.
       [–] Decisions of divers practicall cases. 1649. *See* —Resolu-
       tions and decisions.

378   [–] A defence of the humble remonstrance, against the
       frivolous. *For Nathaniel Butter,* 1641. 4°. L, O, C, ENC,
       DT; CH, CN, MH, NU, WF, Y, ZWT. (var.)

379   [–] The devout soul. *By M. Flesher, for Nat: Butter,* 1644.
       12°. LT, NPL; CLC, NU.

380   [–] —[Anr. ed.] *By W. H. to be sold by George Latham,
       junior,* 1650. 12°. L, C; CH, MH, WF.

380A   [–] —[Anr. ed.] *By W. H. and are to be sold by William
       Hope,* 1658. 12°. IU, MIU, NN, Y.

381   —Divers treatises. Third tome. *By R. H. J. G. and W. H.
       Sold by J. Williams, J. Sweeting, Nath. Brook, and J.
       Place,* 1662. fol. L, C, OU, EN, DT; BN, MH, NR, TO, TSM, Y.

382   —Episcopal admonition. *For C. G.,* 1681. brs. L, O; CH,
       MBA, MH, PU, WF, Y.

382A   —Fanatick moderation. *Printed, and sold by A. Moore,*
       [168–?]. L; NR.

383   —The great mysterie of godliness. *For John Place,* 1652.
       12°. LT, C, SC, ENC, BLH; CLC, CN, NU, WF, Y.

384   — —[Anr. ed.] *By E. Cotes, for John Place,* 1659. 12°. L, O,
       E, BQ; CLC, MH, NCU, NU, WF, Y.

385   [–] The holy order: or, fraternity of the mourners in Sion.
       By J. G. for Nath: Brooke, 1654. 12°. LT; IU, MH, WSC.

385AA [–] —[Anr. ed.] *By J. G. for Nath. Brook,* 1660. 12°. Y.

385A   —Holy raptures. *By E. C. for John Sweeting,* 1652. 12°.
       L; MH.

386   — —[Anr. ed.] —, 1653. 12°. L, NPL; NU.

386A   — —[Anr. ed.] —, 1654. 12°. C.

387   —The invisible world. *By E. Cotes, for John Place,* 1659.
       12°. O, C, LW, NPL, BQ; CLC, MH, NS, NU, WF, Y.

387A   —Jacob's ladder. *For Nath. Crouch,* 1672. 12°. T.C.I 109.
       OSA, CS.

387B ——Second edition. *For N. Crouch, 1676. 12°.* T.C.I 240.
L, O, C; CLC, WF.

387C ——Fifth edition. *For Tho. Guy, 1686. 12°.* CT; Y.

387D ——Seventh edition. *By F. Collins for Tho. Guy, 1690.*
12°. BR.

387E ——Ninth edition. —, *1698. 12°.* T.C.III 99. NU.

388 [–] The lawfulnes and unlawfulnes of an oath. *Printed at*
Oxford [London?] by Leonard Lichfield, 1643. 4°. * MADAN
1448. LT, O, LCL, CT, DC; CH, CLC, MH, MU, WF, Y.

389 —A letter concerning Christmasse. *By E. C. for Francis*
Grove, 1659. 8°. * MH.

389A [–] A letter concerning separation. *For W. D., 1681. fol.* *
L, O; CH, MH, WF, Y, AVP.

390 [–] A letter lately sent by a reverend bishop from the
Tovver. *Printed, 1642. 4°.* * LT, O, C, YM, EN; CH, IU, MH,
NU, WF, Y.

391 [–] —[Anr. ed.] *For Nath: Butter, 1642. 4°.* * LT, O, LSE, CT,
PC; CH, IU, MH, NU, PL, WF.

392 [–] A letter sent to an honourable gentleman, in way of
satisfaction. *[London], printed, 1641. 4°.* * LT, O, LG, LNC,
E; CH, CN, MH, NU, WF, Y.

393 [–] A modest confutation. *[London], printed, 1642. 4°.* *
LT, C, LCL, LNC, EN; CH, MH, NP, WF, Y.

394 [–] A modest offer of some meet considerations. *[London],*
imprinted, 1644. 4°. * LT, O, CT, BC, DT; CH, IU, MH, NU,
WF, Y.

395 ——[Anr. ed.] *Re-printed and are to be sold by Thomas*
Basset, 1660. 4°. * LT, O, C, DU, LSD, DT; CN, MH, NP, TU.

396 [–] —[Anr. ed.] *1695. brs.* LU; MIU.

397 —The old religion. *By M. F. to be sold by William Free-*
man, 1686. 12°. T.C.II 171. L, C, DU, EN, DT; CLC, PL, TSM,
WF, Y.

398 —Osculum pacis. *Per J. Raworth pro N. Butter, 1641. 4°.* *
LW.

399 —Pax terris. *Sumptibus Joannis Bisse, 1648. 12°.* LT, O, C,
OC; CH, IU, NU, WF.

400 —The peace-maker. *By M. Flesher, for Nat: Butter, 1645.*
12°. LT, O, C, EN, BLH; CB, CLC, NU, WF.

401 ——[Anr. ed.] —, *1647. 12°.* L, BR, DCH, LSD, P; CH, CN,
NU, WF, Y.

401A–2 Entries cancelled.

[–] Pscittacorum regia. *1669. See title.*

—Remaining works of. *1660. See*—Shaking of the olive-
tree.

403 —The remedy of discontentment. *By M. F. for Nat.*
Butter, 1645. 12°. LT, O, C, P; CH, MH, NU, WF.

404 ——[Anr. ed.] *By J. G. for Nath: Brooks, 1652. 12°.* L;
CB, CU, IU.

405 ——Fourth edition. *By G. Larkin for Obadiah Blagrave,*
1684. 12°. T.C.II 118. L; IU, TU, Y.

406 [–] Resolutions and decisions of divers practicall cases. *By*
M. F. for Nath. Butter, and are to be sold by Humphrey
Mosley, Abel Roper, and Iohn Sweeting, 1649. 12°. LT, O,
C, EN, DT; CH, IU, MH, TU, WF, Y.

407 ——Second edition. *For N. B. to be sold by R. Royston,*
1650. 12°. L, O, C, AN, DU, BLH; CLC, CN, MH, NU, WF.

408 [–] —[Anr. ed.] *By M. F. for Nath. Butter, to be sold by*
Humphrey Mosley, Abel Roper, and Iohn Sweeting, 1654.
12°. C.

409 ——Third edition. *By R. Hodgkinson, and J. Grismond,*
1654. 12°. C; CLC, IU, LC, MH, MIU, NP, Y.

409A ——Fourth edition. —, *1659. 12°.* BQ; CH, IU.

410 [–] The revelation unrevealed. *By R. L. for John Bisse,*
1650. 12°. LT, O, C, LW, CS, P; CH, MB, NU, VC, WF.

410A [–] Satans fiery darts quenched. *By M. F. for N. Butter. And*
are to be sold by N. Brooks, 1647. 12°. L, O, C, AN; CH,
IU, MH, NU, WF, Y.

411 —Bishops Hall's sayings concerning travellers. *For Will-*
iam Miller, 1674. brs. T.C.I 168. L, LNC; CH.

412 [–] Select thoughts, one century. *By J. L. for N. B. to be*
sold by Nich. Bourn, George Latham, Phil. Stevens, and
Gabriel Bedell, 1648. 12°. LT, O, C; BN, CLC, CU, IU,
MH, Y.

413 ——[Anr. ed.] *For Nath: Brooke, 1654. 12°.* L, C, LSC, NPL;
CLC, IU, MU.

413A ——[Anr. ed.] *By T. M. for Obadiah Blagrave, 1682. 12°.*
T.C.I 477. LG, BLH; WF, Y.

414 —A sermon preach't to his Majesty . . . Aug. 8. *By M.*
Flesher for Nat: Butter, 1641. 8°. LT, CT, DU, ENC, BQ;
CLC, OWC, WF.

414A —Seven irretragable propositions. *[London? 1700.] cap.,*
4°. * L.

415 Entry cancelled. Ghost.

416 — The shaking of the olive-tree. The remaining works of.
By J. Cadwel for J. Crooke, 1660. 4°. LT, O, C, DC, EN;
DT; CH, CN, MH, NU, WF, Y.

417 [–] A short ansvver to the tedious vindication of Smec-
tymnvvs. *For Nathaniel Butter, 1641. 4°.* LT, O, C, NPL,
ENC, DT; CH, CN, MH, NU, WF, Y.

418 [–] A survay of that foolish, seditious, scandalous, prophane libell. *Printed, 1641. 4°.* * LT, O, C, EN, DM; CSS, IU,
MH, NP, NU, WF, Y.

419 —Susurrium cum Deo. *By Will: Hunt, and sold by George*
Lathum, 1651. 12°. L, O, C, DC; CH, CLC, IU, MH, NU,
TSM.

420 ——Second edition. *By Will: Hunt, to be sold by George*
Lathum junior, 1651. 12°. L, O, MR; CLC, NGT, WF, Y.

421 ——Third edition. *By Will: Hunt, 1659. 12°.* C, NPL, BLH;
CLC, CN, IU, NU.

421A ——[Anr. ed.] *By W. H. for Charles Tyus, 1659. 12°.* EN; CH.

422 —Three tractates. *By M. Flesher for Nat. Butter, 1646. 12°.*
L, O, DC; CH, CLC, MH, NCD, NGT, WF, Y.

422A [–] Travels of Don Francisco de Quevedo. *For William*
Grantham, 1684. 12°. L; CLC, CN, IU, MH, MIU, WF.

422B **Hall, Laurence.** The right and due observation of the
Lord's day. *For F. Coles, 1675. 8°.* GU.

423 **[Hall, Ralph.]** Quakers principles quaking. *By R. I. to be*
sold by Edm. Paxton, and Tho. Parkhurst, 1656. 4°. * L,
LF, CT, LCL, YM.

424 Entry cancelled.

[Hall, Richard.] Life & death of . . . John Fisher. *1655.*
See Bayly, Thomas.

Hall, Robert, *pseud. See also* Heylyn, Peter.

424A **H[all], R[obert].** Differences about pre-determination determined. [*London*], *by W. Marshall*, [1700]. sixes.* T.C.III 253. DT; MH.

425 [–] Some arguments and considerations. *For the author, and are to be sold by W. Marshall*, 1699. 12°.* T.C.III 134. O, DT; CH, MH.

425A **Hall, Thomas.** An apologie for the ministry. *By A. W. for Joseph Cranford*, 1600. 4°. L, C, LCL, LLP, BC; CLC, MH.

426 —The beauty of holiness. *By A. M. for John Browne*, 1653. 8°. LT, LW; NU, TO.

426A — —[Anr. ed.] *By Evan Tyler, for John Browne*, 1655. 8°. LCL, LW, CM; MH.

427 —The beauty of magistracy. *By R. W. for Nevil Simmons, in Kederminster, to be sold by Thomas Johnson*, 1660. 4°. L, O, LCL, LW, BLH; CH, IU, MH, NU, WF, Y.

428 —Chiliasto-mastix redivivus. A confutation. *For John Starkey*, 1657. 8°. LT, LW, CCA, BC, SP; IU, NHC, TO, WF.

429 —Comarum ακοσμια. The loathsomnesse of long haire. *By J. G. for Nathanael Webb and William Grantham*, 1654. 8°. LT, O, LCL, CK, DC, EN; CH, CN, MH, WF, Y.

430 —A confutation of the millenarian opinion. 1658. 12°. LW.

431 —An exposition by way of supplement . . . of Amos. *For Henry Mortlock*, 1661. 4°. O, LCL, BC; CH, MH, NU, WF, Y.

432 [–] The font guarded with xx arguments. *By R. W. for Thomas Simmons in Birmingham, and to be sold in London by George Calvert*, 1652. 4°. LT, O, CT, BC, EN; CH, NHC, WF, Y.

433 —Funebria floræ, the downfall. *For Henry Mortlock*, 1660. 4°. LT, O, LG, LLU, BC; CH, IU, MH, TU, WCL, WF, Y.

434 — —Second edition. —, 1661. 4°. L, O, CS, EN, DT; BN, CH, NP, WF, Y.

434A — —Third edition. —, 1661. 4°. L, BIU, DT; TU.

435 Entry cancelled.
—Plain and easy explication. Edinburgh, 1697. *See* Hall, Thomas, *minister at Enver.*

436 —A practical and polemical commentary . . . Timothy. *By E. Tyler, for John Starkey*, 1658. fol. L, C, LCL, LW, BC; CH, MH, NP, NU, WF, Y.

437 [–] The pulpit guarded. *By J. Cottrel, for E. Blackmore*, 1651. 4°. LT, O, C, LCL, YM, DT; CLC, MH, NU, TU, WF, Y.

438 [–] —Third edition. —, 1651. 4°. L, O, C, E, DT; CH, IU, MBA, WF, Y.

439 [–] —Fourth edition. —, 1652. 4°. O, CS, BR, E, DT; CLC, WF.

440 —Samaria's downfall. *By R. I. for Jo. Cranford*, 1660. 4°. L, O, LCL, BC, E, GU; CLC, MB, NU, Y.

441 —Vindiciæ literarum, the schools gvarded. *By W. H. for Nathaniel Webb and William Grantham*, 1654. 8°. L, O, LCL, LSD, EN; CH, MB, MH, NU.

442 — —[Anr. ed.] —, 1655. 8°. L, O, LCL, BC, LLU; CH, CN, MH, NU, WF, Y.

442A **Hall, Thomas,** *minister at Enver.* A plain and easy explication of the Assemblies shorter catechism. *Edinburgh, by George Mosman, and are to be sold by William Dickie, in Glasgow*, 1697. 12°. ALDIS 3667. L, C, EN, ENC.

443 **Hall, Timothy.** A sermon preached . . . April 30. 1684. *For Tho. Parkhurst*, 1684. 4°.* L, O, LG, BLH; TU, Y.

444 —A sermon preached . . . 13th of January, 1688/9. *For Tho. Cockerill*, 1689. 4°.* L, O, OCC, WCA, DT; CLC, WF, Y.

445 **Hall, William,** *barrister.* Mr. Hall's answer to several matters. [*London*, 1695.] fol. L.

445A —Disputatio juridia. *Edinburgh, George Mosman*, 1697. 4°. ALDIS 3667.5. GU.

445B —The King against Reginald Tucker. The case of. [*London*, 1694.] brs. L, LG.

446 **Hall, William,** *fl.* **1642.** A sermon preached . . . xxvii day of March 1642. *By T. Badger, for Samuel Brown*, 1642. 4°.* LT, LSC, CJ, CS, LNC, YM; IU, MM, NU, Y.

447 **Hall, William,** *chaplain.* A sermon preach'd . . . May 9. 1686. *By Henry Hills, for William Grantham*, 1686. 4°.* L, O, LG, MC, DT; CLC, IU, MH, NU, WF, Y.

448 Entry cancelled. Ghost.

449 —A sermon of the general judgment preached before the King . . . on Advent Sunday, 1689. *Dublin, for James Malone*, 1689. 4°.* DIX 236. CD, DN.

Hallelujah, or. 1651. *See* Barton, William.

450 **Hallett, Joseph.** Christ's ascension. *For John Salusbury, and Robert Osborne, in Exon*, 1693. 12°. LCL, LSC; MH.

451 **Halley, Edmund.** Catalogus stellarum Australium. *Typis Thomæ James, impensis R. Harford*, 1679. 4°.* T.C.I 335. L, O, CT, EN, DT; KU, MU, NN, PL, WF.

[–] Ephemeris. 1686. *See* Almanacs.

451A —May it please the Kings most excellent Majesty. [*London*, 1687.] 4°. L, CM.

451B —Mercurii transitus sub solis disco. Oct. 28, 1677. 1679. 8°. NN.

452 [–] A plain declaration of the vulgar new heavens flatform. [*London?* 1679.] 4°. L.

453 —Stell[arum] fixarum hemisphaeriu[m australe]. [*n.p.*, 1690?] brs. O.

454 **Halley, George.** A sermon preached . . . fourteenth of February, 1688/9. *For R. C. to be sold by Rich. Lambert and Francis Hildyard in York*, 1689. 4°.* L, O, C, CE, DT; BBE, INU, NC, NU, WF.

455 —A sermon preach'd . . . 30th of March, 1691. *For Robert Clavel: to be sold by Christopher Welburn, in York*, 1691. 4°.* T.C.II 357. L, O, C, BAMB, YM; CH, CLC, Y.

455A — —[Anr. ed.] *For Christopher Welburn in York*, 1691. 4°.* BAMB; Y.

455B —A sermon preached . . . November 17, 1695. *For Rob. Clark in York*, 1695. 4°.* CLC, MIU, WF.

456 —A sermon preach'd . . . fifth of November, 1697. *Printed for, and sold by Tho. Baxter, York*, 1698. 4°.* L, LSD, NE, YM; MIU, NIC, Y.

456A **Halliman, Peter.** The square and cube root compleated. *By J. Leake for the author, sold at his lodging, and by Edward Poole*, 1686. 8°. L, CM, GU; WF.

456B [**Hallowes, John.**] April the 22th. Nevv and true nevves from Ireland. *For F. Coules*, 1642. 4°.* LT, O, EC, EN, DN, DT; CH, MH, Y.

457 Entry cancelled.
Hallywell, C. Philosophical discourse of earthquakes. 1693. *See* H., C.

458 **Hallywell, Henry.** An account of familism. *For Walter Ketillby*, 1673. 8°. T.C.I 142. O, C, LF, EN, DM; CLC, MH, NU, PH, WF.

459 —A defence of revealed religion. *For Walter Kettilby*. 1694. 8°. T.C.II 509. L, O, LW, NE, DT; CLC, IU.

460 [–] Deus justificatus: or, the divine goodness. *By E. Cotes, for Walter Kettilby*, 1668. 8°. L, O, C, P, E; BN, CLC, IU, MH, NU, WF, Y.

461 [–] A discourse of the excellency of Christianity. *For Walter Kettilby*, 1671. 8°. T.C.I 64. L, O, C, LSD, CD; CH, IU, MH, NGT.

462 —A discourse of the use of reason. *By Hen. Hills, jun. for Walter Kettilby*, 1683. 4°. L, LF, CS; NP.

463 —The excellency of moral vertue. *For James Adamson*, 1692. 8°. T.C.II 422. L, O, C, LF, NE; CLC, WF, MOORE.

463A [–] An improvement of the way of teaching the Latin tongue. *For J. Adamson*, 1690. 8°. T.C.II 339.

464 —Melampronoea: or a discourse. *For Walter Kettilby*, 1681. 8°. T.C.I 464. L, OM, CT, NE, GU; CH, MH, OCI, WF, Y.

465 [–] A private letter of satisfaction to a friend. [*London*], printed, 1667. 8°. L, O, C, OC, E, DT; IU, MH, NGT, WF.

466 —The sacred method. *For Walter Kettilby*, 1677. 8°. T.C.I 266. L, O, C, LW, OM; CLC, NU, WF.

[–] True and lively representation. 1679. *See* Owen, Thankfull.

467 **H[alsey], J[ames].** Divine considerations upon sin. *For R. Royston*, 1676. 12°. T.C.I 265. O, CS, LLU.

468 [–] The vanity of honour. *For J. Magnes, and R. Bentley*, 1678. 12°. T.C.I 318. L, O; CLC, CU.

Halstead, Robert, *pseud*. *See* Peterborough, Henry Mordaunt, *earl of*.

469 **Hamand, Henry.** Ourography; or speculations on the excrements of urine. *For Francis Eglesfield*, 1655. 8°. L, LCS, OR, CS, GU; WSG.

469A ——[Anr. ed.] *By R. D. for Francis Eglesfield, to be sold by William Ballard in Bristow*, 1656. 8°. L; WSG.

470 **[Hamblet, John.]** A famous and joyfull victory obtained by the Earl of Stamfords forces. *Septemb*. 10. [*London*], *for H. Blunen [sic]*, [1642]. 4°.* LT; MM.

471 No entry.

Hambleton, *duke*. *See* H., A.

472 **Hambly, Loveday.** A relation of the last words. *By John Gain*, 1683. 4°.* L, LF, BBN; PH, PSC.

473 **H[ames], R[obert].** Parallels; or, a short discourse. *For the author*, 1675. 8°. C.

474 **Hamey, Baldwin.** Dissertatio epistolaris de juramento medicorum. *Prostat apud Guilielmum Birch*, 1693. 4°.* T.C.II 455. L, C, LR, P, GH; NAM, WSG.

475 **[Hamilton, Alexander.]** A cordial for Christians. *Edinburgh, by George Mosman*, 1696. 8°. ALDIS 3549. L, O, E, EN, GU; CH, CLC, IU, NPT, WF.

[–] Sermon preached in the High-Church. *Edinburgh*, 1690. *See* Meldrum, George.

475A **Hamilton, Alexander,** *merchant*. Articles established by. [*Edinburgh*, 1693.] cap., fol.* ALDIS 3291.7. EN, GU.

475B **Hamilton, Alexander,** *of Kinkel*. To His Grace His Majesties High Commissioner, . . . the petition of. [*Edinburgh*, 1695.] brs. EN.

475C — Unto his Grace, His Majesties High Commissioner, . . . the petition of. [Anr. petition.] [*Edinburgh*, 1690.] brs. EN.

476 **Hamilton, Andrew.** A true relation of the actions of the Inniskilling-men. *For Ric. Chiswell, and are to be sold by Richard Baldwin*, 1690. 4°. T.C.II 300. L, O, C, EN, DT; CH, CN, MH, NU, WF, Y.

477 **[Hamilton, Sir David.]** The private Christian's witness. *For T. Cockerill*, 1697. 8°. T.C.III 4. L, C, ON, SHR, E; TO.

477A **Hamilton, Elizabeth.** To the Parliament of the Common-wealth of England, the humble petition of. [*London*, 1651.] brs. L.

477B **Hamilton, Sir Frederick.** The humble remonstrance of. [*London*, 1643.] 4°.* L; CLC.

478 —The information of. [*London*], *printed*, 1645. 4°. LT, O, A.

479 **Hamilton, James,** *duke*. The copy of a letter from. *For Edward Husband, August 25*, 1648. 4°.* LT, O; CH, MIU, NU.

480 —The declaration . . . 22 July 1648. *Edinburgh, E. Tyler*, 1648. brs. ALDIS 1325. STEELE 3p 1971. L.

481 —A new declaration. *Printed at Edenburgh, reprinted at London*, 1648. 4°.* LT, LVF, MR.

482 —The several speeches of. *For Peter Cole, Francis Tyton, and John Playford*, 1649. 4°.* LT, O, CT, EN, DT; CH, IU, MH, TU, WF, Y. (var.)

482A ——[Anr. ed.] [*London*, 1649.] cap., 4°.* OC; NN, Y.

483 Entry cancelled.

[–] Some farther matter of fact. [n.p., 1679.] *See* title.

484 —The Marqves Hamiltons speech before the Kings . . . *Novem*. 6. 1641. *First printed at Edinburgh, by James Brison, reprinted in London for T. B.*, 1641. 4°.* LT, C, BR, DU, DT; CH, CN, MH, WF, Y.

— Speech made by the . . . Earl of Arran. 1689. *See* Arran, Richard Butler, *earl of*.

485 —A true copie of a paper delivered by. colop: *Hage: by Samuel Broun*, [1649]. cap., 4°.* CJ, LNC, E; Y.

485A **Hamilton, Margaret,** *baroness*. Unto His Grace, His Majesty's High Commissioner . . . the humble petition of. [*Edinburgh*, 1695.] brs. EN.

486 **Hamilton, Sir R[obert].** For the right noble and potent Prince James Duke of Bucclengh [*sic*] . . . Humble supplication. [*Glasgow?* 1679.] brs. ALDIS 2153.8. L, O, EN; CH, MH, Y, ZWT.

487 **Hamilton, Robert.** Schediasmata libero-philosophica. *Edinburgi, excudebat Andreas Anderson*, 1668. 4°.* ALDIS 1850. E.

487A **Hamilton, William,** *2d duke of*. The declaration of. *By Robert Wood*, 1651. 4°.* LT; CH.

487B —A true coppy of a letter . . . to Master William Crofts. *Printed at Leith, by Evan Tyler*, 1651. brs. Y.

488 **[Hamilton, William].** A discourse concerning zeal. *Dublin, by Joseph Ray for Jacob Milner*, 1700. 4°. DIX 322. LW, DI, DN, DT, BLH; Y.

489 **Hamilton, William,** *Gent*. Some necessity of reformation. *For John Sherley*, 1660. 4°.* LT, O, CS, LIU, EN; CLC, IU, MH, NU, WF, Y.

490　**Hammat, John.** A burning and a shining light. *For Nath. Ponder, and Thomas Watson in Newport-Pagnell,* 1685. 4°.* T.C.II 95. LCL, LW, OC, WCA, EN, BLH; CH, NU, WF.

491　Entry cancelled.
　　[**Hammond.**] Gods judgments upon drunkards. 1659. *See* Hammond, Samuel.

491A　[**Hammond, Anthony.**] The gentlemans exercise. *By S. Griffin for William Lee,* 1662. 8°. CH, Y.

491B　**Hammond, Charles.** The credit of Yorkshire. *For Richard Burton,* 1649. brs. MAU.

491C　[–] The divils cruelty. *Lonpuo* [*sic*], *for William Gilbertson,* [1663]. brs. O.

492　—Englnads [*sic*] alarum-bell. *For Richard Burton,* 1652. 8°.* L.

493　—Gods eye from heaven. *Glasgow, by Robert Sanders,* 1664. 8°.* ALDIS 1773.3. L.

493A　——[Anr. ed.] *For T. Coles,* 1675. brs. OP.

494　—Israels just jvdge. *By E. Crowch, for the author,* 1657. 4°.* LT, O; WF.

495　—London's triumphant holiday. *For Francis Grove,* 1660. 4°.* O, CT.

496　—The loyal indigent officer. *By E. C.* [*c.* 1670.] 8°.* DU; CH, CN.

496A　The loyall subject. *For the author in the behulfe of the Indigent party,* 1669. 4°.* NHL.

497　—The old English officer. [*London,* 1679.] 8°.* O.

498　—Truth's discovery. *By Edward Crowch,* 1664. 4°.* L; CH, CLC, CN, MH, WF, Y.

499　—A warning-peece for England. *For Richard Burton in Smithfield,* [1652]. 4°.* L, O; CH.

500　—The worlds timely warning-peece. *For Fr. Grove,* 1660. 8°.* L; CH.
　　Hammond, George. *See also* Hamond, George.

501　Entry cancelled.
　　—Discourse of family-worship. 1694. *See* Hamond, George.

502　—A discovery of the latitude of the loss of the earthly paradise. *By Ro: Ibbitson, for Francis Smith,* 1655. 8°. LT, ORP.

503　Entry cancelled.
　　—Good minister of Jesus Christ. 1693. *See* Hamond, George.

504　—Syons redemption. *By G. Dawson for the author,* 1658. 4°.* LT, O, LCL, LW, LIU, MAB; RBU.

505　—Truth and innocency. *For the author,* 1660. 4°. LT, LW, LIU, MAB, MP.

506　**Hammond, Henry.** The vvorkes of. The first volume. *By Elizabeth Flesher for Richard Royston, and Richard Davis of Oxford,* 1674. fol. T.C.I 165. O, C, BSE, EN, CD; BN, LC, NU, PBL, PPT, WSC.

507　——Fourth volume. *By T. Newcomb and M. Flesher, for Richard Royston, and Richard Davis, in Oxford,* 1684. fol. L, C, WCA, ENC, GU; BN, CLC, MBP, MH, NU, PL, WWC.

508　——First [-4th] volume. Second edition. *For R. Royston, and R. Davis, in Oxford,* 1684. fol. T.C.II 80. L, C, LLP, NE, EN, DT; CLC, IU, MH, NP, WF, Y.

509　—Second volume. Second edition. *For R. Royston; and R. Davis, in Oxford,* 1684. fol. T.C.II 80. L, O, C, ENC, DT; BN, MBP, MH, NP, NU, Y.

510　—An account of Mr. Cawdry's Triplex diatribe. *By J. Flesher, for Richard Royston,* 1655. 4°. LT, O, CS, E, DT; CH, IU, MH, WF, Y.

511　——[Anr. ed.] *By J. Flesher, for Richard Royston, and for Richard Davis in Oxford,* 1655. 4°. GC, LSD; CLC, MH, WG.

512　—Αιεν αληθευειν, or, a brief account. *For Richard Davis, in Oxfor* [*sic*], 1660. 4°.* L, DUS.

512A　——[Anr. ed.] *For Richard Royston,* 1660. 4°.* L, CS; CB, TO, Y.

513　Entry cancelled.
　　—Answer to Mr. Richard Smith's letter, 1684. *See* Smith, Richard. Letter from.

514　—An answer to the animadversions on the dissertations. *By J. G. for Richard Royston,* 1654. 4°. LT, O, C, E, DT; CH, IU, MH, WF, Y.

515　—Αξια Θεου κρισις. Iudgment worthy of God. *Oxford, by H.H. for Ric. Royston and Ric. Davis,* 1665. 12°. MADAN 2702. L, O, CT, YM, DT; BN, CH, CLC, IU, NU, TO, WF.

515A　—The baptizing of infants. *By J. Flesher, for Richard Royston,* 1655. 4°. L, O, CS, EN, DT; CH, IU, MH, NCD, NHC, AVP.

516　——[Anr. ed.] *By J. Flesher, for Richard Royston, and for Richard Davis in Oxford,* 1655. 4°. EC; NU, WF, WG, Y.

517　—Dr. Hammond's brief resolution of that grand case. [*London,* 1689?] cap., 4°.* LL, CT, LSD, MR; Y.

518　—A brief vindication of three passages. *For Richard Royston,* 1648. 4°.* LT, O, C, OC, MR; BN, CLC, IU, MH, NU, WF. (var.)

518A　——[Anr. ed.] *For Rich. Royston,* 1651. 4°. ASU.

519　—Χαρις και ειρηνη, or a pacifick discourse. *For R. Royston,* 1660. 8°. L, O, C, E, DT; CH, CN, MIU, NGT, NU. (var.)

519A　——[Anr. ed.] *For R. Davis, in Oxford,* 1660. 8°. CJ; CN, IU, PL, WF, Y.

520　—The Christians obligations to peace & charity. First edition. *For R. Royston,* 1649. 4°. L, O, C, SC, EN; BN, CH, IU, NU, OCI, WF, Y.

521　——Second edition. —, 1652. 4°. L, O, C, OC, E; BN, CH, CLC, IU, MH, NP, WSC, Y.

522　——[Anr. ed.] —, 1664. fol. O, LLP, CP; CH, MBP, NU, PL, WF.

523　—A collection of severall replies and vindications. *For R. Royston,* 1657. 4°. O, OC, CT.

524　—A collection of such discourses and answers. The first volume. *For R. Royston,* 1657. 4°. O.

524A　——The second volume. —, 1657. 4°. OC; WF.

524B　——The third volume. —, 1657. 4°. WF.

525　[–] Consjderatjons of present use concerning the danger. [*Oxford, by L. Lichfield*], printed 1644[5]. 4°.* MADAN 1711. LT, O, C, MR, DT; CH, MBA, NP, V, Y.

526　[–] —[Anr. ed.] *Printed,* 1644[5]. 4°.* MADAN 1712. L, O, C, DU, DT; CLC, IU, MH, TU, WF, Y.

527　[–] —[Anr. ed.] [*London*], printed, 1646. 4°.* LT, C, OC, EN, DT; CH, CN, MH, NU, Y.

528 [–] —[Anr. ed.] *By T.M. for Fin. Gardiner,* 1682. 4°.* T.C.I 493. L, O, C, LSD; CH, IU, MH, NC, PU, WF.

529 —A continuation of the defence of Hvgo Grotivs. *By J. G. for Richard Royston,* 1657. 4°. L, O, CK, SC, YM; CH, IU, MH, NU, WF.

530 [–] A copy of some papers past at Oxford, betwixt the author of the practicall catechisme, and Mr. Ch. *By R. Cotes for Richard Royston,* 1647. 4°. MADAN 1921. LT, O, C, EN, DT; BN, CH, CN, MH, NU, WF, Y.

531 [–] —Second edition. *By Ja. Flesher for Richard Royston,* 1650. 4°. L, O, CT, YM, E, CD; BN, CLC, IU, NU, WSC, Y.

531A —The daily practice of devotion. *For R. Royston,* 1681. 12°. T.C.I 447. PU.

532 [–] —[Anr. ed.] —, 1684. 12°. O, CS; CLC, LC.

533 —De confirmatione. *Oxoniæ, excudebat Hen. Hall impensis Ric. Royston, Lond. & Ric. Davis, Oxon.,* 1661. 8°. MADAN 2557. L, O, BR, GU, DT; BN, CLC, CU, NU, PL, Y.

533A — —[Anr. ed.] *[London], prostant apud R. Royston,* [1661?]. 8°. O, C, CT, DU; NCD.

533B — —[Anr. ed.] *[n.p.], prostant apud Richardum Davis, Oxoniæ,* 1661. 8°. C; CH.

534 —Δευτεραι φροντιδες, or a review. *By J. Flesher for R. Royston,* 1656. 8°. L, OC, CT, YM, E; CH, IU, MH, WF, Y.

535 — —[Anr. ed.] *By J. Flesher for R. Royston, and R. Davis in Oxford,* 1657. 8°. O, P.

536 —The disarmers dexterities examined. *By J. Flesher, for Richard Royston,* 1656. 4°. LT, O, C, SHR, DT; CLC, IU, NU, WF, WG, Y.

537 —The dispatcher dispatched. *For Richard Royston and Richard Davis in Oxford,* 1659. 4°. LT, O, CS, YM, DT; CH, IU, NU, TO, WF.

538 —Dissertationes quatuor. *Typis J. Flesher, impensis R. Davis in Oxonio,* 1651[2]. 4°. MADAN 2168. LT, OC, CM, LSD, YM; CH, NP, WF.

539 — —[Anr. ed.] *Typis J. Flesher, impensis R. Royston,* 1651[2]. 4°. MADAN 2168n. O, C, NPL, E, DT; BN, CLC, NP, NU, WF, WSC, Y. (var.)

540 —Εκτενεστερον. Or the degrees of ardency. *For R. Royston,* 1656. 4°.* L, O, CT, LW, YM; CH, IU, MH, NU, WF.

541 —Ευσχημονως και κατα ταξιν: or, the grounds of uniformity. *By J. G. for Richard Royston,* 1657. 4°.* L, O, CT, CK, YM; CH, IU, NHC, NU, WF.

542 No entry.

543 —Five propositions to the Kings Majesty. *Cambridge, for Nathaniel Smith,* 1647. 4°.* LT, C, OC, LIU, MR; MB, MH, NU.

544 —Large additions to the practicall catechisme. *By M. F. for R. Royston,* 1646. 4°. L, C, BR, DU, DT; CH, CN, IU, MH, PL, WF, Y.

544A —The last words of. colop: *For Richard Royston,* 1660. 8°.* CH, MH, WF, Y.

544B — —[Anr. ed.] *For Luke Meredith,* 1696. 8°.* C.

545 —A letter of resolution to six quæres. *By J. Flesher for R. Royston,* 1653. 12°. LT, O, C, E, DT; CH, NU, RPJ, WF, Y.

545A — —[Anr. ed.] —, *and R. Davis in Oxford,* 1653. 12°. C, OC.

     [–] Loyall convert. *Oxford,* 1643. *See* Quarles, Francis.

546 [–] Mysterium religionis recognitum. An expedient. *For R. Royston,* 1649. 4°.* LT, O, LCL, CT, DT; BN, IU, MM, NU, WF, Y.

     [–] Observations concerning the originall. 1652. *See* Filmer, Robert.

547 [–] Of a late, or, a death-bed repentance. *Oxford, by Henry Hall,* 1645. 4°.* MADAN 1809. LT, O, CS, WCA, DT; CLC, IU, MH, WF, Y.

548 [–] Of conscience. *Oxford, by Henry Hall,* 1644[5]. 4°.* MADAN 1714. LT, O, C, EN, DT; CLC, IU, NU, WF, Y.

549 — —[Anr. ed.] *For R. Royston,* 1645. 4°.* O, CT, MR, SA, DT; CH, CN, MH, MU, WF.

550 [–] Of conscience, scandall. *Oxford, by Henry Hall,* 1645. 4°. MADAN 1846. LT, O, CT, ENC, DT; CH, CN, MH, NU, WF, Y.

551 [–] —[Anr. ed.] *Printed,* 1646. 4°.* SC; CLC, MH, NU, TSM, WF, Y.

552 — —[Anr. ed.] *By J. G. for R. Royston,* 1650. 4°.* CK, CS, YM; CH, IU, MB, NU, Y.

553 —Of fraternal admonition. *For R. Royston,* 1647. 4°.* LT, O, C, MR, DT; BN, CH, CN, MH, WF, Y.

554 —Of fundamentals in a notion. *By J. Flesher for Richard Royston,* 1654. 12°. L, O, C, E, DT; CH, IU, MH, NU, WF, Y.

555 [–] Of idolatry. *Oxford, by Henry Hall,* 1646. 4°.* MADAN 1874. LT, O, CT, ENC, DT; CH, CU, TU, WF, Y.

555A [–] —[Anr. ed.] —, 1646. 4°.* MADAN 1875. O; MH, Y.

556 [–] Of resisting the lavvfull magistrate. *Printed,* 1643. 4°.* LT, O, CT, SC, DT; CH, IU, MH, NU, Y.

557 [–] —[Anr. ed.] *Oxford, for H. H. and VV. VV,* 1644. 4°. MADAN 1630-1. LT, O, C, ENC, DT; CH, CN, MH, NU, WF, Y. (var.)

557A [–] —[Anr. ed.] *Oxford, for H.H. and W.W.,* 1644. 4°. MADAN 1632. O, BC; INU, IU, NCU, NN, Y.

558 [–] —[Anr. ed.] *Oxford, for H. H. and VV. VV.,* 1646. 4°. NU, ASU.

559 [–] —[Anr. ed.] *[London], printed,* 1647. 4°. L, CK, DU, LIU, DT; BN, CLC, CN, NU, WF, Y.

560 [–] Of scandall. *Oxford, by Henry Hall,* 1644. 4°.* MADAN 1713. LT, O, C, LSD, DT; CH, NU, TU, WF, Y.

561 [–] —[Anr. ed.] —, 1645. 4°. MADAN 1848. LT, O, MR; MIU, NU, Y.

562 [–] —Second edition. —, 1646. 4°.* MADAN 1912. O, BLH; CH, IU, OWC.

562A [–] Of schisme. A defence. *By J. Flesher for Richard Royston,* 1653. 12°. O, C, OC, DU, SC; CH, MWA.

563 — —[Anr. ed.] —, 1654. 12°. L, C, NPL, P, DT; CH, IU, MBC, NU, WF, Y.

564 [–] Of sinnes. *Oxford, by Henry Hall,* 1645. 4°.* MADAN 1817. LT, O, C, E, DT; CH, IU, MH, WWC, Y.

565 — —[Anr. ed.] *Printed,* 1646. 4°.* O, CT, DU, ENC; CH, CN, MH, NU, WF, Y.

566 [–] Of svperstition. *Oxford, by Henry Hall,* 1645. 4°.* MADAN 1849. L, O, CT, E, DT; CH, IU, MH, NU, Y.

567 [–] Of the povver of the keyes. *For Richard Royston,* 1647. 4°. LT, O, C, CT, EN, DT; BN, CH, IU, MH, WF, Y.

568 [–] —[Anr. ed.] *For Richard Royston, and Richard Davis in Oxford,* 1647. 4°. LT, C; NU, WF.

569   [–] —[Anr. ed.] *For Richard Royston,* 1651. 4°. O, C, OC, YM, DT; CU, IU, NP, WSC.

570   [–] Of the reasonableness of Christian religion. *By J. G. for R. Royston,* 1650. 4°. O, CT, DC, DT; IU, NU, WSC.

570A   [–] —Second edition. *By J. F. for R. Royston,* 1650. 4°. LT, LW, CS, LNC; CLC, IU, MH.

570B   [–] —Third edition. *By J. G. for R. Royston,* 1650. 4°. L, O, C, CS, YM; BN, CLC, MB, V, WF, Y.

571   [–] Of vvill-vvorship. *Oxford, by Henry Hall,* 1644. 4°.* MADAN 1735. LT, O, C, CT, DT; CH, IU, MH, NU, TU, Y.

572   —A parænesis. Or, seasonable exhortatory. *By R. N. for Richard Royston,* 1656. 12°. LT, O, C, P, SC; CLC, IU, MH, NU, WF.

573   —A paraphrase, and annotations upon all the books of the New Testament. *By J. Flesher for Richard Royston,* 1653. fol. L, C, CE, DC, DU, E; BN, CH, IU, MBP, NU, WF, WWC.

573A   — —Second edition. —, 1659. fol. L, OC, CCH, EC, DT; MH, NP, PPT, RBU, Y, AVP.

573B   — —"Second" edition. *By J. Flesher for Richard Davis in Oxford,* 1659. fol. OC, GC; MH.

574   — —Third edition. *By J. F. and E. T. for Richard Royston,* 1671. fol. T.C.I 68. L, O, C, LSD, D, DT; BBE, IU, MH, NU, TSM, WWC.

574A   — —"Third" edition. *By J. F. & E. T. for Richard Davis in Oxford,* 1671. fol. L, CM, NPL; NCU.

575   — —Fourth edition. *By E. F. T. R. and J. M. for Ric. Davis in Oxford,* 1675. fol. T.C.I 207. L, CS, LLU, ST. JAMES PARISH, SUFFOLK; NU, PPT, PU, Y, AVP.

575A   — —"Fourth" edition. *By E. F. T. R. and J. M. for R. Royston,* 1675. fol. OC, DUS, LSD, WCA, DT; MH, PBL, PU, SYRACUSE, MOORE.

576   — —Fifth edition. *By J. Macock and M. Flesher for Richard Royston, and Richard Davis in Oxford,* 1681. fol. T.C.I 432. L, C, OH, BC, DU, SHR; BN, CH, IU, PBL, PU, WF.

577   — —Sixth edition. *For Margaret Royston,* 1689. fol. C, LW, BR, DU, EC; CLC, IU, NU, PPT, WWC.

578   Entry cancelled. Ghost.

578A   —A paraphrase, and annotations . . . Psalms. *By R. Norton, for Richard Royston,* 1659. fol. L, OH, CT, P, EC, CD; CH, CN, IU, PL, PPT.

579   — —[Anr. ed.] *By J. Flesher for Richard Royston,* 1659. fol. L, O, BAMB, DC, E, DT; BN, MH, NU, Y.

579A   — —[Anr. ed.] *By R. Norton for Richard Davis in Oxford,* 1659. fol. L, OC, C, LLU, LSD; WF.

580   — —Second edition. *By T. Newcomb and M. Flesher, for Richard Royston, and Richard Davis, in Oxford,* 1683. fol. L, EC, D; PU, WF.

581   [–] A practicall catechisme. *[Oxford, by H. Hall],* printed, 1645. 8°. MADAN 1847. L, O, EC, MR; CH, IU.

581A   — —[Anr. ed.] *By M. F. for Richard Royston,* 1645. 4°. LSC; IU.

582   — —[Anr. ed.] *Oxford, printed,* 1646. 4°. MADAN 1914. LT, O, C, ENC, DT; CH, CN, MH, TU, WF, Y.

583   — —Second edition. *For Ric: Royston,* 1646. 4°. LT, O, DU, SHR, DT; CH, IU, MH, NU, WF.

583A   — —[Anr. ed.] *For Richard Royston,* 1648. 4°. CH, MH.

584   — —Fifth edition. *By M. F. for R. Royston,* 1649. 4°. L, C, ESSEX, NPL, SC; BN, CLC, IU, NU, TSM, WF.

584A   — —"Fifth" edition. *For R. Royston, and for R. Davis in Oxford,* 1649. 4°. IU, TU.

585   — —Third edition. *For Rich: Royston,* 1652. 4°. OC, CK, CT, LLU, P, E; CH, CLC, NU.

586   — —Sixth edition. *By J. F. for R. Royston,* 1655. 12°. L, LIU, SHR; MB, MH, WF, MOORE.

587   — —Seventh edition. —, 1662. 8°. L, C, EC, E, ENC; CLC, IU, TSM, TU, Y.

588   — —"Seventh" edition. *By J. F. for Richard Davis, Oxford,* 1662. 12°. MADAN 2597. L; MH, NP, PU.

589   — —Eighth edition. *By E. T. for R. Royston,* 1668. 8°. C, LLL, BAMB, BANGOR, RPL; BN, FU, IU, PBL, WF, Y.

589A   — —"Eighth" edition. *By E. T. for R. Davis,* 1668. 8°. DL.

590   — —Ninth edition. *By E. Tyler and R. Holt, for Richard Royston,* 1670. 8°. L, C, BANGOR, EC, YM; CLC, MBZ, NHC, TU, Y.

591   — —Tenth edition. *By R. Norton, for R. Royston,* 1674. 8°. L, O, C, BLH, DM; NCU, PL.

591A   — —"Tenth" edition. *By R. Norton for Richard Davis in Oxford,* 1674. 8°. L, OC; ZWT.

592   — —Eleventh edition. *By R. Norton for R. Royston,* 1677. 8°. L, O, BR, D, CD; CB, CLC, TU, Y.

593   — —Twelfth edition. *By M. Flesher, for R. Royston,* 1683. 8°. L, O, C, CT; CH, CU, IU, NCU, TU, Y.

594   — —"Twelfth" edition. *By M. Flesher, for Richard Davis, in Oxford,* 1684. 8°. L, O, BQ; IU.

595   — —Thirteenth edition. *By M. Clark, for Henry Dickenson, and Richard Green, in Cambridge,* 1691. 8°. L, O, C, EN, DT; CH, IU, NIC, RBU, TSM, TU.

596   — —Fourteenth edition. *For Tho. Newborough, J. Nicholson, and Benj. Tooke,* 1700. 8°. T.C.III 200. L, C, OC, BSE, DT; CB, IU, MH, TSM, TU, WF.

597   [–] Private forms of prayer, fitted. *By Tho. Mabb, to be sold by William Not,* 1660. 8°. LT, O; CH.

598   —A reply to the Catholick gentlemans answer. *By J. G. for R. Royston,* 1654. 4°. L, O, CT, E, DT; CH, IU, NU, TU, WG.

598A   [–] The Scriptures plea for magistrates. *Oxford, by Leonard Lichfield,* 1643. 4°.* C; CH, CN, MH, NU, WF.

599   —A second defence of the learned Hvgo Grotivs. *By J. Flesher, for Richard Royston, and for Richard Davis in Oxford,* 1655. 4°.* MADAN 2275n. LT, O, C, SC, YM; CH, IU, NU, WF, Y.

599A   — —[Anr. ed.] *By J. Flesher, for Richard Royston,* 1655. 4°.* L, OC, CS, DU, GC, EN; IU, MH, WG.

600   —Sermons preached. *For Timothy Garthwait,* 1664. fol. L, O, C, AN, RPL, DT; CH, MBP, MU, NU, PL, WF.

601   — —[Anr. ed.] *For Robert Pawlet,* 1675. fol. T.C.I 213. L, C, CS, DC, E, DM; CLC, MH, SW, WF, Y.

602   —Several sermons. *For R. Royston,* 1664. fol. L, C, LS, LW, CD; CH, IU, NU, PL, WF.

603   —Severall tracts. *For Richard Royston,* 1646. 4°. L, O, C, YM, EN; BN, CH, IU, MH, TSM, WF, Y.

604   —Six books of late controversie. *By J. Flesher for Richard Royston,* 1656. 4°. L, LLP, CK, CT, BC; WF.

605 —Some profitable directions. *By J. F. for R. Royston,* 1657. 8°. L, O, CT, E, ENC, BLH; CH, CN, MH, NU, WF, Y.

606 —To the right honourable, the Lord Fairfax. *London, for Richard Royston,* 1649. 4°.* L, O, C, CT, E, DT; CLC, MH, MU, TU, WF, Y. (var.)

607 ——[Anr. ed.] *London. For Richard Royston,* 1649. 4°.* LT, OC, C, MR, YM; CH, CN, MH, NU, WF, Y.

608 [–] Tracts of I. conscience. *Oxford, by Henry Hall,* 1645. 4°. MADAN 1850. O; CLC, TU.

609 [–] A view of some exceptions which have beene made by a Romanist. *[London], printed [at Oxford, by H. Hall] for R. Royston, and R. Davis in Oxford,* 1646. 4°. MADAN 1904. LT, O, C, MR, DT; BN, CH, CN, MH, WF, Y.

609A Entry cancelled.
—View of some exceptions which. [1650.] *See* — View of some exceptions to.

610 [–] —Second edition. *By J. G. for R. Royston,* 1650. 4°. L, O, LIL, CT, E; BN, CLC, IU, MB, MIU, NP, WF.

611 —A view of some exceptions to. *For Rich: Royston,* [1650]. 4°.* L, O, CT; BN, IU, NP, TU, WF, WSC, Y.

612 [–] A view of the nevv directory. *Oxford, by Leonard Lichfield,* 1645. 4°. MADAN 1797. LT, O, C, E, DT; CH, CN, NU, V, WF, Y.

613 [–] —Second edition. *Oxford, by Henry Hall,* 1646. 4°. MADAN 1887. O, LCL, LIU, ENC, DT; CLC, IU, MB, NU, Y.

614 [–] —Third edition. —, 1646. 4°. MADAN 1888. L, O, C, YM, DL, DT; BN, CH, CN, MH, WF, Y. (var.)

614A Entry cancelled.
[–] View of the nevv directory. 1644. *See* [–] Of resisting the lavvfull magistrate.

614B [–] —"Third" edition ["directorie"]. *Oxford, by H. Hall,* 1646. 4°. MADAN 1888*. LIC; BN, CH, CLC, NU, TO, TU. (var.)

615 —A vindication of Dr. Hammonds addresse. *For R. Royston,* 1649. 4°.* LT, O, C, CT, SC; BN, CH, MH, NU, OCI, WF.

616 ——[Anr. ed.] —, 1650. 4°.* LT, O, CT, YM, E; BN, CH, IU, NU, TU, Y.

617 —A vindication of the ancient liturgie. *For Austin Rice,* 1660. 4°. L, O, OC, CP, MR, GU; WF.

618 —A vindication of the dissertations concerning episcopacie. *By J. G. for Richard Royston,* 1654. 4°. L, O, CT, LSD, SC, E; CH, IU, MH, NU, TSM, WF, Y.

619 **Hammond, John.** Hammond versus Heamans. *Printed at London for the use of the author,* [1655]. 4°.* L, LPR; CH, RPJ.

619A —Know thy self. *[London], to be given away by the author,* [n.d.]. brs. O.

620 —Leah and Rachel. *By T. Mabb, and are to be sold by Nich. Bourn,* 1656. 4°.* LT, LG; CH, MH, PL, RPJ, WCL.

621 **Hammond, Robert.** Colonel Hammond's letter sent to William Lenthal. *For Edward Husband, June 26,* 1648. 4°.* LT, KEBLE, CT, MR; CH, CN, CSS, MH, MU, WF.

622 —Colonel Hammond's letter sent to the honorable William Lenthal. *For Edward Husband, July 12,* 1648. 4°.* LT, LLL; CH, CLC, CN, TU, Y.

623 Entry cancelled.
Hammond, Samuel. False Jew. Newcastle, 1653. *See* Welde, Thomas.

623AA [–] Gods judgements upon drunkards. *By E. Tyler,* 1659. 8°. LT; IU.

623BA [–] —[Anr. ed.] *[London], for William London,* 1659. 8°. WF.

623A —The Quaker's house. *Gateside, by Stephen Bulkley,* 1658. 4°.* LF, OQ, CT.

624 **Hammond, Thomas.** Anno 1685. An advertisement of the vertues and use of sundry . . . medicines. *[London,* 1685.] cap., 4°.* L, LG.

625 —The compleat measurer. *By E. O. for Tho. Heath, and W. Crook,* 1669. 8°. T.C.I 5. O; CLC, WF.

625AA —Epilepsys, or convulsion-fits in children effectually cured. [1685.] brs. L.

625A —To all our Friends and brethren. *[London],* 1690. 4°.* LF; CH, PSC.

626 **H[ammond], W[illiam].** Poems. *For Thomas Dring,* 1655. 8°. LT, O, OW, CT; CH, CLC, NCU, WCL, Y.

626A **Hamond, George.** A discourse of family-worship. *For John Lawrence,* 1694. 12°. T.C.II 509. L, O, LCL, LW; TO, WF.

626B —A good minister of Jesus Christ. *For Samuel Sprint, and John Lawrence,* 1693. 8°. T.C.II 437. L, O, LCL, LW; CLC, WF.

627 **Hamond, Walter.** Madagascar. *For Nicolas Bourne,* 1643. 4°.* L, LIU; CH, MH, NHS, Y.
Hampaaneah hammegulleh: or. 1664. *See* Heydon, John.

628 **Hampden, John.** A discreet and learned speech . . . the 4th of Ianuary, 1641. *For I. W.,* 1641[2]. 4°.* LT, C, LL, SP, DT; CSS, MH, MU, TU, WF, Y.

629 ——[Anr. ed.] *For F. Coules,* 1641. 4°.* L.

630 ——[Anr. ed.] *For F. Coules and T. B.,* 1641. 4°.* L, C, OC, DU, DT; CH, CLC, CSS, WF.

631–2A Entries cancelled.
—Mr. Hampdens speech. [n.p., 1643.] *See* Denham, Sir John.
Hampton, Barnabas. Prosodia construed. 1660. *See* Lily, William.

633 **Hampton, Robert.** In great Trinity Lane. *[London,* 1700?] brs. HH.

634 **Hampton, William.** Lachrymæ ecclesiæ; or the mourning of Hadadrimmon. *For VVil. Hope,* 1661. 4°.* LT, CK, DU, MR; CH.

635 —A map of judgement. *By R. I. for H. Brome,* 1667. 4°.* L, O, C, CT; CH, NU.

636 Hampton-Court conspiracy. *[London], printed,* 1647. 4°.* LT, O; CH, CN, CSS, MH, NN, Y.

637 **Hanbury, Nathaniel.** Horologia scioterica. *Apud Awnsham Churchil,* 1683. 4°.* T.C.II 5. L, O, C, E, DT; BN.

638 —Supplementum analyticum. *Cantabrigiæ, ex officina Johann. Hayes. Impensis authoris,* 1691. *Prostant venales per Edwardum Hall.* 4°.* L, O, OC, CT, YM; CSU.

639 **Hanchett, Edward.** To the right honourable the High Court of Parliament, the humble petition of. *[London,* 1654.] brs. LT, LG; MH.

640 **Hancock, Edward.** The pastors last legacy. *Printed,* 1663. 4°.* O, BR; MH.

641 **Hancock, John.** The great duty of thankfulness. *For Jonathan Robinson,* 1698. 4°.* T.C.III 51. L, O, LLP, OC.

642 —A sermon preach'd . . . December 26. 1698. *For B. Aylmer*, 1699. 8°. T.C.III 105. L, O, LLP, LW, OC, EC.

643 **Hancock, Robert.** The loyalty of Popish principles examin'd. *By S. Roycroft, for Thomas Flesher*, 1682. 8°. T.C.I 496. L, O, C, LCL, OC, OU, NE; NU.

644 [–] —[Anr. ed.] *For Thomas Flesher*, 1686. 8°. O, OU.

645 —A sermon preached . . . Septemb. 19. 1680. *By S. Roycroft for Tho. Flesher, and W. Leech*, 1680. 4°.* T.C.I 416. L, O, LG, CT, LSD, NOT; CH, LC, TO, TU, WF.

646 **Hancocke, Thomas.** Succus nutritius. [*Cambridge*], 1696. brs. O.

646A The handycrafts-men of this kingdom. [*London*, 1675.] brs. LPR, LUG.

647 Entry cancelled.
   Handekerchiefe for loyall mourners. 1649. *See* Warmstrey, Thomas.
   Hands of God. [n.p.], 1647. *See* Swadlin, Thomas.

647A **Handson, Ralph.** Analysis or resolution. Fourth edition. *By W. G. for Robert Horne*, 1669. brs. OC.

648 **Hanger, Philip.** A true relation how eighteen men were castaway at sea. *For Charles Harper*, 1675. 4°.* T.C.I 189. L, O, LNC, MR; CH, MH, Y.

649 The hangmans joy. *For John Andrews*, [1660]. 8°.* LT.

650 The hang-mans lamentation for the losse of Sir Arthur Haslerigge. [*London*], *for Tho. Vere, and W. Gilbertson.* 1660. 8°.* LT.

650A The hang-man's lamentation; or the chancellour's farewell. *Printed*, 1689. brs. CN.

651 The hang-mans last will and testament. *For Charls Gustavus.* [1660]. brs. LT; MII.

652 **H[anmer], J[onathan].** Ἀρχαιοσκοπια: or, a vievv. *For Thomas Parkhurst, and Jonathan Robinson*, 1677. 8°. T.C.I 272. L, O, LW, DU, E, DT; CLC, MH, NU, WF, Y.

653 —Τελειωσις: or, an exercitation. *By A. Maxey, for John Rothwell*, 1657. 8°. L, O, LW, CT, P, CD; MH, NU, TO, WF, Y.

654 ——Second edition. *By S. Griffin, for John Rothwell*, 1658. 8°. LT, O, C, LW, GU; CLC, IEG, MH, MWA, NU.

655 **Hannam, Richard.** The speech and confession of. *For G. Horton*, 1656. 4°.* LT.

655A Hannam's last farewell. *For Thomas Vere and William Gilbertson*, 1656. 12°. LT.

656 [**Hannay, Robert.**] A true account of the proceedings, sence and advice. *For R. Levis*, 1694. 4°.* L, O, LF, BAMB, BBN; CH, LC, NN, PH, PHS.

657 **H[annes, Edward].** An account of the dissection of . . . William Duke of Glocester. *For J. Nutt*, 1700. fol.* L, LLP, NE; MMO.

658 [–] Reflections upon Mr. Varillas his History of heresy, book I. [*Amsterdam?*], *printed*, 1688. 12°. LIL, OC, OM, CT; CLC, IU, NU, TU, WF, Y.

659 **Hannis, Richard.** Aime for the archers. *By N. Howell for Robert Minchard and Benjamin Brownsmith*, 1664. 8°. L, O.

659A **Hannott, James.** The right way of seeking God. A sermon preach'd at Great Yarmouth . . . [11 May 1692]. *By Tho. Snowden for Edward Giles*, 1692. 4°.* CH.

660 **Hansard, John.** A book of entries. *By the assigns of Richard and Edward Atkins, for William Crook*, 1685. fol. T.C.II 145. L, LI, LL, LMT, EN, DT; IU, LC, MHL, NCL, WF, YL.

661 **Hansard, William.** To the honourable the knights, citizens and burgesses assembled in the Commons . . . the several petitions of. *Printed at London*, 1646. 4°.* LT, OC, MR, BQ, DN; CH, WF, Y.

662 [**Hansley, John.**] A visitation speech delivered at Colchester. *Printed*, 1662. 4°.* O, MR; CLC.

663 **Hanson, John.** A short treatise shewing the Sabbatharians confuted. [*London*], *by R. D. sold by Livewell Chapman*, 1658. 8°. LCL, CS.

664 **Hanson, Samuel.** The case of. [n.p., 1684?] cap., fol.* L; MU, RPJ.

664A **Hanus, Josephus.** Anni, menses ac dies singuli, quibus natus est, . . . Christus. *Sumptibus authoris, prostant apud Joan. Gailloue, Danielem Du Chemin*, 1696. 8°.* LLP.

665 The happiest newes from Ireland. *For John Greensmith*, 1641. 4°.* LT, O, C, DN; CH, IU, MH, WF, Y.
   Happines of peace. [n.p.], 1641. *See* W., E.

665A Happy be lucky. Or, a catalogue. [*London*, 1693?] 4°.* MH.

665B —Pars secunda. [*London*, 169–?] cap., 4°.* MIU, NU.

665C The happy damsel. [*London*], *for I. Blare*, [1693]. brs. CM.

666 A happy defeat given to the kings forces. *By Andrew Coe*, 1644. 4°.* LT, BC, CD.

667 A happy deliverance, or, a wonderfull preservation. *For John Thomas*, 1641. 4°.* LT, LG, LVF, LNC, ESS; CH, NU, Y.

668 A happy discovery of the strange and fearefull plots. [*London*], *August. 6. for Io. Hundgate*, 1642. 4°.* LT, LIU; OSU.
   Happy future state. 1688. *See* Pett, Sir Peter.

668A The happy greeting of Iohn and Betty. [*London*], *for F. Coles, T. Vere, J. Wright, and J. Clarke*, [1674–79]. brs. O.
   Happy handfull. 1660. *See* Fuller, Thomas.
   Happy, happy, sung by Mrs. Linsey. [1698.] *See* Powell, George.

669 The happy husbandman. [*London*], *for P. Brooksby*, [1687]. brs. EUING 137. L, CM, HH, GU; MH.

669A The happy instruments of Englands preservation. *For Ben: Combe*, [1681]. brs. L.

669B The happy lover. [*London*], *for J. Blare*, [1684–99]. brs. L.

670 The happy lovers. *For C. Dennison*, 1688. brs. O.

671 —[Anr. ed.] [*London*], *for P. Brooksby, J. Deacon, J. Blare, J. Back*, [1688–92]. brs. HH.

671A The happy lovers pastime. [*London*], *for J. H. and sold by F. Coles, T. Vere, J. Wright, and J. Clarke*, [1674–9]. brs. O.

672 —[Anr. ed.] [*London*], *for Charles Passinger*, [1680]. brs. L, O, CM.

672A The happy man. [*London*], *for J. Back*, [1700?]. brs. O.

672B The happy meeting of King William and Queen Mary. [*London*], *by William Bailey*, [1690]. brs. MH.
   Happy newes from Sherborn. 1642. *See* W., J.
   Happy news to England. [n.p.], 1642. *See* Alsted, Johann Heinrich.

673 The happy return of the old Dutch miller. *For Allen Banks*, 1682. brs. O, HH; MH, PU.

674 —[Anr. ed.] [*London*], *for Allen Banks*, 1683. brs. L, MC.

674A The happy return, or an account of . . . Monmouth's sur-
     rendering. colop: *For L. C.*, 1683. brs. L, O; CH, IU, WF, Y.

675 The happy shepheard: or. [*London*], *for C. Bates*, [1695?].
     brs. L, HH.
     Happy slave. 1677. *See* Brémond, Gabriel de.

676 The happy success of the Parliaments armie at Nevvport.
     For John Wright, Novemb. 10. 1643. 4°.* LT; MH, TU.
     Happy union. 1689. *See* W., R.

677 A happy victory obtained by the trained band of Oxford.
     For Thomas Cooke, Sept. 10 [1642]. 4°.* MADAN 1036. LT.

678 Entry cancelled.
     Harangue to the King. 1681. *See* Lombard, André.
     Harbinger for the King. 1672. *See* J., T.

679 **Harbotle, Henry.** To the Parliament. The humble peti-
     tion of. [*London*, 1655.] brs. LT, LG.

680 **Harby, *Sir* Job.** The hvmble manifest of. *Printed*, 1650.
     4°.* LT, O.

681 —To his highness Oliver . . . The humble petition of.
     [*London*, 1658.] 4°.* NC.

681A —To the Parliament of England, the humble petition.
     [*London?* 1660.] brs. LG.

682 **Harby, Thomas.** Divi Arminij mactatorum renata. *By
     Matthew Simmons*, 1642. 4°.* LT, O, LG, EC; IU, NU, TU,
     WF, Y.

683 —The key of sacred Scripture. *For the author*, 1679. 4°. O,
     LW.

684 —The nation's claim of native right. *Printed*, 1650. 4°.
     LCL; WF.

685 —What is truth? *For the author*, 1670. 4°. O, SP.

686 ——[Anr. ed.]—, 1671. 4°. LCL, LW.

687 ——[Anr. ed.]—, 1673. 4°. C, CT, P.

687A ——[Anr. ed.] *Revised by the author, and reprinted for him*,
     1674. 4°. L, C, SHR.

687B ——[Anr. ed.]—, 1675. 4°. C, LNC, EN; WF.

688 ——[Anr. ed.]—, 1678. 4°. L, O, CASTLE ASHBY, YM; Y.

689 ——[Anr. ed.]— 1679. 4°. NU.

690 **Harcourt, Daniel.** The clergies lamentation. [*London*],
     for Henry Shepheard, 1644. 4°.* LT, C; CH, WF, Y.

691 —A hymne called Englands Hosanna. [*London*, 1661.] brs.
     LT.

692 —A new remonstrance from Ireland. *For Henry Shephard*,
     [1643]. 4°.* LT, O, C, MR, DN; CH, CU, LC, MH, NU, WF.

693–4 Entries cancelled.
     [**Harcourt, Henri de.**] French charity. 1655. *See* Cotton,
     Sir Robert Bruce. Answer made by Sr. Robert Cotton.
     [**Harcourt, Henry.**] Englands old religion. Antwerp,
     1658. *See* Beda, *Venerabilis.*

695 **Harcourt, *Sir* Simon.** March 18. A letter sent from . . .
     to a worthy member. *For Joseph Hunscott*, 1641. 4°.*
     LT, O, C, MR, DN, DT; CH.

696 **Harcourt, William.** The Papists new-fashion'd alle-
     giance. [*London*, 1679.] cap., fol.* L, O, C, LNC, MR; CH,
     CN, MIU, WF, Y.

696A The hard case of the glass makers. [*London?* 1697.] brs. L.

697 **H[ardcastle], P[eter].** The Quakers plea, answering. *For
     the author*, 1661. 4°.* L, O, LF, BBN; CH, MH, PH, WF, Y.

697A —A short relation of what is believed. 1666. 8°. LF.

698 —A testimony of Gods love. [*London*], *printed*, 1671. 4°.*
     L, LF, BBN, MR; MH, MM, PH, PSC, WF.

699 **Hardcastle, Thomas.** Christian geography. *For Richard
     Chiswel.* 1674. 8°. T.C.I 168. L, O, LCL, CT, BR; MH, NHC,
     Y.

699A —A sermon preached at Shadwell-Chappell . . . [18 June
     1665]. *Printed*, 1665. 4°.* NU, WF.

699B **Harding, Gideon.** A sermon preach'd before the society
     for reformation of manners. *For Tho. Parkhurst*, 1700.
     8°.* T.C.III 197. L, LW; WF.

700 **Harding, Michael.** Bibliotheca selectissima. [*Oxford,*
     1697.] fol.* L.

700AA **Harding, Thomas.** Annales. An English manuscript.
     [*London*, 1695]. brs. O.

700A **Hardmeat, Tobias.** For the magistrates. [*London?* 1676.]
     4°.* L, LF; MH, PH.

701 No entry.

     Hardouin de Perefixe, *bp*. *See* Perefixe, Hardouin
     Beaumont de, *bp*.

702 **H[ardres], P[eter].** Προσσω και οπισσω, a sermon. [*Lon-
     don?*], *printed*, 1647. 4°.* L, O, C, DC, YM; MH, NGT,
     TSM, WF, Y.

703 **Hardres, *Sir* Thomas.** Reports of cases. *By the assigns of
     Rich. and Edw. Atkins, for Christopher Wilkinson, Samuel
     Heyrick, and Mary Tonson*, 1693. fol. L, O, C, EN, DT; CH,
     LC, NCL, NR, V, WF, YL, AVP.

704 **Hardwick, Humphrey.** The difficvlty of Sions deliv-
     erance. *By I. L. for Christopher Meredith*, 1644. 4°.*
     LT, O, C, EN, DT; CH, IU, MH, NU, WF, Y.

705 —The saints gain by death. *By I. L. for Philemon Stephens*,
     1644. 4°.* O, LLP, LW, CS, GU; CH, MH, NU, WF, Y.

706 **H[ardy], J[ohn], *of the Marygold*.** A description of the
     last voyage to Bermudas. *For Rowland Reynald*, 1671.
     4°.* L; CH, LC, MBA, MH.

707 **Hardy, John, *messenger*.** The last proceedings of the
     Scots. *By Andrew Coe*, 1644. 4°.* LT; CN, MH, WF, Y.

708 **Hardy, Nathaniel.** The apostolical liturgy revived. *By
     A. M. for Joseph Cranford*, 1661. 4°.* O, C, LLP, LW, MR;
     CDA, CLC, CU, MH, WF.

709 —The arraignment of licentious libertie. *By T. R. and
     E. M. for Nat. Webb and Wil. Grantham*, 1647. 4°. LT, O,
     C, EN, DT; CLC, IU, MH, NU, Y.

710 ——[Anr. ed.] *By R. L. for Nathanaell Webb, and William
     Grantham*, 1647. 4°. L, O, C, LW, SHR; CH, IU, MH, NU,
     WF, Y.

711 ——[Anr. ed.] *For Nathanael Webb, and William Gran-
     tham*, 1657. 4°. L; CDA, CLC, MH, NU, WF, Y.

712 —Cardvvs benedictvs, the advantage of affliction. *For
     Joseph Cranford*, 1659. 4°.* L, C, LW; CLC, IU, MH, MWA,
     WF, Y.

713 —The choicest fruit of peace. *By A. M. for Joseph Cran-
     ford*, 1660. 4°.* L, O, C, BC, SP; CH, MH, NU, WF, Y.

714 —Death's alarum. *By J. G. for Nath: Web, and Will:
     Grantham*, 1654. 4°.* LT, O, LW, BQ; CLC, IU, MH, NU,
     WF, Y.

715 —A divine prospective. *For John Clark*, 1649. 4°.* LT, C,
     LW, OM, DU, DT; CLC, IU, NR, NU.

716 ——[Anr. ed.] —, 1654. 4°.* LT, O, LW, OC; CLC, CN, MH, NU, WF, Y.

717 ——[Anr. ed.] —, 1660. 4°.* L, LNC; CDA.

718 —Divinity in mortality. *By A. M. for Nathanael Webb and William Grantham,* 1653. 4°.* LT, O, C, OM, DT; CH, IU, NU, TU, WF, Y.

719 ——[Anr. ed.] *By T. C. for Nathanael Webb and William Grantham,* 1659. 4°.* L, C, LW; CLC, CU, MH, TSM, WF.

720 —The epitaph of a godly man. *By J. G. for Nathanaell Webb and William Grantham,* 1655. 4°.* LT, O, C, YM, DT; CH, IU, MH, NU, WF, Y.

721 —Faiths victory over natvre. *For Nathanael Webb, and William Grantham,* 1648. 4°.* L, O, C, OC, SHR; CLC, IU, NU, TU, WF, Y.

721A ——[Anr. ed.] *By T. C. for Nathannael Webb, and William Grantham,* 1658. 4°.* L, LW; CDA, CH, CLC, IU, MH, NU, TU.

722 —The first general epistle of St. John. First part. *By E. Tyler, for Nathanael Webb and William Grantham,* 1656. 4°. O, CT, SC, ENC, GU; CLC, NN, NU, WF, Y.

723 ——Second part. *For Joseph Cranford,* 1659. 4°. LT, O, LI, CT, SC; CLC, NU, WF, Y.

724 —The hierarchy exalted. *By Abraham Miller for Joseph Cranford,* 1661. 4°.* L, O, C, MR, DT; CDA, CLC, MH, WF.

725 Justice triumphing. *By E. G. for Nathaniel Webb, and William Grantham.* 1647. 4°.* LT, O, LW, CD, DT; CH, MB, MIU, NU, Y.

726 ——[Anr. ed.] *By R. L. for Nathaniel Webb, and William Grantham,* 1648. 4°.* L, C, OM, SHR, DN; CN, IU, NU, WF, Y.

727 ——[Anr. ed.] *For Nathanael Webb, and William Grantham,* 1656. 4°.* L, C, LP, OC, DT; CH, IU, MH, NU, WF.

728 —Lamentation, mourning and woe. *By Tho. Newcomb, for William Grantham,* 1666. 4°.* L, O, LL, CT, LG; CH, CU, MH, WF, Y.

729 —A looking-glasse of hvmane frailty. *By R. D. for Joseph Cranford,* 1659. 8°.* L, LW; CDA, CH, CLC, CN, MH, Y.

730 —A loud call to great mourning. *By Abraham Miller for Joseph Cranford,* 1662. 4°. L, O, C, OC, MR; CH, CLC, NGT.

730A ——[Anr. ed.] —, 1665. 4°.* CDA.

731 ——[Anr. ed.] *For William Grantham,* 1668. 4°.* OC, WCA; CDA, MH, NU, TU, WF, Y.

732 —Love and fear. *By A. M. for Nathanael Webb and William Grantham,* 1653. 4°.* LT, LW, OC, SP, DT; CH, IU, MH, NU, WF, Y.

733 ——[Anr. ed.] *By T. C. for Nathanael Webb and William Grantham,* 1658. 4°.* L, O; CDA, CLC, MH, NU, Y.

734 ——[Anr. ed.] 1675. 4°.* OM.

735 —Mans last journey. *By A. M. for Joseph Cranford,* 1659. 4°.* L, C, LG, LW, YM; CLC, CN, MH, MWA, WF, Y.

736 —Mercy in her beauty. *By J. G. for Nath: Web and Will: Grantham,* 1653. 4°.* L, O, LSC, OC, BQ; CLC, IU, MH, NU, WF, Y.

737 —The olive-branch presented. *By J. G. for John Clark,* 1658. 4°.* L, O, C, LP, LW, MR; CLC, CN, MH, NU, WF, Y.

738 —The pilgrims wish. *By A. M. for Joseph Cranford,* 1659. 4°.* L, LG, LW; CLC, CN, MH, WF, Y.

739 ——[Anr. ed.] *By T. Newcomb, for William Grantham,* 1666. 4°.* L, C, LW, OC, WCA; CDA, WF.

740 —The pious votary. *By J. G. for John Clark,* 1658. 4°. LT, O, LW, CT; CH, CLC, MH, NU, Y.

741 ——[Anr. ed.] —, 1659. 4°. L; CB, MH, NU, WF.

742 —The royal common-wealths man. *[London], in the Savoy, by Tho. Newcomb, for William Grantham,* 1668. 4°.* L, O, C, DU, BLH; CLC, MB, NU, WF, WSC, Y.

743 —A sad prognostick. *By A. M. for Joseph Cranford,* 1658. 8°.* L, O, C, LW, OC, SP; CH, MH, NU, WF, Y.

744 ——[Anr. ed.] 1660. 4°.* L, C; CDA, CLC, MH, NU.

745 —The safest convoy. *For Nathanael Web, and William Grantham,* 1649. 4°.* LT, O, C, MR, DT; CH, CLC, IU, NU, Y.

746 ——[Anr. ed.] —, 1653. 4°.* L, C, LSC, OC; CLC, MH, NU, WF, Y. (var.)

747 —Safety in the midst of danger. *By J. G. for John Clark,* 1656. 4°.* L, O, C, LW; CLC, CN, MH, NU, WF, Y.

747A [–] A sermon preached at St. Gregories Church. 1658. 4°.* EN; CLC.

748 —Several sermons. *By A. M. for Nathanael Webb and William Grantham,* 1653. 4°. CT; NU, PJB.

748aA ——[Anr. ed.] *For Nathanael Webb and William Grantham,* 1656. 4°. OC.

748A ——[Anr. ed.] *For N. Webb,* 1658. 8°. LCL.; CB, CLC, NU.

749 —Thankfulness in grain. *By T. W. for Nath. Webb, and Will. Grantham,* 1654. 4°. LT, O, C, OC; CLC, IU, MH, NU, WF, Y.

750 —Two mites. *By J. G. for Nath: Web and Will: Grantham,* 1653. 4°. L; CB, CDA, CH, CLC, IU, MH, NU.

751 ——[Anr. ed.] *For Nath. Web and Will: Grantham,* 1653. 4°. CH, Y.

752 —VVisdomes character and counterfeit. *By J. G. for John Clark,* 1656. 8°.* L, LW; CLC, IU, MH, NU, WF, Y.

753 —VVisdomes counterfeit. *By J. G. for John Clarke,* 1656. 4°.* L, O, C, EN; CDA, CLC, NU, WF, Y.

753A **[Hardy, Samuel.]** A guide to heaven from the word. *By E. C. for H. Brome,* 1664. 12°. CT; WF.

753B [–] —[Anr. ed.] *For H. Brome,* 1671. 12°. L.

753C [–] —[Anr. ed.] *For H. Brome,* 1673. 24°. T.C.I 241. WU.

753D [–] —[Anr. ed.] *For Awnsham Churchil and Charles Brome,* 1687. 12°. Y.

754 [–] —[Anr. ed.] *Boston, by Samuel Green,* 1689. 24°.* EVANS 469. MB.

755 [–] A guide to scattered flocks. *To be sold by Caleb Swinnock,* 1684. 8°. NU.

755A [–] A second guide to heaven. *For A. Churchill and sold by W. Churchill in Dorset,* 1687. 8°. T.C.II 215. LW; CH, NU.

756 **Hare, Francis.** Posita. *[n.p.],* 1697. brs. O, LLP.

757 —A sermon preach'd . . . January the 6th. *Cambridge, at the University Press, for Edmund Jeffery,* 1700. 4°.* T.C.III 181. L, O, C, CK, LIU, LSD; CH, CLC, CSU, MBA, NGT, WF, Y.

758 ——[Anr. ed.] *Henry Hills,* [1700]. 8°. L, CT.

759 No entry.

[Hare, Henry.] Plaine English. 1643. *See* Bowles, Edward.

760 **Hare, Hugh.** A charge given . . . 5th day of April, 1692. *For John Newton,* 1692. 4°.* T.C.II 413. L, O, CT, DC, MR; CH, CN, MH, PL, WF.

761 — —Second edition. —, 1696. 4°.* L, C, DT; Y.

762 [**Hare, John.**] Englands proper and onely way. *For R. L.,* 1648. 4°.* LT, O, MR; CH, CN, MH, NU, WF, Y.

763 [–] The marine mercury. [*London*], *printed,* 1642. 4°.* LT, O; MH.

764 [–] Plaine English to our wilfull bearers. *For George Whittington,* 1647. 4°.* LT, O, OC, MR; CH, CN, WF, Y.

765 [–] St. Edwards ghost. *For Richard Wodenothe,* 1647. 4°.* LT, O, CS, DU, DT; CH, CN, MH, MIU.

Harflete, Henry. Ἀρωνοφηγματα. An ephemeris. 1651. *See* Almanacs.

766 —A banquet of essayes. *By T. R. & E. M., to be sold by Joseph Barber,* 1653. 8°. LT, O, C; CH, CN, MH, WF, Y.

766A [–] The hunting of the fox, or, flattery displayed. *For Edward Brewster,* 1657. 12°. RHT.

766B [–] —[Anr. ed.] *For Andrew Pennycuik,* 1657. 12°. SP.

—Ουρανοδειξις. 1652. *See* Almanacs.

767 —Vox cœlorum. Predictions. *Imprinted at London for Mat. Walbancke,* [1646]. 8°. LT; Y.

768 [**Harford, Rapha.**] A gospel-engine. *By, and for R. H.,* 1649. 4°.* LT, O, LCL, DC, YM; CLC, CN, CU, NU, WF, Y.

768A **Hargrave, A.** Reason in season: or, a word on the behalf of the non-collegiate physicians. [*London*], *printed,* 1676. 4°.* L, O.

[**Hargrave, Francis.**] Some considerations upon the question. [n.p.], 1676. *See* Holles, Denzil Holles, *lord.*

768B [**Hargreaves, John.**] The world's anatomy. *York, by Stephen Bulkley,* 1675. 4°. Y.

769 **Harington, Henry.** An elegie upon the death of . . . Robert, Lord Brooke. *For H. O.,* 1642. brs. LT.

770 **Harington, *Sir* John.** A briefe view of the state of the Church of England. *For Jos. Kirton,* 1653. 12°. L, O, C, EN, DT; CH, CN, MH, NU, WF, Y.

771 **H[arington], J[ohn].** The Grecian story. *For William Crook,* 1684. 4°. T.C.II 47. L, O, LLU; CH, CN, MH, TU, WCL, Y.

[–] Grounds & reasons. [n.p.], 1650. *See* Hall, John.

772 [–] The history of Polindor and Flostella. *By Tho. Roycroft for Tho: Dring,* 1651. 8°. LT, O, LVD; CH, CLC, CN, MH, WC.

773 — —Third edition. *By T. R. for Thomas Dring,* 1657. 8°. IU, MH, PU, Y.

774 No entry.

[–] Nahash redivivus. 1649. *See* Harrison, John.

775 Entry cancelled.

[–] Politicaster. 1659. *See* Harrington, James, *elder.*

776 **Harlay–Chanvallon, Francois de,** *abp.* The condemnation of Monsieur DuPin his history. *For Charles Brome and William Keblewhite,* 1696. 4°.* T.C.II 580. L, O, CS, AN, DU, DT; CH, CN, LC, NU, Y.

776A —A letter from the arch-bishop of Paris. *Printed and are to be sold by Rich. Baldwin,* 1694. brs. SP, EN; CLC.

777 [**Harley, *Sir* Edward.**] An humble essay toward the settlement of peace and truth. *For N. Simmons, and T. Simmons,* 1681. 4°.* T.C.I 438. L, O, DU, WCA, LW; CN, NU, Y.

778 [–] A scriptural and rational account. *For Jonas Luntley,* 1695. 12°. L, O, LW.

779 — —[Anr. ed.] *For Jonas Luntley,* 1695. 12°. L, LCL, LW; TO, Y.

780 [**Harlowe, Pedaell.**] A detection or, discovery of a notable fravd. *By E. P. for William Leake,* 1641. 4°. L, O, CT, SHR, GU; CH, IU, MH, NU, WF, Y.

781 [**Harmar, John.**] Ad spectatissimum virum, . . . Lambertum Osbalstonum epistola. *Typis,* 1649. [colop: *Venundantur apud Octavian Pullenum.*] 8°. LT, O, C, OC, DU, LSD, DT; CLC, NCD, WF, Y.

782 —Æternitati sacrum. *Typis Joannis Macock,* 1658. brs. O.

783 —Apologia. 1649. L, O.

784 —Χριστολογια μετρικη. Sive hymnus. *Typis Joannis Macock & impensis editoris,* 1658. 8°.* L, O, C, LW, CK; NU, WF.

785 — —[Anr. ed.] *Typis Joannis Macock,* 1660. 8°.* LT, O, LIU; MH, TO.

786 — —[Anr. ed.] *Typis Joannis Heptinstall,* 1698. 8°.* O, EN; CH, IU, MH, NN, WG, Y.

787 —Entry cancelled. Κατηχησις της Χριστιανικης θρησκειας συντομωτερα. 1659. *See* title.

788 — —[Anr. ed.] *Typis Joannis Macock,* 1660. 8°. O, C, LCL, LIU; MH, TO, Y.

789 — —[Anr. ed.] *Prostant venales apud omnes fere bibliopolarum officines,* 1698. 8°. T.C.III 104. O, LCL, EN, GU; CH, IU, MBC, MWA, MH, Y.

790 —Marci Tulii Ciceronis vita. *Oxoniæ, typis A. & L. Lichfield, impensis J. Nixon,* 1662. 8°.* MADAN 2598. O.

791 —Oratio gratulatoria. *Oxoniæ, excudebat A. Lichfield,* 1657. 8°.* MADAN 2323. L, O, C, OB, CK; CLC, NCD, WF.

792 —Oratio Oxoniæ habita. *Typis Guil. Du Gardi,* 1650. 8°. O, C, OB, CK, GU; WF.

792A —Oratio panegyrica in honoram Caroli Secundi. *Typis Thomae Roycroft, pro O.P.,* 1660. 8°. O.

793 — —[Anr. ed.] *Oxoniæ, excudebat W. Hall per autorem,* 1663. 8°. MADAN 2639. O, LW, CCA.

794 —Oratio serenissimi protectoris elogium complectens. *Oxoniæ, excudebat Hen: Hall,* 1654. 4°.* MADAN 2244. LT, O, P, LNC, EN; CH, CLC, MH, TO, WF, Y.

795 —Oratio steliteutica Oxoniæ. *Excudebat Rogerus Daniel,* 1658. 8°.* MADAN 2365. L, O, C, OC, CK, WCA; CLC, NCD, WF.

796 —Serenissimo . . . Olivero. [*London*], 1653. brs. MADAN 2218. O, OB.

797 No entry.

798 —Vindiciæ academiæ Oxoniensis. *Oxoniæ, excudebat A. & L. Lichfield, per J. Nixon,* 1662. 8°. MADAN 2581. O.

799 **Harmar, Samuel.** Vox populi, or, Glostersheres desire. *For Thomas Bates,* 1642. 4°.* LT, MR; CU, MH, Y.

Harmer, Anthony. *See* Wharton, Henry.

799A The harmlesse opinion of the revolution. *For Sarah Howkins,* 1694. 8°.* LSC.

800 No entry.

Harmonia sacra: or. 1688. *See* Playford, Henry.

800A The harmonious consent of the ministers of . . . Lancaster. *By J. Macock, for Luke Fawne*, 1648. 4°.* LT, O, C, SC, DT; CH, MH, MIU, NU, WF.

800AB —[Anr. ed.] *For Luke Fawne and sold by Thomas Smith*, 1648. 4°.* OC; IU.

800B —[Anr. ed.] *Reprinted at Edinburgh by Evan Tyler*, 1648. 4°.* ALDIS 1326. L, EC, MR, EN; MH, Y.

Harmony between the old. 1682. *See* Lobb, Stephen.

Harmony of divine. 1696. *See* Penn, William.

Harmony of divinity. 1684. *See* Hickes, George.

800C A harmany [*sic*] of healths. [*London*], *by John Hamm*[*ond*], [1647]. brs. MAU.

Harmony of natural. 1682. *See* Charleton, Walter.

801 The harmony of ovr oathes. *By T. Pain, and M. Simonds for Thomas Vnderhill*, 1643. 4°.* LT, O, CT, EN, DT; CH, IU, MH, NU, WF, Y.

802 An harmony of the confessions of the faith of the Christian . . . chvrches. *By Iohn Legatt*, 1643. 4°. L, O, CM, LLU, GU, BLH; CH, CLC, IU, MB, NCD, NU, Y.

Harmony of the muses. 1654. *See* C., R.

Harmony of the Old and New. 1694. *See* Tomkins, John.

803 **Haro, Lewis de.** A translate of a letter from. [*London*, 1660.] brs. LT, O, HH, DN; IU, MH.

803A **Harold, Thomas.** Narratio facti. *Parisiis* [*i.e. Dublin*, 1670]. 4°. DIX 361. C, DT.

803B —Tractatus de recursu ad protectionem principium. *Parisiis* [*i.e. Dublin*, 1670]. 4°.* L, O.

803C **Harr., Jo.** A vindication of the armie, from sole calumnious quæres. [*n.p.*, 1647?] cap., 4°.* WF.

803D **H[arrington], Sir J[ames], bart., 1607–1680.** A holy oyl. [*London*], *for the author*, 1669. fol. L, BC.

803E —Horæ consecratæ, or spiritual pastime. *For the author*, 1682. fol. L, O, LW; CH, CN, NCD, NU, WF, Y.

803F —[Anr. ed.] *Printed, and are to be sold by Nath. Ponder, Tho. Symonds, and Jon. Wilkins*, 1682. T.C.I 469. fol. L, LW; CLC, NCD, NU.

803G —Noah's dove. *By T. W. for Ed. Husbands*, 1645. 4°.* L, O, LCL, SP, E; CH, NN, NU, RBU.

804 **Harrington, James, elder.** Aphorisms political. *By J. C. for Henry Fletcher*, [1659]. 4°.* LT, O, LCL, LSD, EN; CLC, CN, MH, WF, Y.

805 ——Second edition. —, 1659. 4°.* O, CK, LLU, BC, CD; CH, MH, MU, PL, Y.

806 —The art of law-giving. *By J. C. for Henry Fletcher*, 1659. 8°. L, O, C, LCL, LI; BN, CH, CN, LC, MH, WF, YL.

806A [–] The benefit of the ballot. [*London?* 1680.] cap., fol.* L, O, LG, OP; CLC, IU, MH, TU, WF, Y.

[–] Brief admonition of some. 1659. *See* Howell, James.

807 [–] Brief directions shewing how a fit and perfect model. colop: *For Daniel Pakeman*, 1659. cap., 4°.* O, CM, MR, SP, DT; IU, MH, WF.

808 [–] The censure of the Rota upon Mr Miltons book. *By Paul Giddy*, 1660. 4°.* LT, O, LUG, OC, CT; CH, CN, MH, NU, WF, Y.

809 [–] The common-wealth of Oceana. *By J. Streater, for Livewell Chapman*, 1656. fol. L, O, C, A, DT; BN, CH, CN, MH, WF, Y.

809A [–] —[Anr. ed.] *For D. Pakeman*, 1656. fol. O, LUG, CM, LIU, E; CH, IU, MB, PL, TSM, Y.

810 — —[Anr. ed.] —, 1658. fol. O, CK; CLC, IU, LC, MH, ZWT.

811 Entry cancelled.

[–] Decrees and orders. 1659. *See title.*

812 —A discourse shewing, that the spirit of Parliaments. *By J. C. for Henry Fletcher*, 1659. 4°.* LT, O, CM, LLU, SP; CH, MH, MU, NU, WF, Y.

813 [–] A discourse upon this saying. *By J. C. for Henry Fletcher*, [1659]. 4°.* LT, O, CM, BC, DT; CH, MH, MU, TU, WF, Y.

813A [–] Half a sheet against Mr. Baxter: or, a paraphase. [*London*, 1658?] brs. MH.

814 Entry cancelled.

—Holy oyl. [*n.p.*], 1669. *See* Harrington, *Sir* James.

814A [–] A letter unto Mr. Stubs in answer to his Oceana weighed. colop: *For J. S.*, 1660. cap., 4°.* LT, CM, SP; CH, INU, MH, WF.

815 Entry cancelled.

—Noah's dove. 1645. *See* Harrington, *Sir* James.

816 —The Oceana of. *Printed*, 1700. fol. T.C.III 188. L, O, C, E, DT; BN, CLC, CN, MBP, MH, MU, NU, WF, Y.

817 —A parallel of the spirit of the people. *By J. C. for Henry Fletcher*, [1659]. 4°.* LT, O, OC, CM, SP; CLC, MH, TO, TU, WF.

817A [–] Pian piano; or intercourse between H. Ferne . . . and J. Harrington. *For Nath. Brook*, 1656. 8°. O, OC; NU.

818 —Political discourses. *By J. C. for Henry Fletcher*, 1660. 4°. L, O, CM; MH, PL, WF.

818A [–] Politicaster: or, a comical discourse. *By J. C. for Henry Fletcher*, 1659. 8°. LT, O, BAMB.

819 [–] Pour enclouer le canon. colop: *For Henry Fletcher*, 1659. cap., 4°.* LT, O, CM, E, DT; CH, MH, TU, WF, Y.

820 —The prerogative of popular government. *For Tho. Brewster*, 1658. 4°. L, O, C, LIU, SP; BN, CLC, CN, LC, MH, NU, WF, Y.

[–] Proposition in order. [*n.p.*, 1659.] *See title.*

821 [–] The Rota: or, a model. *For John Starkey*, 1660. 4°.* LT, O, LUG, CM, LLU, YM; CLC, CN, LC, MH, NU, WF, Y.

822 [–] The stumbling-block of disobedience . . . removed. colop: *For D. Pakeman*, 1658. cap., 4°.* O, C, CM; MH, WF.

823 [–] The vsc and manner of the ballot. [*n.p.*, 1660.] brs. O, CM, MH.

824 —Valerius and Publicola. *By J. C. for Henry Fletcher*, 1659. 4°.* LT, O, CK, CM, LSD; CH, IU, MIU, PL, WF, Y.

825 —The vvayes and meanes. *For J. S.*, 1660. 4°.* LT, O, LUG, CM, MR, SP; CSS, INU, MB, MH, NN, WF.

826 **[Harrington, James], younger.** An account of the proceedings of the right reverend . . . Jonathan . . . Exeter. *Oxford, at the theatre*, 1690. 4°. T.C.II 338. L, O, CT, MR, DT; CH, CN, LC, MH, NU, WF, Y.

827 [–] —Second edition. —, *Sold by Tho. Bennet, London*. 1690. 4°. L, O, OC, BAMB, MR; CH, CN, MH, NU, WF, Y.

828 Entry cancelled.

[–] The benefit of the ballot. 1680. *See* Harrington, James, *elder*.

829   —Catalogue of the library. [*London*], 13 *Feb* 1695. 4°. L.

830   [–] A defence of the proceedings of the right reverend the visitor. *For Tho. Bennet*, 1691. 4°. T.C.II 362. L, O, CS, MR, DT; CLC, MH, NU, WF, Y.

831–2 Entries cancelled.
       —Horæ consecratæ. 1682. *See* Harrington, *Sir* James.

832A   [–] Roger L'estranges queries considered. colop: *For John Palmer*, 1690. cap., 4°.* L, LLP, LIU; CN, MH, PU, WF, Y.

833   Entry cancelled.
       [–] Some queries concerning. 1690. *See* L'Estrange, *Sir* Roger.

834   [–] Some reflexions upon a treatise call'd Pietas romana. *Oxford, at the theater*, 1688. 4°. T.C.II 417. L, O, C, EN, DT; CH, IU, MH, NU, TU, WF, Y.

835   [–] A vindication of Mr. James Colmar. *For Tho. Bennet*, 1691. 4°. T.C.II 362. L, O, CT, MR, DT; CH, MH, NC, WF, Y.

836   [–] A vindication of Protestant charity. *Oxford*, 1688. 4°. MC.

837   **Harris, Anthony.** An account of an apparition. colop: [*London*], *by Nat. Thompson*, 1684. brs. L, O, HH; CH, CLC, MH, Y.

838   **Harris, Batholomew.** The true copy of a letter from. colop: *For Samuel Tidmarsh*, 1688. cap., fol.* L, O, INDIA OFFICE.

       [**Harris, Benjamin.**] Boston almanack. Boston, 1692. *See* Almanacs.

839   No entry.

840   Entry cancelled.
       —Humble petition of. [n.p., 1680.] *See* —To the honourable the Commons.

841   [–] To His most sacred Majesty King William III. A congratulatory poem. *Printed, and sold by B. Harris*, 1697. brs. HH.

842   —To the honourable House of Commons . . . the case and humble petition of. [*London*], 1680/81. fol.* MR; MH, MU.

842A   —To the honourable House of Commons, . . . the case and humble petition of . . . , bookseller lately come from New England. [*London*, 1695?] brs. NN.

842B   —To the honourable the Commons . . . the humble petition of. [*London*, 1680.] brs. LUG, HH.

843   **Harris, Edward.** A trve relation of a company of Brownists. [*London*], *printed*, 1641. 4°.* LT, OW, AN; NU, WF.

844   **Harris, Francis.** Some queries proposed. *For Henry Fletcher*, 1655. 4°. C, LF; PSC.

845   **Harris, John.** The atheistical objections, against the being. *By J. L. for Richard Wilkin*, 1698. 4°. T.C.III 119. O, C, CE, LSD, GU, DT; CH, MH, NU, PL, TU.

846   —The atheist's objection, that. *By J. L. for Richard Wilkin*, 1698. 4°.* T.C.III 62. L, O, C, EN, DT; CH, IU, MH, PL, WF, Y.

847   —The atheist's objections, against the immaterial nature. *By J. L. for Richard Wilkin*, [1698]. 4°. T.C.III 62. L, O, C, LSD, DT; CH, IU, MH, PL, TU, WF, Y.

848–9 Entries cancelled.
       [–] Divine physician. 1676. *See* Harris, John, *M.A.*

850   —Immorality and pride, the great causes of atheism. *By J. L. for Richard Wilkin*, 1698. 4°.* T.C.III 62. L, O, C, LG, DT; CH, CN, MH, PL, WF, WSC, Y.

851   [–] A letter to Dr. T. Robinson. [*London?* 1697.] brs. L, O, LLP.

852   —The notion of a god. *By J. L. for Richard Wilkin*, 1698. 4°.* T.C.III 62. L, O, C, LSD, DT; CLC, MH, PL, TU, WF, Y.

853   —A refutation of the atheistical notion of fate. *By J. L. for Richard Wilkin*, 1698. 4°.* T.C.III 92. L, O, CE, EC, DT; CH, CU, MH, PL, TU, WF, Y.

854   —A refutation of the objections against moral good and evil. *By J. L. for Richard Wilkin*, 1698. 4°.* T.C.III 92. L, O, OC, CE, LSD, DT; CLC, MH, MIU, PL, TU, WF, Y.

855   —A refutation of the objections against the attributes. *By J. L. for Richard Wilkin*, 1698. 4°. T.C.II 92. L, O, CE, EC, DT; CH, MH, MIU, PL, TU, WF, Y.

856   —Remarks on some late papers. *For R. Wilkin*, 1697. 8°. T.C.III 41. L, O, C, AN, SHR, DT; BN, CH, MH, V, WF, WGS, Y.

856A   **Harris, John,** *capt.* To the Parliment of the Commonwealth . . . the humble representation of. [*London*], 1651. cap., 4°.* L.

857   **Harris, John,** *gent.* Englands out-cry. *By T. Forcet, Iuly, 24*, 1644. 4°.* LT, AN, DT; CH. IAU, NU, WF.

858   Entry cancelled.
       [–] Grand designe. 1647. *See* Harris, John, *leveller.*

859   —Peace and not warre. *For Nath. Brook*, 1659. 4°. LT, WCA, BC, DU, CD; CH, IU, MH, WF, Y.

860   —The Pvritanes impvritie. *By T. Favvcet*, 1641. 4°.* LT, O, OC, OW, CCC; MH, NU.

860A   [**Harris, John**], *leveller.* The grand designe: or, a discovery. [*London*], *printed*, 1647. 4°.* LT, E, EN, BLH; CH, CU, MH, MU, WF, Y.

860B   [–] A lash for a lyar. *For J. Hornish, Febr. 22.* 1647. 4°.* LT; CH, MH, NU.

861   [–] The royall quarrell. *For Ja. Hornish, February 9*, 1647. 4°.* LT, O, CS, MR, DT; CB, CLC, CN, IU, MH, NU, WF.

861A   H[arris], J[ohn], *M.A.* The divine physician. [*London*], *for George Rose, in Norwich, to be sold by him there, and by Nath. Brook, and Will. Whitwood, in London*, 1676. 8°. L, O, C, EN; MMO, WSC.

861B   [–] —[Anr. ed.] *By H. B. for Will Whitwood, sold by George Rose in Norwich*, 1676. 8°. T.C.I 245. L, LSC, LWL; WF, WSG, Y.

862   **Harris, John,** *major.* The speech of . . . at the place of execution. *For Nathaniel Bryan*, 1660. 4°.* LT; MH, Y.

863   [**Harris, Joseph.**] The city bride. *For A. Roper and E. Wilkinson, and R. Clavel.* 1696. 4°. L, O, A; CH, CN, LC, NN, WF.

864   [–] Love's lottery. *For Daniel Brown, and Edmund Rumball*, 1699. 4°.* T.C.III 141. L, O, LGI, OW, EN; CH, CN, LC, MH, MU, WF, Y.

865   —The mistakes. *For Jo. Hindmarsh*, 1691. 4°. T.C.II 347. L, O, OW, LLU, EN; CLC, CN, LC, MH, WF, Y.

866–7 Entries cancelled.
       Harris, Mary. *See* Forster, Mary.

867A   **Harris, Renatus.** Renatus Harris, organ-maker, his challenge. [*London?* 1688?] brs. CH.

867B —A song. [*London? 1700.*] brs. L.

868 **Harris, Robert.** The vvorks of. *By James Flesher, for John Bartlet the elder, and John Bartlet the younger,* 1654. fol. L, O, CT, AN, DT; CH, CU, MH, NU, WSC, Y.

869 —Abners funerall. *For Iohn Bartlet,* 1641. 4°.* LT, O, C, ENC, DT; BN, MH, NU, TU, WF, Y.

870 —A brief discourse of mans estate. *By J. Flesher for John Bartlet the elder, and John Bartlet the younger,* 1653. fol.* L; NU, TU.

871 — —[Anr. ed.] —, 1654. 12°. L, LW, DC, SP.

872 —Concio ad clervm. *Excudebat G. M. pro Iohanne Bartlet,* 1641. 4°.* MADAN 968. L, O, C, MR, ENC; BN, IU, MH, NU, WF, Y.

873 — —[Anr. ed.] *Excusum pro Johanne Bartlet,* 1653. fol.* NU, TU, Y.

874 Entry cancelled.
—Judas his miserie. 1653. *See* —Works of.

875 —A sermon preached . . . May, 25. 1642. *By M. F. for Iohn Bartlet,* 1642. 4°. LT, O, CM, AN, ENC, DT; CH, CN, MH, NU, WF, Y.

876 —Severall sermons of. *By James Flesher, for John Bartlet the elder* [*and*] *Jonh* [*sic*] *Bartlet the younger,* 1654. 4°. L; BN, NU.

877 Entry cancelled.
—Treatise. 1653. *See* — Works of.

878 —True religion in the old way. *For John Bartlet,* 1645. 4°.* LT, O, CS, ENC, DT; BN, CLC, IU, MH, NU, WF, Y.

879 —Two letters written by. [*Oxford, by L. Lichfield*], printed, 1648. 4°.* MADAN 1990. LT, O, CJ, LNC; CH, CSS.

880 **Harris, Walter.** De morbis acutis infantum. *Impensis Samuelis Smith,* 1689. 8°. T.C.II 288. L, C, OM, MAU, E; CH, CLC, CJC, MH, NAM, TO, WSG.

[–] Defence of the Scots abdicating. [n.p.], 1700. *See* Hodges, James.

881 [–] The defence of the Scots settlement at Darien, answer'd. *Printed and sold by the booksellers at London and Westminster,* 1699. 12°. L, O, EN, ES, GM; CH, CN, LC, MH, NC, RPJ, WF, Y.

882 —A description of the king's royal palace and gardens at Loo. *By R. Roberts, and sold by J. Nutt,* 1699. 4°. T.C.III 154. L, O, LS, CS, ES; CH, CN, MH, NU, PL.

882A — —[Anr. ed.] *By K. Roberts, and sold by T. Nutt,* 1699. 4°.* L, CS; CLC, MBM, MH, WF, Y.

883 —An exact enquiry into, and cure of the acute diseases of infants. *For Sam. Clement,* 1693. 12°. L, LWL; CH, MBM, NCD, WSG.

883A — —[Anr. ed.] *For S. C. and J. Wyat,* 1694. 12°. T.C.II 493. LWL, GK; TORONTO ACAD. OF MED.

884 [–] A farewel to Popery. *For Walter Kettilby,* 1679. 4°.* T.C.I 1339. L, O, C, LCP, EN; CLC, CN, MH, NU, PL, WF, Y.

885 —Pharmacologia anti-empirica: or a rational discourse. *For Richard Chiswell,* 1683. 8°. T.C.II 16. L, O, C, AM, DT; CH, CNM, MH, NS, WF, HC.

886 **H[arris], Sir W[alter].** Remarks on the affairs and trade of England and Ireland. *For Tho. Parkhurst,* 1691. 4°. T.C.II 339. L, O, C, EN, DT; CH, CN, LC, MH, NC, Y.

887 **Harris, William.** A seasonable exhortation for the inhabitants of Polesworth. [*n.p.*], 1669. PH.

Harrison, Edward. God's revenge. 1692. *See* Harrison, Henry.

888 **Harrison, Edward,** *lieutenant.* Idea longitudinis; being, a brief definition. *For the author, and sold by Mr. Sellers; R. Mount; and P. Lea,* 1696. 8°. L, C, LR, OC, SP; NA.

889 **Harrison, Edward,** *of Keensworth, Herts.* Plain dealing. *For J. Harris,* 1649. 4°.* LT, C, LVF; CH, CN, NHC, NU, WF, Y.

889A **Harrison, Edward,** *fl. 1675.* The properties and portion of the righteous. *Printed in the year* 1675. 8°. ORP.

890 **Harrison, George.** An elegie on the death of the right honourable Robert Blake. [*London*], *for John Bartlet the elder, and John Bartlet the younger,* 1657. brs. LT.

890A **Harrison, [Henry].** God's revenge against murther. [*London,* 1692.] cap., 4°.* L.

891 —The last dying words. *Printed, and are to be sold by Richard Baldwin,* 1692. brs. CM, MC, MR; CLC.

892 —The last words of a dying penitent. *Printed, and are to be sold by Randal Taylor,* 1692. 4°.* L, O, LWI, CM, CT; CH, MH, NU, WF, Y.

893 —A true copy of a letter, written by. *For Randal Taylor,* [1692]. brs. L, CM.

893A [–] The weary traveller. *By A. G. and J. P. for R. Clavell,* 1681. 8°. T.C.I 448. C, CS; LC, WF.

894 **Ha[rrison], Jo[hn].** Nahash redivivus . . . examined and answered. *For Thomas Brewster,* 1649. 4°.* L, O, AN, MR, DT; BN, CH, MH, WF, WU, Y.

895 —A thanksgiving sermon for discovery . . . September 9. 1683. *For W. Crooke,* 1683. 4°.* T.C.II 42. L, O, CS, ENC, DT; CH, CN, IU, WF, Y.

896 —A vindication of the Holy Scriptures. *By J. M. and sold by J. Benson, and J. Playford,* 1656. 12°. LT, C, BLH, WF.

897 **Harrison, Joseph.** A glimpse of divine light. *For N. Brook,* 1655. 4°. LT.

898 —The lamentable cry of oppression. [*London*], *printed,* 1679. 4°.* L, LF, OC, BBN; IE, MH, PH, PSC, WF.

899 [–] The minister of Cirencester's address to the Dissenters. *By T. M., to be sold by Ric. Chiswell; and J. Barksdale,* 1698. 4°.* T.C.III 38. L, O, DU; NU, WF.

899A [–] —[Anr. ed.] *By T. M. to be sold by J. Southby, R. Baldwin, and J. Barksdale in Cirencester,* 1698. 4°.* L, CT, NE.

900 —The Popish proselyte. *For Samuel Tidmarsh,* 1684. 8°. LW, ORP.

900A **Harrison, M[ark].** A narrative of the proceedings of the fleet. *By John Streater,* 1659. 4°.* L, O, C, LG, BC; CH, MB, MH, WF, Y.

901 **Harrison, Michael.** The best match. *For Nathanael Ranew,* 1691. 8°. T.C.II 329. O, LCL; CH, WF.

902 —Christ's righteousness a believer's surest plea. *For Nathanael Ranew,* 1691. 8°. T.C.II 357. O; CH, WF.

903 —Christ's righteousness imputed. *For William and Joseph Marshal,* [1690?]. 4°.* L, O, C.

904 —A gospel church describ'd. *Printed, and sold by T. Pashum in Northampton, and M. Conyers in Newport-Pagnal,* 1700. 12°. O, LCL, LW.

905 —Infant baptism. *For Thom. Cockerill*, 1694. 8°. C.

905A — —Part II. *For Tho. Cockerill, Sen. and Jun.*, 1696. 8°. L; MB.

906 **Harrison, R.** The necessitie of church guides. [*n.p.*], 1675. 4°. LCL.

907 [**Harrison, Richard.**] Irelands misery since the late cessation. *For Henry Shephard, January 26*, 1644. cap., 4°.* LT, LVF, SC, EN, DN, DT; CH, CU, MH, WF, Y.

908 [**Harrison, Robert.**] A strange relation of the suddain and violent tempest. *For Richard Sherlock in Oxford* 1682. 4°.* L, O, OB, OP, CT; CCC, MH, WF, Y.

909 —Two sermons. *Printed, to be sold by Tho. Sawbridge*, 1672. 4°. T.C.I 101. L, O, WCA; NU, WF.

909A — —[Anr. ed.] *Printed, and are to be sold by George Sawbridge, in Melton-Mowbrary, Leicester-shire*, 1672. 4°. WF.

910 **Harrison, Thomas, *Baptist*.** A funeral sermon on Mordecai Abbott . . . April the 7th, 1700. *For D. Brown, and A. Bell*, 1700. 8°. L.

910A —Funeral sermon . . . upon . . . Mrs. Rebecka Goddard. *For J. Harris*, [1692?]. 4°.* L, LG, LW.

911 —A sermon on the decease of Mr. Hanserd Knollys. *For H. Barnard*, 1694. 8°. LW; NHC.

912 —A sermon preach'd . . . March 23, 1694/5. *By J. D. for the author*, 1695. 4°.* L, O, LW; CH, WF.

913 **Harrison, Thomas, *Maj.-Gen*.** A declaration of. *For Nathaniel Tomkins*, 1660. 4°.* LT, O, DU; WF.

913A —The speech of. *For Charles Gustavus*, 1660. 4°.* LT, WF.

914 **Harrison, Thomas, *of St. Dunstan*.** Old Jacobs accompt . . . or a sermon. *By J. Macock, for Lodowick Lloyd & H. Cripps*, 1655. 4°.* LW; CN, MH, MWA, WF.

915 Entry cancelled.
—Rebels no saints. 1661. *See* S., W.

916 —Threni Hybernici: or, Ireland sympathising. *By E. Cotes, and are to be sold by John North at Dublin*, 1659. 4°.* O, C, LVF, DM, DT; CLC, MH, NU, WF.

916A — —For R. Clavell, 1659. 4°.* LW, CD.

917 [–] Topica sacra: spiritual logick. *For Francis Titon*, 1658. 8°. LT, O, LCL, BLH; CH, MM, NU.

917A [**Harrison, Thomas**], ***publisher*.** The doctrine of passive obedience. *For Randal Taylor*, 1689. brs. L, O, C, CS, MC; CLC, CN, MIU, NP, WF, Y.

917B [–] —[Anr. ed.] *Reprinted Edinburgh*, 1689. 4°. ALDIS 2881. EN, AU.

917C [–] Political aphorisms. *For Tho. Harrison*, 1690. 4°.* L, O, C, LVF, EN; CH, IU, MH, PL, WF, Y.

917D [–] —Second edition. —, 1691. 4°.* L, O.

917E [–] —Third edition. —, 1691. 4°. T.C.II 352. O, ENC; CN.

918 **Harrison, William.** The humble petition, or representation of. [*London*], *printed*, 1647. 4°.* LT, DT; CH.

919 **Harriss, Charles.** A Scriptural chronicle of Satans incendiaries. [*London*], *printed*, 1670. 4°.* L, O, C, LF, EN; CH, MH, NU, PH, WF, Y. (var.)

920 —The vvoolf under sheeps-clothing discovered. [*London*], *printed*, 1669. 4°.* L, C, LF, MR, DT; CH, MH, PH, PSC, Y.

Harrisson, John. Syderum secreta, or. 1689. *See* Almanacs.

Harruney, Luke, *pseud*. *See* Diodati, Giovanni.

921 Harry Hangman's honour. [*London*, 1655.] cap., 4°.* LT, NN.

922 **Harsnet, Samuel.** A fvll relation of the defeate given. *By R. Cotes, for Ralph Smith*, 1645. 4°.* LT; WF, Y.

923 **Harst, de.** A panegyrick of the most renowned . . . Princess Christina. *For Thomas Dring*, 1656. 12°. LT, O; MB, MH, TU.

923A **Hart, James.** The anatomie of vrines. *For R. M. to be sold by Samuel Man*, 1652. 4°. LSC, MAU, GU; NAM.

[**Hart, John.**] Black book of conscience. 1658. *See* Jones, Andrew.

923B [–] The burning bush not consumed. [*London*], 1671. 12°. MHS (impf.).

924 [–] —[Anr. ed.] *Edinburgh, Andrew Anderson*, 1674. 12°. ALDIS 2017. L, EN.

925 [–] —[Anr. ed.] *Edinburgh, by the heir of A. Anderson*, 1679. 12°. ALDIS 2146. 5. L.

925A — —[Anr. ed.] [*London*], *by H. S. for J. Clarke, W. Thackery, and T. Passinger*, 1685. 8°. O.

926 [–] The charitable Christian. Third edition. *For John Andrews*, 1658. 8°.* L.

926A [–] —Fifth edition. —, 1659. 8°.* Y.

926B [–] —Seventh edition. 8°.* G.EVANS, HARVARD.

927 [–] —Eighth edition. *For Elizabeth Andrews*, 1662. 8°.* L.

928 [–] —[Anr. ed.] [*London*], *by A. P. and T. H. for W. Thackeray, T. Passinger, P. Brooksby, and J. Williamson*, [167-?]. 8°.* L.

928A [–] —[Anr. ed.] *By E. C. for W. T. sold by John Hose*, 1674. 8°.* L.

928B [–] —[Anr. ed.] *By T. H. sold by J. Wright, J. Clarke, W. Thackeray, and T. Passenger*, 1682. 12°.* CM.

928C [–] —[Anr. ed.] *By H. B. for J. Clark, W. Thackery, and T. Passenger.* 1685. 8°.* O.

929 [–] The Christians best garment. Second edition. *For John Andrews*, 1661. 8°.* L.

930 [–] —[Anr. ed.] *For E. Andrews*, 1664. 8°.* O.

931 [–] —[Anr. ed.] *For William Thackeray, T. Passenger, P. Brooksby, and J. Williamson*, 1678. 8°.* L, O.

932 [–] The Christian's blessed choice. *By J. W. for Eliz. Andrews*, 1668. 8°.* L.

933 [–] —[Anr. ed.] *For W. Thackeray, P. Brooksby, J. Williamson, and J. Hose*, 1676. 8°.* L, O; Y.

933A — —Sixteenth edition. *Printed by J. M. for W. Thackeray, and T. Passinger*, [1676?]. 8°. O.

934 [–] —[Anr. ed.] *For W. Thackeray, T. Passenger, P. Brooksby, and J. Williamson*, 1678. 8°.* L.

935 [–] Christ's first sermon. *For John Andrews*, 1656. 8°.* L.

936 [–] —Fifth edition. —, 1660. 8°.* L.

937 [–] —Eleventh edition. *For Eliz. Andrews*, 1663. 8°.* DT.

938 [–] —Sixteenth edition. *For Will. Thackery, Phil. Brooksby, John Williamson, and John Hose*, 1676. 8°.* L.

938A [–] —"Sixteenth" edition. *By J. N. for W. Thackeray, and T. Passinger*, [1677?]. 8°. O.

939 [–] —Seventeenth edition. *For T. Passinger, Will. Thackery, Phil. Brooksby, and John Williamson*, 1679. 8°.* L.

939A [–] —"Seventeenth" edition. *For E. A., to be sold by T. Vere*, [1680]. 8°. LW.

939B [–] —Twenty-sixth edition. [*London*, 1680?] 12°.* L.
940   [–] —[Anr. ed.] *Glasgow, Sanders*, 1696. 8°. ALDIS 3545. GM.
940A [–] Christ's last sermon. *For Eliz. Andrews*, 1663. 8°. *. DT; Y.
940B [–] —[Anr. ed.] *Edinburgh, A. Anderson*, 1664. 8°. ALDIS 1773.I. EN.
941   [–] —[Anr. ed.] *For Will. Thackery, T. Passenger, Phil. Brooksby, and John Williamson*, 1679. 8°.* L, O, LW.
941A — —[Anr. ed.] [*London*], *by A. M. for W. Thackeray and T. Passinger*, [1679?]. 8°. O.
942   — —Twenty-first edition. *Newcastle; printed and sold by John White*, [1700?]. 8°.* L.
943   — —Twenty-third edition. *By William Dicey*, [1700?]. 12°.* L.
      [–] Death triumphant. 1674. *See* Jones, Andrew.
943A [–] The dreadful character of a drunkard. Tenth edition. *For Eliz. Andrewes*, 1663. 8°. L; CLC.
943B [–] —Seventh edition. *Glasgow, by Robert Sanders*, 1669. 12°.* ALDIS 1865. GU.
943C [–] —[Anr. ed.] *For VV. T. and are to be sold by C. Passing[er]*, 1674. 8°.* Y.
944   [–] —[Anr. ed.] [*London*], *by A. P. & T. H. for W. Thackeray, T. Passenger, P. Brooksby, and J. Williamson*, 1678. 8°.* L; MH, WCL.
944A [–] —Sixth edition. *Edinburgh, by the heir of Andrew Anderson*, 1679. 8°.* ALDIS 2154. EN.
945   [–] —[Anr. ed.] [*London*], *by T. H. for W. Thackeray, T. Passinger, J. Clark, and P. Brooksby*, 1681. 8°.* L.
945A [–] —Thirtieth edition. *For J. Wright, J. Clarke, W. Thackeray, and T. Passenger*, 1682. 8°. O.
945B [–] —[Anr. ed.] [*London*], *by J. M. for J. Clarke, W. Thackeray, and T. Passenger*, 1686. 8°.* O, CM.
945C [–] The dying mans last sermon. Third edition. *For John Andrews*, 1659. 8°.* Y.
945D [–] —Fourth edition. *For John Andrews*, 1661. 8°.* G. EVANS, HARVARD.
945E [–] —Seventh edition. *For Elizabeth Andrews*, 1662. 8°. L.
945F [–] —[Anr. ed.] —, 1665. 8°.* L.
945G [–] —[Anr. ed.] *For W. Thackeray*, 1674. 8°.* Y.
945H [–] —[Anr. ed.] *For W. Thackeray, T. Passenger, P. Brooksby, and J. Williamson*, 1680. 8°.* L.
945I [–] —[Anr. ed.] [*London*], *for W. Thackeray, Phil. Brooksby, John Williamson, and J. Hose*, [1680]. 8°.* WF.
945J [–] —[Anr. ed.] *For J. Wright, J. Clarke, W. Thackeray, and T. Passenger*, [1681–4]. 8°.* LW, OP, CM.
946   [–] Englands faithful physician. *For Eliz. Andrews*, 1666. 8°.* L.
947   [–] —[Anr. ed.] [*London*], *by P. L. for William Thackeray*, 1674. 8°.* L; MH, WCL.
947A [–] —[Anr. ed.] *For W. Thackeray, Phil Brooksby, John Williamson, and J. Hose*, 1676. 8°. OP, GU.
947B [–] —[Anr. ed.] [*London*], *for W. Thackeray, T. Passenger, P. Brooksby, and J. Williamson*, 1680. 12°. L.
948   [–] The everlasting joys of Heaven. *For John Andrews*, 1656. 8°. LT.
949   [–] The firebrand taken out. *For Tho: Mathewes*, 1654. 8°. O; LO, MH, WF, Y.

950   [–] The fort-royal. *By William Leake, for the company of stationers at Edinburgh*, 1649. 12°. ALDIS 1366.5. L, LCL; NU, Y.
950A [–] —[Anr. ed.] *For William Leake*, 1649. 8°. L, C; CH, CLC.
951   [–] —[Anr. ed.] *Edinburgh, by the heires of George Anderson, for Andrew Wilson*, 1649. 12°. ALDIS 1366. L, O, C, EN; CH, IU.
951A [–] —Second edition. *For William Leake*, 1652. 8°. L, OC; CH, CLC, IU, MH, NPT, WF.
952   [–] —Third edition. —, 1655. 8°. L, LLL, LW, E; PL.
953   [–] —"Third" edition. —, 1656. 8°. L, O, C; CLC, MWA, NHC.
953AA [–] A godly sermon. Second edition. *For Eliz. Andrews*, 1663. 8°. L; Y.
953BA [–] —Tenth edition. *For W. Thackeray, sold by I. Hose*, 1675. 8°. L.
953A [–] —Eleventh edition. *For W. Thackeray, and are to be sold by J. Hose* [167–?]. 8°.* MH.
954   [–] —Thirteenth edition. *For VV. Thackery, T. Passenger, P. Brooksby, and J. VVilliamson*, 1680. 8°.* L; NN.
954A [–] —Fourteenth edition. *For J. Wright, J. Clarke, W. Thackeray, and T. Passenger*, 1682. 12°. CM.
955   [–] Heavens glory. 1662. 8°.* LCL.
956   [–] —[Anr. ed.] *For W. Thackeray, T. Passenger, P. Brooksby, and J. Williamson*, 1678. 8°.* L, O.
956A [–] Plain mans plain path-way to heaven. *For Eliz. Andrews*, 1664. 8°. L(t.p.).
957   [–] —Thirty-fourth edition. —, 1665. 8°.* L.
958   [–] —Thirty-fifth edition. *By B. Wood, for Eliz. Andrews*, 1667. 8°.* L.
959   [–] —Fifty-third edition. *For W. Thackeray*, 1675. 8°.* WCL.
959A [–] —Fifty-sixth edition. [*London?* 1680.] 16°. L.
959B [–] —Fifty-seventh edition. [*London*], *for W. Thackeray and T. Passinger*, [1674]. 8°. O, OP.
959C [–] —[Anr. ed.] *Glasgow, Sanders*, 1679. 8°. ALDIS 2156.5. EN.
959D [–] The school of grace. Tenth edition. *For W. Thackeray*, [1675?]. 8°. OP.
959E — —Nineteenth edition. [*London*], *for W. Thackeray, and T. Passinger*, [1686–88]. 8°. O.
960   —Trodden down strength. *By R. Bishop for Stephen Pilkington*, 1647. 8°. LT, O, LCL; CH, CLC, IU, NS, WF, Y.
960A [–] A warning-piece to the sloathful. *For Eliz. Andrews*, 1663. 8°.* Y.
960B [–] —[Anr. ed.] *By G. P. for William Thackeray*, 1671. 8°. A.
961   [–] —[Anr. ed.] *For William Thackeray*, 1678. 8°.* L, O; MH, WCL.

Hart, On-hi, *pseud. See* Hart, John.
962   **Hart, Richard.** Parish churches turn'd into conventicles. *By Ralph Holt, for Obadiah Blagrave*, 1683. 4°.* T.C.II 2. L, O, C, BSM, DU; CH, CLC, CN, NU, SE, TU. [=A31.]
963   **Hart, Thomas.** The foundation and rise of many of the practises. *Printed*, 1659. 4°.* L, LF, BBN; MH, NCD, PH, PSC, Y.
964   No entry.

965 [**Hartcliffe, John.**] A discourse against Purgatory. *For Brabazon Aylmer*, 1685. 4°.* L, O, C, EN, DT; BN, CH, IU, MH, WF, Y. (var.)

966 [–] —[Anr. ed.] *Dvblin, re-printed by Andrew Crook and Samuel Helsham, for Joseph Howes, Samuel Helsham, and Eliphal Dobson*, 1686. 4°.* DIX 219. L, O, DK, DM, DT; NU.

967 —In veritate rerum. [*n.p.*, 1678.] brs. O.

968 —A sermon preached . . . November 29, 1683. *By Ralph Holt, for Samuel Carr*, 1684. 4°.* L, O, C, LG; CH, CLC, NN, WF.

969 —A sermon preached . . . April 11th. 1694. *For Charles Harper*, 1694. 4°.* T.C.II 500. L, O, C, WCA; CH, CLC, WF, Y.

970 —A sermon preached . . . thirtieth of January, 1694/5. *For Charles Harper*, 1695. 4°.* T.C.II 537. L, O, C, DU, DT; CH, IU, MH, NU, WF, Y.

971 —A treatise of moral and intellectual virtues. *For C. Harper*, 1691. 8°. T.C.II 350. L, O, C, BC, EC; CH, IU, LC, MH, TSM, WF, Y.

Hartford, William, *marquis. See* Somerset, William Seymour, *duke of.*

Hartfordshire. *See* Hertfordshire.

972 **Hartgill, George.** Astronomical tables. *For the company of stationers*, [1656]. 4°. L, O, E; CH, MB, MU, WF, WSL.

973 [**Hartley, John.**] Catalogus universalis librorum in omni facultate. *Apud Joannem Hartley*, 1699. 8°. L, O, C, MR, EN; CH, CN, LC, MH, Y.

973A **Hartley, Ralph.** To the right honourable Sir John Houblon . . . the humble petition of. [*London?* 1697.] cap. fol.* OP.

974 **Hartley, William.** Good news to all people. *By John Macock for Lodowick Lloyd, and Henry Cripps*, 1650. 4°.* LT, C, OC, BP, DT; NU, Y.

974A —Infant-baptism none of Christs. *By Henry Hills*, 1652. 4°. BP.

975 —The prerogative priests passing-bell. *By J. M. for H. Cripps, and L. Lloyd*, 1651. 4°.* LT, O; CLC, WF.

976 —The priests patent cancelled. *By G. Dawson for Henry Cripps*, 1649. 4°.* LT, O; CN, CU.

976A **Hartlib, Samuel.** A brief discourse concerning the accomplishment. [*London*, 1647.] cap., 4°.* LT, EN.

977 Entry cancelled.
—Briefe relation. 1641. *See* Dury, John.

978 —Chymical, medicinal, and chyrurgical addresses: made to. *By G. Dawson for Giles Calvert*, 1655. 8°. L, O, MAU, GU; CN, PU, Y, HC.

979 [–] Clavis apocalyptica. *By William Du-Gard for Thomas Matthews, and are to bee sold by Giles Calvert*, 1651. 8°. CE, P, YM; IU, MH.

979A [–] —Second edition. *By W. D. for Tho. Matthewes*, 1651. 8°. LW; CASE WESTERN RES. U., IU, MH.

[–] Common writing. [*n.p.*], 1647. *See* Lodowyck, Francis.

980 —The compleat husband-man. *Printed and are to be sold by Edward Brewster*, 1659. 4°. LT, LS, LUG, CS; BBE, MH, NC.

981 [–] Considerations tending to the happy accomplishment. colop: [*London*], 1647. cap., 4°. LT, O, CT, EN, DT; CSS, IU, MH, NU, WF, Y.

982 [–] Cornu Copia; a miscellanium. [*London*, 1652?] 4°. L, O, LUG, RU; CH, LC, MIU, WF.

983 Entry cancelled.
[–] Description of the famous kingdome of Macaria. 1641. *See* Plattes, Gabriel.

984 [–] A designe for plentie. *For Richard Wodenothe*, [1652?]. 4°.* LT, O, LUG, CT, R, DT; BN, CH, LC, MH, WU, Y.
—A discours of husbandrie. 1605 [i.e. 1650]. *See* Weston, *Sir* Richard.

985 —A discoverie for division. *For Richard Wodenothe*, 1653. 4°.* L, O, CS, R, EN; CH, CN, LC, MH, NC, Y.

985A —Epistola gratulatoria. [*London*, 1655.] 12°. WF.
[–] Essay for advancement of husbandry-learning. 1651. *See* Dymock, Cressy.

986 [–] A faithfvll and seasonable advice. [*London*], by *Iohn Hammond*, 1643. 4°.* LT, O, CT, LNC, DT; HR, CLC, MH, NU, Y.

987 [–] A further discoverie of the office of pvblick addresse. *Printed*, 1648. 4°.* L, O, LUG, CT, LSD; CLC, MH, NU, TU, WF.

988 [–] Glory be to God on high. [*London*], for *Richard Wodenothe*, 1652. 4°.* L; CH, CN, MB, NN, RPJ.

989 —Samuel Hartlib his legacie. *By H. Hills, for Richard Wodenothe*, 1651. 4°. LT, C, LUG, CCO, R; CH, CJC, LC, MH, PL, Y.

990 — —Second edition. *By R. & W. Leybourn, for Richard Wodenothe*, 1652. 4°. L, O, LL, R, RU; BN, CH, IU, MH, NC, WF, Y.

991 — —Third edition. *By J. M. for Richard Wodnothe*, 1655. 4°. L, O, C, BC, R; BN, CH, CN, LC, MH, WF, Y.

992 [–] Londons charitie. *By Robert Ibbitson*, 1649. 4°.* LT, DT; NC.

993 [–] Londons charity inlarged. *By Matth. Symmons, and Robert Ibbitson*, 1650. 4°.* LT, O, LG, LUG, DT; CLC, MH, NC.

994 [–] The necessity of some nearer conjunction. *Printed*, 1644. 4°.* LT, CT, A, DT; NU, WF, Y.

995 Entry cancelled.
—Panegyricus Carolo Gustavo. 1656. *See* Comenius, Johann Amos.

995A [–] The Parliaments reformation. *For Thomas Bates*, 1646. 4°.* LT, LW, BR; MH, NC, WF, Y.

996 Entry cancelled.
—Rare and new discovery. 1652. *See* —Glory be.

997 —The reformed common-wealth of bees. *For Giles Calvert*, 1655. 4°. LT, O, C, CM, R; CH, CN, MH, NN, WF, Y.

998 [–] The reformed husband-man. *By J. C.*, 1651. 4°.* L, LUG, AN, DU, ES, R; CH, CLC, CN, MH, NC, PU, WF.

999 — —[Anr. ed., "reformfd."] —, 1651. 4°.* L, NE, SP, R; LC, MH, Y, ANL.

999A — —[Anr. ed.] *By Hen. Hills*, 1651. 4°.* WCA; NN.
[–] Reformed spiritvall husbandman. 1652. *See* Dury, John.

1000 [–] The reformed Virginian silk-worm. *By John Streater, for Giles Calvert*, 1655. 4°.* LT, O, CM, R; CH, CN, LC, MH, WF, Y.

1001 No entry.
　　　[–] Short letter. 1644. *See* Woodward, Hezekiah.
1002 —The true and readie way to learne the Latine tongue. *By R. and W. Leybourn, 1654.* 4°. L, O, C, LUG; CH, CN, IU, MH, WF.
1003 **Hartman, George.** The family physitian. *For Richard Wellington, 1696.* 8°. T.C.II 602. L, C, LSC, SHR, GU; CH, CLC, CNM, WF.
1003A ——[Anr. ed.] *By H. Hills for the author, 1696.* 8°. CLC, WSG.
1004 —The true preserver and restorer of health. *By T. B. for the author. 1682.* 8°. T.C.II 46. L, C, LCS, LWL, LLU; CH, WSG, WF.
1005 ——Second edition. *By T. B. to be sold by Randol [sic] Taylor, 1684.* 8°. T.C.II 107. L, CT, LLU; LC, WSG.
1006 ——[Anr. ed.] *[n.p.], for A. and J. Churchill, 1695.* 8°. L, CE; CJC.
1006A **Hartman, John.** Praxis chymiatricæ; or the practise of chymistry. *For John Starkey and Thomas Passenger, 1670.* fol. O, GU; PCP, WSG.
1007 **[Hartshorne, Richard.]** A further account of New Jersey. *[London], printed, 1676.* 4°.* L, LF; CH, NN, PL, RPJ.
1007A **Harvard College.** Amplissimo ac celeberrimo . . . theses. *Cantabrigiæ Nov-Anglorum, 1689.* brs. MH.
1008 —Amplissimo, honoratissimo, pariter ac perillustri viro. *Cantabrigiæ [Mass.] Nov-Anglorum tertio nonarum Julii, 1693.* brs. EVANS 638. NN.
1009 Entry cancelled. *See* H1019.
1010 —Amplissimis consultissimis et multifaria virtute . . . Johann. Winthropo, . . . theses. *[Cambridge, Mass., 1647.]* brs. EVANS 22. GH; MHS.
1011 —Authoritatis pondere, iudicii robore, . . . Johanni Endicotto . . . theses. *Cantabrigiæ Nov-Angl: decimo sextilis anno Dom 1653.* brs. GH.
1012 —Catalogus eorum qui in collegio Harvardino. *[Cantabrigiæ, Mass., impensis Samuel Green, 1674.]* fol. EVANS 188. LPR.
1013 Entry cancelled. *See* H1017.
1014 ——[Anr. ed.] *Cantabrigiæ Nov-Anglorum tertio quntilis. 1700.* brs. EVANS 912. MH.
1015 —Clarissimis, dignissimis omnigena virtute consilio, . . . Johanni Endicotto, . . . theses. *Cantabrigiæ Nov-Angliæ quint: id: sextilis anno Dom. 1653.* brs. GH.
1016 —Consultissimo, pariter ac perffonorifico viro, D. Simoni Bradstreeto, . . . theses. *Cantabrigiæ Nov-Anglorum calendis Julii, 1691.* brs. MH.
1017 —Honoratissimo Simoni Bradstreeto. Catalogus. *Bostonæ Nov-Anglorum; die sexto ante idus sextiles. 1682.* brs. MH.
1018 —An humble proposal for the inlargement. *[Cambridge, Mass., by Samuel Green, 1659.]* brs. EVANS 55. MBS.
1019 —Illustrissimis pietate . . . theses. *Cantabrigiæ Nov. Ang. [by Stephen Daye], Mens.8. 1643.* brs. EVANS 12. GH; MHS.
1020 —Illustrissimis viris tam pietate, . . . Johanni Leveretto, . . . theses. *Cantabrigiæ Nov-Anglorum Idibus Sextilis: 1678.* brs. GH; MHS.
1021 Entry cancelled. *See* H1012.
1022 —Præcellenti et illustrissimo viro D. Edmvndo Andros, . . . theses. *Cantabrigiæ Nov-Anglorum, 1687.* brs. MH.
1023 —Qaestiones [sic] in philosophia discutiendæ. *[Cambridge, Mass., Samuel Green, 1653.]* brs. GH.
1024 —Quaestiones in philosophia. 1655. *[Cantabrigiæ, Mass., impensis S. Green, 1655.]* brs. EVANS 41. MH, V.
1025 ——1656. *[Cantabrigiæ, Mass., 1656.]* brs. MH.
1026 ——1658. *[—, 1658.]* brs. GH.
1027 ——1659. *[—, 1659.]* brs. MH.
1028 ——1660. *[Cantabridgiæ, Mass., impensis S. Green, 1660.]* brs. EVANS 59. MH.
1028A ——1663. *[—, 1663.]* brs. MH.
1028B ——1664. *[—, 1664.]* brs. EVANS 92. MH.
1028C ——1665. *[—, 1665.]* brs. EVANS 102. MH.
1028D ——1666. *[—, 1666.]* brs. EVANS 108. MH.
1028E ——1668. *[—, 1668.]* brs. EVANS 123. MH.
1028F —Quæstiones duæ, . . . 1669. *[—, 1669.]* brs. EVANS 140. MH.
1028G —Quæstiones in philosophia, 1673. *[—, 1673.]* brs. MH.
1029 —Quæstiones pro modulo discutiendæ, 1674. *[—, 1674.]* brs. EVANS 189. MH.
1030 ——1675. *[—, 1675.]* brs. EVANS 199. MH.
1031 ——1676. *[—, 1676.]* brs. EVANS 213. MH.
1032 ——1678. *[—, 1678.]* brs. EVANS 248. MH, MHS.
1033 ——1679. *[—, 1679.]* brs. EVANS 270. MH.
1034 ——1680. *[—, 1680.]* brs. EVANS 285. MH.
1035 —Quæstiones in philosophia, 1681. *[—, 1681.]* brs. EVANS 303. MH.
1036 ——1682. *[—, 1682.]* brs. EVANS 315. MH.
1037 —Quæstiones pro modulo discutiendæ, 1684. *[—, 1684.]* brs. EVANS 361. MH.
1037A ——1687. *[—, 1687.]* brs. EVANS 428. MH.
1037B —Quæstiones discutiendæ, . . . 1688. *[—, 1688.]* brs. EVANS 443. MH.
1037C ——1689. *[—, 1689.]* brs. EVANS 470. MH.
1037D ——1690. *[—, 1690.]* brs. EVANS 511. MH.
1037E ——1692. *[—, 1692.]* brs. EVANS 596. MH.
1037F ——1693. *[Boston, impensis Bartholomew Green, 1693.]* brs. MH.
1037G —Quæstiones, quas pro modulo discutiendæ, 1694. *[—, 1694.]* brs. MH.
1038 ——1695. *[—, 1695.]* brs. MH, Y.
1038A ——1696. *[—, 1696.]* brs. MH, Y.
1038B ——1697. *[—, 1697.]* brs. MH.
1038C ——1698. *[—, 1698.]* brs. MH.
1038D —Quæstiones pro modulo discutiendæ, 1699. *[—, 1699.]* brs. MH.
1039 —Quæstiones quas pro modulo, 1700. *[—, 1700.]* brs. MH, Y.
1040 —Spectatissimis integritate, et syncera religione, . . . Johanni Winthropo; . . . theses. *Cantabrigiæ Nov: Ang: Mensi 5. Die. 28. 1646.* brs. GH.
1040A —Theses discvtiendæ, sub. *[Cantabrigiæ, impensis S. Green, 1686.]* brs. EVANS 406. MH.
1041 Entry cancelled.

—Theses philologic. [n.p., 1647.] *See* —Amplissimis consultissimis.

1042 —Viris authoritate praecipuis, . . . Richardo Bellinghamo . . . theses. *Cantabrigia Nov. Anglia [impensis S. Green] die nono Sextilis Anno* 1670. brs. MHS.

Harvest-home. 1674. *See* Bryan, John.

[Harvey, Charles.] Collection of several passages. 1659. *See* Walker, Henry.

1043 **Harvey, Christopher.** Αφηνιαστης: or, the right rebel. *[London], for R. Royston,* 1661. 8°. L, O, SP.

1043A [–] Faction supplanted; or, a caveat. *For R. Royston,* 1663. 8°. MH.

1044 —Self-contradiction censured. *By R. Norton,* 1662. 8°. C, E; MH.

1045 [–] The synagogve. Second edition. *By J. L. for Philemon Stephens,* 1647. 12°. L, O, CT; BN, CH, CN, IU, MH, NP, Y.

1046 [–] —Third edition. *[London], for Philemon Stephens,* 1657. 12°. L, O, C, AN, DC, DT; CH, IU, MH, NP, WF.

1047 [–] —Fourth edition. *For Philemon Stephens,* 1661. 12°. L, O, C, RU; CH, CLC, MH, NGT, NN, TU, Y.

1048 [–] —Fifth edition. —, 1667. 12°. L, O, OM, DT; CH, IU, MH, WF, Y.

1049 [–] —Sixth edition. *For Robert Stephens,* 1673. 12°. L, O, C, LVD, NOT, E; CH, IU, MH, TU, WF, Y.

1050 [–] —Seventh edition. *By S. Roycroft, for R. S. and are to be sold by John Williams junior,* 1679. 12°. L, O, C, LCL, CT; CH, CN, IU, MH, WF, Y.

1051 **Harvey, Edmund.** A letter from. *For John Wright, Novemb.* 11. 1643. 4°.* LT, EN; MH, WF.

1052 —A seasonable speech made. *Printed,* 1642. 4°.* LT, C, LCL, LNC, DT; CN, MBP, MH, MU, NU, RBU.

1052A **Harvey, Gideon.** Against the doctor of Paris. *[London,* 1683.] cap., fol.* DCH.

1053 —Archelogia philosophica nova, or. *By J. H. for Samuel Thomson,* 1663. 4°. L, O, C, LCP, E; CH, IU, LC, MH, WF, Y.

1054 — . . . Ars curandi morbos expectatione. *Prostant venales apud J. Partridge,* 1694. 12°. T.C.II 525. L, CCA.

1055 — —[Anr. ed.] *Impensis Guil. Freeman,* 1696. 12°. C, LWL, AU.

1056 —The art of curing diseases by expectation. *For James Partridge,* 1689. 12°. T.C.II 275. L, O, LCS, MAU, E; CLM, CNM, MU, NAM, Y.

1057 —Casus medico-chirurgicus: or, a most memorable case. *For M. Rooks,* 1678. 8°. T.C.I 358. L, C, LCS, MAU, AU, GH; BN, CH, MU, NAM, WF, WSG.

1058 — —Second edition. *For James Partridge,* 1685. 8°. T.C.II 153. LCS, OB, CCA; WSG.

1059 —The conclave of physicians. *For James Partridge,* 1683. 12°. T.C.II 46. L, O, C, LCS, DUS; BN, CH, LC, MU, PL, JF.

1060 — —Second edition. —, 1686–5. 2 pts. 12°. L, C, LCP, CE, AU, DT; CLC, CNM, MMO, MU, NAM, JF.

1061 —De febribus tractatus. *Impensis Gulielmi Thackeray,* 1672. 8°. T.C.I 120. L, O, LCP, OC, CCA; BN, WSG, ASU.

1062 —A discourse of the plague. *For Nath. Brooke,* 1665. 4°.* L, C, LCS, LG, LWL; CH, MH, PL.

1063 —The disease of London. *By T. James for W. Thackery* 1675. 8°. T.C.I 218. L, O, CCA, MAU, WCA; CH, CNM, MIU, MU, HC.

1063A — —[Anr. ed.] *By B. W. for W. Thackery,* 1684. 8°. WF.

1064 —The family physician. *For T. R.,* 1676. 12°. T.C.I 253. L, OC, CS, CT, MAU; CH, MH, MIU, NAM, WF.

1065 — —Second edition. *For M. R., to be sold by the booksellers of London,* 1678. 12°. T.C.I 315. L, C, OM, GU, LCS; BN, CH, CNM, MBM, MMO, Y, HC.

1066 —The French pox. Fifth edition. *For James Partridge,* 1685. 12°. T.C.II 109. L, LWL, CCA, E; KU, MBM, NAM, WF.

1067 —Great Venus unmasked. Second edition. *By B. G. for Nath. Brook,* 1672. 8°. T.C.I 117. L, LCS, LWL, CT, MAU; CJC, MH, WF.

1068 —Little Venus unmask'd. *For William Thackeray,* 1670. 12°. T.C.I 55. O, LWL.

1069 — —[Anr. ed.] *For J. Partridge,* 1685. 12°. LSC, AU.

1069A — —Sixth edition. *For W. Turner,* 1700. 12°. LCP; MBM.

1070 —Morbus Anglicus, or. *For Nathaniel Brook,* 1666. 8°. LSC, OR; HC.

1071 — —[Anr. ed.] *[London], for William Thackeray,* [1672?]. 24°. T.C.I 55. L, LWL; BN, MBM, NAM, HC.

1072 — —Second edition. *By Thomas Johnson, for Nathanael Brook,* 1672. 8°. L, O, LCS, MAU, GK; CJC, LC, MMO, NAM, WF.

1073 — —[Anr. ed.] —, 1674. 8°. T.C.I 166. C; MBM.

1074 —A new discourse of the small pox. *By H. Hodgskin for James Partridge,* 1685. 12°. T.C.II 71. L, O, LCP, MAU, AU; CLM, CNM, NAM, PL, HC.

1075 Entry cancelled.

—Religio philosophi. 1663. *See* —Archelogia.

1076 —A theoretical and chiefly practical treatise of fevors. *For William Thackeray,* 1674. 8°. T.C.I 177. O, GK; MU, HC.

1077 No entry.

1078 —A treatise of the small-pox. *For James Partridge,* 1696. 12°. C, LCP, LCS; LC.

1078A — —[Anr. ed.] *For W. Freeman,* 1696. 12°. LWL, EN; PU, WF.

1079 —The vanities of philosophy & physick. *For A. Roper, and R. Basset,* 1699. 8°. T.C.III 137. L, O, C, LWL, MAU; CH, CNM, NAM, NP, WU.

1080 — —Second edition. *For W. Turner,* 1700. 8°. L, C, LWL, E; CH, MBM, NAM, NRU, NS, WF.

1080A —Venus vnmasked. *By J. Grismond, for Nath. Brooke,* 1665. 8°. ACADEMY OF MEDICINE OF BROOKLYN LIB.

1081 **Harvey, John.** The histories of Balaam, Jonas. *By E. Cotes, for Nathaniel Brooks,* 1653. 8°. L, O.

1082 —London lawles liberty. *Printed,* 1647. 4°.* LT; CLC, IU, WF.

1083 **Harvey, William.** The anatomical exercises of. *By Francis Leach, for Richard Lowndes,* 1653. 8°. KEYNES 19. LT, O, C, AM, DT; CH, IU, MH, MMO, NAM, WSG, HC.

1084 — —[Anr. ed.] *For Richard Lowndes, and Matth. Gilliflower,* 1673. 12°. T.C.I 123. KEYNES 20. L, O, LCP, CT, E, BQ; CLC, CNM, NAM, WSG, Y, JF.

1085 —Anatomical exercitations, concerning the generation of living creatures. *By James Young, for Octavian Pulleyn*, 1653. 4°. KEYNES 43. LT, O, C, E, GH; CH, CJC, MH, NAM, WF, WSG, HC, AVP.

1086 —De ortu et natura sanguinis. *Ex officina E. T. væneuntque apud Gulielmum Grantham*, 1669. 8°. KEYNES 49. L, LCP.

1087 —Exercitatio anatomica de circulatione sanguinis. *Cantabrigiæ, ex officina Rogeri Danielis*, 1649. 12°. KEYNES 30. L, C, LCP, LCS, GH; MMO, PCP, HC.

1088 ——[Anr. ed.] —, 1649. 12°. KEYNES 31. L, O, C, GU.

1089 —Exercitationes anatomicæ, de motu cordis & sanguinis circulatione. *Ex officina R. Danielis*, 1660. 12°. KEYNES 10. C, LCP, LCS, GH, DT; BN, CLC, CU, MU, NAM, PU.

1090 Entry cancelled. *See preceding entry.*

1091 —Exercitationes de generatione animalivm. *Typis Du-Gardianis; impensis Octaviani Pulleyn*, 1651. 4°. KEYNES 34. L, O, C, GH, DT; BN, CH, CJC, MMO, NAM, Y.

1091A ——[Anr. ed.] *Apud Octavianum Pulleyn*, 1651. 12°. LWL, DUS.

1092 —Two anatomical exercises. *By F. Leach [for R. Field]*, 1653. 8°. LCP, LWL; CLC, IU, MB, MMO, TU, HC.

1092A **Harvey, William,** *of Oldiham, Hants.* A treatise concerning the baptising of infants. *For John Jackson*, 1647. 4°. CS, CT; WF.

1092B **Harvey, William,** *mariner.* Divine meditations upon . . . women. *For the authour*, 1661. 8°. O.

1093 —The marriners card. *Printed*, 1659. 12°. O, LCL, CT; CLC.

1093A —The sectaries downfall. *By T. F. for the author*, 1655. 8°. CT.

1094 —Truth may be blamed. *Printed* 1657. 8°. O, CT.

1094A **Harvy, Edmond.** Rules and directions given by Coll. *By S. Griffin for T. Hewer and Hannah Blacklock*, 1655. 4°. L, O; CH.

1095 **Harward, Michael.** The herds-man's mate. *Dublin, by Benjamin Tooke, to be sold by Joseph Wilde*, 1673. 8°. DIX 151. L.

1096 **Harwood, Sir Edward.** The advice of. *For R. Harford*, 1642. 4°. LT, O, C, LLU, MR; BN, CH, CN, IU, TU, WF, Y.

1096A —Certaine choise and remarkable observations selected. *For J. B.*, 1642. 4°. CN, MH.

1097 **Harwood, James.** A free-wil offering. *Dublin, by J. C.*, 1662. 4°. DIX 116. C, BLH.

1098 —The Lord's Prayer unclasped. *For the author, to be sold by G. and H. Eversden*, 1654. 8°. LT, O, LSC, DC, ENC; NU.

1099 —The minister's office. *By R. W. for the author*, 1659. 12°. LW, DU.

1100 —The passing bell. *[n.p.], printed*, 1655. 8°. CS; NU.

1100A —The passing-bell rung out. *By R. W.*, 1657. CS.

1101 —The plea for the Common Prayer Book. *For the author*, 1654. 8°. NU.

1102 —A plea for the Common Prayer Book. *For the author*, 1657. 8°. L, O, C, CT.

1102AA ——[Anr. ed.] *By R. W. for the author*, 1657. 8°. DU.

1102A **Harwood, John.** The cause, why I deny the authority of George Fox. 1663. 4°. LF.

1103 —A description of the true temple. *For Thomas Simmons*, 1658. 4°. L, O, LF, BBN, MR; MH, PH, PSC.

1103A —The lying prophet discovered. *For Thomas Simmons*, 1659. 4°. L, LF; CH.

1104 —To all people that profess. *[London], printed*, 1663. 4°. L.

1104A [–] A warning from the Lord to the city of Oxford. *[London, 1655.]* cap., 4°. LF; PSC.

1105 [–] A vvarning from the Lord, to the town of Cambridge. *[London, 1655.]* cap., 4°. LT, LF, CS; PSC.

1105A —A warning to the rvlers in Svrrey. *[London], printed for Thee*, 1662. 4°. LF; PSC.

1106 **Harwood, Richard.** King David's sanctuary. *Oxford, for H. Hall and W. Webb*, 1644. 4°. MADAN 1621. L, O, OC, DU, EC, BLH; CH, IU, MH, TSM, WF, Y.

1107 [–] The loyall subiects retiring-roome. *Oxford, by Leonard Lichfield*, 1645. 4°. MADAN 1804. LT, O, DC, MR; CH, IU, NU, WF, Y.

1108 **H[ascard], G[regory].** A discourse about edification. *By Henry Hills, jun. for Fincham Gardiner*, 1683. 4°. T.C.II 14. L, O, C, CT, EN, DT; CH, CN, NU, WF, Y.

1109 [–] —Second edition. *By J. C. and Freeman Collins, for Fincham Gardiner*, 1684. 4°. L, C, OC, LIU, DT; CH, CN, MH, NU, WF, Y.

1110 [–] A discourse about the charge of novelty. *For Robert Horn, and Fincham Gardiner*, 1683. 4°. T.C.II 25. L, O, C, MC, E; CH, IU, MH, NC, NU, TU, Y.

1110A [–] —[Anr. ed.] *For R. H. and F. G., to be sold by Abel Swalle*, 1685. 4°. OH, SHR; CH, CLC, TSM.

1111 [–] —[Anr. ed.] *For T. Basset, and Abel Swalle*, 1685. 4°. L, O, C, EN, DT; BN, CLC, MH, MU, WF, Y.

1112 [–] Gladius justitiæ: a sermon. *By William Godbid, for Nathaniel Brook*, 1668. 4°. L, O, WCA, YM, EN; CLC, Y.

1113 —A sermon preached upon the fifth of November, 1678. *By S. and B. G. for William Crook*, 1679. 4°. T.C.I 341. L, O, CT, LSD, NE; CH, CU, NP, NU, WF, Y.

1114 —A sermon preached . . . feast of St. Michael, 1679. *For William Crooke*, 1680. 4°. T.C.I 366. L, C, LG, CS, DU; CH, CN, IU, NU, WF, Y.

1115 —A sermon preached . . . Tuesday in Easter Week. *For William Crook*, 1685. 4°. T.C.II 123. L, O, C, LSD, WCA; CH, IU, NU, WF, Y.

1116 —A sermon preach'd . . . Novemb. 10. 1695. *For Daniel Brown*, 1696. 4°. T.C.II 567. L, O, LG, CT, SHR; CH, NU, WF, Y.

1117 —A sermon preach'd . . . January the 30th, 1695/6. *For Daniel Brown*, 1696. 4°. T.C.II 567. L, O, C, OM, CT; CH, NU, TU, WF, Y.

1118 No entry.

1119 **[Hasclock, John.]** A letter from Lysbone, directed to Captain Thomas Harrison. *For Lodowick Lloyd and Henry Cripps.* 1650. 4°. LT, O, DT; MH, WF. (var.)

1120 —A true and perfect relation of the surrender of the strong and impregnable garrison, . . . Scillie. *By B. I.*, 1646. 4°. LT, O, DT.

Haslerig, Sir Arthur. Sir Arthur Hesilrigs lamentation. 1660. *See title.*

[–] Sir Arthur Haselrig's last vvill. 1661. *See title.*

1121 —A letter from. *For Edward Husband, July 7.* 1648. 4°.* LT, O, DT; CH.

1122 — —[Same title, 31 October 1650.] *By Edward Husband and John Field,* 1650. 4°.* LT, LLL, MR, EN, DN; CN, Y.

1123 — —[Same title.] *Printed,* 1659. 4°.* L, O, C, MR; CH, CLC, MH, MU, WF.

1124 —Sir Arthur Hesilrige's letter to the honourable committee. *For Edward Husband, August 15,* 1648. 4°.* LT, LLL, MR, GU, DT; CSS, IU, WF.

1125 [–] Lieut. Colonel John Lilb. tryed. *By M. Simmons,* 1653. 4°. LT, CT, DU, E, EN; CLC, MB, MIU, NU, WF, Y.

1125A [–] —[Anr. ed., "Lieut. Colonel J. Lilburn."] *By M: Simmons,* 1653. 4°.* C, OC, MR, DT; CH, CN, MH.

1126 —Sir Arthur Haslerigg his speech in Parliament, the fifth of Ianuary last. *For F. C. and T. B.,* 1641[2]. 4°.* L, O, CCA, BC, MR; MH, PU, WF, Y.

1127 — —[Anr. ed.] *For F. Coules and T. B.,* 1642. 4°.* L, O, OC, CCA, BC; CSS, IU, MH, TU.

1128 —Sir Arthur Haslerigg his speech in Parliament . . . February 21. 1641. *By Iohn Hammond,* 1641. 4°.* L; CH, CN, NPT, WF, Y.

1129 —Sir Arthvr Haslerigg his speech in Parliament . . . 4th of January, 1642. *For F. C. and T. B.,* 1642. 4°.* LT, O, C, BC, LSD, DT; CSS, IU, NU, WF, Y.

1130 — —[Anr. ed.] *For John Wright,* 1642. 4°.* L, O, CT, DU, DT; CH, CN, MH, MU, TU.

1131 Entry cancelled.
—To the right honourable the Parliament of England assembled at Westminster. The humble petition of Sir Arthur Haslerig. [n.p., 1660.] *See title.*
Haslerig & Vain. [1660.] *See* H., T.

1132 **Haslewood, John.** A sermon preached . . . September the 8th, 1700. *For Abel Roper,* 1700. 4°.* L, O, LF, LW, OC; NN, NU, PH.

1133 **Hassal, George.** The designe of God. *Printed,* 1648. 4°.* NU.

1134 [**Hasselwood, Henry.**] Doctor Hill's funeral-sermon. *Printed at London,* 1654. Sold by Richard Moon. 4°.* LT; Y.

1134A The hasty bridegroom. [*London*], *for F. Coles, T. Vere, J. Wright, and J. Clarke,* [1675]. brs. O.

1134B —[Anr. ed.] [*London*], *for J. Wright, John Clarke, William Thackeray and Thomas Passinger,* [1681–4]. brs. CM.

1135 —[Anr. ed.] [*London*], *for A. Milbourn, W. Ownly, and T. Thackeary [sic],* [1695?]. brs. L, O, HH.

1136 The hasty damosel. [*London*], *for P. Brooksby,* [1687?]. brs. O; MH.

1137 The hasty lover. [*London*], *for Charles Barnet,* [1694–1703]. brs. HH.

1138 The hasty virgin. [*London*], *for J. Deacon,* [1685–88]. brs. L, HH; WCL.

1139 The hasty wedding. [*London*], *for, P. Brooksby,* [1680?]. brs. L, O, GU.

1139A **Hatch, John.** A word of peace. *Giles Calvert,* 1646. 16°. L.

1139B **H[atcher], Robert.** Funus corporis. *Excudebat T. R. & E. M. impensis authoris,* 1646. 8°. L, CCA, CM; MB, NN.

1140 [–] Institutio, epithalamium, & militia. *Excudebat T. R. & E. M. impensis authoris.* 1645. 8°. L, CCA; CN, MB, Y.

1140A [–] Paideutica, sive ascetica. *Excudebat R. Raworth,* 1646. 8°. CM; MB, Y.

1141 Entry cancelled.

Hatt, Hannah. *See* Allen, Hannah.

1141A **Hatt, Martha.** To the right honourable the Commons . . . the humble petition. [*London*], 1660. 4°.* O.

1141B —To the right honour:ble the Lords . . . the humble petition. [*London,* 1660.] brs. DN.

Hattecliffe, Vincent, *pseud. See* Spencer, John.

Hattige: or. Amsterdam, 1680. *See* Brémond, Gabriel de.

1142 **Hatton, Sir Christopher.** A treatise concerning statutes. *For Richard Tonson,* 1677. 8°. T.C.I 276. L, O, C, LL, LMT, LNC; CN, MHL, NCL, PU, WF, Y.

Hatton, Edward. Arithmetick. 1699. *See* Recorde, Robert.

1143 —The assessors and collectors companion. [*London*], *for Robert Vincent,* 1697. brs. L, CE; NC.

1144 —Comes commercii: or, the trader's companion. *By J. H. for Chr. Coningsby; J. Nicholson; and Dan. Midwinter and Tho. Leigh,* 1699. 4°. T.C.III 125. L, OC, NPL; UCLA, Y.

1145 —Decimals made easie. *By J. H. for Charles Harper, and William Freeman,* 1699. 4°. L, O, C, AN; CH, CLC, CU, NC, TU, WF.

1146 —An exact table of the weight of gold and silver. *By J. Heptinstall for Chr. Coningsby,* 1696. brs. L, LUG; MH.

1147 —The merchants magazine. *Printed for, and sold by Chr. Coningsby,* 1695. 4°. L, C; NC, Y.

1148 — —Second edition. *By J. Heptinstall, for Chr. Coningsby,* 1697. 4°. L, LUG; CB, NC, RPJ, Y.

1148A — —Third edition. *By J. H. for Chr. Coningsby, and Tho. Leigh, and Dan. Midwinter,* 1699. 4°. T.C.III 145. L, LUG, CCA; CH, CLC, MH, MIU, NC, WF.

1149 **Hatton, Lady Elizabeth.** A true coppy of a letter from. *By R. B. for VVilliam Ley,* 1642. brs. LT, EC.

1150 **Haudicquer de Blancourt, Jean.** The art of glass. *For Dan. Brown; Tho. Bennet, D. Midwinter and Tho. Leigh, and R. Wilkin,* 1699. 8°. T.C.III 143. L, O, C, LG, EN; CH, MH, MU, NP, WF, WGS.

1151 **Haughton, Edward.** The rise, growth, and fall of Antichrist. *By R. W. for Francis Tyton,* 1652. 12°. LT, O, LW, CS; CLC, IU, NU, WF.

1151A The haughty Frenchmens pride abased. *For Rich. Burton,* [1661?]. brs. MH.

1151B **Haukes, Edward.** Hecatonstichon. [*London?* 1662.] brs. MH.

1152 **Hauskins, Thomas.** A sermon preached at Hievvorth . . . 24. of August. 1649. *Oxford, by H. Hall,* 1651. 8°.* MADAN 2169. LT, O; MH, WF.

1153 Entry cancelled. Ghost.

1154 [**Hausted, Peter.**] Ad popvlvm: or, a lecture. [*Oxford, by H. Hall*], *printed,* 1644. 4°.* MADAN 1636. LT, O, C, LSD; CH, CLC, MH, ZWT.

1155 [–] —Sixth edition. [*London*], *printed,* 1660. 8°.* LT, O; NU.

1156   Entry cancelled. *See following entry.*

1156A [–] —[Anr. ed.] *Printed in the late times, and now reprinted,* 1675. 4°.* LG, LLU; CH, CLC, CN, MH, TU, WF, Y.

1156B Entry cancelled.
       [–] —[Anr. ed.] 1678. *See* Cowley, Abraham.

1157   [–] A satyre against Seperatists. *For A. C.,* 1642. 4°.* MADAN 1636. LT, OC, OW, CJ; CH, CU, MH, NU, TU, Y.

1158   [–] —[Anr. ed.][*London*], *printed,* 1660. 4°.* O; NU.
       Hauteville, *pseud. See* Tende, Gaspard de.
       Have among you good women. [1641.] *See* Parker, Martin.

1159   Have amongst you my masters. [*London,* 1647.] brs. LT; CH, Y.

1160   Have-at a venture. [*London*], *for J. Wright, J. Clark, W. Thackery, and T. Passenger,* [1681-4]. brs. L, CM, HH; MH.

1161   Have you any work for a cooper? colop: *For R. H.,* 1681. L, O; CH, CLC, MH, NU, PU, WF, Y.

1162   **Havers, Clopton.** Osteologia nova, or. *For Samuel Smith,* 1691. 8°. T.C.II 334. L, O, C, GH, DT; CH, CNM, MH, MMO, NAM, WF, HC.

1162A **Haviland, James.** The case of. *By T. Sowle,* 1700. brs. LF, MR.

1162B [blank] having declared their intentions. [Quaker marriage certificate.] [*London,* 1697.] brs. OP.
       Having heard. [n.p.], 1659. *See* Nayler, James.

1162C Having laid before this honourable House that the glass manufacture. [*London?* 1697.] brs. L.

1163   **Haward, Lazarus.** The charges issuing forth of the crown revenue of England. *For Iohn Wright,* 1647. 4°. LT, O, C, MR, DT; CH, IU, LC, MH, WF, Y.

1164   — —[Anr. ed.] *For M. Wright,* 1660. 4°. LT, O, CT, EN, DT; CH, CN, LC, MH, TU, WF. (var.)

1165   —A continuation of the last occurrences from Ireland. *For John Thomas,* 1642. 4°.* LT, O, EC.

1166   [–] A few collections for Irelands souldiers. *For John Wright,* 1646 [7]. 4°.* LT, LVF.

1167   —Military and spirituall motions. *By Tho. Harper,* 1645. 4°. DC; CH, MH.

1168   **Hawes, Thomas.** A Christian relation of a Christians affliction. [*London*], *March* 1646. cap., 4°.* LT, DT.

1169   **H[awke], M[ichael].** The grounds of the lawes of England. *For H. Twiford, T, Dring, Jo. Place, and W. Place,* 1657. 8°. LT, O, C, LIL, DT; LC, NCL, NIC, PU, YL.

1170   No entry.

1171   —Killing is murder, and no murder. *For the author; to be sold by the Company of Stationers,* 1657. 4°. CD; CSS, MH, NU, Y.

1171A — —[Anr. ed.] *For the author; and are to be sold at the Stationers shops.* 1657. 4°. L, O, CT, YM, DT; CH, IU, MIU, NU, Y.

1172   [–] The right of dominion. *By T. C., to be sold by John Perry, and by Tho. Bruster,* 1755. 8°. LT, O, LCL, OME, MP; CH, MU, NU, Y.

1172A The hawkers lamentation. *For Langley Curtis,* 1682. O.

1173   **Hawkins, Francis.** A narrative. *For Samuel Carr,* 1681. fol.* L, O, C, CT, LSD, EN; CH, IU, LC, MH, PL, Y.

[–] New additions unto youths behaviour. 1652. *See* Youths behaviour.

1174   **Hawkins, John.** Clavis commercii: or, the key of commerce. *For Sarah Passinger,* 1689. 4°. L; CB, MH, NP, PL, Y.

1174A [–] The clerk's tutor for writing. *For J. Streater, J. Flesher and Hen. Twyford,* 1667. CN.

1175   —The English school-master compleated. *By A. and I. Dawks for the company of stationers,* 1692. 8°. T.C.II 412. L, LIU; WU.

1176   — —Second edition. *By J. Dawks, for the company of stationers,* 1694. 8°. T.C.II 529. L; MU.
       [–] Young clerk's tutor. 1662. *See* Cocker, Edward.

1177   **H[awkins], R[ichard].** A discourse of the nationall excellencies of England. *By Tho. Newcomb, for Henry Fletcher,* 1658. 8°. LT, O, LUG, CS, SP; CH, CN, NP, WF, Y.

1178   Entry cancelled. Ghost.

1179   **Hawkins, Robert.** The perjur'd phanatick. *For Joseph Hindmarsh,* 1685. fol.* T.C.II 112. L, O, LG, BAMB, MR; CH, CN, TO, TU, WF, Y.

1180   **Hawkins, Thomas.** To each gentleman soldier. [*London,* 1691?] brs. L; MH.

1181   **Hawkins, Thomas,** *of Manchester.* A true and perfect relation of the proceedings at Manchester. *October 6.* [*London*], *for H. Blake,* 1642. 4°.* LT; CH.

1182   **Hawkins, William.** Bibliotheca Hawkinsiana, . . . 13 Apr. 1685. 4°. L, O, CS.

1183   **Hawkshaw, Benjamin.** Poems upon several occasions. *By J. Heptinstall, for Henry Dickenson,* 1693. 8°. L, LLL; CH, LC.

1184   No entry.
       Hawkwood, *Sir John.* The honour of the taylors. 1687. *See* title.

1185   [**Hawles,** *Sir John.*] The English-mans right. *For Richard Janeway,* 1680. 4°.* T.C.I 424. L, O, C, AN, BC, DT; CH, CN, MHL, NC, WF, Y.

1186   [–] —[Anr. ed.] *London, for Richard Janeway, & reprinted at Boston, by Benjamin Harris,* 1693. 8°. EVANS 639. L, LL, MR, EN, DT; CH, Y.

1187   [–] The Grand-Jury-man's oath and office explained. *For Langley Curtis,* 1680. 4°.* T.C.I 417. L, O, CT, BC, DU; CLC, MH, MU, NC, WF, Y.

1188   —Remarks upon the tryals of Edward Fitzharris. *For Jacob Tonson,* 1689. fol. L, O, C, MR, EN; BN, CH, CN, LC, MHL, NR, WF, Y.

1189   —A reply to a sheet of paper. *For Israel Harrison, and Jacob Tonson,* 1689. fol.* L, LLP, MR, E; BN, CH, CN, PL, WF, Y.

1190   **H[aworth], S[amuel].** Ανθρωπωλογια or, a philosophic discourse. *For Stephen Foster,* 1680. 12°. T.C.I 383. L, O, LCS, LWL, DUS, GH; CU, NU, WF.

1191   —A description of the Duke's bagnio. *For Sam. Smith,* 1683. 8°. T.C.II 29. L, O, LL, OM, GU; BN, CH, CLC, NAM, WF, HC.

1192   —The true method of curing consumptions. *For Samuel Smith,* 1683. 12°. T.C.I 508. L, O, LCP, MAU, GH; CNM, TORONTO ACAD. OF MED., WF.

1193 **Haworth, William.** Absolute election of persons. *For the author*, 1694. 4°.* L, O, LCL, LW, DT; CLC, NU.

1194 —Animadversions upon a late quibling libel. [*London*], *printed*, 1676. 4°. L, O, LF; MHS, MWA, PH.

1194A —An answer to a sheet entitled the independent agent. [*London*, 1677.] cap., 4°.* MHS.

1195 [–] An antidote against that poysonous and fundamental error. *For Jonathan Robinson*, 1676. 4°. T.C.I 234. O, LF; CH, MHS, PH.

1195A —Jesus of Nazareth not the Quakers Messiah. 1677. 4°. MHS.

1196 —The Quaker converted. *For Jonathan Robinson*, 1674. 4°. T.C.I 185. O, C, LF, LW, BBN; CH, CU, IU, MHS, Y.

1196A ——[Anr. ed.] —, 1690. 4°. O; MWA, PH, PL.

1197 [–] The Quakers creed. *For Jonathan Robinson*, [1679]. 4°.* O, MR.

1198 **Hay, Alexander.** Deo opt. max. auspice, duo antidota. [*Aberdeen, Forbes, younger*], 1675. 4°.* ALDIS 2053. SA.

1199 —Disputatio juridica. *Edinburgh, by the heirs of A. Anderson*, 1697. 4°. ALDIS 3668. EN.

1200 —Tyrocinium pharmaceuticum. *Edinburgi, excudebant hæredes & successores Andreæ Anderson*, 1697. 12°. ALDIS 3669. L, LCP, AM, E, EN; CB, CLC, WSG, WU.

1200A **Hay, *Sir* David.** Unto His Grace, His Majesties High Commissioner . . . the humble petition of. [*Edinburgh*, 1696.] brs. EN.

1201 **Hay, James.** Collonel James Hays speech. [*London*], *printed*, 1655. 4°.* LT, O, C, GU, DT; CH, MH, NU, WF, Y. —See also Carlyle, James Hay, *earl of*.

Hay, John. See Tweeddale, John Hay, *marquis*.

Hay, Paul. The policy and government of the Venetians. 1671. See La Haye, *sieur de*.

1202 [–] The politicks of France. *Printed, and are to be sold by Thomas Sharpe*, 1680. 12°. T.C.I 373. L, C, LW, CM, DT; CN, CSS, LC, MH, NU, Y.

1202A [–] —[Anr. ed.] *Printed and sold by Thomas Orrell*, 1680. 12°. OC; PU.

1202B [–] —Second edition. *For Thomas Basset*, 1691. 12°. T.C.II 387. L, NE; BBE, CH, CLC.

1203 **Hay, T. de.** A letter from Paris. [*London*, 1680.] cap., fol.* L, O, MR, EN; CH, MBA, MH, MIU, WF, Y.

1204 No entry.

1205 Hay any worke for cooper. *Printed in Europe*, [1642]. 4°. LT, AN, DT; CLC, PT.

1206 **Haydock, Roger.** A collection of the Christian writings. *Printed and sold by T. Sowle*, 1700. 8°. L, O, LF, MR, DT; CH, IE, MH, PH, WF, Y.

1207 —A hypocrite unvailed. [*London*], *printed*, 1677. 4°. L, LF, CS, BBN, MR; MM, PH, PSC, Y.

1208 —The skirmisher confounded. [*London*], *printed*, 1676. 4°.* L, LF, OC, BBN, MR; MH, PH, PSC, TU, WF, Y.

1209 Entry cancelled.

Hayles. Speech spoken by. 1687. See Hales, Edward.

[**Hayley, W.**] Remarks upon an essay. 1697. See Burnet, Thomas.

1210 **Hayley, William.** A sermon preached . . . Jan. 30. being Sunday, 1686/7. *For Samuel Smith*, 1687. 4°.* L, OCC, OM, LSD, SC; CH, CLC, MH, NU, WF, Y.

1211 —A sermon preach'd . . . December the 11th, 1695. *For Jacob Tonson*, 1696. 4°.* L, O, C, EN, BLH; CH, IU, MM, NU, WF, Y.

1212 ——Second edition. —, 1696. 4°.* L.

1213 —A sermon preach'd . . . Oct. 3, 1698. *For Jacob Tonson*, 1699. 8°. L, LW, OC, CS, EC, LIU; MH, WF, HC.

1214 —A sermon preached . . . Oct. 30. 1698. *For Jacob Tonson*; 1699. 4°.* L, O, LCP, CS, EC, CD; CH, CLC, WF.

1215 —A sermon preach'd . . . Easter-Tuesday, 1700. *For Jacob Tonson*, 1700. 4°.* L, C, LLP, OC; NU, WF.

1216 **Hayne, Samuel.** An abstract of all the statutes made concerning aliens. [*London*], *by N. T. for the author, to be sold by Walter Davis*, 1685. 4°.* L, O, LUG, LSD; CH, CSS, MH, MIU.

1217 [**Hayne, Thomas.**] Christs kingdome on earth. *By Ric. Cotes for Stephen Bowtell*, 1645. 4°. LT, OC, CT, P, DT; CH, CU, MH, NU, WF, Y.

1218 —The equall wayes of God. Second edition. *For John Clark junior*, 1644. 4°. WF.

1219 —Linguarum cognatio. *Typis Ri. Whitaker*, 1648. 8°. BN; CN, MH.

1220 [–] Of the article of ovr creed. *Printed*, 1642. 4°.* LT, O, C, CT, WCA, BQ; CB.

1221 —To the honourable the Commons of England, a proposal concerning the coin. [*London*, 1696?] brs. L; NC.

1222 [–] Valour crowned. *For Benjamin Allen: Apr. 27.* 1643. 4°.* LT; CH, WF.

H[aynes], J[oseph]. See Haines, Joseph.

1223 No entry.

1224 [**Hayter, Richard.**] The Apocalypse unveyl'd. *By J. R. for T. Rich*, 1676. CS; CH.

1225 —The meaning of the Revelation. *By J. R. for John Williams*, 1675. 4°. L, O, C, DU, P; TSM, WF.

1226 ——[Anr. ed.] *By J. Redmayne for William Crook*, 1676. 8°. T.C.I 233. L, E; NU.

1227 **Hayward, Amey.** The females legacy. *By Benj. Harris, for the author*, 1699. sixes. L.

1228 **Hayward, Edward.** The answer of. *By Peter Cole*, 1656. 4°.* LT.

1229 —The sizes and lengths of riggings. *By Peter Cole*, 1655. fol. L, LR, CM; WF.

1230 ——[Anr. ed.] —, 1660. fol. L, O, CM, DCH, SC; BN, NN, RBU, Y.

1230A ——[Anr. ed.] *For Robert Miller*, 1660. fol. OC.

1231 Entry cancelled.

Hayward, George. Sermon preached . . . January xvj. 1675/6. See Hayward, Roger.

1231A **Hayward, John.** Hell's everlasting flames avoided. Tenth edition. *For Robert Gifford*, 1696. 12°. CLC.

1231B —The horrors and terrors of the hour of death. *For Robert Gifford*, 1690. 12°. WF.

1231C ——[Anr. ed.] —, 1693. tens. Y.

1231D —The precious blood of the son . . . first part. Sixth edition. *For Robert Gifford*, 1696. 12°. CLC.

1231E — —Ninth edition. —, 1698. 12°. GU.

1231F — —Tenth edition. —, 1699. 12°. L.

1232 Entry cancelled.

Hayward, Sir John. History of the life and raigne of Henry the Fourth. 1642. *See* Cotton, *Sir* Robert Bruce.

1233 —The right of succession asserted. *For Mat. Gillyflower, Will. Hensman, and Tho. Fox,* 1683. 8°. T.C.II 9. L, O, C, EN, DT; BN, CH, IU, TU, WF, Y.

1234 —The sanctuarie of a troubled soule. *By Ieane Bell,* 1650. 49. 12°. L, LSC, OC, CS; CLC, IU, PL, WU, Y.

1235 **Hayward, Roger.** A sermon preacht . . . November the xxx, 1673. *For Thomas Basset,* 1673. 4°.* T.C.I 161. L, O, C, LIU, SHR; CH, CN, NU, TSM, WF.

1236 —A sermon preached . . . January xvj. 1675/6. *For Thomas Basset,* 1676. 4°.* T.C.I 226. L, O, C, CT, DT; CH, CLC, NU, TSM, WF.

1237 — —Second edition. —, 1676. 4°.* LW, OC, CS; Y.

1238 **Haywood, William.** A sermon disswading from obloquie . . . Decemb. 7. 1662. *By J. G. for R. Royston,* 1663. 4°.* L, C, LL, OCC, BLH; CH, CN, NU, SE, WF, Y.

1239 —A sermon prepared to be preached. *For Richard Thrale,* 1660. 4°.* LT, LW; CLC, IU, MH, MWA, WF.

1240 —A sermon tending to peace. *By Fr: Neile for Henry Seile,* 1648. 4°.* LT, O, C, OC, DT; CH, MB, MH, NU, WF.

1241 —Tvvo sermons preached. *By I. O. for Henry Seile,* 1642. 4°.* L, O, C, DT; CLC, MH, MWA, NU.

1242 Entry cancelled. Ghost.

He-goats horn broken. 1660. *See* Whitehead, George.

1243 **[Head, Richard.]** The canting academy. *By F. Leach for Mat. Drew,* 1673. 12°. T.C.I 153. O, OC, A; CH, MH, NP, YBA. (var.)

1243A [–] —Second edition. —, 1674. 8°. T.C.I 174. LSC, OB, OW; CLC, CN.

1244 [–] —[Anr. ed.] —["*Der*"], 1675. 12°. MH.

1245 [–] The English rogue, containing a brief discovery. [*London*], *for J. Blare,* 1688. 8°.* O.

1246 [–] The English rogue described. *For Henry Marsh,* 1665. 8°. L; CH, NP.

1247 [–] —Second edition. *For Fra: Kirkman,* 1666. 8°. O; CH, CLC, Y. (var.)

1247A [–] —[Anr. ed.] *For Francis Kirkman,* 1667. 8°. O, DU; MH.

1248 [–] —[Anr. ed.] *For Francis Kirkman, to be sold by him and Thomas Dring the younger,* 1668. 8°. O, DU, E, EN; IU, MH, WF.

1248aA [–] —[Anr. ed.] —, 1669. 8°. LLL, E; Y.

1248bA [–] —[Anr. ed.] *For Francis Kirkman,* 1672. 8°. L, O; PU.

1248cA [–] —[Anr. ed.] —, *to be sold by William Rands,* 1680. 8°. L, O; CLC, CN, MH, OCL, WF.

1248A [–] The English rogue continued, . . . Part two. *For Francis Kirkman,* 1668. 8°. L, O, DU, E; CH, MH.

1249 [–] —[Anr. ed.] —, 1671. 8°. T.C.I 80. L, O; MH, PU, WF, Y.

1249aA [–] —[Anr. ed.] —, *to be sold by William Rands,* 1680. 8°. L, O, OCC; CLC, OCI.

1249A [–] The English rogue continued, . . . Part three. *For Fran. Kirkman,* 1671. 8°. L, O, LSC; CH, CN, WF.

1250 [–] —[Anr. ed.] *By Anne Johnson for Fran. Kirkman,* 1674. 8°. O, DU, EN.

1250A [–] The English rogue continued, . . . Part four. *For Francis Kirkman,* 1671. 8°. L, O, DU; CH, WF, Y.

1251 [–] —[Anr. ed.] *For Francis Kirkman, and are to be sold by William Rands,* 1680. 8°. O, DU, EN; OCI.

1252 [–] The English rogue; or, witty extravagant. *For J. Back,* 1688. 12°. T.C.II 223. O.

1252A Entry cancelled. Ghost.

1253 [–] The floating island. [*London*], *printed,* 1673. 4°.* T.C.I 141. L, O, DU; CH, CLC, CU, LC, MH, WF.

1254 No entry.

1255 —Hic et ubique; or, the humors of Dublin. *By R. D. for the author,* 1663. 4°. L, O, LVD, CS, EC; CH, IU, LC, MH, WF, Y.

1256 [–] Jackson's recantation. *For T. B.,* 1674. 4°.* T.C.I 171. O, LG, DU, SC; CH, CN, IU, MH, NN, TU, WF.

1257 [–] The life and death of Mother Shipton. *For B. Harris,* 1677. 4°. T.C.I 316. L; CH, MH.

1258 [–] —[Anr. ed.] *For Benj. Harris,* 1684. 4°. L, CM.

1259 [–] —[Anr. ed.] *For W. Harris,* 1687. 4°. O, C, LIU, EN; CLC, IU, MB, MH, NCU, NP. [All facsimiles?]

1260 [–] —[Anr. ed.] *For J. Back,* 1694. 4°. T.C.II 514. CT.

1261 [–] —[Anr. ed.] *By W. Onley, for J. Back,* 1697. 4°. MH.

1262 [–] The life and death of the English rogue. *For Charles Passinger,* 1679. 4°. T.C.I 358. L, O, CM, EN; CH.

1263 [–] —[Anr. ed.] *For Eben. Tracy,* [1700?]. 4°. L; CLC.

1264 [–] The miss display'd. *Printed* 1675. 8°. T.C.I 219. O, OC; MH.

1265 [–] —[Anr. ed.], 1683. 8°. O.

1265A [–] Nevvs from the stars . . . by Meriton Latroon. [*n.p.*], 1673. 12°.* NAVAL OBSERVATORY LIBRARY.

1266 [–] Nugæ venales. Second edition. *By W. D.,* 1675. 12°. T.C.I 213. MH, WF.

1267 — —Third edition. *For E. Poole,* 1686. 12°. T.C.II 153. L.

1268 Entry cancelled. Ghost.

1269 [–] O-Brazile. *For William Crook,* 1675. 4°.* L, O, C, SP; MH, NP.

1270 [–] —[Anr. ed.] *Edinburgh, re-printed,* 1675. 4°.* ALDIS 2056.5. EN.

1271 [–] —[Anr. ed.] *By Tho: Newcomb,* 1675. 4°.* CH.

1272 [–] Proteus redivivus: or the art of wheedling. *By W. D.,* 1675. 8°. T.C.I 197. L, O, C, LG, ES; CH, CN, LC, MH, WF, Y.

1273 [–] —[Anr. ed.] —, 1679. 8°. L, O, DML; CH, CSU, IU, MH, NU, WF.

1274 [–] —[Anr. ed.] *For T. D.,* 1684. 12°. T.C.II 54. CH, CU, MB, NP.

1274aA [–] —[Anr. ed.] *For W. D.,* 1684. 12°. L, O; CLC, NC.

1274A [–] —[Anr. ed.] *For Tho. Passinger,* 1684. 12°. LUG; WF.

1275 [–] The Red Sea. *By Peter Lillicrap,* 1666. fol. O.

1276 Entry cancelled.

—Three-fold card, 1647. *See* Head, Richard, *minister.*

1277 [–] The Western wonder: or, O Brazeel. *For N. C.,* 1674. 4°.* L, C; CN, MH, NN, RHT, WF.

1277A **H[ead], R[ichard],** *minister.* The Christians dayly solace. *For Richard Skelton, Isaac Pridmore, and Henry Marsh,* 1659. 8°. AN; CLC.

1277B —A three-fold card. *By E. P. for Fr. Coles*, 1647. 4°. LT, EN, DT; CH, NU.

1278 Entry cancelled.
Head of Nile. 1681. *See* Baker, Thomas.

1279 **Headrich, John.** Arcana philosophia. Or, chymical secrets. *Printed and sold by Henry Hills*, 1697. 8°. T.C.III 26. L, O, C, LCP, LWL; CLC, MH, WF, WU, Y.

1279A ——[Anr. ed., "philosophica."] *Printed by Henry Hills, and sold by Eben. Tracy*, 1697. 8°. L; LC.

1280 Entry cancelled.
Heads and conclusions. [*Edinburgh*], 1680. *See* Church of Scotland.

1280A The heads of a bill for the settling of the river of Wey. [*London*, 1669.] brs. LPR.

1281 The heads of a charge delivered. *Cambridge, by Roger Daniel*, 1647. 4°. C, CT; INU, IU, MH, WF.

1282 The heads of a scheme . . . East India. [*London?* 1696?] brs. L, C; MH.

1282A Heads of agreement assented to. *By R. R. for Tho. Cockerill and Iohn Dunton*, 1691. 4°.* T.C.II 355. L, O, C, BR, E, DT; CH, CN, LC, MH, NU, PL, Y, AVP.

1282AB —[Anr. ed.] *By R. R. for Tho. Cockerill*, 1691. 4°.* IU.

1282B —[Anr. ed.] *Edinburgh, by the heir of Andrew Anderson*, 1691. 4°.* ALDIS 3153. LLP, EN, ES, A.
Heads of all fashions. 1642. *See* Taylor, John.

1283 The heads of all the proceedings in both Houses of Parliament, from the 23. of May to the 30. 1642. *For J. Smith, and A. Coe*, 1642. 4°.* LT, O, OC, EC, EN; MH, Y.

1283A The heads of an act desired . . . for draining Deeping-fenns. [*London?* 1685.] brs. L.

1284 Heads of His Majesties letter and propositions. *By Robert Ibbitson*, 1647. 4°.* LT, O; CH, IU.

1285 The heads of proposals, agreed on. *For George Whittington*, 1647. 4°.* LT, O, OC, LIU, MR; CH, MH, NIC, WF, Y.

1286 Heads of proposals for a more beneficial and equal establishment . . . trade to Africa. [*London*, 1690?] brs. L, LPR; MH.

1287 The heads of reasons, for vvhich a generall councell of Protestants ought to be called. *By E. P. for Nicolas Bourne*, 1641. 4°.* LT, O, C, LIU, DT; CH, CN, MH, NU, WF, Y.

1287A Heads of settlement for the national land-bank. [*London?* 1695.] cap., fol.* MH.

1288 The heads of, severall petitions and complaints made against 1 Sir Iohn Connyers, . . . October 16, 1641. *For Iohn Thomas*, 1641. 4°.* LT, O, DU; CH, MH, TU, WF, Y.

1289 The heads of severall petitions delivered by many of the troopers. *For Iohn Thomas*, 1641. 4°.* LT, O, BR, BC, SP; CH, MBP, MH, WF, Y.

1290-1 Entries cancelled. Serials.

1291A Heads of some of those advantages . . . tobacco trade to Russia. [*London?* 1700.] brs. L, LIU; V.

1291B Heads of the additional bill for paving, cleansing. [*London*, 1672?] brs. LG.

1291C —[Same title.] [*London*, 1674?] brs. LPR.

1292 —[Same title.] [*London*, 1680?] brs. L.

1293 Heads of the charge against the king. *For T. R.*, 1648. 4°.* LT; CH, MIU, WF, Y.

1294 Heads of the expedient proposed in the Parliament at Oxford. colop: *By F. Collins*, 1681. brs. L, O, LIU, LNC, MC; CH, MH, NC, WF, Y.

1295 The heads of the great charge, presented. *For R. Walton, July 8.* 1647. 4°.* LT, LLU, DT; NC.

1296 The heads of the judges arguments. [*London?* 1685.] brs. L, O.

1297 The heads of the petition. 1 That according to our solemne league. [*London*, 1647.] brs. STEELE 2714. LT.

1298 The heads of the present greevances of the county of Glamorgan. [*London*], printed, 1647. 4°.* LT, O, AN, CPL; WF.

1299 The heads of the propositions to be sent. *By B. Alsop*, 1647. 4°.* LT, O, C, AN; NU.

1300 Heads presented by the Army to the Kings most excellent Majestie, on Saturday, June the 19. 1647. [*Cambridge*, 1647.] brs. STEELE 2705. LT, O, LS; MH, WF, Y.

1300A **Heald, Peter.** A sermon preached . . . 23rd day of March 1696/7. *For Elizabeth Janeway in Chichester, and sold by Eben. Tracy*, 1697. 4°.* T.C.III 12. L, O, CT, NE; Y.

1300B [**Heale, William.**] The great advocate. 1682. 12°. T.C.I 510. L, O.
Healing attempt: being. 1689. *See* Humfrey, John.
Healing attempt examined. 1689. *See* Long, Thomas.

1301 The healing balsom of a true lover. [*London*], for F. Cole, T. Vere, J. Wright, J. Clark. W. Thackery and T. Passenger, [1678-80]. brs. L, CM, HH; MH.

1302 A healing motion. [*n.p.*, 1657.] 12°. NU.
Healing paper: or. 1678. *See* Humfrey, John.

1303 Healing qveries for sick chvrches. *Printed*, 1658. 4°.* CH, MBA, NU.
Healing question. [*n.p.*], 1656. *See* Vane, Sir Henry.

1304 A health to all vintners. *For Thomas Bates*, [1642?]. brs. LT, LS.

1304A A health to Caledonia. [*Edinburgh*, 1699.] brs. CN, RPJ.
Health's new store-house. 1661. *See* W., W.
Healy, Richard. Ephemeris. 1658. *See* Almanacs.
—New almanack. 1655. *See* Almanacs.

1305 **Heaman, Roger.** An additional brief narrative. *For Livewell Chapman*, 1655. 4°.* LT.

1306 Heare, heare, heare, a vvord or message from Heaven. *Printed*, 1648. 4°.* LT, C, DT; NU, Y.
Hear this word. [*n.p.*, 1698.] *See* Stafford, Richard.

1307 **Hearne, Robert.** Loyalties severe summons. *By Thomas Milbourn; and are to be sold by Randal Taylor*, 1681. fol.* L, O, CT, LNC, NE, EN; CH, CN, IU, NU, WF, Y.

1308 —Obsequium & veritas: or, a dialogue. colop: *London, printed for the author*, 1681. brs. O, MR; CH, PU, AVP.

1308A ——[Anr. ed.] colop: *For H. R.* 1681. brs. AVP.

1309 [**Hearne, Thomas.**] Ductor historicus: or, a short system of universal history. *For Tim. Childe*, 1698. 8°. T.C.III 93. L, O, CT, GC, E; CH, IU, MH, MIU, WF.

1309A —A seasonable word, or a plain and tender-hearted epistle. *Printed*, 1650. 4°.* LSD; CH.

1309B   **Hearne, William.** An answer to two arguments . . . relating to the line of latitude. *Dublin, by Joseph Ray, and are to be sold by John North,* 1685. fol.* SOUTHAMPTON PUB. LIB.

1310   Heart-bleedings for professors abominations. *For Francis Tyton,* 1650. 4°.* LT, O, DT; CH, NHC.

Heart opened. [n.p., 1654.] *See* Farnworth, Richard.

1311   The heart opened to Christ Jesus. *By John Macock,* 1653. 12°. LT, CASTLE ASHBY.

Heart treasure. 1667. *See* Heywood, Oliver.

1312   Hearth-money. The severall acts of Parliament. [*London*], *in the Savoy, by the assigns of John Bill and Christopher Barker,* 1668. 12°. NC, WF.

1313   —[Anr. ed.] *By Thomas Newcomb and Henry Hills,* 1678. 12°. NC.

1313A   Heartless Harry: or, dolls earnest desire to be marryed. [*London*], *for J. Deacon,* [1695?]. brs. O.

Heart's ease. 1690. *See* Bardwood, James.

Hearty acknowledgment. 1659. *See* Draper, R.

1314   The hearty concurrence of divers citizens. [*London,* 1648.] brs. LT.

1315   —[Anr. ed.] *Reprinted at Edinburgh by Evan Tyler,* 1648. 4°.* ALDIS 1327. O, MR, EN; MH, NU, WF, Y.

1315A   The hearty congratulation and humble petition of . . . Kent. 1659. L.

1315B   [**Heath, Henry.**] Soliloquies. *Doway,* 1674. 24°. L, O, DUS, WARE; CN.

1316   H[eath], J[ames]. An admonition to My Lord Protector and his Council. *Printed in the year,* 1654. 4°.* LT, O, CT, NE, DT; CH, MH, MU, WF, Y.

1317   [–]—[Anr. ed.] *Printed in the yeer,* 1654. 4°.* L, O, CT; MH.

1318   [–] A brief chronicle of all the chief actions. *By J. Best for W. Lee,* 1662. 8°. O.

1318A   [–]—[Anr. ed.] *For William Lee,* 1662. 8°. L, LW, OC; CH, IU, WF, Y.

1319   —A brief chronicle of the late intestine war. Second edition. *By J. B. for W. Lee,* 1663. 8°. L, O, C, MR, EN; BN, CH, IU, LC, MH, NC, WCL, Y.

1320   [–]—Second edition. *By J. Best for William Lee,* 1663. 8°. L, OC, LIU, LLU; CH, IU, MH, WF, Y.

1321   —A chronicle of the late intestine war. Second edition. *By J. C. for Thomas Basset,* 1676. fol. T.C.I 239. L, O, C, EN, DT; BN, CH, CN, LC, MH, WF, Y.

1322   [–] The Commons war. 1646. 8°. L.

1323   —An elegie upon Dr. Tho. Fuller. *Printed,* 1661. brs. O; MH.

1324   —An elegy upon the most lamented death of . . . Dr. John Gauden. *For W. Gilbertson,* 1662. brs. L, MH.

1325   —Englands chronicle. *For Benj. Crayle, N. Bodington, and G. Conyers,* 1689. 12°. T.C.II 287. L, AN; CH, FU, IU, NC, WF.

1326   ——Second edition. *For N. Bodington and G. Conyers,* 1691. 12°. T.C.II 373. O, ES; CLC, IU, LC, WF.

1326A   ——Third edition. *For N. Boddington, and G. Conyers,* 1699. 12°. T.C.III 117. L; CH, IU, MH, WF.

1327   —An essay to the celebration of the anniversary day of His Majesties birth. *Printed,* 1661. brs. L.

1328   [–] Flagellum: or, the life and death of . . . Cromwell. *For L. R.,* 1663. 8°. L, O, LG, CS, BLH; BN, CH, CU, IU, MH, WF.

1329   [–]—Second edition. *For Randall Taylor,* 1663. 8°. L, LLL; CN, NN, NU, OWC, Y.

1330   [–]—Third edition. *By W. G. for Randall Taylor,* 1665. 8°. L, O, CE, DU; BN, CN, NRU, TU, WF, Y.

1331   [–]—Fourth edition. *By E. C. for Randall Taylor,* 1669. 8°. L, LCL, OC, CS, SHR, ES; BN, MBP, MH, MIU, WF, Y.

1332   [–]—[Anr. ed.] *For Randal Taylor,* 1672. 8°. L, O, C, LVF, DT; CH, CU, FU, VC, WF, Y.

1333   ——"Second" edition. —, 1673. 8°. HH (dispersed).

1334   [–]—[Anr. ed.] *For Sam Crouch,* 1679. 8°. L, RU, EN; CH, CLC.

1335   —The glories and magnificent triumphs. *Printed and are to be sold by N. G., R. H. and O. T.,* 1662. 8°. L, O, LI, CT, DUS, MC, CD; BN, CH, CN, MH, PL, WF, Y.

1335A   [–] The history of the life & death of Oliver Cromwell. *For F. Coles,* 1663. 4°.* L; MH, MIU, WCL.

1336   —A new book of loyal English martyrs. *For R. H. and are to be sold by Simon Miller,* [1665?]. 12°. L, O, C, DU, LNC; CH, CLC, IU, LC, MBP, NP, WF.

1337   **Heath, Nicholas,** *abp.* The speech of . . . 1555. *For the author,* 1688. 8°. L, LLP, DU; IU, TU, WF, Y.

1338   Entry cancelled.

Heath, *Sir* Robert. Clarastella. 1650. *See* Heath, Robert.

1339   [–] A Machavillian plot. *Printed,* 1642. 4°.* LT, O, LNC, EN, DT; CH, IU, LC, MH, NU, WF, Y.

1340   —Maxims and rules of pleading. *For Abel Roper,* 1694. 8°. L, O, C, LL, EN; CH, MHL, MIU, WF, YL.

[–] Praxis almæ curiæ. 1694. *See* Brown, William.

1340A   **Heath, Robert.** Clarastella. *For Humph. Moseley,* 1650. 12°. LT, O, LVD, CT, P; CH, CN, MH, NC, Y.

1341   [–] Paradoxical assertions. *By R. W. to be sold by Charles Webb,* 1659. 8°. L, O; IU.

1341A   ——[Anr. ed.] *For I. Crooke,* 1664. 8°. O; CU.

1342   **Heath, Thomas.** Stenographie. *Printed,* 1644. 8°.* CM.

1343   ——[Anr. ed.] *Printed and sold by the author,* 1664. 8°.* O.

1344   [–] Tythes no maintenance. *By R. A. for William Larnar,* 1652. 4°.* NU.

1344A   H[eathcote], *Sir* G[ilbert]. A letter from G. H. to his friend, about his being concerned. [*London,* 1697.] cap., fol.* MH.

Heathcotte, William. Almanack. 1665. *See* Almanacs.

Heathens divinity. [n.p.], 1671. *See* Fox, George.

Heavtonaparnvmenos: or. 1646. *See* Hooker, Thomas.

Heaven opened, and the pains. [n.p.], 1663. *See* Cyprien de Gamaches.

Heaven opened, or, a brief . . . discovery. 1665. *See* Alleine, Richard.

Heaven upon earth. 1667. *See* Janeway, James.

Heavenly child. 1659. *See* Jordan, Timothy.

1345   Entry cancelled.

Heavenly conference between Christ. 1654. *See* Sibbes, Richard.

Heavenly conversation. 1677. *See* S., T.

Heavenly diurnall. 1644. *See* Blackwell, Jonathan.

Heavenly guide. 1641. *See* Walker, Henry.

Heavenly passenger. 1687. *See* M., S.

Heavenly visitation. [n.p., 1685.] *See* Watson, Samuel.

1346   Heavens cry against murder. *For Henry Brome,* 1657. 4°.* LT, C; CSS, Y.

Heavens glory. 1678. *See* Hart, John.

1346aA Heaven's messenger. *For J. Clarke,* [c. 1680.] 8°.* LW, CM.

1346bA The heavy heart, and a light purse. [*London*], *for J. Wright, J. Clark*[,] *W. Thackery, and T, Passinger,* [1681–84]. brs. MH.

1346A **Hebden, Roger.** A plain account of certain Christian experiences. *Printed and sold by T. Sowle,* 1700. 8°. L; CH, CLC, RPJ, Y.

1346B **Hebden, Returne.** The dayly meditations of. 1648. L.

1347   —A guide to the godly. [*London*], *printed,* 1646. 8°. DT; CH.

1348   ——[Anr. ed.] —, 1648. 8°. LT.

1348A **Heblethwait, Robert.** To the honourable House of Commons . . . the humble petition of. *Printed in the year,* 1647. 4°.* O; Y.

1349   The hecatomb, or Presbyterian dinner. [*London,* 1662.] brs. L, LS.

Hectors. 1656. *See* Prestwich, Edmund.

Hédelin, François. *See* Aubignac, François Hédelin, abbé d'.

1350   [**Hedges, *Sir* Charles.**] Reasons for setling admiralty-jurisdiction. [*London*], *printed,* 1690. 4°.* L, LL, MR, DM, DT; CH, CN, MH, NC, WF, Y.

1351   [**Hedworth, Henry.**] Controversy ended. *For Francis Smith,* 1673. 8°. T.C.I 135. L, LF, OC, CT; NU, RPJ.

1352   [–] The spirit of the Quakers tried. *For Maurice Atkins,* 1672. 4°. L, O, LF, BBN, MR; CH, NU, RPJ, WF, Y.

1352A **Hedworth, John.** A copy of a letter written. 1651. cap., 4°.* L, EN; CSS, MH, WF.

1353   —The oppressed man's outcry. *Newcastle,* 1651. 4°.* L, MAU, NE.

1353A ——[Anr. ed.] [n.p., 1651.] cap., 4°.* CSS, WF.

1353B — To the supream authority of this nation . . . the humble petition of. [*London?* 1651.] brs. HH.

1354   **Heereboord, Adrian.** Collegium ethicvm. *Ex officina Rogeri Danielis,* 1658. 8°. O, CT; CH, IU, MH, Y.

1355   —Ερμηνεια logica. *Ex officina Rogeri Danielis,* 1651. 8°. OC, CT, SHR.

1356   ——[Anr. ed.] —, 1562 [i.e. 1662]. 8°. O, C, OC, BC, LLU; LC, NR, PMA, Y.

1357   ——[Anr. ed.] —, 1658. 8°. L, O, BSE, SHR, DT; IU, NPT, TU, WF.

1358   ——[Anr. ed.] *Cantabridgiæ, ex officina Joan. Field,* 1663. 8°. L, C, OC, LLU, GU; CH, CLC, FU, IU, MH, NIC.

1359   ——[Anr. ed.] *Cantabrigiæ, ex officina Joan. Hayes,* 1670. 8°. L,O, C, CT; CH, CLC, MH, NP, TO, WG, Y.

1360   ——[Anr. ed.] *Ex officina J. Redmayne,* 1676. 8°. L, O, D, BQ, EN; IU, MBC, MH, NP, UCLA, Y.

1361   ——[Anr. ed.] *Cantabrigiæ, ex officina Joan. Hayes,* 1680. 8°. L, O, C, BR, DT; CH, IU, MH, PL, WF, Y.

1361A —Meletemata philosophica. *Amstelædami, sumptibus JHenrici Wetstenii.* 1680. *Prostant Londini, apud Abelem Swalle.* 4°. T.C.I 422. C, NPL; MH.

1362   —Adriani Heereboord . . . philosophia naturalis. *Oxoniæ, typis Guil. Hall, venales prostant apud Joh. Crosley,* 1665. 8°. MADAN 2703. O, OC, P; TO, WF.

1362A ——[Anr. ed.] *Oxoniæ, typis Guil. Hall, venales prostant apud Joh. Wilmot,* 1665. 8°. MADAN 2704. CRN, Y.

1362B ——[Anr. ed.] *Oxoniæ, sumptibus Guil. Hall venales prostant apud Joh. Wilmot & Joh. Crosley,* 1665. 8°. CS.

1362C ——[Anr. ed.] *Oxoniæ, typis Guil. Hall venales prostant apud Tho. Bowman,* 1665. 8°. CH.

1363   ——[Anr. ed.] *Oxoniæ, typis Guil. Hall prostant venales apud Johannen Wilmot,* 1668. 8°. MADAN 2803. L, O, CCA; CU.

1364   ——[Anr. ed.] *Oxoniæ, typis Guil. Hall, prostant venales apud Johannem Crosley,* 1668. 8°. MADAN 2803n. L, CT; CLC, NC.

1365   ——[Anr. ed.] *Oxoniæ, typis Hen. Hall prostant venales apud Joh. Wilmot & Joh. Crosley,* 1676. 8°. MADAN 3107; T.C.I 240. L, O, BC; CH, CLC, IU, MH, Y.

1366   ——[Anr. ed.] *Apud Joh. Wilmot & Joh. Crosley,* 1684. 8°. L, LL, LWL, OR, BC, EN; CU, IU, UCLA, WC.

1367   [–] Specimen, tum inscitiæ. *Dicæoploi, apud Verinum Candidum, & Justum Pacium, socios [i.e. Londini, Stewartii et Rivii],* 1648. 4°.* CU.

1368   **Heers, Henry.** The most true and wonderfull narration of two women. *For Tho. Vere and W. Gilbertson,* 1658.* O.

1369   **Hegg, Robert.** In aliquot sacræ paginæ loca lectiones. *Prostant vænales apud Nathanælem Webb, & Guliel. Grantham,* 1647. 4°.* LT, O, CS, BAMB, YM; CLC, NN, NU, Y.

1370   [–] The legend of St. Cuthbert. *For Christopher Eccleston,* 1663. 8°. L, O, C, CM, DU, MR; CH, CLC, CN, MH, NCU, WF.

1370A **Heigham, *Sir* Clement.** A call to a general reformation. *By John Darby for Richard Thurlbourn in Cambridge,* 1700. 4°.* L, CS, CT; CH, Y.

1370B [**Heigham, John.**] The touchstone of the reformed Gospel. *St. Omers,* 1652. 12°. L; MB.

1370C [–]——[Anr. ed.] [n.p., 1674.] 12°. WARE.

1370D [–]——[Anr. ed.] [*St. Omer?*], *permissu superiorum,* 1675. 12°. L, O, DUS; CN, NN, NU.

1370E [–]——[Anr. ed.] [n.p.], 1676. 12°. LLP, DOWNSIDE.

1370F [–]——[Anr. ed.] [n.p.], 1677. 12°. O, LLP.

1370G [–]——[Anr. ed.] [n.p.], 1678. 12°. O.

1370H [–]——[Anr. ed.] [*St. Omer*], *printed,* 1683. 12°. DUS; NGT, Y.

1370I [–]——[Anr. ed.] [*St. Omers*], *superiorum permissu,* 1685. 12°. L, LW.

1370J [–]——[Anr. ed.] [*St. Omers*], *permissu superiorum,* [1685?]. 12°. L; CH, WF.

1370K [–]——[Anr. ed.] *By Henry Hills,* 1687. 12°. L, C.

1370L [–]——[Anr. ed.] *Bordeaux, at Simon Boé's,* 1691. 8°. L.

1371 **Heimbach, Petrus.** Ad serenissimum potentissimum-que principe, Olivarium. *Ex typographiâ Jacobi Cottrellii,* 1656. fol.* LT.

Heinlin, Johann Jacob. *See* Hainlin.

1372 **Heinsius, Daniel.** Crepundia Siliana. *Cantabrigiæ: ex officina R. Daniel.* 1646. 12°. L, O, C, E, DT; CH, CLC, CU, PL, WF, Y.

Helaw, Edward, *pseud. See* Whalley, Edward.

1372A **Heldoren, J. G. van.** An English and Nether-Dutch dictionary. *Amsterdam, by de weduwe Mercy Bruyning,* 1675. 8°. L, EN, CD; NC.

1372B —A new and easy English grammar. *Amsterdam, Mercy Bruining,* 1675. 8°. L, EN, CD; CU, NC, NIC, WF.

1372C — —[Anr. ed.] *For John Miller,* 1690. 12°. L, O.

1373 **Heliodorus, of Emesa.** The Æthiopian history of. *By J. L. for Edward Poole,* 1686. 8°. T.C.II 145. L, CS; CH, IU, LC, MH, NN, ZWT.

1374 [–] The triumphs of love and constancy. Second edition. *By J. Leake, for Edward Poole,* 1687. 8°. T.C.II 189. L; CN, MIU, Y.

1375 Entry cancelled.

Heliodorus, of Larissa. Ἡλιοδώρου. Cantabrigiæ, 1670. *See* Gale, Thomas. Opuscula mythologica.

1376 Hell and death, in the covenant. [*London*], 1647. 4°.* LT, O, OC, DC, AN, EN; CH, MH, NU, TU, WF, Y.

1377 Hell broke loose: or, a catalogue. *For Tho. Underhil, March 9,* 1646. 4°.* LT, O, CK, LNC, DT; CH, IU, NHC, WF, Y.

1378 Hell broke loose: or, an ansvver. *Printed,* 1661. 4°.* O, DU; NU, Y.

1379 Hell broke loose: or, the notorious design. *For Charles Gustavus,* 1651. 4°.* WF, Y.

Hell illuminated. 1679. *See* Aubigné, Théodore Agrippa d'.

Hell in an uproar. 1700. *See* Burridge, Richard.

Hell open'd. 1676. *See* Quicke, John.

Hell reformed. 1641. *See* Quevedo y Villegas, Francisco de.

1380 **Hellier, Henry.** A sermon preached . . . December 4, 1687. *Oxford, at the theater for Richard Chiswel,* 1688. 4°.* L, O, C, BR, DT; CB, MIU, NC, NP, NU, Y.

1380A — —[Anr. ed.] *Oxford, at the theater for John Crosley,* 1688. 4°.* T.C.II 223. OC, OCC, LSD, WCA; CH, CLC, TSM, WF.

1381 —A treatise concerning schism. *By Richard Smith for Jo. Crosley in Oxford,* 1697. 4°. L, O, C, OM, BAMB, EC; CH, TSM, WF.

1382 **Helling, Joseph.** The lambs innocency defended. [*London*], 1658. 4°. L, LF; MIU, Y.

1383 —A salutation from the breathings of the life. *For Robert Wilson,* [1661]. 4°.* L, O, C, LF, BBN; CH, IU, MH, NU, PH, Y.

1384 A hellish murder committed by a French midwife. *For R. Sare, and published by Randal Taylor,* 1688. 4°.* L, O, C, EN, DT; CH, CN, MH, WF, Y.

Hellish Parliament. [n.p.], 1641. *See* Taylor, John.

1385 A hellish plot discovered. *For T. Bates and T. Watson,* 1642. 4°. O, C.

Hell's higher court. 1661. *See* D., I.

1386 Hell's hvrlie-bvrlie. [*London*], *for G. Bishop, Octob. 5.* 1644. 4°.* LT, OW, LLU; CLC, MH.

1386A Hell's master-piece discovered. *For Francis Grove,* [1660?]. brs. EUING 138. GU.

1387 Hells nightwalker. [*London*], *by Charles Barnet,* [1694]. brs. HH.

1388 Hells trienniall Parliament. [*London*], *printed,* 1647. 4°.* LT, MR; CLC, CSS, TU, Y.

1388A **Helme, Carnsew.** Life in death, . . . being a sermon. *Printed,* 1660. 4°.* LW; MH.

[**Helmes, H.**] Gesta Grayorum. 1688. *See* Canning, William.

1389 **Helmes, Thomas.** Davids comfort. *For the authors friends,* 1668. 4°.* L; WF.

Helmet of hope. 1694. *See* Barnett, Andrew.

1390 [**Helmont, Franciscus Mercurius van.**] A cabbalistical dialogue. *For Benjamin Clark,* 1682. 4°. L, O; IU, WF.

1391 Entry cancelled.

—Observations concerning man. 1694. *See* —Seder olam.

1392 [–] One hundred fifty three chymical aphorisms. *For the author, to be sold by W. Cooper; and D. Newman,* 1688. 12°. L, LCP, LCS, GU; PL, WU, Y.

1392A [–] —[Anr. ed.] *For Awnsham Churchill,* 1690. 12°. T.C.II 287. L, OC, CT.

1393 —The paradoxal discourses of. *By J. C. and Freeman Collins, for Robert Kettlewel,* 1685. 8°. T.C.II 137. L, C, OR, CT, GU, DT; CH, CNM, MH, MMO, WF, Y.

1394 —Seder olam: or, the order, . . . of ages. *For T. Howkins,* 1694. 8°. L, O, C, OC, OR; MH, PL, RBU.

1395 —The spirit of diseases. *For Sarah Howkins,* 1694. 8°. L, O, OC, OR, MAU, GU; CH, CJC, LC, NAM, JF.

1396 [–] Two hundred queries. *For Rob. Kettlewell,* 1684. 8°. T.C.II 81. L, O, C, P, E, BQ; CH, CLC, LC, NU, WF.

1397 **Helmont, Jean Baptiste van.** Van Helmont's works. *For Lodowick Lloyd,* 1664. fol. L, LWL; CJC, IU, MMO, PL, Y.

1398 —Deliramenta catarrhi. *By E. G. for William Lee,* 1650. 4°.* LT, O, C, LCS, GU; CH, CNM, LC, MMO, NAM, WF, HC.

1399 —Fons salutis, or the fountain of health opened. *By Andrew Coe, to be sold at Thomas Moulson's house,* [1665]. 8°.* Y.

1400 —Oriatrike or, physick refined. *For Lodowick Loyd,* 1662. fol. L, O, C, LCS, GU; CLC, LC, MH, MU, NAM, Y.

1400A —Præcipiolum; or, the immature-mineral-electrum. 1683. 8°. OR.

1401 —A ternary of paradoxes. *By James Flesher, for William Lee,* 1650. 4°. LT, O, C, LCS, E; CH, IU, LC, MH, MMO, NAM, WF, Y, HC.

1402 — —Second edition. —, 1650. 4°. LCS, LLP, LW, CS, NE; CLC, CNM, LC, MH, NAM, Y.

1403 **Helmont van Valkenburgh, Johannes.** The Dutch prophesie. *By E. C. for John Newton,* 1673. 4°.* L.

Helmont disguised. 1657. *See* Thompson, Ja.

Helpe for young people. *Oxford*, 1649. *See* Lyford, William.

1404 A help to a national reformation. *Printed, and are to be sold by B. Aylmer; W. Rogers; J. Fox; and J. Downing*, 1700. 8°.* L, O, LL.

1404A —[Anr. ed.]. *For D. Brown; B. Aylmer; T. Parkhurst; J. Robinson; R. Sympson; T. Goodwin; W. Rogers; J. Walthoe; Is. Harrison; S. Heyrick; J. Fox; and J. Downing*, 1700. 8°.* BC; CLC, CN.

1404B —[Anr. ed.] *Printed, and are to be sold by D. Brown; B. Aylmer; T. Parkhurst; J. Robinson; W. Rogers; J. Fox; and J. Downing*, 1700. 8°. L; WF.

1404C —[Anr. ed.] *Printed, and are to be sold by J. Downing; B. Aylmer; W. Rogers; D. Brown; and J. Fox*, 1700. 8°. L.

1404D —Third edition. *For D. Brown*, 1700. 4°.* SP.

1404E An help to communicants. *For Tho: Underhill*, 1647. 8°.* PL.

1405 A helpe to discourse, a dialogue. colop: *Printed*, 1681. brs. L, O, LIU, LNC, HH, MC; CH, CLC, MH, NU, PU, WF, Y.
Helpe to discourse. 1648. *See* E., P.
Help to magistrates. 1700. *See* B., P.

1405A An help to prayer. *By M. C. for H. Brome*, 1678. 8°. T.C. I 309. OU; WF.

1405B —Sixth edition. *By F. Leach for Charles Brome*, 1685. 8°. CS.

1406 —[Anr. ed.] *For Charles Brome*, 1686. 8°.* O.

1407 Entry cancelled.
Helpe to the right understanding. 1644. *See* Walwyn, William.

1408 Helter skelter. [*Edinburgh*, 1700?] fol. ALDIS 3970. L.

1409 **Helvetius, Adrien.** A new method of curing all sorts of fevers. *For J. Knapton*, 1694. sixes. T.C.II 579. O; UCLA.

1409A — —Second edition. —, 1695. sixes. T.C.II 552. CLM.

1410 **Helvetius, Johann Friedrich.** The golden calf, . . . transmuting metals. *For John Starkey*, 1670. 12°. T.C.I 56. L, O, C, OC, GU; CH, CLC, PU, WF, WU, Y.

Helwich, Christopher. Familiaria colloquia. Eleventh edition. 1673. *See* Erasmus Desiderius.

1411 —The historical and chronological theatre of. *By M. Flesher, for George West and John Crosley, in Oxford*, 1687. fol. T.C.II 176. L, O, C, NPL, E; CH, CLC, CN, LC, NP, WF, Y.

1412 —Christophori Helvici, v.c. theatrvm historicvm. Fifth edition. *Oxoniæ, excudebat H. Hall, impensis Ioseph: Godwin, Ioh: Adams & Edvard: Forrest*, 1651. fol. MADAN 2170. L, O, C, E, DT; CH, IU, MH, NU, PL, Y.

1413 — —Sixth edition. —, 1662. fol. MADAN 2599. L, O, C, EN, DT; CLC, IU, LC, MB, NC, PL, WF, Y.

1413A **[Helwys, Thomas.]** Persecution for religion judg'd. [*London*], *printed in the years*, 1615. *and* 1620. *And now reprinted*, 1662. 4°. L, LIU, SP; MH, MM, NHC, Y.

1414 **H[ely], J[ames].** A modest representation of the benefits and advantages of making the river Avon navigable. *By John Macock for the author*, 1672. 4°.* L; MH, Y.

1414A **Heming, Edmund.** By virtue of a patent . . . for a new . . . lamps. [*London?* 1691.] brs. LG; MH, WF.

1415 [–] The case of. *Printed*, 1689. 4°.* L, O, LG, DT; WF.

1416 —Objections against Edmund Hemming's proposals . . . answered. [*London*, 1696?] brs. L, O; MH, Y.

1417 —Edward Heming's proposal . . . for raising eight millions. [*London*, 1696?] brs. L, O; MH.

1418 —To the right honourable the knights. [*London*, 1690?] brs. CT; Y.

1419 **Heming, Joseph.** Certain qværies. *Printed*, 1648. 4°.* LT, DT.

1420 —Judas excommvnicated. *For Giles Calvert*, 1649. 4°.* LT, C, CE, ENC, DT; CN.

1421 **Heming, William.** The eunuch. A tragedy. *By J. B. for Dorman Newman, to be sold by Randal Taylor*, 1687. 4°. T.C.II 200. L, O, LVD, LLU, EN; CH, MH, MU, TU, WF, Y.

1421A — —[Anr. ed.] *By J. B., sold by Randal Taylor*, 1687. 4°. CN, PU.

1422 —The fatal contract. *For J. M.*, 1653. 4°. L, O, LVD, OW, CT; CH, CN, LC, MH, TU, WF, Y.

1423 — —[Anr. ed.] *For Andrew Pennycuicke*, 1654. 4°. L, LVD, EC, EN; CH, CSS, MH, TU, WF.

1424 — —[Anr. ed.] *For Richard Gammon*, 1661. 4°. L, O, CCH, DC, EN; CH, CU, MH, TU, WF, Y.

1425 —The Jewes tragedy. *For Matthew Inman, to be sold by Richard Gammon*, 1662. 4°. L, O, LVD, OW, EC; CH, IU, MH, TU, WF, Y.

1426 Hemp for the flaxman. *Leyden, for the benefit of Sweet Singers*, [1682]. brs. L, O; CH, MH, NCD, PU, Y.

1427 **Henchman, Humphrey, bp.** Catalogus librorum. *Venales prostant apuddictum Robert Scott*, 1677. 4°.* L, O, OC, OL, CS, LNC; NG.

1428 **Henchman, Richard.** Ματαιοβραχυτης του βιου: the brevity and vanity of man's life. *By Tho. Roycroft, for William Grantham*, 1661. 8°.* O, E, LW, DU, DT; CLC, CN, Y.

1429 —A peace-offering in the temple. *By Thomas Roycroft, for William Grantham*, 1661. 4°.* LT, LW, EN; CN, MH, NU, WF, Y.

1429A —Preces & lachrymæ arma Christianorum. *For the author*, 1660. 8°. LSC.

1429B **Henden, Simon.** An essay for the discovery . . . new spring schism. *For C. Meredith*, 1652. 4°. O.

1430 —The key of Scripture-prophecies. *By Ja. Cottrel, for Giles Calvert*, 1652. 4°. LT, EN; CH, MM, NU, Y.

Hendericks, Elizabeth. *See* Hendricks, Elizabeth.

1431 **Henderson, Alexander.** The declaration of. [*London*], *printed*, 1648. 4°.* LT, O, C, EN, DT; MBP, MIU, NPT, NU, Y.

1432 [–] The government and order. [*Edinburgh*], *printed*, 1641. 4°. ALDIS 1006. LLP, LW, OCC, LSD, EN, GU; BN, CLC, CN.

1433 [–] —[Anr. ed.] *Edinburgh* [sic], *for Iames Bryson*, 1641. 4°. ALDIS 1005. L, O, C, EN, DT; CH, MIU, NU, PL, WF, Y.

1433A [–] —[Anr. ed.] *Edinburgh, for James Bryson*, 1643. 4°. NN.

1434 [–] —[Anr. ed.] *Edinburgh, by the society of stationers for G. Mosman*, 1690. 8°. ALDIS 3044. LW, EN, GU; CH, CN, WF.

1435   [–] — [Anr. ed.] Edinburgh, for the society of stationers, 1696. 4°. ALDIS 3563.5. CHRISTIE-MILLER.

1436   [–] Reformation of church-government in Scotland. [London], for Robert Bostock, 1644. 4°.* LT, CT, EN, DT; CH, IU, MH, TU, WF, Y.

1437   [–] —[Anr. ed.] Edinburgh, by Evan Tyler, 1644. 4°.* ALDIS 1154. L, MR, AU, EN.

1438   [–] The Scotts declaration, in answer to the declaration. [London], for Edw. Husbands and John Francks, Septem. 1. 1642. 4°.* LT, O, CCA, LNC, DT; CN, CSS, MH, NU, WF.

1438A —A sermon preached . . . before the . . . General Assembly, begun the 12. of August 1639. [n.p.], 1682. 8°. EN.

1439   —A sermon preached . . . December 27. 1643. For Robert Bostock, 1644. 4°.* LT, O, C, EN, DT; BN, CH, CN, MH, WF, Y.

1440   — —[Anr. ed.] Edinburgh, by Evan Tyler, 1644. 4°. ALDIS 1137. L, O, EN, I; CH, IU.

1441   —A sermon preached . . . 18. day of Iuly, 1644. For Robert Bostock, 1644. 4°.* LT, O, C, E, DT; BN, CH, IU, MH, WF, Y.

1442   — —[Anr. ed.] Re-printed at Edinburgh by Evan Tyler, 1644. 4°.* ALDIS 1138. EN; CH, CSS, NGT, NU, Y.

1443   —A sermon preached . . . 28. of May 1645. By F. N. for Robert Bostock, 1645. 4°.* LT, O, C, EN, DT; BN, CH, CN, MH, NU, WF, Y.

1444   [–] The vnlavvfvllnes and danger of limited prelacie. [London], printed, 1641. 4°.* LT, O, C, AU, DT; CH, IU, MH, NU, WF, Y.

1445   [Henderson, Jo.] Mr. Clanny's character. [Edinburgh], printed, 1699. 4°. ALDIS 3874.5. MR, EN.

1446   Henderson, Thomas. Μεγιστα τιμια επαγγελματα: or the vertue, vigour, and efficacy. For Dor. Newman, 1669. 8°. T.C.I 8. O, LSC, LW; CLC.

1447   Hendricks, Elizabeth. An epistle to friends in England. [London], printed, 1672. 4°.* L, O, C, CT, BBN; CH, MB, MH, PL, PSC, WF, Y.

1448   Hendricks, Pieter. The backslider bewailed. [London], printed, 1665. 4°.* L, LF, BBN; MH, NCD, PH, PSC, WF, Y.

1449   Henley, Sir Andrew. A catalogue of the libraries of. [London], 1700. 4°. L, MR; BN.

1450   Hennepin, Louis. A new discovery of a vast country in America. For M. Bentley, I. Tonson, H. Bon/wick, T. Goodwin, and S. Manship, 1698. 8°. T.C.III 38. L, O, CT, ES, DT; CH, CN, LC, MH, MU, NN, RPJ, Y.

1451   — —[Anr. ed.] —"Tonson/", 1698. 8°. L; CH, CN, LC, MH, PBL, SW, WCL, Y.

1452   — —[Anr. ed.] By for [sic] Henry Bonwicke, 1699. 8°. T.C.III 115. L, LW, NE; CH, LC, MH, RPJ, WCL.

1453   The hen-peckt cuckold. For Charles Barnet, [1694–98]. brs. HH.

1453A —[Anr. ed.] [London], printed and sold by J. Millet, [1689–91]. brs. CM.

1454   Henri IV, King of France. A speech of. For Jacob Tonson. 1681. fol.* L, O, C, MR, EN; CLC, MH, MIU, PU, WF, Y.

1455   Henrietta Maria, Queen of England. De boodtschap ende brief van de. Gedruckt by R. Barcker, 1642. 4°.* BN, NN.

       —Copy of I. the letter sent. See title.

1456   —A copie of the Qveen's letter. For Iohn Price, 1642. brs. LT.

       [–] Four letters from the Queen. [n.p., 1651.] See title.

1457   Entry cancelled.
       [–] Qveens majesties declaration and desires. [n.p.], 1642. See title.

1458   —The Queens maiesties gracious answer to the Lord Digbies letter. Printed at London for Tho. Powell, [1642]. 4°.* LT, O, C, EC, MR; CH, CLC, CSS, MH, Y.

1459   —The Queens letter from Holland. For I. Vnderhill, [1643]. 4°.* LT, BC, EC, SP, DT; CH, CLC, WF, Y.

1460   Entry cancelled.
       [–] Queenes letter to the Kings . . . Majesty. [n.p.], 1647. See title.

1461   —The Queens majesties letter to the Parliament. [London], for L. VVhite, [1649]. 4°.* LT; CLC, WF.

1462   —The Queens majesties message and declaration. [London], for L. VVhite, [1649]. 4°.* LT; CSS, MH.

1463   —The Queens majesties message and letter from the Hague. For I. Vnderhill, Octob. 14, [1642]. 4°.* LT, CT, DUC, EC, LNC, DT; HR, CH, WF, Y.

1464   Entry cancelled.
       [–] Queenes Majesties propositions. 1647. See title.

1465   —The Qveenes majesties propositions to the States of Holland. For I. H. and T. R, 1642. June, 30. 4°.* LT, O, EC, LIU, YM; IU.

1466   —The protestation of. Printed at London for John Hancocke, March 9, 1643. brs. LT, LG, LNC; HR, MIU, Y.

1467   —The Queenes speech. [London], 1641. brs. STEELE 1871. L, YM.

1467A — —[Anr. ed.] [London, 1641.] brs. MH.

1468   Henry VIII, King of England. Assertio septem sacramentorum. By Nath. Thompson, 1687. 4°. L, O, CT, E, DT; CH, CN, MH, NU, WF.

1469   — —Second edition. —, 1688. sixes. L, O, LG, CT, DT; CN, MH, PAP, TU, WF, WSC.

1470   —A declaration, containing the just causes. Printed at London, by Tho. Berthelet, 1542. And now reprinted by William Du-Gard, Decemb. 10. 1651. 4°.* MR; CH, CLC, MH, WF, Y.

1471   —A famous speech of . . . 24. of December 1545. Printed, 1642. 4°.* LT, O, C, BC, DT; CH, MH, MU, WF, Y.

1472   —Royal directions. colop: By George Larkin, [1682]. brs. O, OC, HH, EN; CH, CN.

1473   —A speech made by . . . 23. of December, 1546. For Edward Blackmore, 1642. 4°.* LT, C; CH, CN, IU, MH, WF, Y.

1474   H[enry], M[atthew]. A brief enquiry into the true nature of schism. For Tho. Parkhurst, 1690. 8°.* T.C.II 311. L, LCL, LW, OC; MB.

1475   —A discourse concerning meekness. For Tho. Parkhurst, 1699. 8°. T.C.III 121. L, C, LW, OC, MR; CH, NN, NU, TO, WF.

1475A [–] Family-hymns. *For Tho. Parkhurst*, 1695. T.C.II 548. NU.

1476 —A sermon on Acts xxviij. 22. *Printed for, and sold by, Thomas Parkhurst*, 1699. 8°. L, O, OC, MR; CH, NU, RBU, TO, WF.

Henry the second. 1693. *See* Bancroft, John.

1476A **Henryson, Robert.** The testament of Cresseid. [*Glasgow*], *printed*, 1663. 8°.* ALDIS 1754. CT.

1477 **Henshaw, Anne.** To the Parliament of the commonwealth . . . the humble petition of. [*London*, 1654.] brs. LT; MH.

1477A **Henshaw, Joseph, bp.** Daily thoughts. Third edition. *By W. H. for T. A., sold by G. B.*, 1651. 12°. O, C.

1477B ——"Third" edition. 1657. 8°. O.

1477C —Horæ succisivæ, or spare-houres. Sixth edition. *By G. D. and sold by John Sweeting*, 1650. 12°. L.

1477D ——[Anr. ed.] 1659. 4°. P.

1477E ——Seventh edition. *By G. Dawson for I. Sweeting*, 1661. 12°. KU.

1478 [–] Meditations, miscellaneous. 1652. 12°. DC.

1478A [–] —[Anr. ed.] *Printed for the Publique Good*, 1658. 12°. L.

1479 [–] —[Anr. ed.] *By J. H. for Brabazon Aylmer*, 1686. 12°. L, LW, CT.

1480 [–] Miscellanea; or, a mixture. *For Thomas Helder*, 1669. 12°. T.C.I 21. L, O; CH, CN, IU, MH, WF, Y.

1480A [–] —Second edition. —, 1688. 12°. LG.

1481 **Henshaw, Nathaniel.** Aero-chalinos: or, a register for the air. *Dublin, for Samuel Dancer*, 1664. 8°. DIX 126. L, C, LWL, OR, CE, DT; WF, WU, Y, HC.

1482 ——Second edition. *For Benj. Tooke*, 1677. 12°. T.C.I 278. L, O, C, EN, GH; CH, CLC, MH, MMO, WF, JF.

1482A [**Henshaw, Thomas.**] On the most triumphant ceremony . . . Charles II. [*London*, 1661.] fol.* CH.

1483 —A vindication of. colop: [*n.p.*], *Printed at the Spavv*, 1654. cap., 4°.* LT.

1484 **Henson, John.** Ὁ Ἱερευς κατα δυναστευομενος. Or, a narrative of. *By Thomas Creake*, 1659. 4°.* L, LW; CH.

1484A **Henus, Josephus.** Anni menses et dies singuli. *Sumptibus authoris, prostant apud Joan. Cailloué Danielem du Chemin*, 1696. 8°. EC.

1485 **Hepburn, Adam.** Disputatio juridica. *Edinburgh, by the heirs of A. Anderson*, 1696. 4°. ALDIS 3566. EN.

Hepburn, George. Tarrugo unmasked. 1695. *See* title.

1486 **Hepwith, John.** The Calidonian forrest. *By E. G. for R. Best*, 1641. 4°.* L, O, EN; CH, CN, MH, WF, Y.

1487 Heraclitus Christianus: or, the man of sorrow. *By A. M. and R. R. for Brabazon Aylmer*, 1677. 12°. T.C.I 275. L, O, LW, LSD, NE; CN, NU, WF.

1488 Heraclitus derisus, or Ben's monkey stript. colop: *For T. D.*, 1681. brs. L, O; CH, AVP.

1489 Heraclitus dream. *For John Spencer*, 1642. brs. LT.

Heraclitus, his ghost, *pseud.*

1489A **Heraclitus mythologus.** De incredibilibus. *Cantabrigiæ*, 1671. 8°. CCA.

Heraclitus ridens redivivus. [*n.p.*, 1688.] *See* Brown, Thomas.

1490 **Hérard, Claude.** The arguments of. *For C. Broom*, 1699. 8°. O, LW, OC, CK, EN; CH, MH, NIC, WF, Y.

1490A **Herault, Louis.** Harangue prononcée a . . . Guillaume Henry, . . . quatrienne de Novembre. [*London?* 1670.] 4°.* LPR.

1491 —Remerciment faict au roy. *A Londres chez Octavian Pulleyn le jeune*, 1666. fol.* O, C; CN.

1492 —A speech delivered . . . March the 15th. 1665/6. *By Tho: Ratcliffe for Octavian Pulleyn junior*, 1666. fol.* MR, EN.

1493 **Herberay, Nicholas de.** The most excellent history of the . . . knight, Don Flores. Third edition. *For R. I.*, 1664. 4°. L, O, CM; CH, CN.

1494 **Herbert, Mr.** Three elegies upon the much lamented loss of . . . Queen Mary. *By J. Heptinstall, for Henry Playford*, 1695. fol.* L, C, GU, DN; CLC, LC, MH, WF, Y.

Herbert, Arthur. *See* Torrington, Arthur Herbert, earl.

1495 **Herbert, Sir Edward, 1591–1657.** The ansvver of. *Printed at London for George Tomlinson, August 24. 1642.* 4°.* LT, LVF, CCA, AN, DT; CH, CLC, CN, MH, MU, WF, Y.

1496 **Herbert, Sir Edward, 1648–1698.** A short account of the authorities in law. *For M. Clark*, 1688. 4°.* L, O, C, EN, DT; CH, CN, LC, MH, NU, WF, Y.

1497 **Herbert, Edward, lord, of Cherbury.** De causis errorum. 1645. 4°. L, O, C, EN, DT; MH, NU, TU, Y.

1498 ——[Anr. ed.] *Curâ Philemonis Stephani*, 1645. 4°. C, OC, GC, WCA, ENC; MH.

1499 ——[Anr. ed.] *Typis Joannis Raworth*, 1645. 4°. OC; MBP, TU, Y.

1500 ——[Anr. ed.] [*London?*], 1656. 12°. L, O, C, ENC, DL; CH, INU, MH, NP, Y.

1501 —De veritate. Third edition. 1645. 4°. L, O, C, ENC, DT; IU, MBP, NU, TU, Y. (var.)

1502 ——Third edition. [*London?*], 1656. 12°. L, O, C, E, DT; BN, CH, IU, MH, UCLA, TU, Y.

1503 —Expeditio in ream insulam. *Prostant apud Humphredum Moseley*, 1656. 8°. LT, O, C, MR, EN, DT; BN, CH, CN, MH, WF, Y.

1504 —The life and raigne of King Henry the Eighth. *By E. G. for Thomas Whitaker*, 1649. fol. L, O, C, DU, EN; BN, CH, CN, MH, NC, WCL, Y.

1505 —Entry cancelled. Ghost.

1505A ——[Anr. ed.] *By Andr. Clark for S. Mearne*, 1672. fol. LSD, MR; WF.

1505B ——[Anr. ed.] *By Andr. Clark, for J. Martyn, S. Mearne, and H. Herringman*, 1672. fol. T.C.I 113. L, O, C, ES, DT; CH, CN, MH, NP, TSM, Y.

1506 ——[Anr. ed.] *By M. Clark, for Henry Herringman*, 1682. fol. L, C, CT, ENC, GH; CSU, MH, PL.

1506A ——[Anr. ed.] *By M. Clark, for Anne Mearne*, 1682. fol. L, OC, CCH; CH, MH, MU, NCU, PU, WF.

1507 ——[Anr. ed.] *By Mary Clark, for Ann Mearn, to be sold by Tho. Sawbridg* [sic], 1683. fol. T.C.II 52. L, LL, LVD, LVF, DU; CSU, IU, LC, MH, NP, TU.

1507A — —[Anr. ed.] *By M. Clark, for Robert Littlebury, Robert Scott, and George Wells,* 1683. fol. OC, CT, HOUSE OF LORDS; BN, CH, MB, MIU, TO, TU, AVP.

1507AB — —[Anr. ed.] *By M. Clark, for Henry Herringman,* 1683. fol. L; CLC, MH, AUSTRALIAN NATIONAL U.

1507AC — —[Anr. ed.] *By M. Clark, for H. Herringman, sold by T. Passenger,* 1683. fol. L, LU, LIU.

1507B — —[Anr. ed.] *By Mary Clark, for Ann Mearn, to be sold by Geo. Sawbridge,* 1693. fol. Y.

1508 —Occasional verses. *By T. R. for Thomas Dring,* 1665. L, O, C; CH, CLC, MH, RHT, WC, Y.

1509 **Herbert, George.** Jacula prudentum. Or outlandish proverbs. *By T. Maxey for T. Garthwait,* 1651. LT, O, LW, OME, CS; CH, IU, LC, MH, NP, WF, Y.

1509A — —[Anr. ed.] *By T. M. for T. Garthwait,* 1651. 8°. O.

1510–11 Entries cancelled.

—Musæ responsoriæ. Cambridge, 1662. *See* Vivianus, Joannes. Ecclesiastes Solomonis.

—Poemata varii argumenti. 1678. *See* Dillingham, William.

1512 —A priest to the temple. *By T. Maxey for T. Garthwait,* 1652. 8°. L, O, C, LNC, EN; CLC, IU, MH, NP, WC, WF, Y.

1513 — —Second edition. *By T. Roycroft, for Benj. Tooke,* 1671. 8ᵘ. T.C.I 76. L, O, C, EN, DT, GK; CH, IU, MH, NU, WF, Y.

1514 — —Third edition. *By T. R. for Benj. Tooke,* 1675. 12°. T.C.I 208. L, O, CS, D, GK; CH, CN, IU, NU, WF, Y.

1515 —Herbert's remains. *For Timothy Garthwait,* 1652. 12°. LT, O, C, LW, AN, EN; CH, CN, MH, NP, WF, Y.

1515A —Select hymns. *By S. Bridge, for Thomas Parkhurst,* 1697. 8°. T.C.III 24. LW.

1516 —The temple. Sixth edition. *Cambridge, by Roger Daniel,* 1641. 12°. L, O, C, CT, GK; BN, CH, CN, MH, NP, WF, Y.

1517 — —Seventh edition. [*London,* 1647?] 12°. L, O, GK; NP, TU, Y.

1518 — —"Seventh" edition. *By T. R. for Philemon Stephens,* 1656. 12°. L, O, C, DC, DT; BN, CH, IU, MH, NP, WF, Y.

1519 — —Eighth edition. *By R. N. for Philemon Stephens,* 1660. 12°. L, O, C, E, GK; CH, KU, MH, NN, PU, Y.

1520 — —Ninth edition. *By J. M. for Philemon Stephens,* 1667. 12°. O, C, OM, DT, GK; CLC, IU, MH, WF, WSC, Y.

1520A — —"Ninth" edition. —, *and J. Stephens,* 1667. 12°. L.

1521 — —Tenth edition. *By W. Godbid, for R. S., to be sold by John Williams junior,* 1674. 12°. L, O, C, LVD, E; CH, IU, MBP, MH, TU, WF, Y.

1522 — —Eleventh edition. *By S. Roycroft, for R. S., to be sold by John Williams junior,* 1678. 12°. L, O, C, LLU, LSD, GK; CH, CN, MH, NCU, Y.

1523 — —"Eleventh" edition. —, 1679. 12°. L, O, C, CM, LLU; CLC, IU, MH, WF, Y.

1524 — —"Eleventh" edition. *For R. S., to be sold by Richard VVillington,* 1695. 12°. T.C.II 552. O, LU; IU, KYU, MH, Y.

1524AA **Herbert, Henry.** The case of . . . in the election for the town of Bewdley. [*London,* 1677.] brs. LPR.

1524A **Herbert, Sir Percy.** Certaine conceptions. *By E. G. and are to be sold by Richard Tomlins,* 1650. 4°. L; CH.

1525 — —[Anr. ed.] *Printed,* 1651. 4°. L, CT; CLC, CPB, IU, NIC.

1526 — —[Anr. ed.] *By E. G. and are to be sold by Richard Tomlins,* 1652. 4°. LT, O, C, SP; CH, IU, MH, NU, WF, Y.

Herbert, Philip. *See* Pembroke and Montgomery, Philip Herbert, *earl.*

1527 [**Herbert, Thomas.**] An ansvver to the most envious, scandalous, and libellous pamphlet. *Printed,* 1641. 4°.* LT, O, AN, DU; CH, IU, MH, NU, WF. (var.)

1527A [–] —[Anr. ed.] *For T. B.,* 1641. 4°.* MH, Y.

1528 —An elegie vpon the death of Thomas, Earle of Strafford. [*London*], *printed,* 1641. 4°.* L, O, LVF, CS, BC; CH, CU, MH, WF.

1529 —Keep within compasse Dick and Robin. *For Thomas Lambert,* 1641. 8°.* CH.

[–] Letter to the Earle of Pembrooke. [n.p.], 1647. *See* Howell, James.

1530 —Newes newly discovered. [*London*], *for I. Wright,* 1641. 8°.* LT.

1530A —Newes out of Islington. *For Thomas Lambert,* 1641. 8°. AN; CH.

1531 —A reply in the defence of Oxford petition. *Printed,* 1641. 4°.* MADAN 986. L, O, LVF, OC, WCA; CH, MH, TU.

1532 —Secunda vox populi. Or, the Commons gratitude. [*London*], *printed,* 1641. 4°.* L; CH, RHT, WF.

1533 —Vox secvnda popvli. Or, the Commons gratitude. [*London*], *printed,* 1641. 4°.* LT, LG; CH, MH, WF.

1533A **Herbert, Sir Thomas.** Some years travels into divers parts. Third edition. *By J. Best for Andrew Crook,* 1664. fol. OC.

1534 — —"Third" edition. *By J. Best for Andrew Crook and are to be sold by William Crook,* 1665. fol. L, C, LI; CLC, NN, RBU, TU, WF.

1535 — —"Third" edition. *By R. Everingham, for R. Scot, T. Basset, J. Wright, and R. Chiswell,* 1677. fol. L, OR, CPL, DCH, E, BQ; CH, CLC, MBP, WF.

1536 — —Fourth edition. —, 1677. fol. T.C.I 294. L, O, C, EN, DT; BN, CH, CSU, MH, RPJ, WF.

—Speculum anni. [1651.] *See* Almanacs.

Herbert, William. *See also* Pembroke, William Herbert, *earl.*

1537 —Herbert's beleefe and confession of faith. *By Jo. Dever & Robert Ibbitson,* 1646. 12°. LT, BR.

1538 — —Second edition. *By Francis Leach, and are sold by I. Hancock: and by Humphrey Tuckey,* 1648. 8°. LT, O, C, EN; IU.

1539 —Herberts careful father. *By R. A. & J. M. and are to be sold by John Hancock, and by Humphrey Tuckey,* 1648. 8°. LT, O, C, BR, EN; CH, IU, MH, NU, WF, Y.

1540 —Herberts child-bearing woman. *By R. A. & J. M., to be sold by John Hancock, and by Humphrey Tuckey,* 1648. 8°. LT; CH, IU, Y.

1541 [–] Considerations in the behalf of foreiners. colop: *By Sarah Griffin,* 1662. cap., 4°.* L.

1542 —Herberts devotions. *For Simon Miller,* 1657. 8°. O, NPL.

1543 —Herberts French and English dialogues. *By D. Maxwell for T. Davis, & T. Sadler,* 1660. 4°. LT, O, CS.

1544   —Herberts quadripartit devotion. *By J. Y., to be sold by John Hancock, and by Humphrey Tuckey,* 1648. 8°. LT, O, LLP, LW, P; CH, IU, NU, TO, WF.

1545   [–] Reponse aux questions de Mr Despagne. *Chez Jean Baker,* 1657. 4°. LT, C.

1545A An Herculean antidote against the pox. [*London,* 1690?] brs. L.

1546   **Herdson, Henry.** Ars mnemonica. *Typis G. Dawson,* 1651. 8°. LT, O, C, LW, DT; PCP, WF, Y.

1546A —Ars memoriæ. *For William Shears,* 1654. 8°. L; LC, Y.

1546B —Penitent pilgrim. *For William Sheares,* 1652. 12°. C.

Here all may see a clear. [n.p.], 1680. *See* Fox, George.

Here all may see, that. 1656. *See* Fox, George.

Here are several queries. 1657. *See* Fox, George.

1546C Here beginneth the second part of the Fryer and the Boy. *By A. M. and R. R. for Edward Brewster, to be sold by James Gilbertson,* 1680. 8°.* CM.

1547   Here followeth a true relation of some of the sufferings inflicted upon the . . . Quakers. [*London?* 1654.] cap., 4°.* MADAN 2250. L, O, OC; CH, MH, PL, WF.

1547A Here is a true and just account of a . . . plot. colop: *By E. Mallet,* 1683. cap., fol.* L, CH, TU, U.

1547AB —[Anr. ed.] colop: *Reprinted by the heir of Andrew Anderson, Edinburgh,* 1683. fol.* ALDIS 2439.5. L, O, GU; MH, MIU, WF.

1547B Here is a true and perfect account of the proceedings at VVindsor. colop: *For E. Mallet,* 1683. brs. CH.

1548   Here is a true and perfect relation from the Faulcon. [*London*], *for F. Coles, T. Vere, and William Gilbertson,* [1661]. brs. O.

Here is declared. 1658. *See* Fox, George.

1549   Here is great news for England. [*London?* 1700.] brs. LF.

Here is held forth. 1659. *See* Blackborow, Sarah.

1549AA Here is some comfort for poor Cavaleeres. *For F. Grove,* [1660]. brs. EUING 141. GU.

Here is something of concernment. [1660.] *See* Cooke, Edward.

Here you may see. 1660. *See* Fox, George.

Hereby. *See* Herberay.

Herefordshire orchards. 1657. *See* Beale, John.

1549A Here's twenty sworn brethren. *For F. Coles, T. Vere, and J. Wright,* [1663–74]. brs. O.

Heresiography. 1645. *See* Pagitt, Ephraim.

Heresie detected. 1649. *See* Bakewell, Thomas.

Hereticks, sectaries. 1647. *See* Ellyson, John.

1549B **Heriot, Alexander.** A book containing tables for . . . exchange of money. *Edinburgh, by the heirs and successors of Andrew Anderson, sold by J. Vallance,* 1697. 4°. ALDIS 3670. EN, AU, GU.

1549C **Herlackenden, Thomas.** Animadversions on severall material passages in a book. *By Roger Daniel,* 1663. 4°. OC (lost).

1550   **Herle, Charles.** Abrahams offer, Gods offering. *For Peter Cole,* 1644. 4°.* LT, O, LW, LLU, DT; CH, CLC, V, Y.

1551   [–] Ahab's fall. [*London*], *by R. A. for J. Wright,* 1644. 4°.* LT, O, C, CT, AN, DT; CH, CLC, INU, NU, WF, Y.

1552   [–] An answer to Doctor Fernes reply. *By Tho. Brudenell for N. A.,* 1643. 4°. LT, O, C, E, DT; CH, IU, MH, NU, WF, Y.

1553   [–] An answer to mis-led Doctor Fearne. *Printed,* 1642. 4°.* LT, O, CT, EN, DT; CH, IU, MH, LC, NU, WF, Y.

1554   —Davids reserve, and rescue. *For John Wright,* 1645. 4°.* LT, C, LW, OU, LIU, EN, DT; CH, CN, MH, WF, Y.

1555   ——[Anr. ed.] —, 1646. 4°.* O, LW, OCC, DU, MR; MH, NU.

1556   —Davids song of three parts. *By T. Brudenell for N. A.,* 1643. 4°.* LT, O, C, LIU, DT; CH, IU, MH, NU, WF, Y.

1557   No entry.

1558   [–] A fvller ansvver to a treatise vvritten by Doctor Ferne. *For Iohn Bartlet,* 1642. 4°.* LT, O, C, MR, E, DT; CH, CN, MH, NU, WF, Y. (var.)

1559   —The independency on Scriptures. *By Tho. Brudenell for N. A.,* 1643. 4°. LT, O, C, EN, DT; CH, IU, MH, NU, WF, Y.

1560   ——[Anr. ed.] 1655. 4°. LCL.

1561   —A payre of compasses. *By G. M. for Iohn Bartlet,* 1642. 4°.* LT, O, C, EN, DT; CH, MH, MU, NU, WF, Y, AVP.

1562   —Wisdomes tripos. *For Samuel Gellibrand,* 1655. 12°. LT, O, CS, SP, ENC; CH, CN, MH, NU, WF, Y.

1563   ——[Anr. ed.] —, 1670. 12°. L, O, P, DU, EN; BN, CH, MB, MH, Y.

1564   —Worldly policy and moral prudence. *For Sa. Gellibrand,* 1654. 12°. L, CS, SP, E; CH, CN, FU, WCL, WF.

Hermæologium; or. 1659. *See* Jones, Bassett.

1564A **Hermas.** The three books of. *For John White,* 1661. 8°. O, NE.

1565   **Hermes Trismegistus.** The divine Pymander. *By Robert White for Tho. Brewster and Greg. Moule,* 1650. 8°. LT, O, CK, E, GU; CH, IU, MH, MU, NC, WF, Y.

1566   —Hermes Mercurius Trismegistus his divine Pymander. *By J. S. for Thomas Brewster,* 1657. 12°. L, LW, A, GU; IU, LC, NN, MBP, WU.

1567   —His second book. *For Thomas Brewster,* 1657. 12°. L, GU; IU, LC.

Hermetick romance. [n.p.], 1690. *See* Andreae, Johann Valentin.

Hermeticall banqvet. 1652. *See* Vaughan, Thomas.

1568   **Herne, John.** The law of charitable uses. *By T. R. for Timothy Twyford,* 1660. 8°. LT, O, C, LL, NPL; CH, LC, MH, PUL, WF, YL.

1569   ——Second edition. *By J. S. for Timothy Twyford,* 1663. 8°. L, O, LGI, LI, CE; CH, LC, MHL, MU, WF.

1569A ——[Anr. ed.] *By F. S. for T. S. for T. Twyford,* 1663. 8°. LC.

1570   —The law of conveyances. *By T. R. for Hen. Twyford, and Tho. Dring,* 1656. 8°. LT, LIL, OC, CCA, EN; CH, MHL, WF.

1571   ——Second edition. —, 1658. 8°. LT, O, CP, DC, DT; CH, IU, LC, MHL, MU, NCL, WF.

1572   —Lent, 1638. The learned reading of. *For Matthew Walbanke,* 1659. 4°.* L, O, LI, LL, CS; CLC, MHL, NIC, WF, YL.

1573   [–] The modern assurancer, or the clarks directory. *For Henry Twyford, and Nath. Brook,* 1658. 8°. LT, O, BAMB, EN; LC, IU, MHL, NCL, PU, WF.

1574 —The pleader. *For Henry Twyford, Thomas Dring, and Timothy Twyford,* 1657. fol. L, LGI, LL, CS, DT; CH, LC, MHL, MU, NCL, WF, YL.

1575 — —Second edition. 1658. fol. LIL.

1576 **Herne, John,** *mathematician.* Longitude unvailed. *By H. Brugis for the author, to be sold by Robert Starr,* 1678. brs. L.

1576A **H[erne], R.** The history of Genesis. *By J. D. for W. Fisher and R. Mount,* 1690. 8°. T.C.II 321. L.

1577 **Herne, Samuel.** A discourse of divine providence. *By T. Newcomb, for G. Kunholt,* 1679. 4°.* L, O, CT, SHR, WCA; CLC, MB, NU, WF, Y.

1578 —Domus Carthusiana. *By T. R. for Richard Marriott, and Henry Brome,* 1677. 8°. T.C.I 252. L, O, C, EN, DT; CH, IU, LC, MH, NC, Y.

Hero and Leander, in burlesque. 1669. *See* Wycherley, William.

Heroe of Lorenzo. 1652. *See* Gracian, Balthasar.

Herod and Mariamne. 1673. *See* Pordage, Samuel.

Herod and Pilate reconciled. [1647.] *See* Bostock, Robin.

1579 **Herodian.** Ἡρωδιανου ἱστοριων βιβλιαν. Herodiani historiarvm. *Oxoniæ e theatro Sheldoniano,* 1678. 8°. MADAN 3177. L, O, C, LW, DU, DT; CLC, IU, MH, V, WF, Y.

1580 — —[Anr. ed.] —, 1699. 8°. T.C.III 125. L, O, C, CT, D; CH, IU, MBP, WCL, WF, Y.

1580A — —[Anr. ed.] —, *impensis Georg. West & Anth. Peisley,* 1699. 8°. O.

1581 —Herodian's history of the Roman Emperors. *For John Hartley,* 1698. 8°. T.C.III 78. L, O, C, AN, LLU, DT; CH, CN, IU, LC, WF, Y.

1582 —His imperiall history. *By W: Hunt, for the author,* 1652. 4°. LT, OC, CS; CH, CN, Y.

1583 —Herodians of Alexandria his imperiall history. *By W: Hunt, to be sold by Humphrey Moseley,* 1652. 4°. O, DU, LLU; MH.

1584 **Herodotus.** Ἡροδοτου . . . ἱστοριων. . . . Historiarum libri ix. *Typis E. Horton & J. Grover, impensis Johannis Dunmore, Richardi Chiswel, Benjamin Tooke, & Thomæ Sawbridge,* 1679. fol. T.C.I 316. L, O, C, MR, DT; CLC, MH, NC, OCI, PL, WF, Y.

1584A Heroes Davidici. *Oxoniæ, typis Lichfieldianis, & veneunt apud Jo. Crosly,* 1682. 4°.* L, O.

1584B The heroes of France: in a dialogue. *For Abel Roper,* 1694. 12°. CT, P; NN.

Heroick edvcation. 1657. *See* B., I.

Heroick elegie upon the most lamentable death of . . . Madame Isabella Buggs. 1681. *See* I., H.

1585 An heroick elegy upon the most lamented death of that excellent hero Sir Edmund Wyndham. *Printed,* 1680/1. brs. L, MC; MH.

1586 An heroick poem, most humbly dedicated to the sacred majesty of Catharine Queen Dowager. *By Nathaniel Thompson,* 1685. 4°.* L, O; IU, MH, WF, Y.

1587 An heroick poem on her highness the Lady Ann's voyage. colop: *For R. Bently,* 1681. cap., fol.* L, O, LLP; CH, CN, MH, OCI, PU.

1587A An heroick poem on the Observator. *By J. Streater, for H. Million,* 1685. 4°.* L, O; CH, MH.

Heroick poem on the right honourable, . . . Ossory. 1681. *See* Settle, Elkanah.

1588 An heroick poem to the King, upon the arrival of the Morocco . . . embassadors. *For Francis Hicks in Cambridge,* 1682. fol.* T.C.I 495. L, OP, CS, LLU, MR; CH, IU, MH, WF, Y.

1589 An heroic poem upon His Majesties most gratious releasing. *For R. Taylor,* 1689. brs. L, O; CH.

1590 An heroick poem upon His Royal Highnes's arrival. *For J. B.,* 1682. brs. EN; CH, TU.

1591 Entry cancelled.

Heroick poem upon the late horrid rebellion. 1683. *See* Cowley, Abraham.

Heroical panegyrick. 1689. *See* M., *Mrs.* A.

1592 An heroical song on the atchievements of . . . James Duke of York. *By Henry Blunt,* 1660. brs. LT.

1593 An heroical song on the worthy and valiant exploits of . . . Albemarle. *By W. Godbid for John Playford,* 1667. brs. L.

Heroin musqueteer. 1678. *See* Préchac, *sieur de.*

1594 Entry cancelled.

Heron, *Sir* Henry. Late Earle of Lindsey, his title. [n.p., 1661.] *See* Killigrew, *Sir* William.

1595 **Herrick, Robert.** Hesperides: or, the works. *For John Williams, and Francis Eglesfield, to be sold by Tho. Hunt in Exon,* 1648. 8°. LT; CH, CN, IU, WCL.

1596 — —[Anr. ed.] *For John Williams and Francis Eglesfield,* 1648. 8°. L, O, LVD, CE, EC; CH, IU, MH, WF, Y.

1597 [–] His noble numbers. *For John Williams and Francis Eglesfield,* 1647. 4°. LT, O, LVD; CLC, IU, MB, TU, WC, Y.

1598 [–] Poor Robin's visions. *Printed for, and sold by Arthur Boldero,* 1677. 8°. T.C.I 283. L, O, LG, CT; CH, CU, LC, WU, Y.

1599 [–] A song for two voices. [London], *T. Cross,* [1700?]. brs. L.

1600 Entry cancelled.

[Herries, Walter.] Short vindication of Phil Scots defence. 1700. *See* Hodges, James.

1600A **Herring, Anne.** The case of . . . [estate settlement]. [London, 1678.] brs. LPR.

1600B **Herring, Francis.** Preservatives against the plague. *For Jaspar Emerie,* 1641. 4°. NAM, WF, WSG.

1601 — —[Anr. ed.] *For Tho: Pierrepont,* 1665. 4°.* L, O.

1602 —November the 5, 1605. The quintessence of cruelty. *London, by G. M. for R. Harford,* 1641. 8°. LT, O, C, CM, EN; CH, CLC, MBA, WF, Y.

Hertford, William Seymour, *marquess.* *See* Somerset, William Seymour, *duke of.*

Hertford letter. 1699. *See* D., P.

1602A **Hertfordshire.** Hertf. ss. At the general quarter-sessions . . . of Hertford, on the fourteenth and sixteenth days of July . . . [order respecting rogues and vagabonds]. [n.p., 1656.] brs. L.

1602B — —[Same title, order respecting licensing of ale houses.] [n.p., 1656.] brs. L.

1602C   The Hartford-shire damosel. [*London*], *for P. Brooksby*, [1690?]. brs. O.

Hart-fordshire wonder. 1669. *See* Y., M.

1602D   The Hertford-shires murder. [*London*], *for F. Coles, T. Vere, J. Wright, and J. Clarke*, [1674–79]. brs. O.

1603   Hertzbrechendes klag: und leid-geschrey in Gross Brittania. *Gedruckt in Londen*, 1661. 4°.* O.

1604   **Herwig, Henning Michael.** The art of curing sympathetically. *For Tho. Newborough, R. Parker; and P. Buck*, 1700. 12°. T.C.III 185. L, O, C, LL, GU; WF, WSG, HC.

1605   **Hesiod.** Ησιοδου ασκραιου τα ʽευρισκομενα. Hesiodi . . . quæ extant. *Excudebat D. Maxwel, sumptibus Edoardi Brewster & Joannis Baker*, 1659. 8°. O, C; CH, IU, MB, MH, PL, Y.

1606   ——[Anr. ed.] *Cantabrigiæ, ex officina Joann. Hayes*, 1672. 8°. L, CS, CT, LNC, NPL; CLC, CU, MH, RBU, TU.

1607   **Hesketh, Henry.** The case of eating and drinking. *For Walter Kettelby*, 1689. 8°. T.C.II 243. CT, P; NU, WF, Y, MOORE, ZAS.

1608   [–] The charge of scandal. *For Fincham Gardiner*, 1683. 4°. L, O, C, E, GU, DT; CH, IU, MH, NU, WF, Y.

1609   —The dangerous and almost desperate state. *By Tho. James for Will. Leach*, 1679. 4°.* L, C; NU.

1610   —An exhortation to frequent receiving the Holy Sacrament. *For W. Kettilby*, 1684. 8°. T.C.II 58. L; CLC, WF, Y.

1611   —Great mens advantages. *By J. L. for Walter Kettleby*, 1699. 4°.* L, LLP, CT, BAMB, EC; CH, MH, NU, WF, Y.

1612   —The importance of religion. *By H. Hills jun. for Henry Bonwicke*, 1683. 4°.* T.C.II 26. L, O, C, LCL, BLH; CH, CLC, NU, WF, Y, AVP.

1613   —Piety the best rule. *For Walter Kettilby*, 1680. 8°. T.C.I 414. L, O, LLP, OM, CT, DU; CH, CLC, MIU, NU, WF.

1614   —A private peace-offering. *By H. Hills, for Henry Bonwick*, 1684. 4°.* T.C.II 40. L, O, CT, LIU; CH, CSS, IU, NU, WF.

1615   —A sermon preached . . . January 30th 1677/8. *For Will Leach*, 1678. 4°. T.C.I 308. O, C, EC, DT; CH, CLC, NU, WF, Y.

1616   —A sermon preached . . . second of September, 1679. *By A. Godbid, and J. Playford, for Will Leach*, 1679, 4°.* T.C.I 368. L, LG, OC, OU, WCA; CH, CLC, NU, Y.

1617   —A sermon preached . . . September the 2d. 1682. *For Robert Sollers*, 1682. 4°.* T.C.I 503. L, O, C, LL, NE; CH, CLC, NU, WF, Y.

1618   —A sermon preach'd . . . July the 27th 1684. *For Henry Bonwicke*, 1684. 4°.* T.C.II 94. L, O, C, LLP, LSD; CH, CLC, MIU, NU, WF.

1619   —A sermon, preached . . . September the 9th. *By T. M. and J. A. for Henry Bonwicke*, 1684. 4°.* T.C.II 40. L, O, C, BSM, WCA; CH, IU, MIU, NU, WF, Y.

1620   —A sermon preached . . . 26th day of July, 1685. *For Jo. Hindmarsh*, 1685. 4°.* L, O, C, OCC, LSD; CH, CLC, MM, NU, WF, Y.

1621   —A sermon preach'd . . . March 30. 1699. *For Walter Kettilby*, 1699. 4°.* T.C.III 135. L, LLP, BAMB, EC, SHR; NU, WF.

1622   **Heskins, Samuel.** Soul mercies precious. *By J. M. for H. Cripps, and L. Loyd* [*sic*], 1654. 8°. LT.

1622A   **Heskith, Thomas.** The excellency and advantages of religion. *For T. Speed*, 1700. 4°. T.C.III 227. L.

1623   —A sermon preach'd . . . May the 29th and May the 31st, 1699. *For Richard Wilkin*, 1700. 4°.* L; CH, WF, Y.

Heslewood, John. *See* Haslewood, John.

1624   [**Hess, Joannes Armondus de.**] A letter from a Jesuite; or, the mysterie of equivocation. *For W. W.*, 1679. 4°.* L, C, LSD; CH, CLC, MH, MIU, NC, WF, Y.

1624A   [–] —[Anr. ed.] [*Dublin*], reprinted, 1679. 4°.* L, C, CD, DT; NGT.

1625   Entry cancelled.

Hesteau, Clovis. True salt and secret. 1657. *See* Nuisement, Clovis Hesteau, *Sieur de. Sal, lumen & spiritus.*

Hetherington, John. *See* Etherington, John.

1626   [**Hetherington, William.**] The Irish-evidence convicted. *For William Inghal the elder*, 1682. fol.* L, O, DU, LLU, EN, DT; CH, CN, MH, TU, WF, Y.

1627   **Hetley, Sir Thomas.** Reports and cases. *By F. L. for Matthew Walbancke, and Thomas Firby*, 1657. fol. L, O, C, LL, MC, DT; CH, CN, KT, MHL, NCL, WF, YL, AVP.

1627A   **Heusde, Sarah Cornelius de.** Loving reader . . . secret arts for to cure . . . dangerous accidents. [*London*, 1670?] brs. L.

Hew. *See* Hue.

1628   [**Hewat, John.**] A declaration from the Isle of Wyght. *By R. I.*, 1648. 4°.* LT, O, OC, DT; CH, WF.

1629   [–] —[Anr. ed.] *For R. W.*, 1648. 4°.* LT, AN, DT; Y.

1629A   **Hewer.** Mr. Hewer's reply to the petition of the Tanger-inhabitants. [n.p., 1695.] fol. NC.

1630   **Hewerdine, Thomas.** Some plain letters in the defence of infant baptism. *For R. Wilkin*, 1699. 8°. T.C.III 151. L, O, LCL, CS, DT; CH, NHC, NU.

Hewes, Lewis. *See* Hughes, Lewis.

1630A   **Hewetson, Edward.** Advertisement. You may have good drugget. [*London*, 1700?] brs. L.

1630B   [**Hewetson, Michael.**] Ireland's tears. A pindarique poem. *By Nath. Thompson*, 1685. fol.* MH.

1631   **Hewitt, John.** Certain considerations against the vanities. *By Edward Crowch*, 1658. brs. L, LG; MH.

1632   ——[Anr. ed.] *Printed*, 1658. brs. L.

1633   —Dr. Hewit's letter to Dr. Wilde on Monday, June 7. 1658. [*London*, 1658.] brs. LT, O, LL, LS, CS; CLC, MH, MM.

1634   —Nine select sermons. *For Henry Eversden, and Tho. Rooks*, 1658. 8°. LT, O, DU, P, RPL, YM; CLC.

1634A   ——[Anr. ed.] —, [1658]. 8°. WF, ASU.

1635   ——[Anr. ed.] [*London*], *for John Williams*, 1659. 8°. Y.

1636   —Prayers of intercession. *Printed*, 1659. Sixes. L, O, OC, OCC, CS, LNC; CH, INU, IU, NC, TSM, WF.

1637   —Repentance and conversion. *By J. C. to be sold by Samuel Speed*, 1658. 8°. LT, O, C, YM; CLC, LC, NGT, NU.

1637A   ——Second edition. *For Sam. Speed, to be sold by William Thorpe*, 1658. 8°. Y.

1638   —The speech and deportment of. *Printed at London*, 1658. 4°.* O; MM.

1639   —The true and exact speech and prayer of. colop: *Printed,* 1658. cap., 4°.* LT, O, CJ, EN; CH, CN, IU, MH, MM, NU, Y.

1639A   ——[Anr. ed.] [*London,* 1658?] cap., 4°.* LT, O, OC, CJ, BC, DT; CH, CLC, MH, MM, TU, WF.

1640   **Hewitt, Mary.** To the . . . Parliament the . . . petition of. [*London,* 1660.] brs. L; MH.

        Hewitt, Thomas. Annus ab incarnatione. 1654. *See* Almanacs.

1641   Entry cancelled.

        H[ewlett], J. *See* Hewlett, John.

1642   **Hewlett, James.** A true copie of a speech spoken to . . . Charles II. *By James Flesher,* 1661. 4°.* LG.

1643   ——[Anr. ed.] —, 1668. 4°. L, LP; MM.

1643A   **H[ewlett], J[ohn].** The description and use of a quadrant. 1665. 8°. O.

1643B   [–] ——[Anr. ed.] *For the author,* 1672. 8°. L; MH.

1644   Entry cancelled.

        Hewson, John. Colonel Huson's . . . confession. [1659.] *See* title.

1645   —A letter from . . . 14 of March, 1650. *By John Field,* 1651. 4°.* LT, MR, EN, DN.

1646   [**Hewson, M.**] A letter out of Ireland, from an eminent divine. colop: *For Randal Taylor,* 1689. brs. C, DU; CH, MH.

1647   Hewson reduc'd. *For Austine Rice,* 1661. 4°.* O.

        Hexapla Jacobaea. A specimen. Dublin, 1686. *See* Wetenhall, Edward. *bp.*

1648   **Hexham, Henry.** A copious English and Netherduytch dictionarie. *Tot Rotterdam, gedruckt by Aernout Leers,* 1647. 4°. L, O, CT, LNC, MAU; BN, IU, MH.

1649   ——[Anr. ed.] —, 1648. 4°. L, O, C, E, EN; IU, MH, NC, TU, Y.

1649A   ——[Anr. ed.] *Tot Rotterdam: gedruckt by A. Leers,* [1658]. 4°. NN.

1650   ——[Anr. ed., "Englisg."] *Tot Rotterdam, gedruckt by Arnout Leers,* 1660. 4°. L, O, CM, LLU, BQ; CH, MB, NC, PL, WF, Y.

1651   ——[Anr. ed.] *Rotterdam, by the widdow of Arnold Leers,* 1675. 4°. L, CT, DU, EN, GU; BBE, CLC, CN, LC, NC.

1652   —The first part of the principles of the art military. Second edition. *Printed at Delf in Holeand,* 1642. fol. L, O, OC, DCH; MBA, MIU, MU, WF.

1653   —Het groot vvoorden boeck: . . . a large Netherdutch and English dictionarie. *Tot Rotterdam, gedruckt by Arnvt Leers,* 1648. 4°. L, O; CN, IU, MH, NC, TU, ALBERTA.

1653A   ——[Anr. ed.] —, 1658. 4°. CH, CLC, IU, MH, MHS, NN, WF.

1653B   ——[Anr. ed.] —, 1672. 4°. PL.

1653C   ——[Anr. ed.] —, 1678. 4°. LLL; CU, NN.

1654   —The second part of the principles. Second edition. *Printed at Delf in Holeland, by Antony of Heusden,* 1642. fol. L, O, DCH; CN, IU, MBA, MU, WF, Y.

1655   —The third part of the principles. Second edition. *Rotterdam, by James Moxon,* 1643. fol. L, DCH; CN, IU, MU, WF.

1656   —The three parts of the principles of the art military. *For Humphrey Mosley,* 1641. fol. CH, CSS.

1656A   [–] A trve and briefe relation of the bloody battel of Nievport. [*Delft,* 1641.] cap., fol.* MH.

1657   [–] A true and historicall relation of the bloody battell of Nieuport. *Printed in Delff,* 1641. fol.* L, DCH, DT.

1658   **Hext[er], Franc[is].** An elegy. Sacred to the memory of the high-born Prince Henry. *By T. M., and sold by Randal Taylor,* 1690. fol.* MH, Y.

1658A   Hey for Horn Fair. *For F. Coles, T. Vere, and J. Wright,* 1674. 8°. CM; CH.

1658B   Hey for our town. But a fig for Zommerset-shire. [*London*], *for R. Burton,* [1650?]. brs. O.

1659   (Hey hoe, for a husband.) [*London*], *printed,* 1647. 4°.* LT, RU; Y, ZWT.

1660   Hey ho hunt about. [*London*], *for F. Coles, T. Vere, and J. Wright,* [1663–74]. brs. L, O, HH; MH, Y.

1661–2 Entry cancelled.

        Heyden, Hermann van der. *See* Van der Heyden, Hermann.

1663   **Heyden, Sir Christopher.** An astrological discourse. *By J: Macock for Nathaniel Brooks,* 1650. 8°. LT, O, C, LN; CLC, LC.

1663A   ——[Anr. ed.] *By Iohn Macock, for Nathaniel Brooks,* 1650. 8°. L, O, CT, P; CN, CSS, MH, WF, Y.

1664   [**Heydon, John.**] Advice to a daughter. *By J. Moxon for Francis Cossinet,* 1658. 12°. L, C, DC; CH, OCI.

1665   [–] —Second edition. *By T. J. for F. Cossinet,* 1659. 8°. LT; OCI, WCL.

1666   —The English physitians guide. *By T. M. for Samuel Ferris,* 1662. 8°. LWL, E, GU; CH, CPB, CSS, WF, WU.

1667   —Eugenius Theodidactus, the prophetical trumpeter. *By T. Lock for the author, to be sold by Edward Blackmore,* 1655. 8°. LT, LG, GU; CH.

1667A   [–] Hampaaneah hammegulleh: or, the Rosiecrucian crown. *For the author,* 1664. 8°. EN; CRN, MH, WF.

1668   —The harmony of the world. *For H. Brome,* 1662. 8°. L, O, LWL, E; CLC, NP, HC.

1669   —Elhavarevna or, the English physitians tvtor. *For William Gilbertson,* 1665,4. 8°. L, LWL, GU; GH, MH, PL, Y.

1670   —The holy guide. *By T. M. for the author, to be sold by Thomas Whittlesey,* 1662. 8°. L, EN; IU, LC, HC.

1671   —The idea of the law. *For the author,* 1660. 8°. LT, O, SP; CN, LC, NCL, OHU, PU, WF.

1672   —[Hebrew] A new method of Rosie Crucian physick. *For Thomas Lock,* 1658. 4°. LT, O, LCP, LN; CLC, NAM, WU.

1672A   Entry cancelled.

        —Ψονθονφανχια: being. 1664. *See* —Elhavarevna.

1673   —Ψονθονφανχια: or, a quintuple Rosie-crucian scourge. *Printed,* 1665. 4°.* L.

1674   —The Rosie Crucian infallible axiomata. *Printed,* 1660. 8°. L, O, OC, GU.

1675   Entry cancelled.

        —Some gospel truths. 1647. *See* Heydon, John, *minister.*

1676 —Theomagia, or the temple of wisdom. *By T. M. for Henry Brome, and for Tho. Rooks*, 1664–3. 3 pt. 8°. L, O, LWL, E, GU; CLC, MH, WF, Y.

1677 —The wise-mans crown. *For the author; and are to be sold by Samuel Speed*, 1664. 8°. L, O, CT, EN; CH, CPB, MH, MIU, WF, WU.

1678 **Heydon, John, *minister*.** The discovery of the wonderfull preservation of . . . Fairfax. *By M. Simmons*, 1647. 8°.* L; CH, NU, MIU, WF.

1679 —Mans badnes & God's goodnes. *By M. Symmons*, 1647. 8°. L, C.

1679A —Some gospel truths catechistically laid down, . . . vindicated. Third edition. *By Robert Ibbetson*, 1647. 8°. LW; NU.

1680 **Heylyn, Peter.** [Works.] Κειμηλια 'εκκλησιαστικα. *By M. Clark, for Charles Harper*, 1681. fol. T.C.I 454. L, O, C, EN, DT; BN, CH, CN, LC, MH, WF, Y, AVP.

1681 —Ærivs redivivvs: or, the history. *Oxford: for Jo. Crosley, and are to be sold in London by Tho. Basset, and Chr. Wilkinson*, 1670. fol. T.C.I 20; MADAN 2855. L, O, C, EN, BQ; BN, CH, CN, MH, NU, WF, Y.

1681A ——[Anr. ed.] *Oxford, for John Crosley, and are to be sold in London by Thomas Basset*, 1670. fol. L, OH, CK, BAMB, DU; CLC, IU, MH, PBL, WF, Y.

1682 ——Second edition. *By Robert Battersby for Christopher Wilkinson, and Thomas Archer, and John Crosley in Oxford*, 1672. fol. T.C.I 106. L, O, C, ENC, DT; BN, CLC, CU, MH, WF, Y, AVP.

1683 Entry cancelled.
[–] Affairs of church and state. 1661. *See* —Ecclesia restavrata.
[–] Aulicus coquinariæ: or. 1650. *See* Sanderson, *Sir William*.

1684 Entry cancelled.
[–] Bibliotheca regia, or, the royal library. 1659. *See* Charles I.

1685 [–] A briefe relation of the death and svfferings of . . . L. Archbishop of Canterbvry. *Oxford, printed*, 1644[5]. 4°.* MADAN 1722–3. LT, O, CT, EN, DT; CH, CU, MH, TU, WF, Y. (var.)

1686 [–] A briefe relation of the remarkeable occurrences in the northerne parts. [*Oxford*], *by H. Hall*, 1642[3]. 4°.* MADAN 1265. L, O, MR; CN, WF, Y.

1687 —Certamen epistolare, or. *By J. M. for H. Twyford, T. Dring, and J. Place*, 1659. 8°. LT, O, C, EN, DT; CH, CN, MH, NU, WF.

1688 Entry cancelled.
—Church of England justified. 1657. *See* —Ecclesia vindicata.

1689 —Cosmographie. *For Henry Seile*, 1652. fol. L, O, LCP, LMT, CM, DC, DT; CH, CN, LC, MH, NU, WF, Y.

1690 ——Second edition. —, 1657. fol. L, C, OH, DC, GU; CLC, CN, MH, NN, RPJ, WF, Y, AVP. (var. engr. t.p.)

1690A ——Third edition. *For Philipp Chetwind*, 1665. fol. L; PT.

1691 ——"Third" edition. *For Anne Seile*, 1666. fol. L, C, LI, LW, SP, E, EN; BN, CH, IU, LC, MH, RPJ, V, Y.

1691A ——[Anr. ed.] *For Philip Chetwind*, 1666. fol. DU, DL; MHS, Y, YBA.

1692 Entry cancelled. *See following entry.*

1692A ——[Anr. ed.] *For Anne Seile, and are to be sold by George Sawbridg, Thomas Williams, Henry Broom, Thomas Basset, and Richard Chiswell*, 1669. fol. T.C.I 22. L, O, C, AN, NPL; BBE, CDA, IU, PU, TO, TU, WF, Y. (var. engr. t.p.)

1693 ——[Anr. ed.] *For Philip Chetwind*, 1670. fol. L, OME, CCA, WCA; IU, LC, MWA, NN, NP, PL.

1694 ——[Anr. ed.] *For Anne Seile and Philip Chetwind*, 1674. fol. T.C.I 158. L, OC, CJ, AN, DT; CH, MH, MU, RPJ, TU, V.

1694A ——[Anr. ed.] *For Philip Chetwind and Anne Seile*, 1674. fol. CB, NCD, TU, V. (var. engr. t.p.)

1695 ——[Anr. ed.] *By A. C. for P. Chetwind, and A. Seile, to be sold by T. Basset, J. Wright, R. Chiswell, and T. Sawbridge*, 1677. fol. L, O, C, DC, CD; CH, CU, IU, LC, MH, NC, WF, Y.

1696 ——[Anr. ed.] *For P. C. T. Passenger, B. Tooke, T. Sawbridge*, 1682. fol. T.C.I 498. L, O, C, GC, DT; CH, CN, MBP, NR, Y.

1696A–1698A Entries cancelled. Continuous pagination.
——Fourth book. Part II. *See* —Cosmographie.

1699 —Cyprianus Anglicus: or, the history of . . . Laud. *For A. Seile*, 1668. fol. T.C.I 2. L, O, C, EN, DT; CH, CN, MH, WF, Y.

1700 ——[Anr. ed.] *By J. M. for A. Seile, to be sold by George Sawbridge, J. Martyn, T. Williams, J. Place, E. Brewster, J. Starkey, T. Basset, R. Horne, H. Brome, J. Wright, R. Chiswell, R. Boulter, B. Took*, 1671. fol. T.C.I 75. L, O, C, E, DT; BN, CH, LC, MH, MU, NU, WF, Y, AVP.

1701 —Ecclesia restavrata; or, the history. *For H. Twyford, T. Dring, J. Place, W. Palmer*, 1661. fol. L, O, C, BAMB, EN, GK; CH, IU, MH, NU, TO, WF, WG, AVP.

1702 ——Second edition. *For H. Twyford, J. Place, T. Basset, W. Palmer*, 1670. fol. T.C.I 28. L, O, C, DU, DT; CH, CLC, IU, MH, TO, WF.

1703 ——Third edition. *By R. B. for H. Twyford, J. Place, and T. Basset; to be sold by Thomas Randes*, 1674. fol. T.C.I 155. L, O, C, E, DT; BN, CLC, CN, NCU, NU, WF, Y.

1704 —Ecclesia vindicata. *By E. Cotes for Henry Seile*, 1657. 4°. LT, O, C, MC, DT; CH, NU, CN, MB, WF.

1705 No entry.

1706 [–] Examen historicum. *For Henry Seile and Richard Royston*, 1659. 8°. L, CT, AN, DU, EN; BN, CH, CN, LC, MU, WF, Y.

1707 ——[Anr. ed.] —, 1659. 8°. L, O, C, E, DT; MH, MIU, NU, PL, WF, Y.

1708 [–] Extraneus vapulans. *By J. G. for Richard Lowndes*, 1656. 12°. LT, O, C, DU, YM; BN, CH, CN, MH, WF, Y.

1709 [–] The first table, or, a catalogue of all the kings. *For T. Basset and C. Wilkinson*, 1674. 12°. O; WF.

1710 [–] France painted to the life. *For William Leake*, 1656. 8°. L, C, DCH, BQ, GK; CH, CN, MIU, WF, Y.

1711 [–] ——Second edition. —, 1657. 8°. L, O, LLU, SP; CH, CLC, LC, MIU, NCD, WF.

1712 —A full relation of two journeys. *By E. Cotes, for Henry Seile*, 1656. 4°. L, O, CT, EN, DT; CH, CN, IU, MH, WF, Y, AVP.

1713   [–] ʽΗρωολογια Anglorum. Or, an help to English history. *By T. and R. Cotes, for Henry Seile, 1641. 12°.* L, O, C, OC, DU, LLU; CH, IU, MBA, MH, WF, Y. (var.)

1714   ——[Anr. ed.] *By R. Cotes, for Abel Roper, 1642. 12°.* L, DC; CLC.

1715   [–] A help to English history. *For Abel Roper, 1652. 12°.* L, O, DU, WCA; BN, MH, PBL.

1716   ——[Anr. ed.] *For T. Basset, and Chr. Wilkinson, 1669. 12°.* T.C.I 24. NU.

1717   ——[Anr. ed.] —, *1670. 8°.* T.C.I 76. L, O, CS, E, DT; CLC, MIU, TU, WF.

1718   ——[Anr. ed.] *By E. Leach, for T. Basset, and Chr. Wilkinson, 1671. 12°.* L, O, C, BC, YM; BN, CH, CN, IU, MH, WF, Y.

1718A   ——[Anr. ed.] *For T. Basset and C. Wilkinson, 1674. 12°.* CK, BLH; CSU, IU, MBA.

1719   ——[Anr. ed.] *For Tho. Basset, and C. Wilkinson, 1675. 12°.* T.C.I 207. L, C, OC, DUS, EN; CH, IU, NP, TU, TSM, UCLA, AVP.

1720   ——[Anr. ed.] *For T. Basset, and C. Wilkinson, 1680. 12°.* L, O, C, NPL, DT; CH, IU, MBP, MU, V, WF.

1721   —Historia quinqu-articularis: or, a declaration. *By E. C. for Thomas Johnson, 1660. 4°.* LT, O, CT, ENC, DT; BN, CH, IU, NU, WF, Y.

1722   [–] The historie of episcopacie. *For Abel Roper, 1642. 4°.* LT, O, C, LCL, E, CD; CN, MH, NU, WF, Y.

1723   [–] —The second part. *By Richard Hodgkinsonne, 1642. 4°.* LT, O, C, LCL, E, CD; CLC, CN, MH, NU, WF, Y.
    —History of episcopacy. 1657. *See* —Ecclesia vindicata.

1724   [–] A letter from an officer in His Majesties army. [*Oxford, by L. Lichfield*], *printed, 1643. 4°.** MADAN 1350. LT, O, C, LNC, DT; CLC, CN, MH, NC, Y.

1724A   [–] —[Anr. ed.] [*London*], *imprinted, 1643. 4°.** CH, CLC, MH, WF.

1725   [–] A letter to a gentleman of Leicester-shire, shewing. [*Oxford, by H. Hall*], *printed in the yeare, 1643. 4°.* MADAN 1348. LT, O, C, EN, DT; CH, CN, MH, MIU, WF, Y.

1725A   [–] —[Anr. ed.] [*London*], *printed in the yeere, 1643. 4°.** MADAN 1348n. O, MR; CLC, MH.

1726   [–] Lord have mercie upon us. [*Oxford, by H. Hall*], *printed, 1643. 4°.* MADAN 1486. LT, O, C, DC, DT; CH, CN, MH, NU, WF, Y.

1727   [–] Observations on the historie of the reign of King Charles. *For John Clarke, 1656. 8°.* L, O, C, LNC, EN; BN, CH, CN, LC, MH, WF, Y.

1728   Entry cancelled.
    —On the Apostles' creed. 1673. *See* —Theologia vetervm.

1729   —The parable of the tares. *By J. G. for Humphrey Moseley, 1659. 4°.* LT, O, C, E, DT; CH, NU, TSM, WF, Y.

1729A   ——[Anr. ed.] *By J. G. for Richard Marriott, 1659. 4°.* C, EN.

1730   [–] Parliaments power, in lawes for religion. *Oxford, by Henry Hall, 1645. 4°.** MADAN 1806. LT, O, CT, E, DT; CH, CN, MHL, NU, WF, Y.
    [–] Προσσω. [n.p.], 1647. *See* Hardres, Peter.

1731   [–] The rebells catechisme. [*Oxford, by L. Lichfield*], *printed, 1643. 4°.** MADAN 1543. LT, O, CT, AN, EN; CH, CU, LC, MH, NU, TU, WF, Y. (var.)

1731A   [–] —[Anr. ed.] [*London*], *printed 1643. 4°.** L, O, C, EC, LSD, DT; CLC, MH, MIU, TO, WF.

1731B   [–] —[Anr. ed.] [*York*], *printed, 1644. 4°.** LLL, YM; MH.

1732   —Respondet Petrvs: or, the answer of. *For R. Royston, and R. Marriot, 1658. 4°.* LT, O, C, DU, EN; CH, CN, NU, WF, Y.
    [–] Review of the Certamen. 1659. *See* Hickman, Henry.

1733   [–] A second, but more perfect relation of the great victory. [*Oxford*], *by H. Hall for W. Webb, 1642. 4°.** MADAN 1223. O, MR.

1734   —A sermon preached . . . May 29th. 1661. *By E. C. for A. Seile, 1661. 4°.** L, O, CK, SP, YM; CH, IU, NU, TU, WF, Y.

1735   [–] A short view of the life and reign of King Charles. *For Richard Royston, 1658. 12°.* L, O, C, A; CLC, CN, MB, MH, MIU.

1735A   [–] —[Anr. ed., "vievv."] —, *1658. 12°.* LIU, YM; CH, IU, MH, NCD, WF, Y.

1735B   [–] —[Anr. ed.] —, *1658. 8°.* L, O, CT, DU, YM, BQ; MH.

1736   [–] The stumbling-block of disobedience. *By E. Cotes for Henry Seile, 1658. 4°.* LT, O, C, DC, YM; BN, CH, IU, NU, TO, WF, Y.

1737   —A survey of the estate of France. *By E. Cotes for Henry Seile, 1656. 4°.* L, O, LMT, LLU, YM; CH, CN, MIU, WF, Y.

1738   —Theologia veterum, or the summe. *By E. Cotes for Henry Seile, 1654. fol.* L, O, CS, P, EN; BN, CLC, IU, MBA, TU, WF.

1739   ——[Anr. ed.] *By S. Simmons, for A. S., to be sold by Henry Brome, and Benj. Tooke, and Tho. Sawbridge, 1673. fol.* T.C.I 155. L, C, OME, NPL, EN, DT; CH, IU, MH, NU, WF, Y.

1740   [–] Theeves, theeves: or, a relation. [*Oxford, by H. Hall*], *printed, 1643. 4°.** MADAN 1328. LT, O, LLP, DT; NU.

1741   —The vndeceiving of the people . . . tithes. *By M. F., for John Clark, 1648. 4°.** LT, O, C, SC, DT; CH, CU, MH, MU, WF.

1742   ——[Anr. ed.] *By J. G. for John Clark, 1651. 4°.** LT, O, C, LCL, SP; CH, CN, MH, NU, TU, WF, Y.

1743   ——[Anr. ed.] —, *1657. 4°.** LT, LLP, CJ, YM; CH, CN, IU, NGT, WF.

1743A   [–] A view of the proceedings of the western-counties. [*Oxford*], *printed [by L. Lichfield], 1642[3]. 4°.** MADAN 1277. L, O, OL; WF, Y.

1744   [–] The voyage of France. *For William Leake, 1673. 8°.* L, O, E, EN; CLC, CN, NCD, V.

1745   ——[Anr. ed.] *For William Leake and John Leake, 1679. 8°.* L, LW; CH, CLC, WF.

1746   Entry cancelled.
    —Way and manner. 1657. *See* —Ecclesia vindicata.

    Heyman, John. Almanack. [1660.] *See* Almanacs.

1746A   **Heynes, John.** A sermon preached . . . Lord Paget. *For Thomas Fox, 1669 [i.e. 1679]. 4°.* L, O, OC.

1747   **Heynes, Thomas.** The triumphs of royalty. *For W. Freeman, 1683. 4°.* L, LLU; CH, CLC, LC, NC, Y.

1748   **Heyrick, Richard.** Queen Esthers resolves. *By J. Macock, for Lvke Favvne,* 1646. 4°.* LT, O, C, SHR, DT; IU, MB, NU, WF, Y.

1749   ——[Anr. ed.] *For Lvke Favvne, to be sold by Thomas Smith in Manchester,* 1646. 4°.* OCC, MC, MR; CH, CLC, IU, NU.

1750   —Sermon preached . . . 23. of April 1661. *For Ralph Shelmerdine in Manchester,* 1661. 4°.* LT, LLP; IU, NU, Y.

1751   —Three sermons. *By T. B. for L. Fawne,* 1641. 8°. L, O, LW; IU, MH, NU, WF, Y.

1752   **Heyrick, Thomas.** The character of a rebel. *For Samuel Heyricke,* 1685. 4°.* L, O, C, LSD, WCA; IU.

1753   —Miscellany poems. *Cambridge, by John Hayes, for the author, and are to be sold by Francis Hicks and Thomas Basset and Samuel Heyrick in London,* 1691. 4°. T.C.II 336. L, O, C, LVD, EN; CH, CN, LC, NC, TU, WF, Y.

1754   [–] The new Atlantis. A poem. *[London], for the author,* 1687. 4°. L, O, C, LIU, LSD; CH, CN, NP, TU, WF, Y.

1755   —A sermon preached . . . 17th day of February, 1684/5. *for Samuel Heyrick,* 1685. 4°.* O, LSD, WCA; CH, MH, TU.

1756   —A true character of Popery and Jesuitism. *[London], for the author,* 1690. T.C.II 340. L; WF, Y.

1756A   **Heywood, John.** A friendly perswasion and Christian exhortation. 1684. brs. LF; PH.

1757   **Heywood, Nathaniel.** Christ displayed. *For Tho. Parkhurst,* 1679. 12°. T.C.I 415. L, LCL, LW; NU, Y.

1758   **H[eywood], O[liver].** Advice to an only child. *For Tho. Parkhurst,* 1693. 8°. T.C.II 464. L, O; WF.

1759   [–] —[Anr. ed.] —, 1700. 12°. L.

1760   [–] Baptismal bonds renewed. *For Tho. Parkhurst,* 1687. 8°. T.C.II 205. L, O, LCL, LW, ORP, LSD, YM; MH, NHC, NU, RBU, TO, WF, Y.

1761   —The best entail. *For Tho. Parkhurst,* 1693. 8°. L, LCL, LW, EN; IU, RBU.

1762   —Closet-prayer, a Christian duty. *For Tho. Parkhurst,* 1671. 8°. L, O, LCL, LW, YM; CH, IU, NU, WF.

1762A   ——[Anr. ed.] *By A. M. for Tho. Parkhurst,* [1671?]. 12°. ORP; CLC.

1763   ——[Anr. ed.] *For Tho. Parkhurst,* 1687. 8°. T.C.II 235. L, LW, EN; MH.

1764   ——[Anr. ed.] —, 1700. 8°. NU, RBU, Y.

1765   [–] A family-altar erected to the honour of . . . God. *For T. Parkhurst,* 1693. 8°. T.C.II 520. L, O, C, LW, EN; FU, MH, NU, RBU, WF.

1766   —The general assembly. *For Tho. Parkhurst,* 1700. 8°. T.C.III 161. LW, BR.

1767   [–] Heart treasure. *By A. Ibbitson for Thomas Parkhurst,* 1667. 8°. L, O, LW, YM; CH, CLC, CU, IU, NU, RBU, WF.

1767A   —Heavenly converse. *For J. Back for Ephraim Johnston in Manchester,* 1697. 8°. T.C.III 36. MP, YM; MHS.

1768   [–] Israel's lamentation after the Lord. *For Tho. Parkhurst,* 1683. 8°. L, O, LCL, YM.

1769   —Job's appeal. *For B. Aylmer,* 1695. 4°.* L, LW.

1770   —Life in God's favour. *For Dorman Newman,* 1679. 8°. T.C.I 348. L, O, C, LCL, LW, MR; MH, NU, RBU.

1771   —Meetness for Heaven. *[London],* 1679. 12°. LCL.

1771A   [–] A narrative of the holy life, . . . of . . . Mr. John Angier. 1677. 8°. LCL.

1772   [–] —[Anr. ed.] *For Tho. Parkhurst,* 1683. 8°. L; CH, TU.

1773   [–] —[Anr. ed.] —, 1685. 8°. L, C, LCL, LW; IU.

1774   —A new creature. Discourses. *For Tho. Parkhurst,* 1695. 8°. LW, YM; RBU.

1775   —The sure mercies. 1670. 8°. LCL.

1775A   ——[Anr. ed.] 1671. 8°. YM.

1776   ——[Anr. ed.] *By R. W. for Tho. Parkhurst,* 1672. 8°. T.C.I 101. L, O, LCL, LW, LSD, P; CLC, MH, NU, RBU, WF, Y.

1777   **Heywood, Thomas.** The actors vindication. *By G. E. for W. C.,* [1658]. 4°. LT, O, CT, DC, LIU, P; CH, CLC, TU, WF, Y.

1777A   [–] A chronographicall history. *By J. Okes,* 1641. 4°. IU.

1778   Entry cancelled.

      —Common-wealths great ship. 1653. *See title.*

1779   —Englands Elisabeth. *Cambridge: by Roger Daniel: to be sold by J. Sweeting,* 1641. 12°. O, C; CPB, NP, WF.

1780   [–] The famous and remarkable history of Sir Richard Whittington. *By W. Wilson, and are to be sold by Francis Coles,* 1656. 8°. L.

1780A   [–] —[Anr. ed.] *By C. Brown, and T. Norris, for E. Tracy,* [167–?]. 4°. CH.

1781   [–] —[Anr. ed.] *By A. P. and T. H. for T. Vere and J. Wright,* 1678. 4°. L, CS.

1782   [–] —[Anr. ed.] *For W. Thackeray and T. Passinger,* [1686–88]. 4°. O, CM; CH.

1783   —Fortune by land and sea. A tragi-comedy. *For John Sweeting, and Robert Pollard,* 1655. 4°. L, O, LVD, OW, EN; CH, CN, LC, MH, WF, Y.

1784   [–] The generall history of women. *By W. H. for W. H.* 1657. 8°. L, O, C, BC; CH, CN, LC, MH, WF, Y.

1785   [–] Hogs caracter of a projector. *For G. Tomlinson, July* 15, 1642. 4°.* LT; Y.

1785A   [–] —[Anr. ed.] *Printed,* 1642. 4°.* OC; CH, NU.

1786   [–] The life of Merlin. *By J. Okes, to be sold by Jasper Emery,* 1641. 4°. L, O, C, LVD, EN; CH, CN, LC, MH, TU, WCL, WF, Y.

1786A   —Loves mistress. *By John Raworth for John Crouch,* 1640 [i.e., 1662]. 4°. L, O, EC; CH, IU, MH, PU, WF, Y.

1787   [–] Machiavel. As he lately appeared. *By J. O. for Francis Constable,* 1641. 4°.* L, O, C, MR; CH, MH, MIU, WF.

1788   [–] Machiavels ghost. *By J. O. for Francis Constable,* 1641. 4°. O; CH.

1789   [–] Merlins prophesies. *For I. E., and are to be sold by Thomas Pierrepoint,* 1651. 4°. L, C, LLL; CLC, IU, MH, TO, WF, Y.

1790   [–] A preparative to studie or the vertue of sack. *Printed,* 1641. 4°.* LT, LVD, CT; CH, CN, RHT, TU, WCL, WF.

1791   —Reader, here you'l plainly see, iudgement perverted by these three. *[London], printed,* 1641. 4°.* L, O, LVD, LVF; CH, MM, NCD, WCL.

      Hezekiah's return. 1668. *See Littleton, Adam.*

1792   **Hibbert, Henry.** Regina diervm: or, the joyful day. *By Edw. Mottershed,* 1661. 4°.* L, O, C, SP, CD; NU, WF.

1793   —Syntagma theologicvm: or, a treatise. *By E. M. for John Clark,* 1662. fol. L, O, DC, RPL, YM, CD; MH, NU.

1794   —Waters of Marah. *By W. Hunt, to be sold by Francis Coles, and by John Awdley at Hull*, 1654. 8°. L, O.

1795   **Hibner, Israel.** Mysterium sigillorum, herbarum & lapidum. Containing. *By W. Downing, and are to be sold by S. Smith, A. Roper, and P. Buck; W. Battersby; S. Herrick; W. Foltham*, 1698. 8°. L, O, LWL, OR; CH, CLC, MH, WCL.

       Hic, & ubique. 1667. *See* H., B.

1795A **H[ickeringill], E[dmund].** An apology for distressed innocence. *By J. Redmayne, to be sold by W. Granthan*, 1663. 12°. LSC.

1796   —The black Non-Conformist, discover'd. *By G. Larkin, and are to be sold by Richard Janeway*, 1682. fol. L, O, C, EN, DT; CH, CN, MH, TO, TU, WF, Y.

1797   — —Second edition. *By G. Larkin, and are to be sold by Richard Janeway*, 1682. fol. L, LCL, LG, DU, NE; CH, MIU, RPJ, Y, ASU.

1798   —The ceremony-monger. *Printed, and are to be sold by George Larkin*, 1689. 4°. L, O, C, LVF, DT; CH, CN, NU, TO, WF, Y. (var.)

1799   — —[Anr. ed.] *Edinburgh, reprinted*, 1689. 8°. ALDIS 2894. L, C, E, EN; MH.

1800   — —[Anr. ed.] *Reprinted*, 1693. 12°. ENC; CLC, TSM.

1800A — —[Anr. ed.] *For T. C.*, [1696]. CB, WU.

1801   — —[Anr. ed.] *Printed*, [1696?]. 4°. L, LIU, MR, EN, DT; INU, NU, WF.

1802   [–] The character of a sham-plotter. colop: *For Ab. Green*, 1681. brs. L, O, LG, LVF, LIU; CH, MH, WF, Y, ZWT.

1803   —Curse ye Meroz. *By J. R. for J. Williams*, 1680. 4°.* T.C.I 392. L, O, C, E, DT; CH, MH, MU, NU, WF, Y.

1804   —Fourth edition. —, 1680. 4°.* L, O, C, CT, BAMB; IU, NU, TU.

1805   No entry.

1806   [–] The fourth part of Naked truth. *For Richard Janeway*, 1682. fol.* L, LL, O, C, DU, EN; CH, CN, NU, TU, WF, Y.

1807   —The good old cause. *For John Dunton*, 1692. 4°.* T.C.II 390. L, C, LLP, WCA, CD; CH, NC, NU, PU, WF.

1807A [–] Gregory, Father-Greybeard. *By R. Hood, and sold by N. Brooke*, 1672. 8°. NP.

1808   [–] —[Anr. ed.] *By Robin Hood, and sold by Nath. Brooke*, 1673. 8°. T.C.I 142. L, O, C, LLU, YM; CH, CN, MH, TU, WF, Y.

1809   [–] The history of Whiggism. *For E. Smith*, 1682. fol. L, O, C, SP, EN; CH, CN, MH, MM, NU, Y, AVP.

1810   [–] —[Anr. ed.] [*London*], 1684. brs. O.

1811   —The horrid sin of man-catching. *For Francis Smith*, 1681. 4°. L, O, CS, AN, WCA, E; CH, IU, MH, NC, WF, Y.

1812   — —Second edition. —, 1681. 4°.* L, O, CT, LSD, SP; CH, LC, MH, MIU, Y.

1813   — —Third edition. —, 1681. 4°.* CT, DU, WCA, BLH; CLC, NU, ASU.

1814   — —Fourth edition. —, 1682. fol.* L, LCL, LG; CN, LC, MH, NP, RBU, ZWT.

1815   Entry cancelled. Date: 19th century?

1816   [–] Jamaica viewed. *By J. R.*, 1661. 8°. LC, NN, NS, RPJ.

1817   [–] —Second edition. *For Iohn Williams*, 1661. 8°. LT, O, LW, CT, EN; CH, CN, LC, NN, RPJ, WF, Y.

1818   —The lay-clergy. *For John Dunton*, 1695. 4°.* L, O, C, LIU, WCA, EN; CH, NU, WF, Y.

1819   —The most humble confession. colop: *For Benj. Tooke*, 1684. brs. L, O, OC, CS, MC; CH, CN, MH, WF, Y.

1820   [–] The mushroom. *For Fra. Smith, jun.*, 1682. fol.* L, O, LVD, CT, LLU; CH, CN, MH, TU, WF, Y.

1821   [–] The naked truth. The second part. *For Francis Smith*, 1681. fol. L, O, C, BC, DT; CH, CN, LC, MH, TU, Y. (var.)

1822   [–] —Second edition. —, 1681. fol.* L, O, C, LMT, DU; CN, LC, TU, WCA, WF, Y.

1823   Entry cancelled.
       —News from Doctor's Commons. 1681. *See title.*
       [–] Plotters doom. 1680. *See* Palmer, Samuel.

1824   [–] Reflections on a late libel, intituled, Observations. *For John Williams*, 1680. 4°.* T.C.I 406. L, O, C, EN, DT; CH, IU, NU, PL, WF, Y.

1824A [–] —Second edition. —, 1680. 4°.* CS, CT; OSU, PU.

1825   [–] Scandalum magnatum: or the great trial. *For E. Smith*, 1682. fol. L, O, LG, OC, CS, LSD, DT; CH, CN, MH, TU, WF, Y.

1825A [–] —Second edition. —, 1682. fol. L, OC, DU; IU, MH, MIU, PU, WF, Y.

1825B — —Third edition. —, 1[682?]. fol. DT.

1825C [–] The second part of the History of whiggisme. colop: *For E. Smith*. 1682. cap., fol.* L, O, C, CT, SP; CH, KU, MH, WF, Y.

1826   [–] A sermon preach'd on the 30th of January. *Printed, and are sold by J. Nutt*, 1700. 4°.* L, O, C, SP; NN, NU, WF.

1827   —A speech without-doors. *By George Larkin*, 1689. 4°.* L, O, C, EN, DT; CH, IU, MH, NU, WF, Y.

1828   —The test or, tryal of the goodness & value. *By George Larkin, for the assigns of the author*, 1683. fol.* T.C.II 20. L, O, C, EN, CD; BN, CH, IU, NU, TU, WF, Y.

1829   — —Second edition. —, 1683. fol.* L, EN; CN, PU, TU, Y.

1830   [–] The third part of Naked truth. *For Richard Janeway*, 1681. fol.* L, O, OC, CT; CH, IU, MH, NU, WF, Y.

1830A [–] The Trimmer, his friendly debate. *For R. Hall*, 1683. fol.* T.C.II 20. L, O, MR, SP, EN; CH, CN, MIU, WF, Y.

1831   [–] A true table of all such fees. *For H. J., to be sold by R. Janeway*, 1681. brs. L, O; CN.

1831A —A vindication of the late sermon, on Curse ye Meroz. *By J. Redmayne*, 1680. cap., 4°.* O, LLL, CS, DC; CH, IU, WF.

1832   —A vindication of The naked truth. *For Richard Janeway*, 1681. fol.* T.C.I 441. L, O, CT, MR, EN; CH, CN, LC, MH, TU, WF, Y, AVP.

       Hickeringill, Phil, *pseud. See* Hickeringill, Edmund.

1833-5 Entries cancelled.

       [Hickes.] Jacobite principles vindicated. [n.p., 1693.] *See* Lawton, Charlwood.

       [–] Narration of a strange and sudden apparition. [n.p.], 1680/1. *See* Saunders, Jonathan.

1836   **Hickes, Edward.** The righteous judge. *For Benj. Tooke*, 1682. 4°.* T.C.I 492. L, C.

1837   **Hickes, Gaspar.** The advantage of afflictions. *By G. M. for Christopher Meredith*, 1645. 4°.* LT, O, C, BC, GU; CH, IU, NU, WF, Y.

1838 —The glory and beauty of Gods portion. *By G. M. for Christopher Meredith*, 1644. 4°.* LT, O, C, GU, DT; CH, IU, MH, NU, WF, Y.

1839 —The life and death of David. *By G. Miller for Christopher Meredith*, 1645. 4°.* LT, O, C, BR, EN; CH, IU, MBP, MH, NU, WF, Y.

1840 **[Hickes, George.]** An apologetical vindication of the Church of England. *For Walter Kettilby*, 1687. 4°. L, O, C, BSE, EN, DT; CLC, IU, MH, TU, WF, Y.

1841 [–] An apology for the new separation. *Printed*, 1691. 4°.* L, O, C, DU, EN; CH, CN, MM, PL, WF, Y.

1842 [–] The case of infant-baptism. *For Tho. Basset, Benj. Tooke, and F. Gardiner*, 1683. 4°. L, O, C, GU, DT; CH, IU, MH, NU, WF, Y, AVP.

1843 [–] —[Anr. ed.] 1684. 4°. LCL.

1844 [–] —[Anr. ed.] *By T. Hodgkin, for Tho. Basset; Benj. Tooke*, 1685. 4°. L, O, OC, LIU, YM; CH, CN, NU, TU, WF.

[–] Defense of the missionaries arts. 1689. *See* Wake, William, *abp.*

1845 —A discourse of the soveraign power. *For John Baker*, 1682. 4°.* T.C.II 2. L, O, C, MR, DT; CH, CN, NU, WF, Y.

1846 —A discourse to prove. *By W. Godbid, to be sold by Moses Pitt*, 1677. 4°.* T.C.I 272. L, O, C, LLP, YM; CN, MH, NU, TSM, WF, Y.

1847 — —Second edition. *For Walter Kettilby*, 1683. 4°.* T.C.II 9. L, O, C, BAMB, DT; CLC, IU, MH, NU, PL, Y, AVP.

1848–9 Entries cancelled.

[–] Doctrine of passive obedience. 1689. *See* Harrison, Thomas, *publisher.*

1850 [–] The harmony of divinity and law. *By R. E. and are to be sold by Randal Taylor*, 1684. 4°. T.C.II 82. L, O, C, BR, MR, P; CH, CN, MH, NU, WF, Y.

1851 —Institutiones grammaticæ. *Oxoniæ, e theatro Sheldoniano*, 1689. 4°. T.C.II 301. L, O, C, EN, DT; BN, CH, CN, LC, MH, TU, WF, Y. (var.)

1852 [–] Jovian. Or, an answer. *By Sam. Roycroft, for Walter Kettilby*, 1683. 8°. T.C.II 6. L, O, C, E, DT; CH, CN, LC, NU, TU, WF, Y.

1853 [–] —Second edition. *By Samuel Roycroft, for Walter Kettilby*, 1683. 8°. L, O, CT, NE, DT; MH, MIU, NIA, TU, WF.

1854 [–] The judgement of an anonymous writer. Second edition. *By T. B. for Robert Clavell, to be sold by Randolph Taylor*, 1684. 4°.* T.C.II 75. O, CS, P, EN, DT; CH, IU, MH, MIU, NN, SE.

1854A [–] A letter from a person of quality to an eminent dissenter. *By T. B. for Randolph Taylor*, 1685. 4°.* L, O, LSD; CH, NU.

1855 [–] A letter sent from beyond the seas. *[London]*, 1674. 8°.* L, O, C, BSM, DC; CLC, CN, MH, TU, WF, Y. (var.)

1856 [–] A letter to the author of a late paper, entituled, A vindication. *[London], printed* 1689. 4°.* L, O, C, LUG, DC, LSD, AU; CH, MM, NIC.

[–] Missionarie's arts. 1688. *See* Wake, William, *abp.*

1857 —The moral Shechinah. *By J. Wallis, for Walter Kettilby*, 1682. 4°.* T.C.I 504. L, O, C, RU, DT; CH, CLC, IU, MH, WF, Y.

1858 —Peculium Dei, a discourse. *For Walter Kettilby*, 1681. 4°.* T.C.I 439. L, O, C, E, DT; CH, CN, MH, NU, WF, Y.

1859 Entry cancelled.

[–] Plain defence. 1687. *See* Wake, William, *abp.*

1860 [–] Ravillac redivivus. *By Henry Hills*, 1678. 4°. L, O, C, MR, EN; CLC, CN, MH, TU, WF, Y.

1861 [–] —[Anr. ed.] *Reprinted at Dublin*, 1679. 4°. DIX 170. DT, BQ; MHL.

1862 [–] —Second edition. *For Walter Kettilby*, 1682. fol. T.C.I 488. L, O, CS, EN, DT; CH, IU, MIU, WF, Y.

1863 [–] Reflections upon a letter out of the country. *[London, 1689?] cap.*, 4°.* L, C, OC, MR; IU, MBA, MIU, MM.

1864 —A sermon preached . . . 30th. of January, 1681/2. *For Walter Kettilby*, 1682. 4°.* T.C.I 471. L, O, C, EN, DT; CH, CN, MH, NU, WF, Y.

1865 — —[Anr. ed.] —, 1683. 4°.* T.C.II 9. L, O, C, LSD, MR; CH, CLC, IU, MH, NU, WF.

1866 —A sermon preached . . . first of April, 1684. *For W. Kettilby, and R. Kettlewell*, 1684. 4°.* T.C.II 67. L, O, C, AN, DT; CH, CN, MH, NU, WF, Y.

1867 —A sermon preached . . . 29th of May, 1684. *By R. E. for Walter Kettilby, and John Jones in Worcester*, 1684. 4°.* T.C.II 95. L, O, C, BC, EC; CH, CN, MH, NU, WF, Y.

1868 [–] Some discourses upon Dr. Burnet and Dr. Tillotson. *Printed*, 1695. 4°. L, O, C, EN, DT; CH, IU, MH, NU, WF, Y.

1869 [–] Speculum Beatæ Virginis. A discourse. *Printed, and are to be sold by Randal Taylor*, 1686. 4°.* T.C.II 164. L, O, C, E, DT; CH, IU, MH, TU, WF, Y.

1870 [–] —Second edition. —, 1686. 4°.* L, O, C, EN, DT; CH, MIU, NU, WF, Y.

1871 —The spirit of enthusiasm exorcised. *For Walter Kettilby*, 1680. 4°. T.C.I 415. L, O, C, YM, BLH; CH, IU, MH, NU, TU, WF.

1872 — —Second edition. —, 1681. 4°. L, O, LL, LSD, DT; CLC, CN, MH, NU, WF, Y.

1873 — —Third edition. —, 1683. 4°. L, O, C, DU, LSD; CLC, IU, MH, NCU, WF, Y.

1874 [–] The spirit of Popery speaking out of the mouths of phanatical-Protestants. *By H. Hills, and are to be sold by Walter Kittleby [sic]*, 1680. fol. L, O, CT, EN, DT; CH, CN, LC, MH, NU, Y.

1875 —The true notion of persecution. *For Walter Kettilby*, 1681. 4°.* L, O, C, NE, YM; CH, IU, MH, NC, WF.

1876 — —[Anr. ed.] —, 1682. 4°.* T.C.I 458. L, LG, OC, CS, EN, BLH; CH, IU, NU, PU, Y.

1877 — —Second edition. —, 1682. 4°.* L, OB, DT.

1878 [–] A vindication of some among our selves against the false principles of Dr. Sherlock. *Printed*, 1692. 4°. L, O, LW, CT, MR, EN, DT; CH, IU, MH, NU, WF, Y.

1878A [–] Word to the wavering. *Printed*, 1689. 4°.* O, C, OC, CT, LLU, EN; CH, MIU, MM, TU, Y.

1879 **[Hickes, John.]** A discourse of the excellency of the heavenly substance. *Printed*, 1673. 8°. L, LCL, LW, BR; CDA, NU, AVP.

1880 —The last speech of. *[London, 1685.] cap.*, 4°.* L, BANGOR.

1881 [–] A true and faithful narrative of the unjust and illegal sufferings. *[London], printed*, 1671. 4°.* L, O, LCL, LW, OC, DU; CDA, CH, CN, PU, WF, Y.

Hickes, Thomas. *See also* Hicks, Thomas.

1882 **Hickes, Thomas.** A discourse of the souls. *By T. New-comb, to be sold by the author*, 1657. 4°.* LT; CLC, MH.

1883 —A letter or word of advice to the saints. *Printed*, 1653. 4°.* LT.

1884 [**Hickes, William.**] Coffee-house jests. *For Benj. Thrale*, 1677. 12°. T.C.I 292. L, CT.

1885 [–] —Fourth edition. *For Hen. Rhodes*, 1686. 12°. T.C.II 172. L.

1886 [–] —Fifth edition. —, 1688. 12°. T.C.II 235. L.

1887 [–] Grammatical drollery. *For Tho. Fox*, 1682. 8°. L, O; CH, CLC, MH, WCL.

1887A [–] London drollery. *By F. Eglesfield*, 1673. 8°. T.C.I 152. O, OW; CH, CLC.

1888 [–] Oxford drollery. *Oxford, for J. C. to be sold by Thomas Palmer, [London]*, 1671. 8°. T.C.I 66; MADAN 2872. L, O, OW.

1889 [–] —[Anr. ed.] —, 1674. 8°. L.

1890 [–] —[Anr. ed.] *Oxford, by B. G. to be sold by Dan. Major and Tho. Orrel*, 1679. 8°. T.C.I 330; MADAN 3202. L.

1891 —Oxford jests. *For Simon Miller*, 1671. 12°. MADAN 2815. T.C.I 83. CH.

1892 — —[Anr. ed.] —, 1684. 12°. L, O.

1893 Entry cancelled. Date: [1750–60.]
Hickledy-pickledy. [1680?] *See* P., T.

1894 **Hickman, Charles.** Fourteen sermons. *By James Orme, for William Haws*, 1700. 8°. T.C.III 182. L, O, C, LW, DT; CLC, CSB, NPT, WF, Y.

1895 —A sermon preach'd . . . June 27. 1680. *For Henry Brome*, 1680. 4°.* T.C.I 403. L, O, C, LIU, WCA; CH, CLC, IU, NU, WF, Y.

1896 —A sermon preached . . . January 25, 1680. *For Henry Brome*, 1681. 4°.* L, O, C, OC, OM, LSD; CH, NU, WF, Y.

1897 —A sermon preach'd . . . Nov. 21. 1686. *By M. Flesher, for Charles Brome*, 1687. 4°.* T.C.II 186. L, O, LG, OC, OM, LIU, WCA; NGT, NU, TSM, WF, Y.

1898 —A sermon preached . . . 19th of October, 1690. *For Walter Kettilby*, 1690. 4°.* T.C.II 330. L, O, C, OM, BAMB, DT; CH, MH, TSM, WF, Y.

1899 — —Second edition. —, 1690. 4°.* L, C, CT, EC, DT; MH, NC, NU, WF, MONASH.

1900 —A sermon preached . . . 26th of October, 1690. *For Walter Kettilby*, 1690. 4°.* T.C.II 330. L, O, C, EN, DT; CH, IU, MH, TU, WF, Y.

1901 —A sermon preached . . . Octob. 2. 1692. *For Walter Kettilby*, 1692. 4°.* T.C.II 421. L, O, C, EC, DT; CLC, IU, MH, TU, WF, Y. (var.)

1902 —A sermon preached . . . March 15. 1692/3. *For Walter Kettilby*, 1693. 4°.* T.C.II 448. L, O, C, LIU, DT; CLC, INU, NU, WF, Y.

1903 —A sermon preached . . . Nov. 22. 1695. *For Walther Kettelby*, 1696. 4°.* T.C.II 568. L, O, C, DC, DT; CH, IU, LC, MH, MIU, NU, WF, Y.

1904 [**Hickman, Henry.**] Apologia pro ministris. *Eleutheropoli*, 1664. 8°. L, O, OM, SP, BQ; CLC, IU, MB, NU, WF, Y.

1905 [–] —Second edition. *Eleutheropoli, anno æræ Bartholomææ*, 3. [i.e. 1665]. 8°. L, O, LCL, OCC, DU; CLC, IU, MH, NC.

1906 [–] The believer's duty towards the spirit. *For Sa. Gellibrand*, 1665. 8°. L, O, C, LCL; CLC, MH, NU, TO.

1907 — —[Anr. ed.] *For T. Parkhurst*, 1700. 8°. T.C.III 196. L, LCL, LW, GC; MH.

1908 [–] Bonasvs vapvlans. *Printed*, 1672. 12°. L, O, C, LCL, LW, P; MWA, NU, Y.

[–] Χειροθεσια. 1661. *See* Alleine, Richard.

1909 —Historia quinq-articularis exarticulata. *[London], printed*, 1673. 8°. T.C.I 135. L, O, C, DU, E; BN, CH, MH, NU, PL, WF.

1910 — —Second edition. *For Robert Boulter*, 1674. 8°. T.C.I 182. L, O, C, LCL, EN, DT; CH, MIU, NGT, TO.

1910A —Laudensium apostasia, or the Canterburian apostasie. 1654. 4°. P.

1911 —Laudensium apostasia: or a dialogue. *By D. Maxwell, for Sa. Gellibrand*, 1660. 4°. LT, O, C, YM, CD; BN, CLC, MH, MM, NU.

1911A —Πατρο-σχολαστικο-δικαιωσις, or a justification. *Oxford, by A. Lichfield for Joh. Adams and Edw. Forrest*, 1659. 8°. L, LW, OC, LSD, P; MB, TU.

1912 — —Second edition. *Oxford, by Hen. Hall for Joh. Adams and Edw. Forrest*, 1659. 8°. MADAN 2443. L, O, C, LCL, OCC, AN, DM; CH, MB, MH, TO, WF.

1913 [ ] Plvs vltra: or Englands reformation. *For the authors*, 1661. 4°. L, O, C, D, DT; CH, IU, MH, NU, WF, Y.

1914 —Ποθεν ζιζανια. Sive, concio. *Oxoniæ, excudebat A. Lichfield impensis E. Forrest*, 1659. 8°. MADAN 2444. L, O, LW, OC; CH, CLC, WF.

1915 [–] A review of the Certamen epistolare. *For Iohn Adams in Oxford*, 1659. 8°. MADAN 2445. LT, O, OC, OCC, CT, DU; MH, NU, WF, Y.

1916 [–] Speculum Sherlockianum, or. *For Thomas Parkhurst*, 1674. 8°. L, O, LCL, LW, CT; MWA, NCD, TO.

1917 Entry cancelled.
Hickman, William. Spirit of prophecie. 1679. *See* Hughes, William, *hospitaller*.

1917A **Hickock, Richard.** The saints justified. *For Thomas Simmons*, 1660. 4°.* LF; PH.

1918 [–] A testimony against the people, call'd Ranters. colop: *For Thomas Simmons*, 1659. cap., 4°.* O, LF, BBN; CH, MH, PH.

1918A **Hickocks, William.** Strength made perfect. *For Tho. Parkhurst*, 1674. 8°. T.C.I 162. WF.

1918B [**Hicks, Henry.**] A sermon preached at the funeral of . . . Camden. *Oxford, by Leonard Lichfield*, 1681. 4°.* IU, WF.

1919 **Hicks, Thomas.** A continuation of the Dialogue. *For Peter Parker*, 1673. 8°. T.C.I 134. L, C, LF, OH, DT; CH, CN, MH, PH, WF, Y.

1920 Entry cancelled.
[–] Counterfeit Christian. 1674. *See* Penn, William.

1921 [–] A dialogue between a Christian. *[London], Hen. Hills*, 1672. 8°. LF, LSC.

1922 [–] —Second edition. *For Henry Hills, to be sold by Peter Parker*, 1673. 8°. T.C.I 129. L, O, LF, DU, A; CH, CN, MH, NU, PH, WF, Y. (var.)

1923 —The Quaker condemned. *By R. W. for Peter Parker,* 1674. 8°. T.C.I 175. L, C, LF, CT, BBN; CH, CN, MH, PH, RPJ, WF, Y.

1924 [–] The Quakers appeal answer'd. *For Peter Parker,* 1674. 8°. L, O, LF, OC, A; CH, MH, PH, RPJ, TO, WF, Y.

1924A —A rebuke to Tho. Rudyard's folly and impertinencies. [*London,* 1674.] brs. MH.

1925 —Thou shalt fear God. *By R. L.,* 1660. 4°.* LT, EN; NU.

1926 —Three dialogues. *For P. Parker,* 1675. 8°. T.C.I 201. E, EN, GU; MH, PH.

1927 ——[Anr. ed.] *Printed, and are to be sold by Peter Parker,* 1679. 8°. L, LF; CH, PH, RPJ, WF.

1928 **Hicks, William.** Ἀποκάλυψις αποκαλυψεως, or, the Revelation revealed. *By J. Macock, for Daniel White,* 1659. fol. L; NU, TO.

1929 ——[Anr. ed.] *For William Miller,* 1661. fol. SP; NU.

1930 **Hickson, James.** A sermon preached July 26, 1682. *For Richard Lambert in York,* 1682. 4°.* T.C.I 502. MR, YM; IU, NU, WF, Y.

1931 No entry.
Hidden things brought to light. [n.p., 1678.] *See* Rich, Robert.

1931A **Hide, Edmund.** The naked mans peace. *Printed,* 1655. 4°.* NU.

1932 Hie to the fair. [*London,* 1700?] brs. L.
Hieragonisticon: or. 1672. *See* T., D.

1933 **Hierocles.** Ἱεροκλεους . . . Commentarivs in aurea. Pythagoreorum. *Ex officina Rogeri Danielis,* 1654. 2v. 8°. L, O, C, LCP, DU, DT; BN, CH, CU, IU, NP, PL.

1934 ——[Anr. ed.] *Excudebat Rogerus Daniel; et venalis prostat apud Joann. Williams,* 1654. 8°. L, O, C, EC, DT; CN, LC, MH, NCU, Y.

1935 ——[Anr. ed.] *By J. R. for J. Williams, and are to be sold by Henry Dickinson of Cambridge,* 1673. 8°. L, O, C, EN, DT; BN, CH, MH, MU, NU, WF, Y.

1935A ——[Anr. ed.] *Typis J. Redmayne,* 1673. 8°. OC, BAMB.

1935B ——[Anr. ed.] *By J. R. for J. Williams,* 1678. 8°. NC, PL.

1936 —Hierocles de providentia & fato. *Ex officina Rogeri Danielis, et venduntur apud Jo. Williams,* 1655. 8°. L, O, C, DU, DL, DT; CH, CU, IU, MH, NP, WF.

1937 ——[Anr. ed.] *By J. R. for J. Williams, and are to be sold by Henry Dickinson of Cambridge,* 1673. 8°. L, O, C, DUS, DT; CH, IU, MH, MU, NU, WF, Y.

1937A ——[Anr. ed.] *Typis J. Redmayne,* 1673. 8°. OC, BAMB, EN.

1938 —Hierocles upon the golden verses of Pythagoras. *By John Streater for Francis Eaglesfield,* 1657. 8°. LT, O, C, LLL, LW; CH, CN, MH, NC, TO, WF.

1939 ——[Anr. ed.] *By M. Flesher, for Thomas Fickus, in Oxford,* 1682. 8°. T.C.I 486. L, O, C, NOT, EN; CJC, CLC, CN, LC, MH, MU, Y.

1940–1 Entries cancelled.
Hierogliphick. [n.p.], 1688. *See* P., J. More lampoons.
Hierome, Stephen. *See* Jerome, Stephen.

1942 H[ieron], J[ohn]. The way to salvation. *For Nathaniel Ranew, and Jonathan Robinson,* 1668. 8°. L, LCL; MH, WF.

Hieron, Samuel. Careless resident. 1681. *See* —Protestant mirrour.

1942A —The doctrine of the beginning of Christ. *For H. Robinson,* 1658. 8°.* MH.

1943 [–] Fair-play on both sides. *For Richard Head,* 1666. 4°. L; CLC, NU.

1943A —A helpe unto devotion. Twenty-first edition. *For Humphrey Robinson,* 1650. 12°. O.

1943B —The protestant mirrour, . . . or, the careful resident. *For Tho. Cross,* 1681. O, HH; MH.
Ἱερον Σολομωντος. The temple. 1659. *See* Lee, Samuel.
Hierusalem; or the pilgrims. 1684. *See* Patrick, Simon, *bp.*

1944 [**Hierro, Augustin de.**] The process, and pleadings in the court of Spain upon the death of Anthonie Ascham. *By William Du-Gard,* 1651. 4°.* LT, BC, MR, YM; CH, MH, WF, Y.

Higden, Henry. Modern essay on . . . Juvenal. 1686. *See* Juvenal.

1945 —The wary widdow. *For Abell Roper; and Tho. Rainy, in Doncaster,* 1693. 4°. L, O, A; CH, CN, LC, MH, NC, TU, WF, ASU.

1946 **Higford, William.** The institution of a gentleman. *By A. W. for William Lee,* 1660. 8°. L, LG, M; PU, WF.

1947 —Institutions: or, advice. *By Tho. Warren, for Edmund Thorn of Oxford,* 1658. 8°. L, O; CH, CN, MH, OCI, Y.

1948 [**Higgenson, Thomas.**] Glory sometimes afar off. *For Giles Calvert,* 1653. 4°. LT, LF, LW, CT; MB, MH, PH, Y.

1949 —Some legible characters. *By G. D. for Tho. Brewster,* 1659. 4°.* LC, NU.

1950 —A testimony to the true Jesus. *For Thomas Brewster,* 1656. 4°. L, O, LF, CT, BC, MR; TO.

1950A **Higgins, Alexander.** To His Grace, His Majesties High Commissioner, . . . [A petition]. [*Edinburgh,* 1695.] brs. EN.

1951 **Higgins, John.** Christian counsel and advice. [*London*], *printed,* 1663. 4°.* L, C, LF, BBN; CH, IE, PH, PSC, WF, Y.

1952 —A Christian salutation. *For Robert Wilson,* 1663. 4°.* L, O, C, LF, BBN; CH, MH, PH, PSC, WF, Y.

1952A —From Newgate, a prisoner's just cause pleaded. *For Thomas Simmons,* 1661. 4°.* L, LF, MR; CH, IU, MH, PH, PL, RPJ.

1952B —Herein is declared the message of the Lord. [*London*], *printed,* 1658. 4°.* LF.

1952C —To all the inhabitants of the earth. *For Giles Calvert,* 1658. 4°.* L, LF; PH.

1952D ——[Anr. ed.] *Amsterdam,* 1666. 4°.* CSB.

1952E **Higgins, Tobias.** The deafe-man cured. *By T. B. for P. Stephens and C. Meredith,* 1641. 8°. O, LW.

1953 [**Higginson, Francis.**] A brief relation of the irreligion of the Northern Quakers. *By T. R. for H. R.,* 1653. 4°.* L, O, CT, BBN, DT; IU, LC, MB, NU, PL. (var.)

1954 [–] A brief reply to some part of a very scurrilous and lying pamphlet. *By T. R. for H. R.,* 1653. 4°. O, LF, CT; WF.

1955 **Higginson, John.** The cause of God. *Cambridg* [*Mass.*], *by Samuel Green,* 1663. 4°.* EVANS 80. CH, MH, MHS, MU, MWA, NC, RPJ.

1955A [–] A direction for a publick profession. [*Cambridge, Mass., by Samuel Green*, 1665.] cap., 16°.* EVANS 100. MH, MHS, MWA.

1956 —Our dying Saviour's legacy of peace. *Boston, by Samuel Green for John Usher*, 1686. 12°. EVANS 407. MH, MWA, RBU, WCL, Y.

1957 [**Higgons, Thomas.**] The history of Isuf Bassa. *For Robert Kettlewel*, 1684. 8°. T.C.II 84. L, O, DU; CH, CN, LC, MH, NP, WF, ASU.

1957A [–] Ode upon the death of Mr. Cowley. colop: *For H. Herringman*, 1667. cap., fol.* NE; WF, Y.

1958 —A panegyrick to the King. colop: *For Henry Herringman*, 1660. fol.* LT, O, C; CH, CLC, MH, TU, WF, Y.

1959 —The speech of Mr. Higgons in Parliament. *By Roger Norton*, 1661. 4°.* L; MH, TU, Y.

1959A **Higgs, Daniel.** The wonderfull and true relation of the bewitching a young girle. [*n.p.*], 1699. GU.

1960 A high and heavenly eccho. *For John Rothwell*, 1653. brs. LT, LS.

High and mightie commendation. 1642. *See* Randolph, Thomas.

High covrt of justice. [n.p.], 1651. *See* Walker, Clement.

1960aA The high court of justice at Westminster arraigned. *For F. Grove*, [1660]. brs. EUING 139. GU.

1960A The high-Dutch fortune-teller. *By and for W. Onley*, [1700?]. 4°.* L.

1961 The high Dutch Minerva a-la-mode. [*London, printed*, 1680.] sixes. T.C.I 419. L, O, CS; MIU.

1962 The high prized pin-box. [*London*], for J. Wright, J. Clarke, W. Thackery, and T. Passenger, [1681–4]. brs. L, O, CM, HH; MH.

1963 The high-way Hector. [*London*], for W. Gilbertson, [1647–60]. brs. L, HH; MH.

1964 A high way to peace. [*London*], printed, 1643. cap., 4°.* LT, LG, EN; MH, MIU, NU, WF.

High-way to riches. 1664. *See* D., T.

1965 **Higham, John.** Christ's-birth. *Printed* 1652. 4°.* L, C; CLC, WF.

1966 [–] A looking-glass for loyalty. *For Henry Brome*, 1675. 8°. T.C.I 196. L, O, OB, CT, RPL; CLC, IU, WF, Y.

1966A —Loyal sermons in disloyal times. *For Henry Brome*, 1676. 8°. DU.

1967 **Highmore, Nathaniel.** Nathanælis Highmori de hysterica. *Sumptibus Roberti Clavel*, 1670. 4°.* T.C.I 26. L, O, C, MR, GH; CH, CNM, NAM, PU.

1968 —Exercitationes duæ. *Oxon, excudebat A. Lichfield, impensis R. Davis*, 1660. 12°. MADAN 2499. LT, O, C, AU, DT; BN, LC, NAM, PL, TO.

1968A ——Second edition. —, 1660. 12°. OB.

1969 —The history of generation. *By R. N. for John Martin*, 1651. 8°. L, O, C, MAU, GH; BN, CLC, CNM, LC, MMO, NU, WF, JF.

1969A **Hignell, Jeremiah.** Loving and friendly advice and counsel. *Bristol, by Will. Bonny*, [1698]. fol.* LF.

1970 Entry cancelled.

Hilary, St. Saint Hillaries teares. 1642. *See* Taylor, John.

1971 **Hildebrand, Friedrich.** Antiquitates potissimum. Third edition. *Oxon., excudebat Hen: Hall impensis Ric. Davis*, 1673. 8°. T.C.I 157; MADAN 2976. O, CS, P, EN; CH, CLC, Y.

1972 ——"Third" edition. —, 1674. 8°. MADAN 3012. O, OC, DU, NPL; IU, WF, Y.

1973 —Dissertatio theologica. *Oxoniæ, excudebat H. Hall impensis authorem*, 1674. E.

1974 **H[ilder], T[homas].** Conjugall counsell. *For John Stafford*, 1653. 8°. L, OC; CH, CU, MH, PU, WF, Y.

1975 **Hildersam, Arthur.** The canticles. *By L. Milbourn, for Robert Clavel*, 1672. 8°. T.C.I 109. L, O, CS, P; CLC, IU, NU.

1976 —CVIII lectures. Third edition. *By Moses Bell, for Edward Brewster*, 1647. fol. L, C, AN, E, DT; CH, IU, MH, NU, Y.

1977 ——Fourth edition. *For Edward Brewster*, 1656. fol. O, C, LW; IU, NCD, NCU, RPJ, TSM, WF.

1978 —CLII lectures. *By J. Raworth, for Edward Brewster*, 1642. fol. L, O, C, E, DT; CLC, IU, MWA, NU, TSM, WF, Y, AVP.

1979 Entry cancelled. Ghost.

1980 [**Hildesley, Mark.**] Religio jurisprudentis. *For J. Harrison, and R. Taylor*, 1685. 12°. T.C.II 116. L, O, C, LL, GK; CH, MHL, MMO, OCI, WF, JF.

1981 [**Hildyard, Christopher.**] A list or catalogue of all the mayors . . . of Yorke. *York: by Stephen Bulkley*, 1664. 4°. L, YM; WF.

1981A **Hildyard, John.** Reverend brethren. [*London*, 1684.] brs. LG.

1982 —A sermon preached at the funeral of . . . Viscount Yarmouth. *By S. Roycroft, for George Rose in Norwich, and Robert Clavel, in London*, 1683. 4°.* T.C.II 42. L, O, C, CT, BLH; CH, ASU.

1982A ——[Anr. ed.] *For Robert Clavel*, 1683. 4°.* L, C, CS, BP, LSD, WCA; CH, IU, WF.

1983 **Hilgard, nun.** A strange prophecie against bishops. *For John Thomas*, 1641. 4°.* LT, O, LNC, EN; CH, CLC, CU, MH.

1984 [**Hill, A.**] A letter about raising the value of coin. *For Randal Taylor*, 1690. brs. L, LPR.

1984A [–] Sir, the pound weight of standard silver. *Randal Taylor*, 1690. brs. L.

[**Hill, Henry.**] Account of the growth of deism. 1696. *See* Stephens, William.

1985 Entry cancelled.

—Αστρολογια or starry lecture. 1684. *See* Almanacs.

1986 [–] A dialogue between Timotheus & Judas. *For S. Manship*, 1696. 4°. T.C.II 599. O, C, LCL, E; CLC, IU, MH.

1987 [**Hill, Hugh.**] The dying tears of a true lover forsaken. [*London*], for F. Coles, T. Vere, J. Wright, J. Clarke, W. Thackeray, and T. Passenger, [1678–80]. brs. L, CM, HH, GU; MH.

1988 **Hill, John, *astrologer*.** An allarm to Europe. *By H. Brugis for William Thackery*, [1680]. fol. *L, O, EN; CLC, MH, NAM, WF, Y.

1989 **H[ill], J[ohn], *gent*.** The exact dealer: being an useful companion. *For H. Rhodes*, 1688. 12°. T.C.II 219. L; CLC, MH, WF, Y.

1990 [–]—Second edition ["dealer refined"]. *By W. and J. Wilde, for H. Rhodes,* 1691. 8°. O; NC.

1991 [–]—Third edition. *For H. Rhodes,* 1695. 12°. L, C, LW.

1991A ——Fourth edition. —, 1698. 12°. L, LUG, CT, BC; CH, WF.

1991B —The young secretary's guide. *For H. Rodes,* 1687. 12°. T.C.II 201. L.

1991C ——Third edition. *For H. Rhodes,* 1689. 12°. T.C.II 294. CLC.

1992 ——Seventh edition. —, 1696. 12°. L; NC.

1993 ——Eighth edition. —, 1697. 12°. L; CH.

1993A ——Ninth edition. —, 1698. 12°. LIU; MH (impf.).

1994 ——Tenth edition. —, 1699. 12°. T.C.III 146. CN, NIC.

1995 **Hill, John, *of St. Mabyn.*** Ishbibenob defeated and David succoured. *For W. Crooke, and are to be sold by Benj. Smithurst, at Launceston,* 1694. 4°.* T.C.II 475. L, O, C, CT, DC, WCA; CH, WF.

1996 —The grand apostacy of the church of Rome. *For Samuel Heyrick,* 1680. 4°. L, O, C, CT; CH, MM, WF.

1997 **Hill, John, *of York.*** A penny post. *Printed,* 1659. 4°.* L; NN, Y.

1997A **Hill, Sir John, *Colonel.*** Unto the Right Honourable, the . . . Privy Council, the petition of. *[Edinburgh,* 1700?] fol.* EN.

1998 **[Hill, Joseph.]** I Dissertation concerning the antiquity of temples. *For Tho. Parkhurst,* 1696. 4°. L, LCL, LW, CM; IU, NU, WF.

1999 [–] II. Dissertation concerning the antiquity of churches. *For Tho. Parkhurst,* 1698. 4°. LW, CM; NU, WF.

2000 [–] The interest of these United Provinces. *Middelburg, by Thomas Berry,* 1673. 4°. L, O, C, EN, DT; HR, CH, CN, LC, MH, NU, WF, Y. (var.)

2001 —Justitia qua coram Deo. *[n.p.,* 1660.] brs. O.

2001A —Manual lexicon, Greek and Latin. 1663. MB.

2002 —The providence of God. *Rotterdam, by Reinier Leers,* 1685. 4°. L, O, LW, EN; CN, MH, NU, WF.

2003 **Hill, Joshua.** The examination of. *For Edward Husbands, and John Franke,* 1642. brs. LT.

2004 **Hill, Miles.** A true and impartiall account of the plunderings. *By E. G. for L. C.,* 1650. 4°.* LT, O, MR, EN; CLC, CSS, WF, Y.

2004A **Hill, Oliver.** An account of Oliver Hill's agency in Spain. *At Lisbone,* [1691]. 4°. L; WF.

2004B —Epistola ad Anglos. *For T. B.* 1689. 4°. O.

2005 [–] The fifth essay of D. M. *For E. Evetts,* 1700. 12°. L, CT, BAMB, GH; CJC, MMO, JF.

2005AA [–]—[Anr. ed.] *For the author; and are to be sold by Edw. Evetts,* 1700. 8°. L.

2005BA —Remarks of Oliver Hill, upon Mr. Keith's farewell. *[n.p.,* 1698?] 4°.* L (impf.).

2005A **Hill, Robert.** The path-way to pietie. Ninth edition. *By Richard Hodgkinsonne,* 1641. 12°. IU, MH, Y.

2005B **[Hill, Samuel.]** A breif [sic] enquiry into the grounds. *By M. B. for Richard Sare,* 1699. 8°.* T.C.III 136. OC, CM, EC, BP, DT; WF.

2006 [–] The Catholic balance: or a discourse. *For Robert Clavell,* 1687. 4°. L, O, C, E, DT; CH, MH, MU, TU, WF, Y.

2007 —De Presbyteratu dissertatio. *Typis S. Roycroft; impensis R. Clavell,* 1691. 8°. T.C.II 382. L, O, CT, BR, GU; BN, CH, CLC, NU, WF.

2008 —A debate on the justice and piety. *For John Everingham,* 1696. 8°. T.C.II 592. L, O, CM, BAMB, BR, EN; CH, MH, NU, WF, Y.

2009 [–] Municipium ecclesiasticum, or, the rights. *[London],* printed, 1697. 8°. T.C.III 52. L, O, CT, EN, DT; CLC, MIU, NU, PU.

2010 [–] The necessity of heresies asserted. *For Robert Clavel,* 1688. 4°.* L, O, LW, MC, DT; CH, IU, WF, Y.

2011 —The rites of the Christian church. *Sold by the booksellers of London and Westminster,* 1698. 8°. L, O, CT, BAMB, EC, LSD; PU.

2012 [–] Solomon and Abiathar: or the case. *For Ric. Chiswell,* 1692. 4°.* T.C.II 423. L, O, C, EN, DT; CH, MBA, NU, PL, WF, Y.

2013 —A vindication of the primitive fathers. *[London], for J. Whitlock,* 1695. 8°. O, LCL, CE, DU, EN; CH, CLC, NU, WF, Y.

2013A **[Hill, Thomas.]** The doleful dance. *[London], for F. Coles, J. VVright, T. Vere, and VV. Gilbertson,* [1655–8]. brs. O.

2013B [–]—[Anr. ed.] *[London], for F. Coles, T. Vere, and W. Gilbertson,* [1658–64]. brs. O.

2014 [–]—[Anr. ed.] *[London, for F. Coles, T. Vere, I. Wright, J. Clarke, W. Thackeray, and T. Passenger,* 1678–80.] brs. L, CM, HH; MH.

2015 —The gardeners labyrinth. 1651. 4°. LAS.

2016 [–]—[Anr. ed.] *By Jane Bell,* 1652. 4°. LT, LWL, OR, RU, GU; CH, MH, MHO, WF, Y.

2017 [–]—[Anr. ed.] *By J. Bell,* 1656. 4°. L.

2017A [–]—[Anr. ed.] *By H. Bell for Henry Brewster,* 1660. 4°. KEW.

2018 —Natvral and artificiall conclvsions. *By Jane Bell,* 1650. 8°. L, O.

2018A ——[Anr. ed.] *By J. Bell and sold by William Gilbertson,* 1651. 8°. OC.

2019 ——[Anr. ed.] *By A. M. and are to be sold by Edward Brewster,* 1670. 8°. T.C.I 60. L; CH.

2020 ——[Anr. ed.] *By T. J. to be sol* [sic] *by Edward Brewster,* 1684. 8°. T.C.II 52. O.

2021 **Hill, Thomas, *of Trinity College, Cambridge.*** The best and vvorst of Paul. *By Roger Daniel,* [Cambridge], 1648. 4°.* LLP, CS, DT; CLC, IU, MH, NU, WF, Y, ASU.

2022 —God's eternal preparations. *By William Du-gard for Nathanaël Brooks,* 1648. 4°.* O, LLP, MR, DT; CLC, IU, MH, WF, Y, ASU.

2023 —The good old vvay, Gods vvay. *By Ric. Cotes, for John Bellamie and Philemon Stephens,* 1644. 4°. LT, O, C, EN, DT; CH, MH, NU, WF, Y, AVP.

2024 —The militant chvrch. *For John Bellamie and Ralph Smith,* 1643. 4°.* LT, O, C, BR, EN; BN, CH, IU, MH, TU, WF, Y.

2025 —An olive branch of peace. *For Peter Cole,* 1648. 4°.* O, LLP, MR, DT; CLC, MH, MIU, NU, WF, Y, ASU.

2026 —The right separation incovraged. *By R. Cotes, for John Bellamy, and Philemon Stephens,* 1645. 4°.* LT, O, C, EN, DT; CH, CU, MH, NU, WF, Y.

2027 —The season for Englands selfe-reflection. *By Richard Cotes, for John Bellamy, and Philemon Stephens,* 1644. 4°.* LT, O, C, EN, DT; BN, CH, CU, MH, NU, WF, Y.

2028 —Six sermons of. *For Peter Cole, to be sold at his shop, and Richard Westbrook,* 1649. 4°. L, OW, CT, DC, WCA; NU, WF.

2029 —The spring of strengthning grace. *For Peter Cole,* 1648. 4°.* O, LLP, MR, DT; CLC, IU, MH, NU, WF, Y, ASU.

2030 —The strength of the saints. *For Peter Cole,* 1648. 4°.* O, LLP, CM, MR, DT; CLC, IU, MH, NU, WF, Y, ASU.

2031 —The trade of truth advanced . . . July 27. 1642. *By I. L. for Iohn Bellamie, Philemon Stephens, and Ralph Smith,* 1642. 4°. LT, O, C, ENC, DT; CH, CN, MH, NU, WF, Y. (var.)

2032 —Trvth and love happily married. *For Peter Cole,* 1648. 4°.* O, LLP, MR, DT; CLC, IU, MH, NU, WF, Y, ASU.

[**Hill, William.**] Brief narrative of that stupendous tragedie. 1662. *See title.*

2033 [–] Grammaticarum in Dionysii. *Excudebat T. Newcome,* 1658. 8°. L; BN, CH, CLC, IU, MB, WF.

2034   [Anr. ed.] *Ex officina M. Clark,* 1688. 8°. CM, DUS, NE; CH, MB, TO.

2035 [–] A New-Years-gift for women. *By T. N. for the author,* 1660. 8°. LT.

2035A —Omnium febrium causa latet in sanguine. [*Cambridge,* 1681.] brs. MH.

2035AB **Hillenius, Francois.** Den Engelschens ende. *Rotterdam, by Bastiæn Wagens,* 1664. 12°. L; HR, LEIDEN, PL.

2035AC ——[Anr. ed.] —, 1671. 12°. HR, LEIDEN.

2035AD ——[Anr. ed.] —, 1677. 12°. L; HR, Y.

2035AE ——[Anr. ed.] *Rotterdam, by Isaac Næranus,* 1678. 12°. L; WF.

2035AF ——[Anr. ed.] *Rotterdam, by Joannes Borstius,* 1678. 12°. HR.

2035B **Hills, Henry.** A short treatise concerning the propagation of the soul. *For Richard Lowndes, and John Lowndes,* 1667. 8°. L, O, LCL, LSC, CT, P; CLC, NU, Y.

2035C ——[Anr. ed.] *For Richard Lowndes,* 1667. 8°. OH, OU; IU, WF.

2036 **Hilton, John.** Catch that catch can. *For John Benson & John Playford,* 1652. Sixes. L, O, GU, DT; CH, NN, RHT, WF.

2037 ——Second edition. *By W. G. for John Benson, and John Playford,* 1658. obl. 8°. L, GU; LC, WF.

2038 [–] —[Anr. ed.] *By W. G. for John Playford, and Zachariah Watkins,* 1663. obl. 8°. L.

2039 [–] —[Anr. ed.] *By W. Godbid for J. Playford,* 1667. 4°. L, O, GU; CH, CN, IU, LC, MH, NN, PL, WF.

2040 [–] —[Anr. ed.] *By J. P. for John Playford,* 1685. 4°. T.C.II 98. L, O, OCC.

2041 **Hilton, Thomas.** A funeral sermon occasion'd by the death of John Barksdale. *For J. Nutt,* 1700. 4°.* T.C.III 168. L; MBA, WF.

2041A ——[Anr. ed.] *By H. Newman, for John Barksdale in Cirencester,* 1700. 4°. BLH.

2042 Entry cancelled.

Hilton, Walter. Scale. 1659. *See* Hylton, Walter.

2043 **Hilton, William.** A relation of a discovery lately made on the coast of Florida. *By J. C. for Simon Miller,* 1664. 4°.* L, O, EN, GH; CH, LC, MH, MU, NN, RPJ.

2043A ——[Anr. ed.] *By J. C. for Richard Moon, in Bristol,* 1664. 4°.* NN.

2044 Hinc illæ lachrymæ: or, England's miseries. *For J. Johnson,* 1692. 8°. L, OB, CT; CH, CLC, CU, NU, PL, WF, Y.

2045 Hinc illæ lachrymæ, or some pious tears. [*London*], Feb. the 6th. 1684/5. brs. O; MH, Y.

Hinc illæ lachrymæ or the impietie. 1648. *See* Gauden, John, bp.

2045A Entry cancelled.

[**Hinckley, John.**] Epistola veridica. 1659. *See* Dury, John.

2046 —Fasciculus literarum: or, letters. *For Thomas Basset,* 1680. 8°. T.C.I 408. LCL, OC, CS, AN, P, EN; NU, WF, Y.

2047 [–] Πιθαναλογια. Or, a perswasive. *For Thomas Basset,* 1670. 8°. T.C.I 38. L, O, C, DU, P; CH, CLC, MM, NU, WF.

2048 —A sermon preach'd . . . April 21. 1661. *For T. Basset,* 1661. 4°.* O, LW; CH, MH, MWA, WF, Y.

2049 —Two sermons. *Oxford, by Hen: Hall for Ric: Davis,* 1657. 12°. MADAN 2338. L, O, C, LW, SHR; NGT, WF, Y.

2050 [**Hincks, Elizabeth.**] The poor widow's mite. [*London*], printed, 1671. 4°.* L, O, LF, CT, BBN, DUS; CH, IE, PH, PSC, Y.

2051 **Hind, James.** The declaration of. *For G. Horton,* 1651. 4°.* LT, LVF, SP; CH, IU, MHL, MM, NRU, WF.

2052 —The humble petition of. *For G. Horton,* 1651. 4°.* LT, O, DU, SP.

2053 —The trial of. [*London,* 1651.] 4°.* LT.

Hind and the panther. 1687. *See* Dryden, John.

Hind and the panther transvers'd. 1687. *See* Prior, Matthew.

2054 The hind in the toil. *Printed,* 1688. 4°.* O, LVD; CH, CLC, CN, MH, TU, WF, Y.

Hind let loose. [n.p.], 1687. *See* Shields, Alexander.

2055 **H[inde?], J[ohn].** A gagg to Love's advocate. *By William Du-Gard. August 25. 1651.* 4°.* LT, O, CT, AN; CN, CSS, CU, MM, NU, WF, Y.

2055A —The voyce of providence asserted. *Printed for Peter Cole,* 1653. 4°. CLC, WF.

2056 **Hinde, Samuel.** Englands prospective-glasse. *By J. Redmayne for John Crook,* 1663. 4°.* L, O, C, DU, NE; WF, Y, ZWT.

2057 No entry.

2058 [–] Iter lvsitanicvm. *By S. Griffin, for Robert Paulett,* 1662. 4°.* L, O, OB, CS, MR; CH, IU, LC, Y.

2059 ——[Anr. ed.] *Re-printed at Edinburgh,* 1662. 4°.* ALDIS 1737. EN; CH.

2060 Entry cancelled.

[–] The Parliaments reformation. 1646. *See* Hartlib, Samuel.

2061 —A sermon preach't. *Dublin, Benjamin Tooke, 1672.* 4°. DIX 147. DM.

2062 **Hinde, Thomas.** Under God. Humbly desiring his blessing to this . . . cordial drink. [*n,p.,* 1673.] brs. O.

2063 **Hinde, William.** A faithfull remonstrance. *By R. B. for Philemon Stephens, and Christopher Meredith, 1641.* 8°. L, O, C, CT, BC, YM, BLH; BN, CH, IU, TO, WF, Y.

2063A **Hindmarsh, Thomas.** A sermon preach'd . . . August 1, 1680. *For Joseph Hindmarsh, 1680.* 4°.* T.C.I 437. CCA, LSD; CH, Y.

2064 Hinds elder brother, or the master thief discovered. *Imprinted at London by John Clows, 1651.* 4°.* LT.

Hind's ramble. 1651. *See* Fidge, George.

2065 **Hinton, Benjamin.** Eighteen choice and usefull sermons. *By J. C. for Humphrey Moseley, and R. Wodenothe, 1650.* 4°. LT, ENC.

2066 **H[inton], E[dward].** The vanity of self-boasters. *By R. Bishop for S. Gellibrand, 1643.* 4°. LT, O; CLC, MH, NU.

2067 ——[Anr. ed.] *Oxford* [*London*], *for Thom. Robinson, 1651.* 4°. MADAN 2171. L, O, LW, BC, DT; CH, NU, WF, Y.

2068 **Hinton, John.** A sermon preached . . . 26th of July, 1685. *For Walter Kettilby, 1685.* 4°.* T.C.II 141. L, O, OC, CT, BAMB, BR, LSD; CH, NP, NU, WF, Y.

2068aA **Hinton, William.** A survey or account of the most observable passages of my life. *Printed by G. Miller, for the author, 1665.* 4°.* L.

2068A **[Hiobey, William.]** A most certain and true relation of the severall victories . . . in Ireland. *For Joseph Hunscott, 1642.* 8°. EC, DN; CN.

2069 Ἱππ–ανθρωπος: or, an ironicall expostulation. [*London*], *printed, 1648.* 4°.* LT, O; CN, TU.

2069A **Hippen, H.** At the Crown and Golden-Ball . . . liveth H. Hippen . . . . [*London,* 1700?] brs. L.

2070 **Hippisley, Edmund.** The Protestants vvonderment. *For Iohn Franke, 1642.* 4°.* LT; MH, TU, WF, Y.

2071 **Hippocrates.** The aphorisms. *For Humphrey Moseley, 1655.* 12°. L, O, C, MAU, E; CH, CLC, MH.

2072 —The eight sections of Hippocrates aphorisms. *By W. G. for Rob. Crofts, 1665.* 8°. L, O, C, LW, MC; CH, CLC, CNM, MH, WF, HC.

2073 [–] Hippocrates contractus. *Edinburgi, excudebat J. Reid, sumptibus Georgii Mossman, 1685.* 8°. ALDIS 2531. L, O, C, MAU, EN; BN, CLC, IU, MH, TO, WF.

2074 ——[Anr. ed.] *Excus. pro Johan. Malthus, 1686.* 4°. T.C.II 147. L, O, LWL, GU; TO, WSG.

2075 —Manuale medicorum. *Typis Tho. Roycroft, impensis Jo. Martin, Ja. Allestry, & Tho. Dicas. 1659.* 8°. LT, O, C, LW, DUS, P; CH, WSG.

2075A Entry cancelled.

—Presages of. 1655. *See* Lowe, Peter. Discourse.

Hyrelings reward. 1652. *See* T., R.

His Excellencies letter. 1643. *See* Essex, Robert Devereux, 3rd earl.

2075B His Excellency's speech. [*Annapolis, Thomas Reading,* 1700.] cap., fol.* NHS.

His Grace the Duke of Monmouth honoured. 1680. *See* Clark, Henry.

2076 His Grace the Duke of Schomberge's character. colop: *For William Beale,* [1689]. brs. L, OC, DN; CH.

2076A —[Anr. ed.] colop: *Edinburgh, re-printed, 1689.* brs. ALDIS 2895. L, EN.

2076B His Highnesse Prince Rvperts late beating up. *Oxford, by Leonard Lichfield, 1643.* 4°.* MADAN 1400. L, O, C, DU, MR; CH, WF.

2077 His Highnesse Prince Rupert's raising of the siege at Newarke . . . March the 21. 1643. [*Oxford, 1644.*] cap., 4°.* MADAN 1587. LT, MR, DT; IU, Y.

2077A —[Anr. ed., "Newarke upon/Trent."] [*London, 1644.*] 4°.* MADAN 1587n. LT; CH.

His Highnesse the Lord-Protector protected. 1654. *See* Hunton, Samuel.

2078 His Maiesties complaint, occasioned by his late sufferings. [*London*], *printed, 1647.* 4°.* LT.

His Majesties concessions. [*n.p.*], 1648. *See* Vines, Richard.

His Majesty's declaration concerning the charge. [*n.p.*], 1649. *See* Willis, John.

His Majesties declaration defended. 1681. *See* Dryden, John.

2079 His Majesties declaration to the army concerning. *For R. Rishton, 1648.* 4°.* LT; CH, CSS.

His Maiesties demands to Collonel Hammond. 1648. *See* L., J.

2080 His Majesties entertainments. [*n.p.*], 1660. fol. SP, EN.

2081 His Majesties going from the Isle of Wight. *For Richard Robinson, 1648.* 4°.* LT, MR.

2082 His Majesties gracious declaration to the right honorable the Earl of Middlesex. *Imprinted at London, for R. VV. 1648.* 4°.* LT, DT; MIU.

2083 His Majesties gracious message to the army for peace. *Octob. 10. London, for R. Emerson, 1648.* 4°.* LT.

His Majesties gracious message to the citizens. 1648. *See* Ruswel, W.

2083A His Majesties gracious speech to both houses . . . His Majesties speech as printed in Thompsons Domestick. [*London, 1679.*] brs. CN.

His Majesties letter to Lieutenant Generall Cromwell. 1648. *See* Stretton, W.

2084 His Majesties message to the Parliament read in both Houses . . . Novem. 9, 1648. *For C. W. Novemb. 10. 1648.* 4°.* LT, LIU.

His Majesties most gracious speech. [1687–97.] *See* Wagstaffe, Thomas.

2085 His Maiesties passing through the Scots armie. [*Edinburgh?*], *printed, 1641.* 4°.* ALDIS 996.5. LT, C, LLU, MR; CH, MIU, NC.

2086 His Majesties proceedings in Northamptonshire. [*London*], *Aug. 23. for I. Williams, 1642.* 4°.* LT.

His Majesties propriety. 1665. *See* Clavell, Robert.

His Majesties resolution concerning the setting up. [*n.p.*], 1642. *See* Charles I.

His Majesties whole army. 1645. *See* Fairfax, Sir Thomas.

2087 His Majesty having been pleased, of his royal grace and bounty, to renew his brief to the distressed French Protestants. [*London*, 168–?] cap., fol.* O, LPR; CLC, CN, MH, Y.

2088 His most sacred Majesties, and his most honourable Privy Councils letters, relating to the college of physicians. *For Randal Taylor*, 1688. 4°.* O, C, LLP, LWL, CS; CH, CLC, MM, NAM, PL, WF.

His noble numbers. 1647. *See* Herrick, Robert.

2089 His Royal Highness the Duke of York's welcom to London. colop: *For Henry Matthews*, 1682. brs. L, O, MC; CH, MH, Y.

2090 His sacred Majesty Charles the II. his royal title anagramatiz'd. *By T. J.* 1660. brs. LT.

Histoire de la dernière conspiration. 1696. *See* Abbadie, Jacques.

2091 Histoire entière & véritable du procèz de Charles Stuart. *A Londres, par J. G.*, 1650. 8°. LT, O, C, BSM, DT; CH, IU, MBP, MH, MU, WF, Y, ZWT. (var.)

2092 Histoire secrette de la Duchesse de Portsmouth. *Chez Richard Baldwin*, 1690. 12°. CH, CN, IU, MH, WF.

2093 Entry cancelled. Printed in France.

Historia descriptio. Oxoniæ, 1690. *See* Martin, Thomas.

Historia et antiquitates. Oxoniensis, 1673. *See* Wood, Anthony.

Historia histrionica. 1699. *See* Wright, James.

Historia independentiæ. 1648. *See* Walker, Clement.

Historia nuperæ rerum. 1697. *See* Burridge, Ezekiel.

2094 Historiæ Anglicanæ scriptores x. Simeon Monachus Dunelmensis. *Typis Jacobi Flesher, sumptibus Cornelii Bee*, 1652. 2v. fol. L, O, CT, EN, DT; CH, IU, LC, MU, PL, WF, Y, AVP.

2094aA —[Anr. ed.] *Typis Jacobi Flesher, sumptibus Cornelii Bee, 1652. Prostant etians Ludg. Batav. apud Johannem & Danielem Elsevier.* 2v. fol. O, CM; PU.

Historiæ Parliamenti Angliæ. [1650.] *See* May, Thomas.

Historiæ poeticæ. Parisiis, 1675. *See* Gale, Thomas.

Historian unmasked. 1689. *See* Long, Thomas.

2094A The historians guide. *For W. Crook*, 1676. 4°. T.C.I 217. L, O, LG, OC, CT; CH, INU, MB, MH, VC, WF, Y.

2094B —Second edition. —, 1679. 12°. T.C.I 363. L, O, OC, CS, SP, WCA; BN, CH, CN, MH, WF, Y, AMB.

2094C —Third edition. *By W. Horton for W. Crooke*, 1688. sixes. T.C.II 220. L, O, CE, AN, MR; CH, CN, MH, NC, WF, Y.

2094D —[Anr. ed.] *For W. Crook*, 1690. sixes. T.C.II 307. L, SP, E; BN, CLC, MH, TU, WF.

Historical account and defence. 1700. *See* Nye, Stephen.

Historical account of a degradation. [1678.] *See* Boyle, Robert.

2095 An historical account of proceedings betwixt the college of physicians. [*London?* 1690.] fol.* L, O, LPR, MR.

Historical account of some things. 1690. *See* Whitby, Daniel.

Historical account of the antiquity. 1692. *See* Grascombe, Samuel.

2095A An historical account of the ceremonies . . . Pope. [*London?* 1673.] cap., 0°. L.

Historical account of the heroick life. 1683. *See* T., S.

2096 An historical account of the late great frost. *For D. Brown, and J. Waltho*, 1684. 12°. T.C.II 70. L, O, LG, CS, GH; CH.

Historical account of the late troubles. 1686. *See* La Rochefoucauld, Francois, *duc de*.

Historical account of the memorable actions. 1690. *See* J., S.

2097 An historical account of the most remarkable transactions. *For Richard Baldwin*, 1690. 4°.* T.C.II 334. L, O, LIL, OC, CT, DT; CH, CN, MH, PU, TO, WF, Y.

Historical account of the rise. 1690. *See* Thomas, *Sir* Dalby.

2098 An historical account of the rise and progress of addressing. colop: *For R. Janeway*, 1681. brs. O; Y, AVP, ZWT.

Historical account of the wonderful cures. 1680. *See* Simpson, William.

Historical and political discourse, 1682. *See* Selden, John.

Historical and political discourse. 1689.

Historical and political essays. 1698. *See* Briscoe, John.

Historical and political observations. 1683. *See* D., R.

Historical applications. 1670. *See* Berkeley, George, *earl*.

2098A Historical collections concerning church affairs. *Printed*, 1696. 4°. L, O, C, YM, EN, DM; CLC, MM, NU, WF, Y.

Historical collections of the church in Ireland. 1681. *See* Ware, Robert.

2099 Historical collections, or a brief account. *For Simon Neale*, 1681. 8°. T.C.I 440. L, O, RU, DT; CLC, CN, LC, MB, NU, Y.

2100 —Second edition. —, 1682. 8°. LG, LL, RU, SP, E; MHL, OLU, Y.

2101 —"Second" edition. *For S. N. and sold by W. Freeman*, 1685. 8°. T.C.II 130. L, O, C, DU, MR; CH, IU, LC, NC, NU, Y.

Historical collections out of. [n.p.], 1674. *See* Touchet, George.

2102 An historical description of the glorious conquest of . . . Buda. *For Robert Clavell*, 1686. 4°. T.C.II 176. L, O, CT, EN, DT; CLC, CU, MH, NU, WF, Y.

2103 Entry cancelled. Ghost.

2103A An historical dictionary of England and Wales. *For Abel Roper*, 1692. 12°. L, O; CH, CLC, NP, WF.

Historical discourse briefly. 1661. *See* Stephens, John.

Historical discourse concerning. 1688. *See* Allix, Pierre.

2103B An historical discourse of Parliaments. 1656. 12°. NCL.

2103C An historical discourse of the Pope's usurped supremacy. *For C. Harper*, 1678. 12°. T.C.I 338. LLL, EN.

Historicall discourse of the uniformity. 1647. *See* Bacon, Nathaniel.

Historical discourses. 1661. *See* H., J.

Historical epistle. [n.p.], 1652. *See* Smith, Richard.

Historical examination. 1688. *See* Jenkin, Robert.

2104 Historical memoires of the life and death of . . . Prince Rupert. *For Tho. Malthus*, 1683. 8°. T.C.II 3. L, O, CT, DU, A; CH, IU, MH, PBL, WF.

Historical memoires on the reigns. 1658. *See* Osborne, Francis.

2105 Entry cancelled.

Historical narration of the first fourteen years. 1651. *See* Sparke, Michael. Narrative history.

Historicall narration of the judgement. 1645. *See* Ailward, John.

Historical narration of the life. Oxford, 1685. *See* Woodhead, Abraham.

2106 An historicall narrative of the German princess. *For Charles Moulton, 1663. 4°.* L, LG, P; MH.

Historical observations upon the reigns. 1689. *See* Howard, *Sir* Robert.

2106A Historical parts of the Old and New Testaments. *For Sam. Keble, 1694. 16°.* L.

2107 The historicall passages, of England. [*Oxford*], *printed, 1643. 4°.* MADAN 1422. EC; CN.

2108 An historical relation of several great and learned Romanists. *Printed and are to be sold by Richard Baldwin, 1688. 4°.* L, O, CT, EN, DT; CH, CN, MH, NU, WF, Y.

2108A An historical relation of the first discovery of . . . Madera. *For W. Cadman, 1675. 4°.* T.C.I 226. DCH.

Historical relation of the late. 1691. *See* Cockburn, John.

Historical remarques. 1684. *See* Crouch, Nathaniel.

2109 Historical remarques upon the late Revolutions. *In the Savoy, by Tho. Newcomb, to be sold by H. Herringman, 1675. 12°.* L, O, LUG, OC, CS, CT, DU; WF.

Historical review of the late horrid phanatical plot. 1684. *See* W., F. N.

Historical romance. Dublin, 1694. *See* Sergeant, John.

Historical treatise. 1687. *See* DuFour de Longuerue, Louis.

Historicall vindication of the church. 1657. *See* Twysden, Roger.

Historical vindication of the naked gospel. [n.p.], 1690. *See* Le Clerc, Jean.

Historical voyages. 1693. *See* Fer, N. de.

Histories of the gunpowder-treason. 1676. *See* Thou, Jacques Auguste de.

Historie & policie. 1659. *See* Dawbeny, Henry.

History and reasons. 1698. *See* Atwood, William.

2110 This history and transactions of the English nation. *Printed, and are to be sold by Richard Janeway, 1689. fol.* L, O, LL, CT, BR, LSD; CH, Y.

2111 The history of Adam Bell. *Glasgow, by Robert Sanders, 1668.* ALDIS 1842.5. *8°.* L.

2112 —[Anr. ed.] —, *1698. 12°.* ALDIS 3755. RHT.

2113 The history of Adolphvs. *Printed; to be sold by R. T., 1691. 4°.* T.C.II 392. L, O, DT; MH.

History of antient ceremonies. 1669. *See* Porré, Jonas.

History of apparitions. 1658. *See* Bromhall, Thomas.

History of baptism. 1678. *See* St. Nicholas, John.

History of Barbadoes. 1666. *See* Rochefort, Charles de.

2114 The history of Caledonia. *Printed, and sold by John Nutt, 1699. 8°.* L, O, LG, EN; CH, CN, LC, NC, Y.

2115 —[Anr. ed.] *Dublin, re-printed by Stephen Powell, for Josias Shaw, 1699. 8°.* DIX 310. DI, DT; IU, NN, RPJ, WF.

History of Cales passion. 1652. *See* Tooke, George.

2116 The history of Catiline's conspiracy. *By Hen. Hills, jun. for Robert Boulter, 1683. 8°.* L, C.

History of conformity. 1681. *See* Collinges, John.

2116A The histor[y] of Doctor John Favstv[s]. *By E. Cotes and are to be sold b[y] Frances Grove,* [1660]. *8°.* Y.

2117 —[Anr. ed.] *By E. Cotes, to be sold by Charles Tyus, 1664. 8°.* L.

2118 —[Anr. ed.] [*London*], *printed, 1696. 8°.* L.

History of Dorastus. [1700.] *See* Greene, Robert.

History of England. Giving. 1696. *See* Seller, John.

History of episcopacie. 1642. *See* Heylyn, Peter.

2119 Entry cancelled.

History of Europe. 1698. *See* Jones, David. Compleat history.

History of Father La Chaise. 1693. *See* Le Noble, Eustache.

2120 Entry cancelled.

History of feavers. 1674. *See* Πυρετολογια.

2120A The historie of Fryer Bacon. *For M. W. to be sold by D. Newman and B. Alsop, 1683. 12°.* O, CM.

2121 The history of Frier Rush. *By Jane Bell, 1659. 4°.* CH, WF.

History of Gustavus Adolphus. 1689. *See* Prade, Roger de.

History of Henry IV. 1672. *See* Péréfixe, Hardouin de Beaumont de, *abp.*

2122 A history of His Majesties navy royal. 1660. *fol.* O.

History of His sacred Majesty Charles the II. 1660. *See* Dauncey, John.

2122A The history of his Sacred Majesties most wonderfull preservation, after the battle of Worcester. *Printed and are to be sold by Joseph Blacklock and Mr. Michaell, 1660. brs.* L.

History of independency. 1648. *See* Walker, Clement.

2123 No entry.

History of infamous imposters. 1682. *See* Rocoles, Jean Baptiste de.

History of Isuf Bassa. 1684. *See* Higgons, Thomas.

History of jewels. 1671. *See* Chappuzeau, Samuel.

2124 The history of Madamoiselle de St, Phale. *By J. A. for J. Hancock, 1691. 12°.* T.C.II 333. YD.

2124A The history of Mistris Jane Shore. [*n.p.*, 1660?] *8°.* EC.

2124B —[Anr. ed., "M^rs. Iane."] *For F. Coles, T. Vere, and J. Wright,* [1663–1674]. *8°.* CM.

2125 —[Anr. ed., "Mrs. Jane."] *For J. Clarke, W. Thackeray, & T. Passinger,* [1688]. *8°.* O.

2126 Entry cancelled.

History of moderation. 1669. *See* Brathwaite, Richard.

History of monastical conventions. 1686. *See* S., J.

History of most curious manual arts. 1675. *See* Powell, Thomas.

2127 The history of naturalization. [*London*, 1680?] cap., *fol.* L, MR; MH, NC, WF, Y, ANL.

History of New-England. 1654. *See* Johnson, Edward.

2128 The history of Nicerotis. *For R. Bentley and S. Magnes,* 1685. 8°. L; CLC, LC, WF.

2128A The history of Olivaires of Castile. *For A. and J. Churchill, and for Fra. Hildyard in York,* 1695. 12°. L, LLU; CN, Y.

2129 —[Anr. ed.] *For Fra. Hildyard, in York,* 1695. 12°. O.
      History of Oliver Cromwel. 1692. *See* Crouch, Nathaniel.
      History of oracles. 1688. *See* Fontenelle, Bernard Le Bovier de.
      History of passive obedience. Amsterdam, 1689. *See* Seller, Abednego.
      History of philosophy. 1660. *See* Stanley, Thomas.

2130 Entry cancelled.
      History of Philoxypes. 1652. *See* Scudéry, Madeleine de.

2131 Entry cancelled.
      History of plots. 1696. *See* Impartial history of the plots.
      History of Polexander. 1647. *See* Gomberville, Marin le Roy, *sieur* de.
      History of Polindor. 1651. *See* Harington, John.

2132 The history of Pope Joan. Second edition. *Printed,* 1687. 4°.* C; MH.

2133 The history of Popish-sham-plots. *For Richard Janeway,* 1682. 8°. L, LW, MR, SP; CH, CN, MIU, NU, TSM, WF, Y.
      History of Popish transubstantiation. 1679. *See* Cosin, John, *bp.*

2134 Entry cancelled. *See following entry.*

2135 The history of Portugal. *By John Redmayne,* 1662. 12°. O, CT; CN.

2136 The history of Prince Erastus son to the Emperour Dioclesian and those famous philosophers called the seven wise masters of Rome. *By Anne Johnson for Fra. Kirkman,* 1674. 8°. T.C.I 169. L, O, LG; CH, CN, MBP, RHT, TU.
      History of religion. 1694. *See* Howard, *Sir* Robert.

2137 The history of Reynard the fox. [*London*], *printed,* [1700?]. 12°. L.

2138 A history of Robin Hood and the beggar. *Aberdeen, by John Forbes,* 1700. ALDIS 3971. JOHNSTONE.
      History of Scotch-presbytery, 1692. *See* Shields, Alexander.

2138A The history of self-defence. *For D. Newman,* 1689. 4°.* T.C.II 291. L, SP, DT; CH, CSS, CSU.

2138B —[Anr. ed.] —, 1680 [i.e. 1690?]. 4°.* C, OB, OC, CS; CH, CLC, CN, MH, NU, WF, Y.
      History of sin. 1698. *See* Leslie, Charles.

2139 The history of Sir Eger. *Glasgow, by Robert Sanders,* 1669. 4°. ALDIS 1864.7. L.

2140 —[Anr. ed.] [*Glasgow, Robert Sanders?*], *printed,* 1687. 24°. ALDIS 2691.7. CH.
      History of Sr Francis Drake. 1659. *See* Davenant, *Sir* William.

2141 The history of Tarquin and Lucretia. *By T. Leach for C. Wilkinson,* 1669. 4°. L, O; CH, MH.

2142 The history of that most famous Saint & souldier St. George of Cappadocia. *Printed,* 1661. 4°. IT, O, IC; OSU.

2143 Entry cancelled.
      History of the administration of Cardinal Richelieu. 1657. *See* Vialart, Charles. History of the government of France.
      History of the administration of Cardinal Ximenes. 1671. *See* Baudier, Michel.
      History of the affaires. 1690. *See* S., T.

2143A The history of the amours of the French court. *For N. B.,* 1684. 8°. T.C.II 71. CLC.

2143B The history of the amours of the Marshal de Boufflers. *For Edward Mory,* 1697. 8°. L (t.p.); CH, MH.

2144 The history of the association. *For R. Janeway,* 1682. fol.* L, O, CT, LLU, LSD, DU; CH, CN, MH, MM, TU, WF, Y.
      History of the Athenian society. [1691.] *See* Gildon, Charles.

2145 The history of the birth, travels, . . . and death of Fortunatus. *By and for T. Haly,* 1682. 4°. CM; CH, WF.

2146 The history of the blind beggar of Bednal-Green. *For Charles Dennisson,* 1686. 8°. CM.

2146A —[Anr. ed.] [*London*], *for J. Blare,* [1700?]. 4°.* O.
      History of the Bohemian. 1680. *See* Comenius, Johann Amos.
      History of the bucaniers. 1684. *See* Exquemelin, Alexander Olivier.
      History of the cardinals. 1670. *See* Leti, Gregorio. Il cardinalismo.
      History of the Caribby-islands. 1666. *See* Rochefort, Charles de.

2147 The history of the children in the wood. *By I. M. for J. Blare,* 1687. 8°. L, O.
      History of the church of Great Britain, 1674. *See* G[earing], W[illiam].

2148 The history of the church of Malabar. *For Sam. Smith, and Benj. Walford,* 1694. 8°. T.C.II 499. L, O, C, EN, DT; BN, CH, CU, MH, NU, WF, Y.
      History of the civil wars. 1679. *See* Hobbes, Thomas.
      History of the Commons warre. 1662. *See* C., W.

2148A Entry cancelled.
      History of the conquest of Spain. 1687. *See* Luna, Miguel de.

2149–50 Entries cancelled.
      History of the conspiracy. 1675. *See* Saint-Réal, César Vischard de. Conspiracy of the Spaniards.
      History of the coronation of James II. 1687. *See* Sandford, Francis.
      History of the court. 1682. *See* Baudier, Michel.
      History of the creation. 1641. *See* Walker, George.

2151 The historie of the damnable life . . . of Doctor John Faustus. *Printed at London, for Edward Wright,* 1648. 4°. L.

2152 —[Anr. ed.] *For William Whitwood,* 1674. 4°. CM.

2153 —[Anr. ed.] *For Thomas Sawbridge,* 1682. 4°. CH.

2154 —[Anr. ed.] *For W. Whitwood,* [1687?]. 4°. L.

2154A —[Anr. ed.] *By W. H. for William Whitwood,* 1690. 4°. T.C.II 326. A; Y.

2155 —[Anr. ed.] *By W. O. for John Back,* [1696]. 4°. T.C.II 607. L; WF.

2156   —[Anr. ed.] *By C. Brown; for M. Hotham*, [1700?]. 4°. L.

History of the damnable Popish plot. 1680. *See* Care, Henry.

History of the desertion. 1689. *See* Bohun, Edmund.

2157–8 Entries cancelled.

History of the divorce of Henry VIII. [*London?* 1690]. *See* LeGrand, Joachim.

History of the Duke of Guise. 1683. *See* True history.

History of the English & Scotch presbytery. Villa Franca, 1659. *See* Du Moulin, Pierre.

2159   Entry cancelled.

History of the Eucharist. 1684. *See* Laroque, Mathieu de.

History of the ever-renowned. [1680.] *See* Cervantes, Miguel de.

History of the execrable Irish rebellion. 1680. *See* Borlase, Edmund.

History of the famous and passionate love. 1692. *See* Crowne, John.

2160   The history of the famous and renowned knight Sir Bevis of Hampton. *By G. D. for Andrew Crook*, 1662. 4°. O, LLP; WF.

2160A History of the famous and renowned Prince Alfred of England. *By C. Brown, and T. Norris*, [169–?]. 4°. CLC.

History of the famous edict. 1694. *See* Benoit, Elie.

2160B History of the famous exploits of Guy earl of Warwick. [*n.p.*], *printed for Charles Bates*, [1680?]. 4°.* L.

History of the five wise philosophers. 1672. *See* Peachum, Henry.

2161   History of the golden eagle. *For William Thackeray*, 1672. 4°.* L.

2162   —[Anr. ed.] *By William Thackeray.* 1677. 4°.* L, LLL, CM; CN, MH.

History of the government of France. 1657. *See* Vialart, Charles.

History of the grand viziers. 1677. *See* Chassepol, François de.

2163   Entry cancelled.

History of the great level. 1685. *See* History or narrative.

History of the gunpowder-treason. 1678. *See* Williams, John, *bp.*

History of the Holy War. 1686. *See* Maimbourg, Louis de.

History of the House of Esté. 1681. *See* Crauford, James.

History of the House of Orange. 1693. *See* Crouch, Nathaniel.

History of the iconoclasts. [*n.p.*], 1671. *See* Anderton, Thomas.

History of the indulgence. [*n.p.*], 1678. *See* Brown, John.

2164   Entry cancelled.

History of the intrigues. 1697. *See* Frankenstein, Christian Gottfried.

History of the kingdom of Ireland. 1693. *See* Crouch, Nathaniel.

2164A The history of the kingdome of Portugal. *By John Redmayne*, 1661. 12°. L; WF, Y.

History of the Kingdoms of Scotland. 1685. *See* Crouch, Nathaniel.

History of the Kings Majesties affairs. [*n.p.*], 1648. *See* Wishart, George, *bp.*

2165   Entry cancelled.

History of the kings of England. 1692. *See* Short history.

History of the late conspiracy. 1696. *See* Abbadie, Jacques.

History of the late English rebellion. 1665. *See* Younger, William.

2165A The history of the late great revolution in England. *For Thomas Salusbury*, 1690. 8°. T.C.II 351. L, DU, DC; CH, CLC, CN, NRU, NU, TU, WF.

History of the late proceedings. 1681. *See* L., L.

2166   The history of the late revolution in England. *For Tho. Salusbury*, 1689. 8°. T.C.II 286. O, LLP, LIU, MR; CLC, MIU, NP, WF.

2166aA —[Anr. ed.] *Printed*, 1689. 8°. L, LW, DU; NC, PL, Y.

2166A The history of the late war with the Turks. *Printed at Cologn, and re-printed at London, for H. Bonwicke*, 1689. 12°. T.C.II 60. CT; Y.

History of the late warres. 1670. *See* Manley, *Sir* Roger.

History of the life and actions of St. Athanasius. 1664. *See* Bacon, Nathaniel.

History of the life and actions of the Viscount de Turenne. 1686. *See* Courtilz de Sandras, Gatien.

2167   The history of the life and death of Hugh Peters. *For Fr. Coles*, 1661. 4°.* LT; CLC.

History of the life and death of James Arminius. 1672. *See* Bertius, Pierre.

History of the life & death of Oliver Cromwell. 1663. *See* Heath, James.

History of the life and death of Pope Joane. 1663. *See* J., H.

History of the life and death of Sr. Thomas More. 1662. *See* Hoddesdon, John.

2167A The history of the life and death of that antient father … Joh. Tauler. *For Lodowick Lloyd*, 1663. 8°. CN.

2168   The history of the life, bloody reign and death of Queen Mary. *For D. Browne, and T. Benskin*, 1682. 12°. T.C.I 462. L, O, LW; CN, IU, MB, PU, WF.

2168aA —Third edition. —, 1682. 12°. T.C.I.514. Y.

History of the life of Katharine de Medicis. 1693. *See* Estienne, Henri d'.

History of the life of the Duke of Espernon. 1670. *See* Girard, Guillaume.

2168bA The history of the life of the sublime … Joh. Thauler. *By S. Dover for L. Lloyd*, 1660. 8°. EN; CLC, MSL, WF.

History of the life, reign and death of Edward II. 1680. *See* Falkland, Henry Cary, *viscount.*

2168A The history of the life, victorious reign, and death of K. Henry VIII. *Printed, and are to be sold by H. Rodes*, 1682. 12°. T.C.I 472. L, O, LSC, BLH; CH, CLC, MH, WF, Y.

History of the loves of Lysander. 1688. *See* S., T.

History of the managements. 1691. *See* Gualdo Priorato, Galeazzo.

2169   Entry cancelled.

History of the Mareschalless de la Ferté. 1690. *See* Modern novels, Vol. II.

2169A The history of the most famous . . . Janny Geddes. [*Edinburgh?* 1688?] brs. MH.

2170 The history of the most illustrious William, Prince of Orange. [*London*], *printed*, 1688. 12°. T.C.II 249. L, O, C, LW, BAMB; CH, CN, LC, MU, WF, Y.

2171 —Second edition. —, 1689. 12°. L, CS, LIU, LSD; CLC, Y.

History of the most material. 1691. *See* Story, George. True and impartial history.

2172 History of the most remarkable passages. 1680. EN.

History of the most renowned. 1687. *See* Cervantes, Miguel de.

2173 The history of the most renowned Queen Elizabeth. *By W. O. and sold by C. Bates*, [1700]. 4°.* L.

2173AA —[*Anr. ed.*] *By and for C. Brown*, [*c.* 1700]. 4°.* WF.

History of the most unfortunate. 1680. *See* Falkland, Henry Cary, 1st *viscount*.

History of the negotiation. 1690. *See* Teissier, Antoine.

2173A The history of the new plot. *For Randolph Taylor*, 1683. brs. T.C.II 45. L, O, OC; CH.

History of the nine worthies. 1687. *See* Crouch, Nathaniel.

2173B The history of ye Old & New Testament in cutts. [*London*], *Wm. R. for Iohn Williams*, 1671. 8°. L.

History of the Old Testament. 1690. *See* Fontaine, Nicholas.

History of the original. 1685. *See* Simon, Richard.

2173C The history of the Parliament. [*London*], *printed*, 1688. fol. L, BR, DU, LSD, RU, GU; CH, MIU, NN, WF, WG.

History of the persecution. 1688. *See* Burnet, Gilbert, *bp.*

2174 The history of the persecutions of the reformed churches in France. *For Tho. Newborough, and John Nicholson*, 1699. 4°. T.C.II 273. L, LIL, SP, DT; NU, PU, WF.

History of the plot. 1679. *See* L'Estrange, *Sir* Roger.

2175 The history of the plot anatomised. *For M. R.*, 1689. 4°.* T.C.II 255. L, O, CS, EN, DT; CH, IU, MH, WF, Y.

History of the powder-treason. 1681. *See* Williams, John, *bp.*

2176 History of the pretended Prince of Wales. 1696. EN.

History of the principality. 1695. *See* Crouch, Nathaniel.

2176A The history of the reformation of the Church of England. [*Paris*], *printed* 1685. 8°. L, FARM; WF.

Historie of the reformation . . . of the Church of Scotland. 1644. *See* Knox, John.

2177 The history of the revolution in Portugal. *For Mat. Gilliflower, Tim. Goodwin, Mat. Woton, Rich. Parker, and Benj. Tooke*, 1700. 8°. O, CS.

History of the Romish inquisition. 1700. *See* Beaulieu, Luke de.

2177A The history of the rook and turkeys. 1694. 4°. O; LC.

2178 The history of the Royal Congress at the Hague. *Reprinted in London, for Thomas Axe*, 1691. 4°.* LVF, CT, MR, DT; CH, CLC, NGT, NU.

History of the sacred and royal majesty. 1658. *See* Gualdo Priorato, Galeazzo, *conte.*

2179 The history of the second death of the Rump. [*London*, 1660.] brs. LT, O; MH, Y.

History of the Sevarites. 1675. *See* Vairesse d'Allais, Denis.

2180 The history of the seven wise masters of Rome. *By J. C. for E. Blackmore*, 1653. 8°. O.

2180A —[*Anr. ed.*] *By R. I. for E. Blackmore*, 1656. 8°. Y.

2181 —[*Anr. ed.*] *For J. Wright*, 1671. 8°. L.

2181A —Eighth edition. *By E. Crowh* [*sic*] *for J. Wright*, 1673. 8°. MH.

2182 —[*Anr. ed.*] *For J. Wright*, 1677. 8°. CN.

2183 —[*Anr. ed.*] —, 1682. 8°. O.

2184 —[*Anr. ed.*] —, 1684. 12°. L; CH, VC.

2185 —[*Anr. ed.*] *For M. Wotton, and G. Conyers*, 1687. 8°. L, CM, DM; CH.

2185A —[*Anr. ed.*] *For Matt. Wotton and G. Conyers*, 1688. 8°. CN, Y.

2185B —[*Anr. ed.*] —, *and are to be sold by J. Deacon*, 1688. 8°. IU.

2185C —[*Anr. ed.*] *For George Conyers*, 1693. sixes. Y.

2186 —[*Anr. ed.*] *Glasgow, for R. Sanders*, 1693. 8°. ALDIS 3301. L, EN.

2187 —[*Anr. ed.*] *By J. W. for G. Conyers*, 1697. 8°. L.

History of the seven wise mistresses. 1686. *See* Howard, Thomas.

History of the state. 1683. *See* S., J.

History of the successions. 1682. *See* Cooke, Edward.

History of the Tartars. 1679. *See* Palafox y Mendoza, Juan de, *bp.*

History of the three late famous imposters. 1669. *See* Evelyn, John.

History of the thrice illustrious. 1660. *See* Dauncey, John.

History of the transactions. 1664. *See* W., W.

2187A The history of the treaty at Nimueguen. *For Dorman Newman*, 1681. 8°. T.C.I 428. L, LW, OC; CLC, MBA, WF, Y.

History of the triumvirates. 1686. *See* Citri de la Guette, Samuel.

2188 Entry cancelled.

History of the troubles and tryal of William Laud. 1695. *See* Laud, William.

2188A The history of the Turkish wars. *By J. Cottrel and D. Maxwell, sold by Nathanael Brook and Henry Marsh*, 1664. CS.

2188B —[*Anr. ed.*] *By J. Cottrel to be sold by N. Brook.* 1664. LC.

History of the Turks describing. 1683. *See* S., I.

2188C The History of the Turks in the progress. *For W. Whitwood*, 1697. 12°. Y.

2188D The history of the two children in the wood. *By I. M. for J. Blare*, 1687. 8°.* O.

2189 An history of the twofold invention of the cross. *Dublin, printed*, 1686. 8°. DIX 221. L, C; CLC.

History of the two late kings. 1693. *See* Crouch, Nathaniel.

History of the union between. 1698. *See* Taylor, Richard.

History of the union of. 1660. *See* H., M.

History of the valorous. 1652. *See* Cervantes, Miguel de.

2189A The history of the Venetian conquests. *For John Newton,* 1689. 8°. L; CN, FU, WF, Y.

History of the war of Cyprus. 1687. *See* Graziani, Antonio Maria.

2190 The history of the wars in Ireland. *For Benj. Johnson,* 1690. 12°. L, C; CH, CLC, CN, WF.

2190A —Second edition. —, 1691. 12°. L.

2190B The history of the Whiggish-plot. *By T. B. sold by Randal Taylor,* 1684. fol. L, O, LG, LL, OC; BN, CH, MH, WF, Y, AVP.

2191 Entry cancelled.

History of two children. 1687. *See* History of the two children.

History of Whiggism. 1682. *See* Hickeringill, Edmund.

2191A The history of William, Prince of Orange. 1688. 8°. CT.

2192 A history or brief chronicle of the chief matters of the Irish warres. *Printed at London for Robert Ibbitson, to be sold by Peter Stent,* 1650. 4°.* LT, O, C, DN; MIU, WF, Y.

2192A The history or narrative of the great level of the Fenns. *For Moses Pitt,* 1685. 12°. T.C.II 124. LAD; NN.

2192B **Hitcham, *Sir* Robert.** An ordinance for settling . . . Framlingham. *H. Hills & W. DuGard,* 1654. fol. C.

2193 **Hitchcock, John.** The reasonableness and necessity. *By Tho. Warren for Walter Kettilby,* 1697. 4°.* T.C.III 36. L, LW, CT, EC, WCA, EN; NN.

2194 Entry cancelled. Date 1706.

2195 Ho brother Teague. [*London,* 1689?] brs. L; CH.

2195AA **Hoadly, Samuel.** The accidence. *For John Wright,* 1683. 8°. L.

2195A —The natural method of teaching. *By M. F. and are to be sold by B. Aylmer, and A. Swalle,* 1688. 8°. MH.

2195B — —Third edition. *By J. Heptinstall, and are to be sold by B. Aylmer,* 1694. 8°. LLP; CN.

2196 **H[oar], L[eonard].** Index Biblicus. *Cambridge, J. Field,* 1668. 4°. CT.

2197 [–] —[Anr. ed.] *By T. L.,* 1668. 12°. T.C.I 1. L, LW; IU, LC, MB, NN, Y.

2197A [–] —[Anr. ed.] *By Thomas Leach,* 1668. 12°. O.

2198 [–] —[Anr. ed.] —, 1669. 12°. MB, AVP.

2199 [–] —Second edition. *For John Wilkins,* 1672. 8°. T.C.I 122. L, O, LW; CH, CLC, MB, MH, WF, Y.

2200 —The sting of death. *Boston, by John Foster,* 1680. 4°.* EVANS 286. CH, LC, MB, MH, MHS, Y.

2201 [**Hoard, Samuel.**] God's love to mankind. *For John Clark,* 1656. 4°. EC, DT; CLC, PJB.

2202 [–] —[Anr. ed. "man-kinde."] —, 1658. 8°. L, C, BAMB, BR, SHR; CDA, CN, IU, MH, NPT, NU, TO.

2203 [–] —[Anr. ed.] —, 1673. 8°. T.C.I 122. L, O, CT, SA, DT; CLC, IU, LC, PL, WF.

2204 —The soules misery. Second edition. *By J. G. for John Clark,* 1658. 8°. L, C, LCL, LW, BR; CH, CLC, IU, NU.

2205 **Hobart, *Sir* Henry.** The reports of. *By the assignes of Iohn More,* 1641. 4°. L, C, DC, P, EN; CH, CU, LC, NCL.

2206 — —Second edition. *By Iames Flesher, for William Lee and Daniel Pakeman,* 1650. fol. O, NOT, NPL, AN, BQ; LC, MIU, NCL, NCU, V, WF.

2207 —[Anr. ed.] *By R. & W. Leybourn for William Lee and Daniel Pakeman,* 1658. fol. L, LGI, MC, EN, CD; LC, NCL, PL, YL.

2208 — —Third edition. *For William Lee, Allen Banks, & Charls Harper,* 1671. fol. T.C.I 63. L, LL, LMT, CJ, DT; CH, LC, MBP, NCL, PU, WF, YL.

2209 — —Fourth edition. *By G. Sawbridge, W. Rawlins, and S. Roycroft, assigns of Richard and Edward Atkins, for Charles Harper and Tho. Lee,* 1678. fol. L, C, LIL, LMT, OC, BAMB, BC; BN, CH, LC, NCL, NF, NR, PU, WF.

Hobart, Nehemiah. Almanack. *Cambridge* [*Mass.*], 1673. *See* Almanacs.

2210 Entry cancelled.

Hobbes, Thomas. Answer of . . . to Sir William Davenant's preface. *Paris,* 1650. *See* Davenant, *Sir* William. Discourse upon Gondibert.

2211 —Answer to a book published by Dr. Bramhall. *For W. Crooke,* 1682. 8°. LCL; TO, TU, AVP. *See also*—Tracts. 1682.

2212 —The art of rhetoric. *For William Crooke,* 1681. 8°. L, O, C, EN, DT; CH, CN, LC, MH, MU, NU, TU, WF, Y.

2213 —Behemoth. *Printed,* 1679. 12°. L, O, C, EN, DT; CH, IU, LC, NC, RPJ, WF, Y.

2214 [–] —[Anr. ed.] —, 1680. 8°. L, O, C, DC, DU; CLC, CN, LC, NP, NU, PL, Y.

2215 — —[Anr. ed.] *For W. Crooke,* 1682. 8°. L, O, CK, SP, BQ; CH, MH, MU, NU, TSM, WF, Y.

2216 —A catalogue of the works of. [*London*], *for W. Crooke,* [1675]. brs. O.

2217 —Mr Hobbes considered. *For Andrew Crooke,* 1662. 8°. L, O, C, LW, EC; MH.

2218 —Considerations upon the {reputation, loyalty. *For William Crooke,* 1680. 8°. T.C.I 386. L, O, C, AN, EN, DT; BN, CH, CN, MH, NU, WF, Y.

2219 —De corpore politico or the elements of lavv. *For J. Martin, and J. Ridley,* 1650. 12°. LT, O, C, LIU, P; CLC, MH, MIU, WF, Y.

2220 — —[Anr. ed.] *By Tho: Roycroft for John Martin,* 1652. 12°. O, C, LW, OC; BN, MH, NU, TO, WF, Y, YL.

2221 — —[Anr. ed.] *By T. R. for J. Ridley,* 1652. 12°. L, O, CK, GK; CLC, NU.

2222 —De mirabilibus pecci. [*London,* 1666?] cap., 4°.* L, O, BR, EC, LSD, NPL; CLC.

2222A — —Second edition. 1666. 4°.* O, OC.

2223 — —Third edition. colop: *Excudebat J. C. pro Gulielmo Crook,* 1675. 4°.* T.C.I 213. OC, OM, OU, CT, GK; CH, Y.

2224 — —Fourth edition. *For William Crook,* 1678. 8°. T.C.I 296. L, O, C, AN, EN, DT; BN, CH, CN, MH, WF, Y.

2225 — —Fifth edition. —, 1683. 12°. T.C.II 57. L, O, C, E, GK; CH, CLC, IU, MH, NC, WF, Y.

2225A [–] De principiis & ratiocinatione geometrarum. *Apud Andream Crooke,* 1666. 4°. L, O, OC, CK, CS; MH, MU, NN, Y.

2226 —Decameron physiologicum. *By J. C. for W. Crook,* 1678. 8°. T.C.I 293. L, O, C, DU, DT; CH, MH, MU, NU, WF, Y.

2227 No entry.

2228   Entry cancelled.
       —Dialogues of philosophy. 1678. *See* —Decameron.
2229   —Dialogus physicus. *Typis J. B. & prostant venales apud A. Crook*, 1661. 4°.* L, O, LU, CCA, CK; MH, MU, WF, Y.
2230   —Elementorum philosophiæ. *Sumptibus Andreæ Crook*, 1655. 8°. LT, O, C, EN, DT; BN, CLC, CN, MH, TO, WF, Y.
2231   — —Sectio secvnda. *Typis T. C. sumptibus Andr. Crooke*, 1658. 4°. O, LU, OJ, CK, SC, GU; BN, MU, NC, Y.
2232   —Elements of philosophy. The first section. *By R. & W. Leybourn, for Andrew Crooke*, 1656. 4°. L, O, C, LW, SHR; CLC, IU, MH, MU, NU, WF, Y.
2233–4 Entries cancelled.
       —Elements of policy. 1650. *See* —Humane nature.
2235   —Epistola. [*London?* 1674.] brs. MADAN 2998. O, LW, DU; IU, TO.
2236   —Examinatio & emendatio mathematicæ. *Sumptibus Andreæ Crooke*, 1660. 4°. LT, O, LCP, CS, SC; BN, MU, NN, Y.
2237   —Historia ecclesiastica carmine elegiaco concinnata. [*London*], 1688. 8°. L, O, C, P, CD; CH, IU, MH, TU, WF, Y.
2238   —An historical narration concerning heresie. *Printed* 1680. fol.* T.C.I 397. L, O, C, MR, DT; CH, CN, LC, MH, NU, TO, WF, Y.
2239   [–] The history of the civil wars . . . 1640, to 1660. [*London*], *printed*, 1679. 8°. L, O, CT, ENC, BLH; CH, CU, NC, WF, JF.
2240   [–] —Second edition. —, 1679. 12°. L, O, LW, CT, BAMB, DT; CLC, CN, MH, MU, NU, Y.
2241   Entry cancelled. Ghost.
2242   —Humane nature. *By T. Newcomb, for Fra: Bowman of Oxon*, 1650. 12°. MADAN 2021. LT, O, C, BC, AN; CLC, CN, MH, WF, Y.
2243   — —Second edition. *By T. Newcomb for John Holden*, 1651. 12°. LT, O, C, LW, BIU, EN; CLC, NU, TO, WF, Y.
2243A — —"Second" edition. *By T. Newcomb for Francis Bowman*, 1651. 12°. OB.
2244   Entry cancelled.
       — —Third edition. 1684. *See* —Tripos.
2245   —The last sayings. *For the author's executors*, 1680. brs. L, O, C, LNC; CH, MH, TO, WF, Y.
2245A —A letter about liberty. *By J. Grover, for W. Crooke*, 1676. 12°. T.C.I 237. L, O, CT, LNC, SHR; CLC, IU, MBC, MBP, MH, NU, TO, Y.
2245B — —[Anr. ed.] *By J. C. for W. Crook*, 1677. 12°. T.C.I 269. L, O, C, MAU, EN; CN, NS, NU, TO, WF, Y.
2246   —Leviathan . . . civill. *For Andrew Crooke*, 1651. fol. L, O, C, EN, DT; BN, CH, CN, MHL, MU, NU, Y, AVP. (var.)
2247   — —[Anr. ed.] *For Andrew Ckooke [sic]*, 1651. fol. L, O, C, CT, LNC, SP; CH, CN, IU, LC, MH, WF, Y.
2248   — —[Anr. ed., "civil."] *For Andrew Crooke*, 1651 [1680]. fol. L, O, C, CT, LLU, AU; CH, CU, MH, MU, NP, PBL, Y.
2248A —Leviathan, sive de materia. *Apud Johannem Tomsoni*, 1676. 4°. L; NCD.
2249   — —[Anr. ed.]. *Typis Joannis Thomsonii*, 1678. 8°. CU, MH, MHL, PU.
2250   — —[Anr. ed.] *For M. Pardoe*, 1681. 8°. T.C.I 473. MHL.

2251   —The life of . . . by himself. *For A. C.*, 1680. fol.* T.C.I 384. L, O, LLP, CT, LLU; CH, CN, MBP, MH, WF, Y.
2251A —Memorable sayings of. [*London*, 1680.] brs. T.C.I 384. O; MH, WF.
2252   —Of libertie and necessitie. *By W. B. for F. Eaglesfield*. 1654. 12°. O, C, OC, OQ, P, GK; MH, MU, Y.
2252A —Opera philosophica. *Amstelodami, apud Ioannem Blaeu. Prostant etiam Londini apud Cornelium Bee*, 1668. 4°. O, CK, DCH, GK. (var.)
2253   —Philosophicall rudiments. *By J. G. for R. Royston* 1651. 12°. LT, O, C, LL, ES; CH, CN, MH, NU, WF, Y. (var.)
2254   [–] Principia et problemata aliquot geometrica. *Excudebat J. C. pro Gulielmo Crook*, 1674. 4°.* T.C.I 155. L, O, CK, DCH, EN; BN, Y.
2255   [–] Problemata physica. *Apud Andream Crooke*, 1662. 8°. L, LR, OC, CK, DU, EC; NN.
2256   —Quadratura circuli. *Excudebat J. C., sumptibus Andrææ Crooke*, 1669. 4°.* O, LLL, OC, E, DT; BN, MB.
2257   —The questions concerning liberty. *For Andrew Crook*, 1656. 4°. O, C, LW, CK, LNC; CDA, CLC, CN, MIU, NC, TU, Y.
2258   —Rosetum geometricum. *Excudebat J. C. pro Guilielmo Crook*, 1671. 4°. T.C.I 81. L, O, CK, CT, E; BN, MB, MH, MU.
2259   —Seven philosophical problems. *For William Crook*, 1682. 8°. L, O, LCL, P, BQ; CLC, MH, MU, TO, WF, Y.
2260   [–] Six lessons to the professors. *By J. M. for Andrew Crook*, [1656]. 4°. BBE, IU, MU, NU, Y. [With H2232.]
2261   —Στιγμαι 'αγεωμετριας, . . . or markes. *For Andrew Crooke*, 1657. 4°.* O, C, LCP, DU, SHR; BBE, CLC, CSS, Y.
2262   —A supplement to Mr. Hobbes his works. *By J. C. for W. Crooke*, 1675. 4°.* T.C.I 212. LW, CE, CT, DT; BN, CLC, CN, NU, Y.
2263   —Three papers presented to the Royal Society. *For the author*, 1671. 4°.* T.C.I 87. L, O; CH, CSS, MH.
       —To the . . . Royal Society, . . . a confutation. [n.p., 1671.] *See* — Three papers.
       —To the . . . Royal Society, . . . that the quantity of a line. [n.p., 1671.] *See* — Three papers.
       —To the . . . Royal Society, . . . two propositions. [n.p., 1671.] *See* —Three papers.
2264   —Tracts of . . . containing I. his life. *For William Crooke*, 1681. 8°. T.C.I 463. L, C, CK, DU, WCA; CLC, MH, MU, NU, TO, Y.
2265   —Tracts of . . . containing I. Behemoth. *For W. Crooke*, 1682. 8°. L, O, C, EN, CD; BN, CLC, IU, LC, MH, MU, NP, Y.
2266   —Hobbs's tripos. Third edition. *For Matt. Gilliflower, Henry Rogers, and Tho. Fox*, 1684. 8°. T.C.II 89. L, O, C, LVF, ENC, DT; CH, CN, MH, NU, WF, Y.
2267   —Thomæ Hobbesii Malmesburiensis vita. *Typis*, 1679. 4°.* L, O, OC, CK, BAMB; CH, CLC, CN, MH, PL, TO, Y.
2268   —Thomæ Hobbes Angli Malmesburiensis philosophi vita. *Carolopoli, apud Eleutherium Anglicum*, 1681. colop: *Apud Guil. Crooke*. 8°. T.C.I 385. L, O, C, EN, DT; BN, CLC, CN, MH, NU, WF, Y. (var.).
2269   — —[Anr. ed.] —, 1682. 4°. L, O, CT, EN, DT; BN, CLC, CN, CU, MH, TO, WF, AVP.

2270   Entry cancelled.
       [**Hobbes, William.**] De principiis. 1666. *See* Hobbes,
       Thomas.
       Hobbs, Matthew. Almanack. 1693. *See* Almanacs.
       —Chaldæus Anglicanus. 1695. *See* Almanacs.

2271   [**Hobbs, Richard.**] The Quakers looking glass look'd
       upon. *For Francis Smith*, 1673. 4°.* LF.

2272   **Hobson, Paul.** The fallacy of infants baptisme dis-
       covered. *Printed*, 1645. 4°.* LT, CS, GU, DT; CH, CN,
       NHC, NU.

2273   —Fourteen queries and ten absurdities. *By Henry Hills
       for William Hutchison in Durham*, 1655. 8°. LT, O; NHC.

2274   —A garden inclosed. *By Iames and Ioseph Moxon, for
       Henry Overton; and for Giles Calvert*, 1647. 8°. LT, LCL,
       ORP; CH, NU, Y.

2274A [–] Innocency, though under a cloud. *Printed*, 1664. 8°.
       LW.

2275   —Practical divinity. [*London*], *sould by R. Harford*, 1646.
       8°. LT; CH.

2276   —A treatise containing three things. *By M. S. for Tho:
       Brewster*, 1653. 8°. LT, LLP; WF.

2276A ——[Anr. ed.]. *By M. S. for Tho. Brewster, and sold by
       William Hutcheson, in Durham*, 1653. 8°. Y.

2277   **Hobson, Thomas.** The Bristol-narrative. *By William
       Godbid*, 1675. 4°.* L, LPR; Y.

2278   Hobson's choice. A poem. *Printed, and sold by John
       Nutt*, 1700. fol.* CLC, IU, MH, TU, Y.

2279   **Hockin, Thomas.** A discourse of the nature of God's
       decrees. *For Edward Vize.* 1684. 8°. O, C, LW, SP, DT;
       CLC, IU, MB, SE, WF.

2279A Hocus pocus junior. The anatomy of legerdemain.
       Fourth edition. *By G. Dawson, to be sold by Thomas
       Vere*, 1654. 4°. L, LN; NP.

2279B —Fifth edition. —, 1658. 4°. L.

2280   —"Fifth" edition. —, *and Francis Grove*, 1658. 4°. GU;
       CLC.

2281   —Seventh edition. *By G. Purslow, and are to be sold by
       Thomas Vere*, 1671. 4°. LG.

2281A —Eighth edition. [1671?] 4°. NN.

2282   —Ninth edition. *By T. H. and are to be sold by J. Deacon*,
       1682. 4°. GU.

2282A —Tenth edition. —, 1682. 4°. T.C.I 513. DT.

2282AB —"Tenth" edition. *By, and are to be sold by J. Deacon*,
       1683. 4°. L, GU.

2282AC —Eleventh edition. *By J. M. for J. Deacon, sold by J.
       Gilbertson*, 1686. 4°. L, CM.

2282B —Twelfth edition. *By J. M. and are to be sold by J. Deacon*,
       1691. 4°. DT.

2282C —Thirteenth edition. *By W. Onley, to be sold by J.
       Deacon*, 1697. 4°. L.

2283   **Hodden, Richard.** The one good way of God. *By J. C.
       and are to be sold by Richard Moon, in Bristol*, 1661. 4°.
       L, O, LF, BBN, GU, DT; MH, PH, PSC, Y.

2284   **Hodder, James.** Hodder's arithmetick. *By R. Daven-
       port for Tho. Rooks*, 1661. 12°. LT, LU; MB, MH.

2284A ——Second edition. 1663. 12°. LCL.

2284B ——Third edition. *By J. Dover, for Tho. Rooks*, 1664.
       12°. LG, LU.

2285   ——Fourth edition. *By J. Darby, for Tho. Rooks*, 1667.
       12°. C; CH, Y.

2285A ——Ninth edition. *By J. R., for Tho. Rooks*, 1671. 12°.
       T.C.I 90. L, LU.

2286   ——Tenth edition. *By T. J. for Tho. Rooks*, 1672. 12°.
       L, O; CLC, NC, WF.

2286A ——Twelfth edition. *By T. H. for Ric. Chiswell and
       Thomas Sawbridge*, 1678. 12°. T.C.I 314. C; IU, WF.

2287   ——Thirteenth edition. *For R. Chiswell, and T. Saw-
       bridge*, 1681. 12°. T.C.I 446. O, C.

2287A ——Fourteenth edition. *For Ric. Chiswell and Tho.
       Sawbridge*, 1683. 12°. L; CH, NIC.

2288   ——Fifteenth edition. —, 1685. 12°. T.C.II 119. L, O, DU;
       CLC, IU, MU, Y.

2288A ——Seventeenth edition. —, 1690. 12°. LU, LIU.

2289   ——Eighteenth edition. —, 1693. 12°. T.C.II 430. L, O;
       NN.

2289A ——Nineteenth edition. *For Ric. Chiswel, and Geo. Saw-
       bridge*, 1694. 12°. L.

2290   ——Twentieth edition. —, 1697. 12°. L, C, CS; CH, CLC.

2290A ——Twenty-first edition. —, 1699. 12°. GU; MB, RBU.

2291   —Hodder's decimal arithmetick. *By J. C. for Tho:
       Rooks*, 1668. 8°. L, LR, OC; NC, WF.

2292   ——[Anr. ed.] —, 1671. 12°. T.C.I 90. O; NC.

2292A —The pen-man's recreation. [*London*], *sold by Peter
       Stent*, 1659. fol. L.

2292AB ——[Anr. ed.] [*London*, 1660?] obl. fol.* L; IU.

2292AC ——[Anr. ed.] 1667. fol. OP.

2292B ——[Anr. ed.] [*London*], *sold by John Overton*, 1673. fol.
       T.C.I 122. L.

2292C —Hodder's remaines. [*London*], *sold by Iohn Overton*,
       [1675?]. * CN.

2293   **H[oddesdon], J[ohn].** The history of the life and death
       of Sr. Thomas More. *For George Eversden, and Henry
       Eversden*, 1662. 12°. L, O, C, LG, CT, WCA; CH, CSU, IU,
       MH, WF.

2294   —The holy lives of God's prophets. *For Wil: Hope*,
       1654. 8°. LT, O, AN, P; MH, Y.

2295   —Sion and Parnassvs. *By R. Daniel for G. Eversden*, 1650.
       8°. L, O, LG, LW; CH, CLC, IU, LC, MH, WF, Y.

2296   [–] Tho. Mori vita & exitvs. *By E. Cotes, for George
       Eversden*, 1652. 8°. LT, O, LL, CT, EN; CH, CN, MH, MU,
       NC, TU, WF, Y. (var.)

2297   **Hodge, John.** Viro illustrissimo . . . D. Joanni Mid-
       deltonio carmen. *Edinburgi, ex officinâ societatis
       stationariorum*, 1661. 4°. ALDIS 1699. L, AU.

2297A The hodge-podge of this government. [*London?* 1691.]
       brs. HH.

2298   [**Hodges, James.**] A defence of the Scots abdicating
       Darien. [*Edinburgh?*], *printed*, 1700. 8°. ALDIS 3951. L,
       O, C, EN, GU, DT; BN, HR, CH, CN, LC, MH, TU, WF, Y.

2299   [–] The present state of England, as to coin. *For Andr.
       Bell*, 1697. 8°. L, O, EN, GU, DT; CH, IU, LC, MH, NC, Y.

2299A [–] A short vindication of Phil Scots defence. *Printed*
       1700. 8°.* L, O, EN, ES, GU; CH, CN, MH, NC, NN, WF.

2300   [–] A supplement to the present state of England. *For Andr. Bell; and sold by R. Baldwin,* 1697. 8°.* L, LUG, CD; CLC, MH, NC, RPJ, Y.

2301   **Hodges, John.** How to revive the Golden Age. *By H. Bruges for G. Widdows,* [1666?]. brs. L; MH.

2302   [–] The true and onely causes of the great want of moneys. *By P. L. for I. H., and are to be sold by William Whitwood,* 1666. brs. LUG.

2303   — —Second edition ["money"]. *By H. B. and are to be sold by W. Whitwood,* 1673. brs. L; MH, NN.

2304   **Hodges, Nathaniel.** Λοιμολογια. Sive pestis. *Typis Gul. Godbid, sumptibus Josephi Nevill,* 1671. 8°. T.C.I 98. L, GH, DT; NU.

2305   — —[Anr. ed.] —, 1672. 8°. L, O, C, LIU, DT; BN, CH, MH, PL, WF, HC.

2306   —Oratio anniversaria. *Typis J. Playford,* 1684. 4°.* L, LCP, LSC.

2307   —Vindiciæ medicinæ & medicorum: or an apology. *By John Field,* 1665. 8°. O.

2308   — —[Anr. ed.] *By J. F. for Henry Broom,* 1666. 8°. L, LCP, LCS, P, GH; WF, WSG.

2309   **Hodges, Richard.** Enchiridion arithmeticon, or, a manual of millions. Second edition. *By J. F. and are sold by Richard Hodges the author; and by N. Bourn: also by J. Hancock, L. Lloyd, and H. Cripps,* 1651. 8°. NC.

2309A   — —"Second" edition. *By J. Flesher, and are sold by Nicholas Bourn,* 1653. 8°. L; CH, WF.

2310   — —Third edition. *Ellen Cotes,* 1670. 8°. CT, EO.

2310A   — —[Anr. ed.] *By E. Cotes for Robert Horne,* 1670. 8°. T.C.I 22. OC; CU.

2311   —The English primrose. *For Richard Cotes,* 1644. 8°. L, O; CH.

2311A   —Most plain directions for true-writing. *By W. D. for Rich. Hodges to bee sold by him. Also by Nicolas Bourn,* 1653. 8°. OC.

2312   —The plainest directions for the true-writing of English. *By William Du-gard for Thomas Euster,* 1649. 8°. LT, C.

2313   —A special help to orthographie. *For Richard Cotes,* 1643. 4°.* LT, LLL, P; LC, MH.

2314   **Hodges, Thomas,** *of Kensington.* A glimpse of Gods glory. *For Iohn Bartlet,* 1642. 4°.* LT, O, C, EN, DT; CSS, IU, MH, MU, NU, WF, Y.

2315   —The growth and spreading of hæresie. *By T. R. and E. M. for Abel Roper,* 1647. 4°. LT, O, C, EN, DT; CH, IU, MH, NU, WF, Y.

2316   —Inaccessible glory. *For William Leak,* 1655. 4°.* L, O, LW, LSD, EN; WF.

2317   —Sions Halelujah. *By J. Best, for Andrew Crook,* 1660. 4°.* LT, O, LG, LLP, LW, CS, BLH; CU, MH, NN, NU, WF.

2318   **Hodges, Thomas,** *of Soulderne.* A cordiall against the feare of death. *Oxford, by H. H. for Thomas Robinson,* 1659. 4°.* MADAN 2446. L, O, C, LW, CS, DU, DT; MH, MIU, NU, WF.

2319   —The creatures goodness. *For Tho. Parkhurst,* 1675. 4°.* T.C.I 216. L, O, LW, WCA; CH, MH, NU, WF, Y.

2320   —The hoary head crowned. *Oxford, by L. Lichfield for T. Robinson,* 1652. 4°.* MADAN 2195. L, O, C, LW, SP; CLC, NU, TO, WF, Y.

2321   [–] The necessity dignity and duty of gospel ministers. *For William Rogers,* 1685. 4°.* T.C.II 134. L, O, LW, CT, EC, WCA, BLH; CH, CLC, NGT, NU, WF.

2322   —A Scriptvre-catechisme. *Oxford, by H: Hall for T. Robinson,* 1658. 8°. MADAN 2389. L, O, LW; MH, NU, WF, Y.

2323   —A treatise concerning prayer. *By John Grismond,* 1656. 12°. LT, C, P; NU, Y.

2324   [–] A treatise of marriage. *By J. D., to be sold by R. Chiswel,* 1673. 8°. T.C.I 148. L, O, CT, P, SP, ENC; MH, WF.

2324A   [–] —[Anr. ed.] *For W. Rogers,* 1679. CLC.

2324B   —Two consolatory letters. *By A. Maxwell for S. Gellibrand,* 1669. 4°.* O, LW.

2325   [–] The vanity of man. *By J. B. for Tho. Parkhurst,* 1676. 4°. T.C.I 252. L, O, C, CS, WCA, BLH; IU, NU, WF.

2326   Entry cancelled. *See preceding entry.*

2326A   **Hodges, William.** The distressed seamans groans. [*London?* 1696.] cap., fol.* PL.

2327   [–] Great Britain's groans. [*London*], *printed,* 1695. 4°.* L, O, LG, CM, LSD, MR; CH, CSS, CN, NC, WF, Y.

2328   —The groans of the poor. *Printed,* 1696. 4°.* L, O, C, SP, DT; CH, CSS, IU, LC, MH, NC, PU, WF, Y.

2328A   [–] An humble proposal. [*London?* 1693.] cap., fol.* L; MH, NN.

2329   [–] Humble proposals for the relief, encouragement . . ., seamen. [*London*], *printed,* 1695. 4°. L, O, LG, P, SP; CH, IU, MH, NP, WF, Y.

2330   — —[Anr. ed.] —, 1695. 8°. L, O, C; CN, NC.

2331   —An humble representation of the seamens misery. [*London?* 1694/5.] cap., fol.* L, O, LNM, MR.

2332   —Ruin to ruin. *Printed,* 1699. 4°.* L, O, LUG, OC, EN; CH, IU, MH, NC, WF, Y.

2332A   **Hodgeson, Marmaduke.** A treatise of practical gauging. *By J. Richardson for Will. Court,* 1689. 8°. L; CH, WF.

2333   **Hodgkin, Samuel.** A caution to the sons of Sion. *For the author,* 1660. 4°.* LT, O, EN; PH, PSC.

2334   **Hodgkins, John.** A new plot discovered, practised by an assembly of Papists. [*London*], *printed,* 1641. 4°.* LT, O, C, LLL, LVF; CH, MH, TU.

2335   **Hodgson, Mr.** Catalogue of the library. *29 Apr.* 1698. 4°. L.

2335A   [**Hodgson, John.**] A letter from a member of the army, to the Committee of Safety. *For Giles Calvert,* 1659. 4°.* L, LG; INU, MH, PH.

2336   —Love, kindness, and due respect. *For Giles Calvert,* 1659. 4°.* LT, LF; PH.

2337   **Hody, Humfrey.** Anglicani novi schismatis redargutio. *Oxonii, e theatro Sheldoniano,* 1691. 4°. T.C.II 382. L, O, C, EN, DT; CLC, NU, PL, TSM, WF.

2338   [–] Animadversions on two pamphlets lately publish'd. *For John Everingham,* 1696. 4°.* T.C.II 587. L, O, CT, BAMB, EN; CLC, CN, MHL, WF, Y.

2339 —The case of sees vacant. *By J. H. for Henry Mortlock,* 1693. 4°. T.C.II 449. L, O, C, EN, DT; CLC, IU, MH, NU, WF, Y.

2340 —Contra historiam Aristeæ. *Oxonii, typis Leon. Lichfield, impensis Ant. Stephens,* 1684. 8°. L, O, C, AN, EN, DT; BN, CH, CU, MH, OLU, ASU.

2341 ——[Anr. ed.] *Oxonii, typis Leon. Lichfield, prostant venales Londini apud Sam. Smith,* 1685. 8°. T.C.II 128. L, O, C, CT, P, DT; BN, CH, MH, NU, WF, Y.

2342 —A letter from *Oxford, by L. Lichfield, for Ant. Pisly,* 1692. 4°.* L, O, C, EN, DT; CH, LC, MH, NU, PU, WF, Y.

2343 Entry cancelled.
—Oxford-antiquary. 1691. *See title.*

2344 —The resurrection of the same body. *For Awnsham and John Churchill,* 1694. 8°. T.C.II 536. L, O, C, DU, DT; CH, IU, MH, NU, WF, Y.

2345 [–] A short examination of a discourse concerning edification. *Printed: and are to be sold by A. Baldwin,* 1700. 4°.* T.C.III 228. L, O, LW, EC, EN, DT; CLC, IU, MH, NU, TO.

2346 [–] Some thoughts on a convocation. *For Tim. Childe,* 1699. 4°.* T.C.III 92. L, O, C, CT, EC, NPL; Y.
—Unreasonableness of a separation. 1691. *See* Nicephorus.

2347 **Hoffman, Benjamin.** Some considerations of present use. *For F. Gardiner,* 1683. 4°.* T.C.II 13. L, O, C, YM, DT; CH, CLC, Y.

2348 **Hoffman, John.** The principles of Christian religion. *Oxford, by L. Lichfield,* 1653. 8°. L.

2349 ——Second edition. *By T. D. for the author, to be sold by Giles Widdowes,* 1675. 8°. T.C.I 191. O.

2349A [**Hofmann, François.**] A patterne of popish peace. *By L. N. for Richard Whitaker,* 1644. 12°. L, O.

2350 **Hog, William.** Ad Augustissimum, invictissimumque Magnæ Britanniæ, ... Gulielmum III. *Typis F. Collins,* 1697. 4°.* L, O, LW, MR, EN; MH, MM, ZWT.

2351 —Ad virum nobilissimum, ... Carolum Duncombum. *Anno Domini,* 1699. 4°.* L, C; MH, Y.

2352 No entry.

2353 Entry cancelled.
—Cato divinus. 1699. *See* Bible. Latin.

2354 —Descriptio accipitris poetica. [*London,* 1690?] 4°. L.

2355 —In memoriam . . . Mariæ. [*London,* 1695?] cap., fol.* L, LLP, MR; MH.

2356 [–] In obitum Christiani quinti. [*London?* 1699.] 4°.* L, C.

2357 —In obitum illustrissimi Gulielmi, Ducis Glocestriæ. [*London,* 1700.] cap., 4°.* L; MH.

2358 —In obitum præclari Jesu Christi ministri, Gulielmi Batesii. *Impensis autoris,* 1699. fol.* L, LW, MR.

2359 —Paraphrasis in Jobum poetica. *Typis Thomæ Braddyll, & impensis autoris,* 1682. 8°. L, O, C, DCH, RPL; CH, IU, MH, NCD, NP, PU, WF, Y.

2360 ——[Anr. ed.] *Typis H. C. sumptibus Thomæ Malthus.* 1683. 8°. T.C.II 30. L.

2361-3 Entries cancelled.
—Paraphrasis poetica in Ecclesiasten. 1685. *See* —Satyra sacra.

—Paraphrasis poetica in tria. 1690. *See* Milton, John.
—Proverbia Solomonis. 1699. *See* Bible. Latin. Cato divinus.

2364 —Satyra sacra in vanitatem mundi. [*London*], *typis Richardsonianis in usum autoris,* [1685]. 8°. L, C, LLP, LW, OC, DU, P; CH, IU, MB, NP, WF, Y.

2365 [–] Victoria augustissimi Magnæ Britanniæ &c. regis Gulielmi tertii. *Anno Domini,* 1695. 4°.* L, O, LW, EN.

2366 Hogan-moganides: or, the Dutch Hudibras. *For William Cademan,* 1674. 8°. T.C.I 163. L, O, C, LLU, E; CH, CN, LC, MH, MU, TU, WF, Y.

2366A [**Hogarth, Richard.**] Thesaurarium trilingue. *By J. L., to be sold by Randal Taylor,* 1689. 8°. T.C.II 261. OLL, SHREWSBURY SCHOOL; CLC, MH.

2367 **H[ogg], J[ohn].** An answer to a small treatise call'd just measurs. [*London*], *printed,* 1693. 4°. L, O, LF, BP.

2368 [–] An answer to severall material passages. *Printed,* 1691. 4°. LF, O, BBN, P; CH, MHS, PHS.

2368A —Some observations vpon a sermon. [*London*], *printed,* 1675. 4°.* LF.

2368B —Some remains of. *Printed,* 1698. 4°. MH, MWA, Y.

2369 —Something offered to the consideration of Friends. [*London?* 1675.] 4°.* PH.
Hogs caracter [*sic*]. 1642. *See* Heywood, Thomas.

2370 Entry cancelled.
Hojan Effendi. Reign of Sultan Orchan. 1652. *See* Sa'd al-Din ibn Hasanjan.

2371 Holborn-drollery. *For Robert Robinson,* 1673. 8°. T.C.I 127. L; CH, CLC, CN, LC, MH.

2372 The Holbourne Hector. *For C. N.* 1675. 4°.* LG.
[**Holbourne, Richard.**] Free-holders grand inquest. [n.p., 1648.] *See* Filmer, *Sir* Robert.

2372A **Holborne, Sir Robert.** The learned readings of. *For Matt. Gillyflower,* 1680. 8°. LC, MH.

2373 ——[Anr. ed.] *For Sam. Heyrick, and Matthew Gilliflower,* 1681. 8°. T.C.I 450. L, O, LL, LMT, CT; CH, CN, LC, MHL, NCL, WF, YL.

2374 —The reading in Lincolnes-Inne, Feb. 28. 1641. *Oxford: by Leonard Lichfield,* 1642. 4°.* MADAN 1230. LT, O, C, CT, DT; CH, CN, MH, NC, WF, Y.

2374A **H[olcroft], F[rancis].** A vvord to the saints from the watch tower. *Printed,* 1668. 8°.* O.

2375 **Holden, Henry.** The analysis of divine faith. *Printed at Paris,* 1658. 4°. L, O, C, OC, DUS, DT; CLC, NU, TU, WG, Y.

2376 [–] Check: or inquiry. *Printed,* 1662. 4°. L, O, LLP, SP, D, DM; MIU, NU, TU, Y.

2377 —Doctor Holden's letter to a friend of his. [*Douay?* 1657?] cap., 4°.* L; TU.

2378 —A letter written by. [*Douay?* 1657.] 4°.* L.

2379 —A letter written by . . . to Mr. Graunt. *Printed at Paris,* 1661. 4°.* L, LVF, CT, DU, CD.

Holden, Mary. Woman's almanack. 1688. *See* Almanacs.

2380 **Holden, Richard.** The improvement of navigation. *By J. Macock, for John Martyn,* 1680. 4°.* L, C, DT; CH, WF, Y.

2381   **H[olden], S[amuel]**. D. E. defeated. *For R. Royston, to be sold by John Jones in Worcester*, 1662. 4°.* O, LLP, CS; IU, MH, MIU, NU, TU.

2381A   [–] —[Anr. ed.] *For R. Royston*, 1662. 4°.* LLP, OC, MR, SP, DU; MIU, WF.

2382   —Two sermons. *For J. Edwyn*, 1676. 4°. T.C.I 250. L, O, CT, LSD; NU, PL, WF, Y.

2383   **H[older], A[nthony]**. A discovery of two unclean spirits. *For Giles Calvert*, 1657. 4°.* LT, LF, BBN; MH, PH.

2384   **Holder, Christopher**. The faith and testimony of the martyrs. [*London?* 1670.] cap., 4°.* LF, MR; CH, MH, NN, RPJ.

2385   **Holder, William**. A discourse concerning time. *By J. Heptinstall, for L. Meredith*. 1694. 8°. L, O, C, ENC, DT; CH, IU, MH, PL, WF, JF.

2386   —Elements of speech. *By T. N. for J. Martyn*, 1669. 8°. L, O, C, LL, E, CD; BN, CH, IU, LC, MH, NP, WF, Y.

2387   — —[Anr. ed.] *Mark Pardoe*, 1677. 8°. L, LCS; BN.

2388   [–] Introductio ad chronologiam. *Oxoniæ, typis L. Lichfield, Sumptibus Geo. West*, 1691. 8°. O, CT, BC, NE, EN; CH, CLC, MH, WF, Y.

2388A   —A supplement to the philosophical transactions of July, 1670. *For Henry Brome*, 1678. 4°.* L, CS; CLC, CSS, WSG, Y.

2389   —A treatise of the natural grounds, . . . of harmony. *By J. Heptinstall, for the author, and sold by John Carr*, 1694. 8°. T.C.II 533. C, LW, DT; IU.

2389A   — —[Anr. ed.] *By J. Heptinstall, for John Carr*, 1694. 8°. L, O, DT; MBP, Y.

2389B   — —[Anr. ed.] *By J. Heptinstall, and sold by J. Carr, B. Aylmer, W. Hensman, and L. Meredith*, 1694. 8°. L, O, CT; CH, CLC, SE, WF.

2390   No entry.

2391   [**Holding, J.**] The last great and terrible sea-fight between the English and the Dutch. *For G. Horton*, [1652]. 4°.* LT.

2392   **Holdsworth, Richard**. An answer without a question. *Printed*, 1649. 4°.* O; CSS, IU.

2393–5 Entries cancelled.

    —Angell's inspections. 1650. *See* —Valley of vision.

    --David's devotion. 1650. *See* —Valley of vision.

    —Geust-chamber. 1650. *See* —Valley of vision.

2396   —The peoples happinesse. *By Roger Daniel, Cambridge*, 1642. 4°.* O, C, DU; CH, NU, WF, Y.

2397   —Prælectiones theologicæ. *Typis Jacobi Flesher: prostant apud Gul. Wells & Rob. Scott*, 1661. fol. L, O, C, E, DT; BN, CH, NP, NU, WF, Y.

2398   —Quaestiones duæ. *Excudebat G. D. impensis Gulielmi Nealand, Cantabrigiensis*, 1653. 8°.* O, CT.

2399–2400 Entries cancelled.

    —Saints heritage. 1650. *See* —Valley of vision.

    —Saints progresse. 1650. *See* —Valley of vision.

2401   —A sermon preached . . . 27 of March. [*Cambridge*], *by Roger Daniel*, 1642. 4°.* LT, O, C, DU, YM; CH, CSS, IU, MH, NU, TU, WF, Y.

2402   Entry cancelled.

2403   —Sufferers crowne. 1650. *See* —Valley of vision.

2403   —The valley of vision. *By Matthew Simmons*, 1651. 4°. LCL, LW, DT; NU.

2404   — —[Anr. ed.] *By M. S. and are to be sold by R. Tomlins; and Rob. Littlebury*, 1651. 4°. LT, O, C, BC, P; BN, CLC, MH, NU, WF, Y.

2405   — —[Anr. ed.] *For Peter Dring*, 1661. 4°. LLP; MWA, NU.

2406   Entry cancelled.

    —Vigilant servant. 1650. *See* —Valley of vision.

2407   **Holdsworth, Thomas**. Impar conatui: or, Mr. J. B. *For William Keblewhite*, 1695. 4°. L, O, CCA, OCC, WCA, CD; CLC, NU, Y.

2408   **Hole, Matthew**. A correct copy of some letters written to J. M. *For H. Chauklin, in Taunton, and are sold by R. Knaplock*, 1698. 8°. T.C.III 36. L, O, CT, AN, BR; CLC, MH, NR, WF.

2409   —The expediency of a publick liturgy. *For Matt. Wotton*, 1697. 4°.* L, OCC, BR, LIU; NGT, NRU.

2410   —Letters written to J. M. . . . the second part. *For, and to be sold by J. Taylor, and T. Bever in London; H. Clements in Oxon, and J. Miller in Sherborn*, 1699. 8°. L, OCC, CS, LSD; CLC, MBA, WF.

2411   —Our Saviours passion. *For Richard Royston, to be sold by Abisha Brocas in Exon*, 1670. 4°.* O, CS.

2412   —A sermon preached at Taunton. *For Randalph* [*sic*] *Taylor*, 1689. 4°.* L, O, BR; CLC, CN, TSM, WF.

2413   —A sermon preached . . . 19th day of August, 1695. *For Mat. Wotton*. 1696. 4°.* L, O, LW, OCC, BR, LIU; CH, NRU, WF.

2414   —The true reformation of manners. *Oxford, by L. Lichfield, for Henry Clements*, 1699. 4°. L, O, C, BR, CD; CH, CLC, CU, NU, WF, Y.

2415   **Holgate, William**. A brief collection of certain instances. [*London*], *printed*, 1686. 4°.* L, LF, BBN, YM; CH, IU, MH, NU, PH, Y.

2416   —To all who desire satisfaction. *Printed and sold by Andrew Sowle*, 1683. 4°.* L, O, LF, BBN, MR; CLC, MH, NCD, NU, PH, PSC, WF, Y.

    Holl ddled-swydd dyn. 1672. *See* Allestree, Richard.

    Holland. *See* Netherlands.

2417   **H[olland], G[uy]**. The grand prerogative. *By Roger Daniel, to be sold by Antony Williamson*, 1653. 8°. LT, O, C, CT, BSM, SC; CH, WF, WG.

2418   **Holland, Henry Rich, earl of**. The copy of a letter sent from the Earle of Holland. [*London*], *anno Domini* 1641. 4°.* LT, CT, MR, YM; CH, MBP, MIU, MM, NU, WF, Y.

2419   —A declaration made. *For Mathew Walbancke*, 1643. 4°.* LT, O, C, LSD, DT; CH, CN, MH, TU, WF, Y.

2420   Entry cancelled.

    —Lawes and ordinances of warre. 1641. *See* title.

2420A   —The Earle of Hollands letter. [*London*], *printed* 1641. 4°.* OC, ESS; WF, Y.

2421   —The Lord of Hollands letter. [*London*], *printed*, 1641. 4°.* L, O; CH, CN.

2422   —Two speeches . . . 10. of Novemb. *By J. F. for Peter Cole*. 1642. 4°.* LT, O, C, SP, DT; CH, MH, MU, TU, WF, Y.

2423   —A worthy speech spoken. *By T. Fawcet, Iune, 21. 1642.* 4°.* MR, DN; IU.

2423A   ——[*Anr. ed.*] *By T. Fawcet, Iune 22. 1642.* 4°.* CSS, Y.

2424   **Holland, Hezekiah.** Adam's condition in Paradise. *For George Calvert,* 1656, 4°, O; CLC.

2425   —A Christian looking-glasse. *By T. R. & E. M. for George Calvert,* 1649. 8°. LT, O, LCL; IU, NU.

2426   —An exposition or, a short, but full, plaine, . . . revelation of Saint John. *By T. R. and E. M. for George Calvert,* 1650. 4°. LT, O, C, LW, BLH; CLC, MH, NC, NU, WF.

2427   **H[olland], J[ohn].** A short discourse on the present temper of the nation. *Edinburgh, by John Reid, sold by Mrs. Beiglie,* 1696. 4°.* ALDIS 3565. L, LUG, ENC, EN, ES; CLC, IU, MH, RPJ, Y.

2428   **Holland, John,** *porter.* The smoke of the bottomlesse pit. *For John Wright,* 1651. 4°.* LT, OC, BC, DT; NU.

2429   **Holland, Sir John.** Sir Iohn Holland his speech in Parliament. Declaring the great and manifold grievances. [*London*], *printed,* 1641. 4°.* L, O, LNC, E, DT; CH, IU, MH, MU, NU, TU, WF.

2430   —His speech in Parliament. Declaring. *For John Thomas,* 1641. 4°.* LT, SP; WF, Y.

2431   **Holland, Richard.** An explanation of Mr Gunter's quadrant. *Oxford, by Leon. Lichfield,* 1676. 8°.* MADAN 3108. O, OC.

2431A   [–] Globe notes. [*Oxford*], 1666. 8°.* L, LSD; CLC, RPJ.

2432   ——[*Anr. ed.*] *Oxford, by L. Lichfield, for R. Davis,* 1678. 8°.* MADAN 3178. L, O, OM; NN, WF.

2432A   ——[*Anr. ed.*] *For a friend of the authors,* 84 [*i.e.* 1684]. 8°.* O; CH, WF.

2433   —Notes shewing how to get the angle of parallax. *Oxford, by L. Lichfield for Richard Davis,* 1668. 8°.* MADAN 2804. L, O, C, OM, LR.

2434   **Holland, Richard,** *chaplain.* The good Samaritane. *For J. Back,* 1700. 4°.* T.C.III 208. L, LLP, OC, CT, WCA; Y.

2435   —A sermon preached . . . March 19, 1685. *For Walter Kettilby,* 1685. 4°.* T.C.II 123. L, OC, C; CH, CLC, WF, Y.

2436   —A sermon preached . . . February 11th, 1$^{699}_{700}$. *For J. Back; and sold by J. Nutt,* 1700. 4°.* T.C.III 183. L, O, OC, CT, BLH; CH, NPT, PH, PSC, Y.

2436A   ——Second edition. *By J. Richardson for J. Back,* 1700. 4°.* T.C.III 219. C, NE, WCA; NC, WF.

2437   [**Holland, Samuel.**] Don Zara del Fogo. *By T. W. for Tho. Vere,* 1656. 8°. L.

2438   —An elegie humbly offered . . . Earl of Rochester. *For the author,* 1680. brs. L.

2438A   —The muses holocaust. *For the author,* 1662. fol. * CT.

2439   —On the death of my much honoured friend, Colonel Richard Lovelace. An elegie. [*London,* 1660.] brs. C.

2440   —On the untimely and much lamented death of Mrs Anne Gray. [*London,* 1657.] brs. LT.

2441   —A panegyrick on the coronation of . . . Charles II. *For William Plaice,* 1661. fol.* L, C; CH, Y.

2442   —The Phaenix her arrival. *For the author,* 1662. fol.* CH, MH.

2443   —Romancio-mastrix. [*London*], *for the author,* 1660. 8°. L, O, CASTLE ASHBY; CH, CN, MH, Y.

2444   —To the best of monarchs. [*London*], *by S. Griffin, for Matthew Wallbancke,* 1660. brs. LT.

2444A   ——[*Anr. ed.*] *Edinburgh, C. Higgins,* 1660. brs. ALDIS 1645.7. EN.

2445   [–] Wit and fancy in a maze. *By T. W. for Tho. Vere,* 1656. 8°. L, O; CH, WF.

        Holland nightingale. [n.p.], 1672. *See* O., J.

2445A   Holland turn'd to tinder. *By F. Crowch for F. Coles, T. Vere, and J. Wright,* [1666]. brs. EUING 134. GU.

2446   The Hollanders embassage to England. *For Iohn Smith,* 1642. 4°.* LT, O, CT, LNC, CD; CLC, CN, MH, Y.

2446A   **Hollar, Wenceslaus.** Aula veneris. 1644. 12°. NN, UCLA, WF.

2447   —The kingdome of England, & principality of Wales, exactly described. [*London*], *sold by Thomas Ienner,* 1644. fol.* O, C, R; CH, CLC, CN, WF, Y, YBA.

2448   ——[*Anr. ed.*] —, 1671. fol. O, NOT (impf.); CH.

2448A   ——[*Anr. ed.*] *Printed and sold by John Garrett,* 1676. fol. L, O, BC; MIU, NC, WF, Y. (var.)

2449   —Navium variæ figuræ. [*London*], 1647. fol.* O; CH, NP.

2449A   —A new and perfect book of beasts, flowers. *Printed and are to be sould by Iohn Overton,* 1674. fol. ST. BRIDE'S.

2449B   —A new book of flowers & fishes. [*London*], *printed and published by Iohn Overton,* 1671. fol.* CH.

2449C   —Propositions concerning the map of London. [*London,* 1660.] brs. WF.

2450   —Theatrum mulierum. *Printed and sold by Henry Overton,* [1643]. 8°. L, O, C, LG, LLU; CH, CLC, LC, TO.

2450A   ——[*Anr. ed.*] *Sold by R. Sayer,* 1643. 8°. A.

2451   ——[*Anr. ed.*] *By Peter Stent,* [*after* 1643]. O, C; BBE, AVP.

2451A   —A true and exact prospect of . . . London. [*London,* 1666.] brs. WF.

2452   [**Holles, Denzil Holles**], *baron.* The case stated concerning the judicature of the house of peers. [*London?*], *printed,* 1675. 8°. L, O, C, EN, DT; BN, CH, MHL, MU, WF, Y.

2453   [–] The case stated of the jurisdiction. *Printed,* 1676. 8°. L, O, C, EN, DT; BN, CH, CN, LC, MIU, PU, WF, Y.

2454   —The danger of Europe, from the growing power of France. colop: *Printed,* 1681. 4°.* MM.

2455   Entry cancelled.
        —Desires propounded. 1647. *See title.*
        —An exact and true relation of the dangerous . . . fight, . . . neere Kyneton. *See title.*

2456–8 No entries.

2459   [–] The grand question concerning the iudicature. *For Richard Chiswel,* 1669. 8°. L, O, C, NE, DT; BN, CLC, CN, LC, MH, NCL, TO, Y.

2460   —A grave and learned speech, or an apology. [*London*], *printed,* 1647. 4°.* LT, O, C, DT; CH, MH, MU, WF, Y.

2461   [–] A letter of a gentleman to his friend, shewing that the bishops. [*London*], *printed,* 1679. 4°.* 31 pp. O, MR, EN, DT; CH, TO.

2461aA [–]—[*Anr. ed.*] —, 1679. 8°. 119 pp. L, O, C, EN, DT; CN, MHL, NU, TU, Y.

2461A [–] —[Anr. ed.] *For C. R. and to be sold by Thomas Sharp,* 1679. 4°.* T.C.I 375. C, LW, OC, CS; CLC, IU, LC, MH, PL.

2462 [–] A letter to Monsieur Van B— de M— at Amsterdam. [*London,* 1676]. cap., 4°.* L, O, C, MR, EN; CH, CN, MH, MU, WF, Y.

2463 [–] The Long Parliament dissolved. [*London*], *printed,* 1676. 4°.* L, O, CT, MR, DT; CH, CN, NC, PL, WF, Y. (var.)

2464 —Memoirs of. *For Tim. Goodwin,* 1699. 8°. L, O, LVF, CT, EN, DT; BN, CH, CN, LC, MH, MU, NP, NU, TO, TU, Y.

2465 [–] The petition of the members of the House of Commons, who are accused by the army . . . 29. of June 1647. *For Ralph Smith,* 1647. 4°.* LT, O, C, LLU, MR; CH, IU, MH, NU, PT, WF, Y.

2466 —Lord Hollis his remains. *For R. Janeway,* 1682. 8°. L, O, C, LG, EN, DT; BN, CH, CN, LC, MHL, MU, NU, WF, Y.

2467 [–] Some considerations upon the question, whether the Parliament. [*London*], *printed,* 1676. 4°.* L, O, CJ, MR, EN; CH, CN, MH, NC, TU, WF, Y.

2468 —Densell Hollis esq. his speech at the delivery of the protestation . . . 4. May, 1641. [*London*], *for J. A.,* 1641. 4°.* LT, O, LVF, BC, YM; CH, CLC, CN, MH, Y.

2468A ——[Anr. ed.] *Printed,* 1641. 4°.* O, LG, OC, BC, EC, DT; CSS, MH, MM, MU, WF.

2469 —Mr. Hollis, his speech in Parliament; on Munday the 31th of Ianuary, 1642. *By Iohn Hammond,* 1642. 4°.* LT, O, C, LUG, LNC, DT; CH, CN, MH, NC, WF, Y.

2469A ——[Anr. ed., "31. of Ianuarie."] *For C. F.,* 1642. 4°.* L, BC; Y.

2469B ——[Anr. ed.] *For F. C. T. B.,* 1642. 4°.* O.

2469C ——[Anr. ed.] *For F. C.,* 1642. 4°.* NCD.

2470 —Master Hollis his speech in Parliament, the 21. of March, 1642. *For Andrew Coe and Marmaduke Boat,* 1642. 4°.* LT, O, C, BC, MR; CH, CN, CSS, NC, PU, WF, Y.

2471 —Master Hollis his speech in Parliament concerning the Articles . . . the fift of January, 1641. *For Francis Coules and Thomas Banks,* 1641. 4°.* LT, C, BC, DT; CH, CN, MH, MU, WF, Y.

2472 —A speech made by . . . concerning Sir Randol Crew. *By E. G. for L. Blaikelocke,* 1641. 4°.* LT, O, CT, MR, DT; CH, CN, MH, NU, TU, WF, Y.

2472A —A speech, made in Parliament . . . the 5 of January, 1641. *For Iohn Wright,* 1641. 4°.* BC, LNC, CD; CH, CLC, CSS, IU, MH, Y.

2473 —Densell Hollis esq: his speech . . . . 4. May. 1641. *By B. A. and T. F. for J. Hammond,* 1641. 4°.* C; CLC, IU, LC, MU.

2474 —A speech of the honorable . . . 4. May 1641. *By B. A. and T. F. for Iohn Hammond,* 1641. 4°.* L, O, C, EC, DT; CH, CN, CSS, MH, NU, WF, Y. (var.)

2475 —The speech of . . . third of August, 1641. *Printed,* 1641. 4°.* L, BC, MR; CH, CN, MH, NC, TU, WF, Y.

2476 —The speech of . . . 15th. of Iune [1642]. *For Thomas Vnderhill,* 1641. 4°.* LT, O, C, BC, DU; CLC, CN, NU, WF, Y.

2476A ——[Anr. ed.] —, 1642. 4°.* L, O, CCA, BR, DT; CH, IU, LC, MH, MU, TU, WF, Y. (var.)

2477 —Mr. Denzell Hollis, his speech to the Lords, . . . July 9. 1641. *For Francis Constable,* 1641. 4°.* LT, O, LL, LNC, DT; CH, CN, CSS, LC, MH, MU, TU, WF, Y.

2478 —Mr. Hollis his speech to the Lords. *For T. Wright,* 1643. 4°.* LT, O, LUG, CS, DT, CD; CH, CN, MH, MM, WF.

2479 —A true copie of the speech made by. *Printed* 1641. 4°.* L, LL, CT, BC, SP; CH, CN, MH, WF, Y.

2479A —A true relation of the unjust accusation of certain French gentlemen. *By J. Darby and are to be sold by Richard Chiswell,* 1670. 4°.* BP; CN, MHL.

2480 ——[Anr. ed.] —, 1671. 4°.* L, O, C, DU, LSD; CH, IU, MIU, MH, WF, Y.

2481 —The Lord Holles his vindication of himself. *Printed,* 1676. 4°.* L, O, C.

2482 —Densell Hollis Esquire, his worthy and learned speech in Parliament, . . . the thirtieth of December 1641. *For Iohn Thomas, and Thomas Bankes,* 1641. 4°.* LT, O, C, EN, DT; CH, CSS, MH, MU, NU, WF, Y.

2483 ——[Anr. ed., "Decemb. 30. 1631."] *Printed,* 1641. 4°.* L, BC, MR; CH, MH, MIU, MU, TU, Y.

Holliband, Claudius. *See* Sainliens, Claude.

2484 **Hollings, John.** Colores sunt variæ. [*Cambridge*], 1660. brs. L.

2485 **Hollingworth, Richard,** *elder.* An account of the spirits. *For Hen. Brome,* 1680. 4°.* T.C.I 415. L, C, OCC, CT, LSD, SC; NGT.

2486 [–] An answer to a certain writing, entituled, Certain dovbts. *For Luke Fawne,* 1643. Sept. 11. 4°.* LT, CJ, CS, MR; CN, LC, MH, NU, WF.

2487 —The catechist catechized. *By J. M. for Luke Fawn,* 1653. 4°. O, LCL, OC, E, DT; MH, NU.

2487A ——[Anr. ed.] —, and are to be sold by Tho. Smith in Manchester, 1653. 4°. MP; Y.

2488 —Certain queres modestly (though plainly) propounded. *By Ruth Raworth for Luke Fawn,* 1646. 4°.* LT, O, LCL, LW, SC, DT; CH, MH, MWA, RPJ.

2488A ——[Anr. ed.] *By Ruth Raworth for Thomas Smith in Manchester,* 1646. 4°.* MC, MP.

2489–90 Entries cancelled.

—Christian principles. 1681. *See* Hollingworth, Richard, *younger.*

2491 [–] An examination of sundry scriptures. *By J. R. for Luke Fawne,* 1645. 4°.* L, O, C, EN, DT; CH, CU, MWA, NPT, NU.

2492 ——[Anr. ed.] *By J. R. for Tho. Smith,* 1645. 4°.* LT, LSC, OC, MC, MP, DT; WF.

—Exercitation concerning. 1650. *See* Gee, Edward.

2493 Entry cancelled. *See following entry.*

2494 —The Holy Ghost on the bench. *For Luke Fawn, to be sold by Ralph Shelmerdine, in Manchester,* 1656. 8°. L, O, LCL, LW, MC; MH, NU.

2494A ——[Anr. ed.] *By J. M. for Luke Fawne,* 1656. 8°. O; CN, MH.

2494B ——Second edition. —, 1657. 8°. O, CT, MC; CLC, IU.

2494C —The Main pointes of church-government. *By J. M. for Luke Fawne, and are to be sold by Thomas Smith in Manchester,* 1649. 8°. MC.

2495   Entry cancelled.
        —Modest plea. 1676. *See* Hollingworth, Richard, *younger.*

2496   —A rejoynder to Master Samuel Eaton. *By T. R. and E. M. for Luke Fawne,* 1647. 4°. LT, LCL, OM, DT; IU, NU, Y.

2497–8 Entries cancelled.
        —Sermon preached. 1673. *See* Hollingworth, Richard, *younger.*
        —Sermon preached. 1682. *See* Hollingworth, Richard, *younger.*

2499   [–] The true guide: or, a short treatise. *For Henry Shephard,* 1646. 4°.* LT, BC, GU, DT; CH, LC, MH, MM.

2500   **Hollingworth, Richard,** *younger.* The character of King Charles I. *Printed, and are to be sold by R. Tayler,* 1692. 4°.* T.C.II 429. L, O, C, EN, DT; CH, MH, NU, WF, Y.

2500A   —Christian principles. *For Robert Boulter,* 1681. 4°.* L, O, C, EC, E, DT; CH, NU, PU, Y.

2501   —The death of King Charles I, proved a down-right murder. *By R. Norton for Walter Kettilby,* 1693. 4°.* T.C.II 438. L, O, C, EN, DT; CH, CN, LC, MH, NU, WF, Y.

2502   —A defence of King Charles I. *For Samuel Eddowes,* 1692. 4°.* T.C.II 413. L, O, C, EN, DT; CH, CN, MH, NU, WF, Y.

2503   —Dr. Hollingworth's defence of K. Charles the First's holy . . . book. *For Samuel Eddowes,* 1692. 4°.* T.C.II 413. L, O, CE, EN, DT; CH, CN, MH, NU, WF, Y.

2503A   —A modest plea for the church of England. *For R. Royston,* 1676. 8°. T.C.I 234. L, O, CE, SHR; IU.

2504   [–] A second defence of King Charles I. *For S. Eddowes; to be sold by Randal Taylor,* 1692. 4°. T.C.II 413. L, O, CT, EN, DT; CH, CN, MH, NU, WF, Y.

2504A   —A sermon preached . . . July 21. 1673. *For Robert Boulter,* 1673. 4°.* C, SP; NU, Y.

2504B   —A sermon preached . . . November the 5th. 1682. *For Edward Gellibrand, and R. Sollers,* 1682. 4°.* T.C.I 503. L, O, C, LG, BC, EC; CH, CN, NU, WF, Y.

2505   Entry cancelled.
        [–] Vindiciæ Carolinæ. 1692. *See* Wilson, John, *of Lincoln's Inn.*

2506   No entry.

2507   **Hollister, Dennis.** The harlot's vail removed. *For the author,* 1658. 4°. L, LF, BBN, BR, MR; CH, PH, PSC.

2508   —The skirts of the whore discovered. *For Giles Calvert,* 1656. 4°.* LT, LF, BBN; CH, PH, PSC, Y.

2509   **Holloway, James.** The free and voluntary confession and narrative. colop: *For Robert Horn, John Baker and John Redmayne,* 1684. cap., fol.* L, O, C, BR, EN; CH, CN, MH, NU, WF, Y, AVP.

2510   — —[Anr. ed.] colop: *Edinburgh, re-printed by the heir of Andrew Anderson,* 1684. cap., fol.* ALDIS 2456.5. O, EN.

2511   — —[Anr. ed.] colop: *Re-printed, at Dublin, by Mary Crook,* 1684. 4°.* DIX 206. BR, DN; Y.

2512   Entry cancelled.
        [**Hollywell, Henry.**] Improvement of the ways. 1690. *See* Hallywell, Henry.

2512A   **Holme, John.** The Charter-House apothecary's case. [*London,* 1698.] brs. Y.

2513   **Holme, Randle.** The academy of armory. *Chester, for the author,* 1688. fol. L, O, C, MR, E; CH, CN, LC, MH, NN, WF, Y.

2513A   — —[Anr. ed.] *London, for the author, sold by Richard Chiswell,* 1693. fol. T.C.II 454. LIU.

2514   **H[olme], T[homas].** A brief relation of some part of the sufferings of the true Christians. [*n.p.*], *printed,* 1672. 4°. L, O, C, LF, BBN; CH, IE, PSC, WF, Y.

        Holmes, Walter. Annual almanacke. 1649. *See* Almanacs.

2514A   **Holney, John.** A brief account of those . . . pills. [*London?* 1675.] cap.* LG.

2514B   —The catholick or universal pill. [*London,* 1678?] brs. L.

2514C   **Holt, Richard.** Seasonable proposals for a perpetual fund . . . in Dublin. [*Dublin,* 1696?] cap., fol.* DK, DN; Y.

2515   **Holwell, John.** An appendix to Holvvel's Catastrophe mundi. *By J. G. for F. Smith,* 1683. 4°.* L, O, C, EN, GU; CLC, LC, IU, MH, NU, Y, HC. (var.)

2516   —Catastrophe mundi. *For the author,* 1682. 4°. L, O, CT, BAMB, E; CH, IU, LC, MH, WF, Y, AVP.

2517   —Clavis horologiæ: or a key. *For the author; to be sold by Tho. Howkins,* 1686. 4°. T.C.II 146. L, DCH; CLC, MB, MH.

2517A   — —[Anr. ed.] *By Will. Bonny, for Tho. Howkins,* 1686. 4°. L, C; MB, MH.

2517B   — —[Anr. ed.] *By Will. Bonny, for the author, and are to be sold by Tho. Howkins,* 1686. 4°. NE.

2518   —A new prophecy. *At the request of the author,* 1679. fol.* L, O, CT, EN; CH, CLC, MH, WF, Y.

2519   —Holwell's predictions. *Cambridge* [*Mass.*], *by S. G. for Benjamin Harris, at Boston,* 1690. 16°.* EVANS 512. MWA.

2520   —John Holwell's strange and wonderful prophesies. [*torn*], 1696. 8°.* L.

2521   —A sure guide to the practical surveyor. *By W. Godbid, for Christopher Hussey,* 1678. 8°. T.C.I 319. L, O, C, LI; CH, CLC, MH, WF, HC.

2522   —Trigonometry made easie. *For Tho. Howkins,* 1685. 8°. T.C.II 98. O, C, LG, SP.

        Holy and profitable sayings. 1678. *See* S.
        —[Same title.] 1678. *See* V., T.
        —[Same title.] 1678. *See* Gosnold, John.

2523   Entry cancelled.
        Holy breathings of a devout soul. 1695. *See* Arundell, Thomas.

        Holy cheat. 1688. *See* L'Estrange, *Sir* Roger.

2524   An holy defiance to the gates of Hell. *By Matthew Simmons for H. Cripps,* 1648. 4°.* LT, O, DT; CN, IU, NU.

2525   The holy fast of Lent defended. *Printed,* 1677. 4°. T.C.I 280. L, O, C, EC, LSD, DT; CDA, CH, IU, MH, NU, WF, Y.

2526   The holy harmony: or, a plea. *By R. Austin and A. Coe,* 1643. 4°.* LT, LCL, MR; NN.

        Holy inquisition. 1681. *See* Beaulieu, Luke de.
        Holy kiss of peace. 1660. *See* Smith, William, *Quaker.*
        Holy life here. 1652. *See* Stanwix, Richard.

Holy life of Gregory Lopez. [n.p.], 1675. *See* Losa, Francisco.

Holy life of Mrs. Elizabeth Walker. 1690. *See* Walker, Anthony.

Holy life of Philip Nerius. Paris, 1659. *See* Gallonio, Antonio.

Holy lives. 1654. *See* H., J.

2526A Holy meditations, and contemplations. *By Rich. Cotes, for Joh. Sweeting*, 1642. 12°. L.

Holy oyl. [n.p.], 1669. *See* Harrington, *Sir* James, *bart.*

Holy order. 1654. *See* Hall, Joseph, *bp.*

Holy practises. Paris, 1657. *See* More, Gertrude.

2527 The holy rest of God. *By E. P. for Iohn Wright the younger*, 1641. 4°. L, CCA; CH, CLC, MH, NU, WF.

Holy Scripture owned. [n.p.], 1692. *See* B., J.

Holy Scripture the Scripture. 1684. *See* Bampfield, Francis.

Holy Scriptures. 1655. *See* Farnworth, Richard.

2528 The Holy Sisters conspiracy. colop: [*London*], *by T. M.*, 1661. cap., 4°.* LT; MIU.

2528A The holy sister's lamentation. [1699?] brs. L.

Holy things. 1658. *See* Shaw, Samuel.

2529 The holy time of Christmas defended. *Printed*, 1676. 4°.* LLP, CS, LNC; CN, NU.

2530 **Holyday, Barten.** Against disloyalty. *Oxford, by W. H. for S. Pocock*, 1661. 8°. MADAN 2559. O; NU, Y.

[–] Comes facundus. 1658. *See* Edmundson, Henry.

2531 —Motives to a good life. *Oxford, by L. Lichfield for Edward Forrest and Robert Blagrave*, 1657. 4°. MADAN 2339. L, O, C, CT, DC, BLH; CH, CN, IU, NU, TO, WF, Y.

2532 —Of the nature of faith. *By S. G. for W. Lee*, 1654. 4°.* LT, O, LW, BC, BSM; CLC, MH, NU, WF.

2533 —A survey of the world. In ten books. *Oxford, by Will Hall, for the authour*, 1661. 4°. MADAN 2558. L, O, C, OC, LLU; CH, CN, IU, MH, WF, Y.

2534 **Holyoke, Edward.** The doctrine of life. *By T. R. for Nath. Ekins*, 1658. 4°. L, C, LLP; CH, LC, MH, MU, NN, WF, Y, AVP.

2534A **Holyoke, Francis.** Dictionarium etymoligicvm Latinvm. *By Felix Kingston*, 1648. fol. L; CB, MB.

2535 —A large dictionary. *By W. Rawlins, for G. Sawbridge, W. Place, T. Basset, T. Dring, J. Leigh, and J. Place*, 1677. fol. T.C.I 301. L, O, C, EN, DT; BN, CH, IU, LC, MH, TU, WF, Y, AVP.

2536 Entry cancelled. *See preceding entry.*

2536A **Home, *Sir* James Home, *earl of*.** The Lord Hvmes his speech. [*London*], *printed* 1641. 4°.* LT, CT, LNC, EN, ESS; CH, MB, WF, Y.

2536B **Homel, Anne.** French cruelty. [*London*, 1689.] cap., 4°.* Y.

2537 A homely dialogue betwixt a young woman and her sweetheart. [*London?* 1690.] fol. L; MH.

2538 Entry cancelled.

Homer. Homeri . . . gnomologia. Cantabrigæ, 1660. *See* Duport, James.

2539 —Ὁμήρου Ἰλιας. Homeri Ilias. *Cantabrigiæ, ex officina Rogeri Daniel*, 1648. 8°. L, O, C, CT, LLU, CD; IU, Y, AQU.

2540 ——[Anr. ed.] *Cantabrigiæ, excudebat Joannes Field*, 1664. 8°. L, O, C, CT, RU, E; CLC, IU, NC, TO.

2540A ——[Anr. ed.] Ἐν Ὀξονια, ἐκ Θεατρου, 1665. 4°. CU.

2541 ——[Anr. ed.] *Cantabrigiæ, excudebat Joannes Hayes*, 1672. 8°. L, O, CP, CT; CLC, IU, MH.

2542 ——[Anr. ed.] Ἐκ Θεατρου ἐν Ὀξονια, 1676. 8°. MADAN 3109. L, O, C, LIU, DT; BN, CH, CLC, IU, Y.

2543 ——[Anr. ed.] *Cantabrigiæ, excudebat Johannes Hayes*, 1679. 8°. O, C, CT, DC, SHR; BN, CH, IU, MM, PL, Y.

2544 ——[Anr. ed.] *Cantabrigiæ, ex officina Joan. Hayes*, 1686. 8°. L, O, C, NPL, GU; CLC, IU, MBA, NC, OCI.

2544A ——[Anr. ed.] Ἐκ Θεατρου ἐν Ὀξονια, 1688. 8°. PL.

2545 ——[Anr. ed.] *Cantabrigiæ, ex officinâ Joann. Hayes; vendit Ed. Brewster, Londini*, 1689. 4°. T.C.II 239. L, O, C, DC, MR; BN, CH, IU, LC, TU, WF, Y.

2546 ——[Anr. ed.] Ἐκ Θεατρου ἐν Ὀξονια, [1695]. 8°. T.C.II 602. L, OC, BR, LIU, ENC; CH, IU, MH, NRU, Y.

2547 —Iliados liber primus. *Typis Johannis Heptinstall, impensis authoris*, 1685. 8°. L, LW; Y.

2547A ——Second edition. *Typis J. H. impensis Samuelis Smith*, 1686. 8°. Y.

2547B ——"Second" edition. *Impensis Tho. Bennet*, 1687. 8°. T.C.II 295. L; PL.

2547C —The first booke of Homer's Iliads. *By T. Lock, for the author*, 1659. 4°.* WF.

2547D —The first booke of Homers Iliads. *By L. Lock, for the author*, 1660. 4°. L; MH, NIC.

2548 —Homer his Iliads translated. *By Thomas Roycroft*, 1660. fol. L, O, C, GC, MR, CD; CH, CN, IU, MH, TU, WF, Y.

2549 ——[Anr. ed.] *By James Flesher, for the author*, 1669. fol. L, O, C, P, EN, BQ; CSU, IU, MH, NP, TU, Y.

2550 —Homer's Iliads in English. *By J. C. for William Crook*, 1676. 12°. T.C.I 262. L, C, LW, CT; CH, CLC, MH, TU, WCL, Y.

2551 —The Iliads and Odysses of. Second edition. *For Will Crook*, 1677. 12°. T.C.II 56. L, C, LVD, OC, EN, ES; CH, CN, MH, MU, TO, WF, Y.

2552 ——Third edition. *For Will. Crook*, 1686. 12°. T.C.II 171. L, O, C, LVD, LVF, BR, LIU; CH, MH, NP, OCI, TO, WF, Y.

2553 —Homeri Odyssea. *Cantabrigiæ, excudebat Joan. Field*, 1664. 8°. L, O, C, AN, BR, DT; BN, CLC, CN, MH, NC, WF, Y.

2554 —Homer his Odysses. *By Thomas Roycroft, for the author*, 1665. fol. L, O, LCL, CT, MR, EN; BN, CLC, CN, CU, IU, WC, WF, Y.

2555 ——[Anr. ed.] *By James Flesher, for the authour*, 1669. fol. L, O, C, LI, LIU, DT; CH, MBP, NP, TU, Y.

2556 —Homer's Odysses. *By J. C. for W. Crook*, 1675. 12°. T.C.I 197. L, C, CK, P, E; CH, CU, MH, PBL, TO, WCL.

2556A —The third book of Homers Iliads. *By M. I. for the author*, 1660. * MH.

2557 Entry cancelled.

—Translation of Homers works. [n.p., 1660.] *See* Ogilby, John.

2558 —The travels of Ulysses. *By J. C. for William Crook*, 1673. T.C.I 127. L, LLU; CH, MH, Y.

2558A — —Second edition. *By J. C.*, 1674. 12°. L, O, C, CK; CH.
Homer a la mode. Oxford, 1664. *See* Scudamore, James.
Homer and Virgil. 1700. *See* Blackmore, *Sir* Richard.

2559 **Homes, Nathaniel.** The works of. *For the author*, 1652.
fol. L, O, LW, BLH, E; IU, MH, NU, WF.

2560 —Αποκαλυψις αναστασεως. The resurrection revealed.
By Robert Ibbitson, to be sold by Thomas Pierrepont, 1653.
fol. L, LCL, OME, CS, BC, SP, SA; CH, MB, NGT, WF.

2561 — —[Anr. ed.] —, 1654. fol. L, O, C, CP, P; BN, MH, MIU,
NU, RBU.

2562 —Dæmonologie, and theologie. *By Tho: Roycroft, to
be sold by Jo: Martin, and Jo: Ridley*, 1650. 8°. LT, O,
LCL, LW, E; CN, MH, NU, WF, Y.

2563 [–] Ecclesiastica methermeneutica, or church-cases cleered.
By Tho. Roycroft, to be sold by Will. Raybould, 1652.
8°. L, O, LCL, OC; CLC, MBC, NU, TO.

2564 —An essay concerning the Sabbath. *For the author*, 1673.
8°. T.C.I 168. L, CT, E, EN; INU, MH, MWA, NPT.

2565 —God, a rich supply of all good. *By Tho: Roycroft*, 1650.
8°.* LT, O, OB; MH, NU, Y.

2566 [–] Gods gracious thoughts. *Loondon* [*sic*], *By Matthew
Simmons, and are to be sold by John Pounset*, 1647. 4°.*
LT, C, DT; LC, MH, NP, Y.

2567 [–] Gospel musick. *For Henry Overton*, 1644. 4°.* L, O, C,
LCL, BC, EN; CH, MH, MU, NN, TO, Y.

2568 —Miscellanea. *For the author*, 1664. fol. L, LL, LLP.

2569 —The mischiefe of mixt communions. *By Thomas Roycroft, to be sold by William Raybould*, 1650. 4°.* LT, O,
SP, DT; NHC, NU, WF.

2569A — —[Anr. ed., "mischeife."] *By Thomas Roycroft*, 1650.
4°.* CH.

2570 —The nevv vvorld. *By T. P. and M. S. for William
Adderton*, 1641. 4°. LT, O, C, EN, DT; CLC, IU, MH, NU,
WF, Y.

2571 —The peasants price. *By R. O. and G. D. for Benjamin
Allen*, 1642. 4°. LT, O, CT, MR, EN; IU, MH, NHC, NU, WF.

2572 —Plain dealing, or the cause and cure. *For R. I. to be
sold by Anthony Williamson*, 1652. 12°. LT, SP; NHC, Y.

2573 — —[Anr. ed.] *For Robert Ibbitson*, 1652. 8°. LT, O; NU.

2574 —The resurrection-revealed raised. *For the author*, 1661.
fol. L, O, E; MBC, MH, NPT, WF, Y.

2575 —A sermon preached . . . Feb. 2. 1650. *By T. R. and
J. C.*, 1650. 4°.* L, LSC; NU.

2576 —A sermon, preached . . . October the 8. 1650. *By
Thomas Roycroft, to be sold by William Raybould*, 1650.
4°. LT, O, C, LLP, DT, BLH; CH, IU, MB, NU, WF.

2577 —A sermon preached . . . Octob. the 6th. A. D. 1659.
Ptinted [*sic*] *by J. B. for Edward Brewster*, 1660. 4°.* LT,
O, C, CM, DU; MM, NU.

2578 —A vindication of baptizing beleevers infants. *By M.
Simmons, to be sold by Benjamin Allen*, 1646. 4°. LT, O, C,
LW, DT; CSS, NHC, NPT, NU, WF, Y.

2578A — —[Anr. ed.] *By M. Simmons, and are to be sold by
Richard Wodenothe*, 1646. 4°. ORP; BN.

2579 **Homwood, Nicholas.** A word of counsel. [*London*],
printed, 1675. 4°.* L, O, LF, CT, BBN; CH, IE, MH, PH,
RPJ, WF, Y.

2579A — —Second edition. —, 1688. 4°.* LF.
Honest anvver. [1642.] *See* Taylor, John.
Honest citizen. [n.p., 1648.] *See* B., A. J.

2580 An honest commoner's speech. [*London*, 1694.] cap.,
4°.* C, EN; CH, LC, TU, WF, Y.

2581 The honest cryer of London. [*London*], *for George
Thompson*, 1660. brs. LT, O, LG, HH; MH, WF.

2582 The honest design. *For L. Chapman*, 1659. 4°.* LT, O,
LVF, BC; CH, MH, MM, MU, NN, WF.

2583 An honest discourse between three neighbours. *For
Thomas Brewster*, 1655. 4°.* LT, DT; CSS, MH, NU, Y.
Honest ghost. 1658. *See* Brathwaite, Richard.

2584 Honest Hodge and Ralph. *For John Kidgell*, 1680. 4°.*
T.C.I 395. L, O, C, LSD, MR; MIU, WF, Y.

2585 —[Anr. ed., " &."] *For Richard Janeway*, 1680. 4°.* O, OC,
CT, MR; CH, IU, MBA, NC, WF, Y.

2586 The honest informer; or, Tom-tell-troth's observations.
[*London*], *printed*, 1642. 4°.* L, O, CT, LSD, DT; CH, CN,
MH, NU, WF, Y.

2586A Entry cancelled. *See preceding entry.*

2586B Honest invitations, by the unborn doctor. [*London*,
1690?] brs. L.
Honest letter. [n.p.], 1642. *See* W., H.
Honest letetr [*sic*] to a doubtful friend. York, 1642. *See*
R., T.

2587 The honest maidens loyalty. *For Richard Burton*, [1641–
74]. brs. L, HH; MH, Y.
Honest mans delight. [n.p., 1641–74]. *See* J., T.

2587A The honest mans immaginary dreames. [*London*, 1648.]
brs. MAU.

2588 An honest man's wish. [*n.p.*], *printed*, 1688. brs. L, O, C,
OC, HH.

2588A The honest patriot: a short discourse . . . militia. *By
F. G.*, 1659. 8°.* CH.
Honest, plain, down-right-dealing. 1660. *See* Fox,
George, *younger.*

2589 The honest souldier, or, a vindication. *Printed*, 1648.
4°.* LT, MR, DT; CH, MH, WF, Y.

2589A The honest tradesmans honour vindicated. [n.p., 1660].
fol. L.

2590 —[Anr. ed.] *For VV. Thackeray, T. Passenger, and VV.
Whitwood*, [1670–77]. brs. L, CM, HH; MH, Y.
Honest Welch-cobler. [n.p.], 1647. *See* Ward, Nathaniel.
Honesty is the best policy. [n.p., 1689.] *See* Lawton,
Charlwood.
Honesty's best policy. [n.p., 1678.] *See* Nedham, Mar-
chamont.
Honey out of the rock. 1644. *See* Price, John.

2591 The honor and courage of our English Parliaments. *For
John Wickins*, 1681. 4°.* O, CS, YM; CLC, IU, MH, NU, Y.

2592 The honour of a London prentice. *By and for A. M.*,
[1690]. brs. L, O, HH.

2593 —[Anr. ed.] *By and for W. O.*, [1695?]. brs. HH.

2593A The honour of an apprentice of London. [*London*], *for F.
Coles, T. Vere, and VV. Gilbertson*, [1658–64]. brs. O.

2593B —[Anr. ed.] [*London*], *for F. Coles, T. Vere, W. Gilbertson,
and J. Wright*, [1663–65]. brs. EUING 135. GU.

2594–5 Entries cancelled.
　　　Honour of Bristol. [*London*, 1646–80.] *See* Price, Laurence.
　　　Honour of chivalry. 1650. *See* Fernandez, Geronimo *and* Kirkman, Francis.
2595A The honour of great York and Albany. [*London*], by *Nath. Thompson*, 1683. brs. MH.
2596 The honour of London apprentices: exemplified. By *B. A.*, 1647. 4°.* LT, O, LG, BR; CH, WF.
2597 The honour of the English soldiery. By *Tho. Newcomb*, 1651: 4°.* LT; CH, CLC, CN, MIU, TO, WF.
2597A The honour of the gentle-craft. By *A. Clark for T. Passenger*, 1674. 8°. L.
2597B —[Anr. ed.] By *H. B. for John Clark, W. Thackeray, and T. Passenger*, 1685. 12°.* CM.
2598 The honour of the gout. For *A. Baldwin*, 1699. 12°. T.C. III 174. L, LCS; PL, WF, Y.
2599 The honour of the taylors. By *Alexander Milbourn for William Whitwood*, 1687. 4°. T.C.II 198. L, O; CH, CN, MH, NP, WCL, WF, Y.
2600 The honour of Welshmen. By *P. Lillicrap*, 1667. brs. L.
　　　Honor redivivus: or. 1692. *See* Carter, Matthew.
2600A The honourable House of Commons have been pleas'd . . . East India trade. [*London?* 1698.] brs. MH, Y.
2601 The honourable state of matrimony. For *Francis Pearse*, 1685. 12°. L; CN, Y.
2601AA The honourable undertaking; or, five hundred pounds for one shilling. [*n.p.*, 1696?] brs. L.
2601BA Honours invitation, or. By *H. B. for John Clark*, 1673. 4°.* WF.
　　　Honours of the Lords. 1679. *See* Hunt, Thomas.
2601A Honours preservation without blood. For *Philip Brooksby*, 1680. 4°.* T.C.I 397. L, OB; CH.
2602 [**Honyman, Andrew**], *bp.* The seasonable case of submission. *Edinburgh, by Evan Tyler*, 1662. 4°.* ALDIS 1744. BIU, MR, E, EN; CH, IU, MM, NU, TSM, Y.
2603 [–] Survey of Naphtali. Part II. *Edinburgh, by Evan Tyler*, 1669. 4°. ALDIS 1882. EU, ES, EN, GU; CLC, WF.
2604 [–] A survey of the insolent and infamous libel, entituled, Naphtali. [*Edinburgh*], *printed*, 1668. 4°. ALDIS 1852. L, E, EN, GU, SA, DM; CH, IU, NU, WF, Y.
2605 Entry cancelled. Ghost.
2605A [**Hooke, John.**] Catholicism without popery. For *J. Lawrence*, 1699. 8°. T.C.III 120. L, O, LSC, CS, CT; CH, OCI, TO, WF, MOORE.
2606 [**Hooke, Richard.**] The bishop's appeale. *Newcastle, by Stephen Bulkley*, 1661. 4°. O, LLP, NE, YM, DL; Y.
2606A [–] The fatall doom. For *John Williams*, 1655. 12°. LT, O, OC, P; CH, CLC, Y.
2606B [–] —[Anr. ed.] For *Henry Marsh*, 1658. 12°. LSC; MH, MIU.
2606C [–] The good Christian's Heaven. By *William Godbid*, [1660]. 8°. Y.
2607 —The laver of regeneration. [*London*], by *R. A.* to be sold by *Robert Littlebury*, 1653. 4°. O, CS.
2607A [–] —[Anr. ed.] By *H. Hills Jun. for Robert Clavel*, 1684. 8°. CALDERDALE CEN. LIB., HALIFAX.

2607B [–] —[Anr. ed.] —, *and are to be sold by Francis Bently, in Hallifax*, 1684. 8°. HALIFAX ANTIQ. SOC.
2608 —The Non-conformist's champion. For *Tho. Flesher*, 1682. 8°. T.C.I 459. O, LCL, CT, DU, YM, E; CLC, CN, NPT, NU, WF.
2609 —The royal guard. By *W. Godbid*, to be sold by *Ro. Littlebury*, 1662. 8°. L, C, OC.
2610 [–] —[Anr. ed.] By *H. H. jun. for Francis Bently in Hallifax and sold by Rand. Taylor*, 1684. 4°. T.C.II 101. L, O, OC, LSD, DU; CH, CLC, NGT, WF.
2611 **Hooke, Robert.** Animadversions on the first part of the Machina cœlestis. By *T. R. for John Martyn*, 1674. 4°. T.C.I 196. L, O, C, EN, DT; BN, CLC, MH, OCI, WF, Y.
2612 [–] An attempt for the explication of the phænomena. By *J. H. for Sam. Thomson*, 1661. 8°. L, O, CS, EC, DT; CLC, MH, Y.
2613 —An attempt to prove the motion of the earth. By *T. R. for John Martyn*, 1674. 4°.* L, O, C, EN, DT; BN, CH, MWA, OCI, WF, JF.
2613A —Conamen ad motum telluris probandum, e sermone. [*Oxford*], 1679. 4°. L; NN.
2614 —A description of helioscopes. By *T. R. for John Martyn*, 1676. 4°.* T.C.I 220. L, O, C, EN, DT; BN, CH, CLC, MH, MWA, WF.
2615–15A Entries cancelled.
　　　—Fatall doom. 1655. *See* Hooke, Richard.
2616 —Lampas: or, descriptions. For *John Martyn*, 1677. 4°. T.C.I 155. L, O, C, EN, DT; BN, CLC, MB, MH, MWA, WF.
2617 —Lectiones Cutlerianæ: or a collection of lectures. For *John Martyn*, 1679. 4°. T.C.I 341. L, O, OC, RU, E; BN, CLC, MH, NC, JF.
2618 —Lectures and collections. For *J. Martyn*, 1678. 4°. T.C.I 319. L, O, C, EN, DT; BN, CLC, IU, MB, MH, MU, TO, Y.
2619 —Lectures de potentia restitutiva, or of spring. For *John Martyn*, 1678. 4°. T.C.I 332. L, O, C, E, DT; BN, CJC, CLC, MB, MH, TO, WF, JF.
2620 —Micrographia: or some. By *Jo. Martyn and Ja. Allestry*, 1665. fol. L, O, C, MR, EN; BN, CH, LC, IU, MH, NAM, Y, JF, AVP.
2621 ——[Anr. ed.] By *John Martyn*, 1667. fol. L, LCP, OB, RU, DT; IU, LC, MMO, WCL.
2621A ——[Anr. ed.] For *James Allestry*, 1667. fol. LCS, OC, CK, MR, BQ; BN, LC, NCD, WF, WSG, WU.
2621B [**Hooke, Thomas.**] A true relation of a strange monster . . . Ireland. For *Francis Smith*, [1673]. brs. T.C.I 164. DN; BN.
2622 **Hooke, William.** A discourse concerning the witnesses. By *J. Astwood*, for *Thomas Cockeril*, 1681. 4°. L, O, LCL, EN; MB, MH, NN, PL, WF, Y.
2623 —New-Englands sence. For *John Rothwell*, 1645. 4°.* L, O, BC, GH, DT; CH, MH, NU, RPJ, WF.
2624 —New Englands teares. By *E. G. for Iohn Rothwell and Henry Overton*, 1641. 4°.* LT, LW, CM, EN; LC, MH, MU, NU, RPJ, Y.
2625 ——[Anr. ed., "nevv."] By *T. P. for Iohn Rothwell and Henry Overton*, 1641. 4°.* LT, CM; CN, MB, RPJ, WCL, WF.

2626 — —Third edition. *By I. D. for Iohn Rothwell and Henry Overton*, 1641. 4°.* L, OC; CH, MBA, NN, RPJ, V.

2627 —The priviledge of the saints. *For John Allen*, 1673. 12°. L, O, C, LCL; CLC, CN, NU, Y.

2628 — —[Anr. ed.] *For John Wilkins*, 1673. 12°. MH, NGT, RPJ, WF, Y.

2629 —A short discourse. *For John Wilkins*, 1673. 8°. C; MB, NGT, Y.

2629A H[ooker], G. Memorbilia mundi: or, choice memoirs. *For the author, to be sold by F. Smith*, 1670. 8°. L; CH.

2629B **Hooker, John.** The grand balsamici. [*London*, 1690?] brs. L.

2629C —The virtues and happy effects of Bateman's famous spirits. [*London*, 1695?] brs. L.

2630 **Hooker, Richard.** The works of. *By J. Best, for Andrew Crook*, 1662. fol. L, O, C, LIU, E; CH, CU, MH, NC, WF, Y.

2631 — —[Anr. ed.] *By Thomas Newcomb for Andrew Crook*, 1666. fol. L, O, C, DU, DT; BN, CH, IU, LC, MH, NU, WF, Y.

2632 — —[Anr. ed.] *By R. White, for Rob. Scot, Tho. Basset, John Wright, and Rich. Chiswell, and are to be sold by Robert Boulter*, 1676. fol. T.C.I 230. L, O, CT, BR, EN, DT; CLC, CN, IU, MH, NU, WF, Y.

2633 — —[Anr. ed.] *For Robert Scot, Thomas Basset, John Wright and Richard Chiswel*, 1682. fol. T.C.I 513. L, O, C, MR, DT; CLC, IU, LC, NU, WF, Y, AVP.

— —Cœlestis legatus. *Cambridge*, 1668. *See Almanacs.*

[–] Dangers of new discipline. [n.p.], 1642. *See title.*

2634 —Judicious Hooker's illustrations of Holy Scripture. *For the collector*, 1675. 8°. L, OU; CH, Y.

2635 —Of the lawes of ecclesiasticall politie; the sixth and eighth books. *By Richard Bishop, and are to be sold by Iohn Crook*, 1648. 4°. LT, O, C, YM, DT; CH, CU, MH, NU, Y.

2635A — —[Anr. ed.] *By Richard Bishop*, 1648. 4°. C, CK; MB, MM, MU, NCU, NGT.

2635B — —[Anr. ed.] *Printed in the year*, 1648. 4°. Y.

2636 — —[Anr. ed.] *By R. B. and are to be sold by George Badger*, 1651. 4°. L, LCL, CT, GK; CLC, IU.

2637 — —[Anr. ed.] *For Andrew Crooke*, 1666. fol. L, BR, NPL, RPL, SHR; CH, LC, MBA, NPT, Y.

2638 **Hooker, Samuel.** Righteousness rained from Heaven. *Cambridge* [*Mass.*], *by Samuel Green*, 1677. 4°.* EVANS 230. CH, MB, MWA, Y.

2639 **Hooker, Thomas.** The application of redemption. The first eight books. *By Peter Cole*, 1656. 4°. L, LW; LC, WF, Y.

2640 — —The ninth and tenth books. *By Peter Cole*, 1657. 8°. L, LCL, LLP, LW; CLC, LC, NN, PL, Y.

2641 — —Second edition. —, 1659. 4°. LC, MB, MH, NN, Y.

2642 —A briefe exposition of the Lords Prayer. *By Moses Bell for Benjamine Allen*, 1645. 4°. LT, O, DT; CH, MBC, NU, RPJ, WF.

2643 —A comment upon Christ's last prayer. *By Peter Cole*, 1656. 4°. L, LCL, LLP, AN; MH, MU, RPJ, WF, Y.

2644 —The covenant of grace opened. *By G. Dawson*, 1649. 4°. LT, O, C, AN; LC, MH, NP, RPJ, Y.

2645 —The danger of desertion. *By G. M. for George Edwards*, 1641. 4°.* LT, O, LW, EN; CN, LC, MH, NU, RPJ, WF, Y. (var.)

2646 — —Second edition. —, 1641. 4°.* L, CM; CSS, MB.

2647 —An exposition of the principles. *For R. Dawlman*, 1645. 12°. L, O.

2648 —The faithful covenanter. *For Christopher Meredith*, 1644. 4°.* LT, O, MR, DT; INU, MH, Y.

2649 [–] Heavtonaparnvmenos: or a treatise. *By W. Wilson, for Richard Royston*, 1646. 4°. LT, O, C, BC, DT; CLC, MH, NU, WF, Y.

2650 —Heavens treasvry opened. *For R. Dawlman*, 1645. 12°. L, O.

2651 [–] The immortality of the soule. *Printed*, 1645. 4°.* LT, DT; RPJ.

2651A [–] —[Anr. ed.] —, 1646. 4°.* EC, GU; CH, NPT.

2651B —The poor doubting Christian. Sixth edition. *By I. Raworth for Luke Fawne*, 1641. 12°. WF.

2651C — —[Anr. ed.] *For Luke Fawn*, 1652. 12°. LW; AVP.

2651D — —[Anr. ed.] *By John Macock, for Luke Fawne*, 1659. 12°. MB.

2651E — —[Anr. ed.] —, 1664. 12°. YM.

2651F — —[Anr. ed.] *By S. G. for N. Ranew and J. Robinson*, 1667. 12°. LSC; MWA.

2651G — —[Anr. ed.] *By J. M. for Nath. Ranew and J. Robinson*, 1674. T.C.I 166. 12°. Y.

2652 — —[Anr. ed.] *By J. D. for Nath. Ranew, and Jonath. Robinson*, 1684. 12°. T.C.II 64. L, LW; MH, NPT.

2653 — —Twelfth edition. *By R. J. for J. Robinson, A. and J. Churchill, J. Taylor, and J. Wyat*, 1700. 12°. T.C.III 202. RPJ.

2654 —The saints dignitie. *By G. D. for Francis Eglesfield*, 1651. 4°. LT, O, LCL, LSC, ORP; CH, INU, MH, NU, WF, Y.

2655 —The saints guide. *Printed at London for John Stafford*, 1645. 12°. LT, O; CB, CLC, MH, NP, NS, Y.

2656 —The sovles preparation. Sixth edition. *By M. F. for R. Dawlman*, 1643. L, O, LLP, YM.

2657 [–] —Seventh edition. *By J. G. for R. Dawlman, to be sold by Hen. Cripps*, 1658. 12°. C; NU.

2658 —A survey of the summe of church-discipline. *By A. M. for John Bellamy*, 1648. 4°. LT, O, C, E, DT; BN, CH, CN, LC, MH, NU, RPJ, WCL, Y.

2659 **Hookes, Ellis.** A Christian plea. [*London*, 1676?] 8°. L, LF, BBN.

2660 [–] Due order of law and justice. *By Andrew Sowle*, 1680. 4°. L, O, MR, NPL; BN, CH, MH, PL, WF, Y.

2661 [–] For the king and both Houses of Parliament. [*London*], *printed*, 1675. 4°.* L, C, BBN, BR, MR; IE, MH, PH, PSC, RPJ, WF.

2661A [–] A presentation to London. [*London?* 1659.] cap., 4°.* LG, MR; CH, PH, PL, Y.

2661B —The Quakers acquitted. [*London?* 1675.] brs. LF, CM.

2662 —The spirit of Christ. *For Giles Calvert*, 1661. 4°.* L, O, LF, BBN, MR; CH, MH, PH, PSC, Y.

2663 [–] The spirit of the martyrs is risen. *For Thomas Simmons*, [1665]. 4°.* L, LF, BBN; IU, PH, Y.

2663A [–] The spirit of the martyrs revived. [London, 1664.] fol. L, DU; NU, PH.

2663B [–] —[Anr. ed.] [London], printed, 1682. 4°. PH, PSC, WF.

2664 [–] —[Anr. ed.] For T. H., 1683. 4°. L, O, C, LF, P; CH, IE, IU, NGC, PH.

2664A [–] Truth seeks no corners. [London], printed, 1679. 4°.* O; PH, PSC, Y.

2665 **H[ookes], N[icholas].** Amanda. By T. R. and E. M. for Humphrey Tuckey, 1653. 8°. L, O, C, LVD, DC; CH, CN, IU, MH, RHT, WF, Y.

2666 No entry.

2667 **Hoole, Charles.** Centuria epistolarum Anglo-Latinarum; . . . a century. By W. Wilson, for the company of stationers, 1660. 8°. L, CT; CH, CLC.

2668 — —[Anr. ed.] By E. Flesher, for the company of stationers, 1677. 8°. T.C.I 279. O, CS.

2669 — —[Anr. ed.] By T. M. for the company of stationers, 1687. 8°. L; CLC, IU, Y.

2670 — —[Anr. ed.] —, 1700. 8°. L.

2671 —Childrens talke. For the company of stationers, 1659. 8°. L.

2672 — —[Anr. ed.] —, 1673. 8°. Y.

2672A — —[Anr. ed.] —, 1681. 8°. LLU.

2673 — —[Anr. ed.] —, 1697. 8°. L; PL, SMITH, WF.

2674 —The common accidents examined. [London], by E. Tyler for John Saywell, 1656. 8°. O, NOT.

2674A — —[Anr. ed., "accidence."] By T. M., 1659. 8°. L.

2674B — —Fifth edition. By R. D. for John Williams, 1661. 8°. NOT.

2674C — —Seventh edition. By E. Cotes for John Clark, 1667. 8°. O; IU.

2674D — —"Seventh" edition. By E. Cotes for John Clark, 1668. 8°. L; PU.

2675 — —Eighth edition. By A. Clark, for J. Clark, 1671. 8°. L; WF.

2675A — —[Anr. ed.] By A. C. for John Clark, 1673. 8°. OC; MH.

2676 — —[Anr. ed.] —, 1675. 8°. C.

2677 — —[Anr. ed.] By M. C. for John Clark, 1679. 8°. L.

2678 — —[Anr. ed.] For John Clark, 1683. 8°. L, O, C.

2678aA — —[Anr. ed.] By M. C. for John Clark, 1685. 8°. L, O.

2678bA — —[Anr. ed.] —, 1686. 8°. LLU.

2678cA — —[Anr. ed.] By E. Cotes for John Clark, 1688. 8°. LC.

2678A — —[Anr. ed.] By M. C. for John Clark, 1690. 8°. IU.

2678AB — —[Anr. ed.] —, 1695. 8°. L.

2678AC — —[Anr. ed.] By M. C. for A. Armstrong, 1700. 8°. L.

2678B —The common rudiments of Latine grammar. By W. Godbid, for John Saywel, 1657. 8°. O; MH.

2679 — —[Anr. ed.] [London], by T. Mabb, for John Clarke, jun. 1659. 8°. L.

2679A — —[Anr. ed.] for John Clark, 1663. 8°. LLU.

2679B — —[Anr. ed.] By E. Cotes for John Clark, 1667. 8°. CLC, IU.

2679C — —[Anr. ed.] By A. Clark for John Clark, 1671. 8°. LLU.

2680 — —[Anr. ed.] [London], 1674. 8°. CHRISTIE-MILLER.

2681 —An easie entrance to the Latine tongue. By William Du-gard for Joshua Kirton, 1649. 8°. L, O, CT, RPL; IU, WF.

2681A — —Second edition By Thomas Newcomb for Joshuah. Kirton, 1651. 12°. IU.

2682 —Examinatio grammaticæ Latinæ. Typis T. Mabb, veneuntq; apud Johannem Clark, jun. 1660. 8°. LT.

2682A — —[Anr. ed.] Typis Tho. Mabb, 1661. 8°. CLC.

2682B — —[Anr. ed.] Apud Georgium Sawbridge, 1661. 8°. WF.

2683 Entry cancelled.
—Grammatica Latina. Sixth edition. 1670. See —Latine grammar.

2684 —The Latine grammar. By William Du-Gard; to bee sold by John Clark, jun., 1651. 8°. L, O, CH, LLU; Y.

2685 — —Second edition. By William Du-Gard, to bee sold by John Saywell, 1653. 8°. L.

2685A — —Third edition. By T. Mabb to be sold by Henry Mortlocke and Tho. Basset, 1659. 8°. OC, BC; RBU, WF.

2686 — —Fourth edition. By R. J. for F. Smith, 1665. 8°. L; CU, PL.

2687 — —Fifth edition. For Francis Smith, 1669. 8°. T.C.I 15. L.

2687A — —Sixth edition. —, 1670. 12°. LW; IU.

2688 —A new discovery of the old art. By J. T. for Andrew Crook, 1660. 12°. L, O, LU, LW, LLU; CH, IU, MH, NIC.

2688A [–] The petty-schoole. Shewing a way. By J. T. for Andrew Crook, 1659. 12°. O, LLU, M; CH.

2689 —Propria quæ maribus, . . . Englished. By T. H. for John Sayvvell, 1650. 8°. LT, C; WF.

2689A — —[Anr. ed.] By H. T. for John Saywell, 1653. 12°. L (t.p.).

2689B — —[Anr. ed.] By W. G. for John Saywell, 1657. 8°. O.

2689C — —[Anr. ed.] By T. M., 1659. 8°. L.

2690 Entry cancelled.
— —[Anr. ed.] 1683. See —Terminationes.

2691 —Terminationes. Typis T. H. impensis Johannis Sayvvelli, 1650. 8°.* LT, C.

2692 — —[Anr. ed.] Typis G. G. impensis Johannis Saywelli, 1657. 8°. O.

2693 — —[Anr. ed.] Typis T. Mabb, veneuntq; apud Johannem Clark, jun., 1659. 8°. L.

2693A — —[Anr. ed.] Cambridge, by John Field, 1665. 8°. L.

2693B — —[Anr. ed.] Excusum pro J. Clark, 1667. 8°. CLC, IU.

2693C — —[Anr. ed.] Typis E. C. pro J. Clark, 1669. 8°. WF.

2693D — —[Anr. ed.] Typis A. Clark impensis J. Clark, 1672. 8°. OC; MH.

2694 — —[Anr. ed.] Typis A. C. pro J. Clark, 1676. 8°. C.

2694aA — —[Anr. ed.] Typis M. C. pro J. Clark, 1683. 8°. L, O; WF.

2694bA — —[Anr. ed.] —, 1686. 8°. LLU.

2694cA — —[Anr. ed.] —, 1689. 8°. LLU.

2694dA — —[Anr. ed.] —, 1690. 8°. CLC, IU.

2694A — —[Anr. ed.] Typis M. Clark, impensis A. Armstrong, administr. Joannis Clark, 1697. 8°. L; IU, TO.

2694B — —[Anr. ed.] —, 1700. 8°. BC.

2695 —Vocabularium parvum . . . A little vocabulary. For Joshua Kirton, 1657. 12°. L.

2696 — —[Anr. ed.] For William Kirton, 1666. 12°. C; Y.

2696A — —[Anr. ed.] Andre. Clark, 1672. 12°. CP.

2697 — —[Anr. ed.] For Jos. Hindmarsh, 1696. 12°. O.

2698 [**Hooper, George**], *bp.* The Church of England free from the imputation of Popery. *For W. Abington,* 1683. 4°.* L, O, C, OC, LIU; CH, IU, MH, NC, NU, WF, Y.

2699 [–] —[Anr. ed.] *For Ch. Brome,* 1685. 4°. L, LCL, OME, CT, E, DT.

2700 [–] A discourse concerning Lent. *By Tho. Warren. for Walter Kettilby,* 1695. 8°. L, O, C, EN, DT; CH, IEG, NU, WF, Y.

2701 [–] —[Anr. ed.] —, 1696. 8°. L, C, EC; BBE, CH, CLC, TU, ZAS.

2702 No entry.

2703 [–] A fair and methodical discussion. *For R. Chiswell, and R. Bentley,* 1689. 4°. L, O, C, EC, DT; CLC, MH, MM, NU, TU.

2704 [–] The parsons case. *Printed,* 1689. 4°.* L, O, OC, BAMB, LSD, E; CLC, CN, MBA, MH, MM, WF, Y.

2705 —A sermon preach'd . . . 30th, of Octob. 1681. *For Mark Pardoe,* 1682. 4°.* T.C.I 470. L, C, OC, LIU, E; CH, NU, PL, WF, Y.

2706 —A sermon preached . . . fifth of November, 1681. *For Mark Pardoe,* 1682. 4°.* T.C.I 459. L, O, C, BR, DT; CH, IU, NU, WF, Y.

2707 —A sermon preached . . . Jan. 25, 1690/1. *For Walter Kettilby,* 1691. 4°.* T.C.II 355. L, O, C, EN, DT; CH, IU, NU, WF, Y.

2708 —A sermon preach'd . . . January xiv. 1693/4. *By Tho. Warren, for Walter Kettilby,* 1694. 4°.* T.C.II 490. L, O, C, OM, BR, EN; CH, CLC, MH, TO, WF, Y.

2709 —A sermon preach'd . . . Jan. 20. 1695. *By Tho. Warren, for Walter Kettilby,* 1695. 4°.* T.C.II 538. L, O, C, OM, BAMB, LIU; CH, CLC, IU, PL, TSM, WF, Y.

2710 Entry cancelled.

    [**Hoorn, J. G. van.**] Een nieuwe en gemakkelijke. 1690. *See* Heldoren, J. G. van.

2710A **Hooton, Elizabeth.** To the King and both Houses of Parliament. [*London,* 1670.] 4°.* L, LF; PH.

2710B **Hope, Sir Alexander.** Unto His Grace His Majesties High Commissioner, and . . . Parliament. The humble petition of. [*Edinburgh, J. Reid,* 1700.] brs. EN.

2710C **Hope, John.** Disputatio juridica. *Edinburgh, ex officina hæredum A. Anderson,* 1696. 4°.* ALDIS 3566.3. EN, GU.

2711 **Hope, Sir William.** The compleat fencing-master. *For Dorman Newman,* 1691. 8°. T.C.II 350. L, CM; CLC, IAU, MH, NP.

2712 [–] —Second edition. —, 1692. 8°. L, C, EN; MH.

2712A —[Anr. ed.] [*London*], *for Hugh Newman,* 1697. 8°. L (t.p.).

2713 [–] The fencing-master's advice. *Edinbvrgh, by John Reid,* 1692. 8°. ALDIS 3226. L, EN; WF.

2714 [–] The Scots fencing-master. *Edinbvrgh, by John Reid,* 1687. 8°. ALDIS 2690. L, EN; CH, MH, Y.

2715 Entry cancelled.

    —Supplement of horsemanship. [1696.] *See* Solleysell, Jacques de, *sieur de.* Compleat horseman.

2716 [–] The sword-man's vade-mecum. *Edinburgh, by John Reid,* 1691. 12°. ALDIS 3155.5. O, EN; CLC, WF, Y.

2717 ——Second edition. *Printed, and are to be sold by J. Taylor, and S. Holford,* 1694. 8°. T.C.II 493. L, LG, CT; Y.

2717A Hope and peace. In a letter. *For H. Bonwicke,* 1692. 8°. T.C.II 378. O.

2717B Hope farewel, adieu to all pleasure. [*n.p., c.* 1690.] brs. EN.

    Hopefull way to cure. [*n.p.,* 1652.] *See* Younge, Richard.

2718 **H[opkins], C[harles].** The art of love. *For Joseph Wild,* 1700. 8°. T.C.III 173. L, DT; CU, NN, Y.

2719 —Boadicea Queen of Britain. *For Jacob Tonson,* 1697. 4°. L, O, C, LVD, EN; CH, CN, LC, MH, MU, TU, WF, Y, AVP.

2720 —The court-prospect; a poem. [*London*], *sold by John Nutt,* 1699. 4°.* L, O, LW, LIU; CH, CN, MH, MIU, NN.

2721 —Epistolary poems. *By R. E. for Jacob Tonson,* 1694. 8°. L, O, C, OC, DC, DT; CH, CN, CU, MH, WF, Y.

2722 Entry cancelled. Ghost.

2723 —Friendship improv'd. *For Jacob Tonson,* 1700. 4°. L, O, C, LVD, EN; CH, CN, LC, MH, NC, TU, WF, Y.

2724 —The history of love: a poem. *By J. Dawks, for Jacob Tonson,* 1695. 8°. L, O, C, LLU, DT; CH, CN, NN, WF, Y.

2725 [–] Neglected virtue. *For Henry Rhodes, Richard Parker, Sam. Briscoe,* 1696. 4°. L, O, OW, LLU, EN; CH, CN, MH, NC, WCL, WF, Y.

2726 —Pyrrhus king of Epirus. *For Samuel Briscoe, Peter Buck, and Daniel Dring,* 1695. 4°. L, O, C, LVD, EN; CH, CN, LC, MH, NC, TU, WF, Y.

2727 —White-hall. *Dvblin: by Andrew Crook, for William Norman,* 1698. 4°.* DIX 301. L, DT; CN, MH, WF, Y.

2727A **Hopkins, Edward.** To the honorable assembly at the Commons house. [*London,* 1664.] brs. LG.

2728 **Hopkins, Ezekiel,** *bp.* The almost Christian. *For Dorman Newman, Jonathan Robinson, and Tho. Cockeril,* 1693. 8°. T.C.II 462. L, O, C, LG; CLC.

2728A —A blow at profaneness. colop: *For T. Parkhurst,* 1692. 12°.* CT; WF.

2729 —Discourses, or sermons. *For Nathanael Ranew,* 1691. 8°. T.C.II 345. L, O, OC, LSD; CH, NGT, NU.

2730 —An exposition on the Lord's Prayer. *For Nathanael Ranew, and Edward Mory,* 1692. 4°. T.C.II 402. L, O, C, LSD, SC; CH, MBA, MH, NU, WF, Y.

2731 ——Second edition. *For J. Robinson, A. and J. Churchill, J. Taylor, E. Mory, and J. Wyat,* 1698. 8°. O, CT, E, DT; RBU, Y.

2731A —An exposition on the Ten Commandments. *For Nathanael Ranew, Jonathan Robinson, and John Wyat,* 1691. 4°. C.

2732 ——[Anr. ed.] *For Thomas Parkhurst; Nathanael Ranew, and Jonathan Robinson,* 1692. 4°. L, C, OU, LSD, BLH; CH, IU, MBA, MH, VC, WF, Y.

2732A ——[Anr. ed.] *For Nathanael Ranew, Jonathan Robinson, and John Wyat,* 1692. 4°. T.C.II 376. LW, OC, DC, DU, E; NR, NU.

2733 —The first volume of discourses. Second edition. *By J. Wilde, for Nathanael Ranew,* 1694. 8°. T.C.II 495. O; MH, WF.

2734 —The fourth (and last) volume of discourses. *By H. Clark, for J. Robinson, A. and J. Churchill, J. Taylor, and J. Wyat,* 1696. 8°. T.C.II 600. O, BC.

2735 —A second volume of discourses. *By E. H. for Nathanael Ranew*, 1693. 8°. T.C.II 448. L, O, LW, OC, CT; MH, NRU.

2736 —A sermon, preached . . . the 6th. of August, 1662. *By Sarah Griffin, for Nathaniel Ranew*, 1663. 4°. L, O, LW, CT, BC, DT; CH, CU, MH, TU, WF, Y.

2737 Entry cancelled.
      —Sermon preached . . . sixth of August, 1662. 1685. *See* —Vanity of the world.

2738 —A sermon preached at Christ's Church in Dublin, Jan. 31 1669. *Dublin, by Benjamin Tooke, and to be sold by Mary Crooke*, 1671. 4°. T.C.I 65; DIX 142. L, C, OCC, EC, DT; TU.

2739 Entry cancelled.
      —Sermon preached . . . Jan. 31. 1669. . . . 1685. *See* —Vanity of the world.

2740 —A third volume of discourses. *By T. W. for Nathaniel Ranew*, 1694. 8°. T.C.II 490. O, CT, BC.

2741 —The vanity of the world. *For Nathaniel Ranew, and Jonathan Robinson*, 1668. 8°. L, C, LSC; IU, MIU, WF.

2741A ——[Anr. ed.] *For Nathaniel Ranew and Jonathan Robinson*, 1685. 8°. L, O; CH, V, WF, Y.

2742 ——[Anr. ed.] *For Nathanael Ranew, Jonathan Robinson, and Benjamin Tooke*, 1685. 8°. T.C.II 95. L, C; CH, CLC, NU, WF.

2743 **Hopkins, George.** Salvation from sinne. *By J. G. for Nathanael Web, and William Grantham*, 1655. 8°. LT, C, LCL, LW; NU, WF.

2744 **Hopkins, Henry.** A schedule or, list of the prisoners in the Fleet. *By S. G. for Livewell Chapman*, 1653. 4°.* LT, SP; CSS, WF.

2745 **Hopkins, John.** Amasia, or, the works of the muses. *By Tho. Warren for Bennet Banbury*, 1700. 8°. L, C, LVD, LLU, EN; CH, CU, MU, NP, TU, WF, Y.

2746 —Gloria. *For H. Newman*, 1700. fol.* T.C.III 157. MR; MH, NN, NP, TU.

2747 —Milton's Paradise Lost imitated in rhyme. *For Ralph Smith*, 1699. 8°. L, OM; CH, INU, IU, MH, Y, ZWT.
      —Old John Hopkin's, and Tho. Sternhold's petition. 1699. *See* title.

2748 No entry.

2749 —The triumphs of peace. *By B. Motte*, 1698. 8°. L, C, LCL, DT, BLH; CH, MH, NP.

2750 —The victory of death. *By B. M. to be sold by Sam. Buckley; and Rich. Wellington*, 1698. 8°. L, O, C, DT; CLC, MH, NP, TU, WF.

2750A **Hopkins, Marmaduke.** Murmurers reproved. *For Jonathan Robinson*, 1689. 4°.* T.C.II 243. L, CCH; CLC, CSS, PU, WF, Y.

2751 **Hopkins, Matthew.** The discovery of vvitches. *For R. Royston*, 1647. 4°.* LT, GU; CH, MH, WF.

2751A **Hopkins, William.** The flying pen-man. *For Samvel Lee*, [1680?]. 4°.* T.C.I 386. L, O; BBE, CLC, LC.

2752 ——[Anr. ed.] *By C. H. for the author*, 1674. 4°.* T.C.I 198. LNM, LU, MP.

2753 **[Hopkins, William], D. D.** Animadversions on Mr. Johnson's answer to Jovian. *For Walter Kettilby*, 1691. 8°. T.C.II 383. L, O, LCL, CS, BAMB, LSD; CDA, CLC, WF.

2754 —A sermon preached . . . September 3. 1683. *For Walter Kettilby*, 1683. 4°.* T.C.II 37. L, O, C, D; CH, NU, TU, V, WF, Y.

2755 **[Hopkins, William], of Dublin.** A message sent from the kingdom of Ireland. *Imprinted at London, by B. A.*, 1649. 4°.* LT, O, DN; CH, TU, Y.

2756 **[Hopkinson, James.]** The coppie of a letter from Major Generall Poines his quarters. *By B. Alsop, and J. Coe*, 1645. 4°.* LT; MH, Y.

2757 **Hopton, Ralph Hopton, baron.** The declaration of. *[London], printed*, 1650. 4°.* LT, C; CH.

2758 —A declaration sent from. *[London], printed*, 1649. 4°.* LT, C; CH, ZAP.

2759 —A message sent from. *For J. C.*, 1650. 4°.* LT, DT.

2760 Entry cancelled. *See following entry.*

2761 **[Hopton, Susannah.]** Daily devotions. *By A. Maxwell, for Jonathan Edwin*, 1673. 12°. T.C.I 147. L, O, RPL.

2761A **Hopwood, John.** Blessed rest. *For Benj. Harris*, 1676. 12°. O; CH, WF.

2762 **Horace.** Opera. *Edinburgi, excudebat Gideon Lithgo*, 1662. 12°. ALDIS 1737.5. O; NP.

2763 ——[Anr. ed.] *Impensis R. Clavel, H. Mortlock, S. Smith & B. Walford*, 1694. 8°. T.C.II 502. L, O, LCP, CT, DM; CH, IU, MBA, PL, Y.

2764 ——[Anr. ed.] *Cantabrigiæ, typis academicis, impensis Jacobi Tonson*, 1699. 4°. L, O, C, AN, EN, DT; BN, CLC, MH, MU, NP, TO, TU, WF, Y.

2765 ——[Anr. ed.] *Impensis R. Clavel, H. Mortlock, S. Smith & B. Walford*, 1699. 8°. T.C.III 142. O, C, AN, YM, CD; NP, V, Y.

2766 —All Horace his lyrics. *For Henry Herringman*, 1653. 8°. L, O, LVF, MAU; CH, MH, NC, WF.

2767 —All the odes and epodes of. *By Richard Cotes*, 1644. 12°. O.

2768 —Horace's art of poetry. *For Henry Herringman*, 1680. 4°.* T.C.I 394. L, O, CT, EN, CD; CH, CN, MH, TU, WF, Y.

2769 ——[Anr. ed.] *For Henry Herringman, and sold by Joseph Knight and Francis Saunders*, 1684. 4°.* T.C.II 105. L, O, C, ES, DT; CH, IU, MH, NP, WF, Y.

2770 —Horace, the best of lyrick poets. *For W. R. and J. W.*, 1652. 8°. L, O, OC, P, MAU; CN, NN, NP, RPJ, WF.

2771 ——[Anr. ed.] *For W. Webb*, 1652. 8°. MADAN 2195.* O, C; CLC, MH, Y.

2772 —The lyrick poet, odes and satyres. *Southwark, by Henry Hils*, 1649. 8°. L, O, MAU; CH, IU, MH, NP, TO, Y.

2773 —The odes and epodon. *For W. Crooke*, 1684. 8°. T.C.II 47. L, C, LLU, MAU; CH, MH, NN, TU, V, WF, Y.

2774 —The odes, satyrs, and epistles of. *For Jacob Tonson*, 1684. 8°. L, SHR, DT; BN, CLC, IU, MB, NP, RBU, WF, Y.

2774A ——[Anr. ed.] —, *and sold by Tim. Goodwin*, 1684. T.C.II 99. 8°. O, LLU; CDA, CSU, NCD, RBU, TO, Y.

2774B ——[Anr. ed.] *For Jacob Tonson, and Anthony Stephens*, 1684. 8°. O, C, LLU; CH, CLC, NP.

2775 ——Second edition. *For J. T., to be sold by Sam. Manship*, 1688. 8°. T.C.II 235. L; MU.

2776 ——"Second" edition. *For Jacob Tonson*, 1688. 8°. C, CS, BR, MR, E; NCU, PL, RBU, TU, Y.

2777 —Quinti Horatii Flacci poemata, scholiis. Seventh edition. *Typis Joannis Macock, pro Abel Roper*, 1660. 8°. O, C, LNC.

2777A — —[Anr. ed.] *Typis Joannis Macock pro Richardo Tomlins*, 1660. 8°. AN; MH, NP.

2778 — —Eighth edition. *Typis J. Macock, pro A. Roper, R. Tomlins, G. Sawbridge, N. Ranew, & J. Robinson*, 1670. 12°. O, CP, CS, MAU; CLC, PL.

2779 — —[Anr. ed.] *Typis A. C. sumptibus societatis*, 1576 [i.e., 1676]. 12°. T.C.I 239. OC, MAU; BN, CH, FU, Y.

2780 — —[Anr. ed.] *Impensis Abelis Swalle*, 1690. 8°. L, O, C, LLP, E; CN, IU, TSM, WF.

2781 —The poems of Horace. *By E. Cotes for Henry Brome*, 1666. 8°. L, O, LLU, MAU, E; CH, CN, MH, NP, TU, Y.

2782 — —[Anr. ed.] *By E. C. for W. Lee, G. Bedell, H. Heringman [sic], and H. Brome*, 1666. 8°. O, C, LVF, CM, P; IU, WCL, WF, Y.

2783 — —Second edition. *By A. C. for W. Lee, T. Collins, H. Herringman, and H. Brome*, 1671. 8°. L, O, LVD, LW, DT; CU, MH, NNM, NP, WF, Y, ZWT.

2783A — —"Second" edition. *By A. C. for H. Brome*, 1671. 8°. L, O, CM, SHR; CH, CLC, IU, MH, NCD, Y.

2783B — —"Second" edition. *For T. C. and J. F. to be sold by Spencer Hickman*, 1671. 8°. TU.

2784 — —Third edition. *By M. C. for H. Brome*, 1680. 8°. T.C.I 447. L, C, LIU, MAU, D; CH, CN, MH, NN, TU, Y.

2785 —Scholiis commentarii. *For John Seymovr; to be sold by Peter Parker; and Thomas Guy*, 1678. Sixes. L, O, OC; IU, WF, Y.

2786 —Selected parts of Horace. *For M. M. Gabriel Bedell and T. Collins*, 1652. 8°. LT, O, C, LVD, MAU; BN, CH, CN, LC, MH, WF, Y. (var.)

2787 Entry cancelled.
—Some odes of Horace imitated. 1690. *See* Glanvill, John.
Horæ Hebraicæ. 1671. *See* Lightfoot, John.
Horæ subsecivæ: or. 1664. *See* Denton, William.
Horatius. 1656. *See* Corneille, Pierre.

2787A **Horde, Thomas.** The case of Thomas Horde of Aston, . . . Oxon. [*n.p.*, 1670.] brs. LPR.

2788 **Horden, John.** A sermon preached . . . 29th. of May, 1676. *For Henry Brome*, 1676. 4°.* T.C.I 245. L, O, C, LSC, LSD, WCA, CD; NU, Y.

2788A **Horn, Georg.** A full and exact description of the earth. *Amsterdam, for John and Gillis Jansson à Waesberge, and sold at London by Timothy Childe*, 1700. LC.
Horn exalted. 1661. *See* Rogers, George.

2789 **Horne, Andrew.** The booke called, The mirrour of justices. *Imprinted at London, for Matthew Walbancke*, 1646. 8°. L, O, C, LIL, LL; CH, CSU, IU, LC, MHL, NCL, Y.

2789A — —[Anr. ed.] *For H. Marsh*, 1659. 8°. LC, PU.

2790 —La somme appelle Mirroir des iustices. *By E. G. for Matthew Wallbanke and Richard Best*, 1642. 8°. L, O, C, LG, LL; CH, CN, LC, MHL, NCL, NR, PU, TU, WF.

2790A **[Horne, Henry.]** The perfect and compleat bel-man. *For William Holeman*, 1666. 8°. O; WSG, Y.

2791 **Horne, John.** An appeal to the impartial & judicious reader. *For the author*, 1662. 4°. Y.

2792 —Balaam's wish. *Printed*, 1667. 4°. L, NPL.

2793 [–] The best exercise for Christians. *For Thomas Passenger*, 1671. 8°. T.C.I 71. L, O, C, LCL; NU.

2794 —The brazen serpent. *For Benjamin Southwood*, 1673. 4°. T.C.I 140. L, NPL; WF, Y.

2795 —A breife discovery of the people called Quakers. *By J. Brudenell, for the authors*, 1659. 4°. CT, MR.

2795A —Brief instructions for children. Second edition. *By A. C. and are to be sold by Edward Bromly*, 1656. 8°. WF.

2795B —The cause of infants maintained. *For Ben. Southwood*, 1675. 4°. C, CK, CM.

2796 —A caveat against the spirit of Antichrist. *For T. Brewster and G. Moul*, 1651. 8°. LW.

2797 —A comfortable corroborative cordial. *By Tho. Ratcliffe and N. Thompson, for B. Southwood*, 1672. 8°. L; CLC, RBU.

2798 [–] Διατριβη περι παιδο-βαπτισμου, or a consideration. *By J. M. for H. Cripps and L. Lloyd*, 1654. 4°. LT, LB, LCL, NPL, E; MH.

2799 [–] The divine wooer. *For R. Taylor, and T. Sawbridge*, 1673. 8°. T.C.I 151. L, O; CH, CN, IU, Y.

2800 —The efficacy of the true balme. [*London*], *for T. Passenger*, 1669. 8°. L.

2801 [–] Essayes about general and special grace. *By J. Brudenell for the author*, 1659. 4°.* L, O.

2802 — —[Anr. ed.] *For S. Walsall*, 1685. 8°. T.C.II 112. CS, LSC, NPL; NU.

2803 —A gracious reproof. *For Tho. Passenger*, 1668. 12°. O, C.

2804 —The life of faith in death. *By Abraham Miller*, 1649. 4°.* O, C, LW.

2805 —A proposal humbly offered to this honorable House of Commons. [*London*, 1696.] brs. L, LUG.

2806 —Horn's proposals, humbly offered. [*London*, 1696.] brs. L, LUG.

2807 —The Quakers proved deceivers. *For John Allen*, 1660. 4°. LF.

2807A —The reviewer reviewed. *For Austin Rice*, 1667. 4°. CS.

2807B —The reward of the wise. *For B. Southwood*, 1672. 8°. LW.

2808 —The righteovs mans hope. *For Tho. Underhill*, 1649. 4°.* LT, DU, DT; CLC.

2809 —Θυρα 'ανεωγμενη. The open door. *By Robert White, to be sold by Giles Calvert*, 1650. 4°. LT, O, CCA, DC, NPL; NU, Y.

2810 —Truth's triumph over deceit. *For J. Allen*, 1660. 4°. O.

2811 **Horne, Thomas.** Χειραγωγια, sive manuductio. *Excudebat Rob. Young*, 1641. 12°. O, C, LLL, LW; CLC, MH, MWA, WG, HC.

2811A — —[Anr. ed.] *Excudebat Rob. Yong, & venales extant apud Guil. Hope*, 1650. 12°. Y.

2812 — —[Anr. ed.] *Ad insigne bibliorum & coronæ*, 1687. 12°. T.C.II 201. L, LI, EC, CD; BN, CH, IU, LC, NP, Y.

2812A —Janua linguarum, or. Ninth edition. *By James Young, to be sold by John Clark junior*, 1645. 8°. MWA, WF.

2812B —Rhetoricae compendium. *Typis Guil. Dugardi, veneunt apud Franc. Eglesfield*, 1651. 8°.* WF.

2813 —A sermon preached . . . November 18, 1679. *For Samuel Carr*, 1680. 4°.* T.C.I 381. L, C, CK, EC; CLC, CN, WF, Y.

2814 —A sermon preached . . . eighth of February 1684/5. *For Robert Horne*, 1685. 4°.* L, O, C, EC, D; CH, CN, MBA, WF, Y.

2814A **Horne, Willem Adriaan,** *graaf van.* A letter from His Excellency the Heer Van Horne. *For J. G.*, 1674. 4°.* O; HR, CH.

2815 **Horneck, Anthony.** An account of Mr. Edward Sclater's return. [*London*], *in the Savoy: by Edward Jones, for Samuel Lowndes*, 1689. 4°.* L, O, CT, SA, BLH; CH, CN, MH, NU, TU, WF, Y.

2816 ——[Anr. ed.] *London, reprinted Edinburgh*, 1689. 4°. ALDIS 2896. EN.

2817 —An account of what happen'd in . . . Sweden. [*London*], *for S. Lowndes*, 1682. 4°.* O, BAMB, GU; CH, NCU, JF.

2818 Entry cancelled.
—Account of what happen'd in . . . Sweden. 1688. *See* Glanvill, Joseph. Saducismus triumphatus.

2819 —Bibliotheca Hornecciana: a catalogue. [*London*, 1697.] 4°. L, OP.

2820 —The blessed advantages of peace. *For B. Aylmer*, 1697. 8°.* L.

2821 —The crucified Jesus. *For Sam. Lowndes*, 1686. 8°. LW; CLC, MB, NU, WF, Y.

2821A ——[Anr. ed.] —, *sold by Tho. Salusbury and John Salusbury*, 1686. 8°. T.C.II 155. L, NE.

2822 ——Second edition. [*London*], *in the Savoy; by Edw. Jones, for Samuel Lowndes*, 1689. 8°. T.C.II 294. L, LW, OME; FU, Y.

2823 ——Third edition. [*London*], *in the Savoy, for Samuel Lowndes*, 1695. 8°. L, O, LW; CH, CLC, NCU, NGT.

2824 ——Fourth edition. *For S. Lowndes*, 1700. 8°. L, O, C, DC, EN; CLC, IEG, PL.

2824A —Delight and judgment. *By H. Hills jun. for Mark Pardoe*, 1684. 8°. T.C.II 41. L, O, CCA, CS, LLU; CLC, WF, WG.

2825 —The exercise of prayer. *ondon* [*sic*] *for Mark Pardoe*, 1685. 12°. T.C.II 134. L, O; Y.

2825A ——[Anr. ed.] *For Henry Mortlock*, 1697. 12°. T.C.III 3. KEBLE.

2826 —The fire of the altar. [*London*], *by T. N. for Samuel Lowndes*, 1683. 12°. T.C.II 12. O, CT; CH.

2827 ——Second edition. *For Samuel Lowndes*, 1684. 12°. T.C.II 78. L, O; CH.

2827A ——Fourth edition. —, 1688. 12°. WF.

2827B ——"Fourth" edition. —, *to be sold by Henry Rhodes*, 1688. 12°. T.C.II 235. LLP; CLC, Y.

2828 ——Fifth edition. *For Samuel Lowndes, to be sold by Henry Rhodes*, 1690. 12°. T.C.II 308. L, E; CH.

2828A ——Seventh edition. *For Samuel Lowndes*, 1695. 12°. CSE.

2828B ——"Seventh" edition. *For S. L., sold by Tho. Chapman*, 1695. 12°. NE.

2828C ——Eighth edition. *For S. L., sold by T. Bever*, 1698. 12°. CB.

2829 ——Ninth edition. *For Sam Lowndes*, 1700. 12°. L.

2830 —The first fruits of reason. *By F. Collins, for D. Brown; to be sold by John Weld*, 1686. 12°. T.C.II 143. L, O, C, LG, SP, E; CH, CLC, NU, WF.

2831 —Four tracts. *For S. Lownds, W. Hinchman, S. Keble, and D. Browne*, 1697. 8°. T.C.III 22. O, C, LLL, DC, E; CH, CLC, CN, NC.

2831A ——[Anr. ed.] *For S. L. W. H. S. K. and D. B., sold by A. Roper, R. Clavel, and Fr. Coggan*, 1697. 8°. CT, DUS; WF, Y.

2832 —Gods providence. [*London*], *in the Savoy, by T. N. for Samuel Lowndes*, 1682. 4°. T.C.I 471. L, O, LG, CT, DU, DL; CH, CLC, MH, NU, PU, WF, Y.

2833 —The great law of consideration. *By T. N. for Sam. Lownds*, 1677. 8°. T.C.I 251. L, O, LW, AN, MR, AVP.

2834 ——Second edition. —, 1678. 8°. T.C.I 295. L, DC, E, DT; CLC, MIU, NCU, NU, WF.

2835 ——Third edition. —, 1682. 8°. T.C.I 467. C, O, OM; CH, CSU.

2836 ——Fourth edition. *For Samuel Lowndes, to be sold by Tho. Fabian*, 1684. 8°. L, O, C, CCA; CLC, IU, MIU.

2837 ——Fifth edition. *For Samuel Lowndes, to be sold by Henry Rhodes*, 1688. 8°. T.C.II 220. O, LW, EC; CLC, CN, FU, NC.

2837A ——Sixth edition. *For Samuel Lowndes*, 1694. 8°. O, LSC, NE; CDA, CN, PL, Y.

2837B ——Seventh edition. *By Edw. Jones, for Samuel Lowndes*, 1698. 8°. L, CM, SHR; CH, IEG, MH.

2837C ——"Seventh" edition. *By E. Jones for S. L. and sold by W. Hawes*, 1698. 8°. L; WF.

2838 —The happiness of being saved. [*London*], *in the Savoy, by E. Jones, for Sam. Lowndes*, 1695. 4°.* T.C.II 556. L, O, LCL, LW, CT, DU; CB, CLC, FU, NGT, WF.

2839 —The happy ascetick. [*London*], *by T. N. for Henry Mortlock, and Mark Pardoe*, 1681. 8°. T.C.I 413. L, O, CS, LIU, LLU, E; CH, CLC, IU, MBA, MH, Y.

2840 ——Second edition. *For H. M. and M. P. and sold by Joshua Phillips, and Joseph Watts*, 1686. 8°. T.C.II 153. L, CSE, DUS, P, E; CU, CHW, MH, WF.

2840A ——"Second" edition. *For Henry Mortlock and Mark Pardoe*, 1686. 8°. DU; CH, NCU, SE, Y.

2841 ——Third edition. *For Henry Mortlock*, 1693. 8°. T.C.II 458. L, O, C, LNC, SHR; CLC, CN, FU, IU, NC, Y.

2842 ——Fourth edition. —, 1690. 8°. T.C.III 145. L, O; CH, NGT, NU, TSM, AAS.

2843 ——Fifth edition. —, 1693. 8°. LCL, CT.

2844 —The honesty of the Protestant. Second edition. *For James Collins*, 1681. 12°. P; NU, WF, Y.

2845 [-] A letter from a Protestant gentleman to a lady. *For James Collins*, 1678. 12°. L, O, C.

2846 —The nature of true Christian righteousness. [*London*], *in the Savoy, by E. Jones for Sam. Lowndes; and published by R. Taylor*, 1689. 4°.* T.C.II 283. L, O, LLP, OC, YM; CDA, CH, MH, NU, TSM, WF.

2847 —The passion of our blessed Lord. *For S. Bates*, [1700?]. 8°.* L; CLC.

2848 [–] Questions and answers concerning the two religions. *For Sam. Lowndes*, 1688. 8°.* L, O, LLP, OC.

2849 —A sermon preached . . . 24th of June, 1677. *For James Collins*, 1677. 4°.* T.C.I 289. L, O, C, LW, NE; CH, NU, WF, Y.

2850 —A sermon preached . . . Easter-day, MDCLXXXIX. *For Ric. Chiswell*, 1689. 4°.* T.C.II 249. L, O, C, BR, DT; CH, MH, MIU, NU, WF, Y.

2851 —Several sermons upon the fifth of St. Matthew; . . . the first volume. *By J. H. for B. Aylmer*, 1698. 8°. T.C.III 37. O, CT, DUS, RPL, E; CLC, Y, ZAS.

2852 ——Second volume. *For Brabazon Aylmer*, 1698. 8°. T.C.III 72. O, OME, CT, RPL, E; CLC, ZAS.

2853 —The sirenes, or, delight and judgment. Second edition. *By H. Clark for Henry Mortlock*, 1690. 12°. T.C.II 327. LW, MR, NE; CH, LC, Y.

2854 **Horneck, Philip.** A sermon occasioned by the death of Lady Guilford. *For Edmund Rumball*, 1699. 4°.* L, LVF, BP, BLH; CLC, NCD, WF, Y.

Hornworth, Robert. *See* Farnworth, Richard.
Horological dialogues. 1675. *See* Smith, John.
Horological disquisitions. 1694. *See* Smith, John.
Horologium Christianum. Oxoniae, 1689. *See* Lee, Francis.

2855 The horrible and bloody conspiracy vndertaken. *For Tho. Vere, and Wil. Gilbertson*, 1658. 8°.* LT, O.
Horrible and bloody plot. 1646. *See* C., S.

2856 Horrible newes from Colebrooke. *For J. Rich, Nov.* 11. 1642. 4°.* LT; MBP.

2857 Horrible newes from Hvll. *Iuly*, 11. *London for J. H. and T. Ryder*, 1642. 4°.* LT, CD; Y.
Horrible newes from Lancashire. 1642. *See* Williamson, Benjamin.

2858 Horrible nevves from Leicester. *Fo I. Horton, Iune 9.* 1642. 4°.* LT, EC; CH, MH, WF.

2859 Horrible nevves from Warwick-shire. *For T. Rider, Aug.* 20. 1642. 4°.* L; Y.

2860 Horrible news from Yorke. *May 24 [London], for Ioh. Greensmeth. An. Coe*, 1642. 4°.* LT, O, LHO; CH, MBP, MH, WF.

2860A Horrible newes from Yorke. *For T. Ryder*, 1642. *May* 24. 4°.* LT, O; IU, MM, Y.

2861 Horrible news from Yorkshire. *For D. M.* 1676. 4°.* MR.

2862 The horrible persecution of the French Protestants in . . . Poitou. colop: *For Randolph Taylor*, 1681. brs. L, O, C, HH; CH, PL, WF, AVP.
Horrible strategems. 1650. *See* B., A.
Horrible, terrible, troublesome. 1660. *See* Wild, Robert.
Horrible thing committed. 1658. *See* Robertson, Thomas.

2863 The horrid conspiracie of such impenitent traytors as intended a nevv rebellion. *For Samuel Speed*, 1663. 4°.* L, O, C, LSD, EN, BQ; CH, MH, WF, Y.
Horrid, direful, prodigious. 1679. *See* G., E.

2864 Horrid news from St. Martins. *For D. M.*, 1677. 4°.* L.

2865 Horrid news of a barbarous murder. *[London], for John Millet*, [1676]. 4°.* OB, CCH.

2866 The horrid Popish plot happily discover'd. *For R. G.*, 1678. brs. L, HH; MH, Y.
Horrid sin. 1681. *See* S., T.

2867 Entry cancelled.

Horrocks, Jeremiah. Excerpta ex epistolis. 1672. *See following entry.*

2868 —Jeremiæ Horroccii, . . . Opera posthvma. *Typis Gulielmi Godbid, impensis J. Martyn*, 1673-72. 4°. T.C.I 128. L, O, C, E, DT; BN, CH, CU, LC, MH, MU, PL.

2869 ——[Anr. ed.] *Prostant venales apud Mosem Pitt*, 1678. O, CT, DCH, P, EN, CD; IU, V, WCL, WF, Y.

2870 —Jeremiæ Horroccii, . . . Opvscvla astronomica. *Typis W. G. prostant apud Rob. Scott*, 1673. 4°. CPE, P, GU; BN, CLC, MH, NN.
Horse-flesh. 1682. *See* Phillips, John.

2870A The horse-manship of England. *For Thomas Parkhurst*, 1682. 4°.* WF.

2871 [**Horsley, Thomas.**] Strange news from Staffordshire. [*London*, 1679.] cap., fol.* L, LNC; MH.

2871A **Horsman, John.** A plain discourse . . . Lord's Supper. *For E. Richardson*, 1698. 12°. T.C.III 63. L.

2872 [**Horsman, Nicholas.**] The spiritual bee. *Oxford, by A. & L. Lichfield, for Edw. & Joh. Forrest*, 1662. 12°. MADAN 2600. L, O, C, CE, SP; CH, CLC, IU, WF, Y.

2873 [–] —[Anr. ed.] *Oxford, by W. H. for John Crosley*, 1667. 12°. MADAN 2769. L, O, C; NU, PSC.

2874 **Horsman, Robert.** Sionis certamina et trivmphvs. [*London*], 1651. 8°. L, O, CK, WCA.

2874A ——[Anr. ed.] [*London*], 1653. 8°. LT.

Hortolanus, *junior, pseud.*

2875 **Horton, Thomas.** Choice and practical expositions. *By A. Maxwell for Tho. Parkhurst*, 1675. fol. T.C.I 203. L, O, LCL, CE, P, E; IU, MH, NR, NU, TSM, WF, AVP.

2876 —Forty six sermons. *By A. Maxwell for Tho. Parkhurst*, 1674. fol. T.C.I 167. L, O, LW, CS, E; CH, INU, IU, MH, WF, AVP.

2877 —One hundred select sermons. *For Thomas Parkhurst*, 1679. fol. T.C.I 347. L, O, C, MC, E; CLC, WF, Y, AVP.

2878 —The pillar and pattern. *Printed at London by R. I. for Jo. Clark*, 1655. 4°.* LT, O, LG, LW, WCA; CH, NU, WF, Y.

2879 —Rich treasure in earthen vessels. *Printed* 1663. 8°.* L, O, C; CLC, NU, Y.

2880 —The safety of Jerusalem. *For John Clarke*, 1657. 4°.* O, LLP, WCA; CH, MH, NU, WF.

2881 —A sermon preached . . . Febr. 28. 1671. *By W. R. for Ralph Smith*, 1672. 4°.* L, O, LLP, LW, YM; CU, MIU, Y.

2882 —Sinne's discovery and revenge. *By F: Neile for Samuel Gellibrand*, 1646. 4°.* LT, O, C, BP, EN; CH, MH, NP, NU, WF, Y.

2883 —The vnrighteovs Mammon. *By I. R. for John Clark*, 1661. 4°.* O, C, CS, YM; NC, WF.

2884 —Wisdome's jvdgment of folly. *By T. Maxey for Samuel Gellibrand*, 1653. 4°. LT, O, CM, BP, WCA; CLC, MBP, NU, PL, TSM, Y.

2885 —Zion's birth-register unfolded. *For John Clark,* 1656. 4°. LT, O, C, BC, DT; CH, NU, WF, Y.

2886 Entry cancelled.

Horton, Thomas, *Colonel.* Fuller relation of a great victory. 1648. *See title.*

2887 [–] Die Mercurii, 17 Maii, 1648. A true confirmation of the great victory in VVales. *For Edward Husband, May* 18. 1648. 4°.* LT, LLL, AN, LSD; CH, CSS, MH, WF.

Hosannah: a thanksgiving-sermon. Oxford, 1660. *See* Martin, John.

Hosanna: or, a song. [n.p.], 1649. *See* Atkins, *Sir* Thomas.

Hosannah to the son. 1657. *See* Jackson, John.

Hoselock, John. *See* Haslock, John.

2887A **Hoskins, Thomas.** An humble proposal to the . . . house of Commons for raising of large sums of money. [n.p., 1700?] brs. L.

2887B —A proposal for a fund for Greenwich-Hospital and registered seaman. [n.p. 1695?] brs. L; CSS.

2888 **Hospinian, Rodolph Wirth,** *called.* The Jesuit's manner of consecrating. By T. S., 1678. 4°.* T.C.I 332. L, O, OB, LSD, E; CH, NU, PL, WF, Y.

2889 — —[Anr. ed.] *Dublin, reprinted by Joseph Ray, for Joseph Howes and William Winter,* 1681. 4°.* DIX 187. L, DU, DK, DT, BQ; Y.

2889A Hott candle for a lukewarme politician. [*York, by Thomas Broad*], printed 1645. YM.

2890 **Hotchkis, Thomas.** A discourse concerning the imputation. *For Walter Kettilby,* 1675. 8°. T.C.I 215. L, O, C, E, DT; CLC, MB, MH, NCU, NU, WF.

2891 —An exercitation concerning the nature of forgiveness of sin. *By T. M. for Tho. Underhill, and Math. Keinton,* 1655. 12°. LT, O, CK, DT; CLC, IU, MH, NU, Y.

2891A —A postscript. *By S. R. for W. Kettilby,* 1678. 8°. T.C.I 288. L, O, CS, BAMB, DT; CH.

2892 —Reformation or ruine. *For Tho. Parkhurst,* 1675. 12°. T.C.I 216. L, O, C, E; NU.

2893 —The second part of a discourse. *For Walter Kettleby,* 1678. 8°. T.C.I 309. L, O, C, OC, NE, DT; MH.

2894 **Hotham, Charles.** Ad philosophiam Teutonicam manuductio. *Excudit T. W. pro H. Blunden,* 1648. L, O, C, DC, MR; MU, WF.

2895 —Corporations vindicated. *For Giles Calvert,* 1651. 12°. L, O, C, LNC, SP; CH, LC, MH, WF, Y.

2896 —An introduction to the Tevtonick philosophie. *By T. M. & A. C. for Nath. Brooks,* 1650. 12°. L, O, C, YM; CH, WU, Y.

2897 —The petition and argument of. *For Giles Calvert,* 1651. 4°. L, O, C, MR, EN; CH, CSS, LC, WF, Y.

2898 — —[Anr. ed.] [*London*], *printed,* 1651. 12°. SP; CLC, MH.

2899 —To every member of Parliament. [*London,* 1653.] brs. LT.

2900 —A true state of the case of. [*London*], *printed,* 1651. 12°. 93 pp. C, CP, LCL, MR, SP; CH, CLC, MH, Y.

2901 — —[Anr. ed.] [*London*], *printed,* 1651. 4°.* 46 pp. LT, C, LIU, MR; CSS, WF.

2902 Entry cancelled.

[**Hotham, Durand.**] Life of one Jacob Boehmen. 1644. *See title.*

2902A —The life of Jacob Behmen. *For H. Blunden,* 1654. fol.* A–I⁴K². WF.

— —[Anr. ed.] 1654. *See* Böhme, Jacob. Mysterium.

2902B **Hotham, Capt. John.** The declaration of. *For Richard Best, October* 11. 1642. 4°.* LT, EC, YM; CH, MH, MM, TU.

2903 **Hotham, Sir John.** Certaine letters sent from. *Oxford, by Henry Hall,* 1643. 4°.* MADAN 1326. L, O, C, DU, LNC; CH, WF.

2904 Entry cancelled.

—Declaration of. *See* Hotham, *Capt.* John.

2905 —A learned speech made by . . . 23. of May 1642. *For J. Horton,* 1642. *May* 27. 4°.* LT, O, CCA, YM, CD; CH, CN, MH, WF, Y.

2906 —A letter from. *April* 5. *For Edward Husbands,* 1643. brs. STEELE 2402. LT, ES; MH.

2907 —Sir John Hothams letter to a worthy member. *For Edward Husbands,* 1642. brs. LT, O, LG, OC, EC, LNC, YM.

2908 —Reasons why. [*London,* 1642.] cap., 4°.* LT, O, LIU, YM, EN; CH, CN, IU, LC, WF, Y.

2909 —Sir John Hotham's resolution . . . 12 of July, 1642. *For I. Horton, Iuly* 16, 1642. 4°.* LT, EC; Y.

2909A [–] A true and exact relation of all the proceedings. *For Richard Best,* 1643. 4°.* LT, O, CCL, LLU, DT; CH, WF, Y.

2910 —A trve relation of a great discovery intended against Hull. *For F. Coules, and T. Bates, Iune* 4, 1642. 4°.* L; CN, MH, Y.

2910A [**Hotman, François.**] A patterne of Popish peace. *By L. N. for Richard Whitaker,* 1644. 12°. L, LIL; CH, NF, NPT, NU.

2911 **Hough, Ralph.** Catalogue of the library. [*London,* 1699?] 4°. L, O, BR.

2912 **Hough, Roger.** The contents of the history of the five book's [*sic*] of Moses. *For T. Passenger,* 1670. 8°.* L.

2912A Gods hatred against sin. [*London*], *by H. B. for T. Passinger,* 1683. 12°. CM.

2913 —The poor mans misery. *For Tho. Passenger,* 1670. 8°.* L; CSS.

2914 —Saints blessed for ever. *By E. Crouch for T. Vere,* 1667. 8°.* L.

2914A — —[Anr. ed.] *By A. M. for J. Deacon,* [1695]. 8°.* CM.

2914B —Sighs from hell. *For Charles Passinger,* [1680?]. 8°. O.

2915 —A wonder of wonders. *For T. Passenger,* 1666. 8°.* L; CU.

2915A —The young-man's duty. *By W. L. and T. J. for Phillip Brrooksby [sic],* 1677. 8°. GU.

2916 Entry cancelled. Ghost.

2916A **Houghton, Aylmar.** An antidote against Hen. Haggar's poysonous pamphlet. *For Tho. Parkhurst,* 1658. 4°. ORP.

2917 — —[Anr. ed.] *For Tho. Parkhust [sic]* 1659. 4°. LT, CE, CK, BC, E; MM, NHC, Y.

2918 —Clavis εξουσιαριχη: the key of ordination. *Loudon* [*sic*], *by R. I. for Tho. Parkhurst,* 1656. 8°. LT, LLP; MH, MM.

2919 [**Houghton, John.**] An account of a whale. colop: *Printed, to be sold by Randal Taylor*, 1693. brs. C.

2920 —An account of the acres and houses. *For Randal Taylor*, 1693. brs. L, O, LPR; CH, CN, INU, U. OREGON.

2921 No entry.

2922 [–] England's great happiness. *By J. M. for Edward Croft*, 1677. 4°.* T.C.I 283. L, O, CT, EN, DT; CH, CN, MH, NC, WF, Y.

2922A —A proposal for improvement of husbandry. [*London*, 1691.] cap., fol.* L; MH.

2923 **Houghton, Thomas.** The alteration of the coyn. *By W. Downing: to be sold by R. Baldwin*, 1695. 4°. L, O, LG, LUG, CT, EN; CH, CJC, IU, NC, Y.

2923A ——[Anr. ed.] *For the author*, 1695. 4°. L, DT; MH, NN, PU, WF, ANL.

2924 —A book of funds. *For Richard Baldwin.* 1695. 4°.* L, O, CT, ES; NC, WF, Y.

2925 Entry cancelled. *See following entry.*

2925A ——[Anr. ed.] *For the authour*, 1696. 4°.* L, O, LG, CS; CH, IU, MH, NC, PU, WF, ANL.

2926 —The compleat miner. *For William Cooper*, 1688. 12°. L; KQ, WF.

2927 —Europe's glory. *Printed*, 1695. 4°.* L, O, CT, EN, DT; CH, CN, MH, NC, PL, WF, Y.

2928 [–] The golden treasury. *For the author, and sold by J. Marshal*, 1699. IU, NC, WF, Y.

2929 [–] The laws and customs of the miners in the forrest of Dean. *For William Cooper*, 1687. 12°.* T.C.II 199. L, BR, NOT; KQ, WF, Y.

2930 [–] A letter to a member of Parliament: shewing how probably the credit. colop: *For Tho. Cockerill*, 1697. cap., 4°.* OH; NC, Y.

2931 —The loyal and true hearted subjects good will. [*London*], *for Thomas Passenger*, [1680–82]. brs. L, HH; MH.

2931A —A plain and easie method for supplying the scarcity of money. *Sold by E. Whitlock*, 1696. * LUG; PU.

2932 —Proposals for a fund. *Printed*, 1694. 4°.* LUG, ES; LC, MH, NC, NCD, WF, Y.

2933 —Rara avis in terris: or the compleat miner. *Printed*, 1681. LUG, LNC; CH, IU, KQ, MH, NC, PU, Y.

2934 ——[Anr. ed.] *For William Cooper*, 1681. 12°. T.C.I 443. L, O, C, NOT, GU; BN, CH, CLC, MHL, WF, Y.

2935 —Royal institutions. *For the author*, 1694. Sixes. L, C, OC, BC, LUG; BN, CH, CN, LC, MHL, WF, Y.

2936 Entry cancelled.
—Subjects goodwill to king. [1677?]   *See* —Loyal and true hearted subjects good will.

2937 —To the Lords, spiritual and temporal. [*London*, 1694.] brs. L, C.

2937A **Houghton, William.** A discourse concerning Ananias and Saphira. *By J. H. for Nathaniel Webb*, 1661. 4°.* C; WF.

2938 —Preces & lachrymæ. A sermon. *By Roger Daniel, for Samuel Cartwright*, 1650. 4°. LT, ENC, DT; NU, RBU.

2939 **Houlbrook, William.** A black-smith and no Jesuite. *For the author, to be sould by Francis Lash*, 1660. 8°. LT.

2940 —The loyal-blacksmith and no Jesuite. Second edition. *For the author*, 1677. 8°. T.C.I 261. O; CH, WF.

2941 [**Houpreght, John Frederick.**] Aurifontina chymica: or a collection. *For William Cooper*, 1680. 24°. T.C.I 370. L, OC, CT, LLU, GU; CH, CPB, MH, NN, WU, Y.

2942 The hours of daily prayer. Second edition. 1692. brs. L.

2943 **H[ouschone], W[illiam].** The conduct and conveyance of our fathers. [*Scotland*, 1690.] 8°.* EN.

2944 [–] Scotland pulling down the gates. *For Joseph Roberts*, 1683. 4°.* L, O, LSD, EN; NU.

House of wisdom. 1681. *See* Bampfield, Francis.

2945 House-hold observations necessary. *By T. Paine, to be sold by F. Coles*, 1647. brs. LT.

2946 **Houser, Henry.** An exact model. *For Francis Tyton*, 1673. 4°.* T.C.I 116. L, WCA; MH.

2947 Houses insured from loss by fire, by amicable contribution. [*London?* 1695.] brs. MC; NP.

2948 **Houstone, William.** Mr. Houstone's answer. [*Edinburgh*], *Maybol printed*, 1694. brs. ALDIS 3371. EN.

2949 **Houstoun, William.** Disputatio juridica. *Ex typographæo Georgii Mosman, Edinburgi*, 1697. 4°. ALDIS 3671. EN.

2949A [**Hovell, John.**] A discourse on the woollen manufactory of Ireland. [*London*], *printed*, 1698. 4°. L, C, LLP; MERRIMACK VALL. TEXTILE MUS., MH, WF, Y, ANL.

2950 [–] —[Anr. ed.] *Dublin, re-printed by J. B. & S. P., to be sold by Jacob Milner*, 1698. 4°.* DIX 302. L, C, CD, DI, DT; CH, MIU, NC, WU, Y.

2951 **How, Samuel.** The sufficiencie of the spirits teaching. [*London*], *printed*, 1644. 4°. LT, BC, P, SP, DT; MH, NHC, WF, Y.

2952 ——[Anr. ed.] [*London*], *newly printed, and are to be sold by William Larnar*, 1655. 4°.* L, C; MM, PL, PSC, RBU, Y.

2953 ——[Anr. ed.] *By G. L. for Thomas Malthus*, 1683. 4°.* O, P; LC, MBZ, PH, WF.

2954 ——Fifth edition. *For a friend of the author: sold by William and Jos. Marshall*, [1689]. 4°.* O, C, CU, NU.

2955 ——Sixth edition. *For a friend of the author's; and sold by William Marshall*, 1692. 4°.* L, O; NHC, Y.

2956 [**How, William.**] Phytologia Britannica. *Typis Ric. Cotes, impensis Octaviani Pulleyn.* 1650. 8°. L, O, C, MAU, DT; LC, MH, WF.

How all the inhabitants of London . . . coles. [n.p.], 1690. *See* Haddock, Thomas.

2957 How and Rich: an impartial account. colop: *For T.M.*, 1681. brs. L, O, OC, MC; CN, IU, MBA, MH.

2958 How far the clergy and other members of the Church of England ought to communicate. *Printed*, 1690. 4°.* O, LL, OC, BAMB, LSD, YM; CLC, MB, WF, Y.

2959 Entry cancelled.
How far the Romanists may be trusted. 1675. *See* Dodwell, Henry. Some considerations.

How God's people. 1687. *See* Fox, George.

How sin is strengthened. 1657. *See* Nayler, James.

2960 How sweet and lasting are the joys. [*London*], *T. Cross*, [1700?]. brs. L.

How the ground of temptation. [n.p., 1662.] *See* Nayler, James.

How the love of God. [n.p., 166–?] *See* Baker, Richard. *Quaker.*

2961 How the members of the Church of England ought to behave themselves. *Printed, and are to be sold by Randal Taylor,* 1687. 8°. L, O, C, MC, DT; CH, IU, MM, NU, WF, Y.

2962 How to order any land. [*London,* 165–?] 4°.* R; LC.

2963 How without any charge to the publick, to raise four hundred thousand pounds. [*London,* 1696?] brs. L; NC.

2964 **Howar, Thomas.** The poor gift of. *Printed,* 1668. brs. L.

Howard, Charles. *See* Berkshire, Charles Howard, earl of.

Howard, Edward. *See also* Suffolk, Edward Howard, earl of.

2965 —The Brittish princes. *By T. N. for H. Herringman,* 1669. 8°. T.C.I 10. L, O, C, LVD, LLU; CH, CN, MH, TU, WF, Y.

2966 [–] Caroloiades, or, the rebellion. *By J. B. for the author, and publish'd by Randal Taylor,* 1689. 8°. L, LVD, LIU, E, EN; CH, CN, MH, TU, WCL, Y.

2967 [–] —[Anr. ed.] *By J. B. for the author,* 1689. 8°. WF.

2968 [–] Caroloiades redivivus: or, the war. *For George Chapman,* 1695. 8°. L, LLU; CH, CN, MH, OCI, WF, Y.

2969 —The man of Newmarket. *By J. C. for W. Crook,* 1678. 4°. T.C.I 330. L, O, LVD, CS, EN; CH, CN, LC, MH, MU, Y.

2970 —A memorial delivered to his majesty by. [*London,* 1677.] cap., fol.* O.

2971 —A panegyrick to . . . the Duke of York. *For Henry Herringman,* 1666. fol.* CH, CLC, MH.

2972 Entry cancelled. Ghost.

2973 [–] Poems, and essays. *By J. C. for W. Place,* 1673. 8°. T.C.I 152. LIU, CASTLE ASHBY; OSU, RHT, WF, Y.

2973A [–] —[Anr. ed.] *By J. C. for Nicholas Cox,* 1674. 8°. L; WF.

2974 [–] The six days adventure. *For Tho. Dring,* 1671. 4°. T.C.I 80. L, O, LVD, BC, EN; CH, CN, LC, MH, WF, Y.

2975 —The usurper. *For Henry Herringman,* 1668. 4°. L, O, C, OW, EN; CH, CN, MH, MU, TU, WF, Y.

2976 [–] The womens conquest. *By J. M. for H. Herringman,* 1671. 4°. L, O, C, LVD, EN; CH, CN, LC, MH, MU, NC, TU, WCL, WF, Y.

2977 [–] —[Anr. ed.] *For H. Herringman,* 1671. 4°. T.C.I 72. MH.

2978 [**Howard, Edward**], *of Berkshire.* Remarks on the new philosophy of Des-Cartes. *By J. Gardyner, and sold by Richard Ellison,* 1700. 4°. L, DCH, DUS, E.

2978A ——[Anr. ed.] *For T. Ballard,* 1700. 4°. LLU, EN; PU, TU, V, Y.

Howard, Henry. *See* Norfolk, Henry Howard, *duke of.*

2979 **Howard, James.** All mistaken, or the mad couple. A comedy. *By H. Brugis, for James Magnes,* 1672. 4°. T.C.I 103. L, O, LVD, LVF, EN; CH, CN, MH, TU, WF, Y.

2980 —The English mounsieur. A comedy. *By H. Bruges, for J. Magnus,* 1674. 4°. T.C.I 170. L, O, LG, CS, MR; CH, CN, LC, MH, TU, WF, Y.

2981 Entry cancelled.

English monsieur, a comical novel. 1679. *See title.*

2982 **Howard, John.** The evil of our dayes. *For John Lawrence,* 1698. 4°.* L, O, C; CLC, NPT, WF.

2983 —The Trinity asserted. *For J. Lawrence,* 1700. 4°.* L, O, C, LLP, BAMB; CH, IEG, MH, Y.

2984 —The true interest of a nation. *For J. Lawrence,* 1693. 4°.* T.C.II 436. L, O, C, LLP, OM, EC, MR; CH.

2984A **Howard, Luke.** The Devils bow unstringed. *For Thomas Simmons,* 1659. 4°.* LF; PH.

2985 —A few plain words of instruction. *For Thomas Simmons,* 1658. 4°.* L, C, LF, BBN, EN; CH, MH, PH, WF, Y.

2986 —A looking-glass for Baptists. [*London*], *printed,* 1672. 4°.* L; CSS, NHC, PH.

2987 —The seat of the scorner thrown down. [*London*], *printed,* 1673. 4°. L, O, LF, OCC, BBN; CH, PH, PL, WF, Y.

2988 —A warning from the Lord. *For Robert Wilson,* 1661. 4°.* L, LF; PH.

2989 **Howard, Sir Philip.** The new invention of mill'd lead. 1691. 12°. LUS (dispersed).

2990 **Howard, Sir Robert.** An account of the state of His Majesties revenue. *For Thomas Fox,* 1681. fol.* L, O, C, DU, DT; BN, CH, CN, MH, WF, Y.

2991 —The duell of the stags: a poem. [*London*], *in the Savoy, for Henry Herringman,* 1668. 4°.* L, O, C, LVD, EN; CH, IU, MH, TU, WF, Y.

2992 —Five new plays. Second edition. *For Henry Herringman, and are to be sold by Thomas Bennett,* 1692. fol. EN; CH, CN, MU, TO, WF, Y.

2992A —"Second" edition. *For Henry Herringman, and are to be sold by Francis Saunders,* 1692. fol. L, RU; CN.

2993 ——"Second" edition. *For Henry Herringman, and are to be sold by R. Bentley, J. Tonson, F. Saunders, and T. Bennet,* 1692. 4°. L, O, OC, LIU, A; CH, CN, MB, MU, WF, Y.

2994 ——"Second" edition. *For Henry Herringman, and are to be sold by Jacob Tonson, Daniel Browne, Thomas Bennet, and Richard Wellington,* 1700. fol. L, O, C, BC, LLU, DT; CH, CU, LC, MH, TU, WF, Y.

2995 —Four new plays. *For Henry Herringman,* 1665. fol. L, O, C, DU, DT; CH, CN, LC, MH, TU, WF, Y.

2995A [–] A free discourse wherein the doctrines. *For John Lawrence and Richard Baldwin,* 1697. 8°. L, CT, MR; CLC, IU, NP, NR, NU, Y.

2996 —The great favourite. [*London*], *in the Savoy: for Henry Herringman,* 1668. 4°. L, O, CK, EC, LLU; CH, CN, LC, MH, TU, WF, Y.

2997 [–] Historical observations upon the reigns of Edward I. *For J. Partridge and M. Gillyflower,* 1689. 8°. T.C.II 274. L, C, OB, EN, DT; CH, CU, MH, NC, NP, TU, WF, Y.

2998 [–] The history of religion. *Printed,* 1694. 8°. L, C, OH, DC, E; BN, CH, IU, MH, NU, WF, Y.

2999 —The history of the reigns of Edward and Richard II. *By F. Collins, for Thomas Fox,* 1690. 8°. L, O, C, ES, BLH; CH, LC, MH, MU, NU, TU, WSC, Y.

3000 —A letter to Mr. Samuel Johnson. *For Thomas Fox,* 1692. 8°. L, O, CCA, WCA; CH, MU, NC, NP, ANL.

3001 [–] The life and reign of King Richard the Second. *For M. L. and L. C. sold by Langly Curtis,* 1681. 8°. T.C.I 417. L, O, C, OC, AN, EN, DT; BN, CH, CN, MH, TU, WF, Y. (var.)

3002 —A particular accompt of the moneys . . . Exchequer. *For Samuel Hayrick*, 1694. fol. L, C, LUG, DT; BN, LC, WF, Y.

3003 —Poems: viz. 1. a panegyrick. *For Henry Herringman*, 1660. 8°. LT, O, C, LVD, CT; CH, CLC, CN, LC, MH, NC, TU, WC, WF, Y.

3004 —Poems on several occasions. Second edition. *For Francis Saunders*, 1696. 8°. L, LIU; CLC, MH, NP, TU, WF.

3005 —A song in the chances. [*London*, 1700?] brs. L, OM; CLC.

3005A [–] A song in the committee. [*London*], *T. Cross*, [1700?]. brs. L.

3005B —The surprised. *For H. Herringman*, 1668. 8°. EN.

3006 [–] A twofold vindication. *Printed* 1696. 8°. L, O, CS, DU, DM; CU, NCD, NP, RBU, WF, Y.

Howard, Thomas. *See also* Norfolk, Thomas Howard, *duke of.*

3007 —An elegy on the death of the most illustrious Prince Henry. *For W. Gilbertson*, [1660]. brs. L.

3008 [–] The history of the seven wise mistrisses of Rome. *For M. Wright*, 1663. 8°. CH.

3009 [–]—[Anr. ed.] *For M. Wotton, and G. Conyers*, 1686. 8°. L, CM; CN, WF.

3010 [–]—[Anr. ed.] *By W. O. for G. Conyers*, [1700?]. 8°. L.

3011 —An old song of the old courtier. *For F. Coles*, [1670?]. brs. L, O, CM.

3011A —Roman stories. *By T. Sabine*, [1700]. 12°. CH.

Howard, William. *See also* Stafford, William Howard, *viscount.*

3012 **Howard, William Howard, baron.** A letter from. colop: *By Robert Roberts*, 1681. cap., fol.* L, OC, DU, LSD, MR; CH, IU, MH, TU, WF, Y.

3013 —To the king's most excellent majesty. The humble petition of. *For Richard Baldwin*, 1681. brs. L, DU, HH; MH, NC, PU, WF, Y, ZWT.

Howard's retinue. 1670. *See* L., S. Letter from a gentleman.

3014 [**Howe, J.**] To Chloris all soft charms agree. [*London*], *T. Cross*, [1700?]. brs. L.

3014A [**Howe, John.**] An answer to Dr. Stillingfleet's mischief of separation. Second edition. *Printed by S. W. and sold by S. Tydmarsh*, 1680. 4°. T.C.I 413. L, CD.

—'Αρχαιοσκοπια: or. 1677. *See* Hanmer, Jonathan.

3015 —The blessedness of the righteous, discoursed. *Lodon* [*sic*], *by Sarah Griffin, for Samuel Thomson*, 1668. 8°. T.C.I 1. L, O, LCL, BP; CDA, CLC, IU, OLU, WF.

3016 —The blessedness of the righteous opened. *By A. Maxwell, for Sa. Gellibrand*, 1673. 8°. T.C.I 157. L, O, DU, E, DT; IU, NU, TU, UCLA, WF, Y.

3017 ——[Anr. ed.] *By A. Maxwel and R. Roberts, for Ed. Gellibrand*, 1678. 8°. T.C.I 305. L, LW, BR, DL; CH, NGT, NP, NU, RBU.

3017A ——[Anr. ed.] *For Ed. Gellibrand and are to be sold by Robert Boulter*, 1678. 8°. LCL; LC, PPT, WF.

3018 [–] A calm and sober enquiry. *By J. Astwood for Tho. Parkhurst*, 1694. 8°. T.C.II 520. L, O, LCL, GC, MR; CH, CLC, MH, NU, TO, WF.

3019 —The carnality of religious contention. *By J. A. for Tho. Parkhurst*, 1693. 8°. L, LCL, LW, RPL; CH, MBC, NU, WF, Y.

3020 [–] The case of the Protestant Dissenters, represented and argued. colop: *Printed*, 1689. cap., fol.* L, O, DU, EN, GU; CH, IU, NU, WF, Y.

3021 —A discourse concerning the Redeemer's dominion. *For Tho. Parkhurst*, 1699. 8°. T.C.III 136. L, LCL, BC, P, DL; CH, IU, MH, NU, WF, Y.

3022 [–] A discourse of an unconverted man's enmity, against God. *By J. Heptinstall*, 1700. 8°. L; Y.

3023 —A discourse relating to the much-lamented death, . . . of . . . Queen Mary. *For Brabazon Aylmer*, 1695. 4°.* L, O, LW, CT, DT; CH, IU, MH, NU, WF, Y, AVP.

3024 ——Second edition. —, 1695. 4°.* L, C; NP.

3025 —A funeral-sermon for . . . Matthew Mead. *For T. Parkhurst*, 1699. 8°. T.C.III 161. L, C, LCL, LW; MIU, NN, NU, WF.

3026 —A funeral sermon for Mrs. Esther Sampson. *For Thomas Parkhurst*, 1690. 4°.* T.C.II 311. L, O, C, LG, BR, BLH; CH, CN, MH, WF, Y.

3027 —A funeral sermon for . . . Mr Richard Fairclough. *For John Dunton*, 1682. 8°. T.C.II 12. L, LCL; MB, MH, MWA, PJB, PL.

3028 —A funeral-sermon for . . . William Bates. *For T. Parkhurst, and B. Aylmer*, 1699. 8°. T.C.III 161. L, O, C, LCL, LG, ENC; CH, MH, NU, WF, Y.

3029 —A funeral sermon on the death of . . . Mrs. Judith Hamond. *For Tho. Parkhurst*, 1696. 4°.* T.C.III 24. L, LW; CH, CLC, WF.

3030 —A funeral sermon on the decease of . . . Mrs. Margaret Baxter. *For Brabazon Aylmer*, 1681. 4°.* T.C.I 470. L, O, LW, CS, BR, BLH; CH, CN, MH, PL, WF, Y, AVP.

3030A [–] A letter to a friend, concerning a postscript. *By James Astwood for Tho. Parkhurst*, 1694. 8°. L, O, CT, EC, GC; CH, CLC, NPT, NU, TO, WF.

3031 [–] A letter written out of the countrey to a person of quality. *Printed*, 1680. 4°. L, O, C, EN, DT; CH, MH, NC, NU, WF.

3032 —The living temple. *For John Starkey*, 1675. 8°. T.C.I 195. L, O, LCL, CT, AN, E; CH, IU, NU, WG, Y.

3033 —Of charity. *For Tho. Parkhurst*, 1681. 8°. L, O, EC, P, DT; CH, IU, NU, PL, WF, Y.

3034 —Of thoughtfulnes. *For Tho. Parkhurst*, 1681. 8°. L, O, OC, CT, RPL, DT; CH, MB, MIU, NU, WF, Y.

3035 —A post-script to the late letter. *For Brabazon Aylmer*, 1677. 8°. O, C, LW, D; CLC, NGT, NU.

3036 [–] The reconcileableness of God's prescience. *For Brabazon Aylmer*, 1677. 8°. T.C.I 272. L, C, OU, EN, DT; CLC, MBA, NU, WF, JF.

3037 [–] The Redeemer's tears. *By J. Astwood for Thomas Parkhurst*, 1684. 8°. T.C.II 68. L, O, BC; CH, MIU, NU, WF, Y.

3038 —The right use of that argument. *For Brabazon Aylmer*, 1682. 8°. T.C.I 503. L, O, LCL, LW, CT; IU, NU, PL, PU, WF.

3038aA [–] Self-dedication. *For Brabazon Aylmer*, 1682. 12°. L, LSC, LW; CLC.

3038BA [–] A sermon directing what we are to do. *For T. Park-hurst*, 1688. 12°. T.C.II 229. L; WF.

3038A [–] —Second edition. —, 1696. 8°.* CH, NGT, WF.

3039 —A sermon on the much lamented death of . . . Mr. Richard Adams. *By S. Bridge, for Tho. Parkhurst*, 1698. 8°. T.C.III 86. L, LCL, LW, BC; CH, MH, NR, NU.

3040 —A sermon preach'd . . . Decemb. 2. 1697. *By S. Bridge, for Tho. Parkhurst*, 1698. 4°.* L, O, C, SP, EN; CH, MH, NU, PL, TU, WF, AVP.

3041 —A sermon preach'd Febr. 14. 1698. *By S. Bridge, for Tho. Parkhurst*, 1698. 8°. L, LLP, LW, CM, NE; CH, MH, NGT, NU, WF.

3042 Entry cancelled.
—Speech made at the General Quarter Sessions. [1698?] *See title.*

3043 —A treatise of delighting in God. *By A. Maxwell, for Sa. Gellibrand*, 1674. 8°. T.C.I 184. L, O, LCL, CT, EC, E, BQ; CLC, MH, NP, NU, WF, Y.

3044 [–] Two sermons preached at Thurlow. *For Tho. Park-hurst*, 1688. T.C.II 248. L, LW; CH, MH, MIU, NU, WF, Y.

3045 —The vanity of this mortal life. *By A. Maxwell, for Sa: Gellibrand*, 1672. 12°. T.C.I 95. L, O, C, BC; CH, CLC, CU, WF, Y.

3046 Entry cancelled.
— —[Anr. ed.] 1678. *See* —Blessedness of the righteous opened.

3047 [–] A view of that part of the late considerations. *For Thomas Parkhurst*, 1695. 8°. L, LW, CT, EN; NPT, NU, RBU, TO, WF.

3048 [Howe, Josias.] Psal. 4. Vers. 7. Thou hast put glad-nesse. [*Oxford, by Henry Hall*, 1644?] 4°.* MADAN 1751. O.

3049 Howe, Obadiah. Βασιλιδι δωρον: or, the royal pres-ent. *By E. Cotes, for A. Seile*, 1664. 4°.* L, O, LNC, LSD; Y.

3050 —[Hebrew] or, God and the magistrate. *London, for William Mallory at Boston* [*Lincs.*], 1663. 4°. LNC; IU, PU, Y.

3051 —The pagan preacher silenced. *By Th. Maxey for John Rothwell*, 1655. 4°. LT, O, DM, DT; MH, WF.

3052 —The Vniversalist examined and convicted. [*London*], *for John Rothwell*, 1648. 4°. L, O, CM, GU, DT; CLC, NU.

Howell, Humphrey. Duplus annus. Or. 1656. *See* Almanacs.

3053 —Sathan discovered. *By M. S. for George Eversden*, 1656. 4°. YM.

Howell, James. Admonition to my Lord Protector. 1654. *See* Heath, James.

3054 [–] Ah ha; tumulus, thalamus: two. *For Humphrey Moseley*, 1653. 4°.* LT, O; CN, MH, W.

3055 —Angliæ suspiria, & lachrymæ. *Excudit Humphrey Mosley*, 1646. 12°. LT, O; CH, CLC, MH, W.

3056 [–] Bella Scot-Anglica. A brief of all the battells. [*London*], *printed*, 1648. 4°.* LT, O, BC, DU, DT; CH, CN, WF, Y.

3057 [–] A brief account of the royal matches. *By J. G. for H. Brome*, 1662. 4°.* L, O, C, MC, DT, CLC, Y.

3058 [–] A brief admonition of some of the inconveniences. *Printed*, 1659. 4°.* LT, O, CK, BC, LSD; CLC, CN, MH, NU, WF, Y.

3058A [–] A cordial for the Cavaliers. *By* [*H*]*enry Marsh*, 1661. brs. MH.

3059 [–]Δενδρολογια Dodona's grove. Second edition. [*Ox-ford, by H. Hall*], *printed*, 1644. 4°. MADAN 1692. LT, O, C, CT, AN, CD; CH, CU, MH, NP, NU, TU, Y.

3060 — —Third edition. *Cambridge, by R. D. for Humphrey Moseley*, 1645. 12°. L, C, OW, CT, AN; BN, CH, CU, MH, NN, TU, WF, Y.

3061 — —[Anr. ed.] *By T. W. for Humphrey Moseley*, [1649]. 12°. L, O, C, AN, DC; CH, IU, MH, MU, Y.

3062 — —Second part. *By W. H. for Humphrey Moseley*, 1650. 8°. L, O, LVF, CE, AN; CH, CU, MH, NC, NP, TU, WF, Y.

3063 [–] A discourse of Dunkirk. *By J. C. for Samuel Speed*, 1664. 4°.* L, O, OC; MH, WF, W.

3064 [–] —Second edition. —, 1664. 8°.* O; W.

3065 [–] A discours of the empire and of the election of a king of the Romans. *By F. L. for Charles Webb*, 1658. 8°. L, O, C, CM, DT; CN, IU, MH, MIU, W.

3066 [–] —[Anr. ed.] *By F. L. for Rich: Lowndes*, 1658. 8°. LT, AN, SP.

3067 —A discourse of the empire of Germany. Second edi-tion. *For Thomas Davies*, 1659. 8°. C, OC, OW, CH.

3068 —Divers historicall discourses. The first tome. *By J. Grismond*, 1661. 8°. L, O, AN, DU, EN; CN, MB, NN, WF, W.

3069 [–] Dovvn-right dealing. [*London*], *printed*, 1647. 4°.* LT, O, AN, YM, DT; CH, NU, TO, TU, WF, Y. (var.)

3070 [–] England's teares for the present wars. *Printed at Lon-don, by Richard Heron*, 1644. 4°.* LT, O, C, CE, P; CH, CN, MH, TU, WF, Y, W.

3071 [–] Epistolæ Ho-Elianæ. *For Humphrey Moseley*, 1645. 4°. LT, O, C, AN, MR; CH, CN, LC, MH, NC, NP, TU, WF, Y.

3072 — —Second edition. *By W. H. for Humphrey Moseley*, 1650. 8°. L, O, CCH, AN, DC, BLH; BN, CH, IU, MH, WF, Y.

3073 — —Third edition. *For Humphrey Moseley*, 1655. 8°. L, O, CT, AN, DT; CH, CN, MB, NU, WF, Y.

3073A — —[Anr. ed.] —, *sold by Joseph Nevill*, 1655. 8°. CM.

3074 — —Fourth edition. *For Thomas Guy*, 1673. 8°. T.C.I 129. L, O, CM, AN, GU; CH, MB, MBP, NIC, NP, W.

3075 — —Fifth edition. —, 1678. 8°. T.C.I 296. L, O, C, AN, EN; CH, IU, MH, NC, WF, Y.

3076 — —Sixth edition. —, 1688. 8°. T.C.II 220. L, C, BANGOR, EC; CH, LC, MH, MU, TU, WF, Y.

3077 [–] Florus Hungaricus: or the history. *By W. G. for Nath. Brook*, 1664. 4°. L, OC, AN, EN, CD, DT; MU, PL, WF, W.

3077A [–] —[Anr. ed.] *By W. G. for Hen. Marsh*, 1664. 8°. CLC, MH, WCL, W.

3078 —A fourth volume of familiar letters. *For Humphrey Moseley*, 1655. 8°. LT, O, CK; CH, IU, MH, PL, TU, WF, W.

3079 —A German diet. *For Humphrey Moseley*, 1653. fol. L, O, CT, AN, EN; CH, CN, LC, MH, MU, Y.

3080 [–] An inquisition after blood. [*London*], *printed*, 1649. 4°.* LT, O, MR, DT; CH, CN, MH, WF, Y.

3081 —Instructions and directions for forren travell. Second edition. *By W. W. for Humphrey Moseley,* 1650. 12°. LT, O, CE, AN, DU; CH, CN, MH, WF, Y.

3082 [–] Instructions for forreine travell. *By T. B. for Humprey [sic] Mosley,* 1642. 12°. L, O, CT, AN, EN; BN, CH, CN, MH, WF, Y.

3083 [–] The instrvments of a king. *Printed,* 1648. 4°.* LT, O, CE, EN, DT; BN, CH, CN, MH, WF, Y.

3084 [–] The last will and testament of the late renowned Cardinal Mazarin. *By Peter Lillicrap for William Gilbertson,* 1663. 12°. L, O, OC, CT; CH, CLC, MU, Y, W.

3085 [–] A letter to the Earle of Pembrooke. *[London], printed,* 1647. 4°.* LT, O, CT, P, DT; CH, MBP, MH, MIU, WF, Y.

3086 [–] —Second edition. —, 1648. 4°.* CT.

3087 —Lexicon tetraglotton. *By J. G. for Cornelius Bee,* 1660. fol. L, O, CT, EN, DT; BN, CDA, CN, MBP, MH, NN, TU, Y.

3088 — —[Anr. ed.] *By J. G. for Samuel Thomson,* 1660. fol. O, CT, AN, BR, LLU; BN, CH, CLC, MIU, MU, WF.

3089 — —[Anr. ed.] *By Thomas Leach,* 1660. fol. LS, LW, LWL; CH, LC, NCU, NP, WG.

3090 —Londinopolis; an historical discourse. *By J. Streater, for Henry Twiford, George Sawbridge, and John Place,* 1657. fol. L, O, C,, AN, EN; BN, CPB, CN, LC, MB, NN, Y.

3091 — —[Anr. ed.] *By J. Streater, for Henry Twiford, George Sawbridge, Thomas Dring, and John Place,* 1657. fol. L, O, LG, CT, SP; CH, MH, MU, PL, WF, Y.

3092 —Lustra Ludovici: or. *For Humphrey Moseley,* 1646. fol. L, O, C, EN, DT; CH, CN, LC, MH, NC, NP, TU, WF, Y, AVP.

3093 [–] Mercurius Hibernicus. *Printed at Bristoll,* 1644. 4°.* 14 pp. L, O, C, LVF, DU, DT; CLC, CU, IU, WF, Y.

3094 [–] —[Anr. ed.] —, 1644. 4°.* 28 pp. LT, O, C, BR, DT; CH, CSS, MIU, WF, W.

3095 [–] A new English grammar. *For T. Williams, H. Brome, and H. Marsh,* 1662. 8°. L, O, C, AN, GU; CH, CN, MH, WF, Y.

3096 —A new volvme of letters. *By T. W. for Humphrey Moseley,* 1647. 8°. LT, O, CT, AN, MR; CH, CLC, CN, MH, Y.

3096A Entry cancelled.

— —Third edition. 1655. See — Epistolæ Ho-Elianæ.

3097 [–] The nvptialls of Pelevs and Thetis. *For Henry Herringman,* 1654. 4°. LT, O, C, AN, DC; CH, CN, LC, MB, MH, MU, WF, Y.

3098 [–] Παροιμιογραφια. Proverbs. *By J. G.,* 1659. fol. O, LL, CCH, MR, NOT; CH, CN, MH, NCU, NN, Y.

3099 [–] Parables, reflecting upon the times. *Printed at Paris,* 1643. 4°.* LT, O, C, CT, AN, DT; CH, CU, NCU, WF, W.

3100 No entry.

—Perfect description of the people. 1649. *See* Weldon, *Sir* Anthony.

3101 [–] Philanglvs; some sober inspections. Third edition. *By E. C. for H. S.,* 1658. 8°. LT, C, OP, P, AN; CLC, CN, MH, NU, WF, W.

3102 — —Fourth edition. *By T. L. for W. Palmer,* 1660. 8°. L, AN, MR; CH, CLC, CN.

3102A — —"Third" edition. *By E. C.,* 1669. 16°. PUL.

3103 [–] Poems on several choice and various subjects. *By Ja: Cottrell, and are to be sold by S. Speed,* 1663. 8°. L; CH, IU, MH, WCL, W.

3104 —Poems upon divers emergent occasions. Second edition. *By Ja. Cottrel,* 1664. 12°. L, O, AN; CH, MB, MH.

3105 —Mr. Howel's poems. *By James Cottrel,* 1664. 8°. L, LG.

3106 —The preheminence and pedigree of Parlement. *Printed at London, by Richard Heron,* 1644. 4°.* LT, CE, DT; CH, CU, MH, WF, Y.

3106A — —[Anr. ed., "pre-eminence."] *By J. R. For Humphrey Moseley,* 1645. 12°. LSC, AN; NN, Y, W.

3106B — —[Anr. ed.] *By R. R. for Humphrey Moseley,* 1645. 12°.* L; IU, Y.

3107 — —[Anr. ed.] *By W. W. for Humphrey Moseley,* 1649. 8°.* O, BLH, GK; CN, MH, Y.

3108 — —[Anr. ed.] *For Dorman Newman, and Tho. Cockeril,* 1677. 4°.* L, O, C, MR, SP; CH, CN, LC, NN, WF, Y.

3109 [–] Προεδρια-βασιλικη: a discourse. *By Ja. Cottrel for Sam. Speed; and Chr. Eccleston,* 1664. fol. L, C, OW, AN, EN; CH, CU, LC, MH, NC, NP, WF, Y.

3110 — —Second edition. *For Rowland Reynolds,* [1668]. fol. L, AN, SP; CLC, CN, MH, NU, V, WF.

3111 —Προεδρια βασιλικη: dissertatio de praecedentia. *Prostant apud Sam. Thomson; & Sam. Speed,* 1664. 8°. L, O, C, EN, DT; BN, CH, CU, Y, W.

3112 —S. P. Q. V. A survay of the signorie of Venice. *For Richard Lowndes,* 1651. fol. L, O, C, E, CD; BN, CH, CN, LC, MH, MU, NN, NP, WF, Y.

—St. Paul's late progres upon earth. 1644. *See* Pallavicino, Ferrante.

3112A [–] The second part of Massaniello. *For R. Lowndes,* 1650. CB, CLC, INU.

3113 [–] —[Anr. ed.] *By A. M. for Abel Roper, and T. Dring,* 1652. 8°. LT, O, LUG, AN, BQ; CH, IU, MH, WF, Y.

3114 [–] —[Anr. ed.] *By J. M. for A. Roper, and T. Dring, to be sold by Richard Lownds,* 1663. 8°. L, OC, CM, DU, SP; CLC, CN, MB, NN, TU, WF, Y.

3115 —Some of Mr. Howell's minor works. *[London], printed,* 1654. 4°. O.

3116 [–] Som sober inspections made into the carriage. *By E. C. for Henry Seile,* 1655. 8°. LT, O, C, AN, DM; CH, CJC, LC, MH, NC, Y, AVP.

3117 [–] —Second edition. *For Ric. Lownds,* 1656. 8°. L, O, C, LVF, EN, BQ; CH, MB, WF, Y, ZWT.

3118 [–] Som sober inspections made into those ingredients. *For Henry Brome,* 1661. 4°.* LLU; CH, MH, W.

3119 —Θηρολογια. The parly of beasts. *By W. Wilson for William Palmer,* 1660. fol. L, O, CP, AN, LLU, DT; CH, CN, MBP, MH, NN, TU, WF, Y.

3120 [–] A trance: or, newes from Hell. *Printed,* 1649. 4°.* LT, O, LVF, OC, DT; CH, TU, WF.

3121 [–] The true informer, who. *Oxford, printed,* 1643. 4°.* MADAN 1304. O, DC, E, EN, DT; CN, ZWT.

3122 [–] —[Anr. ed., "trve."] *Oxford, by Leonard Lichfield,* 1643. 4°.* MADAN 1305. LT, O, C, LIU, DT; CH, CN, NU, WF, W.

3122A [–]—[Anr. ed.] [London], printed, 1643. 4°.* MADAN 1306. L, O; MH, SCU, W.

3123 —Twelve several treatises. By J. Grismond, 1661. 8°. L, LVF, MR, EN, DT; CLC, CN, CU, NC, WCL, W.

3124 —Two discourses. Second edition. Printed at London, by Richard Heron, 1644. 4°.* O, LL, OC, EN, DT; Y, W.

3125 [–]—Third edition. By R. R. for Humphrey Moseley, 1645. 8°.* L; MH.

3126 Entry cancelled.
—Venice looking-glasse. 1648. See C., J. B.

3127 [–] The vision: or, a dialog. For William Hope, 1651. 8°. LT, O, C, LVF, AN; CH, CN, MH, WF.

3128 [–] The vote, or a poeme royall. By Thomas Badger, 1642. 4°.* LT, O; CH.

3128A [–]—[Anr. ed.] By T. Badger, for Humphrey Mosley, 1642. 4°.* O; MH.

3129 [–] A winter dreame. [London], printed, 1649. 4°.* LT, O, C, LLU, LSD; BN, CH, CN, MH, WF, Y.

3130 **Howell, John.** A discourse on persecution. For Robert Kettlewell, 1685. 4°.* L, O, CS, DU, D; CH, IU, NU, TU, WF, Y.

3130A **[Howell, William], 1656–1714.** The Common Prayer Book the best companion. Printed at Oxford, by Leon. Lichfield, for John Howell, 1686. 12°. T.C.II 164. OC, CS, YM.

3131 [–]—Second edition. Oxford, at the theater, for John Howell, 1687. 8°. T.C.II 183. L, LLP.

3131A [–]—Third edition. —, 1687. 8°. O; MH, WF.

3132 [–]—Fourth edition. —, 1689. 8°. L, O, LLP, OC, CM.

3132A [–]—Fifth edition. Oxford, by Leon. Lichfield for John Howell, 1692. 8°. L, BR; CH, MB.

3132B [–]—Sixth edition. Oxford, by L. L. for John Howell, 1694. 8°. L, O, LLP.

3133 [–]—Seventh edition. Oxford, by L. Lichfield for J. Howell, 1695. 8°. L, O.

3133A [–]—Eighth edition. Dublin, re-printed by J. B. and S. P. and are to be sold by W. Norman, El. Dobson, P. Campbell, and J. Milner, 1699. 8°. WF.

3133B [–]—[Anr. ed.] By J. H. for Henry Mortlock, 1700. 12°. T.C.III 133. CH.

3133C [–] Prayers in the closet. Oxford, at the theater for John Howell, 1689. 8°.* O; NU.

3133D [–]—[Anr. ed.] Oxford, by Leon. Lichfield, for J. Howell, 1692. 8°.* BR; CH.

3133E [–] The word of God the best guide. Oxford, at the Sheldonian Theatre, sold by T. Bennet, 1689. 8°. T.C.II 299. O, LLP.

3133F [–]—[Anr. ed.] Oxford, at the theater, for John Howell, 1689. 8°. OC, CM, CT; NP.

3133G [–]—Second edition. By J. Leake, for Mary Howell, in Oxford, 1698. 8°. T.C.III 85. C; Y.

3134 **Howell, William, 1638?–1683.** Elementa historiæ. Apud. Joh. Martyn, 1671. 12°. T.C.I 67. L, O, C, E, DT; BN, CLC, NN, WF.

3135 —The elements of history. For John King, 1700. 8°. T.C. III 197. L, C, AN; CH, CLC, Y.

3135A —[Anr. ed.] For R. Wellington, A. Bettesworth, and B. Lintott, 1700. 8°. WF.

3136 —An institution of general history. For Henry Herringman, 1661. fol. L, O, LNC, SP, P, E; CH, MH, NU.

3137 ——[Anr. ed.]—, 1662. fol. L, C, CCA, RPL; CLC, WF, Y.

3138 ——Second edition. For Henry Herringman, Thomas Bassett, William Crook, and William Cademan, 1680–85. 4v. fol. T.C.I 403. L, O, C, EN, DT; BN, CH, LC, MH, MU, NC, TU, Y, AVP.

3139 ——[Anr. ed.] For the authors widdow, by Miles Flesher, 1685. fol. L, C, CK, LSD, E, ENC; MBC, MBP.

3139A [–] Medulla historiæ anglicanæ, being. For Abel Swalle, to be sold by him, 1679. 12°. OC, CS; CH, CPB, IU.

3140 [–]—[Anr. ed.] —and Tho. Mercer, 1679. T.C.I 350. L, O, OC; BN, CLC, CN, IU.

3140A [–]—Second edition. For Abel Swalle, 1681. 12°. L, AN; IU, PU, WF.

3141 [–]—"Second" edition. For A. Swalle and S. Tidmarsh, 1683. 12°. T.C.I 480. L; BN, CH.

3142 [–]—Third edition. For Abel Swalle, 1687. 8°. T.C.II 203. L, O, LW, OM, AN, YM; CH, CLC, IU, Y.

3142A [–]—Fourth edition. For Abel Swalle and Timothy Childe, 1694. 8°. T.C.II 515. L, O, LG; CH, CLC, MIU, WF, Y.

3143 Entry cancelled.
[–] Prayers in the closet. Oxford, 1689. See Howell, William, 1656–1714.

3144 **Howell, William, of Fittleworth.** A sermon preached . . . Septemb. 20th. 1675. For William Crook, 1676. 4°.* T.C.I 216. L, O, C, OC, DT; CH, NU, WF, Y.

3145-6 Entries cancelled.
[–] Word of God. Oxford, 1689. See Howell, William, 1656–1714.

3147 **Howes, Edward.** Short arithmetick. By R. Leybourne, for H. Blunden, 1650. 12°. LT; CH.

3148 **Howes, John.** Christ, God-man, set out. For Joseph Nevill, and William Cockrain, in Northampton, 1657. 4°.* L, O, C, OC, CT; TU, WF.

3149 —Real comforts. By S. Griffin, for R. Royston, 1660. 4°. LT, O, C, DT; CH, IU, MH, NU, TU.

3150 —A sermon preached . . . August the 9th. 1669. For William Leake, 1670. 4°.* T.C.I 48. L, O, C, YM, DT; CLC, IU, MH, NC, NU, WF.

3151 **H[owet], H[enoch].** The beast that was, & is not. For Daniel White, 1659. 4°. L, LF, LW, BC.

3151A —Disobedience detected. Printed, 1648. 4°.* NHC.

3152 —Quaking principles dashed in pieces. By Henry Hills, 1655. 4°.* LT.

3153 **Howett, Samuel.** Some few proposals for publick service. [London, 1689.] cap., 4°.* L; WF.

3154 **[Howgill, Francis.]** An answer to a paper; called, A petition of one Thomas Ellyson. Printed, 1654. 4°.* LT, O, LF, BBN, MR; PH.

3155 —The common salvation contended for. For Giles Calvert, [1659–60]. 4°.* LT, O, LF, BBN, MR; CH, PH, PSC.

3155A —A copy of a paper sent to John Otway. [London? 1666?] 4°.* PH.

3156   [–] Darknesse and ignorance expelled. *For Thomas Simmons*, 1659. 4°.* L, LF, BBN; PH, PL, Y.

3157   —The davvnings of the gospel-day. [*London*], printed, 1676. fol. L, O, C, LF, DU, E; BN, CH, CN, MH, WF, Y.

3158   —The deceiver of the nations discovered. *For Thomas Simmons*, 1660. 4°.* LF, BBN, NE; CN, LC, MB, NN, RPJ.

3159   —The fiery darts of the divel quenched. *For Giles Calvert*, 1654. 4°.* LT, O, LF, OC, BBN, MR; NU, PH.

3160   [–] A general epistle to all who have believed. [*London*, 1665.] cap., 4° * L, O, LF, CT, BBN; CH, MH, NU, PH, PSC, Y.

3161   [–] A general epistle to the dispersed and perecvted flock. [*London*], printed, 1665. 4°.* L, LF, OC, BBN, MR; MH, NCD, PH, PL, PSC, Y.

3162   —The glory of the true church. *For Giles Calvert*, 1661. 8°. L, O, C, LF, BBN; MH, PH, PSC, RPJ, Y. (var.)

3163   — —Second edition. *For G. Calvert*, 1662. 8°. C, LF; NU, Y.

3164   — —[Anr. ed.] *For E. Calvert*, 1666. 8°. LF; NU, PL.

3165   [–] The great case of tythes and forced maintenance. [*London*], printed, 1665. 4°. L, O, C, LF, BBN, EN; CH, IU, LC, MH, NU, PH, Y.

3166   —The heart of New-England hardned. *For Thomas Simmons*, 1659. 4°. L, LF; CH, MU, NU, PH, PL.

3167   —An information and also advice. *Printed*, 1659. 4°. L, LF, BBN, LLU; CSS, MIU, PH, PL, PSC, Y.

3168   —The inheritance of Jacob. *For Giles Calvert*, 1656. 4°.* LT, O, BBN, LF, CT; CH, MH, PH, PSC, WF, Y.

3169   —The invisible things of God. *For Thomas Simmons*, 1659. 8°. L, LF, MR; MB, MH, PL, PSC.

3170   —A lamentation for the scattered tribes. *For Giles Calvert*, 1656. 4°.* LT, O, C, LF, BBN; CH, MH, NU, PH, WF, Y.

3171   —The measvring rod of the Lord. *For Giles Calvert*, 1658. 4°.* L, O, C, LF, BBN; CH, IE, MH, NU, PH, Y.

3172   —The mouth of the pit stopped. *For Thomas Simmons*, 1659. 4°.* L, O, LF; CH, PH, PL, PSC, Y.

3173   [–] Mistery Babylon the mother of harlots discovered. *For Thomas Simmons*, 1659. 4°.* L, O, C, LF, BBN; CH, MH, PH, PL, WF, Y.

3174   [–] Oaths no gospel ordinance. [*London*], printed, 1666. 4°. L, LF, MR, YM; CH, MH, NU, PH, PSC.

3175   [–] One of Anti-Christ's voluntiers. *For T: Simmons*, 1660. 4°.* L, O, C, LF, BBN; CH, NCU, NU, PH, PSC.

3176   [–] One warning more unto England. *For Thomas Simmons*, 1660. 4°.* L, LF, CT, BBN, MR; CH, MH, PH, PSC, Y.

3177   —The Popish inquisition. *For Thomas Simmons*, 1659. 4°. L, LF, LW; CH, MH, MU, NN, PSC, Y.

3178   —The rock of ages exalted. *For G. C.*, 1662. 8°. L, LF, LLL; MH, NN, PH, PL, RPJ.

3179   —Some of the misteries of Gods kingdome. *For Thomas Simmons*, 1658. 4°.* L, O, C, LF, BBN; CH, MH, PH, WF, Y.

3180   —Some openings of the womb of the morning. *For Thomas Simmons*, 1661. 4°.* L, LF, BBN, MR, DT; CH, PH, PL, Y.

3181   No entry.

3182   [–] This is onely to goe amongst Friends. colop: *For Thomas Simmons*, 1656. cap., 4°.* LT, LF, BBN, BP, DT; MH, PH, PSC, Y.

3183   —To all you commanders and officers of the army. [*London*, 1657.] 4°.* LF; PH.

3184   [–] To the camp of the Lord. [*London*, 1655.] cap., 4°.* L, C, LF, CT, BBN, BP; PH, PSC, WF.

3185   —The true rule, judge, and guide. [*London*], printed, 1665. 4°. L, LF, BBN, MR, EN; CLC, NCU, NU, PH.

3186   —Truth lifting up its head above slander. [*London*], printed, 1663. 4°.* L, O, LF, BBN; CLC, MH, NCD, PH, PSC, Y.

3187   [–] A visitation of love, peace, and good will. *Printed*, 1664. 4°.* L, O, LF, OC, BBN; CH, MH, NCD, PH, PSC, Y.

3188   [–] The visitation of the rebellious nation of Ireland. *For Giles Calvert*, 1656. 4°.* LT, O, C, BBN, DT; CH, IE, MH, PH, WF, Y.

3189   [–] A woe against the magistrates. *Printed*, 1654. 4°.* LT, O, LF; PH.

3190   [–] The works of darknesse brought to light. *For Thomas Simmons*, 1659. 4°.* L, LF, BBN, E; CH, NCU, PH, PSC, Y.

3191   **Howgill, Mary.** A remarkable letter of. *Printed*, 1657. 4°.* L, LF, OC; CH, CLC, PH, PSC, Y.

3192   [–] The vision of the Lord of hosts. [*London*], printed, 1662. 4°.* L, LF, BBN, MR; CH, IE, MH, PH, WF.

3192A   **Howkins, Thomas.** A catalogue of Friends' books. [*London*, 1687.] 4°.* LF.

3193   Entry cancelled.

3194   **Howldin, J., *pseud.*** See Wildman, John.

3194   **H[owlet], R[obert].** The school of recreation. *For H. Rodes*, 1684. 12°. T.C.II 86. L, O, CK; CH, CN, MH, WF, Y.

3195   [–] —[Anr. ed.] *For H. Rhodes*, 1696. 12°. T.C.II 572. L, O; CLC, IU, WF, Y.

3196   **Howsegoe, Thomas.** The lyer and false accuser made manifest. *For Thomas Simmons*, 1658. 4°.* O, LF.

3197   —A word from the North. *For Giles Calvert*, 1657. 4°.* LT, LF, CT.

        Howseyor, Thomas. See Howsegoe, Thomas.

3197A   **Howson, Robert.** Fifteen questions touching church government. *For the author*, 1685. 4°. OC.

3198   —A sermon preached . . . first of January, 1698. *By W. Downing, for the author*, [1698?]. 4°.* L, C.

3199   [**Hoy, Thomas.**] Agathocles the Sicilian usurper. *For J. C. and are to be sold by Walter Davis*, 1683. fol.* L, O, OC, CS, LLU; CH, IU, MH, NP, TU, WF, Y.

3199A   [–] —[Anr. ed.] *For John Crosley in Oxford*, 1683. fol.* CH, CLC, MU, TU, WF, ASU.

3200   Entry cancelled.

        Hoyle. Rebells warning-piece. [*London*], 1650. See Hoyle, Thomas.

3201   **Hoyle, John.** Bibliotheca Hoyleana: sive catalogus. [*London*], 14 *Nov.* 1692. 4°. L.

3202   No entry.

3203   **H[oyle], J[oshua].** Jehojadahs iustice against Mattan. *By M. Simmons for Henry Overton*, 1645. 4°.* L, O, C, EN, DT; CH, MH, NU, TU, WF, Y.

3204　—A reioynder to Master Malone's reply. *Dvblin, by the societie of stationers,* 1641. 4°. DIX 74. L, O, C, EN, DT; CH, NU, Y.

3204A　**Hoyle, Thomas.** The rebells warning-piece. [*London*], *printed* 1650. 4°.* LT, LIU.

3205　**Huarte Navarro, Juan de Dios.** Examen de ingenios. *For Richard Sare,* 1698. 8°. T.C.III 81. L, O, C, GU, DT; CH, CN, LC, MH, NP, TU, WF, Y.

3206　**Hubbard, Benjamin.** Orthodoxal navigation. *By Thomas Maxey, for William Weekly of Ipswich, to be sold by John Rothwell,* 1656. 8°. L, LR; RPJ.

3207　—Sermo secvlaris. Or, a sermon . . . July 4, 1647. *By R. L. for Nathanael Webb, and William Grantham,* 1648. 4°. LT, O, C, CT; CB, CH, CLC, IU, NU, WF.

3208　**Hubbard, William.** The benefit of a well-ordered conversation. *Printed at Boston by Samuel Green,* 1684. 8°. EVANS 362. LW; LC, MB, MH, MHS, MWA.

3209　—The happiness of a people. *Boston, by John Foster,* 1676. 4°. EVANS 214. L, C, LW; CH, MH, MU, NN, PHS, Y.

3210　—A narrative of the troubles with the Indians. *Boston, by John Foster,* 1677. 4°. EVANS 231. L, C, GH; CH, CN, MB, MH, MHS, RPJ, Y. (var.)

3211　——[Anr. ed., with errata.] —, 1677. 4°. L; CN, LC, PBL, RPJ, WCL, Y.

3212　—The present state of New-England. *For Tho. Parkhurst,* 1677. 4°. L, O, C, DUS, E; CH, LC, MH, MU, RPJ, Y.

3213　**H[ubbersty], S[tephen].** England's lamentation, or her sad estate lamented. [*London*], *printed* 1665. 4°.* L, O, LF, BBN, MR; IE, PH, PSC, WF, Y.

3214　[–] My dearly beloved Friends. [*London,* 1670.] cap., 4°.* L, O, LF; IE, MH, PH, PSC, Y.

3215　**Hubbert, Thomas.** Pilula ad expurgandam hypocrisin. A pill to purge formality. *By Robert White, for Lodowick Lloyd, and Henry Cripps,* 1650. 16°. L, O, C, LW, SP, GU; NCD, NU.

3216　**Hubberthorn, Richard.** [Works.] A collection of the several books and writings of. *Printed, and are to be sold by William Warwick,* 1663. 4°. L, O, C, LF, E; CH, IE, MH, PH, WF, Y.

3216A　—An account from the children of light. *For Thomas Simmons,* 1660. 4°. LF; IE, PH.

3217　—An answer to a book called A just defence. *For Robert Wilson,* 1660. 4°.* L, LF, BBN; PH, PSC.

3218　—An answer to a declaration put forth. *For Thomas Simmons,* 1659. 4°.* L, C, LF, CT, BBN; CH, MH, NU, PH, WF, Y.

　　　—Answer to the oath of allegiance. 1660. *See* Fox, George, *younger.*

3219　—Antichristianism reproved. *Printed,* 1660. 4°.* L, C, LF, CT, BBN; CH, NHC, PH, Y.

3220　—The antipathy betwixt flesh and spirit. *For Giles Calvert,* 1654. 4°.* LT, CT; CH, PH, Y.

3221　——[Anr. ed.] —, 1656. 4°.* L, O, LF, OC, MR; CH, PH, PL, Y.

3222　—The cause of stumbling removed. *For Thomas Simmons,* 1657. 4°.* LT, LF, BBN, LIU; CH, MH, PH, PSC, WF, Y.

3222A　[–] The Common-wealtsh's [*sic*] remembrancer. *For G. Calvert,* 1659. 4°. LF; CH, PH, PL.

3223　—The difference of that call of God to the ministry. *For Thomas Simmons,* 1659. 4°. L, O, C, LF, BBN; CH, MH, NU, PH, PSC, WF, Y.

3223A　[–] The good old cause briefly demonstrated. colop: *For Thomas Simmons,* 1659. cap., 4°.* L, LF, LW, CT, CD; CH, MH, WF.

3224　—The horn of the he-goat broken. *For Giles Calvert,* 1656. 4°.* LT, LF, CT, BBN, MR; MH, PH, PSC, Y.

3225　—The immediate call to the ministery. *For Giles Calvert,* 1654. 4°.* LT, LF, CT, BBN, MR.

3226　[–] The innocency of the righteous seed of God. [*London,* 1655.] cap., 4°.* LT, LF, CT, BBN; CH, MH, PH, PSC, Y.

3227　—The light of Christ within. *For Thomas Simmons,* 1660. 4°.* LT, LF, CT; LC, PH.

3227A　—The Quaker's house built upon the rock Christ. [*London?* 1659.] 4°. LF.

3228　—The real cause, of the nations bondage. *For Thomas Simmons,* 1659. 4°. L, C, LF, CT, BBN; CH, IE, MH, PH, WF, Y.

3229　[–] The rebukes of a reviler. *For Giles Calvert,* 1657. 4°. LT, LF; PH, PSC.

3230　[–] The record of sufferings for tythes in England. *For Tho. Simmons,* 1658. 4°. L, O, CT, LF, YM; CH, CN, MH, NU, PH, WF.

3231　—A reply to a book set forth. *For Giles Calvert,* 1654. 4°.* L, LF, BBN; CH.

3232　—A short ansvver to a book called The fanatick history. *For Giles Calvert,* 1660. 4°.* O, LF, BBN, MR; CH, CN, MH, PH, PL, PSC, Y.

3233　—Something against swearing. *For G. C.,* 1660. brs. LT, LF; MH, NC.

3234　[–] Something that lately passed in discovrse. *By P. L. for G. C.,* 1660. 4°.* L, O, LF, MR; CH, MH, NCD, PH, PSC, WF, Y.

3235　[–] —[Anr. ed.] *By A. W. for G. C.,* 1660. 4°.* L, O, LF; NU, PH, PSC, Y.

3236　—Supplementum sublatum: Iohn Tombes his supplement. *For Robert Wilson,* 1661. 4°.* L, LF, LW, BBN, MR; CH, CLC, LC, MH, PH.

3237　[–] The testimony of the everlasting gospel. [*Norwich?* 1654.] cap., 4°.* LT, LF, OC, BBN, MR; PH, PSC.

3238　[–] A true separation between the power of the spirit. [*London,* 1654.] cap., 4°.* LT, LF, OC, BBN.

3239　[–] A true testimony of obedience to the heavenly call. [*London,* 1654.] cap., 4°.* LT, LF; CH.

3240　—A true testimony of the zeal of Oxford-professors. *For Giles Calvert,* 1654. 4°.* MADAN 2245. LT, O, C, LF, BBN; PH, Y.

3241　—Truth cleared, and the deceit. *Printed,* 1654. 4°.* L, LF, BBN, MR, DT.

3242　—A word of wisdom. *For Thomas Simmons,* 1659. brs. L, LF.

3243　**Hubert, Robert.** A catalogue of many natural rarities. *By Tho. Ratcliffe, for the author,* 1664. 8°. L, O, LCP, CT, RPL, CH, Y.

3244 — —[Anr. ed.] —, 1665. 8°.* O, C, OC, E, EN; CH, WF.

3245 [–] A catalogue of part of those rarities. [London, 166–?] 12°. O, GU.

3246 Entry cancelled.

H[ubert], W[illiam]. The Catholick naked truth. [Half-title to his Puritan convert.] 1676. See following entry.

3246A [–] The puritan convert. [London?], printed 1676. 4°.* L, O, CS, BR, BSM, DT; CH, IU, MH, NU, TO, WF, Y.

3246B Hubert's ghost. For F. Coles, T. Vere, and I. Wright, [1663–74]. brs. O.

3247 —[Anr. ed.] [London], for I. Wright, I. Clarke, W. Thackeray, and T. Passinger, [1681–4]. brs. L.

Huc ades. 1659. See L., T.

3248 Huddleston, Ferdinando. The speech of. [London, 1679.] brs. L, O, HH, LNC; IU, MBA, MH, NC.

3249 Entry cancelled.

Huddleston, John. Usury explained. 1696. See Dormer, John.

Huddleston, Richard. See Hudleston, Richard.

3249A [Hudgebutt, John.] A collection of new ayres. By J. Heptinstall for J. Hudgebutt, 1695. obl. 4°. L.

3250 [–] Thesaurus musicus: being, . . . First book. By J. Heptinstall for John Hudgebut. To be sold by John Carr, and by John Money, 1693. fol.* L, O, LCM, GU; LC, MH, WF.

3251 [–] —Second book. By J. Heptinstall for Henry Playford, and John Money, 1694. fol.* T.C.II 510. L, O, LCM, GU; MH, WF.

3251A [–] — —[Anr. ed.] By J. Heptinstall for John Hudgebutt, to be sold by John Money, 1694. fol.* O, LCM, GU; LC.

3252 [–] —Third book. By J. Heptinstall for John Hudgebutt. To be sold by John Carr, and John Money, 1695. fol.* L, O, LCM, GU; LC, MH, WF.

3253 [–] —Fourth book. By J. Heptinstall for John Hudgebutt. To be sold by John Carr, and Daniel Dring. 1695. fol.* L, O, LCM; LC, MH, WF.

3254 [–] —Fifth book. By J. Heptinstall, for John Hudgebutt, to be sold by Samuel Scott, and Daniel Dring. 1696. fol.* T.C.II 569. L, O, LCM; CLC, LC, MH, WF.

3254A [–] A vade mecum for the lovers of musick. By N. Thompson for John Hudgebut, 1679. 4°. O; CB, LC, NCU.

Hudibras. 1663. See Butler, Samuel.

3255 Hudibras answered, by True de Case. [n.p., 1663.] brs. L, O, LS; MH, Y.

3256 Hvdibras on Calamy's imprisonment. [London, 1663.] brs. L, O, LNC; MH, Y.

3257 Hudleston, Richard. A short and plain way. By Henry Hills, 1688. 4°.* L, O, C, ENC, DT; BN, CH, CN, MH, NU, TU, WF, Y. (var.)

3258 — —[Anr. ed.] Holy-Rood-House, by Mr. P. B., 1688. 12°. ALDIS 2763. SCOTTISH EPISCOPAL CHURCH COLLEGE.

3259 — —[Anr. ed.] Dublin, reprinted for William Weston, 1688. 4°.* DIX 230. L, C, DT.

3260 [Hudson, John.] Geographiæ veteris scriptores. Vol. I. Oxoniæ, e theatro Sheldoniano. 1698. 4°. T.C.III 110. L, O, CT, EN, DT; CLC, IU, MH, MU, NC, WF, Y, AVP.

3261 Hudson, Michael. The divine right of government. [London], printed, 1647. 4°. LT, O, C, SC, DT; CH, CN, MH, NU, WF, Y.

3262 [–] The royall, and the royallists plea. [London], 1647. 4°.* LT, O, C, EN, DT; CH, CN, MH, TU, WF, Y.

3263 Hudson, Samuel. An addition or postscript to the vindication. By J. B. for Andrew Kembe, to be sold at his shop, and by Edward Brewster, and Thomas Basset, 1658. 4°. LT, O, LLP, ORP, NPL; IU, MB, Y.

3264 —David's labour and rest. By James Astwood for Thomas Parkhurst, 1689. 4°.* T.C.II 248. L, LW, WCA, EN, BLH; MWA, NU, WF, Y.

3265 —The essence and unitie of the church Catholike visible. By George Miller for Christopher Meredith, 1645. 4°. LT, O, CT, NPL, DT; CH, CN, MH, NU, WF, Y.

3266 —A vindication of The essence. By A. M. for Christopher Meredith, 1650. 4°. L, O, C, ENC, DT; MH, NR, NU, WF, Y.

3267 — —Second edition. By J. B. for Andrew Kembe, to be sold at his shop, and by Edward Brewster, and Thomas Basset, 1658. 4°. LT, ORP, CT, DU, ENC; CLC, MBA, MU, NU, Y.

3267A Hudson's Bay Company. The Kings of England by right of discovery. [London? 1687.] brs. MIU.

3267B —Upon Wednesday the 18th day of November. The thirteenth day of November, 1696. brs. MIU.

3267C A hue and cry after a Jacobite. 1690. brs. OC; NN.

3268 —[Anr. ed.] colop: Printed at London, and re-printed at Edinburgh, 1690. cap., 4°.* ALDIS 3047. OB, OW, EN, ESS; Y.

Hue and cry after a man-midwife. 1699. See Ward, Edward.

3269 A hue-and-cry after beauty and vertue. [London? 1685.] 4°.* CH.

3270 —[Anr. ed.] [London, 1680.] brs. L, O, LLU; CH, CN, MH, TSM, TU.

3271 A hew and cry after blood & murther. For L. Curtiss, 1681 [2]. brs. L, O, LLP; MH, PU, Y.

3272 A huy [sic] and cry after conscience. colop: Printed, 1667. brs. L.

3273 A hue and crie after Cromwell. Nol-Nod. Printed, 1649. 4°.* LT, O, DU, LLU, DT; CH, CN, MH, TU, WF, Y.

3274 A hue and cry after Dr. T. O. For Alex Banks, 1681. brs. L, O, C, HH; CH, CN, MH, WF, Y.

3275 A hue and cry after Edward Kerby. For Robert Thompson, 1700. brs. L.

3276 The hue and cry after Father Peters. colop: For W. R., 1688. brs. L, C, LG, HH; CH, TO, TSM, WF, Y.

3277 —[Anr. ed.] Reprinted Edinburgh, 1691. brs. ALDIS 3154. EN; CN.

3278 A hue and cry after Good Friday. [Oxford, 1672.] brs. MADAN 2955. L; CCC.

3279 The hue and cry after J— Duke of M—. colop: [London], for B. A., 1683. brs. L, O, OC, HH, EN; CH, CN, LC, MH, WF, Y.

3280 —[Anr. ed.] colop: Edinburgh, reprinted by the heir of Andrew Anderson, 1683. ALDIS 2382.5. L, CT, MC; WF.

3281   A hue-and-cry after Lambert. [*London*, 1660.] brs. O; MIU.

3281A A hue and cry after money. [*London*], *printed*, 1689. 4°.* MH.

3281B A hue-and-cry after Morgan Hews. *For J. Smith*, 1699. brs. MH.

3282   A hue and cry after P. and H. [*London*, 1686.] fol.* L, O, C, OB, LNC; CH, IU, LC, MH, WF, Y.

3282A A hue and crye after passive-obedience. [*London, R. Baldwin*, 1690.] brs. MH.

3283   An hue and cry after R. Lˢ. colop: [*n.p.*], *for Tom. Tell-Troth*, [1680?]. cap., fol.* L, O, CT, MR; CH, CLC, FU, IU, MH, NC, Y.

3284   A hue and cry after religion and justice. [*London*], *printed*, 1649. 4°.* LT, LG; CLC, MH, NU, WF.

3285   Entry cancelled.
       Hue and cry after Sir John Presbyter. [*London*, 1649.] *See* Cleveland, John.

3286   A hue and cry after the abdicated B— of E—. colop: *For E. Golding*, 1691. cap., 4°.* L; CH, CN, WF.

3287   A hue and cry after the devil. *Printed*, 1668. 4°. O; CH, MH.

3287A The hue and cry after the Duke of Berwick, by the discontented Jacobites. colop: *For S. Littleton, February 26th*, 1696. brs. LIU.

3288   A hue and cry after the Dutch fleet. *By L. Miller, for Richard Head*, 1666. brs. O, LPR.

3289   The hue and crie after the Earl of Clarendon. [*London*], *printed*, 1667. brs. L, O.
       Hue and cry after the false prophets. 1661. *See* Burrough, Edward.

3290   No entry.
       Hue-and cry after the fundamental lawes. Europe, [1653]. *See* Lilburne, John.

3291   A hue & crie after the good old cause. [*London*, 1659.] cap., 4°.* O; CH, Y.

3292   A hue and cry after the high court of injustice. *For John Andrews*, 1660. 4°.* LT.

3293   A hue-and-cry after the plot. colop: *For F. Smith*, [1683]. brs. L, O, HH, LLU; CH, IU, MH, NCD.

3293A A hue and cry after the reasons. *Printed at London*, 1679. fol.* L, O, C; CH, CN, INU, MBA, MH, WF, Y.

3293B An hue and cry after the shatter'd French fleet. *For J. Shuter*. 1692. 4°.* NN.

3294   —[Anr. ed.] *Dublin, reprinted for Jacob Miller*, 1692. brs. DIX 377. DI.

3295   The hue and cry after those rambling protonotaries. *By B. Alsop*, 1651. 4°.* LT; MH.

3295A A hue and cry after Tory-honesty. colop: *For N. T.*, 1682. brs. CH, MH.

3296   An hve-and-cry after Vox Popvli. [*London*], *for Edward Martin, in Norwich*, 1646. 4°.* LT, O, C, YM, A, DT; CH, NU, WF.
       Heu [*sic*] and cry: or. [1682.] *See* N., N.

3297   The hue-and-song after patience. [*London*, 1683.] brs. O, EN; CH, CLC, MH.

3298   **Hues, Robert.** A learned treatise of globes. *By J. B. for Andrew Kemb*, 1659. 8°. L, C, OC; MBP, IU, MU, RPJ, WF, Y.

3299   —Tractatus de globis. *Oxoniæ, excudebat W. H. impensis Ed. Forrest*, 1663. 8°. MADAN 2640. L, O, CS, SP; CLC, IU, NN, WF, Y.

3299A ——[Anr. ed.] *Oxford, excudebat H. H. impensis Ed. Forrest*, 1668. 8°. IU.

3300   —Tractatvs dvo mathematici. *Oxoniæ, excudebat L. Lichfield, impensis Ed. Forrest*, 1651. 12°. MADAN 2172. O, LI, CS, NPL, DT; CH, CLC, IU, MH, MU, WF, Y.

3300aA ——[Anr. ed.] —, 1652. 12°. CM, CS; CH.

3300A Entry cancelled. Date after 1700.

3300B **Huet, Pierre Daniel, bp.** De interpretatione. *Prostat apud Abel Swalle*, 1684. 8°. T.C.II 74. LSC, DU, NE, EN.

3301   —A treatise of romances. *By R. Battersby, for S. Heyrick*, 1672. 8°. T.C.I 89. L, O, CM, EN, DT; CH, CN, LC, MH, OCI, Y.

3302   —A treatise of the situation of Paradise. *For James Knapton*, 1694. 12°. T.C.II 482. L, O, C, SHR, SP; CDA, CN, NU, PL, WF, Y.
       [Huetson, Michael.] *See* Hewetson, Michael.

3302A Hugh Peters's dreame. [*London*, 1659.] cap., 4°.* O; CH, MH, MIU, NN, WF.
       Hugh Peters his figaries. 1660. *See* Peters, Hugh.

3303   Hugh Peters last will and testament. [*London*, 1660.] brs. LT, C, EN.
       Hugh Peters's passing-bell. 1660. *See* V., T.

3304   **Hughes, Aud.** Res ab hostibus captae. [*n.p.*, 1662.] brs. O.

3305   **Hughes, George.** An analytical exposition of . . . first book of Moses. [*London*], *printed*, 1672. fol. L, O, C, LCL, E; CLC, CU, MH, PJB, WF, Y.

3306   —Aphorisms. [*London*], *printed*, 1670. 8°. T.C.I 70. L, O, C, DU, E; CH, IU, MH, NU, TU, WF, Y.

3307   —The art of embalming dead saints discovered. *By A. N., for John Rothwell*, 1642. 4°. LT, O, DU, ENC, DT; CH, MWA, NU, WF, Y.

3308   —A dry rod blooming. *By T. Paine for John Rothwell*, 1644. 4°. LT, O, LCL, LW, WCA, E; CLC, NU, Y.

3309   —Sure-footing in Christianity examined. *For Abisha Brocas, in Exon.* 1668. 8°. O, C, LCL, LW; Y.

3309A ——[Anr. ed.] *Printed*, 1668. 8°. CS.

3310   —Væ-euge-tuba. Or, the vvo-ioy-trumpet. *By E. G. for Iohn Rothwell*, 1647. 4°.* LT, O, C, GU, DT; CH, MIU, NU, WF, T. (var.)

3310A **H[ughes], [Iohn], 1615–1686.** Allwydd neu agoriad. *Lvyck* [i.e., *London?*], 1670. 12°. AN; CN, MH, WF, Y.

3311   **Hughes, John, 1677–1720.** The court of Neptune. A poem. *For Jacob Tonson*, 1700. fol.* O, LLU, MR; CH, CLC, CN, MH, TU, WF, Y.

3312   [–] In a grove's forsaken shade. [*London*], *T. Cross*, [1697?]. brs. L.

3312A Entry cancelled.
       —Sermon preach'd. 1683. *See* Hughes, John, *minister*.

3313   [–] The triumph of peace. A poem. *For Jacob Tonson*, 1698. fol.* L, MR; CLC, MH, Y.

3313A **Hughes, John, *minister*.** A sermon preach'd . . . Nov. 18. 1683. *For Fincham Gardner*, 1683. 4°.* LUG, OB, CS, LSD, WCA; CH, CLC, WU, Y.

3314 **Hughes, Lewis.** Certaine grievances. [*London*], printed, 1641. 4°.* LT, O, C, DUS, E; CLC, CN, MH, V, Y.

3314A ——[Anr. ed.] *Printed*, 1642. 4°.* CS; CLC, MH.

3315 ——Fifth edition. *By T. P.*, 1642. 4°. L, OC, CT, EN, DT; NU, PU, WF.

3315A ——Sixth edition. *By T. P. & M. S. for Edward Blackmore*, 1643. 4°. CT, BAMB.

3316 —The errors of the common catechisme. *By Matthew Simmons*, 1645. 4°.* LCL, WCA, YM, E; CH, IU, MH, NU, Y.

3317 [–] A looking-glasse for all trve hearted Christians. *By T. P. and M. S.*, 1642. 4°.* L, LCL, AN; CU, MH.

3318 —Signes from Heaven. *By T. P. and M. S.*, 1642. 4°.* L, CM.

3319 **Hughes, William, *of Clapham*.** Disputationes grammaticles. *Typis G. R. prostantq; venales apud Robertum Boulterum*, 1671. 8°. T.C.I 67. O, C, LW, DUS; LC, U. OREGON.

3319A **Hughes, William, *of Gray's Inn*.** An abridgment of the common law. *By T. R. for H. Twyford, T. Dring, and J. Place*, 1657. 4°. RPL; CH, WF.

3320 Entry cancelled.
[–] Abridgement of the statutes in force. 1663. *See* England. Laws, Statutes. Exact abridgment.
—Abridgement of the three volumes. 1665. *See* Croke, *Sir* George.

3321 [–] Anglo-Jvdævs, or the history. *By T. N. for Thomas Heath*, 1656. 4°. LT, O, C, P, EN; CSS, LC, MH, NC, OHU, Y.

3322 —The commentaries upon original writs. First part. *By Tho. Roycroft, for Henry Twyford, and John Place*, 1655. 4°. L, O, LGI, LL, DT; MHL, PU, WF.

3323 Entry cancelled.
[–] Discourse of pluralities. 1680. *See* Hughes, William, hospitaller.

3324 —The grand abridgment of the law continued. *By J. S. for Henry Twyford, George Sawbridge, Thomas Dring, and John Place*, 1660-3. 3v. 4°. L, O, C, MC, EN; LC, MHL, MU, NCL, WF.

3325 —Nomotomia, in two parts. The first. *By T. R. for H. Twyford, T. Dring, and J. Place*, 1657. 4°. L, O, LW, AN, BC, CD; CH, MHL, PUL.

3326 —The parsons lavv. *For the author*, 1641. 8°. L, C, LI, DC, EN; CH, IU, LC, MHL, NC, NU.

3327 ——Second edition. *For the author, and are to be sold by Tho. Basset, and George Dawes*, 1663. 8°. L, O, OM, CS, BAMB; CH, LC, MHL, PU, TU, WF.

3327A ——Third edition. *By John Streater*, 1663. 8°. L, C, CM; CH, LC, MHL, MU, WF.

3327B ——[Anr. ed.] *By John Streater, Henry Twyford, and Elizabeth Flesher, assigns of Richard Atkins and Edward Atkins*, 1673. 8°. NE, WCA, CD; CLC, IU, MH, PU, WF.

3328 ——"Third" edition. *For W. Leak, T. Basset, S. Heyrick, and G. Dawes*, 1673. 8°. T.C.I 130. L, O, C, LNC, DT; BN, CH, CN, IU, LC, MHL, NCL, YL.

3329 —Hughes's quæries. *For George Dawes*, 1675. 12°. T.C.I 206. L, LGI, LIU; CLC, MHL, MIU, WF, YL.
—Reports and cases of lavv. 1658. *See* Leonard, William.

3330-1 Entries cancelled.
—Reports of certain cases. 1652. *See* Godbolt, John.

3332 **Hughes, William, *horticulturist*.** The American physitian. *By J. C. for William Crook*, 1672. 12°. T.C.I 103. L, O, E, EN, AU; BN, CH, CN, LC, MH, HC.

3333 —The compleat vineyard. *By G. M. for W. Crooke, and John Playfere*, 1665. 4°.* L, O, LG, CAMB. BOTANY; CH, MH, WF, ASU.

3334 ——[Anr. ed.] *By J. C. for Will. Crooke*, 1670. 8°. T.C.I 40. L, O, C, LCP, EN; CH, LC, MHO, WU, Y.

3335 ——Third edition. *For Will Crook*, 1683. 12°. O, LWL; MHO, Y.

3336 [–] The flower-garden. *By H. B. for William Crook*, 1671. 8°.* T.C.I 91. L; CLC, Y.

3337 ——[Anr. ed.] *For William Crook*, 1672. 12°. L, O, KEW, RU; MH, WDA, WF, WU.

3338 ——[Anr. ed.] *For C. Wall*, 1677. 12°. L, OC; IU.

3339 ——Third edition. *For William Crook*, 1683. 12°. T.C.II 57. L, O, LWL; BN, MHO, OSU, WF.

Hughes, William, *hospitaller*. A candid plea. 1684. *See* — Two sermons.

3340 [–] A discourse of pluralities. *For Thomas Parkhurst*, 1680. 4°.* T.C.I 421. L, O, CS, DC, DU; CH, MH, NU, WF, Y.

3341 [–] An endeavour for peace among Protestants. *By T. James for Tho. Parkhurst*: 1680. 4°.* T.C.I 416. L, O, CM, SP; NU, PU, WF.

3342 —Magistracy God's ministry. *By T. M. for George Calvert*, 1652. 4°.* LT, O, C, OC, EC; CH, MM, NU, Y.

3343 [–] The man of sin. *By J. D. for Robert Boulter*, 1677. 4°. T.C.I 275. L, O, C, LIL, EN, CD; CLC, MH, NU, TU, WF, Y.

3344 [–] Munster and Abingdon. *Oxford, by Henry Hall for Robert Blagrave*, 1657. 8°. MADAN 2340-1. L, O, C, DU, SP; CH, IU, NHC, WF, Y. (var.)

3345 —A practical discourse of silence. *By W. Onely, for J. Salusbury*, 1694. 8°. T.C.II 508. L, O, C, LG.

3346 [–] The spirit of prophecy. *For W. Crook*, 1679. 8°. T.C.I 326. L, O, C, SP, DT; CH, IU, MWA, NU, WF. (var.)

3346A [–] —[Anr. ed., "prophesie"] *For Will. Crook*, 1687. 8°. CLC.

3347 —Summons to sinners. *By J. Richardson, for Tho. Parkhurst*, 1681. 8°. T.C.I 483. LSC, LW, NE; NC, NU.

3348 —Two sermons, *By J. A. for Samuel Walsall*, 1684. 4°. T.C.II 94. L, O, WCA, YM; CH, NU.

3348A ——[Anr. ed.] *By Francis Clarke for Samuel Walsall*, 1684. 4°.* O, WCA.

3349 **Hugo, Hermann.** Pia desideria, viz. *Excudit J. C. sumptibus Roberti Pawlet*, 1677. 8°. L, CK, LIU, LSD, EN; CLC, CN, IU, MH, TU, WF, Y.

3349A ——[Anr. ed.] *Excudit H. H. sumptibus Georgii Pawlet*, 1685. 8°. O.

3350 —Pia desideria: or. *For Henry Bonwicke,* 1686. 8°. T.C.II 168. L, O, C, LLU, EN; CH, CLC, CU, MH, NCD, NP.

3351 — —Second edition. *By J. L. for Henry Bonwicke,* 1690. 8°. T.C.II 327. L, O, C, AN, DM; CLC, IU, MH, NU, WF, Y.

3352 **Huise, John.** Florilogivm phrasicωn. or, a survey. *By R. N. for W. Garret,* 1650. 8°. O, C, NOT; CN, MH, NC.

3353 — —[Anr. ed.] *By D. M. for Tho. Davies,* 1659. 8°. L, C, BC, EN; MBA.

3354 **Huish, Alexander.** Musa ruralis. In adventum . . . Caroli II. *Excudebat Thomas Milbourn,* 1660. 4°.* LT, LLP, OB; Y.

3355 [**Huish, Anthony.**] Priscianus ephebus; or. *By Iohn Redmayne, for William Garret,* 1663. 8°. LC.

3356 [–] —[Anr. ed.] —, 1668. 8°. T.C.I 6. L, O, C, LW, BC, LSD; CH, CLC, IU, MH, MU, PU.

3356A [–] —[Anr. ed.] *By Iohn Redmayne for Ralph Needham,* 1669. 8°. PMA, WU.

3357 [–] Priscianus embryo et nascens: being a key. Fourth edition. *For William Garret,* 1670. 8°. L, O, C; CLC, IU, WF.

3358 Entry cancelled. [–] Priscianus ephebus. 1668. *See above* [H3356].

3358A [–] Priscianus nascens or a key to the grammar schoole. *For William Garret,* 1659. 8°. IU.

3358B [–] —[Anr. ed.] —, to be sold by *Timothy Garthwait,* 1660. 8°. L, O; CLC, IU, MB, NC, WF.

3358C [–] —[Anr. ed.] —, 1663. 8°. GU; IU.

3358D [–] —[Anr. ed.] —, 1664. 8°. L.

3359 **Huit, Ephraim.** The whole prophecie of Daniel explained. [*London*], *for Henry Overton,* 1643. 4°. O, BC, E; CN, MH, NU, RPJ, WCL, Y.

3360 — —[Anr. ed.] —, 1644. 4°. LT, O, C, SA, DT; BN, CN, LC, MH, NU, RPJ, Y.

3361 Entry cancelled. **Huit, John.** Prayers of intercession. 1659. *See* Hewitt, John.

3362 Hvlls managing of the kingdoms cause. *For Richard Best,* June 18. 1644. 4°.* LT, O, C, YM, DT; CH, MH, WF, Y. Huls pillar of providence. 1644. *See* Coleman, Thomas.

3363 **Hulsius, Anthony.** The royal joy. *By John Bill,* 1660. 4°.* LT, C; WF. Humane industry. 1661. *See* Powell, Thomas. Humane life: or. 1696. *See* Lucas, Richard. Humane prudence. 1680. *See* Britaine, William de.

3364 Humanum est errare, or false steps. [*London,* 1689?] cap., 4°.* O, LL, LIU, EN; MH, WF, Y.

3365 **H[umberston], H[enry].** A sermon preached . . . 18th. of April, 1686. *For Matthew Turner,* 1686. 4°.* L, O, CS, MC, DT; CH, NU, RBU, WF, Y.

3366 [**Humbie, A.**] A letter from Newcastle. *For Robert Bostock and Samuel Gellibrand,* Octob. 26. 1644. 4°.* LT, O, EN; IU, MH, WF.

3367 The humble acknowledgment and congratulation of many thousands of young-men. *For Laurence Chapman,* 1647. 4°.* LT, LG; CN, MH, MM, WF.

3368 —[Anr. ed.] *For Giles Calvert,* 1647. 4°.* LT, LLU, YM, DT; MH, Y, ZAP.

3369 The humble acknowledgment and petition of divers inhabitants . . . of London. *By M. S. for Henry Overton,* 1646. 4°.* LT, O, CT, SP, DT; CLC, CU, MH, WF, Y.

3369A An humble acknowledgement of His Majesties incomparable grace. *Printed,* 1660. 4°.* GU; WF.

3370 The humble acknowledgment of the inhabitants of Sovth-Wales. *By Edward Husband and John Field,* 1650. 4°.* LT, AN; IU. Humble acknowledgement of the sins. Edinburgh, 1653. *See* Warriston, Archibald Johnston, *lord.* Causes of the Lords vvrath.

3371 Humble address and advice of several of the Peeres. *Printed,* 1679. fol.* L, O, C, LIU, EN; CH, CLC, IU, MH, WF, Y, AVP.

3372 No entry.

3373 The humble address, and hearty desires of the gentlemen, ministers and free-holders of . . . Northampton. [*London,* 1660.] brs. MH.

3374 —[Anr. ed.] *By D. Maxwell,* 1660. brs. LT, O; MH.

3375 The humble address and petition of several peers. [*London,* 1680.] cap., fol.* L, O, LNC, MR, EN; CH, MBA, MH, WF, WU, Y.

3375A The humble address, & c [of 17 peers]. [*London,* 1680.] brs. OC. Humble addresse both of church. [n.p.], 1641. *See* Guild, William.

3376 An humble address from the people of England. *By George Croom,* [1689]. brs. O; Y.

3377 The humble address of the agitators of the army. *For J. Harris,* [1647]. 4°.* LT, O, OC, YM, DT; CH, MH, MU, NU, WF, Y.

3378 The humble address of the archbishop, the bishops, and the rest of the clergy of the Province of Canterbury. *By Charles Bill, and the executrix of Thomas Newcomb,* 1700. fol.* L, LLP, EC, MR; CH, CLC, PL, RPJ, WF, Y.

3379 Entry cancelled. Humble address of the benefic'd clergy. 1689. *See* To the right honourable and honourable the Knights.

3379A The humble address of the corporation of Ripon. *Edinburgh, by the heir of A. Anderson,* 1681. brs. ALDIS 2273. 8. ER.

3379B The humble address of the corporation of Trinity House. colop: *For Rich. Royston,* 1681. brs. CN, AVP.

3380 The humble address of the distressed Protestants. *For N. C.,* 1681. fol.* L, O, SP, EN; CH, CN, PU, WF, Y, AVP.

3380A Humble address of the grand jury of and for . . . Southwark. colop: *For Benj. Tooke,* 1683. brs. CH.

3380AB The humble address of the grand jury of . . . Tamworth. *For C. Mearne,* 1682. brs. O.

3380AC The humble address of the heirs . . . Sir William Courten. [*London,* 1679.] cap., fol.* LUG; WF.

3380B The humble addresse of the Lord Maior, aldermen, . . . 9th of . . . August. *By W. Godbid,* 1659. 4°.* O, OC, LLU; CH, MH, WF.

3381 —13th day of March, 1682. colop: *By Samuel Roycroft,* 1682. brs. L, LG; CH, CU, MH, WF, Y.

3382 Entry cancelled.
Humble address of the Lord Mayor . . . 2 July 1683. *See* To the King's most excellent majesty.

3382A The humble address of the mayor, aldermen . . . Bath. *For Edward Thomas,* 1660. brs. L.

3383 Entry cancelled.
Humble address of the maior, aldermen, ministers . . . of Kingston upon Hull. 1660. *See* To his most excellent majesty Charles the Second . . . The humble address.

3384 The humble addrsse [sic] of the nobility and gentry of . . . Kent. *For Gabriel Bedel, and Thomas Collins,* 1660. brs. L.
Humble address of the Presbyterians. [n.p.], 1687. *See* Alsop, Vincent.

3384A The humble address of the president, vice-president . . . Artillery-Company. *For Walter Davies,* 1681. brs. AVP.

3384B The humble address of the principal and professors [of Edinburgh Univ.]. [*Edinburgh?* 1699.] brs. OP.

3385 An humble addresse of the provinciall synod of Fife. *For George Calvert,* 1660. 4°.* LT, O; CDA, NU, WF.

3386 The humble address of the publicans of New-England. *Printed,* 1691. 4°.* L, EN; CH, LC, MH, MU, NN, RPJ.

3386A —[Anr. ed.] *Printed by James Astwood,* 1691. cap., 4°.* MB.

3386B The humble address of your Majesties Deputy-Lieutenants . . . Glamorgan. *Edinburgh, by the heir of Andrew Anderson,* 1681. brs. EN.

3387 An humble address offer'd to the consideration of the Lords. [*London,* 1695.] 4°.* O, OC, CT, LSD; CH, WF, Y.

3388 An humble address to all the truely loyal Commons. colop: *By D. Mallet,* 1680. cap., fol.* L, O, OC, MR; CH, MIU, WF, Y.

3389 An humble address to the honourable House of Commons, on the behalf of the traders. 1699. brs. LUG.
Humble address to the livery-men. 1682. *See* B., I.

3390 An humble address to the most illustrious . . . James Francis Edward. 1688. brs. MH.

3391 An humble addresse to the right honourable Lords & Commons . . . in vindication of kingly power. *By Peter Lillicrap, for Henry Marsh,* 1660. 4°.* MR; NU, WF.

3391A An humble address to the truly loyal citizens of London. [*London?* 1680.] cap., fol.* O, C.

3392 An humble address with some proposals. *Printed,* 1677. 4°.* L, LUG, CT, DU; LC, MBA, MH, NC, PU, WF, Y.

3392A The humble addreses [sic] of several close prisoners. *Printed,* 1662. 4°.* L, OC, SP; CH, IU, MIU, WF, Y.

3392B An humble adoration of our blessed Lord Jesus. [*London,* 1664.]* O.
Humble advice and earnest desires. 1649. *See* Breedon, Zacheus.

3393 The humble advice, and tender declaration. *By Henry Hills,* [1659]. brs. LT, O, LG; MH, MIU.

3394 No entry.
Humble advice of the Assembly. [1646/7.] *See* Westminster assembly of divines.

3395 Entry cancelled.
Humble advice to His sacred Majesty. Edinburgh, 1683. *See* Cunningham, James.
Humble advice to Protestant dissenters. 1682. *See* Bird, Benjamin.
Humble advice to the conforming. 1672. *See* Fullwood, Francis.

3396 An humble advise to the right honorable the Lord Mayor. [*London,* 1654?] cap., 4°.* MR, SP; CLC, PL, RBU, Y.
Humble and just outcry and appeale of all the inslaved. 1649. *See* F., J.
Humble, and modest proposals tender'd. 1680. *See* Sherlock, William.

3397 The humble and serious testimony . . . Bedford. [*London,* 1657.] brs. L, O, LUG.

3398 The humble and thankful acknowledgement and declaration of the County of Southampton. *For Edward Husband, Jan. 25.* 1647. brs. STEELE 2746. LT, O, LG.

3398A The humble and unanimous answer of the army . . . [10 June 1647]. [*n.p.,* 1647?] brs. INU.
Humble answer of the divines. 1648. *See* Marshall, Stephen.

3399 The humble ansvver of the general councel of officers. *By Matthew Simmons, for Hannah Allen,* 1648. 4°.* LT, O, LLU, YM, DT; CH, IU, TU, WF, Y.

3400 —[Anr. ed.] *For H. Beck,* 1648. 4°.* CLC, MBP.

3401 An humble answer to a petition desiring the regulation of the Biskey trade. [*London,* 1657?] brs. L.

3402 An humble apology for Non-conformists. [*London*], *printed,* 1669. 8°. L, OC, CT, DU, E; IU, MH, NU, WF, Y.

3403 An humble apologie for the ministers of England. *By J. C.,* 1659. 4°. LLP, MR, BQ; CN, WF.

3404 The humble apology of some commonly called Anabaptists. *By Henry Hills, to be sold by Francis Smith,* 1660. 4°.* LT, O, C, LG, DU, LIU; CH, CN, MH, NU, WF, Y.

3405 An humble caution concerning the danger of removing godly and approved ministers. *By Thomas Ratcliffe,* 1660. 4°.* LT, LIU.

3405A The humble confession, and just vindication of them who have suffered much. [*London*], *printed,* 1647. 4°.* Y.

3406 The humble congratulation of the nobility . . . Lincoln. 1660. brs. L.

3407 An humble declaration of the apprentjces. *Printed at London,* 1642. 4°.* LT, O, CJ, LIU, DT; CH, CLC, CN, MH, WF, Y.

3408 The humble declaration, tender, and petition of divers cordiall and wel-affected marriners. *Printed at London for Henry Overton,* 1648. 4°.* LT, BC, MR; CSS, MBP, MH, WF.

3409 An humble defence of the Exeter bill. *For John Martyn,* 1674. 4°. CS; Y.
Humble desired union. 1642. *See* Taylor, John.

3410 The humble desires and proposals of the private agitators. *By I. C.,* 1647. 4°.* LT, CM, MR; CH.

3411 The humble desires of a free svbiect. *For Fr. Coles*, 1659. 4°.* LT, O, LLU; CH, MH, NU, WF, Y.

3412 The humble desires of the citizens, yovng men, and apprentices. *By Richard Cotes*, 1647. 4°.* LT, O, LG, DT; CH, CSS, IU, MH, NU, Y.

3413 The humble desires of the gentlemen, free-holders, and inhabitants, of . . . Durham. *By M. S.*, 1652. brs. L.

3414 The humble desires of the knights, gentlemen, ministers, . . . of Leicester. *For Henry Chase*, 1659. brs. LT, LG; CH, MH.

3415 The humble desires of the loyall hearted, wel-affected free-men. [*London*, 1648.] brs. LT, O, LG; CH, CN, MH.

Humble essay. 1681. *See* Harley, *Sir* Edward.

Humble examination. 1641. *See* Burgess, Cornelius.

3416 The humble gratulation and petition . . . Lancaster. *York; by Robert Barker, and by the assignes of John Bill*, 1642. 4°.* CS, MR; MH, WF, Y.

3417 An humble hint to the king. [*London*], *by Nathaniel Thompson*, 1685. 4°.* O; CH, CLC, WF, Y.

3418 The humble enquiry, by way of catechism. *For Rich: Lowndes*, 1657. 4°.* L; NU.

3419 The humble inquiry, partly approving. *By M. S.*, 1657. 4°.* LT, C; CH.

3420 Humble instructions for the setling of garrisons in Ireland. *For John Field, June 30.* 1646. 4°.* LT, LVF, OC, DN; CH, LC, MH.

Humble letter of loyalty. [n.p.], 1643. *See* T., L.

3421 An humble motion made in the time of . . . Elizabeth. [*London*], *printed* 1590, *reprinted* 1641. 4°.* LT, O, C, BAMB, LNC; CH, CSS, CN, MH, NU, TU, WF, Y.

Humble motion to the Parliament. 1649. *See* Hall, John.

3421A An humble offer at the decision of the question, how the vacant throne. [*London?* 1689.] brs. CH.

Humble offer of the National Land-bank. [*London*, 1696.] *See* Briscoe, John.

3422 Humble offer to the serious consideration of both Houses of Parliament . . . [Weavers company]. [*London*, 1699?] cap., fol.* Y.

3422A The humble penitent. Third edition. *M. G. and W. H.*, 1682. 12°. CLC.

3423 —Fourth edition. *For Matthew Gilliflower*, 1688. 12°. T.C.II 220. O; CLC.

3424 The humble petition and address of divers young men. 1647. 4°. LG (lost).

3425 The humble petition and address of divers young men. [*London*, 1659.] brs. O.

3426 The humble petition and address of the general court sitting at Boston. [*Boston*], *printed*, 1660. 4°.* EVANS 61. LT, O, CT; CH, MH, NN, RPJ, Y.

3427 Entry cancelled.

Humble petition and address of the Lord Mayor. 1680. *See* To the Kings most excellent majesty.

3428 The humble petition and addresse of the officers. *By Henry Hills, for him and Francis Tyton*, 1659. 4°.* LT, O, C, BC, DT; HR, CH, CU, MH, MU, TU, WF, Y.

3429 The humble petition and address of the right honourable the Lord Mayor, . . . of London. colop: *By Samuel Roycroft, London*, 1681. brs. L, O, C, LSD, DT; CH, CN, MH, WF, Y, AVP.

3430 No entry.

3431 The humble petition and case of the tobacco-pipe-makers. [*London*, 1695?] brs. L, LG.

3432 The humble petition and desires of the commanders, masters, mariners, . . . of Thames. *For George Lindsey*, 1648. 4°.* LT, LNM, DT; CN, CSS, MH, MIU.

3433 The humble petition and grateful acknowledgement of the town of Tavnton. *For Edward Husband, Febr.* 17. 1647 [8]. 4°.* LT, DT; MH.

3434 Entry cancelled.

Humble petition and protestation of all the bishops. 1642. *See* To the Kings most excellent Majesty.

3435 The humble petition and protestation of the County of Kent. *By Luke Norton and John Field, for E. Husband and J. Franck, September* 1, 1642. 4°.* LT, O, LG; MH, MU, WF, Y.

3436 The hvmble petition and remonstrance of divers citizens of London. *For Nicholas Manwaring*, 1642. 4°.* LT, LG, OC, MR; IU, MH, NCD, NU, TU.

3437 —[Anr. ed., "divese."] [*Oxford*], *for William Webb*, 1642 [3]. 4°.* MADAN 1209. L, C, LG, OCC, EN; CH, CN, MU, WF, Y.

3438 The humble petition and remonstrance of some hundreds of retaylers. [*London*], *printed*, 1644. 4°.* O, OCC, DT; LC, MH, NC, WF, Y.

3439 An hvmble petition and remonstrance presented . . . concerning the transportation of leather. [*London*], *printed*, 1641. 4°.* LT, O, C, SP, EN; CSS, MH, MIU, NC, NN.

3439A An hvmble petition and remonstrance presented . . . concerning . . . farthing tokens. *Printed*, 1642. 4°.* L, LUG, DT; CH, MH, NU.

3440 The humble petition and representation of many inhabitants of . . . Bvckingham. *For Edward Husband, March* 15. 1647[8]. 4°.* LT, MR; MH, MIU, WF, Y.

3440A The humble petition and representation of several aldermen. *For George Horton*, 1653. 4°.* LT, LG, OC, OJ; CH, CLC, MH, WF.

3441 The humble petition and representation of several churches. *For Francis Tyton and John Playford*, 1649. 4°.* LT, LW, MR, SP; MH, NHC, NU, Y.

3442 The humble petition and representation of the gentry, . . . of Cumberland. *York; by Robert Barker, and by the assignes of John Bill*, 1642. 4°.* L, O, ISD, YM; CN, MH, WF.

3443 —[Anr. ed.] *By Robert Barker, and by the assignes of John Bill*, 1642. 4°.* LT, O, CJ, SP, DT; CH, IU, MH, TU, WF, Y.

3444 The humble petition and representation of the sufferings of several . . . Anabaptists. *For Francis Smith*, 1660. 4°.* O, OC, ORP, SP; CN, MH, MIU, NHC, Y.

3445 The humble petition and resolution of the County of Essex. *Printed June the* 18 *for Joseph Hunscott and John Wright*, 1642. brs. STEELE 2184. O, LG, LS; CH.

3446 The humble petition and resolvtion of the Countie of Kent. [London], *September 1, for John Wright*, 1642. 4°.* L, O, LG, OC, EC, LNC; CH, MH, WF, Y.

3447 The humble petition and resolution of the Deputy-Lieutenants, ... Warwick. *July 11. London, for Joseph Hunscott, and John Wright*, 1642. brs. STEELE 2218. LT, EC, LNC; CH, MH.

3447A —[Anr. ed.] *For Joseph Hunscot and I. Wright*, 1642. brs. WF.

3448 An humble petition for accommodation, presented ... eleventh of December ... Yorke. [London], *Decemb. 17. By T. F. for J. B.* 1642. 4°. O, MR, YM, DT; IU.

3449 Entry cancelled.
Humble petition of aldermen. 1641. *See* To the honourable, the knights, citizens, and burgesses.

3450 The humble petition of all the inhabitants of the town of Old Braintford. *For Edward Husbands and John Frank, November 27,* 1642. 4°.* LT, O, MR; TU, Y.

3451 The humble petition of divers barronets, knights, esquires, ... of Derbie. *By Barnard Alsop,* 1642. 4°.* LT, C, SP; CH, MH, WF.

3452 Entry cancelled.
Humble petition of divers barronets ... of Lincoln. 1642. *See* To the right honourable the house of Commons.

3453 The humble petition of divers baronets, knights, ... of Lincolne. *First printed at Yorke, and now [London] reprinted for Iohn Thomas,* 1642. *August 1.* 4°.* LT, CJ, EC, LNC, DT; CLC, MH, Y.

3454 The humble petition of divers citizens of ... London, to the high and honourable court. [London, 1648.] brs. LT.

3455 The humble petition of divers inhabitants of New England. [London, 1642.] brs. LG.

3456 The humble petition of divers inhabitants of the city of London, and places adjacent. *By John Clowes,* 1648. 4°.* LT, MR; CSS, NC.

3457 The humble petition of divers inhabitants of the County of Hertford. *For Tho. Brewster,* 1659. brs. LT, MH.

3458 The humble petition of divers noblemen and gentlemen. *York, By Robert Barker, and by the assignes of John Bill,* 1642. 4°.* O, C, BR, LLU, YM; CH, MH, WF, Y.

3459 Entry cancelled.
Humble petition of divers of the clergie. 1641. *See* To the right honourable the Lords and Commons.

3460 The humble petition of divers of the knights, gentry, ... of Berkes. *For Thomas Hanson,* 1643. 4°.* LT; MH, WF.

3460A The humble petition of divers persons who have suffered ... in Algeir. [London? 1661.] brs. L.

3461 Entry cancelled.
Humble petition of divers poor prisoners. 1642. *See* To his excellence, the Earl of Forth.

3462 The humble petition of divers well affected magistrates. *For John Wright,* 1648. 4°.* LT, LG, MR; CH, MH, MIU, NU, WF, Y.

3463 The humble petition of divers well-affected persons. *For Thomas Brewster,* 1659. 4°.* LT, O, C, BC, SP; CN, CSS, MH, NC, WF, Y.

3463A The humble petition of 85. gentlemen ... of Chester. *York, by Robert Barker: and by the assignes of John Bill,* 1642. 4°.* C, YM; MBP, WF.

3464 Entry cancelled.
Humble petition of 15,000. 1641. *See* To the honourable the knights, citizens and burgesses.

3465 The humble petition of His Majesties loyall subjects in ... Lincoln. *York, by Robert Barker & by the assigns of John Bill,* 1642. brs. STEELE 2049. L.

3466 Entry cancelled.
Humble petition of His Majesties. [n.p., 1681?]. *See* Humble petitions.

3467 The humble petition of Jock of Bread, Scotland. *For H. Becke,* 1648. 4°.* LT, ES.

3468 The humble petition of knights, esquires, gentlemen, (some of the committee) ... Warwick. *For G. S.* 1644. 4°.* LT, LCL; WF.

3469 The humble petition of many cordial friends, ... in behalf of Mr. Christopher Love. *By J. C.,* 1651. 4°.* LT, LSD.

3470 Entry cancelled.
Humble petition of many hundreds. 1642. *See* To the right honourable, the high Court of Parliament.

3471 The humble petition of many inhabitants in and about the city of London ... May 12. 1659. *For Tho. Brewster & Livewell Chapman,* 1659. 4°.* L, O, CS, LSD, SP; CH, CSS, IU, MH, MU, WF, Y.

3472 The humble petition of many officers lately drawne. *By E. Griffin,* 1647. 4°.* LT, O, YM, DN, DT; CH.

3473 The humble petition of many peaceable citizens. *By Richard Cotes,* 1674. 4°.* LT, BC; WF.

3474 The humble petition of many thousand citizens and inhabitants. *For Livewell Chapman,* 1658[9]. 4°.* LT, O, C, SP, DT; CH, MH, MU, NU, WF, Y.

Humble petition of many thousands, gentlemen. 1652. *See* Baxter, Richard.

3475 The humble petition of many thovsands of wives and matrons. *For Iohn Cookson,* 1643. 4°.* LT, A; CH, CN, MH, MU, WF.

3476 The humble petition of many thousands of yong men. *For William Larnar, July 14.* 1647. 4°.* LT, LG, OC, MR, DT; CSS, MH, NU, Y.

3477 The humble petition of many thousands of young men and apprentices. *For George Whittington,* 1646[7]. 4°.* LT, LUG, LSD, DT; CSS, MH.

3478 The humble petition of many well-affected freemen, and citizens of the city of London. *For Tho: Underhill,* 1646[7]. 4°.* LT; CLC, MH, NU, Y.

3479 The humble petition of many well-affected persons of Somerset. *For Livewel Chapman,* 1659. 4°.* O; MH, NU, WF.

3480 The humble petition of Richard Cromwell. [London, 1659.] brs. L, LS; CH, IU, MH, Y.

3481 The humble petition of some of the inhabitants of the parish of Leonard Shoreditch. *For Iohn Franke*, 1642. 4°.* LT, LLU, MR; CH, MH, NU, WF, Y.

3482 No entry.

3483 Entry cancelled.
Humble petition of the bailifes . . . of Ipswich. 1641. *See* Humble petitions of.

3484 The humble petition of the baronets, esquires, . . . of Lancaster. *By A. N. for I. Franke*, 1642. brs. STEELE 2118. O.

3485 Entry cancelled.
Humble petition of the baronets . . . of Lancaster. 1642. *See* To the Kings most excellent Majestie.

3486 Entry cancelled.
Humble petition of the baronets, . . . of Oxford. [n.p., 1642]. *See* To the honovrable the knights citizens and bvrgesses of the House of Commons.

3487 The hvmble petition of the Brovvnists. [*London*], *printed*, 1641. 4°.* LT.

3488 The humble petition of the captaines, officers, and soldiers of the trayned bands . . . Buckingham. *For Ioseph Hunscott and I. Wright*, [1642]. 4°.* LT, O, MR; MH, WF.

3489 Entry cancelled.
Humble petition of the citizens. [1647.] *See* To the right honourable the Lord Mayor, the right worshipfull the aldermen.

3489A The humble petition of the citizens of London. [*London*, 1659.] brs. L; MH, WF.

3490 The humble petition of the citie of Bristoll. *Printed at Oxford by Leonard Lichfield*, 1643. 4°.* MADAN 1172. LT, CJ, BR.

3491 Entry cancelled.
Humble petition of the clothiers . . . of Suffolk. 1641. *See* To the Kings most excellent majesty.

3492 The humble petition of the committee, gentry, ministry, . . . of Leicester. *For G. Calvert*, 1648. 4°.* LT, C; CSS, MBP, MH, MU, Y.

3492A The humble petition of the common council of the city of London . . . [24 September 1659]. *For John Clark*, 1659. 4°.* CLC.

3493 The humble petition of the common people of England. [*London*, 1646?] 4°.* LL.

3494 —[Same title.] [*London*, 1694?] cap., 4°.* LIU, EN; CH, MH, Y.

3495 The humble petition of the Commons of Kent. *York, by Robert Barker, and by the assignes of John Bill*, 1642. 4°.* L, LG, CCA; MH, NCD.

3495A —[Anr. ed.] *Cambridge, by Roger Daniel*, 1642. 4°.* LG, CT; MH.

3496 —[Anr. ed.] *Printed at Yorke and reprinted at Oxford*, 1642. 4°.* MADAN 1019. O, DT; CH, CSS.

3497 —[Anr. ed.] *By Robert Barker: and by the assigns of John Bill*, 1642. 4°.* LT, SP.

3498 —[Anr. ed.] *First printed at Yorke, and now reprinted at London, for William Smith*, 1642. 4°.* L, LG, CJ, LLU, EN; CH, MH, NCD, OWC, WF, Y.

3499 The humble petition of the Commons of the city of London in common councel. *By Peter Cole, Jan.* 16. 1648. 4°.* LT, O, LG, LIU, DT; CH, MH, MU, NCD, WF, Y.

3500 Entry cancelled.
Humble petition of the Council-general. [n.p., 1698.] *See* Company of Scotland trading to Africa and the Indies. To His Grace.

3501 The humble petition of the Countie of Cornwall . . . 26 June 1642. *By Robert Barker & by the assigns of John Bill*, 1642. brs. STEELE 2203. LT, C; MH, Y.

3501A —[Anr. ed.] *York:*—, 1642. 4°.* MH, WF.

3502 —[Anr. ed.] *For T. Warren*, 1642, 4°.* O, C, CJ; CH, CN, LC, MH, PL, Y.

3502A The humble petition of the county of Derby. *By Barnard Alsop*, 1642. 4°.* LT, C.

3503 The humble petition of the gentry and Commons of the County of York, . . . presented . . . April 22. 1642. *By Robert Barker: and by the assignes of John Bill*, 1642. 4°.* LT, O, CT, EC, EN, DT; CH, IU, MH, TU, WF. (var.)

3504 —[Anr. ed.] *For S. E.*, 1642. 4°.* L, C, OC, LLU, LSD; CH, IU, MBP, MH, MU, Y.

3504A —[Anr. ed.] *For W. J.*, 1642. 4°.* L, LG.

3504B —[Anr. ed.] *For I. T.*, 1642. 4°.* LLU; PU.

3505 The humble petition of the gentry and inhabitants of Holdernes. *By Robert Barker: and by the assignes of John Bill*, 1642. 4°.* LT, O, CJ, EC, YM, DT; CH, CLC, IU, WF.

3506 Entry cancelled.
Humble petition of the gentry, clergie. 1641. *See* To the honorable the knights, citizens, and burgesses.

3507 The humble petition of the gentry, ministers, and commonalty of the Barony of Kendall. *By L. N. and I. F. for Edward Husbands and John Franck, August* 8. 1642. 4°.* LT, O, LG, EC, MR; CU, MH, MIU, WF, Y.

3508 The humble petition of the gentry, ministers, and freeholders of the County of York. *York: by Robert Barker, and by the assignes of John Bill*, 1642. 4°.* LT, OC, CJ, YM, DT; CH, CN, MH, TU, WF.

3508A —[Anr. ed.] *By Robert Barker; and by the assignes of John Bill*, 1642. 4°.* CT; MM, Y.

3508B —[Anr. ed.] *Fifth of April*, 1642. *By Robert Barker*, 1642. 4°.* L.

3509 —[Anr. ed.] *April* 5. 1642. *First printed at York, and now reprinted in London for Charles Greene*, 1642. 4°.* LT, O, C, EC, SP, YM; IU, MH, TU, Y.

3509A —[Anr. ed.] 5. of Aprill, 1642. *Printed first at Yorke, and re-printed at London, for Iohn Wright*, 1642. 4°.* L, C, OC, CJ, YM, DT; CDA, CLC, LC, MH, NCD, WF.

3510 Entry cancelled.
Humble petition of the gentry . . . of Chester. 1642. *See* To the Kings most excellent Majestie.

3511 Entry cancelled.
Humble petition of the Grand-Jury . . . at Chelmsford. 1648. *See* To the right honourable both Houses.

3512 The hvmble petition of the Hartfordshrie-men [*sic*]. *For John Greensmith*, 1641. 4°.* MR; WF.

3513 The hvmble petition of the inhabitants of the County of Bvckingham. *For John [sic] Burroughes, 1641.* brs. STEELE 1937. LT; MH.

3514 Entry cancelled.
Humble petition of the inhabitants . . . of Buckingham. 1641. *See* To the King's most excellent majesty.

3515 The humble petition of the inhabitants of the County of Dorset. *Oxford, by Leonard Lichfield, 1645.* 4°.* MADAN 1796. L, O; WF.

3516 The hvmble petition of the inhabitants of . . . Essex. *For John Thomas, 1641.* brs. STEELE 1944. L, LUG.

3517 The humble / petition / of the inhabi/tants of the Covn/ty of Essex. *Printed at Oxford by Leonard Lichfield, Jan. 11, 1642.* 4°.* MADAN 1177. O, CJ, CT, DT; CH, NU.

3518 The humble/ petition / of the inhabitants / of the Covnty of / Essex. *Printed, at Oxford, Ianuary 11. By Leonard Lichfield, 1642.* 4°.* MADAN 1178. LT, O, BC, LSD, SP; CH, MH, Y.

3519 The humble petition of the inhabitants of the Covnty of Hertford. *Printed at Oxford by Leonard Lichfield, Januar. 7, 1642.* 4°.* MADAN 1168. CJ, CT, MR, DT; CH, MH, Y.

3520 —[Anr. ed.] *Oxford, printed, London reprinted, 1642.* 4°.* L.

3521 —[Anr. ed.] *For Nicholas Vavasour, 1643.* brs. STEELE 2347a. HH.

3522 The humble petition of the inhabitants of the County of Hertford . . . also, . . County of Bedford. *Printed at Oxford by Leonard Lichfield, 1642.* 4°.* MADAN 1174. LT, O, OC, DT; MBP, MH, NCD, WF.

3523 The humble petition of the inhabitants of the County of Oxford. *Printed at Oxford by Leonard Lichfield, February 21, 1642.* 4°.* MADAN 1249. L, O, OCC, OL, DU; MH.

3524 The humble petition of the inhabitants of the County of Suffolke. *For John Wright, 1646.* 4°.* LT, MR, DT; CH, IU, MH, Y.

3524A The humble petition of the inhabitants of the Soake of Peterborow. *[n.p.], May 28. 1650.* 4°.* L.

3525 The humble petition of the knights, esquires, . . . of Lancaster. *For Andrew Coe, 1642.* 4°.* LT, CM, BC, LNC; IAU, MH, WF, Y.

3526 The humble petition of the knights, esquires, . . . of Sommerset. *For W. D., 1642.* brs. STEELE 2181. LT, O, LG, OC, LNC; MH, PU.

3527 The humble petition of the knights, gentlemen, citizens, . . . of Surrey. *Printed, 1648.* 4°.* LT, O, LG, CJ, LSD; CH, IU, MH, WF, Y.

3528 The humble petition of the knights, gentry, . . . of Sussex. *[London], printed, 1648.* 4°.* MIU, WF, Y.

3529 The humble petition of the knights, gentry, . . . of Yorke, . . . April 30, 1642. *By R. O. and G. D. for I. Frank, 1642.* brs. STEELE 2099. LT, OQ.

3530 The humble petition of the knights, ivstices of the peace, . . . of Cornwall. *By R. O. and G. D. for John Bartlet, 1642.* 4°.* LT, C, EC, LNC, MR; CH, MH, MIU, NU, WF, Y.

3531 Entry cancelled.
Humble petition of the lay-Catholiques. 1641. *See* To the honovrable, the knights, citizens and bvrgesses.

3532 The humble petition of the Lord Mayor, . . . 16. of Ianuary 1645. *For John Wright, 17. Ian. 1645[6].* 4°.* LT, O, LG, LSD, DT; CH, MH, MU, TU, WF, Y.

3533 The humble petition of the Lord Major, . . . of London. *By Richard Cotes, 1646.* 4°.* LT, O, C, BC, DT; CH, MH, MU, NU, WF, Y.

3533A 17 Martii, 1646. The humble petition of the Lord Major, alderman . . . to the honorable the Commons. *For Edward Husband, March 18, 1646.* 4°.* CN, MH, Y.

3534 The humble petition of the Lord Major, aldermen, and Commons of . . . London, to the honourable the House of Commons. *By Richard Cotes, London, 1647.* 4°.* LT, O, CM, OC, SP; CH, MH, MU, TU, WF, Y.

3535 The humble petition of the Lord Major, aldermen, . . . to the . . . Lords and Commons . . . With their answer. *By Richard Cotes, London, 1647.* 4°.* LT, O, LG, DC, LIU; CH, MH, NU, WF, Y.

3536 The humble petition of the Lord Major, aldermen, and Commons of the city of London, . . . to the right honourable the Lords and Commons . . . Whereunto is annexed. *By Richard Cotes, London, 1647.* 4°.* LT, OC, CT, BC, DT; CH, CN, MH, WF, Y.

3537 The humble petition of the Lord Major . . . with the answer. *By Richard Cotes, London, [1647].* 4°.* LT, O; CH, MH.

3538 The humble petition of the Lord Major . . . to the . . . Lords and Commons . . . together with their answers. *By Richard Cotes, London, 1648.* 4°.* LT, O, LG, MR; CSS, IU, MBP, MH.

3539 The humble petition of the Lord Major, aldermen, . . . May 9, 1648. *By Richard Cotes, London, 1648.* 4°.* LT, O, MR; CSS, NN.

3540 The humble petition of the Lord Major, aldermen, . . . to the . . . Lords and Commons . . . together with the answers. *By Richard Cotes, London, 1648.* 4°.* LT; CSS, MH, MIU, TO, Y.

3541 —June 27. 1648. *[London], by Richard Cotes, [1648].* 4°.* LT, LG, DU, YM, DT; CH, MH, MIU, NGT, TU, WF, Y.

3542 The humble petition of the Lord Major, . . . with the annexed papers. *[London], by Richard Cotes, July 24. 1648.* 4°.* L, LG, MR; CLC, MH, MU, NU, WF.

3543 The humble petition of the Lord Major, aldermen. *[London], by Richard Cotes, July 31, 1648.* 4°.* LT, OC, SP; CLC, MH, MU, TU, WF, Y.

3544 The humble petition of the Lord Major, aldermen and Commons of the city of London, in Common-Councell . . . [with answer of the Commons]. *[London], by Richard Cotes, August 8. 1648.* 4°.* LT, LG, OC, CJ, LSD; CH, MH, MU, NU, WF, Y.

3545 The humble petition of the Lord Major, aldermen . . . [with answer of the Lords]. *For Edward Husband, August 12. 1648.* 4°.* LT, LG, BC, MR, DT; CH, MIU, MU, WF, Y.

3546 The humble petition of the Lord Major, aldermen, . . . [16 October 1648, for maintenance of godly ministers]. [*London*], *by Richard Cotes, October 17.* 1648. 4°.* LT, MR; CH, MU, WF.

3547 The humble petition of the Lord Major, aldermen, and Commons of the city of London . . . to the right honourable the Lords & Commons. [*London*], *by Richard Cotes*, 1648. 4°.* MR, DT; CH, MH, NU, WF, Y. [Anr. ed. of H3540.]

3548 Entry cancelled.
The humble petition of the Lord Major. *See* — June 27. 1648. [H3541.]

3549 The humble petition of the Lord Major, . . . presented to the Parliament . . . June 2. 1659. *By D. Maxwell*, 1659. 4°.* L, O, LG, BC, LSD; CH, CN, MH, MU, NU, WF, Y.

3550 Entry cancelled.
Humble petition of the Lord Major . . . Jan. 13, 1680. *See* Humble petition of the right honourable.

3551 The humble petition of the Lord Mayor, aldermen, . . . 18th of June, 1683. *By the assigns of John Bill: and by Henry Hills and Thomas Newcomb*, 1683. fol.* L, O, C, DU, SP; CH, IU, MH, WF, Y.

3552 —[Anr. ed.] *Edinburgh, by the heir of A. Anderson*, 1683. fol.* ALDIS 2384. L, EN; BN.

3553 The humble petition of the loyal Dissenters. *For J. Dean*, 1683. brs. LS, EN; WF, Y.

3554 The humble petition of the Major, aldermen, and Commons of the citie of London: and his Majesties gracious answer. *By Robert Barker; and by the assignes of John Bill*, 1642[3]. 4°.* LT, O, LIU, LSD, EN; CH, MH, NCD, TU, WF.

3555 —[Anr. ed.] *Printed, at Oxford Ianuary 5. by Leonard Lichfield*, 1642[3]. 4°.* MADAN 1163. L, LG, DU, MR, DT; CH, CN, WF, Y.

3555A —[Anr. ed.] —, [1642/3.] 4°.* OB, CJ, LIU, LNC.

3556 —[Anr. ed.] *Printed at Oxfokd* [sic] [*London*] *Ianur. 5, by Leonard Lichfield*, 1642[3]. 4°.* MADAN 1164. LT, O, DT; MH, NU.

3556A —[Anr. ed.] — ["*Oxford*"], 1642[3]. 4°.* MM.

3556B —[Anr. ed.] *Shrewsbury, by R. Barker and the assignes of J. Bill*, 1642. 4°.* L, BR.

3557 —[Anr. ed.] *For Humphry Tuckey*, 1643. 4°.* LG, OC, CM, LNC, SP; CLC, CSS, MH. (var.)

3557A —[Anr. ed.] *For Henry Turkey*, 1643. 4°.* O, BC, SP; CSS, IU, MH.

3558 The humble petition of the Major, aldermen, bayliffs, . . . of Oxon. *For Giles Calvert*, 1649. 4°.* MADAN 2011. L, O, MR; CN, CSS, WF, Y.

3559 The humble petition of the many peaceable citizens. *By Richard Cotes*, 1647. 4°.* LG, MR; CH, MH, MU, WF, Y.

3560 Entry cancelled.
Humble petition of the members of the Common Council. 1690. *See* To the honourable the Knights.

3561 The hvmble petition of the merchant-strangers. *For Iohn Wright, Aug. 28.* 1643. 4°.* LUG, MR, DT; MA, MH, NC, WF, Y.

3562 The humble petition of the ministers of the Church of England. [*London*], *printed*, 1641. 4°.* MADAN 980. LT, O, C, E, DT; CH, IU, LC, MH, NU, WF, Y.

3563 The humble petition of the ministers of the Chvrch of England, desiring reformation. *Printed at London*, 1647. 4°.* LT, P, DT; CLC, MH, MU, NU.

3564 The humble petition of the ministers of the counties of Suffolke and Essex, . . . May 29. 1646. *For Iohn Wright, 1 June* 1646. 4°.* LT, O, CJ, SP, DT; CH, IU, MH, MU, NU, WF, Y.

3565 The humble petition of the officers now engaged for Ireland. *For Edward Husband, July 10.* 1649. 4°.* LT, LIU, DN; CH, MH, MU, WF, Y.

3566 The humble petition of the peaceable and well-affected inhabitants of the counties of Norfolk and Suffolk. *For George Whittington*, 1647. 4°.* LT, C; NU, WF, Y.

3567 The hvmble petition of the peacefvll obedient and honest Protestants. *Printed*, 1642. 4°.* LT, O, CJ, EN, DT; LC, MH, NU, TU, Y.

3568 The humble petition of the peacefull, obedient, religious, and honest Protestants. [*London*, 1642.] brs. STEELE 1924. LT, LPR; MH.

3569 —[Anr. ed.] [*London*], *printed*, 1642. 4°.* LT, LG, CT, BR, DU; CH, IU, LC, NU, Y.

3570 The humble petition of the poore distressed prisoners in Ludgate. colop: [*London*], *by M. F.*, 1644. brs. LT, LU.

3570A The humble petition of the poor distressed prisoners in . . . Newgate. *By E. F.*, 1676. brs. LG.

3571 The humble petition of the poor distressed prisoners in the Compter. [*London*], 1666. brs. MC.

3572 The humble petition of the poore distressed prisoners in the hole of the Poultry Compter. colop: [*London*], *by M. F.*, 1644. brs. LT.

3572A The humble petition of the Presbyterian ministers. colop: *Printed at Edinburgh, and re-printed at London by George Croom*, 1690. brs. L; CH.
Humble petition of the prisoners. [n.p.], 1655. *See* Smith, William, *captain.*

3573 The humble petition of the Protestant inhabitants of the Counties of Antrim. *Printed*, 1641. 4°.* LT, O, C, LNC, DT; CH, MH, WF, Y.

3574 —[Anr. ed.] [*London*, 1643.] cap., 4°.* LT; CSS.

3574A The humble petition of the Protestant inhabitants of . . . Ulster. *Printed*, 1641. 4°.* O, LVF.

3575 The humble petition of the Protestants of France. colop: *For L. Curtis*, [1681]. cap., fol.* L, O, CCA, LSD, DU; CH, CN, TO, WF, Y.

3576 —[Anr. ed.] colop: *By N. T. for Andrew Forrester*, 1681. cap., fol.* L, O, OP; CH, IU, Y, AVP.

3576A —[Anr. ed.] [*Dublin?* 1681.] cap., fol.* EN, CD; ZWT.

3577 The humble petition of the right honourable the Lord Mayor, aldermen, . . . of London, . . . thirteenth of January, 1680. *By Samuel Roycroft*, 1680[1]. fol.* L, O, C, DU, MR; CH, IU, MH, TU, WF, Y.

3577A —[Anr. ed.] colop: —, 1680[1]. brs. DT; CN, MH.

3578 The hvmble petition of the Scottish and many others. *Aug. 17. for John Bartlet*, 1642. 4°.* LT, EC, LNC, MR, BQ; CLC, IU.

3579 The humble petition of the serjeants, corporals and others. [*London*, 1700.] brs. LL.

3580 The humble petition of the stationers, printers and booke-sellers of the citie of London. [*London*, 1641.] brs. LS.

3581 An humble petition of the vniversity and city of Oxford. *Printed at Oxford by Leonard Lichfield, and now reprinted at London for Thomas Vincent*, [1644?]. 4°.* MADAN 1754. L, O, LNC, MR, SP; CCC, CH, CSS, MH, MU, WF, Y.

3582 The humble petition of the well-affected Commons. [*London*], *printed*, 1643. 4°.* LT, MR, DT; CLC.

3583 The humble petition of the well-affected of the county of South-Hampton. *For R. Ibbitson*, 1653. 4°.* LT, DT; CH, CLC, WF.

3584 The hvmble petition of the vvell-affected yong men. [*London*, 1643.] brs. LT, LNC.

3585 —[Anr. ed., "yovng."] *For William Lernard*, 1647. 4°.* LT, LG, MR; MH.

3585A The humble petition of the widdows and fatherless children in the West. [*London?* 1689.] brs. L, O; CH, Y.

3586 The humble petition of the vvretched, and most contemptible, the poore Commons of England. *For E. P. and E. B., July 23*, 1642. 4°.* LT, O, MR, SP; CH, MH, WF.

3587 The humble petition of thousands wel-affected persons ... London. [*London*, 1648.] brs. O, LS.

3588 The humble petition of us the Parliaments poore souldiers. *Dublin: by W. B.*, 1648. brs. LT.

3589 Entry cancelled.
Humble petition ... of the inhabitants of Kent. [n.p.], 1641. *See* To the honourable Hovses of Parliament now assembled, the humble.

3589A An humble petition to the present government [Jacobite sentiments]. [*London*, 1691–92.] brs. LPR.

3590 The humble petitions of His Majesties truly loyal Protestant subjects. [*London*, 1680.] brs. L, O, CT, MR, EN; CH, CN, MH, WF, Y.

3590A The humble petitions of the bailifes ... of Ipswich. *For H. Blunden*, 1641[2]. 4°.* LT, LUG, CJ, EC, LNC; CLC, LC, MH, Y.

3591 Entry cancelled.
Humble petitions, serious suggestions. 1648. *See* Ward, Nathaniel. To the high.

3591A The humble presentment of the grand inquest. *Bristol, W. Bonny*, 1696. brs. L.

3591B An humble proposal for national banks. *April 24*, 1696. fol.* LUG.
Humble proposal for the inlargement. [n.p., 1659.] *See* Harvard College.
Humble proposal for the relief. 1671. *See* Culpeper, Sir Thomas, *younger*.

3592 An hvmble proposal of safety to the Parliament. *By T. Pain and M. Simomns* [sic], 1643. 4°.* LT.

3593 An humble proposal of such particular rules ... registry. *For Charles Harper*, 1678. 4°.* L, O, LG.

Humble proposal showing how. 1663. *See* Killigrew, Sir William.

3594 An humble proposal to cause bancrupts make better ... payment. *Printed*, 1679. 4°.* L, LUG, LSD; CLC, MH, PU, Y.

3595 An humble proposal to Parliament, against office-jobbing. [*London*, 1696?] brs. L; MH, Y.

3595A An humble proposal to the Honourable House of Commons, to increase ... customs upon tobacco. [n.p., 1695?] brs. L.
Humble proposal to their most excellent Majesties. [n.p., 1693.] *See* Hodges, William.

3596 An humble proposal, whereby His Majesty may raise ... his credit. [*London*], *in the Savoy, by Thomas Newcomb*, 1673/4. fol.* L, C, LPR, LNC; CH, MH, NC, PU.

3597–8 Entries cancelled.
Humble proposals and desires. 1648. *See* Fairfax, Sir Thomas.
Humble proposals for the relief. [n.p.], 1695. *See* Hodges, William.
Humble proposals of sundry. 1649. *See* Reynolds, Edward, *bp*.

3599 The humble proposalls of the adjutators in the army. *Printed at London by Robert Ibbitson*, 1647. 4°.* LT, O, LLU, DT; CSS, CU, MH, WF.
Humble proposalls to the honorable. 1651. *See* Potter, William.

3600 Humble proposals to the Parliament now assembled. Whereby the ... civil law. *By E. C. for R. Royston*, 1656. 4°.* LL, LSD, EN; NU, WF.

3601 The humble propositions of the agents for the Protestants in Ireland. *By I. N. for Henry Twyford*, 1644. 4°.* MADAN 1644. LT, O, C, DN; CH, CU, MH, WF, Y.
Humble remonstrance against. 1643. *See* Prynne, William.

3602 The humble remonstrance and complaint of all the prisoners. [*London*, 1649.] 4°.* LL.

3603 The humble remonstrance and complaint of many thousands. *Printed at London, for John Gibson, Febr. 3*, 1643. 4°.* LT, DT; CN, NN.

3604 The humble remonstrance and desires of divers officers and souldiers. *By J. C. for G. Horton*, 1647. 4°.* LT, MR, DT; CH, CLC, MH, WF, Y.

3605 The humble remonstrance and petition. [*London*, 1659.] brs. O.

3606 The humble remonstrance and petition of certain churches. [*London*], *printed*, 1653. 4°.* NU.

3607 Entry cancelled.
Humble remonstrance and petition of English Protestants. [n.p., 1677.] *See* To the right honourable the Lords and Commons.

3608 The humble remonstrance and resolves of Col. Overtons regiment. *For Lodowick Lloyd, and Henry Cripps*, 1649. 4°.* LT; CH, MH, ZAP.

3609 Entry cancelled.
Humble remonstrance and supplication. Edinburgh, 1650. *See* To the right honourable the Lords and others of the Committee of Estates.

Humble remonstrance concerning. [n.p., 1690.] *See* Beverley, Thomas.

3610–1 No entries.

3612 An humble remonstrance in the behalfe of the Protestants. *For R. Johnson*, 1643. 4°.* MR; WF, Y.

3613 Entry cancelled.
Humble remonstrance of divers. [n.p.], 1647. *See* Humble remonstrance of the representations.

3614 Entry cancelled.
Humble remonstrance of many thousands. [1653.] *See* To his Excellency, the Lord General Cromwel.

3615 The humble remonstrance of the apprentices. *Printed*, 1647. 4°.* LT, LG, OC, MR; CH, MH, NU, WF, Y.

3616 An humble remonstrance of the batchelors. colop: *Printed for, and sold by the book-selling batchelors*, 1693. cap., 4°.* L; CH, CLC, IU, MH, WF, Y.

3617 An humble remonstrance of the citizens of Edenbvrgh to the convention of the Estates of Scotland. *March* 1. 1648. *by E. T. for . . . the inhabitants of the city of Edenburgh*. 4°.* LT, O, CT, MR, EN; CH, CN, MH, NU, WF, Y.

3618 The humble remonstrance of the commission officers and private soldiers of Major General Goffs regiment. *Printed*, 1659. 4°.* L, O, C, LG, LLU; CH, CSS, MH, NU, Y.

3619 Entry cancelled.
The humble remonstrance of the company of Stationers. [n.p., 1650.] *See* Parker, Henry. To the High Court.

3620 The humble remonstrance of the farmers and adventurers. *Printed*, 1641. brs. STEELE 1873. LT, LS.

3621 The humble remonstrance of the General-Council of officers met at Dalkeith. *Printed at Leith*, 1653. 4°.* STEELE 2100; ALDIS 1477. EN; CH.

3622 —[Anr. ed.] *For Giles Calvert*, 1653. 8°.* LT, O, BC, MR; CH, CLC, MH, WF, Y.

3623 The humble remonstrance of the non-commission officers. *Printed*, 1659. 4°.* LT; MH.

3624 The humble remonstrance of the reduced officers. [*London*], *printed*, 1648. 4°.* LT, CCA, SP; CH, MIU, OWC, WF, Y.

3625 An humble remonstrance of the representations . . . for . . . peace. [*London*], *printed*, 1647. 4°.* LT, O, C, SP, DT; CH, MH, PU, WF.
Hvmble remonstrance to His Maiesty. [n.p.], 1641. *See* Prynne, William.

3625A An humble remonstrance to the King & Parliament. *Printed*, 1675. 4°.* L, LG.

3626 An hvmble remonstrnce [*sic*] to the Kings most excellent Majesty, in vindication . . . of Isaak Pennington. *For T. Wright*, 1643. 4°.* LT, LG, MR; CH, INU, MH, WF, Y.

3626A An humble remonstrance to the Lords and Commons in the present convention assembled. [*n.p.*, 1689.] cap., 4°.* LLP.

3627 An hvmble remonstrance to the right honourable, the Lords in the High Court of Parliament. *Piinted* [*sic*] *and are to be sold by S. B.*, [1641]. 4°.* LT, MR, SP, DN; CH, MH, MIU, WF, Y.

3627A —[Anr. ed.] *Edinburgh, R. Y. & E. T.*, 1641. 4°.* ALDIS 1007.6. L, EN.

3628 Te humple remonstrances of Rice op Meredith, op Morgan. *By Robert Wood*, 1652. 4°.* LT, AN.

3628A The humble reply of the company of white-papermakers. [*London*, 1689–90.] brs. MH, Y.

3629 The humble representation and address of severall churches and Christians in South Wales. *Dublin, By VVilliam Bladen*, 1655. 4°.* DIX 97. L, DN, DT.

3630 The humble representation and address to His Highness of several churches . . . in South-Wales. *By Henry Hills and John Field*, 1656. 4°.* LT, AN, MR; NU, WF, Y.

3631 The humble representation and petition . . . April 6. 1649. *For Giles Calvert*, [1649?]. 4°.* MADAN 2011n. O; CSS, WF, Y.

3632 Entry cancelled.
Humble representation and petition of the Council-General. *Edinburgh*, 1700. *See* Company of Scotland. Representation.

3633 The humble representation and petition of the Justices of Peace, . . . of Chester. *By John Field*, 1651. 4°.* LT; CLC, WF.

3634 The humble representation and petition of the officers of the army. *By Henry Hills*, 1659. 4°.* LT, O, BC, LSD, EN; CH, CN, NU, TU, WF, Y.

3634A —[Anr. ed.] [*London*], *printed* 1659. 4°.* WF, Y.

3635 The humble representation and remonstrance of divers free-men. *Printed*, 1659. 4°.* O; MH, MU, NU.

3636 The humble representation and resolutions of the officers & souldiers of Lieut. Generall Cromwel's regiment. *For Edw. Blackmore*, 1649. 4°.* LT, MR; ZAP.

3637 The humble representation and vindication of many of the messengers. 1654. 4°.* NHC.

3637A —[Anr. ed.], colop: *For Francis Smith*. 1655. 4°.* NU.

3638 The humble representation of his late Majesties and princes domestick servants. [*London*, 1655.] brs. LT.

3639 The humble representation of some officers. [*London*, 1659.] 4°.* LT, O, LG, LSD, DT; CH, CN, MH, WF, Y.

3640 —[Anr. ed.] *London, and reprinted at Edinburgh, by Christopher Higgins*, 1659. 4°.* ALDIS 1601. MR, E, EN; NCD, Y.
Humble representation of the commission. 1648. *See* Gillespie, George.

3641 The humble representation of the committee, gentry, ministry, . . . of Leicester. *For Henry Hood*, 1648. 4°.* LT, LSC, DU, LIU, MR; CH, CU, MH, WF, Y.

3641A The humble representation of the ministers. [*Edinburgh*, 1695.] 4°. ALDIS 3466. EN.

3641B The humble representation of the Protestant purchasers of forfeited lands in Ireland. [*London*, 1699?] brs. DN; CH.

3642 An humble representation of the sad and distressed case . . . seamen. [*London*], 1693. brs. MC.

3643 An humble representation of the sad condition of many of the Kings party. [*London*], *for A. Seile*, 1661. 4°.* L, O, C, DU, LNC; CH, CN, MH, NU, WF, Y.

3644 An humble representation to the honourable the Commons . . sail cloath. [*London*, 1696?] brs. L; Y.

3645 An humble representation upon the perpetual imprisonment. *For John Platt*, 1687. 4°. O, SP.

Humble request of certain. [n.p., 1643.] See Nutt, Thomas.

3646 An humble request to Protestants. For Samuel Crouch, 1688. 4°.* T.C.II 224. L, OC, CS, EN, DN; CLC, MH, NU, TO, Y.

3646A An humble request to the honourable charitable gentry . . . of St Paul's Covent Garden. [London? 1685.] cap., fol.* L.

3647 Humble requests both to Conformists. colop: For Tho. Parkhurst; and sold by Richard Janeway, 1689. fol.* L, O, LUG; CH, PL, WF.

3648 The humble supplication of the Nonconformists. [London, 1679.] brs. STEELE 3p 2462. L, O.

3649 Humble supplication to the King's. [London], reprinted, 1662. 8°. LCL.

3650 The humble tender and declaration of many . . . members of the Trinity House. [London, 1648.] brs. LT, LG, CJ; Y.

3651 The humble wishes of a loyal subject. For A. Banks, 1681. brs. O, MC; MH.

3652 No entry.

3653 **Hume, Alexander.** Disputatio juridica. Edinburgh, heirs of A. Anderson, 1696. 4°. ALDIS 3570. EN.

3654 [–] The flyting betwixt Polwart and Montgomery. [Edinburgh], printed, 1688. 8°.* ALDIS 2760. L, O, E, EN; MH.

3655 **Hume, Andrew.** Disputatio juridica. Edinburgh, heirs of A. Anderson, 1696. 4°. ALDIS 3571. EN.

3656 **Hume, David.** A generall history of Scotland. Third edition. Edinburgh, by Evan Tyler, [1648–1657]. fol. ALDIS 1332. C, MC, EN; IU.

3657 — —Fourth edition. For Simon Miller, 1657. fol. LG, OM, CT, EN; CH, TO, IMPERIAL UNIV. TOKYO.

3657A —The History of the Douglasses, containing the house of Angus. Edinburgh, by Evan Tyler, 1643. fol. DU.

3658 —The history of the houses of Douglas and Angus. Edinburgh, by Evan Tyler, 1644. fol. ALDIS 1141. L, O, C, EN, GU; BN, CLC, MH, TU, WF, Y.

3659 — —Third edition. Edinburgh, by Evan Tyler, to be sold by T. W. at London, 1648. fol. ALDIS 1331. L, O, ES, DT; CH, TU, ZWT.

3660 Entry cancelled.
—Lord Hume his speech. 1641. See Home, Sir James Home, earl of.

Hume, Sir James. See Home, Sir James Home, earl of.

3661 **Hume, John.** Βιος 'επουρανιος, or the character of an heavenly conversation. Cambridge, by John Hayes, 1670. 4°.* C, CE, CT.

3662 —Jachin and Boaz. For Simon Miller, 1676. 8°. T.C.I 250. L, O, C, CS, YM; IEG, NU, TU, Y.

3663 **H[ume], P[atrick].** Annotations on Milton's Paradise Lost. For Jacob Tonson, 1695. fol. O, CT, EC, LLU, E; CH, CN, LC, MH, NC, TU, Y, AVP.

3663A —A poem dedicated to the . . . memory of . . . Q. Mary. For Jacob Tonson, 1695. fol.* L, O, MR; CLC, IU, MH, TU, WF, Y.

[Hume, R.] Parallels; or. 1675. See Hames, Robert.

3663B **Hume, Robert.** A relation of the miraculous cure of Susannah Arch. By J. B. and sold by R. Baldwin, 1695. 8°.* O.

3663C —A sermon preached at the funeral of Mrs. Margaret Hodgson. March 11. 1694. Printed, 1695. 4°.* L.

3664 **Hume, Tobias.** The trve petition of. For Iohn Giles, 1642. 4°.* LT, O, CJ, EC; MH, Y.

3665 **[Humfrey, John.]** Advice before it be too late. [London, 1688.] cap., 4°.* L, O, OC, DU, MR; MH, NU, PL, WF, Y.

3666 —Animadversions. By Tho. Snowden, for Tho. Parkhurst, 1699. * LCL, OC, BAMB, EC, EN; MH, NU.

3666A —Animadversions and considerations. For W. Marshall, 1679. 12°. T.C.I 367. OC.

3667 [–] An answer to Dr. Stillingfleet's book. For Thomas Parkhurst, [1682]. 4°.* T.C.I 426. O, LW, OC, CS, AN, DT; CH, CLC, CN, MH, NU, TU, WF, Y.

3668 [–] An answer to Dr. Stillingfleet's sermon. For J. Janeway, 1680. 4°.* L, O, C, E, DT; CH, CU, MH, NU, WF, Y. (var.)

3668A [–] The association for K. William. colop: For John Littleton, 1696. brs. Y.

3668B [–] —[Anr. ed.] colop: For the author, and reprinted in Dublin, 1696. brs. DN.

3669 [–] The authority of the magistrate. For the author, 1672. 8°. L, O, C, EN, BQ; CH, IU, PU, TU, Y.

3670 [–] The axe laid to the root. By J. Leake, for the author; to be sold by Thomas Parkhurst; and John Southby, 1685. 8°. T.C.II 94. L, O, C, OC, P; CU, NU, Y.

3671 —The βιος παντων ε'ιδεοτος, or [Hebrew] or the vision of eternity. For Giles Calvert, 1657. 4°.* LT, LF; CH, PL, PSC, Y.

3672 [–] A brief receipt moral & Christian. For E. Blackmore, 1658. 12°. LT.

3673 [–] A case of conscience. Whether a Nonconformist. Printed, 1669. 4°.* L, O, LW, OC, BC; CH, CN, NP, NU, WF.

3673A —A case which concerns ministers about the quarterly poll-act. By J. D. sold by A. Baldwin, 1698. 4°.* BAMB; CH.

3674 —Catalogus librorum. Printed, 1682. 4°. L, O, LG, CS, WCA; NG, PL, WF, JF.

[–] Χειροθεσια. 1661. See Alleine, Richard.

3675 [–] Comprehension promoted. [London, 1673?] 4°.* L, O, OC, DU, MR; CN.

3675A [–] Comprehension with indulgence. [London, 1689?] 4°.* IU, WF.

3676 [–] A defence of the proposition. Printed, 1668. 4°. L, O, CT, DU, E; CLC, CN, NU, TO, WF.

3677 —The foure wishes of. [London, 1654.] brs. LT.

3678 —The friendly interposer. For Thomas Parkhurst, 1698. 4°.* LCL, LW, OC, EC, SP; CH, NU.

3678A —Half a sheet of Mr. Humfrey's. For the author Sept. 1st. 1696. brs. BAMB.

3679 [–] The healing attempt: being. For Thomas Parkhurst, 1689. 4°. T.C.II 314. L, OC, P, AU, DT; CLC, IU, MH, NU, WF, Y.

3680 [–] The healing paper: or. *For B. T. and T. M.*, 1678. 4°.*
T.C.I 326. L, O, CS, DU, EN; CH, IU, MH, NU, WF, Y.

3681 —An humble vindication of a free admission. [*London*],
for E. Blackmore, 1651. 8°. L, CT; NU, Y.

3682 ——Second edition. —, 1652. 8°. L, O, ORP, WCA; CLC,
NGT, SE, WF.

3683 ——Third edition. —, 1653. 12°. L, LSC, LW.

3683A ——[Anr. ed.] 1656. 8°. P, SA.

3684 [–] A letter to George Keith, concerning the salvability of
the heathen. *Printed, and sold by the booksellers of London
and Westminster*, 1700. 4°.* L, LF, LW, OC, EC; CLC, PH,
PSC, RPJ, TU.

3685 [–] Materials for union. *Printed, and are to be sold in Oxford*, 1681. 4°.* L, O, LW, OB; MIU, NU, WF.

3686 [–] Mediocria. *For T. Pharkust [sic]*, 1674. 4°. O, LCL, E, GU;
CDA, MM, NU, WF.

3687 ——Second edition. —, 1695. 4°. T.C.II 553. L, LW, OC,
DU, GU; GH, CLC, NU.

3688 ——[Anr. ed.] —, 1698. 4°. T.C.III 23. C, LW, OC, SP; CH.

3689 [–] The middle-way in one paper. *For T. Parkhurst*,
1673. 4°.* T.C.I 117. L, C, EC, NE; CH, IU, MM, NP, NU.

3689A [–] —[Anr. ed.] —, 1674. 4°.* L, OC; Y.

3690 [–] The middle-way . . . of election. *For T. Parkhurst*,
1672. 4°.* T.C.I 117. L, O, OU, E.

3691 [–] The middle-way . . . of justification. *For T. Parkhurst*,
1672. 4°.* L, O, CT, ENC; CH, CLC, MM, NGT, TSM, WF.

3692 [–] The middle-way. Of perfection. *For T. Parkhurst*,
1674. 4°.* L, LCL, BAMB, EC; CH, MM, PH, WF, Y.

3692A [–] The middle way of predetermination. *For Thomas
Parkhurst*, 1679. 4°.* T.C.I 421. CCH, EC; CH, CLC.

3693 [–] The middle-way . . . of the Covenants. *For T. Parkhurst*, 1674. 4°.* T.C.I 171. L, OU, BAMB, EC; CDA, CLC,
MM, NU, WF, Y.

3694 [–] A modest and peaceable inquiry into the design.
For Tho. Parkhurst, 1681. 4°. L, OC, CS, EN, DT; CLC, IU,
MH, NU, WF, Y.

3695 [–] The Nonconformists relief prepared. *For Walter
Kettilby*, 1678. 4°.* O, DU, LNC; CH, CN.

3696 [–] The obligation of human laws discussed. *Printed*,
1671. 8°. O, LW, P; CU, MHL, NU, TU, Y.

3696A —One sheet (or second letter) concerning the difference.
colop: *For T. Parkhurst*, 1695. 4°.* O, BAMB; CH.

3697 —Pacification touching the doctrinal dissent. *For T.
Parkhurst*, 1696. 4°.* T.C.III 23. O, LCL, OC, EC, GU; CH,
MBZ, MH, NU, Y.

3698 [–] A paper to William Penn. *By T. M. for H. Mortlock*,
1700. 4°.* L, LW, OC, BAMB, DT; LC, MU, NN, PSC, RPJ, Y.

3699 —Paulus redivivus: or speculum speculativum. *For
Thomas Pasham*, 1680. 8°. L, SP, ENC; NHC.

3700 [–] Peace at Pinners-Hall wish'd. *Printed and are to be
sold by Randal Taylor*, 1692. 4°.* T.C.II 423. L, O, C,
OC, EC; CN, NN, NU, WF.

3701 [–] The peaceable design. *Printed*, 1675. 8°. L, O, LW, OU;
CLC, MBA, NP.

3702 —Peaceable disquisitions. *For Thomas Parkhurst*, 1678.
4°. T.C.I 328. L, O, C, LCL, EN; CH, IU, MH, NU, WF, Y, AVP.

3703 [–] A peaceable resolution of conscience. *For Robert
Clavel, Thomas Simmons, and Jacob Sampson*, 1680. 8°.
T.C.I 397. L, O, CS, DU, P; WF, Y.

3703A [–] A plea for the Non-conformists. *Printed*, 1674. 8°.
LCL, LW; TO.

3703B [–] A private psalter. *For Thomas Parkhurst and Thomas
Simmons*, 1683. 8°. T.C.II 3. CLC.

[–] Proposition for the safety. 1667. See H., J.

3704 —The question of re-ordination. *For Tho. Williams*,
1661. 8°. O, C, LW, OC, DUS, P, EN; LC, NU.

3705 —A rejoynder to Mr. Drake. *By F. L. for E. Blackmore*,
1654. 8°. LT, O, LW, CT, E, CD; MH, NU.

3706 —A reply to The defence of Dr. Stillingfleet. *For Thomas
Parkhurst*, 1681. 4°. L, LCL, AN, BAMB, MR, DT; NU, WF.

3707 [–] —[Anr. ed.] —, 1682. 4°. T.C.I 484. O, CD; CH, Y.

3708 —The righteousness of God revealed. *For Thomas
Parkhurst*, 1697. 4°. T.C.III 23. L, OC, EC, GU, DT; CH,
CLC, NU, Y.

3709 —A second discourse about re-ordination. *For Tho.
Williams, and Tho. Johnson*, 1662. 4°. L, O, CT, YM, DT;
CH, MH, NU, WF, Y.

3710 —A second vindication of a disciplinary, . . . free admission to the Lords-Supper. *By F. L. for E. Blackmore*, 1656. 8°. LT, O, OC, CS, CD; CH, NU.

3711 —Συμβολη, sive conflictus. [*London*], *for the author*, 1681.
fol.* L.

3712 [–] The third step. *For Tho. Parkhurst*, 1684. 4°.* T.C.II
94. L, O, LW, CT; CLC, WF.

3713 [–] Two points of great moment. [*London*], *printed*, 1672.
12°. OC; NU, TU, Y.

3714 —The two steps of a Nonconformist. *For Thomas Parkhurst*, 1684. 4°.* T.C.II 94. O, LW, CT, BAMB; CLC, CN,
NU, WF.

3715 —Ultima manus, being letters. *For Tho. Parkhurst*, 1698.
T.C.III 86. OC, EC, SP; CH, NU.

3716 [–] Union pursued. *For Rich. Baldwin*, 1691. 4°.* T.C.II
377. L, O, OC, BAMB, DT; CH, CLC, MH, MIU, NU, WF.

3716A [–] A vindication of the Right Reverend Dr. Stillingfleet. 1700. IEG.

3717 [**Humfrey, Thomas.**] A true narrative of God's gracious dealing with the soul of Shalome Ben Shalomoh.
For William Marshal, 1699. 4°.* L, O, LW; CH.

3718 [–] —Second edition. —, 1700. 8°. T.C.III 193. L, O, EN;
PPT.

3718A [–] —Third edition. *Dublin, by John Brocas, for John
Ware*, 1700. 8°.* MH.

Humiliations follow'd. Boston, 1697. See Mather,
Cotton.

Humorous lieutenant. 1697. See Fletcher, John.

3719 The humerous tricks and conceits of Prince Roberts
malignant she-monkey. *For T. Cornish*, [1643]. 4°.*
LT, O; CH, CN, MH.

3720 The humours, and conversations of the town. *For R.
Bentley, and J. Tonson*, 1693. 12°. L, O, LG; CLC, CN,
IU, MH, NCD, WF, Y.

3721 **Humphreys, Humphrey.** A sermon preach'd . . . 30th of January, 1695/6. *For John Everingham,* 1696. 4°.* L, O, C, CT, BAMB, BC; CH, CLC, NN, WF, Y.

3721A —Ymofynion iw hatteb gan brocatorion. 1690. * AN.

3721B **Humphreys, John.** Celeusma: or, truth and her companions triumph. *For the author,* 1680. 4°. PU.

3721C —[Hebrew] Mystery Babylon: or, the whore of Rome. *For W. Marshall,* 1686. 12°. ORP.

3722 —[Hebrew] or, persecution for conscience sake. *For the author,* 1682. 4°.* O, LW.

3722A —[Hebrew] or, the doctrine of the apostles revived. *For William Hull,* 1689. 8°. Y.

3723 —Vindiciæ veritatis. A narrative. *Printed,* 1680. 4°.* L, O, C; CSS, MH, NU, WF, Y.

3723A —The vision of eternity held forth. *For Giles Calvert,* 1657. 4°. LF; PSC.

3724 —The womans priviledges above the man. *For Henry Million,* 1680. MBP.

CXI propositions. Edinburgh, 1647. *See* Gillespie, George.

3725 Entry cancelled.

Hundred and fifty three chymical aphorisms. 1690. *See* Helmont, Franciscus Mercurius *van.*

3726 An hundred godly lessons. *[London], for A. Milbourn,* [1670–97]. brs. L, CM, HH.

3726A —[Anr. ed.] *[London], for F. Coles, T. Vere, J. Wright, and J. Clarke,* [1674–79]. brs. EUING 143. GU.

3726B The Hungarian rebellion. *For William Gilbert, and Tho. Sawbridge,* 1672. 8°. T.C.I 110. L, DUS, SP, CD; CLC, KU, LC, WF.

3727 **Hungerford, *Sir* Edward.** Sir Edward Hvngerfords vindication. *May 6. for Francis Leach,* 1643. 4°.* LT, O, DU, LIU, A, DT; MH.

3728 **Hunscot, Joseph.** The humble petition and information of. *[London,* 1646.] cap., 4°.* LT, DT; NC.

3729 —To the right worshipful Iohn Fowke. *[London,* 1647.] brs. LT.

3729aA **Hunt, Henry.** A collection of some verses out of the Psalms. Second edition. *By J. Heptinstall for Henry Playford; and are to be sold by Anthony Boys,* 1698. 8°. L, O.

3729A ——Third edition. *By J. Heptinstall for Anthony Boys and J. Hare,* 1700. 8°. OH; CLC, IU, PPT.

3730 **[Hunt, James.]** [Glorious light.] *[London,* 1645.] cap., 4°.* LT.

3730A —The Kentjsh petjtjon, set forth, by that divine spirit which God hath given to me. *[London,* 1648?] 4°.* DT.

3730B [–] Now all ye that have a desire. *[n.p.,* 1648.] cap., 4°.* MR.

3731 —A plaine and briefe discovery. *[London], for J. H.,* 1643. 4°.* LT, NE.

3732 —A plaine and perfect touchstone. *[London],* 1643. 4°. MR.

3733 —The sermon and prophecie of. *For Thomas Bates,* 1641. 4°.* LT, LP, LNC; CH, MBZ, Y.

3734 ——[Anr. ed.] *Printed,* 1642. 4°.* LT, O, OW; CH, WF.

3735 —A sermon gathered. *[London,* 1648.] cap., 4°.* LT; NCD.

3736 —The spirituall verses and prose of. *For J. H.,* 1642 [3]. 4°.* CT; CH.

3737 ——[Anr. ed.] —, 1643. 4°.* LT; IU.

3738 ——[Anr. ed.] *[London,* 1648.] cap, 4°.* LT.

3739 —These spirituall verses of. *For Andrew Coe,* 1642. 4°.* LT, LCL, OW, CT; CH, MH.

3739A **Hunt, John.** Infants faith. *R. Janeway,* [1682]. 8°. LW; NHC.

3739B **Hunt, Nicholas.** New recreations. *By J. M. for Luke Fawn,* 1651. 12°. WF.

3740 **Hunt, Raphael.** March 21. Very joyfull news from Ireland. *For Joseph Hunscott,* 1641. brs. STEELE 2057. L, O, C, HH.

3741 **Hunt, Richard.** The bow of Jonathan. *By William Godbid,* 1657. 4°.* L, OCC, CT, BC, DT; MB, MH, MWA, NP, WF.

3742 —A catechisme for Christians. *For Samuel Man,* 1549 [i.e. 1649]. 8°. O, DT.

3743 ——[Anr. ed.] *By R. L. for Samuel Man,* 1649. 8°.* LT, O.

3744 **Hunt, Robert.** The island of Assada. *For Nicholas Bourne,* [1650]. 4°.* LT; CH.

3745 **Hunt, Thomas, *1611–1683*.** Abecedarium scholasticum. Or the grammar-scholars abecedary. *By B. G. for Nath. Brooke,* 1671. 8°. T.C.I 58. L, O; CLC.

3746 ——Second edition. *For Obadiah Blagrave,* 1681. 8°. T.C.I 445. O.

3746A —Libellus orthographicus: or, the diligent school boy's directory. *By T. Johnson, to be sold by John Hancock, and Francis Cossinet,* 1661. 8°. L, O, M; Y.

3747 **Hunt, Thomas, *1627?-1688*.** An apology for the government of England. *By J. Field,* 1686. 8°. L; NU.

3748 [–] An argument for the bishops right in judging. *[London], printed,* 1682. 8°. LCL.

3749 ——[Anr. ed.] *For Thomas Fox,* 1682. 8°. L, O, C, YM, DT; BN, CH, CN, MHL, WF, Y.

3749A —Mr. Hunt's argument for the bishops right. *For the author,* 1682. 8°. L, BC, DU, SP, EN; CLC, CN, LC, MH, Y.

3750 —A defence of the charter. *Printed and are to be sold, by Richard Baldwin.* [1683]. 4°.* L, O, C, EN, DT; CH, CLC, CN, MH, MU, NU, TU, WF, Y.

3751 [–] The great and weighty considerations, relating to the Duke of York. *Printed,* 1680. fol.* 35 [i.e. 31] pp. L, C, MR, EN, DM; CLC, IU, MH, NC, TU, WF, Y.

3752 [–] ——[Anr. ed.] —, 1680. fol.* 37 pp. L, O, C, OC, DU; CH, CN, MH, NU, TU, Y.

3753 [–] ——[Anr. ed.] —, 1680. fol.* 22 pp. LL, SP; CN, MBP, ASU.

3754 [–] ——[Anr. ed.] *[London?* 1681.] fol.* CT; CH, MIU, NP, TU, Y.

3755 [–] The honours of the Lords spiritual asserted. *By Tho. Braddyll, to be sold by Robert Clavel,* 1679. fol.* L, O, C, P, EN; CH, IU, LC, MH, NU, WF, Y.

3756 Entry cancelled. *See* Hunt, Thomas, *1611–1683.*

3757 [–] Mr. Emmertons marriage with Mrs. Bridget Hyde considered. *For the authour, and published by Richard Baldwin,* 1682. 4°.* L, O, CS, MR, E; CH, CN, PL, WF, Y.

3758 —Mr. Hunt's postscript for rectifying some mistakes. *For the author*, 1682. 8°. L, O, C, EN, DT; CH, IU, LC, NU, PL, WF, Y.

3759 [–] The rights of the bishops to judge in capital cases. *By Tho. Braddyll, for Robert Clavel*, 1680. 8°. T.C.I 375. L, O, C, DU, DT; CH, CN, MHL, NU, WF, Y.

3760 Entry cancelled.
[–] Short historical collection. 1680. *See title.*

3761 [–] Two books in defence of the bishops voting. Second edition. *By Tho. Braddyll for Robert Clavell*, 1680. fol.* T.C.I 398. L, O, C, CS, DT; CH, LC, WF.

3761A **Hunt, William.** Claris stereometriae or a key. *By Benj. Motte for the author*, 1691. 12°. L, OC.

3762 —Demonstration of astrology. *For the author; to be sold by George Sawbridge*, 1696. 4°.* L, O, C; CH.

3763 —The gaugers magazine. *By Mary Clark for the author*, 1687. 8°. L, CM, CT; IU, MH, MU, WF, Y.

3763A —A guide for the practical gauger. *By John Darby for Nath. Ponder*, 1673. 8°. L, O, OH; CH, WF, Y.

3764 —A mathematical companion. *By B. M. for R. Wellington*, 1697. 8°. T.C.III 39. C, DUS; CLC, NC.

3764A —Practical gauging epitomizd. *York, by J. White for the author*, 1683. 8°. L; CLC, WF.

3764B **Hunter, Alex.** A treatise of weights, melts, and measures of Scotland. *Edinburgh, re-printed by the heir of Andrew Anderson*, 1690. ALDIS 3047.2. ES, GU.

3764C **Hunter, Alexander, *of Muirhouse*.** Duplys for . . . to the replys. [*Edinburgh*, 1698.] fol. EN.

3764D —Replyes for the creditors of. [*Edinburgh*, 1696.] brs. EN.

3764E —To His Grace, His Majesties High Commissioner, and the . . . Parliament, the petition of. [*Edinburgh*, 1695.] brs. EN.

3764F [–] Unto His Grace, His Majesties High Commissioner, and the Estates of Parliament, the petition of the creditors of. [*Edinburgh*, 1696.] fol. EN.

3765 [**Hunter, Cuthbert.**] Truth cleared from reproaches. *Printed*, 1654. 4°.* LT, LF, MR; PSC.

3765A **Hunter, Jos[iah].** The character of a Christian. *York, printed and sold by Tho: Broad*, 1656. 4°. Y.

3765B —Dorcas revived . . . a sermon. *By Tho. Leach, for Thomas Firby*, 1660. 4°.* O, WCA, YM; IU, Y.

3766 —The dreadfulness of the plagve. *York: by Stephen Bulkley, to be sold by Francis Mawbarne*, 1666. 4°.* LWL, OU, WCA, YM; Y.

3767 —Jvdah's restitution. *York: by Alice Broade*, 1661. 4°.* O; CLC, Y.

3768 [–] Loves companion. *By Francis Leach*, 1656. 4°. O, LW; Y.

Hunter, a discourse. Oxford, 1685. *See* Langbaine, Gerard, *younger.*

Hunting of the fox. 1682. *See* Dean, John.

Hunting of the fox: or flattery. 1657. *See* Harflete, Henry.

3769 The hunting of the fox; or, the sectaries. *Printed*, 1648. 4°.* LT, O, C, P, EN; CH, MB, MH, OWC, TO, WF.

3770 The hunting of the hare. *For Francis Grove*, [1648?]. brs. L.

3770A —[Anr. ed.] *By F. Coles, T. Vere and J. Wright*, [1675]. brs. O.

3770B —[Anr. ed.] [*London*, 1682?] brs. L (impf.).

3770C —[Anr. ed.], [*London*], *for W. Thackeray, and T. Passinger*, 1686–8]. brs. CM.

3771 —[Anr. ed.] *By and for W. O.*, [1695?]. brs. L, HH.

3772 No entry.

3773 **Huntington, Robert.** A charge delivered. *Imprinted at London for G. Wharton*, 1648. 4°.* LT, BR; MH, WF.

3774 —Sundry reasons inducing Major Robert Huntington. [*London*], *printed*, 1648. 4°.* CT, LSC, LIU, MR; CH, IU, MH, NU, WF, Y.

3775 — —[Anr. ed.] *Printed in the yeer*, 1648. 4°.* L, O, LG, BC; CH, CN, MH, TU, WF, Y. (var.)

3776 [**Huntington, Theophilus Hastings**], *earl*. Reasons for the indictment of the D. of York. [*London*, 1680.] brs. L, O, LG, HH, MR; CH, PL, TU, WF, Y.

3777 [–] —[Anr. ed., "inditement."] [*London*, 1680.] brs. EVANS 294. HH; CSS, MH, MHS.

Huntington divertisement. 1678. *See* M., W.

3778 The Huntington-shire plovv-man. [*London*], *for P. Brooksby*, [1685–88]. brs. L, O, CM, HH.

3779 **Huntley, George.** An argvment upon a generall demurrer. *For George Huntley, and are to be sold by Michaell Sparkes*, 1642. 4°. L, O, CE, EN, DT; CLC, CN, MHL, NU, TU, WF, Y.

3780 **Huntly, Lewis Gordon, 3rd marquis.** The declaration and engagement of. *Hagae, by Samuell Broun*, 1650. brs. LT, O, CJ, LNC.

[**Hunton, Philip.**] Jus regum. Or. 1645. *See* Parker, Henry.

3781 [–] A treatise of monarchie. *For John Bellamy, and Ralph Smith*, 1643. 4°. LT, O, C, EN, DT; CH, CN, MH, NU, WF, Y.

3782 [–] —[Anr. ed., "monarchy."] *Printed*, 1680. 8°. L, O, C, DU, DT; CLC, CN, NC, NU, WF.

3783 [–] —[Anr. ed.] *Printed for, and sold by Richard Baldwin*, 1689. 4°. L, O, C, MR, DT; CH, CN, MH, NU, WF, Y.

3783A [–] —[Anr. ed.] *For E. Smith, and are to be sold by Randal Taylor*, 1689. 4°. T.C.II 246. L, O, CT, EC, DT; CH, IU, MH, MIU, TU, WF.

3784 [–] A vindication of the treatise of monarchy. *By G. M. for Iohn Bellamy*, 1644. 4°. LT, O, C, BC, YM; CH, IU, LC, MH, NU, Y.

3785 [–] —[Anr. ed.] *For John Bellamy*, 1651. 4°. CT; WF.

3786 **H[unton], S[amuel].** The army-armed. *For William Ley*, 1653. 4°.* LT, MR; CH, MH, MM, Y.

3786A [–] The golden law. *By J. M. for William Lee*, 1656. 4°. L, O, C; CSS.

3787 [–] His Highnesse the Lord Protector-protected. *For William Ley*, 1654. 4°.* CN, CSS, MH, MIU, TU, WF, Y.

3787A [–] The king of kings. *For the author, and sold by Ralph Hartford*, 1655. 4°. L; CH, MB, MH, NN, PBM, WF, Y.

Huntsmans delight. [n.p., 1670.] *See* Martin, Joseph.

Hurbin, Lionel. *See* Lilburn, John.

3788 Entry cancelled. Date: Nineteenth century.

3789 [**Hursey, Roger.**] Brave newes from Ireland. *For I. G.*, 1641. 4°.* LT, MR.

3790 **Hurst, Henry.** Ἄγνοια του ψυχικου ᾿ανθρωπου. Or, the inability. *Oxford, by Henry Hall for Richard Davis,* 1659. 8°. MADAN 2447. O, C, LCL, SC; MH.

3791 —[Anr. ed.] —, 1660. 8°. MADAN 2500. O, LW, OC, BC; NU, Y.

3792 —᾿Αναμνησις Εὐχαριστικη. The revival of grace. *Printed, to be sold by Tho. Parkhurst,* 1678. 8°. T.C.I 318. O, LCL, LW, P; CH, MH, NU, WF, Y.

3793 —The faithful and diligent servant of the Lord. *For Tho. Parkhurst,* 1677. 4°.* L, O, C, NPL, WCA; CH, CLC, IAU, MB, WF, Y.

3794–6 Entries cancelled.
   [**Hurtado, Luis.**] Famous history of the noble . . . Palmerin. 1664. *See* Moraes, Francisco de.

3797 Entry cancelled.
   [–] Famous history of Valentine and Orson. 1673. *See* Price, Laurence.

3798 **Hurtado de Mendoza, Antonio.** Querer por solo querer: to love only for love sake. *By William Godbid,* 1670. 4°. L, O, LW; CH, LC, MH, WF, Y.

3799 ——[Anr. ed.] *By William Godbid, to be sold by Moses Pitt,* 1671. 4°. T.C.I 86. L, O, C, LLU, EN; CH, CN, MH, WF, TU, Y.

3800 ——[Anr. ed.] *Paris,* 1671. 4°. LSL.

3800A —Zeli Davra, queen of Tartaria. *For, and sold by the booksellers of London and Westminister,* 1679. 4°. TNJ.
   Hurtado de Mendoza, Diego. Lazarillo. 1653. *See* title.

3801 Entry cancelled. Continental printing.

3802 **Hus, Jan.** A seasonable vindication of the supream authority. *By T. Childe, and L. Parry, to be sold by Edward Thomas,* 1660. 4°. LT, O, C, BC, EN; CH, CN, MH, NU, TU, WF, Y.

3803 ——[Anr. ed.] *Printed,* 1668. 4°. L, C; NU, WF.

3804 **Husain ibn ᾿Ali.** [Arabic] Lamiato 'l Ajam, carmen. *Oxonii, apud Ric: Davis excudit Hen: Hall, typis Arabicis Acad.,* 1661. 8°. MADAN 2576. L, O, CT, AN, EN, DT; CH, IU, MH, PL, WF, Y, AVP.

3805 Entry cancelled.
   Husband forc'd to be jealous. 1668. *See* Desjardens, Marie Catherine Hortense.
   Husbandman, farmer, and grasier's compleat instructor. 1697. *See* S., A.

3806 The husbandman's jewel. *For G. Conyers,* [c. 1695]. 12° MH, WF, Y.

3807 The husbandmans plea against tithes. *Printed,* 1647. 4°. LT, C, LW, BP, MR; CSS, MH, NC, NU, WF.

3807A The husband-man's practice. *By W. T. for John Stafford,* 1658. 8°. L (t.p.).

3808 Entry cancelled.
   Husbands, Edward. Collection of all the publicke orders. 1646. *See* England. Laws and statues.

3809–9A Entries cancelled.
   —Exact collection of all remonstrances. 1642. *See* England. Parliament.

3809B The husband's instructions to his family. *By William Downing,* 1685. brs. MH.

3810 **Hushar, Peter.** A catalogue of the library of books. [*London*], 1685. 4°.* L; NG.

3811 **Husnance, Stephen.** Englands faithful monitor. *For the authour,* 1689. 4°. L, O, CK, EN, ES; CH, IAU, MH, WF.

3812 Entry cancelled.
   Hussey, G. Memorbilia mundi. *See* Hooker, G.

3813 **Hussey, Joseph.** The gospel-feast opened. *By J. Astwood for John Salusbury,* 1692. 8°. T.C.II 419. L, O; CH, NU, Y.

3814 ——[Anr. ed.] —, 1693. 8°. L, C, CK, LCL, LW; Y.

3815 **Hussey, William.** An ansvver to Mr. Tombes. *For Iohn Saywell,* 1646. 4°. LT, O, LW, LIU, DT; IAU, NHC, NU, WF.

3816 ——[Anr. ed.] —, 1647. 4°. O.

3817 —A ivst provocation of Master Tombes. *For Iohn Saywell,* 1646. 4°.* LT, O, C, P, DT; WF, Y.

3818 —The magistrates charge. *By Thomas Harper, for Iohn Saywell,* 1647. 4°. LT, C, OCC, GU, DT; CH, IU, MH, NU, WF, Y.

3819 —A plea for Christian magistracie. *For John Saywell,* 1646. 4°. LT, O, C, OC, LIU; CH, CN, MIU, NU, WF, Y.

3820 **Hutcheson, George.** A brief exposition of the prophecies of Haggai. *By T. R. and E. M. for Ralph Smith,* 1654. 8°. LT, O, RPL, DL, E; CH, IU, MH, NU, WF, Y.

3821 —A brief exposition of the prophecies of Obadiah. *By T. R. and E. M. for Ralph Smith,* 1654. 8°. O, LW, AN, EN, GU; IU, NU.

3822 ——Second edition. *For Ralph Smith,* 1654. 8°. LT, O, DL; CH, MH, NU, WF, Y.

3823 —A brief exposition on the xii. smal prophets; the first volume. *For Ralph Smith,* 1655. 8°. LT, O, C, GU, BQ; CH, CLC, IU, MH, NU, Y.

3824 ——Second edition. —, 1657. fol. L, O, LW, P, E; CLC, IU, MH, NP, WF, Y.

3824A —Disputatio juridica. *Edinburgi, ab hæredibus ac successoribus* [sic] *A. Anderson,* 1695. 4°.* ALDIS 3466.5. EN.

3825 —An exposition of the Book of Job. *For Ralph Smith,* 1669. fol. T.C.I 8. L, O, C, GU, E; CLC, MH, NU, TSM, WF, Y.

3826 —An exposition of the gospel of Jesus Christ according to John. *For Ralph Smith,* 1657. fol. L, O, C, E, DT; CLC, MH, NU, TSM, WF, Y, AVP.

3827 —Forty five sermons. *Edinbvrgh, by the heir of Andrew Anderson,* 1691. 8°. ALDIS 3155. L, E, ENC, GU, SA; CH, MH, NGT, NU, Y.

3828 [–] A review and examination of a pamphlet. *Edinburgh, printed,* 1659. 4°. ALDIS 1615. L, O, EN, GU, BLH; CH, NGT, NU, WF, Y.

3828A Entry cancelled.
   Hutchins, Anthony. Caines bloudy race. 1657. *See* title.

3828B [**Hutchinson, Charles.**] Of the authority of councils. *For R. Clavel, W. Rogers, and S. Smith,* 1687. 4°. T.C.II 285. L, O, C, EN, DT; CH, IU, NU, WF, Y.

3829 **Hutchinson, Edward.** A treatise concerning the covenant. *For Francis Smith,* 1676. 8°. L, LCL, ORP, CT, MAB; NHC, NU, WF.

3830　**Hutchinson, Francis, bp.** A sermon preached ... May 27. 1692. *For William Rogers, 1692.* 4°.* L, O, CT; CH, MIU, Y.

3831　——July iij. 1698. *Cambridge, for Edmund Jeffery, 1698.* 4°.* T.C.III 89. L, O, C, OC, MR; CH, IU, NP, WF, Y.

3832　[**Hutchinson, John.**] A discovery of the trecherous attempts of the Cavaliers. *By Richard Bishop, 1643.* 4°.* LT, O; IU, MH.

3833　**Hutchinson, Richard.** The reply of. [*London, 1693/4.*] brs. L, LL.

3834　[–] The warr in New-England visibly ended. *By J. B. for Dorman Newman, 1677.* fol.* L; CH, CN, NN, NP, PL.

3835　[–] —[Anr. ed.] *By J. B. for Francis Smith, 1677.* fol.* CN, MU, RPJ.

3835A　**H[utchinson], S[amuel].** A declaration of a future glorious state. *Printed, 1667.* 4°.* LC, MBA, MWA, TO.

3836　[**Hutchinson, Thomas.**] Forced uniformity neither Christian nor prvdent. [*London, 1675.*] cap., 4°.* L, LF, LG, BBN; CLC, IE, MH, PH, WF, Y.

3837　**Hutchinson, William.** A letter to the Jesuits in prison, colop: *For the author, 1679.* cap., fol.* L, O, C, LNC, MR; CLC, IAU, NC, Y.

3838　[–] A rational discourse concerning transubstantiation. [*London*], *printed, 1676.* 4°.* L, O, CS, DU, P; CH, IU, NCD, WF, Y.

3839　Entry cancelled. Date: 1800.

3840　**Hutton, Charles.** The rebels text opened. *For Walter Kettilby, 1686.* 4°.* T.C.II 156. L, O, OC, BAMB, BR; CH, IU, PU, WF, Y.

3840A　**Hutton, Luke.** Luke Huttons Lamentation. *For F. C. J.W. T.V. W.G.,* [1655–8]. brs. O.

3841　——[Anr. ed.] *For J. Wright, J. Clarke, W. Thackeray, and T. Passenger,* [1681–4]. brs. L, O, CM, HH; MH.

3842　**Hutton, Sir Richard.** The argvments of. *By M. Flesher and R. Young; the assignes of I. More, 1641.* 4°. L, O, C, EN, DT; BN, CH, CN, MH, TU, WF, Y.

3842A　[–] The first part of The young clerks guide. *For Humphry Tuckey, 1649.* 8°. MHL.

3843　—The reports of. *By T. R. for Henry Twyford, and Thomas Dring, 1656.* fol. L, O, C, NPL, DT; CH, MHL, NCL, TU, V, YL.

3844　——Second edition. *By the assigns of Richard and Edward Atkins, for Henry Twyford and Thomas Basset. 1682.* fol. T.C.I 499. L, O, C, LL, EN; CH, MB, NCL, V, WF, YL, AVP.

3845　[–] The second part of The young clerks gvide. *By T. R. & E. M. for Matthew Walbanck, 1652.* 8°. L; CH, CLC, TU, YL.

3845A　[–] —[Anr. ed.] *By T. R. & E. M. for Humfrey Tuckey, 1652.* 8°. MHL.

3845AB　[–] —[Anr. ed.] *For Matthew Walbancke, 1652.* 8°. O.

3845B　[–] —[Anr. ed.] *By H. Hills for Humfry Tuckey, 1653.* 8°. L, DT; MHL, WF.

3845BA　——[Anr. ed.] —, 1655. 8°. L; MHL, YL.

3845BB　[–] —[Anr. ed.] *For Humphrey Tuckey, 1656.* 8°. BC; GU.

3845C　——[Anr. ed.] *For Matthew Walbancke, 1656.* 8°. OC, DUS; MHL, TU.

3846　[–] —[Anr. ed.] —, 1657. 8°. L.

3846A　——[Anr. ed.] *For Humphrey Tuckey, 1659.* 8°. L, CS; MHL.

3846B　——[Anr. ed.] *By T. R. and T. D. for Ambrose Isted, and Samuel Heyrick, 1670.* 8°. CLC, LC, MHL, PUL.

3847　[–] The third part of the young clerks guide. *For Humphrey Tuckey, 1659.* 8°. LT; MHL, TU.

3847A　[–] —[Anr. ed.] *By Thomas Ratcliffe and Thomas Daniel for Ambrose Isted, 1669.* 8°. CLC, LC, MHL, PUL.

3847B　—The young clerks guide. *For Humphrey Tuckey, 1649.* 8°. O.

3848　[–] —Second edition. *By R. L. for Matthew Walbanck, 1650.* 8°. L; LC.

3848AA　[–] —"Second" edition. *By R.L. for Humphry Tuckey, 1650.* 8°. PL.

3848BA　[–] —Third edition. —, 1650. 12°. LSC.

3848CA　[–] —Fourth edition. *For Matthew Walbancke, 1650.* 8°. DC.

3848DA　[–] —"Fourth" edition. *For Humphry Tuckey, 1651.* 8°. CLL.

3848EA　[–] —Fifth edition. —, 1652. 8°. L.

3848A　[–] —Sixth edition. *For Humphry Tuckey, 1653.* 8°. L, LIL, SHR; IU, MHL, WF.

3848AB　[–] —"Sixth" edition. —, 1655. 8°. YL.

3848AC　[–] —"Sixth" edition. *For Matthew Walbank, 1655.* 8°. O.

3848AD　[–] —Seventh edition. *For Humphrey Tuckey, 1656.* 8°. GU.

3848B　[–] —"Seventh" edition. *For Matthew Walbancke, 1656.* 8°. OC, DUS; MHL.

3849　[–] —Eighth edition. —, 1658. 8°. L, O, CP.

3849A　[–] —"Eighth" edition. *For Humphrey Tuckey, 1658.* 8°. PUL.

3850　[–] —Ninth edition. *By Edward Mottershed, for Humphrey Tuckey, 1659.* 8°. L, LG, CCA; LC, NCL, TU.

3851　[–] —Tenth edition. *By E. M. for Humphrey Tuckey, 1659.* 8°. L, DC; CH, IU, MB, MHL.

3852　Entry cancelled. Ghost.

3853　[–] —Twelfth edition. *By T. R. and M. D. for Ambrose Isted, and Samuel Herick, 1670.* 8°. L, C; CLC, LC, MHL, PUL.

3854　[–] —Fourteenth edition. *By T. R. & N. T. for Ambrose Isted and Samuel Heyrick, 1673.* 8°. L, GU; CH, LC, MHL, MU, TU, WF.

3854AA　[–] —Fifteenth edition. *For Thomas Basset and Samuel Heyrick, 1682.* 8°. L, LMT, CP, SA; CU, LC, MHL.

3854A　[–] —"Fifteenth" edition. —, *and Richard Chiswell, 1682.* 8°. T.C.I 477. PU.

3855　[–] —Sixteenth edition. —, 1689. 8°. T.C.II 294. L; CLC, CLL, NCL, PUL, Y.

3855A　[–] —"Sixteenth" edition. *For T. B., S. H., R. C., 1690.* 8°. CM.

3856　**Huxley, George.** A second book of judgements. *By T. R. and N. T. for George Dawes, 1674.* 4°. L, O, LI, LL, CS; CH, LC, MHL, MU, NCL.

3857　——[Anr. ed.] —, 1675. 4°. LL, LMT; CLL, LC, MHL, PUL.

3858　**Huyberts, Adrian.** A corner-stone laid. *For the author, 1675.* 4°.* T.C.I 218. L, O, LG, E, GH; CH, MU, NAM, WF, HC.

3859 **Huygens, Christian.** The celestial worlds discover'd. *For Timothy Childe*, 1698. 8°. T.C.III 96. L, O, C, E, DT; BN, CH, IU, LC, MH, MU, NC, WF, Y.

3860 Hyberniæ lachrymæ, or, a sad contemplation. [*London*, 1648.] brs. LT; TU.

Hyde, Edward. *See also* Clarendon, Edward Hyde, *earl of.*

3861 Entry cancelled.

Hyde, Edward, D. D. Allegiance and conscience. 1662. *See* —True Catholicks tenure.

3862 —Christ and his church. [*London*], *by R. W. for Rich. Davis in Oxford*, 1658. 4°. MADAN 2390. LT, O, CT, DU, E; CH, IU, MH, NU, WF.

3863 —A Christian legacy. [*London*], *by R. W. for R. Davis in Oxford*, 1657. 12°. MADAN 2342. L, OC, CT, LNC; NU.

3864 —A Christian vindication of truth. *By R. White, for Richard Davis in Oxford*, 1659. 12°. MADAN 2447*. L, O, CT, DU, P; NU, WF.

3865 Entry cancelled.

—Debate concerning the English liturgy. 1656. *See* Ley, John.

3866 —The mystery of Christ in us. *By Ja. Cottrel, for Giles Calvert*, 1651. 8°. LT.

3867 Entry cancelled.

[–] Plenvm responsvm. [n.p.], 1648. *See* Clarendon, Edward Hyde, *earl of.*

3868 —The true Catholicks tenure. *Cambridge, by John Field*, 1662. 8°. L, O, C, DU, LNC; CH, CLC, WF.

3869 [–] A wonder and yet no wonder. *By J. Macock, for Giles Calvert*, 1651. 8°. LT.

3870 **Hyde, Sir Henry.** The speech and confession, of. *For G. H.*, 1651. 4°.* LT.

3871 —A true copy of . . . speech on the scaffold . . . 4th of March, 1650. *By Peter Cole*, 1650. 4°.* LT, O, ĆS, DU, DT; CH, CN, MH, TU, WF, Y.

[Hyde, Laurence.] Enjoyment. [n.p.], 1679. *See* Rochester, John Wilmot, *earl of.*

3872 **[Hyde, Thomas.]** An account of the famous Prince Giolo. *Printed and sold by R. Taylor*, 1692. 4°.* T.C.II 424. L, O, CT; MH.

3872A —[Advertisement for his Historia religionis.] [*Oxford*], 1699. brs. L.

3873 —De historia Shahiludii. *Oxonii, e theatro Sheldoniano*, 1689. 4°. L, OM, CS; CLEVELAND PUB. LIB., CN, MH.

3874 —Epistola de mensuris. *Oxoniæ, e theatro Sheldoniano*, 1688. 8°.* L, O, CT, E, DT; NORTHWESTERN, PMA.

3875 —Historia Nerdiludii. *Oxonii, e theatro Sheldoniano*, 1694. 4°. L, O, CT, AN, EN, DT; BN, CH, MH, PL, WF, Y.

3876 —Historia religionis. *Oxonii, e theatro Sheldoniano*, 1700. 4°. L, O, C, EN, DT; BN, CH, LC, MH, NU, Y, AVP.

3877 —Mandragorias. *Oxonii, e theatro Sheldoniano*, 1694. 8°. L, O, C, AN, EN, DT; CH, CN, LC, MH, NC, Y.

3878 Entry cancelled.

—Shahilvdium. 1694. *See* —Mandragorias.

3879 —Specimen libri more Nerochim Maimonidis. [*Oxford*, 1690.] 4°. O.

3879A —[Specimen pages of an Arabic history of Timour.] [*Oxford?* 1675.] fol.* LPR.

3880 Hide Park Camp limned out to the life. *By P. L. for J. P.*, [1665?]. brs. L.

3881 **Hyll, Thomas.** *See* Hill, Thomas.

Hylton, Walter. The scale of perfection. *By G.D., sold by Edward Stanley*, 1653. 12°. E.

3882 —The scale (or ladder) of perfection. *By T. R.*, 1659. 8°. LT, O, C, YM, DL; CLC, CN, WF, WG, Y. (var.)

Hymenaean essay. [n.p.], 1662. *See* Drope, John.

Hymen's præludia. 1652. *See* La Calprenéde, Gaultier de Coste, *seigneur* de.

3883 An hymn to be sung in the procession. [n.p., 1661.] 4°. L, O, LPR; MH, PU, WF.

3884 A hymne to the ark in Newgate. *Printed*, 1663. brs. L, O; MH.

3884A A hymne to the gentle-craft. *For Charles Gustavus*, [1661]. brs. LT, O, OP; MH, WF.

3885 Entry cancelled. Date: 1703.

Hymns and spiritual songs. 1682. *See* Reeve, John.

3886 Hymnus Eucharisticus. [n.p., 1660.] brs. O.

3887 Hypocrisie discovered. [*London*, 1655?] cap., 4°.* BC, DUS, MR; CH, CSS, PL, Y.

3887A An hypocrite unmasked; or, the inside of Colonel Robert Jermye discovered. [n.p., 1659?] brs. L.

3887B The hypocrite unvail'd, and superstition and Deism confuted in sermons. *Printed: sold by Mr. Henry Knox, John Vallange, Thomas Carruthers, and Mrs. Ogston, in Edinburgh*. 1700. 8° in 4s. D (impf.).

3888 Entry cancelled.

Hypo[c]rites unmasked. 1659. *See* Clarges, *Sir* Thomas.

Hypocrites unmasking. 1647. *See* Prynne, William.

3889 The hypocritical Christian. colop: *By George Croom*. 1682. cap., fol.* L, O; CH, MH, NU, WF, Y.

Hypocritical nation. 1657. *See* Patrick, Symon, *bp.*

3890 The hypocritical Whigg displayed. *For C. H.*, 1682. brs. O, MC, EN; CH, MH, PU, WF.

3890A Hypomnemata didactica. *Cantabrigiæ, ex officina Johan. Hayes*. 1690. *Impensis Sam. Simpson*. 8°. C, LLP, CS, NPL; Y.

Hypomnemata logica. Oxoniæ, [1650]. *See* Prideaux, John.

Hypothesis physicæ nova. 1671. *See* Leibnitz, Gottfried.

Hyrelings. *See* T., R.

Hysbys ruwdd. 1693. *See* Almanacs. Morgan, Einon.

3891 **Hyword, Abel.** A famous victory obtained. [*London*], *January 6, for I. H. and T. Finch*, 1643. 4°.* LT.

I

I., A. Hypocrite unvail'd. 1700. *See title.*

1 **I., C.** The Commons petition of long afflicted England. *For Iohn Hammond,* 1642. 4°.* LT, LIU, SP; CH, INU, IU, MH, WF.

2 —The copy of a letter sent from a person of much honour. [*London*], *printed,* 1648. 4°.* LT, O, LLL; CLC, WF, Y.

3 —Iune the second 1642. A new remonstrance of Ireland. *By A. N. for Ed. Blackmore,* 1642. 4°.* LT, O, C, LG, MR; CH, MH, WF.

3A —News from Sr. William Waller. colop: *By E. Mallet,* 1684. brs. O; CH.

4 **I., D.** The glory of our English fleet. *By A. P.,* 1673. fol.* MR.

4A —A letter concerning the witches in the West. [*London?* 1670.] brs. OP.

I., E. Letter sent to an honourable gentleman. [n.p.], 1641. *See* Hall, Joseph, *bp.*

5 —To the honorable committee at Bury. *For Robert Bostocke,* 1643. brs. LT.

I., G. Bemoaning letter. 1700. *See* Mucklow, William.

—Doctrine of the Church of England, established. [n.p.], 1642. *See* Ingoldsby, William.

—Sermon preached at Bugbrook. 1642. *See* Jay, George.

—Spirit of the hat. 1700. *See* Mucklow, William.

I., H. Brief chronicle. 1663. *See* Heath, James.

—Divine contemplations. 1648. *See* Isaacson, Henry.

5A —An heroick elegie upon the most lamentable death of . . . Madame Isabella Buggs. *Printed,* 1681. brs. MH.

—Scripture calendar. 1649. *See* Almanacs. Jessey, Henry.

—Spirituall duell. 1646. *See* Isaacson, Henry.

—Summe and substance. 1647. *See* Isaacson, Henry.

—Treaty of pacification. 1642. *See* Isaacson, Henry.

6 Entry cancelled.

I., H. V. V. The heavenly gvide to trve peace. 1641. *See* Walker, Henry.

7 **I., I.** Reasons why this kingdome, as all others. *Printed at York, by Stephen Bulkley,* 1642. 4°.* LT, OC, CT, MR, DT; CH, CN, MH, NCD, WF, Y.

I., J. Rome is no rule. 1664. *See* Ives, Jeremiah.

8 —A short treatise comprising a brief survey. *Edinburgh, by a society of stationers,* 1661. 4°. ALDIS 1700. E, EN; CH.

9 **I., M.** An order for government of housholds. *For Mary Brusey, to be sold by Iohn Wright iunior,* 1641. brs. L.

I., N. Bentivolio and Urania. 1660. *See* Ingelo, Nathaniel.

I., P. Brief relation of the surprise. 1644. *See* Ince, Peter.

10 Entry cancelled.

—A letter written. 1688. *See* B., T.

I., R. Most pleasant history of Tom a Lincoln. 1655. *See* Johnson, Richard.

10A —A peaceable enquiry into that controversie about re-ordination. *Printed* 1661. 8°. LCL, LW, CS; MB.

11 **I., S. A.** Carminvm proverbalium. *Excudebat R. N. impensis Richardi Thrale,* 1654. 8°. L; CLC, IU, Y.

12 ——[Anr. ed.] *Excudebat E. T. impensis Richardi Thrale.* 1659. 8°. L.

13 ——[Anr. ed.] *Excudebat Gulielm. Godbid, impensis Richardi Thrale,* 1670. 8°. T.C.I 60. L; CH, PBL, WU.

I., T. Apology for private preaching. 1642. *See* Taylor, John.

—Cure for the tongue-evill. 1662. *See* Jordan, Thomas.

13A —An earnest and humble invitation to acts of mercy. *By T. B. for R. Mead,* 1684. brs. DCH.

14 —A perfect narrative of the proceedings of the army under the command of Col. Michael Iones. *For John Wright, Octob.* 17. 1648. 4°.* LT, O, C, LSD, BQ, DN; CLC, MH, Y.

15 No entry.

—Speech to the people. 1642. *See* Jordan, Thomas.

16 —True news from Reading. *For G. L.,* 1688. brs. EN.

17 **I., W.** A confutation of a late paper, entituled, an answer. colop: *For T. D.,* 1681. fol.* L, O, OP, MR, CH, CN, MH, WF, Y, ZWT.

18 —A letter to a gentleman of the insurance office. [*London*], 1681. brs. L, O, MC.

19 —A sermon preached at the fvnerall of Mrs. Alice Bray, . . . March the 2. 1645. *For Mathew Walbancke,* 1646. 4°.* LT; CH, Y.

20 Entry cancelled.

—True gentlewomans delight. 1653. *See* Kent, Elizabeth Grey, *countess of.*

21 —Watch word for Christians. [*London*], *for J. Hose,* [1680?]. brs. L; MH.

21A I. A. B. do sincerely promise and swear. [*n.p.,* 1689.] brs. L, LPR.

I being moved. 1659. *See* Webb, Mary.

I. C. de moribus. Oxoniae, 1665. *See* Casa, Giovanni della.

21B I do as I will. [*London?* 1670.] brs. L.

22 I father a child that's none of my own. [*London*], *for P. Brooksby,* [1680?]. brs. L, O, HH; MH.

23 I marry sir, heere is newes indeed. [*London*], *printed,* 1642. 4°.* LT; TU, Y.

I matter not. [n.p., 1657.] *See* Bateman, Susanna.

23A I thank you I will. 1647. brs. L.

24 I thanke you twice. [*London*], 1647. brs. LT, O, HH; MH.

25 I warrant thee boy, shee's right. *For Tho. Vere.* 1664. brs. HH.

25A I would I were where Helen lies. [*London?* 1690.] brs. L.

26 **Iamblichus.** Ἰαμβλίχου χαλκιδεως της κοιλης Συριας περι μυστηριων λογος. Iamblichi . . . de mysteriis liber. *Oxonii, e theatro Sheldoniano,* 1678. fol. MADAN 3179; T.C.I 335. L, O, C, MR, GU, DT; CH, MH, MU, NC, WF, Y, AVP.

27 **I'anson, Brian.** Nevves ovt of Spaine. *By G. Miller* 1644. 4°.* LT, O, MR; CLC, MH, WF, Y.

Ianson, Sir Henry. See Janson, Sir Henry.

28 **I'anson, Sir Thomas.** Give me kind Heaven. A song. [*London*, 1700?] brs. L.

28A [**Ibbitson, Robert.**] Charitable constructions . . . Sadlers-Hall. *By Peter Ibbitson*, 1647. 8°.* MADAN 1902. LT, C.

28B **Ibeson, James.** To the supreame authority, the Parliament . . . the humble remonstrance. [*London*, 1661.] cap., 4°.* CT.

29 —To the supream authority, the Parliament. A second remonstrance of. [*London*, 1652.] cap., 4°.* LT.

Ibn al-Tufail. See Abu Bakr ibn A Tufail.

30 **Ibrahim.** The Great Turkes letter. *By T. Forcet*, 1645. 4°.* LT, DT.

Ichabod: or, five groans. Cambridge, 1663. See Ken, Thomas, *bp.*

31 Ἰχθυοθήρα, or, the royal trade of fishing. *By J. F. for R. Royston*, 1662. 4°.* L, O, LUG, LNC, EN; CH, CU, MH, WF, Y.

31A Icones Biblicæ . . . figgers of the Bible. *t'Amsterdam by Cornel. Dankertz*, [1659]. 4°. WF.

Iconoclastes: or. [n.p.], 1671. See Fox, George, *elder.*

32 Idea democratica, or, a common-weal platform. *By Tho. Leach*, 1659. 4°.* BP, LUG, SP; CH, CU, MH, MU, NU.

Idea longitudinis; being, 1696. See Harrison, Edward.

Idæa of a perfect princesse. Paris, 1661. See Leslie, William Lewis.

Idea of arithmetick. 1655. See Billingsley, Robert.

Ideæ Cartesianæ. 1698. See Sergeant, John.

32A **Idell, William.** William Idell obtained his majesties order in council. [n.p., 1678.] brs. L.

33 Idem iterum: or, the history of Q. Mary's big-belly. [n.p., 1688?] cap., 4°.* L, O, DU; CH, IU, LC, MH, NU, WF.

Idiota: or. Paris, 1662. See Jordan, Raymond.

34–35 Entries cancelled.

Idman, Nils. Conferences concerning . . . idolatry. 1679. See Stillingfleet, Edward. Several conferences.

—Reply to an answer. 1672. See More, Henry. Brief reply.

Idol of the clownes. 1654. See Cleveland, John.

Idolaters ruine. 1645. See Whitfield, William.

36 An idyll on the peace. *For R. Parker, Peter Buck; and are to be sold by R. Baldwin*, 1697. fol.* L, MR; CLC.

36A If loves a sweet passion. [*London?* 1670.] brs. L.

36B If the English timber-traders to Norway or Gottenberg, object. [*London*, 1670?] brs. LPR.

36C If you find the terror of the Lord upon you this is the sure way to salvation. [n.p., 1700?] 4°.* L.

36D If you love me tell me so. [*London*], *for F. Coles, T. Vere, J. Wright, and J. Clarke*, [1674–79]. brs. O.

37 **Ignatius, Saint.** Ignatii, Polycarpi, et Barnabæ, epistolæ atq, martyria. *Oxoniæ, excudebat Leonardus Lichfield*, 1643. 4°. MADAN 1685. O, C, OB, SC, GU; BN, MH, RBU, SCU.

38 —Appendix Ignatiana. *Excudebat R. B. impensis Georgii Thomasoni*, 1647. 4°. O, C, LIL, SC, DT; BN, CH, IU, NGT, SCU, WF, Y.

39 —Epistolæ genuinæ. Second edition. *Typis Joannis Gellibrand, & Robert Sollers*, 1680. 4°. T.C.I 395. L, O, C, E, DT; BN, CH, CN, MBA, WF, Y, AVP.

40 ——[Anr. ed.] *Oxonii, e theatro Sheldoniano*, 1696. fol. O.

41 Ignativs his prophecie concerning these times. *For Iohn Greensmith*, 1642. 4°.* LT, LNC; CH, NR, WF.

Ignoramus I., pseud.

42 Ignoramus: an excellent new song. *Printed*, 1681. brs. L, O, LSD; CH, MH, PU, TU, WF, Y.

42A —[Anr. ed.] *For A. Banks*, 1681. brs. L, O; MH.

43 The ignoramus ballad. [*London*], *for N. T.* 1681. brs. L, O; CH, MH, PU, Y.

Ignoramus. Comœdia. [n.p.], 1658. See Ruggle, George.

43A An ignoramus found upon the last article of The humble presentment . . . Devon. [*London*], *printed*, 1661. 4°.* L, SC; CH, MH, Y.

44 Ignoramus his conviction. *For R. L.*, 1648. 4°.* LT, O, DT; WF.

45 Ignoramus-justice. *For Allen Banks*, 1682. brs. L, O; CH, CLC.

Ignoramus justices. 1681. See Whitaker, Edward.

46 Ignoramus vindicated. colop: *For William Inghall the elder*, 1681. cap., 4°.* L, O, CT, BC, DU; CH, CN, MHL, WF, Y.

Ignota febris; fevers. [n.p., 1691.] See Maynwaring, Everard.

Ignotus Quidam, pseud.

Ill effects. [n.p.], 1688. See Burnet, Gilbert, *bp.*

47 The ill fortune of a younger brother. [*n.d.*] brs. O.

48 Ill gotten goods seldome thrive. *For W. Gilbertson*, [169–?]. brs. L.

49 I'll hurry thee hence. A song in . . . Justice Buisy. [*London*], *T. Cross*, [1700]. brs. L.

49A I'll make thee b[e] fain to follow me. [*London?* 1670.] brs. L, EN.

49B Ile never love thee more. *For W. Whitwood*, [1670]. brs. O, EN.

50 **Illingworth, James.** A just narrative. *By A. C. for Henry Brome*, 1678. 8°.* T.C.I 289. L, O, LWL, OC; CH, CN, MH, NU, WF, Y.

Illumination to Sion Colledge. 1649. See L., J.

Illustrious history of women. 1686. See Shirley, John.

51 Entry cancelled.

Illustrious lovers. 1686. See Prechac, Jean, *sieur de.*

Illustrious shepherdess. 1656. See Perez de Montalván, Juan.

52 Entry cancelled.

Illustrissimi Domini Roberti Boyle epitaphium. 1692. See Urigny, de.

Illustrissimo Domino. [n.p.], 1653. See Macedo, Francisco.

Illustrissimo heroi, Georgio. [n.p., 1650]. See L., M.

53 The image of jealousie sought out. *For the author*, 1660, 4°. LF; PSC.

53A —[Anr. ed.] —*and are to be sold by Giles Calvert*, 1660. 4°. PL.

54 The image of the malignants peace. [*London?* 1642.] cap., 4°.* LT, O, LG, DU, LIU; CH, MH, NU, WF, Y.

Imago sæcvli: the image. Oxford, 1676. See Williams, Nathaniel.

55 Imitation and caution for Christian women. *By E. M. for George Calvert*, 1659. 4°.* LT, LW; MB, MWA, WF, Y.

Immanuel or. 1667. See Shaw, Samuel.

Immanuel the salvation. 1658. See Perrot, John.

55A The immorality of the English pulpit. *Printed*, 1698. 4°.*
     L, LLP, BC, BSM, LLU; MH.

56   Immortality in mortality magnifi'd. *For Thomas Bates*,
     1647. 4°.* LT, LG; WF.

57   The immortality of mans soule. *By Peter Cole*, 1645. 4°.*
     EC; CLC, MH, NU.

57A Entry cancelled.
     Immortality of the English pulpit. 1698. *See* Immorality.
     Immortality of the human soul. 1657. *See* Charleton,
     Walter.
     Immortality of the soule. 1645. *See* Hooker, Thomas.

58   An impartial account of all the material circumstances re-
     lating to Sir Thomas Armestrong. *For A. Banks*, 1684.
     4°.* O, DU; CH, WF, Y.

59   —[Anr. ed.] *Edinburgh, re-printed by the heir of Andrew
     Anderson*, 1684. 4°.* ALDIS 2457. AU, EN; TU, WF.

60   An impartial account of divers remarkable proceedings.
     Printed, 1679. 12 pp. fol.* L, O, OC, CT, BR, LNC; MIU.

61   —[Anr. ed.] —, 1679. 16 pp. fol.* L, O, C, EN, DT; CH, CN,
     MBP, MH, NU, TU, WF, Y.

62   —[Anr. ed.] —, 1679. 26 pp. fol.* L, O, C, DU, DT; CH, IU,
     MH, WF, Y, AVP.

63   —[Anr. ed.] *For Francis Smith*, 1679. fol.* L, O, BSM; IU,
     U. NEW MEXICO.

64   An impartial account of Richard Duke of York's treasons.
     For Allen Banks, 1682. fol.* L, O, C, DU, LLU; CH, MH, NC,
     TU, WF, Y.

65   An impartial account of some of the transactions in Scot-
     land. *Printed*, 1695. 4°.* L, O, CT, MR, EN; CH, MH, Y.

66   An impartial account of some remarkable passages in the
     life of Arthur Earl of Torrington. *For Robert Fowler*,
     1691. 4°.* L, C, LIU, DN; CH, CN, MH, WF, Y.

67   Impartial account of the arraignment, tryal, . . . Stephen
     Colledge. *For Richard Baldwin*, 1682. fol. O, DC, LLU; CN,
     MH, TU, WF, Y.

68   An impartial account of the arraignment, trial, & con-
     demnation of Thomas late Earl of Strafford. *For Joseph
     Hindmarsh*, 1679. fol. T.C.I 369. L, OJ, CT, MR, DN; CH, CN,
     MH, NU, WF, Y.

69   An impartial account of the behaviour of Sir Thomas
     Armstrong. colop: *By Geo. Croom*, 1684. brs. L, O; CH,
     CSS, INU, IU, WF, ZWT.

69A An impartial account of the doctrines of the Church of
     Rome. *By H. L. and are to be sold by Richard Butler*, 1679.
     fol.* T.C.I 361. OC, SP; CH, IU, WF.

70   An impartial account of the horrid and detestable con-
     spiracy. *For John Salusbury*, 1696. 4°.* L, C, OC, LIU, LSD,
     DN; HR, CH, IU, MH, WF, Y.

70A An impartial account of the late discovery of the persons
     taken . . . Southwark. *For J. C.*, 1688. brs. L, C, DU; CH.

70B An impartial account of the late famous siege . . . of Mons.
     For Richard Waterton, 1694. 4°. L, OC; MM.

71   An impartial account of the misfortune that lately hap-
     pened to . . . Earl of Pembrooke. *For Sam. Miller*, 1680.
     fol.* L, O, CM; MH, WF, Y.

72   An impartial account of the names of His Majesty's . . .
     Privy-Council. *By J. Leake, for Arthur Jones*, 1686. brs.
     L, HH; MH.

73   An impartial account of the nature and tendency of the
     late addresses. *For R. Baldwyn*, 1681. 4°.* 40 pp. L, O, C,
     GU, DT; CH, CN, MH, NU, WF, Y.

73A —[Anr. ed.] colop: *For R. Baldwin*, 1681. fol.* 12 pp. L, CT,
     DU, MR, DT; CSS, IU, MM, TU, WCL, WF.

74   An impartial account of the present state of the Hudson-
     Bay Company. [*London?* 169–.] brs. LPR.

75   An impartial account of the proceedings at Guild-hall the
     5th . . . September, 1683. colop: *By J. Grantham*, 1683.
     brs. O, LG, OC, EN; CH.

76   An impartial account of the proceedings of the common-
     hall of the city of London, . . . June 24, 1682. colop: *For
     Langley Curtis*, 1682. brs. L, O, HH; CH, CN, MH, PL, TU.

76A An impartial account of the several great & successful
     actions. colop: *For R. Hayhurst*, [1691]. brs. CH, Y.

76B An impartial account of the surrender of Charleroy. *For
     A. Roper*, 1693. brs. L; INU, MH.

77   The impartial account of the taking of Luxemburg. colop:
     For A. Bancks, 1684. brs. O.
     Impartial account of the tryal of. [n.p.], 1680. *See* Smith,
     Francis.

78   An impartial account of the trial of the Lord C[or]nwallis
     [*sic*]. *Printed*, 1679. fol.* L, O, CS, BC, DU; CH, CN, MH, TU,
     WF, Y.

78A An impartial account of the word mystery. *Printed*, 1691.
     4°.* L, O, C, E, DT; CH, CN, NU, TU, WF, Y.

79   An impartial and exact accompt of the divers Popish
     books. *For R. G.*, 1678. 4°.* L, O, LIL, LSD; CH, CLC, Y.
     Impartial and full account of the life . . . Lord Russel.
     1684. *See* L., A.
     Impartial and seasonable reflections. 1673. *See* Stubbe,
     Henry.

80   An impartiall and true relation of the great victory. *By
     Edw. Griffin*, July 11. 1648. 4°.* LT, EN; CLC, MH.

80A An impartiall and true relation of the great victory. *By
     Edw. Griffin*, July 12. 1648. 4°.* O; CLC, MH.

81   An impartial character of that famous polititian . . . Car-
     dinal Mazarine. *Printed*, 1661. * LT, OC, LIU; CN, MB, NN.
     Impartial collection. 1679. *See* Burnet, Gilbert, bp.
     Impartial consideration. 1679. *See* Williams, John, bp.
     Impartial disquisition. [1689?] *See* Ghest, Edmund.
     Impartial examination. 1698. *See* C., T.
     Impartial history of the life. 1689. *See* Bent, James.

82   An impartial history of the plots and conspiracies. *By
     W. O. to be sold by E. Whitlock*, 1696. T.C.II 589. LW, CT;
     CH, NU.

83   An impartial enquiry into the administration of affair's in
     England. [*London*], *printed*, 1683. 4°. L, O, LW; CH, CU,
     MH, NCU, WF, Y.

84   An impartial enquiry into the advantages . . . war with
     France. *For Richard Baldwin*, 1693. 4°.* T.C.II 482. L, O,
     LUG, CT, BR; CLC, CN, LC, MH, TO, WF, Y.

85   —Second edition. *Printed*, 1695. 4°.* T.C.II 530. MR; CH, CN,
     WF.

Impartial enquiry into the causes. 1692. *See* Delamere, Henry Booth, *earl.*

86 Entry cancelled. Ghost.

86A —[Anr. ed.] *Dublin, by Andrew Crook, and reprinted at London,* 1691. 16°. L, BLH, DI, DN.

87 An impartiall narration of the management of the late Kentish petition. *Printed,* 1648. 4°.* LT, O, CS.

87A An impartial relation of John Kelly's services. *Printed for the author,* 1699. fol.* L.

Impartial relation of the illegal proceedings. 1689. *See* Fairfax, Henry.

87B An impartial relation of the seizing . . . several high-way-men. *E. Golding,* 1694. brs. CN.

Impartial relation of the surrender and delivery. [1690.] *See* B., W.

Impartial relation of the whole proceedings. [*London*], 1688. *See* Fairfax, Henry.

88 An impartial state of the case of the Earl of Danby. *Printed,* 1679. fol.* L, C, OC, MR, EN; CH, CN, LC, MH, TU, WF, Y.

Impartial survey and comparison. 1685. *See* Burnet, Gilbert, *bp.*

89 An impartial survey of such as are not, . . . fitly qualified. [*London,* 1679?] fol.* L, O, DU, MR; CH, CN, MBA, WF, Y.

Impartial vindication of the clergy. 1680. *See* Rolls, Samuel.

90 An impartial vindication of the English East-India-Company. *By J. Richardson, for Samuel Tidmarsh,* 1688. 8°. T.C.II 225. L, O, C, LUG, EN; CH, CJC, MH, NC, WF, Y.

Impartialist satyre. 1652. *See* Taylor, John.

91 The impeached and imprisoned citizens, aldermen, and members, absolution. [*London,* 1647.] brs. LT.

Impeachment against the bishops. 1641. *See* Wilde, John.

92 The impeachment and articles of complaint against Father Philips. *For A. I.,* 1641. 4°.* LT, O, LFO, CT, MR; CLC, CN, MBP, MH, NU, Y. (var.)

93 —[Anr. ed.] *Printed,* 1641. 4°.* LT, LSE, CT, DN; CH, MH, WF.

94 The impeachment and charge of Mr. Henry Hastings. *July 22. For Iohn Warden,* [1642]. 4°.* LT, O, BAMB, EC; CH, WF, Y.

95 The impeachment by the House of Commons against the Lord Major. *R. Ibbitson,* 1647. 4°.* MR.

96 Entry cancelled.

Impeachment of high treason. 1642. *See* England: Parliament, House of Commons.

97 The impeachment of Sir Edward Harbert. *For Iohn Burroughes, and Iohn Franke,* 1641. 4°.* LT, O, AN, MR; CH, IU, MH, WF, Y.

98 The impeachment of the Duke and Dutchess of Lauderdale. [*Edinburgh?* 1676.] brs. ALDIS 2076.6. L, O, LNC, EN; MBA, MIU, Y.

99 —[Anr. ed.] [*London,* 1679.] cap., fol.* L, O, C, OC, MR; CH, MH, NP, PL, WF.

Imperfect pourtraicture. 1661. *See* Charleton, Walter.

100 Imperial chocolate made by a German lately come into England. [*London,* 1700?] brs. L.

Imperial tragedy. 1669. *See* Killigrew, *Sir* William.

Imperiale, a tragedy, 1655. *See* Freeman, *Sir* Ralph.

Imperious brother. 1656. *See* Perez de Montalvan, Juan.

101 The importance of publick credit. colop: *Printed,* 1699. 4°.* LUG; MH, NC.

101A —[Anr. ed.] [*London?* 1700.] brs. L; MH, Y.

Important considerations. [n.p.], 1688. *See* Watson, William.

102 An important query for Protestants. *For G. L. and J. H.,* 1688. 4°.* L, O, LIL, AU, EN; CLC, IU, MH, NC, TU, Y.

Important questions of state. 1689. *See* Stephens, Edward.

103 Entry cancelled.

Imposter dethron'd. 1658. *See* Farmer, Ralph.

104 The impostor expos'd. *For James Uade,* 1681. 8°. T.C.I 441. L, C, OC, DU, LLU, LNC; Y.

104A —[Anr. ed.] *For J. V., sold by Dan. Brown, and J. Waltho,* 1683. 8°. T.C.II 56. L.

105 Entry cancelled.

Impostor magnus, or. 1654. *See* Taylor, Silas.

Imposture defeated. 1698. *See* Powell, George.

Impotent lover. 1689. *See* Maximianus Etruscus.

Impressio novissima. [n.p., 1677.] *See* Fisher, Payne.

Impressio secunda. [n.p., 1675.] *See* Fisher, Payne.

106 Imprisonment of mens bodyes for debt. [*London*], *printed,* 1641. 4°.* O, LL, MR, P, DT; CH, IU, MH, NU, WF, Y.

107 Impropriations purchased by the Commissioners. *By Richard Cotes,* 1648. 4°.* LT, O, LVF, DU, DT; CLC, INU, MH, MU, PT.

Improvement of the way. 1690. *See* Hallywell, Henry.

108 The impudence of the Romish whore: continued. [*London*], *by Robert Austin.* 1644. 4°.* LT, O, C, EN, DT; CH, MH, WF.

109 In answere to the Earle of Straffords conclvsion. [*London*], *printed,* 1641. 4°.* LT, OC, BC, DU, E; CH, IU, LC, MH, TU, Y. (var.)

109aA In answer to the Earle of Straffords oration. *Printed,* 1641. 4°.* LG, CJ, LIU, LNC; CN, CSS, MIU, WF. (var.)

109bA In Bartholomew-close . . . lives an expert operator. [*London,* 1680?] brs. L.

109cA In Bartholomew fair. At the corner of Hosier-lane . . . a prodigious monster. [*London,* 1685.] brs. L.

109dA In Blackfryers . . . there is a gentlewoman . . . physick. [*London,* 1680?] brs. L.

In Britanniarum reges. 1672. *See* Ferrarius, Gulielmus.

109eA In case any proviso should be offer'd to the bill of naturalization. [*n.p.,* 1698?] brs. L.

109A In commemoration of Mʳ. Christopher Love. [*London,* 1651?] brs. MH.

109AB In Exeter-street . . . liveth a gentlewoman . . . physick. [*London,* 1680?] brs. L.

109AC In Fan-church-street . . . there is an Italian chymist doctor. [*London,* 1670?] brs. L.

109B In Georgium Keithum Caledonium apostatum. [*London*], 1700. fol.* LF; PH.

109C In Great More Fields . . . liveth a physitian. [*London,* 1670?] brs. L.

109D In great Suffolk street . . lives a gentlewoman. [*London,* 1690?] brs. L.

109E In Holborn . . . liveth a physitian. [*London,* 1680?] brs. L.

110 Entry cancelled. Date: 1605.
111 In honovr of the right worshipfvll Doctovr Robert Pinke. [*Oxford, by H. Hall*], 1648. 4°.* MADAN 1972. L, O; MH.
In illustrissimum, ac serenissimum Jacobum II. [*London*, 1685.] *See* Ker, Peter.
111A In James's-street . . . liveth a doctor. [*London*, 1690?] brs. L.
In laudem musices. [*n.p.*, 1672.] *See* Fell, John, *bp.*
112 In Lilium bardum astrologastrum. [*London*, 1650.] brs. LT.
112A In Little Old Baily . . . is resident a licensed physician. [*London*, 1670?] brs. L.
113 In luctrosissimum Mariae . . . obitum. *Edinburgi*, 1695. brs. ALDIS 3466.6. E.
114 In me Orinda has gain'd a heart. [*London*], *T. Cross*, [1700?]. brs. L.
114A In memoriam . . . Roberti Gardiner . . . threnodia. [*London*, 1700?] brs. MH.
115 In memoriam Thomæ Rainsbrough, . . . the epitaph. [*London*, 1648.] brs. LT; MH.
115A In memory of his Highness George Duke of Albemarle. *Printed*, 1669[70]. brs. CH, MH.
115B In memory of L.Coll. Cleaveland. [*Edinburgh?* 1690.] brs. ALDIS 3047.7. L.
116 In memory of that faithful disciple of the Lord William Mecho. [*London*], 1677. 8°.* CLC, MH (impf.).
In memorie of that . . . Mʳˢ Susanna Harris. [*n.p.*, 1649.] *See* Wharton, George.
117 In memory of the truly loyall, and valiant Capt. John George. *Printed*, [1691]. cap., fol.* L.
118 Entry cancelled.
In mortem serenissimæ. 1660. *See* Vliet, Jan van.
118A In natalem augustissimi principis . . . Jacobi Secundi Filii. *Typis Gulielmi Downing*, 1688. brs. MH.
119 In nobile admodum inter gallos. *Oxonii*, 1667. 4°.* L, DT.
In nobilissimi juvenis. [*n.p.*, 1672.] *See* Pugh, Robert.
119A In Northumberland-alley . . . liveth one who . . . cures all violent pains. [*n.p.*, 1670?] brs. L.
In nuperam horrendam montis, 1670. *See* B., D.
In obitum Christiani Quinti. [*n.p.*, 1699.] *See* Hog, William.
In obitum . . . D. Ioannis Lauderi. [*Edinburgh*, 1692.] *See* Deniston, Walter.
119B In obitum & exequis illustrissimæ Mariæ. [*London*], *sold by John Whitlock*, 1695. brs. MH.
119C In obitum eximii clarrissimique viri Georgii Pringli. [*n.p.*, 1689.] brs. EN.
In obitum Mariæ. [*n.p.*, 1694.] *See* Joyner, Edward.
In obitum serenissimi . . . Olivari. 1658. *See* Fisher, Payne.
119D In parishes of about an hundred families, and wherein the registry of the births. [*n.p.*, 1683.] brs. L.
119E In Petty-France . . . is a German who hath a powder. [*London*, 1675?] brs. L.
119F In principem Scotiae. [*Edinburgh?*], 1688. brs. ALDIS 2763. 5. L.
119G In pursuance of His Majesties proclamation . . . [customs form]. [*London*, 1669.] brs. LPR.
120 Entry cancelled.

In pursuance of the order. [*London*, 1648.] *See* London. Common Council.
121 In reges Angliæ a Gulielmo Primo. *Apud Radulphum Needham*, 1671. brs. L.
121A In remembrance of Temperance Aylmer. [*London, B. Aylmer*, 1688.] brs. Y.
122 In sacra Biblia Græca ex versione LXX. interpretum scholia. *Excudebat Rogerus Daniel: prostat autem venale apud Joannem Martin & Jacobum Allestrye*, 1653. 8°. L, O, OC, CS, EC, DL, DM; CH, MIU, TU, WF, Y.
122A In serenissimi Regis Jacobi secundi exilium. *Impensis authoris*, 1690. brs. MH.
In speculo teipsum. Edinburgh, 1692. *See* Brown, Andrew.
122aA In St. Martins Court . . . liveth a gentlewoman. [*London*, 1690?] brs. L.
122B In Surry-street . . . liveth a gentlewoman, who hath a most excellent wash to beautifie the face. [*London*, 1690?] brs. L.
122C In Swan-ally in the Minories, lives a doctor. [*London*, 1670?] brs. L.
123 In the act for raising two millions. [*Edinburgh?* 1698.] brs. ALDIS 3755. 9. LUG, INDIA OFFICE; MH.
124 In the county of Palatine in Durham. 1682. brs. O, DU, EN.
124A In the great levell of the fens . . . are decreed unto the Earl of Bedford. [*n.p.*, 1690.] 4°.* L.
124B In the name . . . of the Commonwealth of England. By the Lords . . . of Newfoundland. [*n.p.*, 1653.] brs. O.
In the 150 page of the book. [*n.p.*, 1645.] *See* Lilburne, John.
124C In the Old-baily . . . sweating-house. [*London*, 1680–1700.] brs. L.
124D In the parable of the marriage feast. Second edition. [*n.p.*], *sold by Samuel Keble*, 1692. brs. L.
125 In tristissimum immanissmumque. [*London*, 1666.] brs. L.
126 In vino veritas: or, a conference. *For J. Nutt*, 1698. 4°.* T.C.III 112. L; NC, WF.
127 Inamorato and Misogamos: or. *For H. Brome*, 1675. brs. L; MH.
Inavgvratio Oliveriana. 1654. *See* Fisher, Payne.
128 I[nce], P[eter]. A brief relation of the surprise of the forts of Weymouth. *For Luke Fawne*, 1644. 4°.* LT; Y.
128A Incestuous marriages, or relations of consanguinity. *For Robert Pawlet*, 1677/8. brs. LWL. [= C5667.]
129 **Inchiquin, Murrough O'Brien, lord.** The declaration and protestation of. [*London*], *printed*, 1648. 4°.* LT, LVF, DT, DN; CH, MH, MIU, Y.
130 —The desires and propositions of. *For R. W.*, 1648. 4°.* LT, O, LVF, OAS, LIU, DN; MH, WF.
131 —A letter from the right honourable the Lord Inchiqvin. *Printed at London by George Miller*, 1644. 4°.* LT, C, LVF, BC, DU, DN; CH, MH, MU, WF, Y.
132 —A letter to . . . Lenthal. *For Edward Husband*, Sept. 28. 1647. 4°.* LT, O, C, MR, DN; CH, CSU, MH, WF, Y.
133 No entry.
134 —More victories lately obtained in Ireland. *For Robert Bostock*, 1647. 4°.* LT, O, MM; NN, WU.

134A   —More victoryes obtained in Ireland. *For Robert Bostock,* 1647. 4°.* C, DN; CH, MH.

135   —The Lord Inchiqvins queries. *Hage: by Samuell Broun,* 1649. 4°.* O, C, SC, DN; MH.

135A   —A trve copy of a letter sent from. *Dublin, by William Bladen,* 1649. 4°.* DIX 347. L, DN; WF.

135B   —A trve copy of a second letter, sent from. *Dublin, by William Bladen,* 1649. 4°.* DIX 347. WF.

136   —A true relation of a great victory. *For Edward Husband, Nov.* 30, 1647. 4°.* LT, O, C, MR, DN; CH, CU, MH, WF.

137   —Two letters sent. *For John Wright,* 1647. 4°.* LT, O, C, LVF, CT, DN; CH, WF, Y.

137A   The inclosing of Jarrow-slike and making a ballast-shore on it. [n.p., 1670.] brs. LPR.

Incognita. 1692. *See* Congreve, William.

138   An incomparable collection of original paintings, . . . 22d . . . February, 1691. [*London*], 1692. 4°.* L.

Incomparable poem Gondibert. [n.p.], 1655. *See* Wild, Robert.

138A   The inconsiderable imployment of people, by the refining of sugar. [*London?* 1695.] brs. LG, LPR.

138B   The inconsistency of mans Dagon. *For Tho. Mitchell,* 1682. 8°. LW.

Inconstant-lover. 1671. *See* Chavigny de la Bretonnière, François de.

139   The inconveniences of a long continuance of the same Parliament. [*London,* 1679/80.] cap., fol.* L, LL, OB, DU, MR; CH, NN, LC, MH, WF, Y.

Inconveniencies of toleration. 1667. *See* Tomkins, Thomas.

140   Inconveniences to the English nation. [n.p.], 1668. fol.* L, O; CLC, MH.

141   **Indagine, Joannes, ab.** The book of palmestry. *By J. Cottrel, for Edw. Blackmore,* 1651. L, E, A; HC.

141A   ——[Anr. ed.] *By R. Ibbitson for Ed. Blackmore,* 1656. 8°. OC; NN. (var.)

141B   ——Fifth edition. *By R. I. for Charls Tyns,* 1664. 8°. PU.

142   ——Sixth edition. *By R. I. for Thomas Passenger,* 1666. 8°. L; CH, WF.

143   ——Seventh edition. *By A. P. for T. Passinger, to be sold by J. Clarke,* 1676. 8°. T.C.I 259. L; NIC, NN.

143A   —"Seventh" edition. *By J. R. for T. Passinger,* 1683. 8°. MH.

143B   ——Ninth edition. *For J. Back,* [1697]. 8°. T.C.III 45. CLC.

144   An indenture, containing a grant of all . . . revenue of Ireland. *Dublin,* 1676. fol. DIX 157. L, O, C, LUG, DK, DT; CLC, WF, ST. PATRICK'S COLL., MANLY, AUSTRALIA.

Independency accused. 1645. *See* P., J.

Independencie Gods veritie. 1647. *See* Goodwin, John.

Independencie no schisme. 1646. *See* Nedham, Marchamont.

145   Independency stript & whipt. [*London*], printed, 1648. 4°.* LT, O, LVF, DT, BLH; CH, NU, Y.

146   The independent catechisme. *For Richard Burton,* 1647. 8°.* LT; CH.

Independants catechism. 1654. *See* C., J.

147   The independents declaration and remonstrance to the Parliament. *Imprinted at London for Nathaniell Gibson,* 1648. 4°.* LT; MH, Y.

148   The independants declaration delivered. *For B. T.,* 1647. 4°.* LT, EN; IU, MH, MM, NU.

149   The independents dream. [*London*], *printed,* 1647. 4°.* LT, MR, DT; WF, Y.

Independent's loyalty. [n.p.], 1648. *See* Osborne, Richard.

Independants militarie entertainment. 1645. *See* L., W.

Index biblicus: or. 1668. *See* Hoar, Leonard.

Index poeticus. 1667. *See* Farnaby, Thomas.

150   An index to the Indian closset . . . to be seen at Leyden. [*London*], *printed* 1688. 4°. LR; CLC, MH.

Index villaris: or. 1690. *See* Adams, John.

Indian dialogues. Cambridge [Mass.], 1671. *See* Eliot, John.

151   The indictment and arraignment of John Price. *For Robert Clavel,* 1689. 4°.* L, O, C, EN, DT; CH, CLC, CN, MHL, WF, Y. (var.)

152   The inditement of tythes. *Printed,* 1646. 4°.* LT, OC, CCA, MR, DT; CH, CSS, MH, NU.

153   The indifferent lover. [*London*], *for Ch Bates,* [1690]. brs. L, CM, HH.

Individual letter. 1651. *See* Burt, Nathaniel.

Inducement to the intrenching. 1642. *See* L., A.

Indvlgence and toleration. 1667. *See* Owen, John.

Indulgence not justified, 1668. *See* Perrinchief, Richard.

154   Indulgence not to be refused. *Printed,* 1672. 4°.* OC, MR; MM, NP, NU.

155   —[Anr. ed.] —, 1673. 4°.* C, CT, EN; NU.

156   Indulgence to Dissenters. 1673. 8°. O, OC; CH, CLC, NSU, WF.

157   Indulgence to tender consciences. *By Henry Hills,* 1687. 4°.* L, O, C, LIL, MR; CN, MH, NGT, NU, WF.

157A   **Inett, John.** A guide to repentance. *For M. Wotton, and T. Walker, in Lincoln,* 1692. 12°. L, O.

157B   —A guide to the devout Christian. *By J. Rawlins, for M. Wotton, and J. Lawson,* 1688. 12°. LLP.

158   ——Second edition. *By J. Richardson, for M. Wotton,* 1691. 12°. O, CS.

158A   ——Third edition. —, 1696. 12°. OC, SHR.

158B   ——Fourth edition. *For M. Wotton,* 1700. 12°. T.C.III 204. Y.

159   —A sermon preached . . . August the first, 1681. *By M. Flesher for Walter Kettilby,* 1681. 4°.* T.C.I 458. L, OCC, C, E, DT; CH, CLC, IU, NU, TSM, WF.

Infallible guide. 1682. *See* H., W.

Infallible way to contentment. 1673. *See* Seller, Abednego.

Infallibility of the Roman. Antwerp, 1674. *See* Worsley, Edward.

160   The infamous history of Sir Simon Synod. [*London*], *printed,* 1647. 4°.* LT, DU; CSS, MH, TU.

Infancy of elders. [n.p.], 1647. *See* S., J.

Infant baptism, and. 1656. *See* Woodward, Hezekiah.

Infant baptism of Christ's. 1687. *See* Petto, Samuel.

Infant-baptism; or. 1700. *See* Rossington, James.

161   Infant's baptism mainteined [sic]. *By William Du-gard for Rob. Beaumont*, 1650. 4°.* LT, O, EN, DT; CH, CSS, IU, MH.

162   Infants baptizing proved lawfull. *By George Miller*, 1644. 4°.* LT, O, LLP, CT, DT; CLC, MH, NHC, NU, WF.

163   The infants lawyer. *By the assigns of R. and E. Atkyns, for Robert Battersby*, 1697. 8°. L, SHR; LC, MHL, NCL, NCU.

Infidelity unmasked. Gant, 1652. *See* Wilson, Matthew.

Information and directions. [n.p., 1684.] *See* Penn, William.

163A   The information and examination of a smith [Jennings]. [*London?* 1680.] brs. L, O, C, LG, LNC; CH, IU, MH, WF, AMB.

Information concerning the present state. 1658. *See* Jessey, Henry.

163B   Information for Aeneus McLeod, town-clerk. [*Edinburgh*, 1695.] fol. EN; CSS.

163C   Information for Dame Helenon, Issobel and Margaret Nicolsons. [*Edinburgh*, 1695.] fol. EN.

164   Information for Gaven Plummer. [n.p., 1700?] brs. RPJ.

164AA Information, for James Mclurg, late dean of guild. [*Edinburgh*, 1694?] cap., fol.* CSS.

164A   Information for John Adam. [*Edinburgh?* 1693.] cap., fol.* L.

164B   Information for John Hamilton . . . against John Weir. [*Edinburgh*, 1695.] fol. EN.

164C   Information for John Ramsay. [*Edinburgh*, 1693.] cap., fol.* ALDIS 3301.5. L.

164D   Information for Lieutenant Collonel Forbes, and John Forbes. [*Edinburgh*, 1700?] fol.* EN.

164E   Information for Lord Basil Hamilton concerning the election of a commissioner. [*Edinburgh*, 1700.] fol. EN.

164F   Information for Mr. Alexander Heriot . . . in relation to the lybel against him. [n.p., 1690.] fol. EN.

164G   Information for Mr. William Erskine. [*Edinburgh?* 1690.] cap., fol.* ALDIS 3047.4. L.

164H   Information for my Lord and Lady Nairn. [*Edinburgh, J. Reid*], 1690. 4°.* EN.

164I   Information for my Lord Hattoun. [*Edinburgh*, 1691–5.] fol. EN.

164J   Information for Sir John Gordon of Park for himself. [*Edinburgh*, 1695.] fol. EN.

164K   Information for Sir John, Hall [sic], Lord Provost of Edinburgh. [*Edinburgh*, 1692.] fol. EN.

164L   Information for Sir Thomas Nicolson. [*Edinburgh*, 1695.] fol. EN.

164M   Information for the Earl and Countess of Southerland. [n.p., 1693?] fol.* O.

164N   Information for the Earl of Argyle against the Duke of Gordon. [*Edinburgh*, 1700.] fol. ALDIS 3974. EN.

164O   Information for the Earl of Roxburgh. [*Edinburgh*, 1700?] fol. EN.

164P   Information for the Earl of Seaforth. [*Edinburgh*, 1697.] fol. EN.

165   Information for the heirs of J. Hay and J. Smart. [n.p., 1690.] fol.* Y.

166   Information for the heritors, elders, . . . against Mr. William Veatch. colop: *Edinburgh, by the heir of Andrew Anderson*, 1690. 4°. ALDIS 3047.5. L, O, ENC.

166A   Information for the Laird of Innes against the Duke of Gordon. [n.p., 1700.] brs. EN.

166B   Information for the Laird of Preston-grainge. [*Edinburgh?* 1695.] brs. ALDIS 3766.55. L.

167   Information for the Lord Blantyre. [n.p., 1696.] fol. EN.

168   Information for the magistrats. [n.p., 1700.] fol. EN.

168A   Information for the ministers in . . . Aberdene. [*Aberdeen?* 1697.] brs. EN.

168B   Information for the moderator of the presbytry of Glasgow. [*Glasgow*, 1698?] fol. EN.

169   Information, for the partners of the manufactory at Leith. [n.p., 1690?] fol.* Y.

169A   Information for Sir John Home of Blackader, against John Doull. [*Edinburgh*, 1692.] fol. EN.

169B   Information for the town of Edinburgh . . . imploying of their poor. [*Edinburgh*, 1700?] cap., fol.* CSS.

169C   Information for Whytefield Hayter and James Chiesly, merchants. [*Edinburgh*, 1695.] brs. EN.

170   An information of the present condition of affairs. *Edinbvrgh, by Evan Tyler*, 1648. 4°.* ALDIS 1333. L, OW, EN, ENC, AU, GM; CH, CLC, MH, NU, WF, Y.

171   God save King Charles. Ane information of the publick proceedings. [*Edinburgh? Tyler*, 1648.] cap., 4°.* ALDIS 1334. MR, D, EN, AU.

171A   Information relating to the mint. [*Edinburgh, by the heir of A. Anderson*, 1686.] fol. * ALDIS 2642. LUG, Y.

Informer: or, a treatise. [n.p.], 1641. *See* C., J.

172   The informers answer to the late character. *For T. C.*, 1675. 4°.* CPB, MH, Y.

Informer's doom. 1683. *See* Dunton, John.

173   The informers lecture to his sons. colop: *For Joseph Collier*, 1682. brs. L, O, LLP, HH, MC; CH, MH.

173A   —[Anr. ed.] *For L. Edwardson*, 1682. 8°. DU, EN.

174   The informers looking-glass. colop: *Printed and are to be sold by Joseph Collier*, 1682. brs. L, O, EN; CH, Y.

175   **Ingelo, Nathaniel.** Bentivolio and Urania. *By J. G. for Richard Marriot*, 1660. fol. L, C, OB, MAU, E, CD; CH, IU, MH, NC, Y. (var.)

176   [–]—Second edition. *For T. Dring, J. Starkey, and T. Basset*, 1669. fol. T.C.I 3. L, BR, DC, EC, MC; CH, CU, NC, WF, Y.

177   ——Third edition. *By T. R. for Richard Marriott, to be sold by Benj. Tooke and Tho. Sawbridge*, 1673. fol. T.C.I 137. L, O, CE, E, EN; BN, CLC, CN, IU, MH, MU, NCD, Y. (var.)

177A   ——"Third" edition. *By T. R. for Richard Marriott, and are to be sold by D. Newman, Benj. Tooke, and Tho. Sawbridge*, 1673. fol. CP; PL, TO.

178   ——Fourth edition. *By A. M. and R. R. for Dorman Newman*, 1682. fol. T.C.I 499. L, O, C, LLP, DT; CH, CLC, CN, IU, PU, WF.

179   ——The second part. *By J. Grismond for Richard Marriott*, 1664. fol. L, O, CT, LLU, MAU, CD; CH, IU, MH, NC, Y.

180   ——Third edition. *By T. R. for Richard Marriott*, 1673. fol. L, O, EN; BN, CLC, MIU, MU, PL, TO.

181 — — —Fourth edition. *By E. T. and R. H. for Dorman Newman*, 1682. fol. L, O, LLP, CCA, DT; CH, CLC, CN, MIU, WF.

182 —A discourse concerning repentance. *By T. R. for Richard Marriott, and sold by William Bromwich*, 1677. 8°. T.C.I 289. L, C, LCL, LW, LSD, CD; CLC, NP, NU, WF.

182A [–] —[Anr. ed.] *By T. R. for Richard Marriott and sold by George Marriott*, 1677. 8°. ORP, DU; PL.

183 —Omnia ad salutem. [*n.p.*, 1658.] brs. O.

184 —The perfection, authority. *By E. T. for Luke Fawn*, 1659. 8°. C, LCL, ESSEX, P.

185 — —Second edition. —, 1659. 8°. LT, O, C, LW, CE; CH, NC, NHC, NU.

186 —A sermon preached at St. Paul's . . . April 17, 1659. *For L. Fawn*, 1659. 8°. LT, LW, P; CH.

Ingenii fructus, or. [*n.p.*], 1700. *See* B., W.

Ingenious and diverting letters. 1692. *See* Aulnoy, Marie Catherine La Mothe, *comtesse*.

187 The ingenious braggadocia. [*London*], *for F. Coles, T. Vere, J. Wright, J. Clarke, W. Thackeray, & T. Passenger*, [1678–80]. brs. L, O, CM, HH; MH.

187A An ingenious contention. *Printed*, 1668. brs. L.

187B **Inglish, Isabella.** Advertisement. At the Hand and Pen . . . true Scots pills. [*London*, 1690?] brs. L.

187C **Inglish, James.** Grand angelica: or the true Scot's pills. [*London*], 1694. brs. L.

188 [**Ingoldsby, William.**] The doctrine of the church of England, established. [*London*], *for William Sheares*, 1642. 4°.* LT, O, LW, CD; CH, CN, MH, NU, WF, Y.

188A [–] Englands oaths. *Printed*, 1642. 4°.* LT, O, OC, CM, BC; CH, IU, MH, NU, WF, Y.

188B Inhuman & cruel bloody news from Leeds. [*London*], *for F. Coles, T. Vere, J. Wright, and J. Clarke*, [1674–79]. brs. O.

Inhumane cardinal. 1696. *See* Pix, Mary.

189 Inimicus patriæ, or a new satyr. colop: *For Joseph Roberts*, 1683. brs. L, MC; CLC, MH.

190 The iniqvity of the late solemne league, or covenant discovered. [*Oxford, by L. Lichfield*], *printed, March 9*, 1643[4]. 4°.* MADAN 1556–6n. LT, O, C, EN, DT; CH, MH, NU, WF, Y.

Injur'd prince vindicated. [*n.p.*, 1688.] *See* James, Elinor.

191 The inn-keeper's complaint. [*London*], *for J. Blare*, [1682–90]. brs. L, HH; MH.

192 **Innes, George.** A militarie rudiment. *Aberdene, by Edward Raban*, 1644. 4°.* ALDIS 1142. EN.

192A **Innes, Sir Harry.** To his grace his majesties high commissioner and the . . . estates. [*Edinburgh?* 1700]. fol. O.

193 [**Innes, James.**] An examination of a printed pamphlet; entituled A narration of the siege. *For Thomas VValkley*, 1465 [i.e. 1645]. 4°.* LT, O, DT; CN, CSS, MH.

193A Innocense clear'd: or a short defence of Mr. [David] Jones's farewel-sermon. *For R. Smith*, 1692. 4°. SP.

194 Innocence unveil'd. [*London*, 1680.] brs. L, O, LG, HH, LLU; CH, CN, MH, TU, WF, Y.

Innocency acknowledg'd. Gavnt, 1645. *See* Ceriziers, René.

Innocency against envy. 1691. *See* Whitehead, George.

Innocency and conscientiousness. 1664. *See* Smith, William.

Innocency and trvth jvstified. [*n.p.*], 1645. *See* Lilburne, John.

Innocency and truth triumphing. 1645. *See* Goodwin, John.

Innocency and truth vindicated. [*n.p.*], 1689. *See* V., P.

195 The innocency asserted. *Printed*, 1664. 4°. CT.

Innocency cleared from lyes. 1658. *See* Boweter, John.

196 Innocency cleared: or the case and vindication of Col. George Gill. [*London*], *printed 10 September*, 1651. 4°.* L, YM; CH, Y.

Innocency cleared; the liberties. [*n.p.*, 1660.] *See* Mason, Martin.

Innocency cleared, true worth. 1645. *See* S., B.

Innocency of the Christian Quakers. [*n.p.*], 1688. *See* Burnyeat, John.

Innocency of the righteous. [*n.p.*, 1655.] *See* Hubberthorne, Richard.

Innocency, though under a cloud. 1664. *See* Hobson, Paul.

Innocency triumphant. 1693. *See* Whitehead, George.

Innocency vindicated. [*n.p.*, 1684.] *See* Bugg, Francis.

197 Innocency vindicated; or, reproach wip'd off. colop: *By J. Darby*, 1689. brs. O, EN; CH.

Innocency with her open face. [*n.p.*], 1669. *See* Penn, William.

198 **Innocent XI, pope.** The Pope's advice to the French King. [*London*, 1688.] brs. L, C, OC; CH, Y.

198A —The Pope's curse. colop: *Printed at Amsterdam*. 1688. *For Jeremiah Lovechurch*. fol.* CB, NU.

199 —A decree made at Rome, second of March, 1679. *For Ric. Chiswell*, 1679. 4°.* T.C.I 351. L, O, CT, EN, DT; CH, IU, NU, PL, WF, Y.

200 —Decrees. *Oxford, by Leonard Lichfield*, 1678. 8°. T.C.I 332; MADAN 3180. O; IU.

201 — —[Anr. ed.] *Oxford, by Leonard Lichfield for Ric. Davis*, 1679. 8°. MADAN 3212. L, O, C, CT, CD; CH, WF, WSL, Y.

201A Entry cancelled.

[–] Letter from His Holiness the Pope. 1682. *See* title.

202 —A letter from the pope to the French King. [*n.p.*, 1680.] cap., fol.* L, LG, OC, LNC, MR; CH, CLC, IU, MBA, PU.

203 —The pope's third breve. *For James Vade*, 1681. 4°.* T.C.I 441. L, O, LW, OC, DU, SP; CH, LC, MIU, VC.

204 —The popes threatning letter to the French king. *For Henry Brome*, 1681. fol.* T.C.I 420. L, O, OB, OC, MR; CH, CN, PU, WF, Y.

204A **Innocent XII, *pope*.** A letter from. [*London*, 1691.] 4°.* O, CT.

204B — —[Anr. ed.] colop: *Dublin, reprinted by Andrew Crook*, [1691?]. cap., fol.* CLC.

204C —The Pope's bull, against the Archbishop of Cambray's book. [*London*, 1700.] cap., 4°.* EN; CLC.

Innocent assemblies. [*n.p.*], 1669. *See* R., J.

205 The innocent cause of the people called Quakers. [*London*, 1676/7.] brs. LF.

Innocent cleared. 1648. *See* Smith, John.

206 The innocent country-maids delight. [*London*], *for P. Brooksby*, [1685?]. brs. L, O, HH; MH, WCL.

207 The innocent countrey-man's reflections. *Edinburgh, by the heir of Andrew Anderson*, 1690. fol. ALDIS 3048. E, EN; CH, WF.

Innocent epicure. 1697. *See* Tate, Nahum.

207A The innocent in prison complayning. [*London*], *printed*, 1646. 4°.* CT; Y.

208 Innocent love in triumph. [*London*], *for P. Brooksby*, [1672–80]. brs. L, O, HH; MH.

209 The innocent shepherd. [*London*], *for C. Dennisson*, [1685–88]. brs. L, HH; MH.

The innocent usurper. 1694. *See* Banks, John.

Innocents no saints. 1658. *See* Dodd, Edward.

209A Entry cancelled.

Innocui sales. A collection. 1694. *See* Killigrew, Henry.

Innovations of popery. 1689. *See* Tomlinson, William.

209B Inquest after blood. Being a relation. *Printed*, 1670. 4°.* LSD; CH, MHL.

209C Enquiries for a parochial visitation. *T. James*, 1685. 4°.* L, LLP.

Inquiries into the causes. [n.p.], 1644. *See* Woodward, Hezekiah.

Inquiries into the general catalogue of diseases. [n.p., 1691.] *See* Maynwaring. Everard.

Enquiries to be propounded. [n.p., 1679.] *See* Plot, Robert.

209D An enquiry after further satisfaction. *For G. T.*, 1649. 4°.* LT, O, C, MR, SP; NHC.

Enquiry after happiness. 1685. *See* Lucas, Richard.

210 An enquiry after plain-dealing. *By J. H. for the author*, 1689. 4°.* L; MH, Y.

211 An enquiry after religion. *For Richard Baldwin*, 1691. 4°.* L, LG, DU, E, CD; CH, NU, TU, WF, Y.

Enquiry after truth. [n.p., 1671.] *See* Penington, Isaac.

Inquiry concerning virtue. 1699. *See* Shaftesbury, Anthony Ashley Cooper, *earl of.*

Enquiry into, and detection. [n.p., 1684.] *See* Ferguson, Robert.

212 An inquiry into the advantages & losses of England, in the French war. *Richard Baldwin*, 1693. 4°.* O.

213 An enquiry into the causes of the miscarriage of the Scots colony at Darien. *Glasgow*. 1700. 8°. ALDIS 3963. L, O, C, MR, EN; CH, CN, MU, NN, TU, WF, Y.

214 Entry cancelled. Ghost.

215 Entry cancelled.

Enquiry into the causes. 1692. *See* Delamere, Henry Booth, *earl of.* Impartial enquiry.

Enquiry into the constitution. 1691. *See* King, Peter, *baron.*

Inquiry into the design. 1681. *See* B., N.

215A An inquiry into the divine right of presbytery. [n.p., 1660?] 4°.* EN.

216 Enquiry into the grounds of a late pamphlet intituled, The mystery. [n.p.], 1676. 4°. LG (lost).

Enquiry into the measures. [n.p., 1688.] *See* Burnet, Gilbert, *bp.*

217 An enquiry into the ministry of Presbyterians. Second edition. *For B. Tooke*, 1678. 12°. T.C.I 335. L, O, C, OC, ORP, SHR.

218 An enquiry into the nature and obligation of legal rights. *By Thomas Hodgkin*, 1693. 4°. T.C.II 466. L, O, CT, AU, CD; CH, CSU, IU, MH, NU, WF.

219 —Second edition. *By R. Roberts*, 1696. 4°. L, CS, EC, LIU, AU; CLC, MH, NC, NP, WF, Y.

Enquiry into the nature, necessity. 1696. *See* Cockburn, John.

Enquiry into the new opinions. 1696. *See* Monro, Alexander.

Enquiry into the occasional conformity. 1697. *See* Defoe, Daniel.

Enquiry into the present state. 1689. *See* Burnet, Gilbert, *bp.*

Enquiry into the reasons. [1688.] *See* Burnet, Gilbert, *bp.*

Inquiry into the remarkable. [n.p., 1690.] *See* Brady, Robert.

219A An enquiry into the vision. 1692. 4°.* LW, GU.

220 An enquiry; or, a discourse between a yeoman of Kent. [*London*, 1693.] cap., 4°.* L, O, CT, LSD, DT; CH, IU, MH, TU, WF, Y.

221 An enquiry, whether it be the interest of the city to insure houses from fire. [*London*, 1680?] cap., fol.* L; LC, MH, NC, Y.

222 An enquiry, whether oral tradition. *For Robert Clavell*, 1684. 8°. T.C.II 92. OCC.

222A —[Anr ed.] —, 1685. 8°. CS, BANGOR, NE, SP; CLC, NU.

Inquisitio Anglicana. 1654. *See* Sadler, Anthony.

222B Inquisitio Anglicana: or, some honest and well intended qvaeres. [*London?* 1654?] cap., 4°. CSS, MH.

223 Inquisitio in naturam. *Impensis R. Cumberland*, 1694. 12°. T.C.II 511 L, O, CT, RPL; WF.

Inquisition after blood. [n.p.], 1649. *See* Howell, James.

223A Inqusition for the blood of our late soveraign. *Printed*, 1660. 8°. L, CPE.

Inquisition of a sermon. Waterford, 1644. *See* C., P.

Inrichment. *See* Enrichment.

224 An inscription intended to be set up for the E—l of R—r. [*London*], *printed*, [1700?]. 4°.* CH, CLC, Y.

In-securitie of princes. [n.p.], 1648. *See* Somner, William.

225 Insigma civicas, or the anti-Royalists, described. colop: *Oxford, by Leonard Lichfield*, 1643. cap., 4°.* MADAN 1477. LT.

225A Insignia præ lustris societatis Scoticanæ, . . . explicata. [*Edinburgh?* 1696.] brs. ALDIS 3571.5. O; MH.

Insinuating bawd. [1699.] *See* Ward, Edward.

226 Insolence and impudence triumphant. [*London*], *printed*, 1669. 4°.* L, O, CT, DU, WCA; CN, NU, PL, WF, Y.

227 The insolency and cruelty of the Cavaliers. *For Robert Wood*, 1643. 4°.* LT, LNC, RU; MH.

228 The instability of the Quakers. *For A. Baldwin*, 1700. brs. O.

229 Entry cancelled.

Installation of Prince George. 1684. *See* King, Gregory. Order of the installation.

230 An instance of Queen Elizabeth's power. *By Henry Hills,* 1687. brs. L, O, C, LG, OC, BSM, EN; MH, Y.

231 An instance of the Church of England's loyalty. *By Henry Hills,* 1687. 4°.* L, O, MR, ENC, DT; CH, CN, MH, NU, WF, Y.

Instance of the repentance. 1690. *See* Pugh, Hugh.

232 Instances of some inconveniences. [*London,* 1680?] brs. L.

232A Institutae ab excellentissimo Comite Cubiliarcho. colop: *Impensis Sterhar: Bowtell,* 1652. 4°.* L.

Institutio, epithalamium. 1645. *See* Hatcher, R.

Institutio . . . Græcæ. 1643. *See* Camden, William.

Institutiones logicæ. Dublini, 1681. *See* Marsh, Narcissus, *abp.*

Institutiones pietatis. [n.p.], 1676. *See* Fox, George.

Institutions, essays. 1695. *See* Quarles, Francis.

233 The institvtions of mathematicall experiments. *For Andrew Crooke,* 1643. 8°. L, O; CH, WF, Y.

233A The institutions of the Congregation. *Printed at Oxford,* 1687. 4°. L, O, OC, OU, DU; Y.

Institutionum ethicarum. 1660. *See* White, Thomas.

234 An instrvction for all those that intend to goe to the . . . Lords Supper. *By Francis Leach,* 1646. brs. LT.

234A Instruction que l'on doit faire lire et apprendre . . . l'Englise Anglicane . . . en . . . Jersey. [*n.p.*], 1649. 12°. L.

Instruction to judges. [1658.] *See* Fox, George.

235 An instruction to performe with fruit the devotion of ten Fridays. [*St. Omers,* 1690.] 12°. L, O; CN, WF, WG.

236–237 Entries cancelled.

Instructions agreed on. 1643. *See* England: Parliament.

238 Berks. Instructions and articles to be duely observed. [*London,* 1658?] brs. L.

Instructions and devotions for the afflicted. [n.p.], 1697. *See* Gother, John.

239 Instructions and propositions drawne up. *For T. Bates, and G. Tomlinson,* 1643. 4°.* LT, LG, DT; CH, MH, NC, TU.

240 Entry cancelled.

Instructions and rules to be duly observed. [n.p.], 1663. *See* James II.

240A Instructions and rules to be observed by the muster-master general. *Dublin, by John Crook, and sold by Samuel Dancer,* 1667. 4°.* C, LPR.

240B Instructions for [blank] collector of . . . customs. [*London,* 1688.] brs. L, OP.

Instructions for a young nobleman. 1683. *See* Trotti de La Chétardie, J.T.

240C Instructions for all buyers and sellers of wares made of gold. *Company of goldsmiths,* [c. 1685]. brs. LG.

241 Entry cancelled.

Instructions for apprentices. 1699. *See* Gother, John.

Instructions for children. [n.p.], 1698. *See* Gother, John.

242–3 Entries cancelled.

Instructions for deputy lieutenants. 1642. *See* England: Parliament, House of Commons.

Instructions for forreine travell. 1642. *See* Howell, James.

Instructions for history. 1680. *See* Rapin, René.

244 Instructions for jury-men. *By T. Leach, for Tho. Johnson,* 1664. 8°. L, O, C, LG; LC, NCL, WF.

245 Entry cancelled.

Instructions for masters, traders. 1699. *See* Gother, John.

Instructions for particular states. [n.p.], 1689. *See* Gother, John.

Instructions for rent-gatherers. 1683. *See* Monteage, Stephen.

Instructions for right spelling. [n.p.], 1673. *See* Fox, George.

245A Instructions for such merchants. [*London,* 1693.] brs. LPR.

245B Instructions for the apprentices. [*London*], *by J. Flesher,* [1670]. brs. L.

245C Instructions for the apprentices in . . . London. [*London?* 1680.] brs. L, LG.

246 Instructions for the commissioners of the militia for the county of [blank]. [*London,* 1650.] brs. LT.

246A Instructions for the committee of sequestrations. [*London,* 1649?] brs. L; MH.

247 Instructions for the more due and regular payment of the quarters of the forces. *C. Bill and the executrix of T. Newcomb,* 1692. brs. C, MC.

248–8A Entries cancelled.

Instructions for the trustees. 1649. *See* England: Parliament.

Instructions for the whole year. [n.p.], 1695. *See* Gother, John.

Instructions for young gentlemen. 1650. *See* Gaetani, Enrico, *Cardinal.*

249 Entry cancelled.

Instructions for youth. 1698. *See* Gother, John.

250 Entry cancelled.

Instructions from the committee. [n.p., 1643.] *See* Scotland. Estates.

251 Instructions given by the commissioners and trustees for improving the fisheries. [*Edinburgh,* 1695.] brs. ALDIS 3466.7. NC.

252 Instrvctions given unto the commissioners. [*London*], *printed,* 1641. 4°.* LT, OC, BC, MR, BLH, DN; WF, Y.

253 Entry cancelled.

Instructions in the art of oratory. 1659. *See* Walker, Obadiah. Some instructions.

Instructions of godliness. [n.p.], 1676. *See* Fox, George.

254 Instructions, rules, & to be observed . . . in the armie. *Edw. Husbands,* [1645]. brs. O.

Instructions to a painter. 1665. *See* Waller, Edmund.

254A Instrvctions to be duly observed by the iudges. *Dvblen [sic], by William Bladen,* 1653. 4°.* DIX 92. DN.

255 Instructions to be held and observed by the surveyors. [*n.p.*], 1697. brs. MC.

255A Instructions to be observed by his Majestie's officers. 1670. 12°. CT.

255B —[Anr. ed.] *Printed,* 1672. 4°.* CLL, NC, WF.

255C Instructions to be observed by the severall collectors. [*London, 1 April,* 1651.] brs. LUG.

Instructions to be observed touching. 1655. *See* Cromwell, Oliver.

Instructor clericalis. 1693. *See* Gardiner, Robert.

256 The instrument; or, vvriting of association. [*London*], *printed*, 1679. fol.* O, CT, BR, LNC, MR; CH, CN, IU, MH, NU, WF, Y.

Instruments of a king. 1648. *See* Howell, James.

257 Instrumentum pacis. *Typis Guil. Du-gard, impensis Sam. Thomson*, 1648. 8°. LT, O, CD, DT; CH, MM.

Insulæ fortunatæ. A discourse. 1675. *See* Allen, Richard.

258 The integrity of the Parliaments army justified. *By Matthew Symmons*, 1647. 4°.* LT, DU, DT; CH, CU.

259 Intelligence from Oxford. *For Thomas Watson*, 1643. 4°.* MADAN 1573. O; MH.

260 Intelligence from Shropshire. *For Thomas Underhill, June 28.* 1645. 4°.* LT, AN; MH.

261 Intelligence from the armie. *For Samuel Gellibrand, June 8*, 1643. 4°.* MADAN 1371. LT, O; CH, MH, MU, NU, WF, Y.

262 No entry.

263 Intelligence from York: relating. [*London*], *August, 25. for H. Blunden*, 1642. 4°.* LT, YM; Y.

Intentions of the armie concerning. [*n.p.*], 1647. *See* Brown, *Sir* Richard, *major-general.*

Intentions of the army discovered. 1647. *See* C., W.

Intentions of the army plainely. [*n.p.*], 1647. *See* R., G.

264 Inter Robertum Williamson, quer' et Mr. Attorn' General, def^t. [*London*, 1699/1700.] brs. LU.

Intercourses of divine love. 1676. *See* Collinges, John.

Interest of creditors. 1673. *See* P., P.

264A The interest of England, as it respects . . . sugar-plantations. *B. Motte*, 1691. 12°.* L.

The interest of England as it stands. 1698. *See* Clement, Simon.

265 Entry cancelled.

Interest of England considered. 1694. *See* Blanch, John.

Interest of England, how it consists. 1642. *See* Constantine, William.

Interest of England in the matter. 1660. *See* Corbet, John.

Interest of England in the present. 1672. *See* Britaine, William de.

Interest of England in the preservation. 1689. *See* Philips, George.

Interest of England in the Protestant cause. 1659. *See* Dury, John.

266 The interest of England maintained. [*London*], *printed, June the 8.* 1646. 4°.* LT, LG, OC, A, DT; CH, LC, MH, NHC, WF.

Interest of England stated. [*n.p.*], 1659. *See* Fell, John, *bp.*

266A Interest of money mistaken. *Printed*, 1668. 4°.* L, O, CK, EN, DT; CH, MH, NC, WF, Y.

Interest of princes. 1680. *See* Bethel, Slingsby.

266B The interest of religion in England: or, a discourse. [*n.p.*, 1690?] cap., 4°.* MM.

Interest of Scotland. [*n.p.*, 1700.] *See* Seton, *Sir* William.

267 The interest of the Church of England. *For G. M.*, 1687. 4°.* O, OB, CS, DT; CLC, NU, WF, Y.

268 The interest of the English nation. *Printed and are to be sold by E. Whitlock*, 1696. 4°.* L, CT, LIU, MR; CH, MH, NP, NU, WF, Y.

269 The interest of the nation. *By B. Motte*, 1691. fol.* L, LUG; MH, MU, RPJ, Y.

270 The interest of the three kingdoms. *For James Vade*, 1680. 4°.* T.C.I 407. OC, DT; CH, LC, MH.

270A —[Anr. ed.] *Printed*, 1680. 4°.* L, O, BC, LSD, SP; CH, CLC, MH, MIU, WF.

270B —Second edition. *For James Vade*, 1680. 4°.* L, CT, DU, MR, SP; TO, Y.

271 The interest of the United Provinces. [*London*], 1653. 4°. LNC, DT.

Interest of these United Provinces. Middelburg, 1673. *See* Hill, Joseph.

Interests of the several princes. 1698. *See* Defoe, Daniel.

Interiour Christian. Antwerp, 1684. *See* Berniers Louvigny, Jean de.

Interpreter. [*n.p.*], 1641. *See* Scott, Thomas.

Interpreter. Oxford, 1643. *See* Scott, Thomas.

Interrogatories on the part and behalf. [*n.p.*, 1689.] *See* G., R.

272 Interrogatories: or, a dialogue between Whig and Tory. *For VV. Brown.* 1681. brs. L, O, MC; CH, MH, TU, WF, Y.

273 Entry cancelled.

Interrogatory, relating. [*n.p.*], 1652. *See* Hartlib, Samuel. Legacie. 1652.

274 Intimation by the town clerk of Edinburgh, . . . [20 Feb.]. [*Edinburgh, by the heir of Andrew Anderson*, 1689.] brs. STEELE 3p 2775; ALDIS 2882. L, EN, ES.

275 An intimation of the deputies of the States General. [*London*, 1680.] cap., fol.* L, O, C, E, DT; HR, CH, CN, MH, PL, TU, WF, Y, AVP.

276 Intolerable oppression. [*n.p.*, 1647.] cap., 4°.* CH, NU.

Intrigues of love. 1689. *See* Conti, Louise Marguerite, *princesse de.*

277 The intrigues of the conclave. *For J. C.*, 1690. 4°.* LIL, LSD; NU, TU, Y.

278 Entry cancelled.

Intrigues of the court of Rome. 1679. *See* Pageau, *abbé.*

279 The intreigues of the French king at Constantinople. *For Dorman Newman*, 1689. 4°.* T.C.II 292. L, O, C, MR, DT; CH, IU, PL, WF, Y.

280 Intrigues of the Popish plot. 1679. fol. EN.

Intrim, lord. See Antrim, Randal MacDonnell, *lord.*

Introductio ad chronologiam. Oxoniæ, 1691. *See* Holder, William.

281 No entry.

Introductio ad lectionem linguarum orientalium. 1655. *See* Walton, Brian, *bp.*

282 Introductio ad sapientiam: enchiridion. *Cantabrigiæ: ex officina Rogeri Danielis*, 1643. 16°. L, C, KEBLE, P, RPL; IU.

283 No entry.

Introduction to algebra. [*n.p.*], 1668. *See* Rahn, Johann Heinrich.

Introduction to astrology. 1661. *See* Phillips, John.

Introduction to the Christian faith. 1646. *See* Wigginton, Giles.

Introduction to the Greeke. 1650. *See* Reeve, Edmund.

Introduction to the holy. 1649. *See* Niclaes, Hendrik.

Introduction to the sacrament. 1682. *See* Addison, Lancelot.

Introduction to the skill. 1655. *See* Playford, John.

Invalidity of John Faldo's. [n.p.], 1673. *See* Penn, William.

Invaluable price. [n.p.], 1681. *See* Baxter, Richard.

284 An invective against the pride of vvomen. [*London*, 1657.] brs. LT.

Invention of engines. 1651. *See* Dymock, Cressy.

285 An inventory of the goods exposed. [*London*, 1664?] fol.* HH (dispersed).

286 The invincible pride of women. [*London*, 1670?] brs. L.

287 —[Anr. ed.] [*London*], *for P. Brooksby, J. Deacon, J. Blare, J. Back*, [1685–92]. brs. CM, HH; MH.

288 The invincible weapon. [*London*], *to be sold by Ro. Walton*, [1648]. brs. LT.

289 No entry.

Invisible John made visible. 1658. *See* Barkstead, John.

Invitation of a seeker. 1670. *See* S., I.

289A An invitation to a solemn day of humiliation. *For Livewell Chapman*, 1657. 4°.* NU.

290 An invitation to Lubberland. [*London*], *for J. Deacon*, [1685?]. brs. L, HH; WCL.

Invitation to Mr. John Garlick's. 1683. *See* Gibbs, Richard.

291 An invitation to the aforementioned society. *For the author*, 1659. 4°.* L, OC, BC; CDA, MH.

292 An invocation to the officers of the army. *Printed*, 1659. 4°.* LT, O, C, BC, SP, DT; CH, MH, MIU, NC, WF.

Inward and spiritual Christian. 1684. *See* Laythes, Thomas.

Inward and spiritual warfare. [n.p.], 1690. *See* Fox, George, *elder*.

293 Iö Carole: or an extract of a letter sent from Parnassus. [*London*], *printed*, 1661. 4°.* L, OB; MH, WF, Y.

Io ruminans: or. [n.p.], 1662. *See* Walden, Richard.

294 [**Ireland, Thomas?**] Momus elencticus or a light come-off. [*London*, 1654.] 4°.* MADAN 2246. L, O, LLU; CH.

295 [-] Speeches spoken to the King and Queen. [*By John Grismond*], *for Richard Royston*, 1663. 4°.* MADAN 2621. L, O, MR; CH, CLC, CN, PL, WF.

296 —Verses spoken at the appearance of the King and Queene. *Oxford, by H. Hall for R. Davis*, 1663. 4°.* MADAN 2622. L, O, OB, EC, LLU; CH, CN, MH, TU, WF, Y.

IRELAND

Note: Entries under the heading "Ireland" are based in large part on Robert Steele, *A Bibliography of Royal Proclamations of the Tudor and Stuart Sovereigns*, Volume II, part I (noted here as STEELE 2p). Official documents issued by groups are listed alphabetically by title, with the introductory phrase usually dropped. Official documents issued by an individual will be found under the individual's name (e.g. James II, Oliver Cromwell, Dublin mayors). Printed items in the Dublin Public Record Office were destroyed in the fire at the Four Courts during the Irish Civil war; where the Dublin Public Record Office held the single known copy, the entry and location have been retained with a note of its loss.

296A An abridgement of an act, for raising one hundred and twenty thousand pounds. *Dublin, by Andrew Crook*, 1699. fol.* L, DN; MHL.

296B An abstract of an act of Parliament made. colop: *Dublin, by Andrew Crook*, 1697. cap., fol.* DIX 293. DI, DN.

297 An account of the sessions of Parliament in Ireland, 1692. *For J. T.*, 1693. 4°.* L, O, MR, EN, DT; CH, CN, MH, WF, Y.

298 An act concerning fines in the County Palatine of Tipperary. *Dublin, by Andrew Crook*, 1695. fol.* DIX 279. L, BQ; CLC, INU, WF.

299 An act declaring which days. *Dublin, by Andrew Crook*, 1695. fol.* DIX 277. L, DN, DT; CLC, WF.

300 An act for avoiding of vexatious delays. *Dublin: by Andrew Crook*, 1697. fol.* DIX 296. L, BLH, BQ, DK, DT; CH, CLC, WF, Y.

301 An act for banishing all Papists. *Dublin, by Andrew Crook*, 1697. fol.* DIX 294. L, BLH, DK, DN, DT; CLC, PU, WF, Y, ZWT.

302 An act for continuing the statute. *Dublin, by Andrew Crook*, 1695. fol.* L, BQ; CLC, WF, Y.

302A An act for dividing the parish of Saint Michan's. *Dublin, by Andrew Crook*, 1697. fol.* DIX 297. DM, DN; Y.

303 An act for incouraging Protestant strangers. *Dublin, by John Crook, sold by Sam. Dancer*, 1662. fol.* DIX 116. O, C.

303A An act for granting a supply. *Dublin, by Andrew Crook*, 1695. fol. DIX 278. DK, DN.

304 —[Same title.] —, 1697. fol. DIX 295. L, BLH, BQ, DK, DT; CH, CLC, WF.

305 An act for granting an additional duty on tobacco. *Dublin: by Andrew Crook*, 1697. fol.* DIX 294. L, BLH, BQ, DK, DT; CH, CLC, WF.

306 An act for granting tales on tryals. *Dublin, by Andrew Crook*, 1695. fol.* DIX 279. L, BQ, DT; CLC, WF.

307 An act for granting unto His Majesty. *Dublin, by Andrew Crook*, 1695. fol.* DIX 278. L, DN, DT; CLC, WF.

307A An act for making the collectors receipts. *Dublin, by Andrew Clark*, 1697. fol.* DIX 295. L, BLH, BQ, DK, DT; CH, CLC, IU, WF, Y.

308 An act for prevention of frauds. *Dublin, by Andrew Crook*, 1695. fol.* L, BQ, DN; CLC, WF, Y.

308A An act for reforming abuses in making of butter-cask. *Dublin: by Andrew Crook*, 1699. fol.* DN; Y.

308B An act for settling the subsidie of povndage. *Dublin, by William Bladen*, 1662. fol. HOUSE OF LORDS, LUG; MH, MHL.

308C —[Same title.] *Dublin, by Benjamin Tooke, for Samuel Dancer*, 1669. 8°.* C; WF, Y.

308D —[Same title.] *Dublin, by Benjamin Took and John Crook, to be sold by Mary Crook and Andrew Crook*, 1682. 12°.* DIX 194. DI, DM, DML, DN.

308E An act for taking away the Court of wards. *By John Crook, and sold by Samuel Dancer*, 1662. 4°.* LPR.

309 An act for taking special bails. *Dublin, by Andrew Crook*, 1695. fol.* DIX 279. L, DN, DT; CLC, WF, Y.

309A An act for the better execution. *Dublin, by Iohn Crook,* 1662. fol. DIX 115. L, O, C, DK, DN; NN, TU, WF.

310 An act for the better observation of the Lords-Day. *Dublin, by Andrew Crook,* 1695. fol.* DIX 278. L, BQ, DN; CLC, WF, Y.

311 An act for the better regulating of measures. *Dublin, by Andrew Crook,* 1695. fol.* DIX 280. L, BQ, DN, DT; CH, CLC, WF, Y.

312 An act for the better securing the government. *Dublin, by Andrew Crook,* 1695. fol.* L, BQ, DN; CH, CLC, MB, WF, Y.

313 An act for the better settleing. *Dublin, by Andrew Crook,* 1695. fol.* L, BQ; MB, Y.

314 An act for the better suppressing Tories. *Dublin, by Andrew Crook,* 1695. fol.* DIX 279. L, BQ, DT; CLC, WF, Y.

315 An act for the confirmation of articles. *Dublin: by Andrew Crook,* 1697. fol.* DIX 294. L, BLH, BQ, DK, DN; CH, CLC, IU, MB, WF, Y.

316 An act for the continuance of the customs. *Dublin, J. Crook,* 1661. brs. STEELE 2p 673. DPR (lost).

316A An act for the inlargement. *Dublin, by John Crook, sold by Sam Dancer,* 1662. fol.* C, LUG.

316B An act for the explaining. *Dublin, by John Crook, to be sold by Samuel Dancer,* 1665. fol. DIX 127. L, O, C, DM, DT; TU, WF.

317 An act for the more easy, and speedy securing. *Dublin: by Andrew Crook,* 1697. fol.* DIX 296. L, LUG, BLH, DK, DT; CH, CLC, IU, WF, Y.

318 An act for the more easy discharging. *Dublin, by Andrew Crook,* 1695. fol.* L, BQ, DN; CLC, WF, Y.

319 An act for the more effectual suppressing. *Dublin, by Andrew Crook,* 1695. fol.* L, BQ, DN; CLC, CN, WF, Y.

320 An act for the more speedy and effectual proceeding. *Dublin, by Andrew Crook,* 1695. fol.* DIX 280. L, DT; CLC, WF, Y.

320A An act for the preservation of the game. *Dublin, by Andrew Crook,* 1699. fol.* DN.

321 An act for the preventing frivolous, . . . law-sutes. *Dublin: by Andrew Crook,* 1697. fol.* DIX 296. L, BLH, BQ, DK, DT; CH, CLC, IU, WF, Y.

322 An act for the prevention of vexations. *Dublin, by Andrew Crook,* 1695. fol.* DIX 281. L, BQ, DN, DT; CLC, WF, Y.

322aA An act for the raising the summ. *Dublin, by Andrew Crook,* 1699. fol.* MB.

322A An act for the relief and release of poor distressed prisoners. *Dublin; by Andrew Crook,* 1699. fol.* DN; WF, Y.

322B An act for the settling of the excize. *Dvblin, by John Crook, and are to be sold by Sam Dancer,* 1662. fol. HOUSE OF LORDS, LUG; MH, MHL.

322C —[Anr. ed.] *Dublin, by Benjamin Tooke and are to be sold by Samuel Dancer,* [1669]. 8°. Y.

322D An act of assesment. *Dublin, by William Bladen,* 1659. fol.* DIX 105. DM.

322E An act of recognition of the . . . rights of His Majesties imperial crown. [*Dublin?* 1689?] fol. L.

323 An act of state, made by the Lords Justices. *Printed at Dublin, by William Bladen, reprinted at London for Edward Husbands.* Novemb. 23, 1642. 4°.* LT, C, LL, EC, LNC, SP, BLH; TU, WF.

324 An act to hinder the reversal. *Dublin: by Andrew Crook,* 1697. fol.* DIX 295. L, BLH, BQ, DK, DT; CH, CLC, IU, MB, WF, Y.

325 An act to prevent frauds. *Dublin: by Andrew Crook,* 1697. fol.* DIX 296. L, BLH, BQ, DK, DT; CH, CLC, IU, WF, Y.

326 An act to prevent Protestants inter-marrying with Papists. *Dublin: by Andrew Crook,* 1697. fol.* DIX 294. L, BLH, BQ, DK, DT; CH, CLC, IU, MB, WF, Y.

327 An act to restrain foreign education. *Dublin, by Andrew Crook,* 1695. fol.* L; MB.

328 An act to supply the defects. *Dublin: by Andrew Crook,* 1697. fol.* DIX 295. L, BLH, BQ, DK, DT; CH, CLC, IU, WF, Y.

329 Acts and statutes made in a Parliament. *Dublin, by Andrew Crook, assignee of Benjamin Tooke,* 1692. fol.* DIX 248. L, BLH, BQ, DN, DT; CH, CLC, NCL, WF, Y.

329aA —[Anr. ed.] *Dublin, by Andrew Crook,* 1695. fol. DIX 275. BLH, DK; CH, IU, MHL, WF.

329A —[Anr. ed.] —, 1697. fol.* DIX 293. BQ, DN, DT; CH, CLC, WF, WU, Y.

329B —[Anr. ed.] —, 1698. fol.* DIX 307. L, C, DN, DT; IU, Y.

330 —[Anr. ed.] —, 1699. fol. DIX 313. L, C, BLH, DT; NR.

331 An addition to the late proclamation . . . 7 February 1644[5]. *Dublin, W. Bladen,* 1644[5]. brs. STEELE 2p 413. DPR (lost).

332 All persons that shall have occasion . . . 29 August 1662. *Dublin, by John Crook, sold by Samuel Dancer,* 1662. brs. STEELE 2p 685. O, LPR.

333 Although by proclamation . . . 15 January 1641[2]. *Dublin,* 1641[2]. brs. STEELE 2p 363. DPR (lost).

334 Although wee find our selves much afflicted . . . 28 July 1648. *Kilkenny,* 1648. brs. STEELE 2p 447. O.

335 As by proclamation bearing . . . 19 August 1665. *Dublin, J. Crook,* 1665. brs. STEELE 2p 746. DPR (lost).

336 As by proclamation dated . . . 7 June 1667. *Dublin, J. Crooke,* 1667. brs. STEELE 2p 784. LPR.

336A An assessment for Ireland for six months. *Dublin, by William Bladen,* 1657. fol.* DIX 100. DM, DN.

336B —[Same title.] —, 1658[9]. fol.* DIX 101. DM.

336C An assessment for Ireland, for three months. *Dublin, by William Bladen,* 1654. fol.* DIX 95. L, LUG, DM.

Assessment upon the precinct. Dublin, 1652. *See title.*

337 At a General Court Martial held at the Inns in Dublin. Whereas information . . . 14 August 1689. *Dublin, Crook & Helsham,* [1689]. brs. STEELE 2p 1053. L, HH.

337aA At the Parliament begun and holden at Dublin, the eight [sic] day of May. *Dublin, by Benjamin Tooke, to be sold by Samuel Dancer,* 1669. fol. DIX 137. L, DI, DN.

337bA At the Parliament begun and holden at Dublin, the sixteenth day of March. *Dublin, by Benjamin Tooke, to be sold by Samuel Dancer,* 1669. fol. DIX 137. L, LUG, DI, DN.

337cA At the Parliament begun at Dublin the seventh day of May. *Dublin, by Andrew Crook and Samuel Halsham,* 1689. fol. L.

337dA By his Highness the Lord Protector's Council . . . The Council duly acknowledging . . . [26 September 1656]. *Dublin, by William Bladen,* 1656. brs. DN.

337A By His Highness the Lord Protector's council . . . A declaration and commission for the assessment. [*Dublin?* 1656.] fol.* MH.

338 By His Majesties commissioners appointed for executing the act of settlement . . . 25 June. colop: *Dublin, J. Crook,* 1666. brs. STEELE 2p 762. DPR (lost).

339 By His Majesties commissioners, appointed for putting in execution. *Dublin, J. Crook,* 1662. fol.* STEELE 2p 690. O, LS, DK.

339A By His Majesties commissioners, for executing the act of settlement . . . 26 of November, 1667. [*Dublin,* 1667.] cap., fol.* DI.

340 By the commissinors [*sic*] apointed for hearing and determining . . . 30 June. *Dublin, B. Tooke,* 1676. brs. STEELE 2p 868. LS.

341 By the commissioners for the settling and securing . . . Ulster. *Dublin, by William Bladen,* 1653. brs. DIX 92. L.

341A By the commissioners. It is ordered . . . 27 March 1654. *Dublin, by VVilliam Bladen,* 1654. brs. PL.

341B —The said commissioners . . . May the eighth, 1654. —, 1654. brs. PL.

341C —Whereas by a declaration . . . 6 May 1653. —, 1653. brs. PL.

341D —Whereas many persons . . . 14 July 1652. —, 1652. brs. STEELE 2p 499. PL.

341E —Whereas several murthers . . . 23 January 1653[4]. —, 1653[4]. brs. PL.

341F —Whereas several persons . . . 24 August 1653. —, 1653. brs. STEELE 2p 524. PL.

341G —Whereas the said commissioners . . . 28 Iuly 1653. —, 1653. brs. PL.

341H —VVhereas the said commissioners . . . [21 October 1653]. *Dublin, by William Bladen,* 1653. brs. DN.

341I —Whereas the said commissioners . . . 12 May 1654. —, 1654. brs. PL.

341J —Whereas there have been . . . 5 November 1652. —, 1652. brs. STEELE 2p 502. PL.

341K By the covncil . . . sixteenth day of December. *Dublin, by VVilliam Bladen,* 1653[4]. brs. PL.

342 By the councell and congregation. Whereas such of the Roman . . . 28 September 1646. *Kilkenny,* 1646. brs. STEELE 2p 440. O.

342A By the Deputy Lieutenants and commissioners of array of the city of Dublin. Whereas by his Majesties special command . . . [raising militia, 30 July 1689]. [*Dublin,* 1689.] brs. DN.

343 By the General Assembly of the confederate Catholicks. Whereas severall declarations . . . 4 July. *Waterford* 1645. *reprinted Kilkenny,* 1646. brs. STEELE 2p 425. O, LPR.

343A By the General Assembly . . . of Ireland mett at the cittie of Kilkenny. *Printed at Kilkenny,* 1646[7]. 4°.* CH.

343B By the Generall Assemblie of the Confederate Catholickes of Ireland. An establishment for the Courte of General Indicature. [*Kilkenny?* 1647.] 4°.* C.

344 By the honourable the Commissioners, appointed to hear . . . 19 September 1697. *Dublin, A. Crook,* 1697. brs. STEELE 2p 1344. HH.

344A By the Lord Deputy and Council . . . nineteenth day of April, 1655. *Dublin, by VVilliam Bladen,* 1655. brs. PL.

344B —the twenty-third day of May. —, 1655. brs. PL.

345–8 Entries cancelled.
By the Lords, Justices, and Councell. Dublin, [1641]. *See* —Whereas a petition hath.
By the Lords Iustices and Councell. [n.p., 1642]. *See* —Whereas many malignant.
By the Lords Iustices and Councell. Dublin, 1643. *See* —We having taken into our.
By the Lord Iustices and Council. Dublin, 1661. *See* —Whereas the Duke of Albemarle.

349 By the Lords Justices general, . . . for the better preserving good order . . . 30 September 1700. *Dublin, A. Crook,* 1700. fol.* STEELE 2p 1424–5. HH.

350 By the Lords Justices general, . . . whereas in and by . . . 26 January 1699. *Dublin, A. Crook,* 1699 [1700]. fol.* STEELE 2p 1413–4. HH.

350A By the Lords-Justices of Ireland. To our trusty . . . [form for appointments]. [*Dublin,* 1690.] brs. DT.

351 Entry cancelled.
By the Lords-Justices of Ireland. Dublin, [1691]. *See* —A proclamation . . . 21 February.

352 By the right honorable the Commissioners . . . 16 July 1690. *Dublin, by Andrew Crook, assignee of Benjamin Tooke,* [1690]. brs. STEELE 2p 1131. DN.

353 By the right honorable the Commissioners . . . 19 July 1690. *Dublin, by Andrew Crook assignee of Benjamin Took,* [1690]. brs. STEELE 2p 1132. DIX 241. L.

353A By the supreame councell of the confederate Catholicks. The deepe sense which we have of the sadd conditions . . . [3 June]. *Kilkenny,* 1648. brs. STEELE 2p 445. O.

354 —Forasmuch as after a long and serious debate . . . [21 September]. *Waterford, Thomas Bourke,* 1643. brs. STEELE 2p 390. O.

355 —Wee the supreame councell . . . [27 May]. *Kilkenny,* 1648. brs. STEELE 2p 444. O.

355A A collection of all the several acts. *Dublin, at His Majesties printing house,* 1684. 12°. DIX 206. L.

356 A collection of all the statutes now in use. *Dvblin, by Benjamin Tooke,* 1678. fol. DIX 163. L, LL, LMT, CCA, DT; CH, CN, MHL, WF, WG, Y.

356A —[Anr. ed.] *Dublin, by Benjamin Took, to be sold by Samuel Helsham, William Norman, Patrick Campbell and William Weston,* 1678. fol. DIX 163. LC.

357 Entry cancelled.
—[Anr. ed.] Dublin, 1684. *See* —Collection of all the several acts.

358 Complaint having been . . . 26 April 1677. *Dublin, B. Tooke,* 1677. cap., fol.* STEELE 2p 877. LS.

359 The copy of a letter written by direction of the Lords . . . 18 April 1644. [*Dublin,* 1644.] brs. STEELE 2p 395. DIX 78. DPR (lost).

360 A declaration . . . 18 July 1687. *Dublin, by Andrew Crook & Samuel Helsham, the assigns of Benjamin Tooke, sold by Andrew Crook, and Samuel Helsham, 1687.* brs. STEELE 2p 981. L, HH, DK, DN.

361 —1 June 1688. —, 1688. brs. STEELE 2p 990. L, HH, DK, DN.

362 —25 September 1688. —, 1688. brs. STEELE 2p 998. L, HH, DK. DN.

363 —29 December 1688. —, 1688. fol. * STEELE 2p 1008. L, HH, DK, DN.

364 —2 February 1688/9. —, 1688[9]. brs. STEELE 2p 1010–1. L, HH, DK, DN, DT.

365 —25 February 1688[9]. —, 1688[9]. brs. STEELE 2p 1017. L, HH, DK, DN.

366 —1 March 1688/9. —, 1688[9]. brs. STEELE 2p 1018–9. L, HH, DK, DN.

367 —20 January 1691[2]. *Dublin, A. Crook, 1691[2].* brs. STEELE 2p 1249. HH.

367A A declaration and commission for the assesment. *Dublin, by William Bladen, 1656.* fol.* DIX 99. L, DM; CLC, MH.

367B A declaration and commission for three months assesment . . . 12th of April. *Dublin, by W. Bladen, 1655.* fol.* CLC.

368 —27 June 1655. —, 1655. brs. STEELE 2p 561. DIX 96. L.

369 —6 September 1655. —, 1655. fol.* STEELE 2p 570. DIX 97. L, DM; CLC.

370 A declaration by the Major-General and Council . . . [9 January 1659/60]. *Dublin, by William Bladen, and re-printed at London, by James Cottrel, 1659.* brs. STEELE 2p 608. LT, O, LG; MH.

371 A declaration concerning the incamping of the horse . . . 28 August. *Dublin. By Andrew Crook & Samuel Helsham, assigns of Benjamin Tooke, 1688.* brs. STEELE 2p 994. L, HH, DK, DN.

372 A declaration concerning the fines to be imposed . . . 11 May. *Dublin, by W. Bladen, 1655.* brs. STEELE 2p 555. L.

373 A declaration concerning the pay, . . . 29 April 1687. *Dublin. By Andrew Crook & Samuel Helsham, assigns of Benjamin Tooke, sold by Andrew Crook, and Samuel Helsham, 1687.* fol.* STEELE 2p 978–9. L, HH, DK, DN.

374 —19 September 1692. *Dublin, A. Crook, 1692.* fol.* STEELE 2p 1267. HH.

375 A declaration directing the officers . . . 12 March. *Dublin, by W. Bladen, 1654[5].* brs. STEELE 2p 549. DIX 94. L.

376 A declaration for making sale of the corn . . . 7 March. *Dublin, by William Bladen, 1654[5].* brs. STEELE 2p 548. DIX 94. L; PL.

376A A a [*sic*] declaration for the destroying of wolves . . . 29 June 1653. *Dublin, by William Bladen, 1653.* brs. STEELE 2p 518. PL.

377 A declaration for the good government . . . 20 July 1688. *Dublin. By Andrew Crook & Samuel Helsham, assigns of Benjamin Tooke, 1688.* fol. * STEELE 2p 992. DIX 231. L, HH, DK, DN.

378 —24 August 1688. —, 1688. fol.* STEELE 2p 993. L, HH, DK, DN.

378A A declaration for the payment of custom. *Dublin, by William Bladen, 1654.* fol.* DIX 95. DM.

379 A declaration of the General Convention of Ireland, . . . 1 May 1660. *Imprinted at Dublin, by William Bladen, 1660.* brs. STEELE 2p 613. DIX 355. O, C.

380 —[Anr. ed.] *Imprinted at Dublin by W. Bladen, and re-printed at London by John Macock, 1660.* brs. STEELE 2p 614. L, HH; MH.

380A —[Anr. ed.] *Printed at Dublyn, and re-printed at London, for Nath. Brooke, 1660.* brs. LG.

380B —[Same title, 12 March, 1659/60.] *Dublin, by William Bladen, 1659.* brs. DN.

381 —[Anr. ed., 12 March 1659/60.] *For Henry Crips, 1660.* 4°.* L, O; MH, MIU, MU, Y.

382 —28 May 1660. *Dublin, by W. Bladen, 1660.* brs. STEELE 2p 618. C.

382A A declaration of the Lord Deputy . . . 9 July 1655. *Dublin, by Will. Bladen, 1655.* fol.* DIX 96. STEELE 2p 562. L, DM.

382B A declaration of the Lord Deputy and Council, for setting apart . . . a day of . . . fasting. *Dublin, by Wil. Bladen, 1658.* fol. L.

383 A declaration of the Lords and Commons concerning ecclesiastical government. *Imprinted at Dublin, by William Bladen, 1661.* brs. STEELE 2p 644. DIX 113. LPR, LS, DI, DN.

384 The declaration of the Lords . . . and Commons . . . concerning His Majesties intended match. *Dublin, by W. Bladen, 1661.* brs. STEELE 2p 646. DPR (lost).

385 —concerning the continuance of the customs . . . [31 July 1661]. *Dublin, John Crook, sold by John North, 1661.* brs. STEELE 2p 650. DPR (lost).

386 —concerning the continuance . . . 7 December 1661. *Dublin, J. Crook, [1661].* brs. STEELE 2p 665. DPR (lost).

387 —concerning the continuance . . . [22 March 1661/2]. *Dublin, J. Crook, 1661[2].* brs. STEELE 2p 675. DPR (lost).

388 —concerning the continuance . . . [21 June]. —, 1662. brs. STEELE 2p 678. DPR (lost).

389 —for the speedy raising of moneys . . . [31 July]. *Dublin, John Crook, 1661.* brs. STEELE 2p 651. DPR (lost).

389A A declaration set forth . . . for vindicating the honour and justice of His Majesties government. *Dublin, by VVilliam Bladen, 1645.* 4°.* CD.

390 A declaration, that all Irish Papists . . . [18 May]. *Dublin, by W. Bladen, 1655.* brs. STEELE 2p 556. L.

391 A declaration, that all persons holding custodiums . . . [21 May]. *Dublin, by W. Bladen, 1655.* brs. STEELE 2p 557. L.

392 A declaration, that no transplanted person . . . [3 April]. *Dublin, by W. Bladen, 1655.* brs. STEELE 2p 551. L.

393 Entry cancelled.
     Deepe sense . . . 3 June. Kilkenny, 1648. *See* By the su-preame councell of the confederate Catholicks.

393A The ensuing declaration of the Lord Nuncio. *Kilkenny, 1648.* brs. STEELE 2p 450. O.
     Exact abridgement of all the publick printed Irish statutes. Dublin, 1700. *See* Meriton, George.

394 Entry cancelled.
     Forasmuch as after a long and serious debate. Waterford, 1643. *See* —By the supreame councell of the con-federate Catholicks.

395   Forasmuch as Almighty God . . . 30 April 1642. *Imprinted at Dublin*, 1642. brs. STEELE 2p 368. DIX 76. DN.

396   Forasmuch as for His Majesties service . . . 22 May 1663. *Dublin, by John Crooke*, 1663. brs. STEELE 2p 703. O, LS, DN.

397   Forasmuch as the infection . . . 28 July 1665. *Dublin, J. Crook*, 1665. cap., fol.* STEELE 2p 744. DPR (lost).

398   Forasmuch as the upholding . . . 7 February 1644[5]. *Dublin, by W. Bladen*, 1644[5]. brs. STEELE 2p 414. DPR (lost).

399   Forasmuch as we judge it fit . . . 24 March 1672. *Dublin, B. Tooke*, 1672. brs. STEELE 2p 839. LS.

400   —27 October 1673. —, 1673. brs. STEELE 2p 843. LPR.

401   Forasmuch as we the Lords . . . 12 March 1660. *Dublin, W. Bladen*, 1660. brs. STEELE 2p 635. DPR (lost).

402   For speciall reasons of state . . . 3 December 1644. *Dublin, by W. Bladen*, 1644. brs. STEELE 2p 407. DPR (lost).

403   —5 January 1666. *Dublin, by John Crook, sold by Samuel Dancer*, 1666[7]. brs. STEELE 2p 775. O, LPR, DN.

404   For stating the accounts of the army . . . 17 February 1690[1]. *Dublin, A. Crook*, [1691]. brs. STEELE 2p 1191. L, HH.

405   For the better destroying of wolves . . . 23 December 1654. *Dublin, by W. Bladen*, 1654. brs. STEELE 2p 542. L.

406   —7 July 1656. *Imprinted at Dublin by William Bladen*, 1656. brs. STEELE 2p 581. DIX 99. L.

407   For the more due and . . . 14 November 1662. *Dublin, J. Crook*, 1662. brs. STEELE 2p 693. LS.

408   For the more ready dispatch of such petitions . . . 30 April 1663. *Dublin, J. Crooke*, 1663. brs. STEELE 2p 699. DPR (lost).

409   For the prevention of all evil . . . 20 November 1678. *Dublin, by Benjamin Tooke, sold by Mary Crook*, 1678. cap., fol.* STEELE 2p 895–6. O, LS, DK, DN.

410   For the quieting of the minds . . . 28 July 1686. *Dublin, by Andrew Crooke and Samuel Helsham, assigns of Benjamin Tooke, sold by Andrew Crook, and Samuel Helsham*, 1686. brs. STEELE 2p 966–7. L, LPR, DK, DN.

411   His Highness Council having taken . . . 7 April 1656. *Dublin, by W. Bladen*, 1656. brs. STEELE 2p 577. L.

412   His Majesties chief commissioner . . . 22 August 1684. *Dublin, B. Took*, 1684. cap., fol.* STEELE 2p 934. LS.

413   His Majesty taking into His . . . 5 January 1660[1]. *Dublin, by W. Bladen*, 1660[1]. brs. STEELE 2p 622. DPR (lost).

414   The hvmble and ivst remonstrance. Of the Knights, citizens, and burgesses, in Ireland. [*London*], *for Hugh Perry*, 1641. 4°.* LT, C, BC, LIU, DN; CN, CSS, MH, TU, WF, Y.

414A   The humble declaration and petition of the Lords . . . and Commons. *For Hum. Blunden, 12. July.* 1642. 4°.* L, LNC, MR, DN; MH, MIU, TU, WF.

415   In pursuance of a proclamation . . . 16 February 1660[1]. *Dublin, by W. Bladen*, 1660[1]. cap., fol.* STEELE 2p 631. DPR (lost).

416   —[Anr. ed.]—, 1660[1]. brs. STEELE 2p 632. DPR (lost).

417   Information haveing been . . . 4 January 1691. *Dublin, A. Crook*, [1691/2]. brs. STEELE 2p 1246. L, HH.

418   Information having been given . . . 21 March 1691/2. *Dublin, A. Crook*, 1691[2]. brs. STEELE 2p 1256. L, HH.

418aA   Instructions for the collectors. *Dublin, by Benjamin Tooke*, 1677. 8°.* DIX 160. DI.

418bA   Instructions for the gaugers. *Dublin, by Benjamin Tooke*, 1677. 8°.* DIX 160. DI.

418cA   Instructions for the several collectors. *Dublin, by Benjamin Tooke*, 1677. 8°.* DIX 160. DI.

418dA   Instructions, for the surveyors. *Dublin, by Benjamin Tooke*, 1677. 8°.* DIX 160. DI.

418A   Irelands excise. *By F. Leache, for Michaell Sparke senior, and iunior*, 1643. *Iuly 29.* 4°.* LT, O, C, LVF, DN; INU, MH, WF, Y.

419   It cannot be expressed . . . 7 July 1648. *Kilkenny*, 1648. brs. STEELE 2p 446. O.

420   It having pleased Almighty God . . . 13 August 1683. *Dublin, by Benjamin Took and John Crook, and are to be sold by Mary Crook and Andrew Crook*, 1683. brs. STEELE 2p 928. LS, EC, DN.

421   It is ordered that any commander . . . 3 March 1645[6]. [*Dublin*, 1645/6.] brs. STEELE 2p 432. O, DT.

421A   It is this day ordered . . . [14 April]. *Dublin, J. Crook*, 1666. brs. STEELE 2p 758. DPR (lost).

422   It is well known to all men . . . 8 February 1641[2]. *Dublin*, 1641. cap., fol.* STEELE 2p 365. DPR (lost).

422A   The journal of the proceedings of the Parliament. *For Robert Clavell*, 1689. 4°.* L, O, C, EN, DT; CH, MIU, MH, WF, Y.

422B   A journal of the proceedings of the pretended Parliament. colop: *By John Wallis*, 1689. brs. L, O, C, HH, DN; CH.

Laws and ordinances of war. Dublin, 1672. *See title.*

Letter from His Grace the Lord and Council. [n.p., 1681.] *See Ormonde, James Butter, duke of.*

423   A letter sent from the Lords of the Councell in Ireland. *By Tho. Paine*, 1641[2]. 4°.* LT, LG, LVF, MR, BLH; CH, MM, WF.

424   Entry cancelled.
The Lord . . . in their late march. Dublin, 1655. *See* —Declaration of the Lord Deputy.
Manifesto, by the General Assemblie. [n.p., 1648.] *See title.*
Manifesto by the Supreme Council. [n.p., 1648.] *See title.*
Order of the General Assemblie. [n.p., 1648.] *See title.*

424A   An order of the right honourable the Commissioners . . . forfeited estates. colop: *Dublin, by the assignees of Benj. Tooke, reprinted by him in London and sold by Randal Taylor*, 1690. brs. Y.

425   Ordered that all persons . . . 2 April 1655. *Dublin, by W. Bladen*, 1655. brs. STEELE 2p 550. L.

426   Entry cancelled.
Ordered that Thursday. Dublin, 1655. *See Cromwell, Oliver. Declaration of . . . inviting the people.*

426aA   Ordered upon question . . . 3 August. *Dublin, J. Crook*, 1666. brs. STEELE 2p 765. LS.

426A   Orders made and established. [*n.p.*, 1642?] 4°.* CH.

426B   Orders, rules, and instructions to be observed by the Muster-master general. *Dublin, by Benjamin Tooke, to be sold by Joseph Wilde*, 1672. 4°.* DIX 144. O, DN.

426C An ordinance for the speedy raising of moneys for. *Dublin, by William Bladen*, 1660[1]. fol.* DIX 109. DM.

426D An ordinance for the speedy raising of moneys towards. *Dublin, by William Bladen*, 1660. fol.* DIX 108. DK, DM.

426E The poll-act abridged. *Dublin, Andrew Crook*, 1695. fol.* DIX 274. L.

427 A proclamation . . . [14 May 1660]. colop: *Dublin, by William Bladen*, 1660. brs. STEELE 2p 615. L, C.

428 — —[Anr. ed.] —, *re-printed at London by Daniel Pakeman*, [1660]. brs. STEELE 2p 616. L, LG.

429 —27 March 1661. *Dublin, by W. Bladen*, 1661. brs. STEELE 2p 637. DIX 113. DK.

430 — —[Anr. ed.] —, *reprinted at London*, 1661. brs. STEELE 2p 638. L, O, LG, OP, DN.

431 —1 April 1661. *Dublin, by W. Bladen*, 1661. brs. STEELE 2p 640; DIX 113. DK.

432 —18 September 1690. *Dublin, A. Crook*, 1690. brs. STEELE 2p 1151. L, HH.

433 — —[Anr. ed.] *Dublin: by Andrew Crooke, assignee of Benj. Tooke; reprinted at London for him*, 1690. brs. STEELE 2p 1152. L; Y.

434 —19 September 1690. *Dublin, A. Crook*, 1690. brs. STEELE 2p 1153. L, HH.

435 — —[Anr. ed.] *Dublin: by Andrew Crooke, assignee of Benj. Tooke; and reprinted at London for him*, 1690. brs. STEELE 2p 1154. L; Y.

436 —26 September 1690. *Dublin, A. Crook*, [1690]. brs. STEELE 2p 1156–7. L, HH. (var.)

437 — —[Anr. ed.] *By Andrew Crook, assignee of Benjamin Tooke*, 1690. brs. STEELE 2p 1158. L, HH, DN.

438 — —[Anr. ed.] *Dublin, E. Jones*, 1690. brs. STEELE 2p 1159. L.

439 —30 September 1690. *Dublin, A. Crook*, 1690. brs. STEELE 2p 1160–1. L, LPR, HH. (var.)

440 —7 October 1690. *Dublin, A. Crook*, [1690]. brs. STEELE 2p 1162. L.

441 —22 October 1690. *Dublin, A. Crook*, 1690. brs. STEELE 2p 1165. L, HH.

442 —14 November 1690. *Dublin, by Andrew Crook, assignee of Benjamin Tooke*, [1690]. brs. STEELE 2p 1169. L, HH, DT.

443 —19 November 1690. *Dublin, A. Crook*, [1690.] brs. STEELE 2p 1170–1. L, HH. (var.)

444 —20 November 1690. *Dublin, A. Crook*, [1690]. brs. STEELE 2p 1172. L, HH.

445 —2 December 1690. *Dublin, A. Crook*, [1690]. brs. STEELE 2p 1173. L, HH.

446 —8 December 1690. *Dublin, A. Crook*, [1690]. brs. STEELE 2p 1174. L, HH.

447 — —[Anr. ed.] —[1690]. brs. STEELE 2p 1175–6. L, HH. (var.)

448 — —[Anr. ed.] —[1690]. brs. STEELE 2p 1177–8. L, HH. (var.)

449 —12 December 1690. *Dublin, A. Crook*, [1690]. brs. STEELE 2p 1179. L, HH.

450 —29 December 1690. *Dublin, A. Crook*, [1690]. brs. STEELE 2p 1180–1. L, HH. (var.)

451 —31 December 1690. *Dublin. A. Crook*, [1690]. brs. STEELE 2p 1182. L, HH.

452 —17 January 1690[1]. *Dublin, A. Crook*, [1691]. brs. STEELE 2p 1183–4. L, HH. (var.)

453 —27 January 1690[1]. *Dublin, A. Crook*, [1691]. fol.* STEELE 2p 1185–6. L, HH. (var.)

454 —6 February 1690[1]. *Dublin, A. Crook*, [1691]. fol.* STEELE 2p 1189–90. L, HH. (var.)

455 —21 February 1690/1. *Dublin, by Andrew Crook, assignee of Benjamin Took*, [1690/1]. brs. STEELE 2p 1192. L, HH.

456 —23 February 1690[1]. *Dublin, A. Crook*, [1691]. brs. STEELE 2p 1193. L, HH.

457 —24 February 1690[1]. *Dublin, A. Crook*, [1691]. brs. STEELE 2p 1195–6. L, HH. (var.)

458 —27 February 1690[1]. *Dublin, A Crook*, [1691]. brs. STEELE 2p 1197–8. L, HH. (var.)

459 —28 February 1690[1]. *Dublin, A. Crook*, [1691]. fol* STEELE 2p 1199–1200. L, HH. (var.)

460 —26 March 1691. *Dublin, A. Crook*, [1691]. brs. STEELE 2p 1201. L, HH.

461 —15 April 1691. *Dublin, A. Crook*, [1691]. brs. STEELE 2p 1202. L, HH.

462 —30 April 1691. *Dublin, A. Crook*, [1691]. brs. STEELE 2p 1205. L, HH.

463 —14 May 1691. *Dublin, A. Crook*, [1691]. brs. STEELE 2p 1208. L, HH.

464 —23 May 1691. *Dublin, A. Crook*, [1691]. brs. STEELE 2p 1209. L, HH.

465 —15 June 1691. *Dublin, A. Crook*, [1691]. fol.* STEELE 2p 1211–2. L, HH. (var.)

466 —17 June 1691 [regulation of sutlers]. *Dublin, A. Crook*, [1691]. fol.* STEELE 2p 1213–4. L, HH. (var.)

467 —[Same date, forbidding intercourse with Lambay.] —, [1691]. brs. STEELE 2p 1215. HH.

468 —22 June 1691 [concerning soldiers absent without leave]. *Dublin, A Crook*, [1691]. brs. STEELE 2p 1216. L, HH.

469 —[Same date, offering amnesty to rebel soldiers.] —, 1691. brs. STEELE 2p 1217–9. HH. (var.)

470 —1 July 1691. *Dublin, A. Crook*, 1691. fol.* STEELE 2p 1221–2. L, HH. (var.)

471 —7 July 1691. [*Dublin*, 1691.] brs. STEELE 2p 1223. DPR (lost).

472 —15 July 1691. *Dublin, A. Crook*, [1691]. fol.* STEELE 2p 1224–5. L, HH. (var.)

473 —16 July 1691. *Dublin, A. Crook*, [1691]. brs. STEELE 2p 1226. L, HH.

474 —24 July 1691. *Dublin, A. Crook*, [1691]. brs. STEELE 2p 1227. L, HH.

475 —4 August 1691. *Dublin, by Andrew Crook, assignee of Benjamin Tooke*, [1691]. brs. STEELE 2p 1228. L, DN.

476 —16 September 1691. *Dublin, A. Crook*, [1691]. brs. STEELE 2p 1229. L, HH.

477 —18 September 1691. *Dublin, A. Crook*, [1691]. fol.* STEELE 2p 1230–1. L, HH. (var.)

478 —25 September 1691. *Dublin, A. Crook*, [1691]. fol.* STEELE 2p 1232–3. L, HH. (var.)

479 —14 October 1691 [oath of fidelity]. *Dublin, A. Crook*, [1691]. brs. STEELE 2p 1234. L.

480 —[Same date, pardon to Rapparees.] —, [1691]. brs.
STEELE 2p 1235–6. L, HH. (var.)

481 —7 November 1691. *Dublin, A. Crook,* [1691]. fol.*
STEELE 2p 1237–8. L, HH. (var.)

482 —9 November 1691 [for discovery of murderers].
Dublin, A. Crook, [1691]. brs. STEELE 2p 1239. L, HH.

483 —[Same date, day of thanksgiving.] —, 1691. brs. STEELE
2p 1240. L, HH.

484 —14 December 1691. *Dublin, A. Crook,* [1691]. brs.
STEELE 2p 1244. L, HH.

485 —16 December 1691. *Dublin, A. Crook,* [1691]. brs.
STEELE 2p 1245. L, HH.

486 —11 January 1691[2]. *Dublin, A. Crook,* 1691[2]. brs.
STEELE 2p 1247–8. L, HH. (var.)

487 —4 February 1691/2. [arms to be surrendered]. *By Andrew
Crook, assignee of Benjamin Tooke,* 1691/2. brs. STEELE
2p 1250–1. LPR, HH. (var.)

488 —[Same date, subjects not to be disturbed.] —, 1691[2].
brs. STEELE 2p 1252. L, HH.

489 —23 March 1691[2]. *Dublin, A. Crook,* 1691[2]. fol.*
STEELE 2p 1257–8. L, HH. (var.)

490 —20 May 1692 [arms to be given up]. *Dublin, by Andrew
Crook, assignee of Benj: Tooke,* 1691[2]. brs. STEELE 2p
1259–60. L, HH, DT. (var.)

491 —[Same date, fishing boats.] —, 1691[2]. brs. STEELE
2p 1261–2. L, HH. (var.)

492 —1 July 1692. *Dublin, by Andrew Crook, assignee of Benjamin Tooke,* 1692. brs. STEELE 2p 1263. L, HH, DN.

493 —7 July 1692. *Dublin, A. Crook,* 1692. brs. STEELE 2p 1264.
L, HH.

494 —21 October 1692. *Dublin, by Andrew Crook, assignee of
Benjamin Tooke,* 1692. fol.* STEELE 2p 1268–9. HH, DN.
(var.)

495 —7 November 1692. *Dublin, by Andrew Crook, assignee of
Benjamin Tooke,* 1692. fol.* STEELE 2p 1270–1. HH, DN.
(var.)

496 —18 November 1692. *Dublin, by Andrew Crook, assignee
of Benjamin Tooke,* 1692. brs. STEELE 2p 1273. LPR, HH.

497 —19 December 1692 [arraying the militia]. *Dublin, by
Andrew Crook, assignee of Benjamin Tooke,* 1692. fol.*
STEELE 2p 1274–5. HH, DN. (var.)

498 —[Same date, no Papists to leave.] —, 1692. brs. STEELE
2p 1276. HH, DN.

499 —2 January 1692[3]. *Dublin, by Andrew Crook, assignee of
Benjamin Tooke,* [1692[3]. fol.* STEELE 2p 1277–8. HH, DN.
(var.)

500 —17 February 1692[3], [currency of halfpence]. *Dublin,
A. Crook,* 1692[3]. brs. STEELE 2p 1279. HH.

501 —[Same date, value of the coin.] —, 1692[3]. brs. STEELE
2p 1280. HH.

502 —27 March 1693. *Dublin, A. Crook,* 1693. brs. STEELE
2p 1281. HH.

503 —8 April 1693. *Dublin, A. Crook,* 1693. brs. STEELE
2p 1282–3. LPR, HH. (var.)

504 —28 April 1693. *Dublin, A. Crook,* 1693. brs. STEELE
2p 1284–5. HH (var.).

505 —3 May 1693. *Dublin, A. Crook,* 1693. fol.* STEELE
2p 1286. HH.

506 —17 May 1693. *Dublin, A. Crook,* 1693. brs. STEELE
2p 1288. HH.

507 —26 June 1693. *Dublin, A. Crook,* 1693. brs. STEELE
2p 1290. HH.

508 —18 August 1693. *Dublin, A. Crook,* 1693. fol.* STEELE
2p 1292–4. LPR, HH. (var.)

509 —18 October 1693. *Dublin, A. Crook,* 1693. fol.* STEELE
2p 1295–6. HH (var.).

510 —19 October 1693. *Dublin, A. Crook,* 1693. brs. STEELE
2p 1297–8. LPR, HH. (var.)

511 —22 November 1693. *Dublin, A. Crook,* 1693. brs. STEELE
2p 1299. HH.

512 —16 February 1693[4]. *Dublin, A. Crook,* 1693[4]. brs.
STEELE 2p 1300. HH.

513 —23 May 1694. *Dublin, A. Crook,* 1694. brs. STEELE
2p 1301. HH.

514 —2 July 1694. *Dublin, A. Crook,* 1694. brs. STEELE 2p 1302.
HH.

515 —19 October 1694. *Dublin, A. Crook,* 1694. brs. STEELE
2p 1303. HH.

516 —10 December 1694. *Dublin, by Andrew Crook,* 1694.
fol.* STEELE 2p 1304. LPR, HH.

517 —18 January 1694[5]. *Dublin, A. Crook,* 1694[5]. brs.
STEELE 2p 1305. HH.

518 —22 February 1694/5. *Dublin, A. Crook,* 1694[5]. brs.
STEELE 2p 1306. HH.

519 —9 December 1695. *Dublin, A. Crook,* 1695. brs. STEELE
2p 1312. HH.

520 —20 January 1695/6. *Dublin, A. Crook,* 1695[6]. brs.
STEELE 2p 1313. HH.

521 —11 February 1695/6 [hearth-money]. *Dublin, A. Crook,*
1695[6]. brs. STEELE 2p 1314. HH.

522 —[Same date, outlaws.] —, 1695[6]. brs. STEELE 2p 1315. HH.

523 —4 March 1695[6]. *Dublin, A. Crook,* 1695[6]. brs. STEELE
2p 1317. HH.

524 —16 March 1695/6. *Dublin, A. Crook,* 1695[6]. brs. STEELE
2p 1318. LPC, HH.

525 —25 April 1696. *Dublin, A. Crook,* 1696. brs. STEELE
2p 1320. HH.

526 —29 June 1696. *Dublin, A. Crook,* 1696. brs. STEELE
2p 1322. HH.

527 —16 July 1696. *Dublin, A. Crook,* 1696. brs. STEELE
2p 1323. HH.

528 —21 August 1696. *Dublin, A. Crook,* 1696. brs. STEELE
2p 1324. DPR (lost).

529 —16 November 1696. *Dublin, A. Crook,* 1696. brs. STEELE
2p 1325. HH.

530 —4 December 1696. *Dublin, A. Crook,* 1696. fol.* STEELE
2p 1326. HH.

531 —12 January 1696[7]. *Dublin, A. Crook,* 1696[7]. fol.*
STEELE 2p 1327. HH.

532 —29 March 1697. *Dublin, A. Crook,* 1697. fol.* STEELE
2p 1328. HH.

533 —18 June 1697. *Dublin, A. Crook,* 1697. brs. STEELE
2p 1329. HH.

534 —22 June 1697. *Dublin, A. Crook*, 1697. brs. STEELE 2p 1330. HH.

535 —26 July 1697. *Dublin, A. Crook*, 1697. brs. STEELE 2p 1331–2. HH. (var.)

536 —13 August 1697. *Dublin, A. Crook*, 1697. brs. STEELE 2p 1334. LPR, HH.

537 —20 August 1697. *Dublin, A. Crook*, 1697. brs. STEELE 2p 1335. HH.

538 —21 August 1697. *Dublin, A. Crook*, 1697. brs. STEELE 2p 1336–7. HH (var.).

539 Entry cancelled.
     —24 September 1697. *See* England: Lords Justices. A Proclamation.

540 —14 October 1697. *Dublin, A. Crook*, 1697. brs. STEELE 2p 1345. HH.

541 —3 November 1697. *Dublin, A. Crook*, 1697. brs. STEELE 2p 1346. HH.

542 —10 December 1697. *Dublin, A. Crook*, 1697. brs. STEELE 2p 1348. HH.

543 —18 December 1697. *Dublin, A. Crook*, 1697. brs. STEELE 2p 1349. HH.

544 —3 January 1697[8]. *Dublin, A. Crook*, 1697[8]. brs. STEELE 2p 1350–1. HH (var.).

545 —8 January 1697/8. *Dublin, A. Crook*, 1697/[8]. brs. STEELE 2p 1352. HH.

546 —27 January 1697[8]. *Dublin, A. Crook*, 1697[8]. brs. STEELE 2p 1353. DPR (lost).

547 —5 February 1697[8]. *Dublin, A. Crook*, 1697[8]. brs. STEELE 2p 1354. HH.

548 —21 February 1697/8, [articles of Limerick]. *Dublin, A. Crook*, 1697[8]. brs. STEELE 2p 1355. HH.

549 —[Same date, weights for coins.] —, 1697[8]. brs. STEELE 2p 1356. DPR(lost).

550 —1 April 1698. *Dublin, A. Crook*, 1698. brs. STEELE 2p 1358–9. HH (var.).

551 —27 April 1698. *Dublin, A. Crook*, 1698. brs. STEELE 2p 1360. HH.

552 —7 May 1698 [against buying debentures]. *Dublin, A. Crook*, 1698. brs. STEELE 2p 1361. HH.

553 —[Same date, against profanity]. —, 1698. brs. STEELE 2p 1362. HH.

554 —23 May 1698. *Dublin, A. Crook*, 1698. brs. STEELE 2p 1363. HH.

555 —2 June 1698. *Dublin, A. Crook*, 1698. brs. STEELE 2p 1364. HH.

556 —16 June 1698. *Dublin, A. Crook*, 1698. brs. STEELE 2p 1365. HH.

557 —27 June 1698 [hearth-money]. *Dublin, A Crook*, 1698. brs. STEELE 2p 1366. HH.

558 —[Same date, popish plots.] —, 1698. brs. STEELE 2p 1367. HH.

559 —30 June 1698. *Dublin, A. Crook*, 1698. brs. STEELE 2p 1368. HH.

560 —12 July 1698. *Dublin, A. Crook*, 1698. brs. STEELE 2p 1369. HH.

561 —14 July 1698 [arrest of outlaws]. *Dublin, A. Crook*, 1698. fol.* STEELE 2p 1370–1. HH (var.).

562 —[Same date, discovery of concealments.] —, 1698. fol.* STEELE 2p 1372–3. HH (var.).

563 —[Same date, against export of wool.] —, 1698. fol.* STEELE 2p 1374–5. HH (var.).

564 —22 August 1698. *Dublin, A. Crook*, 1698. brs. STEELE 2p 1376. HH.

565 —29 August 1698. *Dublin, A. Crook*, 1698. brs. STEELE 2p 1377. HH.

566 —12 September 1698. *Dublin, A. Crook*, 1698. brs. STEELE 2p 1378. HH.

567 —7 October 1698. *Dublin, A. Crook*, 1698. brs. STEELE 2p 1379. HH.

568 —8 October 1698. *Dublin, A. Crook*, 1698. brs. STEELE 2p 1380. HH.

569 —19 October 1698. *Dublin, A. Crook*, 1698. brs. STEELE 2p 1381. HH.

570 —29 October 1698. *Dublin, A. Crook*, 1698. fol.* STEELE 2p 1382. HH.

571 —18 November 1698. *Dublin, A. Crook*, 1698. brs. STEELE 2p 1383. HH.

572 —24 November 1698. *Dublin, A. Crook*, 1698. brs. STEELE 2p 1384. HH.

573 —3 December 1698. *Dublin, A. Crook*, 1698. brs. STEELE 2p 1385. HH.

574 —7 December 1698. *Dublin, A. Crook*, 1698. brs. STEELE 2p 1386. HH.

575 —23 January 1698[9]. *Dublin, A. Crook*, 1698[9]. fol.* STEELE 2p 1387–8. HH (var.).

576 —7 February 1698[9]. *Dublin, A. Crook*, 1698[9]. fol.* STEELE 2p 1389. HH.

577 —3 April 1699. *Dublin, A. Crook*, 1699. fol.* STEELE 2p 1390. HH.

578 —5 April 1699. *Dublin, A. Crook*, 1699. brs. STEELE 2p 1391. HH.

579 —17 April 1699. *Dublin, A. Crook*, 1699. fol.* STEELE 2p 1392. HH.

580 —1 May 1699. *Dublin, A. Crook*, 1699. brs. STEELE 2p 1394. HH.

581 —4 May 1699. *Dublin, A. Crook*, 1699. brs. STEELE 2p 1395–6. HH (var.).

582 —12 May 1699. *Dublin, A. Crook*, 1699. brs. STEELE 2p 1397. HH.

583 —14 June 1699. *Dublin, A. Crook*, 1699. brs. STEELE 2p 1398. HH.

584 —5 July 1699. *Dublin, A. Crook*, 1699. brs. STEELE 2p 1399. HH.

585 —19 July 1699. *Dublin, A. Crook*, 1699. fol.* STEELE 2p 1400. HH.

586 —14 August 1699. *Dublin, A. Crook*, 1699. brs. STEELE 2p 1401. HH.

587 —13 September 1699. *Dublin, A. Crook*, 1699. fol.* STEELE 2p 1404–5. HH (var.).

588 —5 October 1699. *Dublin, A. Crook*, 1699. brs. STEELE 2p 1406. HH.

589 —20 October 1699. *Dublin, A. Crook*, 1699. fol.* STEELE 2p 1407–8. HH (var.).

590 —30 October 1699. *Dublin, A. Crook,* 1699. brs. STEELE 2p 1409. HH.

591 —29 November 1699. *Dublin, A. Crook,* 1699. brs. STEELE 2p 1410. HH.

592 —29 December 1699. *Dublin, A. Crook,* 1699. fol.* STEELE 2p 1411–2. HH (var.).

593 —19 February 1699[1700]. *Dublin, A. Crook,* 1699 [1700]. fol.* STEELE 2p 1415–6. HH (var.).

594 —18 March 1699[1700]. *Dublin, A. Crook,* 1699[1700]. fol.* STEELE 2p 1417. HH.

595 —26 April 1700. *Dublin, A. Crook,* 1700. brs. STEELE 2p 1418–9. HH (var.).

596 —17 May 1700. *Dublin, A. Crook,* 1700. fol.* STEELE 2p 1420–1. HH (var.).

597 —24 June 1700. *Dublin, A. Crook,* 1700. brs. STEELE 2p 1422. HH.

598 —26 June 1700. *Dublin, A. Crook,* 1700. fol.* STEELE 2p 1423. DPR (lost).

599 —12 December 1700. *Dublin, A. Crook,* 1700. brs. STEELE 2p 1427. HH.

600 —against duelling . . . 23 February. *Dublin, A. Crook,* [1691]. brs. STEELE 2p 1194. L, HH.

601 —appointing the time . . . 23 September 1662. *Dublin, J. Crook,* 1662. brs. STEELE 2p 689. LS.

602 —concerning a Parliament . . . 26 March 1661. *Dublin, by W. Bladen,* 1661. brs. STEELE 2p 636. DPR (lost).

603 —concerning a Parliament . . . 17 July. *Dublin, by Andrew Crook,* 1695. brs. STEELE 2p 1310. LPR, HH.

604 —concerning a cessation of armes. *Printed at Dublin, by William Bladen,* 1643. 4°.* DIX 77. LT, O, C, AU, DI; CH, Y.

605 — —[Anr. ed.] *Dublin by William Bladen; reprinted at London for Edw. Husbands, October 21.* 1643. 4°.* LT, O, C, MR, BLH; CH, CSU, MH, MIU, WF, Y. [=C2560.]

605A — —[Anr. ed.] *[Edinburgh, Evan Tyler],* 1643. 4°.* CT.

606 —concerning gun-powder . . . 10 October 1661. *Dublin, J. Crook,* 1661. fol.* STEELE 2p 659. DPR (lost).

607 —concerning gun-powder . . . 14 October 1661. *Dublin, J. Crook,* 1661. fol.* STEELE 2p 660. LS.

608 —concerning licences . . . 26 August 1663. *Dublin, J. Crooke,* 1663. brs. STEELE 2p 712. DPR (lost).

609 —concerning passes for ships . . . 10 January 1676/7. *Dublin, B. Tooke,* 1676[7]. fol.* STEELE 2p 873. LS.

610 —for a day of humiliation . . . 21 January 1660[1]. *Dublin, by W. Bladen,* 1660[1]. brs. STEELE 2p 627. LPR.

611 —for a general fast . . . 24 June 1695. *Dublin, A. Crook,* 1695. brs. STEELE 2p 1309. HH.

612 —for a general fast . . . 17 June 1696. *Dublin, A. Crook,* 1696. brs. STEELE 2p 1321. HH.

613 —for a publique fast . . . 27 November 1641. *[Dublin,* 1641.] brs. STEELE 2p 356. DPR (lost).

614 —for a publick thanksgiving . . . 30 September 1695. *Dublin, A. Crook,* 1695. brs. STEELE 2p 1311. HH.

615 —for a solemn and publick thanksgiving . . . 10 August 1685. *Dublin, by Benjamin Tooke, sold by Andrew Crook, and Samuel Helsham,* 1685. fol.* STEELE 2p 956. L, HH, DK, DN.

616 —for a thanksgiving . . . 22 June 1665. *Dublin, J. Crook,* 1665. cap., fol.* STEELE 2p 740. LS.

617 —for a thanksgiving . . . 15 August 1666. *Dublin, J. Crook,* 1666. cap., fol.* STEELE 2p 768. DPR (lost).

618 —for a thanksgiving . . . 6 April. *Dublin, A. Crook,* 1696. brs. STEELE 2p 1319. HH.

619 —for a thanksgiving . . . 30 November. *Dublin, A. Crook,* 1697. brs. STEELE 2p 1347. HH.

619A —for an imposition . . . [9 December 1644]. *Dublin, by William Bladen,* 1644. 4°.* CH.

619B —for an imposition . . . [9 May 1645]. *Dublin, by William Bladen,* 1645. 4°.* DIX 79. C; MBA.

620 Entry cancelled.

—for apprehending and securing. 1695. *See* England: Lords Justices.

621 —for assembling of both Houses . . . 22 November. *Dublin,* 1641. brs. STEELE 2p 352. DPR (lost).

622 —for bringing in a proportion of corn . . . 11 February. *Dublin, J. Crooke,* 1666[7]. cap., fol.* STEELE 2p 778. LPR.

623 —for preventing disorders . . . 18 March. *Dublin, A. Crook,* 1697[8]. brs. STEELE 2p 1357. DPR (lost).

624 —for publique prayer . . . 24 July 1665. *Dublin, J. Crook,* 1665. cap., fol.* STEELE 2p 741. DPR (lost).

625 —for publishing an act . . . 22 February. *Dublin, by John Crooke, sold Samuel Dancer.* 1666[7]. cap., fol.* STEELE 2p 779. LPR, LS, DN.

625A —for publishing the peace. *[Dublin, by J. Brent, J. Brocas, and S. Powell,* 1697.] brs. DIX 291. DI.

626 —for securing mens estates . . . 23 September. *Dublin, society of stationers,* 1641. brs. STEELE 2p 339. DPR (lost).

626A —for the apprehension of the chiefe rebels . . . 8 February 1641/2. *For Henry Shepheard,* 1641. 4°.* LT, DN; WF, NN. [=E931A.]

627 —for the disbanding of the New Irish Army . . . 21 May. *Dublin, society of stationers,* 1641. brs. STEELE 2p 337. DPR (lost).

628 —for the due and speedy execution . . . 23 February. *Dublin, by W. Bladen,* 1660[1]. brs. STEELE 2p 634. DPR (lost).

629 —for the encouragement of sutlers . . . 27 April 1691. *Dublin, by Andrew Crook assignee of Benjamin Tooke,* [1691]. brs. STEELE 2p 1204. HH; PL.

630 —for the further adjournment . . . 27 October 1641. *Dublin, society of stationers,* 1641. fol.* STEELE 2p 342. DPR (lost).

631 —for the immediate fortifying . . . 22 November. *Dublin,* 1641. brs. STEELE 2p 353. DPR (lost).

632 — —[Anr. ed.] *Imprinted first at Dublin, and reimprinted at London, to be sold by Henry Walker,* 1641. STEELE 2p 354. O, LS, CT.

633 —for the prorogation of the Parliament . . . 27 October. *Dublin, society of stationers,* 1641. brs. STEELE 2p 341. DPR (lost).

634 — —27 December 1641. *Dublin,* 1641. brs. STEELE 2p 359. DPR (lost).

635 —for the publishing . . . 22 February 1695/6. *Dublin, A. Crook,* 1695[6]. brs. STEELE 2p 1316. HH.

636 —for the raising of coyn . . . 29 May 1695. *Dublin, by Andrew Crook*, 1695. fol.* STEELE 2p 1307–8. LPR, HH, DN. (var.)

637 —for the suppressing of unlawful assemblies . . . 12 November 1662. *Dublin, J. Crook*, 1662. fol.* STEELE 2p 692. DPR (lost).

638 —having . . . 6 November 1678. *Dublin, by Benjamin Tooke, sold by Mary Crook*, 1678. cap., fol.* STEELE 2p 892. DN.

639 —published by the Lords Justices and Councell of Ireland. *Printed at Dublin by William Bladen, reprinted at London for Edward Husbands*, 1642. 4°.* LT, O, C, EC, DN; CH, CLC, LC, MH, WF.

639A —to restrain the landing of men . . . plague . . . [29 August 1664]. *Dvblin, by John Crook, sold by Samuel Dancer*, 1664. brs. DN.

640 —requireing all officers . . . 23 July 1692. *Dublin, A. Crook*, 1692. fol.* STEELE 2p 1265–6. L, HH. (var.)

641 The propositions sent by the Irish Parliament held at Kilkenny. *For I. H.* 1647. 4°.* LT, LG, LVF, DN; CH, MH, MU, WF, Y.

642 The protestation and declaration of the Lords . . . 17 November. *Dublin*, 1641. brs. STEELE 2p 351. DIX 75. DPR (lost).

642A May 18. Remarkable propositions. *London, for W. G. to be sold by T. Bates*, 1642. 4°.* LT, O, C, OC, EC; CLC, CN, MH, WF, Y.

642B A remonstrance. *Dublin, by William Bladen*, 1646. 4°.* DIX 80. LT, OC, C, DN, DT.

643 Right trusty and entirely . . . 21 May 1646. *Dublin, by W. Bladen*, 1646. brs. STEELE 2p 434. L, O.

643A Rules and orders appointed to be used. *Dublin, for Will. Winter*, 1685. 8°.* WF.

643B Rules and orders to be observed. *Dublin, by William Bladen*, 1659. 4°. DIX 102. DUBLIN LAW LIB.; PUL.

644 Rules and orders to be observed. *Dublin, A. Crook*, 1697. brs. STEELE 2p 1339–40. HH (var.).

645 Rules, orders, and declarations. *Dublin, A. Crook*, 1697. brs. STEELE 2p 1338. HH.

645A Rules, orders, and directions agreed. *Dublin, by John Crook, to be sold by Sam. Dancer*, [1662]. fol.* DIX 114. LUG, DN.

646 Rules, orders, and directions appointed. *Dublin, by John Crook*, 1666. fol.* DIX 130. LPR, LUG, DT; WF.

647 Rules, orders, and directions, made and establish'd. [*Dublin*, 1672.] fol.* STEELE 2p 831. DIX 144. L, LPR, OC, DI, DT.

647A Rules, orders, and directions ["for the better regulating of all such cities"], 16 Sept. 1672. *Dublin, by Benjamin Tooke, to be sold by Joseph Wilde*, 1672. fol.* DIX 144. L, LPR, DK, DN, DT; MHL.

647B —["several cities"], 23 Sept. 1672. —, 1672. fol.* DIX 145. DI, DM, DN, DT; MHL.

647C —["Drogheda"], 25 Sept. 1672. —, 1672. fol.* DIX 363. DI, DM, DN, DT; MHL.

647D —["Dublin"], 24 Sept. 1672. —, 1672. fol.* DIX 363. LPR, DI, DM, DN, DT; MHL.

647E ——[Anr. ed.] *Dublin, by Benjamin Took, aud [sic] John Crook: sold by Mary Crook and Andrew Crook*, 1681. fol.* MR.

647F —["Gallway"], 23 Sept. 1672. *By Benjamin Tooke, sold by Joseph Wilde*, 1672. fol.* DIX 363. LPR, DI, DM, DN, DT; MHL.

647G —["Lymerick"], 23 Sept. 1672. —, 1672. fol.* DIX 363. DI, DM, DN, DT; MHL.

648 Rules, orders, and directions . . . 4 September. *Dublin, A. Crook*, 1699. fol.* STEEL 2p 1402–3. HH (var.).

649 Rules, orders, and instructions. *Dublin, A. Crook*, 1700. fol.* STEELE 2p 1426. HH.

650 Rules to be observed . . . 9 October 1690. *Dublin, Joseph Ray*, 1690. brs. STEELE 2p 1163. L.

651 —29 July 1697. *Dublin, by A. Crook*, 1697. fol.* STEELE 2p 1333. DIX 382. MR.

652 Sixteene qveres propounded by the Parliament of Ireland. [*London*], printed, 1641. 4°.* LT, O, C, ESS, DN; CH, CN, MH, WF, Y.

Speaker's speech to . . . the Lord Justices . . . third of December, 1697. Dublin, [1697]. *See* Rochfort, Robert.

652A The substance of an act of Parliament. colop: *Dublin, by Andrew Crook*, 1695. cap., fol.* DIX 274. LPR, DI, DN.

652B Summer assizes, 1694. *Dublin, by Andrew Crook*, 1694. brs. LPR.

652C Their excellencies the Lords Justices speech. *Dublin, by Andrew Crook*, 1697. brs. HH.

653 These are to make knowne . . . 23 October 1641. *Dublin, society of stationers*, 1641. brs. STEELE 2p 340. DPR (lost).

653A —[Anr. ed.] *For Tho. Walkley*, 1641. brs. LNC.

654 This assembly taking seriously into consideration . . . 30 September 1648. *Kilkenny*, [1648]. brs. STEELE 2p 453. O.

654A To His Excellency Henry, Lord Viscount Sidney; . . . the humble address of the . . . Parliament. *Dublin, by Joseph Ray for William Norman*, 1692. brs. DIX 248. CD, DN.

654B To the King's most excellent majesty. The humble address of . . . Parliament. *Dublin, by and for Andrew Crook, and for Jacob Milner*, 1695. brs. DIX 273. DI.

654C A true account of the whole proceedings of the Parliament in Ireland. *For R. Clavell*, 1689. 4°. T.C.II 286. L; CLC, VILLANOVA.

654D Two acts. I. An act for reviving two statutes. *Dublin*, 1695. fol.* L.

654E Two acts. I. An act for taking away the writt. *Dublin*, 1695. fol. L.

654F Two acts. I. An act to take away damage. *Dublin*, 1695. fol. L.

655 Vpon consideration had . . . 12 February 1654[5]. *Dublin, by W. Bladen*, 1654[5]. brs. STEELE 2p 546. L.

656 —10 December 1679. *Dublin, Took & Crook*, 1679. brs. STEELE 2p 909. LS.

657 Vpon consideration of the . . . 5 September 1644. *Dublin, by W. Bladen*, 1644. cap., fol.* STEELE 2p 402. O.

658 —18 November 1644. *Dublin, by W. Bladen*, 1644. brs. STEELE 2p 406. O.

659 Vpon consideration of the annexed . . . 13 January 1644[5]. *Dublin, by W. Bladen*, 1644[5]. brs. STEELE 2p 412. DPR (lost).

660 —2 April 1645. —, 1645. brs. STEELE 2p 417. DPR (lost)

661 —22 April 1645. —, 1645. brs. STEELE 2p 419. DPR (lost).

662 —22 May 1645. —, 1645. brs. STEELE 2p 420. DPR (lost).

663 —4 June 1645. —, 1645. brs. STEELE 2p 421. DPR (lost).

664 —21 June 1645. —, 1645. brs. STEELE 2p 423. DPR (lost).

665 —30 June 1645. —, 1645. brs. STEELE 2p 424. DPR (lost).

666 —24 July 1645. —, 1645. brs. STEELE 2p 427. O.

667 —29 July 1645. —, 1645. brs. STEELE 2p 428. O.

668 We . . . being deeply sensible . . . 14 May 1679. *Dublin, Took & Crook*, 1679. cap., fol.* STEELE 2p 905. DPR (lost).

669 We cannot but call to mind . . . 29 June 1663. *Dublin, J. Crooke*, 1663. cap., fol.* STEELE 2p 708. O.

670 We . . . considering that at this . . . 26 July 1665. *Dublin, J. Crook*, 1665. cap., fol.* STEELE 2p 743. DPR (lost).

671 We . . . considering the duty incumbent . . . 13 December 1662. *Dublin, J. Crook*, 1662. cap., fol.* STEELE 2p 694. LS.

672 We . . . doe by this proclamation . . . 29 May 1643 *Dublin, by W. Bladen*, 1643. brs. STEELE 2p 381. DPR (lost).

673 We doe by this proclamation . . . 2 August 1643. *Dublin, by W. Bladen*, 1643. brs. STEELE 2p 384. DPR (lost).

674 Wee . . . doe by this proclamation . . . 20 September 1644. *Dublin, by W. Bladen*, 1644. brs. STEELE 2p 403. DPR (lost).

675 We . . . do command and . . . 27 March 1672. *Dublin, B. Tooke*, 1672. brs. STEELE 2p 823. LS.

676 Wee doe hereby declare and . . . 4 December 1644. *Dublin, by W. Bladen*, 1644. brs. STEELE 2p 408. DPR (lost).

676A Wee doe hereby declare and publish . . . 14. of April, 1646 . . . [provisions]. *Imprinted at Dublin, by William Bladen*, 1646. brs. STEELE 2p 433a. DN.

677 We doe hereby in His . . . 18 January 1641[2]. *Dublin*, 1641[2]. brs. STEELE 2p 364. DPR (lost).

678 We . . . do order, command, . . . 8 June 1666. *Dublin, J. Crooke*, 1666. brs. STEELE 2p 761. LS.

679 We finding great abuse in the . . . 7 February, 1644[5]. *Dublin, by W. Bladen*, 1644[5]. brs. STEELE 2p 415. DPR (lost).

680 We . . . for prevention of . . . 2 September 1670. *Dublin, B. Tooke*, 1670. brs. STEELE 2p 816. DPR (lost).

681 We . . . having received His Majesties . . . 8 July 1643. *Dublin, by W. Bladen*, 1643. cap., fol.* STEELE 2p 383. DPR (lost).

682 We . . . having taken into consideration . . . 1 April 1643. *Dublin, by W. Bladen*, 1643. brs. STEELE 2p 380. DPR (lost).

683 We having taken into our . . . 24 June 1643. *Dublin, by W. Bladen*, 1643. cap., fol.* STEELE 2p 382. DIX 77. L, DI.

684 We having taken into our serious . . . 19 August 1643 . . . [impost at Drogheda]. *Dublin, by W. Bladen*, 1643. cap., fol.* STEELE 2p 385. DPR (lost).

685 —[Same date, impost at Trim.] — 1643. cap., fol.* STEELE 2p 386. DPR (lost).

686 —[Same date, impost on tobacco.] — 1643. brs. STEELE 2p 387. DPR (lost).

687 —20 May 1644. *Dublin, by W. Bladen*, 1644. cap., fol.* STEELE 2p 397. DPR (lost).

688 —12 October 1644. *Dublin, by W. Bladen*, 1644. cap., fol.* STEELE 2p 404. DPR (lost).

689 We hereby think fit . . . 10 February 1684/5. *Dublin, B. Took* [1684/5]. brs. STEELE 2p 937. L, LS, HH, DK.

690 We judging it requisite . . . 22 November 1672. *Dublin, B. Tooke*, 1672. brs. STEELE 2p 834. LS.

691 —14 October 1678. *Dublin, by Benjamin Tooke, sold by Mary Crook*, 1678. brs. STEELE 2p 888. LS, DN.

692 We . . . taking into our consideration . . . 11 April 1661. *Dublin, by W. Bladen*, 1661. brs. STEELE 2p 641. DPR (lost).

693 Wee the Lord Lieutenant . . . 7 January 1666[7]. *Dublin, J. Crook*, 1666[7]. brs. STEELE 2p 776. DPR (lost).

694 —23 August 1676. *Dublin, by Benjamin Tooke, sold by Joseph Wilde*, 1676. cap., fol.* STEELE 2p 871. LS, DN.

695 We the Lord Lieutenant and . . . 20 November 1678. *Dublin, by Benjamin Tooke, sold by Mary Crook*, 1687 [i.e. 1678]. brs. STEELE 2p 897. LS, DK, DN.

696 We the Lords Iustices and Councell . . . 9 February 1642[3]. *Dublin, by W. Bladen*, 1642/3. brs. STEELE 2p 377. DPR (lost).

697 —15 January 1660[1]. *Dublin, by W. Bladen*, 1660[1]. brs. STEELE 2p 625. LPR.

698 Entry cancelled.
Wee the supreame Councell . . . 27 May 1648. *See* —By the supreame councell of the confederate Catholicks.

699 Whereas a committee of the General . . . 23 February 1660[1]. *Dublin, by W. Bladen*, 1600[1]. brs. STEELE 2p 633. DPR (lost).

700 Whereas a committee of the . . . 21 June 1661. *Dublin, by W. Bladen*, 1661. brs. STEELE 2p 647. DPR (lost).

701 Whereas a late proclamation . . . 21 February 1686[7]. *Dublin, by Andrew Crook and Samuel Helsham, assigns of Benjamin Tooke, sold by Andrew Crook, and Samuel Helsham*, 1686[7]. cap., fol.* STEELE 2p 970. L, HH, DK, DN.

702 Whereas a most barbarous . . . 19 October 1677. [*Dublin*, 1677.] cap., fol.* STEELE 2p 880. LS.

703 Whereas a petition hath . . . 29 October 1641. *Dublin, society of stationers*, 1641. brs. STEELE 2p 343. DPR (lost).

703A —[Anr. ed.] *Imprinted at Dublin, by the Society of Stationers*, 1641. brs. STEELE 2p 344. LT.

704 Whereas a petition was . . . 2 May 1687. *Dublin, by Andrew Crook and Samuel Helsham, assigns of Benjamin Tooke, sold by Andrew Crook, and Samuel Helsham*, 1687. cap., fol.* STEELE 2p 980. L, HH, DK, DN.

705 Whereas a proclamation . . . 16 January 1687[8]. *Dublin, by Andrew Crooke and Samuel Helsham, assigns of Benjamin Tooke, sold by Andrew Crook, and Samuel Helsham*, 1687[8]. cap., fol.* STEELE 2p 984–5. L, HH, DK, DN. (var.)

706 Whereas a writing under . . . 16 May 1666. *Dublin, J. Crooke,* 1666. cap., fol.* STEELE 2p 760. DPR (lost).

707 Whereas amongst many other . . . 17 August 1661. *Dublin, J. Crook,* 1661. brs. STEELE 2p 653. DPR (lost).

708 Whereas amongst many other . . . 13 September 1661. *Dublin, J. Crook,* 1661. brs. STEELE 2p 657. DPR (lost).

709 Whereas an act lately . . . 16 August 1665. *Dublin, J. Crook,* 1665. cap., fol.* STEELE 2p 745. LS.

710 Whereas an act of Council . . . 18 July 1687. *Dublin, by Andrew Crook and Samuel Helsham, assigns of Benjamin Tooke, sold by Andrew Crook, and Samuel Helsham,* 1687. cap., fol.* STEELE 2p 982. L, HH, DK, DN.

711 Whereas application hath . . . 21 May 1677. *Dublin, B. Tooke,* 1677. cap., fol.* STEELE 2p 878. LS.

711A Whereas Art Roe Magenis . . . [15 November 1666]. *Dublin, by John Crook, sold by Samuel Dancer,* 1666. brs. LPR.

712 Whereas articles of peace . . . 30 July 1646. *Kilkenny,* 1646. brs. STEELE 2p 436. LPR.

713 Whereas articles of peace are made . . . 17 January 1648[9]. *Kilkenny, William Smith,* 1648[9]. brs. STEELE 2p 455. LPR.

714 Whereas at the Parliament . . . 24 March 1661[2]. *Dublin, T. Crook,* 1661[2]. brs. STEELE 2p 676. LS.

715 Whereas by a clause in the . . . 15 October 1667. *Dublin, J. Crook,* 1667. cap., fol.* STEELE 2p 791. LS.

716 Whereas by a clause . . . 30 June 1676. *Dublin, by Benjamin Tooke, sold by Joseph Wilde,* 16[76]. cap., fol.* STEELE 2p 870. LS.

717 Whereas by a declaration. *Dublin, by W. Bladen,* 1656. cap., fol.* STEELE 2p 580. L (impf.).

718 Whereas by a proclamation . . . 29 April 1667 . . . [wheat]. *Dublin, J. Crooke,* 1667. fol.* STEELE 2p 782. DPR (lost).

719 Whereas by act of Council . . . 29 April 1667 . . . [payment of moiety]. *Dublin, J. Crooke,* 1667. brs. STEELE 2p 783. DPR (lost).

720 Whereas by an act made . . . 27 May 1663. *Dublin, J. Crook,* 1663. cap., fol.* STEELE 2p 705. O, DI.

721 —3 June 1663. *Dublin, J. Crooke,* 1663. cap., fol.* STEELE 2p 706. DPR (lost).

722 Whereas by act of Parliament . . . 23 June 1662. *Dublin, J. Crook,* 1662. cap., fol.* STEELE 2p 679. DPR (lost).

723 Whereas by an act of . . . 15 August 1666. *Dublin, J. Crook,* 1666. cap., fol.* STEELE 2p 770. DPR (lost).

724 Whereas by an act . . . 17 September 1666. *Dublin, J. Crook,* 1666. cap., fol.* STEELE 2p 772. LS.

725 Whereas by an order . . . 27 February 1654[5]. *Dublin, by W. Bladen,* 1654[5]. brs. STEELE 2p 547. L.

726 Whereas by direction . . . 15 August 1666. *Dublin, by John Crook, sold by Samuel Dancer,* 1666. brs. STEELE 2p 769. LPR, DN.

727 Whereas by former orders made . . . 14 December 1644. *Dublin, by W. Bladen,* 1644. brs. STEELE 2p 410. DPR (lost).

728 Whereas by former orders, . . . 7 November 1681. *Dublin, by Benjamin Took & John Crook, sold by Mary Crook, and Andrew Crook,* 1681. brs. STEELE 2p 921. DN.

728A Whereas by his Majesties authoritie there are articles of peace . . . [19 August 1646]. *Imprinted at Dublin, by VVilliam Bladen,* 1646. brs. STEELE 2p 437a.

729 Whereas by occasion of the . . . 23 July 1662. *Dublin, J. Crook,* 1662. brs. STEELE 2p 681. DPR (lost).

730 Whereas by occasion of the backwardness . . . 11 September 1667. *Dublin, J. Crook,* 1667. cap., fol.* STEELE 2p 789. O, LPR.

731 Whereas by one act of Parliament . . . 17 October 1662. *Dublin, J. Crook,* 1662. cap., fol.* STEELE 2p 691. DPR (lost).

732 —18 March 1662[3]. *Dublin, J. Crook, sold by S. Dancer,* 1663. cap., fol.* STEELE 2p 697. DPR (lost).

733 Whereas by one clause . . . 6 July 1670. *Dublin, B. Tooke,* 1670. cap., fol.* STEELE 2p 814. DPR (lost).

734 Whereas by order, . . . 28 March 1678. *Dublin, B. Tooke,* 1678. cap., fol.* STEELE 2p 885. DPR (lost).

735 Whereas by our late proclamation . . . 13 August 1648. *Kilkenny, Thomas Bourke,* [1648]. brs. STEELE 2p 448. O.

736 Whereas by our proclamation . . . 10 April 1663. *Dublin, J. Crook,* 1663. cap., fol.* STEELE 2p 698. LS.

737 —19 February 1676[7]. *Dublin, B. Tooke,* 1676[7]. cap., fol.* STEELE 2p 875. LS.

738 —26 March 1679. *Dublin, by Benjamin Took, sold by Mary Crook,* 1679. cap., fol.* STEELE 2p 903. LS, DK, DN.

739 —25 June 1691. *Dublin, A. Crook,* 1691. brs. STEELE 2p 1220. L, HH.

740 —2 September 1697. *Dublin, A. Crook,* 1697. fol.* STEELE 2p 1341–3. HH (var.).

741 Whereas by proclamation . . . 6 March 1642[3]. *Dublin, by W. Bladen,* 1642[3]. brs. STEELE 2p 379. DPR (lost).

742 —19 September 1662. *Dublin, J. Crook,* 1662. cap., fol.* STEELE 2p 686. DPR (lost).

743 —14 September 1668. *Dublin, J. Crook,* 1668. brs. STEELE 2p 797. LS, DN (impf.).

744 —14 December 1674. *Dublin, by Benjamin Tooke, sold by Joseph Wilde,* 1674. cap., fol.* STEELE 2p 854. LS, DN.

745 —bearing . . . 12 December 1678. *Dublin, by Benjamin Tooke, sold by Mary Crook,* 1678. cap., fol.* STEELE 2p 898. O, DK, DN.

746 —26 April 1680. *Dublin, Took & Crook,* 1680. brs. STEELE 2p 913. LS.

747 Whereas by proclamation . . . 21 June 1684. *Dublin, B. Took,* [1684]. brs. STEELE 2p 933. LS.

748 —16 October 1685. *Dublin, by Benjamin Tooke, sold by Andrew Crook, and Samuel Helsham,* [1685]. cap., fol.* STEELE 2p 958. L, HH, DK, DN.

749 Whereas by reason that diverse . . . 15 August 1661. *Dublin, J. Crook, sold by John North,* 1661. cap., fol.* STEELE 2p 652. DPR (lost).

750 Whereas by several proclamations . . . 29 November 1680. *Dublin, Took & Crook,* 1680. cap., fol.* STEELE 2p 917. LS, DK.

751 Whereas by severall warrants . . . 31 December 1642. *Dublin, by W. Bladen,* 1642. brs. STEELE 2p 375. DPR (lost).

752 Whereas by some letters . . . 13 December 1678. *Dublin, by Benjamin Tooke, sold by Mary Crook*, 1678. brs. STEELE 2p 899. LS, DN.

753 Whereas by the act intituled . . . 19 September 1662. *Dublin, J. Crook*, 1662. cap., fol.* STEELE 2p 687. DPR (lost).

754 Whereas by the act . . . 3 January 1665[6]. *Dublin, J. Crook*, 1665[6]. brs. STEELE 2p 751. DPR (lost).

755 Whereas by the antient . . . 9 July 1672. *Dublin, B. Tooke*, 1672. cap., fol.* STEELE 2p 824. LS.

756 Whereas by the ancient laws . . . 10 July 1685. *Dublin, by Benjamin Tooke, sold by Andrew Crook, and Samuel Helsham*, 1685. cap., fol.* STEELE 2p 952. L, HH, DK, DN.

757 —15 October 1688. *Dublin, by Andrew Crook & Samuel Helsham, assigns of Benjamin Tooke*, 1688. cap., fol.* STEELE 2p 1000–1. L, HH, DN. (var.)

758 Whereas, by the direction . . . 5 August 1663. *Dublin, J. Crooke*, 1663. cap., fol.* STEELE 2p 711. O.

759 Whereas by the frequent concourse . . . 28 December 1641. *Dublin*, 1641. brs. STEELE 2p 360. DPR (lost).

760 Whereas by the good and . . . 19 December 1677. *Dublin, B. Took*, 1677. cap., fol.* STEELE 2p 881. LS.

761 Whereas by two several . . . 16 October 1678. *Dublin, by Benjamin Tooke, sold by Mary Crook*, 1678. cap., fol.* STEELE 2p 889. LG, LS, DN.

762 Whereas certain wicked persons . . . 21 May 1663. *Dublin, by John Crooke, and sold by Samuel Dancer*, 1663. cap., fol.* STEELE 2p 700. O, OC.

763 Whereas Colonell Owen ONeill, coming into this kingdome, . . . 30 September 1648. [*Dublin*, 1648.] brs. STEELE 2p 452. O.

764 Whereas Dermott Riane . . . 15 April 1656. *Dublin, by W. Bladen*, 1656. brs. STEELE 2p 579. L.

765 Whereas divers complaints . . . 15 October 1667. *Dublin, J. Crook*, 1667. brs. STEELE 2p 792. DPR (lost).

766 Whereas divers disloyal . . . 10 June 1675. *Dublin, by Benjamin Tooke, sold by Joseph Wilde*, 1675. cap., fol.* STEELE 2p 859. LS, DN.

767 Whereas divers ill affected to the government . . . 14 September 1648. *Kilkenny*, 1648. brs. STEELE 2p 451. O.

768 Whereas divers officers of His Majesties . . . 29 November 1680. *Dublin, Took & Crook*, 1680. cap., fol.* STEELE 2p 916. O.

769 Whereas divers persons in seveal [*sic*] . . . 19 January 1660[1]. *Dublin, By W. Bladen*, 1660[1]. brs. STEELE 2p 626. LPR.

770 Whereas divers persons . . . 26 November 1669. *Dublin, B. Tooke*, [1669]. brs. STEELE 2p 804. DPR (lost).

771 —28 March 1670. *Dublin, B. Tooke*, 1670. brs. STEELE 2p 807. LS.

772 —17 October 1673. *Dublin, by Benjamin Tooke, sold by Joseph Wilde*, 1673. brs. STEELE 2p 842. LS, DN.

773 —9 December 1691. *Dublin, A. Crook*, [1691]. brs. STEELE 2p 1243. L, HH.

774 Whereas Donnell ODowd . . . 2 March 1673[4]. *Dublin, B. Tooke*, 1673[4]. cap., fol.* STEELE 2p 849. DPR (lost).

775 Whereas Dualtagh . . . 25 June 1666. *Dublin, J. Crook*, 1666. cap., fol.* STEELE 2p 763. O, LS.

776 Whereas Edmund mac Gilaspy . . . 1 June 1670. *Dublin, B. Tooke*, 1670. cap., fol.* STEELE 2p 809. DPR (lost).

777 Whereas for speciall reasons of state . . . 10 June 1642. *Dublin, by William Bladen*, 1642. cap., fol.* STEELE 2p 369. DPR (lost).

778 Whereas for sundry good causes and . . . 10 December 1661. *Dublin, J. Crook*, 1661. brs. STEELE 2p 666. LS.

779 —20 January 1661[2]. *Dublin, J. Crook*, 1661[2]. brs. STEELE 2p 669. DPR (lost).

780 —19 February 1661[2]. *Dublin, J. Crook*, 1661[2]. brs. STEELE 2p 671. DPR (lost).

781 Whereas for the better enabling . . . 7 February 1660[1]. *Dublin, by W. Bladen*, 1660[1]. brs. STEELE 2p 630. DPR (lost).

782 Whereas for the better . . . 12 July 1666. *Dublin, J. Crook*, 1666. cap., fol.* STEELE 2p 764. DPR (lost).

783 Whereas great complaint is made . . . 25 November 1654. *Dublin, by VVilliam Bladen*, 1654. brs. STEELE 2p 539. DT.

784 Whereas . . . Halsey and Walter Butler. . . . 10 September 1661. *Dublin, J. Crook*, 1661. brs. STEELE 2p 655. DPR (lost).

785 Whereas his highness . . . 1 January 1654[5]. *Dublin, by W. Bladen*, 1654[5]. brs. STEELE 2p 544. L.

786 —7 August 1655. *Dublin, by W. Bladen*, 1655. brs. STEELE 2p 566. L.

787 Whereas His Majestie . . . 4 September 1666. *Dublin, J. Crook*, 1666. cap., fol.* STEELE 2p 771. DPR (lost).

788 Whereas His Majesties . . . 31 July 1667. *Dublin, J. Crooke*, 1667. cap., fol.* STEELE 2p 785. DPR (lost).

789 Whereas His Majesty . . . 9 October 1671. *Dublin, B. Tooke*, 1671. cap., fol.* STEELE 2p 818. DK.

790 Whereas His Majestie being . . . 4 June 1684. *Dublin, B. Took*, [1684]. cap., fol.* STEELE 2p 931. L, DK.

791 Whereas His Majesty being informed . . . 11 August 1685. *Dublin, by Benjamin Tooke, sold by Andrew Crook, and Samuel Helsham*, 1685. brs. STEELE 2p 957. L, HH, DK, DN.

792 Whereas His Majesty by His . . . 20 October 1671. *Dublin, B. Tooke*, 1671. cap., fol.* STEELE 2p 819. DPR (lost).

793 Whereas His Majestie by his letters . . . 29 July 1672. *Dublin, B. Tooke*, 1672. cap., fol.* STEELE 2p 825–6. L (var.).

794 —[Anr. ed.] *Dublin, by Benjamin Tooke, sold by Joseph Wilde*, 1676. cap. fol.* STEELE 2p 827. DN.

795 Whereas His Majesty by his . . . 9 January 1660[1]. *Dublin, by W. Bladen*, 1660[1]. brs. STEELE 2p 624. DPR (lost).

796 —24 January 1672[3]. *Dublin, by Benjamin Tooke, sold by Joseph Wilde*, 1672[3]. cap., fol.* STEELE 2p 835. LPR, LS.

797 Whereas His Majesty by . . . 7 February 1672[3]. *Dublin, B. Tooke*, 1672[3]. brs. STEELE 2p 837. LS.

798 —1 March 1674[5]. *Dublin, B. Tooke*, 1674[5]. cap., fol.* STEELE 2p 857. LS, DN.

799 —20 December 1675. *Dublin, by Benjamin Tooke, sold by Joseph Wilde*, 1675. brs. STEELE 2p 864. LS, DN.

800 —26 May 1676. *Dublin, B. Tooke*, 1676. cap., fol.* STEELE 2p 865. LS.

801 —26 June 1676 [quit rents]. *Dublin, by Benjamin Tooke, sold by Joseph Wilde*, 1676. cap., fol.* STEELE 2p 866. DN.

802 —[Same date, transplanted persons.] —, 1676. cap., fol.* STEELE 2p 867. LS, DN.

803 —12 April 1678. *Dublin, B. Tooke*, 1678. brs. STEELE 2p 886. DK.

804 Whereas His Maistie is at . . . 18 November 1642. [*Dublin*, 1642.] brs. STEELE 2p 374. LPR, DN.

805 Whereas his Majestie (out of . . .) . . . 30 March 1661. *Dublin, by W. Bladen*, 1661. brs. STEELE 2p 639. DPR (lost).

806 Whereas his Majestie upon . . . 30 June 1676. *Dublin, by Benjamin Tooke, sold by Joseph Wilde*, 1676. cap., fol.* STEELE 2p 869. DN.

807 Whereas His Majesty . . . 19 July 1680. *Dublin, Tooke & Crook*, 1680. cap., fol.* STEELE 2p 914. LS.

808 —15 November 1680. *Dublin, Took & Crook*, 1680. cap., fol.* STEELE 2p 915. LS.

809 Entry cancelled.
Whereas His Majesty . . . 14 April 1690. [n.p., 1690.] *See* MacDermott, Terence.

809A Whereas His Majesties commissioners . . . 9 April 1666. *Dublin, by John Crooke*, 1666. fol.* DIX 131. DM.

810 Whereas His Most Excellent . . . 21 March 1669[70]. *Dublin, B. Tooke*, 1669[70]. brs. STEELE 2p 805. DPR (lost).

811 Whereas His Sacred Majesty . . . 4 April 1688. *Dublin, by Andrew Crooke and Samuel Helsham, assigns of Benjamin Tooke, sold by Andrew Crook, and Samuel Helsham*, 1688. cap., fol.* STEELE 2p 987–8. L, HH, DK, DN. (var.)

812 Whereas I am informed . . . 8 December 1649. *Cork*, 1649. brs. STEELE 2p 460. HODGKIN.

813 Whereas in an act . . . 27 February 1663[4]. *Dublin, J. Crooke*, 1663[4]. cap., fol.* STEELE 2p 723. LS.

814 Whereas in an act intituled . . . 11 November 1663. *Dublin, J. Crooke*, 1663. cap., fol.* STEELE 2p 718. DPR (lost).

815 Whereas in an act lately . . . 28 January 1662[3]. *Dublin, J. Crook, sold by S. Dancer*, 1662[3]. cap., fol.* STEELE 2p 696. DPR (lost).

816 Whereas in an act . . . 23 January 1666[7]. *Dublin, J. Crooke*, 1666[7]. brs. STEELE 2p 777. LS.

817 Whereas in an act of . . . 26 August 1669. *Dublin, B. Tooke*, 1669. brs. STEELE 2p 801. DPR (lost).

818 Whereas in an act . . . 15 February 1674[5]. *Dublin, by Benjamin Tooke, sold by Joseph Wilde*, 1674[5]. fol. STEELE 2p 856. DT.

819 Whereas in and by an act . . . 29 January 1657[8]. *Dublin, by W. Bladen*, 1657[8]. brs. STEELE 2p 596. DK, DT.

820 Whereas in expectation of . . . 30 April 1662. *Dublin, J. Crook*, 1662. brs. STEELE 2p 677. O, LS.

821 Whereas in pursuance of . . . 14 July 1655. *Dublin, by W. Bladen*, 1655. brs. STEELE 2p 563. L.

822 —20 January 1657[8]. *Imprinted at Dublin, by VVilliam Bladen*, 1657[8]. brs. STEELE 2p 595. DT.

823 —21 March 1669[70]. *Dublin, B. Tooke*, 1669[70]. brs. STEELE 2p 806. DPR (lost).

824 —29 November 1673. *Dublin, by Benjamin Tooke, sold by Joseph Wilde*, 1673. cap., fol.* STEELE 2p 847. DN.

825 Whereas in pursuance to a . . . 29 June 1661. *Dublin, by W. Bladen*, 1661. brs. STEELE 2p 648. DPR (lost).

826 Whereas in the act intituled . . . 9 September 1663. *Dublin, J. Crooke*, 1663. cap., fol.* STEELE 2p 716. DPR (lost).

827 Whereas in the act, entituled, . . . 10 July 1668. *Dublin, J. Crook*, 1668. cap., fol.* STEELE 2p 796. DPR (lost).

828 Whereas in the beginning of . . . 19 August 1642. *Dublin, by W. Bladen*, 1642. brs. STEELE 2p 371. DPR (lost).

829 Whereas in the present treaty . . . 8 January 1644[5]. [*Dublin*, 1644/5.] brs. STEELE 2p 411. O.

830 Whereas in the tenth . . . 15 August 1666. *Dublin, J. Crook*, 1666. cap., fol.* STEELE 2p 767. LS.

831 Whereas in the twenty . . . 7 July 1675. *Dublin, by Benjamin Tooke, sold by Joseph Wilde*, 1675. cap., fol.* STEELE 2p 860. LPR, LS, DN.

832 Whereas information hath been given . . . 8 November 1673. *Dublin, by Benjamin Tooke, sold by Joseph Wilde*, 1673. cap., fol.* STEELE 2p 845. LPR, LS, DN.

833 Whereas information hath been made . . . 15 April 1671. *Dublin, B. Tooke*, 1671. brs. STEELE 2p 817. DPR (lost).

834 Whereas information is given . . . 28 July 1673. *Dublin, B. Tooke*, 1673. cap., fol.* STEELE 2p 840–1. DPR (lost).

835 Whereas information is . . . 26 July 1675. *Dublin, by Benjamin Tooke, sold by Joseph Wilde*, 1675. cap., fol.* STEELE 2p 861. LS, DN.

835A Whereas it appears by examinations . . . 10 February 1685[6]. *Dublin, by Benjamin Tooke, to be sold by Andrew Crook and Samuel Helsham*, 1685[6]. fol.* STEELE 2p 963–4. L (var.).

836 Whereas it appears by the examination . . . 14 April 1679. *B. Tooke & J. Crook*, 1679. cap., fol.* STEELE 2p 904. O, LS.

837 Whereas it appears by . . . 23 December 1685. *Dublin, by Benjamin Tooke, sold by Andrew Crook, and Samuel Helsham*, 1685. cap., fol.* STEELE 2p 959–60. L, HH, DK, DN.

837A Whereas it hath been a. . . . 31 October 1687. *Dublin, by Andrew Crook & Samuel Helsham, assigns of Benjamin Tooke, sold by Andrew Crook, and Samuel Helsham*, 1687. brs. STEELE 2p 983. L, HH, DK, DN.

838 Whereas it hath been by many . . . 14 April 1656. *Dublin, by W. Bladen*, 1656. cap., fol.* STEELE 2p 578. L.

839 Whereas it hath pleased . . . 11 February 1684[5]. *Dublin, by Benjamin Tooke, sold by Andrew Crook and Samuel Helsham*, 1684[5]. cap., fol.* STEELE 2p 938–9. L, HH, DK, DN. (var.)

840 Entry cancelled.
Whereas it hath pleased Almighty God. *Edinburgh*, 1685. *See* England: Privy Council.

841 Whereas it hath pleased . . . 8 February 1687[8]. *Dublin, by Andrew Crook and Samuel Helsham, assigns of Benjamin Tooke, sold by Andrew Crook, and Samuel Helsham*, 1687[8]. cap., fol.* STEELE 2p 986. L, HH, DK, DN.

842 —23 June 1688. *Dublin, by Andrew Crook and Samuel Helsham, assigns of Benjamin Tooke, sold by Andrew Crook, and Samuel Helsham,* 1698. cap., fol.* STEELE 2p 991. L, HH, DK, DN.

843 Whereas it is a certain truth . . . 15 April 1661. *Dublin, by W. Bladen,* 1661. brs. STEELE 2p 642. DPR (lost).

844 Whereas it is observed . . . 14 January 1641[2]. [*Dublin,* 1642.] brs. STEELE 2p 362. DPR (lost).

845 Whereas it is observed that . . . 21 June 1642. *Dublin, by W. Bladen,* 1642. brs. STEELE 2p 370. DPR (lost).

846 Whereas it is of great importance . . . 16 September 1690. *Dublin, A. Crook,* [1690]. brs. STEELE 2p 1148–9. L, HH.

847 —[Anr. ed.] *Dublin, by Andrew Crook, assignee of Benj. Tooke; and re-printed at London for him,* 1690. brs. STEELE 2p 1150. L, HH.

848 Whereas many and . . . 6 June 1683. *Dublin, Tooke & Crooke,* 1683. cap., fol.* STEELE 2p 926. L, LS, DK.

849 Whereas many malignant . . . 14 October 1642. *Printed at Dublin by William Bladen,* 1642. brs. STEELE 2p 373. L, LPR, DN.

850 Whereas not only the pious . . . 27 January 1685[6]. *Dublin, by Benjamin Tooke, sold by Andrew Crooke, and Samuel Helsham,* 1685[6]. cap., fol* STEELE 2p 961–2. L, HH, DK, DN. (var.)

851 Whereas notwithstanding . . . 15 April 1665. *Dublin, J. Crook,* 1665. cap., fol.* STEELE 2p 736. DN (impf.), DPR (lost).

851A —19 Apr. 1655. *Dublin, by William Bladen,* 1655. brs. STEELE 2p 553. PL.

852 —16 September 1665. *Dublin, J. Crook,* 1665. fol.* STEELE 2p 748. DPR (lost).

853 Whereas on the nineteenth of . . . 7 November 1661. *Dublin, J. Crook,* 1661. fol.* STEELE 2p 662. DPR (lost).

854 Whereas on the second day . . . 22 September 1666. *Dublin, J. Crook,* 1666. cap., fol.* STEELE 2p 773. DPR (lost).

855 Whereas on the seventh day . . . 27 February 1661[2]. *Dublin, J. Crook,* 1661[2]. cap., fol.* STEELE 2p 672. LS.

856 Whereas our very good Lord . . . 18 February 1672[3]. *Dublin, B. Tooke,* 1672[3]. cap., fol.* STEELE 2p 838. LS.

857 Whereas Popish priests, friers, . . . 17 March 1661[2]. *Dublin, J. Crook,* 1661[2]. brs. STEELE 2p 674. DPR (lost).

858 Whereas Redmond OHanlon . . . 14 December 1674. *Dublin, by Benjamin Tooke, sold by Joseph Wilde,* 1674. cap., fol.* STEELE 2p 853. LS, DN.

859 —16 October 1676. *Dublin, B. Tooke,* 1676. cap., fol.* STEELE 2p 872. LS.

860 —21 January 1679[80]. *Dublin, Took & Crook,* 1679[80]. cap., fol.* STEELE 2p 911. LS.

861 Whereas Richard Power, late . . . 17 July 1685. *Dublin, by Benjamin Tooke, sold by Andrew Crook, and Samuel Helsham,* [1685]. brs. STEELE 2p 953–4. L, HH, DK, DN.

862 Whereas Robert Brown vicar of . . . 16 July 1662. *Dublin, John Crook,* 1662. brs. STEELE 2p 680. LS.

863 Whereas Robert Robinson late of . . . 2 July 1683. *Dublin, Took & Crook,* 1683. cap., fol.* STEELE 2p 927. LS.

864 Whereas Rory macRandal . . . 3 June 1668. *Dublin, J. Crook,* 1668. cap., fol.* STEELE 2p 794. LS.

865 Whereas Rory mac Randall . . . 29 April 1670. *Dublin, B. Tooke, sold by Mary Crooke,* 1670. cap., fol.* STEELE 2p 808. LS.

866 Whereas several complaints . . . 14 September 1667. *Dublin, J. Crook,* 1667. brs. STEELE 2p 790. LS.

867 Entry cancelled.
Whereas severall declarations and protestations. Waterford, 1646. *See* —By the General assembly of the Confederate Catholicks.

868 Whereas several felonies, . . . 24 March 1665[6]. *Dublin, J. Crooke,* 1665[6]. cap., fol.* STEELE 2p 755. DPR (lost).

869 Whereas several merchants . . . 7 March 1686[7]. *Dublin, by Andrew Crooke and Samuel Helsham, assigns of Benjamin Tooke, sold by Andrew Crook, and Samuel Helsham,* 1686[7]. brs. STEELE 2p 972. L, O, HH, DK, DN.

870 Whereas several murthers, . . . 24 January 1654[5]. *Dublin, by W. Bladen,* 1654[5]. brs. STEELE 2p 545. L.

871 —28 May 1655. —, 1655. brs. STEELE 2p 559. L.

872 Whereas several of the . . . 12 June 1685. *Dublin, by Benjamin Tooke, sold by Samuel Helsham,* [1685]. fol.* STEELE 2p 942–3. L, HH, DK, DN. (var.)

873 Whereas several officers and . . . 27 July 1655. *Dublin, by W. Bladen,* 1655. brs. STEELE 2p 565. L.

874 Whereas several persons . . . 20 September 1688. *Dublin, by Andrew Crooke and Samuel Helsham, assigns of Benjamin Tooke, sold by Andrew Crook, and Samuel Helsham,* 1688. cap., fol.* STEELE 2p 995. L, HH, DK, DN.

875 ——[Anr. ed.] —, [1688]. brs. STEELE 2p 996. DPR (lost).

876 —7 December 1688. *Dublin, by Andrew Crooke and Samuel Helsham, assigns of Benjamin Tooke, sold by Andrew Crook, and Samuel Helsham,* 1688. cap., fol.* STEELE 2p 1004–5. L, HH, DK, DN. (var.)

877 ——[Anr. ed.] *Dublin, by Andrew Crook and Samuel Helsham; and re-printed at London by George Croom,* 1688. brs. STEELE 2p 1006. O; CH, MH.

878 —25 January 1688[9]. *Dublin, by Andrew Crook & Samuel Helsham, assigns of Benjamin Tooke,* 1688[9]. cap., fol.* STEELE 2p 1009. L, HH, DK, DN, DT; INU.

878A ——[Anr. ed.] *Dublin, by Andrew Crook and Samuel Helsham; re-printed at London by George Croom,* 1689. brs. LG, OC, DN.

879 —7 March 1688[9]. *Dublin, by Andrew Crook & Samuel Helsham, assigns of Benjamin Tooke,* 1689. brs. STEELE 2p 1020–1. L, HH, DK, DN. (var.)

880 ——[Anr. ed.] *Reprinted, for T. G., sold by R. Baldwin,* 1689. brs. STEELE 2p 1022. L, LPR, OP, EN; INU.

881 Whereas several proclamations . . . 3 August 1669. *Dublin, Benjamin Tooke,* 1669. brs. STEELE 2p 799. DPR (lost).

882 Whereas several rolls . . . 1 October 1669. *Dublin, B. Tooke,* [1669]. brs. STEELE 2p 802. O.

883 Whereas several soldiers . . . 5 March 1691 [2]. *Dublin, A. Crook,* 1691[2]. brs. STEELE 2p 1255. L, HH.

884 Whereas since His Majesties . . . 28 August 1663. *Dublin, J. Crook,* 1663. cap., fol. STEELE 2p 713. DPR (lost).

885 Entry cancelled.

Whereas such of the Roman. Kilkenny, 1646. *See* —By the Councell and Congregation.

886   Whereas sundry lands, tenements . . . 11 November 1644. *Dublin, by W. Bladen*, 1644. brs. STEELE 2p 405. DPR (lost).

887   Whereas sundrie persons have . . . 16 November 1641. [*Dublin*, 1641.] brs. STEELE 2p 349. O.

888   Whereas sundry persons who . . . 28 August 1644. *Dublin, by W. Bladen*, 1644. brs. STEELE 2p 401. DPR (lost).

889   Whereas the city of Dublin . . . 16 September 1690. *Dublin, A. Crook*, 1690. brs. STEELE 2p 1145–6. L, HH.

890   —[Anr. ed.] *Dublin, by Andrew Crook, assignee of Benj. Tooke; and re-printed at London for him*, 1690. brs. STEELE 2p 1147. L, HH.

891   Whereas the commissioned . . . 24 November 1671. *Dublin, B. Tooke*, 1671. cap., fol.* STEELE 2p 820. DPR (lost).

892   Whereas the commissioners . . . 22 January 1665[6]. *Dublin, J. Crooke*, 1665[6]. cap., fol.* STEELE 2p 752. DPR (lost).

893   —26 March 1666. *Dvblin, by John Crooke, sold by Samuel Dancer*, 1666. cap., fol.* STEELE 2p 756. DN.

894   —27 April 1666. —, 1666. cap., fol.* STEELE 2p 759. DPR (lost).

895   —29 October, 1669. *Dublin, B. Tooke*, [1669]. cap., fol.* STEELE 2p 803. LS.

896   —15 January 1682[3]. *Dublin, Tooke & Crooke*, 1682[3]. cap., fol.* STEELE 2p 925. LS.

897   —11 April 1687. *Dublin, by Andrew Crook and Samuel Helsham, assigns of Benjamin Tooke, sold by Andrew Crook, and Samuel Helsham*, 1687. cap., fol.* STEELE 2p 977. L, HH, DK, DN.

898   Whereas the Duke of Albemarle . . . 17 April 1661. *Dublin, by William Bladen*, 1661. brs. STEELE 2p 643. L, DK.

899   Whereas the farmers of his . . . 5 February 1676[7]. *Dublin, B. Tooke*, 1676[7]. cap., fol.* STEELE 2p 874. LS.

899A   Whereas the inhabitants of Athlone . . . 30 November 1697. *Dublin, by Andrew Crook*, 1697. brs. DN.

900   Whereas the kings most excellent Maiesty . . . 29 January 1660[1]. *Dublin, by W. Bladen*, 1660[1]. brs. STEELE 2p 629. LPR.

901   —20 August. *Dublin, J. Crook*, 1661. fol.* STEELE 2p 654. DPR (lost).

902   —7 January 1664[5]. —, 1664[5]. cap., fol.* STEELE 2p 731. LS.

903   —15 December 1675. *Dublin, by Benjamin Tooke, sold by Joseph Wilde*, 1675. brs. STEELE 2p 862–3. LS, DN. (var.)

904   —6 February 1684[5]. *Dublin, by Andrew Crook, sold by Samuel Helsham*, 1684[5]. brs. STEELE 2p 935. L, HH, DK, DN.

905   Whereas the late commissioners . . . 21 May 1655. *Dublin, by W. Bladen*, 1655. brs. STEELE 2p 558. L.

906   Whereas the late farmers of his . . . 12 January 1682[3]. *Dublin, Tooke & Crooke*, 1682[3]. brs. STEELE 2p 924. LS.

907   Whereas the late General Convention . . . 2 January 1660[1]. *Dublin, by W. Bladen*, 1660[1]. brs. STEELE 2p 621. DPR (lost).

908   Whereas the late horrid plot . . . 10 December 1679. *Dublin, Took & Crook*, 1679. cap., fol.* STEELE 2p 908. LS.

909   Whereas the late Lord Deputy . . . 19 October 1665. *Dublin, J. Crook*, 1665. cap., fol.* STEELE 2p 750. DPR (lost).

910   Whereas the late Lords Justices . . . 20 May 1644. *Dublin, by W. Bladen*, 1644. cap., fol.* STEELE 2p 399. DPR (lost).

911   —15 August 1662. *Dublin, J. Crook*, 1662. cap., fol.* STEELE 2p 683. DPR (lost).

911A   Whereas the Lords . . . [24 September 1660, excise and customs]. *Printed at Dublin by William Bladen*, 1660. brs. STEELE 2p 620a. DN.

912   Whereas the Lords of his . . . 9 August 1669. *Dublin, B. Tooke*, 1669. cap., fol.* STEELE 2p 800. DPR (lost).

913   —27 October 1673. —, 1673. cap., fol.* STEELE 2p 844. LPR.

914   Whereas the lords spiritual . . . 20 November, 1661. *Dublin, J. Crook, sold by S. Dancer*, 1661. fol.* STEELE 2p 663. DPR (lost).

915   Entry cancelled.

Whereas the master-posters . . . 31 May 1688. [n.p., 1688.] *See* Smith, John, *Lord Mayor of Dublin*.

916   Whereas the Parliament is prorogued . . . 22 February 1663[4]. *Dublin, J. Crook*, 1663[4]. brs. STEELE 2p 722. DPR (lost).

917   Whereas the Parliament stands . . . 12 September 1664. *Dublin, J. Crooke*, 1664. brs. STEELE 2p 726. LS.

918   —13 October 1664. —, 1664. brs. STEELE 2p 728. DPR (lost).

919   —17 November 1664. —, 1664. brs. STEELE 2p 729. LS.

920   —19 December 1664. —, 1664. brs. STEELE 2p 730. LS.

921   —10 February 1664[5]. —, 1664[5]. brs. STEELE 2p 733. LS.

922   —30 March 1665. —, 1665. brs. STEELE 2p 735. LS.

923   —18 April 1665. —, 1665. brs. STEELE 2p 737. DPR (lost).

924   —18 May 1665. —, 1665. brs. STEELE 2p 738. DPR (lost).

925   —22 June 1665. —, 1665. brs. STEELE 2p 739. LS.

926   —24 July 1665. —, 1665. brs. STEELE 2p 742. LS.

927   —21 August 1665. —, 1665. brs. STEELE 2p 747. DPR (lost).

928   —18 September 1665. —, 1665. brs. STEELE 2p 749. DPR (lost).

929   Whereas the persons to . . . 10 February 1642[3]. *Dublin, by W. Bladen*, 1642[3]. brs. STEELE 2p 378. DPR (lost).

930   Whereas the present condition . . . 16 November 1641. *Imprinted at Dublin*, 1641. brs. STEELE 2p 350. O.

931   Whereas the present Parliament . . . 21 May 1663. *Dublin, J. Crook*, 1663. brs. STEELE 2p 701. O.

932   —1 July 1663. —, 1663. brs. STEELE 2p 709. DPR (lost).

933   —3 August 1663. —, 1663. brs. STEELE 2p 710. DPR (lost).

934   —4 September 1663. —, 1663. brs. STEELE 2p 714. DPR (lost).

935   —31 October 1663. —, 1663. brs. STEELE 2p 717. DPR (lost).

936 —19 December 1663. —, 1663. brs. STEELE 2p 719. DPR (lost).

937 —22 January 1663[4]. —, 1663[4]. brs. STEELE 2p 720. LS.

938 —6 February 1663[4]. —, 1663[4]. brs. STEELE 2p 721. DPR (lost).

939 Whereas the process of His . . . 27 April 1678. *Dublin, B. Tooke, sold by Joseph Wilde,* 1678. brs. STEELE 2p 887. LS.

940 Whereas the several . . . 24 July 1690. *Dublin, E. Jones.* 1690. brs. STEELE 2p 1133. DPR (lost).

941 Whereas the sins of . . . 8 February 1665[6]. *Dublin, J. Crooke,* 1665[6]. brs. STEELE 2p 753. LS.

942 Whereas the wives children and family . . . 26 September 1690. *Dublin, A. Crook,* 1690. brs. STEELE 2p 1155. L, HH.

943 Whereas there hath been a . . . 30 June 1679. *Dublin, Tooke & Crook,* [1679]. cap., fol.* STEELE 2p 906. O.

944 Whereas there have been . . . 8 December 1686. *Dublin, by Andrew Crooke and Samuel Helsham, assigns of Benjamin Tooke, sold by Andrew Crook, and Samuel Helsham,* 1686. cap., fol.* STEELE 2p 968. L, HH, DK, DN.

945 Whereas there was a letter . . . 24 December 1661. *Dublin, J. Crook,* 1661. brs. STEELE 2p 668. DPR (lost).

946 Whereas there was an ordinance . . . 13 February 1661[2]. *Dublin, J. Crook,* 1661[2]. brs. STEELE 2p 670. LS.

947 Whereas this house have taken notice . . . 12 April 1666. *Dublin, J. Crooke,* 1666. brs. STEELE 2p 757. DPR (lost).

948 Whereas Thurloe Boyle, Thurloe . . . 17 August 1670. *Dublin, B. Tooke,* 1670. cap., fol.* STEELE 2p 815. DPR (lost).

949 Whereas, tobacco is one of . . . 21 July 1679. *Dublin, Tooke & Crook,* 1679. cap., fol.* STEELE 2p 907. DPR (lost).

950 Whereas upon information . . . 20 June 1685. *Dublin, by Benjamin Tooke, sold by Andrew Crook, and Samuel Helsham,* [1685]. fol.* STEELE 2p 947–8. L, DK, DN.

951 Whereas upon the French . . . 28 February 1665[6]. *Dublin, J. Crooke,* 1665[6]. cap., fol.* STEELE 2p 754. LS.

952 Whereas upon the humble application . . . 7 January 1660[1]. *Dublin, by W. Bladen,* 1660[1]. brs. STEELE 2p 623. DPR (lost).

953 Whereas wee . . . 23 June 1647. *Dublin, by W. Bladen,* 1647. brs. STEELE 2p 443. O, LPR.

954 Whereas we are authorized . . . 16 August 1677. *Dublin, B. Tooke,* 1677. cap., fol.* STEELE 2p 879. LS, DK.

955 Whereas we are given to understand by . . . 22 January 1660[1]. *Dublin, by W. Bladen,* 1660[1]. brs. STEELE 2p 628. L, LPR.

956 Whereas we are highly sensible . . . 22 June 1670. *Dublin, B. Tooke, sold by Joseph Wilde,* 1670. cap., fol.* STEELE 2p 810. LPR.

957 —[Anr. ed.] *Dublin, B. Tooke, sold by Mary Crooke,* [1670]. brs. STEELE 2p 811–3. LS, DN. (var.)

958 Whereas wee are informed . . . 29 March 1644. *Dublin, by W. Bladen,* 1644. brs. STEELE 2p 393. DPR (lost).

959 —12 April 1644. —, 1644. brs. STEELE 2p 394. DPR (lost).

959A —3 April 1647. *Imprinted at Dublin, by VVilliam Bladen,* 1647. brs. DN.

960 —10 September 1661. *Dublin, J. Crook,* 1661. brs. STEELE 2p 656. DPR (lost).

961 Whereas we are informed, and . . . 16 September 1661. *Dublin, T. Crook,* 1661. brs. STEELE 2p 658. DPR (lost).

962 Whereas we are informed that . . . 7 November 1661. *Dublin, J. Crook,* 1661. brs. STEELE 2p 661. DPR (lost).

963 Whereas we are informed . . . 4 August 1662. *Dublin, J. Crook,* 1662. cap., fol.* STEELE 2p 682. LS.

964 —22 September 1662. *Dublin, J. Crook,* 1662. brs. STEELE 2p 688. DPR (lost).

965 Whereas we are informed, that . . . 18 December 1662. *Dublin, J. Crook,* 1662. brs. STEELE 2p 695. O.

966 Whereas we are informed . . . 8 September 1663. *Dublin, J. Crook,* 1663. brs. STEELE 2p 715. DPR (lost).

967 —27 May 1664. *Dublin, by John Crooke, sold by Sam. Dancer,* 1664. brs. STEELE 2p 725. O, DN.

968 —1 October 1664. —, 1664. brs. STEELE 2p 727. O, LS, DN.

969 —29 January 1668[9]. [*Dublin, J. Crook,* 1669.] brs. STEELE 2p 798. LS.

970 —25 October 1672. *Dublin, B. Took,* 1672. cap., fol.* STEELE 2p 833. LS.

971 —4 February 1672[3]. [*Dublin,* 1673.] brs. STEELE 2p 836. DPR (lost).

972 —18 May 1674. *Dublin, B. Tooke,* 1674. cap., fol.* STEELE 2p 851. LS.

973 —9 April 1677. —, 1677. cap., fol.* STEELE 2p 876. LS.

974 —9 January 1677[8]. *Dublin, by Benjamin Tooke, sold by Joseph Wilde,* 1677[8]. cap., fol.* STEELE 2p 882. DN.

975 —22 March 1677[8]. —, 1677[8]. brs. STEELE 2p 884. LS.

976 —26 March 1679. —, 1679. cap., fol.* STEELE 2p 902. LS, DK.

977 —24 March 1679[80]. *Dublin, Took & Crook,* 1679[80]. brs. STEELE 2p 912. LS.

978 —1 July 1681. —, 1681. brs. STEELE 2p 920. LS.

978A —19 March 1682. *Dublin, by Benjamin Tooke and John Crooke, sold by Mary Crooke and Andrew Crooke,* 1682. brs. 1682.

979 —5 May 1684. *Dublin, B. Took [sold by Mary Crook],* [1684]. brs. STEELE 2p 930. LS.

980 —9 June 1684. *Dublin, B. Took,* [1684]. cap., fol.* STEELE 2p 932. LS.

981 —24 July 1685. *Dublin, by Benjamin Tooke, sold by Andrew Crook, and Samuel Helsham,* [1685]. cap., fol.* STEELE 2p 955. L, HH, DK, DN.

982 —21 February 1686[7]. *Dublin, by Andrew Crooke and Samuel Helsham, assigns of Benjamin Tooke, sold by Andrew Crook, and Samuel Helsham,* 1686[7]. cap., fol.* STEELE 2p 969. L, HH, DK, DN.

983 — —[Anr. ed.] *Edinburgh, by the heir of A. Anderson,* 1687. brs. STEELE 3p 2688; ALDIS 2710. HH, EN, ER.

984 —4 April 1687. *Dublin, by Andrew Crook and Samuel Helsham, assigns of Benjamin Tooke, sold by Andrew Crook, and Samuel Helsham,* 1687. brs. STEELE 2p 976. L, HH, DK, DN.

985 Whereas we formerly issued a . . . 22 November 1661. *Dublin, J. Crook,* 1661. fol.* STEELE 2p 664. DPR (lost).

986 Whereas we have . . . 28 December 1688. *Dublin, by Andrew Crook and Samuel Helsham, assigns of Benjamin Tooke*, 1688. cap., fol.* STEELE 2p 1007. L, HH, DK, DN.

987 Whereas we have been necessarily . . . 21 March 1666[7]. *Dublin, J. Crooke*, 1666[7]. cap., fol.* STEELE 2p 780. LS.

988 Whereas, we have by the blessing . . . 23 May 1663. *Dublin, J. Crooke*, 1663. cap., fol.* STEELE 2p 704. O, LS.

989 Whereas we . . . have issued . . . 1 November 1641. *Dublin, society of stationers*, 1641. brs. STEELE 2p 346. DPR (lost).

990 Whereas we . . . have lately found . . . 30 October 1641. [*Dublin, society of stationers*, 1641.] brs. STEELE 2p 345. DPR (lost).

991 Whereas we have lately seen . . . 18 December 1643. *Dublin, by W. Bladen*, 1644. brs. STEELE 2p 391. O.

992 Whereas we have received . . . 2 November 1678. *Dublin, by Benjamin Tooke, sold by Mary Crook*, 1678. cap., fol.* STEELE 2p 891. DN; Y.

993 —23 December 1679. *Dublin, Took & Crook*, 1679. cap., fol.* STEELE 2p 910. LS.

994 —12 October 1683. —, [1683]. cap., fol.* STEELE 2p 929. LS.

995 Whereas we have seen a . . . 26 June 1663. *Dublin, J. Crook*, 1663. brs. STEELE 2p 707. DPR (lost).

996 Whereas we have sent our . . . 9 May 1691. *Dublin, A. Crook*, [1691]. brs. STEELE 2p 1206. HH.

997 Whereas we held it necessary . . . 5 October 1674. *Dublin, B. Tooke*, 1674. cap., fol.* STEELE 2p 852. DPR (lost).

998 Whereas wee issued a proclamation . . . 17 July 1645. *Dublin, by W. Bladen*, 1645. brs. STEELE 2p 426. DPR (lost).

999 —13 January 1645[6]. —, 1645 [6]. brs. STEELE 2p 431. DPR (lost).

1000 Whereas we observe that . . . 20 May 1644. *Dublin, by W. Bladen*, 1644. brs. STEELE 2p 398. DPR (lost).

1001 Whereas we observe that these . . . 16 April 1645. *Dublin, by W. Bladen*, 1645. brs. STEELE 2p 418. DPR (lost).

1002 Whereas we take notice . . . 9 May 1659. *London reprinted*, [1659]. brs. STEELE 2p 604. L, O, LG.

1003 Whereas we the Lord Lieutenant . . . 26 September 1666. *Dublin, J. Crook*, 1666. cap., fol.* STEELE 2p 774. DPR (lost).

1004 —8 March 1671[2]. *Dublin, B. Tooke, sold by Joseph Wilde*, 1671[2]. cap., fol.* STEELE 2p 821. LPR, LS.

1005 —21 October 1672. *Dublin, B. Took*, 1672. cap., fol.* STEELE 2p 832. LPR, LS.

1006 —27 April 1674. *Dublin, by Benjamin Tooke, sold by Joseph Wilde*, 1674. cap., fol.* STEELE 2p 850. LS, DN.

1007 —10 April 1682. *Dublin, by Benjamin Took & John Crook, sold by Mary Crook, and Andrew Crook*, 1682. cap., fol.* STEELE 2p 922. DN.

1008 —11 February 1684[5]. *Dublin, by Benjamin Tooke, sold by Andrew Crook, and Samuel Helsham*, 1684[5]. brs. STEELE 2p 940–1. L, HH, DK, DN. (var.)

1009 Whereas we the Lords Justices . . . 14 January 1642[3]. *Dublin, by W. Bladen*, 1642/3. brs. STEELE 2p 376. DPR (lost).

1010 —10 December 1661. *Dublin, J. Crook*, 1661. cap., fol.* STEELE 2p 667. DPR (lost).

1011 —22 June 1685 [against Monmouth]. *Dublin, by Benjamin Tooke, sold by Andrew Crook, and Samuel Helsham*, [1685]. cap., fol.* STEELE 2p 949. L, HH, DK, DN.

1012 —[Same date, against Monmouth's Declaration.] —, [1685]. cap., fol.* STEELE 2p 950. L, HH, DK.

1013 —[Same date, reward for Monmouth.] —, [1685]. brs. STEELE 2p 951. L, HH, DK.

1014 Whereas we understand . . . 18 August 1662. *Dublin, J. Crook*, 1662. brs. STEELE 2p 684. DPR (lost).

1015 William . . . Whereas it has been humbly . . . 17 April 1699. *Dublin, A. Crook*, 1699. cap., fol.* STEELE 2p 1393. HH.

1016 Ireland, or a booke: together with an exact mappe. *For Iohn Rothwell*, 1647. 8°.* LT, O; WF.

Irelands advocate. 1641. *See* Goodwin, John.

1017 Irelands amazement. *For John Thomas*, 1641[2]. 4°.* LT, DN.

1018 Irelands ambition taxed. [*London?*], printed 1659. 4°. O, C; CSS.

Ireland's case. [n.p.], 1695. *See* Reily, Hugh.

1018A Irelands complaint against Sir George Ratcliffe. *For Iohn Thomas*, 1641. 4°.* LVF, DN.

1019 Ireland's complaint, and Englands pitie. *For John Greensmith*, 1641. 4°.* LT, LVF, MR, DN; Y.

1020 Irelands complaint of the armies hypocrisie. [*London*, 1647.] brs. LT, HH.

1021 Entry cancelled. *See following entry*.

1022 Ireland's declaration: being a remonstrance [acknowledging Charles II]. [*London*, 1660.] brs. LT, O, LG; MH.

1023 No entry.

1024 Irelands fidelity to the Parliament of England. *By Tho. Newcomb*, 1660. 4°.* LT, LVF, BQ; WF, Y.

Ireland's ingratitude. 1643. *See* Crawford, Laurence.

1025 Ireland's lamentation: being a short, but perfect, full, and true account. *By J. D. and sold by Rich. Janeway*, 1689. 4°.* L, O, LVF, BAMB, DT; CH, CN, MH, TU, WF, Y.

Irelands misery. 1644. *See* Harrison, Richard.

Irelands sad lamentation. [n.p., 1680.] *See* L., F.

Ireland's tears. A pindarique poem. 1685. *See* Hewetson, Michael.

1026 Ireland's tears. To the sacred memory of . . . King Charles II. colop. *By Nath. Thompson*, 1685. fol.* O, LLP, LLU; CH, CLC, IU, PU.

Irelands tragical tyrannie. 1642. *See* Robinson, John.

Irelands trve divrnall. 1641. *See* Bladen, William.

Ireland's wonders from the skies. *See* Lord Chancellor's petition. 1688.

1027 Irena, a tragedy. *By Robert White for Octavian Pulleyn, junior*, 1664. 4°. O; CH.

Irenæus, jr. *pseud.*

1028 **Irenæus.** Proposals for subscriptions to a new edition of Irenæus. [*Thomas Bennet*, 1699?] brs. OP.

Irenicon. [n.p., 1674.] *See* Sherwin, William. Προδρομος.

Irenicum: in quo casus. 1654. *See* Durie, John.

Irenicum irenicorum, seu. 1658. *See* Zwicker, Daniel.

1029   Irenicum magnum: the gospel terms. *For A. Baldwin,*
        1700. 8°. T.C.III 196. L, O, C, EN, DT; TO, WF.
        Irenicum; or. 1659. *See* Newcomen, Matthew.
        Irenodia gratulatoria. [*n.p.*], 1652. *See* Fisher, Payne.

1030   **Ireton, Henry.** A declaration and prolcamation [*sic*] of
        the Deputy-General of Ireland . . . concerning . . . the
        plague. *Printed at Cork,* 1650. *Reprinted at London by
        John Field,* [1650?]. 4°.* LT, O, C, OME, DN; CH, MH, Y.

1030A   — —[Anr. ed.] *Imprinted at Dublin,* 1650. 4°.* CD.

1031   —A declaration of the Lord Lieutenant of Ireland. *For
        the undeceiving. Corke, reprinted at London, by E. Grif-
        fin, March* 21. 1650. 4°.* LT, C, DN; CH, CSS, WF, WU, Y.

1031A   — —[Anr. ed.] *Corke, re-printed at London by E. G.
        March* 21, 1650. 4°.* OC; MH.

1032   —A letter from the Lord Deputy-General of Ireland,
        unto the Honorable William Lenthal. *By John Field,*
        1651. 4°.* LT, O, OC, SP, DN, DT; CH, Y.

1032A   —Propositions approved and granted by . . . [25 Feb-
        ruary 1650]. 1650/1. DN.

1033   —Sad nevves from Ireland. *For Robert Ibbitson,* 1651.
        4°.* LT, SP, DN; MBA, MIU, Y.

1034   [–] The true copy of a petition presented to the Lord
        General. *Printed* 1648. 4°.* O; WF.

1035   **Ireton, Sir John.** Mr. Iohn Iretons oration. [*London,*
        1659.] cap., 4°.* LT, O; CH, CLC, MH, MIU, NU, Y.

1036   **Irish, David.** Levamen infirmi: or, cordial counsel to
        the sick. *For the author: to be sold by Isaac Walker, in
        Guildford,* 1700. 8°. L, LWL, GU; NAM.
        Irish cabinet. 1645. *See* Cole, William.
        Irish colours displayed. 1662. *See* Orrery, Roger Boyle,
        earl of.
        Irish colours folded. 1662. *See* Walsh, Peter.

1037   An Jrish declaration from the viscounts, earles, barons,
        . . . in Ireland. *For I. Horton, Iune,* 24. 1642. 4°.* LT,
        MR, DN.

1038   Entry cancelled.
        The Irish-evidence. 1682. *See* Hetherington, William.
        Irish footmans poetry. [n.p.], 1641. *See* Taylor, John.

1038A   The Irish forfeitures now lying before a committee of
        the . . . House of Commons. [*n.p.,* 1690.] brs. L.

1038B   The Irish garland. *For P. Brooksby,* [*c.* 1689]. 8°. O.
        Irish Hudibras. 1689. *See* Farewell, James.

1039   The Irish lasses letter. [1688.] brs. O.

1040   The Irish martyr. *For F. C. and T. V.,* 1641. 4°.* LT, MR,
        DN; CN.
        Irish massacre. [1646.] *See* Parker, Henry.

1041   The Irish occurrences. Comfortable nevvs. *For R. H.,*
        1642. 4°.* LT, DN, DT; MIU.

1042   The Irish occurrences, or, a true relation. *By A. N. for
        H. T.* 1642. 4°.* OC, DN; MH.
        Irish papers. 1646. *See* Bristol, George Digby, *earl of.*

1043   The Irish petition to this Parliament. *Imprinted at Dublin,
        and now reprinted at London for for* [*sic*] *Daniell Williams,*
        1641. 4°.* L, O, C, SP, DN.

1044   The Irish rendezvous. *For Randal Taylor,* 1689. fol.*
        L, C; MH, Y.

1045   The Irish rogue. *For G. Conyers,* [1690]. 12°. T.C.II
        333. L; MH.

1046   The Irsih [*sic*] treaty. *By T. Harper for H. Shepheard, to be
        sold by G. Tomlinson,* 1643. 4°.* LT, O, DN; CH, MH.

1047   An iron rod for the Naylors. [*London,* 1655.] brs. LT.

1048   **Ironside, Gilbert, *bp.*** A sermon preached . . . May 15,
        1660. *For Robert Clavell,* 1660. 4°.* LT, O, LLP; NU.

1049   — —November 23. 1684. *Oxford, by Leonard Lichfield,
        for James Good,* 1685. 4°.* L, O, CT, LIU, LSD; CH, IU, NU,
        TU, WF, Y.

1049A   The irregular and disorderly state of the plantation trade.
        [*London?* 1695.] cap., fol.* L; MH, NC.
        Irregularitie of a private prayer. [n.p.], 1674. *See* Sher-
        lock, Richard, *bp.*

1050   [**Irvine, Alexander.**] A dialogue between A. and B.
        Printed, 1694. 4°. L, O, C, EN, DT; CH, IU, MBA, MM, NP,
        WF, Y.

        [**Irvine, Christopher.**] Bellum grammaticale. Edin-
        burgh, 1652. *See* Guarna, Andreas.

1051   —Historiæ Scoticæ. *Edinbruchii, sumptibus Gideonis
        Schaw, typisq; Andersonianis regiis,* 1682. 8°. ALDIS 2333.
        L, O, C, AN, EN, DT; CH, CLC, IU, LC, TU, WF, Y.

1052   — —[Anr. ed.] *Edinburgi, sumptibus quorundum bibliopol-
        arum Edinburgensium; typisque Jacobi Watson,* 1697. 4°.
        ALDIS 3673. L, O, EN, ENC, DT; BN, CLC, IU, MH, NC, NU,
        WF, Y.

1053   —Medicina magnetica. [*Edinburgh, C. Higgins*], printed,
        1656. 8°. ALDIS 1545. LT, O, C, EN, AM; CH, MH, NA, WF.

1054   Entry cancelled. Ghost.

1055   **Irving, George.** Disputatio juridica. *Edinburgh, Watson,*
        1698. 4°. ALDIS 3756. EN.
        Iryngio, C. de. *See* Irvine, Christopher.

1056   Is not the hand of Joab in all this? [*n.p.*], printed, 1676.
        4°.* L, LG, LUG, LSD; CSS, MH, NC, WF.

1057   **Isaac, Israel.** Christ Jesus, the true Messiah, delineated.
        By E. Tyler, and R. Holt, for the author; 1682. 4°.* O,
        LLU, CD, DT.
        Isaac, Thomas. *See* Isacius, Thomas.

1057A   I[saacson], H[enry]. Divine contemplations. *For
        Richard Thrale,* 1648. 12°. O.

1058   —An exact narration of the life and death of . . . Lancelot
        Andrewes. *For John Stafford,* 1650[1]. 4°.* LT, O, CK,
        EC, EN; MM, NU, PL.

1059   [–] A spirituall duell between a Christian and Satan. *By
        W. Wilson, for Richard Thrale,* 1646. 12°. L, O, LCL, P;
        MM, NU, WF.

1059A   [–] The summe and substance of Christian religion.
        Printed 1646. 8°. Y.

1060   [–] —[Anr. ed.] *By W. Wilson, to be sold by Richard
        Thrale,* 1647. 8°. O, CS; PL.

1061   [–] A treaty of pacification or conditions. 1642. *London,
        for R. Thral.* 12°. LT, C, DC; CH, WF.

1061A   [–] —Second edition. *By J. R. for Richard Thrale,* 1645.
        12°. O.

1061B   [–] —Fourth edition. —, 1648. 12°. CLC.

1061C **Isacius, Thomas.** Methodus cognascendi caussas. *Typis Guil. Du-gardi, veneunt apud Octavian Pulleyn,* 1650. 12°. L, O, CP; WF.

1062   [**Isack, I.**] A famous victory obtained by {Sir William Brewerton. *By B. Alsop, Febr. the 2d.* 1644. 4°.* LT.

Isagoge ad Dei providentiam: or. 1672. *See* Crane, Thomas.

Isaiah, Paul, *pseud.*

Iscanus, Theophilus, *pseud. See* Du Moulin, Louis.

1063   I'se no more to shady coverts. [*London,* 1697.] brs. L.

1064   **Isendoorn, Gisbert.** Cursus logicus. *Oxonii, typis Gulielmi Hall, impensis Rob. Blagrave,* 1658. 12°. MADAN 2391. L, O; TO, Y.

1065   Entry cancelled.

[**Isham, John.**] *See* Isham, Zacheus.

1066   [**Isham, Zacheus.**] The catechism of the church: with proofs. *For R. Clavel,* 1694. 8°. T.C.II 520. O.

1067   [–] —Second edition. —, 1695. 8°. L, OC; IU.

1067A [–] —Third edition. —, 1696. 8°. O.

1067B [–] —Fourth edition. —, 1699. 8°. ORP.

1067C [–] A daily office for the sick. *By S. Roycroft, for Robert Clavell,* 1694. 8°. T.C.II 506. O, C, LLP, MR, NL; IU.

1067D — —Second edition. —, 1699. 8°. L, C, AN, EC, NL; WF.

1068   —A sermon preached . . . March 15. 1694/5. *For Walter Kettilby,* 1695. 4°.* T.C.II 547. L, O, C, OC, EC; CH, MH, NU, TU, WF, Y.

1069   — —Second edition. —, 1695. 4°.* L, C, OC, BC, MR; CLC, IU, Y.

1070   —A sermon preach'd . . . Decemb. 3. 1696. *By J. L. for Walter Kettilby,* 1697. 4°.* T.C.III 4. L, O, C, CT, BAMB; CH, CLC, IU, NU, Y.

1071   —A sermon preached before the . . . Lord-Mayor, . . . Wednesday in Easter week, MDCC. *For Walter Kettleby,* 1700. 4°.* T.C.III 182. L, O, C, LLP, OCC; CH, NGT, NU, Y.

Island princess. 1669. *See* Fletcher, John.

Isle of man. 1648. *See* Bernard, Richard.

Isle of pines. 1668. *See* Neville, Henry.

1072   Islington Wells a song. *For J. Dean,* 1684. brs. L.

Islington-wells. 1691. *See* Ames, Richard.

1073   **Isma'il Ibn' Ali.** Chorasmiæ et Mawaralnahræ. 1650. 4°. L, O, SC, EN, DT; BN, CH, MH, NP, OCI, PL, WF, Y.

1074   **Isocrates.** Epistolæ. *Typis J. Heptinstall,* 1685. 12°. CT; Y.

1075   —Orationes duæ. *Sumptibus authoris. Prostant venales apud Johannem Baker. Et apud Richardum Jones.* 1676. 4°. L, O, C; CLC, PL.

1076   — —Second edition. *Oxonii. Excudit H. H., sumptibus authoris.* 1677. 4°. L, O, C, LL, LW, CS, LLU; WF.

1076A — —[Anr. ed.] *Sumptibus Johannes Baker,* 1680. 8°. T.C.I 387. L; CLC, PL, Y.

1076B —Orationes et epistolae. *Excudebat Joannes Field,* 1665. 12°. ASU.

1077   — —[Anr. ed.] *Cantabrigiæ, ex officina Johan. Hayes,* 1686. 12°. L, O, C, LL, LW, GU; CH, CLC, IU, PL, WF, Y.

1077A —Orationes tres. *Typis Johannis Macock pro societate stationorum,* 1668. 8°. O.

1077B — —[Anr. ed.] *Typis M. Clark, pro societate stationariorum,* 1682. 8°. AVP.

1078   —Parænesis. *Cantabrigiæ, per Thomam Buck,* 1653. 12°. O, C, CCA, BC, EC, NPL; WF.

1078AA — —[Anr. ed.] *Typis J. Redmayne, pro societat[e] stationarum,* 1669. 12°. L; PL.

1078A — —[Anr. ed.] —, 1680. 12°. CS; CH, MH, Y.

1078B — —[Anr. ed.] *Typis F. Heptinstall, pro societate stationariorum,* 1699. 12°. O, EN; IU, LC, MWA.

1078C Entry cancelled.

Israël, Joseph ben. Converted Jew. [n.p.], 1653. *See* Welde, Thomas. False Jew.

Israel's condition. 1656. *See* L., D.

Israel's lamentation. 1683. *See* Heywood, Oliver.

1079   Israel's reformation. *Printed,* 1698. fol.* L, LLP; Y.

1080   Istleworth-Syons peace. *By W. Godbid,* 1657. 4°. L, LG, LL; CH, CLC, MH, WF.

1080A It being the laudable custom . . . western counties. [*London,* 1659.] brs. L.

1081   It has been observed, that nothing has been so destructive to the peace . . . *Pirnted* [sic] *for N. Ponder, and S. Lee,* [1680?]. brs. CH.

1081A It having pleased Almighty God . . . [dinner at Haberdasher's Hall]. 1682. brs. LG, LPR.

1082   It is conceived by the judgement of many that if the courtiers. [*London,* 1644.] cap., 4°.* LT; CSS.

1083   Entry cancelled.

15. Iune, 1645. It is desired that all ministers. [n.p., 1645.] *See* London. Lord Mayor.

1083A It is humbly offered, by some uninterested persons, that the laying a greater duty on low-wines. [*London,* 1690.] brs. LPR.

1084   It is humbly proposed on the behalf of the purchasers. [*London,* 1660.] brs. LT.

1085   It is humbly proposed, that all plate receive a stamp, or mark. [*London?* 1695.] brs. LG, LPR, LUG.

1086   It is ordered, that notwithstanding the additionall . . . 8 May 1654. [*London,* 1654.] STEELE 3036. brs. L, LPR.

1087   It is this day resolved upon the question . . . 4 July 1642. *By L. N. and J. F. for Husbands & Franck,* 12 July 1642. brs. STEELE 2213. O, EC.

1088   It is thought fit by divers persons of quality. [*London*], 16 of August, 1644. brs. LT.

1088AA It must be acknowledged, that an act to prevent stock-jobbing. [*London?* 1697.] brs. MH.

1088bA It was little expected by the College of Physicians. [*London,* 1694.] brs. L.

Italian convert. 1655. *See* Balbani, Niccolo.

Italian song call'd Pastorella. [n.p., 1699.] *See* Bononcini, Giovanni Battista.

Italy, in its original glory. 1660. *See* Schott, Frans.

Item against sacriledge. 1653. *See* Clarke, Samuel.

1088A An item for England in some honest intimations. colop: *Printed,* 1655. 4°. CSS.

1089   An item to His Maiestie. [*London*], *printed,* 1642. 4°.* LT, LLU, MR, SP; CH, MH, MIU, NN, WF, Y.

Iter Australe, a. [n.p., 1660.] *See* Bispham, Thomas.

1090 Iter Australe: attempting . . . By a loyal pen. *By Tho. Leach,* 1660. 4°.* L, EN; MH, WF, Y.

Iter Boreale attempting. 1660. *See* Wild, Robert.

1091 Iter Boreale his country clown. *For the author,* 1665. brs. O, LS; MH.

1092 Iter Boreale: or Esq; Spare-penny's departure. *By the assigns of Col. Hewson, for the cobler of Agawam,* 1682. brs. L, O, EN; CH, MH.

Iter Boreale, or, Tyburn. 1682. *See* Dean, John.

Iter Boreale. The second part. 1660. *See* H., T.

1092A Iter Boreale, to the Presbyterian party. *Printed,* 1663. brs. MH.

Iter Carolinum, being. *See* Walker, *Sir* Edward.

Iter Lvsitanicvm. 1662. *See* Hinde, Samuel.

1093 Iter Oxoniense. [*London,* 1681.] brs. L, O; CH, CN, MH, NCD, PU, Y.

1094 **Ives, Jeremiah.** Confidence encountred. *Printed at London; and are to be sold by Dan. White; or may be had at the authors house,* 1658. 4°. LT, O, CS, MR, SP; CLC, NU, WF.

1095 —Confidence questioned. *For Daniel White,* 1658. 4°.* LT, LW.

1095A —A contention for truth. *Printed,* 1672. 8°. O, LCL.

1096 —Contest for Christianity. *For F. Smith, and Jonathan Robinson,* 1674. 8°. LF.

1097 [–] The corrector corrected. 1672. 8°. T.C.I 110. LCL.

1098 —Eighteen questions. *By G. D. for Francis Smith,* 1659. 4°.* LT, CS, MR; CH, CLC, INU, WF.

1099 —The great case of conscience opened. *By S. D. for Francis Smith,* 1660[1]. 4°.* LT, LCL; CH, CLC, MB, NHC, NU, WF.

1100 —Infants-baptism disproved. *Printed at London for Richard Moone,* 1655. 4°. L, O, C.

1101 Entry cancelled. *See preceding entry.*

1102 —Innocency above impudency. *By J. Cottrel for R. Moon,* 1656. 4°. LT, C, LCL, LF, DT; NU, PH, PL.

1102A —Quakers no Christians. *For F. Smith,* 1674. brs. TO; MH.

1103 —The Quakers quaking. *By J. Cottrel, for R. Moon,* 1656. 4°. LT, O, C, LCL, LF; PH.

1103A —Questions for the Quakers. *For Francis Smith,* 1674. 4°.* NHC.

1103B [–] Rome is no rule. *By T.M. for Livewel Chapman,* 1664. 8°. O; IU.

1104 —Saturday no Sabbath. *For Dan. White, and Fran. Smith,* 1659. 8°. L, O, C, LCL, ORP; CH, CLC, MH, NHC, NU.

1105 —A sober request to the Quakers. *For F. Smith,* 1674. brs. O.

1106 —A stop to a lying pamphlet. *For the author,* 1656. 4°.* C.

1106A [–] Vindiciæ veritatis; or, an impartial account. *Printed,* 1672. 8°. T.C.I 101. L, O, CS.

1107 **Ives, John.** One trumpet more sounded. [*London*], *printed,* 1664. 4°. L, O, LF, BBN, MR; MH, PH, PL.

1107A **Ivie, John.** A declaration written by. *For the author,* 1661. 4°.* OB.

1108 **Ivie, Thomas.** Alimony arraign'd. *Printed,* 1654. 4°. LT, O, CCO, MR, EN; CH, CJC, MHL, WF, Y.

1108A —The declaration of. [*London,* 1661.] brs. LG.

1109 —The humble appeal and remonstrance of. [*London,* 1654.] 4°. C.

Ivory, J. Continuation of the names. Cambridge, 1675. *See* Langbaine, Gerard, *elder.*

1110 **Izacke, Richard.** Antiquities of the city of Exeter. *By E. Tyler and R. Holt, for Richard Marriott; sold by George Marriott,* 1677. 8°. T.C.I 266. L, O, C, MC, DT; CH, CN, MBP, WF, Y.

1111 —Remarkable antiquities of the city of Exeter. *For Rowland Reynolds.* 1681. 8°. T.C.I 419. L, O, C, WCA, EN; CLC, IU, MH, NN, WF, Y.

—Foundation of the university. Cambridge, 1672. *See* Langbaine, Gerard, *elder.*

J

1 **J.** A practical grammar, or, the easiest and shortest way. *By Henry Hills, for Thomas Cockerill,* 1682. 8°. T.C.I 511. L; WF.

1A — —Second edition. *For Thomas Cockerill,* 1698. 8°. T.C.III 68. L.

J., A. Miraculum basilicon, or. 1664. *See* Jennings, Abraham.

J., B. Alchemist. [1680.] *See* Jonson, Ben.

—Cataline his conspiracy. 1669. *See* Jonson, Ben.

—Herm'ælogium; or. 1659. *See* Jones, Bassett.

—Jus primogeniti: or. [n.p., 1699.] *See* Brydall, John.

2 —A letter from a gentleman in the countrey to a member. [*London?* 1696.] brs. L.

3 Entry cancelled.

—Letter to a gentleman of note. 1690. *See* Jenks, Benjamin.

4 —A summary account of the proceedings upon the happy discovery of the Jacobite conspiracy. [*London,* 1696.] cap., fol.* L, C; CH, CN, WF, Y.

5 —The tragical history, admirable atchievements . . . of Guy Earl of Warwick, a tragedy. *For Thomas Vere and William Gilbertson,* 1661. 4°.* L, O, LVD, OW, A; CH, CN, CU, WF.

5A —Two letters written to a gentleman of note guilty of common swearing. *For Benj. Tooke,* 1691. 8°. L.

J., C. Cluster of sweetest grapes. 1664. *See* Jelinger, Christopher.

5B — A net for the fishers of men. [*London*], *printed,* 1686. 24°. LLP, MC.

5C ——[Anr. ed.] [*London*], 1687. sixes. FARM.

6 —One of George Keith's friends serious enquiry. *For B. Aylmer, and C. Brome*, 1700. 4°. LF.

7 **J., D.** King Charles I no such saint. 1698. 4°. L, O, C, LVF, EN, BLH, DT; CH, MIU, WF.

—Looking-glasse for the Parliament. [n.p.], 1648. *See* Jenkins, David.

—Short, sure and conscientious expedient. [n.p.], 1648. *See* Jenkins, David.

—Wars and causes. 1695. *See* Jones, David.

J., Da. Preparative to the treaty. [n.p.], 1648. *See* Jenkins, David.

J., E. An injur'd prince vindicated. [n.p., 1688?] *See* James, Elinor.

8 —A new answer to a speech. [*n.p.*, 1681.] brs. L, O, EN; CH, CN, MH, Y.

J., G. Englands oaths. 1642. *See* Ingoldsby, William.

9 —Letter sent into France to the Lord Duke of Buckingham. [*London*], imprinted, 1649. 4°.* L, O, YM.

—Νεοφυτο-αστρολογος: the. 1660. *See* Gadbury, John.

10 Entry cancelled.

—Ψευδο-αστρολογος. Or, the spurious prognosticator. 1660. *See* Gadbury, John.

11 —A second letter to the Lord Duke of Buckingham. [*London*], imprinted, 1649. 4°.* L.

—Spirit of the hat. 1673. *See* Mucklow, William.

12 Entry cancelled.

—Treaty of pacification. 1645. *See* Isaacson, Henry.

J., H. Calculation for . . . 1645. [1645.] *See* Almanacs: Jessop, Henry.

13 —Exceeding good nevves from Ireland. *By B. A.*, May 30, 1647. 4°.* LT, O, OC; Y.

14 —The history of the life and death of Pope Joane. *For F. Coles*, 1663. 4°. O.

15 —A letter from a gentleman in the country to his friend in the city. *By G. C. for William Miller*, 1691. 4°.* T.C.II 385. L, LUG, CT, BR; CH, CJC, MH, NC, WF, Y.

—Lords loud call. 1660. *See* Jessey, Henry.

16 Entry cancelled.

—Modell of a Christian society. Cambridge, 1647. *See* H., J.

—Scripture almanack. [n.p., 1648.] *See* Almanacs: Jessey, Henry.

17 —To the most excellent princesse the Dutchesse of New-castle. *By Sarah Griffin*, 1667. brs. L.

—Treaty of pacification. 1645. *See* Isaacson, Henry.

J., J. Churches ardent love to Christ. 1687. *See* Jordan, Joshua.

—Essay of the form. 1700. *See title.*

—Heaven upon earth. 1667. *See* Janeway, James.

—Ingeniossimo humanissimoque. [n.p., 1685.] *See* Jones, J.

18 —The resolvtion of the armie concerning the citizens of London. [*London*], printed, 1648. 4°.* LT, O; BBE, WF, Y.

19 —The resurrection of dead bones. *For Giles Calvert*, 1655. 8°. LT; MH.

20 Entry cancelled.

—Rome is no rule. 1664. *See* Ives, Jeremiah.

21 —A strange and terrible sight foreseene. *For Ed. Blackmore, and Tho. Banks*, 1643. 4°.* LT; WF.

—Strength in weakness. 1655. *See* Jackson, John, *lover of truth.*

22 **J., M.** Some proposals by a well-wisher. [*London*, 1653.] brs. LT.

23 **J., N.** A letter from N. J. to E. T. [*n.p.*, 1690.] 4°. O, LL, LUG, CT, LSD; CH, INU, NC, WF.

24 **J., P.** An addition to the relation of some passages. *For Robert Bostocke*, 1643[4]. 4°.* LT, O, LVF, AN; CH, INU, MH.

25 —An answer to another letter from Legorn. colop: *London, printed, and are to be sold by Richard Janeway*, 1680. fol.* L, O, LUG, LNC, MR; CH, CU, MH, PU, WF, Y.

25A —A sermon preached Septem. the 5th. . . . wherein is set forth the Kings due. *Imprinted*, 1647. 4°.* MM.

26 **J., P. H.** The absolution of a penitent. colop: *By J. Dawks*, 1696. cap. 4°.* MR; CLC, WF.

27 **J., R.** Compunction, or pricking of heart. *By Ruth Raworth for Thomas Whitaker*, 1648. 4°. LSC, E; Y.

28 —Dives and Lazarus. Twenty-first edition. *For W. Thackeray*, 1677. 8°.* L.

28A ——Twenty-second edition. *By H. B. for W. Thackeray*, 1684. 8°. O, LW.

—Faithfull depositaty [*sic*]. Newcastle, 1649. *See* Jenison, Robert.

29 —A letter of advice to a friend about the currency of clipt-money. *For Edw. Castle*, 1696. 8° in 4s.* L, O, LUG, EN; CH, INU, LC, MH, NC, Y, ANL.

29A ——Second edition. *For Edw. Castle*, 1696. 8° in 4s.* T.C.II 580. CM; MH, NCD, PU, WF.

30 ——"Second" edition. *For A. and J. Churchill*, 1696. 8° in 4s.* T.C.III 6. L, OC, LUG; CH, IU, MH.

31 —Nineteen arguments proving circumcision no seal. *Printed*, 1645[6]. 4°.* LT, CS, MR, E, GU; CH, NHC, WF.

31A **J., S.** At a meeting held at Turner's hall . . . January 1699. By George Keith. [*London*, 1700.] brs. L.

—Daniel in the den. 1682. *See* Jay, Stephen.

32 —England's new remembrancer. *By W. and J. Wilde for H. Rhodes*, 1691. 12°. T.C.II 348. O; NP, Y.

—Daniel in the den. 1682. *See* Jay, Stephen.

32A —An historical account of the memorable actions . . . William Henry. *For R.H.*, 1689. 12°. ORP; CLC.

32B —An historical account of the memorable actions . . . William III. *Printed, and sold by H. Rhodes*, 1689. 12°. T.C.II 273. L, NPL, AU; CLC, Y.

33 ——Third edition. *For H. Rhodes*, 1690. 12°. T.C.II 293. L, LLP, LIU, AU; CH, NC, WF.

33A Entry cancelled.

—Letter to the clergy of the diocess of Norfolk. [n.p., 1699.] *See* Field, John.

33AB —The relation of a gentlewoman long under the persecution of the bishops. *At the cost of S. J.* 1642. 12°. ZWT.

33B Entry cancelled.

—Second letter to the clergy . . . of Norfolk. [n.p., 1699.] *See* Field, John.

—To Sions lovers. [n.p.], 1644. *See* Jones, *Mrs.* Sarah.

34 —A true copy of a letter sent by. colop: *For A. Bancks*,
     1684. brs. O, EN; CH, WF.

35 **J., T.** A brief representation and discovery of the notorious
     falshood. *By J. L. for Philemon Stephens*, 1649. 4°.* LT, O,
     OC, NPL; CH.
     —Choice banquet. 1665. *See* Armstrong, Archibald.
     —Christian souldier. 1642. *See* Jordan, Thomas.
     —Diurnall of dangers. [1642.] *See* Jordan, Thomas.

36 —A glimps [*sic*] of the King of Glory. *Printed*, 1672. 8°. Y.

37 —An harbinger for the King of Glory. *Printed*, 1672. 8°.
     ORP; Y.
     —Heavenly child. 1659. *See* Jordan, Timothy.
     —Honest ansvver. [n.p., 1642.] *See* Taylor, John.

37A —An honest mans delight. *For R. Burton*, [1641–74]. brs. O.
     —Jewels of ingenvity. [*London*, 166–?] *See* Jordan, Thomas.

38 —A letter of advice to His Excellency the Lord General
     Monck. [*London*], *printed*, 1659[60]. 4°.* LT, O, MR; CH,
     MH, MIU, WF, Y.

38A ——[Anr. ed.] [*London*], *printed*, 1660. 4°.* O, LG.

39 —A letter sent from a merchant in Dublin. *For Thomas
     Pool*, 1659[60]. brs. LT, O, C, LG; MH.
     —Looking-glass for a covetous miser. [1670–77.] *See*
     Jordan, Thomas.

39A —The love-sick young man, and witty maid. [*London*], *for
     W. Thackeray*, [1688–89]. brs. O.

39B —A loyal subjects admonition. *For F. Grove*, [1660?]. brs.
     EUING 160. GU.
     —Medicine for the times. 1641. *See* Jordan, Thomas.

40 —A merry dialogue between a doctor. [*London*], *for R.
     Burton*, [1670?]. brs. L.

40A —The merry mans resolution. [*London*], *for J. Williamson*,
     [1665]. brs. L, CM, HH; MH.

40B ——[Anr. ed.][*London*], *for Richard Burton*, [1655]. brs. O.

41 —The nature, nobility, character, . . . of money. *For
     William Thackeray*, 1684. brs. L, O, MC; CLC, MH, PU, Y.
     —Of the heart. 1678. *See* Jones, Thomas.

42 —On the death of the Lord General Monck. *For William
     Thackeray*, 1669[70]. brs. L; MH.

43 —On the death of the renowned General George Duke of
     Albemarle. *For Robert Clavel*, 1670. brs. L; MH.
     —Pictures of passions. 1641. *See* Jordan, Thomas.
     —Piety, and poesy. 1642. *See* Jordan, Thomas.

44 —A poore scholar's thred-bare suit. *For William Gilbertson*,
     1663. brs. L.

45 ——[Anr. ed.] *For William Whitwood*, 1668. brs. L.
     —Roaring black smiths. [1655.] *See* Jordan, Thomas.

45A —Satan deluding by feigned miracles. *By R.I. for Philemon
     Stephens*, 1655. 4°. YM.
     —Selfe; or, a riddle. 1668. *See* Jordan, Thomas.
     —Vindication of the Surey demoniack. 1698. *See* Jollie,
     Thomas.

45B —The way to Christ. *Printed*, 1674. 8°. BR; Y.
     —The world turn'd upside down. 1647. *See* Jordan,
     Thomas.
     J., Tho. Royal arbor. 1664. *See* Jordan, Thomas.

46 **J., W.** The cause of our divisions searched out. *Peter Cole*,
     1657. 8°. NU.

47 —A collection of seven and fifty approved receipts. *By
     Peter Lillicrap, for John Wingfield*, 1665. 4°.* LL; MBM,
     ZDU.

48 —A dissection of all governments. *Printed*, 1649. 4°.*
     LT, C, DT; CH, NU, Y.
     —Ductor historicus: or. 1698. *See* Hearne, Thomas.

49 [–] An exact list of their Majesties forces now in . . . Ireland.
     colop: *For Richard Baldwin*, 1690. brs. C, DN; CH, Y.

49A ——[Anr. ed.] colop: *Edinburgh, re-printed by the heir of
     Andrew Anderson*, 1690. brs. ALDIS 3039. EN; FU, WF.

50 —The jubilie of England. *For J. Bartlet*, 1646. 4°.* LT, O, EN.
     —Lawfulnes of tythes. 1675. *See* Jeffrey, William.

51 —A letter from an ignoramus to his correspondent.
     December 6th, 1682. colop: *For Richard Janeway*, 1682.
     cap., fol.* L, O, OP, EN; CH, MH, MM, NN, PU, WF, Y.

52 —Obedience active and passive due to the svpream povver.
     Oxford, by Leonard Litchfeild, 1643. 4°.* MADAN 1251.
     LT, O, C, GU, DT; CH, CN, MH, WF, Y.
     —Remembrance of former times. Boston, 1697. *See*
     Jameson, William.

53 —The third letter from W. J. to . . . Dr. Wallis. *Printed*,
     1693. 4°. L, O, C, LCP, LLP, LW, WCA; MB, MU.
     J. F. Didascaliæ; discourses. [n.p.], 1643. *See* Ferret, John.
     J. P. the follower. 1660. *See* Perrot, John.

54 **Jabir ibn Haiyan.** The works of Geber. *For N. E. by
     Thomas James; to be sold by Robert Clavel*, 1678. 8°. L,
     LW, LLU, DU, GU; IU, NAM, NN, Y.

54A ——[Anr. ed.] *For N. E. by Thomas James*, 1678. 8°. OC,
     LC, WU.

55 ——[Anr. ed.] *For William Cooper*, 1686. 8°. L, OR; MH,
     NC, PL, Y.
     Jaccheus. *See* Jack.

56 Entry cancelled.
     [**Jack, Gilbert.**] Grammatica rationis. Oxonii, 1675. *See*
     Fell, John.

57 —Primæ philosophiæ. *Cantabrigiæ, ex officina Rogeri
     Danielis*, 1649. 12°. OJ, CT, BC, DUS, DT; CLC, MH, WF.

58 **Jack, Thomas.** Onomasticon poeticum. *Cantabrigiæ; ex
     academiæ typographeo*, 1654. 8°. C, CT.

59 Jack Catch his Bridewel oration. colop: *For D. M.*, 1686.
     brs. O.

60 Jack Had-lands lamentation. [*London*], *for P. Brooksby*,
     [1685–88]. brs. L, O, CM, HH; MH.

61 Jack Presbiter. [*n.p.*], *printed*, 1690. brs. L.
     Jack Pudding: or. 1654. *See* Erbery, William.

62 Jack the cobler's caution. colop: *For T. S.*, 1682. brs. O;
     CH, CN, WF.
     Jack the plough-lads lamentation. 1654. *See* Robins,
     Thomas.

62A **Jackett, William.** To the most honorable the Council of
     State, the humble petition of. [*London*, 1650?] cap., 4°.*
     CSS.

63 **Jackman, A.** Syons calamitye or Englands miserye.
     [*n.p.*], *sold by Nathaniell Gilbye*, [1643]. brs. LT.

63A **Jackson, Abraham.** Seasonable advice to the apprentices.
     Simon Miller, 1659. 12°. LU.

64 **Jackson, Arthur.** Annotations upon the five books, . . . Iob, the Psalms, . . . the third part. *By Roger Daniel, for the authour,* 1658. 4°. LT, O, LCL, MC, CD; IU, MH, NU, Y.

65 —Annotations upon the remaining historicall part. *Cambridge, by Roger Daniel,* 1646. 4°. L, OC, CS, MC, EN, CD; CH, MH, MM, TU, Y.

66 —Annotations upon the whole book of Isaiah. *For Tho. Parkhurst,* 1682. 4°. T.C.I 505. L, C, CT, E, CD; CH, CLC, NU, PPT, Y.

67 —A help for the understanding. *By Roger Daniel, of Cambridge,* 1643. 4°. L, O, C, EN, DM; CH, MH, NU, TU, WF, WSC, Y.

68 **Jackson, Christopher.** The magistrate's duty. *York: be* [*sic*] *Jo. White for Francis Hildyard,* 1685. 4°.* T.C.II 155. L, WCA, YM; CH, NN, NU, Y.

68A **Jackson, Henry.** Short memorable sentences. *For Anna Brewster,* 1668. brs. MH.

69 —A testimony of truth. colop: [*London*], *for M. W.,* [1662]. cap., 4°.* L, LF, BBN; IU, MH, NP, PH, PSC.

70 —Unnatural son. *For R. Brown,* 1700. 8°. CT.

71 —A visitation of love. *Printed,* 1663. 4°.* L, O, C, LF, BBN; MH, NC, NU, PH.

72 **Jackson, J.** A discourse on God's foreknowledge. 1697. 8°. LCL.

73 **Jackson, James.** The friendly enquirer's doubts . . . answered. *Printed and sold by T. Sowle,* 1698. 12°. T.C.III 170. L, LF, OC, BBN, MR; MH, PH, PSC, WF, Y.

74 —The malice of the rebellious husband-men. [*London*], *printed,* 1676. 4°.* L, C, LF, BBN; CLC, MH, PH, PSC.

75 —The strong man armed, cast out. [*London*], *printed,* 1674. 4°.* L, O, LF, BBN, MR; MH, NC, PH, Y.

75A —The strong man armed, cloathed. [*London*], *printed,* 1674. 4°.* MH.

75B **Jackson, John,** *of Kilgraves, York.* An abridgment of the histories of Noah. *By John Legatt,* 1647, 8°. Y.

75C —The pedigree and peregrination of Israel. *By M. Simmons, for John Wilcox,* 1649. 8°. L.

76 **Jackson, John,** *minister of gospel in London.* The booke of conscience opened and read. *By F. K. for R. M. to be sold by Daniel Milbourne,* 1642. 12°. L, O, LG, LW.

76A —The lyon and the lamb reconciled. *For Austin Rice,* 1660. 12°. CLC.

76B —The true evangelical temper. *By M. Flesher, for R. Milbourne,* 1641. 8°. L, O, CE, CT; NU, IU.

77 **Jackson, John,** *fl. 1648.* Επιτομη Ὑγιαινοντων λογων or a taste. *By A. M. for Christopher Meredith,* 1648. 8°. O.

78 [**Jackson, John**], *lover of truth.* Hosannah to the son of David. *By William Godbid,* 1657. 4°. LT, LF; CH.

78A [–] A sober word to a serious people. *By J. Cottrel, for James Noell; to be sold by Giles Calvert,* 1651. 4°. LT, O, LF, CT, BC; CH, NHC, NU, PH, Y.

78B [–] Strength in weakness; or. *By J. Macock,* 1655. 4°.* L, LF.

79 **Jackson, John,** *of Queens College, Cambridge.* Index Biblicus: or an exact concordance. *Cambridge: by John Field,* 1668. 4°. L, O, C, E, ENC; CH, IU, NN, TO, V, WF, Y.

80–2 Entries cancelled.

—Pedigree and peregrination. 1649. *See* Jackson, John, *of Kilgraves, York.*

[–] Sober word. 1651. *See* Jackson, John, *lover of truth.*

[–] Strength in weakness; or. 1655. *See* Jackson, John, *lover of truth.*

83 **Jackson, John,** *of St. John's, Cambridge.* A treatise concerning mans future eternity. *By M. Inman, to be sold by Nath. Ranew, and by Tho. Forde; and by Iohn Greenwood,* 1661. 12°. L; NU.

84 Entry cancelled.

—True evangelical temper. 1641. *See* Jackson, John, *minister of gospel in London.*

85 **Jackson, Joseph.** Enchiridion medicum. *Excudebat, T. Sowle,* 1695. sixes. L, GH; PL.

85A [–] An essay concerning a vacuum. *For Andrew Bell,* 1697. 8°. L, DU, E, EN; WU.

86 **Jackson, Nicholas.** An account of the late bloody sea-fight. colop: *For Joseph Robinson,* [1690]. brs. L; CH.

86A [**Jackson, Richard.**] A New Years-gift to a notable grandee. *For the author,* 1662. MBA.

87 [–] Qværies proposd for the agitators. colop: *Imprinted at London,* 1647. cap., 4°.* LT, EC, DT; CH, INU, MH, WF, Y.

87A —A suddain essay, with a sincere desire to vindicate Christianity. *By Tho. Harper,* 1655. 4°.* MH, MWA.

87B **Jackson, Richard,** *quack.* Advertisement. There is lately found . . . an excellent purging water. [*London,* 1675?] brs. L.

88 **Jackson, Thomas.** A collection of the works of. *By R. Norton for Timothy Garthwait.* 1653. fol. L, O, CK, YM, EN; CLC, MBP, PL, TO, WF.

89 —An exact collection of the works of. [Commentaries on the Apostles Creed, Bk. 10.] *By R. Norton for Timothie Garthwait,* 1654. fol. L, O, CS, SC, DT; MIU, NU, TO, WF.

90 —The works of. *By Andrew Clark, for John Martyn, Richard Chiswell, and Joseph Clark,* 1673. 3v. fol. T.C.I 137. L, O, C, E, DT; BN, CH, IEG, MH, NU, PL, WF, Y.

91 —The eternal trvth of scriptures. *By R. Norton, for T. Garthwait,* 1653. fol. L; PL.

91A —Excerpta quædam. *For Robert Clavell,* 1672. 8°. T.C.I 98. L.

91B — —[Anr. ed.] *Impensis authoris,* 1672. 8°. CS.

92 —Μαραν αθα: or Dominus veniet. Commentaries. *By A. Maxey for Timothy Garthwait,* 1657. fol. L, O, CT, NPL, EN; NU, PL, TO, WF.

—Speculum perspicuum. 1653. *See* Almanacs.

93 **Jackson, William.** The free-born English mans plea. *By Edward Cole,* 1660. 4°.* LT; MH, MM.

93A —An introduction of the first grounds . . . of arithmetick. *By R. I. for F. Smith,* 1660. 12°. MIU, NC.

94 — —[Anr. ed.] —, 1661. 12°. LT, OC.

95 —Of the rule of faith. *Cambridge, by John Hayes for Henry Dickinson, and to be sold by R. Chiswel, in London,* 1675. 4°.* T.C.I 195. L, O, C, CT, DC, LSD; CH, MH, NU, WF, Y.

Jackson's recantation. 1674. *See* Head, Richard.

96 **Jacob, Henry.** Kneeling in the act of eating. *Printed,* 1641. 8°. LT.

97 —Philologiæ ἀνακαλυπτηριον oratione. *Oxoniæ, ex-cudebat H. Hall*, 1652. 4°. MADAN 2184–5. L, O, OM, CT, DT; NPT, Y.

98 **Jacob, John.** [Hebrew] the Jevv turned Christian. *By A. M. and R. R. for Tho. Cockerill*, 1678/9. 4°.* T.C.I 340. L, O, C, CE, P; CH, NGT, NN, NU, WF.

99 —Publicanus vindicatus: or, a short narrative. *Printed*, 1654. 4°.* L; Y.

[–] Two conferences. 1678. *See* Mayo, Richard.

99A [**Jacob, Joseph.**] The covenant and catechism of the church . . . Horsly-Down. *Printed* 1700. 8°. L, LCL, ORP, E; MHS, NHC.

100 [–] The covenant to be the Lord's people . . . Horsly-Down. *Printed*, 1700. 8°.* L, O, LCL, ORP; MHS, NHC.

Jacob at his journeys end. 1665. *See* B., A.

Jacob wrestling. 1663. *See* Taylor, Thomas.

Jacobite conventicle. 1692. *See* Ames, Richard.

Jacobite principles. [n.p., 1693.] *See* Lawton, Charlwood.

101 The Jacobite tossed in a blanket. *[London], for J. Conyers, and J. Conyers*, [1688–91]. brs. HH.

101A The Jacobite's badge. *For the use of the successor of Jack Adams and Hobody Boody*, 1697. brs. MH.

102 The Jacobites exultation. *[n.p., 1692.]* brs. HH; MH.

103 The Jacobite's hopes frustrated. *For Jeremiah Wilkins*, 1690. 4°.* L; MIU.

104 The Jacobites Hvdibras. *For Abel Roper*, 1692. 4°.* L, CT, AU; CH, CN, MH, NCU, NN, WF, Y.

105 The Jacobites invitation to the French king. *For F. Weekly*, 1692. brs. L.

106 The Jacobites lamentation. *Printed*, 1696. brs. L.

107 The Jacobite's new creed. *For E. Golding*, 1693. 8°.* EN.

108 No entry.

109 **Jacombe, Samuel.** Moses his death. *For Adoniram Byfield*, 1657. 4°. LT, O, C, ENC, BLH; CF, MH, NU, WF, Y.

109A [–] A short and plaine catechisme. Second edition. *For Adoniram Byfield*, 1657. 8°.* CM.

109B [–] —Fourth edition. *For Francis Tyton*, 1668. 8°.* L, C; NU.

109C [–] —Fifth edition. —, 1672. 8°.* T.C.I 479. NGT.

109D [–] —Sixth edition. —, 1682. 8°.* OC; WF.

110 — —[Anr. ed.] *For Ric. Chiswel*, 1694. 12°.* T.C.II 514. L, CT; NU.

111 **Jacombe, Thomas.** Abraham's death. *For Brabrazon Aylmer*, 1682. 4°. L, LSC, LW, WCA, YM; CH, CLC, MH, NU, WF, Y.

112 —The active and publick spirit. *By T. R. for Philemon Stephens, and Abel Roper*, 1657. 4°. LT, O, LP, CS, DT; CH, CLC, MH, NU, WF.

113 —Bibliotheca Jacombiana. 31 Oct. 1687. 4°. L, O, C, BC, DM; CN, NG, WF, JF.

114 —Οἱ ἐλεημονες ἐλεη θησονται, or Gods mercy. *For Philemon Stephens*, 1657. 4°. LT, O, C; CLC, MH, NU, WF, Y.

115 —Enochs walk and change. *By T. R. and E. M. for Ralph Smith*, 1656. 4°. L, O, LCL, LW, OC; CH, MIU, NU, WF, Y.

115A — —Second edition. —, 1656. 4°. CDA, CLC.

116 — —"Second" edition. *By T. R. and E. M. for Abel Roper*, 1656. 4°. LT, O, C, E, DT; CN, MH, NU, TU, WF.

117 — —Third edition. *By Sarah Griffin, for Abel Roper*, 1657. 4°. O, BC, MR, ENC, DT; CLC, MH, NU, TU, WF.

118 —Ὁσιος ἐγκαινισμος. Or a treatise. *For Ralph Smith and Samuel Gellibrand*, 1668. 8°. T.C.I 1. L, O, C, LG, BLH; CH, MH, NU, WF, Y.

119 —Several sermons preach'd. *By W. Godbid, to be sold by M. Pitt, and R. Chiswel, and J. Robinson*, 1672. 4°. T.C.I 115. L, O, LCL, LW, E, BLH; CLC, IU, MH, NU, WF, Y.

120 —The upright man's peace. *For Daniel Brown*, 1682. 4°.* T.C.I 470. L, LG, LW, CS, WCA; CB, CLC, PU, Y.

120A **Jacque, W.** Dr. Jacque's vindication against Mr. Kirkwood's defamation. *[Edinburgh, 1698.]* 4°.* EN.

121 **Ja'far Agha, haji.** The speech of. colop: *By T. B. for Richard Mead*, 1684. brs. L, O, EN; PU, Y.

122 **Jaffray, Andrew.** A serious and earnest exhortation. *[London, 1677.]* 4°.* L, LF, BBN.

122A **Jagel, Abraham.** Catechismus Judæorum. *For S. Carr*, 1679. 8°. T.C.I 360. O, LLP, BAMB, YM, DL.

122B — —[Anr. ed.] *Typis A. Godbid & J. Playford, pro S. Carr*, 1679. BAMB, DU; LC, MH, NN.

122C [–] The Jews catechism. *For Benjamin Harris*, 1680. 12°.* WF.

123 **Jager, Robert.** Artificial arithmetick in decimals. *By Robert and William Leybourn, for Humphrey Moseley*: 1651. 8°. L, O, C, OC, DC; CH, CLC, MIU, NC, NN.

123A **Jamaica.** The continuation of the laws of. *For Charles Harper and Samuel Crouch*, 1698. fol. PHS.

124 —The laws of Jamaica. *By H. Hills for Charles Harper*, 1683. 8°. T.C.II 101. L, C, AU; CN, LC, MHL, NCL, PHS, RPJ.

125 — —[Same title.] *By H. H., jun. for Charles Harper*, 1684–98. fol. T.C.II 101. L, O, C, AU, DT; MHL, NCL, PHS, RPJ, TU, Y.

Jamaica viewed. 1661. *See* Hickeringill, Edmund.

125A [**Jamby, Pedro de.**] A true narrative of the great and bloody fight . . . French and Dutch. *For D. M.*, 1674. 4°.* NN.

126 **James I, *King of England.*** King James his apology for the oath of allegiance. *For Henry Eversden*, 1660. 12°. EN; NF, ZWT.

127 —King James his apothegmes. *By B. W.*, 1643. 4°.* L, O, LW, YM, EN; BN, CH, MH, NNM.

128 —Βασιλικον δωρον. Or, King James's instructions. *By M. Flesher, for Joseph Hindmarsh*, 1682. 8°. T.C.I 478. L, O, LL, LIU, EN; CH, IU, LC, MH, NU, V, WF, Y.

128A — —[Anr. ed.] *By M. Flesher, for Samuel Mearne*, 1682. 8°. LW; CH, MH, NNM.

129 —King James his charge to the judges. *For Langly Curtise*, 1679. 4°.* O; CH, IU, MH, PU.

130 —A commission with instrvctions and directions. *By Bonham Norton and Iohn Bill*, 1622. Reprinted for H. H., 1643. 4°.* LT; CH, NN, YL.

131 —King James his counterblast to tobacco. *For John Hancock*, 1672. 4°. T.C.I 118. L, O, MR; MH, MIU, NC, NN, WF.

132 —A declaration made by. *[London], for Matthew Walbancke*, 1646. 4°.* LT, CT, P, EN, GU, CD; BN, CH, Y.

133 —His Majesties declaration, touching his proceedings. *Printed*, 1642. 4°. LT, CSSX, MR; CLC, MH, WF, Y.

134   —King James his divine prophecie. *For R. Austin.* 1645. 4°.* LT, O, DT; MH, TU, Y.

135   —The dutie of a king. *For I. B.,* 1642. 4°.* LT, O, BC, LIU; CH, CN, NU, TU, WF, Y.

136   —King Iames his iudgment by way of counsell. colop: *Printed at London for Thomas Cooke,* 1642. 4°.* LT, O, C, MR, ENC; CH, MH, TU, WF, Y.

137   —King Iames his iudgement of a king. [*London,* 1642.] cap., 4°.* LT, O, C, ENC, CD; CH, CN, LC, MH, TU, Y. (var.)

138   —King James his learned and wise speech. *For I. T.,* 1645. 4°. DT; MH, TU.

139   —King James, his letter and directions. [*London*], *for Thomas Walkeley,* 1642. 4°. LT, O, C, EN, DT; BN, CH, CN, MH, TU, WF, Y.

140   —King James his opinion and iudgement. colop: [*London*], *printed,* 1647. cap. 4°.* LT, O, MR, CD, DT; CH, WF, Y.

141   —K. James's opinion of a king, of a tyrant. colop: *For R. Baldwin,* 1689. cap. 4°.* O, OC, BANGOR, EN; CH, MII, MM, NP, WF, Y.

142   —A Puritane set forth. *For N. B.,* 1642. 4°. LT, LG; NU, TU, Y.

143   —Regales aphorismi: or a royal chain of golden sentences. *By B. A.,* 1650. 12°. LT, LG, RU; CH, IU, Y.

144   —The speech of . . . 22th. [*sic*] Martii, 1603. *For Richard Baldwin,* 1689. fol.* O, C; Y.

144A   —The touchstone or, trial of tobacco. *Printed,* 1676. 4°. CLC, NN, WF, Y.

145   —The trve lavv of free monarchy. *Printed, and are to be sold by T. P.,* 1642. 4°.* LT, LL, BC, EN, DT; IC, NC, NP, NU, WF.

146   —A true relation of the commissions and warrants. *For Michael Spark,* 1651. 4°. L; NN.

147   [–] Two broad-sides against tobacco. *For John Hancock,* 1672. 4°. L, O, C, MR; CH, LC, NN, RPJ, WF.

148   —Vox regis: or, the difference. *For Francis Smith,* 1681. 4°.* L, O, CT, LSD, DT; CH, CN, MH, NU, WF, Y.

149   —Wittie observations. [*London,* 1643.] 4°.* LT; CH, WF.

149A   **James II,** *King of England.* An abreviation of a grant . . . to John Earle. [*London?* 1685.] brs. L.

150   —An account of what His Majesty said. *By the assigns of John Bill; and by Henry Hills and Thomas Newcomb,* 1684[5]. brs. STEELE 3767–71. L, O, LPR, MC, DT; CH, MBP, MH, PU, WF, Y. (var.)

151   ——[Anr. ed.] *Dublin, reprinted by Benjamin Tooke, sold by Mary Crook,* 1684[5]. brs. STEELE 2p 936. L, DN.

152   —James . . . After so long, and ruinous . . . 8 June 1697. [*London,* 1697.] brs. STEELE 4228. O.

153   —Articles of peace and commerce between the most serene . . . James II. . . . And the most illustrious Lords, the Douletli Basha, . . . of Algiers. [*London*], *by Thomas Newcomb in the Savoy,* 1687. 4°.* L, O, C, WCA, DT; CH, LC, MB, PBL, WCL, WF, Y.

154   —His Majesty at his first sitting . . . 6 February 1684/5. *Edinburgh, reprinted by the heir of Andrew Anderson,* 1685. brs. STEELE 3p 2582–3; ALDIS 2553. HH, EN, ER. (var.)

154A   —His Majesty being given to understand. [*London,* 1684/ 5.] brs. MH.

155   —His Majesties commission for the rebuilding of . . . S. Paul. *By Charles Bill, Henry Hills, and Thomas Newcomb,* 1685[6]. fol.* L, P; CH, CN, TU.

155A   —The late King James's commission to his privateers. colop: *For P. Smart,* 1692. brs. MH.

155B   —A copy of the late King James's letter. colop: *For A. Johnson,* 1692. brs. L, EN; CN, LC.

155C   —A copy of the late King James II his letter to the convention. *For R. Baldwin,* 1689. brs. L, C, EN; NCD.

156   —A declaration . . . 25 August 1685. *By the assigns of John Bill; and by Henry Hills, and Thomas Newcomb,* 1685. brs. STEELE 3815–6. L, O, LPR, LS, MC; CH, PU, WF. (var.)

157   —By the king, a declaration . . . 2 September 1688. *By Charles Bill, Henry Hills, and Thomas Newcomb,* 1688. brs. STEELE 3871. L, O, LG, LS, DC; MH, NP, WF.

158   —A declaration . . . 21 September 1688. —, 1688. brs. STEELE 3873–4. L, O, C, LG, LPR; MH, WF. (var.)

159   ——[Anr. ed.] *Dublin, re-printed by Andrew Crook & Samuel Helsham, assigns of Benjamin Tooke,* 1688. brs. STEELE 2p 997. L, DM, DN.

160   ——[Anr. ed.] *Holy-Rood-House, by Mr. P. B.,* 1688. brs. STEELE 3p 2727. ALDIS 2764.5. OP, CCA, EN, ER, ES; IU, MH.

161   ——6 November 1688. *By Charles Bill, Henry Hills, & Thomas Newcomb,* 1688. brs. STEELE 3893–6. L, O, LPR, LS, MC; MH, NP, PU, TSM, WF. (var.)

162   ———[Anr. ed.] *Dublin, re-printed by Andrew Crook & Samuel Helsham, assigns of Benjamin Tooke,* 1688. brs. STEELE 2p 1002. DN.

163   ———[Anr. ed.] *Holy-Rood-House, by Mr. P. B.,* 1688. brs. STEELE 3p 2742; ALDIS 2801. L, HH, EN, ER, ES.

164   ——1 April 1689. *Dublin, by Andrew Crook & Samuel Helsham, assigns of Benjamin Tooke,* 1689. brs. STEELE 2p 1033–5. L, DN. (var.)

165   ——eighth of May, 1689. [*London,* 1689.] brs. STEELE 4002–4. L, LIU, LS, HH; CH. (var.)

166   ——28 June 1689. *Dublin, by Andrew Crook & Samuel Helsham, assigns of Benjamin Tooke,* 1689. fol.* STEELE 2p 1041. L, HH, DK, DN.

167   ——27 July 1689. —, 1689. brs. STEELE 2p 1047–8. L, HH, DK, DN. (var.)

168   ——18 August 1689. —, 1689. STEELE 2p 1054. L, HH, DK, DN.

169   ——2 September 1689. —, 1689. brs. STEELE 2p 1061. L, HH, DK, DN.

170   ——3 September 1689, [property of rebels]. —, 1689. brs. STEELE 2p 1062. L, HH, DK, DN.

171   ——[Same date, offering pardon.] —, 1689. brs. STEELE 2p 1063–4. L, HH, DK, DN. (var.)

172   ——12 November 1689. *Dublin, by Andrew Crook the assign of Benjamin Tooke,* 1689. brs. STEELE 2p 1079. L, HH, DK, DN.

173   ——24 November 1689. —, 1689. brs. STEELE 2p 1081. L, HH, DK, DN.

173A   ——20 December 1689. colop: —, 1689. brs. STEELE 2p 1085–6. L, HH, DK, DN; PL. (var.)

174   ——24 January 1689[90]. —, 1689[90]. brs. STEELE 2p 1095. L, HH, DK, DN.

175   ——14 February 1689[90]. *Dublin, for James Malone,*
      1689[90]. brs. STEELE 2p 1099. L, HH, DK.

176   ——18 February 1689[90]. colop: *Dublin, for James*
      Malone, 1689[90]. fol.* STEELE 2p 1100. L, HH, DT; PL.

177   ——28 February 1689[90]. colop: *Dublin, for James*
      Malone, to [be] sold at his shop. And by Andrew Crook,
      1689[90]. brs. STEELE 2p 1101. L, HH, DK, DN.

178   ——19 March 1689[90]. —, *1689[90].* brs. STEELE 2p 1103.
      L, HH, DK, DN.

179   ——25 April 1690. *Dublin, for James Malone,* [1690]. brs.
      STEELE 2p 1110. L, HH, DK, DN.

180   ——9 June 1690. —, [1690]. brs. STEELE 2p 1112. L, HH,
      DK, DN.

181   Entry cancelled.
      —Declaration for the better government. Dublin, 1689.
      See —A declaration . . . 20 December.

181A —The declaration of His Royal Highness James Duke of
      York . . . Governour, and the rest of the Royal African
      Company . . . to all . . . subjects . . . inhabiting the
      plantations in America . . . [10 December 1672, prices
      for slaves]. [*London,* 1672.] brs. LPR.

182   Entry cancelled.
      —Directions concerning preachers. Dublin, 1686. *See title.*

183   —An excellent speech spoken by. *Printed at Oxford for*
      Edward Benington. 1647. 4°.* MADAN 1945 *. O.

184   —A gallant speech spoken by. *Printed at Oxford for*
      Edward Benington, 1647. 4°.* MADAN 1945. LT, O.

184A —Gan fod y ffurf Gweddi gyda Diolch. [*n.p.*], 1685. brs. AN.

184B —James Duke of York . . . general instructions. [*London,*
      1670?] cap., fol.* L; NCD.

185   —His Majesties gracious answer to the letter . . . [6
      October]. *Edinburgh, by the heir of Andrew Anderson,*
      1688. brs STEELE 3p 2735; ALDIS 2764. EN, ER, ES; MH, Y.

186   —His majesties gracious declaration to all his loving sub-
      jects for liberty of conscience . . . fourth day of April,
      1687. colop: *By Charles Bill, Henry Hills, and Thomas*
      Newcomb, 1687. cap., fol.* STEELE 3843. L, O, C, DC, EN;
      CH, CN, MH, TU, WF, Y.

187   ——[Anr. ed.] *Dublin, re-printed by Andr. Crook and Sam.*
      Helsham, assigns of Benjamin Tooke, sold by Andrew
      Crook, and Samuel Helsham, 1687. fol.* DIX 226; STEELE
      2p 973–5. L, HH, DN, DCA; PL. (var.)

188   ——[Anr. ed.] *Edinburgh, by the heir of Andrew Anderson,*
      1687. fol.* STEELE 3p 2692; ALDIS 2711. L, EN, ER, AU;
      CSS, WF.

189   Entry cancelled. *See* J186.

189A ——[Anr. ed.] colop: *By Charles Bill, Henry Hills, and*
      Thomas Newcomb, 1687. Edinburgh, re-printed at Holy-
      Rood-House, by James Watson, 1687. cap., fol.* ALDIS
      2711.5. EN.

190   ——[Anr. ed.] *By Charles Bill, Henry Hills, and Thomas*
      Newcomb, 1688. fol.* 7 pp. LW, OC, CT, MR, EN; CH, CLC,
      MH, NU, PL, TU, WF.

191   —His Majestie's gracious declartion [*sic*]. James R. Ovr
      conduct . . . 27 April, 1688. *By Charles Bill, Henry Hills,*
      and Thomas Newcomb, 1687/8. fol.* 4 pp. STEELE 3864.
      L, LL, OP, C; CLC, CN, MH, WF, Y. (var.)

191A–2 Entries cancelled. *See* J191; J189A.

193   —His Majesties gracious declaration . . . seventh day
      of April, 1688. colop: *Holy-Rood-House, re-printed by*
      Mr. P. B., 1688. cap., fol.* STEELE 3p 2710; ALDIS 2765.
      L, O, EN, ER; CDA, MH.

193A —His Majesties gracious letter (the 12th day of April,
      1686.) [*London*], *in the Savoy, by T. Newcomb, for A.*
      Oswald, 1686. fol.* L.

194   —His Majesties gracious letter to the Lord Provost.
      Edinburgh, by the heir of Andrew Anderson, 1685. brs.
      ALDIS 2551. L, EN; MH.

194A ——[Anr. ed.] [*Edinburgh?* 1685.] brs. EN.

195   —His Majesties gracious letter to the Parliament of
      Scotland. *By Thomas Newcomb in the Savoy; and re-*
      printed Edinburgh, by the heir of Andrew Anderson, 1685.
      fol.* ALDIS 2552. L, EN; CH, CSS; MH, WF.

195A —Instructions and rules to be duly observed by each and
      every master-gunner. [*London,* 1663.] brs. O, LPR.

195B —James, Duke of York . . . Instructions for the . . . fleet.
      [*London?* 1660.] cap., fol.* L.

196   —His Majesties late letter in vindication of himself.
      colop: [*London*], *for John Flemming,* 1688/9. cap., 4°.*
      L, O, C, MR, EN, DM; CH, CN, MH, MM, NU.

197   ——[Anr. ed.] [*London?* 1689.] cap., 4°.* L; CN.

198   ——[Anr. ed.] [*London*], *re-printed,* 1689. 4°.* L, EN, ESS;
      CLC, CN, MH, TO, WF, Y.

199   —His Majesties letter from St. Germans. [*London,*
      1689.] cap., fol.* L, OC, MR; WF.

200   —His Majesties letter to his honourable Privy Council
      of Scotland. *Printed at London and re-printed at Edinburgh,*
      by the heir of Andrew Anderson, 1687. brs. ALDIS 2693. L,
      EN, AU; CH, MH.

201   —His Majesty's letter to his Privy Council in Scotland.
      Dublin, by Andrew Crook and Samuel Helsham, 1686.
      4°.* DIX 222. L, DCA.

202   —The late King James his letter to his Privy Council
      . . . [12 Feb. 1687]. colop: *Re-printed at Edinburgh,* 1689.
      brs. ALDIS 2897. L, O, EN; IU, MH.

203   Entry cancelled.
      [–] Late King James's letter to his Privy Counsellors.
      With just reflections. 1692. *See title.*

204   —His Majesties letter to sundry of the Lords . . . [2 April].
      [*London,* 1692.] brs. STEELE 4082. L, O, LPR, HH; Y.

204A —The Kings letter to the Earl of Feversham. *Printed,*
      1688. brs. L, O, IG, CK, DU, EN; INU, Y.

205   —The King's letter to the general of his army . . . [11
      December]. [*London,* 1688.] brs. STEELE 3917. L, O, C, EN;
      CH, WF, Y.

206   —The King's letter to the great council of peers. *For W.*
      Thomson, 1688. brs. L, O, LG, DU, HH, MC; CH.

207   —His Majesties letter to the House of Lords . . . [3
      February]. [*London,* 1688/9.] brs. STEELE 3954. L, LG, LS,
      HH, EN; INU, LC, MH, Y.

208   —His Majesty's letter to the lords . . . 4/14 January 1688/9.
      [*London,* 1688/9.] brs. STEELE 3943–4. L, O, C, LG, MC, EN;
      INU. (var.)

209 — —1 March. [*Edinburgh*, 1689.] 4°. STEELE 3p 2777. brs.
HAMILTON; CH.

210 —A letter written by King James to His Holiness the
Pope, . . . [Nov. 26, 1689]. *Printed at London, re-printed
Edinburgh*, 1691. brs. ALDIS 3156. EN; Y.

211 Entry cancelled.
—Late King James's manifesto. 1697. *See* title.

212 —His Majesty's most gracious and free-pardon, . . . 21
March 1684/5. *By George Croom*, 1685. brs. L, O, LG,
HH; CH, Y.

212A — —[27 August.] *By George Croom*, 1685. brs. O.

213 —His Majesties most gracious and general pardon . . . 27
September 1688. *By Charles Bill, Henry Hills, and
Thomas Newcomb*, 1688. brs. STEELE 3875. L, O, LG, EN,
DT; MH, WF.

214 — —[Anr. ed.] *Holy-Rood-House, by Mr. P. B.*, 1688.
brs. STEELE 3p 2730; ALDIS 2796. HH, EN, ER, ES; MH, WF.

215 — —2 October 1688. *By Charles Bill, Henry Hills, and
Thomam [sic] Newcomb*, 1688. brs. STEELE 3879–80. L, LG,
LPR, OQ, HH; INU, MH. (var.)

215A —His Majesties most gracious ansvver to the letter from
the arch-bishops . . . [15 November 1688]. *Edinburgh, by
the heir of Andrew Anderson*, 1688. brs. EN.

216 —His Majesties most gracious declaration to all . . .
[20 April 1692]. [*London?* 1692.] 4°.* STEELE 4086. L, O,
MR, EN; INU, NC, WF, Y.

216A — —[Anr. ed.] *St. Germains, by Thomas Heles*, 1692. fol. O.

217 —His Majesties most gratious declaration . . . 17 April
1693. [*London?* 1693.] 4°.* STEELE 4119. L, O, MR.

217A — —[Anr. ed.] [*n.p.*,1693.] brs. STEELE 4120. LS, CT, LSD,
MR, EN; CH, CSS, WF, Y.

218 —His Majesties most gracious declaration to his good
people . . . [20 April]. [*Edinburgh*, 1692.] fol.* STEELE 3p
2933. O.

219 —His Majesties most gracious letter to the Parliament of
Scotland. [*London*] *in the Savoy: by Tho: Newcomb, for
Andrew Oswald*, 1686. fol.* L, O, C, OC, LIU; CH, INU,
MH, NP, TU, WF, Y.

219A — —[Anr. ed.] [*Edinburgh*, 1686.] cap., fol.* ALDIS 2643.
L, EN, AU; MH.

220 — —[Anr. ed.] *Dublin, re-printed by Andrew Crook and
Samuel Helsham, assigns of Benjamin Took*, 1686. 4°.*
DIX 222. DCA, DK, DN.

221 —His Majesties most gracious pardon, pleaded at Justice-
Hall . . . 7th. of March, . . . 1687. *By D. Mallet*, [1687/8].
brs. L, O, LS.

222 — —21st. of March, 1687/8. *By George Croom*, 1688. brs.
L, O, HH.

222A —His Majesties most gracious pardon, to several prisoners
in Newgate. *By George Croom*, 1685. brs. L.

223 —His Majesties most gracious pardon, to the poor prisoners . . . 26th. of February, 1685/6. *By E. Mallot,
for D. Mallet*, [1686]. brs. O, LPR, HH.

224 —His Majesties most gracious pardon vvhich was
pleaded . . . 26 July. colop: *By D. Mallet*, 1686. brs. L, O.

225 —His Majesties most gracious speech to both Houses . . .
22th of May, 1685. *By the assigns of John Bill: and by
Henry Hills, and Thomas Newcomb*, 1685. fol.* L, O, C,
CS, EN, CD; CH, INU, MH, NC, WF, Y.

226 — —[Anr. ed.] —, and re-printed *Edinburgh, by the heir of
Andrew Anderson*, 1685. fol.* ALDIS 2554. BR, EN; MH.

227 — —[Anr. ed.] *Dublin, re-printed by Benjamin Tooke, to be
sold by Samuel Helsham*, 1685. fol.* DIX 212. L, DM, DT;
CH.

228 — —30th of May, 1685. *By the assigns of John Bill; and by
Henry Hills, and Thomas Newcomb*, 1685. fol.* L, OC,
EN; CLC, CN, MH, NC, WF, Y.

228A — — —[Anr. ed.] *Dublin, reprinted by Benjamin Took, sold
by Samuel Helsham*, 1685. fol.* L.

229 — —9th of November 1685. *By the assigns of John Bill: and
by Henry Hills, and Thomas Newcomb*, 1685. fol.* L, O,
C, OC, DC; CH, NC, TU, WF, Y. (var.)

230 — — —[Anr. ed.] *Dublin, reprinted by Benjamin Took, to be
sold by Andrew Crook, and Samuel Helsham*, 1685. fol.* L.

231 — — —[Anr. ed.] *London, reprinted Edinburgh, by the heir of
Andrew Anderson*, 1685. fol. ALDIS 2556. L, EN.

231A Entry cancelled.
— —sixteenth of March, 1688[9]. *See* William III.

232 — —seventh of May, 1689. *Dublin, Dublin [sic], by
Andrew Crook and Samuel Helsham, assigns of Benjamin
Tooke*, 1689. fol.* L.

233 Entry cancelled.
—Order in Council. Dublin, 1688. *See* England. Privy
Council. At the Council-Chamber . . . 22th. of
October.

234 —An order . . . 23 August 1689. *Dublin, by Andrew Crook
and Samuel Helsham, assigns of Benjamin Tooke*, 1689.
brs. STEELE 2p 1056. L, HH, DK, DN.

235 Entry cancelled.
—Orders concerning preachers. 1685. *See* —To the
most reverend fathers.

236 —His Majesties orders for regulation of the musters.
colop: *By Charles Bill, Henry Hills, and Thomas Newcomb*, 1686/7. cap., fol.* O, LL, LIU, EN; CH, CN, WF, Y.

237 —Our will and pleasure is that you . . . 25 August 1689.
*Dublin, by Andrew Crook and Samuel Helsham, assigns of
Benjamin Tooke*, 1689. brs. STEELE 2p 1057. L, HH, DK, DN.

238 —A proclamation . . . 6 February. *By the assigns of John
Bill and by Henry Hills, and Thomas Newcomb*, 1684[5].
brs. STEELE 3774. L, O, LG, CCA, MC, DT; CH, IU, MH, MHS,
PU, TSM.

239 — —16 February 1684/5. —, 1684/5. brs. STEELE 3783–4.
L, O, LG, LPR, LS; CH, MH, PU, Y. (var.)

240 — —13 June 1685. —, 1685. brs. STEELE 3794–8. L, O, LPR,
MC, DT; CH, MH, PU. (var.)

241 — — —[Anr. ed.] *Dublin, B. Tooke*, 1685. fol.* STEELE 2p
944. L, DN.

242 — — —[Anr. ed.] *Edinburgh, by the heir of Andrew Anderson*, 1685. brs. STEELE 3p 2627. ALDIS 2587. EN, ER.

243 — —16 June 1685. *By the assigns of John Bill, and by
Henry Hills and Thomas Newcomb*, 1685. brs. STEELE
3803–5. L, O, C, LG, MC, DT; CH, MH, PU. (var.)

244 ———[Anr. ed.] *Dublin, B. Tooke, 1685. 4°.** STEELE 2p 946. L, DN.

245 ———[Anr. ed.] *By the assigns of John Bill, and by Henry Hills and Thomas Newcomb. Edinburgh, re-printed by the heir of Andrew Anderson, 1685.* brs. STEELE 3p 2629; ALDIS 2589. ER, EN.

246 ——19 July 1685. *By the assigns of John Bill; and by Henry Hills, and Thomas Newcomb, 1685.* brs. STEELE 3809–11. L, O, LPR, LS, DT; CH, MH, PU, WF. (var.)

247 ——7 September 1685. —, 1685. brs. STEELE 3817. L, O, LPR, MC, DT; CH, MH.

248 ——eighth day of January 1685/6. *By the assigns of John Bill; and by Henry Hills, and Thomas Newcomb, 1685/6.* brs. STEELE 3825. L, O, LPR, MC, DT; CH, MH, PU, WF.

249 ——12 February 1687. *Edinburgh, by the heir of Andrew Anderson, 1687.* fol. STEELE 3p 2684–5; ALDIS 2709. L, HH, EN, ER; MH. (var.)

250 ———[Anr. ed.] —, 1687. *[London], by George Croom. 1686/7.* brs. STEELE 3p 2686. L, O, OP, DM; CH, MH, WF.

251 ———[Anr. ed.] *By George Croom, 1687.* brs. STEELE 3p 2687. L, LPC, HH; CH, WF.

252 ——28 June 1687. *Edinburgh, by the heir of Andrew Anderson, 1687.* brs. STEELE 3p 2693; ALDIS 2712. L, HH, EN, ER, ES; CH, NN, WF.

253 ———[Anr. ed.] —, *reprinted [London] by T. Newcomb for S. Forrester, 1687.* brs. STEELE 3p 2694. L, O, LG, BR, EN; CH, INU.

254 ——11 July 1687. *By Charles Bill, Henry Hills, and Thomas Newcomb, 1687.* fol.* STEELE 3847. L, O, LPR, MC, DT; CH, MH.

255 ——7 May 1688. *Edinburgh, by the heir of Andrew Anderson, 1688.* fol.* STEELE 3p 2711–2; ALDIS 2783. L, EN, ER, ES; CH. (var.)

256 ———[Anr. ed.] —*reprinted at London by George Croom, 1688.* brs. STEELE 3p 2713. L, LG.

257 ——10 June 1688. *By Charles Bill, Henry Hills, and Thomas Newcomb, 1688.* brs. STEELE 3866. L, O, C, LG, LPR, DT; MH, WF, Y.

258 ——29th of June 1688. —, 1688. brs. STEELE 3867. L, O, LG, LPR, DT; CH, MH, TSM, WF.

259 ——12 August 1688. —, 1688. brs. STEELE 3870. L, O, LG, LPR, DT; CH, MH, Y.

260 ——28th day of September 1688. —, 1688. brs. STEELE 3876–8. L, O, LG, CCA, DT; MH, TSM, WF, Y. (var.)

261 ———[Anr. ed.] *Dublin, by Andrew Crook & Samuel Helsham, 1688.* brs. STEELE 2p 999. DPR (lost).

262 ——20 October 1688. *By Charles Bill, Henry Hills, and Thomas Newcomb, 1688.* brs. STEELE 3886–7. L, O, LG, LPR, CCA; MH, NP, WF. (var.)

263 ——2d day of November, 1688. —, 1688. brs. STEELE 3891–2. L, O, LG, LPR, DT; MH, WF, Y. (var.)

264 Entry cancelled.
——6th day of November. 1688. *See* —Declaration.

265 ——25 March 1689 [forbidding plundering]. colop: *Dublin, by Andrew Crook and Samuel Helsham, assigns of Benjamin Tooke, 1689.* brs. STEELE 2p 1023–4. L, HH, DK, DN. (var.)

266 ———[Anr. ed.] —; *and re-printed at London, 1689.* brs. STEELE 2p 1025. L, C, EN.

267 ——[Same date; summoning Irish Parliament.] *Dublin; by Andrew Crook and Samuel Helsham, assigns of Benjamin Tooke, sold by Andrew Crook, and Samuel Helsham, 1689.* brs. STEELE 2p 1026–7. L, HH, DK, DN. (var.)

268 ———[Anr. ed.] —; *and re-printed at London, 1689.* brs. STEELE 2p 1028. L, C; CLC.

269 ——[Same date; free exercise of religion.] *Dublin, by Andrew Crook & Samuel Helsham, assigns of Benjamin Tooke, 1689.* brs. STEELE 2p 1029–30. L, HH, DK, DN. (var.)

270 ———[Anr. ed.] 1689. brs. STEELE 2p 1031. L.

271 ——[Same date; raising value of coin.] colop: *Dublin, by Andrew Crook and Samuel Helsham, assigns of Benjamin Tooke, 1689.* fol.* STEELE 2p 1032. L, HH, DK, DN.

272 ——1 April 1689. *Dublin, by Andrew Crook and Samuel Helsham, assigns of Benjamin Tooke, 1689.* fol.* STEELE 3p 2794–5. L, O, HH, DK, DN. (var.)

273 ——4 May 1689 [against adherents of the Prince of Orange]. colop: —, 1689. brs. STEELE 3p 2813. L, C, HH, DK, DN.

274 ——[Same date; coinage.] *Dublin, by Andrew Crook and Samuel Helsham, assigns of Benjamin Tooke, 1689.* brs. STEELE 2p 1036. L, C, HH, DK, DN.

275 ——14 June 1689. colop: *Dublin, by Andrew Crook and Samuel Helsham, assigns of Benjamin Tooke, 1689.* brs. STEELE 2p 1037. L, HH, DK, DN.

276 ——18 June 1689. —, 1689. fol.* STEELE 2p 1038. L, HH, DK, DN.

277 ——24 June 1689. —, 1689. brs. STEELE 2p 1039. L, HH, DK, DN; INU.

278 ——27 June 1689. —, 1689. fol.* STEELE 2p 1040. L, HH, DK, DN.

279 ——20 July 1689 [Protestants to give up arms]. —, 1689. brs. STEELE 2p 1043. L, HH, DK, DN.

280 ——[Same date; Protestants to leave Dublin.] —, 1689. brs. STEELE 2p 1042. L, HH, DK, DN; PL.

281 ——26 July 1689 [duty on wines]. —, 1689. brs. STEELE 2p 1044. L, HH, DK, DN.

282 ——[Same date; Protestants not to leave parishes.] —, 1689. brs. STEELE 2p 1045–6. L, HH, DK, DN. (var.)

283 Entry cancelled.
——27th day of July. Dublin, 1689. *See* —Declaration.

284 ——30 July 1689. —, 1689. brs. STEELE 2p 1049–50. L, HH, DK, DN. (var.)

285 ——5 August 1689. —, 1689. brs. STEELE 2p 1051. L, HH, DK, DN.

286 ——20 August. —, 1689. brs. STEELE 2p 1055. L, HH, DK, DN.

287 ——31 October 1689 [officers not to be absent]. *Dublin, by Andrew Crook the assign of Benjamin Tooke, 1689.* brs. STEELE 2p 1076. L, HH, DK, DN.

288 ——[Same date; horses not to be seized.] —, 1689. brs. STEELE 2p 1077. L, HH, DK, DN.

289 ——18 November 1689. —, 1689. brs. STEELE 2p 1080. L, HH, DK, DN.

290   ——29 November 1689. —, 1689. brs. STEELE 2p 1082.
       L, HH, DK, DN.

291   ——30 November 1689. —, 1689. brs. STEELE 2p 1083. L,
       HH, DK, DN.

292   ——13 December 1689. —, 1689. brs. STEELE 2p 1084–4a.
       L, C, HH, DK, DN; WF.

293   ——27 December 1689. *Dublin, by Andrew Crook the
       assignee of Benjamin Tooke, to be sold by Andrew Crook,*
       1689. brs. STEELE 2p 1089. L, HH, DK, DN.

294   ——3 January 1689[90]. —, 1689[90]. brs. STEELE 2p 1090.
       L, HH, DK, DN.

295   ——10 January 1689[90]. —, 1689[90]. brs. STEELE 2p 1091.
       L, HH, DK, DN.

296   ——21 January 1689[90], [to encourage tillage]. colop:
       Dublin, by Andrew Crook the assignee of Benjamin Tooke,
       1689[90]. brs. STEELE 2p 1093. L, HH, DK, DN.

297   ——[Same date; against high prices of butchers.] —,
       1689[90]. brs. STEELE 2p 1094. L, HH, DK, DN.

298   ——4 February 1689[90], [copper and brass money].
       Dublin, for James Malone, 1689[90]. brs. STEELE 2p 1096.
       L, HH, DK, DN.

299   ——[Same date, levy of £20,000.] colop: *Dublin, for
       James Malone,* 1689[90]. brs. STEELE 2p 1097–8. L, HH,
       DK, DN. (var.)

300   ——28 February 1689[90]. *Dublin, for James Malone,*
       1689[90]. fol.* STEELE 2p 1102. L, O, HH, DK, DN.

301   ——25th day of March 1690. *Dublin, for James Malone;
       to [be] sold at his shop, and by Andrew Crook,* 1690. fol.*
       STEELE 2p 1104. L, HH, DN.

302   ——28 March 1690. —, 1689[90]. brs. STEELE 2p 1105.
       L, HH, DK, DN.

303   ——4 April 1690. —, 1690. brs. STEELE 2p 1106. L, HH, DK,
       DN.

304   ——15 April 1690. —, 1690. brs. STEELE 2p 1108. L, HH,
       DK, DN.

305   ——21 April 1690. —, 1690. fol.* STEELE 2p 1109. L, HH,
       DK, DN.

306   ——13 June 1690. *Dublin, for James Malone,* 1690. brs.
       STEELE 2p 1114. L, HH, DK, DN.

307   ——15 June 1690 [against buying gold at high rates]. —,
       1690. brs. STEELE 2p 1115. L, HH, DK, DN.

308   ——[Same date; for crown pieces of copper and brass.]
       —, 1690. brs. STEELE 2p 1116–7. L, HH, DK, DN. (var.)

309   ——[Same date; calling in copper half crowns.] —,
       [1690]. brs. STEELE 2p 1118. L, HH, DK, DN.

309A–C Entries cancelled.
       —Proclamation adjourning the meeting. 1685. *See* Scot-
       land. Privy Council.
       ——against all persons. 1685. *See* Scotland. Privy Council.
       ——against slanderers. 1686. *See* Scotland. Privy Council.

310   —A proclamation against spreading . . . [15 June]. *By the
       assigns of John Bill, and by Henry Hills, and Thomas New-
       comb,* 1685. brs. STEELE 3799–802. L, O, LPR, MC, DT; CH,
       INU, MH, PU. (var.)

311   ——[Anr. ed.] *Dublin, B. Tooke,* 1685. fol.* STEELE 2p
       945. L, DN.

312   ——[Anr. ed.] *London reprinted Edinburgh, by the heir of
       Andrew Anderson,* 1685. brs. STEELE 3p 2628; ALDIS 2588.
       HH, EN, ER.

313   ——appointing a time . . . [23 December]. *By Charles
       Bill, Henry Hills, and Thomas Newcomb,* 1687. brs.
       STEELE 3855. L, O, CCA, MC, DT; CH, CN, MH, WF, Y.

314   ———[Anr. ed.] *Reprinted Edinburgh, by the heir of
       Andrew Anderson,* 1688. brs. STEELE 3p 2701; ALDIS 2780.
       HH, EN, ER.

315   ——calling a Parliament for April 9 . . . [16 February
       1684/5]. *Edinburgh, by the heir of Andrew Anderson,* 1685.
       brs. STEELE 3p 2591; ALDIS 2577. HH, EN, ER, AU; CH.

316   ———[Anr. ed.] —, *and reprinted at London for L. Curtiss,*
       1685. brs. STEELE 3p 2592. L, LG, LPC, HH; MH, WF.

317   ——commanding the return . . . [14 March 1687/8]. *By
       Charles Bill, Henry Hills, and Thomas Newcomb,* 1687/8.
       brs. STEELE 3861. L, O, C, LPR, EN; CH, INU, MH, MU, WF.

317A   Entry cancelled.
       ——commanding the return . . . [22 March]. Edinburgh,
       1688. *See* Scotland. Privy Council.

318   ——concerning the persons . . . [25 May]. *Edinburgh, by
       the heir of Andrew Anderson,* 1688. brs. STEELE 3p 2714;
       ALDIS 2785. HH, EN, ER; CH, MH.

319   ——containing His Majesties gracious and ample in-
       demnity . . . [25 September]. *Edinburgh, by the heir of
       Andrew Anderson,* 1688. brs. STEELE 3p 2728; ALDIS 2795.
       LLP, HH, EN, ER, ES; MH, WF.

320   ———[Anr. ed.] —, 1688. *Reprinted at London by John
       Wallis,* 1688. brs. STEELE 3p 2729. L, O, LPR, EN.

321   ——containing His Majesties gracious indemnity . . . [26
       February 1684/5]. *Edinburgh; by the heir of Andrew Ander-
       son,* 1685. brs. STEELE 3p 2593; ALDIS 2578. OP, EN, ER; WF.

322   ———[Anr. ed.] —, *reprinted at London by George Croom,*
       1685. brs. STEELE 3p 2594. L, LG, HH; CH, WF.

323   ———[Anr. ed.] *London reprint, L. Curtis,* 1685. brs.
       STEELE 3p 2595. HH.

324   ———[Anr. ed.] *London reprint, L. Curtiss,* 1685. brs.
       STEELE 3p 2596. O, LPC.

324A–B Entries cancelled.
       ——containing His Majesties gracious pardon. 1686. *See*
       Scotland. Privy Council.
       ——continuing the adjournment. 1686. *See* Scotland.
       Privy Council.

325   ——declaring His Majesty's pleasure . . . [6 March
       1684/5]. *By the assigns of John Bill: and by Henry Hills,
       and Thomas Newcomb,* 1684/5. brs. STEELE 3787–9. L, O,
       LPR, MC, DT; CH, PU. (var.)

326   ———[Anr. ed.] *Edinburgh reprinted by the heir of Andrew
       Anderson,* 1685. brs. STEELE 3p 2597; ALDIS 2579. HH,
       EN, ER.

326A   Entry cancelled.
       ——discharging forraign copper-coyn. 1686. *See* Scot-
       land. Privy Council.

327   ——for a solemn . . . thanksgiving . . . [11 July 1685]. *By
       the assigns of John Bill, and by Henry Hills and Thomas
       Newcomb,* 1685. brs. STEELE 3806–8. L, O, LPR, MC, DT;
       CH, MH, PU. (var.)

327A–C Entries cancelled.
———for a thanksgiving. 1685. *See* Scotland. Privy Council.
———for an anniversary thanksgiving. 1685. *See* Scotland. Privy Council.
———for apprehending several traitors. 1685. *See* Scotland. Privy Council.

328 ———for continuing the collection . . . [9 February 1684/5]. *By the assigns of John Bill; and by Henry Hills and Thomas Newcomb*, 1684[5]. brs. STEELE 3775–9. L, O, LPR, MC, DT; CH, MH, PU, WF, Y. (var.)

329 ———[Anr. ed.] *Reprinted Edinburgh, by the heir of Andrew Anderson*, 1685. brs. STEELE 3p 2587; ALDIS 2576. HH, EN, ER, ES.

330–1 Entries cancelled.
———for discovering such as own. Edinburgh, 1685. *See* Scotland. Privy Council.

332 ———for dissolving this present Parliament . . . [2 July]. *By Charles Bill, Henry Hills, & Thomas Newcomb*, 1687. brs. STEELE 3845–6. L, O, LPR, MC, DT; CH, MH, Y. (var.)

333 ———for enforcing the due execution . . . [7 September]. *By the assigns of John Bill; and by Henry Hills and Thomas Newcomb*, 1685. brs. STEELE 3818. L, O, MC, EN, DT; CH, CLC, MH, PU.

334 ———for further proroguing of the Parliament . . . [7 January]. *By Charles Bill, Henry Hills, and Thomas Newcomb*, 1686/7. brs. STEELE 3839–40. L, O, LPR, MC, DT; CH, MH, PU, WF. (var.)

335 ———for further proroguing the Parliament . . . [18 March 1686/7]. —, 1686/7. brs. STEELE 3841–2. L, O, LPR, EN, DT; CH, PU, WF. (var.)

336 ———for prizing of Canary wines . . . [16 December]. —, 1687. brs. STEELE 3853. L, O, MC, EN, DT; CH, KU, MH, WF.

337 ———for prohibiting the transportation of frames for knitting . . . [24 October]. —, 1686. brs. STEELE 3837. L, O, LG, LPR, DT; CH, MH, MIU, PU.

338 ———for proroguing of the Parliament . . . [8 October]. —, 1686. brs. STEELE 3835–6. L, O, LPR, EN, DT; CH, MH, PU, WF. (var.)

339 ———for protecting and securing the patentees . . . [19 December]. —, 1687. brs. STEELE 3854. L, O, LPC, EN, DT; CH, CLC, MH.

340 ———for putting in execution the additional act . . . [4 November]. —, 1687. fol.* STEELE 3850. L, O, MC, EN, DT; CH, MH, NC, WF.

341 ———for putting in execution the law . . . [18 November]. —, 1687. brs. STEELE 3851. L, O, LPR, LS, DT; CH.

341A Entry cancelled.
———for putting the Kingdom of Scotland. 1685. *See* Scotland. Privy Council.

342 ———for quieting the post-master-general . . . [7 September]. *By the assigns of John Bill, and Henry Hills and Thomas Newcomb*, 1685. brs. STEELE 3819–20. L, O, LPR, LS, MC; CH, MH, PU. (var.)

343 ———[Anr. ed.] *Reprinted Edinburgh, by the heir of Andrew Anderson*, 1685. brs. STEELE 3p 2655; ALDIS 2600. EN, ER.

344 ———for restoring corporations . . . [17 October]. *By Charles Bill, Henry Hills, and Thomas Newcomb*, 1688. brs. STEELE 3881–3. L, O, CCA, EN, DT; MH, WF. (var.)

345 ———[Anr. ed.] *Holy-Rood-House, by Mr. P. B.*, 1688. brs. STEELE 3p 2737; ALDIS 2799. HH, EN, ER, ES.

346 ———for restraining all His Majesties subjects . . . [1 April]. *By the assigns of John Bill, and by Henry Hills, and Thomas Newcomb*, 1685. brs. STEELE 3790. L, O, LG, LPC, LPR; CH, MH, MIU, PU, Y.

347 ———for restraining the number . . . of hackney coaches . . . [25 November]. *By Charles Bill, Henry Hills, and Thomas Newcomb*, 1687. brs. STEELE 3852. L, O, MC, EN, DT; CH, MH.

347A Entry cancelled.
———for securing the peace of the Highlands. 1685. *See* Scotland. Privy Council.

348 ———for suppressing and preventing . . . books . . . [10 February]. —, 1687/8. brs. STEELE 3859. L, O, LPR, MC, DT; CH, MIU, WF.

349 ———for the better execution . . . [30 April]. —, 1687. brs. STEELE 3831. L, O, LPC, MC, DT; MH, Y.

350 ———for the better government . . . [23 December]. *Dublin, by Andrew Crook the assignee of Benjamin Tooke*, 1689. fol.* STEELE 2p 1087–8. L, HH, DK, DN; PL. (var.)

351 ———for the better putting in execution . . . [13 January]. *By Charles Bill, Henry Hills, & Thomas Newcomb*, 1687[8]. brs. STEELE 3856. L, O, LG, LPR, OQ, DT.

352 ———for the careful custody . . . [5 March]. —, 1685/6. fol.* STEELE 3827. L, LG, OQ, DT; CH, PU, WF.

353 ———for the encouraging . . . manufacture of white paper . . . [29 April]. —, 1687. brs. STEELE 3844. L, O, LPR, MC, DT; CH, MH, NC, PU, WF.

354 ———for the meeting of the Parliament . . . [11 October]. *By the assigns of John Bill and by Henry Hills and Thomas Newcomb*, 1685. brs. STEELE 3822–3. L, O, MC, EN, DT; CH, MH, PU, WF. (var.)

355 ———for the more effectual reducing . . . [20 January]. *By Charles Bill, Henry Hills, and Thomas Newcomb*, 1687/8. fol.* STEELE 3857. L, O, LPR, MC, DT; CH, MIU, RPJ.

356 ———for the putting in execution . . . [6 April]. —, 1688. brs. STEELE 3863. L, O, LG, LPR, DT; CH, MH, MIU, NC.

357 ———for the recalling all His Majesties subjects . . . [17 July]. —, 1686. brs. STEELE 3833–4. L, O, LPR, MC, DT; CH, MIU, PU, WF. (var.)

358 ———for the speedy calling of a Parliament . . . [30 November]. —, 1688. brs. STEELE 3909–12. L, O, MC, EN, DT; INU, MH, TO, WF, Y. (var.)

359 ———[Anr. ed.] *Dublin, re-printed by Andrew Crook & Samuel Helsham, assigns of Benjamin Tooke*, 1688. brs. STEELE 2p 1003. DN.

360 ———[Anr. ed.] *Reprinted Edinburgh, by the heir of Andrew Anderson*, 1688. brs. STEELE 3p 2748; ALDIS 2804. HH, EN, ER, ES; CH.

361 ———inhibiting all persons . . . [7 May]. *By Charles Bill, Henry Hills, and Thomas Newcomb*, 1686. fol.* STEELE 3832. L, O, LPR, MC, EN; CH, MH, PU, WF.

361A ——of pardon . . . [24 June]. *By the assigns of John Bill; and by Henry Hills, and Thomas Newcomb*, 1685. brs. OC.

362 ——22 November. *By Charles Bill, Henry Hills, and Thomas Newcomb*, 1688. brs. STEELE 3904–5. L, LPR, OQ, EN, DT; MH, WF, Y. (var.)

363 ——of the Kings Majesties . . . pardon . . . [10 March]. —, 1685[6]. brs. STEELE 3828–9. L, O, MC, EN, DT; CH, INU, MH, PU. (var.)

364 ———[Anr. ed.] *Dublin, by Andrew Crook & Samuel Helsham, sold by Samuel Helsham, Joseph Howes, and Eliphal Dopson*, 1686. brs. STEELE 2p 965. MIU.

365 ——prohibiting His Majesties subjects to enter . . . [2 March]. *By Charles Bill, Henry Hills, & Thomas Newcomb*, 1687/8. brs. STEELE 3860. L, O, LPR, EN, DT; CH, MH.

366 ——prohibiting His Majesties subjects to trade . . . [31 March]. —, 1688. brs. STEELE 3862. L, O, LPR, EN, DT; CH, MH, RPJ.

367 ——prohibiting the importation of foreign needles . . . [14 August]. —, 1687. brs. STEELE 3849. L, LPR, OQ, MC, DT; MH, Y.

368 ——prohibiting the keeping of Exeter Fair . . . [16 November]. —, 1688. brs. STEELE 3899–3900. L, O, LG, LPR, DT; MH, Y. (var.)

368A–D Entries cancelled.
——requiring all heretors and freeholders. Edinburgh, 1685. *See* Scotland. Privy Council.
——requiring all the members. 1685. *See* Scotland. Privy Council.

369 ——signifying His Majesties pleasure . . . [6 February]. *By the assigns of John Bill, and by Henry Hills, and Thomas Newcomb*, 1684[5]. brs. STEELE 3772–3. L, O, LPR, MC, DT; CH, IU, MH, PU, WF, Y. (var.)

370 ———[Anr. ed.] —, 1684, *Edinburgh [re]printed, by the heir of Andrew Anderson*, 1685. brs. STEELE 3p 2584. HH, E, EN, ER.

371 ——to prohibit His Majesties subjects . . . [1 April]. *By the assigns of John Bill, and by Henry Hills and Thomas Newcomb*, 1685. brs. STEELE 3791. L, O, LG, LPR, DT; CH, MH, MIU, PU, ANL.

372 ——to restrain the spreading of false news . . . [26 October]. *By Charles Bill, Henry Hills, and Thomas Newcomb*, 1688. brs. STEELE 3888–9. L, LPR, OQ, EN, DT; INU, WF, Y. (var.)

373 ——to summon in George Speake . . . [26 July]. *By the assigns of John Bill; and by Henry Hills, and Thomas Newcomb*, 1685. brs. STEELE 3812–4. L, O, LPR, MC, DT; CH, MH, PU, WF, Y. (var.)

374 ——whereas an humble address. —, 1685. brs. L.

375 Entry cancelled.
——Publication of the royal authority. 1685. *See* Scotland. Privy Council.

375A —The late King James's reasons for signing Sir G. Barclay's commission. *Sold by Eliz Whitlock*, 1696. 4°. CT.

376 —His Majesties reasons for withdrawing himself from Rochester . . . [22 December]. [*Rochester*, 1688.] brs. STEELE 3932. L, O, C, EN, DM; BN, CH, CN, MH, WF, Y.

376A ——[Anr. ed.] *Dublin, Andrew Crook and Samuel Helsham, assigns of Benjamin Tooke*, 1688. fol.* DM.

376B ——[Anr. ed.] [*Edinburgh*], *printed*, 1689. 4°.* ALDIS 2897.5. L, DL, E, EN; Y.

377 ——[Anr. ed.] [*Rochester?*], *printed*, 1689. cap., 4°.* L, O, LG, DU, E; CLC, CN, INU, MH, NC, WF.

378 Entry cancelled.
——[Anr. ed.] 1696. *See* —Late King James's reasons.

379 —His Majesties regulation in the business of plate-carriage. [*London*, 1686.] cap., fol.* O.

380 —His Majesties resolution for the calling of a free Parliament. [*London*, 1688.] brs. O, DU; CH.

381 —The royal charter of confirmation . . . to the society of the Trinity-House of Deptford-strond. *Printed*, 1685. 8°. L, LG, CM; CH, CLC, MBP, WF.

382 —His Majesties royal letter to his Privy Council . . . [31 March]. *Edinburgh, at Holy-Rood-House by James Watson*, 1687. brs. STEELE 3p 2689; ALDIS 2694. AU, EN, ER; MH, NP, TU.

383 ——[Anr. ed.] [*Edinburgh*], *printed at Holy-Rood-House, by James Watson, reprinted* [*London*] *by G. Croom*, 1687. brs. STEELE 3p 2690–1. O, LG, LS; NP, TU.

384 —Royal tracts. In two parts. *At Paris, for Estiene Lucas*, 1692. 12°. L, O, C, DU, AU; CH, CN, MH, NU, WF, Y.

385 Entry cancelled.
—Rules and articles for the . . . land-forces. 1685. *See title.*

386–6A Entries cancelled.
—Late King James's second manifesto. 1697. *See title.*

386B —Septima pars patentium de anno regni regis Jacobi Secundi quarto. [*London?* 1688.] cap., fol.* MH, NN, NP, RPJ, V.

387 —The speech of His royal Highness James Duke of York and Albany, . . . July 28, 1681. colop: *By N. T.*, 1681 brs. L, O, OP; Y.

388 —His Majesties speech, with the journal . . . May 30th. *Edinburgh, by the heir of Andrew Anderson*, 1685. fol. ALDIS 2555. EN.

388aA —Three proclamations. The one for the seizing of . . . Monmouth. *Dublin, reprinted by Benjamin Tooke; to be sold by Andrew Crooke and Samuel Helsham*, 1685. 4°.* L, DN.

388A–B Entries cancelled.
—To all and singular archbishops, bishops. 1687/8. *See* —Whereas by our letters patents.
—To all and sundry our good subjects. 1685. *See* —Proclamation calling a Parliament.
—To all . . . archbishops . . . and others our officers . . . [6 May 1687]. *By Tho. Milbourn*, 1687. brs. L.

389 —To the most reverend fathers in God, William . . . [5 March]. colop: *By Charles Bill, Henry Hills, and Thomas Newcomb*, 1685[6]. cap., 4°.* L, O, C, MR, DT; CH, IU, MH, NU, TU, WF, Y. (var.)

390 ——[Anr. ed.] colop: *Printed at London: and reprinted at Edinburgh, by the heir of Andrew Anderson*, 1686. cap., fol.* ALDIS 2644. EN; CH, MH.

391 [-]——[Anr. ed.] colop: *Dublin, re-printed by Andrew Crook, and Samuel Helsham, assigns of Benjamin Tooke, to be sold by Andrew Crook, and Samuel Helsham*, 1686. cap., 8°.* C.

391A [–] —[Anr. ed.] *Dublin, re-printed by Joseph Ray, for Robert Thornton, 1686.* cap., 4°.* DN, DT.

391B —James the second . . . To our trusty and well beloved [blank]. Greetings. This to autorize you to be Leivtenant to that troop of horse. [*St. Germains, 1692.*] brs. LPR.

392 —Tractatus pacis, . . . Jacobum II, . . . Ludovicum XIV. *Typis Thomæ Newcomb, 1686.* 4°.* L, LIU; CH, NN, RPJ, Y.

393 —Treaty of peace, good correspondence & neutrality in America, between . . . James II . . . and . . . Lewis XIV. [*London*], *in the Savoy: by Thomas Newcomb, 1686.* 4°.* L, O, OC, LSD, DT; CH, FU, LC, MH, RPJ, Y. (var.)

394 —A true coppy of His Majesties proclamation . . . 28 Sept. *Holy-rood-house, by Mr. P. B., 1688.* brs. STEELE 3p 2731; ALDIS 2797. L, O, MC, EN, ES; CH.

395 —A true copy of the letters patents . . . 4 September. [*London, 1688.*] brs. STEELE 3872. L.

396 —A true representation of His Majesty's Declaration. colop. *Printed, and sold by R. Janeway, 1688.* brs. L, O, HH, DUS, EN; CH, CN, WF.

396A —Jacobus Secundus . . . The twenty fifth day of August [1687] . . . Company of free fishermen of the river of Thames . . . [ordinances]. *By Charles Bill, Henry Hills, and Thomas Newcomb, 1687.* brs. L.

397 Entry cancelled.
—King James the Second's warrant. 1688. *See* England: King in Council. Whereas in the charters.

398 —We are graciously pleased to declare . . . 2 September. [*Dublin, 1689.*] brs. STEELE 2p 1059–60. L, HH, DK, DN.

399 —We having thought fit . . . 10 June 1690. *Dublin, by Andrew Crook,* [1690]. brs. STEELE 2p 1113. L, HH, DK, DN.

400 —Whereas all reasonable means are . . . 14 September 1689. *Dublin by Andrew Crook and Samuel Helsham, assigns of Benj. Tooke, 1689.* brs. STEELE 2p 1069–70. L, HH, DK, DN. (var.)

401 —Whereas an address hath been . . . 5 August 1689. *Dublin, by Andrew Crook and Samuel Helsham, assigns of Benjamin Tooke, 1689.* brs. STEELE 2p 1052. L, HH, DK, DN.

402 —Whereas by Our letters patents, . . . 31 January. [*London*], *in the Savoy, by Thomas Newcomb, 1687/8.* brs. STEELE 3858. L, LG, LPR, LS, DM; MH.

403 —Whereas great disorders have been . . . 24 September 1689. *Dublin, by Andrew Crook and Samuel Helsham, assigns of Benjamin Tooke, 1689.* brs. STEELE 2p 1072. L, HH, DK, DN.

404 —Whereas His Majesty hath been certainly . . . 30 July 1687. *By Charles Bill, Henry Hills, and Thomas Newcomb, 1687.* brs. STEELE 3848. L, O, LG, MC, DT; MH.

405 —Whereas it hath pleased God . . . [6 February 1684/5]. *Edinbrugh, by the heir of Andrew Anderson, 1685.* brs. STEELE 3p 2585; ALDIS 2574. EN, ER.

406 ——[Anr. ed.] *London, reprint, by T. Newcomb for S. Forrester, 1685.* brs. STEELE 3p 2586. L, O, LS, HH.

407 —Whereas it is the highest prerogative . . . 5 March. [*London*], *in the Savoy, by Thomas Newcomb, 1685*[6]. brs. STEELE 3826. L, O, CM; CH, WF.

408 —Whereas several of our troops of horse . . . 2 November 1689. *Dublin, by Andrew Crook, assign of Benjamin Tooke, 1689.* brs. STEELE 2p 1078. L, HH, DK, DN.

409 —Whereas we are informed that . . . 24 September 1689. *Dublin, by Andrew Crook and Samuel Helsham, assigns of Benjamin Tooke, 1689.* brs. STEELE 2p 1071. L, HH, DK, DN.

410 —Whereas we have issued a proclamation . . . 8 October 1689. *Dublin, by Andrew Crook and Samuel Helsham, assigns of Benj. Tooke, 1689.* brs. STEELE 2p 1074. L, HH, DK, DN.

411 —Whereas we have prorogued the . . . 17 October 1689. *Dublin, by Andrew Crook, the assign of Benjamin Tooke, 1689.* brs. STEELE 2p 1075. L, HH, DK, DN.

412 **James V, of Scotland.** A ballad of a countrey vvedding. [*London*, 1660.] brs. LT.

413 [–] Christ's kirk on the green. [*London*], *for Richard Royston, 1663.* brs. O, LNC, MC, EN; MH, Y.

413A [–] —[Anr. ed.] [*London, c. 1670.*] brs. EN; MH.

414 **James, Christian.** A wonderful prophesie. [*London*], *for George Conyers,* [1690–99]. brs. L, HH.

414A ——[Anr. ed.] *For J. Wright,* [1656]. brs. EUING 400. GU.

414B ——[Anr. ed.] [*London*], *for J. Clarke, W. Thackeray, and T. Passenger,* [1690]. brs. CM.

415 **James, Elinor.** Mrs. James's advice to the citizens of London. [*London? 1688.*] brs. L, O, C, LG; CH.

415A —Mrs. Jame's apology. [*London, 1694.*] brs. L.

415B —Mrs. James's application to the . . . Commons. [*London? 1695.*] brs. HH.

416 —The case between a father and his children. *By Tho. James, 1682.* brs. EN, CH; IU, Y.

416A —Dear sovereign. [*London, 1687.*] brs. OC.

417 —Mrs. James's defence of the Church of England, [*London*], *for me Elinor James, 1687.* 4°.* L, O, LG, CS, DC, LSD, DT; IU, MM, NU, PH.

417AA —Mrs. James's humble letter. [*London? 1699.*] brs. HH.

417BA —I can assure your honours . . . East-India-Company. [*London, 1699?*] brs. INDIA OFFICE.

417A [–] An injur'd prince vindicated. [*London? 1688.*] brs. MH.

417AB —May it please your honours, . . . East India Company. [*London, 1699?*] brs. INDIA OFFICE.

417AC —May it please your Majesty, to accept my thanks. [*London, 1689.*] brs. LG.

417B —May it please your most sacred Majesty, seriously to consider my great zeal. [*London, 1685.*] brs. CM, HH; MH, Y.

417C —Most dear Soveraign, I cannot but love. [*London, 1689.*] brs. CH, MH, Y.

418 —My Lord, I thought it my bound duty. [*London, 1687.*] brs. O, MH.

419 —My Lords, I can assure. [*London, 1688.*] brs. L, LPR.

419A —My Lords, I did not think. [*London? 1690.*] brs. CN.

419B —My Lords, you can't but be sensible. [*London? 1688.*] brs. L; CN, INU.

420 —Mrs. James her new answer to a speech. [*London, 1681.*] brs. O, LG.

421 —Sir, my Lord Major. [*London, 1690?*] brs. L.

421aA —This being your Majesty's birth-day. [*London*, 1690.] brs. L, OC.

421A —To the honourable convention, Gentlemen, you seem. [*London?* 1688.] brs. L; CH.

421B —To the honourable House of Commons . . . [payment of King's debts]. [*London?* 1685.] brs. HH.

421C — —[Same title, East India Co.] [*London?* 1699.] brs. HH.

422 —To the Honourable the House of Commons . . . I am very sorry. [*London?* 1696.] brs. LUG, CM, DC, HH; CLC.

422aA —To the Kings most excellent majesty. [*London*, 1685.] brs. L, OC, CM, DU; MH, Y.

422bA —To the right honourable Convention. Gentlemen, though you have a new name. [*London?* 1688.] brs. L, INU.

422A —To the right honourable the House of Lords. My lords. [*London?* 1688.] brs. O; MH.

422B —To the right honourable, the Lord Mayor . . . and all the rest of the loyal citizens. [*London*, 1683.] brs. MH.

423 —Mrs. James's vindication of the Church of England. *For me Elinor James*, 1687. 4°.* L, O, C, LIU, EN; CLC, CN, MH, NU, WF, Y.

424 **James, Francis.** A proclamation to the king. *Printed at London by John Hammond*, 1647. 4°.* LT, C, DU, LSD, DT; MM, NU, WF.

425 **James, Haestrect.** A poem upon the conclusion of the peace of Europe. *By W. Onley, and are to be sold by E. Whitlock*, 1698. fol.* T.C.III 55. O; MH, Y.

426 **James, Henry.** A sermon preached . . . October 11. 1674. *By W. Godbid, to be sold by M. Pitt*, 1674. 4°.* T.C.I 196. L, O, C, EN, BLH; CLC, MIU, NU, TSM, WF, Y.

426A — —[Anr. ed.] *By William Godbid*, 1674. 4°.* CT; IU, MH.

427 **James, John,** *of Latimers*. Ad clerum. A visitation sermon. *By T. H. for R. Chiswel*, 1678. 4°.* T.C.I 319. L, O, C, BR, WCA; CH, Y.

427A —The different end of the wicked. *For William Court*, 1689. 4°.* LW, WCA; WF.

428 —A sermon preached . . . Decemb. 24. 1682. *For Richard Chiswell*, 1683. 4°.* L, O, LG, OCC, WCA; CH, NGT, NU, TU, WF, Y.

429 **James, John,** *weaver*. The last words and actions of. *R. Vaughan*, 1661. 4°.* C, OB, MR; PL, WF.

430 —The speech and declaration of. *For George Horton*, 1661. 4°.* L, C; WF.

431 —The true and perfect speech of. *For George Horton*, 1661. 4°.* L.

432 **James, Marmaduke.** The best fee-simple. *By J. M. for J. Martin, J. Allestry, T. Dicas*, 1659. 4°. LT, O, SP.

432A —A narrative of the unfaithful and vexatious practises of Nicholas Clark attorney [*sic*]. *Printed*, 1673. 4°.* O.

433 **James, Ralph.** The Quakers subterfuge. *For Francis Smith*, 1672. 4°.* L, LF, LW, MR.

434 **James, Thomas.** Bellvm papale, sive, concordia. *Impensis Joh. Dunmore*, 1678. 12°. T.C.I 321. L, O, C, EN, DT; CH, MH, NU, TU, WF, Y.

435 —Spira's despair revived. *For T. Parkhurst*, 1694. 12°. T.C.II 521. LCL.

435A — —[Anr. ed.] *For R. Baldwin*, 1694. 8°. O; Y.

436 —A treatise of the corruption of Scripture. *For Josh. Phillips, and Joseph Watts*, 1688. 8°. T.C.II 243. L, O, CE, MR, EN, CD; CH, IU, PL, TU, WF, Y.

437 —A vindication of that part of Spira's despair. *For John Lawrence*, 1695. 4°.* NU.

438 **James, William,** *1635?–1663*. Ἐισαγωγη in linguam Chaldaeam. *Ex officina Roger Daniel*, 1651. 8°. L, CT; OHU.

439 **James, William.** *fl. 1689*. England interest: or, means to promote . . . wooll. 1689. brs. C, LG, LUG.

440 —An explanation of the proposal. [*London?* 1696.] brs. LUG.

441 —Proposals humbly offered to the . . . Commons. [*London?* 1696.] brs. L, LUG, GH; NC.

442 **Jameson, John.** Rebellio debellata. *Edinbvrgh, by a society of stationers*, 1661. 8°. ALDIS 1701. L, SP, E, EN; MH.

443 **Jameson, William.** Nazianzeni querela. *Glasgow, by Robert Sanders, for the author*, 1697. 4°. ALDIS 3674. L, C, LCL, EN, DT; CH, CN, MH, NU, TU, WF, Y.

444 [–] A remembrance of former times for this generation. *Boston, by B. Green, and J. Allen, for Duncan Campbel*, 1697. 4°.* EVANS 784. MB, MHS, MWA.

445 —Verus Patroclus: or, the weapons of Quakerism. *Edinburgh, printed*, 1689. 8°. ALDIS 2898. L, LF, E, EN, ENC; CH, MB, PH, PSC, WF.

446 [**Jamieson, Alexander.**] Apology for, or vindication of, the oppressed persecuted ministers. [*Edinburgh?*], 1677. 8°. ALDIS 2093. L, LW, E, EN, SA; CLC, IU, MH, NP, NU.

447 **Jan III Sobieski.** Copia literarum. *For R. H. to be sold by Randal Taylor*, 1685. brs. O, LG, HH; CH.

448 —A letter from the King of Poland to His Queen. colop: *For R. Baldwin*, 1683. brs. O, LSD; CH, IU, Y.

449 —A letter from the King of Poland. *Dublin, reprinted*, 1683. fol.* DIX 202. DT; NC.

450 —The letter of the King of Poland. colop: *Printed, to be sold by Walter Davis*, 1683. cap., fol.* O; CH, Y.

450A —The speech delivered by. *By Nat. Thompson*, 1683. brs. DCH.

451 [**Jane, Joseph**], *bp*. Εικων ακλαστος the image vnbroaken. [*London*], *printed*, 1651. 4°. ALMACK 74. L, OC, CS, E, DT; CH, CN, MH, NU, WF, Y, AVP.

451A —Salmasius his dissection. *For J. G. B.*, 1660. 4°. LC, MH, WF.

452 [**Jane, William.**] A letter to a friend, containing some queries. [*London*], 1689. brs. LLP, EN; CN.

453 [–] —[Anr. ed.] [*London*, 1689.] cap., 4°.* L, OC, CT, MR, DT; CH, CN, NU, TU, WF, Y.

454 [–] The present separation self-condemned. *For Edward Croft*, 1678. 4°. T.C.I 319. L, O, C, BAMB, LSD, DM; CH, CLC, NPT, NU, Y.

455 —A sermon preached . . . December 6. 1674. *By W. Godbid, and are to be sold by R. Littlebury*, 1675. 4°.* T.C.I 194. L, O, C, CT, E, DM; CH, CN, NU, TU, WF, Y.

456 — —April the 11th. 1679. *By M. C. for Henry Brome and Richard Chiswel*, 1679. 4°. L, O, C, DL, DT; CH, CN, MH, NU, TU, WF, Y.

457 ——the 26th of November, 1691. *Oxford, at the theater, for Thomas Bennet, London,* 1691. 4°.* L, O, C, NE, DT; CH, CN, LC, NU, TSM, WF, Y.

458 ——in November, 1692. *Oxford, at the theater, for Thomas Bennet, London,* 1692. 4°.* T.C.II 437. L, O, C, DU, DT; CH, CN, NU, TSM, WF, Y.

459 **Janeway, James.** Death unstung. *For Dorman Newman,* 1669. 8°. L, C; CLC, Y.

460 ——[Anr. ed.] *For Iohn Wilkins,* 1671. 8°. L, O; NU.

460A ——[Anr. ed.] *For Dorman Newman,* 1671. 8°. BC.

461 ——[Anr. ed.] *By T. Milbourn for Dorman Newman,* 1672. 8°. L, C, LCL; MH.

462 ——[Anr. ed.] —, 1673. 8°. L; MH.

463 ——[Anr. ed.] *By T. Milbourn, for Dorman Newman, to be sold by Henry Hallett,* 1677. 8°. L, C.

464 [–] Heaven upon earth. *Printed,* 1667. 8°. CLC, NU.

465 ——[Anr. ed.] *For D. Newman,* 1669. 8°. T.C.I 23. LCL.

466 ——Third edition. *By T. Milbourn, for D. Newman,* 1671. 8°. T.C.I 91. L, LW, BC; TO.

467 ——Fourth edition. —, 1673. 8°. L; MH.

468 ——Sixth edition. *By T. Milbourn, for D. Newman, to be sold by Henry Hallett,* 1677. 8°. L, O, C; CH, NF.

469 ——Seventh edition. *For D. Newman,* 1685. 8°. NU.

470 —Invisibles, realities, demonstrated. *For Tho. Parkhurst,* 1673. 8°. T.C.I 125. L, O, C, LW, CK; CH, MH, MIU, NU, Y.

471 ——[Anr. ed.] —, 1674. 8°. L, CK; NF, NGT, WF.

471A ——[Anr. ed.] —, 1677. 8°. DU; CLC.

471B ——[Anr. ed.] —, 1678. 8°. L.

471C ——[Anr. ed.] —, 1684. 12°. T.C.II 77. LW.

472 ——Second edition. —, 1690. 8°. T.C.II 343. C, LCL; Y.

472A ——Third edition. —, 1698. 8°. T.C.III 136. C, CS.

473 —Mr. James Janeway's legacy. *For Dorman Newman,* 1674. 8°. T.C.I 167. L, CT, BR; NN, RPJ.

474 ——[Anr. ed.] —, 1675. 8°. L, O, C; CN, CU, MH, NP, RPJ.

474A ——[Anr. ed.] —, 1680. 8°. T.C.I 409. MB.

475 ——[Anr. ed.] *For Dorman Newman, and to be sold by Thomas Maltbus* [sic], 1683. 12°. T.C.II 2. LCL; CN, MH, NP, WF, Y.

475A —Memento mori. Man's last end. *For C. Passinger,* [1674]. 8°. CT.

476 —The saints incouragement. *By A. M. for Tho. Parkhurst,* 1674. 8°. T.C.I 146. L, O, C, LCL; CH, MH.

477 —Mr. Janeway's sayings. *For A. Purslow,* 1674. brs. L.

477A —A token for children. *Edinburgh, A. Anderson,* 1672. 12°. ALDIS 1946. I.

478 ——[Anr. ed.] *For Dorman Newman,* 1676. 12°. O, C.

479 ——[Anr. ed.] 1679. 12°. LCL.

480 ——[Anr. ed.] *Boston in N.E., for Nicholas Boone,* 1700. EVANS 914. MWA.

480AA ——The second part. *For D. Newman,* 1673. 12°. C. Jani Anglorum. [*n.p.*], 1680. *See* Atwood, William.

480A **Janney, Thomas.** An epistle from. colop: *Printed and sold by T. Sowle,* 1694. 4°.* LF, MR; CH, NPT, NS.

481 [**Janson, Sir Henry.**] Jonas redux. *For Henry Brome,* 1672. 4°.* L, O, CT, MR, DT; LC, MH, NPT, WF.

482 [–] Philanax Anglicus: or a Christian caveat. *For Theo: Sadler,* 1663. 8°. L, C, DU, EN, DM; BN, CH, MH, NU, WF, Y.

483 [–] ——Second edition. —, 1663. 8°. O, C, LLP, BSM, DU; CH, CN, CU, MH, TU, Y.

484 ——[Anr. ed.] *W. Cademan,* 1670. 8°. E, LNC; CLC.

485 [**Jansse, Lucas.**] Le miracle du Père Veron. *Pour D. Du Chemin,* 1699. 12°. O.

485A [**Janssen, Sir Theodore.**] A discourse concerning banks. colop: *For James Knapton,* 1697. cap., 4°.* L, LUG; CH, CU, MH, NC, WF.

486 [–] A second part to a discourse concerning banks. [*London,* 1697.] cap., fol.* L; CH, MH, NC, Y.

487 Ianuaries accovnt, giving a full and true relation. colop: *For Richard Harper,* 1645. cap., 4°.* LT; MH, Y.

Iarmin. *See* Jermyn.

488 [**Jarrige, Pierre.**] A further discovery of the mystery of Jesuitisme. *For T. Dring,* 1658. 8°. L, O, C, NE, DT; CLC, IU, MH, NU, PU, WF.

488A [–] ——[Anr. ed.] —, 1648 [*i.e.* 1658]. 8°. TU.

489 [–] ——[Anr. ed.] *For R. Royston,* 1658. 12°. LT, OCC, CT, SP, BQ; CH, CN, MIU, RPJ, TU, Y.

489A ——[Anr. ed.] *For G. Sawbridge,* 1658. 8°. OU, MR, P; CN, TO.

490 —The Jesuites displayed. *Printed at London, to be sold by W. Gilbertson,* 1658. 8°. O, LCL, LLP, SP; NU, WF, Y.

491 **Jasz-Berenyi, Pál.** Examen doctrinæ Ariano-Socinianæ. *Sumptibus Samuelis Broun,* 1662. 8°. L, O, C, SC, YM; BN, LC, OHU, Y.

492 —Fax nova linguæ Latinæ. *By R. Wood, to be sold by Nath. Brooke,* 1664. 8°. L, O, C, P; CH, IU, Y.

493 ——Second edition. *By B. Wood, sold by R. L. & Nath. Brooke,* 1666. 8°. L, O, C, LLP; BN, CLC, IU, LC, MIU.

494 ——Fourth edition. *Impressi pro, prostantque venales apud Nath. Brooke,* 1670. 8°. T.C.I 27. L, O, C, DC, E; WF.

494A —Institvtionum grammaticorum. *Ex officina R. W. prostantque venales apud Nath. Brooke,* 1663. 8°. L, O, C, GU; CH, Y.

495 ——[Anr. ed.] —, 1666. 8°. O, C; BN.

495A ——[Anr. ed.] *Ex officina J. G. prostantque venales apud Nath. Brooke,* 1666. 8°. CLC, IU, LC.

495B ——[Anr. ed.] *Ex officina B. W. prostantque venales apud Nath. Brooke,* 1667. 8°. L, O; IU, LC, MIU.

495C ——[Anr. ed.] *Ex officina E. T. prostantque venales apud Nath. Brooke,* 1669. 8°. L, O, OC; IU, WF.

495D —A new torch to the Latine tongue. Third edition. *London, N. Brooke,* 1667. 8°. LC.

495E Jatropoton, or, a most grateful and wholesome corrective. [*London,* 1700?] brs. L.

496 **J[ay], G[eorge].** A sermon preached at Bugbrook in Northamptonshire, May 15. 1642. *By Tho. Harper,* 1642. 4°.* O.

497 **J[ay], S[tephen].** Daniel in the den. *By J. A. for John Dunton,* 1682. 4°.* T.C.II 12. L, O, C, EN, DT; CH, CN, NU, WF, Y.

498 —Τα καννακου: The tragedies of sin. *By J. Astwood, for John Dunton,* 1689. 8°. T.C.II 283. L, O, C, LLL, OC; BN, NU.

498A —To the right honourable His Majesties judges, now sitting in Oxon, &c. The humble petition of. [*Oxford?* 1680?] brs. MH.

499 **Jeake, Samuel.** Λογιστικη λογια, or, arithmetick sur-
     veighed. *By J. R. & J. D. for Walter Kettilby, and
     Richard Mount,* 1696. fol. L, CT, SP; CLC, LC, NC, WF, Y.
     Jealous husbands. 1679. *See* Leanerd, John.

500 The jealous lover satisfy'd. *[London], for J. Blare,* [1685].
     brs. L, O, HH; MH, Y.

501 Entry cancelled.
     Jealous lover's complaint. [n.p., 168–?] *See* Shepher'ds
     lamentation.

502 The jealous old dotard. *[London], for P. Brooksby,* [1672–
     80]. brs. L, HH; MH.

503 [**Jeamson, Thomas.**] Artificiall embellishments. *Oxford,
     by William Hall,* 1665. 8°. MADAN 2705. L, O, CM, LLU,
     GU; CH, CLC, MH, PU, WF, Y.

504 Entry cancelled.
     Jeanes, Henry. Certain letters. 1660. *See* —Second part.

505 —Dr. Creed's voluminous defence. *For Edward Brewster,*
     1661. 4°. O, BC, BR, MR; CLC, NU.

506 —Doctor Hammond his Εκτενεστερον. *Oxford, by
     Henry Hall, for Thomas Robinson,* 1657. 4°.* MADAN
     2343. LT, O, LW, OC, CT, MR; CII, MII, NU, WF, Y.

507 —A mixtvre of scholasticall divinity. *Oxford, by H. Hall,
     for Thomas Robinson.* 1656. 4°. MADAN 2299. LT, O, C,
     GU, DT; CH, IU, MH, NU, WF, Y.

508 —A second part of The mixtvre of scholasticall divinity.
     Oxford, by H. Hall, for Thomas Robinson. 1660. 4°.
     MADAN 2501. LT, O, DC, BR, DT; CLC, IU, MH, NU, TO, WF.

509 Entry cancelled.
     [–] Treatise concerning the indifference. *Oxford,* 1659.
     See —Second part of the mixtvre.

509A —A treatise of the excellency of praise. *By G. D. and are
     to be sold by Samuel Gellibrand,* [n.d.]. 4°. BAMB.
     ——[Anr. ed.] [1656.] *See* —A mixtvre.

510 —Uniformity in humane doctrinall ceremonies. *Oxford,
     by A. Lichfield, for Tho. Robinson,* 1660. 4°. LT, O, LCL,
     BC, BR, DT; CLC, IU, NU, TO, WF.

511 —The want of church-government no warrant. *For
     Samuel Gellibrand,* 1650. 4°. LT, O, C, E, DT; CH, CLC, NU,
     WF, Y.

512 ——[Anr. ed.] *Oxford, by H. Hall, for Th. Robinson,* 1653.
     8°. MADAN 2229. LT, O, CM, BC, DT; CLC, MH, NU, WF.

513 —The vvorke of heaven upon earth. *By G. D. for Francis
     Eglesfield, and are to be sold by George Treagle in Taunton,*
     1649. 4°. L, C, LW, BR; CH, IU, MH, Y.

513A ——[Anr. ed., "vvorks."] *By G. D. for Francis Eglesfield,*
     1649. 4°. O, NU.

514 **Jeckell, Robert.** A lively testimony. *Printed,* 1676. 4°.*
     L, LF; MH, PH, PSC, Y.

514A [**Jeffery, John.**] The dangerous imposture of Quakerism.
     For Ann Baldwin, 1698. fol. O, LSC, CT; PH.

514B [–] —[Anr. ed.] —, 1699. cap., 8°.* CT; TU.

515 —The duty & encouragement of religious artificers.
     Cambridge, by John Hayes, for Samuel Oliver in Norwich,
     1693. 4°.* O, C, BAMB, BC, NPL; Y.

516 —A plain and short discourse concerning the . . . Lord's
     Supper. *For W. Rogers,* 1699. 8°.* T.C.III 122. L, O, C,
     LW, EC, LSD; NIA.

517 —Proposals made. *For Tho. Goddard, in Norwich,* 1700.
     12°.* O, NPL.

518 —Religion the perfection of man. *For Walter Kettilby,*
     1689. 12°. T.C.II 237. L, O, C, LLP, CT, P, DT; CLC, NU.

519 —A sermon preached . . . May 18, 1692. *By Samuel Roy-
     croft, for Robert Clavell,* 1692. 4°.* L, C, CT, LSD; CH,
     WF.

520 ——June xx. 1693. *For James Adamson,* 1693. 4°.* L, O,
     C, BAMB; CLC, WF.

521 ——March 8th. 1695/6. *For William Rogers,* 1696. 4°.*
     T.C.II 584. L, O, CT, EC, NPL; WF, Y.

522 **Jeffery, William.** Antichrist made known. *By R. I. for
     Francis Smith,* 1656. 4°.* LT, O, LF.

522A —The gospel declared in truth. *[London], for G. Calvert,*
     1650. 8°. L(t.p.).

523 [–]—The lawfulnes of tithes. *For John VVilliams,* 1675.
     4°.* L, O, C, LF, EN; CH.

523A [–] —[Anr. ed.] *By J. R. for John Whitlocke,* 1676. 4°.*
     T.C.I 228. LLP; WF.

524 —The whole faith of man. Second edition. *By G. Daw-
     son, for Francis Smith, and Stephen Dagnal, of Alisbury,*
     1659. 8°. LT, LCL; NHC.

525 **Jeffreys, George Jeffrey, baron.** The chancellor's ad-
     dress & confession. colop: *Printed,* 1689. cap., 4°.* L,
     O; CH.

526 —The argument of . . . concerning the great case of
     monopolies. *Printed, and are sold by Randal Taylor,* 1689.
     fol.* T.C.II 251. L, O, CT, EN, DT; CN, LC, MHL, NC, PL, Y.

527 —The charge given by. *[London?* 1685.] cap., fol.* L, O,
     BR; CH, CLC, IU, WF, Y.

528–8A Entries cancelled. Lord Chancellor's petition. 1688. *See
     title.*

529 —To His Highness William Henrick, Prince of Orange,
     the most humble petition of. *Boston, by S. G. for
     Samuel Phillips,* 1689. brs. EVANS 471. LC, MHS, MU.

530 **Jegon, William.** The damning nature of rebellion. *For
     Will. Oliver, in Norwich,* 1685. 4°.* T.C.II 143. L, O; CH,
     CLC, CN, MH, WF.
     Jehojadahs iustice. 1645. *See* Hoyle, Joshua.
     Jehoshaphats going forth. [n.p., 1642.] *See* Ward, R.

531 Iehovah Iireh: or, Gods providence. *By Rich. Coles, for
     Michael Sparkes senior,* 1643. 4°.* L.
     Jehavah Jireh merito audiens. 1642. *See* Tuke, Edward.

531A **Jekyll, Thomas.** A brief and plain exposition of the
     church-catechism. *In the Savoy, by Edw. Jones, for
     Joseph Watts,* 1690. 8°. L, LLP.

531B ——[Anr. ed.] *For Rich. Cumberland,* 1696. 8°. IU.

531C ——Second edition. *By K. Astwood, for B. Barker,* 1700.
     8°. OC.

532 ——Third edition. —, 1700. 8°. O.

533 —Peace and love. *By Thomas Milbourn, for Dorman New-
     man,* 1675. 4°.* T.C.I 210. L, OCC, CT, BR, EC; CH, CLC,
     IU, NU, WF, Y.

534 —Popery a great mystery. *For Jonathan Robinson,* 1681.
     4°.* T.C.I 435. L, O, OM, CS, BLH; CLC, IU, TU, WF, Y.

535 —Publick charity. *For John Everingham,* 1697. 4°.* T.C.III
     12. L, O, C, CS, BAMB, DM; CH, CLC, NU, WF.

536 —Righteousness and peace. *For Jonathan Robinson, 1681.* 4°.* T.C.I 458. L, O, C, LG, DM; CH, IU, NU, TU, WF, Y.

537 ——Second edition. —, 1681. 4°.* T.C.I 478. O, LSD; PU.

538 —A sermon preach'd . . . June 27, 1698. *By R. and T. Mead, for Ralph Simpson, and Richard Cumberland, 1698.* 8°.* T.C.III 75. L, O, CM, BAMB, EC; MH, NU.

539 —True religion makes the best loyalty. *For Jonathan Robinson, 1682.* 4°.* T.C.I 493. L, O, CT, WCA, DT; CH, CLC, IU, NU, WF, Y.

540 **Jelinger, Christopher.** Christ and his saints. [*London*], *for Edward Brewster, 1656.* 12°. O; CH.

541 [–] A cluster of sweetest grapes. *Printed, 1664.* 8°. L, LCL; Y.

542 —The excellency of Christ. *By I. L. for Fran. Eglesfield, and are to be sold by William Russell in Plimouth, 1641.* 8°. L, O, LSC, OME; MH.

542A ——[Anr. ed.] *By I. L. for Tho. Nickols, 1641.* 8°. L.

543 —Heaven won by violence. *Printed, 1665.* 8°. O, AN; WF.

544 —A nevv Canaan. [*London*], *printed, 1664.* 8°. O, LCL, AN; WF.

545 —The resolution-table. *For E. Brewster, 1676.* brs. L; MH.

546 —Sacra unio, or, an holy union. *By M. White, for John Wright, and Jacob Sampson, 1681.* 8°. T.C.I 427. L, LCL, LW, OU, SP; CN, NU, Y.

547 —Three treatises: I. The spirituall merchant. [*London*], *1676.* 12°. L, LCL, LW.

548 —The usefulnesse and excellency of Christ. *For F. Eglesfield, to be sold by Tho. Hunt in Exeter, 1647.* 12°. LCL, NU.

549 —Usury stated overthrown. *For J. Wright and J. Sampson,* [*1679?*] 8°. LUG, OU, CT, P, SP; CH, CJC, MB, NC, WF, Y.

550 **Jemmat, Samuel.** A sermon preached . . . March the nineteenth, 1682/3. *Oxford, by Leonard Lichfield, for George Teonge, in Warwick, 1683.* 4°.* T.C.II 39. L, O, CT, BC, WCA; CLC, IU, WF.

550A **Jemmat, William.** Now and ever; shewing. *L. Miller for J. Chandler, 1666.* 4°.* EN.

550B —A practical exposition of . . . Jonah. *By L. Miller, for John Chandler, 1666.* 4°. L, LSC, P.

551 —The rocke. *For Samuel Enderby, 1644.* 12°. O; Y.

552 —A vvatch-word for Kent. *Printed at London for Matthew Walbanke, 1643.* 4°.* LT, LG.

552A ——[Anr. ed.] *Printed at London for Fulke Clifton, 1643.* 4°.* Y.

553 Jemmy and Anthony. [*London*], *for R. Shuter, 1682.* brs. L.

554 Jemmy returned. [*London*], *for J. Conyers,* [*1682*]. brs. O.

555 Entry cancelled.

[**Jemson, Nathaniel.**] True and perfect account. 1672. *See* Pye, John.

555A **Jenings, Abraham.** Digitus Dei, or an horrid murther. *By Abraham Jenings, 1664.* 4°.* CH.

556 **Jenings, Francis.** The faithful description of pure love. *By J.B. and may be had at Simon Orchard's house, 1659.* 4°. E.

556A [–] Some queries, proposed to discover the necessity of magistrates. *Printed, 1661.* 4°.* O.

557-8 Entries cancelled.

Jenings. Samuel. Truth rescued. Philadelphia, 1699. *See* Jennings, Samuel.

559 **J[enison], R[obert], 1649-88.** Faithfull depositaty. Newcastle, 1649. *See* Jenison, Robert, 1584-1642.

——The information of. *By the assigns of John Bill, Thomas Newcomb, and Henry Hills, 1680.* fol.* L, O, CT, EN, DT; CH, MBP, MU, TU, WF, Y.

560 —The informations of. *For Thomas Basset, and Richard Tonson, 1680.* fol.* L, O, C, MR, DT; CH, CN, MH, TU, WF, Y, AVP.

561 —The narrative of. *For F. Smith, T. Basset, J. Wright, R. Chiswel and S. Heyrick, 1679.* fol. L, O, C, EN, DT; CH, CN, MH, TU, WF, Y.

562 ——[Anr. ed.] *Dublin, reprinted, 1679.* 4°.* DIX 171. C, CD, DT; CLC, PL, WF, Y.

562A **J[enison], R[obert], 1584-1652.** The faithfull depositaty [*sic*]. *Newcastle, by S. B., 1649.* 4°. O, CT, NE, EN; WF, Y.

563 —The return of the sword. *By John Macock, for Luke Favvne, 1648.* 4°.* LT, O, C, YM, DT; CH, MB, NU, WF, Y.

564 —Solid comfort. [*London*], *printed, 1641.* 4°. LW, MR; CH.

564A —A treatise of contrition. *For Joseph Kirton, 1655.* CS.

565 —Two treatises. *By E. G. for L. Blaiklock, 1642.* 12°. LSC, LW, SHR; CH.

[**Jenkin, Robert.**] Ansvver to a treatise. 1691. *See* Bisbie, Nathaniel.

566 [–] An answer to the vindication of the letter from a person of quality in the north. *Printed, 1690.* 4°.* L, O, OB, CT, MR; WF, Y.

567 [–] A defence of the profession. *Printed, 1690.* 4°. L, O, C, MR, EN, DM; CLC, CN, MH, NU, TU, WF, Y.

568 [–] An historical examination of the authority. *For Henry Mortlock, 1688.* 4°. L, O, C, E, DT; CH, CN, MH, TU, WF, Y.

569 [–] ——Second edition. —, 1688. 4°. L, O, C, EN, DT; CLC, MH, NU, WF, Y.

570 —The reasonableness and certainty of the Christian religion. *For Peter Buck, 1698.* 8°. L, LW, CT, NPL, D, DT; MH, NPT, NU.

571 ——Second edition. *For P. B. and R. Wellington, 1700.* 8°. T.C.III 168. L, C, OC, BP, DUS, LIU; MH, NU.

571A ——Book II. *For Peter Buck, 1700.* 8°. C, LW, BP, NPL, D, DM; MH, NPT, NU.

572 [–] The title of a thorough settlement examined. *Printed, to be sold by John Wells, 1691.* 4°. T.C.II 361. L, O, C, MR, AU; CH, CN, MH, NC, WF, Y.

573 [–] The title of an usurper. *Printed, 1690.* 4°. L, OC, CT, LIU, LSD, MR; CH, CLC, MM.

574 **Jenkins, David.** The vvorks of. *For I. Gyles, 1648.* 12°. LT, O, C, EN, DT; CH, CN, MHL, NU, TU, WF, Y.

575 ——[Anr. ed., "works."] *For I. Gyles, 1648.* 12°. LG, CT, AN, DU; CH, IU, LC, MM, PU, Y, AVP.

576 ——[Anr. ed.] *For J. Gyles, 1648.* 12°. OC, AN; LC, NCL, TO.

577 ——[Anr. ed.] *For M. Walbanck and J. Gyles, 1648.* 12°. L, AN. (var.)

578 ——[Anr. ed.] —, 1661. 12°. LGI.

579 ——[Anr. ed.] *By Samuel Roycroft, for Samuel Heyrick,* [*1681*]. 12°. L, O, LG, BR, AN; CH, MHL, MIU, NCL, WF, Y.

580 [–] All is not govld that glisters. *Printed at London, 1648.* 4°.* LT, C, DT; MH, Y.

581 —The answer of. [*London*], *printed*, 1648. 4°.* LT, O, C, AN, EN, DT; CH, CLC, MH, MM, WF, Y.

582 [–] An apology for the army, touching. [*London*], *printed in the yeare*, 1647. 4°.* LT, C, OC, AN, DT; CH, CLC, IU, MM, NU, TU, WF.

583 ——[Anr. ed.] *Printed*, 1647. 4°.* LT, O, C, EN, DT; BN, CLC, CN, MBP, MH, TU, WF, Y.

584 [–] The armies indemnity. [*London*], *printed*, 1647. 4°.* LT, O, C, AN, DT; BN, CH, MBP, MH, TU, WF, Y. (var.)

585 —The cordiall of. [*London*], *printed*, 1647. 4°.* 14 pp. L, O, CCA, AN, DU, DT; BN, CSS, MH, MU, TU, Y.

586 ——[Anr. ed.] —, 1647. 4°.* 24 pp. LT, O, C, AN, DT; CH, CLC, CN, NU, PU, WF.

587 Entry cancelled.
     [–] Cordial of . . . answered. 1647. *See* Parker, Henry.

588 —A declaration of. [*London*, 1647.] brs. L, O, LS, CT, AN; CH, MHL, WF.

589 ——[Anr. ed.] [*London*], *printed*, 1648. 4°.* LT, C, AN.

590 —A discourse touching the inconveniencies of a long continued Parliament. [*London*], *printed*, 1647. 4°.* LT, O, C, AN, DT; BN, CH, CN, MH, TU, WF, Y.

591 [–] God and the king: or, the divine constitution. [*London*], *printed*, 1649. 4°.* LT, O, OC, LSD, MR; CH, CLC, MH, NU, WF, Y.

592 —Jenkinsius redivivus. *For Jo. Hindmarsh*, 1681. 12°. T.C.I 439. L, O, C, AN, EN, CD; CH, CN, LC, MH, NP, NR, WF, Y.

592A [–] The King's prerogative. *Printed* 1680. fol.* T.C.I 386. L, O, OC, OM, CT, DU, DT; CH, CN, MBA, MH, WF, Y.

592B [–]—[Anr. ed.] *For J. Walthoe*, 1684. 8°. T.C.II 50. L, O, CS, DT; CLC, MU.

593 —Lex terræ. *For Iohn Gyles*, 1647. 4°.* LT, O, C, MR, DT; BN, CN, CSS, MIU, NN, Y.

594 —Lex terræ, or, a briefe discourse of law. *For Jo. Gyles*, 1648. 4°. O, CPL; CN, MHL, NU.

595 [–] A looking-glasse for the Parliament. [*London*], *printed*, 1648. 4°.* LT, O, OC, LLU, MR; CH, CN, NU, TU, WF, Y.

596 —Davidis Ienkins ivdicis in VValliæ principatu lex terræ. 1648. 4°.* O, OB, DU, DT; MIU, NU, WF, Y.

597 —Pacis consultum: a directory. *Printed at London, by J. C. for H. Fletcher*, 1657. 8°. LT, O, DC, EN, DT; CH, LC, MHL, NCL, YL.

598 —Judge Jenkin's [*sic*] plea. [*London*], *printed*, 1647[8]. 4°.* LT, O, C, AN, LIU; CH, MH, MU, WF, Y.

599 ——[Anr. ed.] —, 1648. 4°.* LT, AN, MR; CH, MBP, PU, WF, Y.

600 [–] A preparative to the treaty. [*London*], *printed*, 1648. 4°.* LT, DT; WF.

601–2 Entries cancelled.
     [–] Proposition for the safety & happiness of the King. 1667. *See* H., J.

603 —A recantation of. [*London*, 1647.] brs. LT, O, LPR, CJ, AN; CH, IU, MH.
     —M. Jenkin's recantation. 1651. *See* Jenkyn, William.

604 —Iudge Ienkins remonstrance to the Lords and Commons. [*London*], *printed*, 1647[8]. 4°.* L, O, CT, AN, MR; BN, CH, MH, MU, WF, Y.

605 ——[Anr. ed.] *Reprinted*, 1660. 4°.* LT, MR; PL, TU.

606 —Rerum judicatarum centuriæ octo. *For Henry Seile*, 1661. fol. L, LL, CT, AN, DT; CB, MH, NCL, PU.

607 —A scourge for the directorie. *For J. B.*, 1647. 4°.* LT, O, AN; CSS, IU, NU, Y.

608 —Severall papers lately vvritten. [*London*], *anno*, 1647. 4°. L, CT, AN, LIU, P; BN, CLL, MM, TU, YL.

609 [–] A short, sure and conscientious expedient. [*London*], *for I. G.*, 1648. 4°.* LT, O; CSS, NU, WF.

610 —To the honorable societies of Gray's Inne, . . . Lex terræ . . . 28° Aprilis 1647. [*London*, 1647.] 4°.* O, CT, AN, DU; CH, MH, MIU, NU, TU.

611 ——Apriles 1647. [*London*, 1647.] cap., 4°.* L, AN; MM, WF.

612 ——28, Aprilis 1647. [*London*, 1647.] 4°.* LT, O, OC, CT, AN, DT; CLC, NU, PU, TU, WF.

613 [–] A vindication of Judge Jenkins. [*London*, 1647.] cap., 4°.* LT, O, C, AN, DT; BN, CH, CN, MH, TU, WF, Y. (var.)

614 [**Jenkins, Leoline.**] A letter to the King, when Duke of York. [*London*, 1685?] cap., 4°.* L, DT; CLC, IU, MH, NU, TU.

615 [–]—[Anr. ed.] colop: *Printed, and are to be sold by Richard Janeway*, 1688. cap., 4°.* L, O, CT, BP, EC; CH, IU, MH, NU, WF, Y.

616 **Jenkins, Walter.** The law given forth out of Sion. *For R. Wilson*, 1663. 4°.* L, C, LF, BBN; PH, PSC, WF, Y.

617 [**Jenkinson, William.**] Lamentable and sad newes from the north. *For G. Thomlinson, and T. Watson*, 1642. 4°.* LT, LE, CD.

618 **Jenks, Benjamin.** The bell rung to prayers. *For Will. Rogers, and Benj. Tooke*, 1699. 12°. T.C.III 119. SHR; NU, WF.

618A [–] A letter to a gentleman of note. *For Randall Taylor*, 1690. 4°.* L, LL, BC, BR; CH, MH, NPT, NU, Y.

619 [–] The liberty of prayer asserted. *By R. Roberts*, 1695. 8°. T.C.II 547. O, C, LLP, RPL, DT; IEG, WF.

619A [–]—[Anr. ed.] —, 1696. 8°. CN.

620 —Prayers and offices of devotion. *For Will Rogers; and Benj. Tooke*, 1697. 8°. T.C.III 11. L, O, LLP, SHR.

620A ——Second edition. —, 1700. 12°. T.C.III 178. RPL.

621 —A sermon preach'd . . . December 2, 1697. *For Will. Rogers; and Benj. Tooke*, 1697. 4°.* L, O, SHR.

622 —Submission to the righteousness of God. *For W. Rogers; and B. Tooke*, 1700. 8°. T.C.III 193. L, O, RPL, GU; CLC, WF.

623 —A thanksgiving sermon, . . . fifth of November, 1689. *For Benj. Tooke, to be sold by R. Taylor*, 1689. 4°.* T.C.II 284. O, P; NPT, NU, WF.

624 **Jenks, Edward.** Ten articles already proved. [*London*, 1649.] brs. LT, OC.

625 [–]—[Anr. ed.] [*London*, 1649.] brs. LT, LUG.

626 —To all the people of England. [*London*, 1649.] brs. LT.

627 **Jenks, Francis.** Mr. Francis Jenk's speech spoken in a common hall, the 24th of June 1679. [*London*, 1679.] brs. L, O, C, LG, LW; CH, CN, MH, WF, Y.

628 **Jenks, Henry.** The Christian tutor. *For Henry Faithorne, and John Kersey*, 1683. 8°. T.C.II 11. L, O, C, CE, LSD; CLC, NGT, WF, Y.

629   **[Jenks, Silvester.]** The blind obedience of an humble penitent. [*London*], 1698. 12°. L, O, WARE.

629A   [–] —Second edition. [*Paris?*], 1699. 12°. L, LLP, BSM, DUS; CLC, CN, MSL, TU, WF; Y.

629B   [–] A contrite and humble heart. *Paris*, 1692. 12°. WARE; CN, MBJ, Y.

630   [–] —Second edition. [*Louvain?*], 1693. 8°.* L, O, DUS; CLC, TU, WF.

630A   [–] —"Second" edition. [*Louvain?*], 1697. 8°. L, O.

630B   [–] —Fourth edition. *Printed*, 1698. 12°. WARE; CLC, CN.

630C   [–] A letter concerning the Council of Trent. [*n.p.*], 1686. 12°.* L; MSL.

630D   [–] Practical discourses upon the morality of the Gospel. [*London*], 1699. 12°. O, WARE.

630E   [–] —Part II. [*n.p.*], 1700. 12°. O, WARE; WF, WG.

630F   [–] Three sermons upon the sacrament. *Printed*, 1688. 12°. O, C, DUS; IU, WF.

631   **Jenkyn, Pathericke.** Amorea. The lost lover. *For William Leake*, 1661. 8°. L, OW; NCU.

632   **Jenkyn, William.** Ἀλλοτριοεπισκοπος. The busie bishop. *By A. M. for Christopher Meredith, and Tho. Vnderhill*, 1648. 4°. LT, O, C, EN, DT; BN, CH, IU, NC, NU, WF, Y.

633   —The burning, yet un-consumed bush. *Printed*, 1662. 4°.* LW; NU.

634   [–] Celeusma, seu clamor. *Printed*, 1679. 4°. T.C.I 424. L, O, C, E, DT; CH, MH, NU, WF, Y.

635   —Certaine conscientious queries from. [*London*], sold by *R. Harford*, 1651. 4°.* L, O, AN, DC, DU; CH, CU, MBP, MH, NU, WF.

636   —De memoriâ. *Excudebat R. White, inpensis Sa. Gellibrand*, 1659. 4°. LT, O, C, BC, P; BN, CH, MB, LC, NU, WF.

637   —Mr. Jenkins dying thoughts. *For Edward Goldwin*, 1685. brs. L, O, LG.

638   —Exodus: or. *For Edward Brewster and William Cooper*, 1675. 4°. L, O, C, BR, CD; CH, IU, MH, NU, TU, WF, Y, AVP.

639   —An exposition of the epistle of Jude. First part. *By Th. Maxey, for Samuel Gellibrand*, 1652. 4°. O, LCL, CS, MC, GU; CH, IU, MH, NF, NU, WF.

640   — —[Anr. ed.] —, 1653. 4°. LT; MIU.

641   — —Second edition. *By Tho. Maxey, for Sa. Gellibrand*, 1656. fol. L, O, LCL, CCH, ENC; CH, MH, PPT, TSM, WF, Y.

642   — —The second part. *By Tho. Maxey, for Samuel Gellibrand*, 1654. 4°. LT, LLP, CS, AN; IU, MH, NF, NU, PPT, WF.

643   —The humble and penitent petition of. *Printed*, 1660. 4°.* LT, O, LLP, MR, WCA; CSS, NU, WF, Y.

643A   —The humble petition of. *Printed*, 1651. 4°.* NU, Y.

644   — —[Anr. ed.] [*London*, 1652?] brs. L.

645   —Ὁ δηγος τυφλος The blinde guide. *Printed at London by M. B. for Christopher Meredith*, [1648]. 4°. L, O, C, BC, BLH; BN, CSS, IU, MH, NC, NU, TO, Y.

646   —The policy of princes. *By A. M. for Samuel Gellebrand*, 1656. 4°. C, LCL, LW, BC, E, DT; CLC, MH, MIU, NU, Y.

647   — —[Anr. ed.] *By A. M. for John Dallam*, 1656. 4°. LT, O, LLP; BN, CH, CLC, NN.

648   Entry cancelled.

—Present separation self-condemned. 1678. *See* Jane, William.

649   —Mr. Jenkins recantation. *Printed*, 1651. 4°.* LT, CPL, SP.

650   —Reformation's remora. *By G. M. for Christopher Meredith*, 1646. 4°.* LT, O, C, BR, DT; CH, CU, MH, NU, WF, Y.

650A   —Refutatio cujusdam scripti. [*London*], *prostat apud Ben. Alsop*, 1681. 4°.* L, LW, CT, DM; CLC, MH, MWA.

650B   —The saints worth. *Printed*, 1662. 4°.* WCA.

651   —A sermon preached . . . 5. day of November, 1651. *By R. Wood, for G. Horton*, 1651. 4°.* LT; CLC, NU.

652   — —[Anr. ed.] *By T. R. for W. R.*, 1652. 4°.* LT, O, LG, CM, DT; CLC, NU, WF.

653   —A shock of corn. *For Samuel Gellibrand*, 1654. 4°. LT, O, CK, SP, E, ENC; CH, CN, MH, NU, TU, WF, Y. (var.)

654   —A sleeping sicknes. *By W. Wilson, for Christopher Meredith*, 1647. 4°.* LT, O, C, MR, WCA; CH, MB, MH, NU, WF, Y.

655   —The stil-destroyer. *For Christopher Meredith*, 1645. 4°. LT, O, C, EN, DT; CH, IU, MH, NU, WF, Y.

656   **[Jenner, David.]** Beavfrons; or, a new-discovery. *London, for Charles Morden, in Cambridge*, 1682. 4°.* NU.

657   [–] —[Anr. ed.] —, 1683. 4°.* L, O, C, OC, CT, DUS; CSS, NPT.

658   — —[Anr. ed.] *For Charles Morden in Cambridge, and are to be sold by Joseph Hindmarsh*, 1685. 4°.* T.C.II 102. O, CT, DM; CH, CLC, IU, MIU.

658A   —Cain's mark. *By J. R. for John Williams*, 1680. 4°.* O, OCC; MH, PL, WF, Y.

659   — —[Anr. ed.] —, 1681. 4°.* L, SHR; CH, NU.

659A   — —[Anr. ed.] —, 1682. 4°.* V.

660   —The life & death of S. Luke. *For J. Williams*, 1676. 4°.* T.C.I 226. L, O, C, DU, BLH; CLC, NU, PL, WF, Y.

661   —The prerogative of primogeniture. *For J. Hindmarsh*, 1685. 8°. T.C.II 102. L, O, C, P, DT; BN, CH, LC, NU, TU, Y.

661A   **[Jenner, Thomas.]** The ages of sin. *By Thomas Jenner*, [1655]. 4°.* L; CH, MH, Y.

661B   [–] A book of drawing, limning, washing. *By James and Joseph Moxon, for Thomas Jenner*, 1647. fol. PL.

662   Entry cancelled.

     [–] —[Anr. ed.] 1652. *See* Albert Durer revived.

663   [–] —[Anr. ed.] *By M. Simmons for T. Jenner*, 1660. fol.* LT; Y.

664   Entry cancelled.

     [–] —[Anr. ed.] 1666. *See* Albert Durer revived.

665-6   No entries.

     —Former ages never heard of. 1656. *See* Vicars, John.

667   —Londons blame. [*London*], *for T. J.*, 1651. 4°.* LT, O, LG, LUG, EN; CH, CN, MH, MIU, WF, Y.

667A   —A new booke of mapps. [*London*], *Tho. Jenner*, [1645?]. fol. LG; LC.

667B   [–] The path of life. *By M. S. for Thomas Jenner*, 1656. 4°. L; Y.

     —Work for none but angels. 1653. *See* Davies, *Sir* John.

668   **Jenner, Thomas, of Catherlough.** Quakerism anatomis'd and confuted. [*Dublin*], *printed*, 1670. 8°. DIX 140. L, O, LW, CT, DN, DT; NN, NU, PSC, WF.

668A   **Jenney, Henry.** A caveat or information. *By S. G. for Tho. Firby*, 1656. 4°.* L.

669 J[ennings], A[braham]. Miraculum basilicon. Or the royal miracle. *Printed*, 1664. 8°. L, CM, BC, CUC; NU.

670 Jennings, Samuel. The state of the case briefly. *Printed and sold by T. Sowle*, 1694. 8°. O, LF; CH, LC, NN, PHS, RPJ.

670A —Truth rescued from forgery. *Printed at Philadelphia by Reynier Jansen*, 1699. 4°.* EVANS 865. PHS.

671 Jennings, Theodore. The right vvay to peace. *For Giles Calvert*, 1647. 4°.* LT, O, MR, DT; CH, IU, NU, WF.

672 —Truths returne. *By J. C.*, 1646. 4°.* LT, MR; CLC, MH.

673 Jennison, William. A lash for a lyar. *By E. Cotes for John Clark, and for Will Hall*, 1658. 4°. EN; CINCINNATI PUB. LIB., MB.

673A Jenny, John. A sermon preached at the funeral of . . . Lady Frances Paget. *By J. D. for Nevil Simmons*, 1673. 4°.* T.C.I 125. L, WCA; CH, CLC, WF.

674 Ienny, Ienny; or, the false-hearted knight. [*London*], *for F. Coles, T. Vere, J. Wright, and J. Clarke*, [1678]. brs. L, O, HH; MH.

674A —[Anr. ed.] [*London*], *for J. Clarke*, [1680?]. brs. O.

675 Jennies answer to Sawny. [*London*], *for P. Brooksby*, [1682]. brs. L, HH; MH.

676 Jenneys lamentation. *For A. Banks*, [168–?]. brs. O.

677 Jenny's lamentation for the loss of her Jemmy. [*London*], *for P. Brooksby*, [1682]. brs. L, HH; MH.

677A Jephcott, John. A sermon of good works. *For John Jones in Worcester*, 1698. 4°.* T.C.III 51. L, CT, MC, SHR.

678 Jephson, Michael. A sermon preached . . . 23nd of October, 1690. [*Dublin*], *by Joseph Ray*, 1690. 4°.* DIX 240. CD, DT.

679 Jephson, William. A sermon preached . . . the 5th of November, 1698. *Dublin, by Andrew Crook*, 1698. 4°.* DIX 304. L, DN, DT.

679A Jephthah's rash vow. *By and for W. O. and sold by C. Bates*, [1700?]. brs. NNM.

679B Jeremiah in Baca. *For John Watson*, 1688. 12°. L, CT; CLC, WF.

Ieremiah revived. [n.p.], 1648. *See* P., N.

Jeremias redevivus: or. [n.p.], 1649. *See* Montague, Walter.

Jeremy Ives's sober request. [n.p., 1674.] *See* Penn, William.

680 A jerk for the Jacks. *Printed*, 1696. 4°.* O, LUG, CT; CH, MB.

681 Jermin, Michael. The father's institution to his childe. *By Ralph Wood for John Wright*, 1658. 8°. LCL.

681aA Jermy, John. Nature confin'd. *H. Eversden*, 1667. 12°. L; PH.

Jermyn, Henry. *See* St. Albans, Henry Jermyn, *earl of.*

681bA Jermyn, *Lady* Rebecca. A true state of the right and claime of . . . to the Registers office in Chancery. [*London*, 1655.] brs. LPR.

681cA [Jerome, Steven.] A ministers mite. *By T. H., to be sold by John Saywell*, 1650. 8°. LT, C; WF.

681dA [–] Treason in Ireland. *For Salomon Johnson*, 1641. 4°. L, O, C, EC, DN; WF.

681A Jerubbaal, John. The danger of innovations. *For Jonathan Robinson*, 1697. 4°.* O, LLP, MR, NE; CLC, MH, NN, Y.

Jerub-baal, being a three-penny answer. 1697. *See* P., E.

Jerrubbaal justified. 1663. *See* S., R.

Jerubbaal: or, a vindication. 1668. *See* Brown, Robert.

Jerubbaal, or the pleader. 1662. *See* P., T.

Jerub-baal redivivus: or. 1663. *See* P., T.

Jerusalem and Babel. 1653. *See* Patteson, Matthew.

681B Hierusalem; or the pilgrim and his guide. *By J. and J. How, for the author, and are to be sold by John Barksdale*, 1684. 12°. L.

Jerusalems glory. [*London*], 1675. *See* Burroughes, Jeremiah.

682 [Jervis, Humphrey.] Whereas great numbers . . . 12 May 1682. [*Dublin*, 1682.] brs. STEELE 2p 923. DN.

683 Jervis, William. A brief vindication of. [*London*, 1653.] fol.* LT.

684 —Drury-House nobly declared. [*London*, 1656?] cap., fol.* C.

685 [Jesland, Thomas.] A trve and fvll relation, of the trovbles in Lancashjere. *For Edward Blackmoore, December the 9th.* 1642. 4°.* LT; MH, MIU.

685A [Jesop, William.] A more exact and full relation of many admirable passages. [*London*], *June 19. For Mathew Walbanke*, 1644. 4°.* LT; INU, WF.

686 Jesserson, *Mrs.* Susanna. A bargain for bachelors. [*London*], *for E. A.*, 1675. 4°.* Y.

686A Jessey, H[enry]. A catechisme for babes. *By Henry Hills*, 1652. 12°.* MH.

—Description and explanation. 1654. *See* Adrichomius, Christianus.

[–] English-Greek lexicon. 1661. *See* Caryll, Joseph.

687 —The exceeding riches of grace advanced. *By Matthew Simmons for Henry Overton, and Hannah Allen*, 1647. 8°. L, O, C, LB, ORP; Y.

688 — —Second edition. —, 1647. 8°. O, C, LCL.

689 — —Third edition. —, 1648. 8°. L, ORP, ENC; IU, NHC.

690 — —Fourth edition. —, 1648. 8°. C.

691 — —Sixth edition. *By J. M. for Henry Cripps, Lodowick Lloyd, and Livewell Chapman*, 1652. 8°. LT.

692 — —Seventh edition. *By J. C. for Henry Mortlock*, 1658. 8°. C, LCL, LW; CLC, MH, NU, WF.

692A — —[Anr. ed.] *For H. Cripps*, 1658. 8°. CS.

692B — —"Seventh" edition. *For P. Parker*, 1666. 8°. LSC.

692C [–] An information concerning the present state of the Jewish nation. *By R. W. for Thomas Brewster*, 1658. 4°.* L, O; CH, MH, OHU.

693 Entry cancelled.

—Looking-glass for children. 1673. *See* P., H.

694 [–] The Lords loud call to England. *For L. Chapman, and for Fr. Smith*, 1660. 4°. MADAN 2472. LT, O, C, MP, DT; CH, CU, MH, NU, WF, Y.

695 —Miscellanea sacra: or. *By T. M. for Livewell Chapman*, 1665. 8°. L, LCL, LSC, ORP, DC; NHC.

696 [–] A narrative of the late proceed's [*sic*] at White-Hall, concerning the Jews. *For L. Chapman*, 1656. 4°.* L, O; HR, CH, MIU, NN, RPJ, Y.

697 Entry cancelled.

—Of the conversion. 1650. *See* Sibelius, Casper.

[–] Scripture almanack. [1648.] *See* Almanacs.

[–] Scripture kalendar. 1650. *See* Almanacs.

698 —A storehovse of provision. *By Charles Sumptner for T. Brewster, and G. Mould,* 1650. 8°. L, LCL, LW, SP; MH, NHC, NU, RBU, WF.

699 **Jessop, Constant.** The angel of the church of Ephesus no bishop. *By G. M. for Christopher Meredith,* 1644. 4°. LT, O, C, EN, DM; CH, CLC, IU, MH, MM, NU, WF.

700 ——[Anr. ed.] *Printed,* 1660. 4°. O, LW, EN, GU, DT; MH, NN, NU, Y.

701 **Jessop, Francis.** Propositiones hydrostaticæ. *Prostant apud Sam. Smith & Hen. Faithorn,* 1687. 4°.* T.C.II 218. L, O, C, OC, YM; CLC, CSU, MIU, MU, WF, Y.

J[essop], H[enry]. Calculation. [1645.] *See* Almanacs.

701A **Jessop, Thomas.** Catalogus variorum librorum. 21 *Feb.* 1680/1. 4°.* OP.

702 A jest; or, Master Constable. *For Francis Grove,* [1662?]. brs. L.

703 The Jesuite and priest discovered. *Printed,* 1663. 4°.* C; CSS, NU, Y.

Jesuite countermined. 1679. *See* Bradshaw, John.

Jesuite discovered. 1659. *See* S., J.

704 The Jesuite in masquerade. *For C. Mearne,* 1681. fol.* L, O, C, LG, DU; CH, MH, NN, PL, WF, Y, AVP.

704A —[Anr. ed.] —, 1682. fol.* MIU.

705 The Jesuite in the pound. *For S. M.,* 1688. brs. L, O, C, LG, DU; CH, MH.

706 The Jesuite unmasqued. *For S. Walsal,* 1689. 4°.* L, O, LIL, DU, MR; CH, IU, MH, PL, WF, Y.

707–8 Entries cancelled.

Jesuita vapulans: or. [n.p. 1681.] *See* N., C.

709 Jesuitical aphorismes. *By R. E. for John Starkey,* 1679. 4°.* T.C.I 332. L, O, OC, BAMB, EN, DM; CH, MH, NU, WF, Y.

Jesuitical design discovered. [1674.] *See* Moone, John.

Jesuitismus detectus. 1689. *See* T., H.

710 The Jesuites advice to the painter. colop: *For T. Davies,* 1681. cap., fol.* L, O; CN, CU, MU, NP, TU, Y.

710A The Jesuits cabinet broken up. *Dublin, by J. Brocas, sold by Math. Gunne and Rob. Thornton,* 1700. 8°. CT, DN.

Jesuits' catechism. 1679. *See* H., A.

711 The Iesuits character. Or, a description. *By Edw. Griffin,* 1642. 4°.* LT, MR; CH, MH.

712 The Jesuits character. Written. *Printed,* 1679. 4°. brs. L, O; CLC, MH, TSM, WG, Y.

713 The Iesuits creed. [*London*], *printed, Ian.* 26. 1641[2]. brs. LT; MH.

714 The Jesuits exaltation. [*n.p.*], 1688. brs. O.

715 The Jesuites firing-plot revived. colop: *For L. Curtiss,* 1680. cap., fol.* L, O, OP, LNC; CH, TU, WF, Y.

715A The Jesuits Ghost; with the prayer. *By J. M. for the author,* 1689. 4°.* C; PL, WF, Y.

715B —[Anr. ed.] *By John Wallis for the author,* 1689. 4°.* CLC.

716 The Jesuites ghostly wayes. *For Will. Bowtel,* 1679. 4°. T.C.I 342. L, DT; CH, CSS, PL, WF, AMB.

716A The Jesuits' gospel according to Saint Ignatius Loiola. *For Norman Nelson,* 1679. fol.* L, LNC; CH, MH, WF, Y.

Jesuits grand design. [n.p., 1660.] *See* Peirce, *Sir* Edmond.

717 The Jesuites intrigues. *For Benjamin Tooke,* 1669. 4°. T.C.I 9. L, O, C, SP, DT; CH, CU, LC, MH, NU, Y.

717A —Second edition. *For Ric. Chiswell,* 1679. 4°. WF.

718 The Jesuits justification. [*London?* 1679.] brs. L, O, C, LG, LLU, LNC; CH, CN, MH, PU, TU, WF, Y.

719 The Jesuites lamentation. [*London,* 1680.] brs. L, O; CN, MH, Y.

719A The Jesuits last farewell. *Printed,* 1674. CS.

720 The Jesuits letter of thanks. *Printed,* 1679. 4°. O.

721 —Second edition. —, 1679. 4°. L, LIL, CS, LSD; MB, NU, WF.

Jesuits loyalty. 1677. *See* Stillingfleet, Edward, *bp.*

Jesuit's manner of consecrating. 1678. *See* Hospinian, Rodolph Wirth, *called.*

Jesuit's memorial. 1690. *See* Persons, Robert.

Jesuits morals. 1670. *See* Perrault, Nicolas.

721A The Jesuits morals condemned. *For Walter Kettilby,* 1680. fol. WF.

721B The Jesuites new discovery. [*London*], *printed,* 1679. fol.* O, LSD; IU.

721C —[Anr. ed.] [*London?* 1682.] brs. O, HH.

722 The Jesuites plea. *Printed,* 1679. 4°.* L, LIL; MIU, NC, WF, Y.

723 The Iesvites plot discovered. [*London*], *printed,* 1641. 4°.* LT, LG; MH, NU, WF, Y.

724 Jesvites plots and counsels plainly discovered. *For John Bartlet,* 1642. 4°.* LT, O, MR; CH, INU.

724A —[Anr. ed.] *Printed,* 1642. 4°.* O, DT; MH, MM.

Jesuites policy. [n.p.], 1669. *See* Derby, Charles Stanley, *earl.*

725–6 Entries cancelled.

Jesuite's reasons unreasonable. 1662. *See* Sergeant, John.

727 The Jesuits speak their merits. [*London,* 1679?] brs. L.

728 The Jesuits unmasked. *For Henry Brome,* 1679. 4°.* T.C.I 331. L, O, C, MR, ENC; CH, IU, MH, NU, TU, WF, Y.

728A Iesus Christ manifested. *For Giles Calvert,* 1648. 4°.* MR.

Jesus, Maria, Joseph; or. Amsterdam, 1657. *See* Crowther, Arthur Anselm.

Jesu-worship confuted. 1660. *See* Burton, Henry.

729 **Jevon, Rachel.** Carmen θριαμβευτικον. *Typis Joannis Macock,* 1660. fol.* LT, O, LL, CS; CH, MH, WF, Y.

730 —Exultationis carmen. *By John Macock,* 1660. fol.* L, O, LL, CS; CH, MH, WF, Y.

731 [**Jevon, Thomas.**] The devil of a wife. *By J. Heptinstall, for J. Eaglesfield,* 1686. 4°. T.C.II 168. L; CH, LC, MH, MU, TU, Y.

731A ——[Anr. ed.] *For James Knapton,* 1693. 4°. L, LIU; CH, CN, MH, TU, WF, Y.

732 [–] —Second edition. —, 1695. 4°. L, O, OW, EC, A; CH, CU, LC, MH, TU, Y.

732A **Jewel, Edward.** A brief account of the qualifications. [*London,* 1680?] brs. L.

732B —A brief discourse of the stomach. *Printed,* 1678. 4°.* L.

733 **Jewel, John,** *bp.* Apologia ecclesiæ Anglicanæ. *Cantabrigiæ, excudebat Joannes Hayes; impensis Joannis Creed,* 1683. 12°. T.C.I 514. L, O, C, CT, DU; CH, LC, MIU, TU, WF, Y.

734 ——[Anr. ed.] *Impensis Tho. Dring,* 1692. 12°. T.C.II 411. L, C, OC, LSD, DT; CH, CLC, MSL, NPT, NU, TU.

735　—An apology for the Church of England. *By R. R., to be sold by Randall Taylor,* 1685. 4°. T.C.II 134. L, O, C, EN, DT; CLC, MIU, NU, PL, PU.

736　—The apology of the Church of England. *By T. H. for Richard Chiswell,* 1685. 8°. L, O, CS, MR, D, DT; CH, CN, MH, TU, WF, Y.

737　—Certaine frivolovs obiections. *By T. Cotes,* 1641. 4°.* O, OCC, BAMB, LNC, YM; CH, CN, MH, NU, WF, Y.

738　—Dadseiniad meibion y daran. *Printiedig yn Rhydychen* [Oxford] *gan W. H. ac a werthir gan lyfrwyr Gwrecsam, a Llanfyllin,* 1671. 8°. MADAN 2889. L, O, AN, LSD; CN, WF, Y.

739　—A sermon preached before Q. Elizabeth. [London], *printed,* 1641. 4°. LT, O, OC, CK, LLU, SC; CH, CLC, MH, NU, WF, Y.

　　Jewell of earthly joy. 1660. *See* P., W.

　　Jewels of ingenvity [166–?] *See* Jordan, Thomas.

　　Jewish kalender. [1699.] *See* Almanacs. Abendano, Isaac.

740　The Jews' case. [*n.p.*], 1697. brs. MC.

　　Jews catechism. 1680. *See* Jagel, Abraham.

741　The Jewes high commendation. [London], *for F. Coles, T. Vere, and W. Gilbertson,* [1680]. brs. O.

742　The Jews jubilee. *For Randall Taylor,* 1688. 4°.* L, O, LG; CH, MH, OHU, WF, Y.

743　The Jewes message. [London], *for George Freeman,* 1665. 4°.* O; MH.

　　Jinner, Sarah. Almanack. [1658.] *See* Almanacs.

743A　**Jo, Ja.** A warning-peece to all back-sliding Protestants. [London], *printed,* 1644. 4°.* LLL, EN; MH, NU, WF.

　　Joannes, Antiochenus. *See* Joannes, Malalas.

744　**Joannes de Bado Aureo.** Tractatus de armis. *Typis R. Norton,* 1654. LMT, DUS; NP, Y.

744A　**Joannes,** *Evangelista.* The kingdome of God in the sovle. *Printed at Antwerpe by Henry Artsens. Now printed in English at Paris by Lewis De La Fosse,* 1657. 12°. L, O, C, BSM, DU, DL; CH, CN, NU, TU, WF, Y.

745　**Joannes,** *Malalas.* Ιωαννου . . . Joannis Antiocheni cogonmento Malalæ historia chronica. *Oxonii e Theatro Sheldoniano,* 1691. 8°. T.C.II 425. L, O, CS, AN, EN, DT; BN, CU, MBP, MH, NU, WF, Y.

746　**Joannes, Parisiensis.** Determinatio. *Excudebat B. G. impensis J. Cailloue,* 1686. 8°. L, O, CS, EN, DT; IU, NU, PL, WF, Y.

747　**Joannes,** *Scotus, Erigena.* Joannis Scoti Erigenæ de divisione naturæ. *Oxonii, e Theatro Sheldoniano,* 1681. fol. T.C.I 512. L, O, CCA, AN, EC, P, E; CLC, MH, MIU, HC.

748　Joannes Nisbetus eques, agri dirlitonii quondam dominus, Gulielmo Nisbeto Adolescenti. [London, 1687.] 4°.* L.

　　Joannis Bidelli vita. 1682. *See* Farrington, John.

749　Entry cancelled.

　　Joannots, Du Vignan, *sieur des. See* DuVignan, *sieur des* Joannots.

750　Joan's ale is new. [London], *for F. Coles, T. Vere, J. Wright, J. Clarke, W. Thackeray, & T. Passinger,* [1680]. brs. L, O, HH.

750A　—[Anr. ed.] *For T. Vere,* [*n.d.*]. brs. O.

751　Joan's sorrowfull lamentation: or. [London], *for P. Brooksby,* [1675?]. brs. L, CM, HH.

752　Joan's sorrowful lamentation to Roger. [London,] *for P. Brooksby, J. Deacon, J. Blare, J. Back,* [1685–92]. brs. O, HH.

753　Joans victory over her fellow-servants. [London], *for P. Brooksby,* [1672–95]. brs. L, O, HH; MH, Y.

754　A job for a joyner. *For F. Coles, T. Vere, and J. Wright,* [1663–74]. brs. O.

754A　A job for a journeyman joyner. [London], *for J. Deacon,* [1695?].

755　[**Jobert, Louis.**] The knowledge of medals. *For William Rogers,* 1697. 8°. T.C.III 4. L, O, CS, E, DT; CH, MH, PL, WF, Y.

　　Iobvs triumphans. [London], 1651. *See* Oxenden, Henry.

756　**Joceline, Elizabeth.** The mother's legacy. *Oxford, at the Theater, and are to be sold by Jo. Wilmot,* 1684. 8°. T.C.II 112. L, O, CT, DC; CH, CLC, NP, Y.

757　[**Joceline, Nathaniel.**] Parliament physick. *For E. Blackmore,* 1644. 4°. LT, MR, SC, YM, DT; CH, NU.

758　Jockey and Willy. [London], *for P. Brooksby, J. Deacon, J. Blare, J. Back,* [1689–92]. brs. HH.

758A　Jockeys complaint for want of his Jenny. [London], *For T. Vere,* [*n.d.*]. brs. O.

　　Jockey's down-fall. 1679. *See* Philipps, John.

758B　Jockey's escape from bonny Dundee. [London, 1689?] brs. L, O, CM.

　　Jockey's farewel. [*n.p.*, 1670.] *See* Philipps, John.

758C　Jockey's lamentation turn'd into joy. [London], *for J. Jordan,* [1682?]. brs. WF.

759　Jockey's lamentation turn'd to joy. [London], *for J. Deacon,* [1690?]. brs. L, O.

759A　Jockie's lamentation, whose seditious work. *For Francis Grove,* [1657?]. brs. O.

759B　—[Anr. ed.] [London], *for J. Wright, J. Clarke, W. Thackeray, and T. Passenger,* [1681–4].

　　Joco-serio. Strange news. 1661. *See* Wither, George.

760　Entry cancelled.

　　Johannes, Fr. De modo existendi corporis Christi. 1686. *See* Joannes, Parisiensis. Determinatio.

760A　**Johan,** *duke of Lignitz.* Prince Johan, Christian duke of Lignitz . . . had a discourse. [London? 1680.] brs. HH, EN.

　　John. To the Prince of Venice. 1661. *See* Perrot, John.

761　No entry.

　　John of Austria. A declaration to the English nation. 1649. *See* Clare, R.

　　John de Werstaonnay. *See* LeNoir, Jean.

　　John, Gabriel, *pseud. See* D'Urfey, Thomas.

762　**John, Theodore.** An account of the conversion of Theodore John. *For John Dunton,* 1693. Sixes. T.C.II 463. L, O, C, LLP, ORP; WF.

762A　John and his mistris. *Published by J. Deacon,* [c. 1685]. 8°.* CM.

　　John and Joan. [1641.] *See* Parker, Martin.

　　Iohn Armstrongs last good night. [1658.] *See* R., T.

763　John Lilburne. Anagram. [London, 1653.] brs. LT.

763A　Iohn Robinsons park. [London? 1700.] brs. EUING 144. GU.

　　John the Baptist, forerunner. [*n.p.*, 1644.] *See* Robinson, Henry.

John the divine's divinity. 1649. *See* F. J.

763B John the glover, and Jane his servant. *[London], for I. Deacon,* [1690?]. brs. O.

John, the prisoner, to the risen seed. [n.p., 1660.] *See* Perrot, John.

John, to all God's imprisoned. 1660. *See* Perrot, John.

764 Johnny Armstrong's last goodnight. *[London], by and for A. Milbourn,* [1680]. brs. HH; MH.

764A —[Anr. ed.] *For F. Coles, T. Vere, I. Wright, and I. Clarke,* [1674–79]. brs. OC.

765 —[Anr. ed.] *For and by W. O.* [1670–80]. brs. L, HH, GU.

766 **[Johns, William.]** The traitor to himself, or mans heart his greatest enemy. *Oxford, by L. L. and are to be sold by Edward Forrest, and Hugh Keat, in Evesham,* 1678. 4°. T.C.I 320; MADAN 3181. L, O, RU; CH, IU, MH, WF, Y.

767 Johns earnest request. *[London], for P. Brooksby,* [1685–88]. brs. L, CM, HH; MH.

768 **Johnsen, H.** Anti-Merlinus: or a confvtation of Mr William Lillies predictions. *[London], printed,* 1648. 8°. LT; Y.

769 **Johnson, Mr.** Plain dealing: in a dialogue. colop: *For S. Eddowes,* 1691. cap., 4°.* L; MH, NC, PL, WF, Y.

770 **Johnson, Archibald.** A letter to the House, from the Laird Wareston. *By Edward Mason,* 1659[60]. brs. LT; MIU.

770aA **Johnson, Christopher.** A sermon preached . . . Dec. 2nd 1697. *By F. Collins, for S. Buckley,* 1698. 4°.* C.

770bA —Three sermons. *For Samuel Buckley,* 1696. 4°. L, LLP.

770cA **[Johnson, E.]** A short answer to a book lately . . . Chancery. *Printed,* 1654. 4°.* P; NP.

770dA **Johnson, Edward.** The benefit of affliction. *By Ralph Wood for the author,* [1657]. 8°. P.

770A —An examination of the essay. *For W. Thomas,* 1659. 4°.* O, LLP, LIU, LLU; CH, IU, MH, Y.

771 **[Johnson, Edward,]** *1599?–1672.* A history of New-England. *For Nath. Brooke,* 1654[53]. 4°. LT, O, LCL, E, GH; CH, CN, LC, MH, MU, NN, RPJ, Y.

772 **Johnson, Francis,** *Brownist.* A brief treatise, containing. *By M. S. for B. Allen,* 1645. 8°.* LT; CH, NU.

773 **Johnson, Francis,** *Franciscan.* A narrative of the proceedings and tryal of. *[London, 1679.]* fol.* L, O, CM, MR, DT; CH, IEG, MBP, TU, WF, Y.

774 —Mr. Johnson's speech. *[London, 1679.]* fol.* L, CM, BAMB, MR; MBP, MH, MHL, PU, WF, Y.

775 —A true copy of the speech of. *[London, 1679.]* cap., fol.* L, O, LNC, MR, EN; CH, CLC, WF, Y.

Johnson, G. Account astrologicall. 1659. *See* Almanacs.

776 **Johnson, J.** A copy book. *By H. Brugis, for Iohn Overton,* 1669. 4°.* L, C.

776A —The vvriting school-master. *By S. Griffin for John Overton,* 1667. * CN.

777 **Johnson, James.** The judge's authority. *Cambridge, by John Hayes, for Samuel Simpson in Cambridge,* 1670. 4°.* L, C, OCC, WCA, YM, EN; CH, CLC, NU, WF.

778 —Nature inverted. *Cambridge, by John Hayes, for Samuel Simpson,* 1670. 4°.* L, C, OCC, YM, EN; CH, NU, Y.

778aA **Johnson, John.** Johnsons arithmetick. Fourth edition. *By R. Cotes for Sam. Enderby, and John Sweeting,* 1646. 12°. O.

778A —Johnsons arithmetick. Fift [*sic*] edition. *By R. C. for John Sweeting,* 1649. 12°. L; MU.

778B — —Sixth edition. *By T. N. for J. Sweeting,* 1655. 12°. GU.

779 — —Seventh edition. *By R. & W. Leyborn for I. Sweeting,* 1657. 12°. MU, WF, Y.

780 — —Ninth edition. *By J. Flesher, for Robert Horn,* 1671. 12°. T.C.I 91. OC; CLC, IU, NC.

781 — —"Ninth" edition. *By A. Clark for Robert Horn,* 1677. 12°. L, CT; PL, V.

781A **Johnson, John,** *of Methley, Yorks.* Balsamum Britannicum, Brittains balm: . . . preached in a sermon . . . 21 March, 1647. *Printed at York by Tho: Broad,* 1648. 8°. OU.

782 **Johnson, John,** *Gent.* The academy of love. *For H. Blunden,* 1641. 4°. L, LL, P; CH, CN, IU, WF, Y.

783 **Johnson, John,** *New College fellow.* Εκλαμψις των δικαιων; or, the shining forth. *For the author, and sold by Tho. Parkhurst, Will. Miller, and Benj. Alsop,* 1680. 4°.* L, O, C, OC, BR; CH, CN, LC, MH, NU, WF, Y.

784 **Johnson, Jonathan.** The Quaker quasht. *For Francis Smith,* 1659. 4°. LT.

784A **Johnson, M[armaduke].** Ludgate, what it is. *By and for Tho. Johnson, and are to be sold by Fr. Cossinet,* 1659. 8°. MHL.

785 Entry cancelled.

[Johnson, Nathaniel.] Auction. [1693.] *See* Johnston, Nathaniel.

Johnson, R. Almanack. 1683. *See* Almanacs.

785A **Johnson, Ra[lph].** Ancilla grammaticae, or short rules of spelling. *By Tho. Pierrepont,* 1662. 8°. O.

786 —The scholars guide. *For Tho. Pierrepont,* 1665. 4°.* MADAN 2690n. L, O, C; CSS, MH, WF.

787 Entry cancelled. Ghost.

788 — —[Anr. ed.] *By A. C. for Henry Brome,* 1677. 8°. T.C.I 277. L, C, EN; MB, MH.

789 — —Fourth edition. *By M. C. for Henry Brome,* 1679. 8°. T.C.I 336. L; CLC, IU.

790 — —Fifth edition. *For Ch. Brome,* 1699. 8°. T.C.III 128. LL, CS; COLBY, Y.

791 **Johnson, Richard.** The crown garland. *For W. Gilbertson,* 1659. 8°. L.

792 — —[Anr. ed.] *By J. M. for W. and T. Thackeray,* 1662. 8°. O; CH, MBP, WCL.

793 — —[Anr. ed.] *For W. W. and are to be sold by Tho. Passenger,* 1680. 8°. CLC.

794 — —[Anr. ed.] *For M. W. and are to be sold by Dorman Newman, and Ben. Alsop,* 1683. 8°. L, CM; MH, RHT.

795 — —[Anr. ed.] *By J. M. for W. and T. Thackeray,* 1692. 8°. L, O; WF.

795A [–] The famous history of the seven champions. *By R. Bishop,* [1641–54]. L, U. BRISTOL; WF, ZAP.

796 — —[Anr. ed.] *By J. B. for Andrew Crook,* [1660]. 4°. L, O; LC.

797 — —[Anr. ed.] *By G. P. for Andrew Crook,* 1670. 4°. L, O; CLC, IU, MBP, NP, Y.

797A — —Ninth edition. *By R. B. for A. Crook,* [1670?]. 4°. CN.

798 [–] —[Anr. ed.] *By R. W. for T. Bassett, J. Wright, and R. Chiswell,* [1680]. 4°. CU, MH, TO.

798A [–] —[Anr. ed.] *For R. Scot, T. Basset, J. Wright, and R. Chiswell,* [1680]. 4°. CU, MH, TO.

799 [–] —[Anr. ed.] *For R. Scot, Tho. Basset, Ric. Chiswell, M. Wotton, and G. Conyers,* 1687. 4°. L, CM; CU, IU, WF, Y.

800 — —[Anr. ed.] *For Ric. Chiswell, M. Wotton, G. Conyers, and B. Walford,* 1696. 4°. L, C; CH, IU, MH, NU, WF, Y.

801 [–] —Second part. *By G. Dawson, to be sold by Andrew Crook,* [1660]. 4°. LC.

802 [–] — —[Anr. ed.] *By Ed. Crowch for Andrew Crook,* 1670. 4°. L; CLC, IU, MBP, NP, Y.

802A [–] — —[Anr. ed.] *For R. Scot, T. Basset, J. Wright, and R. Chiswell,* 1680. 4°. MH.

803 [–] — —[Anr. ed.] *By W. Onley, for Ric. Chiswell, M. Wotton, G. Conyers, and B. Walford,* 1696. 4°. L, C; CH, CN, MH, WF, Y.

804 [–] —Third part. *For John Back,* 1696. 4°. L; CH, IU, MH, OLU, Y.

804A —The golden garland of princely delight. Thirteenth edition. *[London], for J. Deacon,* [1690]. 8°. T.C.II 397. L, CT; MH, WF.

804B [–] The life and death of the famous Thomas Stukely. *For F. Coles,* [1670?]. brs. L, O.

804BA [–] —[Anr. ed.] *[London], for Clarke, Thackeray, and Passenger,* [1684–86]. brs. CM.

804C [–] —[Anr. ed.] *[London], for A. M., W. O. and T. Thackeray,* [1694]. brs. L, HH; MH.

804CA [–] —[Anr. ed.] *By and for W. O.,* [1695]. brs. L.

804D [–] —[Anr. ed.] colop: *[London], by and for C. B. and sold by J. Walter,* [c. 1700]. brs. WF.

804E [–] —[Anr. ed.] colop: *[London], by L. How,* [c. 1700]. brs. WF.

804F [–] —[Anr. ed.] colop: *Printed and sold in Bow-Church-yard,* [c. 1700]. brs. WF.

805 [–] The most famous history of the seven champions. *For R. Scot. T. Basset, J. Wright, and R. Chiswell,* 1680. 2v. 4°. L.

806 [–] — . . . vol. 3. *By J. R. for B. Harris,* 1686. 4°. CM.

806A [–] The most illustrious history of the seven champions. *For W. Gilbertson,* 1661. 4°.* Y.

806B [–] —[Anr. ed.] *For William Whitwood,* 1675. 4°. CT.

807 [–] The most pleasant history of Tom A Lincoln. Ninth edition. *By T. R. & E. M. for Francis Coles,* 1655. 4°. L.

807A [–] —Tenth edition. *By G. Purslow, for F. Coles,* 1668. Y.

808 [–] —Twelfth edition. *By H. Brugis for W. Thackery,* 1682. 4°. O, CM.

809 [–] —[Anr. ed.] *By H. B. for W. Thackeray,* 1682. 4°. O.

809A [–] The pleasant conceites of old Hobson the merry Londoner. *For W. Gilbertson,* [1649?]. 8°. C.

809B [–] The renowned history of the seven champions. *By Tho. Norris,* [1700?]. 4°.* IU.

810–11 Entries cancelled. *See* J807A and J806B.

812 **[Johnson, Richard]**, *of the Parliamentary army.* Good and trve nevves from Ireland. *For H. Blunden,* 1642. 4°.* LT, EC, MR, DN; CH, CLC, MH.

813 [–] The last intelligence from Ireland, received February the first. 1641[2]. *For H. Blunden,* 1642. 4°.* LT, LNC, LVF, DN; TU.

814 [–] A letter from the head-qvarters, at St. Albanes. *[London], printed,* 1648. 4°.* LT; CLC, MH.

815 Entry cancelled.

Johnson, Robert. Letter from. 1642. *See* Johnston, Robert.

815A **Johnson, Robert.** A letter from Dublin. colop: *[London], for Richard Newcome,* 1690. brs. C, MC, DN; Y.

815B —Great news from Ireland. colop: *[London], sold by R. Janeway,* 1690. brs. DN.

816 **Johnson, Robert, M.D.** Enchiridion medicum: or a manual of physick. *By J. Heptinstall, for Brabazon Aylmer,* 1684. 8°. T.C.II 46. L, C, LW, OM, MAU; WF, WSG, JF.

816A — —Second edition. —, 1684. 8°. WSG.

817 —Praxis medicinæ reformata: or, the practice. *For Brabazon Aylmer,* 1700. 8°. T.C.III 171. L, LCS, AM; WU.

818 **Johnson, Robert, Rev.** Lux & lex. *By A. Miller, for Philemon Stephens,* 1647. 4°.* LT, O, C, E, DT; CH, CN, MH, NU, WF, Y.

819 **[Johnson, Samuel.]** The absolute impossibility of transubstantiation. *For William Rogers,* 1688. 4°. T.C.I 285. L, O, C, E, DT; CLC, CN, NU, TU, WF, Y.

820 [–] —Second edition. —, 1688. 4°. L, O, SP, DL, E; CU, MH, NU, TU, WF, Y.

821 —An argument proving. *For the author.* 1692. 4°.* L, O, C, E, DT; CH, CN, LC, MH, NU, Y.

821A — —[Anr. ed.] *For the author: and are to be sold by Richard Baldwin,* 1692. 4°. L, LLP, LW, LIU, WCA; CSU, LC, MH, MU, TU.

822 — —Fourth edition. *For the author,* 1692. 4°. L, O, C, ENC, DT; HR, CH, LC, NP, NU, Y.

823 — —Fifth edition. *By J. D. for the author, and are to be sold by Richard Baldwin,* 1693. 8°. L, O, NE; MBA, NC, Y.

823A — —"Fifth" edition. *For the author,* 1693. 4°. L, O, LW, DU, LIU; CH, MH, MIU, TU, Y.

824 [–] A confutation of a late pamphlet intituled, A letter ballancing the necessity. *For A. Baldwin,* 1698. 4°.* L, O, C, MR, EN; CH, CN, MH, TU, WF, Y.

825 [–] —Second edition. *For A. Baldwin,* 1698. 4°.* L, LUG, CS, MR, DT; CLC, IU, MH, RPJ, TU, WF, Y.

825A [–] Disswasive from popery, and from countenancing . . . papists. colop: *For Sam. Clark,* [1685]. brs. DU.

826 —An essay concerning Parliaments. *For the author,* 1693. 4°. L, O, C, LG, MR, DT; CH, CN, MH, NC, TU, WF, Y.

826A — —Second edition. —, 1694. 4°. LSD.

827 — —"Second" edition. *For the author; to be sold by Richard Baldwin,* 1694. 4°.* L, O, CT, LIU, LSD; CH, MH, MU, NC, WF, Y.

828 — —Third edition. —, 1694. 4°.* L, O, C, BC, DT; CH, IU, LC, MH, WF, Y.

828A [–] Godly and wholsome doctrine. colop: *For Sam. Thomason,* 1685. brs. L, O; PL.

829 [–] Jvlian the apostate: being a short account of his life. *For Langley Curtis*, 1682. 12°. 94 pp. L, O, C, DC, DT; CLC, CN, MH, TO, TSM, WF, WSC, Y.

830 [–] —[Anr. ed.] —, 1682. 8°. 172 pp. L, O, CT, DU, BQ; CH, CN, NU, PL, TU, WF, Y.

830A [–] —[Anr. ed.] 1683. 8°. CCH.

830B — —Third edition. *For Richard Chiswell*, 1688. 12°. L.

831 — —Fourth edition. *For Richard Chiswell*, 1689. 8°. L, O, OC, NE, BLH; CDA, CLC, IU, FLORIDA STATE, PL.

832 —Jvlian's arts to undermine . . . Christianity. *By J. D. for the author, to be sold by Richard Chiswell, and Jonathan Robinson*, 1689. 8°. L, O, C, E, DM; CH, IU, MH, NU, TU, WF, Y.

833 — —[Anr. ed.] *By J. D.*, 1699. 8°. KANSAS STATE.

834 [–] A letter from a freeholder, to the rest. [*London*, 1689.] cap., 4°.* L, O, C, BC, DM; CH, CN, LC, MH, NU, TU, Y. (var.)

834A [–] A letter of advice to all protestant soldiers, and seamen. *Printed*, 1688. brs. L.

835 —Notes upon the Phœnix edition of the pastoral letter. Part I. *For the author*, 1694. 4°. L, O, C, P, E, DT; CH, CN, LC, MH, NP, NU, TU, Y.

835A [–] Of majestracy. [*London*, 1688.] 4°.* CT; MBA, MH, WF.

836 [–] The opinion is this. colop: *For J. Watts*. 1689. cap., 4°.* L, O, C, MR, AU, DT; CH, CN, LC, MH, NU, TU, Y.

837 [–] Purgatory prov'd by miracles. *For Richard Baldwin*, 1688. 4°. L, O, C, E, DT; CH, CU, MH, TU, WF, Y.

838 —Reflections on the history of passive obedience. colop: *for Richard Baldwin*, 1689. cap., 4°.* L, O, CJ, EN, DT; CLC, CN, MH, NU, WF, Y.

839 —Remarks upon Dr. Sherlock's book . . . resistance. *For the author, to be sold by Richard Baldwin*, 1689. 8°. L, O, LCL, LSD, AU; CLC, MH, NU, WF, Y.

840 [–] —[Same title, "allegiance."] *For J. Humphries*, 1690. 4°.* L, C, OB, MR, GU, DT; CH, IU, MH, TU, WF, Y.

841 — —Second edition. —, 1690. 4°.* L, O, CS, AU, DT; CDA, CN, MH, NU, TU, WF, Y.

842 [–] —Second edition. *Edinburgh re-printed*, 1691. 4°. ALDIS 3193. L, EN, A; OSU.

843 —A second five year's struggle. *For the author, to be sold by Richard Baldwin*, 1689. 8°. L, O, C, DU, BQ; CH, CU, MH, NU, WF, Y.

844 [–] The second part of the confutation. *For A. Baldwin*, 1700. 4°. T.C.III 188. L, O, C, LSD, ESS; CH, IU, NU, WF, Y.

845 —A sermon preach'd . . . Palm-Sunday, 1679. *For the author, to be sold by Richard Baldwin*, 1684. 4°.* L, O, C, LLU, LSD; CH, CN, NU, PL, WF, Y.

846 [–] The tryal and examination of a late libel, intituled, A new test. [*London*, 1687?] cap., 4°.* L, O, LL, OC, LSD; CH, MIU, TU, WF, Y.

847 [–] The true mother church. *For Brabazon Aylmer*, 1688. 12°.* O, LW, OC, DU, NE; CH, IU, NU, WF, Y. (var.)

847A [–] The way to peace. *For Richard Baldwin*, 1688. 4°. L, O, CT, MR, DT; CH, CN, MH, WF, Y.

848 **Johnson, Stephen.** Exceeding good newes from the neweries in Ireland. *By T. F. for I. H.*, 1642. 4°.* LT, O, C, EC, DN.

849 [**Johnson, Thomas**], *hackney coachman*. The case of several of Their Majesties loyal subjects very much oppressed. [*London*, 169–?] brs. CH.

849A [**Johnson, Thomas**], *merchant*. A discourse, consisting of motives for the enlargement . . . of trade. *By Richard Bishop for Stephen Bowtell*, 1645. 4°. LT, LG, LUG, EN, DT; CH, CU, MH, WF, Y.

850 —A plea for free-mens liberties. [*London*], *printed 1646 to be sold in London*. 4°.* LT, LUG, OH, DT; CH, MH, PU.

851 [**Johnson, Thomas**], *of Samburne*. Some speciall passages from Warwickshire. *For Iohn Bull*. 1642. 4°.* LT, O, SC, ESS; IU, MH, Y.

852 [**Johnson, Thomas**], *fl. 1643*. A trve relation of Gods providence in the province of Mvnster. *By L. N. for William Ley*, 1642. 4°.* LT, DN; BN.

853 [–] Victorious newes from Ireland. [*London*], *Aug. 27. for I. Rider*, 1642. 4°.* C; MH.

853A [**Johnson, Thomas**], *fl. 1696*. A general proposal for the building of granaries. [*London*, 1696.] cap., 4°.* MH.

853B [**Johnson, Thomas**], *fl. 1718*. Novus Græcorum epigrammatum. *For S. Smith and B. Walford*, 1699. 8°. T.C. III 157. O.

854 **Johnson, William**, *chemist*. Αγυρτο-μαστιξ. Or, some brief animadversions. *By T. Mabb, for Henry Brome*, 1665. 8°. L, O, LG, CCA, GU; NAM.

855 —Lexicon chymicum. *Excudebat G. D., impensis Gulielmi Nealand*, 1652–3. 8°. 2 pts. L, O, C, EN, DM; BN, CJC, LC, MH, WSG, WU.

856 — —[Anr. ed.] —, 1657. 8°. L, C, CT, LIU, GU; BN, CH, CJC, MH, WF, Y.

857 — —[Anr. ed.] —, 1660. 8°. L, O, DCH, GU; BN, CLC, NAM, WSG, WU.

858 **Johnson, William**, D. D. Deus nobiscum, or a sermon. *By J. Flesher for Octavian Pullyn*, 1659. 8°. CLC.

859 — —Second edition. *For John Crook*, 1664. 8°. L, O, C, OC, P; CH, IU.

860 —Deus nobiscum. A narrative. Third edition. *By T. R. for Ben. Tooke*, 1672. 8°. T.C.I 106. L, O, C, WCA; NN, TU, WF, Y.

861 **Johnson, William**, *priest*. Novelty represt. *Paris, for E. C.*, 1661. 8°. L, C, LCL, BSM, DU; CH, CN, NU, TU, WF.

862 Entry cancelled. Ghost.

863 [**Johnson, William**], *of Lurgyshall*. The resolution of the gentry and comonalty in the county of Nottingham. *For Henry Fowler, Septem. 15*. 1642. 4°.* LT, LNC, LSD.

Johnston, Archibald. *See* Warriston, Archibald Johnston, *lord*.

864 Entry cancelled.

Johnston, Arthur. Epigrams. *Aberdeen*, 1685. *See* Skene, Alexander. Memorialls.

865 —Paraphrasis pœtica Psalmorum Davidis. *Excudebat R. Daniel, & venalis prostat apud S. Thomson*, 1657. 8° LT, O; BN, CLC, IU, KQ, MBC, Y.

866 **Johnston, Sir John.** A brief history. [*London*], *for J. Millet*, 1690. 8°.* L.

866A — —[Anr. ed.] *Edinburgh, J. Reid*, 1694. 8°. EN.

867 —Capt. Johnsons last farewel. [*London*], *for Charles Bates*,
       [1690?]. brs. L.
868 [**Johnston, Joseph**.] A full answer to The second defence.
       colop: *By Henry Hills*, 1687. cap., 4°.* O, LLP, DUS, MC,
       AU; CH, CLC, MBA, NN, WF, Y.
869 [–] A letter from the vindicator of the Bishop of Condom.
       colop: *By Henry Hills*, 1687. cap., 4°.* L, O, C, OC, MR;
       CH, MH, MIU, MM, Y.
869A [–] A reply to the defence of the exposition. *By Henry
       Hills*, 1686. 4°. O.
870 [–]—[Anr. ed.] —, 1687. 4°. L, O, C, MC, EN, DT; CH, MH,
       MU, NU, WF, Y.
871 [–] A vindication of the Bishop of Condom's exposition.
       By Henry Hills, 1686. 4°. L, O, CT, MC, EN, DT; CH, CU,
       MH, NU, WF, Y. (var.)
872 **Johnston, Nathaniel.** The assurance of abby and other
       church-lands. *By Henry Hills*, 1687. 8°. L, O, C, EN, DT;
       CH, CN, LC, MHL, NU, Y.
873 [–] The auction: or, a catalogue of some useful books. *For
       Robert Hardy*, [1693]. cap., 4°.* L, O, C, MR, EN; CH, CN,
       MH, WF.
874 [–] The dear bargain. [*London*, 1688.] cap., 4°.* O, C, OC,
       MR, EN; CH, MBA, MIU, NU, WF, Y.
875 [–] —[Anr. ed.] [*London*], 1690. fol.* LL, LUG.
876 —The excellency of monarchical government. 1685. fol. LL.
877 ——[Anr. ed.] *By T. B. for Robert Clavel*, 1686. fol. T.C.II
       156. L, O, C, EN, DT; BN, CH, CN, LC, MH, TU, WF.
877A ——[Anr. ed.] *For R. Clavel*, 1686. fol. CDA, LC, Y.
878 —Enquiries for information. [*London?* 1685.] brs. L.
879 —The King's visitatorial power asserted. *By Henry Hills*,
       1688. 4°. L, O, C, DU, DT; CH, MHL, NAM, NCL, WF, Y.
879A **Johnston, Patrick.** Unto the right honourable, the
       lords of His Majesties Privie Conncil [*sic*], the petition.
       [*Edinburgh*, 1697.] brs. CSS.
880 **Johnston, Robert.** The historie of Scotland. *By W.
       Wilson, for Abel Roper*, 1646. 12°. L, O, C, E, DT; CH, CN,
       LC, MH, NU, WSC, Y.
881 Entry cancelled. Ghost.
882 —A letter from . . . directed to Master William Agard.
       For T. How, 1642. 4°.* LT, LNC, MR, DT; CH.
882A ——[Anr. ed.] *For T. B.*, 1642. 4°.* WF, Y.
883 The joynt declaration of the seve[r]all counties of Kent.
       [*London*, 1648.] brs. LT, LG; IU, MIU, Y.
884 Entry cancelled.
       Joynt resolvtion. 1649. *See* England. Parliament.
885 The joint-testimonie of the ministers of Devon. *By
       William Du-gard for Ralph Smith*, 1648. 4°.* LT, O, C,
       EN, DT; CH, MH, MIU, NU, WF, Y.
886 **Jole, Robert.** Arithmetick. *By H. B. for R. Jole*, 1677.
       12°. L; V.
887 **Jole, William.** Comfortable words. *By John Winter for
       Samuel Homes*, 1671. 8°. O, LCL; IU, MH.
887A —The pious mans kallender. *J. Bradford*, [1690?]. 12°.* L.
888 —A vvarning to drunkards. *For N. P. and sold by Rich.
       Janua*, 1680. 4°.* L, LG, EN.

889 **Jollie, T[homas].** A vindication of The Svrey demoni-
       ack. *For Nevill Simmons, in Sheffield, Yorkshire: and sold
       by G. Conyers*, 1698. 4°. T.C.III 97. L, O, C, EN, A; CH, MH,
       NIC, WF, Y.
890 ——[Anr. ed.] *For Nevill Simmons, in Sheffield, Yorkshire:
       and sold by A. Baldwin*, 1698. 4°. LW, OB, MR; IU, MH.
891 The jolly chair-men. [*London*], *for P. Brooksby, J. Deacon,
       J. Blare, and J. Back*, [168–?]. brs. L, HH.
891A The jolly cheese-monger; or, the Presbyterian follies.
       [*London*], *for J. Knight*, [1690?]. brs. NNM.
892 The jolly coach-man. [*London*], *for P. Brooksby*, 1685. brs.
       L, HH.
892A A jolly company of jovial blades. *For F. Coles, T. Vere,
       and J. W[r]ight*, [1663–74]. brs. EUING 152. O, GU.
892B —[Anr. ed.] [*London*, 1663–70.] brs. EUING 153. GU.
893 The jolly gentleman's frolick. [*London*], *for C. Bates,
       at the White-Hart*, [1685]. brs. L, O, CM, HH; MH.
894 —[Anr. ed.] *For C. Bates at the Sun and Bible*, [1688]. brs.
       HH.
894A Jolly Jack of all trades, or, the cries of London city.
       [*London*], *for J. Conyers*, [1695?]. brs. O.
895 The jolly pinder of Wakefield. [*London*], *for W. Thackeray,
       J. M. and A. M.*, [1689–92]. brs. L, HH.
895A —[Anr. ed.] [*London*], *for F. Coles, T. Vere, and W.
       Gilbertson*, [1658–64]. brs. O.
896 —[Anr. ed.] *For F. Coles, T. Vere, and J. Wright*, [1663–
       74]. brs. L.
896A —[Anr. ed.] [*London*], *for F. Coles, T. Vere, J. Wright, and
       J. Clarke*, [1674–9]. brs. O.
897 —[Anr. ed.] [*London*], *by and for W. O.*, [1690]. brs. L, HH.
897A —[Anr. ed.] [*London*], *for Alex Milbourne*, [1693]. brs. CM.
897B The jolly shepherd, and jovial shepherdess. [*London*], *for
       F. Coles, T. Vere, J. Wright and J. Clarke*, [1674–79]. brs.
       O.
898 The jolly Welsh-woman. [*London*], *for P. Brooksby, J.
       Deacon, J. Blare, and J. Back*, [1688–92]. brs. L, CM, HH;
       MH.
899 Entry cancelled.
       Joma. Codex Talmudicus. *See* Mishnah. 1648.
899A Jonæ philologi lepidi ac festivi. *Edinburghi, ex officina G.
       Mosman*, 1692. ALDIS 3229. EN.
       Jonas, Runolphus. *See* Jonsson, Runolfur.
       Jonas redux. 1672. *See* Janson, *Sir* Henry.
900–3 Entries cancelled.
       Jones. Jones of Hatton-garden. [n.p., 1673.] *See* Jones,
       George, *of Hatton Garden*.
       Jones, Captain. A letter from. 1644. *See* Jones, John,
       Captain.
       [–] Plain English: or, the sectaries. 1646. *See* Jones, John,
       Captain.
903A [**Jones, Adam**.] Nevves from Leicester. *For I. Horton.*
       Iune 10. 1642. 4°.* MH.
904 **Jones, Andrew.** The black book of conscience. Sixth
       edition. 1658. 8°.* L.
905 ——Thirteenth edition. *For John Andrews*, 1660. 8°.* Y.
905A ——Seventeenth edition. —, 1661. 8°.* G. EVANS (HAR-
       VARD).

906 — —Twenty-second edition. *For Eliz. Andrews*, 1663.
8°.* L; Y.

907 — —Twenty-ninth edition. *By B. W. for Eliz. Andrews,*
1666. 8°.* L.

907A — —Thirty-third edition. *For W. Thackeray, Phil.*
Brooksby, John Williamson, and J. Hose, 1676. 8°.* Y.

908 — —Thirty-sixth edition. *For Will. Thackery, T. Pas-*
senger, Phil. Brooksby, and John Williamson, 1679. 8°.*
MH.

908A — —Thirty-seventh edition. *For W. Thackeray*, 1681. 8°.
OP.

908B — —Forty-second edition. [*London*], *for J. Clark, W.*
Thackeray, & T. Passinger, [1680?]. 8°.* LW, CM.

908C — —Forty-third edition. [*London*], *for W. Thackeray &*
T. Passinger, [1664–92]. 8°.* O.

908D — —Twenty-fourth edition. *Edinburgh*, 1687. 12°. GU.

908E — —Forty-fifth edition. *By and for W. O.*, [1698]. 8°.* L.

909 — —Fifty-fourth edition.[*London*, 1700?] 4°.* OP.

910 —Death triumphant. Fifth edition. *For Will. Thackery,*
1674. 8°.* MH.

910A — —Sixth edition. *For I. Clarke, W. Thackeray, and T.*
Passinger, [1680]. 8°.* CM.

910B — —Eighth edition. *For Will. Thackery*, 1681. 8°. OP;
CLC.

911 —Dooms-day: or, the great day. *For John Andrews*, 1660.
8°.* L; G. EVANS [HARVARD].

912 — —Twenty-second edition. *For W. Thackeray*, 1674.
8°.* L; Y.

913 — —Twenty-fifth edition. *For W. Thackeray, T. Pas-*
singer, P. Brooksby and J. Williamson, 1678. 8°.* L, O; CH,
MH.

913A — —Thirtieth edition. *For J. Wright, J. Clark, W.*
Thackeray & T. Passenger, 1682. 8°.* O.

914–920 Entries cancelled.
—Dreadful character of a drunkard. 1663. *See* Hart, John.
—Dying mans last sermon. 1659. *See* Hart, John.

920A —Morbus satanicus. The devil's disease. Fifth edition.
For John Andrews, [1656?]. 8°.* CH.

920B — —Eighth edition. —, 1662. 8°.* *For John Andrews,*
1662. 8°.* G. EVANS, HARVARD.

921 — —Tenth edition. *For Elizabeth Andrews*, 1662. 8°.* L.

922 — —Sixteenth edition. *For Eliz. Andrews*, 1667. 8°.* O.

923 — —Twenty-first edition. *For VV. Thacke[r]ay*, 1674.
8°.* Y.

923A — —Twenty-fifth edition. *By W. L. and T. J. for W.*
Thackery, Phil. Brooksby, John Williamson, and J. Hose.
1677. 8°.* MH.

923B — —Twenty-seventh edition. *By W. L. and T. J. for W.*
Thackeray, T. Passenger, P. Brooksby, and J. Williamson,
1677. 8°.* WF.

923C — —Thirty-sixth edition. *By H. B. for J. Clark, W.*
Thackeray and T. Passenger, 1681. 8°.* L, LG, OP.

923D — —"Thirty-sixth" edition. —, 1685. 8°.* O, LW.

923E — —Fourteenth edition. *Edinburgh, printed*, 1699. 8°.* Y.

924 **Jones, Bassett.** The copy of a petition presented to . . .
Protector. [*London*], *printed*, 1654. 4°.* LT, AN, FONMON;
CSS, Y.

925 [–] Herm'ælogium; or, an essay. *By R. W. for T. Basset,*
1659. 8°. LT, O, LU, AN, E; CU, MH.

926 —Lapis chymicvs philosophorum. *Oxoniæ, excudebat*
Hen: Hall, 1648. 8°. MADAN 2005. L, GU; Y.

927 **[Jones, David]**, *fl. 1676–1720.* A compleat history of
Europe . . . from 1676 to . . . 1697. *For John Harris, John*
Nicholson, and Andrew Bell, 1698. 8°. L, OC, AN, DC, E, DT;
CH, CN, MB, PL, Y.

928 [–] —[Anr. ed.] *By T. Mead for John Nicholson, C. Harris,*
and Andrew Bell, 1699. 8°. L, GU; BN, CH, CU, NR, PL, WF.

929 —A continuation of The secret history of White-Hall.
Printed, and are to be sold by R. Baldwin, 1697. 8°. T.C.III
13. L, O, C, E, DT; CLC, CN, LC, MH, NF, NU, TU, Y.

930–3 Entries cancelled.
—A farewel-sermon. 1692. *See* Jones, David, *1663–1724?*

933A [–] The late history of Europe. *Edinburgh, by George Mos-*
man, 1698. 8°. CLC.

934 —The secret history of White-Hall. *Printed, and are to be*
sold by R. Baldwin, 1697. 8°. T.C.III 5. L, O, C, E, DT; CLC,
IU, LC, MH, NC, NF, NU, Y.

934A —A theatre of wars, between England and France. *For W.*
Whitwood, 1698. 8°. CN, MH, WF.

934B —The tragicall history of the Stuarts. *Printed*, 1697. 8°.
L, C, DU, LSD, GU; CH, CN, MBP, PL, TU, WF, Y.

934C — . . . Vindication against the Athenian Mercury concerning vsury. *By Richard Baldwin*, 1692. 4°.* L, LUG, CS.

934D **Jones, David, *1663–1724?.*** A brief vindication of the
late farewell-sermon. 1692. 4°.* LUG.

934E —A farewel-sermon. *For Thomas Parkhurst; and Brab.*
Aylmer, 1692. 4°.* 40 pp. T.C.II 391. L, O, C, LUG, AN; NC.

934F — —[Anr. ed.] —, 1692. 4°.* 41 pp. L, O, OM, LSD, MR;
CN, NU, WF, Y.

934G — —Third edition. —, 1692. 4°.* OC; CH, TSM, WF.

934H — —Fourth edition. —, 1692. 4°.* L; MIU, NU, TU, WF, Y.

935 —A sermon against swearing. *For Tho. Parkhurst*, 1699.
4°.* T.C.III 160. L, O, OC, CT, EN; CSU, WF, Y.

936 —A sermon of the absolute necessity. *For Thomas Park-*
hurst; and Brab. Aylmer, 1692. 4°.* T.C.II 391. L, O, C, LG,
EC, MR; CH, NPT, TSM, WF, Y.

937 —A sermon preached . . . November the 2d 1690. *Printed*
and are to be sold by Rich. Humpheries, 1690. 4°.* L, O, LG,
OC, DT; CH, CN, MH, NU, WF, Y.

938 —A sermon preach'd before the University of Oxford.
For Brab. Aylmer, 1698. 4°.* T.C.III 89. L, O, C, CT; CH,
CLC, NGT, WF, Y.

939 —A sermon upon Ember-Week. *For Tho. Parkhurst*, 1699.
4°.* T.C.III 121. L, C, OC, AN, EC; CH, CLC, IEG, MB, WF, Y.

939AA — —[Anr. ed.] —, *and re-printed* [*Dublin*] *by John Brocas,*
for Josias Shaw, 1699. 8°.* DERRY DIOCESAN LIB.

939A–40 Entries cancelled.
—Theatre of war. 1698. *See* Jones, David, *fl. 1676–1720.*
—Tragicall history. 1697. *See* Jones, David, *fl. 1676–1720.*

941 **[Jones, Evan.]** Londons remembrancer. *Printed*, 1670.
4°.* L, LF, BBN, MR; CH, MH, PH.

941A —Deceivers made manifest. [*London*], 1672. brs. LF.

941AB **Jones, [George], *of Hatton Garden.*** . . . His book of
cures. [*London*, 1673.] cap., 4°.* L.

941AC — —[Anr. ed.] [London, 1674?] 4°.* L.

941AD — —[Anr. ed., "mighty cures."] [London? 1675.] 4°.* L.

941AE —The English physitian giveth notice. Printed, May the 20th, 1674. 12°.* L.

941AF —Hells Cabal, or the devilish plots . . . discovered. [London, 1674?] brs. MH.

941AG — . . . I have practiced above thirty years. [London, 1675.] 4°. L.

941AH —George Jones . . . is now resident. [London, 1675?] cap., fol.* LWL.

941AI — . . . This is to give you notice of my friendly pill. Printed October the 15th 1674. 12°.* L.

941B [Jones, George], d. 1704. The future state. For J. Greenwood, 1683. 8°. T.C.II 24. L, O, C, DU, DT; CH, MH, NU, WF, Y.

942 [Jones, George], of Chester. A letter of a sad tragedy by Prince Griffin at Sayton. For A. C. and A. W., 1648. 4°.* LT, AN; MH.

942A [Jones, Henry], bp. A perfect relation of the beginning . . . Irish-rebellion. By J. R., 1641[2]. 4°.* LT, O, C; CH, CLC, MH, NR, WF, Y.

942B —A relation of the beginnings . . . of the rebellion in . . . Cavan. For Godfrey Emerson, 1642. 4°.* C, DM.

943 —A remonstrance of divers remarkeable passages concerning the church and kingdome of Ireland. For Godfrey Emerson, and William Bladen, 1642. 4°. LT, O, C, EN, DT; CH, CN, MH, NU, WF, Y.

944 —A remonstrance of the beginnings. August 11. London, for Godfrey Emerson, 1642. 4°.* LT, O, C, DU, DN; CH, CN, WF.

945 —The royal patient traveller. [London], for the authour, [1660]. brs. O, LLP.

946 —Saint Patricks purgatory. For Richard Royston, 1647. 4°. L, O, C, OC, DT.

947 —A sermon at the funeral of James Margetson. For Nathanael Ranew, 1679. 4°.* T.C.I 341. L, O, C, LSD, DT; CH, MH, NU, TU, WF, Y.

948 —A sermon preached at the consecration of . . . Ambrose Lord Bishop of Kildare . . . June 29, 1667. Dublin, by John Crook and sold by Samuel Dancer, 1667. 4°. DIX 134. C, BLH, CD, DN, DT; IU, WF.

949 —A sermon of antiChrist, preached . . . Novemb. 12. 1676. Dvblin, at His Majesties printing-house, 1676. 4°.* DIX 158. L, O, C, DM, DT; CDA, NU, WF.

950 — —Second edition. Reprinted at London for Nathaniel Ponder, 1679. 4°.* L, O, C, WCA, DT; CH, MB, WF, Y.

951 — —"Second" edition. Reprinted at London, and published by Randal Taylor, 1686. 4°.* L, BLH; CLC.

952 —A sermon preach't . . . before the generall convention . . . May 24. 1660. By J. C. for J. Crook, 1660. 4°.* LT, C, WCA; LC, TSM.

953 No entry.

954 Jones, Inigo. The most notable antiquity of Great Britain . . . Stone-Heng. By James Flesher, for Daniel Pakeman, and Laurence Chapman, 1655. fol. L, O, C, E, DT; BN, CH. MH, MU, WF, Y.

955 Jones, Isaac. Good newes from Ireland. For Robort [sic] Howes and Thomas Bates, 1642, August the 4. 4°.* LT, C, EC, DN.

955A J[ones], J. Ingeniossimo humanissimoque viro D. Jo. Cotesworth, M. D. Carmen gratulatorum. [n.p., 1685.] fol.* DU.

956 Jones, J. Catalogue of stock. [London], 1699. 4°. L.

956A Jones, James. The grand case of subjection . . . in matters of religion, resolved. By George Larkin, 1684. fol.* L, O; CH.

957 —Modesty and faithfulness. For Thomas Malthus, 1683. fol.* T.C.II 18. L, O, BR, DU, EN, DM; CH, CLC, MH.

958 —Nonconformity not inconsistent with loyalty. For the author, and are to be sold by William Bateman, 1684. fol.* L, O, BR, SP; CLC, MH, NU, Y.

959 —A plea for liberty of conscience. By George Larkin, 1684. fol.* L, O, BR; CH, CLC, TO, WF, Y.

960 —A token of Christian love. colop: For Tho. Malthus, 1683. brs. L, O, EN; IU, TU, Y.

961 [Jones, John], bp. Christvs Dei, or, a theologicall discourse. Oxford, by H. Hall, 1642. 4°.* MADAN 1098. LT, O, CT, LNC; CLC, MM, Y, ASU.

961A [–] —[Anr. ed.] Printed at Oxford, 1643. 4°.* MADAN 1099. LT, O, C, MR, DT; CH, MIU, NU, WF, Y. (var.)

961B Jones, John, Captain. A letter from. By A. Coe, 1644. 4°.* LT; CH.

961C [–] Plain English: or, the sectaries anatomized. By T. R. and E. M. for Ralph Smith, 1646. 4°.* LT, O, SP, A, DT; CH, MH, NU, WF, Y.

962 Jones, John, gent. The works of. [London, 1650.] 12°. L, DC.

963 — —[Anr. ed.] 1651. 8°. LG, LMT.

964 —The crie of bloud. By W. D. for Tho. Matthews, 1651. 12°. LT, O, AN.

964A — —[Anr. ed.] By William Du-gard, for Thomas Matthews, 1651. 12°. MHL, WF.

964B — —[Anr. ed.] For Thomas Matthews, 1653. 12°. MHL.

965 —Eight observable points of law. [London, 1645?] brs. L.

966 Entry cancelled.

[–] Elegies. Dublin, 1661. See Jones, John, of Trinity College, Dublin.

967 —Every mans case, or, lawyers routed. Printed, 1652. Sixes.* LT; WF.

968 [–] An examination of the observations vpon His Majesties answers. [Oxford, by H. Hall] printed, 1643. 4°.* MADAN 1423. L, O, CT, AN, DT; CH, CU, MH, NU, WF, Y.

969 Entry cancelled.

—Judges judged. 1650. See Coke, Sir Edward.

970 —Jurors judges of law and fact. By W. D. for T. B. & G. M., [1650]. 12°. LT, AN; MHL, NU, WF.

971 Entry cancelled.

—Lachrymae Hungaricæ. [1664.] See Schilling, P.

971A —Lawyers vnmask'd. For Thomas Matthewes, 1653. 12°. MHL.

972 —The new returna brevium. By William Du-gard, 1650. 12°. LT, O, CCA, AN; CH, MHL, WF, Y.

972A — —[Anr. ed.] For Tho. Matthewes, 1653. 12°. MHL.

973 —The peace of justice. *By W. Bentley, for W. Shears,* 1650. 12°.* L, LG, CCA, AN; MHL, WF.

974 **Jones, John, M.D.** De febribus intermittentibus. *Typis H. H.,* 1683. 8°. LW, OR, AU, DT.

975 —De morbis Hibernorum. *Impensis S. Keble,* 1698. 4°. T.C.III 66. L, OC, LSD, DT; MM, PL.

976 —The mysteries of opium reveal'd. *For Richard Smith,* 1700. 8°. L, O, OR, CCA, AN, DT; CLC, IU, LC, MH, MMO, Y.

977 —Novarum dissertationum de morbis. *Typis H. H. impensis Gualteri Kettilby,* 1683. 8°. T.C.II 47. L, O, C, LCP, CT, MAU; MMO, NAM, WF, JF.

977A **[Jones, John],** *of Trinity College, Dublin.* Elegies on the much lamented death of the . . . Earl of Mountrath [Chas. Coote]. *Dublin, by John Crook, sold by Samuel Dancer,* 1661. 4°.* DIX 112. DT.

978 —Oratio funebris . . . Mauritii Eustace, . . . 5° Julii 1665. *Dublin,* 1665. 4°.* DIX 128. C, DM; CH.

979 —Threnodia in obitum . . . Wentworthii Kildariae. *Dudlini [sic], typis Joannis Crooke, prostantque venales apud Sam. Dancer,* 1664. 4°.* DIX 124. DT.

980 **[Jones, John],** *of Merionethshire.* The great duty of conformity. *For Tho. Mercer,* 1684. 8°. T.C.II 68. L, O, LW, OC, RPL; NU.

981 ——[Anr. ed.] —, 1693. 8°. OM, BANGOR, DM.

982 **[Jones, John],** *of St. Alban's.* Fanum Sti. Albani poema. *Impensis authoris,* 1683. 4°.* L, O; CPB, WF.

982A **Jones, John,** *fl. 1688.* An exact copy of a letter dropt. *[London],* 1688. brs. L, OC, HH, DU; Y.

982B **Jones, John.** Phono-graphy. colop: 1698. cap., fol.* L.

983 **Jones, Michael.** Lieut: General Jones's letter to the Councel of state. *For Edward Husband, August 11.* 1649. 4°.* LT, O, C, LVF, BLH, DT; CH, CN, MH, MU, WF. (var.)

983A **Jones, Dr. Michael.** The case of Dr. Michael Jones [for lands in Ireland]. *[London, 1695?]* brs. DN.

984 **Jones, Nathaniel.** To the Parliament of the Commonwealth . . . the humble petition of. *[London, 1654.]* brs. LT.

985 **Jones, Richard.** Perl y Cymro: neu, cofiadur y Beibl. *Printiedig yn Ghaer Ludd [London] gan T. H. ar gôst yr Awdur, ac ydynt i werth gan E. Brewster,* 1655. 8°. L, O, AN.

986 —Testûn testament newydd ein Harglwydd. *Ag iw werthu gan John Brown,* 1653. 4°. L, O, AN.

987 **[Jones, Robert.]** A great and bloody fight in Shropshire. *For A. H.,* 1648. 4°.* LT; MH, MU, Y.

—Resurrection rescued. 1659. *See* Lushington, Thomas.

988 **[Jones, Roger.]** Mene Tekel; or, the downfal. *[n.p.] printed,* 1663. 4°. O, C, EN; CLC, NC, NU, PU, Y.

989 **Jones, Mrs. Sarah.** This is light's appearance. *[London?* 1650.] 4°.* LF; PH.

990 **[-]** To Sions lovers. *[London], printed,* 1644. 4°.* LT, DT; NU, WF.

990A **Jones, Simon.** A guide to the young-gager. *By J. D. for J. Coniers,* 1670. 12°. T.C.I 26. C.

Jones, Thomas. Almanack. 1681. *See* Almanacs.

990B —An astrological speculation. *For the author,* 1681. 4°. L, LSD.

991 **Jones, Thomas,** *1618-1665.* De origine Dominii. *Oxoniæ, excudebat H. H. impensis R. Davis,* 1660. 8°. MADAN 2503. L, O, C, LL, DC.

991A —Prolusiones academicæ, in duas partes distributæ. *Oxoniæ, typis H. Hall impensis Rich. Davis,* 1660. 8°. MADAN 2502. O, C, LL, DC, YM; BN, DICKINSON.

992 **Jones, Thomas, D.D.** Elymas the sorcerer. *For H. Jones,* 1682. fol.* L, O, C, DU, EN; CH, IU, MH, NU, TU, WF, Y.

992A **Jones, Thomas,** *of Hereford.* An antidote for troubled soules. *For John Wright, the younger,* 1641. 8°.* NPT.

993 ——[Anr. ed.] *For John Wright,* 1646. 8°.* L; CH.

993A —Mercy triumphing over judgement. *By E. P. for Iohn Wright the younger,* [1641?]. 8°. OW; WF.

994 —A new love-song. *For Richard Burton,* [1641–60]. brs. HH.

995 **[Jones, Thomas],** *of Llandyrnos.* A sermon preached (December 23. 1680.) . . . at the funeral of Ezerel Tonge. *By N. T. to be sold by T. Parkhurst, B. Shirley, and W. Hnchiman,* 1681. 4°.* L, O, LW, DU; CLC, NGT, WF.

996 **[-]** Of the heart, and its right soveraign: and Rome no mother-church. *For Edw. Foulkes, to be sold by T. Basset,* 1678. 8°. T.C.I 302. L, O, C, LSD, DT; CH, MBP, MH, NU, TSM, WF.

996A **Jones, Thomas,** *of Shrewsbury.* Carolau, a dyriau duwiol. *[Shrewsbury?], Thomas Jones,* 1696. 8°. AN, CPL.

997 —Y Gymræg yn ei disgleirdeb. *Argraffwŷd* 1688, *yng Haerlydd gan Mr. Lawrence Baskervile tân Lun [London], a chan Mr. John Marsh.* 8°. L, O, C, MR, AN; CN, MH, NC, PL, WF, Y.

998 —Yr hen llfyr plygain. *Thomas Jones,* 1683. 24°. AN.

999 **Jones, Sir Thomas.** Les reports de divers special cases. *By the assigns of Rich. and Edw. Atkins, for Samuel Keble,* 1695. fol. T.C.II 558. L, O, C, MC, DT; CH, LC, MH, NN, NP, WF.

[Jones, William], *of London.* Animadversions upon a letter. *[n.p.],* 1656. *See* Sedgwick, William.

1000 **[-]** Ecclesia reviviscens. A poem. *For Tho. Salusbury,* 1691. 4°.* T.C.II 377. L, O, LVD; CLC, CU, MB, MH, Y.

1001 No entry.

—Morbus Satanicus. 1677. *See* Jones, Andrew.

1002 **[-]** Work for a cooper. *By J. C. for S. C[rouch],* 1679. 4°.* T.C.I 331. L, O, LF, AN; CH, CLC, IU, PH, PHS.

[Jones, Sir William.] Design of enslaving. 1689. *See* Ferguson, Robert.

[-] Just and modest vindication. *[n.p.,* 1682.] *See* Ferguson, Robert.

1003 —Les reports de . . . de divers special cases. *By T. R. and N. T. for Thomas Basset and Richard Chiswel,* 1675. fol. T.C.I 190. L, O, C, EN, DT; BN, CH, LC, MHL, NCL, YL.

1004 Entry cancelled. Ghost.

1005 **Jones, William,** *minister.* Y trydydd ar pedwaredd gorchymynnion. *For John Williams,* 1656[55]. 4°.* LT, AN.

1006 **Jonson, Ben.** The works of. *By Thomas Hodgkin, for H. Herringman, E. Brewster, T. Bassett, R. Chiswell, M. Wotton, G. Conyers,* 1692. fol. T.C.II 414. L, O, C, MR, DT; BN, CH, CN, MH, NP, TU, WF, Y.

1007 **[-]** The alchemist. *Printed and sold by the booksellers,* [1680]. 8°. L; INU, IU, Y.

1008   [–] Catiline his conspiracy. A tragœdie. *For A. C. and are to be sold by William Cademan*, 1669. 4°. T.C.I 7. L, OW, CK; CH, CU, LC, MH, NP, PU, WF, Y.

1009   [–] —[Anr. ed.] —, 1674. 4°. T.C.I 179. L, C; CH, CN, LC, MH, TU, Y.

1010   [–] —[Anr. ed.] *For William Crook*, 1674. 4°. L; CU, MH, OCI, WF.

1011   —The divell is an asse. *Imprinted at London*, 1641. fol. L, O, C; CH, CU, TU, WF, Y.

1012   [–] A strange banquet, or, the divels entertainment. [*London*], *for W. Gilbertson*, [1685?]. brs. L.

1013   [–] —[Anr. ed.] *By and for W. O. for A. M. to be sold by J. Deacon*, [1684–95]. brs. EUING 343. L, O, CM, HH, GU.

1014   [–] —[Anr. ed.] [*London*], *for F. Coles, T. Vere, I. Wright, J. Clarke, W. Thackeray, and T. Passenger*, [1678–80]. brs. O.

1015   —The widdow a comedie. *For Humphrey Moseley*, 1652. 4°. L, O, LVD, CT, LIU, EN; CH, CN, LC, MH, TU, WF, Y.

1015aA **Jonsson, Runolfur.** Recentissima antiquissimæ linguæ . . . incunabula. *Oxoniæ, e theatro Sheldoniano*, 1688. 4°. L, CT, MR; MB, NN, PL.

1015A **Jonston, John.** A description of the nature of four-footed beasts. *Amsterdam, for the widow of John Jacobsen Schipper, and Stephen Swart*, 1678. fol. L; CLC, MH, NC, PL.

1015B   —[Anr. ed.] *For Moses Pitt*, 1678. fol. T.C.I 358. RU; WF, WU.

1016   —An history of the constancy of nature. *For John Streater, London*, 1657. 8°. LT, O, C, CE, GU; CLC, IU, MH, MIU, PU.

1017   —An history of the wonderful things of nature. *By John Streater*, 1657. fol. L, O, CT, MR, E; CH, CN, LC, MH, WCL, Y.

1018   —The idea of practical physick. *By Peter Cole*, 1657. fol. L, LWL; CH, LC, WSG, HC.

1018A   ——Second edition. *By Peter and Edward Cole*, 1661. fol. LWL; WSG.

1018B   ——"Second" edition. *By Peter Cole*, 1663. fol. NAM.

1018C **Jordaine, Joshua.** Duodecimal arithmetick. *By John Richardson for the author*, 1687. 8°. RBU.

1018D   ——[Anr. ed.] —, *to be sold by John Taylor*, 1687. 8°. L, OC; PL.

1018E **[Jordan, Joshua]**, *fl. 1687*. The churches ardent love to Christ. *For John Taylor*, 1687. brs. MH.

1019   **[Jordan, Raymond.]** Idiota: or, Duns contemplations of divine love. *Printed at Paris*, 1662. 12°. L, E.

1019A   **[Jordan, Thomas.]** The anarchie; or the blessed reformation. [*London*, 1648.] brs. LT.

1019B   ——[Anr. ed., "blest."] [*London*, 1648.] brs. LT.

1019C   [–] Bacchus festival. [*London*], 1660. brs. LT; MH.

1020   —A box of spikenard. Second edition. *For the author*, 1661. 8°. L, O.

1021   [–] The careless gallant. [*London*], *for F. Coles, T. Vere, J. Wright, and J. Clarke*, [1675–80]. brs. L, O, CM, HH.

       [–] Choice banquet. 1665. *See* Armstrong, Archibald.

1022   [–] The Christian souldier. *For Edward Christopher*, 1642. 4°.* LT, O; CH, CU.

1023   —Claraphil and Clarinda. *By R. Wood*, [1650?]. 8°. L, O, CT; CH, CN, MH.

1024   [–] A cure for the tongue-evill. *For Christopher Ecclestone*, 1662. 4°. L; CH.

       —Death dis-sected. [n.p., 1649.] *See* Buckler, Edward.

1025   [–] The debtors apologie. [*London*], 1644. 4°.* CH.

1026   [–] A dialogue betwixt Tom and Dick. [*London*, 1659–60.] brs. HH.

1027   [–] A diurnall of dangers. *Printed at London for E. Christopher*, [1642]. 4°.* LT, OC, CJ; Y.

1028   —Divine raptvres or, piety in poesie. *Printed by authoritie, for the use of the author*, 1646. 4°. L; CH, MH.

1029   Entry cancelled. Ghost.

1030   —Divinity and morality. *By R. A.*, [1660?]. 8°.* L, O; CH, IU, MH.

1031   —Fancy's festivals: a masque. *By Tho. Wilson*, 1657. 4°. L, O; CH, CLC, PU, WF.

1032   ——[Anr. ed.] *For Andr. Pennycuicke*, 1657. 4°. L, LVD; CLC, WF.

1033   —The goldsmiths jubile: or. *By W. Godbid, for John Playford*, 1674. 4°.* L, O, LG; CH, RHT, Y.

1033A   [–] Jewels of ingenvity. *By J. M.*, [166–?]. 8°.* CH.

1033B   [–] A letany for the nevv-year. [*London*, 1660.] brs. LT, O.

1034   —London in its splendor. *By W. G. for Nath. Brook and John Playford*, 1673. 4°.* L, O, LG, CE; Y.

1035   —London in luster. *For John Playford*, 1679. 4°.* L, O, LG, LSD, DT; CH, CN, LC, MH, WF, Y.

1036   —London triumphant. *By W. G. for Nath. Brook and John Playford*, 1672. 4°.* L, O, LG, LI; CH, CLC, CU, MH, Y.

1037   —London's glory. *For John and Henry Playford*, 1680. 4°.* L, O, LG, LSD; CH, CN, LC, MH.

1038   —London's joy or the Lord Mayor's show. *For John and Henry Playford*, 1681. 4°. L, O, LG, LSD, EN; CH, CN, MB, Y.

1039   [–] Londons ioyfull gratulation. *By Iohn Iohnson*, 1642. 4°.* LT; CH.

1040   —London's resurrection to joy and triumph. *For Henry Brome*, 1671. 4°.* L, O, LG, CS; CH, CLC, MH, NC, NNM.

1041   —London's royal triumph. *For John and Henry Playford*, 1684. 4°.* L, O, LG, LUG, LSD; CH.

1042   —London's triumphs: express'd. *For John Playford*, 1676. 4°. LG, MR; CH.

1043   —Londons triumphs: illustrated. *For John Playford*, 1677. 4°.* L, O, LG, LPR, LSD; CH, CN, LC, WF.

1044   [–] A looking-glass for a covetous miser. *For W. Thackeray, T. Passinger, and W. Whitwood*, [1670–77]. brs. L, HH; MH.

1044A   [–] The Lord Mayor's show. *For T. Burnel* [sic], 1682. 4°.* L, O, LG, LSD; CH, WF.

1045   —Love's dialect. *For the use of the author*, 1646. 4°. O, EN.

1046   [–] A medicine for the times. *For Robert Wood*, 1641. 4°.* LT, O, C, LG, OW, MR, YM; CH, CLC, CN, MH, NU, WF, Y.

1047   —Money is an asse. *By Peter Lillicrap for Fra. Kirkman*, 1668. 4°. L, O, LLU, LVD; CH, IU, LC, MH, WC, WF, Y.

1048   —The muses melody. *By J. C.*, [1680?]. 8°.* L, O, OB; MH.

1049   —Musick & poetry, mixed. *For the author*, [after 1660]. 8°. WF.

1050   —A new droll: or the counter-scuffle. *Printed*, 1663. 4°.* O; WF, Y.

1051   —A nursery of novelties. *For the author*, [1665?]. 8°. L, O, OW; CH.

1052   [–] Pictures of passions. *For Robert Wood*, 1641. 8°. L.

1053   — —[Anr. ed.] *By R. Wood*, [1641]. 8°. O; CH, Y.

1054   [–] Piety, and poesy. Contracted. *For Rob: Wood*, 1643. 8°.* L, LG, OW.

1054A   [–] —[Anr. ed.] —, [166–?]. 8°.* O, CT; CH, MH.

1054B   [–] A pleasant dialogue between the country-man and citizen. [*London*, 1660.] brs. LT.

1055   [–] The prodigals resolution. [*London*], *for F. Coles, T. Vere, J. Wright, and J. Clarke*, [1680]. brs. L, CM, HH; MH.

1056   —The roaring black-smiths resolution. *For Richard Burton*, [1655]. brs. L.

1057   —A rosary of rarities. *For the author*, [1663–4]. 8°. O.

1058   —A royal arbor of loyal poesie. *By R. W. for Eliz. Andrews*, 1663. 8°. O; WF.

1059   [–] —[Anr. ed.] *By R. Wood for Eliz. Andrews*, 1664. 8°. L.

1060   —Rvles to know a royall king. *For Robert Wood and Edward Christopher*, 1642. 4°.* LT, O, LG, LHO, DT; BN, CH, CN, LC, TSM, WCL, WF, Y.

1061   — —[Anr. ed.] *For Tho: Bankes*, 1647. 4°.* LT, DT; CH.

1061A   [–] Selfe; or, a riddle, called the monster. *By E. C. for T. Vere and W. Thackeray*, 1668. fol. OP; CH.

1061B   [–] A song to his excellency . . . Monck. *For William Anderson*, 1660. brs. L, HH.

1061C   [–] A speech made to his excellency . . . Monck . . . 28th of March, 1660. *For Henry Broome*, 1660. brs. LT, HH; CH.

1062   —A speech made to his excellency the Lord General Monck . . . tenth day of April. *For H. B.*, 1660. brs. LT, O, HH; Y.

1063   — —[Same title, "twelfth day of Aprill."] [*London*, 1660.] brs. LT, O, LG, HH, MC; Y.

1064   — —[Same title, "thirteenth day of April."] *London, by W. Godbid*, 1660. brs. L, HH, MC; CH, MH, WF, Y.

1065   [–] A speech made to the Lord General Monck . . . 13 of March. [*London*, 1659–60.] brs. LT, O, LG, HH; MH, Y.

1066   —A speech spoken to . . . General Monck . . . thirteenth of April. *By W. Godbid*, 1660. brs. L, O; CN.

1066A   [–] —[Same title, "4th. of April."] *By Thomas Leach*, [1660]. brs. L; MH, Y.

1066AB [–] —[Same title, "April the tenth."] *For John Towers*, 1660. brs. LT.

1066B   [–] A speech to the people. *For H. B.*, 1642. 4°.* LT, LG, BC; CH, CN, MH, NCD, NN, WF, Y.

1067   —Tricks of youth. *For the use of the author*, [1663?]. 4°. L; CH, WF.

1068   —The triumphs of London; performed on Friday. *By J. Macock, for John Playford*, 1675. 4°.* L, O, LG, MR; CH, CLC, CN.

1069   [–] The triumphs of London; performed on Monday. *For John and Henry Playford*, 1683. 4°.* L, LG; CH, CU, IU.

1070   —The triumphs of London: performed on Tuesday. *For John Playford*, 1678. 4°.* L, O, LG; CH, MH.

1071   —The walks of Islington and Hogsdon. *By Tho. Wilson*, 1657. 4°. LT, O, LG, OW, EN; CH, CN, LC, MH, WF, Y.

1071A   —Wealth out-witted. *For the use of the author*, [1668?]. 4°. L.

1072   —VVit in a wildernesse of promiscuous poesie. *By R. A.*, [1665?]. 8°.* L; CH, MH.

1072A   [–] The world turn'd upside down. *For John Smith*, 1647. 4°.* LT; CH.

1073   **J[ordan], T[imothy].** A heavenly child, born. *By R. I. for L. Chapman*, 1659. 8°. LCL, ORP.

1074   **Jorden, Edward.** A discourse of natural bathes. Third edition. *Imprinted at London, and are to be sold by Thomas Salmon, in Bathe*, 1669. 8°. L, O, AM, AU, DT; CH, MH, MIU, PL, WF.

1075   — —Fourth edition. *Imprinted at London, for George Sawbridge, and Thomas Salmon, in Bathe*, 1673. 8°. T.C.I 156. L, O, C, OC, BR; CB, CLC, IU, NAM, NCD, WSG.

Joseph, ben Gorion. See Josippon.

1076   **Josephus, Flavius.** The famous and memorable works of. *By J. L. for Anne Hood*, 1655–56. fol. L, LLP, LSD, BQ.

1076A   — —[Anr. ed.] *By J. L. for Richard Tomlins*, 1655. fol. FU, NC.

1076B   — —[Anr. ed.] *By J. L. for Abel Roper*, 1655–56. fol. CDA, CLC, CU, INU, OCI, OHU, Y.

1076C   — —[Anr. ed.] *By J. L. for Luke Faune*, 1655. fol. IU.

1077   — —[Anr. ed.] *By T. R. for Nathaniel Ranew, and Jonathan Robinson*, 1670. fol. T.C.I 28. L, MC; CN, Y, AVP.

1077A   — —[Anr. ed.] *By T. R. and T. D. for Nathaniel Ranew, and Jonathan Robinson*, 1670. fol. C (impf.); OHU.

1077B   — —[Anr. ed.] *By T. R. and T. D. for Abel Roper*, 1670. fol. BC, LIU.

1078   —The works of. *For Abel Roper*, 1676. fol. T.C.I 241. L, O, C, LLP, CK, E; CH, NN, RBU, Y, ZAP.

1078A   — —[Anr. ed.] *For Nath. Ranew*, 1676. fol. L, IU, NR.

1078B   — —[Anr. ed.] *For Jonath. Robinson*, 1676. fol. OHU.

1078C   — —[Anr. ed.] *For Thomas Fabian*, 1676. fol. SHR; PL, ZAP.

1079   — —[Anr. ed.] *For H. Herringman; to be sold by T. Passenger, and T. Sawbridge*, 1683. fol. T.C.II 33. L, LL, LLP; MB, PBM.

1079A   — —[Anr. ed.] *For H. Herringman, T. Basset, N. Ranew, R. Chiswell, J. Wright, and J. Robinson*, 1683. fol. L, LSD; CH, CLC, OHU, WF, Y.

1079B   — —[Anr. ed.] *For H. Herringman, T. Basset, N. Ranew, J. Wright, and J. Robinson*, 1683. fol. CS.

1080   — —[Anr. ed.] *For T. Basset, N. Ranew, R. Chiswell, J. Wright, J. Robinson, M. Wotton, and G. Connyers*, 1693. fol. T.C.II 446. L, O, C, OC, OM; CLC, CU, MH, OCI, Y.

1080A   — —[Anr. ed.] *For Abel Roper, and are to be sold by George Sawbridge*, 1693. fol. L, O, CT, GC, EN, DM; MH.

1080B   — —[Anr. ed.] *For A. Roper & R. Basset*, 1699. 8°. L, CT, EN.

1080C   — —[Anr. ed.] *For A. R. and R. B. and sold by W. Turner*, 1700. T.C.III 219. 8°. NCD, Y.

1080D —Flavii Josephi antiquitatem Judaicarum liber primus [specimen sheet]. [*Oxford*, 1691.] brs. LPR.

1081 —Josephi antiquitatum judaicarum libri quatuor priores. *Oxoniæ, e Theatro Sheldoniano*, 1700. fol. L, O, C, EC, WCA, DT, DM; CDA, LC, MH, NU, OHU, Y.

1082 —Josephi antiquitatem judaicarum specimen. [*Oxford*, 1694.] brs. O.

1082A —Josephi historiarum de bello Judaico. *Oxonii, e theatro Sheldoniano*, 1687. fol. OC.

Josephus redivivus: or. 1660. *See* Roberts, Hugh.

1083 [**Josippon.**] The vvonderful, and most deplorable history ... of the Jews. *For John Stafford, and by Humphrey Moseley*, 1652. 8°. LT; BBE, LC, Y.

1083A [–] —[Anr. ed.] *For John Stafford, to be sold at the George, and by John Holden*, 1652. 8°. W.

1084 [–] —[Anr. ed.] *By J. L. for John Stafford*, 1653. 8°. O; IU, Y.

1085 — —[Anr. ed.] *For Christopher Eccleston*, 1662. 8°. L, O, AN; CH, Y.

1086 — —[Anr. ed.] *For John Syms*, 1669. 8°. T.C.I 22. L, O; OHU, W.

1086A — —[Anr. ed.] —, 1671. 8°. C, CASTLE ASHBY.

1087 [–] —[Anr. ed.] 1673. 8°. E.

1088 — —[Anr. ed.] *For William Thackeray*, 1684. 8°. T.C.II 65. L, O; CLC.

1088A — —[Anr. ed.] *For W. Thackeray, sold by James Gilbertson*, 1688. 8°. O.

1088B — —[Anr. ed.] *By J. Wilde, for T. Thackeray*, 1694. 8°. T.C.II 530. OHU, W.

1088C — —[Anr. ed.] *London*, [*c.* 1698]. 8°. L.

1089 — —[Anr. ed.] *By W. Wilde, for H. Rhodes*, 1699. 8°. T.C.III 139. L, DT; IU, WF.

1090 [–] —[Anr. ed.] *For H. Rhodes*, 1699. 8°. T.C.III 164. LW.

Joshua's resolution. 1663. *See* Gouge, Thomas.

1091 **Josselyn, John.** An account of two voyages to New-England. *For Giles Widdows*, 1674. 8°. T.C.I 177. L, O, MR, EN, CD; CH, CN, LC, MH, MU, NN, RPJ, Y.

1092 — —Second edition. *For G. Widdowes*, 1675. 8°. E; MH, RPJ.

1093 —New-Englands rarities. *For G. Widdowes*, 1672. 8°. T.C.I 112. L, O, C, E, EN; BN, CH, CN, LC, MH, MU, HC.

1094 — —Second edition. —, 1675. 8°. CH, RPJ, Y.

1095 **Josselyn, Ralph.** The state of saints departed. *By A. M. for Christopher Meredith*, 1652. 8°. L, LW.

Journall of all proceedings. 1659. *See* H., H.

1096 A journal of all that happen'd in the march of the Vaudois. colop: *For Ben Griffin*, 1689. brs. OC; CH.

1097 —[Anr. ed.] *Edinburgh, re-printed*, 1689. brs. ALDIS 2899. HH.

Journal of meditations. [n.p.], 1699. *See* Bacon, Nathaniel.

1097AA A journal of several remarkable passages. [*London?* 1693.] 4°. L, LUG; MH, MIU, WF.

1097A A journal of the expedition of Monsieur de la Fueillade. *For T. Williams and J. Starkey*, 1670. 8°. O; CLC, MH.

1098 A journal of the Kings march from Hilsbourgh. colop: *For R. Baldwin*, 1690. brs. C, OC, MC, DN.

1099 A journal of the late motions and actions of the confederate forces against the French. *Printed, and are to be sold by Richard Baldwin*, 1690. 4°.* T.C.II 312. L, O; CH, LC, MM, TU, WF, Y.

1100 A iovrnall of the most memorable passages in Ireland. *For T. S. October* 19, 1642. 4°.* LT, C, EC, DN; Y.

1101 Entry cancelled.

Journal of the most remarkable occurrences. Dublin, [1689]. *See* Nihell, James.

1102 A journal of the proceedings in the late expedition to Port-Royal. *Boston in New-England, for Benjamin Harris*, 1690. 4°.* EVANS 513. LPR.

1103 A journal of the residence. *Hague*, 1660. fol. O.

1104 Entry cancelled.

Journal of the siege and taking of Buda. 1687. *See* Richards, Jacob.

1105 A journal of the siege of London Derry. colop: *For Richard Chiswell*, 1689. brs. L, O, C, OC, MC; CH, CN, Y.

1106 A journal of the siege of Mentz. *For R. Bentley, and are to be sold by R. Baldwin*, 1689. 4°.* T.C.II 287. L; CLC, WF, Y.

1107 A journal of the Venetian campaigne. *By H. C. and sold by R. Taylor*, 1688. 4°. L, O, CS, BAMB; CH, INU, LC, MH, WF, Y.

1108 Entry cancelled.

Journal of the victorious expedition. 1695. *See* Exact journal.

1109 A journal of the war with Holland. *Oxford, at the theatre*, 1673. 8°. MADAN 2978; T.C.I 133. L, O, C, OC, NE; WF, Y.

1110 A journal of what has past in the north of Ireland. colop: *For E. Goldin*, 1689. brs. L, O, OC, MC, DN.

1111 A journal of what passed in the expedition of . . . Benjamin Fletcher. colop: *New York, by Wm. Bradford*, 1696. 4°.* EVANS 743. L, OC.

1112 A journal: or a most particular account of all that passed . . . Vienna. *For H. Rogers, and M. Gylliflower; to be sold by Walter Davis*, 1684. 8°. L, C, OC, LLU, NE; CH, CN, MH, TU, WF, Y.

1113 A iovrnall, or, a trve and exact relation of each dayes passage. *For Hugh Perry*, 1644. 4°.* LT, LLU, YM; CH, CSS, Y.

Journal or diary. 1656. *See* Beadle, John.

Journey into Spain. 1670. *See* Brunel, Antoine de.

Journey into the country. 1675. *See* Creamer, Charles.

Journey to England. 1700. *See* Evelyn, John.

Journey to Hell. 1700. *See* Ward, Edward.

Journey to Jerusalem. 1672. *See* Crouch, Nathaniel.

Journey to London. 1698. *See* King, William.

Journey to Scotland. 1699. *See* Ward, Edward.

1114 The jovial beggars merry crew. [*London*], *for I. Deacon*, [1684?]. brs. L.

1115 The jovial companions. [*London*], *by C. Bates*, [1670?]. brs. L.

Joviall crew, 1651. *See* Sheppard, Samuel.

1115A The joviall crew, or, Beggers-bush. *For William Gilbertson*, [1660–65]. brs. EUING 150. GU.

1116 —[Anr. ed.] *For W. Thackeray, T. Passenger, and W. Whitwood, [before 1672].* brs. L, O, HH; MH, Y.

1116A —[Anr. ed.] *For John Hose, [1660–75].* brs. O.

1116B The jovial garland. *Sold by T. Passenger, 1677.* T.C.I 295. L.

1116C The joviall lasse. 1675. brs. CM.

Jovial marriner. [1670.] *See* Playford, John.

1117 The jovial may-pole dancers. *[London], for I. Deacon, [1684–95].* brs. L, HH; MH.

1117A The jovial pedler. *For Richard Harper, [1633–52].* brs. L.

1118 The jovial tinker; or. *For Eliz. Andrews, [168–?].* brs. O.

1119 The joviall tinker of England. *For John Hickman, 1648.* 4°.* LT, O, OC, EC, ESS; CH, MH, NU, TU, WF, Y.

1119A Jovial Tom of all trads [sic]. *For J. Back [1687?].* brs. MH.

Jovian. Or, an answer. 1683. *See* Hickes, George.

1120 **Joy, George.** Innocency's complaint. *[Boston, by John Foster], 1677.* brs. EVANS 232. CH, MHS.

Joy after sorrow. [1648.] *See* Price, Laurence.

1120A Joy and honour. *[London], for John Williamson, [1670–78].* brs. O.

1120B Joy to the person of my love. *[London? 1670.]* brs. L.

1121 **Joyce, George.** A letter or epistle to all well-minded people. *By J. C., 1651.* 4°.* LT; CN, MH, Y.

1122 —New propositions from the armie. *For Robert Ellson, July 17. 1647.* 4°.* LT, MR; CH, MH.

1123 [–] A true impartiall narration, concerning the armies preservation of the King. *[London, 1647.]* cap., 4°.* LT, O, C, CT, DT; CH, CN, MH, WF, Y.

1124 —A true narrative of the occasions and causes. *[London, 1659.]* fol.* LT, O; CH, MIU, WF, Y.

1125 [–] A vindication of His Majesty and the army. *For John Benson, 1647.* 4°.* LT, OC, CS, SP; CH, CLC, CN, MH, MIU, WF.

1125A **Joyce, Thomas.** The case of Thomas Joyce appellant. *[London, 1690?]* brs. LG.

1125B —Thomas Joyce, appellant. Richard Fowkes [et. al.], respond. *[London, 1691.]* brs. LG.

1126 Joyfull & happy news from Iredand [sic]. *For Edw. Blackmore, 1643.* 4°.* LT, LLP, DN, DT; CH, CU, Y.

Joyfull and happie newes from the west. 1642. *See* St. Leger, Sir William.

1126A A ioyful and true relation of the great victory obtained by . . . Faireax [sic] . . . against the Irish. *By Andrew Coe, 1644.* 4°.* LNC.

1127 Joyfull and welcome nevves from Shrevvesbury. *[London], for Th. Rider, October 7. 1642.* 4°.* LT; MH.

1127A Joyful cuckoldom. *By J. Heptinstall for Henry Playford, 1671[1695?].* 4°. L.

1127B The joyfull meeting betwixt John. 1675. brs. O.

Joyfull message for all loyall subjects. 1647. *See* Godfrey, N.

1128 Entry cancelled.

Joyfull message sent from both houses. [1642.] *See* England: Parliament.

1129 A joyfull message sent from the citizens of London. *For R. Williamson, 1648.* 4°.* LT; MH.

1130 Entry cancelled.

Joyfull message sent from the House of Commons. 1642. *See* England: Parliament, Commons.

1131 Joyful news for all Christendom. *For J. Jones, 1661.* 4°.* LT, O; WF.

1132 Joyfull nevves for England. *Imprinted at London, 1648.* 4°.* LT.

1132A —and all other parts. *[London], F. Coles, J. Wright, Tho. Vere, and W. Gilbertson, [1654].* brs. L.

1132B Joyfull newes for England, or. *By Peter Lillicrap for Richard Head, 1666.* brs. L.

1133 Joyful news for maids. *[London], for P. Brooksby, J. Deacon, J. Blare, and J. Back, [1688–92].* brs. HH; MH.

1134 Joyfull nevves for the citizens of London from the princes fleet at sea. *[London], printed, 1649.* 4°.* LT, DT; MH.

Joyfull newes from Captain Marro. *[n.p.], 1642. See* Damon, John.

1135 Joyfull nevves from Colchester. *Printed, 1648.* 4°.* LT.

1136 Joyfull newes from Holland. *By Robert Wood, 1651.* 4°.* LT.

1136A Joyfull newes from Hull. *[London], August 2. For Thomas Baley, 1642.* 4°.* L, YM; MIU.

1137 Joyfull newes from Ireland, being a relation. *For John Greensmith, 1641.* 4°.* LT, SP, DN; MH.

Ioyfull nevves from Ireland, or. 1642. *See* Loftus, Edward.

1137A Joyfull newes from Lancashire. *[London], for T. Rider, 1642.* 4°.* CD.

1138 Ioyfull newes from Lichfield. *For Thomas Watson, 1643.* 4°.* LT, CD.

1139 Joyfvll nevves from Nevvcastle. *[London], for B. A., February 1. [1647].* 4°.* LT, MR.

1140 Joyfull nevves from Norvvich. *For T. Rider, Aug. 17. 16426 [sic].* 4°.* LT.

1141 Joyfull nevves from Plimouth. *For Leonard Smith, 1643.* 4°.* LT, MR.

1142 Ioyfull newes from Portsmouth. *[London], for Iohn Iones August 8, 1642.* 4°.* LT.

1143 Ioyfull news from Portugal. *For J. J., 1661.* 4°.* L.

1144 Ioyfvll nevves from sea: or good tidings. *Printed at London for William Ley, 1642.* 4°.* LT, SP; WF.

1144A Joyfull newes from the Earle of VVarwick. *[London], for Th. Cooke, October 4. 1642.* 4°.* LNC; CH, MH, WF, Y.

1145 Joyfull newes from the Isle of Ely. *[London], for W. B., Septemb. 2. 1642.* 4°.* LT, EC.

1146 Joyfvll nevves from the King, being a perfect relation. *For Elizabeth Alsop, 1647.* 4°.* LT, DT.

1147 Joyfull newes from the King. *For J. Baitman, 1648.* 4°.* LT, CT, EN; MH, MU.

1147A Joyfull newes from the King, or, the true proceedings. *For Henry Fowler, Septemb. 2 1642.* 4°.* L, CD; INU, MH, OCI, WF.

1148 Joyfull nevves from the Kings Majesty. *September 4. [London], for G. W., 1648.* 4°.* LT; CH, WF.

1149 Joyfull nevves from the Marquesse of Ormond. *Imprinted at London for R. W., August 15. 1649.* 4°.* LT, C; Y.

1150   Joyfull nevves from the Princes fleet at sea. *Aprill 12, for R. Williamson,* 1649. 4°.* LT, LNM.

1151   Joyfull nevves from the treaty containing. *Octob.* 10, *for R. W.,* 1648. 4°.* LT; IU, MH.

1152   Joyfull newes from Wells. *For Henry Fowler, Aug.* 12, 1642. 4°.* LT.

Joyful news of opening. 1677. *See* Turnor, Thomas.

Joyfull newes of the Kings Majesties safe arrival. 1647. *See* Whalley, Edward.

1153   Joyfull newes of the Kings most certaine resolution. *For Th. Hoverton, October* 12. 1642. 4°.* LT, O; WF, Y.

1154   Ioyfull tydings to all true Christians. *For Iohn Hammond,* 1642. 4°.* LT, O, MR; CH, NC.

Joyfull tidings to the begotten. [n.p.], 1664. *See* Smith, William, *Quaker of Besthorp.*

1155   The joyfullest newes from Hvll. [*London*], *August 17, by T. Fawcet for T. R.,* [1642]. 4°.* LT.

1156   [**Joyner, Edward.**] Armante Gulielmo. [*Oxford, 1692.*] brs. O.

1157   [–] In obitum Mariæ. [*Oxford, 1694.*] brs. O.

1158   Entry cancelled. Ghost.

1159   **Joyner, William.** The Roman empress. [*London*], *in the Savoy, by T. N. for Henry Herringman,* 1671. 4°. T.C.I 56. L, O, OW, CT, DU, A; CH, CN, LC, MH, TU, WF, Y.

1160   [–] Some observations upon the life of Reginaldus Polus. *For Mathew Turner,* 1686. 8°. L, O, C, DU, DM; CH, CN, MH, PBL, TU, WF, WG, Y.

1160A   **Joynes, Clement.** Montanism revived, . . . confuted. *For the author,* 1700. 8°.* LF.

1161   **Joynes, John.** A sermon preached . . . 1650. January 9. *By T. N. for Edward Man,* 1668. 4°. L, O, LLP, LW, BLH; NU, WF, Y.

Joys of vertuous love. [n.p., 1685–88.] *See* D'Urfey. Thomas.

1162   [**Juan de Santa Maria**], *fray.* Policie vnveiled. *For H. Moseley,* 1650. L, O; CLC, LC, NCD, NP.

1163   **Jubbes, John.** An apology unto the honorable and other the honored. [*London,* 1649.] cap., 4°.* LT, MR; CN, INU, MH, NU, WF.

1164   —A briefe vindication of the religion and governmet [*sic*] of New-England. [*n.p., c.* 1649–50.] cap., 4°.* CN.

Jubilie of England. 1646. *See* J., W.

1165   Judah betrayed: or, the Egyptian plot. *For J. Witty,* 1682. 4°.* L; MH, PU, WF, Y.

Judas his thirty pieces. [n.p., 1668.] *See* Bolton, John.

1166   Ivdas justified by his brother Scot. [*London*], *printed,* 1647. brs. LT.

1167   The ivdges ivdgement. A speech. [*London*], *printed,* 1641. 4°.* LT, O, C; CSS, MH, NU, TU, WF, Y.

1168   —[Anr. ed.] [*London*], *for John Aston,* 1641. 4°.* L, O, C, BC, MR; CH, CN, MH, NU, Y.

1169   The judges opinions concerning petitions. *For Thomas Burrell,* 1679. brs. L, O, HH, MC, EN; CH, MH, PU, WF, Y.

1169A   The judges opinions delivered . . . in the case between John St. Leger. [n.p., 1685.] fol.* L.

Judges resolution. 1642. *See* Berkeley, *Sir* Robert.

1170   The iudges resolvtions. *Printed at London by Tho. & Rich. Cotes, for Will. Cooke,* 1641. 4°.* LT, C; NC.

1171   A judgment & condemnation of the fifth-monarchy. men. *Printed,* 1661. 4°.* LT, O.

1172   The judgment and doctrine of the clergy of the Church of England. *For J. H. and T. S.,* [1687]. 4°.* L, O, CS, E, DT; HR, CH, CU, MH, TU, FW, Y.

1173   The judgment given forth by twenty eight Quakers against George Keith. *Printed at Pensilvania; and now re-printed at London, for Richard Baldwin,* 1694. 4°.* T.C.II 471. L, O, LF, GU; MU, NNM, PH, PHS, RPJ, WCL.

Judgment of a disinterested person. 1696. *See* Bury, Arthur.

1174   The judgment of a good subject. *By T. N.,* 1672. 4°.* O, OC; CH, WF.

Judgement of an anonymous writer. 1684. *See* Hickes, George.

1175   The ivdgement of an old grand-jvry-man of Oxford-shire. *Oxford, by Leonard Lichfield,* 1645. 4°.* MADAN 1777. LT, O, CT, BC, EN, DT; CH, CN, CSS, Y.

1175A   The judgment of antiquitie, concerning . . . Easter. [*London?* 1650.] cap., 4°.* CJ.

1176   The judgement of foraign divines. *Printed,* 1660. 4°.* LT, O, CS, AN, EN, DT; CH, IU, MII, NU, TU, WF, Y.

1177   —[Anr. ed.] *Printed, and are to be sold by Richard Baldwin,* 1690. 4°.* L, OB; MH, NGT, NU, Y.

1177A   The judgement of God shewed upon one John Faustus. [*London*], *for F. Coles, T. Vere, and W. Gilbertson,* [1658–64]. brs. EUING 145. O, GU.

1177B   —[Anr. ed., "judgment."] [*London*], *for W. Thackeray, T. Passinger,* [1686–8]. brs. CM.

1178   —[Anr. ed.] [*London*], *by and for A. M.,* [1693?]. brs. L.

1179   —[Anr. ed.] *By W. O.,* [1695?]. brs. L.

1180   —[Anr. ed.] [*London*], *for A. M. W. O. and Tho. Thackeray,* [1695]. brs. L, O; MH.

Judgment of non-conformists, of the interest. 1676. *See* Baxter, Richard.

Judgment of several eminent divines. Boston, 1693. *See* Mather, Increase.

Judgment of the ancient Jewish church. 1699. *See* Allix, Pierre.

Judgment of the comet. Dublin, 1682. *See* Wetenhall, Edward.

1181   The judgement of the court of King's bench. [*London*], *for N. T.,* 1686. MC.

1182   The iudgement of the court of warre. *Printed at Oxford by Leonard Lichfield,* 1643. brs. STEELE 2449; MADAN 1397. LT.

Judgment of the fathers. 1695. *See* Smalbroke, Thomas.

Judgment of the foreign reformed churches. 1690. *See* Willis, John.

1183   The judgment of the old nonconformists. [*n.p.*], *re-printed,* 1662. 4°.* O, LIU; NGT.

1184   The judgment of the reformed churches. *For Andrew Crook,* 1652. 4°. O, LSD; WF.

Judgment on Alexander. 1672. *See* Saint Evremond, Charles Marguetel.

Ivdgment, or a definition. [n.p.], 1641. *See* D., J.

1184aA The judgment or resolution of all the Lords. [*London?* 1679.*] brs. L, O, LG, HH, LNC; CN, MH, WF, Y.

1184A The judgement upon the arguments, for and against the charter of London. colop: *By George Croom*, 1683. brs. DU, LSD; CH, WF.

1185 Judgements as they were upon solemne arguments given. [*London*], *by Thomas Roycroft*, 1655. 12°. L, O, LGI, CS, DT; CU, LC, MHL, NCL, PU.

Judgments of God. 1668. *See* B., F.

1186 The iudiciall arraignment, condemnation, execution & interment of the . . . Dutch devil excize. [*London*, 1653.*] cap., 4°.* LT.

Judicial astrologers. [n.p.], 1659. *See* Allen, John, *bookseller*.

Judiciall astrologie. 1652. *See* Rowland, William.

Judicious observation. 1683. *See* Wiswall, Ichabod.

1187 A judicious vievv of the businesses which are at this time between France and . . . Austria. *By W. Wilson, for Henry Herringman*, 1657. 8°. LT; Y.

Judicium discretionis:or. 1667. *See* Wilson, Thomas.

Judicium vniversitatis. [n.p.], 1648. *See* Sanderson, Robert.

Jugulum causæ. [n.p.], 1671. *See* Du Moulin, Louis.

Julian and Gregorian year. 1700. *See* Willis, John.

Julian the apostate. 1682. *See* Johnson, Samuel.

1188 Entry cancelled.

Juliana, *of Norwich.* XVI revelations. 1670. *See* Cressy, Hugh Paulin.

1189 **Julius II,** *Pope.* . . . Dialogus. *Oxoniæ, excudebat H. Hall, impensis Th. Gilbert*, 1669. 8°. MADAN 2827. L, O, BAMB, P; MH.

1190 — —[Anr. ed.] *Oxonii*, 1680. [*sic.*] 8°. MADAN 3265. L, O, LW, OC; CH, LC, MB, NU, TO, Y.

1191 **Juniper, William.** The strange and wonderfull visions. *For J. Davies, to be sold by Simon Miller*, 1662. 4°.* L, O, C; CN, MH, WF.

1192 A juniper lecture. *For William Ley*, 1652. 12°. LT.

1193 The juniper lecturer corrected. *Printed*, 1662. 4°.* L; MH.

1194 **Junius, Franciscus.** De pictura veterum. *Prostant apud Sam. Smith & Benj. Walford*, 1694. fol. T.C.II 512. O, LL, OB, CCA, EC, LLU; CH, WF, Y.

Junius, R., *pseud. See* Younge, Richard.

1195 Jupiter: Doctor Stillingfleet's true god. [*n.p.*, 1674?] 8°. O.

Jura cleri: or. Oxford, 1661. *See* Carpender, William.

Jura coronæ. 1680. *See* Brydall, John.

1196 **Jurieu, Pierre.** The accomplishment of the scripture prophecies. In two parts. *Printed*, 1687. 8°. T.C.II 272. L, O, CE, E, DT; CH, LC, MH, MU, NU, WF.

1197 —M. Jurieu the famous French protestant divine, his account. [*London?* 1690.] brs. L, HH.

1198 —Account of the present persecution. *London, reprinted Glasgow, Sanders*, 1698. brs. ALDIS 3757. EN.

1199 —L'ame affligée. *A Londres, et se vend par C. Lucas*, 1695. 4°.* L (lost).

1200 —A continuation of the accomplishment. *Printed*, 1688. 8°. LCL, LW, DUS, E, DT; CH, MH, NU, PL, WF.

1200A [–] A defence of Their Majesties King William and Queen Mary. *For John Taylor, and publish't by R. Baldwin*, 1689. 4°. T.C.II 289. L, OC, CT, E, DT; CH, MU, NU, WF, Y.

1201 [–] Le dragon missionaire: or, the dragoon turn'd apostle. [*n.p.*], *printed*, 1686. 4°.* LG, MR; CN, WF.

1202 [–] Eclaircissements sur les scandales. *Chez Ant. Hill*, 1687. 12°. LSC; BN, CN.

1203 —The history of the council of Trent. *By J. Heptinstall, for Edward Evets, and Henry Faithorne and John Kersey*, 1684. 8°. T.C.II 84. L, O, C, E, DT; CH, CN, MBC, MH, NU, WF, Y.

1204 —Monsieur Jurieu's judgment upon the question of defending our religion. *For John Lawrence, to be sold by Richard Baldwin*, 1689. 4°.* T.C.II 277. L, O, C, EN, DT; CLC, CN, NU, PL, WF, Y.

1205 [–] The last efforts of afflicted innocence. *For M. Magnes and R. Bentley*, 1682. 8°. T.C.I 512. L, OJ, AN, ENC; CH, CLC, NU, WF, Y.

1206 —A pastoral letter written. *For Daniel Brown: and Richard Baldwin*, 1695. 4°.* L, O, C, LW, CT; CH, IU, MH, NU, WF, Y.

1207 —Monsieur Jurieu's pastoral letters. *For Jo. Hindmarsh*, 1688. 4°.* LIL, OM, LSD, SP; CH, CLC, NN, PL, Y.

1208 — —[Anr. ed., twenty-four letters.] *For T. Fabian; and J. Hindmarsh*, 1689. 8°. T.C.II 261. L, O, C, LIU, E; CLC, MBC, NP, NU, WF.

1208A — —[Anr. ed.] *For Tho. Fabian*, 1691. 8°. CLC, TU.

1208B — —[Anr. ed.] *For T. Fabian; and J. Hindmarsh*, 1699. 8°. BC.

1209 —A plain method of Christian devotion. *For C. Harper*. 1692. 12°. T.C.II 418. L, O, C, EC, ESSEX; CLC, WF, Y.

1210 [–] The policy of the clergy of France. *For R. Bentley, and M. Magnes*, 1681. 8°. T.C.I 442. L, O, C, E, DT; CH, CN, NU, PL, WF.

1211 —A preservative against the change of religion. *By S. Roycroft, for Thomas Cockerill*, 1683. 8°. O, C, NE, P, DT; NU.

1212 —The reflections of . . . upon the strange . . . exstasies of Isabel Vincent. *For Richard Baldwin*, 1689. 4°. T.C.II 259. L, O, C, EN, DT; BN, CH, CN, MH, WF, Y.

1213 —Seasonable advice to all Protestants in Europe. *For R. Baldwin*, 1689. 4°.* T.C.II 269. L, O, C, BR, EN; CH, MH, NU, WF, Y.

1213A **Jurin, Jean.** A true and exact relation of the difference between Mr. Christopher Cisner . . . and John Jurin. *By William Bentley*, 1657. 4°. LLP, MR; CN.

Ivris et ivdicii fecialis. Oxoniæ, 1650. *See* Zouche, Richard.

Jury-man charged. 1664. *See* E., H.

1214 A jury-man's judgement upon the case of Lieut. Col. John Lilburn. [*London*, 1653.] cap., 4°.* LT, O, OC, ORP, LIU; CH, LC, MIU, NU, Y.

1215 The ivry of inqvisition. [*London*], *printed*, 1641. 4°.* L, C, BR, MR, DT; CH, CSS, MIU, NU, VC, WF.

1215A The juries right. *H. J.*, 1654. 4°. L; CLC.

Jus anglorum. 1681. *See* Atwood, William.

1216 Jus divinum ministerii evangelici. Or the divine right.
      *For G. Latham, J. Rothwell, S. Gellibrand, T. Vnderhill,
      and J. Cranford,* 1654. 4°. LT, O, C, NPL, EN, DT; CH, IU,
      MH, NU, TU, WF, Y.

1216A —[Anr. ed.] *By John Legat and Abraham Miller,* 1654. 4°.
      CH.

      Jus divinum of presbyterie. [n.p.], 1646. *See* Writer,
      Clement.

1217 Jus divinum regiminis ecclesiastici: or, the divine right.
      By J. Y. for Joseph Hunscot and George Calvert, 1646.
      4°. LT, C, LL, MR, EN, DT; CH, CN, IU, LC, MH, NU, Y.

1218 —Second edition. —, 1647. 4°. LT, C, OU, E, DT; CLC, IU,
      MBC, MH, NU, WSC, Y.

1219 —Third edition. *By R. W. for George Calvert,* 1654. 4°.
      L, O, C, SC, D; CH, IU, MBC, MH, NP, NU.

      Jus gentium or. 1660. *See* P., S.

      Jus populi or. 1644. *See* Parker, Henry.

      Jus populi vindicatum. [n.p.], 1669. *See* Stewart, James.

      Jus primatiale; or. [n.p.], 1672. *See* Plunkett, Oliver.

      Jus primogeniti: or. 1699. *See* Brydall, John.

      Jus regiminis: being. 1689. *See* Denton, William.

      Jus regum. Or. 1645. *See* Parker, Henry.

      Jus sigilli: or. 1673. *See* Brydall, John.

      Just account upon the account. 1656. *See* Woodward,
      Hezekiah.

1220 A just and cleere refutation. *For the author,* 1665. 4°.* O;
      CH.

      Just and lawful trial of the Foxonian. 1657. *See* Crisp,
      Thomas.

      Just and lawful trial of the teachers. 1657. *See* Burrough,
      Edward.

1221 Just and legal exceptions against the late act. [London,
      1657?] cap., 4°.* LUG; MH, Y.

      Just and modest reproof. Edinburgh, 1693. *See* Rule,
      Gilbert.

1222 A just and modest vindication of his Royal Highness the
      Duke of York. *For Thomas Benskin,* 1680. 4°.* O, LL,
      LSD, MR, EN; CH, CLC, IU, MH, MM, WF, Y.

1223 A just and modest vindication of the many thousand
      loyal apprentices. colop: *For R. Goodfellow,* 1681. brs.
      L, O, LG; CH, MH, NC, AVP.

      Just and modest vindication of the proceedings. [n.p.,
      1681.] *See* Ferguson, Robert.

1224 A just and modest vindication of the Protestants of
      Ireland. *For Tim. Goodwin,* 1689. 4°.* T.C.II 323. L, O,
      DN; CH, MM, WF, Y.

      A just and modest vindication of the Scots design.
      [n.p.], 1699. *See* Ferguson, Robert.

      Just and necessary apology. 1646. *See* Calamy, Edmund.

1225 Just and reasonable desires . . . Gateshead. [London, 1657.]
      cap., 4°.* CT.

      A just and seasonable reprehension of naked breasts.
      1678. *See* Boileau, Jacques.

      Just and sober vindication. 1694. *See* Gailhard, John.

      Just and solemn protestation. 1648. *See* Prynne, William.

1226 A just and solemn protestation of the free-born people
      of England. [London, 1647.] brs. LT, LG, OC; WF.

1227 A just and true account of the malt lottery tickets.
      Printed and sold by Freeman Collins, 1697. fol.* MR.

1228 Entry cancelled.

      Iust and true remonstrance. 1641. *See* Bushell, Thomas.

      Just apologie for an abvsed armie. 1646. *See* G., W.

      Just apology for His sacred Majestie. [n.p.], 1642. *See*
      Lake, *Sir* Edward.

      Just appeal. [n.p., 1683.] *See* Bampfield, Francis.

1228A Just at St. Andrews wardrobe church . . . liveth a
      physician. [London, 1675?] brs. L.

1229 A just balance. *By Ja: Cottrel, for Giles Calvert,* 1651. 4°.*
      LT, O, CPL, DC, DU; CSS, IU, MM, NU, WF, Y.

1229A A just censure of a seditious pamphlet. *By T. Newcomb,*
      1660. 4°.* Y.

      Just censure of Francis Bugg's. 1699. *See* Penn, William.

1230 A just censure of the answer to Vox cleri. *Printed,* 1690.
      4°.* O, LLP, OCC, CS, EC, SP, CD; CLC, NU, PL, Y.

1231 Just complaint of the oppressed. [London, 1684?] 4°. L,
      LF; CH, IE, KQ, MH, PH.

1232 A ivst complaint, or lovd crie. *Printed,* 1642[3]. 4°.* LT,
      C, LG, CT, LIU, LSD, EN; CN, CSS, Y, ASP, ZWT.

      Just correction. 1647. *See* Vicars, John.

      Just defence and vindication. 1660. *See* Gaskin, John.

      Ivst defence of John Bastwick. 1645. *See* Bastwick, John.

1233 Entry cancelled.

      Just defence of John Lilburne. [n.p., 1653.] *See* Lilburne,
      John.

      Just defence of the royal martyr. 1699. *See* Baron,
      William.

      Just devil of Woodstock. [1660.] *See* Widdows, Thomas.

      Just discharge. Paris, 1677. *See* Godden, Thomas.

      Just enquiry. 1693. *See* Whitehead, George.

1234 Entry cancelled.

      Ivst man in bonds. [n.p., 1646.] *See* Lilburne, John.

      Just measure. [n.p.], 1648. *See* M., R.

      Just measures in an epistle. 1692. *See* Penn, William.

      Just measures of the pious. Edinburgh, 1700. *See* Monro,
      George.

1235 A just narrative of the hellish new counter-plots of the
      Papists. *For Dorman Newman,* 1679. fol.* L, O, C, DC,
      EN; CH, CN, MH, NU, TU, WF, Y. (var.)

1236 Just principles of complying. *For J. Lawrence,* 1689. 4°.
      T.C.II 303. L, C, LLP.

1236A —[Anr. ed.] *For Richard Baldwin,* 1689. 4°. CLC, IU, TU.

1237 A just rebuke of a late unmannerly libel. *Printed,* 1699.
      4°.* L, O, CT, MR, CD; CDA, CH, CLC, MM, WF, Y.

1238 A just reproof to Mr. Richard Baxter. *Printed,* 1680. fol.*
      L, O, OB, LSD, MR; CH, LC, MH, WF.

1238A A just request of the officers, and souldiers . . . under . . .
      Fairfax. [London, 1647.] 4°.* CH.

1239 A just reward for unreasonable service. *Printed,* 1675.
      8°. L, O; CLC.

1240 The just reward of a debauched cavalier. [London], *May
      13. for I. Jackson,* 1643. 4°.* LT; CH.

1240A The just reward of perjury. *For J. Deacon,* [1687?]. brs.
      MH.

1241 The iust reward of rebels. *Printed at London for F. Couls, I. Wright, T. Banks and T. Bates,* 1642. 4°.* LT, LG.
Just vindication of learning. 1679. *See* Blount, Charles.

1242 A just vindication of Mr. Poole's designe. [*London,* 1667.] 4°.* L.
Just vindication of my earnest. 1696. *See* Keith, George.

1243 A just vindication of the honour of King James. colop: *London, R. Oswell,* [1683]. cap., fol.* L, O, EN; CH, CN, MH, MU, WF, Y.

1244 A just vindication of the principal officers. *For Nathanael Brooke,* 1674. 4°.* T.C.I 164. L, O, C, LSD, DT; CH, MH, MM, WF, Y.

1245 A just vindication of the reputation of Mr. VVhite Alderman of . . . Exon. *For Iohn Rothwell,* 1649. 4°.* LT, DT; CH, MH.

1246 A just vindication on the behalf of Iohn Eliot. [*London*], *imprinted,* 1648. 4°.* MH.

1246A Just weights and measures. [*n.p.,* 1690?] brs. L; Y.

1247 Justa sive interiæ regicidarum: or, Tybvrns revels. *For R. B.,* 1660[1]. brs. LT.

1248 Justice in masquerade. A poem. [*London,* 1680.] brs. L, MR; CN, MH, TSM, Y.

1249 The justice of our cause. [*n.p.,* 1699.] cap., 4°.* O, CT, BAMB; CLC, MM.

1250 Entry cancelled.
Justice of peace his calling. 1684. *See* Bohun, Edmund.

1251 Entry cancelled.
Justice of peace restored. Third edition. 1671. *See* Justice restored.
Justice of the army. 1649. *See* L., R.
Justice of the Parliament. 1689. *See* Shower, *Sir* Bartholomew.

1251A The justice of the peace; or a vindication. *Printed,* 1697. 4°.* CH.
Justice perverted. 1695. *See* Crosfeild, Robert.

1251B Justice restored: or, a guide for . . . justices of peace. *By T. R. for H. Twyford, T. Dring, and J. Place,* 1660. 12°. L; MHL, WF.

1252 —Second edition. *By Th. Roycroft, for H. Twyford, T. Dring, and J. Place,* 1661. 12°. LT, O, LLP, DC, NPL; CH, IU, LC, MHL.

1253 —Third edition. *By John Streater, one of the assigns of Rich. and Edw. Atkins,* 1671. 12°. LLP; LC, NCL.
Justice revived. 1661. *See* Wingate, Edward.
Justice the best support. 1697. *See* Crosfeild, Robert.

1253A Justice trymphant [*sic*]. 1683. brs. CLC.

1254 Justices plea, or, a serious, seasonable and most submissive motion. [*London,* 1644.] cap., 4°.* LT, O, DT; CH, CSS.

1255 Ivsticia prestigiosa, or ivdges tvrned ivglers. *Printed,* 1644. 4°.* LT.
Justificatio gratuita. 1685. *See* Gataker, Charles.
Justification justified. 1674. *See* Rolle, Samuel.

1256 The justification of a safe and wel-grounded answer. *By A. Griffin,* 1646. 4°.* LT, LVF, SP, EN, DT; CH, IU, MH, NPT, NU, WF, Y.
Justification of a sinner. 1650. *See* Crell, Johan.

1257 A justification of our brethren of Scotland. [*London*], *anno,* 1647. brs. LT, HH.

1258 The justification of the assertion of the burgomasters . . . of Amsterdam. *Printed, and are to be sold by Richard Baldwin,* 1690. 4°.* L, O, LL, LPR, OM, MR; HR, CH, CN, MH, TU, WF, Y.

1258A A justification of the directors of the Netherlands East-India Company. 1687. 8°. L.

1259 —[Anr. ed.] *For S. Tidmarsh,* 1688. 8°. L, LLL, LUG, OH, EN; CLC, NC, NIC, WF, Y.

1260 A justification of the late act of Parliament. colop: *For R. Baldwin,* 1689. brs. L, C, HH; CH, PL, WF, Y.

1261 A jvstyfycatjon of the mad crew. [*London*], *printed,* 1650. 4°.* LT; CLC.

1261A A justification of the members within doors. [*London?* 168–?] brs. CH.
Justification of the paper. 1681. *See* Whitaker, Edward.
Justification of the present war. 1672. *See* Stubbe, Henry.

1262 Entry cancelled.
Justification of the Prince of Orange's descent. 1689. *See* Ferguson, Robert. Brief justification.

1262A A justification of the proceedings of the French-church. [*London,* 1656.] 4°. LG, P.

1263 A iustification of the synod of Sion Colledge. [*London*], *printed,* 1647. brs. LT; CH.

1264 A justification of the whole proceedings of Their Majesties. *For Randal Taylor,* 1689. 4°.* T.C.II 256. L, O, C, LVF, EN, DT; CH, CN, MH, MU, TU, WF, Y.
Justification of two points. 1646. *See* Bakewell, Thomas.
Justifying faith. 1679. *See* Ellis, Clement.

1265 **Justinus,** *martyr.* Του αγιου Ιουστινου απολογια. Εκ Θεατρου Οξονια, [1700]. 8°. L, O, C, MR, DT; CH, CLC, MH, NC, NP, Y.

1265A **Justinus, Marcus Junianus.** Justini ex Trogi Pompeii historiis externis. *Excusi pro Felice Kingstonio & veneunt per Gulielmum Gilbertson,* 1651. 8°. CS, LLU; NN, Y.

1265B ——[Anr. ed.] *Excusi per Robertum White, & veneunt per Gulielmum Gilbertson,* 1659. 8°. O.

1265C ——[Anr. ed.] *Excusum pro Gulielmo Gilbertson,* 1664. 8°. L; CH.

1265D ——[Anr. ed.] *Excusum pro Gulielmo Whitwood,* 1668. 8°. L.

1266 ——[Anr. ed.] *Oxonii,* [*excudebat Gul. Hall*]*per Fran. Oxlad senior & junior,* 1669. 12°. MADAN 2832. L, O, DU, LSD, CD; CLC.

1266A ——[Anr. ed.] *Excusum pro Gulielmo Whitwood,* 1671. 8°. TO, TSM.

1267 ——[Anr. ed.] [*Oxford*], *e Theatro Sheldoniano,* 1674. 12°. MADAN 3014. L, O, C, CT, YM, DM; CLC, NC, Y.

1268 ——[Anr. ed.] *G. Whitwood,* 1675. 12°. L.

1268A ——[Anr. ed.] *Excusum pro Gulielmi Whitwood,* 1677. 8°. T.C.I 277. O, C.

1269 ——[Anr. ed.] [*Oxford*], *e theatro Sheldoniano,* 1684. 12°. L, OC, EC, NE; CLC, PU.

1270 — —[Anr. ed.] *Excudebat E. Horton, impensis W. Whit-wood,* 1686. 12°. T.C.II 168. L, FONMON, NPL; IU, MBC, WF.

1270aA — —[Anr. ed.] *Excudebat W. Horton, impensis W. Whit-wood,* 1687. 12°. CH.

1270bA — —[Anr. ed.] —, 1688. 12°. L.

1270A — —[Anr. ed.] *Pro societate sationariorum* [sic], 1695. 8°. T.C.II 582. MH.

1270B — —[Anr. ed.] *Pro societate stationarium,* 1700. 8°. MB.

1271 —The history of. *For William Gilbertson,* 1654. 8°. L, BC, BSO, LLU, NOT; CH, CN, MIU, RBU, Y.

1272 — —Second edition. —, 1664. 8°. L, LLU; CH, CLC, FU, IU, NC, OCL.

1273 — — —Third edition. *For W. Whitwood,* 1671. 8°. T.C.I 99. L; WF.

1273A — —"Third" edition. *For William Whitwood,* 1672. 8°. CLC, WF.

1273B — —"Third" edition. *For W. W. to be sold by Edward Thomas,* 1672. 8°. L; TU.

1274 — —Fourth edition. *For William Whitwood,* 1682. 12°. T.C.I 479. L; CLC, TO, V, WCL, WF.

1275 — —Fifth edition. —, 1688. 12°. T.C.II 227. LL, CS; CLC, LC, MU, NC.

1276 **Juvenal.** Decimus Junius Juvenalis, and Aulus Persius Flaccus translated. *Oxford, by W. Downing, for F. Oxlad senior, J. Adams, and F. Oxlad junior,* 1673. fol. T.C.I 134; MADAN 2979. L, O, C, EN, DT; CH, CN, MH, MU, NC, NP, TU, WF, Y. (var.)

1277 —The first six satyrs of. *Oxford, by Henry Hall, for Thomas Robinson,* 1644. 8°. MADAN 1752. O; CH, IU, MH, Y.

1278 —A modern essay on the tenth satyr of Juvenal. *By T. M. and are to be sold by Randal Taylor,* 1687. 4°. L, O, LIU, LLU, MAU; CH, CLC, IU, MH, PL, WF, Y.

1278A — —[Anr. ed.] *By T. M. for the author, and sold by R. Bentley, Joseph Hindmarsh, John Newton, and by Randal Taylor,* 1687. 4°. CN, MH.

1278B — —[Anr. ed.] *For T. Milbourn,* 1687. 4°. O.

1279 —A modern essay on the thirteenth satyr of Juvenal. *For Jacob Tonson,* 1686. 4°. L, O, OC, MAU, DT; CH, MH, MIU, PL, WF, Y.

1280 —Mores hominum, the manners of men. *By R. Hodg-kinsonne,* 1660. fol. L, O, CCA, EN, DT; BN, CLC, CN, MH, WF, Y.

1281 —The satyrs. *For Humphrey Moseley,* 1646. 8°. CK; CH, IU, MH, Y.

1282 —Satyræ. Fourth edition. *Excudebat Ioannes Legat, impensis Christophori Meredith,* 1648. 8°. O, C; NC, VC, Y.

1283 — —[Anr. ed.] *Typis Rogeri Danielis, vænales apud T. Garthwait,* 1656. 12°. O; IU, WF.

1283A — —[Anr. ed.] *Typis H. L. & R. V. & sumptibus Andrae Kembe,* 1660. 12°. L, LLU; NC.

1283B — —[Anr. ed.] *Ex officina Johannis Redmayne,* 1668. 12°. L, OC, EN; WF.

1284 — —[Anr. ed.] *Ex officina E. Tyler. Sumptibus Nath. Brook & Edw. Thomas,* 1669. 12°. O, AN, RPL; CB, CLC, Y.

1284aA — —[Anr. ed.] *officinâ Joannis Redmayne,* 1677. 12°. Y (impcf.).

1284bA — —[Anr. ed.] *Typis E. Redmayne,* 1686. 12°. IU, NIA.

1284A — —[Anr. ed.] *Impensis Tho. Basset, Ric. Chiswell, Matt. Wotton, & Geo. Conyers,* 1689. 12°. O; CN, MH, Y.

1285 — —[Anr. ed.] *Impensis Tho. Dring, & Abel Swalle,* 1691. 8°. T.C.II 370. L, O, C, AN, BR, EC; CH, IU, MH, WF, Y.

1286 — —[Anr. ed.] *Impensis R. Clavel, J. Sprint, J. Nicholson, and T. Child,* 1699. 8°. T.C.III 158. L, O, C, LW, AN; BN, CH, IU, MH, PPT, TU, SELWYN COLL. DUNEDIN.

1286A — —[Anr. ed.] *Impensis R. Clavel; J. Sprint; & J. Nichol-son,* 1699. 8°. L; PU, SW.

1287 — —[Anr. ed.] *Impensis Tim Childe,* 1700. 8°. C, LLU.

1288 —The satires of Decimus Junius Juvenalis. *For Jacob Tonson,* 1693. fol. L, O, C, E, DT; BN, CH, CN, MH, MU, NP, TU, WF, Y.

1289 — —Second edition. —, 1697. 8°. L, O, CS, LLU, DT; CLC, LC, MH, NP, Y.

1290 — —Third edition. *For Jacob Tonson; to be sold by Robert Knaplock,* 1697. T.C.II 602. 8°. L, O, DC, NOT, D; CLC, IU, MH, TSM, WF, Y.

1291 —Juvenal's sixteen satyrs. *For Humphery Moseley,* 1647. 8°. L, O, C, MAU, EN; CH, CN, LC, MH, MU, NP, TU, WF, Y.

1292 — —[Anr. ed.] *For Peter Parker, to be sold at his shop, and Thomas Guy,* 1673. 8°. T.C.I 129. L, OC, BAMB, BC, RU, DT; CLC, CN, MH, PL, WF, Y.

1292A —The tenth satyr of. *For Gabriel Collins,* 1678 [1687]. 4°.* MH.

1293 — —[Anr. ed.] *By D. Mallet for Gabriel Collins,* 1687. 4°. T.C.II 200. L, O, LVD, LLU, MAU; CLC, CN, TU, WC, WCL, WF, Y.

1294 — —[Same title.] *For Richard Baldwin,* [1693?]. 4°.* T.C.II 465. L, O, C; CLC.

1295 —The vvish, being the tenth satyr of. *Dublin, by Benjamin Tooke,* 1675. 4°.* T.C.I 205; DIX 155. L, O, OC, LLU, DN, DT; CH, MH, PU, WF, Y.

Juvenalis redivivus; or. [n.p.], 1683. *See* Wood, Thomas.

Juvenilia sacra. 1664. *See* B., P.

[Juxon, William.] Χαρις και ειρηνη: or. 1662. *See* Gauden, John, *bp.*

1296 Entry cancelled.

—Subjects sorrovv. 1649. *See* Brown, Robert.

Juxta suorum cineres. [n.p.], 1690. *See* Fisher, Payne.

K

K., A. Contemplation on Bassets down-hill. [n.p., 1658.] *See* Kemp, *Mrs.* Anne.

1 Entry cancelled.

—A visitation of tender love. [n.p., 1662.] *See* Rigge, Ambrose.

K., B. Appendix to. 1692. *See* Keach, Benjamin.

—Darkness vanquished. 1675. *See* Keach, Benjamin.

—Elegy on the death of that . . . John Norcot. 1676. *See* Keach, Benjamin.

—Glorious lover. 1679. *See* Keach, Benjamin.

—Grand impostor discovered. 1675. *See* Keach, Benjamin.

—Laying on of hands. 1698. *See* Keach, Benjamin.

—Progress of sin. 1684. *See* Keach, Benjamin.

—Travels of true godliness. 1683. *See* Keach, Benjamin.

—Τροποσχημαλογια: tropes. 1682. *See* Keach, Benjamin.

—War with the devil. 1673. *See* Keach, Benjamin.

2 **K., C.** Art's master-piece, or a companion. *For G. Conyers, and J. Sprint,* 1697. 12°. T.C.III 7. L; NP.

2A ——Third edition. *For G. Conyers,* [1698?]. 12°. PFL.

3 ——Fourth edition. *For G. Conyers, and J. Sprint,* [1700]. 12°. O; W.

4 —Propositions agreed upon by the estates. *By John Clowes,* 1648. 4°.* LT, EN; MH.

5 —Some seasonable and modest thoughts. [*Edinburgh*], *printed,* 1696. 4°.* ALDIS 3632.5. O, LG, LUG, AU, ES; CH, MH, NN, WF, Y.

6 [-]—[Anr. ed.] *Edinburgh, re-printed by George Mosman,* 1696. 4°.* ALDIS 3632. L, LUG, D, EN, ES; CH, CLC, NC, PU, WF, Y.

K., D. Cathedrall and conventuall churches. [n.p.], 1656. *See* King, Daniel.

K., D. H. Deepe groane. [n.p.], 1649. *See* King, Henry, *bp.*

6A **K., E.** That neither temporallities nor tyths. [*London*], *printed,* 1672. 4°. O, LLP, SP; WF.

7 Entry cancelled.

K., F. Counterfeit lady. 1673. *See* Kirkman, Francis.

—Leoline and Sydanis. 1642. *See* Kynaston, *Sir* Francis.

7A —A little grammar. *Hamburg, Georg König,* 1699. 8°. L.

8 —The present great interest both of king and people. [*London?* 1679.] cap., fol.* L, O, C, LL, MR, EN; CH, INU, MBA, MH, WF, Y.

—Unlucky citizen. 1673. *See* Kirkman, Francis.

K., G. Christian faith. Philadelphia. 1692. *See* Keith, George.

—Divine immediate revelation. 1684. *See* Keith, George.

—An essay for the discovery of some new geometrical problems. 1697. *See* Keith, George.

—False judgments. [n.p., 1692.] *See* Keith, George.

—Plain discovery of many. [n.p., 168–?] *See* Keith, George.

—Plain short catechism. Philadelphia, 1690. *See* Keith, George.

—Pretended antidote. Philadelphia, 1690. *See* Keith, George.

—Serious appeal. Philadelphia, 1692. *See* Keith, George.

9 Entry cancelled.

—Supplement to a late treatise. [n.p., 1697?] *See* Keith, George.

—Truths defence: or. 1682. *See* Keith, George.

K., H. Apocalyptical mysteries. 1667. *See* Knollys, Hanserd.

10 —An arrest on the East India privatier. [*London,* 1681.] 4°.* L, INDIA OFFICE, OJ, LSD; CSS, MH, WF.

—Exposition of the whole book. 1689. *See* Knollys, Hanserd.

—Monumenta Westmonasteriensia: or. 1682. *See* Keepe, Henry.

—Sermon preached before the kings. Oxford, 1643. *See* Killigrew, Henry.

10A **K., I.** A further evidence of the aforementioned Thomas Hewet. *For Thomas Simmons,* 1659. 4°.* L, LF; CH.

11 **K., J.** A catechisme for the times. *By G. Miller,* 1645. 8°.* LT, O, MR.

—Rational compendious way. [n.p.], 1674. *See* Keynes, John.

12 —A scripture catechisme very usefull. *By T. R. and E. M. for John Bellamie,* 1646. 8°.* LT, O; NU.

13 —Scripture security for conscience. *By T. R. and E. M. for John Bellamie,* 1646. 4°.* LT, O; CH, NU.

14 —A sermon preached before Sir Marmadvke Langdale. [*London*], *printed,* 1648. 4°.* L; CH, CLC, NU.

K., P. Elegy on the deplorable, and never enough. 1685. *See* Ker, Patrick.

—Flosculum poeticum. Poems. 1684. *See* Ker, Patrick.

—In illustrissimum, ac serenissimum Jacobum II. [*London,* 1685.] *See* Ker, Peter.

—Λογομαχια: or. 1690. *See* Ker, Patrick.

—Mournful elegy. 1685. *See* Ker, Patrick.

14A —Nomenclatura trilinguis. *For Benjamin Crayle; and George Conyers,* 1688. 8°. T.C.II 224. L, DUS, NOT.

15 ——Third edition. *For George Conyers,* 1697. 8°. T.C.III 39. NOT; MBC, WF.

15A —A poem on the coronation of James the II. *By George Croom.* 1685. brs. CH, MH, Y.

15B —Rudimenta grammatices. *Edinburgh, a society of stationers,* 1658. 8°. ALDIS 1583.5. EH.

15C ——[Anr. ed.] *Edinburgh, A. Anderson,* 1670. 12°. ALDIS 1913. EH.

16 ——[Anr. ed.] *By F. C. for Thomas Sawbridge,* 1686. 8°. O, C.

17 ——[Anr. ed.] *Glasguæ. Excudebat Robertus Sanders,* 1693. 8°.* ALDIS 3338. GU.

17A ——[Anr. ed.] *Edinburgh,* 1699. 12°. ALDIS 3902. A.

18 —The scholar's instructor. *For George Conyers,* [1700?]. 4°. L.

—Surfeit to A.B.C. 1656. *See* King, Philip.

K., R. Catena, sive. 1647. *See* King, Robert.

—God's sovereignty. 1688. *See* Kingston, Richard.

—True history of the several designs. 1698. *See* Kingston, Richard.

19   **K., S.** A true relation of the taking of the city of Yorke. *For Thomas Cooke, Sept.* 20, 1642. 4°.* LT, LIU.

20   **K., T.** The kitchin-physician. *For Samuel Lee,* 1680. 12°. T.C.I 370. L, O; CH, WSG.

21   —News from Yorke: sent. [*London,* 1643.] brs. LT.

22   [–] The Pope's pedigree. [*n.p.*], *printed,* 1664. 8°.* O.

—Royal sufferer. [*n.p.*], 1699. *See* Ken, Thomas, *bp.*

23   —Terrible newes from York. [*London*], *for Iohn Gee,* 1642. 4°.* LT, O, YM; MM.

—Veritas evangelica, or. 1687. *See* Kemeys, Thomas.

23A   **K., W.** The devil's last legacy. *Printed* 1642. 4°.* L, OW; CH.

—Dialogue between two friends. 1689. *See* Kennet, White, *bp.*

23B   —An English answer to the Scotch speech. *By T. N. for Edward Man,* 1668. 4°.* CCA, CT, MR; MM.

24   —Good news for England. *For Randal Taylor,* 1689. 4°.* L, C, EN.

25   —Letter from a gentleman to his friend, on the treaty. colop: *For J. Nutt,* 1700. brs. INU, MH.

26   Entry cancelled.

—Letter on George Keith's advertisement. 1697. *See title.*

26A   —Newes from Hereford. [*London*], *for F. Coles, T. Vere, and W. Gilbertson,* [1661]. brs. O.

—State of the Protestants. 1691. *See* King, William, *abp.*

26B   K. William and Q. Mary's kind iuvitation [*sic*] to London's triumph. *For T. B.,* 1689. PU.

27   K. William, or K. Lewis. Wherein is set forth the inevitable necessity. *For Ric. Chiswell.* 1689. 4°.* L, O, LVF, CT, EN, DT; CH, CN, MH, TU, WF, Y.

28   Ka mee, and I'le ka thee. [*London*], *printed,* 1649. 4°.* LVF, CT, ENC; CLC, IU, WF, Y.

28AA   **Kaiserstein, Salomon A.** . . . de Monarchie Jesuelitica. *Mense Octobri,* 1682. 8°. L; CN, IU, PL.

Kalendarium catholicum. [*n.p.*], 1686. *See* Almanacs. Blount, Thomas.

Kalendarium Julianum. [1666.] *See* Almanacs. B., G.

28A   Κατηχησις, . . . Catechismus. *Prostant apud Sam. Carr,* 1685. 12°. Y.

28B   —[Anr. ed.] —, 1686. 12°. PL.

29   Entry cancelled.

Κατηχησεις της Χριστιανικης πιστεως. *Cantabrigiæ,* 1648. *See* Catechesis.

29A   Ἡ κατηχησις της Χριστιανικης θρησκειας. *Typis Joannis Macock & impensis J. H.,* 1659. 8°. L, O, C, LW, AU, GU; NPT, NU, WF.

30   —[Anr. ed.] *Typis Joannis Macock,* 1660. 12°. O, C, E, SA.

30A   —[Anr. ed.] *Prostant venales,* 1698. 12°. O, EN; NU.

Τω καθολικω Stillingfleeton. Or. Bruges, 1672. *See* Canes, John Vincent.

31   **Kaye, Stephen.** Εισοπτρον του χριστιανισμου, or a discourse. *York: by Jo. White, for Robert Clarke,* 1686. 8°. T.C.II 155. LSC, YM; CLC, IU, WF.

32   **Kaye, William.** Baptism without bason. *By Ja. Cottrel, for Rich. Moon,* 1653. 4°. LT, O, LBU.

33   —The doctrine of our martyres remembred. *For Martha Harrison,* 1655. 4°.* LT.

34   —A free, plain, and just way concerning communion. [*London*], *printed,* 1655. 4°.* LT.

35   —God's gracious presence. *By J. Bell for Thomas Parkhurst,* 1655. 4°. L.

36   [–] —[Anr. ed.] —, 1658. 4°.* C; Y.

37   —Gods presence with the present government. *By T. Mabb, for R. Moon,* 1655. 4°.* Y.

38   —A plain answer to the eighteen quaeries. *For N:E:,* 1654. 4°. O, LF, CT, DT.

39   [–] The reformation, in which is reconciliation. *For M. I. to be sold by Toh.* [*sic*] *Parkhurst,* 1658. 8°. LT.

40   [–] The reformed protestant's catechism. *For M. I. to be sold by Tho. Parkhurst,* 1658. 8°. LT, RBC.

40A   —Satisfaction for all such as oppose reformation. *Yorke, by Tho. Broad, and to be sold by Nathanniel Brookes in London,* 1647. 4°.* CH, Y.

41   —Satisfaction for such as oppose reformation. *Printed at Yorke by Tho. Broad,* 1645. 4°.* YM.

42   —A tripartite remonstrance. *Printed at London, by J. C. for John Place,* 1657. 4°.* O, LLP, NE.

42A   —An united profession of faithfulness. *Printed at London, by James Cottrel,* 1657. brs. MM.

43   **Kea, James.** A sermon preached at Glascow. [*London?* 1680.] cap., fol.* ALDIS 2199.7. L, C, OC, EN, DT; CH, CN, MH, TU, WF, Y.

43A   **Keach, Benjamin.** An answer to Mr. Marlow's appendix. *For the author, and sold by John Hancock, and by the author,* 1691. 8°. L, ORP; MH, NHC, NU.

44   —Antichrist stormed. *For Nath. Crouch,* 1689. 12°. T.C.II 246. L, LCL; CH, CLC, MH, NHC, NU, TO, WF, Y.

45   [–] An appendix to the answer unto two Athenian mercuries. 1692. 4°. O; CH.

46   —The articles of the faith. *Printed,* 1697. 4°. ORP; NHC, NU.

47   —The ax laid to the root: . . . Part I. *For the author, to be sold by John Harris,* 1693. 4°. T.C.II 449. L, O, C, ORP; MH, MIU, NHC, NU, Y.

48   — —Part II. —, 1693. 4°. L, O, ORP; MH, MIU, NHC, NU, Y.

49   —The banquetting-house. *By J. A. for H. Barnard,* 1692. 12°. T.C.II 394. L.

50   —The breach repaired. *For the author, and sold by John Hancock, and by the author,* 1691. 8°. L, O, LW, ORP; CLC, CU, MH, NHC, NU, PPT, WF.

51   — —Second edition. *By John Marshall,* 1700. 8°. T.C.III 163. L, O, ORP, EN; NHC.

52   —A call to weeping. *For, and sold by John Marshall,* 1699. 8°. T.C.III 15. LCL, LF; NHC.

53   —Christ alone the way to Heaven. *Printed, and sold by Benja. Harris,* 1698. 8°. T.C.III 35. O, LCL, ORP; NHC, NU.

54   —A counter-antidote. *For H. Bernard,* 1694. 4°. L, O, C, ORP; CH, NHC, NU.

55   —The counterfeit Christian. *Printed, and are sold by John Pike; and by the author,* 1691. 4°. LW, ORP, MR; CH, MH, NHC, NU, Y.

56   Entry cancelled.
       [–] Covenant and catechism. 1700. *See* Jacob, Joseph.

57   [–] Darkness vanquished. 1675. 8°. LB, LCL.

58   —The display of glorious grace. *By S. Bridge, and sold by Mary Fabian: and William Marshall,* 1698. 8°. T.C.III 75. L, LCL, LW, MR, ENC; NHC, NU.

59   ——[Anr. ed.] *By S. Bridge, and sold by Mary Fabian: and Joseph Collier; and William Marshall,* 1698. 8°. ORP; MH, NHC, NU, WU, AVP.

60   —Distressed Sion relieved. *For Nath. Crouch,* 1689. 8°. T.C.II 253. L, O, BC, LLU, EN; CH, LC, MH, NHC, NU, WF, Y.

61   [–] An elegy on the death of that most laborious . . . John Norcot. *For Ben. Harris,* 1676. brs. L; MH.

62   —The everlasting covenant. *For H. Barnard,* 1693. 4°. L, LSC, LW, ORP, GU; CH, MH, NHC, NU, WF.

63   [–] A feast of fat things. *By B. H.,* 1696. 12°. L.

64   [–] The glorious lover. *By J. D. for Christopher Hussey,* 1679. 8°. T.C.I 350. L, LG, LVD, LLU; CH, MH, WF, Y.

64A   ——Second edition. *By F. L. for Christopher Hussey,* 1685. 8°. O, LW; CLC, NHC.

64B   ——Third edition. —, 1685. 12°. O, GU.

65   ——Fourth edition. *For Christopher Hussey,* 1696. 8°. T.C.II 594. L, LCL, A, EN; CH, LC, NC, NHC, NP.

66   —The glory of a true church. *Printed,* 1697. 12°. L, O, LG, ORP; MH, NHC, NU.

67   —God acknowledged. *For William Marshal, and John Marshal,* 1696. 4°.* T.C.II 585. L, O, LCL, LF; NHC.

68   —Gold refin'd. *For the author, and are to be sold by Nathaniel Crouch,* 1689. 8°. L, C; MH, NHC, NU.

69   —A golden mine opened. *Printed, and sold by the author, and William Marshall,* 1694. 8°. T.C.II 555. L, LCL, ENC; CH, MH, NHC, NU, WF.

70   ——[Anr. ed.] *For William Marshall,* 1694. 4°. MH.

70A   ——[Anr. ed.] *Printed, and sold by the author,* 1694. 8°. ORP.

71   —Golevni gwedi forri. *Ac ydynt ar werth gan William Marshal.* 1696. 8°. L, AN; Y.

72   [–] Grand impostor discovered. *For B. Harris,* 1675. 8°. T.C.I 221. O, C, LF; CH, MH, NHC, NU, PH, WF. (sometimes part of 103A.)

72A   —Instructions for children. *By Will. Bradford, New York,* 1695. MWA.

73   —The Jewish sabbath abrogated. *Printed and sold by John Marshall,* 1700. 8°. T.C.III 170. L, O, C, DU, EN; MH, NHC, NU, WF, Y.

73A   ——[Anr. ed.] *Printed and sold by William Marshall,* 1700. 8°. CLC.

74   [–] Laying on of hands. *Printed, and are to be sold by Benj. Harris,* 1698. 12°. L, LW; NU.

75   —Light broke forth in Wales. *Printed, and sold by William Marshal,* 1696. 8°. L, O, AN, MR, DT; CLC, MH, NU, WF, Y.

76   —The marrow of true justification. *For Dorman Newman,* 1692. 4°.* L, LW, ORP, E, EN, DT; CH, MH, NHC, NU, WF.

77   —A medium betwixt two extremes. *For Andrew Bell,* 1698. 4°. LW, ORP; NHC, NU.

78   Entry cancelled. *See following entry.*

79   [–] Pedo-baptism disproved. Second edition. *For the author, and sold by John Harris,* 1691. 4°.* ORP, MAB, EN; CH, MH, MIU, NHC, TO, WF.

80   [–] The progress of sin. *For John Dunton,* 1684. 12°. O, LF; CLC, IU, MH, NHC, NU, WF, Y.

80A   ——Second edition. —, 1684. 12°. T.C.II 118. Y.

81   Entry cancelled. Ghost.

82   ——Third edition. *For Nicholas Boddington,* 1700. 12°. T.C.III 204. L (lost); NN, PH.

83   Entry cancelled.
       [–] Protestant tutor. Boston, 1685. *See title.*

84   —The rector rectified. *Printed and sold by John Harris; and at the author's house, Southwark,* 1692. 16°. L, ORP; NHC, NU, TO, Y.

85   Entry cancelled.
       —Scripture metaphors. 1681. *See* Delaune, Thomas. Τροπολογια.

86   [–] A short confession of faith. *Printed,* 1697. 4°. L, O, ORP; NHC, NU, RBU.

87   [–] Sion in distress. *By George Larkin, for Enoch Prosser,* 1681. 8°. L, LCL, LVD, LW; CLC, MH, NHC, NU, WF, Y. (var.)

88   [–] —Second edition. —, 1681. 8°. L, O, A; CH, CN, NGT, NU, WF.

89   [–] — "Second" edition. —, 1682. 8°. L, O, DU, LLU, EN; CLC, IU, MH, NHC, WF, Y.

90   ——Third edition. *Boston in New-England, by S. G. for Samuel Philips,* 1683. 8°. EVANS 344. MWA.

91   ——"Third" edition. *Boston in New-England, by S. G. for Thomas Baker,* 1683. 8°. EVANS 345. CH, LC, MH, MWA, V.

92   [–] —[Anr. ed.] *For G. Larkin and J. How,* 1691. 12°. L; CLC.

92A   [–] —[Anr. ed.] *Printed,* 1692. 12°. L, O, ORP; CLC, CU, INU, MH, WF.

93   —Spiritual melody. *For John Hancock,* 1691. 12°. O, LCL, LF, ORP; LC, MBA, NHC.

94   —Spiritual songs. Second edition. *For John Marshal,* 1700. 12°. T.C.III 163. L, O, ORP.

95   —A summons to the grave. *For Ben. Harris,* 1676. 8°. T.C.I 244. LW; CLC, NHC, NU.

96   —The travels of sin. 1699. 8°. LCL.

97   [–] The travels of true godliness. *For John Dunton,* 1683. 8°. T.C.II 24. L (lost).

98   [–] —Third edition. —, 1684. 12°. O; NHC, NU, WF.

99   [–] —Fifth edition. —, 1684. 12°. LSC.

99A   [–] —Sixth edition. —, 1684. 12°. NHC.

100   ——Fourth edition. *By I. Dawks, for N. Boddington,* 1700. 12°. T.C.III 204. L (lost); NHC, PPT.
       —Τροπολογια: a key. 1682. *See* Delaune, Thomas.

101   [–]Τροποσχημαλογια: tropes and figures. *By J. D. for John Hancock, and Benj. Alsop,* 1682. fol. T.C.II 1. L, OW, CS, AN, P, ENC; CLC, IU, NPT, NU, TSM, WF, Y.

101A   ——[Anr. ed.] *By John Darby for the author,* 1682. fol. LW, LIU; CLC.

102   —A trumpet blown in Zion. *Printed,* 1694. 4°. L, ORP; NU.

103   [–] War with the devil. *For Benjamin Harris,* 1673. 8°. Y.

103AA   [–] —[Anr. ed.] —, 1674. 8°. T.C.I 147. Y.

103A   [–] —Third edition. —, 1675. 8°. L; NHC, WF.

104 [–]—Fourth edition. —, 1676. 8°. L, O, C, ORP; CLC, MB, MH, NHC, Y.

104A ——Fifth edition. —, 1678. 8°. T.C.I 305. L; OCI.

105 [–]—Seventh edition. —, 1683. 8°. L, C; CH, CN, LC, NC, Y.

106 [–]—Eighth edition. —, 1684. 8°. L; CH, CLC, IU, MIU, NU.

106A ——"Eighth" edition. *For S. Harris, to be sold by Peter Parker,* 1691. 8°. T.C.II 416. LW; Y.

106B ——Tenth edition. *Printed and sold by B. Harris,* 1700. 8°. L, C; Y.

107 ——[Anr. ed.] *Belfast, by Patrick Neill & company,* 1700. 12°. O, BLH, DN.

108 [–] Zion in distress: or, the sad and lamentable complaint. *Printed,* [1670]. 8°. Y.

108A **Keach, Elias.** A banquetting-house. *By Benja. Harris for the author,* 1696. 12°. L, ORP; NHC.

108B —A discourse of the nature and excellence of . . . patience. *For the author, and sold by John Marshall,* 1699. 8°. ORP.

109 —The glory and ornament. *Printed,* 1697. 12°. L; NHC, RBU.

110 —A plain and familiar discourse on justification. *For John Harris,* 1694. 4°.* L, O, C.

111–2 Entries cancelled.

[**Kearnie, P.**] By the generall assemblie of the confederate Catholics. Kilkenny, 1646. *See* Ireland.

113 **Keble, Joseph.** An assistance to justices of the peace. *By W. Rawlins, S. Roycroft, and H. Sawbridge, assigns of Richard and Edward Atkins; for Tho. Dring,* 1683. fol. O, C, LL, LMT, EN; CLC, LC, NCD, NCL, PUL, YL.

113A ——[Anr. ed.] *By W. Rawlins, S. Roycroft, and H. Sawbridge, assigns of Richard and Edward Atkins, for Ch. Harper,* 1683. fol. L, DUS, NOT, WCA; CLL, LC, MHL.

113B ——[Anr. ed.] *By W. Rawlins, S. Roycroft, and H. Sawbridge assigns of Richard and Edward Atkins; for Samuel Keble,* 1683. fol. OC, BR, NL, RU; KU, YL.

114 ——[Anr. ed.] *By W. Rawlins, S. Roycroft, and H. Sawbridge, assigns of Richard and Edward Atkins, for Tho. Dring, Cha. Harper, and Sam Keble,* 1689. T.C.II 4. fol. L, BP, FONMON; MHL, MIU, NIC, PU, WF.

115 —An explanation of the laws against recusants, . . . abridged. *For Samuel Keble,* 1681. 8°. T.C.I 450. L, O, CJ, DU, RU; BN, CB, CH, MHL, NCL, WF.

116 —Reports in the court of King's Bench. *By W. Rawlins, S. Roycroft and M. Flesher, assigns of Richard and Edward Atkins, for Thomas Dring, Charles Harper, Samuel Keble, and William Freeman,* 1685. fol. T.C.II 136. L, O, C, LGI, LL, MC, DT; KT, MHL, NCL, NR, V, AVP.

117–120 Entries cancelled.

—Statutes at large. 1676. *See* England. Laws.

121 **Keble, Samuel.** An account of the several impressions. [*London,* 1693.] fol.* O, EN.

121A —A catalogue of some books, printed for. *For Samuel Keble,* [1700?]. brs. L.

121B [–] Restitution to the royal authour. *For Samuel Keble,* 1691. fol.* T.C.II 370. L, OC, CS, LIC, E; CH, IU, MH, NU, WF, Y.

122 [**Keck, Sir Anthony.**] Cases argued and decreed in the high court of chancery. *By the assigns of Rich. and Edw. Atkins, for John Walthoe,* 1697. fol. T.C.III 4. L, LL, BAMB, LLU, DT; CH, IU, LC, NP, WF, Y.

123 **Keckermann, Bartholomæus.** Systema compendiosum. *Oxonii, excudebat Gulielmus Hall pro Francisco Oxlad,* 1661. 8°. MADAN 2560. O, C, OC, CT, GU; BN, CH, CLC, IU, MB, NC, Y.

Kedarminster-stuff. 1681. *See* Browne, John.

124 [**Keeling, Josias.**] The Queenes proceedings in Holland. *Decemb. 30, by T. F. for I. M.,* 1642. 4°.* LT, MR, SP; HR, CH, CN, MH.

Keepe thy head. 1641. *See* Lookes, John.

124A [**Keepe, Henry.**] The genealogies of the high-born prince. [*London*], *by N. Thompson,* 1684. 8°. O, MC, SP; CH, CLC, WF, Y.

125 —By Henry Keepe, . . . Having in the year 1681. published. [*n.p.,* 1683.] brs. O.

126 [–] Monumenta Westmonasteriensia: or an historical account. *For C. Wilkinson and T. Dring,* 1682. 8°. T.C.I 494. L, O, C, MR, EN, CD; CH, CN, LC, MH, TU, Y.

127 [–] —[Anr. ed.] —, 1683. 8°. L, O, C, BAMB; BN, CH, CLC, IU, NCD, OLU, TU, Y.

128 —A true and perfect narrative of . . . finding the crucifix. *By J. B. to be sold by Randal Taylor,* 1688. 4°.* L, O, LIL, OBL, DU, MC; CH, CLC, IU, MH, TU, WF, Y.

129 The keepers of the liberties of England by authority of Parliament, . . . whereas at the Gaol-delivery. [*London,* 1653.] brs. LT.

130 —whereas at the generall quarter sessions. [*London,* 1653.] brs. LT.

131 [**Keill, James.**] The anatomy of the humane body abridged. *For William Keblewhite,* 1698. 12°. T.C.III 102. L, LCP, OM, CT, DT; CH, CLM, OLU, TU, WF.

132 **Keill, John.** An examination of Dr. Burnet's theory of the earth. *Oxford, at the Theater,* 1698. 8°. T.C.III 66. L, O, C, EN, DT; BN, CH, CJC, MH, NU, WF, Y.

133 —An examination of the reflections. *Oxford, at the Theater for Henry Clemens,* 1699. 8°. L, O, C, EN, DT; CH, CSU, MH, WF.

134 **Keilwey, Robert.** Reports d'ascuns cases. Third edition. *For Charles Harper, William Crooke and Richard Tonson,* 1688. fol. T.C.II 216. L, O, C, EN, DT; CLL, LC, MHL, NCL, V, YL, AVP.

135 **Keith, George.** Mr. George Keith's account of a national church. *Printed,* 1700. 4°.* L, O, LF, SP, BLH; CH, MH, PH, PSC, RPJ.

136 [–] An account of the great divisions, amongst the Quakers. *Printed for, to be sold, by John Gwillim, and Rich. Baldwin,* 1692. 4°.* L, O, C, LF, GU; CH, LC, MH, MU, PH, RPJ, Y.

137 —An account of the Quakers politicks. *By W. Redmayne for Brab. Aylmer and Charles Brome,* 1700. 4°.* L, O, C, LCF, LF, BBN, MR, SP; PH, PSC, RPJ, WF, Y.

137A —Advertisement . . . [for 11 January]. [*London*], 1700. brs. OC.

137B —An advertisement of a meeting. [*London*, 1696.] cap., 4°.* oc.

137C —An advertisement of an intended meeting. [*London*, 1697.] brs. c; NN.

138 —The Anti-Christs and Sadducees. *For the author*, [1696]. 4°.* L, O, C, LF, AU; CH, LC, MU, PHS, RPJ.

138A —Antwoord op elf vragen, . . . An answer to eleven questions. *Rotterdam*, 1680. 4°.* L, LF.

139 [–] An appeal from the twenty-eight judges. [*Philadelphia*, *by William Bradford*, 1692.] brs. EVANS 597. LF; FRIENDS LIB., PHILA.

140 [–] —Second edition. [—, 1692.] 4°.* EVANS 598. PHS.

141 [–] —Third edition. [—, 1692.] cap., 4°.* EVANS 599. CH, LC, PHS.

142 —The arguments of the Quakers. *For C. Brome*, 1698. 4°. T.C.III 63. L, O, C, LF, CT, AU; CH, LC, MH, NU, PH, RPJ, Y.

143 —The arraignment of worldly philosophy. *For R. Levis*, 1694. 4°.* O, LF, EN; CLC, PH, PSC, RPJ, Y.

144 —The benefit, advantage and glory of silent meetings. *Printed*, 1670. 4°.* L, LF, LLP, MR, EN; CH, MH, PH, PSC, RPJ, Y.

145 — —[Anr. ed.] *Printed, by Andrew Sowle*, 1687. 4°.* L, O, LF, BBN; LC, MU, NU, PH, PSC, RPJ.

146-7 Entries cancelled. Ghosts.

148 —Bristol Quakerism expos'd. *For John Gwillim*, 1700. 4°.* L, O, C, LF, LLP, BAMB, BR; CH, PHS, PSC.

149 —The causeless ground of surmises. colop: *For R. Levis*, 1694. cap., 4°.* L, O, LF, GU; PHS, RPJ, WCL.

150 —A Christian catechisme. *For Brabazon Aylmer*, 1698. 8°. T.C.III 90. L, O, C, LF, LW; CH, MH, PH, PSC, WF, Y.

150A [–] The Christian faith and profession of the . . . Quakers. [*London?* 1694.] brs. CT.

151 [–] The Christian faith of the people of God. *Printed and sold by William Bradford, at Philadelphia*, 1692. 4°.* EVANS 600. LC, MWA, PHS, RPJ, V.

152 Entry cancelled. Ghost.

153 —The Christian Quaker. *Printed in Pensilvania, and re-printed in London, for Benjamin [i.e. Elias] Keach, to be sold by him; and John Harris*, 1693. 4°.* L, O, LF, LW, BBN; LC, MB, MU, PHS, RPJ, WCL.

154 [–] A chronological account of the several ages of the vvorld. [*New York*], *printed*, 1694. 4°.* EVANS 691. L, O, LF; CH, MWA, PHS, RPJ, V.

155 —George Keith's complaint against the Quakers. *Printed and sold by the booksellers of London and Westminster*, 1700. 4°. L, LF, NE.

156 —The deism of William Penn. *For Brab. Aylmer*, 1699. 8°. T.C.III 122. L, O, C, LF, BBN, DT; CH, LC, MU, PH, PSC, RPJ, Y.

157 —A discovery of the mystery of iniquity. [*Philadelphia*, *by William Bradford*, 1692.] 4°.* EVANS 602. O, BAMB; CH, PHS.

157A [–] Divine immediate revelation. *Printed*, 1684. 8°. LF, MR; MH, PH, PSC, RPJ, TU.

158 [–] —Second part. Second edition. 1685. 8°. O.

159 [–] —Second part. *Printed*, 1684. 8°. RPJ.

160 [–] An essay for the discovery of some new geometrical problems. *Printed 1697, and are to be sold by the author; and by B. Aylmer.* 4°.* LW, OC, AU; Y.

161 —An exact narrative of the proceedings. *For B. Aylmer, and J. Dunton*, 1696. 4°. T.C.II 587. L, O, C, LF, AU, DT; CLC, CN, LC, MH, PH, RPJ, Y.

162 [–] An exhortation & caution to friends concerning buy-ing or keeping of negroes. [*New-York: by William Bradford*, 1693.] 4°.* EVANS 636. LF; CH, WF.

163 —George Keith's explications. *For B. Aylmer, and Rich. Baldwin, and are to be sold by the author*, 1697. 4°.* L, O, LF, MR, GU; CH, MH, PH, PSC.

164 [–] False judgments reprehended. [*Philadelphia, by William Bradford*, 1692.] 4°.* EVANS 611. LC, MU, PHS, RPJ.

165 —Mr. George Keith's farewel sermon. *For the author*; 1700. 4°.* L, O, LF, LG, MR, EN; MH, PH, PSC, WF, Y.

166 [–] A farther account of the great divisions. *For J. Dunton*, 1693. 4°.* L, O, C, LF, GU; CH, LC, MU, PH, PHS, TU.

167 —George Keith's fourth narrative. *For Brabazon Aylmer*, 1700. 4°. T.C.III 181. L, O, C, LF, CT, AU; CLC, CN, LC, MH, NU, PH, RPJ, Y.

168 —The fundamental truths of Christianity. *Printed*, 1688. 8°.* L, C, LF, LW, LLP; CH, NU, PH, PSC, RPJ, WF, Y.

169 — —[Anr. ed.] *Printed at London, 1688, and re-printed at Philadelphia by William Bradford*, 1692. 4°.* EVANS 603. LC, PH, FRIENDS LIB., PHILA.

170 [–] A further discovery of the spirit of falshood. colop: *For R. Levis*, 1694. cap., 4°. L, O, LF, BAMB; CH, INU, PH, PHS, RPJ.

171 [–] A general epistle to Friends. [*Aberdeen?*], *printed*, 1671. 4°.* ALDIS 1923.4. L, O, LF, CT, BBN; CLC, LC, MH, MU, PH, Y.

171A —The great doctrine of Christ crucified. *For Nath. Crouch*, 1694. 8°. T.C.II 518. C, LSC, OC; PH.

172 —Gross error and hypocrisie detected. *For Walter Kettilby*, 1695. 4°.* L, O, LF, CT, BBN, AU; CLC, MH, PH, PSC, RPJ, Y.

173 —Help in time of need. [*Aberdeen*], *printed*, 1665. 4°. ALDIS 1793. L, O, LF, BBN, AU; CH, MH, PH, RPJ, Y.

174 —The heresie and hatred. *Printed and sold by William Bradford at Philadelphia*, 1693. 4°.* EVANS 641. O, LF; CH, LC, MWA, PHS, RPJ.

175 —Immediate revelation. [*Aberdeen*], *printed*, 1668. 4°. ALDIS 1843. L, O, LF, MR, GU, EN; CH, MH, PH, PSC, RPJ, Y.

176 — —Second edition. [*London*], *printed*, 1675. 8°. L, C, LF, P; BN, CLC, LC, NU, PH, RPJ, WF, Y.

177 — —"Second" edition. [*London*], *printed*, 1676. 8°. L, RPL; CLC, LC, MH, NU, PH, RPJ, WSC.

178 [–] A just vindication of my earnest expostulation. colop: *By J. Bradford*, 1696. cap., 4°.* O; CH, NN.

179 —The light of truth. [*London*], *printed*, 1670. 4°.* C, LF, OC, BBN, MR; CH, MH, MU, PH, RPJ, Y.

180 —A looking-glass for all those. *Printed*, 1674. 8°.* L, LF; NN, PH, PHS.

181 [–] A loving epistle to all the moderate. [*London?* 1694.] 4°.* LF.

182 —More divisions. *First printed beyond sea, and now reprinted, and are to be sold by Richard Baldwin*, 1693. 4°.* T.C.II 474. L, O, LF, OC, GU; CH, LC, NN, PH, RPJ, WCL.

183 Entry cancelled.
—More work for. 1696. *See* Penn, William.

184 —A narrative of the proceedings of . . . at Coopers Hall. *For the author*, 1700. 8°. CT.

185 —[Anr. ed.] *For J. Gwillim*, 1700. 4°.* L, O, LF, LLP, BAMB; MH, PH, PSC, RPJ.

186 —New-England's spirit of persecution transmitted to Pennsilvania. [*Philadelphia*], *printed* [*by William Bradford*], 1693. 4°.* EVANS 642. O, LF, CT, BAMB, EN; MWA, NN, PHS, RPJ, V.

187 [–] A plain discovery of many gross cheats. [*London*, 168–?] cap., 4°.* L.

188 [–] A plain short catechism. *Printed and sold by William Bradford at Philadelphia*, 1690. 8°. EVANS 514. LF, BBN; PHS.

189 —The plea of the innocent. [*Philadelphia, by William Bradford*, 1692.] 4°.* EVANS 612. C, LF; CH, INU, LC, MWA, PHS.

190 —The Presbyterian and independent visible churches. *Philadelphia, printed and sold by Will. Bradford*, 1689. 8°. EVANS 472. LF; CH, LC, MB, MHS, NN, PHS.

191 ——[Anr. ed.] *For Thomas Northcott*, 1691. 8°. L, O, LCL, LF, MR; CH, CN, LC, MH, NU, PH, RPJ, Y.

192 [–] The pretended antidote proved poyson. *Philadelphia, by Will. Bradford*, 1690. 8°. EVANS 515. LF, MB, MWA, PL.

192A [–] —[Anr. ed., "antidoe."] —, 1690. 8°. LC, RPJ.

193 [–] The pretended yearly meeting of the Quakers. [*London*], *for R. Levis*, 1695. 4°.* O, LF, LLP, CT, BAMB; LC, MWA, NN, PHS, RPJ.

194 —Quakerism no popery. [*London*], *printed*, 1675. 8°. C, LF, MR, AU; BN, MB, MH, PH, PHS, PSC.

195 —The Quakers creed. colop: *For Jonathan Robinson*, [1678?]. cap., 4°.* L, O.

196 —The Quakers proved apostats. colop: *For Brabazon Aylmer, and Charles Brome*, 1700. 4°.* O, LF, LLP, NE; PL, RPJ, WF.

197 No entry.
—Mr. George Keith's reasons for renouncing Quakerism. 1700. *See* title.

198 —The rector corrected. *Printed*, 1680. 8°. O, C, LF, AU; BN, CH, LC, NCD, NHC, NU, PH, RPJ, Y.

199 —A refutation of three opposers. *Philadelphia, printed and sold by William Bradford*, 1690. 8°. EVANS 516. LF; MWA, PRF.

200 No entry.

201 [–] A rod for Trepidantium Malleus. *Printed, and sold by M. Fabian*, 1700. 4°.* L, O, LW, SP; WF.

202 —A salutation of dear and tender love. [*Aberdeen*], *printed*, 1665. 4°.* L, O, LF, BBN, AU, EN; PH, PHS, RPJ.

203 —A seasonable information and caveat. *For R. Levis*, 1694. 4°.* O, C, LF, OC, BAMB; LC, PH, PSC, RPJ.

204 —A second narrative. *For B. Aylmer*, 1697. 4°.* T.C.III 21. L, O, C, AU, GU; CH, LC, MU, PH, RPJ, Y.

205 [–] A serious appeal to all the more sober, impartial & judicious people in New-England. *Printed and sold by William Bradford at Philadelphia*, 1692. 4°. EVANS 605. LF; CH, MWA, PHS, PRF.

206 —A serious call to the Quakers. *For W. Haws*, 1700. fol. L, O, LF, OC.

206A ——Second edition. [*London*], *sold by B. Aylmer, and C. Brome*, 1700. brs. L, O, LF, LG, OC, CS, MR; PH, TSM.

206B [–] —[Anr. ed.] *Dublin, re-printed*, 1700. 4°.* DT; Y.

207 [–] A serious dialogue betwixt a church-man and a Quaker. *For Brab. Aylmer*, 1699. 8°.* O, C, LF, SP, CD; MH, PH, PSC, RPJ, WF, Y.

208 —A sermon preached at the meeting . . . 16th of the second month, 1696. *For B. Aylmer*, 1696. 4°.* T.C.II 576. O, C, LF, CT, SP, CD; MH, NU, PH, PSC, RPJ, WF, Y.

209 —A sermon preach'd at Turners-hall . . . the 5th. of May, 1700. *By W. Bowyer, for Brab. Aylmer, and Char.* [*sic.*] *Brome*, 1700. 4°.* T.C.III 195. L, O, C, LF, GM; CLC, IU, MH, NU, RPJ, WF, Y.

209A ——Second edition. —, 1700. 4°.* O, LF, CD; LC, PH, PSC, RPJ, TU.

210 —Mr Keith's sermon, preach'd on May the 12th, 1700. *For the author*, 1700. 4°.* L, O, LLP, EN, AU; RPJ.

211 —A sermon preach'd . . . May the 19th, 1700. *For J. Gwillim*, 1700. 4°.* L, O, LF, LSD, NE; CH, MH, PH, RPJ, WF, Y.

212 —A short Christian catechisme. *For Brabazon Aylmer*, [1698]. 8°.* T.C.III 105. O, C, LF, OC, BC; CH, MH, WF.

213 [–] Some of the fundamental truths of Christianity. Third edition. [*Philadelphia, by William Bradford*, 1692.] 4°.* LC, PHS, RPJ.

214 —Some of the many fallacies of William Penn. *For Benj. Tooke*, 1699. 8°.* T.C.III 120. O, LF, LLP, OC; PSC, Y.
[–] Some of the Quakers principles. 1693. *See* Bugg, Francis.

215 [–] Some reasons and causes of the late seperation [*sic*]. [*Philadelphia, by William Bradford*, 1692.] 4°.* EVANS 606. L, LF, BBN; CH, IE, LC, MWA, PHS, RPJ. (var.)

216 —Sophistry detected. *Bristol, printed and sold by W. Bonny*, 1699. 4°. O.

216A —A supplement to a late treatise called An essay. colop: *for the author*, [1697?]. 4°.* L, O, OC.

217 —A testimony against that false & absurd opinion. [*Philadelphia, by William Bradford*, 1692.] 4°.* EVANS 607. LF; CH, LC, MWA, PHS, PRF.

218 —A third narrative. *For C. Brome*, 1698. 4°. T.C.III 63. L, O, CT, BBN, AU; CLC, CN, LC, MH, PH, RPJ, Y.

219 —A true Christ owned. [*London*], *printed*, 1679. 8°. LF, MR, EN; CH, MWA, NHC, NU, PH, PSC.

220 —The true copy of a paper. *For R. Levis*, 1695. 4°.* O, LF, LLP, CT, BAMB; LC, PH, PHS, RPJ, Y.

221 Entry cancelled.
—True copy of three judgments. [*Philadelphia*, 1692.] *See* Budd, Thomas.

222 —A true relation of a conference. *For Brab. Aylmer*, 1699. 4°. L, O, C, LF, LLP, BR; INU, IU, PH.

223 —Truth advanced. [*New York*], *printed* [*by William Brad-ford*], 1694. 4°. L, O, C, LF, LLP; CH, MWA, NHS, PHS, RPJ.

224 —Truth and innocency defended. [*Philadelphia, by William Bradford, 1692.*] cap., 4°.* EVANS 609. LF; CH, LC, MH, MWA, PHS, RPJ.

225 [–] Truths defence: or. *For Benjamin Clark, 1682.* 8°. L, LF, DU, MR, E; CH, LC, NHC, NU, PH, RPJ, Y.

226 —Two sermons. *By W. Bowyer, for Brab. Aylmer, and Char.* [*sic*] *Brome, 1700.* 4°.* L, O, C, EN, CD; CH, MH, MU, PH, RPJ, TU, Y.

227 ——Second edition. —, 1700. 4°.* T.C.III 195. L, C, LF, LW, CS; CH, NP, RPJ, WF.

228 —The universall free grace of the gospell. [*Holland*], *printed*, 1671. 4°. L, O, C, BBN, EN; BN, CH, LC, MH, MU, Y.

229 —George Keith's vindication. [*London*], *printed*, 1674. 8°.* L, LF, OC; MWA, PH, PHS.

230 [–] A vision concerning the mischievous seperation among friends. *Printed and sold by Will. Bradford at Philadelphia, 1692.* 4°.* EVANS 610. L, LF, BBN; CH, LC, MWA, PHS, RPJ.

231–2 Entries cancelled. *See following entry.*

233 ——[Anr. ed.] colop: [*Aberdeen*], *printed*, 1677. 8°. ALDIS 2101. L, O, LF, LW, AU, ENC; BN, CH, LC, MH, NU, PH, PSC, RPJ, Y.

234 Entry cancelled. *See preceding entry.*

235 —The way to the city of God described. [*Aberdeen*], *printed*, 1678. 8°. L, O, C, LF, DU, AU; CH, LC, MH, NU, PH, PSC, RPJ, Y.

236 —The woman-preacher of Samaria. [*London*], *printed*, 1674. 4°.* L, O, LF, BBN, SP; BN, CLC, LC, MH, MU, PH, RPJ.

237 **Keith, Robert.** Theses philosophicæ. *Abredeis, excudebat Ioannes Forbesius, 1687.* 4°.* ALDIS 2724. L, O.

Kekatihw, Drawde, *pseud.* See Whitaker, Edward.

Kellet, Joseph. Faithful discovery. 1653. See Feake, Christopher.

237A **Kellett.** Mr. Kelletts case with the society of Clements-Inn. *For Rich. Baldwin, 1682.* fol.* DCH, EN.

238 **Kellett, Edward.** Tricœnium Christi, . . . The three-fold supper of Christ. *By Thomas Cotes for Andrew Crooke, 1641.* fol. L, O, C, LI, DC, LNC; BN, NGT, NU, TO, WF.

238A **Kellie, Alexander.** Truths plea for infants. *By T. R., sold by Nath. Brooks, 1656.* 4°. L.

239 **Kellison, Matthew.** A deuout paraphrase on the 50th Psalme. *Printed at Paris, 1655.* 8°. LT; TU.

239A ——[Anr. ed.] *For Henry Herringman, 1655.* 8°. CLC.

240–246 Entries cancelled.

[–] Touchstone of the reformed gospel. 1652. See Heigham, John.

246A **Kelsall, John.** A testimony against gaming. 1682. brs. LF.

246B ——[Anr. ed.] *Reprinted by John Bringhurst,* [1682?]. brs. LF.

246C ——[Anr. ed.] *By T. Sowle, 1696.* brs. LF.

247 **Kelsey, Joseph.** Christ crucified. A sermon. *For Walter Kettilby, 1691.* 4°.* T.C.II 377. L, O, C, BAMB, EN; CH, CLC, IU, MH, TU, WF, Y.

248 —Μελχισεδεκ. Concio. *Impensis Gualteri Kettilby, 1691.* 4°.* T.C.II 360. L, O, CT, BAMB, YM; CH, IU, Y.

249 —A sermon preached . . . 25th of September, 1673. *For Jonathan Edwin, 1674.* 4°.* T.C.I 161. L, O, C, MR, D; CH, MIU, NU, TU, WF, Y.

250 **Kem, Samuel.** The King of Kings His privie marks. *For John Field, May 4, 1646.* 4°.* LT, CS, BR, DT; CH, CLC, IU, MH, MM, WF.

251 —King Solomon's infallible expedient. *By J S. for G. Sawbridge, 1660.* 4°.* LT, O, OC, BLH.

252 —The messengers preparation for an address. *By Robert Austin, 1644.* 4°.* MADAN 1696. LT, O, CT, YM, DT; CH, CN, MH, NU, TU, WF, Y. (var.)

253 —An olive branch. *By J. D. & R. I. for Andrew Kembe, 1647.* 4°.* LT, O, CS, YM; CH, IU, MH, MM, NU, WF, Y.

254 —Orders given out; the word, stand fast. *By I. M. for Michael Spark, 1647.* 4°.* LT, O, OC, CS, BR, P; CH, NGT, WF, Y.

255 —A sermon preached before the commissioners. *For R. Austin, 1646.* 4°.* LT, O, BLH, DT; CH, MH, NU, WF.

256 **K[emeys], T[homas].** Veritas evangelica, or the gospel-truth. *By Nat. Thompson, 1687.* 4°. L, O, CS, E, DT; CLC, CN, MH, NU, WF, Y.

257 **K[emp], Mrs. A[nne].** A contemplation on Bassets down-hill. [*Oxford, by H. Hall, 1658?*] brs. MADAN 2392. O.

258 **Kemp, Edward.** Reasons for the sole use of the churches prayers. *Cambridge, by John Field, 1668, to be sold by Edward Story in Cambridge.* 4°.* L, O, C, BP, EC; CLC, NU, WF, Y.

259 —A sermon preached . . . September the 6. 1668. *Cambridge, by John Field, 1668. To be sold by Edward Story.* 4°. L, O, C, CT, DU, DT; CH, NGT, TSM, WF.

260 **Kemp, W[illiam].** A brief treatise of the nature . . . of the pestilence. *Printed for, and are to be sold by D. Kemp, 1665.* 4°. L, O, C, MAU, GH; CH, MH, NN, PL, WF, Y.

Kempis, Thomas á. See Thomas á Kempis.

260A **[Ken, Thomas], bp.** Directions for prayer. [*London, for Charles Brome, 1686.*] cap., 8°.* T.C.II 156. L, LLP, CS, EN; CDA, MH, NCD, WF, Y.

260B —Esponiad ar gatechism. *Rhydnchen, 1688.* 8°. AN.

261 [–] An exposition on the church-catechism. *For Charles Brome; and William Clarke, in Winchester, 1685.* 8°. L, O, OC, CT, BC; CH, IU, MB, NC, NR, WF, Y.

262 [–] —[Anr. ed.] —, 1686. 8°. L, O, C, LSD, DT; CH, CSB, IU, NU, TU, WF.

263 [–] —[Anr. ed.] *London, for Charles Brome and William Clarke in Winchester, 1685. Boston in New-England, re-printed by Richard Pierce, 1688.* 4°. EVANS 445. CH, MB, MWA, V.

264 [–] —[Anr. ed.] *For Charles Brome; and William Clarke, 1696.* 8°. L, C, CS, LIU; IU, NP, WF.

264A [–?] Ichabod: or, five groans. *Cambridge, for J. Greaves, 1663.* 4°. L, O, CT, DU, EN, DT; CH, MBP, MH, NU, WF, Y.

264B [–?] —[Anr. ed.] *For J. Harris, 1691.* 4°.* T.C.II 345. L, O, C, CT, BAMB, DT; CH, TO.

264C [–] Lacrymæ ecclesiæ Anglicanæ: or, a serious and passionate address. [*London*], *printed*, 1689. 4°. L, O, C, LSD, YM, DT; CH, IU, MH, NU, WF.

265 [–] A letter to the author of a sermon, entitled, A sermon preach'd at the funeral of Her late Majesty. [London, 1695.] 4°.* L, O, C, OC, MR, DT; CH, CN, NU, WF, Y.

266 [–] A manual of prayers for . . . Winchester College. For John Martyn, 1674. 8°. T.C.I 168. L, OC, CT; CH, MH, UCLA.

267 [–] —[Anr. ed.] —, 1675. 8°. L, O, C.

268 [–] —[Anr. ed.] —, 1677. 8°. L, SP.

269 [–] —[Anr. ed.] —, 1679. 8°. O; IU.

270 [–] —[Anr. ed.] For Henry Brome, and William Clarke, 1681. 8°. T.C.I 447. L, LLP; CH.

271 Entry cancelled.
     [–] —[Anr. ed.] Paris, 1682. See Manual of prayers and litanies.

271A [–] —Sixth edition. For W. Abington, and W. Clarke in Winchester, 1684. 12°. LLU; MH.

271B [–] —[Anr. ed.] Paris, 1685. 12°. GU.

272 Entry cancelled.
     [–] —[Anr. ed.] 1686. See Manual of prayers and other Christian devotions.

273 [–] —"Sixth" edition. London, for Charles Brome, and Will. Clark in Winchester, 1687. 12°. L, OC; WF.

273A [–] —[Anr. ed.] For Charles Brome, and are to be sold by Tho. Bennet, 1687. 12°. C; Y.

274 [–] —Seventh edition. For Charles Brome, and Will. Clark in Winchester, 1692. 12°. T.C.II 529. L, O; CH.

274AA [–] —[Anr. ed.] For Charles Brome, [1695?]. 12°. NNM.

274A [–] —[Anr. ed.] For Charles Brome, 1697. 12°. T.C.II 607. L; CLC, MB, WF, Y.

275 [–] —"Second" edition. For A. Bettesworth, 1700. 12°. T.C.III 221. L, LW, RPL, DT.

275A —[Anr. ed.] For Charles Brome, 1700. 12°. L.

276 —A pastoral letter from. London, for Charles Brome, and W. Clark, in Winchester, 1688. 4°.* T.C.II 222. L, O, C, BR, EN, CD; CH, MH, NU, WF, Y.

276A [–] —[Anr. ed.] London, for C. Brome, 1688, reprinted 1692. brs. OP, EN.

277 [–] Prayers for the use of all persons who come to the Bath. For C. Brome, 1692. 12°. T.C.II 418. L, O, BR; CH, MMO, TU.

278 [–] The royal sufferer. [n.p.], printed, 1699. 8°. L, O, C, CM, NE; CLC, CN, Y.

279 —A sermon preached . . . 30th of June, 1682. London, by M. Flesher, for Joanna Brome; and William Clarke in Winchester, 1682. 4°.* T.C.II 227. L, O, C, BR, YM; CH, IU, NU, V, WF, WSC, Y.

280 —Third edition. London, for Charles Brome; and William Clarke in Winchester, 1688. 4°.* L, BR; CH, RBU, WF.

280A [–] All glory be to God. Reverend brother, the time of Lent. [London, 1687.] cap., 4°.* CS.

281 —All glory be to God. Sir, His Majesty in these His letters patents. [n.p.], 1686. brs. O, BR.

281aA —All glory be to God. Thomas unworthy bishop. For Charles Brome, 1685. 4°. C.

281bA —[Anr. ed.] —, 1688. 4°. O, BR; IU, MH.

281cA —Three hymns. For C. Broome, 1700. 8°.* EN.

281dA —To the poor inhabitants within the diocese of Bath. [London? 1686.] cap., 8°. OC.

281A Kendal, John. Χρονομετρια or, the measure of time. By J. Playford for C. Hussey, 1684. 8°. T.C.II 44. L, O, CT, GU; CLC, NC, NN, WF, Y.

Kendal, Roger. Ephemeris. 1700. See Almanacs.

282 Kendall, George, clerk. The clerk of the surveigh surveighed. [London], for the author, 1656. 4°.* L.

282A —A reply to a paper called, Mr. Haywards answer. For the author G. Kendal, 1656. 4°. PL.

283 Kendall, George, M.A. An appendix to The unlearned alchimist. For Joseph Leigh, to be sold at his shop and by the author, [1664?]. 8°. L, C, E; CRN, MBM, MH, WF, WU.

284 Kendall, George, D.D. Fur pro tribunali. Oxoniæ, excudebat Hen. Hall, impensis Tho. Robinson, 1657. 8°. MADAN 2344. LT, O, C, BC, SC; BN, NN, NP, NU, Y.

285 — —[Anr. ed.] Oxoniæ, 1662. 16°. LCL.

286 —Sancti sanciti. Or, the common doctrine. By Tho. Ratcliffe, and Edw. Mottershed, 1654. fol. L, O, C, EN, DT; IEG, MB, MH, NU, WF, Y.

287 —Θεοκρατια: or, a vindication. By Tho: Ratcliffe and Edw. Mottershed, 1653. fol. L, O, C, E, DT; CH, IU, MH, NP, NU, WF.

288 Entry cancelled.
     —Verdict in the case depending. 1654. See Howe, Obadiah. Pagan preacher.

288A Kendall, Nicholas. A sermon preached . . . 18 March, 1685. For R. Royston; sold by Geo. May, Exeter, 1686. 4°. T.C.II 165. WF.

289 Kenmuir, John, Viscount. Last and heavenly speeches. Edinburgh, Tyler, 1649. 4°. ALDIS 1371. L, EN, I.

289A Kennedy, Cornelius. Disputatio juridica. Edinburgi, ex officina hærendum A. Anderson, 1700. 4°.* ALDIS 3976.5. EN.

290 Kennedy, David. The late history of Europe. Edinburgh, by George Mosman, 1698. 8°. ALDIS 3758. L, O, EN; CH, CLC, WF, Y.

290A Kennedy, Herbert. Theses . . . nasce philosophicas. Edinburgi, ex officinâ typographicâ Georgii Mosman, 1694. brs. ALDIS 3410. GU.

291 Kennedy, Hubert. Amplissimis . . . viris D. Joanni Hall. Edinburgi, hæres A. Anderson, 1690. brs. ALDIS 3098. E.

292 —Nobilissimis . . . viris D. T. Kennedy. Edinburgi, J. Reid, 1686. brs. ALDIS 2674. E.

293 Kennedy, Sir James. Æneas Britannicus. [Aberdeen, John Forbes], 1663. 4°. ALDIS 1754.7. AU, E(both fragments).

294 —Διαδημα και μιτρα. Seu Daphnidis et Drvydvm reditus. Aberdoniæ, excudebat Ioannes Forbesius, 1662. 4°.* ALDIS 1739. L, AU, E, EN; Y.

295 —Γαμηλιον δωρον. Edinburgi, ex officina societatis stationariorum, 1662. 4°.* ALDIS 1738. E, EN; CN, Y.

296 Kennedy, Thomas. Disputatio juridica. Edinburgh, heirs of A. Anderson, 1696. 4°. ALDIS 3572. EN.

297 Kennett, Basil. The lives and characters of the ancient Grecian poets. For Abel Swall, 1697. 8°. L, O, C, EN, DT; BN, CLC, CN, LC, MH, NC, WF, Y.

298 —Romæ antiquæ notitia: or, the antiquities. *For A. Swall and T. Child*, 1696. 8°. L, O, C, ENC, DT; CH, CN, NR, WF, Y.

299 ——Second edition. *For Timothy Child. And Robert Knaplock*, 1699. 8°. T.C.III 129. L, LW, CS, LLU, RPL; CLC, LC, PU, TU, WF.

300 **K[ennet], W[hite], bp.** A dialogue between two friends. *For Ric. Chiswell*, 1689. 4°.* L, O, CT, EN, DT; CH, CN, MH, NU, TU, WF, Y.

301 [–] A letter from a student at Oxford to a friend in the country. *For John Seeres*, 1681. 4°.* L, O, LL; CH, MH, NU, WF, Y, AVP,

302 —Parochial antiquities. *Oxford, at the Theater*, 1695. 4°. T.C.II 601. L, O, C, EN, DT; BN, CLC, CN, LC, MH, WF, Y, AVP.

303 —The righteous taken away from the evil to come. *Oxford, by Leonard Lichfield, for George West*, 1695. 4°.* T.C.II 547. L, O, CS, AN, BC; CH, IU, MH, NU, WF, Y.

304 [–] Some remarks on the life, death, and burial of Mr. Henry Cornish. *For John Nutt*, 1699. 4°.* L, O, OC, CS, MR; NU.

305 [–] To Mr. E. L. on his Majesties dissolving the late Parliament. *[London?], printed*, 1681. brs. L, O; MH.

306 **[Kenrick.]** The great good man. *[London], T. Cross*, [1700?]. fol.* L.

306A **[Kenrick, Daniel.]** A new session of the poets. *For A. Baldwin*, 1700. fol.* L, O, LVD, MR, DT; MB, MH, MU, NP, WF, Y.

307 —A sermon preached . . . April 7th, 1688. *By David Mallet*, 1688. 4°.* L, O, OC, OM, CT; CLC, Y.

308 **Kent, Dixey.** An abstract of a proposal. *[London? 1694.]* brs. LUG; NC.

309 —To the honourable, the House of Commons . . . . Proposals humbly offered. *[London? 1694.]* brs. L, LUG; MH, Y.

310 **Kent, Elizabeth Grey, countess of.** A choice manuall, or rare and select secrets. *By G. D.*, 1653. 12°. L, O, LG, LWL, CE; VC.

310A ——[Anr. ed.] *By R. Norton*, 1653. 12°. L, LLU.

310B [–]—[Anr. ed., "of rare."] *By G. D. and are to be sold by William Shears*, 1653. 8°. LWL; Y.

311 ——Second edition. 1653. 12°. L, C, LLU, E, GU; CH, LC, NN, VC, WSG, AVP.

312 ——Fourth edition. —, 1654. 12°. C, LWL, GU; WSG.

312A ——[Anr. ed.] —, 1655. 12°. NAM.

312B ——Ninth edition. *By Gartrude Dawson*, 1656. 12°. LLU.

313 ——Eleventh edition. *By Gartrude Dawson, and are to be sold by Will. Shears*, 1659. 12°. LWL, CCH, LLU, MR, GU; LC, NN.

313A ——Twelfth edition. *By Gartrude Dawson, and are to be sold by William Shears*, 1659. 12°. GU.

313B ——Thirteenth edition. —, 1661. 12°. WF.

314 ——Fourteenth edition. *By Gartrude Dawson, to be sold by Margaret Shears*, 1663. 12°. L.

315 ——Fifteenth edition. *Edinburgh, by a society of stationers*, 1664. 12°. O, LWL.

315A ——"Fifteenth" edition. *By Gertrude Dawson to be sold by Margaret Shears*, 1667. 12°. L, LWL, GU.

315B ——Sixteenth edition. *By A. M. for Margaret Shears*, 1671. 12°. LWL; CLC.

316 ——Eighteenth edition. *For Henry Mortlock*, 1682. 12°. L; WF.

317 ——Nineteenth edition. —, 1687. 12°. T.C.II 212. L, LCS, AN, GU; CJC.

317A [–] A true gentlewomans delight. *By G. D. to be sold by William Shears*, 1653. 12°. L, O, C, LCP, LLU, GU; Y.

317B [–] —[Anr. ed.] *By R. Norton*, 1653. 12°. VC.

317C [–] —[Anr. ed.] *By A. M. for Margaret Shears*, 1671. 12°. LC.

317D [–] —[Anr. ed.] *For H. Mortlock*, 1687. 12°. CJC.

318 **[Kent, Thomas.]** The fall of man declared. *For Thomas Simmons*, 1661. 4°.* L, LF, BBN, MR; IU, MH.

319 **Kentish, Richard.** Καθ' ὑπερβολην οδος: or, the way of love. *[London], for Hannah Allen*, 1649. 4°.* LT, DU, DT; PAP, WF.

320 —A sure stay for a sinking state. *By A. M. for Henry Overton*, 1648. 4°.* LT, O, C, BLH, DT; CH, MH, NU, WF, Y.

321 **Kentish, Thomas.** Tho. Kentish a trustee for certain indigent poor, his complaint. *[London, 1689.]* brs. L.

321A —Φιλανθρωποφαχια delineated. *Printed*, 1661. 4°. L; WF.

322 The Kentish conspiracy. *By R. Cotes, for Michael Spark, Junior*, 1645. 4°.* LT, LG, LSD, SP, DT; CH, IU, MH, MIU, Y.

323 Kentish Dick. *[London], for J. Deacon*, [1690?]. brs. L, O, HH, GU; MH.

324 The Kentish fayre. *Printed at Rochester [London]*, 1648. 4°.* LT, O; CH, CN, MH, TU, Y.

324A The Kentish frollick; or, sport. *[London], for C. Tracey*, [1689–93]. brs. CM.

324B The Kentish frolick, or, the tanner. *[London], by I. Blare*, [1685–88]. brs. O.

325 Kentish long-tayles and Essex calves. *Printed at London for R. M.*, 1648. 4°.* LT, O, LG; CN, IU, MIU, Y.

326 The Kentish maiden. *[London], for J. Back*, [1690?]. brs. L, CM, HH; MH.

327 The Kentish miracle. *[London], for J. Deacon*, [1684]. brs. L, CM, HH, GU.

328 The Kentish petition: to. *[London], for Hannah Allen*, 1648. brs. STEELE 2813. LT, O, LS, DT; MIU.

328A The Kentish Sampson. *[London], for B. Deacon*, 1699. 8°.* L.

329 The Kentish wonder. *For P. Brooksby*, [1672–80]. brs. L, HH.

330 **Kephale, Richard.** Medela pestilentiæ; wherein. *By J. C. for Samuel Speed*, 1665. 4°. L, O, C, LCP, LIU; MH, MIU, NN, WSG, HC.

331 Entry cancelled.

Kepler, John. His reconcilings of Scripture texts. 1661. *See* Salusbury, Thomas. Mathematical collections.

332 —Tabulæ Rudolphinæ, or the Rudolphine tables. *Printed*, 1675. 4°. L, O, DT; CH, CSU, IU, LC, MH, PL, HC.

332A **Kepple, Joseph.** The maiden-head lost by moon-light. *For Nathaniel Brooke*, 1672. 4°.* MH.

333 **[Ker, Andrew.]** A brotherly exhortation from the general assembly. [6 Aug.] *Edinburgh, by Evan Tyler*, 1649. 4°.* ALDIS 1359. L, MR, EN; WF.

334 [–]—[Anr. ed., 16 Aug.] —, 1649. 4°. ALDIS 1360. L, EN.

335 [–] —[Anr. ed.] *Edinburgh, by Evan Tyler*, 1649. *Re-printed at London*. 4°.* LT, C, MR, DT; NU, Y.

335A —*Edinburgh* 5 January 1647. The commission of the General Assembly, . . . distressed people in Argyle. [*Edinburgh*, 1647.] brs. Y.

336 [–] A solemne and seasonable warning to all estates. *Edinburgh: by Evan Tyler*, 1646. 4°.* STEELE 3p 1921. ALDIS 1236. LT, OW, AU, EN, GM; NU, WF.

336A — —[Anr. ed.] *First printed at Edinburgh by Evan Tyler and re-printed at London by John Dever & Robert Ibbitson for John Bellamy, Janua. 4*, 1647. 4°.* OC; CLC.

336B **Ker, Gilbert.** A letter sent from. [*Edinburgh*, 1649.] 4°.* MR, EN.

337 **K[er], P[atrick].** An elegy on the deplorable, and never enough to be lamented death, of . . . Charles the II. *By George Croom*, 1685. brs. L; CLC.

338 [–] Flosculum poeticum. Poems. *For Benjamin Billingsley*, 1684. 8°. T.C.II 98. L, O, LG; CH, CN, MH, WF, Y.

339 Entry cancelled.
—Λογομαχια: or the conquest. 1690. *See* —Πολιτικος.

340 [–] The map of man's misery. *For John Lawrence*, 1690. 12°. T.C.II 297. L; WF.

341 [–] —[Anr. ed.] *Boston, for Samuel Phillips*, [1700]. 12°. EVANS 615. CHS, MWA.

341A [–] A mournful elegy, on . . . Charles the II. *By George Croom*, 1685. brs. L, OP; MH.

342 [–] Πολιτικος μεγας: the grand politician. *For T. Howkins*, 1690. 8°. T.C.II 338. OM, CT; CN.

342A [–] —[Anr. ed.] *For Tho. Howkins*, 1691. 8°. L; IU, WF, Y.

343 **Ker, Peter.** The mournful mite. *By G. C. for T. P.*, 1685. fol.* O; MH, IU, PU.

344 —In illustrissimum, ac serenissimum Jacobum II. [*London*, 1685.] brs. L, O; CH, CN, MH, WF, Y.

345 [**Ker, Walter.**] A blasphemous and treasonable paper. *Edinburgh, heir of A. Anderson*, 1681. fol. ALDIS 2251. L, EN.

346 [**Ker, William.**] The sober conformists answer. [*Edinburgh*], *printed*, 1689. 4°.* ALDIS 2974.7. L, O, DU, A, E; CLC, CN, NU, PU, WF, Y.

346A **Kerhuel, Jean de.** Idea eloquentiae. *Venalis extat* [*sic*] *apud S. Lowndes*, 1673. 8°. T.C.I 143. O, OC; WF.

347 [**Keriff, Ismael.**] Letter sent by the Emperor of Morocco. colop: *For H. Jones*, 1682. brs. HH; CH, TU, AVP.

Kerr, Robert. *See* Lothian, Robert Kerr, earl of.

348–50 Entries cancelled.
[**Kerr, Thomas**], *bp.* Ichabod. *Cambridge*, 1663. *See* Ken, Thomas, *bp.*
[–] Lacrymæ ecclesiæ Anglicanæ. 1689. *See* Ken, Thomas, *bp.*

351 **Kersey, John.** A brief narrative or the remonstrance of. *Printed*, 1677. 4°.* O.

352 —The elements of that mathematical art . . . algebra. *By William Godbid, for Thomas Passinger, and Benjamin Hurlock*, 1673-4. fol. T.C.I 134. L, O, C, E, DT; BN, CH, MU, NC, PL, WF, Y.

353 —The third & fourth books of the elements of algebra. *By William Godbid for Thomas Passinger*, 1674. fol. T.C.I 187. L, O, C, E, DT; BN, CLC, NC, PL, TO, WF, Y.

353A **Kerswell, John.** Speculum gratitudinis; or David's thankfulness. *For the author*, 1665. 4°.* L, LW.

354 **Ketch, John.** The apologie of. colop: *For John Brown*, 1683. brs. L, O, OC, MC; CH, MH, NP, PU.

355 —The man of destiny's hard fortune: or, Squire Ketch's declaration. *For T. M.*, 1679. 4°.* L, O; Y.

356 Entry cancelled.
—Romanists best doctor. 1680. *See title.*

356A **Kettilby, Walter.** Books printed for. [*London?* 1688.] 4°.* OC.

357 Entry cancelled.
[**Kettlewell, John.**] Christian prudence. 1691. *See* —Of Christian prudence.

358 [–] Christianity, a doctrine of the cross. *For Jos. Hindmarsh, and Rob. Kettlewell*, 1691. 4°. T.C.II 384. L, O, C, EN, DT; CH, NU, OCI, PL, TSM, WF, Y.

359 — —[Anr. ed.] *For Jos. Hindmarsh*, 1695. 4°. L, O, CT; LC.

360 —A companion for the penitent. *For Robert Kettlewell, and sold by Benj. Bragg*, 1694. 12°. T.C.II 508. L, O, C, LLP, OC; CH, CLC, OLU, Y.

361 — —[Anr. ed.] *For R. K. to be sold by Sam. Keble*, 1696. 12°. L; Y.

361A — —[Anr. ed.] *For Robert Kettlewell, and sold by Benj. Bragg*, 1700. 12°. L.

362 [–] A companion for the persecuted. [*London*], *printed*, 1693. sixes. T.C.II 508. L, O, C, LW, OC; CLC, NU, TU, WF, Y.

363 —Death made comfortable. *For Robert Kettlewell, to be sold by Sam. Keble*, 1695. 12°. T.C.II 519. L, O, C, BC, P; CH, CLC, FU, IU, WF, Y.

364 —The declaration and profession of. [*London*, 1694/5.] brs. O, LCL, LL, OM, CT, HH.

365 —A discourse explaining the nature of edification. *For Robert Kettlewell*, 1684. 4°.* T.C.II 92. L, O, C, OM, DT; CH, CLC, IU, NN, WF, Y.

366 [–] The duty of allegiance settled. *Printed*, 1691. 4°. L, O, C, MR, DT; CH, MB, NU, WF, Y.

367 —Five discourses. *For A. and J. Churchil*, 1696. 8°. T.C.II 568. L, O, LW, CT, EN; CH, MU, NU, PL, TU, WF, Y.

367A —Four several tracts. *Printed*, 1695. 4°. O, BC.

368 —A funeral sermon . . . 29th of September, 1684. *For Robert Kettlewell*, 1684. 4°.* T.C.II 92. L, O, C, AN, BLH; CH, IU, NU, WF, Y.

369 —An help and exhortation. *By R. E. for Robert Kettlewell*, 1683. 12°. T.C.II 41. L, O, C, YM, DT; CH, CLC, WF, Y.

370 — —Second edition. *By H. C. for Robert Kettlewell*, 1686. 12°. T.C.II 295. L, C, LLP, CT, CD; CH, CLC, NU, Y.

370A — —"Second" edition. *For Thomas Chapman*, 1687. 12°. LLP.

371 — —Third edition. *For Alex. Bosvile*, 1699. 12°. T.C.II 606. L, C; CH, CLC.

372 —The measures of Christian obedience. *By J. Macock, for Robert Kettlewell*, 1681. 4°. T.C.I 448. L, O, C, OC, DT; CH, IU, NP, PL, PU, WF.

373 — —Second edition. *By B. White for Robert Kettlewell*, 1684. 4°. L, O, C, NPL, D, DT; CH, LC, NU, PL, Y.

374 — —"Second" edition. *For Thomas Chapman*, 1687. 4°. L, O, C, CT, RPL; CH.

375 — —Third edition. *By H. C. for Tho. Newborough*, 1696. 8°. L, O, LW, LSD, ENC, CD; CLC, MBA, NPT, PL.

376 — —Fourth edition. *By J. H. for Tho. Newborough*, 1700. 8°. T.C.III 191. L, C, OU, BC, DU, DT; MH, NCU, V, Y.

377 [–] Of Christian communion. *[London], printed*, 1693. 4°. L, O, C, EN, DT; CH, CN, NU, WF, Y.

378 [–] Of Christian prudence. *For Jo. Hindmarsh*, 1691. 8°. T.C.II 355. L, O, C, CD, DT; CH, NU, TSM, WF, Y.

379 —An office for prisoners for crimes. *By A. and J. Churchill*, 1697. 12°. T.C.III 22. L, O, LLP, DT; CH, WF.

380 [–] The practical believer. *For Robert Kettlewell*, 1688. 8°. T.C.II 284. L, O, C, LW, P, DT; CLC, NU, PL, WF, Y.

380A — —Part II. *For Robert Kettlewell, and are to be sold by R. Clavell and W. Rogers*, 1689. 8°. L, O, C, LW, P, DT; CLC, NU, PL, WF, Y.

381 —The religious loyalist. *For Robert Kettlewell*, 1686. 4°.* T.C.II 165. L, O, C, OC, EC, LSD; CDA, CH, NU, WF, Y.

382 —A sermon preached . . . January 24, 1685. *For Robert Kettlewell*, 1686. 4°.* T.C.II 166. L, O, C, BC, BLH; CH, IU, MH, NU, WF, Y.

383 —Two sermons preached on the . . . death of the Lord and Lady Digby. *Printed and are to be sold by Abel Roper*, 1688. 4°. T.C.II 229. MR; Y.

383A **Key, Leonard.** Here is a further discovery. *[London, 1685.]* cap., 4°.* LF, OC.

383B —The lybeller carracteriz'd. *[London, 1684.]* 4°.* LF, OC.

Key for Horn fair. 1674. *See* R., T.

Key of knowledge. 1660. *See* Whitehead, George.

Key of knowledge. Dublin, 1696. *See* Ammonet, S.

383C Key of paradise. *[Paris, 1662.]* 12°. FARM (lacks t.p.).

383D —[Anr. ed.] *[Rouen], by David Maurry, [c.* 1674]. 12°. ROGERS.

383E —[Anr. ed.] *[St. Omer]*, 1674. sixes. STONYHURST.

384 —[Anr. ed.] *At S. Omers. Permissu superior*. 1675. 12°. L, O, LLP; TU.

384A —[Anr. ed.] *Paris*, 1681. 18°. C, DUS.

384B The key of true policy. *Printed at London by J. F.* 1652. 4°.* EN (impf.); MM.

Key of wealth. 1650. *See* Potter, William.

Key opening a way. 1693. *See* Penn, William.

385 A key to catechisms. *For Richard Chiswell, to be sold by Robert Eveleigh in Exon*, 1682. 8°.* L.

Key to Helmont. 1682. *See* Bacon, William.

Key to open scripture. 1681. *See* Delaune, Thomas. Τροπολογια.

386 Entry cancelled.

Key to open the way. 1693. *See* Penn, William. Key, opening.

387 A key to the cabinet of the Parliament. *[London], printed*, 1648. 4°.* LT, O, OC, EC, DT; CH, MH, NU, WF.

Key to the Epsom love-letter. [n.p., 1675.] *See* C., L.

Key to the Kings cabinet. Oxford, 1645. *See* Browne, Thomas, *canon of Windsor*.

388 The key to the Kings cabinet-counsell. *By Bernard Alsop*, 1644. 4°.* LT; CH, CN, MH, NU, TU, WF, Y.

Key (with the whip). [n.p.], 1682. *See* Nesse, Christopher.

389 **[Keymor, John.]** A cleare and evident way for enriching the nations of England and Ireland. *By T. M. & A. C. & are to be sold by John Saywell*, 1650. 4°.* LT, LUG, DU, DT; INU, LC, MH, NC, WF, Y.

390 —John Keymors observation made upon the Dutch fishing. *For Sir Edward Ford*, 1664. 4°.* L, O, LUG, CT, DT; HR, IU, MH, MIU, WF, Y.

391 [–] Sir Walter Raleigh's observations, touching trade. *By T. H. and are to be sold by William Sheeres*, 1653. 12°. L, C, LUG; CLC, CN, MH, WF, Y.

392 Entry cancelled.

Keynes, George. Roman martyrologe. St. Omers, 1667. *See title*.

393 **K[eynes], J[ohn].** A rational compendious way to convince. *[London], printed*, 1674. 12°. L, O, CS, BSM, LNC, D, GK; CLC, CN, WF, Y.

394 **Khrypffs, Nicolaus,** *cardinal.* The idiot in four books. *For VVilliam Leake*, 1650. 12°. LT, C, LW, LWL, SP; CH, CSS, MH, PU, WF, HC.

395 —Οφθαλμος ἁπλους or the single eye. *For John Streater*, 1646. 12°. LT, P; CLC, NU.

396 **[Kidder, Richard],** *bp.* The charge of . . . June 2. 1692. *By J. H. for Brab. Aylmer*, 1693. 4°.* T.C.II 436. L, O, C, AN, DT; CH, MH, NU, WF, Y.

397 —Charity directed. *For Thomas Parkhurst*, 1676. 4°.* T.C.I 252. L, O, LC, EN, DT; NC, NU, WF, Y.

398 —The Christian sufferer supported. *For W. Kettilby*, 1680. 8°. T.C.I 391. L, O, LW, AN, E, DT; CH, CLC, NGT, NIA, PL, Y.

399 —A commentary on the five books of Moses. *By J. Heptinstall, for William Rogers*, 1694. 2v. 8°. T.C.II 498. L, O, CT, NPL, GU, DT; CH, MH, MU, NU, Y.

400 —Convivium cœleste. A plain and familiar discourse. *By A. Maxwell, for Tho. Parkhurst*, 1674. 8°. T.C.I 167. L, O, LLP; CLC.

401 — —Second edition. *By John Richardson, for Tho. Parkhurst; to be sold by Edward Giles, in Norwich*, 1684. 8°. T.C.II 77. L, CE.

401A — —"Second" edition. *By John Richardson, for Tho. Parkhurst*, 1684. 8°. O, LW, CS, CD; CH, LC, MIU, NIA, WF, Y.

402 —A demonstration of the Messias . . . part I. *By J. Heptinstall, for B. Aylmer*, 1684. 8°. T.C.II 93. L, O, C, LW, DT; CH, MH, NGT, NU, WF, Y.

403 — —part II. *By J. H. for W. Rogers, and M. Wotton*, 1699. 8°. T.C.III 89. L, O, C, LW, DU, DT; CLC, MH, NU, PPT, WF.

404 — —part III. —, 1700. 8°. T.C.III 167. O, C, LW, MC, DT; CLC, MH, NGT, NU, PPT, WF.

404A —A discourse concerning the education of youth in religion. *For Tho. Parkhurst*, 1672. 8°. T.C.I 115. CLC.

405 —The duty of the rich. *By J H. for Barbazon Aylmer*, 1690. 4°.* L, O, C, LLP, OC, EC; CLC, WF, Y.

406 —The judgment of private discretion. *For Brabazon Aylmer*, 1687. 4°.* L, O, C, EN, DT; CLC, IU, MH, NU, TU, WF, Y.

[–] Letter to a friend relating. 1690. *See* Prideaux, Humphrey.

407 —The life of the Reverend Anthony Horneck. *By J. H. for B. Aylmer*, 1698. 8°. L, O, C, BR, DT; CH, CLC, NU, OCI, Y.

408 —Of fasting: a sermon. *By J. H. for Brabazon Aylmer*, 1694. 4°.* T.C.II 507. L, C, OC, AN, BR; CH, PL, TSM, WF, Y.

409 Entry cancelled.
[–] Protestants letter. 1690. *See title.*

410 —Reflections on a French testament. *For Walter Kettilby*, 1690. 4°.* T.C.II 329. L, O, C, SP, DT; CH, MH, NU, TU, WF.

411 [–] A second dialogue between a new Catholick convert. *For B. Aylmer*, 1687. 4°.* L, O, CS, E, DT; CLC, IU, MH, NU, TU, WF, Y.

412 —A sermon preached . . . July the 16th. 1682. *By H. H. for Walter Kettilby*, 1682. 4°.* T.C.I 504. L, C, CT, BAMB, BR; NU, Y.

413 —A sermon preached . . . August 17, 1686. *For Walter Kettilby*, 1686. 4°.* T.C.II 175. L, O, C, LIU, BLH; HM, IU, WF.

414 —A sermon preached . . . 30th. of January, 1691/2. *By J. H. for B. Aylmer*, 1692. 4°.* T.C.II 390. L, O, C, EN, DT; CLC, WF, Y.

415 —A sermon preached . . . fifth of November, 1692. *For Tho. Parkhurst*, 1693. 4°.* L, O, C, BAMB, EN, BLH; WF.

416 —A sermon preached . . . March 12. 1692[3]. *By J. H. for Brab. Aylmer*, 1693. 4°.* T.C.II 450. L, O, OC, BR, BAMB; CLC, MBZ, PL, RBU, WF, Y.

416A —A sermon preached before the Queen . . . May 23, 1694. *By J. H. for Brabazon Aylmer*, 1694. 4°. CH.

417 —A sermon upon the resurrection. *By J. H. for William Rogers*, 1694. 4°.* T.C.II 498. L, O, C, LG, EC; CLC, IEG, PL, WF, Y.

418 —Twelve sermons preach'd. *By J. H. for B. Aylmer, and M. Wotton*, 1697. 8°. L, O, LW, DU; NU, TU.

419 —The vanity of man. *For Thomas Parkhurst*, 1673. 4°.* L, LW, CS; MB, NU, Y.

420 —The young man's duty. *By H. L. for G. Calvert and S. Sprint*, 1671. 12°. L, LW.

421 — —Fourth edition. *For George Calvert*, 1677. 12°. T.C.I 262. C.

421aA — —Sixth edition. *By J. Rawlins for R. Simpson*, 1690. 12°. T.C.II 318. LLP, NE; CLC.

421A The kid-napper trapan'd. *For P. B.*, 1675. 4°.* NCU, NN.

422 **Kidner, Thomas.** Catalogus variorum & insignium librorum. [*London*], 6 Feb. 1676/7. 4°. L, O, OL, CE, CS, LNC; NG.

423 **Kiffin, William.** A briefe remonstrance. [*London*], printed, 1645. 4°.* LT, DT; CU, NU, RBU.

423A —Certaine observations upon Hosez. *For William Larner*, 1642. 4°. O, LSC.

424 —A discovrse between. *Printed at London*, 1654. 4°.* LT.
[–] Glimpse of Sions glory. 1641. *See* Goodwin, Thomas.

425 —A sober discourse of right. *By Geo. Larkin, for Enoch Prosser*, 1681. 8°. L, O, ORP; CLC, NU, RBU.

426 —To Mr. Thomas Edwards. Sir you stand as one professing. [*London*], Novemb. 15. 1644. brs. LT.
[–] VValwins vviles. [1649.] *See* Price, John.

427 **Kightley, Edward.** A full and true relation. *Printed, November the 4*, 1642. 4°.* LT, BC.

428 **Kilburne, Richard.** A brief survey of the county of Kent. *By Thomas Mabb for Henry Atkinson*, 1657. fol.* L; WF.

428A —Choice presidents. *By the assigns of Richard and Edw. Atkins, for Richard Tonson*, 1680. 12°. T.C.I 384. CB, MHL.

429 — —Second edition. —, 1681. 12°. T.C.I 454. L, LSC; BN, CLC, PUL.

430 — —Third edition. *By the assigns of Rich. and Edw. Atkins, for Richard Tonson*, 1685. 12°. T.C.II 106. L, CP; CLC, CN, LC, MHL, MIU, NCL.

431 — —Fourth edition. *For Richard Tonson*, 1690. 12°. L, OC, CJ; CH, LC, MHL.

432 — —Fifth edition. *For Mary Tonson*, 1694. 12°. L, CT, DUS, DT; MHL, NCL, PUL.

433 — —Sixth edition. —, 1700. 8°. L, O, C; BN, HM, MHL, NCL, TU, WF.

434 —A topographie . . . of Kent. *By Thomas Mabb, for Henry Atkinson*, 1659. 4°. L, O, C, EN, DT; BN, CLC, CN, LC, MH, MU, Y.

435 **Kilburne, William.** Dangerous errors in several late printed Bibles. *Printed at Finsbury* [*London*], 1659. 4°.* L, O, CT, EN; CSS, IU, MH, NU.

436 —A New-Years-gift for Mercurius Politicus. *By Thomas Milbourn*, [1659]. brs. LT, O.

436A —To the supreme authority, the Parliament . . . . An humble addresse . . . concerning the . . . several errone-ous Bibles. [*London*], 1659. cap., 4°. L (t.p.).

436B [**Kilby, Richard.**] The burden of a loaden conscience. *For A. Baldwin*, 1699. 4°. T.C.III 181. L, LW; MIU.

437 **Killcop, Thomas.** Ancient and durable gospel. *By H. H. to be sold by Giles Calvert*, 1648. 8°. LT, C.

438 —The pathway to justification. *Printed*, 1660. 4°.* LT, C.

439 —Seekers svpplyed. *By Tho. Paine for George Whittington*, 1646. 4°.* LT, DT; CH, NU.

440 [–] A short treatise of baptisme. *Printed*, 1642. 8°.* LT, CT.

441 —The unlimited authority of Christs disciples cleared. *By J. C.*, 1651. 8°. LT.

442 **Killigrew, Mrs. Anne.** Poems. *For Samuel Lowndes*, 1686. 4°. T.C.II 147. L, O, LVD, CT, LLU; CH, CN, LC, MH, TU, Y.

443 [**Killigrew, Henry.**] A book of new epigrams. *For Henry Bonwicke*, 1695. 8°. L, LVD; CH, CN, LC, MH, MIU, TU, WF, Y.

443A [–] A court of judicature. *For Henry Bonwicke*, 1697. 8°. T.C.III 15. L; MH, AVP.

443B [–] Innocui sales. A collection of new epigrams. *By T. Hodgkin, to be sold by Matth. Gillyflower*, 1694. 8°. WF.

444 —Pallantus and Eudora, a tragœdie. *For Iohn Hardesty*, 1653. fol. L, O, C, LVD; CH, LC, MH, MIU, NC, NP, WF, Y.

444A — —[Anr. ed.] *Printed in the year*, 1653. fol. CH, MH, WF.

445 [–] A sermon preached before the Kings most excellent Majesty at Oxford. *Oxford, for W. Web*, 1643. 4°.* MADAN 1272. LT, O, CS, EN, DT; CH, WF.

445A [–] —[Anr. ed.] —*and now reprinted at London for G. T.*, 1643. 4°.* Y.

446 —A sermon preach'd . . . the first Sunday of Advent, 1666. *By Tho. Roycroft for Thomas Hacker*, 1666. 4°.* L, O, DC, LSD, OC; CLC, NC, NU, WF.

446A   — —[Anr. ed.] *For H. R.*, 1668. 4°.* CM, CT.

446B   — —[Anr. ed.] —, 1669. 4°.* WCA.

447   —A sermon preach'd . . . May 29th, 1668. *By T. R. for R. Royston*, 1668. 4°.* L, O, LL, EC, BR; CH, NU, TU, WF, Y.

448   —A sermon preach'd the Sunday before Easter in West-minster-Abby. [*London*], *in the Savoy: by E. Jones, for Samuel Lowndes*, 1689. 4°.* T.C.II 245. L, O; NC, Y.

449   —Sermons preached. *By J. M. for R. Royston*, 1685. 4°. T.C.II 122. O, C, LVF, RPL; CH, IU, WF.

449A   —Twenty two sermons. *Printed and are to be sold by John Whitlock*, 1695. 4°. O, LSD; CH, PL, WF.

       [**Killigrew, Sir Peter.**] King's Majesties most gracious message to the Parliament. 1647. *See* Sharpe, W.

450   **Killigrew, Thomas.** Comedies and tragedies. *For Henry Herringman*, 1664. fol. L, O, C, EN, DT; CH, CN, LC, MH, TU, Y.

451   [–] Foole that I was. [*London*, 1642.] brs. LT.

452   —The prisoners and Claracilla. *By T. Cotes for Andrew Crooke*, 1641. 12°. L, O, CE, LIU, EN; CH, CN, MH, WF, Y.

453   **Killigrew, Sir William.** . . . His answer to the fenne mens objections. *Printed at London*, 1649. 4°.* L, O, CT; CSS, MH, WF.

454   —An answer to such objections as were made by some commoners. *For the author*, 1647. 4°. C, NOT.

455   —The artless midnight thoughts. Second edition. *For Thomas Howkins*, 1684. 12°. L; CH, MH.

456   —A breviate of the cause. [*London*, 1651?] 4°. LT.

456A   —The draining of Lindsey Level. [*London*, 1678.] cap., fol.* L, LPR.

457   —The Earle of Lindsey his title . . . fennes. [*London*, 1654.] brs. L; CH, WF.

458   —Fovr nevv playes. *Oxford, by Hen: Hall for Ric: Davis*, 1666. fol. MADAN 2746. L, O, C, LVD, E; CH, CN, MH, TU, WF, Y.

459   Entry cancelled.
       [–] Humble proposal. 1663. *See* [–] To the King's.

460   [–] The imperial tragedy. *For Will. Wells and Rob. Scott*, 1669. fol. T.C.I 10. L, O, LVD, LLU; CH, CN, LC, MH, WF, Y.

460A   —The late Earle of Lindsey, his title. [*London*, 1661.] brs. L, LUG.

460B   — —[Anr. ed.] [*London*, 1663.] cap., fol.* LPR.
       —Love and friendship. Oxford, 1666. *See* —Fovr nevv playes.

461   —Mid-night and daily thoughts. *For Thomas Bennet*, 1694. 8°. L; CH, IU, MH, TU, WF, Y.

462   — —[Anr. ed.] *For Randal Taylor*, 1694. 8°. L, O, OW, CT, LLU; CH, CLC, MH, RHT, WCL, Y.

462A   — —Part IV. *For the author*, 1695. 8° in 4s.* IU.

462B   [–] Mid-night thoughts. *For Benjamin Clark*, 1681. 12°. MH, PL.

463   [–] —[Anr. ed.] *Benj. Clark*, 1682. 12°. T.C.I 459. L, OCC; CN, NU.
       [–] Ormasdes. 1665. *See* —Three playes.

464   [–] Pandora: a comedy. *By T. Mabb for John Pleyfere and Tho. Hors-man*, 1664. 8°. O, CT; CLC, MH, TU, WCL, Y.
       — —[Anr. ed.] Oxford, 1666. *See* —Fovr nevv playes.

465   —A paper delivered and dispersed by. [*London*, 1651.] brs. LT; MH, Y.

466   —A proposal, shewing how this nation may be vast gainers. [*London*, 1696.] 4°.* L, LLP, LUG, LLU; CH, MH, NC, TO, WF, Y.

467   —The rioters in Lindsey Levell. [*London*, 1655.] brs. LT, MH.
       —Seege of Urbin. Oxford, 1666. *See* —Fovr nevv playes.
       —Selindra, 1665. *See* —Three playes.
       — —[Anr. ed.] Oxford, 1666. *See* —Fovr nevv playes.

468   [–] A short answer to a paper, intituled, Reasons. [*London*, 1698.] cap., fol.* O.

469   —Three new playes. *For Simon Neale*, 1674. 8°. L; CH, CLC, MH, MU, WF, Y.

470   —Three playes. *By T. Mabb; for John Playfere, and Thomas Horsman*, 1665. 8°. L, O, LVF, OW, LLU; CH, CN, LC, MH, TU, Y.

470A   —To shew the countreys consent. [*London?* 1671.] brs. L.

471   [–] To the King's and Queen's . . . An humble proposal. [*London*, 1690.] 4°.* C, LUG; CH, MH, NC, PU, WF, Y.

472   —Whereas it has been often said. [*London*, 1650?] brs. L.

473   [**Killin, Margaret.**] A warning from the Lord to the teachers. *For Giles Calvert*, 1656. 4°.* LT, O, C, LF, DT; CH, CN, MH, PH, PSC, TU, Y.

473A   Killing is murder. *For Joseph Moor*, 1657. 4°. LT, O, C, DU, BQ; CH, IU, MH, NU, TSM, WF, Y.
       Killing is murder, and no murder. 1657. *See* Hawke, Michael.

474   Entry cancelled.
       Killing noe murder. [*n.p.*, 1657.] *See* Titus, Silas.

474A   **Killingworth, Edmund.** A poem on the peace. *For E. Whitlock*, 1697. fol.* LLP, MR; CN.
       Killiray, Matthew. Christians comfort. 1673. *See* title.

474B   —Every man's duty. *For W. Thackeray*, 1673. 8°.* CH.

475   —The godly mans gain. *For W. Thackeray*, 1665. 8°.* L.

475A   — —[Anr. ed.] *For William Thackeray*, 1674. 8°. BLH; CH.

475B   —A new book containing sundry set-forms of prayers. *For Wm. Thackaray* [*sic*], 1673. 8°.* CH.

475C   —The pathway to saving knowledge. *For W. Thackeray*, 1673. 8°.* CH.

475D   —The ready way to get riches. *For W. Thackeray*, 1673. 8°.* CH.

475E   [–] —[Anr. ed.] —, 1681. 8°.* LW.

475F   —A short and sure way to grace. *For W. Thackeray*, 1674. 8°.* CH.

475G   —The sinners sobs. *For William Thackeray*, 1667. 8°. L.

475H   — —[Anr. ed.] *For William Thackaray* [*sic*], 1673. 8°.* CH.

475I   —The swearer and the drunkard. *For W. Thackeray*, 1673. 8°.* CH.

475J   —Ten sermons. *For William Thackeray*, 1675. 8°. CH.

475K   —The touchstone of a Christian. *For W. Thackeray*, 1675. 8°.* CH.

475L   —The way to heaven made playn. *For W. Thackery*, 1674. 8°.* CH.

476   Killycrankie to be sung. [*n.p.*, 1689.] brs. EN.

477   [**Kilvert, Richard.**] A discourse of a true English-man. *Printed at London for Thomas Walkley*, 1644. 4°.* LT, O, MR; LEIDEN, CDA, CH, CLC, CN, NU, WF.

[–] Last discourse. [n.p.], 1641. *See* Abell, William.

478 [–] A reply to a most untrue relation made and set forth . . . by certaine vintners. [*London*], *printed*, 1641. 4°.* LT, LG, CT, LSD; IU, NC, Y.

479 **Kimberley, Jonathan.** Of obedience for conscience-sake. *By J. H. for Benj. Tooke and John Smith*, 1683. 4°. T.C.II 37. LSC, OC, CT, BC, LSD; CH, WF, Y.

Kimbolton. *See* Manchester.

479A A kind congratulation between Queen Elizabeth, and the late Queen Mary II. *By R. Smith*, 1695. brs. MH.

479B The kind hearted maidens resolution. [*London*], *for J. Clarke*, [1650–71]. brs. EUING 149. GU.

479C —[Anr. ed.] *For F. Coles, T. Vere, J. Wright, and J. Clarke*, [1675]. 4°.* OP.

479D A kind husband. [*London*], *for P. Brooksby*, [1677]. brs. O.

A kind invitation to the people called Quakers. [*London*], 1697. *See* Stephens, Edward.

Kind lady. [n.p., 1683.] *See* D'Urfey, Thomas.

480 The kind mistress. [*London*, 1673?] brs. L.

480A —[Anr. ed.] *By and for W. O. for A. M. and are to be sold by C. Bates*, [169–?]. brs. MH.

480B The kind shepherd and amorous shepherdess. [*London*], *for J. Clarke, W. Thackeray, and T. Passenger*, [1684–86]. brs. O.

481 The kind virgin's complaint. [*London*], *for A. M., W. O., and T. Thackeray*, [1700?]. brs. L, O.

481A —[Anr. ed.] [*London*], *for J. Clarke, William Thackeray, and Thomas Passinger*, [1684–6]. brs. CM.

Kind William. [*London*, 1684.] *See* Bowne, Tobias.

482 The kind young man's answer. [168–?] brs. O.

483 **Kinder, Phil.** Pietati sacrum. H.S.E. [*London*, 1650.] LT, O.

Kindersley, Robert. Martial horse, 1652. *See* Elslyot, Thomas.

484 **K[ing], D[aniel], *of Chester*.** The cathedrall and conventuall churches. [*London*], *printed and sold by Iohn Overton, anno* 1656. fol. L, O, C, CM, DU; CH, CN, LC, MH, NC.

485 [–] —[Anr. ed.] [*London*], 1656. 4°. L.

485A [–] —[Anr. ed.] [*London*], *printed and sould by Iohn Ouerton*, 1656 [1666–1671]. 4°. O, SP.

486 — —Second edition. [*London*], 1672, *sould by Io: Overton*. fol. T.C.I 22. O, DUS.

487 Entry cancelled.

—On St. Pavl's cathedrall. [n.p.], 1658. *See* title.

488 —The vale-royall of England. *By John Streater*, 1656. fol. L, O, C, MR, ES, DT; BN, CH, CN, LC, MH, Y.

489 **King, Daniel, *preacher*.** A discovery of some troublesome thoughts. *Printed*, 1651. 4°. L, CT, SP; CB.

489A —Self the grand enemy of Jesus Christ. *For Francis Smith*, [1660?]. 12°. LW, ORP.

490 —A way to Sion sovght ovt. *By Charles Sumptner, for Hanna Allen*, 1650. 4°. LT, O, LW, ORP, CT, MAB; NHC, NU.

491 — —Second edition. *Printed at London, and reprinted, Edinburgh, by Christopher Higgins*, 1656. 4°. ALDIS 1546.6. E; WF.

492 **King, Edward.** A discovery of the arbitrary, tyrannicall, and illegall actions. *Printed*, 1647. 4°.* LT, LL; CH, WF, Y.

492A —To the honourable the committee of Parliament for grievances, the humble petition of. [*n.p.*, 1666.] brs. L.

493 —To the Honourable the House of Commons, the humble petition of. [*London*, 1646.] brs. LT, LNC.

493A —A true account of the reduction. *For Richard Baldwin*, 1689. brs. HH; Y.

494 **[King, Gregory.]** The order of the installation of Henry Duke of Norfolk. *For Robert Clavel*, 1685. fol.* T.C.II 149. L, O, OP, MR, SP; CH, MH, TO, WF, Y.

495 [–] The order of the installation of Prince George of Denmark. *For Benjamin Tooke*, 1684. fol.* L, O, LG, CT, DU; CH, CLC, PL, WF, Y.

496 —A scheme of the rates and duties granted to His Majesty. *By Charles Bill, and the executrix of Thomas Newcomb*, 1695. brs. L, EN; WF.

497 **King, Henry, *bp*.** Ben Johnson's poems, elegies. *Printed and sold by the booksellers*, 1700. 8°. KEYNES 5. OC; CH, NC.

498 [–] A deepe groane, fetch'd at the funerall of . . . Charles the First. [*London*], *printed*, 1649. 4°.* KEYNES 2. LT, O, LLU, YM, DT; BN, CH, CN, MH, NCD, WF, Y.

499 [–] An elegy upon the most incomparable K. Charls the I. [*London*, 1660?] 4°.* KEYNES 6. L, O, YM, GK; CH, CU, MH, WF, Y.

499A [–] —[Anr. ed.] *For Henry Herringman*, 1661. 4°.* DU, EXETER CATH.; Y.

500 [–] A groane at the fvnerall. [*London*], *printed*, 1649. 4°.* KEYNES 1. O; MH.

501 [–] Poems, elegies, paradoxes, and sonnets. *By J. G. for Rich: Marriot and Hen: Herringman*, 1657. 8°. KEYNES 3. LT, O, OC, OW, EN; CH, IU, MH, NC, WCL, Y.

502 — —[Anr. ed.] *For Henry Herringman*, 1664. 8°. KEYNES 4. L, O, LW, LIU, MR, GK; CH, CN, MH, WF, Y.

503 Entry cancelled.

[–] Sermon preached before the Kings . . . Majesty at Oxford. 1643. *See* Killigrew, Henry.

504 —A sermon preached . . . the 29th of May. *For Henry Herringman*, 1661. 4°.* KEYNES 55. L, O, LL, LLP, GK; CH, LC, NU, TU, WF, Y.

505 [–] A sermon preached . . . April 24. 1662. *For Henry Herringman*, 1662. 4°.* KEYNES 57. L, O, C, LW, BLH, GK; CH, MH, MIU, NU, WF, Y.

506 —A sermon preached . . . Octob. 8. 1662. *For Henry Herringman*, 1663. 4°.* KEYNES 59. L, O, LLP, WCA, CD; CH, CLC, IU.

507 —A sermon preached the 30th of January . . . 1664. *For Henry Herringman*, 1665. 4°.* KEYNES 60. L, O, C, LL, CT; CH, CLC, NU, WF, Y.

508 **King, John, *d. 1679*.** The last speeches of. [*Edinburgh?*], *printed*, 1680. 4°.* ALDIS 2200. L, O, C, MR, EN, DT; CH, IU, NU, PU, WF, Y.

509 **King, John, *fl. 1661*.** A sermon on the 30th of January. *For John Playford*, 1661. 12°. O.

510 **King, John,** *1652–1732.* A sermon preached . . . Dec. 12, 1697. *For Thomas Bennet,* 1697. 4°.* T.C.III 52. L, LW, CS; CH, WF.

510A **King, Josiah.** The afternoon tryall of old Father Christmas. *By E. C. for John Ratcliff,* 1658. 8°. O.

510B —The examination and tryall of old Father Christmas. *For Thomas Johnson,* 1658. 8°. O.

511 — —[Anr. ed.] *For H. Brome, T. Basset and J. Wright,* 1678. 12°. L, O; CH, TU, WCL.

511A — —[Anr. ed.] *For Charles Brome,* 1687. 12°. WF.

512 —Mr. Blount's oracles of reason, examined. *Exon, by S. Darker, for Ch. Yeo, J. Pearce and Ph. Bishop,* 1698. 8°. O, LLP, OC, CD, DT; CLC, IU, MBA, NU.

512A — —[Anr. ed.] *Exeter, by S. Darker, for Philip Bishop,* 1698. 8°. L, DU, NE, GU; CH, LC, IAU, MH, WF.

512AB **King, Manasseth.** A new and useful catechism. Third edition. *Printed* 1693. 8°. OC.

512B — —Fourth edition. —, 1699. 8°. MH.

513 [**King, Peter**], *baron.* An enquiry into the constitution. *For Jonathan Robinson, and John Wyat,* 1691. 8°. T.C.II 376. L, C, DU, E, DT; CH, CN, NU, TU, WF, Y, AVP.

514 [–] — —[Anr. ed.] —, 1692. 8°. O, C; CN.

515 [**King, Philip.**] The surfeit to A. B. C. *For Ewd. Dod,* 1656. 12°. O; CH.

516 **K[ing], R[obert].** Catena, sive elegiæ. *Typis J. Y. & impensis A.B.,* 1647. 4°.* L, O, C, MR, DN; CH, IU, MH, WF, Y.

517 —A second booke of songs. [*London,* 1695.] fol. L, CM; MB.

518 —Songs for one two and three voices. [*London,* 1692.] 4°.* L, LG, CM; CN.

519 — —[Anr. ed.] [*London*], *sold by Iohn Crouch,* [1692]. 4°.* O, OC, GU; LC.

520 **King, William,** *abp.* An admonition to the dissenting inhabitants of . . . Derry. *Dublin, by Andrew Crook,* 1694. 4°. DIX 261. O, DI, DK, DN, DT, BQ.

521 — —[Anr. ed.] *For William Keblewhite,* 1694. 8°. T.C.II 554. L, C, LCL, MR, ENC, DT; CH, CLC, NU, WF, Y.

522 Entry cancelled. —Animadversions on a pretended Account of Danmark. *See* King, William, 1663–1712.

522A [–] An answer to a book which will be published. colop: *For Randal Taylor,* [1693]. 4°. OC.

523 —An answer to the considerations which obliged Peter Manby. *For R. Taylor,* 1687. 4°. T.C.II 245. L, O, C, EN, DT; CH, CU, MH, NU, WF, Y.

524 — —[Anr. ed.] *Dublin, by Joseph Ray, sold by John North,* 1687. 4°. DIX 225. L, O, CT, CD, DT; CH.

524A — —[Anr. ed.] *Dublin, by Joseph Ray, sold by John Norton,* 1687. 4°. CD.

524B —The Lord Bishop of Londonderry's case . . . to induce the Lords of England. [*n.p.,* 1698.] brs. O.

525 —Catholick religion asserted. *Printed at Dublin, and reprinted at London, for William Whitwood,* 1686. 4°.* DIX 216. MC; CLC.

526 —A discourse concerning the inventions. *For William Keblewhite,* 1694. 8°. T.C.II 490. L, O, C, YM, D; CH, NCD, NU, WF, Y.

527 — —Second edition. —, 1694. 8°. T.C.II 514. C, OC, OM, EN, DT; CH, CLC, CN, NU, SW.

528 — —[Anr. ed.] *Dublin, for the author, by Andrew Crook,* 1694. 4°. DIX 261. O, C, LW, LIU, CD, DM, DN, DT; WF.

529 — —"Second" edition. *By Andrew Crook,* 1694. 8°. DIX 261. O, LW, EN, CD.

529A — —[Anr. ed.] *Dublin, by Andrew Crook, sold by Eliphal Dobson,* 1694. 8°. DT.

530 — —Third edition. *For William Keblewhite,* 1696. 8°. T.C.II 573. L, LCL, EC, YM; CH, LC, WF, Y.

531 — —Fourth edition. —, 1697. 8°. T.C.III 44. L, BLH, BQ; CB, CH, LC, NU, Y.

532 —Europe's deliverance. *Printed at Dublin, and reprinted at London for Tim. Goodwin,* 1691. 4°.* L, CT, LLP, LIU, DT; CH, MIU, NU, WF, Y.

533 —A second admonition. *Dublin, by Andrew Crook,* 1695. 4°. DIX 269. L, CD, DI, DN, DT; WF.

534 — —[Anr. ed.] *For R. Clavel,* 1696. 8°. T.C.II 567. L, O, C, LW, CT, BLH; CH, NU, Y.

535 —A sermon preached . . . 16th of Novr., 1690. *Dublin, Joseph Ray,* 1691. 4°.* DIX 245. O, CD, DT; WF.

536 — —[Anr. ed.] *Printed at Dublin. And reprinted at London for Tim. Goodwin,* 1691. 4°.* L, O, C.

537 — —[Anr. ed.] *For Robert Clavel,* 1691. 12°.* T.C.II 345. L, O, C, LW, OC, NPL, BLH; CH, CLC, NGT, NU, Y.

538 [–] The state of the Protestants of Ireland. *For Robert Clavell,* 1691. 4°. T.C.II 379. L, O, C, EN, DT; CH, MH, MU, NU, PL, WF, Y, AVP.

539 [–] —Third edition. *By Samuel Roycroft for Robert Clavell,* 1692. 8°. T.C.II 405. L, O, C, NOT, GU, DT; CH, CLC, IU, NC, NCU, WF, Y.

540 [–] —Fourth edition. —, 1692. 8°. T.C.II 432. L, C, LIU, E, DT; CH, CN, LC, PBL, TU, Y.

541 —A vindication of the answer. *Dublin, by Joseph Ray, to be sold by William Norman,* 1688. 4°.* DIX 228. L, O, C, DU, DN, DT; CDA, CLC.

542 [–] A vindication of the Christian religion. [*Dublin?*], *printed* 1688. 4°.* DIX 230. L, BANGOR, DM, DT, BLH; CLC, WF, Y, AVP.

542A —William, Lord Bishop of Derry, appellant. The society . . . for the new plantations in Ulster, respondents. [*Dublin,* 1697.] cap., fol.* DI.

543 **King, William,** *1624–1680.* Poems of Mr. Covvley and others. *Oxford, by William Hall, for the author,* 1668. fol. MADAN 2805. L, O, OCC, CM, GU; CN, MH, Y, ZWT.

543A [**King, William**], *1663–1712.* Animadversions on a pretended Account of Danmark [*by Robt. Molesworth*]. *For Tho. Bennet,* 1694. 8°. T.C.II 522. O, OC, CE, CD; BN, CH, IU, MBP, NN, WF, Y.

544 [–] Dialogues of the dead. *Printed, and sold by A. Baldwin,* 1699. 8°.* T.C.III 159. L, O, C, E, DT; CH, CN, NCD, WF, Y.

545 [–] The furmetary. *Printed, and sold by A. Baldwin,* 1699. 8°.* T.C.III 141. L, AN, LSD, MR, DT; CH, MH, NN, TU, Y.

545A [–] A journey to London. *Printed, and sold by A. Baldwin,* 1698. 8°.* T.C.III 155. L, O, C, E, GH; BN, CH, IU, MBM, MMO, NCD, Y.

545B [–] —Second edition. —, 1699. 8°.* OB, BAMB, DC; CLC, CN, MH, WF, HC.

546 [–] The transactioneer with some of his philosophical fancies. *Printed*, 1700. 8°. T.C.III 176. L, CS, LSD, GH, DT; CH, CLC, MH, INU, WF.

547 The King advancing, or. *For Charles Prince*, 1660. 4°.* LT, O; MH, AVP.

King and a poor northern man. 1673. *See* Parker, Martin.

548 The King and Parliament. *For James Dean*, 1685. brs. O.

549 No entry.

550 The King and the bishop. [*London*], *by and for Alexander Milbourne*, [1670–97]. brs. L, O, CM, HH; CSB.

551 —[Anr. ed.] *For F. Coles, T. Vere, and J. Wright*, [1663–74]. brs. L, O.

551A The King and the cobler. *For C. Dennisson*, [1670?]. 12°.* CM.

551B The King and the farmers of excise against the merchants importers of brandy. [*London*, 1670.] brs. LPR.

551C The King and the forrester. [*London?* 1696.] brs. L.

551D The King being seized in fee in right of Dutchy of Lancaster . . . Fennes . . . [case of patentees to reap their corn]. [*London*, 1641.] brs. LPR.

King Charles I his imitation. 1660. *See* W., J.
King Charles I no such saint. 1698. *See* J., D.
King Charles his entertainment. 1641. *See* H., J.

552 King Charles his farewell. *For K. G.*, 1649. 4°.* ALMACK p. 74. LT.

553 King Charles his glory and rebells shame. [*London*, 1660.] brs. L, DN.

554 King Charles his royall welcome. *For G. R.*, 1647. 4°.* LT, O, EN, DT.

554A King Charles his speech, and last farewell. [*London*, 1649.] brs. MAU.

King Charls, his starre. [n.p.] 1654. *See* Evans, Rhys.

555 No entry.

King Charls his tryal: or a perfect narrative. 1649. *See* W., C.

556 King Charls his tryal at the high court. Second edition. *By J. M. for Peter Cole, Francis Tyton, and John Playford*, 1650. 8°. LT, LG, AN, DT; CH.

557 —Third edition. *For John Playford*, 1655. 12°. Y.

King Charles the first, no man. [n.p.], 1649. *See* Philipps, Fabian.

558 King Charles the second's restoration. [*London*, 1661.] L.

559 King Charles vindicated. *Printed*, 1648. 4°.* LT, DT; CH, MBP, MH, NU, WF, Y.

560 —Second edition. *Imprinted*, 1648. 4°.* LT, IAU, MH, NU.
King Charles vindicated. [n.p.], 1660. *See* L., W.
King Edward the third. 1691. *See* Bancroft, John.
King enjoyes his own. [n.p., 1660–65.] *See* Parker, Martin.
King found at Southvvell. 1646. *See* Lloyd, M.

560AA King Jame's letter to the French king. An excellent new song. [n.p., 1692.] brs. EN.

560BA King James's royal victory. [*London*], *for J. Clarke, W. Thackeray, and T. Passinger*, [1685]. brs. CM.

560CA King Josiah commanding. *For James Watts*, 1686. brs. Y.

560A Entry cancelled.

King-killing doctrine. 1679. *See* Arnauld, Antoine.

561 King Lewis of France, the hector. *For Richard Baldwin*, 1690. 4°. T.C.II 323. O; CLC, WF, Y.

562 The King no tyrant. *For Laurence Chapman*, 1643. 4°.* LT, EN; CH, INU, MH, MM, TU, Y.

563 The King of Denmarck, the King of France. *For J. Bandon*, 1642. 4°.* LT, MR; CN.

564 The king of good-fellows. [*London*], *for J. Jordan*, [1684?]. brs. L.

565–7 No entries.

King of hearts. 1690. *See* Mainwaring, Arthur.
The King of Kings his privie marks. 1646. *See* Kem, Samuel.
King of hearts. 1690. *See* Mainwaring, Arthur.

568 The King of Morocco's letter. colop: *For Richard Janeway*, 1682. brs. L, O, LNM, EN; CH, Y.

568A —[Anr. ed.] [*Edinburgh?* 1682.] brs. ALDIS 2333.5. L.

569 The King of Poland's ghost. colop: *For Jos. Hindmarsh*, 1683. brs. L, O, LLP, HH, EN; CH, MH, NCD, TU, Y.

570 The King of Poland's last speech. *For J. P.*, 1682. brs. L, O, MC; CH, MH, NCD, PU, WF, Y.

570A —[Anr. ed.] [n.p., 1682?] brs. L.

571 The King of Scotland's negotiations at Rome. *By William Du-gard*, 1650. 4°.* LT, O, CM, LIU, DT; HR, CH, IU, MH, NU, WF, Y.

572 —[Anr. ed.] *Edinburgh, by Evan Tyler*, 1650. 4°.* ALDIS 1413. DU, MR, EN, ES; MBP.

573 Entry cancelled. Ghost.

574 The King of Spains cabinet council divulged. *By J. H. for J. S. to be sold by Simon Miller*, 1658. 8°. LT, CCA, SP; CLC, CN, WF, Y.

575 The King of Vtopia, his letter. *Printed at Cosmopolis in 7461, and reprinted at London*, 1647. cap., 4°.* LT, MR; MIU.

King on his throne. York, 1643. *See* Mossom, Robert.
King Richard the third revived. 1657. *See* Prynne, William.

575A King Solomons experimental observations. *By G. C. and are to be sold by Randal Taylor*, 1687. 12°.* T.C.II 202. MH.

576 The King the good-fellows. [*London*, 1684?] brs. L.

576A King William and his forrester. *Printed and sold by J. Bradford*, [1690]. brs. L.

King William and Queen Mary. 1693. *See* Blount, Charles.

576B King William, and Queen Mary, at White-hall. *For Robert Clavel*, 1689. brs. L.

577 Entry cancelled.

King William or K. Lewis. 1689. *See* K. William.

578 King William's courage [*London*], *for P. Brooksby, J. Deacon, J. Blare, and J. Back*, [1690–92]. brs. L, CM, HH.

579 King William's march. [*London*], *for Ch. Bates*, [1690–1]. brs. HH.

579A King William's statue. [*Dublin*], *by J. Ray*, [1698]. brs. C.

580 King William's toleration: being an explanation. *For Robert Hayhurst*, 1689. 4°.* L, O, LSD, SP, DT; CH, CN, MH, MM, TU, WF.

580A King William's welcome to London: being a joyful congratulation. colop: *By W. Downing*, 1695. brs. MH.

Kingdom of darkness. 1688. *See* Crouch, Nathaniel.

Kingdome of England and principality of Wales. [*London*], 1676. *See* Hollar, Wenceslaus.

581 Entry cancelled.

Kingdom of Sweden restored. 1682. *See* Saint Paul, *d.* 1684?

Kingdome saved. 1663. *See* Lloyd, David.

582 The kingdomes briefe ansvver, to the late declaration. *Printed*, 1648. 4°.* LT, O, C, AN, MR, DT; CH, CN, MH, NU, TU, WF, Y.

583 The kingdomes case; or, the question resolved. *For Iohn Wright*, May 1. 1643. 4°.* LT, O, LNC, EN, DT; CH, CN, MH, MU, NU, TU, Y.

584 —[Anr. ed.] *For John VVright*, 1649. 4°.* LT, O, OC; CH, MB, WF.

585 The Kingdomes grand qvere. What. *By M. S. for H. Cripps*, 1648. 4°.* LT, MR, CD; CSS, MB, MH, NU, WF.

586 The kingdomes hvmble remonstrance. [*London*], *printed*, 1648. 4°.* LT, MR; INU, MIU.

587 The kingdomes monster vncloaked from Heaven. [*London*], *printed*, 1643. brs. LT; NCD.

588 The kingly myrrour. *For C. V.*, 1649. 12°.* ALMACK p. 74. LT.

588A **Kings, William.** A sermon preached . . . April the 14th, 1667. *By T. R. for Nath. Brook*, 1667. 4°.* L; Y.

589 The Kings [Richard II] articles and the Parliaments honovr. [*London*], *August 1, for Thomas Baley*, 1642. 4°.* LT.

590 The kings-bench cabal. *For J. Dean*, 1684. brs. L; MH.

591 Entry cancelled.

Kings cabinet opened. 1645. *See* Charles I.

Kings cavse. [n.p.], 1644. *See* Doughty, John.

Kings disguise. [n.p., 1647.] *See* Cleveland, John.

592 The King's dispensing power. colop: *Printed, and sold by R. Janeway*, [1687?]. cap., fol.* L, O, C, BR, DUS; CH, CN, MH, TU, WF, Y.

592A The Kings ecclesiastical commission. [*London? 1686.*] fol. O, P.

593 The Kings estate at present. *Printed*, 1647. 4°.* LT, MR, DT; CLC, MH, NU, TU, WF, Y.

King's evidence justified. 1679. *See* Dangerfield, Thomas.

594 The Kings evidence vindicated. colop: *For R. Janeway*, 1680. cap., fol.* L, O, OP; CH, CN, WF, Y.

595 The Kings forces totally rovted. [*London*], *for Edward Husband, Sept.* 29, 1645. 4°.* LT, O, CCL, EN, DT; CLC, CN, MH, WF, Y.

King's grant. 1669. *See* Atkyns, Richard.

596 Entry cancelled.

King's health. 1682. *See* D'Urfey, Thomas.

597 The Kings last farewell to the world. *For Robert Ibbitson*, 1648[9]. brs. LT, HH; CH, TU.

597A The Kings letter intercepted coming from Oxford. *By Andrew Coe*, 1644. 4°.* CH.

King's life-guard. 1665. *See* Griffith, Matthew.

598 Entry cancelled.

Kings maiesties alarum for open war. 1642. *See* Charles I.

King's majesties desires. 1647. *See* Williamson, Robert.

Kings Majesties last propositions. [n.p.], 1648. *See* Wilson, John, *of Breadon*.

Kings Majesties letter intercepted. 1647. *See* Sammel, L.

Kings Majesties letter to the Queen. 1648. *See* Charles I.

599 The Kings Majesties letter to His son. *For R. W.*, 1648. 4°.* LT.

600 The Kings Majesties love to London. *By John Best*, 1665. brs. L.

601 The Kings Majesties message to . . . the Prince of Wales. [*London*], *for G. VVharton*, 1648. 4°.* LT.

602 The Kings Maiestjes most gracjous speech, declaring His desires. *For I. Ianes, July* 24. 1648. 4°.* LT, LG, DT; MH, Y.

603 The Kings Majesties prophecie concerning the army. [*London*], *printed*, 1648. 4°.* LT.

King's Majesties propositions. [n.p.], 1647. *See* Fornace, W.

Kings Maiesties receiving. [n.p.], 1646. *See* N., D.

Kings Majesties resolvtion concerning York-shire. 1642. *See* Sanders, Edward.

Kings march. 1646. *See* R., S.

603A The Kings medicines for the plague. *For F. Coles, T. Vere, R. Gilbertson and J. Wright*, 1665. 8°. * L.

603B —[Anr. ed.] *For F. Coles, and T. Vere*, 1664. 8°.* LWL.

Kings most gracious messages. [n.p.], 1648. *See* Symmons, Edward.

Kings noble entertainment. 1641. *See* Rigby, Sir Nathaniel.

604 Entry cancelled.

King's possessions. 1647. *See* Charles I.

605 The King's power in ecclesiastical matters truly stated. [*n.p.*, 1688.] cap., 4°.* L, O, CT, LIU, EN; CN, MHL, PL, WF, Y.

King's prerogative. 1680. *See* Jenkins, David.

605A The Kings primer. *By T. J. for Sam Speed*, 1669. 12°.* Y.

606 The Kings psalter. *For Sam. Speed*, 1670. 8°. L; MH.

606A —[Anr. ed.] [1670?] 8°. O (impf.)

607 —[Anr. ed.] *For S. S. and sold by Tho. Hartley*, 1671. 8°. L, O.

607A The King's reasons (with some reflections upon them). [*London*, 1689.] brs. C, LG; IU, WF, Y, ZWT.

King's right of indulgence. 1688. *See* Anglesey, Arthur Annesley, *earl*.

608 The King's tryal. Together, with the manner. *For Thomas Williams*, [1649]. 4°.* LT; CH, MHL.

609 **Kingsnorth, Richard.** The true tything of the gospel-ministers. *By G. Dawson, for Francis Smith*, 1657. 4°.* MH, Y.

610 **Kingston, Richard.** The cause & cure of offences. *For Daniel Brown*, 1682. 8°. T.C.I 482. O, LSC, CP, DM, DT.

611 [–] God's sovereignty and man's duty asserted. *By John Richardson for the author*, 1688. 4°.* L, BLH.

612 —Impudence, lying and forgery, detected. *Printed*, 1700. 8°.* L, O; MU, WF.

613 —A modest answer to Captain Smith's immodest memoirs. *For John Nutt*, 1700. 8°.* L, O, CT, BAMB, LIU; BN, CH, CN, NU, WF, Y.

614 —Pillulæ pestilentiales: or a spiritual receipt. *By W. G. for Edw. Brewster*, 1665. 8°. L, O, LG, LP, LSC; CH, WF.

615   [–] A true history of the several designs. *For the author, and sold by Abel Roper*, 1698. 8°. L, O, C, ES, DT; BN, CH, CN, MH, NU, WF, Y.

616   —Tyranny detected. *For John Nutt*, 1699. 8°. L, C OH, LIU, AU; CH, CN, NU, WF, Y.

617   —Vivat Rex. A sermon. *For Joseph Hindmarsh*, 1683. 4°.* T.C.II 39. O, C, BR, LSD, DT; CH, NU, WF, Y.

618   **Kinnaird, Charles.** Reverendissimo in Christi patri Arthuro. [*Edinburgi*, 1686.] brs. ALDIS 2674.3. E.

618A   **Kinnaston, Edward.** The case of . . . relating to his election . . . Shrewsbury. [*London*, 1678.] brs. LPR.

      Kiranus, *pseud.*

619   **Kirby, Richard.** Catastrophe Galliæ, & Hiberniæ restitutio, an impartial judgement. *For Tho. Howkins*, 1690. 4°.* L, O, C, BQ, DT; VILLANOVA, Y.

620   —A diurnal speculum. *By John Bringhurst*, 1684. 8°.* O.

621   —Dreadful news from Wapping. *By W. D.*, 1693. 8°.* O.

      —Ephemeris. 1681. *See* Almanacs.

622   —The marrow of astrology. *By Joseph Streater, for the authors, to be sold by John Southby.* 1687. 4°. T.C.II 177. L, O, LW, MC; CLC, MBA, WF.

623   —Vates astrologicus: or, England's astrological prophet. *For Thomas Malthus*, 1683. 4°. T.C.II 18. L, O, EN, DM; CH, CSS, MIU, NN, WSG.

624   **Kircher, Athanasius.** The vulcano's. *By J. Darby for John Allen, to be sold by him; and by Benjamin Billingsly*, 1669. 4°. T.C.I 21. L, C, MR, P, DT; CH, CLC, IU, MH, PL, WF, Y.

625   **Kirk, Edmund.** The sufferers legacy. *By Geo. Croom.* 1684. brs. L, LG, HH; WF.

625A   —A true paper delivered by. colop: *For Langley Curtis*, 1684. brs. O.

      [**Kirk, Patrick.**] Λογομαχια: or. 1690. *See* Ker, Patrick. Πολιτικος.

625B   **Kirke, Percy.** A letter from. [*London*], *for J. M.*, 1690. brs. C.

626   —Major-General Kirk's letter to his Grace the Duke of Hamilton, . . . August the 5, 1689. colop: *Edinburgh, by the heir of Andrew Anderson*, 1689. brs. ALDIS 2901. L, O, C, E, EN; CN.

626A   —A particular account from Collonel Kirke, of the state of London-Derry. colop: *For J. Wilson*, 1689. brs. L, C; CH, MH.

627   —A true account from Coll. Kirke of the relieving of London-Derry, brought by Mr. Beale. *For James Partridge*, 1689. brs. MC, DN; MH.

628   ——[Anr. ed.] *Edinburgh, re-printed*, 1689. brs. ALDIS 2900. L, HH, E, EN; CH, TU.

629   [**Kirke, Thomas.**] A modern account of Scotland. [*London*], *printed*, 1679. 4°.* T.C.I 362. L, O, CT, MP, EN; CH, CN, MH, WF, Y.

630   Entry cancelled.
      Kirk of Scotlands conclusion. 1646. *See* Church of Scotland.

      Kirkby, Christopher. Compleat and true narrative. 1679. *See* B., J.

630A   **K[irkman], F[rancis].** The counterfeit lady unveiled. *For Peter Parker*, 1673. 8°. T.C.I 126. O; CH, CN, NHS, WF.

630B   [–] —[Anr. ed.] —, 1679. 12°. L.

631–2   Entries cancelled.
      [–] English rogue continued. 1668. *See* Head, Richard.

632A   [–] Famous and delectable history of Don Bellianis. *For Francis Kirkman*, 1673. 4°.* L, O, C, E; CLC, CN, MH, TU, Y.

633   [–] The honour of chivalry: . . . the second part. *By Tho. Johnson, to be sold by Andrew Kembe*, 1664. 4°. OC; CH.

633A   [–] —[Parts 1 and 2.] *By Tho. Johnson, for Fran. Kirkman*, 1671. 4°. T.C.I 100. L, O; CLC, IU, TU, ZAP.

633B   [–] The honour of chivalry: . . . the second part. *By Tho. Johnson, for Fran. Kirkman*, 1671. 4°. L, O; CLC, INU, MH, TU, Y.

634   —The honour of chivalry: . . . the third part. *By Ed. Okes, for Fran. Kirkman*, 1672. 4°. L, O; CH, CN, INU, TU, Y.

635   [–] The Presbyterian lash. . . . Part 1. *For the use of Mr. Noctroffs friends*, 1661. 4°.* LT, O, OW, EC; CH, CN, IU, WF, Y.

636   [–] —[Anr. ed.] —, 1666. 4°. L, LVD.

637   [–] A true, perfect and exact catalogue of all the comedies, tragedies. [*London*], 1661. 4°.* L, O, C, CT; CN, MB, NN, WF.

637A   — —[Anr. ed.] [*London*, 1671]. 4°.* O, BC; CH, MB, MH, OSU, TU, WF.

638   [–] The unlucky citizen. *By Anne Johnson, for Fra. Kirkman*, 1673. 8°. T.C.I 152. L, O, LG, A; CH, CN, CU, MH, PU, WF.

639   No entry.
      [–] The wits; or, sport upon sport . . . Part I. 1662. *See* title.

639A   **Kirkwood, James.** Account of Mr. Kirkwood's plea against the Kirk-session of Kelso. [*n.p.*, 1693?] cap., 4°.* NN.

640–2   Entries cancelled.
      —Advice to children. 1690. *See* —True interest *and* —New family-book.

642A   —All the examples. *Edinburgh, by George Swintoun and James Glen*, 1676. 8°. ALDIS 2076.9. EN, GU; CH, CLC.

643   —Grammatica delineata. Third edition. *Typis G. Godbid, prostant venales Edinburgi apud Henry Leslie*, 1677. 8°. ALDIS 2102. L, C, E, EN, GU; BN, WF.

643A   —Grammatica Despauteriana. *Edinburgi, Mosman*, 1695. 8°. ALDIS 3466.8. EN.

644   — —[Anr. ed.] *Edinburgi, ex officina Georgii Mosman*, 1696. 4°. ALDIS 3573. SA, E, EN; NC, WF.

644A   — —[Anr. ed.] *Edinburgi, ex typographoeo Georgii Mosman, apud quam venales prostant, & Joannem Vallange*, 1700. 12°. ALDIS 3977. PL.

645   —Grammatica facilis. *Edinburgi, excudebant*, 1674. 12°. ALDIS 2022. EN.

646   — —[Anr. ed.] *Glasguæ, excudebat Robertus Sanders*, 1674. 8°. ALDIS 2023. L, EN; CH.

646A   — —[Anr. ed.] [*n.p.*], *printed*, 1674. 12°. TO.

646B   [–] Libel and complaint before Their Majesties secret council. [*Edinburgh*, 1692?] cap., fol. NE.

647 —A new family-book. Second edition. *For J. Taylor, and J. Everingham, 1693.* 12°. T.C.II 449. L, O, NE, RPL; CH, CLC, MM.

648 [–] An overture for founding & maintaining of bibliothecks in every paroch. *[Edinburgh], printed, 1699.* 4°.* ALDIS 3877. WF.

649 —Mr. Kirkwood's plea. *By D. E. for the author, 1698.* 4°. L, OM, NE, A, EN, CD; INU, WF.

649A —Prima pars grammaticae in metrum redacta. *Edinburgi, excudebant Georgius Swintoun, et Jacobus Glen, 1675.* ALDIS 2054. 8°. EN, GU; CH, CLC.

649B —Rhetoricæ compendium. *Edinburgi, haeres typographi regii, prostant G. Lesly & A. Hyslop, 1678.* 12°. ALDIS 2130. O, EN.

650 — —Second edition. *Edinburgii, ex officina Georgii Mosman, 1696.* 12°.* ALDIS 3574. AU, E, EN.

650aA —Secunda pars grammaticae. Second edition. *Edinburgi, excudebant Georgius Swintoun et Jacobus Glen, 1676.* 12°. ALDIS 2076.95. EN, GU; CH.

650bA —Tertia pars grammaticæ. Second edition. *Edinburgi, excudebant Georgius Swintoun & Jacobus Glen, 1676.* 12°. ALDIS 2076. 96. GU; CH.

650A [–] The true interest of families. *For S. Lowndes, 1690.* 12°. T.C.II 319. NE.

651 [–] —[Anr. ed.] *For J. Taylor; and J. Everingham, 1692.* 12°. T.C.II 409. L, O; CH.

652 Entry cancelled.
[–] True interest of families. Second edition. 1693. See — New family-book.

653 **Kirle, R.** A coppy of a letter writ from. *[London, 1643.]* cap., 4°.* LT, O, C, DU, LIU; CH, MH, NU, WF, Y.
Kiss of a sea-man's. 1655. See Smithson, Samuel.

653A Kissing goes by favour. *[London], for Thomas Vere, [1650–56].* brs. L.

654 The kitchin-maids answer to the London apprentice's word. *For W. Rayner, 1691.* 4°.* O, LLP, DU, DT; CH, CN, NP, Y.
Kitchin-physick. 1676. See Cock, Thomas.
Kitchin-physician. 1680. See K., T.

655 **Kitchin, John.** The grand statute. *For Francis Kitchin and John Garway, 1660.* 4°.* LT, O, LW, SP; MH, MWA, Y.

656 —Jurisdictions. *By T: Roycroft, for M: Walbancke, and H: Twyford, 1651.* 8°. LT; CLL, LC, MHL, NCL, PUL, TU.

657 — —Second edition. *For M: Walbancke, and H. Twyford, and J. Place, 1653.* 8°. L, O, CCA, LLU; CH, CLC, LC, MHL, NCL, PUL.

658 — —Third edition. —, 1656. 8°. L, C, LMT, DT; LC, MHL, MU, NCL, PUL.

658A — —"Third" edition. —, 1657. 8°. O, EN; LC.

659 — —Fourth edition. *By J. Streater, for Hen. Twyford, 1663.* 8°. L, LIL, CP, DC, CD; CLL, LC, MHL, NCL, WF, YL.

659A — —"Fourth" edition. *By J. Streater, for John Place, 1663.* 8°. LIU; PL, TU.

660 — —Fifth edition. *For Hen. Twyford, and Sam. Heyrick, 1675.* 8°. T.C.I 201. L, O, LIL, CS, NE; CH, IU, MHL, NCL, WF, YL.

661 **Kittermaster, Thomas.** A vvonderfull deliverance. *By T. F. for I. H., October 20, 1642.* 4°.* LT, O.
X[i.e., K]λεις ευαγγελιου. 1672. See Sherwin, William.

662 Κλεις προφητειας. Or, the key of prophecie. *[London], printed, 1660.* 4°.* LT, O, MR; MH, WF, Y.

662A **Knaggs, Thomas.** An assize-sermon . . . March the 23d, 1696/7. *For Jonas Luntley, 1697.* 4°. NE.

663 —An exhortation to a personal . . . repentance. *For John Barnes, to be sold by A. Baldwin, 1699.* 4°. L, LLP, CT, ASSINGTON PARISH, SUFFOLK; CH, IU, Y.

663A —A help to prayer. *For J. Luntley, to be sold by Andrew Dell, 1697.* 12°. OC.

663B —A sermon preached . . . 19th day of June, 1689. *For Richard Randell and Peter Maplisden, in New-Castle upon Tine, 1689.* 4°.* NE; Y.

663C —A sermon preached before the mayor . . . fifth of November, 1691. *For Joseph Hall, Newcastle, 1691.* 4°. NE.

663D —A sermon preached . . . November the fifth, 1693. *For Ric. Chiswell, 1693.* 4°.* T.C.II 457. L, BANGOR, NE, SHR, WCA; CHW, Y.

663E —A sermon preach'd . . . 22d of September 1695. *For Richard Baldwin, 1695.* MIU, WF.

664 —A sermon preached . . . 16th day of April, 1696. *For Richard Baldwin, 1696.* 4°.* L, O; CLC, Y.

664A —A sermon preached . . . June the 21th 1698. *By Jer. Wilkins, and sold by J. Wells, [1698].* 4°.* Y.

665 **Knap, John.** An encomium upon that most accomplish'd gentleman, Stephen Mosdel. *[London], printed, 1671.* 8°. DT; MH.

666 —Englands sorrow. *By George Croom, 1685.* brs. L, O, MC; CH, IU, MH, WF.

667 **Knapp, William.** Abraham's image. *By Peter Cole, 1658.* 4°.* LT, OB, NPL, BLH; MH, MWA.

667A —Θεοφιλιας λογισμος: or, an account. *For John Southby, 1685.* 8°. CT.

668 **Knatchbull, Sir Norton.** Animadversiones in libros Novi Testament. *Typis Guil. Godbid, 1659.* 8°. LT, O, C, LNC, EN; BN, NGT, NU, TO, WF.

669 [–] —Second edition. —, 1672. 8°. T.C.I 114. L, OM, CS; IU, Y.

670 — —[Anr. ed.] *Oxoniæ, excudebat Henricus Hall impensis Ric. Davis, 1676.* 8°. T.C.I 258; MADAN 3112. O, AN, CD.

671 — —Third edition. *Oxoniæ, excudebat Henric. Hall impensis R. Davis, 1677.* 8°. MADAN 3143. L, O, C, DU, DT; BN, CH, PPT, WF, WSC, Y.

672 —Annotations upon some difficult texts. *Cambridge, by J. Hayes, for W. Graves, 1693.* 8°. T.C.II 451. L, O, C, NPL, E, DT; CH, IU, MH, NU, PL, WF, Y.

673 —The library of. *[London], 22 June 1698.* 4°.* L, OC; MH.

674 The knave of clubs. 1643. 4°.* LT, O; CH, NCD, TU.

675 The knave uncloak'd. *For Tho. Parkhurst, 1679.* 4°.* L, C, ORP, EN, DT; CH, IU, MBA, NU, WF, Y.
Knavery in all trades. 1664. See Tatham, John.

676 The knavery of astrology discover'd. *For T. B. and R. E., 1680.* 4°.* L, LN, LSD; CH, MH, MBA.
Knaves and fooles. 1648. See H., S.
Knaves are no honest men. [n.p., 1672.] See L., J.

677 The knavish merchant. *[London], printed, [1661].* 4°.* LT.

678   **Knell, Paul.** Five seasonable sermons. *Printed*, 1660[1]. 8°. LT, O, C, LCL, DC, DU; CLC, WF.

679   —Israel and England paralelled. *Printed*, 1648. 4°.* LT, O, C, WCA, DT; CH, CN, NU, WF, Y.

680   ——[Anr. ed.] *Printed, 1648. And now reprinted. Sold by Randal Tayler and Robert Stephens*, 1681. 4°.* L, O, C, BLH; NN, NPT, PL.

681   ——[Anr. ed.] *Printed, 1648, and now reprinted*, 1695. 4°.* L, LLP, CT; MH, NU.

682   —The life-guard of a loyall Christian. *Printed*, 1648. 4°.* LT, O, C, YM, DT; CH, CN, MH, NU, Y.

683   —A looking-glasse for Levellers. *Printed*, 1648. 4°.* LT, C, LG, CT, LSD; CH, IU, NU, TSM, WF, Y.

684   **Knight, Arthur.** The speech and confession of. *Imprinted at London, for G. Horton*, 1653. 4°.* LT, MR; CU.

685   —The speech of. *For Tho. Heath*, [1653]. 4°.* LT, O; CU, MH.

686   **Knight, *Sir* John.** The following speech. [*London*, 1694.] cap., 4°.* LLP, OC, CS, EC, MR; CH, MH, MM, NU, WF.

687   —Order by John Knight, Mayor, for restraining blasphemy. [*Bristol*, 1670?] brs. L.

687A   —A speech in the House of Commons. colop: [*London*], *printed*, 1693. 4°.* L, O, LCL, DT; CH, NN.

687B   —The speech of . . . against the bill. [*n.p.*, 1694?] 8°. L, BR; NC, NCD.

688   **Knight, John, D.D.** The Samaritan rebels perjured. [*London*], *for William Thorp in Banbury, to be sold by Randal Taylor*, 1682. 4°.* L, O, OC, CT, E; CH, MIU, NU, PL, V, WF.

689   —A sermon preach'd . . . Nov. 18. 1699. *London, for George Thorp, in Banbury*, 1700. 4°.* L, O, C, BAMB, DU; CH, CLC, TU, WF, Y.

690   Entry cancelled.
       Knight, *Sir* John. Speech. 1693. *See above* [K687A].

691   **Knight, Nicholas.** A comparison between the true and false ministers. [*London*], *printed*, 1675. 4°.* L, O, LF, BBN; CH, IE, MH, PH, WF.

691A   —Something concerning the mystery of godliness. [*London*, 1676.] cap., 4°.* L, LF; MH, PH.

692   **Knight, R.** A letter from. [*London*], *printed*, 1647. *July 22.* 4°.* LT, LVF, DN; CH.

693   **Knight, Valentine.** Proposalls of a new modell for rebuilding . . . London. *By T. Leach, for Samuel Speed*, 1666. brs. L, O, LG, LPR.

694   ——[Anr. ed.] *By H. Bruges, for Samuel Speed*, 1666. brs. O; MH.

694A   ——[Anr. ed.] [*London*, 1666.] brs. CH, YBA.

694B   **Knight, William.** The case and vindication of. *Printed*, 1653. 4°.* WF.

695   —A declaration of the treacherous procedings [*sic*] of the Lord of Inchequin. *Printed*, 1648[9]. 4°.* LT; CN, MH, NN.

695A   —Mr. Knight's strange . . . prophecy. *By John Harrison* 1699. WF.

695B   —Vox luminarium. *Benj. Harris*, 1699. 4°.* L.

696   —Vox stellarum: or, the voyce of the stars. *By E. T. and R. H. for Thomas Passinger*, 1681. 12°. T.C.I 429. L, C; LC.

697   The knight adventurer: or the infamous and abominable history of . . . Sir Firedrake. *By R. I.*, 1663. 8°.* CH.

697A   The knight and the beggar-wench. *For F. Coles, M. Wright, T. Vere, and W. Gilbertson*, [1658]. brs. GU.

697B   ——[Anr. ed.] *For F. Coles, T. Vere, and J. Wright*, [1675]. brs. O.

697C   ——[Anr. ed.] *For F. Coles, T. Vere, J. Wright, Clarke, Thackeray and Passinger*, [1678–80]. brs. CM.

697D   ——[Anr. ed.] *For A.M.*, [1685?]. brs. L.

698   ——[Anr. ed.] *By and for W. O. for A. M. and sold by C. Bates*, [1690]. brs. L, HH; MH.

       Knight errant. 1652. See B., J.

699   Knight-errantry; or, Don Quixote encountring the wind mill. colop: [*London*], *printed*, 1695. cap., fol.* LLP, LLU, EN; NCD, Y.

700   The knitters jobb. [*London*], *for P. Brooksby*, [1675–80]. brs. L, O, HH; MH.

700A   A knock at the door of Christless ones. *For T. Passenger*, 1683. 12°. CM.

701   **Knolles, Richard.** Proposals for subscribing the famous history of the Turks. [*London*], 1687. brs. LG (lost).

702   —The Turkish history. Sixth edition. *For Tho. Basset*, 1687. 2v. fol. T.C.II 210. L, O, C, EN, DT; IU, LC, MH, NN, PL, TU, Y.

703   ——*For Awnsham Churchill*, 1687. 2v. fol. BN, NN.

703A   ——*For Robert Clavell*, 1687. 2v. fol. CS, WCA; AVP.

703B   ——*For Jonathan Robinson*, 1687. 2v. fol. LW, NE, DL; CN.

       ——Vol. II, parts ii and iii; vol. III. 1687. *See* Rycaut, *Sir* Paul.

703C   [**Knollys, Hanserd.**] An answer to a brief discourse concerning singing. *Printed for the author H. K.* 1691. WF.

704   [–] Apocalyptical mysteries. *Printed*, 1667. 8°. L, ORP; CU, MH, NHC, Y.

705   [–] The Baptists answer. *For Francis Smith*, 1675. 8°.* L, O, ORP; MH, NHC, NU, TO, WF.

706   —Christ exalted. *Printed*, 1645. 4°.* LT, C, OC, MR; Y.

707   ——[Anr. ed.] *By Jane Coe*, 1646. 4°.* LT, LW, BC, DT; CH, NHC, NU, Y.

708   —An exposition of the eleventh chapter of the Revelation. [*London*?], *printed*, 1679. 4°. L, LSC; CH, MWA.

709   —An exposition of the first chapter of the Song of Solomon. *By W. Godbid, to be sold by Livewel Chapman*, 1656. 4°. O, LB, OME, ORP, LIU.

710   [–] An exposition of the whole Book of the Revelation. *For the author; to be sold by William Marshall*, 1689. 8°. T.C.II 331. L, LCL, LW, ORP, AN; CLC, LC, MBC, NU, TO, Y.

711   Entry cancelled.
       —Glimpse of Sions glory. 1641. *See* Goodwin, Thomas.

711A   —The gospel minister's maintenance vindicated. *Printed, and are to be sold by John Harris*, 1689. 12°. ORP; MH, NHC.

712   —Grammaticæ Græcæ compendium. 1664. 12°. L, O; CLC, IU, WF.

713   —Grammaticæ Latinæ compendium, or. *Printed*, 1664. 12°. L, O; CLC, IU, WF.

714 —Grammaticæ Latinæ, Græcæ, & Hebraicæ. *Typis Tho. Roycroft*, 1665. 12°. L, O, ORP; CH, CLC, IU, NHC, RBU, WF.

715 —The life and death of. *For John Harris*, 1692. 8°. L, C, LCL, LF, LW; CH, CLC, CN.

716 —Linguæ Hebricæ delineatio. 1664. 12°.* L, O; CLC, IU, WF.

717 —A moderate answer vnto Dr. Bastvvicks book. *By Iane Coe*, 1645. 4°.* LT, O, LCL, SC, DT; MH, NHC, WF, Y.

718 —Mystical Babylon vnvailed. [London], *printed*, 1679. 4°.* L, O; CH, MH, WF, Y.

719 —The parable of the Kingdom of Heaven expounded. *For Benjamin Harris*, 1674. 8°. T.C.I 195. L, LB, ORP, AN; CU, MH, OHU, WF, Y.

720 —Petition for the prelates. 1641. 4°. LCL.

721 —Radices Hebraicæ omnes. 1664. 12°. L, O; CLC, IU, WF.

722 —Radices simplicium vocum. 1664. 12°.* L, O; CLC, IU, WF.

723 —Rhetoricae adumbratio. 1663. 12°.* L; CLC, IU, WF.

724 —The rudiments of the Hebrew grammar. *By M. B.*, 1648. 8°.* LT, ORP, EN, DT; CH, CLC, CU, MB, MH, WF.

724A ——[Anr. ed.] *By Moses Bell, for William Larnar, and George Whittington*, 1648. 8°. MH (t.p.).

725 —The shining of a flaming-fire in Zion. *By Jane Coe*, 1646. 4°.* LT, O, LCL, MAB, DT; CH, NHC, NU, PL, WF, Y.

726 —The world that now is. *By Tho. Snowden*, 1681. 8°. L, O, ORP, AN.

726A [Knorr von Rosenroth, Christian.] A genuine explication of the visions of . . . Revelation. *By W. G. sold by Moses Pitt*, [1670?]. 8°. T.C.I 78. L; IU.

Knot of fooles. 1658. *See* Brewer, Thomas.

727 A knot untied. *For Henry Eversden*, 1660[1]. 4°.* LT, LG; CH, CLC, NU.

Knot unty'd. 1682. *See* Ferguson, Robert.

728 No entry.

[Knott, Edward.] Protestancy condemned. Doway. 1654. *See* Wilson, Matthias.

728aA Know all men by these presents, that [blank] holden. *Boston, for John Usher*, [1689?]. brs. LC.

728bA —[Anr. ed.] [London, 1693.] brs. OP.

728cA —[Anr. ed.] [New York, William Bradford, 1695?] brs. RPJ.

728dA Knowing the great abuses . . . I infallibly cure the veneral pox. [London, 1685?] brs. L.

Knowledge of medals. 1697. *See* Jobert, Louis.

728A Entry cancelled.

Knowledge of the world. [1694.] *See* Chevremont, Jean Baptiste de.

729 **Knowles, John.** An answer to Mr. Ferguson's book. [London?], *for J. J. and sold by P. P. and W. C.*, [1668?]. 8°. L, LW, OC, CT, SP, E; MH, NU, WF.

730 —A modest plea for private mens preaching. *Printed*, 1648. 4°.* LT, C, LIU, EN; CLC.

731 **Knowles, William.** A godly gift. *For Fr. Coles*, 1663. 8°.* DT.

732 —The great assizes or generall day of judgement. *For Fr. Coles*, 1662. 8°.* L.

733 —The great assizes. *By E. O. for F. Coles*, 1668. 8°.* L.

733A ——[Anr. ed.] *By H. Brugis for W. Thackeray*, 1681. 12°. CM.

734 —Great Brittains warning piece. *For F. Coles*, 1662. 8°.* L.

734A —A serious call to obstinate sinners. *For Fr. Coles*, 1677. 8°.* Y.

734B ——[Anr. ed.] *By H. B. for W. Thackeray*, 1684. 12°. CM.

735 —Truth reignes conquerour. *For Fr. Coles*, 1662. 8°.* L.

736 Knovvne lavves. *Printed*, 1643. 4°.* LT, O, CT, EN, DT; CH, CN, LC, MH, NU, Y.

737 The known saying in the New Testament. [London, 1688?] cap., 4°.* EC; NU.

738 [Knox, John.] The historie of the reformation of the Church of Scotland. *By John Raworth, for George Thomason and Octavian Pullen*, 1644. fol. L, O, C, EN, DT; BN, CH, CN, MH, NN, NU, WF, Y.

739 [–] —[Anr. ed.] *Printed at London for G. T. and O. P. and reprinted at Edinburgh by Robert Bryson*, 1644. 4°. ALDIS 1143. L, O, C, E, GU; BN, CH, IU, TO, WF, VICTORIA U., NZ.

740 No entry.

741 Entry cancelled. Ghost.

742 **Knox, Robert.** An historical relation of the island Ceylon. *By Richard Chiswell*, 1681. fol. T.C.I 461. L, O, C, EN, DT; BN, CH, MH, MU, WF, Y.

742A ——[Anr. ed.] —, 1682. fol. L (t.p.).

742B **Knox, *Sir* W.** Thursday noon, being Feb (26) 84/85. My dearest soul. colop: *Printed*, 1689. brs. CN, Y.

743 **Knutton, Immanuel.** Four sermons. *For George Sawbridge*, 1655. 12°. O, LW.

744 —Seven qvestions abovt the controversie. *By Tho: Paine, to be sold by Andrew Kembe*, 1645. 4°.* LT, C, CE, YM, EN; NHC, NU, Y.

745 **Königsmark, Karl Johann, *grefre*.** Count Conningsmarck's letter to the Lady Ogle. *For J. S.*, 1682. brs. O, EN; CH.

746 Κολλουριον, or eye salve to anoint the eyes. *By G. Dawson for Henry Cripps*, 1649. 4°.* LT, LG, MR; CN, MM, Y.

Komenski. *See* Comenius.

747 **KORAN.** The Alcoran of Mahomet. *Printed*, 1649. 4°. LT, O, C, E, AU; CH, CN, LC, MH, NU, Y.

747A ——[Anr. ed.] —, 1649. 8°. L, MR; CLC, CN, MH, NU, PL.

748 ——[Anr. ed.] *Printed, and are to be sold by Randal Taylor*, 1688. fol. T.C.II 210. L, O, CS, E, DT; CH, IU, NCD, NN, Y.

749 **Kornmann, Heinrich.** Sibylla trig-Andriana, seu de virginitate. *Prostant venales apud Ed: Forrest, Oxon*. 1669. 12°. T.C.I 10; MADAN 2833. L, O, MR, GH; NCD, WF.

Κοσμοβρεφια, or. 1658. *See* Billingsly, Nicholas.

750 **Kotter, Christopher.** The prophecies of. *For Robert Pawlet*, 1664. 12°. O, C, SHR; CH, MH.

750A ——Second edition. *For Robert Pawlet*, 1664. 8°. O; LC.

750B **Krainski, John de Kraino.** A relation of the distressed state of the church . . . Lithuania. *Printed*, 1661. 4°.* CS; MIU, WF.

750C **Kuhlmann, Quirin.** Cyrus refrigeratorius Jerusalemitanus. [London], *juxta exemplar Genevense excudebat Johannes Gain*, 1682. 8°.* L; PL.

751 —Kircheriana de arte magna sciendi. *Imprimuntur a Johan. Gain, pro authore, ac prostant apud Gulielmum Cooper*, 1681. 8°.* L; CLC, NA, PL.

752 —Constantinopolitana de conversione Turcarum. *Excudebat Johannes Gain*, 1682. 8°.* L; PL.

753 —Des Christen des Jesuelitens. *Vor den Author Johannes Gain in Mai*, 1681. 8°. L.

753A [–] . . . The Earle of Holland, chief of adepts, his . . . wonder-revalation. *Amsterdam, for the author*, 1684. 8°. WF.

754 —A Z The general London epistle of. *For The author*, 1679. 8°. L, O, C, DUS; CLC, NCU, NU, WF, Y.

754A —. . . Heptaglotta . . . opera suorum juvenilium. [*London*], 1683. 8°. WF.

755 —Mysterium viginti unarum. *Excudebat Johannes Gain*, 1682. 8°.* L, O; PL.

756 —Quinarius suorum lapidum. *Londini, Oxoniique, pro authore excudebatur*, 1683. 8°. L, O; PL.

757 — . . . His quinary of slingstones. *London and Oxford, for the author*, 1683. 8°.* L; PL.

757A —Responsaria de sapientia. *Excudit Johann Gain pro authore, mense Majo & prostant apud Guilelmum Cooper*, 1681. 8°. PL.

757B —Salmon a Kaiserstein cosmopolita. *Mense Octobri*, 1682. 8°.* PL.

758 —Testimonia humana. *Imprimuntur a Johanne Gain pro authore, et prostant apvd Gulielmum Cooper*, 1683. 8°. L; WF.

Kunckel, Johann. *See* Loewenstein, Johann Kunckel, baron.

759 **Kynaston, *Sir* Francis.** Leoline and Sydanis. *By Ric. Hearne*, 1642. 4°. L, O, OC; CH, CN, WCL, WF, Y.

760 [–] —[Second edition.] *By Ric. Heron to be sold by Thomas Slater*, 1646. 4°. L, LG, OW.

761 **Kynaston, Thomas.** To the King's most excellent Majesty. The humble petition of . . . [againt East India Co. of the Netherlands]. [*London*, 1677.] brs. CSS.

L

1 **L.** A letter intercepted at a court-guard. *For Edw: Husbands, February* 28. 1642[3]. 4°.* LT, O, LP, MR, LSD; CSS, LC, MH, NU, TU, WF, Y.
—Red-shankes sermon. 1642. *See* Row, James.

2 Entry cancelled. Ghost.

2A **L., A.** Dictionarium Latino-barbarum. *Typis J. C., impensis Johannis Wright, & Richardi Chiswel*, 1677. 4°. L.
—Hezekiah's return. 1668. *See* Littleton, Adam.

3 —An impartial and full account of the life and death of William Lord Russel. *For Caleb Swinock*, 1684. 12°. L, O, C, LG, DU; CH, NRU, WF, Y.

3A —An inducement to the intrenching of . . . York. 1642. 4°. L.

4 [–] A letter from a French lawyer. *For Ric. Chiswell*, 1689. 4°.* T.C.II 277. L, O, C, EN, DT; CH, CN, MH, NU, TU, WF, Y.

4A —A letter to a friend touching Dr. Jeremy Taylor's Disswasive. *Printed*, 1665. 4°.* L, O, LLP, OC, DU, DM; CLC.

5 —A question deeply concerning married persons. *For Tho. Underhill*, 1653. 4°.* L.
—Scripture-terms of Church-union. [1700?] *See* L'Ortie, Andre.
—Solomon's gate. 1662. *See* Littleton, Adam.

6 —To all the honest, wise and grave citizens. [*London*, 1648.] brs. LT.

7 —A true relation of the late expedition of the . . . Earl of Ormond. *For Joseph Hunscott*, 1642. 4°.* LT, LG, LL, OC, EC, DN; IU, MH, Y.

7A **L., B.** England's happiness: in a discourse . . . on the . . . coronation. [*London*], *for J. Blare*, 1689. 12°.* L.
—Shiboleth of priest-hood. [n.p.], 1678. *See* Lindley, Benjamin.
—Treatise of election. 1700. *See* Lindley, Benjamin.

8 —A true and faithful coppy of a real letter. [*London*, 1679?] cap., fol.* L, O, DU, LNC, MR; CH, MH, NC, TU, WF, Y.

8A —A true coppy of a second letter, from a friend. [*London*, 1679.] cap., fol.* L; CH, CLC.

L., C. Christians combat. 1664. *See* Love, Christopher.

9 **L., D.** Israel's condition and cause pleaded. *By P. W. For William Larnar and Jonathan Ball*, 1656. 8°. LT; CH, MB.
—Lettera esortatoria. [n.p.], 1667. *See* Loftus, Dudley.
—Most exact and accurate map. 1676. *See* Lupton, Donald.

10 —The Scots scovts discoveries. *For William Sheares*, 1642. 4°.* LT, O, CT, EN, DT; CH, CN, MBP, MH, WF, Y.

11 ——[Anr. ed.] *Printed*, 1642. 4°.* L, O, LNC, MR, EN; MH, NU, SCU, TU.
—Temple of vvisdom. Philadelphia, 1688. *See* Leeds, Daniel.

11A —A true account of the behaviour, confession . . . of the condemned pirates . . . [13 November 1700]. colop: *For Ed. Malletrat* [*sic*], 1700. brs. MR.

12–13 Entries cancelled.

L., E. Descent upon France. 1693. *See* Littleton, Edward.
—Discourse about keeping our money. 1696. *See* Littleton, Edward. Short discourse.
—Divine meditations. York, 1650. *See* Llewellin, Edward.
—English examples. 1676. *See* Leedes, Edward.

14 Entry cancelled.
—Funerall sermon. Paris, 1675. *See* Lutton, Edward.
—Just apology. [n.p.], 1642. *See* Lake, *Sir* Edward.
—Parochial queries. [n.p., 1697.] *See* Lhuyd, Edward.
—Philologicall commentary. 1652. *See* Leigh, Edward.

15 Entry cancelled.
—Preservative for our money. 1696. *See* Littleton, Edward, *fl.* 1694.
—Prodigal return'd home. [n.p.], 1684. *See* Lydeott, E.

16 —Proposals by E. L. to raise one million three hundred thousand pounds. [*London?* 1700.] brs. L; MH, Y.
—Review of some short directions. Oxford, 1664. *See* Lowe, Edward.
—Short direction. Oxford, 1661. *See* Lowe, Edward.

17 Entry cancelled.
—Short discourse. 1696. *See* Littleton, Edward.
—Supply to a draught. [n.p.], 1653. *See title.*
—Taste of the everlasting. [1670.] *See* Lane, Edward.

17A **L., Elizabeth.** Short remains of a dead gentlewoman. [*n.p.*, 1690?] fol.* WF.

18 **L., F.** Irelands sad lamentation: discovering its present danger. colop: *Printed*, 1680. brs. L, O, C, MC, EN; CH, MBA, MH, MU, Y.
—Present state of New-England. [n.p., 1689.] *See* Palmer, John.

18A **[L., G.]** The amorous gallant's tongue tipt with golden expressions. *For Robert Gifford*, 1698. 12°. LLU.
—Caledonias covenant. [n.p.], 1641. *See* Lauder, George.
—Debauched cavalleer. 1642. *See* Lawrence, George.
—Divine meditations; or. 1700. *See* Liddell, George.
—Epistle declaratorie. [n.p.], 1657. *See* Leyburn, George.

19 —Eubulus. Or, a free and loyal discourse. [*London*], 1660. 4°. E.

20 —The gentleman's new jockey. *By W. W. for Nicholas Boddington*, 1687. 12°. T.C.II 188. L; WF, Y.

20aA — —Second edition. *By W. Wilde for Nicholas Boddington*, 1691. 12°. L, EN.

20A — —Third edition. *By W. Onley, for Nicholas Boddington*, 1696. 12°. T.C.II 571. CLC, MH.

20B — —Fourth edition. —, 1700. 12°. CH.
—Glories of Heaven. 1699. *See* Larkin, George. World to come.
—Hypothesis physica nova. 1671. *See* Leibnitz, Gottfried.
—Letter written by. [n.p., 1657.] *See* Leyburn, George.

21 —Love's advocate, or certain arguments. *By James Moxon*, 1651. 4°.* LT, LG; CU, WF, Y.
—Some observations upon the life of Reginaldus Polus. 1686. *See* Joyner, William.
—World to come. 1699. *See* Larkin, George.

21A **L., H.** A circular letter to the clergy of Essex. colop: *Printed*, 1690. brs. L; WF, Y.

21B —A divine horn-book. *For the author*, 1688. 4°.* L.

21C —Reasons humbly offer'd against grafting upon or confirming the present East-India Company. [*London*, 1699?] brs. INDIA OFFICE.
—Replies made. 1657. *See* Lavor, Henry.

22 **L., I.** A discourse concerning the great benefit of drayning. [*n.p.*], *by G. M.*, 1641. 4°.* L, O; CLC, MH, Y.

23 —A divine balsam to cure the bleeding wounds. *For Robert Wood.* 1642. 4°.* LT, EC, LIU, E, DT; CH, MH, NU, PU, WF, Y.

24 —A mournefull epitaph upon . . . Iohn Rogers. [*London*], *printed*, 1642. brs. L.
L., J. Alarvm to poets. 1648. *See* Lane, John.

25 —An alarm to vvarre. *By H. I.*, 1642. 4°.* LT, DN; Y.

26 —Animadversions on the Scotch covenant. *For Nath. Brook*, 1662. 4°.* O, SP; MH, Y.

27 Entry cancelled.
—Apology for His Majestie. [n.p.], 1642. *See* Lake, Sir Edward. A just apology.
—Calendarium lunæ. Glasguæ, 1699. *See* Law, John.

27A —The Christian warfare. *Printed and sold by John Gain*, 1680. 4°. L, DU; CH, IU, MH, WF.

27B —The double eternity. *By M. Clark for the author.* 1695. fol.* L; Y.

28 —Englands doxologie. *Imprinted at London, by Barnard Alsop*, 1641. 4°.* LT, O, EC, SC, EN; CLC, IAU, NU, WF, Y.
—Epitaph on the late deceased. 1655. *See* Longe, J.
—Εναγγελιογραφα, or. 1656. *See* Lewis, John.

28A —A full and true account of a bloody and dismal fight. colop: *For Richard Pardoe.* [1690.] brs. MH.
—Good help. 1671. *See* Lloyd, John.

29 —Good news from Scotland, being. *For Giles Calvert*, 1648. 4°.* LT, O, EN, DT; Y.

30 —His Maiesties demands to Collonel Hammond. *By I. C. for R. W.*, 1648. 4°.* LT, AN.

31 —Illumination to Sion Colledge. *By Matthew Simmons, to be sold by Giles Calvert, June 1*, 1649. 4°.* LT, CT, DT; CN, CSS, Y.
—Just apology for His Sacred Majestie. 1642. *See* Lake, Sir Edward.

32 —Knaves are no honest men. [*London*], *printed*, [1672?]. 8°.* L, C.

33 —A letter from an English reformed Quaker. [*London, T. Sowle*, 1700.] cap., 4°.* L, EN; CH, NU, Y.

33A —A letter from on board Their Majesties fleet. colop: *For James Partridge*, 1689. brs. OC, DN; CH, Y.
—Metellus his dialogues. 1693. *See* Lewkenor, John.

34 —The new disease. *For W. T.* 1676. 4°.* L, O; MH, NAM.

35 —Old sayings and predictions verified. *Printed*, 1651. brs. LT; MH.

36 Entry cancelled.
—Only way to rest. [n.p.], 1657. *See* Lewgar, John.
—Papist mis-represented. [n.p.], 1665[*i.e.* 1685]. *See* Gother, John.
—Plaine truth without feare. [n.p.], 1647. *See* Lilburne, John.
—Plea for common-right. 1648. *See* Lilburne, John.

37 —A poem royal to the sacred maiesty of Charles the II. *For Giles Calvert*, 1662. brs. L.
—Revelation of revelations. 1683. *See* Lead, Jane.

38 —The Scotch covenant condemned. *For the author*, 1660. 4°.* LT, O, OB, EN; CLC, MH, NU, WF, Y.

38A —A sermon preached on January the 1st 1680/1 . . . in Jamaica. *By Nathaniel Thompson*, 1681. 4°.* WF.

39 —A small mite, in memory of . . . Mr. William Erbery. [*London*], *April 20*, 1654. 8°.* LT, O.

39A —To his mistress. [*n.p.*, 1646?] cap., fol.* OC, LLU.
—To the Pope, and all his cardinals. [n.p.], 1671. *See* Lancaster, James.
—Treatise of the souls union. 1680. *See* Lougher, John.
—Vanity of the creature. 1684. *See* Allestree, Richard.

L., **Jo.** Good help for weak memories. 1671. *See* Lloyd, John.

40 L., **L.** Evagoras: a romance. *For Rob. Clavel, and Tho. More,* 1677. 8°. T.C.I 266. L, O; CH, CLC, CN, CU, MH, Y.

41 —The history of the late proceedings of the students of . . . Edenborough. *For Richard Janeway,* 1681. fol.* T.C.I 428. L, O, LG, MR, E; CH, CN, MH, NU, Y.

42 —A letter written to a member. *Printed,* 1660. 4°.* O, MR; CN, NN, PL.

42A —Scotland against Popery. [*London,* 1680.] brs. L, LL.

43 — —[Anr. ed.] *For Richard Janeway,* 1681. fol.* L, LNC, LSD, EN; CH, MIU, NU, PU, Y.

44 —A true relation of the taking of Sherburne Castle. *For Samuel Gellibrand,* 1643. 4°.* LT, O.

L., **M.** Albion's congratulatory. Edinburgh, 1680. *See* Livingston, Michael.

—Albion's elegie. Edinburgh, 1680. *See* Livingston, Michael.

45 Entry cancelled.

—Dissertatio medicinalis de calculo humano. 1696. *See* Lister, Martin.

—For the Parliament sitting. [n.p., 1659?] *See* Lynam, Margaret.

45A —Illustrissimo heroi, Georgio [L]immuchi comitis . . . excomiaticon. [*n.p.,* 1650.] brs. EN.

—Patronus redux: or. Edinburgh, 1682. *See* Livingston, Michael.

45B L., **N.** Delaun reviv'd, viz. a plain . . . discourse of that famous doctor's pills. [*London,* 1680?] 4°.* LWL.

46 [–] A letter from a minister in the country, to a member. *For Richard Baldwin,* 1689. 4°.* T.C.II 291. L, O, C, E, DT; CH, LC, MH, MU, NU, Y.

47 —A letter sent from Portsmouth. [*London,* 1659.] brs. LT, O, CJ; CH.

48 —Proposals for regulating the coin. [*London?* 1695.] cap., 4°.* LUG; MH, NC.

49 —The way to good success. *York, by John White, to be sold by Thomas Clark in Hull,* 1685. 4°.* L, O, OCC, LSD.

50 L., **P.** The English academy. *For Dixy Page,* 1672. 8°. T.C.I 119. O.

51 —A true and faithful narrative of the late barbarous cruelties . . . at Rochel. colop: *By D. Mallet,* 1681. cap., fol.* L, O, OP; CH, WF.

52 —The true coppy of a letter written by a gentleman in Brussells. *For L. Curtis,* 1684. brs. O; TU, WF.

L., **P. D.** Princely way. 1677. *See* Lainé, Pierre de.

L., **R.** Citt and Bumpkin. 1680. *See* L'Estrange, Sir Roger.

53 —A confutation of the solemne league. *Printed,* 1648. 4°.* LT, OC, EN; CU, Y.

—Dialogue between. 1689. *See* L'Estrange, Sir Roger.

53A [–] A fight in Ireland between . . . Cromwels forces and . . . Inchequeens. [*London,*] *for B.A.,* [1649]. 4°.* DN; MH.

54 —The free mans plea for freedom. *For Robert White,* 1648. 4°.* LT, LUG, DT; CSS, MH, MU, Y.

—God save the King. Edinburgh, 1660. *See* Lawrie, Robert.

—Gospel-separation. 1657. *See* Lawrence, Richard.

—History of the Athenian society. [1691.] *See* Gildon, Charles.

55 [–] The iustice of the army against evill-doers vindicated. *By T. Paine,* 1649. 4°.* LT, O, LG, MR; CH, WF.

55A [–] —[Anr. ed.] *By Thomas Paine, for Giles Calvert,* 1649. 4°.* IU.

—Latine grammar. 1659. *See* Lloyd, Richard.

—Letter of advice to a young gentleman. Dublin, 1670. *See* Lingard, Richard.

—Letter out of Scotland. [n.p., 1681.] *See* L'Estrange, Sir Roger.

56 Entry cancelled.

—Pia fraus. 1684. *See* Lawe, Robert.

56A [–] Two sallies forth by the Lord Goring. *By B. A.,* 1648. 4°.* L; CH.

—School-masters auxiliaries. 1659. *See* Lloyd, Richard.

56B —The taking of Wexford. *For Francis Leach,* 1649. 4°.* LT, LVF, OC, DN; CH, Y.

56C —A thanksgiving sermon for His Majesty's safe return . . . 2nd of December 1697. *For the author,* 1697. 4°.* BAMB.

56D —The visitation: or, long look'd-for . . . submission of M. Baxter. *Printed in August,* 1662. 8°.* L, MR; OSU.

57 L., **S.** An account of the secret services. *Ratisbone* [*Amsterdam?*], 1683. 12°. L; CH, CLC, MIU, WF.

58 —A catechisme shorter than the short catechisme. *By A. M. for Tho. Underhill,* 1649. 4°.* L.

59 —Considerable considerations to be considered of. [*London*], *printed,* 1654. 4°.* LT, O, MR, SP, DT; CN, Y.

—Dangerous rule. 1658. *See* Ladyman, Samuel.

60 Entry cancelled.

—Donation of Canaan. 1677. *See* Fletcher, Giles. Israel redux.

—Ecclesia gemens: or. 1677. *See* Lee, Samuel.

61 —A letter from a gentleman of the Lord Ambassador Howard's retinue, to his friend in London. *By W. G. for Moses Pitt,* 1670. 4°.* T.C.I 38. L, O, SC, SP, EN, DM; CH, CN, MH, WF, Y.

62 —A letter to the Right Honorable the Lord Lambert. [*London*], *printed,* 1659. 4°.* LT, O, CS, EN, BQ; CH, CU, MH, WF, Y.

63 —A particular church of Christ's institution. *For the author,* 1690. 8°. L, O.

64 Entry cancelled.

[–] Remarques on the humours and conversations of the town. *See title.*

65 [–] Remarques on the humours and conversations of the gallants. Third edition. *For Allen Banks,* 1673. 12°. T.C.I 137. L, O, OC, SP, DT; PL.

66 —Three sermons, viz. Davids tears. *By T. C. and L. P. for Robert Crofts,* 1660. 8°. LT.

—Vindication of free-grace. 1645. *See* Lane, Samuel.

67 L., **T.** Annotations upon the late protestation. [*London,* 1642.] cap., 4°.* LT, EC, MR, DT; CH, MH, MIU, NU, WF, Y.

—Appeal to the Parliament. 1660. *See* Lawson, Thomas.

68 —Babylon is fallen. *By M. S.,* 1651. 8°.* O, DU, SHR; CH, CU, NU, TO, WF.

68A —A breife exposition of the xi. xii and xiii. chapters of The Revelation. *By M. Simmons,* 1651. 8°. O; MH, NU, TO, WF.

69 Entry cancelled.
—Child's delight. [1695.] *See* Lye, Thomas.

70 —Comfortable nevves from Breda. *For Henry Seile, May 4,* 1660. brs. LT, LS; Y.

71 —Considerations humbly proposed. *Printed,* 1658. 4°.* L, MR; CH, MH, NN, WF, ZWT.

72 —De fide ejus-què ortu. *Excudebat Matthæus Simmons.* 1653. 8°. L, O, DU, SHR, EN; CLC, MH, NU, TO, WF, Y.

73 —A discourse of fines. [*London,* 1670?] cap., fol.* L, LL, LLP, BR; CH, MH, WF.
—Discourse of paying of tithes. 1656. *See* Larkham, Thomas.
—Discourse of subterraneal treasure. 1668. *See* Lawrence, Thomas.
—England's almanack. 1700. *See* Almanacs.

73A —Extent of the sword. [*London?* 1653.] cap., 4°.* O, SP; NU.

74 Entry cancelled.
—Fair maids choice. [n.p., 1670?] *See* Lanfiere, Thomas.
—Gallant seamans return. [n.p., 1678–80.] *See* Lanfiere, Thomas.
—Grief allayed. 1682. *See* Laxton, Thomas.

75 —Huc ades, hæc animo. Or a serious. *Printed,* 1659. 4°.* LT, O, LLU, DT; CH, MH, MU, NC, WF, Y.

76 —A letter to the Right Honorable William Lenthall. *By Francis Leach,* 1651. 4°.* CT, BC, EN; CH, CN, WF, Y.

77 —The life and reign of Innocent XI. *For Abel Roper,* 1690. 4°. T.C.II 286. L, O, MR, EN; CH, CN, MH, NU, TU, WF, Y.
—Looking-glass for a bad husband. [1680.] *See* Lanfiere, Thomas.
—Memorials of the royal martyr. 1670. *See* Lambert, Thomas. Sad memorials.

78 —Πολυπενθεος θρηνωδια. The mourners song. *By M. S.,* 1651. 8°. L.

79 No entry.
—Sad memorials. 1670. *See* Lambert, Thomas.
—Taunton maids delight. [n.p., 1680–85.] *See* Lanfiere, Thomas.

80 —To the Church of Rome. *First printed,* 1588, *and sundry times since,* [1651]. 4°.* O, DU; CH, CLC, NU, WF.

81 —Trve nevves from Norvvich. *For Benjamin Allen, and T.B.,* 1641[2]. 4°.* LT, O, EC, NPL; Y.

82 —The true notion of government. *For Edward Gellibrand,* 1681. 4°.* T.C.I 452. L, O, DU, LSD, EN; CH, CN, PL, WF, Y.

83 —A voyce out of the wildernes crying. *By M. S.* 1651. 8°. L, O, C, DU, P; CH, CLC, MH, NU, TO.

83A ——[Anr. ed.] *Printed* 1661. 8°. O, LSC, DU; NU, WF.
—The wonder of wonders. [n.p., 1675?] *See* Lanfiere, Thomas.

83B **L., T. R. d.** The all-conquering genius of . . . James II. *By John Harefinch,* 1685. 4°.* L; WF.

83C **L., T. V.** The copy of a letter from Min Heer T. V. L. [*Amsterdam,* 1689.] brs. OC; CLC.
L., W. Art of numbring. 1667. *See* Leybourn, William.

84 —The bramble berry. *Printed at London by Richard Cotes,* 1643. 4°.* LT, O, CT, EN, DT; CH, MB, MH, NU, Y.

84A —A brief account of the most remarkable prodigies. [*London*], *printed and sold by J. Bradford,* 1696. brs. MH.
—Catalogue of new books. 1660. *See* London, William.

85 —A certaine relation of the Earle of Ormonds nine dayes passage. *For Iohn Franke,* 1642. 4°.* LT, C, CT, EC, LNC, DN; MM, WF, Y.
—Conflict in conscience. Edinburgh, 1664. *See* Livingstone, William.

86 —The covrts of ivstice corrected. *For George Lindsey,* 1642. 4°.* LT, LG, EC, DT; CH, MH, MM, WF.
—Further essay. 1695. *See* Lowndes, William.
—Glorious truth. 1653. *See* Levitt, William.
—Gods judgements. 1659. *See* Hammond, Samuel.

87 —Good newes from the Netherlands. [*London,* 1660.] brs. LT.
—Helpe for young people. Oxford, 1649. *See* Lyford, William.

88 —The Independants militarie entertainment. *For Henry Overton,* 1645. 4°.* LT, O; CH, PL, Y.

89 —King Charles vindicated, or the grand cheats. [*London*], *for Theodorus Microcosmus,* 1660. 4°.* LT, O, BC, LSD, GU; CH, CN, MH, MIU, WF.

89A —King William's welcome. *Printed and sold by J. Bradford,* [1692.] brs. L.

90 —A letter from an impartial hater of the Papists. [*London,* 1680.] brs. L, HH, EN; CH, CLC, INU, NC, PU, Y.

91 —A letter from one of the persons under censure of Parliament. *For William Shears,* 1660. 4°.* LT, O; MH.

92 —A medecine for malignancy. *Printed at London for Ralph Smith,* 1644. 4°. LT, EC, MR, SP; CH, CU, MH, MM, TU, WF, Y.
—Merlinus Anglicus junior. 1644. *See* Almanacs. Lilly, William.

93 —Newes from Tvrkie. *For H.B.,* 1648. 4°.* LT, LIU; MH, Y.

94 ——[Anr. ed.] *For Humphrey Blunden,* 1648. 4°.* O; CH, NP.
—Plantation work. 1682. *See* Loddington, William.
—Preservative against the major part. [n.p., 1650.] *See* Leach, William.
—Proposalls for an act. 1649. *See* Leach, William.
—Quakerism no paganism. 1674. *See* Loddington, William.

95 Entry cancelled.
—Romes A B C. [n.p.], 1641. *See* title.

96 —The sacramental stvmbling-block removed. *By James and Joseph Moxon; for Henry Overton,* 1648. 4°. LT, O, LLP, LSC, CT, ENC, DT; NU, WF.
—Strange newes from the east. 1677. *See* Lilly, William.
—Thanksgiving sermon. Dublin, 1661. *See* Lightburn, William.
—Twelve pagan principles. [n.p., 1674.] *See* Loddington, William.

97 Entry cancelled.
—Two great questions determined. 1681. *See* Lawrence, William.

97A   Entry cancelled.
      —Two great questions whereon. 1681. *See* Lawrence, William.
      —Use of the semicircle. [1680.] *See* Leybourn, William.
98   —The wood-mongers remonstrance. *Printed*, 1649. 4°.*
      L, O, LUG; CSS, NC.
99   Entry cancelled. Date: 1869.
      L. C. his lamentation. 1684. *See* Curtis, Langley.
99A   Entry cancelled.
      Labadie, de. Mr. de Labadie's letter. [n.p.], 1696. *See title.*
      [La Barre, François Poulain de.] *See* Poulain de la Barre, François.
100   **La Bastide, Marc Antoine de.** An answer to the Bishop of Condom's book. *Dublin, Benjamin Tooke, sold by Joseph Wilde*, 1676. 12°. T.C.I 256; DIX 157. LLP, LW, CT, GU, DK, DT.
101   **La Bizadière, Michel David de.** An historical account of the divisions in Poland. *For H. Rhodes; T. Bennet; A. Bell; and D. Midwinter and T. Leigh*, 1700. 8°. T.C.III 155. L, O, LLU, EN, GU, CD; CH, CN, MH, WF, Y.
102   Labour in vain. [*London*], *for P. Brooksby, J. Deacon, J. Blare, J. Back*, [1688–92]. brs. HH.
      Labour in vain. 1700. *See* Ward, Edward.
      Labouring persons. Oxford, 1690. *See* Lee, Francis.
103   **[La Brune, Jean de.]** The life of that most illustrious Prince Charles V. [*London*], *by Edw. Jones, and published by Randal Taylor*, 1691. 8°. T.C.II 347. L, CT, LLU; CH, CN, LC, MB, PL, Y.
103A [–] —[Anr. ed.] [*London*], *for Francis Saunders*, 1691. 8°. L, NE, CD; CLC, NP, TU.
104   **La Bruyère, Jean de.** The characters. *For John Bullord, and sold by Matt. Gilliflower; Ben. Tooke; Christopher Bateman; and Richard Parker*, 1699. 8°. T.C.III 126. L, O, CT, MR, EN; CH, LC, MH, PL, Y.
105   — —Second edition. *For John Bullord, and sold by John Nicholson; and Tho. Newborough*, 1700. 8°. T.C.III 189. L, O, C, LLU, DT; CH, CN, PL, TU, WF, Y.
105A Labyrinte de Versailles. *Amsterdam, N. Visscher*, [1682?]. WF.
      Labyrinthvs Cantvariensis: or. Paris, 1658. *See* Carwell, Thomas.
106   **[La Calprenède, Gaultier de Coste]**, *seigneur de.* Cassandra. *For Humphrey Moseley*, 1652. 8°. L, O, CASTLE ASHBY; CH, CN, LC, NP, PU, WF, Y.
106A [–] —[Anr. ed.] *For Humphrey Moseley, William Bentley, and Thomas Heath*, 1652. fol. L, O, C; IU, MH, MIU, NCU, TO.
107   [–] —[Anr. ed.] *For Humphrey Moseley*, 1661. fol. L, O, LLU, LSD; CH, CN, LC, MH, TU.
108   [–] —[Anr. ed.] *For A. Moseley*, 1664. fol. L, O, LLP, BC, NOT; CLC, IU, LC, NP, TU, V.
109   [–] —[Anr. ed.] —, 1667. fol. L, O, LLL, E; CH, CN, IU, NC.
109A [–] —[Anr. ed.] —, *and are to be sold by Robert Littlebury and Moses Pitt*, 1667. fol. FU, PU.
110   [–] —[Anr. ed.] *For Peter Parker*, 1676. fol. T.C.I 224. L, O, AN, LLU; CH, CN, IU, MH, NCD, TU.
110A [–] Cleopatra. *For Humphrey Moseley and John Holden*, 1652. 8°. O; IU, MH.

111   [–] Hymen's præludia . . . first part. *For George Thompson*, 1652. 12°. LT; CH, LC, PU, Y.
112   [–] — —[Anr. ed.] *By J. G. for R. Lowndes*, 1654. 8°. L, O; CH, CN, IU, MH, PBM, WF, Y.
112A [–] — —[Anr. ed.] *By F. L. for R. Lowndes*, 1657. 8°. O; MH, NP, RBU, Y.
112B [–] — —[Anr. ed.] *By R. D. for Rich. Lownds*, 1663. 8°. MH, NCU, Y.
113   [–] —Second part. *By J. G. for R. Lowndes*, 1654[3]. 8°. LT, O; CH, CN, IU, MH, Y.
113A [–] — —[Anr. ed.] *By Elizabeth Brudenell, for Richard Lowndes*, 1657. 8°. NP.
113B [–] — —[Anr. ed.] *By R. D. for Rich. Lowndes*, 1663. 8°. MH, NCU, Y.
114   [–] —Third part. *By J. G. for R. Lowndes*, 1655. 8°. LT, O; CH, IU, MH, NP, PBM, Y.
114A [–] — —[Anr. ed.] *By R. D. for Rich. Lownds*, 1663. 8°. MH, NCU, Y.
115   [–] —Fourth part. *By J. G. for R. Lowndes*, 1656. 8°. L, O, LLU; CH, IU, MH, NCU, NP, WF.
116   [–] —Fifth part. *For J. G. and R. Lowndes*, 1656. 8°. L, O, LLU; CH, IU, MH, NCU, OSU, WF.
116A [–] —Sixth part. *By F. Leach, for R. Lowndes*, 1658. 8°. L, O; CH, IU, MH, NCU.
117   [–] —Seventh part. *For Humphrey Moseley and John Crook*, 1658. 8°. LT, O, LLL; CH, IU.
117A [–] — —[Anr. ed.] *For Humphrey Moseley*, 1658. 8°. MH, V.
118   [–] —Eighth part. —, 1658. 8°. LT, O, LLL; CH, MH.
119   [–] —Ninth, and tenth part. *For Humphrey Moseley and John Crook*, 1659. fol. L, O; CH, CN, MH, NC, NCU.
120   [–] —Eleventh, twelfth and last parts. *For Humphrey Moseley*, 1659. fol. L, O; CLC, IU, LC, MH, NC, NCU.
121   Entry cancelled.
      [–] —[Anr. ed.] 1663. *See* — —First part; — —Second part; — —Third part.
122   [–] —In twelve parts [parts 1–6]. *By R. D. for A. Mosely and J. Crooke*, 1665. fol. L, O, LLU, EN; CLC.
122A [–] — —[Anr. ed.] —, 1668. fol. CLC, KYU, MH.
122B [–] —Six last parts [parts 7–8]. *By E. M. for A. Moseley*, 1663. O, EN; CLC, CN, KYU, MH, PU.
123   [–] —[Anr. ed. Parts 1–12.] *By W. R. and J. R. and are to be sold by Peter Parker, and Thomas Guy*, 1674. fol. T.C.I 155. L, O, CP, E; CH, CN, MH, TU, Y.
124   [–] —[Anr. ed.] *By F. Collins for Thomas Fabian*, 1687. fol. L, O, AN, LIU, RU; CLC, CN, MBA, PU, V, WF, Y, AVP.
124A [–] —[Anr. ed.] *For Ralph Smith*, 1698. fol. L, O, LLL; CN.
125   [–] Pharamond. *By Ja: Cottrell, for Samuel Speed*, 1662. fol. L, O; CLC, IU, MH, MIU, PU.
126   [–] —[Anr. ed.] *For T. Bassett, T. Dring, and W. Cademan*, 1677. fol. T.C.I 280. L, O, C, BP, EN; CH, CN, MH, MU, TU, WF, Y.
      La Chaise, Francois de. The Jesuite unmasqued. 1689. *See title.*
127   —Father La Chaise's project for the extirpation of hereticks. [*London*, 1688.] 4°.* L, O, LIL, BP, AU; CH, IU, MH, MM, NC, NU, Y.

128   **La Chambre, Marin Cureau de.** The art how to know men. *By T. R. for Thomas Dring*, 1665. 8°. L, O, CT, AN, DU; CH, IU, MH, NAM, WF, Y.

128A   — —[Anr. ed.] *For Thomas Basset*, 1670. 8°. O; CN.

129   —The characters of the passions. *By Tho. Newcomb, for John Holden*, 1650. 8°. LT, O, CT, E, DT; CLC, CN, CU, WF, Y.

130   Entry cancelled.

     — —[Anr. ed.] 1661. See —Discourse upon the passions.

130A   — —Second edition. *For H. Herringman; sold by R. Bentley and Daniel Brown*, 1693. 8°. T.C.II 467. DT.

131   —A discourse of the knowledg of beasts. *By Tho. Newcomb for Humphrey Moseley*, 1657. 8°. LT, O, CT, DUS, DT; CH, CLM, CN, LC, MH, Y.

131A   —A discourse on the principles of chiromancy. *By Tho. Newcomb, to be sold by Tho. Basset*, 1658. 8°. L; CLC, WSG.

131B   [–] A discourse upon the passions. *By Tho. Newcomb for Hen. Herringman*, 1661. 8°. DT, CASTLE ASHBY; IU, PL, Y.

132   [–] A physical discourse touching the nature. *By Tho. Newcomb, to be sold by Tho. Basset*, 1658. 8°. O, CT.

132A   —The second part of the passions. *By T. Newcomb, for H. Herringman*, 1661. 8°. OC; WG, Y.

133   **[La Chappelle, Jean de.]** The unequal match. *For Charles Blount, and Richard Butt*, 1681. 12°. T.C.I 461. L, O; CLC, CN, IU, RBU.

134   [–] — . . . second and last part. *For R. Bentley*, 1683. 12°. T.C.II 27. L, O, CS; CLC, CN.

134A   **La Charrière, Joseph de.** A treatise of chirurgical operations. *For Dan. Brown*, 1695. 12°. L, O, LCS, P; MBM, PCP, WSG, HC.

     [La Chétardie, Trotti de.] *See* Trotti de la Chétardie.

134B   Lachrymae Anglicanae, or England's tears for the dissolution of the Parliament. *[London], for R. J.*, 1681. brs. DU, LNC; AVP.

     Lachrymæ ecclesiæ. [n.p.], 1689. See Ken, Thomas, bp.

135   Lachrymæ Hungaricæ. *Apud Nath. Brook*, [1664]. brs. L.

     Lachrymæ musarum. 1649. See Brome, Richard.

136   Lachrymæ philosophiæ: or an elegy on the . . . death of . . . Robert Boyle. *For Richard Baldwin*, 1691/2. fol.* LLU; JF.

136A   **LaCroze, Jean Cornand de.** An historical and geographical description of France. *For T. Salusbury*, 1694. 12°. T.C.II 494. L, O, CT; CH, CLC, MH, WF, Y.

137–8   Entries cancelled. Serials.

138A   —A letter from. *Printed* 1693. 8°.* O, OC.

138B   —A new exact geographical description of France. *For J. Salusbury*, 1695. 12°. O; CU, LC.

139   **Lactantius.** Lucii Cœlii Lactantii Firmiani opera quæ extant. *Oxonii, e theatro Sheldoniano*, 1684. 4°. L, O, C, AN, YM, EN, CD; BN, CH, CLC, MH, MU, NC, WF, Y.

140   — —[Anr. ed.] *Cantabrigiæ, ex officinâ Johan. Hayes, impensis Hen. Dickinson, & Rich. Green*, 1685. 8°. T.C.II 115. L, O, C, DUS, ENC, DT; BN, CH, IU, MH, NU, TU, WF, Y.

141   —Lucii Cæcilii Firmiani Lactantii de mortibus persecutorum liber. *Oxonii, e Theatro Sheldoniano*, 1680. 12°. T.C.I 445. MADAN 3269. L, O, C, DU, DT; CH, CLC, IU, MH, WF, Y.

142   —A relation of the death of the primitive persecutors. *Amsterdam, for J. S.*, 1687. 12°. L, O, C, DU, AU; CH, CN, KT, NU, WF, Y.

142A   **[Lacy, John.]** The arraignment of Thomas Howard. *[London], by Nathaniel Thompson*, 1685. 4°.* CH.

143   —The dumb lady. *For Thomas Dring*, 1672. 4°. T.C.I 103. L, O, LVD, OW, EN; CH, CN, LC, MH, TU, WF, Y.

144   —The old troop. *For William Crook and Thomas Dring*, 1672. 4°.* T.C.I III. L, LVD, OW, LLU, EN; CH, CN, MH, MU, WF, Y.

145   — —[Anr. ed.] *For Benj. Tooke*, 1698. 4°.* T.C.III 54. L, O, C, EC, EN; CH, CN, LC, MH, WF, Y.

146   —Sauny the Scott: or, the taming of the shrew. *Printed and sold by E. Whitlock*, 1698. 4°. T.C.III 65. L, O, OW, EN, DT; CH, CU, MH, TU, WF, Y.

147   —Sʳ. Hercules Buffoon. *For Jo. Hindmarsh*, 1684. 4°. T.C.II 99. L, O, C, EN, DT; CH, CU, LC, MH, WF, Y.

147A   [–] A song in the Taming the shrew. *[London*, 1699?] brs. WF.

148   [–] 'Twas in the month of May. *William Pearson*, 1699. brs. L; WF.

148A   **Lacy, John,** merchant. Tobacco, a poem. *[London*, 1669.] brs. L.

     Ladensium αυτο κατακρισις. [n.p.], 1641. See Baillie, Robert.

149   **[La Devéze, Abel Rodolphe de.]** The life and death of Monsieur Claude. *For Thomas Dring*. 1688. 4°. T.C.II 223. L, O, C, EN, DT; CH, IU, MH, NU, TU, WF, Y.

     Ladies, a second time. [n.p.], 1647. See Neville, Henry.

     Ladies answer. [n.p.], 1670. See Cellier, Elizabeth.

150   The ladies behaviour. A dialogue. *Printed, and are to be sold by Randall Taylor*, 1693. 8°. T.C.II 427. L, O.

     Ladie's blush. 1673. See V., W.

     Ladies cabinet. 1654. See B., M.

     Ladies calling. Oxford, 1673. See Allestree, Richard.

151   The ladies champion. *[London], printed*, 1660. 4°.* LT.

152   The ladies companion, or, a table furnished with sundry sorts of pies and tarts. *By W. Bentley, to be sold by W. Shears*, 1654. 12°. LT, OC; WF.

153   The ladies delight. *For Charles Tyus*, [1659–63]. brs. HH.

154   —[Anr. ed.] *For W. Thackeray, T. Passenger, and W. Whitwood*, [1670–77]. brs. L, HH; MH.

     Ladies dictionary. 1694. See H., N.

     Ladies dispensatory. 1652. See Sowerby, Leonard.

     The ladies dressing-room unlock'd. 1700. See Evelyn, Mary.

154AA   The lady's garland. *[London?* 1700.] brs. L.

154A   The ladies invention. *[London*, 1698.] brs. LLL; CH.

155   The ladies lamentation. *For Richard Burton*, 1651. brs. L.

155A   The lady's lamentation for Sir John Fenwick. *For C. Barnet*, 1697. brs. OP.

155B   The ladies lamentation, or, the commanders last farewel. *[London?* 1692.] brs. L.

156   The ladies losse at the adventures of five hours. *[London], printed*, 1663. 4°.* O; IU, TU.

     Ladies milk-house. 1684. See B., W.

Lady's New-Years gift. 1688. *See* Halifax, George Savile, *marquess*.

157 The ladies of London's petition. [*London*], *for Josiah Blare*, [1684–88]. brs. HH; MH.

Ladies Parliament. [n.p., 1647.] *See* Neville, Henry.

158 The ladies preparation to the monthly sacrament. *For S. Neale*, 1691. 8°. T.C.II 355. O.

159 A lady's religion. *By Tho. Warren for Richard Baldwin*, 1697. 12°. LLP, GK; MIU.

160 The ladies remonstrance. *Imprinted at London for Virgin Want; to be sold by John Satisfie*, [1659.] 4°.* O; TU.

161 The lady's tragedy. [*London*], *for J. Deacon*, [1684–95]. brs. HH.

162 The ladyes vindication. *For William Gilbertson*, [1662.] brs. L.

162A Lady Alimony. *For Tho. Vere and William Gilbertson*, 1659. 4°. L, O, LVD, OW, EN; CH, CN, MH, NRU, WF, Y.

163 The Lady Bark or, new upstart-lady. [*Aberdeen, Forbes*, 1680?] 4°.* ALDIS 2199.9. EN; IU, MH, NP.

163A The lady besieged. A new song. [*London*, 1670?] brs. L.

164 The Lady Dacre's case. [*London?* 1690.] brs. LUG.

165 The Lady Gray vindicated. colop: *Printed*, 1681. brs. L, O, LL, LN, LNC; CH, MBA, MH, MU, PU, Y.

165A The Lady Isabella's tragedy. *For Eliz. Andrews*, [1664?]. brs. O.

166 —[Anr. ed.] [*London*], *for P. Brooksby*, [1672–96]. brs. L, O, CM, HH, GU.

166A —[Anr. ed.] [*London*], *for E. Brooksby*, [1700?]. brs. HH.

166B —[Anr. ed.] *By and for W. O.*, [1700?]. brs. L.

166C The Lady Ivy [claim to lands]. [n.p., 1696.] fol.* L.

167 The lady of pleasure. [*London*], *for J. Back*, [1685?]. L, O, HH; MH.

168 **L[adyman], S[amuel].** The dangerous rule. *By J. C. for Tho. Newbery*, 1658. 12°. C.

Laertius, Diogenes. *See* Diogenes Laertius.

168A Lætitæ Caledonicæ, or, Scotland's raptures upon . . . Charles the Second. [*Edinburgh*, 1660.] brs. ALDIS 1646.3. EN.

169 **[La Fayette, Marie Madeleine de La Vergne]**, *comtesse de.* The Princess of Cleves. *For R. Bentley and M. Magnes*, 1679. 8°. T.C.I 349. L, O, C, LLU; CH, CLC, CN, MH, Y.

170 [–] —[Anr. ed.] *For R. Bentley and S. Magnes*, 1688. 12°. T.C.II 238. L; CH, CLC, CN, PU, WF, Y.

171 [–] The Princess of Monpensier. *Printed*, 1666. 8°. L; CLC, CN, CU, MH.

172 —Zayde, a Spanish history. *By T. Milbourn for William Cademan*, 1678. 8°. L, O; CN, WF, Y, ZAP.

172A — — [Anr. ed.] *For William Cademan*, 1678. 8°. L, O; CH.

173 — — Second edition. *For Francis Saunders*, 1690. 8°. L; CH, CLC, CN, MH, MIU, Y.

173A —— Second and last part. *By T. M. for W. Cademan*, 1678. 8°. L, O; CN, WF, Y, ZAP.

174–175 Entries cancelled.

La Fin. *See* La Fin, Charles de.

176 **[La Fin, Charles de.]** A letter written upon occasion from the Low-Countries. *For Nath: Butter, March 22*, 1641[2]. 4°.* LT, O, EC; CSS, LC, MIU, WF.

176A —Sermo mirabilis: or the silent language. *For Tho. Salusbury, and sold by Randal Taylor*, 1692. 4°.* T.C.II 488. L; WF.

176B ——Second edition. *For Tho. Salusbury*, 1693. 12°.* T.C.II 433. EN.

176C ——Third edition. *For J. Salusbury*, 1696. 12°.* L, OC; WSG.

177 **La Fite, Daniel.** A friendly discourse. *For Ric. Northcott*, 1691. 12°. T.C.II 345. O, OC, EN.

177A — —[Anr. ed.] *For W. Whitwood*, 1697. 12°. T.C.II 573. O.

178 **La Fontaine, *sieur de.*** The military duties of the officers of cavalry. *For Robert Harford*, 1678. 8°. T.C.I 313. L, O, OC, ES; CH, MH, MU, TO, WF, Y.

LaFontaine, Jean Baptiste de, *pseud.* *See* Courtilz de Sandras, Gatien.

LaFountaine, Edward. *See* Fountaine, Edward.

179 **La Framboisière, Nicolas Abraham de.** The art of physick. *By H. C. for Dorman Newman*, 1684. 12°. T.C.II 61. L, O, OC; PCP, HC.

179A **[LaGrancour, Albert Eugene de.]** Serenissimorum principum Jacobi Stuarti. *Typis Tho. Newcombe*, 1673. 4°.* L; Y.

180 Entry cancelled.

La Grange, *prince de.* Ἐγκυκλεοχρεια or universal motion. 1662. *See title.*

La Guard, Theodore de, *pseud.* *See* Ward, Nathaniel.

La Guarden, Theodore de, *pseud.* *See* Ward, Nathaniel.

La Guilletière, de. *See* Guillet de Saint-George, Georges.

180A **LaHaye, *sieur de.*** The policy and government of the Venetians. *For John Starkey*, 1671. 12°. T.C.I 65. L, O, CT, LLU, EN; CLC, MU, NIC, NN, WF, Y.

181 **[La Haye, Carolus de.]** Doctrinæ antiquæ de natura animæ. *Excudebat R. Norton, & prostant venales apud Johannem Martin & Jacobum Alestrey*, 1654. 12°. NU.

181A **La Hire, Philippe de.** Gnomoniques, or the art of drawing sun-dials. *For Rich. Northcott*, 1685. 8°. T.C.II 114. L, LIU; MB, MH, MU, NC, WU.

181B ——Second edition. *For J. Moxon*, 1693. 8°. L, OC.

La Houssaye, Amelot de. *See* Amelot de la Houssaye, Abraham Nicholas.

Laick, Will. *See* Ridpath, George.

182 **Lainé, Pierre de.** A compendious introduction to the French tongue. *By T. N. for Anthony Williamson*, 1655. 8°. LT, CS.

182A [–] The princely way to the French tongue. *For Henry Herringman*, 1667. 8°. CS.

183 [–] —Second edition. *By J. Macock for H. Herringman*, 1677. 8°. T.C.I 269. L, C; CH, IU, WF.

184 The Laird of Dysarts dreame. [*Edinburgh, c.* 1700.] brs. ALDIS 3978. HH.

185 **Lake, Arthur, bp.** Ten sermons. *By Thomas Badger, for Humphrey Mosley*, 1641. 4°. L, O, C, LLP, CT; CLC, CU, IU, NU, Y.

186   **Lake, Clement.** Something by way of testimony concerning. *Printed and sold by T. Sowle*, 1692. 4°.* L, LF, BBN; PH, PSC, Y.

186A   **Lake, Sir Edward.** The answer of . . . to the petition and articles given in against him . . . by Edward Kinge. [*London*, 1665?] cap., fol.* L, LNC, MR.

187   [–] A just apology for His Sacred Majestie. *Iuly 8. [London], for Robert Wood*, 1642. 4°.* LT, CT, EC, LIU, DT; CH, IU, MH, OWC, Y.

188   —Memoranda: touching the oath ex officio. *For R. Royston*, 1662. 4°. L, O, CE, LNC, EN; CH, MHL, NCL, NU, WF, Y.

188A   **Lake, Edward.** Officium eucharisticum. A preparatory service. *By T. Milbourn, for Christopher Wilkinson*, 1673. 8°. T.C.I 138. P; WF.

188B   [–] —Second edition. —, 1674. 8°. T.C.I 181. CS, CT.

188C   [–] —Third edition. *For Christopher Wilkinson*, 1677. 12°. T.C.I 296. OC; CLC.

188D   [–] —Fourth edition. —, 1678. 8°. ZWT.

188E   [–] —Fifth edition. —, 1679. 12°. T.C.I 376. WF.

189   — —Sixth edition. 1681. 8°. OME, LNC.

189A   [–] —Seventh edition. *For C. Wilkinson*, 1682. 12°. T.C.I 498. DU, RPL.

190   [–] — Eighth edition. *For Christopher Wilkinson*, 1683. 12°. L, OC, CT.

191   [–] —"Eighth" edition. *Dublin, by Joseph Ray, for Robert Thornton*, 1683. 8°. DIX 201. DT.

192   [–] —Twelfth edition. *For Christopher Wilkinson*, 1687. 12°. L (lost).

192A   [–] —Thirteenth edition. —, 1689. 12°. DU.

192B   — —Fourteenth edition. —, 1690. 12°. LSC.

192C   [–] —Sixteenth edition. *For E. Wilkinson, sold by her and A. Roper*, 1695. 8°. CLC.

192D   — —Eighteenth edition. *A. Roper*, 1699. 8°. LLP.

193   —A sermon preached . . . thirtieth of January, M DC LXXXIII. *By M. C. for C. Wilkinson*, 1684. 4°.* T.C.II 67. L, O, C, YM, DT; CH, MH, NU, WF, Y. (var.)

194   —A sermon preach'd . . . December the 7th, 1693. *By J. Leake for Henry Bonwicke*, 1694. 4°.* T.C.II 490. L, O, LLP, OC, CT, MR, WCA; CH, NGT, Y.

195   **Lake, John, bp.** Catalogus librorum. [*London, 27 April* 1691.] 4°.* L; MH.

195A   —The character of a true Christian. *For Obadiah Blagrave*, [1690]. 4°.* T.C.II 298. WF.

196   —The declaration of. [*London*, 1689.] brs. L, O, C, LCL, HH; CH, CLC, INU, Y.

197   —A sermon preached . . . 29th of May, 1670. *Savoy: By Tho. Newcomb for William Grantham*, 1670. 4°. T.C.I 64. L, O, C, P, WCA, DT; CH, CLC, NC, NU, WF.

198   —Στεφανος πιστου: or the true Christians character. *By William Godbid, for Nathaniel Brooke*, 1671. 4°.* L, O, C, LL, DU, YM; WSC.

199   **Lake, S.** A sermon preached . . . December 15, 1664. *Roger Daniel*, 1664. 4°. CT.

200   **Lakin, Daniel.** A miraculous cure of the Prusian Swallow-knife. *By I. Okes*, 1642. 4°. L, O, OB, GH; NAM, PCP, WSG, JF.

200A   **Lallemont, Pierre.** The holy desires of death. [*London*], *printed*, 1678. 12°. L, DUS, WARE; CN, Y.

201   **La Loubere, Simon de.** A new historical relation of the Kingdom of Siam. *By F. L. for Tho. Horne, Francis Saunders, and Tho. Bennet*, 1693. fol. T.C.II 439. L, O, C, E, DT; CH, CN, LC, MH, NC, Y.

202   Entry cancelled.

     La March, John de. *See* De La March, John.

203   **La Martelière, Pierre de.** The argument of. *For James Adamson*, 1689. 4°. T.C.II 259. L, O, C, CT, WCA; CH, MIU, NU, TU, WF, Y.

204   **La Martiniere, Pierre Martin de.** A new voyage into the northern countries. *For John Starkey*, 1674. 12°. T.C.I 162. L, O, C, OC, EN; MIU, NP, PL, RPJ, WF, Y.

205   The Lama-sabachthani, or, cry of the Son of God. *By E. Jones, for Samuel Lowndes*, 1689. 12°. T.C.II 245. L, O, C; WF.

205A   —Second edition. *By Edw. Jones, for Samuel Lowndes*, 1691. 12°. T.C.II 352. L; Y.

205B   [Anr. ed.] *Printed and sold by Benja. Harris*, 1700. 8°. CLC.

205C   [**Lamb, Catharine.**] A full discovery of the false evidence. *For John and Thomas Lane*, 1688. 4°.* O, OC, LCL, CS, NE, DT; CH, IU, MH, WF, Y.

205D   [**Lamb, Francis.**] Astroscopium: or two hemispheres. *By William Leybourn, for the author, sold by R. Morden*, 1673. 8°. T.C.I 141. L, O, C, CS.

205E   [–] —Second edition. *By Phillip Lea*, 1700. 4°. CLC.

205F   —A geographical description of . . . Ireland. [1685?] 12°. O; LC, WAYNE ST. U.

206   **Lamb, Philip.** A funeral sermon after the interment of Mrs. Sarah Lye. *Printed*, 1679. 8°. L, LCL, LW.

207   —A funeral sernom [*sic*], delivered upon . . . John Gould. *By M. C. for John Smith*, 1679. 8°. L, OC.

207AA   —A new year's gift, as a true portraiture. *For Thomas Parkhurst*, 1680. 8°. T.C.I 449. CS.

207A   —The royal presence, or . . . a farewell sermon. *Printed*, 1662. 4°.* L; Y.

207B   —A sermon, preached at the funeral of Mrs. Hanah Butler . . . July the 29th, 1675. *For Tho. Taylor*, 1675. 4°.* T.C.I 216. L; Y.

208   **Lamb, Thomas.** Absolute freedom from sin. *By H. H. for the authour, and are to be sold by him, and also by William Larnar, and by Giles Calvert, and by Richard Moon, and by Thomas Brewster*, 1656. 4°. L, O, ORP; MH, NHC, NU.

     [–] Appeal to the Parliament. 1660. *See* Lawson, Thomas.

208A   —Christ crucified. [*London*], 1646. 4°. NHC.

209   —A confutation of infants baptisme. [*London*], *seen, and allowed by us and printed*, 1643. 4°. CS, DT; MU, NHC, RPJ.

210   [–] A fresh suit against independency. *For Walter Kettilby*, 1677. 8°. L, O, LW, CS, DU, NPL; CH, MBA, NU, WF, Y.

211   [–] A stop to the course. *For Walter Kettilby*, 1672. 8°. C, LW, OC, CT, AN, BR; CLC, WF.

212   [–] —Second edition. —, 1693. 8°. T.C.II 445. DC; MBA.

212A   —A treatise of particular predestination. *Printed*, 1642. 4°.* CT; Y.

213 —Truth prevailing. *By G. Dawson, to be sold by Francis Smith,* 1655. 4°. L, ORP.

Lamb and his day. [1660/1.] *See* Smith, Humphry.

213A The lamb calling his followers. *Printed,* 1662. 8°. LCL, DU.

214 **Lamball, William.** Something in answer to Thomas Curtis. [*London,* 1686.] cap., 4°.* BBN; CH, PH.

215 —A stop to the false characterizers. [*London*], *by Andrew Sowle,* 1685. 4°.* BBN.

215A **Lambard, William.** The duty and office of high-constables. *By Joh. Streater, Hen. Twyford, and Eliz. Flesher, the assigns of R. and E. Atkins,* 1671. 12°. CS; CH, IU, MHL, WF.

215B ——[Anr. ed.] *By G. Sawbridge, T. Roycroft, and W. Rawlins, the assigns of R. Atkins and E. Atkins,* 1677. 12°. O, LLL.

216 —The perambulation of Kent. *For Matthew Walbancke, and Dan Pakeman,* 1656. 8°. L, O, C, DC, EN, GH; BBE, CH, MHL, WF, Y.

217 **Lambe, John.** A dialogue between a minister. *For Walter Kettilby,* 1690. 8°. T.C.II 310. L, O, C, LLP, CD.

218 —The liberty of human nature. *For Walter Kettilby,* 1684. 4°.* T.C.II 95. L, C, LUG, BAMB, WCA; CLC, MH, NU, WF, Y.

219 —A sermon preached . . . 23. of March 1672/3. *By T. R. and N. T. for Robert Boulter,* 1673. 4°.* T.C.I 133. L, O, C, LG, WCA; CH, NU, TU, WF, Y.

220 —A sermon preached . . . Jvne 13. 1680. *For Walter Kettilby,* 1680. 4°.* T.C.I 415. L, O, C, NE, DT; CH, MH, NP, NU, WF.

221 —A sermon preached, . . . fifth of February, 1681/2. *For Walter Kettilby,* 1682. 4°.* T.C.I 493. L, O, C, CT, DT; CLC, IU, MH, NU, TSM, WF, Y.

222 —A sermon preached . . . Jan. 19. 1689. *For Walter Kettilby,* 1690. 4°.* T.C.II 297. L, O, C, LLP, LSD; CLC, IU, MH, NP, WF, Y.

223 —A sermon preached . . . Jan. 24. 1690/1. *For Walter Kettilby,* 1691. 4°.* T.C.II 355. L, O, C, EN, DT; CH, IU, MH, NU, WF, Y.

224 —A sermon preached . . . Jan. 15. 1692. *By Tho. Warren for Walter Kettilby,* 1693. 4°.* T.C.II 437. L, O, C, EN, DT; CLC, IU, MH, NU, WF, Y.

225 —A sermon preached . . . March 22. 1692. *By Tho. Warren for Walter Kettilby,* 1693. 4°.* T.C.II 448. L, O, C, LLP, DT; CH, MH, NU, WF, Y.

226 —A sermon preach'd . . . January 13. 1694/5. *For Walter Kettilby,* 1695. 4°.* L, C, CT, BAMB, DT; IEG, MH, NCD, NU, WF, Y.

227 —A sermon preached . . . Jan. 19th, 1695/6. *For Walter Kettilby,* 1696. 4°.* T.C.II 567. L, C, CT, BAMB, DT; CH, IEG, MH, NU, Y.

228 **Lambe, Samuel.** The humble representation of. [*London?* 1658.] brs. L, LUG; WF.

229 —Seasonable observations. colop: *Printed at the authors charge, to be sold by William Hope,* 1657. cap., fol.* L, O, LG, DC; MH, NC, PU, WF, ANL.

Lambe, Thomas. *See* Lamb, Thomas.

229A **Lambermont, Ludovicus, lord.** Ακεστοριαϛανθολογια. *Excudebat R. Nortonus,* 1654. 12°.* L, OB.

230 Entry cancelled.

Lambert, Lady. To His Excellency General Monck. [1660.] *See* title.

231 **Lambert, James.** The countryman's treasure. *For Henry Twyford,* 1676. 8°. T.C.I 237. L; WF.

232 ——[Anr. ed.] *For Henry Twyford; and Obadiah Blagrave,* 1683. 8°. T.C.II 19. L, LWL, R; BN, MH, TO, Y.

233 **Lambert, John.** By Major Generall Lambert, . . . 4 Jan. 1648[9]. [*London,* 1649.] brs. STEELE 2815. O.

233A —By Major-General Lambert . . . whereas complaints. *Printed at Leith by Evan Tyler,* 1651. brs. Y.

234 Entry cancelled.

—Curtain conference. [1660.] *See* title.

234A —Forasmuch, as I am credibly informed. *Edinburgh, by Evan Tyler,* 1651. brs. Y.

235 Entry cancelled.

[–] Letter from Kendall. 1648. *See* Rushworth, John. Severall fights.

236 —A letter from . . . to General Monck. *Printed,* 1659. 4°.* LT, O, C, BC, E; CH, MH, MU, WF, Y.

237 —The Lord Lambert's letter to the right honorable the speaker. *By Tho. Newcomb,* 1659[60]. 4°.* L, O, C, AN, MR; CH, CN, MH, MU, WF.

238–240 Entries cancelled.

—Lord Lambert's letter to the speaker. 1659. *See* title.

—Message of. 1660. *See* title.

—Poor John: or, a Lenten dish. [n.p., 1660.] *See* title.

—Prayer of. 1660. *See* title.

241 —A proclamation published through every regiment. *Printed at London by Robert Ibbitson,* 1648. 4°.* LT; CH, MIU.

242 —A second, and a third letter from. *By Tho. Newcomb,* 1659. 4°.* L, O, BC, SP; CH, CN, MH, MIU, MU, WF.

243 —Colonell Iohn Lambert's speech at the Council of State. *By Iohn Redmayne.* 1659[60]. 4°.* LT, O, LIU, LSD, BLH; CLC, CSS, MH, WF.

243A **Lambert, Ralph.** A sermon preach'd at the funeral of Ann Margetson. *For Peter Buck,* 1693. 4°. O.

244 **L[ambert], T[homas].** Sad memorials of the royal martyr. *By Tho. Milbourn for Robert Clavel,* 1670. 4°.* T.C.I 35. L, O, C, DU, DT; CH, CN, NU, WF.

245 Lamberts last game plaid. [*London*], *for Richard Andrew,* 1660. 4°.* LT, O, MR; CN, MB.

245A —[Anr. ed.] *Printed,* 1660. 4°.* MIU, WF.

246 Lambeth faire, vvherein. [*London*], *printed,* 1641. 4°.* LT, O, LLP, OC, LLU; CH, CN, MH, NU, TU, WF, Y. (var.)

247 —[Anr. ed.] *By Ry. Et.,* 1641. 4°.* O, LG, LVF, YM, EN; CH, CSS.

248 Lambeth faire's ended. [*London*], *printed,* 1641. 4°.* L, O, LVF, OW, EN; CH, Y.

249 The lambs defence against lyes. *For Giles Calvert,* 1656. 4°.* LT, O, C, MR, DT; CH, MH, NCD, PSC, WF, Y. (var.)

Lambs of Christ. 1692. *See* Ellis, Clement.

Lambs officer. 1659. *See* Fox, George.

Lambs warre. 1657. *See* Nayler, James.

249A The lame crew. [*London*], *by P. Stent*, [1640–67]. brs. LG.

250 Lamentable account of the murther of Sir William Hescot. 1684. brs. LG(lost).

251 The lamentable and bloody murder of . . . Lieutenant Dallison. *For B. H.*, 1678. 4°.* C; NU.

Lamentable and sad newes. 1642. *See* Jenkinson, William.

252 The lamentable and tragical history of Titus Andronicus. [*London*], *for F. Coles, T. Vere, J. Wright, & J. Clarke*, [1675]. brs. L.

252A —[Anr. ed.] *For F. Coles, T. Vere, and W. Gilbertson*, [1658–64]. brs. WF.

253 —[Anr. ed.] [*London*], *by and for A. M.*, [1690?]. brs. L.

254 —[Anr. ed.] *By and for W. O.*, [1700?]. brs. L; MB.

254A A lamentable ballad, of a combate. [*London*], *F. C. J. W. T. V. W. G.*, [1655–58]. brs. L.

254B —[Anr. ed.] *For Francis Coles, T. Vere, and W. Gilbertson*, [1658–64]. brs. O.

254C —[Anr. ed.] *For F. Coles, T. Vere, and J. Wright*, [1663–74]. brs. EUING 194. GU.

254D —[Anr. ed.] *Printed at London for F. C.*, [1687–91]. brs. EUING 195. GU.

255 —[Anr. ed.] *For A. M. W. O. and T. Thackeray*, [1695?]. brs. L, O, HH.

255A A lamentable ballad of fair Rosamond. *By and for W. O.*, [1695?]. brs. EUING 238. GU.

256 A lamentable ballad of Little Musgrove. *For A. M. W. O. and T. Thackeray*, [1695?]. brs. L, O, CM, HH.

—[Anr. ed.] [1674–9.] *See* Lamentable ballad of the little Musgrove.

256A —[Anr. ed.] *By and for W. O.*, [1695?]. brs. L.

256B A lamentable ballad of the ladies fall. [*London*], *for F. Coles, T. Vere, and William Gilbertson*, [1658–64]. brs. EUING 196. GU.

257 —[Anr. ed., "lady's."]. *By and for W. O. for A. M.*, [1695?]. brs. HH.

258 —[Anr. ed.] [*London*], *by and for W. O. and sold by J. Walter*, [1700?]. brs. MH.

259 —[Anr. ed.] [*London*], *for W. Thackeray, E. M. and A. M.* [1692]. brs. MH.

260 —[Anr. ed.] [*London*], *by and for A. Milbourn*, [1693?]. brs. L, O, CM, HH.

261 —[Anr. ed., "ladies."] [*London*], *for F. Coles, T. Vere, J. Wright, and J. Clarke*, [1674–79]. brs. L.

261A [A] lamentable ballad of the little Musgrove. *For F. Coles, T. Vere, and J. Wright*, [1663–74]. O.

262 —[Anr. ed.]. *For F. Coles, T. Vere, J. Wright, and J. Clarke*, [1675]. brs. L, O, CM.

262A A lamentable ballad of the tragical end of a gallant lord. [*London*], *For F. Coles, T. Vere, and W. Gilbertson*, [1658–64]. brs. EUING 197. GU.

263 —[Anr. ed.] *By and for W. O. and sold by B. Deacon*, [1700?]. brs. L, O.

264 —[Anr. ed.] *By and for A. Milbourn*, [1693?]. brs. L, HH.

265 —[Anr. ed.] [*London*], *for W. Thackeray, J. M. and A. M.* [1689–92]. brs. L, O, CM, HH.

266 A lamentable ballad on the Earl of Essex's death. [*London*], *for A. M. W. O. and T. Thackeray*, [1695]. brs. EUING 199. L, CM, HH, GU.

266A —[Anr. ed.] [*London*], *by and for A. M.*, [1700]. brs. L.

Lamentable complaint. 1645. *See* H., T.

267 The lamentable complaints of Hop the Brewer. [*London*], *printed*, 1641. 4°.* L; CH, Y (trimmed).

268 The lamentable complaints of Nick Froth. [*London*], *printed*, 1641. 4°.* LT; MH, Y.

269 A lamentable ditty composed upon the death of Robert, Lord Devereux. [*London*, 1670?] brs. EUING 199. L, O, GU.

269A —[Anr. ed.] [*London*], *for A. M., W. O., and T. Thackeray*, [1695?]. brs. L, CM, HH.

270 The lamentable ditty of the Mousgrove. *For F. Coles, T. Vere and W. Gilbertson*, [1658–64]. brs. O.

271 The lamentable estate and distressed case of the deceased Sr. William Dick. [*London*, 1657.] fol.* LT; CH, Y.

271A The lamentable fall of Queen Elenor. [*London*], *for F. Coles, T. Vere, and W. Gilbertson*, [1658–64]. EUING 184. GU.

271B —[Anr. ed.] *For F. Coles, T. Vere, and J. Wright*, [1663–74]. brs. O.

272 A lamentable narration of the sad disaster . . . of the Spanish plate-fleet. *By T. F. for N. B.*, [1658.] brs. LT.

273 A lamentable new ballad upon the Earle of Essex his death. [1685.] brs. O.

274 Entry cancelled. Date: 1630? [STC 23291].

275 Lamentable newes from Ireland. *June 8. For I. Green and A. Coe*, 1642. 4°.* LT, C, DN.

275A —[Anr. ed.] *For I. G. and A. C.*, 1642. 4°.* OC.

276 —[Anr. ed.] *For I. G. Smith, and A. Coe*, 1642. 4°.* LT, EC.

276A Lamentable news from sea; . . . being a true relation of . . . the Cherry. 1677. 4°.* LPR.

276B Lamentable news from Southwark. *Printed*, 1675. 4°.* Y.

Lamentable representation. 1656. *See* T., U.

Lamentable sufferings. 1659. *See* Curtis, Samuel.

277 Lamentatio civitatis; or. *For Robert Rogers, to be sold at his house or at the Glassbrook*, 1665. 4°.* L, C, LG; NN.

278 The lamentation. *Printed*, 1679. brs. OC, HH; CH, MIU, NCD.

279 —[Anr. ed.] *For T. D.*, 1679. brs. L, O, OC, MR; CLC, CN, MH, TSM, Y.

Lamentation for the deceived. [n.p., 1657.] *See* Bettris, Jeane.

280 A lamentation for the reigning abomination of pride. [*London? 1680.*] cap., 4°.* L.

281 The lamentation of a bad market: or, knaves. *Printed at the charge of John Lambert, Charles Fleetwood, Arthur Hesilrig, and—Hewson the Cobbler*, 1660. 4°.* LT, MR; CH, MIU.

282 Entry cancelled.

—[Anr. ed.] [n.p., 1674–79.] *See* Lamentation of a bad market, or the drownding.

283 Entry cancelled.

—[Anr. ed.] 1660. *See* Lamentation of a bad market: or, the disbanded souldier.

284 The lamentation of a bad market: or, the disbanded souldier. *For Charles Gustavus*, 1660. brs. LT.

284A The lamentation of a bad market, or the drownding of three children. [*London*], *for F. Coles, T. Vere, J. Wright, and J. Clarke*, [1674–79]. brs. L, CM, HH; MH, Y.

284B The lamentation of a sinner, or Bradshavv's horrid farevvel. *Printed*, 1659. 4°.* L, OB; CH, MH, MIU.

285 The lamentation of Cloris. [*London*], *for F. Coles, T. Vere, I. Wright, I. Clarke, W. Thackeray, & T. Passinger*, [1678–80]. brs. EUING 193. L, CM, HH, GU; MH.

285AA The lamentation of Mary Butcher, now . . . in Worcester city-goal. [*n.p.*, 1700?] brs. L.

285A–286 Entries cancelled.

Lamentation of Mr. Pages wife. [1670.] *See* Deloney, Thomas.

287 The lamentation of seven journey men taylors. [*London*], *for I. Deacon*, [1684–95]. brs. L, O, CM, HH; MH.

288 The lamentation of the ruling lay-elders. [*London*], *printed*, 1647. 4°.* LT, O, C, DU, YM; CH, CSS, MIU, NU, PT.

289 The lamentation of the safe committee. *For William Gilbertson*, 1660. 8°.* LT; CLC.

Lamentation over England, because of. [n.p., 1665.] *See* Rigge, Ambrose.

Lamentation over England, from. [*n.p.*], 1664. *See* Watkins, Morgan.

290 A lamentation over the house of Israel. [*London*, 1664?] 4°.* LF.

Lamentation over thee. 1665. *See* Crane, Richard.

Lamentation unto this nation. [1660.] *See* White, Dorothy.

Lamentation with a call to mourning. [1659?] *See* Penington, Isaac.

Lamentationes obscurorom vivorum epistola. 1689. *See* Gratius, Ortuinus.

290A The Lamentations of Jeremiah in meeter. *By R. I. for Stephen Bowtell*, 1652. 8°.* LT.

290B The Lamentations of the prophet Jeremiah, paraphras'd. *Printed Nov.* 11, 1647. 4°. L.

291 Lamentations vpon the never enough bewailed death of the Reverend Mr. John Reiner. [*Cambridge, Mass.*, 1676.] brs. MBA.

292 The lamented lovers. [*London*], *for P. Brooksby, J. Deacon, J. Blare, and J. Back*, [1685–92]. brs. EUING 190. L, CM, HH, GU; MH.

293 The lamenting lady's farewel. [*London*, 1700?] brs. L.

294 The lamenting ladies last farewel. [*London*], *for T. Vere*, [1650?]. brs. L, O.

295 —[Anr. ed.] *For Tho. Vere*, [1656?]. brs. EUING 183. L, GU.

295A —[Anr. ed.] [*London*], *for T.V., sold by F. Coles*, [1660?]. brs. O.

296 —[Anr. ed.] *For W. Thackeray*, [1685]. brs. L, HH; MH.

296A —[Anr. ed.] [*London*], *for J. Wright, J. Clarke, W. Thackeray, and T. Passinger*, [1681–84]. brs. CM.

297 A lamenting vvord shewing. *For Thomas Brewster*, 1657. 4°.* CT, BC; NU, PL, WF, Y.

La Millitière, Theophile Brachet de. *See* Brachet de la Millitière, Theophile.

297A La Molliere, **monsieur de**. A Portuguez grammar; or, rules. *By Da. Maxwell for Samuel Brown*, 1662. obl. 8°. LIU.

La More, **Thomas de, *pseud.***

298 Lamothe, **Claude Grostête de**. The inspiration of the New Testament. *For Tho. Bennet*, 1694. 8°. T.C.II 490. L, O, C, ENC, DT; CH, IU, MH, NU, WF, Y.

299 [–] Two discourses concerning the divinity. *For Richard Baldwin*, 1693. 4°. L, O, CT, E, DT; Y.

300 La Mothe Le Vayer, **Francois de**. The great prerogative of a private life. *By J. C. for L. C. and sold by Charles Blount*, 1678. 12°. T.C.I 302. L, O, C; CU, Y.

301 —Notitia historicorum selectorum, or animadversions. *Oxford, by Leon Lichfield for Ric. Davis*, 1678. 12°. T.C.I 322; MADAN 3182–3. L, O, C, E, DT; CH, CN, LC, MH, MIU, Y. (var.)

302 [–] Of liberty and servitude. *For M. Meighen, and G. Bedell*, 1649. 12°. L, O, LW, OC, GK; CLC, IU, MH, NNM, WF.

303 La Motte, **Francois de**. The abominations of the Church of Rome. *By W. G. to be sold by Moses Pitt*, 1675. 4°. T.C.I 204. L, O, C, DU, EN; CH, CN, NU, WF, Y.

304 —Les motifs de la conversion. *A Londres, se vendent chez Moyse Pitt*, 1675. 4°. T.C.I 213. L, CCA; CLC, IU.

304A Lamplugh, **Thomas, *abp.*** [A letter to the clergy from the bishops about Irish protestant refugees]. 1689. brs. LG.

304B —[A pastoral letter to clergy of the diocese of Exeter about catechisms.] [167–?] 4°.* NU.

305 —A sermon preached . . . the fifth of November. [*London*], *in the Savoy, by Tho. Newcomb, to be sold by Henry Brome*, 1678. 4°.* T.C.I 347. L, O, C, LSD, BLH; CH, CN, MH, NU, WF, Y. (var.)

306 ——[Anr. ed.] [*London*], *in the Savoy, by Thomas Newcomb*, 1678. 4°. LL, CT; CH, Y.

306A Lampoons. [*London?* 1687.] brs. L, O, LG, OC, LLU; CH, CLC, CN, MH, NCD, Y.

307 Lamport, **John, *alias* Lampard**. A direct method of ordering and curing . . . the small pox. *By J. Gain, for the author, to be sold by Samuel Crouch*, 1685. 4°.T.C.II 157. L, LWL; CH, PL, WF.

Lamps of the law. 1658. *See* Blount, Thomas.

La Musse, **Margaret**. Triumphs of grace. 1687. *See* title.

307A [Lamy, **Bernard**.] The art of speaking. *By W. Godbid, sold by Moses Pitt*, 1676. 8°. T.C.I 257. L, O, C, AN, E; CH, CU, MH, WF, Y.

307B [–] —[Anr. ed.] *For T. Bennet*, 1696. 8°. T.C.II 592. L, AN, RPL; CH, IU, MH, PL, Y.

308 Lamzweerde, **Jan Baptist van**. Historia naturalis. Molarum uteri. 1687. AU, GH.

309 The Lancashire cuckold. *For J. Blare*, [1690?]. brs. EUING 200. L, GU.

310 The Lancashire Levite rubuk'd: or, a farther vindication. *By R. J. and sold by A. Baldwin*, 1698. 4°.* L, CS; MH.

Lancashire Levite rebuk'd: or, a vindication. 1698. *See* Carrington, John.

310AA The Lancashire lovers. [*London*], *for J. Wright, J. Clarke, W. Thackeray, and T. Passinger*, [1681–84]. brs. O.

310A The Lancashire sham-plot. [*London*, 1693 *or* 4.] brs. MH.
310B Lancashire's glory. [*London*], *printed for E. Oliver*, [*n.d.*]. brs. O.
      Lancashires valley. 1643. *See* Angier, John.
311   **L[ancaster], J[ames].** To the Pope, and all his cardinals. [*London*], *printed*, 1671. 4°. L, O, LF, BBN, MR; MH, PH, PSC.
312   [**Lancaster, Nathaniel.**] A true relation of a great victory obtained (through Gods providence) by the Parliaments forces in Cheshire. *For Edward Husband, Novemb.* 5, 1645. 4°.* LT, O, AN; MH, WF.
313   **Lancaster, Robert.** Vindiciæ evangelii: or, a vindication. *For a friend of the authors, and sold by Will. Marshall*, 1694. 4°. L, O, GU; CH, CLC, NU, TO.
314   **Lancaster, William.** William Lancaster's queries to the Quakers. [*New York, by William Bradford*], 1693. PHS (frag.).
315   —A sermon preached . . . 30th of January, 1696/7. *For Walter Kettilby*, 1697. 4°.* T.C.III 3. L, O, C, BAMB, NE; CH, CLC, MH, NU, TSM, WF, Y.
      Lancasters massacre. 1643. *See* H., J.
      [**Lancelot, C.**] Epigrammatum delectus. 1683. *See* Nicole, Pierre.
316–17 Entries cancelled.
      Lanceter. *See* Lanseter.
317A **Lancton, Thomas.** Dublin, Ianuary, 31. 1641, Exceeding good newes from Ireland. *For Iohn Thomas*, 1641. 4°.* LNC, MR.
318   —Exceeding joyfull newes from Ireland. *By T. F. for J. Thomas*, 1641[2]. 4°.* L, O, LNC, EN; MH, INU, WF.
319   —Dvblin Febr. 7. 1641[2] or, the last true newes from Ireland. *For John Thomas*, 1641[2]. 4°.* LT, O; INU, WF.
320   Land and houses belonging to Benjamin Hinton's estate. [*London*, 1687.] brs. LG.
321   The land of Canaan as it was possessed. *By M. Simmons for Thomas Jenner*, 1652. 4°.* LT; CLC, NP.
      Land of promise. 1641. *See* E., I.
      Land-tempest. 1644. *See* P., W.
321A **Lander, Thomas.** The information of. *For Thomas Simmons*, 1681. fol.* L, O; CLC, NN, PU, WF, Y.
      Landgartha. Dublin, 1641. *See* Burnell, Henry.
321B The landing of His Sacred Maiesty King Charles at Dover. [*London*], *for H. Seamer*, [1660]. 4°.* LIU.
322   The landing of the forces in Kent. [*London*], *printed*, 1648. 4°.* LT, LG, CD; MH, Y.
323   A land-mark for all true English loyal subjects. colop: *For Francis Smith*, 1681. brs. L, O, LG, DU, MC; CH, CN, MH, WF, Y, AVP.
323A **Lands, Heber.** A short treatise of practical gauging. *By W. Horton for George Sawbridge*, 1694. 12°. CLC.
324   A landskip: or a brief prospective. [*London*], *printed*, 1660. 4°.* LT, O, CM, BC, YM; CH, CLC, IU, NU, WF.
325   **Lane, Archibald.** A key to the art of letters. *For A. and J. Churchil, and J. Wild*, 1700. 8°. L, O, LU, CQ, LLP; CLC, IU, NC, WF.

326   —A rational and speedy method of attaining to the Latin tongue. *By J. D. for the author*, 1695. 8°. O, LW, EN; CH, CLC, WF, Y.
327   ——[Anr. ed.] *For J. Harris, and A. Bell*, 1698. 8°. T.C.III 42. L.
328   [**Lane, Bartholomew.**] An appeal to the conscience. *By J. G. for John Walthoe*, 1684. 4°.* T.C.II 86. L, O, C, SP, DT; CH, CLC, INU, KYU, NU.
329   —A modest vindication of the hermite of the Sounding Island. *By T. Snowden, for the author*, 1683. fol.* T.C.II 33. L, O, CS, MR; CH, IU, MBA, PU, WF, Y.
330   —The prerogative of the monarchs. *For William Bateman*, 1684. 8°. T.C.II 87. O; CLC, LC.
331   **Lane, Edward.** Du Moulin's reflections reverberated. *For William Crook*, 1681. 4°. T.C.I 452. L, OB, CCH, E, DT; CH, PU, WF.
332   —Look unto Jesus. *By Thomas Roycroft for the authour to be sold by Humphrey Tuckey, and by William Taylor in Winchester*, 1663. 4°. L, LLP, LW, CS; CLC, MH, NU, WF, Y.
333   —Mercy triumphant. *For William Crooke*, 1680. 4°. L, O, CT, P; CH, CLC, MBZ, PU, WF.
334   [–] A taste of the everlasting ffeast. [1670?] 4°. L.
335   **Lane, Edward, *Col.*** An image of our reforming times. *For L. Chapman*, 1654. 4°. LT, CJ, A, DT; CLC, CN, MH, NU, WF, Y.
336   **Lane, Erasmus.** Divinitas Christi. [*Cambridge*], 1670. brs. L.
337   **L[ane], J[ohn].** Alarvm to poets. *Printed*, 1648. 4°.* O; CH, INU, Y.
338   —Persecution detected. *For the author*, 1652. 4°.* L, LCL; WF.
339   No entry.
      Lane, Moses. Protestant school. 1681. *See* Ussher, James, *abp.*
340   **Lane, Richard.** Reports in the Court of Exchequer. *For W. Lee, D. Pakeman, and G. Bedell*, 1657. fol. L, O, C, EN, DT; CH, LC, MHL, MIU, V, Y, AVP.
341   **L[ane], S[amuel].** A vindication of free-grace. *By John Macock, for Michael Spark junior*, 1645. 4°. LT, O, CS, LIU, DT; CH, MH, WF, NU, Y.
      Lane, *Sir* Thomas. Lane Mayor. 1694. *See* London. Lord Mayor.
341A —The speech of. colop: *For Thomas Cockerill*, 1694. brs. WF.
      La Neuville. *See* Foy de la Neuville.
      La Neuville, Balthasar Hezeneil de. *See* Baillet, Adrien.
342   **Laney, Benjamin, *bp.*** Five sermons. *For Timothy Garthwait*, 1669. 4°. L, O, C, LCL, DU; CH, MH, NGT, NU, TSM.
343–4 Entries cancelled.
      —Letter about liberty. 1676. *See* Hobbes, Thomas.
345   —A sermon preached . . . March 9th. 1661. *By R. N. for Timothy Garthwaite*, 1662. 4°.* L, O, C, DU, LNC; CLC, CN, NGT, NU, WF, Y.
346   —A sermon preached . . . April 5. 1663. *For Timothy Garthwait*, 1663. 4°.* L, O, C, DU, DT; CH, CLC, NU, WF, Y.

347 —A sermon preached . . . March 12. 1664/5. *For Timothy Garthwait*, 1665. 4°.* L, O, C, DU, LNC; CH, IEG, MH, NU, TSM, WF, Y.

348 —A sermon preached . . . March 27th 1664. *For Timothy Garthwait*, 1665. 4°.* L, O, C, YM, DT; CLC, IU, MH, NU, WF, Y.

349 —A sermon preached . . . March 18. 1665/6. *For Timothy Garthwait*, 1666. 4°.* L, O, C, YM, BLH; CH, CLC, IU, NU, WF, Y.

350 —A sermon preached before the King at White-Hall. *For Henry Brome*, 1675. 4°.* T.C.I 209. L, O, C, OM, LNC; CH, CN, MH, NU, TSM, WF, Y.

351 [–] The shepherd. *For Timothy Garthwait*, 1668. 4°.* OC, OU, DU; CH, CLC, IU, MH, NU, PU.

351A —Six sermons. *For Henry Brome and Walter Kettilby*, 1675. 4°. C, CS, BAMB.

351B —Two sermons. *For Timothy Garthwait*, 1665. 4°. CS, LNC.

352 [–] —[Anr. ed.] *For T. Garthwait*, 1668. 4°. L, C, OC, DU, LNC; CH, IU, MH, NU, PU.

352A **Lanfiere, Thomas.** A caveat for a spendthrift. *For W. Thackeray, T. Passenger, and W. Whitwood*, [1670–77]. brs. L, HH.

353 —The citty prophisier. [*London*], *for F. Coles, T. Vere, J. Wright, and J. Clarke*, [1674–79]. brs. O.

354 —The clothiers delight. [*London*], *for F. Coles, T. Vere, I. Wright, and I. Clarke*, [1674–79]. brs. L.

355 —A discription of plain-dealing. [*London*], *for F. Coles, T. Vere, J. Wright, and J. Clarke*, [1674–79]. brs. L, HH; MH, Y.

355A [–] The fair maids choice. [*London*], *for F. Coles, T. Vere, J. Wright, and J. Clarke*, [1674–79]. brs. L.

356 [–] The gallant seamans return. [*London*], *for F. Cole, T. Vere, J. Wright, and J. Clarke. W. Thackery, T. Passenger*, [1678–80]. brs. L, O, CM, HH; MH, Y.

356A [–] —[Anr. ed.] [*London*], *for W. Thackery, and T. Passenger*, [1686–88]. brs. O.

356B —The garland of love and mirth. *For I. Deacon, sold by R. Kell*, [1685]. 8°.* CM.

357 —Good fellovvs consideration. [*London*], *for P. Brooksby*, [1685?]. brs. EUING 133. L, HH, GU.

358 [–] The good fellows frolick. [*London*], *for J. Coniers*, [1682]. brs. L, O, CM, HH; MH.

359 —The good-fellow's resolution. [*London*], *for F. Coles, T. Vere, J. Wright, J. Clarke, W. Thackeray, and T. Passinger*, [1678–80]. brs. L, HH.

360 [–] A looking-glass for a bad husband. *For W. Thackeray, T. Passenger, and W. Whitwood*, [1670–77]. brs. L, HH; MH.

361 [–] The Taunton maids delight. [*London*], *for P. Brooksby*, [1680–85]. brs. HH; MH.

361A —The true lovers lamentation. [*London*], *for J. Clarke*, [1680]. brs. O.

362 [–] A warning-piece for all wicked livers. [*London*], *for I. Wright, I. Clark, W. Thackeray, and T. Passenger*, [1681–84]. brs. L, O, HH, DU; MH.

362A [–] —[Anr. ed.] [*London*], *for I. Wright, I. Clarke, W. T. and T. Passenger*, [1681–84]. brs. HH; MH.

362B [–] The wonder of wonders. [*London*], *for J. Hose, and E. Oliver*, [1675?]. brs. O.

363 [**Langbaine, Gerard**], *elder.* The ansvver of the Chancellor, masters and scholars. *Oxford, by H. Hall*, 1649. 4°.* MADAN 2019. O, P; WF.

364 [–] —Second edition. *Oxford, by H. Hall and are to be sold by Ric: Davis*, 1678. 4°.* MADAN 3184. L, O, C, P, YM; CH, CN, MH, NU, WF, Y.

365 Entry cancelled.
—Broken title. 1642. *See* Burgess, Cornelius.

365A [–] A continuation of the names of all such noble persons as have been chancellour. [*Cambridge*], *by John Hayes, for John Ivory*, 1675. brs. O.

366 [–] A defence of the rights and priviledges of the University of Oxford. *Oxford, at the Theater*, 1690. 4°. T.C.II 323. L, O, CT, MR, DT; CH, CN, MH, NU, WF, Y.

366A [–] —[Anr. ed.] *Oxford, at the theater*, 1690. fol. O; Y.

367 [–] Episcopall inheritance. *Oxford, by Leonard Lichfield*, 1641. 4°. MADAN 999. LT, O, C, EN, DT; CLC, IEG, MH, NPT, NU, WF, Y.

368 [–] The foundation of the Universitie of Cambridge. *By M. S. for Thomas Jenner*, 1651. 4°.* LT, O, CT, MR, DT; CH, CN, MH, MU, WF, Y.

369 [–] —[Anr. ed.] *Cambridge, by John Hayes, for John Ivory*, 1672. brs. L, C, LG, LNC; Y.

370 [–] The foundation of the Universitie of Oxford. *By M. S., for Thomas Jenner*, 1651. 4°.* MADAN 2150. LT, O, CT, MR, DT; CH, CN, MH, TU, WF, Y.

370A —Philosophiæ moralis compendium. *Impensis Rich. Sare*, 1698. 12°. T.C.III 82. LLP, OC, GU; IU, Y.

371 [–] A review of the covenant. [*Oxford, by L. Lichfield.*] *Printed*, 1644[5]. 4°. MADAN 1716. LT, O, CS, AN, DT; CH, CU, MH, NU, TU.

372 [–] —[Anr. ed.] *For Humphrey Robinson*, 1661. 4°. L, O, C, EN, DT; CH, CU, MH, NU, WF, Y.

373 **Langbaine, Gerard,** *younger.* An account of the English dramatick poets. *Oxford, by L. L. for George West and Henry Clements*, 1691. 8°. T.C.II 358. L, O, CT, AN, EN, DT; CH, CN, LC, MH, WC, WF, Y, AVP.

373A [–] An exact catalogue of all the comedies. *Oxon, by L. Lichfield for Nicholas Cox*, 1680. 4°.* MADAN 3276. L, O, OB; LC, MB, WF.

373B Entry cancelled.
[–] —[Anr. ed.] 1688. *See* —Momus triumphans.

374 [–] The hunter. A discourse. *Oxford, by L. Lichfield, for Nicholas Cox.* 1685. 8°. L, O, LAS; CH, IU, LC, MH, WF, Y.

375 —The lives and characters of the English dramatick poets. *For Tho. Leigh and William Turner*, [1699]. 8°. T.C.III 96. L, O, LVD, CT, EN, BQ; CH, CN, MH, NP, TU, WF, Y.

376 — —[Anr. ed.] *For William Turner*, 1699. 8°. L, CCA, ES; CH, MB, MH, NCU, PU, TU, Y.

376A — —[Anr. ed.] *For N. Cox and W. Turner*, 1699. TO, WF.

377 —Momus triumphans, or. *For N. C., sold by Sam. Holford*, 1688 [1687]. 4°.* T.C.II 239. L, O, CT, BAMB, BC, EN; CH, CN, LC, TU, WF, Y.

377A   ——[Anr. ed.] *For Nicolas Cox, and are to be sold by him in Oxford*, 1688 [1687]. 4°. T.C.III 239. LLU; CLC, MB, MH, PU, WF.

377B   —A new catalogue of English plays. *For Nicholas Cox, and are to be sold by him in Oxford*, 1688 [1687]. 4°. O, OC; CLC, MH, NCD.

378   **Langdale, Marmaduke, *baron.*** De Verclarringe van, . . . the declaration of . . . general of the northerne parts. *Printed*, 1648. 4°. O, LNC; BN, CH, MH.

379   —The declaration of . . . generall of the gentlemen. *Printed*, 1648. 4°.* LT, CS, MR; CSS, IU, MH, MIU.

380   —A declaration of . . . in vindication of James, Earle of Darby. *Printed*, 1649. 4°.* LT; CH, WF.

381   —An impartiall relation of the late fight at Preston. [*London*], *printed*, 1648. 4°.* LT, O, LLL; MH.

382   —A letter from. *Printed*, 1648. 4°.* LT; MH, WF.

383   —The resolution of. *For G. N.*, 1648. 4°.* LT, OB; WF.

384   **Langford, Charles.** Gods wonderful mercy. *For Anna Brewster*, 1672. 12°. L, LCL, LW.

385   Entry cancelled.
    —Recover'd captive. 1672. *See* —Gods wonderful.

386   **Langford, Emanuel.** A sermon preach'd before the Honourable House of Commons. *For Thomas Bennet*, 1698. 4°.* T.C.III 52. L, O, C, NE, EN; CH, CLC, NU, WF, Y.

387   **Langford, John.** A just and cleere refutation. *For the author*, 1655. 4°.* LT, O; CH, MBA, MU, NS, RPJ.

388   **Langford, T.** Plain and full instructions to raise all sorts of fruit-trees. *By J. M. for Rich. Chiswel*, 1681. 8°. T.C.I 419. L, O, CS, DU, CD; CH, IU, LC, MH, PL, WDA, HC.

389   ——Second edition. *For Richard Chiswell*, 1696. 8°. T.C.III 100. L, O, LCS, CT, EN; CLC, MH, NR, PL, WF.

390   ——"Second" edition. *For R. Chiswell, and sold by D. Midwinter and T. Leigh*, 1699. 8°. L; CH, MHO, PL.

390A   **Langham, W.** Admirable snuff. [*London*, 1675?] brs. L.

391   **Langhorne, Daniel.** Appendix ad elenchum. [*Londini*], *excusa*, 1674. 4°. T.C.I 206. L, O, C, CK, EN; CLC, MH, PL, WF.

392   —Chronicon regum Anglorum. *Typis E. F. impensis Benj. Tooke*, 1679. 8°. T.C.I 334. L, O, C, EN, DT; BN, CH, CN, TU, WF, Y.

393   —Elenchus antiquitatum. *Typis B. G. impensis Ben. Took*, 1673. 8°. T.C.I 155. L, O, CP, MR, EN, DT; BN, CH, CN, LC, NP, Y, AVP.

394   ——[Anr. ed.] *Excudebat Benja. Tooke*, 1675. 8°. L, O, C, CK, DU; MH, WF.

395   —An introduction to the history of England. *For Charles Harper, and John Amery*, 1676. 8°. T.C.I 218. L, O, C, DU, EN; CH, CLC, CU, MH, WF, Y.

396   **Langhorne, Richard.** Considerations touching the great question. *By H. H. for the assigns of R. Langhorne and sould by N. Thompson and M. Turner*, 1687. fol.* L, O, CS, DU, EN; BN, CH, CN, TU, WF, Y.

396A   ——[Anr. ed.] *For Richard Langhorn*, 1687. fol.* CN.

397   —Mr. Langhorn's memoires. [*London*], *printed*, 1679. fol. * L, O, C, DU, MR; BN, CH, CU, MH, WF, Y.

398   —The petition and declaration of. [*London*, 1679.] cap., fol.* L, O, C, LNC, MR; BN, CH, IU, MH, NU, TU, Y.

399   —The speech of. [*London*, 1679.] cap., fol.* L, O, C, LNC, MR; BN, CH, CN, MH, WF, Y.

400   **Langhorne, Rowland.** The declaration and propositions of. *For R. W.*, 1648. 4°.* LT, AN.

401   —A declaration by. *For Laurence Chapman, May 15*, 1648. 4°.* LT, O, AN, LIU, MR; CH, IU, PT, WF, Y.

402   —Major Generall Laughorn's [*sic*] letter to the Honourable William Lenthall. *For Edward Husband, Octob. 28*, 1645. 4°.* LT, O, AN, SP, DT; CH, IU, MH, Y.

402AA   [–] A true relation of the late successe of the . . . forces in Pembroke-shire. *For Edward Husband, Aug. 25.* 1645. 4°.* LT, AN, CPL; WF.

402A   —Two letters sent to the honoble William Lenthal. *For Edward Husband*, 1645[6]. 4°.* LT, LLU, CD; CH, CN.

402B   **Langhorne, William.** Considerations humbly tendered . . . East-India Company. [*London?* 1688.] cap., fol.* L.

402C   —Some considerations relating to the East-India trade. [*London?* 1694.] cap., fol.* LUG, INDIA OFFICE; CSS, WF.

Langlade, James de. *See* Saumieres, Jacques de Langlade de.

403   **L'Angle, Samuel de.** A letter. *By A. W. for Joshua Kirton*, 1660. 4°.* LT, OB, BC, YM; CH, IU, MM, PL, WF, Y.

404   **Langley, John.** Gemitus columbæ: the mournfull note of the dove. *By Joh. Raworth for Philemon Stephens*, 1644. 4°.* LT, O, C, EN, BLH; CH, CN, MH, NU, WF, Y.

404A   [–] Totius rhetoricæ adumbratio. In usum Paulinæ Scholæ. *Cantabrigiæ: ex officina Rogeri Daniel.* 1644. 8°.* C.

404B   ——[Anr. ed.] *Cambridge*, 1650. 8°.* ST. PAUL'S SCHOOL, LONDON.

404C   [–] —Third edition. *Ex officina Rogeri Danielis*, 1659. 8°.* L, CT.

405   **Langley, Samuel.** Suspension reviewed. *By J. Hayes for Thomas Underhill*, 1658. 8°. LT, O, LCL, LW, CS; CLC, IU, NU, TO, WF.

Langley, Thomas. New almanack. [1641.] *See* Almanacs.

406   **Langley, William.** The death of Charles the First lamented. *By T. R. for R. Lowndes, and Sym. Gape*, [1660]. 8°. DC; NC, NU.

407   ——[Anr. ed.] *By T. R. for R. Lowndes, and Sym. Gape*, 1660. 8°. LT, EN; CH, PFL, WF, Y.

408   —The persecuted minister. *By J. G. for Richard Royston*, 1656. 4°. LT, O, C, BSE, E; CH, CLC, IU, NHC, NU, TSM.

409   **Langrish, Hercules, *major.*** To the right honorable the Lords & Commons . . . the humble petition of. [*n.p.*, 1644?] cap., 4°. L.

410   **Langston, John.** Εγχειριδιον ποιητικον, sive poesews Græcæ medulla. *Excudebant E. Tyler & R. Holt impensis Thomæ Cockerill.* 1679. 8°. T.C.I 343. L, O, C, LW; PL, WF.

411   —Lusus poeticus Latino-Anglicanus. *For Henry Eversden*, 1675. 8°. T.C.I 213. L, CK, DU, NOT, ES; CH, IU, MH, TU, Y.

412   ——Second edition. *For William Leach*, 1679. 8°. T.C.I 377. O, C; CU, IU, PL.

413   ——Third edition. *By John Richardson*, 1688. 12°. T.C.II 234. L, O, LW, RPL, EN; IU, MIU, NC, NCU, WF, Y.

414   [**Languet, Hubert.**] Vindiciæ contra tyrannos: a defence. *For Matthew Simmons and Robert Wilson*, 1648. 4°. LT, O, LSC, LW; MH, NU, PMA.

415   [–] —[Anr. ed.] *By Matthew Simmons, and Robert Ibbitson*, 1648. 4°. L, CD; CH, CLC, NN, WF.

415A   [–] —[Anr. ed.] *Edinburgh*, 1679. 8°. C.

416   [–] —[Anr. ed.] *For Richard Baldwin*, 1689. 4°. T.C.II 257. L, O, BAMB, LLU, AU, EN; CH, CN, MH, NU, WF, Y.

Languish, Hercules, *pseud.*

417   The languishing lady. [*London*], *for C. Bates*, [1695?]. brs. L, HH.

418   The languishing shepherd. [*London*], *for P. Brooksby, J. Deacon, J. Blare, J. Back*, [1688–92]. brs. L, HH.

418A   The languishing state of our woollen manufacture. [*London*, 1695?] brs. L.

419   The languishing swain. [*London*], *for J. Deacon*, [1685–88]. brs. L, HH; MH, WCL.

420   The languishing young man. [*London*], *for J. Deacon*, [1690]. brs. L, O, CM, HH.

421   Lanii triumphantes, or the butchers prize. *By J. B. for William Crook*, 1665. 4°.* L, OB; MH.

422   **Lansdowne, George Granville, baron.** Heroick love. *For F. Saunders, H. Playford and B. Tooke*, 1698. 4°. T.C.III 55. L, O, C, A, DT; CH, CN, LC, MII, TU, Y.

423   [–] The she-gallants: a comedy. *For Henry Playford, and Benj. Tooke*, 1696. 4°. T.C.II 569. L, O, C, OW, EN; CH, CN, LC, MH, TU, WF, Y.

424   ——[Anr. ed.] *For J. Conyers*, 1700. 4°. O.

425   [–] So well Corinna like's the joy. [*London*], *T. Cross*, [1697?]. brs. L; WF.

425A   [–] A song on a ladys. [*London*, 1700?] brs. CH.

425B   **Lanseter, John.** Lanseters lance, for Edwards'es gangrene. *Printed*, 1646. 4°.* LT, MR, GU, DT; CH, MH, TO, Y.

425C   [**Lanseter, R.**] Gallicantus, seu præcursor Gallicinii primus. Containing two addresses. *For Nathaniel Ranew*, 1659. 4°.* O.

425D   ——[Anr. ed.] —, 1660. 4°.* LT, O; MBP, Y.

426   Entry cancelled.

Lant, Benjamin. *See* Laney, Benjamin.

427   [**La Peyrère, Isaac de.**] Men before Adam. *Printed*, 1656. 8°. L, O, C, BSM, E, CD; CH, MH, MU, NU, WF, Y.

428   Entry cancelled. *See preceding entry.*

429   [**LaPlacette, Jean.**] Of the incurable scepticism of the Church of Rome. *For Ric. Chiswel*, 1588 [*i.e.* 1688]. 4°. T.C.II 270. L, O, C, DC, MC, E, DT; CH, CU, MH, WF, Y.

430   [–] Six conferences concerning the Eucharist. *For Richard Chiswell*, 1687. 4°. T.C.II 270. L, O, C, E, DT; CH, IU, MH, NU, TU, WF, Y.

431   **La Quintinie, Jean de.** The compleat gard'ner. *For Matthew Gillyflower, and James Partridge*, 1693. fol. T.C.II 456. L, O, C, E, DT; CH, CN, LC, MH, MU, NC, Y, AVP.

432   ——[Anr. ed.] *For M. Gillyflower*, 1699. 8°. L, GC, NE, RU, DT; CLC, CN, MH, TU, WF.

432A   ——Second edition. —, *sold by Andrew Bell*, 1699. 8°. T.C.III 145. CH, MB, MH, NIC.

432B   —Directions concerning melons. [*London?* 1693.] fol. L.

432C   [**La Ramée, Pierre de.**] Art of persuasion, or a compendium of logick. *By T. Maxey*, 1651. 16°. O.

433   —A compendium of the art of logick. *By Thomas Maxey*, 1651. 12°. O, C, MAU; CN, TO.

434   —P. Rami . . . dialecticæ libro duo. *Ex officina Johannis Redmayne, & venuent per Robertum Nicholson & Henricum Dickinson Cantabrigiæ*, 1669. 8°. C, LW, MAU, E, BQ; MB, MH, NC, RBU, Y.

434A   ——[Anr. ed.] *Ex officina Johannis Redmayne & veneunt per Henricum Dickinson*, 1669. 8°. CS; CH, WF.

435   ——[Anr. ed.] *Cantabrigiæ, ex officina Joann. Hayes, impensis G. Morden*, 1672. 8°. T.C.I 129. C, LW, OC, LSD, MAU, GU; CLC, IU, MB, NP, V, WF, Y.

436   **Lardner, James.** Of earnestly contending. *For B. Aylmer*, 1700. 4°.* T.C.III 208. L, O, LLP, CT; WF, Y.

Large and particular relation of the affairs of Ireland. 1689. *See* M., J.

437   Large and sure foundations. *Printed*, 1693. fol.* L; CH, WF, Y.

438   A large relation of the fight at Leith. *By Ed. Griffin*, 1650. 4°.* LT; CH, CN, MH, WF.

Large scriptural catechisme. 1672. *See* Petto, Samuel.

439   A large summary of the doctrines. [*n.p.*], *for A. L.*, 1675. 8°. L, DUS; NU, TU.

Large supplement. [*n.p.*], 1641. *See* Baillie, Robert.

440   The larger and shorter catechisms. 1650. 8°. O.

441   **Larkham, Thomas.** The attributes of God vnfolded. *For Francis Eglesfield*, 1656. 4°. LT, LCL, AN; IU, NCU, NN, NU, OSU, WF.

441A   [–] A discourse of paying of tithes. *By T. P. & E. M., to be sold by Francis Eglesfield*, 1656. 8°. IU.

441B   —The parable of the wedding-supper. Second edition. *For Francis Eglesfield*, 1656. 8°. IU.

442   —The wedding supper. *Printed, and are to be sold by Giles Calvert*, 1652. 12°. O, LCL, LW, ORP; MBA.

443   **Larkin, Edward.** A catalogue of English books. [*London*, 1689.] 4°.* JF.

444   —Speculum patrum: a looking-glasse of the fathers. *For Henry Eversden*, 1659. 8°. LT, O, C, EN, DT; CH, LC, MH, MIU, NU, TU, Y.

444A   ——[Anr. ed.] *For H. E. and are to be sold by Iohn Sprat*, 1659. 8°. WF.

445   —The true effigies. *By E. Cotes, for Henry Eversden*, 1659. 8°. LT, O, CK, EN, DT; CLC, CN, MH, NU, TU, WF.

445AA   L[arkin], G[eorge]. The world to come. The glories of heaven. *For John Gwillim*, 1699. 12°. CLC, NU.

445A   **Larner, William.** A vindication of every free-mans libertie. [*London*, 1646.] cap., 4°.* MH.

445B   **La Roberdière, Alexandre de.** Les stratagemes d' amour. *A Londres, imprimé*, 1680. 8°. CN.

445C   —Love victorious. *For R. Bentley and S. Magnes*, 1684. 12°. T.C.II 70. MH.

445D   [–] Voyage de l'amour en Angleterre. *A Paris et se vend a Londres, chez Richard Bentley*, 1680. 8°. CN, Y.

446   [**La Roche-Guilhem**], **Mlle. Anne de.** Almanzor and Almanzaida. *For J. Magnes and R. Bentley*, 1678. 12°. T.C.I 320. L, O; CH, CLC, MH, Y.

447 [–] Asteria and Tamberlain. *For Robert Sollers*, 1677. 12°. T.C.I 281. O; CN, IU, MH, Y.

[–] Great Scanderbeg. 1690. *See* Chevreau, Urbain.

448 [–] Rare en tout. Comedie. *Chez Jacques Magnes, & Richard Bentley*, 1677. 4°. L, EN; CN, Y.

449 [–] Royal lovers: or, the unhappy prince. A novel. *For Robert Sollers*, 1680. 8°. T.C.I 369. L, O.

449A [–] Taxila, or love prefer'd. *For T. Salusbury*, 1692. 12°. T.C.II 410. L, O; CLC, Y.

450 [–] Zingis: a Tartarian history. *For Francis Saunders, and Richard Parker*, 1692. 12°. L; CH, CN, INU, MH, NP, PU, Y.

451 **La Rochefoucauld, Francois, duc de.** Epictetus junior. *For T. Bassett*, 1670. 12°. T.C.I 32. L, O, CS, CPL, DU; CLC, LC, MH, WF, Y.

451aA —An historical account of the late troubles. *For Henry Chapman*, 1686. 8°. T.C.II 136. L; CLC, LC, WF, Y.

451A —The memoirs of. *For James Partridge*, 1683. 8°. T.C.II 44. LSC, CS, LLU, CD; CH, CLC, IU, MH, WF, Y.

451B — —[Anr. ed.] —, 1684. 8°. L, LSD, Y.

452 —Moral maxims and reflections. *For M. Gillyflower, R. Sare and J. Everingham*, 1694. 12°. T.C.II 493. L, O, LLU, EN, DT; CH, LC, MBA, MH, WF, Y.

453 **Larroque, Matthieu de.** Conformity of the ecclesiastical discipline. *For Tho. Cockerill*, 1691. OC, LW, E, GU, DT; IU, KYU, NU, TU, WF.

454 —The history of the Eucharist. *For George Downes*, 1684. 4°. T.C.II 81. L, O, CE, D, DT; CLC, IU, KT, NU, WF, Y.

455 **La Rue, Charles de.** A funeral oration or sermon. *Printed and sold by Richard Baldwin*, 1695. 4°.* L, CT, EC, LSD, WCA, DT; MB, MH, NU, U. OREGON, WF. (var.)

456 Entry cancelled.

LaSalle, Jean Baptiste de, *pseud.* Paradoxes. 1653. *See* Hall, John.

456A **Lascary, Mercurius.** To His Grace James Duke of Ormonde. [*Dublin*, 1677.] brs. DI.

Las Casas, Bartholome de. *See* Casas, Bartholome de las, *bp.*

Las Coveras, Francisco de. *See* Quintana, Francisco de.

457 **La Serre, Jean Puget de.** Ethice Christiana, or the school of wisdom. *By D. M. for Henry Marsh*, 1664. 8°. L, O, P; OCI, WF, Y.

458 —The mirrour which flatters not. *By E. T. for R. Thrale*, 1658. LW, D, E; CH, CLC, CSU, IU, Y.

458A — —[Anr. ed.] *By E. Tyler for R. Thrale and J. Thrale*, 1664. 12°. CH, CLC, Y.

459 — —[Anr. ed.] *By E. T. and R. H. for R. Thrale*, 1673. 12°. T.C.I 138. L, LW, BR; IU, LC, WF.

460 —The secretary in fashion. *For Humphrey Moseley*, 1654. 8°. LT, O, C; CH, MH, TU, Y.

461 — —Second edition. —, 1658. 8°. L, O; IU, WF, Y.

461A — —Fourth edition. *For J. M., to be sold by Rowland Reynolds*, 1668. 8°. L; WF.

462 — —Fifth edition. *For Peter Parker*, 1673. 8°. T.C.I 137. L; CH, CLC, CU, MBA.

462aA — —Sixth edition. *For John Cripps*, 1683. 8°. L; CU, MBP, WF.

462A A lash for the parable-makers. colop: *For C. B. and are to be sold by Randal Taylor*, 1691. cap., 4°.* L, O; CH, MH.

462B A lash to disloyalty. colop: [*London*], *by N. T.* 1983 [*i.e.*, 1683]. brs. L; CLC, MH.

462C **Lasher, Joshua.** Pharmacopœus et chymicus symmystæ. *Impensis Tho. Speed*, 1698. 8°. L, O, CCA; TO, WSG.

462D The lass of Cumberland. [*London*], *for F. Coles, T. Vere, J. VVright, and J. Clarke*, [1674–79]. brs. O.

462E The lass of Lynn's new joy. [*London*], *printed and sold by J. Millet*, [1685–90]. brs. L.

462F **Lassels, Richard.** An excellent way of hearing mass. Fifth edition. *Printed* 1686. 12°. DUS; CLC.

462G —An Italian voyage. *For Richard Wellington and B. Barnard Lintott*, 1697. 8°. CT; KU, MIU, NN.

463 — —Second edition. *For Richard Wellington, and are to be sold by Percivall Gilbourne*, 1698. 8°. T.C.III 59. L, O, C, LWL, ENC, DT; CH, CN, LC, MH, NP, Y.

463A [–] A most excellent way of hearing mass. [*London*], *by T.G.* 1687. 12°. O, DOUAI ABBEY.

464 —The voyage of Italy. *Printed at Paris, by Vincent dv Movtier*, 1670. 12°. L, O, CS, P, ES; BN, CLC, CN, LC, MH, Y.

465 — —[Anr. ed.] *Newly printed at Paris, to be sold in London, by John Starkey*, 1670. 12°. T.C.I 30. L, O, C, EN, DT; CH, MU, NC, TU, WF, Y.

466 — —[Anr. ed.] *For R. C. J. R. and A. C., and are to be sold by Charles Shortgrave*, 1686. 8°. O, OC, DU, LLU, MR; CH, KU, LC, MH, Y.

466A — —[Anr. ed.] *For R. C. J. R. and A. C.*, 1686. 8°. PL.

466B — —[Anr. ed.] *For Robert Clavel, and Jonathan Robinson, and Awnsham Churchill*, 1686. 8°. L, DUS, NE; NC, WF.

466C The lasses of Kinghorn. [*n.p.*, 1700?] brs. EN.

467 The last account from Fez. colop: *For Walter Davis*, [1682/3]. cap., fol.* L, O; CH, CN, PU, WF, Y.

468 The last advice of William Lavd. *For J. B.* 1645. 4°.* LT, O, DT; MH, MIU.

469 The last and best edition of new songs. *Printed*, 1677. 8°. T.C.I 255. O; CH, RHT.

470 The last and best newes from Ireland: declaring. *For F. Coules and T. Bates*, 1641. 4°.* LT, BLH, DN; CN.

470A —[Anr. ed.] *For F. Coules*, 1641. 4°.* WF.

471 The last and most exact edition of new songs. *Printed*, 1678. 8°. T.C.I 310. RHT.

472 The last, and now only, compleat collection, of the newest and choisest songs and poems. Second edition. [*London*], *for Will. Gilbert, and Tho. Sawbridge*, 1672. 8°. T.C.I 130. O; CH, WF.

473 The last and truest discovery of the Popish-plot. colop: [*London*], *by N. T.*, 1683. brs. O; CLC, MH, TU.

Last and truest intelligence. [*n.p.*], 1642. *See* Cox, Owen.

474 The last answer February 22. of the London and Scots commissioners. *Oxford, by Leonard Lichfield*, 1644[5]. 4°.* MADAN 1730. LT, O, CJ, BAMB, DT; CH, CSS, NU, WF.

475 The last articles of peace made, concluded, accorded and agreed upon the 30. day of Iuly, 1646. *Imprinted first at Dublin by William Bladen; and now reprinted at London for Edw. Husband, Sept. 7*. 1646. 4°.* LT, O, C, LSD, DT, BLH; CH, CLC, MH, WF, WU, Y.

476 The last, best, and truest nevves from Ireland. *By Thomas Harper, March* 18. 1641[2]. 4°.* LT, C.

477   The last bloudy fight at sea, between the English and the Dutch. *For George Horton*, 1652. 4°.* LT.

478   The last conclave, containing a relation. *By Stephen Bulkley, for Henry Seile*, 1642. 8°.* C; CH.

479   Entry cancelled.

Last conflicts and death of Mr. Thomas Peacock. 1646. *See* Bagshaw, Edward, *younger*.

Last counsel. 1660. *See* Gregory, Francis.

480   The last damnable designe of Cromwell. [*London*, 1649.] brs. LT.

481   Entry cancelled.

Last discourse betwixt Master Abel. [n.p.], 1641. *See* Abell, William.

481A The last dying speeches and confession of the six prisoners. *For T. Davies*, 1680. fol.* NP, WF.

482   The last dying speeches and confessions of the prisoners . . . twenty second of . . . October. colop: *For T. Davies*, 1680. fol.* O; MH.

482A The last dying speeches and confessions of the three notorious malefactors . . . executed [4 March]. colop: [*London*], *for T. B.*, 1681. cap., fol.* MH, PU.

482B The last dying speeches, confessions and execution of John Stokes. colop: [*London*], *for L. Curtis*, 1684. fol.* L, O; WF.

482C The last dying speeches, confession and execution of Rice Evans. colop: *By George Croom*, 1684. cap., fol.* L, O, DCH; WF.

483   The last dying words and execution of Jonathan Tue. *By Eliz. Mallet*, 1684. fol.* L.

Last efforts. 1682. *See* Jurieu, Pierre.

484   The last endeavour to preserve the committee of safety. [*London*, 1648.] brs. LT.

485   The last farewel to the rebellious sect called the Fifth Monarchy-men. *Printed*, 1661. 4°.* LT.

486   The last great and blovdy fight in Ireland. *For Robert Williamson, the 4. of September*, 1649. 4°.* LT, C, DN.

487   The last great and bloudy fight between the English and the Dutch. *For G. Horton*, 1652. 4°.* LT.

Last great and terrible sea-fight. [1652.] *See* Holding, J.

Last instructions to a painter. [1667.] *See* Marvell, Andrew.

Last intelligence from Ireland received. 1642. *See* Johnson, Richard.

The last ioyfull intelligence, 1643. *See* Alexander, John, *Parliamentary man*.

Last joyfull newes from Ireland. 1642. *See* R., P.

Iune the 24. 1642. Last joyfull newes from Ireland. 1642. *See* Smith, Samuel, *waggon maker*.

488   The last lamentation, of the languishing squire. [*London*], *for P. Brooksby, J. Deacon, J. Blare, J. Black* [*sic.*], [1685–92]. brs. L, O, CM, HH; MH.

489   Entry cancelled.

Last letters to the London merchants. [n.p.], 1665. *See* Serarius, Petrus.

490   The last memorial of the agent. colop: *For R. H.*, 1683. brs. L, O, LG, OC, HH, EN; CH, MH, Y.

Last memorial of the Spanish ambassador. 1681. *See* Ronquillo, Pedro.

490A The last national address. [*Edinburgh*], 1700. WF.

491   The last news from France. *For W. Thackeray, T. Passinger, and W. Whitwood*, [1677?]. brs. L, O.

491A —[Anr. ed.] *For W. Gilbertson*, [1647–65]. brs. EUING 181. GU.

491B —[Anr. ed.] [*London*], *for F. Coles, T. Vere, J. Wright, and J. Clark*, [1674–79]. brs. CM.

492   The last nevves from Ireland being a relation. *For John Thomas*, 1641. 4°.* LT, O, C, DN; INU, Y.

493   The last nevves from Ireland; or, a trve relation of the sad estate. *For VV.L.*, 1641. 4°.* LT, C, EC, MR, DN; Y.

494   The last newes from Ireland. *June 13. London, for I. Green, and A. Coe*, 1642. 4°.* L, O, C, LVF; NU.

495   The last nevves from Kent. *By B. A.*, 1648. 4°.* LT, LG, DT; MIU.

Last nevves from the armie. 1647. *See* Michel, Thomas.

496   The last nevves from the King of Scots. *Imprinted at London for G. Wharton*, 1651. 4°.* LT; Y.

497   The last newes from the Kings Majesties army now at Maidenhead. *Novemb. 11. for T. Watson and J. Jackson*, 1642. 4°.* LT, O; NHS.

Last newes from the North. 1646. *See* H., J.

Last nevves from the Prince. 1648. *See* N., P.

Last nevves from Yorke. 1642. *See* H., T.

498   The last nevvs in London. *For R. R.*, 1642. 4°.* LT, OC, DT; MH, MM.

498A Whitehall, October 18. 1697. Last night came in two mails from Holland. [*London*], *in the Savoy, by E. Jones*, 1697. brs. EN.

498B The last offers of the noblemen . . . now in armes for the Covenant. [*Edinburgh*], *by Evan Tyler*, 1648. brs. ALDIS 1334. 3. EN, Y.

499   The last paper of advice from Ireland. colop: *For D. Newman*, 1690. brs. MC; CH, Y.

500   Entry cancelled.

Last papers betwixt His Maiesty. 1648. *See* Charles I.

Last proceedings of the Scots. 1644. *See* Hardy, John.

501   The last propositions proposed betwixt the Kings most excellent Majesty. *Printed*, 1647. 4°.* LT, DT.

Last Protestant almanack. [n.p.], 1680. *See* Almanacs.

501A The last resolutions of Mounson, Mildman, and Wallop. *For Tho. Davis*, 1661. 4°.* MH, Y.

502   The last sayings of a mouse lately starved in a cupboard. colop: [*London*], *for S. P. Q. L.*, 1681. brs. L, O, LLP; CH, CN, MH, MIU, NCD, PU, WF, Y.

Last search after claret. 1691. *See* Ames, Richard.

503   The last sham of Edward Fitzharris. 1681. brs. LG (lost).

504   The last speech & behaviour of William . . . Russell. *By J. C. and F. C. for Thomas Fox*, 1683. fol.* L, O, C, DU, LSD; CH, CN, MH, NU, TU, WF, Y, AVP.

504A —[Anr. ed.] *Edinburgh, D. Lindsay*, 1683. fol.* ALDIS 2386. MR, EN.

504B —[Anr. ed.] colop: *Dublin, at His Majesties printing-house, to be sold by Joseph Wilde*, 1683. fol.* DIX 201. L, DI, DK, DT.

504C The last speech and carriage of the Lord Russel. [*London*, 1683.] cap., fol.* L, O, BC; CH, WF, Y.

504D —[Anr. ed.] *Edinburgh, reprinted*, 1683. fol.* ALDIS 2387. L, EN; CLC, CSS, IU.

504E The last speech and confession of Charles Obrian and Daniel Cary. colop: *By George Croom*, 1688. cap., fol.* Y.

504F The last speech and confession of Sarah Elstone. [*London*], *for T. D.*, 1678. 4°.* LW.

505 The last speech and confession of the whore of Babylon. *For K. B.*, 1673. 4°.* L, DU; CH, Y.

505aA The last speech and dying words of Thomas . . . Pride. *For C. W.*, 1680. 8°.* L, O, C, LG, MR; CLC, LC, MIU, TU, Y.

505bA The last speech, confession and execution of John Smith. *By E. Mallet*, 1684. cap., fol.* WF.

505cA The last speech, confession, and execution of the two prisoners at Tyburn [John Gower and Fran. Robinson]. [*London*], *by E. M.*, 1684. fol.* L.

505dA The last speech of Thomas Thwing. [1680.] brs. O.

505A The last speeches and confessions of Captain Thomas Walcott. colop: [*London*], *for J. Coniers*, [1683?]. cap., fol.* CH.

505B —[Anr. ed., "The last speeches, behaviour and prayers."] *Reprinted Edinburgh by the heir of A. Anderson*, 1683. fol. ALDIS 2388. L, O, EN; CLC, MIU.

506 The last speeches of the five notorious traitors and Jesuits. [*London*, 1679.] cap., fol.* L, O, C, DU, EN; BN, CH, CN, MH, TU, WF, Y.

506A —[Anr. ed., "speech."] [*Dublin*, 1679.] cap., 4°.* DT.

507 The last speeches of three priests. [*London*, 1679.] brs. L.

507A Last Sundays night frollick. *For H. Marston*, 1695. brs. MH.

507B The last time I came o'er the moor. [*London?* 1670.] brs. L.

508 The last true and joyfull newes from Ireland declaring. *September 22. for Thomas Cook*, 1642. 4°.* LT, DN.

508A The last true and new intelligence from Scotland . . . overthrow of the rebels. [*London*, 1679.] 4°.* EN (impf.).

Last trve intelligence from Ireland. 1642. *See* Cole, Robert.

509 The last true intelligence from Ireland. *Decemb. 14. for L. Wright*, 1642. 4°.* LT, DN; Y.

510 The last true intelligence from Warwick. *Octob.* 31. *for Thomas Watson*, 1642. 4°. LT, BC.

Last true newes from Ireland, being. 1642. *See* P., W.

510A The last true newes from Ireland, March 4, 1641. [*n.p.*, 1641/2]. cap., 4°.* INU.

Last true newes from Yorke. 1642. *See* Dickenson, Henry.

Last visitation. 1660. *See* Bagshaw, Edward, *younger*.

511 The last votes from the armie, June 26, 1647. *For Thomas Watson, June 28*, 1647. 4°.* LT, O, LG, DC, DT; CSS.

512 The last warning to all the inhabitants of London. [*London, Larner's last press*, 1645/6.] cap., 4°.* LT, LG, OC, A, DT; CH, CN, MH, NU, Y.

513 The last weeks proceedings of the Lord Brooke. *By R. O. and G. D., March* 1, 1642[3]. 4°.* LT, O, DT; MH.

513A The last will and testament of a Jacobite. *For W. Penn*, 1692. brs. CN.

513B The last will & testament of Anthony earl of Shaftsbury, elect King of Poland. [*London*, 1682]. brs. Y.

514 The last will and testament of Anthony King of Poland. colop: [*London*], *for S. Ward*, 1682. fol.* L, O, LL, DU, LLU; CH, CN, MH, PU, TU, WF, Y.

514aA —[Anr. ed.] colop: [*London*], *for S. Ward*, 1682. brs. MH, NCD, WF.

514A Entry cancelled.

Last will and testament of . . . Cardinal Mazarin. 1663. *See* Howell, James.

515 The last will and testament of Carolus Gustavus. [*n.p.*] *for William Leadsom*, 1660. 4°.* LT; CSS, MIU.

516 The last vvill and testament of Charjng Crosse. [*London*], *printed*, 1646. 4°.* LT, MR; CH, CSS, Y.

517 The last vvill and testament of Dr. John Donne. *Printed*, 1663. 4°.* GK.

518 The last will and testament of Doctors Commons. [*London*], *printed*, 1641. 4°.* O, LG, OW, MR; CN.

518A The last will and testament of Father Petre's. *Printed*, 1688. brs. C; MH.

518B —[Anr. ed., "Peters."] [*London*, 1689.] cap. fol.* L, CT; CN.

519 The last will and testament of H—r Augustina. 1687. fol. LG (lost).

520 The last will and testament of James Hynd. *For I. H.*, 1651. 4°.* LT.

521 The last will and testament of lieut. col. John Lilburne. [*London*], *printed*, 1654. 4°.* LT.

522 Entry cancelled.

Last vvill & testament. 1648. *See* Lieutenant Generall Cromwell's.

523 The last vvill and testament of P. Rvpert. *Printed*, 1645. *October* 7. 4°.* LT, DT; CH, TU, WF.

524 The last vvill and testament of Philip Herbert. *Nod-Nol, printed*, 1650. 4°.* LT, O, CSSX, EN; CH, MH, MIU, WF, Y.

525 The last vvill and testament of Sir James Independent. [*London*], *printed*, 1647. 4°.* LT, MR; CH, CN, MH, TU, WF, Y.

526 The last vvill and testament of Sir Iohn Presbyter. [*London*], *printed*, 1647. 4°.* LT, O, CJ, DU, MR; CH, CN, MH, NU, TU, WF, Y. (var.)

527 —Second edition. *Printed*, 1647. 4°. O; CH, MIU, PT, TU.

528 —Third edition. [*London*], *printed*, 1647. 4°.* O, C, MR.

528aA —[Same title.] *For Samuel Birdet* [*i.e. Burdet*], 1661. brs. MH.

528A The last will and testament of Squire Dun. *For George Horton*, [1663.] 4°.* CH.

Last will and testament of superstition. 1642. *See* B., J.

529 The last vvill and testament of that monstrous, bloudy . . . Parliament . . . 15 of May: 1648. [*London*], *printed*, 1648. 4°.* L, O, OC, MR; CN, CSS, MH, MIU, NP, NU, Y.

530 —[Anr. ed.] [*London*, 1660.] brs. O, LL.

530A —[Anr. ed.] [*London*], *reprinted for Gabriel Townsend*, [1681]. brs. O; CH, CN, MH, WF.

531 The last will and testament of the charter of London. colop: *For John Owsley*, 1683. brs. L, O, LG, HH; CH, IU, NCD, WF.

531A The last will and testament of the Earl of Pembroke. [*London?* 1679.] cap., fol.* L, O; CH, MH, WF, Y.

532 The last will and testament of the late deceased French jackanapes. *For May-day, to be sold in Hide-Park,* 1661. 4°.* L; Y.

532A The last will and testament of the late Lord Chancellour. [*London*], *for W. Thompson,* 1689. brs. CN, Y.

Last will and testament of the late renowned Cardinal Mazarin. 1663. *See* Howell, James.

532B The last will and testament of Thomas Harrison. *For J. G.,* 1660. 4°.* MIU.

533 The last will and testament of Tom Fairfax. [*London*], *printed,* 1648. 4°.* LT; CSS, TU, Y.

534 The last words and sayings of the true-Protestant Elm-Board. colop: *For F. Shepherd,* 1682. brs. L, O, C, MC, EN; CH, IU, MH, TU, WF, Y.

534A The last words of Thomas, Lord Pride. [*London,* 1659?] cap., 4°.* O, LG, OC, BC, LSD, MR; CH, MH, MIU, TU, Y.

535 Entry cancelled.

Last years intelligencer. 1663. *See* Sixteen hundred and sixty-two.

536 The last years transactions vindicated. *For Richard Baldwin,* 1690. 4°.* T.C.II 303. L, O, C, MR, EN, DT; CH, CN, MH, NU, TU, WF, Y.

Lasting almanack. [1660.] *See* Almanacs.

537 **Latch, John.** Plusieurs tres-bons cases. *By T. R. for H. Twyford, T. Dring, and J. Place,* 1661. fol. L, O, C, MC, NPL, CD; BN, CH, KT, LC, MHL, NCL, YL, AVP.

538 ——[Anr. ed.] —, 1662, fol. L, O, LL, EN, DT; CLL, LC, NCD, NCL, V.

Late act of the convocation. Rouen, 1652. *See* Rowland, William.

539 Late and lamentable news from Ireland, wherein. *For Ioseph Huuskott* [*sic*], 1641. 4°.* LT, O, SP, DN; CH, PT.

540 ——[Anr. ed.] *Imprinted first at London, and re-imprinted by R. Y. and E. T. and are to be sold by Andro Wilson, in Edinburgh,* 641 [i.e. 1641]. 4°.* ALDIS 1008. EN, D, DT.

541 A late and trve relation from Ireland: of the vvarlike. *For Iohn Thomas,* 1641. 4°.* LT, C, DN; Y.

Late apology. 1667. *See* Lloyd, William, *bp.*

Late assembly. 1651. *See* Parker, William.

541A The late barbarous and inhumane cruelties . . . Quakers. *For Benjamin Clark,* 1682. 4°.* L; CH, MH, PHS, Y.

542 The late bloody fight in Flanders. [*London*], *for P. Brooksby,* [1688–95]. brs. L, HH; WCL.

Late censors. 1698. *See* Groenevelt, Johann.

543 The late conference held between the Master of the Temple and the author of Jovian. *By the assigns of William King and John Kid, sold by J. Humphries,* 1690. 4°.* MR.

Late conflagration consumed. [1667.] *See* Rookes, Thomas.

Late converts. 1690. *See* Brown, Thomas.

544 The late covenant asserted. [*London*], *printed,* 1643, *for Thomas Underhill.* 4°.* MADAN 1435. LT, O, CS, EC, EN, DT; CH, MH, NU, WF, Y.

Late dialogue. 1644. *See* Gillespie, George.

544A The late dreadful and most admired calamity of a parcel of land . . . Bulkley. *For Tho. Vere, and William Gilbertson,* 1657. 8°.* L.

545 The late Duke of Monmouth's lamentation. [*London*], *for P. Brooksby,* [1685]. brs. L, CM, HH; MH.

546 The late eclipse unclasped. [*London,* 1652.] 4°.* LT; CH, CSS.

547 The late famous tryal of Mr. Hickeringill. *For Fr. Smith,* 1681. fol.* L, O, C, LG, DU; CH, CN, LC, NU, MH, Y.

548 The late famous victory: obtained by Captaine Lan[g]ley. *For Thomas Rider,* 1643. 4°.* LT, O; INU.

549 The late keepers of the English liberties drawn to the life. *Printed,* 1680. 4°.* T.C.I 397. L, O, CT, LSD, MR; CH, CN, MB, NU, WF, Y.

549A The late King James's letter to his privy-counsellors. With just reflections upon it. *For Ric. Chiswell,* 1692. 4°.* T.C.II 427. L, C, LIU, MR, DT; CH, CLC, CN, MH, NU, WF, Y.

550 The late King James's manifesto answer'd. *Printed, and are to be sold by Richard Baldwin,* 1697. 4°. L, O, C, MR, EN, DT; HR, CH, IU, LC, MH, NU, TU, Y.

551 ——[Anr. ed.] *Dublin: re-printed by Andrew Crook, for William Norman, Eliphal Dobson, Patrick Campbell, and Jacob Milner,* 1697. 4°.* DIX 290. L, BC, BLH, DK, DN, DT.

552 The late King James's second manifesto . . . answered. *For Richard Baldwin,* 1697. 4°.* L, O, C, MR, AU; CH, MB, MIU, NU, TSM, WF, Y.

553 ——[Anr. ed.] *Dublin, reprinted by Andrew Crooke, for William Norman, Eliphal Dobson, Patrick Campbell, and Jacob Milner,* 1697. 4°.* DIX 291. BLH, BQ, DI, DK, DT; Y.

The late King of Spain's will. Dublin, 1700. *See* Carlos III.

554 A late letter concerning the sufferings of the Episcopal clergy in Scotland. *For Robert Clavel,* 1691. 4°.* T.C.II 350. L, O, C, DU, EN, CD; CH, CN, MH, NU, WF, Y.

Late letter from Sir Thomas Fairfax's army. 1645. *See* Rushworth, John.

Late libeller's folly. 1694. *See* Gouldney, Henry.

554A The late Lord Russels case with observations. *A. Churchill,* 1689. 4°.* DCH.

Late newes or. 1660. *See* Evelyn, John.

555 The late plot on the fleet, detected. [*London,* 1689.] cap., 4°.* L, C, OC, BC, LSD, CD; CH, CN, NN, Y.

556 ——[Anr. ed.] *Printed at London, and reprinted at Edinburgh,* 1690. 4°.* ALDIS 3050. L, O, EN, AU, ESS; CN, WF.

The late prints for a standing army. 1698. *See* Orme, Thomas.

Late proceedings and votes. Glasgow, 1689. *See* Ferguson, Robert.

557 The late proceedings of the Scottish army. *By M. B. for Robert Bostock,* 28. *July.* 1645. 4°.* LT, O, DT; CSS, MH, TU, Y.

Late proposal of union. 1679. *See* Womock, Laurence.

Late prosperous proceedings. 1643. *See* E., E.

558 The late revolution. *Printed, and are to be sold by Richard Baldwin,* 1690. 4°. T.C.II 313. L, O, LVD, OW, MR; CH, LC, MH, MU, NC, WF, Y.

559 The late storie of Mr. VVilliam Lilly. *Printed, January,* 1647/8. 4°.* LT, O, YM; MH, MIU, WF, Y.

559A The late successful proceedings of the army. *For J. M.*, 1647. 4°.* LT, O, DN; CH, MH, NN.

560 The late victorious proceedings of Sir Thomas Fairfax. *For Matthew Walbancke, 9 March*, 1645[6]. 4°.* LT, O; CH, WF.

Late victory obtayned by the Parliaments forces. 1646. *See Payne, George.*

561 The late Viscount Stafford found more guilty. colop: *For Benjamin Harris*, 1680. brs. L, O, LIU, MR; CDA, CH, IEG, MH, NU, WF, Y.

561A A late voyage to Holland. *[London], for John Humphrey*, 1691. 8°.* L.

562 The late will and testament of the Doctors Commons. *[London]*, 1641. brs. LT; MH.

Latest and truest newes. 1642. *See Loftus, Edward.*

563 The latest intelligence of Prince Ruperts proceeding. *Printed February 2.* 1642[3]. 4°.* LT, LHO, DT; Y.

564 December 22. 1642. The latest printed newes from Chichester. *For T. Underhill*, 1642. 4°.* LT; INU.

565 The latest remarkable truths, (not before printed) from Chester. *For Thomas Vnderhill, October 4*, 1642. 4°.* LT, LLL, BC, EC, LNC, CD; CH, MH, Y.

566 The latest remarkable truths from Worcester. *For T. Vnderhill*, 1642. 4°.* LT, O, EC, YM; Y.

[**Latey, Gilbert.**] Declaration from the people. [n.p.], 1660. *See Burrough, Edward.*

[–] Good council and advice. [n.p.], 1676. *See title.*

567 [–] To all you taylors and brokers who lyes [*sic*] in wickedness. *For Robert Wilson*, 1660. 4°.* L, LF, BBN; MH, PH, PSC.

568 **Latham, Simon.** Latham's faulconry. Fourth edition. *By Ric. Hodgkinsonne, for Thomas Rooks*, 1658. 8°. LT, O, CK, DCH, ESSEX, E; CH, CLC, INU, WF, Y.

569 —Latham's new and second book of faulconry. *By R. H. for Thomas Rooks*, 1658. 8°. LT, O, OR, CK; CH, CLC, INU, WF, Y.

570 —The whole work of Mr. Latham's books of faulconry. *By Sarah Griffin, for William Lee*, 1662. 8°. 3 pts. CH, LC, WF.

Latham spaw. 1670. *See Borlase, Edmund.*

571 [**Lathbury, Thomas.**] A letter or declaration, sent from the King of Scots. *For G. Orton*, 1650. 4°.* LT; CH, MH, Y.

572 **Lathom, Paul.** Christ crvcified. *By Tho. Milbourn.* 1666. 8°. L, O, LCL, LLL; CH, MH.

572A —Christian religion asserted. *For Obadiah Blagrave*, 1678. CS.

572B ——[Anr. ed.] *For Robert Harford*, 1678. PACIFIC SCH. OF RELIGION.

573 —God manifested by his works. *For Rich. Royston*, 1678. 4°.* L, O, C, OM; CH, CSU, NU, WF, Y.

574 —The power of kings. *By M. Clarke, for Joanna Brome*, 1683. 4°.* L, O, EN; CH, MH, NU, V, WF, Y.

575 —Victory over death. A sermon. *By H. C. for Edward Gellibrand*, 1676. 4°.* T.C.I 244. L, O, AN, LSD, WCA; CH, CLC, NGT, WF, Y.

576 **Latimer, Hugh.** The preaching bishop. *Printed*, 1661. 8°. LLP, OC, CT; DETROIT PUB. LIB.

Latine grammar. 1659. *See Lloyd, Richard.*

576A The Latin prophecy. *For Thomas Fox*, 1684. brs. O, LLP; CH.

Latitudinarius orthodoxus. 1697. *See Bury, Arthur.*

Latium & Lyceum. Oxoniæ, 1654. *See Wickers, Robert.*

577 Entry cancelled.

578 **La Tour d'Auvergne, Anne de.** Certain letters evidencing. 1660. *See title.*

La Tour, Filliberto Sallier de. The speech of. *Edinburgh, re-printed by the heir of Andrew Anderson*, 1690. brs. ALDIS 3049. O, LIU, EN; CN.

579 **Laud, William, abp.** A commemoration of King Charles. *By M. B.*, 1645. 4°.* LT, O, OC, YM, DT; CH, CN, WF.

580 —The coppy of a letter sent by. *[London], printed*, 1641. 4°.* L, O; IU, MIU, NU.

581 —The copie of a letter sent from . . . the 28. of June 1641, unto the Universitie of Oxford. *[Oxford], printed*, 1641. 4°.* MADAN 971. LT, O, DU, EN, DT; CH, MH, MIU, WF, Y.

582 —The copy of the petition presented to the Honourable Houses of Parliament. *For Io. Smith*, 1643. 4°.* LT, O, C; MH, WF.

583 —The daily office. Fourth edition. *For Matthew Gillyflower and William Hensman*, 1683. 12°. T.C.II 9. L, OC; IU, Y.

583A ——Fifth edition. *For T. B., M. G. and W. H., to be sold by Richard Heavisid*, 1687. 12°. O, BANGOR, EN; CH, Y.

584 ——"Fifth" edition. *Printed and are to be sold by John Walthoe, and Robert Vincent*, 1688. 12°. L, YM; NGT.

585 No entry.

586 —The history of the troubles and tryal. *For Ri. Chiswell*, 1695. fol. L, O, C, AN, D, DT; BN, CH, CN, MH, NU, TU, WF, Y, AVP.

587 Entry cancelled.

——[Anr. ed.] 1700. *See*—Second volume of the remains.

588 —The Bishop of Canterbury his last speech . . . [10 January 1644]. *[London], printed*, 1644. 4°.* LCL; TO.

589 —A letter from. *[London], printed*, 1641. 4°.* MADAN 972. O, LVF, CJ; WF, Y.

590 —A letter sent by. *[London], printed*, 1641. 4°.* MADAN 969. LT, O, LVF, DU, RU; CH, CN, MH, MIU, NU, WF, Y.

591 —A letter sent from. *Ordered to be printed, first at Oxford by Leonard Lichfield, and now re-printed at London for Edward Vere*, [1642]. 4°.* MADAN 1141. LT, DU, SP; CH, CLC, CN, INU, MH, Y.

591A —The Arch-Bishop of Canterbury his letter to the King. *[London, 1695/6.]* brs. HH; MH.

592 —Officium quotidianum: or a manval. *For Jo. Martin, and Jo. Ridley*, 1650. 12°. LT, CT, DU.

593 ——Second edition. *For Robert Crofts*, 1663. 12°. O, OC; CLC, Y.

594 —A relation of the conference between William Laud, . . . and Mr. Fisher the Jesuite. Third edition. *By J. C. for Tho. Bassett, T. Dring and J. Leigh*, 1673. fol. T.C.I 143. L, O, C, E, DT; CH, CN, MBP, NC, Y.

595 ——Fourth edition. *By Ralph Holt for Thomas Bassett, Thomas Dring, and John Leigh*, 1686. fol. T.C.II 171. L, O, C, BC, DT; CH, MH, MU, NF, NU, TU, WF, Y.

596 —The second volume of the remains of. *For Sam. Keble, Dan. Brown, Will. Hensman, Matt. Wotton, and R. Knaplock,* 1700. fol. L, O, C, NPL, EN; CH, MBP, MH, NU, TU, WF, Y, AVP.

597 —The sermon, last speech and prayers of. colop: *For J. Jones,* 1660. cap., 4°.* LT, LHO, EN; Y.

598 —Seven sermons preached upon severall occasions. *For R. Lowndes,* 1651. 12°. LT, O, C, E, DT; CH, CN, MH, NU, WF, Y.

599 —The archbishop of Canterbury's speech: or his funerall sermon. *By Peter Cole,* 1644/5. 4°.* LT, O, C, EN, DT; CH, IU, MH, NU, TU, WF, Y. (var.)

599A ——[Anr. ed.] *Printed with license,* [1645?]. 4°.* L, DU, D, EN.

600 —A summarie of devotions. *Oxford, by William Hall,* 1667. 8°. MADAN 2770. L, O, C, EN, DT; CH, IU, MH, NU, TSM, WF, Y.

600A ——[Anr. ed.] *Printed,* 1667. 12°. CT, LIU; CLC, CU, WF.

601 —The trve copie of a letter sent from. *Oxford, by Leonard Lichfield,* 1641. 4°.* MADAN 970. LT, O, CT, YM, DT; CH, MH, MIU, MU, WF, Y.

602 —A trve copy of certain passages of . . . his speech. *Oxford, by Leonard Lichfield,* 1644[5]. 4°.* MADAN 1719. L, O, MR, YM, EN; NCD, WF, Y.

602A Laudanum helmontii . . . elixir proprietatis . . . spirit of harts-horn. *[London,* 1666?] brs. MH.

603 L[auder], G[eorge]. Caledonias covenant. *[Edinburgh?],* printed, 641. 8°.* ALDIS 1007. 95. L; CH.

604 —Hecatombe Christiana; or Christian meditations. *[n.p.],* 1661. 4°. E.

604A —A horse or a new-yeares gift to . . . Sir Phillip Balfour. *At Middelbrugh, by James Fierens,* 1646. 4°.* L.

605 **Lauderdale, John Maitland,** *duke of.* Bibliotheca instructissima ex bibliothecis duorum . . . theologorum Londinensium. 1691/2. 4°.* L, ST. EDMUND HALL; CLC, MH.

606 —Bibliotheca selectissima, diversorum librorum. *[London],* 18 *Apr.* 1687. 4°.* L, O, C, LR, OP, MR, EN; CH, NG, Y, JF.

607 —Bibliotheque de feu Monseigneur le duc de. *[London],* 1690. 4°.* L, O; MH, JF.

608–9 Entries cancelled.
—Catalogus librorum. *[n.p.,* 1688.] *See* Lauderdale, Richard Maitland, *earl of.*

610 —Catalogus variorum. *[London],* 26 *Martii,* [1691]. fol. L, O, OP; MH.

610A —A dialogue between L. and D. *[London?* 1679.] brs. L.

611 —The English part of the library of. *[London],* 1690. 4°.* O; CN, MH, JF.

612 Entry cancelled.
—Remainder of prints. *[n.p.,* 1689.] *See* Lauderdale, Richard Maitland, *earl of.*

613 Entry cancelled.
—Speech of . . . [19 October]. *[n.p.],* 1669. *See* Charles II. Letter to his Parliament.

613A Entry cancelled.
——[Anr. ed.] *Edinburgh,* 1669. *See* Charles II. Letter to his Parliament in Scotland.

614 —The speech of . . . twelfth of November, 1673. *In the Savoy: by Thomas Newcomb,* 1673. fol.* L, O, C, MR, EN; CLC.

615 **[Lauderdale, Richard Maitland],** *earl of.* Catalogus librorum instructissimæ bibliothecæ. *[London,* 30 *October* 1688.] 4°. L, O, C, LV, OC; CN, MH, NG, WF, JF.

616 [–] —[Anr. ed.] *[London,* 8 *April* 1689.] 4°. O, C, OP, OW, EN; WF, JF.

617 —Remainder of prints. *[London,* 28 *October* 1689.] 4°. L, C, LV, OC, OP; NG.

Lawd's labyrinth. *Paris,* 1668. *See* Carwell, Thomas. Labyrinthvs.

617A Laugh and lie down. *[London],* for J. Shooter, [1691]. brs. CM.

Laugharne, Rowland. *See* Langhorn, Rowland.

618 **Laughton, Jo.** Princeps. *[n.p.],* 1698. brs. O.

619 **Launcelot, Bulkeley.** A prayer ordered to be used by the Earle of Ormonde, Feb. 28th. *Dublin,* 1642. DIX 76. O, DM.

620 **Launoy, Jean de.** Elogium. *Typis J. Playford, pro. R. Littlebury,* 1685. 8°. L, C, LW, OC, P, DT; WF.

621 —Joannis Launoii epistolæ omnes. *Cantabrigæ, ex officina Joan. Hayes, impensis Edvardi Hall,* 1689. fol. O, C, LIL, MR, EN, DT; BN, CH, CLC, MH, MU, WF.

Laureat. Jack Squabb's history. *[n.p.,* 1687.] *See* Gould, Robert.

622 The laurel. *For Benj. Tooke,* 1685. 4°.* T.C.II 114. L, O, C, LVD, LSD; CH, MH, MU, TU, WF, Y.

623 Entry cancelled. Date: [1710?].

623A A laurell of metaphysicke. *[London],* to be sold by Ro. Walton, [1655]. brs. O; Y.

Laurence, George. *See* Lawrence, George.

Laurence, Richard. *See* Lawrence, Richard.

623B **[Laurence, Sir Thomas.]** Verses spoken to the King. *[Oxford, by H. Hall, for R. Davis,* 1663.] 4°.* MADAN 2623. L, O, LLU; WF, Y.

623C **Laussac, D'Astor de.** The character of the true church. *For Matt. Wotton and sold by A. Baldwin,* 1700. 4°. T.C.III 169. OC, BAMB; WF.

623D ——[Anr. ed.] *For Matt. Wotton,* 1700. 4°.* LLP.

623E —Sermon prononce dans l'eglise francoise de la Savoye, le 20 Novemb. 1697. *A Londres, Ches la veuve Marret & Henry Ribotteau,* 1698. 8°.* LLP.

623F **La Vallette, M. de.** Lettre de Monsieur de la Vallette . . . sur son changement de religion. *Londres, D. du Chemin,* 1700. 12°. WF.

623G **La Valliére, Lousie Françoise,** *duchesse de.* The penitent lady. *For Dorman Newman,* 1684. 12°. T.C.II 69. L, LSC; CLC, WF, Y.

623H ——Second edition. —, 1685. 12°. OC.

624 **La Varenne, Francois Pierre de.** The French cook. *For Charls Adams,* 1653. 12°. LT; CJC, MH, PFL.

625 ——[Anr. ed.] —, 1654. 12°. O, LCP; NN, WF.

625A ——Third edition. *For Thomas Dring and John Leigh,* 1673. 8°. T.C.I 156. LWL, LLU, EN; CH, WC.

626   **La Vauguion.** A compleat body of chirurgical opera-
       tions. *For Henry Bonwick, T. Goodwin, M. Wotton,
       B. Took, and S. Manship,* 1699. 8°. T.C.III 137. L, O, C,
       NPL, GH; CLC, LC, MIU, NAM, WF.
626A   **Laverenst, Anne.** In Holbourn . . . liveth. [*London,*
       1700?] brs. L (var.).
       —To ladies, . . . cure any distemper incident to woman-
       kind. [*London,* 1700?] brs. L.
627   **Lavor, Henry.** Predestination handled. *By I. Coe,* 1646.
       8°.* LT, O, C, CE; NU.
628   [–] Replies made to the antiquaries. *For Dan. White,* 1657
       [8]. 4°. LT, O, LF; IE, PH, PSC.
629   **L[aw], J[ohn].** Calendarium lunæ perpetuum. *Glasguæ,
       excudebat Robertus Sanders,* 1699. 4°. ALDIS 3860. OC, EN,
       GU.
629A   —Theses philosophicae. *Glasguæ, excudebant Robertus
       Sanders,* 1698. brs. GU.
630   **Law, Kentigern.** Disputatio juridica, de legibus.
       Edinburgi, excudebat Jacobus Watson, 1699. 4°. ALDIS
       3861. EN.
631   **Law, Thomas.** Thomas Law his Christmas greeting.
       Printed, 1661. brs. L.
631A   —Natural experiments. *By R. D. sold by Edward Farnham,*
       1657. 12°. L, C.
631B   —Ζυγοστατης, or the false ballance. 1658. 12°. P.
631C   **Law, William.** Theses. *Edinburgi, ex typographeo Georgii
       Mosman,* 1697. brs. ALDIS 3713. GU.
       Law against bankrupts. 1693. *See* Goodinge, Thomas.
632   A law against cuckoldom. *Printed,* 1700. fol.* LLU, MR;
       MH, MIU, NN, TU, WF, Y.
632A   The law and methods of proceeding upon forgeries in
       Scotland. [*n.p.,* 1700?] brs. Y.
633   Law lies a bleeding. 1659. brs. O.
634   The law of commons and commoners. *By the assigns of
       Richard and Edward Atkins; for John Walthoe,* 1698. 8°.
       L, O, C, LL; CH, IU, MHL, NCL, PU, WF, YL.
635   The law of ejectments. *For John Deeve,* 1700. 8°. BAMB,
       FONMON, MR; LC, MHL, PU, WF.
       Law of obligations. 1693. *See* Ashe, Thomas.
       Law-power. 1656. *See* Woodward, Hezekiah.
       Law read June the 10. [1656.] *See* Prynne, William.
636   Law unknown, or, judgement unjust. [*London*], *printed,*
       1662. 4°.* L, OC; MHL, TU, WF, YL.
637   [**Lawcey, Will.**] Sir Phillip Stapleton dead. *Printed at
       London by Robert Ibbitson,* 1647. 4°.* LT, O, DT; MH.
637A   **L[awe], R[obert].** Pia fraus: or, Absalom's theft. *By
       J. C. and F. Collins,* 1684. 4°.* WCA, DT; CH.
638   **Lawes, Henry.** Ayres and dialogues. *By T. H. for John
       Playford,* 1653. fol. L, O, CK, BQ; CH, IU, LC, MH, NN, WF.
639   —Ayres, and dialogues . . . third book. *By W. Godbid for
       John Playford.* 1658. fol. L, O, CK, GU, BQ; CH, LC, MH,
       NN, WF.
640   —Choice psalmes put into musick. *By James Young for
       Humphrey Moseley and Richard Wodenothe,* 1648. 4°.
       L, O, OM; CH, INU, MH, PL, WF, Y.
641   —The second book of Ayres, and dialogues. *By T. H. for
       Jo. Playford,* 1655. fol. L, O, CK, BQ; CH, LC, MH, NN, WF.

642   —Select ayres and dialogues . . . third book. *By William
       Godbid for John Playford,* 1669. fol. T.C.I 15. L, O, CM, CT,
       GU; LC, NN, WF, Y.
643   —Select ayres and dialogues . . . second book. *By William
       Godbid for John Playford,* 1669. fol. T.C.I 15. L, O, C, CT, E,
       GU; LC, NN, WF.
644   Entry cancelled.
       —Third book of ayres. 1658. *See*—Ayres, and dialogues
       . . . third book.
645   —The treasury of musick. *By William Godbid for John
       Playford,* 1669. fol. T.C.I 15. L, O, CM, CT, GU; CLC, IU,
       LC, NN, WF.
646   A lawfull league and covenent, to bee entred into.
       [*London*], *printed,* 1648. 4°.* LT, C, DT; CLC.
       Lawfulnes and unlawfulnes. Oxford, 1643. *See* Hall,
       Joseph, *bp.*
       Lawfulnes of mixt-marriage. 1681. *See* Denn, John.
       Lavvfulnes of obeying. 1649. *See* Rous, Francis.
       Lawfulness of taking the new oaths. 1689. *See* Maurice,
       Henry.
647   The lawfulness of the late passages of the army . . . exam-
       ined. *Printed,* 1647. 4°.* LT, MR, SP, DT; CH, CN, MH, MU,
       NU, WF, Y.
       Lawfulness of the oath. 1662. *See* Nye, Philip.
       Lawfulness of tithes. 1675. *See* Jeffrey, William.
648   **Lawkerry, Nehemiah.** A motion propounded. *Printed
       at London, by Robert Ibbitson,* 1648. 4°.* LT, O, LUG, BC;
       CSS, MH, MM, TU, Y.
       Lawles tythe-robbers. 1655. *See* Culmer, Richard.
       Lawmind, John. *See* Wildman, John.
649   **Lawrence, Alexander.** An answer to a book published
       by Richard Smith. [*London*], *printed,* 1677. 4°.* L, LF;
       CH, MH, PH, PSC, WF, Y.
650   —A faithful warning. [*London*], *printed,* 1675. 4°.* L, C,
       LF; IE, MH, PH, PSC.
650A   —Something by way of rejoinder. [*London*], *printed,*
       1678. 4°.* LF; PH.
651   **Lawrence, Anthony.** Nurseries, orchards, profitable
       gardens. *For Henry Brome,* 1677. 4°.* T.C.I 257. L, O,
       LG, LUG, OC, R; CH, CLC, PL, WF, Y.
651A   **Lawrence, Benjamin.** Concerning marriage. [*London*],
       1663. 4°.* L; WESTERN RESERVE HIST. SOC.
652   **Lawrence, Edward.** Christs power over bodily dis-
       eases. *By R. VV. for Francis Tyton,* 1662. 8°. O, LCL; CLC,
       MH, NAM, NU, WF.
653   ——Second edition. *By J. C. for Francis Tyton,* 1672. 8°.
       T.C.I 106. L, LCL, LW; CH.
654   —Parents groans over their wicked children. *For Thomas
       Parkhurst and Joseph Collier,* 1681. 8°. T.C.I 449. L, LCL,
       EN, M; CU, NU, Y.
655   —Two funeral sermons. *By J. R. for T. Parkhurst,* 1690.
       12°. LW.
656   **L[awrence], G[eorge].** The debauched cavalleer. *By
       L. N. for Henry Overton,* 1642. 4°.* LT, O, DU, EN, DT;
       CH, CN, CSS, MH, WF, Y.
657   —Gospel separation separated. 1657. 12°. LCL.

658   —Laurentius Lutherizans. Or the protestation of. *For R. Harford,* 1642. 4°.* LT, O, LG, MR, E; CH, MM, NU.

659   —Peplum Olivarii, or a good prince bewailed. *By E. M. for Samuel Thomson,* 1658. 4°.* LT, O, LCL, LW; CH, CN, WF, Y.

659A **Lawrence, Henry.** The doctrine of baptisme truly stated. *By M. Simmons, for John Blague and Samuel Howes,* 1652. 8°. CD.

660   —An history of angells. *By M. S. to be sold by William Nealand,* 1649. 4°. C.

661   — —[Anr. ed.] *By Matthew Simmons, to be sold by Thomas Huntington,* 1650. 4°. ORP, MR; CLC, IU, LC, NU.

662   —Militia spiritualis. Or a treatise of angels. *By M. Simmons for John Blague, and Samuel Howes,* 1652. 4°. DC, P; CH, MH.

663   [–] Of baptisme. *[Amsterdam?],* printed, 1646. 8°. LT, C, LCL, ORP; NHC, NU, RBU, WF, Y.

664   [–] —[Anr. ed.] *By J. Macock,* 1659. 8°. NHC, NU.

665   [–] Of our communion and warre with angels. *[Amsterdam?],* printed, 1646. 4°. LT, LCL, BC; CH, CLC, IU, MH, NU, TO, Y.

666   [–] —[Anr. ed.] *[Amsterdam?], for Giles Calvert,* 1646. 4°. L, O, C, LW, GU; CH, CN, MU, NHC, WF. (var.)

667   —A pious and learned treatise of baptisme. *Printed, and are to be sold by William Nealand,* 1649. 12°. O, LCL, P; NHC, NPT.

668   —A plea for the vse of gospell ordinances. *By M. S. for Livewell Chapman,* 1652. 4°. LT, SA; NHC, NU, Y.

669   [–] Some considerations. *By M. Symmons, for Hanna Allen,* 1649. 4°. LT, O, LF, CT, DT; IU, NHC, NU.

670   [**Lawrence, John.**] Orbis imperantis tabellæ. *Apud I. Lawrence,* 1685. 8°. L, O, C; LC, MBA.

671   Entry cancelled.
      Lawrence, Sir John. Order conceived. [1665.] *See* London. Court of Aldermen.

672   [**Lawrence, Leonard.**] Epithalamium: or. *Printed,* 1650. 4°.* IU.

673   **Lawrence, Matthew.** The use and practice of faith. *By A. Maxey for Willian [sic] Weekly at Ipswich, and are to be sold by John Rothwel; and by Robert Littleberry,* 1657. 4°. LT, LCL, LLP, MC, P; CLC, IU, MH, NU, WF, Y.

674   **Lawrence, Richard.** The antichristian presbyter. *[London], printed,* 1647. 4°.* LT, O, C, MR, DT; CH, MH, MU, NU, WF, Y.

675   [–] England's great interest in the well planting of Ireland. Second edition. *Dublin, Wil. Bladen,* 1656. 4°.* DIX 98. DK, DN.

676   [–] Gospel-separation separated. *For Giles Calvert,* 1657. 8°. LT, LW; CH, NPT, NU, TO, WF.

677   —The interest of England. *By Henry Hills,* 1455 [i.e. 1655]. 4°.* LT, DT; CH, CN, MH, WF, Y.

678   — —[Anr. ed.] 1555 [i.e. 1655]. 4°. LCP.

679   — —[Anr. ed.] *Dublin, by Wil. Bladen,* 1655. 4°.* DIX 96. L, C, EN, DN.

680   Entry cancelled. *See following three entries.*

680A —The interest of Ireland. *Dublin, by Jos. Ray, for Jos. Howes, and are to be sold by Awnsham Churchill, London,* 1682. 8°. T.C.I 512. L, C, OC, MC, BQ, DN; CH, CN, MH, MU, PL, WF, Y.

680B — —[Anr. ed.] *Dublin, by Jos. Ray, for Jo. North, Sam. Helsham, Jos. Hawes, W. Winter, El. Dobson and Will. Norman,* 1682. 8°. IU, PU.

681   — —Part II. *Dublin, by Jos. Ray for Jo. North, Sam. Helsham, J. Howes, W. Winter, and El. Dobson,* 1682. 8°. DIX 192; T.C.I 512. L, C, OQ, EN, DT; BN, CH, CN, LC, MH, NC, Y.

682   —The wolf stript. *Printed,* 1647. 4°.* LT, CT, BR, SC, DT; CH, LC, NU.

683   **L[awrence], T[homas], 1645–1714.** A brief answer to three books. *[London, 1674–81?]* cap., 4°.* L, LF, BBN; CH, PH, PSC, Y.

684   [–] Concerning marriage. A letter. *[London], printed,* 1663. 4°.* LF, CT, BBN; CLC, PH, PSC, RPJ.

685   Entry cancelled.
      [–] Discourse of subterraneal treasure. 1668. *See* Lawrence, Thomas, A.M.

685A —Hypocrisie detected. *By Andrew Sowle,* 1681. 8°.* LF.

686–7 Entries cancelled.
      —Mercurius centralis. 1664. *See* Lawrence, Thomas, A.M.
      [–] Sad memorials. 1670. *See* Lambert, Thomas.

687A [–] Some pity on the poor. *[London? 1675?]* cap., 4°.* LUG; CSS, WF, Y.

688   —The streight gate. *[London, 1673?]* 4°.* L, LF, BBN; PSC.

689   Entry cancelled.
      —Verses spoken to the King. [n.p., 1663]. *See* Laurence, Sir Thomas.

689A —William Rogers's Christian Quaker manifested. *For Benjamin Clark,* 1681. 8°.* LF; PH.

689B **L[awrence], T[homas], A.M.** A discourse of subterraneal treasure. *For J. Collins,* 1668. 8°. O, C, NPL; WF.

689C —Mercurius centralis. *By J. G. for R. Royston,* 1664. 12°. L, O, OB, NPL, GK; HC.

689D — —[Anr. ed.] *By J.G. for J. Collins,* 1664. C, LWL (lacks t.p.), CM, NPL, GK; CH, IU, MH, PL, WF, Y.

690   **Lawrence, William.** Marriage by the morall law of God. *[London],* 1680. 4°. L, O, C, DU, E; CH, MBP, MIU, WF, Y.

691   [–] The right of primogeniture. *For the author,* 1681. 4°. L, O, DU, E, ES; BN, CH, IU, MBP, NHL, WF, Y.

692   —To the Honourable, the referrees of his Highnesse . . . the petition of. *[London, 1654.]* brs. LT; MH.

692A [–] Two great questions determined. *For Richard Janeway,* 1681. fol.* T.C.I 441. L, O, C, BAMB, LLU; CH, CN, MIU, NU, WF, Y.

693   [–] The two great questions, whereon. *For the author,* 1681. 4°.* L, O, LLP, E, SA; BN, CH, MBP, MM, PU, WF, Y.

693A [–] —[Anr. ed.] *For A.C.,* 1681. 4°.* L; CLC, MH, WF.

694   **L[awrie], R[obert].** God save the King. *Edinburgh, C. Higgins,* 1660. 4°.* ALDIS 1646. EN, GU; IU.

694AA The lawes against witches, and coniuration. *For R. W.,* 1645. 4°.* O.

694BA Laws & articles of war, for . . . forces within . . . Scotland. *Edinburgh, by E. Tyler,* 1667. 4°. EN.

Laws and customs. 1687. *See* Houghton, Thomas.

Lawes and orders of warre. Dublin, 1641. *See* Ormonde, James Butler, *duke*.

694CA Lavves and ordinances of the sea. *For Matthew Walbancke.* 1644. brs. LPR.

694A Lawes and ordinances of warre. *By Robert Barker, and by the assignes of John Bill,* 1641. 4°.* O, CT; CH, WF.

695 —[Anr. ed.] *For John Wright.* [1642]. 4°.* L, O, LLU; CDA.

—[Anr. ed.] 1642. *See* Essex, Robert Devereux, *earl.*

695A —[Anr. ed.] *For Laurence Chapman,* 1642. 4°.* LT, LG, CT, DT; CH, MU, WF.

696 Entry cancelled.

—[Anr. ed.] Waterford, 1643. *See* Ormonde, James Butler, *duke.*

—[Anr. ed.] 1646. *See* Essex, Robert Devereux, *earl.*

696A —[Anr. ed.] *Dublin, by William Bladen,* 1647. 4°.* CH.

696B —[Anr. ed.] *Dublin, reprinted,* 1651. 4°.* INU.

696C —[Anr. ed.] *Dublin, by William Bladen,* 1652. 4°.* DIX 320. CD.

696D —[Anr. ed.] *Dublin, by John Crook, sold by Samuel Dancer,* 1662. 4°.* LPR, OC.

696E —[Anr. ed.] *Dublin, by Benjamin Tooke; and are to be sold by Joseph Wilde,* 1672. 4°.* DIX 147. DN, EN.

696F —[Anr. ed.] *Dublin, by Benjamin Took; to be sold by Joseph Wilde,* 1677. 4°.* DIX 159. DI.

Laws and ordinances touching. Edinburgh, 1691. *See* Scotland. Privy Council.

697 The lawes and statutes of Geneva. *By Tho. Fawcet, for Mathew Wallbanck, and Lawrence Chapman,* 1643. 4°. LT, LIU, E, EN, DT; CH, CN, MH, TU, WF, Y.

698 The lavves and statutes of God, concerning the punishment . . . murderers. *By Matthew Simmons for Benjamin Allen,* 1646. 4°.* LT, O, DT; CH, MBP, MH.

Law's discovery. 1653. *See* F., J.

698A The laws in Venice for prohibition of foreign cloth. [*n.p.,* 1661?] brs. L.

699 Entry cancelled.

Lawes of God. 1646. *See* Lavves and statutes.

700 The laws of honor; or, an account of the suppression of duels in France. *For Thomas Flesher,* 1685. 12°. T.C.II 159. L, O, C, LLP, LW; CH, CLC, MIU, OCI, WF, Y.

Laws of paradise. 1695. *See* Lead, Jane.

Lawes of Virginia. 1662. *See* Moryson, Francis.

701 Laws of vvar and ordinances of the sea. *By John Field,* 1652. 4°.* LT, CCA; CN, MHL, WF.

701AA —[Anr. ed., "Lavvs of war."] *By Sarah Griffin,* 1659. 4°.* BC.

701A The lawes, orders, and statutes . . . for the citizens of London. *For G. Horton,* 1662. 4°.* CH, MU, WF.

701B Laws, ordinances, and decrees made . . . [Bedford Level]. [*London,* 1666.] cap., 4°.* L.

Lawes subversion. [*n.p.*], 1648. *See* Wildman, *Sir* John.

702 **Lawson, Deodat.** A brief and true narrative. *Boston, for Benjamin Harris,* 1692. 12°.* EVANS 613. MHS, MIU.

703 —Christ's fidelity the only shield. *Boston, by B. Harris, & sold by Nicholas Buttolph,* 1693. 8°. EVANS 643. CH, MB, MHS, MWA, V.

704 —The duty & property of a religious householder. *Boston, by Bartholomew Green, and sold by Samuel Phillips,* 1693. 8°. EVANS 644. LC, MB, MHS, MWA, Y.

[–] Further account of the tryals. 1693. *See title.*

705 **Lawson, George.** Catalogus liborum. [*London*], 31 *May* 1681. 4°. L, O, OP, CS; NG, NPT.

706 —An examination of the political part of Mr. Hobbs his Leviathan. *By R. White, for Francis Tyton,* 1657. 8°. LT, O, C, GU, BQ; CLC, IU, MH, NC, WF, Y.

707 —An exposition of the Epistle to the Hebrewes. *By J. S. for George Sawbridge,* 1662. fol. L, O, C, P, E; CLC, IEG, MH, WF, Y.

707A —Magna charta ecclesiæ universalis: the grand charter. *By G. Miller for Joseph Leigh,* 1665. 8°. SC; CLC.

708 ——Second edition. *By T. M. for Jeremiah Lawson; to be sold by Tho. Newborough,* 1686. 8°. T.C.II 172. L, O, C, LW, SP.

709 ——Third edition. *For Thomas Parkhurst,* 1687. 12°. T.C.II 212. L, C, LW; MWA, NU.

710 —Politica sacra & civilis: . . . the first part. *For John Starkey,* 1660. 4°. LT, O, C, OC, BQ; BN, LC, NU.

711 ——Second edition. *For J. S. to be sold by T. Goodwin,* 1689. 8°. T.C.II 256. L, OC, CS, DU, E, DT; BN, CH, IU, NU, TO, WF, Y.

712 —Theo-politica: or, a body of divinity. *By J. Streater, for Francis Tyton,* 1659. fol. L, O, C, SP, E; IEG, MH, WES, WF.

713 **Lawson, Jeremy.** Lawson of oathes and witnesses. colop: [*London*], *for Jeremy Lawson,* 1681. brs. L, O; WF, AVP.

714 **Lawson, John, M.D.** Upon the blessed retvrn of . . . Charles the Second. *By Thomas Ratcliffe,* 1660. brs. LT; MH.

715 **Lawson, John, *schoolmaster.*** For the Sabbath. *By J. L. for Christopher Meredith,* 1644. 12°.* O; CH, CLC.

716 —Gleanings and expositions of some. *By T. R. and E. M. for Nath. Webb and Will. Grantham,* 1646. 4°. LT, O, C, LCL, OC, DU; CLC, MB, NU, TU, WF.

717 [–] Truth cleared. [*London*], *printed,* 1654. 4°.* LF; PSC.

718 **Lawson, *Sir* John, *vice-admiral.*** A declaration of . . . [13 December]. [*London,* 1659.] brs. L, O, LG, CCA, DN; CH, MH, Y.

719 ——[Anr. ed.] [*London*], 1659. 4°.* L, O, MR.

719A ——[Anr. ed.] *Edinburgh, C. Higgins,* 1660. brs. EN.

719B [–] A great and bloudy fight at sea. *For J. Fielding,* 1652. 4°.* LT.

720 —Two letters from Vice-Admiral. *By John Streater,* 1659. brs. L, O, LG, LS; CDA, MH, Y.

721 ——[Anr. ed.] [*London,* 1659.] brs. LT, O, LG.

721A **Lawson, Thomas.** Eine antwort auf ein buch . . . An answer to a book. [*London*], 1668. 8°. PH.

722 [–] An appeal to the Parliament. colop: *For Robert Wilson,* 1660. cap., 4°.* L, O, LF, LL, BBN; CH, MH, PSC, WF, Y.

723 —Βαπτισμαλογια or a treatise. [*London*], *printed* 1677/8. 4°. L, O, LF, CS, BBN; BN, CH, IE, MH, PH, Y.

724 —Dagon's fall before the Ark. [*London*], *printed,* 1679. 8°. L, O, LF, BBN; LC, MIU, PH, PSC, WF.

725   —The lip of truth opened. *For Giles Calvert, 1656. 4°.*
      LT, LF, BBN, MR; PH, PSC, Y.

726   —A mite into the treasury. *By Andrew Sowle, 1680. 4°.*
      L, O, LF, MR, E; CLC, MB, MH, PSC, PU, WF, Y.

726A — —[Anr. ed.] *By Andrew Sowle, and are sold at his shop,*
      1680. 4°. BR; IE, MH, PH.

727   —A serious remembrancer to live well. *Printed, 1684. 8°.**
      L, LF; NU, PH, WF, Y.

728   —A treatise relating to the call, work & vvages of the
      ministers. *For Benjamin Clark, 1680. 4°.* L, O, BBN, MR,
      E; BN, CLC, IU, MB, MH, PH, Y.

729   —An untaught teacher witnessed against. *For Giles*
      Calvert, 1655. 4°.* LT, LF, MR; CH.

730   **Lawson, William.** A new orchard. Second edition. *By*
      W. Wilson, for John Harison, 1648. 4°. L, O, LWL, CK, EN;
      CLM, LC, MH, MU, PL, Y.

731   — —"Second "edition. *By W. Wilson, for E. Brewster,*
      and George Sawbridge, 1653. 4°. L, LWL; IU, MB, MH, PT,
      WF, Y.

732   — —"Second" edition. —, *1656. 4°.* L, R; BN, CLC, MH,
      NC, NN, PT, Y.

733   — —Third edition. *By William Wilson, for George*
      Sawbridge, 1660. 4°. L, RU, E; CH, CLC, LC, MH, WF, Y.

734   — —"Third" edition. —, *1665. 4°.* L, O.

735   — —Fifth edition. *For George Sawbridge, 1668. 4°.* L, O,
      LWL; MH, MHS, Y.

736   — —Sixth edition. —, *1676. 4°.* L, LAS, LWL, OH, EN; CLC,
      CN, MH, PL, WDA, Y.

737   — —"Sixth" edition. *For Hannah Sawbridge, 1683. 4°.*
      L, O, NOT, R; CH, IU, MHO, NC, PBL, WDA, Y.

738   Entry cancelled. Ghost.

739   **[Lawton, Charlwood.]** A French conquest neither de-
      sirable nor practicable. *By His Majesty's servants, 1693.*
      4°.* L, O, C, MR, AU; CH, CN, NU, TU, WF, Y.

739A [–] Honesty is the best policy. *[London, 1689.] fol.** MH, Y.

739B [–] The Jacobite principles vindicated. *[London, 1693.] 4°.**
      O, LLP, OC, CS, MR, EN; CN, TU, WF, Y.

739C [–] —[Anr. ed.] *Reprinted, 1693. 4°.** O, LVF, CT, MR, EN;
      NGT, WF, Y.

739D [–] A short state of our condition. *[London, 1693.] cap.,*
      4°.* L, O, LUG, CT, MR; CH, LC, MIU, NP, TU, Y.

739E [–] The vindication of the dead. *[London, 1691.] cap., 4°.**
      O, LL, CS, MR, EN; CN, WF, Y.

      Lavvyer of Lincolnes-Inne. [n.p.], 1647. *See* Nedham,
      Marchamont.

      Lawyer outlaw'd. [n.p.], 1683. *See* L'Estrange, *Sir* Roger.

      Lawyer's bane. 1647. *See* Nicholson, Benjamin.

739F The lawyers clarke trappand. *For John Johnson, 1663. 4°.**
      O; MH, NC.

740   The lawyers demurrer. colop: *For Richard Janeway,*
      1681. brs. L, O, C, MC, DT; CH, CN, MH, MU, TU, Y, AVP.

740A The lawyers demurrer argued. *For A. B., [1681]. brs.* L;
      CH, MH, NCD.

740B The lawyers disbanded. *For J. Perry, [1680?]. 4°.** CLC, MU.

741   The lawyer's duel. *[London, 1655?] fol.** L.

742   The lawyers last farewell. *For Robert Eles, 1652. 4°.** O, BC.

743   The lawyer's plea, in the behalf. *[London, 1665?] brs.* L.

      Lawyerus bootatus. 1691. *See* Ames, Richard.

744   **L[axton], T[homas].** Grief allayed, death sweetned. *By*
      S. Roycroft, for Robert Clavell, 1682. 4°.* T.C.I 482. L,
      LSD, MR; CH, IU, V, WF.

      Lay by your pleading. 1685. *See* Richards, James.

      Lay-Christians obligation. 1687. *See* Stratford, Nicholas.

745   The lay-divine: or. colop: *For W. Ley, 1647. cap., 4°.**
      LT, OC; CH, CN, Y.

746   **[Layer, John.]** The office and dvtie of constables.
      Cambridge, by Roger Daniel, and are to be sold by Francis
      Eaglesfield [London], 1641. 8°. O, DC; IU, MHL, PUL.

      Laying on of hands. 1698. *See* Keach, Benjamin.

747   The lay-man's ansvver to the lay-mans opinion. *Printed,*
      1687. 4°.* L, O, C, EN, DT; CH, MH, NU, TU, WF, Y.

      Lay-mans opinion. [n.p.], 1687. *See* Darrell, William.

748   The lay-man's religion. *By Eliz. Holt for Walter Kettilby,*
      1690. 4°. T.C.II 330. L, O, CK, CS, GK; CH, IEG, MH, NP,
      NU, WF. (var.)

749   — —Second edition. —, *1690. 4°.* L, OC, CT, GK; CH, MB,
      MH, Y.

      Laymans manual. [n.p.], 1698. *See* Tootell, Christopher.

750   Lay-preaching vnmasked. *For W. L., 1644. 4°.** LT, SP;
      CH, CU, MH, NU.

751   **[Laythes, Thomas.]** The exercise of the spirit. *[London],*
      printed, 1686. 4°.* LF, BBN, MR; CH, PH, PSC.

752   [–] The inward and spiritual Christian. *Printed, 1684.*
      4°.* LF, BBN, MR; MH, MM, PSC.

752A [–] A sober warning to people. *Printed and sold by T.*
      Sowle, 1696. fol.* LF.

753   [–] Some questions and answers. *[London, 1691.] brs.* LF,
      BBN; PL.

753A — —[Anr. ed.] *For Thomas Northcott, [1691]. brs.* MR.

754   [–] Something concerning my convincement. *[London,*
      1686.] cap., 4°.* LF, MR; CH, MH, PH, PSC, WF, Y.

755   [–] Something concerning the two births. *[London, 1686.]*
      4°.* LF; Y.

755A **[Layton, Henry.]** An argument concerning the human
      souls seperate subsistance. *[London? 1699.] cap., 4°.**
      L; MH.

755B [–] Observations concerning money and coin. *For Peter*
      Buck, 1697. 4°. L, LUG, BAMB, BP, DT; IU, MH, NC, WF, Y.

756   [–] Observations upon a sermon intituled, A confutation
      of atheism. *[London, 1695?] cap., 4°.** L, O, ORP, CQ,
      BAMB; LC, MH, MHL, PU, TU. (var.)

757   [–] Observations upon a short treatise, written by Mr.
      Timothy Manlove. *[London, 1698?] cap., 4°.* L, O, ORP,
      EC; LC, MH, PU.

758   [–] Observations upon Mr. Wadsworth's book. *[London,*
      1690?] cap., 4°. L, O, ORP, EC; LC, MH, PU.

759   [–] A search after souls. *[London? 1700.] cap., 4°.* L, O, ORP,
      EC; LC, PU.

760   **Layton, John.** A sermon preached . . . November 22,
      1683. For Sam Carr, 1684. 4°. CT.

761   Lazarillo, or the excellent history. *For William Leake,*
      1653. 8°. L, DU, A; CH, CLC, IU, MH, WF, Y.

761A —[Anr. ed.] *By R. Hodgkinsonne*, 1655. 8°. O, CASTLE ASHBY; IU, MU, NP, Y.

762 —[Anr. ed.] *By B. G. for William Leake*, 1669. 8°. T.C.I 32. L, DU; CN, TO.

763 —[Anr. ed.] *For Eliz. Hodgkinson*, 1677. 8°. T.C.I 316. L, O, AU; CH, CN, FU, NN, WF, Y.

763A Lazarus and his sisters discoursing. [1655.] 4°.* L; MH.
Lazarus redivivus. 1671. *See* Blake, Nicholas.
Lazarus's sores licked. 1650. *See* Hall, Edmund.

764 **Lea, Francis.** Judgment brought forth unto victory. [*London*], *printed*, 1671. 8°. L, LF; PSC.

765 —A looking-glass for the Episcopal people. [*London*], *printed*, 1674. 4°.* L, C, LF, BBN, BP; MM, NU, PH, WF.

766 [–] Some breathings of the Father's love. [*London*, 1673.] cap., 4°.* L, LF, BBN; PH, PL, PSC, Y.

767 **Lea, Philip.** Hydrographia universalia, or. [*London*, 1700.*] 16°. LC.
—London almanack. [*n.p.*, 1680.] *See* Almanacs.

767A **Leach, Edmund.** Deceptio intelectus & visus. Or the lawyers vviles unmasked. [*London?* 1652.] 4°.* WF.

768 —The down-fall of the vnjust lawyers. *By E. Cotes*, 1652[3]. 4°.* LT.

769 —A short supply or amendment to the propositions. *By John Macock, and are to be sold by Lodowick Lloyd.* 1651. 4°.* LT; MB, Y.

770 **Leach, William.** An abatement of most of the motions. *By E. Cotes*, 1652. 4°.* L, MR; WF.

771 —Bills proposed for acts. *By F. L. to be sold by G. B.*, 1651. 4°. LT, LW, CS, DT; CSS, LC, MB, MHL, MM.

772 —The bribe-takers of jury-men. *By E. Cotes*, 1652. 4°.* LT, MR; CH, CLC, CSS.

773 —First, a bitt and a knock for vnder-sheriffs. *By E. Cotes*, 1652. 4°.* LT, CS.

774 —First a safe guard. *By E. Coates*, 1652. 4°.* LL; CSS, YL.

775 —Funerall of symonie. 1653. LCL.

775A [–] A new Parliament. *Printed*, 1651. 4°.* L, CCA, BC; MH, MB, MIU.

776 [–] A preservative against the major part. [*London*, 1650?] 4°.* L.

777 [–] Proposalls for an act for speedy setting at large all prisoners. *By F. Leach*, 1649. 4°.* LT, LUG; CH, INU, MB, MH.

778 —Proposals for an act for the more speedy satisfaction of creditors. *By John Macock, for the author*, 1650. 4°.* LT, LUG, DU, DT; CSS, MB, MH, Y.

779 —Proposalls for an act for prevention. *By F. Leach, to be sold by Lawrence Blaicklock*, [1650]. 4°.* LT, LW, DT; CSS, MB, MH.

780 —Propositions I. For recording. *By W: H: to be sold by G: B:*, 1651. 4°.* LT, LG, CT, EN; CH, CLC, NCL.

781 [–?] Reasons offered in order to the passing. [*n.p.*, 1661.] 4°. O.

782 [**Lead, Jane.**] The ascent to the mount of vision. *Printed*, 1699. 4°.* L, LLP; WF.

783 —The Enochian walks with God. [*London*], *printed, and sold by D. Edwards*, 1694. 4°.* L, LW; CLC, NC, Y.

783AA —A fountain of gardens. *Printed and sold by J. Bradford*, 1696. 8°. L.

783BA ——[Anr. ed.] [*London*], 1697. 8°. CLC.

783A ——[Anr. ed.] *Printed and are to be sold by the book-sellers*, 1697. 8°. LLP, LW, EN; CLC, WF, Y.

783B ——Vol. II. *Printed, and sold by the booksellers*, 1697. 8°. L, LW, OH; CLC.

784 ——vol. III, part I. [*London*], *printed*, 1700. 8°. T.C.III 21. L, LW.

785 —The heavenly cloud. *For the author*, 1681. 4°.* L, LW; CH, FU, MH, NU, WF, Y.

786 [–] The laws of paradise. *Printed and sold by T. Sowle*, 1695. 8°. L, LW; CLC, LC, PSC.

787 —A message to the Philadelphian Society. *Printed and sold by J. Bradford*, 1696. 8°. L, LLP; CLC, LC, NC.

788 —A messenger of an universal peace. *Printed*, 1698. 12°. L; LC, WF.

789 [–] The revelation of revelations. *Printed and sold by A. Sowle. Also by J. Lead*, 1683. 4°. L, O, LLL, LW, BC; CH, CLC, IU, MH, NU, WF, Y.

789A [–] A revelation of the everlasting gospel-message. *London, printed*, 1697. 8°. L.

790 —The signs of the times. *Printed*, 1699. 4°.* L, LLP; WF.

791 —The tree of faith. *Printed and sold by J. Bradford*, 1696. 8°. L; CLC.

791A —The wars of David. *By J. Bradford*, 1700. 4°. WF.

792 —The wonders of God's creation manifested. *Printed, and sold by T. Sowle*, [1695?]. 8°. L, LW; CLC, CN, LC, WF.

792A **Leadbetter, Arthur.** Arithmetical rules. *By Edw. Jones, for Thomas Salusbury*, 1691. 12°. T.C.II 368. L, O.

793 **Leader, Thomas.** The wounded-heart. *Printed*, 1665. 4°.* L, O, BBN, MR, EN; CH, MH, RPJ, WF, Y.

794 [**Leanerd, John.**] The counterfeits. *For Jacob Tonson*, 1679. 4°. T.C.I 331. L, O, OW, LLU, EN; CH, CN, LC, MH, TU, WF, Y.

795 —The country innocence. *For Charles Harper*, 1677. 4°. T.C.I 273. L, O, LF, OW, EN; CH, CN, LC, MH, WF, Y.

796 Entry cancelled. Ghost.

796A [–] The jealous husbands. *For T. Norman*, 1680. 4°. CH, CN.

797 [–] The rambling justice. *By E. F. for Thomas Orrell and James Vade*, 1678. 4°. T.C.I 320. L, O, OW; CH, LC, MH, MU, WCL, WF, Y.

798 ——[Anr. ed.] —, 1678. 4°. L, O; CH, CLC, CN, MH, WF.

798A ——Second edition. *By Tho. Bennet*, 1694. 4°. WF.

798B Leaping of the lords. [*n.p.*, 1700?] brs. L.
Learne of a Turke. 1660. *See* B., M.
Learn to lye warm. 1672. *See* B., A.
Learned and exceeding well-compiled vindication. [*n.p.*], 1646. *See* Crell, Johann.
Learned and necessary argument. 1641. *See* Yelverton, Sir Henry.

799 A learned and witty conference, lately betwixt a Protestant and a Papist. *For Iohn Thomas*, 1641. 4°.* LT, O; CLC, MH, MM, NU, WF.
Learned discourse. 1685. *See* Sheridan, Thomas.
Learners help. 1658. *See* Ross, Alexander.

800 Leather-more: or advice concerning gaming. Second edition. 1668. 4°.* O, LNC; CH.

801 **Le Blanc, Vincent.** The world surveyed. *For John Starkey,* 1660. fol. L, O, C, LL, DM; CH, CN, LC, MBP, MH, RPJ, WF, Y.

801A [–] —[Anr. ed.] *For Francis Smith,* 1672. PHS.

802 **Le Blanc de Beaulieu, Ludovicus.** Theses theologicæ. *Prostant venales apud Mosem Pitt,* 1675. fol. T.C.I 213. L, O, C, EN, DT; CH, CLC, MH, NP, TO.

803 ——Third edition. —, 1683. fol. T.C.II 8. L, O, C, ENC, DT; CLC, MBA, NP, NU, PL, WF.

803A **LeBoe, Franz.** A new idea of the practice of physiq. *For B. Aylmer,* 1675. 8°. T.C.I 187. LW, E, GK; CLC, NAM, PCP, WSG, WU.

803B —Of children's diseases. *For George Downs,* 1682. 12°. T.C.I 460. L, OC, P; WSG.

804 **Le Bossu, Renè.** Monsieur Bossu's treatise of the epick poem. *For Tho. Bennet,* 1695. 8°. L, O, C, E, DT; CH, CN, LC, NP, TU, WF, Y.

805 **Le Brun, Bonaventure.** A true and exact copy of the several articles . . . imposed upon the French Prottestants. *Dublin, for John Bentley,* 1685. fol.* DIX 215. DT.

806 **Le Camus, Etienne, bp.** A pastoral letter. *By Nath. Thompson,* 1687. 4°.* L, O, C, OME, DT; CLC, MB, NU, PL, TU, WF, Y.

807 **Lecester, John.** Englands miraculous preservation. *For John Hancock,* 1646[7]. brs. LT; WCL.

808 The leacherous Anabaptist. *For Benjamin Harris,* 1681. brs. L, O, LG, HH; CH, MH, TU.

809 [**Lechford, Thomas.**] New-Englands advice to Old-England. [London], *printed,* 1644. 4°. LT, LNC; CH, MBJ, NN, RPJ.

810 —Plain dealing: or, nevves from New-England. *By W. E. and I. G. for Nath: Butter,* 1642. 4°. LT, C, CE, LNC; BN, CH, CN, LC, MH, NN, RPJ, Y.

Lechmere, Edmund. *See* Stratford, Edmund.

810A **Le Clerc, Daniel.** The compleat surgeon. *For M. Gillyflower, T. Goodwin; M. Wotton, J. Walthoe, and R. Parker,* 1696. 12°. T.C.III 13. L, LCS; NAM, WF.

811 —The history of physick. *For D. Brown, A. Roper, T. Leigh and D. Midwinter,* 1699. 8°. T.C.III 138. L, O, C, GU, DT; CH, CNM, LC, MB, NAM, HC.

812 **Le Clerc, Jean.** Joannis Clerici ars critica. *Apud Rob. Clavel, Timoth. Childe, & Andream Bell,* 1698. 8°. T.C.III 56. L, O, C, EN, DT; CH, MBP, MH, NC, WF, Y.

812A ——[Anr. ed.] *Typis excusum Roberto Clavel & prostant venales per Josephum Ray, Dublinia,* [1696]. 8°. CPE, DT.

813 Entry cancelled. Serial.

814 —A compendium of universal history. *For M. Gilliflower, J. Tonson, W. Freeman, J. Walthoe, and R. Parker,* 1699. 8°. T.C.III 171. L, AN, SHR; CLC, CN, CU, WF, Y.

815 [–] Five letters concerning the inspiration of the Holy Scriptures. [London], *printed,* 1690. 8°. L, O, C, ENC, DT; CH, CSU, IU, MH, NU, WF, Y.

816 [–] An historical vindication of The naked gospel. [London], *printed,* 1690. 4°. L, O, C, BAMB, DT; CH, CN, NU, TU, WF, Y.

817 [–] —[Anr. ed.] *For E. Reyner,* 1691. 4°. L, SHR; MM, TU, WF.

818 [–] The life and the famous cardinal-Duke De Richlieu . . . vol. I. *For M. Gillyflower; W. Freeman; J. Walthoe; and R. Parker,* 1695. 8°. T.C.II 557. L, O, LL, BAMB, E; CH, CLC, IU, MBC, MH, WF, Y.

819 [–] —Vol. II. *For Matth. Gillyflower, Will. Freeman, J. Walthoe, and R. Parker,* 1695. 8°. T.C.II 557. L, O, LL, BAMB, E; CH, CLC, IU, MIU, WF, Y.

820 —The lives of Clemens Alexandrinus. *For Richard Baldwin,* 1696. 8°. L, O, C, DU, DT; CH, OCI, PL, WF, Y.

821 —Logica: sive, ars ratiocinandi. *Impensis Awnsham & Johan. Churchill.* 1692. 12°. T.C.II 425. L, O, C, BAMB, EN; CH, CU, MH, NC, WG, Y.

822 —Memoirs of Emeric Count Teckely. *For Tim. Goodwin,* 1693. 12°. T.C.II 439. L, O, C, LLU, SP; CH, IU, LC, MH, PL, Y.

—Ontologica. 1692. *See* —Logica.

823 —Parrhasiana: or, thoughts upon several subjects. *For A. and J. Churchil,* 1700. 8°. T.C.III 174. L, O, C, EN, DT; CH, CU, MH, PL, TU, Y.

823A —Joan. Clerici Physica. *Impensis A. Swalle & T. Childe,* 1696. 12°. T.C.II 570. L, BAMB, NPL, SA, BQ; CH, LC, MU, PL, WF, Y.

824 ——[Anr. ed.] *Cantabrigiæ, typis academicis, sumtibus Timothei Child, & Roberti Knaplock, Londini,* 1700. 12°. T.C.III 216. L, C, CT, GU; CH, CU, NP, TO, WU.

825 —Reflections upon what the world commonly call good-luck. *For Matth. Gilliflower, Tim. Goodwin, Matth. Wotton, and B. Tooke,* 1699. 12°. T.C.III 126. L, O, C, BAMB, EN; CH, IU, LC, MH, NC, TU, Y.

826 —A supplement to Dr. Hammond's paraphrase. *For Sam. Buckley,* 1699. 4°. T.C.III 119. L, O, C, AN, EN, DT; CH, NU, TU, WF, Y.

827 —A treatise of the causes of incredulity. *For Awnsham and John Churchill,* 1697. 8°. T.C.III 1. L, O, C, E, DT; CDA, CH, CLC, MH, NU.

827A ——[Anr. ed.] —, *sold by Edward Castle,* 1697. 8°. WF.

828 —Twelve dissertations. *Printed and are to be sold by R. Baldwin,* 1696. 8°. L, O, C, CT, E; CH, MH, MU, NU, WF.

829 [**Le Clerc, Sebastien.**] Magnum in parvo; or, the practice of geometry. *For Robert Prick,* 1671. 12°. O; MH, YBA.

830 [–] —[Anr. ed.] —, 1672. 8°. T.C.I 173. L, O, C, AN; CH, MH, NC, NRU, WF, Y.

831 **Le Comte, Louis Daniel.** Memoirs and observations topographical, . . . China. *For Benj. Tooke, and Sam. Buckley,* 1697. 8°. T.C.III 13. L, O, C, LW, DT; CH, IU, LC, MH, PL, TU, Y.

831A ——Second edition. *For Benjamin Tooke,* 1698. 8°. C, CD; CLC, MU, WF, Y.

832 ——"Second" edition. *For Benj. Tooke, to be sold by Geo. Huddleston,* 1698. 8°. T.C.III 46. L, C, OH, BC, GU, DT; CH, IU, MB, NC, NP, TU.

833 ——Third edition. *For Benjamin Tooke*, 1699. 8°.
T.C.III 113. L, C, CT, E, DT; BN, CH, MH, MIU, NC, WF.

834 A lecture for all sects. *For F. Grove*, [1680?]. brs. O.

834A A lecture held forth at a conventicle. colop: [*London*], *Printed and sold by N. T.* [1683]. brs. L, O, DU; CH, CN, Y.

834B [**Ledeatt, Simon.**] Oratio habita in scholâ Christi orphanotrophii. *Typis Gulielmi Godbid*, 1675. 8°. LG, DM; NAM.

835 **Lederer, John.** The discoveries of. *By J. C. for Samuel Heyrick*, 1672. 4°.* T.C.I 89. L, O, LCP, CM, E; CH, CN, LC, MH, V, Y.

836 **Ledgingham, Robert.** The humble recital of. [*London*, 1699?] brs. LG (lost).

837 —To the honourable the Commons . . . reasons for using the new-invented chainpumps. [*London*, 1698?] brs. LG.

837A —To the honourable the Commons . . . the humble representation of. [*London?* 1698.] brs. L.

837B —The uses and conveniences of Mr. Ledgingham's new-invented chain pumps. [*London?* 1700.] brs. L.

837C **LeDuke, John.** Arithmetical questions. *Da. Maxwell, to be sold by Sa. Gellibrand; and by William Hall, in Colchester*, 1663. Y.

837D —Tables for the ready casting up. *By D. Maxwel; sold by Sa. Gellibrand; and William Hall*, 1664. 8°. L.

838 **Lee, Sir Charles.** Notes of the evidence. colop: *For S. Carr*, 1681. brs. L, O, C, HH, EN; CH, CN, MBA, WF, Y.

839 [**Lee, E.**] Legenda lignea: with an answer. *Printed*, 1653. 8°. LT, O, C, E, DT; CLC, CN, MH, TU, WF, Y.

840 [**Lee, Francis.**] Horologium Christianum. *Oxoniæ, typis L. Lichfield*, 1689. 12°. L, O; CLC, WF, Y.

841 [–] The labouring persons remembrancer. *Oxford, by L. Lichfield*, 1690. 8°.* L, O, LW, NE.

842 [–] The state of the Philadelphian Society. *For the booksellers*, 1697. 4°.* L, LW, BAMB; WF.

843 [**Lee, Joseph.**] Considerations concerning common fields. *For Abel Roper*, 1654. 8°.* LT, O, C, CT, MR, R; CH, CN, MH, NC, WF.

843A —Ευταξια του αγρου; or, a vindication of a regulated inclosure. *By E. C. and are to be sold by Thomas Williams*, 1656. 4°.* L, LUG, LLU; MH.

844 **Lee, Leonard.** A remonstrance humbly presented. *By E. G. for John Rothwell*, 1644[5]. 4°.* LT, LW, MR, EN, DT; MH, NC, WF.

845 **Lee, Nathaniel.** The works of. *For Richard Bentley and S. Magnes*, 1687. 4°. CLC, UCLA, WF.

845A ——[Anr. ed.] *For R. Bentley*, 1694. 4°. O, LVD, LLU, DT; IAU, MH, NC, Y.

846 —Cæsar Borgia, . . . a tragedy. *By R. E. for R. Bentley, and M. Magnes*, 1680. 4°. T.C.I 370. L, O, LVF, CT, EN; CH, CN, LC, MH, TU, WF, Y.

847 ——[Anr. ed.] *For R. Bentley*, 1696. 4°. L, OW, CT, LLU, EN; CLC, CU, MH, TU, WF, Y.

848 —Constantine the Great. *By H. Hills jun. for R. Bently and J. Tonson*, 1684. 4°. L, O, LVF, CT, EN; CH, CN, LC, MH, TU, WF, Y, AVP.

849 —Gloriana. *For J. Magnes and R. Bentley*, 1676. 4°. T.C.I 236. L, O, OW, CK, EN; CH, CN, LC, MH, TU, Y.

850 ——[Anr. ed.] *For R. Wellington, and E. Rumball*, 1699. 4°. T.C.III 128. L, O, OW, CT, E; CH, CU, MH, TU, WF, Y.

851 [–] Loves boundless power. [*London*], *for J. Deacon*, [1680–1]. brs. HH.

852 —Lucius Junius Brutus. *For Richard Tonson and Jacob Tonson*, 1681. 4°. T.C.I 451. L, O, C, LVD, EN; CH, CN, LC, MH, TU, WF, Y.

853 —The massacre of Paris. *For R. Bentley and M. Magnes*, 1690. 4°. T.C.II 288. L, O, CT, EN, DT; CH, CN, LC, MH, NP, TU, WF, Y.

854 —Mithridates King of Pontus. *By R. E. for James Magnes and Rich. Bentley*, 1678. 4°. T.C.I 320. L, O, C, CK, EN; CH, CN, LC, MH, TU, Y.

855 ——Second edition. *By R. E. for Rich. Bentley and S. Magnes*, 1685. 4°. T.C.II 118. L, BC, LSD, EN; CH, IU, MH, NC, TU, WF, Y.

856 ——[Anr. ed.] *For R. Bentley*, 1693. 4°. L, O, LVD, CT, EN; CH, MH, MU, TU, WF, Y.

857 —On the death of Mrs. Behn. *For Abel Roper*, 1689. brs. TU.

858 —On their Majesties coronation. colop: *For Abel Roper*, 1689. brs. TU, Y.

859 No entry.

[–] Piso's conspiracy. 1676. *See title.*

860 —The Princess of Cleve. *Printed*, 1689. 4°. L, O, LVF, OW, LLU; CH, CN, LC, MH, TU, WF, Y.

861 ——[Anr. ed.] *For Abel Roper*, 1689. 4°. T.C.II 253. L; LC, MH, Y.

862 ——Second edition. *By J. O. for R. Wellington*, 1697. 4°. T.C.III 27. L, O, C, OW, EN; CH, CU, MH, TU, WF, Y.

863 No entry.

864 Entry cancelled.

—Prologue spoken at Mithridates. [n.p., 1682]. *See* Dryden, John.

865 —The rival queens. *For James Magnes and Richard Bentley*, 1677. 4°. T.C.I 291. L, O, OW, LLU, EN; CH, CN, LC, MH, TU, WF, Y.

866 ——[Anr. ed.] *By J. Gain for Richard Bentley*, 1684. 4°. T.C.II 118. L, C, LVF, LLU, LSD; CH, CN, MH, TU, WF, Y.

867 ——[Anr. ed.] *For Richard Bentley*, 1690. 4°. T.C.II 325. L, O, CCA, EN; CH, CU, MH, TU, WF, Y.

868 ——Second edition. *For R. Bently*, 1694. 4°. T.C.II 515. L, O, OW, LLU, EN; CH, CU, MH, TU, WF, Y.

869 ——Third edition. *For R. Wellington, and E. Rumbal*, 1699. 4°. T.C.III 141. L, OW, CT, EN; CH, CN, IU, MH, WF.

870 —Sophonisba. *For J. Magnes and R. Bentley*, 1676. 4°. T.C.I 218. L, O, OW, LLU, EN; CH, CN, LC, MH, TU, WF, Y.

871 ——[Anr. ed.] *For R. Bently and M. Magnes*, 1681. 4°. T.C.I 446. O, C, LLU, EN; CLC, CU, LC, MH, WF, Y.

872 ——[Anr. ed.] *For R. Bently and S. Magnes*, 1685. 4°. L, O, CT, LSD, EN; CH, CLC, NCD, TU, WF, Y.

873 ——Third edition. *For Sam. Brisco*, 1691. 4°. T.C.II 387. L, LVD, CCC; CH, CLC, IU, MH, TU, Y.

874 ——[Anr. ed.] *For R. Bently*, 1691. 4°. LVD, CCA; CLC, CN, IU, OCI, WF.

874A ——[Anr. ed.] *For R. Bentley*, 1693. 4°. L; WF.

875 ——[Anr. ed.] *For Tho. Chapman*, 1693. 4°. L, O, LLU; BN, CH, IU, MH, TU, WF, Y.

876 — —[Anr. ed.] —, 1697. 4°. L, O, C, EN, CD; CLC, MH, MU, TU, WF, Y.

877 —Theodosius: or. *For R. Bentley and M. Magnes,* 1680. 4°. T.C.I 418. L, O, CCA, LLU, EN; CH, CN, LC, MH, TU, WF, Y.

878 — —Second edition. *For R. Bentley and S. Magnes,* 1684. 4°. T.C.II 118. L, C, LVF, LLU, LSD; CH, CU, MH, TU, WF, Y.

879 — —[Anr. ed.] *For Tho. Chapman,* 1692. 4°. L, O, LVD, OW, LLU; CH, CN, MB, TU, WF, Y.

880 — —[Anr. ed.] *For R. Bentley,* 1697. 4°. L, O, CT, BC, EN; CLC, MH, MU, TU, WF, Y.

881 [–] Thy genius lo! [*London*], *Tho. Cross,* [1697?]. brs. L.

882 —To the Duke on his return. [*London*], *for J. Tonson,* 1682. brs. L, O, HH; CH, TU, WF, Y.

883 —The tragedy of Nero. *By T. R. and N. T. for James Magnus and Richard Bentley,* 1675. 4°. T.C.I 211. L, O, CCA, LLU, EN; CH, CN, LC, MH, TU, Y.

884 — –[Anr. ed.] *For R. Bentley,* 1696. 4°.* L, O, CT, LI U, EN; CLC, MH, MU, NC, WF, Y. (var.)

885 [–] The true lovers tragedy. [*London*], *for P. Brooksby,* [1680–82]. brs. L, CM, HH; MH.

885A [–] —[Anr. ed.] [*London*], *for T. Vere,* [1680–82]. brs. O.

885B **Lee, Obadiah.** A sermon preached . . . the xxvi of July, 1685. *Printed for, and sold by Elizabeth Richardson in Wakefield,* 1685. 4°.* Y.

886 **Lee, Richard.** A catalogue of the library of choice books. 28 *Apr.* 1685. 4°. L, O.

887 No entry.

888 —Cor humiliatum & contritum. A sermon. [*London*], *for R. Royston, J. Williams, T. Garthwait,* 1663. 4°. L, O, C, E, DT; CH, IU, MH, NU, WF, Y.

889 — —[Anr. ed.] *For John Williams,* 1664. 4°. L, O, LW, CS, DT; NU, PU.

889A [–] This most deplorable case. 1678. 4°.* L; MH.

890 Entry cancelled.

[**Lee, Samuel.**] Antichristi excidium. 1667. *See* Leigh, Edward.

891 —Χαρα της πιστεως. The joy of faith. *Boston, by Samuel Green,* 1687. 8°. EVANS 429. L, LCL, LW; CH, MH, NU, WF, Y.

892 —Contemplations on mortality. 1669. 12°. LCL, LG; LC.

893 — —[Anr. ed.] *Boston in N. E. re-printed, by B. Green and J. Allen, for Samuel Phillips,* 1698. 8°. T.C.III 120; EVANS 820. MB, MH, MWA, RPJ, Y.

894 [–] Ecclesia gemens: or, two discourses. *For John Hancock,* 1677. 8°. T.C.I 340. L, O, C, CK, SP; CH, IU, MH, NU, WF, Y.

895 [–] Ελεοθριαμβος; Or, the triumph of mercy. *For John Hancock,* 1677. 12°. T.C.I 271. L, O, LCL, CK; CH, MH, NU, RPJ, WF, Y.

896 —The great day of judgment. *Boston in New-England, by Bartholomew Green, for Nicholas Buttolph,* 1692. 12°.* EVANS 614. L; CHW, MWA.

897 [–] Ιερον Σολομωντος. The temple of Solomon. *By John Streater, for Francis Tyton,* 1659. fol. LWL; RPJ.

898 Entry cancelled.

—Israel redux. 1677. *See* Fletcher, Giles.

899 —The library of the late reverend and learned Mr. Samuel Lee . . . exposed . . . to sale, by Duncan Campbell. *Boston: by Benjamin Harris for Duncan Cambell,* 1693. 4°.* EVANS 645. MB.

900 [–] Orbis miraculum, or the Temple of Solomon. *By John Streater, for Humphrey Moseley,* 1659. fol. L, LCL, LI; LC, NU, RPJ, TSM, WSC, AVP.

901 [–] —[Anr. ed.] *By John Streater, for Abell Roper,* 1659. fol. NU.

902 [–] —[Anr. ed.] *By John Streater, for Giles Calvert,* 1659. fol. O; CLC, CN, OHU, NU.

902A — —[Anr. ed.] *By John Streater,* [*for Luke Fawne,* 1659 (in ms.)]. fol. NNM.

903 — —[Anr. ed.] *By John Streater, for Luke Fawn,* 1659. fol. L, C, E, DT; CH, Y.

903A — —[Anr. ed.] *By John Streater, for George Lee,* 1659. fol. WES.

903B [–] —[Anr. ed.] *By John Streater, for Thomas Basset,* 1659. fol. LLP, LSC; IU, WF.

903C [–] —[Anr. ed.] *By John Streater, for George Sawbridge,* 1659. fol. L, CCA, SHR; FU.

903D [–] —[Anr. ed.] *By John Streater, for John Field,* 1659. fol. BQ; NN.

903E [ ] —[Anr. ed.] *By John Streater, for Francis Titon,* 1659. fol. IU, LC, RBU.

903F [–] —[Anr. ed.] *For F. Tyton and Tho. Basset,* 1665. fol. L.

904 **Leech, David.** Parerga Davidis Leochæi . . . operis pars prior. *Excudebat Franciscus Leach,* 1657. 8°. CT, DT; WF.

905 **Leech, Jeremiah.** St. Pavls challenge. *By Thomas Paine, and are to be sold by Francis Eglesfield,* 1644. 4°.* LT, O, BC, P, EN; CH, IU, MWA, NU, WF.

906 **Leech, John.** A booke of grammar questions. Fourth edition. *By Tho. Harper, to be sold by John Hardisty,* 1650. 8°. L, O.

906A — —"Fourth" edition. —, 1651. 8°. L (t.p.).

906B **Leech, Richard.** To each gentleman soldier. [1690?] brs. L.

907 **Leedes, Edward.** Ad prima rudimenta Græcæ linguæ. *Typis Benj. Motte, impensis Johan. Chamberlayne, Buriensis,* 1693. 4°. O, C; MB.

908 [–] English examples. *For Nevil Simmons, and Thomas Simmons,* 1676. 8°. T.C.I 237. O, C.

908A [–] —Second edition. —, 1677. 12°. T.C.I 269. L.

908B [–] —Fourth edition. *For Thomas Simmons,* 1681. 12°. T.C.I 433. WF.

908C [–] —Seventh edition. *For Thomas Simmons, to be sold by Ben. Cox,* 1685. 12°. T.C.II 153. CLC.

908D [–] —Eighth edition. *For B. G., T. S. and Ben. Cox,* 1687. 12°. O.

908E [–] —Twelfth edition. *Dublin, by John Brocas and Cornelius Carter for William Norman, Eliphel Dobson, Patrick Campbell, and Jacob Millner,* 1697. 12°. DIX 382. L (t.p.).

908F [–] —[Anr. ed.] *For Charles Harper, Sam. Smith and Benj. Walford, and J. Slatter at Eaton,* 1699. 12°. T.C.III 112. PL.

909 —Methodus Græcam linguam docendi. *Impensis J. Chamberlain, Buriensis,* 1690. 8°. O, C, CT; IU, MB.

910 ——[Anr. ed.] *Cantabrigiæ, ex officina Johan. Hayes. Impensis Joh. Chamberlayne, Buriensis. Et prostant venales apud Pet. Parker, Londini,* 1699. 8°. T.C.II 322. L, C, CT; CLC, IU, NNM, WF.

910A [–] More English examples. Third edition. *For J. C., to be sold by Peter Parker,* 1692. 12°. T.C.II 415. CH.

910B [–] ——Fifth edition. ——, 1699. 12°. IU.

910C [–] New English examples. *For J. Chamberlain in Bury, and B. Aylmer,* 1685. 12°. T.C.II 128. CLC.

911 Entry cancelled.

——Vossius in supplementum. 1665. *See* Voss, Gerard Johann.

Leeds, Daniel. Almanack. Philadelphia, 1687. *See* Almanacs.

911A [–] The case put & decided by George Fox, George Whitehead, Stephen Crisp. [*New York, by William Bradford,* 1699.] 4°.* EVANS 822. NJH.

912 ——A challenge to Caleb Pusey. [*New-York, by William Bradford,* 1700?] 4°.* EVANS 916. MWA.

913 ——The innocent vindicated. [*New York*], *printed,* 1695. CH, MWA.

914 ——News of a trumpet. *Printed and sold by William Bradford in New-York,* 1697. 8°. EVANS 786. OC; CH, NN, PHS, RPJ, TU.

915 [–] The temple of vvisdom. *Printed and sold by William Bradford in Philadelphia,* 1688. 8°. EVANS 447. MH, NN, PHS.

916 ——A trumpet sounded. *Printed by William Bradford, in New York; to be sold by B. Aylmer, and C. Brome, London,* 1699. 8°. L, O; NN.

917 **Leeds, Peregrine Osborne, *duke of.*** A journal of the Brest-expedition. *For Randal Taylor,* 1694. 4°.* L, O, C, CT, LIU; CH, CN, RPJ, WF, Y.

917A ——[Anr. ed.] ——, *and re-printed in Dublin by Andrew Crook,* 1694. 4°.* ST. COLUMBA'S CATHEDRAL, DERRY.

918 **Leeds, Thomas Osborne, *duke of.*** An account at large of the . . . Earl of Danby's arguments. *For Charles Mearue,* [*sic*], 1682. fol.* L, O, C, MR, DT; CH, CN, LC, MH, TU, Y.

919 ——Second edition. *For Charles Mearne,* 1682. fol.* O, C, LL, LSD, DT; CH, IU, MH, PL, TU, WF, Y.

920 ——The ansvver of. *By E. R. to be sold by Randal Taylor,* 1680. fol.* T.C.I 407. L, O, C, DU, DT; BN, CH, CN, LC, MH, Y.

921 ——The Earl of Danby's answer to Sr. Robert Howards. *For Randall Tayler,* 1680. fol.* L, O, LUG, DU, LSD; BN, CH, CN, MH, TU, WF, Y.

922 ——The arguments of the Right Honourable the Earl of Danby the second time. *For Richard Tonson,* 1682. fol.* L, O, CT, DU, DT; BN, CH, CU, MH, TU, WF, Y.

923 ——An explanation of the Lord Treasurer's letter. [*London*], *printed,* 1679. fol.* L, O, OC, BP, NE; CH, CN, MH, NU, TU, WF, Y.

923A [–] The thoughts of a private person. [*London*], *printed,* 1689. 4°.* T.C.II 277. L, OC, CT, MR, DT; CH, IU, MH, NU, WF, Y. (var.)

924 [**Le Faucheur, Michel.**] An essay upon the action of an orator. *For Nich. Cox,* [?1680.] 12°. L, O, E; CH, CLC, U, NU, WF.

924A **Le Fèvre, Nicolas.** A compendious body of chymistry. *For Tho. Davis and Theo. Sadler,* 1662. 4°. NL, GU; MIU.

924B ——[Anr. ed.] *By Tho. Ratcliffe for Octavian Pulleyn, Junior,* 1664. 4°. L.

925 ——A compleat body of chymistry. *By Tho. Ratcliffe for Octavian Pulleyn, junior,* 1664. 4°. L, C, LIU, GU; CU, LC, MH, TO, WSG, Y.

926 ——[Anr. ed.] *For O. Pulleyn, junior and are to be sold by John Wright,* 1670. 4°. T.C.I 32. L, O, C, GU, DT; CH, CNM, MH, WF, Y. (var.)

927 ——Discours sur le grand cordial de Sr. Walter Rawleigh. *Chez Octavian Pulleyn le jeune,* 1665. 12°. L, LCP, GU; BN, CH, CLC, HC.

928 ——A discourse upon Sr Walter Rawleigh's great cordial. [Anr. ed.] *By J. F. for Octavian Pulleyn junior,* 1664. 8°. L, O, C, GU; CH, CLC, INU, MH, PCP, WF, WSG.

929 [**Lefevre, Raoul.**] The destruction of Troy. Seventh edition. *By R. I. for S. S. to bee sold by F. Coles, and C. Tyus,* 1663. 4°. L, LSD; CLC, MIU, Y.

930 [–] ——Eighth edition. *For T. Passenger,* 1670. 4°. L, CT; CH, CLC, IU, MIU, Y.

931 [–] ——Ninth edition. ——, 1676. 4°. T.C.I 230. L, O; CH, LC, MH, NP, TU, WF, Y.

932 [–] ——Tenth edition. ——, 1680. 4°. T.C.I 434. L; CH, CLC.

933 [–] ——Eleventh edition. ——, 1684. 4°. L, O, CM, DU, E; CH, CN, IU, MH, NCD.

933A [–] ——, an essay upon the second book. *By Humphrey Moseley,* 1656. 4°.* O.

934 [–] The destruction of Troy, the second book. *By R. I. for Samuel Speed,* 1663. 4°. L, LSD; CLC, MIU, Y.

935 [–] ——[Anr. ed.] *By T. J. for Samuel Speed,* 1670. 4°. T.C.I 51. L; CH, CLC, IU, MIU, Y.

936 [–] ——[Anr. ed.] *For Thomas Passinger,* 1676. 4°. L, O; CH, LC, MBP, MH, TU, Y.

937 [–] ——[Anr. ed.] ——, 1680. 4°. L; CH, CLC.

937A [–] ——[Anr. ed.] ——, 1684. 4°. L, O, CM, DU, E; CH, CN, IU, NCD, MH.

938 [–] ——the third book. *By R. I. for Samuel Speed,* 1663. 4°. L, LSD; CLC, MIU, Y.

939 [–] ——[Anr. ed.] *By E. T. and R. H. for Thomas Passenger,* 1670. 4°. L, CT; CH, CLC, IU, MIU, Y.

940 [–] ——[Anr. ed.] *For Thomas Passenger,* 1676. 4°. L, O; CH, LC, MBP, MH, TU, Y.

941 [–] ——[Anr. ed.] ——, 1680. 4°. L; CH, CLC.

941A [–] ——[Anr. ed.] ——, 1684. 4°. L, O, CM, DU, E; CH, CN, IU, NCD, MH.

942 **Le Franc, James.** Ο βασανος της αληθειας, or the touch-stone of truth. *Cambridge, by John Field,* 1662. 8°. O, C, CT, NPL.

942A ——Corpus animatum. *Excudebat R. Davenport, veneuntq; apud Thomam Dicas,* 1664. 8°. L, BC.

Legacie left. Dowa [*sic*], 1654. *See* Bayly, Thomas.

Legal and other reasons. 1675. *See* Cole, William.

943　A legal examination of abuses of law. *Printed and sold by Andrew Sowle,* 1682. 4°.* L, LF; CH, LC, MH, PSC, Y.
　　Legality of the court. 1688. *See* Care, Henry.

943AA　Legatio regis psittacorum e terra. Magellanica. [*Londini*], 1658. 24°. LC, MH.
　　Legend of Brita-Mart. 1646. *See* Tooke, George.
　　Legend of Captaine Iones. 1648. *See* Lloyd, David.
　　Legend of St. Cuthbert. 1663. *See* Hegg, Robert.
　　Legenda lignea: with. 1653. *See* Lee, E.

943A　**Le Gendre, *sieur de.*** The manner of ordering fruit-trees. *For Humphrey Moseley,* 1660. 12°. L, R, GK; CH, CLC, MH, WU, ZAP.

944　**Le Gendre, Louis.** The history of the reign of Lewis the Great. *For D. Brown; Th. Leigh and D. Midwinter, and Robert Knaplock,* 1699. 8°. L, CE, DT; CLC, CN, TU, WF, Y.

　　Legge, George. *See* Dartmouth, George Legge, *baron.*
　　Legis fluvius: or. 1658. *See* G., A.
　　Legislative povver. 1656. *See* Aspinwall, William.

945　**Le Grand, Antoine.** Antonii Le Grand apologia pro Renato Descartes. *Typis M. Clark,* 1679. 8°. T.C.I 360. L, O, C, P, EN; BN, CB, NC, NIC, PU, UCLA, Y.

946　—Censura justissima responsi. *Anno,* 1698. 8°. DUS; Y.

947　—Dissertatio de carentia. *Apud J. Martyn,* 1675. 12°. T.C.I 199. L, O, C, EN, DT; BN, CLC, CU, MH, WF, Y.

948　—Dissertatio de ratione cognoscendi. *Apud Joannem Hartley,* 1698. 8°. T.C.III 56. DUS, P; Y.

949　—The divine Epicurus. *By H. Bruges for M. Widdows,* 1676. 8°. T.C.I 228. L, LW, DUS, LLU, EN; CH, CLC, IU, LC, PU, TU, Y.

950　—An entire body of philosophy. *By Samuel Roycroft, and sold by the undertaker Richard Blome: and Mr. Horn and Mr. Southby; Mr. Chiswell, Mr. Clavell and Mr. Brome; Mr. Tonson; Mr. Saunders; Mr. Gilliflower; and Mr. Richards,* 1694. fol. L, O, CT, D, BQ; CLC, LC, MH, MU, Y.

950A　——[Anr. ed.] *By Samuel Roycroft, and sold by the undertaker Richard Blome,* 1694. fol. L, OC, CM; CH, PL, TU.

951　—Historia naturæ. *Apud J. Martyn,* 1673. 8°. T.C.I 136. L, O, C, AN, E, DT; BN, CH, CLC, CNM, MH, MM, OCI.

952　——Second edition. —, 1680. 4°. T.C.I 398. L, C, LW, EN, DT; BN, CH, NAM, PL, WF, Y.

953　—Historia sacra. *Impensis Henrici Faithorne & Joannis Kersey,* 1685. 8°. T.C.II 139. L, O, C, EC, GU; BN, CH, CLC, PL, WF, Y.

954　—Institutio philosophiæ. *Apud J. Martyn,* 1672. 8°. T.C.I 97. L, O, C, OM, AN, DUS, ENC; MB, U. SOUTHERN CAL., Y, ZDU.

955　——Third edition. —, 1675. 8°. T.C.I 191. L, C, LW, NOT, E; BN, CH, CLC, OHU, RBU, UCLA, Y.

956　——[Anr. ed.] —, 1678. 8°. CJC, LC, MH, MU.

957　——Fourth edition. *Typis M. Clark, impensis J. Martyn,* 1680. 4°. T.C.I 398. L, O, C, EN, DT; BN, CLC, IU, MH, V, WF.

958　—Man without passion. *For C. Harper, and J. Amery,* 1675. 8°. T.C.I 198. L, O, C, LLU, EN; CH, CN, LC, MH, NU, Y.

959　—Philosophia veterum. *Apud J. Martyn,* 1671. 12°. T.C.I 74. L, O, C; CLC, MB, UCLA.

959A　[–] Proposals for the printing Le Grand's histories of nature. [*London,* 1693.] fol.* L.

960　[**Le Grand, Joachim.**] The history of the divorce of Henry VIII. [*London?* 1690.] cap., 4°.* L, O, C, DU, CD; CH, CN, MH, NU, WF, Y.

960A　**LeGrosse, Robert.** Iter Australe. *Excudebat T. Milbourn,* 1667. 4°.* L, CCA, LNC; Y.

961　—Sionis reductio, & exultatio. Or, Sions return. *By Tho: Leach,* 1662. 4°. O, CCA, WCA; MM, WF.

962　**L[eibnitz], G[ottfried Wilhelm von].** Hypothesis physica nova. *Impensis J. Martyn,* 1671. 12°. T.C.I 81. L, O, C, LR, CCH, NE; MH.

　　Leycester, John, *pseud.*

963　**Leicester, John.** An elegiacall epitaph upon . . . Iohn Hampden. *By Bernard Alsop.* 1643. brs. LT.

964　Entry cancelled.

　　Leicester, Sir Peter. Historical antiquities. 1673. *See* Leycester, Sir Peter.

965　[**Leicester, Philip Sidney**], *earl of.* An armie for Ireland. *For John Greensmith,* 1642. 4°.* LT, O, SC, BLH, DN.

966　—The great and famous collection of . . . Italian drawings. [*London?* 1698.] 4°.* HH (dispersed).

967　**Leicester, Robert Dudley,** *earl.* A letter from. *For Iohn Wright, Septemb. 27.* 1642. 4°.* LT, O, C, LNC, DT; CH, CSS, MH, MU, WF, Y.

968　Leycesters common-wealth: conceived. [*London*], *printed,* 1641. 4°. LT, O, CT, NOT, EN; BN, CSS, CN, MH, WF, Y.

969　Leicester's common-wealth: conceived, spoken. *Printed Anno Dom.* 1641. 8°. L, O, CT, BC, DC; CH, IU, MH, NP, WF.

969AA　—[Anr. ed., "Leycesters."] [*London*], *printed,* 1641. 8°. LG; INU, MH, WF, Y.

969A　Leicestors common-vvealth fully epitomiz'd. [*London?*], *printed,* 1641. 4°.* L; CH, CN, MH, WF, TSM.

970　Entry cancelled.

　　Leycester's ghost. [n.p.], 1641. *See* Rogers, Thomas.

971　A Leicester-shire frolick. [*London*], *for P. Brooksby,* [1680?]. brs. L, O, HH.

971A　—[Anr. ed.] [*London*], *for R. Burton,* [1641–74]. brs. O.

972　The Leicester-shire tragedy. [*London*], *for P. Brooksby,* [1685?]. brs. L, CM, HH.

973　Leycestershires petition. *For T. B.,* 1642. 4°.* LT, LE, LNC, MR; MBP, NU, WF, Y.

974　**Leigh, Charles.** Exercitationes quinque. *Oxonii, typis L. Lichfield; impensis T. Bennet,* 1697. 4°. T.C.III 55. L, O, LCS, OR, MAU, MC; BN, PL.

974A　——[Anr. ed.] *Oxonii, typis L. Lichfiel* [*sic*], *impensis Ephr. Johnson & T. Bennet,* 1697. WSG.

975　—The natural history of Lancashire. *Oxford, for the author, and to be had at Mr. George West's, and Mr. Henry Clement's there; Mr. Edward Evet's; and Mr. John Nicholson, London,* 1700. fol. L, O, C, NOT, EN, DT; BN, CH, CJC, LC, MH, TU, Y, AVP.

976　—Phthisiologia Lancastriensis. *Impensis Sam. Smith et Benj. Walford,* 1694. 8°. T.C.II 493. L, O, C, E, DT; BN, CLC, PL, WF, HC.

977   [–] Remarks on Mr. Richard Bolton's piece. *Printed; and sold by John Shelmerdine, in Manchester,* 1698. 8°.* L, OC.

978   —A reply to John Colebatch. *Printed; and sold by John Shelmerdine, in Manchester,* 1698. sixes.* L, O; WF.

979   —A reply to Mr. Richard Bolton. *For John Sprint,* 1698. 8°.* L.

980   **Leigh, Dorothy.** The mother's blessing. *By E. Cotes for Andrew Crooke,* 1656. 12°. L.

981   ——[Anr. ed.] —, 1663. 12°. L.

981A   ——[Anr. ed.] *By E. Cotes for Andrew Crook.* 1667. 12°. IU.

982   ——[Anr. ed.] *By S. & B. G. for Andrew Crook,* 1674. 12°. L.

983   **Leigh, Edward.** Analecta de XII. Primis Caesaribus. Select and choyce observations. Second edition. *Printed at London by Moses Bell for Mathew Walbancke,* 1647. 8°. L, O, C; CH, CN, MH, WF, Y.

984   — Analecta Cæsarum romanorum. Or, select observations. Fourth edition. *By R. D. for John Williams,* 1664. 8°. L, O; CLC, MH, NCU, OCI, WF, Y, AVP.

985   —Annotations on five poetical books. *By A. M. for T. Pierpoint, E. Brewster, and M. Keinton,* 1657. fol. L, O, C, E, DT; CH, NU, PU, WF, Y.

986   —Annotations upon all the New Testament. *By W. W. and E. G. for William Lee,* 1650. fol. L, O, C, AN, E, BQ; BN, CLC, IU, MH, NU, WF, Y.

986A   [–] Antichristi excidium. *Typis Johannis Streater,* 1664. 8°. L, O, LW, BAMB, P; LC, MB, MH, RBU, WF.

987   —Choice observations of all the Kings. *By Joseph Cranford,* 1661. 8°. L, O, C, WCA, EN; CH, CLC, CN, WF, Y.

988   —Critica sacra. Observations. *By G. M. for Thomas Vnderhill,* 1641. 4°. L, O, LW, LSD, GU; CH, MWA, NU, OHU, WF, Y.

989   ——[Anr. ed.] —, 1642. 4°. L, LLP, BAMB, YM, DT; CN, MBP, NRU, WF, Y.

990   —Critica sacra; or, philologicall. Second edition. *By James Young, for Thomas Underhill,* 1646, 4°. LT, O, C, LLP, E, DT; BN, CH, CN, MH, TU, WF.

990A   ——; or observations. Second edition. *By A. Miller for Thomas Underhill,* 1650. fol. OW, CS, DU, DUS, LIU; MH, WF, Y.

991   ——in two parts. Third edition. *By Abraham Miller and Roger Daniel for Thomas Underhill,* 1650. fol. L, O, C, ENC, DT; CLC, IU, MH, NU, WF, Y, AVP.

991A   ——: or, philologicall. Third edition. *By Roger Daniel, for Thomas Underhill,* 1650. fol. CSE, DUS; MH.

991B   ——: or observations. Third edition. *By A. M.,* 1662. 4°. MH, Y.

992   ——in two parts. Fourth edition. *By Abraham Miller and Roger Daniel,* 1662. fol. L, O, C, LW, E; BN, CH, IU, MBC, NC, NU, TO.

993   ——; or, philologicall. Fourth edition. *By John Redmayne,* 1662. fol. CH, MH, NU, Y, ASU.

993A   ——in two parts. "Fourth" edition. *For William Crook,* 1664. fol. OC; MH.

994   —England described. *By A. M. for Henry Marsh,* 1659. 8°. LT, O, C, AN, DU, EN; CH, CN, LC, PL, Y.

995   —Fœlix consortium; or, a fit conjuncture. *For Charles Adams,* 1663. fol. L, O, LCL, WCA, ENC; CLC, IU, MB, NCU, NU.

996   —The gentlemans guide. *For William Whitwood,* 1680. 8°. T.C.I 396. BC, LIU, DM; CH, LC, WF.

997   [–] A philologicall commentary. *By T. Mabb for Charles Adams,* 1652. 8°. LT, O, C, LL, EN; CH, FU, LC, MHL, NN, YL.

998   [–] ——[Anr. ed.] —, 1653. 8°. LT.

999   ——Second edition. *By A. M. for Charles Adams,* 1658. 8°. L, LL, LLU; CH, CLL, NCL, WF, YL.

1000   —The saints encouragement. *By A. M. for William Lee and Thomas Underhill,* 1648. 12°. O, CS, DC.

1001   ——Second edition. *By Abraham Miller for William Lee and Thomas Underhill,* 1651. 12°. LT, C, LCL; CLC, IU, MH, NU, WF.

1002   —Second considerations concerning the high court of Chancery. *By J. G. for Rich. Marriot,* 1658. 4°.* O, LLL.

1003   —Select and choyce observations. *By Roger Daniel, for John Williams,* 1657. 8°. L, O, C, LLL; CLC, CN, MH, NR, TU, WF, Y.

1004   ——Second edition. *By R. Davenport for John Williams,* 1663. 8°. L, LLP, CCO, AN; CH, IU, TU, Y.

1005   ——Third edition. *For J. Williams, and are to be sold by Amos Curteyne, in Oxford,* 1670. 8°. T.C.I 45; MADAN 2855n. L, O, DU, YM, EN; CH, CN, MH, NC, TU, WF.

1006   —A speech, of . . . thirtieth of Septem. 1644. *By F. L. for Matthew VValbancke,* 1644. 4°.* LT, C, SP, SS, DT; IU, MH.

1007   —A supplement to the critica sacra. *For Andrew Crook, and Edward Brewster,* 1662. fol. EC, WCA; MBC, MH, NU, PL, Y.

1008   —A system or body of divinity. *By A. M. for William Lee,* 1654. fol. L, O, C, AN, DC, ENC; CLC, IU, NU, PPT, V, Y.

1009   ——Second edition. —, 1662. fol. L, OM, CT, SP, E; CH, IU, MH, NCD, PPT, WF.

1010   —Three diatribes. *For William Whitwood,* 1671. 8°. T.C.I 58. L, O, C, LUG, LLU; CH, CJC, MH, NC, TU, WF, Y.

1011   —A treatise of divinity. *By E. Griffin for William Lee,* 1646. 4°. O, LCL, CS, AN, ES; CDA, NU, PPT, WF.

1012   ——[Anr. ed.] —, 1647. 4°. LT, O, LW, ENC, DT; IU, LC, NCD, Y.

1013   —A treatise of religion & learning. *By A. M. for Charles Adams,* 1656. fol. MADAN 2217. L, O, C, E, CD; BN, CLC, IU, LC, MBC, MH, Y.

1014   —A treatise of the divine promises. Second edition. *By George Miller, to be sold by Thomas Underhill,* 1641. 12°. L, O, C, AN, BC; CLC, IU, WF, WU.

1015   ——Third edition. *By A. Miller for Thomas Underhill,* 1650. 12°. L, O, E; IU, MBA, AVP.

1016   ——Fourth edition. *By A. Miller, for Henry Mortlocke,* 1657. 8°. LT, O, C, DC, ENC; CLC, FU, MIU, NU, PPT, TO, Y.

1017   **Leigh, Henry.** Urinæ. [*n.p.*], 1697. brs. O.

1017A   **Leigh, John.** The saints rest and reward. *By J. G. for Tho: Heath,* 1654. 4°.* L, C, WCA, YM.

1017B   **Leigh, Philip *alias* Metcalfe.** A sermon preached . . . 29th of January 1687/8. *For Henry Hills,* 1688. 8°. Y.

1018   [**Leigh, Richard.**] The censvre of the Rota. *Oxford, by H. H. for Fran. Oxlad junior,* 1673. 4°.* MADAN 2980. L, O, C, LVD, MR, A; CH, CN, MH, MU, TU, WF, Y.

1019   [–] Poems, upon several occasions. *By Andr. Clark for William Hensman,* 1675. 8°. MADAN 3038. L, O, LVD, LLU; CH, CN, IU, MH, TU.

1020   [–] The transproser rehears'd. *Oxford, for the assignes of Hugo Grotius, and Jacob Van Harmine,* 1673. 8°. MADAN 2981; T.C.I 135. L, O, C, LNC, E; CLC, CN, MH, NU, WF, Y.

1021   **Leigh, Thomas.** The keeping of holy days. *By H. Hills jun. for Walter Kettilby,* 1684. 4°.* T.C.II 95. L, O, C, BAMB, YM, D; CH, CLC, NCD, NGT, WF, Y.

1022   **Leighton, Alexander.** An appeal to the Parliament. Second edition. [*Amsterdam?* 1644?] 4°. L, O, C, OW, BLH; CH, CU, MH, WF, Y. (var.)

1023   [–] A decade of grievances. [*London*], printed, 1641. 4°.* LT, O, LVF, YM, F, EN; CH, CU, MH, NU, WF, Y.

1024   —An epitome or briefe discoverie. *By I. D.,* 1646. 4°. LT, O, C, DT; CH, LC, NU, WF, Y.

1025   **Leighton, Sir Ellis.** The speech . . . April the 4th, 1672. *Dublin, by Benjamin Tooke, sold by Joseph Wilde,* 1672. 4°.* DIX 147. O, OC, DML.

1026   **Leighton, Henry.** Linguæ Gallicæ addiscendæ regulæ. *Oxoniæ, excudebat H. H. impensis authoris,* 1659. 12°.* MADAN 2448. O, C, OB.

1027   ——[Anr. ed.] —, 1662. 8°.* MADAN 2601. O, LW, OC.

1027A ——[Anr. ed.] *Oxoniæ, excudebat A. & L. Lichfield,* 1662. 8°.* CH, CLC, Y.

1027B **Leighton, John.** A cordial for drooping sinners. *For the author to be sold by Jonathan Greenwood,* 1691. WF.

1027C [**Leighton, Robert**], *abp.* The case of the accomodation lately proposed. [*Edinburgh*], printed 1671. 4°. ALDIS 1927.97. O, DU, EN, ENC, GU; CLC, CN, IU, NU, WF, Y.

1027D —Mr. Lighton's catechism for children. *Edinburgh,* [*J. Watson,* 1695]. 8°.* EN.

1028   —A practical commentary upon the two first chapters . . . of St. Peter. *York: by J. White,* 1693. 4°. L, O, C, YM, E; CLC, MBA, NU, VC, WF.

1028A ——[Anr. ed.] —, *and are to be sold by Sam. Keble,* 1693. 4°. LW, DL; NGT.

1029   —A practical commentary, . . . vol. II. *By B. G. for Sam. Keble,* 1694. 4°. C, LW, SHR, E; MBA, NU.

1030   —Prælectiones theologicæ. *Typis exousæ* [*sic*] *B. Griffin, venales prostant apud Sam. Keble,* 1693. 4°. T.C.II 481. L, O, C, LW, DL, E; CLC, KQ, MBA, MH, NU, WF.

1031   —Sermons preached by. *For S. K., to be sold by Awnsham and John Churchill,* 1692. 8°. T.C.II 423. L, LLP, LW, EN, BQ; CH, CLC, MH, NU.

1031A ——[Anr. ed.] *For Sam. Keble,* 1692. 8°. L, CS, CT, DU, DL; CLC, Y.

1031B ——Second edition. *For Sam. Keble, to be sold by Awnsham and John Churchill,* 1692. 8°. DL; PL.

1032   **Leightonhouse, Walter.** The duty and benefit of frequent communion. *For W. Crook,* 1689. 4°. T.C.II 243. O, WCA; CH, CLC.

1032A —Hope in God. *For Awnsham and John Churchill,* 1695. 4°. CLC, NGT.

1032B —A sermon preached . . . March 6th, 1691/2. *For W. Crook,* 1692. 4°.* T.C.II 400. L, O, C, LLP, WCA; CH, CLC, NU, WF.

1033   —Twelve sermons. *London, for Joh. Knight at Lincoln; and are to be sold by A. and J. Churchill,* 1697. 8°. T.C.III 23. L, LNC, SHR; CH, CLC, MBA, Y.

       Leinsula, Franciscus, *pseud. See* Lisle, Francis.

1034–34A Entries cancelled.

       Leishley, Henry. Coppy of a letter. [n.p.], 1641. *See* Leven, Alexander Leslie, *earl.*

1035   **Leith, Patrick.** Disputatio juridica, de furtis. *Edinburgi, excudebat Jacobus Watson,* 1699. 4°.* ALDIS 3862. E, EN.

1035A **Leithe, Patt.** The noble resolution. 1647. 4°.* CT.

1036   **Leland, John.** Κυκνειον ασμα. Cygnea cantio. *Typis & expensis Johannis Streater,* 1658. 8°. L, O, C, MR, E; BN, CH, CN, MH, WF, Y.

1036A ——[Anr. ed.] —, [1658?]. 8°. MH.

1036B [**Lely, Peter.**] Advertissement du vendu par auction publiq; des desseins italiens. [*London,* 1688?] brs. L.

       LeMaire, Jacques Joseph. Voyage of. 1696. *See* title.

1037   **LeMedde, Theodore.** Elixyrlogia. *Henry Eversden,* 1665. 4°.* L, LCP.

1037A **Lemery, Nicolas.** An appendix to a course of chymistry. *For Walter Kettilby,* 1680. 8°. T.C.I 393. L, OB, LLU, GU; MH, PU, WSG, WU, HC.

1038   —A course of chymistry. *For Walter Kettilby,* 1677. 8°. T.C.I 290. L, O, LCP, CCA, GU, DT; CNM, MB, NC, WU, Y.

1038A ——[Anr. ed.] —, 1680. 8°. LC.

1039   ——Second edition. *By R. N. for Walter Kettilby,* 1686. 8°. T.C.II 151. L, O, C, LLU, DT; CH, IU, MH, NAM, HC.

1040   ——Third edition. —, 1698. 8°. T.C.III 44. L, O, C, GU, DT; CLC, MBC, MH, TU, WF, HC.

1040A ——"Third" edition. *For W. Kettilby, and sold by James Bonwicke,* 1698. 8°. C, CT; IU, PL.

1041   —Modern curiosities. *For Matthew Gilliflower and James Partridge,* 1685. 12°. T.C.II 138. L, O, C; CLC, CRN, NN, WU, Y.

1042   —Pharmacopæia Lemeriana contracta: Lemery's universal pharmacopiœa abridg'd. *For Walter Kettilby,* 1700. 12°. T.C.III 214. L, C, BC.

1043   Lemmata meditationum. *Dvblin, to be sold by Joseph Wilde,* 1672. 8°. DIX 363. L, DT; TO.

1043A **Lemnius, Levinus.** A discourse [*sic*] touching generation. *By John Streater,* 1664. 8°. O.

1043B ——[Anr. ed.] —, 1667. 8°. WF, WSG.

1044   —The secret miracles of nature. *By Jo. Streater, to be sold by Humphrey Moseley, John Sweeting, John Clark, and George Sawbridge,* 1658. fol. L, O, C, E, GU; CH, CLC, NCD, TU, WF, HC.

1044A **LeMort, Jacques.** Pharmacia medico-physica. *Apud Abel Swalle,* 1684. 8°. T.C.II 74. CCA, MAU; WU.

1045   **Le Moyne, Pierre.** The gallery of heroick women. *By R. Norton for Henry Seile,* 1652. fol. L, C, OC, LSD, E; CH, CN, LC, MH, NC, Y.

1046 —Of the art both of writing & judging of history. *For R. Sare and J. Hindmarsh*, 1695. 12°. L, O, C, E, DT; CH, CLC, CN, LC, NP, SE, TU, Y.

1047 **Le Muet, Pierre.** The art of fair building. *For Robert Pricke*, 1670. T.C.I 130. L, C, EN; CH, LC, MU, YBA.

1048 — —Second edition. —, 1675. fol. T.C.I 201. L, C, DCH; CH, CLC, FU, NC, Y.

1049 **Leng, John, bp.** Fides in SS. Trinitatem. [*Cambridge*], 1698. brs. O, C.

1050 —A sermon preach'd . . . 16th day of April. 1699. *Cambridge, at the University Press, for R. Clavel, London, and Edmund Jeffery in Cambridge*, 1699. 4°.* T.C.III 122. L, O, C, BAMB, EC, CD; CH, CN, NP, TO, WF, Y.

Lennox, James Stuart, duke of. *See* Richmond, James Stuart, *duke of.*

1051 **Le Noble, Eustache.** Abra-mulé, or a true history. *For R. Clavel*, 1696. 8°. L, LLP, CS, EN; CH, CN, IU, LC, MH.

1051A [–] The cabinet open'd. *For Richard Baldwin*, 1690. 12°. T.C.II 313. L, CT; CLC, NCD.

1052 [–] The history of Father La Chaise. *By J. Wilde for Henry Rhodes*, 1693. 8°. T.C.II 477. L, O, CT, P, AU; CH, CLC, LC, WF.

1052A [–] The second volume of the History of Father La Chaise. *For John Harris*, 1695. 8°. O; WF.

1053 **[Le Noir, Jean.]** The new politick lights. *By W. Godbid, to be sold by T. Flesher, and by R. Sollers, and by H. Bonwick*, 1678. 8°. T.C.I 294. L, O, CT, P, CD; CH, CLC, NU, WF.

1054 [–] Rome a la mode. *Printed, and are to be sold by H. Bonwicke*, 1678. 8°. T.C.I 321. ENC; NU.

1054A [–] —[Anr. ed.] *Printed and are to be sold by R. Sollers*, 1678. 8°. TU.

1054B [–] —[Anr. ed.] *Printed and are to be sold by T. Flesher*. 1678. DL; WF.

1054C [–] Le voyage de Cromvvel en l'autre monde. Second edition. *Par R. Daniel pour Iean Clark*, 1690. 8°. LG, EN; WG, Y.

Lenox, duke of. *See* Richmond, James Stuart, *duke of.*

1055 **Lens, B.** At the drawing-school. [*n.p.*], 1697. brs. L.

1056 Lent. Here Lent and Shrovetyde, claime. *By M. S. for Thomas Jenner*, 1660[1]. brs. LT.

1056A Lent preachers, appointed by. [*London*, 1679/80.] brs. MH.

1057 Lent preachers appointed to. *London, for Samuel Mearne*, [1680]. brs. MH.

1057A —[Same title.] *London, for Charles Mearne*, [1681]. brs. MH.

1057AB —[Same title.] *For Samuel Mearne*, [1682]. brs. OC.

1057B —[Same title.] [*London*], *for Charles Mearne*, [1684]. brs. O, DCH.

1058 —[Same title.] —, [1685]. brs. O, LG, HH.

1059 —[Same title.] *For Walter Kettilby*, [1685]. brs. O, LG.

1060 —[Same title.] —, 1686. brs. O, LG, HH; CH.

1061 —[Same title.] [*London*], *for Sam. Carr*, 1687. brs. O.

1062 —[Same title.] —, 1688. brs. O.

1063 —[Same title.] —, [1690]. brs. O, OC; PL.

1063A —[Same title.] —, 1692. brs. OC.

1064 Lent-Preachers at court. [*London*], *sold by T. Garthwait*, 1661. brs. LT, LPR.

1064A —[Anr. ed.] —, 1662. brs. CS.

1064B —[Anr. ed.] *For James Collins*, 1675. brs. LNC.

Lenten litany. 1698. *See* Coward, William.

Lenten prologue refus'd. [*n.p.*, 1683.] *See* Shadwell, Thomas.

1065 **Lenthall, Sir John.** A coppy of the speech made by. *By Tho. Leach*, 1659. 4°.* L, O; NU, Y.

1066 Entry cancelled.
—List of all the prisoners. 1653. *See* title.

1066A —To the right honourable the Commons . . . The humble petition of. [*London*, 1658?] brs. MH.

1067 —A representation of the case of. [*London*], *printed*, 2654 [1654]. 4°.* L.

1067A **Lenthall, William, Mr.** Mr. Lenthalls answer, to a paper. [*London*, 1699?] brs. WF.

1068 **Lenthall, William, speaker.** A copie of a letter sent by . . . 28 January 1641[2]. [*London*, 1642.] brs. STEELE 1964. L.

1069 —A copie of a letter sent by Mr. Speaker. *For Robert Hodgekinsonne*, 1642. 4°.* LT, O, CT, EC; CH, CLC, Y.

1070 —A copy of the Speakers letter. *Oxford, by Leonard Lichfield*, 1642. 4°.* MADAN 974. O, LLP, OB; MM, NU, Y.

1071 —A declaration of. *By M. S. for George Whittington*, 1647. 4°.* LT, LG, KEBLE, SP, DT; BN, CLC, MH, TU, WF, Y.

1071A — —[Anr. ed.] *For George Whittington*, 1647. 4°.* L, O, OC, BC; CH, IU, INU, MH, PT, TU.

1072 — —[Anr. ed.] *Oxford, by J. Harris and H. Hills*, 1647. 4°.* MADAN 1949. L, O, MR; CH, WF, Y.

1073 —A letter from the Speaker. *By L. N. and J. F. for E. Husbands and J. Franck, September 8*, 1642. 4°.* L, O, LLU, LNC, YM; CH, WF.

1074 —Master Speakers letter ordered. *For John Franck*, 1641[2]. 4°.* LT, O, CT, SP, YM; CH, CSS, INU, IU, WF.

1075 Entry cancelled.
—Letter sent from the Speakers. 1648. *See* England: Parliament.

1076 —Mr. Speakers letter to the Kings . . . Majestie, Febr. 16, 1641[2]. *For John Thomas*, 1641[2]. 4°.* L, O, LPR, EC, MR; CLC, CSS, PU, WF, Y.

1077 [–] Reasons humbly offer'd why the name of. [*London*, 1660.] brs. L, O.

1078 —Mr. Speakers speech before His Majestie, . . . 2. of December. *For John Greensmith*, 1641. 4°.* L; CN, CSS, MH, WF, Y.

1079 —Mr. Speakers speech before the King . . . July 3. 1641. [*London*], *printed*, 1641. 4°.* LT, O, C, BC, YM; CH, MH, MU, NU, WF, Y. (var.)

1080 — —[Anr. ed., "July the third."] *Printed*, 1641. 4°.* LT, O, C, YM, EN; CH, CN, MH, TU, WF, Y.

1081 —Mr. Speaker's speech in the Lord's House . . . June 22, 1641. [*London*, 1641.] cap., 4°.* L, O; CLC, NP.

1082 —The speech of Master Speaker . . . 2. of December. *By A. N. for Henry Twyford*, 1641. 4°.* OC, MR, DN; CLC, IU, MIU, NP, Y.

1083 — —[Anr. ed.] *For Henry Twyford*, 1641. 4°.* LT; CH, IU, LC, MH, WF, Y.

1084   [–] Mr. Speakers speech on Thursday, the thirteenth of May, 1641. *For Francis Constable*, 1641. 4°.* LT, O, CT, DU, LIU; CSS, IU, MH, NP, WF, Y.

1085   [–] Master Speaker his speech to His Majestie, . . . fifth day of November, 1640. *For William Sheares*, 1660. 4°.* EC, NE; MH, TU, WF, Y.

1086   [–] Mr. Speaker his speech to his Mtie. the thirteenth of May, 1641. [*London*, 1641?] brs. WF.

1087-8   Entries cancelled.
    —Speech which the Speaker made . . . thirteenth day of September. 1660. *See* Grimston, *Sir Harbottle.*
    ——November 9. 1660. *See* Grimston, *Sir Harbottle.*

1089   —Mr. Speakers speech, with His Majesties speech . . . 22. June 1641. [*London*], *printed*, 1641. 4°.* LT, O, C, AN, DT; CH, CN, MH, TU, WF, Y.

1090   —To his very loving friends. The High Sherife. [*London*, 1642.] brs. STEELE 1945. LT.

1091   —The trve coppy of a letter sent by. [*London*], *for Iohn Thomas*, 1641. 4°.* C; CN, MH, Y.

1092   ——[Anr. ed.] [*London*], *printed*, 1641. 4°.* LT, MR; CH, INU, MH, WF.

1093   —A true narrative of. *Printed*, 1660. 4°.* CLC, MH, NU.

1094   —Two letters of note. *For F. Coules*, 1641[2]. 4°.* LT, LLP, EC, MR; CH, WF, Y.

1095   [**Lenton, Francis.**] Characters: or, wit and the world. *For Samuel Speed*, 1663. 12°. L.

1095A   —Lentons characters. *For Richard Harper*, 1653. 12°. OW.

1095B   **Lenton, John.** A consort of musick. [*London*], *R. Brett*, 1692. obl. 4°. L.

1095C   **Lentulus, Publius.** An epistle of Publius Lentulus written to the Senate. [*London*, 1650?] brs. L.

1095D   —Publius Lentulus his news to the Senate of Rome. [*London?* 1700.] brs. HH; Y.

1096   —His report to the Senate of Rome concerning Jesus Christ. *For Francis Smith*, [1677]. brs. L, LL, HH; CH.

1097   **Leo, of St. Mary Magdalen.** Pious instructions, in Meeter. *Printed*, 1693. 4°. O; CH.

1098   Entry cancelled.
    Leo, William. Sermon preached . . . April 21. 1645. *See* Loe, William.
    Leoline and Sydanis. 1642. *See* Kynaston, *Sir Francis.*

1099   **Leon of Modena.** The history of the rites, customes, . . . of the present Jews. *By J. L., to be sold by Jo: Martin; and Jo: Ridley*, 1650. 8°. LT, O, C, EC, RPL, DM; CH, MH.

1099A   ——[Anr. ed.] *For Jo: Martin, and Jo: Ridley*, 1650. 8°. CS, CD; CLC, CN, OHU, WF, Y.

1100   **Leon, Jacob Judah Aryeh.** A relation of the most memorable thinges in the Tabernacle of Moses. *Amsterdam, by Peter Messchaert*, 1675. 4°.* LG, OC, P, SP; MH, OHU, PL, WF, Y.

1100A   [**Léonard, T.**] Memorable accidents, and unheard of transactions. *For Nath. Crouch*, 1693. 12°. T.C.II 409. L, O, CT, A; CN, Y.

1101   **Leonard, William.** The fourth part of The reports. *For William Lee and Abel Roper*, 1675. fol. T.C.I 206. L, O, C, OC, DT; CLC, NCL, PUL.

1102   ——[Anr. ed.] *By the assigns of Richard and Edward Atkins; for Henry Herringman, Ben. Griffin, Charles Harper, and Samuel Keble*, 1687. fol. L, C, LGI, LL; BN, MHL, NCL, PUL, WF, AMB, AVP.

1103   —Reports and cases of lavv. *By Tho. Roycroft, for Nath. Ekins*, 1658. fol. L, O, C, NOT, DT; CH, KT, LC, NCL, YL.

1104   ——Second edition. *By William Rawlins, Samuel Roycroft, and Miles Flesher, assigns of Richard and Edward Atkins. For H. Twyford, H. Herringman, T. Basset, R. Chiswell, B. Griffin, C. Harper, T. Sawbridge, J. Place, and S. Keble*, 1687. fol. T.C.II 199. L, O, C, LG, MC; BN, CH, MHL, NCL, NP, PUL, V, WF, AVP.

1104A   —The second part of reports. *By Tho. Roycroft for Nath. Ekins*, 1659. fol. L, CS, CD, DT; CLC, PUL.

1105   ——[Anr. ed.] *By the assigns of R. and E. Atkins, for R. Chiswell and Tho. Sawbridge*, 1687. fol. L, C, LG, LGI, LL; BN, CH, MHL, NCL, PUL, WF, AVP.

1105A   —The third part of the reports. *By John Streater, to be sold by Henry Twyford, Thomas Dring, John Place, and William Place*, 1663. fol. OC, CS, DT; CLC, PUL.

1106   ——[Anr. ed.] *By the assigns of Richard and Edward Atkins; for Henry Twyford, Thomas Basset, William Rawlins, and John Place*, 1686. fol. L, O, C, LGI, CD; BN, CH, MHL, NCL, PUL, WF, AVP.

1107   Entry cancelled.
    Leopold, *Duke of Albany*. Act by his Royal Highness. Edinburgh, 1681. *See* Scotland: Privy Council.

1108   **Leopold I, *emperor of Germany*.** The Emperors answer to the French King's manifesto. *For Brabazon Aylmer*, 1688. 4°.* L, O, C, MR, DT; CH, CN, MH, NU, TU, WF, Y.

1108A   —Articles of peace between the Emperour . . . and France, . . . Reswick. *Printed, and are to be sold by E. Whitlock*, 1697. 4°.* INU, MH, WF, Y.

1108B   —The chief articles of the peace . . . France. *Edinburgh, by the heirs and successors of Andrew Anderson*, 1697. brs. ALDIS 3657.5. EN; CSS.

1109   —The Emperours concessions. colop: *For Richard Baldwin*, 1681. brs. L; MBA, MH.

1110   —The Emperor's letter to James II. 6th of February 1688/9. [*London*, 1688/9.] brs. L, O, OC, HH, EN.

1110A   —The Emperor's letter to James 2d. . . . 9 of April, 1689. [*London*, 1689]. brs. L; MM.

1111   —The Emperor's letter to his own subjects. colop: *For R. Clavel*, 1689. cap., 4°.* T.C.II 276. L, MR, WCA; CH, LC, MH, WF, Y.

1111A   —His Imperial Majesty's letter to the Pope. *For Richard Baldwin*, 1691. brs. CLC, CN.

1112   ——[Anr. ed.] *Edinburgh, re-printed by the heir of A. Anderson*, 1692. brs. ALDIS 3227. HH, EN.

1112A   —The Emperors letter to William III. colop: [*London*], *for Robert Clavel*, 1689. brs. C, WCA; CLC, CN, NCD.

1113   —A letter written by the Emperor to the late King James. *For Ric. Chiswell*, 1689. 4°.* T.C.II 255. L, O, CT, EN, DT; CH, CN, MH, RPJ, TU, WF, Y.

1113A   —The Emperor's new declaration. *For Richard Baldwin*, 1689. brs. C, LPR.

1114   —A proclamation: being His Imperial Majesty's Act of oblivion. *For James Partridge*, 1684. brs. L, O, LG; CH.

1114A —A true copy of the imperial decree. colop: *By John Wallis*, 1688. brs. L; CH, CN.

1115   [**Le Pays, René.**] The drudge. *For Henry Herringman*, 1673. 8°. T.C.I 119. L, O, CT, LLU, E; CH, CN, MH, WF, Y.

1116   **Le Prestre de Vauban, Sébastien.** The new method of fortification. *For Abel Swall*, 1691. 8°. T.C.II 360. L, O, C, OC, NE; CLC, CN, MH, MU, U. ALBERTA, Y.

1116A ——Second edition. —, *sold by W. Freeman*, 1693. 8°. T.C.II 444. L, O, WCA, GU; CH, LC, MH, MIU, WF.

1117   **L'Epy, Heliogenes de.** A voyage into Tartary. *By T. Hodgkin, to be sold by Randal Taylor*, 1689. 12°. T.C.II 238. L, O, C, LLU, EN; BN, CLC, MIU, SE, WF.

1117A **Le Ragois, Claude.** Instruction sur l'histoire de France. *A Londres, chez Pierre de Varennes*, 1694. 12°. UCLA.

1118   **Le Roy *called des Brosses*, Gabriel.** Homilie sur l'Evangile. *Imprime a Londres, par Tho. Newcomen*, 1654. 8°.* LT.

1119   No entry.

1120   [**Leslie, Charles.**] An answer to a book intituled The state of the Protestants. *Printed*, 1692. 4°. L, C, OM, EN, DT; CH, IU, LC, NU, TU, Y.

1120A —Mr. Leslie's answer to the remarks. [*London?* 1697.] cap., 4°.* CT.

       [–] Axe laid to the root. 1685. See Humfrey, John.

1121   [–] A brief account of the Socinian trinity. *For Charles Brome*, 1695. 8°.* T.C.II 537. L, O, C, EN, DT; CLC, NU, ZWT.

1122   Entry cancelled.

       [–] —[Anr. ed.] 1700. See —Discourse; shewing. 1700.

1123   [–] The case of the regale and of the pontificat stated. [*Oxford?*], *New-Years-day.* 1700. 12°. L, O, C, ENC, DT; CH, CN, LC, MH, NU, Y.

1124   [–] The charge of Socinianism against Dr. Tillotson. *Edenbvrgh: printed* 1695. 4°.* ALDIS 3449. L, O, C, CT, MR, EN; CH, MH, NC, MU, WF, Y.

1125   [–] Considerations of importance to Ireland. [*London*], *printed* 1698. 4°.* C, LUG, LSD, MR.

1126   [–] A defence of a book intituled, the snake in the grass. *By M. Bennet, for C. Brome, W. Keblewhite. And Geo. Strahan*, 1700. 8°. T.C.III 159. L, O, CT, E, DT; CH, CN, MH, NU, WF, Y.

       [–] Delenda Carthago. [n.p.], 1694. See Shaftesbury, Anthony Ashley Cooper, *earl of*.

1127   No entry.

1128   [–] A discourse proving the divine institution. *For C. Brome, W. Keblewhite, and H. Hindmarsh*, 1697. 4°. T.C.II 599. L, O, C, AN, DT; CLC, CN, LC, MH, NU, PSC, Y.

1129   No entry.

1130   [–] A discourse; shewing, who they are that are now qualify'd to administer baptism. *For C. Brome; W. Keblewhite; and H. Hindmarsh*, 1698. 4°. T.C.III 34. L, O, CT, EN, DT; CLC, MH, NU, TSM, WF, Y.

1131   [–] —[Anr. ed.] *By W. Redmayne for C. Brome, W. Keblewhite, and G. Strachan*, 1700. 8°. O, OC, BLH; CH, CN, MH, NU, PH.

1132   [–] An essay concerning the divine right of tythes. *For C. Brome, W. Keblewhite; E. Pool, and G. Strahan*, 1700. 8°. T.C.III 181. L, O, C, BSE, DT; CLC, LC, MHL, MU, NU, TU, Y.

1133   [–] Five discourses, . . . viz. on water-baptism. *For C. Brome, W. Keblewhite, and G. Strahan*, 1700. 8°. T.C.III 181. L, O, C, YM, DT; CH, MH, MU, NU, WF, Y.

1134   [–] Gallienus redivivus, or, murther will out. *Printed at Edinburgh*, 1695. 4°.* ALDIS 3462. L, O, C, MR, EN; CH, CN, MH, NU, TU, WF, Y.

1134A [–] —[Anr. ed.] *Edinburgh, printed*, 1695. 4°.* ALDIS 3463. O, DU, MR, D, EN; IU, MM, Y.

1135   [–] The history of sin and heresie attempted. *For H. Hindmarsh*, 1698. 4°. L, O, C, EN, DT; CH, CN, MU, NU, WF, Y.

1136   [–] A letter of advice to a friend, upon the modern argument . . . fornication. *For William Keblewhite*, 1696. 4°.* T.C.II 598. L, O, OC, CT, MR, NE; PL, WF, Y.

1137   [–] Liturgy's vindicated. *For C. Brome*, 1700. 8°. T.C.III 181. LCL; NU.

1138   [–] Now or never. [*London*, 1696.] cap., 4°.* O, LL, OC, MR, EN; CH, NU, Y.

1139   Entry cancelled.

       [–] Parallel between the faith. 1700. *See title*.

1140   [–] Primitive heresie revived. *For C. Brome, W. Keblewhite. And H. Hindmarsh*, 1698. 4°.* T.C.III 36. L, O, C, EN, DT; CH, MH, MU, NU, WF, Y, AVP. (var.)

1141   Entry cancelled.

       [–] —Second edition. 1700. See —Discourse; shewing. 1700; —Five discourses, 1700.

1142   [–] Querela temporum: or, the danger of the Church of England. [*London*, 1694.] cap., 4°.* L, C, LLP, OC, MR; CH, WF.

1143   [–] —[Anr. ed.] colop: *Printed*, 1695. 4°.* L, O, CS, MR, YM; CH, CLC, NC, NP, NU.

1144   Entry cancelled.

       [–] Reflections upon a libel. 1696. *See title*.

1145   [–] A religious conference between a minister and parishioner. *For Awnsham and John Churchill*, 1696. 4°.* T.C.III I 1. L, O, CT, DT.

1146   [–] —[Anr. ed.] *For Charles Brome*, 1698. 4°. T.C.III 91. L, O, LF, CT, DT; CLC, CN, NHC, NU, WF.

1147   [–] Remarks on some late sermons. [*London*, 1695.] 4°. L, O, CT, MR, EN, DT; CN, MB, MH, TSM, WF.

1148   [–] —Second edition. *Printed*, 1695. 4°. L, O, CT, BP, YM, D; CH, MH, NP, NU, TU, WF, Y.

1149   [–] Satan dis-rob'd from his diguise of light. *For C. Brome; and H. Hindmarsh*, 1697. 4°. O, LCL; RPJ.

1149A [–] —[Anr. ed.] *For C. Brome, W. Keblewhite, and H. Hindmarsh*, 1697. 4°. C, OC, CT, LSD, MR; CH, CN, MH, PHS, WF.

1150   [–] —[Anr. ed.] —, 1698. 4°. T.C.II 599. L, LF, CT, LSD, GU; IU, MH, PH, PSC.

1151   [–] —Second edition. —, 1698. 4°. T.C.III 103. L, O, C, EN, DT; CH, LC, MH, RPJ, TU, Y.

1152 [-] A short and easie method with the Deists. *By W.*
      Onley, for H. Hindmarsh, 1698. 8°.* L, LL, OC, CT, LSD;
      MH, NN, TU.

1153 [-] —[Anr. ed.] *London, reprinted Edinburgh, John Reid,*
      1698. 8°.* ALDIS 3803. EN; CDA.

1154 [-] —Second edition. *For C. Brome, W. Keblewhite, E.*
      Poole, and George Strahan, 1699. 12°. T.C.III 128. L, O,
      LW, CS, SC, DT; CLC, NU, OCI, TSM, Y.

1154A [-] —[Anr. ed.] *For C. Brome, H. Hindmarsh, and E.*
      Poole, 1699. 12°. OC; CH.

1154B ——"Second" edition. *For C. Brome, W. Keblewhite,*
      H. Hindmarsh, and E. Poole. 1699. 12°. CP, DUS, MR, CD;
      MH, OHU, OSU, WF.

1155 [-] —[Anr. ed.] *Dublin, re-printed, and sold by Andrew*
      Crook, 1699. 8°.* DIX 311. CD, DI, DK.

1156 [-] The snake in the grass: or, Satan. *For Charles Brome,*
      1696. 8°. T.C.II 577. L, O, C, BC, YM; CH, MH, RPJ, WF, Y.

1157 [-] —Second edition. —, 1697. T.C.III 17. L, O, CS, E, DT;
      CH, CN, LC, MH, NU, PH, V.

1158 [-] —Third edition. —, 1698. 8°. T.C.III 59. L, O, C, GM,
      DT; CH, LC, MU, NU, PH, TU, Y.

1159 [-] Some seasonable reflections upon the Quakers. *For*
      Charles Brome, 1697. 4°.* T.C.III 12. L, O, C, LF, CT, GM;
      CLC, PH, PL, RPJ, Y.

1160 [-] Tempora mutantur. Or, the great change. colop:
      [*London*], *printed,* 1694. 4°.* L, O, C, MR, EN; CH, INU, TU.

      Leslie, David. *See* Newark, David Leslie, *baron.*

      Leslie, George. *See* Lesly, George.

1161 **Leslie, Henry, *bp*.** The blessing of Ivdah explained.
      Oxford, by Leonard Lichfield, 1644. 4°.* MADAN 1604.
      L, O, C, LLP, OM, MR, DT; CB.

1162 —A discourse of praying. *For John Crooke,* 1660. 4°.* LT,
      OCC, DN, DT; IU.

1163 —The martyrdome of King Charles. *Hage, by Samuel*
      Broun, 1649. 4°.* LT, O, C, LSC, AN; CH, CLC, CN, CSS,
      WF.

1164 [-] —[Anr. ed.] —, 1649. 4°.* L, O, C, DU, DT; BN, CN,
      IU, MH, Y.

1165 ——[Anr. ed.] *Printed at the Hague, by Samuel Brown,*
      and re-printed at London, 1649. 4°.* L, O, CT, EN, DT;
      CH, CN, MH, MIU, TU, WF.

1166 ——[Anr. ed., "Charls."] *Printed at the Hage 1649, and*
      reprinted at London by W. Godbid, 1660. 4°.* LT, OU,
      WCA; CB, CH, CLC.

1167 [-] A sermon preached . . . ninth of Feb. *Oxford, by*
      Leonard Lichfield, 1643. 4°.* MADAN 1546. LT, O, C,
      LLP, DT; CH, CN, MH, TU, WF, Y.

1168 —A sermon preached . . . the 4th of July, 1695. *Dublin,*
      for Matthew Gunne, 1695. 4°.* DIX 271. DT.

1169 **Leslie, James.** Ο αστηρ ορθρινος απολαμπει —seu
      natalis Domini. *Aberdoniis, F. V.,* 1661. 4°.* ALDIS
      1703. C, D, EN, AU, SA; INU.

1170 **Leslie, John, *bp*.** Articles to be enquired of. *Dublin,*
      by John Crooke, to be sold by Samuel Dancer, 1667. 4°.*
      DIX 134. DT.

1170A —De origine moribus. *Excusum pro Roberto Boulter,* 1677.
      4°. T.C.I 284. WF.

1171 **Leslie, John, *minister*.** The parasynagogue para-
      gorized. *By Thomas Maxey,* 1655. 12°. L, LSC, LW, CS;
      MH, NU.

1172 **Leslie, John, *fl. 1675*.** A true and faithful accompt of
      the most material passages of a dispute. 8°. *Printed,*
      1675. EN; PH, PHS.

1173 [**Leslie, William Lewis.**] The idæa of a perfect prin-
      cesse. *Paris,* 1661. 8°. L, CT, AN, DU, GM, EN; CLC, CN,
      TU, WF, Y.

1174 **Lesly, George.** Divine dialogues. *For Charles Smith,*
      1678. 8°. T.C.I 309. LW, E; IU.

1175 ——Second edition. *For Nicholas Woolfe,* 1684. 8°.
      T.C.II 64. L; CH, CU, MH, WF, Y.

1176 —Israel's troubles and triumph. *For the author, and sold by*
      Nicholas Woolf, 1699. 8°. L, LCL, LLU, EN; CN, MH, Y.

1177 —Joseph reviv'd. *For the author, and are to be sold by*
      Charles Smith, 1676. T.C.I 236. C, LW, GM; CH.

1177A ——[Anr. ed.] —, 1678. 8°. CH, IU.

1178 —A sermon preached March 12. 1689. *For Benjamin*
      Cox, 1690. 4°.* L; CLC.

1178A —The universal medicine: a sermon. *For C. Smith,* 1678.
      8°. T.C.I 309. LW.

1179 ——Second edition. *For Nicholas Woolfe,* 1684. 8°.
      T.C.II 64. L.

1179A **Lessius, Leonard.** A consultation about religion.
      Printed 1693. 4°. C, LLL; CN, NU, TU.

1180 —Sir Walter Rawleigh's ghost. *By Tho. Newcomb, for*
      John Holden, 1651. 12°. LT, O, C, EN, DT; CH, IU, MH,
      NU, WF, Y.

1181 —The temperate man. *By J. R. for John Starkey,* 1678.
      8°. T.C.I 322. L, C, LSC, DC, LLU, D; CH, CN, MH, WF, Y.

      Lesson for all. [1670.] *See* C., J.

1182 Lessons for the recorder. [*London?* 1680.] brs. L.

1183 **L'Estrange, Hamon.** The alliance of divine offices. *For*
      Henry Broom, 1659. fol. L, O, CE, DL, DT; BN, CH, CN,
      TU, WF, Y.

1184 ——Second edition. *For Charles Brome,* 1690. fol. T.C.II
      306. L, O, C, NPL, ENC; CH, CLC, IU, MH, NP, WF.

1185 ——Third edition. —, 1699. fol. T.C.III 115. L, O, LCL,
      DU, EN; CN, CSU, TSM, Y, MOORE.

1186 —Americans no Iewes. *By W. W. for Henry Seile,* 1652.
      4°. LT, O, C, OCC, LNC; CH, CN, LC, MH, Y.

1187 —An answer to the Marques of Worcester's last paper.
      By Robert Wood for Henry Seile, 1651. 8°. LT, O, C, DU,
      DT; CH, CU, NU, TU, WF, Y.

1188 —Gods Sabbath ⎱before⎰ the law. *Cambridge, by Roger*
                      ⎰under ⎰
      Daniel, 1641. 4°. LT, O, C, EN, CD; CH, CN, MH, NU, WF, Y.

      [-] Life and reigne of King Charls. 1651. *See* title.

1188A [-] The observator observ'd. *By T. C. for Edw. Dod,*
      1656. fol. O, DU, DT; MBP, NIC, WF, Y.

1189 [-] The reign of King Charles. *By E. C. for Edward Dod,*
      and Henry Seile the younger, 1655. fol. L, O, CT, E, DT;
      BN, CH, LC, MH, MU, Y.

1190 [-] —Second edition. *By F. L. and J. G. for Hen. Seile*
      senior & junior and Edw. Dod, 1656. L, O, C, EN, DT; BN,
      CH, CN, LC, MBP, MH, TO, TU.

1190A [–] —[Anr. ed.] *By F. L. and J. G. for Edward Dod, and Henry Seile the younger, 1656.* fol. PU, Y.

1191 [–] Smectymnuo-mastix: or, short animadversions. *By Robert Wood for Henry Seile, 1651.* 4°.* LT, O, DU; CLC, IU, NU.

1192 **L'Estrange, *Sir* Roger.** The accompt clear'd. *For Joanna Brome, 1682.* 4°.* T.C.I 512. L, O, C, DUS, EN; CH, CN, MHL, NU, PL, WF, Y.

1193 [–] An account of the growth of knavery. *By H. H. for Henry Brome, 1678.* T.C.I 313. L, O, C, MR, DT; BN, CH, CU, MH, TU, WF, Y.

1194 ——Second edition. *By T. B. for Henry Brome, 1681.* 4°.* L, O, C, EN, DT; CH, CN, MH, NU, TU, WF.

1195 —An answer to a Letter to a dissenter. *For R. Sare, 1687.* 4°. T.C.II 209. L, O, C, EN, DT; BN, CH, CN, MH, WF, Y.

1196 [–] —[Same title.] *Printed anno 1687.* 4°.* L, OB, OC, LIU; CH, MIU, NN, WF.

1197 [–] An answer to The appeal from the country to the city. *By M. C. for Henry Brome, 1679.* 4°.* T.C.I 374. L, O, C, EN, DT; CH, CN, MU, NU, TU, WF, Y.

1198 ——[Anr. ed.] *By T. B. for Henry Brome, 1681.* 4°.* L, O, LG, E, DT; CH, CN, MH, NU, TU, WF.

1199 ——[Anr. ed.] —, *1684.* 4°.* L.

1200 —L'Estrange his apology: with a short view. *For Henry Brome, 1660.* 4°. LT, O, CT, DC, DT; BN, CLC, MH, NU, WF, Y.

1201 —L'Estrange his appeale from the Covrt Martiall. *[London], printed, 1647.* 4°.* LT, LCL, OC, LLU, DT; CH.

1202 —L'Estrange his appeal humbly submitted. *For Henry Brome, 1681.* 4°.* T.C.I 420. L, O, C, EN, DT; CH, CN, MH, NU, TU, WF, Y.

[–] Appeale in the case. [n.p.], 1660. *See* Peirce, *Sir* Edmond.

1203 [–] A brief history of the times. *For Charles Brome, 1687–88.* 3v. 8°. T.C.II 193. L, O, C, DU, DT; BN, CH, CN, LC, NC, TU, Y.

1203A [–] —[Anr. ed.] *By J. Bennet, for Charles Brome, 1687.* fol.* CCA, CT, GC, NE, SP; CLC, CN, MH, PU, WF.

1204 —L'Estrange's case in a civil dialogue. *For H. Brome, 1680.* 4°.* L, O, C, MR, EN; BN, CH, CN, LC, MH, Y. (var.)

1205 ——Second edition. —, *1680.* 4°.* L, O, C, EN, DT; IU, LC, MH, TU, WF, Y.

1206 [–] The case put, concerning the succession. *By M. Clark, for Henry Brome, 1679.* 4°.* T.C.I 374. L, O, C, EN, DT; CH, IU, MH, NC, TU, WF, Y.

1207 [–] —Second edition. *By M. C. for Henry Brome, 1679.* 4°.* T.C.I 399. L, O, C, DU, LSD; CH, MH, MU, NU, WF, Y.

1208 ——Third edition. *For H. Brome, 1680.* 4°.* T.C.I 420. L, O, C, E, DT; CH, CN, MH, NU, TU, WF.

1209 —The casuist uncas'd. Second edition. *For H. Brome, 1680.* 4°. L, O, C, EN, DT; CH, MH, NC, TU, WF, Y.

1210 ——[Anr. ed.] *For Henry Brome, 1681.* 4°. L, O, C, MR, YM; CH, CN, MH, NU, TU, Y.

1211 [–] A caveat to the Cavaliers. *For Henry Brome, 1661.* 4°.* L, O, CT, LNC, DT; BN, CH, MH, NC, NU, WF.

1212 [–] —Second edition. —, *August the 13. 1661.* 8°. L, O, OC; CLC, TO, WF, Y.

1213 [–] —Third edition. —, *August the 21. 1661.* 8°. L, OC, LLU, LSD, A; CLC, IU, MH.

1214 [–] —Fourth edition. —, *September the 18th. 1661.* 8°. L, O, CT, YM, ENC; CH, MH, MIU, NU, WF, Y.

1215 [–] The character of a Papist in masquerade. *For H. Brome, 1681.* 4°. T.C.I 443. L, O, C, EN, DT; BN, CH, CN, MH, WF, Y.

1216 [–] Citt and Bumpkin. In a dialogue. *For Henry Brome, 1680.* 4°.* T.C.I 396. L, O, C, LNC, DU; CH, CN, MH, NU, WF, Y. (var.)

1217 [–] —Second edition. —, *1680.* 4°.* L, LG; MH, MIU.

1218 [–] —Third edition. —, *1680.* 4°.* L, O, C, BC, EN; CH, MH, MM, WF.

1219 [–] —Fourth edition. —, *1680.* 4°.* T.C.I 409. L, O, C, E, DT; CSS, MBP, MH, MU, NC, TU, Y. (var.)

1220 [–] — . . . the first part. Fifth edition. *For Joanna Brome, 1681.* 4°.* T.C.I 478. L, O, CT, EN, DT; KU, NGT, TO, ZWT.

1221 [–] Citt and Bumpkin. Or, a learned discourse . . . second part. *For Henry Brome, 1680.* 4°.* T.C.I 396. L, O, C, SP, E; CH, IU, MH, NU, PL, Y.

1222 [–] —Second edition. —, *1680.* 4°.* L, O, OB, OC, EN; CH, MH, NC, TU, WF, Y.

1223 [–] —Third edition. —, *1680.* 4°.* T.C.I 409. L, O, C, BC, WCA, CD; IU, MH, MU, TU, Y.

1224 [–] —Fourth edition. *For Joanna Brome, 1681.* 4°.* T.C.I 478. L, O, CT, EN; CLC, NGT, ZWT.

1225 —A collection of several tracts in quarto. *By T. B. for Henry Brome, 1681.* 4°. C, CS, NPL; CH, CLC, MBA, NP.

1225AA ——[Anr. ed.] *For Henry Brome, 1681.* 4°. CD.

1225A ——[Anr. ed.] *For Joanna Brome, 1682.* 4°. T.C.I 424. **DT**; NU.

1226 [–] The committee: or, Popery in masquerade. *By Mary Clark for Henry Brome, 1680.* brs. T.C.I 398. L, O, OC, OP; CH, MH.

1226A [–] —[Anr. ed.] *For Henry Brome, 1680.* brs. EC.

1227 [–] —[Anr. ed.] *By Mary Clarke, for Henry Brome, 1681.* brs. L; TU, WF, ZWT.

1227A [–] —[Anr. ed.] *[London, 1681?]* brs. O.

1228 [–] A compendious history of the most remarkable passages of the last fourteen years. *By A. Godbid, and J. Playford, and are sold by S. Neale, 1680.* 8°. T.C.I 382. L, O, C, DU, LLU; CH, CN, MH, WF, Y.

1229 —Considerations and proposals in order to the regulation of the press. *By A. C. June 3d. 1663.* 4°.* L, O, CT, MR, ES; CH, CN, NR, NU, TU, Y.

1230 [–] Considerations upon a printed sheet. *By T. B. for Joanna Brome, 1683.* 4°. L, O, C, EN, DT; CH, CN, MH, TU, WF, Y.

1231 [–] —[Anr. ed.] *Edinburgh, re-printed by the heir of Andrew Anderson, 1683.* 4°.* ALDIS 2374. EN; IU, PU, TO, Y.

1232 [–] —Third edition. *By T. B. for Joanna Brome, 1683.* 4°. L, O, CCA, MR, DT; IU, MH, MM, NP, TSM, WF.

1233 [–] —Fourth edition. —, *1683.* 4°. L, C, OU, BAMB, LSD, EN; CH, CN, MBA, TU, Y.

1234 Entry cancelled.

[–] Crack upon crack. [n.p., 1680.] *See title.*

1235   [–] A dialogue between Sir R. L. and T. O. D. [Oates]. *For R. Waston*, 1689. 4°.* L, O, C, LG, DC; CH, CU, Y.

1235A [–] A dialogue between Tom and Dick. *[London], printed* 1680. 4°.* T.C.I 422. L, O, CT, EN; CH, MBP, MH, WF, Y.

1236   —A discourse of the fishery. *For Henry Brome*, 1674. 4°.* T.C.I 163. L, O, C, SP, EN; CH, CN, MH, NC, WF, Y.

1237   ——[Anr. ed.] *For Charles Brome*, 1695. 8°.* L, LUG, D, ES; BN, CLC, MH, NC, WF, Y.

1238   —Discovery upon discovery. *For Henry Brome*, 1680. 4°.* T.C.I 397. L, O, C, DU, MR; BN, CH, CN, MH, NU, TU, Y. (var.)

1239   ——Second edition. —, 1680. 4°.* L, O, CT, EN, DT; CLC, MH, MU, NC, TU, WF, Y.

1240   —The dissenter's sayings. *For Henry Brome*, 1681. 4°. T.C.I 443. L, O, C, LIU, BLH; CH, IU, MH, NC, TU, WF, Y.

1241   ——Second edition. —, 1681. 4°. L, O, C, DU, DT; CLC, CN, MH, TU, WF, Y, AVP.

1242   ——Third edition. *For Joanna Brome*, 1681. 4°. T.C.I 466. L, O, C, EN, DT; CH, CN, MBP, NF, NU, VC.

1243   ——Fourth edition. —, 1683. 4°. L, C, ORP, EN, DT; IU, MH, MM, NPT, NU.

1244   ——[Anr. ed.] *For Charles Brome*, 1685. 4°. L, C, LLL; CLC, CN, MB, NU, WF, Y.

1245   ——The second part. *For Joanna Brome*, 1681. 4°. T.C.I 464. L, O, C, EN, DT; CH, MH, MU, NU, TU, WF, Y, AVP.

1246   ———Second edition. —, 1681. 4°. L, O, C, EN, DT; CH, CN, MBP, MH, NU, TU, Y.

1246A [–] Double your guards. *Printed* 1660. 4°. LT, O, OC; CN, ZWT.

1246B [–] The engagement and remonstrance of the city of London. *[London*, 1659.] brs. LT, O, LG, OC; CH.

1247   —Fables and storyes moralized. *By R. Sare*, 1699. fol. T.C.III 159. L, C, LSD, EN, DT; CH, CN, LC, MH, NP, TU, Y.

1247A [–] The fanatique powder-plot. *[London*, 1660.] brs. LT, O, LS; MH, MIU, Y.

1247B [–] The final protest, and sense of the citie. *[London*, 1659.] brs. LT, O, LG; CH, MH.

1247C [–]—[Anr. ed., "sence."] *[London*, 1659.] brs. MH.

1247D [–] For His Excellency Gen. Monck. *Printed at Oxford for N. O.*, 1660. brs. MADAN 2508. L, OC, LS; CH, MH.

1248   [–] The free-born subject. *For Henry Brome*, 1679. 4°.* L, O, C, LIU, MR; CH, MH, MU, NU, TU, WF, Y.

1249   ——Second edition. —, 1680. 4°.* T.C.I 399. L, O, C, DU, EN, CD; CH, CN, MBP, MH, MU, NU, TU.

1250   ——Third edition. —, 1681. 4°.* L, LG, LLL, OB, DT; CDA, NU, TO, WF, Y.

1250A [–]—[Anr. ed.] *For B.C.*, 1688. 4°.* L, LSD; TU.

1250B [–] A free Parliament proposed. *[London*, 1660.] brs. LT, O, LG, OC.

1251   [–] A further discovery of the plot, drawn from . . . Oates. *For Henry Brome*, 1680. fol.* C, OC, MR, SA; CH, CLC, MH, MM, PU.

1252   [–] A further discovery of the plot: dedicated to . . . Oates. —, 1680. 4°.* L, O, C, MR, EN; CH, CN, MH, TU, WF, Y.

1253   ——Second edition. —, 1680. 4°.* L, O, C, LCL, DC; BN, CH, MH, MIU, NCD, TU.

1254   —Third edition. —, 1680. 4°.* T.C.I 399. L, O, LW, CJ, CD; CB, MBP, NC, TU, Y. (var.)

1254A ——[Anr. ed.] *Reprinted Edinburgh, by the heir of Andrew Anderson*, 1680. fol. ALDIS 2199. EN.

1255   —Fourth edition. *For Henry Brome*, 1681. 4°.* L, C, E, EN, DT; CH, CN, NP, TU, Y.

1255A [–] Goodman Country: To his Worship the City of London. colop: *[London], by M. Clark for Walter Kettilby*, 1680. cap., fol.* LLU, MR, SP, DT; CH, CLC.

1255B [–]—[Anr. ed.] *[London*, 1680.] fol.* L, LG, OC, CS, DU; CB, CN, CU, LC, MH, Y. (var.)

1256   [–] The growth of knavery and Popery. *For Henry Brome*, 1678. 4°. T.C.I 366. L, O, DU, NE, EN; CH, Y.

1257   —Histoire de la conspiration. *Chés Richard Bentley, & chés Marc Pardoe*, 1679. sixes. C, CT, LLU; CLC, MH.

1258   [–] The history of the plot. *For Richard Tonson*, 1679. fol. T.C.I 369. L, O, C, EN, DT; CH, CN, MHL, NU, WF, Y.

1259   ——Second edition. *For Henry Brome, and Richard Tonson*, 1680. fol. T.C.I 410. L, CS; CLC, MM, NU.

1259A [–]—[Anr. ed.] *For M. R.*, 1689. *. LLP.

1260   —The holy cheat. Fourth edition. *Printed* 1662. *And now reprinted for Joanna Brome*, 1682. 4°. T.C.I 479. L, O, C, YM, EN; CH, CN, MH, NU, TU, WF, Y.

1260A [–]—[Anr. ed.] *For B. C.*, 1688. 4°. DT; Y.

1261   —Interest mistaken. *For Henry Brome*, 1661. 4°. O, C, LLP, LLU, LSD; BN, CLC, MH, NC, NU, WF, Y.

1262   ——Second edition. —, 1661. 8°. L, O, LCL, DC, ENC; CLC, MIU, TO, WF, Y.

1263   ——Third edition. —, 1662. 8°. L, C, OC, EN, DT; CH, IU, LC, MH, NU, Y.

1264   ——Fourth edition. —, 1662. 8°. L, O; CLC, IU, NC, Y.

1265   Entry cancelled.
       ——"Fourth" edition. 1682. *See* —Holy cheat.
       [–] Judgement of an anonymous. 1684. *See* Hickes, George.

1266   [–] The lawyer outlaw'd. *[London], by N. T. for the author*, 1683. 4°.* L, O, C, EN, DT; CH, CN, MH, NU, WF, Y.

1266A [–]—[Anr. ed.] *[London], by N. T.*, 1683. 4°.* LG, LW; CH, MH, Y.

1266B [–]—[Anr. ed.] *Printed* 1683. 4°.* CCA; CH.

1267   —L'Estrange no Papist: in answer. *By T. B. for H. Brome*, 1681. 4°.* T.C.I 430. L, O, C, EN, DT; CH, CN, MH, NU, TU, WF, Y. (var.)

1267A–68 Entries cancelled.
       [–] L'Estrange no Papist. 1681. *See title.*

1269   [–] A letter out of Scotland. colop: *[London], for N. F.*, 1681. cap., fol.* L, O, LG, DU, DT; CH, CN, MBA, MH, Y.

1270   —A memento: directed . . . The first part. *For Henry Brome, Aprill the* 11. 1662. 4°. L, O, C, DU, YM; CH, CN, MH, NU, WF, Y.

1271   —A memento. Treating, of the rise, progress, and remedies of seditions. Second edition. *[London], printed* 1642, *and now reprinted for Joanna Brome*, 1682. 4°. T.C.I 480. L, O, C, EN, BLH; CH, CU, MH, NU, WF, Y.

1272   —A modest plea both for the caveat. *Aug.* 28. 1661. *For Henry Brome*. 8°.* L, O, OC, LSD, A; CLC, IU, WF, ZAP.

1273 — —Second edition. *For Henry Brome, September 7. 1661.* 8°.* L, O, LVF, CT, LLU, NOT; CH, CN, MH, MIU, NU, Y.

1274 — —Third edition. *For Henry Brome, 1662.* 8°. L, O, EN, ENC; CLC, IU, MIU, NC, NIC.

1275 —L'Estrange's narrative of the plot. *By J. B. for Hen. Brome, 1680.* 4°.* T.C.I 404. L, O, C, LIU, EN; BN, CH, CN, MBP, MH, NC, TU, WF, Y.

1276 — —Second edition. —, *1680.* 4°.* L, O, C, OC, DT; CH, MU, PL, TU, Y.

1277 — —Third edition. —, *1680.* 4°.* T.C.I 424. L, O, C, EN, DT; CH, CN, MH, MIU, TU, Y.

1277A [–] A necessary and seasonable caution. [*London, 1660.*] brs. LT, LS.

1278 Entry cancelled. Serial.

1279 [–] No blinde guides. *For Henry Broome April 20, 1660.* 4°.* L, O, C, EN, DT; BN, CH, CN, MH, TU, WF, Y.

1279A [–] No fool to the old fool. [*London, 1659/60.*] brs. LT, O, OC; MH, MIU, Y.

1280 —Le non-conformiste Anglois dans ses écris. *Pour la Veuve du Henry Brome, 1683.* 4°. T.C.II 30. L, O, C, OC, LLU; BN, CH, Y.

1281 —Notes upon Stephen College. *For Joanna Brome, 1681.* 4°. T.C.I 464. L, O, CT, LSD, EN; CH, IU, MH, NU, TU, WF, Y.

1282 — —Second edition. —, *1681.* 4°. L, O, C, E, DT; BN, CLC, CN, MH, WF, Y.

1283 [–] The Observator defended. *For Charles Brome, 1685.* 4°.* L, O, C, EN, DT; CH, CU, MH, NC, WF, Y.

1283A [–] The Observator's observation how narrowly he scap'd hanging. colop: *Dublin. Reprinted by Andrew Crook and Samuel Helsham; sold by William Weston,* [*1685*]. cap., 4°.* L.

1283B [–] The Observator's observations upon the bill of exclusion. colop: *Dublin. Reprinted by Andrew Crook and Samuel Helsham; sold by William Weston,* [*1685*]. cap., 4°.* L, LIU.

1283C [–] Otes his case, character, person and plot. colop: *Dublin, reprinted for William Weston,* [*1685*]. cap., 4°.* L, LIU.

1284 [–] The parallel; or, an an [*sic*] account. *For Henry Brome, 1679.* fol.* T.C.I 374. L, O, CT, BP, LNC; CH, CN, LC, MH, NU, TU, Y.

1284A [–] Peace to the nation. [*London, 1660.*] brs. LT; MH, MIU.

1284B [–] Physician cure thy self. *For H. B., 1660.* 4°.* LT, O, C, CT, DC, LIU; CH, INU, NP, NU, WF, HC.

1285 [–] A plea for limited monarchy. *By T. M. for William Shears, 1660.* 4°.* L, O, LG, BC, YM; CH, CU, MH, WF, Y.

1285A [–] —[Anr. ed.] *Printed, 1660.* 4°. O; PU.

1286 [–] The Presbyterian sham. *Printed, 1680.* 4°.* L, CT, LSD, SP, E, DT; CH, IU, MH, NC, WF, Y.

1287 [–] The reformation reform'd. *For Joanna Brome, 1681.* 4°.* T.C.I 464. L, O, C, EN, BLH; CH, CN, MH, NU, TU, WF, Y.

1288 [–] —[Anr. ed.] *For B. C., 1688.* 4°.* L, LLL; CLC, NU, Y.

1289 [–] The reformed Catholique. *For Henry Brome, 1679.* 4°.* T.C.I 373. L, O, C, DC, DT; CH, CN, MH, NU, PU, TU.

1290 [–] —Second edition. —, *1679.* 4°.* T.C.I 399. L, O, C, EN, DT; CDA, IU, MBP, MH, NC, TU, WF, Y.

1291 [–] —[Anr. ed.] *Dublin, reprinted, 1679.* 4°.* DIX 169. DT, BLH.

1292 Entry cancelled.
[–] Register of the nativity. 1678. *See title.*

1293 —The relaps'd apostate. *For Henry Brome, 1641* [*i.e. 1661*]. 4°. L, O, C, DU, E; CH, CN, MH, NU, TU, Y.

1294 — —Second edition. —, *1661.* 8°. L, C, OU, DU, EN; CH, IU, LC, MH, NU, Y.

1295 — —Third edition. —, *1681.* 4°. T.C.I 423. L, O, C, LIU, DT; CH, CN, MH, NU, TU, WF, Y.

1296 [–] Remarks on the grovvth. *For Walter Kettilby, 1682.* 4°. T.C.I 486. L, O, C, LSD, EN, CD; CH, IU, MH, NU, WF, Y.

1297 [–] A reply to the reasons of the Oxford-clergy. *By Henry Hills, 1687.* 4°.* L, O, CT, MR, DT; CLC, CN, MH, NU, TU, WF, Y.

1298 —A reply to the Second part of the Character of a Popish svccessor. *For Joanna Brome, 1681.* 4°.* T.C.I 464. L, O, C, EN, DT; BN, CH, CN, MH, NU, TU, WF, Y.

1299 [–] The resolve of the citie. [*London, 1659.*] brs. LT, LG; CH.

1299A [–] A rope for Pol, or, a hue and cry after Marchemont Nedham. *Printed, 1660.* 4°.* LT, O, C, OC, SP; CH, CLC, IU, MIU, WF.

1300 [–] Rump enough. *Printed March 14, 1659[60].* 4°.* LT, O, LG, MR; CN, NN, NU.

1301 [–] A seasonable memorial in some historical notes. *For Henry Brome, 1680.* 4°.* T.C.I 396. L, O, C, DU, SA; CH, IU, LC, MH, NU, TU, Y.

1302 [–] —[Anr. ed.] *Reprinted Edinburgh, by the heir of Andrew Anderson, 1680.* 4°.* ALDIS 2224. O, DU, EN; WWC.

1303 [–] —Second edition. *For Henry Brome, 1680.* 4°.* L, O, CS, DU, EN; CH, MBP, MH, MU, NP.

1304 — —Third edition. *By J. Bennet for Henry Brome, 1681.* 4°.* L, O, C, E, DT; CH, CN, MH, NU, TU, WF, Y.

1305 Entry cancelled.
—Sermon prepar'd to be preach'd. 1682. *See title.*

1306 —The shammer shamm'd. *For Joanna Brome, 1681.* 4°.* T.C.I 486. L, O, C, EN, DT; BN, CH, CN, MH, WF, Y.

1307 —A short ansvver to a whole litter of libellers. *By J. B. for Hen. Brome, 1680.* 4°.* T.C.I 407. L, O, C, DU, EN; BN, CLC, CU, MH, NU, PL, WF, Y.

1307A —A short ansvver to a whole litter of libels. *By J. B. for Hen. Brome, 1680.* 4°.* L, O, LSD, NPL, CD; CH, CN, MBA, MH, TU, Y.

1308 —A short view. *For H. Brome, 1660.* 4°. LCL, LLL, OC, YM; CN, WF, Y, ZWT.

1308A [–] Sir Politique uncased. *Printed 1660.* 4°.* LT, O, LSD, MR; CLC, CN, TU.

1308B [–] Some queries concerning the election. *Printed 1690.* 4°.* L, O, CT, LSD, MR; CH, CN, MH, TU, WF, Y.

1309 [–] The state and interest of the nation. *Printed, 1680.* 4°.* T.C.I 397. L, O, DU, LNC, MR; CH, IU, LC, MM, WF, Y.

1310 —State-divinity. *For Henry Brome, 1661.* 8°. O, C, LCL, DU, EN; CH, CN, LC, MH, NR, NU, Y.

1311 — —[Anr. ed.] —, *1661.* 4°.* L, OC, LLU, LSD, CD; CH, MH, NU, TO, Y.

1312   [–] Theosebia, or the churches advocate. *For Walter Davis*, 1683. 4°.* T.C.II 49. O, OC, DU, EN; CH, MH, NU, PU, Y.

1313   —Roger Lestrange to a gentleman. [*London*, 1646.] brs. LT, LG, LS.

1313A   [–] To his Excellency General Monck. *For Y. E.*, 1660. brs. LT, C; CH, CSS, IU, MH.

1314   —To the Reverend Dr. Thomas Ken. [*London*, 1682?] brs. L, O; MH.

1314A   —To the right honorable Edward earl of Clarenden. *For Henry Brome*, 1661. 4°.* L, O, C, LSD, ENC; CH, MH, NR, NU, Y.

1315   —Toleration discuss'd. *For Henry Brome*, 1663. 4°. L, O, C, DC, E; BN, CH, CN, MH, TU, WF, Y.

1316   [–] —[Same title.] *By E. C. and A. C. for Henry Brome*, 1670. 8°. T.C.I 20. L, O, C, E, DT; CH, CLC, CN, MH, NU, Y.

1317   — —Second edition. *By A. C. for Henry Brome*, 1673. 8°. L, C; NF.

1318   — —Third edition. *For H. Brome*, 1681. 4°. T.C.I 399. L, O, C, EN, DT; CH, CN, MU, NU, TU, WF, Y.

1318A   [–] Treason arraigned. *Printed*, 1660. 4°.* LT, O, SP; CLC, MH, NC, TU, Y.

1319   Entry cancelled.
      [–] Treatise of wool. 1677. *See* Clarke, George.

1320   —Truth and loyalty vindicated. *For H. Brome and A. Seile, June the 7th.* 1662. 4°. L, O, C, EN, CD; CH, IU, MH, NU, WF, Y.

1320A   [–] Two cases submitted to consideration. colop: *For R. Sare, and published by Randal Taylor*, 1687. brs. L, O, C, LG; CN, TSM, WF, Y.

1320B   [–] —[Anr. ed.] [*Edinburgh*], *printed at Holy-Rood-House*, 1687. brs. CSS.

1321   [–] Tyranny and Popery lording it. *For Henry Brome*, 1678. 4°. T.C.I 313. L, O, CT, MR, ENC; CH, IU, MH, NU, TU, WF.

1321A   [–] —[Anr. ed.] *By H. H. for Henry Brome*, 1678. 4°. O, C, CS, BC, CD; MIU.

1322   — —Second edition. *For Henry Brome*, 1680. 4°. T.C.I 399. L, O, C, BP, EN; CH, CN, MBP, NC, Y.

1323   — —"Second" edition. —, 1681. 4°.* T.C.I 466. L, OB, MR, E, DT; CDA, CN, IU, NU, WF.

1323A   [–] —[Anr. ed.] *For B. C.*, 1688. 4°.* TU.

1324   —L'Estrange his vindication to Kent. [*London*], *printed*, 1649. 4°.* L, DU, LNC, MR.

1324A   —L'Estrange his vindication, from the calumnies . . . in Kent. [*London*], *printed*, 1649. 4°.* Y.
      [–] Visitation: or. 1661. *See* L., R.

1325   —A whipp a whipp. *For Henry Brome, February the 7th* 1662. 4°. L, O, C, LNC, EN; CH, MH, NU, PL, WF, Y.

1325A   —A whipp for the animadverter. *For Henry Brome, February the 12th.* 1662. 4°. OC, CJ, CS, LIU, MR; MIU, WF.

1325B   —A whipp for the schismaticall animadverter [Bagshaw]. Second edition. *For Henry Brome, February the 7th.* 1662. 4°. WF.

1326   — —Second edition. *For Henry Brome, February the 12th,* 1662. 4°. O, LCL, CCH, SP, DT; CLC, IU, MH, NC, WF, Y.

1327   —A word concerning libels and libellers. *For Joanna Brome*, 1681. 4°.* T.C.I 476. L, O, C, E, BLH; BN, CH, CN, MH, NU, TU, WF.

1328   — —Second edition. —, 1681. 4°.* I, O, C, DUS, EN; CN, TO, WSL, Y.

1328A   [–] A word in season. *Printed at the Hague for S. B.*, 1660. brs. LT, O; CH, MH, MIU, Y.

1328B   L'Estrange no papist nor Jesuite. *For Henry Brome*, 1681. 4°.* L, OC, DU, LSD, MR; CH, MH, PL, WF, Y.

1328C   L'Estrange no papist. Odi profanum. *By F. Leach for Charles Brome*, 1685. 4°.* LSD; BN, CH, Y.

1329   Let me speake too? Or, eleven queries. *Printed*, 1659. 4°.* L, O, BC, LNC, LSD; HR, CH, CN, MH, WF, Y.

1329A   **[Leti, Gregorio.]** The amours of Charles Duke of Mantua. Second edition. [*London*], *for H. Herringman, sold by J. Knight and F. Saunders*, 1685. 8°. T.C.II 130. WF.

1330   [–] Il cardinalismo di Santa Chiesa; or the history of the cardinals. *For John Starkey*, 1670. fol. T.C.I 19. L, O, C, EN, DT; CH, CN, NU, WF, Y.

1330A   [–] —[Anr. ed.] *For J. S. and are to be sold by Dorman Newman*, 1670. fol. O, CS, EN, CD; IU, TU.

1330B   [–] —[Anr. ed.] *For John Starkey, and are to be sold by Dorman Newman*, 1670. fol. CT.

1330C   [–] The ceremonies of the vacant see. *By H. L. and R. B. for Tho. Basset*, 1671. 8°. L, O, C, OC, CE, SP; CH, FU, WF.

1331   [–] Del teatro Brittanico. *Da Roberto Scott*, 1683. 4°. 2v. L, O, C, LG, DT; CLC.

1331A   [–] A letter to a friend, upon the dissolving. colop: *Printed* 1690. brs. L, O, C, MR; CH, MH, NC, WF, Y.

1332   —The life of Donna Olimpia. *By W. G. to be sold by Robert Littlebury*, 1666. 8°. L, O, OC, CK, WCA; CH, CLC, IU, LC.

1333   [–] —[Anr. ed.] *By W. Godbid, and are to be sold by Robert Littlebury*, 1666. 8°. L, CK; LC.

1334   [–] —[Anr. ed.] —, 1667. 8°. L, O, C, LNC, EN; BBE, CH, CN, NN, WF, Y.

1334A   [–] —[Anr. ed.] *By W. G., sold by Robert Littlebury*, 1667. 8°. CM; MIU, PL.

1334B   [–] —[Anr. ed.] *For R. Littlebury, sold by Tho. Cockerill*, 1678. 8°. T.C.I 323. L, O, DU, P; CH, SYRACUSE.

1334C   [–] The new Pope. *Printed*, 1677. 8°. T.C.I 252. L, O, C, OC, P; CH, CN, NU, TSM, WF, Y.

1334D   [–] —[Anr. ed.] *For Tho. Basset*, 1689. 8°. L.

1335   [–] Il nipotismo di Roma; or, the history. *For John Starkey*, 1669. 8°. T.C.I 2. L, O, C, DU, E; CH, CN, NU, PL, TU, Y, AVP. (var.)

1336   [–] —[Anr. ed.] —, 1673. 8°. L; LC.

1337   [–] —[Anr. ed.] *For John Starkey, to be sold by Thomas Archer*, 1673. 8°. T.C.I 130. O, C, EN, BLH, DT; CH, CN, LC, MH, WF, Y, AVP.

1338   [–] The present state of Geneva. *For William Cademan*, 1681. 8°. T.C.I 450. L, CT, BAMB, LIU, SP; CH, MB, MM, WF.

1339   [–] —[Anr. ed.] *For Randall Taylor*, 1687. 8°. L, OC, E, EN, GU; NC.

1339A   [–] —[Anr. ed.] *For Will. Whitwood*, 1689. 8°. L; IU.

1340 [–] Il puttanismo Romano. *Per Tomaso Buet*, 1669. 8°.
L, E; CH, NC.

1340A [–] —[Anr. ed.] *Printed*, 1670. 8°. L, DU; CH, TO, WF.

1341 [–] —[Anr. ed.] *In London[Geneva?], per Tomaso Bret*,
1675. 8°. L.

Letten, Nathaniel. July 18, 1671. On a tryal. 1671. *See
title.*

Letter about raising. 1690. *See* Hill, A.

1342 Letter about the election. 1690. brs. LG (lost).

1343 A letter advising in this extraordinary juncture. 1689.
brs. LG (lost).

1344 A letter agreed unto, and subscribed by, the gentlemen,
ministers, freeholders . . . of Suffolk. Presented to . . .
Lord Mayor. *For Thomas Dring*, 1659[60]. brs. LT, O,
DN; CH, MH, WF.

1344A —[Same title.] Presented to . . . Monck. *For Thomas
Dring*, 1659[60]. brs. L, DN; CH, MH, WF.

1344B A letter and declaration of the gentry of . . . Norfolk . . .
[to Monck]. *For John Place*, 1660. brs. L, O, LG, DN; MH.

1345 A letter and declaration of the nobility and gentry of
. . . York, to . . . Monck. *Printed at York, and re-printed
at London for John Starkey*, 1659[60]. brs. STEELE 3153.
LT, O, LG, MC, DN; MH, TU.

1345A —[Anr. ed.] *For John Starkey*, 1659. brs. LLU.

1345B —[Anr. ed.] *Edinburgh, by C. Higgins*, 1660. brs. EN.

1346 A letter and declaration of the lords, knights, . . . of
York. *For John Starkey*, 1659[60]. brs. STEELE 3154. L,
CJ, DN.

1346A Letter and relation of the victory of York. *Edinburgh,
Tyler*, 1644. 4°. ALDIS 1144. E.

Letter &c. Gentlemen. [n.p., 1688.] *See* William III.

Letter, ballancing. [n.p.], 1697. *See* Somers, John Somers,
baron.

1347 A letter: being a full relation of the siege of Banbury
Castle. *For Iohn Wright, Septemb. 4*. 1644. 4°.* LT, O;
MH, WF.

Letter by the Lord Generals direction. 1644. *See* Carre,
James.

Letter concerning confession. 1650. *See* S., T.

Letter concerning events. [n.p.], 1649. *See* R., J.

1348 Letter concerning guards and garrisons. 1699. LUS (lost).

1349 Entry cancelled.

Letter concerning separation. 1681. *See* Hall, Joseph, *bp.*

Letter concerning Sir William. [n.p., 1694.] *See* N., H.

Letter concerning the coin. 1695. *See* Woods, Thomas.

1350 Entry cancelled.

Letter concerning the colledg. [n.p., 1688.] *See* Cellier,
Elizabeth. To Dr. —.

Letter concerning the Council. [n.p., 1686.] *See* Jenks,
Sylvester.

1351 A letter concerning the disabling clauses. *To be sold by
Randall Taylor*, 1690. 4°.* T.C.II 304. L, O, C, EN, DT;
CH, CN, MH, NC, TU, WF, Y. (var.)

1351A A letter concerning the East India trade. colop: *Printed*,
1698. cap., fol.* MH, MIU.

1352 A letter concerning the Iesuites. [*Douai?*], 1661. 4°. L,
O, DT; CH, CSS.

1353 A letter concerning the matter of the present excom-
munications. *For Benjamin Alsop*, 1683. 4°.* L, O, C,
CS, DU; CH, CLC, MH, NU, WF, Y.

Letter concerning the present state of physick. 1665. *See*
Merret, Christopher.

Letter concerning the present state of religion. [n.p.,
1656.] *See* Thorndike, Herbert.

1354 A letter concerning the present troubles in England.
Oxford, by Henry Hall, 1645. 4°. MADAN 1812. LT, O, P,
DT; CH, NU.

1355 A letter concerning the souldiers and their orders. *For
R. Smithurst*, 1648. 4°.* LT, O, DU, MR, DT; IU, MH, MU,
NU, Y.

Letter concerning the storming. 1645. *See* Norton,
Ralph.

Letter concerning the test. 1687. *See* H., W.

1356 A letter concerning the tryal at Oxford of Stephen
College. *For W. Davies*, 1681. brs. L, O, C; CH, MH, Y.

Letter concerning the witches in the West. [1670?] *See* I.,
D.

Letter concerning toleration. 1689. *See* Locke, John.

1357 A letter containing an humble and serious advice. [*Edinburgh*], *printed* [*Tyler*], 1661. 4°.* ALDIS 1704. O, EN;
MIU, TU, WF.

1357A A letter containing some reflection, on a discourse, called
Good advice. [*London*, 1688.] cap., 4°.* EN; PU.

Letter containing some reflections. [n.p., 1689.] *See*
Burnet, Gilbert, *bp.*

Letter, containing some remarks. [n.p., 1686.] *See*
Burnet, Gilbert, *bp.*

1358 A letter declaratorie . . . Kent. [*London*], *printed*, 1648.
brs. LT.

Letter desiring a just. [n.p., 1662.] *See* Walsh, Peter.

Letter desiring information. 1687. *See* Meredith, Edward.

1359–61 Entries cancelled.

Letter directed from the Council of Scotland. [1680.]
See Scotland. Privy Council.

Letter directed to Master Bridgeman. 1642. *See* E., R.

Letter directed to the right honourable the Earle of
Perth. 1700. *See* Melfort, John Drummond, *earl of.*

Letter. Dunkirke. [n.p., 1688.] *See* S., R.

Letter for a Christian family. [n.p., 1680.] *See* Vicars, John.

Letter for toleration. 1689. *See* Long, Thomas.

1362 A letter formerly sent to Dr. Tillotson. [*London*, 169–?]
cap., 4°.* L, CS, DU; TU, WF, Y.

1363 A letter formerly written to Mr. Tichborne. *By D.
Maxwell*, 1662. 4°. LG; CLC.

1364 A letter found in Utopia. *Printed*, 1675. 4°.* T.C.I 220.
CH, NU.

1365 Entry cancelled.

Letter from — to his friend concerning . . . Glasgow.
[1700]. *See* Letter from [blank].

1365A A letter from a bishop to a lord. [*London*], 1689. fol. * LLP.

1366 A letter from a captain of the Army, to an honourable
member of Parliament. *By John Streater, and John
Macock*, 1659[60]. 4°.* LT, O, LLU, SP; CLC, CSS, MH, WF.

Letter from a Catholick gentleman. 1678. *See* R., B.

Letter from a Christian friend. [n.p., 1655.] *See* Bl., Ro.

Letter from a citizen in London. [n.p., 1695.] *See* D., C.

Letter from a citizen of Glasgow. [n.p.], 1700. *See* B., J.

Letter from a citizen of London. [1692.] *See* W., J.

Letter from a citizen of Oxford. [n.p., 1681.] *See* P., T.

Letter from a city-minister. 1689. *See* Whitby, Daniel.

1367   Entry cancelled. Date: 1763?

Letter from a clergy-man in the city. [n.p., 1688.] *See* Sherlock, William.

1368   A letter from a clergy-man in the country, to a minister. *Printed*, 1689. 4°.* L, O, C, LSD, DT; CH, CU, MH, NU, WF, Y.

1369   —[Anr. ed.] *Edinburgh, re-printed*, 1689. cap., 4°.* ALDIS 2905. L, O, EN; CLC, Y.

1369A   Entry cancelled.

Letter from a clergy-man in the country to the clergy-man in the city. 1688. *See* Cartwright, Thomas, *bp*.

1370   A letter from a clergy-man of the Church of England to an eminent divine. [n.p., 1689.] cap., fol.* O.

Letter from a councellor. 1685. *See* D., P.

1371   A letter from a country curate to Mr. Henry Care. colop: *Printed, and are to be sold by Randal Taylor*, 1688. cap., 4°.* O, OC, DT; CN, MIU, NP.

Letter from a country gentleman. [n.p., 1692.] *See* N., W.

Letter from a country gentleman to a member. [169-?] *See* T., T.

1372   March the 27th. 1684. A letter from a country minister. *For Walter Kettilby*, 1684. brs. L, O, LG; WF.

Letter from a Dissenter. 1689. *See* N., N.

1372aA A letter from a Dissenter in the country. [*London?* 1689.] brs. HH.

Letter from a Dissenter to the divines. 1687. *See* Gother, John.

1372bA A letter from a Dissenter to the petitioning bishops. colop: *For N. D.*, 1688. brs. L, O, LG; MIU, Y.

Letter from a Dutchman. 1673. *See* C., F. Two letters.

1372cA Letter from a freeholder in the county of Edinburgh. [n.p., 169-?] fol.* NP.

1372A   A letter from a freeholder of Buckinghamshire. [*London?* 1679.] cap., fol.* L, O, C, OP, LNC, DT; CH, IU, MH, WF, Y.

Letter from a freeholder, to the rest. [n.p., 1689.] *See* Johnson, Samuel.

Letter from a French lawyer. 1689. *See* L., A.

1373   A letter from a French Protestant to a friend. *Dublin, printed*, 1681. fol.* DIX 184. DN; TU.

Letter from a friend in Abingdon. [n.p., 1679.] *See* B., A.

1374   A letter from a friend in London, to another at Salamanca. colop: *For J. C.*, 1681. cap., fol.* L, O, EN; MBA, PU, WF, Y.

1374A   —[Anr. ed.] colop: *For Wal. Davies*, 1681. cap., fol.* MR; PU.

Letter from a friend in Shropshire. 1681. *See* M., J.

1375   A letter from a friend in the countrey: to a member. [*London*], *printed*, 1643. 4°.* LT, LG, CJ, BC, DT; CH, CU, MH, NU, WF.

Letter from a friend in the north. [n.p., 1690?] *See* S., T.

1376   A letter from a friend, occasioned by the receipt of His Majesties most gracious expresses. [*London*], *printed*, 1660. 4°.* LT, O, MR; CN, MH, NC, WF, Y.

Letter from a friend to a loyal subject. 1680. *See* V., J.

1377   A letter from a friend, to a person of quality: in answer to a letter from a person of quality, to his friend; about abhorrers and addressers. colop: [*London*], *for T. Davies*, 1682. brs. L, O, OC, CT, HH; CH, MBA, PU, Y.

1377A   —[Anr. ed.] colop: [*London*], *for J. Tonson*, 1682. brs. DCH; MIU, WF.

1378   A letter from a friend to the wise and learned, in England. colop: *Printed 1680, by Tho. James*. 4°.* O; Y.

1378A   A letter from a general officer to a colonel. [*London*, 1692?] brs. CH.

Letter from a gentleman at Fez. 1682. *See* B., A.

1379   A letter from a gentleman at London, to his friend in the countrey. [*London*, 1676.] cap., 4°.* O, MR; CH.

1379aA A letter from a gentleman at London to his friend at Edinburgh. [*London?* 1700.] brs. EN; CH, MIU, NN, Y.

1379A   Entry cancelled.

Letter from a gentleman at New-Market. 1683. *See* S., J.

1380   A letter from a gentleman at St. Germains. [*London*, 1692?] brs. L.

1381   —[Anr. ed.] [*London*], *printed*, 1697. 4°.* L, O, C, LG, LUG; CH, IU, MB, MH, WF, Y.

1382   A letter from a gentleman from the city of New York. *Printed and sold by William Bradford in New-York*, 1698. 4°.* RPJ.

1382A   A letter from a gentleman in America to his friend in Scotland. [*London*, 1699.] brs. MIU, RPJ.

Letter from a gentleman in answer to Mr. Mayor. [n.p., 1648.] *See* H., G.

1382B   A letter from a gentleman in Ardmagh, . . . giving an account of the Rapparees. [*Dublin*, 1697?] brs. DN.

1382C   A letter from a gentleman in Buckinghamshire. *For Randal Taylor*, 1694. 4°. L, O; INU.

1382D   A letter from a gentlemen in camp, . . . unto his friend at Dublin. [*Dublin*], *sold by John Foster*, [1690]. brs. DT.

Letter from a gentleman in Colchester. [n.p., 1648.] *See* B., I.

1382E   A letter from a gentleman in Exeter. [*London*], *printed*, 1688. brs. C, HH, EN.

1383   A letter from a gentleman in Flanders. [n.p., 1690.] brs. L, O; TU.

Letter from a gentleman in Germany. 1684. *See* Vandenberg, Abraham.

1384   A letter from a gentleman, in Glocestershire. [n.p., 1678.] 4°.* L, O.

Letter from a gentleman in Grayes-inn. [n.p.], 1662. *See* A., F.

1385   Entry cancelled.

Letter from a gentleman in Ireland, to his brother. 1677. *See* Marvell, Andrew.

1386   A letter from a gentleman in Ireland to his friend in London. *Dublin, printed*, 1688. 4°.* DIX 232. C, LLP, LVF, ES, DI; CH, MIU, WF, Y.

Letter from a gentleman in Kent. 1648. *See* B., A.

Letter from a gentleman in London. [n.p., 1681.] *See* P., R.

Letter from a gentleman in Manchester. 1694. *See* B., T.

1387   A letter from a gentleman in the city, to a clergy-man. *For D. C.*, 1688. 4°.* L, O, LSD; CH, PHS, PL, VC.

1388   A letter from a gentleman in the city to a gentleman in the country, about the odiousness of persecution occasioned. [*London*], *printed*, 1677. 4°.* LLP, CS, DT; NU, PH, PSC, WF.

1388A   Entry cancelled.

Letter from a gentleman in the city to a gentleman in the country, about the odiousness of persecution. [*London*], 1687. *See* N., A.

1389   A letter from a gentleman in the city to a lord. [*London*], *printed*, 1691. 4°. L, O, LLP, OC, CT; MBA, NC, WF.

1389A   A letter from a gentlemen in the city, to his friend in the country. [169–?] 4°.* NC.

1390   A letter from a gentleman in the city, to one in the covntry; concerning the bill. *Printed*, 1680. 4°.* L, O, CT, EN, DT; CH, CN, LC, MH, NU, TU, Y. (var.)

Letter from a gentleman in the country, to a member. Dublin, 1697. *See* B., F.

—[Same title.] [n.p., 1695.] *See* J., B.

1391   A letter from a gentleman in the country to a person of honour in London. colop: *For J. H.*, 1680. cap., fol.* L, OB, OC, LNC, MR; CH, CLC, MH, WF, Y.

1392   A letter from a gentleman in the country to his correspondent. [n.p., 1689.] brs. O.

1393   A letter from a gentleman in the country to his friend at Edinburgh. *Edinbvrgh, by George Mosman*, 1696. fol.* ALDIS 3575. L, LUG, MR, EN; MH, MIU, RPJ, WF.

Letter from a gentleman in the country to his friend at London. [n.p.] 1698. *See* D., W.

1393A   A letter from a gentleman in the country, to his friend in London. [*London*, 1679.] cap., fol.* L, OC; CH.

1393B   —[Same title. Begins: "Sir, In the prints." About East-India trade.] [*London*, 1700?] brs. INDIA OFFICE.

Letter from a gentleman in the country to his friend in the city. 1691. *See* J., H.

1393C   A letter from a gentleman in the country to his friend in the city. My dear friend. [*London*, 1682.] brs. CH.

Letter form [*sic*] a gentleman in the country, to his friends. [n.p.], 1687. *See* Penn, William.

1394   A letter from a gentleman in the country to his representative in Parliament. colop: *For R. Baldwin*, [1686?]. brs. L, O, C, LG; MH.

1395   Entry cancelled.

Letter from a gentleman in the countrey to some. 1679. *See* N., N.

1396   A letter from a gentleman in Yorkshire, to his countryman. *Printed*, 1695. 4°.* L, CS, LLU, LSD, SP; CH, CN, MH, WF, Y.

Letter from a gentleman of quality. [n.p.], 1679. *See* F., E.

1397   A letter from a gentleman of the city of New York. *Printed and sold by William Bradford in New-York*, 1698. 4°.* EVANS 823. O, LPR, LSD; CH, NHS, NN, RPJ.

1398   A letter from a gentleman of the Isle of Ely. [*London*, 1679.] cap., fol.* L, O, LLL, CS, MR; CH, CN, MBA, TU, WF, Y.

Letter from a gentleman of the Lord Ambassador Howard's retinue. 1670. *See* L., S.

1399   A letter from a gentleman of the Romish religion, to his brother. *For John Starkey*, 1674. 4°.* T.C.I 179. L, O, CT, BR, DU; HR, CH, NC, NU, WF, Y.

1400   —[Anr. ed.] 1679. 4°.* O, LL.

Letter from a gentleman of worth. 1642. *See* B., J.

1401   A letter from a gentleman to an East-India merchant. colop: *Printed, and sold by John Nutt*, 1698. cap., fol.* L; MH, NC.

Letter from a gentleman to his friend, by way. [n.p.], 1692. *See* S., R.

1402   A letter from a gentleman to his friend concerning the second edition of The declaration. *Printed*, 1699. 8°.* LL, LW.

Letter from a gentleman to his friend in London. [n.p.], 1660. *See* R., T.

Letter from a gentleman to his friend, on the treaty. 1700. *See* K., W.

1402A   A letter from a gentleman to some divines of the Church of England. colop: *For J. C.*, 1689. brs. C; CH.

Letter from a gentleman to the honourable Ed. Howard. [n.p.], 1668. *See* F., R.

1403   A letter from a grave gentleman once a member. [*Oxford, by L. Lichfield.*] *Printed*, 1643. 4°.* MADAN 1349. L, O, C, DU, DT; CH, MH, NU, WF, Y.

1404   A letter from a grave gentleman. *York, Stephen Bulkeley*, [1643]. 4°. CT.

Letter from a Jesuit at Paris. 1679. *See* Nalson, John.

Letter from a Jesuite: or. 1679. *See* Hess, Joannes Armondus de.

1405   A letter from a Justice of Peace to a counsellor. [*London?* 1680.] cap., 4°.* L, O, DU, LNC, CD; CH, CN, MH, PL, WF.

1406   —[Anr. ed.] colop: *For T. Pikes*, 1681. brs. L; CN, Y.

1407   —[Anr. ed.] colop: *For Jonathan Low*, 1681. cap., 4°.* L, LW, MR; CH, CN, MH, MIU, WF.

1408   A letter from a lawyer in the countrey. colop: *For Richard Janeway*, 1689. cap., fol.* MR, EN; CH, MM, PL, WF, Y.

1409   A letter from a lawyer of the Inner Temple. *Printed*, 1698. 4°.* L, OH, LUG, LSD, EN, DT; CLC, IU, MH, NC, WF, Y.

Letter from a London minister. 1659. *See* Poole, Matthew.

Letter from a lover. [n.p., 1660.] *See* O., H.

1410   A letter from a loyal member of the Church of England. *Printed*, 1689. 4°.* L, O, CT, DU, MR; CH, MM, TU, WF, Y.

Letter from a matron. [n.p.], 1682. *See* B., M.

Letter from a member of the army. 1659. *See* Hodgson, John.

1411   A letter from a member of the Hovse of Commons, to a gentleman. *Oxford, by H. Hall*, 1644. 4°.* MADAN 1625. LT, O, CJ, DC, EC, DT; CH, CN, MH, NU, WF.

1412   A letter from a member of the House of Commons to
        his friend. [*London?* 1689.] brs. L, MR; TU.

1412A   A letter from a member of the Parliament of Scotland.
        Printed, and are to be sold by John Whitlock, 1695. fol.*
        L, CCA, INDIA OFFICE; IU, MH, Y.

1413   —[Anr. ed.] colop: *Printed at London and re-printed at
        Edinburgh, by the heirs and successors of Andrew Anderson,*
        1696. 4°.* ALDIS 3576. O, LUG, EN, ES; MIU, NN, RPJ.

1414   A letter from a merchant in London. [*London?* 1690.]
        cap., fol.* TU, Y.

1414A   A letter from a merchant in Scotland ... Scotch-
        Linnen. [*Edinburgh,* 1700.] 4°.* NC.

1414B   A letter from a minister in Norfolk. *For D. Midwinter
        and T. Leigh,* 1700. 8°.* T.C.III 207, L, LLL, LLP, OC; WF.
        Letter from a minister in the country. 1689. *See* L., N.

1414C   A letter from a minister in the country, to a minister in
        London. *Brab. Aylmer,* [1697]. fol.* L.

1415   A letter from a minister of the Church of England,
        communicated. [*London,* 1679?] brs. L, OB, OC, HH; CH,
        MH, PU, Y, AMB.

1416   A letter from a minister of the Church of England to a
        gentleman in the countrt [*sic*]. *Printed,* 1695. 4°.* L,
        O, OC, CT, MR; CH, INU, MH, PU, WF, Y.

1417   A letter from a minister of the Church of England, to
        the pretended Baptist [Comber]. [*London*], 1688. 4°.*
        L, O, OC, MR; MIU, MU, PL, RPJ, WF.
        Letter from a minister to a person. [n.p., 1679.] *See* B., A.

1418   A letter from a minister to his friend, concerning ...
        chesse. *For Thomas Parkhurst, and Joseph Collier,*
        1680. brs. L.

1418A   —[Anr. ed.] *For Thomas Parkhurst,* 1680. brs. MH.
        Letter from a nobleman in London. [n.p., 1690.] *See*
        Halifax, George Savile, *marquess.*

1419   A letter from a noble-man of this kingdome. *Printed,*
        1648. 4°.* LT, O; CH, MH, NU.
        Letter from a Parliament man. [n.p.], 1675. *See* Shaftes-
        bury, Anthony Ashley Cooper, *earl of.*

1420   A letter from a person in the countrey to his friend in
        the city: giving his judgement. [*London,* 1656.] cap.,
        4°.* LT, O, MR, SP, DT; CLC, CSS, NU, PL, WF, Y.

1420A   A letter from a person of honour at London in answer
        to his friend in Oxfordshire. [*London,* 1690.] brs. O.
        Letter from a person of honour in France. 1659. *See* E., S.
        Letter from a person of honour in the country. 1681.
        See Anglesey, Arthur Annesley, *earl of.*

1421   A letter from a person of honour, reconciling the dis-
        senting brethren. *By R. A.,* 1645. 4°.* LT, MR; NU.

1422   A letter from a person of honour, relating the slaughter.
        Printed, 1648. brs. LT.

1423   A letter from a person of quality in Edenburgh to an
        officer of the army. *By Sarah Griffin, for Thomas Hewer,*
        [1659]. brs. LT; MH, Y.

1424   A letter from a person of quality in Scotland, to a per-
        son of honour in London. colop: [*London*], *for Joseph
        Heath-coat,* 1681. brs. L, O; CH, CN, MBA, MH, Y.
        Letter from a person of quality in the North. 1689.
        See Eyre, *Mrs.* Elizabeth.

        Letter, from a person of quality in the Parliaments army.
        1647. *See* M., B.
        Letter from a person of quality on board. 1676. *See* F., T.

1425   No entry.
        A letter from a person of quality residing in Kinsale.
        1646. *See* S., B.

1426   Entry cancelled.
        Letter from a person of quality to a principal peer. [1661.]
        See H., J.
        A letter from a person of quality to an eminent dis-
        senter. 1685. *See* Hickes, George.

1427   A letter from a person of quality to his friend, about
        abhorrers and addressers, &c. colop: *For John Frith,*
        1682. brs. L, O, C, BR, MC; CH, IU, MH, NC, TU, WF, Y.

1428   A letter from a person of quality to his friend concerning
        His Majesties late declaration. [*London,* 1681.] 4°.*
        L, O, C, LIU, MR; CH, MH, PL, TU, WF, Y.
        Letter from a person of quality, to his friend in the
        country. [n.p.], 1675. *See* Shaftesbury, Anthony
        Ashley Cooper, *earl of.*

1429   A letter from a Presbyterian minister. [*Edinburgh,* 1693?]
        cap., 4°.* ALDIS 3303.5. L, EN; WF.

1430   A letter from a Presbyterian of qvalitie. *Printed,* 1648.
        4°.* LT, MR; CH, CLC, MH, NU.

1431   A letter from a private gentleman. [*n.p.*], 1642. 4°. L, O,
        SC; WF.
        Letter from a Protestant gentleman. 1678. *See* Horneck,
        Anthony.

1432   A letter from a Protestant in Ireland, to a member.
        [*Oxford, by L. Lichfield*], *printed,* 1643. 4°.* MADAN
        1485. LT, O, C, LIU, BLH; CH, CLC, MH, WF, Y.
        Letter from a Protestant of integrity. 1661. *See* D., L.

1433   Entry cancelled.
        Letter from a Protestant, to a peer. 1661. *See* D., L.
        Letter from a Protestant of integrity.

1434   A letter from a Roman Catholick to one of his friends
        at Amsterdam. *For R. Baldwin,* 1689. brs. CH.

1435   A letter from a scholar in Oxford, to his friend in the
        countrey. [*London*], *printed,* 1647. 4°.* MADAN 1936.
        L, O, OC, CS, DU; IU, MH, TU, WF, Y.

1436   A letter from a scholler in Oxford-shire to his Vnkle.
        [*Oxford*], *printed,* 1642[3]. 4°.* MADAN 1166. L, O, CJ,
        DU, EN; CLC, MU, TU, WF, Y.
        Letter from a soldier in the royal camp. 1690. *See* P., T.

1436A   A letter from a stranger to a minister, clearly showing ...
        what sin is. [*London,* 16—?] 4°.* LLP.
        Letter from a student at Oxford. 1681. *See* Kennett,
        White.
        Letter from a trooper. [n.p., 1695.] *See* Sergeant, John.
        Letter from a true and lawfull member. [n.p.], 1656. *See*
        Clarendon, Edward Hyde, *earl of.*

1437   A letter from a true Dutchman. colop: [*London*], *Randal
        Taylor,* 1693. 4°.* DC, DT; NR.
        Letter from a worthy gentleman. 1642. *See* R., R.

1438   A letter from Amsterdam conteining [*sic*] the full rela-
        tion. *By Bernard Alsop for T. P.,* 1650. 4°.* LT, BC.

1439 A letter from Amsterdam, to a friend in England. *For G. H.*, 1678. 4°.* L, O, C, MR, EN; HR, CH, CN, MH, WF, Y.

1439A A letter from Amsterdam to a friend in Paris. [*London*, 1679.] 4°. L.

Letter from Amsterdam, to J. P. 1673. *See* D., T.

1440 A letter from Amsterdam to M. C. in London. colop: *For J. S.*, 1684. brs. L, HH; TO, WF, Y.

1441 Entry cancelled. *See following entry.*

1442 A letter from an absent lord. [*n.p.*, 1688/9.] cap., fol.* L, O, EN; Y.

Letter from an anti-hierarchical divine. 1661. *See* S., P.

Letter from an anti-phanatique. 1660. *See* Morley, Henry.

Letter from an ejected member. [n.p.], 1648. *See* S., G.

1443 A letter from an eminent merchant in Constantinople. colop: *For A. Jones*, 1683. brs. L, O.

1444 A letter from an eminent merchant in Ostend. colop: *For J. Stans, and sold by R. Janeway*, 1682. brs. L; CH.

1445 A letter from an eminent person in Gloucester. *By James Cottrel*, 1660. 4°.* LT, O.

1445A A letter from an eminent person in the northerne army. *Printed at London, by Robert Ibbitson*, 1648. 4°.* LT, C; CH, MH, Y.

Letter from an English merchant. [1688.] *See* M., G.

Letter from an English merchant at Amsterdam. 1695. *See* D., P.

1446 A letter from an English merchant, who left Holland. [*n.p.*, 1691.] brs. O, OC; CH.

1446A A letter from an English officer. colop: *For Richard Baldwin*, 1690. brs. L, C, DN; Y.

A letter from an English Reformed Quaker. [1700.] *See* L., J.

Letter from an honourable gentleman. [n.p.], 1647. *See* B., I.

Letter from an honourable person in London. [1660.] *See* G., J.

Letter from an ignoramus. 1682. *See* J., W.

Letter from an impartial hater. [n.p., 1680.] *See* L., W.

1447 A letter from an Independent to his honoured friend. [*London*, 1645.] cap., 4°.* L, C, OC, MR; CN, MH, MM, WF.

1448 A letter from an officer belonging to the ordnance. colop: *For Ric. Chiswell*, 1689. brs. L, OC, MC; Y.

1449 —[Anr. ed.] *Edinburgh, re-printed*, 1689. brs. ALDIS 2907. L, EN.

Letter from an officer in His Majesties army. [n.p.], 1643. *See* Heylyn, Peter.

1449A A letter from an officer of quallitie. *By T. Paine, August 26.* 1647. 4°.* DN; MH.

1450 A letter from an officer of the army in Ireland. [*London?* 1659.] brs. LT; MH, Y.

Letter from an old common-council-man. 1681. *See* N., D.

1451 Entry cancelled.

Letter from Artemiza. [n.p., 1679.] *See* Rochester, John Wilmot, *earl of.*

Letter from B. W. 1683. *See* W., B.

Letter from Barwick. 1659. *See* M., J.

1451A Letter from [blank] to his friend concerning . . . Glasgow's business. [*Glasgow*, 1699.] cap., 4°. ALDIS 3862.5. O, EN.

1452 Letter from Chester. [*n.p.*], 1642. LVF.

1452A A letter from Chester of the twenty second instant [July] . . . Ireland. *For D. K.*, 1689. brs. CH, Y.

1452B A letter from Chester of the 29th of July. colop: *For John Amery, to be sold by Randal Taylor*, 1689. brs. DN; Y.

1452C A letter from Chester of the 24th of August. colop: *For Randal Taylor*, 1689. brs. DN; Y.

1453 A letter from Colchester, to the disperst bretheren. colop: *For A. Banks*, 1682. brs. O; CH, CU, PU, Y.

1454 A letter from Constantinople. 1685/6. fol. LG (lost).

1455 A letter from Count Teckely. *For Charles Corbet*, 1683. brs. O, EN.

1456 A letter from divers ministers about Colchester. 1645. brs. LG (lost).

1457 A letter from divers of the gentry of the County of Lincolne to . . . Monck. *For Richard Lowndes*, 1659[60]. brs. LT, O, LS.

Letter from Dr. P. 1696. *See* Payne, William.

1458 Letter from Dublin, by an officer. 1642. LVF.

1459 A letter from Dublin in Ireland, containing. colop: *For Richard Baldwin*, 1690. brs. MC; CH, Y.

1460 Entry cancelled.

Letter from Dublin; of April. 1690. *See* Johnson, Robert.

1461 A letter from Duke Schomberge's camp. *For Tho. Parkhurst: and published by Randal Taylor*, 1689. 4°.* L, C, BQ; CH, CN, INU, MM, WF, Y.

Letter from Dundalk. 1689. *See* W., J.

Letter from Edenbrough. [n.p., 1681/2.] *See* D., T.

Letter from Edinburgh, concerning. [n.p., 1649.] *See* S., I.

1462 A letter from Edinburgh, containing a true . . . relation. [*Edinburgh*], 1648. 4°. ALDIS 1334.7. E.

1463 A letter from Edinburgh, November 30, 1643. [*London?* 1643.] 4°.* MR; MM, WF, Y.

1463A A letter from Edinburgh. To one in London. colop: *Edinburgh, by the heir of Andrew Anderson*, 1690. cap., 4°. NN.

1464 A letter from Exeter, advertizing the state of affairs there. *For Thomas Creake*, [1660]. brs. LT, O, LG; Y.

Letter from Exon. 1690. *See* W., J.

1465 A letter from Father La Chaise. *Printed in Philadelphia* [*i.e., London*], [1688]. 4°.* EVANS 438. MH, NN, PHS, Y.

1466 A letter from Feversham. [*London*], *for I. H.*, 1688. brs. L, O; CH, CN.

Letter from G. H. [n.p., 1697.] *See* Heathcote, *Sir* Gilbert.

1467 A letter from General Blake's fleet. *For Robert Ibbitson*, 1652. 4°.* LT, LG, BLH.

1468 Entry cancelled.

Letter from Generall Leven. Edinburgh, 1644. *See* Leven, Alexander Leslie.

1469   A letter from General Ludlow to Dr. Hollingworth. *Amsterdam, printed*, 1692. 4°. L, O, C, EN, DT; CH, CN, MH, NU, TU, WF, Y, ZWT. (var.)

1470   A letter from Hampton-Covrt. *For V, V.*, 1647. 4°.* LT, SP; IAU, MH, WF.

1471   A letter from Hampton Court: of 600 horse and foot. *Printed*, 1648. 4°.* LT, O, LLL; MH, NN.
       Letter from His Excellencies qvarters. 1646. *See* C., W.

1472   No entry.

1473   A letter from His Holiness the Pope, to . . . Monmovth. colop: *For J. Johnson*. 1682. brs. O; CH, MH, MU, TU, Y.

1474   A letter from His Holiness the Pope of Rome, to . . . the Prince of Orange. *Edinburgh, re-printed* 1689. 4°.* ALDIS 2911. L, O, LIL, EN; CH, CN, NC, WF.
       Letter from His Majetties [*sic*] covrt at Holmbie. 1647. *See* Corbet, Roger.

1475   A letter from His Majesties court in the Isle of Wight. *For R. W.*, 1648. 4°.* LT, LLL.
       Letter from His Majesties quarters at Newcastle. 1646. *See* A., E.
       Letter from Holland. [1673.] *See* C., D.

1476   A letter from Holland: being a true relation. [*London*], *printed*, 1648. Octob. 12. 4°.* LT, MR; MH, NU.

1477   A letter from Holland, relating the designes of the Scotch Presbyter. colop: *Printed at Rotterdam*, 1650[1]. cap., 4°.* LT; Y.
       Letter from Holland, touching. [n.p.], 1688. *See* Witt, Cornelius de.
       Letter from Horsum. [n.p., 1648.] *See* T., R.

1478   A letter from Ireland concerning the late trayterous conspiracie. *For Hen. Marsh*, 1663. 4°.* Y.

1479   A letter from Ireland, giving an account of a bloody engagement. *For A. R.*, 1689. brs. CH, Y.
       A letter from Ireland to an honourable citizen of London [n.p., 1660.] *See* P., W.
       Letter from J. B. [n.p., 1679.] *See* B., J.

1480   A letter from Jack the Cobler, to any body. [*London*, 1680.] brs. L, O; CH, CN, MH, WF, Y.

1481   A letter from Jamaica. [n.p., 1682.] brs. O, C; NN, OLU, RPJ.
       Letter from Kendall. 1648. *See* Lambert, John.

1482   A letter from Kent: of the rising at Rochester. *Printed at London by Robert Ibbitson*, 1648. 4°.* LT; CH, MH, MIU, MU, Y.

1483   A letter from Kinsale to a gentleman in Dublin. *Dublin, printed*, 1696. brs. DIX 282. LVF, DN.

1484   Entry cancelled.
       Letter from Leghorn. 1691. *See* M., W.

1484A A letter from Legorn. Decem 1, 1679. From aboard the Van-herring. [*London*, 1680.] fol.* L, O, LLU, MR, DT; CH, CN, MBA, NP, WF.

1485   Entry cancelled. Ghost.

1486   A letter from Liverpool. *For J. C.*, 1689. brs. L, DN; Y.

1487   A letter from Levvis the Great. [*London*, 1689–90.] brs. L, HH; MH.

1487A A letter from London to a friend in Westminster . . . relating to the coyn. *R. Baldwin*, 1695. brs. LUG.

1488   A letter from Lucifer. colop: *For Charles Lee*. 1682. fol.* L, O, DU, MC; MH, Y.
       Letter from Lysbone. 1650. *See* Hasclock, John.

1489   A letter from Major General Ludlow to Sir E[dward] S[eymour]. *Amsterdam, printed*, 1691. 4°.* L, O, C, EN, DT; CH, CN, MH, TU, WF, Y.
       Letter from Mercurius civicus. [n.p.], 1643. *See* Butler, Samuel.
       Letter from N. J. [n.p., 1690.] *See* J., N.
       Letter from Newcastle. 1644. *See* Humbie, A.
       Letter from New-Castle, containing. 1646. *See* N., E.
       Letter from Newcastle of the commissiones. 1647. *See* Sitrauk, W.

1490   A letter from Newcastle, shewing. *For Thomas Hewer*. 1646. 4°.* LT, CT, DT.
       Letter from New-England. 1682. *See* W., J.

1491   A letter from No Body in the city, to No Body in the covntrey. *For Some-Body*, 1679. 4°.* C, LVF, CT, LSD, YM, CD; CH, IU, MH, NU, WF, Y.

1492   A letter from no far countrey. [*London*], 1660. 4°.* L, DUS, MR; CSS, NN, WF, ZWT.

1493   Entry cancelled.
       Letter from on board Major-General Kirke. 1689. *See* Billing, R.

1494   A letter from on board the York-Frigat. [n.p., 1689.] brs. C, MC.
       Letter from on board Their Majesties fleet near Ushant. 1689. *See* L., J.

1494A A letter from one in the country, concerning some of the present differences. [*Boston, by Bartholomew Green and John Allin*, 1700?] cap., 4°.* MH, NN.

1495   A letter from one in the country, to a Member of Parliament. [*Edinburgh*, 1700.] 4°.* ALDIS 3979. EN; CSS, NC.
       Letter from one of the persons. 1660. *See* L., W.

1495A A letter from one of the principal officers of the Grand Vizir. *For Walter Davis*, 1684. 4°. OC.
       Letter from one of the trained-bands. [n.p.], 1643. *See* W., A.
       Letter from Oxford. Oxford, 1693. *See* N., N.
       Letter from Paris. [n.p., 1680.] *See* Hay, T. de.

1495B A letter from Paris from Sir George Wakeman. colop: [*London*], *for T. B.*, 1681. brs. L, O, C, HH; CH, MH, WF, AVP.

1496   A letter from Plymouth. *For A. N.*, Novemb. 4. 1643. 4°.* LT; Y.
       Letter from Rhoan. [n.p.], 1641. *See* Taylor, John.

1497   A letter from Rochel in France to Mr. Demevare. colop: *For R. Bentley*, 1681. brs. HH, MC, EN; MH, WF.

1498   Entry cancelled.
       Letter from Rome to a friend. [n.p., 1679.] *See* W., T.

1498A A letter from Rome, written by a Roman Catholick. [*London*, 1689.] brs. CN.

1499   —[Anr. ed.] colop: *Reprinted at Edinburgh*, 1689. brs. ALDIS 2908. L, EN; CN.

1500   A letter from Rotterdam, touching the Scotch affaires, since November, 1650. [*London*, 1650.] cap., 4°.* O; Y.

Letter from St. Omars. 1679. *See* G., D.

Letter from St. Omers. [1681.] *See* B., B.

1501   A letter from Scotland: and the votes of the Parliament. [*London*], printed, 1649. 4°.* LT; MBP, MH, Y.

1502   A letter from Scotland, giving a full and impartiall relation. [*London*, 1649.] brs. LT.

1502A   A letter from Scotland, giving a true relation. *For J. Morice*, 1682. brs. DCH; CN.

1502B   —[Same title, "of the present posture."] *For Tim Goodwin*, [1692]. brs. OC; CN.

1502C   A letter from Scotland, to a gentleman at court. *By R. Roberts*, 1690. brs. HH; INU, WF.

1503   A letter from Scotland, with observations. colop: *For E. C.*, 1682. brs. L, O; CH, MH, Y.

1504   Entry cancelled.

Letter from Scotland: written. [n.p., 1681.] *See* Roscommon, Wentworth Dillon, *earl of.*

1505   A letter from several ministers in and about Edinburgh. *Printed at Edinburgh for Christopher Higgens, and reprinted at London for Richard Hills*, 1659[60]. 4°.* LT, O; CLC, MH, NU, Y.

1505A   A letter from several of the Protestant clergie in Chesire. [*London*, 1659.] brs. MH (var.).

1506   A letter from Shrewsbury. *For T. H.*, [1660]. brs. LT, O.

1507   Die Lunæ, 3° April, 1643. A letter from Sir John Hotham from Hull. *April 5. London, for Edward Husbands*, 1643. brs. LT.

1508   Entry cancelled.

Letter from Sir Thomas Fairfax's army. 1645. *See* Late letter.

1509   A letter from sixteen gentlemen of Kent. *For R. White, Decemb.* 19, 1648. 4°.* LT, LG, BR; CH, CSS, WF, Y.

1510   A letter from Some-Body in the country. *For D. M.*, 1679. 4°.* O, LSD, YM; CH, CLC, CN, IU, NU.

1511   A letter from some officers of the army at Whitehall. *Edinburgh, by Christopher Higgins*, 1659. 4°. ALDIS 1603. MR, EN; Y.

1512   Entry cancelled.

—[Anr. ed.] *Edinburgh*, 1659. *See* Letter from the officers.

1513   A letter from some thousands of the gentry. [*London*], 1659. brs. L.

Letter from Tangier concerning. [n.p., 1682.] *See* Franklin, William.

Letter from Tangier, to a friend. 1683. *See* Poseley, M.

Letter from the Arch-bishop of Paris. 1694. *See* Harlay-Chanvallon, François de.

1513A   A letter from the Arch-bishops and Bishops. colop: *Edinburgh, by the heir of Andrew Anderson*, 1688. brs. ALDIS 2767. L, MR, EN; CH, WF.

1514   A letter from the armie, concerning the Kings Majesty. *Printed at London by R. I.*, 1647. 4°.* LT; CH, MIU, Y.

A letter from the atturney of Ireland. 1649. *See* Basill, William.

Letter from the author of the argument. 1697. *See* Trenchard, John.

1514A   A letter from the bishops of Scotland, to the bishops of England. [*Edinburgh*, 1689.] brs. GU; WF.

Letter from the camp. 1674. *See* M., R.

1514B   A letter from the Church of Christ at Dartford. 1656. 4°.* Y.

1515   A letter from the clergy of France. *For Joanna Brome*, 1682. 4°.* T.C.I 497. L, O, CT, MR, DT; CN, MH, NC, NU, WF, Y.

1516   A letter from the commanders and officers of the fleet. *By Sarah Griffin, for Thomas Hewer*, 1659. 4°.* L, O, LLU, LSD, YM; MIU, NN, PL, WF, Y.

1516A   A letter from the commissioners of the militia of Westminster . . . to Fleetwood. [*London*, 1659.] brs. WF.

Letter from the councel of officers at Whitehall to Colonel Lilburne. Leith, 1653. *See* England. Privy Council.

1517   A letter from the Devil to the Pope. [*London?* 1670.] cap., fol.* L, C, MR; CH, MH, NU, AMB.

1518   A letter from the Dutch. of Portsmouth to Madam Gwyn. colop: *For J. S.*, 1682. brs. L, O, LG, EN; CH, MH, RHT, WF, Y.

1519   A letter from the Earl of Norwich. *Printed at London by B.A.*, 1648. 4°.* LT, O, AN; Y.

1520   A letter from the fleet, with a divrnal account. *By J. C.*, [1653]. 4°.* LT; WF.

1520A   A letter from the French King to the Great Turk, lamenting the woful loss of his noble fleet. [*London*, 1692.] brs. CN.

1521   A letter from the general meeting of officers of the army. *By Henry Hills, to be sold by him, and by Thomas Brewster*, 1652[3]. brs. LT, O.

1521A   A letter from the governor of Algier. *By Tho. Hodgkin, sold by J. Whitlock*, 1695. brs. CN.

1522   A letter from the grand-jury of Oxford. colop: *For Al. Banks*, 1681. brs. L, O, C, MC; CH, CN, MH, NP, WF, Y.

Letter from the head-qvarters. [n.p.], 1648. *See* Johnson, Richard.

1523   A letter from the Isle of VVight, of the designe. *For H. Becke*, 1648. 4°.* LT, LLL; CH, CN, MH.

Letter from the Jesuits. [n.p.], 1688. *See* P., R.

1524   A letter from the King of Denmark. *For Gustavus Montelion*, 1660. 4°.* LT, O, MR.

1525   A letter from the King of Morocco. *For Rowland Reynolds*, 1680. fol.* L, O, LNM, LUG; CH, MH, WF, Y.

1526   A letter from the Kings Majesties court at Hampton. *For John Wilson*, 1647. 4°.* LT, MR; WF.

1527   A letter from the Kings Majesties court at Oatelands. *Cambridge, for Nathaniel Smith*, 1647. 4°.* LT, O, C, LG, MR; CLC, LC, NC, WF.

1528   A letter from the Kings Majesties court, of the Kings comming. *By Robert Ibbitson*, 1647. 4°.* LT, LLU; CSS, Y.

1529   A letter from the Lady Creswell [*pseud.*] to Madam C. the Midwife. [n.p., 1680.] cap., fol.* L, O, LLU; CH, IU, MH, MM, NU, WF.

Letter from the Leaguer. 1648. *See* Rushworth, John.

1529A   A letter from the Lord Chancellor of Poland to General Teckley. [*London?*], *for P. Brooksby*, 1684. brs. O; CH, MH.

Letter from the Lord Lieutenant. 1650. *See* Cromwell, Oliver.

1530   A letter from the Lord Major, aldermen and common-councel of London, to His Excellency Sir Tho: Fairfax. *For Laurence Chapman, Novem.* 27. 1647. 4°.* LT, LG, OC, LLU, MR; CH, CN, MH, MU, Y.

1531   A letter from the Lord Mayor, aldermen, . . . in answer to a letter. *For A. R.*, 1648. 4°.* LT.

Letter from the member of Parliament. [n.p., 1689.] *See* M., M.

1532   A letter from the navy vvith the Earle of Warwick. *For Lawrence Blaikloke*, 1648. 4°.* LT, LNM; CSS, MH.

1533   A letter from the nobility. *Edinburgh, re-printed*, 1689. 4°.* ALDIS 2910. L, O, LIU, E, EN; CH, CSU, IU, MM, NU, Y.

1534   —[Anr. ed.] *Impressum juxta typum nuper Edinburgi excusum anno*, 1700. 4°.* O, EN; CH, WF.

1534A   A letter from the noblemen, gentlemen, justices, and free-holders of . . . Fife, to . . . Monck. [*London*, 1659.] brs. L, O; MH.

1535   A letter from the North. Loving friends. [*London*, 1653.] brs. LT.

1535A   A letter from the officers at White-hall. *Printed at Edinburgh, by Christopher Higgins*, 1659. 4°. ALDIS 1604. CT, E, EN; MBP, MH, Y.

1536   —[Anr. ed.] —, *and reprinted in London*, 1659. 4°. L, LIU; CH, MH, WF, Y.

1537   A letter from the Pope, to His distresed [*sic*] sons. *Printed*, 1674. 4°.* L, BC; NC, Y.

1537A   A letter from the Pope to the French King. [*n.p.*, 1672]. brs. L.

1538   A letter from the protesters, with an answer. [*Edinburgh*], *printed* [*by Andrew Anderson*], 1653. 4°.* ALDIS 1479. L, O, E, EN; CH, CLC, NU, WF.

1539   A letter from the Quakers to the mayor. colop: *For T. Knowlis*, 1682. brs. BR, EN; CH.

1540   A letter from the states of Holland. *By Will. Bonny*, 1693. brs. O; CN.

1541   A letter from the Synod of Zeland. *Printed at Edinburgh by Evan Tyler*, 1643. 4°.* ALDIS 1087. L, O, CT, MR, EN; CH, CN, MH, NU, WF, Y.

1542   —[Anr. ed.] *Printed at Edinburgh, and now reprinted at London for Edward Brewster*, 1643. 4°.* LT, EC, BLH; MH, MU, NN, Y.

1543   A letter from the town of Newcastle. [*n.p.*, 1680.] brs. O.

1544   A letter from the University of Cambridge. *Cambridge*, 1649. brs. O.

1545   A letter from the University of Oxford to the ministers. [*n.p.*], 1649. brs. O.

Letter from the vindicator. 1687. *See* Johnston, Joseph.

1546   A letter from the West to a member. [*Edinburgh*, 1689.] cap., 4°.* ALDIS 2911.5. L, C, AU, E, EN, CD; CLC, MH, Y.

1547   A letter from two Protestant ministers in England. [*Edinburgh*], 1692. brs. ALDIS 3230. EN; WF.

Letter from Utercht[*sic*]. [*n.p.*], 1648. *See* Spelman, Clement.

Letter from W. B. 1683. *See* B., W.

1548   A letter from Winchester. colop: *For Allen Banks*, 1681. fol.* L, O, BR; CH, LC, PU, WF, Y.

1549   A letter, giving a description of the Isthmus of Darien. *Edinburgh, for John Mackie and James Wardlaw*, 1699. 4°.* ALDIS 3865. L, O, EN; CN, LC, MB, NN, RPJ.

1549A   A letter giving a particular account . . . of the Scots Parliament. colop: *Printed*, 1695. cap., 4°.* CT; WF.

1549B   A letter giving an account of the manner of chusing Joseph King of Hungaria. *For R. Bently, and are to be sold by R. Baldwin*, 1690. 4°.* L, O; CSS.

1550   A letter giving ane short and true accompt. [*n.p.*], 1686. O, EN.

1551   Entry cancelled.

Letter humbly addrest. 1698. *See* Stephens, William.

1552   A letter humbly offer'd to the consideration of all gentlemen. *For E. Whitlock*, 1696. 4°.* LUG, EN; CH, MH, NC, PU, Y.

1553   A letter in answer to a city friend. *Printed and are to be sold by Randal Taylor*, 1687. 4°.* L, O, LIL, LLP, EN; CB, CH, IU, MIU.

1554   A letter in answer to a Dissenter. [*London*, 1687.] fol. LG (lost).

1555   A letter in answer to a friend, upon notice of a book entituled. A short view. colop: *For Randall Taylor*, 1681. cap., fol.* L, OP, DU; CH, CN, NN, PU, Y.

Letter, in answer to divers curious. 1671. *See* Charant, Antoine.

1555A   A letter in answer to the late dispensers of Pope Benedict. *Paris, by E. A.*, 1659. 8°. Y.

Letter in answer to two. 1687. *See* G., T.

1556   A letter in nature of an appeale. *Printed at Kilkenny*, 1648. 4°.* DIX.

1557   A letter, in which the argvments of the annotator. [*Oxford, by H. Hall.*] *Printed*, 1645. 4°.* MADAN 1800. LT, O, C, LNC, DT; CH, MH, MIU, NU, WF.

1558   —Second edition. *Oxford, by Henry Hall*, 1645. 4°.* MADAN 1801. O, CT.

Letter intercepted at a court-guard. 1642. *See* L.

1559   A letter intercepted from a confident. [*London?* 1689.] brs. L.

1560   A letter intercepted, from the Popish-printer in Fetter-Lane. colop: *For Jonathan Low.* 1681. brs. O, EN; CH, MH, WF, Y.

Letter intercepted printed. 1660. *See* D., N.

Letter lately sent. 1642. *See* Hall, Joseph, *bp.*

1561   Entry cancelled.

Letter occasioned by a letter of my Lord Howard. 1681. *See* A letter to a friend, occasioned.

Letter occasioned by the second letter. 1685. *See* Burnet, Gilbert, *bp.*

1562   A letter of a French Protestant. *By A. M.*, 1688. 4°.* CJ; Y.

Letter of a gentleman. [*n.p.*], 1679. *See* Holles, Denzil Holles, *baron.*

1563   Entry cancelled.

Letter of a great victory. 1648. *See* Haslerig, *Sir* Arthur,
A letter from.
1563A A letter of a Jesuit of Liege. [*London*, 1687.] cap., 4°.* L.
Letter of a sad tragedy. 1648. *See* Jones, George.
1564 A letter of addresse from the officers of the army in
Scotland. *By John Field*, 1659. 4°.* L, O, C, BC, DU; CH,
CU, LC, MH, Y.
Letter of addresse to the Protector. [n.p., 1657.] *See* F., D.
Letter of advice concerning marriage. 1676. *See* B., A.
Letter of advice from a friend. 1684. *See* T., N.
1564A A letter of advice from a Protestant out of Ireland. *For
Robert Smith*, 1689. brs. CH, Y.
Letter of advice. From a secluded member. [n.p.], 1649.
See S., E.
Letter of advice sent. [n.p.], 1688. *See* O., A.
1565 A letter of advice sent to Sir Thomas Armstrong. 1684.
fol. LG (lost).
Letter of advice to a friend about the currency. 1696.
See J., R.
Letter of advice to a friend, upon. 1696. *See* Leslie,
Charles.
Letter of advice to a young gentleman. Dublin, 1670.
See Lingard, Richard.
1566 A letter of advice to a young gentleman of an honour-
able family, now in his travels. *For R. Clavell*, 1688.
8°. T.C.II 259. L, O, C, AN; CB, MH, MU, WF.
1567 A letter of advice to a young lady. *Printed, and are to be
sold by Richard Baldwin*, 1688. 8°.* L, LLP, BAMB; CLC,
MH, MIU, WF, Y.
1567A A letter of advice to all Protestant soldiers. *Printed*, 1688.
brs. L.
1568 A letter of advice to all the members of the Church of
England. *For Samuel Keble*, 1688. 4°.* L, O, C, E, DT;
CH, IU, MM, NC, NU, PU, Y.
Letter of advice to His Excellency. [n.p.], 1659. *See* J., T.
Letter of advice to the churches. 1700. *See* Mather,
Cotton.
Letter of advice to the Londoners. [n.p., 1643.] *See*
A., P.
1569 A letter of advice to the petitioning apprentices. colop:
By N. Thompson, 1681. brs. L, O, C; CH, MH, MU, AVP.
1570 A letter of advice vnto the ministers assembled. [*London*,
1646.] 4°.* LT, LW, OC, MR; CSS, WF, Y.
Letter of an Independent. [n.p.], 1645. *See* Swadlin,
Thomas.
1571 A letter of an Independent, to his honoured friend in
London. [*London*, 1647.] cap., 4°.* LT, OC, DT; CH, MH,
NU, WF.
1572 A letter of comfort to Richard Cromwell. *Printed* 1659.
4°.* LT, OC, MR, SP, DT; HR, CH, CN, MH, WF, Y.
Letter of due censure. 1650. *See* Parker, Henry.
Letter of examination. [n.p.], 1672. *See* Edmondson,
William.
Letter of friendly admonition. [n.p.], 1647. *See* Halifax,
George Savile, *marquess*.
1573 A letter of high consequence, principally. [*London*],
printed, 1642. 4°.* LT, LG; CLC, IU, MH, TU, WF, Y.

Letter of enquiry. 1689. *See* Taylor, James.
Letter of love. [n.p., 1669.] *See* Penn, William.
1573A A letter of many ministers. *For Thomas Vnderhill*, 1643.
4°. LT, O, C, BC, GU; CH, CN, LC, MH, NN, RPJ, Y.
1573B Entry cancelled. Ghost. *See previous entry.*
1573C A letter of November the 16th. [*London?*], *printed in the
year* 1659. 4°.* LLU, ESS; CH, CSS, MH, WF, Y.
Letter of queries. 1682. *See* M., T.
1574 A letter of religion to the Protestant-dissenters. *By F.
Leach, for Chr. Wilkinson*, 1675. 4°.* T.C.I 205. L, O,
OCC, CS; CASE WESTERN, CH, NU, Y.
1574A —[Anr. ed.] *For Chr. Wilkinson*, 1675. 4°.* LNC; CLC.
Letter of remarks. 1683. *See* Anglesey, Arthur Annesley,
earl.
Letter of resolution concerning Origen. 1661. *See* Rust,
George, *bp.*
Letter of resolution concerning the doctrines. [n.p.,
1691.] *See* Nye, Stephen.
1575 A letter of several French ministers. [*London*, 1688.] cap.,
4°.* L, O, CCA, MR, EN, DT; CH, CN, MH, NU, TU, WF, Y.
1576 A letter of spirituall advice. [*Oxford*], *by Henry Hall*.
1643. 4°.* MADAN 1298. O, DC, EN; CH, NU.
1576A —[Anr. ed.] [*London*], *printed*, 1643. 4°.* MADAN 1298n.
O, OC, MR, NE; CH, CN, TU, WF, Y.
Letter of thanks. Paris, 1666. *See* Sergeant, John.
1577 A letter of the apprentices of the city of Bristoll. *For
I. Pridmore*, 1660. 4°.* LT, O; CSS, PL, Y.
1578 A letter of the ministers of the city of London, presented
the first of Ian. 1645. *For Samuel Gellibrand*, 1645[6].
4°.* LT, O, MR, EN, DT; CH, CN, MH, TU, WF, Y.
1579 A letter of the officers of the army in Scotland . . . [Oct.
22]. *Edinburgh, by Christopher Higgins*, 1659. 4°.* ALDIS
1605. L, O, MR, EN; MIU, Y.
1580 —[Anr. ed.] colop: *Edinburgh, by Christopher Higgins, and
re-printed at London*, 1659. cap., 4°.* LT, O, LG, SP, BLH,
DT; CH, CLC, MH, PL, WF.
1581 A letter of the Presbyterian ministers. *For J. Johnson*,
1668. 4°.* O, OC, CJ, DU, MR, CD; CH, CN, NU, WF, Y.
1582 A letter of the svrrender of Sterling-Castle. *For Francis
Leach*, 1651. 4°.* LT; CH, WF.
1583 Letter of the 22 of December, 1659. 1659. LUS (dispersed).
Letter of vnity. 1648. *See* W., S.
1583A A letter on George Keith's advertisement. *Printed and
sold by T. Sowle*, 1697. 4°.* L, LF, LSD; MH, NN, PH.
1584 A letter on the subject of the succession. *Printed at
London*, 1679. fol.* LT, O, C, MR, DU; CH, CN, LC, MH,
NU, Y.
1584A A letter or an epistle to all well-minded men. *Printed*
1649. 4°.* DU; CSS, MIU, Y.
Letter or declaration, sent. 1650. *See* Lathbury, Thomas.
Letter out of Flanders. 1660. *See* S., G.
Letter out of France. 1672. *See* F., J.
1584B A letter out of Holland, dated April 30. *By J. C. for
R. Robinson*, 1672. 4°.* LPR; CH, CN, LC, MH, Y.
Letter out of Ireland, from an eminent divine. 1689.
See Hewson, M.

Letter out of Lancashire. [n.p.], 1694. *See* Wagstaffe, Thomas.

Letter out of Scotland. 1681. *See* L'Estrange, *Sir* Roger.

Letter out of Suffolk. 1694. *See* Wagstaffe, Thomas.

1585   A letter out of the countrey, to a friend. *For Jacob Tonson*, 1695. 4°.* L, OC, CS, BAMB; CH, NU, WF.

Letter out of the country, to a member. 1689. *See* Maurice, Henry.

Letter out of the country, to the clergy. [n.p., 1692.] *See* B., A.

1586   Entry cancelled. Ghost.

1587   A letter really written by a moderate Cavallier. *Printed*, 1647. 4°.* LT, O, MR, DT; NU, WF, Y.

1588   A letter respecting an act for continuing several duties. *For E. Whitlock*, 1696. brs. MC.

Letter sent by a Yorkshire gentleman. [n.p., 1642.] *See* Bourchier, *Sir* John.

1589   A letter sent by an Oxford scholler to his quondam schoolemaster. [*Oxford*], *for W. Webb*, 1642[3]. 4°.* MADAN 1259. O, OC, DU, LNC, DT; CH, CCC, CLC.

1590   Entry cancelled.

Letter sent by order of both Houses. 1642. *See* England. Parliament.

1591   A letter sent by Sir Iohn Svckling from France. *Imprinted at London*, 1641. 4°.* LT, O, OQ, LLU; CH, IU, MH, TU, WF, Y.

1592   A letter sent by the commissioners of the kingdome of Scotland. 1647. 4°.* OB, CM, MR; CSS, MH, WF.

Letter sent by the Emperor of Morocco. 1682. *See* Keriff, Ismael.

Letter sent by the Grand Visier. 1687. *See* Azen, Solyman Mahomet.

1593   Entry cancelled.

Letter sent by those assembled. 1641. *See* Coppy of I. The letter.

1594   A letter sent from a countrey gentleman to a friend, a member. [*Oxford, H. Hall*], *printed*, 1642. 4°.* MADAN 1128. L, O, OC; CH, WF.

Letter sent from a gentleman in the Hague. [n.p., 1649.] *See* G., R.

1595   A letter sent from a gentleman in Oxford, to his friend in London. [*Oxford, by L. Lichfield*], 1646. 4°.* MADAN 1860. LG, OCC, OL, EN; CSS, IU, NU.

1596   A letter sent from a gentleman at Beverley. *For Tho. Banks and William Lee*, July 21. 1642. brs. LT, O, EC.

Letter sent from a gentleman to Mr. Henry Martin. 1642. *See* Copley, Lionel.

Letter sent from a merchant. 1659. *See* J., T.

Letter sent from a private gentleman to a friend in London. [n.p.], 1642. *See* F.

1597   A letter sent from a worthy divine, to the Right Honorable the Lord Mayor of the city of London. *Octob.* 27. *for Robert Wood*, 1642. 4°.* LT, O, LG; WF.

1598   A letter sent from a worthy divine. *Printed at London by Richard Cotes*, 1642. brs. L, CJ.

Letter sent from aboard. 1648. *See* B., C.

Letter sent from beyond. [n.p.], 1674. *See* Hickes, George.

Letter sent from Constantinople. 1685/6. *See* R., P. A copy of.

1599   A letter sent from His Excellency Generall Blake. *For D. G.*, 1652. 4°.* LT.

1600   No entry.

1601   Letter sent from Ireland, dated. *By John Streater, and John Macock*, 1659[60]. 4°.* LT, O, DN; CSS, MH, MU, V.

1602   No entry.

1603   A letter sent from Newport. [*London*], *printed*, 1648. 4°.* LT, O, MR; CLC, CSS, MH, MU, Y.

Letter sent from Portsmouth. [n.p., 1659.] *See* L., N.

1604   A letter sent from several agitators. *For John Harris*. 1647. 4°.* LT, O, MR; CH, MH, NU, WF, Y.

1605   A letter sent from the agitators of the army. *Oxford, by J.H. and H.H.*, 1647. 4°.* MADAN 1942. OW, AN, YM, ESS, EN.

1606   Entry cancelled.

Letter sent from the commissioners of Scotland. 1660. *See* Scotland. Commissioners.

1607   A letter sent from the court of his Royal Maiesty the King of France. *For Sam: Cotton*, 1652. 4°.* LT; CH.

1608   A letter sent from the devises in Wiltshire. [*London*], *for W. Webb*, 1643. 4°.* Y.

1609   A letter sent from the inhabitants of Hull. *For F. B., May 12*. 1642. 4°.* LT, O, LL, SP, YM; CH, CSS, NU, Y.

1609A   —[Anr. ed.] *Printed* 1642. 4°.* O, C, LLU; MH, WF.

1609AB   —[Anr. ed.] *For Ed. Blackmore, May 13*, 1642. 4°.* CJ; CLC.

Letter sent from the Leagver. [1642.] *See* S., T.

1609B   A letter sent from the Lord Goring directed to the Lord Maior. *By B.A.*, 1648. 4°.* CT; CH, MIU.

1609C   A letter sent from the Maior, burgesses . . . Hull. *For I. T. Iune 17*. 1642. 4°.* MH.

Letter sent from the provost vice-chancellour of Oxford. 1642. *See* Pinke, Robert.

1610   A letter sent from the Queen of England. *For Nathaniel Williamson*, 1648. 4°.* LT, O; MH, MU.

1611   A letter sent trom [*sic*] the states of Holland. *For R. VV.*, 1648. 4°.* LT.

1612   A letter sent from the states of Holland to the King of Scots, imploring. *For George Horton*, 1652. 4°.* LT.

1613   A letter sent from those lords, whose names. [*London*, 1642.] brs. STEELE 2172. LT, BR, LNC; CH, MH, MU, Y.

Letter sent into France. [n.p.], 1649. *See* J., G.

1614   A letter sent out of Holland. *For Thomas Johnson*, 1642. 4°.* LT, LG, OC, OW; CH, IU, Y.

Letter sent ovt of Ireland. 1642. *See* Farmer, Jacob.

Letter sent to a friend. [n.p.], 1675. *See* Stopford, Joshua.

1614A   A letter sent to a noble lord . . . of a great miracle. *Imprinted*, 1649. 4°.* MIU, TORONTO ACAD. OF MED.

Letter sent to a worthy member. 1642. *See* Giffard, John.

Letter sent to an honourable gentleman. [n.p.], 1641. *See* Hall, Joseph, *bp.*

1615   A letter sent to D[uke]. L[auderdale]. [*London*, 1679.] cap., 4°.* L, MR; PL, Y.

1616   A letter sent to Dr. Tillotson several months ago. [*London?* 1690.] cap., 4°.* L, O, CT, LSD, MR; CLC, CN, MH, NP, WF, Y.

Letter sent to General Monk. 1659. *See* Nichols, Henry.

1617   A letter sent to George Wither, poetica licentia. 1646. cap., 4°.* LT, DT.

1618   A letter sent to His Majestie, from a honorable member of . . . Commons. *For Richard Bartlet:* 1643. 4°.* LT, MR, SP, DT; MH, WF, Y.

1619   A letter sent to His Majestie, from the lords justices, and councell in Ireland, April 23. 1642. *By Robert Barker; and by the assignes of John Bill,* 1642. 4°.* LT, O, C, DN, DT; CH, MH, MU, NCD, WF, Y. (var.)

Letter sent to London. [n.p.], 1643. *See* Taylor, John.

1620   A letter sent to Master Speaker, from the knights, esqvires, . . . of Lincoln. *Printed at York, by Stephen Bulkley for Marke Foster,* 28 July 1642. brs. STEELE 2224. L.

Letter sent to Mr. Garway. [n.p., 1673]. *See* N., H.

Letter sent to Mr. Speaker. 1642. *See* Brookhaven, John.

Letter sent to my Lord Maior. 1642. *See* Streater, Aaron.

Letter sent to the Earl. 1648. *See* Ascue, George.

1621   A letter sent to the Honourable George Lord Digby. *Printed at London for R. J.,* 1641[2]. 4°.* LT, O, CT, DT; CLC, MU, NU, WF, Y.

Letter sent to the Honourable William Lenthall. 1644. *See* Pindar, Martin.

—[Same title.] 1645. *See* Rushworth, John.

Letter sent to the King. [n.p., 1666.] *See* Fell, Margaret.

Letter sent to the Right Honourable Edward Earle of Manchester. [n.p.], 1648. *See* Fortescue, Anthony.

1622   A letter sent to the right honourable the Lord Mayor. *For George Whittington,* [1647]. 4°.* LT, LG, LL, DC, DT; CH, MH, MIU, MU, NN.

1623   A letter sent to the Right Honourable, the Lord Mayor of . . . London. *By Henry Hills,* 1659[60]. brs. LT, LG.

1624   Entry cancelled.

Letter sent to the right honourable William Lenthal. 1659. *See* Butler, John.

1625   A letter sent to the Right Honourable William Lenthall . . . concerning the raising. *By Edward Husbands, Iuly* 10, 1645. 4°.* LT, O, BR, LSD, MR; MH, NN.

1626   A letter sent to the Right Honourable Wm. Lenthall . . . concerning the routing of Col: Gorings army. *For John Field, Iuly* 22. 1645. 4°.* LT, O, BR; MH.

1627–8   Entries cancelled.

Letter shewing that a restraint. 1698. *See* A letter to a member of Parliament shewing.

Letter shewing the necessity. Oxford, 1699. *See* Defoe, Daniel. A letter to a member.

1629   A letter to A. B. C. D. E. F &c. *For Dan Brown,* 1698. 4°.* T.C.III 56. L, O, C, EN; CU.

1630   —[Anr. ed.] *For D. Brown, and R. Smith, sold by E. VVhitlock,* 1698. 4°.* L, DT; CH, CN, MB, MIU, TO, WF, Y.

1631   A letter to a baron of England. *Printed,* 1679. fol.* L, O, C, OC; CH, INU, MH, WF, Y.

Letter to a bishop concerning. 1689. *See* Comber, Thomas.

Letter to a bishop from. 1691. *See* W., F.

1631A   A letter to a citizen of London, from his friend in the country. colop: *Printed,* 1689. cap., 4°.* MH.

Letter to a convocation-man. 1697. *See* Shower, *Sir* Bartholomew.

Letter to a country-gentleman. 1698. *See* W., G.

Letter to a deist. 1677. *See* Stillingfleet, Edward, *bp.*

Letter to a Dissenter. [n.p., 1687.] *See* Halifax, George Savile, *marquess.*

1632   A letter to a Dissenter, concerning the necessity. [*London*], *printed,* 1689. 4°.* L, O, OC; CH, CN, MH, NU, WF, Y.

1633   Entry cancelled.

Letter to a Dissenter from his friend. Hague, 1688. See Defoe, Daniel.

1634   A letter to a dissenting clergy-man. *For Richard Baldwin,* 1690. 4°.* T.C.II 339. L, O, CT, LSD, DT; CH, CN, MH, NU, TSM, WF, Y.

1635   A letter to a foreigner. *For Dan. Brown,* 1698. 4°.* T.C.III 56. L, O, CT, LIU, EN; CH, CN, MB, TU, WF, Y.

1636   A letter to a friend. [*London,* 1689?] brs. L, MR; CN, IU.

1637   A letter to a friend, about the late proclamation on the 11th. of December, 1679. *Printed,* 1679. 4°.* T.C.I 407. L, O, C, DU, EN, DT; CH, CN, NC, WF, Y.

1638   A letter to a friend, advising. *For Abel Roper,* 1689. brs. L, C, LG, HH, EN; CH, CN.

Letter to a friend: being. [1684.] *See* B., A.

Letter to a friend, concerning a French. 1692. *See* Sherlock, William.

1638A   A letter to a friend, concerning a late pamphlet. *Printed,* 1696. 4°.* LUG, CT; CH, MH, MIU.

1639   Entry cancelled.

Letter to a friend, concerning a postscript. 1694. See Howe, John.

1639A   A letter to a friend concerning credit. *For Andr. Bell,* 1697. cap., 4°.* L; CH, CSS, NIC, WF.

Letter to a friend, concerning his. 1692. *See* Davies, Rowland.

Letter to a friend concerning some. 1670. *See* Vernon, George.

1639B   Letter to a friend concerning the Bank of England. 1696. *See* P., S.

Letter to a friend concerning the behaviour. 1693. *See* Allix, Pierre.

Letter to a friend concerning the bill. [n.p.], 1700. *See* E., R.

1640   A letter to a friend, concerning the credit of the nation. *For E. Whitlock,* 1697. 4°.* L, O, LUG; CH, CSS, MH, Y.

1640A   —[Anr. ed.] *Printed,* 1697. 4°.* IU, MH, NC, P U.WF,

1641   A letter to a friend, concerning the Duke of Norfolk's bill. [*London,* 1700?] cap., fol.* LC, NP, Y.

1642   A letter to a friend. Concerning the East-India trade. *Printed, and are to be sold by E. Whitlock,* 1696. 4°.* L, O, LG, LUG, EN, DT; CH, IU, MH, NC, NR, WF, Y.

Letter to a friend concerning the late answers. [n.p.], 1687. *See* F., S.

1643   A letter to a friend, concerning the nature of the divine
       persons in the Holy Trinity. *For S. Manship*, 1698.
       4°.* L, O, CS, BAMB, LSD; CLC, MBA.

1644   A letter to a friend concerning the next Parliament's
       sitting. [*London*], *for J. K.*, 1681. brs. L, O; CH, MH.

1644A A letter to a friend concerning the partition treaty.
       [*London*, 1700?] cap., fol.* MH, NC, Y.

1645   A letter to a friend, concerning the present proposal.
       [*London?* 1699.] brs. L; MIU, Y.

1645A A letter to a friend concerning the present state of
       affairs. [*London*, 1693.] cap., 4°.* L; MM, WF, Y.

1645B Belfast, May 8. 1690. A letter to a friend, concerning the
       present state of the army in Ireland. *For Robert Clavell*,
       1690. brs. C, DN; CH, Y.

       Letter to a friend concerning the sickness. [1700.] *See* P., B.

       Letter to a friend concerning usury. 1690. *See*, C., R.

1645C A letter to a friend, containing certain observations. *For
       Benjamin Tooke*, 1682. 4°.* T.C.I 486. L, O, C, MR, EN,
       DT; CH, CN, MH, WF, Y.

1645D —[Anr. ed., "freind."] *Dublin*, re-printed 1682. 4°.* DIX
       196. L, OCC, DU; CH, MB.

       Letter to a friend, containing some queries. [n.p.], 1689.
       See Jane, William.

       Letter to a friend, giving. 1692. *See* Monro, Alexander.

1646   A letter to a friend, in answer to a letter to a dissenter.
       colop: *For J. Harris*, 1687. brs. O, OC, CS, DU; CH, CN,
       MU, WF, Y.

       Letter to a friend, in answer to a letter. 1688. *See* Gras-
       combe, Samuel.

1647   A letter to a friend in answer to the enquiry into the
       present state of affairs. [*London*, 1690?] 4°.* LL, OC, CT,
       WCA.

       Letter to a friend in the country, being. [n.p.], 1680.
       See P., J.

1648   A letter to a friend in the country, concerning his Grace
       the Duke of Buckingham. [*London*, 1679.] cap., fol.*
       EN; CH, MH, WF, Y.

1649   A letter to a friend in the country, concerning the pro-
       rogation. [*London*, 1681.] brs. L, O, OP; CH, MBA, MH, Y.

1650   A letter to a friend in the country, concerning the use
       of instrumental musick. *For A. Baldwin*, 1698. 4°.
       L, O, C, LLP, OC, CT, CD; LC, WF, Y.

1650A A letter to a friend in the country. Giving an account.
       [*London*, 1696.] brs. C.

1651   A letter to a friend in the country. Sir, you are pleased.
       colop: *Printed*, 1695. cap., 4°.* L, OC, CT, LSD, MR; CLC,
       IU, MH, MM, NP, WF, Y.

1652   A letter to a friend in the country, touching. [*London*,
       1680.] fol.* L, O, LNC, MR; CH, MH, WF.

1653   A letter to a friend, in vindication of the proceedings
       against Sir John Fenwick. *For Samuel Heyrick*, 1697.
       4°.* L, C, LLP, MR, LSD; CH, CN, MB, WF, Y.

1654   A letter to a friend, occasioned by my Lord Howard of
       Escricks letter. colop: *For A. B.*, 1681. cap., fol.*
       L, O, LL, DU, MR; CH, CN, MH, TU, WF, Y.

       Letter to a friend, occasion'd by the surrender. 1691.
       See Wetenhall, Edward.

1654A A letter to a friend. Perhaps mankind might not be
       worse. [*London*, 1691.] 4°.* CS, LSD, MR; CH, CN, NC,
       TU, WF. (var.)

       Letter to a friend, reflecting on. 1687. *See* Ellis, Clement.

       A letter to a friend, reflecting upon the present condi-
       tion. [n.p., 1680?] *See* P.

       Letter to a friend relating. 1690. *See* Prideaux, Hum-
       phrey.

1655   A letter to a friend. Shewing from scripture, fathers, and
       reason. *Printed*, 1679. fol.* T.C.I 397. L, O, DU, LNC, MR;
       CH, MH, NU, WF, Y.

       Letter to a freind [*sic*], shewing the illegal. 1645. *See*
       C., A.

       Letter to a friend to vindicate. 1645. *See* Lilburne,
       Robert.

       Letter to a friend touching. 1678. *See* Troughton, John.

1655A Entry cancelled.

       Letter to a friend, touching Dr. Jeremy Taylor's Dissuas-
       ive. 1665. *See* L., A.

1656   A letter to a friend, upon the dissolution of the late
       Parliament. colop: *Printed*, 1690. brs. L, O, LIU, MC, EN;
       CH, CN, PL, TU, WF, Y. (var.)

1657   Entry cancelled.

       Letter to a friend, upon the dissolving. 1690. *See* Leti,
       Gregorio.

       Letter to a friend: with remarks. 1700. *See* B., A.

1657A A letter to a gentleman about the election . . . Cam-
       bridge. colop: *Printed* 1690. brs. L, C, OC; PL.

1658   A letter to a gentleman at Brussels. *Printed*, 1689. 4°.*
       L, O, C, DU, EN; CH, IU, LC, MM, NC, TU, Y.

       Letter to a gentleman elected. [n.p., 1694.] *See* Wag-
       staffe, Thomas.

1659   A letter to a gentleman in answer to a late book, en-
       tituled, A discourse concerning the period of humane
       life. *Printed and are to be sold by Enoch Wyer*, 1677. 4°.*
       T.C.I 293. L, O, CCH, SP; CH, NC.

1660   A letter to a gentleman in the commission of the peace.
       For Benj. Tooke, 1695. 8°. LLP; MH.

1661   Letter to a gentleman in the country concerning the
       price of guineas. [*London*, 1695/6.] fol.* NC, Y.

1661A A letter to a gentleman in the country concerning the
       project . . . coin. [*London?* 1695.] brs. HH; Y.

       Letter to a gentleman in the country, giving. 1684. *See*
       Barbon, Nicholas.

1661B A letter to a gentleman in the country, in answer to
       W. H. *For the author*, 1682. 4°.* DUS; MIU, Y.

       Letter to a gentleman of Leicester-shire. [n.p.], 1643.
       See Heylyn, Peter.

       Letter to a gentleman of note. 1690. *See* Jenks, Benjamin.

       A letter to a gentleman of the insurance office. [n.p.],
       1681. *See* I., W.

       Letter to a gentleman touching. 1690. *See* N., N.

1661C A letter to a gentleman upon a royal fishery. colop: *For
       E. Whitlock*, 1698. brs. MH, WF.

1662   A letter to a gentleman upon occasion of some new
       opinions. *For Walter Kettilby*, 1696. 4°.* L, O, C, LW,
       LIU; CLC, MIU, NU, TSM, WF, Y.

1663   A letter to a gentlewoman concerning government. *Printed: and sold by E. Whitlocke*, 1697. 4°.* L, D; CLC, MB, WF, Y.

A letter to A. H. Esq: concerning the stage. 1698. *See* Milbourne, Luke.

Letter to a lady concerning. 1696. *See* Stephens, Edward.

Letter to a lady, furnishing. 1688. *See* Barecroft, Charles.

1664   A letter to a lawyer. *For John Eglesfeild*, 1685. 4°.* L, O, LLL, LSD, DT; CH, CLC, IU, MH, AVP.

1665   Entry cancelled.

Letter to a livery-man. [n.p., 1695.] *See* H., R.

Letter to a lord concerning a bill. [1698?] *See* N., N.

1666   A letter to a lord, in answer to a late pamphlet. *For Tho. Bennet*, 1692. 4°.* T.C.II 427. L, O, C, LLU, CD; HR, CH, CLC, IU, NU, PU, WF, Y.

Letter to A. M. 1698. *See* B., F.

Letter to a member of Parliament concerning. 1699/1700. *See* B., J.

1667   A letter to a member of Parliament concerning clandestine trade. *Printed, and sold by A. Baldwin*, 1700. 4°.* T.C.III 188. L, LLP, LUG; HR, CN, LC, MH, NC, PL, Y.

1668   A letter to a member of Parliament concerning guards and garisons. *For A. Baldwin*, 1699. 4°.* L, O, LIU, AU, DT; CH, CN, MH, PL, TU, WF, Y.

1669   A letter to a member of Parliament concerning the bank. *Edinburgh, by John Reid, to be sold by Robert Allan*, 1696. 4°.* ALDIS 3577. L, LUG, ES, AU; NC, RPJ.

1670   A letter to a member of Parliament concerning the four regiments commonly called Mariners. *For A. Baldwin*, 1699. 4°.* L, O, LUG, LIU, DT; CH, CN, MH, WF, Y.

1671   A letter to a member of Parliament for liberty of conscience. colop: *By Rich. Baldwin*, 1689. cap., fol.* L, O; CH, MB, WF, Y.

Letter to a member of Parliament for settling guineas. [n.p., 1696.] *See* H., G.

1672   Entry cancelled.

Letter to a member of Parliament, from a wel-wisher. [n.p., 1697.] *See* Donaldson, James.

Letter to a member of Parliament, from his friend. [n.p., 1696.] *See* R., S.

1673   Letter to a member of Parliament, Honoured Sir, it cannot. [London, 169–?] cap., 4°.* Y.

Letter to a member of Parliament, in favour. 1689. *See* N., N.

1674   A letter to a member of Parliament in the country, concerning the present posture of affairs in Christendom. *Printed*, 1700. 4°.* L, O, C, LLU, EN; CH, CN, MHL, TU, WF, Y.

1675   —Second edition. —, 1700. 4°.* L, O, CS, CD, DT; HR, CLC, MH, NC, TU, WF, Y.

1676   A letter to a member of Parliament, now in the country. *Printed, and sold by John Nutt*, 1700. 8°.* O, C.

Letter to a member of Parliament; occasioned by a letter. 1697. *See* Wright, William.

1677   A letter to a member of Parliament, occasioned, by the growing poverty of the nation. *Edinburgh, printed*, 1700. 4°.* ALDIS 3980. L, LUG; CH, LC, MH, NC, WF, Y.

1678   A letter to a member of Parliament, occasion'd by the votes. *Printed* 1695. 4°.* L, O, C, LUG, CT; CH, CN, MM, TU, WF, Y.

1679   A letter to a member of Parliament on the account of some present transactions. colop: *By F. Leach*, 1689. brs. L, O, C, LG, HH; CH, CN, MH, TU, WF, Y. (var.)

Letter to a member of Parliament; shewing. 1697. *See* Houghton, Thomas.

1680   A letter to a member of Parliament, shewing, that a restraint on the press. *By J. Darby, sold by Andr. Bell*, 1698. 4°.* L, LLP, OP, CT, DUS, DT; CH, LC, MH, NC, TU, Y.

1681   —[Anr. ed.] *By J. Darby, and sold by A. B.*, 1700. 4°. T.C.III 188. O, EN; WF.

Letter to a member of Parliament, shewing the necessity. *Oxford*, 1699. *See* Defoe, Daniel.

1681A   A letter to a member of Parliament. Sir, I heartily congratulate. [*London*, 1693.] fol.* OP.

1682   A letter to a member of Parliament. With two discourses. [*London*], *printed*, 1675. 4°.* L, O, CJ, E; CH, MH, WF, Y.

Letter to a member of Parliament, written. 1699. *See* H., H.

1683   A letter to a member of the Gommittee [sic] of Grievances. [n.p., 1690.] brs. L, O, LLP, OC, CS; CH, WF.

1684   Entry cancelled.

Letter to a member of the convention. [n.p., 1688.] *See* Sherlock, William.

Letter to a member of the convocation. 1699. *See* Usher, Charles.

1684A   A letter to a member of the high and honourable court of Parliament. [*London*], *sold by Randal Taylor*, 1689. 4°.* LLL, LLP, EC; CSU, NP, NU.

1685   A letter to a member of the honourable House of Commons; in answer to three queries. *Printed, and are to be sold by E. Whitlock*, 1697. 8°.* L, O, LUG, CT, SP; CH, MH, NC, PU, WF, Y.

1686   A letter to a member of the honourable House of Commons, speaking his humble desires. colop: *Printed*, 1660. cap., 4°.* LT, O, CD; CH, MH, PL.

Letter to a member of the House of Commons, concerning the bishops. 1689. *See* Maurice, Henry.

1686A   A letter to a member of the House of Commons, concerning the proceedings. [*London*, 1699?] 4°. CS, MR; MH.

1686B   A letter to a member of the House of Commons, in answer to a book. *Printed*, 1647. 4°.* SP; MH, Y.

1687   A letter to a member of the late Parliament. [n.p.], *printed*, 1700. 4°.* O, CS, EC, LSD, EN; MH, NC, WF, WSL.

1688   A letter to a member of this present Parliament. *Printed*, 1688. 4°.* L, C, CT, SP; CH, IU, MBA, NC, NU, WF, Y.

1689   A letter to a noble lord at London from a friend at Oxford. *Oxford*[by L. Lichfield], *printed*, 1643. 4°.* MADAN 1396. L, O, OC, DC, EN, DT; CH, CLC.

1690   —[Anr. ed.] [*London*], *printed*, 1643. 4°.* LT, O, CJ, EC, DT; CH, CLC, MH, NU, WF, Y.

1691   —[Anr. ed.] [*Oxford, by L. Lichfield*], *printed, February* 22, 1643[4]. 4°.* MADAN 1538. O, OC, BC, EN; CH, CLC, CU.

Letter to a noble lord concerning. [n.p., 1681.] *See* M., D.

Letter to a noble peer. [n.p., 1681.] *See* S., L.

Letter to a non-conformist. 1677. *See* Calder, Robert.

1692   Entry cancelled.

Letter to a parliament-man. 1649. *See* Letter written out of the countrey.

Letter to a peer of the Church of England. 1687. *See* Sabran, Lewis.

Letter to a person of honour, concerning. [n.p., 1680.] *See* Ferguson, Robert.

Letter to a person of honour in London. 1663. *See* M., H.

Letter to a person of quality, concerning. 1668. *See* Du Moulin, Peter.

1692A   A letter to a person of quality, concerning the Archbishop of Canterbury's sentence. *Printed*, 1699. 4°.* L, CS, DU, LSD; NN, Y.

1692B   A letter to a person of quality, occasioned by a printed libel. [*London?* 1678.] cap., 4°.* O.

1693   A letter to a person of quality, occasioned by the burning. [*London*, 1681.] brs. L.

Letter to a person of quality, occasion'd by the news. [n.p., 1688.] *See* S., R.

1694   A letter to a physician concerning acid and alkali. *For Andrew Bell*, 1700. 8°. T.C.III 185. LCS; HC.

1695   A letter to a priest of the Roman Church. *By Andrew Clark, for Henry Brome*, 1675. 4°.* T.C.I 188. L, O, LLP, CM, DT; CH, IU, MH, NU, WF.

1696   A letter to a reverend minister of the Gospel. [*Edinburgh*, 1689.] cap., 4°.* ALDIS 2913.5. L, O, A, E, EN; CLC, IU, MH, NPT, WF, Y.

1697   A letter to a virtuous lady. colop: *For John Harris*, 1686. brs. O; CH, CN, MH, Y.

Letter to young divine. 1692. *See* Prince, J.

1698   A letter to an eminent member of Parliament, about the present rate of guineas. [*London*, 1695.] cap., fol.* L, LUG, OC, MR; CH, MH, NC, PL, WF, Y.

Letter to an honest citizen. [n.p., 1692.] *See* S., T.

Letter to an honourable member of Parliament. [n.p., 1700.] *See* W., R.

1699   A letter to an honourable member of the House of Commons; in the vindication of the Protestant Reformed Church. *Printed*, 1679[80]. 4°.* L, O, LL, LSD, P; CH, CLC, IU, MH, VC, WF, Y.

Letter to Ann, Duchess of York. [n.p.], 1670. *See* Morley, George, *bp.*

Letter to Anonymus. 1683. *See* Sherlock, William.

Letter to both Houses. Paris, 1679. *See* P., E.

Letter to Doctor Bates. 1695. *See* Lobb, Stephen.

Letter to Dr. Bvrnet. [n.p., 1685.] *See* Lowth, Simon.

1700   A letter to Dr. du Moulin. *Printed*, 1680. fol.* L, O, BC, LSD, MR; CH, MH, PU, WF, Y.

Letter to Dr. E. Hyde. [n.p., 1655.] *See* Ley, John.

Letter to Dr. E. S., 1687. *See* Meredith, Edward.

1701   A letter to Doctor Lancaster, wherein. *Printed*, 1697. 4°.* L, C; MH, NC, NS, WF, Y.

Letter to Dr. Samuel Turner. 1647. *See* Fountaine, John.

Letter to Dr. Sherlock. 1691. *See* Lloyd, William, *bp.*

Letter to Dr. T. Robinson. [n.p., 1697.] *See* Harris, John.

Letter to Dr. W. Payne. [n.p., 1689.] *See* Grascombe, Samuel.

Letter to Dr. William Needham. 1688. *See* Sabran, Lewis.

Letter to Father Lewis Sabran 1688. *See* Gee, Edward, *younger.*

1702   A letter to Father Petre. *For Randal Taylor*, 1691. 4°.* NE, P; CN, CSS, IU.

1702A   A letter to Father Petres from the Devil. colop: *For R. M.*, 1689. brs. CT; Y.

1703   A letter to Ferguson. *For Joseph Hindmarsh*, 1684. fol.* L, O, LLP, EN; CH, CLC, NCD.

1704   A letter to General Monk, expressing. [*London*, 1660.] brs. LT; CH, MH.

Letter to General Monck, in answer. 1659. *See* Morris, Richard.

1704A   A letter to George Keith, concerning his late religious differences with William Pen and his party. colop: *For R. Baldwin*, 1696. cap., 4°.* NN, RPJ.

Letter to George Keith concerning the salvability of the heathen. 1700. *See* Humfrey, John.

1705   A letter to Hilton, the Grand Informer. colop: *For R. Lee*. 1682. brs. O, C; CH, IU, MH, Y.

Letter to his Excellency. 1659. *See* S., T.

Letter to his Excellency. [n.p., 1660.] *See* Maudit, John.

Letter to his Grace the D. of Monmouth. [n.p., 1680.] *See* F., C.

1706   A letter to His Highness the Prince of Orange. *For R.J.*, 1689. 4°.* OC, LSD; Y.

Letter to his most excellent Majesty. 1699. *See* Stephens, William.

1707   A letter to his Royal Highness the Duke of York. colop: *For William Inghall*, 1681. fol.* L, O, CT, BR, DT; CH, IU, LC, MH, TU, Y.

Letter to his worthy friend. 1696. *See* Connor, Bernard.

1708   A letter to J. C. Esq.; upon Mr. Toland's book. *Dublin*, 1697. fol.* DIX 292. DT.

1709   A letter to Lieutenant Collonel John Lilburn. colop: *By Henry Hills*, 1653. cap., 4°.* LT, CT, MR; WF.

1710   Entry cancelled.

Letter to Lord Digby. 1641. *See* A letter sent to the Honourable George Lord Digby.

Letter to Mr. Braine. [n.p., 1650.] *See* Chamberlen, Peter.

1711   Entry cancelled. *See* L1713A.

1712   Letter to Mr. Congreve, occasion'd. *For E. Whitlock*, 1698. fol.* LVF; CLC, Y.

1713   Entry cancelled. Ghost.

1713A   A letter to Mr. Congreve on his pretended amendments. *For Samuel Keble*, 1698. 4°.* L, O, C, CS, LSD, DT; CLC, CN, MB, MH, PU, TU, WF, Y.

Letter to Mr. G. 1687. *See* Stillingfleet, Edward.

1713B   A letter to Mr. Henry Stubs concerning his censure. *For Octavian Pullen*, 1670. 4°.* L, O, CS, NPL, DT; CH, MIU, WF, WSG.

1714 A letter to Mr. James Parkinson. *For Robert Clavel, 1691.* 4°.* T C.II 362. O, DU, WCA, CD; CH, NC, NU . . .

1715 A letter to Mr. Marriot from a friend. *For the friends of Mr. Marriot, 1652.* 4°.* LT.

Letter to Mr. Miles Prance. [n.p., 1682.] *See* Everett, George.

1716 Entry cancelled.

Letter to Mr. Nathaniel Tenche. 1689. *See* White, George.

Letter to Mr. Penn. 1688. *See* Popple, *Sir* William.

1717 A letter to Mr. Robert Bridgman. [*London*], *printed and sold by the booksellers of London and Westminster, 1700.* 4°. L, LF, DU; PH, PHS.

Letter to Mr. Robert Burscough. 1700. *See* Stoddon, Samuel.

1718 A letter to Mr. S. a Romish priest. [*London, 1672.*] cap., fol.* L, O, C, LNC, LSD; CH, CN, MH, WF, Y.

1719 A letter to Mr. Samuel Johnson, occasion'd by his argument. [*London, 1692.*] 4°.* L, O, CT, LSD, MR; CN, TU, Y.

Letter to Mr. Secretary Trenchard. [n.p., 1694.] *See* Ferguson, Robert.

1720 No entry.

A letter to Mr. Settle. [n.p.], 1683. *See* S., W.

Letter . . . to Mr. Simon Lowth. 1685. *See* Burnet, Gilbert, *bp.*

Letter to Mr. Speaker Lenthal. [n.p.], 1646. *See* Warwick, *Sir* Philip.

1721 A letter to Mr. Tho. Edwards. *For Tho. Veere, 1647.* 4°.* LT, DT; MB, MH, WF, Y.

Letter to Monsieur Van B——. [n.p., 1676.] *See* Holles, Denzil Holles, *baron.*

1722 Letter to Nicholas Ridley Bishop of London for the taking downe of altars. 1641. 4°.* CHRISTIE-MILLER.

Letter to one of the chief. [n.p.], 1674. *See* Pettus, *Sir* John.

1722A A letter to S. C. M. a member of Parliament . . . Barbadoes. [*London?* 1700.] cap., 4°.* RPJ.

Letter to Sir Thomas Osborn. 1672. *See* Buckingham, George Villiers, *2d duke of.*

Letter to some divines. 1695. *See* P., J. W.

1723 A letter to the admired fraternity of the Order of R. C. *By J. C. for William Ley, 1655.* 4°.* LT.

Letter to the answerer. [n.p., 1667.] *See* M., P.

Letter to the arch-bishops. [n.p., 1697.] *See* Bugg, Francis.

Letter to the author of a book. [n.p., 1694.] *See* Elys, Edmund.

Letter to the author of a late. [n.p.], 1689. *See* Hickes, George.

Letter to the author of a sermon. [n.p., 1695.] *See* Ken, Thomas, *bp.*

Letter to the author of Milton's life. 1699. *See* C., J.

1724 A letter to the author of the Dutch design, anatomized. colop: [*London*], *November the 8th, 1688.* fol.* LL, OC, EN; MH, MM, NP, TU, WF, Y.

1725 —[Anr. ed.] [*London, 1689.*] 4°.* L, OC, MR; CH, MH, NU, WF.

Letter to the author of the late letter. [n.p., 1690.] *See* Wagstaffe, Thomas.

1726 Entry cancelled.

Letter to the author of the preparation. 1682. *See* Letter to the late author.

Letter to the author of the reply. 1687. *See* Darrell, William.

1727 A letter to the author of the vindication of the ecclesiastical commissioners. [*Oxford, 1688.*] cap., 4°.* L, OC, CS, EC, EN; CH, CN, MH, TU, WF, Y.

1728 A letter to the author of the vindication of the proceedings. *Printed Eleutheropolis.* [*Oxford, 1688.*] 4°.* L, O, CT, DU, DT; CH, MH, MU, TU, NU, WF, Y.

1728A A letter to the authors of the answers to the case of the allegiance. colop: *For Randal Taylor, 1691.* cap., 4°.* T.C.II 364. L, CT, BAMB; CH, CLC, MBA, MH.

1728B —[Anr. ed.] colop: *For Robert Clavell, 1691.* cap., 4°.* CH, MB.

1729 A letter to the Bishop of Munster. *Printed, 1666.* 4°.* L, O.

Letter . . . to the Bishop of R——. 1696. *See* Payne, William.

Letter to the Bishop of Sarum. [n.p.], 1690. *See* Lowthorp, Jonathan.

1730 Entry cancelled.

Letter to the clergy of both universities. 1694. *See,* Tindal, Matthew. Letter to the reverend the clergy.

Letter to the clergy of the diocess of Norfolk. [n.p., 1699.] *See* Field, John.

Letter to the D. of P. 1687. *See* Sergeant, John.

Letter to the deists. 1696. *See* Prideux, Humphrey.

1731 A letter to the distressed reformed churches of France. *Dublin, for Joseph Howes, 1686.* 4°.* DIX 223. DU, DI, DM, DT; LC.

1732 Entry cancelled.

Letter to the Duke of York. 1681. *See* Letter to His Royal Highness.

1733 A letter to the Earl of Manchester. [*London*], *printed, 1648.* 4°.* LT, O, CS, BC, DU; CH, CN, MH, NU, WF, Y.

Letter of the Earle of Pembrooke. [n.p.], 1647. *See* Howell, James.

1734 A letter to the Earl of Shaftsbury this 9th. of July, 1680. [*London, 1680.*] cap., fol.* L, O, CT, BC, LSD; CH, CN, MH, TU, WF, Y.

Letter to the honourable Collonel Okey. 1659. *See* B., A.

Letter to the honourable Major Slingsby. [n.p., 1688.] *See* Beaumont, John.

1735 No entry.

1736 Entry cancelled.

Letter to the Honorable William Lenthal. 1646. *See* Mitton, Thomas.

1737 A letter to the hono[ble] William Lenthal . . . from the commissioners. *For Edw. Husband, April 6. 1646.* 4°.* LT, O, C, CT, LSD, DT; CH, CLC, MH, WF.

1737A A letter to the House, from the Laird Wareston. *By Edward Mason, 1659[60].* brs. L, LG; MH, MIU.

Letter to the King, when Duke. [n.p., 1685.] *See* Jenkins, Leoline.

1738   A letter to the kindome [*sic*] of England, to stand. *By R. O. & G. D.*, 1642. brs. LT, LG, EC.

1739   Entry cancelled.

Letter to the Kings most Excellent Majesty. 1660. *See* England: Parliament. House of Commons.

1739A   A letter to the late author of The preparation for martyrdom. *By T. N. for Samuel Lowndes*, 1682. 4°.* T.C.I 504. LW, DC, DT; CLC, IU, Y.

Letter to the late Lord Bishop. 1699. *See* D., E.

1740   A letter to the Lord Chancellour. colop: *Printed*, 1689. brs. L, O, C; CH, MH.

1741   A letter to the Lord Fleetwood. *Edinburgh, by Christopher Higgins*, 1659. 4°.* ALDIS 1606. MR, EN; Y.

Letter to the Lord General Monck. [1660.] *See* E., C.

Letter to the Lord Grey. [n.p.], 1644. *See* Grey, Henry.

1742   Letter to the Lord Mayor from the committee. 1659. brs. LG (lost).

1743   A letter to the Lord Mayor of London [from Charles II] for raising. 1661. brs. O.

1743A   A letter to the loyal apprentices in and about London. *By E. Whitlocke*, 1697. brs. CN.

1743B   A letter to the members of Parliament . . . concerning the triennial bill. [*London?* 1694.] cap., 4°.* LSD; TU.

Letter to the misrepresenter. 1687. *See* Taylor, James.

Letter to the most illustrious Lord. 1664. *See* D., N. R.

1744   A letter to the officers and souldiers. *Dublin, for James Malone*, 1689. brs. DIX 236. DN.

1745   A letter to the Paris Gazetteer. *For Richard Baldwin*, 1695. 4°.* L, LLL; WF, Y.

Letter to the parishioners. 1700. *See* Brewster, S.

Letter to the Quakers. 1690. *See* Bugg, Francis.

1746   A letter to the Reverend Dr. Bentley. *Printed, and sold by J. Nutt*, 1699. 4°.* L, C, LSD, MR; MIU, MM.

1746A   A letter to the Reverend Doctor South. *For John Newton*, 1693. 4°.* T.C.II 482. L, OC, CS, LLU, P; MH, MM, WF.

Letter to the reverend the clergy. [n.p.], 1694. *See* Tindal, Matthew.

1747   A letter to the Right Honorable A. Earl of Essex, from Dublin. *For Langley Curtis*. 1679. 4°.* L, O, C, DU, DT; CH, MH, MIU, TSM, WF, Y.

1747A   —[Anr. ed.] *By Tho. Newcomb*, 1679. 4°.* O.

1748   A letter to the Right Honovrable, Alderman Warner. [*London*], *printed*, 1648. 4°.* LT, C, DT; CH, CN, MH, MIU, NU.

1749   A letter to the Right Honourable, and Right Reverend the Generall Assembly. *Printed at London for S. B.*, July 6. 1648. brs. LT; MH, NU.

Letter to the right honorable my Lord Chief Justice. [n.p., 1694.] *See* Ferguson, Robert.

Letter to the right honorable the Lord Lambert. [n.p.], 1659. *See* L., S.

1750   A letter to the Right Honourable Thomas Alyn Lord Mayor of . . . London. *By I. C.*, [1659]. brs. LT, LG; MH.

Letter to the right honorable William Lenthall. 1651. *See* L., T.

Letter to the right worshipful T.S. 1675. *See* B., W.D.

Letter to the superiours. 1688. *See* Gee, Edward, *younger*.

1751   A letter to the three absolvers, Mr. Cook. *For R. Baldwin*, 1696. fol.* T.C.II 594. L, O, C, LG; CH, MBP, MIU, NU, TU, WF, Y.

1752   A letter to the unknown author of Jus populi. [*n.p.*], 1671. 8°. L, EN; WF.

Letter to Thomas Curtis. [n.p., 1697.] *See* Sandilands, Robert.

1753   A letter to two Members of Parliament. [*London?* 1696.] brs. LUG; MH.

Letter torn in pieces. 1692. *See* Elys, Edmund.

Letter touching a colledge. [n.p.], 1675. *See* C., B.

1754   Entry cancelled.

Letter touching predestination. 1679. *See* A sober letter.

1755   Letter touching the last engagement. 1653. 8°. LUS (dispersed).

1755A   A letter touching the present state of affairs. *For John Wells*, 1685. 8°.* CH, WF.

Letter unto a person of honour. 1662. *See* Bagshaw, Edward, *younger*.

1756   Entry cancelled.

Letter unto Mr. Stubs. 1660. *See* Harrington, James, *elder*.

Letter wherein is shewed. 1680. *See* B., S.

Letter which was sent. 1689. *See* N., N.

Letter with a narrative. 1659. *See* Butter, Nathaniel.

Letter with animadversions. 1661. *See* Collop, John.

1757   A letter withovt any superscription. [*London*], *printed*, 1643. 4°.* LT, C, OC, EC, LSD; CH, CN, MH, MU, WF, Y.

1758   A letter writ by a clergy-man to his neighbour. *For Ric. Chiswell*, 1689. 4°.* T.C.II 255. L, O, C, DU, BLH; CH, CN, MH, NU, TU, WF, Y.

1759   The letter writ by the last Assembly General of the clergy of France. *For Richard Chiswell*, 1683. 8°. T.C.I 509. L, O, C, ENC, DT; CH, CN, NU, WF, Y.

Letter writ to an atheistical. 1691. *See* Shannon, Francis Boyle, *viscount*.

1760   A letter written & presented to the late Lord Protector. *By J. C. for the authour*, 1659. brs. LT.

Letter written by a Iesvite. [1642.] *See* C., M.

1761   A letter written by a learned and reverent divine, to William Laud. [*London*], *printed*, [1643]. 4°.* LT, LSC, CK, DT; NU.

Letter written by a minister. 1686. *See* B., T.

Letter written by G. L. [n.p., 1657.] *See* Leyburn, George.

1762   A letter written by the Grand Vizier. *Printed at London, and reprented at Holy-Rood-House*, 1687. brs. ALDIS 2697. HH.

1763   A letter written from a person of worth. *Printed*, 1647. 4°.* LT, MR; CH, MH, MIU.

Letter written from Dover. 1660. *See* Price, John *of Dover*.

1763A   A letter writen from Hamborough. colop: *by J. C. for John Crooke*, 1659. cap., 4°.* WF, Y.

1763B   A letter written from Rome. 1691. fol.* O.

1764   A letter written from Walshall. [*Oxford, by H. Hall*], *printed*, 1643. 4°.* MADAN 1308*. LT, O, CJ, LNC, DT.

1765   A letter written in high-Dutch by a Danish gentleman. [*London*], *printed*, 1676. 4°.* O.

1766   A letter written out of Bedfordshire unto the Earle of Manchester. [*Oxford, by L. Lichfield*, 1643.] brs. MADAN 1413. LT, OCC, CT.

1766A   A letter written out of the countrey to a friend in London concerning Easter-day. *For Timothy Garthwait*, 1664. 4°.* DU.

1767   A letter written out of the countrey to a Parliament-man. *Printed*, 1649. 4°.* L, O, MR, SP, E; CH, MIU, NN, WF, Y.

       Letter written out of the countrey to a person. 1680. *See* Howe, John.

       Letter vvritten out of the country to Mʳ Iohn Pym. [n.p.], 1642. *See* E., R.

1767A   A letter written to a Christian friend . . . tythes. *Printed the sixth day of the tenth month*, 1653. 4°.* OC, EN; Y.

       Letter written to a friend, a member. 1661. *See* H., R.

       Letter written to a friend concerning. 1674. *See* Croft, Herbert, *bp.*

1768   A letter vvritten to a friend, declaring his opinion. [*London*], *printed*, 1643. 4°.* LT, CT, LLU, YM, DT; MH, NU.

       Letter written to a friend in the countrey. [n.p., 1692.] *See* Brown, Andrew.

       Letter written to a friend in Wilts. 1666. *See* Tully, Thomas.

       Letter written to a gentleman. 1653. *See* Hall, John.

       Letter written to a member. 1660. *See* L., L.

1769   A letter, written to a member of Parliament concerning the East-India trade. [*London*, 1693.] cap., 4°.* INDIA OFFICE, CT; NC, WF.

1770   A letter written to an honorable member of the House of Commons, Sir, the jealousies. [*London*, 1648.] brs. LT, OC, HH; MH.

       Letter written to Dr. Burnet. 1685. *See* Coventry, *Sir* William.

1771   A letter written to one of the members. *Printed*, 1692. 4°.* L, O, LIU; HR, CH, CN, NU, TU, WF, Y.

1772   A letter written to the French King by the lords. [*London*, 1680.] cap., fol.* L, O; WF.

       Letter written upon occasion. 1641. *See* LaFin, Charles de.

       Letter, written upon the discovery. 1678. *See* Burnet, Gilbert, *bp.*

       Lettera esortatoria. [n.p.], 1667. *See* Loftus, Dudley.

       Letters and essays. 1696. *See* Gildon, Charles.

1773   Letters, and other curious pieces. *For Jonathan Edwin*, 1672. fol.* L, O, DU, SP, EN; CH, IU, MH, WF, Y.

       Letters and poems. 1692. *See* Walsh, William.

1774   Letters and poems in honour of . . . Margaret, Dutchess of Newcastle. [*London*], *in the Savoy: by Thomas Newcombe*, 1676. fol. L, O, CS, CT; MH, NC, OCI, ASU.

       Letters at the instance of Sir George Mackenzie. Edinburgh, 1682. *See* Scotland. Privy Council.

1775   Letters by which it is certified, that Sir Samuell Luke tooke at Islip. Fiftie Horse. *By F. L. May* 28. 1644. 4°.* LT; IU, MH.

1776   The letters, commissions and other papers . . . July 31. 1648. *For Edward Husband, August* 4. 1648. 4°.* LT, C, OC, DU, MR; CH, CLC, IU, MH, MM, NU, TU.

1776A   Letters concerning . . . Dr. Brown's vindicatory schedule. *Edinburgh, by the heir of A. Anderson*, 1692. 8°. ALDIS 3231.5. EN.

1777   Letters concerning the persecution of the Episcopal clergy. [*n.p.*], 1689. 4°. ENC.

1778   Letters from Ireland, relating. *By John Field for Edward Husband*, 1649. 4°.* LT, O, C, BC, DT; CH, CN, MH, MU, WF, Y.

1779   Letters from Lieutenant General Crumwels quarters. *For R. Smithurst*, 1648. 4°.* LT, MR; MH, TU.

1780   Letters from Paris. *By Matthew Simmons*, 1648[9]. 4°.* LT, O, LVF, MR, DT; CH, MH, Y.

       Letters from Saffron-Walden. 1647. *See* W., T.

1781   Letters from the fleet at sea. 1653. 8°. LUS (dispersed).

1782   Letters from the head-quarters of our army in Scotland. *By E. G.*, 1650. 4°.* LT, DT; CH, MH, MU, NN.

1782A   Letters from the Lord Generall his qvarters. *By Jane Coe.* 1644. 4°.* O; MH, Y.

1782B   Letters of advice from two reverend divines. *For J. Collins and D. Newman*, 1676. 12°. T.C.I 225. OC.

       Letters of advice: touching. [*n.p.*], 1644. *See* Wither, George.

1783   Letters of consequence from Scotland. *For Robert Bostock*, 1643. 4°.* LT, O, ESS, DN, DT; CH, CN, MH, TU, WF, Y.

1784   Letters of love and gallantry . . . Vol. I. *For S. Briscoe*, 1693. 12°. T.C.II 466. O.

1785   —. . . Vol. II. —, 1694. 12°. O; CH.

       Letters of publication. Edinburgh, 1687. *See* Scotland. Privy Council.

1786   Letters of religion and vertue. *For Henry Bonwicke*, 1695. 12°. T.C.III 21. L, O, C, CT; CLC, NBL, WF, Y.

       Letters three. [*n.p.*, 1680.] *See* S., M.

       Letters to a sick friend. 1682. *See* Marloe, John.

1787   Letters to the Council of State, from the commissioners of the militia. *By Abel Roper and Thomas Collins*, 1660. 4°.* CH, IU, TU, Y, ZWT.

       Letters written by a French gentleman. 1695. *See* Levassor, Michael.

1787A   Lettre a Monsieur l'Eveque de Meaux. *Chez la veuve Jean Smith*, 1686. 4°.* O; IU, WF.

1787B   Lettre au gazettier de Paris sur le siége de Namur. *Chez Edouard Jones*, 1695. 12°. OC.

1787C   Lettre contenant quelques pensées. *Pour l'auteur*, 1699. 8°.* CJ.

1788   Lettre d'un Protestant de France, a un de ses amis. *Imprimée a Londres l'anné*, 1668. 4°.* Y.

       Lettre écrite à un nonconformiste. 1687. *See* Halifax, George Savile, *marquess.*

1789   Lettres & memoires sur l'excommunication. *A Londres, pour Thomas Parkhurst*, 1698. 4°.* O, C, EN; CH, WF.

1789A Lettres patentes . . . pour la compagnie du commerce de l'Afrique & des Indes. [*Edinburgh?*], *imprimé pour la Compagnie*, 1697. 4°.* MIU.

1790 [**Leurechon, Jean.**] Mathematicall recreations. *For William Leake*, 1653. 8°. L, O, C, BC, DT; CLC, LC, MU, NC, Y.

1791 [–] —[Anr. ed.] —, *and John Leake*, 1674. 8°. T.C.I 174. L, O, C, BR, GU; CH, CLC, IU, MH, NA, NC, VC.

1792 **Leusden, John.** Compendium Græcum Novi Testamenti. Fourth edition. *Sumptibus Samuelis Smith*, 1688. 12°. C, GU.

1793 ——Fifth edition. *Apud Rob. Clavel, Hen. Mortlock & Sam. Smith*, 1691. 8°. T.C.II 382. L, O, C, LCP, CD; CLC, MB, TU, WF, Y.

1793A —A short Hebrew and Caldaick grammar. *Printed at Utrecht, for Samuel Smith, at London*. 1686. 12°. CH, WF, Y.

1793B ——[Anr. ed.] *Printed at Utrecht, by Francis Halma*, 1686. 8°. PMA.

1793C ——[Anr. ed.] *Utrecht, for Thomas Malthus at London*, 1686. 8°. AVP.

1794 **Levassor, Michel.** The history of the reign of Lewis XIII. *For Thomas Cockerill*, 1700. 8°. T.C.III 185. L, O, C, P, GU; CH, CN, LC, MB, WF, Y.

1794A ——[Anr. ed.] *Printed, and are to be sold by John Nutt*, 1700. 8°. LLU; CLC, PL.

1795 [–] Letters written by a French gentleman. *Printed, and sold by R. Baldwin*, 1695. 4°. T.C.II 551. L, O, BANGOR; CH, CLC, MB, MH, PL, WF, Y.

1796 [–] The sighs of France in slavery. [First and second memorial.] *For D. Newman*, 1689. 4°.* T.C.II 291. L, O, CT, EN, DT; CN, MBA, MH, NU, WF, Y.

1796A [–] —Third [and fourth] memorial. *For D. Newman*, 1689. 4°.* L, O, LG, EN, DT; CLC, MBA.

1796B [–] —Fifth [and sixth] memorial. *For D. Newman*, 1690. 4°.* L, LG; CH, CLC, MBA.

1797 [**Le Vayer de Boutigny, Roland.**] The famous romance of Tarsis and Zelie. *For Nathanael Ponder*, 1685. fol. T.C.II 96. L, O, CT, LLU, A; CH, CN, MH, TSM, WF, Y.

1797A [–] Tarsis and Zelie. *For Nathanael Ponder*, 1685. fol. O, CT; MU, NP.

1798 [**Leveck, Joseph.**] A true accompt of the late reducement of the Isles of Scilly. *By J. M. for Giles Calvert*, 1651. 4°.* LT; WF.

1799 The Leveller: or, the principles & maxims. *For Thomas Brewster*, 1659. 4°.* LT, O, C, EN, DT; CH, CN, MH, WF, Y.

1800 The Levellers directory. [*London*], *printed*, 1648. 4°.* TU.

1800A The Levellers (falsly so called) vindicated. [*London*, 1649.] cap., 4°.* LT, O, DU, LLU, MR; CH, CU, MH, MIU, WF.

1801 The Levellers institvtions for a good people. *For W. B.* 1648. 4°.* LT; NU, PT.

       Levellers levell'd. [n.p.], 1647. *See* Nedham, Marchamont.

1802 Entry cancelled.
       Levellers new remonstrance, concerning. 1649. *See* Levellers remonstrance, concerning.

1803 The Levellers new remonstrance or declaration. *Printen* [*sic*], 1649. 4°.* LT; MH.

1803A The Levellers remonstrance, concerning. *Imprinted at London, for R. W.*, May 10, 1649. 4°.* LT; MH.

1804 Entry cancelled.
       Levellers remonstrance, sent. 1652. *See* Lilburne, John.

1805–7 Entries cancelled.
       Leven, Alexander Leslie, *1st earl of*. Articles and ordinances of warre. 1644. *See* Scotland. Estates.
       —Bloudy fight in Scotland. 1649. *See* title.
       —Camp discipline. 1642. *See* Newark, David Leslie, baron.

1807A —The coppy of a letter sent from Generall Leishley. [*London*], *printed*, 1641. 4°.* LT, O, LNC, YM, BLH; CH, MH, TU, WF, Y. (var.)

1807B ——[Anr. ed., "copy."]. —, 1641. 4°.* L, EN; MH, TU.

1807C ——[Anr. ed., "copie," "Lesley."] [*London*, 1641.] brs. L, O, LG.

1808 —The declaration and propositions of. *For R. W.*, 1648. 4°.* LT, MR, SP; CII, IU, MII, WF, Y.

1809 Entry cancelled.
       —Declaration of. [n.p., 1645]. *See following entry.*

1810 —A declaration of . . . concerning the rising of the Scotish army. *By M. B. for Robert Bostock*, 11. Sep. 1645. 4°.* LT, O, C, LVF, DT; WF.

1811 ——[Anr. ed.] —, 14. Sep. 1645. 4°.* LT, O, MR; CLC, MH, TU, WF, Y.

1812 —The declaration of His Excellency. *For Laurence Chapman*, July 6, 1646. 4°.* LT, O, CT, EN, DT; CLC, IU, MH, TU, Y.

1813 —The declaration of the Lord Generall, . . . 27 June 1646. *Edinburgh, by E. Tyler*, 1646. 4°.* STEELE 3p 1915; ALDIS 1223. EN; CH.

1814–15 No entries.

1816 —A letter from Generall Leven. *For Edw. Husbands*, July 12. 1644. 4°.* L, O, LLU, DT; CH, MH, MU, WF, Y.

1817 ——[Anr. ed.] *Re-printed at Edinburgh by Evan Tyler*, 1644. 4°.* ALDIS 1144.3. O, E, EN; NU, WF.

1818 [–] A true relation of the totall routing of the Lord George Digby. *By M. B. for Robert Bostock*, 1645. 4°.* LT, O; CSS, NC, Y.

1819 **Levens, Peter.** The path-vvay to health. *For J. W. to be sold by John Andrews*, 1654. 8°. LT; TO, WF.

1819A ——[Anr. ed., "pathway."] *For J. W. to bee sold by Charles Tyus*, 1664. 12°. L, LWL, GU; NN, WSG.

1820 **Leveridge, Richard.** [A new book of songs. *Printed and sold by John Walsh and J[ohn] Hare*, 1697.] fol. * O (lacks t.p.).

1820A —A new song set by Mr. Leveridge, sung att the theater in Dublin. [*London*, 1700?] fol.* LC, MH.

1821 —A second book of songs. *Sould by I. Walsh, & I. Hare, & I. Young*, [1699]. fol.* LCM.

1822 —[Anr. ed.] *Sould by I. Hare, & I. Walsh, & I. Young*, [1699]. fol.* O; NN.

1822A —[Anr. ed.] [*London*, 1699?] fol.* TO.

1822B **Levet, John.** To the high and honourable House of Peers . . . the humble petition of . . . and Mary his wife. [*London*, 1645?] fol.* L, CASTLE ASHBY, LNC.
       Leviathan drawn out. 1653. *See* Ross, Alexander.

1823 **Le Vince.** A catalogue of choice prints and drawings, . . . 9th . . . December, 1691. [*London*], 1691. fol.* L.

1824 **Levingston, Anne,** *Mrs.* The state of the case in brief, between the Countess of Sterlin, and. [*London*, 1654.] brs. LT; MH.

1825 —A true narrative of the case. [*London?* 1655?] fol. L.

1825A **Levingston, Thomas.** Some considerations humbly proposed to the worthy members of Parliament by . . ., and Anne his wife. [*London*, 1654.] brs. LUG; MH.

1826 **Levinz, William.** Bibliotheca Levinziana sive catalogus. [*London*], 29 *June* 1698. 4°. L, OC, OW, CS; BN, NG.

1826A **Levison, Richard.** Untimely repentence. A sermon preach'd before . . . Lord Petre . . . April the 1st, 1688. *By Mary Thompson*, 1688. 4°.* IU.

1827 The Levites lamentations. [*London?* 1642.] 4°.* O, MR.

1828 **L[evitt], W[illiam].** The glorious truth of redemption. *For the author*, 1653. 8°.* LT.

1829 —The Samaritans box newly opened. *By James and Joseph Moxon*, 1647. 4°.* LT, E, DT; IU, MM.

1830 **[Lewes, Daniel.]** The literal mans learning. [*London*], *for the author*, [1657]. cap., 4°.* LT; WF.

1831 **Lewgar, John.** Erastus junior. Or, a fatal blow . . . In two parts. *Printed, and are to be sold by Livewell Chapman*, 1660. 4°.* LT, O, C, P, YM; CH, MIU, NU, WF.

1832 [–] Erastus senior. [*London*], *printed*, 1662. 8°. L, O, C, LCL, DU; BN, CH, CN, NU, TU, WF, Y.

1832A [–] The only way to rest of soule. [*n.p.*], *for the author*, 1657. 12°. L, CS, DC, DUS, LNC; TU, WG.

1833 **Le White, Thomas.** An ansvver to a letter sent to a gentleman of the Middle-Temple. *By J. Clowes*, 1659. 4°. LT; CH, CSS, Y.

1833A —A brief character of Englands distraction. *Printed*, 1660 [1659]. 4°.* MR; MH.

1834 —Considerations by way. *For the author*, 1660. brs. LT; MH.

1835 **Lewin, John.** The man-child brought forth in us. *For G. C.*, [1648?]. 8°.* CT; NU.

1836 **Lewis, David.** The last speech of. [*London*, 1679.] cap., fol.* L, OB, CM; CH, LC, MH, PU, WF, Y.

1837 —A narrative of the imprisonment. [*London?* 1679.] cap., fol.* L, CM, BAMB, MR, DT; CH, LC, MIU, PU, TU, Y.

1838 Entry cancelled.

Lewis, John. Abstract of proposals. [n.p., 1695]. *See* Lewis, John, 1675–1747.

1839 [–] Contemplations upon these times. *By R. VV. for Nath. VVebb, and W. Grantham*, 1646. 4°.* LT, AN, MR, DT; CH, MM, WF.

1840 [–] Ευαγγελιογραφα, or, some seasonable. *By R. I. for N. Ekins*, 1656. 4°.* L, O.

1840A ——[Anr. ed.] *For N. Ekins*, 1659. 4°.* L.

1840B **Lewis, John,** *1675–1747.* An abstract of proposals. [*London?* 1695.] brs. L, LUG.

1840C —A proposal to prevent the corruption of the coyn. [*London*, 1695.] brs. L, LUG.

1841 Entry cancelled. *See following entry.*

1842 **Lewis, Mark.** An essay to facilitate the education of youth. *For Thomas Parkhurst*, 1674. 8°. T.C.I 188. L (impf.), O, C, LSC, LW; CH, WU, Y (impf.).

1842A —Institutio grammaticæ pueriles. *Printed*, 1661.

1843 ——[Anr. ed.] *By Tho. Roycroft, for the author*, 1670. 8°.* L, C, OC; WF.

1843A ——[Anr. ed.] *Printed*, 1671. 8°. WF.

1844 [–] A model for a school for the better education of youth. [*London*, 1675?] 8°. L; IU.

1845 —Plain, and short rules. [*London*, 1675?] cap., 8°.* L, O, LSD; CH, WF.

1846 —Proposals to increase trade. *For Henry Million*, 1677. 8°.* L, O, LLP, LPR, LUG; CLC, IU, NC, NN, PL, WF, Y.

1847 —Proposals to the King and Parliament, how this tax. *Printed*, 1677. 4°.* L, O, LG, CT, MR, EN; IU, NC, PL.

1848 [–] Proposals to the King and Parliament, or a large model. *For Henry Million*, 1678. 4°.* L, C, LVF, OH, EN; CH, CN, MH, NCD, WF, Y.

1849 —A short model of a bank. [*London*, 1678.] 8°.* L, O, LG, LPR, LNC; Y.

1850 —Vestibulum technicum: or, an artificial vestibulum. *For Thomas Parkhurst*, 1675. 8°.* T.C.I 228. L; PL, Y.

1851 **Lewis, William.** The information of. *For Randal Taylor*, 1680. fol.* L, O, C, EN, DT; CH, MH, MU, TU, WF, Y.

1851A Lewis his second letter to James. [*London*, 1689.] brs. L.

1852 **L[ewkenor], J[ohn].** Metellus his dialogues: the first part. *By Tho. Warren for N. Rolls*, 1693. 8°. L, LVD, OC, LLU; CH, CN, NP, PU, WF, Y.

1853 **[Le Wright, Raoul.]** Nuncius propheticus. 1642. 4°. LT, O, C, EN, DT; CH, IU, WF, WU, Y.

1853A **L'W[right], T[homas].** A more exact character . . . Oliver Cromvvell. *For J. Jones*, 1658. 4°.* L, O; Y.

1854 **Lewthwat, Richard.** A justification of set forms of prayer. *By A. Godbid and J. Playford, for Robert Clavel*, 1679. 8°. T.C.I 368. C, LSC, OM, SP, DT; CLC.

1855 —Vindiciæ Christi, . . . A plea for Christ. *By R. W. for Nath. Webb, and VVilliam Grantham*, 1655. 4°.* LT, LSC; MM, WF.

Lex custumaria: or. 1696. *See* Carter, Samuel.

1856 Lex exlex: or the dovvnfall of the law. [*London*], *for the authour*, [1652]. 4°. LT, CT, DU; PL, Y.

1857 Lex forcia: being a sensible address to the Parliament. *For R. C. and are to be sold by Eliz. Whitelock*, 1698. 4°.* L, O, C, LLP, BAMB; CH, CLC, MH, TULANE, WF.

1857A —[Anr. ed.] *Printed*, 1699. 4°.* OC, EN; CN, PL.

1858 Lex Londinensis; or, the city law. *By S. Roycroft for Henry Twyford*, 1680. 8°. T.C.I 417. L, O, LG, LL, DUS; CH, MHL, MU, NCL, WF, Y.

1859 Lex Parlamentorum; or, an abstract. *Printed*, 1648. 4°.* LT, LIU, MR, DT; CLC, IU, MH, Y.

Lex Parliamentaria: or. 1690. *See* Petyt, George.

Lex, rex. 1644. *See* Rutherford, Samuel.

1860 Lex talionis. Neque est lex . . . poor Robin turn'd Robin the devil. colop: *Printed*, 1680. brs. L, HH, LNC; CH, CLC, IU, MH, PU, WF.

1861   Lex talionis. Or, a declamation. [*London*], *printed*, 1647.
       4°.* LT, O, C, DU, EN; CH, CN, MH, NU, WF, Y.

1862   Lex talionis, or, a receipt. [*London*, 1685?] brs. L, C, OP,
       HH, LIU; CH, INU, MBA, MH, Y, ZWT.

1863   Entry cancelled.
       Lex talionis: or, an enquiry. 1698. *See* Defoe, Daniel.

1864   Lex talionis: or, London revived. [*London*, 1647.] brs.
       LT, LVF, CE.
       Lex talionis: or, the author. 1676. *See* Fell, Philip.
       Lex talionis: or the law. 1682. *See* Carew, George.

1865   Entry cancelled.
       Lex talionis: poor Robin. 1680. *See* Lex talionis. Neque.
       Lex talionis; sive. 1670. *See* Stubbe, Henry.

1866–7 No entries.
       Ley, James. *See* Marlborough, James Ley, *earl of*.

1868   **Ley, John.** An acquittance or discharge from D^r. E. H.
       Printed, 1654. 4°.* LT, O, C, OME, DT; MH.

1869   — —[Anr. ed.] *For F. Brewster*, 1655. 4°.* NU.

1870   [–] An after-reckoning with Mr Saltmarsh. *For Chris-
       topher Meredith*, 1646. 4°. LT, O, LCL, DT; CH, MH, NU,
       WF, Y.
       [–] Annotations upon all the books. 1645. *See* Dow-
       name, John.

1871   —A case of conscience. *By R. H. for George Lathum*,
       1641. 4°.* L, C, LCL, LI, MR; CLC, MM, NGT, NU, WF, Y.

1872   —A comparison of the Parliamentary protestation. *By
       G. M. for Thomas Vnderhill*, 1641. 4°. LT, O, C, MR, DT;
       CH, CLC, NCD, NU, WF, Y.

1873   —A debate concerning the English liturgy. *By A. M.
       for Edward Brewster*, 1656. 4°. L, O, C, BC, DT; IEG, NU,
       WF, Y.

1874   —Defensive doubts. *By R. Young, for G. Lathum*, 1641.
       4°. L, O, C, E, DT; CLC, CN, NU, SE, WF, Y.

1875   [–] A discovrse concerning Puritans. A vindication.
       [*London*], *for Robert Bostock*, 1641. 4°. LT, O, C, SC, DT;
       CH, CU, MH, NU, WF, Y.

1876   [–] —Second edition. *For Robert Bostock*, 1641. 4°. O, OB,
       CJ, DT; CH, IAU, LC, MH, NU, Y.

1877   —A discourse of disputations. *For Nath: Webb and Will:
       Grantham*, 1658. 4°. LT, C, LW, CT, BC, P; CH, IU, NU.

1878   [–] Exceptions many and jvst against two injurious
       petitions. *Oxford, by L. Lichfield, for Tho. Robinson*,
       1653. 4°. MADAN 2230. LT, O, C, DU, P; CH, CU, MH, NU,
       WF, Y.

1879   —The ^a fvry of vvarre, and ^b folly of sinne. *By G. M.
       for Christopher Meredith*, 1643. 4°. LT, O, C, EN, DT; CH,
       CN, MH, NU, TU, WF, Y, AVP.

1880   —General reasons. *For Edward Brewster*, 1655. 4°.* L, O;
       MM.

1881   —A letter (against the erection of an altar). *For George
       Lathum*, 1641. 4°.* L, C, LCL, BAMB, MR; CDA, MH, NGT,
       NU, WF, Y.

1882   [–] A letter to Dr. E. Hyde. [*London*, 1655.] cap., 4°.*
       L, O, SP; NU.

1883   —Light for smoke. *By I. L. for Christopher Meredith*,
       1646. 4°. LT, O, C, YM, DT; CH, CLC, IU, NGT, NU, Y.

1884   —A monitor of mortalitie. *By G. M. for Christopher
       Meredith*, 1643. 4°. L, O, C, ENC, DT; CLC, NGT, NU, WF, Y.

1884A —A monitor of mortalitie, the second sermon. *For
       Christopher Meredith*, 1643. 4°.* LW, CS.

1885   —The nevv qvere. *For C. Meredith*, 1646. 4°. LT, O, C,
       ENC, DT; CH, MH, MU, NU, WF, Y.

1886   —Sunday a sabbath. *By R. Young, for George Lathum*,
       1641. 4°. L, O, C, EN, DT; CH, IU, NF, NU, WF, Y.

1887   **Ley, William.** A brief plat-form. *By William Du-gard,
       to be sold by Nathanaël Brooks*, 1648. 4°.* LT, DT; CLC,
       MHS.

1888   —῾Υπερασπιστης; or, a bvckler. *Oxford, by Leon.
       Lichfield, for Tho. Robinson*, 1656. 4°.* MADAN 2300.
       LT, O; NHC, NR, NU, OWC, Y.

1889   —Reports. *Thomas Roycroft*, 1659. fol. CT.

1890   Entry cancelled.
       L[eybourn], G[eorge]. Letter written by. [n.p., 1657.]
       See Leyburn, George.
       Leyborn, William. Almanack. 1651. *See* Almanacs.

1891   —Arithmetick; vulgar. *By R. and W. Leybourn, to be
       sold by G. Sawbridge*, 1657. 8°. L, C; CH.

1892   — —[Anr. ed.] *By R. and W. Leybourn, to be sold by
       George Sawbridge*, 1659. 8°. L.

1893   — —Third edition. —, 1660. 8°. LT, O, CM; MU, Y.

1893A — —"Third" edition. *By J. Streater for George Sawbridge*,
       1668. 8°. O, OC, CP; CH, CLC, WU.

1893B — —"Third" edition. —, [1668?]. 8°. L.

1894   — —Fourth edition. *By Tho. James for George Saw-
       bridge*, 1678. 8°. T.C.I 324. L, O, C; CB, MB, WCL.

1895   Entry cancelled.
       — —[Anr. ed.] 1666. *See* — —Third edition. 1660.

1895A — —Fifth edition. *By T. B. for Hannah Sawbridge*, 1684.
       8°. T.C.II 107. WF.

1895B — —Sixth edition. *For A. and J. Churchill*, 1693. 8°.
       T.C.II 467. BC; PBL.

1896   — —Seventh edition. *By J. Matthews, for Awnsham and
       John Churchill*, 1700. 8°. T.C.III 234. L, O, CT, BAMB, BC;
       CU, INU, IU, MU.

1897   —Arithmetical recreations. *By J. C. for Hen. Brome and
       Sam. Speed*, 1667. 12°. CT.

1898   — —Second edition. *For Hen. Brome*, 1676. 12°. T.C.I
       241. L, O, NOT; CLC.

1899   — —Third edition. *For Ch. Brome*, 1699. 12°. T.C.III
       162. O, INU.

1900   —The art of dialling. *By S. G. and B. G. for Benjamin
       Tooke and Thomas Sawbridge*, 1669. 4°. T.C.I 18. L, O, C,
       EN, GU; CH, CLC, LC, MB, NC, PL.

1901   — —Second edition. *By J. Grover, for Thomas Sawbridge*,
       1681. 4°. T.C.I 446. L, BC; MH, WF, HC.

1901A — —Third edition. *For Thomas Sawbridge*, 1690. 4°.
       T.C.II 295. L; WCL.

1902   — —"Third" edition. *For Thomas Braddyll*, 1700. 4°.
       L, LWL, FONMON; CJC, WU, Y.

1903   —The art of measuring. *For Richard Jones*, 1669. 8°.
       T.C.I 19. L, C, OC.

1903A — —Third edition. *For Rich. Northcott*, 1681. 8°. T.C.I
       490. L.

1904   [–] The art of numbring. *For G. Sawbridge*, 1667. 12°.
       L, O, OC, CM, CS, LIU.

1904A [–] —[Anr. ed.] *For W. Hayes*, 1667. 12°. OB; WCL, WU, Y.

1905   [–] —[Anr. ed.] *For G. Sawbridge*, 1667. 16°. L, E.

1906   [–] —[Anr. ed.] *By T. B. for H. Sawbridge*, 1685. 12°. L,
       BC, DC, DCH; CH, CLC, MH, PL, WF.

1907   —The compleat surveyor. *By R. & W. Leybourn, for
       E. Brewster and G. Sawbridge*, 1653. fol. L, C, DU, YM,
       DM; CH, IU, MH, NN, TU, Y.

1908   — —Second edition. *By R. and W. Leybourn, for G.
       Sawbridge*, 1657. L, C, LIB, R, E; CB, CJC, LC, MH, NC, PL.

1909   — —Third edition. *By E. Flesher for George Sawbridge*,
       1674. fol. T.C.I 173. L, O, C, LIB, EN; CH, CLC, MH, NC, PBL.

1910   — —Fourth edition. —, 1679. fol. T.C.I 362. L, C, AN,
       GU, DT; BN, CLC, IU, MH, NSU, PBL, WF.

1911   —Cursus mathematicus. Mathematical sciences. *For
       Thomas Basset, Benjamin Tooke, Thomas Sawbridge,
       Awnsham and John Churchill*, 1690. fol. T.C.II 335.
       L, O, C, LW, DUS; BN, CH, IU, LC, MH, NC, Y.

       [–] Description and use of a portable instrument. 1685.
       See Gunter, Edmund.

1912   —Dialing. *For Awnsham Churchill*, 1682. fol. T.C.I 460.
       L, C, DCH, LIU, DT; CH, LC, MH, NC, PL, PU, WF, HC.

1913   — —Second edition. *By J. Matthews, for Awnsham and
       John Churchill*, 1700. fol. L, O, LWL, OC, DT; CH, LC,
       MH, NP, TU, Y.

1914   —Four tables of accompts. *Printed, and are to be sold by
       Robert Walton*, [169 -?]. brs. O.

1915   —An introduction to astronomy. *By J. C. for Robert
       Morden and William Berry*, 1675. 8°. T.C.I 205. L, LW,
       OC, CT; CH, CLC, LC, MU, NP, Y.

1916   —The line of proportion. *By J. S. for G. Sawbridge*, 1667.
       12°. L, OC, CM.

1916A — —Second edition. —, 1668. 12°. C, CS.

1917   — —[Anr. ed.] —, 1673. 12°. T.C.I 155. L, O; WCL.

1918   — —[Anr. ed.] *By J. M. for G. Sawbridge*, 1675. 12°. L,
       BC; OLU, PU.

1919   Entry cancelled.
       — — . . . second part. 1677. *See*—Line of proportion,
       commonly called.

1920   — —[Anr. ed.] *By J. M. for G. Sawbridge*, 1678. 12°. L,
       CS, E; CH, LC, WF.

1921   — —[Anr. ed.] *For Hannah Sawbridge*, 1684. 12°. L, O;
       CH, NC.

1922   — —Sixth edition. *For A. and J. Churchill*, 1698. 12°.
       T.C.III 57. DUS; CH, MU, WU.

1923   Entry cancelled. Date: [1726].

1923A —The line of proportion, commonly called . . . a
       second part. *By W. L. and T. J. for George Sawbridge*,
       1677. 12°. T.C.I 281. L, O, E; CLC, NC, OLU.

1924   —Nine geometricall exercises. *By J. Flesher, for W.
       Hayes*, 1669. L, C; MU.

1925   — —[Anr. ed.] *James Flesher for George Sawbridge*, 1669.
       4°. T.C.I 5. BN, CLC, MH.

1926   —Panarithmologia, being a mirror. *By T. J. for John
       Dunton, and John Harris*, 1693. 8°. T.C.II 479. L, O, C,
       LUG; CH, NCU, WF, Y.

1927   Entry cancelled. Date: [1710?].

1928   —Panorganon: or, a universal instrument. *For William
       Birch*, 1672. 4°. T.C.I 104. L, O, C, E, DT; CH, LC, MH,
       MU, NC, WF, Y.

1928A —Planometria. *For Nathanael Brooks*, 1650. 8°. L, LIU, P;
       CH, CLC, MH, WF, WU, Y.

1929   —A platform for purchasers. *For Thomas Raw, of Bath:
       and sold by Obadiah Blagrave*, 1685. 8°. T.C.II 120. L, LIB,
       BC; CH, CLC, MH, NC, PU, Y.

1930   —A platform guide, mate, for purchasers. *By Thomas
       Ratcliffe and Thomas Daniel for Nathaniel Brooks*, 1668.
       8°. T.C.I 5. L, O, C, LIB; LC, PU, Y.

1931   —Pleasure with profit. *For Richard Baldwin, and John
       Dunton*, 1694. fol. L, O, C, AN, EO, DT; CH, MU, NC, PL,
       WF.

1932   — —[Anr. ed.] *For Nathaniel Rolls*, 1695. fol. T.C.II 524.
       L, O, LWL, EO, GU, BQ; TO.

1933   —A president for purchasers. *For William Jacob; and
       Langley Curtis*, 1678. brs. T.C.I 304. O; MH.

1934   —Proposals for the printing . . . Pleasure with profit. *For
       John Dunton*, 1693. brs. O; WES.

       —Speculum anni. 1648. *See* Almanacs.

1934A —A supplement to geometrical dialling. *For Thomas
       Sawbridge*, 1689. 4°.* L; WCL.

1935   [–] The use of the semicircle. *By W. G. for Walter Hayes*,
       [1680?]. 12°. L.

1936   **Leyburn, George.** Dᵣ. Leybvrns encyclical ansvver.
       At Doway, by L. Kellam, 1661. 4°. L, DUS.

1937   [–] An epistle declaratorie, or manifest. [*Douay*], *by the
       Widdowe of Marke Wyon*, 1657. 4°. L.

1938   —Holy characters. *Printed at Doway, by Baltazar Bellier*,
       1662. 8°. L, O, C, LSC, BSM, P; CH, CN, NU, TU, WF, Y.

1938A [–] A letter written by. [*Douay? 1657.*] 12°.* L.

1939   —The summe of Doctor Leyburnes answere. [*Doway?*],
       by the Widdowe of Mark Wyon, 1657. 16°.* L.

1940   —To Her Most Excellent Maiestie Henrietta Maria.
       [*Doway? 1660.*] cap., 4°.* L, DUS.

       [**Leyburn, John.**] Papists protesting. 1686. *See* Gother,
       John.

1940A Entry cancelled.
       [–] Pastoral letter from the four Catholic bishops.
       [n.p.], 1688. *See title.*

1941   Entry cancelled.
       [–] A reply to the answer made upon the three royal
       papers. *See title.*

       Leycester, John, *pseud. See* Roe, Sir Thomas.

1941A **Leycester, Sir Peter.** An answer to Sir Thomas
       Mainwaring's book, intituled, —An admonition.
       [*London*], *printed*, 1677. 8°.* L.

1942   —An answer to the book of Sir Thomas Manwaringe.
       [*London*], *Anno Dom*, 1673. 8°. L, O, AN, RU, EN; WF.

1943   —Historical antiquities. *By W. L. for Robert Clavell*,
       1673. T.C.I 126. fol. L, O, C, EN, DT; BN, CH, CN, LC, PL, Y.

1944   —A reply to Sᵣ Thomas Manwaring's answer. *Printed*,
       1676. 8°. MH, WF, Y.

1944A —Two books: the first being styled a reply. [*London*],
       printed, 1674. 8°. L; CH, WF.

Leyden University. A catalogue of all the cheifest rarities. Leiden, 1683. *See* Schuyl, Frans.

L – – gley C – – – s his lamentation. 1684. *See* Curtis, Langley.

1944B **Lhuyd, Edward.** A design of a British dictionary. [*Oxford*, 1695.] brs. OP; MH, Y.

1945 Entry cancelled. *See following entry.*

1946 —Edvardi Luidii, . . . lithophylacii Britannici ichnogaphia. *Ex officina M. C.*, 1699. 8°. T.C.III 110. L, O, C, AN, GU, DT; BN, IU, MH, MU, PL.

1947 [–] Parochial queries in order to a geographical dictionary, . . . of Wales. [*London*, 1697.] cap., fol.* O, OP; MH.

1948 The lier laid open in a letter. *Printed*, 1648. 4°.* LT, O, DU, SC, E, DT; CH, NC, Y.

Liar; or, a contradiction. [n.p.], 1641. *See* Taylor, John.

Libel and complaint. [n.p., 1692?] *See* Kirkwood, James.

1949 The libel issu'd out of the Chancellor's court. [*London*, 1693.] fol.* O, OP, MR.

Libeller characteriz'd. [n.p.], 1671. *See* Rudyard, Thomas.

1950 Liber assisarum, or le livre. 1679. fol. LMT; CLC, MHL.

1951 Liber placitandi. A book of special pleadings. *For John Place and Thomas Basset*, 1674. fol. T.C.I 173. O, LI, LL, LMT, DT; CH, MHL, MU, NCL, YL, AVP.

1951A —[Anr. ed.] *For J. Place and T. Basset. And for H. Twyford, G. Sawbridge, J. Bellinger, W. Place, R. Pawlet, C. Wilkinson, T, Dring, W. Jacob, C. Harper, J. Amery, J. Leigh, J. Williams, and J. Poole*, 1674. fol. CS, LIU; PU, WF.

1952–7 Entries cancelled.

Liber precvm pvblicarvm. Oxoniæ, 1660. *See* Oxford University. Christ Church.

1958 Libertatis amator: a litany. [*London?* 1681.] brs. HH.

1958A The liberties and customes of the miners. [*London*], by R. A., 1645. 4°.* MH.

1959 —[Anr. ed.] [*London*], by E. G., 1649. 4°.* L, O; NC, WF.

Liberties, usages, and customes. 1642. *See* Calthrop, Sir Henry.

1959A The libertines lampoone. [*London*, 1674.] brs. L.

Liberty of an apostate. 1683. *See* Cater, Samuel.

1960 Liberty of conscience asserted, and several reasons. *For Robert Wilson, in Martins Le Grand*, 1661. 4°.* L, O, C, BP, GU; CH, IE, MH, NU, PH, TU, WF.

1961 —[Anr. ed.] —, at the sign . . . , 1661. 4°.* LF; NU, PH, PSC, TU, WF, Y.

Liberty of conscience asserted and vindicated. 1689. *See* Care, George.

1962 Liberty of conscience asserted. Or persecution for religion. *For R. A.*, 1649. 4°.* LT, DT; Y.

1963 Liberty of conscience confuted. [*London*], *printed*, 1648. 4°.* LT, OC; CH, MH, NU, WF.

1964 Liberty of conscience explicated. *For John Lawrence, and are to be sold by Richard Baldwin*, 1689. 4°.* T.C.II 277. L, LLP, EN, DT; CN, CSU, MH, NU, WF.

1965 Liberty of conscience in its order to universal peace. *For Thomas Parkhurst.* 1681. 4°. T.C.I 416 L, O, C, LW, MR, EN; PL, MM, TO, WF, Y.

Liberty of conscience: or. [n.p.], 1643. *See* Robinson, Henry.

Liberty of conscience, the. 1668. *See* Wolseley, Sir Charles.

Liberty of conscience upon. 1668. *See* Wolseley, Sir Charles.

1966 Liberty of philosophizing. 1689. 8°. LL.

Liberty of prayer. 1695. *See* Jenks, Benjamin.

1967 No entry.

Liberty of the imprisoned Royallist. [n.p., 1647.] *See* Lovelace, Richard.

Liberty of the subject. [n.p.], 1664. *See* Farnworth, Richard.

Liberty vindicated. [n.p.], 1646. *See* Lilburne, John.

1968 The library of a late eminent sergeant of the law. [*London*], 30 *Aug* 1697. 4°. L, CD.

1969 The library of a reverend divine. [*London*, 1700.] 4°. L; JF.

1969A Libri novissimé. *Prostant venales apud Sam. Smith & Benj. Walford*, 1695. fol. OC.

Libro delle preghiere. 1685. *See* Church of England.

1970 Entry cancelled.

Librorum manuscriptorum. Oxonii, 1692. *See* Tenison, Thomas, *abp.*

1971 **Liby, W.** Merlinus democritus: or, the merry-conceited prognosticator. *For G. Horton*, 1656. 4°.* LT.

1971A **Lichtenberger, Johann.** Spectators, make a ring. *For the author, to be sold by Henry Brome*, 1663. brs. L.

1972 **Liddel, Duncan.** Artis conservandi sanitatem. *Aberdoniæ, excudebat Iacobus Brounus*, 1651. 8°. ALDIS 1447. L, O, AM, E, EN; IU, NAM, WF.

1973 **Liddell, George.** Certaman mathematicum, or, a mathematicall–dispute. *Aberdeen, by Iohn Forbes, December 4th. 1684, to be sold by Andrew Dumbar, in Edinburgh.* 8°.* ALDIS 2449. AU, ES.

1974 [–] Divine meditations; or a honey-comb. Second edition. *For John Marshall*, 1700. 12°.* L, E; NN.

1974A —A honey-comb to refresh weary travellers. *By R. Janeway, jun. for John Marshall*, 1700. sixes.* Y.

1975 —The solution of the five problems. *Aberdeen, by Iohn Forbes*, 15 *February* 1685. 8°.* ALDIS 2610. ES.

1975A —The traveller's song. *For the author*, 1699. 12°. EN.

1976 **Lidderdale, Robert.** Theses philosophicæ. *Edinburgh, by the heir of A. Anderson*, 1685. brs. ALDIS 2613. E.

1977 **Lidgould, Charles.** Charity to our poor persecuted brethren abroad . . . April 5. 1699. *For Joseph Wilde*, 1699. 4°.* L, O, LLP, CT, BP; CH, WF.

1978 —A sermon preach'd . . . July the 24th, 1698. *For Joseph Wild*, 1699. 4°.* L, O, LLP, CT; CH, WF.

Lieut. Colonel J. Lilburn tryed. 1653. *See* Haselrig, Sir Arthur.

1979 Lieutenant Generall Cromwell's last vvill & testament. *Printed*, 1648. 4°.* LT, O, DT; CLC, INU, MH, MIU, Y.

1979A Die Sabbatti, 20 Januarii, 1649. Lieutenant General Hammond, Colonel Okey, . . . presented a petition to the House. [*London*, 1649.] brs. O, AN.

1980   The life and actions of the late renowned prelate & souldier Christopher Bernard van Gale. *For Benj. Tooke, Rob. Harford, and Sam. Carr.* 1680. 8°. T.C.I 403. L, C, LLP, OC, DU, CD; CH, CLC, MIU, PL, WF, Y.

1981   The life and acts of the most famous . . . Sir William Wallace. *Edinburgh, by Robert Bryson,* 1645. 8°. ALDIS 1189. O, EN.

1982   —[Anr. ed.] *Edinburgh, by Gideon Lithgovv,* 1648. 8°. ALDIS 1328. E, EN.

1983   —Seventh edition. —, 1661. 8°. ALDIS 1697. EN, GU; WC.

1984   —[Anr. ed.] *Edinburgh, a society of stationers,* 1661. 8°. ALDIS 1698. EN.

1985   —[Anr. ed.] *Glasgow, by Robert Sanders,* 1665. 8°. ALDIS 1791. L, O, EN; IU.

1986   —[Anr. ed.] *Edinburgh, by Andro Anderson,* 1666. 12°. ALDIS 1816. E.

1987   —[Anr. ed.] *Edinburgh, by Andrew Anderson,* 1673. 12°. ALDIS 1988. CM, EN.

1987A   —[Anr. ed.] *Glasgow, by Robert Sanders,* 1685. 12°. ALDIS 2550. EN; MH.

1987B   —[Anr. ed.] —, 1699. 12°. ALDIS 3854. GU.

1988   The life and amours of Charles Lewis Elector Palatin. *For Thomas Nott; and are to be sold by Randal Taylor,* 1692. 12°. L; CH, CLC, WF, Y.

1989   The life and approaching death of William Kiffin. *For Thomas Bateman,* 1659[60]. 4°.* LT, MR; CLC, NHC.

1990   Entry cancelled. Date: 1732.

1990A   The life and conversation of Temperance Floyd. *By J. W.,* 1687. 8°.* O.

1991   The life and conversation of the pretended Captain Charles Newery. *For the author,* 1700. fol.* L, LUG.

    Life and death of Alexander. 1661. *See* Curtius Rufus, Quintus.

1992   The life & death of Captain William Bedloe. *By George Larkin, for John Hancock and Enoch Prosser,* 1681. 8°. T.C.I 461. L, O, CT, P, EN; CN, MH, NN, WF, Y.

1992A   The life and death of Charles the first. *By J. Bradford,* [1690?]. 8°.* L, O; CN.

1992B   The life and death of Damaris Page. *For R. Burton,* 1669. 4°.* L.

    Life and death of Dr. Martin Lvther. 1641. *See* Adamus, Melchior.

    Life & death of Edmvnd Stavnton. 1673. *See* Mayo, Richard.

1992C   The life and death of famous Thomas Stukeley. *For F. Coles,* [1670?]. brs. O.

1993   The life and death of George of Oxford. *[London], for P. Brooksby,* [1683]. brs. L, CM, HH; MH, NNM, Y. (var.)

1994   Entry cancelled.

    Life and death of . . . Hanserd Knollys. 1692. *See* Knollys, Hanserd.

1994A   The life and death of Henrietta Maria. *For Sam. Speed,* 1669. 12°. L; WCL.

1995   —[Anr. ed.] *For Dorman Newman,* 1685. 8°. T.C.II 113. L, EN; CH, MIU, Y.

1996   The life and death of Jabez-Eliezer Russel. *Printed,* 1672. 4°.* LW.

    The life and death of James Arminius. 1672. *See* Bertius, Pierre.

1997   The life and death of James, commonly called Collonel Turner. *For T. J.,* 1663. 4°.* L, O, LG, CT; MM, WF.

1998-9   Entries cancelled.

    Life and death of John Angier. 1677. *See* Heywood, Oliver. Narrative.

2000   The life and death of John Atherton. *Printed,* 1641. 4°.* LT, C, E; CLC, CN, INU, NCD, NP, Y.

2001   The life and death of King Charles the Martyr, parallel'd with our Saviour. *Printed,* 1649. 4°.* LT, CT, MR, YM; NCD.

2002   The life and death of King Richard the second. *For G. Tomlinson, and T. Watson,* 1642. 4°.* LT, CT, EC, LLU, EN; CH, MH, MU, NU, WF, Y.

    Life and death of Major Clancie. 1680. *See* Settle, Elkanah.

    Life and death of Monsieur Claude. 1688. *See* La Deveze, Abel Rodolpe de.

    Life and death of Mother Shipton. 1677. *See* Head, Richard.

    Life and death of Mr. Henry Jessey. [n.p.], 1671. *See* Whiston, Edward.

    Life and death of Mr. John Rowe. 1673. *See* Gale, Theophilus.

    Life and death of Mr. Joseph Alleine. [n.p.], 1671. *See* Alleine, *Mrs.* Theodosia.

    Life and death of Mr. Thomas Wilson. [n.p.], 1672. *See* Swinnock, George.

2003   The life and death of Mr. Vavasor Powell. *[London], printed,* 1671. 8°. L, O, CPL, DU, LSD; CH, MH, NHC, NU, WF.

2004   The life and death of Mrs. Margaret Andrews. *For Nath. Ponder,* 1680. T.C.II 430. LCL; CN, Y.

2005   The life and death of Mrs. Mary Frith. *For W. Gilbertson,* 1662. 12°. L.

2006   The life and death of Mris Rump. *For Theodorus Microcosmus,* 1660. brs. LT, O.

2007   The life and death of Philip Herbert. *[London], printed,* [1650]. 4°.* LT, MR; CH.

2008   The life and death of Ralph Wallis. *By E. Okes, for William Whitwood,* 1670. 4°. L, O, SP; CH, MH, MIU, NU, WF, Y.

2009   The life and death of Rosamond. *[London], for F. Coles, T. Vere, and J. Wright,* [c. 1670]. 8°.* MH.

2009A   —[Anr. ed.] *For F. Coles, T. Vere, J. Wright, J. Clarke, W. Thackeray, & T. Passinger,* [1678-80]. 8°.* CM.

2009B   —[Anr. ed.] *For W. Thackeray and T. Passenger,* [1686-88]. 8°. O.

2009C   The life and death of Sheffery ap Morgan. *[London], for J. Deacon,* 1683. 8°.* O, CM.

2009D   —[Anr. ed.] *By C. Brown for S. Deacon,* [c. 1700]. 8°.* AN.

    Life and death of Sir Henry Vane. [n.p.], 1662. *See* Sykes, George.

2010   The life and death of Sir Hugh of the Grime. *[London], for P. Brooksby,* [1672-95]. brs. L, O, CM, HH; MH.

Life and death of Sr Thomas Moore. [n.p.], 1642. *See* More, Cresacre.

2011   The life & death of Stephen Marshal. *Printed*, 1680. 4°.*
L, O, LG, OB; CH, CN, MH, MIU, NU.

Life and death of that holy. 1662. *See* Cawton, Thomas.

Life and death of that judicious. 1660. *See* Durham, William.

2012   The life and death of that matchless mirrour . . . Henrietta Maria. *For S. Speed*, 1669. 12°. L, O, CT, LNC; CLC, WCL.

2013   The life & death of that pious, reverend, learned, Richard Baxter. *For Randal Taylor*, 1692. 4°.* T.C.II 402. L, LW.

Life & death of that renowned John Fisher. 1655. *See* Bayly, Thomas.

Life and death of that reverend. Oxford. 1662. *See* Fell, John.

2014   No entry.

Life and death of the B. Virgin. 1688. *See* Fleetwood, William.

Life and death of the eminently learned Dr. Samuel Winter. 1671. *See* W., J.

Life and death of the English rogue. 1679. *See* Head, Richard.

2015   The life and death of the famous champion of England, S. George. [London], *for F. Coles, T. Vere, and W. Gilbertson*, [1660]. 8°. PFORZHEIMER.

2015A —[Anr. ed.] [London], *for F. Coles, T. Vere, J. Wright, and J. Clark*, [1674–79]. 8°. CT.

2016   —[Anr. ed.] *By J. M. for J. Clarke, W. Thackeray and T. Passinger*, [1685?]. 12°. CM.

2016A —[Anr. ed.] *For W. Thackeray*, [1688–89]. 8°. O.

The life and death of the famous Thomas Stukely. [1670.] *See* Johnson, Richard.

Life and death of the godly. 1676. *See* Bragge, Robert.

2017   Life & death of the incomparable and indefatigable Tory Redmond O Hanlyn. [Dublin], *for J. Foster*, 1682. 4°.* DIX 194. L, BQ.

Life and death of the pyper. [n.p., c. 1690.] *See* Sempill, Robert.

2018   The life and death of the Right Honourable Robert, Earle of Essex. *For J. Pots*, 1646. brs. LT; CN, INU, MIU.

Life and death of Thomas Tregosse. 1671. *See* Gale, Theophilus.

Life and death of Thomas Woolsey. 1667. *See* Cavendish, George.

Life and death of William Lawd. 1645. *See* Woodward, Hezekiah.

Life & death offered. 1662. *See* Carter, R.

2019   The life and death, travels and sufferings of Robert VVidders. *Printed*, 1688. 4°.* L, LF, D; MH, PH, RPJ, WF.

Life and doctrine. Gant, 1656. *See* More, Henry, *of the Society of Jesus*.

Life and gests. Gant. 1674. *See* Strange, Richard.

2020   The life and light of a man in Christ. *By Thomas Pain*, 1647. 12°. LT.

2020A The life and pranks of long Meg of Westminster. [n.p., c. 1680.] 8°. L, O (frag.).

Life and reign of Innocent XI. 1690. *See* L., T.

2020B The life and reigne of King Charls. *For W. Reybold*, 1651. LT, O, CPE, DU, EN, CD; CH, CLC, CN, MH, NU, Y.

2020C —[Anr. ed.] *For W. Reybould*, [1651]. 8°. DU; WF.

Life and reigne of . . . King Charles the II. 1660. *See* Eglesfield, Francis.

Life and reign of King Richard II. 1681. *See* Howard, Sir Robert.

2021   The life and travels of our Blessed Lord . . . Jesus Christ. [London], *for P. Brooksby*, [1685–88]. brs. L.

Life of a satyrical puppy. 1657. *See* May, Thomas.

2022   The life of Æsop of Tunbridge . . . Part I. *For John Wells*, 1698. 4°.* Y.

2023   —. . . Part II. —, 1698. 8°.* L.

2024   The life of Boetius, recommended to the author of the Life of Julian. *Printed, and are to be sold by W. Davis*, 1683. 8°. T.C.I 512. L, O, LW, CS, SP; CLC, MH, NU, WF, Y.

2025   Entry cancelled.

Life of Caleb Vernon. 1666. *See* Vernon, John. Compleat scholler.

2025A The life of Captain James Whitney. *For A. R.*, 1692/3. 4°.* EC; CH.

2025B Entry cancelled.

Life of Carolvs Gustavvs. 1688. *See* Prade, Jean Le Royer, *sieur* de. History of Gustavus Adolphus.

2025C The life of Christ magnified. *For John Bringhurst*, 1681. 8°.* LF.

2025D The life of Cornelius van Tromp. *By J. Orme, for R. Clavel, J. Sturton and A. Bosvile, and J. Cater*, 1697. 8°. L, O, LG, LSC, CT, DU, EN, DM; CH, CN, PL, WF, Y.

Life of Count Olfeld. 1695. *See* Rousseau de la Valette, Michel.

2026   The life of Deval. [London], *by W. R.*, 1669. 4°.* L, EN; MIU, Y.

Life of Dr. Thomas Morton. York. 1669. *See* Baddeley, Richard.

Life of Donna Olimpia. 1666. *See* Leti, Gregorio.

Life of Donna Rosina. [1700.] *See* Castillo Solorzano. Alonso de.

Life of Enoch. 1662. *See* Bayly, William.

2027–9 Entries cancelled.

Life of Francis of Lorrain. 1681. *See* Valincour, Jean Baptiste.

Life of God. 1677. *See* Scougal, Henry.

Life of Gregory Lopez. 1675. *See* Losa, Francisco. Holy life.

2029A The life of H[enry] H[ills]. *For T. S.*, 1688. 8°. L; MH, TU.

2030   The life of Henry the Second. *Printed at London for H.B.*, 1642. 4°.* LT, DT; CH, CN, CSS, MH, WF, Y.

2031   The life of Herod the Great. *For Enoch Wyer*, 1678. 4°.* T.C.I 290. L, P; CH, MIU, WF, Y.

2032   Entry cancelled.

Life of Innocent XI. 1683. *See* Nesse, Christopher. Devil's patriarck.

2033   The life of John Machin. 1671. 12°. LW, P.

Life of John Milton. 1699. *See* Toland, John.

Life of Lewis. 1693. *See* Coste, Pierre.

2033A The life of long Meg of Westminster. *By J. M. for G. Conyers*, [1690?]. 12°.* CM.

2034 The life of love. [*London*], *for P. Brooksby*, [1685–88]. brs. EUING 180. L, CM, HH, GU.

Life of Merlin. 1641. *See* Heywood, Thomas.

2035 Life of Michael Adrian de Rvyter. *By J. B. for Dorman Newman*, 1677. 12°. L, LLL, OH, CT; CH, CLC, CN, MH, WF.

Life of Mr. Thomas Firmin. 1698. *See* Nye, Stephen.

The life of Monsieur Des Cartes. 1693. *See* Baillet, Adrien.

2035A The life of Monsieur L'Arroque. [*London*, 1684?] 4°.* EN.

Life of Mother Shipton. [1660.] *See* Thompson, Thomas.

2035B The life of one Jacob Boehmen. *By L. N. for Richard Whitaker*, 1644. 4°.* LT, CT; MH.

2035C The life of St. Anthony of Padoua. *Printed at Paris*, 1660. 12°. L, O; WF.

Life of St. Mary. 1687. *See* Puccini, Vincentio.

Life of Sir Henry Wotton. 1670. *See* Walton, Izaak.

Life of Tamerlane. 1653. *See* Clarke, Samuel, *of St. Bennet Fink*.

Life of that incomparable man. 1643. *See* Przypkowski, Samuel.

2036 The life of that incomparable Princess Mary. *For Daniel Dring*, 1695. 12°. L, DCH, LLU; CH, CN, MB, PL, WF, Y.

Life of that most illustrious. 1691. *See* La Brune, Jean de.

Life of that reverend . . . Thomas Fuller. 1661. *See* Fell, John.

Life of the blessed St. Agnes. 1677. *See* Pratt, Daniel.

Life of the famous Cardinal. 1695. *See* Le Clerc, Jean.

Life of the famous John Baptiste Colbert. 1695. *See* Courtilz de Sandras, Gatien.

Life of the holy mother. [n.p.], 1671. *See* Teresa, *saint*.

Life of the Lady Warner. [n.p.], 1691. *See* Carisbrick, Edward.

Life of the learned . . . Smith. 1698. *See* Strype, John.

2036A Entry cancelled.

Life of the most illustrious monarch Almanzor. 1693. *See* Luna, Miguel de.

Life of the most learned Father Paul. 1651. *See* Micanzio, Fulgenzio.

Life of the most learned . . . Hammond. 1661. *See* Fell, John.

Life of the renowned. 1679. *See* Bouhours, Dominique.

Life of the right reverend. 1688. *See* Banks, Jonathan.

Life of the valiant . . . Sir Walter Raleigh. 1677. *See* Shirley, John, 1648–1679.

2037 The life of Titus Oats from his cradle. colop: *By E. Mallet*, 1685. cap., fol.* O, MC, MR, SP; CH, MH, TU, Y.

2038 —[Anr. ed.] colop: *By E. Mallet*, 1685. *Reprinted at Edinburgh, by the heir of Andrew Anderson*, 1685. cap., fol.* ALDIS 2557. L, EN.

Life of Tomaso. [n.p.], 1667. *See* Flecknoe, Richard.

Life of William Bedell. 1685. *See* Burnet, Gilbert, *bp*.

2039 The life of William Fuller. *For Abel Roper*, 1692. 4°.* L, OC, CM, CT, MR; CH, MH, PL, WF, Y.

2040 The life of William now Ld Arch-Bishop of Canterbury, examined. *For N. B.*, 1643. 4°. LT, LLP.

2041 Entry cancelled.

Life of William Prince of Orange. 1688. *See* History of the most illustrious William.

2042 Life of William Simpson. [n.p.], *printed*, 1671. PSC.

2043 **Liford, R.** England's fair warning. *For J. Blare*, 1693. 8°.* L; NC.

2044 No entry.

Light for the ignorant. [n.p.], 1641. *See* Lilburne, John.

Light for the Iews. 1656. *See* Evans, Rhys.

Light from the sun. [n.p.], 1672. *See* Grigg, Henry.

2045 Light in darknesse. Or, a clear and impartial discovery. [*London*], 1656. 4°.* MR, YM; NN, WF.

Light in darkness; or, a consideration. 1669. *See* Phelpes, Charles.

2046 Light in darkness, or a modest enquiry . . . cure of Mariane Maillard. *For Tho. Parkhurst*, 1694. 8°.* O, EN; MH.

Light manifesting. Aberdene, 1670. *See* Mitchell, William.

Light risen. 1654. *See* Farnworth, Richard.

2046A Light shining in Bvckingham-shire, or, a discovery. [*London*], *printed*, 1648. 4°.* L, O, RU; CN, MH, WF.

2047 —. . . the first part. [*London*], *printed*, 1648. 4°.* LT, O, C, YM, EN; MH, NC, RBU, WF.

Light shining out. 1659. *See* Stubbs, Henry.

Light to grammar. 1641. *See* Woodward, Hezekiah.

Light upon the candlestick. 1663. *See* Ames, William, *Quaker*.

2047A **Lightbody, George.** Quæstiones grammaticæ. *Edinburgi, Gideon Lithgo*, 1660. 8°. ALDIS 1647. EN, GU.

2048 **Lightbody, James.** Every man his own gauger. *For G.C.*, [*c.* 1695]. 12°. CH, WF, Y.

2048A ——[Anr. ed.] *For Hugh Newman*, 1695. 12°. T.C.II 524. CS.

2048B ——[Anr. ed., "gauge."]. *Printed and sold by A. Baldwin*, [1695]. 12°. L.

2049 —The gauger and measurer's companion. *For J. Everingham*, 1694. T.C.II 500. L, O, OB; LC.

2049A —The mariners jewel. *For Robert Whitledge, and sold by Alexander Sims*, 1695. 12°. L; WF.

2049B ——Second edition. *For Robert Whitledge and sold by Alexander Sims and Rich. Mount*, 1697. 12°. CLC, MWA.

2050 **L[ightburn], W[illiam].** A Thanksgiving sermon. *Dublin, by John Crook: to be sold by Samuel Dancer*, 1661. 4°.* DIX 113. L, DM.

2051 **Lightfoot, John.** The works of. *By W. R. for Robert Scot, Thomas Basset, Richard Chiswell, John Wright*, 1684. 2v. fol. T.C.II 110. L, O, C, EN, DT; BN, CH, IU, MH, NU, PL, Y, AVP.

2052 —A commentary upon the Acts of the Apostles. *By R. C. for Andrew Crooke*, 1645. 4°. L, O, C, E, DT; CH, IU, MH, NU, PL, WF, AVP.

2053 —Elias redivivus: a sermon. *By R. Cotes, for Andrew Crooke*, 1643. 4°. LT, O, C, E, DT; CH, IU, MH, NU, TU, WF, Y, AVP.

2054 —A few, and new observations. *By T. Badger*, 1642. 4°.* LT, O, C, DUS, SS; CH, MH, NR, NU, WF, Y.

2055 —An handfvll of gleanings. *By R. Cotes, for Andrew Crooke*, 1643. 4°. L, O, C, SS, YM; CH, IU, MH, TU, WF, Y.

2055A ——[Anr. ed.] *By G. Dawson for Andrew Crook*, 1658. 4°. OC.

2056 —The harmony, chronicle and order of the Old Testament. *By R. Cotes for John Clark*, 1647. 4°. LT, O, C, E, DT; CH, IU, MH, NU, TU, WF, Y.

2057 —The harmony, chronicle and order of the New Testament. *By A. M. for Simon Miller*, 1655. fol. L, O, CCH, ENC, DT; CH, IU, MH, NU, WF, Y.

2058 —The harmony of the foure evangelists. *By R. Cotes for Andrew Crooke*, 1644. 4°. LT, O, C, CT, DC; CLC, IU, MH, NU, TU, Y.

2059 ——Second part. *By R. Cotes for John Clark*, 1647. 4°. L, O, C, OC, SP, DL; CLC, IU, MH, NU, TU, WF, Y.

2060 —— . . . the Third part. *By R. C. for Andrew Crook*, 1650. 4°. L, O, OC, CT; CDA, CH, NCU, PJB, WF.

2060A ———[Anr. ed.] *By G. Dawson for Andrew Crook*, 1658. 4°. OC, SP; WF.

2060B —Horæ Hebraicæ & Talmudicæ in Acta S. Apostolorum. *Hagae-Comitis, et vaeneunt Londini*, 1678. 4°. NU.

2061 —Horæ Hebraicæ et Talmudicæ. Impensæ I. In chorographiam . . . S. Matthæi. *Cantabrigiæ, excudebat Joannes Field, impensis Edovardi Story*, 1658. 4°. L, O, C, E, DT; BN, CH, CLC, IU, LC, NU, PU, Y.

2062 [–] Horæ Hebraicæ et Talmudicæ, impensæ in Evangelium S. Joannis. *Imprimebat Thomas Roycroft; prostant venales apud Benjamin Tooke*, 1671. 4°. L, O, C, E, DT; BN, CH, IU, MBC, WF, Y.

2063 [–] Horæ Hebraicæ et Talmudicæ. Impensæ in Evangelium S. Lucæ. *Cantabrigiæ, ex officina Johan. Hayes, impensis Ed. Story*, 1674. 4°. O, C, LLP, E, DT; BN, CH, IU, MBC, NU, PL, WF.

2064 [–] —[Anr. ed.] *Sumptibus E. S. & venales prostant ad officinum Roberti Boulter*, 1674. 4°. T.C.I 180. WCA, EN; BN, CH, CLC, IU, Y.

2065 [–] Horæ Hebraicæ et Talmudicæ. . . . Sancti Marci. *Cantabrigiæ, excudebat Johannes Field, prostant apud Thomam Danks*, 1663. 4°. L, O, C, CT, DL, DT; BN, CLC, NU, PPT, Y.

2065A [–] —[Anr. ed.] *Cantabrigiæ: excudebat Joannes Field*, 1663. 4°. CT; CH.

2066 —In Evangelium sancti Matthæi. *Cantabrigiæ: excudebat Joannes Field*, 1658. 4°. LVF, LW, LNC, MC, SA; IU,NU, WU.

2067 —Horæ . . . ad Corinthios. *Cantabrigiæ, excudebat Joan. Field*, 1664. 4°. O, LW, OC, CT.

2068 —A sermon preached . . . 26 day of August 1645. *By R. C. for Andrew Crook*, 1645. 4°.* LT, O, C, EN, DT; CH, IU, MH, NU, WF, Y, AVP.

2069 —A sermon preached . . . Febr. 24, 1646/47. *By S. I. for Andrew Crooke*, 1647. 4°.* LT, O, C, SS, DT; CH, MH, NU, WF, Y, AVP.

2070 —Some genuine remains of. *By R. J. for J. Robinson: and J. Wyat*, 1700. 8°. T.C.III 196. L, O, C, EN, DT; CLC, IU, MH, NU, WF, Y, AVP.

2071 —The temple: especially. *By R. C. for Andrew Crook*, 1650. 4°. L, O, CT, SA, DT; CDA, IU, MH, NC, WF, Y, AVP.

2072 —The temple service. *By R. Cotes for Andrevv Crooke*, [1649]. 4°. LT, O, C, YM, E; BN, CH, IU, MH, NU, WF.

2073 **Lightfoot, Peter.** A battell with a vvaspes nest. *Printed*, 1649. 4°. LCL, YM, DT; CLC, Y.

2074 Entry cancelled.

Lightless starre. 1652. *See* Resbury, Richard.

Lightning colomne. Amsterdam, 1662. *See* Colom, Jacob.

2075 **Ligon, Richard.** A trve & exact history of the Island of Barbados. *For Humphrey Moseley*, 1657. fol. L, O, C, E, DT; CH, LC, MH, MU, RPJ, WF, Y.

2076 ——[Anr. ed.] *Printed and are to be sold by Peter Parker, and Thomas Guy*, 1673. fol. T.C.I 129. L, O, C, EN, DT; CLC, CN, LC, MH, RPJ, V, WCL, AVP.

2077 **Lilburne, Elizabeth.** To the chosen and betrusted knights, . . . the humble petition of. [*London*, 1646.] brs. LT, LG, CS, DT; MIU, NN, WF.

2077aA **Lilburne, Elizabeth, fl. 1696.** Elizabeth Lilburne . . . against William Carr . . . The case. [*n.p.*, 1696.] brs. L.

2077A **Lilburne, George.** To every individuall member . . . Commons. [*London*, 1649.] cap., 4°.* O; CH.

2078 **Lilburne, John.** The afflicted mans out-cry. [*London*, 1653.] cap., 4°.* LT, CT; WF, Y.

2079 —An agreement of the free people of England. colop: *For Gyles Calvert*, [1649.] cap., 4°.* LT, O, C, MR, EN, DT; CH, CN, NU, PH, WF.

2080 —An anatomy of the Lords tyranny. [*London*, 1646.] cap., 4°.* LT, O, C, EN, DT; CH, CU, MH, NU, TU, WF.

2081 —An answer, to Nine arguments. *Printed*, 1645. 4°.* LT, O, DT; CN, WF.

2082 —L. Colonel John Lilbvrne his apologetical narration. *Amsterdam, printed, Aprill.*, 1652. by L. I. 4°. LT, DT; CSS.

2083 ——[Anr. ed.] [*Amsterdam*, 1652.] 4°. L; NU.

2084 —As you were. [*Amsterdam?*], *printed May* 1652. 4°.* L, CJ, DT; IU, NU.

2085 —The banished mans suit. *By Tho. Newcomb*, [1653]. brs. LT, O; MH.

2086 —The case of the tenants of the Mannor of Epworth. [*London*, 1651.] cap., 4°.* LT, O; CN, MH.

2087 —The charters of London. *Printed at London, Decemb.* 18. 1646. 4°. LT, O, DT; CH, CN, MH, NC, WF.

2088 Entry cancelled. Ghost. *See following entry.*

2089 —The Christian mans triall. Second edition. *For William Larnar*, 1641. 4°.* LT, O, OW, SP; CH, NHC, NU, PH, WF, Y.

2089A [–] A conference with the souldiers. [*London*, 1653.] cap., 4°.* LT, CT; PSC.

2090   —The copy of a letter, from . . . to a freind [*sic*]. [*London, Larner's press at Goodman's Fields*, 1645.] cap., 4°.* LT, O, C, EN, DT; CH, CU, MH, WF, Y. (var.)

2091   —A coppy of a letter sent by . . . to Mr. Wollaston. [*London*, 1646.] brs. LT, O, OL, HH.

2092   —A copie of a letter, written by . . . to Mr. William Prinne Esq. [*London*, 1645.] cap., 4°.* LT, O, C, EC, DT; IU, MH, MIU, PSC, Y.

2093   —A copy of a letter written to Coll. Henry Marten. [*London*, 1647.] brs. LT, OW.

2094   —The copie of a letter written to the general. [*London*, 1649.] brs. LT, C; CH, MH.

2095   —A declaration of . . . to the free-born people of England. *For G. Horton*, 1651 [2]. 4°.* LT, MR.

2096   [–] —[Anr. ed.] *For George Horton*, 1654. 4°.* LT.

2097   —A defencive declaration of L. Col. [*Amsterdam*, 1653.] cap., 4°.* MR, EN.

2098   — —[Anr. ed., "defensive."] [*London*, 1653.] cap., 4°.* LT, ORP, BAMB, BC, LIU; BBE, CSS, MIU, PSC, WF.

        [–] Defiance against all. [n.p.], 1646. *See* Overton, Richard.

2099   —A defiance to tyrants. *Printed, Jan.* 1648. 4°.* LT, O; CN, CU, Y.

2100   —A discourse betwixt Lieutenant Colonel Iohn Lilburn, close prisoner. *Printed*, 1649. 4°.* LT, C, LG, LVF, DUS; CLC, CU, IU, MH, PH, WF.

2100A   — —[Anr. ed., "discovrse."] —, 1649. 4°.* L, O, C, CT; CH, MH, MIU, NU, Y.

2101   —The engagement vindicated. *By John Clowes*, 1650. 4°.* LT, O, BC, DU, DT; CH, CN, MH, NU, PSC, WF, Y. (var.)

2102   [–] Englands birth-right justified. [*London, Larner's press at Goodman's Fields*, 1645.] cap., 4°. LT, C, LLL, OC, CJ; CH, NU, WF.

2103   — —[Anr. ed.] colop: [*London*], *printed, Octob.* 1645. cap., 4°. LT, C, LCL, EC, LIU, DT; CH, CSS, NP, PT, WF.

2103A   — —Second edition. colop: [*London*], *printed, Novem.* 1645. 4°. CT, MR; BBE, MWA, PT, ANL.

2104–5 Entries cancelled.

        —Englands lamentable slaverie. [n.p.], 1645. *See* Walwyn, Williams.

        [–] Englands miserie. [n.p., 1645.] *See* Overton, Richard.

2106   —Englands new chains discovered. [*London*, 1649.] cap., 4°.* LT, O, C, EN, CD; BN, CH, CU, MBP, MH, NU, PH, WF, Y.

2107   —Englands weeping spectacle. [*London*], *printed*, 1648. 4°.* LT, LVF; MIU, NU.

2108   —The exceptions of. *For Richard Moon*, 1653. 4°.* LT, O, OC, CT, LIU, CD; CH, CN, MH, NU, WF, Y. (var.)

2109   [–] For every individuall member of the honourable House of Commons. [*London*, 1647.] cap., 4°.* LT, MR; CSS, WF.

2109A   —For the worshipful, Mr. Steel. [*London*, 1653.] cap., 4°.* L; NU.

2110   [–] Foundations of freedom. *For R. Smithurst*, 1648. 4°.* O, MR, ESS, EN; CLC, CU, NU, WF, Y.

2110A   [–] —[Anr. ed.] *Published*, 1648. 4°.* L, O, C, BR, LIU; CH, CN, MH, TU, WF, Y.

2111   —The free-mans freedome vindicated. [*London*, 1646.] cap., 4°.* LT, O, CS, EN, DT; CH, IU, MH, NU, PH, WF.

2112   —The grand plea of. [*London*, 1647.] 16 pp. cap., 4°.* LT, O, C, LF, DU; CH, CU, MH, NU, PSC, WF, Y.

2112A   — —[Anr. ed.] [*London*, 1647.] 24 pp. cap., 4°.* O, C, LIU, MR, DT; MH, MIU, WF.

2113   [–] An hue-and cry after the fundamental lawes. *Europe, printed*, [1653.] 4°.* LT, O, OW.

2114   —The humble and further demand of. [*London*, 1653.] cap., 4°.* LT, O, OW, MR; NU, WF.

2115   —The hunting of the foxes from New-Market. [*London*], *printed in a corner of Freedome, right opposite to the Councel of Warre, anno Domini*, 1649. 4°.* LT, O, C, EN, DT; BN, CH, CN, MH, WF, Y. (var.)

2116   —An impeachment of high treason. *Imprinted at London*, 1649. 4°. LT, O, C, MR, EN; BN, CH, CN, MH, WF, Y.

2117   [–] In the 150 page of the book called, An exact collection. [*London*, 1645.] brs. LT, OC; Y.

2118   —Innocency and trvth jvstified. [*London*], *printed*, 1645 [6]. 2 pts. 4°. LT, O, C, LCL, DUS, DT; CH, CSS, CU, NU, Y.

2119   —The innocent man's first proffer. [*London*, 1649.] brs. LT.

2120   —The innocent man's second proffer. [*London*, 1649.] brs. LT; MIU.

2121   Entry cancelled.

        —John Lilburne. Anagram. O! J burn in helL. [n.p., 1653.] *See title.*

2122   —Ionahs cry out of the whales belly. [*London*, 1647.] cap., 4°.* LT, O, C, EN, DT; CH, CN, NU, TU, WF, Y.

2123   —The ivglers discovered. [*London*, 1647.] cap., 4°.* LT, BC, LLU, MR, EN; CH, CN, NU, WF, Y.

2123A   [–] The just defence of. [*London*, 1653.] cap., 4°.* LT, CT, MR; MIU, WF.

2124   —The ivst man in bonds. [*London*, 1646.] cap., 4°.* LT, DT; CN, MH, MIU, NP, PH.

2125   —The ivst mans ivstification. [*London*, 1646.] cap., 4°.* LT, OC, MR, EN, DT; CN, MH, NU, PT, WF.

2126   — —Second edition. [*London*, 1647.] cap., 4°.* LT, OC, DUS, MR; CH, KQ, TU, WF, ANL.

2127   —A iust reproof to Haberdashers-Hall. [*London*, 1651.] 4°.* LT, OC, LIU, EN; CSS, NU, PSC, WF, Y.

2128   —L. Colonel John Lilburne revived. [*Amsterdam?*], *printed*, 1653. *In March.* 4°.* LT.

2129   No entry.

2130   —The lawes funerall. [*London*, 1648.] cap., 4°.* LT, O, CT, DUS, EN; NU, PH, MK, Y, ANL.

2131   —The legall fundamentall liberties of the people of England revived. *Printed*, 1649. 4°. LT, O, C, MR, EN; BN, CH, CN, MH, WF, Y.

2132   — —Second edition. *Reprinted*, 1649. 4°. LT, O, C, OW, LIU; CH, CU, MH, NC, NU, WF.

2133   —A letter of . . . 31. of March 1651. [*London*, 1651.] cap., 4°.* LT, OW, MR; MIU.

2134   —A letter sent from. *For Iames Rogers.* 1643. 4°.* LT, O, MR; CLC, MBP, MH, NU.

2135   Entry cancelled.
        —Col: Lilburnes letter to a friend. 1645. *See* Lilburne,
        Robert.
2136   —L. Colonel John Lilburne his letter to his . . . wife.
        colop: *Amsterdam, L. I.,* 1652. cap., 4°.* MR, DT.
2136A   [–] The Levellers remonstrance, sent. *For George Horton,*
        1652. 4°.* LT, O; Y.
2137   [–] Liberty vindicated against slavery. [*London*], *printed,*
        1646. 4°.* LT, O, CCA, EN, DT; CH, CN, MH, PSC, WF, Y.
2138   [–] A light for the ignorant. [*London*], *printed,* 1641.
        4°.* O, DT; CSS, MH, MWA, NU.
2139   —Londons liberty in chains discovered. [*London,* 1646.]
        cap., 4°. L, O, CT, EN, CD; CH, CN, MH, TU, WF, Y.
2140   No entry.
2141   —Malice detected. *Printed at London,* 1653. 4°.* LT, CT,
        BSO, MR; CH, MIU, NU.
2142   —A manifestation from. *For W. Larner, April* 14, 1649.
        4°.* L, LC, CT, MR, EN; BN, CU, MH, MU, NC.
2143   — —[Anr. ed.] [*London*], *printed,* 1649. 4°.* LT, O, C,
        BAMB, MR, CD; CH, CN, PSC, WF, Y.
2144   —A more full relation of the great battell. *By T. Forcet
        for Peter Cole.* 1645. 4°.* LT, O, CT, BR; MH, WF.
2145   —More light to Mr John Lilburnes jury. *Printed, August*
        16, 1653. cap., 4°. L, LF, CT, MR; CH, WF.
2146   —A new bull-bayting. *Nod-Nol, printed,* 1649. 4°.* LT;
        CH.
2147   —A new complaint of an old grievance. [*London,* 1647.]
        4°.* LT, O; MH, WF.
2148   —The oppressed mans importunate and mournfull
        cryes. [*London,* 1648.] cap., 4°.* L, MR; CH, MH, MIU,
        WF.
2149   —The oppressed mans oppressions declared. [*London,*
        1646/7.] 28 pp. cap., 4°.* O, LF, CT, EN, DT; CH, CU, PH,
        TU, Y.
2149A   — —[Anr. ed.] — 39 pp. 4°.* LT, O, CT, LIU, DT; CH, MH,
        MIU, NP, WF.
2150   —The out-cryes of oppressed Commons. [*London,*
        1647.] cap., 4°.* LT, O, CS, MR, DT; CSS, CU, MH, NU,
        TU, Y.
2151   — —Second edition. [*n.p.,* 1647.] cap., 4°.* L, O, BP, MR,
        EN; CSS, NC, WF.
2152   [–] An out cry of the youngmen and apprentices. [*Lon-
        don,* 1649.] cap., 4°.* LT, LVF, OC, BR, MR; MIU, IU, WF,
        Y.
2153   —The peoples prerogative and priviledges. *Printed,*
        1647[8]. 4°. LT, C, LVF, EN, DT; CH, NC, NU, WF, Y.
2154   —The picture of the Councel of State. [*London*], *printed,
        Year,* 1649. 4°. LT, O, C, EN, DT; BN, CH, CN, MH, WF, Y.
2155   — —Second edition. —, *yeer,* 1649. 4°.* LG, LUG, CT, E;
        CH, NC, NU, PH, Y.
2156   [–] Plaine truth without feare or flattery. [*London*],
        printed, 1647. 4°.* O, C, DU, GU, DT; BBE, CN, MH, NU.
2157   [–] —[Anr. ed., "vvithout."] —, 1647. 4°.* O; CH, NU.
        [–] —[Anr. ed., "Plain."] [*n.p.*], 1647. *See* Wilbee, Amon.
2158   —A plea at large, for. [*London,* 1653.] cap., 4°.* LT, DT;
        NU, WF.

2159   —A plea for common-right. *By Ja. and Jo. Moxon, for
        Will. Larner,* 1648. 4°.* LT, LLU, MR; BBE, CH, MIU, PT,
        Y.
2159A   —Lieu. Col. John Lilburn's plea in law. [*London, June*
        28, 1653.] cap., 4°.* LIU.
2160   — —Second edition. [*London, July* 2, 1653.] cap., 4°.*
        LT, LF, LG, ORP, CT, MR; CSS, MH, MU, WF.
2161   —A plea, or protest, made by VVilliam Prynne. [*Lon-
        don*], *for Iah. Hornish,* 1648. 4°.* LT, C, OC, MR, DT; CH,
        LC, MH, NU, TU, Y.
2162   —A preparative to an hue and cry. [*London,* 1649.] cap.,
        4°.* LT, O, CT, DUS, EN; CH, MIU, NU, TU, WF, Y.
2163   —The prisoner's most mournful cry. [*London,* 1653.]
        cap., 4°.* LT, O, ORP, OW, MR; CSS, MH, NU, TU, WF.
2164   —The prisoners mournfull cry. [*London,* 1648.] cap.,
        4°.* LT, O, LF, CT, MR; MH, MU, NCD, NU, WF, Y.
2165   —The prisoners plea. [*London,* 1648.] cap., 4°.* LT, LCL,
        OC, DT; CH, MH, MIU, PT, WF.
2166   —The proposition of. [*London,* 1647.] brs. O.
2167   —Rash oaths unwarrantable. [*London,* 1647.] cap., 4°.
        LT, O, LG, CT, BC, EN, CD; CH, CN, NU, PH, TU, WF, Y.
2168   —The reasons of Lieu. Col. Lilbournes sending his
        letter. colop: [*London*], *printed* 13 *June,* 1645. 4°.* LT, O,
        CS, BP, EN, DT; WF.
2169   — —[Anr. ed.][*London*], 1647. cap., 4°. LT.
2170   Entry cancelled.
        —Reasons upon which. 1650. *See* —Engagement
        vindicated.
2171   —The recantation of. [*London*], *printed,* 1647. 4°.* LT,
        O, LVF, OC, MR, DT; CN, MH, NU, PH, WF.
2172   [–] Regall tyrannie discovered. *Printed,* 1647. 4°. LT, O,
        LVF, CT, MR, DT; CH, CN, LC, MH, NU, Y.
2173   —A remonstrance of. *Imprinted at London, for G. Hor-
        ton,* 1652. 4°.* LT, LVF; CN, NU.
2174   —The resolved mans resolution. [*London,* 1647.] cap.,
        4°.* LT, O, CT, LIU, EN; CH, CN, MH, NU, TU, WF, Y.
2175   —The resurrection of. *For Giles Calvert,* 1656. 4°.* LT,
        O, LF, EN; CH, CN, IE, PSC, WF.
2176   — —Second edition. —, 1656. 4°.* LT, O, LF, LL, CT, DU;
        NU, PH, Y.
2177   —A salva libertate, sent to Collonell Francis West.
        [*London,* 1649.] brs. LT, OW, DT.
2178   —A second address. *By Tho. Newcomb,* [1653]. brs. LT,
        LVF; TU.
2179   —The second letter from. *Printed,* 1653. 4°.* LT, O, LVF,
        CT, MR; WF.
2180   [–] The second part of Englands new-chaines dis-
        covered. *Printed,* 1649. 4°.* LT, O, OC, LIU, MR; CH, MH,
        MU, WF, Y.
2181   — —[Anr. ed.] —, 1649. 4°.* LT, LF, LG, SP, EN; BBE, CN,
        MIU, MM, NN, NU.
2181A   [–] —[Anr. ed.] [*n.p.,* 1649.] cap., 4°. O; IAU.
2182   —Strength out of vveaknesse. *Printed,* 1649. 4°.* LT,
        LVF, EN, DT; CH, CN, MIU, WF.
2183   —A third address. *By Tho. Newcomb,* [1653]. brs. LT; MH.
2183A   —To all the affectors and approvers in England. [*London,*
        1649.] cap., 4°.* L, LG, OC.

2184 —To every individuall member of . . . Commons: the humble remembrance of. [*London*, 1648.] cap., 4°.* LT, O, CT; CLC, CU, NU, WF.

2185 —To every individuall member of the supreame authority. [*London*, 1650.] brs. LT; MH.

2186 ——[Anr. ed.] [*London*, 1651.] cap., 4°.* LT, MR, DU; CSS.

2186A —To his honored friend, Mr. Cornelius Holland. [*London*, 1649.] cap., 4°.* LVF, OC; MIU.

2187 —To the hon^ble the House of Commons. [*London*, 1645.] brs. LL.

2187A —To the right honourable the chosen and representative body . . . the humble petition of. [*London*, 1646.] 4°.* L.

2188 [–] To the Right Honovrable the Commons of England; . . . the humble petition of thousands wel-affected persons. [*London*, 1648.] brs. STEELE 2794. LT, O, LG, DU, LNC; CLC, Y.

2189 —To the supreme authority for the Common-wealth. [*London*, 1653.] brs. L; WF, Y.

2190 —To the supreme authority, the people . . . the humble petition of. [*London*, 1650.] 4°.* LT, LF, LS; MIU, NU.

2191 —A true relation of the materiall passages. [*London*, 1646.] cap., 4°.* LT, OC, CT, MR, DT; CN, CSS, MH, MIU, WF, Y.

2191A [–] Truth's victory over tyrants. [*London*], *printed*, 1649. 4°.* LT; WF.

2192 —Two letters: the one from. [*London*, 1647.] cap., 4°.* L; MIU.

2193 —Tvvo letters vvrit by. [*London*, 1647.] cap., 4°.* LT, O, C, EN, DT; CH, CU, NU, TU, WF, Y.

2194 [–] Two petitions presented to the supreme authority. *By J. B.*, 1650. 4°.* O, LUG; CN, MH.

2195 [–] An vnhappy game at Scotch and Engljsh. *Edinbvrgh, by Evan Tyler*, 1646. 4°.* ALDIS 1242-3. LT, O, C, EN, DT; CH, CN, MH, MM, NU, TU, WF, Y. (var.)

2196 —The upright man's vindication. [*London*], 1646. 4°. LCL.

2197 ——[Anr. ed.] [*London*, 1653.] 4°.* LT, CT, DT; CH, MH, NP, NU, PH, WF.

2198 —A whip for the present House of Lords. [*London*, 1648.] 4°.* LT, O, CT, LIU, EN; CH, MH, NU, WF.

2199 **Lilburne, Robert.** Col: Lilburnes letter to a friend: published. *For Peter Cole, Sept.* 23, 1645. 4°.* LT, BAMB, MR.

2200 —Two letters from. *For Robert Ibbitson*, 1651. 4°.* LT, GC, LNC; CLC, CN, MIU, WF.

2201 —By the commander in chief . . . Whereas (amongst other things) . . . 7 *April* 1654. *Printed at Leith.* 1654. brs. STEELE 3p2110. ALDIS 1494.5. L, O, EN; VC.

2201A —By the commander in chief . . . Whereas his excellency by his proclamation. [Restrictions on travel, 27 September.] *Printed at Leith*, 1653. brs. STEELE 3p 2105. ALDIS 1482.3. EN.

2202 Lilbvrns ghost, with a whip. *For Livewell Chapman*, 1659. 4°.* LT, DU, MR; MH, MU, WF.

2203 Lillies ape whipt. [*London*], *for W. I. C. I. G. W.*, [1652]. 4°.* LT, O; CSS, MIU, WF, Y.

2204 Lillies banquet: or, the Star-gazers feast. *For R. Eels*, [1653]. brs. LT.

2205 Lillies invitation to those. *Printed*, 1668. brs. L.

2206 Lillyes lamentations or. *For R. Eeles*, [1652]. 4°.* LT; Y.

Lilly, William. Anglicanus. 1646. *See* Almanacs.

2207 —Anglicus, peace, or no peace. *By J. R. for John Partridge and Humphrey Blunden*, 1645. 4°. L, O, C, MR, DT; CLC, CN, MH, TU, WF, Y.

2208 —Anima astrologiæ: or, a guide. *For B. Harris*, 1676. 8°. L, O, LWL, NE; CLC, CN, INU, MH, MU, NAM, NCD, NS, WF.

2208A ——Second edition. *For Benj. Harris*, 1683. 8°. MB.

2209 —Annus tenebrosus, or the dark year. *For the company of stationers, and H. Blunden*, 1652. 4°. LT, O, C, E; CH, CLC, CN, MH, WF, Y.

2210 —Astrological judgments for 1682. [*London*], 1682. 8°. L, MR.

2211 —An astrologicall prediction . . . 1648 . . . 1650. *By T. B. for John Parttridge* [sic] *and Humfrey Blunden*, 1648. 4°. LT, O, C, EN, DT; BN, CH, CN, MH, WF, Y. (var.)

2212 —Astrological predictions for 1654. [*London*, 1654.] 8°. GU.

2213 —Mr. Lillie's astrological predictions for 1677. [*London*], *for T. Passinger*, [1676]. 4°.* L, O, MR, A; INU.

2214 [–] Catastrophe mundi: or, Merlin reviv'd. *Printed and are to be sold by John How and Thomas Malthus*, 1683. 8°. T.C.II 7. L, O, CT, CPL, DU; CH, CN, MH, NU, WF, Y.

2215 —Christian astrology. *By Tho. Brudenell for John Partridge and Humph. Blunden*, 1647. 4°. L, O, C, MC, E; CH, IU, LC, MH, TU, Y. (var.)

2216 ——Second edition. *By John Macock*, 1659. 4°. L, LWL, ES, GU; CLC, MIU, PBL, PL, TSM, WF, Y, AVP.

2217 —A collection of ancient and moderne prophesies. *For John Partridge and Humphry Blunden*, 1645. 4°. LT, O, C, EN, DT; CH, CU, MH, NU, TU, WF, Y.

2218 —The dangerous condition of the Vnited Provinces prognosticated. *For W. Whitwood*, 1672. 4°.* L, LG, OC, NE; HR, CLC, CSS, WF, ZAP.

2219 —An easie and familiar method whereby to iudge. *For the company of stationers, and H. Blunden*, 1652. 4°.* LT, O, C; CH, CN, MH, NCD, WF, Y.

2220 —Englands monethly observations. [*London*], *for W. Gilbertson*, [1653]. brs. L.

2221 —Englands propheticall Merline. *By John Raworth, for John Partridge*, 1644. 4°. LT, O, C, E, DT; CH, CN, MH, WF, Y.

—English ephemeris. 1650. *See* Almanacs.

2222 Entry cancelled.

—Fore-warn'd, fore-arm'd. 1682. *See* title.

2223 —The great and wonderful predictions of. *For Josh. Conyers*, 1683. 4°.* L, O.

2224 [–] A groatsworth of wit for a penny. [*London*], *for W. T. and sold by Ionah Deacon*, [c. 1670]. 8°.* CM; CH.

2224A —Doctor Lillys last legacy. Seventh edition. *For Richard Baker*, 1683. 4°.* L.

2225 —Mr. Lillies late prophecy come to pass. [*London*], *by A. Purslow*, 1673. 4°.* L; INU.

2226   Entry cancelled.
        —Late storie of. 1647/8. *See title.*
        —Merlini Anglici ephemeris. [n.p.], 1647. *See* Almanacs.
        —Merlinus Anglicus junior. 1644. *See* Almanacs.

2226A   —Mirror of natural astrology; or, a new book of fortune. *For W. Thackeray and sold by J. Deacon,* [1675?]. 8°. CM.

2227   —Monarchy ofte geen monarchy. [*London*], *ghedruckt by Humfrey Blunden,* 1653. 4°. O, LNC; CLC, IU, MIU, WF, Y.

2228   —Monarchy or no monarchy in England. *For Humfrey Blunden,* 1651. 4°. LT, O, C, YM, EN; CH, CN, LC, MH, NC, TU, Y. (var.)

2228A   — —[Anr. ed.] *For Henry Cripps & Lodowick Lloyd,* 1655. 4°. CH, CLC.

2228B   —Lilly's new Erra Pater. *Published by J. Conyers,* [1695?]. 12°.* CM.

2229   —Mr. Lillies new prophesie of a general peace. [*London?*], *for M. B.,* 1674. 4°.* L.

2230   —Mr. Lilly's new prophecy: or, certain notable passages. *For L. C.,* 1678. 4°.* L, O, EN; CH, MH.

2231   —Mr. Lilly's new prophecy: or, several strange. *For J. Heathcoat,* 1681. 4°.* LG; CH, PU, Y.

2232   —Mr. Lillies nevv prophecy. Or; sober predictions. [*London*], *for John Clarke,* [1675]. 4°.* L; CH, CN, MH, Y.

2233   —Lillies new prophecy; or, strange and wonderful predictions. [*London*], *by A. P. and T. H. for Phillip Brooksby.* 1678. 4°.* L; MH.

2234   —Mr. Lillies new prophecy, or the White Easter. *For Phillip Brooksby,* 1673. 4°. EN.

2235   —Mr. Lilly's new prophecy, touching the notable actions. *Printed,* 1679. 4°.* MH.

2235A   —News from the heavens: or, new prophesies. [*London*], *by A. Purslow,* 1673. 4°. CSS.

2235B   —Observations for this present year. [*London*], *printed,* 1667. 8°.* WF.

2236   —William Lilly student in astrologie, his past and present opinions. *Printed,* 1660. 4°.* LT; MH.

2237   —A peculiar prognostication. [*London*], *published,* 1649. 4°.* LT, LVF, CT, DU, DT; TU, WF.

2238   —Mr. Lillie's predictions concerning the many lamentable fires. [*London*], *for P. Brooksby, in West Smithfield,* 1676. 4°.* L, OB, MR; WF.

2239   —Mr Lillyes prognostications of 1667. [*London*], *printed,* 1667. 4°.* L, O, E; MH, Y.

2240   —A prophecy of the White King. *By G. M. and are to be sold by John Sherley and Thomas Vnderhill,* 1644. 4°.* LT, O, C, EN, DT; CH, IU, MH, NU, WF, Y.

2241   —Lillies prophetick occurences. colop: *For L. Curtis,* 1682. brs. O, C, LG; CH, CN, INU.

2242   [–] Lilli's propheticall history of . . . 1642. *Printed,* 1642. 4°.* LT, LNC; CH, MH, WF.

2243   Entry cancelled.
        —Several observations on the life and death of King Charles I. 1651. *See* —Monarchy or no monarchy in England.

2244   [–] Some further remarks upon Mr Gadbury's defence. [*London*], *printed,* 1676. 8°.* L, O; CLC.

2245   —The starry messenger. *For John Partridge and Humphry Blunden,* 1645. 4°. LT, O, C, E, DT; CH, CN, MH, NU, WF, Y.

2246   —Lillys strange and wonderful prognostication . . . 1681. *Dublin, reprinted for George Foster,* 1681. 4°.* DIX 188. C, CD; VC.

2247   —Lilly's strange and wonderful prophecy. [*London*], *for P. Brooksby,* 1680. 4°.* BR, EN; VC.

2248   [–] Strange news from the East. *For B. H.,* 1677. 4°.* L, O, BC; CH, WF.

2249   —Svpernatvrall sights and apparitions. *For T. V. and are to be sold by I. S.,* 1644. 4°.* LT, O, C, LG, DT; CH, CN, LC, MH, NU, Y.

2250   —Two famous prophesies. [*London,* 1688?] cap., 4°.* L, EN; MH, NU.

2250A   —A very strange prediction of liberty of conscience. *Printed and sold by Andrew Sowle,* 1688. brs. MH, NN.

2251   Entry cancelled.
        —Vox cœlorum. Predictions. [1646.] *See* Harflete, Henry.

2252   —The vvorlds catastrophe. *For John Partridge, and Humphrey Blunden,* 1647. 4°. LT, O, C, EN, DT; CH, CN, MH, MU, WF, Y.

2253   Lilly lash't vvith his ovvn rod. [*London*], *printed,* 1660. brs. LT; MH, OLU.

2254   **Lily, William.** A breviate of our Kings whole Latin grammar . . . called, Lillies. *By W. H. for Richard Thrale,* [1660]. 8°. L, O; CU.

2255–7 Entries cancelled.
        —Brevissima institutio. Oxonii, 1651. *See* —Short introduction. 1651.
        — —[Anr. ed.] 1668. *See* —Short introduction. 1668.
        — —[Anr. ed.] Dublin, 1671. *See* —Short introduction. 1672.

2258   — —[Anr. ed.] *Oxonii, e Theatro Sheldoniano,* 1672. 12°. MADAN 2929. O, C, OC, NOT; CH, CN, IU, WU, Y.

2258A   Entry cancelled.
        — —[Anr. ed.] 1681. *See* —Short introduction. 1681.

2259   [–] —[Anr. ed.] *Oxonii, e Theatro Sheldoniano,* 1687. 12°. L; CH, IU, WF, WU, Y.

2260   — —[Anr. ed.] —, 1692. 12°. L, LP, CK, CT, LIU; CH, CLC, CN, NC, NCD, Y.

2261   [–] —[Anr. ed.] —, 1699. 8°. L, LP, AN, LLU; CH, IU, TU, WF, Y.

2262   —An English grammar. *By Felix Kyngston for Mathew Walbank and Laurence Chapman.* 1641. 8°. L, O, LI, LSC, GU; CH, CN, MH, NC, PL, WF, Y.
        —Janua clavis, or Lily's syntax explained. 1679. *See* Banks, Jonathan.

2263   —Lily, improved, corrected, and explained. *For R. Bentley,* 1696. 4°. T.C.II 591. L.

2264   —Lilies lillies. *By Roger Norton,* 1655. 8°. O.

2265   Entry cancelled.
        —Latine grammar. Fourth edition. 1665. *See* Hoole, Charles.

2265A   [–] Prosoda construed. *By Roger Norton,* 1660. 8°.* CT.

2265B   [–] —[Anr. ed.] —, 1672. 8°.* IU.

2265C [–] —[Anr. ed.] —, 1674. 8°.* WF.

2265D [–] —[Anr. ed.] —, 1680. 8°.* IU, MH, TO.

2265E [–] —[Anr. ed.] —, 1683. 8°.* L.

2265F [–] —[Anr. ed.] —, 1697. 8°.* LIU.

2266 —The royal grammar. *By Edward Jones, for the author, and sold by Thomas Flesher,* 1685. 8°. T.C.II 138. L; NIC, WF, Y, AMB.

2267 ——[Anr. ed.] *For Awnsham Churchill,* 1688. 8°. T.C.II 233. L, C; IU, PU.

2268 —Lillies rvles constrved. *Printed at London,* 1641. 8°. L, LLU.

2269 ——[Anr. ed., "Ljljes rvles."] *By the assignes of Roger Norton,* 1642. 8°. L, NOT.

2270 ——[Anr. ed.] *Printed,* 1653. 8°. L.

2270A ——[Anr. ed.] *By Roger Norton,* 1654. 32°. L.

2270B ——[Anr. ed.] —, 1660. 8°. MAGDALEN COLL. SCH., OXFORD; IU.

2270C ——[Anr. ed.] —, 1662. 8°. LSD; TU.

2270D ——[Anr. ed.] —, 1663. 8°. CN.

2270E ——[Anr. ed.] —, 1668. 8°. EN.

2271 ——[Anr. ed.] —, 1671. 8°. L.

2271A ——[Anr. ed.] —, 1676. 8°. WF.

2272 ——[Anr. ed.] —, 1678. 8°. L, C; CLC, IU, NRU.

2272A ——[Anr. ed.] —, 1679. 8°. IU, TO.

2273 ——[Anr. ed.] —, 1685. 8°. L.

2273aA ——[Anr. ed.] —, 1686. 8°. L.

2273A ——[Anr. ed.] —, 1687. 8°. MH.

2274 ——[Anr. ed.] —, 1689. 8°. L, C; VC.

2274A ——[Anr. ed.] —, 1691. 8°. IU.

2274B ——[Anr. ed.] —, 1693. 8°. CH.

2274C ——[Anr. ed.] —, 1694. 8°. O.

2274D ——[Anr. ed.] —, 1695. 8°. IU.

2274E ——[Anr. ed.] —, 1699. 8°. LIU; IU.

2274F [–] A short introduction of grammar. *By the printers of London,* 1641. 8°. L, LLU; Y.

2274G ——[Anr. ed.] *By Miles Flesher, Robert Young, and R. Hodgkinson,* 1641. 8°. IU, U. ALBERTA.

2275 ——[Anr. ed.] *Printed,* 1642. 8°. L; IU.

2276 ——[Anr. ed.] *For Roger Norton,* 1645. 8°. L, O; BN, CLC, IU.

2277 ——[Anr. ed.] *By Roger Norton,* 1650. 8°. LIU; BN, IU.

2278 [–] —[Anr. ed.] *Oxford, by L. L. and H. H.,* 1651. 8°. MADAN 2173. O; IU, MH, NC, Y.

2279 [–] —[Anr. ed.] —, 1653. 8°. L, OM.

2279A [–] —[Anr. ed.] *By Roger Norton,* 1653. 8°. L; IU.

2279B [–] —[Anr. ed.] *Cambridge, by Thomas Buck,* 1653. 8°. L, LLU, RU.

2279C [–] —[Anr. ed.] *Oxford, by L. L. and H. H.,* 1654. 8°. L; IU.

2280 [–] —[Anr. ed.] —, 1655, 8°. LP.

2280aA [–] —[Anr. ed.] *By Roger Norton,* 1657. 8°. EC; IU.

2280bA [–] —[Anr. ed.] —, 1658. 8°. O; WU.

2280A [–] —[Anr. ed.] *Oxford, by A. L. and H. H.* 1659. 8°. MADAN 2449. L; Y.

2280B [–] —[Anr. ed.] *Cambridge, by John Field,* 1660. 8°. LAWS-HALL PARISH, SUFFOLK.

2281 [–] —[Anr. ed.] *By Roger Norton,* 1661. 8°. L, O.

2282 [–] —[Anr. ed.] *Cambridge, by John Field,* 1661. 8°. C, CK, BSE; IU.

2283 [–] —[Anr. ed.] *By Roger Norton,* 1662. 8°. O, CM; CLC, INU, MH, NN.

2283A [–] —[Anr. ed.] —, 1663. 8°. TU.

2283B [–] —[Anr. ed.] —, 1664. 8°. L.

2284 [–] —[Anr. ed.] *Cambridge, by John Field,* 1666. 8°. CCA; IU, NC, WF.

2284A [–] —[Anr. ed.] *By R. Norton,* 1667. 8°. IU.

2285 Entry cancelled.

[–] —[Anr. ed.] 1669. See —1669.

2286 [–] —[Anr. ed.] *By Rog. Norton,* 1668. 8°. EN; IU, LC, NC.

2287 ——[Anr. ed.] *Cambridge, by John Field,* 1668. 8°. L, O, CCA; BN.

2288 [–] —[Anr. ed.] *By Rog. Norton,* 1669. 8°. O; CLC, SW.

2288A [–] —[Anr. ed.] —, 1670. 8°. LLL.

2289 [–] —[Anr. ed.] —, 1671. 8°. L, CS; IU.

2290 ——[Anr. ed.] *Cambridge, by John Hayes,* 1671. 8°. CT; WG.

2290A [–] —[Anr. ed.] *By Rog. Norton,* 1672. 8°. CT; IU, MH.

2290B [–] —[Anr. ed.] *Dublin, by Benjamin Tooke, to be sold by Joseph Wilde,* 1672. 8°. CD, DN.

2291 [–] —[Anr. ed.] *By Rog. Norton,* 1673. 8°. LP, NOT; TU.

2292 [–] —[Anr. ed.] *Cambridge, by John Hayes,* 1673. 8°. C.

2293 [–] —[Anr. ed.] *Oxford, at the Theater,* 1673. 12°. MADAN 2982. L, O, C, LL, EC, NOT, DM; CH, CN, IU, WU, Y.

2294 [–] —Second edition. —, 1675. 12°. MADAN 3063. L, O, LW, OC, NOT, E; CLC, PL, TO.

2294A [–] —[Anr. ed.] *By Roger Norton,* 1675. 8°. L, LLL.

2294B [–] —[Anr. ed.] *Cambridge, J. Hayes,* 1677. 8°. WU.

2294C [–] —[Anr. ed.] *Oxford, at the Theater,* 1678. 12°. ST. PAUL'S SCHOOL, LONDON.

2295 [–] —[Anr. ed.] *By Rog. Norton,* 1678. 8°. C; CLC.

2295A [–] —[Anr. ed.] —, 1679. 8°. BR; IU.

2296 [–] —Third edition. *Oxford, at the Theater,* 1679. 8°. MADAN 3213. L, O, C, LP, LLU; CLC, CU, IU, OLU, TO.

2296A [–] —[Anr. ed.] *By Rog. Norton,* 1680. 8°. L, O, LIU.

2296B [–] —[Anr. ed.] —, 1681. 8°. L, DM.

2297 [–] —[Anr. ed.] *Cambridge, by John Hayes,* 1681. 8°. C, YM, EN; CN.

2297A [–] —[Anr. ed.] *By Rog. Norton,* 1682. 8°. O; NN.

2298 [–] —[Anr. ed.] *Oxford, at the Theater,* 1683. 8°. O.

2298aA [–] —[Anr. ed.] *By Rog. Norton,* 1684. 8°. L.

2298A [–] —[Anr. ed.] *Cambridge, by John Hayes,* 1685. 8°. L; MH.

2299 [–] —[Anr. ed.] *Oxford, at the Theater,* 1687. 8°. T.C.II 227. L, O, LP; IU, U. NEW MEXICO, WF, WU, Y.

2299A [–] —[Anr. ed.] *By Rog. Norton,* 1687. 8°. UNIVERSITY OF PUERTO RICO.

2299B [–] —[Anr. ed.] *Cambridge, by John Hayes,* 1687. 8°. IU.

2299C [–] —[Anr. ed.] —, 1689. 8°. C.

2299D [–] —[Anr. ed.] *By Rog. Norton,* 1690. 8°. L, EN; VC.

2299E [–] —[Anr. ed.] —, 1691. 8°. CH.

2300 [–] —[Anr. ed.] *Oxford, at the Theater,* 1692. 12°. T.C.I 430. L, O, C, LP, CT, LIU; CH, CN, IU, NC, NCD, PU, Y.

2300A [–] —[Anr. ed.] *By Rog. Norton,* 1693. 8°. IU.

2300B [–] —[Anr. ed.] *Cambridge, by John Hayes,* 1693. 8°. O.

2300C [–] —[Anr. ed.] *By Roger Norton, 1695.* 8°. TU.

2301 [–] —[Anr. ed.] *Cambridge, by John Hayes, 1695.* 8°. C.

2302 [–] —[Anr. ed.] *Dublin, printed & sold by A. C., likewise sold by W. N. E. D. P. C. and J. M., 1969.* DIX 286. M. POLLARD.

2302A [–] —[Anr. ed.] *By Rog. Norton, 1697.* 8°. GU.

2303 [–] —[Anr. ed.] *Oxford, at the Theater, 1699.* 8°. L, O, AN, E, LW, DT; CH, CLC, IU, TU, WF, Y.

2304 [–] —[Anr. ed.] *By Rog. Norton, 1699.* 8°. O, LIU.

2304A [–] —[Anr. ed.] *By Will. Norton, 1699.* 8°. IU.

2304B [–] —[Anr. ed.] *Cambridge, by John Hayes, 1699.* 8°. CLC.

2304C —Shorter examples. *For Charles Harper, Sam. Smith, and Benj. Walford and J. Slatter, Eton, 1700.* 12°. EC.

2304D —A synopsis of Lillies grammar. Second edition. *Oxford, by H. Hall: for Thomas Hancox, in Hereford, 1675.* 8°. LSD.

2304E **Limborch, Philipp.** De veritate religionis. *1691.* 4°. ENC.

2305 —Theologia Christiana. Third edition. *Amstelaedami: apud Sebastianum Petzoldum; et prostant Londini, apud S. Smith and B. Walford, 1700.* fol. T.C.III 186. LIL, GC, LSD, CD.

2306 **Limojon de Saint Didier, Alexandre Toussaint.** The city and republick of Venice. *For Char. Brome, 1699.* 8°. T.C.III 108. L, LL, DU, DT; CLC, CN, MH, WF, Y.

2307 Entry cancelled.

Lin, Francis. Sharp, but short noise. 1650. *See* Hall, Francis.

2308 **Linch, Samuel.** Rebellion painted to the life. *For Robert Crofts, 1662.* 12°. L, LCL.

2309 **Lindeman, Michel.** A prophesie, of a countryman. *Edinburgh, re-printed, 1700.* brs. ALDIS 3981. EN; CN, MH.

2310 **Lindesay, Thomas.** A sermon preached . . . Dec. 1. 1691. *For J. Miller, 1692.* 4°.* L, O, C, OC, CT; CLC, WF.

2311 **L[indley], B[enjamin].** The Shiboleth of priest-hood. *[London], printed, 1678.* 4°.* L, LF, OC, BBN, MR; CH, MH, PH, WF, Y.

2312 [–] A treatise of election. *Printed and sold by T. Sowle, 1700.* 4°. LF, BBN, DU; IE, MBA, MH, PH, PSC.

2313 **Lindsay, *Sir* David.** The vvorkes of. *Edinburgh, by Gedeon Lithgovv, 1648.* 8°. ALDIS 1336. L, O, EN; CH, MB, WF.

2314 ——[Anr. ed.] *Glasgow, by Robert Sanders, 1656.* 12°. ALDIS 1546.9. MH, TU.

2315 ——[Anr. ed.] —, *1665.* 12°. ALDIS 1794. L; WCL.

2316 ——[Anr. ed.] *Edinburgh, by Andrew Anderson, 1670.* 12°. ALDIS 1905. L, O, EN; CH, NCU, WF.

2317 ——[Anr. ed.] *Glasgow, by Robert Sanders, 1672.* 12°. ALDIS 1947. O, EN, GU.

2318 ——[Anr. ed.] —, *1683.* 12°. ALDIS 2389. L, EN; CH, CLC, IU, WF, Y.

2319 ——[Anr. ed.] —, *1686.* 12°. ALDIS 2644.5. GU.

2320 ——[Anr. ed.] —, *1696.* 12°. ALDIS 3578. L, O, A, EN; CH, CN, IU, MH, WF.

2321 —The converts cordiall. *Aberdene, by Edward Raban, 1644.* 4°.* ALDIS 1145. HH (dispersed).

2321A —The history of the noble and valiant Squyer William Meldrum. *Glasgow, by Robert Sanders, 1669.* 12°.* L.

2322 ——[Anr. ed.] —, *1683.* 4°. ALDIS 2390.5. O.

2323 —Information for the Earl of Crawfurd. *[Edinburgh, 1680?]* fol. L.

2323A —A supplication. *[Edinburgh, 1690.]* brs. ALDIS 3051. EN.

2323B **Lindsay, John Lindsay, *earl of*.** The Earles of Lindsey and Cumberlands petition. *For J. Harrison, 1642.* 4°.* L.

2324 —The Earle of Craford his speech before the Parliament in Scotland, October the 25. 1641. *For John Thomas, 1641.* 4°.* LT, O, LNC, EN, BLH; CH, MH, TU, WF, Y.

2325 **Lindsay, William Crawford, *earl*.** The speech of. *J. C., 1690.* brs. L.

2326 ——[Anr. ed.] *Edinburgh, by the heir of Andrew Anderson, 1690.* fol.* ALDIS 3031. L, MR, EN; CH, LC, WF, Y.

2327 ——[Anr. ed.] colop: *At Edinburgh, and reprinted at London by George Croom, 1690.* fol.* CII.

2328 **Lindsey, *Major*.** Maior Lindsey's legacie. *[London], by T. Paine, 1645.* brs. LT.

2329 **Lindsey, Montagu Bertie, *earl of*.** A declaration and iustification, of the Earle of Lindsey. *Oxford [London], by Leonard Leychfield, [1642/3].* 4°.* MADAN 1218. LT, O, CT, BC; CH, MH, Y.

2330 —The Earle of Lindsey his declaration and iustification. *[Oxford?], 1642.* 4°.* MADAN 1217. O, OC, OME, CT.

2330A **Lindsey, Robert Bertie, *earl of*.** A relation of the proceedings. *[London? 1650.]* cap., 4°.* C; CN.

Line, Francis. *See* Hall, Francis.

Line of righteousness. 1661. *See* Fox, George.

2330B The lineage of locusts. *[London, 1641.]* brs. LT.

2331 **Lineall, John.** Itur [*sic*] Mediteranium. *For the author, and to be sold by John Felton in Stafford, 1658.* 4°.* L, O; CH.

2331A —To his highness Oliver Cromwell. *[London, 1655.]* brs. O.

2331B —A true accompt of the proceedings of the right Honourable Lord Glynne. *1658.* 4°.* O.

2332 The linnen and woollen manufactory discoursed. *Printed, to be sold by Thomas Mercer, 1691.* fol.* L, O, DU, EN; MERRIMACK VALL. TEXTILE MUS., MH, NC.

2333 —[Anr. ed.] *For Geo. Huddleston, 1698.* 4°. O; MH, MIU, NC, WF, ANL.

2334 The linnen drapers' answer to that part of Mr. Cary his essay on trade. *[London? 1700.]* fol. L; NC.

Lines to Mrs. Mary Moore. *[n.p.], 1674. See* W., R.

2334A **[Linfield, E.]** The answer of his Excellencie Sir Thomas Fairfax. *For Robert Williamson. 1647.* 4°.* LT, C, OC, DT; CH.

2335 **Linfield, James.** Idea positiva. *[n.p.], Jul. 1 1679.* brs. L, O, LNC; CH.

Linford, Thomas. *See* Lynford, Thomas.

2335A **Ling, John.** A short answer of . . . about Christmas. *[London], 1648.* CSS.

2336 **Ling, Nicholas.** Politeuphuia. *By R. Young for J. Smethwick, 1641.* 12°. L, O, CK, DT; CH, IU, MH, TU, WSC.

2336A [–] —[Anr. ed.] *By M. Flesher, and are to be sold by George Badger, 1647.* 12°. CH, CN, IU, NN, WF.

2337 [–] —[Anr. ed.] *By Ja. Flesher, and are to be sold by Richard Royston, 1650.* 12°. L, CT; CH, FU, MB, MH, PBL, WF, Y.

2338 [–] —[Anr. ed.] *By James Flesher, and are to be sold by Richard Royston, 1653.* 12°. O; CH, CN, CSU, IU, MH.

2339 [–] —[Anr. ed.] —, *1655.* 12°. L; CH, MH, NP, OCI, Y.

2339A [–] —[Anr. ed.] —, *1661.* 12°. C; CLC, IU, WF.

2340 [–] —[Anr. ed.] —, *1663.* 12°. L, O; IU, Y.

2341 [–] —[Anr. ed.] *By J. Flesher for R. Royston, 1667.* 12°. O; CLC, IU, MH, OLU, TU.

2342 [–] —[Anr. ed.] *By J. Flesher, to be sold by R. Royston, 1669.* 12°. L, LLL, DU; INU, IU, MU, NCD, WF.

2342A [–] —[Anr. ed.] *By E. Flesher for Nathaniel Hook, 1671.* 12°. L, LIU.

2343 [–] —[Anr. ed.] —, *to be sold by James Collins, 1671.* 12°. CH, CLC, IU, TU, WF, Y.

2344 [–] —[Anr. ed.] *By E. Flesher, and are to be sold by Edward Brewster, 1674.* 12°. L, NOT; CLC, LC, MH, MIU, PBL, Y.

2345 [–] —[Anr. ed.] —, *1678.* 12°. L, LLU, GK; CH, IU, LC, NU, PU, WF.

2346 [–] —[Anr. ed.] *By E. Flesher, 1684.* 12°. OP, LIU; CH, INU, MH, OCI, WF.

2347 [–] —[Anr. ed.] *For E. Flesher, 1688.* 12°. L, RPL; CH, IAU, IU, MH, TO, WF.

2348 [–] —[Anr. ed.] *By J. H. for W. Freeman, 1699.* 12°. T.C.III 98. L, C; CN, LC, OSU, WF, Y.

2349 **L[ingard], R[ichard].** A letter of advice to a young gentleman leaving the university. *Dublin, by Benjamin Tooke, to be sold by Mary Crook, 1670.* 12°. T.C.I 50; DIX 361. L, CE; CH, WF.

2350 — —[Anr. ed.] *For Benjamin Tooke, 1671.* sixes. L, O, OC.

2351 — —[Anr. ed.] —, *1673.* sixes. T.C.I 157. O, OCC, OM, P; MH.

2352 [–] —[Anr. ed.] *New York, printed and sold by VV. Bradford, 1696.* sixes. EVANS 745. NC, NN.

2353 —A sermon preached . . . July 26. 1668. *By J. M. for John Crook, 1668.* 4°.* L, O, C, DU, DT; BBE, CH, TU, WF, Y.

Lingua; or the combat. 1657. *See* Tomkis, Thomas.
Lingva testivm. [n.p.], 1651. *See* Hall, Edmund.

2354 Entry cancelled.
Linguæ Romanæ dictionarium. Cambridge, 1693. *See* Littleton, Adam.

Linus, Franciscus. *See* Hall, Francis.

2354A Linx Britannicus, or contemplations. [*London?* 1658.] cap., 4°.* OC; CSS.
Lyon disturbed. Amsterdam, 1672. *See* Grybius, Johannes.

2355 Entry cancelled. Amsterdam printing.

2356 The lions elegy. *For T. B. 1681.* brs. L, O; CH, CN, MH, PU, TU, Y.

[Lipeat, Thomas.] Divell in Kent. 1647. *See* Mowlin, John.

2357 —A true ministry anatomized. *By J. C., 1651.* 8°.* LT; MH.

2358 **Lips, Joest.** Justi Lipsii de constantia. *Oxonii, typis Will. Hall, 1663.* 12°. MADAN 2641. L, O, OC, CK, DUS; CLC, WF.

2359 —A discourse of constancy. *For Humphrey Moseley, 1654.* 12°. L, O, BC, SHR, DT; IU, MMO, NPT, NU, TU, WF.

2360 — —[Anr. ed.] *By J. Redmayne, for James Allestry, 1670.* 8°. T.C.I 27. L, O, C, BC, RPL; IAU, LC, MB, MH, NP, Y.

2361 —Miracles of the B. Virgin. *Printed, 1688.* 4°.* L, O, CT, ENC, DT; CH, CN, MH, NU, TU, WF, Y.

2362 —Justi Lipsii Roma illustrata. *Impensis Abelis Swalle & Tim. Childe, 1692.* 8°. L, O, CS, BAMB, EN, DT; CH, LC, MB, MU, NC, WF, Y. (var.)

2363 — —[Anr. ed.] *Impensis Gulielmi Whitwood, 1698.* 8°. L, C, NE; BN.

2364 —Two bookes of constancy. *Printed 1653.* NC, Y.

2365 [–] War and peace reconciled. *Printed, and sold by R. Royston, 1672.* 8°. L, O; CH, CLC, CN, WF.

2365A **Lipsius, Jacobus.** Jacobus Lipsij omnen anagrammaticum ex augusto nomine . . . Carolus Secundus. *Oxoniæ. Typis A. & L. Lichfield, 1663.* LC.

2366 —Serenissimo . . . domino Carolos. *Typis. T. Regirost [Roycroft], 1661.* 4°.* CB.

Lipsius, Justus. *See* Lips, Joest.
Liquor alchahest, or. 1675. *See* Starkey, George.

2366aA **Lira, Mareschalck.** A brief relation of several remarkable passages of the Jevves. [*London*], *printed, 1666.* 4°.* LUC; NN.

2366A Lisander or the souldier of fortune. *By H. H. for Henry Faithorne and John Kersey, 1681.* 12°. T.C.I 450. L; CLC, CN, PU.
Lisarda. 1690. *See* Cox, H.

2367 **Liset, Abraham.** Amphithalami, or, the accomptants closet. *By James Flesher, for Nicholas Bourne, 1660.* fol. L, CM; CU, MH, NC, WF, Y.

2368 — —[Anr. ed.] *By Miles Flesher for Robert Horne, 1684.* fol. LLL, LMT, NE, CD; IU, MB, MHL, NN, PL.

Lisieux, Zichare de. *See* Fontaines, Louis.

2369 **Lisle, Francis.** The kingdoms divisions. *By John Clowes, for Hannah Allen, 1649.* 4°.* LT, O; CLC, MB, MH, MU, NU, ZAP.

2370 **[Lisola, Francois Paul], baron de.** The buckler of state and justice. *By James Flesher, for Richard Royston, 1667.* 8°. L, O, C, NE, DM; CH, CN, MHL, TU, WF, Y.

2371 [–] —Second edition. *For Richard Royston, to be sold by Richard Chiswell, 1673.* 8°. T.C.I 165. L, O, C, SC, DT; CH, CU, MIU, Y.

2371A [–] —"Second" edition. *For Richard Chiswell, 1677.* 8°. T.C.I 279. O, DT; MH.

2372 [–] Englands appeal from the private cabal. [*London*], *anno. 1673.* 4°. O, C, EN, GU, DT; IU, MH, NCU.

2372A [–] —[Anr. ed.] [*London*], *anno 1673.* 4°. L, O, C, LG, DU, MR; CDA, CN, CU, MHS, MM, WF, Y. (var.)

2372B [–] —[Anr. ed., last word is "Ninis."] [*Scotland?*], *anno 1673.* 4°. DU, DT; MH, NN.

2372C [–] —[Anr. ed., "appeal, from . . . caballe."] [*London*], *anno 1673.* 4°. O, C, LIU; CH, MU, NU, PL, TU, WF.

2373 [–] —[Anr. ed., "appeale."] *Anno 1673.* 4°. L, O, EN; MB.

2374   [-] Observations on the letter written by the Duke of Buckingham. *Printed*, 1689. 8°. O; CH, CLC.

2375   [-] Observations on the letter written to Sir Thomas Osborn. *For J. B.*, 1673. 4°.* L, O, C, DU, LIU; CH, CN, MH, WF, Y.

2376   A list of abhorrors. [*London*], *by Benjamin Harris*, [1681]. brs. L, O, LG, DU, LNC; CH, MH, MU, PU, Y.

2377   A list of all the adventurers in the mine-adventure. colop: *By F. Collins*, 1700. cap., fol.* L, O, LUG, EC; INU, MH, NC, Y.

2377A   A list of all the commissioners names. *Printed*, 1697. brs. MH.

2378   A list of all the conspirators that have been seiz'd. [*London*, 1683?] brs. L, O, OC, DU, EN; CH, CN, MH, TU, Y.

2379   —Second edition. [*London*, 1683?] brs. L; CH.

2380   List of all the forces sent upon the expedition for the relief of Candia. 1669. 4°. WF.

2380A   A list of all the Irish army in Ireland. colop: *For William Faulkner*, 1690. brs. DN; CH, Y.

2380B   A list of all the land-forces. *By Edward Jones in the Savoy*, 1698. brs. NCD, TU.

2380C   A list of all the offices and places within the city of London. *Printed*, 1697. 12°.* WF.

2381   A list of all the prisoners in the Upper Bench Prison . . . third of May, 1653. *For Livewell Chapman*, 1653. 4°.* LT, O, C, LG, SP, EN; CH, CLC, MH, MU, WF.

2382   A list of all the ships and frigots of England. *By M. Simmons, and are to be sold by Thomas Jenner*, 1660. 4°.* L, LNM, LPR; RPJ.

2383   A list of all the victories. *By Robert Ibbitson*, 1651. brs. LT.

2384   A list of all those that were committed to the Tower. [*London*], *printed*, 1696. brs. O, OP, HH.

2385   A list of both houses of Parliament, prorogued to the 26th of January, 1679. *For Thomas Newcomb and John Starkey*, 1679[80]. brs. L, O, OP, HH; MR, CH, MH, NN, WF, Y.

2385A   —[Anr. ed.] *Dublin, re-printed*, 1679[80]. fol.* DIX 175. CD.

2385B   A list of both houses of Parliament summoned by . . . King James the Second. *For A. Green*, 1685. brs. MH.

2386   List of diamond rings. 1687. fol. LG (lost).

2387-8 Entries cancelled.
        List of directors elected in January. [n.p., 1696.] *See* National land-bank.
        List of directors elected in October. [n.p., 1695.] *See* Drapers-hall.

2389   A list of divers persons whose names. *For V, V.*, 1647. 4°.* LT, CT, DU, MR, DT; CH, MH, MIU, MU, WF.

2390   A list of His late Majesties unjvst judges. *For John Stafford and Edward Thomas*, 1660. brs. LT.

2391   A list of His Majesties navie. *For W. Reynor*, March 4 1641[2]. brs. O, LG, LL, LS, EC.

2392   A list of his Majesties navie royall. [*London*], *for John Rothwell*, 1641[2]. brs. STEELE 2011. LT.

2393   —[Anr. ed.] [*London*], *for Lawrence Blaiklock*, 1643. brs. LT.

2394   —[Anr. ed.] *For Laurence Blaiklock*, 1644. brs. LT; Y.

2395   —[Anr. ed.] *By E. Crowch, for Thomas Vere*, 1672. brs. L, OC, HH, LNC; CH, WF.

2396   —[Anr. ed.] *Edinburgh*, 1672. brs. ALDIS 1948. EN.

2396A   —[Anr. ed.] *Reprinted at Dublin by Benjamin Tooke*, 1672. brs. EN.

2397   A list of His Majesties regalia, besides plate . . . at the jewel-house in the Tower. [*London*, 169-?] brs. L, OP; CH.

2397A   A list of His Majesty's ships. 1660. fol.* LAD.

2398   Entry cancelled.
        List of King James's Irish . . . forces. 1697. *See* H., I.

2399   A list of knights & burgesses for several covnties. *By Francis Leach*, 1654. 4°.* LT, O, OC, CS, DU; CH, WF.

2400   A list of knights made since . . . May 29. 1660. *By S. Griffin*, 1660. brs. LT, O, LG.

2401   No entry.

2402   A list of officers claiming to the sixty thousand pounds. *For Henry Brome and Ann Seile*, 1663. 4°. L, O, C, DU, SP; CH, CN, WF.

2403   A list of one unanimous club of voters. [*London*, 1679.] cap., fol.* L, O, C, MR, EN, DT; CH, MH, MU, WF, Y. (var.)

2404   A list of persons, thieves, . . . within . . . Striviling. *Edinburgh, by the heir of A. Anderson*, 1683. brs. ALDIS 2391. EN; MH.

2405   A list of several ships belonging to English merchants. *Amsterdam, printed*, 1677. 4°.* L, O, C, LSD, DT; CN, CSS, MH, WF, Y.

2405A   A list of several sorts of silks. [*London*, 1696.] brs. L; MH.

2405B   A list of ships taken since July 1677 . . . Algier. *For Richard Janeway*, 1682. brs. O (impf.).

2405C   A list of Sir Peter Lely's great collection. 1682. fol.* DCH.

2406   A list of some of the grand blasphemers. *By Robert Ibbitson*, 1654. brs. LT, MR; MH.

2407   Entry cancelled.
        List of subscribers. [n.p., 1696.] *See* Company of Scotland.

2408   A list of such English and Scotch commanders. *For Robert Wood*, 1642. brs. LT.

2409   A list of such of the names of the nobility, gentry and commonalty of England and Ireland, . . . attainted of high treason. *For R. Clavel, and J. Watts*, 1690. 4°. T.C.II 315. L, C, OC, P, DT, BLH; CH, CU, MH, WF, Y.

2410   A list of such of the navy royall. *For Laurence Blaiklock*, 1645. brs. STEELE 2619. LT; NN.

2411   A list of svch ships and friggotts. [*London*], *for Ed. Hvsband, Aprill.* 21, 1646. brs. STEELE 2560. LT; MH, NN.

2412   —[Anr. ed.] *For Edward Husband, May* 20. 1647. brs. STEELE 2687. LT; NN.

2412A   A list of the adventurers of England, trading into Hudson's Bay. *Thirteenth of November*, 1696. brs. LPR.

2412B   A list of the adventurers in the mine-adventure. *By F. Collins*, 1699. brs. MH.

2412C   A list of the adventurers in the stock of the . . . East-India Company. [*London*, 1682.] brs. LPR.

2413   The list of the army raised under the command of . . . Robert, Earle of Essex. *For John Partridge*, 1642. 4°.* LT, O, CM, DU, SS, DT; CH, CN, CU, WF, Y.

2414　A list of the chairman, treasurer, and committee elected . . . [Glass sellers]. [*London*, 1693.] brs. LG.

2415　A list of the chaplains. [*London*], *for William Nott*, 1688[9]. brs. O, OC; CH, MH.

2415A　A list of the clergy of Hempshire. *Printed*, 1662. 4°.* C.

2416　Entry cancelled. Date: 1640. [STC 19616.]

2416A　A list of the commissioners of lieutenancy . . . of London. [*London*, 1690.] brs. L; MIU, Y.

2417　A list of the common-wealth of Englands navie at sea. *By M. Simmons, to be sould at his house, and by Tho: Jenner*, 1653. brs. LT, O; CH, RPJ, WF, Y.

2417A　A list of the company of the royal fishery. *C. Brome*, 1697. brs. MH.

2418　A list of the conventicles. *By Nat. Thompson*, 1683. brs. L, O; CH, IU, Y.

2418A　A list of the court of aldermen. *By John Darby*, 1693. brs. LG.

　　　　List of the divers commanders. 1644. *See* M., T. Particular list.

2419　List of the doctors and masters appointed. [n.p.], 1687. brs. O.

2419A　A list of the dukes, marqvesses. *For John Starkey*, 1681. brs. O; CH, MH.

2420　A list of the earls and lords. *For Isaac Pridmore*, 1660. brs. L, O; MH, Y.

2420A　A list of the English and Dutch men of war. *For R. Bentley*, 1691. brs. CN.

2421　A list of the English redeemed out of slavery. *For Daniel Slater, and sold by Randle Taylor*, 1681. brs. O; Y.

2422　The list of the English royal navy. *For John Amery, and sold by R. Taylor*, 1694. brs. L.

2422A　List of the fellows and other members of the Royal College of Physicians. *Printed*, 1688. brs. L.

2423　List of the fellovvs of the Royal Society. [*London*, 1663.] brs. O, OB, CT.

2423A　—[Anr. ed. "fellows"] 1664. brs. L.

2424　—[Anr. ed.] 1666. brs. L, O.

2425　—[Anr. ed.] 1667. brs. L, O.

2425A　—[Anr. ed.] 1668. brs. L, LPR.

2425B　—[Anr. ed.] 1669. brs. L.

2425C　—[Anr. ed.] 1670. brs. L, LPR.

2426　—[Anr. ed.] 1671. brs. L, O.

2426A　—[Anr. ed.] 1672. brs. L, LPR.

2427　—[Anr. ed.] 1674. brs. L, O.

2428　—[Anr. ed.] [1675.] brs. O.

2429　—[Anr. ed.] 1677. brs. L, O.

2430　—[Anr. ed.] 1678. brs. L, O.

2430A　—[Anr. ed.] 1679. brs. L.

2431　—[Anr. ed.] 1680. brs. L, O.

2431A　—[Anr. ed.] 1681. brs. L.

2432　—[Anr. ed.] 1682. brs. L, O.

2433　—[Anr. ed.] 1683. brs. L, O.

2434　—[Anr. ed.] 1684. brs. O.

2435　—[Anr. ed.] [1686.] brs. L, O.

2436　—[Anr. ed.] 1687. brs. L, O.

2437　—[Anr. ed., Nov. 30, 1687.] 1688. brs. O.

2438　—[Anr. ed., Nov. 30, 1688.] 1688. brs. L, O.

2438A　—[Anr. ed.] 1689. brs. L.

2438B　—[Anr. ed.] 1690. brs. L.

2439　—[Anr. ed.] 1691. L, O, LPR.

2439A　—[Anr. ed.] 1692. brs. L.

2440　—[Anr. ed.] 1694. brs. O.

2440A　—[Anr. ed.] 1695. brs. L.

2440B　—[Anr. ed.] 1696. brs. L.

2440C　—[Anr. ed.] 1697. brs. L.

2440D　—[Anr. ed.] 1698. brs. L.

2440E　—[Anr. ed.] 1699. brs. L.

2441　A list of the field-officers chosen. 1641. brs. LT.

2442　A list of the field-officers. *For Edward Paxton, Iune* 11. 1642. brs. LT.

2442A　—[Anr. ed.] —, *June* 13. 1642. brs. L, OC, EC.

2442B　A list of the forces for the year 1691. *For Richard Baldwin*, 1691. brs. L, LG, DU, HH.

2442C　A list of the forts and castles. [*London?* 1698.] brs. L; Y.

2442D　A list of the fortunate adventurers in the mine-adventure. *By F. Collins and are to be sold by A. Baldwin*, 1699. brs. L.

2442E　A list of the 400 hackney-coaches. *By Tho. Leach*, 1662. 4°.* WF.

2443　—[Anr. ed.] 1664. 4°. LG.

2443A　A list of the French fleet. *For B. G.*, 1690. brs. Y.

2444　A list of the French kings fleet. *For Robert Hayhurst*, 1689. brs. L, O, C; CH, CN.

2444A　A list of the French men of war. *For J. Smith*, 1691. brs. CN.

2445　List of the governour, deputy-governour, and directors for the 1698. [*London*, 1698.] brs. LG.

2446　A list of the horse under the command of William Earl of Bedford. *August* 16. *London, for J. Partridge*, 1642. brs. LT; Y.

2447　A list of the horse races that are to be run . . . at Newmarket. [*London*], *Feb.* 1679. brs. O.

2447A　A list of the House of Lords. *For Nathaniel Ponder*, 1681. brs. C; CH.

2447B　—[Anr. ed.] —, *and Richard Davis in Oxford*, 1681. brs. O.

2448　A list of the imperial forces in . . . Hungary. [*London*], *by G. Croom*, [1687]. brs. O.

2449　A list of the imprisoned and secluded members. [*London*, 1648.] brs. LT, C, LG, CT; CH, MH, WF.

2449A　A list of the Irish killed in the battaile. *For Laurence Chapman*, 1647. brs. CH.

2450　A list of the knights, citizens, and burgesses. *For Nathaniel Brooks*, 1661. brs. O.

2451　—[Anr. ed.] *For Henry Eversden*, 1661. brs. L, HH; TU.

2452　A list of the knights, citizens, burgesses, and barons of the Cinque Ports. *For Nathaniel Ponder, and Nathaniel Thompson*, 1679. brs. L, O, CM, DU, MR; CLC, MH, WF, Y.

2452A　A list of the knights, citizens and burgesses of the new Parliament. *Printed, and are to be sold by Eliz. Whitlock*, 1698. brs. CH.

2452B　A list of the Lent preachers. *For Samuel Mearne*, [1681]. brs. MH.

2452C　—[Same title, "Lent-preachers."] *For Thomas Jones*, 1691. brs. OC.

2453   A list of the lodgers, together. [*London*, 1659.] brs. HR, MH.

2453A   A list of the lords that enter'd their protest. *Printed*, 1689. brs. L, C, HH; CLC, ZWT.

2454   A list of the members elected for the Parliament. *For Thomas Poole*, 1661. brs. O.

2454A   A list of the members of the company of apothecaries. [*London?* 1700.] brs. L.

2454B   A list of the members of the . . . corporation for the linnen manufacture. [*London*, 1691.] brs. L.

2454C   A list of the members of the House of Commons, [*London?* 1648.] brs. OP.

2455   List of the members of the Kings College of Physicians. [*London*], 1673. brs. O.

2456   —[Anr. ed.] [*London*], 1676. brs. O.

2457   —[Anr. ed.] [*London*], 1683. brs. O.

2458   A list of the members returned to serve in this present convocation. *For Jacob Tonson*, 1689. brs. O, LLP, OP; CH, IU, MH.

2458A   A list of the monasterys, nunnerys, and colleges, . . . beyond sea. *For A. Baldwin*, 1700. 4°.* L, LIL, MR, SP; CH, CN, INU, PU, WF, Y.

2458B   A list of the names and sir-names of the Lords Spiritual. *For Richard Wier*, 1689. brs. MH.

2459   A list of the names and stocks, of the governour and company of . . . Hudsons-Bay. [*London*, 1673.] brs. L.

2459A   A list of the names and sums of all the new subscribers. [*London*, 1697?] cap., fol.* MH.

2459B   A list of the names of all the adventurers . . . to East-India. [*London*, 1657?] brs. MH.

2459C   A list of the names of all the adventurers . . . April 1684. [*London*, 1684.] cap., fol.* Y.

2460   A list of the names of all the adventurers in the . . . East India Company. 18th day of April. [*London*, 1691.] cap., fol.* LG, LUG; MH, ANL.

2460A   —21th. of May 169[6?]. [*London*, 1696?] cap., fol.* INDIA OFFICE.

2460B   —10th. of April, 1697. [*London*, 1697.] cap., fol.* INDIA OFFICE.

2460C   A list of the names of all the adventurers . . . East Indies, the 4th of April, 1700. [*London*, 1700.] cap., fol.* WF.

2460D   A list of the names of all the adventurers of the Royal Affrican-Company. [*London*, 1675/6.] brs. LPR.

2460E   —[Anr. ed.] [*London*, 1677/8.] brs. LPR.

2460F   —[Anr. ed.] [*London*, 1697.] brs. LPR.

2461   A list of the names of all the aldermen. [*London*], 1692. brs. L, O, HH; NN.

2462   The list of the names of all the commanders, and other gentlemen of note. *For J. R.*, 1642. *Decemb.* 19. brs. LT, EC.

2463   A list of the names of all the members. *By R. Ibbitson*, 1653. brs. LT, O, LNC; NR.

2463A   A list of the names of all the partners in the lead mines. [*London?* 1694.] brs. L.

2463B   A list of the names of all the proprietors in the Bank of England, March 18, 1698. [*London*, 1699.] cap., fol.* LG.

2464   A list of the names of all the subscribers to the Bank of England. [1694.] brs. O, DM; MH.

2464A   A list of the names of His Majesty of Great Britain's subjects . . . at Maccaness. *By H. Newman, November* 1698. brs. OC.

2464B   A list of the names of such lieutenants . . . fleet. 1700. fol.* LAD.

2464C   A list of the names of such of the subscribers of land and money. [*London*, 1695?] brs. EN.

2465   A list of the names of such persons who are thought fit. *For John Avstin, June* 16. 1642. brs. LT, HH.

2465A   A list of the names of the adventurers in the Bank of Scotland. *Edinburgh, by the heirs and successors of A. Anderson*, 1696. brs. EN.

2465B   A list of the names of the commissioners . . . land-bank. [*London*, 1696.] brs. LG.

2466   List of the names of the corporation of the Kings College of Physitians. colop: *For Samuel Tidmarsh*, 1681. brs. LG; WF.

2466A   A list of the names of the court of aldermen . . . London. *By G. C. for Joseph Harrison*, 1690. brs. L, LG.

2466B   —[Same title.] *For R. Baldwin*, 1690. brs. T.C.II 324. LG.

2466C   A list of the names of the field officers, captains. [*London*, 1681.] brs. L.

2467   —[Anr. ed.] [*London*, 1683.] brs. L.

2468   —[Anr. ed.] *For W. Bonny and R. H.*, 1690. brs. L, LG, HH; CH, CN.

2468A   A list of the names of the Irish prisoners. *For Ed. Golding*, 1691. brs. Y.

2469   —[Anr. ed.] *London, reprinted Edinburgh*, 1691. brs. ALDIS 3157. EN.

2470   A list of the names of the iudges of the High Court of Justice, for the tryall of James, Earl of Cambridge. *For William Wright*, 1648[9]. brs. LT, O, LS, BR, DT; MH, MHS, MIU, WF, Y.

2471   A list of the names of the iudges of the High Court of Iustice, for triall of the King. *Printed at London for R. J.* 1649. brs. LT, O, LS, SP, YM; CH, IU, MH, MIU, WF.

2472   A list of the names of the knights, citizens, burgesses, and barons of the Cinque ports. *For Robert Pawley*, 1660. brs. O.

2473   —[Anr. ed.] [*London*, 1679.] brs. L, O, C, LNC; Y.

2473A   —[Anr. ed.] *For Thomas Newcomb, John Starkey, and Robert Pawlet*, 1679. brs. L, LG, HH; CH, WF, Y.

2473B   —[Anr. ed.] colop: *Reprinted at Dublin, and sold by Mary Crook*, 1679. cap., 8°.* C.

2474   —[Anr. ed.] [*London*, 1681.] cap., fol.* L, C, OP, DU, LIU; CH, MH, PL, RBU, Y.

2475   A list of the names of the Long Parliament, anno 1640. *Printed*, 1659. 8°. MADAN 2427. LT, BC; CLC, MB, RBU.

List of the names of the members. [n.p., 1648.] *See* Elsynge, Henry.

2476   A list of the names of the rebells. *By E. Mallet*, 1686. brs. L, O, OB, DCH, HH.

2477   A list of the names of the severall colonells. *For Henry Overton*, 1642. brs. STEELE 2077. LT, O, LG.

2478   Entry cancelled.

List of the names of the subscribers of land and money. [n.p., 1695.] *See* Briscoe, John.

2478aA A list of the names of the subscribers of the Land-Bank. *July 23.* 1695. [*London*], 1695. brs. LG, LLU.

2478bA —[Same title, Sept. 1695.] colop: [*London*], *For T. Cockerill and E. Jones*, 1695. cap., fol.* LG, EN.

2478cA —[Same title, Nov.] colop: *By J. D.*, 1695. cap., fol.* LG.

2478dA A list of the names of the subscribers to a loan. [*London*, 1698.] cap., fol.* MH.

2478A A list of the names of those pretended judges. [*London*, 1649.] brs. CH.

2479 Entry cancelled.
List of the officers claiming. 1663. *See* List of officers.

2480 A list of the old and new regiments of horse. *Jun. 15. London, for T. Walkley*, [1642]. 4°.* LT, LVF, BLH, DT; CSS.

2480A —[Anr. ed.] *For T. Walkley*, [1642]. 4°.* MR.

2481 A list of the Parliament of women. *For T. N.*, 1679. brs. CH, MH, Y.

2481A A list of the perticulars [*sic*] of His Majesties fleet. *Printed* 1665. brs. L; Y.

2482 —[Anr. ed.] *Printed at London, and reprinted at Edinburgh*, 1665. brs. ALDIS 1795. EN.

2483 A list of the persons intercommuned. [*Edinburgh, after* 1674.] brs. STEELE 3p 2397. ALDIS 2054.8. EN, ER; CH, MH.

2484 A list of the persons to whom lycences . . . 22 February 1691/2. [*Dublin*, 1691/2.] fol.* STEELE 2p 1253. DT.

2485 A list of the poll of the several companies. *For Walter Davis*, 1682. brs. L, O, C; CN.

2486 A list of the præbendaries. 1685. brs. O.

2487 —[Same title.] 1687. brs. O.

2488 —[Same title.] *For Walter Kettilby*, 1688. brs. L, O, EC.

2489 —[Same title.] —, 1693. brs. O.

2490 A list of the preachers appointed. 1686. brs. LG (lost).

2491 —[Same title.] 1687. brs. O.

2492 —[Same title.] 1688. brs. O.

2492A —[Same title.] *For Walter Kettilby*, 1689. brs. OC; MH.

2493 —[Same title.] —, 1690. brs. L, O.

2493A —[Same title.] —, 1691. brs. OC.

2493B —[Same title.] —, 1692. brs. OC.

2493C A list of the present arch-bishops. *For T. Hawkins*, 1691. brs. L.

2494 A list of the princes, dukes, earls. *By Robert Ibbitson*, 1652. brs. LT; Y.

2494A A list of the princes present at the congress at the Hague. *for J. Tonson*, 1691. brs. L, DU, HH.

2495 —[Anr. ed.] *Edinburgh, re-printed*, 1691. brs. ALDIS 3159.5. EN; CN, WF.

2496 A list of the prisoners of the Vpper Bench Prison. *By T. Mabb, for Livewell Chapman*, 1653. 4°.* LT, O, LG, OC; NC.

2497 A list of the prisoners of vvar, vvho are officers. *By John Field*, 1651. 4°.* LT, OC, BC, GC, MR; CH, CN, MH, WF, Y.

2498 A list of the prisoners taken, and those that were slain by Collonell Horton. *Printed at London, by Robert Ibbitson in Smithfield*, 1648. 4°.* LT, AN.

2498A A list of the prizes taken . . . by His Highness Royal, . . . June 3. [*Edinburgh?* 1665.] brs. EN.

2498B A list of the rooms and offices bought. [*London?* 1696.] brs. LG; RBU.

2498C A list of the Royal Adventurers of England trading into Africa. [*London*, 1663?] brs. LPR.

2498D —[Same title.] [*London*, 1671?] brs. LPR.

2498E A list of the Royal Society. 30 *Nov.* 1663. brs. JF.

2499 —[Same title.] *For John Martyn*, 1667. brs. O, LPR.

2499A —[Same title.] —*and James Allestry.* 1669. brs. MH.

2499B —[Same title.] *For John Martyn*, 1673. brs. L.

2500 —[Same title.] —, 1674. brs. O.

2500A —[Same title.] —, 1677. brs. MMO.

2500B —[Same title.] 1682. brs. LPR.

2500C —[Same title.] 1684. brs. ZAS.

2501 —[Same title.] *By Tho. James*, 1690. brs. O.

2501A —[Same title.] —, 1693. brs. NN.

2502 —[Same title.] —, 1694. brs. O, LPR.

2503 —[Same title.] —, 1695. brs. O.

2504 —[Same title.] —, 1699. brs. MC.

2504A A list of the seven thousand men. [*London*], *for A. Baldwin*, 1699. brs. CH, MH.

2504B A list of the several persons in civil offices. colop: *For John Amery, to be sold by Randal Taylor*, 1689. brs. C, DN; CH.

2505 A list of the severall regiments and chief officers of the Scottish army. *For Robert Bostock and Samuel Gellibrand*, 1644. brs. LT, LG, HH; Y.

2506 A list of the several reversionary annuities. [*London*, 1696.] cap., fol.* L.

2506A A list of the ships belonging to His Majesties navy-royal. *For G. Horton*, 1666. brs. L, LPR.

2507 A list of the ships taken. *By M. S.*, 1652. brs. LT.

2507A —[Same title.] *For Rich. Janeway*, 1682. brs. DCH.

2507B A list of their Majesties royal fleet. *For John Amery, to be sold by Randal Taylor*, 1689. brs. C, LG, OC.

2508 —[Same title.] *London, reprinted Edinburgh*, 1689. brs. ALDIS 2915. EN.

2509 —[Same title.] *For Robert Hayhurst*, 1691. brs. O, C, OC, MC.

2509A —[Same title.] *For R. Bentley*, 1691. brs. OC, HH.

2510 —[Same title.] *Printed at London, and re-printed at Edinburgh by the heir of A. Anderson*, 1691. brs. ALDIS 3158. E, EN; TU, Y.

2511 —[Same title.] 1693. brs. MC.

2512 —[Same title.] 1696. brs. MC.

2513 A list of their Majesties royal forces. *Edinburgh, by the heir of Andrew Anderson*, 1691. brs. ALDIS 3159. EN.

2513A A list of their names who by their adventures are capable of being chosen committees. [*London?* 1674?] brs. L.

2513B [Anr. ed.] [*London*, 1675.] brs. Y.

2513C [Anr. ed.] [*London?* 1676?] brs. L.

2514 —[Anr. ed.] [*London*, 1679.] brs. O.

2514A —[Anr. ed.] [*London*, 1681.] brs. CN.

2514B A list of their names who were taken out of the House. [*London*, 1657.] 4°.* CM.

List or catalogue of all the mayors. York, 1664. *See* Hildyard, Christopher.

2514C **Lister, Martin.** Appendix ad historiæ animalium Angliæ, tres tractatus. *Eboraci* [*York*], *sumptibus authoris,* 1681. 4°.* O, LCS, NE, GK.

2515 Entry cancelled.
——[Anr. ed.] 1685. *See* Goedaert, Johannes. De insectis.

2516 —Martini Lister conchyliorum bivalvium. *Sumptibus authoris,* 1696. 4°. L, O, LCS, CS, MR; BN, CH, IU, MH, MMO, WGS, AAS.

2517 —De cochleis. *Sumptibus authoris,* 1685. 4°. L, O, LR, E.

2518 —De fontibus medicatis Angliæ. *Eboraci* [*York*], *sumptibus authoris,* 1682. 8°. O, LR; BN.

2519 ——Second edition. *Impensis Walteri Kettilby,* 1684. 8°. T.C.II 73. L, O, C, AM, DT; BN, CH, CNM, PL, TO, WF.
—Dissertatio medicinalis de calculo humano. 1696. *See* —Conchyliorum bivalvium.

2520 —Martini Lister exercitatio anatomica. *Sumptibus Sam. Smith & Benj. Walford,* 1694. 8°. T.C.II 493. L, O, C, AN, RU, AU; BN, CH, IU, MH, NAM, WF, HC.

2521 —Exercitatio anatomica altera. *Apud Sam. Smith et Benj. Walford,* 1695. 8°. T.C.II 559. L, O, C, RU, E; BN, CH, CLM, CNM, PBL, WF.

2522 —Exercitationes & descriptiones. *By R. E. for Walteri Kettilbii,* 1686. 12°. GK.

2523 —Martini Lister . . . historiæ animalium Angliæ. *Apud Joh. Martyn,* 1678. 4°. T.C.I 320. L, O, C, AN, EN, DT; BN, CH, IU, LC, MH, NC, HC.

2523A —Martini Lister historiæ conchyliorum. *Sumptibus authoris,* 1685–92. 6 pts. fol. L, O, C, AU, DT; BN, CLC, CU, LC, MMO, Y.

2524 —Martini Lister historiæ sive synopsis methodicæ conchyliorum. *Sumptibus authoris,* 1685–92. fol. L, O, CS, EN, DT; BN, MMO, WF, Y.

2524A —A journey to Paris in the year 1698. *For Jacob Tonson,* 1698. 8°. GK; MBM.

2525 ——[Anr. ed.] *For Jacob Tonson,* 1699. 8°. L, O, C, E, DT; CH, CN, MMO, NAM, WF, Y.

2526 ——Second edition. —, 1699. 8°. L, O, C, DU, MAU; BN, CLC, CN, LC, MH, MMO, Y.

2527 ——Third edition. —, 1699. 8°. L, O, C, EN, DT; CH, CLC, MBM, MMO, WF.

2528 —Letters, and divers other mixt discourses. *York, by John White for the author,* 1683. 4°. L, O, YM; CH.

2529 —Novæ ac curiosæ exercitationes. *Impensis Walteri Kettilbii,* 1686. 12°. O, GK; CH, CLC, MH, MMO, WF, WU.

2530 —Octo exercitationes. Second edition. *Apud Sam. Smith et Benj. Walford,* 1697. 8°. T.C.II 603. L, O, C, E, GH; BN, CH, CNM, NAM, WF, HC.

2531 —Sex exercitationes. *Impensis S. Smith et B. Walford,* 1694. 8°. T.C.II 512. L, O, C, AN, MAU, GH; BN, CH, NC, PL, WF, WSG.

2532 A letany for St. Omers. colop: *For W. Richard,* 1682. brs. L, O, LLU; CH, CN, MH, NCD, WF, Y.

2533 —Part II. —, 1682. brs. L, O, LLU, MC; CH, MH, NCD, NP.

2533A A litany for the fast. [*London?* 1682.] brs. L; MH, PU.

2534 Entry cancelled.

Letany for the nevv-year. [n.p., 1660.] *See* Jordan, Thomas.

2535 A litany from Geneva, in answer. *Printed,* 1682. brs. L, O, C, MC; CH, IU, MH, NP, WF.

2536 The litany. Of the D. of B. [*London, c.* 1679–80.] brs. L, O, HH; CH, MH, TU, WF, Y.

Litchfield to be surrendred. 1646. *See* Dyot, Richard.

2537 No entry.

Literæ a conventu theologorum in Anglia. 1644. *See* Westminster assembly.

2538 Entry cancelled.

Literæ capitaneorum Bohemia. 1690. *See* Gratius, Orthwinus. Fasciculus.

2539 Litteræ consolatoriæ; from the author. *For Rowland Reynolds,* 1669. brs. L.

2540 Entry cancelled.

Literæ patentes. Edinburgh, 1695. *See* Company of Scotland.

Literæ pseudo-senatus. [n.p.], 1676. *See* Milton, John.

Literal mans learning. [n.p., 1657.] *See* Lewes, Daniel.

2541 **Lithgow, William.** Lithgow's nineteen years travels. *For John Wright, and Thomas Passinger,* 1682. 8°. T.C.I 499. L, O, CT, LLU, EN; CLC, CN, MU, NCD, WF.

2542 ——Tenth edition. *By J. Millet, for M. Wotton, G. Conyers, and T. Passinger,* 1692. 8°. T.C.II 431. L, O, OC, CK, LLU, NOT; CB, WF, Y.

2543 —The present surveigh of London. *By J. O.,* 1643. 4°.* L, E, A, AU.

2544 [–] Scotland's parænesis to her dread soveraign King Charles II. [n.p.], *printed,* 1660. 4°. E, EN; MH, Y.

2545 —A true experimentall and exact relation upon . . . seige of Newcastle. *Edinburgh, by Robert Bryson,* 1645. 4°.* ALDIS 1191. LT, O, EN, A; CH, IU.

Lithobolia. 1698. *See* Chamberlayne, Richard.

2546 **Litsfield, Edmund.** Τριαμβισις celsissimi domini Oliverii Cromvvelli. *Excudebat Jacobus Moxon,* 1654. fol.* LT.

2546A The little barly-corne. *For E. B.,* [1645?]. brs. L.

Little Beniamin. 1648. *See* Reading, John.

2547 Entry cancelled.

Little catechism. 1692. *See* Mason, John.

2548 A little eye-salve. colop: [*London*], *printed,* 1647. 4°.* LT, O, LG, CT, DT; CH, CN, MH, NU, TU, WF, Y.

Little grammar. Hamburg, 1699. *See* K., F.

2549 Entry cancelled.

Little horns doom. 1651. *See* Cary, Mary.

2550 The little infant Titus. *By George Croom,* 1685. brs. O; CH, MH.

2551 Little John and the four beggars. *For W. Thackeray, T. Passenger, and W. Whitwood,* [1670?]. brs. L, CM.

2551A —[Anr. ed.] *William Gilbertson,* 1657. brs. O.

Little manvel. Paris, 1669. *See* Clifford, William.

2552 Little Non-such: or, certaine new questions. *For H. P.,* 1646. 4°.* LT, OC, CT, MR, DT; NGT, NU, TU, Y.

2552A —[Anr. ed.] —, 1657. 4°.* LLP; MM.

Little peace-maker. 1674. *See* Morton, Charles.

2553 A little true forraine nevves. *For Nathanael Butter,* 1641[2]. 4°.* LT; INU, NN, NU, RPJ.
Little-vvits protestation. 1642. *See* G., I.

2554 **Littlebury, Robert.** Bibliopoli Littleburiani. [*London*], 30 *Mar* 1696. 4°. L, LR, LV, OC, OP.

2555 ——. . . Pars secunda. [*London*], 11 *May* 1696. 4°. L, O, LR, LV, OP.

2556 ——Pars tertia. [*London*], 15 *Feb* 1697. 4°. L, O, LR, LV.

2557 ——Pars quarta. [15 *March,* 1697.] 4°.* L, O, LR, LV.

2558 ——Pars quinta, & ultima. 29 *Nov.* 1697. fol.* L, O, C, LR, OP.

2558A —Catalogue des livres Francois qui se trouuent. *A Londres, chez Ro. Littlebury,* 1678. 4°.* DL; NG.

2558B —Catalogus librorum ex Gallia. [*London,* 1676.] cap., fol.* WCA.

2559 **Littleton, Adam.** Bibliotheca Littletoniana. The library of. [*London*], 15 *Apr* 1695. 4°. L; MH.

2560 —The churches peace asserted. *For Philip Chetwind,* 1669. 4°.* L, O, CT, BAMB, EN; CH, MIU, NU, TU, WF, Y.

2561 —Elementa religionis. 1658. LCL.

2562 [–] Hezekiah's return of praise. *By E. Cotes, for Samuel Tomson,* 1668. 4°.* L, O, CS, MR, WCA; CH, IU, NU.

2563 —Linguæ Latinæ liber dictionarius . . . A Latine dictionary. *For T. Basset, J. Wright, and R. Chiswell,* 1678. 4°. T.C.I 301. L, O, C, GU, DT; BN, CH, IU, MH, TU, WF, Y.

2564 ——Fourth edition. —, 1684. 4°. T.C.II 117. L, O, C, AN, BQ; BN, CH, CN, MBP, TO, Y.

2565 —Linguæ Romanæ dictionarium . . . A new dictionary. *Cambridge, for W. Rawlins, T. Dring, R. Chiswell, C. Harper, W. Crook, J. Place, and the executors of S. Leigh* [*London*], 1693. 4°. T.C.II 440. L, O, EC, LSD, NPL; CH, IU, MBP, MH, NP, TU, WF, Y.

2566 —Pasor metricus, sive voces. *Ex officina Rogeri Danielis,* 1658. 4°. L, O, CK, P, EN; IU.

2567 —A sermon at a solemn meeting, . . . June 24. 1680. *For William Birch, to be sold by John Crump,* 1680. 4°.* L, O; CH, IU, NPT, Y.

2568 —A sermon at the funeral of the . . . Lady Jane . . . Cheyne. *By John Macock,* 1669. 4°. L, BLH; CH, WF.

2569 —A sermon preached . . . Feb. 7. 1670. *By John Macock,* 1671. 4°.* L, O, CT; CH.

2570 —A sermon preached . . . March 8th 1670/1. *By J. Macock for R. Davis of Oxon,* 1671. 4°.* T.C.I 78; MADAN 2890. L, C, BR, DU, LSD; CH, WF.

2571 —A sermon before the . . . Lord Mayor . . . Febr. 29. 1679/80. *By S. Roycroft, for Rich. Marriott, to be sold by Walter Kettleby,* 1680. 4°.* T.C.I 391. L, O, LG, OM, CCC; CH, NU, TU, WF, Y.

2572 —Sixty one sermons. *By S. Roycroft for Richard Marriott,* 1680. fol. T.C.I 380. L, O, CT, DU, EN; CLC, MH, NC, TSM, WF.

2573 [–] Solomon's gate. *By R. Daniel,* 1662. 8°. L, O, C, LCL; NGT, WF, Y.

2574 [–] Tragi-comœdia Oxoniensis. [*Oxford, by H. Hall,* 1648.] 4°.* MADAN 1989. L, O, C, OH; BN, CH, CN, IU, MH, NC, Y.

2575 **Littleton, Edward,** *of All Souls.* De juventute. *Typis Abrahami Miller apud Gulielimum Lee,* 1664. 4°. O, OC, EN; PPT.

2576 ——[Anr. ed.] *Prostant apud Tho. Newborough,* 1689. 4°. L, O, DU, P, EN; CLC, MH, Y.

2576A **L[ittleton], E[dward],** *fl.* **1694.** The descent upon France. colop: *For Rich. Baldwin,* 1693. cap., 4°.* O, C; CH, WF, Y.

2577 [–] The groans of the plantations. *By M. Clark,* 1689. 4°.* L, O, OC, YM, EN, DT; CH, LC, MH, MU, NC, Y.

2578 [–]——[Anr. ed.] *By M. Clark,* 1689, *reprinted,* 1698. 4°.* L, O, C, E, EN; CN, LC, MB, MU, NCD, Y.

2579 [–] The management of the present war. *For R. Clavel, C. Wilkinson and J. Hindmarsh, and are to be sold by Randal Taylor,* 1690. 4°.* L, O, BAMB, LIU, P; CH, CN, MH, NU, TU, WF, Y.

2580 [–] Observations upon the warre of Hungary. *Printed, and are to be sold by Randall Taylor; and Tho. Newborough,* 1689. 4°. L, O, BAMB; CH, MH, WF.

2580A [–] A preservative for our money. *By B. Motte, sold by E. Whitlock,* 1696. 4°.* L, O, LUG; IU, MH, NC, WF, Y, ANL.

2581 [–] A project of a descent upon France. *Printed; and are to be sold by Rich. Baldwin,* 1691. 4°.* L, O, CT, LIU, DT; CH, MH, MIU, MM, WF.

2582 —A proposal for maintaining and repairing the high ways. *Printed and are to be sold by Randal Taylor,* 1692. 4°.* L, O, C, LLP; LC, WF, Y.

2582A [–] A short discourse about our keeping our money. *By B. Motte, to be sold by John Whitlock,* 1696. 4°.* L, LG, LL, LUG; IU, MH, NC, NR, PU, WF, Y, ANL.

2583 **Littleton, Edward,** *baron.* Les reports des tres honorable . . . en le courts del Common Banck. *By W. Rawlins, S. Roycroft, and H. Sawbridge, assigns of Richard and Edward Atkins. For Thomas Bassett, Samuel Heyrick, William Crooke, and William Hensman,* 1683. fol. T.C.II 29. L, O, C, EN, DT; CB, LC, MB, MHL, NCL, YL.

2584 ——[Anr. ed.] *By W. Rawlins, S. Roycroft, and H. Sawbridge, assigns of Richard and Edward Atkins. For Tho. Dring and Charles Harper,* 1683. fol. KT, V, WF.

2584A —The Lord Keepers speech to the . . . Commons. *For Iohn Burroughes, and Iohn Franke,* 1641[2]. 4°.* LT, O, LUG, MR; CLC, CN, MH, NN, WF, Y. (var.)

2585 —A svbmissive and petitionary letter. [*London,* 1642.] cap., 4°.* LT, MR, DT; CH, MB, WF, Y.

2586 **Littleton, Sir Thomas.** Littletons tenures in English. Fifth edition. *For the company of stationers,* 1656. 8°. L, CS, AN, DU, BQ; LC, MHL, MIU, NCL, TU.

2587 ——[Anr. ed.] —, 1661. 8°. L, BR, LIU; CLC, CLL, LC, MHL, NCL.

2588 —Littleton's tenures, in French and English. *By John Streater, James Flesher, and Henry Twyford, assigns of Richard Atkins, and Edward Atkins, and are to be sold by George Sawbridge, John Place, John Bellinger, William Place,* 1671. sixes T.C.I 77. L, O, CJ, AN, EN, DT; CH, LC, MHL, NCL, TU, WG, YL.

Liturgia, seu liber precum. 1670. *See* Church of England.

2589   Liturgia tigurina: or, the book of common prayers. *For D. Newman, R. Baldwin, J. Dunton,* 1693. 12°. T.C.II 450. L, O, NPL, MR, ENC, DT; CH, IU, MH, NU, WF, Y.

Litvrgical considerator. 1661. *See* Firmin, Giles.

Liturgical discourse. [n.p.], 1670. *See* Mason, Richard Angelus.

Liturgie, c'est a dire. 1667. *See* Durel, Jean.

Liturgy of the ancients. 1696. *See* Stephens, Edward.

Liturgy's vindicated. 1700. *See* Leslie, Charles.

2590   The lively character of a contented and discontented cockold. colop: 1700. 4°.* L; NN.

2591   A lively character of His Maiesties wisdome. [*London*], *printed,* 1647. 4°.* LT, C, OC, MR, DT; CH, CSS, LC, MH, Y.

2592   A lively character of some pretending grandees. *Printed,* 1659. 4°.* LT, O, C; CLC, CSS, MH, MU, WF.

2593   The lively character of the malignant partie. [*London*], *published and printed,* 1642. 4°.* LT, O, MR; CLC, CN, MH, NU, TU, Y.

Lively oracles. Oxford, 1678. *See* Allestree, Richard.

2593A   The lively picture of Levvis du Moulin. *For Rich. Royston,* 1680. 4°.* T.C.I 396. L, O, C, DC, YM, DT; CH, CLC, NU, PL, Y.

2594   A lively pourtraict of our new-cavaliers. *Printed,* 1661. 4°.* O, LL, CT, DU, P; CH, MH, NU, WF, Y.

2594A   A lively pourtraicture of the face of this Commonwealth. [*London?*], *printed,* 1659. 4°.* L, O, BAMB, BC, LLU; CLC, CN, MH, NP, WF, Y.

2594B   Liveries and fees anciently given, . . . by the city of London. [*London,* 1692?] brs. CM.

2594C   The livery-mans advice to his brethren. colop: *For Langley Curtiss,* 1690. brs. PL.

Lives & deaths of the holy apostles. 1685. *See* D., P.

Lives of holy saints. 1681. *See* Marbeck, John.

Lives of sundry notorious villains. 1678. *See* Behn, *Mrs.* Aphra.

Lives of ten excellent men. 1677. *See* Barksdale, Clement.

Lives of the prophets. 1695. *See* M., R.

2594D   **Livesey, James.** Catastrophe magnatum: funeral sermon. [*London*], 1657. 8°. MRL.

2594E   —Enchiridion judicum; or Jehosaphat's charge. *By R. I. for Tho. Parkhurst,* 1657. 8°. LT, MC; MB, Y.

2595   —Πνευματ-απολογια. Or, an apology for the power *By A. M. for Robert Clavel,* 1674. 8°. L, O, LW, BLH; IU, WF.

2595A   [–] Ψυχησημια: or the greatest loss. *By J. B. for Tho. Parkhurst,* 1660. 4°. LT, LW, MC, MRL; Y.

2595B   —The spirit of the Lord. *By F. M. for Robert Clavel,* 1674. 8°. CLC.

2596–7   Entries cancelled.

Livesey, John. Enchiridion. 1657. *See* Livesey, James.

[–] Ψυχησημια. 1660. *See* Livesey, James.

[**Livie, J.**] Bloody almanack. 1654. *See* Almanacs.

2598   A living epitaph upon the crown'd women. [*London?* 1700.] brs. L.

2598A   A living testimony from the power and spirit of our Lord Jesus Christ. [*London,* 1685.] cap., 4°.* L, O, LF, OC; CH, PH, PL, PSC, Y.

2599   **Livingston, John.** A letter, written . . . October 7, 1671. [n.p.], 1671. 4°. L, O, EN.

2600   **L[ivingston], M[ichael].** Albion's congratulatory. *Edinburgh, by the heir of Andrew Anderson.* 1680. fol. ALDIS 2203. EN; CH.

2601   [–] Albion's elegie. *Edinburgh, by the heir of Andrew Anderson,* 1680. 4°.* ALDIS 2203.5. L.

2602   —Augustis ac præpotentibus heroibus, Jacobo et Mariæ. [n.p., 1680.] brs. EN.

2603   —Celsissimo principi, Gulielmo. [n.p., 1680.] brs. EN.

2604   —Patronus redux: or, our protectour. *Edinburgh, by the heir of Andrew Anderson,* 1682. 4°. ALDIS 2337. L, EN; CH.

2605   **Livingstone, Patrick.** Plain and downright-dealing. *Printed,* 1667. 4°.* L, O, LF, BBN, AU; CH, MH, PH, PSC, WF, Y.

2606   —To all friends everywhere. [*London,* 1670.] cap., 4°.* L, O, C, BBN, AU; CH, IE, MH, PH, WF, Y.

2606A   —To the King and both houses of Parliament. [*London,* 1670.] brs. MH.

2607   —Truth owned. *Printed,* 1667. 4°. L, O, LF, BBN, MR; CH, MH, PH, PL, PSC.

2608–9   Entries cancelled.

Livingstone, *Sir* Thomas. Exercise of the foot. Edinburgh. 1693. *See* Teviot, Thomas Levingston, *viscount.*

—True and real account. [1690.] *See* Teviot, Thomas Levingston, *viscount.*

2610   **L[ivingstone], W[illiam].** The conflict in conscience of a dear Christian, named Bessie Clerkson. *Edinburgh, by Andrew Anderson,* 1664. 12°.* ALDIS 1770. L.

2610A   [–] —[Anr. ed.] *Edinburgh,* 1681. 8°. ALDIS 2261.5. EN.

2610B   [–] —[Anr. ed.] *Glasgow, by Robert Sanders,* 1685. 8°.* ALDIS 2537.3. EN.

2611   [–] —[Anr. ed.] —, 1698, 8°.* ALDIS 3740. O, EN.

2612   **Livius, Titus.** Qui extant historiarum libri. *Cantabrigiæ, ex officina Joan. Hayes. Impensis Joan. Creed & Henr. Dickinson,* 1679. 2v. 8°. T.C.I 360. C, CK, DC, LIU, NPL; CLC, NN, OCI, PL, WF, Y.

2613   —The Romane history. *By W. Hunt for Gabriel Bedell,* 1659. fol. L, O, C, NOT; CH, IU, MWA, NRU, TU, WF.

2613A   — —[Anr. ed.] *By W. Hunt for George Sawbridge,* 1659. fol. CP, CS; MB, TO, WF.

2613B   — —[Anr. ed.] *By W. Hunt, for Joshua Kirton,* 1659. fol. IU, AVP.

2614   — —[Anr. ed.] *By W. Hunt for Abel Roper,* 1659. fol. L.

2615   — —[Anr. ed.] *For Awnsham Churchill,* 1686. fol. L, O, C, E, DT; CLC, MH, MU, V, WF, Y, AVP.

2616   Le livre des assises. *By George Sawbridge, William Rawlins, and Samuel Roycroft, assigns of Richard and Edward Atkins. To be sold by H. Twyford, F. Tyton, J. Bellinger, W. Place, T. Basset, R. Pawlet, S. Heyrick, C. Wilkinson, T. Dring, W. Jacob, C. Harper, J. Leigh, J. Amery, J. Place, and J. Poole,* 1679. fol. L, O, C, CS, BAMB, GU; CU, MHL, TO, V, WF.

2617 O livro da oração commum. *Oxford, na estampa do Teatro,* 1695. fol. L, O, C, OC, DUS, EC, DT; CH, CU, Y.

2617A **Ll., J.** The death of God's Moses's considered. *For, and sold by Thomas Parkhurst,* 1678. 4°.* L, LW, DU, WCA; CH, CLC, WF, Y.

Ll., M. Men-miracles. [n.p.], 1646. *See* Llewellyn, Martin.

Ll., N. Letter written to a gentleman. 1653. *See* Hall, John.

2618 Entry cancelled.
—True account and character. [n.p., 1647.] *See* Hall, John, *poet.*

2618A **Ll., O.** A despised virgin beautified. *By Henry Hills,* 1653. 4°.* DT.

Ll., R. Artis poeticæ. 1653. *See* Lloyd, Richard.

2619 **Llanvædonon, William.** A brief exposition upon the second Psalme. *For Livewell Chapman,* 1655. 4°. LT, O, C.

2620 **Llewelin, David.** A sermon preach'd . . . August 13. 1677. *For Samuel Carr,* 1678. 4°.* T.C.I 288. L, O, C, BAMB, RPL; CH, CLC, NGT, WF.

2621 **L[lewellin], E[dward].** Divine meditations grounded. *York: by Tho. Broad,* 1650. 4°. YM; WF.

2622 ——[Anr. ed.] *York, by Tho: Broad, to be sold in London by Nath: Brooks,* 1650. 4°. LT.

2623 **Llewellyn, Martin.** An elegie on the death of . . . Henry Duke of Glocester. *Oxford, by Hen. Hall, for Ric. Davis,* 1660. fol.* MADAN 2504. LT, O, LL, LLP, MR; CH, IU, MH, WF, Y.

2624 —The marrow of the muses. *For William Sheares,* 1661. 8°. O; MH.

2625 [–] Men-miracles. With other poemes. [*Oxford, by H. Hall*], *printed,* 1646. 8°. MADAN 1884. LT, O, LIU, LLU, EN; CH, IU, MH, NC, TU, WF, Y.

2626 [–] —Second edition. *For Will. Shears junior.* 1656. 8°. L, O, LVD, CS, EC, LLU; CH, CN, MH, MMO, Y.

2627 [–] —[Anr. ed.] *Printed, and are to be sold by Peter Parker,* 1679. 8°. EN, GK; MB, MH, NN.

2627A [–] A satyr occasioned by the author's survey of a scandalous pamphlet. *Oxford, by Leonard Lichfield,* 1645. 4°.* MADAN 1799. LT, O, CT, DT; CH, MH.

2628 [–] To the Kings most excellent Majesty. colop: *For J. Martin, Ja. Allestry, T. Dicas,* 1660. fol.* LT, O, EC, LLU; CH, CU, MH, TU, WF.

2628A [–] —[Anr. ed.] [*London,* 1660.] fol.* L, OB; Y.

2629 [–] Wickham wakened. [*Oxford, by William Hall*], *printed,* 1672. 4°.* MADAN 2952. O, LF, LLU; CH, MH, PH, Y.

2630 **[Lloyd, David],** *1597-1663.* The legend of Captaine Iones. *By M. F. for Richard Marriot,* 1648. 4°. LT, O; CH, CN, MH, Y.

2631 [–] —[Anr. ed.] *For Richard Marriot,* 1656. 8°. L, O; CH, CLC, MB, NN, PU, Y.

2632 [–] —[Anr. ed.] *For Humphrey Moseley,* 1659. 4°. LT, O, LVD, CK, AN; CLC, CN, MH, NP, RPJ, Y.

2633 [–] —[Anr. ed.] *For E. Okes and Francis Haley,* 1671. 8°. T.C.I 74. L, CK, CM, LLU, A; CH, MH, MU, WF, Y.

2634 [–] —[Anr. ed.] *For Francis Haley,* 1671. 8°. RPJ.

2635 [–] —: continued from his first-part. *By M. F. for Richard Marriot,* 1648. 4°. L, O; CH, MH, Y.

[Lloyd, David], *1635-1692.* Cabala, or an impartial account. 1663. *See* Birkenhead, *Sir* John.

2636 —Cabala: or, the mystery of conventicles unvail'd. *For Thomas Holmwood,* 1664. 4°. L, O, C, MR, EN; CLC, MBA, NU, WF, Y.

2637 —Dying and dead mens living words. *For John Amery,* 1668. 12°. CS, DC, DU; CH, CLC.

2638 ——[Anr. ed.] —, 1673. 12°. T.C.I 143. L, O, CPL, SP, EN; BN, CB, CH, CLC, NCD.

2639 ——[Anr. ed.] —, 1682. 12°. T.C.I 479. L, CP; CH, CLC, NU, WF.

2640 —Εικων βασιλικη. Or, the true pourtraicture of . . . Charles the II. In three books. *For H. Brome, and H. Marsh,* 1660. 3 pts. 8°. LT, O, C, OC; CH, CN, MH, NU, WF, Y. (var.)

2640A [–] Fair warnings to a careless world. *For Samuel Speed,* 1665. 4°. NC.

2640B [–] —[Anr. ed.] *York, by Stephen Bulkley and are to be sold by Francis Mawbarne,* 1666. 24°. LC.

2641 [–] The kingdome saved. *Printed,* 1663. 8°. V, Y.

2642 —Memoires of the lives, actions. *For Samuel Speed: sold by him: by John Wright: John Symmes: and James Collins,* 1668. fol. L, O, C, EN, DT; BN, CH, CN, NU, TU, WF, Y.

2643 ——[Anr. ed.] *For Dorman Newman,* 1677. fol. L.

2644 —Modern policy compleated. *By J. B. for Henry Marsh,* 1660. 8°. L, O, BR, DU, ES; CH, CN, NU, WF, Y.

2645 [–] Never faile: or, that sure way of thriving. *For Henry Marsh,* 1663. 8°. C, DU; NU.

[–] Restauration of . . . Charles the II. 1660. *See* —Εικων βασιλικη [Book three].

2646 [–] State-worthies. Second edition. *By Thomas Milbourn for Samuel Speed,* 1670. 8°. T.C.I 52. L, C, AN, LIU, E, DT; BN, CH, CN, MH, NU, TU, WF, Y.

2647 [–] —"Second" edition. *For Peter Parker,* 1679. 8°. L; CH, IAU, MH, NC, NN, WF.

2648 [–] The states-men and favourites of England. *By J. C. for Samuel Speed,* 1665. 8°. L, C, MR, EN, BQ; CH, IU, MBP, MH, PL, TU, WF, Y.

2649 [–] Wonders no miracles. *For Sam. Speed,* 1666. 4°.* L, O, CS, DU, EN; CH, LC, MH, NU, WF.

2650 Entry cancelled.
Lloyd, Edward. Design of a British dictionary. [n.p., 1695.] *See* Lhuyd, Edward.

2651 Entry cancelled.
Lloyd, Hugh, *bp.* Articles of visitation and enquiry. 1662. *See* Church of England.

2652 —Phrases elegantiores ex Cæsaris. *Oxoniæ, excudebat Hen. Hall, impensis Joseph Godwin,* 1654. 8°. MADAN 2256. O, C, LL; BN, CH, WF.

2653 **Lloyd, Jenkin.** Christ's valedictions. *By D. M. for D. Pakeman,* 1658. 12°. LT, LSC.

2654 **Lloyd, John,** *rector.* Bibliotheca Lloydiana. [*London*], *Dec.* 3 1683. 4°. L, O, OP, CS; MH, NG.

2655 [–] A good help for weak memories. *For Thomas Helder,* 1671. 8°. T.C.I 78. L, C, SP; CH, CU, IU, WF.

2655A —A treatise of the Episcopacy. *By W. G. for John Sherley, and Robert Littlebury,* 1660. 4°. O, C, OC, BP, DT; CH, CN, NU, WF, Y.

2656 **Lloyd, John, bp.** The library of . . . sixth of February. [*London*], 1699. 8°. L, O, OAS, CS; BN, MH, NN, Y.

2657–8 No entries.

2659 Entry cancelled.
—Treatise of the Episcopacy. 1660. *See* Lloyd, John, *rector.*

2660 **Lloyd, Lodowick.** The marrow of history. *By E. Alsop,* 1653. 4°. L, O, C, AN, YM; CH, MH, MU, TU, WG, Y.

2661 ——[Anr. ed.] *For John Andrews,* 1659. 4°. L.

2662 [**Lloyd, M.**] The king found at Southvvell. *For F. L.,* 1646. 4°.* MADAN 1863. LT, O, OC.

2663 **Lloyd, Morgan.** Nevves from VVales. [*London*], *for J. G. and A. C.,* 1642. 4°.* LT, AN; WF.

2664 **Lloyd, Nicholas.** Catalogus librorum. [*London*], 4 *July* 1681. 4°. L, O, OP; LC, NG.

2664A Entry cancelled.
—Dictionarium historicum. 1686. *See* Estienne, Charles.

2665 [**Lloyd, Owen.**] The panther-prophecy. [*London*], *printed,* 1662. fol.* L, LW, AN; CH, MH, WF.

2666 **Ll[oyd], R[ichard],** *1595-1659.* Artis poeticæ, musarum. *Typis T. R.,* 1653. 8°. L.

2667 Entry cancelled.
—Case of the merchants. [n.p., 1680?] *See* Lloyd, Sir Richard.

2668 —An English grammar. *For the author,* 1652. 8°. CHRISTIE-MILLER.

2669 —The Latine grammar. *By Thomas Roycroft for the author,* 1653. 8°. L.

2670 [–] —[Anr. ed.] *By T. R.,* 1659. 8°. LT.

2671 [–] The schoole-masters auxiliaries. *By T. R. for the author,* 1654. 8°. L.

2672 [–] —[Anr. ed.] *By T. R.,* 1659. 8°. LT.

2672A **Lloyd, Sir Richard.** The case of the merchants. [*London*, 1680?] fol. L, LPR.

2673 [**Lloyd, William**], **bp.** An answer to the Bishop of Oxford's [S. Parker's] reasons. *Printed,* 1688. 4°. L, O, C, MC, EN, DT; CH, CN, MH, NC, WF, Y. (var.)

2673A —Articlau o Ymweliad. *Printiedig yn y Theater yn Rhydychen,* 1685. 4°.* ST. ASAPH CATH.

2674 —A chronological account of the life of Pythagoras. *By J. H. for H. Mortlock and J. Hartley,* 1699. 8°. T.C.III 138. L, O, C, MR, DT; BN, CH, CLC, CN, TO, WF, Y.

2675 [–] A conference between two Protestants and a Papist. [*London*], 1673. 4°.* L, C, OC, DU, LSD, DT; CH, CN, NU, TU, WF, Y.

2676 [–] Considerations touching the true way to suppress Popery. *For Henry Brome,* 1677. 4°. T.C.I 267. L, O, C, EN, DT; CH, IEG, LC, MH, NU, TU, Y.

2677 [–] The difference between the church and court of Rome. *By Andrew Clark for Henry Brome,* 1674. 4°.* L, O, C, EN, DT; CH, CN, MH, NU, TU, WF, Y.

2678 [–] —Second edition. —, 1674. 4°.* T.C.II 81. L, O, C, LNC, DT; CLC, LC, MBA, TO, TU, Y.

2679 —A discourse of God's ways . . . Part I. *By H. Hills for Thomas Jones,* 1691. 4°. L, O, C, AN, MR, DT; CH, CN, MH, NU, TU, WF, Y.

2680 ——Second edition. —, 1691. 4°. L, O, BC, E, DT; CN, IEG, MBA.

2680A —An exposition of the prophecy of seventy weeks. [*n.p.,* 1690.] 4°. L, BAMB.

2681 —An historical account of church-government. *For Charles Brome,* 1684. 8°. L, O, C, MR, EN, BLH; CH, CN, MU, NU, TU, Y, AVP.

2682 ——Second edition. *By M. Flesher, for Charles Brome,* 1684. 8°. T.C.II 67. L, C, OC, BC, SA, DT; BN, CLC, MIU, NU, PL, TSM, WF, Y.

2683 [–] The late apology in behalf of the Papists re-printed and ansvvered. *For M. N.,* 1667. 4°.* L, O, C, EN, DT; CH, IU, MH, NU, TU, WF, Y.

2684 [–] —[Anr. ed.] *For Henry Brome,* 1673. 4°.* T.C.I 192. OC, OME, BAMB; CLC, LC, WF.

2685 [–] —Fourth edition. —, 1675. 4°.* L, O, C, SC, DT; CLC, MBA, MH, NU, TO, TU.

2686 [–] A letter to Dr. Sherlock. *For Thomas Jones,* 1691. 4°.* L, O, CS, LSD, MR; CH, CU, MH, NU, TU, WF, Y.

2687 [–] —Second edition. —, 1691. 4°.* L, O, C, D, DT; CH, IU, NC, NP, TU, WF, Y.

[–] Lex talionis: or, the author. 1676. *See* Fell, Philip.

2688 [–] Papists no Catholicks. *For the author,* 1677. 4°.* L, O, LLP, BC, MC; CH, TU, WU, Y.

2689 [–] —Second edition. *For Henry Brome,* 1679. 4°. T.C.I 268. L, O, C, EN, DT; CLC, CN, NGT, NU, WF, Y.

2689A [–] —[Anr. ed.] *Printed* 1686. 4°.* L, OC; CH.

2690 [–] The pretences of the French invasion examined. *For R. Clavel,* 1692. 4°.* T.C.II 412. L, O, C, MR, DT; CH, CN, MH, NU, TU, WF, Y.

2691 [–] —[Anr. ed.] *Dublin, re-printed for William Norman, Eliphal Dobson, and Patrick Campbel,* 1692. 4°.* DIX 252. L, LIU, DN, DT; Y.

2692 [–] A reasonable defence of the seasonable discourse. *For H. Brome,* 1674. 4°.* T.C.I 153. L, C, OME, EN, DT; CH, MH, NU, TU, WF, Y.

2692A [–] Seasonable advice to all Protestant people. *For Randal Taylor,* 1681. 4°.* T.C.I 444. L, O, DT; CH, CU, WF.

2692B [–] A seasonable advice to Protestants. *For Charles Brome,* 1688. 4°.* L, LL, CT, DU, EN; CH, MH, NU, WF, Y.

2693 [–] A seasonable discourse shewing the necessity. *For Henry Brome,* 1673. 4°.* L, O, C, MR, EN; CH, MIU, NU, PL, TU, WF.

2694 [–] —Second edition. —, 1673. 4°.* L, C, OC, BR, LSD, CD; CDA, CU, MH, NC, TU, V.

2695 [–] —Third edition. — 1673. 4°.* L, O, CT, BAMB, DT; CH, CN, MH, NU, PL, TU, Y.

2696 [–] —Fourth edition. —, 1673. 4°.* L, O, C, DUS, LSD; CH, CN, MH, NU, PL, TU, Y.

2697 [–] —Fifth edition. —, 1673. 4°.* L, O, C, SC, DT; CH, CN, MH, NU, TU, WF, Y.

2698 Entry cancelled.

—Series chronologica. Oxoniæ, 1700. *See* Lloyd, William, 1674–1719.

2699 —A sermon at the funeral of Sir Edmund-Bury Godfrey, . . . last day of Octob. 1678. *By M. Clark, for Henry Brome*, 1678. 4°.* L, OC, CS, CPL, LIU; CH, CLC, MU, TO, TU, WF, Y. (var.)

2700 ——[Anr. ed.] *By Tho. Newcomb, for Henry Brome*, 1678. 4°.* T.C.I 326. L, C, OM, DC, DT; CH, CN, MH, MU, NU, TU, WSC, Y.

2701 ——[Anr. ed.] *Dublin, by Benjamin Tooke, to be sold by Mary Crook*, 1678. 8°.* DIX 163. L, DN.

2702 —A sermon preached . . . Decemb. 1. M.DC.LXVII. *By E. Cotes, for Henry Brome*, 1668. 4°.* L, O, C, DU, DT; CH, CN, MH, NU, TU, WF, Y.

2702aA ——[Anr. ed.] *By A. C. for Henry Brome*, 1674. 4°. MR; IU, NP, PL.

2702A —A sermon preached . . . 24th of July, 1671. *By Thomas Milbourn, for Thomas Johnson*, 1671. 4°.* L, C, LSD, WCA; CH, CLC.

2703 —A sermon preached . . . 12 of December, 1672. *By A. C. for Henry Brome*, 1672. 4°.* L, O, C, DU, DT; CH, CN, NU, TU, WF, Y.

2704 ——[Anr. ed.] *For Joanna Brome*, 1673. 8°. L, LLP, CT, D, DT; BN, CLC, IU.

2705 ——[Anr. ed.] *For Henry Brome*, 1675. 8°. T.C.I 125. L, O, LLP, LLU; CH, CLC, HM, NR, JF.

2705A ——[Anr. ed.] *For Henry Brome*, 1678. 4°.* ASSINGTON PARISH, SUFFOLK.

2706 ——[Anr. ed.] *For Charles Brome*, 1694. 4°. BC, BQ; CH, NN, NU, PPT, WF.

2707 ——[Anr. ed.] —, 1698. 8°. DT; BN, CLC, MH.

2708 —A sermon preached . . . March 6. 1673/4. *By Andrew Clark, for Henry Brome*, 1674. 4°.* T.C.I 167. L, O, C, DU, DT; CH, MH, MIU, NU, TU, WF, Y.

2709 —A sermon preached . . . November the fifth, 1678. *By T. N. for Henry Brome*, 1679. 4°.* T.C.I 347. L, O, C, AN, BLH; CH, CN, NU, TU, WF, Y.

2710 —A sermon preached . . . 24th of Novemb. 1678. *By M. C. for Henry Brome*, 1678. 4°. T.C.I 347. L, LLP, CT, BAMB, NOT; WF.

2711 ——[Anr. ed.] —, 1679. 4°. L, O, C, DC, DT; CH, CN, NU, TU, WF, Y.

2712 —A sermon preached . . . November 5. 1680. *By M. C. for Henry Brome*, 1680. 4°.* T.C.I 423. L, O, C, LNC, DT; CH, CN, MH, NU, TU, WF, Y.

2713 —A sermon preached . . . fifth day of November, 1689. *For Robert Clavell*, 1689. 4°.* T.C.II 283. L, O, C, CPL, DT; CH, CN, NU, TU, WF, Y.

2714 —A sermon preached . . . March the twelfth, 1689/90. *For Robert Clavell*, 1690. 4°.* T.C.II 312. L, O, C, EN, DT; CH, CLC, CN, NU, TU, WF, Y.

2715 —A sermon preached . . . January the 30th. *For Thomas Jones*, 1691. 4°.* L, O, BAMB, EN, DT; CH, CLC, WF, Y.

2716 —A sermon preached . . . May 29. *For Thomas Jones*, 1692. 4°.* L, O, C, SHR, BLH; CH, CLC, NGT, TSM, WF, Y.

2717 —A sermon preach'd . . . 30th of January, 1696/7. *For John Everingham*, 1697. 4°.* L, O, C, BAMB, MR; CH, CN, NU, TU, WF, Y.

2718 [–] Several tracts against Popery. *For Charles Brome*, 1689. 4°. T.C.II 263. C.

2719–20 Entries cancelled.

—Utrum horum. 1691. *See* title.

2720A **Lloyd, William,** *reverend.* The last speech of. [*London*, 1679.] brs. L; MU.

2720B **Lloyd, William, 1674–1719.** Series chronologica, Olympiadum. *Oxoniæ, e theatro Sheldoniano*, 1700. fol. T.C.III 173. L, O, C, BAMB, GU, DT; IU, LC, MBA, PL, WF, Y.

Lluelyn, Martin. *See* Llewellyn, Martin.

2720C **Llwyd, Morgan.** Cyfarwyddid ir cymru. *Printiedig*, 1657. 12°.* AN, CPL. [Part of B3427A.]

2720D [–] Dirgelwch i rai iw ddeall. *Gan James Flesher, ac a werthir gan Thomas Brewster*, [1653.]. 8°. AN.

2720E —Gwyddor vchod. *Printiedig*, 1657. 12°.* AN, CPL. [Part of B3427A.]

Llyfr gweddi gyffredin. *See* Book of Common Prayer.

2720F —[Anr. ed.] *Rhydychen* [Oxford], *yn y Flwyddyn*, 1683. 12°. AN.

2720G —[Anr. ed.] *Argraphwyd yng Haerlûdd dros Thomas Jones*, 1687, *gan Mr. Charles Beard . . . a Mr. John Marsh, yn Llundain.* 8°. AN.

2720H —[Anr. ed.] *Rhydychain, gan Leon. Lichfield, dros Joan Howel*, 1693. 8°. OC, AN.

2720I —[Anr. ed.] [*Shrewsbury?*], *dros Thomas Jones*, 1700. 8°. AN, BANGOR, CPL.

2721 Entry cancelled.

Y llyfr plygain. 1683. *See* Jones, Thomas, *of Shrewsbury.* Yr hen llyfrplygain.

Llyfr y resolusion. 1684. *See* Parsons, Robert, S. J.

Lobb, Emmanuel, *pseud. See* Sergeant, John.

[**Lobb, Samuel.**] Healing attempt. 1689. *See* Humfrey, John.

2721A **Lobb, Stephen.** An appeal to the Right Reverend Edward Lord Bishop of Worcester. *For Nath. Hiller*, 1698. 8°. O, LCL, ENC, GU; CLC, MH, NPT, WF.

2721B —Cranmer redivivus. 1683. 4°. P.

2722 [–] A defence of the Report. *For Nath. Hiller*, 1698. 8°. L, LCL, DU, ENC, GU; MH, MWA, Y.

2723 —A dreadful oration deliver'd by. [*London*], *by N. T.*, 1683. 4°.* L, O, OC; CH, IEG, WF, Y.

2724 [–] A further defence of the Report. *For N. Hiller*, 1698. 8°. L, LCL, ON, ENC, GU; CLC.

2724A —The glory of free-grace display'd. *For Benjamin Alsop*, 1680. 8°. T.C.I 438. MBA, MH.

2724B [–] —[Anr. ed.] *By T. S. for B. Alsop*, 1680. 8°. LW; TO.

2725 [–] The growth of error. *For John Salusbury*, 1697. 8°. O, C, LW, NE, ENC, DT; CLC, IU, NU, TO, AVP.

2726 [–] The harmony between the old and present nonconformists principles. *Printed and are to be sold by Joseph Collier*, 1682. 4°. T.C.I 483. L, O, CT, DU, E; CH, CN, MH, NU, WF, Y.

2727   [–] A letter to Doctor Bates. *For Nathaniel Hiller*, 1695. 4°.* L, O, LCL, LUG, LW, GU; NU, WF.

2728   —A peaceable enquiry . . . part I. *For John Dunton*, 1693. 8°. T.C.II 472. L, O, LCL; MH, NCU, TO, WF, Y.

2729   [–] A report of the present state of the differences. *For Nath. Hiller*, 1697. 8°.* L, LCL, DU, ENC, GU; CH, MH, NU.

2729A [–] A second letter to a Dissenter. *For John Harris*, 1687. cap., 4°.* L, O, CS, BR, DU; CLC, CN, MH, NU, WF, Y.

2730   [–] The true dissenter. [*London*], *printed*, 1685. 8°. L, O, LW, P, CD; CSB, IU, MH, MWA, NU, TO, Y.

2731   **Lobeira, Vasco.** The fifth book of the most pleasant . . . history of Amadis de Gaul. *By T. J. for Andrew Kembe and Charls Tyus*, 1664. 4°. L, O, C, LG; CH, MH, WF, WU.

2731A ——Sixt part. *By Jane Bell*, 1652. 4°. L, O; CH, MH, NP, CLEVELAND PUB. LIB.

2732   **L'Obel, Matthew de.** Stirpium illustrationes. *Typis Tho: Warren, impensis Jos: Kirton*, 1655. 4°. LT, O, C, OM, DT; BN, CH, CLC, LC, MB, MH.

2733   [**Lobo, Jeronymo.**] A short relation of the River Nile. *For John Martyn*, 1669. 8°. T.C.I 9. L, LG, OC, CCA, WCA; CH, LC, MH, PL, WCL, Y.

2734   [–] —[Anr. ed.] —, 1673. 8°. T.C.I 138. L, O, GH; CLC, MH, NCD, TU, Y.

2735   **Locke, John.** An abridgment of Mr. Locke's essay. *For A. and J. Churchill, and Edw. Castle*, 1696. 8°. T.C.II 571. L, O, C, GU, DT, BQ; CH, CN, MH, NU, WF, Y.

2736   ——Second edition. *For A. and J. Churchil*, 1700. 8°. L, C, OC, AN, EN, DT; CH, CN, MH, PL, WF, Y.

       — Account of Mr. Lock's religion. 1700. *See* Milner, John.

2737   [–?] A common-place book to the Holy Bible. *By Edw. Jones, for Awnsham and John Churchil*, 1697. 4°. T.C.III 22. L, O, C, NPL, E; CH, CN, MH, NU, WF, Y.

2738   [–] An essay concerning humane understanding. *By Eliz. Holt, for Thomas Basset*, 1690. fol. T.C.II 302. L, O, C, EN, DT; CH, CN, MH, MMO, NU, TU, WF, Y. (var.)

2739   [–] —[Anr. ed.] *For Tho. Basset, and sold by Edw. Mory*, 1690. fol. L, CK, CS, EC, GU; CH, INU, MH, NN, TSM, Y, AVP.

2740   ——Second edition. *For Awnsham and John Churchill; and Samuel Manship*, 1694. fol. T.C.II 541. L, O, C, DU, DT; BN, CH, IU, MH, NU, TU, WF, Y. AVP.

2740A ——"Second" edition. *For Thomas Dring and Samuel Manship*, 1694. fol. O, AN, SA; MB, MH, PL, TO, Y. (var.)

2741   ——Third edition. *For Awnsham and John Churchil; and Samuel Manship*, 1695. fol. L, O, C, BR, E; CLC, IU, MH, NP, WF, Y.

2742   ——Fourth edition. —, 1700. fol. T.C.III 176. L, O, C, EN, DT; CH, CU, MH, PL, TU, WF, Y, AVP.

2743   Entry cancelled. Ghost.

2743A [–?] The fundamental constitutions of Carolina. [*London*, 1670.] cap., fol.* LPR; CH, LC, MH, NCU, NN, PHS, RPJ.

2744   [–?] —[Anr. ed.] [*London*, 1682.] fol.* NN.

2745   [–] Further considerations concerning raising the value of money. *For A. and J. Churchil*, 1695. 8°. T.C.II 571. L, O, LUG, CT, EN; CH, MH, MMO, NP, WF, Y.

2746   [–] —Second edition. —, 1695. 8°. L, O, CT, EN, BQ; CH, MH, NP, WF, Y. (var.)

2746A [–] —"Second" edition. *For Awnsham and John Churchil*, 1696. 8°. L, O, CK; CN, NC.

2746B [–?] Γραφανταρκεια, or, the Scriptures. *For Sampson Evans, in Worcester*, 1676. 4°. T.C.I 250. L, C, LCL, BSO, GC; MBA, NU.

2746C [–?] —[Anr. ed.] —, and sold by H. Sawbridge, 1684. 4°. T.C.II 39. L, OW; CLC.

2747   [–] A letter concerning toleration. *For Awnsham Churchill*, 1689. 4°. T.C.II 284. L, O, C, EN, DT; BN, CH, LC, MH, MIU, TU, Y.

2748   [–] —Second edition. —, 1690. 12°. T.C.II 305. L, O, C, LW, DT; CH, CN, MH, PL, TU, WF, HC.

       [–] Letter from a person of quality, to his friend. [n.p.], 1675. *See* Shaftesbury, Anthony Ashley Cooper.

2748A —A letter to Edward Lᵈ Bishop of Worcester. *For A. and J. Churchill*, 1697. 8°. CS, LLU, WINCHESTER CATH.; CN, MH, NRU.

2749   —A letter to the Right Reverend Edward Lᵈ Bishop of Worcester. *By H. Clark, for A. and J. Churchill; and Edw. Castle*, 1697. 8°. T.C.III 23. L, O, C, AN, EN, DT; BN, CH, CU, MMO, MU, NAM, NU, TU, Y.

2750   Entry cancelled.
       [–] Reason and religion. 1694. *See title.*

2751   [ ] The reasonableness of Christianity. *For Awnsham and John Churchill*, 1695. 8°. T.C.II 568. L, O, CT, E, DT; BN, CH, CN, MH, NU, WF, Y. (var.)

2752   [–] —Second edition. —, 1696. 8°. T.C.II 596. L, O, CK, CT, GU; BN, CLC, CN, MH, NCD, NU, WF, Y.

2753   —Mr. Locke's reply to the Right Reverend the Lord Bishop of Worcester's answer to his letter. *By H. Clark, for A. and J. Churchill, and E. Castle*, 1697. 8°. T.C.III 51. L, O, C, EN, DT; BN, CH, MH, MIU, PL, WF, Y.

2754   ——[Same title.] . . . to his second letter. *By H. C. for A. and J. Churchill; and E. Castle*, 1699. 8°. T.C.III 105. L, O, C, EN, DT; BN, CH, MH, MIU, NU, TU, WF, Y.

2755   [–] A second letter concerning toleration. *For Awnsham and John Churchill*, 1690. 4°. T.C.II 323. L, O, C, E, DT; BN, CH, CN, MH, NU, WF, Y.

2756   [–] A second vindication of The reasonableness of Christianity. *For A. and J. Churchill, and Edward Castle*, 1697. 8°. L, O, C, MR, CD; BN, CLC, CU, MH, NU, TSM, WF, Y.

2756A [–] —[Anr. ed.] *For A. and J. Churchill*, 1697. 8°. T.C.III 23. OJ, GU; NU, PL.

2757   —Several papers relating to money. *For A. and J. Churchill*, 1696. 8°. T.C.II 596. L, O, C, EN, DT; BN, CH, CJC, LC, MH, NC, Y. (var.)

2758   [–] Short observations on a printed paper, intituled, For encouraging the coining. *For A. and J. Churchill*, 1695. cap., 8°.* T.C.II 540. L, O, CT, EN, BQ; CH, IU, MH, NC, WF, Y.

2759   Entry cancelled.
       —Short observations. 1696. *See* —Several papers relating to money.

2760   [–] Some considerations of the consequences. *For Awnsham and John Churchill*, 1692. 8°. T.C.II 413. L, O, C, CT, EN, BQ; CH, IU, MH, NC, WF, Y, AVP.

2761 ——Second edition. —, 1696. 8°. O, OC, CT, DUS, M; CLC, CN, MIU, WF, Y.

2762 [–] Some thoughts concerning education. *For A. and J. Churchill,* 1693. 8°. T.C.II 467. L, O, CK, CT, DU, LIU; CH, LC, MH, MMO, NU, WCL, Y. (A3v, line 19: "patronage.")

2762A [–] [Second edition?] —, 1693. 8°. O, CK; CN, IU, MH, TO. ("patronnge.")

2763 [–] —Third edition. —, 1695. 8°. L, O, C, LLU, EN; BN, CLC, MH, MIU, NC, TU, Y, AVP.

2764 [–] —Fourth edition. —, 1699. 8°. T.C.III 113. L, O, C, CK, BC; BN, CH, CU, MH, TU, WF, Y.

2765 [–] A third letter for toleration. *For Awnsham and John Churchill,* 1692. 4°. T.C.II 423. L, O, C, EN, DT; CH, CN, MH, MMO, WF, Y.

2766 [–] Two treatises of government. *For Awnsham Churchill,* 1690. 8°. T.C.II 292. L, O, C, CK, BAMB, DT; CLC, CN, LC, MH, MMO, NCD, NU, Y. (var.)

2767 [–] —Second edition. *For Awnsham and John Churchill,* 1694. 8°. T.C.II 541. L, O, CM, D, DM; CH, CN, MH, NAM, NC, TU, Y.

2768 [–] —[Anr. ed.] —, 1698. 8°. T.C.III 57. L, O, C, GU, DT; CH, CN, MH, NC, WF, Y.

2769 [–] A vindication of The reasonableness. *For Awnsham and John Churchil,* 1695. 8°.* T.C.II 568. L, O, CT, GU, DT; CH, CN, MH, NU, WF, Y.

2770 **Locke, Matthew.** The English opera. *By T. Ratcliff, and N. Thompson for the author, and are to be sold by John Carr,* 1675. 4°. L, O, LLU, GU; CH, CN, LC, MH, WF, Y.

2771 —His little consort of three parts: . . . bassus. *By W. Godbid for John Playford,* 1656. obl. 4°.* L, O.

2772 ——. . . treble. —, 1656. fol.* O.

2773 ——. . . treble and tenor. —, 1656. fol.* O.

2774 —Melothesia: or certain general rules for playing upon a continued-bass. *For J. Carr,* 1673. 4°. T.C.I 151. L, C, GU; IAU, INU, LC.

2775 —Modern church-musick pre-accus'd. [*London,* 1666.] fol. L.

2776 —Observations upon a late book, entituled, An essay. *By W..G. to be sold by John Playford,* 1672. 8°.* T.C.I 111. L, O, CM; CH, CINCINNATI PUB., LC.

2777 —The present practice of musick vindicated. *For N. Brooke, and J. Playford,* 1673. 8°. T.C.I 127. L, O, C, CT; CH, IU, LC, MU, Y.

2777A [**Lockhart, George.**] A further account of East-New-Jarsey. *Edinburgh, by John Reid,* 1683. 4°.* ALDIS 2380.5. E, EN; RPJ.

2778 —To his grace James, Duke of Queensberry, . . . the representation. [*n.p.,* 1700.] brs. EN.

2779 **Lockhart, Sir William.** A letter sent from Col. Will. Lockhart, . . . Decemb. 31, 1659. *By John Streater, and John Macock,* 1659[60]. 4°.* LT, O, LIU, MR; CH, CLC, MH, MU, WF, Y.

2780 Entry cancelled.
[**Lockier.**] Character. [n.p., 1652.] *See* Lockyer, Lionel.

2781 **Lockyer, Lionel.** An advertisement, concerning those most excellent pills, called, Pillulæ radijs solis extractæ. [*London,* 1664.] cap., 4°.* L, O; WF.

2781A ——[Anr. ed.][*London,* 1667.] 4°.* C.

2781B ——[Anr. ed.][*London,* 1676.] 4°.* C.

2781C ——[Anr. ed.][*London,* 1680.] 4°.* L.

2781D [–] The character of a time-serving saint. [*London,* 1652.] brs. LT.

2781E —Dr. Lockyer's vindication. *For the author,* 1658. 8°. OC.

2782 **Lockyer, Nicholas.** The workes of. *By I. D. for Iohn Rothwell,* 1644. 8°. L, LSC, DCH, EC; IU, NU.

2783 —Baulme for bleeding England. *By E. G. for John Rothwell,* 1643. 8°. L, O; CH, CLC, IU, MH, WF.

2783A ——[Anr. ed.] *By John Raworth for John Rothwell,* 1643. 8°. L, C, LCL, DC, E, GU; CLC, CN, NU, OWC, TU.

2784 ——[Anr. ed.] *By J. D. for Iohn Rothwell,* 1644. 8°. L, O, C, ENC, DT, BLH; CLC, IU, MH, NF, NU, Y.

2785 ——[Anr. ed.] *By E. G. for John Rothwell,* 1646. 4°. L, O, LCL, CT, EC, GU; IU, MIU, NU, Y.

2786 ——[Anr. ed.] —, 1649. 4°. LW, EC; CLC, CN, MH, NU, WF.

2786A —Christs commvnion with His Chvrch militant. Second edition. *By R. H. for Iohn Rothwell,* 1641. 12°. EC; Y.

2786B ——Third edition. *By R. H. for John Rothwell,* 1643. 12°. C.

2787 ——[Anr. ed.] *By I. N. for Iohn Rothwell,* 1644. 8°. L, O, C, BLH; CH, IU, MH, NU.

2788 ——[Anr. ed.] *Cambridge, for J. Rothwell,* 1645. 12°. L, CE, LNC, GU.

2788A ——[Anr. ed.] *By T. F. for John Rothwell,* 1646. 8°. GU; Y.

2789 ——[Anr. ed.] —, 1650. 8°. LT, LCL, LW, EC; CLC, CN, MH, NGT, NU, WF.

2789A ——Fifth edition. *By T. C. for J. Rothwell,* 1654. 8°. ORP.

2789B ——Sixth edition. *By S. G. for J. Rothwel,* 1656. 12°. CLC.

2790 ——"Fifth" edition. *For J. Hancock sen. & jun.,* 1672. 12°. T.C.I 122. O, C.

2791 —A divine discovery of sincerity. *By E. G. for John Rothwell,* 1643. 8°. L, C, BLH, BQ; CLC, LC, NU.

2792 ——[Anr. ed.] *By Edward Griffin for Iohn Rothwell,* 1645. 8°. GU; CH, CLC, MH, Y.

2793 ——[Anr. ed.] *For John Rothwell,* 1649. 8°. L, O, LW, EC; CLC, CN, MH, NGT, NU, WF, Y.

2794 —England faithfully watcht with, in her wounds. *By M. S. for John Rothwell, and Ben. Allen,* 1646. 8°. LT, O, LCL, EC, GU; CH, CN, MH, NU, WF, Y, AVP.

2795 —Englands warning-piece. *Printed,* 1659. 8°. O, DC, EC.

2796 —A litle stone, out of the mountain. *Printed at Leith by Evan Tyler,* 1652. 12°. ALDIS 1462.9. LCL, LW, E, ENC; MH.

2797 —A memorial of God's judgments. *For Dorman Newman,* 1671. 8°. T.C.I 84. L, O, C, LCL, LW; CH, IU, MH, NU, WF, Y.

2798 —An olive-leafe. [*London*], *by E. G. for J. Rothwell,* 1650. 8°. O, LCL, LSC, LW, EC; CLC, IU, MH, NU, WF.

2799 [–] Queries upon the late act against conventicles. 1670. 4°.* O, ORP, DT; PSC.

2800 —A sermon preached . . . Octob. 28, 1646. *By Matthew Simmons, for John Rothwell, and Han. Allen*, 1646. 4°.* LT, O, C, EN, DT; CH, MH, MIU, NU, TU, WF, Y.

2801 [–] Some seasonable and serious queries. [*London*], *printed*, 1670. 4°.* L, O, C, DU, DT; CH, MH, MU, NU, WF, Y. (var.)

2802 [**Loddington, William.**] The Christian a Quaker. *Printed*, 1674. 8°. L, C, LF, OC; MH, NHC, PH, PSC.

2803 —The good order of truth justified. [*London*], *printed and sold by Andrew Sowle*, 1685. 4°.* LF; CH, PSC, Y.

2804 [–] Plantation work. *For Benjamin Clark*, 1682. 4°.* L, LF; CH, LC, PH, RPJ, Y.

2805 [–] Quakerism no paganism. *Printed*, 1674. 8°. L, LF, OC, EN; BN, PH, PSC.

2806 —A salutation to the Church of God. *For Tho. Cooke*, 1682. 8°.* L, LF; PH, Y.

2807 [–] The twelve pagan principles. [*London*], *printed*, 1674. 8°.* L, LF, OC, BBN; MH, PH, PSC.

2808 —Tythe no gospel maintenance. *Printed and sold by T. Sowle*, 1695. 8°.* LF, BBN; PH, PSC.

2809 **Lodge, Robert.** A salutation of love. [*London*], *printed*, 1665. 4°.* L, C, LF, BBN; MH, PH, PL, PSC, Y.

2810 **Lodge, Thomas.** Euphues golden legacie. *For Francis Smethwicke*, 1642. 4°. L; MH, WF.

2811 No entry.
[–] Lady Alimony. 1659. *See title.*

2812 **Lodington, Thomas.** The honour of the clergy vindicated. *By John Macock for Joseph Clarke*, 1674. 4°. T.C.I 176. L, O, C, OC, CT, LSD; CLC, MIU, NN, TSM, WF, Y.

2812A —The honour of the magistrate asserted. *For Robert Clavel*, 1674. 4°.* L, OC, OU, CM, NE, WCA; MIU, WF.

2813 **Lodowick, Christian.** A letter from. [*Philadelphia*, 1692.] cap., 8°.* EVANS 552. MH, MHS, MWA, NN.
—New-England almanack. Boston, 1695. *See Almanacs.*

2814 [**Lodowyck, Francis.**] A common writing. [*London*], *for the author*, 1647. 4°.* LT, O, CM, DT; CH, IU, LC, NN.

2815 [–] An essay towards an universal alphabet. [*London*, 1686.] cap., 4°.* O; CLC.

2816 [–] The ground-work or foundation laid. [*London*], *printed*, 1652. 4°.* L, O, AN; MH, MU, NN.

2817 **Loe, William.** A sermon preached at Lambeth, April 21. 1645. *For Richard Royston*, 1645. 4°.* L, O, LW, CE, DT; CH, IU, MH, NU, WF, Y.

2818 **Loeffs, Isaac.** The soul's ascension. *For N. Ranew and J. Robinson*, 1670. 8°. T.C.I 25. O, LCL, P; NGT, Y.

2818A **Loewenstein, Johann Kunckel, baron.** Observationes chymicae. *Londini & Roterodami, apud Henricum Wilsonium & consortes*, 1678. 12°. L, GU.

2818B —Utiles observationes. —, 1678. 12°. L, GU.

2818C **Lofting, John.** The answer of . . . to a paper . . . by George Oldner. [*London*, 1693?] brs. LG.

2818D —The new sukeing worme engine. [*London*, 1689–94.] brs. L.

2819 **Loftus, Dudley.** Anaphora. *Dublini, impressa typis Josephi Ray, prostat apud Gulielmum Norman*, 1693. 4°.* DIX 256. DM.

2820 —The case of Ware and Sherley. *Dublin, by Benjamin Tooke to be sold by Samuel Dancer*, 1669. 4°.* DIX 137. L, O, LLP, BC, DN, DT; CN, MH.

2821 —Διγαμιας αδικια: or, the first marriage of Katherine Fitzgerald. *Printed*, 1677. 4°.* L, CE, E, BQ, DT; CN, WF.

2822 Entry cancelled.
—History of the twofold invention. Dublin, 1686. *See title.*

2822A [–] Lettera esortatoria. [*Dublin*], *stampata*, 1667. 4°. DT.

2822B [–] —Second edition. [*Dublin*], *stampata*, 1667. 4°. DM.

2823 Entry cancelled.
—Logica. Dublin, 1657. *See Aristotle.*

2824 —Oratio funebris . . . Johannis Archepiscopi Armachani, . . . XVI die Julii, 1663. *Dublinii, typis Johannis Crooke*, 1663. 4°.* DIX 118. L, C, OC, DM, DT.

2825 Entry cancelled.
—L'oratione. Dublin, 1664. *See Ormond, James Butler, marquis.*

2826 —The proceedings observed in order to, and in the consecration of the twelve bishops. *By J. C. for John Crook*, 1661. 4°.* LT, O.

2827 —Reductio litium. [*Dublin*], 1670. 4°.* DIX 140. O, DT.

2828 [–] Speech delivered at a visitation held in the diocese of Clogher . . . Septr. 27. 1671. *Dublin, by Benjamin Tooke, sold by Joseph Wilde*, 1671. fol.* DIX 142. DT.

2829 Entry cancelled.
—Sponsa nondum uxor. 1677. *See Thompson, Robert.*

2829A [–] The vindication of an injured lady. *London [i.e. Dublin]*, *printed*, 1667. 4°.* O, DT.

2830 [**Loftus, Edward.**] Approved, good and happy newes from Ireland. *For Iohn Wright*, 1641[2]. 4°.* LT, MR, DT; MH.

2830A [–] —[Anr. ed., "ioyfull newes."] —, 1641. 4°.* O, C, EC; WF.

2831 [–] Ioyfull nevves from Ireland, or. *For Iohn Franke*, 1642. 4°.* LT, O, LSD, DN; MIU, Y.

2832 [–] The latest and truest newes from Ireland. *For H. S. and W. Ley*, 1642. 4°.* LT, O, C, DN.

2832A **Loftus, Nicholas.** To the honourable House of Commons . . . the humble answer of. *By John [. . .] and Robert Ibbitson*, 1646. brs. WF.

2833 Entry cancelled. Date: 1640 [STC 3090].

2834 [**Logan, John.**] Analogia honorum: or, a treatise. *By Tho. Roycroft*, 1677. AN, EC, LIU, BLH; CLC, LC, NC, PL, Y, AVP.

2835 Entry cancelled.
—Treatise of honour. 1679. *See Guillim, John. Display of heraldry.*

2836 **Loggan, David.** Cantabrigia illustrata. *Cantabrigiæ*, 1688. fol. LIB, CK, DCH, NPL; YBA.

2837 —[Anr. ed.] *Cantabrigiæ*, [1690?]. fol. L, O, C, GH, DT; BN, CH, CLC, IU, MBA, MH, PU, WF, Y.

2838 —Oxonia illustrata. *Oxoniæ, e theatro Sheldoniano*, 1675. fol.* MADAN 3035. L, O, C, E, DT; BN, CH, CN, LC, MH, NC, Y.

Logic; or. 1685. *See Arnauld, Antoine.*
Logick primer. [n.p.], 1672. *See Eliot, John.*

Logicke unfolded. 1656. *See* Spencer, Thomas.

Logica, sive. 1674. *See* Arnauld, Antoine.

2838A Logicæ institutiones in usum Academicæ Dubliniensis. *Dublin*, 1697. 12°. DRS.

Logicæ summa. 1685. 8°. *See* Sterne, Richard. Summa logicæ.

2839 A logical demonstration of the lawfulness of subscribing. *By John Macock for Giles Calvert*, 1650. 4°.* LT, O, LVF, NOT, DT; CH, CLC, CN, IU, MH, NU.

2840 **Logie, Andrew.** Cum bono deo. A remonstrance. [*Aberdeen*], *printed*, [*Iames Brown*], 1661. 4°.* ALDIS 1705. EN, EUF.

2841 Λογικη λατρεια. The reasonableness of divine service. *Printed, and are to be sold by Tho. Basset*, 1661. 4°. L, O, DUS, LIU, DT; CH, MH, MIU, NU, WF.

Λογοι απολογητικοι. Foure. [n.p.], 1649. *See* B., T.

Λογοι ευκαιροι. Essayes. 1653. *See* Master, William.

Λογομαχια: or. 1690. *See* Ker, Patrick. Πολιτικος.

2842 Λογος αυτοπαστος, or. *For Edward Brewster, to be sold at Mr. Marriotts*, 1667. 12°. L, C, SP, DT.

Λογου θρησκεια: or. 1670. *See* Glanvill, Joseph.

Loiola. 1648. *See* Hacket, John, *bp.*

2842A **Lomax, Nathaniel.** Launceus redivivus: or. [*London*], *by J. C. for the author*, 1675. 8°.* L.

2842B [**Lombard, André.**] Harangue au Roy . . . 19 d' Octobre 1681. *A Londres*, 1681. 4°.* O, CS, LSD.

2842C [–] An harangue to the King. colop: *For R. Bentley and M. Magnes*, 1681. brs. L, O, CS, HH, MC; CH, CN, WCL, WF, Y.

2843 —A speech delivered to His Majesty. *By Tho. Newcomb.* 1665. fol.* L, O, C, LPR, SP; Y.

2844 [–] A speech to the King: . . . the 19th of October 1681. *Dublin, by Joseph Ray, for William Mendey*, 1681. 4°.* DIX 185. C, DU, BLH, DN, DM, DT; IU.

2844A The Lombard-street lecturer's late farewell sermon, answer'd. *For the assigns of John Bastwick and sold by T. J.*, 1692. 4°.* L, LUG; IU, WF, Y.

2845 [**Lombe, Henry.**] An exhortation given forth. colop: *By T. Sowle*, 1694. cap., 4°.* L, LF, BBN, MR; CH, CN, MH, NCD, NR, WF, Y.

Londinatus, Christianus, *pseud.*

2846 Entry cancelled.

Londinensis lex. 1680. *See* Lex Londinensis.

2847 Londini lachrymæ, or Londons complaint. *By R. D.*, 1665. brs. L, LS.

Londini quod reliqvvm. Or. 1667. *See* Ford, Simon.

Londini renascentis. 1668. *See* Ford, Simon.

Londinum triumphans. 1682. *See* Gough, William.

2848 **L[ondon], W[illiam].** A catalogue of new books, by way of supplement. *By A. M., sold by Luke Fawn and Francis Tyton*, 1660. 4°.* LT, DU; CH, CN, LC, NG, NP.

2849 [–] A catalogue of the most vendible books. *Printed*, 1657. 4°. L, O, C, DM, DT; PU, UCLA.

2850 [–] —[Anr. ed.] —, 1658. 4°. LT, O, C, E, DT; CH, CN, LC, MH, TU, NC, Y. (var.)

2851 [–] The civil wars of France, during . . . Charls the Ninth. *By H. H. for W. London*, 1655. 12°. LT, O, LLP, CM, SP; NC, TO, WF.

[–] Gods judgements upon drunkards. [n.p.], 1659. *See* Hammond, Samuel.

LONDON

NOTE: Entries in the "London" section are listed chronologically under sub-headings. Petitions, addresses, declarations and accounts of meetings are listed at title.

2851A **London. Commissioners of Lieutenancy.** Guild Hall London. December the 11th, 1688. By the commissioners of lieutenancy . . . Ordered, that Sir Robert Clayton . . . be a committee. [*London*, 1688.] brs. O, C, LG; CH.

2851B **London. Commissioners of Sewers.** At a court of sewers held at the Guild Hall. *By Hen. Hills for John Bellinger*, [1653]. brs. LT.

—By the commissioners appointed . . . for the repairing the highways. [1662.] *See title.*

—At a meeting of the commissioners. [1667.] *See title.*

2851C —Rules and directions prescribed and made for the pitching and levelling the streets. [*London*], *for N. Brooke*, 1667. brs. L, LG.

2851D ——[Same title, 16 March 1667/8.] [*London*], *for Nath. Brooke*, 1668. brs. MH.

2851E —Ford. Mayor. At a meeting of the Commissioners and Surveyors. *For Nathaniel Brooke*, 1670. brs. L.

2851F —[13 November 1671.] By the commissioners. [Order to provide names of paviers.] [*London*], *by Andrew Clark*, 1671. brs. LG.

2851G —[7 April 1673.] By the commissioners for sewers. *By Andrew Clark*, [1673]. brs. L.

—Heads of the additional bill for paving. [*London*, 1680?] *See title.*

2851H **London. Committee for the Militia.** September 29. 1642. The persons to whom the militia of the citie of London is committed . . . hereby declare. [*London*, 1642.] brs. LT, HH; MH, Y.

—The 21. of August. 1643. Whereas the committee for the militia in the city of London. 1643. *See* England: Parliament.

2851I —Whereas the committee for the militia of London, taking into consideration. [4 April 1644]. [*London*, 1644.] brs. MH.

2851J —May 11. 1644. The committee of the militia of the city of London, and parts adjacent. [*London*, 1644.] brs. MH.

2851K —The committee of the militia of the city of London, having taken knowledge . . . [11 May 1644]. [*London*, 1644.] brs. MH.

2851L —Orders to be observed in the marching . . . May 23. 1644. *Printed* 1644. 4°.* LT, DT; MH, NU.

2851M —23 julii. 1644. At the sub-committee at Salters hall in Breadstreet. Whereas by ordinance. [*London*, 1644.] brs. MH.

—At the committee of the militia . . . the 3d of Iune, 1648. [1648.] *See title.*

—Committee of the militia London. [n.p., 1648.] *See title.*

—Committee of the militia of London. [n.p., 1648.] *See title.*

—At the committee of the militia . . . by vertue of . . . an act. [n.p.], 1650. *See title.*

2851N **London. Common Council.** A Common Councell, held . . . [31 December 1641. Control of crowds]. *By Robert Barker: and by the assignes of John Bill,* 1641. 4°.* LT, O, LG, DU, ESS, DT; CH, CN, MH, NU, WF, Y.

—Propositions agreed upon at a Court of Common Councell. 1642. *See title.*

—Cities propositions. 1642. *See title.*

2851O —An act of Common-Councell concerning the collecting and gathering of the fifteenes. [7 April 1643.] [*London*], *by Richard Cotes,* [1643]. brs. LT, LG; MH.

2851P —An act of Common Councell, for the prohibiting of all persons . . . from . . . putting to sale . . . any pamphlets, books, or papers. [9 October 1643.] *By Richard Cotes,* [1643]. brs. LT; CLEVELAND PUB. LIB.

2851Q —An act of Common-Covncel for the well-ordering . . . of the watches. [9 October 1643.] —, 1643. 4°.* LT; CSS, TU.

2851R —May 11, 1644. The Common councell of the city of London, (having taken knowledge . . .). [*London,* 1644.] brs. MH.

2851S —The ansvver of the right honourable the Lord Major, aldermen, and commons . . . to a letter . . . from . . . Fairfax. [12 June 1647.] [*London*], *by Richard Cotes,* 1647. 4°.* LT, O, LG, DC, DT; CH, CN, MH, TU, WF, Y.

—Two letters, the one, from the right honorable the Lord Major. 1647. *See title.*

—Letter from the Lord Major, aldermen & Common-Councel . . . to . . . Sir Tho: Fairfax. 1647. *See title.*

—Sir, you are desired to be at a court of Common Councell. [n.p., 1648.] *See title.*

2852 —An act and declaration of the Common Covncel . . . touching the late insurrection. *For Edward Husband,* April 14. 1648. 4°.* LT, LG, BC, MR; CH, CLC, CN, MH, WF.

2852A —Commune concilium tent' . . . [27 July 1648] . . . Forasmuch as this court did apprehend. [*London*], *by Richard Cotes,* 1648. brs. DT; MH.

2852B — —[Anr. ed.] —, 1648. brs. STEELE 2783. LT, HH; MH.

—At a generall meeting of the committee for arrears. [13 September.] [n.p., 1648.] *See title.*

2852C —In pursuance of the order of the honorable committee . . . [9 November 1648. Order for return of lands]. [*London,* 1648.] brs. LT.

—Letter from the Lord Major, aldermen, . . . in answer to a letter. 1648. *See title.*

—At a meeting of the committee of arrears. [11 December.] [n.p., 1648.] *See title.*

2852CA —Commune concilium tent. . . . [24 May 1649, repayment of debt]. [*London*], *by Richard Cotes,* [1649]. brs. O.

2852D —At a meeting of the committee for arrears, . . . [5 June]. [*London,* 1649.] brs. L.

2852E —Foot, Major. At a Common-Councel held . . . [20 August 1650]. It is ordered. [*London,* 1650.] brs. LT.

2852F —Directions of the Right Honourable the Lord Major, aldermen and commons . . . To the severall ministers . . . [16 February 1649/50. Poor relief]. [*London*], *by Richard Cotes,* [1650]. brs. MH.

—At a Common-Councell held in Guildhall . . . Aprill 24, 1655. [*London*], 1655. *See title.*

2852G —An act of Common-Councell made the eleventh day of September, . . . 1655. For the better avoiding. [*London*], *by James Flesher,* 1655. 4°.* LT, LG, OC, E; MH.

—At a Common Councell there held the two and twentieth day of August. [n.p., 1656.] *See* Gloucester, City of.

2852H —An act of Common-Councell made Oct. 6, 1646, . . . for reformation of sundry abuses. *By James Flesher,* 1656. 12°. L.

2852I —Tichborne, Mayor. At a Common Councell holden . . . [1 March 1656/7. Order for poor relief]. —, [1656/7]. brs. L.

2852J —A Common Councell holden . . . [8 July 1657. Order regarding markets]. [*London*], *by James Flesher,* [1657]. brs. LG.

2852JA —London, March 15. 1658. The Lord Mayor, Alderman, and Commons . . . [petition to Cromwell]. [*London,* 1658.] brs. CN.

2852K —An act of Common Councell, made 1 July. For the better rule . . . of the carrs. —, 1658. 4°.* LG.

2852L —Aleyn, Mayor. At a Common-Councel . . . [23 November 1659. Order for a fast day]. —, [1659]. brs. LT, O, LG; Y.

2852M — —[14 December 1659. Order for preserving the peace.] —, [1659]. brs. LT, O, LG; CH, MH, Y. (var.)

2852N — —[20 December 1659. Defense of mayor.] —, 1659. brs. LT, O, LG, CJ; CH, MH.

2852O —A Common Council holden . . . [29 December 1659. Report by Alderman Fowke]. [*London,* 1659.] brs. L, O, CJ. [=new E2902.]

2852P — —[Anr. ed.] [*London,* 1659.] brs. LT.

—True copy of the letter sent from the Lord Mayor . . . to . . . Moncke. 1659. *See title.*

—Two letters, the one, sent by the Lord Mayor. 1659. *See title.*

2852Q —Aleyn, Mayor. A Common-Councell holden . . . [1 May 1660. Order concerning the King's letter]. [*London*], *by James Flesher,* 1660. 4°.* L, O, LG, OC, DU, LSD, CD; CH, CN, MH, NU, TU, WF, Y.

2852R —The ansvver of the right honourable the Lord Mayor, aldermen, and Common-Council . . . to His Majesties . . . letter. *For Samuel Styles,* [1660]. 4°.* LT, LPR; NU, Y.

2852S —A Common-Councell holden . . . [21 May 1660. Restoration of King]. [*London*], *by James Flesher,* 1660. 4°.* C; CH, CLC, MH, NC, PL, WF. [=E2901.]

—City's remonstrance. 1661. *See title.*

2852T —Commune Concilium tentum . . . [17 October 1662. Addition to Newgate market]. [*London*, 1662.] brs. L.

2852U ——[20 October 1662. Act concerning the herb market.] *By James Flesher*, [1662]. brs. L.

2852V ——[23 May 1663] . . . An act for the translation of all persons that keep inns. [*London*, 1663.] brs. LG.

2852W —Robinson, Mayor. Commune Concilium tentum . . . [10 October 1663. Act for regulating traffic]. [*London*, 1663.] brs. L.

2852X —An act of Common Council [1551] concerning orphans. [*London*], *J. Flesher*, 1663. 8°. L.

2852Y —Commune Concilium . . . [21 June 1665. Act relating to "carrs"]. *William Godbid for the use of Christ's Hospital*, 1665. fol.* LG; WF.

2852Z —Commune Concilium tentum . . . [4 July 1665. Act regarding cloth]. [*London*], *by James Flesher*, 1665. fol.* LC.

2852ZA ——[21 March 1666/7. Rebuilding of London.] —, [1666/7]. fol.* STEELE 3488. L, O, C, LPR, HH.

2853 ——[29 April 1667. Act enlarging certain streets destroyed by fire.] —, [1667]. fol.* STEELE 3491. L, O, LG, HH, EN; CH.

2853A —Peake Mayor . . . [1 September 1668] . . . Whereas by an order of His Majesty . . . [for apprehending sellers of scandalous pamphlets]. —, [1668]. brs. L; CH.

2854 —An act for preventing and suppressing of fires. [15 November 1668.] *For Nath. Brook*, 1668. 4°.* L, LG, LNC, LSD, GH; CH, NN, OCI, TU, WF.

2854A —Turner Mayor . . . [26 January 1668] . . . This court having received . . . complaints from many . . . citizens . . . that frequent the burse Royal Exchange. *By James Flesher*, [1668/9]. fol. L.

2854B —An act of Common-Council for the better regulation of the courts of law. [*London*], *by James Flesher*, 1669. 4°.* LG; CH, WF.

2854C —Commune Concilium tentum . . . [24 March 1669] . . . An act appointing the exchange-hours. [*London*], *by Andrew Clark*, [1669]. brs. L, LG.

2854D —Whereas by an act of Common-Council the 4th of July, 1665 . . . it was enacted . . . that all . . . clothes . . . called Coventry . . . October, 11. 1670. [*London*, 1670.] brs. L.

2854E —Commune Concilium tentum . . . [27 October 1671] . . . An act for setling of lay-stalls. *By Andrew Clark*, 1671. fol. L.

2854F ——[27 October 1671] . . . An act for setling the standing of cars. —, 1671. brs. L.

2854G —Commune Concilium tent' . . . decimo tertio die Octobris, anno regni Eduardi sexti. [Act concerning orphans.] colop: [*London*], *by Andrew Clark*, 1671. 8°.* L, LG.

2854H —An act of Common Council [27 October 1671]: together with certain orders . . . touching the paving and cleansing the streets. [*London*], *by Andrew Clark*, 1671 [2]. 8°.* L, LG; MBP, WF.

2854I —Commune Concilium tentum . . . [5 September 1672] . . . An act for the settlement . . . of several publick markets. colop: —, 1672. fol.* L, LG.

2854J ——[11 October 1669] . . . An act for the better regulation of the courts of law of Guildhall. *By Andrew Clark*, 1672. brs. L.

2854K ——[23 October 1672] . . . An act for the weighing of goods. colop: [*London*], *by Andrew Clark*, 1672. fol.* LG.

2854L ——[21 February 1673/4] . . . An act for regulation of the brokers upon the Royal Exchange. [*London*], *by Andrew Clark*, [1674]. fol.* L, O, LG, OP.

2854M ——[17 September 1674] . . . An act for the settlement . . . of . . . publick markets. —, 1674. fol. L, LG.

—Proposals for subscription of money . . . reported to the . . . Lord Major. 1674. *See* Cardonel, Philip de.

—Proposals for increase of wealth by subscriptions. 1675. *See* Cardonel, Philip de.

2854N —Lawrence, Mayor. Com. Concil. tent. . . . [27 January 1664. Collection of acts concerning woodmongers]. [*London*, 1675?] 4°. L.

2855 Entry cancelled. *See* L2851O.

2856 Entry cancelled. *See* L2861H.

2856A —An act for preventing and suppressing of fires. [*London*], *by Andrew Clark*, 1676. 4°.* LG.

2856B —An act of Common-Council for the government of cars. [2 April 1677.] *By Andrew Clark*, 1677. fol.* L.

2856C —An act for preventing and suppressing of fires. —, 1677. 4°.* L, LG.

2857 —An act of Common-Council for regulation of Blackwell-Hall. *By Anne Godbid*, 1678. fol.* L, O.

2857A —An act of Common-Council . . . [1554-5] . . . for retrenching of the expences of the Lord Mayor. *For Fr. Smith*, 1680. fol.* LG, MR, SP; CH, CN, MH, WF, Y.

2857B —Commune Concilium tentum . . . [13 January 1680/1] . . . This day the members that serve. [*London*, 1681.] 8°.* OP.

2857C —A brief account of what pass'd at the Common Council . . . [13 May 1681]. colop: *For VValter Davis*, 1681. brs. L, O, LG, OC, HH; CH, CN, MH, PU, Y, AVP.

2857D —An act of Common-Council, for the government of Carrs . . . [15 October 1681.] *Printed for Christ-Hospital*, 1681. fol.* L, LUG.

2857E —Moore, Mayor. At a Common Council . . . [16 November 1681. Proposals for fire insurance]. [*London*, 1681.] brs. L, O, LG; Y.

—England's interest; or, the great. 1682. *See* Verney, Robert.

2857F —Prichard, mayor. Cur' special' tent' . . . [29 January 1682/3] . . . This court being . . . assembled to consider of some effectual course . . . for suppressing of all conventicles. [*London*], *by Samuel Roycroft*, [1683]. brs. LG.

2857G —An act of Common Council for the better regulation of hackney-coaches. [13 March 1683.] *By Samuel Roycroft*, 1683. fol.* L; IU.

2858 —An act of Common Council for regulating the election of sheriffs. [6 June 1683]. *By Samuel Roycroft*, 1683. fol.* L, O, LG, CS, DU, EN; CH, CN, WF.

2858A Entry cancelled. *See* L2857A.
—To the Kings most excellent Majesty, the humble petition of the Lord Mayor, aldermen. [2 July 1683.] 1683. *See title.*

2858B —Address of the Lord Mayor, aldermen, and commons . . . [2 July 1683, to the King]. *Edinburgh reprinted by the heir of Andrew Anderson*, 1683. brs. STEELE 3p 2545. ALDIS 2364.5. EN, ER.
—To His Highness the Prince of Orange. The humble address of. 1688. *See title.*

2858C —The address of the Lord Mayor, aldermen, and Common-Council . . . [8 March 1688/9, to the Lords]. colop: *By James Partridge, Matthew Gillyflower, and Samuel Heyrick*, 1688/9. brs. L, O, C, LG, HH; CH, MIU, PL, WF, V, Y. (var.)

2859 Entry cancelled. *See* L2857G.

2859A —The address of the Lord Mayor, Aldermen and Common-Council . . . [13 March 1688/9, to the Commons]. *For Joseph Watts*, 1689. brs. L, C, HH; CH, CLC, CSS, MIU, PL.

2859B ——[Anr. ed.] —, 1689. fol.* CH; MR.

2859C —Pilkington Mayor. Commune concil' tent . . . [10 March 1689/90. Vote of thanks to city M.P.'s]. [*London*], *by Samuel Roycroft*, [1689/90]. brs. L.

2859D —An act of Common Council for regulating the election of sheriffs . . . [6 June 1683]. *Reprinted by Samuel Roycroft*, 1690. fol.* WF.

2860 —Entry cancelled. *See* L2856B.

2860A —An act of Common Council for the settlement and well-ordering of publick markets . . . [17 September 1674]. [*London*], *by Samuel Roycroft*, 1690. fol.* L, LG; CH.

2861 —An act of Common Council, for the nomination of aldermen . . . [26 October 1692]. —, 1692. fol.* L, C.
—Right of the city of London. 1692/3. *See title.*

2861A —The address of the Lord Mayor, aldermen . . . August 17. 1693. [*London*], *by Edward Jones*, 1693. brs. HH; MH.

2861B —Com' Concil' tent' . . . [26 October 1694] . . . an act for licensing carts, to be used by the freemen, woodmongers or traders in fuel. colop: [*London*], *by Samuel Roycroft*, 1694. fol.* WF.

2861C —Com' Concil' tent' . . . [15 June 1694. Act relating to election of sheriffs]. colop: —, 1694. fol.* L, LG; CSS.

2861D ——[11 September 1694] . . . An act . . . for regulating the company of masons. [*London*], *by Samuel Roycroft*, 1694. fol.* L, LG.

2861E ——[11 September 1694] . . . An act . . . for regulating the company of plaisteerers. —, 1694. fol.* L, LG.

2861F ——[19 October 1694] . . . An act . . . for regulating the company of joyners and ceilers. colop: —, 1694. fol.* LG.

2861G ——[21 June 1695] . . . An act . . . for setling the methods of calling, adjourning and dissolving the common-halls. colop: —, 1695. fol.* LG.

2861H —Lane Mayor. An act of Common Council for lighting the streets . . . [25 October 1695]. *By Samuel Roycroft*, 1695. brs. L.

2861I —Houblon, mayor. Wednesday, [5 August 1696] . . . at a committee . . . held for the publick markets. [*London*], —, 1696. brs. LG.
—Copy of the report of the committee of Common Council. [n.p., 1696.] *See title.*
—Copy of an award referring to the public markets. 1697. *See title.*

2861J —An act of Common Council for the better regulation of weighing of goods . . . [18 November 1698]. [*London*], *by Samuel Roycroft*, 1698. fol.* L, LG; NC.

2861K —An act of Common Council for the better relief of the poor . . . [8 December 1698]. —, 1698. fol.* L, LG.

2861L —Com' Concil' tent' . . . [7 June 1700. Order to print two acts concerning election of sheriffs]. —, 1700. fol.* L, LG.

London. Common Hall. Account of the proceedings at Guild-hall . . . 24th. of June 1676. [n.p., 1676.] *See title.*
—Account of the proceedings at the Guild-Hall . . . September 12, 1679. [n.p., 1679.] *See title.*
—True account of the proceedings at the Common-hall . . . 24th of June. [n.p., 1680.] *See title.*
—Proceedings at the Guild-hall in London . . . July the 29th, 1680. [n.p., 1680.] *See title.*
—My lord, we the Commons of London, in Common-hall assembled. [October.] [n.p., 1680.] *See title.*
—Proceedings of the Common-hall of London the 24th of June, 1681. 1681. *See title.*
—Impartial account of the proceedings of the Common-hall . . . June 24 1682. 1682. *See title.*
—True account of the proceedings of the Common Hall. [24 June.] 1689. *See title.*
—At a Common-hall. July 5 1695. [n.p., 1695.] *See title.*
—London. The 29th day of September, 1696. This day the citizens being met. 1696. *See title.*

London. Corporation. Liberties, usages, and customes of the city of London. 1642. *See* Calthorp, *Sir* Henry.

2861M —The laws of the market. [*London*], *by James Flesher*, 1653. 8°. LG.

2861N ——[Same title.] —, 1668. 8°. L, LG.

2861O ——[Same title.] *By Andrew Clark*, 1677. 8°. L.

2861P —The order of my Lord Mayor, the aldermen, and sheriffes, for their meetinges and wearing of their apparell. *By J. Flesher*, 1655. 8°.* L.

2861Q ——[Same title.] [*London*], —, 1656. 8°.* L, LG.

2861R ——[Same title.] —, 1669. 8°. O.

2861S ——[Same title.] [*London*], *by Andrew Clark*, 1673. 8°. LG.

2861T ——[Same title.] [*London*], *by Samuel Roycroft*, 1680. 8°. LG.

2861U ——[Same title.] —, 1682. 8°.* L, LG.

2861V ——[Same title.] —, 1687. 8°. LG.

2861W ——[Same title.] —, 1692. 8°.* L, LG; CH, WF.

2861X ——[Same title.] —, 1696. 8°.* L.

2861Y ——[Same title.] —, 1700. 8°.* L.

——Lawes, orders, and statutes . . . for the citizens of London. 1662. See title.

2861Z —The answer on behalf of the city of London, to the reasons of the County of Middlesex. [Concerning abatement of assessments.] [London, 1675?] brs. LUG.

——Lex Londinensis. 1680. See title.

——Royal charter of confirmation. [1680.] See title.

2862 Entry cancelled. See L2851P.

2862A Entry cancelled. See L2860A.

2863 Entry cancelled. See L2851Q.

2864 Entry cancelled. See L2852G.

2864A **London. Court of Aldermen.** A warrant sent from the Lord Maior and aldermen, to all the trained bands. Septemb. 23. For Francis Coules, 1642. 4°.* LT, LG; Y.

2864B —Orders formerly conceived and agreed to be published by the Lord Major. By Richard Cotes, 1646. 4°.* LT, DT; CN, CSS, WF.

2864C —May 11. 1647. Orders set dovvne by the court of Lord Major and aldermen . . . concerning the rates of carriages. [London, 1647.] brs. MH.

2864D —Ten severall orders to be put in execution by the Lord Major. By Bernard Alsop, 1647. 4°.* LT, LG, DT; CN, NC, NP.

——Articles of the charge of the VVardmote enquest. [1649.] See title.

2864E —Rules, directions, and by-laws, devised . . . for regulation of hackney coachmen. colop: [London], by James Flesher, [1654. cap., fol.* LT, O; CH, MH. (var.)

2864F —Pack, mayor . . . [2 January 1654/5] . . . Ordered, that such of the rules . . . made by this court . . . for regulation of hackney coachmen. colop: —, 1655. 4°. LG, LPR.

2864FA —February 15. 1654. Orders set down by the court of Lord Mayor and Aldermen . . . concerning the rates of carriages with carrs. [London], by James Flesher, [1655]. brs. O.

2864G —Tichborne, maior . . . [9 June 1657. Order preventing the holding of a vegetable market]. [London], by James Flesher, [1657]. brs. LG.

——Chiverton, Mayor. Tuesday, the eighth day of December, 1657. An order. [1657.] See Chiverton, Sir Richard.

2864H —Chiverton mayor . . . 4th of February 1657. My Lord Mayor and this Court . . . taking into consideration the wants . . . of the . . . poore. [London], by James Flesher, [1657/8]. brs. LG, EN.

2864I —The orders and directions of the right honourable the Lord Mayor . . . plague. [London], for George Horton, [1665]. 4°.* LP, LWL.

2864J —Orders conceived and published by the Lord Major . . . concerning the . . . plague. [London], by James Flesher, [1665]. 4°.* L, O, LG, LWL, OC; CH, MIU, WF, Y, ZDU.

2864K —Turner, mayor . . . [25 February 1668. Report on the petition of poor women]. [London, 1668.] brs. L.

2864L —Peake Mayor . . . [28 April 1668] . . . This day the President. [Orders to the governors of Christs-hospital.] [London, 1668.] fol.* L, LG.

2864M —Ford. Mayor . . . [17 January 1670/1] . . . Whereas the fish-market at Billingsgate. [London], by Andrew Clark, [1671]. brs. LG.

2864N —Ford Mayor . . . [7 September 1671] . . . Whereas this court having received . . . complaints of the . . . demands made by water-men. By Andrew Clark, 1671. brs. L.

2864O —Hanson maior . . . [6 April 1673] . . . Whereas in and by the additional act of Parliament . . . [order for removal of temporary shops built after the fire]. [London], —, [1673]. brs. LG.

2864P —Hooker Maior . . . [17 March 1673/4] . . . This court taking into their consideration . . . [order to remove sheds erected since the fire]. —, [1674]. brs. L, LG.

——At the committee appointed to consider the rates of wharfage. [1674.] See title.

2864Q —By the Mayor. The right honourable the Lord Mayor . . . minding to discover . . . those manifold corruptions. [17 November 1676.] [London], by Andrew Clark, 1676. brs. LG; MH.

——Account of the proceedings at the Guild-hall. [n.p., 1679.] See title.

2864R —Edwards Mayor . . . [7 August 1679] . . . Whereas this city and liberties . . . are much pestered with . . . hawkers. [London], by Samuel Roycroft, [1679]. brs. WCL.

2864S —Clayton, Mayor . . . [16 September 1680] . . . This court now considering . . . [order concerning official processions]. —, 1680. brs. L, LG; MH.

2864T —Ward, mayor . . . [20 October 1681] . . . For prevention of many incumbrances . . . [order against disorderly standing cars]. [London, 1681.] brs. LG.

2864U —By the Lord Mayor and the Court of Aldermen. Whereas an indignity. [27 January 1681/2.] [London], S. Roycroft, [1681/2]. brs. STEELE 3732. L, HH.

——Brief collection out of the records. [n.p.], 1682. See title.

2864V —Pritchard, Mayor . . . [21 November 1682] . . . Whereas this city . . . [order against selling books in the streets]. [London], by Samuel Roycroft, 1682. brs. LG.

2864W —Short instructions for the executors . . . securing orphans portions. —, 1682. 8°. L, LG.

2864X —Tulse Mayor . . . [21 October 1684] . . . It is ordered . . . [servants not to be held without testimonials]. —, [1684]. brs. L, HH; CH.

2864Y —Shorter mayor . . . [27 March 1688] . . . Whereas the right honourable . . . [order concerning the paving of streets]. —, [1688]. brs. L, LG.

——Order of the hospitalls of K. Henry the viijth. [n.p.], 1557 [i.e., 169–?]. See title.

——Case of the city of London. In reference to the debt. 1691. See title.

2865 Entry cancelled. See L2852K.

2865A —Pilkington, Mayor. [6 July 1691. Order enforcing rules for hackney coaches.] *Samuel Roycroft*, 1691. brs. L.

2865B —Pilkington mayor . . . [30 July 1691] . . . Upon the humble petition . . . [order concerning St. Bartholomew Fair]. *By Samuel Roycroft*, [1691]. brs. L.

2865C —Stamp Mayor . . . [10 November 1691] . . . This court having received frequent complaints of . . . foreign-buying. [*London*], *by S. Roycroft*, [1691]. brs. L, LG, OP; CH, MH.

2865D —Stamp mayor . . . [13 August 1692] . . . This court considering . . . [order requiring certain officers to attend the Lord Mayor and aldermen]. [*London*], *by Samuel Roycroft*, 1692. brs. L, LG.

2865E —Fleet mayor . . . [1 December 1692] . . . This court this day taking notice . . . [order forbidding bets on outcome of the war]. —, 1692. brs. LG; MH.

2865F —Edwin mayor . . . [12 May 1698] . . . This day an order and report . . . touching several duties . . . at Billingsgate, was presented. [*London*, 1698.] brs. LG.

2865G —Child, mayor . . . [15 June 1699] . . . Whereas by the ancient laws . . . [order against unmarked weights]. [*London*], *by Samuel Roycroft*, 1699. brs. LG.

2865H —Levett mayor . . . [14 December 1699] . . . Whereas notwithstanding several good . . . orders . . . for the prevention of . . . abuses in the fishmarket. —, 1699. brs. L, LG; MH.

2865I —Levett, mayor . . . [25 June 1700] . . . The King's most excellent Majesty . . . as also the . . . Parliament, having frequently express'd their great sense of the deplorable increase of prophaneness. —, 1700. brs. L, O, LG; MH, MIU.

2865J —Levett Mayor . . . [10 October 1700] . . . Upon reading the humble petition . . . [order that Exchange brokers should not do business in Exchange Alley]. —, 1700. brs. L, LG.

2865K **London.** *Deputy Lieutenants.* His Majesties Lieutenants for the City of London . . . do will and require . . . [3 November 1662, order to draw up roll of militias]. [*London*, 1662.] brs. LPR.

2865L —To the end you may be in better capacity . . . [4 November 1662, suppression of insurrections]. [*London*, 1662.] brs. LPR.

2866 Entry cancelled. *See* L2852Y.

2867 Entry cancelled. *See* L2858B.

2868 Entry cancelled. *See* L2858C.

2868A Entry cancelled. *See* L2859A.

2869 Entry cancelled. *See* L2851S.

2870 Entry cancelled. *See* L2852R.

2871 Entry cancelled. *See* L2852E.

2872 Entry cancelled. *See* L2852M.

2873 Entry cancelled. *See* L2852N.

2874 Entry cancelled. *See* L2852L.

2875 Entry cancelled.
—At a Common Councell there held. [n.p., 1656.] *See* Gloucester, City of.

2876 Entry cancelled. *See* L2877C.

2877 Entry cancelled. *See* L2851B.

2877A **London. Governors for the Poor.** Severall propositions tendered by the corporation for the imploying the poor. [18 September 1650.] *By Richard Cotes*, 1650. brs. CH.

2877B —. . . The report of the governours of the corporation for imploying . . . the poor. [*London*], *by James Flesher*, 1655. brs. L; MH.
—[10 April 1655.] A true report of the great number. [n.p., 1655.] *See title*.

2877C —At a court held by the . . . Lord Mayor president, and the rest of the governors . . . the 6th of February. —, 1655[6]. brs. LT, LG.
—The 7 of Aprill 1658. A true report of the president and governours of the corporation for the poore. [n.p., 1658.] *See title*.

2878 —At a court of the right honourable the president and governors for the poor. [*London*, 1699] brs. L.
London. Lord Mayor. [Gurney, *Sir* Richard.] Lord Maior of Londons letter to the King . . . Iune 22. [n.p., 1642.] *See* Gurney, *Sir* Richard.

2878A —[Pennington, *Sir* Isaac.] Novemb. 12. 1642. You are to give notice in your pulpit. [Order directing London ministers to announce instructions for soldiers.] [*London*, 1642.] brs. LG.

2878B —[–] Februar. 18. 1642. Whereas the Lords and Commons . . . made request . . . for the loane. [*London*, 1643.] brs. LT, LG; MH.

2878C —[–] April 15. 1643. [Order to London ministers to support Parliament's army.] [*London*, 1643.] brs. LG.

2878D —[–] By the Mayor. Whereas the Lords Day. [Proclamation regulating sale of milk on sabbath. 19 June 1643.] [*London*, 1643.] brs. LT; MH.

2878E —[Wollaston, *Sir* John.] By the Mayor. To the Aldermen of the ward of [blank]. [Order for proper observance of the sabbath. 2 November 1643.] *By Richard Cotes*, [1643]. brs. LT; MH.

2878F —[–] By the mayor. To every minister within . . . London . . . The extraordinary blessing of God upon the forces . . . of Sir William Waller. [30 March 1644.] [*London*], —, [1644]. brs. MH.

2879 Entry cancelled. *See* L2851E.

2880 Entry cancelled. *See* L2887A.

2881 Entry cancelled. *See* L2887B.

2882 Entry cancelled. *See* L2857C.

2882A Entry cancelled. *See* L2851A.

2882B —[Wollaston, *Sir* John.] By the Major. A proclamation for the bringing into the port of London, . . . fewell. [27 June 1644.] [*London*], *by Richard Cotes*, [1644]. brs. LT; Y.

2882C —[Atkins, *Sir* Thomas.] 15. Iune, 1645. It is desired that all ministers. [Order for a thanksgiving prayer.] [*London*, 1645.] brs. LT.
—[–] By the Mayor. Whereas the slow comming in of the moneys. [20 June 1645.] 1645. *See* Atkin, Thomas.
—[Adams, *Sir* Thomas.] The Lord Mayor's farewell. 1646. *See title*.

2882D —[Warner, *Sir* John.] By the Major. Forasmuch as it is conceived . . . that the city . . . is in great danger . . . 25 of Aprill, 1648. [*London*], *by Richard Cotes*, [1648]. brs. L; CH, MH.

2882E —[–] By the Major. [Order for the defense of the city. 29 April 1648.] *By Richard Cotes*, 1648. brs. L.

2882F —[–] By the Major. Forasmuch as to the court of Common-Councell. [Order concerning the trained bands. 24 May 1648.] [*London*], —, 1648. brs. STEELE 2766. LT, O, LG, HH.

2882G —[–] By the Major. Forasmuch as notwithstanding divers good acts. [Order to observe properly the Lord's Day. 8 August 1648.] *By Richard Cotes*, [1648]. brs. LT.

2882H —[–] By the Major. Whereas by severall orders. [Collection of arrears for the army. 29 August 1648.] —, 1648. brs. LT.

2882I —[–] By the Major. Whereas by a precept. [Collection of arrears for the army. 4 September 1648.] —, 1648. brs. LT.

2882J —[Reynardson, *Sir* Abraham.] By the Major. [Order concerning assessments for the army. 2 December 1648.] —, 1648. brs. LT.

2882K —[–] By the Major. [Instructions to the aldermen. 12 December 1648.] —, [1648]. fol. LT.

2882L —[–] By the Major. To the aldermen of the ward of [blank]. Whereas . . . [order for the apprehension of rogues. 22 March 1649]. [*London*], 1649. brs. LT.

2883 —[Andrewes, Thomas.] By the Mayor. Whereas by an act of Parliament. [Order against unlicensed books. 9 October 1649.] [*London*], *by Richard Cotes*, 1649. brs. LT; NU.

2883A Entry cancelled. *See* L2885U.

2883B —[Andrewes, Thomas.] By the Mayor. [Order for better observance of the Lord's Day.] [*London*], *by Richard Cotes*, 1649. brs. LG.

2883C —[Foote, Thomas.] By the Major. We charge and command you, that upon S. Thomas day. colop: *Printed at London, by Richard Cotes*, [1649]. fol.* LT.

2883D —[–] By the Major. We charge and command you, that upon the twenty first. [Instructions to the aldermen. 21 December 1649.] colop: —, [1649]. fol.* LT.

2883E —[Kendrick, *Sir* John.] By the Major: Whereas divers good laws . . . have been made . . . to prevent the prophanation of the Lords day. [13 November 1651.] *By Richard Cotes*, 1651. brs. L.

2883F —[Fowke, *Sir* John.] Whereas the Lord Generall hath received a message. [Notice to collect old linen for soldiers. 6 August 1653.] [*London*, 1653.] brs. LT.

2883FA —[Vyner, Thomas.] By the Mayor. To the alderman of the ward of [blank]. Whereas by an ordinance. [For improving streets. 25 April 1654.] [*London*], *by James Flesher*, [1654]. brs. O.

2883G —[–] By the Mayor. To the alderman of the ward of [blank]. Whereas divers good laws . . . have been made for the due observation of the Lords day. [15 May 1654.] *By James Flesher*, [1654]. brs. L, O.

2883GA —[–] By the Mayor. To the alderman of the ward of [blank]. Whereas according to the directions. [Street repair. 28 June 1654.] [*London*], *by James Flesher*, [1654].

2883H —[–] By the Mayor. To the alderman of the ward of [blank]. [Order concerning night watches. 7 November 1654.] [*London*, 1654.] brs. LT.

2883I —[Pack, *Sir* Christopher.] By the Mayor. Whereas by neglect. *By James Flesher*, [1655]. brs. LT, CM.

2883J —[Dethick, John.] By the Mayor. Whereas by neglect of executing good lawes . . . against rogues. [23 January 1655/6.] [*London*], —, [1656]. brs. L, LG.

2883K —[–] By the Mayor. Whereas by oft and sad experience. [Order for better observance of Lord's Day. 18 March 1656.] —, [1656]. brs. L, LG.

2883L —[Tichborne, *Sir* Robert.] London &c. Forasmuch as notwithstanding divers good acts. [Order for better observance of the Lord's Day. 12 November 1656.] [*London*, 1656.] brs. LT.

2883M —[–] Tichborne, Mayor . . . [26 May 1657]. Whereas the late ordinances touching hackney coaches. [*London*], *by James Flesher*, [1657]. brs. LG.

2883N —[–] By the Mayor. To the alderman of the ward of [blank]. Whereas by an act of Parliament. [Order concerning poor relief. 18 June 1657.] *By James Flesher*, [1657]. [The imprint date is altered in ink to 1658.] brs. L.

2883O —[–] By the Maior. To the alderman of the ward of [blank] or to his deputie. Whereas the Common Councell. [Order concerning poor relief. 5 August 1657.] —, [1657]. brs. L.

2883P —[Chiverton, Richard.] By the Mayor. To the alderman of the ward of [blank]. Whereas oftentimes heretofore. [Order to punish vagrants. 14 November 1657.] —, [1657]. brs. L.

2883Q —[Ireton, *Sir* John.] By the Mayor. To the alderman of the ward of [blank]. Whereas oftentimes heretofore. [Order concerning vagrants. 15 November 1658.] —, [1658]. brs. L.

2883R —By the Mayor. To the alderman of the ward of [blank]. [Precept for holding the wardmote on St. Thomas's day.] [*London*], —, [166–?]. brs. LG.

2884 Entry cancelled. *See* L2885C.

2884A Entry cancelled. *See* L2886D.
       —[Browne, *Sir* Richard.] By the mayor. Whereas I have this day received an order. [Poor relief.] [n.p., 1661.] *See* Browne, *Sir* Richard, lord mayor.

2885 —[–] By the Mayor. Whereas by an ancient law . . . it is provided, that no fairs . . . be kept in church-yards. [19 October 1661.] [*London*], *by James Flesher*, [1661]. brs. L, O.

2885A Entry cancelled. *See* L2886G.

2885B —[Frederick, *Sir* John.] By the Mayor. [Order against using St. Paul's churchyard as a market place. 22 November 1661.] *By James Flesher*, [1661]. brs. L.

2885C —[–] By the Mayor. To the alderman of the ward of [blank]. Whereas by a late act of Parliament, for repairing . . . sewers. [22 July 1662.] —, [1662]. brs. L, O.

2885D —[–] By the Mayor. Whereas for remedies of many . . . dangers. [22 October 1662.] —, [1662]. brs. L.

2885E —[Robinson, *Sir* John.] By the Mayor. Whereas the unruly and meaner sort of people . . . [order to control hackney coachmen, 3 March 1662/3]. [*London*], —, [1662/3]. brs. LPR.

—[Bateman, *Sir* Anthony.] By the Mayor. Whereas at a meeting. [Order regulating price of sea-coals. 24 March 1664.] [n.p., 1664.] *See* Bateman, *Sir* Anthony.

2885F —[Lawrence, *Sir* John.] By the Mayor. Whereas it hath pleased God. [Order for preventing spread of plague.] *By James Flesher*, [1665.] brs. L.

2885G —[–] By the Mayor. To the alderman of the ward of [blank]. As a farther means . . . to obviate the increase of the plague. [4 July 1665.] —, [1665]. brs. L.

2885H —[–] By the Mayor. To the alderman of the ward of [blank]. Whereas my self and my brethen [sic] . . . have made choice of two able . . . physicians. [13 July 1665.] —, [1665]. brs. L.

2885I —[–] By the Mayor. His Majesty taking notice of the vast sums. [Order to encourage home manufactures. 27 October 1665.] —, [1665]. brs. L.

2885J —[Bludworth, *Sir* Thomas.] By the Mayor. Whereas in order to the rebuilding of the city. [10 October 1666.] [*London*], —, [1666]. brs. STEELE 3477. L, LG, HH.

2885K —By the Mayor. To all constables. [Order to apprehend persons defacing proclamations.] [*London*, 1667?] brs. LG.

2885L —[Turner, *Sir* William.] By the Mayor. The right honourable the Lord Mayor, considering how far the evil temper . . . hath prevailed. [11 November 1668.] *By James Flesher*, [1668]. brs. L.

2885M —[–] By the mayor . . . [9 March 1668] . . . It is thought fit . . . that in the appointment of appraisers. [*London*, 1668.] brs. MH.

2885N —[Starling, *Sir* Samuel.] By the Mayor. The right honourable the Lord Mayor . . . remembering the many . . . grievous judgements. [Order against cursing. 18 November 1669.] *By James Flesher*, [1669]. brs. L.

2885O —By the Mayor. To the alderman of the [blank] ward. We charge and command you . . . [form for calling wardmotes]. [*London*, 1670?] brs. LPR.

2885P —[Ford, *Sir* Richard.] By the Mayor. Whereas several notorious riots. [6 June 1671.] *By Andrew Clark*, [1671]. brs. OP.

2885Q —[–] By the Maior. The right honourable the Lord Maior, minding . . . to discover . . . corruptions. [7 November 1671.] *By Andrew Clark*, 1671. fol. L.

2885R —[Hanson, *Sir* Robert.] By the Maior. The right honourable the Lord Maior . . . doth . . . think it fit to . . . declare. [Order to observe the laws. 23 December 1672.] [*London*], —, 1672. brs. L, O, LG; MH.

2885S —[Hooker, *Sir* William.] By the Maior. Whereas divers persons rudely disposed. [Order to all persons to behave themselves in an orderly manner. 20 March 1673.] —, [1673]. brs. LG.

2885T —[–] By the Maior. The right honourable the Lord Maior deeply weighing. [Order for precautions on the watch because of street outrages. 10 March 1673/4.] —, [1673/4]. brs. LG.

2885U —[–] By the Maior. Whereas divers rude and disordered young-men . . . do . . . throw about squibs. [3 November 1674.] —, 1674. brs. L, LG, OP; CLC, CN, MH.

—[Davies, *Sir* Thomas.] By the Mayor. [17 November 1676.] 1676. *See* Davies, *Sir* Thomas.

—[–] By the Mayor. [7 December 1676.] [*London*], 1676. *See* Davies, *Sir* Thomas.

2885V —[–] By the Mayor. The right honourable the Lord Mayor . . . taking especial notice of the inordinate liberty now used by vagrants. [13 October 1676.] [*London*], *by Andrew Clark*, [1676]. brs. LG.

2885W —[Clayton, *Sir* Robert.] By the Major. The right honourable the Lord Major having taken into his serious consideration the many dreadful afflictions. [Order against drunkenness. 29 November 1679.] colop: [*London*], *by Samuel Roycroft*, 1679. brs. L, O, LG; CH, MH, NC, WF.

2885X —[–] By the mayor. The right honourable the Lord Mayor (by and with the advice of the aldermen . . .) doth hereby . . . declare. [Order to obey laws. 31 January 1679/80.] [*London*], *by Samuel Roycroft*, 1679. brs. LG; MH.

—[–] By the Mayor. [To] the alderman of the ward of [blank]. Whereas the night watches. [23 March 1680.] [n.p.], 1680. *See* Clayton, *Sir* Robert.

—[–] By the Mayor. Whereas it appears. [Order against riotous assemblies. 30 March 1680.] [n.p., 1680.] *See* Clayton, *Sir* Robert.

—[–] By the Major. To the alderman of the ward of [blank]. [Order to punish vagrants. 15 June 1680.] [n.p.], 1680. *See* Clayton, *Sir* Robert.

2885Y —[Ward, *Sir* Patience.] By the Mayor. Whereas by the laws. [Order to seize all billets. 2 April 1681.] [*London*], *by Samuel Roycroft*, 1681. brs. L, LG.

2885Z —[–] By the Mayor. To the alderman of the ward of [blank]. Whereas among the many enormities. [Observance of the Lord's Day. 2 November 1681.] —, 1681. brs. O, LG; CH, MH.

2886   Entry cancelled.
—By the right worshipful the mayor and aldermen. These are to give notice. Bristol, 1696. *See* These are to give notice.

2886A Entry cancelled. *See* L2851N.

2886B —By the Mayor. To the alderman of the ward of [blank]. [Proclamation forbidding bonfires and fireworks.] [*London*, 1682?] brs. LG.

2886C —[Moore, *Sir* John.] By the Mayor. Whereas I have received. *By Samuel Roycroft*, 1682. brs. L.

2886D —[–] By the Mayor. To the alderman of the ward of [blank]. Whereas the last Lords Day there were great tumults. [20 June 1682.] colop: [*London*], —, 1682. brs. L, O, LG, LPR, OP; CH, MH.

2886E —[Pritchard, *Sir* William.] By the Mayor. To the alderman of the ward of [blank]. [Order to prevent tumults on holidays. 14 November 1682.] *By Samuel Roycroft,* 1682. brs. L.

2886F —[–] By the Mayor. To the alderman of the ward of [blank]. Whereas by the laws. [Order prohibting drinking in taverns on the Lord's Day. 15 February 1683.] [*London*], —, [1683]. brs. L, O, LG; MH.

2886G —[Tulse, *Sir* Henry.] By the Mayor. Whereas the Lord Mayor and aldermen. [Suppression of conventicles. 15 January 1683/4.] —, [1683]. brs. O, LG, OC; CH, CN, MH, SE, Y.

2886H —[–] By the Mayor. To the alderman of the ward of [blank]. [Order against throwing squibs. 25 October 1684.] —, 1684. brs. L, LG.

2886I —[Jeffrey, *Sir* Robert.] By the Mayor. To the alderman of the ward of [blank]. [Order prohibiting tippling in victualling-houses. 9 February 1685/6.] —, [1686]. brs. L.

2886J —[Peake, *Sir* John.] By the Mayor. To the ward of [blank]. Whereas divers good laws. [Order to punish vagrants. 15 March 1686/7.] —, [1687]. brs. LG.

2886K —[–] By the Maior. To the alderman of the ward of [blank]. Whereas divers good laws. [Order against profanation of the Lord's Day. 8 November 1687.] [*London*, 1687.] fol.* L, LG, OP.

2886L —[–] —[Anr. ed.] colop: *By S. Roycroft,* 1687. fol.* CH.

2886M —[Pilkington, *Sir* Thomas.] By the Mayor. To the alderman of the ward of [blank]. [Proclamation forbidding tumultuous meetings on pretence of petitioning Parliament. 3 February 1688/9.] [*London*], *by Samuel Roycroft,* [1689]. brs. L, C, LG.

2886N —[–] By the Maior. To the alderman of the ward of [blank]. Whereas divers good laws . . . the Prince of Orange. [3 February 1688/9.] colop: *By Samuel Roycroft,* [1689]. cap. fol.* L.

2886O —[–] By the Mayor. To the alderman of the ward of [blank]. Whereas I lately recommended . . . the strict execution of the laws for . . . the Lord's day. [19 November 1689.] [*London*], *by Samuel Roycroft,* 1689. brs. L, O, LG.

2886P —[–] By the Mayor. To the alderman of the ward of [blank]. We charge. [Order concerning the Wardmote. 15 December 1689.] —, 1689. fol.* L.

2886Q —[–] By the Mayor. To the alderman of the ward of [blank]. Whereas the frequenting and tipling in taverns. [*London*], —, 1669. brs. LG. [Date altered in ink to 1689.]

2886R —Lane, Mayor. The right honourable the Lord Mayor having a deep sense of the duty . . . for the suppression of prophaneness. —, 1694. brs. L, O, LG, OP; MH.

2886S —By the Mayor. [Order to decorate houses for the King's return.] —, 1697. brs. LG.

     —[Clarke, *Sir* Edward.] By the Mayor. To the alderman of the ward of [blank]. [Order against throwing fireworks. 13 October 1697.] [n.p.], 1697. *See* Clarke, *Sir* Edward.

2886T —Child. Mayor. Forasmuch as the general corruption. [1 March 1698/9.] [*London*], *by Samuel Roycroft,* 1698[9]. brs. LG.

2887   Entry cancelled. *See* L2852Q.

     London. Sessions. London ss. Ad deliberationem Gaolæ. [16 April 1645. Order concerning city watches.] [1645.] *See* Ad deliberationem.

2887A —At the general quarter-sessions of the publick peace holden . . . [12 January 1652/3. Order fixing the price of coal and wood]. [*London*], *by James Flesher,* [1653]. brs. LT; Y.

2887B —At the generall sessions of the publike peace holden . . . [16 August 1654. Order regulating ale-houses]. [*London,* 1654.] brs. LT.

2887C —Whereas at the open generall quarter sessions of the publick peace holden . . . [23 April 1655. Order regulating prices and wages]. colop: [*London*], *by James Flesher,* [1655]. fol.* LT, LUG.

2887D —London ss. At the generall quarter sessions of the publick peace holden . . . [8 April 1657]. *By James Flesher,* [1657]. brs. L.

2887E —London ss. At the generall quarter sessions holden . . . [8 April 1657. Order licensing ale-houses]. [*London,* 1657.] brs. L.

2887F —[A table of rates for carriage of all commodities within London.] [*London*], *by James Flesher,* [166–?]. brs. LG (impf.).

2887FA —London ss. Whereas by the laws . . . all private meetings and unlawfull assemblies are prohibited . . . [6 November 1662]. [*London,* 1662.] brs. LPR.

2887G —At a meeting of the Lord Mayor and others His Majesties Justices of the Peace for . . . London . . . Middlesex . . . Surrey . . . [20 March 1664. Order regulating coal prices]. *By James Flesher,* [1664]. brs. L.

2887H —Ad session' Oier et Terminer . . . tent' . . . [17 June 1667. Order for prevention of disorders among carmen]. [*London,* 1667.] brs. L.

2887I —London ss. Ad general quarterial' session' pacis . . . [16 October 1672] . . . Whereas daily complaints are made . . . of the excessive rates demanded by . . . carmen. *By Andrew Clark,* [1672]. brs. L.

2887J ——[Same title. 15 October 1673.] —, 1673. brs. L.

     —London ss. Ad generalem quarterial sessionem . . . [21 October 1677. Order fixing rates for horsemeat]. [n.p.], 1677. *See* Ad generalem.

2887K —Anno vicesimo primo Jacobi regis, &c. An act to prevent the destroying and murthering of bastard children. Whereas many lewd women. [*London*], *by Samuel Roycroft,* 1680. brs. LG.

2887L —At the general sessions of the peace . . . [31 August 1681. Charging N. Thompson, B. Tooke, and J. Brome with seditious publications]. colop: *For Rich. Janeway,* 1681. brs. CH, MH, WF.

2887M —London ss. Ad session' oyer et terminer et general' quarterial' session' pacis . . . [13–25 October 1682. Order concerning ale-houses]. [*London*], *by Samuel Roycroft,* [1682]. brs. L, O, LG.

2887N —London ss. Be it remembered that Robert Sawyer. [*London*, 1682.] brs. CS.

28870 —London ss. Ad general' quarterial' session' pacis . . . [11 October 1683] . . . Whereas daily complaints are made by merchants. [Rates for car-men.] *By William Godbid*, [1683]. brs. L.

2887P —Lane, mayor. London ss. Ad generalem session' pacis . . . [8 May 1695. Order concerning public houses]. [*London*], *by Samuel Roycroft*, brs. L, LG; MH.

2887Q —Abney mayor. Ad general quarterial' session' . . . Whereas many murders. —, 1700. brs. L.

2888–9 Entries cancelled.
—Royal charter of confirmation. [1680.] *See title*.
London almanack. 1673. *See* Almanacs.

2889A London and England triumphant. *For F. Grove*, [1660]. brs. EUING 167. GU.

2890 The London bully, or the prodigal son. *By Hen. Clark, for Tho. Malthus*, 1683. 12°. T.C.II 28. O.

2891 Entry cancelled.
London c — ds. 1682. *See* London cuckolds.

2891A London. Cargoe of the Martha arrived . . . 25th. of September, 1696. [*London*, 1696?] brs. MH.

2892 London, cargoe, of the Rochester, arrived . . . 21th . . . of October, 1689. [*London*, 1689.] brs. L.

2893 The London chaunticleres. *For Simon Miller*, 1659. 4°.* L, O, LVD, OW; CH, IU, LC, WF, Y.

2894 The London cuckold. [*London*], *printed J. Back* [*sic*], [1688]. brs. L, O, CM, HH; MH.

2894A The London cuckolds. colop: *For C. Tebrooke*, 1682. brs. O, MC; CH, MH.

2895 The London damsels fate. [*London*], *for P. Brooksby*, [1672–95]. brs. O, HH; MH.
London drollery. 1673. *See* Hickes, William.

2896 The London intelligence being a full and true account. [*London*, 1697.] brs. L.

2897 London jests: or, a collection. *For Dorman Newman.* 1684. 12°. T.C.II 76. L.

2897A —[Anr. ed.] —, 1685. 12°. WF.

2897B The London jilt. *For Hen. Rhodes*, 1683. 12°. T.C.II 5. MH.

2897C —Second part. —, 1683. 12°. MH.

2898 The London jilts lamentation. [*London*], *for J. Deacon*, [1685–88]. brs. HH.
London, King Charles his Augusta, 1648. *See* Davenant, *Sir* William.

2899 The London ladies vindication of top-knots. [*London*], *for P. Brooksby, J. Deacon, J. Blare, J. Back*, [1688–92]. brs. L, CM, HH.

2900 The London lads lamentation to Cupid. [*London*], *for I. Back*, [1685–88]. brs. L, O, CM, HH, GU; MH.

2901 The London lasses folly. [*London*], *for C. Dennisson*, [1685]. brs. CM.

2902 The London lasses hue-and-cry. [*London*], *for P. Brooksby, J. Deacon, J. Blare, and J. Back*, [1685–92]. brs. L, HH; MH, Y.

2903 The London lasses lamentation. [*London*], *for P. Brooksby, J. Deacon, J. Blare, and J. Back*, [1685–92]. brs. L, O, CM, HH.

2904 Entry cancelled. Same as previous entry.

2905 The London-libertine. *For J. Science*, [1690?]. brs. L, CM, HH.
London-master. Dublin, 1694. *See* Orpen, Richard.

2905A The London-ministers legacy . . . farewel-sermons. Second edition. [*London*], 1662. 8°. L.

2906 The London printers lamentation. [*London*, 1660.] cap., 4°.* LT, LLP.

2907 The London prodigal. *By J. W. for R. C.*, 1673. brs. L.

2908 The London-spaw advertisement. [*London*, 1685.] brs. L.

2909 The London taylors misfortune. [*London*], *for J. Back*, [1685–88]. brs. O, HH.

2909A London, the fourth of March, 1689. Pol'd for members. [*London*, 1689.] brs. L, C.

2910 A London Tory vying in cruelty. colop: *For Ellis Brand*, 1691. brs. L.

2911 London undone. *By E. C. for H. Eversden, and H. Brome*, 1666. brs. L.

2912 The London vocabulary. *By P. Toolsey for H. Walwyn*, [1700?]. 12°. L, O.

2912A The Londoner's answer to downright Dick. [*London*], *for J. Black*, [1685–88]. brs. CM.

2912B The Londoners lamentation. *For J. Clark*, [1666]. brs. EUING 170. GU.

2913 The Londoners last warning. [*London*, 1659.] cap., 4°.* LT, O; CH, MH.

2914 The Londoners petition. To the Right Honorable the Lords and Commons. *For Adam Bell*, [1642]. brs. STEELE 2329. LT; MH.

2915 London's account: or. [*London*], *imprinted*, 1647. 4°.* LT, O, C, LG, LIU; CH, CN, MH, NU, WF, Y. (var.)

2916 Londons alacritie. [*London*], *for Thomas Lambert*, 1643. brs. L.

2917 Londons allarum; or, England toss'd in a blanket. [*London*], *for Tom-tell-truth*, [1659]. cap., 4°.* L, MR; CH, WF.

2918 Londons allarum: or, the great and bloody plot. *For G. Horton*, 1661. 4°.* C; CN, WF.

2919 Londons ancient priviledges unvailed. [*London*, 1648.] brs. LT.
Londons charitie. 1649. *See* Hartlib, Samuel.
Londons choice. [n.p., 1679.] *See* E., E.

2920 London's complaint against Oxford. 1666. brs. MADAN 2734*. L.

2921 Londons complaint and lamentation. [*London*, 1644.] brs. MADAN 1642. LT.

2922 Londons declaration, in the defence of the citisens. *For Iohn Greensmith*, 1642. 4°.* LT, O, MR, SC, EN; CH, CN, MH, NU, TU, WF, Y.

2923 Londons defiance to Rome. [*London*, 1679.] fol.* L, O, LG, OH, MR; CH, CLC, IU, MBA, WF, Y.

2924 Londons desire and direction to all. *For T. I.*, 1642. 4°.* LT, MR; CN, NU, Y.

2925 Entry cancelled.

Londons destroyer detected. 1666. *See* N., E.

2926 Entry cancelled.

London's dreadful visitation. 1665. *See* Graunt, John, *of Bucklersbury.*

Londons drollery. [n.p., 1680.] *See* Settle, Elkanah.

2927 Londons flames: being. *Printed*, 1679. 4°.* L, LG, LSD, MR, YM; CH, CN, MH, NU, WF, Y.

2928 Londons flames discovered. *Printed*, 1667. 4°.* L, O, LG, MR, GH; CH, CN, MH, NU, WF, Y.

2929 London's flames reviv'd. *For Nathanael Ranew, and Jonathan Robinson*, 1689. 4°.* T.C.II 264. L, O, C, LIU, EN; CH, CU, MH, NC, WF, Y.

London's gate. 1647. *See* Fisher, Edward.

2930 Londons glory, and Whittingtons renown. *For R. Burton*, [1641]. brs. L.

London's glory: or the history of the . . . London-prentice. [1700?] *See* Shirley, John, 1680–1702.

2931 Londons glory, or, the riot and ruine of the fifth monarchy men. [*London*], *for C. D.*, 1661. 8°.* LT.

Londons glory represented. 1660. *See* Tatham, John.

London's great jubilee restor'd. 1689. *See* Taubman, Matthew.

Londons improvement. 1680. *See* Newbold, A.

2932 London's index or some reflexions. *Printed*, 1676. brs. L.

2933 London's joy and loyalty. *By Nathaniel Thompson*, 1682. brs. O.

2933A Londons joy and tryumph. *Printed*, 1682. brs. LG; CH.

Londons ioyfull gratulation. 1642. *See* Jordan, Thomas.

2933B London's lamentation on its destruction by . . . fire. [*n.p.*], 1666. brs. LPR.

2934 London's lamentation, or, a fit admonition. *By E. P. for John Wright junior*, 1641. 4°.* LT; CH.

2935 London's lamentation: or, an excellent new song. [*London*], *by N. T.*, [1683]. brs. L, O, LG, HH; CH, CLC, MH, Y.

2936 London's lamentations for the losse of their charter. *For A. Banks*, 1683. brs. L, O; CH.

London's lamentations: or. 1666. *See* P., R.

2936A London's liberties; or a learned argvment. *By Ja. Cottrel for Gyles Calvert*, 1651. 4°.* LT, O, LG, CM, DT; CH, MB, MH, MIU, NU, WF.

2936B —[Anr. ed.] *For R. Read*, 1682. fol.* T.C.I 517. L, O, LG, LLU, EN; CH, CN, MH, TU, WF, Y.

2936C Londons liberties: or the opinions. Second edition. *For Tho. Simmons*, 1683. fol. * LG; IU, MH.

2937 Londons Lord have mercy upon us. *For Francis Coles, Thomas Vere, and John Wright*, [1665]. brs. L, LG, LU, HH.

2937A —[Anr. ed] [*London*, 1665?] brs. L.

2937B —[Anr. ed.] [*London*], 1665. brs. MIU.

2937C —[Anr. ed.] *Edinburgh, Society of Stationers*, 1665. brs. ALDIS 1795.5. EN.

2938 Londons loud cryes to the Lord. *By T. Mabb, for R. Burton, and R. Gilberson* [sic], [1665]. brs. L.

2939 Londons love, or, the entertainment of the Parliament. *For John Thomas*, 1641[2]. 4°.* LT, C, LG; CH, INU, Y.

Londons love to her neighbours. [n.p.], 1643. *See* Williams, John, *capt.*

2940 Londons loyalty to their King. [*London*, 1679.] brs. L, LG, OC, HH, LNC; CH, IU, MH, PU, WF, Y.

2941 London metamorphosis or, a dialogue. [*London*], *printed*, 1647. 4°.* LT; CSS, MH.

London's mortality. [n.p., 1665.] *See* Baxter, Richard.

2942 Londons new colours displaid. [*London*, 1648.] cap., 4°.* LT, MR, SP, ESS; CN, IU, MH, NU.

2943 London's new cry. *For J. Shooter*, [1697–99]. brs. HH.

2944 Londons new recorder. [*London*], *printed*, 1647. brs. LT, O, LG, OC; Y.

2945 London's nevv wonder: or, the great sleeper. *For George Horton*, 1659. 4°.* O.

2946 Londons-Nonsuch; or, the glory of the Royal Exchange. *By S. S.*, 1668. fol.* L, O; CH, WF.

2946A Londons nonsuch surveyed. *For the author*, 1668. fol.* NN.

2947 Londons ordinary. [*London*], *for F. Coles, T. Vere, J. Wright, and J. Clarke*, [1674–79]. brs. EUING 169. L, O, CM, HH, GU.

2948 London's outcry to her sister-cities. [*London*, 1659.] brs. LT, LG.

2949 London's plague from Holland. [*London*, 1684?] brs. L.

London's plague-sore. 1665. *See* N., E.

2949A Londons praise, or, the glory of the city. [*London*], *for J. Hose*, [1660–75]. brs. O.

Londons remembrancer. 1670. *See* Jones, Evan.

2950 Londons remembrancer: or, a timely admonition. [*London*], *printed*, 1648. 4°.* LT, MR; CN, MH, MU.

Londons remonstrance. 1642. *See* H., I.

Londons resurrection. 1669. *See* Ford, Simon.

2951 London's sighs for her worthy patriot . . . Sir Richard Ford. *For L. C.* 1678. brs. L; MH.

London's sins. [n.p.], 1665. *See* N., E.

2951A Londons speech to His Royal Highness the Prince of Orange. *For J. G.*, 1688. brs. TO, Y.

2951B —[Anr. ed.] [*London*, 1688.] brs. MH, WF.

2952 Londons teares, vpon the never too much to be lamented death of . . . S[r]. Richard Wiseman. *For John Greensmith*, P642 [i.e. 1642]. brs. LT, O, LUG; MH.

Londons triumph. 1656. *See* Brewer, Thomas, *poet.*

London's tryumph, celebrated. 1659. *See* Tatham, John.

Londons triumph, or, his. 1673. *See* H., G.

2953 London's triumph; or, the magnificent glory. [*London*], *for P. Brooksby, J. Deacon, J. Blare, and J. Back*, [1691?]. fol. L.

Londons triumph: or, the solemn. 1656. *See* Bulteel, John, *younger.*

Londons triumph: presented. 1662. *See* Tatham, John.

2954 Entry cancelled.

London's triumphant holiday. 1660. *See* Hammond, Charles.

London's tryumph celebrated. 1657. *See* Tatham, John.

2955 Londons warning-peece, being, the common-prayers complaint. *Yorke, by Stephen Buckley*, 1643. brs. LT, O, HH; CH.

2956 Londons wonder; being a description. [*London*], *for J. Deacon*, [1685]. brs. L.

2957 Londons wonder. Being a most true and positive relation . . . of a great whale. *For Francis Grove*, 1658. 8°.* LT, O.

2957A Londons wonders: or, London's warning. *By A. P.*, 1673. 4°.* LG.

2957B **Long, Henry.** The case of. [*London*, 1694.] brs. WF.

2957C **Long, Richard.** Mr. Richard Long's case. [*n.p.*, 1687?] brs. L.

2958 **Long, Thomas.** An answer to a Socinian treatise [by A. Bury]. *By Freeman Collins, to be sold by Randal Taylor*, 1691. 4°. L, O, OC, LLP, NE; CH, CU, NU, WF, Y.

2959 —Apostolical communion. *Printed*, 1673. 8°. L, O, E.

2960 [–] Calvinus redivivus; or, conformity. *By J. M. for John Martyn*, 1673. 8°. T.C.I 136. L, O, C, AN, DT; NU, PBL, PH.

2961 [–] The case of persecution, charg'd. *By Freeman Collins; to be sold by Richard Baldwin*, 1689. 4°. L, O, C, MR, DT; CH, MH, NU, V, WF.

2962 —The character of a separatist. *For Walter Kettilby*, 1677. 8°. T.C.I 288. O, LCL, CT, EN, DT; CH, NU, WF, Y.

2963 —A compendious history of all the Popish . . . plots. *For D. Brown, and T. Goodwin*, 1684. 8°. T.C.II 84. L, O, CS, EN, DT; CH, IU, MH, NC, NU, TU, WF, Y.

2964 [–] A continuation and vindication of the defence. *For R. Chiswell*, 1682. 8°. L, C, ON, DU, P, DT; CSB, MBA, MH, NU, WF.

2964A [–] —[Anr. ed.] —, *sold by F. Gardiner*, 1682. T.C.II 492. CLC.

2965 —Dr. Walker's true, modest, and faithful account. *Printed and are to be sold by R. Talor*, 1693. 4°. T.C.II 427. L, O, C, CT, LIU, LSD; CH, CN, MH, WF, Y.

2966 —An exercitation concerning the frequent use of our Lords Prayer. *By J. G. for R. Marriot*, 1658. 8°. L, O, LCL, CT, YM, E; CLC, NU, TO.

2967 [–] A full answer to all the popular objections. *Printed, and are to be sold by R. Baldwin*, 1689. 4°. T.C.II 291. L, O, C, AU, DT; CH, CN, MH, NU, TU, WF, Y.

2968 [–] The healing attempt examined. *By Freeman Collins, to be sold by Richard Baldwin*, 1689. 4°.* T.C.II 283. L, O, C, LLP, AU, DT; CH, CLC, MH, NU, WF.

2969 [–] The historian vnmask'd. *Printed, and are to be sold by Richard Baldwin*, 1689. 4°. T.C.II 291. L, O, C, BAMB, BC, CD; CH, CN, MH, NU, TU, WF, Y.

2970 —The history of Joshua. *By J. C. and F. C. for Daniel Brown*, 1684. 4°.* L.

2971 —The history of the Donatists. *For Walter Kettilby*, 1677. 8°. T.C.I 272. L, O, C, EN, DT; CH, IU, MH, NU, WF, Y.

2972 —King David's danger. *By J. C. and Freeman Collins, for Fincham Gardiner, to be sold by Walter Davies*, 1683. 4°.* T.C.II 40. L, O, CT, YM, BLH; CH, CN, NU, WF, Y.

2973 [–] The letter for toleration decipher'd. *By Freeman Collins, and are to be sold by R. Baldwin*, 1689. 4°.* T.C.II 283. L, O, LLP, DT, M; MM, NN, NU, WF.

2974 —Mr. Hales's Treatise of schism. *For Walter Kettilby*, 1678. 8°. T.C.I 309. O, C, SP, EN, DT; CH, NCD, NU, WF, Y.

2974A —Moses and the royal martyr. *By J. C. and F. Collins, for Daniel Brown*, 1684. 4°.* IEG.

2975 [Anr. ed.] —, *to be sold by Walter Davies*, 1684. 4°.* T.C.II 83. L; CH.

2976 [–] No Protestant, but the dissenters plot. *By J. C. and Freeman Collins, for Daniel Brown*, 1682. 8°. T.C.I 487. L, O, LCL, CT, DU, EN; CH, CLC, CN, NU, WF.

2977 [–] The nonconformists plea for peace impleaded. *For Walter Kettilby*, 1680. 8°. O, LVF, CS, NE; CLC, NPT.

2978 —The original of war. *By J. C. and F. Collins, for Daniel Brown; to be sold by Walter Davies*, 1684. 4°.* T.C.II 83. L, O; CH, NU, WF, Y.

2979 [–] Reflections upon a late book, entituled, The case of allegiance consider'd. *For Richard Baldwin*, 1689. 4°.* L, O, C, AU, DM; CH, MM, NP, NU, WF, Y.

2980 [–] A resolution of certain queries concerning submission. *Printed, and are to be sold by R. Baldwin*, 1689. 4°. L, O, C, DU, LIU, DT; CH, CN, MH, NU, TU, WF, Y.

2981 —A review of Mr. Richard Baxter's life. *By F. C. to be sold by E. Whitlock*, 1697. 8°. L, O, CT, E, CD; NU, WF, Y.

2982 —A sermon against murmuring. *For Richard Royston, to be sold by George May, in Exon*, 1680. 4°.* T.C.I 403. MR; NU, WF, Y.

2982A — —[Anr. ed.] *For Richard Royston*, 1680. 4°.* L; TU.

2983 —The unreasonableness of rebellion. *By J. C. and Freeman Collins, to be sold by Randal Taylor*, 1685. 4°.* L, O, LSD; NP, NU, WF.

2984 [–] The vnreasonableness of separation: the second part. *By J. C. and F. Collins, for Daniel Brown*, 1682. 8°. O, C, LW, BR, SC, DT; CH, NU, PL, PU, WF.

2985 [–] A vindication of the primitive Christians. *By J. C. and Freeman Collins, sold by Robert Kettlewell*, 1683. 8°. L, O, CT, AN, E, EN; BN, CH, CN, NU, WF, Y. (var.)

2986 [–] Vox cleri. *Printed, and are to be sold by R. Taylor*, 1690. 4°. T.C.II 204. L, O, C, EN, DT; CH, CN, MH, TU, WF, Y.

2987 [–] —Second edition. —, 1690. 4°. O, C, DU, MR, DT; CLC, IU, NU, TO, PU, WF, Y.

2987A [–] Vox regis & regni: or a protest. *For G. C. and are to be sold by Richard Baldwin*, 1690. 4°.* L, O, CT, EN, DT; CH, CN, NU, TU, WF, Y.

2987B Long Lent, 1685. Or, a vindication of the feasts. [*Edinburgh*, 1685.] brs. EN.

2988 Long lookt for come at last. *Printed*, 1667. brs. L.

2989 Long lookt for is come at last. [*London*], *for F. Coles, T. Vere, J. Wright, J. Clark, W. T. and T. P.*, [1680?]. brs. L.

2990 The long-nos'd lass. [*London*], *for P. Brooksby*, [1685–88]. brs. L, HH; MH.

2991 The Long Parliament as it acted in the year 1641, 1642, & 1643. [*London*], 1661. 4°. DU; MBP, NU, Y.

Long Parliament dissolved. [*n.p.*], 1676. *See* Holles, Denzil Holles, *baron.*

Long Parliament is not revived. 1660. *See* C., R.

Long Parliament revived. 1661. *See* Drake, *Sir* William.

Long Parliament. Tvvice defunct. 1660. *See* Prynne, William.

2992 Long Parliament-vvork. *By T. L. for G. Calvert*, 1659. 4°.* LT, O, MR, E; HR, CH, CN, MH, WF, Y.

2993 A long-winded lay-lecture. [*London*], *printed*, 1647. 4°.* LT; MU, WF.

2994 **L[onge], J.** An epitaph on the late deceased, . . . Elizabeth Cromwel. *By James Cottrel*, 1655. brs. LT.

2995 **Longeville, Charles.** To the Kings Most Excellent Majesty, the humble petition of. [*London*, 1685.] brs. O.

2995A The longing lasses letter to her love. [*London*], *for J. Deacon*, [1690?]. brs. O.

2995B The longing maid. [*London*], *for F. Coles, T. Vere, J. Wright, and J. Clarke*, [1674–79]. brs. O.

Longing shepherdess. [1680?] *See* Guy, Robert.

2996 The longing virgins choice. [*London*], *for P. Brooksby*, [1672–95]. brs. L, O, HH; MH.

2997 **Longinus, Dionysius.** An essay upon sublime. *Oxford: by Leon. Lichfield*, 1698. 8°. CH, WF, Y.

2998 ——[Anr. ed.] *Oxford, by L. L. for T. Leigh, London*, 1698. 8°. T.C.III 81. L, O; CLC, MH, TO.

2999 —Περι ὑψους or. *By Roger Daniel for Francis Eaglesfield*, 1652. 8°. LT, O, C, LW, DU; CH, IU, MH, NN, WF, Y.

3000 —Διονυσιου Λογγινος Ρητυρος περι . . . Liber de grandi loquentia. *Oxonii, impensis Guil. Webb*, 1650. 12°. MADAN 2036. L.

3000A ——[Anr. ed.] *Oxonii, excud. G. T. impensis Guil. Webb*, 1650. 8°. DU.

3001 —A treatise of the loftiness or elegancy of speech. *By N. T. for John Holford*, 1680. 12°. L, O, CCH, LIU; CLC, IU, LC, MH, WF.

Longitude found. 1676. *See* Bond, Henry.

Longitudinis inventæ. 1699. *See* Fyler, Samuel.

3002 **Longland, Thomas.** Quatuor novissima: or, meditations upon the four last things. *By A. Maxey, for J. Rothwell*, 1657. 12°. LT, CS.

3003 [**Longus.**] Daphnis and Chloe. A most sweet, and pleasant pastorall romance. *For John Garfield*, 1657. 8°. LT; CH, CLC, CSU, WCL.

3004 Entry cancelled.

Looke about you. 1641. *See* Contzen, Adam.

3005 Look about you: a discovrse. *For Tho. Wilkinson, Ian. 21.* 1643. 4°.* LT, O, LG, DT; CH, MH, MU, WF, Y.

3006 Look abovt you now or never, or, two groats-worth of good councel. [*London*], *for G. Horton*, [1654]. brs. LT.

3007 Look abovt yov: or, a groatsworth of good councel. *For G. Horton*, 1654. brs. LT.

3008 Looke about you: or, a word in season. *For Robert Bostock*, 1647. 4°.* LT, DT; CH, MH, NU, WF.

3009 Looke about you, or the fault-finder. [*London*, 1647.] cap., 4°.* LT, O, DT; TU.

Looke not upon me. [n.p.], 1648. *See* Fornis, Edward.

3010 Look to it London, threatned. [*London*, 1648.] cap., 4°.* O, LG; CN, MH, NU, WF.

3010A [**Lookes, John.**] Keepe thy head on thy shoulders. *For Thomas Lambert*, 1641. brs. MAU.

3010B —The rag-man. *For Fr. Grove*, [1652?]. brs. L; MU.

3011 —The two converted theeves. *For Francis Grove*, 1641. 8°.* Y.

Looking-glass for a bad husband. [1670.] *See* Lanfiere, Thomas.

3011A A looking-glass for a Christian family. [*London*], *for R. Burton*, [1641–74]. brs. O.

3012 —[Anr. ed.] [*London*], *for F. Coles, T. Vere, I. Wright, I. Clarke, VV. Thackeray, and T. Passenger.* [1678–80]. brs. L, O, CM, HH; MH.

3012A —[Anr. ed.] *For J. Wright, J. Clarke, W. Thackeray, and T. Passenger*, [1681–84]. brs. L, HH.

Looking-glass for a covetous miser. [1670.] *See* Jordan, Thomas.

3013 A looking-glasse for a drunkard. *For J. D. to be sold by George Wilford*, 1652. brs. LT.

3014 —[Anr. ed.] *By H. Brugis for W. Whitwood*, [1670?]. brs. L, O.

3015 A looking-glasse for a Tory. colop: *For L. C.*, 1682. brs. L, O; MH, NCD, WF, Y.

3016 A looking-glasse for all proud, ambitious, covetous and corrupt lavvyers. [*London*, 1646.] cap., 4°.* LT, O, LL.

3016A A looking-glasse for all trve Christians. *For F. Coles, T. Vere, W. Gilbertson*, [1658–64]. brs. EUING 164. GU.

3016B —[Anr. ed.] [*London*], *for F. Coles, T. Vere, and J. Wright*, [1663–74]. brs. O.

Looking-glasse for all trve hearted. 1642. *See* Hughes, Lewis.

Looking-glass for children. 1672. *See* P., H.

3016C A looking-glass for drunkards. *For Richard Burton*, [1641–74]. brs. O.

3017 A looking-glass for England. Being an abstract. *Printed*, 1667. 4°.* L, O, C, LVF, DT; CH, CN, MH, NU, WF, Y.

3018 Entry cancelled.

Looking-glasse for England wherein. 1646. *See* Snell, George.

3018A A looking-glass for kidnappers. [Advert.] *Printed, and sold by A. Baldwin*, 1698. 4°. L (t.p.).

3019 A looking-glass for King-opposers. *For Edward Thomas*, 1660. 4°.* L, CD; CH, Y.

3020 A looking-glass for ladies. [*London*], *for F. Coles, T, Vere, J. Wright, and J. Clarke*, [1674–79]. brs. L, O, CM, HH; MH, Y.

3020A A looking-glass for loyallists. *For T. S.*, 1682. brs. CH.

Looking-glass for loyalty. 1675. *See* Higham, John.

3021 A looking-glass for maids. *For Tho. Vere.* [167–?] brs. EUING 163. L, O, GU.

3022 —[Anr. ed.] [*London*], *for F. Coles, T. Vere, J. Wright, J. Clarke, W. Thhckeray [sic], & T. Passinger*, [1678–80]. brs. L, HH; MH.

3023 A looking-glasse for, or an awakening word. [*London*, 1656.] 4°. LT, O; CH, CLC, NC, PL, WF, Y.

3024 A looking-glasse for rebells. *Oxford, for William Web*, 1643. 4°.* MADAN 1440. LT, O, MR; CH, NU, WF.

3025 A lookjng-glas for sectaryes. *For M. S.*, 1647. 4°.* LT, DU, DT; CN.

3026   A looking-glasse for sope-patentees. *Printed*, 1646. 4°.*
LT, O, C, LG, LUG; INU, NC, WCL.

3027   A looking-glasse for statesmen. [*London*], *for I. H.*, 1648.
brs. L, LS.

Looking-glass for the Jews. [n.p.], 1674. *See* Fox, George.

3027A A looking-glass for the Lord Chancellor. [*London?*
1688.*] brs. C; CH, MH.

3027B A looking-glass for the members of the Bank of England. [*London*, 1696?] brs. MH.

3028   A looking glasse for the Oxford Jvncto. *By E. F. for
Thomas Vere, Novemb.* 3. 1645. 4°.* MADAN 1822.
LT, O, YM; NU, WF.

Looking-glasse for the Parliament. [n.p.], 1648. *See*
Jenkins, David.

3029   A looking-glasse for the Popish garrisons. *Printed at
London by W. W.* 1645. 4°.* LT, DT; MH.

3030   A looking-glas for the Presbitary government. *By B.A.*,
1645. 4°.* LT, BR, MR; MH, NU, Y.

Looking-glasse for the Quakers. 1657. *See* Collier,
Thomas.

—[Same title.] 1689. *See* Pennyman, Joseph.

3031   A looking-glasse for the Ranters. *By T. M. for Richard
Moon*, 1653. 4°.* L; NU.

Looking-glass for the Recorder. [n.p., 1682.] *See*
Docwra, Anne.

3032   A looking glasse for the soule. [*London*], *by Tho: Paine
and Math: Symmons, September* 19, 1643. brs. LT, LS.

3032A A looking-glass for the times. *Printed*, 1689. 4°.* BC; MM,
WF.

Looking-glass for the unmarried. 1697. *See* Bury,
Edward.

3033   A looking-glasse for the vvell-affected in the city of
London. [*London*], *printed*, 1648. 4°.* LT, OB, MR; CN,
MIU.

3033A A lookinglass for the Whigs: or, down with common-
wealthsmen. *For W. Kent*, [c. 1685]. brs. MH.

3034   A looking-glass for traytors. *For Thomas Vere and
William Gilbertson*, 1660. brs. LT.

3034A —[Anr. ed.] [*London*], *for F. Coles, T. Vere, J. Wright and
J. Clarke*, [1678]. brs. O.

3035   A looking-glass for wanton women. [1680?] brs. O.

Looking-glasse for vvomen. 1644. *See* H., T.

3036   A looking-glasse for young-men and maids. *For Tho:
Vere*, [1655?]. brs. L.

3037   A looking-glasse of the world. *By F. N.* 1644. 4°.*
LT, DN; CH, CLC, MH, TU, WF.

Looking-glasse or paralel. [n.p., 1661.] *See* Shaw,
Samuel.

3038   A looking-glass (or vvarning-peece) for all such as
prophane churches. *For Richard Burton*, 1652. brs. LT.

3039   A looking-glasse. Wherein is discovered the face of
distraction. *By G. W., Feb.* 3. 1642[3]. 4°.* LT, CK;
CLC, LC, Y.

[**Loots–man, Jacob.**] The Zea-atlas or the water-world.
Amsterdam, 1698. *See* title.

3040   The Lord Baltamore's case. *Printed*, 1653. 4°.* L; NN, RPJ.

Lord, John. Almanack. 1678. *See* Almanacs.

3041   The Lord Bishop of Londonderry's case. [*n.p.*, 1698.]
cap., fol.* O; Y.

3041A The Lord Bruce and . . . his wife, desire a bill may be
passed in Parliament. [*London?* 1680.] brs. L.

3042   The Lord Chancellors discovery and confession. colop:
For R. Lee, 1689. brs. L, O, C, OP, HH; CH, WF.

3042A The Lord Chancellors petition. *For S. M.*, 1688. brs. L,
C, LG, OC, BR; CH.

3042B —[Anr. ed.] colop: [*Edinburgh*], *printed*, 1689. cap., 4°.*
ALDIS 2915.5. L, O, C, EN; MB, MIU, TO, Y.

3043   The Lord Chancellors villanies. *Printed*, 1689. brs. O;
MH, PU.

Lord Chief Justice Herbert's account examin'd. 1689.
See Atwood, William.

3044   The Lord Craven's case, as to. *By William Du-Gard*,
1653. fol. LT; WF.

3045   The Lord Craven's case, briefly stated. *By Tho. Newcomb*, 1654. 4°.* LT, CCO, BC, DT; CH, CLC, IU, MH, WF, Y.

3045A The Lord Cravens case briefly stated . . . with observations. *By T. L. for T. H.*, 1654. 4°.* CH.

3045B The Lord Craven's case. Considerations humbly offered.
[*London?* 1659.] fol. L.

3045C The Lord Craven's case. The Lord Craven by leave.
[*London?* 1660.] fol.* L.

3046   The Lord Generall Cromwell his march to Sterling.
By E. G., 1650. 4°.* LT, GC, MR; MH.

Lord George Digby's cabinet. 1646. *See* Bristol, George
Digby, *earl*.

Lord have mercie upon us. [n.p.], 1643. *See* Heylyn,
Peter.

3047   Lord have mercy upon us, or the visitation at Oxford.
[*London*], *printed at Pembrook and Mongomery* [i.e.
Oxford], 1648. 4°.* MADAN 1981. LT, O, AN, DU, MR;
CLC, MH, MIU, TU, WF, Y.

3047A The Lord Henry Cromvvels speech in the Hovse.
[*London*], *printed*, 1659. 4°.* LT, O; CN, MIU, WF, Y.

Lord Keepers speech to the House of Commons. 1641[2].
See Littleton, Edward Littleton, *baron*.

3048   The Lord Lambert's letter to the Speaker. *Printed*,
1659[60]. 4°.* LT, O, C, BC, SP; CN, MH, MIU, WF, Y.

Lord Loudouns speech. 1648. *See* Rosse, William.

Lord Maior of Londons letter to the King. [n.p., 1642.]
See Gurney, *Sir* Richard.

3049   The Lord Mayor of London's vindication. colop: *For
E. Smith*, 1682. 4°.* L, O, LG; CH, MH, MIU, NU, Y.

3050   The Lord Mayor's farewell from his office of mayor-
altie. 1646. cap., 4°.* LT, O, OC, GU, EN; IU, NHC.

3051   The Lord Mayor's right of electing a sheriff asserted.
colop: [*London*], *for Joanna Brome*, 1682. cap., fol.*
T.C.I497. L, O, OC, CT, MR; CH, MBA, PL, WF, Y.

3052   No entry.

Lord Mayor's show. 1682. *See* Jordan, Thomas.

3053   The Lord Merlins prophecy. *By J. C. for G. Horton*,
1651. 4°.* LT, O; CH, MH, Y.

3054   The Lord Osmonds overthrovv. *For Iohn Greensmith*,
1642. 4°.* LT, LVF; MIU.

Lord Russels farewel. [n.p., 1683.] *See* Dean, John.

3055   The Lord Russels last farewell. *For J. Dean,* 1683. brs. O;
       CH, MH.

3055A The Lord Russel's speech vindicated. colop: *For Will.
       Crook,* 1683. brs. O; CH, MB, Y.
       Lord Stafford's ghost. [n.p.], 1680. *See* Nesse, Chris-
       topher.

3056   Lord Thomas and fair Elinor. *For A. M. W. O. and T.
       Thackeray,* [1694?]. brs. L, HH.

3057   The Lord Viscount Stafford found more guilty. colop:
       For Benjamin Harris, 1680. brs. L, O.

3058   Lord Willoughby: being. *For A. M. W. O. and T.
       Thackeray,* [1694?]. brs. L, O, CM, HH; MH.

3058A —[Anr. ed.] *By and for W. O.,* [1700]. brs. L.

3059   Lord Willoughby. Or, a true relation. [*London*], *for F.
       Coles,* [n.d.]. brs. L, O.

3060   A lordly prelate. [n.p.], *printed,* 1641. 4°.* CH, NU.
       Lords and Commons first love. 1647. *See* Prynne,
       William.

3060A The Lords & Commons reasons and justifications for
       the deprivation . . . of James II. colop: *For Thomas
       Tilliar,* 1689. 4°.* L, CS, LSD, CD, DT; CH, CN, MH, NU,
       WF, Y.

3060B —[Anr. ed.] colop: *Edinburgh, re-printed,* 1689. brs. ALDIS
       2917. L, EN; CSS, MH, Y.
       Lords-day. Or. 1672. *See* Young, Thomas.

3060C The Lord's-day to be kept holy. *For William Marshal,*
       1694. 8°.* WF.
       Lords-day vindicated. 1692. *See* Trosse, George.
       Lord's free prisoner. [n.p., 1683.] *See* Bampfield,
       Francis.
       Lords loud call. 1660. *See* Jessey, Henry.

3061   Entry cancelled.
       Lord's prayer unclasped. 1654. *See* Harwood, James.

3062   A Lord's speech without doors. [*London,* 1689.] cap., fol.*
       OC, CS, DU, MR; CDA, IU, MH, NP, PL, Y.

3062A —[Anr. ed.] colop: [*London*], *printed,* 1689. cap., 4°.* L,
       C, MR, AU, EN; CH, CN, INU, NN.

3062B —[Anr. ed.] colop: [*Edinburgh, Reid?*], *printed,* 1689. 4°.*
       ALDIS 2916. AU, EN.
       Lords table. 1656. *See* Woodward, Hezekiah.
       Lord's trumpet. [n.p., 1700?] *See* Peden, Alexander.

3063   The Lords voice crying to England. *For Tho. Parkhurst,*
       1680. 4°.* T.C.I 416. EN; CLC, MH, Y.

3064   **Loredano, Giovanni Francesco.** Accademical dis-
       courses. *By Tho. Mabb, for John Playfere, and Margaret
       Shears,* 1664. 8°. L, O; CH, CN, MH, WF.

3065   —The ascents of the soul. *By A. G. and J. P. for Robert
       Harford,* 1681. fol. L, O, C, AU, E; CH, IU, MH, NU, WF, Y.

3066   —Dianea: an excellent new romance. *For Humphrey
       Moseley,* 1654. 8°. LT, O; CLC, CN, CU, IU, Y.

3067   —The life of Adam. *For Humphrey Moseley,* 1659. 8°.
       LT, O; CLC, NC, WF.

3068   —The novells of. *For Thomas Fox and Henry Lord,* 1682.
       12°. L; Y.

3069   Entry cancelled.
       —La scala santa. 1681. *See* Coleraine, Henry Hare,
       baron.

3070   No entry.

3071   Loretto and Winifred. [n.p., 1688.] brs. O.

3072   **Lorimer, James.** Theoremata. *Abredoniæ, excudebat
       Joannes Forbesius,* 1683. brs. ALDIS 2433.5. AU.

3073   [**Lorimer, William.**] An apology for the ministers who
       subscribed. *For John Lawrence,* 1694. 4°. T.C.II 475.
       L, O, C, EN, GU; LC, NU, TO, WF.

3074   —Remarks on the R. Mr. Goodwins discourse. *For
       John Lawrence,* 1696. 4°. T.C.II 594. L, O, LCL, EN, GU;
       NC, NU, PPT, TO, WF, Y.

3074A **Lorrain, Paul.** An account of the behaviour and con-
       fessions of the condemn'd criminals . . . [6 November
       1700]. colop: *For E. Mallet,* 1700. brs. MR.

3074B — —condemn'd pirates . . . [13 November 1700]. colop:
       For E. Mallet, 1700. brs. MR.

3074C — —condemn'd criminals . . . [20 December 1700].
       colop: *For E. Mallet,* 1700. brs. MR.

3075   —A guide to salvation. *For L. Meredith,* 1693. 12°. T.C.II
       438. O; CLC, NP.

3076   **Lort, Roger.** Epigrammatum . . . liber primus. *Typis
       R. A. sumptibus Johannis Wright,* 1646. 4°.* L; Y.

3077   **Lortie, André.** Grace & paix. *Se vend chez François
       Bureau,* 1684. 4°. OCC, DT.

3078   —A practical discourse concerning repentance. *For
       Will. Rogers,* 1693. 12°. T.C.II 436. L, O.

3078A [–] The scripture terms of Church-union. [1700?] 4°. LLP.

3079   [–] A treatise of the Holy Communion. *By W. Godbid,*
       1677. 12°. T.C.I 280. C, OC, SHR.

3080   [**Losa, Francisco.**] The holy life of Gregory Lopez.
       Second edition. [*London*], *printed,* 1675. 8°. L, O, LW,
       BC, SHR; CH, CN, MH, PL, RPJ, Y.

3080AA [–] —"Second" edition. *For W. C.,* 1686. 8°. LSC, DUS;
       CN, LC, WF.

3080BA [–] —[Anr. ed.] [n.p., n.d.] 8°. DUS.

3080A **Loss, Friedrich.** Conciliorum: sive, de morborum
       curationibus. *Apud Awnsham Churchill,* 1684. 8°.
       T.C.II 86. L, O, OB, P, MC; CLC, CNM, NAM, WSG.

3080B —Observationum medicinalium. *Typis E. Flesher &
       prostant apud Gualterium Kettilby,* 1672. 8°. T.C.I 121.
       L, O, OB, CCA; CU, PL, WF, WSG.

3081   The lost maidenhead. *For H. Smith,* 1691. 4°.* T.C.II
       360. DU; CLC, WF.
       Lost sheep is found. 1642. *See* Agar, Benjamin.

3082   **Lothian, Robert Kerr,** *earl.* The Earl of Lothian . . .
       his discourse to the Lords, . . . January the 27th, 1690.
       Edinburgh, Society of Stationers, 1690. brs. ALDIS 3052.
       EN, ES; CSS.

3083   —The discourse of . . . 16th day of January, 1692. *Edin-
       burgh, by the heir of Andrew Anderson,* 1692. fol.* ALDIS
       3232. MR, EN; WF, Y.

3083A —The speech of . . . 16th day of January. *Printed at
       Edinburgh and reprinted at the Savoy by Edw. Jones,*
       [1692]. brs. OC, HH.

3083B —The Earl of Lothian's speech to the General Assembly.
       *Edenburgh, by the heir of Andrew Anderson and re-printed
       at London by G. Croom,* 1692. brs. GU; Y.

3084   **Lotius, Eleasar.** Allocvtio D. D. Lotii. [*London*],
       1649. 4°.* LT, O, C, DU, E; CH, MH, MM, Y.
       [**Loubayssin de la Marca, Francisco.**] Don Henriquez
       de Castro. [1686.] *See title.*

3085   **Loudoun, John Campbell,** *earl.* The Lord Lowden
       his learned and wise speech . . . September 9, 1641.
       For Iohn Thomas, 1641. 4°.* LT, C, MR, BLH; CH, CN,
       IU, MH, WF, Y.

3086   —A second speech made by . . . 24 of Septemb. 1641.
       By A. N. for I. M., 1641. 4°.* LT, O, MR; MH, MU, WF, Y.

3087   Entry cancelled.
       —Severall speeches spoken by. Edinburgh, 1646. *See*
       Scotland. Estates. Some papers given in.

3088   —A speech made by . . . 20 of Septemb. *Printed,* 1641.
       4°.* L, O, C, MR, ESS; CH, CLC, LC, MH, NP, Y.

3089   Entry cancelled.
       —His speech . . . September 9. 1641. *See* —The Lord
       Lowden his learned.

3090   —A speech of . . . to a grand committee . . . 12 of
       September, 1645. *Printed at London by E. P. for Hugh
       Perrey,* 1645. 4°.* LT, O, C, A, DT; CSS, INU, MH, MU,
       WF, Y.
       —Speech to the English commissioners. 1648. *See*
       Rosse, William.

3091   —The Lord Chancellor of Scotland his speech . . . Jvly,
       1646. *By Mathew Simmons for Rich. Tomlines,* 1646.
       4°.* OW, EN; MH, MM, NU.

3091A ——[Anr. ed.] *By Mathew Simmons for John Tomlines,*
       1646. 4°.* LT, DT; CH, WF.

3092   Entry cancelled.
       —Theses philosophicæ. Edinburgh, 1697. *See* Loudoun,
       John.

3093   [–] Two speeches of the Lord Chancellour of Scotland.
       For T. H., Novemb. 9. 1646. 4°.* LT; CH, MH, TU, WF.

3093A **Loudoun, John.** Theses philosophicæ. *Edinburgi, ex
       typographæo Georgii Mosman,* 1697. 4°.* ALDIS 3711.
       EN, SA.

3093B **Lougher, John.** Precious promises. *By M. Maxwell, and
       R. Roberts, for Edw. Giles, in Norwich,* 1681. 12°. L, NPL.

3093C —Sermons. *By T. S. for E. Giles, in Norwich,* 1685. 8°.
       T.C.II 134. EN, NPL.

3094   [–] A treatise of the souls union with Christ. *For J.
       Hancock,* 1680. 8°. T.C.I 398. L; CLC, LC, MH, Y.

3095   **Louis IV,** *King of France.* Elegant apothegms in the
       speech of Lewis IV. colop: [*London*], *by N. T.,* 1685.
       fol.* L, O, MR; CB, CH, CLC, WF.

3096   Entry cancelled.
       —Lively pourtraicture. 1659. *See title.*

3097   **Louis XIII,** *King of France.* A letter written by the
       French King. *For Nath. Butter, March,* 18. 1642. 4°.*
       O, EC, DU, E; MIU, NU, WF.

3097A —The King of France his message to the Queene of
       England. *Decemb.* 9, *for T. Wright,* 1642. 4°.* EC.

3098   Entry cancelled.
       —Royal letter. 1641. *See title.*

3098A **Louis XIV,** *King of France.* An abstract of the consul-
       tations. 1695. 4°.* L; MH.

3099   [–] The French King's answer to Mons. Tyrconnel's
       letter. colop: *For R. Baldwin,* 1690. cap., 4°.* L, C; CH,
       MM.

3100   —The French King's appeal from the proceedings of
       the Pope. *For Richard Baldwin,* 1688. 4°.* O, LLP, OC,
       EC, BP; CH, MM, WF, Y.

3101   —The articles of agreement between. *For H. S.* 1649.
       4°.* LT, O, LUG, DT; CSS, MH, MU, SYRACUSE.

3102   —Articles of agreement concluded between His Most
       Christian Majesty, and the Republik of Geneva. colop:
       By George Croom, 1685. cap., fol. *O, LSD, MR; CH,
       NP.

3103   —Articles of peace between the two crowns of France
       and Spain. *By E. O. for William Crook,* 1668. 4°.*
       L, O, MR; CH, IU, MH, TU, WF, Y.

3103A —Articles of peace offered [to Great Britain] by the
       Crown of France. 1696. brs. EN.

3104   —A copy of a letter from. colop: *For J. Hawkins,* 1692.
       brs. O, EN; Y.

3105   —A copy of the French King's declaration. 1694. brs.
       MC.

3105A —A copy of the French King's letter to the Archbishop
       of Paris. *For B. Aylmer, and sold by R. Baldwin,* 1696.
       brs. HH.

3105B —The French King's declaration . . . [12 October 1700].
       By J. Wilkins, 1700. brs. L.

3105C —The French King's declaration enjoining the execu-
       tion. [*London*], *by John Nutt,* 1698. 4°.* CS; INU, MB,
       WF.

3106   Entry cancelled. *See next entry.*

3107   —The French King's declaration for settling the general
       poll-tax: together with his edict. *For Richard Baldwin,*
       1695. 4°.* L, O, C, LPR, CT; CH, MB, MIU, PL, WF.

3108   —The declaration of . . . against the most horrid pro-
       ceedings. [*London,* 1649.] brs. L, LG; CH, CN, MH, MIU.

3108A Entry cancelled. Same as previous.

3108B —A declaration of . . . declaring the reasons. *Printed,*
       1649. 4°.* LT, O, LPR; CH, MIU, NN, WF.

3109   —The declaration of . . . to all. colop: [*London*], *for R.
       Royston, April* 9. 1649. cap., 4°.* LT, C, OC, MR, SP; CSS,
       MH.

3110   —A declaration of the Most Christian King, shewing
       the reasons. *In the Savoy, by Tho: Newcombe,* 1674.
       fol.* L, O, LL, OC, LNC; CH, MHL, MIU, WF, Y.

3111   ——[Anr. ed.] *Edinburgh, reprinted by Andrew Anderson,*
       [1674]. fol.* ALDIS 2020. EN; MH.

3112   —The French Kings declaration of a war against
       England. *By Tho. Newcomb,* 1666. 4°.* L, O, OC, CT,
       LNC, MR; CH, IU, MH, WF, Y.

3112A —The French King's declaration of war by sea and land
       against the Spaniards. colop. [*London*], *printed,* 1689.
       brs. L, C, CS; MH, WF, Y.

3113   —The French King's declaration of war against the
       Hollanders. *Dublin; re-printed;* 1688. brs. L.

3114   —The most Christian Kings declaration of warr against
       the States-Generall. *In the Savoy, by Tho: Newcomb,*
       1672. fol.* L, O, C, SP, EN; CH, MH, MIU, TU, V, Y.

3114A — —[Anr. ed.] *Edinburgh, re-printed by Evan Tyler, 1672.* brs. ALDIS 1951. HH, EN; MH, WF.

3115 — —[Anr. ed.] *In the Savoy, by Thomas Newcomb, and reprinted at Dublin by Benjamin Tooke, and are to be sold by Joseph Wilde, 1672.* fol.* MH.

3115A —The French King's declaration of war against . . . Spain. *[London], in the Savoy, by Edward Jones, 1689.* brs. L, O; CH, WF.

3115AB — —[Anr. ed., "Spaniards."] *[n.p., 1689.]* fol. L.

3115B Entry cancelled.
— —[Anr. ed.] Edinburgh, [1674]. *See* — . . . declaration of warr against the States-Generall. Edinburgh, 1672.

3116 —The French King's declaration, that the children of those of the pretended reformed religion may change. *Printed at London for Andrew Forrester, 1681.* brs. C; CH, CN, MB, Y, AVP.

3116A —The French King's declaration to prevent the Assemblies. *Printed at Paris: and reprinted at London, for Richard Baldwin, 1689.* brs. HH; IU, MHS, WF.

3117 —The French King's decree against Protestants. *For the author, 1689.* 4°.* T.C.II 259. L, BAMB, AU; CH, CLC, MH, NU, WF.

3118 [–] Dialogue between the King of France and the late King James. *For Richard Baldwin, 1695.* 4°.* L, O, C, LIU, AU; CH, CN, MB, MH, PBM, WF, Y.

3118A [–] —Second edition. —, *1697.* 8°. O; Y.

3119 —An edict of . . . prohibiting. *[London], by G. M., 1686.* 4°.* L, O, MC, P; CH, CN, MH, NC, WF.

3120 — —Second edition. —, *1686.* 4°.* L, O, C, EC, DT; CH, CN, MH, NU, WF, Y.

3120A —The most Christian Kings edict or proclamation. *By the assigns of John Bill and Christopher Barker, 1676.* brs. L, O, C, OC, HH; CH, MH. (var.)

3120B — —[Anr. ed.] *Edinburgh, re-printed by the heir of Andrew Anderson, 1676.* brs. ALDIS 2079. EN.

3121 Entry cancelled.
—French King's edict, ordering. 1695. *See* — . . . Declaration for settling the general poll-tax.

3122 —The French King's edict upon the delcaration made by the clergy of France. *Printed, 1682.* fol.* L, O, CT, LSD, DT; CH, NU, PU, WF, Y.

3122A — —[Anr. ed.] *For Robert Clavell, 1682.* fol.* T.C.I 486. O, BAMB, LSD; CH, IU, MH, WF, Y.

3122B — —[Anr. ed.] *[Dublin, 1682.]* cap., fol.* DT; ZWT.

3123 — —[Anr. ed.] *Reprinted Edinburgh, by the heir of A. Anderson, 1682.* fol.* ALDIS 2332. L, EN, AU; NP.
—French King's lamentation. 1691. *See title.*

3124 —The last resolution of. colop: *By George Croom, 1683.* cap., fol.* L, O, OP; WF, Y.

3124A — —[Anr. ed.] *Reprinted at London, by C. C., 1683.* cap., fol. CH.

3125 — —[Anr. ed.] *Reprinted Edinburgh, by the heir of Andrew Anderson, 1683.* fol.* ALDIS 2385. L, EN; IU.

3125A —The late treaty made between . . . and the States General. *For Randal Taylor, 1691.* fol.* O.
—Letter from the French King. 1692. *See title.*

3126 Entry cancelled.

—French King's letter to Monsieur the Cardinal D'Estrees. [1688?] *See*—French King's memorial to the Pope.

3127 —The King of France's letter to the Earl of Tyrconnel. *For T. P., 1688.* brs. O, HH, MC, DN; Y.

3127A —The French King's letter to the Pope. *[London], sold by Randal Taylor, 1689.* brs. OC, C; Y.

3127B —The French King's manifesto. colop: *For J. Wallis, 1693.* brs. L.

3128 —A memorial from . . . to the States General. *Printed, and sold by J. Nutt, 1700.* 4°.* L, O, C, LSD, EN, DT; CLC, CN, MB, NC, WF, Y.

3128A — —Second edition. —, *1700.* 4°.* L; CH, CN, INU, PU.

3128B — —"Second" edition. *Dublin, reprinted by C. Carter, 1700.* 4°.* DIX 323. DI, DK.

3129 —The French King's memorial to the emperor of Germany. *For Joseph Hindmarsh, 1688.* 4°.* T.C.II 256. L, O, C, DU, AU, CD; CH, CN, MH, NC, TU, WF, Y.

3130 —The French King's memorial to the Pope. *For Joseph Hindmarsh, 1688.* 4°.* T.C.II 256. L, O, C, EN, DT; CH, CN, MH, TU, WF, Y.

3131 —The French King's new declaration, imparting. *Printed at Paris, and reprinted at London for Richard Baldwin, 1689.* brs. MC; MH.

3131A —The French King's new declaration, in favour of the troopers. *For Richard Baldwin, 1689.* brs. O; Y.

3132 —The French King's new declaration. An edict. *For Ben. Griffin, 1689.* brs. L.

3132A —The French Kings new declaration trans. from the original. colop: *For T. Vray, 1696.* 4°.* SP, EN.

3132B —The French Kings new declaration. colop: *Printed, and sold by R. Baldwin, 1696.* 4°.* WF.

3133 —The French Kings new declaration, published at Paris, [26 September 1699]. *For J. Harrison, 1699.* brs. CH.

3134 —The King of France his nevv order to his subjects. colop: *For Jonathan Robinson, 1681.* cap., fol.* T.C.I 464. L, O, C, OP; CH, CLC, PU, WF, Y.

3135 Entry cancelled.
—Ordonnance du roy tres-Chretien. Edinburgh, 1676. *See* —Most Christian Kings edict or proclamation.

3136 —An ordonance of the most Christian King forbidding . . . commerce with the Spaniards. *In the Savoy, by Tho. Newcomb, 1673.* fol.* L, LPR, MR; TU.

3136A —Preliminary articles (or propositions for a general peace) between His Most Christian Majesty and the several allies. *Sold by E. Whitlock, 1696.* brs. CN.

3137 Entry cancelled. Date: [1706?].

3137A —The French King's proposals for a peace. 1696. brs. EN.
—Lewis his second letter to James. [n.p., 1689.] *See title.*

3138 —The French King's speech to the Queen of England. *[London, 1689.]* cap., 4°.* MR; LC, Y.

3139 —The treaty betwixt the most Christian King . . . and the States General. *For A. Baldwin, 1700.* 4°. L, O, C, LSD, EN, DT; CH, CLC, CN, MH, TU, WF, Y.

3139A —A treaty made between . . . States General. *For Randal Taylor, 1691.* 4°.* L, O, LSD; CH, MHL.

3139AB —A treaty of commerce, navigation and marine affairs. *Printed, and sold by A. Baldwin,* 1699. 4°.* WF, Y.

3139B —The treaty of peace between the crowns of France & Spain. *By Tho. Newcomb, and are to be sold by G. Bedell and T. Collins,* 1660. 4°.* LT, O, C, CT, MR, DT; CLC, MH, NCL, WF, Y.

3140 —The treaty of peace, called the Pyrenæan treaty. *For T. Collins, J. Wright, T. Sawbridge, and M. Pitt,* 1678. 4°.* T.C.I 306. L, OC, CCA, EN, DT; CH, MB, MH, PU, WF, Y.

3140A —The treaty of Pyrennes. *For W. Drury,* [1659]. cap., 4°.* L; MH.

3141 **Love, Mrs.** Loves name lives. *Printed,* 1651. 4°.* O, LG, LW, CT, DU, BLH; CN, MIU, NS, NU, WF, AVP.

3142 ——[Anr. ed.] —, 1663. 4°.* L, O, LW, WCA, AN; CH, CU, Y.

3142A **Love, Barry.** The catechism of the church resolved. Second edition. *For W. Rogers,* 1699. 8°. L, LIU; Y.

3143 **Love, Christopher.** Mr. Love's case. *For R. W. and Peter Cole,* 1651. 4°. LT, O, C, LW, AN, DT; CH, CN, CU, MH, NU, TU, WF, Y.

3144 [–] The Christians combat. *For Charles Tyus,* 1664. 8°.* L.

3145 —The Christians directory. *For John Rothwell,* 1653. 4°. LT, O, LCL, AN, LLU; CH, CN, INU, NU, TU.

3146 ——[Anr. ed.] *By Iohn Owsley, for Iohn Rothwell,* 1658. 4°. O, CPL; IU, MH, NGT, WF, Y, AVP.

3147 —A Christians duty and safety. *For E. Brewster and George Sawbridge,* 1653. 8°. LT, O, LCL, LW; CLC, IU, MH, NU, PU, Y.

3148 —A cleare and necessary vindication of the principles and practices of me. *Printed,* 1651. 4°.* LT, O, C, LCL, AN, BLH; CH, CU, NU, WF, Y, AVP.

3149 —The combate between the flesh and spirit. *By T. R. ana E. M. for John Rothwell,* 1654. 4°. LT, O, C, AN, YM; CH, CN, MH, NU, TU, WF.

3150 ——Second edition. *By D. Maxwell for John Rothwell,* 1658. 4°. L, O, CPL, DC, E, ENC; INU, IU, NGT, Y, AVP.

3151 —The dejected soules cure. *For John Rothwell,* 1657. 4°. L, O, LCL, AN, E, BLH; CN, CU, MH, NU, WF, Y, AVP.

3152 —Englands distemper. *By John Macock, for Michael Spark junior,* 1645. 4°.* LT, O, C, AN, E, DT; CH, CN, NC, TO, Y.

3153 ——[Anr. ed.] —, 1651. 4°.* L, C; CLC, CSS, MBP, NWA, PL.

3154 —His funeral sermon, preached by himself. *By Robert Wood,* 1651. 4°.* LT.

3155 —Grace. *By T. R. and E. M. for John Rothwell,* 1652. 8°. LT, O, OME, DC, AN; CB, CH, NU, WF, Y.

3156 ——[Anr. ed.] *By E. G. for J. Rothwell,* 1652. 8°. L, O; CU, NU, TU, Y.

3157 ——[Anr. ed.] 1653. 8°. LCL.

3158 ——Second edition. *For John Rothwell,* 1654. 4°. L, C, LCL, AN, LLU; CN, CU, IU, TSM, WSC.

3159 ——Third edition. *By W. H. for Iohn Rothwell,* 1657. 4°. O, LW, AN, CPL, ENC, BLH; CN, IU, FU, WF.

3159A ——[Anr. ed.] *For G. Eversden and sold by R. Lowndes,* 1676. 8°. T.C.I 231. C, EN; MH, NHC.

3159B ——[Anr. ed.] *For Sam. Sprint,* 1677. 8°. MH.

3160 —The hearers duty. *By E. C. for George and Henry Eversden,* 1653. 8°.* L, AN; CH, NU, WF, Y.

3161 —Heavens glory, Hells terror. *For John Rothwell,* 1653. 4°. LT, C, LCL, LW, AN, E; CH, CN, NHC, NU, TO, WF, Y.

3162 ——[Anr. ed.] —, 1655. 4°. L, CPL; CN, INU, MH, OWC, PL.

3163 ——[Anr. ed.] *By S. G. for John Rothwell,* 1658. 4°. L, O, LCL, AN, ENC; IU, MH, NCD, WF, Y.

3164 ——[Anr. ed.] *For Peter Parker,* 1671. 8°. T.C.I 75. LW, CPL, DU, YM; CH, CLC, NU, Y.

3164A ——[Anr. ed.] —, 1679. 8°. L, CPL; Y.

3165 Entry cancelled.
—Hell's terror. 1653. *See* —Heavens glory.

3166 —Love's letters, his and hers. [*London*], *printed,* 1651. 4°.* LT, LIU, GK.

3167 [–] The main points of church-government. *By J. M. for Luke Favvne,* 1648[9]. 8°. LT, O, CM, YM.

3168 [–] A modest and clear vindication of the serious representation. *For Stephen Bowtell,* 1649. 4°. LT, O, OC, CS, P, DT; CH, CU, NC, NU, WF, Y.

3168A —The mortified Christian. *For Francis Eglesfield,* 1654. 8°. L, GU; WF.

3168B —The naturall mans case stated. *By E. Cotes, for George Eversden,* 1652. 8°. O, CPL; Y.

3169 ——Second edition. —, 1652. 8°. L, O, DC, DCH, RU; CB, MH, WF, Y.

3169A ——Third edition. *By E. Cotes, for George Eversden,* 1653. 8°. O; Y.

3170 ——[Anr. ed.] *By E. Cotes, for Henry Eversden,* 1658. 8°. LW, BC; CLC, IU, NU.

3170A ——[Anr. ed.] *By E. Cotes for George Eversden,* 1658. 8°. CN, MH.

3171 —The penitent pardoned. *For John Rothwell, and for Nathanael Brooks,* 1657. 4°. L, LW, CPL, ENC; CH, NU, TO, WF, Y.

3172 —Scripture rules. [*London,* 1652.] brs. L, EN.

3173 ——[Anr. ed.] *For John Rothwell,* 1653. brs. LT, LS.

3173A ——[Anr. ed.] [*London,* 1696.] brs. Y.

3174 —Short and plaine animadversions on some passages in Mr. Dels sermon. *By M. Bell for Iohn Bellamy,* 1646. 4°. LT, O, C, AN, DT; CH, CU, MH, MU, NU, WF, Y.

3175 ——Second edition. *By R. Cotes, for Iohn Bellamie;* 1647. 4°. L, O, C, OC, CCA, E; BBE, MB, NHC.

3175A —The sinners legacy. 1657. 4°. LCL.

3176 —The souls cordiall . . . the third volum. *For Nathaniel Brooke,* 1653. 8°. LT, O, LCL, LSC, CPL; NU, WF, Y.

3177 —Mr. Love's speech made on the scaffold. [*London,* 1651.] cap., 4°.* LT, O; Y.

3177A —The strange and wonderful predictions of. [1651?] 8°. E, DT.

3178 —A treatise of effectual calling and election. *For John Rothwell, to be sold by John Clark,* 1653. 4°. LT, C, OH, CK, AN, YM; CLC, MH, NP, NU, Y.

3179 ——Second edition. *For John Rothwell,* 1655. 4°. LCL, LW, CPL; CN, MH, INU, PL, Y.

3180 ——[Anr. ed.] *By I. Owsley for Iohn Rothwell,* 1658. 4°. L, O, BR, E, ENC; CH, CN, MH, NU, WF, Y.

3181 —A true and exact copie of Mr. Love's speech. [*London*, 1651.] cap., 4°.* LT, O, C, AN, SP; CN, CU, MB, MIU, NU.

3182 —The true and perfect speech of . . . on the scaffold. *Imprinted at London by John Clowes, 1651.* 4°.* LT; INU, WF, Y.

3183 —The true doctrine of mortification. *By E. Cotes, 1654.* 8°. LCL, LW, AN, MR; CH, NU.

3184 —A vindication of. *By R. Wood, 1651.* 4°.* L, O, LG, MR.

3185 —The zealous Christian. *By R. and W. Leybourn, for John Rothwell, 1653.* 8°. O, C, LCL, LW, ENC; CH, CLC, NU, TU, Y.

3186 — —Second edition. *For John Rothwell, 1654.* 4°. L, LCL, AN, LLU; CH, CN, IU, MH, WF.

3187 — —[Anr. ed.] —, *1657.* 4°. L, O, LLP, AN, E, ENC; CH, IU, MH, NGT, NU, Y, AVP.

   [**Love, James.**] Mariners jewel. 1695. *See* Lightbody, James.

3187A **Love, Jeremiah.** Clavis medicinae; or. *For Henry Brome, 1674.* 8°. T.C.I 177. WF.

3188 — —[Anr. ed.] *By J. R. for W. B., 1675.* 8°. L, O, C; WSG.

3189 —The practice of physick reformed. *For Henry Brome, 1675.* 8°.* L; WSG.

3190 [**Love, John**], *Quaker.* An epistle to all young convinced friends. *Printed and sold by T. Sowle, 1696.* 4°.* L, LF, BBN, MR; CLC, NPT, PH, PSC.

3191 **Love, John,** *surveyor.* Geodæsia: or, the art of surveying. *For John Taylor, 1688.* 4°. T.C.II 224. L, O, MC, DT; CH, CLC, MH, MU, RPJ, Y.

3192 **Love, Richard.** Oratio habita in academia Cantabrigiensi. *Cantabrigiæ, excudebat Joannes Field, 1660.* 4°.* L, O, LNC, SP; CH, MH, NU, TU, WF, Y.

3192A — —Second edition. —, *1660.* 4°.* L, C, OB, CS, CT.

3193 —The vvatchmans vvatchvvord. *By Roger Daniel of Cambridge, 1642.* 4°.* LT, O, C, LCL, YM; CH, CU, MH, NU, TU, WF, Y.

   Love a la mode. 1663. *See* Southland, Thomas.

3194 Love and constancy. *For John Hose, [1665?].* brs. L.

3195 The love and faithfulnes of the Scottish nation. *By F: Neile for Tho: Vnderhill, 1646.* 4°.* LT, MR, EN, DT; CH, IU, MH, MM, NU, Y.

3196 Love and gallantry. [*London*], *for Phillip Brooksby, [1674?].* brs. L.

3197 Love and honesty, or, the modish courtier. [*London*], *for E. Oliver, [1676].* brs. L, O.

3198 Love and honour. [*London*], *for P. Brooksby, [1672].* brs. L, O, HH; MH.

3199 —[Anr. ed.] *For E. Brooksby, [1695–1703].* brs. L, O, HH.

3200 Love and honour: or, the lover's farewel. *By W. O. for J. Foster, [1695?].* brs. L.

   Love and jealousie. 1683. *See* Dryden, John.

3201 Love and loyalty. [*London*], *for P. Brooksby, J. Deacon, J. Blare, and J. Back, [1688–92].* brs. L, O, CM, HH.

3202 Love and loyalty well met. [*London*], *for J. Blare, [1684–5].* brs. L, HH; MH.

   Love and truth. 1680. *See* Walton, Isaak.

3203 Love crownd with victory. *For P. Brooksby, [1672–95].* brs. L, O, HH; MH.

   Love given o're. 1683. *See* Gould, Robert.

3204–5 No entries.

3206 Love in a barn. [*London?* 1670.] brs. L.

3207 Love in a bush. [*London*], *for James Bissel, [1685–88].* brs. L, CM, HH; MH.

3208 Love in a maze. [*London*], *by and for Alex. Milbourn, [1690?].* brs. EUING 177. L, GU; CH.

3208A —[Anr. ed.] *By and for A. M. [1690].* brs. L.

3208B —[Anr. ed.] *For J. Hose, [1660–80].* brs. EUING 178. GU.

3208C —[Anr. ed.] *For R. B., sold by F. Coles, [1670?].* brs. O.

3209 —[Anr. ed.] [*London*], *for W. Thackeray, [1688–89].* brs. L, CM, HH.

3210 Love in a mist. [*London*], *for I. Deacon, [1684–95].* brs. L, O, HH; MH.

3210A Love in distress: or, the lucky discovery. A novel. *By W. Onley, for H. Newman, S. Briscoe, and H. Nelme, 1697.* 12°. CN.

   Love in its extasie. 1649. *See* Peaps, William.

   Love in the blossome. [1672.] *See* Playford, John.

3211 Love is a god. [*London*], *T. Cross, [1700?].* brs. L.

3211A Love is the cause of my mourning. [*London?* 1670.] brs. L.

3211B —[Anr. ed.] [*London?* 1700.] brs. L.

   Love letters between. 1684. *See* Behn, *Mrs.* Aphra.

3211C Love lies a bleeding. *For F. G., [1653?].* brs. EUING 174. GU.

   Love of the soul. St. Omers, 1652. *See* Martin, Gregory.

   Love one another. [n.p., 1643.] *See* Taylor, John.

3212 The love-sick lady. [*London*], *for P. Brooksby, J. Deacon, J. Blare, J. Back, [1688–92].* brs. L, CM, HH.

3213 Entry cancelled.

   Love-sick maid. [1670–90.] *See* Love-sick maid: or Cordelia's.

3214 The love-sick maid of Portsmouth. [*London*], *for I. Blare, [1680?].* brs. L.

3215 The lovesick maid of Waping. [*London*], *for J. Conyers, [1682–88].* brs. L, HH; MH.

3216 The love-sick maid: or, Cordelia's. *For W. Thackeray, T. Passenger, and W. Whitwood, [1670?].* brs. L.

3216A —[Anr. ed.] [*London*], *by and for A. M., [1693?].* L, O, CM, HH, GU; MH.

3217 The love-sick maid quickly revived. *For Phil. Brooksby, [1672–95].* brs. L, HH.

3218 The love-sick serving-man. [*London*], *for P. Brooksby, J. Deacon, J. Blare, J. Back, [1684].* brs. L, O, CM, HH; MH.

3219 The love-sick shepheard. *For Richard Burton, [1641–74].* brs. O.

3220 The love-sick soldier. [*London*], *for P. Brooksby, [1690?].* brs. L, CM, HH.

   Love-sick young man. [n.p., 1688–89.] *See* J., T.

3221 The love sports of wanton Jemmy. *For Phil. Brooksby, [1675–80].* brs. L, HH.

3221A —[Anr. ed.] *For P. Brooksby, [1680?].* brs. O.

3222 Love the pretiovs oyntment. *For John Wright, 1654.* 4°.* L, LW; NU.

3223 —[Anr. ed.] *London; reprinted at Leith, 1654.* 4°.* ALDIS 1492. L, EN.

Love to the captives. 1656. *See* Rofe, George.

Love to the life. 1674. *See* Mayhew, Richard.

Love to the lost. [n.p.], 1665. *See* Nayler, James.

Love tricks. 1667. *See* Shirley, James.

Love will finde out. 1661. *See* Shirley, James.

3223A Love vvithout blemish. [*London*], *for J. Wright, J. Cl[a]rk, W. Thackeray, and T. Passenger*, [1681–84]. brs. O.

Love without interest. 1699. *See* Penkethman, William.

3224 Love without measure. [*London*], *for VV. Thackery, and T. Passinger*, [1686–88]. brs. L, CM, HH; MH.

3225 **Loveday, Robert.** Loveday's letters domestick and forrein. *By J. G. for Nath. Brook*, 1659. 8°. LT, O, C, EC, EN; BBE, CH, IU, MH, TU, WF, Y. (var.)

3226 ——Second edition. —, 1662. 8°. L, C, RU, GK; CLC, CN, NCD, NNM, WF, Y.

3227 ——[Anr. ed.]. *For Nath. Brook, and William Cartwright*, 1663. 8°. CLC, MH, PU, Y.

3228 ——Fourth edition. *For N. B. to be sold by Benjamin Billingsley*, 1669. 8°. T.C.I 24. L, O, CS; CLC, NP.

3228A ——"Fourth" edition. *By S. G. and B. G. for Nath. Brooks*, 1669. 8°. OP, LSD; IU.

3229 ——Fifth edition. *By E. Tyler and R. Holt, for Nathaniel Brooke*, 1673. 8°. T.C.I 122. L, O; CN, CU, IU, WF.

3229A ——Sixth edition. *By J. Macock for Nathaniel Brooke*, 1676. 8°. T.C.I 262. Y.

3229B ——"Sixth" edition. *For Obadiah Blagrave*, 1677. 8°. T.C.I 284. L, O; IU, NIC, Y.

3230 ——Seventh edition. *By J. Rawlins for Obadiah Blagrave*, 1684. 8°. L, O, LW, CP, A; CLC, CN, CU, MH, MIU, OLU.

3231 **Loveday, Samuel.** An alarm for slumbring Christians. *For Francis Smith*, 1675. 8°. T.C.I 195. L, C, ORP, ENC; MH.

3232 —An answer to the lamentation of Cheap-side Crosse. *For T. A.*, [1642]. 4°.* LT, LG, OW; CH, LC, MH, WF.

3233 —The hatred of Esau. [*London*], *by John Clowes, for Gieles [sic] Calvert*, [1650]. 8°. LT.

3234 Entry cancelled. *See following entry.*

3235 —Personal reprobation reprobated. *For the authour, to be sold by him, and Francis Smith, and P. Parker*, 1676. 8°. T.C.I 233. O, LCL, ORP, E, ENC; CH, CU, MH, NHC, NU, ASU.

3235A **Loveday, Thomas.** The custom of the mannor of Paynswicke. *Printed*, 1688. 12°. LC, WF.

3236 **Lovel, Henry.** Horrid and strange news from Ireland. *By Tho. Harper*. 1643. 4°.* LT, GU; CH, MH.

3237 Entry cancelled.

[**Lovelace, Dudley Posthumous.**] Elegies. 1660. *See* Lovelace, Richard. Lucasta. 1659.

3238 **Lovelace, Francis.** The speech of . . . 27 day October, 1660. *By S. Griffin, for Matthew Walbancke*, 1660. 4°.* LT; MH, Y.

3239 —The speech of . . . to His Majestie, . . . 25th day of May, 1660. —, 1660. 4°.* L, O, CS, DU, EN; CH, CLC, WF, Y.

3239A [**Lovelace, Richard.**] The liberty of the imprisoned Royallist. [*London*, 1647.] cap., 4°.* LT; CH, WF.

3240 —Lucasta: epodes. *By Tho. Harper, to be sold by Tho. Evvster*, 1649. 8°. LT, O, CE, DU, LLU; CH, IU, MH, TU, WCL, Y.

3241 —Lucasta. Posthume poems. *By William Godbid for Clement Darby*, 1659. 8°. L, O, LVD, CT; CH, CN, MH, NCD, WF, Y.

[**Lovell.**] Papists protesting. 1686. *See* Gother, John.

3242 [**Lovell, Archibald.**] A summary of material heads. *By T. B.*, 1696. 4°.* L, O, NE, EN; CH, MBA, NU, WF, Y.

3243 **Lovell, Robert.** Παμβοτανολογια, sive enchiridion . . . or a compleat herball. *Oxford, by William Hall for Ric. Davis*, 1659. 8°. MADAN 2450. LT, O, CT, E, DT; CH, MH, MIU, NN.

3244 ——Second edition. *Oxford: by W. H. for Ric. Davis*, 1665. 12°. MADAN 2706. L, O, C, GU, DT; CH, CJC, MH, MU, WF, Y.

3245 —Πανορυκτολογια. Sive pammineralogicon. Or an universal history of mineralls. *Oxford, by W. Hall, for Joseph Godwin*, 1661. 8°. MADAN 2561. L, O, C, DC, LLU; CH, IU, MBP, MH, NR, PL, WF, HC, AVP.

3246 —Πανζωορυκτολογια. Sive panzoologicomineralogia. *Oxford, by Hen: Hall, for Jos: Godwin.* 1661. 8°. MADAN 2562. LT, O, C, GU, E; CH, CJC, MBP, MH, WGS, Y, AVP.

3246A **Lovell, William.** Approved receipts. *For Charles Tyus*, 1663. 8°.* WU.

3246B —The Duke's desk broken up. *For the author*, 1660. 8°. WU.

3247 ——[Anr. ed.] *Yorke: by Alice Broade, to be sold by Francis Mawburne*, 1661. 24°.* YM.

3247A —The Dukes desk newly broken up. *For John Garway*, 1661. 8°. L; PCP.

3247B ——[Anr. ed.] *For J. Garway & sold by J. Andrews*, [1661?]. 8°. LWL.

3247C ——[Anr. ed.] *By T. Leach for F. Coles*, 1665. 8°.* L (lost).

3247D ——[Anr. ed.] *By E. C.*, 1672. 8°.* L (lost).

3247E The lovely London lass. *For F. Coles, T. Vere and J. Wright*, [1663–74]. brs. O.

3247F The lovely Northern lass. [*London*], *for F. Coles, T. Vere, and J. Wright*, [1663–74]. brs. L, O.

Lovely Polander. [1681.] *See* Préchac.

3248 **Lover, Thomas.** The true gospel-faith witnessed. *For Francis Smith*, 1654. 8°.* LT, OC.

3249 A lover complimenting his mistriss. [*London*, 1670?] brs. L.

3250 A lover forsaken. *Printed at London, by G. P.*, [1650?]. brs. EUING 188. L, GU.

3251 The lovers academy. *For T. Passinger*, [c. 1680]. 12°.* CM.

Lovers battle. [n.p., 1670.] *See* Robins, Thomas.

3252 A lovers desire. [*London*, 1650?] brs. L.

3253 The lovers fancy. *For F. Coles, T. Vere, J. Wright, and J. Clarke*, [1674–79]. brs. L.

3254 The lovers farewell. *For John Andrewes*, [1655?]. brs. L.

3254A —[Anr. ed.] *For Fr. Coles, Tho. Vere, Jo. Wright, and Jo. Clarke*, [1647–79]. brs. O.

3254B The lovers final farewel. [*London*], *for Eliz. Andrews*, [1663–4]. brs. O.

3254C   The lover's happinesse. *For F. Coles, T. Vere, I. Wright, and I. Clark,* 1678. brs. O.

3254D   —[Anr. ed.] [*London*], *for R. Burton,* [1641–74]. brs. O.

        Lovers joy and grief. [1641.] *See* Parker, Martin.

3254E   The lover's mad fits. *For F. Coles, T. Vere, W. Gilbertson, and J. Wright,* [1663–5]. brs. O.

3255   —[Anr. ed.]. *By A. P. for F. Coles, T. Vere, J. Wright, and J. Clarke,* [1675?]. brs. L, O, CM.

3255A   Lovers paradice. [*London*], *for I. Jordan,* [1680–82]. brs. O.

3256   The lovers pastime. *For R. Burton,* [1680?]. brs. O.

3257   The lovers prophesie. [*London*], *for P. Brooksby,* [1680–85]. brs. HH.

3257A   The lovers quarrel, or Cupids. *By A. P.* [*for*] *F. Coles, T. Vere, and J. Wright,* [1663–74]. 8°.* L.

3257B   —[Anr. ed.]. *For F. Coles, T. Vere, J. Wright, and J. Clarke,* 1677. 8°.* O.

3257C   —[Anr. ed.] *For J. M., & sold by W. T. & T. Passinger,* [1685?]. 12°.* CM.

3258   The lover's secretary. *For R. Bentley,* 1692. 12°. T.C.II 513. L, O.

        Lovers teares. [1641.] *See* P., M.

3258A   The lover's tragedy; or, parents cruelty. [*London*], *for P. Brooksby,* [1685–88]. brs. EUING 186. GU.

3259   The lovers victory. [*London,* 1680?] brs. O.

        Love's a lottery. 1699. *See* Harris, Joseph.

        Love's advocate. 1651. *See* L., G.

3260   The loves and adventures of Clerio and Lozia. *By J. M. and are to be sold by William Ley,* 1652. 8°. LT; CH, CN.

3261   Loves better then gold. [*London*], *for P. Brooksby,* [*c.* 1676]. brs. L, O, HH; MH.

3261A   Loves boundless power. [*London*], *for T. Vere,* [1660?]. brs. O.

3262   —[Anr. ed.] [*London*], *for I. Deacon,* [1690?]. brs. L; MH, Y.

3262A   Loves captivity and liberty. *For F. Coles, T. Vere, J. Wright, and J. Clarke,* [1674–79]. brs. O.

3263   Loves carouse. *For Fra. Grove,* [1660?]. brs. L.

3263A   Loves conquest, or, take her in the humour. [*London*], *for P. Broksby* [sic], [1690?]. brs. O.

3263B   Loves conquest over death. [*London*], *for C. Passenger,* [1680?]. brs. O.

        Love's dominion. 1654. *See* Flecknoe, Richard.

3264   Love's downfal. [*London*], *for A. M. W. O. and T. Thackeray,* [1684.] brs. L, O, CM, HH.

3264aA   —[Anr. ed.] *For R. Burton,* [1641–74]. brs. O.

3264bA   —[Anr. ed.] [*London*], *for F. Coles, T. Vere, J. Wright, I. Clarke, W. Thackeray, and T. Passinger,* [1678–80]. brs. O.

3264cA   —[Anr. ed.] [*London*], *for W. Thackeray, T. Passinger, and W. Whitwood,* [1678]. brs. O.

3264A   Entry cancelled.

        Love's empire. 1682. *Se* Bussy, Roger de Rabutin, conte de.

3265   Loves extasie. [1687.] brs. O.

3266   Loves fancy. *For F. Coles, T. Vere, and I. Wright,* [1675?]. brs. O.

        Loves fierce desire. [n.p., 1670.] *See* Price, Laurence.

3266A   Loves fierce dispute. [*London?* 1670.] brs. L.

3266B   Love's fortune. *Thomas Jenkins,* 1656. brs. CM.

3267   —[Anr. ed.] [*London*], *for F. Coles, T. Vere, J. Wright, J. Clark, W. Thackeray, and T. Passinger,* [1680–82]. brs. HH; MH.

3268   Loves garland or posies. *Printed at London by R. C. to be sold by F. G.,* 1648. 8°.* L.

3269   —[Anr. ed.] *By Andrew Clark, to be sold by Tho. Passenger,* 1674. 8°.* L.

        Love's journal. 1671. *See* Desjardins, Marie Catherine Hortense de, *Mme.* de Villedieu.

3270   Loves lamentable tragedy. [*London*], *for I. Deacon,* [1682/3]. brs. L, CM, HH.

3270A   —[Anr. ed.] [n.p., 1682.] brs. L.

3271   Loves master-piece. *For F. Coles, T. Vere, and J. Wright,* [1663–74]. brs. O.

3271A   —[Anr. ed.] *By H. B. for P. Brooksby,* 1683. 12°.* CM.

3272   Loves mistress. *For F. Coles, T. Vere, J. Wright, and J. Clarke,* [1675]. brs. O.

3273   Loves mistery. *For William Kenrick,* [1663?]. brs. L.

        Love's name lives. 1651. *See* Love, Mrs.

3274   The loves of Charles, Duke of Mantva. [*London*], *in the Savoy for Henry Herringman,* 1669. 8° T.C.I 2. L, O; CH, CN, CU, MH, WF, Y.

3275   The loves of Damon and Sappho. [*London*], *for F. Coles, T. Vere, J. Wright, J. Clarke, W. Thackeray, and T. Passinger,* [1680]. brs. L, HH; MH.

3276   The loves of Hero and Leander. A mock poem. *Printed at London,* 1651. 8°. LT, AN.

3277   The loves of Hero and Leander: . . . with marginal notes. *Printed at London,* 1653. 8°. L, O; WF, Y.

3278   —[Anr. ed., "marginall."] —, 1653. 8°. CH, CLC, MH, Y.

3279   The loves of Jockey and Jenny. [*London*], *for P. Brooksby,* [1684–5]. brs. EUING 173. L, CM, HH, GU; MH.

        Loves of sundry philosophers. 1673. *See* Desjardins, Marie Catherine Hortense de, *Mme.* de Villedieu.

3280   Loves overthrow. [*London*], *for P. Brooksby,* [1672–95]. brs. L, HH; MH.

        Loves paradice. [1663.] *See* P., J.

3281   Love's posie. *For Joseph Hindmarsh,* 1686. 12°. T.C.II 159. L, P; CLC.

3281A   Love's power. [*London,* 1685.] brs. L.

3282   Loves power and greatness. *For Phillip Brooksby,* [1672–95]. brs. L, HH.

        Love's return. [n.p., 1655.] *See* S., S.

3283   Loves school, or a new merry book of complements. *For W. Thackery,* 1674. 8°.* CH.

3283A   —[Anr. ed.] —, *T. Passinger, P. Brooksby, and J. Clarke,* 1682. 8°.* CM.

3283B   Love's secret wound. [*London*], *for J. Blare,* [1685]. brs. O.

3283C   Loves tide. [*London*], *for F. Coles, T. Vere, J. Wright, and J. Clarke,* [1674–79]. brs. O.

3284   Loves torments eased by death. [*London*], *for P. Brooksby,* [1672–95]. brs. EUING 172. L, HH, GU; MH.

3285   Love's triumph. *For D. M.,* 1676. brs. L.

3286   Loves triumph over bashfulness. [*London*], *for P. Brooksby,* [1672–95]. brs. L, O, HH; MH.

3287 Love's tyrannick conquest. [London], for C. Hussey, [1680?]. brs. L.

3288 Loves tyranny. [London], for C. Passinger, [1678–82]. brs. L, O, HH; MH.

3289 Loves unspeakable passion. [London] for J. Deacon, [1684]. brs. L, O, HH; MH.

3290 Loves victory obtained [sic]. [London], for F. Coles, [1655–60]. brs. L, CM, HH; MH.

3291 Loves wound, and loves cure. For F. Coles, T. Vere, and J. Wright, [1663–74]. brs. O.

3292 **Lovewell, John.** A complaint of the oppressed. Printed, 1661. 4°.* L, O, LF, MR, EN; MH, PH.

Loving & friendly invitation. 1683. See Taylor, John, Quaker.

3293 The loving chamber-maid. [London], for Phil. Brooksby, [1675?]. brs. EUING 179. L, O, HH, GU.

Loving epistle to all. [n.p., 1694.] See Keith, George.

3294 The loving lad, and the coy lass. [London], for J. Wright, J. Clarke, W. Thackeray, and T. Passinger, [1681–84]. brs. L, CM, HH; MH.

3294A —[Anr. ed.] By E. C., for F. Coles, T. Vere, and J. Wright, [1663–74]. brs. O.

Loving salutation to all Friends. [n.p., 1662.] See Brend, William.

Loving salutation to the seed. 1657. See Fell, Margaret.

Loving salutation with [n.p.], 1665. See Farnworth, Richard.

3295 The loving shepherd. [London,] For P. Brooksby, I. Deacon, I. Blare, and I. Back, [1680?]. brs. L, CM; MH.

3296 The loving young couple. For F. Coles, T. Vere, J. Wright, and J. Clarke, [1674–79]. brs. O.

Low, Emmanuel, pseud. See Simons, Joseph.

3297 The low-country soldier. [London], for C. Bates, [1685]. brs. EUING 162. L, O, CM, HH, GU; MH.

Lovv Dutch character'd. 1658. See P., T.

3298 Entry cancelled.

Low estate of the low-countrey Countess of Holland. 1672. See Stevenson, Matthew.

3299 **Lowde, James.** A discourse concerning the nature of man. By T. Warren, for Walter Kettilby, 1694. 8°. T.C.II 482. L, O, C, LW, YM, DT, CH, CN, LC, MH, NU, Y.

3300 Entry cancelled. Ghost. See previous entry.

3301 —Moral essays. York, by J. White for Fra. Hildyard, to be sold by Brab. Aylmer, and Tho. Bennet, London, 1699. 12°. L, C, SHR; MH, NORTHWESTERN.

3302 —The reasonableness of the Christian religion. For Walter Kettilby, 1684. 4°. T.C.II 82. L, O, C, BR, YM; MBA, WF, Y.

Lowden, lord. See Loudoun, John Campbell, earl.

3303 Entry cancelled.

Lowe, Christopher. Scripture rules to be observed in buying and selling. 1653. See Love, Christopher.

3304 L[owe], E[dward]. A revievv of some short directions. Second edition. Oxford, by W. Hall for R. Davis, 1664. 12°. MADAN 2662–3. O, YM; CLC, LC. (var.)

3305 [–] A short direction for the performance of Cathedrall service. Oxford, by William Hall for Richard Davis, 1661. 8°.* MADAN 2563. LT, LLP; CB, CH, MB, MH, NC.

3306 **Lowe, Peter.** A discourse of the whole art of chyrurgery. Fourth edition. By R. Hodgkinsonne, 1654. 4°. L, C, LCS, GU, E; MMO, NRU, U. ALABAMA, HC.

3307 Entry cancelled.

Lowell, Percival. Funeral elegie vpon . . . John Winthrop. [n.p., 1676.] See title.

3307A [**Lower, Richard.**] A brief account of the virtues of . . . Astrop. Printed, 1668. 4°.* L, LWL, OC.

3308 —Diatribae Thomæ Willisii . . . de febribus. Apud Jo. Martyn & Ja. Allestry, 1665. 8°. L, O, C, LCP, DT; BN, CLC, NIC, WSG, JF. (var.)

3309 —Dr. Lowers, and several other eminent physicians receipts. For John Nutt, 1700. 12°. T.C.III 198. L, C, LCS, LSM, MAU; CJC, U. BRITISH COLUMBIA, WF.

3310 —Tractatus de corde. Typis Jo. Redmayne, impensis Jacobi Allestry, 1669. 8°. T.C.I 10. L, O, C, GH, DT; BN, CLC, INU, MB, MU, WSG, JF.

3311 — —Second edition. Typis Jo. Redmayne & impensis Jacobum Allestry, 1670. 8°. T.C.I 52. LW, CT, NPL, GK; PL, RICHMOND ACAD. OF MED., HC.

3312 — —Fourth edition. Typis M. C. impensis J. Martyn, 1680. 8°. T.C.I 398. L, O, C, GU, BQ; BN, CH, MBM, NC, PL, WSG, JF.

3313 [–] Willisius male vindicatvs. Dublini, 1667. 8°. L, O.

Lower, Sir William. Amorous fantasme. 1660. See Quinault, Philippe.

3314 —The enchanted lovers. Hage: by Adrian Vlack, 1658. 12°. LT; CH, CLC, CN, CU, WF, Y.

3315 — —[Anr. ed.] For Henry Herringman, 1659. 12°. LVD.

3316 — —[Anr. ed.] For Fr. Kirkman, 1661. 12°. L.

3317 —A funeral elegy on her illustrious Highnesse the Princesse Royal of Orange. [London? 1661.] brs. MH.

3318 No entry.

—Noble ingratitude. Hague, 1659. See Quinault, Philippe.

3319 —Three new playes. For Franc. Kirkman, 1661. 12°. L, O; CU, LC.

3319A — —[Anr. ed.] For F. Kirkman, 1661. 12°. OW, EC; CH.

3320 **Lowick, Thomas.** The history of the life & martyrdom of St. George. By J. Best for William Crook, 1664. 4°.* L, O; CH, NP, Y.

3321 **Lowman, R.** An exact narrative and description of the . . . fire-works. colop: By N. Thompson, 1685. fol. L, O; MH.

3321A **Lowndes, Ralph.** The penitential declaration of. [Chester? 1690.] brs. HH.

3321B **Lowndes, William.** A copy of a letter . . . July 29, 1696. [London, 1696.] brs. L.

3322 [–] A further essay for the amendment of the gold and silver coins. By T. Hodgkin, and sold by Richard Baldwin, 1695. 4°.* L, LI, CT, EN; IU, LC, NC, NP, PU, WF, Y.

3323 [–] A report containing an essay for the amendment of the silver coins. *By Charles Bill, and the executrix of Thomas Newcomb, 1695.* 8°. L, O, C, EN, DT; BN, CH, LC, MH, MIU, NC, NR, Y.

3323A **Lownds, T.** A funeral elegy . . . Oliver. *By T. Johnson for F. Corrinet, 1658.* brs. L.

3324 **Lowth, Simon.** Catechetical questions. *For Chr. Wilkinson, and Tho. Burrel, 1673.* 12°. T.C.I 126. L, O, C, OC, LNC.

3325 — —Second edition. *For W. G. and are to be sold by Chr. Wilkinson, and Tho. Burrel, 1674.* 12°. T.C.I 181. L, CS, YM; MH.

3326 Entry cancelled.
    [–] Historical collections concerning church affairs 1696. *See title.*
    [–] Letter to a friend, in answer. 1688. *See* Grascome, Samuel.

3327 [–] A letter to Dr. Bvrnet, occasioned by his late letter to Mr. Lowth. colop: *For Randal Taylor, 1685.* cap., 4°.* L, O, EC, LLU, WCA, DT; CH, CN, MH, NU, WF, Y, AVP.

3328 —A letter to Edw. Stillingfleet. *By J. L. to be sold by Randal Taylor, 1687.* 4°. T.C.II 175. L, O, C, ENC, DT; CH, IU, NCD, NP, NU, WF, Y.

3329 —Of the subject of church-power. *For Benj. Tooke, 1685.* 8°. T.C.II 91. L, O, C, EN, DT; BN, CH, CN, MH, NU, WF.

3330 **Lowth, William.** A vindication of the divine authority. *Oxford, at the theater. And are to be sold by John Wilmot, 1692.* 8°. T.C.II 421. L, O, C, ENC, DT; CH, IU, MH, NU, PL, TSM, Y.

3331 — —Second edition. *London, by William Horton, for John Wilmot in Oxford, 1699.* 8°. T.C.III 148. L, O, CT, ENC, DT; CH, INU, NCD, PL, WF.

3332 [–] —[Anr. ed.] *[Boston: by B. Green and J. Allen, 1700.]* 8°.* EVANS 957. MB, MH, MHS, Y.

3332A Entry cancelled.
    Lowther, *Sir John.* Effect of what was spoken by. 1689. *See title.*

3333 [**Lowther, Luke.**] By the Lord Mayor of . . . Dublin. *[Dublin, 1680.]* brs. STEELE 2p 918. LS.

3334 [**Lowthorp, Jonathan.**] A letter to the Bishop of Sarum. *[London], printed, 1690.* 4°.* O, LL, OC, CS, LLU; CH, IEG, NU, WF, Y.

3335 The loyal address of the eminent town of Lynn-Regis. *[London, 1681.]* brs. L, O, HH; CH, IU, PU, WF, Y, AVP.

3336 The loyal addresse of the gentry of Gloucestershire. *For Humphrey Tuckey, 1660.* brs. LT, LG.

3336A A loyale anagrame on the Duke of Albany. *[n.p., 1688.]* brs. L.

3336B A loyal anagram on the Prince . . . born the 10th of June. *Holy-Rood-House, P. B., 1688.* brs. ALDIS 2767.5. EN.
    Loyal and impartial satyrist. 1694. *See* Rogers, Thomas.

3337 Loyal and ingenuous returns. *For A. Seile, 1661.* 4°.* O, LUG, LNC; Y.
    Loyal appeal. [n.p.] 1681. *See* R., W.

3338 The loyal apprentices protestation. *[London], by A. B. and sold by Randal Taylor, 1681.* brs. L, O, LG; CH, MH, PU, WF, Y.

3339 The loyal British fighting in Flanders. *[London? 1694.]* brs. L.

3339A The loyal bumper: or, England's comfort. *[London, 1689?]* brs. MH.

3339B The loyal caution to all the Kings friends. *For J. Dean, [1683?].* brs. MH, Y.
    Loyal citizen. 1682. *See* D., J.
    Loyal citizen revived. 1643. *See* Garway, *Sir* Henry.

3340 The loyal city of Bristol. *[n.p.], for J. Davies, 1681.* 4°.* EN; IU, WF.

3341 A loyal congratulation to . . . Shaftesbury. *For Charles Leigh, 1681.* brs. L; CH, MH, PU, Y.

3342 Entry cancelled.
    Loyal conquest. 1683. *See* Dean, John.

3343 Loyal constancy. *[London], for P. Brooksby, [1680].* brs. O, HH; MH.
    Loyall convert. Oxford, 1643. *See* Quarles, Francis.

3344 The loyall covenanter. *[n.p.], printed, 1648.* 4°. L, O, NE, DT; CH, WF, Y.

3345 The loyal English man's wish. *Printed and sold by T. Moore, 1692.* brs. HH; CH.

3346 The loyal feast, design'd. *For Allen Banks, 1682.* brs. O, LG; CH, MH, Y.

3346A The loyal forrister, or, royal pastime. *[London], for C. Bates, [1690–94].* brs. EUING 156. GU.
    Loyal garland. 1671. *See* M., S.

3347 The loyal health. *For A. Banks, 1682.* brs. L, O, LG, OC; CH, MH, TU, Y.
    Loyal health. [n.p.], 1684. *See* R., W.
    Loyal incendiary. 1684. *See* Pordage, Samuel.

3348 The loyal letany. *[London, 1681.]* brs. L, O, C; CDA, CH, MH, NCD, NP, PU, WF.

3349 The loyal livery-mens hue and cry. *For Robert Miller, 1683.* brs. L; Y, ZWT.

3350 The loyal London prentice. *For Richard Hill, 1681.* brs. L, O; MH.

3350A A loyal love-letter. *[London], for R. Burton, [1641–74].* brs. O.

3351 The loyal lovers farewel. *[London], for J. Blare, [1684–90].* brs. HH; MH.

3352 The loyal maids good counsel. *[London], for P. Brooksby, [1685–88].* brs. L, O, HH; MH, Y.

3353 The loyal man's letany. *By George Croom, 1685.* brs. L, O, CT, HH; CH, MH, NCD, Y.

3353A The loyal martyr vindicated. *[London, 1691?]* 4°. L, O, CT, DU, LSD, MR; CH, CLC, CN, MH, WF, Y.

3353B Loyal martyrs, or, the bloody inquisiror [sic]. *[n.p., 1700?]* brs. L.

3354 The loyal medal vindicated. *For R. Janeway, 1682.* fol.* L, O, LLU; CH, CN, MH, MU, TU, WF, Y.

3355 The loyal Nevv-Years gift. *By George Croom, 1685.* brs. O; MH.
    Loyal nonconformist. [n.p.], 1666. *See* Wild, Robert.

Loyal non-conformist: or, the religious subject. 1644.
    See Palk, Thomas.

3356   The loyal Observator. colop: For W. Hammond, 1683.
        4°.* L, O, CS, LSD, SP; CH, MH, NC, WF, Y.

3357   A loyal paper of verses. colop: For Francis Ellis, 1687.
        brs. O.

Loyal poems. 1685. See Taubman, Matthew.

3358   The loyal Presbyterian. For G. Egerton, 1666. 4°. EN;
        NPT.

3358A   The loyall Protestants association. [London, 1679.] brs.
        O, LIU; CH, MH.

3359   The loyal Protestant's new litany. For T. Davis, 1680.
        brs. L, O, LLU, MC; CH, MH, PU, WF, Y.

3360   The loyal Protestants vindication. For Walter Kettilby,
        1680. fol.* T.C.I 387. L, O, C, MR, EN; CH, MH, NC, TU,
        WF, Y.

3361   Loyal queries, humbly tendred to the serious consider-
        ation of the Parliament. Printed, 1659. 4°.* LT, O, MR,
        CD, DT; CH, CU, MH, NU, WF, Y.

Loyal remembrancer. 1660. See Crown, S.

3362   The loyal remonstrance. For William Palmer, 1661. brs.
        L.

3363   May, the 10. 1642. The loyall resolution of the gentry
        . . . of Yorke. May 16. for Iohn Richman, 1642. 4°.*
        LT, O, MR, YM; CLC, MB, Y.

3364   The loyall sacrifice. [London], printed, 1648. 12°. LT, O, CT,
        LLU, LNC; CH, CN, NN, WF, Y.

3365   A loyal satyr against Whiggism. colop: For C. B. to be
        sold by W. Davis, 1682. cap., fol.* L, O, LLU; CH, TU, Y,
        ASU.

3366   The loyal Scot [with music]. For Alexander Banks, 1682.
        brs. L, O, MC; MH, PU.

3367   —[Anr. ed., without music.] —, 1682. brs. MC; CH, MH,
        Y.

3368   The loyal sherifs of London. For M. Thompson, 1682.
        brs. L, O; MH.

3369   The loyal soldier of Flanders. [London], for P. Brooksby,
        J. Deacon, J. Blare, J. Back, [1688–92]. brs. EUING 165.
        L, O, CM, HH, GU; MH.

3370   The loyal soldiers courtship. [London], for P. Brooksby,
        J. Deacon, J. Blare, and J. Back, [1689–90]. brs. L, O, HH.

3371   The loyal soldiers of Flanders. [London], for C. Bates,
        [1690–95]. brs. HH.

Loyall song. [n.p., 1647.] See Wortley, Sir Francis.

Loyall subject. 1660. See Thomson, R.

3371A   The loyal subject (as it is . . .). By E. C. for F. Coles, T.
        Vere, and J. Wright, [1663–70]. brs. O.

3371B   —[Anr. ed.] [London], for I. Wright, I. Clarke, W.
        Thackeray and T. Passinger, [1681–84]. brs. O.

3371C   The loyal subject resolution. By T. Mabb for Richard
        Burton, [1660–65]. brs. EUING 161. GU.

Loyall subjects admonition. [1660?] See J., T.

3371D   The loyal subjects exultation, for the coronation. For F.
        Grove, [1660]. brs. EUING 158. GU.

Loyal subjects hearty wishes. [1660.] See P., J.

Loyall subjects joy. [1660.] See Robins, Thomas.

3372   The loyal subjects jubilee. [London, 1649.] brs. LT; CH.

Loyall subjects lamentation. 1661. See Rise, Augustin.

3373   The loyal subjects littany. Printed, 1680. brs. L, O, HH,
        LLU; CH, MH, PU, WF, Y.

3373A   —[Anr. ed.] For B. Tooke, 1680. brs. O.

Loyal subjects loveing advice. 1685. See Pike, John.

Loyall subiects retiring-roome. Oxford, 1645. See Har-
    wood, Richard.

3374   The loyal subjects teares. For Charles King, 1660. 4°.*
        LT; WF.

3374A   The loyall subjects well wishing. For Richard Burton,
        1647. brs. BARNBOUGLE CASTLE [EN has film].

Loyal tear dropt. 1667. See Glanvill, Joseph.

3375   Loyal tears poured on the herse of . . . Henry Duke of
        Gloucester. By W. G., 1660. brs. L; MH.

3376   The loyal Tories delight. For R. Shuter, [1680]. brs. L.

3377   A loyal vote for the happy birth. For William Hensman,
        1688. brs. O; MH.

3378   The loyalist setting forth. colop: For C. Tebroc, 1682.
        brs. O; MH.

Loyalists reasons. Edinburgh, 1689. See Cullen, Francis
    Grant, lord.

Loyalties tears. [n.p., 1649.] See Birkenhead, Sir John.

3379   The loyalty and glory of the city of Bath. By A. Mil-
        bourn, [1689]. brs. O; MH.

3379A   Loyalty and nonconformity. Printed, 1669. 4°.* L, O;
        CH, CLC, WF.

3379B   Loyalty asserted, or the protestation of the English.
        [London, 1648?] cap., 4°.* MR.

Loyalty banished. [n.p.], 1659. See Prynne, William.

3380   Loyalty in grain. colop: [London], published by Langley
        Curtiss, 1682. brs. DU; CH, WF, Y.

Loyalty of Popish principles. 1682. See Hancock,
    Robert.

Loyalty of the last long Parliament. 1681. See B., T.

3381   Loyalty rewarded; or, a poem. colop: For R. W., 1681.
        brs. L, C, MC; CH, MH, WF, Y.

Loyalty speakes truth. [n.p., 1648.] See Nedham,
    Marchamont.

3382   Loyalty triumphant; or a poem. colop: For William
        Grace, 1681. brs. L, O, C; CH, MH, TU, WF, Y.

3382A   Loyalty triumphant, on the confirmation of Mr. North.
        By Nath. Thompson, 1682. brs. LG; CH, MH.

3382B   Loyalty triumphant, or a looking-glass for deceivers.
        For W. Giles, 1682. brs. CH.

3382C   Loyalty triumphant: or, phanaticism display'd. [Lon-
        don], for C. Corbet, 1684. brs. L; CH, CLC.

3383   Loyalty unfeigned. [London], for P. Brooksby, [1682]. brs.
        L, HH; MH.

3384   Loyalty vindicated, being an answer. Boston, By B.
        Green and J. Allen, 1698. 4°.* EVANS 824. LPR; CH, NHS.

3385   Loyalty vindicated from the calumnies cast upon it by
        Richard Janeway. colop: For H. Jones, 1681. brs. L;
        CH, CN, PU, Y, AVP.

Loyola's disloyalty. 1643. See Crashaw, William.

3386   **Lubin, Eilhard.** Clavis Græcæ lingvæ. In officina Roberti
        White, sumptibus Johannis Partridge, 1647. 8°. CT, DU,
        LLU, LSD; CH, CLC, IU, MH.

3386A ——[Anr. ed.] *Impensis Abelis Roper*, 1662. 8°. IU, MB.

3386B ——[Anr. ed.] *Typis Johannis Macock, impensis Abelis Roper*, 1669. 8°. T.C.I 15. L, O; IU, MB, PL.

3387 **Lucan.** Lucans Pharsalia. Fourth edition. *By William Bentley for William Shears*, 1650. 12°. L, O, CE, LIU, BQ; CH, CN, MH, TU, WF, Y.

3388 ——[Anr. ed.] *For William Shears*, 1659. 8°. L, CCH; IU, NN, NP, Y.

3389 ——[Anr. ed.] *For Peter Parker*, 1679. 8°. L, O, DT; PL.

3390 **Lucas, *Sir* Charles.** His last speech. *For R. Smithurst*, 1648. 4°.* LT; INU, MIU.

3391 **Lucas, John Lucas, *baron*.** My Lord Lucas his speech in the House of Peers, Feb. the 22. 1670/1. *Middleburg, printed*, 1673. 4°.* L, O, C, YM, DT; CH, MH, MU, NU, WF, Y. (var.)

3392 —My Lord Lucas his speech . . . Feb. the 22. 1670/1. *Printed*, 1670[1]. 4°.* L, LW, DU, EN, DT; CH, CN, MH, MU, NU, Y.

3393 **Lucas, John.** The exceeding abundant grace of God. *By Tho. Snowden for Edward Giles in Norwich*, 1696. 4°.* C, DT.

3394 **Lucas, Richard.** The Christian race: a sermon. *For Samuel Smith*, 1692. 4°.* T.C.II 420. L, O, C, OM, SC; CH, NU, PL, WF, Y.

3395 —Devotion & charity. *For Samuel Smith*, 1692. 4°.* T.C.II 401. L, O, C, LW, OM; CH, MH, NU, PL, Y.

3396 [–] The duty of servants. *For Sam. Smith*, 1685. 8°. T.C.II 142. L, LLP, CT, BC, DUS; CH, MH, NC, Y.

3397 [–] —Second edition. *For S. Smith and B. Walford*, 1699. 12°. T.C.III 148. LW.

3398 —Humane life. *For George Pawlet and Samuel Smith*, 1690. 8°. L, CS, DUS, LLU, NPL; CH, CN, MH, TU, WF, Y.

3398A ——[Anr. ed.] *For George Pawlet*, 1690. 8°. DUS.

3399 [–] —Third edition. *For Sam. Smith, and Ben. Walford, and Edw. Pawlet*, 1696. 8°. L, O, BSE, EC, EN; NIA, NU, TU, Y.

3400 [–] —Fourth edition. —, 1700. 8°. O, LIU, MR, NE; CN, MH, WF, Y.

3401 —The incomprehensibleness of God. *For S. Smith, and B. Walford*, 1694. 4°.* T.C.II 491. L, O, C, BR, SHR; CH, MBZ, NCD, NU, PL, WF, Y.

3402 [–] An enquiry after happiness . . . vol. 1. *For G. Pawlet and S. Smith*, 1685. 8°. T.C.II 96. L, C, OM, EN, DT; CH, CLC, CU.

3403 [–] —Second edition. *For Samuel Smith and Edward Pawlett*, 1692. 12°. L, O, C, OC, DUS; CLC, MH, NIA, Y.

3404 [–] —Third edition. *For S. Smith and B. Walford, and Edw. Pawlett*, 1697. 8°. T.C.III 45. L, O, LW, EC, DT; MIU, NCU, NU, TU, WF.

3405 —Nabal's apology. *For S. Smith and B. Walford*, 1696. 4°.* L, O, C, LG, CS; NU, WF, Y.

3406 [–] The plain man's guide to Heaven. *For Samuel Smith*. 1692. 12°. T.C.II 401. L, O, LLP; CH, CLC.

3407 [–] —Second edition. *For S. Smith and B. Walford*, 1697. 8°. T.C.III 17. O, CS, NE.

3408 [–] Practical Christianity. *By S. and B. G. for R. Pawlet*, 1677. 8°. T.C.I 300. O, C, OC, LLU, DT; IEG, TSM.

3409 [–] —Second edition. *By B. Griffin for R. Pawlett*, 1681. 8°. L, C, CT, DU; CLC, TU.

3410 ——Third edition. *By M. Flesher for George Pawlet*, 1685. 8°. L, BSE, D; MH, NU.

3411 ——Fourth edition. *For Edward Pawlett*, 1693. 8°. L, O, LW, D, DT; CDA, NHS, NIA, NU, WF, Y.

3412 ——Fifth edition. —, *sold by Henry Bonwick*, 1700. 8°. T.C.III 189. L, C, OC, BSE, SHR; CH, CLC, TU.

3413 —Reformation. *For Sam. Smith, and Benj. Walford*, 1697. 4°.* T.C.III 34. L, O, C, LLP, CT, LIU, CD; NU, WF, Y.

3414 [–] Religious perfection. Or, a third part. *For Sam. Smith and Benj. Walford*, 1696. 8°. T.C.II 568. L, O, OC, CS, NPL; CLC, IU, MH, NR, WF.

3415 [–] —Second edition. —, 1697. 8°. L, O, C, CT, EC; CH, FU, NU, TU, Y.

3416 —The righteous man's support. A sermon. *For S. Smith and B. Walford*, 1693. 4°.* T.C.II 462. L, O, C, MR, SC; CH, MBZ, NU, PL, WF, Y.

3417 —A sermon preacht . . . July 23. 1686. *For Sam. Smith*. 1686. 4°.* L, O, CS, EC, BLH; CH, CLC, WF, Y.

3418 —A sermon preached . . . August 23d. 1691. *For Samuel Smith*, 1691. 4°.* T.C.II 376. L, O, OM, EC, LSD; CH, NU, PL, TU, Y.

3419 Entry cancelled.
—Sermon preach'd . . . June 14. 1693. *See* —Righteous man's support.

3420 —A sermon preach'd . . . 16th of February, 1698/9. *For S. Smith and B. Walford*, 1699. 4°.* L, O, LLP, CS, EC; CLC, Y.

3421 —Twelve sermons. *For Sam. Smith and B. Walford*, 1699. 8°. T.C.III 89. O, LW, CT, LSD, D, DT; CLC, NGT, WF, Y.

3422 —Unity and peace. *By H. Hills, for Robert Pawlet*, 1683. 4°.* T.C.II 13. L, O, C, LSD, GU; CH, NC, NU, WF, Y.

3423 **Lucas, *Sir* Thomas.** Admirable good newes againe from Ireland. *By T. F. for I. Thomas*, 1641[2]. 4°.* LT, O, C, LVF, LNC, MR; CH, INU, TU, WF.

Lvcas redivivvs or. 1655. *See* Anthony, John.

3423A **Luce, Richard.** Christian liberty. *For Rowland Reynolds*, 1673. 4°.* T.C.I 125. L, O, WCA; CH, CLC.

Lucerna scholastica. Or, the scholar's companion. 1680. *See* B., J.

3424 **Lucian.** Lucian's works. *By Henry Clark, for W. Benbrige*, 1684–85. 5v. 8°. T.C.II 102. L, O, CS, E, EN; BN, CH, CN, MH, TU, WF, Y.

—Burlesque upon burlesque. 1675. *See* Cotton, Charles.

3425 —Certaine select dialogues. [*London*], *for Richard Davis in Oxford*, 1663. fol. MADAN 2642. OC, OM, CCH, BAMB; CH, IEG, MBC, MH, WF, Y.

3426 Entry cancelled. Ghost.

3426A —Lucian's Charon. *For Loudon Farrow*, [1700?]. 8°. L.

3426B —Dialogi selecti. *Typis Henric. Hillii junioris impensis authoris*, 1684. 12°. TU.

3426C ——Second edition. *Typis J. Heptinstall, impensis authors*, 1684. 12°. LLU, RIPON CATH; U. TASMANIA.

3427 —Dialogorum selectorum. *Typis Guil. Dugardi, impensis Godofredi Emmersoni*, 1649. 12°. L, DC; CH.

3427A — —[Anr. ed.] *Impensis Andreæ Crook*, 1655. 12°. L, DL; CH.

3427B — —[Anr. ed.] —, 1664. 12°. C, DU; MH, Y.

3427C — —[Anr. ed.] —, 1667. 12°. BAMB, CH, IU, Y.

3428 — —[Anr. ed.] —, 1671. 12°. NPL, D, DT.

3428A — —[Anr. ed.] *Typis E. Hodgkinson & T. Hodgkin, impensis R. Scot, T. Basset, J. Wright, & R. Chiswel,* 1677. 12°. T.C.I 261. L, O, C; CH, IU, WF, Y.

3429 — —[Anr. ed.] *Typis J. Redmayne, impensis R. Scot, T. Basset, J. Wright, & R. Chiswel,* 1685. 12°. L, O, RU, DT; CH, IU.

3429A — —[Anr. ed.] *Typis T. Hodgkin, impensis T. Basset, R. Chiswell, S. Smith, B. Walford, M. Wotton & G. Conyers,* 1694. 12°. L, O, CT; CH, CLC, IU, PAP, Y.

3429B — —[Anr. ed.] *Typis T. Hodgkin, impensis R. Chiswell, W. Batersby, S. Smith, B. Walford, M. Wotton, & G. Conyers,* 1700. 12°. CS.

3430 —Lucian's Δραπεται Englished. [*London*], printed, 1648. 8°. CH.

3431 —Nonnulli e Luciani dialogis selecti. *Excudebat Sam. Roycroft, & prostant venales apud Nevil Simmons, & Thomam Simmons, Buriensem,* 1678. 12°. T.C.I 303. L, O, C; CH, IU, MB, TO.

3432 —Lucian's dialogues, (not) from the Greek; . . . the second part. *For William Bateman,* 1684. fol.* O; CH, CLC.

3433 Entry cancelled. Ghost.

3434 —Part of Lucian made English. *Oxford, by H. Hall for R. Davis,* 1663. fol. MADAN 2642. O, LU, CT, LIU, RPL; CLC, CU, MH, NGT, TU, WF.

3435 — —[Anr. ed.] —, 1664. fol. MADAN 2664. L, O, C, DU, EN; CH, CN, MBC, MH, MU, WF, Y.

3436 Entry cancelled.

—Religious impostor. [1700.] *See* Smith, Sebastian.

3437 Entry cancelled.

Lucian's ghost. 1684. *See* Fontenelle, Bernard le Bouvier.

Lucida intervalla. 1679. *See* Carkesse, James.

3438 Lucifer faln. [*London?* 1672.] brs. L.

3439 Lucifer's bull to the Pope. [*London,* 1680.] cap., fol.* L; IU, Y.

Lvcifers lacky. 1641. *See* Taylor, John.

3440 Lucifers life-guard. *Printed,* 1660. brs. LT, O, DN; MH, NHC, Y.

3441 Lucilla and Elizabeth, or, Donatist and Protestant schism parallel'd. colop: *By Henry Hills,* 1686. cap., 4°.* L, O, CS, EN, DT; CH, IU, MH, NGT, WF, Y.

Luckey chance. 1687. *See* Behn, Mrs. Aphra.

3442 **Lucretius.** De rerum natura. *Cantabrigiæ, ex officina Joann. Hayes,* 1675. *Impensis W. Morden.* 12°. L, O, C, EN, DM; CH, FU, IU, MH, NC, NP, PL, WF, Y.

3443 Entry cancelled.

— —[Anr. ed.] *Oxoniæ,* 1682. *See* —T. Lucretius Carus.

3444 — —[Anr. ed.] *Cantabridgiæ, ex officina Joann. Hayes,* 1686. *Impensis H. Dickinson,* 12°. L, O, C, CT, DC; BN, CLC, MH, NN, TU, V, Y.

3445 — —[Anr. ed.] *Oxonii, e theatro Sheldoniano, impensis Ab. Swall & Tim. Child,* 1695. 8°. L, O, C, EN, BQ; BN, CH, MH, MU, WF, Y.

3446 —An essay on the first book of. *For Gabriel Bedle, and Thomas Collins,* 1656. 8°. LT, O, C, DC, EN; BN, CH, CN, MH, MU, TU, WF, Y.

3447 —T. Lucretius Carus the Epicurean philosopher, his six books De natura rerum. *Oxford, by L. Lichfield, for Anthony Stephens,* 1682. 8°. L, O, C, LLU, EN; CH, CN, LC, MH, NC, NCD, Y.

3448 — —Second edition. *Oxford, by L. Lichfield, for Anthony Stephens,* 1683. 8°. T.C.II 6. L, O, CS, BC, DT; BN, CH, CU, MH, V, WF, Y.

3449 — —Third edition. *For Thomas Sawbridge, and Anthony Stephens,* 1683. 8°. T.C.II 54. L, O, C, EN, CD; BN, CH, IU, LC, MH, NC, Y.

3449A Entry cancelled. *See previous entry.*

3449B — —"Third" edition. *For Anthony Stephens,* 1683. 8°. L, CM, GK; CLC, CN, IU, MH, NP, WF.

3449C — —Fourth edition. *For T. Braddyl,* 1699. 8°. L, O, CS, DT; CH, IU, LC, MH, PL, Y.

3450 — —[Anr. ed.] *Printed,* 1700. 8° fours. L, O, C, MC, GU, BQ; CH, IU, MH, MMO, PU, WF, Y.

3451 Luctus Britannici: or the tears of the British muses. *For Henry Playford, and Abel Roper: and sold by John Nutt,* 1700. L, O, CS, LLU, MR; CH, CN, MH, TU, WF, Y.

3451A Lucubratincula poetica de moribus rite instituendis. *Edinburgi, excudebant haeredes A. Anderson,* 1700. 8°. ALDIS 3982. EN.

3452 **Lucy, William, bp.** An answer to Mr. Hobbs his Leviathan. *By S. G. and B. G. for Edward Man,* 1673. LW, OC, CK, CT, AN, EN; CLC, NP, NU, TU, WF, Y.

3452A [–] Examinations, censures, and confutations of . . . Leviathan. *By Philip Wattleworth for William Hope,* 1650 [*i.e.* 1658]. 12°. LT.

3452B [–] —[Anr. ed.] —, 1656. 12°. LT, CS; CN.

3453 [–] Observations, censvres and confutations of . . . Leviathan. *By T. F. for H. Robinson,* 1657. 12°. LT, O, CS, DU, SC.

3454 — —[Anr. ed.] *By J. G. for Nath. Brooke,* 1663. 4°. L, O, C, DU, E; CH, CLC, IAU, NU, RBU, WF.

3454A —A second part of Observations. *By S. G. and B. G. for Edward Man,* 1673. 12°. CS.

3455 [–] A treatise of the nature of a minister. *By Thomas Ratcliffe for the author, and are to be sold by Edward Man,* 1670. 4°. T.C.I 42. L, C, DU, ESSEX, DT.

3456 — —[Anr. ed.] *By T. R. and M. D. and are to be sold by Edward Man,* 1670. 4°. L, O, C, E, DT; CLC, IU, MH, NU, WF, Y.

3456A **Ludgater, Robert.** The presbyter's antidote. 1669. brs. LF.

3457 Ludgates late petition. [*London*], printed, 1659. 4°.* LT, LLU; MH.

3458 Entry cancelled.

[**Ludkin.**] Some observations made upon the Calumba Wood. 1682. *See* Peachie, John.

3459 No entry.

3460 **Ludlow, Edmund.** Memoirs of . . . in two volumes. *Switzerland, printed at Vivay,* 1698. T.C.III 77. L, O, C, EN, DT; BN, CH, CN, LC, MH, NP, Y.

3461 Entry cancelled.
— —Vol. II. Vevay, 1698. *See previous entry.*

3462 — —. . . third and last part. —, 1699. 8°. L, O, C, DU, DT; CH, CN, LC, MH, TU, Y.

Ludlow no lyar. Amsterdam. 1692. *See* Bethel, Slingsby.

Ludlow Redivivus, *pseud.*

3463 **Ludolf, Heinrich Wilhelm.** Henrici Wilhelmi Ludolfi grammatica Russica. *Oxonii, e theatro Sheldoniano,* 1696. 8°. T.C.II 591. L, O, C, MR, DT; CH, CN, MH, WF, Y.

3464 [–] Meditations upon retirement. *Printed,* 1691. fol.* T.C.II 366. L, O.

3465 **Ludolf, Hiob.** Confessio fidei Claudii regis Æthiopiæ. *Apud Thomam Roycroft,* 1661. 4°.* CS, LNC, EN; CH, CLC, MB, PL, TU, WF.

3466 —Grammatica Æthiopia. *Apud Thomam Roycroft,* 1661. 4°. L, O, C, EN, DT; CH, MB, MIU, PL, TU, WF.

3467 —[Æthopic] Lexicon Æthiopico-Latinum. *Apud Thomam Roycroft,* 1661. 4°. L, O, C, EN, DT; CH, CN, LC, MH, TU, Y.

3468 —A new history of Ethiopia. *For Samuel Smith,* 1682. fol. T.C.I 484. L, O, C, GU, DT; CH, CN, LC, MH, PL, TU, Y.

3468A — —[Anr. ed.] *By A. Godbid and J. Playford for Samuel Smith,* 1682. fol. C, DUS.

3469 — —Second edition. *For Sam. Smith,* 1684. fol. T.C.II 51. L, C, NE; NC, PL, WF, Y.

3470 — —"Second" edition. *For Samuel Smith,* 1684. fol. L, O, LWL, OC, BC, ENC; CH, CLC, MBA, MU, NN, TU, WF.

3471 **Ludovico, Prince.** An auction of paintings . . . 22d . . . January. [*London,* 1692.] 4°.* L.

Ludovicus á Fonte Virgineo, *pseud. See* Maidwell, Lewis.

Ludus literarum, the sporting. 1674. *See* B., J.

Ludus ludi literarii: or. 1672. *See* S., R.

Ludus mathematicus: or. 1654. *See* Wingate, Edmund.

3471A Ludus Scacchiæ, a satyr. *For Rob. Clavell,* 1675. 8°. T.C.I 218. O.

3471B —[Anr. ed.] —, 1676. 8°. CH.

3471C **Luis, of Grenada.** A memorial of a Christian life. *For Mat. Turner,* 1688. 8°. L, O, BSM, DUS; CLC, TU, WF, WG, Y.

3471D — —Second volume. [*London*], *printed* 1699. 8°. WARE; TU, WF, WG.

3471E — —Second part. *Mat. Turner,* 1699. 8°. L.

3472 **Luke, John.** A sermon preached . . . Decemb. 15. 1664. *By R. Daniel,* 1664. 4°.* L, O, CT; CH.

Luke Huttons lamentation. [1655–8.] *See* Hutton, Luke.

3473 **Lukin, Henry.** The chief interest of man. *By R. D. for T. Basset,* 1665. 12°. L, O.

3474 — —Second edition. *By J. C. for T. Basset,* 1670. 12°. T.C.I 39. L, LCL, LW, P; TO, WF.

3474A —The good and faithful servant. *For Tho. Parkhurst,* 1696. 8°. T.C.III 24. LCL, LW; WF.

3475 —The interest of the spirit in prayer. *By J. D. for Brabazon Aylmer,* 1674. 12°. T.C.I 146. O, LW, P; CLC.

3476 —An introduction to the Holy Scripture. *By S. G. for Allen Banks and Charles Harper,* 1669. 8°. T.C.I 1. L, O, C, LIC, YM; CH, IU, MH, NU, TO, WF, WSC, Y. (var.)

3477 —The life of faith. *By J. H. for John Allen,* 1660. 12°. L, LW, CS, P; CLC, IU, TO.

3478 —The practice of godlines. *By A. M. for Tho. Underhill,* 1658. 12°. P; NU.

3479 — —Second edition. —, 1659. 12°. LT, EN.

3480 — —Third edition. *For John Dunton,* 1690. 12°. T.C.II 307. LW; CLC, Y.

3481 —A remedy against spiritual trouble. *For Thomas Cockerill,* 1694. 8°. O, C, LW; NU.

3482 A lullaby, come little babe. *By and for A. M.,* [1670]. brs. L.

Lumen de lumine: or. 1651. *See* Vaughan, Thomas.

3483 **Lumley, Pain.** Good news: or wine and oil. 1661. LCL.

3484 [**Lumsden, Alexander.**] A brief account of the proceedings against the six Popish priests. [*London,* 1680.] fol.* L, OB, DU, LNC; CH, WF, Y.

3484A [**Luna, Miguel de.**] The history of the conquest of Spain by the Moors. *By F. Leach for S. H., sold by T. Fox,* 1687. 8°. L, OM, CM, DU, LLU; CH, MB, WF.

3484B [–] —[Anr. ed.] *By F. Leach for Tho. Fox,* 1687. 8°. OC; CN.

3484C [–] The life of the most illustrious monarch Almanzor. *For Dan. Brown, and Isaac Cleave,* 1693. 8°. L, O; CLC, CN, MH, NHS, PL, Y.

3485 The lunatick lover. [*London*], *for P. Brooksby,* [1688–95]. brs. L, CM, HH.

3486 Lunaticus inamoratus or, the mad lover. *By Sarah Griffin,* 1667. brs. L.

3486A **Lundius, Nicolaus.** Regi serenissimo & potentissimo Carolo Secundo. [*Londoni,* 1660.] fol.* MH.

3487 **Lunsford, Sir Thomas.** An ansvver to a letter written from Cambridge. [*London*], *printed,* 1647. 4°.* LT, SP; CH.

3487A —Collonel Lunsford his petition. *For Lavrence Horton,* 1641[2]. 4°.* L, LG, EC, SP; CH, CN, MH, OWC, Y.

3488 —A speech made by. *Printed,* 1642. 4°.* LT, O, LVF; CN, CSS, INU, MH, MIU.

3489 **Lupton, Donald.** Englands command on the seas. *For Jos. Blaik-lock,* 1653. 8°. L, LNM; CSS, NN, Y.

3490 [–] Flanders. Or, an exact . . . description. *By Thomas Ratcliffe,* 1658. 4°.* L, C; BN, CH, MH, MU, WF.

3491 —The freedom of preaching. *By R. W. for R. Harford,* 1652. 8°.* LT.

3492 [–] A most exact and accurate map of the whole world. *For John Garrett,* 1676. 4°. T.C.I 227. L, LW, CJ; CN, MU, WF.

3493 [–] The quacking mountebank. *For E. B.,* 1655. 4°.* LT, O, C, BBN, YM; NU, PH, PSC.

3494 —The two main qvestions resolved. *By R. W. for R. Harford,* 1652. 8°.* LT.

3495 —The tythe-takers cart overthrown. *By J. M. for R. Harford,* 1652. 8°. LT; WF.

3496 [–] A warre-like treatise of the pike. *By Richard Hodgkinsonne,* 1642. 12°. L, DC; CH, MU, WF.

3497 [**Lupton, Thomas.**] A thousand notable things. *For John Wright,* 1650. 8°. MAU; BN, CLC, MH, Y.

3498 [–] —[Anr. ed.] *For M. Wright,* 1660. 8°. LT, O, LWL, CT, LLU; CH.

3499 [–] —[Anr. ed.] *By Edward Crowch for John Wright,* 1670. 8°. T.C.I 23. CH, NR.

3500 [–] —[Anr. ed.] *By Henry Bruges for John Wright,* 1675. 8°. L, O, GU; CLC, WF.

3501 [–] —[Anr. ed.] *For M. Wotton and G. Conyers,* 1686. 8°. L, LNC; CH, CLC, OCI.

3501aA [–] —[Anr. ed.] *For G. Conyers,* [1700]. 12°. L; CLC, CU.

3501A Entry cancelled.

Lushington, Thomas. Expiation of a sinner. 1646. *See* Crell, Johann.

3502 —Logica analytica. *Typis Abrahami Miller,* 1650. 8°. L, LW, OC, CT, DT.

3503 [–] The resurrection rescued. *For Richard Lowndes,* 1659. 12°. MADAN 2425. LT, O, C, CM, DU; CH, Y.

3503A Entry cancelled.

[Lusignano, Steffani.] History of the war of Cyprus. 1687. *See* Graziani, Antonio Maria.

Lusoria: or occasional pieces. 1661. *See* Feltham, Owen.

3504 The lustful fryar. [1689.] 8°. L.

3504A Lusts dominion. *For F. K. and are to be sold by Robert Pollard,* 1657. 12°. L, O, LVD, EN; CH, CN, LC, MH, Y.

3504AB —[Anr. ed.] *For F. K.,* 1657. 12°. LC.

3504B —[Anr. ed.] *For Fr. Kirkman,* 1661. 12°. LVD, EN; CH, LC.

3505 The lusty fryer of Flanders. [*London*], *for J. Blare,* [1688]. brs. L, O, CM.

3506 The lusty lad of London. *For J. Deacon,* [1700?]. brs. L, CM, HH.

3507 The lusty miller's recreation. [*London*], *for P. Brooksby,* [1672–95]. brs. EUING 157. L, O, HH, GU; MH.

Lusus amatorius. 1694. *See* Musæus.

Lusus fortunæ: the play. [n.p.], 1649. *See* Forde, Thomas.

3507A Lusuum poeticorum sylva. *Typis E. C.,* 1667. 12°. L.

3508 **Luther, Martin.** An abstract of a commentarie by. *For Henry Atkinson,* [1642]. 4°.* LT, O; CH.

3509 Entry cancelled. LCL copy lacks t.p. Same as next.

3510 —Dris Martini Lutheri colloquia mensalia: or, Dr. Martin Luther's divine discourses. *By William Du-Gard,* 1652. fol. L, O, C, E, DT; CH, CN, MH, WF, Y.

3510A ——Second edition. *By William Du-Gard for William Throppe,* 1659. fol. O; MH, WF.

3510B —A commentarie of. *By George Miller,* 1644. 4°. L, O, OC, AN, BC, BR; CH, CN, MH, TO, TSM, WF.

3511 —Martin Luther's declaration to his countrimen. [*London,* 1643.] cap., 4°.* LT, LIU, DT; CLC, MIU, Y.

3512 —Loci communes. *Typis R. H. & W. E. impensis Gulielmi Wells; & Joshuæ Kirton,* 1651. 4°. L, O, C, ENC, DT; CLC, MH, NCU, WF, Y.

3513 —The prophecyes of. *For Andrew Kembe and Edward Thomas,* 1664. 4°. L, CT, EN; CH, CLC, MH, NN, WF.

3514 —Dr. Martin Luthers prophecies of the destruction of Rome. *For W. W.,* [1679]. 4°.* O, CT, EN; VC, WF, Y.

3514A ——[Anr. ed.] *Edinburgh, reprinted* 1679. 4°.* ALDIS 2152.3. L, EN.

3514B ——[Anr. ed.] [*Dublin*], *reprinted,* 1679. 4°.* CD, DK, DT; WF.

3515 —Several choice prophecyes of. *For Edward Thomas,* 1666. 4°.* O, YM; WF.

3516 —The signs of Christs coming. *Printed,* 1661. 4°.* L, O, LCP, LW, SP, E, CD; CH, MH, NU, WF, Y.

3517 —Thirtie fovre special and chosen sermons of. *By Tho. Paine, to be sold by Francis Tyton,* 1649. 8°. L, O, C, LCL, MR; CH, MBZ, MIU, MU, NCD, NU, Y. (var.)

3518 ——[Anr. ed.] *By Tho. Paine, and sold by E. Dod and N. Ekins,* 1652. 8°. L, O; CLC, WF.

3519 —A word in season: being the commentary of. *By George Larkin,* 1685. 4°. O, LW.

Lutheri posthuma. 1650. *See* Bell, Henry.

3519A **L[utton], E[dward].** The funerall sermon of Mr. Miles Pinckency. *At Paris, by Vincent DuMoutier,* 1675. 4°.* L; Y.

3520 Entry cancelled. Printed in [Amsterdam?]

Lux in tenebris, or. 1654. *See* Fauntleroy, Thomas.

Lux mathematica. 1672. *See* R., R.

3521 Lvx matvtina: or, some beams. [*London*], *printed,* 1662. 4°. L, LW, YM; NU, TO.

Lux occidentalis: or. 1689. *See* Rogers, Thomas.

Lux orientalis, or. 1662. *See* Glanvill, Joseph.

3521aA **Luxemburg, François Henri de Montmorency-Bouteville, duc de.** A letter from . . . to the French king. *For Daniel Lyford,* 1693. brs. CN.

3521A —A perfect account of the taking . . . Bodegrave. [*London*], *in the Savoy, by Thomas Newcomb,* 1672/3. fol.* L, O; CH, MH.

Luzancy, Hippolite de. *See* Du Chastelet de Luzancy, Hippolite.

3522 Entry cancelled.

[L] W[right], T[homas]. More exact character . . . Cromvell. 1658. *See* LeWright, Thomas.

Lycidus. 1688. *See* Tallement, Paul.

3523 **Lycophron.** Λυκοφρονος . . . Lycophronis Chalchidensis Alexandra. *Oxonii, e theatro Sheldoniano,* 1697. fol. T.C.III 79. L, O, C, E, DT; BN, CH, LC, MH, MU, OCI, Y.

3524 **Lyde, Robert.** A true and exact account of the retaking of a ship. *For R. Baldwin,* 1693. 4°.* T.C.II 452. L, O, C, LG, CT, DC; MH, PU, Y.

Lyde, William. *See* Joyner, William.

3525 **L[ydeott], E.** The prodigal return'd home. [*n.p.*], *printed,* 1684. 8°. L, O, C, DUS, LLP, YM; CH, CN, MSL, WF.

Lydia's heart opened. 1675. *See* Strong, James.

3525A **Lydiat, Simon.** Εταχυολογια. Spicilegium. *Prostant apud H. Bonwick,* 1696. 8°. T.C.II 570. L; PL, WF, Y.

3526 **Lydiat, Thomas.** Thomae Lydiat canones, chronologici. *Oxonii, e theatro Sheldoniano,* 1675. 8°. MADAN 3064. L, O, C, AN, MR, DT; CH, IU, NC, PL, WF, Y.

3527 Entry cancelled. Date: 1607. STC 17040.

3527A **Lydius, Johannes.** Christelyke religie voorgedyelt. [*New York, by William Bradford,* 1700.] 8°. CH, PHS.

3527B **Lye, Thomas.** The Assemblies shorter catechism. *Printed,* 1672. 8°. L; OBERLIN, WF.

3528 ——[Anr. ed.] —, 1674. 4°. L, O; NU.

3529 —Catalogus variorum librorum. 17 *Nov.* 1684. 4°. L, O.

3530 —The childs delight. *By S. Simmons, for Tho. Parkhurst,* 1671. 8°. T.C.I 67. MH, NC, Y.

3530A [–] —[Anr. ed.] [London? 1695.] 8°. LL.

3531 —Death the sweetest sleep. By J. R. for Thomas Parkhurst, 1681. 4°.* L, O, LW; CH, LC, WF, Y.

3532 —An explanation of the shorter catechism. By A. M.
for Tho. Parkhurst, 1675. 8°. L, LCL, LW, ENC; CLC, IU,
NU, TO, Y.

3533 ——[Anr. ed.] —, 1676. 8°. L, O, C, BR, ENC; MB, NGT,
NU, WF.

3533A ——[Anr. ed.] Edinburgh, by the heirs of A. Anderson,
1678. 12°. ALDIS 2131.5. EN.

3534 Entry cancelled.
——[Anr. ed.] 1683. See—Plain and familiar method.
Dublin, 1683.

3535 ——[Anr. ed.] By J. Astwood for Tho. Parkhurst, 1688.
8°. T.C.II 265. L.

3536 ——[Anr. ed.] —, 1689. 8°. L, LCL; NU.

3537 —The fixed saint held forth. [London], printed, 1662.
4°.* L, O, C, LW, MR; Y.

3538 —The king of terrors' metamorphosis. By M. S. for
Henry Cripps, 1660. 4°.* LT, O, LW, ENC; CLC, WF, Y.

3539 —A new spelling book. Second edition. For Tho. Parkhurst, 1677. 12°. L, O; TO.

3539A ——[Anr. ed.] —, 1696. 8°. HAMBURG, RHT.

3540 —A plain and familiar method. Parker, 1662. 12°.* DC.

3540A ——[Anr. ed.] Printed and to be sold by Tho. Parkhurst,
1672. 8°.* L, O; CH, CLC, WF, Y.

3540B ——[Anr. ed.] Printed and are to be sold by Peter Parker,
1672. 8°.* WF.

3541 ——[Anr. ed., "plaine."] For Peter Parker, 1673. 12°.* L,
O; NU.

3541A ——[Anr. ed.] Dublin, by J. Ray for J. Howes, 1683. 8°.
LW.

3542 —Reading and spelling English made easie. By A. Maxwell, for Tho. Parkhurst, 1673. 8°. T.C.I 128. IU, Y.

3543 **Lyford, Edward.** [Hebrew] or, the true interpretation
and etymologie of Christian names. By T. W. for
George Sawbridge, 1655. 12°. LT, O, CT, BC, SP; LC, MH,
TO, WF, Y.

3544 **Lyford, William.** An apologie for our publick ministerie. By William Du-gard, 1652. 4°. O, LW; CH, MH.

3545 ——[Anr. ed.] By William Du-gard, to bee sold by
Joseph Cranford, 1653. 4°. LT, O, C, SS, DT; IU, NHC,
NU, WF, Y.

3546 ——Third edition. For Richard Royston, 1657. 4°. L, MR,
BLH; MH, NU, Y.

3546A —Conscience informed. For Brome, 1661. 12°. LSC, P.

3546B [–] An helpe for young people. Oxford, by Leonard Lichfield, 1649. 8°.* MADAN 2024. CH, Y.

3547 —Lyford's legacie: or. For Richard Royston, 1656. 12°.
LT, O, CT; CN, NU, WF.

3548 ——Second edition. 1658. 12°. LCL.

3549 —The matching of the magistrates authority. London,
for R. Royston, to be sold by Tho: Miller in Sherborne,
1654. 4°.* O, LW, OC, ENC; NU, Y.

3549A ——[Anr. ed.] By J. G. for R. Royston, 1654. 4°.* C, LW,
CS, CT; CSS, MM, TO.

3550 —The plain mans senses exercised. London, for Richard
Royston, and Edward Forrest in Oxford, 1655. 4°. L, O,
LCL, E, DT; MB, NU, TO, WF, WSC, Y.

3550A ——[Anr. ed.] For Richard Royston, 1655. 4°. L, CS, AN,
LSD, MR; CLC, MH.

3551 ——[Anr. ed.] —, 1657. 4°. MR, P, ENC, BLH; NHC.

3552 —Principles of faith & good conscience. [London], by
T. Harper, and are to be sold by P. Nevil, 1642. 8°. O,
LCL, LW, DT; NU, TO.

3553 ——Second edition. Printed at Oxford by L. Lichfield,
for Ed. Forrest and John Adams, 1650. 8°. MADAN 2037.
CT; Y.

3554 ——Third edition. Oxford, by Leonard Lichfield for John
Adams and Edward Forrest, 1652. 8°. MADAN 2197.
L, O; NU, WF.

3555 ——Fourth edition. Oxford, by Henry Hall for John
Adams and Edward Forrest, 1655. 8°. MADAN 2276. L, O;
CH, CLC, Y.

3556 ——Fifth edition. —, 1658. 8°. MADAN 2394. L, LSC.

3557 —Three sermons. Oxford, by H. Hall, for Edward Forrest,
1654. 4°. MADAN 2257. L, O, LW, BC, MR; CH, NU.

3558 —The translation of a sinner. Oxford, by Leonard Lichfield, for Edward Forrest, junior, 1648. 4°.* MADAN
2006. L, O, C, DC, YM; NP, NU, WF, Y.

3559 —The triall of a Christian's sincere love. 1650. 12°.
LCL.

3560 [**Lygon, Richard.**] Several circircumstances [sic] to
prove that Mris. Jane Berkeley. [London, 1654.] cap.,
4°.* LT.

3561 Entry cancelled. See following entry.

3562 Lying allowable with Papists. [London, 1680.] cap., fol.*
L, O, C, LG, LNC; CH, CN, MH, TU, WF, Y.

Lying spirit. 1658. See Smith, William, Quaker.

Lying spirit. [n.p.], 1673. See Willsford, John.

3562A The lying Whig drawn in his own colours. [London,
1685.] brs. MH.

Lying wonder discovered. 1659. See Blackley, James.

3563 Entry cancelled.

Lying-vvonders. 1660. See Clark, Robert.

3564 [**Lynam, Margaret.**] The controversie of the Lord.
[London], printed, 1676. 4°.* L, C, LF, BBN; CH, MH, PH,
PL, PSC, Y.

3564aA [–] For the Parliament sitting at Westminster. [London?,
1659.] brs. PL.

3564A Entry cancelled.

Lynch, James. Sermon preach'd . . . Octob. 23, 1689.
1689. See Vesey, John, abp.

3564B **Lynde, Sir Humphrey.** The ancient doctrine of the
Church of England. For Austin Rice, 1660. 4°. WF.

Lyndsay, Sir David. See Lindsay, Sir David.

3564C [**Lyndwood, William.**] Provinciale vetus provinciæ
cantuariensis [ecclesiæ Anglicanæ]. Oxoniæ, excudebat
Hen: Hall, impensis Ri: Davis, 1664. 12°. MADAN 2669.
L, O, CT, DU, E, DT; CH, KQ, TO, WF.

3565 [–] Provinciale (seu . . .). Oxoniæ, excudebat H. Hall,
impensis Ric. Davis, 1679. fol. T.C.I 345; MADAN 3221.
L, O, C, EN, DT; BN, CH, CN, LC, MH, Y, AVP.

3566 **Lynford, Thomas.** God's providence the cities safety. *For Walter Kettilby,* 1689. 4°.* T.C.II 243. L, O, C, BAMB, WCA; CLC, NU, TSM, WF, Y.

3567 —A sermon concerning the worship of God. *For James Adamson,* 1691. 4°.* T.C.II 366. L, O, CS, LIU, DT; CLC, MU, NU, TU, WF, Y.

3568 —A sermon preached . . . Novem. xvi. 1679. *For Walter Kettilby,* 1679. 4°.* T.C.I 367. L, O, C, LSD, YM; CH, MH, NU, TSM, WF, Y.

3569 —A sermon preached . . . Easter week, 1698. *For Walter Kettilby,* 1698. 4°.* T.C.III 72. L, O, C, DU, NE; CH, MH, NU, WF, Y.

3570 [–] Some dialogues between Mr. G. and others. *For Randall Taylor,* 1687. 8°. T.C.II 285. L, O, OC, DU, DT; CLC, WF, Y.

3571 **Lyngue, John.** Davids deliverance. *For John Clark,* 1661. 4°.* L, O, EC; MWA, Y.

3571aA The Lyn persecution. 1692/3. 8°.* O.

3571A [**Lynne, M.**] The nevvest intelligence from the army in Ireland. *Printed February 17.* 1642[3]. 4°.* LT, MR; CH.

3571B **Lyon, John.** The Exchequer Gallon vindicated. *J. Macock,* 1659. 4°. L.

Lysimachus, Irenaeus, *pseud.*

3572 **Lyster, Thomas.** The blessings of eighty eight. *By J. Matthews, for George Huddleston,* 1698. 8°. L; CH, MH, NU, WF.

3572A **Lytcott,** *Sir* **George.** To my posterity, 1675. [*n.p.,* 1675.] 8°.* L.

3573 **Lytler, Richard.** The reformed Presbyterian. *By J. G. for Nath. Brooks,* 1662. 8°. O, C, LCL, LW, DU; CH, CLC, NC, NU, TO, WF.

Lyttleton. *See* Littleton.

M

M., A. Anatomical account. 1682. *See* Mullen, Allan.

1 —Christian divrnall. *By T. H. for Tho. Rawe,* 1650. 12°. L, LSC; NPT.

—Collection of poems on affairs. 1689. *See* title.

—Country almanack. 1675. *See* Almanacs.

—A cry, a cry. 1678. *See* Mudd, Ann.

—Description of a plain instrument. 1668. *See* Martindale, Adam.

2 —An heroical panegyrick, humbly dedicated to . . . Bishop of Salisbury. *For Richard Baldwin,* 1689. fol.* O, LLP, OB, EC, E; MH, Y.

—Enquiry into the new opinions. 1696. *See* Monro, Alexander.

—Last instructions to a painter. [1667.] *See* Marvell, Andrew.

3 —A most choice historical compendium. *For John Weld,* 1692. 12°. T.C.II 393. L, O, CT.

4 —The original, succession, and progeny of the Lombard kings. *By H. Brugis,* 1681. fol.* L; CLC, CN, MH.

—Πηγιαμα 1668. *See* Mure, Andrew.

4A —Plain-dealing: or, a full . . . examination. *By Andr. Clark, for Henry Dickinson in Cambridge,* 1675. 12°. L, O, C, EC, P; CLC, CN, MH, NCU, NU, VC.

4B ——[Anr. ed.] *Cambridge: by J. Hayes, for Henry Dickinson,* 1675. 12°. O, C, LLP, OC, NE; CH, IU, NP, NU, TU.

5 Entry cancelled.

—Present state of Scotland. 1682. *See* Mudie, Alexander. Scotiæ Indiculum.

5A —Queen Elizabeths closset of physical secrets. *For Will. Sheares junior,* 1652. 4°. GU.

5B ——[Anr. ed.] —, 1656. 4°. TORONTO ACAD. OF MED., HC.

6 —The reformed gentleman. *For T. Salusbury,* 1693. 8°. T.C.II 441. L, O; CH, CLC, CN, WF, Y.

—Relation of new anatomical. 1682. *See* Mullen, Allan. Anatomical account.

7 —A rich closet of physical secrets. *By Gartrude Dawson, to be sold by William Nealand,* 1652. 4°. LT, C, LG, GU; HC.

7A ——[Anr. ed.] *By Gartrude Dawson, to be sold by John Saywell,* 1653. 4°. LWL; WF.

7B ——[Anr. ed.] *By Gartrude Dawson, and are to be sold by* [sic], [1653]. 4°. CH, CRN.

—Scotiæ indiculum. 1682. *See* Mudie, Alexander.

—Second part of the collection of poems. 1689. *See* title.

8 **M., B.** A letter, from a person of quality in the Parliaments army. *For H. T.,* 1647. 4°.* LT, C; MH, Y.

—Oratio dominica. 1700. *See* Motte, B.

9 —Sabaudiensis in reformatam religionem . . . narratio. *Typis Tho: Newcomb, impensis authoris,* 1655. 4°.* LT, O, CSSX, DU, EN; CH, NU, WF.

10 [**M., C.**] The case of the coin fairly represented. [*Dublin?* 1697.] cap., 4°.* L.

10A —A faithful account of a great engagement. colop: *For R. Hayhurst,* 1690. brs. C, OC; CH, MH.

11 —Newes from the citie of Norwich. *For Th. Clapham, Aug. 26.,* [1642.] 4°.* LT, LNC, NPL; MH, WF.

—Plain and candid account. [1681.] *See* Marshall, Charles.

12 —The prancing swearer. *By T. M.,* 1686. brs. MH, Y.

12A —A true account of the tryals . . . at Salem. *For J. Conyers,* [1693]. 4°.* NN, RPJ.

M., D. Fifth essay of. 1700. *See* Hill, Oliver.

—Gardeners labyrinth. 1652. *See* Hill, Thomas.

13 —A letter to a noble lord concerning a late prophane pamphlet entituled, The Presbyterians pater noster. [*London*, 1681.] brs. L, O, C, HH, LNC, EN; CH, CN, IU, MH, WF, Y.

13A ——[Anr. ed.] colop: [*London*], *reprinted*, 1681. brs. PU.

14 —A new and perfect relation of the takeing . . . five pyrates. [*London*], *for I. Conniers*, [1670]. 4°.* L, O, MR.

14A **M., E.** An achrostickal epitaph on S[ir Edward Sprague]. [*London*, 1673.] brs. O; MH.

—Ashrea. 1665. *See* Manning, Edward.

15 —A brief ansvver unto the Cambridge moddel. *For Thomas Simmons*, 1658. 4°.* L, O, C, LF, BBN; CH, MH, PH, PSC, Y.

—Commentarie, or exposition. 1652. *See* Marbury, Edward.

—Converted twins. 1667. *See* Medbourne, Matthew.

16 —A copy of a letter sent from a person that was present at the apprehension of Mr. Meade. colop: *By R. W.*, 1683. brs. O, EN; CH, CLC, MH, NN, PU, Y.

—Covenant acknowledged. 1660. *See* Mason, E. M.

17 —E. M. A long imprisoned malignant, his humble svbmission. [*London*], *printed*, 1647. 4°.* LT, C, OC, MR, ENC; CH, IU, NU, WF, Y.

—Free trade. 1651. *See* Misselden, E.

—Ignota febris; fevers. [1691.] *See* Maynwaring, Everard.

—Inquiries into the general catalogue. [n.p., 1691.] *See* Maynwaring, Everard.

—Letter to Dr. E. S. 1687. *See* Meredith, Edward.

18 —Mercvrivs pacificvs, or, vox tvrtvris. *Printed*, 1644. 4°.* LT, O, C, OB, MR; CH, MH, MIU, NU, TU, WF, Y.

19 —The present danger of Tangier. [*London?* 1679.] cap., fol.* L, O, OC, LLU; CH, CLC, MH, NC, WF, Y.

20 —Protection perswading subjection. *By Henry Hills*, 1653[4]. 4°.* LT, MR; CH, NC, NN.

—St. Cecily: or, the converted twins. 1666. *See* Medbourne, Matthew.

—Serious debate. 1689. *See* Maynwaring, Everard.

20A —A sermon of thanksgiving for . . . Charles the Second. *Rotterdam, for P. K., to be sold by William Weston in Dublin*, [1683?]. 4°.* L.

—Test and tryal. 1690. *See* Maynwaring, Everard.

20B —The universal scorbutick pills. *For the undertakers*, 1675. brs. L.

—Vox turturis. 1647. *See* Marbury, Edward.

21 **M., F.** A narrative of the causes and events of civil-war. *For the authour*, 1659. 4°.* CH, CSS, MH.

21A [–] Proposals most humbly offered for raising . . . five millions of money. 1696. cap., 4°.* PU.

—To the Kings most excellent majesty. [n.p., 1699.] *See* Monck, Franz.

22 **M., G.** The case of the afflicted clergy . . . Scotland. [*London*, 1691.] cap., 4°. OB, OC; MIU, NIC, TO.

23 —The citizens complaint for want of trade. *Printed*, 1663. 4°.* L; NC.

24 Entry cancelled.

—Collections of scripture. 1695. *See* —Some collections.

—Country contentments. 1649. *See* Markham, Gervase.

25 —Delight and pastime. 1697. *See* Miège, Guy.

—The distressed oppressed condition of . . . South-Wales. colop: *Published by G. M.*, [1655]. 4°.* O, OC, AN, DT; CSS.

—English house-wife. 1649. *See* Markham, Gervase.

—Inrichment of the weald. 1656. *See* Markham, Gervase.

—Expiation of a sinner. 1646. *See* Crellius.

26 —A letter from an English merchant in London. colop: *For R. C. and H. L.*, [1688]. cap., fol.* L, O, C, LG, MR; CLC, MIU, Y.

—Love of the soul. St. Omers, 1652. *See* Martin, Gregory.

—Miscellanea: or, a choice. 1694. *See* Miège, Guy.

27 —Mortality represented. *Edinburgh, by the heir of Andrew Anderson*, 1687. 8°.* ALDIS 2697.7. EN.

—New state of England. 1691. *See* Miège, Guy.

27A —Oedipus: or, the resolver. *For Nath. Brookes*, 1650. 12°. L; WF.

—Praise of Yorkshire ale. York, 1685. *See* Meriton, George.

—Religious stoic. Edinburgh, 1685. *See* Mackenzie, *Sir* George.

27B —Some collections of Scripture. *For the author*, 1695. 12°. LW.

27C —To the honourable the Commons . . . from the collector . . . at Bristol. [*London?* 1700.] brs. L; CH.

M., H. Ah, ha; tumulus. 1653. *See* Howell, James.

28 —The armies dutie. *Printed*, 1659. 4°.* LT, O, C, BC, MR; CH, CU, MH, NU, TU, WF, Y.

—Enchiridion metaphysicum. 1671. *See* More, Henry.

—England's glory; or, the great. 1694. *See* Mackworth, *Sir* Humphrey.

—God the protector. 1641. *See* Miller, Henry.

29 —A letter to a person of honour in London, from an old Cavalier. *Printed*, 1663. 4°.* L, CT, DU, WCA; CH, CLC, MIU, NU, TU, WF, Y.

—Life and doctrine. Gant, 1656. *See* More, Henry, *of the Society of Jesus.*

30 —A pair of spectacles for this purblinde nation. *Printed*, 1659. 4°.* LT, O, LG, EN, DT; CH, CN, MH, MU, NU, Y.

—Ψυχοδια platonica: or. Cambridge, 1642. *See* More, Henry.

—Psychozoia. Cambridge, 1647. *See* More, Henry.

31 —A true relation of the proceedings from York and Beverley. *Aug. 3. For John Johnson*, 1642. 4°.* LT, O, EC, LNC; MM, WF, Y.

M., I. Brief discourse concerning singing. 1690. *See* Marlow, Isaac.

31A —Corpus sine capite visibili, an aenigmaticall emblem. *By Luke Norton*, 1642. 4°.* LNC; CH.

31B —An exact delineation of . . . Bristoll. *Bristoll, for the author and sold by Mr. Tho: Wall*, 1671. brs. O.

31C —New conceited letters, newly laid open. *For John Stafford*, 1662. 4°. CM.

32 —A wipe for Iter-Boreale Wilde. *Printed*, 1670. brs. L, O; MH.

M., J. Accedence commenc't grammar. 1669. *See* Milton, John.

—Argument or, debate. 1642. *See* March, John.

33 —The atheist silenced. *By T. R. & N. T. for Daniel Brown,*
1672. 8°. T.C.I 104. L, OC, CS, P; CLC, MHS, NU.
—Brief notes. 1660. *See* Milton, John.
—Brief rule of life. 1669. *See* Morton, John.
—Catholike scriptvrist. Gant, 1662. *See* Mumford, James.

33A —The Church of England vindicated. *For C. Wilkinson,*
T. Dring, and C. Harper, 1680. 4°. T.C.I 402. CLC.
—City match. Oxford, 1659. *See* Mayne, Jasper.
—Collection of the church-history. 1688. *See* Milner, John.
—Compendium linguæ. 1679. *See* Taylor, Christopher.
Compendium trium.
—Considerations touching the likeliest. 1659. *See* Milton,
John.

34 —A contract answer to a correct copy of letters. *For John*
Roberts, to be sold by him in Bridgewater and by Tho.
Cockerill, 1698. 8°. L, O; NU.
—Copy of a letter addressed. 1643. *See* Maynard, *Sir* John.
—Difference abovt church government. 1646. *See* Mayne,
Jasper.

35 —A discovery, or, certaine observations. [*Amsterdam?*],
printed, 1657. 4°. L; CLC.
—Doctrine and discipline. 1643. *See* Milton, John.

35A —An elegiack essay upon the death of the Reverend Mr.
Thomas Gouge. *For John Marshall,* 1700. 8°.* LW; CLC,
MH.

36 —An essay of moral rules. *Printed Tho. Cockeril,* 1677.
12°. L.

36A —God and his cloud of providences. *By J. Clowes, to be sold*
by John Hancock, 1652. 4°. SP.

36B —Great news from Dublin. *For W. Downing,* 1689. brs. O.

37 Entry cancelled.
—Guide to English juries. 1682. *See title.*
—Heads of all fashions. 1642. *See* Taylor, John.
—Hosannah: a thanksgiving-sermon. Oxford, 1660. *See*
Martin, John.
—Huntsmans delight. [n.p., 1670?] *See* Martin, Joseph.
—Index horarius. 1662. *See* Marcus, Joannes.
—Jesuitical design. [1674.] *See* Moon, John.
—Jesuits grand design. [n.p., 1660.] *See* Peirce, *Sir* Edmond.

37A —A large and particular relation of the affairs of Ireland.
colop: *For Randal Taylor,* 1689. brs. O, C, DUS, DN; CH, Y.

38 —A letter from a friend in Shropshire. colop: *For Al.*
Banks, 1681. brs. L, O, HH; CH, MH, AVP.

39 —A letter from Barwick. *Printed,* 1659. 4°.* O; CH, MM.

40 Entry cancelled.
—Letters to a sick friend. 1682. *See* Marloe, John.
—Lives of holy saints. 1681. *See* Marbeck, John.
—Midnight-cry. 1691. *See* Mason, John.

41 —Murther unparalel'd. *For the author, J. M.,* 1682. brs.
O; CH.
—Musarum deliciæ. 1655. *See* Mennes, *Sir* John.

42 —Neutrality is malignancy. [*London*], *printed,* 1648. 4°.*
LT, SP; CH, NU, WF.

42A —Newes from Hell. Rome. [*London*], *printed* 1641. 4°.*
L; CLC, MH, WF, Y.

42B ——[Anr. ed., "nevvs."] —, 1642. 4°.* LT, LF, OC; CH,
MH, NU, TU, WF.

43 —A notable plot discovered in a letter. [*London*], *printed,*
[1649]. 4°.* LT, LUG; CH, MH.
—Of true religion. 1673. *See* Milton, John.

44 —On the never too much lamented death of . . . Henrietta
Maria. *Printed,* 1670. brs. L; MH.

45 —Φαρμακα γρανοθεν The shadow of the tree of life. *For*
John Wilkins, 1673. 12°. Y.

45A ——[Anr. ed.] *For John Wright,* 1674. 12°. T.C.I 186. P.

46 Entry cancelled.
—Proposals. 1696. *See* —To the honourable.

47 —The ranters last sermon. *By J. C.,* 1654. 4°.* LT.
—Readie & easie vvay. 1660. *See* Milton, John.
—Remembrance for the living. Paris, 1660. *See* Mumford,
James.
—Reply to the answer printed. 1642. *See title.*

47A —Schoole-lawes. *Printed* 1650. 8°.* L.
—Sermon preached before the worshipful mayor. 1699.
See Moore, John, *of Bridgwater.*

47B —A soveraigne salve to cure the blind. *By T. P. and M. S.*
1643. 4°.* LT, O, C, BR, DT; CH, MH, NU, TU, WF, Y.

48 —Sports and pastimes: or, sport for the city. *By H. B.*
for John Clark, 1676. 4°.* CH.

48A ——[Anr. ed.] *By A. M. for W. Thackeray and J. Deacon,*
[c. 1680]. 4°.* CM.
—Supplement to Dr. Du Moulin. 1680. *See* Milton, John.
—Tenure of kings. 1649. *See* Milton, John.
—Tetrachordon. 1645. *See* Milton, John.

49 —To the honourable the knights, citizens, and burgesses
of the House of Commons . . . proposals most humbly
offered. *For the author,* 1696. 4°.* CH, NC, PU, Y, ANL.

50 —The traveller's guide. *By the assigns of Richard and*
Edward Atkins, for Langley Curtis and Thomas Simons,
1683. 12°. T.C.II 7. L, LSC, CT; CLC, MIU, TU, WF, Y.

50A ——[Anr. ed.] *For L. C. and T. S. and to be sold by D.*
Brown, and J. Walthoe, 1692. 12°. T.C.II 413. CH.
—Treatise of civil power. 1659. *See* Milton, John.
—True light. [n.p., 1658.] *See* Moon, John.

51 —A true relation of the gelding. colop: [*London*], *printed,*
and are to be sold by Richard Janeway, 1680. fol.* O, MR;
MH, TU.
—Two plaies. Oxford, 1658. *See* Mayne, Jasper.

52 —A vindication of the loyal London-apprentices: against
. . . Richard Janeway. [*London,* 1681.] brs. L, O, LG; CH,
IU, AVP.

52A —Vitiorum enormitas: or, a discourse. *By J. R. for the*
author, 1691. 8°. O, OBL, DUS.
—Wit and drollery. 1656. *See title.*

M., L. After-reckoning. 1646. *See* Ley, John.

53 —The Papists designe against the Parliament. [*London*], *for*
H. F., 1642. 4°.* LT, O, LG; CN, MH, NU, TSM, WF, Y.

54 —A perfect relation of the horrible plot, and bloudy conspiracie. *For I. Iohnson,* 1647. 4°.* LT, DT; IU.

M., M. All the chief points. 1697. *See* Marsin, M.
—Appendix to Solomon's. 1667. *See* Mead, Matthew.
—Clear and brief explanation. 1697. *See* Marsin, M.
—Coppie of a letter sent from one of the Qveenes servants.
1642. *See title.*

55 [-] Good nevvs to the good women. *Printed and sold by S. Darker, and at John Gouges, and at Elizabeth Degrate's,* 1700. 8°. O.

55A —Guglielmo Augusto, Britanniarum regi . . . adreneris omne. *Excudebat G. Croom et prostant apud R. Baldwin,* 1696. brs. HH.

56 —A letter from the member of Parliament, in answer to the letter of the divine [N.N.]. [*London,* 1689?] cap., 4°.* L, OC, DU, EC, LSD; CH, CN, NU, WF, Y.

57 No entry.
—The near aproach of Christ's kingdom. 1696. *See* Marsin, M.
—On the death. [n.p., 1679.] *See* Murray, Mungo.

57A —The pious man's directions. Second edition. *By A. & I. Dawks for B. Allport,* 1691. 12°. L.

58 —A practical treatise; shewing when a believer. *For M. M., sold by E. Whitlock, J. Clark, and W. Reddish,* 1696. 8°. T.C.III 3. L, O, LLP; CH.
—Solomon's prescription. 1665. *See* Mead, Matthew.
—Song of Sion. [n.p.], 1662. *See* Grave, John.
—Treatise of sacramental covenanting. 1667. *See* Rawlet, John.

59 —A treatise proving three worlds. *For M. M., sold by E. Whitlock, J. Clark, and W. Reddish,* 1696. 8°. T.C.III 3. O.

60 No entry.
—The womans advocate. [n.p.], 1697. *See* Marsin, M.

61 **M., M. V.** Satyra Manneiana. [*Oxford?*], 1650. 4°. O, LCP, DU; WF.

62 **M., N.** A modest apology for the students of Edenburgh. *For Richard Janeway,* 1681. fol.* L, O, MR, E; CH, IU, MH, WF, Y.

63 **M., N. N.** The defeat of the Barbary fleet. *For Richard Lowndes,* 1657. 4°.* LT, SP; CH.

64 **M., P.** A brief enquiry into leagues and confederacies. *For J. Tonson,* 1682. 4°. L, O, MR, P, SP; INU, MH, PU, TSM, WF, Y.

65 —The Church of England, and the continuation of the ceremonies thereof. *For S. Cook,* 1690. 4°. L, O, CS, DU, NPL, WCA; CH, NU, Y.

65A —A letter to the answerer of The apology for the Catholicks. [*London?* 1667.] cap., 4°.* LSD; CH, TU, WF, Y.

66 —A sermon preached . . . the thirtieth of January, 1670. *Dublin, by Benjamin Tooke, and are to be sold by Joseph Wilde,* 1671. 12°. DIX 362. DN.
—Some queries . . . concerning the English reformation. 1688. *See* Manby, Peter.

66A —The speech of a fife laird. [*Edinburgh?* 1670.] brs. L.
66B — [Anr. ed.] [*Scotland, c.* 1680.] brs. EN.
66C [-] —[Anr. ed.] [*Scotland, c.* 1690.] brs. CH.
67 Entry cancelled.
—True intelligence. 1642. *See* P., M.

68 —The vanity, mischief and danger. *Printed, and are to be sold by Rich. Baldwin,* 1690. 4°.* L, O, CT, EN, DT; CH, IU, LC, MH, NU, TU, WF, Y.
M., P. D. Jerusalem and Babel. 1653. *See* Patteson, *master.*

69 **M., R.** An ansvver to a lawless pamphlet. *By I. N. for Henry Seile,* 1641. 4°.* LT, O, AN, LLU, LNC; MH, WF, Y.

—Anti-paræus. York, 1642. *See* Owen, David.
70 —The best schoole of war. *For R. H.,* 1642. 4°.* HUTH.
70A —The church-catechism enlarged. *For Thomas Parkhurst,* 1697. 8°. LW.
—Commentariorum. 1686. *See* Manley, Sir Roger.
71 —A compleat schoole of vvarre. *Printed at London for Richard Harper,* 1642. 4°.* LT, O, LNC; CH, MH.
—England's looking in. 1641. *See* Maddison, Sir Ralph.
—History of the late warres. 1670. *See* Manley, Sir Roger.
72 —The just measure of a personall treatie. *Printed,* 1648. 4°.* LT, O, CT, MR, DT; CH, CLC, MH, MM, NC, WF.
—King on his throne. York, 1643. *See* Mossom, Robert, *bp.*
72A —Letter from the camp near the river Ricton. *Printed,* 1674. brs. L; MH.
—Letter to General Monck. 1659. *See* Morris, Richard.
—Lives of holy saints. 1681. *See* Marbeck, John.
72B —The lives of the prophets. *For Nathaniel Rolls,* 1695. 4°. OC.
—Love to the life. 1674. *See* Mayhew, Richard.
73 [-] The parsons vade mecum. *For T. Salusbury,* 1693. 12°. T.C.II 442. L, LLP, CE, YM; CH, IAU, NC, TSM, WF, WWC.
74 Entry cancelled.
—Perfect conveyancer. 1655. *See* title.
—Plant of paradise. 1660. *See* Mossom, Robert, *bp.*
—Poema mortuale: or. [n.p.], 1679. *See* Mayhew, Richard.
75-6 Entries cancelled.
—Russian impostor. 1674. *See* Manley, Sir Roger.
—Scarronides: or. 1665. *See* Monsey, R.
—Sichah: or. 1683. *See* Mayhew, Richard.
—Sion's prospect. 1651. *See* Mossom, Robert, *bp.*
77 —Speculum libertatis Angliæ re restitutæ: or. *By J. B. to be sold by Richard Skelton,* 1659. 4°.* LT, BC, DU, LLU; CH, CLC, CSS, IU, MH. (var.)
78 —A watchword to the saints. *By D. Maxwell for Will. Weekly of Ipswich, sold by John Rothwell,* 1660. 4°.* CCC; NHC.
78A —A word to the Royalists, or Caveliers. [*London,* 166-?] cap., 4°.* LF; PL, MH, Y.
M., S. Cupids courtship. 1666. *See* Marmion, Shackerley.
78B —The golden drops of Christian comfort. [*London, by J.M.*] *for J. Blare,* 1687. 8°. CM.
79 —The heavenly passenger. *For J. Deacon,* 1687. 4°.* T.C.II 178. L; CM.
79A —The loyal garland. Fourth edition. *By T. Johnson for T. Passenger,* 1671. 8°. O.
79B — —"Fourth" edition. —, 1673. 8°. O.
79C — —[Anr. ed.] *By J. M. for I. Deacon,* 1685. 8°. O, CM.
79D — —Fifth edition. *By J. R. for T. Passinger,* 1686. 8°. L, O, LG; WF.
—Prognosticon posthumum. 1643. *See* Morgan, Sylvanus.
—Θεοσπλαγχναποδοσις or. 1647. *See* Moore, Samuel.
79E —The true tryal of understanding; or wit. *By I. M. for I. Deacon,* 1687. 12°.* CM.
M., S. W. Caledons complaint. [n.p., 1641.] *See* Moore, Sir William.
M., T. Admonition to the reader. [n.p.], 1676. *See* Mainwaring, Sir Thomas.

—Anatomy of Lievt. Col. John Lilbvrn's spirit. 1649. *See* Sydenham, Cuthbert.

—Blood for blood. Oxford, 1661. *See* Reynolds, John.

—Box of spikenard. [1659.] *See* Malpas, Thomas.

—Breviary of the history. 1650. *See* May, Thomas.

80   —Certain information from Devon and Dorset. [*London*], *August, 27. for H. Blunden,* 1642. 4°.* LT, LNC; MH.

81   —Certaine observations upon some texts of scripture. [*London*], *printed,* 1648. 4°.* L, O, C, DC, SP; CH, NU, WF, Y.

—Cloud of witnesses. 1665. *See* Mall, Thomas.

81A —A copy of a letter written by. [*n.p.,* 1699.] 8°.* O.

—Exact account of Romish doctrine. 1679. *See* Morton, Thomas.

—Funeral sermon preached upon the death. 1692. *See* Milway, Thomas.

—Grammaticall miscellanies. Oxford, 1660. *See* Merriott, Thomas.

—Historiæ Parliamenti Angliæ. [1650.] *See* May, Thomas.

81B —The history of independency. The fourth and last part. *For H. Brome; and H. Marsh,* 1660. 4°. LT, O, C, EN, DT; CH, CN, MH, NU, TU, WF, Y.

81C —Letter concerning the present state of physick. *For Jo. Martyn and Ja. Allestry,* 1665. 4°. L, O, C, LWL, CU; BN, CN, KU, WF, WSG.

82   —A letter of queries to the Popish brethren of the association. colop: *For A. Banks,* 1682. brs. O, C, LG; CH, TU, WF, Y.

—Life and death of Mother Shipton. 1687. *See* Head, Richard.

82A —The life of a satyrical pvppy, called Nim. *By for* [sic] *Humphrey Moseley,* 1657. 8°. L, O; CH, CN, MH, WF, Y.

83   Entry cancelled.

—List of the divers commanders. 1644. *See* —Particvlar list.

—Mensa lubrica Montgom. Oxford, 1651. *See* Masters, Thomas.

83A —An Oxford elegie. [*London?* 1658?] brs. MH.

84   —A particvlar list of divers of the commanders. *For Ralph Rounthwait,* 1644. 4°.* LT, O; WF.

—Penitent bandito. 1663. *See* title.

84A —The Princes standard set up. *For R. A.,* 1648. 4°.* CH, CSS, MH.

—Short view of the lives. 1661. *See* Manley, Thomas.

85   —Sir Thomas Fairfaxes taking of Dennis Castle. [*London*], *for Matthew Walbanke, March 26,* 1646. 4°.* LT, O, CT, DT; CSS.

—Sollicitor. 1663. *See* Manley, Thomas.

86   —A treatise of the new heavens. *Printed,* 1680. 4°.* L, O.

—Veni; vidi; vici. 1652. *See* Fisher, Payne.

—Vvlgaria sive. Oxoniæ, 1652. *See* Merriot, Thomas.

—Wandring lover. 1658. *See* Meriton, Thomas.

87   Entry cancelled.

—Young accountants remembrancer. 1692. *See* Mercer, Thomas.

M., W. Brief character of the antient. 1695. *See* Mather, William.

—Brief narrative of the second meeting. [n.p.], 1674. *See* Mead, William.

88   —The compleat cook. *For Nath. Brook,* 1655. 12°. LT, AM; LC, NN, WU.

89   ——[Anr. ed.] *By T. C. for Nath. Brook,* 1656. 12°. LWL; LC, MH.

90   ——[Anr. ed.] *By E. B. for Nath. Brook,* 1658. 12°. L; MH, NN.

91   ——[Anr. ed.] *For Nath. Brook,* 1659. 12°. C, LLU; CH, LC, NN, Y.

92   ——[Anr. ed.] *For Nath. Brooke,* 1662. 12°. LWL; PL, Y.

92A ——[Anr. ed.] *By J. G. for Nath. Brook,* 1663. 12°. LLU.

93   ——[Anr. ed.] *By J. Winter for Nath. Brooke,* 1668. 12°. WF.

94   ——[Anr. ed.] *By E. Tyler, and R. Holt, for Nath. Brooke,* 1671. 12°. L, LG, LWL; NN, Y.

94A ——[Anr. ed.] *For Obadiah Blagrave, and R. Harford,* 1679. 12°. L; NAM.

94B ——[Anr. ed.] *Printed and sold by G. Conyers,* 1694. 12°. PBL.

95   —Huntington divertisement. *By J. Bennet,* 1678. 4°. L, O, C; CH, CU. (var.)

95A —A letter from Leghorn, March the twenty foureh [sic]. colop: *For L. C.,* 1691. cap., 4°.* CH.

95B Entry cancelled.

—Middle way of predetermination. 1679. *See* Humfrey, John.

—Of the Quakers. 1700. *See* Mather, William.

96   —The Queens closet opened. [*London*], *for Nathaniel Brook;* 1655. 12°. LT, LWL, LLU, E, GU; CLC, LC, NCD, NN, WG, WU.

97   ——[Anr. ed.] *For Nath. Brook,* 1656. 12°. LCS, LWL; LC, MH.

98   ——Fourth edition. *For Nathaniel Brooks,* 1658. 8°. L, O, LWL, LLU, AM; MH, WF, WSG.

99   ——[Anr. ed.] *For Nath. Brooke,* 1659. 12°. C.

99A ——[Anr. ed.] *For Peter Dring,* 1661. 12°. LWL, CCH; CH, MH.

100 ——[Anr. ed.] *For Christ. Eccleston,* 1662. 12°. L, LWI; BBE, PL, Y.

100A ——[Anr. ed.] *For N. Brooke,* 1662. 12°. CJC.

100B ——[Anr. ed.] *By J. G. for Nath. Brook,* 1664. 12°. NCD, RHT.

100C ——[Anr. ed.] *By J. W. for Nath. Brooke,* 1668. 12°. L, LLU; U. DELAWARE.

101 ——[Anr. ed.] *For N. Brooke, to be sold by Charles Harper,* 1671. 12°. T.C.I 92. L, O, LG, LWL, LLU, GU; MB, NN.

102 ——[Anr. ed.] *For Nath. Brooke, to be sold by Tho. Guy,* 1674. 12°. L, C, LLU, MAU; WSG.

103 ——[Anr. ed.] *For Obadiah Blagrave,* 1679. 12°. T.C.I 363. L, LLU, GU.

104 ——[Anr. ed.] —, 1683. 12°. C, GU; CH, PCP, WSG.

104A ——[Anr. ed.] *For Benjamin Crayle,* 1684. 12°. T.C.II 76. GU.

105 ——Tenth edition. *For R. Bentley, J. Phillips, H. Rhodes, and J. Taylor,* 1696. 12°. T.C.II 572. L, C, LCP, LG, GU.

105A ——"Tenth" edition. *For E. Blagrave and are to be sold by the booksellers of London and Westminster,* 1696. 12°. L, C, LWL; NN, WF.

106 ——"Tenth" edition. *For J. Phillips, H. Rhodes, J. Taylor, and K. Bentley*, 1698. 8°. O; WF.

107 —A satyrical poem on the most horrid . . . Jesuitish plot. *For Tho. Cockerill*, 1679. fol.* L, O, LG, DU, LLU; CLC, CN, IU, MH, MU, Y.

108 Entry cancelled.
—Sermon preach'd. 1687. *See* Wall, William.
M., Z. Snare broken. [n.p.], 1692. *See* Mayne, Zachary.

109 Entry cancelled.
—VVhole triall of Connor Lord Macguire. 1645. *See title.*

110 M. Deputy Recorders speech at the Chequer Barr to Baron Trever. *For Daniell Bradley*, 1642. brs. LT; Y.
M. Harrington's parallel. [n.p., 1659.] *See* Rogers, John.

111 M. Lewes Hewes his dialogve ansvvered. *For I. M.*, 1641. 4°. C, MR, E; NU, WF, Y.
M.S. to A.S. with a plea. 1644. *See* S., M.
M. Whitebread's contemplations. 1679. *See* White, Thomas, *Roman Catholic.*

112 **Mabbatt, John.** A briefe or generall reply, unto Mr. Knuttons answers. [n.p.], printed, 1645. 4°.* NU, Y.

113 **[Mabbut, George.]** Tables for renewing. *Cambridge, by John Hayes*, 1686. 8°. T.C.II 149. O, LLP, CT, BAMB, LIU, DT; CH, MH, WF, Y.

113A **[–]** —Second edition. —, 1700. *To be sold by Ed. Hall.* 8°. T.C.III 173. L, C, CT; WF.

113B **Macallo, J.** XCIX canons, or rules . . . physick. *By J. Grismond*, 1659. 12°. L, O, LWL.
Macbeth. A tragedy. 1687. *See* Shakespeare, William.

114 **[Mac Bride, John.]** Animadversions on the defence of the answer. [Belfast], 1697. 4°. LVF, EN, DN, DT.

115 —A sermon before the provincial synod . . . June 1. 1698. [Belfast?], printed, 1698. 4°.* L, C, LLP, EN, CD.

116 **McCarmick, William.** A farther impartial account of the actions of the Inniskilling-men. *For Ric. Chiswell.* 1691. 4°. T.C.II 379. L, O, C, LVF, EN, DT; CN, IU, MIU, WF, Y.

116A **Macclesfield, Charles Gerard, earl of.** The answer of . . . to . . . Alexander Fytton. [n.p., 1685.] fol.* O.

117 **Mac Connor, Dermond.** The copy of a letter. *For R. Harford*, 1642. 4°.* LT, O, LNC, MR, DT; CH, MH, WF, Y.

118 **Maccov, Johannes.** Johannis Maccovii . . . distinctiones et regulæ. *Oxoniæ, ex officina Hen. Hall, impensis Roberti Blagravii*, 1656. 12°. MADAN 2301. L, O, OC, CCA, EC, NE, GU.

118A **MacCulloch, Sir Godfrey.** The last speech of. *Edinburgh, J. Reid*, 1697. brs. ALDIS 3674.5. EN.

118B **MacDermott, Terence.** By the Lord Mayor. Whereas His Majesty . . . 14 April 1690. [Dublin, 1690.] brs. STEELE 2p 1107. L, HH, DK, DN.

118C **McDonald, John.** To his grace, His Majesties high commissioner, and the . . . Estates of Parliament. The humble supplication of. [Edinburgh, 1695.] brs. EN.

119 Entry cancelled.
MacDonnell, Sir William. Anglia liberta. 1651. *See title.*

120 **Mace, Thomas.** Musick's monument. *By T. Ratcliffe and N. Thompson, for the author, and are to be sold by himself, in Cambridge, and by John Carr* [London], 1676. fol. T.C.I 246. L, O, C, EN, DT; BN, CH, CN, LC, MH, MU, Y, AVP. (var.)

121 **[–]** Profit, conveniency, and pleasure, to the whole nation. [London], printed, 1675. 4°.* L, LUG, LLU, DT; CH, IU, NC, WF, Y.

121A —Riddles, mervels, and rarities. *For the author*, 1698. 4°.* YM; WF.

121B **[Macedo, Francisco.]** Domus sadica. *Typis Gulielmi Du-Gard*, 1653. fol. WF.

122 **[–]** Illustrissimo domino, dom. Israel: La Gherfelt. [London], 1653. fol.* LT.

123 —Lituus Lusitanus. *Excudebat R. Norton*, 1654. 4°. CT, EN, GU; BN, Y.

124 —Mens divinitus inspirata. *Excudebat R. Nortonus*, 1653. 4°. LT, CK, CT, DT; NU, Y.

125 —Scrinium divi Augustini. *Typis T. Roycroft*, 1654. 4°. CT, EN, GU; BN, TU, Y.

126 —Tessera Romana authoritatis pontificiæ. *Excudebat R. Norton*, 1654. 4°. O, CT, EN, GU; Y.
Mac Flecknoe. 1682. *See* Dryden, John.

126A **McGrigor, Evan.** To His Majesties high commissioner. [Edinburgh, 1695.] brs. ALDIS 3468.2. L.
Mac Guire, Connor. *See* Enniskillen, Connor Maguire, baron.

127 **Mac Guire, Francis.** The copy of two letters sent from Rome. *For Marmaduke Boat*, 1642. July 2. 4°.* LT; CH.

127A **Macham, N.** The vindication of ordinary and publick preaching. *For Thomas Bassett*, 1658. 8°. O, LCL, BC.

127B **[Machell, Thomas.]** That the Northern counties. [Oxford, by H. Hall, 1677.] cap., fol.* MADAN 3145. O.
Machiavel. As he lately appeared. 1641. *See* Heywood, Thomas.
Matchiavel junior. 1683. *See* S., W.

128 **Machiavelli, Niccolo.** The works of. *For J. S., to be sold by Robert Boulter*, 1675. fol. T.C.I 199. L, O, LW, E, DT; CLC, CN, IU, MH, MU, WF, Y.

128A ——[Anr. ed.] *For John Starkey*, 1675. fol. LG, OC, CK, CT, BC, EN; CH, MH, MIU, PL, TU, Y.

129 ——[Anr. ed.] *For John Starkey, Charles Harper and John Amery*, 1680. fol. T.C.I 453. L, C, LL, BAMB, DT; CH, CN, MBP, MH, MU, NU, Y, AVP.

130 ——[Anr. ed.] *For R. Clavel, Cha. Harper, Jonathan Robinson. Joh. Amery, A. and J. Churchil*, 1694. fol. T.C.II 532. L, C, NE, GU; CH, CLC, IU, WF.

131 ——[Anr. ed.] *For R. Clavel, C. Harper, J. Amery, J. Robinson, A. and J. Churchil, sold by Cha. Harper and A. and J. Churchil*, 1695. fol. T.C.II 541. L, CE, DU, E, DT; CH, IU, MH, NP, WF, Y.

132 —Machiavil's advice to his son. colop: *For T. Burrel*, [1681]. cap., fol.* L, O, LLP, LLU; CH, MIU, PU, WF, Y.

132A —A caveat for wives. *Printed*, 1660. 4°.* WF.

133 **[–]** The divell a married man. [London, 1647.] cap., 4°.* LT; CH, MH.

134 —Machivael's [sic] discourses. *By T. N. for Daniel Pake-man*, 1663. 12°. L, C, LVF, BC, ENC; CH, MH, NP, WF, Y.

134aA ——[Anr. ed.] *For G. Bedell, and T. Collins*, 1663. 12°. MH.

134A ——[Anr. ed., "Machiavell's."] *For Tho. Dring*, 1663. 12°. L, O; IU.

135 ——Second edition. *For Charles Harper, and John Amery, and are to be sold by Thomas Burrell and William Hensman*, 1674. 8°. T.C.I 158. O, C, OM, P, E, DT; CH, CN, MH, NC, TU, WF, Y.

135A ——[Anr. ed.] *For Charles Harper and John Amery*, 1674. 8°. L; MH, PU, WF, Y.

136 —The Florentine history in viii. books. *For Charles Harper, and John Amery, and by them sold*, 1674. 8°. T.C.I 187. L, O, C, ENC, DT; CH, IU, LC, MH, TU, WF, Y.

—Nicholas Machiavel's letter. [n.p., 1688.] *See* Wharton, Thomas, *marquess*.

—Marriage of Belphegor. 1671. *See* Salas Barbadillo, Alonso Jeronimo de. Novels of Quevedo.

137 Entry cancelled.

—Nicholas Machiavel's prince. 1661. *See* —Discourses. 1663.

138 Entry cancelled. Foreign printing.

139 —The publisher or translator of Nicholas Machiavels whole works. [*London*], *printed*, 1688. 8°.* L; MH.

140 —Nicholas Machiavel . . . his testimony against the Pope. [*n.p.*], *re-printed in the year* 1689. 8°. EN.

141 —A true copy of a letter written by. *For R. Bentley*, 1691. 4°.* T.C.II 383. L, O, C, MR, YM; CH, CN, MH, NU, WF, Y.

142 —Machiavel's vindication of himself. [*London*, 1691.] cap., 4°.* L, O, LSD, CD; CH, CLC, IU, PL, WF, Y.

143 Entry cancelled.

Machivilian Cromwellist. 1648. *See* Prynne, William.

Machiavillian plot. 1642. *See* Heath, *Sir* Robert.

Machiavels ghost. 1641. *See* Heywood, Thomas.

143A **McIntosh, Lauchlin.** Unto his grace His Majesties High Commissioner . . . petition of. [*Edinburgh*, 1690.] brs. ALDIS 3106.5. EN.

144 **Mackaile, Matthew.** The diversitie of salts. *Aberdeen, by Iohn Forbes*, 1683. 8°. ALDIS 2392. L, O, C, EN, AM; CH, MH, PU, WF, WU.

145 [–] Fons Moffetensis. *Edinburgi, excudebat Christophorus Higgins pro Roberto Brown*, 1659. 8°. ALDIS 1607. L, O, E, AM, EN, GU; CH, CN, WF.

146 Entry cancelled. Same as previous entry.

147 —Macis macerata. *Aberdene, by Iohn Forbes*, 1677. 12°. ALDIS 2103. L, AM, EN, GU; CN.

148 —Moffet-well. *Edinburgh, for Robert Brown*, 1664. 8°. ALDIS 1775. L, O, E, EN, GU; CH, CLC, WF, WSG, HC.

149 —Terrae prodromus theoricus. *Aberdeen, by Iohn Forbes. For George Mosman, at Edinburgh*, 1691. 4°. ALDIS 3160. L, EN, GU, SA; CH, WF.

Mackenzie, George. *See also* Cromarty, George Mackenzie, *earl of*.

150 **Mackenzie, Sir George.** The antiquity of the royal line. *For Joseph Hindmarsh*, 1686. 8°. T.C.II 157. L, O, C, MR, EN, CD; CH, CLC, IU, LC, MH, NU, Y, AVP.

151 [–] Aretina; or, the serious romance . . . part first. *Edinburgh, for Robert Broun, [by Evan Tyler?]*, 1660. 8°. ALDIS 1623. L, EN; WF, U. WASHINGTON.

152 [–] ——[Anr. ed.] *For Ralph Smith*, 1661. 8°. ALDIS 1688.3. O, EN; WF.

153 [–] ——[Anr. ed.] *For George S[awbridge*, 1661]. 8°. ALDIS 1688.7. Y.

154 —A defence of the antiquity. *Edinburgh, by the heir of Andrew Anderson*, 1685. 8°. ALDIS 2558. L, CE, E, EN, AU; CH, CLC, IU, NP, WF, Y.

154A ——[Anr. ed.] *For Abel Swalle*, 1685. 8°. CH.

155 ——[Anr. ed.] *For R. C. and are to be sold by Abell Swalle*, 1685. 8°. T.C.II 138. L, O, C, EN, DT; CLC, CN, TSM, WF, Y.

156 ——[Anr. ed.] *For Richard Chiswell*, 1685. 8°. L, O, CT, WCA, EN; BN, CH, CLC, LC, MIU, NU, WF, AVP.

157 —Idea eloquentiæ. *Edinburgi, excudebat hæres Andreæ Anderson*, 1681. 8°. T.C.I 466. ALDIS 2274. L, O, C, EN, GU; BN, CH, CLC, CU, TO, WF, Y.

158 —The institutions of the law of Scotland. *Edinburgh, by John Reid*, 1684. 12°. ALDIS 2459. L, O, C, EN, GU; BN, CLC, IU, MIU.

159 ——Second edition. *Edinburgh, by John Reid, for Thomas Broun*, 1688. 12°. ALDIS 2768. L, C, DU, EN, CD; CLC, IU, LC, MHL, MU, NP.

160 ——Third edition. *For Andrew Bell and Jonas Luntley*. 1694. 8°. L, O, C, EN, DT; BN, CH, IU, LC, MHL, MU, YL.

161 ——"Third" edition. *Edinburgh, for Thomas Broun*, 1699. 8°. ALDIS 3865.7. L, EN, D; CH, IU.

162 —Jvs regium: or, the just. *Edinburgh, by the heir of Andrew Anderson*, 1684. 4°. ALDIS 2460. L, O, E, EN, DL; CLC, IU, NN, OCI, WF.

163 ——[Anr. ed.]. *For Richard Chiswel*, 1684. 8°. T.C.II 86. L, OB, CT, EN, DT; CLC, CU, LC, MH, TU, Y.

164 ——[Anr. ed.] *For R. Chiswel*, 1684. 8°. L, O, CS, E, CD; CH, CN, MHL, NC, NU, TU, WF.

165 —The laws and customes of Scotland. *Edinburgh, by George Swintoun*, 1678. 4°. ALDIS 2133. L, O, C, EN, GU, AU; CLC, LC, MHL, NN, OCI, WF, YL.

166 ——[Anr. ed.] *Edinburgh, by James Glen*, 1678. 4°. ALDIS 2133.1. L, O, C, E, GU; CN, LC, NCL, OCI, PT.

167 ——[Anr. ed.] *Edinburgh, by Thomas Brown*, 1678. 4°. ALDIS 2132. L, C, CCA, EN, GU, BLH; CH, LC, MWA, NN, Y.

168 ——"Second" edition. *Edinburgh, by the heirs and successors of Andrew Anderson. For Mr. Andrew Symson*. 1699. fol. ALDIS 3866. L, O, MR, EN, D; CH, IU, LC, MHL, NCL, WF, YL.

— Letters, at the instance of. Edinburgh, 1682. *See* Scotland. Privy Council.

169 [–] A memorial for His Highness the Prince of Orange, in relation to the affairs of Scotland. *For Randal Taylor*, 1689. 4°.* T.C.II 256. L, O, C, MR, EN, DT; CH, CN, MH, NU, WF, Y.

170 [–] A moral essay. *Edinburh* [sic], *for Robert Brown*, [1665]. 8°. ALDIS 1796.5. EN, ES, DL; CLC.

171 [–] ——[Anr. ed.] —, 1665. 8°. ALDIS 1796. O, LUG, EN, ES, GK; CH, CN, NCU, WF, Y.

172 ——[Anr. ed.] *Edinburgh, for Robert Broun, 1666.* 8°. ALDIS 1817. EN, GK; CH, OCI.

173 ——[Anr. ed.] *By W. W. and are to be sold by H. Sawbridge, 1685.* 8°. T.C.II 153. L, O, C, EN, DT; BN, CH, LC, MH, NU, TU, Y.

174 ——"Second" edition. *For S. Briscoe, 1693.* 8°. T.C.II 468. L; CLC, CN, FU, OCI, JF.

175 —Moral gallantry. A discourse. *Edinburgh, for Robert Broun, 1667.* 8°. ALDIS 1838. L, O, AU, EN, I; CLC, IU, NCD, NN, NU.

176 ——Second edition ["that Point"]. *Printed at Edenburgh, and re-printed at London, by J. Streater, 1669.* 12°. T.C.I 5. L, O, CE, EN, DT; CLC, CN, MH, TU, WF, WSC, Y.

177 ——[Anr. ed., "That point."] —, *1669.* 12°. L, CT, LIU, WCA, AU, GU.

178 ——[Anr. ed.] *For Hanna Sawbrige. 1685.* 12°. T.C.II 108. L, O, C, EN, DT; CLC, CN, IU, MH, NCD, WF, Y.

179 —The moral history of frugality. *For J. Hindmarsh, 1691.* 8°. T.C.II 361. L, O, C, CT, EN, DT; CH, CJC, MH, NU, WF, Y.

180 ——[Anr. ed.] *Edinburgh, re printed for Andrew Chalmers and John Vallenge, 1691.* 4°.* ALDIS 3161. L, D, EN, GK; IU.

181 —A moral paradox. *Edinburgh, for Robert Broun, 1667.* 8°. L, O, EN, AU; IU, NN, NU.

182–3 Entries cancelled.
—Moral paradox. 1669. See—Moral gallantry.

184 —Observations on the acts of Parliament. *Edinburgh, by the heir of Andrew Anderson, 1686.* fol. ALDIS 2645. L, O, C, E, EN, GU; CH, CN, LC, MHL, NU, TU, Y.

185 ——[Anr. ed.] *Edinburgh, by the heir of Andrew Anderson, to be sold by Thomas Brown, 1687.* fol. ALDIS 2698. L, O, DU, EN, ES, SA; CLC, LC, MHL, NCL, YL.

186 —Observations upon the laws and customs of nations. *Edinburgh, by the heir of Andrew Anderson, 1680.* fol. T.C.I 511; ALDIS 2204. L, O, C, EN, GM; CH, CN, MHL, MU, NC, NCD, WF.

187 —Observations upon the 28. [18] act, 23. Parl. *Edinburgh, by His Majesties printers, 1675.* 8°. ALDIS 2055. L, O, EN; CH, CLC, MHL, WF.

188 ——Second edition ["18. Act"]. *Edinburgh, by the heirs and successors of Andrew Anderson. For Mr. Andrew Symson, 1698.* 8°. ALDIS 3758.7. EN; CLL, LC, WF.

189 —Observations upon the XVIII. act. *Edinburgh, by the heirs and successors of Andrew Anderson. For Mr. Andrew Symson, 1699.* fol. ALDIS 3866.5. L, MR, EN, ES, GM, D; CH, CLC, IU, LC, MHL, NCL, WF, Y.

190 —Oratio inauguralis. *1689.* 8°.* T.C.II 302. L, O, EN; CH, LC, WF.

191 —Pleadings, in some remarkable cases. *Edinburgh, by George Swintoun, James Glen, and Thomas Brown, 1672.* 4°. ALDIS 1949. L, O, LW, EN, AB; CLC, LC, MHL, PU, WF.

192 [–] —[Anr. ed.] —, *1673.* 4°. ALDIS 1990. L, C, EN, ES, GU; CH, LC, NIC, PU, TO.

193 —Reason. An essay. *For Jacob Tonson, 1690.* 12°. L, O, CS, AU, M; CH, CLC, NU, TU, VC, Y.

194 ——[Anr. ed.] *For Joseph Hindmarsh and Rich. Sare, 1695.* 12°. T.C.II 526. L, C, OM, EN, DT; CLC, CU, MU, WF, Y, JF.

195 [–] Religio stoici. *Edinburgh, for Robert Brown, 1663.* 8°. ALDIS 1762. EN, AU, GK; CU.

196 [–] —[Anr. ed.] *For George Sawbridge, 1663.* 8°. GK.

197 [–] —[Anr. ed.] *Edinburgh, For R. Broun, 1663.* 8°. L, O; MMO, NU.

198 [–] —[Anr. ed., "friendly."] *Edenburgh [i.e. London]: for R. Broun, 1665.* 8°. ALDIS 1797. O, CT, DC, DU, EN; BN, CH, CN, MH, PL, WF, HC.

199 [–] —[Anr. ed., "Friendly."] —, *1665.* 8°. O, C, LW, LIU, ES; CLC, IU, MH, MMO, WF, Y.

200 [–] The religious stoic. *Edinburgh printed, and reprinted at London, and are to be sold by R. Taylor, 1685.* 8°. T.C.II 150, L, O, CT, A, EN, GK; CLC.

200A [–] —[Anr. ed.] *By T. B., to be sold by R. Taylor, 1685.* 8°. SP, EN; OCI, WF.

201 ——Second edition. *For S. Briscoe, 1693.* 8°. T.C.II 468. L, C, LW, GU, GK; CLC, IU.

202 Entry cancelled. Ghost.

203 Entry cancelled.
[–] Representation to the high court of Parliament. [n.p., 1686.] See title.

204 [–] The science of herauldry. *Edinburgh, by the heir of Andrew Anderson, 1680.* fol. ALDIS 2205. L, O, C, EN, BLH; BN, CLC, CN, MHL, NCD, WF, Y.

205 Entry cancelled.
—Solitude preferable. 1685. See—Moral essay.

206 —That the lawful successor cannot be debarr'd. *Edinburgh, by the heir of Andrew Anderson, 1684.* 8°. ALDIS 2461. L, O, E, EN, D; CLC, IU, NC, OCI, WF.

207 Entry cancelled.
[–] Tryal and process of high treason . . . against Mr. Robert Baillie. 1685. See—True and plain account.

208 [–] —[Anr. ed.] *Edinburgh, by the heir of Andrew Anderson, 1685.* fol.* ALDIS 2621. O, SP, A, EN, GU; CH, CLC, CN, NU, TO, WF.

209 [–] A true and plain account of the discoveries made in Scotland. *Edinburgh, by the heir of Andrew Anderson, 1685.* fol. ALDIS 2619. O, A, EN, GU; CH, CLC, CN, NU, TO, Y.

210 [–] —[Anr. ed.] *Reprinted at London, by Thomas Newcomb, for Susanna Forrester, 1685.* fol. L, O, CS, DU, EN; CH, CLC, CN, PU, WF, Y.

211 [–] A vindication of His Majesties government. *Edinburgh, by the heir of Andrew Anderson, 1683.* 4°. ALDIS 2442. L, MR, P, EN; CLC, IU, MH, WU.

212 [–] —[Anr. ed.] *Printed at Edinburgh: and re-printed at London, by Nathaniel Thompson, for Susanna Forrester, 1683.* 4°.* L, CS, MR, EN, DT; CH, CN, NU, WF, Y.

213 —A vindication of the government. *For J. Hindmarsh, 1691.* 4°. T.C.II 384. L, O, C, EN, DT; CH, CN, NU, TU, WF, Y.

214 Entry cancelled.
—Virtuoso. 1675. See—Religio stoici.

214A **Mackenzie, George,** *subtacksman.* Unto his Grace . . . High Commissioner . . . the petition of. [*Edinburgh? 1697.*] fol.* ALDIS 3714.5. EN.

215 **Mackenzie, John.** Dr. Walker's invisible champion foyl'd. *For the author, 1690.* 4°.* T.C.II 333. L, O, C, LVF, MR, CD; CLC, CN, MH.

216 —A narrative of the siege of London-derry. *For the author, and are to be sold by Richard Baldwin,* 1690. 4°. T.C.II 333. L, O, C, EN, DT; CH, CN, MH, NC, WF, Y.

217 **Mackenzie, Simon.** Disputatio juridica. *Edinburgi, apud Joannem Reid,* 1693. 4°.* ALDIS 3305.5. EN.

Mackqueen, John. *See* MacQueen, John.

218 **M[ackworth],** *Sir* H[umphrey]. England's glory; or, the great improvement of trade. *By T. W. for Tho. Bever,* 1694. 8°. T.C.II 513. L, O, C, LG, EN; CLC, IU, LC, MH, NC, Y.

218A —Gentlemen, these are to give you notice of a charity. [*London,* 1698.] brs. MH.

219 —The mine-adventure. *For Freeman Collins,* 1698. fol.* L, O, LL; MH, NC.

220 — —[Anr. ed.] [*London,* 1698.] cap., fol.* L, O; MH.

220A [–] A new abstract of the mine-adventure. [*London?* 1698.] brs. L; MH, Y.

221 [**Macky, John.**] A view of the court of St. Germain. *For R. Baldwin,* 1696. 4°.* L, O, CT, EN, CD; CLC, IU, MH, NU, TU, WF, Y. (var.)

221A [–] —[Anr. ed.] *Dublin, re-printed by Andrew Crook,* 1696. 4°.* DIX 283. L, O, C, LIL, EN, DN, DT; MH, NU.

221B [–] —[Anr. ed.] *—and again re-printed at Glasgow, by Robert Sanders,* 1696. 8°.* ALDIS 3639. EN, GU.

222 **McMath, James.** The expert mid-wife. *Edinburgh, by George Mosman,* 1694. 8°. ALDIS 3375. L, LWL, MAU, GH; OCI, RICHMOND ACAD. OF MED.

223 **Macmordaci, Gilbert.** Theses philosophicæ. *Edinburgh, by the heir of Andrew Anderson,* 1682. brs. ALDIS 2361. E.

224 **MacNamara, John.** The information of. *For Randolph Taylor,* 1680. fol.* L, O, C, DU, EN, DT; CH, CN, MBC, MH, WF, Y.

Mac O Bonniclabbero, *pseud.*

224A **MacOlero.** Rapparee saint. A funeral sermon upon M. St. Ruth. *Edinburgh,* 1691. 4°. ALDIS 3188. EN.

Macollo, J. *See* Macallo, J.

225 **MacQueen, John.** A divine and moral essay. *For Daniel Brown, and Richard Smith,* 1699. 8°. T.C.III 93. L, C, LLP, OC, E, CD; CH, CLC, Y.

226 [–] Gods interest in the King. *London, by Nath. Thompson, And sold by Alexander Ogston . . . at Edingurgh* [sic], 1687. 4°.* L, O, DUS, EN, DL; CH, CLC, IU.

227 —The good patriot. *Edinburgh, by John Reid,* 1694. 4°. ALDIS 3376. O, OC, EN, ENC; CH, WF.

228 —The magistrate's dignity. *By J. D., sold by John Vallange, Edinburgh,* 1693. ALDIS 3306. LCL, EN; CH, WF.

229 **Macrobius, Ambrosius Aurelius Theodosius.** Opera. *Typis M. C. & B. M. Impensis T. Dring & C. Harper,* 1694. 8°. T.C.II 480. L, O, C, E, DT; CH, MH, MU, NC, TU, WF, Y.

229A **Macropedius, Georgius.** Methodus de conscribendis epistolis. *Excudebat Abraham Miller,* 1649. 8°. CT; MH.

230 [**Mac Ward, Robert.**] The banders disbanded. [*Edinburgh*], *printed* 1681. 4°. ALDIS 2276. O, EN, ENC; CLC, MH, NU, Y.

231 Entry cancelled.

232 [–] Case of the accomodation. 1671. *See* Leighton, Robert.

232 [–] The English ballance. [*London*], *printed,* 1672. 4°. L, LUG, EN; HR, CH, MM, NN, WF.

233 [–] The poor man's cup. [*Edinburgh*], *printed,* 1678. 4°.* ALDIS 2136. L, LPR, EN; CH, CLC, IU, Y.

234 [–] —[Anr. ed.] [*Edinburgh*], *printed,* 1681. 4°.* ALDIS 2285.5. EN, ENC; WF.

235 [–] The true non-conformist. [*n.p.*], *printed,* 1671. 8°. L, O, LW, EN, ES, BLH; CLC, MH, NU, WF, Y.

236 A mad designe: or, a description of the King of Scots. *By Robert Ibbitson,* 1651. brs. LT, LS.

237 The mad dog rebellion. [*London,* 1648.] cap., 4°.* LT, LHO, BC; CASE WESTERN, CSS, MH, NU, Y.

238 Entry cancelled.

Mad man's morice. [1670?] *See* Crouch, Humphrey.

238A —[Anr. ed., "Mad-man's."] *For Francis Coles,* [1641–81]. brs. EUING 201. GU.

238B —[Anr. ed.] [*n.p.*], *for F. Coles,* [1667–80]. brs. EUING 202. GU.

239 —[Anr. ed., "Mad mans."] [1675?] brs. L.

Madman's plea. 1653. *See* Erbery, William.

240 A mad marriage. [*London*], *for I. Deacon,* [1680?]. brs. L, O.

241 The mad-men's hospital. colop: *By N. T.,* 1681. brs. L, O, MC; CH, IU, MH, NU, WF, Y.

Mad-merry Merlin. 1653. *See* Almanacs.

241A The mad merry pranks of Robin Good-Fellow. *For F. Coles, T. Vere, and J. Wright,* [1663–74]. brs. EUING 203. GU.

241B —[Anr. ed.] [*n.p.*], *for F. Coles, T. Vere, J. Wright, J. Clark, W. Thackeray, and T. Passinger,* [1680]. brs. EUING 204. GU.

242 —[Anr. ed.] *By and for W. O. Sold by C. Bates,* [1690?]. brs. L.

242A —[Anr. ed.] *By and for W. O. and sold by the booksellers,* [1690?]. brs. L.

Mad Tom a Bedlams desires. 1648. *See* Wortley, Sir Francis.

Madam, although my former freedom. [*n.p.,* 1645.] *See* Durie, John.

Madam, ever since I. [*n.p.,* 1645.] *See* Durie, John.

243 Madam Gwins ansvver to the Dutches of Portsmouths letter. colop: *For J. Johnson,* [1682]. brs. CH, MH, RHT, WF, Y. (var.)

243A —[Anr. ed.] *By and for W.O.,* [1690?]. brs. L.

Madam Semphronia's farewel. [*n.p.,* 1682.] *See* P., D.

244 **Madan, Patrick.** A philosophical and medicinal essay of the waters of Tunbridge. *For the author,* 1687. 4°.* L, O, C, LCS, LSC; CLC, WF.

244A **Maddison,** *Sir* **Ralph.** England's looking in and out. *By T. Badger for H. Mosley,* 1641. 4°. L.

245 —Great Britains remembrancer. *By Tho. Newcomb, to be sold by Humphrey Moseley,* 1655. 4°.* LT, O, C, NOT, EN; CH, CU, MH, NU, WF, Y.

246 **Maddocks, John.** Gangrænachrestum, or, a plaister. *Oxford,* [*by H. Hall*], 1646. 4°.* MADAN 1901. LT, CS, DT; CH.

Madruddyn. 1651. *See* Fisher, Edward.

247 **Magaillans, Gabriel de.** A new history of China. *For Thomas Newborough*, 1688. 8°. T.C.II 230. L, O, C, LW, MR, DT; CH, CN, MH, NC, WF, Y.

248 A magazine of scandall. *Printed at London for R. H.*, 1642. 4°.* LT, O, C, MR, A; CH, MH, WF.

Maggots: or poems. 1685. *See* Wesley, Samuel.

Magia Adamica: or. 1650. *See* Vaughan, Thomas.

Magia coelestis. 1673. *See* Benlowes, Edward.

249 The magick of Kirani. [*London*], printed, 1685. 8°. L, LSC, LWL, GU; MIU, NP, WF.

250 A magical vision, or a perfect discovery. *For Thomas Palmer*, 1673. 12°.* L, LN, A, GU; CH.

251 **Magirus, Johann.** Physiologiæ peripateticæ libri sex. *Cantabrigiae: ex officina R. Danielis*, 1642. 8°. L, O, C, P, EN; CH, CLC, IU, MB, NAM, WF, Y.

Magistracy and government. 1689. *See* Shower, *Sir* Bartholomew.

Magistrates ministery. Cambridge, 1655. *See* C., J.

252 The magistrates monitor. colop: *For Richard Janeway*, 1682. cap., 4°.* L, O, DU, MR, YM; CN, MH, NU, WF, Y.

Magna charta: containing. 1659. *See* C., J.

253 **Magna Carta.** Magna Charta, made in the ninth year of King Henry the third. *By the assignees of Richard and Edward Atkins, for Thomas Simmons*, 1680. 4°. T.C.I 405. 68pp. L, O, C, MR, EN; CH, IU, MH, NCL, WF, Y.

253A ——[Anr. ed.] —, 1680. 8°. 108pp. L, O; LC, MIU, MWA, PUL, YL.

253B ——[Anr. ed.] —, 1680. 8°. 79pp. EN.

254 Magna & antiqua charta Quinque Portuum. *Cantabrigiæ, excudebatur pro Majore & Juratis Hastingiæ*, 1675. 8°. L, C, LL, LLP, OM; CH, MBP, MIU, NCL, WF.

255 Magnalia Dei. A relation of some of the many remarkable passages in Cheshire. *For Robert Bostock*, 1644. 4°.* LT, O, OC, CT, MR, DT; CH, CLC, IU, MH, WF, Y.

Magnalia naturæ: or. 1686. *See* Becher, Johann Joachim.

255A **Magnen, Jean Chrysostome.** Democritus reviviscens. *Ex officina Rogeri Danielis*, 1658. 12°. O, CS, LNC; Y.

256 Magni sylvii sal volatile oleosvm. *Printed*, 1674. 4°.* NU.

Magnificentiss. dominis. [n.p.], 1651.] *See* S., A.

Magnum in parvo: or. 1671. *See* Le Clerc, Sebastien.

Magnum in parvo. Or a receipt. 1689. *See* S., T.

257 **Magnus, Olaus, abp.** A compendious history of the Goths. *By J. Streater, and are to be sold by Humphrey Mosely, George Sawbridge, Henry Twiford, Tho: Dring, John Place, and Henry Haringman*, 1658. fol. L, O, C, E, DT; CH, CN, LC, MH, NCL, WF, Y.

258 **Magnus, Valerian.** Brevis disqvisitio. *Eleutheropoli* [*London*], *typis Godfridi Philadelphi*, 1650[1]. 12°. LT, O;NU. [–] ——[Anr. ed.] 1653. *See* Biddle, John.

258A **Magrath, James.** The vindication of James Magrath, in a letter to a friend. colop: [*n.p.*], *for the authour*, 1682. brs. NIC.

259 No entry.

Maguire, Connor, lord. *See* Enniskillen, Connor Maguire, *baron.*

Maguire, Francis. *See* MacGuire, Francis.

260 Entry cancelled.

Maguotus. Ad prima rudimenta. 1693. *See* Leedes, Edward.

261 Entry cancelled.

Mahmud, Shah-Kuljl. Astronomica. 1652. *See* Cholgius, *shah.*

262 **Mahomet IV, sultan.** The great Turks declaration of war. colop: *By G. C. for John Mumford*, 1683. brs. O; WF.

262A ——[Anr. ed.] [*Edinburgh?* 1683.] brs. ALDIS 2382.3. L, HH.

263 —A declaration or denouncing of war. colop: *For Langley Curtis*, 1683. brs. O, HH.

264 —A defiance and indiction of war. colop: *For A. Banks*, 1683. brs. O; CH.

—Great Turkes letter. 1653. *See* Ibrahim, *sultan.*

264A The maid is the best that lies alone. [*London*], *for R. H. & J. Williamson*, [1675?]. brs. O.

Maiden-warrier. [n.p., 1689.] *See* D'Urfey, Thomas.

264B A maidenhead ill-bestowed. [*London*], *for R. Burton*, [1679]. brs. O.

265 The maiden's answer to the young-men's request. [*London*, 1685?] brs. L.

266 The maidens best adorning. *By George Larkin*, 1687. brs. L.

267 The maiden's choice. *R. Burton*, [1655?]. brs. L.

267A The maidens complaint against coffee. *For J. Jones*, 1663. 4°.* OC; MH.

268 The maidens counsellor. [*London*], *for P. Brooksby*, [1685–88]. brs. L, HH.

Maidens delight. [1656.] *See* Price, Laurence.

268A The maiden's desire. [*London?* 1700.] brs. L.

269 The maidens frollick. [*London*], *for P. Brooksby, J. Deacon, J. Blare, J. Back*, [1686–92]. brs. L, O, CM, HH.

269A The maidens garland. [*London*], *for J. Back*, [1685?]. 8°.* CM.

270 The maidens lamentation. [1680?] brs. O.

271 Entry cancelled.

Maidens nay. [1663–74.] *See* H., R.

Maydens of Londons brave adventures. [1655.] *See* Price, Laurence.

271A The maidens plea: or, her defence. *By G. Croom, for the author*, 1684. 4°.* CN.

272 The maidens reply to the young mans resolution. [*London*], *for J. Williamson*, [1665]. brs. L, HH; MH.

Maidens sad complaint. 1678. *See* W., L.

273 The maidens tragedy. [*London*], *for P. Brooksby, J. Deacon, J. Blare, and J. Back*, [1685–92.] brs. L, HH; MH.

274 —[Anr. ed.] [*London*], *for J. Deacon*, [1688–95]. brs. L, CM, HH.

275 The maids ansvver to the batchelors ballad. [*London*], *for P. Brooksby*, [1678–85]. brs. L, O, HH; MH.

276 The maids complaint against the batchelors. *For J. Coniers*, 1675. 4°.* O; CH, MH, Y.

277 The maids complaint for want of a dill doul. [*London*], *for V. Wentbridg*, [1680–90]. brs. L, O, CM, HH.

277A —[Anr. ed.] [*London*], *for J. Wiight* [*sic*], *J. Clark, W. Thackeray, & T. Passenger*, [1690?]. brs. L.

278   The maids delight. 1670. brs. L.

278A   The maid's kind answer. [London], for P. Brooksby; J.
       Deacon; J. Blare; J. Back, [1684–90]. brs. CM.

279   Maids lamentation. [London], for P. Brooksby, [1680?].
       brs. L, HH; WCL.

279A   The maid's lamentation for want of Tochar-good. [Scot-
       land, 1700?] brs. NN.

280   The maids petition. For A. L., 1647. 4°.* LT, LG, OC, LLU,
       LNC; CH, CSS, MH, Y, ZWT.

281   The maids prophecies. [London, 1648.] cap., 4°.* LT, LLU,
       DT.

       Maids revenge upon Cupid. [1662.] See Price, Laurence.

282   The maid's twitcher. [London, 1700?] brs. L.

283   The maids unhappinesse. [London], for J. Wright, J. Clark,
       W. Thackery and T. Passenger, [1683?]. brs. L.

284   **Maidwell, Lewis.** The loving enemies. For John Guy,
       1680. 4°. T.C.I 394. L, O, C, LGI, OW; CH, CN, LC, MH, NC,
       TU, WF, Y.

284A   —A pindarick poem . . . to . . . William Fox. [London,
       1680.] cap., fol.* OC.

285   —Proposals reviv'd, of establishing . . . a public scholc.
       [London, 1699.] brs. L, O; Y.

285A   [–] A scheme for a public academy. [London, 1700.] fol.*
       L; CH, WF.

285B   [–] A scheme of learning propos'd. [London, 1700?] fol.*
       Y.

285C   [–] Soteria regi, et ecclesia Anglicanæ. [London, 1678–91.]
       cap., fol.* CH.

286   **Maier, Michael.** Lvsvs serivs: or, serious passe-time. For
       Humphrey Moseley, and Tho: Heath, 1654. 12°. L, O,
       GU; CLC, CPB, OSU, WF, WU, Y.

287   —Themis aurea. The laws of the . . . Rosie Crosse. For N.
       Brooke, 1656. 8°. L, O, LLP, OC, GU, DT; CH, CLC, MH, PL,
       WF, WU.

288   [**Maijole, J. B. Primi- Visconti**], *count de.* An account
       of the reasons which induced Charles II . . . to declare
       war. For Richard Baldwin, 1689. fol.* T.C.II 255. L, O, C,
       OC, DU, LIU; CH, MIU, TU, WF, Y.

288A   Whitehall, June 7. 1697. The mail from Holland of
       Friday. [London], in the Savoy, by E. Jones, 1697. brs. EN.

288B   [**Maimbourg, Louis.**] A discourse concerning the
       foundation. For Jos. Hindmarsh, 1688. 8°. WF.

289   —An historical treatise of the foundation. For Jos. Hind-
       marsh, 1685. 8°. T.C.II 113. L, O, C, MC, GU; CH, CN, MIU,
       TU, Y.

290   —The history of the Crusade. By R. H. for Thomas Dring,
       1685. fol. T.C.II 124. L, O, C, LNC, EN; BN, CH, CN, LC,
       MH, WF, Y.

291   [–] The history of the Holy War. By R. H. for Arthur
       Jones, 1686. fol. L, DU, DT; CLC, SCU.

291A   [–] —[Anr. ed.] By R. H. for Thomas Dring, 1686. fol. BBE,
       WF.

292   —The history of the League. By M. Flesher for Jacob
       Tonson, 1684. 8°. L, O, C, EN, DT; CH, CN, MH, TU, WF, Y.
       (var.)

293   —A peaceable method. Printed at Paris, 1671. 8°. L, O, C,
       DUS, DT; CH, MIU, TU, VC, WF, Y. (var.)

294   —[Anr. ed.] [London], for G. W., 1686. 4°. L, O, CT, MC,
       EN; CH, CLC, MH, MIU, NU, TU, WF, Y.

Maimonides, Moses. See Moses ben Maimon.

Main points. 1648. See Love, Christopher.

294A   **Maine, Province.** By Thomas Danforth . . . with the
       consent of the council . . . Octob. 1682. [Order for
       thanksgiving.] brs. MHS (imp.).

295   The maintenance of the sanctuary. By A. N. for Iohn
       Maynard, 1642. 4°. LT, O, LNC, P, E, DT; NU, WF.

295A   [**Mainwaring, Arthur.**] The King of hearts. Sondon
       [sic], printed, 1690. brs. L, O, C; CLC, NP, MH, Y.

295B   [–] —[Anr. ed.] [London, 1690.] cap., fol.* L; MH, PL, ASU.

295BA —Tarquin and Tullia. [London, 1689.] brs. OC; MH.

295C   Entry cancelled.

Mainwaring, Matthew. Vienna. No art. 1650. See title.

296   Entry cancelled.

Mainwaring, Randall. Case of Mainwaring. [n.p.],
       1646. See title.

296A   —The protestation of . . . to clear his innocency. [London?
       1646.] brs. LG.

297   **M[ainwaring], Sir T[homas].** An admonition to the
       reader of Sir Peter Leicester's books. [London], printed,
       1676. 8°.* L, CT; CLC, Y.

298   —An answer to Sir Peter Leicester's addenda. For
       Samuel Lowndes, 1673/4. 8°. L, O; ARIZONA ST.

299   —An answer to two books. For Sam: Lowndes, 1675.
       8°. L, O, CT.

300   —A defence of Amicia. For Sam. Lowndes, 1673. 8°.
       T.C.I 133. L, O, C, LIU, EN; CH, CLC, LC, MH, TSM, WF, Y.

301   —The legitimacy of Amicia. For Sam. Lowndes, 1679. 8°.
       L, O, C, LI, DU, EN; CH, CLC, CN, MIU, WF, Y.

302   Entry cancelled. See next entry.

303   —A reply to an answer to the defence. For S. Lowndes, 1673.
       8°. T.C.I 149. L, O, C, DU, EN; CH, MH, MIU, TSM, WF, Y.

304   **Maisterson, Henry.** A sermon preached at St. Pauls.
       [Cambridge], by Roger Daniel, 1641. 4°.* C, LW, CT, LNC;
       CH, IU, Y.

Maitland, John. See Lauderdale, John Maitland, earl of.

Majestas intemerata. Or. [n.p.], 1649. See Cleveland, John.

Majesty in misery. [n.p.], 1681. See Charles I.

305   **Major, Elizabeth.** Honey on the rod. By Tho: Maxey,
       1656. 12°. L; CLC.

306   **Major, William.** A copy of verses presented. By John
       Wallis, 1689. brs. O.

307   **Makemie, Francis.** An answer to George Keith's libel.
       Boston, by Benjamin Harris, 1694. 8°. EVANS 693. C, LW;
       MBJ, MHS, MWA, NHS, NN, RPJ, V.

308   —Truths in a true light. Edinbvrgh, by the successors of
       Andrew Anderson, 1699. 8°.* ALDIS 3866.7. MH, NN, NU.

309   [**Makin, Mrs. Bathshua.**] An essay to revive the antient
       education of gentlewomen. By J. D. to be sold by Tho.
       Parkhurst, 1673. 4°.* L, LU, LW; CH, CN, WF.

310   The malady and remedy of vexations. Printed September
       24. 1646. 4°.* LT; CH, MHL, RBU.

Malala, Joannes. See Joannes, Malalas.

311   **Malbon, Samuel.** Christs glorious appearance. By John
       Hancock sen. and jun., 1673. 8°.* T.C.I 168. O, C; MWA, TO.

312 —Death and life. *For John Allen*, 1669. 8°. T.C.I 13. ASSING-
TON PARISH, SUFFOLK; MH, MWA, NU, TO.

Malecontent; a satyr. 1684. *See* D'Urfey, Thomas.

313 The male and female husband. [*London*], *for P. Brooksby*,
[1672–95]. brs. L, HH; MH.

314 **Malebranche, Nicolas.** Christian conferences. *Printed
and are to be sold by J. Whitlock*, 1695. 8°. T.C.II 554. L, CS,
DUS, NE, CD; CH, LC, MH, NU, WF, ASU.

314A —De inquirenda veritate libri sex. *Apud Abel Swalle*, 1687.
4°. L.

315 —Malebranche's search after truth. Vol. I. *For J. Dunton,
and S. Manship*, 1694. 8°. T.C.II 556. L, O, C, LL, DUS, E;
CH, MBC, MH, MIU, TU, WF, Y.

316 ——Vol. II. *For S. Manship*, 1695. 8°. T.C.II 556. L, DUS,
LIU, MRL, E; MH, SW, WF.

316A ——[Anr. ed.] *For J. Dunton*, 1695. 8°. LSD, NE; CH, CLC,
MIU, PU, Y.

317 —Father Malebranche's treatise concerning the search
after truth. *Oxford, by L. Lichfield, for Thomas Bennet,
London*, 1694. fol. L, O, C, ES, BQ; CH, CN, MH, NP, TU, WG.

318 ——Second edition. *By W. Bowyer, for Thomas Bennet,
T. Leigh and W. Midwinter*, 1700. fol. O, CSSX, E, DT; CH,
LC, MH, MU, NU, OCI, Y.

318A ——"Second" edition. *By W. Bowyer, for Thomas Bennet,
T. Leigh and D. Midwinter*, 1700. fol. T.C.III 164. L, BAMB,
LIU, MR, CD; CDA, CLC, MU, NCU, TO, WF.

319 —A treatise of morality. *For James Knapton*, 1699. 8°.
T.C.III 96. L, O, C, CK, DU, DT; CLC, LC, MH, NU, OCI, Y.

320 [–] A treatise of nature and grace. *Printed, and are to be
sold by John Whitlock*, 1695. 8°. L, C, DUS, P, E; CLC, MH,
RBU, Y, ASU.

[Maleverer, John.] 'Επινίχιον. Sive. [n.p., 1690?] *See*
title.

Malice of the independent-agent. [n.p., 1678.] *See* Stout,
Henry.

320A A malicious man makes reasons. To the honourable the
knights. [*London*, 1700?] brs. L; MH.

320B —[Anr. ed., "The humble petition of Prince Butler."]
[*London*, 1700?] brs. L; MH.

321 A malicious rich man makes acceptable pleasant reasons
. . . assembled. The humble petition. [*London?* 1700.]
brs. HH; MH.

321A —[Anr. ed., "assembled, the humble petition."] [*London*,
1700?] brs. HH; MH.

Malignancy un-masked. 1642. *See* S., J.

322 Entry cancelled.

Malignants conventicle. 1643. *See* Webb, M.

323 The malignants inqvest. *By B. A.*, March 17, 1646. 4°.*
MADAN 1839. LT, O; NU.

324 The malignants lamentation. *By J. M.* 1645. 4°.* LT, O,
MR, YM, DT; MH, MIU, WF.

325 Malignants remember Rochell. *By J. M. and are to be
sold by M. S.*, 1645. 4°.* LT, DT; CH, MH, NU, Y.

326 The malignants trecherous and bloody plot. [*London*],
sould by Io. Hancock, [1643]. brs. LT; Y.

327 **Malkin, Gilbert.** A good-work for bad times. 1697.
4°.* L; CH, NC, WF.

327A —The humble proposal of. [*London?* 1694?] brs. O; MH, Y.

327B [–] A proposal humbly presented to the . . . Commons.
[*London?* 1697.] brs. L; MH.

328 **Mall, Thomas.** The axe at the root. *For Tho. Parkhurst*,
1668. 4°. L, O, LCL.

328A ——[Anr. ed.] *For John Weeks in Tiverton*, 1668. 4°.* L,
O.

329 [–] A cloud of vvitnesses. *For the author, to be sold by Robert
Boulter*, 1665. 8°. L, O, C, LCL, DU, E; CLC, CU, NGT, WF, Y.

330 [–] —[Anr. ed.] *For Robert Boulter*, 1670. 8°. T.C.I 52. L, O,
C, LW; CH, MH, NCD, NGT, WF.

331 [–] — . . . Second part. *For the author, and are to be sold by
Robert Boulter*, 1665. 8°. LW, DU; CU, MBA, MH, NCD.

332 [–] ——[Anr. ed.] *For Robert Boulter*, 1677. 8°. T.C.I 278. L,
LW, DU; CH, MH, NP, WF, WSC.

333 [–] — . . . third and last part. *For the author, to be sold by
Robert Boulter*, 1665. 8°. L, LW, DU; CH, CU, MH, NCD,
NU, PL, WF.

334 [–] Of holy living. *London, for William Grantham, to
be sold by Robert Eveleigh, in Exon.*, 1668. 12°. O.

334A [–] An offer of farther help. *For the Authour, and are to be
sold by Robert Boulter*, 1665. 8°. L, LCL, LW, DU, GU; CH,
MH, NGT, NU. (var.)

335 —A serious exhortation to holy living. *London, for
William Grantham, to be sold by Robert Eveleigh, in
Exon*, 1668. 12°. L, O, LCL, LSC, LW.

335A [–] A true account of what was done . . . in Exon. *By R. W.
for Mathew Keinton*, 1658. 8°. L, LCL; WF.

The mall. 1674. *See* Dryden, John.

336 Mall and her master: or, a dialogue between a Quaker
and his maid. [1675.] 4°.* O; CLC, MH, Y.

337 **Mallery, Thomas.** The inseparable communion. *For
R. D.*, 1674. 8°. O, LSC, SP; NU.

338 **Mallet, *Sir* John.** Concerning penal laws. *For Thomas
Cockeril*, 1680. fol.* L, O, DU, LSD, DT; CH, MHL, MIU, WF,
Y.

339 **Malory, *Sir* Thomas.** Brittains glory. *By H. B. for
J. Wright, J. Clark, W. Thackeray, and T. Passinger*,
1684. 4°. CM.

340 **M[alpas], T[homas].** A box of spikenard newly broken.
By J. S. for George Sawbridge, 1659. 8°. LT, LSC; CLC.

340A [–] —Second edition. *For the author*, 1661. 8°. L; MH.

341 —Monarchiæ encomium . . . or a congratulation. *London,
by T. Leach, to be sold by William Palmer, and by Joan
Malpas, in Sturbridg*, 1661. 8°. LT.

342 **Malpighi, Marcello.** Opera omnia. *Prostant apud
Robertum Scott , & Georgium Wells*, 1686. fol. T.C.II 179.
L, O, LN, MAU, EN, BQ; CNM, MMO, NAM, NCD.

342A ——[Anr. ed.] *Prostant apud Robertum Scott*, 1686. fol.
LSC, CCA, LLU, NE, CD; MH, NAM.

342B ——[Anr. ed.] *Apud Thomam Sawbridge*, 1686. fol. OC,
CM, CP; MH, PBL, PL, HC, ZDU.

343 ——[Anr. ed.] *Apud Robertum Littlebury*, 1687. fol.
L, C, OME, GH, DT; BN, CH, TO, WCL, WF.

344 —Operum tomus secundus. *Typis M. F. Impensis R.
Littlebury, R. Scott, Tho. Sawbridge, & G. Wells*, 1686.
fol. L, O, C, GH, DT; BN, CLC, MH, PL, WCL, WF.

345 —Anatome plantarum. *Impensis Johannis Martyn*, 1675–9. 2v. fol. T.C.I 229. L, O, C, RU, E; BN, CH, CJC, LC, MH, WF, Y.

346 —De structurâ glandularum. *Apud Richardum Chiswell*, 1689. 4°.* T.C.II 254. L, O, C, LCS, OM; NIC, HC.

347 ——[Anr. ed.] —, 1697. fol.* L, C, OM, NE, GH; CH, MH, MU, PL, WF, WU.

348 —De viscerum structurâ. *Typis T. R. Impensis Jo. Martyn*, 1669. 12°. T.C.I 10. L, O, C, GH, DT; BN, CLC, INU, NAM, PL, WF, HC.

349 —Dissertatio epistolica de Bombyce. *Apud Joannem Martyn & Jacobum Allestry*, 1669. 4°. T.C.I 21. L, O, LCS, CT, MR; BN, CH, CJC, CLC, MH, TO, WDA, HC.

350 —Dissertatio epistolica de formatione pulli in ovo. *Apud Joannem Martyn*, 1673. 4°.* T.C.I 129. L, O, C, MR, EN, BQ; CU, MH, PL, TU, WSG, Y, HC.

351 —Dissertationes epistolicæ duæ, una de formatione. *Impensis Joannis Martyn*, 1673. 4°. LCS, OC, CM, MR; MMO, PL, TO.

352 —Opera posthuma. *Impensis A. & J. Churchill*, 1697. fol. T.C.III 6. L, O, C, EN, DT; BN, CH, MH, MU, NAM, WF, Y.

353 The maltster caught in a trap. [*London*], *for P. Brooksby*, [1672–95]. brs. L, HH; MH.

354 The maltster's daughter of Marlborough. *For J. Blare*, [1684–98]. brs. HH.

355 **Malvezzi, Virgilio, *marchese*.** The chiefe events of the monarchie of Spaine. *By T. W. for Humphrey Moseley*, 1647. 12°. LT, O, CT, LLU, SP; CH, CN, IU, MH, WF, Y.

356 —Considerations upon the lives of Alcibiades and Corialanus [*sic*]. *By William Wilson for Humphrey Moseley*, 1650. 12°. L, O, LLU, SP, CU; CH, CU, IU, MH, TU, WF, Y.

357 —Il Davide perseguitato. David persecuted. *For Humphrey Mosely*, 1647. 12°. LT, O, C, OM, SP; CH, CN, IU, MH, TU, WF, WG, Y.

358 ——[Anr. ed.] —, 1650. 12°. L, O, DC; CU.

359 —Discovrses upon Cornelius Tacitus. *By E. G. for R. Whitaker, and Tho. Whitaker*, 1642. fol. L, O, C, AN, E, DT; CH, CN, LC, MH, MU, OCI, WF, Y, AVP.

360 —The pourtract of the politicke Christian-favourite. *For M. Meighen and G. Bedell*, 1647. 12°. L, O, C, CE, LSD, P; BN, CH, CN, MU, PL, WF, WG, Y.

361 —Romvlvs and Tarqvin. Third edition. *For Humphrey Moseley*, 1648. 12°. L, O, C, DC, E; BN, CH, CN, LC, MH, WF, Y.

362 —Stoa triumphans: or, two sober paradoxes. *By J. G.*, 1651. 12°. LT, O, C, LW, CE; CN, NR.

363 Entry cancelled.

[**Malynes, Gerard.**] Advice concerning bills. 1655. *See* Marius, John.

364 —Consuetudo: vel, lex mercatoria, or, the ancient law-merchant. *By William Hunt for Nicolas Bourne*, 1656. fol. L, LCP, LL, LUG, CM; BN, CB, CU, MHL, NCL, PL, WF.

364A ——[Anr. ed.] *By J. Redmayne, for T. Basset; and R. Smith*, 1685. fol. NN, SE.

365 ——Third edition. *For T. Basset, R. Chiswell, M. Horne, and E. Smith*, 1686. fol. T.C.II 184. L, CT, MC, EN, DT; BN, CH, IU, MHL, NCD, WF, YL.

Mamamouchi; or. 1675. *See* Molière, Jean Baptiste Poquelin.

Man, John. Edinburghs true almanack. Edinburgh, 1696. *See* Almanacs.

366 —Unto the Right Honourable George Hume. *Edinburgh, John Reid*, 1699. brs. ALDIS 3868.5. E.

367 **Man, Thomas.** Prodigia. [*n.p.*], 1680. brs. L, O.

368 Man considered. *By James Cottrel*, [1652.] 8°.* LT.

Man hath had his day. [n.p.], 1663. *See* Perrot, John.

369 The man-hunter. colop: *For the author*, 1690. cap., 4°.* L, LLP, LIU, MR; CH, CN, INU, PL, WF.

370 A man in favour. [*London*], *for J. H.*, 1688. brs. L, O, HH.

Man in paradise. [1656.] *See* Bunworth, Richard.

Man in the moone. 1657. *See* Godwin, Francis.

Man in the moon. [n.p.], 1676. *See* S., J.

Man in the moone discovering. 1657. *See* S., S.

370A The man in the moon drinks claret. [*London*], *for F. Coles, T. Vere, and W. Gilbertson*, [1658–64]. brs. EUING 207. GU.

371 —[Anr. ed.] [*London*], *for W. Thackeray, and T. Passinger*, [1686–88]. brs. L, CM, IIII.

Man-mouse taken. 1650. *See* Vaughan, Thomas.

372 The man of destiny's hard fortune. *For T. M.*, 1679. 4°.* O; CN, Y.

Man of honour. [n.p., 1689.] *See* Halifax, Charles Montagu, *earl of.*

Man of Newmarket. 1678. *See* Howard, Edward.

Man of sin. 1677. *See* Hughes, William, *hospitaller.*

Man wholly mortal. 1655. *See* Overton, Richard.

Management of the present war. 1690. *See* Littleton, Edward.

373 Entry cancelled.

Manasseh Ben Israel. Anglo-Judævs, or the history. 1656. *See* Hughes, William, *of Gray's Inn.*

374 —De termino vitæ; or the term of life. *For W. Whitwood*, 1700. 8°. L, LWL; OHU, Y.

375 —The hope of Israel. *Printed at London by R. I. for Hannah Allen*, 1650. 8°. LT, LW, CT, DT; CH, MH.

376 ——Second edition. *By R. I. for Livewell Chapman*, 1651. 4°. LT, C, LG, OC, DT; CN, MU, NN, NU.

377 ——"Second" edition. —, 1652. 4°. L, C, E; LC, MH.

378 Entry cancelled.

—Narrative of the late proceeds. 1656. *See* Jessey, Henry.

—Of the term of life. *Printed and sold by J. Nutt.* 1699. 8°.

378A T.C.III 121. LUC, DU, NE; LC, NN, RBU.

379 —To His Highnesse the Lord Protector . . . the humble addresses of. [*London*, 1655.] 4°.* 26 pp. L, C, OCC, LNC, SP, DM; CH, CLC, CSS, OHU.

380 ——[Anr. ed.] [*London*, 1655.] 4°.* 23pp. LT, CT; CDA, CSS, LC, Y.

381 —Vindiciæ Judæorum, or a letter. [*London*], *by R. D.*, 1656. 4°.* LT, LW, CT, P, SP; CLC, MH, MIU, NN, OHU, WF.

382 **Manby, Peter.** A brief and practical discourse of abstinence. *Dublin, by Joseph Ray, for William Winter*, 1682. 4°.* DIX 193. L, O, DI, DT; WF.

383 —The considerations which obliged. *Dublin, for Christopher Ians*, 1687. 4°.* L, O, LP, EN, CD, DT; CLC, WF.

383A ——[Anr. ed.] *[Dublin], for Christopher I'anes,* 1687. 4°.* DIX 225. DN.

384 ——[Anr. ed.] *Re-printed for Nath. Thompson,* 1687. 4°.* L, O, LW, MC, DT; CH, MH, NP, NU, Y.

384A ——[Anr. ed.] *Printed for Nathaniel Thompson,* 1687. 4°. L, BLH, BQ; CLC, MH.

385 —A letter from a Protestant in London. *Dublin,* 1690. brs. DIX 375. LG (lost).

386 —A letter to a friend. *Dublin,* 1688. 4°.* DIX 229. DM.

387 —A reformed catechism. *Dublin, by Jos. Ray, for Rich. I'ans,* 1687. 4°. DIX 226. L, O, OBL, BQ, DN, DT.

387A ——[Anr. ed.] *Dublin, by Jos. Ray, for Christ. I'ans,* 1687. 4°. CD, DM, DN, DT.

388 ——[Anr. ed.] *[London], by Nathaniel Thompson,* 1687. 4°. L, O, LW, DU, DT; CH, MH, NU, Y.

388A [-] Some queries . . . concerning the English Reformation. *For the author,* 1688. 4°.* L, OC, MR.

Manby, Thomas. Collection of all the statutes. 1670. *See* England. Laws, Statutes.

—Collection of the statutes. 1667. *See* England. Laws, statutes.

—Exact abridgment of all the statutes. 1674. *See* England. Laws, statutes.

389 [**Manby, William.**] Some considerations towards peace. *[n.p.], printed,* 1680. 4°.* LLP; MIU, NU.

389A **Manchester, Edward Montagu, earl of.** According to His Majesties especial command to me signified for avoiding . . . fire [at Whitehall]. *[London,* 1662.] brs. LPR.

390 —A jvdicious speech made by. *Printed at London for I. W.,* 1642. 4°.* C, OC, BR, LNC, DT; CLC, CSS, IU, MH, NU, WF, Y.

391 Entry cancelled.

—Letter. 1643. *See* Letter written out of Bedfordshire.

392 Entry cancelled.

—Letter from . . . tenth of June. 1647. *See* Montagu, Edward Montagu, *second baron.*

393 —Reasons delivered by. *Printed at London by Robert Ibbitson,* 1647. 4°.* LT, O, OC; CN, WF.

394 —Manchesters resolvtion against the Lord Strange. *Iuly 12. for A. Coe,* 1642. 4°.* LT, AN; CSS, IU, MH.

395 —The Right Honovrable the Lord Kimbolton his speech in Parliament, Ian. 3. 1641. *For Iohn Thomas,* 1641[2]. 4°.* LT, O, MR, CD; CH, CSS, IU, MH, WF, Y.

396 ——[Anr. ed.] *For F. C. and T. B.,* 1642. 4°.* L, O, BC, BR, SP; CLC, IU, MH, TU, WF, Y.

397 —The Earl of Manchester's speech to His Maiesty, . . . 29th of May, 1660. *By John Macock, and Francis Tyton,* 1660. 4°.* LT, O, C, LIU, SP; CH, CN, MH, NU, TU, WF.

398 —The speech of . . . first day of Dec. *For Nath. Brook,* 1664. fol.* L, O, LG, MR, EN; CLC, CSS, NS, WF, Y.

398A ——[Anr. ed.] *Edinburgh, reprinted,* 1664. 4°.* ALDIS 1775.3. CLC.

399 —The Earl of Manchester's speech to His Majesty, . . . 29 May 1660. *Edinburgh, reprinted by Christopher Higgins,* 1660. brs. STEELE 3p 2174. ALDIS 1648. EN, ES; Y.

399A Entry cancelled.

—Three speeches delivered. [1643.] *See* title.

399B —To the church wardens and constables. *[London,* 1644.] brs. CT.

400 —Tvvo speeches . . . 13. of Ianuarie 1642. *For Iohn Norman,* 1642[3]. 4°.* L, O, CS; CH, CLC, CN, MH, MU, Y.

400aA ——[Anr. ed.] *For Peter Parker,* 1642[3]. 4°.* O.

400bA ——[Anr. ed.] *For Peter Cole,* 1642[3]. 4°.* BC, BR; CDA, CSS, MIU, WF.

400A ——[Anr. ed.] *Sold by William Sheares,* 1643. 4°.* L, OC, CT, BR, LNC; CH, CLC, CN, MH, MU, TU.

401 —Two speeches . . . 25. of Nov. 1642. *By J. F. for Peter Cole,* 1642. 4°.* LT, C, OC, BC, LNC; CH, CN, MH, NU, WF, Y.

402 —Tvvo speeches spoken . . 13th of January, 1642. *For Peter Cole,* 1643. 4°.* LT, C, LG, DU, EN, DT; CH, CN, LC, MU, NU, TU, WF, Y.

403 Entry cancelled.

—Two speeches made by the speakers. 1647. *See* England. Parliament.

404 **Manchester, Henry Montagu, earl of.** Manchester al mondo. Fifth edition. *By Richard Bishop, for Francis Constable,* 1642. 12°. L, OC, DU, NPL, SHR; CH.

404A ——[Anr. ed.] *For Rich: Thral,* [1648]. 12°. CLC.

405 ——Sixth edition. *By T. R. and E. M. for Richard Thrale,* 1655. 12°. L, BSM, CASTLE ASHBY; CLC, IU, NCD.

406 ——Seventh edition. *By Evan Tyler for Richard Thrale,* 1658. 12°. L, O, LW, GK; MH, WF, Y.

407 ——Eighth edition. —, 1661. 12°. L, CT; CH, CLC, SE.

407A ——Ninth edition. *By William Godbid for Richard Thrale and James Thrale,* 1666. 12°. O.

408 ——"Ninth" edition. —, 1667. 12°. L, O, C, DU; CH, NPT.

408A ——[Anr. ed.] *By B. G. for Richard Thrale,* 1670. 12°. OC.

409 ——"Third" edition. *By J. Haviland, for F. Constable,* 1676. 12°. CN, CU.

409A ——[Anr. ed.] *For Richard Thrale,* 1676. 12°. L; CLC, CN.

410 ——Fifteenth edition. *For Brabazon Aylmer,* 1688. 12°. T.C.II 308. L, LIU; CH, CLC, Y.

411 Manchesters ioy, for Derbies overthrow. *[London], for Bernard Hayward,* 1643. 4°.* LT, CD.

Manchini, Maria, pseud. *See* Brémond, Gabriel de.

Mancini, Hortense. *See* Saint Real, Caesar Vischard de.

412 **Mandeville, Sir John.** The voyages and travels. *By R. B., sold by Edward Dod and Nathaniel Ekins,* 1650. 4°. CM, MR, EN.

413 ——[Anr. ed.] *By R. B., and are to sold [sic] by A. Crooke,* 1657. 4°. L.

414 ——[Anr. ed.] *For A. Crooke,* 1670. 4°. L.

415 ——[Anr. ed.] *For R. Scott, T. Basset, J. Wright, and R. Chiswel,* 1677. 4°. T.C.I 284. L, CM; CH.

416 ——[Anr. ed.] —, 1684. 4°. L, LLU; CH, TO.

417 ——[Anr. ed.] *For Rich. Chiswell, B. Walford, Mat. Wotton, and Geo. Conyers,* 1696. 4°. T.C.II 593. L; CLC, NN, RHT, WF, WSG.

418 **Mandey, Venterus.** Mechanick-powers. *For the authors, and sold by Ven. Mandey, and James Moxon, and R. Clavel,* 1696. 4°. L, LG, GC, DT; CH, MH, NCU, NN, WF, Y.

419 ——[Anr. ed.] —, [1696?]. 4°. L, OC, CT, DCH, GH; PU, WCL, Y.

420 ——Second "edetion." *Printed and sold by Ven. Mandey, and James Moxon,* 1699. 4°. O.

420A ——Mellificium mensionis: or, the marrow of measuring. *For the author, and sold by Richard Chiswel and Benjamin Clark, and by the author,* 1682. 8°. T.C.I 473. L, O, C, DU; CH, TO, YBA.

420B ——Second edition. *For Thomas Hawkins,* 1685. 8°. T.C.II 152. L; CLC, PU, TO.

420C ——[Anr. ed.] *Printed, sold by Samuel Clark,* 1698. 8°. TO.

421 Manes Presbyteriani: or the monuments of the kirk. *For the Reverend C. Lasses,* 1661. 4°. L, O, DU, P, A; CH, MH, NU, Y.

Manifest and breife discovery. 1646. *See* A., I.

422 The manifest of the county of Kent. [*London,* 1648.] brs. LT, CJ; MH, MIU, WF, Y.

423 The manifest presented to the Parliament in Scotland in regard of the present troubles. [*London,* 1648.] cap., 4°.* LT.

423A A manifest publist to their brethren by the . . . Catholick English clergy. [*London?* 1661.] cap., 4°.* L; CN.

Manifest touching M. W. P. 1650. *See* P., W.

Manifest truths. 1646. *See* Bowles, Edward.

424 A manifestation directed to the honourable houses of Parliament. *For J. Wright, August* 10. 1644. 4°.* LT, O, C, GU, DT; CH, MH, MU, TU, WF, Y. (var.)

Manifestation of divine love. 1660. *See* Salthouse, Thomas.

Manifestation of prayer. 1663. *See* Smith, William, *of Besthorp.*

Manifestation of the love of God. [n.p., 1663.] *See* Smith, William, *of Besthorp.*

424A Le manifeste de Jaques II, avec la response. *A Londres: se vend par C. Lucas,* 1697. 12°. WF.

425 Manifeste ou declaration des royaumes d'Angleterre & d'Escosse. *Imprimé, Februier.* 1/11. 1643/4. 4°.* LT.

426 Manifesto, by the general assemblie of the Confederate Catholiques . . . against the declaration. [*Kilkenny,* 1648.] brs. O.

427 Manifesto by the supreme council . . . against the Lord Nuncio. [*Kilkenny,* 1648.] brs. O.

428 The manifesto, of near 150 knights. [*n.p.,* 1697.] brs. MC; NC.

428aA ——[Anr. ed.] 1697. fol.* L.

428A A manifesto: or an account of the state of the present differences between . . . Denmark and Norway. [*London?*], *printed,* 1677. 4°. L, C, OC, BC; CH, LC, MH, WF, Y.

429 A manifesto or declaration, set forth by the undertakers. *Boston: by B. Green and J. Allen,* 1699. fol.* EVANS 859. O; MBA, MH, MHS.

Manifold miseries of civill warre. 1642. *See* Parker, Henry.

Manifold practises. 1648. *See* Nedham, Marchamont.

430 **Manilius, Marcus.** The five books of. *For Jacob Tonson,* 1697. 8°. L, O, C, DU, E, DT; CH, MH, MU, NCD, NP, WF, Y.

431 ——[Anr. ed.] *Printed,* 1700. 8°. L, O, C, MC, GU; CJC, CLC, MB, MH, TO, Y.

432 ——The sphere of. *For Nathanael Brooke,* 1675. fol. T.C.I 196. L, O, C, LVD, DT; CH, IU, LC, MH, MU, NCD, WF, Y, AVP.

433 Mankind displayed. *By H. C. for Thomas Northcott,* 1690. 12°. T.C.II 304. L, LW; CLC.

433A ——[Anr. ed.] *By H. C., and sold by James Adamson,* 1690. 12°. PU.

434 **Manley, *Mrs.* Mary de la Rivière.** Letters writen by. *For R. B.,* 1696. 12°. T.C.II 591. L; CLC, CN, WF, Y.

435 ——The lost lover. *For R. Bently; F. Saunders; J. Knapton, and R. Wellington,* 1696. 4°. T.C.II 590. L, O, LVD, EN, DT; CH, CN, LC, MH, TU, WCL, WF, Y.

436 ——The royal mischief. *For R. Bentley, F. Saunders, and J. Knapton,* 1696. 4°. T.C.II 590. L, O, LVD, OW, EN; CH, CN, LC, MH, TU, WCL, WF, Y.

437 **M[anley], *Sir* R[oger].** Commentariorum de rebellione Anglicana. *Impensis L. Meredith & T. Newborough.* 1686. 8°. T.C.II 179. L, O, CT, DU, EN; BN, CH, CLC, IU, WF, Y.

438 ——[Anr. ed.] *Typis E. Horton et R. Holt,* 1686. 8°. L, C, OM, EN, DT; Y.

439 [-] The history of the late warres in Denmark. *For Thomas Basset,* 1670. fol. T.C.I 19. L, O, CCA, MR, DT; BN, CH, CN, IU, LC, NCD, WF.

439A ——Second edition. —, 1683. fol. T.C.II 56. MC; Y.

440 ——The history of the rebellions. *For L. Meredith, and T. Newborough,* 1691. 8°. T.C.II 346. L, O, C, EN, DT; CH, CN, LC, MH, PL, TU, WF, Y.

440A [-] The Russian impostor. *By J. C. for Thomas Bassett,* 1674. 8°. T.C.I 177. L, O, CE, CT, ESSEX; CH, CLC, WF, Y.

440B [-] ——Second edition. *For Tho. Basset,* 1677. 8°. T.C.I 284. L, C, DT; NN.

441 **Manley, Thomas.** The affliction and deliverance of the saints. *By W. H. for Iohn Tey,* 1652. 8°. LT; CH, IU.

442 ——An appendix to the office and duty of an executor. *For Henry Twyford,* 1676. 8°. L, DU; WF.

443 ——The clerks guide, leading into three parts. *By John Streater, Henry Twyford, and E. Flesher, assigns of Richard and Edward Atkyns,* 1672. 8°. T.C.I 124. OM; BN, CB, CH, FU, LC, MHL.

444 ——A discourse shewing that the exportation of wooll is destructive. *For Samuel Crouch,* 1677. 4°.* T.C.I 274. L, LUG, OC, ES; IU, LC, MH, NC, PU, WF, Y.

——Exact abridgment. 1670. *See* Coke, *Sir* Edward.

[-] Iter Carolinum. 1660. *See* Walker, *Sir* Edward.

445 ——The present state of Europe. *For Richard Baldwin,* 1689. 4°.* T.C.II 302. L, O, CE, EC, LSD, EN, DT; CH, CU, NC, WF, Y.

446 [-] A short view of the lives of those illustrious princes, Henry, Duke of Gloucester, and Mary. *For a society of stationers,* 1661. 8°. L, O, C, DU, EN; CH, CLC, MH, WF.

447 [-] ——[Anr. ed.] *For Henry Brome,* 1661. 8°. O, LNC.

448 [-] The sollicitor. Second edition. *By J. Streater,* 1663. 12°. L, O, LL, LSC, CCA, NPL; CU, LC, MHL.

448A [-] ——[Anr. ed.] *By J. C. for Hen. Marsh,* 1663. 8°. GU.

449 ——Temporis Augustiæ: stollen houres recreations. *For John Stephenson,* 1649. 12°. LT; WF.

450 —Usury at six per cent. examined. *By Thomas Ratcliffe, and Thomas Daniel, and are to be sold by Ambrose Isted,* 1669. 4°. L, OB, CS, MR, EN, DT; CH, CJC, LC, MH, NC, NCD, Y.

451 Entry cancelled.

[-] Veni: vidi: vici. 1652. *See* Fisher, Payne.

452 **Manlove, Edward.** Divine contentment. *For Richard Mills,* 1667. 8°. L, O, C, DERBY FREE LIB.; MH, Y.

453 —The liberties and cvstomes of the lead-mines. First edition. *Printed,* 1653. 4°.* L, O, C, LUG, E; CH.

453A ——[Anr. ed.] *For Thomas Johnson,* 1657. 4°.* LNC.

454 **Manlove, Timothy.** The immortality of the soul asserted. *London: by R. Roberts for Nevill Simmons, in Sheffield. And sold by George Coniers,* 1697. 8°. T.C.II 600. L, C, LCL, MR, E; BN, CH, IU, NU, Y.

455 —Præparatio evangelica: or, a plain and practical discourse. *London, for Nevill Simmons, in Sheffield, Yorkshire: and sold by George Coniers,* [London], 1698. T.C.III 92. L, LCL, LW; CH, CLC, MH, NU, WF, Y.

455A **[Mann, Nicholas.]** Critical notes on some passages of Scripture. *For C. Davis,* 1647. 8°. CLC.

456 The manner and good svccesse of the Lord Brookes forces. *For Humphrey Blunden,* 1642. brs. LT, LUG, HH.

457 The manner how the prisoners are to be brought into the city. *By T. F. and J. Coe,* 1645. 4°.* LT.

458 The manner of creating the knights of the ancient . . . Order of the Bath. *For Phil. Stephens,* 1661. 4°.* LT, O, LL, CT, MC; CH, CN, CSS, MB.

459 The manner of electing and enstalling the knights of . . . the Garter. *For James Thrale,* [1661]. 4°.* L, MR; Y.

459A The manner of His Majesties curing the disease. *For D. Newman,* 1679. brs. O, OP.

Manner of holding Parliaments. [n.p.], 1641. *See* Hakewill, William.

Manner of making of coffee. 1685. *See* Dufour, Sylvestre.

459B The manner of performing the novena. [*St. Omers,* 1690.] 12°. L; WG.

460 The manner of procession to the Parliament House in Scotland. colop: *Dublin, re-printed for Andrew Crook, and Samuel Helsham,* 1685. 4°.* DIX 214. C, LIU.

461 The maner [*sic*] of siting [*sic*] of the Parlament. *By R. I. for Peter Stent,* 1653. brs. LT.

462 The manner of the arraignment of those twenty eight persons. *For J. S. and Edward Thomas,* 1660. 4°.* LT, MR; MIU, Y.

463 The manner of the barbarous murther of James [Sharp]. *For J. S. and B. H.,* 1679. brs. L, O; CH, MH.

Manner of the beheading. [1648.] *See* Sibbald, James.

463A The manner of the burning the Pope in effigies in London. *For D. M.,* 1678. 4°.* MH.

464 The manner of the coronation of the present Pope Alexander VIII. colop: [*London*], *for J. Millet,* 1689. brs. CH.

465 The manner of the deposition of Charles Stevvart, King. [*London*], *printed,* 1649. 4°.* LT; MH, Y.

466 The manner of the discovering the King at Southwell. *By Bernard Alsop and J. Coe,* 1646. 4°.* LT, O, OC, CT; Y.

467 The manner of the election of Philip Herbert. [*London*], *printed,* 1649. 4°.* LT; CH, CLC, CN, MH, Y.

468 The manner of the election of the honourable . . . Sir Harbottle Grimston. colop: *For Rich. Janeway.* 1681. brs. L, O, DU, LNC; CH, MH, WF, Y.

469 Entry cancelled. Ghost.

470 The manner of the execution of eleven notorious offenders. colop: *For Langley Curtis,* [1682]. fol.* L.

471 The manner of the execution of the five notorious Jesuits. colop: [*London,* 1679.] cap., fol.* L, O; CH, MH.

471A The manner of the execution of William Howard, late Earl of Stafford. colop: *By D. Mallet,* 1680. cap., fol.* CH, WF, Y.

471B The manner of the impeachment of the XII. bishops. [*London*], *printed in the yeare* 1641. brs. IU.

472 —[Anr. ed.] *Printed,* 1642. 4°.* L, LHO; CH, CLC, CN, MH, MU, NU, Y.

473 —[Anr. ed.] *For Iohn Thomas,* 1642. 4°.* O, MR; MH.

474 —[Anr. ed.] *For Joseph Hunscott.* 1642. 4°.* LT, O, CJ, BR, DT; CH, IU, MH, MU, NCD, WF, Y.

475 —[Anr. ed.] *Printed at London, and re-printed at Edinburgh,* [1641]. 4°.* ALDIS 1009. EN; MM.

475aA The manner of the killing Pensionary de Witt. [*London*], *sold by John Overton, and Dorman Newman,* 1673. brs. NN.

475bA The manner of the Kings tryal. *For F. Coles,* [1648-80]. brs. O.

475A —[Anr. ed.] [*London*], *by and for C. B. and sold by J. Walter,* [1682?]. brs. MH.

475B —[Anr. ed.] [*London*], *for W. Thackeray and T. Passinger,* [1686-88]. brs. O, CM.

476 The manner of the march and embattelling. *Printed,* 1643. 4°.* LT, O.

Manner of the proceedings. 1653. *See* Vaughan, Rice.

476A The manner of the proclaiming of King William. *For Robert Clavel,* 1689. brs. L, O, LG, CT; CH, NP.

476B —[Anr. ed., "proclaiming King."] *Printed,* 1689. brs. L; MH.

477 —[Anr. ed., "proclaiming of."] *Edinburgh reprinted by the* [*heir of Andrew Anderson?*], 1689. brs. ALDIS 2920; STEELE 3p 2773. EN, ER, ES.

478 —[Anr. ed.] *Glasgow reprinted,* 1689. brs. STEELE 3p 2774; ALDIS 2921. EN.

479 The manner of the solemnity of the coronation. *By T. C. to be sold by W. Gilbertson,* 1660. brs. LT, O.

480 The manner of the taking of Newarke. *For I. Walton,* Mar. 7, 1643. 4°.* EN, CD; IU.

481 Entry cancelled.

Manner of visiting the monasteries. 1669. *See* Teresa, saint. Works.

Manners of the Israelites. 1683. *See* Fleury, Claude.

482 **M[anning], E[dward].** Ashrea: or, the grove of beatitudes. *For W. P.,* 1665. 12°. L, O; CLC, IU, Y.

483 [-]—[Anr. ed.] *By J. M. for W. Place,* 1665. 12°. CLC, CU, IU, WF, Y.

484 —The mask'd devil, or Quaker. *Printed,* 1664. 4°. L, O, LF; WF.

485 **Manning, Francis.** A congratulatory poem; . . . Namur. *For Peter Buck,* 1695. fol.* L; Y.

486 —The generous choice. A comedy. *For R. Wellington: and A. Bettesworth,* 1700. 4°. L, O, OW, A, EN; CH, CU, LC, MH, TU, WF, Y, AVP.

487 —Greenwich-Hill. A poem. *By Tho. Warren, for Francis Saunders,* 1697. fol.* L, O, LLU; CLC, MH, Y.

488 —A pastoral essay, lamenting . . . Queen Mary. *For J. Weld: to be sold by J. Whitlock,* 1695. fol.* L, O, C, MR, AU; CLC, IU, NP, TU, WF, Y.

488A —Sylvana, a pastoral. Second edition. *For J. Weld,* 1695. IU.

489 —To His sacred Majesty, King William III. *For J. Weld,* 1698. fol.* MR; TU.

489A ——[Anr. ed.] —, *and are to be sold by E. Whitlock,* 1698. fol.* NP.

490 ——Second edition. *For J. Weld,* 1698. fol.* CH, PBL, Y.

491 **Manning, William.** Catholick religion. *For Dorman Newman,* 1686. 12°. T.C.II 163. L, LCL, LSC, LW, P.

492 **Manningham, Thomas, *bp.*** A comparison between a sincere penitent. *For W. Crooke; and S. Smith,* 1693. 4°.* T.C.II 448. L, O, C, BC, CD; CH, MBZ, NGT, TSM, WF, Y.

493 —The nature and effects of superstition. *By Thomas Braddyll and Robert Everingham,* 1692. 4°.* L, O, C, OC, BLH; CH, CN, MH, NU, WF, Y.

494 —Of religious prudence. *For William Crooke,* 1694. 4°.* T.C.II 475. L, O, C, LLP, CD; CLC, MH, NU, TO, WF, Y.

495 Entry cancelled.
      —One hundred and ninety sermons. 1681. *See* Manton, Thomas.

496 —Praise and adoration. *For William Crook,* [1681]. 4°.* L, C, CD, DT; CH, CN, PL, PU, WF, Y.

497 ——[Anr. ed.] *London: for William Crooke, and William Cadman, also sold by R. Davis in Oxford,* 1682. 4°.* T.C.I 503. L, O, C, BC, LSD; CH, CLC, MH, NU, TSM, WF, Y.

498 —A sermon at the funeral of Sir John Norton. *For William Crooke,* 1687. 4°.* T.C.II 186. L, O, C, LIU, DT; CH, CN, IU, NU, WF, Y.

499 —A sermon concerning publick worship . . . 23d of March, 1691/2. *For W. Crook, and S. Smith,* 1692. 4°.* T.C.II 401. L, O, C, EC, CD; CH, CN, MH, NU, TSM, WF, Y.

500 —A sermon on the sincerity. *For S. Smith, and B. Walford,* 1694. 4°.* L, O, C, LLP, OC, CT; CH, CLC, MBZ, NU, WF, Y.

501 —A sermon preach'd . . . December 7. 1679. *For Will. Crook,* [1679]. 4°.* T.C.I 380. L, O, C, YM, DT; CH, CN, NU, WF, Y.

502 ——[Anr. ed.] *For William Crooke,* 1680. 4°.* T.C.I 399. L, O, C, OC, OM, LSD; CH, CLC, MH, NU, WF.

503 —A sermon preached . . . Feb. 16. 1685/6. *By F. Collins, for W. Crooke,* 1686. 4°.* T.C.II 163. L, O, C, LSD, DT; CH, IU, MH, NU, WF, Y.

504 —A sermon preach'd . . . 30th of December, 1694. *For Sam. Smith and Benj. Walford; and Eliz. Crooke.* 1695. 4°.* T.C.II 537. L, O, C, LG, MR; CH, IU, MH, NU, TU, WF, Y.

505 ——Second edition. —, 1695. 4°.* L, O, C, CT; CDA, CH, CLC, NN, TU, Y.

506 ——Third edition. —, 1695. 4°.* L, C; INU.

507 [–] A short view of the most gracious providence. *For William Crook,* 1685. 4°.* T.C.II 135. L, O, C, EN, DT; CH, CN, NU, WF, Y.

508 —Six sermons preached. *For Will. Crook,* [1687]. 4°. T.C.II 196. L, OC, CT, MR, CD; CH, CN, IU, NU, WF.

509 [–] A solemn humiliation. *By F. Collins for W. Crooke,* 1686. 4°.* T.C.II 156. L, O, C, EN, DT; CH, CN, MH, NU, TU, WF, Y.

510 —Two discourses: the first, shewing. *For Will. Cademan,* 1681. 8°. T.C.I 451. L, O, CT, DU, LSD; CU, PU, WF, Y.

510A ——[Anr. ed.] —, 1682. 8°. OC.

511 —Two discourses: the first concerning truth. *For W. Crooke, and sold by J. Bird,* 1689. 8°. T.C.II 243. DT; LC, Y.

511A Mans amazement. [*London*], *for J. Deacon,* [1684]. brs. CM.

      Man's felicity. [n.p., 1663–74.] *See* P., M.

      Mans master-piece. 1658. *See* Temple, *Sir* Peter.

      Mans mortallitie. Amsterdam, 1643. *See* Overton, Richard.

512 **Mansell, John.** A sermon preached . . . October the 10th. 1694. *By J. Richardson, for Brabazon Aylmer,* 1695. 4°.* L, O, C, SP, WCA; CH, LC, NU, WF.

513 —Two sermons. *By J. Richardson, for Brabazon Aylmer,* 1695. 4°. T.C.II 518. L, O, C, SP, WCA; LC, NU, WF.

513A **Mansell, *Sir* Robert.** The true state of the businesse of glasse. [*London,* 1641.] brs. LT; MH.

514 **Mansell, Roderick.** An exact and true narrative of the late Popish intrigue. *For Tho. Cockerill and Benj. Alsop,* 1680. fol. L, O, C, EN, DT; BN, CH, CN, MH, TU, WF, Y.

515 —A poem upon the coronation of . . . King James II. *For J. Hindley,* 1685. fol.* L, O, LLU; CH, CN, IU, MH, WF, Y.

516 **Mantell, Walter.** A short treatise of the lawes of England. *By Richard Cotes,* 1644. 4°.* LT, CS, BC, MR, EN; CH, IU, MHL, NU.

      Mantle thrown off. 1689. *See* B., H.

517 **Manton, Thomas.** Advice to mourners. *By J. D. for Jonathan Robinson,* 1694. 8°. L, O, C, LCL, LW; MH, NU, ZDU.

518 —The blessed estate. *For Robert Gibbs,* 1656. 4°.* L, O, C, LCL, LW, ENC, BLH; IU, NP, NU, WF, Y.

519 —Catalogus variorum. [*London*], 25 *Mar.* 1678. 4°. L, O, OL, CE, LNC.

520 —Christs eternal existence. *Printed,* 1685. 8°. L, O, LW; CDA, IU, MH, NU, WF, Y.

521 —Christs temptation and transfiguration. *Printed,* 1685. 8°. L, O, LW, DU; CDA, IU, MH, NU, WF, Y.

522 —XVIII sermons. *By J. D. for J. Robinson; and B. Aylmer,* 1679. 8°. T.C.I 368. L, O, LW, CT, P; CLC, LC, MH, NU, Y.

523 —Englands spirituall languishing. *By R. Cotes for John Clarke,* 1648. 4°.* LT, O, C, E, DT; BN, CH, CN, MH, TU, WF, Y.

524 —A fourth volume. *By J. D. to be sold by Jonathan Robinson,* 1693. fol. T.C.II 451. L, O, C, P, ENC; CH, IU, KYU, MH, NU, TO, Y.

525 —Meate out of the eater. *By M. S. for Hanna Allen,* 1647. 4°. LT, O, C, E, ENC, BLH, DT; BN, CH, MH, NU, WF, Y.

526 —One hundred and ninety sermons. *For Tho. Parkhurst, Jonathan Robinson, Brabazon Aylmer, and Benjamin Alsop,* 1681. fol. T.C.I 426. L, O, C, GC, ENC; IU, MBP, MH, NCD, NU, Y, AVP.

526A — —[Anr. ed.] *For T. P. and are to be sold by Michael Hide in Exon,* 1681. fol. CH, IU, WF, MOORE.

527 —A practical commentary, or an exposition . . . James. *By J. Macock, for Luke Favvne,* 1651. 4°. L, O, LW, NPL, E; CH, MH, NU, TU, Y.

528 — —Second edition. *By John Macock, for Luke Favvne,* 1653. 4°. LT, OC, CS, ENC, DT; CH, IU, MH, NU, WF, Y.

529 — —Third edition. *By J. Macock, for Luke Favvn,* 1657. 4°. L, C, LCL, CT, AN, ES, DT; CH, MB, NP, NU, TU, WF, Y.

530 —A practical commentary, or an exposition with notes on the Epistle of Jude. *By J. M. for Luke Fawn,* 1658. 4°. LT, O, LCL, AN, BC, E; CH, IU, MH, NU, TU, WF, Y, AVP.

531 — —Second edition. —, 1662. 4°. LW, ENC, ES; PL, Y.

532 —A practical exposition of the Lord's-Prayer. *By J. D. and are to be sold by Jonathan Robinson,* 1684. 8°. T.C.II 58. L, O, LCL, LW, MC, ENC, BLH; CH, MH, NCD, NU, WF.

533 —Proposals concerning the printing a volume of elaborate sermons. [*London, Thomas Parkhurst, Jonathan Robinson, Brabazon Aylmer, Benjamin Alsop,* 1681.] brs. OP.

534 —A second volume of sermons. *By J. Astwood for Jonathan Robinson,* 1684. 2pts. fol. T.C.II 92. L, O, CS, LSD, P, ENC; CH, IU, MH, NU, TO, Y.

534A — —[Anr. ed.] *By R. Roberts for Jonathan Robinson,* 1684. fol. GC.

534B — —[Anr. ed.] *By J. Astwood for J. R., and are to be sold by Michael Hide.* 1684. fol. MOORE.

535 —A sermon preached . . . August, 25. 1651. *By J. B.,* 1651. 4°.* LT, C, LG, LW, DT; NU.

536 —Sermons preached by. *For Brabazon Aylmer,* 1678. 4°. L, O, LCL, LW, P, SHR; CH, IU, MB, MH, NU, WF, AVP.

537 —Several discourses tending to promote peace. *For Jonathan Robinson,* 1685. 8°. L, O, CT, P, SP; CH, MH, NU, TO, WF, Y, AVP.

538 —Sfveral [*sic*] discovrses. *For J. R. to be sold by John Weld,* 1685. 8°. MH.

539 —A third volume of sermons. *By J. D. to be sold by William Marshal,* 1689. fol. T.C.II 242. L, O, LCL, AN, LSD, RPL, ENC; IU, NU, WF, Y.

539A — —[Anr. ed.] *By J. D. for Thomas Parkhurst, and Jonathan Robinson,* 1689. fol. GC, P; CH, MB, MH, TO.

539B — —[Anr. ed.] *By J. D. to be sold by Michael Hide, at Exeter,* 1689. fol. L; MOORE.

540 —Words of peace. *By A. P. and T. H. for P. Brooksby,* 1677. brs. L, IS.

Mantuan. *See* Spagnuoli, Baptista.

541 Entry cancelled.

Mantuan English'd, and paraphras'd. [1679.] *See* Spagnuoli, Baptista.

541A A manual for husbands. *Printed and sold by Robert Barnham,* 1697. 8°. Y.

541B A manual for parents. *For J. Cranford,* 1660. 12°. ASSINGTON PARISH, SUFFOLK.

Manual of controversies. Doway, 1654. *See* Turberville, Henry.

541C A manuall of devotions. [*London?* 1644.] 8°. L.

541D —[Same title.] *For J. Nutt,* 1698. 8°. O.

541E A manuel of devout prayers. *Gant, R. Walker,* 1670. 12°. LSC.

542 —[Anr. ed.] *Paris,* 1671. 12°. C.

542A —[Anr. ed.] *Paris,* 1675. 24°. L, LLP.

542B —[Anr. ed.] [*London*], *printed,* 1686. 8°. LLP; Y.

542C —[Anr. ed.] *At Paris, in the year* 1686. 8°. Y.

542D —[Anr. ed.] *By N. Thompson,* 1687. 24°. CK.

543 —[Anr. ed.] *By Henry Hills,* 1688. 18°. L.

544 —[Anr. ed.] *Holy-Rood-House, by Mr. P. B.,* 1688. 12°. ALDIS 2769. L, EN, DL; WF.

544A —[Anr. ed.] [*London*], *Mary Thompson,* 1688. 12°. FARM.

544B —[Anr. ed.] [*n.p.*], 1696. 18°. L.

544C A manual of godly praiers. *To Antworpe, by the widowe of Iohn Gnobbart for James Thompson,* 1650. 12°. O, WARE.

544D —[Anr. ed.] *S. Omers,* 1652. 12°. FARM.

544E —[Anr. ed.] *Antwerp, by Michael Cnobbaert,* 1671. 12°. O; TU.

544F —[Anr. ed.] [*n.p.*], *printed,* 1686. 12°. O.

544G A manual of prayers and litanies. *At Antwerp, by Michael Cnobbart* [*sic*], 1658. 12°. EC, WARE; CN.

544H —[Anr. ed.] *Paris,* 1662. 8°. YM.

544I —[Anr. ed.] *Printed at Roan,* 1665. 12°. VC.

544J —[Anr. ed.] *Paris,* 1670. 12°. DUS, FARM.

544K —[Anr. ed.] *Printed at Paris,* 1674. 12°. L, DUS; NN.

544L —[Anr. ed.] *Paris,* 1682. 12°. LLP.

544M —[Anr. ed.] *Paris,* 1686. 12°. LLP.

544N —[Anr. ed.] [*n.p.*], 1688. 12°. EC, WARE, CN.

Manvall of prayers, collected. Oxford, 1462 [*i.e.* 1642]. *See* C., W.

5440 A manual of prayers and other Christian devotions. *By Henry Hills,* 1686. 12°. C, LLP, FARM.

544P —[Anr. ed.] *Paris, printed,* 1692. 12°. LLP.

544Q —[Anr. ed.] [*London*], *printed,* 1698. 8°. WARE.

Manual of prayers for. 1674. *See* Ken, Thomas, *bp.*

Manvell of the arch-confraternite. Doway, 1654. *See* Mason, Richard.

544R A manual of the practical part of a Christian religion. *For Henry Brome,* 1670. 8°. T.C.I 54. WF.

Manual 1 of the third order. Doway, 1643. *See* Mason, Richard Angelus.

545 A manuell, or a justice of peace his vade-mecum. *By Roger Daniel, Cambridge,* 1641. 8°. C; WF.

545AA —[Anr. ed.] *By M. Flesher & R. Young,* 1641. 12°. CT.

545A —[Anr. ed.] *By T. Badger, for Mat. Walbanck,* 1642. 8°. CLC, MHL; MOUNT HOLYOKE.

545B A manuall or analecta. *By Miles Flesher and Robert Young,* 1641. 12°. L, OC; CH, MIU, PL, WF, Y.

545C —[Anr. ed.] —, 1642. 12°. LLP; WF.

546 —[Anr. ed.] *Printed,* 1646. 12°. DC, DUS.

547 —Sixth edition. *For W. L. and D. P.,* 1648. 12°. L, C, EN, CD; LC, MHL, WF, UCLA.

547A —[Anr. ed.] *By James Flesher for William Lee and Daniel Pakeman,* 1660. 12°. L.

548 **[Manuche, Cosmo.]** The bastard: a tragedy. *For M. M., T. Collins, and Gabriell Bedell*, 1652. 4°. L, O, LVD, OW, BC; CH, CN, LC, MH, WC, WCL, WF, Y.

549 —The just general a tragi: comedy. *For M. M., T. C. and G. Bedell*, 1652. 4°. L, O, LVD, OW; CH, CN, MH, WC, WF, Y.

550 —The loyal lovers. *For Thomas Eglesfield*, 1652. 4°. L, O, LVD, CT; CH, CU, MH, TU, WC, WF.

Manuductio apographia or. 1680. *See* R., F.

Manuductio: or. 1656. *See* S., J.

Manuel, Francisco. *See* Mello, Francisco Manuel de.

Manus testium movens: or. [n.p.], 1651. *See* Hall, Edmund.

551 **Manwaring, Sir Henry.** The sea-mans dictionary. *By G. M. for John Bellamy*, 1644. 4°. LT, O, CT, DT; IU, RPJ, WF, Y.

551A ——[Anr. ed.] 1666. 4°. LNM.

551B ——[Anr. ed.] *By W. Godbid for G. Hurlock*, 1667. 4°. L, O, C, CM.

552 ——[Anr. ed.] *By W. Godbid for Benjamin Hurlock*, 1670. 4°. L, O, OC, CE, CASTLE ASHBY; CH.

553 **Manwood, John.** An abridgment of Manwood's forrest laws. *For Nath. Rolls*, 1696. L; CH, MH, MIU, NN, WF.

554 —A treatise of the lavvs of the forest. Third edition. *For the company of stationers*, 1665. 4°. L, O, LI, LNC, EN; BN, CH, CLC, IU, MH, NCL, NP, WF, YL.

554A The many advantages the Bank of the City of London will afford. [*London, John Gain*, 1682.] brs. L, LUG.

Many deep considerations. [n.p., 1664.] *See* Penington, Isaac.

Many strong reasons confounded. 1657. *See* Burrough, Edward.

Many sufferings of an undone gentleman. [n.p., 1648.] *See* Coningsby, Thomas.

554B Many waters cannot quench love. *Printed*, 1659. 4°. CN, TO.

555 Many vvonderfvl and very remakeable [*sic*] passages. *For George Thompson*, 1642. 4°.* LT, O, LVF; CH, CSS, MH, Y.

556 **Manzini, Giovanni Battista.** The loving husband, and prudent wife. *For J. Martin, and J. Allestrye*, 1657. 12°. L, O.

557 —Manzinie his exquisite academicall discourses. *By Thomas Harper*, 1654. 4°. L, O, OB; CSU, IU, LC.

558 ——[Anr. ed., "; his most."] *For Humphrey Moseley*, 1655. 4°. LT, O, C, YM; CH, CN, MH, MU, WF, Y.

Map of man's misery. 1690. *See* Ker, Patrick.

Mappe of mischiefe. [n.p.], 1641. *See* V.

Map of misery. 1650. *See* Tooker, Giles.

559 A map of ye kingdome of Ireland. [*Oxford*], *sovld by Will: Webb*, 1641 [1642?]. brs. MADAN 998. LT.

559A A map of the whole world. *For Thomas Jenner*, 1668. 4°. CH, Y.

560 A map or groundplott of . . . London. [*London*], *sould by Nathanael Brooke*, [1666]. CT.

561 **Maplet, John.** Epistolarum medicarum specimen. *Typis Francisci Leach, impensis editoris*, 1694. 4°.* L, O, OR; WU.

562 **[Mapletoft, John.]** A perswasive to the consciencious frequenting. *By A. G. for Walter Kettilby*, 1687. 4°.* L, O, C, OC, EC, BLH; CH, IU, NU, TU, WF, Y, AVP.

563 —The rich man's bounty. *For Brabazon Aylmer*, 1695. 4°.* T.C.II 548. L, O, C, LLP, OC, OP; CH, CLC, NU, TU, WF.

564 —A sermon preach'd . . . January the 1st. 1700. *For B. Aylmer*, 1700. 4°.* T.C.III 168. L, O, C, EC, MR; CLC, CU, NU, WF.

Mar., Ch. Tragicall history. [n.p.], 1663. *See* Marlowe, Christopher.

565 **[Marana, Giovanni Paolo.]** The amours of Edward the IV. *For Richard Sare*, 1700. 12°. L, O; CN, MIU, Y.

565A Entry cancelled. *See* M565 BC.

565B [–] Letters writ by a Turkish spy. *By J. L.*, 1687. 12°. O; CN, MH.

565BA [–] The first volume of letters. *By J. Leake, and are to be sold by Henry Rhodes*, 1687. 12°. T.C.II 209. CS; CH.

565BB [–] —Second edition. *For Henry Rhodes*, 1691. 12°. L, CT; CLC, IU, PU, SE.

565BC [–] —Third edition. —, 1691. 12°. T.C.II 373. O, LLP, DU; CLC, MH.

565BD [–] —Fourth edition. —, 1692. 12°. O; CH, CN, IU, WF, Y.

565BE [–] —Fifth edition. *By J. Leake for Henry Rhodes*, 1693. 12°. O.

565BF [–] —Sixth edition. *For Joseph Hindmarsh and Richard Sare*, 1694. 12°. L, O, CM; MH, PL.

565BG [–] The second volume of letters. *By J. Leake, for Henry Rhodes*, 1691. T.C.II 348. 12°. L; CH, CLC, PU, SE.

565C [–] —Second edition. —, 1691. 12°. L, O, RPL; CH, CN, IU, MH.

565CA [–] —Third edition. —, 1692. 12°. O; IU, WF, Y.

565CB [–] —Fourth edition. —, 1693. 12°. L, O; WF.

565CC [–] —"Fourth" edition. *By E. Holt for Joseph Hindmarsh and Richard Sare*, 1694. 12°. O, OC, CM; PL.

565CD [–] The third volume of letters. *By J. Leake for Henry Rhodes*, 1691. 12°. L, O, CS; CLC, CN, IU, MH, SE.

565CE [–] —Second edition. —, 1692. 12°. O, CM, CT; CH, IU, MH, WF, Y.

565CF [–] —Third edition. —, 1692. 12°. L, O.

565CG [–] —Fourth edition. *For J. Hindmarsh and R. Sare*, 1694. 12°. L, O, OC, CM; PL.

565CH [–] The fourth volume of letters. *By J. Leake, for Henry Rhodes*, 1692. 12°. O, CS, CT; CH, CLC, CN, IU, MH, SE, WF, WG, Y. (var.)

565CI [–] —Second edition. —, 1692. 12°. L, O, CM; PL.

565CJ [–] —Third edition. *By H. Clark for J. Hindmarsh and R. Sare*, 1694. 12°. L, O, OC; PL.

565CK [–] The fifth volume of letters. *By J. Leake for Henry Rhodes*, 1691. 12°. CS; CLC, CN.

565CL [–] —[Anr. ed.] —, 1692. 12°. L, O; CH, IU, MH, SE, WF.

565CM [–] —Second edition. —, 1693. 12°. O, CM; PL, Y.

565CN [–] —[Anr. ed.] *For Joseph Hindmarsh and Richard Sare*, 1694. 12°. OC; Y.

565D [–] —The sixth volume of letters. *By J. Leake, for Henry Rhodes*, 1693. 12°. L, O, CT, P; CH, CLC, CN, IU, MH, SE, WF, Y. (var.)

565DA [–] —[Anr. ed.] *By J. R. for J. Hindmarsh and R. Sare*, 1694. 12°. O, OC, CM.

565DB [–] —[Anr. ed.] *For H. Rhodes, R. Sare, and H. Hindmarsh*, 1698. 12°. Y.

565DC [–] The seventh volume of letters. *For Henry Rhodes*, 1694. 12°. L, O, CM, CS, CT, DUS; CH, CLC, IU, MH, SE, WF.

565E [–] —Second edition. *By J. R. for J. Hindmarsh and R. Sare*, 1694. 12°. L, O, OC; CN, MH, WF.

565EA [–] The eighth and last volume. *By J. R. for J. Hindmarsh and R. Sare*, 1694. 12°. T.C.II 491. O, OC, CT; CH, CLC, CN, IU, MH, WF. (var.)

565EB [–] The eight volumes of letters. *For H. Rhodes, J. Hindmarsh, and R. Sare*, 1694. 12°. L, O, CM; MH, PL.

565EC [–] —[Anr. ed.] *For Joseph Hindmarsh and Richard Sare*, 1694. 12°. OC.

565F **M[arbeck, John].** The lives of holy Saints. *By R. N. for John Williams*, 1681. 4°. L, OM, CS; CDA, CLC, CN, CU, MH.

565G [–] —Second edition. *Printed* 1685. 4°. L, OC, LSD; CLC, MH, WF.

566 **Marbury, Edward.** A brief commentarie or exposition upon . . . Obadiah. *By T. R. and E. M. for George Calvert*, 1649[50]. 4°.* LT, O, LSC, SHR, DT; CLC, IU, MH, NU, PPT.

567 —A brief commentarie, or exposition upon . . . Habakkuk. *By T. R. and E. M. for George Calvert*, 1643. 4°. IU, MBP.

568 ——[Anr. ed.] *By T. R. and E. M. for Octavian Pullen*, 1650. 4°. L, O, LSC, SHR, P; CLC, LC, MH, VC, WF.

569 [–] —[Anr. ed., "A commentarie."] *For Samuel Man*, 1652. 4°. L, LCL, ENC; IU, NU.

570 [–] Vox turturis vel columba alba albionis. The voice. *For T. W.* 1647. 4°. LT, C, OC, DT; CPB, CN, IU, MH, NU, Y.

Marcelia; or. 1669. *See* Boothby, *Mrs.* Frances.

571 **March, John,** *of Gray's Inn.* Actions for slander. *By F. L., for M. Walbank and R. Best*, 1647. 8°. O, CT; CLL, CU, LC, MHL, WF, YL.

572 ——[Anr. ed.] *By I. C. for Mathew Walbanck, & Richard Best*, 1648. 8°. L, DC, LIU; CH, LC, MHL, NCL, PL.

572A ——[Anr. ed.] *For Mathew Walbancke, and Richard Best*, 1655. 8°. LIU; BBE, CH, CSU, MHL, YL.

573 ——[Anr. ed.] *For Elizabeth Walbanck*, 1674. 8°. T.C.I 165. O, LIL, CS, EN, CD; CLC, MHL, MU, WF, YL.

574 —Amicus reipublicæ. The common-wealths friend. *By Will. Bentley, for Francis Eglesfield*, 1651. 8°. LT, O, C, LCL, LGI, GU, CD; BN, CH, CLC, LC, MBP, MHL, PUL.

575 [–] An argument or, debate in law. *By Tho. Paine, and M. Simmons, for Tho. Vnderhill*, 1642. 4°.* LT, O, C, EC, DT; CH, CN, IU, MH, TU, WF, Y.

576 —Reports: or, new cases. *By M. F. for W. Lee, M. Walbanke, D. Pakeman and G. Beadel*, 1648. 4°. L, O, LMT, CT, MR; CH, LC, MHL, MIU, YL.

577 ——Second edition. *By J. C. for Samuel Heyrick*, 1675. 4°. T.C.I 201. L, O, C, DU, EN; CH, CLC, LC, MHL, NCL, TU, WF, YL.

578 —The second part of Actions for slanders. *For Mathew Walbancke*, 1649. 8°. L; CH, LC, PL.

579 **March, John,** *B. D.* Th' encænia of St. Ann's Chappel. *London, for Richard Randal and Peter Maplisden, in Newcastle upon Tyne*, 1682. 4°.* L, OC, CT, DU, YM; IU, MB, NU, V, WF, Y.

580 —The false prophet unmask't. *London, by J. R. for Richard Randell, and Peter Maplesden, in New-Castle upon Tyne*, 1683. 4°.* T.C.II 13. L, O, DU, NE, YM; CH, CLC, Y.

581 —A sermon preached . . . 30th of January, 1676/7. *London, by Thomas Hodgkin, for Richard Randell, and Pet. Maplisden, in Newcastle upon Tyne.* 1677. 4°.* L, O, CT, WCA, YM, BLH; CH, MH, Y.

581A —A sermon preach'd before the . . . Mayor . . . of Newcastle . . . May 29. 1684. *By T. Hodgkin, for R. Randell and P. Maplisden in Newcastle upon Tyne.* 1684. 4°.* MR, NE; CH.

582 —Sermons. *For Robert Clavell, sold by Joseph Hall in New-Castle upon Tine*, 1693. 8°. T.C.II 473. L, O, DT; CB, NU, WF.

583 ——Second edition. *For Robert Clavell*, 1699. 8°. T.C.III 99. L, LW, CT, NE; IU, WF, Y.

584 No entry.

585 **Marchant, Hugh.** Marchants water-works. [*n.p.*, 1700?] brs. L.

586 **Marchmont, Patrick,** *earl.* The speech of . . . 19th of July, 1698. colop: *Edinburgh, by the heirs and successors of Andrew Anderson*, 1698. fol. ALDIS 3760. EN, ES; WF.

586A —The speech of . . . 22 of August 1698. *Edinburgh, by the heirs and successors of Andrew Anderson*, 1698. brs. ALDIS 3760.3. EN; WF.

586B —The speech of . . . first of September 1698. colop: *Edinburgh, by the heirs and successors of Andrew Anderson*, 1698. brs. ALDIS 3760.6. EN; CSS, WF.

587 —The speech of . . . 21. May 1700. colop: *Edinburgh, by the heirs and successors of Andrew Anderson*, 1700. cap., fol.* ALDIS 3983. EN; IU, MH, MIU, WF.

588 —The speech of . . . 29 October, 1700. colop: *Edinburgh, by the heirs and successors of Andrew Anderson*, 1700. brs. ALDIS 3984. LU, EN.

Marciano, or. Edinburgh, 1663. *See* Clark, William.

588A **M[arcus], J[oannes].** Index horarius in tres libros. *Apud Gulielmum Leybourn*, 1662. 8°. L, LR, EN; NN, WF.

589 Mardike Fort, with its out-works as it now is. *By M. S. for Thomas Jenner*, 1658. brs. LT.

589A Mardike, or the soldier's sonnet to his sword. *For James Goodman*, 1660. brs. L.

589B **Mare, Richard.** God's dreadful judgement upon an eminent person . . . transformed into a dog. *For D.M.*, 1675. 4°.* L.

Mare clausum: or. 1666. *See* Settle, Elkanah.

Margarita in Anglia. [*n.p.*], 1660. *See* Fox, George.

590 Margery Good-covv, that gave a gallon. *Printed*, 1659. 4°.* LT, O, OC, MR; HR, CN, CSS, MH, NN, Y.

591 **[Margetts, Thomas.]** A bloody fight in Scotland. *Edenburgh, by Evan Tylar, re-printed at London, by Robert Ibbitson*, 1648. 4°.* ALDIS 1309. LT, MR, EN.

592 Entry cancelled.

Marguerite de Navarre. Grand cabinet-counsels. 1658. *See* Marguerite de Valois.

593 —Heptameron, or. *By F. L. for Nath: Ekins*, 1654. 8°. LT, O, DC, EC; CLC, MH, ZWT.

593aA **Marguerite de Valois.** The workes of. *By I. C.*, 1642. 8°. OC.

593bA —The grand cabinet-counsels unlocked. *By R. M.* 1656. 8°. CLC.

593cA ——[Anr. ed.] *By R.H.*, 1658. 8°. L, O; CH, CLC.

593dA ——[Anr. ed.] —1660. 8°. MBZ.

593A —The history of. *By R. H.*, 1649. 8°. CH.

594 ——[Anr. ed.] —, 1650. 8°. L.

594A ——[Anr. ed.] *Printed*, 1653. 8°. CN.

594B ——[Anr. ed.] —, 1654. 8°. WF.

594C —The history or memorials of. [*London*], *for R. H.*, 1648. 8°. O, EN, DT.

595 —The memorialls of. *By R. H.*, 1641. 8°. L, O, CS, DU, E, EN; CH, TU.

596 ——[Anr. ed.] —, 1645. 8°. LC.

596A ——Second edition. —, 1647. 8°. DC; CH.

596B ——[Anr. ed.] —, 1662. 8°. L, O, CASTLE ASHBY; Y.

596C ——[Anr. ed.] —, 1664. 8°. WF.

597 ——[Anr. ed.] 1665. 8°. BN.

597A Maria misera miseranda: or, a brief relation. *For R. T.*, 1674. 4°.* CH.

598 Maria to Henric, and Henric to Maria. *For Joseph Knight*, 1691. fol.* L, O; CH, CLC, MH, NP, WF, Y.

599 **Mariana, Juan de.** The general history of Spain. *For Richard Sare, Francis Saunders and Thomas Bennet*, 1699. fol. T.C.III 154. L, O, C, A, DT; BN, CLC, CN, LC, MH, MU, TU, WF, Y, AVP.

600 Marianus, or, loves heroick champion. *By B. Alsop and T. Fawcet, to be sold by Iames Becket*, 1641. 12°. L; CN, MIU, PU, Y.

Marine mercury. [n.p.], 1642. *See* Hare, John.

601 The mariners delight. [*London*], *for J. Conyers*, [1682–88]. brs. L, O, HH; MH.

Mariners jewel. 1695. *See* Lightbody, James.

601A The mariner's misfortune. [*London*], *for J. Blare*, [1684–94]. brs. L.

602 **Marino, Giovanni Battista.** The slaughter of the innocents by Herod. *By Andrew Clark, for Samuel Mearne*, 1675. 8°. T.C.I 194. L, LCL, CS; CH, NCD, NP, TO, WF, Y.

Mariot. *See* Marriot.

602A **Maris, Elizabeth.** At the Blew-Ball . . . liveth [advert.]. [*London*, 1700?] brs. L.

602B **Maris, Peter.** Advertisement. At the Crown . . . doctor. [*London*, 1700?] brs. L.

602C —Advertisement. It is well known. [*London*, 1700?] brs. L.

603 **Marius, John.** Advice concerning bills of exchange. *By I. G. to be sold by Nich. Bourne*, 1651. 12°. LT.

604 ——Second edition. *By W. H. to be sold by Nicolas Bourne*, 1655. 8°. LT, LUG; CLC, LC, MH, MU.

604A ——"Second" edition. *By William Hunt, to be sold by Nicholas Bourne*, 1655. fol. L, LCP, LL, LUG; BN, CB, CU, MHL, PL, WF.

605 ——"Second" edition. *For J. Clark, and are to be sold by W. Hope*, 1670. 8°. T.C.I 51. L, LIL, YM; CH, IU.

606 ——Third edition. *For Robert Horne*, 1674. 8°. T.C.I 172. LGI, LUG, EN, DT; LC, MH, NC, NP, NR, WF.

607 ——Fourth edition. —, 1684. fol.* L, LMT, BAMB, NE, CD; BN, IU, MB, MHL, NN, PL, SE, V.

608 ——[Anr. ed.] *For Tho. Horne*, 1700. fol.* L, O, DT; CH, CN, NCD, RPJ, WF, Y.

609 Mark Noble's frollick. [*London*], *for B. Deacon*, [1670?]. brs. L.

610 —[Anr. ed.] [*London*], *for P. Brooksby, J. Deacon, J. Blare, and J. Back*, [1688–92]. brs. L, CM, HH; MH.

Markham, George. Almanack. 1656. *See* Almanacs.

611 [**Markham, Gervase.**] Cheape and good husbandry. Seventh edition. *Printed at London by Bernard Alsop; for Iohn Harrison*, 1648. 4°. L, O, LUG, LWL, CK; CH, IU, MH, TU, Y.

612 [–] —Eighth edition. *By Thomas Harper, for John Harrison*, 1653. 4°.* L, O, LWL; BN, CLC, CPB, IU, MB, MH, Y.

613 [–] —Ninth edition. *By W. Wilson, for E. Brewster, and George Sawbridge*, 1657. 4°. L, O, R; BN, MH, NC, Y.

614 [–] —Tenth edition. *By W. Wilson, for George Sawbridge*, 1660. 4°. L, LCS, CCA, R; CJC, CLC, MH, NIC, WSG, Y.

615 [–] —Eleventh edition. —, 1664. 4°. L, O, LUG; CLC, IU, MH, NN, OSU.

616 [–] —Twelfth edition. *By John Streater, for George Sawbridge*, 1668. 4°. L, LWL, DUS, R; CLC, MH, NR, WF, Y.

617 [–] —Thirteenth edition. *By E. H. for George Sawbridge*, 1676. 4°. L, LWL, OH, R, EN; CB, CN, MH, NIC, PL, PU, Y.

618 [ ] —Fourteenth edition. *By T. B. for Hannah Sawbridge*, 1683. 4°. L, O, NOT, R; CH, IU, MH, NCD, Y.

619 —The compleat husbandman. *For G. Conyers*, [1695]. 12°.* WF, Y.

620 [–] Country contentments. Sixth edition. *By William Wilson for Iohn Harison*, 1649. 4°. L, O, LUG, LWL, CK, AN; BN, CH, IU, MB, MH, TU, Y.

621 [–] —Seventh edition. *By W. Wilson, for E. Brewster, and George Sawbridge*, 1654. 4°. LWL, R; CLM, IU, MB, MH, Y.

622 [–] —Eighth edition. *By W. Wilson for E. Brewster, and George Sawbridge*, 1656. 4°. L, O, R, MR; CU, MH, MU, NC, Y.

623 [–] —Ninth edition. *By William Wilson, for George Sawbridge*, 1660. 4°. L, O, R; CJC, CLC, MH, MIU, NP, Y.

624 [–] —Tenth edition. —, 1664. 4°. L, O; NN.

625–7 Entries cancelled.

[–] —"Tenth" edition. 1668. *See* —Way to get wealth. 1668.

——Eleventh edition. 1675. *See* —Way to get wealth. 1676.

——"Eleventh" edition. 1683. *See* —Way to get wealth. 1683.

628 Entry cancelled.

[–] Country house-wife's garden. 1676. *See* Lawson, William. New orchard.

629 [–] The English house-wife. Fifth edition. *By B. Alsop for John Harison*, 1649. 4°. L, O, LWL, CK, LLU, R; BN, CH, IU, LC, MH, TU, WF, Y.

630 [–] —"Fifth" edition. *By W. Wilson, for E. Brewster, and George Sawbridge*, 1653. 4°. LWL; IU, MB, MH, NR, Y.

631 [–] —Sixth edition. —, 1656. 4°. L, O, LLU, R; BN, MH, NC, PT, Y.

632 [–] —Seventh edition. —, 1660. 4°. L; CJC, CLC, MH, Y.

633 [–] —Eighth edition. *By W. Wilson, for George Sawbridge*, 1664. 4°. L, O.

634–6 Entries cancelled.

    [–] —"Eighth" edition. 1668. *See* —Way to get wealth. 1668.

    — —"Eighth" edition. 1675. *See* —Way to get wealth. 1676.

    — —Ninth edition. 1683. *See* —Way to get wealth. 1683.

637 —The inrichment of the weald of Kent. *By Eliz. Purslow, for John Harrison*, 1649. 4°.* L, O, LLP, LWL, CK, AN; BN, CH, IU, MB, MH, TU, Y.

638 [–] —[Anr. ed.] *By W. Wilson, for E. Brewster, and George Sawbridge*, 1653. 4°. LWL; CLC, IU, MB, MH, WF, Y.

639 [–] —[Anr. ed.] —, 1656. 4°.* L, LAS, LLP, LUG, R; BN, MH, NC, PT, Y.

640 [–] —[Anr. ed.] *By William Wilson, for George Sawbridge*, 1660. 4°.* L, EN; CH, CLC, IU, MH, WF, Y.

641 [–] —[Anr. ed.] *By W. Wilson, for George Sawbridge*, 1664. 4°.* O; MA, NN.

642–5 Entries cancelled.

    [–] —[Anr. ed.] 1668. *See* —Way to get wealth. 1668.

    — —[Anr. ed.] 1675. *See* —Way to get wealth. 1676.

    — —[Anr. ed.] 1676. *See* —Way to get wealth. 1676.

    — —[Anr. ed.] 1683. *See* —Way to get wealth. 1683.

645A —Markham's faithfvll farrier. *By R. Coles for Fulke Clifton*, 1647. 4°. L; Y.

646 — —[Anr. ed.] *For Thomas Vere*, 1656. 8°. L; IU.

646A — —[Anr. ed.] —, 1661. 8°. WF.

646B — —[Anr. ed.] *By J. Millet, for J. Deacon*, 1686. 8°. Y.

646C — —[Anr. ed.] *For J. Deacon, to be sold by W. Thackeray*, 1686. 8°. CLC.

647 — —[Anr. ed.] —, 1687. 8°. T.C.II 183. C.

647A — —[Anr. ed.] *By J. Mallet, for J. Deacon*, 1687. 8°. ROYAL VET. COLLEGE.

648 —Markhams farewell to hvsbandry. Fourth edition. *By William Wilson for Iohn Harison*, 1649. 4°. L, O, CK, AN, R; BN, CH, IU, MH, NC, TU, Y.

649–52 Entries cancelled.

    [–] —Fifth edition. 1653. *See* —Inrichment. 1653.

    — —Sixth edition. 1656. *See* —Inrichment. 1656.

    — —Seventh edition. 1660. *See* —Inrichment. 1660.

    — —Eighth edition. 1664. *See* —Inrichment. 1664.

653 — —Ninth edition. *By E. O. for George Sawbridge*, 1668. 4°. L, LWL, DUS; CLC, MH, PU, Y.

654 — —Tenth edition. *For George Sawbridge*, 1676. 4°. L, LWL, OH, R, EN, DT; CLC, CN, MH, NR, WDA, Y.

655 — —Eleventh edition. *For Hannah Sawbridge*, 1684. 4°. L, O, LUG, NOT, R; CH, IU, NS, PBL, TO, Y.

656 Entry cancelled. Ghost.

657 —Hungers prevention. Second edition. *For Francis Grove, and are to be sold by Martha Harrison*, 1655. 8°. L, O, LWL, E, EN; CH, IU, MU, WF, Y. (var.)

658 —Markhams maister-peece. Sixth edition. *By John Okes*, 1643. 4°. L, LWL, OB, CCO; CB, CH, CLC, IU, WSG.

659 — —Seventh edition. *By William Wilson*, 1651. 4°. LWL, R; CJC, MIU, NN, WSG, Y.

660 — —Eighth edition. *By W. Wilson, to be sold by George Sawbridge*, 1656. 4°. L, O, LAS, LWL, AN, R; CLC, IU, NN.

661 — —Ninth edition ["master-piece."] *By William Wilson, for George Sawbridge*, 1662. 4°. L, LG, LWL, R, EN; IU, NN.

662 — —Tenth edition. *By Edward Okes, and are to be sold by Thomas Passenger*, 1668. 4°. L, R, EN; IU, NN, PU, WF, Y.

663 — —Eleventh edition. *By Andrew Clark for Thomas Passenger*, 1675. 4°. T.C.I 214. L, O, R, GU; CLC, AMB.

664 — —Twelfth edition. *By Evan Tyler and Ralph Holt, for John Wright and Thomas Passenger*, 1681. 4°. T.C.I 434. L, DUS, R; INU, Y.

664A — —Thirteenth edition. *For John Wright and Thomas Passinger*, 1683. 4°. O, LWL; IU, MU, Y.

665 — —Fourteenth edition. *By John Richardson for Tho. Passinger, and M. Wotton and George Coniers*, 1688. 4°. L, C, LWL; CNM, MBM, MU, Y.

665A — —Fifteenth edition. *By John Richardson for M. Wotton and George Coniers*, 1694. 4°. L, LWL, CCA; CLC, WF, WSG, Y.

666 —Markhams method. Seventh edition. *By Iohn Okes for Iohn Harison*, 1641. 8°. L, C; WU.

667 — —"Seventh" edition. *By Ja. Cottrel, for John Harrison*, 1650. 8°. C.

668 — —Tenth edition. *For William Thackeray*, 1671. 8°. L.

669 — —Eleventh edition. —, 1684. 8°. C; CLC.

670 —The perfect horseman. *For Humphrey Moseley*, 1655. 8°. L; WF, Y.

671 — —Second edition. —, 1656. 8°. O; BN, CH, IU.

672 — —[Anr. ed.] —, 1660. 4°. LWL; CLC, MICHIGAN ST.

672A — —[Anr. ed.] *For Richard Chiswell*, 1668. 8°. ROYAL VET. COLLEGE.

672B — —[Anr. ed.] *By J. D. for Richard Chiswell*, 1671. 8°. L, LWL; CB, CLC.

673 — —[Anr. ed.] *By J. D. for Richard Chiswel*, 1680. 8°. T.C.I 423. L, R; IU, Y.

673A — —[Anr. ed.] *By B. W. for Richard Chiswel*, 1684. 8°. T.C.II 88. Y.

674 —The souldiers exercise. Third edition. *By John Dawson, to be sold by Lawrence Blaiklock*, 1643. 4°. O; CH, CN, MU, NCD.

675 —A way to get wealth. Seventh edition. *By B. A. for Iohn Harison*, 1648[9]. 4°. L, O, LWL, CK, GU; CH, IU, MH, TU, Y.

676 [–] —Eighth edition. *For E. Brewster, and George Sawbridge*, 1653. 4°. LUG, LWL, LLU; CPB, IU, MB, MH, Y.

676A [–] —[Anr. ed.] *By T. Harper, for J. Harrison*, 1653. 4°. MU.

677 [–] —Ninth edition. *By W. Wilson for E. Brewster and George Sawbridge*, 1657. 4°. L, CT, R, EN; CDA, MH, MIU, NC, NCU, Y.

678 [–] —Tenth edition. *By William Wilson for George Sawbridge*, 1660. 4°. L, C, LUG; CLC, LC, MH, NS, Y.

679 [–] —Eleventh edition. —, 1660. 4°. L, O, C, BC, R; LC.

680   ——Twelfth edition. *By John Streater for George Saw-bridge*, 1668. 4°. L, C, LG, LWL, R; CB, MH, Y.

681   [–] ——Thirteenth edition. *By E. H. for George Sawbridge*, 1676. 4°. L, C, LAS, LWL, LLU, EN; CLC, CN, MH, PL, WF, Y.

682   [–] ——Fourteenth edition. *By T. B. for Hannah Sawbridge*, 1683. 4°. T.C.II 52. O, LLU, R, DT; CH, MH, VC, WDA, Y.

683   [–] ——Fifteenth edition. *For A. and J. Churchill*, 1695. 4°. L; OSU.

      Markham, *Sir Robert.* The case of Sir Robert Markham . . . concerning his election as burgess. [*London*, 1678.] brs. LPR.

684   **Markland, Abraham.** Poems on His Majestie's birth. *By James Cotterel*, 1667. 4°. L, LG, LLU; CLC, IU, WF, Y.

685   —A sermon preached . . . Octob. 29. 1682. *For Brabazon Aylmer*, 1683. 4°.* T.C.II 13. L, C, LG, OCC, WCA; NP, NU, V, WF.

      Marks of the apocalyptical beast. 1667. *See* Bagshaw, Edward, *younger.*

685A **Marlborough, James Ley, *earl.*** A copy of the Earl of Marlborough's letter to Sir Hugh P[ollard] . . . . April 24, 1665. *For G. Bedell and T. Collins*, 1665. brs. C.

686   —Fair warnings to a careless world. *For Samuel Speed*, 1665. 4°.* L, O, OC, DU; CLC, MM, WF, Y.

687   —A learned treatise concerning wards. *By G. Bishop and R. White, for Henry Shepheard, and Henry Twyford*, 1642. 8°. L, O, C, CT, DC, EN; CH, MBP, PU, TU, WF, Y.

688   —Reports of divers resolutions in lavv. *By Tho. Roycroft for H. Twyford, Tho. Dring, and Jo. Place*, 1659. fol. L, O, C, LG, DT; CH, KT, MHL, NCL, WF.

689   —The two noble converts. *By J. D. and sold by Randal Taylor*, 1680. brs. L, O, LS, CK; CH, INU, MH, WF, Y.

690   ——[*Anr. ed.*] *Reprinted Edinburgh, by J. S.* 1680. brs. ALDIS 2233. EN.

691   **Marlborough, John Churchill, *duke.*** The Lord Churchill's letter. [*n.p.*, 1688.] brs. L, O, C, CS, EN; CH, MH, TU, WF, Y. (var.)

      Marleborovves miseries. 1643. *See* B., T.

691A **M[arloe], J[ohn].** Letters to a sick friend. *By J. A. for Thomas Parkhurst*, 1682. 8°. T.C.I 483. L, LW, LWL; UCLA.

691B [**Marlow, Isaac.**] An account of the unjust proceedings. [*London*, 1697.] 8°. O, EN.

692   —An answer to a deceitful book. *For the author*, 1698, 8°. O.

692A [–] A brief discourse concerning singing. *For the author*, 1690. 8°.* O, EN.

692B —A clear confutation of Mr. Richard Allen. [*London*, 1696.] 8°. EN.

693   —The controversie of singing. *For the author*, 1696. 8°. L, O, LG, EN; LC, RBU.

693A —Prelimited forms of praising God. *For the author*, 1691. 8°. ORP, EN.

694   —The purity of gospel-communion. *By J. Astwood for the author*, 1694. 8°. O, EN.

694A —Some brief remarks on a paper printed. [*n.p.*, 1692.] cap., 8°.* O, ORP.

694B [–] Some short observations made on a book . . . by Mr. Benjamin Keach. colop: *For the author*, 1691. cap., 8°.* LL, ORP.

695   —A tract on the Sabbath-day. *By J. A. and sold by H. Barnard, and by Hannah Smith*, 1693/4. 4°. L, O, C, MR, EN; NHC.

696   —A treatise of the Holy Trinunity [*sic*]. *For the author, to be sold by Richard Baldwin*, 1690. 12°. T.C.II 319. L, O, LLL, CT, LNC; NHC, NPT.

697   —Truth soberly defended. *Printed*, 1692. 8°. L, ORP.

698   **Marlow, Jeremiah.** A book of cyphers. *For W. Rogers*, 1683. 8°. T.C.II 30. L, O, C, CM; CH, CLC, CN, WF, Y, YBA.

699   No entry.

      Marlowe, Christopher. Lusts dominion. 1657. *See* title.

700   [–] A tragicall history of . . . Doctor Faustus. [*London*], *for W. Gilbertson*, 1663. 4°. L, O, LVD, OW, EC; CH, MH, RHT, Y.

700A **Marmet, Ezekiel.** Sermon de feu Mr. Marmet. *Imprimé a Londres par T. Forcet*, 1645. 8°.* O; Y.

701   **Marmet, Pierre de.** Entertainments of the cours. *By T. C.*, 1658. 8°. LT, O, CT, LLU, EN; CH, CLC, CN, PU, WF, Y.

702   Entry cancelled.
      —Sermon. 1645. *See* Marmet, Ezekiel.

703   **Marmion, Shackerley.** The antiquary. A comedy. *By F. K. for I. W. and F. E.*, 1641. 4°. L, O, LVD, CK, EN; CH, CN, LC, MH, TU, WF, Y.

703A [–] Cupid's courtship. *By E. O. for Richard Head*, 1666. 8°. CH, MH.

704   [–] ——Second edition. *By E. O. for Thomas Dring*, 1666. 8°. L.

705   Marmor in quo legitur sequens. [*n.p.*], 1680. brs. L.

      Marmora Oxoniensia. Oxonii, 1676. *See* Oxford University.

706   **Marnetté.** The perfect cook. *Printed at London for Nath. Brooks*, 1656. 12°. LT, O; NN.

706A ——[*Anr. ed.*] *For Obadiah Blagrave*, 1686. 12°. T.C.II 202. NN.

      Maronides. 1672. *See* Phillips, John.

706B **Marott, Louis.** A narrative of the adventures of. *For Edward Brewster*, 1677. 8°. T.C.I 281. L, O; MH.

707   The Marques of Clanrickards engagement. [*Kilkenny*, 1646.] 4°.* C.

708   **Marr, John.** Navigation in coasting. *Aberdeen, by Iohn Forbes, and are to be sold in Dundee*, 1683. 8°. ALDIS 2393. E, EN; CH.

709   Marriage asserted. *For Henry Herringman*, 1674. 8°. T.C.I 189. L, O; CLC, MH, NN, NP.

      Marriage by the morall law. [*n.p.*], 1680. *See* Lawrence, William.

      Marriage-musick. [*n.p.*, 1670.] *See* C., Z.

      Marriage of armes. 1651. *See* Whitehall, Robert. Τεχνη πολιμογαμια.

710   Marriage promoted. In a discourse. *For Richard Baldwin*, 1690. 4°. T.C.II 314. L, O, CS, EN, DT; CH, CN, MH, NU, WF, Y.

      Marriages of cousin germans. Oxford, 1673. *See* Dugard, Samuel.

711   The married-mans best portion. *For W. Thackeray, T. Passenger, and W. Whitwood*, [1670–77]. brs. O, HH.

712 The married mens feast. *By Peter Lillicrap for John Clark*, 1671. 4°.* O; CH.

713 The married wives complaint. *For P. Brooksby*, [1680?]. brs. O.

714 **Marriot, John.** The English mountebank. *For George Horton*, 1652. 4°.* LT.

715 **Marriott, Robert.** A sermon in commemoration of . . . Mᴿⁱˢ. Elizabeth Dering. *By E. P. for N. Bourne*, 1641. 4°.* L, O, LW; MH, Y.

716 **Marriott, Thomas.** The danger of division. *For Walter Kettilby*, 1689. 4°.* T.C.I 284. L, CT; CH, CLC, MH, WF.

717 —Rebellion unmasked. *By I. R. for Thomas Iohnson*, 1661. 4°.* LT, C, BLH.

718 —A sermon preached . . . Easter-day, 1689. *For Walter Kettilby*, 1689. 4°.* T.C.II 268. L, O, CT, EC, BR, DT; CLC, MH, NU, WF.

Marrow of alchemy. 1654. *See* Starkey, George.

Marrow of chymical physick. 1669. *See* Thrasher, William.

719 The marrovv of complements. *For Humphrey Moseley*, 1655. 12°. LT, O.

Marrow of modern divinity. 1645. *See* Fisher, Edward.

Marrow of physicke. 1648. *See* Brugis, Thomas.

720 **Marryat, Richard.** A short treatise. *For William Larnar*, 1642. 4°.* LT, DT; NU.

Mars, Richard. God's dreadful judgement. 1675. *See* Mare, Richard.

721 Mars and Venus: or, the amorous combatants. [*London*], *for J. Wright, J. Clarke, W. Thackera* [*sic*] *and T. Passenger*, [1681–84]. brs. CM, HH; MH.

722 Mars Christianissimus. *For R. Bentley, and S. Magnes*, 1684. 12°. T.C.II 116. L, CT, SP; CLC, Y.

Mars his triumph. 1661. *See* Barriffe, William. Military discipline.

723 **Marsal, Richard.** Fifteen considerations. *By Bernard Alsop*, 1645. 8°.* LT.

724 —XXIX. Directions. *By Bernard Alsop*, 1647. 8°.* LT.

725 **Marsden, Thomas.** Roman Catholicks uncertain. *For Walter Kettilby*, 1688. 4°. L, O, C, EN, DT; CH, MH, MIU, TU, WF, Y.

726 **Marsh, A.** The confession of the new married couple. *Printed*, 1683. 12°. T.C.II 51. L, O, A; CH, NN.

727 —The ten pleasures of marriage. *Printed*, 1682. 12°. T.C.II 32. L, O; CH, NN, PU.

728 **Marsh, Francis,** *abp.* An address given in to the late King James, by the titular Archbishop of Dublin. *For Ric. Baldwin*, 1690. 4°.* CT; Y.

729 [**Marsh, Henry.**] A new survey of the Turkish Empire. *By Ja: Cottrel, for Hen. Marsh*, 1663. 12°. O, C, OM; PL.

729A [–] —[Anr. ed.] *For Henry Marsh*, 1663. 12°. L; CLC, LC.

730 [–] —Second edition. *By Ja: Cottrel, for Hen. Marsh*, 1663. 12°. L; CH, CN, MIU, NP, WF.

731 [–] —[Anr. ed.] *By J. Best for John Williams*, 1664. 8°. OB; MH.

732 — —[Anr. ed.] *By J. B. for Samuel Bolton*, 1664. 8°. L, LW, CT, CD; KU, LC, WF, Y.

732A —The second part of the new survey. *By J. Best for H. Marsh*, 1664. 12°. LC.

733 **Marsh, John.** Marsh his mickle monument raised on shepherds talkings. [*London*], 1645. 4°. LT, O; CH.

734 **Marsh, Narcissus,** *abp.* The charge given . . . July 27, 1692. *Dublin, by Joseph Ray*, 1694. 4°. DIX 262. BR, CD, DT.

735 —The charge given . . . June the 27th, 1694. *Dublin, by Joseph Ray*, 1694. 4°. DIX 263. CD, DI, DM.

735A —The charge given by . . . to the clergy . . . of Leinster. *Dublin, by Joseph Ray*, 1694. 4°. CD, DT.

735B —Institutio logicæ in usum juventis academicæ Dubliniensis. *Dublini, apud Sam: Helsham*, 1679. 8°. DT.

736 [–] Institutiones logicæ. *Dublini, apud S. Helsham*, 1681. 8°. DIX 181. O, C, DM, DN, DT; CB, WF.

737 [–] —[Anr. ed.] *Dublini, apud J. North, E. Dobson, and M. Gunn*, 1697. 8°. DIX 287. DN.

738 **Marsh, Richard.** The vanity and danger of modern theories. *Cambridge, at the University press, for Edmund Jeffery, in Cambridge*, 1699. 4°.* T.C.III 151. L, O, C, CT, DU, E; CH, CLC, CN, NU, WF, Y.

739 Entry cancelled.

Marsh, William. Sermon preach'd. 1687. *See* Wall, William.

739A **Marshall, Charles.** An epistle to Friends coming forth. [*London?* 1680.] 8°.* LF; CDA, IE, MU, PH, PSC, WF.

740 —An epistle to the flock of Christ Jesus. [*London*], *printed*, 1672. 4°.* L, C, LF, BBN, BR; CLC, MH, NR, PH, Y.

740AA — —Second edition. *Printed and sold by T. Sowle*, 1697. 12°. PSC.

740A —A general epistle to Friends, and professors of the truth. [*London*, 1680.] brs. LF.

740B —On the 24th of the 5th month, 1674. as I lay in my bed. [*London*, 1647.] brs. MR.

741 [–] A plain and candid account of the nature . . . certain experienced medicines. [*London*], *for the author, by T. Sowle*, [*c.* 1681]. 8°.* L, O, LF, BBN; PH, PHS.

741A —A plain and candid relation of the nature . . . spiritus mandus. [*n.p., c.* 1681.] brs. O.

742 —A second epistle. [*London*], *printed*, 1673. 4°.* L O, LF, BBN; CLC, IE, MH, NCD, PH, PL, PSC, Y.

743 [–] Some testimonies of the life, death, and sufferings of Amariah Drewet. *By Andrew Sowle*, 1687. 4°.* L, LF, MR; MH, PH, PSC.

744 —A tender visitation in the love of God. *Printed and sold by Andrew Sowle*, 1684. 4°.* L, O, LF, BBN; CLC, MH, PH, PL, PSC, Y.

745 —The trumpet of the Lord. [*London*], *printed*, 1675. 4°.* L, O, C, LF, BBN; CH, IE, MH, PH, PSC, WF, Y.

746 —The way of life revealed. [*London*], *printed*, 1674. 4°.* L, O, LF, BBN, BR; CLC, IE, MH, PH, PSC, WF, Y. (var.)

746AA **Marshall, John.** The three regiments. [*London*, 1681.] brs. O.

746A **Marshall, Marmaduke.** Certain proposalls in all humblenesse presented. [*London?* 1649.] brs. Y.

747 **Marshall, Stephen.** The works of . . . first part. *By Peter Cole, and Edward Cole*, 1661. 4°. O; MWA, Y.

748 [–] An answer to a booke entitvled, An hvmble remonstrance. *For I. Rothwell, and are to be sold by T. N.*, 1641. 4°. LT, O, CT, DU, E, DT; CH, CN, MH, NU, TU, JF.

748A [–] —[Anr. ed.] [*London*], *printed*, 1641. 4°. O, C, LW, CT, SP, DT; CH, CN, IU, MH, TU, WF.

748B [–] —[Anr. ed.] *By Tho: Paine, for J. R. and M. S., and are to be sold by T. N.*, 1641. 4°. LIU.

749 —A copy of a letter written by. *For Samuel Gellibrand*, 1643. 4°.* LT, O, C, MR, SP; CH, LC, MH, MU, NU, TU, Y.

750 ——[Anr. ed.] *For John Rothwell*, 1643. 4°.* LT, LCL, LW, OC, LSD, MR; CLC, IU, MH, NU, WF.

751 —A defence of infant-baptism. *Printed at London by Ric. Cotes, for Steven Bowtell*, 1646. 4°. LT, O, C, EN, DT; CH, IU, MH, NU, WF, Y, AVP. (var.)

752 —A divine proiect. *By Richard Cotes, for Stephen Bowtell*, 1644. 4°. LT, O, C, LLU, DT; CH, MIU, NU, WF, Y.

753 —Emmanuel. *By R. Cotes for Stephen Bowtell*, 1648. 4°.* LT, O, C, OCC, AN; CH, IU, MH, NU, WF, Y.

754 [–] An expedient to preserve peace. *Printed*, 1647. 4°.* LT, CK, DT; CH, IU, NU, WF.

754A [–] —[Anr. ed.] *For H. R.*, 1647. 4°.* OC, CCC; WF, Y.

755 Entry cancelled.

[–] Godly man's. 1680. *See title.*

756 —Gods master-piece. *By Richard Cotes, for Stephen Bowtell*, 1645. 4°. LT, O, C, EN, DT; CH, IU, MH, NU, WF, Y, AVP.

757 [–] The humble answer of the divines . . . Octob. 6. 1648. *For Abel Roper*, 1648. 4°.* LT, O, C, DU, EN, DT; CH, IU, MH, NU, TU, WF, Y.

758 [–] —[Anr. ed.] —, 1660[1]. 4°.* LT, O, OC, AN, BC; CLC, MIU, NU, PL, TU, WF, Y.

759 —A letter from. *For John Bellamy and Ralph Smith.* 1643. 4°.* L, O, C, EN, DT; CH, MH, NU, TU, WF, Y.

760–1 Entries cancelled.

—Letter of spiritual advice. Oxford, 1643. *See title.*

—Letter written by. 1643. *See* —Copy of a letter.

761A —Meroz curse for not helping the Lord. *Printed*, 1641. 4°.* L, LW, CT, DU; IU, Y.

761B ——[Anr. ed.] *For F. C. and T. B.*, 1641. 4°.* CLC.

761C ——[Anr. ed.] *For Iohn Wright junior*, 1641. 4°.* CT; Y.

762 —Meroz cursed, or, a sermon. *By R. Badger, for Samuel Gellibrand*, 1641[2]. 4°. LT, O, C, ENC, DT; CH, CN, MH, MU, NU, TU, WF, Y. (var.)

763 ——[Anr. ed.] 1642. 4°. BC.

764 ——[Anr. ed.] *By J. R. for Samuel Gellibrand*, 1645. 4°. O, LSC, LW, BC, DU; CSS, IU, MBP, MH, NU, WF, Y, AVP.

765 —A most true and succinct relation of the late battell. *For H. S., Novemb. 3. 1642.* brs. LT.

766 —A peace-offering to God. *By T. P. and M. S. for Samuel Man*, 1641. 4°. LT, O, C, NOT, EN, DT; CH, CN, MH, TU, WF, Y, AVP. (var.)

767 —A plea for defensive armes. *For Samuel Gellibrand*, 1642. 4°.* NU.

768 ——[Anr. ed.] —, 1643. 4°.* AU; CH, Y.

769 —The power of the civil magistrate. *For Nathaniel Webb, and William Grantham*, 1657. 8°. L, O, BC, E, DT; CLC, IAU, NU, V, WF.

770 —Reformation and desolation. *For Samuel Gellibrand*, 1642. 4°. LT, O, C, EN, DT; CH, CN, MH, TU, WF, Y. (var.)

771 —The right vnderstanding of the times. *By Richard Cotes, for Stephen Bowtell*, 1647. 4°. LT, O, C, BC, DT; CH, CN, MH, NU, WF, Y, AVP.

772 —A sacred panegyrick, or a sermon. *For Stephen Bowtell*, 1644. 4°.* LT, O, C, EN, DT; CLC, CN, MH, TU, WF, Y.

773 —A sacred record. *By Rich. Cotes for Stephen Bowtell*, [1645]. 4°.* LT, O, C, EN, DT; CH, CN, MH, NU, WF, Y.

774 —A sermon of the baptizing of infants. *By Richard Cotes for Stephen Bowtell*, 1644. 4°. LT, O, CK, EN, DT; CH, IU, MH, NU, WF, Y, AVP. (var.)

775 ——[Anr. ed.] —, 1645. 4°. LW, CT, BAMB, LLU, SA; MH, NU, TO, TSM, Y.

776 —A sermon preached . . . November 17, 1640. *By J. Okes, for Samuel Man*, 1641. 4°. C, LW, MR, NE, SHR; IU, MH, Y, MOORE.

776A ——[Anr. ed.] *By I. Okes for Samuel Man*, 1641. 4°. LT, O, C, OC, EN, DT; CH, CN, MH, TU, WF, Y.

777 ——[Anr. ed.] *For Samvel Man*, 1645. 4°. L, O, C, DC, MR; CH, IU, MH, NU, TU, WF, Y.

778 No entry.

779 —A sermon preached . . . Aug. 12. 1647. *By R. Cotes for Stephen Bowtell*, 1647. 4°.* LT, O, C, BC, DT; CH, CN, MH, NU, WF, Y.

780 —A sermon preached . . . Januar. 26. 1647[8]. *By Richard Cotes for Steven Bowtell*, 1647[8]. 4°.* LT, O, C, BC, DT; CH, IU, MH, NU, WF, Y.

781 —A sermon preached . . . Easter Monday April 1652. *By R. I. for Stephen Bowtel*, 1652. 4°.* O, MR, ENC; MB, NGT, NU, WF.

782 ——Second edition. —, 1653. 4°.* LT, O, LW, BC, MR; CH, IU, MH, NU, Y.

783 —The sinne of hardnesse of heart. *By R. Cotes, for Stephen Bowtell*, 1648. 4°.* LT, O, C, BC, BLH; CH, IU, MB, NU, WF, Y.

784 [–] Smectymnuus redivivus. *By T. C. for John Rothwell*, 1654. 4°. L, O, C, NPL, EN, BQ; CLC, IU, MH, NU, RPJ, TU, Y.

785 [–] —[Anr. ed.] *For John Rothwell, and now republished*, 1660. 4°. O, MR; CU, IU, NORTHWESTERN, NU.

786 [–] —[Anr. ed.] *For John Rothwell*, 1660. 4°. L, OC, CSE, EC; IU, NU, WF.

787 [–] —Fifth edition. —, 1661. 4°. OC, NE, SP, GU; CB, MIU, RPJ.

788 Entry cancelled. Ghost.

789 —The song of Moses. *For Sam: Man and Sam: Gellibrand*, 1643. 4°. LT, O, C, DU, DT; CH, CN, MH, NU, TU, WF, Y.

790 —The strong helper. *By Richard Cotes, for Stephen Bowtell*, 1645. 4°. LT, O, C, EN, DT; CH, CN, MH, NU, WF, Y, AVP.

791 —A thanksgiving sermon. *By R. Cotes. for Stephen Bowtell*, 1648. 4°.* LT, O, C, MR, DT; CLC, IU, MB, NU, Y.

792 —Θρηνωδια a sermon. *For Stephen Bowtell*, 1644. 4°.* LT, O, C, ENC, DT; CN, MH, NR, NU, WF, Y.

793 —Θρηνωδια. The chvrches lamentation. *Printed at London for Stephen Bowtell*, 1644. 4°.* L, O, C, DU, EN; CLC, CN, MH, NCD, NU, WF, Y.

794 ——[Anr. ed.] *For Stephen Bowtell*, 1644. 4°.* L, C, OB, DU, EC, DT; CH, MH, MU, TU, VC, WF, Y, AVP.

795   Entry cancelled.
      —True and succinct relation of the late battel. 1642. *See*
      —Most true.

796   —The true copy of the letter. *For Samuel Gellibrand,*
      Septemb. 8. 1643. 4°.* LT, C, CM; TU, WF, Y.

797   —A tvvo-edged svvord. *By R. Cotes for Stephen Bowtell,*
      1646. 4°.* LT, O, C, YM, DT; CH, MH, NU, WF, Y.

798   [–] A vindication of the ansvver to the hvmble remon-
      strance. *For Iohn Rothwell, 1641.* 4°. LT, O, CT, DUS, DL,
      DT; CH, CN, MH, NU, TU, WF, JF.

798A [–] —[Anr. ed.] *Printed, 1641.* 4°. LW, OC, CT, DU, LIU; CH,
      IU, ZWT.

799   [–] —[Anr. ed.] *For John Rothwell,* [1654]. 4°. CS, NPL; CH,
      IU, MIU, NGT, PPT, RPJ.

800   **[Marshall, Thomas]**, *1621–1685.* The catechism set
      forth. *At the theater in Oxford, 1679.* 8°. T.C.I 366;
      MADAN 3216. L, O, C, OC, OM; CH, WF, Y.

801   [–] —Second edition. —, *1680.* 8°. MADAN 3270. L, OC.

801A [–] —Fourth edition. *1683.* 8°. OCC.

802   [–] —Fifth edition. *At the theater in Oxford, 1683.* 8°. L, O,
      CS, LSD; Y.

803   [–] —Sixth edition. —, *1684.* 8°. L, O, LLP, OU, CT; NU.

803A [–] —Seventh edition. —, *1686.* 8°. OC; CLC, Y.

804   [–] —Eighth edition. —, *1689.* 4°. CH, NU.

805   [–] —Ninth edition. —, *1692.* 8°. T.C.II 430. O, OC, EC.

806   [–] —Tenth edition. *Oxford, at the theater for T. Bennet,*
      London, 1698. 4°. O.

807   [–] —Eleventh edition. *Oxford, at the theater, 1700.* 4°. O.

807A [–] Y catechism a osodwyd allan yn llyfr gweddi
      gyffredin. *Rhydychen* [*Oxford*], *1682.* 8°. WF.

808   **Marshall, Thomas,** *minister.* The Kings censure upon
      recusants. *For Francis Cowles, 1654.* 4°. LT, O, CT, EN;
      MIU, NU, WF.

809   **Marshall, Walter.** The gospel-mystery of sanctification.
      For T. Parkhurst, 1692. 8°. T.C.II 419. L, O, C, LW, E; CH,
      IU, MH, NU, WF, Y.

809A **Marshall, William.** Answers upon several heads in
      philosophy. *By T. L. for Nathaniel Brooke, 1670.* 8°.
      T.C.I 27. L, O; CLC, IU, WF.

809B —Philosophy delineated. *For Obadiah Blagrave, 1678.* 8°.
      L, CS; PCP.

810   **Marsham,** *Sir John.* Chronicus canon. *Excudebat Tho.*
      Roycroft, prostant apud Guliel. Wells & Rob. Scott, 1672.
      fol. T.C.I 120. L, O, C, E, DT; BN, CH, CN, MH, NCD, WF, Y.

810A ——[Anr. ed.] *Excudebat Thomas Roycroft, 1672.* fol. OC,
      CP, GC; PU, TO.

811   —Diatriba chronologica. *Typis Jacobi Flesher, 1649.* 4°.
      L, O, C, LNC, DT; BN, CH, CN, IU, TU, WF, Y.

812   **M[arsin], M.** All the chief points contained in the
      Christian religion. *Printed and are to be sold by J. Clark,*
      E. Whitlock, and W. Reddish, 1697. 8°.* O, C, LSC, OC;
      MBP, MH.

812aA [–] —[Anr. ed.] *1699.* 8°.* L.

812A [–] A clear and brief explanation upon the chief points.
      Printed and sold by John Clarke, John Gwillim, Mrs.
      Mitchell, and Mr. Garin, 1697. 8°. T.C.III 92. L, LLL; CH,
      MH, WF, Y.

813   —The figurative speeches. *Printed and sold by John Clarke,*
      John Guillim, Mrs. Mitchel, and Mr. Garin, 1697. 8°.
      LLP, OC; MBP, MH. (var.)

813A —The first book . . . the seventh book. *Printed and sold*
      by Edward Pool; John Gwillim; Mrs. Mitchell. By Abel
      Roper, 1698. 8°. MH.

813B —A full and clear account the Scripture gives. *Printed,*
      and sold by John Gouge, at Mrs. Fabian, at John Clarks,
      and at John Gwillim's, 1700. T.C.III 196. L, O, WCA;
      CH, MH, WF.

813C [–] The near aproach[*sic*] of Christ's Kingdom. *For M. M.*
      and are to be sold by Tho. Fabian, 1696. 8°. T.C.III 3.
      L, O, LLP, OC; CH, MH, NU, WF.

813CA [–] A rehearsal of the covenant by Moses. [*London, 1697.*]
      8°.* MH.

813CB [–] Some of the chief heads of the most miraculous
      wonders. [*London, 1694?*] cap., 8°.* O; CH.

      [–] This treatise proving three worlds. 1696. *See* —First
      book.

813D —Truth vindicated. Second edition. *Printed and sold*
      by John Goudge, at Mrs. Fabian, and at John Clarks, 1700.
      8°. L; CH, MH, WF.

813E —Two sorts of latter days. *Printed and sold by J. Bradford,*
      Mrs. Michael. At John Gwillum's, 1699. 8°.* T.C.III 121.
      L, O, LLL; CH, MH, WF.

813EA [–] The womens advocate. Second edition. *For Benjamin*
      Alsop and Thomas Malthus, 1683. 12°. T.C.II 20. CN.

813EB [–] —[Anr. ed.] —, *1687.* 12°. CN.

813F [–] —[Anr. ed.] colop: [*London*], *sold by J. Clark, 1697.*
      cap., 8°.* O, CT; CH, MH, NU, WF.

814   **Marston, Edward.** A sermon of simony. *For the author,*
      1699. 4°.* L, O, C, LLP, BAMB.

815   **Marston, Humphrey.** The confession of. *For G. Horton,*
      1654. 4°.* LT; CH.

816   **Marston, John.** Comedies, tragi-comedies; & tragedies.
      Printed, 1652. 4°. CH.

817   **Marston, John,** *minister.* A sermon preached at St.
      Margaretts in VVestminster, sixt of February. *By F. L.*
      for Io. Burroughes, and Io. Franke, 1642. 4°.* LT, O, C, CJ,
      GU; IU, NGT, NP, RBU, WF, Y.

      Marston-moor. [n.p.], 1650. *See* Fisher, Payne.

817A **Martel, Margaret.** A true copy of the paper delivered
      by. *By Mary Edwards,* [1697]. brs. CN.

817B —A true translation of a paper . . . delivered by. *For E.*
      Mallet, 1697. brs. CN.

818   **[Marten, Henry.]** A corrector of the ansvverer to the
      speech out of doores. *Edinburgh. By Evan Tyler, 1646.*
      4°.* ALDIS 1220. LT, O, C, EN, DT; CH, CU, MU, NU, WF, Y.

819   —Coll: Henry Marten's familiar letters. *Bellositi Do-*
      bunorum [*Oxford, by A. Lichfield*] *for Richard Davis, 1662.*
      4°. MADAN 2602. L, O, C, LLU, YM; CH, MH, WF.

819A ——[Anr. ed.] *Oxford, for Richard Davis, 1662.* 4°. O.

820   ——[Anr. ed.] *Bellositi Dobunorum* [*Oxford*] *for Richard*
      Davis, 1663. 4°. MADAN 2643. L, O, C, LVF, MR, DT; CN,
      MH, NPT, OWC, WF.

821   —The familiar epistles of. Second edition. *For Jo. Hind-*
      marsh, 1685. 4°. T.C.II 106. L, O, LLU; CH, CN, CSS, WF, Y.

822 —The independency of England. *For Peter Cole, and John Sweeting,* 1648. 4°.* LT, O, C, BC, DT; CH, CN, MH, NU, WF, Y.

822A ——[Anr. ed.] [*n.p.,* 1648.] cap., 4°.* DU.
[–] Manifest truths. 1646. *See* Bowles, Edward.

823 —The Parliaments proceedings justified. *For John Sweeting,* 1648. 4°.* LT, O, C, EN, DT; CH, CN, MH, NU, WF, Y.

824 —Friday 22 October 1652. Col. Martin reports from the Councell of State propositions touching the Isle of Jersey. [*n.p.,* 1652.] brs. L.

824A [–] A resolve of the person of the King. *Edinburgh* [*i.e. London?*], *as truly printed by Evan Tyler . . . as were the Scotish papers,* 1646. 4°.* ALDIS 1235.5. LSE, EN; CH, CSS, WF.

825 [–] A word to Mr. VVil. Prynn Esq. *For T. Brewster,* 1649. 4°.* LT, O, CCA, DU, LSD; CH, IU, MH, NU, WF.

825A **Martial.** Epigrammata. *Ex officina Rogeri Danielis,* 1655. 12°. L, IU.

825B ——[Anr. ed.] —, 1661. 12°. C, DL.

825C ——[Anr. ed.] *Ex officina J. Redmayne,* 1668. 12°. WF, Y.

825D ——[Anr. ed.] —, *et prostant venalia apud Gulielmum Birch,* 1668. 12°. IU.

826 ——[Anr. ed.] *Ex officina J. Redmayne,* 1670. 12°. O; IU.

826A ——[Anr. ed.] *Excudebat T. R. impensis Roberti Stephani,* 1673. 12°. T.C.I 144. L, O, CP, AN, LLU; IU, Y.

827 ——[Anr. ed.] *Ex officina J. Redmayne,* 1675. 12°. L, LSD; IU.

828 ——[Anr. ed.] —, 1677. 12°. C, OC, YM; IU, PL.

829 ——[Anr. ed.] *Ex officinâ Eliz. Redmayne,* 1689. 12°. T.C.II 281. L, CT; IU.

830 —Epigrams of Martial, Englished. Second edition. *For Henry Bonwicke,* 1695. T.C.II 558. L, O, LVD, LLU, DT; CH, CN, IU, LC, MH, NCD, TU, WF, Y.

831 —Ex otio negotium. Or, Martiall his epigrams. *By T. Mabb, for William Shears,* 1656. 8°. LT, O, C, LIU, EN; CH, CN, IU, LC, MH, TU, WF, Y.

832 No entry.

833 —Select epigrams of Martial, Englished. First edition. *In the Savoy: by Edward Jones, for Samuel Lowndes,* 1689. 8°. T.C.II 275. L, O, LL, GC, LLU; CH, CLC, IU, TU, WF, Y.

834 —M. Val. Martialis. Spectaculorum liber. Paraphrais'd. *By H. Bruges, for Giles Widdowes,* 1674. 8°. T.C.I 170. CH, MH.

835 No entry.
[**Martin.**] History of antient ceremonies. 1669. *See* Porré, Jonas.

836 **Martin, Lieut. Col.** A relation of the great victories and successes of the garrison of Plymouth. *By T. P., June 4th.* 1644. 4°.* LT; CH, MH, WF.

837 **Martin, Edward.** . . . His opinion concerning the difference between the Church of England and Geneva. *Printed,* 1662. 8°. L, O, C, LW, OC, DU, DT; NIA, TO, Y.

837A **M[artin], G[regory].** The love of the soul. *St. Omers,* 1652. 12°. L.

838 **Martin, James.** Positiones philosophicæ. colop: *Edinburgh, excudebat hæres Andreæ Anderson,* 1681. cap., 4°.* ALDIS 2277. E, SA, DT.

839 ——[Same title.] *Edinburgh,* 1686. brs. ALDIS 2652.7. SA.

[**Martin, John.**] An account of Mr. Lock's religion. 1700. *See* Milner, John.

840 [–] Go in peace. containing. *By A. M. for Richard Royston,* 1674. 8°. T.C.I 186. L, O, C; CH, CLC, NP, WF, Y.

841 [–] —[Anr. ed.] *By J. L. for Luke Meredith,* 1687. 12°. T.C.II 212. L, O, LSD, NE; CLC, IU.

842 [–] Hosannah: a thanksgiving-sermon. *Oxford, by H. Hall, for Rich. Davis,* 1660. 4°.* MADAN 2505. LT, C, LW, D; NU, WF, ZWT.

843 —Lex pacifica: or Gods own law. *London, by J. G. for Richard Royston, to be sold by John Courtney in Salisbury.* 1664. 4°.* L, LLP; CLC, MIU, NU.

843aA ——[Anr. ed.] *By J. G. for Richard Royston,* 1664. 4°.* O; CLC, WF.

843A Entry cancelled.
—Preacher sent. 1658. *See title.*

843B **M[artin], Joseph].** The huntsmans delight. [*London*], *for W. Thackeray and T. Passinger,* [1686–88]. brs. CM.

844 [–] —[Anr. ed.] *By and for A.M.,* [1693?]. brs. L.

844A [–] —[Anr. ed.] *For W.O.,* [1700?]. brs. O.

845 —The seamans folly. *For P. Brooksby,* [1685–90]. brs. L, HH.

846 **Martin, L.** Father Peter's birth. [*n.p.,* 1688–9.] brs. HH.

847 **Martin, Martin.** A late voyage to St. Kilda. *For D. Brown and T. Goodwin,* 1698. 8°. T.C.III 77. L, O, C, MR, E, BQ; BN, CH, CN, IU, LC, Y.

848 **Martin, Richard.** A speech delivered. *Printed at Oxford for William Webb; and reprinted for Anthony Vinson* [*London*], 1643. 4°.* MADAN 1225. LT, O, OC, BR, DU, DT; CH, CLC, MH, WF, Y.

849 Entry cancelled. Date: 1639. STC 17514.

849A **Martin, Robert.** Catalogus librorum ex præcipuis Italiæ. [*Londini*], *typis Thomæ Harper,* 1650. 4°.* O.

850 [**Martin, T.**] Mary Magdalen's tears wipt off. *By J. C. for T. Garthwait,* 1659. 8°. LT, O, CSE, BR, P; CH, CLC, CN, WF.

850A [–] —[Anr. ed.] *By J. C. and are to be sold by J. Courtney, in Salsbury,* 1659. 8°. CCA; CLC, MH.

851 [–] —[Anr. ed.] *For Robert Pawlett,* 1676. 8°. T.C.I 234. L, O, CP, DU; CH, CLC, MM, NU, WF, Y.

852 [**Martin, Thomas.**] Historica descriptio complectens vitam, . . . Gulielmi Wicami. *Oxoniæ, e theatro Sheldoniano,* 1690. 4°. L, O, CT, MR, DT; CH, CN, TU, WF, Y.

852A **Martin, William.** Unto the right honourable, the Lords of Council and session. The petition of. [*Edinburgh, c.* 1695.] fol. EN.

853 [**Martindale, Adam.**] An antidote against the poyson of the times. *London, for Luke Fawn, to be sold by Thomas Smith in Manchester,* 1653. 8°.* LT.

854 —The countrey-survey-book. *By A. G. and J. P. for R. Clavel,* 1682. sixes. T.C.I 460. L, O; MU, WF.

854A ——Second edition. *For R. Clavell and T. Sawbridge,* 1692. sixes. T.C.II 431. L; CLC.

855 [–] The description of a plain instrument. *For J. Coniers,* 1668. 8°.* L; CH.

856 —Divinity-knots unloosed. *For John Hancock*, 1649. 8°. LT, C, DT.

857 **[Martindall, Anne.]** A relation of the labour, travail and suffering of . . . Alice Curwen. [*London*], *printed*, 1680. 4°. LF, MR; MH, MU, NR, PH, RPJ, Y.

858 **Martini, Martino.** Bellum Tartaricum, or the conquest of . . . China. *For John Crook*, 1654. 8°. LT, O, CT; CLC, CN, NN, NP, SE, WF.

858A **Martini, Pedro.** [Hebrew] that is the key of the holy tongue. *Amsterdam, for C.P.*, 1645. 8°. MH, RBU.

858B — —Second edition. *Amsterdam, for C. P., to be sold by Daniel Frere*, 1648. 8°. CT; MH, RBU, ZAP.

858C — —[Anr. ed.] *Amsterdam, to be sold by Laurence Sadler and Gabriell Bedell*, 1650. 8°. L, LSD; IU, Y.

Martinius, Henricus. Bloody almanack. 1661. *See* Almanacs. Martin, Henry.

Martin's echo. [n.p., 1645.] *See* Overton, Richard.

858D **Martyn, John.** Mensuration made easie. *By James Cottrel*, 1661. 8°. NC.

858E **Martyn, John,** *bookseller*. A catalogue of some books printed for, colop. *By T.N. for J. Martyn*, 1670. 4°.* L; LC.

859 The martyr of the people. *Printed*, 1649. 4°.* LT, SP; CSS, WF.

Martyrdome of King Charles. Hage, 1649. *See* Leslie, Henry, *bp*.

Martyrdom of Theodora. 1687. *See* Boyle, Robert.

Μαρτυριον Χριστιανον, or. 1664. *See* Douglas, Thomas.

Μαρτυρολογια. 1677. *See* Foxe, John.

860 **[Marvell, Andrew.]** An account of the growth of Popery. *Amsterdam, printed*, 1677. 4°. L, O, CCH, MR, EN; CH, CN, NU, TU, WF, Y, AVP. (var.)

861 — —[Anr. ed.] *Printed at Amsterdam* [*London*, 1678]. fol. L, O, DC, LSD, EN, DT; CH, MH, TU, WF, Y.

862 Entry cancelled. Ghost.

863–5 Entries cancelled.

[–] Advice to a painter. [n.p., 1666.] *See* Savile, Henry. Advice. [1679.]

[–] —[Anr. ed.] [n.p., 1679.] *See* Savile, Henry.

[–] —[Anr. ed.] 1681. *See* Advice to a painter in a poem.

866 —Mr. Andrew Marvell's character of Popery. *For Richard Baldwin*, 1689. 4°.* L, O, CT, LIU, MR; CH, CN, CU, PU, TU, WF.

867 [–] The character of Holland. colop: *By T. Mabb for Robert Horn*, 1665. cap., fol.* LNC; CH, TU.

868 [–] —[Anr. ed.] *For Rob. Horn*, 1672. 4°.*, L, LPR, MR, SP; CH, LC, Y.

[–] Collection of poems on affairs of state. 1689. *See title*.

869 [–] A common-place-book out of The rehearsal transpros'd. *For Henry Brome*, 1673. 8°. T.C.I 128. L, O, CT; CH, CN, MH, WF, Y.

869A [–] Directions to a painter. [*London*], *printed*, 1667. 8°.* t.p., B–G⁴. L, O, C, LG, DC; CH, IU, MH, NCD, PL, WF.

869B [–] —[Anr. ed.] —, 1667. 8°.* A–C⁸. CH.

869C [–] —[Anr. ed.] 1689. 8°.* EN.

870 [–] An elegy upon the death of my Lord Francis Vjlljers. [*London*, 1648.] 4°.* OW; OWC.

871 [–] The first anniversary of the government under His Highness the Lord Protector. *By Thomas Newcomb, to be sold by Samuel Gellibrand*, 1655. 4°.* LT, O, LW, LSD; CH, CLC, CN, NRU, Y.

871A [–] The last instructions to a painter. [*London*, 1667.] cap., 8°.* PL.

871B [–] A letter from a gentleman in Ireland. *Printed, and are to be sold by Langley Curtiss*, 1677. 4°.* L, O, C, MR, EN, DT; CH, CU, MH, NCD, WF, Y.

872 —Miscellaneous poems. *For Robert Boulter*, 1681. fol. T.C.I 432. L, O, LVF, CT, EN; CH, CN, IU, LC, MH, TU, WF, Y. (var.)

873 [–] Mr. Smirke: or, the divine in mode: . . . animadversions on. [*London*], *printed*, 1676. 4°. L, O, DU, EN, DT; CLC, IU, TO, WF.

873A [–] —[Anr. ed., "Mr. Smirke; or."] [*London*], *printed*, 1676. 4°. L, C, DU, MR, DT; CH, CN, IU, MH, TO, Y.

873B [–] —[Anr. ed., "Mr. Smirke. Or . . . animadversions of."] [*London*], *printed*, 1676. 4°. O, LW, SP, EN, DT; CH, MR, NP, NU, TU, WF, Y.

874 Entry cancelled. Ghost.

875–7 Entries cancelled.

[–] New advice to a painter, &c. [n.p., 1679/80.] *See title*

[–] Plain-dealing. 1675. *See* M., A.

878 [–] The rehearsal transpros'd. *By A. B. for the assigns of John Calvin and Theodore Beza*, 1672. 8°. L, O, C, SP, ENC; CH, IU, MH, NU, TU, WF, Y.

878A [–] —Second edition. —["assings"], 1672. 12°. O, LLP, OC, OU, CT; TU, WF, Y.

879 [–] —"Second" edition. *By J. D. for the assigns of John Calvin and Theodore Beza; sould by N. Ponder*, 1672. 8°. L, O, C, BP, DU, P, BQ; CLC, CN, MH, MU, TU, WF, Y. (var.)

880 [–] —[Anr. ed.] *Printed*, 1672. 8°. L, O, C, LLU, ENC; CH, CN, MH, NU, TU, WF, Y. (var.)

881 Entry cancelled. [=M879]

881aA [–] —"Second" edition. 1673. 12°. NE; CLC, WF.

881A [–] —[Anr. ed.] *By J. X. for the assigns of John Calvin and Theodore Beza*, 1673. 12°. L, CT, DC; MWA.

882 — —the second part. *For Nathaniel Ponder*, 1673. 8°. L, O, C, MR, EN; CH, CU, MH, NU, TU, WF, Y.

882A — — —[Anr. ed.] —, 1673. 12°. L.

883 — — —[Anr. ed.] —, 1674. 12°. L, O, C, LIU, E, DT; CH, MH, NU, TU, WF.

884 [–] Remarks upon a late disingenuous discourse, . . . by T. D. *Printed and are to be sold by Christopher Hussey*, 1678. 8°. T.C.I 308. L, O, LW, OC, CT, P; NP, TU, WF.

885 [–] A seasonable argument to perswade all the grand juries. *Amsterdam, printed*, 1677. 4°. L, O, CJ, DU, WCA; CH, CN, MH, NU, WF, Y.

886 Entry cancelled.

[–] Seasonable question and an usefull answer. 1676. *See* P., H.

886A [–] The second advice to a painter. [*London*], *printed*, 1667. 8°.* L; NN, TSM.

887 Entry cancelled.

[–] Second advice to the painter. [n.p., 1679.] *See title*.

887A [–] The second, and third advice to a painter. *A. Breda*, 1667. 8°.* L, O (impf.); NCD, TU (impf.).

888 —A short historical essay. *Printed*, 1680. 4°.* T.C.I 382. L, O, C, DU, LNC, MR, EN, CD; CH, CN, MH, MU, NU, TU, WF, Y.

889 ——[Anr. ed.] *For R. Baldwin*, 1687. 4°.* L, O, C, LLU, ENC; CH, CU, MH, TU, WF, Y.

890–2 Entries cancelled.

   [–] S'too him bayes. Oxon, 1673. *See title*.

   [–] Third part of advice. 1684. *See title*.

   [–] Third advice. [n.p., 1679.] *See title*.

   Marvellous history intituled Beware the cat. 1652. *See* Baldwin, William.

893 A marvelous medicine. [*London*], *for F. Coles, T. Vere, and VV. Gilbertson*, [1658–64]. brs. L, O, CM.

893A —[Anr. ed.] *For F. Coles, T. Vere, and J. Wright*, [1663–74]. brs. O.

893B Marvels ghost: being the true copy of a letter sent to the A.B. of C. [*London*, 1688.] cap., 4°.* LG, OB, EN, MH.

894 Mary Aubrey: or, hellish murder. 1688. 4°. LG (lost).

   Mary Magdalen's tears. 1659. *See* Martin, T.

895 Entry cancelled. Date: [1711].

896 **Maryland.** The charter of Mary-land. [*London, c.* 1679.] cap., 4°.* RPJ.

896A ——[Anr. ed.] [*London, c.* 1685.] cap., 8°.* PL, RPJ.

896B —[A complete body of the laws of Maryland. *Annapolis, by Thomas Reading*, 1700.] fol. LC (lacks t.p.).

897 —A law of Maryland concerning religion. [*n.p.*, 1689.] brs. LPR; NN. (var.)

   Mary's choice. 1674. *See* Watkinson, Peter.

898 **Mascall, Leonard.** The countreyman's jewel. *For William Thackery*, 1680. 8°. L, LLL, R, RU; CH, Y.

899–901 Entries cancelled.

   —Counrty-man's [sic] new art of planting. 1651. *See* Brossard, Davy.

902 —The government of cattell. *By Thomas Harper, for Martha Harrison*, 1653. 4°. L, O, C, DC, R; CH, IU, NS, Y.

903 ——[Anr. ed.] *For J. Stafford and W. Gilbertson*, 1662. 4°. BC, P, R; WDA.

903A ——[Anr. ed.] *For John Stafford and W. G.*, 1662. 4°. L, LWL, GU.

903B ——[Anr. ed.] *For William Gilbertson and John Stafford*, 1662. 4°. L, MAU; CLC, WF, Y.

903C **Mascall, William.** A new and true Mercurius. *For the author*, 1661. 4°.* L.

904 **Mascardi, Agostino.** An historical relation of the conspiracy of John Lewis Count de Fieschi. *For John Newton*, 1693. 8°. T.C.II 424. L, O, C, CT, BAMB, DC; CH, IU, PL, WF, Y.

905 [**Masham, Damaris**], *lady*. A discourse concerning the love of God. *For Awnsham & John Churchil*, 1696. 12°. T.C.III 1. L, O, C, LLP, LW; CLC, MIU.

905A [–] ——[Anr. ed.] —, 1697. 8°. LW.

906 The mask taken off. *For John Gwillim*, 1700. 8°. O, LF.

907 **Mason.** Ecclesia potestatem habet. [*n.p.*, 1661.] brs. O.

908 [**Mason, Abel.**] Sad and fearfull newes from Beverley. *July 26. London, for I. Harnom*, [1642]. 4°.* LT, O, CD; IU.

909 **Mason, Charles.** The day of the Lord. *For the author, to be sold by John Williams, and Benj. Teuke*, 1676. 4°.* L, LW, YM; NU.

910 —Miles Christianus. A sermon. *For Benjamin Tooke*, 1673. 4°.* T.C.I 147. L, LL, CK, CS, SP; CH, NU, Y.

911 [–] Officium ministri, vel. *Typis R. Davenport vaeneuntque apud Ioh. Williams*, 1663. 4°.* LSC, CT, DU, LIU, P; CLC, PU.

912 [–] Solus Christus totius mundi episcopus. *Excudebat J. R. prostat autem venale apud J. Williams, & B. Took*, 1677. 4°.* T.C.I 276. L, LW, CT; CH, CLC, NU, Y.

913 **Mason, E. M.** The covenant acknowledged. *For John Marriot*, 1660. 4°.* CH, MH, NU, WF.

913A **Mason, Francis.** Vindiciae ecclesiae Anglicanae. Third edition. *Typis Felicis Kingstoni, sumptibus Dan. Frere*, 1646. fol. L, SA.

913B **Mason, Henry.** Foure treatises. *For Robert Clark*, 1653. 12°. WF.

914 —Four usefull and profitable treatises. *For John Clark*, 1656. 12°. C, LSC; MB, NU.

915 —Hearing and doing. *For John Clark*, 1656. 12°. C; NU.

916 **Mason, John**, *of Fordham*. Mentis humanæ metamorphosis; . . . the history. *By F. L. for B. Harris*, 1676. 8°. T.C.I 221. L, O, LCL, ORP; CLC, CN, IU, WF, Y.

916A [–] War with the devil, the second part. *Printed for Benjamin Harris*, 1683. 8°. Y.

916B **Mason, John**, *1646?–1694*. A little catechism, with little verses. *For John Lawrence*, 1692. 8°. T.C.II 436. L, O.

917 [–] The midnight-cry. *For Nathanael Ranew*, 1691. 4°.* T.C.II 329. L, O; IU, SE, WF.

917A [–] ——Second edition. —, 1691. 4°.* T.C.II 352. GU; CH, MWA, Y.

918 [–] ——Fourth edition. —, 1692. 4°. T.C.II 405. C, LW, DU.

919 [–] ——Fifth edition. —, 1694. 4°. L, LLP, CT; MH.

   [–] Penitential cries. 1696. *See title*.

920 Entry cancelled.

   [–] Princeps rhetoricus. 1648. *See* Mason, John, *of Cambridge*.

921 [–] Spiritual songs, or, songs of praise. *For Richard Northcott*, 1683. 8°. T.C.II 29. L, O, LLP; MH, Y.

921A [–] ——Second edition. —, 1685. 8°. L, LLL, EN; NPT.

921B [–] ——Third edition. —, 1691. 8°. GU.

921C [–] ——Fourth edition. *For Thomas Parkhurst*, 1694. 8°. T.C.II 521. MH.

922 [–] ——Fifth edition. —, 1696. 8°. T.C.III 30. C; CLC, CN, IU, LC.

922A [–] ——Sixth edition. *For Tho. Parkhurst*, 1699. 8°. L.

923 —The waters of Marah sweetned. *For John Macock*, 1671. 4°.* LW, CT; CH.

923A [**Mason, John**], *of Cambridge*. Princeps rhetoricus or πιλομαχια. Ye combat of caps. *For H. R.*, 1648. 4°.* LT, O; SR, CH, IU, WF.

923B **Mason, John**, *fl. 1659*. Blood-thirsty Cyrus unsatisfied with blood. *Printed*, 1659. 4°. O.

   Mason, Margery, *pseud*.

924 **Mason, Martin.** The boasting Baptist dismovnted. *For Giles Calvert*, 1656. 4°.* LT, LF, MR; CH, PH.

925 —Charles, King of England, the infinite eternal being. *For Robert Wilson*, 1660. brs. LT, LF, CT; PSC, WF.

926 [-] A check to the loftie linguist. *For Giles Calvert*, 1655. 4°.* LT, LF, BBN; WF.

927 —A faithful warning. *For Robert Wilson*, [1660]. 4°.* LT, C, LF, OC, BBN; CH, IE, MH, NCD, PH, PSC, WF, Y.

928 — —[Anr. ed.] —, [1661?]. 4°.* L, LF, BBN; CH, MH, PHS, PSC.

929 —A friendly admonition. *[London], printed*, 1662. 4°.* L, LF, BBN, BP; CH, PH.

930 [-] Innocency cleared; the liberties. *[London*, 1660?] cap., 4°.* L, LF, OC, BBN, MR; CH, IE, MH, NCD, PH, PSC, WF, Y.

930A —Love and good-will to all. *Printed*, 1665. brs. MH.

931 —A loving invitation. *For Robert Wilson*, [1660]. 4°.* L, O, C, LF, BBN; CH, IE, MH, NCD, PH, PSC, WF, Y.

932 [-] One mite more. *Printed*, 1665. 4°.* L, LF, BBN, MR, GU; CH, IE, MH, NCD, PH, PSC, Y.

933 —The proud Pharisee reproved. *Printed*, 1655. 4°. LT, O, C, LF, MR; PH, PSC.

933A [-] Sion's enemy discovered. *[London*, 1659.] 4°.* LF.

934 —To both houses of Parliament. *For Robert Wilson*, 1660. brs. LT, LF; PH, PSC.

935 **Mason, Philip.** A catalogue of . . . Latin and English books. *[London*, 1691.] 4°.* L.

936 [**Mason, Richard Angelus.**] A liturgical discourse of the holy sacrifice of the mass . . . first part. *[London], printed*, 1670. 8°. L, O, C, LSD, P; CLC, CN, TU, WF, WG.

937 [-] — . . . second part. —, 1669. 8°. L, O, C, DUS, LSD; CLC, CN, TU, WF, WG.

938 [-] —[Anr. ed.] —, 1675. 12°. L, DUS; CLC, MSL, WF, Y.

939 [-] A manvell of the arch-confraternitie. Second edition. *At Doway, by Baltasar Bellers*, 1654. 12°. L, O, LLP, WARE; CLC, CN, NU, Y.

939A [-] A manvall of the third order of . . . S. Francis. *At Doway, by the widow of Marke Wyon*, 1643. 12°. O, OG, DUS; Y.

939B [-] The rule of penance. *At Doway, by the widdow of Marke Wyon*, 1644. 12°. L, O, OG, WARE; CN.

940 [**Mason, Robert.**] The English and Scottish Protestants happy tryumph. *For J. Horton*, 1642. *June* 4. 4°.* LT, C, EC, DN; WF, Y.

941 **Mason, William.** Arts advancement. *[London], for the author: sold by Mʳ. Benj. Alsop, Mʳ. Wilkins, Mʳ. Jacob Sampson, Mʳ. Thom: Fox*, 1682. 8°.* T.C.I 507. L, O, CM, MC, EN; CLC, MH, NN, WF, Y.

941A — —[Anr. ed.] *For the author, sold by Mʳ. Benj. Alsop, Mʳ. Wilkins, Mʳ. Ben: Harris, Mʳ. Thom: Fox*, 1682. 8°.* LU.

942 — —Third edition. *For the author*, 1687. 16°.* T.C.II 220. LU; CH, CN, NN, Y.

943 — — "Third" edition. *For the author*, 1699. T.C.II 562. L, LU, EN; IU, LC, NN, WF, Y.

944 —Aurea clavis: or, a golden key. *Printed for, and sold by, the author: also by C. Coningsby, R. Cumberland, J. Back*, 1695. 8°. T.C.II 562. LU, LW.

945 —A pen pluck'd from an eagle's wing. *By J. Darby, for the author*, 1672. 16°. T.C.I 105. L, O, LU, CM, MC; CH.

945A — —[Anr. ed., "plvk'd."] —, 1672. 16°. NN, Y.

946 — —Second edition. *For and sold by the author: also by Chr. Coningsby, John Back, R. Cumberland*, 1695. 8°. T.C.II 562. LU, EN; NN, Y.

947 —A regular and easie table of natural contractions. *[London*, 1695.] brs. T.C.II 562. L, LG, LU, MP; NN.

948 **Mason, William, *Anabaptist.*** A little starre. *By G. D. for Giles Calvert*, [1653]. 8°. LT, LCL.

948A The masse priests lamentation. *For Richard Burton*, 1641. brs. MH.

949 **Massachusetts Bay Colony.** Acts and laws, of His Majesties province of the Massachusetts-Bay. *Boston, by Bartholomew Green, and John Allen, for and sold by Michael Perry, and Benjamin Eliot*, 1699. fol. EVANS 867. L, LL; CH, CN, LC, MH, SE, PHS, Y.

950 —Acts and laws, passed by the great and general court . . . of the Massachusetts-Bay. *Boston, by Benjamin Harris*, 1692. fol. EVANS 618. CH, LC, MB, NN, PHS.

951 —Acts and laws, passed . . . eighth of February. *Boston, by Benjamin Harris*, 1693. fol.* EVANS 647. MBA, MWA, PHS.

952 —Acts and laws, passed . . . 31 May. *Boston, by Bartholomew Green, and sold by Samuel Phillips*, 1693. 4pp. fol.* CH, MHS, MWA, NN, PHS.

953 — —[Anr. ed.] —, 1693. 15pp. fol.* EVANS 649. CH, MBA, MHS, NN, PHS.

954 —Acts and laws, passed . . . sixth day of July. *Boston, by Bartholomew Green, and sold by Samuel Phillips*, 1693. fol.* EVANS 650. MBA, MHS, PHS.

954A Entry cancelled. Continuation of EVANS 649–50.

954B Entry cancelled. pp. 141–50.

955–5A Entries cancelled. pp. 159–76; pp. 177–92.

956 —Anno 1697 [election of councillors]. *[Boston*, 1697.] brs. MBS.

957 —Anno regni regis & reginæ . . . By the Governour, & council. *Whereas. Boston [by Samuel Green], March* 24, 1689/90. brs. EVANS 519. MHS, MU.

958 —The answer of the House of Representatives, to His Excellency the Earl of Bellomont's speech. colop: *Boston, by Bartholomew Green, and John Allen*, 1699. fol.* LPR.

958A —At a convention of the representatives . . . May 24, 1689. *Boston, Richard Pierce*, [1689]. brs. LPR.

959 —At a council held at Boston, March 10, 1668. A proclamation. *[Cambridge, Mass.*, 1669.] brs. EVANS 141. NN.

960 —At a council held at Boston Septemb. 8, 1670. *[Cambridge, Mass.*, 1670.] brs. EVANS 149. MBS.

960A —At a council held at Boston the 25th of June, 1675. *[Boston*, 1675.] brs. MHS.

961 —At a council held in Boston August the thirtieth, 1675. An order. *[Cambridge, Mass., by Samuel Green*, 1675]. brs. EVANS 205. MBA.

961A —At a council held at Boston, September the seventeenth, 1675. *[Boston*, 1675.] brs. MHS.

962 —At a council held at Boston April the 4th. 1676. *[Cambridge, Mass.*, 1677.] brs. EVANS 215. MBA.

963 —At a council, held at Charlestown, June the 20th, 1676. [*Cambridge, Mass.*, 1676.] brs. EVANS 216. MHS.

963A —At a council held at Boston January the third 1677. [*Boston*, 1678.] brs. MHS.

964 —At a council held at Boston the 9th. of April, 1677. *Cambridge* [*Mass.*], *by Samuel Green*, 1677. brs. EVANS 234. MBA.

965 —At a council held at Boston, March 28. 1678. *Cambridge* [*Mass.*], *by Samuel Green*, 1678. brs. EVANS 249. MBA.

966 —At a council held at Boston the 22d. of August 1678. *Boston, John Foster*, [1678]. brs. MHS.

966A —At a council held at Boston . . . January 6. 1679. [*Boston, by John Foster*, 1680.] brs. MH.

966AB —At a council held at Boston March 8, 1679. [*Boston*, 1680.] brs. NP.

966B —At a court held at Boston in Nevv-England the 29th of March, 1677. *Cambridge* [*Mass.*], *by Samuel Green*, 1677. brs. EVANS 233. MBA.

967 —At a general court held at Boston in the year [blank]. [*Cambridge*, 1668?] brs. MH.

967A —At a general court held at Boston, March the eleventh. [*Cambridge, Mass.*, 1674.] brs. MHS.

967B —At a general court held at Boston, February the 21st, 1675. [*Boston*, 1676.] brs. MHS.

967C —At a general court held at Boston the 11th of October, 1675. [*Boston*, 1675.] brs. BBE, MHS.

968 Entry cancelled. *See* next entry.

968A —At a general court held at Boston the 3ᵈ. of May 1676 for defraying the charges. [*Boston, by John Foster*, 1676.] brs. MBA, MH.

969 —At a general court held at Boston May the 3d, 1676. For the preventing. [*Cambridge, Mass., by Samuel Green*, 1676.] brs. EVANS 217. MBA, MH.

969A —At a general court held at Boston, the eleventh of October, 1676. [*Boston*, 1676.] brs. MHS.

970 —At a general court held at Boston May 8. 1678. [*Boston?* 1678.] brs. EVANS 252. MHS.

971 —At a general court held at Boston in New-England the second day of October 1678. A proclamation. *Cambridge* [*Mass.*], *by Samuel Green*, 1678. brs. EVANS 250. NN.

971A —At a general court held at Boston, October 15. 1679. [*Boston, by John Foster*, 1679.] brs. EVANS 273. MH.

972 —At a general court held at Boston the 16th of March 1680-1. [*Cambridge, Mass.*, 1681.] brs. EVANS 304. MWA.

973 —At a general court held at Boston; May 24th, 1682. *Cambridge* [*Mass.*], *by Samuel Green*, 1682. brs. EVANS 316. MB, MBA.

973A —At a general court . . . March 14, 1682[3]. [*Boston*, 1683.] brs. LPR.

974 —At a general court held at Boston May. 16. 1683. *Cambridge* [*Mass.*], *by Samuel Green*, 1683. brs. EVANS 346. MBA.

975 —At a general court on adjournment, held at Boston Feb. 13 1683/4. *Cambridge* [*Mass.*]: *by Samuel Green*, 1684. brs. EVANS 365. MBA.

976 —At a general court held at Boston, January 28, 1684. *Cambridge* [*Mass.*], *by Samuel Green*, 1684. brs. EVANS 364. MBA.

977 —At a general court held at Charlstown . . . Feb. 12th 1689/90. *Boston: by Samuel Green*, [1690]. brs. EVANS 529. MHS.

978 —At a general court for Their Majesties colony . . . December 22th [*sic*]. 1691. [*Boston*, 1691.] brs. EVANS 554. MBS, MHS.

979 —At a great and general court or assembly . . . an act for granting. colop: *Boston, B. Allen & J. Allen*, 1700. fol.* EVANS 920. PHS.

979A — —[Same title.] colop: *Boston, by Bartholomew Green and John Allen*, 1700. fol.* EVANS 919. PHS.

979B —At a meeting of the council . . . March the fourth. [*Cambridge, Mass.*, 1675.] brs. MHS.

980 —At a second sessions of the general court held at Boston . . . [2 October 1678]. [*Boston?* 1678.] brs. EVANS 251. MHS.

980A —At a sessions of the general court held at Boston the 3rd of November, 1675. [*Boston*, 1675.] brs. MHS.

981 —At a sessions of the General Court held at Boston the 4th of March 1680. [*Cambridge, by Samuel Green, Mass.*, 1681.] brs. EVANS 288. MBA.

982 —At a session of the General Court . . . 28th of May. 1690. [*Boston*, 1690.] brs. EVANS 520. MHS.

983 —At a special General Court held at Boston Novemb. 7. 1683. *Cambridge* [*Mass.*], *by Samuel Green*, 1683. brs. EVANS 347. MBA.

983A —At the convention of the governour and council . . . [22 June]. [*Cambridge, by Samuel Green*, 1689.] brs. EVANS 475. MBS.

984 —At the convention of the governour and council, . . . June 22, 1689. [*Boston*, 1689.] brs. MBS.

985 —At the convention of the governour and council . . . September 7, 1689. [*Boston*, 1689.] brs. EVANS 482. BC; MBS.

986 —At the general court of Their Majesties colony. *Cambridge* [*Mass.*]: *by Samuel Green*, 1690. EVANS 521. brs. CH, MBS.

987 —The book of the general lavvues and libertyes. *Cambridge* [*Mass.*] *according to order of the General Court* [*by Matthew Day*], 1648. *To be sold* [*by*] *Hezekiah Usher in Boston*. fol. EVANS 28. CH.

988 —The book of the general lavvues. *Cambridge* [*Mass.*]: *printed* [*by Samuel Green*], 1660. fol. EVANS 60. CH, MBA, MHL, MHS, MWA, NN, PHS.

989 —Boston in New-England August 9th, 1667. The governour, deputy governour . . . do judge meet. [*Cambridge, Mass., by Samuel Green*, 1667.] brs. EVANS 115. CH, MBS.

990 —Boston, March 22, 1672,3. An order. [*Cambridge, Mass.*, 1673.] brs. EVANS 176. MBS.

990A —Boston 3d. December 1689. At the convention. [*Boston?* 1689.] brs. LPR.

990B —By his excellency, a proclamation . . . [16 October 1689.] *Boston, Richard Pierce*, [1689]. brs. MHS, NHS.

990C — . . . By his excellency and council . . . a day of prayer. [20 December 1692.] [*Boston*, 1692.] brs. LPR.

991 —By his excellency the governour, a proclamation. *Boston: by Benjamin Harris*, 1692. brs. EVANS 619. MHS.

992 —By his excellency the governour. Whereas. [*Boston*], *by Benjamin Harris*, 1692. brs. L; MHS.

992A —By the council and representatives of the colony. [*Boston*, 1689.] brs. LPR.

992B —By the general court . . . October the tenth, 1677. [*Boston*, 1677.] brs. LPR.

993 —By the governour and council assembled at Boston the 2d. of April, 1685. *Cambridge [Mass.]: by Samuel Green*, 1685. brs. EVANS 391. MBA.

993A —By the governour and company . . . at a general court . . . Feb. 16th 1685. [*Boston, by John Foster*, 1686.] brs. MH.

994 —By the governour & General Court. *Boston: by Samuel Green*, [1690]. brs. EVANS 530. MHS.

994A —By the governour and council . . . third day of December 1689. [*Boston*, 1689.] brs. LPR.

995 —By the governour & council . . . September 29, 1690. [*Boston*, 1690.] brs. EVANS 533. MHS, MWA.

995A —By the governour and council. A proclamation. [23 April.] [*Cambridge, by Bartholomew Green*, 1691.] brs. EVANS 557. MBS.

996 —By the governour, Council, and Representatives, . . . 8th of June, 1692. [*Boston*, 1692.] brs. EVANS 620. MHS, V.

997 —By the president and Council . . . June 8, 1686. *Boston, by Richard Pierce*, [1686]. brs. EVANS 410. MHS.

997A —The charter granted by Their Majesties . . . to the inhabitants. *Printed*, 1692. fol.* NN.

998 — —[Anr. ed.] *Printed at London, and re-printed at Boston, by Benjamin Harris*, 1692. fol.* EVANS 616. MBA, MWA.

999 — —[Anr. ed.] *Boston in New-England, by Bartholomew Green and John Allen, for and sold by Michael Perry, and Benjamin Eliot*. 1699. fol.* EVANS 868. L; CH, CN, LC, MH, NN, PHS, SE, V, Y.

1000 —A copy of the Kings Majesties charter. *Boston in New-England, by S. Green, for Benj. Harris*, 1689. 4°.* EVANS 474. L; MB, MBA, MH, MHS, MWA.

1001 —A declaration of the General Court . . . October 18. 1659. [*Printed in New-England.*] *Reprinted in London*, 1659. brs. L, O, LG; CH, MH.

1002 —The General Courts answer to Joseph Dudley. *Boston, by Richard Pierce*, 1686. brs. EVANS 412. MBS.

1003 —The general laws and liberties of the Massachusetts Colony. *Cambridge [Mass.] by Samuel Green, for John Usher of Boston*, 1672. fol. EVANS 168. L, O; CH, LC, MH, MU, NN, Y.

1004 —The general laws and liberties. *Cambridge in New-England, by Samuel Greene, for John Usher of Boston, and are to be sold by Richard Chiswel, London*, 1675. fol. T.C.I 206; EVANS 200. L, C; MWA, PHS, RPJ.

1005 —The governour and company of . . . at a General Court held at Boston. [*Cambridge, Mass.*, 1684.] brs. MB.

—Humble petition and address of the General Court. [n.p.], 1660. *See title.*

1006 —Letters of administration. [*Boston*, 1700.] brs. MBS.

1007 —Naval office at Boston, in Their Majesties province . . . these are to certifie. [*Boston*, 1692.] brs. MBS.

—Oath of allegiance. [n.p., 1678.] *See title.*

1008 —An order for regulating constables payments. *Cambridge [Mass.], by Samuel Green*, 1682. brs. EVANS 317. MBA.

1008A —An order of the General Court. [*Cambridge, by Samuel Green*, 1678.] brs. MHS.

1009 —Orders, made at a General Court. [*Cambridge, Mass.*, 1674.] brs. EVANS 178. MBA.

1009A —A proclamation. [For a fast, 6 June.] [*Cambridge, by Samuel Green*, 1678.] brs. EVANS 252. MHS.

1010 —A proclamation. [For a fast, 11 December.] *Cambridge [Mass.]: by Samuel Green*, 1679. brs. EVANS 273. CHS.

1011 —A proclamation. [For a fast, 15 April.] *Cambridge [Mass.], by Samuel Green*, 1680. brs. EVANS 287. MWA.

1011A —A proclamation. [For a fast, 21 April.] [*Cambridge, by Samuel Green*, 1681.] brs. EVANS 304. MWA.

1011B —A proclamation. [Claims in Narragansett.] [*Cambridge, by Samuel Green*, 1683.] brs. EVANS 348. MHS.

1011C —A proclamation by the president and council . . . May 25, 1686. *Boston, by Richard Pierce*, 1686. brs. LPR; CH.

1012 —A proclamation by the president . . . May 28, 1686. *Boston, in N. E. by Richard Pierce*, [1686]. brs. EVANS 409. CH, MHS.

1013 —A proclamation by the president . . . May 29, 1686. *Boston, by Richard Pierce*, 1686. brs. EVANS 411. MHS.

1014 —Province of the Massachusetts-Bay [arms]. By the honorable, the Lieutenant Governour. [27 May 1696.] *Boston; by Bartholomew Green and John Allen*, [1696]. brs. EVANS 751. MB.

1014A —Province of the Massachusetts-Bay . . . By the honorable, the Lieutenant Governor . . . a proclamation. Whereas the Indians. [9 February 1698.] *Boston, Bartholomew Green and John Allen*, 1698. brs. LC.

1014B —Province of the Massachusetts-Bay ss. By the honorable, the Lieutenant Governour . . . a proclamation. [16 June 1698.] *Boston in New England, by Bartholomew Green, and John Allen*, 1698. brs. MH.

1015 —Province of the Massachusetts-Bay. ss. By virtue of an act. [*Boston*, 1692.] brs. SE.

1016 —Several acts and laws. *Boston, by Benjamin Harris*, 1692. fol.* EVANS 617. L; MBA, MWA, NN, PHS.

1017 —Severall lavvs and orders made at severall General Courts. [*Cambridge, Mass.: by Samuel Green*, 1663.] fol.* EVANS 81. MHL, MHS, MWA.

1018 — —[Same title.] —, [1664.] fol.* EVANS 88. MHS, MWA.

1019 — —[Same title.] —, [1665.] fol.* EVANS 103. MHL, MWA.

1020 — —[Same title.] —, [1666.] fol.* EVANS 109. MHL, MWA.

1021 — —[Same title, "seveval."] —, [1668.] fol.* EVANS 124. MWA.

1022 —Several laws and orders made . . . 15th of May, 1672. [*Cambridge, Mass., by Samuel Green*, 1672.] fol.* EVANS 169. O; CH, LC, MHL, MU, MWA, NN, RPJ, Y.

1022A–23 Entries cancelled. Continous pagination.

1023A —Severall laws and ordinances of war . . . made [26 October 1675]. [*Boston, by John Foster, 1675.*] brs. LC, MH.

1024 —Sundry laws made. *Cambridge [Mass.]; by Samuel Green,* 1677. fol.* EVANS 237. MBA, MHS.

1024A —To the constables and select men of [blank.] [*Boston, 1677.*] brs. MWA.

1024B ——[Same title.] [*Boston, 1679.*] brs. MB.

1025 —To the elders and ministers of every town. [*Cambridge, Mass., by Marmaduke Johnson?* 1668.] brs. EVANS 126. MHS.

1025A —Two addresses from the governour, council, and convention. colop: *For Richard Baldwin,* 1689. cap., fol.* L, GU; CN, MB, MHS, V.

1026 —Whereas the lawes published. [*Cambridge, Mass.,* 1668.] brs. MBS.

Massachusetts or the first planters. Boston, 1696. *See* Scottow, Joshua.

1027 [**Massard, Jacques.**] Remarks upon the dream of the late abdicated queen. *For Tho. Salusbury, and are to be sold by R. Baldwin,* 1690. 4°.* T.C.II 324. L, O, AU; CB, CH, CLC, IU, MM, WF.

1027A [–] A treatise of the vertues and uses of several panacea's. *For the author,* 1685. 12°. L, O.

1028 **Massarius, Alexander.** De morbis fœmineis, the womans counsellour. *For John Streater,* 1657. 8°. LT.

1029 **Massauve.** Bibliotheca Massoviana: sive catalogus. [*London*], 1 Feb. 1687/8. 4°. L, O, C, LWL, OC, OP; BN, CLC, CN, MH, NG, WF, JF.

1030 **Massey, Christopher.** Microcosmography: or specvlvm mvndi. *By Richard Cotes,* 1650. 4°.* L, O; FU, MH.

1031 **Massey, Sir Edward.** A copie of Collnel Massey's letter. *By Tho: Forcet,* 1645. 4°.* LT, Y.

—Declaration and speech of . . . concerning the inthroning. 1650. *See* H., J.

1032 —The declaration of . . . shewing the true grounds. *For J. L.,* 1647. 4°.* LT, OC, MR, EN; CH, CN, MH, MM, WF, Y.

1033 —The declaration of . . . concerning his comming into England. [*London*], printed, [1648]. 4°.* LT, OC; CU, MH.

1034 —The declaration of . . . And eighty other English officers. [*London*], printed, 1650. 4°.* LT; CH, CSS, Y.

1035 —The declaration of . . . upon his death-bed. *For George Wharton,* 1651. 4°.* LT.

1036 —A declaration to the city. [*London*], *for C. VV.,* 1648. 4°.* LT, LIU, MR, DT; MH, TU.

1037 —A letter from. *For Thomas Bateman,* 1659. 4°.* OC; BBE, CH, MIU, WF, Y.

1038 —A short declaration by. *Printed,* 1649. 4°.* LT, CJ, DU, LIU, E; BBE, CH, MH, OWC, WF.

1039 **Massey, Isaac.** Midsvmmer's prognostication. *By Edward Griffin,* 1642. 4°.* LT, O; CH, MH, TO, WF, Y.

1039A **Massey, Robert.** The examination, and correction of a paper. *By Gartrude Dawson, May the 5.* 1649. 4°.* L; MH, MIU, OWC.

Massie. *See also* Massey.

1040 **Massie, Andrew.** Clarissimo, generosissimo, ac colendissimo domino, D. Thomæ Kennedy. *Edinburgi, excudebat hæres Andreæ Anderson,* 1687. brs. ALDIS 2725. E.

1041 Entry cancelled. *See next entry.*

1042 —Nobilissimo potentissimoque heroi, ac domino D. Georgio. *Edinburgi, excudebat Ioannes Reid,* 1683. brs. ALDIS 2435. E, AU.

1042A —Theses philosophicæ. *Edinburgi, excudebant hæredes et successores Andreæ Anderson,* 1695. brs. ALDIS 3511. GU.

1042B ——[Anr. ed.] *Edinburgi, excudebant hæredes Andreæ Anderson,* 1698. brs. GU.

1043 Massinello: or, a satyr. *For James Norris,* 1683. 4°.* T.C.II 5. L, LVD, OC, LLU, DT; CH, CLC, IU, MH, TU, WF, Y.

1044 **Massingberd, Henry.** The counsell and admonition of. *By A. M.,* 1656. fol. CH.

1045 No entry.

1046 **Massinger, Philip.** The city madam. *For Andrew Pennycuicke,* 1658. 4°. L, O; CH, CU, MH, NP, Y.

1047 ——[Anr. ed., "city-madam."] —, 1659. 4°. L, O, LVF, OW, EN; CH, LC, MH, MU, TU, WF, Y.

1048 —The excellent comedy, called The old law. *For Edward Archer,* 1656. 4°. L, O, LVD, CT, LIU; CH, CN, MH, NP, TU, WF, Y.

1049 No entry.

1050 —Three new playes. *For Humphrey Moseley,* 1655. 8°. LT, O, LVD, LVF, OC; CH, CN, LC, MH, TU, WF, Y.

1051 No entry.

1052 —The virgin-martyr: a tragedie. *By B. A.,* 1651. 4°. LT, O, OW, EC; CH, CN, MH, WF, Y.

1053 No entry.

1054 ——[Anr. ed., "virgin martyr."] *For William Sheares,* 1661. 4°. L, O, C; CH, CN, LC, MH, WF, Y.

Massy, Isaac. *See* Massey, Isaac.

1055 **Master, Thomas.** Tho: Masteri μακαριτου . . . Iter boreale. [*Oxford, by Henry Hall*], 1675. 4°.* MADAN 3065. L, O, OB, OC, BAMB; CH, CN, WF, Y.

—Mensa lubrica. [n.p., 1690?] *See* Masters, Thomas.

1056 —Monarchia Britannica. *Oxonii, excudebat Will. Hall, impensis Joseph Godwin,* 1661. 4°.* MADAN 2565. L, O, CT, DU, E, EN; CH, IU, NN, PU, WF, Y.

1057 ——[Anr. ed.] *Oxonii, e theatro Sheldoniano,* 1681. 4°. O, CT, WCA; CCC, CLC, Y.

1058 —The Virgin Mary. A sermon. *By Robert White, for Octavian Pulleyn, junior,* 1665. 4°.* LW; IU, Y.

1058A [**Master, William.**] Drops of myrrhe. *By R. W. for Rich. Davis in Oxon.,* 1653. 8°.* O, AN; CLC.

1059 [–] ——[Anr. ed.] —, 1654. 8°.* LT, EN; MBJ, NU, Y.

1060 [–] Λογοι ευκαιροι. Essayes. *By R. W. for R. Davis, in Oxon,* 1653. 8°. MADAN 2231. O, CT, EN; CLC, MBJ, NU.

1060A [–] ——[Anr. ed.] —, 1654. 8°.* LT; Y.

Master Clark defended. [n.p., 1691.] *See* Clark, James.

1061 Master Edmund Calamies leading case. *Printed,* 1663. 4°.* L, O, LL, CCA, MR, SP; IU, NU, TO. [= C258.]

1062 Master John Goodwins quere's [sic] questioned. *For Tho Vnderhill*, 1653. 4°.* LT, LSD, MR, SP, E; CH, CU, MH, NU, WF.

Master of the temple as bad. 1696. *See* Shower, *Sir Bartholomew.*

1063 Entry cancelled.

Masterman, G. Triumph stain'd. 1647. *See* Masterson, George.

1064 The master-piece of love-songs. *For A. M. W. O. and Tho. Thackeray*, [c. 1695]. brs. EUING 208. L, O, HH, GU; MH.

1065 —[Anr. ed.] [*London?* 1695.] brs. L.

1066 The master-piece of Round-heads. [*London*, 1643.] cap., 4°.* LT, OC, OW, CM, DT; CH, CN.

1066A The master, wardens, and assistants of the Company of Vinteners . . . [order to abide by price regulation]. [*London*, 1665?] brs. LPR.

1067 [**Masters, Samuel.**] The case of allegiance in our present circumstances consider'd. *For Ric. Chiswell*, 1689. 4°.* T.C.II 255. L, O, C, EN, DT; CH, CN, MH, NU, TU, WF, Y. (var.)

1068 —The Christian temper. *For Awnsham Churchill*, 1690. 4°.* T.C.II 312. L, O, OC, LSD; MH, MIU, NU, Y.

1069 —A discourse of friendship. *By T. B. for Marm. Foster and Awnsham Churchill*, 1685. 4°.* L, O, LG, OCC, CS; CH, CLC, IU, PU, WF, Y.

1070 —The duty of submission. *For Awnsham Churchill*, 1689. 8°. T.C.II 284. O; MB, NU.

1070A **Masters, Thomas.** Mensa lubrica; Anglice shovel-board. [*Oxford*, 1690?] 4°.* O; MH.

1071 [–] Mensa lubrica Montgom. *Oxoniæ, excudebat L. Lichfield*, 1651. brs. MADAN 2154. O.

1072 **Masterson, George.** Ανθρωπασθενες. A good ground. *For Edward Husband*, 1651. 4°.* L, LLP, LW, OC, LIU, EN; CH.

1072A —Milk for babes. *By A. M. for the author*, 1654. 8°. CT.

1073 —The spiritual house. [*London*], *for Philemon Stephens, the younger*, 1661. 8°. L, O, LSC, DC, EN; CH, CLC, NU, WF.

1074 —The triumph stain'd. *By John Field*, 1647[8]. 4°.* LT, O, CT, BAMB, LLU, DT; CH, CU, MH, NU, Y.

1075 Entry cancelled.

Mat, Ed. King Charles the II. 1660. *See* Mathews, Edward.

1075A Mat month: or, sergeant fierifacias. [n.p., 1690?] brs. L.

1076 A match at a venture. [*London*], *for I. Deacon*, [1680?]. brs. L.

1077 Match me these two: or the conviciton [sic]. [*London*], *printed*, 1647. 4°.* LT, O, CS, DU, DT; CH, INU, MH, Y.

Matchlesse crueltie. 1655. *See* Perrin, Jean Paul.

1078 The matchless murder. [*London*], *for J. Conyers*, [1682]. brs. L, O.

Matchless picaro. 1680. *See* Cellier, Elizabeth.

1079 Entry cancelled.

Matchless rogue. 1680. *See* Cellier, Elizabeth.

Matchless shepard. [1656.] *See* Price, Laurence.

1079AA A mate for mariners, and a treasure for travellers. *By B. Alsop and T. Fawcet, for William Lugger*, 1641. 4°. DUS; NN.

Materials for union. Oxford, 1681. *See* Humfrey, John.

1079A Entry cancelled.

M[atern], J[ohn]. Compendium linguæ Græcæ. 1679. *See* Taylor, Christopher. Compendium trium linguarum.

1080 The mathematicall divine. *For William Sheares*, 1642. 4°.* LT, O, DT; IU, WF.

Mathematicall magick. 1648. *See* Wilkins, John, *bp.*

Mathematicall recreations. 1653. *See* Leurechon, Jean.

1081 **Mather, Cotton.** Addresses to old men. *Boston: by R. Pierce, for Nicholas Buttolph*, 1690. 8°. EVANS 534. MB, MBA, MH, MHS, V.

1082 —Balsamum vulnerarium. *Boston: by Bartholomew Green, and John Allen, for Nicholas Buttolph*, 1692. 12°. EVANS 559. MHS, NN, RPJ.

1083 —Batteries upon the kingdom of the Devil. *For Nath. Hiller*, 1695. 8°. L; CH, LC, MB, NN, RPJ, WF, Y.

1084 —Blessed unions. *Boston, by B. Green & J. Allen, for Samuel Phillips*, 1692. 12°. EVANS 621. LC, MB, MH, MHS, MWA, RPJ, V.

—Boston ephemeris. Boston, 1683. *See* Almanacs.

1085 —The Bostonian Ebenezer. *Boston, by B. Green & J. Allen, for Samuel Phillips*, 1698. 12°. EVANS 827. LC, MB, SE.

1086 —Brontologia sacra: the voice of the glorious God. *By John Astwood*, 1695. 4°.* MB, MHS, MWA, RPJ.

1087 Entry cancelled.

—Call of the Gospel. Boston, [1686]. *See* Mather, Increase. Sermon occasioned.

1088 No entry.

1089 —The Christian thank-offering. *Boston, in N. E., by B. Green & J. Allen, for Michael Perry*, 1696. 8°.* EVANS 752. RPJ.

1090 [–] A cloud of witnesses. [*Boston? by B. Green & J. Allen?*, 1700?] cap., 4°.* EVANS 921. Y.

1091 —A companion for communicants. *Printed at Boston by Samuel Green for Benjamin Harris*, 1690. 8°. EVANS 535. LC, MB, MH, MU, NU, RPJ, V, Y.

1092 —The day, & the work of the day. *Boston, by B. Harris, for Samuel Phillips*, 1693. sixes. EVANS 652. L; MB.

1093 —Decennium luctuosum. An history. *Boston in New-England, by B. Green and J. Allen, for Samuel Phillips*, 1699. EVANS 873. O; CN, MB, MBA, MWA, NN, V.

1094 [–] The declaration, of the gentlemen, merchants, and inhabitants of Boston. colop: *Boston, by Samuel Green, and sold by Benjamin Harris*, 1689. fol.* EVANS 491. LPR; CH, LC, MBS, MH, MHS.

1095 —Durable riches. *Boston, by John Allen, for Vavasour Harris*, 1695. sixes. EVANS 722. CH, MB, MH, MHS, MWA, NU, RPJ.

1096 [–] Early piety. *By J. Astwood, for J. Dunton*, 1689. 8°. T.C.II 268. CN, MB, MWA, NN, RPJ, Y.

1097 — —[Anr. ed.] —, 1689. 8°. O; MH.

1097A   ——Second edition. *By J. Astwood for John Dunton,* 1689. L, O, LW; CH, CN, LC, MH, RPJ.

1098   —Early religion urged. *Boston, by B. H. for Michael Perry,* 1694. 8°. EVANS 698. MH, MHS, MWA, V.

1099   —Ecclesiastes. The life of . . . Jonathan Mitchel. *Massachvset; by B. Green and J. Allen,* 1697. 8°. EVANS 790. L, LW; CH, CN, MH, MWA, NN, RPJ, SE, Y. (var.)

1100   [–] An elegy on the much-to-be-deplored death of . . . Nathanael Collins. *Boston in New-England, by Richard Pierce for Obadiah Gill,* 1685. 8°.* EVANS 392. CH, NN, RBU.

1101   [–] Eleutheria: or, an idea of the reformation. *For J. R. and sold by A. Baldwin,* 1698. 8°. L, LW, ORP, BSO; MB, MHS, MU, MWA, V.

1102   [–] —[Anr. ed.] *For J. R. and sold by John Mackie, in Edinburgh,* 1698. 8°. ALDIS 3760.9. EN; V.

1103   [–] —[Anr. ed.] *London, for J. R. and sold by Sam. Philips at Boston,* 1698. 8°. LCL, LW, E, ENC; MB, MH, MHS, MWA, WF, Y.

1103A   Entry cancelled. =M1102.

1104   —The everlasting Gospel. *Boston, by B. Green and J. Allen, for Nicholas Buttolph,* 1700. 12°. EVANS 923. CH, LC, MB, MH, NN, Y.

1105   —Fair weather. *Boston, by Bartholomew Green, and John Allen, for Benjamin Harris,* 1692. 12°. EVANS 560. MH, MWA.

1106   ——[Anr. ed.] *Boston: by Bartholomew Green and John Allen, for Nicholas Buttolph,* 1692. 12°. EVANS 561. MH, MHS, Y.

1107   —Faith at work. *Boston in New England, by B. Green and J. Allen,* 1697. 8°.* EVANS 791. MH, NNM, V.

1108   —The faith of the fathers. *Boston in New-England, by B. Green, and J. Allen,* 1699. 8°* EVANS 874. O; CH, MB, MH, MHS, RPJ, V.

1109   —The family well-ordered. *Boston, by B. Green, & J. Allen, for Michael Perry: & Benjamin Eliot,* 1699. 12°. EVANS 875. L; LC, MB, MH, MHS, MWA, RPJ, SE, V.

1110   —La fe del Christiano. *Boston [by B. Green and J. Allen],* 1699. 8°.* EVANS 876. MH, MWA, NN.

1111   —A good man making a good end. *Boston in N.E., by B. Green, and J. Allen, for Michael Perry,* 1698. 8°. EVANS 828. LW; CH, LC, MBA, MH, MWA, NN, RPJ, V.

1112   —A good master well served. *Boston in New-England, by B. Green, and J. Allen,* 1696. 8°. EVANS 754. CN, MH, MHS.

1113   [–] Grace triumphant. *Boston, in N.E., by T. Green, sold by Benjamin Eliot,* 1700. 12°.* EVANS 925. MWA.

1114   [–] The great physician. *Boston in N. E. Printed and sold by Timothy Green,* 1700. 12°. EVANS 926. Y.

1115   —Help for distressed parents. *Boston, by John Allen, for Vavasour Harris,* 1695. 12°. EVANS 723. MBA, MHS, V.

1116   [–] Humiliations follow'd with deliverances. *Boston in N. E., by B. Green, & J. Allen, for Samuel Phillips,* 1697. 12°. CH, LC.

1117   —Johannes in Eremo. *[Boston], for and sold by Michael Perry,* 1695. 8°. EVANS 724. LW, OB, CS; CH, CN, LC, MH, NN, RPJ, SE, TU, V, Y.

1118   —Late memorable providences. Second edition. *For Tho. Parkhurst,* 1691. 8°. T.C.II 342. L, O, LCL, LW, GU; CH, LC, MH, NN, RPJ, Y.

1119   [–] A letter of advice to the churches. *Printed, and sold by A. Baldwin,* 1700. 4°.* T.C.III 228. L, O, NE, EN, DT; MBA, MH, MHS, MWA, NU, RPJ, WF, V.

1120   —Life and death of the renown'd Mr. John Eliot. Second edition. *For John Dunton,* 1691. 8°. L, O, LLL, EN; CH, CN, LC, MH, MU, MWA, NN, RPJ, V, Y.

1121   ——Third edition. —, 1694. 12°. T.C.II 474. L, O, CS, CD; CLC, CN, LC, MH, NN, RPJ, WF, V, Y.

1122   —Little flocks guarded. *Boston, by Benjamin Harris, & John Allen,* 1691. 8°. EVANS 563. MH, MHS, MWA, V, Y.

1123   —Memorable providences. *Printed at Boston in N. England by R. P.,* 1689. *Sold by Joseph Brunning.* 8°. EVANS 486. L; CH, LC, MB, MH, MWA, RPJ, V.

1124   ——[Anr. ed.] *Printed at Boston in New-England, and reprinted at Edinburgh by the heirs and successors of Andrew Anderson,* 1697. 12°. ALDIS 3678. A, GU; CH, LC, RPJ, V.

1125   —Memoria Wilsoniana. *Printed for and sold by Michael Perry, in Boston, in N. E.* 1695. 8°.* EVANS 725. MHS, MWA.

1126   —Mens sana in corpore sano. *Boston in N. E., by B. Green, and J. Allen, for Samuel Phillips,* 1698. 12°. EVANS 829. MH.

1127   —A midnight cry. *Boston; by John Allen, for Samuel Phillips,* 1692. 12°. EVANS 622. MB, MHS, MWA, RPJ, V.

1128   —Military dvties. *Boston in New-England, by Richard Pierce: and are to be sold by Joseph Brunning,* 1687. 8°. EVANS 431. L; CH, MH, MHS, MWA, V, Y.

1129   [–] A monitory, and hortatory letter. *Boston, N. E. printed,* 1700. 8°.* EVANS 928. LC, MB, MH, MWA.

1130   [–] —[Anr. ed.] *Boston, in N. E. printed,* 1700. 8°.* EVANS 927. L; MH, SE.

    —Observable things. Boston, 1699. See—Decennium.

1131   —Observanda. *Boston in N. E., by B. Green, for Samuel Phillips,* 1695. 8°. EVANS 726. MHS, MWA, NPT, V.

1132   [–] The old principles of New-England. *[Boston; by B. Green and J. Allen,* 1700.] 8°.* EVANS 929. CHW, MWA.

1133   —Optanda. Good men described. *Boston, printed and sold by Benjamin Harris,* 1692. 8°. EVANS 623. LW; MH, MHS, V.

1134   —Ornaments for the daughters of Zion. *Cambridge [Mass.]: by S. G. & B. G. for Samuel Phillips at Boston,* 1691[2]. 12°. MB, MHS.

1135   ——[Anr. ed.] —, 1692. 12°. EVANS 624. MBA, MH, MWA, NN, RPJ, V.

1136   ——[Anr. ed.] *For Tho. Parkhurst,* 1694. 12°. T.C.II 521. L, O; MB, MH, MHS, MU, V, WF.

1137   [–] A pastoral letter to the English captives. *Boston, by B. Green, and J. Allen,* 1698. 8°.* EVANS 830. CH, MH.

1138   [–] Pietas in patriam: the life . . . Sir William Phips. *By Sam. Bridge, for Nath. Hiller,* 1697. 12°. L, LG; CH, CN, LC, MH, NN, RPJ, Y.

1139   —A pillar of gratitude. *Boston, by B. Green, & J. Allen,* 1700. 12°.* EVANS 930. MH, MHS, MWA.

1140 —Pillars of salt. *Boston in New-England, by B. Green, and J. Allen, for Samuel Phillips,* 1699. 8°. EVANS 877. CH, MB, MH, MWA, Y.

1141 —Piscator evangelicus. *[Boston], printed [for Michael Perry],* 1695. 8°.* EVANS 727. CH, CN, LC, MB, NU, V, Y.

1142 —A poem dedicated to the memory of ... Urian Oakes. *Boston in New-England, for John Ratcliff,* 1682. 4°.* EVANS 319. CH, MH, RBU.

1142A —[Present] from a farr countrey. *Boston, by B. Green and J. Allen for Michael Perry,* 1698. 8°. MWA, RPJ.

1143 —The present state of New-England. *Boston, by Samuel Green,* 1690. 8°. EVANS 537. CH, LC, MH, MHS, MWA, NN, RPJ, V, Y.

[–] Principles of the Protestant religion. Boston, 1690. *See* Allen, James.

1144 —Reasonable religion. *Boston in N. E., by T. Green, for Benjamin Eliot,* 1700. 12°. EVANS 931. MB, MHS, MWA, V.

1145 [–] The religious marriner. *Boston in New-England, by B. Green, and J. Allen, for Samuel Phillips,* 1700. 8°.* EVANS 932. O; MHS.

1146 [–] The resolved Christian. *[n.p.], to be sold by Nicholas Boone, in Boston,* 1700. 8°. EVANS 933. RPJ.

1147 [–] Right thoughts in sad hours. *By James Astwood,* 1689. 8°. O; LC, MB, MBA, NU, V.

1148 —A scriptural catechism. *Boston, by R. Pierce, for Nicholas Buttolph,* 1691. 8°.* EVANS 565. MBA, MH, MHS, MWA, V.

1149 [–] The serious Christian. *By Benj. Harris,* 1699. 12°. MB, V.

1150 —The serviceable man. *Boston, by Samuel Green, for Joseph Browning,* 1690. 8°. EVANS 538. MH, MHS, MWA, NPT, RPJ, Y.

1151 —Seven select lectures. *For Nath. Hiller,* 1695. 8°. MH, RPJ.

1152 —The short history of New-England. *Boston, by B. Green, for Samuel Phillips,* 1694. 4°. EVANS 700. MWA, RPJ.

1153 [–] Small offers towards the service of the tabernacle. *[n.p.], by R. Pierce. Sold by Jos. Brunning in Boston,* 1689. 8°. EVANS 487. L; CH, LC, MH, MWA, NN, V.

1154 —Souldiers counselled and comforted. *Boston, by Samuel Green.* 1689. 8°.* EVANS 488. CN, LC, MH, MWA, RPJ, Y.

1155 [–] Some considerations on the bills of credit. *Boston: by Benjamin Harris and John Allen,* 1691. 8°.* EVANS 566. O; CHW, MBA.

1156 —Speedy repentance urged. *Boston, by Samuel Green, and sold by Joseph Browning, and Benj. Harris,* 1690. 8°. EVANS 539. LC, MB, MH, MWA, RPJ, Y.

1157 —[Terribilia Dei. Remarkable judgments of God.] *[Boston: by B. Green and J. Allen,* 1697.] 8°. EVANS 795. MH.

1158 —Things for a distress'd people to think upon. *Boston in N. E., by B. Green and J. Allen, for Duncan Campbel,* 1696. 8°. EVANS 755. MB, MH, MWA, RPJ, Y.

1158A —Things that young people should think upon. *Boston in N. E., by B. Green & J. Allen,* 1700. 8°.* EVANS 934. MWA.

1159 —Things to be look'd for. *Cambridge [Mass.]: by Samuel Green, & Barth. Green, for Nicholas Buttolph, in Boston,* 1691. 8°. EVANS 567. CH, MH, RPJ, V.

1160 [–] Thirty important cases. *Boston, by Bartholomew Green, & John Allen,* 1699. 8°. EVANS 878. LC, MB, MH, MHS, MWA, NN, RPJ, V.

1161 —The thoughts of a dying man. *Boston, in N. E., by B. Green & J. Allen for J. Wheeler,* 1697. 12°.* EVANS 796. MH, MWA, NN.

1161A [–] To his excellency, Richard, Earl of Bellomont ... The address. *Boston, by Bartholomew Green and John Allen,* 1699. brs. EVANS 872. MHS.

1162 [–] A token, for the children of New-England. *Boston, in N. E., by Timothy Green, for Benjamin Eliot,* 1700. 12°.* MWA, NN, RPJ, WF, Y.

1163 —The triumphs of the reformed religion, in America. *Boston, by Benjamin Harris, and John Allen, for Joseph Brunning,* 1691. 8°. EVANS 568. L, LG; CH, LC, MH, MU, NN, RPJ, SE, V, Y.

1164 —Unum necessarium. *Boston, by B. H. for Duncan Campbell,* 1693. 8°. EVANS 654. MWA, NN, V, Y.

1165 —A warning to the flocks. *Boston, printed [by B. Green and J. Allen],* 1700. 8°. EVANS 935. INU, MB, MH, MWA, RPJ, V.

1166 —Warnings from the dead. *Boston in New-England: by Bartholomew Green, for Samuel Phillips,* 1693. 12°. EVANS 655. MHS, MWA, V.

1167 —The way to excel. *Boston, in N.E., by B. Green. and J. Allen,* 1697. 8°.* EVANS 797. MHS.

1168 —The way to prosperity. *Boston, by Richard Pierce, for Benjamin Harris,* 1690. 8°. EVANS 540. MB, MH, MHS, RPJ, Y.

1169 ——[Anr. ed.] *Boston, by R. Pierce for Joseph Brunning, Obadiah Gill, and James Woode,* 1690. 8°. EVANS 541. LC, MH, MHS, MWA, NN, V.

1170 —Winter meditations. *Boston, printed and sold by Benj. Harris,* 1693. 8°. EVANS 656. CH, MB, MBA, MWA, NN, SE, V, Y.

1171 —The wonderful works of God. *Printed at Boston by S. Green, & sold by Joseph Browning, and Benj. Harris,* 1690. EVANS 540. CH, LC, MB, MH, MWA, NN, V, Y.

1172 —The wonders of the invisible world. *Boston, by Benj. Harris for Sam. Phillips,* 1693. 8°. EVANS 657. L, O, A; CH, MB, MHS, NN, SE, V.

1173 ——[Anr. ed.] *Boston, printed, and sold by Benjamin Harris,* 1693. 8°. O, A; MH, MWA, RPJ.

1174 ——[Anr. ed.] *Printed first at Bostun [sic] in New-England; and reprinted at London, for John Dunton,* 1693. 4°. L, MR, A, GU; CH, LC, MH, MU, NN, V, Y. (var.)

1175 ——Second edition. *Printed first, at Boston, —,* 1693. 4°. O, C, LW, OC; CN, MB, MH, NN, WCL, Y.

1176 ——Third edition. —, 1693. 4°. L, O, C, BAMB, EN; CH, MH, NN, SYRACUSE, V.

1177 —Work upon the ark. *Boston, by Samuel Green and sold by Joseph Brunning,* 1689. 16°. EVANS 489. MWA, RPJ, V, Y.

1178 —Wussukwhonk en Christianeue. *Mushauwomuk, nashpe Bartholomew Green, kah John Allen,* 1700. 8°.* EVANS 936. CH, CHW, MH, NHS, NN.

1179 **Mather, Eleazar.** A serious exhortation. *Cambridge [Mass.]: by S. G. and M. J.,* 1671. 4°.* HOLMES MMIOA; EVANS 162. L, O; CH, LC, MB, NN, RPJ, V.

1180 ——Second edition. *Boston, by John Foster,* 1678, 4°.* HOLMES MMIOB; EVANS 254. LC, MB, MH, MWA, NN, V.

1181 **Mather, Increase.** Angelographia, or a discourse. *Boston in N. E., by B. Green & J. Allen, for Samuel Phillips,* 1696. 8°. EVANS 756. L, LCL, LW; CH, LC, MH, MWA, RPJ, Y.

1182 [–] The answer of several ministers. *Boston in N. E., printed and sold by Bartholomew Green,* 1695. 12°.* EVANS 729. LW; LC, MB, MH, MWA, NN, V.

1183 [–] An arrow against profane and promiscuous dancing. *Boston, by Samuel Green, and are to be sold by Joseph Brunning,* 1684 [*i.e.* 1685]. 12°.* EVANS 370. MB, MCL, MHS, NN, V.

1184 [–] A brief account concerning several of the agents of New-England. *Printed,* 1691. 4°.* O; CH, MBA, MH, MHS, RPJ, V.

1185 [–] A brief discourse concerning the unlawfulness of the common prayer worship. *[Cambridge, Mass.], printed, [Samuel Green,* 1686]. 8°.* EVANS 490. O; CH, MB, MHS, MWA.

1186 [–] ——Second edition. *Reprinted at London,* 1689. 8°.* O; MB, MWA.

1187 —A brief history of the vvarr with the Indians. *Boston, printed and sold by John Foster,* 1676. EVANS 220. GU; CH, LC, MH, MWA, NN, PHS, V.

1188 ——[Anr. ed.] *London, for Richard Chiswell, . . . according to the original copy printed in New-England,* 1676. 4°. T.C.I 266. L, O, CQ, EN, DT; CH, CN, LC, MH, MU, MWA, RPJ, V, Y.

1189 [–] A brief relation of the state of New England. *For Richard Baldwine,* 1689. 4°.* L, O, OC, GH, GU; CH, CN, LC, MH, NN, V.

1190 —A call from Heaven. *Boston, by John Foster,* 1679. 8°. EVANS 274. O; MB, MH, NN, RPJ, V, Y.

1190A ——[Anr. ed.] —, *sold by John Ratcliff,* 1679. 8°. CH, MHS, MWA, V.

1191 ——Second edition. *Boston, by R. P. for I. Brunning,* 1685. 8°. EVANS 393. CH, CSL, MB, MH, MWA, RPJ, V.

1192 [–] A case of conscience concerning eating of blood. colop: *Boston in New-England, by B. Green, and J. Allen,* 1697. cap., 12°.* EVANS 798. NN.

1193 —Cases of conscience concerning evil spirits. *Boston printed, and sold by Benjamin Harris,* 1693. 8°. EVANS 658. L, O, EN; CH, MB, MH, MU, MWA, NN, RPJ, V.

1194 No entry.
——[Anr. ed.] 1693. *See* Further account of the tryals.

1195 —David serving his generation. *Boston, by B. Green, & J. Allen,* 1698. 8°.* EVANS 831. LW; CH, LC, MH, MHS, MWA, NN, RPJ, V, Y.

1196 —The day of trouble is near. *Cambridge [Mass.]: by Marmaduke Johnson,* 1674. 4°.* EVANS 192. CH, LC, MB, NS, RPJ, V.

1196A —De successu evangelij. *[Boston,* 1687.] 16°.* MHS.

1197 —[Anr. ed.] *Typis J. G.,* 1688. 8°.* L, O, C, LLP; CH, CN, LC, MH, MWA, RPJ. (var.)

1198–9A Entries cancelled.
—Declaration, of the gentlemen. Boston, 1689. *See* Mather, Cotton.
—Discourse concerning the danger. Boston, 1679. *See* — Call from Heaven.

1200 —A discourse concerning the subject of baptisme. *Cambridge [Mass.], by Samuel Green.* 1675. 4°. EVANS 207. L, O, GH, GU; CH, LC, MH, MHS, MU, NU, V, Y.

1201 —A discourse concerning the uncertainty of the times of men. *Boston in New England, by B. Green and J. Allen, for Samuel Phillips,* 1697. 12°.* EVANS 799. MH, NN.

1202 Entry cancelled.
—Disquisition. Boston, 1696. *See* —Angelographia.

1203 —The divine right of infant-baptisme asserted. *Boston, by John Foster,* 1680. 4°.* EVANS 292. L, BC; CH, LC, MH, MWA, RPJ, V.

1204 —The doctrine of divine providence. *Boston in New-England [sic] by Richard Pierce for Joseph Brunning,* 1684. 8°. EVANS 371. O; CH, LC, MH, MU, MWA, RPJ, Y.

1205 —An earnest exhortation. *Boston, by John Foster,* 1676. 12°.* EVANS 221. CH, MH, MHS, MWA, RPJ, V.

1206 —An / essay / for the recording of / illustrious / providences. *Boston in New-England, by Samuel Green for Joseph Browning,* 1684. 8°. L, LF, CS, GU; CH, LC, MB, MH, Y.

1207 ——[Anr. ed., "An essay/."] *Boston in New-England, by Samuel Green for Joseph Browning, . . . Town-House,* 1684. EVANS 372. O; CH, MHS, MWA, NN, RPJ.

1208 ——[Anr. ed.] *Printed at Boston, to be sold by George Calvert, London,* 1684. 8°. EVANS 373. L, O; CN, LC, MH, MU, MWA, V, Y.

1209 ——[Anr. ed.] *Printed at Boston, to be sold by Tho. Parkhurst [London],* 1687. 8°. CH, CLC, V.

1210 Entry cancelled.
[–] Faithful advice. [n.p., 1699.] *See* Mather, Cotton. Warning to the flocks.

1211 —The first principles of New-England. *Cambridge [Mass.], by Samuel Green,* 1675, 4°, EVANS 208. L, O; CH, LC, MH, MWA, NN, V, Y.

1212 —The folly of sinning. *Boston, by B. Green, & J. Allen, for Michael Perry, and Nicholas Buttolph,* 1699. 12°. EVANS 879. LC, MB, MCL, MH, MWA.

1213 Entry cancelled.
[–] Further account of the tryals. 1693. *See* title.

1214 [–] A further vindication of New-England. *[London,* 1689.] brs. V.

1215 —The great blessing. *Boston, printed and sold, by Benjamin Harris,* 1693. fol.* EVANS 659. LW; LC, MH, MWA, NU, RPJ, V, Y.

1216 —The greatest sinners exhorted. *Boston in N. E. by R. P. for Joseph Brunning,* 1686. 8°. EVANS 415. LC, MCL, MWA, NC, Y.

1217 —Heavens alarm to the world. *Boston; by John Foster,*
1681. 8°.* EVANS 306. CH, MH, MHS, MWA, NN, Y.

1218 ——Second edition. *Boston in New-England, for Samuel*
Sewall. And are to be sold by Joseph Browning, 1682. 8°.
EVANS 320. CN, LC, MH, MHS, MWA, NN, V, Y.

1219 ——"Second" edition. *Boston in New-England, for*
Samuel Sewall. And are to be sold by John [sic] Browning,
1682. 8°. MH, PL, V, WCL, Y.

1220 —An historical discourse concerning the prevalency of
prayer. *Boston, printed and sold by John Foster, 1677.*
EVANS 238. 8°.* L, O, GU; CH, LC, MH, MU, NN, RPJ, V.

1221 Entry cancelled. See previous entry.

1222 Entry cancelled.
—Honoratissimo Simoni Bradstreeto. *Bostonæ, 1682.*
See Harvard College.

1223 —The judgment of several eminent divines. *Boston, by*
Benjamin Harris, and are to be sold by Richard Wilkins,
1693. 8°.* EVANS 660. O; MB, MHS, MWA, Y.

1224 —Κομητογραφια. Or a discourse. *Boston in New-*
England, by S. G. for S. S. And sold by J. Browning,
1683. 8°. EVANS 352. L; CH, CN, LC, MH, MU, MWA,
NN, V, Y.

1225 Entry cancelled.
—Letter concerning the success. *1689. See* —Brief
relation.
[–] Letter of advice to the churches. *1700. See* Mather,
Cotton.

1226 —The life and death of that reverend man of God, Mr.
Richard Mather. *Cambridge [Mass.]: by S. G. and*
M. J. 1670. 4°.* EVANS 150. L, GH, GU; CH, MH, MU,
MWA, NN, PHS, RPJ, V.

1227 —Masukkenukeeg matcheseaenvog. *Bostonut, nashpe*
Bartholomew Green, kah John. Allen, 1698. 8°. EVANS
832. CH, MB, MWA, NN, Y.

1228 —The mystery of Christ opened. *Printed at Boston in*
New-England, 1686. 8°. EVANS 416. L, O, EN; CH, LC,
MH, MU, NN, V, Y.

1229 ——[Anr. ed.] *[Boston], printed, 1686.* 8°. L, LCL; MB,
MWA, NU, RPJ, TSM.

1230 —The mystery of Israel's salvation. *For John Allen,*
1669. 8°. EVANS 143. L, LW, E; CH, CN, MB, V, Y.

1230A ——[Anr. ed.] *[London], printed in the year 1669.* 8°.
EVANS 143. O, LCL, E; CH, LC, MH, MWA, V, Y.

1231 [–] A narrative of the miseries. *[London, for Richard*
Baldwin? 1688]. cap., 4°.* GH; CH, MH, MHS, RPJ, V,
WCL.

1231A [–] ——[Anr. ed.] *London, for Richard Janeway. And reprinted*
at Boston in New-England, by Richard Pierce. 1688. cap.,
4°.* MB.

1232 [–] The necessity of reformation. *Boston; by John Foster,*
1679. 4°.* EVANS 263. O; LC, MH, MWA, NN, RPJ, V.

1233 [–] New England vindicated. *[London, 1689.]* cap., 4°.*
L; LC, MHS, MWA, RPJ, V.

1234 —The order of the Gospel. *Boston, by B. Green, & J.*
Allen for Nicholas Buttolph, 1700. 12°. EVANS 939.
LCL; CH, MB, MH, MWA, NPT, V, Y. (var.)

1235 ——[Anr. ed.] *Boston, by B. Green, & J. Allen, for*
Benjamin Eliot, 1700. 12°. EVANS 938. O; LC, MH, MWA,
NN, RPJ, V, Y.

1236 ——[Anr. ed.] *Printed at Boston in New-England, and*
reprinted at London, and sold by A. Baldwin, 1700. 8°.
L, O, LSC, ENC, GU; LC, MH, MU, NN, RPJ, V, Y.

1237 —Practical truths tending. *Boston in New-England, by*
Samuel Green upon Assign/ment of Samuel Sewall, 1682.
12°. EVANS 322. CH, LC, MH, MWA, NN, RPJ, V.

1238 —Pray for the rising generation. *Cambridge [Mass.]: by*
Samuel Green, and sold by Edmund Ranger in Boston,
1678. 4°.* EVANS 255. O; CH, CN, MB, MWA, RPJ, V, Y.

1239 ——Second edition. *Boston, by John Foster, 1679.* 8°.*
EVANS 275. O; CH, MB, MH, MHS, MWA, RPJ, Y.

1240 —The present state of the New-English affairs. colop:
Boston, printed and sold by Samuel Green, 1689. brs.
EVANS 492. MBS, MWA.

1241 [–] Reasons for the confirmation of the charter. *[London,*
1690/1.] cap., 4°.* MBA, MHS.

1242 [–] ——[Anr. ed., "charters."] *[London, 1690/1.]* cap., 4°.*
MHS.

1243 —A relation of the troubles. *Boston; printed and sold by*
John Foster. 1677. 4°. EVANS 238. L, O, GH, GU; CH, CN,
LC, MH, NN, RPJ, V, Y. (var.)

1244 —Renewal of covenant. *Boston; by J. F. for Henry*
Phillips, 1677. 4°.* EVANS 239. CH, MH, MWA, NU, V.

1245 —Returning unto God. *By John Foster, 1680.* 4°.*
EVANS 293. L; CH, LC, MB, MWA, RPJ, SE, V, Y.

1246 —A sermon occasioned by the execution of a man.
Boston, for John Dunton, 1686. 8°.* NHS.

1247 ——[Anr. ed.] *Boston, for Joseph Brunning, 1686.* 8°.*
EVANS 417. MH, MWA, RPJ, Y.

1248 ——Second edition. *Boston, by R. P. Sold by J. Brunning,*
1687. 8°. EVANS 432. L; MB, MH, MWA, NN, RPJ, Y.

1249 Entry cancelled.
——[Anr. ed.] *1691. See* Wonders of free-grace. *1690.*

1250 —A sermon (preached . . . the 18th of the 1. moneth
1674). Second edition. *[Boston], by R. P. for J. Brunning*
in Boston, 1685. 8°.* EVANS 394. INU, LC, MB, MH, MHS,
MWA, RPJ, V.

1251 —A sermon wherein is shewed. *Boston in New-England:*
for Samuel Sewall, 1682. 4°.* EVANS 324. O, LW; CH,
LC, MH, RPJ, V, Y.

1252 —Solemn advice to young men. *Boston in New-England,*
by Bartholomew Green. Sold by Samuel Phillips, 1695.
8°. EVANS 728. MB, MH, MWA, RPJ.

1253 —Some important truths. *For Richard Chiswell, 1674.*
8°. T.C.I 168. O, E, ENC; CH, MB, MWA, NN, RPJ, V.

1254 ——Second edition. *Printed at Boston in New-England by*
Samuel Green for John Griffin, 1684. 8°. EVANS 374.
MHS.

1255 —The surest way to the greatest honour. *Boston, by*
Bartholomew Green, & John Allen, for Samuel Phillips,
1699. 8°. EVANS 880. LLP; MB, MHS, MWA, NHS, RPJ, V.

1256 —A testimony against several prophane . . . customs.
Printed, 1687. 8°.* O; CH, MB, MH, MWA, PL, RPJ.

1257 —The times of men are in the hand of God. *Boston, by John Foster, 1675.* 4°.* EVANS 209. CH, LC, MB, MHS, MWA, V.

1258 —Two plain and practical discourses. *London: for J. Robinson, to be sold by Samuel Phillips, in Boston, in New-England, 1699.* 12°. T.C.III 135. L, LW; CH, LC, MHS, MWA, V.

1259 Entry cancelled.
[–] Vindication of Nevv-England. [n.p., 1690.] *See title.*

1260 —The wicked mans portion. *Boston, by John Foster. 1675.* 4°.* EVANS 210. O; CH, INU, LC, MH, MWA, NN, RPJ, V.

1261 —Wo to drunkards. *Cambridge [Mass.]: by Marmaduke Johnson, 1673. And sold by Edmund Ranger in Boston.* 4°.* EVANS 179. LC, MB, MH, MWA, RPJ, SE, V.

1262 Entry cancelled.
[–] Wonders of free-grace. 1690. *See title.*
Mather, Nathaniel. Boston ephemeris. *Boston, 1685. See* Almanacs.

1263 —A discussion of the lawfulness. *For Nath. Hiller, 1698.* 12°. HOLMES MM22A. L, O, C, LCL, LW; CLC, LC, MB, MH, RPJ, NN, V.

1264 No entry.

1265 The righteousness of God. *For Nathanael Hiller, 1694.* 4°. HOLMES MM27A. L, O, C, LCL, GU; CH, CN, MH, NU, WF, Y.

1266 —A 'sermon wherein is shewed. *Printed at Boston in New-England by R. P. For Joseph Browning, 1684.* 8°.* EVANS 375; HOLMES MM29. O; CH, LC, MB, MH, MU, RPJ, V, Y.

1267 **[Mather, Richard.]** An apologie of the chvrches in New-England. *By T. P. and M. S. for Benjamin Allen, 1643.* 4°. HOLMES MM3. LT, O, NE, DT; CH, CN, MH, MU, NN, RPJ, V, Y.

1268 —A catechisme or, the grounds. *For Iohn Rothwell, 1650.* 8°. HOLMES MM36. O; MWA, PL.

1269 [–] Church-government and church-covenant discvssed. *By R. O. and G. D. for Benjamin Allen, 1643.* 4°. HOLMES MM38. LT, O, C, GH, DT; CH, MH, MU, NU, RPJ, V, Y.

1270 [–] —[Anr. ed.] *By R. O. and G. D. for Benjamin Allen, to be sold . . . , 1643.* 4°. HOLMES MM38. CH, CN, MH, MWA, RPJ, V, Y.

1271 [–] A defence of the answer and arguments of the synod. *Cambridge [Mass.]: by S. Green and M. Johnson for Hezekiah Usher of Boston. 1664.* 4°. HOLMES MM39; EVANS 89. L, EN, DM; CH, CN, MH, NN, RPJ, V, Y.

1271A [–] A disputation concerning church-members. *By J. Hayes, for Samuel Thomson, 1659.* 4°.* HOLMES MM40. LT, LW, OC; IU, MH, MWA, RPJ, V, Y.

1272 —A farewel exhortation. *By Samuel Green at Cambridg in New-England, 1657.* 4°.* HOLMES MM41; EVANS 47. CH, LC, MB, MH, MWA.

1273 —An heart-melting exhortation. *By A. M. for I. Rothwell, 1650.* 12°. HOLMES MM42. L, O; Y.

1274 —A modest & brotherly ansvver. *For Henry Overton, 1644.* 4°. HOLMES MM50. LT, O, CT, MR, DT; CH, CN, MH, MWA, NN, RPJ, V, WF, Y.

1275 —A reply to Mr Rutherfurd. *For J. Rothwell and H. Allen, 1647.* 4°. HOLMES MM54. LT, O, LCL, EN, DT; LC, MH, NN, V, WCL, Y.

1276 —The summe of certain sermons. *By Samuel Green at Cambridg in New-England, 1652.* 4°. HOLMES MM55; EVANS 35. CH, LC, MHS.

1277 **Mather, Samuel, *1651–1728*.** A dead faith anatomized. *Boston in New England, by Bartholomew Green, and John Allen, 1697.* 8°. HOLMES MM98A; EVANS 800. CHW, MB, MBC, MHS, MWA.

1278 **[Mather, Samuel], *1626–1671*.** A defence of the Protestant Christian religion against Popery. *[Dublin], printed, 1672.* 4°. DIX 148. L, EN, ENC, DT; MBA, WF.

1279 —The figures or types. *[Dublin], printed, 1683.* 4°. DIX 204. HOLMES MM90A. L, OM, CS, GU, DN; MBA, MH, MWA, NU, RPJ, TO, WF, AVP.

1280 — —[Anr. ed.] *Dublin, printed, 1685. Sold at London by H. Sawbridge, and A. Churchill.* 4°. HOLMES MM90B; DIX 211. O, DN; CH, MB, MH, MWA, PL, Y.

1281 — —[Anr. ed.] *For Nath. Hiller, 1695.* 4°. HOLMES MM90C. CII, CLC, NU.

1282 —Irenicum: or an essay for union. *By Thomas Snowden, 1680.* 4°.* HOLMES MM91. O, LCL, LW, CD, DT; CH, NU, PL, V.

1283 —A testimony from the scripture. *[Cambridge, Mass., S. G. and M. J., 1672?]* 4°. HOLMES MM94A; EVANS 151. CH, LC, MB, MBA, MH, MHS, NN.

1284 **Mather, William.** An answer to the switch for the snake. *[London], printed, 1700.* 4°. L, LF, LSC; PH.

1284A [–] A brief character of the antient Christian Quakers. *For S. Clarke, 1695.* 8°.* LF.

1284AB —Directions to parents. *For D. Brown, A. Roper and H. Newman, 1697.* 12°. M.

1284B —An instrument from that little stone. *For Sarah Howkins, 1694.* 4°.* LF.

1284C —A novelty: or, a government of women. *For Sarah Howkins, [1694?].* 4°.* LF; PH.

1285 —Of repairing and mending the highways. *For Samuel Clark, 1696.* 8°. L.

1285A [–] Of the Quakers despising the Holy Scriptures. *For B. Aylmer, and C.Brome, 1700.* brs. C, LF; CH, MH, PH.

1285B — —Third edition. —, *1700.* brs. OC.

1286 —A very useful manual. *By T. Snowden, 1681.* 12°. L; MH, NN.

1287 —The young man's companion. Second edition. *For Thomas Howkins, 1685.* 12°. T.C.II 105. L, LF, CS.

1287A — —Third edition. *By Tho. Howkins, 1692.* 12°. DT; NC.

1287B — —Fourth edition. *For Sarah Howkins, 1695.* 12°. CLC.

1287C — —[Anr. ed.] *By J. Mayos for S. Clarke, 1699.* 12°. LF, LUC.

Mathers, Patrick, *pseud*. *See* Gregory, James.

1287D **[Mathew, Francis.]** Of the opening of rivers. *By James Cottrell, 1655.* 4°.* L, DT.

1287E [–] —[Anr. ed.] *By G. Dawson*, 1656. 4°.* L, LUG, BR, EN;
CLC, WF, Y.

1287F [–] —[Anr. ed.] —, 1660. 4°.* L.

1287G [–] To his highness, Oliver, . . . a Mediterranean passage.
By Gartrude Dawson, 1656. 4°.* L, O, NPL, EN; CLC,
WF, Y.

1287H —To the Kings most excellent Majesty, . . . a Mediterranean passage. *By Thomas Newcomb*, 1670. 4°.* L, O,
LPR, LUG, BR; CH, IU, MU, WF, Y.

1288 **[Mathew, John.]** Certain material and useful considerations about the laws. *For R. Harford*, 1680. fol.*
T.C.I 373. L, O, LL; Y.

1288A [–] —[Anr. ed.] *Printed at London*, 1680. fol.* L, O, C, OC,
CS, DU; CH, CLC, MH, PU, TU, WF.

1288B **Mathew, N. A.** A catechism, being an enlargement. *By
J. D. for Jonathan Robinson*, 1677. 8°.* T.C.I 327. O, LLP.

1288C ——[Anr. ed.] —, 1679. 8°.* LLP.

1288D **Mat[hews], Ed[ward].** King Charles the II. His restitution. *Printed* 1660. 4°.* LT, O; CH, CN, WF, UCLA.

1289 **Mathews, Lemuel.** A pandarique [*sic*] elegie upon the
death of . . . Jeremy [Taylor]. *Dublin, by John Crook, to
be sold by Samuel Dancer*, 1667. 4°.* DIX 134. L, C.

1290 **Mathews, Richard.** The unlearned alchymist his antidote. *For Joseph Leigh, and are to be sold by Giles
Calvert, and Livewell Chapman*, 1660. 8°. O; CLC, MH, WU.

1290A ——[Anr. ed.] *For Joseph Leigh*, 1662. 12°. L, LW,
LWL; NAM, JF.

1290B ——[Anr. ed.] —, *and are there to be sold, and by Giles
Calvert*, 1662. 8°. L; CH, LC, MH, Y.

1291 ——[Anr. ed.] *For Joseph Leigh*, 1663. 8°. L, LWL, MAU,
E, GU; CRN, WF, WSG, WU, Y.

1292 **Mathuradasa.** The copy of a letter writ to . . . Edward
Littleton. [*London?* 1695.] brs. L, C; Y.

1292A **Matlock, John.** Fax nova artis scribendi, or an introduction. *By John Leake, for the author; and are to be
sold by Luke Meredith*, 1685. 4°. T.C.II 114. O; CH, CN.

1292B —Method and practice defended. *For the author, and
are to be sold by Thomas Sawbridge, and Luke Meredith*,
1685. 4°.* CH.

1293 **Maton, Robert.** Christs personall reigne on earth.
Printed, and are to be sold by John Hancock, 1652. 4°.
L, O, CS; CN, MH, NU, PT.

1294 —Israel's redemption. *For Daniel Frere*, 1642. 8°. LT, O,
LWL, OC, CM, P; NN, Y.

1295 —Israel's redemption redeemed. *By Matthew Simmons,
to be sold by George VVhittington*, 1646. 4°. LT, LCL, LSC,
LW, CM; NU.

1296 —A treatise of the fifth monarchy. *For John Hancock*,
1655. 8°. NU.

Matrimonial customs. 1687. *See* Gaya, Louis de.

Matrimonial honovr. 1642. *See* Rogers, Daniel.

1297 Matrimonii pensitatio: or, no joynture. *For the author,
and are to be sold by Norman Nelson*, 1679. 4°.* L, O,
LG, MR; CH, CN, MH, NP, TU, Y.

Matrona Ephesia. 1665. *See* Charleton, Walter.

1298 **Matteis, Nicola.** Ayrs for the violin. [*London*], 1685.
4°. L; CN, IU, NN.

1299 —Arie diverse per il violino. [*London*], 1688. 4°. L.

1300 —A collection of new songs. *Printed for and sold by
John Walsh, and likewise at Mr. Hare's shop*, 1696. fol.*
T.C.II 589. L, O, CK; NN, WF.

1301 — . . . Second book. *Printed for & sould by I: Walsh*,
[1699]. fol.* T.C.II 139. CH, NN, WF.

1301A —The false consonances of musick. [*London*, 1690.] NN
(film).

1302 —The second treble of the third and fourth parts.
[*London*], 1687. 4°. L.

1303 The matter of fact a la mode de France. [*London*],
printed, 1680. fol.* L, O, OC, LNC, MR; CH, MBA, MH,
WF, Y, ZWT. (var.)

1303A The matter of fact of Sir Richard Temple's case.
[*London?* 1690.] brs. CH.

1304 The matters of fact in the present election of sheriffs.
colop: *For J. Johnson*, 1682. cap., fol.* L, O, C, LG, MC,
DT; CH, CN, MBA, MH, PL, WF, Y. (var.)

1305 Matters of great consequence, and worthy of note.
Printed at London for F. Coules and Tho. Bankes, 1642.
4°.* LT, O, CT; HR, CH, CLC, MH, MIU, NCD, WF, Y.

1306 March 2. Matters of great note and consequence. *For
George Thompson*, 1641[2]. 4°.* LT, O, OC, BR, LNC; CH,
TU, WF, Y.

1306A Matters of great note and high consequence . . . Aprill,
19. [*London*], *for Iohn Wels*, 1642. 4°.* CJ; CLC, Y.

1307 Matters of high consequence concerning the great affairs
of the kingdome. *By T. P. and M. S. for W. Gaye*, 11.
of June. 1642. 4°.* MR; Y.

1308 Matters of note made known to all true Protestants.
For Fr. Coles, 1641[2]. 4°.* LT, O, C, LG, BC; CH, MIU,
MM, OWC, Y.

1309 **Matthew, Edward.** Καρολου τρισμεγιστου επιφανια.
The most glorious star. *For J. Stafford and Edw.
Thomas*, 1660. 12°. L, ES; CH, MH, WF.

1310 ——[Anr. ed.] *For the use and benefit of William Byron*,
1661. 12°. L, OW, CT; CH, CLC, LC.

1311 ——[Anr. ed.] —, 1662. 12°. O, LW; MIU, NR, PL, SE.

1312 ——[Anr. ed.] —, 1663. 12°. L.

1313 ——[Anr. ed.] —, 1664. 12°. L; IU, Y.

1314 ——[Anr. ed.] —, 1665. 12°. O.

1315–1318 Entries cancelled.

[Matthew, Francis.] *See* Mathew, Francis.

1319 **Matthew, Sir Tobie.** A collection of letters. *For
Henry Herringman*, 1660. 8°. LT, O, C, ES, DT; BN, CH,
CN, MH, NCD, WF, Y.

1320 Entry cancelled. *See next entry.*

1321 ——[Anr. ed.] *For Tho. Horne, Tho. Bennet, and Francis
Saunders*, 1692. 8°. O, C, CT, EC, ES; CH, MH.

1322 [–] A missive of consolation. *At Louain*, 1647. 8°. L, O,
C, BSM, DU; BN, CH, CN, MH, TU, WF, Y.

—The penitent bandito. 1663. *See* Biondo, Giuseppe.

1323 **Matthews, Mr.** A catalogue of the libraries of books
of. [*London*], 28 *January*, 1688/9. 4°.* O, LV, OC.

1324 **Matthews, Marmaduke.** The Messiah magnified. *By
A. M. for Simon Miller*, 1659. 8°. L; CH.

1325 —The rending church-member regularly call'd back. *By A. M. for Simon Miller*, 1659. 8°. O.

Matthews, Roger. Letter to General Monck. 1659. *See* Morris, Richard.

1326 **Mauclerc, Julien.** A new treatise of architecture. *By J. Darby, and are to be sold by Robert Pricke*, 1669. fol. T.C.I 19. L, C, DCH; CH, MBP, NC, TO, WF, Y.

1327 [**Maudit, John.**] Αντιπροβολη, or a defence. *By T. R. for the author*, 1660. 12°. L.

1328 —The Christian sovldiers great engine. *Oxford, by Leonard Lichfield*, 1649. 4°.* MADAN 2016. LT, O, CT, BC, DT; CLC, IU, NP, WF, Y.

1329 [–] A letter to His Excellency the Lord General Monk containing. [*London*, 1660.] cap., 4°.* LT, O, LCL, DU; MH, Y.

1330 [–] The practises of the Earl of Leycester. *By T. R. for the author*, 1660. 12°.* L.

1330A —A vvarning piece to afflicted England. *By D. Maxwell for Sa. Gellibrand*, 1659. 4°.* CSS, MH, WF.

1331 Maudlin, the merchants daughter of Bristol. [*London*], *by and for W. O.*, [1690?]. brs. EUING 209. L, GU.

1332 —[Anr. ed.] [1670?] brs. L, HH.

1333 —[Anr. ed.] [1675?] brs. L.

Mauduit. *See also* Maudit.

1333A **Mauduit, Isaac.** A sermon preach'd . . . May 13th, 1700. *For Eben. Tracy*, 1700. 8°. T.C.III 193. L, LW; MH.

1334 —Tri-unity. *By Hannah Clark, for John Dunton*, 1694. 4°. O, LW; NU.

1335 **Mauger, Claude.** French and English letters. Second edition. *By Tho. Roycroft, to be sold by Samuel Lawndes* [sic], 1676. 8°. T.C.I 222. L, O, LLU; BN, CH, CLC, CSU, IU, WF.

1336 —Mr. Mauger's French grammar enriched. Second edition. *By R. D. for Iohn Martin, and Iames Allestree*, 1656. 8°. LT, O, CE; CLC.

1337 — —Third edition. *For John Martin, James Allestree, and Thomas Dicas*, 1658. 8°. OB, CM; BN, IU.

1337A — —Fourth edition. —, 1662. 8°. LLP, CCA, NOT, DL; IU.

1338 — —Fifth edition. *For John Martyn, James Allestry, and Thomas Dicas*, 1667. 8°. LLU, SA; BN, MBC.

1339 — —Sixth edition. *By T. R. for John Martyn, and James Allestry*, 1670. 8°. T.C.I 52. O, CT.

1340 — —Seventh edition. *By T. R. for John Martyn*, 1673. 8°. T.C.I 166. L, O, E; CLC, TU.

1340aA — —Eighth edition. *By T. Roycroft for John Martyn*, 1676. 8°. T.C.I 241. L.

1340bA — —Ninth edition. *By S. Roycroft for John Martyn*, 1679. 8°. L, O.

1340cA — —"Ninth" edition. 1681. BN.

1340dA — —Tenth edition. *By R. E. for R. Bentley and M. Magnes*, 1684. 8°. CLC, IU.

1340eA — —Eleventh edition. *By R. E. for R. Bentley and S. Magnes*, 1684. 8°. CLC, IU.

1340fA — —"Eleventh" edition. *For R. B. and are to be sold by Tho. Harrison*, 1684. 8°. DC; BN, Y.

1340gA — —Twelfth edition. *By R. E. for R. Bentley & S. Magnes*, 1686. 8°. L, O.

1340hA — —Thirteenth edition. —, 1688. 8°. L; CH, IU.

1340iA — —"Thirteenth" edition. —, *to be sold by Tho. Guy*, 1688. 8°. T.C.II 221. NE; TO, Y.

1340jA — —Fourteenth edition. *By R. E. for R. Bentley and S. Magnes*, 1689. 8°. O; TU.

1340A — —Fifteenth edition. *By R. E. for R. Bentley, to be sold by Tho. Guy*, 1693. 8°. CH, NP.

1340B — —"Fifteenth" edition. *By R. E. for R. Bentley and S. Magnes*, 1693. 8°. IU.

1340C — —"Fifteenth" edition. —, 1694. 8°. EN.

1341 — —Sixteenth edition. *By R. E. for R. Bentley*, 1694. 8°. L; PBM.

1341A — —"Sixteenth" edition. 1696. LSC.

1341B — —Eighteenth edition. *By R. E. for K. Bentley*, 1698. 8°. T.C.III 99. CS; WF.

1342 —Grammaire Angloise. *Chez John Edwark*, 1699. 8°. C; BN.

1343–6 Entries cancelled.

—Grammaire Francoise. *See*—French grammar.

1347 —Mauger's letters written upon several subjects. *By Tho. Roycroft*, 1671. 8°. L, O; BN, CH, U. OREGON, WF.

1348 Entry cancelled.

—Lettres Francoises. 1676. *See*—French and English letters.

1349 —Nouvelle double grammaire . . . New double grammar. *A La Haye, chez Adrian Moetjens*, 1693. 12°. O; MH.

1350 — —[Anr. ed.] —, 1696. 12°. C; BN, NC.

1351 —Oliva pacis in . . . pacem. [1660?] brs. L.

1351A —Le tableau du jugement universel. *Par T. D. & se vendent chez Mathieu Turner*, 1675. 8°. LCP.

1352 —The true advancement of the French tongue. *By Tho: Roycroft, for J. Martin, and J. Allestrye*, 1653. 8°. LT; PMA.

1353 [**Maule, Thomas.**] Nevv-England pe[r]secutors mauld. [*New York, William Bradford*, 1697.] 4°. EVANS 801. LF; CH, MH, MHS, NN, PH, PSC, RPJ, SE. (var.)

1354 —Truth held forth. [*New York*], *printed* [*by William Bradford*], 1695. 4°. EVANS 730. LF; MH, RPJ, SE, V.

1355 **Maulyverer, John.** Suppositis particularis striatis. [*n.p.*, 1671.] brs. O.

1356 **Maundrell, Henry.** A sermon preach'd . . . Dec. 15. 1695. *For Daniel Brown*, 1696. 4°.* T.C.II 567. L, O, C, OM, LSD; CLC, CN, NGT, NU, WF, Y.

1357 **Maurice,** *prince.* Articles of agreement betweene his excellency Prince Maurice, and the Earle of Stamford. *For Tho. Walkley*, 1643. 4°.* LT, O, LSD, DT; CH, CN, MH, MU, WF, Y.

1357A **Maurice, David.** The bruised reed. *Oxford, printed at the Theater*, 1700. 4°.* L, O, CPL.

1358 **Maurice, Henry,** *1650?–1699.* An impartial account of Mr. John Mason. *By Tho. Warren, for Walter Kettilby*, 1695. 4°. T.C.II 539. L, O, C, BAMB, LSD; CH, MH, MIU, NU, WF, Y.

1359 **Maurice, Henry,** *1648–1691.* The Antithelemite. *For Sam. Smith*, 1685. 4°. T.C.II 135. L, O, C, DU, EN; CH, CN, MH, RPJ, WF, Y.

1360 —A defence of diocesan Episcopacy. *By Hannah Clark, for James Adamson*, 1691. 8°. T.C.II 355. L, O, C, ENC, DT; CH, CLC, NU, PBL, WF, Y.

1361 ——Second edition. *For H. Bonwick, T. Newborough, and R. Wilkin*, 1700. 8°. T.C.III 201. L, O, C, DU, D, CD; CLC, CN, NU, PBL, Y.

1362 [–] Doubts concerning the Roman infallibility. *For James Adamson*, 1688. 4°.* L, O, C, EN, DT; CLC, MH, MIU, NU, TU, WF, Y.

1362A [–] Falshood detected. *For Awnsham Churchill*, 1690. 4°.* T.C.II 314. L, O, LLP, CS, CT; CH, MBA, MIU, NU, WF, Y.

1363 Entry cancelled.
——Impartial account. 1695. *See* Maurice, Henry, 1650?–1699.

1364 [–] The lawfulness of taking the new oaths. *For J. Mills, to be sold by Randal Taylor*, 1689. 4°.* L, O, C, AU, DT; CH, LC, MH, MU, NCD, NU, WF, Y.

1365 [–] A letter out of the country, to a member. *For Awnsham Churchill*, 1689. 4°.* T.C.II 292. L, O, CT, DU, AU, DT; CH, CN, MH, NU, TU, WF, Y.

1366 [–] A letter to a member of the House of Commons, concerning the bishops. *Printed*, 1689. 4°.* L, O, CT, E, DT; CH, CLC, CN, MH, TU, WF, Y. (var.)

1367 —Preparatio evangelica; a plain and practical discourse. 1698. 8°. LCL.

1368 [–] The project for repealing the penal laws. [*London*, 1688.] cap., 4°.* L, OC, CCA, WCA, EN; CH, CN, LC, NU, TU, WF, Y.

1369 [–] Remarks from the country. *Printed*, 1689/90. 4°.* L, O, CT, E, DT; CH, CLC, CN, MH, NU, TU, WF, Y. (var.)

1370 —A sermon preached . . . January the 30th, 1681. *By Samuel Roycroft, for Robert Clavell*, 1682. 4°.* T.C.I 482. L, O, C, LSD, DT; CH, NU, PU, TU, WF, Y.

1371 [–] A vindication of the primitive church. *For Moses Pitt*, 1682. 8°. T.C.I 457. L, O, C, E, DT; BN, CH, CN, NU, WF, Y.

1371A **Mauriceau, Francois.** The accomplisht midwife. *By John Darby to be sold by Benjamin Billingsley*, 1673. 8°. L, LWL; MBM, NAM, TO.

1371B —The diseases of women with child. *By John Darby; to be sold by R. Clavel, and W. Cooper; by Benj. Billingsly, and W. Cadman*, 1672. 8°. T.C.I 103. GU; MBM.

1372 ——Second edition. *By John Darby*, 1683. 8°. T.C.II 56. L, C, LCS, LWL; TO, U. WASHINGTON, WF.

1372A ——"Second" edition. *By J. D. to be sold by Andrew Bell*, 1696. 8°. CPA; KU, MBM.

1373 ——Third edition. *For A. Bell*, 1697. 8°. T.C.III 32. L, LCS, LWL, OR; MBM, MU, WSG, HC.

Maurier, Louis Aubery de. *See* Aubery de Maurier, Louis.

1373A **Maxey, Anthony.** Certain sermons. Seventh edition. *By T. H. and T. K., part of the impression for Edward Minshew*, 1656. CS, DU.

1373B [**Maximianus Etrusius.**] The impotent lover. *For B. Crayle*, 1689. 8°. DT; LC, MH, WF.

1374 The maximes of mix[t] monarchy. [*London*, 1643.] cap., 4°.* LT, CT, LNC, MR; CSS, MH, NP, NU, WF, Y.
Maximes of reason, 1658. *See* Wingate, Edmund.

1375 Maximes unfolded. [*London*, 1643.] 4°.* LT, O, CT, BP, AU; CH, CN, MH, PL, TU, WF, Y.

1376 **Maximus Tyrius.** Τοῦ Μαξιμου Τυριου λογοι. Maximi Tyrii dissertationes. *Oxoniæ, e theatro Sheldoniano*, 1677. 12°. MADAN 3146. L, O, C, AN, DT; BN, CH, CN, LC, MH, WF, Y.

1376A **Maxsey, Andrew.** A copy of verses. [*London*], *by H. Brugis for Andrew Maxsey*, 1680. brs. O.

1377 [**Maxwell, John**], *abp.* An answer by letter to a worthy gentleman. [*Oxford, by L. Lichfield*], *printed*, 1644. 4°. MADAN 1684. LT, O, CT, E, DT; CH, CU, MH, NU, WF, Y.

1378 Entry cancelled. *See preceding entry.*

1379 [–] The burthen of Issachar. [*London*], *printed*, 1646. 4°. LT, O, CT, DU, EN; CH, CN, MH, NCD, NU, WF, Y.

1379A [–] —[Anr. ed., "bvrden."] —, 1646. 4°. L, O, CT, BC, DT; CLC, CN, NU, WF, Y.

1380 [–] Episcopacie not abivred. [*Dublin*], *printed*, 1641. 4°. O, CT, DU, P, EN, DT; CH, CN, Y.

1381 [–] Presbytery display'd. *For Henry Brome*, 1663. 4°. L, O, C, DU, EN; CH, MBP, MH, MIU, NCD, NU, PL, WF, Y.

1382 [–] —Second edition. —, 1668. 4°. L, C, MR, EN, DT; CH.

1383 [–] —Fourth edition. —, 1681. 4°. L, O, OC, CS, MR; CLC, WF.

1384 [–] Sacro-sancta regum majestas: or, the sacred and royall prerogative. *Printed at Oxford* [*by H. Hall*], 1644. 4°. MADAN 1523. LT, O, C, EN, DT; CH, CN, MH, NU, WF, Y.

1385 [–] —[Anr. ed.] *For Tho. Dring*, 1680. 8°. L, CS, MC, SP, E; CLC.

1386 [–] —Second edition. *For T. Dring*, 1686. 8°. T.C.II 161. L, DT; CU, NS, TU.

1387 **Maxwell, Robert**, *bp.* In obitum Richardi Pepys. *Dublinii*, 1658. brs. L.

[**Maxwell, William.**] Medicina magnetica. [n.p.], 1656. *See* Irvine, Christopher.

1388 **May, Edward.** A most certaine and true relation . . . monster. 1685. 8°. LCP.

1388A **May, George.** The vvhite-powder plot discovered *Sold by Francis Grove and Francis Mawborn in York*, 1662. 4°.* L.

1389 **May, Henry.** XXX. Christian and politick reasons. *By M. S. and R. I.*, 1652. 4°.* LT.

1390 **May, Joseph.** Epaphras. A sermon. *By T. H. for Humphrey Robinson*, 1641. 4°.* L, O.

1391 **May, Robert.** The accomplisht cook. *By R. W. for Nath. Brooke*, 1660. 8°. LT; CB, LC.

1392 ——Second edition. *By R. Wood, for Nath. Brooke*, 1665. 8°. O, LLU; LC.

1393 ——Third edition. *By J. Winter, for Nath. Brooke*, 1671. 8°. T.C.I 68. L, LLU; LC, NN.

1393AA ——"Third" edition. —, *sold by Tho. Archer*, 1671. 8°. L.

1393A ——Fourth edition. *For Robert Hartford*, 1678. 8°. L, LLU; MH.

1393B ——"Fourth" edition. *For Obadiah Blagrave*, 1678. T.C.I 306. LWL; CH, LC.

1394 ——Fifth edition. *For Obadiah Blagrave*, 1685. 8°. T.C.II 119. L, O, C, LCP, LLU; LC, MBA, NN, WF, Y.

1395 **M[ay], T[homas].** A breviary of the history of the Parliament. *By Rob. White, for Thomas Brewster and Gregory Moule,* 1650. 8°. LT, O, CT, DT; CH, CN, MH, NU, WF.

1396 ——Second edition. *By J. Cottrel, for Thomas Brewster,* 1655. 8°. L, O, LL, LMT, GU; IU, LC, MH, TO.

1397 ——[Anr. ed.] *For Anne Brewster,* 1680. 8°. L, O, C, OC, DU, RU; CH, CN, LC, MH, NU, PL, TU, WF.

1398 ——[Anr. ed.] —, 1689. 8°. T.C.II 287. O; CU, IU, NC, Y.

1399 [–] The changeable covenant. *By G. D. for Thomas Brewster and Gregory Moule,* 1650. 4°.* LT, LW, OC, DC, EN; CH, CLC, MM, MH.

1400 [–] The character of a right malignant. [*London,* 1644/5]. 4°.* LT, OW, MR, DT; MH, TU.

1401 —A continuation of Lvcans historicall poem. Fourth edition. [*London*], *for Will. Sheares,* 1650. 12°. O; CH, CN, MH, TU, Y.

1402 [–] —[Anr. ed., "A continuation of the svbiect of Lucans."] *For William Shears,* 1567 [*i.e.* 1657.] 8°. L, O, CCH, LIU; CH, CU, PL, WF, Y.

1403 [–] —[Anr. ed.] —, 1657. 24°. C, MAU, P; CH, IU, MH, PL, TO, WCL.

1404 [–] A discovrse concerning the svccesse of former Parliaments. *Imprinted at London,* 1642. 4°.* LT, O, CT, EN, DT; CII, CN, MII, NU, TU, WF, Y.

1405 ——Second edition. *By T. F. for Thomas Wakeley,* 1644. 4°.* O, SP; CH, MH, PUL, Y.

1406-7 Entries cancelled.
      —Epitome of English history. 1690. *See* May, *Sir* Thomas.

1408 [–] Historiæ Parliamenti Angliæ. *Typis Caroli Snmptner* [sic] *prostant venales officina Thomæ Brusteri,* [1650]. 8°. LT, O, C, LVD, CK; CH, CLC, IU, WF, WG.

1409 [–] —[Anr. ed.] *Typis Caroli Sumptner,* 1651. 12°. L, CS, LLU, E, DT; CH, CLC, CN, LC, MHL, NP, Y.

1410 —The history of the Parliament of England. *By Moses Bell, for George Thomason,* 1647. fol. L, O, C, EN, DT; BN, CH, CN, LC, MH, NU, TU, WF, Y.

1411 Entry cancelled.
      [–] Life of a satyrical pvppy. 1657. *See* M., T.

1411A [–] Observations vpon the effects of former Parljaments. [*London,* 1642.] 4°.* LT, O, DT, MR, CD; CH, CSS, MH, MM, NCD, WF, Y.

1411B [–] The observator, upon the success of former Parliaments. *For I. H. and H. VVhite.* 1643. 4°.* CH, CSS, NC.

1412 —The old couple. A comedy. *By J. Cottrel, for Samuel Speed,* 1658. 4°. L, O, LVD, CK, EN; CH, CN, LC, MH, TU, WF, Y.

1413 —Supplementum Lvcani. Second edition. *Typis M. Flesher, sumptibus D. Frere,* 1646. 12°. L, O, CT; BN, CLC, MBP, MH, NCD, JF.

1414 No entry.

1415 [–] A true relation from Hvll. *By G. Dexter, for Iohn Bull.* 1643. Sept. 30. 4°.* LT, MR, YM; MH, TU, WF.

1416 —Two tragedies. *For Humphrey Moseley,* 1654. 12°. L, O; CH, MB, NC, NP, PU, WF.

1416A [**May,** *Sir* **Thomas.**] Arbitrary government displayed to the life. *For Charles Leigh,* 1682. 8°. L, O, C, LG, OB; CH, CLC, MBP, MH, NU, WF.

1416B [–] —Second edition. *For William Cademan,* 1683. 8°. O, OC, SP; CU, MBP, NP.

1416C [–] —[Anr. ed.] *For Joseph Hindmarsh,* 1683. 12°. T.C.II 19. L, CT, AN; CH, CN, NGT, WU, Y.

1416D —An epitome of English history. Third edition. *For W. C.,* 1690. 12°. L, ES.

1416E ——"Third" edition. *For N. Boddington,* 1690. 12°. L, O, AU; CH, MH, WF, Y.

1416F **May, William.** To the King's most excellent Majesty, . . . the case of . . . [piracy]. [*London,* 1696.] brs. LPR.

1417 The May-Day country mirth. [*London*], *for J. Deacon,* [1684–95]. brs. L, O, HH; MH.

1417A —[Anr. ed.] [*London*], *for W. Thackeray,* [1688–89]. brs. CM.

1417B May it please you sir to take notice . . . [Charity Commissioners]. [*Oxford?* 1667.] brs. L, O.

1417C May it please your Lordship, we the embroiderers . . . East-India silks. [*n.p.,* 1697?] brs. Y.

1418 May it please your Majesty, we your Majesties most loyal subjects. *For H. Jones,* 1688. brs. MH.

1419 May it please your most excellent Maiesty. . . . Northampton. *For John Martin, James Allestry, and Thomas Dicas,* [1660]. brs. LT; MH.

1419A The May-pole dancers. [*London*], *for J. Deacon,* [1682–1700]. brs. HUTH.

1419B The May-poles motto. [*London?* 1661.] brs. L.

1419C May we say, Honoured Sir, that what Salomon said . . . [petition by Merchant Adventurers to Cromwell for repayment of public debts, 25 August 1652]. [*London,* 1652.] brs. MH.

1420 **Maydman, Henry.** Naval speculations. *By William Bonny, and sold by Sam. Manship, and J. Fisher, and A. Feltham, and M. Gillyflower,* 1691. 8°. T.C.II 361. L, O, C, LUG, EN; CH, CN, MH, TU, WF, Y.

1421 **Mayer, John.** Christian liberty vindicated. *By Eliz. Purslow, for Matthew Welbancke,* 1647. 4°.* LT, O, CS, MR, DT; CLC, CSS, IU, NU, WF, Y.

1422 —A commentary upon all the prophets. *By Abraham Miller and Ellen Cotes,* 1652. fol. L, O, CT, LSD, BQ; CH, CLC, MH, NU, WF, Y, AVP.

1423 —A commentary upon the holy vvritings of Job. *For Robert Ibbitson and Thomas Roycroft,* 1653. fol. L, O, CS, LCL, NE; CLC, MH, TSM, WF, ZWT, AVP.

1424 —A commentary vpon the whole Old Testament. *By Robert and William Leybourn,* 1653. fol. L, LCL, LSC, CS, MC; MH, VICTORIA U., N.Z.

1424A ——[Anr. ed.] *By R. L. and R. I., sold by Edward Dod,* 1654. fol. CSE.

1425 —Many commentaries in one. *By John Legatt, and Richard Cotes; to be sold by William Leak,* 1647. fol. L, LCL, LW, CS, P; CLC, FU, IU, MH, NN, WF, AVP.

1426 —Unity restor'd to the church. *For A. Rice,* 1661. 4°. L, CS; MH.

1427 **Mayerne, Sir Theodore Turquet.** Archimagruis Anglo-Gallicus; or, excellent . . . receipts. [*London*], *for G. Bedell, and T. Collins*, 1658. 12°. L; NAM, NN.
— [–] Compleat midwifes practice. 1663. *See* Chamberlaine, Thomas.

1427A —Consilia, epistolae et observationes. *Impensis Sam. Smith & Benj. Walford*, 1695. fol. CS; NAM.

1428 —Medicinal councels or advices. *For N. Ponder*, 1677. 8°. T.C.I 253, L, O, C, LCP, LCS; KU, MMO, WSG, HC.

1429 Entry cancelled.
— —Murderous midwife. [n.p.], 1673. *See title.*

1430 —Opera medica. *Typis R. E.*, 1700. fol. O, C, LCP, OC, AU; TO, WSG.

1431 —Praxeos Mayernianæ in morbis. *Impensis Sam. Smith*, 1690. 8°. T.C.II 337. L, O, C, GH, DT; CH, MMO, NAM, PL, WF, HC.

1432 ——[Anr. ed.] *Impensis Sam. Smith et Benj. Walford*, 1695. 8°. BN, PBL, PL, WSG.

1433 ——[Anr. ed.] —, 1696. 8°. L, O, C, GH, DT; CLC, NAM, TO, WF.

1434 —Theod. Turqueti D. de Mayerne, . . . Tractatus de arthritide. *Impensis Mosis Pitt*, 1676. 8°. T.C.I 248. O, C, LL, LWL, OC, E; BN, LC, WSG.

1435 —A treatise of the gout. *For D. Newman*, 1676. 12°. T.C.I 253. L, O, LWL, DT; CLC, NAM, PCP, WSG, HC.

Mayerus, Michael. *See* Maier, Michael.

1436 **Mayhew, Matthew.** A brief narrative of the success which the Gospel hath had. *Boston, by Bartholomew Green, sold by Michael Perry*, 1694. 8°. EVANS 701. O, LW; MHS.

1437 —The conquests and triumphs of grace. *For Nath. Hiller*, 1695. 8°. LW; CH, PRF, RPJ, V.

1438 **Mayhew, Richard.** Χαρισμα πατρικον; a paternal gift. *For John Hancock*, 1676. 8°. L; NU.

1439 —Εσχατος εχθρος. Or the death of death. *By Thomas Snowden, for the author*, 1679. 8°. L, LCL, ENC; CLC, MH, WF.

1440 [–] Love to the life. *For B. Harris*, 1674. 12°. T.C.I 195. L.

1441 [–] Poema mortuale; or, an elegy. [*n.p.*], 1679. 8°.* ENC; CLC.

1442 [–] Sichah: or, a continued tract . . . second part. *By Th. Dawks, for the author*, 1683. 8°. L.

1443 [–] Sichah: or a tract of meditation. . . first part. *For J. Phillips*, 1682. 8°. L, LCL, LSC.

1444 —Tria sunt omnia: or a necessary narration. *By Thomas Snowden, for the author*, 1680. LCL, LW, SP; CH, NU.

1445 —The young man's guide to blessedness. *For J. Hancock*, 1677. 8°. T.C.I 251. LCL; CLC.

1445A **Mayhew, Thomas.** Upon the death of his late Highness, Oliver . . . an elegie. *For Edward Husbands*, 1658. brs. MH.

1446 —Upon the joyfull and welcome return of His Sacred Majestie, Charls the Second. *For Abel Roper*, 1660. 4°.* LT, O, OH, MR, EN; CH, IU, MH, TU, WF, Y.

1447 **Maylins, Robert.** A letter which was delivered to the King . . . from the Barbadoes. *For Giles Calvert*, 1661. brs. LF; LC.

1448 **Maynard, John,** *of Mayfield.* The beauty and order of the creation. *By T. M. for Henry Eversden*, 1668. 12°. LCL, LW, P; NU.

1449 —Bibliotheca Maynardiana. 13 *June* 1687. 4°. L, O, LR, LV.

1450 —The law of God ratified. *For Francis Tyton*, 1674. 8°. T.C.I 167. L, O; NU, WF.

1451 —A memento to young and old. *For Thomas Parkhurst*, 1669. 8°. LCL; CLC.

1452 —A sermon preached . . . Feb. 26, 1644. *By George Bishop for Samuel Gellibrand*, 1645. 4°.* LT, O, C, MR, EN; CH, CN, MH, NU, TU, WF, Y.

1453 —A shadovv of the victory of Christ. *By F: Neile for Samuel Gellibrand*, 1646. 4°.* LT, O, C, DU, DT; CH, IU, MH, NU, WF, Y.

1454 [**Maynard, Sir John.**] The copy of a letter addressed to the Father Rector at Brussels. *For Ralph Rounthwait*, 1643. 4°.* LT, C, SP, YM; CH, CLC, MIU, NU, WF.

1455 —England's champion. [*London*, 1648.] brs. LT; CLC, MH.

1456 —The humble plea and protest, of. [*London*, 1648.] brs. LT, LG, LPR.

1457 —The picklock of the old fenne project. *By J. B.*, 1650. 4°.* LT, LG; CLC, CN, CSS.

1458 [–] A speech spoken by an honorable knight . . . 27 of June, 1648. *Printed*, 1648. 4°.* LT; IU, MH, NU, TU, Y.

1459 —A speech spoken in the honourable House of Commons. *For I. Harris, Aug.* 11. 1648. 4°.* LT, EC, MR, YM; CN, CSS, INU, MIU, PH, Y.

1459A **Maynard, Sir John,** *judge.* A judicious answer to six queries concerning the Jews. *For Sam. Speed*, 1666. 4°.* DU.

1460 —Les reports des cases. *By George Sawbridge, William Rawlins and Samuel Roycroft, assigns of Richard and Edward Atkyns, for T. Basset, J. Wright, and James Collins*, 1678. fol. T.C.I 321. L, O, LI, CJ, DT; CLL, LC, MHL, NCU, NN, WF.

1461 —Master Meynard his speech at the committee at Guild Hall . . . January 6. [*London*], *printed*, 1642. 4°.* LT, O, C, LNC, DT; CH, MH, MU, NCD, NU, WF, Y.

1462 —Mr. Maynards speech before both Houses. . . . the xxiiijth. of March. [*London*], *printed*, 1641. 4°.* LT, O, C, DU, DT; CH, CLC, MH, MU, WF, Y. (var.)

1462A **Maynard, Josias.** A tyrall [sic] skill. [*London*, 1652.] brs. Y.

1463 [**Mayne, Jasper.**] The amorovs warre. [*London*], *printed*, 1648. 4°. L, O, LVF, OW, A, DT; CH, IU, MH, TU, WCL, WF, Y.

1464 [–] —[Anr. ed.] *Oxford, by Henry Hall, for Ric. Davis*, 1659. 4°. MADAN 2451. L, O, BC; CH, CN, MH, MU, PBL, Y.

1465 [–] —[Anr. ed.] —, 1659. 8°. MADAN 2452. L, O, LVD, OC, LLU, EN, DT; CLC, LC, MH, MU, WF, Y.

1466 —Certaine sermons and letters. *For R. Royston*, 1653. 4°. L, O, YM; NU, WF.

1467 [–] The city match. Third edition. *Oxford, by Henry Hall for Rich: Davis*, 1659. 8°. MADAN 2453. L, O, LVD, OC, EC, EN, DT; CLC, CN, CU, MH, WF, Y.

1468 Entry cancelled. *See previous entry.*

1469 —Concio ad academiam Oxoniensem. *Typis J. Grismond, & prostant apud R. Royston*, 1662. 4°.* L, O, C, DU, NPL; CLC, IU, NU, TU.

1470 [–] The difference abovt church government ended. *By R. L. for William Leake*, 1646. 4°.* LT, O, C, P, DT; CLC, MH, MU, NU, WF, Y.

1471 —A late printed sermon against false prophets. [*London*], printed, 1647. 4°. MADAN 1932. LT, O, C, DU, BLH; CH, CU, MBP, MH, NU, WF, Y.

1472 —Οχλο-μαχια. Or the peoples war. [*Oxford, by L. Lichfield*], printed, 1647. 4°.* MADAN 1941. LT, O, C, LNC, DT; CH, CN, MH, MU, NU, TU, WF, Y.

1472A —Pregeth yn erbyn schism. *Gan Jo. Straeter, tros Phil. Chetwinde*, 1658. 4°.* AN.

1473 —A sermon against false prophets. [*Oxford, by L. Lichfield*], printed, 1646[7]. 4°.* MADAN 1910. LT, O, C, BC, BLH; CDA, CH, CLC, TU, Y.

1474 ——[Anr. ed.] [*London*], printed, 1647. 4°.* L, OC, CK, MR, DT; CLC, MH, MU, NU, WF, Y.

1475 —A sermon against schisme. *For R. Royston*, 1652. 4°.* L, O, C, DU, EN; CH, CU, MH, NU, WF, Y.

1476 [–] A sermon concerning unity & agreement. Preached at Carfax Chvrch in Oxford, August 9. 1646. [*Oxford, by L. Lichfield*], printed, 1646. 4°. MADAN 1903. LT, OC, CS, BR, DT; CH, CN, MH, TU, WF, Y.

1477 ——[Anr. ed.] [*Oxford*], printed, 1647. 4°.* L, C, OC, CK, EN; CLC, CU, MH, NU, Y.

1478 —A sermon preached at the consecration . . . Herbert [Croft]. *For R. Royston*, 1662. 4°. L, O, C, DU, DT; CH, IU, NCD, NU, WF, Y.

1479 [–] To His Royal Highnesse the Duke of Yorke. On our late sea-fight. colop: *Oxford, by Henry Hall for Ric: Davis*, 1665. fol.* MADAN 2710. L, O; CLC, MH, Y.

1480 [–] Two plaies the city match. "Second" edition. *Oxford, re-printed by Hen. Hall for Ric. Davis*, 1658. 4°. MADAN 2395. L, O, OW, EC; CH, CN, MBP, MH, WF, Y.

1481 [–] Ymddiffyniad rhag pla o schism. *Printiedig ynghaer Ludd gan Joa. Streater, tros Philip Chetwinde*, 1658. 8°.* L, O; CN.

1482 [**Mayne, John.**] Arithmetick: (vulgar, decimal, & algebraical.) *For J. A.*, 1675. 8°. L; WF.

1483 —The practical gauger. *By W. G. for N. Brooke*, 1676. 12°. T.C.I 197. O, OB, OC.

1483A ——Fifth edition. *For J. Phillips; H. Rhodes; & J. Taylor*, 1699. T.C.III 114. 12°. WF.

1484 —Socius mercatoris: or the merchant's companion. *By W. G. for N. Crouch*, 1674. 8°. T.C.I 150. O, LR, OC, CT; NBL.

1485 **Mayne, Zachary.** St. Paul's travailing-pangs. *By M. I. for Ioseph Leigh, and Henry Cripys*, 1662. 8°. C, LW; NU, Y.

1486 —Sanctification by faith vindicated. *London, by W. O. for John Salusbury, and sold by Walter Dight in Exon*, 1693. 4°. T.C.II 473. L, O, EC; CLC, MH, WF.

1487 ——[Anr. ed.] *By W. O. for John Salusbury*, 1693. 4°.* L, C.

1488 [–] The snare broken. [*n.p.*], printed, 1692. 4°. O.

1489 [–] —[Anr. ed.] [*n.p.*], printed, 1694. 4°.* CS, DU, WCA; MIU, NU, TO.

1489A **Maynforth, Robert.** An exhortation to all people in general. *For T. Sowle*, 1691. 8°.* LF.

1490 [**Maynwaring, Everard.**] The Catholick medicine and sovereign healer. *For R. Horne, T. Basset, and C. Blount*, 1684. 4°. T.C.II 97. O; CSS.

1491 —The efficacy and extent of true purgation. *For D. Browne, and R. Clavel*, 1696. 4°.* CS, GH; NU, WSG.

1492 —The frequent, but unsuspected progress of pains. *By J. M. for Henry Bonwicke*, 1679. T.C.I 333. LCP, LWL, CE, AM; BN.

1493 —The history and mystery of venereal lues. *By J. M. and sold by the booksellers*, 1673. 8°. T.C.I 127. LCS, LWL, AN, AM; BN, CLC, NAM.

1494 [–] Ignota febris; fevers mistaken. colop: *For the booksellers*, [1691]. 4°.* T.C.II 360. O; WF, WSG.

1495 ——[Anr. ed.] *By J. Dawks, to be sold by D. Brown*, 1698. 8°. L, MAU; WSG.

1496 [–] Inquiries into the general catalogue of diseases. [*London, 1691.*] cap., 4°.* T.C.II 346. L, C; CH, CN, MH, WF.

1497 —Medicus absolutus . . . the compleat physitian. *For the booksellers*, 1668. 8°. L, O, LCP, CE, GU; CH, MIU, WF, HC.

1498 The method and means of enjoying health. *By J. M. for Dorman Newman*, 1683. 8°. T.C.I 508. L, O, LCS, CS, MAU, D; BN, CLM, LC, MH, WSG.

1498A ——[Anr. ed.] *By J. M. for the booksellers*, 1683. 8°. WF.

1499 —Monarchia microcosmi: the origin. *For John Everingham*, 1692. 12°. T.C.II 403. L, O, C, OC; MH, WF, WSG.

1500 —Morbus polyrhizos . . . a treatise of the scurvy. *By R. D. for T. Basset*, 1665. 8°. O, OC, CCA, WCA; MB, HC.

1500A ——Second edition. *By J. D. for H. Broom*, 1666. 8°. WSG.

1501 ——"Second" edition. *By J. D. for S. Thompson*, 1666. 8°. CE; MMO.

1502 ——"Second" edition. *By J. D. for G. Sawbridge*, 1666. 8°. LWL; MMO.

1503 ——Third edition. *Printed: sold by H. Eversden*, 1669. 8°. T.C.16. L; WF, HC.

1503A ——"Third" edition. *Sold by G. Sawbridge*, 1669. 8°. WSG.

1503B ——"Third" edition. *Printed: and are to be sold by the booksellers*, 1669. 8°. O; CLC, NN.

1504 ——Fourth edition. *By J. M. to be sold by Peter Parker*, 1672. 8°. T.C.I 93. L, O, LCS, LWL, CS; CH, INU, MIU, WF, WSG.

1505 ——"Fourth" edition. —, 1679. 8°. O; BN.

1506 —The mystery of curing. *For the booksellers*, 1693. 4°.* T.C.II 438. L, O; WF.

1507 ——Second edition. *Printed, and sold by W. Crook; and J. Everingham*, 1694. 4°.* T.C.II 503. L, LWL, OC; WSG, Y.

1508 —Nova medendi ratio, a short and easie method of curing. *By J. Dover, for Henry Broome*, 1666. 4°.* L, O, GH.

1508A ——[Anr. ed.] *By J. Dover for M. Speed.* 1666. 4°.* O; WSG.

1509   —Pains afflicting humane bodies. *For Henry Bonwicke,* 1682. 8°. T.C.I 485. L, O, LCS, CS.

1510   Entry cancelled.
        —Pharmacopœia domestica. 1672. *See*—Morbus poly-rhizos. Fourth edition.

1511   No entry.
        —Pharmacopœian physician's repository. 1670. *See*—Vita sana.

1512   —Praxis medicorum. *By J. M. to be sold by T. Archer,* 1671. 4°. T.C.I 71. L, O, LWL, LSD; CH, WF.

1512A   —A serious debate . . . health and sickness. *For Thomas Basset and Thomas Horne,* 1689. 8°.* T.C.II 287. O; WSG.

1513   —Solamen ægrorum. *Excusum per G. M. pro Gulielmo Crooke,* 1665. 8°. L, O, LWL.

1514   —Tabidorum narratio: a treatise of consumptions. *For T. Basset,* 1667. 12°. L, LCP, LWL, OC, WCA; WF, HC.

1515   [-] The test and tryal of medicines. colop: *For Thomas Basset; and Thomas Horne,* 1690. cap., 4°.* L.

1516   —A treatise of consumptions. Second edition. *By Anne Maxwell, to be sold by Tho. Basset,* 1668. 12°. LM.

1516A   —Tutela sanitatis sive vita protracta. *By Peter Lillicrap. And sold by S. Thompson: T. Basset,* 1663. 8°. LWL, WCA; NAM.

1517   —[Anr. ed.] —, 1664. 8°. L, O, LCS, LWL; MIU.

1518   —Useful discoveries. *By A. M. for T. Basset,* 1668. 12°. L, LCP, LWL, WCA; MIU, PCP, HC.

1519   —Vita sana & longa. The preservation. *By J. D.,* 1669. 8°. T.C.I 26. L, O, LCS, LSC; CLC, NCD, NRU, WSG, WU.

1520   ——[Anr. ed.] —, 1670. 8°. LCP, LWL, CS, LIU, MAU, E; BN, CH, MH, NAM, WF, HC.

1520A   **Mayo, Daniel.** A sermon preach'd . . . July 14th 1700. *For J. Lawrence,* 1700. 8°. LW, GU.

1521   **Mayo, Richard.** The cause and cure of strife. *For Thomas Parkhurst,* 1695. 4°.* T.C.II 548. L, LW; CH, LC, WF, Y, AVP.

1522   [-] A conference betwixt a Papist and a Jew. *By A. M. and R. R. for Tho. Parkhurst,* 1678. 4°.* 34 pp. L, O, C, DU, BLH; CH, CN, LC, NU, Y.

1523   [-] A conference betwixt a Protestant and a Jevv. *For Tho. Parkhurst,* 1678. 4°.* T.C.I 318. L, O, BC, DU, BLH; CH, CN, MH, NU, WF.

1523A   [-] —[Anr. ed.] —, 1687. 4°. MH.

1524   —Κρυπτευχολογια: or, a plain answer. *By D. Maxwel for Thomas Parkhurst,* 1664. 4°.* LW, LNC, EN; NU, WF, Y.

1525   ——[Anr. ed.] *By T. M. for Thomas Parkhurst,* 1673. 8°.* O, LW; MH.

1526   ——[Anr. ed.] *For Thomas Parkhurst,* 1677. 8°.* T.C.I 271. L, O, C, DT.

1527   ——[Anr. ed.] —, 1687. 8°.* O, LW; CLC.

1528   [-] The life & death of Edmund Staunton. *For Th. Parkhurst,* 1673. 8°. T.C.I 125. L, O, C, DU, DT; NGT, NU, WF, Y.

1529   [-] A present for servants. *By T. Warren, for Nath. Ranew,* 1693. 12°.* T.C.II 438. L, O.

1530   [-] Two conferences: one betwixt a Papist and a Jew. *For Tho. Parkhurst,* 1678. 4°. T.C.I 337. L, LW, OC, CT; MIU.

1531   [-] —[Anr. ed.] *For Thomas Parkhurst,* 1679. 4°. LIL, DT; CLC, MH, MIU, MWA.

1532   [-] —[Anr. ed.] *For Thos. Parkhurst,* 1699. 12°. EN.

1533   **Mayow, John.** The mothers family physician. *Oxford, by L. Lichfield for J. Cox,* 1687. 12°. WSG.

1534   —Ραχιτιδολογια or a tract. *Oxford, by L. L. for Th. Fickus,* 1685. 12°. L, O, CS; WSG, JF.

1535   —Tractatvs dvo. *Oxon: excudebat Hen: Hall, impensis Ric: Davis,* 1668. 8°. T.C.I 6. LCS, OB, CT; CJC, PCP.

1536   ——[Anr. ed.] *Oxon: excudebat Hen. Hall impensis Ric. Davis,* 1669. 8°. MADAN 2834. O, C, LCS, AM, GH; BN, MMO, MU, JF.

1537   —Tractatus quinque medico-physici. *Oxonii, e theatro Sheldoniano,* 1674. 8°. T.C.I 183; MADAN 3015. L, O, C, LCS, MAU, EN, DT; BN, CH, MMO, NAM, PL, WSG, HC.

1537A   Entry cancelled.
        Mazarin, Armand. The arguments of. 1699. *See* Hérard, Claude.

1538-8A Entries cancelled.
        Mazarin, Hortense Mancini, *duchesse de*. The memoires of. 1676. *See* Saint Réal, César Vischard de.

1539   **Mazarin, Jules, *cardinal*.** The declaration of. *For M. M.,* 1652. 4°.* LT, MR.

1540   —Cardinal Mazarin's letters to Lewis XIV. *For R. Bentley,* 1691. 12°. T.C.II 383. L, O, C, CT, E; CH, CLC, CN, MH, WF, Y.

1541   Entry cancelled.
        —News from France. 1652. *See* Naude, Gabriel.

1541A   The maze: contrived, digested and couched. [*n.p.*], *printed,* 1659. 4°. L, O.

1542   **Mazzella, Scipio.** Parthenopoeia, or the history of. *For Humphrey Moseley,* 1654. fol. L, O, C, AN, LIU, DL, DT; CH, LC, MB, MH, MU, NC, NCD, WF, Y.

1542A   **Mead, E.** A copy of a letter, containing an account . . . of Capt. Robert Mead. colop: *For S. M.,* 1692. brs. L.

1543   **Mead, Matthew.** The almost Christian discovered. *Belfast, by Patrick Neill and Company,* 1700. 12°. O, BLH.

1544   [-] An appendix to Solomon's prescription. [*n.p.*], 1667. 8°. L, LW, LWL; CH, IU, WSG.

1545   —Comfort in death. *By S. Bridge, for Tho. Parkhurst: and John Lawrence,* 1698. 4°.* T.C.III 86. L, O, CS, WCA, E; CH, CLC, MH, NU, TU, WF, Y.

1546   —Εν ολιγω χριστιανος. The almost Christian discovered. *For Tho. Parkhurst,* 1662. 8°. L, LCL, AN, BR, BLH; CH, CLC, IU, MB, NF, NU, Y.

1547   ——[Anr. ed.] *By J. Best, for Thomas Parkhurst,* 1664. 12°. L, O, LCL; IU, ZAS.

1547A   ——[Anr. ed.] *By R. I. for Thomas Parkhurst,* 1666. 12°. WF.

1547B   ——[Anr. ed.] *By R. W. for T. Parkhurst,* 1668. 12°. CLC.

1548   ——[Anr. ed.] *By A. M. for Thomas Parkhurst,* 1670. 12°. NU.

1549   ——[Anr. ed.] —, 1671. 12°. LW.

1550   ——[Anr. ed.] *Glasgow, by Robert Sanders,* 1672. 12°. ALDIS 1950.5. I.

1551   ——[Anr. ed.] *Sold by Geo. Swinnock,* 1675. 12°. T.C.I 201. LW; MBC.

1551A   — —[Anr. ed.] *For Thomas Parkhurst*, 1677. 12°. CN.

1552   — —[Anr. ed.] *Glasgow, by Robert Sanders*, 1678. 12°. ALDIS 2133.2. L.

1552AA   — —Sixth edition. *For Thomas Parkhurst*, 1679. 12°. IU.

1552A   — —[Anr. ed.] *For Thomas Parkhurst*, 1683. 12°. T.C.II 21. MIU, NHC.

1553   — —Eighth edition. *By J. A. for Thomas Parkhurst*, 1684. 12°. L; ASU.

1553A   — —Ninth edition. *By T. S. for Thomas Parkhurst*, 1691. 12°. MH.

1553B   — —Tenth edition. *By T. M. for Thomas Parkhurst*, 1694. 12°. NPL.

1553C   — —Eleventh edition. *By J. Brudenell for Thomas Parkhurst*, 1700. 8°. T.C.II 166. L, O; WF.

1554   —A funeral sermon preached upon . . . Mr. Thomas Rosewell. *For John Lawrence*, 1692. 4°.* T.C.II 407. L, O, C, LW, BR, E; CLC, LC, PL.

1555   —The good of early obedience. *For Nath. Ponder*, 1683. 8°. T.C.II 12. L, O, LCL, LW, ENC; CH, MH, MIU, NU, TSM, WF, Y.

1556   —The pastors valediction. *Printed*, 1662. 4°.* O, BR; NP.

1557   [–] Solomon's prescription. *Printed*, 1665. 4°. L; LC, MH, MIU, NU.

1558   [–] —[Anr. ed.] —, 1666. 4°. L, O, LW, LWL, P; CLC, MH, WF, JF.

1558A   [–] —[Anr. ed.] —, 1667. 8°. L, LW; CH, CLC.

1559   —Spiritual vvisdom improved. *For Thomas Parkhurst*, 1660. 4°.* LT, C, LW, BC, LIU; CLC, MH, NU, TU, WF, Y.

1559A   — —Second edition. —, 1661. 4°.* LW; Y.

1560   — —Third edition. *For Tho. Parkhurst*, 1676. 4°.* NU.

1561   — —Fourth edition. —, 1678. 12°.* L.

1562   —Two sticks made one. *For Tho. Parkhurst*, 1691. 4°.* T.C.II 358. L, O, C, LCL, EN, BLH; CH, CLC, MH, NU, WF, Y, AVP.

1563   —The vision of the vvheels. *For Tho. Parkhurst*, 1689. 4°. T.C.II 247. L, O, C, DU, EN; CH, MB, NU, TU, WF, Y.

1563A   —The young man's remembrancer. *For John Marshall*, 1700. 12°. T.C.III 222. TO, AVP.

1564   **Mead, Robert.** The combat of love and friendship. *For M. M., G. Bedell, and T. Collins*, 1654. 4°. MADAN 2247. LT, O, C, OW, GH; CH, CN, MH, LC, WF, Y.

1565   **Mead, William.** A brief account of the most material passages. [*London*, 1674.] 8°.* L, LF, OC; PH, PSC, Y.

1565A   —A brief narrative of the second meeting. [*London*], *printed* 1674. 8°. L; CN, PHS.

1566   **Meadows, Sir Philip.** A narrative of the principal actions. *By A. C. for H. Brome*, 1677. 12°. T.C.I 289. L, O, C, WCA, BQ, DT; CH, CN, PL, WF, Y.

1566A   [–] —[Anr. ed.] —, 1678. 12°. DU.

1567   —Observations concerning the dominion. *In the Savoy: by Edw. Jones, and sold by Samuel Lowndes; and by Edward Jones*, 1689. 4°.* T.C.II 258. L, O, C, LLP, LIU, DT; CH, CN, MH, WF, Y.

1567A   — —[Anr. ed.] *Printed and sold by Edward Jones*, 1689. 4°. OC.

1567B   —The wars betwixt Sweden and Denmark. *For Henry Brome*, 1680. 12°. T.C.I 410. DU.

1568   **Meager, Leonard.** The English gardener. *For P. Parker*, 1670. 4°. T.C.I 38. L, O, R; CB, CH, WU, Y.

1569   — —[Anr. ed.] *For T. Pierrepoint*, 1682. 4°. MHO, PL, WDA.

1570   — —[Anr. ed.] *For J. Wright*, 1683. 4°. L, CT, R, RU; MB, MH.

1570A   — —[Anr. ed.] *For J. Wright, and sold by John Hancock*, [1683]. 4°. SE.

1571   — —[Anr. ed.] *By J. Rawlins for M. Wotton and G. Conyers*, 1688. 4°. L, R; CDA, CLC, CH, MH, NR, Y.

1572   — —Ninth edition. *By J. Dawks for M. Wotton, and G. Conyers*, 1699. 4°. T.C.III 101. L, OR, LLU, RU; NP, WF.

1572A   — —"Ninth" edition. *By J. Dawks, for M. Wotton, and B. Conyers*, 1699. 4°. CH, CSU, LC.

1573   —The mystery of husbandry. *London: by W. Onley, to be sold by Will. Majore, in Newport, Cornwall*, 1697. 12°. L, O, LUG, R; NC, WDA.

1573A   — —[Anr. ed.] *By W. Onley for Henry Nelme*, 1697. 12°. LWL, OXF. AGRICULTURE, RU; CH, MH, WF, WU, Y.

1573B   Entry cancelled. Date: [1720].

1574   — —Second edition. *For Henry Nelme*, 1697. 12°. L; MH, MHO, WDA.

1575   — —[Anr. ed.] *For Peter Parker*, 1699. 8°. L, O; MHO, NDL, Y.

Means of preventing. 1665. *See* R., M.

Means to free Europe. 1689. *See* B., P.

Meanes to prevent perishing. 1658. *See* S., W.

Meanes to reconcile. 1648. *See* Anderson, Henry.

Mean-well, Ralph, *pseud.*

1576   Entry cancelled.

Meara, Dermod. Pathologia. 1665. *Part of next entry.*

1577   **Meara, Edmund.** Examen diatribæ Thomæ Willisii, . . . de febribus. *Typis J. Flesher: prostat venale apud Octav. Pulleyn juniorem*, 1665. 8°. L, O, C, MAU, E, DM; CLM, NIC, PCP, WF, HC.

1578   Entry cancelled.

[**Meare.**] Some observations made upon the Molucco nutts. [n.p.], 1672. *See* Peachie, John.

1579   **Mearne, Charles.** Appendix to catalogue. [*London*], 22 *Feb.* 1687. 4°.* L.

1580   —A catalogue of English books. [*London*], 17 *Feb.* 1687. 4°.* L, O; CN, MH, JF.

1581   —A catalogue of the French books of. [*London*, 26 *Jan.* 1686/7.] 4°.* L, OC; MH, NG, JF.

1582   Entry cancelled.

Measure of the earth. 1688. *See* Perrault, Claude. Memoir's for a natural history.

Measuring-rule concerning liberty. [n.p., 1661.] *See* Fox, George.

1583   **Meath, Edward Brabazon,** *earl.* To the Parliament of the common-wealths . . . the humble petition of. [*London*, 1654.] brs. LT, C; MH.

The medall. 1682. *See* Dryden, John.

Medal of John Bayes. 1682. *See* Shadwell, Thomas.

Medal revers'd. 1682. *See* Pordage, Samuel.

1583A   [**Medbourne, Matthew.**] The converted twins. *For Robert Pawlett*, 1667. 4°. L, O, OW; CH, CLC, MH, Y.

1583B [–] St. Cecily: or, the converted twins. *By J. Streator,* 1666. 4°. O, C, LVF, CCA; CH, CN, LC, NC, PU, WF.

1583C **Medburn, J.** A measuring line, or, a rule for saints. *By R. I. for F. Smith,* [1657?]. 8°. ORP (inc.).

1583D **Medcalf, Augustine.** A sermon. *Printed,* 1679. 4°. WF.

1584 **Meddens, John.** Tabellæ dialectorum. 1691. 8°. OM.

1585 **Mede, Joseph.** The vvorks of. *By M. F. for John Clark,* 1648. 4°. L, C, OC, BANGOR; BN, CH, IU, MH, NCD, NU, Y. (var.)

1586 ——Second edition. *By James Flesher, for Richard Royston,* 1664. fol. L, O, C, E, DT; CLC, IEG, MWA, NU, PL, WF, Y.

1587 Entry cancelled. Ghost.

1588 ——Third edition. *By Roger Norton, for Richard Royston,* 1672. fol. T.C.I 106. L, O, CT, ENC, DT; CLC, CN, MH, NU, Y.

1589 ——Fourth edition. —, 1677. fol. L, O, CT, EN, DT; BN, CH, IU, MH, NCD, NR, NU, WF.

1590 —The apostasy of the latter times. *By Richard Bishop for Samuel Man,* 1641. 4°. LT, O, C, CT, BP, LSD; CLC, IU, MH, NU, WF, Y.

1591 ——[Anr. ed.] —, 1642. 4°. L, O, C, SA, EN; CH, CLC, MH, NU, TU, WF.

1592 ——"Second" edition. *By L. N. for Samvel Man,* 1644. 4°. L, O, C, LNC, EN; CH, CN, MH, NU, TU, WF, Y.

1593 ——Third edition. *By T. R. for Samvel Man,* 1654. 4°. O, LLP; CB, CLC, IU.

1593A ——"Third" edition. —, 1655. 4°. L, OC, DUS, SP; IEG.

1594 —Clavis apocalyptica. *Cantabrigiæ, apud R. Daniel,* 1649. 4°. L, O, C, CT, DU, SC; BN, CH, CLC, MIU, TSM, Y.

1595 —Daniels vveekes. *By M. F. for John Clark,* 1643. 4°. LT, O, C, LSD, SC, EN; CH, CN, MH, NU, TU, WF, Y.

1596 —Diatribæ. Discovrses. *By M. F. for John Clark,* 1642. 4°. LT, O, C, AN, E; CH, IU, NU, PL, TU, WF, Y.

1597 ——Second edition. —, 1648. 4°. L, C, DUS, DL, BLH; CH, CLC, IU, MH, PL, TSM, WF.

1598 ——Pars IV. *By J. F. for John Clark,* 1652. 8°. LT, O, C, LNC, GU, DT; CH, IU, MH, NU, WF, Y.

1599 —Dissertationum ecclesiasticarum triga. *Typis Tho: Roycroft: impensis Jo. Martin, Jac. Allestrye, & Tim. Garthwait,* 1653. 4°. L, O, CS, LSD, SC; BN, CH, CLC, IU, NU, RBU, WF.

1600 —The key of the Revelation. *Printed at London by R. B. for Phil. Stephens,* 1643. 4°. LT, O, CK, LSD, EN; CH, MH, MU, NCD, NU, Y.

1601 ——Second edition. *Printed at London by J. L. for Phil. Stephens,* 1650. 4°. L, O, C, DUS, SA; CH, CN, NU, PL, WF.

1602 Entry cancelled.
—Name altar. 1648. *See*—VVorkes. 1648.

1603 —Josephi Medi, . . . opvscvla Latina. *Cantabrigiæ: per Thomam Buck, impensis Gulielmi Morden,* 1652. 4°. L, O, C, E, DT; BN, CH, CLC, IU, MH, PU, WF.

1604 —Παραλειπομενα. Remaines. *By J. G. for John Clarke,* 1650. 4°. L, O, C, AN, BLH; CH, IU, MH, NU, WF, Y.

1605 —A paraphrase and exposition of the prophesie of Saint Peter. *By R. Bishop, for Samuel Man,* 1642. 4°.* LT, O, C, LNC, E; CH, IU, MH, NU, PL, TU, WF.

1606 ——Second edition. *By R. Leybourn, for Samuel Man,* 1649. 4°.* O, CS, SHR, BLH; CH, MH, NU, WF, Y.

1607 ——[Anr. ed.] —, 1650. 4°.* EN; WF.

1608 ——Third edition. *By T. Maxey for Samuel Man,* 1652. 4°.* L, C, OC; CH, IU, TU.

——[Anr. ed.] 1653. *See*—Apostasy. Third edition. 1654.

Medela medicinæ. A plea. 1665. *See* Nedham, Marchamont.

Medela medicorum; or. 1678. *See* Staines, William.

Medicæ dissertationes tres. 1680. *See* Morton, Thomas.

Medicaster medicatus, or a remedy. 1685. *See* Yonge, James.

Medice, cura teipsum. 1671. *See* Stubbe, Henry.

Medici catholicon, or. 1656. *See* Collop, John.

1608A Medicina in manu imperiti . . . a licensed physician. [*London,* 1680?] brs. L.

Medecine for malignancy. 1644. *See* L., W.

Medicine for the times. 1641. *See* Jordan, Thomas.

1609 Medecines against the pest. *Edinburgh, J. Lindesay,* 1645. 8°. ALDIS 1192. EN.

Medico-mastix or. [n.p.], 1645. *See* A., E.

Mediocria. 1674. *See* Humfrey, John.

Meditation for the 30th day of January. [n.p.], 1660. *See* R., M. de.

1609A A meditation meete for a Christian. [*London?* 1645.] brs. L.

1610 Entry cancelled.

Meditation vpon the history of Pekah. 1650. *See* Pertinent and profitable meditation.

Meditations and prayers. 1682. *See* Northumberland, Elizabeth Percy.

1611 Entry cancelled.

Meditations collected and ordered. 1663. *See* Daniel, Edward.

Meditations divine. 1659. *See* Tubbe, Henry.

Meditations in my confinement. 1666. *See* Clarke, Thomas.

Meditations, miscellaneous. 1652. *See* Henshaw, Joseph, bp.

Meditations of an humble heart. 1661. *See* Smith, Humphrey.

Meditations upon a seige. [n.p.], 1646. *See* Peake, Humphrey.

Meditations upon retirement. 1691. *See* Ludolf, Heinrich Wilhelm.

Meditations upon the Lords Prayer. 1665. *See* Wither, George.

Meditations upon the marks. Paris, 1655. *See* Wilkinson, Henry.

Mediterranean passage. 1670. *See* Mathew, Francis. To the kings most excellent majesty.

1612 **Medley, William.** A standard set up. [*London*], *printed,* 1657. 4°.* LT, O, BC, DU, SP; CH, CSS, NU, WF, Y.

Medow. *See* Meadows.

Medulla historiæ Anglicanæ. 1679. *See* Howell, William.

Medulla historiæ Scoticæ. Being. 1685. *See* Alexander, William.

1613-4 Entries cancelled.

[**Mee, Dr.**] Character of a compleat physician. [1680?] *See* Merret, Christopher.

M[eed], W[illiam]. *See* Mead, William.

1615 **Meeke, William.** The faithfull scout. *Printed at Yorke by Tho. Broad, to be sold by Nathanniel [sic] Brookes in London,* 1646. 4°. O, YM; CH.

1616 ——[Anr. ed.] —, 1647. 4°. CH.

1616A Meeting accidently at a coffee-house. [*London,* 169–?] brs. O.

Meetness for Heaven. 1679. *See* Heywood, Oliver.

1617 **Meggot, Richard.** Bibliotheca Meggotiana. Catalogue of the library. [*London*], 6 Nov. 1693. 4°. L, O, OP.

1618 —The new-cured criple's caveat. *By T. M. for Peter Dring,* 1662. 4°.* L, O, C; CH, MH, NGT, WF, Y.

1619 —The rib restored. *By J. G. for Nath: Webb, and Wil: Grantham,* 1656. 4°.* L, O, LSC, DT; NU, WF.

1620 —A sermon preached . . . June 9th. 1670. *By E. Tyler and R. Holt, for Joseph Clark,* 1670. 4°.* T.C.I 48. L, O, C, D, BLH; CH, CN, MH, NU, WF, Y.

1621 —A sermon preached . . . January the 30th, 1673/4. *For Nathaniel Brooke,* [1674]. 4°. T.C.I 168. L, O, C, MR, WCA; CH, IU, MH, NU, TU, WF, Y.

1622 —A sermon preached . . . Avgvst 15. 1675. *For Nathanael Brooke,* 1675. 4°.* 35 pp. T.C.I 225. L, O, C, LNC, LSD; CH, NU, MIU, TU, WF, Y.

1623 ——[Anr. ed.] —, 1675. 4°.* 38 pp. Y.

1624 —A sermon preached . . . on St. Paul's Day, 1675/6. *For John Baker,* 1676. 4°.* T.C.I 226. L, O, C, CT, DT; CSU, MH, NU, TU, WF, Y.

1625 —A sermon preached . . . September 13. 1676. *For Nathanael Brooke,* 1676. 4°.* T.C.I 251. L, O, C, LL, LLP; CH, MH, NU, TU, WF, Y.

1626 —A sermon preached . . . March 23. 1681/2. *By A. Grover, for Thomas Rowe jun.* 1682. 4°.* L, O, C, BR, EC; CH, IU, NU, V, WF, Y.

1627 —A sermon preached . . . March the 16. 1682/3. *For Walter Kettilby,* 1683. 4°.* T.C.II 14. L, O, C, BAMB, EC; CH, IU, MH, NU, V, WF, Y.

1628 —A sermon preached . . . July 14th. 1689. *For Tho. Bennet,* 1689. 4°.* L, C, OM, EC, WCA; CH, MH, NU, WF, Y.

1629 —A sermon preached . . . Sept. 21. 1690. *For Tho. Bennet,* 1690. 4°.* T.C.II 331. L, O, OM, EC, WCA, DT; CH, CN, MU, NU, WF, Y.

1630 —A sermon preached . . . Jvly 5. 1691. *For Tho. Bennet,* 1691. 4°.* L, O, C, EC, DT; CLC, MU, NU, WF, Y.

1630A —A sermon preached . . . July 15. 1691. *For Tho. Bennet,* 1691. 4°.* LLP, OC, EC, WCA.

1631 —A sermon preached . . . July 19. 1691. *For Tho. Bennet,* 1691. 4°.* L, O, C, EC, LSD; CLC, MU, NU, TSM, WF, Y.

1632 —A sermon preached . . . March 11th, 1691/2. *For Tho. Bennett,* 1692. 4°.* L, C, OC, LIU, DT; CH, MU, NU, WF, Y.

1633 —Ten sermons upon several occasions. *For Tho. Bennet,* 1696. 8°. L, O, LLP, LW, CS, LSD; CH, NGT, TU, WF.

Meir of Collingtoun. [n.p.], 1695. *See* D., P.

Melancholy cavalier. [n.p.], 1654. *See* Rowlands, Samuel.

1634 The melancholy complaint of D. Otes. *For Charles Brome,* 1684. fol.* T.C.II 128. L, O, C, LLL, MR; CH, CN, MH, TU, WF, Y.

1635 **Melancthon, Philipp.** Epistolarvm. *Excudebant M. Flesher & R. Young. Prostant apud Cornelium Bee,* 1642. fol. L, O, C, OB, BAMB, DT; BN, CH, IU, MH, NP, PL, WF.

1635A ——[Anr. ed.] *Excudebant M. Flesher & R. Young,* 1642. *Sumptibus Adriani Vlacq.* fol. C, CM; PL.

[**Meldrum, George.**] Letter to a friend, giving. 1692. *See* Monro, Alexander.

1636 —A sermon preached . . . April 27. 1690. *Edinburgh, by the heir of Andrew Anderson,* 1690. 4°.* ALDIS 3053. O, E, EN, GU.

1637 —A sermon concerning zeal. *Printed at Edenburgh: and reprinted at London, for Richard Baldwin,* 1690. 4°.* T.C.II 319. MR, E, AU; NU, WF.

1638 [–] A sermon preached in the High-Church of Edinburgh. *Edinburgh, by the heir of Andrew Anderson,* 1690. 4°.* ALDIS 3094. L, EN, SA.

1639 —Theses philosophicæ. *Abredoniis, e typographæo Jacobi Broun,* 1659. 4°. ALDIS 1618. O, AU.

1640 **Meldrum, Sir John.** The copy of a letter sent to the King by. *For Joseph Hunscott. Octob.* 18. 1642. 4°.* LT, O, DU, EC, DT; CN, CSS, IU, LC, MH, NCD, NU, Y.

1641 **Melfort, John Drummond, earl of.** The Earle of Melfort's letter. [*Edinburgh?* 1687.] cap., 4°.* L, OJ, LSD, AU, DT; CH, CN, MH, WF, Y.

1642-3 Entries cancelled. Date: 1700[1].

1644 **Melish, Stephen.** England's warning. *Imprinted at London,* 1664. 4°. L, O, OC, MR.

1645 —XII visions of. *For the author,* 1663. 4°.* L, LF; CLC.

1646 A melius inquirendum into the birth. *For J. Wilks,* 1689. fol.* L, LIL, MR, CD, DT; CH, MIU, NU, WF, Y.

1647 Melius inquirendum: or a further modest and impartial enquiry. *London, for Jonathan Robinson. Sold by Clement Elis, in Mansfield,* 1689. 4°.* T.C.II 278. L, C, OC, CCH; CH, CN, NU, WF.

1647A ——[Anr. ed.] *For Jonathan Robinson,* 1689. 4°.* L, O, OC, BANGOR, DT; CLC, IU, MH, PL, WF, Y.

Melius inquirendum. Or a sober. [n.p.], 1678. *See* Alsop, Vincent.

Melius inquirendum: or, an answer. Edinburgh, 1699. *See* Eizat, *Sir* Edward.

Melius inquirendum; or, an impartial. 1688. *See* E., W.

1647B **Mellidge, Anthony.** If the measure of my sufferings. [*London,* 1659.] brs. LF, OP.

1648 —A true relation of the former faithful . . . service, . . . of. [n.p., 1656.] cap., 4°.* L, LF; PH.

1648A **Mello, Francisco Manuel de.** The government of a wife. *For Jacob Tonson, and R. Knaplock,* 1697. 8°. T.C. III 42. L; CH, CN, MB, TU, WF, Y.

1648B **Meloniere, general.** A letter from . . . August the 12th. *For El. Jones,* 1690. brs. HH.

Melpomene: or. 1678. *See* Bulteel, John, *younger.*

1649 **Melvill, Elizabeth, Lady Culross.** A godly dream. *Aberdene, by E. Raban,* 1644. 12°.* ALDIS 1146. L.

1649A ——[Anr. ed.] [*Glasgow, Sanders? 1686.*] 8°. ALDIS 2645.
5. EN.

1650 ——[Anr. ed.] *Glasgow, by Robert Sanders, 1698.* 8°.*
ALDIS 3762. HUTH.

1651 **Melville, George, earl.** The speech of . . . April 15,
1690. colop: [*London*], *by Edward Jones in the Savoy,*
1690. brs. L, C, O, OC, MC, EN; CH, CLC, TU, Y.

1652 ——[Anr. ed.] *Edinburgh, by the heir of Andrew Anderson,*
1690. fol.* ALDIS 3054. O, MR, EN; CH, WF, Y.

1652A —To his grace Their Majesties high commissioner,
and . . . parliament . . . [petition for restoration of
property]. [*Edinburgh, 1690–94.*] brs. DL.

1653 Entry cancelled. Ghost.

1654 **Melville, Sir James.** The memoires of. *By E. H. for
Robert Boulter, 1683.* fol. T.C.II 4. L, O, C, EN, DT; BN,
CH, CN, LC, MH, WF, Y.

1655 **Melville, James.** Ad serenissimum Jacobum primvm.
*Excudebat J. R. pro Georgio Thomason & Octaviano
Pullen, 1645.* 4°. LT, C, NE, EN, DT; CH, WF, Y.

1656 **Melvin, John.** Good company. *For Tho. Parkhurst,*
1659. 8°. LT.

1656A The member of Parliament's answer. [*London? 1700.*]
brs. HH.

1656B The members' justification. [*London, 1647.*] brs. L.

1656C The members of the court of assistants of the Royal-
African Company. [*London, 1694.*] brs. LPR.

1657 A memento for all freeholders. [*London, 1690.*] brs. L.

1658 Entry cancelled.
Memento for English Protestants. 1680. *See* Amy, S.

1659 A memento for Holland. *By James Moxon, 1653.* 8°. LT.

1660 A memento for the people, about their elections. *For
Rich. Moone, 1654.* brs. LT, O.

1661 A memento for yeomen. *August 23. 1642. London, for
Nathaniel Allen,* 4°.* LT, EC; IU, MH, NC, WF, Y.

1662 Memento mori, a full and true relation. *Printed and
sold by J. Read, 1698.* brs. L.
Memento mori, or a word. Edinburgh, 1699. *See* Clark,
James.

1663 A memento to English-men for the special service of
K. William and Q. Mary. [*London? 1691.*] cap., 4°.*
DU, MR; HR, CN, WF, Y.

1664 A memento to the East-India Companies. *Printed, 1700.*
8°.* L, C, LUG, OC; MH, MIU.

1665 July, 25. 1643. Memento to the Londoners. [*London,*
1643.] brs. LT; MH.
Memento's to the world. [n.p.], 1680. *See* Greene,
William.

1666 Memoires concerning the campagne of three Kings.
For Ric. Baldwin, 1693. 12°. T.C.II 439. O; CH.

1667 Entry cancelled.
Memoir's for a natural history. 1688. *See* Perrault,
Claude.

1668 Memoirs of Charles V late Duke of Lorrain. *For W.
Chandler, to be sold by R. Baldwin, 1694.* 12°. L, O; WF.
Memoirs of Denmark. 1700. *See* Crull, Jodocus.
Memoirs of Emeric. 1693. *See* Le Clerc, Jean.
Memoires of Mary Carleton. 1673. *See* G., J.

Memoires of Monsieur Du-Vall. 1670. *See* Pope,
Walter.

1669 Memoirs of Queen Mary's days. [*London, 1679.*] cap.,
fol.* L, O, CT, LNC, MR; CH, CLC, MH, TU, WF, Y.

1669AA Memoires of the affairs of France. *By J. C. for Tho.
Dring, 1675.* 8°. T.C.I 217. L, DUS; WF, Y.
Memoirs of the court of France. 1692. *See* Aulnoy,
Marie Cathérine, *comtesse d'.*
Memoirs of the court of Spain. 1692. *See* Aulnoy,
Marie Cathérine, *comtesse d'.*
Memoires of the Dutchess Mazarine, 1676. *See* Saint
Réal, César Vischard de.
Memoires of the family. 1683. *See* Watson, John.
Memoires of the life and actions. Edinburgh, 1685. *See*
Tyler, Alexander.
Memoires of the life and death of Sir Edmondbury
Godfrey. 1682. *See* Tuke, Richard.

1669A Memoires of the life and death of that matchless mirrour
. . . Henrietta Maria. . *Printed 1671.* 8°. L; CN, CU, NRU.

1670 Memoirs of the life and death of the famous Madam
Charlton. *For Phillip Brooksby, 1673.* 4°. LG; CLC, CN,
MH, Y.
Memoires of the life, and rare adventures. 1672. *See*
Desjardins, Marie Cathérine Hortense de.

1671 Memoires of the life of Anthony late Earl of Shaftsbury. *For Walter Davis, 1682/3.* fol.* T.C.II 4. L, O, CT,
BSM, MR; CH, MBA, MH, MIU, TO, WF, Y.

1672 Memoirs of the most remarkable enterprises and actions
of James Duke of York. *For Richard Janeway, 1681.*
fol.* L, O, C, DU, LLU; CH, CLC, IU, MH, PU, TO, WF, Y.
Memoires of the Sieur de Pontis. 1694. *See* Pontis, Louis
de.

1673 Memoires of the transactions in Savoy. *For M. Gylliflower, W. Freeman, M. Wotton, J. Waltho, and R.
Parker, 1697.* 12°. T.C.III 24. L, O, CT, NE; CH, INU, MU, Y.

1674 The memoires of Titus Oates. *For Thomas Graves,*
1685. 4°.* L, O, OCC, DC, MR; CH, IU, MH, WCL, WF, Y.
Memoirs of what past. 1692. *See* Temple, *Sir* William.
Memoires relating. [n.p.], 1690. *See* Pepys, Samuel.
Memorabilia mundi: or. 1670. *See* Hooker, G.
Memorable accidents. 1693. *See* Leonard, T.

1675 The memorable battle fought at Killy Crankie. [*London,*
1689.] brs. L; MH.

1676 The memorable case of Denzil Onslow. colop: *For R.
Baldwyn, 1681.* cap., fol.* L, O, C, OP; CH, CN, MIU,
NCD, WF, Y, AVP.

1677 Entry cancelled.
Memorable dayes and workes of God. 1646. *See* Caryl,
Joseph.

1677A Memorable song on the unhappie hunting in Chevie-
Chase. *For E. Wright, [1645?].* brs. MRL.

1677B —[Anr. ed., "unhappy."] *For J. Wright, [1650?].* brs. CH.

1677C —[Anr. ed., "memoriable."] [*London*], *for F. Coles, T.
Vere, and W. Gilbertson, [1658–64].* brs. EUING 212-3.
O, GU. (var.)

1678 —[Anr. ed.] [*London*], *for F. Coles, T. Vere, and J. Wright,*
[1663–74]. brs. L.

Memorables of the life. 1690. *See* Baxter, Richard.

1679   Memorandums for London. *By G. M.*, [1644]. brs. LT; MH, Y.

1680   Memorandums for those that go into the country. [*London?* 1688.] 4°.* L, O, OC, CS, LIU; CH, CN, MH, TU, WF, Y.

1681   Memorandums of the conferences held. *By William Du-gard* 1650. 4°.* LT, C, BC, SP, DT; CH, MH, MU, NU, WF, Y.

1682   Memorare novissima. Third edition. *Oxford, by Leonard Lichfield for William Smart,* 1671. brs. MADAN 2888. O.

    Memoria Balfouriana. Edinburghi. 1699. *See* Sibbald, Robert.

1682A   Memoriæ sacrum Edvardi comitis Sandovici. *Typis Johannis Redmayne,* 1672. brs. O, OC; MH.

1682B   Memoriæ sacrum Lancelot: Dawes. [1654.] brs. O.

1683   Memoriæ sacrum. Resiste viator, paucis te volo: Robertvs Chester. [*n.p.,* 1659.] brs. O.

1684   Entry cancelled.
    Memorial . . . yearly sallary. [n.p., 1698.] *See* Memorial to his grace.

1684A   Memorial against an overture of an act for statuting. [*Edinburgh,* 1698.] brs. ALDIS 3762.3. EN.

1685   A memorial between jest and earnest. *Philadelphia* [*London*] *by Philaletes for the author,* 1691. 4°.* EVANS 569. O, MR; PHS.

    Memorial delivered to His Majesty. 1664. *See* Van Gogh, Michiel.

    Memorial for His Highness the Prince of Orange. 1689. *See* Mackenzie, George.

1685A   Memorial for the burghs of regalities. [*Edinburgh,* 1698.] brs. ALDIS 3762.7. EN.

    Memorial for the learned. 1686. *See* Davies, John.

1686   A memorial from the English protestants. [*London,* 1688.] fol.* L, O, C, BR, MR, DT; CH, CN, MH, NCD, WF, Y. (var.)

1687   —[Anr. ed.] colop: [*London*], *printed,* 1689. cap., 4°.* I, DU, A; CLC, MH, TSM, WF, Y.

1688   A memorial given in to the Senate of the city of Hamburgh. [*Edinburgh,* 1697.] brs. ALDIS 3678.5. EN; MH, RPJ.

1688A   —[Anr. ed., "with the Senate's answer."] colop: *Edinburg, printed,* 1697. brs. RPJ.

1689   Memoriall. Henry Parker having served. [*London,* 1647.] brs. LT.

    Memorial humbly presented. 1690. *See* Turner, John.

1689A   Memorial humbly presented to His Majesties Commissioner . . . by the administrator's of Heriot's hospital. [*Edinburgh,* 1695.] brs. ALDIS 3468.7. L.

1689B   Memorial in behalf of the purchasers of forfeited lands in Ireland. [*London,* 1699?] brs. CH.

1690   A memoriall intended to be delivered to the Lords States. *Printed,* 1662. 4°.* OC, MR, SP, BLH; CH, NU.

1691   A memorial of God's last twenty nine years wonders. *By J. Rawlins, and sold by R. Janeway,* 1689. 4°. T.C.II 290. L, O, CT, EC, EN; CLC, CN, LC, MH, NU, TU, Y.

1691A   A memorial of the demands made by the confederate princes. *For W. R., and are to be sold by E. Whitlock,* 1697. brs. HH.

1692   A memorial of the deplorable case of the Protestant purchasers. [*n.p.,* 1699?] brs. L, LL.

1692A   A memorial of the late and present popish plots. [*London,* 1680.] cap., fol.* MR; PU.

1693   A memorial of the Protestants of the Church of England, presented to their Royal Highnesses. [*London,* 1688.] brs. L, O, C, LPR, HH; CH, IU, MH, PL, WF, Y. (var.)

1693A   A memorial on the behalf of Mr. Hartlib. [*London,* 1647.] cap., 4°.* LUG.

1694   A memorial on the death of that faithful servant . . . Nathaniel Strange. *Printed,* 1666. brs. L.

1695   Memorial presented to the Lord Chief Justice. 1690. 4°. LG (lost).

1695A   Memorial to his grace, His Majesties high commissioner . . . concerning a fond for a yearly sallary to the judge of the high court of Admiralty. [*Edinburgh,* 1698.] brs. ALDIS 3763. HH, EN.

1696   A memoriall to preserve vnspotted to posterity the name . . . of Doctor Crispe. *Printed at London for John Sweeting.* 1643. brs. LT, HH; MH.

1697   Memorial to the Lords of His Majesties Privy Council. [*Edinburgh,* 1695?] cap., fol.* ALDIS 3469b. L, LUG; Y.

1698   Memorial to the members of Parliament of the court party. [*Edinburgh,* 1700.] 4°.* ALDIS 34692. L, EN; CH, RPJ, WF, Y.

    Memorialls for the government. Aberdeen, 1685. *See* Skene, Alexander.

    Memorials lately presented by the French . . . ambassadors. [n.p., 1688.] *See* Avaux, Jean Antoine de Mesmes, *comte d'*.

    Memorials of Alderman Whitmore. 1681. *See* Barksdale, Clement.

    Memorials of the English affairs. 1682. *See* Whitelock, *Sir* Bulstrode.

    Memorials of the method. 1656. *See* Scobell, Henry.

1699   Memoriam vesperiarum et comitiorum in Theatro Oxoniensi . . . Paulo Brand. [*n.p.,* 1677.] brs. O.

1700   Memories of the life of the famous Madam Charlton. *For Philip Brooksby,* 1673. 4°.* T.C.I 126. L, O; CH, MH, MHL.

1701   Entry cancelled.
    Memory of that faithful man of God, Thomas Stordy. 1692. *See* Wilkinson, John.

1701A   The memory of that faithful servant of Christ, William Carter. *For Thomas Northcott,* 1690. 4°.* LF; CH, IE, PH.

1702   Entry cancelled.
    Memory of that servant of God, John Story. 1683. *See* Wilkinson, John.

1702A   The memory of the just is blessed . . . Thomas Wadsworth. [*London,* 1676.] brs. MH.

    Men before Adam. 1656. *See* La Peyrère, Isaac de.

    Men-miracles. [n.p.], 1646. *See* Llewellyn, Martin.

    Men, women, or children. [n.p., 1690.] *See* Collings, Richard.

Menasseh, *ben Israel*. *See* Manasseh.

1703 **Mence, Francis.** Vindiciæ fœderis: or, a vindication. *London, for the author, to be sold by John Lawrence, by Mrs. Mary Gurnel, and Mr. William Wingod, in Wapping,* 1694. 12°. L, C, LCL, ORP; NHC, NU, TO, Y.

1704 Mendacimastix or, a whip. colop: [*London*], *by D. Mallet.* 1680. cap., fol.* L, O, EN; MH, PU.

1705 **Mendes Pinto, Fernando.** The voyages and adventures of. *By J. Macock, for Henry Cripps and Lodowick Lloyd,* 1653. fol. L, O, BAMB, SP, WCA; CH, CLC, IU, MH, TU, WF, Y, AVP.

1706 ——[Anr. ed.] *By J. Macock, to be sold by Henry Herringman,* 1663. fol. L, O, CM, BC, A; CLC, CN, MBA, MIU, MU, Y.

1706A ——Second edition. *By J. Macock for Henry Herringman,* 1663. fol. NCU.

1707 ——Third edition. *For Richard Bently, Jacob Tonson, Francis Saunders, and Tho. Bennet,* 1692. fol. L; CH, LC, NP.

1707A The mending of a clause, in the bill relating to the Irish forfeitures. [*London,* 1699?] brs. CH.

1708 Entry cancelled.
       Mendoza, Antonio de. *See* Hurtado de Mendoza, Antonio.
       Mene mene, tekel upharsin. 1689. *See* Partridge, John.
       Mene tekel being. [1688.] *See* Partridge, John.
       Mene tekel; or. [n.p.], 1663. *See* Jones, Roger.

1709 Mene tekel to fifth monarchy. *Printed,* 1665. brs. L.
       Menippeus rusticus. 1698. *See* S., C.

1710 **M[ennes], Sir J[ohn].** Musarum deliciæ. *For Henry Herringman,* 1655. 8°. LT, O, C; CH, CN, MH, WF, Y.

1711 [–]—Second edition. *By J. G. for Henry Herringman,* 1656. 8°. LT, O, CT, EC, LLU; BN, CH, LC, MH, MU, WF, Y.

1712 [–] Recreation for ingenious head-peeces. Third edition. *By R. Cotes for H. B.,* 1645. 8°. L; WF, Y.

1713 [–]—[Anr. ed.] *By M. Simmons, to be sold by John Hancock,* 1650. 8°. L; CN, IU, WF.

1714 [–]—[Anr. ed.] *By M: Simmons,* 1654. 8°. L, OP, GK; CH, IU, LC, MB, NN, WCL, WF.

1715 [–]—[Anr. ed.] *By S. Simmons,* 1663. 8°. L, O; CH, LC, WF.

1715A [–]—[Anr. ed.] *For J. Stafford,* 1665. 8°. NN, WF.

1716 [–]—[Anr. ed.] *By S. Simmons,* 1667. 8°. L; IU, MH.

1717 [–]—[Anr. ed.] *By S. Simmons, to be sold by Thomas Helder,* 1667. 8°. L; CH, MH, WF, Y.

1718 [–]—[Anr. ed.] *For John Hancock,* 1683. 8°. MH.
       [–] Wit and drollery. 1656. *See* title.

1719 [–] Wit restor'd, in severall select poems. *For R. Pollard, N. Brooks, and T. Dring,* 1658. 8°. L, O, OW, LLU; CH, IU, MH, RHT, WF.

1720 [–] Wits recreations containing. *By Thomas Cotes, for Humphry Blunden,* 1641. 8°. L, O, BLH; CH, MH, TU, WF, Y.

1721 The mens answer to the womens petition against coffee. *Printed* 1674. 4°.* L; MH, WF, Y.
       Mensa lubrica Montgom. Oxford, 1651. *See* Masters, Thomas.
       Mensa mystica; or. 1676. *See* Patrick, Symon, *bp.*

1722 No entry.

1723 **Menzies, Alexander.** Disputatio juridica. *Edinburgi, ex officina hæredum A. Anderson,* 1700. 4°.* ALDIS 3984.5. EN.

1724 **Menzies, John.** Britannia rediviva. *Aberdene, by James Brown,* 1660. 4°.* ALDIS 1649. EN, AU, GU; WF.

1725 —Papismus Lucifugus. *Aberdene, by Iohn Forbes younger,* 1668. 4°. ALDIS 1846. L, O, C, EN, GU; CH, IU, NPT, NU, TU, WF, Y.

1726 —Positiones aliquot theologicæ. [*Aberdeen*], 1674. 4°. ALDIS 2023.3. E.

1727 —Roma mendax. *For Abel Roper,* 1675. 4°. T.C.I 198. L, O, C, DU, E, GU; IU, NU, TO, WF, Y.

1728 —A sermon, preached . . . 20. of July [1681]. *Edinbvrgh, by the heir of Andrew Anderson,* 1681. 4°.* ALDIS 2278. L, EN; MH, NU, WSG.
       Mephibosheth and Ziba. 1689. *See* B., H.

1728AA **Mercator, George.** Atlas or a geographicke description, of the . . . world. *Sumptibus & typis Henrici Hondij, Amsterodami,* 1641. 2 v. fol. RPJ.

1728A **Mercator, Nicolaus.** Nicolai Mercatoris hypothesis astronomica nova. *Ex officina Leybourniana,* 1664. fol.* SC; MU.

1728B —In geometriam introductio brevis. 1678. 12°. SC.

1729 —Nicolai Mercatoris . . . institutionum astronomicarum libri duo. *Typis Gulielmi Godbid, sumptibus Samuelis Simpson, Cantabrigiensis* 1676. 8°. T.C.I 248. L, O, C, BAMB, E, DT; BN, CH, MBA, MU, WF, HC.

1730 —Logarithmo-technia. *Typis Guilielmi Godbid, impensis Mosis Pitt,* 1668. 4°. T.C.I 6. L, O, C, DT, EN; BN, IU, MB, NN, PL, WF.

1731 The mercenary sovldier. [*London,* 1646.] brs. LT.

1732 [**Mercer, Richard.**] A further discovery of the mystery of the last times. *For W. Roybould,* 1651. 4°. LT, LSC; NHC.

1733 [–] Some discoveries of the mystery of the last times. *For Giles Calvert,* 1649. 4°.* LT, C; NHC.

1734 **Mercer, Thomas.** A speech of . . . spoken . . . the 27. of May, 1645. *By Peter Cole,* 1645. 4°.* LT, LG, DT; CH, INU, MH, MU, PU.

1734A [–] The young accountants remembrancer. *For the author T. M.,* 1692. fol.* O.

1734B [–]—Third edition. —, 1697. brs. LG.

1735 **Mercer, William.** Angliæ speculum. *By Tho: Paine, and are to be sold by Lawrence Chapman,* 1646. 4°. LT, O; CH, CN, MH, WF, Y.

1736 —An elegie, on the death of the thrice valiant . . . John Luttrell. [*London*], *by T. Paine,* 1645. brs. L.

1737 —An elegie in memorie, . . . of . . . Sir Henrie Mervyn. *By Jane Coe,* 1646. brs. L; MH.

1738 —An elegie vpon the death of . . . Essex. *By I. C.,* 1646. brs. LT.

1739 [–] The moderate cavalier. [*Cork?*], *printed,* 1675. 4°.* L; CH.

1740 —News from Parnassus. *By M. W. for the author,* 1682. 8°. EN.

1741 [–] A welcom in a poem. *Dublin, by Iosiah Windsor, for Robert Howes,* 1669. 4°.* DIX 139. L; CH.

[Menton, L.] *See* Meriton, L.

Merchant man and the fidler's wife. 1678. *See* P., J.

1742   The merchant of Scotland. [*London*], *for E. Oliver*, [1695?]. brs. L.

Merchant royal. 1682. *See* Wilkinson, Robert.

Merchant Taylors' School. Election. [n.p., 1682.] *See* title.

1743   —Election . . . on St. Barnabas day. [*London*, 1687.] fol.* LG (lost).

1744   —XIX election . . . June X. [*London*, 1680.] brs. LG (lost).

1744A —III. election . . . Juniis 11. 1664. [*London*, 1664?] brs. O.

Merchant's dayly companion. 1684. *See* P., J.

1745   The merchants daughter of Bristow. *For F. Coles, T. Vere, and W. Gilbertson*, [1658–64]. brs. EUING 210. O, GU.

1745A —[Anr. ed.] *For F. Coles, T. Vere, and J. Wright*, [1663–74]. fol.* OC.

1746   Entry cancelled.

Merchant's humble petition. 1659. *See* Baker, Richard, *merchant*.

Merchants remonstrance. 1644. *See* Battie, I.

Merchant's ware-house. 1696. *See* F., J.

1746A The merciful father. [*London*], *for P. Brooksby*, [1683]. brs. CM.

1747   Mercvries message defended. *Printed*, 1641. 4°.* LT, O, LVF, OC, AN; CLC, MH, TU, WF, Y, ZWT.

1748   Mercvries message, or the coppy of a letter sent to William Laud. [*London*], *printed*, 1641. 4°.* L, O, CT, DU, EN; CH, IU, MH, NU, TU, WF, Y. (var.)

Mercurio-cœlico mastix. Or. [n.p.], 1644. *See* Wharton, *Sir* George.

1749   No entry.

Mercurius academicus. [n.p.], 1648. *See* Swadlin, Thomas.

1750   Mercurius alethes: or, an humble petition. *Printed*, 1653. 4°.* LT, C; CLC.

1751   Mercurius Anglicus: or Englands Merlin. *By R. Wood*, 1653. 4°.* L, LWL; CH.

Mercurius anti-mechanicus. 1648. *See* Ward, Nathaniel.

1752   Mercurius anti Mercvrivs. [*London*, 1648.] 4°.* LT, O; CH.

Mercvrivs aqvaticvs; or. [n.p.], 1643. *See* Taylor, John.

1753   Mercurius Belgicus: or, a briefe chronology. [*London*], *printed*, 1685. CCA, CK, AN; MBP, WF, Ƴ.

1754   No entry.

1755   Mercurius benevolens. Not prag. nor pol. *For Hen. Brome*, 1661. 4°.* LT; MH, Y.

1756   Mercurius Britanicus, his apologie. *For R. W.* 1645. 4°.* LT, C, CT, MR, DT; MH, MIU, PL, Y.

1757   Mercurius Britannicus his spectacles. [*London*, 1647.] cap., 4°.* LT; CSS, Y.

1758   Mercurius Britanicus his vision. *For W. Ley*, 1647. 4°.* LT, DT.

Mercurius Britanicus his welcome. [n.p.], 1647. *See* Wortley, *Sir* Francis.

Mercurivs Britannicvs judicialis. [n.p., 1641.] *See* Brathwait, Richard.

Mercurius Britanicus, or. [n.p.], 1641. *See* Brathwait, Richard.

1759   Mercurius Calidonivs, presenting. [*Edinburgh*], *printed*, 1648. 4°.* ALDIS 1336.5. LT, CT, ES; Y.

Mercurius Cambro-Britannicus. 1652. *See* Griffith, Alexander.

1760   Entry cancelled. Serial.

Mercurius civicus. Or. 1674. *See* Almanacs.

Mercurius cœlicus: or. 1644. *See* Wharton, *Sir* George.

1761   Mercurius Davidicus, or a patterne of loyall devotion. *Oxford, by Leonard Leichfield*, 1634 [*i.e.* 1643]. 8°.* MADAN 1464. LT, O, CT, DU, LSD, SA; CH. (var.)

1762   Numb. 1. Mercurius deformatus: or the true observator. colop: *Printed, and sold by the Mercury Women*, 1691. brs. L.

1763   Mercurius Democritus, his last will. *Printed*, 1652. 4°.* LT, MR.

1764   Mercvrius diaboljcus, or Hells intelligencer. [*London*], *printed*, 1647. 4°.* LT; MH, MIU, Y.

1764A —[Anr. ed.] —, 1650. 4°.* BLH.

1765   Mercurius ecclesiasticus: or, Doctor Cozens his visitation. [*London*], *printed*, 1645. 4°.* LT; TU.

Mercurius Hibernicus: or. Bristoll, 1644. *See* Howell, James.

1766   Entry cancelled.

Mercurius Lepidus. 1652. *See* News from the lowe countreys.

1766A Mercurius matrimonialis. [*London*, 1691.] brs. L, HH; CN, MH, PL.

Mercurius melancholicus, *pseud.*

Mercurius menippeus. The loyal satyrist. 1682. *See* Butler, Samuel.

1767   Mercurius Mercuriorum stultissimus, vvritten. [*London*], *printed*, 1647. 4°.* LT; CH, MIU, WF, Y.

1768   Mercurius militans, with his hags haunting cruelty. [*London*], *printed*, 1648. cap., 4°.* LT, O.

Mercvrivs pacificvs, or. 1644. *See* M., E.

Mercurius pacificus. With. [n.p., 1650.] *See* Taylor, John.

Mercurius panegyricus. [n.p., 1683.] *See* Panegyrick mercury.

1768A Mercurius politicus: a private conference between Scot & Needham. *Printed*, 1660. 4°. L, MR; KU, MIU, ZWT.

1769   Mercurius propheticus. Or, —a collection. [*London*], *printed*, 1643[4]. 4°.* LT, O, CT, MR; CH, LC, MH, MIU, TU, Y.

1770   Mercurius Radamanthus. [*London*, 1653.] cap., 4°.* LT.

1770A Mercurius religiosus: faithfully communicating . . . the vanity of Christmas. colop: *Printed at London for Robert Ibbitson*, 1651. cap., 4°.* CSS.

Mercurius rusticus. 1685. *See* Ryves, Bruno.

Mercurius rusticus: or, a. [n.p., 1643.] *See* Wither, George.

1771   Mercurius rusticus: the downfall of tythes. [*London*, 1653.] cap., 4°.* LT; CN.

1772   Mercurius Scoticus, giving. *Rotterdam, by P. C. and are to be sold by Gysbert van Roon*, 1650. 4°.* L,LNC, SC, DT; MH.

1773   Mercurius Somniosus commvnicating his packet of intelligence. *By Jane Coe*. 1644. 4°.* LT; CSS, WF.

1774 Mercurius urbanicus. Or, newes from London. [*London*], *printed*, 1648. 4°.* LT, O; CH.

1775 Mercurius vapulans, or Naworth stript. [*London*], *for I. F. March 4*, 1644. 4°.* LT, C, MR; WF, Y.

1776 Mercurius venereus, wherein. [*n.p.*], 1649. 4°. O; CN.

1777 Mercurius verax, or truth appearing. [*London*, 1649.] cap., 4°.* LT.

Mercurius verax; or. 1675. *See* Phillips, John.

1778 Hebdomas prima. Mercurius zeteticus. The theme, Scoto-Presbyter. [*London*, 1652.] cap., 4°.* LT, O.

Mercury, or the secret. 1641. *See* Wilkins, John, *bp*.

1779 The Mercury-gallant. *By T. R. and N. T. for Dorman Newman*, 1673. 8°. T.C.I 128. CT, CASTLE ASHBY; BBE, CLC, CN, WF, Y.

1780 Mercy and truth, righteovsness and peace. [*London*], 1642[3]. 4°.* LT, O, LG, EC, DT; CDA, CH, IU, MH, NN, WF.

Mercy in her exaltation. 1655. *See* Goodwin, John.

Mercy triumphant. 1696. *See* D., W.

1781 **[Meredith, Edward.]** A letter desiring information of the conference. colop: *By Henry Hills*, 1687. cap., 4°.* L, O, LSD, E, DT; CH, IU, MH, TU, WF, Y.

1782 [–] A letter to Dr. E. S[tillingfleet] concerning his late letter. *By Henry Hills*, 1687. 4°.* L, O, CT, E, DT; CH, IU, MH, NU, TU, WF, Y. (var.)

1783 —Some farther remarks on the late account given by Dr. Tenison. *By Henry Hills*, 1688. 4°. L, O, C, EN, DT; BN, CH, MH, NU, TU, WF, Y.

1784 [–] Some remarques upon a late popular piece of non-sence called Julian the Apostate. *For T. Davies*, 1682. fol.* L, O, CT, LSD, P; CH, MH, NU, WF, Y.

1785 **Meredith, Walter.** The fidelity, obedience, and valour. *By E. Griffin*. 1642. 4°.* LT, C, LVF, CT, BLH; CH, LC, MH, MIU, WF, Y.

1786 The merit and honour of the old English clergy. *For R. Royston*, 1662. 8°. L, O, CT, DU, DL; CLC, MM, NU.

1787 **Meriton, George.** Anglorum gesta; or, a brief history of England. *By T. Dawks, for Tho: Basset*, 1675. 12°. T.C.I 210. L, O, C; CH, CLC, CN, CPB, IU, LC, NCU, WF.

1788 ——Second edition. —, 1678. 12°. T.C.I 297. L, LI, LW, OM, DU; CH, CLC, IU, Y.

1789 —An exact abridgement of all the publick printed Irish statutes. *Dublin, by and for Andrew Crook, for Matthew Gunne and Eliphal Dobson*, 1700. 8°. DIX 320. L, CD, DK, DM, DT; CLC, LC, MHL, MIU, WF.

1790 [–] A geographicall description of the world. *For William Leake*, 1671. 8°. T.C.I 66. L, O, C, BC; CH, IU, RPJ, Y.

1791 ——Second edition. *For William Leake, and John Leake*, 1674. 12°. T.C.I 157. L, OC; CH, IU, MH, MU, NN, Y.

1792 ——Third edition. —, 1679. 12°. T.C.I 362. L, C; CLC, NN, TU, WF.

1793 —A guide for constables. *For A. Crook, W. Leak, A. Roper, F. Tyton, G. Sawbridge, J. Place, W. Place, J. Starkey, T. Basset, R. Pawley, & S. Heyrick*, 1669. 12°. T.C.I 10. L, LUG, CS, DC; FU, IU, MHL, PUL.

1793A ——Second edition. —, 1671. 12°. MM.

1794 ——Third edition. —, 1671. 12°. T.C.I 77. L, WCA; BN, MHI, MU.

1795 ——Fourth edition. *For Geo. Sawbridge, A. Crook, W. Leak, A. Roper, F. Tyton, J. Place, W. Place, J. Starky, T. Basset, R. Pawlet, and S. Heyrick*, 1674. 12°. T.C.I 193. L, P; CH, MHL, Y.

1795A ——Fifth edition. *For G. Sawbridge, A. Roper, F. Tyton, W. Place, J. Starkey, T. Bassett, R. Pawlet, S. Heyrick, J. Place, and W. and J. Leake*, 1677. 12°. T.C.I 263. MHL, V.

1796 ——Sixth edition. *For G. Sawbridge, A. Roper, F. Tyton, J. Starky, T. Basset, R. Pawlet, S. Heyrick, W. R. J. Place, and W. and J. Leak*, 1679. 12°. T.C.I 363. L, O, LI, DU, YM; CLC, MH, TO.

1797 ——"Sixth" edition. *For John Norton*, 1681. 12°. L, O, OM; BN, Y.

1797A ——Seventh edition. *For H. Herringman, H. Sawbridge, F. Tyton, J. Starky, T. Basset, R. Pawlet, S. Heyrick, W. R. J. Place, and W. Leak*, 1682. 12°. L, LG, LUG, EC; LC, MHL, MIU.

1798 ——[Anr. ed.] *By the assigns of Richard and Edward Atkins, for Langley Curtis and Thomas Simons*, 1683. 12°. CT.

1798A ——Eighth edition. *By the assigns of Richard and Edward Atkins*, 1685. 12°. L, O, CT, NPL; CN, WF.

1799 —A guide to surveyors. *London, by W. Rawlins and S. Roycroft, assigns of Rich. and Edw. Atkins: for A. and J. Churchill, and Fr. Hildyard in York*, 1694. 8°. T.C.II 492. L, O, LGI, OM, YM; CH, CLC, LC, WF.

1800 —Immorality, debauchery, and profaneness, exposed. *For John Harris and Andrew Bell*, 1698. 8°. T.C.III 74. L, O, LUG, NE, EN; CH, TO.

1801 ——Second edition. —, 1698, 8°. L; MH.

1802 —Land-lords law. *By the assigns of John More*, 1665. 12°. L, CT; PUL.

1803 ——[Anr. ed.] *For Henry Twyford, Thomas Dring, and John Place*, 1665. 12°. L, O, LUG, CCA; CH, LC, MHL, MIU, PUL, WF, YL.

1803A ——[Anr. ed.] *For T. D. and J. P.*, 1668. 8°. L, LUG; LC.

1804 ——Third edition. *For John Place, and Thomas Basset*, 1669. 12°. T.C.I 15. L, CS, DC, NE; CSU, MHL, MIU, NCL, TO.

1805 ——Fourth edition. *For T. Basset and J. Place*, 1681. 12°. T.C.I 447. L, C, LMT, CP, DU; CH, CLC, MHL, NCL.

1806 ——Fifth edition. *For W. Battersby, and John Place*, 1697. 12°. L, O, LUG, EN; CH, LC, MHL, PUL, WF.

—New guide for constables. [1692.] *See* P., J.

1807 —Nomenclatura clericalis: or, the young clerk's vocabulary. *London, for Richard Lambert, in York, and are to sold* [sic] *by the booksellers of London*. 1685. 8°. T.C.II 113. L, O, LL, DU, LLU; CH, IU, MH, PUL, WF.

1808 —The parson's monitor. *By the assigns of Richard and Edw. Atkins, for Richard Tonson*, 1681. 12°. T.C.I 450. L, O, C, CE, BLH; CH, LC, PU, WF, Y.

1809 [–] The praise of Yorkshire ale. *York: by J. White, for Francis Hildyard*, 1685. 8°. L, O, LLU, YM, EN; CH, CN, LC, NP.

1810 [–] —Third edition. —, 1697. 8°. L, O, LU, LVD, CT; CH, CN, MH, TU, WF, Y.

1811 —The touchstone of wills. *For W. Leak, A. Roper, F. Tyton, T. Dring, J. Place, W. Place, J. Starkey, T. Basset, R. Pawlet, & S. Herrick,* 1668. 8°. C; MHL, NRU, PUL.

1812 — —Second edition. *For W. Leak, A. Roper, F. Tyton, J. Place, W. Place, J. Starkey, T. Basset, R. Pawlet, and S. Herrick,* 1671. 12°. T.C.I 77. L, LGI, CJ, P; MHL, WF.

1813 — —Third edition. —, 1674. 12°. T.C.I 193. L, O; CH, LC, MHL, NCL, PUL, YL.

1814 [–] A York-shire dialogue. *York, by John White, and are to be sold by Richard Lambert,* 1683. 4°. L, O, CT, NPL; MH, Y.

1814A Entry cancelled.
—York-shire dialogue. York, 1697. *See* —Praise of Yorkshire ale.

1814B **Meriton, Henry.** A sermon preacht . . . 11th of April, 1696. *For George Rose,* 1695 [sic]. 4°.* NPL; Y.

1814C — —[Anr. ed.] —, *in Norwich,* 1696. 4°.* NE.

1815 —A sermon preacht . . . 11th of April, 1696. *Printed, and are to be sold by Eliz. Whitlock,* 1696. 4°.* L, O, C, OC; CB.

1816 **Meriton, John,** *1662-1717.* An antidote against the venom of Quakerism. *For the author: and are to be sold by J. Robinson, and H. Rhodes,* 1699. 8°.* L, O, C, LF, OC; PL, RPJ.

1817 **Meriton, John,** *1636-1704.* Curse not the King. *By J. Macock for Henry Herringman,* 1660[1]. 4°.* LT, O, CT, MR, SC; CH, NGT, NU, WF.

1818 —Forms of prayer. *By H. H. for Robert Boulter,* 1682. 8°. O, C, LW; CLC.

1819 Entry cancelled.
—Obligation. 1670. *See* Meriton, John, b. 1629.

1820 —Religio militis. A sermon. *For Ralph Smith,* 1672. 4°.* T.C.I 125. L, O, C, OC, SP; CN, MIU.

1820A **Meriton, John,** *b. 1629.* The obligation of a good conscience. *By S. G. and B. G. for Francis Eglesfield,* 1670. 4°.* T.C.I 65. L, O, C, DU, WCA.

1821 —A sermon preached . . . July 30. 1676. *For Simon Miller,* 1677. 4°.* T.C.I 250. L, O, C, LL, LSD; CH, CLC, MIU, V, WF, Y.

1821A [**Meriton, L.**] Pecuniae obediunt omnia. *York: by John White for the author, and sold by Tho: Baxter,* 1696. 8°. L, O; CH, MH, NN, WCL, Y.

1821B [–] —Second edition. *Printed, and sold by the booksellers of London and Westminster,* 1698. 8°. L, O, LLU; CH, IU, MH, NN, WF, Y.

1822 **Meriton, Thomas.** Love and war. *For Charles Webb,* 1658. 4°. L, O, OW, EC, EN; CH, CN, LC, MH, WF, Y.

1823 —A sermon preached . . . July 22. 1690. *Printed,* 1690. 4°.* L, C.

1824 [–] The wandring lover. *By T. L. for T. C. and W. Burden,* 1658. 4°. L, O, LVD, OW, CS; CH, CU, LC, WF, Y.

1825 The merits of the election between the Honourable Craven Howard. [1699.] fol.* LL.

1825AA Munday, November 24. The merits of the election for the city of Chester. [*London,* 1690.] brs. LPR.

1825A The merits of the election of Richard Williams. [*London?* 168–?] brs. CH.

1825B Entry cancelled.
Merke, Thomas, bp. Character of. [n.p., 1689.] *See* Godwin, Francis, *bp.*

1826 —A pious and learned speech. *For N. V. and J. B.,* [1642?]. 4°.* LT, O, C, MR, EN, DT; CH, CN, MH, TU, WF, Y.

1827 —The Bishop of Carlile's speech in Parliament, concerning deposing of princes. *Printed,* 1679. fol.* LT, O, C, MR, EN; CH, CN, LC, MBA, MH, WF, Y.
—Speech spoken by . . . with some observations. [n.p., 1689.] *See* title.

1828 Merlin reviv'd: or, an old prophecy. *For S. S.,* 1681. brs. L, O, C, LLU; CH, CLC, CN, MH, WF, Y.

1829 —[Anr. ed.] [1681.] brs. O, LL; CH.

1830 —[Anr. ed.] [*London,* 1682.] brs. L, O, OP, HH; CN, MH, TSM, TU, Y, ASU.

1831 Entry cancelled. Ghost.

1831A Merlini Anglici errata. [*London*], *printed,* 1697. 8°. L.

1832 Merlini liberati errata; or. *For G. C.,* 1692. 4°.* O, C; Y.
Merlins prophesies. 1651. *See* Heywood, Thomas.
Merlinus Anglicus junior. 1644. *See* Almanacs. Lilly, William.
Merlinus Anglicus, or. 1650. *See* Almanacs. A., M.
Merlinus liberatus. [1690.] *See* Almanacs. Partridge, John.
Merlinus Scotus. Edinburgh, 1698. *See* Almanacs. T., J.
Merlinus verax: or. 1687. *See* Almanacs.

1833 No entry.

1834 Meroveus, a prince. *For R. Bentley and M. Magnes,* 1682. 12°. T.C.I 461. L; CLC, CN, NCD, NCU, WF.

1835 [**Merret, Christopher.**] The accomplisht physician. *Printed,* 1670. 4°. T.C.I 48. L, LWL, OR, CCA; CH, CJC, NAM, PCP, WF, HC.

1835A —Catalogus librorum. [15 *December* 1660.] 4°. L.

1835B [–] The character of a compleat physician. colop: *For E. H.,* [1680?]. 4°.* L, O, LCS; CSS.

1835C [–] —[Anr. ed.] [n.p., 1680?] 4°.* O, LWL; WSG.

1836 —A collection of acts of Parliament. [*London*], *Anno Dom.,* 1660. 4°. L, O, LCP, GH, DT; CH, NAM, WF, HC.

1836A —Dr. Merrett aged 81 and upwards . . . this proposition. [*London,* 1695.] brs. O.

1837 Entry cancelled. [–] Letter concerning the present state. *See* M., T.
[–] Lex talionis. 1679. *See* Stubbe, Henry.

1838 Entry cancelled.
[–] Medice, cura teipsum. 1671. *See* Stubbe, Henry.

1839 —Pinax rerum naturalium. *Impensis Cave Pulleyn, typis F. & T. Warren,* 1666. 8°. L, O, LR, LSC, MC; CH, CLC, MH, MMO.

1840 — —Second edition. *Typis T. Roycroft, impensis Cave Pulleyn,* 1667. 8°. L, O, CT, MAU, E, AM; BN, CH, CJC, MH, NAM, WDA.

1840A — —"Second" edition. —, *prostant apud Sam. Thompson*, 1667. 8°. L, O, C, SHR.

1841 —Self-conviction; or an enumeration of the absurdities. *For James Allestry*, 1670. 4°.* T.C.I 38. L, O, C, LCP, SA; BN, CH, CN, LC, MH, MIU, HC.

1842 —A short reply to the postscript. *By T. R. for J. Allestry*, 1670. 4°.* L, O, LCP, LWL, GU; BN, LC, TO.

1843 —A short view of the fravds. *For James Allestry*, 1669. 4°. T.C.I 26. L, O, C, LCS, GU; CH, MH, MIU, MMO, TO, Y.

1844 — —Second edition. —, 1670. 4°. T.C.I 40. L, O, C, GU, DT; BN, CLC, LC, MH, NU, TU, WF.

1845 **Merrifield, John.** Catastasis mvndi: or the true state. *For Rowland Reynolds*, 1684. 4°.* T.C.II 87. L, O, DU, P, EN; CH, MH, MIU, HC.

1845A —Catastrophe Galliæ: or the French king's fatal downfal. *Rowland Reynolds*, 1691. 4°. CN.

1846 **M[erriott], T[homas].** Grammaticall miscellanies. *Oxford, by A. Lichfield*, 1660. 8°. MADAN 2507. L, O, C, EC.

1847 [–] Vvlgaria sive miscellanea. *Oxoniæ, excudebat L. Lichfield, impensis authoris*, 1652. 8°. MADAN 2198. LT, O; WF, Y.

1848 **Merry, Nat.** Cure for the dogmatical incurables. colop: *By T. James*, 1682. brs. L.

1848A —Evident satisfaction to the sick. [*London*, 1682?] brs. L.

1848B —A friendly and seasonable advertisement concerning the dog-days. [*London*, 1682?] brs. L.

1849 —A plea for the chymists or non-colegiats. colop: *For the author Nat. Merry*, 1683. brs. L.

1849A A merry and pleasant discourse. *For W. Thacery* [*sic*] *and W. Whitwood*, [1666–92]. brs. O.

    Merry Andrew. Edinburgh, 1699. See Almanacs.

1850 The merry bag-pipes. [*London*], *for C. Bates*, [1688–92]. brs. L, CM, HH; MH.

1851 A merrie ballad, called, Christs Kirk on the green. [*London*], *for Patrick Wilson*, 1643. brs. LT; MH.

    Merry bell-man's out-cryes. [n.p.], 1655. See C., J.

1852 The merry boys of Christmas. [*London*, 1660?] brs. L.

1853 The merry boys of Europe. [*London*], *for J. Clarke*, [1682?]. brs. L.

1854 A merry conceited fortune-teller. *For John Andrews*, 1662. 12°. L.

    Merry conceited humors of Bottom. 1661. See Shakespeare, William.

    Merry conceits and passages. [1685.] See P., J.

1855 The merry country maids answer. *For R. Burton*, [168–?]. brs. O, CM.

1856 The merry devil of Edmonton. *For William Gilbertson*, 1655. 4°.* L, LVD, CT; CH, NNM, WF, Y.

1856A A merry dialogue between a maid. *For F. Coles, T. Vere, and J. Wright*, [1663–74]. brs. O.

    Merry dialogue between Andrew. [1680.] See W., L.

1857 A merry dialogue between Band, Cuff, and Ruff. *For F. K.*, 1661. 4°.* L; CH, LC, MH.

    Merry dialogue between a doctor. [n.p., 1670.] See J., T.

1858 A merry dialogue between Thomas and John. [*London*], *for J. Williamson*, [1665]. brs. L, O.

1858A A merry dialogue between Tom the taylor. *For I. Clarke*, 1684. 8°.* CM.

1858B A merry discourse between Billy and his mistris. [*London*], *for F. Jordan*, [1684]. brs. L.

1859 The merry discourse between two lovers. *For John Clarke*, [168–?]. brs. O.

1860 Merry drollery, . . . the first part. *By J. W. for P. H.*, [1661?]. 8°. O; Y.

1861 Merry drollery complete. *For Simon Miller*, 1670. 8°. T.C.I 22. O; CH, Y.

1862 —[Anr. ed.] *For William Miller*, 1691. 8°. T.C.II 397. L, O.

1863 The merry Dutch miller. *By E. Crowch, for F. Coles, T. Vere, and J. Wright*, 1672. 8°. L.

1864 The merry gossips vindication. [*London*], *for P. Brooksby*, [1672–95]. brs. L, HH.

1864A The merry hay-makers. *For C. B.*, [1689–94]. brs. EUING 215. GU.

    Merry hoastess. [1660.] See Robins, Thomas.

1864B A merry life and a short. [*London*], *for P. Brooksby*, [1672–96]. brs. O.

1865 The merry maid of Middlesex. *By E. Crowch, for F. Coles, T. Vere, & J. Wright*, [1663–74]. brs. O, HH; MH.

1866 The merry maid of Shoreditch. [*London*], *for J. Deacon*, [1680–90]. brs. O, HH; MH.

    Merry mans resolution; or, his last farewel. [1655.] See Price, Laurence.

1867 Entry cancelled.

    Merry mans resolution, or, a London frolick. [1665.] See J., T.

1868 The merry milk-maid. [*London*], *for P. Brooksby, J. Deacon, J. Blare, and J. Back*, [1688–92]. brs. HH; MH.

1869 The merry milkmaid of Islington. *For Dan. Browne, Dan. Major, and James Vade*, 1680. 4°.* T.C.I 440. L, O, LG; CH.

1870 The merry milk-maids. *For J. Deacon*, [1688–92]. brs. L, O, HH.

1870A A merry new ballad, both pleasant and sweete. [*London?* 1650.] brs. L.

1871 A merry new dialogue, between a courteous young knight. *For W. Thackery*, [1688–9]. brs. O.

    Merry new song. [n.p., 1660.] See H., C.

1872 Merry nevves from Epsom-Wells. *For G. Kendal*, 1663. 4°.* L.

1872AA The merry Oxford knight. *By A. M. for James Bissel*, [c. 1690]. CM.

1872A A merry, pleasant, and delectable history, between K. Edward the fourth. *For F. Cole*, [1680?]. 8°.* CH.

1873 The merry plow-man. [*London*], *for I. Deacon*, [1684–95]. brs. L, CM, HH; MH.

    Merry tales. [n.p., 1690.] See Borde, Andrew.

1873A Merry Tom of all trades. [*London*], *Fran. Coles, John Wright, Tho. Vere, and William Gilbertson*, 1656. brs. O, CM, HH.

1873B —[Anr. ed.] [*London*], *for F. Coles, T. Vere, and W. Gilbertson*, [1658–64]. brs. O.

1873C —[Anr. ed.] [*London*], *for F. Coles, T. Vere, I. Wright, and I. Clarke*, [1674–79]. brs. O.

1874   —[Anr. ed.] *[London], for I. Wright, I. Clarke, W. Thackeray, and T. Passinger*, [1681–84]. brs. L, HH.

1874A A merry vvedding, or, O brave Arthur. *For F. Coles, T. Vere, J. Wright, and J. Clarke*, [1674–79]. brs. O.

1875   —[Anr. ed.] *By and for W. O. for A. M. and sold by J. Deacon*, [1695]. brs. HH; MH.

1875A —[Anr. ed.] *[n.p., n.d.]* brs. EUING 214. GU.

1876   The merry wives of Wapping. *For F. Coles, T. Vere, J. Wright, and J. Clarke*, [1674–79?]. brs. O.

1876A —[Anr. ed.] *[n.p., 1700?]* brs. L.

1877   The merry wooing of Robin & Joan. *[London], for J. Conyers, [c. 1695]*. brs. L, CM.

1877A [**Merryweather, John.**] Directions for the Latine tongue. *For Benj. Tooke*, 1681. 8°. T.C.I 429. O, GK; CH, WF.

   Mersen. *See* Marsin.

1878   **Mervault, Pierre de.** The last famous siege of . . . Rochel. *For John Wickins*, 1679. 8°. T.C.I 369. L, O, DU; BBE, PL.

1879   ——[Anr. ed.] —, 1680. 8°. C, CM, P, CD, DT; CH, CLC, INU, MH, PL, WF, Y.

1880   **Mervyn, Sir Audeley.** An exact relation of all svch occurrences. *For Tho. Downes and William Bladen*, 1642. 4°.* LT, O, C, EC, LIU, SP, CD; CH, CN, Y.

1880A ——[Anr. ed.] —, [1642]. 4°.* L, O, DT; MH.

1881   ——[Anr. ed.] *By Luke Norton and John Field, for Ralph Rounthwait*, [1642]. 4°.* MR, BQ; CLC, NU, WF.

1882   —Irelands complaint. *For John Thomas*. 1641. 4°.* LT, O, C, LVF, OC, BLH; CN, IU, MBP, MH, Y.

1883   —A speech delivered . . . to . . . Duke of Ormond . . . the 29. of July 1662. *Dublin, by VViliam [sic] Bladen*, 1662. 4°.* DIX 115. C, DT.

1884   ——Second edition. *Dublin, by W. B.*, 1662. 4°.* DIX 114. DN.

1885   —A speech delivered to the Duke of Ormond. *Dublin, Printed by J. Crook, reprinted at London*, 1665. fol. DIX 129. O.

1886   Entry cancelled.
   —Capt. Audley Mervin's speech. 1641. *See* England. Parliament. Speeches and passages.

1887   —Captaine Audley Mervin's speech delivered . . . to the Lords . . . May 24. 1641. Concerning the judicature. *For R. Royston*, 1641. 4°* LT, O, C, MR, BQ; CH, CN, MH, TU, WF, Y.

1888   ——[Anr. ed.] *Dublin, printed*, 1641. 4°.* DIX 74. C, EN, CD.

1888A —A speech made before the Lords . . . March the 4th. 1640. *[London], printed*, 1641. 4°.* L, O, DN; BBE, CH, CN, MH, NN, TU, WF, Y.

1889   —A speech made by . . . March 4, 1640. *[London], for Hugh Perry*, 1641. 4°.* LT, O, C, MR, DT; BN, CH, CN, MH, TU, WF, Y. (var.)

1890   —A speech made by . . . the 11th day of May. *Dublin, by William Bladen*, 1661. 4°.* DIX 111. L, O, C, EN, DT; CLC, CSS, MH.

1891   ——[Anr. ed.] *Printed at Dublin, by William Bladen. and re-printed at London by J. Streater*, 1661. 4°.* L, O; CN, MH, Y.

1892   —The speech of . . . delivered to . . . James Duke of Ormond, . . . the 13 day of February 1662. *Dublin, by W. B.*, 1662. 4°.* DIX 114. L, C, LPR, P, DN.

1892A ——[Anr. ed.] *Dublin, by William Bladen*, 1662. 4°.* BQ, DT.

1893   ——[Anr. ed.] *Printed at Dublin; and reprinted at London by J. Streater*, 1662. 4°.* L, O, C, MR, BLH, DT; CH, LC, MH, MU, WF, Y.

1894   ——[Anr. ed.] *Dublin, for Samuel Dancer*, 1663. 4°.* DIX 118. L, LI, LW, CD, DT; CN, MM.

1895   ——[Anr. ed.] *Dublin, for William Bladen*, 1663. 4°.* DIX 118. L, C, LVF, OB, BLH, DK; CN, WF, Y.

1895A ——[Anr. ed.] *[London], printed*, 1668. 4°.* L, C; CSS, MB.

1896   —Two speeches; the one. *For Samuel Speed*, 1662. fol.* C, MR.

1897   A messe of pottage, well seasoned. *[London*, 1643?] 4°.* L; LC.

1898   A message brought to the Parliament. *[London], for R. Smithurst*, 1648. 4°.* LT, CJ, LIU, MR, DT; IU, LC, MH, MU.

   Message for instruction. 1658. *See* Burrough, Edward.

   Message from the Estates. 1648. *See* Rosse, William.

1899   A message from the Isle of Wight, brought by Major Cromwell. *[London], for R. Smithurst*, 1648. 4°.* LT, LIU; IU, MH, WF, Y.

   Message from the King of Scotland. 1650. *See* Rishton, A.

1900   A message from the King of Scots: and the full and perfect relation. *For George Horton*, 1651. 4°.* Y.

1900A A message from the King of Scots, to his sister. *For George Horton*, 1651. 4°.* CH.

   Message from the Lord General Crumwel. 1650. *See* B., T.

   Message from the Lord, to all. 1653. *See* Farnworth, Richard.

1901   Entry cancelled.
   Message from the royall prisoner at Windsor. 1648. *See* Charles I.

   Message from the spirit. 1658. *See* Nayler, James.

   Message from Tory-land. [n.p.], 1682. *See* S., R.

1902   The message of John Lambert. *For Iames Dukeson*, 1660. brs. LT, O; CH, MH.

   Message of peace. 1642. *See* R., T.

1903   Entry cancelled.
   Message of thankes. 1642. *See* Pym, John.

   Message proclaimed. [1658.] *See* Burrough, Edward.

   Message sent forth. [n.p.], 1662. *See* Bayly, William.

   Message sent from his Highnesse. [n.p.], 1648. *See* Green, Robert.

1904   A message sent from the city of London, to the King. *[London], printed*, 1648. 4°.* LT, LIU.

   Message sent from the kingdom of Ireland. 1649. *See* Hopkins, William, *of Dublin*.

1905   A message sent from the kingdom of Scotland, . . . Octob. 18. *For R. VVilliamson*, 1648. 4°.* LT, LIU, DT; MH, WF, Y.

   Message sent from the kingdom of Scotland and to his. 1648. *See* Byfield, Richard.

1906   A message sent from the kingdome of Scotand [*sic*], to Major Generall Massey. *For R. W.*, 1648. 4°.* LT, MR, DT; Y.

Message sent from the Lord Hopton. 1650. *See* S., T.

1907   A message sent from the officers & souldiers in the army. *For R. Williamson*, 1648. 4°.* LT; MH.

1908   A message sent from the Princes court in Holland. *Imprinted at London, for G. Laurenson, Aprill* 5. 1649. 4°.* LT, LIU; MH, MU.

1909   A message sent to the King . . . 15 Novemb. 1648. *For H. Becke*, 1648. 4°.* LT; CN, CSS.

1910   A message sent to the L. Admiral Vantrump. *By E. C.*, 1652. 4°.* LT.

1911   Entry cancelled.

Message sent to the Parliament. [n.p.], 1642. *See* England. Parliament. Commons.

Message to all kings and rulers. [n.p., 1659.] *See* Burrough, Edward.

1912   A message to both houses of Parliament, for a personall treaty. *By Robert Ibbitson*, 1647. 4°.* LT, CM, MR; CH, CSS, IU, MH, MIU.

Messenger from the dead. 1658. *See* Perrinchief, Richard.

1913   A messenger of truth from the Common Hall. *For John Whitlock*, 1689. brs. CLC.

1914   Die 16. Octob. 1648. A messenger sent to the city of London. *For R. M.*, 1648. 4°.* LT; CLC.

Messiah found. 1656. *See* W., R.

Messias of the Christians. 1655. *See* Münster, Sebastian.

Messie, Petrus. *See* Mexia, Pedro.

1915   **Mestrezat, Jean.** Conference touchant le pedobaptesme. *Imprimé a Londres, par Thomas Creake*, 1654. 4°. LT.

1916   Metal for metal: or, a proposal. [*London?* 1694.] brs. NC.

Metamorphos'd beau. 1700. *See* Ward, Edward.

1917   Metamorphosis Anglorum, or, reflections historical. *For William Palmer*, 1660. 12°. LT; CLC.

1917A   —[Anr. ed.] *Printed*, 1660. 12°. CS; CH, CN, Y.

Metamorphosis Christiana. 1679. *See* Beare, Nicholas.

1918   **Metcalfe.** March 21th, 1641. A continuation of the good newes from Ireland. *For John Thomas*, 1641. 4°.* L, O, C, EC, SP.

1919   **Metcalfe, Francis.** Cortex Peruvianus. [*Cambridge*], 1663. brs. L.

—Hemerologeion. [1654.] *See* Almanacs.

1920   Entry cancelled. Ghost.

1921-2   No entries.

1923   **Metcalfe, Theophilus.** A school-master to radio-stenography. *Printed, and are to be sold by John Hancock*, 1649. 8°. LU.

1924   — —[Anr. ed.]—, 1668. 8°.* LU, MC, EN.

1925   —Short writing. Sixth edition. *For the author. Sould at his house. & at Mr. Simpsons*, 1645. 12°.* L; BN.

1926   — —"Sixth" edition. *For Io: Hancock*, 1646. 12°.* L, LU; BN.

1927   — —Seventh edition. *Printed, and are to be sold by John Hancock*, 1650. 8°. * L (lost).

1928   — —Eighth edition. —, 1652. 16°.* L, LU; NN.

1928A   — —Ninth edition. —, 1657. 8°. LU.

1929   — —[Anr. ed.]—, 1660. 8°. L; WF.

1930   — —[Anr. ed.]—, 1668. 8°. LC, NN.

1931   — —"Ninth" edition. —, 1669. 8°. L, MC, EN; Y.

1932   — —[Anr. ed.] —, 1674. 16°. T.C.I 191. O, LU; CH, LC, MWA, NN.

1933   — —[Anr. ed.] —, 1679. 8°. L, C, LNM, LU, EN; NN.

1934   — —Tenth edition.—, 1681. 8°. LU; CLC.

1935   — —[Anr. ed.] —, 1690. 8°.* T.C.II 341. LU, CM; Y.

1936   — —[Anr. ed.] *For John Hancock*, 1698. 8°. L, O, LU; MH.

Metellus his dialogues. 1693. *See* Lewkenor, John.

Μετεμψυχωσις, or. 1692. *See* Bulstrode, Whitelocke.

Meteors: or. 1654. *See* Fulke, William.

1937   **Metford, James.** A discourse of licenses to preach. *For H. Hindmarsh*, 1698. 4°.* L, O, CT, BAMB, EC; MH, NR, Y.

1938   —A general discourse of simony. *London, for Joseph Lawson, in Lincoln; and sold by R. Chiswel, and T. Sawbridge*, 1682. 8°. T.C.I 509. L, O, C, DU, DT; CH, CLC, MH, PU, WF, Y.

1939   Methinks the poor town has been troubled. [*n.p.*], *printed*, 1673. 8°.* L, O, OC; CN.

1940   —Second edition. —, 1673. 8°.* MH.

1941   Entry cancelled.

Method concerning the relief. 1699. *See* Child, *Sir* Josiah.

1942   Entry cancelled.

Method for an immediate coinage. [n.p., 1695.] *See* Slaney, Abel.

Method for executing. 1684. *See* N., F.

1942A   A method how to offer up mass. *By T. H.*, 1694. FARM, WARE.

Method of a synod. 1642. *See* T., G.

1943   The method of chemical philosophie and physick. *By J. G. for Nath. Brook*, 1664. 8°. L, O, LWL, GU; CH, WF, HC.

Method of conversing with God. 1692. *See* Boutauld, Michel.

1944   A method of curing the French pox. *For John Taylor, and Thomas Newborough*, 1690. 12°. LM (dispersed).

1945   A method of gaining the whole Christian world to be converts. colop: *By Henry Hills*, 1687. brs. L, SP; CH, CN, MH, TU, WF, Y.

A method of pleading by rule. 1697. *See* Gardiner, Robert.

1946   The method of saying the rosary. [*London*], *printed*, 1669. 16°. O, LLP, DOWNSIDE.

1947   —[Anr. ed.] [n.p.], 1684. 12°. EN, CD.

1947A   —[Anr. ed.] *Duaci apud B. Bellerum*, 1684. 24°. L.

1947B   —Sixteenth edition. *By N. T.*, 1686. 8°.* Y.

1947C   —"Sixteenth" edition. *Printed*, 1686. 12°.* L, LLP.

1947D   —Seventeenth edition. *Printed*, 1686. 16°. LLP, OC, CS; CH.

1947E   —"Seventeenth" edition. *By N. T.*, 1687. 8°. DOUAI ABBEY, BERKS.

1948   The method of turning the militia of Scotland. colop: *Reprinted at London (according to . . . Edinburgh) for John Gay and William English*, 1680. cap., fol.* L, O, C, OP, MR; CH, CSS, MH, WF, Y.

1948A The method, orders, and rulles . . . appointed . . . plantation in Ulster. [*London*, 1690.] brs. LG.

1949 A method proposed for the regulating the coin. [*London?* 1696.] brs. LUG; MH.

1949A A method proposed to the Honourable House of Commons for ordering and collecting the duties to be paid . . . upon births, marriages. [*London*, 1694.] brs. L.

Method to arrive. [n.p., 1671.] *See* Sergeant, John.

Methode to gain satisfaction. 1673. *See* P., J.

Method to science. 1696. *See* Sergeant, John.

1949B Methods to prevent smuggling in Great Britain. [*n.p.*, 168–?] cap., fol.* NC.

Methodus concionandi. 1648. *See* Chappell, William, *bp.*

Methodus novissima. 1699. *See* Brown, William.

1949C **Meurisse, F. M.** A laurell of metaphysicke. [*London*], *are to be sold by Ro: Walton*, [1650?]. brs. MH.

1950 **Mewe, William.** The robbing and spoiling of Jacob and Israel. *Printed at London for Christopher Meredith*, 1643. 4°. LT, O, C, E, DT; CH, IU, MH, NCD, NU, WF, Y.

1951 [**Mews, Peter**], *bp.* An account of the late visitation at St. Mary Magdal. Colledge . . . 24th of October 1688. colop: *For Randal Taylor*, 1688. cap., fol.* L, O, C, OC, MR; CH, CN, MH, MIU, WF, Y.

1952 [–] The ex-ale-tation of ale. *By T. Badger*, 1646. 8°.* LT.

1952A [–] —[Anr. ed.] *By M. I. for F. Coles*, 1663. brs. O.

1953 [–] —[Anr. ed.] *By J. R.*, 1668. 8°.* L; TU.

1954 [–] —[Anr. ed.] —, 1671. 8°.* O, LVD, LLU, GH; CH, MH, WF.

1955 [–] Exaltatio alæ. The ex-ale-tation of ale. [*London*], 1666. 8°.* L, O; PU, Y.

1956 **Mexia, Pedro.** The rarities of the world. *By B. A.*, 1651. cap., 4°. L, CE, BC, EN, CD; CLC, INU, MH, MIU, TO, Y.

1957 —The wonders of the world. *For John Andrews*, 1656. 4°. L.

1958 **Mézeray, Francois-Eudes de.** A general chronological history of France. *By T. N. for Thomas Basset, Samuel Lowndes, Christopher Wilkinson, William Cademan, and Jacob Tonson*, 1683. fol. T.C.II 28. L, O, C, EN, DT; CH, CU, MH, MU, NCD, Y.

1959 [**Micanzio, Fulgenzio.**] The life of the most learned Father Paul. *For Humphrey Moseley, and Richard Marriot*, 1651. 8°. L, O, C, LW, EN, DT; CLC, CN, MMO, NU, TU, WF, Y.

1960 No entry.

1961 Entry cancelled.

Michael opposing the dragon. 1659. *See* Coppin, Richard.

1961A Michaelmass term: the citizens kind welcome. [*London*], *for F. Coles, J. W., T. Vere, W. Gilbertson*, [1655–8.] brs. L.

1961B —[Anr. ed.] [*London*], *for F. Coles, T. Vere, and J. Wright*, [1663–74]. brs. O.

1962 **Michel, James.** The spovse rejoycing. *Printed*, 1654. 8°.* LT.

1963 [**Michel, Peter.**] A victory obtained by Lieut: Gen: David Lesley. *By Robert Wood*, 1650. 4°.* LT, DT; CLC.

1964 [**Michel, Thomas.**] The last nevves from the armie: June the twentieth, 1647. *For James Neale, June 21.* 1647. 4°.* MADAN 1935. LT, O, ESS; NN, Y.

1965 [**Michelborne, John.**] An account of the transactions in the north of Ireland. 1692. 4°. L, O, BLH, DT; CH, CN, WF.

Micro-chronicon: or. [n.p.], 1647. *See* Ryves, Bruno.

Μικροκοσμογραφια. A description. 1654. *See* Turner, Robert.

Micro-cosmographie. 1650. *See* Earle, John.

1966–9 No entries.

Middle state of souls. [n.p.], 1659. *See* White, Thomas, *Catholic.*

Middle-way. 1672. *See* Humfrey, John.

1969A **Middlesex.** At the general quarter sessions . . . rates of wages for labourers. [*London*, 1665?] fol. L.

1969B —Midd. ss. As generalem sessionem pacis . . . [8 December 1673, order estreating fines]. [*London*, 1673.] brs. L.

—Mid. ss. Ad general. quarterial. sessionem . . . [14 October 1681] . . . VVereas by a statute . . . [suppression of conventicles]. [n.p., 1681.] *See* Ad general.

1969C —Mid. ss. Ad general. quarterial. sessionem . . . [18 October 1681] . . . In pursuance of an order . . . [suppression of conventicles]. [*London*, 1681.] brs. CH.

1969D —Midd. ss. Ad general. sessionem pacis . . . [5 December] . . . directed Sir William Smith to speak. [*London*, 1681.] fol. LSD.

—Midd. ss. Ad generalem sessionem . . . [22 December 1681] . . . Whereas by an order . . . [suppression of conventicles]. 1681. *See* Ad generalem.

—Midd. ss. Ad general. quarterial. sessionem . . . [13 January 1681/2] . . . VVhereas at a sessions . . . [against dissenting preachers]. 1682. *See* Ad general.

1969E —Midd. s.s. By their Majesties commissioners . . . these are to certifie . . . [poll tax]. [*London*, 169–?] brs. OP.

—Mid. ss. Ad general. quarterial. session . . . [order about vice]. 1691. *See* Ad general.

1969F —Midd. ss. Ad general' quarterial' session' pacis . . . [10 July 1691. Reformation of manners]. 1691. brs. L.

—Midd. ss. Ad generalem sessionem pacis . . . [14 October 1692. Order about vice]. [n.p., 1692.] *See* Ad generalem.

1969G —Middl'ss. Ad generalem quarterialem sessionem pacis . . . [order concerning convex lights]. [*London*, 1694.] brs. LG.

1970 Middles[ex]. These are to will and require you. [*London*, 1658.] brs. LT.

1971 **Middleton, George.** Theses philosophicæ. *Abredoniæ, excudebat Ioannes Forbesius iunior*, 1675. 4°.* ALDIS 2066. E.

1972 Entry cancelled.

[**Middleton, John Middleton**], *earl.* Academiæ Edinburgenæ gratulatio. Edinburgh, 1661. *See* Edinburgh University.

1973 —Die Saturn: 13 Junii 1685. The Earl of Middleton acquaints the House. *Edinburgh, heir of A. Anderson*, 1685. brs. ALDIS 2541. EN.

1974 —An exact [sic] of Lievtenant Generall Middletons letter. *By G. Bishop, August.* 28. 1644. 4°.* LT, O, MR; MH, NN, WF.

1975 —For the good of the publick. *Edinburgh, for the author,* [1700?]. 4°.* ALDIS 3985. L.

1976 —A letter from His Majesties quarters. *By E. G.,* 1646. 4°.* L.

1977 [–] Scholæ Edinensis in Caroli II . . . Ode. *Edinburgi, excudebat Gideon Lithgo,* 1661. 4°. ALDIS 1718. ES.

1978 **Middleton, John,** *astrologer.* Practical astrology. *By J. C. for Richard Preston,* 1679. 8°. T.C.I 343. L, O, C; CLC, CN, CU, MH, WF, HC.

1978A **Middleton, Richard.** The true way to compass heaven on earth. *For J. Williams,* 1641. 12°. LSC.

1979 **Middleton, Thomas.** Any thing for a quiet life. A comedy. *By Tho. Johnson for Francis Kirkman, and Henry Marsh,* 1662. 4°. L, O, LVD, LIU, EN; CH, LC, MH, WCL, WF, Y.

1980 —The changeling. *For Humphrey Moseley,* 1653. 4°. L, O, LVD, CK, LIU, EN; CH, IU, LC, MH, TU, WF, Y.

1981 ——[Anr. ed.] *Printed,* 1653. 4°. O, CT; CH, WCL.

1982 [–]——[Anr. ed.] *For A. M. and sold by Thomas Dring,* 1668. 4°. L, O, LG, OC; CH, CN, MH, WF, Y.

1983 [–] The counterfeit bridegroom. *For Langley Curtiss,* 1677. 4°. T.C.I 291. L, O, LVD, OW, EN; CH, CN, LC, MH, WCL, WF, Y.

1984 —The mayor of Quinborough: a comedy. *For Henry Herringman,* 1661. 4°. L, O, LVD, CK, EN; CH, CN, MH, TU, WF, Y.

1984A ——[Anr. ed., "a tragedy."] —, 1661. 4°. EN; CH.

1985 —No $\left\{ \begin{array}{c} \text{wit} \\ \text{help} \end{array} \right\}$ like a woman's. A comedy. *For Humphrey Moseley,* 1657. 8°. L, O, LVD, OW, LIU; CH, CN, LC, MH, WCL, WF, Y.

1986 —The Spanish gipsie. *By I. G. for Richard Marriot,* 1653. 4°. L, O, LVD, CT, IIU, EN; CH, CN, MH, WF, Y.

1987 ——Second edition. *By T. C. and L. P. for Robert Crofts,* 1661. 4°. L, O, OC, OW, EN; CH, CN, LC, MH, TU, WF, Y.

1988 ——[Anr. ed.] *By T. C. and L. P. for Francis Kirkman,* 1661. 4°. LVD, EN; CH, LC, WF, Y.

1989 —Two new playes, viz. More dissemblers besides women. Women beware women. *For Humphrey Moseley,* 1657. 8°. L, O, LVD, CT, LIU; CH, CN, LC, MH, TU, WCL, WF, Y.

1990 [**Middleton, Thomas**], *divine.* An appendix to the history of the Church of Scotland. *By E. Flesher, for R. Royston,* 1677. 47 pp. fol. L, O, C, EN, GU; CH, CN, MH, TO, TU, WF.

1991 [–]——[Anr. ed.] —, 1677. 77 pp. 4°. L, LW, MR, E, AU; CH, CLC, IU, MH, NU, WF.

1992 **Middleton, Sir Thomas.** A copy of a letter sent from. *For Edward Husbands, July* 10. 1644. 4°.* LT, O, OB, AN; CH, IU, WF, Y.

1993 —A declaration, pvblished by . . . setting forth the illegality. *For Io. Thomas,* 1644. 4°.* L, C, AN, A, DT; CH, CN, MH, WF, Y.

1994 **Midgley, Robert.** Geographia universalis, or. 1694. 8°. OME.

1995 [–] A new treatise of natural philosophy. *By R. E. for J. Hindmarsh,* 1687. 12°. T.C.II 188. L, CM, LLU, P; CH, MH, MMO, PL, SE, WF, WU, HC.

1995A —Popery banished. *Edinburgh, reprinted,* 1689. 4°.* L; Y.

1996 **Midhope, Stephen.** Deaths advantage. *By L. N. for Francis Eglesfield,* 1644. 4°.* LT, O, C, LW, WCA; CH, MH, WF.

Midnight-cry. 1691. *See* Mason, John.

1997 A midnight ramble to a catch. *[London], for Charles Corbet,* [c. 1683]. brs. MH.

1998 Entry cancelled.

Mid-night thoughts. 1682. *See* Killigrew, *Sir* William.

1999 A midnight touch at an unlicens'd pamphlet called, A vindication of the arch-bishop. *[London,* 1690.] brs. L, OC; CLC, TU.

2000 The mid-nights watch. *For George Lindsey,* 1643. 4°.* LT, OC, DT; CH, WF, Y.

2001 The midshipman's garland. *For J. Walter,* [1694?]. brs. L.

Midsummer-moone. [n.p.], 1648. *See* Winyard, Thomas.

2001A The midsummer wish. *[n.p.,* 1670?] brs. L.

2002 The midwife unmask'd. colop: *For T. Davies,* 1680. cap., fol.* L, O, DU, MR; CH, MH, NP, NU, WF, Y.

2003 [The midwi]ves ghost. *For T. Vere,* 1680. brs. O.

2004 The mid-wives just complaint. *For T. S.,* 1646. 4°.* LT; NC, WSG.

2005 The mid-wives just petition. *Printed at London,* 1643. 4°.* LT, O, LWL, OW; CLC, INU, NC, TO.

2006 Entry cancelled. Ghost.

2006A [**Miege, Guy.**] Compleat guide to the English tongue. *For R. Wild,* 1689. 8°. T.C.II 279. HAMBURG.

2007 [–] A complete history of the late revolution. *For Samuel Clement,* 1691. 4°. L, LW, BC, DU, EN; HR, CH, CN, MH, WF, Y.

2008 [–] Delight and pastime. *For J. Sprint, and G. Conyers,* 1697. 8°. T.C.II 7. L, O; IU, WCL, WF, Y.

2009 Entry cancelled.

—Dictionary of barbarous French. 1679. *See* Cotgrave, Randle.

2010 —The English grammar. *By J. Redmayne, for the author,* 1688. 8°. T.C.II 233. C, LSC, AN.

2011 ——Second edition. *For John Wyat and Samuel Clement,* 1691. 8°. T.C.II 363. O, GU; CLC, IU.

2012 —The great French dictionary. *By J. Redmayne, for Tho. Basset,* 1688. fol. T.C.II 224. L, O, C, GU, DT; CH, CU, LC, MH, PL, TU, WF, Y.

2013 —The grounds of the French tongue. *For T. Basset,* 1687. 8°. T.C.II 194. L, C.

2013A —Miege's last and best French grammar. *For William Freeman and Abel Roper,* 1698. 8°. T.C.III 67. 8°. WF.

2013B —Methode abbregee. *For William Freeman and Abel Roper,* 1698. 8°. IU.

2014 [–] Miscellanea: or, a choice collection. *For William Lindsey,* 1694. 8°. L, O, C, LG, A; CH, CN, MH.

2015 —A new cosmography. *For Thomas Basset,* 1682. 8°. T.C.I 486. L, MR; CH, MH, RPJ, SYRACUSE.

2016 —A new dictionary French and English. *By Tho. Dawks for Thomas Basset*, 1677. 4°. T.C.I 267. L, O, C, E, DT; IU, PL.

2017 ——[Anr. ed.] *For Thomas Basset*, 1679. 4°. L, O, C, BR, DT; BN, CH, CN, IU, MH, Y.

2018 —A new French grammar. *For Thomas Bassett*, 1678. 8°. T.C.I 322. L, O, C, OC, BC; CLC, PL.

2019 [–] The new state of England. *By H. C. for John Wyat*, 1691. 12°. T.C.II 333. I, O, CS, AU, E; CH, CLC, TU, WF, Y.

2019A [–] —[Anr. ed.] *By H. C. for Jonathan Robinson*, 1691. 12°. L, NOT; CH, CN, LC, MH, PL.

2020 [–] —Second edition. *For R. Clavell, H. Mortlock and J. Robinson*, 1693. 12°. L, O, LUG, CS; CH, CN, MB, TU, Y.

2021 [–] —"Second" edition. —, 1694. 12°. BN, CLC, NN.

2022 [–] —Third edition. —, 1699. 8°. T.C.III 145. L, O; CH, CLC, NCD, NU, TU, Y.

2023 —Nouvelle methode pour apprendre l'Anglois. *A Londres, for Thomas Basset*, 1685. 8°. T.C.II 158. L, LW.

2024 The present state of Denmark. *For Tho. Basset*, 1683. 8°. T.C.II 44. L, O, NE, SP, DM.

2025 [–] A relation of three embassies . . . performed by the Earle of Carlisle. *For John Starkey*, 1669. T.C.I 13. L, O, LW, CT, ES, CD; CH, CN, MH, NCD, NN, PU, WF, Y.

2025A —A short and easie French grammar. *For Tho. Basset*, 1682. 8°. T.C.I 477. LLP; CH, WF, Y.

2026 —A short dictionary English and French. *For Tho. Basset*, 1684. 8°. L, O, DC, CD; CH, MIU, NCU, NN, WF, Y.

2027 ——Second edition. —, 1685. 8°. T.C.II 160. NE; BN, CLC, CU, MH, TU, Y.

2028 —The short French dictionary. Third edition. *For Thomas Basset*, 1690. 8°. T.C.II 340. L, O, LLU, DT; CN, MH, WF.

2029 ——"Third" edition. *Hague, by Henry van Bulderen*, 1691. 8°. L, C, GU, DT; CB, CH, LC, TU, Y.

2029A ——Fourth edition. —, 1699. 8°. YM; MH.

Mighty victory in Ireland. 1647. *See* More, Will.

Mighty victory over the Irish. Dublin, 1647. *See* Moore, Robert.

2029B **Milbourne, Luke.** The catechisme of the Church of England explain'd. *Rotterdam, Yvans*, 1700. 8°. LLP.

2030 Entry cancelled.

—Christian pattern paraphrased. 1697. *See* Thomas à Kempis.

2031 —A false faith. *By R. R. for W. Kettelby and B. Aylmer*: 1698. 4°.* T.C.III 90. L, O, C, LLP, BLH, DT; CH, IU, NU, TU, WF.

2032 —A farewel sermon. *For Brabazon Aylmer*, 1699. 4°.* T.C.III 168. L, LLP, OC, NE, BLH; CH, CLC, NU, Y.

2033 [–] A letter to A. H. Esq; concerning the stage. *For A. Baldwin*, 1698. 4°.* L, O, OC; CH, MH, MU, NIC.

2034 —Mysteries in religion vindicated. *For Walter Kettilby*, 1692. 8°. T.C.II 401. L, O, C, AN, EN; CH, LC, MH, PU, WF.

2035 —Notes on Dryden's Virgil. *For R. Clavill*, 1698. 8°. T.C.III 66. L, O, C, EN, DT; CH, CN, MH, MU, TU, WF, Y.

2036 —The originals of rebellion. *By J. Wallis, for Walter Kettilby*, 1683. 4°. T.C.II 14. L, O, OC, CT, BC, NPL, DT; CH, MH, NU, WF, Y.

2037 —Samaritanism reviv'd. *By Samuel Roycroft, for Walter Kettilby*, 1683. 4°. T.C.II 38. L, O, C, CT, BAMB, LSD; CDA, CLC, NU, WF.

2038 [–] A short defence of the orders of the Church of England. *Printed, and are to be sold by Randal Taylor*, 1688. 4°.* L, O, C, E, DT; CH, CLC, IU, MH, NU, TU, WF, Y.

2038A [–] —[Anr. ed.] *For William Redmaine, of Great Yarmouth, and Tho. Bennet*, 1688. 4°.* LLP, BAMB; PU.

2039 A mild, but searching expostulatory letter from the poor and plain-dealing farmers. [*London*, 1679.] brs. L, O, C, LW, LLU, EN; CH, IU, MBA, MH, TO, WF, Y.

2040 **Mildmay.** Lex naturæ est indispensabilis. [*n.p.*, 1650.] brs. O.

2040A **Mildmay, William.** The case of. [*London*, 1676?] brs. MH.

2040B **Mildmay family.** Robert Baron Fitswalter . . . [genealogical table]. [*London*, 1667.] brs. LPR.

2041 **Miles, Abraham.** The countrymans friend. *For E. Andrews*, 1662. 8°.* L.

2042 —The dub'd knight. [*London*], *for W. Whitwood*, [1660–70]. brs. L, HH, GU; MH.

2042A —The last farewel of three bould traytors. *For John Andrews*, [1661]. brs. MH.

2043 —Mirth for citizens. [*London*], *for P. Brooksby*, [1673?]. brs. L, CM, HH; MH.

2044 —A sad and true relation of a great fire. *For E. Andrews*, [1662]. brs. O.

2045 — A vvonder of vvonders: being. [*London*], *for William Gilbertson*, [1662]. brs. O.

2046 **Miles, John.** A letter from on board His Majesties ship, the Pearl. 1684. brs. LG (lost).

2047 [–] A true relation of the great victory, obtained by the King of the Abissines. colop: *By G. Croom*, 1684. brs. O; CH, MU.

2048 ——[Anr. ed.] *Edinburgh, re-printed by John Reid, and are to be sold by James Mein*, 1684. brs. ALDIS 2462. HH, EN.

2048A Miles Prance his farewel. [*London, sold by N. Thompson*], 1686. brs. Y.

2049 Entry cancelled.

Militant Christian. 1669. *See* Coven, Stephen.

Military and maritime [*sic*] discipline. 1672. *See* Venn, Thomas.

2050 Entry cancelled.

Military articles of Lymerick. Dublin, 1692. *See* Civil articles.

Military discipline; or. [*n.p.*, 1685.] *See* S., J.

2050A The military discipline wherein is martially showne. *Sold by Tho. Jenner*, 1642. 4°.* L; MH.

Military instructions. Cambridge, 1644. *See* Cruso, John.

2051 Milites cavsæ: the souldiers of right. [*London*], *printed*, 1648. 4°.* C, MR; CN.

2052 Militia old and new. *Printed 18 August 2642 [i.e. 1642]*. 4°.* LT, O, C, SP, DT; CH, MH, MU, NCD, NU, WF, Y.

2053 No entry.

Militia reform'd. 1698. *See* Toland, John.

Militiere, Theophile Brachet de la. *See* Brachet de la Militiere, Theophile.

Milk for babes. 1661. *See* Nayler, James.

2053A The milking pail. [*London?* 1670.] brs. L.

2054 The milkmaids resolution. [*London*], *for P. Brooksby*, [1672–95]. brs. L, HH; MH.

2055 Entry cancelled.

Mill, Adiel. Catalogus. 1691. *See* Catalogus variorum & insignium tam antiquorum.

2056 **Mill, Henry.** A funerall elegy upon . . . Essex. *By John Macock for William Ley*, 1646. brs. LT.

2057 **Mill, Humphrey.** The nights search. *For William Ley*, 1652. 8°. L; CH, CN.

2058 —The second part of the nights search. *For Henry Shepheard, and William Ley*, 1646. 8°. L, O, OW; CH, CN, MB, MH, WF.

2059 **Mill, John.** A sermon preached on the Feast of the Annunciation. *In the Savoy: by Tho. Newcomb*, 1676. 4°.* L, O, LL, OB, LIU; MIU, MM, WF, Y.

Mill'd lead demonstrated. 1695. *See* Hale, Thomas.

Mill'd lead sheathing. 1695/6. *See* Hale, Charles.

2060 Millennianism: or, Christ's thousand years. *For W. Crook*, 1693. 8°. T.C.II 448. L, O, CT, MR; CLC, CN, NU, WF.

2060A **Miller, Henry.** God the protector of Israel. *By A. N. for Thomas Warren*, 1641. 4°.* MH, MWA.

2061 **Miller, Joshua.** Antichrist in man the Quakers idol. *By J. Macock, for L. Lloyd*, 1655. 4°.* LT, LF, CT, AN; NU, PH.

2062 —A beame of light darted. *For H. C. & L. L.*, 1650. 8°. NU.

2063 **Miller, Robert.** The English-French-mans address. *Printed*, 1666. brs. L.

2063aA **Miller, Thomas.** The compleat modellist. Second edition. *By W. Leybourn for George Hurlock*, 1664. 4°.* LNM, CM.

2063A ——Third edition. *By W. G. for George Hurlock*, 1667. 4°. MIT, WPO.

2064 ——Fourth edition. *For William Fisher, and Eliz. Hurlock*, 1676. 4°.* T.C.I 224. L, O; CLC, WF, Y.

2065 ——[Anr. ed.] *For William Fisher*, 1684. 4°. L.

2065A ——[Anr. ed.] *For Richard Mount*, 1699. 4°. SE.

2066 **Miller, William.** Catalogue of papers. [1695?] 4°. L; NG.

2067 —A curious collection of books. [1695?] 4°. L, O, LV; CH.

2067A —The famous collection of papers and pamphlets. [*London*, 1695?] 4°. MH.

2067B The miller of Essex. [*London?* 1700.] brs. L.

2068 [**Milles, Thomas.**] Remarks upon the occasional paper, number VIII. [*London*, 1697?] 4°.* CT, EC; Y.

2069 **Millet, John.** A sermon preached . . . on the 9 of November 1648. *Oxford, by H. Hall*, 1652. 4°.* MADAN 2199. O, LW, DC, DT; CH, NU, TU, WF.

2070 ——[Anr. ed.] *Oxford, by H. Hall for R. Davis*, 1652. 4°.* MADAN 2199n. LT, OC, WCA; CLC, MH, NGT, Y.

Millinton, *Mr.* Die veneris 8 martii 1649[50]. Mr Millington reports. 1649. *See* Mr. Millington.

2071 **Millington, Edward.** Auctio Millingtoniana picturarum omnigenarum, &c. A collection . . . 13th . . . August. 1691. [*London*], 1691. fol.* L.

2071A Entry cancelled.

—Bibliotheca selectissima, diversorum librorum. 1687. *See* Lauderdale, John Maitland, *Duke of.*

—Catalogue of valuable books. 1689. *See title.*

2071B Entry cancelled.

—Catalogus librorum bibliothecas. 1681. *See* Button, Ralph.

2071C The million act modestly calculated. *For Randal Taylor*, 1693. brs. MH.

2072 [**Mills, John.**] The desires and propositions proposed to Sir John Hotham. *July 19. London, for Edward Iohnson*, [1642]. 4°.* LT, O, YM, CD; CLC, WF, Y.

2073 **Mills, Thomas.** The history of the holy war. *For Tho. Malthus*, 1685. 8°. T.C.II 96. L, C; LC, WF.

2074 **Millwater, Lewis.** The cure of ruptures. *Printed*, 1651. 4°.* LT.

2075 [**Milner, John.**] An account of Mr. Lock's religion. *Printed and sold by J. Nutt*, 1700. 8°. T.C.III 176. L, O, CT, EN, DT; CLC, CU, LC, MH, NU, WF, Y.

[–] Answer to the vindication of the letter. Oxford, 1690. *See* Wellwood, James.

2076 [–] A brief examination of some passages. *Printed and sold by Ronald Taylor*, [1700?]. 8°.* L, C, OC, YM; CU, NU, WF, Y.

2077 [–] A collection of the church-history of Palestine. *For Thomas Dring*, 1688. 4°. T.C.II 206. L, O, C, E, DT; CH, CSU, MIU, Y.

2078 —Conjectanea in Isa. IX. I, II. *Typis Robert. White*, 1673. 4°.* L, O, OC, CT, BAMB, LNC; CH, WF.

2078A ——[Anr. ed.] *Typis R. White, prostat venale apud H. Dickinson, Cantabrigiæ*, 1673. 4°.* CT.

2079 —De Nethinim sive Nethinæis. *Cantabrigiæ, ex officina Johann. Hayes*, 1690. *Impensis Caroli Brown*. 4°.* O, C, OM, CT, BAMB, CD; BN, CH, MH, Y, ZWT.

2080 —A defence of Arch-Bishop Usher. *Cambridge, by J. Hayes for Benj. Tooke, to be sold by W. Graves in Cambridge*, 1694. 8°. T.C.II 483. L, O, C, OM, SP, DT; CH, WF.

2081 [–] A short dissertation concerning the four last kings of Judah. *For Charles Brome*, 1689. 4°.* L, O, CT, DU, E; CH, CLC, WF.

2082 [–] A view of the dissertation upon the epistles of Phalaris. *By H. C. for John Jones*, 1698. 8°. L, O, C, LL, LVD; CLC, CSB, MH, MIU, NU, WF.

2083 [**Milner, Richard.**] A few words to the King. [*London*], *printed*, 1675. brs. LF, BBN.

2084 **Milner, William.** A sermon at the funeral of Mrs. Elizabeth Fisher, . . . June the 2d. 1698. *For Thomas Speed*, 1698. 4°.* T.C.III 72. L, C, CS, BLH; CH, CLC, WF, Y.

2085 [**Milton, Christopher.**] The state of church-affairs. *By Nat. Thompson for the author*, 1687. fol. L, O, MR, EN, DT; CH, CLC, CN, IU, NU.

2086 **Milton, John.** The works of. [*London*], *printed*, 1697. fol. L, O, C, BC, E; CH, CN, IU, LC, MH, TU, WF, Y.

2087   —A complete collection of the historical. *Amsterdam,* [*London*], *finish'd,* 1698. fol. L, O, C, EN, DT; BN, CLC, CN, IU, MH, TU, WF, Y, AVP.

2088   [–] Accedence commenc't grammar. *For S. S. and are to be sold by John Starkey,* 1669. 12°. T.C.I 14. L, O, LL, CT, CCH, GU; CH, IU, MH, NC, NN, PRF.

2088A [–] —[Anr. ed.] *By S. Simmons,* 1669. 12°. L, O, LU; INU, IU, MH, TEXAS CHRISTIAN, WF, Y.

2089   [–] Animadversions upon the remonstrants defence. *For Thomas Vnderhill,* 1641. 4°. LT, O, C, EN, DT; CH, CN, IU, MH, NU, TU, WF, Y.

     [–] Answer to a printed book. Oxford, 1642. *See* Digges, Dudley.

2090   [–] An apology against a pamphlet call'd A modest confutation. *By E. G. for Iohn Rothwell,* 1642. 4°. LT, O, C, GU, DT; CH, CN, IU, MH, NU, TU, WF, Y.

2091   —An apology for Smectymnuus. *For John Rothwell,* [1654]. 4°. C, LU, NPL, E, CD; IU, NC, PPT, RPJ, TU, WF.

2092   —Areopagitica. *Printed,* 1644. 4°.* LT, O, C, EN, DT; CH, IU, LC, MH, NN, TU, WF, Y.

     [–] Argument or, debate. 1642. *See* March, John.

2093   —Artis logicæ plenior institutio. *Impensis Spencer Hickman,* 1672. 12°. T.C.I 105. L, O, C, MAU, EN, DT; BN, CH, CN, IU, MII, TU, WF, Y.

2094   — —[Anr. ed.] *Impensis S. H. prostant pro R. Boulter,* 1673. 12°. T.C.I 128. LW, CCH, SA; CLC, IU, MH.

2095   Entry cancelled. *Error for 1673 edition.*

2096   —A brief history of Moscovia. *By M. Flesher, for Brabazon Aylmer,* 1682. 8°. T.C.I 472. L, O, C, MR, E; CH, CN, IU, MH, TU, WF, Y.

2097   [–] Brief notes upon a late sermon, titl'd, The fear of God. *Printed,* 1660. 4°.* L, O, C, MR, WCA; CH, CN, IU, MH, NN, Y.

2098   —Mr John Miltons character of the Long Parliament. *For Henry Brome,* 1681. 4°.* L, O, C, EN, DT; CH, CN, IU, LC, MH, TU, WF, Y, AVP.

2099   [–] Colasterion. [*London*], *printed,* 1645. 4°.* LT, O, C, MR, DT; CH, IU, MH, MU, TU, WF, Y.

2100   —Comœdia Joannis Miltoni. *Anno Domini,* 1698. 4°. L, O, LVD, CQ, MC; CH, MH, Y.

2101   [–] Considerations touching the likeliest means to remove hirelings. *By T. N. for L. Chapman,* 1659. 12°. LT, O, C, CCH, EN; CH, CN, IU, MH, NU, WCL, Y.

2102–3 Entries cancelled.

     [–] Copy of a letter from an officer. [n.p., 1656.] *See* G., R.

     [–] Copy of a letter written to an officer. 1656. *See* title.

2104   —A defence of the people of England. [*Amsterdam?*], *printed,* 1692. 8°. L, O, CCH, EN, BLH; CH, IU, LC, MH, NU, TU, Y, AVP.

2104A — —[Anr. ed.] [*London*], *printed,* 1695. 8°. L, O, DUS; CB, INU, IU, MH.

2105   — —[Anr. ed.] *For Nathaniel Rolls,* 1695. 8°. Y.

2106   —Defensio pro populo anglicano. *Typis Du Gardianis,* 1651. 4°. MADAN 3. L, O, C, CK, AN, YM; CH, CSU, IU, LC, MH, PL, TU, Y.

2107   Entry cancelled.

     [–] Discourse shewing in what state. [n.p.], 1641. *See* title.

2108   [–] The doctrine and discipline of divorce. *By T. P. and M.S.,* 1643. 4°. LT, O, C, E, DT; BN, CH, IU, LC, MH, NU, TU, Y.

2109   [–] —Second edition. *Imprinted,* 1644. 4°. LT, O, C, E, DT; CH, IU, MH, TU, WF, Y.

2110   [–] —[Anr. ed., "Year 1645," no errata.] —, 1645. 4°. L, O, CCH, EN, DT; CB, IU, LC, MH, MU, TU, Y.

2111   [–] —[Anr. ed., "yeare 1645," with errata.]—, 1645. 4°. L, O, C, LCL, GM; CH, INU, IU, MH, NP, TU, Y.

2112   [–] Εικονοκλαστης in answer. *By Matthew Simmons,* 1649. 4°. LT, O, C, AN, EN, DT; CH, IU, LC, MH, NU, TU, Y, AVP.

2113   [–] —Second edition. *By T. N., and are to be sold by Tho. Brewster and G. Moule,* 1650. 4°. L, C, CCH, CE, CT; BN, IU, MH, NP, TU, Y.

2114   [–] —"Second" edition. *By Thomas Newcomb,* 1650. 4°. L, O, CANTERBURY CATH.; INU, WF.

2115   — —[Anr. ed.] *Amsterdam, printed,* 1690. 8°. L, O, C, DU, EN, CD; CH, IU, LC, MH, NU, Y, AVP. (var.)

2116   — —'ou réponse. *A Londres, par Guill. Du-Gard,* 1652. *Et se vend par Nicolas Bourne.* 8°. L, O, C, LLU, AU; BN, CH, INU, IU, MH, WF, Y.

2117   —Epistolarum familiarium liber unus. *Impensis Brabazoni Aylmeri,* 1674. 8°. L, O, C, MR, EN, DM; BN, CH, CN, IU, MH, TU, WF, Y.

2118   Entry cancelled.

     [–] Grand case of conscience concerning. 1650. *See* title.

2119   —The history of Britain. *By J. M. for James Allestry,* 1670. 4°. L, O, C, EN, DT; BN, CH, IU, MH, NU, TU, WF, Y.

2120   — —[Anr. ed.] *By J. M. for Spencer Hickman,* 1671. 4°. T.C.I 56. L, O, C, AN, E; CLC, CN, INU, IU, MH, NCD, Y.

2121   — —Second edition. *By J. M. for John Martyn,* 1677. 8°. T.C.I 277. L, O, C, DU, LIU; CLC, IU, MH, TU, WF, Y.

2122   — —"Second" edition. *By J. M. for Mark Pardoe,* 1678. 8°. L, O, BIU, D; INU, IU, MH, PU, RBU, TO, WF.

2123   — — [Anr. ed.] *For Ri. Chiswell. Sold by Nath. Roles,* 1695. 8°. T.C.II 531. L, O, CCH, BC, CD; BN, CLC, INU, IU, MBP, MH, WF, Y.

2124   — —[Anr. ed.] *By R. E. for R. Scot, R. Chiswell, R. Bently, G. Sawbridge; to be sold by A. Swall, and T. Child,* 1695. 8°. L, O, CCH, CPL; BN, CH, IU, NP, PL, Y.

2125   No entry.

     [–] Letter written to a gentleman. 1653. *See* Hall, John.

2126   —Letters of state. *Printed,* 1694. 12°. L, O, C, LVD, AN, E; BN, CH, IU, MH, NU, TU, WF, Y.

2127   Entry cancelled.

     [–] Life and reigne of King Charls. 1651. *See* title.

2128   —Literæ pseudo-senatus Anglicani, Cromwellii. [*n.p.*], *impressæ anno,* 1676. 12°. L, O, C, MR, BQ; CLC, CN, IU, MH, MU, NN, NP, TU, Y, AVP. [Fruit as t.p. device.]

2129   — —[Anr. ed., face as t.p. device.] —, 1676. 12°. L, O, C, EN, DT; CH, IU, MH, NN, PL, Y.

2130–1 Entries cancelled.

     [–] Newes from Hell. Rome. [n.p.], 1641. *See* M., J.

     [–] Novæ Solymæ. [n.p.], 1648. *See* Gott, Samuel.

2132   [–] Of education. [*London: Thomas Underhill,* 1644.] cap., 4°.* LT, O, C, LW, CCH, DM; CH, CLC, INU, IU, MH, NU, Y.

2133 [–] Of prelatical Episcopacy. *By R. O. & G. D. for Thomas Vnderhill*, 1641. 4°.* LT, O, C, EN, DT; CH, IU, MH, MU, TU, WF, Y.

2134 [–] Of reformation. *[London], for Thomas Underhill*, 1641. 4°. LT, O, C, EN, DT; BN, CH, IU, MH, NU, TU, WF, Y.

2135 [–] Of true religion. *Printed*, 1673. 4°.* T.C.I 135. L, O, C, LNC, AU, DM; CH, IU, LC, MH, TU, WCL, Y, AVP.

2136 —Paradise lost. *Printed and are to be sold by Peter Parker and by Robert Boulter and Matthias Walker*, 1667. 4°. L, CT, MR, P, EN; CH, CN, IU, MH, NN, TU, Y.

2137 — —[Second title-page.] —, 1667. 4°. L, CCH, LNC; CH, IU, MH, NN, TU, WCL, Y.

2138 — —[Third title-page.] —, 1668. 4°. L, LCL, CT, MR, DT; CH, IU, MH, NN, TU, Y, AVP.

2139 — —[Fourth title-page.] *By S. Simmons, and are to be sold by S. Thomson, H. Mortlack, M. Walker, and R. Boulter*, 1668. 4°. L, O, C, MR, AN, EN; BN, CH, IU, MH, NN, TU, WCL, Y.

2140–1 Entries cancelled. Ghosts.

2142 — —[Fifth title-page.] *By S. Simmons, and are to be sold by T. Helder*, 1669. 4°. L, O, CT, MR, EN; CH, IU, LC, MH, WCL, Y. (var.)

2143 — —[Sixth title-page.] —, 1669. 4°. L, O, C, CCH, MR; CH, IU, MH, NCD, NP, WC, Y, AVP.

2144 — —Second edition. *By S. Simmons*, 1674. 8°. T.C.I 181. L, O, C, EN, DT; BN, CH, IU, LC, MH, MU, RPJ, TU, Y, AVP.

2144A — —[Anr. ed.] —, *and to be sold by T. Helder*, 1675. 8°. IU.

2145 — —Third edition. *By S. Simmons*, 1678. 8°. L, O, C, MR, EN; CH, IU, MH, TU, WF, Y, AVP.

2146 — —Fourth edition. *By Miles Flesher, for Richard Bently, and Jacob Tonson*, 1688. fol. L, CS, CT, CPL; CH, IU, MH, MU, TU, WSC, Y.

2147 — —"Fourth" edition. *By Miles Flesher, for Jacob Tonson*, 1688. fol. L, C, OC, CT, AN, EN; CLC, IU, MH, PBM, WF.

2148 — —"Fourth" edition. *By Miles Flesher, for Richard Bently*, 1688. fol. L, O, LVD, CS; CLC, IU, LC, MB, TU, VC.

2149 — —Fifth edition. *For Richard Bently, and Jacob Tonson*, 1691. fol. O, LUC, CT, RPL, DT; CLC, CN, INU, IU, MH, TU, AVP.

2150 — —"Fifth" edition. *For Jacob Tonson*, 1692. fol. O, LUC, CJ, CQ, MR, DT; CH, INU, IU, MH, MU, WF.

2150A — —"Fourth" edition. *By R. E. for J. Tonson*, 1693. fol. U. SUSSEX; IU.

2151 — —Sixth edition. *By Tho. Hodgkin for Jacob Tonson*, 1695. fol. L, OC, CT, AN, E; CB, IU, LC, MH, PU.

2152 —Paradise regain'd. *By J. M. for John Starkey*, 1671. 8°. T.C.I 56. L, O, C, MR, EN; CH, CN, IU, MH, TU, WF, Y.

2153 — —Second edition. *For John Starkey*, 1680. 8°. T.C.I 453. L, O, C, LVD, MR; CH, CN, IU, MH, TU, WF, Y.

2154 — —Third edition. *By R. E. and are to be sold by Randal Taylor*, 1688. fol. L, O, C, AN, E; CH, IU, MH, TU, WF, Y.

2155 —Paradisus amissa. *Impensis Thomæ Dring*, 1686. 4°.* L, O, LW, LSD; CLC, CN, IU, MH, NN, Y.

2156 —Johannis Miltoni paradisi amissi. *Cantabrigiæ, ex officina Jo. Hayes, impensis Sam. Simpson*, 1691. 4°.* L, O, C, BAMB, EN; BN, CH, INU, MH, NC, Y.

2157 —Paraphrasis Latina. *For the author*, 1694. 4°.* L, O, CCH, BLH; INU, IU, MBA, MH, ZWT.

2158 —Paraphrasis poetica. *Typis Johannis Darby*, 1690. 8°. L, O, C, LVD, AN, EN, DM; BN, CH, CN, IU, MH, TU, WF, Y.

2159 —Joannis Miltoni Londinensis poemata. *Typis R. R. prostant apud Humphredum Moseley*, 1645. 8°. LT, O, LVF, LSD, AU; CB, IU, MB, MH, NP, TU, Y, AVP.

2160 —Poems. *By Ruth Raworth for Humphrey Moseley*, 1645. 8°. LT, O, C, MR, ES; CH, IU, MH, TU, WF, Y, AVP.

2161 — —Second edition. *For Tho. Dring . . . White Lion*, 1673. 8°. T.C.I 151. L, O, CCH, AN, EN; BN, CH, IU, MH, TU, WF, Y, AVP.

2161A — —[Anr. ed.] *For Tho. Dring . . . Blew Anchor*, 1673. 8°. L, O, C, CCH, MR; CH, IU, MR, NN, Y.

2162 — —Third edition. *For Jacob Tonson*, 1695. fol. L, O, C, EN, DT; CH, IU, MH, TU, WF, Y.

2163 —The poetical works of. *For Jacob Tonson*, 1695. fol. L, O, C, EN, DT; CH, IU, LC, MH, MU, TU, Y, AVP.

2164 [–] Pro populo adversus tyrannos. *Printed*, 1689. 4°.* L, O, C, YM, EN, DT; CH, CN, IU, LC, MH, NU, PL, WF, Y.

2165 —Ioannis Miltoni Angli pro popvlo Anglicano defensio. *Typis Dv Gardianis*, 1650. 12°. MADAN 4. L, O, C, BR, MR; CH, IU, LC, MH, NP, TU, Y.

2166 — —[Anr. ed.] *Typis Du Gardianis*, 1651. 4°. MADAN I. L, O, C, LSD, GU; CH, IU, MH, NN, WF, Y. (var.)

2167 — —[Anr. ed.] —, 1651. fol. MADAN 2. L, O, C, DU, DT; CH, IU, MB, MH, NN, Y.

2168 Entry cancelled.

— —[Anr. ed.] 1651. *See* —Defensio pro populo.

2168A — —[Anr. ed.] *Typis Du-Gardianis*, 1651. 12°. MADAN 5. L, O, C, EN, DN; CH, IU, MH, NN, TU, Y.

2168B — —[Anr. ed.] —, 1651. 12°. MADAN 6. LT, O, C, SA, DT; CH, CN, IU, MH, NU, WF, Y, AVP.

2168C — —[Anr. ed.] —, 1651. 12°. MADAN 7. L, O, C, LG, BC, ENC; CB, CH, IU, MB, MH, TU, WF, Y.

2168D — —[Anr. ed.] —, 1651. 12°. MADAN 9. L, O, LLL, RU, BQ; CLC, IU, MH, NC, TU, Y, AVP.

2168E — —[Anr. ed.] —, 1651. 12°. MADAN 10. L; IU, MH, MWA, NN.

2169 — —[Anr. ed.] —, 1652. 12°. MADAN 12. L, O, C, GM, DT; CH, IU, MH, MU, NU, WF, Y.

2169A — —[Anr. ed.] —, 1652. 12°. MADAN 13. L, O, C, GU, DT; CH, IU, MH, PL, TU, Y.

2170 — —[Anr. ed.] *Typis Neucombianis*, 1658. 12°. MADAN 14. LT, SHEFFIELD; MH, NC.

2171 —Joannis Miltoni Angli pro populo Anglicano defensio secunda. *Typis Neucomianis*, 1654. 8°. LT, O, C, AN, ENC, BQ; BN, CH, IU, MH, MU, TU, WCL, Y.

2172 —Joannis Miltoni pro se defensio contra Alexandrum Morum. *Typis Neucomianis*, 1655. 8°. LT, O, CT, MR, E, BQ; BN, CH, CN, IU, MH, NCD, WF, Y, AVP.

2173 [–] The readie and easie vvay. *By T. N. and are to be sold by Livewell Chapman*, 1660. 4°.* LT, O, C, CCH, YM; CH, IU, MH, NP, TU, Y.

2174 [–] —Second edition. *For the author*, 1660. 12°. BN, IU, MH.

2174A Entry cancelled. Ghost.

2175   —The reason of church-governement. *By E. G. for Iohn Rothwell*, 1641. 4°. LT, O, C, EN, DT; CH, IU, LC, MH, NU, TU, Y, AVP.

2176–6A Entries cancelled.

[–] Reply to the answer (printed . . .). 1642/3. *See title*.

2176B —Miltons Republican-letters. [*Amsterdam?*], *printed*, 1682. 4°. L, CCH; IU.

2177   —Samson agonistes. *Printed, and are to be sold by Randal Taylor*, 1688. fol. L, O, C, BC, LIU; CH, IU, MH, TU, WF, Y.

2178   No entry.

2179   Entry cancelled.

[–] Soveraigne salve. 1643. *See M., J*.

2180   [–] A supplement to Dr. Du Moulin. *Printed*, 1680. fol.* L, O, LUC, SP; IU, MH, NNM, WF. (var.)

2181   [–] The tenure of kings and magistrates. *By Matthew Simmons*, 1649. 4°. LT, O, C, AN, GM, DN, DT; BN, CH, CN, IU, MH, NN, TU, Y.

2182   [–] —Second edition. —, 1649. 4°. L, O, C, E, DM; CH, IU, MH, NP, TU. (var.)

2183   [–] —[Anr. ed.] —, 1650. 4°. L, O, C, EN, DT; CH, IU, MH, NN, Y.

2184   [–] Tetrachordon. *Printed*, 1645. 4°. LT, O, C, E, DT; BN, CH, IU, MH, NU, TU, WF, Y, AVP.

2185   [–] A treatise of civil power in ecclesiastical causes. *By Tho. Newcomb*, 1659. 12°. L, O, C, LVD, MR; CH, CN, IU, MH, NP, WF, Y.

2186   **Milward, Matthias.** The souldiers trivmph. *By W. E. and I. G. for Iohn Clark*, 1641. 4°.* LT, CM, DT; CH, CLC, MH, MWA, NU.

2187   —The svvord-bearer. *By Iohn Norton for Samuel Man*, 1641. 4°.* L, CJ, CT, P, DC, DT; MH, MWA, WF.

2187A **Milward, William.** The case of. [*London*, 1661.] brs. LG.

2188   **M[ilway], T[homas].** A funeral sermon preached upon the death of . . . Francis Holcroft. *For William Marshall*, 1692. 4°.* T.C.II 422. L, O, LCL, LW, CS.

2189   **Minderer, Raymond.** Medicina militaris: or, a body of military medicines. *By William Godbid, to be sold by Moses Pitt*, 1674. 8°. T.C.I 169. L, O, LWL, OR, MAU, E; MIU, WF, WSG, HC.

Minerva, or. 1677. *See C., R*.

2190   Minerva. The High-Dutch grammer. *For Will. Cooper*, 1685. 12°. T.C.II 128. L; CLC, PU, Y.

Minerva's check. 1680. *See B., T*.

Minerva's triumph. 1680. *See Shaw, Samuel*.

2190A **Minge, Thomas.** Gospel-baptism or, plain proof. *By K. Astwood, and sold by William Marshall, and John Marshal*, 1700. 12°. L, ORP.

2191   **Mingzeis, Alexander.** A confvtation of the new Presbyterian error. [*London*], *printed*, 1648. 8°.* LT, DT.

2192   —The down-fall of Babylon. [*London*], *printed*, 1647. 8°.* LT; CH.

2192A —England's alarum. *For F. Coles*, 1666. 8°. C.

2192B —England's caveat. *Thomas Harper*, 1647. 8°.* L.

2193   —The way to thrive. *Printed*, 1653. 8°.* LT.

2194   **Minis.** Englands ioyalty. *By R. H. for J. H.*, 1641. 4°.* LT, O, DT.

2194A —[Anr. ed.] *For John Harison*, 1641. 4°.* O; Y.

Minister of Cirencester's address. 1698. *See Harrison, Joseph*.

Minister of Richmond's reasons. 1696. *See Borfet, Abiel*.

Ministers dvty. 1656. *See Woodward, Hezekiah*.

Ministers mite. 1650. *See Jerome, Steven*.

2195   The minister's reasons. colop: *By G. Larkin*, 1688. cap., 4°.* L, O, DU, MR, EN; CH, CLC, IU, MH, NU, TU, WF, Y.

Ministery of Christ. [n.p.], 1658. *See Brown, Robert*.

2196   Entry cancelled.

Minority of St. Lewis. 1685. *See Phillips, Edward*.

Minors no senators. 1646. *See Prynne, William*.

2197   The mint and exchequer united. [*London?* 1695.] brs. LUG, HH.

2197A **Minutius, Cassid Aureus.** Colloquium Davidis. [*Impe*]*nsis Thomæ Burrell*, 1679. fol.* L.

2198   **Minucius Felix, Marcus.** Octavius. *Cantabrigiæ, ex Officina R. D[aniel]*, 1643. 16°. L, C, KEBLE, CT; KT, MB.

2199   —Marci Minvcii Felicis equitis Romani Octavius. *Oxoniæ, typis W. Hall impensis Ric. Davis*, 1662. 12°. MADAN 2593. L, O, LSD, P, EN; CH, IU, MH, PL, TU, Y.

2200   — —[Anr. ed.] *Oxoniæ, typis L. Lichfieid [sic] impensis Ric. Davis*, 1678. Sixes. MADAN 3175. L, O, C, MR, GU; CH, CN, TU, V, Y.

2201   — —[Anr. ed.] *By J. M. for R. Royston*, 1682. 8°. I, O, CM, EC, SP; CH, MH, NU, PL, TSM, WF, Y.

2202   — —[Anr. ed.] *Printed, and are to be sold by John Whitlock*, 1695. 8°. LW, DUS; NU, PU, WF.

Mirabile pecci: or. 1669. *See A., H*.

2203   No entry.

Mirabilis annus. [n.p.], 1661. *See Ενιαυτος τεραστιος*.

2204   Mirabilis annus secundus: or, the second part of the second years prodigies. [*London*], *printed*, 1662. 4°. L, O, CCH, MR, DT; CH, CLC, CN, MH, NHC, Y.

2205   Mirabilis annus secundus; or, the second year of prodigies. [*London*], *printed*, 1662. 4°. O, LVF, CT, BC, MR, CD; CH, CLC, CN, MH, NHC, PU, Y.

2206   A miracle: an honest broker. *Printed at London*, 1642[3]. 4°.* LT, O, C, EN, DT; CH, CU, MH, NU, TU, WF, Y.

Miracle du père Veron. 1699. *See Jansse, Lucas*.

2207   A miracle of miracles wrought by the blood of King Charles. *Printed*, 1649. 4°.* LT, CT, DT; CH, TORONTO ACAD. OF MED., WF.

2207A The miracle of nature. [*London*, 1670?] brs. L.

Miracles, no violations. 1683. *See Blount, Charles*.

Miracles not ceas'd. 1663. *See Digby, J*.

Miracles of art. 1678. *See Crouch, Nathaniel*.

Miracles perform'd. 1692. *See Ward, Edward*.

2208   Miracles reviv'd. [*London*], *for A. Banks*, [1682]. brs. L, OC, CS, HH, LSD; CLC, TU, WF, Y.

2209   —[Anr. ed.] colop: —, 1682. brs. O, MC, MR; CLC, MIU, Y.

2209A —[Anr. ed.] colop: *Edinburgh, reprinted by the heir of Andrew Anderson*, 1682. brs. Y.

2210   Miracles upon miracles. *For A. C.*, 1687. brs. MC.

Miracles work's above. 1683. *See* Browne, Thomas, *fellow of St. John's.*

Miracula mundi. To the King. Edinburgh, 1683. *See* Cunningham, James.

2211 Miracula naturæ: or, a miracle of nature. [*n.p., n.d.*] brs. L; CH.

2212 The miraculous child: or, wonderful news from Manchester. *For F. L.* 1679. 4°.* L, O; TORONTO ACAD. OF MED.

2213 —[Anr. ed.] [*Dublin*], *reprinted*, 1679. 4°.* CD, DT; CH, WF.

2214 No entry.

Miraculous conformist. Oxford, 1666. *See* Stubbe, Henry.

2214A A miraculous cure for witchcraft. [*n.p.,* 1670?] brs. L.

2215 The miraculous fasting of the naked-man [Jos. Wright]. *For J. Nutt,* 1700. brs. O; MH.

2216 Entry cancelled.

Miraculous origin. Bononiæ, 1678. *See* Teramano, Pietro.

2216A A miraculous proof of the resurrection. *By T. Dawks,* [1680]. fol.* O.

2217 The miraculous recovery of a dumb man at Lambeth. *For D. M.,* 1676. 4°.* L, O, LR, LSD, MR.

2218 Entry cancelled.

Miraculous victory obtained. [n.p.], 1643. *See* Fairfax, Ferdinando.

Miraculum basilicon. Or. 1664. *See* Jennings, Abraham.

2218A Miraculum signum coeleste: a discourse. [*London*], *printed,* 1658. 8°. WF.

Mirana. A funeral eclogue: sacred to . . . Countess of Abingdon. 1691. *See* Gould, Robert.

2219 **Mirandula, Octavian.** Illustrium poetarum flores. *Imprimebat T. Newcomb pro societate bibliopolarium,* 1651. 12°. O, LW, D; CH, IU, KYU, NU, Y.

2220 ——[Anr. ed.] *Imprimebat E. Tyler,* 1667. 12°. C, CT; IU, MBJ, TU, WF, ZWT.

2221 The mirrour of allegiance. [*London*], *printed,* 1647. 4°. LT, O, CT, SP, CD; CH, CN, MH, TU, WF, Y.

2222 The mirrour of Christian piety. *For Langley Curtiss,* 1679. 12°. T.C.I 329. L, O, C, LW; CLC, NBL.

Mirrour of Christianity. 1669. *See* Boreman, Robert.

2223 The mirrour of complements. Fourth edition. *By T. H. and are to bee sold by F. Coles, R. Harper, and W. Gilbertson,* 1650. 8°. O; CH.

2223A The mirrour of cruelty. [*London*], *for I. Deacon,* [1683]. 4°.* Y.

Mirrour of government. 1658. *See* Rocket, John.

Mirror of martyrs. 1685. *See* Cotton, Clement.

Mirrovr of mercy. 1655. *See* Boreman, Robert.

Mirror of truth. 1672. *See* S., B.P.

2224 Entry cancelled.

—[Anr. ed.] 1688. *See* S., B.P.

2225 A mirror; wherein the rumpers and fanaticks. *For Robert Pawley,* 1660. 4°.* LT; MH, MIU, OWC, Y.

2226 Entry cancelled.

Mirth for citizens. [n.p., 1673.] *See* Miles, Abraham.

2227 Mirt[h] in abundance. *For Francis Grove,* 1659. 8°.* L.

Mirza: a tragedie. [1647.] *See* Baron, Robert, *of Gray's Inn.*

Misaurus, Philander, *pseud.*

Miscellanea: consisting. 1670. *See* H., D. N.

Miscellanea. I A survey. 1680. *See* Temple, *Sir* William.

2228 Miscellanea magna, or industrious collections. *For G. T.,* 1653. brs. LT; MH.

Miscelanea medica: or. 1675. *See* Cocke, Thomas.

Miscellanea of morall. [n.p.], 1650. *See* Done, John.

Miscellanea: or, a choice. 1694. *See* Miège, Guy.

Miscellanea; or, a mixture. 1669. *See* Henshaw, Joseph, *bp.*

2228A Miscellanea Parliamentaria. *For Matthew Gilliflower,* 1685. 12°. MHL, NCL, PUL.

Miscellanae sacra, containing. 1692. *See* Farrah, Benjamin.

2228B A miscellaneous catalogue of . . . experiments. colop: *Dublin, by Joseph Ray,* [1690?]. cap., fol.* L.

2229 Miscellaneous poems upon several occasions. *Printen* [sic] *for H. Hindmarsh,* 1698. 8°. DT; Y.

2230 Miscellany, being a collection. *For J. Hindmarsh,* 1685. 8°. T.C.II 127. L, O, C, EN, DT; CH, CN, MH, TU, WF, Y.

2231 Entry cancelled. Ghost.

Miscellany of divers problems. 1662. *See* Pellisson, George.

Miscellany of poems. 1689. *See* Steevens, Thomas.

2232 Miscellany poems and translations. *London, for Anthony Stephens, in Oxford,* 1685. 8°. L, O, CT, DU, LLU; CH, CN, MH, TU, WF, Y.

Miscellany poems. Containing. 1684. *See* Dryden, John.

Miscellany poems upon several occasions. 1692. *See* Gildon, Charles.

2232A Miscellany. Poems; [with the cure of love]. *For Will. Rogers: and Fr. Hicks in Cambridge,* 1697. 8°. T.C.III 27. L; O, MB, MH.

2232B Miscellany poems. With the temple of death. *For Gilbert Cownly,* 1685. 8°. LLU.

Miscellany poems. Written by R. W. 1700. *See* Warren, Robert.

2233 The mischief of cabals. *Printed, and are to be sold by Randal Taylor,* 1685. 4°.* L, O, C, LUG, DU; CH, CN, MH, NU, WF, Y.

Mischief of dissensions. 1681. *See* E., A.

Mischief of impositions. 1680. *See* Alsop, Vincent.

2234 The mischief of intemperance. *For J. Deacon and are to be sold by Godfrey Bouchier . . . in Peterborough,* 1691. 8°.* T.C.II 411. MH.

2235 The mischief of persecution exemplified. *For Tho. Fabian,* 1688. 4°. T.C.II 222. L, O, LW, BP, DT; CH, NHC, PU, WF, Y.

2235A The mischief of the five shillings tax upon coal. *By H. Hills, for Edward Poole,* 1698. 4°.* CN.

2236 —[Anr. ed.] —, 1699. 4°.* L, LUG; CU, MH, NC, PU, WF, Y.

2237 The mischief that falls on the freeholders of England . . . wooll. [*London,* 168–?] cap., fol.* L; CH, MERRIMACK VALLEY TEXTILE MUS., NC.

2238 The mischiefs and unreasonableness of endeavouring to deprive His Majesty. *Dublin, by Joseph Ray for Samuel Helsham*, 1681. 4°.* T.C.I 464; DIX 187. L, O, C, MR, DT; CDA, CH, PU, WF, Y.

2238A The mischiefs of rebellion. *For William Abington*, 1684. 8°. T.C.II 63. OC, BANGOR; WF.

2239 The miser mump'd of his gold. [*London*], *for P. Brooksby, J. Deacon, J. Blare, J. Back*, [1688–92]. brs. L, CM, HH; MH.

2240 The miser, written. colop: [*London*], *by J. P. for Charles Brome*, 1685. brs. O; CH, CLC, MH.

2241 The miserable case of the poor glass-makers and families. [*London, c. 1696.*] brs. L, LL.

2242 The miserable case of the poor glass-makers, artificers. [*London, c. 1696.*] brs. L, LL.

2243 The miserable maulster. [*London*], *for J. Raven*, [*c. 1690*]. brs. HH.

2244 The miserable mountebank. [*London*], *for J. Deacon*, [1685–88]. brs. IIII.

2245 Entry cancelled.

Misericordium volo. 1677. *See* Long, Thomas. Character of a Separatist.

2246 The miseries of vvar. [*London*], *for Nicholas Vavasor*, 1643. 4°.* LT, O, MR, DT; CLC, TU, WF, Y.

2246A The miseries which must fall upon the glass-makers. [*London? 1695.*] brs. L.

2247 Misery to bee lamented. *For F. G.*, [1661]. brs. O.

2248 Misery upon misery. A more full and particular relation. [*London, 1695.*] brs. L.

2248A The misfortunes of St. Paul's cathedral. [*London, 1678.*] cap., 4°.* O, LG; IU.

2248B **Mishnah.** Joma. Codex Talmudicus. *Typis J. Junii*, 1648. 4°. C, LW, OC, DU, WCA, DT; MBP, MH, NN, OHU, Y.

2249 Entry cancelled.

—[Hebrew] Capitula patrum. 1651. *See* Taylor, Francis.

2250 —Misnæ pars: ordinis primi. *Oxoniæ, e theatro Sheldoniano*, 1690. 4°. L, O, LW, CT, DT; NP, OHU, WF.

2250A The misleading of the common people. *For the author*, 1685. 4°.* MM.

2251 A mis-led king, and a memorable Parliament. [*London*, 1643.*] 4°.* LT, CCA, DT; Y.

Misopappas, Philanax, *pseud.*
Misopormist; or. 1667. *See* B., W.

Misorcus, *pseud.*
The miss display'd. 1675. *See* Head, Richard.
Missa triumphans. *Louain*, 1675. *See* Collins, William.
Missale Romanvm vindicatvm. Or. [n.p.], 1674. *See* Fuller, Robert.

2252 **M[isselden], E[dward].** Free trade. Second edition. *For William Hope*, 1651. 8°. L.
Mission of consolation. 1653. *See* Slingsby, William.
Missionarie's arts. 1688. *See* Wake, William, *abp.*
Missive of consolation. *Louain*, 1647. *See* Matthew, Sir Tobie.

2253 **Misson, François Maximilien.** A new voyage to Italy. *For R. Bently; M. Gillyflower, T. Goodwin, and M. Wotton; and S. Manship*, 1695. 2v. 8°. L, C, BQ; CN, MH, TU.

2253A ——[Anr. ed.] *For R. Bently, T. Goodwin, and M. Wotton*, 1695. 2v. 8°. PU.

2253B ——[Anr. ed.] —, *and S. Manship*, 1695. 2v. 8°. O, LLU, NE; WF, YBA.

2254 ——Second edition. *For T. Goodwin; M. Wotton; S. Manship; and B. Took*, 1699. 2v. 8°. T.C.III 146. L, O, C, BAMB, DT; CLC, LC, TU, WF, Y.

Missonne, François. Merlinus Gallicus. 1660. *See* Almanacs.

2255 The mistake of the times. *For George Linsey*, 1647. 4°.* LT, DT; MH.
Mistaken advantage. *Edinburgh*, 1695. *See* Cromarty, George Mackenzie, *earl.*
Mistaken beauty. 1685. *See* Corneille, Pierre.

2256 The mistaken bride. [*London*], *for J. Conyers*, [1688–91]. brs. L, HH, GU; MH.
Mistaken husband. 1675. *See* Dryden, John.

2256A Mistaken justice: or, innocence condemn'd . . . Francis Newland executed. *For Richard Smith*, 1695. 4°. L; CH, CLC, MB, MHL.

2257 The mistaken lover. [*London*], *for C. Dennisson*, [1685–88]. brs. HH; MH.

2257AA The mistaken mid-wife. [*London*], *for F. Coles, T. Vere, J. Wright, and J. Clarke*, [1674–79], brs. O.

2257BA The mistaken murderer: . . . William Lewis. *Printed and sold by Edw. Poole*, 1698. cap., 4°.* LSD.

2257CA Mr. — a member of the House of Commons his speech. [*London? 1690.*] cap., 4°.* TU.

2257DA Mr. Allen's vindication; or remarks. *Printed*, 1700. brs. CN.
Mr. Anthony. 1690. *See* Orrery, Roger Boyle, *earl of.*
Mrs. Anthony Sadler examined. 1654. *See* Nye, John. Mr. Sadler.

2257A Mr. Ashtons ghost to his late companion in the Tower. colop: *For T. Axe*, 1691. cap., 4°.* CH.
Mr. Baxter baptised. 1673. *See* Baxter, Benjamin.

2257B Mr. Cecill Boothe's case . . . against George Earl of Warrington. [*London, 1696?*] brs. Y.
Mr. Chillingworth's book. 1687. *See* Patrick, John.
Mr. Clanny's character. [n.p.], 1699. *See* Henderson, Jo.

2258 Mr. Coleman's legacies. *For D. M.*, 1679. fol.* O; CN, Y.

2258A Mr. [William] Cooke's case. [*London, 1679.*] brs. MH.

2258B Mr. Cotton Mather opposed. [*Boston? 1690.*] 8°.* MCL.
Mr. Courten's catastrophe. 1652. *See* Darell, John.

2259 Mr. Cowley's verses in praise of Mr. Hobbes, oppos'd. *Printed*, 1680. 4°.* L, O, OC, CS, SP; CH, CLC, MH, TO, Y.

2260 Mr. Croftons case soberly considered. *For the authours*, 1661. 4°.* L, LCL, BP, DU, P; CLC, MM, NU.

2261 Mr Davis his case. [1671.] brs. L, O, NPL.

2261A Mr. De Labadie's letter to his daughter. [*London*], *printed*, 1696. 8° in 4s.* L, LG, CCA, EN; CH, CN, MH, TU, WF, Y.

2262 Mr De la Rue's case. [*London, 1700?*] brs. LL.
Mr. Dreyden vindicated. 1673. *See* Blount, Charles.

2262A Mr [Thomas] Duckets case. [*London, 1676?*] brs. MH.

2263 Mr [Charles] Duncomb's case. [*London, 1698?*] brs. LG, LL; Y.

2264   Mr. Emerton's cause now depending . . . stated. colop:
        For R. Dew, 1682. cap., fol.* L, O, LL, CT, LSD; CH,
        PL, TU, WF, Y. (var.)
        Mr. Emmertons marriage. 1682. *See* Hunt, Thomas.

2264A   Mr. Ferguson's lamentation. *For J. Smith*, 1683. 4°.* L,
        O, LSD, SP, E; CH, WF.

2265   Mr. Fitz-Harris (now prisoner in the Tower) his case
        truly stated. colop: *For John Smith*, 1681. cap., fol.*
        L, O, LL, OC, MR; WF, Y, ZWT.

2265AA Mr. Garret . . . being lately deceased, the same little pots
        of pomatum. [*London*, 1680?] brs. L.
        Mr. George Keith, at Turners-Hall. 1696. *See* C., W.

2265A   Mr. George Keith's reasons for renouncing Quakerism.
        Printed, 1700. 8°* L, O, C, LF, DUS; CH, IU, MH, NN, PHS,
        WF.
        Mr. Hall's answer. [n.p., 1695.] *See* Hall, William.

2266   Entry cancelled.
        Mr Hampdens speech. [1643.] *See* Denham, *Sir* John.

2267   Mr. Harringtons case. [*London*, 1679.] cap., 4°.* L, LUG,
        CT, DU, MR, DT; CH, IU, MIU, WF, Y.
        Mr. Haynes his recantation-prologue. [*London*, 1689.]
        See Brown, Thomas.

2267A   Mr. Henry Martin his speech . . . June 8. 1648. [*London*],
        printed, 1648. 4°.* LT, O; CSS, INU, MIU, NN, OWC.

2268   Entry cancelled.
        Mr Hobbes considered. 1662. *See* Hobbes, Thomas.
        Mr. Hobbs's state. 1672. *See* Eachard, John.

2269   Entry cancelled.
        Mr. John Asgill his plagiarism. 1696. *See* Briscoe, John.

2269A   Mr John Herberts case, touching the custos brevium
        office. [*n.p.*, 1659?] brs. L.
        Mr John Mackenzyes narrative. 1690. *See* Clark, W. J.
        Mr John Miltons character. 1681. *See* Milton, John.
        Mr. Keith. No Presbyterian. 1696. *See* C., W.

2269B   Mr Lee's case . . . concerning the Lord Stawell's estate.
        [*n.p.*, 1695?] brs. L.
        Mr L'Estrange refuted. 1681. *See* P., J.

2270   Entry cancelled.
        Mr Lewes Hewes. 1641. *See* M. Lewes.

2271   Die veneris, 8 Martii, 1649. Mr. Millington reports.
        By Edward Husband and Iohn Field, 1649[50]. brs. STEELE
        2891. LT, O, LUG, EN, DT; MH, V, WF, Y.

2271A   Mr Prinn's answer to Mr Howe's printed case. [*n.p.*,
        1700?] brs. L.
        Mr. Pryn's good old cause. 1659. *See* Rogers, John.
        Mr. Pulton consider'd. 1687. *See* Tenison, Thomas, *abp.*

2272   Entry cancelled.
        Mr. [Joseph] Read's case. 1682. *See* Read, Joseph.
        Mr. Recorder's speech 1653. *See* Steele, William.

2272A   Mr. Richard Long's case. [*n.p.*, 1687?] brs. L.

2273   Mr. Rider's answer to the false and scandalous reflec-
        tions. [*London, c.* 1699–1700.] brs. LL.

2274   Mr. Rider's case. [*London, c.* 1699–1700.] brs. L, LL; CH.

2274AA Mr Rider's reply to Warner's answer. [*n.p.*, 1695?] brs.
        L.

2274A   Mr. Roger Le Stranges sayings. colop: *For Langley
        Curtis*. 1681. cap., fol.* L, O, CT; CH, IU, MH, NC, WF, Y.

2274B   Mr. Rotherham's case. [*London?* 1680.] brs. MH.
        Mr Sadler re-examined. 1654. *See* Nye, John.

2274BA Mr. Sadler, saddled, in the vindication of Mr. R. Cran-
        mer. *By Thomas Mabb*, 1664. colop: *Printed*, 1665. 4°.*
        L, C.
        Mr St. John's case. [n.p., 1658?] *See* St. John, Oliver.

2274BB Mr. [Henry] Serles case. [*London*, 1685?] brs. L.

2274C   Entry cancelled.
        Mr. Sidney his self-conviction. 1684. *See* Sidney,
        Algernon.
        Mr. Smirke. [n.p.], 1676. *See* Marvell, Andrew.

2275   Mr. Smyth's discovery of the Popish sham-plot in Ire-
        land. colop: *For R. Baldwin*, 1681. cap., fol.* L, O, OC,
        MR, DT; CH, CN, MH, TU, WF, Y.

2276   Wednesday the 27 August 1651. Mr. Speaker, by way
        of report. [*London*, 1651.] brs. STEELE 2948. LT, LNC.
        Mr. Toland's Clito. 1700. *See* F., S.

2277   Mr. Turbulent. *For Simon Neal*, 1682. 4°. L, O; MB.
        Mr. Vice-Chancellors. *See* Pinke, Robert.

2278   Mr. VVilliam Prynn his defence of stage-plays. *Printed*,
        1649. 4°.* LT, C, LCL, LG, LL; NU, VC, WF.
        Mr. William Wheelers case. [n.p., 1645.] *See* Parker,
        Henry.

2279   Mr [Richard] Woollaston's case. [*London*, 1698.] brs.
        L, LL.

2280   Mrs. Abigail. *For A. Baldwin*, 1700. 4°*. O, LW; IU, WF,
        Y.

2280A   Mrs. Mehetabel Holt. A person of early piety . . .
        [*Boston, S. Green*, 1690?] brs. MHS.

2280B   Mrs Page's complaint for causing her husband to be
        murthered. [*London*], *by and for W. D.*, [1670?]. brs. L.

2281   Mistris Parliament brought to bed. [*London*], *printed*,
        1648. 4°.* LT, O, LVF, AN; CLC, CN, MH, NU, PU, Y.

2282   Mistris Parliament her gossipping. [*London*], *printed*,
        1648. 4°.* LT, O, LVD, LVF, AN; CH, CLC, MH, Y.

2283   Mrs Parliament her invitation. [*London*], *printed*, 1648.
        4°.* LT, O, LG, AN; MB, Y.

2284   Mistris Parliament presented in her bed. [*London*],
        printed, 1648. 4°.* LT, O, AN; CH, MB, MBP, MH, WF, Y.

2285   Mris. Rump brought to bed of a monster. [*London*], *by
        Portcullis Damgate for Theod. Microcosmus*, 1660. brs.
        LT, OC; MH, MIU, Y. (var.)

2286   Entry cancelled.
        Mrs [Hester] Shaw's innocency restored. 1653. *See* Shaw,
        Mrs Hester.

2287   Entry cancelled.
        Mistris Shawes tombstone. 1658. *See* Shaw, John.
        Mrs. Warden's observations. [n.p., 1642.] *See* B., J.

2287A   **Mitchel, Edward.** A brief survey of all the reigns of . . .
        kings of this isle. *For William Sherwin*, 1674. brs. L.

2287B   **Mitchell, John.** The way to true honour. *By I. Dawks,
        for B. Barker*, 1697. 8°. LLP.

2288   ——[Anr. ed.] *Edinbvrgh, by the heirs of A. Anderson*,
        1699. 12°.* ALDIS 3873. L, EN; Y.

2289   **Mitchel, Jonathan.** A discourse of the glory. *For
        Nathaniel Ponder*, 1677. 8°. T.C.I 288. L, O, C, ORP; MH,
        MWA, PT, RPJ, V, Y.

2290   —Nehemiah on the vvall. *Cambridge* [*Mass.*]: *by S. G. and
       M. F.,* 1671. 4°.* EVANS 163. LW; CH, MH, MWA, RPJ, Y.

2291   [–] Propositions concerning the subject of baptism.
       [*London*], *printed,* 1662. 4°. L, O; MH, MWA, RPJ, V, Y.

2292   [–] —[Anr. ed.] *Cambridge* [*Mass.*]: *by S. G. for Hezekiah
       Usher at Boston,* 1662. 4°.* EVANS 68. L, DM; CH, MB,
       MWA, NN, NPT, SE, V.

2293   [**Mitchell, William.**] Light manifesting darknes. *Aber-
       dene, by John Forbes younger,* 1670. 8°. ALDIS 1904. HH.

2294   —A sober ansvvere. *Aberdene, by Iohn Forbes,* 1671. 8°.
       ALDIS 1924. LF, AU, E, GU, SA, DM; CN, PH, WF.

2294aA **Mitchelson, John.** Disputatio juridica. *Edinburgh, ex
       officina G. Mosman,* 1694. 4°.* ALDIS 3376.3. EN, GU.

2294A A mite from a mourner. *Printed,* 1676. brs. MH.
       Mite from three mourners. [n.p., 1666.] *See* C., A.
       Mite into the treasury. 1680. *See* Lawson, Thomas.
       Mite of affection. 1659. *See* Billing, Edward.
       Mite to the treasvry. 1653. *See* W., J.

2295   **Mitton, Peter.** Edicts upon the ordaining. *By J. R. to
       be sold by Peter Mitton,* 1645. 8°. LT.

2296   [**Mitton, Thomas.**] A letter to the Honorable William
       Lenthal . . . concerning the svrrender of Ruthin-Castle.
       For Edw. Husband, April 14. 1646. 4°.* LT, O, AN, DT; Y.

2297   —Colonell Mittons reply. colop: [*London*], *by R. Austin.*
       [1645.] cap., 4°.* LT, AN; CH, CSS, MH.

2298   Entry cancelled.
       —Two great victories: on [sic] obtained. 1644. *See title.*
       Mixt poem. 1660. *See* Crouch, John.

2298A **Moalamb, John.** The reprobate reproved. *By J. C. for
       R. Moore,* 1655. 8°. NE.
       Mock-Clelia. 1678. *See* Subligny, Adrien Thomas
       Perdou de.
       Mock-duellist. 1675. *See* Bellon, Peter.
       Mock-elogie on the funeral of Mr. Caryl. [n.p., 1673.]
       See H., E.

2298B The mock expedition or, the women in breeches.
       Wapping [*London*], *for Moll Tarr Breeches.* [1695?] brs. MH.
       Mock-majesty. 1644. *See* Phillippson, J.
       Mock poem, or. 1681. *See* Colvill, Samuel.

2299   The mock-press. colop: *For C. B.* 1681. brs. O; CH, MH,
       NCD.

2299A —[Anr. ed.] —, [1681]. brs. MH.

2300   A mock-song: or, love. [*London*], *for P. Brooksby,*
       [1672–95]. brs. L, HH; MH.

2301   Mock songs and joking poems. *For William Birtch,*
       1675. 8°. T.C.I 197; MADAN 3039. L, O, OW; MH, NN.

2302   [**Mocket, Richard.**] God and the King. *Imprinted,* 1663.
       4°.* L, O, CT, ES, DT; CH, CN, LC, MH, NU, TU, Y. (var.)

2302A [–] —[Anr. ed.] *York, printed,* 1663. 8°. YM; WF.

2303   [–] Tractatus de politia. *Excudebat S. Roycroft, impensis
       Rob. Clavel,* 1683. 8°. L, O, CS, EN, DT; BN, CLC, CN,
       MHL, NU, WF, Y.

2303A [**Mockett, Thomas.**] Christian advice both to old and
       young. *For Edw. Brewster,* 1671. 12°. T.C.I 54. L; CLC.

2304   —Christmas, the Christians grand feast. *For Richard
       Wodenoth,* 1651. 4°.* LT, O, C, LW, DT; CH, CSS, IAU,
       NU, PL.

2305   —The chvrches trovbles. *For Christopher Meredith,*
       1642. 4°. LT, O, LW, MR; IU, MH, NU, WF, Y, AVP.

2305A —The covenanters looking-glasse. *For C. Meredith,*
       1644. 4°. O, LSC; Y.

2306   —Gospell duty and dignity. *By A. M. for Christopher
       Meredith,* 1648. 4°. L, O, C; IU, LC, NU, Y.

2307   —The nationall covenant. *By J. R. for Chr. Meredith,*
       1642. 4°. LT, O, C, BC, EN; CLC, IU, MH, NU, WF, Y.

2308   —A new catechisme. *By A. M. for Christopher Meredith,*
       1647. 12°.* O.

2309   —A vievv of the solemn leagve and covenant. *For
       Christopher Meredith,* 1644. 4°. LT, O, CE, EN, DT; CH,
       CN, NU, WF, Y.

2310   **Mocquet, Jean.** Travels and voyages into Africa. *For
       William Newton; and Joseph Shelton; and William
       Chandler,* 1696. 8°. T.C.II 588. L, O, LA, LNM, E; CH, CN,
       LC, MBP, MH, RPJ, Y.

2311   A mode: the cities profound policie. [*London*], *printed,*
       1647. brs. LT, O, LVF; CH, TU.
       Model for a school. [n.p., 1675.] *See* Lewis, Mark.

2312   A model for erecting a bank of credit. *By J. A. for
       Thomas Cockeril,* 1688. 8°.* L, LG; MB, MBA, RPJ.

2313   A modal [sic] for the French King. *For R. Baldwin,* 1682.
       fol.* L, O, OP, CS, DU; CH, MM, WF.
       Model for the maintaining. 1648. *See* Poole, Matthew.
       Modell of a Christian society. Cambridge, 1647. *See*
       H., J.

2314   A model of a college to be settled in the university.
       [n.p., 1689.] brs. L, O, LG, OC; Y.

2315   A model of a democraticall government. *For W. P.,*
       1659. 4°.* LT, O, LUG; CLC, CU, MH, MU, WF, Y.

2316   The model of a design to reprint Stow's survey. [n.p.],
       1694. brs. O.

2317   A model of a new representative. *For Giles Calvert,* 1651.
       4°.* LT; CLC, MM.

2317A The model of Papal supremacy. colop: *For Jonathan
       Edwin,* 1679. brs. L, O, LNC; CH, CN, MH, WF.

2318   The model of Presbytery. *For Jonathan Edwin,* 1677.
       brs. L, LNC; CH, CN, MH, WF.
       A modell of the fire-workes. 1647. *See* Browne, George.
       Model of the gospel-sanctification. [n.p., 1693.] *See*
       Beverley, Thomas.
       Modell of the government of the church. 1646. *See*
       Walker, George.
       Model of the government of the province. Edinburgh,
       [1685]. *See* Scott, George.

2319   A modell of trvths. [*London*], *printed,* 1642. 4°.* L, O, OC,
       LNC, DT; MH, OCI, TU, WF, Y.
       Modena, Leon. *See* Léon de Modena.

2320   A moderate and cleer relation of the private souldierie
       of Colonell Scroops. *By James and Joseph Moxon, for
       William Larnar,* 1648. 4°.* LT, KEBLE, MR; MH, NR, WF,
       Y.

2320A A moderate and most proper reply to a declaration.
       Printed, 1642. 4°.* L, LIU; CH, LC, WF.

2321   —[Anr. ed.] *Printed,* 1643. 4°.* MADAN 1109n. LT, O, CT,
       YM, DT; CLC, IU, MH, NC, Y.

2322 A moderate and safe expedient to remove jealousies. [*London*], *printed*, 1646. 4°.* L, O, LIL; CN, MH, NU, RPJ.

2323 A moderate answer to a late printed pamphlet. *Printed*, 1647. 4°.* LT, DC, MR, DT; CH, MH, NU, Y.

Moderate answer to a pamphlet. 1646. *See* E., O.

Moderate answer to Mr. Prins. 1645. *See* Robinson, Henry.

Moderate ansvver to these. 1645. *See* Blake, Thomas.

Moderate cavalier. [n.p.], 1675. *See* Mercer, William.

2323A A moderate computation of what the water-tax. [*London?* 1697.] brs. MH.

2323B A moderate decision of the point of succession. colop: *For R. Janeway*, 1681. 4°.* O, OC; CH, MM, PL.

2324 A moderate expedient for preventing of popery. [*London?* 1680.] fol.* L, O, CT, DU, MR; CH, CN, MH, TU, WF, Y.

2325 The moderate independent. *Printed*, 1660. 4°.* O, DU, WCA, CD, DT; CH, MH, NU.

Moderate enquirer. 1659. *See* Caton, William.

2326 The moderate man's proposall. *By A. W. for Giles Calvert*, 1659. 4°.* LT, O, C, LIU, MR; MH, NU, WF.

Moderate Parliament considered. [n.p., 1679.] *See* P., G.

2327 The moderate Presbyter. *Printed at London for Richard Cotes*, 1646. 4°.* LT, O, CT, EN, DT; CH, IU, MH, NGT, NU.

2328 Entry cancelled. Ghost.

2329 The moderate Presbyterian. *By R. B. for Luke Fawne*, 1645. 4°.* LT, O, BC, MR, E; MH, NU, RPJ.

2329A The moderate Presbyterian. London, the third of April, 1662. [n.p.], *printed*, 1662. brs. EN.

2330 A moderate reply to His Majesties answer . . ; January 13. 1643. *Printed, Jan.* 13. 1643. 4°.* MADAN 1163n. O, LIU, LNC, EN; CSS, MH, MIU, MU, NU, Y.

2331–1A Entries cancelled.

Moderate reply to the citie-remonstrance. 1646. *See* Price, John, *of London*.

2331B Moderation a vertue: or, a vindication of the . . . moderate divines. *For Jonathan Robinson*, 1683. 4°. T.C.II 27. L, O, CT, DU, EN; CH, MH, PL, WF, Y.

2332 Moderation. Name and thing. *For Robert Bostock*, 1647. 4°.* LT, O; MIU, Y.

Moderation: or, arguments. 1660. *See* T., S.

Moderation's commendation. 1677. *See* S., N.

2333 Entry cancelled.

Moderator: endeavoring. 1652. *See* Caryl, Joseph.

Moderator expecting. 1642. *See* Povey, Thomas.

2334 The moderator: in reply to Mr. Thomas Chaloners speech. *By Francis Leach*, 1646. 4°.* LT, O, CT, BC, DT; CH, CN, MH, MU, NU, WF, Y.

2335 The moderator's pax vobis. *For B. Alsop*, 1647. 4°.* LT, MR, EN.

Modern account of Scotland. [n.p.], 1679. *See* Kirke, Thomas.

Modern assurancer. 1658. *See* Herne, John.

2336 The modern conveyancer. *By the assigns of Richard and Ed: Atkyns for John Walthoe*, 1695. 8°. T.C.II 523. L, C, EN; MH, MIU, PUL, WF, YL.

2337 —Second edition. *By the assigns of Richard and Edward Atkins, for John Walthoe and are to be sold by W. Lindsey*, 1697. 8°. L, LGI; MHL.

2338 The modern fanatical reformer. *For Rich. Kell*, 1693. brs. L.

2339 Modern novels: in XII volumes. Vol. I. *For R. Bentley*, 1692. 12°. L, MR; CLC.

2339A —Vol. II. —, 1692. 12°. L; CLC.

2340 —Vol. III. —, 1692. 12°. L; CLC.

2341 —Vol. IV. —, 1692. 12°. L; CLC.

2342 —Vol. V. —, 1692. 12°. L; CLC.

2343 —Vol. VI. —, 1692. 12°. L; CLC.

2344 —Vol. VII. —, 1692. 12°. L; CLC.

2345 —Vol. VIII. —, 1692. 12°. L; CLC.

2346 —Vol. IX. —, 1692. 12°. L; CLC.

2346A —Vol. X. —, 1692. 12°. L; CLC.

2346B —Vol. XI. —, 1692. 12°. L; CLC.

2347 —Vol. XII. —, 1692. 12°. L; CLC.

Modern pleas. 1675. *See* Tomkins, Thomas.

Modern policies. 1652. *See* Sancroft, William, *abp*.

Modern religion. 1699. *See* Ward, Edward.

Modern reports. 1682. *See* Colquitt, Anthony.

Modern statesman. 1654. *See* Wither, George.

2348 Entry cancelled.

Modern whore. [n.p.], 1675. *See* Modish.

Modest account from Pensylvania. 1696. *See* Pusey, Caleb.

2348A A modest account of that most dreadful fire . . . at Wapping. *By D. Mallet*, 1682. brs. O; CH.

2349 A modest account of the present posture of affairs. *For Richard Baldwin*, 1682. fol.* T.C.I 487. L, O, C, CT, DU; CH, CU, MH, NU, TU, WF, Y.

2350 A modest account of the vvicked life of that grand impostor Lodowick Muggleton. *Printed at London for B. H.*, 1676. 4°.* C; CN.

2351 —[Anr. ed., "Lo. Mugleton."] *For B. H.* 1676. 4°.* L, LF, DU, MR; MH, NU, PH, WF.

2352 A modest address to the livery-men of London, . . . June 24. 1681. colop: *For Richard Janeway*, 1681. brs. L, O, LG, HH; CH, MH, MU, NN, Y.

Modest advertisement. 1641. *See* Morley, George, *bp*.

Modest and clear vindication. 1649. *See* Love, Christopher.

Modest and free conference. [n.p.], 1669. *See* Burnet, Gilbert, *bp*.

2353 A modest and impartial narrative of several grievances. *Printed at New-York, and re-printed at London*, 1690. 4°.* L, O, LPR.

2354 —[Anr. ed.] [*Philadelphia, by William Bradford*, 1691.] cap., 12°.* EVANS 570. MHS.

Modest and just apology . . . East India Company. 1690. *See* T., N.

Modest and peaceable inquiry. 1681. *See* Humfrey, John.

Modest and peaceable letter. 1668. *See* P., B.

Modest and true account of the chief. Antwerp, 1696. *See* Colson, Nicholas.

Modest and true account of the proceedings. 1694. *See* Praed, John.

2355 A modest answer to a printed pamphlet, entituled, A speech. [*London*, 1681?] fol.* L, O, C, OC; CH, CN, MH, TU, WF, Y.

2355A —[Anr. ed.] [*London?* 1681.] brs. MR; CH, NC, NP, WF.

2356 A modest answer to Dr. Dove's sermon. *For R. Rabnutt*, 1682. 4°.* L, O, LG, OC, MR, SP; WF.

Modest answer to Dr. Stillingfleet's. 1680. *See* Rule, Gilbert.

2357 A modest apology for the loyal Protestant subjects. [*London*, 1692.] 4°.* O, LL, OC, CT; MH, TU, WF, Y.

Modest apology for the students. 1681. *See* M., N.

2358 A modest apology for the suspended bishops. *By T. B. and are to be sold by Randolph Taylor*, 1690. 4°.* T.C.II 351. L, O, C, AN, DU, MR, CD; CH, CN, MH, NU, WF, Y.

Modest apology occasioned. Glasgow, 1696. *See* Craghead, Robert.

2359 A modest attempt for healing. *For R. Janeway*, 1690. 4°.* T.C.II 339. L, O, LSD, WCA, EN, CD; CH, CN, MH, NU, TU, WF, Y.

Modest cavallieres advice. [n.p.], 1647. *See* Gerbier, Charles.

Modest censure. 1687. *See* N., T.

2359A A modest computation of the loss . . . in Chancery. [*London?* 1700.] brs. L.

Modest confutation. [n.p.], 1642. *See* Hall, Joseph, *bp*.

Modest critick. 1689. *See* Rapin, René.

2360 A modest defence of the clergy. *For John Nutt*, 1699. 4°. O, OC, CS, BAMB, NPL; CH, INU, TU, WF, Ÿ.

Modest detection. 1696. *See* Penington, Edward.

2361 A modest discourse concerning the ceremonies. *By T.R. for Nathanael Webb*, 1660. 4°.* LT, O, OC, CCH, DU, P, DM; MH, MIU, NU, TO, WF.

2362 A modest essay in vindication of the Right Honourable Sir Thomas Lane. colop: *For John Whitlock*, 1695. cap., fol.* Y.

Modest examination. [n.p.], 1696. *See* Eizat, Sir Edward.

2363 A modest examination of the new oath of allegiance. *For Randal Taylor*, 1689. 4°.* L, O, CT, E, DT; CH, MH, NU, WF, Y.

2364 A modest examination of the resolution. *For Thomas Parkhurst*, 1683. 4°.* L, O, LW, CT, LSD, WCA, DT; CH, CN, NN, PU, WF.

2365 A modest enquiry concerning the election of the sheriffs. *For Henry Mead*, 1682. 4°.* L, O, LG, LW, SP, DT; CH, CN, MH, NU, WF, Y.

2366 A modest inquiry into the carriage of some of the dissenting bishops. colop: *For J. K.*, 1691. cap., 4°.* L, O, LL, LLP, OC; CH, MH, PL, WF, Y.

2367 A modest enquiry into the causes of the present disasters. *For Richard Baldwin*, 1690. 4°.* L, O, CT, EC, MR, DT; CH, CN, MH, NCD, NU, WF, Y.

2367A A modest inquiry into the meaning of the revelation. *Printed*, 1688. 4°.* T.C.II 238. L, O, DU; LC, TO.

Modest enquiry whether. 1687. *See* Care, Henry.

2367B A modest motion for a moderate monarchy. *For the author*, 1660. 4°. MH.

Modest observations. 1684. *See* Tryon, Thomas.

Modest offer. [n.p.], 1644. *See* Hall, Joseph, *bp*.

2367C A modest offer of some meet considerations . . . East India. [*London?*], 1695. brs. LUG; MH, MIU.

2368 A modest petition, for a happy peace. *For Robert Bostock, Decemb. 13*. 1642. 4°.* LT, EC, SP, DT; CLC, CN, MH, TU, WF, Y.

Modest plea for an equal. 1659. *See* Sprigg, William.

Modest plea for infants. Cambridge, 1677. *See* Walker, William.

Modest plea for the clergy. 1677. *See* Addison, Lancelot.

Modest plea for the Lord's day. 1669. *See* Collinges, John.

2369 A modest proposal for the more certain and yet more easie provision . . . poor. *For J. Southby*, 1695/6. 4°.* L, LUG; IU, MH, NC, NCD, Y, ANL.

2370 Entry cancelled.

Modest reflections upon the commitment of the Earl of Shaftsbury. 1681. *See* Some modest reflections.

Modest reply humbly offered. 1692. *See* Acton, Samuel.

2371 A modest reply, in answer to the modest plea. *Printed*, 1659. 4°.* LT, O, OC, CT; CH, MH, MU, WF, Y.

2371A The modest reply of J. Blackstone examined. [*London*, 169–?] brs. O.

2372 A modest reply to a too hasty and malicious libel. colop: *For R. Janeway*, 1681. brs. L, O, CT; CH, MH, NCD, PU, Y.

2372A A modest reply to the city-reasons against the apothecaries bill. [*London?* 1694.] brs. L; O.

Modest representation. 1672. *See* Hely, James.

Modest survey. 1676. *See* Burnet, Gilbert, *bp*.

2373 Entry cancelled.

Modest vindication of Henry VValker. 1642. *See* Walker, Henry.

2374 A modest vindication of Oliver Cromwell. *Printed*, 1698. 4°. T.C.III 67. L, O, LG, DU, MR, DT; CH, CN, MIU, WF, Y.

2375 A modest vindication of the Earl of S⸺y. colop: *For Smith*, 1681. cap., fol.* L, O, CT, DU, EN, CD; CH, MH, MIU, TU, WF, Y, AVP.

2375A —[Anr. ed., "Shaftsbury."] *For Francis Smith*, 1681. fol.* WF.

2375B —[Anr. ed.] *Reprinted Edinburgh, by the heir of A. Anderson*, 1681. 4°. ALDIS 2278.3. EN; MH.

2376 A modest vindication of the petition of the Lords spiritual and temporal. [*London*, 1688.] brs. L, C, OC, BR, HH; CH, MH, TU, WF, Y.

2377 A modest vindication of the proceedings of the late Grand-Jury of the Old Baily. colop: *For N. Thompson*, 1681. brs. L, O, LL; CH, MBA, MH, PU, WF, Y.

2378 Modesty amazed. [*London*], *for J. Deacon*, [1685–88]. brs. EUING 218. L, CM, HH, GU; MH. (var.)

2379 Modesty triumphing over impudence. *For Jonathan Wilkins*, 1680. fol.* L, O, C, CT, LIU, DT; CH, MH, NCD, NU, WF, Y, AVP.

2380   The modish London life. [1688.] brs. O.

2380A   The modish whore; or, wee'l raise. [London], for Philip
        Brooksby, 1675.

        Modus tenendi Parliamenta. Dublin, [1692]. See Scobell,
        Henry.

2381   **Moellenbrook, Valentin Andreas.** Cochlearia curiosa.
        By S. and B. Griffin, for William Cademan, 1676. 8°.
        T.C.I 236. L, O, LWL, OC, AU; LC, NAM, SE, WDA, WF, Y.

2381A   —The curiosities of scurvy-grass. For William Whitwood,
        1689. 12°. L (t.p.).

2381B   —The history of scurvy-grass. By S. and B. G. for W.
        Cademan, 1677. 8°. WDA.

2382   **Moffet, Thomas.** Healths improvement. By Tho.
        Newcomb for Samuel Thomson, 1655. 4°. LT, O, C, MAU,
        EN; CH, CJC, LC, MH, MMO, NAM, HC.

2382AA [**Mogridge, Anthony.**] Ex nihilo omnia: or, the saints
        companion. By J. Orme for Thomas Jones, 1692. 4°. L,
        LLL.

2382BA [–] —[Anr. ed.] —, 1693. 4°. O, EN; NN.

        Moir, Alexander. See More, Alexander.

        Mola asinaria. 1659. See Butler, Samuel.

2382A   [**Molesworth, Robert Molesworth**], *viscount*. An
        account of Denmark. Printed, 1694. 8°. L, O, C, SP, DT;
        CH, CN, MH, TU, WF, Y, AVP. (var.)

2383   [–] —Third edition. For Timothy Goodwin, 1694. 8°.
        T.C.II 477. L, O, CM, MR, DT; CH, CN, LC, MB, NCD, NF, Y.

        [–] Denmark vindicated. 1694. See Crull, Jodocus.

2383AA [–] Etat present de Danemarc. Chez Thomas Fuller, 1694.
        8°. O; WF, Y.

        Moliere, Henrietta Sylvia. Memoirs. 1672. See Des-
        jardins, Marie Catherine.

2383A   **Molière, Jean Baptiste Poquelin.** The citizen turn'd
        gentleman. For Thomas Dring, 1672. 4°. T.C.I 118.
        L, O, LV, OW, EN; CH, CU, MH, WCL, WF, Y.

2384   —Mamamouchi. For Thomas Dring, 1675. 4°. T.C.I 219.
        L, O, LVD, OW, LLU; CH, CN, MH, TU, WF, Y.

2385   —Tartuffe. By H. L. and R. B. for James Magnus, 1670.
        4°. T.C.I 50. L, O, LLU, A; CH, LC, MH, NN, WF, Y.

2386   **Molina, Miguel de.** The Spanish Otes. By J. Bennet, to
        be sold by Walter Davis, 1685. 4°.* L, O, MR; CH, CLC.

        Molinæus, Ludovicus. See Du Moulin, Louis.

        [**Molines.**] Comical history. 1655. See Sorel, Charles.

        M[olines], A[llan]. Anatomical account. 1682. See
        Mullen, Allan.

2387   **Molinos, Miguel de.** The spiritual guide. [London],
        printed, 1688. 12°. L, O, C, GU, DT; CH, CN, MH, NU, TU, Y.

2387A   ——Second edition. For Tho. Fabian, 1688. 12°. T.C.II
        222. DUS.

2387B   ——[Anr. ed.] [London], printed, 1689. 12°. CDA.

2388   ——[Anr. ed.] —, 1699. 12°. L, CCH; CH, CLC, WF, Y.

2389   **Molins, William.** Μυσκοτομια: or, the anatomical
        administration of all the muscles. By John Field for
        Edward Husband, 1648. 8°. C, LWL, GH; BN, WSG.

2390   ——[Anr. ed., "Μυοτομια."] For Abel Roper, 1676. 8°.
        T.C.I 269. L, O, LCS, LSC, CCA; CLC, NAM, WF.

2391   ——[Anr. ed.] Printed for and sold by W. Rogers, 1680.
        12°. T.C.I 400. LCP, GH; MBM, HC.

2392   **Mollet, André.** The garden of pleasure. In the Savoy,
        by T. N. for John Martyn, and Henry Herringman,
        1670. T.C.I 26. C; CH, LC, MHO.

2393   **Mollineux, Henry.** Antichrist unvailed. Printed and
        sold by T. Sowle, 1695. 8°. L, O, LF, ORP, MR; CH, IE, PH,
        PSC, WF.

2394   —An invitation from the spirit of Christ. Printed and
        sold by T. Sowle, 1696. 12°. L, O, LF, MR; MH, PH, PSC.

2395   [**Molloy, Charles.**] De jure maritimo et navali: or, a
        treatise. For John Bellinger; and George Dawes; and
        Robert Boulter, 1676. 8°. T.C.I 227. L, O, P, E, CD; CJC,
        CLC, MH, MIU, NCL, V.

2396   [–] —Second edition. For John Bellinger; George Dawes;
        and Robert Boulter, 1677. 8°. T.C.I 284. LL, CT, GC; CH,
        MH, MU, NCL, TU, WF, Y.

2397   ——Third edition. For John Bellinger, and George Dawes,
        1682. 8°. T.C.I 480. L, C, OM, LIU, DT; BN, CLC, CN, LC,
        MHL, NCL, Y.

2397A   ——"Third" edition. For Thomas Passinger, 1682. 4°.
        CH, TO, WG.

2398   ——Fourth edition. For John Bellinger; and John
        Walthoe, 1688. 8°. T.C.II 234. L, O, C, LUG, BR; BN, CH,
        MH, MU, TU, WCL.

2399   ——"Fourth" edition. Printed, and are to be sold by Abel
        Swalle, 1690. 8°. L; CH, CJC, MHL, NCL.

2400   —Hollands ingratitude. By T. J. for Fr. K., 1666. 4°.*
        L, C, CT, DU; CH, INU, MH, NC, NP, Y.

        M[olyneux], A[llan]. Anatomical account. 1682. See
        Mullen, Allan.

2401   Entry cancelled.

        —Relation of new anatomical observations. 1682. See
        Mullen, Allan. Anatomical account.

2402   **Molyneux, William.** The case of Ireland's being
        bound. Dublin, by Joseph Ray, 1698. 8°. DIX 298. L, O,
        C, EN, DT; CH, MHL, MU, NCL, TU, Y.

2403   ——[Anr. ed.] Dublin, by and for J. R. and are to be sold
        by Rob. Clavel and A. and J. Churchil, in London, 1698.
        8°. DIX 298. L, C, LUG, CS, LLU, DT; BN, CN, LC, MBA,
        MHL.

2404   Entry cancelled. Date: 1720.

2405   —Dioptrica nova. A treatise of dioptricks. For Benj.
        Tooke, 1692. 4°. T.C.II 381. L, O, C, GU, DT; CH, CJC,
        MH, PL, WF.

2406   —Sciothericum telescopicum. Dublin, by Andrew Crook
        and Samuel Helsham, for William Norman, Samuel
        Helsham and Eliphal Dobson, 1686. 4°. OC, ARMAGH; Y.

2406A   ——[Anr. ed.] Dublin, by Andrew Crook and Samuel Hel-
        sham, and are to be sold by W. Norman and S. Helsham
        and El. Dobson, 1686. 4°. DIX 220. T.C.II 216. L, O, C,
        EN, DT; CH, CLC, MWA, WF, Y.

2407   —Whereas there is an accurate account and description
        of Ireland. [Dublin, 1682.] brs. O.

        Momus elencticus or. [n.p., 1654.] See Ireland, Thomas.

2408   Monarchia transformata in respublicam deformatam:
        or, a jury of twelve impossibilities. [London, 1649.]
        brs. LT.

        Monarchia triumphans, or. 1666. See Dormer, P.

Monarchy asserted. 1660. *See* Whitelock, Bulstrode.

Monarchy revived. 1661. *See* Eglesfield, Francis.

Monarchy triumphing. 1661. *See* Sheldon, Gilbert.

Monastichon Britanicum; *or*. 1655. *See* Broughton, Richard.

2409   Monasticon, or London's gratulation. *Printed at London,* 1660. brs. L.

Moncayo, De Castell. *See* Castel Moncayo, *marquis.*

2409A   M[onck], F[ranz]. To the King's most excellent majesty . . . the following reasons. [*London?* 1699.] brs. L.

Monck, George. *See* Albemarle, George Monck, *duke of.*

2410   **Monck, Thomas.** A cure for the cankering error. *For the author,* 1673. 8°. L, C, LCL, LW, ORP; NHC.

2411   [**Moncrief, Jo.**] A seasonable admonition and exhortation. *Edinbvrgh, by George Mosman,* 1699. 8°.* ALDIS 3905. L, EN, ENC; CLC, NN, NU.

2411A   **Moncrieff, Patrick.** Disputatio juridica. *Edinburgi, ex officina hæredum A. Anderson,* 1700. 4°.* ALDIS 3986.5. EN.

Monenda: or the antiquity. 1663. *See* Philipps, Fabian.

2412   [**Money, William.**] To the members of both Houses of Parliament. For their serious consideration. [*London,* 1685.] 4°.* LF; IE, PU, Y.

2412A   Money makes the mare to go. [*London*], *for I. Deacon,* [1680?]. brs. MH.

2413   Money [required?] for the public and future ease. [*London,* 1696?] brs. L.

2414   The money that makes a man. [*London*], *for F. Coles. T. Vere, J. Wright, J. Clarke, W. Thackery, and T. Passinger,* [1680?]. brs. L.

2414A   Money well bestowed: or, a new-fashion spit. [*London?* 1680.] brs. MH.

2415   Moneys mischievous pilgrimage. [*London,* 1697?] cap., 4°.* L, CT; MH, PU, Y.

2416   [**Monginot, François de.**] A new mystery in physick discovered. *For Will. Crook,* 1681. 12°. T.C.I 439. L, O, C, LCS, GU, DT; BN, MH, WF, WU, HC.

2417   —A resolution of doubts. *By T. N. for T. Heath,* 1654. 12°. C; BN.

2418   [–] The true Protestant sovldier. *By G. M. for William Lee,* 1642. 4°.* L, ORP; MH, TU.

2419   **Monier, Pierre.** The history of painting. *For T. Bennet, D. Midwinter, and T. Leigh; and R. Knaplock,* 1699. 8°. T.C.III 144. L, O, C, BAMB, BR; CH, CN, LC, MH, TU, Y.

2420   [**Monipennie, John.**] The abridgement or summarie of the Scots chronicles. *Edinburgh: by the heires of George Anderson, for the Company of Stationers,* 1650. 12°. ALDIS 1394. L, O; IU, WF.

2421   [–] —[Anr. ed.] *Edinburgh, by a Society of Stationers,* 1662. 12°. ALDIS 1727. L, EN; CLC, IU, Y.

2422   [–] —[Anr. ed.] *Edinburgh, by George Swintoun and James Glen, and are to be sold by them, and by Thomas Brown and David Trench,* 1671. 12°. ALDIS 1917. L, O, CM, E, EN, BLH; IU, MM.

2423   [–] —[Anr. ed.] *Glasgow, by Robert Sanders,* 1671. 12°. ALDIS 1918. GM, EN.

Monitory and hortatory letter. *Boston,* 1700. *See* Mather, Cotton.

Monitory letter about the maintenance. *Boston,* 1700. *See* Mather, Cotton.

2423A   A monitory letter to Mr. Williams. *Printed,* 1699. 4°.* LLP, ST. EDMUND HALL, OXF., DC; NHC, WF.

Monk, George. *See also* Albemarle, George Monck, *duke of.*

[**Monk, George.**] The Christians victory over death. 1670. *See* Ward, Seth.

2424   Entry cancelled.

Monk, W. M. Sermon preach'd . . . Oct. 24, 1686. 1687. *See* Wall, William.

Monk unvail'd. 1678. *See* Dupré, *abbe.*

Monk's hood. 1671. *See* Du Moulin, Pierre.

2425   **Monmouth, Henry Carey, earl of.** A speech made in the House of Peeres, . . . 13. of Ianuary. 1641. *Printed at London, for I. Benson,* 1641[2]. 4°.* L, O, C, LNC; CH, MH, MU, NU, WF, Y.

2426   ——[Anr. ed.] *Printed,* 1641[2]. 4°.* LT, C, OH, CT; IU, MH, WF.

2427   **Monmouth, James Scott, duke of.** An abridgment of the English military discipline. *Printed at London; Reprinted at Boston by Samuel Green and sold by Benjamin Harris,* 1690. 8°. EVANS 508. MWA, NN.

2428   —A copy of the late Duke of Monmouth's letter to the Duke of Albemarle. colop: *By George Croom,* 1685. brs. L, O, LL, DCH, DU; CH, CLC, INU, MH, MIU, WF, Y.

2429   —The declaration of. [*London,* 1685.] 4°.* STEELE 3793. L, O; CH, MIU, WF.

2429A   Monmouth again at court. [*London?* 1683.] brs. O.

2429B   Monmouth and Bucleugh's welcome from the north. [*n.p.,* 1678.] brs. EN.

2430   —[Anr. ed.] *For Tho. Johnson,* 1682. brs. L, O; CH, MH, Y.

2431   Monmouth degraded. *For James Dean,* 1685. brs. O; MH.

2432   Monmouth routed. *For James Dean,* 1685. brs. O, CM, BR.

2433   —[Anr. ed.] [*London*], *for P. B.,* 1688. brs. CM, HH.

2433AA   Monmouth worsted in the West. [*London*], *for G. H.,* 1688. brs. O, CM.

2433A   Monmouth's downfal. *For Nicholas Woolfe,* 1685. brs. MH.

2434   Monmouth's return. [*London*], *For C. Corbet,* 1683. brs. O, EN; CH, CLC, MH, Y.

2434A   Monmouth's saying in the West. [*London*], *for B. J.,* [1688]. brs. CM.

Monomachia: or a duel. [n.p.], 1687. *See* Ward, Thomas.

2435   [**Monpersan, Louis de.**] La politique des Jesuites. 1688. 12°. L, O, LLL, DT; CH, CLC, MH, WF, HC.

2435A   **Monro, Alexander, of Bearcrofts.** To his grace, His Majesties high commissioner . . . information for. [*n.p., c.* 1680.] 4°.* WF.

2436   **M[onro,] A[lexander], d. 1715?** An advertisement by. [*Edinburgh?* 1695.] 4°.* ALDIS 3468. LLP, LW, OC, MR; MIU.

2437   [–] An apology for the clergy of Scotland. *For Jos. Hindmarsh,* 1693. 4°. T.C.II 423. L, O, C, DU, EN; CH, CN, MH, NU, TU, WF, Y.

—Collection of all the acts. 1693. *See* England: Laws, statutes.

2437A [–] A collection of tracts. *For Joseph Hindmarsh, 1692.* 4°. T.C.II 428. NN, NU.

2438 Entry cancelled.
[–] History of Scotch-Presbytery. 1692. *See* Shields, Alexander.

2439 [–] An enquiry into the new opinions. *For Walter Kettilby, 1696.* 8°. L, O, C, E, AU; CH, CLC, NU, Y.

2440 [–] A letter to a friend, giving an account. *For Joseph Hindmarsh, 1692.* 4°.* T.C.II 428. L, O, C, YM, EN, CD; CH, CN, MH, NU, TU, WF, Y.

2441 —A letter to the Honourable Sir Robert Howard. *For E. Whitlock, 1696.* 4°.* L, O, CT, EN; WF.

2442 —The prelatical church-man. 1690. 4°.* EU.

2443 [–] Presbyterian inquisition. *For J. Hindmarsh, 1691.* 4°. T.C.II 396. L, O, C, EN, DT; CH, CN, MH, NU, WF, Y.

2444 —Sermons preached. *For Joseph Hindmarsh, 1693.* 8°. T.C.II 462. L, O, C, E, EN; CN, IEG, NU.

2445 Entry cancelled. *See previous entry.*
[–] Some remarks upon a late pamphlet. 1694. *See* Strachan, William.

2446 [–] The spirit of calumny. *For Joseph Hindmarsh, 1693.* 4°. L, O, C, E, EN, CD; CH, CN, MH, NGT, NU, WF, Y.

2446A **Monro, Andrew.** Compendium rhetoricæ. *Typis G. Wilde, impensis autoris prostat vænale apud S. Crouch & apud B. Crayle, 1688.* 8°.* T.C.II 232. LSD.

2447 —Institutio grammaticæ. *Excudebat Freeman Collins, prostatque venalis apud Johannem Lawrence, 1690.* 8°. L, EN.

2448 **[Monro, George.]** The just measures of the pious institution of youth. *Edinburgh, by John Reid, 1700.* 12°. ALDIS 3976. L, E, LSD, GU, M; CH.

2449 **Monro, John.** Illustrissimo & nobilissimo domino D. Georgio Vicecomiti de Tarbat, . . . positiones hasce philosophicas, . . . theses. colop: *Edinburgi, excudebat Joannes Reid, 1686.* brs. ALDIS 2674.6. AU.

2450 —Nova & artificiosa methodus docendi. *Prostant apud Georgium Wells, & Abel Swalle, 1687.* 4°. L, O, C; IU, MBC.

2451 Entry cancelled.
—Positiones. *Edinburgi, 1686. See* —Illustrissimo.

2452 **Monro, Robert.** Disputatio juridica. *Edinburgi, apud successores Andreæ Anderson, 1693.* 4°.* ALDIS 3307.5. EN.

2453 **Monro, Robert, lord.** A letter of great consequence. [*London*], *for Edward Husbands. July 8. 1643.* 4°.* LT, O, C, LVF, BLH, DN; CH, IU, MH, WF, Y.

2454 —The resolution of Major-Generall [Robert] Monro. [*London*], *printed,* [1648]. 4°.* LT, MR; CH, MU, Y.

2454A —The Scotch military discipline. *For William Ley, 1644.* fol. BC, NL, EN; CLEVELAND PUB. LIB., MU, WF.

2455 **M[onsey], R.** Scarronides: or Virgile travestie. *By Thomas Mabb, for Robert Clavel, 1665.* 8°. L, O, C, DT; CH, CLC, IU, MH, NP, WF.
[–] Scarronides . . . in imitation. 1665. *See also* Cotton, Charles.

2456 M. Colbert's ghost. *Cologn, chez Pierre Marteau, 1684.* 12°. DU, SP; CH, CN, IU, WF, Y.

2456A —[Anr. ed., "Monsieur."] *For Edward Golden, 1684.* 24°. T.C.II 75. LUG; MH.

2457 Monsievr Covenant's last vvill and testament. [*London, 1662.*] cap., 4°.* MIU, NU.

2458 Monsieur in a mouse-trap. colop: *For Tho. Hinton, 1691.* cap., 4°.* L, O, LLU; CH, MH, WF, Y.

2459 —[Anr. ed.] [*Edinburgh*], *reprinted, 1691.* brs. ALDIS 3163.3. MC, EN; CN.

2460 The monsieur: or, a letter. colop: *For Rich. Janeway, 1681.* brs. L, O, HH; CH, CN, MH, MIU, MU, ZWT, AVP.

2461 **[Monson, Sir John.]** An antidote against the errour in opinion. *By E. Griffin, 1647.* 8°. L, C, LNC, P, YM; CDA, CH, CLC, WF.

2462 [–] A discourse concerning supreme power. *For R. Chiswell, 1680.* 8°. T.C.I 375. L, O, C, NOT, CD; CH, NS, NU, WF, Y.

2462A Entry cancelled. Date: [1640].

2462B [–] Since the recommitment of Sir J. Monsons bill. [*London, c. 1662.*] brs. L.

2463 [–] A short answer to several questions. *Printed, 1678.* 4°. O, SP.

2464 [–] A short essay of afflictions. *By E. G., 1647.* 8°. L, O, C, LCL, NOT, YM; CDA, CH, CLC, WF, Y.

2465 **Monson, Sir William.** Megalopsychy. *For W. Crooke, and sold by W. Davis, 1682.* fol. T.C.I 472. L, O, C, DU, LIU; CH, CN, LC, NU, PL, WF, Y.

2466 —A true and exact account of the wars with Spain. *For W. Crooke, and sold by W. Davis, 1682.* fol. T.C.I 472. L, O, CCA, DU, EN; CH, LC, MU, WF, Y.

2467 A monstrous birth. *For Livewel Chapman, 1657.* 4°.* L.
Monstrous devourer. 1675. *See* W., L.

Montagu, Edward. *See* Manchester, Edward Montagu, *earl.*

2467A **Montagu, Edward Montagu, 2nd baron.** A letter from . . . tenth of June. 1647. *For John Wright, 1647.* 4°.* LT, O, OC, LSD, DT; CH, CLC, MH, WF, Y.

Montagu, Henry. *See* Manchester, Henry Montagu, *earl.*

2468 **Montagu, Ralph Montagu, duke.** Two letters from . . . to the Ld. Treasurer. *Printed, and are to be sold by Jonathan Edwin, 1679.* 4°.* LT, O, C, MR, CD; CH, CN, MH, NP, WF, Y. (var.)

2468A ——[Anr. ed.] [*Dublin*], *reprinted 1679.* 4°.* DIX 164. CD, DT.

2469 **Montagu, Richard, bp.** The acts and monuments of the church. *By Miles Flesher and Robert Young, 1642.* fol. L, O, C, E, DT; BN, CH, IU, MBA, NU, TU, WF, Y.

2470 —Θεανθρωπικον; seu, de vita Jesu Christi. 1641. fol. EN.

2471 ——[Anr. ed.] *Typis M. Flesher et R. Young, 1648.* fol. BN.

2472 **Montagu, Walter.** The coppy of a letter sent from France. [*London*], *imprinted, 1641.* 4°.* LT, O, C, BR, DU; CH, MH, MU, TU, WF, Y.

2472A [–] Jeremias redevivus; or, an elegiacall lamentation. [*London?*], *printed 1649.* 4°.* LT; CH.

2473 —Miscellanea spiritualia. *For W. Lee, D. Pakeman, and G. Bedell,* 1648. 4°. LT, O, C, E, GU; BN, CH, CN, LC, MH, NU, TU, WF, Y.

2474 — — . . . the second part. *For John Crook, Gabriel Bedell, and partners,* 1654. 4°. LT, O, CS, DUS, DL; BN, CLC, CN, MH, NU, TU, WF, Y.

2475 —The shepheard's paradise. *For Thomas Dring,* 1629. [1659]. 8°. L, O, LVD, OW, CK; CH, MH, PU, WCL, WF, Y.

2476 — —[Anr. ed.] *For John Starkey,* 1659. 8°. L, LLL, CT, LIU, EN; CH, CN, LC, MH, Y.

2477 **Montague, William.** The delights of Holland. *For John Sturton: and A. Bosvile,* 1696. 8°. L, LUG, LIU, LLU; CLC, NN, TO, WU, Y.

2478 **Montagu, Zacheus.** The jus divinum of government. *By A. M. for Abel Roper,* 1652. 12°. LT, LSC, E.

2479 **Montaigne, Michel de.** Essays of. *For T. Basset, and M. Gilliflower, and W. Hensman,* 1685–6. 3v. 8°. T.C.II 116. L, O, LVF, EC, DT; BN, CLC, CN, MH, WF, Y.

2480 — —Second edition. —, 1693. 3v. 8°. L, O, CT, AN, BR; BN, CLC, MU, NCU, NP, WG, Y.

2480A — —"Second" edition. *For M. Gilliflower and W. Hensman, R. Bently, and J. Hindmarsh,* 1693. 3v. 8°. L, CM; MH.

2481 — —Third edition. *For M. Gilliflower and W. Hensman, R. Wellington and H. Hindmarsh,* 1700. 3v. 8°. L, LW, CM, LLU, DT; BN, CH, CN, MB, PBM, WF, Y, AVP.

2482 **Montalvan, Francisco Baltheo.** Naked truth. *For Thomas Palmer,* 1672. 12°. CHRISTIE-MILLER.

2483 — —[Anr. ed.] *For T. Palmer,* 1673. L; CN.

Montalvan, Juan Perez de. *See* Pérez de Montalván, Juan.

2484 Entry cancelled.

Montanus, Arnoldus. Atlas Chinensis. 1671. *See* Dapper, Olfert.

2485 —Atlas Japannensis. *By Tho. Johnson for the author,* 1670. fol. L, O, C, BR, EN; BN, CH, CN, LC, MH, NU, WF, Y.

2486 Entry cancelled.
       —Embassy. 1670. *See* —Atlas Japannensis.

2486A —Remarkable addresses by way of embassy from the East-India Company. *Printed by the author [i.e. J. Ogilby], and are to be had at his house,* 1671. fol. OM.

Montanus, Benedictus Arias. *See* Arias Montanus, Benedictus.

2486B **Montauban, *Monsieur de.*** A relation of a voyage . . . on the coast of Guinea. 1698. 12°.* LNM.

Montault de Bénac, Philippe. *See* Navailles, Philippe Montault de Bénac, *duc de.*

2487 **Monteage, Stephen.** Debtor and creditor. *By J. R., to be sold by Ben. Billingsley,* 1675. 4°. T.C.I 205. L.

2488 — —Second edition. *By J. Richardson for B. Billingsley,* 1682. 4°. T.C.I 498. C; CLC, LC.

2489 — —Third edition. —, 1690. 4°. LUG, CT, E; CB, WF.

2490 [–] Instructions for rent-gatherers accompts. *By J. Richardson for Benj. Billingsley,* 1683. 4°.* T.C.II 49. L, LUG, CT, E, DT; LC, MB, WF.

2490A **Monteith, Robert.** An exact table, shewing . . . legal registration. *Edinburgh,* [1700?]. brs. EN.

2491 **[Montelion.]** Don Juan Lamberto, or, a comical history . . . first part. *Sold by Henry Marsh,* 1661. 4°. LT, O, C, MR; CLC, MB, MH, MIU, NP, WF.

2492 [–] —Second edition. *By J. Brudenell, for Henry Marsh,* 1661. 4°. L, O, CT; CLC, CN, IU, NN, NP, ZWT.

2492A [–] —Third edition. *For Henry Marsh,* 1664. 4°.* L; CH, CN, MH, Y.

2492AB [–] —"Third" edition. *For Henry Marsh,* 1665. 4°.* CSS, MU.

Montelion, 1660. [n.p., 1659.] *See* Almanacs. Phillips, John.

2492B Montelions predictions. *By S. and B. Griffin, for Thomas Palmer,* 1672. 4°. L, LIU, NPL; CH.

2493 Entry cancelled.

Montespan. Amorous conquests. 1685. *See* Courtilz, Gatien de.

Montesperato, Ludovicus de, *pseud.* *See* Conring, Hermann.

2494–6A Entries cancelled.

Montfaucon de Villars. *See* Villars, de Montfaucon, abbé de.

Montfort. *See* Bremond, Gabriel de.

2497 **Montgomerie, Alexander.** Cerasum et sylvestre prunum. *Edinburgi, excudebant hæredes & successores Andreæ Anderson.* 1696. *Et vænales prostant ex officinâ M. Hen. Knox.* 4°.* ALDIS 3585. L, O, C, E, EN, DT; CH, CLC, IU, WF. (var.)

2498 —The cherrie and the slae. *Aberdene, by Edward Raban,* 1645. 8°. ALDIS 1193. L.

2498A — —[Anr. ed.] *For I. D.,* 1646. 8°. OW.

2498B — —[Anr. ed.] *Edinburgh, by the heires of Robert Bryson,* 1646. 12°. LSD.

2498C — —[Anr. ed.] *Glasgow, by Robert Sanders,* 1668. 16°. ALDIS 1847. L (impf.).

2499 — —[Anr. ed.] *Edinburgh, by Andrew Anderson,* 1675. 16°. ALDIS 2056. MR; MH.

2499A — —[Anr. ed.] *Edinburgh, by the heir of Andrew Anderson,* 1680. 12°. ALDIS 2206.3. CM, EN.

2500 — —[Anr. ed.] *Edinburgh, by the heir of Andrew Anderson,* 1682. 12°. ALDIS 2338.5. L, EN.

2501 — —[Anr. ed.] *Edinburgh, by John Reid,* 1691. 8°. ALDIS 3163.7. EN.

2502 — —[Anr. ed.] *Glasgow, by Robert Sanders,* 1698. 8°. ALDIS 3766. O, EN.

2503 — —[Anr. ed.] *Belfast, printe [sic] and sold by Patrick Neill,* 1700. 8°.* LC.

[–] Flyting betwixt Polwart. [n.p.], 1688. *See* Hume, Alexander.

2504 **[Montgomery, James.]** Great Britain's just complaint. *[London], printed,* 1692. 4°. L, O, CT, YM, EN, DT; CH, IU, MH, TU, WF, Y.

2505 [–] —Second edition. *Oxford: printed* 1692. 4°. L, OC, CS, MR, EN, CD; CLC, CN, MH, NU, TU, Y.

2505A A monthly intelligence, relating the affaires of . . . Quakers. *For the author,* 1662. 4°.* L; MH, NN, PH, Y.

Monthly observations. 1688. *See* Tryon, Thomas.

Monthly preparations. 1696. *See* Baxter, Richard.

2506 **Montluc, Blaise de.** The commentaries of. *By Andrew Clark, for Henry Brome,* 1674. fol. T.C.I 148. L, O, C, ES, DT; CLC, CN, LC, MH, NCD, WF, Y.

2506A — —[Anr. ed.] *For Charles Brome,* 1688. fol. NN.

2507 **[Montpensier, Anne Marie Louise d' Orleans], duchesse de.** The characters or pourtraits of the present court of France. *By J. C. for Thomas Palmer,* 1668. 8°. L, C, OB, CT; CLC, CN, IU, LC, MH, WF, Y.

Montre. 1686. *See* Bonnecorse, Balthazar de.

2508 **Montrose, James Graham, marquis.** Certaine instrvctions given by the L. Montrose. *Printed,* 1641. 4°.* LT, O, LNC, EC, MR; CH, IU, MBP, MH, WF, Y.

2509 Entry cancelled. *See* M2514.

2510 —The declaration of . . . However the justice of His Majesties cause. [*London*], *for Matthew Simmons,* [1649]. brs. STEELE 3p 2033. L; HR.

2511 —Declaration of . . . November 1649. *Paris, G. Sassier,* [1649]. 4°.* BN.

2512 Entry cancelled. *See* M2514A.

2513 —Declaration of . . . Though it may seem. *Gottenberge,* 1649. 8°.* STEELE 3p 2030. L, CT; WF.

2514 — —[Anr. ed.] [*Gottenberg*], 1649. 16°.* STEELE 3p 2031. LT.

2514A — —[Anr. ed.] [*Scotland*], 1649. brs. STEELE 3p 2032. L.

2515 Entry cancelled. *See following entry.*

2516 —A declaration of . . . 9 July 1649. *Printed,* 1649. 4°.* STEELE 3p 2023. LT; CH, CSS, LC.

2516A —The declaration of. *For Matthew Simmons,* 1649. 4°.* CT, MR; CH, CSS, MIU, Y.

2517 — —[Anr. ed.] —, 1650. 4°.* LT, O, CT, DC, SP; CH, LC, MH, MU, Y.

2518 —Disputatio juridica . . . de aleatoribus. *Edinburgi, officium hæredum Andreæ Anderson,* 1698. 4°.* ALDIS 3752. EN; WF.

2519 —A proper new ballad, to the tune of I'll never love thee more. [*n.p.,* 1690?] brs. L.

Montrose redivivus. 1652. *See* Wishart, George.

Montrosse totally routed. 1645. *See* Thompson, William.

2520 The monvment of Charles the First. [*London,* 1649.] brs. LT; CH, MH.

Monumenta Westmonasteriensia: or. 1682. *See* Keepe, Henry.

Monumentum regale or. [*n.p.*], 1649. *See* Cleveland, John.

2521 **Moody, Joshua.** The believers happy change. *Boston, by B. Green and J. Allen,* 1697. 8°.* EVANS 802. MB, MWA.

2522 —The great sin of formality. *Boston: by Benjamin Harris and J. Allen. And are to be sold by Richard Wilkins,* 1691. 8°.* EVANS 571. MB, MH, NN.

2522A —Lamentations upon the never enough bewailed death of . . . John Reiner. [*Boston,* 1676.] brs. MBA (frag.).

2523 —A practical discourse. *Boston in New-England by Richard Pierce for Joseph Brunning,* 1685. 8°. EVANS 396. CH, MB, MHS, MWA, NC, NP, RPJ, SE.

2524 —Sovldiery spiritvalized. *Cambridge* [*Mass.*]: *by Samuel Green,* 1674. 4°. EVANS 193. CH, MB, MH, MWA, NN.

2524A **[Moon, John.]** Great trumpet of the Lord. [*London?* 1660.] cap., 4°.* L, LF, MR; CH, MH, PH, WF.

2524B [–] A Jesuitical design discovered. [*London,* 1674.] brs. MH.

2525 —The revelation of Jesus Christ. *For Thomas Simmons,* 1658. 4°.* L, O, LF, MR; CH, IE, MH, PH, WF, Y.

2526 —The true light hath made. *For G. Calvert,* 1657. 4°.* LT, LF.

2527 [–] The true light, which shines. [*London?* 1658.] brs. L, LF, BBN; PH.

2527A **[Moone, Paul.]** A visitation of love to all people. *For Benjamin Clark,* 1681. 4°.* L, LF, MR; PH, PHS, PSC.

Moon-shine. 1672. *See* Achard, J.

2528 **Moor, Edmund.** A catalogue of Mr. Edmund Moors library. [*London*], 1689. 4°.* OC; JF.

2529 **Moore, Adam.** Bread for the poor. *By R. & W. Leybourn for Nicholas Bourn,* 1653. 4°. L, O, C, R, EN; CH, IU, MH, NC, WF, Y.

2530 **Moore, Andrew.** A compendious history of the Turks. *By John Streater,* 1660. 8°. LT, LSC, P; BN, LC, MH, MU, WF.

2531 — —Second edition. —, 1663. 8°. C, EN; CLC, Y.

2532–3 Entries cancelled.

—Πηγιαμα. Aberdene, 1668. *See* Mure, Andrew.

2533A **Moore, Andrew, fl. 1698.** Of churches and meeting-houses, . . . in a dialogue. [*n.p.*], *printed for the author,* 1698. 4°.* NPT.

2534 **Moore, Charles, viscount.** A certificate from. *For Joseph Hunscott,* 1642. 4°.* LT, O, C, SP, DN; MH.

2535 **Moore, Sir Francis.** Cases collect & report. *By R. Norton for Robert Pawlet,* 1663. fol. L, O, C, EN, CD; CH, IU, KT, LC, NCL, V.

2536 — —Second edition. *For Robert Pawlet,* 1675. fol. T.C.I 213. L, O, LGI, CT, DT; LC, MHL, NCL, WF, YL.

2537 — —"Second" edition. *For G. Pawlet, to be sold by Mat. Wotton,* 1688. fol. L, O, LG, LL, NPL; LC, MHL, MIU, NCL, V, WF.

2538 —An exact abridgement in English, of the cases. *For John Starkey, Thomas Basset, and Samuel Speed,* 1665. 8°. L, O, LL, CS, GU; CH, MHL, NCL, WF.

2539 —The law of charitable uses. *For Henry Twyford,* 1676. fol. T.C.I 232. L, O, C, LL, EN; CH, LC, MHL, NCL, YL.

2540 Entry cancelled. *See preceding entry.*

2541 **[Moore, Francis.]** A gallant victory obtained by . . . Inchiqveen. *For W. S.,* 1647. 4°.* LT, C, DN.

2542 Entry cancelled.

—Kalendarium ecclesiasticum. 1699. *See* Almanacs.

2543 **Moore, Francis, of Highwech.** Nature's goodnight. *By J. G. to be sold by Francis Eglesfield,* 1656. 4°.* L, O, LW, BLH; CLC, TU, WF, Y.

2544 **Moore, John, curate.** The banner of Corah. *Bristoll: by W. Bonny, for the author,* 1696. 8°. L, O, LLP, BR; CH, NU, WF, Y.

2545 **Moore, John, bp.** Of patience. *For R. Royston; and Walter Kettilby,* 1684. 4°. T.C.II 82. L, O, C, BAMB, WCA; CLC, CN, NU, PL, TU, WF, Y.

2546   [–] Of religious melancholy. *For William Rogers, 1692.* 4°.* T.C.II 400. L, O, C, LIU, DT; CH, CN, NU, TU, WF, Y.

2547   ——Second edition. —, 1692. 4°.* L, C, BLH; CH, LC, PL, Y.

2547A   ——Third edition. —, 1692. 4°.* C, OU, NPL; TSM.

2547B   ——"Third" edition. —, 1693. 4°.* LW, OU.

2548   Entry cancelled. Date: post-1700.

2549   [–] —Fourth edition. —, 1699. 8°.* T.C.III 131. L, C, LSD, NE; MWA.

2550   [–] Of the immortality of the soul. *For William Rogers, 1694.* 4°.* T.C.II 498. L, O, C, MR, CD; CH, CN, NGT, TSM, WF, Y.

2551   —Of the wisdom and goodness of providence. *For W. Rogers, 1690.* 4°. T.C.II 329. L, O, C, LSD, CD; CH, MIU, TSM, WF, Y.

2552   —A sermon preach'd . . . 28th of May, 1682. *For Walter Kettilby, 1682.* 4°. L, O, C, P, WCA; CH, CN, NU, PL, V, WF, Y.

2553   —A sermon preached on the 28th of June. *For William Rogers, 1691.* 4°.* T.C.II 376. L, O, C, LIU, DT; CH, CN, MH, NU, TSM, WF, Y.

2554   [–] A sermon preach'd . . . April 16. 1696. *For Will. Rogers, 1696.* 4°.* T.C.II 576. L, O, C, OM, CT; CH, MH, NU, WF, Y.

2555   [–] A sermon preach'd . . . January 31. 1697. *By R. R. for W. Rogers, 1697.* 4°.* T.C.III 49. L, O, C, SP, DT; CH, CLC, LC, WF, Y.

2555AA   **M[oore], J[ohn],** *of Bridgwater.* A sermon preached before the worshipful mayor. *For the author, 1699.* 8°.* BR.

2555A   Entry cancelled.

       Moore, Sir John. Moore, mayor. At a Common Council holden in the Chamber of the Guildhall . . . 16th of Novemb. 1681. [n.p., 1681.] *See* London. Court of Common Council.

2556   —The speech of . . . Sept. 29, 1681. *For Jonathan Robinson, 1681.* brs. LG, OC; CH, CN, MH, WF, Y.

2557   ——[Anr. ed.] colop: *For R. Read, 1682.* brs. L, O, DU; CH, CN, MBA, WF.

2557A   **Moore, John,** *of Edinburgh.* For the right honourable, my lord provost . . . a table to find the true hour of the day. *Edinburgh, by J. Swintoun, 1681.* brs. EN.

       Moore, John, *of Knaptoft.* Considerations concerning common fields. 1654. *See* Lee, Joseph.

2558   —The crying sin of England. *By T. M. for Antony Williamson, 1653.* 4°.* LT, O, C, LUG, LW; CU, MH, NC, NU, WF.

2559   —A scripture-vvord against inclosure. *For Anthony Williamson, 1656.* 4°.* L, C; NN.

2560   **Moore, John,** *of Wechicombe.* A leaf pull'd from the tree of life. *For E. Brewster, 1660.* 4°.* LT, LSD; LC, NU.

2561   **Moore, John,** *of West Cowes.* Moses revived. *Printed, and are to be sold by Gyles Meddowes, 1669.* 8°. T.C.I 4. L, O, C, AN, EN; NHC, NU.

2561A   ——[Anr. ed.] *For E. Brewster, to be sold by W. Keblewhite, 1669.* 8°. LSC; CLC.

2562   **Moore, John,** *Puritan.* Protection proclaimed. *By J. C. for Henry Fletcher, 1656.* 4°.* LT, CCA, MR; MH.

2563   **Moore, Sir Jonas.** Moores arithmetick. *By Thomas Harper for Nathaniel Brookes, 1650.* 8°. L, C, LLL, OC, CT; CH, IU, MB, MU, NCD.

2564   ——[Anr. ed.] *By J. G. for Nath. Brook, 1660.* 8°. LT, O, C, OC, CCA; CH, CLC, LC, MU, WCL, WF.

2565   Entry cancelled.

       [–] Moor's arithmetick. 1681. *See* —New systeme.

2566   ——Third edition. *By R. H. for Obadiah Blagrave, 1688.* 8°. T.C.II 211. L, C, LW, BAMB; CH, LC, MU, NC, PL.

       [–] Arithmetick in species. 1680. *See* Perkins.

2567   —Bibliotheca mathematica. [*London, 3 Nov. 1684.*] 4°.* L, O, CS; BN, CN, MH, NG.

2568   Entry cancelled.

       [–] Doctrine of surds. 1680. *See* Perkins. Arithmetick.

2568A   [–] Englands interest and the farmers friend. *Printed and sold by J. How, 1697.* 12°. OB.

2569   —An excellent table for the finding the periferies. [*London*], *1674.* brs. L.

2570   ——[Anr. ed.] *By W. G. for N. Brooke, 1676.* brs. O.

2571   —The history or narrative of . . . Bedford Level. *For Moses Pitt, 1685.* 8°.* L, O, C, CT, R, DT; BN, CH, CU, MH, WF, Y.

       [–] Index horarius. 1662. *See* Marcus, Joannes.

2572   —A mathematical compendium. *Printed and sold by Nathanael Brooke, 1674.* sixes. T.C.I 188. L, O, LR; CLC, MH, MU. (var.)

2573   ——Second edition. *For Robert Harford, 1681.* sixes. L, O, C, OC, DT; CH, MB, MU, NC, WF, Y.

2573A   ——Third edition. *For Obadiah Blagrave, 1690.* 12°. CLC, IU.

2574   ——"Third" edition. *For Richard Mount, 1693.* 12°. LW, OC, EC; CH, SMITH COLL.

2575   ——"Third" edition. *For J. Lawrence, 1695.* 16°. T.C.II 562. C, EO.

2576   —Modern fortification. *By W. Godbid, for Nathaniel Brooke, 1673.* 8°. T.C.I 134. L, O, CK, MC, DT; CH, CLC, MIU, TO.

2577   ——[Anr. ed.] *For Obadiah Blagrave, 1689.* 8°. T.C.II 265. L, C, OC, CT, NE; CN, MIU, MU, PL, WF.

2578   —A new geography. *For Robert Scott, 1681.* 4°. NE, EN; CLC, LC, SCU, WF.

2579   —A new systeme of the mathematicks. *By A. Godbid and J. Playford, for Robert Scott, 1681.* 4°. T.C.I 431. L, O, C, EN, DT; BN, CJC, CLC, MH, MU, PL, SCU.

2580   —Resolutio triplex. *Typis J. G. prostant venales . . . per Nath. Brookes, 1658.* 4°.* O, CT.

2580A   —A short introduction into the art of species. *Printed and sold by Joseph Moxon, 1660.* 8°.* CLC.

2581   [**Moore, Mary.**] Wonderfull news from the North. Or, a true relation. *By T. H., to be sold by Richard Harper, 1650.* 4°.* LT, O; MH.

2582   **Moore, Peter.** The apprentices warning-piece. *Printed and sold by Henry Walker, 1641.* 4°.* LT, MR; WF.

2583   **Moore, Richard.** ῾Ο θησαυρος εν οστρακινος σκευεσιν. A pearl in an oyster-shel. *By A. M. for Tho. Parkhusrt, 1675.* 8°. L, O, LCL, BC; CLC, WF, Y.

2584 —The redemption of the seed of God. [*London*], *printed*, 1677. 8°. L, BBN, BR; BN, CLC, IU, MH, PH, PSC.

2585 **[Moore, Robert.]** A mighty victory over the Irish rebels obtained by Colonell Jones. *Dublin, for Charles Ryley*, 1647. 4°.* DIX 81. LT, O, C, CT, CD; CH, WF.

2586 Entry cancelled.

Moore, Samuel. Ανω Θεοκρυπτα. 1647. *See* — Θεοσπλαγχναποδοσις.

2586A —An heavenly wonder. *By Matthew Simmons*, 1650. 8°. CH, CLC.

2587 Entry cancelled.

—Σπλαγχναποδοσις. 1647. *See next entry.*

2588 [–] Θεοσπλαγχναποδοσις or, the yernings of Christs bowels. *By Matthew Symmons*, 1647. L, DT; CLC, CU, IU, NCD, NU, Y.

2589 [–] —[Anr. ed.] *By M. S. to be sold by Hanna Allen*, 1648. 8°. LT, LCL, LSC; CB, CH, MH, NCD, WF.

2589A **Moore, Thomas, elder.** An address for submissive, peaceable and loving living. *By James Cottrel*, 1656. 4°.* MH, WF.

2590 —A brief declaration of Jesus Christ. *Delft*, 1647. 12°. LCL; CH.

2591 —A brief discourse about baptisme. *By Gar: Dawson, for Tho: Brewster and G: Moule*, 1649. 4°.* LT, O, LCL, LW; IAU, NHC.

2592 —A discovrse about the pretious blood. [*London, Nov. 6, 1646.*] 4°. LT, C, DT; NP.

2593 —A discovery of sedvcers. [*London*], *printed*, 1646. 4°.* LT, O, ORP, CT, DT; CH, MH, NHC.

2593A —An explicite declaration. *By James Cottrel*, 1656. 4°. ORP, ENC; CH, MH.

2593B — —[Anr. ed.] *By J. C. for Livewel Chapman*, 1656. 4°. WF.

2594 —A treatise of the person of Christ. *By J. C. for Livewel Chapman*, 1657. 4°. L.

2594A A treatise, shewing the liberty and bondage of the will. *By W. C. for Anthony Nicolson in Cambridge*, 1652. 4°.* O; NHC.

2595 —An vncovering of mysteriovs deceits. *Printed*, 1647. SA, DT; NHC, NU.

2596 [–] The vniversallity of God's free-grace. *Printed*, 1646. 4°. LT, LCL, CM, ENC, DT; IU, MH, NPT, NU.

2597 **Moore, Thomas, younger.** An antidote against the spreading infections. *Printed at London, by R. Ibbitson for Livewell Chapman*, 1655. 4°. L, LF, CCA; NU.

2598 —Breach upon breach. *By J. B. for the author*, 1659. 4°. L, O, LF; CH.

2599 Entry cancelled.

—Clavis aurea. 1695. *See* Moore, Thomas, *fl.* 1695–1700.

2600 —A defence against the poyson of Satan's designe. *For Livewel Chapman*, 1656. 4°. L.

2601 Entry cancelled.

—Explicite declaration. 1656. *See* Moore, Thomas, *elder.*

2601A —Fornication condemn'd. *By Ja. Cotterel, for the author; to be sold by Nath. Crouch*, 1667. 4°. CLC, MM, NN, Y.

2602 —A fuller discovery of the dangerous principles . . . Quakers. *For John Allein*, 1660. 4°. O; NU, Y.

2603 —Instruction to the living. *By E. Brudenell, for John Allen*, 1659. 4°. L, O, LF.

2604 —A lamentation over the dead in Christ. *Printed at London by R. I. for Livewell Chapman*, 1657. 4°. O, LF, SP.

2605 —Mercies for men. *By R. I.*, 1654. 4°. LT, LF.

2606 —A motive to have salt always in our selves. *By H. Brugis for B. Southwood*, 1671. 8°. C.

2607 Entry cancelled.

—Second addition. 1697. *See* Moore, Thomas, *fl.* 1695–1700.

2608 —Truth, vindicating it self. *For the author*, 1661. 4°.* Y.

2608aA **Moore, Thomas, fl. 1695-1700.** An addition to the Clavis aurea. *Printed*, 1696. 8°.* O, LLP; WF.

2608bA —Clavis aurea; or, a golden key. *Printed*, 1695. 8°.* L, O, LLP; MH, WF.

2608cA —A disputation: whether Elijah. *Printed*, 1695. 8°. LLP.

2608A —The doctrin [*sic*] of transubstantiation. *Printed; and sold by W. Marshall*, 1700. 8°.* MH.

2608B —A second addition to the Clavis aurea. *Printed*, 1697. 8°.* O, C, LLP; WF.

2609 **M[oore], S[ir] W[illiam].** Caledons complaint against infamous libells. [*Edinburgh*, 1641.] 4°. C, E, EN, ES; CLC.

2610 —The cry of blood. *Edinburgh, by the heires of George Anderson*, 1650. 4°.* ALDIS 1414. L, EN, ES; CH.

2611 **Moore, William, of Whalley.** The grand inquiry who is the righteous man. *London, by E. Cotes, for Ralph Shelmerdine in Manchester*, 1657. 8°. L, LSC.

2612 — —[Anr. ed.] *By E. Cotes, for Henry Eversden*, 1658. 8°. O.

2613 **Moorhead, William.** Lachrimæ sive valedictio Scotiæ . . . the tears and valediction of Scotland. *By H. Brugis, for the author*, 1660. 4°.* O, CT; CH, MH.

Moores baffled. 1681. *See* Addison, Lancelot.

2613A **[Moraes, Francisco de.]** The famous history of the noble and valiant Prince Palmerin . . . first part. *By R. I. for S. S. to be sold by Charles Tyus*, 1664. 4°. L; CH, CLC, CN, FU, NP, WF, Y.

2613B [–] —Second part. —, 1664. 4°. L; CLC, CN, NP, WF, Y.

2613C [–] —[Anr. ed.] *For William Thackeray and Thomas Passinger*, 1685. 4°. T.C.II 151. CM; MH.

2613D **Morains, Francois de.** The perfect major: shewing the easiest way of handling arms. *By B. Griffin for the author*, 1686. 8°. L.

Moral discourse. 1690. *See* Abercromby, David.

Morall discourses. 1655. *See* Culpeper, Sir Thomas.

Moral essay. Edinburgh, [1665]. *See* Mackenzie, Sir George.

2614 A moral essay concerning . . . pride. *For Joseph Hindmarsh*, 1689. 8°. T.C.II 304. L, CM, CT, DT; CB, CLC, Y.

2615 A moral essay upon the soul of man. *By H. Hills, jun. for H. Faithorne*, 1687. 8°. L, O, DUS, BQ; CLC, IAU, LC.

2616 —[Anr. ed.] *For Tho. Jones*, 1690. 8°. L, O, P; IU, LC, MU, TO, WF.

Moral essays and discourses. 1690. *See* Shannon, Francis Boyle, *viscount.*

Moral essays; contain'd. 1677. *See* Nicole, Pierre.

2617 Entry cancelled.

Moral instructions. 1683. *See* Dufour, Sylvestre.

Moral practice. 1670. *See* DuCambout de Pont Chateau, S.J.

Moral treatise. 1694. *See* Cassagnes, Jacques.

Moralist: or a satyr. 1691. *See* Brown, Thomas.

2617A The moralitie of the fourth commandment. [*London*, 165–?] EN; NU.

Morality of the seventh-day-sabbath. 1683. *See* B., J.

Morality represented. Edinburgh, 1687. *See* M., G.

Moray. *See* Murray.

Morbvs epidemius. Oxford, 1643. *See* Greaves, Sir Edward.

2617B **Morden, *Sir John*.** Sir John Morden's case, as to his election for Colchester. [*n.p.*, 1696.] brs. L.

2617C **Morden, Robert.** Atlas terrestris. [*London*], *sold by Robt. Morden*, [*c.* 1690]. 8°. LC, RPJ.

2618 Entry cancelled.
—Fortification. 1688. *See* S., J.

2619 —Geography rectified. *For Robert Morden and Thomas Cockeril.* 1680. 4°. T.C.I 404. L, O; CLC, LC, MU, RPJ, Y.

2620 — —Second edition. —["*Cockerill*"], 1688. 4°. T.C.II 225. L, C, BC, LLP, DT; CN, LC, NCD, NU, PU, RPJ, WF, YBA.

2621 — —Third edition. —, 1693. 4°. T.C.II 459. L, O, C, LW, OC, AN; CH, IU, LC, MB, NN, RPJ.

2622 — —Fourth edition. *For R. Morden and T. Cockerill, to be sold by M. Fabian, and Ralph Smith,* 1700. 4°. T.C.III 200. L, FONMON; MIU, MWA, PL, RPJ, WF, Y.

2622A — —"Fourth" edition. *By R. R. for Robert Morden and Thomas Cockerill,* 1700. 4°. C, CT; LC, MBA, MH, SYRACUSE.

2623 —A pocket book of all the countries of England. [*London*], *sold by Robert Morden and Joseph Pask,* [1680]. 8°. L.

2623A —A prospect of London. colop: *For R. Morden and P. Lee,* 1700. fol.* LG; CLC.

2624 **Mordington, James Douglas, *baron*.** The humble proposals of. [*London,* 1690?] brs. L.

2625 —A proposal humbly offered. [*London,* 1670?] brs. L, HH; BN.

2626 **More, Alexander.** Alexandri Mori Ad quædam loca novi fœderis notæ. *Typis Jacobi Flesher: prostant apud Gul. Wells & Rob. Scott,* 1661. 8°. L, O, CS, E, DM; MH, WF, Y.

2627 —A sermon preach'd at the Hague . . . 1650. *By J. D. for Roger Clavel,* 1694. 4°.* L, O, LW, CT, EN; U. OREGON, WF.

2628 —Theses philosophicæ. *Abredeis,* 1691. 4°.* ALDIS 3202.7. AU.

2629 — —[Anr. ed.] *Abredeis, excudebat Ioannes Forbesius,* 1699. 4°.* ALDIS 3911. O.

More, Caleb. War in New-England visibly ended. 1677. *See* Hutchinson, Richard.

2630 [**More, Cresacre.**] The life and death of Sᵣ. Thomas Moore. [*n.p.*], *for N. V.,* 1642. 4°. L, O, C, CT, EN; CLC, MH, NU, WF.

2631 Entry cancelled.

[**More, *Sir Francis*.**] Exact abridgment. 1665. *See* Moore, Sir Francis.

2631A **More, Gertrude.** The holy practises. *Printed at Paris by Lewis de la Fosse,* 1657. 12°. L, O, C, LW; CLC, CN, TU.

2632 —The spiritval exercises. *Printed at Paris, by Lewis de la Fosse,* 1658. 12°. L, O, LW, BSM, DUS; BN, CH, TU, WF, Y.

2633 **More, Henry.** Henrici Mori Cantabrigiensis opera omnia. *Typis impressa J. Macock, sumptibus autem J. Martyn, & Gualt. Kettilby,* 1679. fol. T.C.I 371. L, O, C, GC, EN; BN, MB, NU, OCI, UCLA, WF, Y.

2633A — —[Anr. ed.] *Typis R. Norton impensis J. Martyn & Gualt. Kettilby,* 1679. fol. MIU.

2634 —Opera philosophica. *Typis J. Macock, impensis Johan Martyn & Gualteri Kettilby,* 1679. fol. LLP, LW, BAMB, ES; CLC, Y.

2635 Entry cancelled. Ghost.

2636 —Opera theologica. *Typis J. Macock, impensis Johan. Martyn & Gualteri Kettilby,* 1675. fol. T.C.I 213. L, O, C, EN, DT; BN, CN, CU, IU, MBA, Y.

2636A — —[Anr. ed.] *Impensis Gualteri Kettilby,* 1700. fol. PL.

2637 —An account of virtue: or, Dr. Henry More's abridgment of morals. *For Benj. Tooke,* 1690. 8°. T.C.II 337. L, O, C, LLP, CK, AN; CLC, CN, MH, WF, Y.

2638 [–] Annotations upon the two foregoing treatises, Lux orientalis. *For J. Collins, and S. Lounds,* 1682. 8°. OU, BC, DUS, EC, BLH; CLC, CN, MBA, NC, NU, PL, Y.

2639 —An antidote against atheisme. *By Roger Daniel,* 1653. 8°. L, O, C, LCL, DC, P; CH, MH, NU, WF, Y, HC.

2640 — —Second edition. *By J: Flesher, to be sold by William Morden in Cambridge,* 1655. 8°. LT, O, C, OC, CK; CLC, CN, MIU, NU, TU, WF.

2641 —Apocalypsis apocalypseos; or the revelation. *By J. N. for J. Martyn, and W. Kettilby,* 1680. 4°. T.C.I 380. L, O, C, BC, EN; CLC, MBA, MH, MU, NU, WF, Y.

2642 [–] Appendix to the late antidote. *By I. R. for Walter Kettilby,* 1673. 8°. T.C.I 135. O, LW, CT, NPL, P; CLC, WF, Y.

2643 [–] A brief discourse of the real presence. *For Walter Kettilby,* 1686. 4°. L, O, C, EN, DT; CH, IU, MH, NU, TU, WF, Y.

2644 [–] —Second edition. —, 1686. 4°. L, O, C, EN, DT; CDA, MH, NU, PL, WF, Y.

2645 —A brief reply to a late answer to. *By J. Redmayne, for Walter Kettilby,* 1672. 8°. T.C.I 125. L, O, C, SP, E; CLC, MBA, NU, WF, Y.

2645A [–] —[Anr. ed.] *By I. Redmayne, for Walter Kettilby,* 1673. 8°. DUS.

2646 —A collection of several philosophical vvritings of. Second edition. *London, by James Flesher, for William Morden in Cambridge,* 1662. fol. L, O, C, EN, DT; BN, CH, CN, LC, MH, NP, NU, V, Y.

2647 —Conjectura cabbalistica. Or, a conjectural essay. *London, by James Flesher, to be sold by William Morden, in Cambridge,* 1653. 8°. LT, O, CT, DUS, GU; CH, MH, MU, NCD, NU, WF, Y.

2648 —Democritus Platonissans. *Cambridge, by Roger Daniel,* 1646. 8°. L, O, C; CH, CN, Y.

2649 —Discourses on several texts. *By J. R., to be sold by Brabazon Aylmer, 1692.* 8°. T.C.II 422. L, O, C, SHR, EN; CLC, CN, MH, NCD, NU, WF, Y.

2650 [–] Divine dialogues, . . . God. *By James Flesher, 1668.* 8°. T.C.I I. L, O, C, E, DT; CH, CN, MH, NU, WF, Y.

2651 [–] —[Anr. ed., "God and."] —, 1668. 8°. L, O, CT, E, DT; CH, CN, MH, WF, Y.

2652 —Enchiridion ethicum. *Excudebat J. Flesher, venale autem habetur apud Gulielmum Morden, Cantabrigiensem, 1668.* 8°. L, O, LW, CT, SHR, E; BN, CH, CLC, MBC, MIU, Y.

2653 — —Second edition. —["*Guilielmum*"], 1669. 8°. L, O, C, SA, BQ, DT; CH, CN, MH, WF, Y.

2653A — —[Anr. ed.] *Amsteloedami, apud Joannem Paullium. Prostant venales apud Guil. Graves, Cantab., 1685.* 12°. O, CK; NU.

2654 [–] Enchiridion metaphysicum: . . . pars prima. *Typis E. Flesher. Prostat apud Guilielmum Morden, Cantabrigiensem, 1671.* 4°. T.C.I 81. L, O, C, E, DT; BN, CH, LC, MBA, MH, MIU, Y.

2655 [–] Enthusiasmus triumphatus, or, a discourse. *By J. Flesher, and are to be sold by W. Morden in Cambridge, 1656.* 8°. LT, O, CT, GU, DT; CH, CU, MH, NU, WF.

2656 —Epistola H. Mori ad V. C. *Typis J. Flesher, & venalis prostat apud G. Morden, Cantabrigiensem, 1664.* 8°.* L, O, C, LNC, SC; BN, CLC, CN, MH, NCU, WF.

2657 No entry.

2658 —An explanation of the grand mystery of godliness. *By J. Flesher, for W. Morden, in Cambridge, 1660.* fol. L, O, C, E, DT; CLC, CU, MH, NCD, NU, PH, WF, Y.

2659 Entry cancelled.
—Exposition of . . . Daniel. 1681. *See* —Plain and continued exposition.

2660 —An exposition of the seven epistles. *By James Flesher, 1669.* 8°. T.C.I 12. L, O, C, E, DT; CLC, MH, NU, OCI, WF.

2661 Entry cancelled.
[–] Free Parliament proposed. [*London, 1660.*] *See* L'Estrange, Sir Roger.

2661A [–] Free-Parliament quæres. [*London*], *printed 1660.* 4°.* LT, O, OC, LSD, MR; CH, MIU, NGT, WF, ZWT.

2662 —An illustration of those two . . . Daniel. *By M. Flesher, for Walter Kettilby, 1685.* 4°. T.C.II 141. L, O, C, BC, P; CLC, MBA, NU, PL, Y.

2663 —The immortality of the soul. *By J. Flesher, for William Morden in Cambridge, 1659.* 8°. L, O, OC, CT, BAMB; CH, CN, MH, TU, WF, Y.

2664 —Letters on several subjects. *By W. Onely, for John Everingham, 1694.* 8°. T.C.II 498. L, O, C, LCL, LW; CH, IU, NU, WF, Y.

2665 Entry cancelled.
—Life and doctrine. Gant, 1656. *See* More, Henry, *of the Society of Jesus.*

2666 —A modest enquiry into the mystery of iniquity. *By J. Flesher for W. Morden in Cambridge, 1664.* fol. L, O, C, EN, DT; CLC, CN, MH, NU, TU, WF, Y.

2667 [–] Observations upon Anthroposophia theomagica. *Parrhesia* [*London*], *but are to be sold, by O. Pullen, 1650.* 8°. L, O, C, E, GU; CH, MH, WF, WU, Y.

2668 Entry cancelled.
—On fluid bodies, 1676. *See* —Remarks.

2669 —Paralipomena prophetica containing several supplements. *For Walter Kettilby, 1685.* 4°. T.C.II 141. L, O, C, CT, BAMB; CH, MBA, MIU, NP, PL, Y.

2670 —Philosophicall poems. *Cambridge, by Roger Daniel, 1647.* 8°. L, O, C, LIU, BQ; CH, CN, MBP, MH, TU, WF, Y.

2671–2 Entries cancelled.
— —[Anr. ed.] 1653. *See preceding entry.*
—Philosophical writings. 1662. *See* —Collection of several philosophical writings.

2673 —A plain and continued exposition of . . . Daniel. *By M. F. for Walter Kettilby, 1681.* 4°. T.C.I 436. L, O, C, CT, EN; CH, IU, MBA, PL, WF, WSC.

2674 [–] Ψυχωδια Platonica: or a Platonicall song of the soul. *Cambridge, by Roger Daniel, 1642.* 8°. LT, O, C, E, ES; CH, CN, MH, WF, Y.

2674A [–] —[Anr. ed., "A platonick song of the soul."] —, 1647. 8°. CPB.

2675 —Remarks upon two late ingenious discourses. *For Walter Kettilby, 1676.* 8°. T.C.I 228. L, O, C, OM, GU; BN, CLC, MH, PL, WF, Y.

2676 —Scriptorum philosophicorum tomus alter. *Typis R. Norton, impensis J. Martyn & Gualt. Kettilby, 1679.* fol. L, O, OC, BAMB, EC; MBA, PL, Y.

2677 [–] The second lash of Alazonomastix. [*Cambridge*], *by the printers to the University of Cambridge, 1651.* 12°. L, C, OB, SC, E; BBE, CH, CLC, MH, Y.

2677A [–] Some cursory reflexions impartially made upon Mr. Richard Baxter. *For Walter Kettilby, 1685.* 4°.* T.C.II 124. L, O, CS, BC, WCA; MHS, MIU, WF.

2678 —Some few more remarkable and true stories. 1688. LMT.

2679 —Tetractys anti-astrologica, or, the four chapters. *By J. M. for Walter Kettilby, 1681.* 4°. T.C.I 430. L, O, C, LWL, OME, BAMB; CH, CU, MH, TSM, WF, Y.

2680 [–] The two last dialogues. *By J. Flesher, 1668.* 12°. EC, NE; CLC, NU, WF, Y.

2680A **M[ore], H[enry],** *of the Society of Jesus.* The life and doctrine of ovr saviovr Iesvs Christ. *Gant, by Maximiliaen Graet, 1656.* 8°. L, O, DUS; CH, CLC, CN, NU, WF, Y.

2681 **More, John.** A generall exhortation. *By G. D., 1652.* 8°. L; Y.

2682 —A lost ordinance restored. colop: *For Richard Moone, 1653[4].* cap., 4°.* LT.
—Protection proclaimed. 1656. *See* Moore, John, Puritan.

2683 —A trumpet sounded. [*London*], *printed, 1654.* 4°. L, LCL; MM, Y.

2684 **More, Nicholas.** A letter from Doctor More. [*London*], *printed, 1687.* 4°.* L; CH, MU, PSC, PSCO, RPJ.

2685 **More, Richard.** A true relation of the murders committed in . . . Clunne. *By T. B. for P. Stephens & C. Meredith, 1641.* 12°. L, O; CLC.

2685A **More, Robert.** The writing masters assistant. *Sold by the author and John Barnes, [1696?].* 4°.* L, CM.

2686 Entry cancelled.

[**More, S. J.**] England's true interest. 1697. *See* Moore, *Sir* Jonas.

2687 **More, Stephen.** The wise Gospel preacher. *For the author*, [*c.* 1650]. 8°. O, LCL; CLC, CN, NGT.

2687A ——[Anr. ed.] *For the author*, 1673. 8°. WF.

2688 **More, *Sir* Thomas.** The historie of the pitifvll life, and vnfortunate death of Edward the Fifth. *By Thomas Payne for the Company of Stationers, and are to be sold by Mich: Young*, 1641. 12°. L, O, C, CT, DT; CH, CN, MH, WCL, WF, Y.

2688A ——[Anr. ed.] *By Thomas Payne for William Sheares, to be sold by Michael Young*, 1641. 12°. L, LG, OCC, CK, DU, E; CLC, CN, Y.

2689 ——[Anr. ed.] *For William Sheares*, 1651. 12°. O, LLP, LUC, CK, ESSEX; CLC.

2690 —Thomæ Mori Utopia. *Oxonii, typis W. Hall, impensis Fran. Oxlad*, 1663. 24°.* MADAN 2643. L, O, C, EN, BLH; CH, IU, MH, NP, WF, Y.

2691 —Utopia. *For Richard Chiswell*, 1684. 8°. L, O, C, EN, DT; CH, IU, MH, TU, WF, Y.

2692 ——[Anr. ed.] *For Richard Chiswell, and to be sold by George Powell*, 1685. 8°. T.C.II 148. L, O, MAU, ES, DT; CH, CN, LC, MH, NU, Y.

2692A **More, Thomas.** A funerall ovation . . . Cromwell. [*London*, 1658.] cap. LG.

2693 [**More, William.**] A mighty victory in Ireland: obtained. *Printed at London by Robert Ibbitson*, 1647. 4°.* LT, O, C, DN, DT; CH, WF, WU.

2694 —A short and plain tractate. *By T. H. for Charles Green*, 1645. 8°. O.

2694A [–] Very good nevves from Ireland. *For V, V.*, 1647. 4°.* LT, DN; CH, MH.

2694B **More, *Sir* William.** Sir William More's case. [*London*, 1675.] brs. MH.

2694C More bloody newes from Essex. *For D. M.*, 1677. 4°.* O.

2695–6 Entries cancelled.

More brave, and good newes. 1641. *See* Turner, Ambrose.

More cheap riches. 1660. *See* Church, Nathaniel.

More divisions among the Quakers. [n.p.], 1693. *See* Keith, George.

More English examples. 1692. *See* Leedes, Edward.

A more exact and full relation of many admirable passages. [*London*], 1644. *See* Jesop, William.

2697 A more exact and full relation of the horrid and cruel murther . . . Cossuma Albertus. *Printed, and are to be sold by R. Vaughan*. 1661. 4°.* CLC, MH, Y.

2697A A more exact and necessary catalogue of pensioners in the Long Parliament. [*London*], *Printed*, 1648. brs. O.

2698 —[Anr. ed.] [*London, c.* 1660.] brs. L, LL, OC, HH; CH, CN, MH, PU, WF, Y.

A more exact and particvlar relation of the taking of Shrevvsbury. 1645. *See* Reinking, William.

2699 A more exact and perfect relation of the great victory. *Imprinted at London for John Wright*, 1645. 4°.* LT, O, DT.

2699A A more exact and perfect relation of the treachery . . . of Francis Pitt. *For John Field, Octob.* 18. 1644. 4°.* MH, WF.

More exact character. 1658. *See* L' Wright, Thomas.

More exact relation of the great defeat given to Gorings' army. 1645. *See* Blackwell, John, *capt.*

More exact relation of the late. 1644. *See* Watson, Lion.

More exact way. Dublin, 1654. *See* Osborne, Henry.

2700 The more excellent way. *For Giles Calvert*, 1650. 8°.* LT, C.

2700A A more full and exact account of that most dreadful fire. colop: *By D. Mallet*, 1682. cap., fol.* L; CH.

More full and exact relation (being). 1645. *See* Rushworth, John.

More full and exact relation from Reading. 1643. *See* C., T.

More full relation of the continved svccesses. 1645. *See* C., W.

More full relation of the great victory obtained by our forces near Worcester. 1651. *See* Stapleton, Robert.

2700B A more fuller and exact account of the tryals . . . Old Bayly . . . [19, 20, 22 February]. 1674. 4°.* L (lost).

2700C More glorious, joyfull and renowned newes from Ireland. [*n.p.*, 1642.] 4°.* INU.

More good newes from Ireland. 1642. *See* W., D.

2701 More good news from Ireland, giving a faithful account. colop: *For R. Baldwin*, 1689. brs. C, OC, MC, DN; CH, Y.

2702 More happy and joyfull nevves from Ireland. *For H. Luudon*, 1642. 4°.* LT, O, EC, DN; INU, MH, MIU.

2703 More happy newes from Ireland. *For Iohn Greensmith*, 1641. 4°. MR; CLC, MH.

2703A More haste, than good speed. *For G. Tompson*, 1659. 4°.* MH.

2704 The more haste, the worst speed. [*London*], *for P. Brooksby*, [1680?]. brs. L.

2704A More joyfull newes from Hull . . . set in a letter from Sir John Hotham. [*London*], *August* 2. *Printed for J. Wels*, 1642. 4°.* L, LIU; CH.

More joyfull newes from Ireland. 1642. *See* Poole, Ensign.

2705 Entry cancelled.

More lampoons. [n.p.], 1688. *See* P., J.

2706 More last words and sayings of the true Protestant Elm-Board. [*London*], *for S. Hadwel*, 1682. brs. L, O, OC; Y.

2707 More later and trver newes from Somersetshire. *For Rich. Abbis.*, *August* 16, 1642. 4°.* LT, BR; Y.

2708 More letters from Scotland. *By F: Neile*, 1651. 4°.* LT, MR.

2709 More light shining in Buckingham-shire: . . . the second part. *Printed*, 1649. 4°.* LT, O, YM, EN; RBU.

2710 More light to Mr. John Lilburnes jury. colop: *Printed*, 1653. *August* 16. cap., 4°.* LT.

2711 More newes from Hvll. *For Richard Cooper*, 1642. 4°.* LT, O.

2712 More newes from Ireland; or, the bloody practices. *For Iohn Thomas*, 1641. 4°.* LT, LLL, MR, DN; MIU.

More news from Rome. 1666. *See* Wallis, Ralph.

2712aA More news from the fleat. *For T. Passenger,* [1664–88]. brs. O.

2712A More nevvs from Virginia. [*London*], *for W. Harris,* 1677. 4°.* V.

More particular and exact account. [n.p.], 1659. *See* B., J.

More particvlar and exact relation. 1645. *See* Bishop, George, *capt.*

2712B A more particular relation of the victory . . . of Prince Lewis of Baden. colop: [*London*], *by Edw. Jones in the Savoy,* 1691. brs. OC; MH, PL.

2713 A more perfect and exact relation of the last great and terrible sea-fight neer the Downs. *Imprinted at London for Geo. Horton,* 1652. 4°.* LT.

More perfect and particular relation. 1645. *See* H., W.

2714 More plots found out, and plotters apprehended. *For Henry Overton,* 1643. 4°.* LT, O, DU, MR, YM; CH, CN, MH, WF, Y.

2714A More reasons humbly offer'd to the . . . Commons, for the bill for encouraging learning. [*London,* 1698?] brs. L.

2714B More reasons humbly offered to the . . . Commons, for the bill . . . for securing property of . . . books. [*London,* 1698?] brs. L.

2715 More sad and lamentable news from Bristol. *For John Moderation,* 1682. 4°.* LF, BR; PH.

More than conqueror. Dublin, 1673. *See* Parry, Benjamin, *bp.*

More true and an exacter relation. [n.p.], 1642. *See* C., T.

2716 More true and exceeding joyfull newes from Ireland. *For I. H.* 1642. 4°.* LT, O, C, LLL, MR, DN; MH, NN, WF.

2717 More warning yet. Being a true relation. *Printed at London, by J. Cottrell; and are to be sold by Richard Moone,* [1654]. 4°.* LT; CH, CSS.

More work for George Keith. 1696. *See* Penn, William.

2718 More work for the Popish implements. colop: *For J. B.,* 1682. fol. * L, O, MR; CH, NIC, NN, PU, WF, Y.

2719 **Morel, Pierre.** The expert doctor's dispensatory. The whole art of physick. *For N. Brook,* 1657. 8°. LT, O, LWL, OB, GU; NAM, WF, WSG, HC. (var.)

2720 **Morel, Theodorius.** Enchiridion dvplex. *Typis Guil. Du-gard; impensis Andr. Crook,* 1650. 8°. L, O, CT, AU, E; MH, IU, TO, TU, WF.

2720A ——[Anr. ed.] *Typis Tho. Newcomb, impensis Andr. Crook,* 1664. 8°. L.

Moreland. *See* Morland.

2721 [**Morellet, Laurent.**] An historical explication of what there is most remarkable . . . at Versailles. *For Matthew Turner,* 1684. 12°. T.C.II 124. L, O; NN, WF, Y.

2722 [**Morer, Thomas.**] An account of the present persecution of the church in Scotland. *For S. Cook,* 1690. 4°. T.C.II 314. L, O, C, DU, EN, DT; CH, CN, NP, NU, WF.

2722A [–] —[Anr. ed.] *Printed,* 1690. 4°. L, O, C, OC, MR; IU, MH, MIU, WF, Y.

2723 —A sermon preach'd . . . May 29. 1699. *For James Bonwicke,* 1699. 4°.* T.C.II 134. O, LP, OC; Y.

2724 —A sermon preach'd . . . Novemb. 5. 1699. *By T. Mead, for James Bonwicke,* 1699. 4°.* T.C.III 151. L, O, LP; CH, Y.

2725 **Moreri, Louis.** The great historical, geographical and poetical dictionary. Sixth edition. *For Henry Rhodes; Luke Meredith; John Harris; and Thomas Newborough,* 1694. fol. T.C.II 481. L, O, C, NPL, E; CLC, CN, LC, PL, WF, Y.

2725A **Moret, François.** A genealogy of . . . Kings of Spain. [*London?* 1700.] brs. L.

Moreton, *bp. See* Morton.

2726 **Moretti, Tomaso.** A general treatise of artillery. *By A. G. and J. P. for Obadiah Blagrave,* 1683. 8°. T.C.II 6. L, C, CT, NE; CLC, CN, MIU, PL, WF.

2726aA —A treatise of artillery. *By William Godbid, to be sold by N. Brooke,* 1673. 8°. CH.

2726A [**Morey, Dewance.**] A true and faithful warning from the Lord God. [n.p., 1665.] cap., 8°.* L, DT; CLC.

2727 **Morford, Thomas.** The Baptist and Independent churches. *For Robert Wilson,* 1660. 4°.* L, O, LF, BBN, BR; LC, MH, NHC, PH, PSC.

2728 —The cry of oppression. *Printed,* 1659. 4°.* LT, LF, BBN, BR, MR; CH, MH, PH, PSC, Y.

2729 **Morgan.** A collection of new songs. *Sould by I: Walsh, and I. Hare,* 1697. fol.* L.

2730 **Morgan, Edward.** Edvvard Morgan, a priest, his letter. *For T. B.* 1642. 4°.* L, O, EC; CH, CLC, IU, MH, MM, Y.

2731 [–] A prisoners letter to the Kings most excellent Maiesty. *Printed,* 1641[2]. 4°.* LT.

2731A **Morgan, Einion.** Hysbys rwidd a di honglad. *For the author,* 1693. 8°. AN.

2732 [**Morgan, Matthew.**] An elegy on the death of the Honourable Mr. Robert Boyle. *Oxford, by Leonard Lichfield,* 1692. fol.* L, O, LCL, OM, MR; Y.

2733 [–] —[Anr. ed.] *Oxford, by L. Lichfield, for Chr. Coningsby, London,* 1692. fol.* O; CH, MH, Y.

2734 —Eugenia: or, an elegy. *Oxford, by Leonard Lichfield,* 1694. 4°. L; MH, Y.

2735 [–] A poem to the Queen. *Oxford, by Leonard Lichfield for John Wilmot,* 1691. fol.* T.C.II 360. L, O, LCL, MR; AU; CH, CN, LC, MH, NP, PU, Y.

2736 —A poem to the King. *For E. Whitlock,* 1698. fol.* LCL, LVF, MR; MH, WF.

2737 —A poem upon the late victory. *Printed,* 1692. 4°.* T.C.II 411. L, O, C; INU, IU, MH, WCL, Y.

Morgan, Rice op Meredith op, *pseud.*

Morgan, Shinkin ap, *pseud.*

Morgan, Shon ap, *pseud.*

2738 **Morgan, Sylvanus.** Armilogia. *By T. Hewer, for Nathaniel Brook, and Henry Eversden,* 1666. 4°. L, O, AN, MR, EN, BLH; CH, CN, PL, WF, Y.

2739 —Catalogue of the library. [*London*], 5 Apr 1693. 4°.* L.

2740 —Heraldry epitomiz'd. *Printed and are to be sold by William Bromwich,* 1679. brs. T.C.I 372. O; CH.

2741 —Horologiographia optica. Dialling. *By R. & W. Leybourn, for Andrew Kemb, and Robert Boydell,* 1652. 4°. LT, O, C, P, EN; CH, CLC, MU, WF, Y.

2742 [–] Prognosticon posthumum. 1643/4. Printed, 1643[4]. 4°.* LT, O, LN, LIU; CH.

2743 —The sphere of gentry. By William Leybourn, for the author, 1661. fol. L, O, C, MR, EN; CH, CN, LC, MH, NCD, Y.

2744 **Morgan, T.** The Welchmens ivbilee. For I. Harrison, [1642]. 4°.* LT, O, OW, AN; INU.

2744A **Morgan, Sir Thomas.** By the commander in chief of His Majesties forces in Scotland. Whereas I have received . . . [16 July 1660. Order to arrest Lord Warriston]. Edinburgh, by C. Higgins, 1660. brs. EN.

2745 —Hereford taken. For Jane Coe, 1645. 4°.* DT; Y.

2746 —Collonel Morgans letter concerning his taking . . . Kildrummie. By F. Neile, 1654. 4°.* LT, O.

2747 —Col: Morgan Governor of Glocester's letter to . . . Lenthal. For Edw. Husband, March 24, 1645[6]. 4°.* LT, O, DT; CH, NU, WF, Y.

2748 —A letter to the Honorable William Lenthal. [London], for E. Husband, [1646]. 4°.* LT, AN, DU, DT; IU, MH.

2749 —Severall letters from. Imprinted at London, for John Wright, 24. Decemb. 1645. 4°.* LT, O, AN, YM, DT; MH, MM, Y.

2749A —A true and just relation of Major General Sir Morgan's progress in France. For J. Nutt, 1699. 4°. L; CLC.

2750 —A trve relation by Colonell Morgan. For Matthew Walbanck, March 24, 1645[6]. 4°.* LT, SP; IU.

2751 —Two letters from . . . to severall members. For T. Bates, 1645. 4°.* LT, O; Y.

2752 — —[Anr. ed.] For Thomas Bates, 1645. 4°.* L, O, AN, DT.

2753 —Two letters sent to the Honorable W. Lenthall. For Edw. Husband, December 22, 1645. 4°.* LT, O; CN.

2754 [**Morgan, Thomas**], of Oxford. Allegations in behalf of the high and mighty Princess the Lady Mary, now Queen of Scots. By J. D., 1690. fol.* L, E, DT; LC, MH, WCL, Y.

      Morgan, William. The Kings coronation. 1685. See Ogilby, John.

2755 —Proposals by . . . for vending Mr. Ogilby's works in a standing lottery. [London, 1676/7.] brs. O; MH.

2756 —Proposals for a general sale of maps . . . May 17. [London, 1687.] brs. LG (lost).

2757 — —[Same title, November 8.] [London, 1687.] brs. LG (lost).

2757A —Proposals for publishing the actual survey of London. [London? 1680.] brs. LG.

2758 —Religio militis: or, a soldier's religion. For Daniel Dring, and sold by John VVhitlock, 1695. 4°.* T.C.II 555. C, OC, EN; MIU.

2758A —A second proposal by . . . for a general sale of Mr. Ogilby's books. [London, 1677.] brs. MH.

2759 —The Welchmans inventory. For Thomas Lambert, 1641. brs. LS.

2760 Entry cancelled.
      Morbus epidemicus. Oxford, 1643. See Greaves, Sir Edward.

2761 **M[orice], Sir W[illiam].** Animadversions upon Generall Monck's letter. [London], printed, 1659[60]. 4°.* LT, O, MR; CH, MH, MM, NN, Y.

2762 —Coena quasi Κοινη: the new-inclosvres broken down. By W. Godbid, for Richard Thrale, 1657. 4°. LT, O, C, ENC, DT; CH, IU, MH, NU.

2763 — —Second edition. By R. Norton for Richard Royston, 1660. fol. L, O, C, LL, LW, DU, CD; MH, NRU, NU, Y.

2763A — —"Second" edition. For R. Roiston, 1660. fol.* OC.

      [–] Letter to General Monck. 1659. See Morris, Richard.

2764 **Morin, Jean Baptiste.** Antiquitates ecclesiae Orientalis. Prostant apud Geo. Wells, 1682. 8°. L, O, CS, ENC, DT; BN, CH, CLC, NCD, PL, WF, Y.

2765 —Factum du. [London, 1685.] 4°. L.

2766 **Morin, Lucas.** Dilucidatio articulorum. Excudebat T. C. pro H. Robinson, [1658]. 12°. LT, O, CT; WF.

2767 **Morin, Thomas.** A proposal for the incouragement of seamen. [London, 1697.] cap., 4°.* L, EN; MBP, MH, Y.

2768 **Morison, James.** Disputatio juridica inauguralis de pactis. Edinburgh, Watson, 1697. 4°. ALDIS 3679. EN.

2769 —The everlasting Gospel. [Edinburgh], 1668. 8°. ALDIS 1847.3. L.

2770 **Morison, Robert.** Hortus regius. Typis Tho. Roycroft, impensis Jacobi Allestree, 1669. 8°. T.C.I 10. L, O, C, EN, AU, DT; BN, CLC, MH, WDA, WF.

2771 —Plantarum historiae . . . pars secunda. Oxonii, e theatro Sheldoniano, 1680. fol. T.C.I 445; MADAN 3271. L, O, C, EN, AM, DT; BN, CLC, IU, MH, WDA, WSC, HC.

2772 — — . . . pars tertia. Oxonii, e theatro Sheldoniano, 1699. fol. L, O, C, EN, AM, DT; BN, CLC, CSU, MH, PL, WDA.

2773 —Plantarum umbelliferarum. Oxonii, e theatro Sheldoniano, 1672. fol. MADAN 2917. L, O, C, EN, DT; BN, CSU, IU, MH, MHO, PL, WDA, WF.

2774 [**Morisot, Claude Barthelemy.**] Carolvs I. Britanniarvm Rex. A secvri et calamo Miltonii vindicatvs. Dublini, apud libervm correctorem, 1652. 8°. DIX 90. L, C, DT; CH, PH, Y.

2775 **Morland, Israel.** A short description of Sion's inhabitants. For the author, 1690. 4°. L, LCL; CLC, LC, Y.

2776 **Morland, Sir Samuel.** Sir Samuel Morland's answer to several papers. [London, 1677?] brs. L, LPR.

2777 —The description and use of two arithmetick instruments. Printed, and are to be sold by Moses Pitt, 1673. 8°. T.C.I 135. L, O, C, LIU, DT; CH, CU, MH, MU, WF.

2778 —The doctrine of interest. Printed at London, by A. Godbid and J. Playford, and are sold by Robert Boulter, 1679. 8°. T.C.I 350. L, O, C, E, GU; CLC, RBU, WF.

2779 —The history of the evangelical churches of . . . Piemont. By Henry Hills, for Adoniram Byfield, 1658. fol. L, O, C, E, DT; BN, CH, LC, MH, MU, NU, WCL, Y.

2780 —Hydrostaticks. For John Lawrence, 1697. 12°. T.C.III 39. L, DCH; FRANKLIN INST., MU, WF.

2781 —A new, and most useful instrument for addition. [London], made publick 1672. 8°. CM, DT; WU.

2781A —A new method of cryptography. [London, 1666.] cap., fol.* WF, YBA.

2781B —The poor man's dyal. 1689. 4°.* LLP.

2782 —Sir Samuel Morland having made a final agreement. [London, 1670?] brs. L, LPR.

2783 —Tuba stentoro-phonica. *By W. Godbid, to be sold by M. Pitt*, 1671. fol.* L, DCH; BN, CH, CLC, INU, LC.

2784 — —[Anr. ed.] —, 1672. fol.* T.C.I 97. L, C, OC, LNC, P; CH, LC, MH, WF, YBA.

2785 —The urim of conscience. *By J. M. and B. B. for A. Roper, E. Wilkinson and R. Clavel*, 1695. 8°. L, O, LW, CE, ENC; CLC, IU, MH, NCD, NU, WF, Y.

2785A **Morley, Benjamin.** A vindication of . . . the laying on of hands. *By Henry Mills and disposed of by Francis Smith*, 1653. 8°. OC.

2786 **Morley, Charles.** Scorbutus. [n.p.], 1698. brs. O.

2787 **Morley, Christopher Love.** De morbo epidemico. [*London*, 1679.] 8°. L.

2788 — —[Anr. ed.] *Impensis Johannis Gay*, 1680. 8°. C, LCP, LWL, OC, OR, GH; BN, CLC, TO, WF, WSG.

      Morley, George. Ad cl. virium janum ultium epistolae duae. 1683. *See* —Several treatises.

      [–] Character of Charles the Second, written. 1660. *See* Tuke, *Sir* Samuel.

      —Epistola ad virum clarissimum. 1683. *See* —Several treatises.

2789 —Epistola apologetica. *Apud Timotheum Garthwait*, 1663. 4°.* O, C, MR, P, SP.

      —Letter from Father Cressey. 1683. *See* —Several treatises.

2790 —The Bishop of VVorcester's letter to a friend. *By R. Norton for Timothy Garthwait*, 1662. 4°. L, O, C, AN, EN, DT; CH, IU, MH, NU, TU, WF, Y. (var.)

2791 Entry cancelled. Ghost.

2792 Entry cancelled.

      —Letter written . . . to her Highness the Dutchess of York. 1683. *See* —Several treatises.

2793 [–] A modest advertisement concerning the present controversie. *For Robert Bostock*, 1641. 4°.* LT, O, C, EN, DT; CH, CN, MH, NCD, NU, WF, Y, AVP.

2794 —A sermon preached . . . the 23d of April, . . . 1661. *By R. Norton for T. Garthwait*, 1661. 4°. LT, O, C, LL, EN, DT; CH, IU, MH, NU, TU, WF, Y. (var.)

2795 Entry cancelled.

      —Sermon preached . . . November 5. 1667. 1683. *See* —Several treatises.

2796 —Several treatises. *For Joanna Brome*, 1683. 4°. T.C.I 505. L, O, C, EN, DT; CH, CN, NU, TU, WF, Y.

      —Three letters. 1682. *See* —Several treatises.

2797 [–] The Bishop of Winchester's vindication of himself. *By M. Flesher for Joanna Brome*, 1683. 4°. T.C.II 24. L, O, C, YM, DT; CH, CN, NCD, NU, WF, Y.

2797A [**Morley, Henry.**] A letter from an anti-phanatique. *Printed*, 1660. 4°.* CH, PL.

2798 **Morley, Thomas.** A congratulatory poem. *By W. Downing*, [1688/9]. brs. C, HH.

2799 Entry cancelled.

      —Psalms with singing tunes. 1688. *See* Bible. English. Psalms. Whole book of psalms [B2565A].

2800 **Morley, Thomas, of Coughes.** A remonstrance of the barbarous cruelties. *By E. G.*, 12 June 1644. 4°.* LT, O, C, LVF, LW, DU, SP, DT; CH, MH, WF, WU, Y.

Mormonostolismos, sive. [n.p.], 1691. *See* Steward, *Sir* Simeon.

2800A **Mornay, Philippe de.** Contemplations upon life and death. *For G. Larkin*, 1697. 4°.* L, MR.

2801 —A pious and Christian consideration of life. *By J. L. for Luke Meredith*, 1699. 8°. T.C.III 117. L, LSC; CLC, Y.

2802 —The soules own evidence. *By M. S. for Henry Overton*, 1646. 4°. LT, LSC, DT; CU, MH, MWA, NU.

Morning alarum. 1651. *See* R., D.

2803 Morning and evening prayers. *Edinburgh, by His Majestie's printers*, 1674. 8°.* ALDIS 2023.7. EN.

2803A —as they are used in the New-Colledge of Cobham. [*London*], *printed*, 1687. 4°.* L; Y.

Morning-exercise against popery. 1675. *See* Vincent, Nathaniel.

Morning exercise at Cripplegate. 1661. *See* Annesley, Samuel.

Morning exercise methodized. 1660. *See* Case, Thomas.

2804 Entry cancelled. Ghost.

Morning ramble. 1673. *See* Payne, Henry Neville.

2805 The morning-star out of the north. *For B. H.*, 1680. 4°.* LSC, LSD, EN; CLC, WF.

2806 A mornings ramble. *By George Croom, for the author.* 1684. brs. O, LG, HH; CLC, MH, Y.

2807 Moro-mastix: Mr Iohn Goodwin whipt. *For Tho. Underhill*, 1647. 4°.* LT, O, LIU, LLU, DT; CH, MH, NU, TU, Y.

2807A [**Morrell, William.**] Diego redivivus, or the last will. *For Abel Roper*, 1692. 4°.* L, EN; CH, CLC, WF.

2808 **Morris, Anthony.** A general testimony from the . . . Quakers. [*Philadelphia?* 1691.] brs. PHS.

2809 **M[orris], R[ichard].** A letter to General Monck, in answer. *For R. Lowndes*, 1659[60]. 4°.* LT, O, CT, BC, MR, CD; CH, MH, MU, WF, Y.

2810 **Morris, Samuel.** A looking-glasse for the Quakers. *For Edward Thomas*, 1655. 4°.* LT, LF.

2811 **Morris, Thomas, *Baptist.*** A messenger sent. *For R. E. to be sold by Richard Moon*, 1655. 4°.* LT.

2812 **Morris, Thomas.** A sermon preached . . . 18th [October] . . . 1679. *By J. M. for John Wickins*, 1681. 4°.* L; CH, WF.

2813 **Morris, William.** To the supream authoritie (under God) of the Common-wealth . . . the true and faithfull testimony. *For Thomas Simmons*, 1659. 4°.* L, LF; CH, NP, PH, PL, Y.

2813A —Tithes no gospel-ordinance. [*London*], 1680. 4°.* LF; PH.

Mors, Roderick, *pseud.* *See* Brinkelow, Henry.

2814 Entry cancelled. Ghost.

2815 **Morse, Robert.** The clergyman's office. *London: for Tho. Bennet, and Henry Clements, in Oxford*, 1699. 4°.* T.C.III 134. L, OM, CS; NU, Y.

Mort du juste. 1693. *See* Abbadie, Jacques d'.

2816 Entry cancelled. *See* M2826A.

2817 **Morton, Anne Douglas, *countess of.*** The Countess of Morton's daily exercise. *For R. Royston*, 1666. 12°. L.

2817A — —Ninth edition. —, 1679. 12°. L (impf.).

2818 — —Fourteenth edition. *For Luke Meredith*, 1689. 12°. T.C.II 325. L; NGT.

2818A — —Fifteenth edition. —, 1692. 24°. T.C.II 433. CLC.

2819 — —Seventeenth edition. *By J. H. for Luke Meredith*, 1696. 12°. T. C.II 605. L, C; WF.

2820 **Morton, Arthur.** The touch-stone of conversion. *By Fr: Neile for Tho: Underhill*, 1647. 12°. LT, O, EN, DT; WF.

2821 [**Morton, Charles.**] Debts discharge. *For Tho. Cockerill*, 1684. 8°. LCL; MB, MWA.

2822 [–] A discourse concerning a lumber-office. *By Sam. Darker, for J. Lawrence*, 1696. 4°.* L.

2823 [–] The gaming-humour considered. *For Tho. Cockerill*, 1684. 8°. L, LCL; IU, MB, MWA, NP, Y.

2824 [–] Little peace-maker. *For Tho. Parkhurst*, 1674. 8°. T.C.I 185. L, LCL, SP; CLC, INU, MB, MWA, V.

2824A [–] Some meditations on . . . Exodus. [*London*, 168–?] 8°.* MH, MWA.

2825 —The spirit of man. *Boston; by B. Harris, for Duncan Campbell*, 1693. EVANS 661. L, O, LCL; CH, CN, MB, MH, RPJ, V.

2826 [–] The way of good men. *For Benjamin Alsop*, 1681. 8°. T.C.I 465. L, LCL; CLC, MB, MWA, V.

2826A **Morton, David.** Sacris ordinibus non rite initiate. [*Cambridge*], 1633 [1663]. brs. L.

2826B [**Morton, John.**] A brief rule of life. *By J. C. for Hen. Brome*, 1662. 8°.* Y.

2826C [–] —[Anr. ed.] *For H. Brome*, 1669. 12°. L (impf.).

2826D [–] —[Anr. ed.] —, 1672. 24°. WU.

2826E [–] —[Ninth edition.] *For Charles Brome*, 1684. 24°. CT.

2827 **Morton, Nathaniel.** New-Englands memoriall. *Cambridge* [*Mass.*]*: by S. G. and M. J. for John Vsher of Boston*, 1669. 4°. EVANS 144; T.C.I 38. L, O, LW, CU; CH, CN, LC, MH, MWA, NN, Y.

2828–9 Entries cancelled.

Morton, Richard. De febribus inflammatoris. 1694. *See —Πυρετολογια pars altera*.

—De morbis acutis. 1692. *See —Πυρετολογια*.

2830 —Phthisiologia: or, a treatise of consumptions. *For Sam. Smith and Benj. Walford*, 1694. 8°. T.C.II 501. L, O, C, LCP, CT; CLC, MBM, NP, PL, WF, HC.

2831 —Phthisiologia seu exercitationes. *Impensis Samuelis Smith*, 1689. 8°. T.C.II 288. L, O, C, AM, DT; CLM, NAM, PL, WF, HC.

2832 —Πυρετολογια. *Impensis Samuelis Smith*, 1692. 8°. L, O, C, LCP, MAU, GH; BN, CLM, MB, NAM, WF, HC.

2833 — —pars altera. *Impensis Sam. Smith & Benj. Walford*, 1694. 8°. L, C, OME, GH, DT; BN, CH, CLM, NP, PL, WF, WSG.

Morton, Robert. Ephemeris. 1662. *See* Almanacs.

2834 —The nature, quality . . . of coffee. [*London*, 1670?] brs. L; CLC.

[**Morton, Thomas**], **bp.** Christvs Dei, the Lords annoynted. 1643. *See* Jones, John, *bp.*

2835 [–] Confessions and proofes of Protestant divines. *Oxford, by Henry Hall*, 1644. 4°. MADAN 1657. LT, O, CT, EN, DT; CH, IU, MH, NU, WF, Y.

2836 [–] —[Anr. ed.] [*London*], *printed*, 1662. L, DU, MR, EN; NU, TU.

2837 —Englands warning-piece. *By T. Favvcet, Aug. 5.* 1642. 4°.* LT.

2838 —Επισκοπος αποστολικος, or the Episcopacy. *For J. Collins*, 1670. 8°. T.C.I 25. L, O, CE, DU, WCA; CH, NSU, NU, WF, Y.

2839 [–] An exact account of Romish doctrine. *For John Starkey*, 1679. 4°.* L, O, C, NPL, DT; CH, CN, MH, WF, Y.

2840 [–] Ezekiel's vvheels. *By J. G. for Richard Royston*, 1653. 8°. LT, O, C, DU, SC; CH, MH, NU, WF, Y.

2840A —The Lord's Supper; or, a vindication. Second edition. *For R. M., part of the impression to be vended for Edward Minshaw*, 1652. fol. LSC, CCO.

2840B — —"Second" edition. —, 1656. fol. O.

2841 [–] Medicæ dissertationes tres. 1680. brs. O.

2842 [–] The necessity of Christian subjection. *Oxford, printed*, [1642/3.] 4°.* MADAN 1258. L, O, LW, CT; CH, MM, NU, WF, Y.

2843 [–] —[Anr. ed.] —, 1643. 4°.* MADAN 1258*. LT, O, C, DU, DT; CH, MIU, NN, WF.

2844 [–] —[Anr. ed.] —, 1643. 4°.* MADAN 1421. LT, O, C, CT, WCA; CH, MIU, NU, WF.

2845 —The presentment of a schismaticke. *By I. Okes, for R. Whitaker, and S. Broun*, 1642. 4°.* L, O, C, LSD, CD; CH, MBZ, NR, NU, WF.

2846 — —[Anr. ed.] *By T. Badger, for R. Whitaker, and S. Broun*, 1642. 4°.* LT, O, C, BR, DU; CH, MIU, MM, OSU, Y.

2847 [–] Tractatus de febribus intermittentibus. 1680. brs. O.

2848 [–] A vindication of the Bishop of Dvrham. *By Richard Cotes, for Robert Milborne*, 1641. 4°.* LT, ORP, MR, YM, DT; CH, MIU, NU, WF.

2849 [**Moryson, Francis.**] The lawes of Virginia now in force. *By E. Cotes, for A. Seile*, 1662. fol. L, O; CH, LC, RPJ.

2850 [–] —[Anr. ed.] *Printed*, 1662. fol. NN, PHS.

2850A **Mosan, Jacob.** The general practice of physick. Fourth edition. *For F. L. Henry Hood, Abel Roper, and Richard Tomlins*, 1654. MWA.

2851 **Moscheni, Carlo.** Brutes turn'd criticks. *For Daniel Dring*, 1695. 12°. L, O, C; CLC, CU, MH, WF, Y.

2852 **Moseley, Humphrey.** Φυλλον θεραπευτικον: an healing leaf. *By D. Maxwell for Sa. Gellibrand*, 1658. 4°.* L, O, C, BC, BP, LLU, DT; NU.

2853 **Moses ben Maimon.** R. Moses Maimonides de jure pauperis. *Oxonii, e Theatro Sheldoniano apud Mosem Pit*, [*London*], 1679. 4°. T.C.I 371; MADAN 3215. L, O, CT, E, DT; CU, IU, MH, NU, Y.

2854 — . . . De sacrificiis liber. *Typis Milonis Flesher, sumptibus auctoris: prostat apud Mosem Pitt, & apud Brabazonum Aylmer*, 1683. 4°. L, O, CT, EN, DT; CLC, CU, MH, NU, WF, Y.

2855 —[Hebrew] Porta Mosis sive dissertationes. *Oxoniæ, excudebat H. Hall, impensis R. Davis*, 1655. 4°. MADAN 2277. L, O, C, E, DT; CH, CU, MH, NU, WF, Y.

2856 —Specimen libri more norochim. [*Oxford*, 1690.] 4°.* O.

Moses and Aaron. 1675. *See* Womock, Laurence, *bp.*

Moses message to Pharaoh. [n.p., 1653.] *See* Farnworth, Richard.

Moses returned. Edinburgh. 1660. *See* Ramsay, James.

2857 **Mosley, Nicholas.** Ψυχοσοφια: or, natural & divine contemplations. *For Humphrey Mosley,* 1653. 8°. LT, O, OC, BR, DC, BLH; CH, CLC, IU, NN, WF, Y.

2857AA **Mosman, John.** The Christian's companion under soul-exercise. [*Edinburgh?* 1678.] 4°. ALDIS 2133.25. D, EN.

2857BA **Moss, John.** The thorough-base to the lessons on the basse-viol. *By W. Godbid for the author, to be sold by John Playford,* 1671. obl. 4°. T.C.I 66. CK.

2857CA **Moss, Rob.** Transubstantio non est æque credibilis . . . Jul. 7. 1696. [*Cambridge,* 1696.] brs. C.

2857A **Mosse, John.** Religious meditations on Ecclesiastes. *Printed,* 1699. 8°. LF.

2858 **Mossom, Charles.** An account of the disposal of the money. [*London,* 1687/8.] cap., fol.* C; Y.

2859 Entry cancelled.
   M[ossom], R[obert], bp. Anti-Parœus. York, 1642. *See* Owen, David.

2860 —An apology in the behalf of the seqvestred clergy. *For William Grantham,* 1660. 4°.* LT, O, C, E, DT; CH, CN, MH, WF, Y.

2861 —Englands' gratulation. *By Tho: Newcomb, for William Grantham,* 1660. 4°.* LT, O, C, AN, YM; CH, CN, MH, MIU, NU, Y. (var.)

2862 [–] The King on his throne. *Printed at York, by Stephen Bulkley,* 1642. 4°.* L, O, LCL, YM, BQ; Y.

2862A [–] —[Anr. ed.] —, 1643. 4°.* L; CH.

2863 [–] —[Anr. ed.] *Printed at York,* 1643. 4°.* LT, O, CT, LLU, YM, DT; CLC, CU, MBZ, NU, WF.

2864 —A narrative panegyrical. *By Tho. Newcomb, to be sold by Timothy Garthwait,* 1665/6. 4°.* L, O, LW, EN, DN; Y.

2865 [–] A plant of paradise. *By R. N.,* 1660. 4°.* LT, O, LW; CN, IU, MH, WF, Y.

2866 —The preacher's tripartite. *By Thomas Newcomb,* 1657. fol. L, O, CP, CT, LSD, YM; CH, IEG, NPT, NU, WF, Y.

2866A — —Second edition. *For L. Meredith,* 1685. fol. T.C.II 120. YM.

2867 [–] Sion's prospect. *By Thomas Newcomb,* 1651. 4°. L, O, YM; CH, CU, IU, MH, Y.

2868 [–] —[Anr. ed.] *By T: N: for Humphrey Moseley,* 1653. 4°. LT, O, LW, CP, BLH; CLC, NU, WF.

2868A The most acceptable and faithful account of the capitulation . . . of Charlemont. *For L. C.,* 1690. brs. DN; CH, MH.

2868B A most barbarous murther being a true relation. *For E. Horton,* 1672. 4°.* L, DT.

2869 The most blessed and truest newes from Ireland. *For T. W. and G. H.,* 1642, 4°.* LT, C, MR, YM, DN.

Most blessed and truest newes, that. 1642. *See* Barry, John.

Most certain and true relation. 1642. *See* Hiobey, William.

2870 A most certain, strange, and true discovery of a vvitch. [*London*], *by John Hammond,* 1643. 4°.* LT, O, GU; MH.

Most choice historical compendium. 1692. *See* M., A.

2870A The most Christian Turk. *For Henry Rhodes,* 1690. 12°. T.C.II 300. L, O; CN.

2870B A most cruel and terrible engagement. 1691. 4°.* CH.

Most curious Mercurius Britannicus. [n.p., 164–?] *See* Taylor, John.

2871 Entry cancelled. *See following entry.*

2872 Most damnable and hellish plot. *Dublin, by William Bladen, now reprinted at London by Thomas Bates,* 1642. 4°.* DIX 76. LT, O, C, OQ, MR; Y.

Most dear soveraign, I cannot. [n.p., 1689.] *See* James, Elinor.

Most delectable history of Reynard. 1650. *See* Shirley, John.

Most delightful and pleasant history. 1661. *See* Sorel, Charles.

Most delightful history of . . . Jack of Newbery. 1684. *See* Deloney, Thomas.

Most delightful history of . . . Reynard. 1681. *See* Shirley, John.

2872A The most deplorable case of the . . . distressed planters. [*London,* 1690?] brs. L, INDIA OFFICE.

2873 The most deplorable case of the orphans. [*London,* 1692?] brs. LL.

2873A A most devout prayer unto . . . Virgin Mary. [*London*], *printed,* 1686. 12°.* L; Y.

Most easy and exact manner. 1650. *See* Urquhart, Sir Thomas.

Most easie method. 1687. *See* Worlidge, John.

Most easie way. 1641. *See* W., N.

2874 The most equal and easie method of raising a sufficient fund. *For Randal Taylor,* 1691. 4°.* O, C; CH, NC, PU, WF.

Most exact and accurate map. 1676. *See* Lupton, Donald.

2875 A most exact and true relation extracted out of the registers. *By J. C. for John Crooke,* 1659. 4°. LT, O, OC, CT; WF.

2876 A most exact and true relation of the proceedings of His Maiesties armie at Shelborne [*sic*]. *For R. M. and G. B.,* 1642. 4°.* LT, LSD, MR; MH.

Most exact letter. [n.p., 1653.] *See* Violet, Thomas.

2876A A most exact list of the names of the Knights . . . of the Cinque-Ports. *For Tho. Walkley,* 1661. 4°. O.

2876B —[Anr. ed.] *For Tho. Walkeley,* 1663. 4°. CS.

Most exact relation. 1642. *See* Whetcombe, Tristram.

Most excellent and approved medicines. 1652. *See* Read, Alexander.

2876C Most excellent and delightful history of Fortunatus. *By A. M. for J. Conyers & J. Blare,* [1690]. 12°. *CM.

2877 The most excellent and famous history of . . . Amadis of Greece. *For J. Deacon and J. Blare,* 1693. 4°. T.C.II 477. PL, WF, ZAP.

2877A —Second edition. —, 1694. 4°. L, O, DC; CH, CN, MBA, MU, Y.

2878 A most excellent and rare discourse. *Thom. Roycroft,* 1656. 4°. L; CN.

Most excellent and rare drink. [n.p., 1650.] *See* H., J.

2878A A most excellent ballad of an old man and his wife. *For F. Coles, T. Vere, and W. Gilbertson*, [1658–64]. brs. EUING 221. GU.

2878B —[Anr. ed.] *For F. Coles, J. Wright, and J. Clarke*, [1675?]. brs. O.

2879 —[Anr. ed.] [*London*], *for F. Coles, T. Vere, I. Wright, J. Clarke, W. Thackeray, and T. Passenger*, [1678–80]. brs. L, O.

2880 A most excellent ballad of Ioseph the Carpenter. [*London*], *for F. Coles, T. Vere and J. Wright*, [1663–74]. brs. L, O, CM.

2880A A most excellent ballad of S. George for England. [*London*], *for F. Coles, T. Vere, and W. Gilbertson*, [1658–64]. brs. EUING 92. O, GU.

2880B —[Anr. ed.] [*London*], *for F. Coles, T. Vere, and J. Wright*, [1670]. brs. EUING 222. O, GU.

2881 —[Anr. ed.] [*London*], *for J. C. W. T. and T. Passenger*, [1684–86]. brs. O.

Most excellent eloquent speech. [n.p.], 1683. *See* Severus, Alexander.

2882 The most excellent history of Antonius and Aurelia. *By T. Haley, and are to be sold by J. Wright, J. Clarke, W. Thackeray, and T. Passenger*, 1682. 4°. O, CM.

Most excellent history of Argalus. 1672. *See* Quarles, Francis.

Most excellent, profitable, and pleasant book. 1649. *See* Roussat, Richard.

2882A A most excellent song of the love of young Palmus. [*London*], *for I. W.*, [1655?]. brs. L.

2882B —[Anr. ed.] *For F. Coles, T. Vere, and J. Wright*, [1663–74]. brs. EUING 219. GU.

2883 —[Anr. ed.] [*London*], *for F. Coles, T. Vere, I. Wright, and I. Clark*, [1675?]. brs. L, O.

2884 —[Anr. ed.] [*London*], *for W. Thackerey, J. M. and A. M.*, [1689–92]. brs. L, CM, HH.

2884A —[Anr. ed.] [*London*]. *By and for Alex Milbourn*, [1690?]. brs. L.

2884B The most excellent spirit of ground-ivey. [*London*, 1680?] brs. L.

2884C The most excellent universal pill. [*London*, 1670?] brs. L.

Most excellent way of learning masse. 1683. *See* Lassels, Richard.

2885 A most execrable and barbarovs mvrder done by an East-Indian devil. *For T. Banks, July the 18.* 1642. 4°.* LT.

2885A The most famous and experienced operator, D. Jarco, lately here arrived. [*London*, 1690?] brs. L.

2886 A most faithfull relation of two vvonderful passages. *By James Cottrel*, 1650. 4°.* LT; MH.

Most famous, delectable, and pleasant history. 1649. *See* Forde, Emanuel.

2887 The most famous history of the learned Fryer Bacon. *For Tho. Norris*, [c. 1700]. 4°. C, LN; CN, CRN, Y.

Most famous history of the seven champions. 1680. *See* Johnson, Richard.

2888 A most famous victory obtained by that vallant [*sic*] religious gentleman, Collonell Venne. *For J. Rich, Nov.* 10. 1642. 4°.* LT, O, EC; NU.

2889 Most fearefull and strange newes. *For Iohn Thomas*, 1641. 4°.* LT, O, EC; WF.

2890 A most glorious representation of the incomparable free grace of Christ. *By M: Symmons*, 1650. 4°. LT, ORP, DT.

2891 A most godly and comfortable ballad of the glorious resurrection. *For F. Coles, T. Vere, and W. Gilbertson*, [1658–64]. brs. EUING 224. L, GU.

2892 —[Anr. ed.] [*London*], *for W. Thackeray*, [1688–89]. brs. L, CM, HH.

2892A —[Anr. ed.] [*London*], *by and for A. M. and sold by the booksellers*, [1693?]. brs. L.

Most gracious message. 1648. *See* R., E.

2893 A most grave and modest confutation. *For Edward Brewster and George Badger*, 1644. 4°. O, C; CN.

2894 The most hearty and unspeakable rejoycings. *By George Croom*, 1688. brs. O.

2895 A most horrid and bloody murther committed at Islington. colop: *By E. Mallet*, 1683. fol.* L, LG; MH.

2896 A most horrid but true copy of a publick confession of faith, . . . Hungaria. *For R. G.*, 1679. 4°.* CH, IU, LC, NR.

2897 The most humble, and joyfull congratulatory address. *For Henry Seile*, 1660. brs. L.

Most humble remonstrance. [n.p., 1696.] *See* Chabbert, John.

Most humble representation. [n.p., 1698.] *See* Beverley, Thomas.

Most illustrious history of the seven champions. 1661. *See* Johnson, Richard.

2897A A most impartial account sent in a letter. colop: *By D. Edwards*, 1699. brs. L.

2898 The most indigent poor prisoners letter to a worthy member. [*London?* 1697.] brs. L, LG, LUG.

2899 —[Anr. ed.] colop: *By Fr. Wilkins*, 1700. fol. L; PU, WF.

2900 Most joyfull newes by sea and land. *For John Hunt, Novemb.* 3. 1642. 4°.* MADAN 1052. LT, YM.

2901 The most lamentable and deplorable accident which on Friday last June 22. befell Laurence Cawthorn. *For W. Gilbertson*, 1661. 8°.* L.

2901A The most lamentable and deplorable history of the two children in the wood. *By and for W. O.*, [1700?]. 4°.* L, O.

2902 A most lamentable information of part of the grievances of Mugleswick. [*London*, 1642.] brs. LT, O, EC, YM.

2903 A most learned & eloquent speech . . . 23th [*sic*] June 1647. [*London*, 1647?] cap., 4°.* LT, O, CJ, MR, DT; CH, LC, MH, MU, TU, WF, Y.

2903A —[Anr. ed.] [*London*, 1680.] fol.* O; MH.

2904 —[Anr. ed.] colop: *For A. Banks*, 1681. fol.* O, MR; CH, NP, WF.

2905–7 Entries cancelled.

Most learned, conscientious and devout exercise. 1649. *See* Cromwell, Oliver.

2908 A most miraculous and happy victory obtained by James Chudlegh. [*London*], *printed this 29. Aprill, for R. D.* 1643. 4°.* LT, O, DT; CU, MH.

2909   A most miraculous and unheard of relation. *For Charles Tyus*, 1660. 4°.* MR.

Most natural and easie way. 1698. *See* Ainsworth, Robert.

2909A   A most notaple [*sic*] example of an ungracious son. *For F. Coles, T. Vere and W. Gilbertson*, [1658–64]. brs. EUING 227. GU.

2909B   —[Anr. ed., "notable."] *For F. Coles, T. Vere, and I. Wright*, [1663–74]. brs. EUING 225. GU

2909C   —[Anr. ed.] *For F. Coles, T. Vere, J. Wright, and J. Clarke*, [1674–79]. brs. EUING 226. GU.

2910   —[Anr. ed.] [*London*], *for Alex. Milbourn*, [1693?]. brs. L, CM, HH.

2911   —[Anr. ed.] [*London*], *by and for A. M.*, [1693?]. brs. HH.

Most pithy exhortation. [n.p.], 1649. *See* Nedham, Marchamont.

2911A   The most pleasant and delightful art of palmistry. *By A. M. for J. Deacon and C. Dennison*, [c. 1680]. 8°.* CM.

2911B   The most pleasant and delightful history of Argalus. *By J. M. for Eben. Tracy, sold by J. Blare*, 1691. 4°. L.

2912   The most pleasant and delightful history of Reynard the Fox. The second part. *By A. M. and R. R. for Edward Brewster*, 1681. 4°. L, O, CK, CT; CLC, CN, IAU, WF, Y.

2913   A most pleasant but true description . . . old and new Jacobites. *Printed*, 1691. 4°.* T.C.II 384. L, O; PU, Y.

Most pleasant comedy of Mucedorus. [1656.] *See* Greene, Robert.

2914   The most pleasant history of Bovinian. *For J. Stafford*, 1656. 4°. L.

Most pleasant history of Ornatus. 1683. *See* Forde, Emanuel.

2914A   The most pleasant history of Reynard the Fox. [*London*], *for J. Conyers, and are to be sold by J. Blare*, [1700?]. 8°.* O.

Most pleasant history of Tom a Lincoln. 1655. *See* Johnson, Richard.

2914B   The most pleasing and delightful history of Reynard the fox. *By W. Onley, sold by H. Nelme*, 1697. 8°. WCL.

Most rare and excellent history. [n.p., 1685.] *See* Deloney, Thomas.

2915   The most remarkable passages from most parts of Christendome. *Nath. Butter*, 1642. 4°. L, MR, GH.

2916   Entry cancelled.

Most remarkable passages of. 1675. *See* Grueber, Johann. China and France. 1676.

2917   The most remarkable trials of Nathaniel Thompson. colop: *For L. Curtiss*, [1682]. brs. O, C, DU, HH; CH, MH, MIU, WF.

Most renowned and pleasant history. 1677. *See* Forde, Emanuel.

Most sacred and divine science. 1680. *See* Butler, J. Ἁγιαστρολογια.

2918   The most sad and lamentable narration of the death of Michael Berkley. *For Tho. Vere, and Wil. Gilbert*, 1658. 8°.* O.

2919   A most sad and serious lamentation. *For G. Thompson*, 1642. 4°.* LT, MR; CH, MH, MIU, Y.

Most safe and effectual cure for the rickets. [1676?] *See* Care, Henry.

2919A   A most serious expostulation. [*London*, 1680?] fol.* L, O, LL, CS, MR, EN; CH, CN, MH, TU, WF, Y.

2920   A most strange and dreadful apparition of several spirits. *For J. Clarke*, 1680. 4°.* L, O; MH.

2921   The most strange and wovnderfvll apperation. [*sic*] of blood in a poole at Garraton. *Printed at London by I. H.*, [1645]. 4°.* LT, LWL; CH.

2921AA   Most strange and wonderful news from . . . Leister. *For T. M.*, [1694]. brs. L; CN.

2921A   Most strange and wonderful nfws [*sic*] from North-Wales. colop: [*London*], *for B. Lyford*, 1694. brs. L; MH.

2922   The most strange and wonderful predictions of Cleombrotus an heathen Jew. *For Langley Curtis*, 1679. 4°.* O, CT, MR; MBA, MH, NU, TU, WF.

Most strange and wonderful, tho' true. 1693. *See* D., M.

2923   A most strange letter: which was found in the Old-Change. *For I. R.*, 1642. 4°.* LT, O; CH.

2923A   —[Anr. ed.] *For Iohn Greensmith*, 1642. 4°.* CT; MH, MIU, WF, Y.

2923B   The most strange, wonderful and surprizing apparition. [*London*? 1680.] brs. CH.

Most sweet, and pleasant pastorall. 1657. *See* Longus. Daphnis and Chloe.

2923C   A most sweet song of an English merchant. [*London*], *for F. Coles, T. Vere, and W. Gilbertson*, [1658–64]. brs. EUING 232. O, GU.

2923D   —[Anr. ed.] *For F. Coles, T. Vere, and J. Wright*, [1663–1674]. brs. EUING 230. GU.

2923E   —[Anr. ed.] [*London*], *by J. Clarke, W. Thackeray, and T. Passinger*, [1684–86]. brs. CM.

2924   —[Anr. ed.] *For A. M. W. O. and T. Thackeray*, [1695]. brs. L, O, CM, HH.

2924A   —[Anr. ed.] [*London*], *by and for W. O.*, [1697–1700?]. brs. EUING 231. GU; MH. (var.)

2925   Entry cancelled.

Most true and exact relation of that expedition of Kent. [n.p.], 1650. *See* Carter, Matthew.

2926   Entry cancelled.

Most true and succinct relation of the late battell. 1642. *See* Marshall, Stephen.

Most true and wonderfull narration of two women. 1658. *See* Heers, Henry.

2927   The most true and wonderful relation of a starre. *For F. Coles*, 1658. 4°. O; CSS.

2927AA   A most true but dreadful account from Shoreditch. [*London*? 1700.] cap., fol.* L.

2927A   A most true relation of a vvonderful victory. *By R. Oulton and G. Dexter for Ioseph Hnnscott* [*sic*] *July 7.* 1642. 4°.* C, OC, EC, BLH, DN; CH, MH.

2928   A most true relation of divers notable passages of divine providence. *For Laurence Blaikelocke*, 1643. 4°.* LT, O, SP, EN; CH, MH, MU, WF, Y.

2928A   A most true relation of the attachment . . . Will Waller. [*London*], *printed* 1641. 4°.* L, DU; WF.

2929   A most true relation of the great and bloody battell fought by Capt. Hotham. [*London*], *Decemb. 7. for L. Wright*, 1642. 4°.* LT, O; Y.

2930   A most true relation of the great and bloody battell. [*London*], *Decemb. 8. for L. Wright*, 1642. 4°.* LT, O, LNM, MR, EN; NN.

       A most true relation of the last weekes. 1642. *See* W., G.

2931   A most trve relation of the present state of His Majesties army. *For I. C.*, 1642. 4°.* BC, LSD, SP; MH.

2931aA   —[Anr. ed.] *For I. E.*, 1642. 4°.* LT, O, CS, LIU, MR; CH, WF, Y.

2931bA   Aug. 7: 1670. A most useful sermon preached in London. [*London*], *printed*, 1671. 8°.* MH.

2931cA   —[Anr. ed.] *Reprinted for J. Johnson*, 1682. 8°.* LW.

2931A   The most vile and lamentable confession of Hugh Peters. *For John Andrews*, [1660]. 12°.* LT.

2931B   Most welcome news from York. *For William Arding*, *June 23*, 1642. 4°.* INU, OSU, WF.

2932   Most wicked, cruel, bloody and barbarous newes from Northampton. *For Thomas Smith*, 1676. 4°.* L, MR; Y.

2933   A most wonderful and sad judgement of God upon one Dorothy Mattley. [*London*], *for VV. Gilbertson*, [1661]. brs. O.

2934   The most wonderfvl and true relation of Master John Macklain. [*London*], *for T. Vere & W. Gilbertson*, 1657. 8°.* LT.

2935   A most wonderful and true relation of one Mr. Philips. *Printed and sold by J. Bradford*, 1698. brs. L.

2936   The mother and daughter. [*London*], *for P. Brooksby*, [1672–95]. brs. L, O, HH; MH.

2936A   Mother Bunch's closet newly broke open. *By A. M. for P. Brooksby*, 1685. 12°.* CM.

2936B   Mother damnable. *Printed*, 1676. brs. L.

       Mother's blessing. 1656. *See* Leigh, Dorothy.

2937   The mother's blessing. [*London*], *by I. M. for I. Clarke, W. Thackeray, and T. Passinger*, 1685. 12°.* L, O, CM.

2938   A motion from the armie of their severall requests. *For R. Simpson*, 1667 [*i.e.* 1647]. 4°.* LT, O, DC, DT; MH, WF.

2939   A motion humbly presented to the consideration of the . . . committee. [*London*], *for H. Walker*, 1641. 4°.* LT, C, DT; CH, MH, MU, NU, WF, Y.

2940   A motion humbly presented to the consideration of the High Court. *For Richard Smithers*, 1641. 4°.* LT, C, LSC, MR; WF.

       Motions to this present Parliament. [n.p.], 1641. *See* DuMoulin, Louis.

2941   Motives and reasons, concerning His Highnesse the Prince Elector Palatines [Charles Louis] comming. *By Jane Coe*, 1644. 4°.* LT, O, MR, EN, DT; CH, MH, WF, Y.

2942   Motives grounded upon the word of God. *Printed at London*, 1647. 4°.* LT, DT.

2942A   Motives to godly mourning and rejoycing. *For the author*, 1698. 4°.* LW; WF.

       Motives to holy living. Oxford, 1688. *See* Woodhead, Abraham.

       Motives to induce. 1641. *See* Dury, John.

2943   Motives to perswade people to abstain from one meals-meat. [*London*, 1646.] cap., 4°.* MADAN 1902. LT.

2944   **M[otte], B.** Oratio dominica. *Prostant apud Dan. Brown, & W. Keblewhite*, 1700. 4°. L, O, CCO, AN, E; CH, CN, MH, TU, WF.

2945   **Motteux, Peter.** Beauty in distress. *For Daniel Brown; and Rich. Parker*, 1698. 4°. T.C.III 79. L, O, C, DC, DT; CH, CN, LC, MH, TU, WCL, WF, Y.

2946   [–] A dialogue between a widow and a rake in the Island Princess. [*n.p.*], 1699. brs. L, MC.

2946A   [–] A dialogue in ye 3d act of ye island princess. [*London*, 1700.] fol.* NN, WF.

2946B   [–] An enthusiastick song in the island princess. [*London*, 1700.] cap., fol.* L; LC, WF.

2947   [–] The epilogue in the island-princess. [*London*, 1698.] brs. MC.

2948   —Europes revels. *For J. Tonson*, 1697. 4°.* L, C, LG, A, DT; CH, CN, CU, LC, V.

2949   —The island princess. *For Richard Wellington, and sold by Bernard Lintott*, 1699. 4°. T.C.III 124. L, O, OW, CT, EN; CH, CN, LC, MH, NP, WF, Y.

2950   [–] The jolly, jolly swains. [*London*], *T. Cross*, [1700]. brs. L.

2951   [–] The loud alarms of war. [*London*, 1700?] brs. L.

2952   [–] Lovely charmer, dearest creature. [*London*], *T. Cross*, [1700]. brs. L; CH, MH.

2953   —Love's a jest. *For Peter Buck, John Sturton, and Alexander Bosvil*, 1696. 4°. T.C.II 602. L, O, LVF, CCA, EN; CH, CN, LC, MH, TU, WF, Y.

2954   —The loves of Mars & Venus. *Printed*, 1696. 4°.* L, O, OW, CT, LLU, EN; CH, CLC, MB, MH, PU, WF, Y.

2955   ——[Anr. ed.] —, 1697. 4°.* L, O, C, OW, EN; CH, CN, MH, TU, WF.

2956   —Maria. A poem. *For Peter Buck*, 1695. fol.* L, C, CT, LLU; CH, CN, LC, MH, TU, WF, Y.

2957   [–] Must then a faithful lover go. [*London*], *T. Cross*, [1700?]. L.

2958   —The novelty. *For Rich. Parker, and Peter Buck*, 1697. 4°. L, O, OC, OW, LLU, EN; CH, CN, LC, MH, TU, WF, Y.

2959   [–] The prologue, in the island-princess. [*London*, 1698.] brs. L; NN.

2960   [–] Rouse ye gods of ye main. [*London*, 1700.] fol.* L.

2961   [–] Single songs, and dialogues, in the musical play of Mars & Venus. *By J. Heptinstall, for the authors, and sold by John Hare. And by John Welch*, 1697. fol.* L, LCM; CLC, LC, WF.

2961A   [–] A song in the mad lover. [*London*, 1700?] brs. CLC.

2962   [–] A song in the opera call'd the island princess. 1699. brs. L, MC; LC, WF.

2962A   [–] A song in the second act of the island princess. [*London*, 1700.] brs. L.

2963   [–] The town rak's. [*London*], *Tho. Cross*, [1696?]. brs. L.

2963A   [–] A two part song. [*London*, 1700.] brs. L; WF.

2964   —Words for a musical entertainment . . . taking of Namur. [1695?] brs. L.

2965   —Words for an entertainment at the music feast. 1695. brs. MC.

2966   —The words of a new interlude, called The four seasons. *For R. Basset*, 1699. 4°.* T.C.III 109. L, LLU, ES; MB, Y.

2967   **Moulton, Thomas.** The compleat bone-setter. *By J. C. for Martha Harison*, 1656[7]. 8°. LT, LCS, AM, GU; CN, WF, WSG.

2968   — —Second edition. *For Tho: Rooks*, 1665. 8°. L, LCS, MAU; HC.

2968A   — —"Second" edition. *Nath: Crouch*, 1666. 8°. WSG.

2968B   **Mount, Mr.** A full account from Ireland, of the maid at Dublin. [*London*], *For P. Brooksby, and sold by R. Kell*, [1700?]. 8°.* L; MIU.

2969   Mount Aetna's flames. [*London*], *for F. Coles, T. Vere, and J. Wright*, [1669]. brs. O.

2970   Entry cancelled.
        Mount of spirits. 1691. *See* Wolseley, *Sir* Charles.
        Movnt Pisgah. 1689. *See* Flavell, John.

2970A   Mount Sion or a treatise shewing to a protestant. *Doway*, 1658. STONYHURST.

2971   Entry cancelled.
        [**Mountacute, Walter.**] *See* Montagu, Walter.
        Mountagu(e). *See* Montagu(e).
        Mountain, Didymus, *pseud.*

2972   No entry.

2973   **Mountfort, William.** Greenwich-Park. *For Jo. Hindmarsh, R. Bentley, and A. Roper*, 1691. *Sold by Randal Taylor*. 4°. T.C.II 360. L, O, LLU, EN, DT; CH, CN, LC, TU, WF, Y.
        [–] Henry the second. 1693. *See* Bancroft, John.

2974   —The injur'd lovers. *For Sam Manship*, 1688. 4°. T.C.II 223. L, O, CT, A, DT; CH, CN, LC, MH, TU, WF, Y.
        —King Edward the third. 1691. *See* Bancroft, John.

2975   —The liee [*sic*] and death of Doctor Faustus. *Printed and sold by E. Whitlock*, 1697. 4°.* L, O, MR, E; CH, CN, MH, WF.

2976   [–] Prologue to the injur'd lovers. colop: *For Sam. Manship*, 1687. brs. O; CH, CLC.

2977   —The successfull straingers. *For James Blackwell, and sold by Randal Taylor*, 1690. 4°. T.C.II 301. L, O, LVD, CT, EN; CH, CN, LC, MH, WF, Y.

2978   — —[Anr. ed.] *For W. Freeman*, 1696. 4°. T.C.II 579. L, OC, OW; CU, LC, MH, WF, Y.

2979   **Mountrath, Charles Coote, earl of.** The declaration of. *Dublin, by William Bladen*, 1659[60]. brs. BLH; IU, MH.

2979A   — —[Anr. ed.] —, 1660. 4°.* DIX 106. OW.

2980   — —[Anr. ed.] *Dublin, by William Bladen, and reprinted at London by J. Macock*, 1659[60]. 4°.* LT, O, C, CCA, DT; CH, IU, WF, WU.

2981   — —[Anr. ed.] *For Tho. Vere, and W. Gilbertson*, 1660. 4°.* LT, O, SP, BLH, DN.

2982   — —[Anr. ed.] *By D. Maxwell*, 1660. 4°.* C; MH, Y.

2983   —Two letters from. *Printed at London for Robert Ibbitson*, 1650. 4°.* L, C, LVF, DN; CH, IU.

2984   A mournful caral or an elegy. [*London*], *for M. Coles, T. Vere, J. Wright, I. Clarke, W. Thackeray, and T. Passenger*, [1680–82]. brs. L, CM.

2984A   —[Anr. ed., "mournfull carroll, elegie."] [*London*], *for William Gilbertson*, 1656. brs. O.

2985   The mournfull cryes of many thousand poore tradesmen. [*London*, 1648.] brs. LT; NC, Y.

2986   A mournful ditty of the Lady Rosamond. *For F. Coles, Tho. Vere and W. Gilbertson*, [1658–64]. brs. O.

2986A   A mournfull elegie, in pious and perpetuall memory … Robert, Earle of Essex. *For Thomas Banks*, 1646. 4°.* GU.
        Mournful elegy, on the deplorable. 1685. *See* Ker, Patrick.

2987   A mournful elegy upon the three renowned vvorthies, Duke Hamilton. [*London*], *printed*, 1649. brs. LT; MH.
        Mournefull epitaph. [n.p.], 1642. *See* L., I.

2988   The mournful maid of Berkshire. *For J. Deacon*, [1684–95]. brs. L, CM, HH.

2988A   The mournful maidens complaint. [*London*], *for J. Hose*, [1660–75]. brs. O.

2989   The mournful shepherd. [*London*], *for P. Brooksby*, [1683]. brs. EUING 234. L, O, CM, HH; GU; MH.

2990   The mournful subjects or, the whole nations lamentation. [*London*], *for J. Deacon*, [1685?]. brs. L, CM.

2991   The mourning conquest. [*London*], *for J. Wright, J. Clarke, W. Thackeray, and T. Passenger*, [1681–84]. brs. L, O, CM.

2991A   The mourning court: or, … funeral of … Mary. *Printed*, 1695. brs. O.

2991B   The mourning cross. *By Tho. Milbourn*, 1665. brs. LG; MH.

2992   The mourning lady. *For J. Deacon*, [1694–5]. brs. HH.

2993   The mourning poets. *For J. Whitlock*, 1695. fol.* L, O, CS, LLU, MR; CH, CN, MH, TU, WF, Y.
        Mourning-ring. 1692. *See* Dunton, John.

2994   **Mowbray, Laurence.** The narrative of. *For Thomas Simmons, and Jacob Sampson*, 1680. fol.* T.C.I 382. L, C, OB, DU, EN, DT; CH, MH, MU, TU, WF, Y.

2995   [–] The pourtraicture of Roger L'Estrange. *Printed*, 1681. fol.* L, O; CH, MH, TO, WF, Y. (var.)

2995A   **Mowbray, Thomas.** The honour of Kings vindicated. *Middelburg, T. Berry*, 1663. 4°.* L, GU.

2996   The mowing-devil. *For H. T.*, 1678. 4°.* L; NR, Y.

2997   [**Mowlin, John.**] The divell in Kent. *Printed*, 1647. 4°.* LT; CSS, MB, Y.
        Moxon, Joseph. Advertisement. There is invented … a new kind of globe. [1679.] *See* Castlemaine, Roger Palmer, *earl of*.

2998   —A book of sea-plats. *Sold at his shop*, 1665. *London*. fol.* O.

2999   —A brief discourse of a passage by the North-pole. *For Joseph Moxon*, 1674. 4°. T.C.I 178. L, O, LCP, LR, CT; NC, NN, PL, RPJ, Y.

3000   — —Second edition. *By J. Moxon*, 1697. 4°.* L, OM, CS.

3000A   —A catalogue of globes. [*London?* 1680.] cap.* CM; MU.

3000B   —A collection of some attempts made to the north-east. *For Joseph Moxon, and* [*sold*] *by James Moxon*, 1676. brs. O, INDIA OFFICE.

3001   Entry cancelled.
        —Ductor ad ast. 1659. *See* —Tutor to astronomie.
        —English globe. 1679. *See* Castlemaine, Roger Palmer, *earl of*.

3002   [-] An epitome of the whole art of war. *For J. Moxon,* 1692. 8°. L, NE.

3003   [-] —[Anr. ed.] *For Tho. Axe, Philip Lee, and Edward Pool,* 1692. 8°. T.C.II 394. L(t.p.).

3004   —A map of the River Thames, merrily cald Blanket Fair. *To be sold by Joseph Moxon,* [1683/4]. brs. O.

3005   Entry cancelled. Ghost.

3006   —Mathematicks made easie. *For Joseph Moxon,* 1679. 8°. T.C.I 341. L, O, C, LIU; CH, CLC, CU, MU, NC, PBL.

3007   — —Second edition. —, 1692. 8°. L, O, C, LLU, EN; BN, CH, LC, MH, MU, WF, Y.

3008   — —Third edition. *For J. Moxon, and Tho. Tuttell,* 1700. 8°. L, C, CM; CLC, IU, MH, NN, TO, V.

3009   —Mechanick dyalling. *For Joseph Moxon,* 1668 [1678]. 4°. L, O, C, OC, CT, GC; CH, CSS, MBA, MH, MU.

3010   — —[Anr. ed.] *P. Lea,* [1690]. 4°. CJC, WPO.

3011   — —Second edition. *For James Moxon,* 1692. 4°. L, LG; NC, Y.

3012   — —Third edition. —, 1697. 4°. O, C, OM, CT, BC; CLC, MB, NN, WF.

3012A   — —"Third" edition. —, 1698. 4°. L.

3013   —Mechanick exercises. *For Joseph Moxon,* 1677. 4°. T.C.I 302. L, O, C, CT, BAMB, DM; CH, MH, NC, PUL, V, Y.

3014   — —Second volume. —, 1683. 4°. T.C.II 33. L, C, OM, MR, E, DM; BN, CH, CN, MBA, V, WF, AVP.

3015   — —Second edition. *Printed and sold by J. Moxon,* 1693. 4°. L, C, BC, ES, GU; MBA, WF, Y, YBA.

3016   — —"Second" edition. —, 1694 [1700]. 4°. L, O, BC; KU, LC, RPJ, Y.

3016A   — —[Anr. ed.] —, 1695. 4°. CLC, MIU.

3017   — —Third edition. —, 1700. 4°. O, BC; MH, YBA.

3018   —Practical perspective. *By Joseph Moxon,* 1670. fol. T.C.I 30. L, O, C, EN, DT; BBE, CH, MH, NN, RPJ, WF.

3018A   —Proves of the several sorts of letters cast by. *Westminster, by Joseph Moxon,* 1669. brs. L, CM.

3019   —Regulæ trium ordinum . . . or the rules of . . . print letters. *For Joseph Moxon,* 1676. 4°. T.C.I 247. L, O, C, LW, MR; CH, CN, LC, MB.

3020   — —Second edition. —, 1693. 4°. BN, LC.

      [-] Sacred geographie. 1671. *See title.*

3021   —A tutor to astronomie and geographie: or an easie and speedy way. *By Joseph Moxon,* 1659. 4°. L, O, C, BC, NPL; CLC, CU, MH, MU, PL, Y.

3022   Entry cancelled.

      — —[Anr. ed.] 1665. *See*—Tutor to astronomy and geography, or the use.

3023   — —Second edition. —, 1670. 4°. T.C.I 27. L, O, C, DC, E, BQ; CLC, CN, LC, MH, NC, RPJ, WSC, Y.

3024   — —Third edition. *By Tho. Roycroft, for Joseph Moxon,* 1674. T.C.I 181. L, O, C, EN, DT; CLC, CN, LC, MH, HC.

3025   — —Fourth edition. *By S. Roycroft for Joseph Moxon,* 1686. 4°. L, O, C, GC, MR, EN; CH, LC, MH, MU, NC, TU, Y.

3026   Entry cancelled. Ghost.

3026A   — —Fifth edition. *For James Moxon,* 1698. 4°. L, OC, DT, EN; CLC, PU, Y.

3027   — —"Fifth" edition. *For W. Hawes,* 1699. 4°. L, BC, NE, RPL; CH, CLC, IU, MBA, MBC, PL.

3027aA   — —"Fifth" edition. *Sold by Phillip Lea,* [1699]. 8°. L, O; CLC, RPJ.

3027bA   —A tutor to astronomy and geography, or the use of copernican spheres. *For Joseph Moxon,* 1665. 4°. L, O, LCP, OB, CM; CLC, LC, MH, PL, HC.

3027cA   —The use of the astronomical playing-cards. *Sold by Joseph Moxon,* 1676. 8°. T.C.I 257. OC; CLC, Y.

3027A   — —[Anr. ed.] *By J. Moxon,* 1692. 8°. CH, MH, MU, Y.

3027B   **Moyer, Samuel.** The case of. [*London?* 1691.] brs. HH.

3028   **Moyle, John.** Abstractum chirurgiæ marinæ. Or, an abstract. *By J. Richardson for Tho. Passinger,* 1686. 12°. T.C.II 193. L; MU.

3028A   —Chirurgus marinus; or, the sea chirurgion. *For Eben. Tracy, and H. Barnard,* 1693. 12°. L, LCS.

3029   **Moyle, Robert.** An exact book of entries. *For Robert Crofts,* 1658. 4°. LT, O, LGI, LL, NPL; LC, MHL, NCL, NP, PUL.

      M[oyle], W[alter]. Discourse upon improving the revenue. 1697. *See* Davenant, Charles. Discourses.

3030   [-] The second part of an argument, shewing that a standing army is inconsistent. *Printed,* 1697. 4°.* L, O, C, LLU, AU, DT; CH, CN, MH, TU, WF, Y.

3031   Much a-do about nothing. *For T. Vere,* [1660]. brs. O.

3032   —[Anr. ed.] *For Tho. Vere,* 1664. brs. L.

      Much-esteemed history of . . . Don Quixote. 1699. *See* Cervantes Saavedra, Miguel de.

3033   [**Mucklow, William.**] A bemoaning letter. *For A. Baldwin,* 1700. 8°.* T.C.III 187. O, MR; RPJ.

3034   —Liberty of conscience asserted. *Printed,* 1673/4. brs. L.

3035   [-] The spirit of the hat. *For F. Smith,* 1673. 8°.* T.C.I 142. L, O, C, LF, OC, BAMB, A; CH, NU.

3035A   [-] —[Anr. ed.] *For A. Baldwin,* 1700. 8°.* CH.

3036   [-] Tyranny and hypocrisy detected. *For Fr. Smith,* 1673. 8°. T.C.I 154. L, O, LF, OC; NU.

3037   **M[udd], A[nn].** A cry, a cry: a sensible cry. colop: *Printed,* 1678. 4°.* L, C, LF; MB, MH, PH, PSC, Y.

3038   **M[udie], A[lexander].** Scoitæ indiculum. *For Jonathan Wilkins,* 1682. 12°. L, O, C, EN, DT; CH, CN, LC, MH, NN, TU, WF, Y.

3039   Entry cancelled.

      Müller, Johann. Εσοπτρον αστρολογικον. [1655.] *See* Engel, Johann.

3039A   **Münster, Sebastian.** The Messias of the Christians. *By William Hunt,* 1655. 8°. L, OC, CS, CT, P; CH, IU, MB, MH, OHU, WF.

      Muffet, Thomas. *See* Moffett, Thomas.

3040   **Muggleton, Lodowick.** The acts of the witnesses of the spirit. *Printed,* 1699. 4°. L, O, LF, CT, LLU; CH, CN, NCD, NU, PH, WF, Y.

3041   —The answer to William Penn. *Printed,* 1673. L, C, LF, NPL, DT; CH, CLC, IU, NU, WF, Y.

3042   —A discourse between John Reeve and Richard Leader. [*London,* 1682.] cap., 4°.* L, O, MR; MB, NU, WF, Y.

3043   —The prophet Muggleton's epistle to the believers. [*London?* 1690.] cap., 4°.* L; IU, WF.

3044   —A letter sent to Thomas Taylor. [*London?*], *printed,* 1665. 4°.* L, C, LF, OC, BLH; CH, CN, MH, NU, PH, WF, Y.

3045 Entry cancelled. Date: [1719].

3046 —A looking-glass for George Fox. [*London?*], *printed*, 1667. 4°. L, LLP, OC, NPL, BLH; CH, IU, NU, PL, WF, Y.

3047 ——[Anr. ed.] —, 1668. 4°. LF, LPR; PH.

3048 —The neck of the Quakers broken. *Amsterdam* [*London?*]: *printed*, 1663 [1667?]. 4°. L, O, C, LF, CD; CH, IU, MH, NU, PH, WF, Y.

3049 —A true interpretation of all the chief texts. *Printed*, 1665, *for the author*. 4°. L, O, C, LF, CD; CH, IU, MH, NC, NU, WF.

3050 —A true interpretation of the eleventh chapter of . . . Revelation. [*London*], *printed*, 1662, *for the author*. 4°. L, C, LF, LLP, OC, CD; CH, IU, MBP, MH, NU, WF.

3051 —A true interpretation of the witch of Endor. *Printed*, 1669. 4°. L, O, OC, GU, BLH; CH, CN, NU, SE, WF, Y.

3052 Muggleton reviv'd. *For D. M.*, 1677. 4°.* NU, PH.

Muggletonians principles. [n.p.], 1695. *See* Tomkinson, Thomas.

Muggleton's last will. 1679. *See* B., J.

3053 **Mulerius, Carolus.** Linguæ Italicæ. *Oxonii, impensis Joh. Crosley*, 1667. 8°.* MADAN 2771. O, OC, LSD.

3054 Entry cancelled.

Mulgrave, John Sheffield, earl. *See* Buckingham, John Sheffield, *duke of*.

3055 **Mullard, Joshua.** Celestial soliloquies. 1651. 12°. DC.

3056 —Medicina animæ: or, the lamentation. *By Tho. Harper*, 1652. 12°. LT.

3057 **M[ullen], A[llan].** An anatomical account of the elephant. *For Sam. Smith*, 1682. 4°. T.C.I 508. L, O, C, GH, DT; CLM, MH, NAM, PL, WF, HC.

3058 **Mullenaux, Samuel.** A journal of the three months royal campaign. *For P. Lee*, 1690. 4°. L, O, C, LIU, BQ; CH, TU, WF, Y.

3058A ——[Anr. ed.] —, *Boston, re-printed by R. P. for Benjamin Harris*, 1691. cap., 4°.* LC.

3058B **Mullinax, John.** Symplegades antrum. [*London*, 1660.] 4°. MH.

3059 **Mulliner, John.** A testimony against perriwigs. [*London*], *printed*, 1677. cap., 4°.* L, LF, OP, CS, BBN; MB, MH, PH, PSC.

3060 Entry cancelled.

[**Mullins, James.**] Some observations made upon the cylonian plant. 1695. *See* Peachie, John.

Multum in parvo. 1687. *See* Pennyman, John.

3061 Multum in parvo, aut vox veritatis: wherein. *For Rich. Janeway*, 1681. fol. L, O, LSD, EN, DT; CH, MH, MU, NU, WF, Y.

Multum in parvo: lately. [n.p.], 1688. *See* P., T.

3062 Multum in parvo: or, a summary. *For J. H.*, 1653. 4°.* LT, O, MR; CSS, MH.

3063 **M[umford], J[ames].** The Catholike scriptvrist. *Printed in Gant, by Maximilian Graet*, 1662. 8°. L, C, DUS; NU, WF.

3064 ——Second edition. *For Matthew Turner*, 1686. 12°. L, O, C, DUS, MC, DT; CH, CLC, CN, MSL, Y.

3065 ——Third edition. *Holy-Rood-House* [*Edinburgh*], *by James Watson*, 1687. 8°. ALDIS 2699. L, C, E, EN, GU; TU, WCL, WF.

3066 [–] The qvestion of qvestions. *Printed in Gant, by Maximilian Graet*, 1658. 4°. L, O, CT, DUS, NPL; CH, CU, NU, WF, Y.

3067 [–] —[Anr. ed.] [*London*], *printed*, 1686. 4°. LSC, DUS, MC, E; MSL, NGT, NU, TU, ST. PATRICK'S COLL., AUSTRALIA.

3068 —— Second edition. *By Henry Hills, for him and Matt. Turner*, 1686/7. 12°. L, O, C, EN, DT; CH, CLC, CN, MBP, MIU, TU.

3069 [–] A remembrance for the living to pray for the dead. [*St. Omer*], 1641. 12°. L, DUS; CN, NU.

3070 [–] —[Anr. ed.] *Printed at Paris*, 1660. 8°. L, O, LSC, MC; CH, CN, NU, TU, WF, WG, Y.

3071 [–] —Second part. Second edition. [*London*], *anno*. 1661. 8°. L, FARM, DUS; MSL, TU.

3071A [–] A vindication of St. Gregorie his dialogues. *For Ja. Crook*, 1660. 4°.* O, DU.

3072 **Mun, Thomas.** England's benefit and advantage by foreign trade. *By E. J. for Tho. Horne*, 1698. 8°. L, LUG, E, EN, CD; CH, MH, MU, NC, PL, WF.

3073 —England's treasure by forraign trade. *By J. G. for Thomas Clark*, 1664. 8°. L, O, C, E, DT; BN, CH, LC, MH, MU, Y.

3074 —— Second edition. *By J. Flesher for Robert Horne*, 1669. 8°. T.C.I 27. L, O, C, LUG, DT; BN, CSS, LC, MH, MU, WF, Y.

3075 [**Muncaster, Randal.**] A true representation of the state of the bordering customary tenants. [*London*, 1654.] cap., 4°.* LT, MR.

Mundorum explicatio or. 1661. *See* Pordage, Samuel.

3076 Mundus foppensis: or, the fop display'd. *For John Harris*, 1691. 4°.* T.C.II 337. L, O, CT; CLC, LC, MH, WF, Y.

Mundus muliebris: or. 1690. *See* Evelyn, Mary.

3077 **Mundy, Henry.** Βιοχρηστολογια seu commentarii de aere vitali. *Oxonii* [*exc. H. Hall*] *impensis Jo. Crosley*, 1680. 8°. T.C.I 418; MADAN 3272. L, O, C, MAU, E, DT; DICKINSON COLL.

3078 ——[Anr. ed.] *Oxoniæ*, 1685. 12°. L.

Municipium ecclesiasticum. Or. [n.p.], 1697. *See* Hill, Samuel.

3079 **Munning, Humphrey.** A. pious sermon preached. *Cambridge, by Roger Daniel*, 1641. 4°.* L; TU, ZWT.

3080 **Munro, Dr.** Advertisement by. [*Edinburgh*, 1693.] brs. ALDIS 3287. OC, HH, BLH.

3081 Munster paralleld. *By T. M. for T. B.*, 1661. 4°. NU.

Murat, comtesse de. *See* Desjardins, Marie Catherine Hortense.

3082 **Murcot, John.** Saving faith. *By T. R. & E. M. for Tho. Underhill*, 1656. 4°.* L, O, C, LSC, BC; WF, Y.

3083 —Several works of. *By R. White, for Francis Tyton*, 1657. 4°. LT, LCL, LW, P, E, DT; CH, MH, NU, TU, WF, Y.

3084 Murther, murther, or, a bloody relation. *Printed at London, for Tho. Bates*, 1641. 4°.* LT, LG, EN; CH, Y.

3085 Murder out at last. [*London*], *by N. T.*, 1683. brs. L, O; CH, CLC, MH, NCD.

3086 —[Anr. ed.] *Edinburgh re-printed*, 1683. brs. ALDIS 2394. L, O, EN.

3087 Mvrther revealed. *Printed*, 1659. 4°.* LG, OC; CSS, MH.

Murther unparalel'd. 1682. *See* M., J.

3088   Murther upon murther: being a full and true relation. colop: *By G. Croom,* 1691. brs. L, HH; CH, CN.

3089   Murder upon murder, committed. *For T. Langley, and are to be sold by Thomas Lambert,* [1680?]. brs. O.

3090   Murther upon murther: or a true and faithful relation. *By W. D. for J. Conyers,* 1684. 4°.* WF.

   Murther will out. [n.p., 1692.] *See* Braddon, Laurence.

3090A Murder will out, an impartial narrative. *Ed. Golding,* 1692. fol.* CN.

3091   Murder will out: being a relation of the late Earl of Essex's ghost. [*London?* 1683.] brs. C, HH; CH, CN, PU, MH.

3092   Entry cancelled.

   Murder will out: or, a clear and full discovery. 1689. *See* Danvers, Henry.

3093   Murther will out, or, a true and faithful relation. *For C. Passinger,* [1675]. 4°.* L.

3093A Murther will out; or, an unrighteous discharge. *Printed* 1662. 4°.* L, OC.

3094   Murther will out. Or, honest-men look to your selves. [*London*], *printed,* 1648. 4°.* LT; TU, Y.

   Murder will out: or, the King's letter. 1663. *See* Charles II.

3095   —[Anr. ed.] *Printed,* 1689. 4°.* L, O, C, AN, MC, DT; CLC, CN, MB, WF, Y.

3095A —[Anr. ed.] *Printed* 1698. 4°.* C, BAMB, GU, DN; IU, WF.

3095B The murtherer justly condemned. [*London*], *for John Foster,* [1697]. brs. EUING 223B. GU.

   Murderer punished. 1668. *See* Alleine, Richard.

3096   The murtherer turned true penitent. [*London*], *for P. Brooksby,* [1688]. 8°.* O.

3097   The murderous midwife. [*London*], *printed,* 1673. 4°.* LG; MIU.

3097A Murthers reward. *By A. M. for W. Thackeray and T. Passinger,* [c. 1685]. 8°.* CM.

3097B M[ure], A[ndrew]. Πηγιαμα, or the vertues of . . . water at Peterhead. *Aberdene, by Iohn Forbes younger,* 1668. brs. O.

   Mure, *Sir* William. *See* Moore, *Sir* William.

3098   **Muret, Pierre.** Rites of funeral. *For R. Royston,* 1683. 8°. T.C.I 502. L, O, C, SP, EN; CLC, CN, MH, MU, NCU, NU, WF, Y. (var.)

3099   — —[Anr. ed.] *Printed and are to be sold by John Whitlock,* 1695. 8°. LW, EN; MBP, MIU, WF.

   Murford, James. *See* Mumford, James.

3100   **Murford, Nicholas.** Fragmenta poetica. *For Humphrey Moseley,* 1650. 12°. L, O, NPL; CH, CLC.

3101   [**Murford, Peter.**] Nevves from Sovthampton. *For Henry Overton,* 1644. 4°.* LT, O; Y.

3102   Entry cancelled. *See preceding entry.*

3103   The murmurers. A poem. *For R. Baldwin,* 1689. fol.* L, O, C, DU, E, ES; CLC, CN, MH, TU, WF, Y.

   Murnival of knaves. 1683. *See* Norris, John.

3104   **Murphy, Edmund.** The present state and condition of Ireland. *For R. Boulter, and Benj. Alsop,* 1681. fol.* L, O, C, DU, DT; CH, CN, LC, MH, WF, Y.

3105   [**Murray.**] A review of Mr. M. H.'s new notion. *For Edward Mory,* 1692. 4°. T.C.II 401. L, LG, OU, LIU, MR, DT; CLC, NU, WF, Y.

3106   **Murray, Alexander Stewart, *earl of.*** The speech of . . . 29th of April, 1686. *Edinburgh, by the heir of Andrew Anderson,* 1686. fol.* ALDIS 2646. L, MR, AU, EN; CH, CLC, CSS, MH, WF.

3106A **Murray, Charles.** Unto the right honourable the lords of His Majesties treasury and exchequer. The petition of. [*Edinburgh, after* 1687.] brs. EN.

3107   **Murray, Janet.** Unto the lords of council and session, the petition of. [*Edinburgh,* 1700.] brs. ALDIS 3987. O.

   Murray, John. *See* Tullibardine, John Murray, *earl of.*

3108   **M[urray], M[ungo].** On the death and horrid murther of . . . James [Sharp]. [*Edinburgh,* 1679.] brs. ALDIS 2155. EN.

3109   [–] On the death of his grace John Duke of Rothes. [*Edinburgh?* 1681.] brs. ALDIS 2275.5. EN.

3110   [–] On the death of the illustrious David Earle of Wemyss. [*Edinburgh,* 1679.] brs. ALDIS 2154.2. EN.

3111   [–] On the death of the most sadly, . . . James Duke of Montrose. [*Edinburgh?* 1684.] brs. ALDIS 2456.5. EN.

3112   [–] To . . . James Earl of Perth. [*Edinburgh?* 1685?] brs. ALDIS 2557.5. EN.

3113   [–] To . . . John Earle of Lauderdale. [*Edinburgh?* 1670.] brs. ALDIS 1913.7. EN.

3114   [**Murray, Robert.**] An account of the constitution and security of the general bank of credit. *By John Gain,* 1683. 4°.* L, O, LG, EN, DT; CH, CN, LC, MH, NR, WF, Y.

3115   [–] An advertisement for the more easie and speedy collecting of debts. [*London,* 1682.] brs. O, LPR.

3116   [–] Corporation-credit. *By John Gain, for the office,* 1682. 4°.* L, O, LG, LUG, MR, EN; CJC, CSS, LC, MH, NC, WF, Y.

3116A —Letters and pacquets not exceeding a pound weight. 1680/1. brs. L.

3116B —A proposal for a national bank. *For the proposer,* 1695. 4°.* OH; CSS, MH.

3117   — —[Anr. ed.] *For the proposer,* 1695/6. 4°.* L, O, C, LG, EN, DT; BN, CH, LC, NC, NCD, PU, Y.

3117A — —[Anr. ed.] *By G. L. for the proposer,* 1696. 4°.* NP.

3118   [–] A proposal for the advancement of trade. *By A. M. and R. R. for Dorman Newman, and Jonathan Edwin,* 1676. fol.* T.C.I 238. L, C, LPR, OC, LSD; MH.

3119   — —[Anr. ed.] colop: *For Jonathan Edwin,* 1676. cap., fol.* L, LUG; IU, NC.

3120   —A proposal for the better securing our wooll. [*London,* 1695?] cap., 4°.* L, O, LUG, BR, EN; BN, MH, MIU, NC, NCD.

3121   —A proposal for the more easie advancing to the crown. [*London,* 1696.] cap., 4°.* L, O, LUG, LVF, LSD, EN; CH, CU, MH, NC, WF.

3122   —A proposal for translating the duty of excise, from malt-drinks. [*London,* 1696?] cap., 4°.* L, LUG; MH.

3123   —Reasons humbly offer'd. . . . For translating the duty. [*London,* 1696?] cap., 4°.* L, LUG, OH, BP, EN; MH, NC, NCD, NCL.

3124 **Murrell, John.** A new booke of cookerie. Sixth edition. *J. Marriot,* 1641. 12°. L; LC.

3125 —Murrels two bookes of cookerie and carving. Fifth edition. *By M. F. for Iohn Marriott,* 1641. 8°. L, O; BN, CJC.

3126 ——Seventh edition. *By Ja. Fl. for R. Marriot,* 1650. 8°. L.

3126A ——Eighth edition ["Murrell's cookery"]. *By D. Maxwell, and are to be sold by Robert Horn,* 1659. 8°. L(t.p.).

3127 **Murtadhá ibn al Khafíf.** The Egyptian history. *By R: B. for W. Battersby,* 1672. 8°. T.C.I 86. L, O, C, E, DT; CLC, LC, WF.

3128 ——[Anr. ed.] *By R: B. for Thomas Basset,* 1672. 8°. O, LWL, AN, DU, LIU; CH, MH, MIU, WF, Y.

Murther. *See* Murder.

3128A Mus rusticus. [1680?] brs. O.

3129 Musa præfica. The London poem. *For T. M. and John Holford,* 1685. fol.* T.C.II 138. L, O; CH, MH, NP, TU, WF, Y.

Musæ subsecivæ. Cantabrigiæ, 1676. *See* Duport, James.

Musæum regalis societatis; or a catalogue. 1681. *See* Grew, Nehemiah.

3130 **Musæus.** Musæi, Moschi & Bionis, quæ extant. *Typis Thomæ Roycroftii impensis authoris,* 1655. 4°. L, C, MR, NPL, GH, DT; CH, CLC, MU, TU, WF, Y.

3131 ——[Anr. ed.] *Typis Thomæ Roycroftii, impensis Jo. Martin, Jac. Allestrye, & Tho. Dicas,* 1659. 4°. L, O, C, EN, GH; CH, CLC, IU, MH, Y.

3132 —Ερωτοπαιγνιον. The loves of Hero and Leander. *Oxford, by Henry Hall,* 1645. 4°.* MADAN 1851. O, EN.

3133 —Lusus amatorius. *Prostant venales apud Thomam Speed,* 1694. 4°.* L, O; CLC, IU, NIC, WF, Y.

3133A ——[Anr. ed.] *Impensis Thomae Speed,* 1699. 4°. T.C.III 141. O, CT, BAMB.

3134 — . . . On the loves of { Hero and Leander: *By F. B. for Humphrey Moseley,* 1647. 12°. LT, O, LW, DC, LLU; CH, CN, MH, TU, WF, Y.

3135 Musarum Anglicanarum analecta: . . . Vol. I. *Oxon. E theatro Sheldoniano. Impensis Joh. Crosley & Sam. Smith,* 1692. 8°. T.C.II 382. L, O, C, GC, DT; CH, MH, TU, WF, Y.

3135A —Second edition. —, 1699. 8°. O.

3136 —Second edition. *Oxon. E Theatro Sheldoniano, impensis Joh. Crosley,* 1699. 8°. L, O, C, EN, DT; CH, CLC, CN, MH, TU, Y.

3137 — . . . Vol. II. —, 1699. 8°. L, O, C, MR, DT; CH, CN, MH, TU, WF.

3137A ——[Anr. ed.] *Oxon, e theatro Sheldoniano, impensis Tim Childe,* 1699. 8°. T.C.III 110. O; CH, PU, Y.

Musarum deliciæ. 1655. *See* Mennis, *Sir* John.

3138 **Muschamp, A.** Fvrther intelligence from Ireland. *By R. Oulton & G. Dexter, for Henry Overton,* 1642. 4°.* LT, O, LW, EC, DN; WF.

3138A The Muscovy operator. [n.p., 1700?] brs. L.

Muse de cavalier. 1685. *See* Cutts, John.

3139 The muse of New-Market. *For Dan. Browne, Dan. Major, and James Vade,* 1680. 4°. L, O, A; CH, LC, MB, MH, WF.

Muses cabinet. 1655. *See* Winstanley, William.

Muses congratulatory address. [n.p., 1660.] *See* B., T.

3140 The muses farewel to Popery and slavery. *For N. R. H. F. and J. K.,* 1689. 8°. L, O, CCH, AU, E, DT; CH, CN, LC, MH, TU, WF, Y.

3141 —Second edition. *For S. Burgess,* 1690. 8°.* L, O, C, DU, DT; CH, CN, CU, MH, TU, Y.

3142 The muses fire-works. *For William Miller,* [1680?]. brs. L; MU.

Muses joy. 1661. *See* Crouch, John.

Muses looking-glasse. 1643. *See* Randolph, Thomas.

Muses mistresse. 1660. *See* Cotgrave, John.

3143 **Musgrave, Christopher.** Motives and reasons. *For John Harefinch,* 1688. 4°.* T.C.II 236. O, OB, OC, DU, MR; CLC, MH, MIU, PL.

3144 **Musgrave, John.** Another word to the wise. [*London,*] *printed,* 1646. 4°.* LT, OC, DT; CH, CSS, MH, WF.

3145 —The conscience pleading. *Printed,* 1647. 4°.* NU, WF.

3146 [–] A cry of blovd of an innocent Abel. *Printed,* 1654. 4°.* LT, EN; CH.

3147 —A declaration of. *For John Musgrave,* 1647. 4°.* LT, DT; CH.

3148 [–] A fourth word to the wise. [*London,* 1647.] cap., 4°.* LT, DT; MIU, WF.

3149 Entry cancelled.

[–] Good covnsel in bad times. 1647. *See* title.

3150 —The humble address of. [*London,* 1651.] cap., 4°.* MH.

3151 —The lamentation of. [*London,*] *for J. Wright, J. Clark, W. Thackeray, and T. Passenger,* [1683?]. brs. L, O, HH.

3152 —Musgraves musle broken. [*London,*] *printed,* 1651. 4°.* LT, C, MR; CH, Y.

3153 —A true and exact relation of the great and heavy pressures. *Printed,* 1650. 4°. LT, O, C, LIU, EN; IU, MIU, MM.

3154 —A word to the wise. [*London,* 1646.] cap., 4°.* LT, A, DT; CH, MH.

3155 —Yet another word to the wise. [*London,*] *printed,* 1646. 4°.* LT, LIU, MR, DT; CH, WF.

3156 Musgrave muzzled: or the traducer gagg'd. *Newcastle, by S. B.,* 1650. 4°. EN.

3157 —[Anr. ed.] *By John Macock, for L. Lloyd, and H. Cripps,* 1651. 4°.* LT, LSC, EN, DT; WF.

Mushroom. 1682. *See* Hickeringill, Edmund.

3157A Music; or, a parley of instruments. *Printed,* 1676. 4°.* L; CH.

3158 Musick and mirth. *By T. H. for John Benson, and John Playford,* 1651. 12°.* O.

Musica Oxoniensis. A collection. Oxford, 1698. *See* Smith, Francis.

3159–61 Entries cancelled.

Musicall banquet. 1651. *See* Playford, John.

Musical companion. 1673. *See* Playford, John.

3162 The musicall compass. [*London,*] *for J. Gillibrand,* 1684. 4°.* L, O.

Musical entertainment perform'd. 1684. *See* Fishburn, C.

Musical shepherdess. [n.p., 1676.] *See* Pope, Walter.

Musicks hand-maide. 1663. *See* Playford, John.

Musicks recreation. 165[2?]. *See* Playford, John.

3163 **Mussell, Francis.** Good nevves for all true hearted subjects. [*London*], by R. H. for T. B., 1641. brs. LT, HH.

3164 —The prisoners observation. [*London*], *printed*, Feb. 4. 1645. brs. LT.

Mustur roll. 1655. *See* Brathwait, Richard.

Mutatus polemo revised. 1650. *See* C., P.

Mutatus polemo. The horrible. 1650. *See* B., A.

Mutiny maintained. [n.p., 1660.] *See* N., N.

Muttredas. Copy of a letter. [n.p., 1693.] *See* Mathuradasa.

3165 **Muys, Jan.** A rational practice of chyrurgery. *By F. Collins for Sam. Crouch*, 1686. 8°. T.C.II 157. L, C, LCS, LWL, MAU, GH; PCP, TORONTO ACAD. OF MED., WSG.

3166 A muzzle for Cerberus. *For R. Smithurst*, 1648. 4°.* LT, AN; CH, IU, WF, Y.

3167 The muzled ox. *For W. Hope*, 1650. 4°.* LT, LUG, OC, CK; CH, CLC, CU, MB, NU, WF.

3168 My bonny dear Shonny. [*London?* 1683.] brs. MH.

My dearly beloved Friends. [n.p., 1670.] *See* Hubbersty, Stephen.

3168A My dog and I. [*London*], *for F. Coles, T. Vere, J. Wright, and J. Clarke*, [1675]. brs. O.

My edict royal. [n.p., 1655.] *See* Thau.

3169 My Lord Dursley's answer to a paper, called, Mr. Cook's case. [*London*, 1679.] brs. MH.

3169A My Lord of Pembrokes speech to His Maiesty. [*London*], *printed*, 1648. 4°.* LT; CH.

3170 My lord, this paper comes to your lordship's hands. [*London*, 1689.] brs. L; MH.

3171 My lord, We the Commons of London, in Common-hall assembled, being deeply sensible. [*London*, 1680.] brs. L, C, LG, HH; MH.

3171A My wife. *For R. Marriot*, 1660. 8°.* C.

3171B My wife will be my master. [*London*], *for F. Coles, T. Vere, J. Wright, and J. Clark*, [1674–79]. brs. O.

3172 —[Anr. ed.] [*London*], *for F. Coles, T. Vere, I. Wright, J. Clarke, W. Thackeray, and T. Passenger*, [1678–80]. brs. L, CM, HH; MH.

3172A —[Anr. ed.] [n.p., 1690?] brs. L.

3173 **Myers, George.** A serious examination of a pretended answer. [*London*], *printed*, 1686. 4°.* L, LF; PSC.

3174 —The spiritual worship exalted. [n.p., 1687.] 8°. O, LF, MR.

3175 **Myhill, Samuel.** A proposal for raising the annual sum. [*London*, 1690?] brs. LG; Y.

3176 **Myles, Samuel.** A sermon preach't . . . December 20th. 1698. *Boston, by B. Green, and J. Allen*, 1698. 16°.* EVANS 833. MWA.

Myn heer. T. van C's answer. [n.p., 1690.] *See* C, T. van.

3177 **Mynsicht, Adrian Von.** Thesaurus & armamentarium medico-chymicum: or a treasury. *By J. M. for Awnsham Churchill*, 1682. 8°. T.C.I 495. C, LCS, GU; CLM, MH, WF, WSG, WU, HC.

3178 Mysogynus: or, a satyr upon women. *London, for John Langly, in Oxford*, 1682. 4°.* L, O; CLC, MH, NP.

3179 The mysteries of God finished. *For John Marshal*, 1699. 4°. L, OC, ORP; CLC, NU, WF, Y.

Mysteries of love. 1658. *See* Phillips, Edward.

Mysteries of Mount Calvary. 1686. *See* V., J.

Μυστηριον της ανομιας. That is. 1664. *See* Arnauld, Antoine.

Mysterium religionis. 1649. *See* Hammond, Henry.

Mistery Babylon. 1659. *See* Howgil, Francis.

3180 The mistery discovered. [*London*], *for I. Wright, J. Clark, W. Thackeray, and T. Passinger*, [1681–84]. brs. L, HH.

Mystery of afflictions. York, 1668. *See* Shipton, William.

3181 The mystery of Ambras Merlins. colop: *For the author, and sold by Benj. Billingsley*, [1683]. cap., fol.* L, O, EN; IU.

3182 —[Anr. ed.] colop: *For Benj. Billingsley*, 1683. cap., fol.* L, CM; CH, MH, MU, WF.

Mystery of astronomy. 1655. *See* Bagwell, William.

3183 The mystery of atheism. *For A. and J. Churchil, and sold by Rich. Gravell*, 1699. 8°. T.C.III 168. OCC, CS, MAU, NE, P; CH, IU, PPT, WF.

Mystery of godlines. [1654.] *See* C., I.

3184 A mystery of godlinesse. *Printed*, 1663. 4°.* O, LNC; CU, NU, WF.

Mysterie of iniquite. 1643. *See* Bowles, Edward.

3184A The mysterie of iniquitie, or, a remarkable relation. *Printed in February*, 1655. 4°.* HUTH.

Mystery of iniquity unfolded. 1675. *See* Allen, William.

3185 The mistery of iniquity unfolded: or the reason why all those Jesuits. [*London*, 1680.] cap., fol.* L, O, C, LG, MR; CH, LC, NU, PU, WF.

3186 The mystery of iniquity working. [*London*], *printed*, 1689. 4°.* T.C.II 258. L, O, C, MR, AU, DT; CLC, CU, MH, NU, WF, Y.

Mysterie of iniqvity yet working. 1643. *See* Bowles, Edward.

3187 Entry cancelled.

Mystery of Jesuitism. 1658. *See* Pascal, Blaise. Les provinciales.

Mystery of Jesuitism. 1679. *See* Pascal, Blaise.

3188 The mysterie of magistracy unvailed. *Printed*, 1663. 4°. L, O, C, LVF; CLC, MH, NU, PL.

3189 The mystery of mony-catching or the character of an importunate-dunn. *For D. M.*, 1678. 4°.* CN, MH, Y.

Mystery of phanaticism. 1698. *See* B., A.

3190 The mystery of prophesies revealed. *Printed*, 1660. 4°.* LT, O.

Mysterie of rhetorique. 1665. *See* Smith, John, *of Montague Close.*

3191 The mystery of the good old cause briefly unfolded. *Printed*, 1660. 8°. LT, C, OB, BC, DU; CH, MH, NCD, NU, WF, Y. (var.)

Mystery of the marriage song. 1656. *See* Troughton, William.

Mystery of the new fashioned goldsmiths. [n.p.], 1676.
See R., J.

Mystery of the temple. 1677. *See* Allen, William, *vicar of Bridgewater.*

Mysterie of the two ivnto's. [n.p.], 1647. *See* Walker, Clement.

Mystery of the vialls. 1651. *See* Parker, Robert.

3192 A mystery which the angels desired to look into. [*London*, 1647.] cap., 4°.* LT, CT; CH.

Mysticall wolfe. 1645. *See* Pagitt, Ephraim.

Μυθολογια. 1693. *See* C., R.

N

1 **N.** An epistle narrative of the barbarous assault and illegal arrest of Freder. Turvill. *Printed*, 1660. 4°.* LT, MR; CH, ZWT.

2 **N., A.** England's advocate. *By George Larkin, jun. to be sold by J. Nut*, 1699. 8°. L, LUG; CU, MH, MU, NC, WF.

2A Entry cancelled. Ghost.

3 [–] A letter from a gentleman in the city to a gentleman in the country about the odiousness of persecution. [*London*], *printed*, 1687. 4°.* L, O, CT, EN, DT; CN, MH, MWA, NR, Y.

3A ——[Anr. ed.] *Edinburgh, by John Reid*, 1688. 12°.* ALDIS 2766. EN; WF.

—Londons improvement. 1680. *See* Newbold, A.

N., B. Englands selected characters. 1643. *See* Breton, Nicholas.

4 —The true character tending to love. [*London*], *for R. Wodenothe*, 1647. 4°.* LT, DT; CH, CLC, CSS, MM, NC.

N., C. Cabinet of hell. 1696. *See* Nicholetts, Charles.

5 —The Duke of Monmouth, and Earl of Essex. [*n.p.*, 1680.] brs. O; CN, MBA.

—Dying man's destiny. 1682. *See* Nicholetts, Charles.

—Full and true account of the late blazing star. 1680. *See* Nesse, Christopher.

5A —Jesuita vapulans: or a whip for the fool's back. [*London*, 1681.] brs. O, C, MR; CH, CN, MH, WF, Y.

—Peace-offerings. 1666. *See* Nesse, Christopher.

6 —Reasons why the supreme authority of the three nations. *Printed at London, to be sold by Rich. Moone*, 1653. 4°.* LT, BC, DU, MR; CH, CN, IU, NC, TO, WF.

—Signs of the times. 1681. *See* Nesse, Christopher.

—True account of this present blasing-star. 1682. *See* Nesse, Christopher.

7 **N., D.** The figure of six. *For John Wright*, 1652. 12°.* CH.

7A ——[Anr. ed.] —, 1654. 12°.* CH.

8 —The Kings Maiesties receiving of the propositions for peace. [*London*], *by Jane Coe*, 1646. 4°.* LT, MR, DT.

9 —A letter from an old Common-Council-man to one of the new Common-Council. colop: *For W. Inghall*, 1681. cap., fol.* L, O, LG; CH, CN, MH, WF, Y.

10 Entry cancelled.

—Sir Politique uncased. 1660. *See* L'Estrange, *Sir* Roger.

11 **N., E.** The copy of a letter from Newcastle. *For E. E.*, 1646. 4°.* LT, DU, DT.

12 ——[Anr. ed.] *By John Field, for P. S., Febr.* 11, 1646/7. 4°.* LT, MR, EN, DT.

13 —A letter from New-Castle. *For E. E. the* 15. *of September*, 1646. 4°.* LT, O, OC, DT; Y.

13A —London's destroyer detected. *Printed*, 1666. 4°.* O, LG.

14 —London's plague-sore discovered. *For the author*, 1665. 4°.* L, O.

14A —London's sins reproved. *Printed*, 1665. brs. MH.

15 —Offices and places of trust not to be boucht [*sic*] or sold. *For Richard Marriot*, 1660. 4°.* L, O, LG, LL, LUG; CH, CSS, MH, WF, Y.

15A —Truth is strongest. 1672. 4°.* ORP; NHC, ZAP.

16 **N., F.** A method for executing the powers, relating to the militia. *For John Smith*, 1684. 8°.* L, LG, OC; CH, WF, Y.

—Narrative of the Earl of Clarendon's. Lovain, 1668. *See* French, Nicholas, *bp.*

16A **N., G.** The close hypocrite discovered. *Printed* 1654. 4°.* Y.

17 —A declaration to all His Majesties loving subjects. *Imprinted at York by Tho: Broad, reprinted at London*, 1648. 4°.* LT; MH, MIU, Y.

18 —A geographicall description of the Kingdom of Ireland. *By I. R. for Godfrey Emerson*, 1642. 4°. LT, O, C, LW, LIU, BLH; CH, IAU.

N., G. D. L. M. French alphabet. 1647. *See* DeLaMothe, G.

N., H. Evangelium regni. 1652. *See* Niclas, Hendrik.

—Figure of the true. 1655. *See* Niclas, Hendrik.

—First epistle. [n.p.], 1648. *See* Niclas, Hendrik.

—First exhortation. 1656. *See* Niclas, Hendrik.

—Introduction to the holy. 1649. *See* Niclas, Hendrik.

19 —A letter concerning Sir William Whitlock's bill. [*London*, 1694?] 4°.* L, O, CT, LSD, MR; CH, NGT.

—Letter sent to General Monk. 1659. *See* Nichols, Henry.

19A —A letter sent to Mʳ. Garway. [*London?* 1673.] cap., fol.* LUG, MC; MH.

20 —An observation and comparison between the idolatrous Israelites. *For L. Chapman*, 1659. 4°.* LT, O, OC, DUS; CSS, MH, NHC, NU, WF, Y.

—Plvs vltra: or Englands. 1661. *See* Hickman, Henry.

—Prophecy of the spirit. 1649. *See* Niclas, Hendrik.

—Revelatio Dei. 1649. *See* Niclas, Hendrik.

—Terra pacis. 1649. *See* Niclas, Hendrik.

—Yea and nay almanack. 1678. *See* Almanacs.

N., I. Vindication of truth. 1656. *See* Nayler, James.

N., J. Accomplished lady. 1684. *See* Norris, James.

20A —An account of the gaines of . . . William Lenthall. [*London*], *printed*, 1660. 4°.* WF.

—Ansvver to twenty eight queries. 1655. *See* Nayler, James.

—Behold you rulers. 1658. *See* Nayler, James.

—Cases of conscience. 1673. *See* Norman, John.

—Compleat arithmetician. 1691. *See* Newton, John.

—Door opened. 1667. *See* Nayler, James.

—King's prerogative. 1684. *See* Jenkins, David.

—Love to the lost. [n.p.], 1665. *See* Nayler, James.

—Milk for babes. 1661. *See* Nayler, James.

21 —A perfect catalogue of all the Knights of the . . . Garter. *For Anne Seile*, 1661. 4°.* LT, O, LL, LUG, CJ; CH, CN, MHL, NU, WF, Y.

22 —The plain mans defence against Popery. *For Tho. Parkhurst*, 1675. 8°. T.C.I 217. CII, CLC.

23 —Proh tempora! Proh mores! Or an unfained caveat. *By T. N.*, 1654. 4°.* LT; MH, WF, Y.

—Psalm of thanksgiving. [n.p.], 1659. *See* Nayler, James.

—Royall law and covenant. 1655. *See* Nayler, James.

—Salutation to the seed. 1665. *See* Nayler, James.

—Several papers. [n.p., 1659.] *See* Nayler, James.

23A —Strange news from Westminster of a monstrous . . . child. *For J. N.*, 1674. 4°. ASU.

23B —Threnos militarius. *Excudebat T. M.*, 1690. fol.* WF.

—To those who were in authority. 1660. *See* Nayler, James.

—What the possession. 1664. *See* Nayler, James.

N., L. Voice of the rod. 1668. *See* Stodden, Samuel.

N., M. Case of the kingdom. 1647. *See* Nedham, Marchamont.

—Discourse concerning schools. 1663. *See* Nedham, Marchamont.

—Independencie no schisme. 1646. *See* Nedham, Marchamont.

—Medela medicinæ. A plea. 1665. *See* Nedham, Marchamont.

—Ob pacem toti ferè Christiano orbi. 1679. *See* Newport, Maurice.

—Sereniss. Principi Carolo. 1665. *See* Newport, Maurice.

24 **N., N.** An account of the defeat of Count Teckely. colop: *By E. Mallet*, 1683. brs. L; CH.

25 —An account of the late proposals of the Archbishop. [*London*, 1688.] cap., 4°.* L, O, C, MR, EN, DT; CH, CN, MH, TU, WF, Y.

25A —An account of the proposals of the Arch-bishop of Canterbury. [*London*, 1688.] brs. L, O, C, HH, LIU; CH, MBA, MH.

26 —America: or an exact description of the West-Indies. *By Ric. Hodgkinsonne for Edw. Dod*, 1655. 8°. LT, O, LW, E, EN; CH, CN, LC, MH, NN, TU, RPJ, Y. (var.)

26A ——[Anr. ed.] *By R. H. for Edw. Dod*, 1657. 8°. L; MU, NHS, V.

27 —An answer to Monsieur De Rodon's Funeral of the mass. *At Douay*, 1681. 8°. L, O, LLP, DUS, E; CLC, CN, MBA, NU, TU.

28 —The blatant beast muzzl'd. [*London*], *printed*, 1691. 12°. L, O, C, AN, AU, ES; BBE, CH, CLC, LC, NRU, Y.

28A —The blessed martyrs in flames. *For John Dunton*, 1683. 12°. T.C.II 12. DU.

29 —A brief account, and seasonable improvement of the late earthquake. colop: *For Nathaniel Ponder*, [1675/6]. cap., 4°.* O.

30 —The Catholick answer to the seekers request. *For John and Thomas Lane*, 1687. 4°.* L, O, CT, MR, DT; CH, MH, MIU, NU, WF, Y. (var.)

31 ——[Anr. ed.] *Re-printed at Holy-Rood-House* [*Edinburgh*], 1687. 4°.* ALDIS 2683. EN, AU; CLC.

32 —The Catholick letter to the seeker. *For John Lane*, 1688. 4°.* L, O, LIL, CT, DT; CH, IEG, MH, NN, WF, Y.

33 Entry cancelled.

—Daily exercises. Paris, 1684. *See* Nepveu, Francois.

—Discourse concerning the rise. 1699. *See* Calamy, Edmund, *younger*.

—Dolefull fall of Andrew Sall. [n.p.], 1674. *See* French, Nicholas.

—English nunne. [n.p.], 1642. *See* Anderton, Lawrence.

—Examination of Tilenvs. 1658. *See* Womock, Laurence, *bp.*

—Expedition of His Highness. 1688. *See* Burnet, Gilbert, *bp.*

—Few plain reasons. 1688. *See* Barlow, Thomas, *bp.*

—French conquest. 1693. *See* Lawton, Charlwood.

34 —From a gentleman of Boston to a friend in the country. *Boston: by Samuel Green*, 1689. brs. EVANS 493. LPR; MBS.

35 Entry cancelled.

—Garland of pious and godly songs. Ghent, 1684. *See* Wadding, Luke. Small garland.

36 —The heu [*sic*] and cry: or, a relation. *For Roger Catflogger*, [1682?]. L, O, LSD, SP, DT; CH, CLC, KU.

—History of the Bohemian. 1650. *See* Comenius, Johann Amos.

—Lancashire Levite. 1698. *See* Carrington, John.

—Letter concerning the council. [n.p., 1686.] *See* Jenks, Silvester.

37 —A letter from a dissenter to his friend. *For W. Crooke*, 1689. 4°.* L, O, LW; CH, CN, MIU, NP, WF, Y.

38 ——[Anr. ed.] colop: [*Edinburgh?*], *re-printed*, 1689. 4°.* ALDIS 2906. EN; CH, CLC, NGT, NU.

39 —A letter from a gentleman in the countrey to some of his familiar friends. *Printed*, 1679. fol.* CT; CH, IU, MH, NU, WF, Y.

40 —A letter from Oxford, concerning Mr. Samvel Johnson's late book. *Oxford, printed*, 1693. 4°.* L, O, CS, EN, DM; CH, CN, MH, NU, TU, WF, Y.

41 Entry cancelled.

—Letter of advice to all the members. 1688. *See* title.

42 —A letter to a gentleman touching the treatise. *For A. Churchill*, 1690. 8°. T.C.II 284. L, O; CLC.

42A —A letter to a lord concerning a bill . . . East-India Company. [*London?* 1698.] brs. L, INDIA OFFICE; Y.

43 —A letter to a member of Parliament, in favour of the bill. *Printed, and are to be sold by Randal Taylor*, 1689. 4°.* L, O, OC, EC, LSD; CH, CN, MH, NU, TU, WF, Y.

44 [–] The letter which was sent to the author of The doctrine of passive obedience . . . answered. *For Tho. Harrison*, 1689. 4°.* T.C.II 352. L, O, C, DC, DT; CH, CN, NU, WF, Y.

45 [–] —Second edition. —, 1689. 4°.* DT; CLC, CN.
—Life of the Lady Warner. 1691. *See* Carisbrick, Edward.
—Modest apology for the students. 1681. *See* M., N.

46 —Mutiny maintained. [*London*, 1660.] 4°.* LT, O, LSD; CLC, MH.

46A —A narrative of all the proceedings in the drayning. *By A. W. for the use of the author*, 1661. 4°.* L.
—Nullity of the prelatique clergy. Antwerp, 1659. *See* Talbot, Peter.

47 —Old Popery as good as new. [*London*], *printed*, 1688. 4°.* L, O, C, DU, LSD, DT; CN, INU, IU, WF, Y.

48 —Old Popery as good, or rather then new. [*London*], 1688. 4°.* L, O, LIL, LW, DT.

49 Entry cancelled.
—Origo Protestantium. 1677. *See* Shaw, John, *of Whalton*.
—Polititians cathechisme. Antworp [*sic*], 1658. *See* Talbot, Peter, *abp*.
—Present interest of England. 1683. *See* Nalson, John.
—Refin'd courtier. 1679. *See* Casa, Giovanni della, *abp*.

50 No entry.

51 —Reflections upon Mʳ. Baxter's last book. *For Robert Clavil*, 1689. 4°.* T.C.II 305. L, O, C, EC, P; CH, CN, NU, WF, Y.

52 —Romes follies, or the amorous fryars. *For N. Nowell*, 1681. 4°.* L, O, BAMB, EN; CH, CN, LC, MB, MU, WF, Y.

53 —The scarlet gown, or the history of all the present cardinals. *For Humphrey Moseley*, 1653. 8°. LT, O, OC, CS, RPL, BQ; CH, CN, LC, MH, NU, TU, WF, Y.

54 ——[Anr. ed.] —, 1660. 8°. LT, C, NE, DT; LC, MB, MBA, MH, WF, Y.

55 —The sentiments of. *For Henry Brome*, 1679. 4°.* T.C.I 374. LG, OC, SC, EN, DT; CH, MH, NU, PL, WF, Y.

56 —Several letters written by some French Protestants now refug'd in Germany. *Printed, and are to be sold by Langley Curtiss*, 1690. 4°.* L, O, C, DU, EN; CH, IU, MH, NU, WF, Y.

57 —A short account of the present state of New-England, Anno Domini 1690. [*London*, 1690.] cap., 4°.* O, LLP; RPJ.

58 —Some reasons for annual Parliaments. [*London*, 1693?] cap., 4°.* L, O, BC, DT; CH, CLC, NU, WF, Y.

59 —Some remarks on Mr. Bois book. colop: *Printed and are to be sold by Randle Taylor*, 1689. cap., fol.* C, LLP, MC, DN, DT.

60 Entry cancelled.
—Three sermons. 1688. *See* Jenks, Silvester.
—Threefold alphabet. 1681. *See title*.

61 —A treatise concerning estates tayle. *For Iohn Grove*, 1641. 4°.* L, O, CT, MR, DT; CH, CLC, CSS, MH, MIU, WF.
—Treatise of the nature. Rouen, 1657. *See* Talbot, Peter.

62 —A true and perfect relation of the late and dreadful inundation. *Printed*, 1675. 4°.* L, O, MR; CH.

63 —Vox clamantis; or, a cry. *For W. H. to be sold by Richard Janaway*, 1683. 4°. T.C.II 6. L, O, OCC, CS, P; CH, MIU, PU, WF, Y.

N., O. Roman-church's devotions. [n.p.], 1672. *See* Woodhead, Abraham.

N., P. Bank of England. 1697. *See* H., P.

64 —An exact abridgment of all the trials. *By J. D. for Jonathan Robinson*, 1690. 8°. T.C.II 287. L, O, C, LIU, MR; CH, CN, NCL, TU, WF.

64A ——[Anr. ed.] *By J. D. for Awnsham Churchill*, 1690. 8°. CT, DU; CN, INU, MB, MIU, Y.

65 —The last nevves from the Prince of Wales. *Printed*, 1648. 4°.* LT, O, OC; MH, MU.

N., S. Abraham in arms. Boston, 1678. *See* Nowell, Samuel.
—Aula lucis, or. 1652. *See* Vaughan, Thomas.

66 —A call to all the shepherds of Israel. *For John Norris*, [1681]. 4°. T.C.I 494. O, D; MH, PU.

67 —A catalogue of the names of all His Majesties justices. *For W. Davies*, 1680. fol.* T.C.I 421. L, LVF, BC, DU, MR; CH, CN, MH, NCD, WF, Y.

68 —Certain queries humbly proposed. *For P. L.*, 1658. * L; CH, CLC, CU, INU, TU, WF.
—Concordance to the Holy Scriptures. Cambridge, 1662. *See* Newman, Samuel.
—Discourse concerning natural. 1696. *See* Nye, Stephen.

69-71 Entries cancelled.
—Loyal garland. 1671. *See* M., S.

72 —Rawleigh redivivus or the life & death of . . . Shaftsbury. *For Thomas Malthus*, 1683. 8°. T.C.II 15. L, LLU, E, EN, DT; CH, CN, MH, NU, TU.

73 ——Second edition. —, 1683. 12°. T.C.II 35. L, OC, CS; CH, CN, MH, NP, WF, Y.

N., T. Best way of disposing. 1696/7. *See* Neale, Thomas.

74 —A brief narration of the tryall of Captain Clement Nedham. *By H. Hills, to be sold at his house and at Mrs. Michels shop*, 1653. 4°.* LT, O, MR.
—Choice collection. 1684. *See* Thompson, Nathaniel.

75 Entry cancelled.
—For supplying five milions. [n.p., 1696.] *See* Neale, Thomas.
—Gemmarius fidelis; or. 1659. *See* Nicols, Thomas.
—Letter to the right hononrable [*sic*], my Lord. [n.p., 1694.] *See* Ferguson, Robert.
—Medulla historiæ. 1687. *See* Howell, William.
—A modest and just apology for, or, defence . . . East-India Company. 1690. *See* T., N.

76 —A modest censure of the immodest letter to a dissenter. *Printed, and are to be sold by Randal Taylor*, 1687. 4°.* L, O, C, MC, EN, DT; CH, CN, MH, NU, WF, Y.
—Nineteen humble propositions. [n.p., 1643]. *See* Nutt, Thomas.

77 —Palæmon, or, the grand reconciler. [*London*], anno 1646. 4°.* L, O, CT, EN, DT; CH, CN, MH, NU, WF, Y.

78 —A poem on the Queen. *For Richard Baldwin*, 1695. fol.* L, O, CT, E; CLC, CN, MH, TU, WF, Y.

79 —The Pope's supremacy destroyed. colop: *For J. Wilkins*, 1682. cap., fol.* L, O, LG, MC, EN; CH, MH, PU, Y.
—Profitable adventure. 1693/4. *See* Neale, Thomas.
—Proposal concerning the coin. [n.p., 1695.] *See* Neale, Thomas.

80 Entry cancelled.
—Second part of the narrative. 1648. *See* title.
—Way humbly proposed. [n.p.], 1695. *See* Neale, Thomas.
—Way to make plenty. [n.p., 1696.] *See* Neale, Thomas.

81 **N., W.** A full relation of the great defeat given to the Cornish cavilliers. *For Edward Blackmore, May* 3, 1643. 4°.* LT.

82 —A letter from a country gentleman, to an eminent. [*London*, 1692.] brs. L, O, C, DC, HH; MH, NN, WF.
—Treatise of the principall grounds. 1641. *See* Noye, William.

82A —Dublin. January the 28th. A trve and perfect occurrence of . . . Dvblin. *For George Thompson*, 1642. 4°.* DN; MH.

83 —Trvth in two letters. *Printed*, 1642. 4°.* LT, O; CH, CLC, MH, MU.
Naboth's vinyard: or, the innocent traytor. 1679. *See* Caryll, John.

84 Nahash revived: or, the Church of Englands love to dissenters. colop: *Printed*, 1688. 4°.* O.
Nahash redivivus. 1649. *See* Harrison, John.

85 **Nailour, William.** A commemoration sermon, . . . Feb. 18, 1674[5]. *By Andrew Clark, for Henry Brome*, 1675. 4°.* T.C.I 203. L, O, C, LL, SC; CH, MH, NU, WF, Y.
Naked gospel. [n.p.], 1690. *See* Bury, Arthur.
Naked Popery. 1677. *See* Baxter, Richard.
Naked truth; the first part. [n.p.], 1680. *See* Croft, Herbert, *bp*.
Naked truth. The second part. 1681. *See* Hickeringill, Edmund.

86 Entry cancelled.
Naked truth, in an essay. 1696. *See* Blanch, John.

87 The naked truth of the distillers case. [1698?] brs. LL.

88 The naked-truth; or, a new song. [*London*], *for J. Blare*, [1684–85]. brs. EUING 236. L, GU; MH.

89 Naked truth: or, a vvay. [*London*], *printed*, 1648. 4°.* LT, O, DT; CU, MIU, NU, Y.

90 Entry cancelled. Ghost.
Naked vvoman. 1652. *See* Brown, David.
[**Nalson, John.**] Animadversions upon a paper. [n.p., 1683.] *See* Settle, Elkanah.

91 [–] The character of a rebellion. *For Benj. Tooke*, 1681. fol.* L, O, LG, CS, MR, EN; CH, CU, MH, NU, WF, Y, AVP.

92 —The common interest. *For Jonathan Edwin*, 1677. 8°. T.C.I 293. L, C, OM, CS, DT; CH, CLC, MH, MIU, NS.

93 — —[Anr. ed.] —, 1678. 8°. L, O, C, YM, EN, CD; CH, CN, MH, NU, WF, Y.

94 [–] The complaint of liberty & property. *For Robert Steel*, 1681. fol.* L, O, C, MR, SP; CH, CN, MH, WF, Y, AVP.

95 [–] —[Anr. ed.] *Edinbvrgh, re-printed*, 1681. 4°.* ALDIS 2260. AU, E; IU, MH, WF.

96 [–] The countermine. *For Jonathan Edwin*, 1677. 8°. T.C.I 274. L, O, C, CE, DT; BN, CH, CN, LC, NU, TU, Y.

97 [–] —Second edition. —, 1677. 8°. L, O, CJ, E, DT; CLC, MB, MH, NU, TU, WF.

98 [–] —Third edition. —, 1678. 8°. T.C.I 315. L, O, C, DU, EN; CH, CLC, MM, NR, NU, PU, Y.

99 [–] —Fourth edition. *For Tho. Dring and John Leigh*, 1684. 8°. T.C.II 51. L, LW, CT; CH, CLC, MBA.

99A — —"Fourth" edition. —, *and are to be sold by Jos. Hindmarsh*, 1684. 8°. O, C; BN.

100 — —"Fourth" edition. *By H. Hills jun. for Tho. Dring, and John Leigh*, 1684. 8°. L, C, OM; CH.

101 [–] England bought and sold. *For T. O.*, 1681. fol.* T.C.I 441. L, O, CT, SP, GU; CH, CN, MH, PU, TU, WF, Y, AVP.

101A [–] —[Anr. ed.] [*Edinburgh*], *re-printed*, 1681. fol.* ALDIS 2265.9. L.

101B [–] An essay upon the change of manners. *For H. Rodes*, 1681. brs. O, LG; CN, MH.

102 [–] Foxes and fire-brands. *For Benjamin Tooke*, 1680. 4°.* T.C.I 406. L, O, C, EN, DT; CH, IU, MH, NU, PSC, WF, Y.

103 [–] —Second edition. —, 1681. 4°.* T.C.I 453. L, O, C, LF, DT; CLC, CU, MH, NHC, NP, TU, Y, AVP.

104 [–] — "Second" edition. *Dublin, by Joseph Ray for a Society of Stationers*, 1682. 4°. DIX 192. L, O, C, LF, DT; CN, NU, TO, TU, VC, Y.

105 [ ] "Second" edition. *Dublin, by Jos. Ray, for Jos. Howes, and are to be sold by Awnsham Churchill* [*London*], 1682. 8°. DIX 192. L, O, C, YM, DT; CH, CN, MH, NU, TU, WF, Y. (var.)
[–] —Third and last part. 1689. *See* Ware, Robert.

106 —An impartial collection . . . vol. I. *For S. Mearne, T. Dring, B. Tooke, T. Sawbridge, and C. Mearne*, 1682. fol. T.C.I 471. L, O, C, EN, DT; BN, CH, CN, LC, MH, NU, TU, WSC, Y, AVP.

106A — —[Anr. ed.] *For Thomas Dring*, 1682. fol. CP, CD; SYRACUSE.

107 — — . . . vol. II. *For S. Mearne, T. Dring, B. Tooke, T. Sawbridge, and C. Mearne*, 1683. fol. T.C.II 27. L, O, EN, DT; BN, CH, CN, LC, MH, NCD, NU, WSC, Y, AVP.

107A — — —[Anr. ed.] *For Tho. Dring, Benj. Tooke, Ch. Harper, Tho. Sawbridge, and Jo. Amery*, 1683. fol. CJ, DU, MR; NIA, PU, TU.

107B — — —[Anr. ed.] *For Thomas Dring, Benjamin Tooke, and Tho. Sawbridge*, 1683. fol. SYRACUSE.

108–9 Entries cancelled.
[–] King's prerogative. 1680. *See* Jenkins, David.

110 [–] A letter from a Jesuit at Paris. *Printed, and are to be sold by Jonathan Edwin*, 1679. 4°.* L, O, C, MR, DT; CH, IU, MH, NU, WF, Y.

110A [–] —[Anr. ed.] [*Dublin*], *reprinted* 1679. 4°.* CS, CD, DM, DT.

111 [–] The present interest of England; or, a confutation. *For Thomas Dring*, 1683. 4°.* T.C.II 63. L, O, CT, EN, DT; CH, CN, LC, MH, NC, TU, WF, Y.

112 [–] —Second edition. 1685. 4°.* LLL, LUG.

113 [–] The project of peace. *For Jonathan Edwin*, 1678. 8°. T.C.I 342. L, O, C, MR, EN; CH, CN, NU, TU, WF, Y.

114 [–] Reflections upon Coll. Sidney's Arcadia. *For Thomas Dring*, 1684. fol.* T.C.II 63. L, O, CS, DC, LLU; CH, CN, MH, TU, WF, Y.

115   [–] Toleration and liberty of conscience considered. *For Thomas Dring*, 1685. 4°.* T.C.II 123. L, O, CS, DU, EN; CLC, CU, MH, NU, TU, WF, Y.

116   —A true copy of the journal of the high court of justice. *By H. C. for Thomas Dring*, 1684. fol. T.C.II 83. L, O, CE, ES, DT; BN, CH, IAU, MH, NU, TU, WF, Y.

117   [–] The true liberty & dominion of conscience vindicated. *In the Savoy, by Tho: Newcomb, for Jonathan Edwin*, 1677. 8°. T.C.I 271. O, C, BC, E, DT; CH, MU, WF.

118   [–] —Second edition. *By Henry Hills, for Jonathan Edwin*, 1678. 8°. T.C.I 335. L, O, C, YM, DT; CLC, CN, MM, NU, TU, Y.

119   [–] The true Protestants appeal to the city. colop: *Printed*, 1681. cap., fol.* L, O, C, DU, MC; CLC, CN, MH, TU, WF, Y.

120   [–] —[Anr. ed.] colop: *Edinburgh, reprinted*, 1681. cap., fol.* ALDIS 2317. L, MR, EN.

121   [–] Vox populi, fax populi. Or, a discovery. *By S. R. for Benj. Tooke*, 1681. 4°.* T.C.I 441. L, O, LG, LSD, SP; CLC, MH, MM, WF, Y.

121A   **Nalton, James.** The cross crowned. *By D. M. for Sa. Gellibrand*, 1661. 8°. LW, OC; CLC, NN.

122   —Delay of reformation. *For Samuel Gellibrand*, 1646. 4°. L, O, C, EN, DT; CH, CN, MH, NU, WF, Y.

122A   —Gods great care of his good people. *By A. M. for Nathanael Webb*, 1665. 12°. CLC.

123   —Twenty sermons. *By R. H. and M. S. for Dorman Newman*, 1664. 8°. LCL, LW; MH, NU.

124   — —[Anr. ed.] *For Dorman Newman*, 1677. 8°. L, LCL, CT; MH.

    Name, an after-one. 1681. *See* Bampfield, Francis.

    Names, dignities, and places. 1642. *See* B., W.

125   The names of all the knights and burgesses in the House of parl: Nov. 3. 1640. [*London*, 1654?] cap., 4°.* CH, WF, Y.

126   Names of all the parishes. 1657. 4°. LW, LNC.

127   Entry cancelled.

    Names of 51 persons. [*London*, 1695.] *See* Briscoe, John.

127A   The names of several persons trading in . . . Exon. [*London?* 1698.] brs. L; MH.

128   The names of such members of the Commons. *Printed at London for John Francks.* 1642. brs. STEELE 2072. LT, O; MH, MHS.

129   —[Anr. ed.] *By A. N. for John Franck*, 1642. brs. STEELE 2073. L, LNC; CH, MH, Y.

129A   The names of the aldermen . . . of London. colop: *For William Leach*, 1681. brs. O; WF.

129B   The names of the benefactors . . . to the Isle of Man. *For Joseph Clark*, 1674. brs. L, LNC.

129C   The names of the commissioners appointed. [*London*, 1698.] brs. MH.

130   The names of the committee of the House of Commons. *By B. Alsop*, 1641. 4°.* LT, LG, CT; CSS, WF, Y.

131   Entry cancelled.

    Names of the divines. 1642. *See* Names of the orthodox divines.

132   The names of the fellows of the King's College of Physicians. *Printed*, 1683. brs. L, O.

132A   The names of the field officers, captains. [*London*, 1680.] brs. LG, HH; MH.

132B   The names of the gentlemen elected by the petitioners for . . . Surrey. [*London*, 1648.] brs. MH.

132C   Yorkshire. ss. The names of the jury. [*London*, 1654.] brs. OP.

133   The names of the ivstices of peace. *For Thomas Walkley*, 1650. 8°. LT, O, C, OC; MHL, WF.

134   The names of the knights, citizens and burgesses of the House of Commons . . . 3 Novem. 1640 . . . until this present 11 of July 1648. *For John Wright.* 1648. 4°.* LT, O, C, DU, DT; CH, MH, NC, WF, Y.

135   The names of the knights, citizens, and burgesses, of the Parliament. *For Thomas Walkley*, 1652. 8°.* LT, O.

136   The names of the knights, citizens and burgesses. *Dublin, by Joseph Ray, for Robert Thornton*, 1695. brs. DIX 272. L, OQ, DT.

136A   The names of the knights of the counties, citizens . . . and barons. *By Richard Hodgkinson*, 1661. 8°. L.

137   The names of the Lord Lievtenants of every county. *Printed*, 1641[2]. brs. LT, LS, OC.

138   The names of the Lords and Commons assembled in the pretended Parliament. *By Tho. Harper, for Thomas Walkley*, 1646. 4°.* MADAN 1915. O; CH, IU, WF, Y.

139   The names of the lords and other the commissioners for Greenwich Hospital. colop: *By Charles Bill, and the executrix of Thomas Newcomb*, 1695. fol.* O.

139aA   —[Anr. ed.] [*London*, 1699.] fol.* L.

139A   The names of the lords of His Majesty's most honourable Privy-Council. *For T. M. Anno Dom.* 1688. brs. L, O, C; CH, INU.

139B   —[Anr. ed.] colop: *For T. M.*, 1689. brs. L, DU; WF.

140   The names of the Lords of His Majesties Privy Council. 1686. brs. LG (lost).

141   The names of the lords spiritual and temporal, who deserted. *For J. Nenton* [sic], 1688/9. brs. L, LPR; CH, CN, MH, PL, WF.

141A   —[Anr. ed.] [*Edinburgh*], re-printed, 1689. brs. ALDIS 2921.5. L, EN.

141B   —[Anr. ed.] The names of the Lords temporal in this present Parliament. [*London*, 1661.] 4°.* LPR; MIU.

142   The names of the members of Parliament. *By M. Simmons, for Tho. Jenner*, 1654. 4°. L, O, C, MR; CH, CN, MH, TU, WF, Y.

142A   The names of the members of the fishing society . . . [*Scotland*]. [*n.p.*, 1670.] brs. LUG, EN.

143   The names of the orthodox divines. *Printed at London for G. W.*, 1642. brs. O, LG, CJ; MH, NU.

143A   —[Anr. ed.] *Printed at London for John Franck*, 1642. brs. O; MH, MHS, WF.

143B   The names of the persons to be a new council of state . . . Feb. 23. *By Thomas Leach*, 1659. brs. O.

143C   The names of the towns and parishes in North and South-Wales wherein poor children. [*n.p.*], *by I. R.*, 1684. brs. L.

144   The names of those divines. *For Ioseph Hunscot and Edward Blackmore*, [1642]. brs. L, O, LUG; CH, MH, Y.

145   **Nanfan, Bridgis.** Essays divine and moral. *For William Leach*, 1680. 8°. T.C.I 373. L, LCL, DU; CLC, CN, NU, WF, Y.

145A ——[Anr. ed.] *For Sams. Evans,* 1680. 8°. wf.

146 ——[Anr. ed.] *London, for Sampson Evans, in Worcester.* 1681. 8°. L; CH, CN, NU.

147 ——Second edition. *London, for William Leach, and Sampson Evans in Worcester,* 1682. 8°. O.

148 **Nanfan, John.** An answer to a passage in Mr. Baxter's book. *London, for John Jones in Worcester,* [1660?]. 4°. L, CT, MR, SP; CLC, NU.

149 —By the honourable . . . a proclamation . . . August 29, 1699. *By W. Bradford, in New-York,* 1699. brs. EVANS 886. LPR.

150 —By the honourable. . . . a proclamation . . . September 22. 1699. *By W. Bradford, in New-York,* 1699. brs. EVANS 887. LPR; CN.

151 **Nani, Giovanni Battista.** The history of the affairs of Europe. *By J. M. for John Starkey,* 1673. fol. T.C.I 126. L, O, CE, E, DT; CH, CN, LC, MH, TU, WF, Y

    Naphtali; or. [n.p.], 1667. *See* Stirling, James.

    [**Napier, John.**] Bloody almanack. 1643. *See* Almanacs.

152 —A plaine discovery of the whole revelation of St. John. Fifth edition. *Edinbvrgh, for Andro Wilson,* 1645. 4°. ALDIS 1194. LT, O, C, BC, EN, BLH; CH, CN, NU, WF, Y.

153 [John] Napiers narration: or, an epitome. *By R. O. and G. D. for Giles Calvert,* 1641[2]. 4°.* LT, O, P; CH, MIU, NU, WCL, Y.

    Naps upon Parnassus. 1658. *See* Flatman, Thomas.

154 **Narborough, *Sir* John.** An account of several late voyages. *For Sam. Smith and Benj. Walford,* 1694. 8°. T.C.II 501. L, O, C, EN, DT; CH, LC, RPJ, WCL, WF, Y.

155 —A particular narrative of the burning in the port of Tripoli. *In the Savoy, by Tho: Newcomb,* 1676. fol.* L, LNM, OC, MR; CH, CN, Y.

    Narjann, Thomas, *pseud.* *See* Tanner, Thomas.

156 No entry.

    Narration of some church courses. 1644. *See* R., W.

157 Entry cancelled.

    Narration of the carriage and successe. 1643. *See* Briefe narration.

158 A narration of the expedition to Taunton. *For Samuel Gellibrand, May 23.* 1645. 4°.* LT; CSS, Y.

159 A narration of the great victory, (through Gods providence). [*London*], *for Edw. Husbands, Dec. 16.* [1643]. 4°.* LT, O; MH, NN, WF, Y.

    Narration of the grievovs visitation. 1641. *See* C., J.

160 Entry cancelled.

    Narration of the life of Mr. Henry Burton. 1643. *See* Burton, Henry.

161 A narration of the most material Parliamentary proceedings. *For Th. Jenner,* 1651[2]. 4°.* L, O, C, AN, DU, EN; CH, LC, MH, MIU, WF, Y.

162 A narration of the siege and taking of the town of Leicester. *By G. Miller,* 1645. 4°.* LT, O, MR, DT; CLC, Y.

163 Entry cancelled.

    Narration; or (second part). 1665. *See* Darell, John. True and compendious.

164 The narrative. [Begins] Come prick up your ears. *For Anthony Jackson,* 1681. brs. EN; CH, MH, NCD, Y.

165 A narrative, and an accompt concerning the hospital on Oxnontown-Green, Dublin. *Dublin, by Benjamin Tooke,* 1673. 4°. DIX 150. O, DI, DK, DN, DT; WF.

166 A narrative and declaration of the dangerous design. *For Edward Husband, June 8.* 1648. 4°.* LT, LG, BC, MR, ESS; CH, MH, MU, NU, WF, Y.

167 A narrative and testimony concerning Grace Watson. *For Thomas Northcott,* 1690. 4°.* LF; PH, PSC.

    Narrative history of King James. 1651. *See* Sparke, Michael.

168 Narrative of a great and bloudy fight at sea. 1652. 8°. LUS (dispersed).

168A A narrative of a maid lately burnt to death . . . by the force of a chymical spirit. *D. M.,* 1678. 4°.* LWL.

    Narrative of a strange and sudden apparition. [n.p.], 1680/1. *See* Saunders, Jonathan.

    Narrative of affares [*sic*] in the west. [n.p.], 1647. *See* Grenville, *Sir* Richard.

169 A narrative of affairs lately received from . . . Jamaica. *For Randal Taylor,* 1683. fol.* T.C.II 19. L, O, OC, CCA; CH, MB, MU, RPJ, Y.

    Narrative of all the proceedings. 1661. *See* N., N.

170 A narrative of an ill favoured attempt. [*London,* 1654.] cap., 4°.* MR; OWC, TO.

171 The narrative of Colonel Tho. Blood. *By R. Everingham,* 1680. fol.* L, C, LG, OC, BC; CH, CN, MH, PU, WF, Y.

172 Narrative of Edmond Nangle of Cloandaran. [*Dublin?*], 1665. 4°.* DIX 129. DN, DT.

173 Entry cancelled.

    Narrative of how things were carried. [n.p.], 1660. *See* Brief narrative how.

    Narrative of Mr. John Fitz-Gerrald. 1681. *See* P., H.

    Narrative of Mr. John Smith. 1679. *See* Smith, John, *of Walworth.*

    Narrative of Popish plots. 1678. *See* W., D. W.

    Narative [*sic*] of some of the sufferings. 1661. *See* Perrot, John.

    Narrative of some passages. 1670. *See* North, Francis Dudley, *baron.*

174 A narrative of the adventures of Lewis Marott. *For Edward Brewster,* 1677. 8°. L, O; MB, MH, WF.

175 A narrative of the apprehending, commitment, arraignment, . . . of John James. *Printed,* 1662. 4°.* L, C, AN, BAMB, MP, ENC; CH, IU, LC, MH, NU, TU, WF, Y.

176 A narrative of the apprehending of the arch-jesuite Blundel. [*London,* 1680?] cap., fol.* L, O, LLU; CLC, WF, Y.

177 Narrative of the apprehension, tryal, and confession of the five several persons. [*London*], 1677. 4°. LL.

178 Entry cancelled.

    Narrative of the battles. 1685. *See* Narrative of the late dreadful battels.

    Narrative of the cause. Amsterdam, 1677. *See* E., J.

    Narrative of the causes and events. 1659. *See* M., F.

179 A narrative of the cruelties & abuses acted by Isaac Dennis keeper. [*London,* 1684.] cap., 4°.* L, BR, DT: CH, MH, PH, PL, WF, Y.

180 A narrative of the demon of Spraiton [*i.e.* Spreyton]. *For Daniel Brown, and Thomas Malthus,* 1683. 4°.* T.C.II 28. L, O, C, OB, GU; WF.

181 Entry cancelled.
Narrative of the discovery of a college. 1679. *See* Croft, Herbert, *bp.* Short narrative.

182 No entry.

183 A narrative of the disease and death of . . . John Pym. *For Iohn Bartlet,* 1643. 4°.* LT, O, LW, BC, LSD; MH, NC, WF, Y.

183A A narrative of the dreyning of the . . . fenns. [*London?* 1660.] brs. L.
Narrative of the Earl of Clarendon's. Lovain, 1668. *See* French, Nicholas, *bp.*

183B Narrative of the election of Dr. Hough . . . Magdalen. colop: *For R. Baldwin,* 1688. cap., 4°. MB.

184 Entry cancelled.
Narrative of the engagement between His Majesties Fleet. 1666. *See* True narrative.

185 A narrative of the excommunication of Sir John Pettus. [*London*], *printed,* 1674. 4°.* L, O, C.

186 Entry cancelled.
Narrative of the fire of London. 1667. *See* Waterhouse, Edward. Short narrative.

187 A narrative of the great and bloody fight. *For T. M.,* 1677. fol.* L, LNC, SP; CH, CSS.
Narrative of the great success. 1658. *See* Doyley, Edward.

188 A narrative of the great victory obtained by the Lord Generall in Kent. *Printed at London by Robert Ibbitson,* 1648. 4°.* LT, LG; MH, MIU.

189 Entry cancelled.
Narrative of the hellish. 1679. *See* A just narrative.
Narrative of the holy life. 1683. *See* Heywood, Oliver.

189A A narrative of the horrid murther . . . James [Sharp]. [*London*], *for P. Brooksby,* 1679. 4°.* L.

190 A narrative of the late action between the French. *For Phillip Brooksby,* 1674. fol.* L, MR; CN, NP.

191 Entry cancelled.
Narrative of the late design. 1679. *See* Bury, John. True narrative.

191A A narrative of the late dreadful battels . . . Prince de l'Or. colop: *For R. Rumball,* 1685. brs. O, HH; MH.

192 Narrative of the late engagement between His Majesties fleet. [*London*], *by A. Purslow,* 1673. 8°. HR, NN, WF.

193 A narrative of the late extraordinary cure wrought . . . upon Mrs. Eliz Savage. *For John Dunton, and John Harris,* 1694. 8°.* L, O, CT, BAMB, GH; CH, CLC, NN, PBL, WSG, JF.

194 A narrative of the late Parliament, (so called) their election. [*London*], 1657[8]. 4°.* LT, O, CCA, LLU, BQ; CH, CN, MH, NU, WF, Y.

194A A narrative of the late proceedings of some justices . . . Lewes. [*London*], *printed,* 1670. 4°.* WF; ZWT.
Narrative of the late proceeds. 1656. *See* Jessey, Henry.

195 Narrative of the late success of the fleet. 1656. fol. O, LPR.

196 Entry cancelled.
Narrative of the late treacherous and horrid designe. 1643. *See* Brief narrative.

197 Entry cancelled. Ghost.

198 A narrative of the life, apprehension, imprisonment, and condemnation of Richard Dudly. *Printed,* 1669. 4°.* EN; CH.

199 A narrative of the meeting of some gentlemen, . . . Canterbury. [*London,* 1660.] brs. MIU.
Narrative of the miseries of New England. [n.p., 1688.] *See* Mather, Increase.

199A A narrative of the most deplorable death . . . Capt. William Bedlow. [*London*], *for P. Brooksby,* [1680]. 4°.* L.

199B The narrative of the most dreadful tempest . . . in Holland. *Cambridge* [*Mass.*], *by S*[*amuel*] *G*[*reen*] *for John Ratcliffe,* 1674. 4°.* MHS.

199C A narrative of the most material proceedings . . . against John Giles. [*London,* 1680.] cap., fol.* TU, WF.

200 Entry cancelled.
Narrative of the . . . murder committed on John Knight. 1657. *See* Full and the truest narrative.

201 A narrative of the northern affairs. [*London*], *printed,* 1659. 4°.* LT, O, BC, ESS; CLC.
Narrative of the planting. Boston, 1694. *See* Scottow, Joshua.

202 Narrative of the plotting. 1650. EN.

203 Entry cancelled.
Narrative of the Popes late fireworks. [1679.] *See* Bedloe, William. Narrative and impartial discovery.

204 A narrative of the Popish-plot. colop: [*London*], *for the information of all anti-plotters,* 1681. brs. OC; MH, Y.

204A A narrative of the proceedings against the vice-chancellor . . . of Cambridge. 1689. fol. O, BAMB.

205 Entry cancelled.
Narrative of the proceedings and tryal. [n.p., 1679.] *See* Johnson, Francis.

206 Narrative of the proceedings at Surry-Assizes. [*n.p.,* 1679.] fol. LL.

207 Entry cancelled.
Narrative of the proceedings at the assizes holden for . . . Surrey. [1679.] *See* True narrative.

208 Entry cancelled.
Narrative of the proceedings at the Old-Baily. 1679. *See* True narrative of the proceedings at the sessions-house . . . 30th of April.

209 A narrative of the proceedings at the sessions for London . . . 10th of December, 1679. [*London,* 1679?] cap., fol.* LG, MR; MH.

210 A narrative of the proceedings at the sessions, held in Justice-Hall. [*London*], *for John Millet,* 1676. 4°. MR.

210A A narrative of the proceedings at the sessions-house . . . [7–10 July]. D.M., 1675. 4°.* LG.

210B —[13–16 October 1675.] [*London*], *printed in the year,* 1675. 4°.* OB.

211 A narrative of the proceedings at the sessions-house. 1679. fol. EN.

212 A narrative of the proceedings at the sessions-house for London and Middlesex. Giving an account. colop: *For T. Davies,* 1680. fol.* LNC, MR; MH, WF.

212A —[Anr. ed.] colop: *For L. Curtis*, 1680. fol.* PU.

213 A narrative of the proceedings at the sessions-house in the Old-Bailey, April 21, 1680. [*London*, 1680.] fol.* L, LNC, MR.

213A A narrative of the proceedings in Ireland about Mr. Edward Bagshaw. [*London?* 1662.] cap., 4°. C.

Narrative of the proceedings of Sir Edmond Androsse. [n.p.], 1691. *See* Stoughton, William.

214 A narrative of the proceedings of . . . Fairfax. *Oxford, by H. H.*, 1649. 4°.* MADAN 2013. OW, CT; CSS.

215 A narrative of the proceedings of the committee of the militia of London. [*London*, 1659.] brs. LT, O; CH, CLC, MH.

215A A narrative of the proceedings of the elders, messengers . . . Bristol. *Printed*, 1694. 4°.* BB.

Narrative of the proceedings of the fleet. 1659. *See* Harrison, Mark.

216 A narrative of the proceedings of the General Assembly. 1689. 4°.* L; NHC, TO.

216A —[Anr. ed.] 1690. 4°.* NHC.

217 —[Anr. ed.] 1691. 4°.* L; NHC.

218 —[Anr. ed.] 1692. 4°.* L; NHC.

219 Entry cancelled.

Narrative of the proceedings of the northern armies. 1659. *See* G., H.

220 A narrative of the process against Madam Brinvilliers. *For Jonathan Edwyn*, 1676. 4°.* L, OB, MR, GU, DM; CH, CLC, MBM.

221 A narrative of the progress of his most Christian Majesties armes against the Dutch. *In the Savoy: by Tho. Newcomb.* 1672. fol.* L, O, LL, DU, SP; HR, CH, CN, MH, WF, Y.

222 —[Anr. ed.] *Reprinted Edinburgh*, 1672. 4°.* ALDIS 1952. EN.

Narrative of the royal fishings. 1661. *See* Smith, Simon.

223 A narrative of the sessions.[*London*], *for P. Brooksby*, 1673. 4°.* NU.

224 The narrative of the sessions. February 26, 1678/9. *For L. C.*, 1678–9. 4°.* NR, NU.

Narrative of the settlement. Lovain. 1668. *See* French, Nicholas, *bp.*

225 A narrative of the siege and surrender of Maestricht. *In the Savoy: by Tho. Newcomb.* 1673. fol.* L, O, OC, LNC, LSD; CH, CN, LC, PU, WF, Y.

225A —[Anr. ed.] *Reprinted at Dublin by Benjamin Tooke*, 1673. 4°.* HR.

226 A narrative of the state of the case between John Cromwel . . . and . . . his wife. *Printed*, 1652. 4°.* L, O, C.

227 A narrative of the success of the voyage of . . . Heneage Finch. *By I. R.*, 1661. 4°.* L, CS; CN, NN, WF.

228 Entry cancelled.

Narrative of the sufferings. Edinburgh, 1698. *See* Cullen, Francis Grant, *lord.* True narrative.

229 Entry cancelled.

Narrative of the unjust. [n.p.], 1671. *See* Hickes, John. True and faithful.

Narrative of the wicked plots. 1679. *See* Scott, Thomas.

230 A narrative, or journal of the proceedings . . . Breda. *In the Savoy, by Tho. Newcomb, and are to be sold by Robert Pawlet*, 1667. 4°. L, BC, DM; HR, CH, CN, MH, TU, WF, Y.

230A A narrative, or resumption of the severall proceedings in the . . . Admiralty. *Printed*, 1653. 4°.* L, LUG; MH.

231 A narrative presented to the Right Honovrable the Lord Major. *By Richard Cotes*, 1647. 4°.* LT, O, LG, DC, DT; CH, CLC, MH, NU, Y.

Narrative, together with letters. 1648. *See* Taylor, *capt.*

231A A narrative, wherein is faithfully set forth the sufferings of John Canne. *Printed*, 1658. 4°.* L, LG, LW; CH, NHC, VC, WF, Y.

232 The narrow way. *For James Vade*, 1681. 4°. L, O, BC; CH, NU, WF.

232A **Nash, John.** A poem, condoling the death of K. Charles II. *For Randal Taylor*, 1684/5. fol.* L, O, OP; CH, CLC, WF, Y.

233 **Nasir Al-Din, Muhammad ibn Muhammad al-Tusi.** *Binæ tabulæ geographicæ. Typis Jacobi Flesher: prostant apud Cornelium Bee*, 1652. 4°. L, O, EN, GH, DT; CH, MU, NN, WF, Y.

233A **Nasmyth, Arthur.** Divine poems. *Edinbvrgh, for James Miller*, 1665. 8°. ALDIS 1798. L, O, EN, GU; MH.

233B **Nathan, Isaac, *rabbi*.** [Hebrew] Tractatus de patribus. *Typis E. Cotes impensis G. and H. Eversden*, 1654. 4°. O, CCA, SHR, WCA, A; OHU, Y.

234 Entry cancelled.

Nationall assembly of Scotland. 1641. *See* Church of Scotland.

235 A national catechism. 1687. 12°. L.

National covenant. Edinburgh, 1660. *See* Church of Scotland.

235aA National land-bank in Exchange-ally . . . January the 23d, 1695. [List of directors.] [*London*, 1696.] brs. LG.

235A The nations address to the committee of grievances. *For R. Hayhurst*, 1689. brs. O; CH, MH, Y.

236 The nations agrievance. [*London*, 1679.] cap., fol.* L, C, LG, MR; CH, INU, MBA, MH, WF, Y.

236A The nations interest humbly offered. Briefly shewing . . . wool-manufacture. [n.p., 1677.] brs. MH.

237 The nations interest: in relation to . . . the Duke of York. *For James Vade*, 1680. 4°.* L, O, CT, BP, SP; CH, CN, MH, PU, WF.

238 The natives: an answer to the foreigners. *Sold by John Nutt*, [1700]. fol.* T.C.III 215. L, MR; CLC, CN, MH, TU, WF, Y.

239–40 Entries cancelled.

Nativity of Sir John Presbyter. [n.p.], 1645. *See* Overton, Richard.

Nativity of that most illustrious . . . Carolus Gustavus. 1659. *See* Gadbury, John.

Nativity of the most valiant. 1680. *See* Gadbury, John.

241 Natura exenterata: or nature unbowelled. *Printed for, and are to be sold by H. Twiford, G. Bedell and N. Ekins*, 1655. 8°. LT, O, LWL, LNC, E, AM, GU; CH, CU, NAM, WF, Y.

241A Natura lugens: or an elegy on . . . Robert Boyle. *For John Taylor*, 1692. brs. T.C.II 394. MH.

Natural allegiance. 1688. *See* Northleigh, John.

242 Entry cancelled.

Natvral and artificiall conclvsions. 1650. *See* Hill, Thomas.

Natural history of coffee. 1682. *See* Chamberlayne, John.

Natural history of Oxford-shire. Oxford, [1676]. *See* Plot, Robert.

Natural history of the passions. [n.p.], 1674. *See* Charleton, Walter.

Natural-philosophy improven. [n.p.], 1683. *See* Sinclair, George.

243 Entry cancelled.

Nature and power. 1668. *See* Owen, John. Nature, power.

Nature, nobility, character. 1684. *See* J., T.

244 The nature of a common-hall briefly stated. colop: *For J. Johnson*, 1682. brs. L, LG, MC, DT; MBA, MH, MU, PL.

Nature of church-government. [1690.] *See* Burthogge, Richard.

Nature of the drink. Oxford, 1659. *See* David, *Antiochenus.*

Nature, power, deceit. 1668. *See* Owen, John.

245 Entry cancelled.

Nature's cabinet unlock'd. 1657. *See* Brown, Thomas.

Natures dowrie. 1652. *See* S., L.

Nature's paradox. 1656. *See* Camus, Jean Pierre.

245A Natures wonder. [*London*], *Novemb. 12th.* 1664. *For E. Andrews.* brs. EUING 237. GU.

246 **Naudé, Gabriel.** The history of magick. *For John Streater*, 1657. 8°. LT, O, C, GU, DM; CH, CN, LC, MH, MMO, NP, TU, WF, HC.

247 —Instructions concerning erecting of a library. *For G. Bedle, and T. Collins, and J. Crook*, 1661. 8°. L, O, C, E, DT; CH, IU, LC, MH, NG, PL, Y, AVP.

248 —News from France. Or, a description of the library of Cardinall Mazarini. *For Timothy Garthwait*, 1652. 4°.* L, O, CT; CSS, MH, WF, Y.

Naufragia publicanorum. 1657. *See* C., J.

249 **Naunton, Sir Robert.** Fragmenta regalia. Written by. [*London*], *printed anno*, 1641. 4°.* L, O, C, DUS, EN; CH, IU, MH, PL, WF, Y.

250 —Fragmenta regalia, or observations. [*London*], *printed*, 1641. 4°.* L, O, C, DT; CH, IU, MH, PL, PU, WF, Y.

251 ——Third edition. —, 1642. 4°.* L, O, C, A, DT; CH, MH, NU, TU, WF.

252 ——[Anr. ed.] *By T. Mab and A. Coles, for W. Sheares*, 1650. 12°. L, O, MR; CH, CLC, IU, WF.

253 ——[Anr. ed.] *By G. Dawson, for William Sheares*, 1653. 12°. L, O, C, OC, E; CH, WF.

254 **Navailles, Philippe Montault de Bénac, duc de.** An exact account of the late engagement. *In the Savoy, by Tho. Newcomb*, 1669. 4°.* L, YM; CH, Y.

254A ——[Anr. ed.] *Edinburgh, A. Anderson*, 1669. 4°.* ALDIS 1869.5. EN.

255 The navall expedition, of the right honourable Robert, Earl of Warwick. *By Matthew Simons, for Hannah Allen*, 1648[9]. 4°.* LT, OC; CH, RPJ, WF.

Naworth, George, *pseud. See* Wharton, George.

256 **N[ayler], J[ames].** An account from the children of light. *For Thomas Simmons*, 1660. 8°. L, LF, OC; IE, MU, PH, PHS.

257 —All vain janglers. [*London*, 1654?] cap., 4°.* LT, O, LF, AN, BBN; MH, NCD, NU, PH, PSC, Y. (var.)

258 —An answer to a book called The Quakers catechism. *Printed*, 1655. 4°. LT, O, C, LF, AN, MR; NU, PH, PSC.

259 [–] —[Anr. ed.] —, 1656. colop: *For Giles Calvert.* 4°. L, O, LF, LIU, DT; CH, LC, MH, NCD, NU, PH, Y.

260 [–] An ansvver to some qveries put out by one John Pendarves. *For Giles Calvert*, 1656. 4°.* LT, O, LF, CT, BBN, AN, MR; MH, NU, PH, PSC, Y.

261 —An answer to the booke called the perfect Pharisee. [*London*, 1653.] 4°.* LT, LF, BBN, MR, EN; PH, PHS, PL, Y.

262 [–] An ansvver to twenty eight queries. *For Giles Calvert*, 1655. 4°.* LT, O, C, AN, LF, BBN, MR; CH, MH, MU, NCD, PH, PSC, Y.

263 —Antichrist in man. *For Giles Calvert*, 1656. 4°.* LT, O, C, LF, AN, BBN, MR; CH, MH, NCD, PH, PSC, WF, Y.

264 [–] Behold you rulers. colop: *For Thomas Simmons*, 1658. cap., 4°.* L, O, C, LF, OC, AN, MR; CLC, MH, Y.

265 [–] —[Anr. ed.] colop: *For Thomas Simmons*, 1660. cap., 4°.* LT, O, LF; CH, MH, NCD, NU, PH, PL, Y.

266 —The boaster bared. *For G. Calvert*, 1655. 4°.* LT, O, LF, AN, BBN; CH, CU, PH, PSC.

267 —Chvrches gathered against Christ. *For Giles Calvert*, 1654. 4°.* LT, LF, BBN; CH, PH, PHS, PL.

268 Entry cancelled.

[–] Copies of some few of the papers. [n.p., 1656.] *See* title.

269 —Deceit brought to day-light. *By T. L. for Giles Calvert*, 1656. 4°.* LT, O, C, LF, AN, BBN; CH, LC, MH, NCD, PH, Y.

270 Entry cancelled.

—Discovery of faith. 1653. *See* Farnworth, Richard.

270A —A discovery of the beast. *Printed*, 1655. 4°.* O; CH, MH.

271 ——[Anr. ed.] —, 1655, *for Giles Calvert.* 4°.* LT, C, LF, AN, BBN, MR; MH, PH, PL, PSC.

272 —A discovery of the first wisdom. *For Giles Calvert*, 1653. 4°.* LT, O, LF; MH, PH, WSG, Y.

273 ——[Anr. ed.] *For Giles Calvert*, 1653. *And now reprinted for Thomas Simmons*, 1656. 4°.* L, O, C, LF, AN, EN; CH, IU, MH, PH, PSC, WF, Y.

274 —The discovery of the man of sin. *For Giles Calvert*, 1654. 4°. LT, AN, BBN; CH, PL.

274A ——[Anr. ed.] —, 1655. 4°. O, LF, BR, MR; MH, NCD, PH, PSC.

275 —A dispute between. *For Gyles Calvert*, 1655. cap., 4°.* L, LF, OC, BBN; MH, NC, PH.

276 —A door opened to the imprisoned seed. *For Thomas Simmons*, 1659. 8°. L, O, LF.

276A ——[Anr. ed.] *Printed*, 1659. 4°. PH, PSC.

277 [–] —Second edition. —, 1667. 4°.* L, O, CJ, AN, BP, MR; BN, CH, MH, NU, WF, Y.

278 —A few words in answer. *For Thomas Simmons*, 1659. 4°.* L, LF, CT, BBN; CH, MH, PSC.

279 —A few words occasioned. [*London*, 1654.] 4°.* LT, O, LF, AN, MR; CH, PH, PL.

280   —A foole answered. *Printed and are to be sold by Giles Calvert*, 1655. 4°.* LT, O, LF, AN, BBN, MR; CH, IU, MH, PH, WF, Y.

281   —Foot yet in the snare. *For Giles Calvert*, 1656. 4°.* LT, O, LF, AN, MR; CH, MH, NCD, NU, PH, PSC, WF, Y.

281A [–] Give ear you gathered-churches. [*London*, 1660.] cap., 4°.* LF, LLP, OC, AN, LIU, MR; CH, MH, NCD, PH, PL, WF.

282   [–] Glory to God almighty. colop: *For Thomas Simmons*, [1659]. cap., 4°.* L, O, LF, CT, BBN, LIU; CH, MH, PH, PSC, RPJ, Y.

283   Entry cancelled.

       [–] Grand imposter examined. 1656. *See* Deacon, John.

284   [–] Having heard that some have wronged my words. colop: *For Thomas Simmons*, 1659. cap., 4°.* L, O, C, LF, BBN; CH, IE, MH, NU, PH, PSC, WF, Y. (var.)

285   —How sin is strengthned. colop: *For Thomas Simmons*, 1657. cap., 4°.* L, LF, OC, AN; IAU, MH, PH, PSC, Y.

286   ——[Anr. ed.] —, 1658. cap., 4°.* LF, MR; MH, PH, Y.

287   [–] —[Anr. ed.] —, 1660. 8°.* L, O, C, LF, BC; Y.

288   [–] —[Anr. ed.] [*London*, 1664–5?] cap., 4°.* L, O, LF; CH, MH, NC, PH, WF, Y.

289   [–] How the ground of temptation. [*London*, 1662?] cap., 4°.* L, LF; CH.

290   [–] The lambs warre. colop: *For Thomas Simmons*, 1657. cap., 4°.* L, O, LF; CH, MH, NU.

291   [–] —[Anr. ed.] *For Thomas Simmons*, 1658. 4°.* L, LF, OC, AN, BBN, MR; CH, MH, NCD, PH, PSC, WF, Y.

292   —A lamentacion (by one . . .). *For Tho. Wayt, in York*, 1653[4]. 4°.* LT, O, LF, OC, BBN; CH, PH, PSC, RPJ.

292A —A letter written by. *Printed*, 1660. 4°.* O, LF.

293   —The light of Christ. *For Giles Calvert*, 1656. 4°.* LT, O, C, LF, OC, AN, BBN; PH, PSC.

294   —Love to the lost. *For Giles Calvert*, 1656. 4°. LT, LF, OC, AN, LIU, MR; CH, IU, LC, PH, Y.

295   ——Second edition. —, 1656, 4°. L, O, C, LF, MR; CH, MH, NCD, PH, PL, Y. (var.)

296   [–] —[Anr. ed.] [*London*], *printed*, 1665. 4°. L, O, C, LF, AN, MR; CH, MH, NCD, NHC, PH, WF, Y.

297   [–] —[Anr. ed.] —, 1671. 4°. L, LF, DU; CH, MH, NCD, NU, PH, WF, Y.

297A [–] —[Anr. ed.] [*London*, 1671?] 4°. MH.

298   [–] A message from the spirit of truth. *For Thomas Simmons*, 1658. 4°.* L, LF, OC, AN, BBN, BP, DT; CH, CN, MH, NCD, NU, PH, WF, Y. (var.)

299   [–] Milk for babes. *For Robert Wilson*, 1661. 4°.* LT, O, LF, CT, BP; CH, MH, NU, PH, WF, Y.

300   ——Second edition. [*London*], *printed*, 1665. 4°.* L, C, LCL, LF, LIU; CH, MH, MIU, PH, PHS.

301   ——Third edition. *Printed*, 1668. 4°.* L, O, LF, AN, BR, DU; CH, CN, MH, NC, PH, TU, WF.

302   —The power and glory of the Lord. *For Giles Calvert*, 1653. 4°.* LT, C, LF; CLC, MH, PH, PSC, Y.

303   ——Second edition. —, 1656. 4°.* L, O, LF, OC, CT, AN; CH, CLC, MH, PH, PSC, WF.

304   [–] A psalm of thanksgiving. [*n.p.*], 1659. 4°.* LF, BBN.

305   —A publike discovery. *For Giles Calvert*, 1656. 4°.* LT, O, C, LF, AN, BBN, MR, DT; CH, LC, MH, NCD, PH, PSC, Y.

306   —The railer rebuked. [*London*, 1655?] cap., 4°.* LT, O, LF, AN, BBN, MR; CH, MH, NU, PH, PSC, RBU.

307   —James Nailor's recantation. *For Edward Farnham*, 1659. 4°.* LT, C, LF, OB, BR; CH.

308   [–] The royall law and covenant. *For Giles Calvert*, 1655. 4°.* L, O, LF, OC, CT, AN, MR; CH, MH, PH, PSC, WF, Y.

308A —Une salutation a la semence de Dieu. *Imprimé pour Robert Wilson*, 1661. 4°.* LLP.

309   —A salutation to the seede of God. *For Giles Calvert*, 1655. 4°.* L, LF, LG, OC, MR; CH, MH, PSC, WF, Y.

310   ——Second edition. —, 1655. 4°.* LT, LF; PL, PSC.

311   ——Third edition. —, 1656. 4°.* L, O, C, LF, CT, AN; LC, NU, PH, WF, Y.

311A ——Fourth edition. —, 1656. 8°. LF; CLC, IE, PH, PSC.

312   [–] —[Anr. ed.] *Printed*, 1665. 4°.* L, O, LF, AN, LIU, MR; CH, IE, NN, PH, PSC, WF, Y.

313   —Satans design discovered. *For Giles Calvert*, 1655. 4°.* LT, O, LF, BBN, MR; CH, MH, MU, PH, Y.

       [–] Saul's errand. 1653. *See* Fox, George.

314   —A second answer to Thomas Moore. *For Giles Calvert*, 1655[6]. 4°.* LT, O, LF, MR; CH, MU, PH, PSC, Y.

315   —The secret shooting. [*London*, 1655.] brs. LT, LF.

316   [–] Several papers of confessions. [*London*, 1659?] 4°.* LF, BBN; PSC.

316A —Several petitions answered. *For Giles Calvert*, 1653. 4°. O, LF, OC, MR; CH, MH, PH, PSC, Y.

317   —A short ansvver to a book. *For Giles Calvert*, 1660. 4°.* L, LF; NU, PH.

317A —Sinne kept out of the kingdome. [*London*, 1653.] brs. LF.

318   [–] Something further in answer. [*London*, 1655.] cap., 4°.* LT, O, LF, AN, BBN, MR; PH, PSC.

319   [–] Spirituall wickednesse. [*London*, 1654.] cap., 4°.* LT, LF, BBN.

320   [–] To all the people of the Lord. colop: *Printed*, 1659. cap., 4°.* O, LF, BBN; NU, Y.

321   —To the life of God in all. colop: *For Thomas Simmons*, 1659. cap., 4°.* L, O, LF, CT, BBN; CLC, IE, MH, PH, PSC, Y.

321A [–] To those who were in authority. *For Thomas Simmons*, 1660. brs. L, LF, DN; CLC, PH, PL.

322   [–] A true discoverie of faith. *For Giles Calvert*, [1655]. 4°.* LT; CH.

323   ——[Anr. ed.] —, 1655. 4°.* L, LF, AN, OC, CT; MU, PH, PSC.

324   —Truth cleared from scandals. [*London*], *printed*, 1654. 4°.* L, BBN.

324A ——[Anr. ed.] [*London*, 1654.] cap., 4°.* LF; PHS.

325   —Two epistles of. colop: [*London*], *printed*, 1654. cap., 4°.* L, LF, BBN; IE, NU, PHS, PSC.

326   [–] A vindication of truth. *For Giles Calvert*, 1656. 4°. LT, O, C, LF, AN, BBN; CU, IE, MH, NCD, PH, PSC, Y.

327   —Weaknes above wickednes. *For Giles Calvert*, 1656. 4°.* L, O, LF, AN, BBN, MR; LC, MH, PH, PSC, WF, Y.

328   —What the possession of the living faith is. *For Thomas Simmons*, 1659. 4°. LT, O, C, LF, MR; CH, IU, MH, NU, PH, WF, Y.

329   [–] —Second edition. *Printed*, 1664. 4°.* L, O, C, AN, MR, LF; CH, IE, LC, MH, NCD, PH, Y.

329A ——[Anr. ed.] 1676. 8°. PSC.

330   — —[Anr. ed.] [*London*], *printed*, 1676. 4°. L, LF; CH, MH, NN, WU, Y.

331   —Wickedness weighed. *For Giles Calvert*, 1656. 4°.* LT, O, C, LF, AN, BBN, MR; CH, IE, LC, MH, NCD, PH, PSC, Y.
Nayler's blasphemies. 1657. *See* Deacon, John.

332   **Naylier, John.** The new made Colonel. *By J. M.*, 1649. 4°.* LT; CH, CN, WF, Y.

333   **Naylor, James.** The right way. *For Tho. Parkhurst*, 1699. 8°. T.C.III 121. L, LW.

333A **Neale, J.** Good news from Heaven. *For W. Gilbertson*, 1664. NPT.

334   [**Neale, R.**] Foure propositions propounded by the Royalists in . . . Oxford. *For G. Cotton*, 1647. 4°.* MADAN 1933. LT, O, DU, MR; WF.

335   **Neale, Thomas.** About mending the coyn. colop: *By F. Collins*, 1695. brs. L, LUG; MH, NC.

336   [-] The best way of disposing of hammer'd money. colop: [*London*], *reprinted Feb.* 20. 1696/7. brs. L, MC, GH.

337   [-] —Second edition. colop: [*London*], *printed Feb.* 4. 1696/7. *Reprinted, with amendments, Feb.* 20. 1696/7. brs. L.

338   [-] —Third edition. colop: [*London*], *printed Feb.* 4. 1696/7. *Reprinted, with amendments, Feb.* 20. 1696/7. *And now printed again, March* 18. 1696/7. brs. L; MH, Y.

338A —For supplying five milions [sic] of money. [*London*, 1696.] brs. LPR; NC, Y.

339   —Fourteen hundred thousand pound. [*London*, 1697.] brs. L, DT.

340   —A further account of the proposals. colop: *By Freeman Collins*, 1695. cap., fol.* L.

340A —A million lottery was proposed. [*London*, 1694.] cap., fol.* WF.

341   —The national land-bank, together with money. [*London?* 1695/6.] brs. LG, LUG.

342   Entry cancelled.
[-] New abstract of the mine-adventure. [n.p., 1694.] *See* Mackworth, *Sir* Humphrey.

343   [-] A profitable adventure to the fortunate, and can be. colop: *By F. Collins*, 1693/4. brs. L, O, MC; MH, Y.

344   —The profitable adventure to the fortunate. Erected by. colop: *By F. Collins*, 1694. cap., fol.* L.

345   —The profitable adventure to the fortunate: lately begun [24 July]. *By F. Collins*, 1694. brs. L.

345A — —[Anr. ed., 22 August.] colop: *By F. Collins*, 1694. brs. L.

346   —A profitable and golden adventure. [*London*], 1695. brs. Y.

347   — —[Anr. ed.] [*London*, 1695.] brs. Y.

348   [-] A proposal concerning the coin. [*London?* 1695.] brs. L, LUG; NC.

349   [-] A proposal for amending the silver coins. *For the author, sold by R. Baldwin*, 1696. 8°. LUG, CT, LIU, GH; BN, IU, LC, MH, NC, PU, Y.

349A [-] A proposal for raising a million. 1694. fol.* LPR, LUG, EN.

349B [-] [A proposal, showing how clipt money] may pass, in an adventure. [*London*, 1695?] brs. L.

350   —Proposals of an adventure for the fortunate in fifty thousand tickets. 1693. brs. MC.

351   —The second drawing of the blank tickets. [*London*, 1695.] brs. L.

352   —A second profitable adventure. [*London?*], *reprinted March* 12, 1695. brs. L, LUG; MH, NC, Y.

352A — —[Anr. ed.] [*London*], *re-printed Novemb.* 2d. 1696. brs. LPR.

352B [-] Suppose for the year 1695. wanting five or six millions. [*London*, 1694.] fol.* NC.

352C —There is granted to their Majesties. colop: *By F. Collins*, 1694. cap., fol.* OC.

353   [-] To preserve the East-India trade. [*London?* 1692.] cap., fol.* BN, CH, MH, MIU, NC, WF, Y.

353A [-] —[Anr. ed.] colop: *By Freeman Collins*, 1695. fol.* L, C; MH, MIU.

353B [-] A translation of the articles established by . . . exchequer of Venice. [*London*, 1693.] fol.* CN, MH, Y.

354   [-] A way to supply the King's occasions. [*London*], *reprinted, Dec.* 28, 1694. brs. Y.

354A [-] —[Anr. ed.] colop: [*London*], *reprinted Decemb.* 23, 1695. brs. MH.

355   [-] —[Anr. ed.] colop: [*London*], *reprinted Feb.* 6th, 1695. brs. O; MH, NC, Y.

356   [-] A way humbly proposed on a fund. [*London*], 1695. brs. O, LUG; NC.

357   [-] A way to make plenty of money. [*London?* 1696.] brs. L, LUG; MH.

358   **Neale, Thomas,** *of Warneford*. A treatise of direction. *For Humphrey Robinson*, 1643. 12°. L, O; MH, WF.

359   — —[Anr. ed.] —, 1664. 12°. L.

360   **Neale, Walter.** A sermon preached . . . 23d of April, 1696. *For Abel Swall and Tim. Child*, 1696. 4°.* C, BLH, DT; WF.

361   The Neopolitan. *For R. Bentley*, 1683. 12°. T.C.II 27. L; CLC, CN, CU.
Near aproach. 1696. *See* Marsin, M.

362   Near Charing Cross. *By T. James*, 1687. brs. L.

363   **Neau, Elie.** An account of the sufferings of the French Protestants. *For Richard Parker, and sold by A. Baldwin*, 1699. fol.* L, O, LLP, ENC, DT; CH, CLC, MB, WF, Y.

363A A necessary abstract of the laws relating to the militia. *For Robert Vincent*, 1691. 8°. WF.

364   A necessary advice for profitably reading books of controversie. [1690.] * O, C, LL, LLP, CS, BAMB.

365   Entry cancelled.
Necessary and seasonable caution. [n.p., 1660.] *See* L'Estrange, *Sir* Roger.

366   A necessary and seasonable testimony against toleration. *By A. M. for Tho. Vnderhill*, 1649. 4°.* LT, O, CT, BC, SP, DT; IU, MH, MU, NU, WF, Y.

366A —[Anr. ed.] [*Edinburgh*, 1649.] 4°.* ALDIS 1375. L (impf.).

367   Entry cancelled.
Necessary companion or. 1685. *See* Reynell, Carew.

368   A necessary examination of a dangerous design and practice. *Printed at London by Tho. Brudenell*, 1649. 4°.* LT, C, DT; CH, MH, WF, Y.

Necessary family book. 1688. *See* W., R.

369   A necessary warning to the ministerie. *Edinburgh, by Evan Tyler,* 1643. 4°.* ALDIS 1088. L, CT, MR, EN, GM; CH, CN, NU, WF, Y.

369A A necessitated appeal. *Imprinted at London, May* 1645. 4°.* OC.

369B The necessitated virgin. [*London*], *for J. Deacon,* [1685?]. brs. O.

Necessity dignity and duty. 1685. *See* Hodges, Thomas, *of Soulderne.*

Necessity of a well experienced souldiery. Cambridg [*Mass.*], 1679. *See* Richardson, John.

Necessity of altering. [1690?] *See* A., W.

Necessity of Christian subjection. Oxford, 1642/3. *See* Morton, Thomas, *bp.*

Necessity of heresies. 1688. *See* Hill, Samuel.

Necessity of keeping still. 1698. *See* Stafford, Richard.

370   The necessity of monarchy. colop: *For W. Davis,* 1681. brs. L, O, MC; CH, CN, MH, PU, WF, Y.

371   The necessity of Parliaments. *Printed, and sold by Rich. Janeway,* 1689. 4°.* T.C.II 259. L, C, CCA, DU, E; CN, MH, MM, WF, Y.

371A —[Anr. ed., "by Rich. January."] —, 1689. 4°.* CH.

Necessity of reformation. Boston, 1679. *See* Mather, Increase.

Necessity of reformation, . . . second part. 1686. *See* Stratford, Nicholas, *bp.*

372   The necessity of setling the crown of England. colop: *Printed* 1689. cap., fol.* L, O, LG, MR; CLC, MH, WF.

372A —[Anr. ed.] [*Edinburgh*], *printed,* 1689. 4°.* ALDIS 2923. Y.

Necessity of some nearer. 1644. *See* Hartlib, Samuel.

Necessity of the absolute power. 1648. *See* Filmer, *Sir* Robert.

373   The necessity of the speedy calling a common-hall. [*London*], *printed,* 1648. 4°.* LT, O, LUG, CT, MR; CH, CN, MBP, MH, Y.

374   [**Nedham, Marchamont.**] An ansvver to a declaration of the Lords and Commons. [*London*], *for J. S.* 1648. 4°.* L, O; CH, MH, WF, Y.

375   [–] Anti-Machiavell. [*London*], *printed,* 1647. 4°.* LT, OC, CT, E, DT; CH, CU, MH, NU, WF, Y.

376   —The case of the common-vvealth of England, stated. *For E. Blackmore, and R. Lowndes,* [1650]. 4°. LT, O, C, CT, BC, P, DT; CH, CN, LC, MH, NU, TU, WF, Y.

377   ——Second edition. —, 1650. 4°. L, O, C, LNC, EN; HR, CH, IU, LC, MHL, NU, Y.

378   [–] The case of the kingdom stated. *Printed,* 1647. 4°.* LT, O, C, DU, EN; BN, CH, CN, MH, NU, TU, WF, Y.

379   [–] —Second edition. —, 1647. 4°.* L, O; CH, IU.

380   [–] —Third edition. —, 1647. 4°. LT, O, C, DU, EC, DT; IU, MH, Y, JF.

381   —Certain considerations tendered in all humility. *Printed,* 1649. 4°.* O, CASTLE ASHBY; MB, TU.

382   [–] A check to the checker of Britannicus. *By Andrew Coe,* 1644. 4°.* LT, O, CT, BR, DT; CH, CU, MH, NU, WF, Y.

383   [–] Christianissimus christianandus. Or, reason for the reduction. *By Henry Hills, and are to be sold by Jonathan Edwin,* 1678. 4°. L, O, C, EN, DT; CH, CN, MH, NU, WF, Y.

383A [–] —[Anr. ed.] *By Henry Hills, for Jonathan Edwin,* 1678. 4°. T.C.I 302. L, O, CS, DU, LNC, DT; CLC, MH, MU, PL, WF.

384   ——[Anr. ed.] *Printed* 1678, *and reprinted for Rich. Baldwin,* 1692. 4°. T.C.II 386. L, O, OC, LIU, DT; CH, MB, MIU, TU.

385   —The cities feast. *For Henry Marsh,* 1661. brs. LT.

386   [–] Digitus Dei: or, God's justice. *Imprinted at London,* 1649. 4°.* LT, O, C, EN, DT; BN, CH, CN, MBP, MH, NU, TU, WF, Y. (var.)

387   [–] A discourse concerning schools. *For H. H.,* 1663. 4°.* L, O, C, DU, EN; CH, MH, WF, Y.

388   [–] The excellencie of a free-state. *For Thomas Brewster,* 1656. 8°. LT, O, C, SP, EN; CLC, CN, MH, PU, WF, Y.

389   —The great accuser cast down. *By Tho. Newcomb, for George Sawbridge,* 1657. 4°. LT, O, LW, CT, BC; CH, MH, NU, WF, Y.

390   [–] Honesty's best policy. [*London,* 1678.] cap., 4°.* L, O, CT, DU, EN, DT; CH, CN, MII, NU, TU, WF, Y.

391   [–] Independencie no schisme. *For Rob. White,* 1646. 4°.* LT, CT, MR, DT; CH, MH, MWA, NU, Y.

392   —Interest will not lie. *By Tho. Newcomb,* 1659. 4°. LT, O, C, DU, EN; HR, CH, CN, MH, NU, WF, Y. (var.)

393   [–] The lavvyer of Lincolnes-Inne reformed. [*London*], *printed,* 1647. 4°.* LT, O, CS, AN, DU, DT; CH, CN, MH, NU, WF, Y.

394   [–] The levellers levell'd. [*London*], *printed,* 1647. 4°.* LT, O, LVD, OC, OW; CH, CU, MH, NU, PU, Y.

395   [–] Loyalty speakes truth. [*London,* 1648.] cap., 4°.* LT; CU, MH, Y.

396   [–] The manifold practises and attempts of the Hamiltons. *Printed at London,* 1648. 4°.* LT, O, CT, YM, EN, DT; CH, MBP, MH, MU, WF, Y.

397   [–] Medela medicinæ. A plea. *For Richard Lownds,* 1665. 8°. L, O, C, MAU, E, DT; BN, CH, CLC, NAM, WF, Y, HC.

397A [–] A most pithy exhortation delivered. [*London*], *printed,* 1649. 4°. LT; CH, CU, MH, NN, WF.

398   [–] News from Brussels, in a letter. [*London*], *printed,* 1660. 4°.* LT, O, C, BC, DU; CH, CN, MH, TU, Y.

398A [–] —[Anr. ed., "newes."] —, 1660. 4°.* L, OC; CSS, MH, PL, WF.

399   [–] The pacquet-boat advice. *For Jonathan Edwin,* 1678. 4°.* L, O, CT, MR, EN; CLC, CN, MH, NU, WF, JF.

400   [–] A pacquet of advices and animadversions. *Printed,* 1676. 4°. 50 pp. L, O, C, DU, MR, GU; CH, CN, LC, MH, TU, Y.

401   [–] —[Anr. ed.] —, 1676. 4°. 74 pp. C, LW, DU, WCA, EN; CH, CN, MU, TU, WF, Y. (var.)

402   [–] A plea for the King, and kingdome. [*London*], *printed,* 1648. 4°.* LT, O, C, BC, DU; CH, CN, MH, NU, WF, Y.

403   [–] A second pacquet of advices. *Printed at London, and are to be sold by Jonathan Edwin,* 1677. 4°. L, O, C, MR, EN; CH, CN, LC, MH, NP, NU, TU, WF, Y.

404   —A short history of the English rebellion. *Printed,* 1661. 4°.* L, O, LVF, OC, CT, CD; CH, IU, MH, TU, WF, Y.

405 —The solemn league and covenant, commonly call'd the Scotch covenant. [*London*, 1680.] brs. L, LG, OB, HH, LNC; CH, CLC, MH, WF, Y.

406 [–] The true character of a rigid presbyter: . . . to which is added, a short history of the English rebellion: compiled in verse. *By the assignes of J. Calvin, and are to be sold by Z. Crofton*, 1661. 4°. L, O, LLP, MR, EN; CLC, IU, MH, NPT, JF.

407 [–] —Second edition. —, 1661. 4°. L, OB, DU; CH, NP.

408 **Nedham, Thomas.** A treatise of a consumption. *For the author, to be sold at his house; and Eliz. Harris*, 1700. sixes. T.C.III 172. L, OR; NAM.

Needful corrective. [n.p., 1659.] *See* Vane, *Sir* Henry.

409 Entry cancelled.

Needham, G. *See* Needham, Walter.

410 **Needham, Robert.** Six sermons. *By M. Clark for Walter Kettilby*, 1679. 8°. T.C.I 339. L, O, C, DU, LSD; PL, WF, Y.

411 **Needham, Walter.** Disquisitio anatomica. *Typis Gulielmi Godbid, venales apud Radulphum Needham*, 1667. 8°. L, O, C, E, DT; BN, CLC, CU, MIU, NRU, PL.

412 **Needler, Benjamin.** Expository notes, . . . Genesis. *By T. R. & E. M. for Nathanael Webb and William Grantham*, 1655. 8°. LT, O, C; CLC, MH.

413 Entry cancelled.

Neesham, T. *See* Nesham, Thomas.

414 A negative voyce. [*London*], *printed*, 1659. 4°.* LT, O, LSD; CH, CN, MH, MIU, NU, Y.

Neglected virtue. 1696. *See* Hopkins, Charles.

Negotiations of the embassadors. 1691. *See* Boyer, Pierre.

Negotiations of Thomas Woolsey. 1641. *See* Cavendish, George.

Nehemiah, or. Oxford, 1670. *See* Parry, John, *bp.*

414A Prov. 22.6. Nehtupeh peisses ut mayut. [*Cambridge, Mass.: Samuel Green*, 1687?] 8°. MHS.

Nehushtan: or, a sober. 1668. *See* Wilson, Joseph.

Nehvshtan: or, John Elliot's. 1694. *See* Forbes, James.

414B Neighbours farewel to his friends. [*n.p.*, 1670.] brs. L.

414C **Neile, Sir Paul.** It is desired by . . . [disputed election]. [*London*, 1677.] brs. LPR.

415 **Nelme, John.** England's royal stone. *By Ja: Cottrel, for Henry Fletcher*, 1660. 4°.* LT; MWA, NU, Y.

416 **Nelson, Abraham.** A perfect description of Antichrist. *By T. F.*, 1660. 4°. O, EN; CH, CU, NU.

417 [**Nelson, Robert.**] Transubstantiation contrary to scripture. *For Dorman Newman*, 1688. 4°.* T.C.II 247. L, O, C, E, DT; CH, MIU, NU, TU, WF, Y.

418 **Nemesius, bp.** The character of man. *For Rob. Crofts*, 1657. 12°. L, LW, OC, DC; WF.

419 —Νεμεσιου . . . Περι φυσεως ανθρωπου βιβλιον . . . de natura hominis. *Oxonii, e theatro Sheldoniano*, 1671. 8°. MADAN 2891. L, O, C, EN, DT; BN, CH, MH, MMO, WF, Y.

420 **Nendick, Humphrey.** A book of directions. [*London*, 1677?] cap., 4°.* L.

421 —A compendium of the operations . . . of . . . the popular-pill. For its speciall vertues. [*London*, 1675?] cap., 4°.* L; WF.

422 —A compendium of the operations, . . . of . . . the popular-pill. Which hath. [*London*, 1676?] cap., 4°.* L.

423 —A compendium of the vertues, . . . of . . . Nendicks-popular-pill. *Printed*, 1674. 4°.* L.

423A —Nendick's popular-pill. [*London*, 1670?] brs. L.

423B —The vertues of . . . Nendick's popular-pill. [*London*, 1670.] brs. L. (var.)

Νεοφυτω-αστρολογος: the. 1660. *See* Gadbury, John.

Νεοφυτοπρεσβυτερος, or. [n.p.], 1648. *See* Goodwin, John.

Neuporto. *See* Newport.

424 [**Nepos, Cornelius.**] Collections out of the late Lord Chief Justice Hale's Pomponius Atticus. *Printed*, 1689. fol.* L, O; Y.

425 —. . . De vita excellentium imperatorum. *Impensis Abelis Swalle, & prostant venales apud Staffordum Anson*, 1691. 8°. C, LW, AN, EC, GU, DT; CLC, IU, MB, NCD, WF, Y.

425A ——[Anr. ed.] *Impensis Abelis Swalle*, 1691. 8°. CS.

426 ——[Anr. ed.] *Prostant apud Joannem Jones*, 1699. 8°. C.

426A ——[Anr. ed.] *Prostant apud S. & J. Sprint, & J. Nicholson*, 1700. 8°. L; MH.

426B —Excellentium imperatorum vitæ. *Oxoniæ, e theatro Sheldoniano*, 1697. *Excudebat Johan. Crooke*. 8°. AN, DCH, MC, MR; CLC, FU, MH, VC.

427 —The life & death of Pomponius Atticus. *By W. Godbid, for W. Shrowsbury*, 1677. 8°. T.C.I 272. L, O, C, NPL, DT; CH, CLC, CN, INU, LC, NCD, Y.

428 —The lives of illustrious men. *Oxon, for Hen. Cruttenden, to be sold by Anth. Stephens*, 1684. 8°. L, O, C, OM, MR; CH, CN, OCI, TU, WF, Y.

429 ——Second edition. *For John Weld*, 1685. 8°. T.C.II 139. L, O, CT, DT; CH, IU, PL, NP, PBM, PL.

429A ——Third edition. *For J. Weld*, 1699. 8°. CDA, WF.

430 —Cornelii Nepotis vitæ excellentium imperatorum. *Oxonii, e theatro Sheldoniano*, 1675. sixes. MADAN 3066. L, O, DT; CCC, PL.

431 ——[Anr. ed.] —, 1678. 12°. MADAN 3185. L, C.

432 ——[Anr. ed.] —, 1687. 12°. T.C.II 224. L, O; OLU, Y.

433 ——[Anr. ed.] *Apud Sam. Smith*, 1688. 12°. T.C.II 232. L, CT.

434 ——[Anr. ed.] *Oxoniæ, e theatro Sheldoniano*, 1697. *Excudebat Johan Crooke*. 8°. L, O, LW, CT, AN, MR; CLC, Y.

Neptunes address. 1661. *See* Tatham, John.

435 Neptunes fair garland. *By I. M. for I. Deacon*, 1676. 8°.* CM.

436–7 Entries cancelled.

Neptune's raging fury. [1695?] *See* Parker, Martin.

437A [**Nepveu, François.**] The daily exercises of a Christian life. *Printed at Paris* 1684. 8°. L, O, C, DUS, WARE; CLC, CN, TU, WF, WG. (var.)

437B [–] —Second edition. *Printed at S. Omers, by Ludovicus Carlier*, 1689. 12°. FARM; TU, WF.

437C —The method of mental prayer. [*St. Omer*], *by Thomas Hales*, 1694. 12°. L, DU, FARM, WARE; Y.

438 **Neri, Antonio.** The art of glass. *By A. W. for Octavian Pulleyn*, 1662. 8°. L, O, C, AN, EN, DT; BN, CH, CLC, IU, MH, WF, Y.

439   Nero Gallicanus; or, the true pourtraicture of Lewis XIV. *Printed, and are to be sold by Randal Taylor*, 1690. 4°. L, O, CT, SP; CH, LC, V, WF, Y.

440   **Nesbitt, John.** A funeral sermon preached upon the death of . . . Mr. Thomas Gouge. *For John Marshall*, 1700. 8°. T.C.III 170. L, C, LCL, LW; CLC, MH.

440A **Nesham, Thomas.** A sermon preached. *By Tho: Brudenell, for John Benson*, 1642. 4°.* LW, CT, MH, MWA.

441   **Nesse, Christopher.** An antidote against Arminianism. *By R. Tookey, for Tho. Cockerill*, 1700. 12°. T.C.III 211. L, LCL, CS, RPL; MH, NU, Y.

441A [–] An astrological and theologigal [sic] discourse. *For Langley Curtis*, 1681. 4°.* O; MH.

442   No entry.

443   —A Christians walk and work. [London], *for Dorman Newman*, 1678. 8°. T.C.I 310. L, LCL, CS, ENC; CLC, MH, NU, WF, Y.

444   ——Second edition. *Printed and are to be sold by John Harding*, 1678. 8°. L, LW, GU; Y.

444A ——"Second" edition. —, 1679. 8°. T.C.I 336. L.

445   —A chrystal mirror. *By J. C. for the author, and to be sold by him*. 1679. 8°. L, LCL, LW, CS, AN; MB, MH, NU, WF.

446   —A compleat and compendious church-history. *By T. H. to be sold by Jacob Sampson: and by Jonathan Wilkins*, 1680. T.C.I 404. CS, EN; CH, NU, WF, Y.

447   ——Second edition. *For the author*, 1681. 8°. T.C.I 433. L, LCL, LG, DM, DT; CLC, CU, IU, MH.

448   —A compleat history and mystery . . . first volume. *For the author; sold by Tho. Parkhurst*, 1690. fol. T.C.II 329. LCL, CS, BR, MR; CH, IU, NU, PPT, RBU, Y.

449   —A compleat history and mystery of the Old and New Testament. *By Tho. Snowden, to be sold by Tho. Parkhurst: and Jonathan Robinson*, 1696. fol. L, BR, MR; CLC, IU, MH, NU, V, Y.

450   [–] The crown and glory of a Christian. *For D. Newman*, 1676. 8°. T.C.I 250. O, C.

451   [–] —Third edition. *Boston: by Samuel Green for John Griffin*, 1684. 8°. EVANS 358. LC, V.

451A [–] —"Third" edition. *Boston in New England, by Samuel Green for Thomas Adams*, 1684. 8°. SE.

452   [–] The devils patriarck. *For John Dunton*, 1683. 8°. T.C.II 15. L, O, LW, CT, DU; CH, CN, MH, NU, TU, WF, Y.

453   —A distinct discourse and discovery. *For the author, and are to be sold by him*. 1679. 8°. L, O, C, LW; CU, MH, NU, RBU, WF.

454   —A divine legacy. *By T. S. and sold by T. Parkhurst, and J. Robinson*, 1700. 8°. LW; MH, NU, WF, Y.

455   —The fourth volume of the sacred history . . . New-Testament. *By Thomas Snowden for the author*, 1696. fol. L, LW, CS, MR; KQ, MH, NU, PPT, Y, AVP.

456   [–] A full and true account of the late blazing star. colop: *For J. Wilkins, and J. Sampson*, 1680. cap., 4°.* L, O, YM; CLC, MH, WF.

457   [–] A key (with the whip) to open the mystery. [London], *by Richard Janeway*, 1682. 4°.* L, O, LVD, OB; CLC, MH, NR, Y.

457A [–] —[Anr. ed.] [London], *by T. Snowden for the author*, 1682. 4°.* WF.

457B [–] —[Anr. ed.] [London], *By F. Saunders for the author*, 1682. 4°.* PU.

458   [–] The Lord Stafford's ghost. [London], *printed*, 1680. fol.* L, O, CS, MC, MR; CN, IU, MH, Y.

458A [–] —[Anr. ed.] [London], *for T. Benskin*, [1680]. fol.* O, MR; CN.

459   [–] [Hebrew] Peace-offerings and lamentations. *For the author*, 1666. 4°.* L, O, LW; MBA.

460   —A philosophical and divine discourse blazoning. *For L. Curtiss*, 1681. 4°.* O, CASTLE ASHBY; CLC, LC, MBA, Y.

461   —A Protestant antidote. *For Dorman Newman*, 1679. 8°. T.C.I 357. O, LCL, CS, EN; CLC, IU, MH, NU, PU, WF.

462   —The second volume of the sacred history and mystery. *By Thomas Snowden for the author*, 1695. fol. L, LW, CS, MR; CH, MH, NU, PPT, Y.

463   [ ] The signs of the times. *For the author. And published by Langley Curtiss*, 1681. 4°. T.C.I 452. L, O, LCL, CT, YM; CLC, MH, NU, WF, Y.

464   —A spiritual legacy. *By H. Clark, for the author, and are to be sold by L. Curtis*, 1684. 12°. L, LCL, LW, CS, DT; CLC, MH, NU.

465   [–] A strange and wonderful Trinity. *For Langley Curtiss*, 1683. 4°.* L, O, MR, EN; CLC, WF, Y.

466   [–] A true account of this present blasing-star. colop: *For L. Curtis*, 1682. brs. L, O; CH, MH, PT, Y.

      [–] A whip for the fools back. 1681. *See* —A key (with the whip).

467   A nest of nunnes egges. *Printed at London for J. T.*, [1680?]. brs. L.

468   A nest of perfidious vipers. *For G. Bishop, Septemb. 21.* 1644. 4°.* LT, LW, OW; CH, CLC, MH, NU, Y.

469   A nest of plots discovered. [London], *printed*, 1679. brs. O; MH, Y.

470   A nest of serpents discovered . . . the Adamites. [London], *printed*, 1641. 4°.* LT, LCL, LG, OC, CJ, AN; IU, NU.

470A A net for a night-raven. [London], *for F. Coles, T. Vere, and J. Wright*, [1674-79]. brs. O; NN.

      Net for the fishers of men. 1686. *See* J., C.

471   The Netherland-historian. *Amsterdam, by Stephen Swart*, 1675. 8°. L, O, CT, MC, E, CD; CH, CN, LC, PL, WF, Y.

472   **Netherlands.** An account of the passages in the Assembly of. *Printed, and are to be sold by Richard Baldwin*, 1690. 4°.* T.C.II 299. L, O, CT, DU, LIU; CH, CLC, IU, NU, TO, WF, Y.

473   —The answer and resolvtion of the states of Holland. *Iuly, 12. London for J. H. and T. Ryder*, 1642. 4°.* LT.

474   —The answer of the States Generall . . . to the declaration of warr. *Hague*, 1674. 4°.* L, O, C, DU, EN; HR, CH, MBA, OSU, PU.

474A —An answer of the States-General . . . to the memorial . . . Novemb. the 17th 1674. [n.p., 1674.] 4°.* WF.

475   Entry cancelled.
      —Declaration of the Confederate princes. 1689. *See* New declaration.

476 —A declaration of the high and mighty lords, the states of Holland. *For G. Horton,* 1652. 4°.* LT.

477 Entry cancelled.
—Declaration of the lords. 1652. *See* —A declaration or manifest.

478 —A declaration of war . . . against . . . Sweden. *In the Savoy: by Tho. Newcomb,* 1675. fol.* L, O, OC, DU, LNC; CH, MIU, NC, NCD, TU.

479 —A declaration of war, by the States General, against the French. *Re-printed at Edinburgh,* 1689. brs. ALDIS 2880. L, HH, EN.

480 —A declaration or manifest of the high and mighty lords of the States Generall of the United Netherland provinces. *Amsterdam, by the widdow and heires of Hillebrandt Jacobsz van Wouw,* 1652. 4°.* LT, O, LL, CJ, BC, DT; HR, CH, CN, MH, WF, Y.

480A —A deduction penned to informe the King of Great Brittanie. *At the Hague. In the moneth of December* 1664. 4°. MH.

481 —An extract of the registers of the resolutions of the high and mighty lords, the States General of the united provinces, of the Netherlands . . . 14th. October. 1688. [*London,* 1688.] brs. L, O, CCA, MC, EN; CH, CN, MH, WF, Y.

482 —Extract of the States General their resolution. . . . 28th. October. 1688. [*London,* 1688.] brs. L, O, C, EC, HH; CH, CN, MH, TU, WF, Y.

483 [–] An extract out of the register, of the resolutions of the lords. *For Edward Husband, March* 30. 1649. 4°.* LT, O, MR; CH, MH, WF, WSC.

483aA —The generall exercise, ordered by . . . the Prince of Orange . . . infantrie. *Printed at the Hague by Jacob Scheltus,* 1688. 4°.* WF.

483A ——[Anr. ed.] *For William Marshall,* 1689. 4°.* L, O, MR, EN; CSS, IU, MH, MM.

483B ——[Anr. ed.] [*n.p.*], *reprinted,* 1689. 4°.* EN; WF.
—Laws and ordinances touching military discipline. Edinburgh, 1691. *See* Scotland. Privy Council.

484 —A letter from the States General. *At the Hague, anno* 1673. 4°.* L, O, C, CDC; HR, CH, MM, NP, OSU, WF, Y.

485 —The letter sent by the States General of the United Provinces. *By the assigns of John Bill and Christopher Barker,* 1673. fol.* L, O, C, DU, E; CH, CN, MH, TU, WF, Y.

486 ——[Anr. ed.] *Edinburgh, re-printed by His Majesties printers,* 1673. fol. ALDIS 1989. O, EN; MH.

486A ——[Anr. ed.] *Reprinted at Dublin by Benjamin Tooke, to be sold by Joseph Wilde,* 1673. 4°.* DIX 151. DK, DN.

486B —The letters patents of . . . granted to William Walcot. [*London,* 1693.] cap., fol.* L; CH, TU.

487 —La lettre des Estats Generaux. *Des assignés de Jean Bill et Christophle Barker,* 1673. fol.* LPR, MR; CH, MM.

487A —The lords ambassadours . . . propositions. *For H. T.,* 1644. brs. L, LG, EC; LEIDEN U., Y.

488 —An ordinance and instructions. *By T. M. for D. Newman,* 1674. 4°.* L, LPR, LUG; MH, NC.

489 —A placat of the high and mighty lords the States General. colop: *The Hague, by Jacobus Scheltus,* 1672. fol.* L, O, OC, MR; CH, CLC, CSS, Y.

489A —De propositien van . . . Ambassadeeren Extraordinair. *Ghedruct door M.B. voor Robbert Costock, 16. April* 1645. 4°.* WF.
—Propositions of the ambassadors. 1644. *See title.*

490 —Reply of the States General. [*Hague*], 1673. 4°. OJ, DU, EN.

491 —The resolvtion of the Estates. *By B. A. for R. VV.* 1648[9]. 4°.* LT, O, DN; MH.

492 —The treaty and articles of agreement between. *By J. Clowes.* 1650. 4°.* LT; HR.

492A —Two letters, one from the States-General. *For Jonathan Edwin,* 1672. fol.* L, O, LG, OC, MR; HR, CH, MH, MIU, NN, NS, WF, Y.

492B ——[Anr. ed.] *Edinburgh, re-printed by Evan Tyler,* 1672. 4°.* ALDIS 1965. EN; NN.

492C ——[Anr. ed.] *Reprinted at Dublin by Benjamin Tooke; to be sold by Joseph Wilde,* 1672. 4°.* DIX 148. DK.

493 **Nethersole, Sir Francis.** An addresse to the Lord Mayor. *Printed,* 1659.* CU.

494 [–] Another parcell of problems. [*London*], *printed,* 1648. 4°.* LT, C, LUG, LW, DT; CH, IU, MH, NU, TU, Y.

495 —Ὁ αυτο-κατακριτος. The self-condemned. *Printed* 1648. 4°.* LT, C, P, GU, DT; CH, IU, MH, NU, WF, Y. (var.)
[–] Αυτοκατακριτοι. Or. 1679. *See* Greene, Martin.

495A [–] Considerations upon the present state. *Printed,* 1642. 4°.* LT, C, LG, EC, DT; CH, CN, MH, TU, WF, Y.

496 [–] Parables reflecting upon the times. [*London*], *printed* 1648. 4°.* LT, O, LW, GU, DT; CH, CN, NU, Y.

497 [–] Problemes necessary to be determined. [*London*], *printed,* 1648. 4°.* LT, O, C, GU, DT; CH, CN, MH, NU, Y.

498 [–] A project for an equitable and lasting peace. [*London*], *printed,* 1648. 4°.* LT, O, C, LUG, DT; CH, CN, MH, NU, WF, Y.

499 [–] A strong motive to the passing of a generall pardon. [*London*], *printed,* 1648. 4°.* LT, C, LUG, GU, DT; CH, CU, LC, MH, NU, TU.

499A **Neurenberg, Frederick van.** There is lately arrived . . . a faithful physician. *Printed,* 1698. brs. L.

500 Neutrality condemned. colop: *For Henry Overton, December [i.e. January] 6.* 1642[3]. cap., 4°.* LT, O, LIU, LNC, DT; CN, MBP, MH, MIU, ZWT.
Neutrality is malignancy. [*n.p.*], 1648. *See* M., J.

501 **Nevay, David.** Nobiliss. ampliss. illustriss. dominis, D. Gilberto Erroliæ . . . theses. *Edinburgi, excudebat Gideon Lithgow,* 1648. brs. ALDIS 1346. E.
Neve, John. New almanack. [1641.] *See* Almanacs.

501A **Neve, R[ichard].** Nox & avrora Britannica. *Apud Jo. Martin, Ja. Allestry, Tho. Dicas,* 1661. 8°. L; CLC, Y.
Neve, Robert. New almanacke. 1664. *See* Almanacs.
Never faile. 1663. *See* Lloyd, David.

501B **Nevett, Thomas.** A treatise of consumptions. *By John Astwood: sold by Thomas Parkhurst and Brabazon Aylmer,* 1697. 8°. L.
Neville, Edward, *alias. See* Carisbrick, Edward.

502   [**Neville, Francis de.**] The Christian and Catholike ver-
        itie. *By T. P. and M. S. for H. Blunden,* 1642. 4°. LT, O,
        C, DU, P, DT; CLC, IU, MH, NU, WF, Y.

503   [–] The convertion of. *For H. B.,* 1644. 4°. L, YM; NU, Y.

503A **Neville, Henry.** Discourses concerning government.
        Printed, and sold by A. Baldwin, 1698. 8°. T.C.III 116. L, P;
        CLC, MH, NC, PL, WF.

504   [–] An exact diurnall of the parliament of ladyes. [*London*],
        printed, 1647. 4°.* MADAN 1922 . LT, O, EN; CH, Y.

505   [–] The Isle of Pines, or, a late discovery. *By S. G. for Allen
        Banks and Charles Harper,* 1668. 4°.* L, OC, BAMB, LNC,
        EN; CH, CN, LC, MH, RPJ, WSL.

506   [–] —[Anr. ed.] *For Allen Banks and Charles Harper,* 1668.
        4°.* L, O, C, CM, E; LC, MH, NP, RPJ, ZWT.

506A [–] —[Anr. ed.] *Reprinted at Dublin by Samuel Dancer,*
        [1668]. 4°.* SOUTHAMPTON PUB. LIB.

507   [–] The ladies, a second time, assembled in Parliament.
        [*London*], *printed,* 1647. 4°.* LT, O, CT, MR, EN; CH, CN,
        MH, MIU, WF, Y.

508   [–] The ladies parliament. [*London,* 1647.] cap., 8°.* LT,
        OB, CJ.

508A [–] Nevill versus Strood. The state of the case. [*n.p.,* 1656.]
        brs. L.

509   [–] A new and further discovery of the Islle [*sic*] of Pines.
        For Allen Bankes and Charles Harper, 1668. 4°.* L, C, OC,
        P; CH, MH, RPJ, Y, ZWT.

510   [–] Newes from the new exchange. *Printed,* 1650. 4°.* LT,
        O, LG, LSD, MR; CH, CN, MH, WF, Y. (var.)

511   [–] The parliament of ladies. Or divers. [*London*], *pinted*
        [*sic*] *in the yeare,* 1647. 4°.* LT, O, LVF, CJ, MR; CH, CLC,
        MH, Y.

512   [–] —Second edition. —, 1647. 4°.* LT, CT, EC, MR; EN;
        CJC, NN. (var.)

512A [–] A parliament of ladies: with their lawes. [*London*],
        1647. 4°. L, O; CH, CLC, MH, Y, ZWT.

513   [–] Plato redivivus: or. *For S. I.,* 1681[80]. 8°. L, O, C, AN,
        BC, LLU, CD; CH, CJC, LC, MH, NCD, NP, TO.

514   [–] —[Anr. ed.] *For S. I. and sold by R. Dow,* 1681. 8°.
        T.C.I 443. L, O, C, EN, DT; CN, MB, MHL.

515   [–] —Second edition. *For S. I. and sold by R. Dew,* 1681.
        8°. L, O, CS, DUS, LIU; CH, CN, MB, NU, TU, WF.

516   No entry.
        [–] Publisher or translator. [*London*], 1688. *See* Machiavelli,
        Niccolo.

517   [–] Shufling, cutting, and dealing. [*London*], *printed,* 1659,
        4°.* LT, O, C, DU, EN; HR, CH, CN, MH, WF, Y.

518   **Neville, Robert.** The absolute and peremptory decree.
        For Benj. Billingsley, 1682. T.C.II 1. L, O, C, CT, DT; CLC,
        MH, NU.

519   —An English inquisition. *By S. and B. G. for Benj. Tooke,*
        1673. 4°.* T.C.I 125. O, C, LL, CS; CN, WF.

520   —Goodness proved. *For Benj. Billingsley,* 1687. 4°.*
        T.C.II 205. L, CK, SC; CH.

521   —The great excellency. *For Benjamin Billingsley,* 1681.
        4°.* T.C.I 458. L, O, C, CK, DU, EC; CH, CLC, CU, PL, WF.

522   —The nature & causes of hardness of heart. *For Benj.
        Billingsley,* 1683. 4°.* T.C.II I L, C, CK, BANGOR, SHR; CH,
        NU, PL.

523   —The necessity of receiving the Holy Sacrament. *By
        J. D. for Benj. Billingsly,* 1679. 4°.* T.C.I 356. L, C, CK,
        LSD, MR; CH, NU, TSM, WF, Y.

524   —The poor scholar. *By Tho. Johnson, for Francis Kirkman
        and Henry Marsh,* 1662. 4°. L, O, C, LVD, DU; CH, CU, LC,
        MU, WF, Y.

525   —A sermon preached . . . August 18. 1678. *For Benj.
        Billingsley,* 1679. 4°.* T.C.I 327. L, O, LSD; NU, Y.

526   —Τα ανω the things above. *By J. R. for Benjamin Bill-
        ingsly,* 1683. 4°.* T.C.II I. L, C, CK, EC; NU, PL.

527   Entry cancelled. Date: after 1700.

528   **Neville, Thomas.** To the High Court of Parliament . . .
        the humble petition of. [*London,* 1654.] brs. LT.

        New abstract of the mine-adventure. [1698.] *See* Mack-
        worth, *Sir* Humphrey.

529   The new academy of complements. *For Samuel Speed,*
        1669. 12°. T.C.I 7. WF.

530   —[Anr. ed.] *For Tho. Rooks,* 1671. 12°. L; CN.

530A —[Anr. ed.] *Joshua Conyers,* [1680]. 8°. CM.

531   —[Anr. ed.] *For George Sawbridge,* 1681. 12°. CH.

531A —[Anr. ed.] *By I. Dawks, for Awnsham and John Churchill,*
        1698. 12°. L.

532   A new academy: or, the accomplish'd secretary. Second
        edition. *For Roger Clavill, and sold by T. Leigh and D.
        Midwinter,* 1699. 12°. T.C.III 100. O.

        New account of the alterations. [1700.] *See* Parker,
        Gustavus.

        New account of the present. 1688. *See* DuVignan, *sieur*
        des Joannots.

        New additions. 1675. *See* Blagrave, Joseph.

532A The new adventurers account given in by them . . .
        [draining fens]. [*London,* 1663.] fol.* LPR.

533   New advice to a painter. *Printed,* 1673. brs. L, LLU; CN,
        MH, WF.

533A New advice to a painter, &c. [*London,* 1679/80.] fol.* L,
        O, LLU, DT; CH, CLC, CN, MH, TU, WF, Y.

        New ayres and dialogues. 1678. *See* Simpson, Christopher.
        A compendium.

534   Entry cancelled. *See next entry.*

535   The new alleigeance; or. [*London*], *printed,* 1648. 4°.* LT,
        CT, DT; MH, NN.

        New almanack, after. 1663. *See* Almanacs. Blount,
        Thomas.

        New almanack. Aberdeen, 1690. *See* Almanacs.

536   A new anatomie: or character of a Christian. *For Robert
        Leybourne,* 1645. 4°.* LT, O; CH.

537   A new and accurate map of the world. [*London*], *to be sold
        by Tho: Jenner,* 1641. brs. O.

538   The new and better art of agriculture. [*London,* 1668?]
        brs. L, LPR.

539   A new and delightful ballad, called, Debauchery scared.
        [*London*], *for J. Bissel,* [1685?]. brs. L.

        New and easy English grammar. Amsterdam, 1675. *See*
        Heldoren, J. G. van.

New and easie institution. 1647. *See* Taylor, Jeremy, *bp.*

540　A new and easie method to learn to sing by book. *For William Rogers, 1686. 8°.* T.C.II 167. L, O, C, BAMB, DT; CH, CN, LC, MB, NN, Y.

New and easy method to understand. 1695. *See* Fourcroy, *abbé.*

541　A new and exact description of Muscovy. *For R. Baldwin, 1698. 4°.** L, O, LUG; CH, CN, LC, MH, PL, WF.

542　A new and exact draught, describing ye late sea-engagement. *Printed and sold by P. Lea, and by M. Tauuel,* [1692]. brs. O.

New and exact prognostication. Aberdeen, 1681. *See* Almanacs.

543　A new and further discovery of another great and bloody plot against . . . the Lord Protector. *For George Horton, 1655. 4°.** LT.

New and further discovery. 1668. *See* Neville, Henry.

New and further narrative. 1676. *See* S., N.

New and most exact account. Dublin, 1683. *See* Crafford, John.

New and needful treatise. 1668. *See* Feyens, Joannes.

New and perfect relation. [n.p., 1670.] *See* M., D.

544　A new and profitable invention for drying malt. [*London,* 1695?] brs. L.

545　The new and strange imprisonment of the . . . Quakers in . . . Bristol. [*London,* 1682.] 4°.* L, LF; PH, PSC.

546　A new (and too true) description of England. *Printed,* 1643. 4°.* LT, OC, BC, MR; CH, NCD, TU, WF, Y.

547　A new and true ballad of the poet's complaint. [*London*], *for F. Coles, T. Vere, J. VVright, and J. Clarke,* [1655–74]. brs. L, O, HH; MH.

548　A new and true declaration of the false treachery of the Scots. *For J. H.,* 1651. 4°.* LT, O, MR; WF, Y.

New and true description of the world. 1673. *See* C., S.

549　A new and true eccho. [*London,* 1648.] cap., 4°.* LT; Y.

549A　A new and true list of the House of Lords. *By Richard Baldwin,* 1680[1]. brs. C, CN, WF.

549B　—[Anr. ed.] *For Richard Davis, in Oxford,* 1681. brs. AVP.

550　Entry cancelled.

Aprill the 22th. Nevv and true nevves from Ireland. 1642. *See* Hallowes, John.

New and useful concordance. 1673. *See* Powell, Vavasor.

550A　A new and useful invention for light. [*London*], 1685/6. brs. EN.

New answer. [n.p., 1681.] *See* J., E.

New answer to an argument. [n.p., 1697.] *See* Prior, Matthew.

551　Entry cancelled.

New apparition of S. Edmund-bery Godfrey's ghost. 1681. *See* Pordage, Samuel.

Nevv army. 1645. *See* Brandon, John, *gent.*

New art of brewing. 1690. *See* Tryon, Thomas.

552　The new art of gardening. colop: *Printed, sold by E. Whitlock,* 1696. cap., 4°.* O.

New art of making . . . wines. 1691. *See* Y-Worth, William.

552A　The new art of thriving. Or, the way to get and keep money. [*London*], *by H. Brugis for J. Conyers,* [1689?]. brs. CSS.

553　—[Anr. ed.] *Worcester, S. Gamidge,* [1700?]. brs. L.

554　The new art to live without money. *For D. M.,* 1676. 4°.* MH.

New articles for peace. 1648. *See* S., R.

New Athenian comedy. 1693. *See* Settle, Elkanah.

New Athenians. 1692. *See* Penn, William.

New Atlantis. [n.p.], 1687. *See* Heyrick, Thomas.

New atlas: or. 1698. *See* C., T.

New-Babel's confusion. 1647. *See* Prynne, William.

554A　A new ballad being a comparison between one that cut off his own nose. [*London?* 1681.] brs. O; CH.

555　A new ballad, called a review of the rebellion. [*London,* 1647.] brs. LT, C.

555A　A new ballad, called Simony Fair. [n.p., 1675?] brs. L.

556　A new ballad, call'd The Greenwich hunting-match. [*London,* 1700.] brs. HH.

556A　A new ballad, called the Protestants prophesie. *For F. Coles, T. Vere, J. Wright, & F. Clarke,* [1676]. brs. L, O.

557　A new ballad, called, Trap. [1675.] brs. O.

557A　A new ballad, composed by a lover. [*London, c.* 1679.] brs. L.

557B　A new ballad declaring the excellent parable of the prodigal child. [n.p.], *for F. Coles, T. Vere, and J. Wright,* [1663–74]. brs. EUING 240. GU.

557C　—[Anr. ed.] *By and for A. M.,* [1690?]. brs. L.

557D　A new ballad for you. [*London?* 1650.] brs. L.

557E　—[Anr. ed.] [*London?* 1690.] brs. L.

558　A nevv ballad from Whigg-land. *For N. Whigg,* 1682. brs. L, O, MC, EN; CH, MH, NCD.

559　Entry cancelled. Date: [1625?] STC 1331.3.

560　A new ballad, intituled, A warning to youth. [*London,* 1690?] brs. O; MH.

560A　A new ballad intituled the stout cripple. [*London*], *for F. Coles, T. Vere, and W. Gilbertson,* [1658–64]. brs. EUING 241. GU.

560B　—[Anr. ed.] [*London*], *for F. Coles, T. Vere, and J. Wright,* [1663–74]. brs. EUING 242. GU.

561　—[Anr. ed.] [*London*], *by and for A. M.,* [1693]. brs. L.

New ballad of a famous German prince. 1666. *See* Birkenhead, *Sir* John.

561A　A new ballad of an amourous coachman. [*London*], *for P. Brooksby,* [1690?]. brs. O.

562　A new ballad of bold Robin Hood. *By and for W. O.,* [1695?]. brs. L.

563　A new ballad, of Jocky's iourney into England. *For P. M. and M. R.,* 1681. brs. L.

New ballad of King Edward. 1671. *See* Butler, Samuel.

564　A new ballad of King John. [*London*], *for P. Brooksby,* [1672–85]. brs. L, CM, HH.

565　A new ballad, of Londons loyalty. [*London,* 1680.] brs. O.

566　—[Anr. ed.] *For Richard Sanders,* 1681. brs. L, O, MC; MH, Y.

567　A new ballad of Robin Hood. *For A. M. W. O. and T. Thackeray,* [1695]. brs. L, CM, HH.

568   A new ballad of St. George and the dragon. *By and for W. O. and sold by J. Blare*, [*c.* 1700]. brs. L, O, HH.

568AA —[*Anr. ed.*] *By and for W. O.*, [1700]. brs. L.

568BA The new ballad, of the lass of Peaties mill. [*Scotland*, 1700?] brs. EN.

568A A new ballad of the Protestant joyner. [*London*], *for J. Clark*, [1681]. brs. MH.

568B A new ballad of the souldier and Peggy. [*London*], *for F. Coles, T. Vere, and W. Gilbertson*, [1658–64]. brs. O; MH.

568C —[*Anr. ed.*] [*London*], *for F. Coles, T. Vere, and* [*J.*] *Wright*, [1663–74]. brs. O.

569   A new ballad of the three merry butchers. *For J. Bissel*, [1685–95]. brs. EUING 235. CM, GU.

569A —[*Anr. ed.*] *For J. Bisset, and sold by J. Foster*, [1685–95]. brs. L.

570   A new ballad on the great victory at sea. *For A. B. and sold by Richard Baldwin*, [1692]. brs. HH.

571   A new ballad, or, the true-blew-Protestant dissenter. [*London*], *for W. Davis*, 1682. brs. L, O; MH.

572   A new ballad shewing how a prince of England. [*London*], *for F. Coles, T. Vere, and W. Gilbertson*, [1658–64]. brs. EUING 245. GU.

572A —[*Anr. ed.*] [*London*], *for F. Coles, T. Vere, and J. Wright*, [1663–1674]. brs. O.

573   A new ballad. The triumph of justice. [*London*, 1688?] brs. L, HH, DU.

574   A new ballade, to an old tune. [*London*, 1660.] brs. LT, O; MH.

575   —[*Anr. ed.*] *Printed at the Hague for S. Browne*, [1670?]. brs. L.

575A A new ballad to the praise of James D. of Monmouth. *Printed and sold by J. Grantham*, 1682. brs. CH, MH, OCI.

576   A new ballad, to the tune of, Good people. [*London*, 1680–85.] brs. L, C, HH; Y.

577   A new ballad, to the tune of, I'll tell thee, Dick. [*London*, 1684.] brs. L, O; CLC, MH.

578   A new ballad upon Dᵣ. Oates his retreat. colop: *For W. Brown*, 1681. brs. L, O; MH, Y.

579   A new ballad upon the land-bank. [*London*, 1696.] brs. L, HH; MH.

579A A new ballad upon the present conspiracy of the Papists. *For N. M.*, 1679. brs. MH.

579B A new ballad, with the definition of the word Tory. *For R. Lett*, 1682. brs. L; MH.

580   The new balovv. [*London*, 1670?] brs. L.

580A Nevv Bartholmevv fayrings: presented to several members of the juncto. *Printed*, 1649. 4°.* O.

580B A new bill drawn up . . . in reply to the ladies and batchelors petition. [*n.p.*, 1693.] cap., 4°.* L; IU, MH, WF, Y.

New birth. 1654. *See* Bartlet, Richard.

581   A new birth of the city-remonstrance. *For John Pounset*, 1646. 4°.* LT, DT; WF.

New bloody almanack. 1643. *See* Almanacs. Booker, John.

New book for children. 1681. *See* Crisp, Stephen.

582   New booke of common prayer. According to . . . Scotland. [*London*], *by Iohn Ioness*, 1644. 8°.* LT, O, E, EN; Y.

583   A new booke of common-prayer. [*London*, 1647.] cap., 4°.* LT, O, DU.

583A A new book of cyphers. *Sold by J. Nutting*, [1700?]. 4°. L.

584   A new book of instruments. *For W. Jacobs, and T. Dring*, 1680. 8°. T.C.I 405. O; CLL, LC, MHL, NCL.

584A —[*Anr. ed.*] *For William Jacob*, 1680. 8°. CP; CH, WF.

585   A new book of knowledge. *For G. Conyers*, 1697. 8°.* LLL, GU; CLC, MH, TU, WF, Y.

585A A new booke of merry riddles. *For C. Bates*, [1660]. cap., 12°.* CH.

585B —[*Anr. ed.*] [*London*], *sold by S. Lyne*, [1665]. 12°.* WF.

586   The new brawle, or Turnmill-street against Rosemary Lane. *Printed at London by Nan Quiet*, 1654. 8°.* LT.

586A The new broome. *For F. Coles*, [1641–80]. brs. CM.

587   Entry cancelled.

New bull-bayting. Nod-nol, 1649. *See* Overton, Richard.

588   A nevv carroll compyled by a burgesse of Perth. [*London*, 1641.] brs. L.

589   New carolls for this merry time of Christmas. *By H. B. for Andrew Kemb*, 1661. 12°.* O.

590   A new case put to an old lawyer. *For William Ley*, 1656. 4°.* LT, OC; CSS, PU.

New catalovge of the dvkes. 1644. *See* Walkley, Thomas.

591   A new catalogve of the names of the knights. Fifth edition. *For Thomas Walkley*, 1644. 8°.* LT, O, CT, DT, E; CH.

592   A new catch in praise of the reverend bishops. [*London*, 1690–91.] brs. HH; MH.

New catechisme; according. [*n.p.*], 1644. *See* Goode, William.

New catechisme commanded to be set forth, for the instruction of all those. 1647. *See also* C., E.

592A A new catechisme commanded to be set forth for the instructing of youth in . . . religion. *For H. P. sold by Francis Coles*, 1645. 8°.* CH.

593   The new Catholick ballad. *For E. Rydal*, 1681. brs. O; CH, MH, Y.

594   A new charge against J. C. [*London*], *printed*, 1647[8]. 4°.* LT.

595   New Christmas carrols. *By J. M. to be sold by W. Thackeray and T. Passinger*, [1662?]. 12°.* O.

596   —[*Anr. ed.*] *By T. H. for F. Coles, T. Vere, J. Wright, J. Clark, W. Thackeray, and T. Passinger*, 1681. 12°.* NNM.

596A The new claret-club. [*Edinburgh*], 1669. 4°. EN.

New collection of new songs. 1674. *See* Bulteel, John.

New collection of poems. 1674. *See* Bulteel, John.

597   A nevv collection of the choicest songs. [*London*], *printed*, 1676. 8°. T.C.I 246. O; CH, RHT, Y.

598   —[*Anr. ed.*] *For D. Brown, and T. Benskin*, 1682. 4°.* T.C.I 463. MH.

599   —[*Anr. ed.*] *By T. Haley*, 1682. 8°. MH.

600   A new-come guest to the tovvne. *For Matthew Walbancke, Iune the 5th.* 1644. 4°.* LT, YM; CH, CLC, WF, Y.

New conceited letters. 1662. *See* M., I.

600A A new copy of verses about interlopers. [*London*, 1681?] brs. MH.

600B A new copy of verses call'd The heiress's lamentation. *For J. Richardson*, [*c*. 1690]. brs. MH.

601 The new corant. *For F. Coles, T. Vere, J. Wright, and J. Clark*, [1674–79]. brs. O.

New court-contrivances. 1693. *See* Grascome, Samuel.

New court-songs. 1672. *See* Veel, Robert.

601A The new courtier. [*London*], *for F. Coles, T. Vere, and J. Wright*, [1663–74]. brs. O.

601B —[Anr. ed.] *By P. L. for F. Coles, T. Vere, and J. Wright*, [1663–74]. brs. O.

602 —[Anr. ed.] [*London*], *for F. Coles, T. Vere, J. Wright, J. Clarke, W. Thackeray, and T. Passinger*, [1678–80]. brs. EUING 246. L, O, CM, GU; MH.

603 A new creed. Consisting. [*London*], *printed*, 1642. 4°.* NU.

604 —[Anr. ed.] —, 1648. 4°.* LT; CH, MIU, MM, WF, Y.

604A The new crown garland. *For J. Back*, 1689. 8°. O.

605 A new declaration and engagement. *Printed at Dublin, and re-printed by W. Godbid*, 1660. brs. L, O, C, LG.

606 A new declaration and message presented to the Kings Majesty. *For C. Withrington*, 1648. 4°.* LT; NU.

607 A new declaration from eight regiments. *By J. C. and A. C. for G. Horton*, 1647. 4°.* LT, O, LG, MR; CU.

608 A new declaration erom [*sic*] the armie under . . . Fairfax. *For George Pleydell*, 1647. 4°.* LT, DT; CSS.

609 Entry cancelled.

New declaration in favour of the troopers. 1689. *See* Louis XIV.

610 Entry cancelled. *See next entry.*

610A A nevv declaration of the citizens of London to . . . Monck. *For G. Horton*, 1660. 4°. * L, O; MH.

611 A new declaration of the confederate princes. *For Tim. Goodwin*, 1689. 4°.* T.C.II 292. L, O, C, SP, DT; CH, MH, MU, TU, WF, Y.

612 A new declaration of the Generall Assembly. [*London*], *for G. W.*, 1648. 4°.* LT, O, AN, DT.

612A A new declaration of the Kings Majesties going to the Isle of Weight. *For G. Horton*, 1647. LSE; MH.

613 A nevv declaration of the last affairs in Ireland, . . . 2, of May, 1642. *By A. N. for John Franck*, 1642. 4°.* LT, O, LL, MR, DN; MH, MU, Y.

614 A new declaration out of Orient. *By R. A. and A. C.*, 1643. 4°.* LT, O; Y.

615 —[Anr. ed.] *Printed*, 1647. 4°.* LT; WF.

New declaration presented. Oxford, 1647. *See* Gardiner, James.

616 A new delightful ballad, called, Debauchery scared. [*London*], *for J. Bissel*, [1685–88]. brs. L, CM; MH.

New description of Paris. 1687. *See* Brice, G.

New dialogue between a burgermaster. 1697. *See* Puckle, James.

617 A new dialogue between Alice & Betrice. [*London*], *for J. Blare*, [1685–88]. brs. L, HH.

618 A new dialogue between Mr. Woodbee. colop: [*London*], *for T. Benskin*, 1681. brs. L, O; CH, MH, NC, AVP.

618A A new dialogue between Squire Ketch. *For A. H.*, 1699. brs. CN.

619 A new dialogue betwixt Heraclitus & Towzer. colop: *For T. B.*, [1681?]. brs. L, O; MH.

619A A new dialogue, or, a brief discourse between two travellers. *For Tho. Vere*, 1648. 8°.* WF.

New dialogues of the dead. 1683. *See* Fontenelle, Bernard Le Bouvier de.

New dictionary in five alphabets. *Cambridge*, 1693. *See* Littleton, Adam. Linguæ romanæ.

New dictionary of the terms. 1699. *See* E., B.

620 A new directory: compiled by these most grave, . . . divines. [*London*], *printed*, 1647. 4°.* LT; CH, TU, Y.

621 A new discourse about the fire of London. colop: *For R. Janeway*, 1682. cap., fol.* L, O; MH, NIC, Y.

622 A new discovery of a designe of the French. *For Ioseph Watson*, 1642. 4°.* LT, EC; WF.

623 A new discovery of a great and bloody plot. *For R. Smithurst*, 1648. 4°.* LT.

New discovery of an old intreague. [n.p.], 1691. *See* Defoe, Daniel.

624 A new discoverie of an old traveller. *Printed*, 1676. 4°.* Y.

625 A new discovery of hidden secrets. *For John Wright*, 1645. cap., 4°.* LT, YM, DT; CSS.

626 A new discoverie of Mr. Jermyn's conspiracye. *By T. F. for D. C., Iuly, 21*. 1642. 4°.* LT, EC.

627 A new discovery of old England. [*London*, 1648.] cap., 4°.* LT, OC, DT; CH, MH, MIU, NU, WF, Y.

New discovery of old pontificall practises. 1643. *See* Udall, John.

New discovery of severall passages. 1642. *See* S., W.

New discovery of terra incognita. 1693. *See* Foigny, Gabriel de.

New discovery of the horrid association. 1690. *See* G., J.

New discovery of the prelates. 1641. *See* Prynne, William.

628 A new discovery of the private methods of France. *For J. Weld*, 1691. 4°.* T.C.II 361. L, O, SP, DT; CH, CLC, MH, Y.

629 Entry cancelled.

New discovery of the sham-Presbyterian plot. 1681. *See* Carrol, James.

New disease. 1676. *See* L., J.

629A Entry cancelled.

New disorders of love. 1687. *See* Gibbs, Richard.

New disputation. 1642. *See* Price, Laurence.

Nevv distemper. Oxford, 1645. *See* Quarles, Francis.

New distemper. 1680. *See* Tomkins, Thomas.

629B A new ditty of the saylor and his love. *John Wright*, 1656. brs. CM.

630 A new ditty, shewing. [*London*], *for J. W., J. C., W. T., and T. P.*, [1681–84]. brs. L, CM.

631 A new diurnall of passages more exactly drawne up then heretofore. colop: *Printed at Oxford for H. H.*, 1643. 4°.* MADAN 1365. O, OC, LSD; CH.

632 A new Dutch song. [n.p., 1688.] brs. EN; MH.

633 A new elegie in memory of the right valiant, . . . Col. Rainsborough. *For Henry Cripps*, 1648. brs. LT; MH, Y.

634 A new engagement, or, manifesto. [*London*], *printed*, 1648. brs. LT, O; CH, MH.

635 New-England a degenerate plant. *Printed*, 1659. 4°.* O; LC, PH, RPJ, V, Y.

New-England almanack. Cambridge, [Mass.], 1685. *See* Almanacs. Danforth, Samuel.

Nevv-England pesecutors [*sic*]. [n.p., 1697.] *See* Maule, Thomas.

New England vindicated. [n.p., 1689.] *See* Mather, Increase.

New-Englands advice. [n.p.], 1644. *See* Lechford, Thomas.

New Englands crisis. Boston, 1676. *See* Tompson, Benjamin.

636 New-England's ensigne. *By T. L. for G. Calvert*, 1659. 4°. L, CT, BBN; CH, MH, MU, NN, RPJ, WCL, Y.

New-England's faction. 1690. *See* D., C.

New Englands first fruits. 1643. *See* Eliot, John.

New-England's present sufferings. 1675. *See* Wharton, Edward.

637 Entry cancelled.

New England's pretended Christians. 1660. *See* Smith, Humphrey. To New-England's.

New-England's tears. 1676. *See* Tompson, Benjamin.

637A A new English dictionary. *For Timothy Childe*, 1691. 8°. T.C.II 340. L, O, AN, LSC, AU; CH, CN, NN, TU, WF.

New English examples. 1685. *See* Leedes, Edward.

New English grammar. 1662. *See* Howell, James.

637B A new essay towards a true ecclesiastical history. 1679. 4°. ENC.

638 A new, exact, and most expeditious method of . . . fortifications. *Printed*, 1666. fol.* L, CASTLE ASHBY; Y.

638A A new expedient to raise money to carry on a vigorous war. [*London*, 1696?] brs. EN.

New experiments. [n.p.], 1683. *See* Grew, Nehemiah.

639 A new express from Ireland. *Reprinted Edinburgh, by the heir of Andrew Anderson*, 1690. brs. ALDIS 3058. L, EN.

New fairing. 1688. *See* Phillips, William.

640 A new-fashioned marigold. *For F. Coles, T. Vere, J. Wright, and J. Clarke*, [1674–79]. brs. L, O, HH.

New fiction. 1661. *See* Croxton, James.

641 A new found stratagem. [*London?*], *published*, 1647. 4°.* LT, O, C, MR, DT; MH.

New fund. [n.p., 1690.] *See* Roots, Thomas.

642 A new game at cards. [*London*], *for Francis Coles, John Wright, Tho. Vere, and William Gilbertson*, [1655–58]. brs. O.

642A A new garland, composed of fifteen . . . songs. [*London*], *published by J. Conyers*, [*c.* 1690]. 12°.* CM.

643 The new garland of delight compo,'d [*sic*] of wit. [*London*], *for J. Deacon*, [*c.* 1690]. 8°.* CHRISTIE-MILLER.

644 The new German doctor. [*London*], *for J. Deacon*, [1688–92]. brs. L, O, HH; MH.

New guide for constables. [1692.] *See* P., J.

645 **New Hampshire Province.** Acts and laws. *Boston, by Bartholomew Green, and John Allen*, 1699. fol.* EVANS 882. PHS.

645A —The answer of the House of Representatives to . . . the Earl of Bellomont's speech. *Boston, Bartholomew Green and John Allen*, 1699. brs. LPR.

645B New Haven's settling in New-England. *By M. S. for Livewell Chapman*, 1656. 4°. MWA, NN.

New help to discourse. 1669. *See* Winstanley, William.

New heresie. 1662. *See* Arnauld, Antoine.

New history of the Roman conclave. 1691. *See* B., W.

646 A new history of the succession. *For Ric. Chiswell*, 1690. 4°. T.C.II 320. L, O, C, DU, MC, CD; CH, IU, MH, NU, WF, Y.

647 A new hve and cry after Maior General Massey. *Printed at London*, 1652. 4°.* LT, OC.

648 A new ignoramus. *For Charles Leigh*, 1681. brs. L, O, LSD; CH, MH, TU, WF, Y.

New instructions to the guardians. 1694. *See* Penton, Stephen.

648A The new instructions to the officers . . . hearth-money. *For T. Basset*, 1685. 12°. O.

649 New intelligence from Ireland. *For Edward Blackmore, June 22*. 1642. 4°.* LT, O, C, EC, LNC, DN; CH, NN, WF, Y.

New invention for the sheathing. [n.p., 1675.] *See* Rastel, Thomas.

650 A nevv invention; or, a paire of cristall spectacles. [*London*], *for G. Bishop, June 7*. 1644. 4°.* LT, O, C, YM, AU; CH, CU, MH, WF, Y.

651 The new Irish Christmas box. [*London*], *for B. Deacon*, [1700?]. brs. L.

New Jerusalem. 1652. *See* Reeve, Edmund.

651AA The new jovial garland. *For J. Conyers*, 1688. 8°. O.

651A A new King anointed: with the manner. *For Liveill Chapwell* [*sic*], 1659. 4°.* SP; CLC, CSS, MH, MIU.

New Lambeth fayre. 1642. *See* Overton, Richard.

New letter from Aberdeen. 1665. *See* R., R.

New letter from Leghorn. 1681. *See* S., J.

652 A new letter from London-Derry. colop: *By W. Downing*, 1689. brs. L, O; Y.

New letter from Windsor. 1681. *See* Freeman, John.

New letter to all drunkards. 1696. *See* F., J.

Nevv light-house. [n.p.], 1650. *See* Beech, William.

New light of alchymy. 1674. *See* Sendivogius, Michael.

New light, or tub-lecture. 1664. *See* C., W.

652A A new list of all the conspirators that have been seiz'd . . . [Rye House] plot. Third edition. colop: [*London*], *to be sold* [*by N. Thompson*, 1683]. brs. MR.

653 A new list of all the members. [*London*], *by Robert Ibbitson*, [1653]. brs. LT, O, DT.

653A A new list of fifty two ships. [*London*, 1700?] brs. L, INDIA OFFICE; MH, Y.

654 A new list of the offices and officers. *For Edward Castle*, 1697. 12°. T.C.III 53. L, LG, LLL, CM, CT, AN; MH, NP, TU, WF.

New littany designed. 1684. *See* Durfey, Thomas.

654A A new letanie for our new Lent. [*London*, 1646.] cap., 4°.* L; CH, MH, PL. (var.)

654B A new letany for the general fast day. [*London*, 1690.] brs. MH.

655 A new litany for the holy time of Lent. *Oxford, by H. Cruttenden*, [c. 1688]. brs. O; TU.

656 A new letany for these times. 1659. 4°. O.

657 —[Anr. ed.] *Printed*, [1660?]. 4°. L, MR, LLU; CH, MH, Y.

658 The new letany. From a senseless mayor. [*London*, 1659.] brs. LT.

659 The nevv letanie. [begins] From an extemporary prayer. [*London*, 1647.] brs. LT; MH, MIU.

659A The new London drollery. [*London*,] *by A. M. for P. Brooksby*, [1687.] 12°.* CM.

660 A new looking-glass for the kingdom. Wherein. colop: *For J. C.*, 1690. brs. L, OP, MC; CH.

New lord's winding-sheet. [n.p.], 1659. *See* Barkstead, John.

661 New mad Tom of Bedlam. [*London*], *for W. Thackeray and T. Passinger*, [1686–88]. brs. L, CM, HH.

662 —[Anr. ed.] [*London*, 1690?] brs. EUING 248. L, GU; MH.

662A —[Anr. ed.] [*London*], *by W. O.*, [1695?]. brs. L.

New made gentlewoman. [1675.] *See* W., L.

663–4 No entries.

New Magna Charta. [n.p.], 1648. *See* Prynne, William.

Nevv map of England. 1659. *See* B., I.

New-market song. 1684. *See* D'Urfey, Thomas.

665 A new marriage, between Mr. King, and Mrs. Parliament. [*London*], *printed*, 1648. 4°.* LT; CN. (var.)

665A The new married couple. [*London*], *for P. Brooksby*, [1675]. brs. O.

666 The new married Scotch couple. [*London*], *for VV. Thackeray, T. Passinger, and VV. VVhitwood*, [1685?]. brs. L.

New martyrology. 1689. *See* Tutchin, John.

Nevv matters of high and great consequence. 1642. *See* Charles I.

667 New matters of note made known. *For J. W.*, 1641[2]. 4°.* LT, DU; CN, OWC.

668 The new medley. *For Fran. Grove*, [1680?]. brs. O.

669 A new meeting of ghosts at Tybvrn. *Printed*, 1660[1]. 4°.* LT, OC; CN.

670 A new Mercury, called Mercurius Problematicus. *By B. A.*, 1644. 4°.* LT, O, MR, DT; MH, MM.

New merry dialogve. [1656.] *See* Price, Laurence.

670A A new merry song of Robin Hood. *For W. Thackeray, T. Passenger, and W. Whitwood*, [1685?]. brs. L, O.

671 New message to the Royalists of . . . England & Scotland. *For J. J.*, 1648. 4°.* LT, MR; CH, MH.

672 A new method of curing the French pox. *For John Taylor and Thomas Newborough*, 1690–89. 4 pts. 12°. T.C.II 287. L, O, LWL, OR; WF.

New method of writing. [1700.] *See* Parker, Henry.

673 A new miracle or Dr. Norman's safe return. *For J. Dean*, [1684]. brs. O, LG; CLC.

673A The nevv mode. Or, we'l raise up our honour again. *For Phillip Brooksby*, [1672–96]. brs. O.

674 A new modell hvmbly proposed. *By Francis Leach*, 1653. 4°.* LT, DU, MR; CU, MH, MU, WF, Y.

675 The new model of a part of the militia. [*Edinburgh, by the heir of Andrew Anderson*, 1680.] cap., fol.* ALDIS 2207. MR, EN; CSS.

676 A new moddell: or the conversion. *For G. T.*, 1652. brs. LT, O; IU, MH.

677 A new modell or the conversion of the infidell terms. [*London*], *printed*, 1652 [*i.e.* 1659]. 4°.* LT, OC, BAMB; Y.

New mystery. 1681. *See* Monginot, Francois de.

678 A new narrative of a gent. of Grays Inn. colop: *For the author*, 1680. cap., fol.* L, O, OC, LIU, MR; CH, TU, WF, Y.

679 A new narrative of the old plot. *For Charles Corbet*, 1683. brs. L, O, LLU, MC; CH, CLC, IU, MH, Y.

679A —[Anr. ed.] *For J. Dean*, 1684. brs. L, O, LLP; CLC, MH.

679B —[Anr. ed.] *For John Moxon*, 1684. brs. L.

680 Entry cancelled.

New narrative of the Popish plot. [n.p., 1680.] *See*, Gadbury, John.

680A A new-naturalized work of a learned stranger . . . geometrie. *By M. S. for Thomas Jenner*, 1657. fol.* WF, Y, YBA.

681 Entry cancelled.

New, new, new Bartholomew fayring. 1649. *See* Nevv Bartholomevv.

682 New news, and strange news from Babylon. [*London*], *for John Thomas*, 1641. 4°.* LT, LLU; Y.

683 A new news-book. colop: [*London*], *by Richard Janeway*, 1681. brs. O; CH, Y.

684 New news from Babylon. [*London*], *for John Thomas*, 1641. 4°. LT.

685 New news from Bedlam. *For the author, and published by Langley Curtis*, 1682. 4°. L, C; CH, CN, MH, MM, Y.

686 New news from Cornvvall. *Octob. 27. London, for Ioshua Kirton*, 1642. 4°.* LT, EC; Y.

687 New news from the old exchange. [*London*, 1650.] 4°.* LT.

New news from Tory-land. 1682. *See* Phillips, John.

688 Nevv nevvs of a strange monster. [*London*, 1679.] fol.* L, C, LNC; CH, CLC, MH, WF, Y.

New non-conformist. 1654. *See* Feake, Christopher.

689 The new nonconformist: or, Dr. Sherlock's case. *Printed*, 1690. 4°.* T.C.II 315. L, O, C, LIU, EN, DT; CLC, MH, NCD, NU, WF, Y.

690 The new oath examined. [*London*, 1689–90.] brs. HH; MH.

691 The new oath of allegiance justified. *Printed, and are to be sold by Randal Taylor*, 1689. 4°.* L, O, CT, GU, DT; CH, CN, MH, NU, TU, WF, Y.

692 The nevv oath or covenant to be taken by all persons. *For Philip Lane, September 4.* 1643. 4°.* L, O, C, BC, DT; CH, CN, MH, TU, WF, Y.

New observations. [n.p.], 1642. *See* B., J.

New opera. 1697. *See* Powell, George.

New orchard. 1683. *See* Lawson, William.

693 New orders new. *For T. V.*, 1642. 4°.* LT, O, OW, CJ, MR; CH, CN, MIU, NU, WF, Y.

694 The new orders of His Majesty's justices of the peace. [*London*, 1681–2.] brs. L, O, LF; CH, WF.

695 A nevv ordinance made of an old declaration. *Printed*, 1648. 4°.* LT; IU.

696 A nevv paire of spectacles. *By Robert Ibbitson*, 1648[9].
    4°.* LT, O, OC, CT, DT; CH, CN, MH, TU, WF, Y.
    New papers. 1647. *See* Burfoit, T.
    New Parliament. 1651. *See* Leach, William.

697 A new petition: earnestly entreating subscription. *By
    Matth. Symmons*, 1646. 4°.* LT, LG, CCC, A, DT; MH, WF.

698 A new petition of the Papists. [*London*], *printed*, 1641. 4°.*
    LT, O, NPL; CLC, CN, INU, MH, Y.

699 Entry cancelled. Ghost.

700 A new petition. To the Kings most excellent Majesty.
    The humble petition of the knights, gentry, . . . of
    Yorke. *For Iohn Wright*, [1642]. brs. STEELE 2100. L, O,
    LS, EC, LNC, YM; CLC, IU.

701 —[Anr. ed.] *Imprinted at London by R. O. and G. D. for
    Iohn Frank*, 1642. brs. LT, LG, YM; CLC, MH.

702 A new play called Canterburie his change of diot. [*Lon-
    don*], *printed*, 1641. 4°.* LT, O, CT; CH, CSS, MB, MH, MIU,
    Y.

703 Entry cancelled. Ghost.

704 A new plea for the Parliament: and the reserved man
    resolved. colop: *Imprinted at London, for Henry Overton*,
    1642[3]. 4°.* LT, O, C, EN, DT; CH, CN, CSS, LC, MH,
    NU, WF, Y. (var.)

704A —[Anr. ed.] [*London*, 1643.] 4°.* O, MR; MH, WF.

705 A nevv plot agianst [*sic*] Hvll. *May 30.* [*London*], *for
    I. Smith, and Rich. Cocks*, 1642. 4°.* LT, CT; MH.

706 A new plot against the Parliament. Englands deliverance.
    For John Greensmith, 1641. 4°.* LT, LG, LNC, DT; IU,
    MBP, Y.

706A —[Anr. ed.] *For H. E.*, 1641. 4°.* WF.

707 Entry cancelled.
    New plot discovered. 1641. *See* Hodgkins, John.

707A A new plot newly discovered. [*London?*], *for J. Conyers*,
    [1680?]. 4°.* L.

708 —[Anr. ed.] [*London*], *for J. Conyers*, 1686. 4°.* CN.
    New plot of the Papists. 1679. *See* Dormer, John.

709 A new plot, or the Whig and Tory united. *D. Mallet*,
    1686. fol.* O, MR.

709A New plots discovered, against the Parliament. *By T.
    Favvcet, for J. R. Nov. 3.* 1642. 4°.* LT; IU, MH, MIU.

710 Entry cancelled.
    New Plymouth colony. Address presented to the King,
    August 7th. 1689. Boston, 1690. *See* title.

711 —The book of the general laws of the inhabitants of the
    jurisdiction of New-Plimouth. *Cambridge* [*Mass.*]: *by
    Samuel Green.* 1672. fol. EVANS 171. LC, MHL, MHS, SE.

711A ——[Anr. ed.] *Boston in New-England: by Samuel Green*,
    1685. 4°. EVANS 397. L; CH, LC, MBA, MH, MHS.

712 A new poem on the dreadful death of the Earl of Essex.
    For E. Cart, 1683. brs. O.

713 —[Anr. ed.] [*London*, 1683.] brs. L; MH, TU, Y.

713A A new poem on the excellency and antiquity of law. *By
    G. C. for the author*, 1682. brs. L; CH, MH, Y.
    New poem on the late illustrious congress. 1691. *See*
    Sault, Richard.

714 A new poem on the Lord Mayor. *For J. Hindley*, 1682.
    brs. EN; CH, MH, PU, WF.

714A —[Anr. ed.] *For J. H.*, 1682. brs. O, LG; MH, PU.
    New poem. To condole. [n.p., 1682.] *See* Waller, *Sir
    William.*

715 Nevv poems upon the death of that eminent servant of
    God, . . . Stephen Charnock. *By Thomas Snowden*,
    1680. brs. L; MH, Y.
    New politick lights. 1678. *See* Le Noir, Jean.

715A The new politicks of the Court of France. *For Henry
    Rhodes and John Harris*, 1695. 8°. T.C.II 528. RPL; CLC,
    IU, WF.

715B A new poll-bill for raising the sum of seven hundred
    thousand pound. [*London*, 1689–94.] cap., fol.* LPR; Y.

716-7 Entries cancelled.
    New Pope. 1677. *See* Leti, Gregorio.

718 The new Popish sham-plot, discovered. colop: *For T.
    Davies*, 1681. brs. L, O, HH, MC, DT; CH, CN, MH, WF, Y.

718A —[Anr. ed.] —, [1681]. brs. LSD; MH.
    New prayers for K. William. 1693. *See* Bleming, John.
    New preachers, new. [n.p.], 1641. *See* Taylor, John.

719 New predictions of the fate of all the princes. [*London*],
    printed, 1688. 4°.* L, O; CH, MU.

720 A new Presbyterian ballad. [*London*], *printed*, 1681. brs.
    L, O; CII, MH, Y.
    New Presbyterian light. 1647. *See* Prynne, William.
    New primmer. New York, 1698. *See* Pastorius, Franz
    Daniel.

720A The new proceedings of the English affairs in Ireland.
    colop: *For Dorman Newman*, 1690. brs. CH, MH.
    New proclamation, in answer. 1649. *See* Douglas, *Lady*
    Eleanor.
    New proclamation: or. 1653. *See* F., I.
    New prognostication. Glasgow, 1667. *See* Almanacs.
    H., J.
    New prognostication. Aberdeen, 1651. *See* Almanacs.

721 A new project humbly offer'd to the consideration of the
    honourable House of Commons. [*London?* 1695.]
    brs. LUG.

722 The new projector. [*London*], *for William Gilbertson*,
    [1662?]. brs. L.

723 A new prophesie. *For Richard Burton*, [1657]. brs. L.

724 A new prophecy of several strange . . . revolutions.
    Printed and sold by John Mayor, 1697. brs. CH.

724A A new proposal for raising more money . . . Ireland.
    [*London*, 1689.] cap., fol.* L; MH.

725 New propositions for peace presented. *For R. VVells*,
    1648. 4°.* LT.

726 New propositions from the armie. *For R. W.*, 1648.
    4°.* LT, O, LIU; CH, CSS, NU, Y.

727 New propositions from the King of Scotland to the
    Parliament. *For E. Cotton, Aug.* 17, 1649. 4°.* LT; CH,
    MH.

728 New propositions from the King, to . . . Fairfax. *For
    W. Fielding*, 1648. 4°.* LT.

729 New propositions from the Kingdom of Scotland. [*Lon-
    don*], *printed*, 1648. 4°.* LT, O, OC, DT.
    New propositions from the parliament of Scotland. 1648.
    See Scotland. Estates.

New propositions from the souldiery. 1647. *See* Rushton, R.

730 New propositions propounded at the Kings royall court at Holmby. *For F. F.*, Feb. 26, 1647. 4°.* LT, O, LIU, DT; NU.

731 Entry cancelled.
New propositions propounded. 1642. *See* England: Parliament.
New Protestant almanack. 1677. *See* Almanacs.

732 A new Protestant ballad. [*London*, 1690?] brs. HH.

733 A nevv Protestant litany. colop: *Printed*, 1689. 4°.* L, LLL; CLC, CN, MH, Y.

734 A new protestation against the Parliament. *For John Thomas*, 1641. 4°.* LT, O, C, MR, BLH, DN; IU, Y.
New quadrant. 1649. *See* Brookes, Christopher.

735 Nevv quæres of conscience. colop: *Oxford, for William Web*, 1643. 4°.* MADAN 1437. LT, O, EC, MR, DT; CH, MH, NU, TU, WF.

736 Nevv questions resolved. [*London*, 1648.] cap., 4°.* MH, NU, WF.

737 A new, rare, and exellent [*sic*] sonnet. *For F. C. J. W. T. V. W. G.*, [1656?]. brs. L.

738 A new relation of a great and happy victory. 1642. L.

739 Entry cancelled.
New relation of Rome. 1664. *See* Corraro, Angelo.

740 A new remonstrance and declaration from the army. *Sent Novemb.* 18. to be printed, [1648]. 4°.* LT; IU, TU, WF.
New remonstrance from Ireland. 1642. *See* Emitie, Thomas.
New remonstrance from the Kings. 1648. *See* S., W.

741 A new remonstrance from the souldiery, to . . . Fairfax. *For Robert VVilliamson*, 1648. 4°.* LT, OB, DT; CH, MH, NC.
New remonstrance of Ireland. 1642. *See* I., C.

742 A new remonstrance of severall matters of consequence [*sic*]. *For I. Horton*, June 25. 1642. 4°.* L, O; Y.

743 A nevv remonstrance of the eleven impeached members. [*London*], *printed*, 1647. 4°.* LT, LLU, LNC, DT; CH, CN, MH, NN, Y.

744 A new remonstrance of the free-born people. *For G. Horton*, 1651. 4°.* LT, MR; MB.

745 A nevv remonstrance wherein is declared who are the malignant party. *For Hen. Fowler, and Dan. Williams*, 1642. 4°.* LT, O, C, CJ, LIU; INU, NN, NU.

745A A new revolution, or, the high flyer turned Whig. [*n.p.*, 1700?] brs. EN.

746 A new rising by divers knights. *Printed*, 1648. 4°.* LT, EN.

747 The new royal march. [1686.] brs. O.

747A An ew [*sic*] satyr written against lying. *By G. C. for the author*, 1682. L, O; CH, MH.

748 A new satyricall ballad of the licentiousness of the times. *Printed*, 1679. brs. L, HH; MH, TU, Y.

748A The new school of education. *By J. M. for T. Passinger*, [*c.* 1680]. 12°.* CM.

749 A new Scotch ballad: call'd Bothwel-Bridge. *For T. B.*, 1679. brs. L, O; MH, RHT, TU.

750 A new Scotch ballad of jealous Nanny. [*London*], *for P. Brooksby*, [1672-95]. brs. EUING 249. L, O, HH, GU; MH.

751 —[Anr. ed.] —, [1680?]. brs. L.

752 The new Scotch-jigg. *For W. Thackerary, T. Passenger, and W. Whitwood*, [1690?]. brs. L, O, CM; MH.

752A A new Scotch whim. *Edinburgh, printed*, 1693. brs. MH.
New sect of religion. [*n.p.*], 1641. *See* Bray, Thomas.

753 Entry cancelled.
New session of the poets. 1700. *See* Kenrick, Daniel.

753A A new shining light. *Rotterdam, sould by Pieter van Alphen*, 1662. 4°. CM.

754 Entry cancelled.
New song. [*n.p.*, 1688.] *See* Wharton, Thomas.

754A A new song. [begins] Thanks to our good K—— William. *Printed*, 1693. brs. L; MH, NNM.

754B A new song. [begins] Wou'd you bee a man off favour. [*London*, 1683.] brs. MH.

755 A new song: being a dialogue between a Whig and Tory. *For T. P.*, 1682. brs. L, O, EN; CH.

755A A new song, being the Tories imploration. *For J. D.*, 1682. brs. O; MH, NCD, PU.

755B —[Anr. ed.] *For W. D.*, 1682. brs. L.

756 A new song, being the Tories tryumph. *For J. D.*, 1682. brs. L, O; CH, IU, MH, PU, Y.

757 A new song between Whig and Tory. *For J. Dean*, 1683. brs. MC.

758 A new song called Love in a tub. *For Absalon Chamberlain*, [1683]. brs. HH.

759 A new song, called, Parthenia's complaint. [*London*], *for P. Brooksby*, [1687?]. brs. L, HH.

760 A new song, called The lover's tragedy. [*London*], *for P. Brooksby*, [1685-88]. brs. L, HH; MH.

760A A new song called the Salamanca doctors glister-pipe. [*London*], *for R. I.*, 1683. brs. MH.

761 Entry cancelled.
New song: Ho, brother Teague. [*n.p.*, 1689.] *See* Wharton, Thomas, *marquis*.

761A A new song in praise of the loyal Company of Stationers. [*London*], *by N. T.*, 1684. brs. O; CLC.

762 A new song lately come from Ireland. [*London*, 1688.] brs. EN; MH.

763 A nevv song made by a person of quality, and sung befor [*sic*] His Majesty. *Printed*, 1683. brs. L, O; CLC, MH, Y.

764 A new song of a new wonder. *For S. D.*, 1688. brs. L, O, C; MH, Y.

765 A new song of an orange. [*London*, 1688.] brs. O, C, EN; CLC, MH, TU.

765A —[Anr. ed.] *Printed*, 1688. brs. CH, MH, Y.

765AB —[Anr. ed.] *For A. B.*, 1689. brs. O.

765B A new song of lulla by, or, Father Peter's policy discovered. [*London*], *printed*, 1688. brs. O; MH.

765C A new song of Mallinger, or, the female-dear-joy. [*n.p.*, 1700?] brs. EN.

766 A new song of Moggies jealousie. [*London*], *for J. Deacon*, [1682?]. brs. L, O, CM; CH, MH.

767 A new song of the French king's fear. [*London*, 1689.] brs. L, O.

767AA A new song of the misfortunes of an old whore. [*London*, 1688.] brs. C.

767A A new song. On King William. *For E. Hawkins*, 1689. brs. MH.

768 A new song on the arrival of Prince George. [*London*], *by Nath. Thompson*, 1683. brs. EN; CLC.

769 A new song on the calling of a free Parliament. [*London*, 1689.] brs. HH.

770 A new song, on the strange and wonderful groaning board. *For T. P.* 1682. brs. L, O; CH, IU, MH, NCD, WF, Y.

771 A new song. Or, Englands outcry against . . . Jefferies. [*London*, 1688–9.] brs. MH.

New song: or, the old womans wish. 1684. *See* P., S.

771A A new song: or the Whigs hard hearts. *By George Croom*, 1684. brs. LG.

772 A new song, shewing the crueltie of Gernutus. [1680?] brs. O.

773 A new song: since Jenny. [*London?* 1700.] brs. L.

New song sung before. 1683. *See* Settle, Elkanah.

New song sung in Abdelazar. [n.p., 1695.] *See* Behn, Mrs. Aphra.

New song, sung in The Spanish frier. [n.p., 1690.] *See* Dryden, John.

773A A new song to drive away cold winter. *For F. Grove*, [1641–60]. brs. O.

774 —[Anr. ed.] *For F. Coles, T. Vere, J. Wright, J. Clarke, W. Thackeray, and T. Passinger*, [1680?]. brs. L, O, CM.

774AA A new song. To the tune of, A beggar. [*London*, 1687?] brs. MH.

774A A new song. To the tune of, Lay by your pleading. [*London*, 1689?] brs. LLP; MH.

774B A new song. To the tune of Robin Goodfellow. colop: *For C. Tebroc*, 1682. brs. O; CH, MH, Y.

775 A new song to the tune of the Grenadeers march. [*Dublin*, 1685.] brs. L.

776 A new song upon the coronation of King James II. *For James Dean*, 1685. brs. MH, Y.

776A A new song upon the Council of six. 1689. brs. MH.

776B A new song upon the Hogen Mogen's. [*London*, 1688.] brs. MH, Y.

776C A new song upon the K—g of Poland, and the Prince. colop: [*London*], *for the Polonian King*, 164800 [*i.e.* 1682]. brs. CH, MH, Y.

New songs. 1677. *See* W., P.

776D A new sonnet, shewing how the Goddesse Diana transformed Acteon. *For J. W.*, [1650?]. brs. MRL.

776E —[Anr. ed.] [*London*], *for F. Coles, T. Vere, J. Wright, and J. Clarke*, [1674–79]. brs. EUING 251. GU.

776F —[Anr. ed.] [n.p., 1680?] brs. L.

776G —[Anr. ed.] [*London*], *for J. Clarke, W. Thackeray, and T. Passenger*, [1684–6]. brs. CM.

777 A new Spanish tragedy. [1641.] brs. O.

New state of England. 1691. *See* Miège, Guy.

778 A new summons to Horn-Fair. [*London*], *printed and sold by H. H.*, [1700?]. brs. L; WCL.

778A A new summons, to warn all the bawds and whores. *For P. Smart*, 1695. brs. MH.

779 A new survey of the Book of common prayer. *For the author*, 1690. 4°. T.C.II 332. L, LCL, LLP; CH, NU, WF, Y.

New survey of the justice. 1659. *See* Sheppard, William.

New survey of the Turkish empire. 1663. *See* Marsh, Henry.

780 A new systeme of the Apocalypse. *Printed*, 1688. 12°. L, O, LW, BR, GU, E; CH, MH, NU, TU, WF, Y.

New test in lieu. 1688. *See* Shute, Giles.

781 The new test of the Church of England's loyalty, examined. *By R. G.*, 1687. 4°.* L, O, CS, MR, DT; CH, MH, MU, NU, WF, Y.

782 A new test of the Church of England's loyalty, published. *Printed*, 1687. 4°.* L, LIL, LL, DC, MC; CH, MM, NU, PU.

783 A new test of the Church of Englands loyalty. With allowance. *For N. T.*, 1687. 4°.* L, O, CT, DU, EN, DT; CH, CN, MH, NU, TU, WF, Y. (var.)

783A —[Anr. ed.] *Printed* 1687. 4°.* TO, Y.

784 The New Testament sabbath. *Printed*, 1696. 12°. O, EN; NU.

785 A nevv-thing, of nothing. *For Tho. Vere*, 1664. brs. L, O, CK; MH, WF.

786 A new touch of the times. [*London*, 1690?] brs. O.

New touch-stone. 1679. *See* Badcock, William.

787 New treason plotted in France. [*London*], *June 25 for I. Tompson and A. Coe.* 1642. 4°.* LT, O, EC; CSS, MH, Y.

788 The new treasury of musick. *For Henry Playford*, 1695. fol. T.C.II 550. L.

New treatise of algebra. [1694.] *See* Sault, Richard.

New treatise of artificial wines. [n.p.], 1690. *See* Y-Worth, William.

New treatise of natural philosophy. 1687. *See* Midgley, Robert.

New trial of the ladies. 1658. *See* Blake, William.

789 A new tricke to take townes. *By E. G.*, 1645[6]. 4°.* LT, MR; Y.

790 Entry cancelled. Date: after 1700.

New verses concerning the plot. 1680. *See* Taylor, John.

791 A new vision of the Lady Gr s. colop: *For J. Smith*, 1682. brs. L; MH.

New votes. 1642. *See* England. Parliament.

New voyage. 1674. *See* La Martinière, Pierre Martin de.

792 A new way of hunting. *By E. C. for F. Coles, T. Vere, and J. Wrig[h]t*, 1671. brs. O.

792A The new way of love. [*London?* 1700.] brs. L.

793 The nevv way of marriage. [*London*], *for P. Prooksby [sic]*, [1672–95]. brs. L, O; MH.

New way of reading. [n.p., 1699.] *See* Gouldney, Henry.

794 A new way, to pay old debts: or, the law and freedom. *Imprinted at London, for George Horton*, 1652. 4°.* LT, C.

795 Entry cancelled. Ghost.

795A A new way to play an old game. [*London*], *for C. Corbet*, 1683. brs. O; CLC, MH.

795B A new wedding. *For F. Coles, T. Vere and J. Wright*, [1663–74]. brs. O.

New Westminster wedding. [n.p., 1693.] *See* P., J.

796   The new wife of Beath, much better reformed. *Glasgow, by Robert Sanders*, 1700. 12°.* ALDIS 3988. L, EN.

797   A nevv vvind-mil, a new. *At Oxford, by Leonard Lichfield*, 1643. 4°.* MADAN 1389. LT, O, LG; CH, CU, NN, WF, Y.

New witnesses proved.[n.p.], 1672. *See* Penn, William.

797AA   A new wonder: or, a strange and true account . . . storm. [*London*], *for F. Coles, T. Vere, J. Wright, J. Clarke, W. Thackeray, and T. Passenger*, 1681. brs. O.

New world of English words. 1658. *See* Phillips, Edward.

797BA   A New Years gift. [63] Articles of impeachment against Edward Seymour. *For John Wright and Richard Chiswell*, 1680. brs. HH.

797CA   The New-Years gift: being a paraphrase. *For the author*, 1690. brs. O.

797A   A New-Years gift: being a poem dedicated to . . . Titus Oates. [*London*], 1680. brs. L; CH, MH.

New-years gift: being an help. 1690. *See* C., J.

797B   The new year's gift, complete: in six parts. *For Henry Mortlock*, 1693. 12°. L.

797C   —[Anr. ed.] —, 1696. 24°. T.C.II 572. L; WF.

797D   A New-Years-gift composed of prayers. Second edition. *For Simon Neale*, 1681. 12°. T.C.I 433. CLC.

797E   —Third edition. —, 1683. 24°. L.

797F   —Fourth edition. *For S. N.*, 1685. 24°. T.C.II 130. L.

798   A New-Year's gift for Dr. [Peter] Birch. *Printed*, 1696. 4°.* L, O, LLP, LVF, WCA; CH, MB, WF.

Nevv-yeers-gift for England. 1653. *See* Burt, Nathaniel.

799   A Nevv-yeares-gift for His Maiesty. [*London*], *printed*, 1644. 4°.* LT; LC, MH, MM.

800   A New-Years-gift for Papists. 1667. brs. L.

801   —[Anr. ed.] *For L. Curtis*, 1677. brs. L.

802   A New-Years-gift for plotters. colop: [*London*], *for J. K.*, 1681. brs. L, O, MC; CH, CLC, CN, MH, PU, Y.

802A   A new-years-gift for Protestants. *For R. Taylor*, 1691. 4°.* LSC.

802B   New Year's gift for Sir Bartholomew Shower. [*n.p.*, 1696.] brs. L.

803   Entry cancelled.

New years gift for the Antinomians. 1699. *See* Young, Samuel.

New-years-gift for the anti-prerogative-men. 1682. *See* Brydall, John.

804   A New-Years-gift for the dispensing judges. *Printed*, 1689. brs. L.

805   A New-yeers gift for the Kings most excellent Majesty. *For T. G.*, 1649. 4°.* LT; DT; CSS.

806   A New-Years-gift for the late Rapparees. A satyr. *For E. Smith*, 1691. 4°.* L, O, LG, LIU, DT; CH, MH, NP, WF, Y.

807   A New-Years-gift for the Lord Chief in Justice Sc[rog]gs. [*London*, 1679.] cap., fol.* L, O, C, MR, DU, DT; CH, MH, MU, NU, TU, WF, Y. (var.)

808   A New-Years-gift for the Rump. *Printed at Oxford, for G. H.*, [1660]. brs. MADAN 2511. LT, O; MH.

809   —[Anr. ed.] [*Oxford?* 1660.] brs. L, O; CLC, MH, Y.

810   A New-yeers gift for the saints at Westminster. [*London*], *printed*, 1648. 4°.* LT, LG; CSS, MH, Y.

811   A New-Years-gift for the Tories alias Rapperrees. [*London*, 1690?] brs. L, LG.

812   A New-Years gift for the Whigs. [*London*], *for J. Deane*, [1684]. brs. O, HH; CLC.

813   A New-Years-gift for Towzer. colop: *For E. Harrison*, 1682. cap., fol.* L, O, EN; MH, NN, PU, WF, Y.

New-years-gift for women. 1660. *See* Hill, William.

813A   A New years-gift, or a token of love. colop: *For Thomas Whitledge*, 1693. cap., 4°.* WF.

New-years gift: or, advice. 1696. *See* A., P.

814   A New-Years gift, or, the Covent-Garden adventure. colop: [*London*], *for R. T.*, 1689. brs. TU.

814A   A New-Year's gift; or, the devout Christian's manual. *By W. Onely and are to be sold by R. Baldwin*, 1694. 12°. LLP.

815   Entry cancelled.

New-years gift; presented by Tho. Lord Fairfax. 1648[9]. *See* Fairfax, *Sir* Thomas.

New Years-gift to a notable grandee. 1662. *See* Jackson, Richard.

816   A New-Years-gift to be presented to the Kings most excellent Majestie. colop: *For T. B.*, 1647. 4°.* LT, O, DT; MH.

816A   A New-Years gift to dissenters. *Printed*, 1688. brs. MH.

817   A New-years gift to His Majestie. colop: *For W. C.*, 1688. brs. O.

818   A New-years gift to impostors. [*London*, 1697?] cap., fol.* O, LL, CS, MR; CN.

818A   A New-years-gift to the honourable Admiral Russel. [*London?* 1692.] cap., 4°.* CLC.

818B   —[Anr. ed.] *Printed and sold by T. Moore*, 1693. 4°.* L.

819   A New-years guift [*sic*] to the Templers. [*London*], *by Nat. Thompson*, [1683]. brs. O; CH, MH, WF, Y.

820   A New-Years-gift to the Tories. *For Francis Smith sen.*, 1682/3. brs. L, O, C, HH, EN; CH, MH, MU, Y.

820A   A Nevv-Years-gift to youth. *By George Croom*, 1685. brs. HH; CH, MH.

820B   A new-years offering to . . . King William III. colop: *For R. Baldwin*, 1697. brs. L; CH, MH.

821   The new yeares wonder. [*London*], *for Robert Ellit*, [1643]. 4°.* LT.

822   **New York. Province. General Assembly.** An act for granting to their Majesties the rate. [*New York, William Bradford*, 1693.] cap., fol.* EVANS 665. CH, NN, PHS.

823   —Anno Regni Gulielmi . . . quinto . . . an act for raising six thousand pound . . . 1693. colop: *Printed and sold by William Bradford, of New-York*, 1693. cap., fol.* EVANS 667. CH, NHS, NN.

824   ——[Anr. ed., "1694."] —, 1693. fol.* EVANS 666. NYSOC.

825   —Anno Regni Gulielmi . . . quinto. An act for restraining and punishing privateers. colop: *New York: William Bradford*, 1693. cap., fol.* EVANS 663. CH, NN.

825AA   ——[Anr. ed.] [*New York*, 1693.] cap., fol.* EVANS 664. CH, NHS.

825A   —An act passed the 12th of September 1693 . . . for settling a ministry. [*New York*, 1693.] cap., fol.* LPR.

825B —An act passed the 12th of September, 1693 . . . A petition of the church-wardens . . . [*New York*, 1695.] cap., fol.* LPR.

826 —Acts made the 5th Assembly, 4th session. [*New York, by William Bradford*, 1696.] fol.* EVANS 758. CH, LC, NN.

827 —Acts made the 5th Assembly, 5th sessions. [*New York, by William Bradford*, 1697.] fol.* EVANS 803. CH, LC, NN, PHS.

828 —The charter of the city of New-York. *New-York, by William Bradford*, 1694. cap., fol.* EVANS 706. LPR; CH.

829 —The fifth Assembly, third sessions. Beginning the 25th day of March, and ending the 24th day of April. *By William Bradford, in New-York*, 1696. fol.* EVANS 757. CH, NN.

830 —A catalogue of fees established. colop: *Printed and sold by William Bradford, in New York*, 1693. fol.* EVANS 673. LPR; CH, MU, NN, PHS.

830A —The journal of the House of Representatives. *Printed and sold by William Bradford*, 1695. fol.* EVANS 735. LPR.

831 —The laws & acts of the General Assembly. *At New-York, printed and sold by William Bradford*, 1694. fol. EVANS 703. CH, LC, NN, PHS.

832 —An ordinance established by the mayor. [*New York?* 1700.] brs. LPR.

833 —An ordinance of His Excellency and Council for the establishing courts of judicature. [*New York, by William Bradford*, 1699.] cap., fol.* EVANS 889. CH, LC, MHL, NN, PHS.

834 —The remonstrance of several of the representatives. *Printed and sold by William Bradford of New-York*, 1698. fol.* EVANS 846. LPR.

835 —Votes of the House of Representatives . . . May 19– June 14. 1698. [*By William Bradford of New-York*, 1698.] fol.* EVANS 849. O, LPR; MHS.

835A The new youth's behaviour. *By B. G. for Sam. Keble*, 1684. 8°. T.C.II 91. LSC.

835B **Newall, W.** The merchant's companion. *By J. D. to be sold by the author, and W. Wilson, of Dumfries*, 1692. O; WF.

835C **Newark, David Leslie, baron.** Camp discipline. *For Jo. Rothwell, tenth of August*, 1642. 4°.* LT, O, LL, EC, YM; CLC, MH, PHS, PL, WF.

836 —A coppy of Generall Lesley's letter to . . . Suckling. [*London*], *printed*, 1641. 4°.* L, LG, SP; CLC, MH, MM, WF, Y.

837 —Generall Lessley's direction and order. *By Richard Badger, for L. Blaikelock.* 1642. 4°.* LT, CT, EC; MH, WF.

838 —A most worthy speech spoken by. *For James Douglas*, 1647. 4°.* LT, DT; IU.

839 —Generall Lesley's speech in the Parliament of Scotland. *Printed at London for T. B.*, 1641. 4°.* LT, DU, MR, ESS; CH, MB, NN, WF, Y.

840 — —[Anr. ed.] [*London*, 1641.] 4°.* LT, C; MBP, MH.
841–2 No entries.
    —My Lord Newarks speech to the trained-bands. 1642. *See* Dorchester, Henry Pierepont, *marquis*.

843 —Two letters from. *For Robert Bostock*, 1646. 4°.* LT, O, MR, YM, DT; CH, MH, NN, TU.

844 No entry.
Newark, Henry Pierpoint, viscount. *See* Dorchester, Henry Pierpont, *marquis*.

845 **Newbery, William.** A letter to Dr. Fowler. *Printed*, 1685. fol.* L, O, C, MR, EN; CH, CN, MH, WF, Y.

846 **N[ewbold], A.** Londons improvement and the builder's security asserted. *For the author, by Thomas Milbourn*, 1680. fol.* L, O; CH, NP, TU, Y.

847 **Newbury, Nathanael.** The yeomans prerogative. *By J. Moxon, for J. N.*, 1652[3]. 4°.* LT, C, LW, WCA, EN; CLC, WF, Y.

848 **Newcastle, Margaret Cavendish, duchess of.** De vita et rebus gestis. *Excudebat T. M.*, 1668. fol. L, O, C, OC, E; CLC, LC.

849 —Description of a new world. *By A. Maxwell*, 1666. fol. L, LVD, LLU, GH; CLC, IU, MH, Y.

850 — —[Anr. ed.] —, 1668, fol. L, DUS; CLC, CN, IU, WF.

851 —Grounds of natural philosophy. Second edition. *By A. Maxwell*, 1668. fol. L, O, C, CK, CT, DUS; CH, MH, MU, NP, OCI.

852 Entry cancelled.
    —Letters and poems in honour. 1676. *See title.*

853 —The life of . . . William Cavendishe. *By A. Maxwell*, 1667. fol. L, O, C, LVD, E; CH, CN, MH, WF, Y.

854 — —Second edition. —, 1675. 4°. L, CASTLE ASHBY; CH, MH, PL, WCL, WF, Y.

855 —Natures pictures. *For J. Martin and J. Allestrye*, 1656. fol. L, O, C, OB, E, BLH; CB, CH, MH, NC, WF.

856 — —Second edition. *By A. Maxwell*, 1671. fol. L, O, LVD; CH, CLC, FU.

857 —Observations upon experimental philosophy. *By A. Maxwell*, 1666. fol. L, LVD, LLU, GH; CLC, IU, NP, WF, Y.

858 — —Second edition. —, 1668. fol. O, C, CT, DUS, YM, DT; CLC, CN, MU, NP, OCI, VC.

859 —Orations of divers sorts. *Printed*, 1662. fol. L, O, C, LVF, OC, NE; CH, CLC, CN, MH, WCL.

860 — —Second edition. —, 1662. fol. L.

861 — —[Anr. ed.] —, 1663. fol. DU, LVD; CH, MH.

862 — —"Second" edition. *By A. Maxwell*, 1668. fol. YM, E; CLC, MIU, NP, WF, Y.

863 —The philosophical and physical opinions. *For J. Martin and J. Allestrye*, 1655. fol. L, O, C, CK, BC, E; BN, CH, CLC, CN, NCD, Y.

864 — —[Anr. ed.] *By William Wilson*, 1663. fol. L, O, C, OC, DU; BN, CH, CLC, MH, OCI, WF.

865 —Philosophicall fancies. *By Tho: Roycroft for J. Martin, and J. Allestrye*, 1653. 8°. LT, O, LVD; CH, CLC, MH.

866 —Philosophical letters. *Printed*, 1664. fol. L, O, C, DU, A; BN, CLC, CU, NCU, TO, TU, WF, Y.

867 —Plays, never before printed. *By A. Maxwell*, 1668. fol. L, C, OW, AN, YM, ES; BN, CH, CN, LC, MH, WF, Y.

868 —Playes written. *By A. Warren, for John Martyn, James Allestry, and Tho. Dicas*, 1662. fol. L, O, C, LVD, EN; CH, CN, MH, WCL, WF, Y.

869 —Poems, and fancies. *By T. R. for J. Martin, and J. Allestrye*, 1653. fol. L, O, C, LVF, GH; CH, CN, MH, WC, Y.

870   ——Second edition. *By William Wilson*, 1664. fol. L, O,
       C, DU, MR; CH, NCU, PBL, WF, Y.

871   ——Third edition. *By A. Maxwell*, 1668. L, LVD, CT, YM;
       CH, MH, NP, ASU.

872   —CCXI sociable letters. *By William Wilson*, 1664. fol.
       L, O, C, LVD, E; CH, CN, MH, WF, Y.

873   —The worlds olio. *For J. Martin and J. Allestrye*, 1655.
       fol. L, O, C, LVD, E; CH, CLC, MH, NC, WF, Y.

874   ——Second edition. *By A. Maxwell*, 1671. fol. L, YM; CH,
       CLC, MH, OCL, Y.

874A   **Newcastle, William Cavendish,** *duke of.* Answer of.
       York, by Stephen Bulkley, 1643. 4°.* CJ, CT, YM; CLC.

875   —An answer of . . . to the six groundlesse aspersions.
       Printed at York, and reprinted at Oxford by H. H., 1642
       [3]. 4°.* MADAN 1235. L, O, CT, BC, LLU; CH, CLC, Y.

875A   ——[Anr. ed.] *Printed at Oxford, and reprinted at Shrews-*
       bury, 1642. 4°.* MH.

876   —Being commanded by . . . to publish the following
       articles for his new course. [*Oxford*, 1662.] brs. O.

877   [–] The country captaine. *For Hum: Robinson and Hum:*
       Moseley, 1649. 12°. L, O, LVD, LIU, LLU; CH, CN, LC, MH,
       TU, WF, Y. (var.)

878   —A declaration and svmmons sent by. *For Peter Cole,*
       July 15, 1643. 4°.* LT, C; CH, WF.

879   —A declaration made by. *Printed at York, by Stephen*
       Bulkley, 1642. 4°.* L, CT, LNC, YM, D; CLC, MM, TO, Y.

880   ——[Anr. ed.] *Printed at York, and now re-printed at Lon-*
       don, 1642. 4°.* LT, OC, CS, LLU, DT; CH, CN, MH, MU,
       NCD, WF, Y.

881   ——[Anr .ed.] [*Oxford*], *for W. Webb*, 1643. 4°.* MADAN
       1568. O, MR; CH, MH.

882   —A declaration of the right honourable the. *Printed at*
       York by Stephen Bulkley, 1642[3]. 4°.* LT, C, OC, CJ, YM,
       DT; BN, CH, CN, MH, TU, WCL, WF, Y. (var.)

883   —The humorous lovers. *By J. M. for H. Herringman*,
       1677. 4°. T.C.I 267. L, LVD, OW, CS, A; CH, CU, LC, MH,
       TU, WF, Y.

884   —Methode nouvelle. *Chez Thos. Milbourn*, 1671. fol.
       CT, AM; CH.

885   ——[Anr. ed.] *J. Melbourn*, [1672]. fol. BN.

886   No entry.

887   —A new method . . . to dress horses. *By Tho. Milbourn*,
       1667. fol. L, O, C, R, E; CH, CJC, MH, TU, WF, Y.

888   —Observations. *Printed*, 1643. 4°. CT, DT; CH.

889   —A proclamation by. *Printed at York by Stephen Bulkley*,
       1642[3]. brs. STEELE 2401. HH.

890   —Sir, the apparent danger. [*n.p.*], 1642. brs. O.

891   —The triumphant widow. *By J. M. for H. Herringman*,
       1677. 4°. T.C.I 267. L, O, LVD, LIU, EN; CH, CN, LC, MH,
       TU, WF, Y.

       —Varietie. 1649. *See* —Country captaine.

891A   The Newcastle associators. [*London*], *by Nath. Thompson*,
       [1684?]. brs. MH.

892   Newcastle upon Tyne, Sept. 26th. 1670. At a court held
       in the Guildhall, within the town of Newcastle upon
       Tyne. [*n.p.*, 1670.] brs. L, LPR.

893   **Newcome, Henry,** *1650–1713.* The compleat mother.
       For J. Wyat, 1695. 8°. T.C.II 526. L, LWL, OC; WSG.

894   [**Newcome, Henry**], *1627–1695.* The covenant of grace
       effectually remembred. *By A. M. and R. R. for Richard*
       Janeway, 1682. 4°.* L, LW; NU.

895   —The divine goodness a pattern. *By J. D. for Jonathan*
       Robinson, 1689. 4°.* T.C.II 284. L, O, LIU, DT; Y.

896   [–] A faithful narrative of the life and death of . . . Mr.
       John Machin. *For Nevill Simmons*, 1671. 8°. T.C.I 73.
       L, O, LW, CT, BR, P; CLC, IU, TO, Y.

897   —An help to the duty in and right improvement of sick-
       ness. *For Thomas Parkhurst*, 1685. 8°. LCL, LW.

898   —A plain discourse about rash and sinful anger. *For Tho.*
       Parkhurst, 1693. 8°. LCL, LW; CLC, MH, WF.

899   —The sinner's hope. *By E. C. for George Eversden*, 1660.
       8°. LT, LCL, LW, OC, MR; IU.

900   —Usurpation defeated. *For Ralph Shelmerdine in Man-*
       chester, 1660. 8°. LCL, LW, MC, MP.

900A   ——[Anr. ed.] *For Henry Eversden*, 1660. 8°. IU.

901   **Newcome, Peter.** A catechetical course of sermons. *By*
       J. R. for John Wyat, 1700. 2 v. 8°. T.C.III 224. O, C, OME,
       RPL, ENC; CB, NU, WF, Y.

902   —Peccata in deliciis. A discourse. *By J. D. for Jonathan*
       Robinson, 1686. 4°.* T.C.II 175. L, O, C, EC, DT; IU, NC,
       NU, WF.

903   —A sermon preached . . . April 16. 1696. *For John Wyat*,
       1696. 4°.* T.C.II 577. L, O, C; CLC.

904   **Newcomen, Matthew.** The all-seeing vnseen eye of
       God. *By A. M. for Christopher Meredith*, 1647. 4°. LT, O,
       C, BAMB, DT; CH, IU, MH, NU, WF, Y.

905   —The best acquaintance. *For Peter Parker*, 1668. 8°. T.C.I
       4. LCL, GU; NU.

906   ——[Anr. ed.] *P. Parker*, 1679. 12°. LCL, LSC.

907   —The craft and crvelty. *By G. M. for Christopher Mered-*
       ith, 1643. 4°. 70 pp. LT, O, LLP, LNC, RU; CLC, NU, WF, AVP.

908   ——[Anr. ed.] —, 1643. 4°. 48 pp. L, O, C, EN, DT; CH, CN,
       MBP, MH, NU, TU, WF, Y, AVP.

908A   ——[Anr. ed.] *By G. M. and are to be sold by Peter Cole*,
       1643. 4. OC; BBE, CH, CSS, MB, MH, NCD.

908B   ——[Anr. ed.] *For Peter Cole*, 1643. 4°.* L, LLP, LW, CM,
       LSD; MH, NP, OWC.

909   —The dvty of such as would walke worthy of the Gospel.
       By G. M. for Christopher Meredith, 1646. 4°. LT, O, C,
       LCL, DT; CH, IU, MH, MWA, NU, WF, Y.

910   [–] Irenicvm; or, an essay. *For Nathanael Webb and*
       William Grantham, 1659. 4°. LT, O, LW, OC, BC; CH, MH,
       NU, W, Y.

911   —Jervsalems vvatch-men. *By M. F. for Christopher*
       Meredith, 1643. 4°.* LT, O, C, EN, DT; CH, MH, MU, NCD,
       NU, WF, Y.

912   —A sermon preached at the funerals of . . . Samvel
       Collins. *London, by D. Maxwell for W. Weekley at*
       Ipswich, to be sold by J. Rothwel, and Rich. Tomlins,
       1658. 8°. L, LCL, OCC, CT; NU.

913   —A sermon, tending to set forth. *By George Miller for*
       Christopher Meredith, 1644. 4°.* LT, O, C, BR, EN; CH,
       IU, MH, NU, WF, Y.

914 —Ultimum vale. *Printed*, 1663. 8°. L, O, C, AN, BC, DU; MH, NU, WF, Y.

Newest and best newes. 1642. *See* Plunket, Richard.

Nevvest and trvest. [n.p.], 1642. *See* W., A.

915 The newest collection of the choicest songs. *By T. Haly, for D. Brown, and T. Benskin*, 1683. 8°. T.C.I 509. L, O; CN, MH, WF.

The nevvest intelligence from the army in Ireland. 1642[3]. *See* Lynne, M.

916 Entry cancelled.

Newest proceedings in Ireland. [n.p.], 1642. *See* Walsgrave, J.

917 **Newey, Charles.** Captain Charles Newy's case. *For the author*, 1700. fol.* L; WF.

918 —Captain Charles Newey's vvonderful discovery. colop: *By Jer. Wilkins*, 1700. brs. CH, MH.

918A The Newgate salutation: or, a dialogue. *For the use of the students in Whittington's Colledge*, [1681?]. brs. L, O, C; CH, CLC, MH, NCD, Y.

919 Newgates remonstrance to His Excellency the Lord Gen: Cromwel. *For G. Horton*, 1653. 4°.* LT.

920 **Newhouse, Daniel.** The vvhole art of navigation. *For the author*, 1685. 4°. L, C, CM, MR; CH.

921 ——[Anr. ed.] *For Tho. Passinger, and Tho. Sawbridge and E. Playford*, 1686. 4°. T.C.II 146. L, OC, CCA, GU; WF.

922 ——[Anr. ed.] *For Rich. Mount*, 1698. 4°. CT; NN.

923 **Newman.** An hundred and six lessons, or Christian directions. *Printed at York by Tho: Broad*, 1646. brs. LT, LS.

Newman, Henry. Vt fluctus. [n.p.], 1691. *See* Almanacs.

—Harvard's ephemeris. Cambridge [Mass.], 1690. *See* Almanacs.

923A **Newman, John.** The light within. 1668. LCL.

923B **Newman, John, doctor.** By His Majesties authority. These are to give notice . . . practitioner in physick. [London, 1680.] brs. L.

924 **Newman, Richard.** A sermon preached . . . 30th. of January, 1693/4. *For Randal Taylor*, 1694. 4°.* L, O, C.

925 **N[ewman], S[amuel].** A concordance to the Holy Scriptures. *Cambridge, by John Field*, 1662. fol. L, O, C, MR, ENC; CH, IU, MH, PL, WG, Y.

926 [–] —Second edition. *Cambridge, by John Hayes: for George Sawbridge. And also to be sold by John Martin, Robert Horne, Henry Brome, Richard Chiswell, Robert Boulter, John Wright, and William Jacob, in London*, 1672. fol. L, O, C, D, DT; CH, CLC, IU, NU, TU, Y.

927 [–] —Third edition. *Cambridge, by John Hayes: for Hannah Sawbridge in London*, 1682. fol. L, O, C, EN, DT; CLC, NN, NP, PL, WF.

927A [–] —[Anr. ed.] *Cambridge, by John Hayes for H. Sawbridge; to be sold by John Harris in London*, 1685. fol. O.

928 ——Fourth edition. *Cambridge, by John Hayes: for Awnsham and John Churchill, London*, 1698. fol. T.C.III 57. L, O, C, EC, BQ; CH, IU, MB, MH, NCD, NU, WF, AVP.

929 —A large and complete concordance to the Bible. *For Thomas Dovvnes and James Young*, 1643. fol. L, O, CT, NPL, AU, DT; CLC, NN, RPJ, TSM, Y.

930 ——Second edition. *For Thomas Downes, and Andrew Crook*, 1650. fol. L, O, C, E, GH; CH, LC, MH, NN, RPJ, Y.

931 ——Third edition. *For Thomas Dovvnes, and Andrevv Crook*, 1658. fol. L, O, C, LW, YM, SA; MBA, MU, RPJ, TU, Y.

932–3 Entries cancelled.

New-market song. 1684. *See* D'Urfey, Thomas.

934 **Newnam, Richard.** The complaint of English subjects. *For the author*, 1699. 8°. CLC, NU.

935 ——[Anr. ed.] *Printed*, 1700. 8°. L, DU; MH.

936 **Newness, J.** What charming sounds are these. [London, 1700?] brs. L.

937 Entry cancelled.

Newport, Francis, lord. A declaration of the gentry of the county of Salop. 1660. *See* title.

938 **Newport, Maurice.** By the commissioners appointed by his Majesty, for the repairing the high-wayes. [London], *for J. G.*, 1662. brs. STEELE 3366. L.

[–] Double eternity. 1695. *See* L., J.

938A [–] Ob pacem toti fere Christiano orbi. *Typis Roberti Carnii*, 1679. 4°. L; WF.

939 [–] Sereniss. Principi Carolo secundo . . . Votum candidum, vivat rex. *Typis Roberti Viti*, 1665. 4°. L; MH.

939A ——Second edition. *Typis Neucomianis*, 1669. 8°. L, O, C, DU, E, EN; CH, CLC, CN, TU, WF, Y.

939B ——Third edition. *Anno Dom.* 1676. 8°. L, LLL, CT, E; CH, NP, NU, WF.

940 **Newport, William.** The fall of man. *By L. N. for Richard Wodenoth*, 1644. 4°.* O, C, LW; NU.

941 **Newrobe, Richard.** Delightfull nevves to all loyall subiects. *Printed at London for Iohn Howell*, 1642. 4°.* C, EN, GU, DN; CH, MH, Y.

942 —Farewell myter or, Canterburies meditations. [London], *for William Larnar*, 1641[2]. 4°.* LT, LSC; MIU, NU, Y.

943 —The Kings favovr. *By Iohn Hammond*, 1641[2]. 4°.* LT, OC, EC; CN, Y.

944 —The mvtvall ioyes of the King. *For John Howell*, 1642. 4°.* LT, O, C, DN; CH, MH, Y.

Newes coming up. 1654. *See* Fox, George.

945 News for the curious. *For M. Pardoe, G. Downes, and B. Aylmer*, 1684. 8°. T.C.II 73. C.

946 News for youngmen and maids. *For W. Thacery* [sic], *and W. Whitwood*, [1675?] brs. L.

946A News from Bartholomew-fair. [London? 166–?] 4°. LG.

947 News from Basing-stoak of one Mrs. Blunden. [London], *for John Millet*, [1680?]. 4°.* L.

948 News from Bath. *For R. Baldwin*, 1689. brs. O, C; CH.

948A News from Bedlam. *For B. H.*, 1674. 8°. OC.

948B News from Bishops-gate-street. colop: *For Stephen Draper*, [1689]. cap., 4°.* L, O; CH.

949 Nevves from Black-Heath. *For Henrie Andrews.* 1642. 4°.* LT, LG, EC; INU, MH, WF, Y. (var.)

950 Nevves from Bowe. *By B. A.*, 1648. 4°.* LT, LG; MIU, Y.

950A News from Braband; or, an account . . . April 1. *Edinburgh, re-printed* 1691. brs. CN.

News from Brussels. [n.p.], 1660. *See* Nedham, Marchamont.

951 Newes from Cambridge. [n.p.], *Sept 2nd* 1642. 4°. O.

951A   News from Cambridge. Or a brief relation. *For R. B.,* 1675. 4°.* cs.

951B   News from Chelmsford. *For D. M.,* 1678. 4°.* wf.

952   Entry cancelled.

News from Cheshire. [1688.] *See* P., J.

News from Chester 1689. *See* P., J.

News from Colchester. 1681. *See* B., A.

953   News from Covent-Garden. *For J. T.,* 1675. 4°.* L; MH, Y.

Newes from Dennington Castle. [n.p.], 1646. *See* Ryves, William.

954   News from Doctor's Commons. colop: *For R. Janeway,* 1681. cap., fol.* T.C.I 453. L, O, CT, DU, EN, DT; CH, CN, MH, NU, TU, WF, Y, AVP.

News from Dublin. 1647. *See* C., H.

Nevves from Dvnkirke. [1642.] *See* H., G.

955   News from Dunkirk-house. [*London,* 1667.] brs. L, O, LVF, LNC, MC; CH, WF.

956   News from Epsom. [*n.p.*], 1679. 4°. E.

957   News from Fleetstreet: or. *For William Powel,* 1675. 4°.* LG; CH.

957A   Nevves from forraigne parts. *Printed at London for Nath. Butler, March 5.* 1641. 4°.* O; MH, WF, Y.

Newes from France. [1642.] *See* S., W.

News from France: in a letter. 1682. *See* Burnet, Gilbert, *bp.*

957B   News from Frost-fair. [*London*], *for I. Wright, I. Clark, W. Thackeray, and T. Passinger,* [1683]. brs. MH.

958   News from Gaunt. *For William Thackeray and William Whitwood,* 1678. 4°.* HUTH.

959   News from Germanie. *December the 10th, printed,* 1642. 4°.* LT, MR; MIU.

960   News from Goodman's fields. 1675. 4°. LG (lost).

961   Newes from Guild-Hall. Or, a premonition. [*London,* 1650.] cap., 4°.* LT, LG; CH, CN, CU, MB, NU.

961A   News from Guild-hall: or an answer. [*London,* 1680.] cap., fol.* O, C, LG, LLU, EN; MH, WF.

962   News from Guild-Hall, or the combate. [*London,* 1683.] cap., fol.* L, O, MC; CH, Y.

963   Entry cancelled. *See previous entry.*

Newes from Heaven both good. 1641. *See* F., E.

964   News from Heaven: or, a dialogue. [*London,* 1679.] cap., fol.* L, O, C, MR, SP, DN; CH, CLC, IU, MH, PU, WF, Y.

News from Hell. 1680. *See* Panton, Edward.

News from Hell; or the devils court. 1673. *See* V., S.

965   News from Hell; or the relation of a vision. [*London,* 1660.] brs. LT.

News from Hell, Rome. [n.p.], 1641. *See* M., J.

966   Entry cancelled.

News from Hereford. [n.p., 1661] *See* K., W.

967   News from Holland: of the entertainment. *For Ed. Blackmore, May the 20th* 1642. 4°.* LT, O; CH, TU, Y.

968   Nevves from Holland; or, a short relation. *Printed at Amsterdam.* 1647. *And reprinted at London by T. W. for H. B.,* 1648. 4°.* LT, LW, MR; CN, NU.

969   Newes from Hull. *For Thomas Baker,* 1642. 4°.* L, O, EC.

970   Newes from Hide-Parke. *For William Gilbertson,* [1640–43]. brs. L, O, CM, HH.

971   —[Anr. ed.] *for F. Coles, T, Vere, and J. Wright,* [1663–74]. brs. EUING 250. HH, GU.

971A   —[Anr. ed.] *By E. Crouch, —,* [1663–74]. brs. O.

Nevves from Ipswich. [n.p.], 1641. *See* Prynne, William.

972   News from Ireland. Being the examination . . . of William Kelso. [*London*], *printed,* 1679. fol.* L, O, C, MR, BQ; CH, MH, PU, WF, Y.

973   Nevvs from Ireland concerning the proceedings of the presbytery. *By Edward Husband and John Field,* 1650. 4°.* LT, BLH, DN.

974   July 12th. 1642. Newes from Ireland, relating. *For John Sweeting, July 12.* 1642. 4°.* LT, O, C, LVF; CH.

975   Entry cancelled.

News from Ireland, touching. 1682. *See* Smith, William, *prisoner.*

Newes from Ireland, wherein is related. 1641. *See* Cole, Robert.

976   News from Islington: or. 1674. 4°.* LG.

976A   News from Jamaica. *For N. T.,* 1677. brs. LNC.

976B   News from Jamaica in a letter from Port Royal. *By Peter Lillicrap, for Philip Brigs,* 1671. 4°.* NN.

977   Newes from Kent. A true and most exact relation. *By R. I. for George Hutton,* 1648. 4°.* LT, LG, SP; MIU.

978   Newes from Kent, vvherein. *For Robert White,* 1648. 4°.* LT, O, LG; MIU, Y.

979   Newes from Kingstone assizes. *Printed,* 1676. 4°. MR.

979A   Entry cancelled.

Nevves from Leicester. 1642. *See* Jones, Adam.

979B   News from Maidstone: or, a true narrative. *For D. M.,* 1678. 4°. LC.

980   Newes from Manchester. Being a true relation. *For Richard Best,* 1642. 4°.* LT, LNC, SC, EC.

981   News from Morefields. *For J. Hose,* [1690?]. brs. O.

982   Newes from More-lane. *For William Gammon,* [1665?]. brs. L.

983   News from New-England, being. *For J. Coniers,* 1676. 4°.* L, O, MR; CH, CN, MU, NN, RPJ, WCL.

983A   News from New-England: in a letter. colop: *For John Dunton,* 1690. brs. CN, V.

984   Newes from New-England: of a most strange and prodigious birth. colop: *For John G. Smith,* 1642. 4°.* LT, O; Y.

News from Newcastle. 1651. *See* Cleveland, John.

985   News from Newgate: a gaol-delivery [3–10 September]. *For R. Vaughan,* 1673. 4°.* LG, LPR.

985A   News from Newgate: or, an exact . . . [29–30 April, 1–2 May]. *For R.V.,* 1674. 4°.* CH.

986   News from Newgate: or, a true relation. *For D. M.,* 1677. 4°.* L.

987   News from Newgate: or, the female Muggleton. *For P.B.,* 1678. 4°.* O; NU.

987A   News from old Gravel-lane. [*London*], *printed,* 1675. 4°.* L.

987B   Nevvs from Ostend. *For F. Coles, T. Vere, J. Wright, and J. Clark,* [1674–79]. brs. O.

988   News from Pannier-Alley. *Printed, and published by Randal Taylor,* 1687. 4°.* L, O; MH.

989   Newes from Pauls, containing a relation. *Printed,* 1642. 4°.* LT, LG, LP, OW; CH, LC.

990   Newes from Powles, or. [*London*], *printed*, 1649. 4°.* LP, OC, DU; CN, NHC.

Nevves from Pembroke. Mongomery, 1648. *See* Birkenhead, *Sir* John.

990A Newes from Pontefract. [*York*], *printed*, 1645. 4°.* YM.

991   Newes from Prince Rvpert. *By F. L.* May 25. 1644. 4°.* LT, O, CDC; MH.

992   News from Puddle-Dock. *For R. O.*, 1674. 4°.* LG; MH.

993   News from Purgatory. [*London*, 1679?] cap., fol.* L, O, C, DU; CH, MH, PU, WF, Y.

993A News from Ring-Cross. [*London*], *For George King*, 1675. 4°.* Y.

994   Entry cancelled.

Nevves from Rome. [n.p.], 1641. *See* B., T.

994A News from Rome, being a dialogue between the Pope and the devil. [*London*], *published by Martin Marpope*, [1677?]. 4°.* MH.

995   News from Rome, or, a dialogue between His Holinesse. [*London*, 1680.] cap., fol.* L, O, LLU, MR; CN, MH, MU, TU, WF, Y.

Nevves from Rome, or a trve. 1641. *See* B., T.

996   News from St. John Street. *For D. W.*, 1676. 4°.* O.

997   Newes from Sally. [*London*], *printed*, 1642. 4°.* LT, O; CH.

Newes from Scotland. His Majesties manifest. 1641. *See* Charles I.

News from Scotland: or. [1648.] *See* D., A.

997A News from Scotland: two acts of the Parliament. *By D. Maxwell for T. Garthwait*, 1662. 4°.* O.

998   News from sea. *For R. W.*, 1674. 4°.* L.

999   News from sea; or a true relation brought from Dover. *For D. M.*, [1676]. 4°.* L, MR.

1000 Newes from sea, concerning Prince Rupert. *For J. C.*, 1650. 4°.* L, LNM; MH, NN.

1001 News from Sherburn-Castle. colop: *For P. T.*, 1688. brs. L, LG; NP.

1002 Nevves from Sir John Svcklin. *For M. Rookes*, 1641. 4°.* LT; INU, MM, RHT.

News from Sr. William Waller. 1684. *See* I., C.

Newes from Smith. 1645. *See* Birkenhead, *Sir* John.

1003 News from So – – – Ho. colop: *By E. Mallet*, 1683. brs. L, O, EN; CH, TU, WF, ZWT.

Nevves from Sovthampton. 1644. *See* Murford, Peter.

1004 Newes from Svnderland. [*London*, 1648.] brs. LT, OC.

1004A News from Sussex. *For D. M.*, 1676. 4°.* L.

1005 News from the camp, on Black Heath. *For Thomas Vere*, 1673. brs. L.

News from the channel. 1673. *See* Wearis, F.

Newes from the citie of Norwich. [1642.] *See* M., C.

1005A News from the coast of Spain. [*London*], *for F. Coles, T. Vere, J. Wright, and J. Clark*, [1674–79]. brs. O.

1006 News from the Coffe-House. *By E. Crouch for Thomas Vere*, 1667. brs. L.

Newes from the dead. Oxford, 1651. *See* Watkins, Richard.

1007 News from the East-Indies. [*London?* 1691.] brs. L, LUG; CH, MH, MIU, WF.

1007A Newes from the Exchange. *For P. D.*, 1674. 4°.* L, LG; MH.

1007B News from the fens, or, an answer. *Printed*, 1654. 4°. L.

News from the fleet being a full account. 1690. *See* R., N.

1007C News from the fleet. Being a true account. *For Richard Baldwin*, 1689. brs. CN.

News from the goldsmiths. 1678. *See* Tovey, W.

1008 Nevves from the great Turke. *For Jo. Handcock*, 1645. 4°.* LT; NU, Y.

News from the Jews. 1671. *See* Gorion ben Syrach.

Newes from the Kings bath. Bristoll, 1645. *See* Pricket, Robert.

1008A Entry cancelled. Serial.

1009 News from the lowe countreys. *For W. N.*, 1652. 8°.* LT, O.

Nevves from the narrovv seas. 1642. *See* D., Em.

1009A News form [*sic*] the Netherlands. [*London*], *for F. Coles, T. Vere, J. Wright, and J. Clarke*, [1678–9]. brs. O.

Newes from the new exchange. 1650. *See* Neville, Henry.

News from the New-Jerusalem. 1649. *See* D., S. P.

1010 Nevves from the North. [*n.p.*], *printed*, 1641. 4°.* L, YM, DT; MH, WF.

1011 News from the North, a poem. colop: *For J. Dean*, 1683. brs. MC; CH, CLC, Y.

1012 Newes from the North: being. *Decemb.* 3. *for J. Usher*, 1642. 4°.* LT.

News from the North; or, 1648. *See* H., H.

1012A Newes from the North: or a relation of a great robberie . . . nere Swanton. *Printed* 1641. 4°.* OC; INU.

1013 News from the press. [*London*], *printed*, 1673. 4°.* L.

1013A News from the river of Thames. [*London*], *by E. and A. Milbourn, S. Hinch, J. Mason*, 1683. brs. MH.

1014 News from the Royall Exchange. *For Charles King.* 1660. brs. LT, O; MH, Y.

1014A Entry cancelled.

News from the session-house. 1689. *See* News from the Sessions house. The tryal.

1015 Nevvs from the sessions; or, a true relation . . . Sep. 9th. [*London*], *for Philip Brooksby*, 1674. 4°.* NU.

1016 Nevvs from the sessions. Or, the whole tryal of George Allen. [*London*], *for George Smith*, 1675. 4°.* NU.

1017 News from the Sessions house in the Old Bailey. *By and for P. Lillicrap*, 1674. 4°.* L, CD.

1017A —[Same title.] *Printed*, 1675. 4°.* LG.

1017B —[Same title.] *For D. M.*, 1676. 4°.* LG.

1018 News from the sessions-house . . . Lodowick Muggleton. *For B. H.*, 1676. 4°.* L, MR; MH.

1019 News from the sessions-house in the Old-Baily: being a true relation. *For Jo. Connyers*, 1678. 4°.* NU.

1019A News from the Sessions house. The tryal, conviction . . . Popery. colop: *By E. Webster, for J. Gibbs*, 1689. cap., fol.* CH, Y.

1019B —[Anr. ed.] colop: *By William Beale for J. Gibbs*, 1689. cap., fol.* CH, WF.

1020 Nevves from the siege before Yorke. *By M. O. for H. S.*, Iune. 24. 1644. 4°.* LT, DT.

1021 Entry cancelled. Ghost.

1021A News from the Strand; or, the Duke of Grafton present'd. *For S. M.*, 1688. fol.* L.

1022 Nevvs from the Thames. colop: *By T. Snowden, January 30*. 1684. brs. L, O, LG, LLP; CLC, MH, Y.

1022A Nevves from the Tovver. [*London*], *imprinted*, 1642. 4°.* MH.

News from the West of Ireland. 1642. *See* Aston, Thomas, *capt.*

1023 News from the West: or, a pleasant relation. [*London*], *for P. Brooksby*, [1685?]. brs. O.

Newes from Turkie. 1648. *See* L., W.

1024 News from Tyburn: or, a full. *For D. M.*, 1674. 4°.* LG.

1025 News from Tyburn: or a true relation. 1676. 4°. LG (lost).

1026 News from Tybourn: or, the confession. *For D. M.*, 1675. 4°.* L, LG, OB.

1026A News from Vienna. colop: *Printed*, 1683. brs. L.

1026B News from White-hall. [*London*, 1688.] brs. L, OC, EC.

1027 News from Windsor. [*London?* 1679.] cap., fol.* O; LC, WF, Y.

1027A Newes from York and the North. *For Francis Coules*, 1642. 4°.* L, O; IU.

1028 News from Yorke being a true relation. *For Richard Best*, 1642. brs. LT, LG, LS, EC.

1029 —[Anr. ed., "nevves."] —, 1642[3]. 4°.* LT, YM; IU, WF, Y.

News from Yorke: sent. [n.p., 1643.] *See* K., T.

1030 Newes from Yorke, with His Majesties propositions. [*London*], *for Hugh Perry*, 1642. brs. LT, LS, EC, HH, LNC.

1031 News indeed: Winchester taken. *For Laurance Blaiklock*, 1644. 4°.* LT, O; CH.

News of a new world from. 1676. *See* S., J.

1032 News of a new world: or. *Printed*, 1663. 4°. L, LF.

1033 Newes out of Ireland. *For Richard Best*, 1642. 4°.* AN; CLC, IU, NU.

1034 Newes ovt of Ireland concerning the warlike affaires. *By G. M.*, 1642. 4°.* LT, LVF, DN.

1035 Entry cancelled.

Newes out of the East. 1664. *See* Philly, John.

1036 Nevves ovt of the Lovv-covntries. *First printed at Oxford for William Webb, and since reprinted in London*, 1643.4°.* MADAN 1203. LT, O, LLL, LPR; HR, CH, Y.

1036aA News out of the Strand. *For Francis Grove*, [1662]. brs. EUING 252. GU.

1036A Newes out of the West. [*London*], *printed*, 1647. 4°.* L; CH, NN.

1037 Nevves, true newes, laudable newes, citie newes. *For F. Cowles, T. Bates, and T. Banks*, 1642. 4°.* LT, OC; CH, CLC, LC.

1038 —[Anr. ed.] *For R. G.* 1679. 4°.* CD; MH.

1038A —[Anr. ed.] [*Dublin*], *reprinted* 1679. 4°.* CD; MIU.

1039 Entry cancelled.

[**Newsam, Thomas.**] Thoughts of a private person. 1689. *See* Leeds, Thomas Osborne, *duke of.*

1040 **Newte, John.** The lawfulness and use of organs. *London: by Freeman Collins, to be sold by William Rogers; and by Humphry Burton in Tiverton*, 1696. 4°. T.C.II 598. L, C, LLP, OC, EC; CH, NU, WF, Y.

1041 Entry cancelled.

[–] Letter to a friend in the country, concerning the use. 1698. *See* title.

1042 [**Newton, Archbald.**] Uldericus veridicus. *Eleutheropoli Natiliæ* [*Edinburgh*], *excudebat Calabricus Neapolitanus*, 1657. 4°.* ALDIS 1571.5. L, C, DU, EN; CH, NP, NU, WF, Y.

1043 **Newton, Francis.** To the right honourable the Lords and Commons . . . the humble petition of. *By Richard Cotes*, 1648[9]. brs. LT.

1044 **Newton, George.** An exposition with notes, . . . John 17th. *By R. W. for Edward Brewster*, 1660. fol. LCL, LW, BR, DT; MH.

1044A — —[Anr. ed.] —, *and sold by Edw. Rosseter*, 1660. fol. CS.

1044B — —[Anr. ed.] *By R. W. for W. R., to be sold by Joseph Cranford*, 1660. fol. LW; CH, IU, WCL.

1045 —Men's wrath and God's praise. *London, by W. Wilson, for Francis Eglesfield, and are to be sold by George Treagle in Taunton*, 1646. 4°.* LT, O, BR, DT; FU.

1045A — —[Anr. ed.] *By W. Wilson, for Francis Eglesfield*, 1646. 4°.* CH, MH, NU.

1046 —A sermon preached the 11. of May 1652. *London, for William Roybould, to be sold by George Treagle in Taunton*, 1652. 4°.* LT, O; IAU, TU.

1047 —A sermon preached at the funeral of Mr. Joseph Alleine. *Printed and are to be sold by Nevil Simmons*, 1672. 8°.* L, O, C, LCL, BR, DU; CH, MH, NU, TSM, WF, Y. (var.)

1047A — —[Anr. ed.] *Nevil Simmons and Dorman Newman*, 1673. 8°.* L, LIC.

1048 **Newton, *Sir* Isaac.** Philosophiæ naturalis principia mathematica. *Jussu Societatis Regiæ ac typis Josephi Streater. Prostat apud plures bibliopalas.* 1687. 4°. L, O, C, E, DT; BN, CH, IU, LC, MH, TU, WF, Y, AVP.

1049 — —[Anr. ed.] *Jussu Societatis Regiæ ac typis Josephi Streater. Prostant venales apud Sam. Smith*, 1687. 4°. O, C, LR, CK, MC, ENC, DM; INU, MMO, MU, NN, NP, Y.

1050–51 Entries cancelled.

[–] Tables for renewing. Cambridge, 1686. *See* Mabbut, George.

1051A **Newton, James.** They that have any friends distracted or melancholy . . . may be cured by my means. [*London*, 1675.] brs. L.

1051B **Newton, John.** The art of natural arithmetick. *By E. T. and R. H., to be sold by Rob. Walton*, [1671]. 8°. T.C.I 89. CS; CLC.

1052 —The art of practical gauging. *For D. Page*, 1669. 8°. T.C.I 13. L, O, C, OB; BN.

[–] Artist's vade mecum. 1698. *See* Colton, *Dr.*

1053 —Astronomia Britannica, exhibiting the doctrine. *For the author, by R. and W. Leybourn, to be sold by Thomas Pierrepont*, 1657. 4°.* L, O, C, EN, DT; CH, IU, MH, PL, TU, WF.

1054 [–] The compleat arithmetician. *For John Taylor, and Christopher Browne*, 1691. 8°. T.C.II 368. L, O.

1055   —Cosmographia, or a view. *For Thomas Passinger, 1679.* 8°. T.C.I 333. L, O, C, OC, DU, E; BN, LC, MB, MU, NP, Y.

1056   —The countrey school-master. *Printed and to be sold by Rob. Walton, 1673.* 4°. T.C.I 152. O.

1056A [–] —[Anr. ed., "country school master."] *Printed for and sold by Chr. Coningsby,* [1695]. 8°. CM.

1057   —The English academy. *By W. Godbid, for Tho. Passinger, 1677.* 8°. T.C.I 257. L, O, C, LUC; BN, CLC, CU, NC.

1058   ——Second edition. *By A. Milbourn, for Tho. Passenger, 1693.* 12°. T.C.II 431. L, C, OAS; MB, MIU, NP, WF, Y.

1058A —An ephemeris ordiary. *Printed, 1667.* C.

1059   —Geometrical trigonometry. *For George Hurlock, and Thomas Pierrepont, 1659.* 12°. O, OC, SC; MU.

1060   —A help to calculation. *By Ioseph Moxon, 1657.* 4°. L, C, LR, OC, DCH; BBE, CH, CLC, IU, MU, NC.

1061   —Institutio mathematica. Or, a mathematical institution. *By R. & W. Leyburn, for George Hurlock, and Robert Boydel, 1654.* 12°. L, O, LW, CT, SC; CH, CJC, CLC, WF.

1062   ——[Anr. ed.] *For W. Fisher, 1671.* 12°. L, LR, EN; CH, MU.

1063   —An introduction to the art of logick. *By E. T. and R. H. for Thomas Passenger, 1671.* 12°. T.C.I 73. L, O, OC, DT; CN, IU.

1064   ——Second edition. *By A. P. and T. H. for T. Passenger, 1678.* 12°. T.C.I 337. O, E; BN, CH, CLC, MH, WF, AMB.

1065   —An introduction to the art of rhetorick. *By E. T. and R. H. for Thomas Passenger, and Ben. Hurlock, 1671.* 12°. T.C.I 88. L, O, NOT, E; BN, CH, CN, IU, MH, MU, WF.

1065A —Mathematical elements. 1657. 4°. CASTLE ASHBY.

1066   ——[Anr. ed.] *By R. & W. Leybourne for Robert Horn, 1660.* 4°. O, C, LR, OB, OC, DT; RBU.

1067   —The scale of interest. *For Dixy Page, 1668.* 8°. L; BN, IU, PL.

1067A ——[Anr. ed.] —*and Allen Bancks, 1668.* 8°. O, LW, SP, DT; CLC, WF.

1067B ——[Anr. ed.] *By E. C. for Dixy Page, 1668.* 8°. C, OC.

1068   —School pastime. *Printed, and are to be sold by Robert Walton,* [1669]. 8°. T.C.I 9. L, C.

1069   —— . . . second part. —, [1669]. 8°. L.

1070   —Sixteen pence in the pound. *Printed, 1658.* 8°.* LT.

1071   —Tabulæ mathematicæ: or, tables. *By R. & W. Leybourn, to be sold by George Hurlock, and by Robert Boydell, 1654.* 12°. L, O, OC, DCH, SC; CH, WF.

1071A ——[Anr. ed.] *For William Fisher, 1671.* 12°. MU.

1072   —Trigonometria Britanica. *By R. and W. Leyburn, to be sold by George Hurlock, Joshua Kirton, and Thomas Pierrepont, and William Fisher, 1658.* fol. L, O, C, EN, DT; BN, CH, CJC, CLC, MB, MU, RBU.

1073 **Newton, John,** *of St. Martin's.* The penitent recognition. *For Richard Chiswel, 1684.* 4°.* T.C.II 80. L, O, C, LW, EN; CH, MBA, MHL, WF, Y.

1073A ——[Anr. ed.] —, *and sold by William Atkins in Chicester, 1684.* 4°.* WCA, BLH.

1074 **Newton, Samuel.** An idea of geography. *London, for Christopher Hussey, sold likewise by M. Marlo in Wapping, by W. Court, by B. Billingsly and R. Parker, and by R. Cumberland, 1695.* 8°. L, LWL, CM.

1075 **Newton, William.** The copy of a letter written by. [*London,* 1642.] brs. LT, O, LG, LS, EC, HH; CLC, Y.

Newy, Charles. *See* Newey, Charles.

1075A The next door to the Castle-Tavern . . . liveth a gentle-woman . . . [advert.] [*London,* 1685?] brs. L.

1075B Next door to the Still . . . liveth a gentlewoman, who cutteth . . . hair. [*London,* 1700?] brs. L.

Next way to France. 1651. *See* P., H.

Nicanor, Lysimachus, *pseud.* *See* Corbet, John.

1076 **Nicephorus.** The unreasonableness of a separation. *By J. Heptinstall, for Henry Mortlock, 1691.* 4°.* T.C.II 367. L, O, C, DU, EN, DT; CH, LC, MH, MU, NCD, NU, Y.

1077 **Nicholas, Abraham.** Thoographia, or, a new art of shorthand. *Printed and sold by H. Mortlock, W. Freeman, S. Manship, and J. Garret, 1692.* 8°. T.C.II 427. L, LU, CM, CQ, MC; LC, NN.

1078   ——Second edition. *Printed and sold by Henry Mortlock, and W. Freeman, 1697.* 8°. NN.

1079   ——Fourth edition. *For William Davis, 1699.* 8°. NN.

1080 **Nicholas, Edward.** Apologia por la noble nacion. *Impresa en casa de Juan Field, en Londres, 1649.* 8°.* MB, MH, Y.

1081   —An apology for the honorable nation of the Jews. *By John Field, 1648[9].* 4°.* LT, O, LF, DT; CH, MH, OHU.

1082 **Nicholas, Jerome.** Nevvs certain and terrible from . . . Poland. *For Andrew Coe, 1642.* 4°.* LT, O, EC; CN.

1082A **Nicholas, John.** Sir, I do most earnestly desire. [*Oxford,* 1678.] brs. MADAN 3189. O.

Nicholas Machiavel's letter. [n.p., 1688.] *See* Wharton, Thomas, *marquis.*

1083 **Nicholes, M.** A catechisme, composed. Fifth edition. *By E. G. for Anne Boler, 1642.* 8°. O.

1084 **Nicholetts, Charles.** A burning yet unconsumed bush, exemplified. *Printed and sold by B. Harris, 1700.* 12°. L, O.

1085 [–] The cabinet of Hell unlocked. *For William Marshall, and John Marshall, 1696.* 4°.* T.C.II 586. O, CT.

[–] Dialogue between Simeon and Levi. 1688. *See title.*

1086 —The dissenters' jubilee. *By G. Larkin, 1687.* 4°. L, O, C, LW, OC, BLH; NU, WF.

1087 [–] The dying man's destiny. *For Dorman Newman, 1682.* 4°.* T.C.I 494. L, O, LL, LW; CDA, CLC, NAM, WF, Y.

1088 —The great work of God. *By Hugh Newman, 1698.* 4°.* T.C.III 64. L.

1089 **Nicholl, Henry.** Argumenta. [n.p.], 1678. brs. O.

1089A **Nicholls, Nicholas.** To the Kinge's most excellent Majestie. The humble petition of. [*London,* 1665.] brs. LPR.

1090 **Nicholls, William.** The advantage of a learned education. *By W. Redmayne for Fran. Saunders, and Benj. Tooke, 1697/8.* 4°.* T.C.III 49. L, O, C, RU, DT; MH, NU, SE, Y.

1091 —An answer to an heretical book called The naked Gospel. *For Walter Kettilby,* 1691. 4°. T.C.II 356. L, O, C, DU, WCA; CH, IU, MH, NU, PL, WF, Y.

1092 —A conference with a theist. *By T. W. for Francis Saunders; and Tho. Bennet,* 1696. 8°. T.C.II 577. L, O, C, AN, E, GU, CD; CH, IU, MH, NU, PL, WF, Y.

1093 ——Second edition. *By T. W. Francis Saunders; and Thomas Bennet,* 1698. 8°. L, CP, BC, DC, EN, DT; CB, IU, MIU, NPT, Y.

1094 ——Part II. —, 1697. 8°. T.C.III 12. L, O, CS, EN, DT; CB, MH, MIU, PL, Y.

1094A ———Second edition. —, 1699. 8°. BC.

1095 ——Part III. *By S. Budge, for E. Whitlock,* 1698. 8°. T.C.III 105. L, O, C, BSE, EN, DT; CB, MH, MIU.

1096 ——Part IV, and last. *By S. Budge, for F. Saunders; and T. Bennet,* 1699. 8°. T.C.II 105. L, O, CT, EN, DT; CB, MH, MIU, WF, Y.

1097 —An essay on the contempt of the world. *In the Savoy: by E. Jones, for Francis Saunders,* 1694. 8°. T.C.II 499. L, O, OB, OC, NE, EN; CH, WF, Y.

1098 —A practical essay of the contempt of the world. *By S. Bridge, for Francis Saunders,* 1698. 8°. L, LLP, LW, CE, NPL, E; CLC, MH, WF, Y.

1099 **Nichols, Charles.** The hue and cry after the priests. *For Livewell Chapman,* 1651. 4°. LW, E, EN.

1099A —The seamans summons. *For L. Chapman,* 1655. 4°.* LW.

1100 **N[ichols], H[enry].** A letter sent to General Monk, to St. Albons [*sic*] the 29 of January. *For the author,* 1659[60]. 4°.* LT, C, LG; CH, INU, MH, MIU, NN, PL.

1101 —The shield single. *By J. M. for H. Cripps, and L. Lloyd,* 1653. 4°. LT.

1102 Entry cancelled.

Nichols, Philip. Sir Francis Drake revived. 1653. See D., R.

1103 [**Nichols, T.**] A conference betwixt the Kings most excellent majesty and Mr. Peters. *By B. A., Iuue [sic] 22,* 1647. 4°.* LT; CLC, MH, MU, NN.

1103A [**Nichols, William.**] Great news from Dublin. colop: *For John Palmer,* 1690. brs. L, DN; CH, Y.

1104 **Nicholson, Benjamin.** A blast from the Lord. *For Giles Calvert,* 1653. 4°.* LT, AN; PH.

1105 [-] The lawyer's bane. *For George Whittington,* 1647. 4°.* LT, O, LL, DT; CH, CLC, MHL.

1106 —Some returns to a letter. *For Giles Calvert,* 1653. 4°.* LT, LF, BBN, MR, YM; CH, CU, NU, PH.

1107 [-] Truths defence against lies. [*London,* 1655.] cap., 4°.* LT, O, LF, BBN, MR; CH, MH, PH, PSC, Y.

1108 **Nicholson, Francis.** The confession of. colop: [*London*], *printed, and are to be sold by Richard Janeway,* 1680. cap., fol.* L; MH.

1109 **Nicholson, Joseph.** The standard of the Lord lifted up in New-England. *For Robert Wilson,* 1660. 4°.* L, LF; CH, MB, MU, PH, RPJ.

1110 **Nicholson, William, bp.** An apology for the discipline of the ancient church. *For William Leake,* 1659 [58]. 4°. LT, O, CS, DU, P, CD; CH, CLC, IU, NU, TO, WF.

1111 —David's harp strung and tuned. *For William Leake,* 1662. fol. L, O, C, AN, DU, CD; CLC, IU, NU, WF, WWC, Y.

1112 —Εκθεσις πιστεως or an exposition. *For VVilliam Leake,* 1661. fol. L, O, CT, NPL, DT; CH, CSU, IU, NU.

1113 —A plain, but full exposition of the catechisme. *By Evan Tyler, and are to be sold by Nathanael Web and William Grantham,* 1655. 4°. L, OME, CJ; MH, NU, Y.

1114 ——[Anr. ed.] *For Nathanael Webb, and William Grantham,* 1661. 4°. L, O, CT, P; CH, CN, MB, NU, TU, WF.

1115 ——[Anr. ed.] —, 1662. 4°. L, O, C, YM, SP; NU, TO.

1116 ——[Anr. ed.] —, 1663. 4°. L, O, C, LSD, DT; CDA, CH, CLC, MBP, WWC.

1117 ——[Anr. ed.] *For William Grantham,* 1671. 4°. L, O, C, OC, BSE; CH, IU.

1118 [-] —[Anr. ed.] *For William Miller,* 1676. 4°. L, C, OJ, D; CLC, WF.

1119 [-] —[Anr. ed.] *For R. Chiswell, and Benj. Tooke, and T. Sawbridge,* 1678. 4°. T.C.I 314. L, O, C, LSD, CD; CH, CLC, IU, TU, Y.

1120 ——[Anr. ed.] *By T. H. and W. H.,* 1686. 8°. L, LLP, OC, OME, DT; CH, CLC, NCU, Y.

1120A ——[Anr. ed.] —, 1689. 8°. LSD.

1121 Nick and Froth. [*London*], *for R. Burton,* [1641-74]. brs. L, HH; MH.

1121A The nicker nicked. Third edition. [*London*], *printed,* 1669. 4°.* L, O.

1122 [**Niclas, Hendrik.**] An apology for the service of love. *For Giles Calvert,* 1656. 12°. LT, LCL; NU.

1123 [-] Evangelium regni. *For Giles Calvert,* 1652. 8°. HH (dispersed).

1124 [-] —[Anr. ed.] *Imprinted at London,* 1652. 8°. O, C, CT; CLC, LC, NU, WF, Y.

1125 [-] A figure of the true & spiritual tabernacle. *For Giles Calvert,* 1655. 8°. LT, O, LLP, CT, BC; CDA, LC, MWA, NU, PH.

1126 [-] . . . The first epistle. A crying voice. [*London*], *printed,* 1648. 8°. LT; LC, WU.

1127 [-] The first exhortation of. *For Giles Calvert: and John Allen,* 1656. 8°. LT, LLP, OC, NE; CLC, NU, PH, WU.

1128 [-] An introduction to the holy understanding. *For George Whittington,* 1649. 8°. LT, O, CT; CB, CDA, CLC, LC, NU, WU.

1129 [-] The prophecy of the spirit of love. *For Giles Calvert,* 1649. L, O, C; CLC, LC, MWA, NU, WU.

1130 [-] Revelatio Dei. The revelation of God. *For Giles Calvert,* 1649. 8°. LT, O, LLP, OC, CT; CDA, CH, LC, NU, WSC, Y.

1131 [-] Terra pacis. A true testification. *For Samuel Satterthwaite,* 1649. 8°. O, CT; CLC, LC, MWA, NU.

1131A Nicodemus his gospel. [*n.p.*], 1646. 8°. O.

Nicola. See Matteis, Nicola.

1131B **Nicolas, *of the Holy Cross.*** Pious reflections. *Doway, by M. Mairesse,* 1695. 8°. L; Y.

1132 [**Nicole, Pierre.**] Epigrammatum delectus. *Impensis Mosis Pitt,* 1683. 8°. T.C.II 17. L, O, C, E, DT; CLC, CN, NP, TU, Y.

1133 [-] —[Anr. ed.] *Sumptibus Sam. Smith,* 1686. 8°. T.C.II 169. L, O, C, CT, DU, RPL; CH, CLC, IU, NC, WF, Y.

1134 [–] —[Anr. ed.] —, 1689. 12°. L, O, C, CT, NOT; CH, CU, MH, PL, WF.

1135 [–] —[Anr. ed.] *Sumptibus S. Smith & B. Walford*, 1699. 12°. T.C.III 42. L, C, BC, CASTLE ASHBY; CLC, PU, WF.

1136 [–] Moral essays. *For J. Magnes and R. Bentley*, 1677. 12°. T.C.I 267. L, O, CK, P, SP; CH, CLC, CU, IU, MU.

1137 [–] —Third edition. *For Sam. Manship*, 1696. 8°. T.C.II 583. L, LW, CS, LLU, GU; CH, CN, MH, PL, WF, Y.
    [–] —Second volume. 1678. *See* —Of the education.

1137AA [–] — —[Anr. ed.] *For R. Bentley and S. Magnes*, 1684. 12°. CK; CH, WF.

1137A [–] — —Second edition. *For Samuel Manship*, 1696. 8°. L, CS, DUS, LLU, GU; CH, CLC, IU, MH, NN, PL, WF, Y.

1137AB [–] —Third volume. *For R. Bentley & M. Magnes*, 1680. 12°. T.C.I 397. OC; CLC.

1137B [–] — —Third edition. *For Sam. Manship*, 1696. 8°. DUS, NE; CH, CLC, IU, MH, NN, PL.

1137BA [–] —Fourth volume. *For R. Bentley and M. Magnes*, 1682. 12°. OC; CLC.

1137C [–] — —[Anr. ed.] *For Samuel Manship*, 1696. 8°. DUS, NE, SHR; CH, CLC, IU, MH, NN, PL.

1137D [–] Of the education of a prince. *For James Magnes and Richard Bentley*, 1678. 12°. T.C.I 293. L, C, OC, NE; CLC, CN, PU, WF, Y.

1138 [–] The pernicious consequences of the new heresie of the Jesuites. *By J. Flesher, for Richard Royston*, 1666. 8°. L, O, C, OC, CT, P; CH, MH, WF, Y.

1139 **Nicolls, Ferdinando.** The life and death of Mr Ignatius Jurdain. *For Tho. Newberry*, 1654[5]. 4°.* LT, O, C, CT, YM, E; BN, CH, MH, WF.

1140 — —Second edition. *For Thomas Newberry*, 1655. 12°. L, O, LW; CH, Y.

1141 **Nicolls, R.** The conditions for new-planters. [*Cambridge, Mass., by Samuel Green*, 1665.] brs. EVANS 98. MHS.

1142 **Nicols, Daniel.** A sermon preach'd . . . July XVIII. 1681. *London, by A. G. and J. P. for Joseph Lawson, in Lincoln; and sold by Richard Chiswell; and Thomas Sawbridge*, 1681. 4°.* T.C.I 470. L, C, LSD; CH.

1142A **Nicols, Francis.** This most precious balsome . . . like a plaister. [*London*, 1650.] brs. MH.

1143 **Nicols, Thomas.** Arcula gemmea: or, a cabinet of jewels. *For Nath. Brooke*, 1653. 4°. LT, CT, BC, EN, DT; CH, IU, LC, WF, WU.

1144 [–] Gemmarius fidelius; or, the faithful lapidary. *For Henry Marsh*, 1659. 4°. L, O, LWL, CM; MH, WGS.

1145 —A lapidary. *Cambridge: by Thomas Buck*, 1652. 4°. LT, O, C, E, DT; CH, LC, MH, MU, PL, WF, JF.

1146 **Nicolson, William,** *abp.* The English historical library. *For Abel Swall and T. Child*, 1696. 8°. T.C.II 588. L, O, C, E, DT; CLC, CN, MH, NU, TU, WF, Y.

1146A — —[Anr. ed.] *For Abel Swall and T. Child, and are to be sold by Roger Clavel, and Francis Mills and W. Turner*, [1697?]. 8°. CK, CS, EC, LLU, P; CH, IU, MH, NU, TU, Y.

1147 — —Part II. *For Abel Swall*, 1697. 8°. L, O, C, E, DT; CLC, CN, MH, NU, V, WF.

1148 — —Part III. *For Timothy Childe*, 1699. 8°. T.C.III 138. L, O, C, E, DT; CH, CLC, IU, MH, NR, TU, V, WF, Y.

1148A [–] Of the medals and coins of Scotland. [*London?* 1700.] cap., 4°.* LUG.

1149 —A sermon preach'd . . . Feb. 15. 1684/5. *For John Gellibrand*, 1685. 4°.* L, O, LW, DU, LSD; CN, MH, PPT, Y.
    Niemant mijns gelijck. [n.p., 1695?] *See* Gerardts, Gonsale.

1149AA **Nieremberg, Juan Eusebio.** Contemplations of the state of man. *For John Kidgell, to be sold by Dormna* [sic] *Newman*, 1684. 8°. T.C.II 59. L, O, C, CT, LLP, P, D; CLC, CSU, IU, NP, WF, Y.

1149BA [–] —Fourth edition. *For John Kidgell, to be sold by Randall Taylor*, 1692. 8°. CLC, NU, VC, WF, Y, ZAS.

1149CA [–] —"Fifth" edition. *By H. Newman, for him, and E. R. and sold by R. Smith*, 1699. 8°. L, O, C, EN; CH, CLC.

1149A Entry cancelled.
    —Flores solitudinis. 1654. *See* Vaughan, Henry.

1150 —A meditation of life and death. *Oxford, by L. L., for Tho. Fickus*, 1682. 8°.* L, LIU; CASE WESTERN, WF, Y.

1150A —Of adoration in spirit. [*St. Omers*], printed, 1673. 8°. L, O, DUS, HEYTHROP, WARE, CD; TU, WF.

1150B [–] Prudential reflections. *By Ja: Cotterel, for R. Robinson*, 1674. 12°. T.C.I 164. L, LLU; CLC.

1151 —A treatise of the difference betwixt the temporal and eternal. [*London*], printed, 1672. 8°. T.C.I 109. L, O, C, EN, DT; CH, CU, MH, OCI, WF, Y.
    Niessen, Gertrude. *See* Dirrecks, Gertrude Niessen.

1152 **Nieuhof, Johan.** An embassy from the East-India Company. *By John Macock, for the author*, 1669. fol. L, C, OQ, CT, DT; CH, CN, MH, PL, WG, Y.

1153 — —Second edition. *By the author* [i.e., *John Ogilby*], 1673. fol. L, O, OC, CK, DT; BN, CH, CN, MH, NF, WF.
    Een nieuwe en gemakkelijke Engelsche spraak-konst. 1690. *See* Heldoren, J. G. van.

1153A The night-bell-man of Pickadilly. [*London*, 1693.] brs. L, EN; MH, Y.

1154 The night-walker of Bloomsbury. *By J. Grantham*, 1683. brs. L, O, LLU, MC; CH, MB, MBA, MH, WF, ZWT.

1155 The night-vvalkers. [*London*], *for P. Brooksby*, 1682. brs. L, HH.

1156 The night-walkers declaration. *For D. M.*, 1676. 4°.* L, MR.

1157 The night-walkers: or, the loyal huzza. [*London*], *for P. Brooksby*, 1682. brs. L.
    Nightingale, Robert. Mercurius philastrogus. [n.p., 1653.] *See* Almanacs.

1157A The nightingales song. 1675. brs. O.

1157B **Nihell, James.** A journal of the most remarkable occurrences . . . army. *Dublin, for James Malone*, [1689]. fol.* O.

1157C Nihil absque Deo. Try the preserving of health. [*London*, 1680?] brs. L.
    Nil dictum quod. 1681. *See* Disney, William.

1158 Nil probas: or, a discovery. *For Giles Calvert*, 1646. 4°.* LT, O, LNC, SC, DT; MM, OHU, OSU, WF.

1158A Nine canons added to those of the Church of England. [*London?* 1690.] brs. HH.

1158B The nine mortal weapons. [*London*, 1650?] brs. L.

1159 The nine muses. *For Richard Basset*, 1700. fol.* L, LVD, LLU; CLC, MH, NP, OSU, WF, Y.

1160 Nine notable prophesies. [*London*], *for Richard Harper*, 1644. 4°. O.

IX proposals. 1647. *See* Prynne, William.

1160A Nine proposals of religion. [*London*], *printed*, 1689. brs. HH.

IX qveries. 1647. *See* Prynne, William.

1161 Nine quotable prophesies. [*n.p.*], 1644. 4°. O.

1162 Nine speciall passages, concerning the militia. *For Edward Blackmore, June* 11, 1642. 4°.* L, OP, MR, SP, YM; CH, CSS, WF, Y.

Nineteen arguments. 1645. *See* J., R.

1163 Nineteen cases of conscience. *Printed*, 1659. 4°.* LT, O, LW, EC, LSD, DT; CH, CN, MH, NU, WF, Y.

Nineteen humble propositions. [*n.p.*, 1643.] *See* Nutt, Thomas.

1163A Nineteen quaeries tending to unbeguile a Protestant. [*London?* 1680.] 4°.* MR; CH, WF.

1164 A ninth collection of papers relating to the present juncture. *Printed, to be sold by Richard Janeway*, 1689. 4°.* L, OC, CM, BR, BLH; CH, IU, MH, NU, WF, Y.

Il nipotismo. 1669. *See* Leti, Gregorio.

1165 **Nisbet, Alexander, 1623-1669.** A brief exposition of the first and second epistles general of Peter. *Edinburgh, by Christopher Higgins*, 1658. 8°. ALDIS 1579. L, O, EN, ENC, GU; CLC, NU, WF.

1166 ——[Anr. ed.] *For the Company of Stationers*, 1658. 8°. LT, O; MH, TO.

1167 Entry cancelled.

——Essay. Edinburgh, 1700. *See* Nisbet, Alexander, 1657-1725.

1168 ——An exposition with practical observations upon . . . Ecclesiastes. *Edinbvrgh, by George Mosman*, 1694. 4°. ALDIS 3378. L, C, LW, ENC, SA; CH, IU, MH, NU, WF, Y.

1168A **Nisbet, Alexander, 1657-1725.** An essay on additional figures. *Edinburgh*, 1700. 12°. ALDIS 3989. ES.

1169 **Nisbet, John.** Epicedium nobilissimi et inclyti herois, Dni Roberti Devereux, Comitis Essexiæ. [*London*, 1646.] brs. LT, SS.

1170 Entry cancelled.

Nisbet, Sir John. *See* Dirltoun, John Nisbet, lord.

1171 **Nisbet, William.** A golden chaine of time. *Printed at Edinburgh by the heires of George Anderson, for the Company of Stationers*, 1650. 8°. ALDIS 1415. L, EN, GU, I; Y.

1172 ——A scripture chronology. *For Joshua Kirton*, 1655. 8°. LT, O; NU.

1172A **Niven, William.** To the King's most sacred Majesty, upon the happy birth of the Prince. colop: *By Mary Thompson*, 1688. brs. O; MH.

1173 No age like unto his age: or, times unparallel'd oppression. *By J. C.* 1653. 4°.* LT, O, BC, LSC; CH, MH.

1174 No antiquity for transubstantiation. *Printed*, 1688. 4°.* T.C.II 244. L, NPL; NU, Y.

No blinde guides. 1660. *See* L'Estrange, *Sir* Roger.

1174A No creature is so false as man. [*n.p.*, 1670?] brs. L.

1175 No droll, but a rational account. *For Y. E.* colop: *For Henry Brome*, [1660]. 4°.* LT, O; CH, CN.

1175A ——[Anr. ed.] *For Y.E.*, 1660. colop: *For Henry Brome.* 4°.* C, LUG, OC, MR, E; CLC, MH, Y.

1175B ——[Anr. ed.] —["*YE.*"], [1660]. 4°.* O; MH, MM, NN, WF.

No evidence. 1681. *See* Clarkson, David.

No fool to the old fool. [n.p.], 1659. *See* L'Estrange, *Sir* Roger.

1176 No interest beyond the principall. *For H. Becke*, 1648. 4°.* LT, O, MR, DT; CH, INU, MH, MM, WF.

1177 No jest like a true jest. *For J. Deacon*, [1672]. 8°. O, CM, EN.

1177A ——[Anr. ed.] *For Tho. Vere and William Gilbertson*, [1660?]. 8°.* CH.

1178 ——[Anr. ed.] *By A. P. for T. Vere*, 1674. 8°.* CH.

1179 ——[Anr. ed.] *By T. H. for T. Vere*, 1680. 12°.* CN.

1180 No King but the old Kings son. *For Theophilus Microcosmus*, 1660. brs. LT, O, OC.

1181 No love, no life. [*London*], *for J. Deacon*, [1684]. brs. L, O, CM.

No martiall law. [n.p.], 1648. *See* Whittington, John.

1182 No money, no friend. [*London*], *for F. Coles, T. Vere, J. VVright, J. Clarke, VV, Thackeray, and T. Passinger*, [1680?]. brs. L, CM, HH; MH.

1183 No new Parliament. *Printed*, 1660. 4°.* LT, O, OC, LSD, MR; CH, CLC, MH, MIU, MU.

No nevvs, but a letter. [n.p., 1648.] *See* W., R.

1184 No pamphlet, bvt a detestation against all such. *Printed*, 1642. 4°.* LT, CT, DN; CLC, Y.

1185 No Papist nor Presbyterian. [*London*], *published*, 1649[48]. 4°.* LT, C, DT; CH, MH, NU, WF, ZAP.

No Parliament but the old. 1659. *See* R., W.

1185A No Parliament, no penny. [*London*], *for a lover of his country*, [c. 1660]. 4°.* MB.

1186 No Parliament without a king. *Oxford* [*London*], *for Leonard Lichfield*, 1642[3]. 4°.* MADAN 1207. LT, O, CT, SP, DT; CH, CN, MH, NU, WF, Y.

No peace. Oxford, 1645. *See* Arnway, John.

1187 No Popery, or a catechism. *For the author, and sold by Tho. Parkhurst*, 1682. 8°. C; NU, TO, WF.

1188 ——[Anr. ed.] *Edinburgh, by the heir of Andrew Anderson*, 1683. 12°. ALDIS 2398. L.

1188A ——[Anr. ed.] *Edinburgh, J. Reid*, 1683. 8°. ALDIS 2399. EN.

1189 ——[Anr. ed.] *Glasgow, by Robert Sanders*, 1683. 8°. ALDIS 2400. EN.

No post from Heaven. Oxford, 1643. *See* A., G.

No præexistence. 1667. *See* Warren, Edward.

No Protestant, but the dissenters plot. 1682. *See* Long, Thomas.

No Protestant-plot. 1681. *See* Ferguson, Robert.

1190 No Protestant plot, or, the Whigs loyalty. [*London*], *for Charles Corbet*, 1683. brs. O; CH, CLC, MH, NCD, TU, Y.

No remission. [n.p.], 1665. *See* Whitehead, George.

1191 No retvrn to monarchy. *For Thomas Brewster*, 1659. 4°.* LT, O; CSS, MH, MU, NN, RBU, WF.

1191A No ring, no vvedding. *By John Hamond*, [1656]. brs. MAU.
       No sacrilege. 1659. *See* Burgess, Cornelius.
1192   No stopping of the coin. *J. Whitlock*, 1695. brs. LG, LUG;
       MH, PU.
1192A Noah's dove: with a green olive-leaf, or, the national
       covenant. [*Scotland?* 1687.] brs. EN; CSS.
1192B Noah's flood revived, or a second deluge . . . [4 Novem-
       ber 1675]. [*London*], *printed*, 1675. 4°.* OB.
1193   [**Nobbes, Robert.**] The compleat troller. *By T. James
       for Tho. Helder*, 1682. 8°. T.C.I 487. L; CH, MH, NN, PU,
       WF, Y.
       Nobilis pharmacopola. 1693. *See* Villiers, Jacob de.
       Nobilissima disceptatio. 1690. *See* Wingfeld, Robert.
1194   Entry cancelled.
       Noble. Visions. 1700. *See* Noble, David.
1195   **Noble, Charles.** The inexpediency of the expedient.
       For Tho. Pierrepont, 1659. 4°.* C, MR, DT; CH, NP, WF.
1196   —A moderate answer to certain immoderate quæries.
       For Henry Marsh, 1659. 4°.* LT, C; CSS, MH.
1196A **Noble, David.** The visions & prophecies of Daniel.
       For Nevil Simmons in Sheffield, 1700. 8°. C, LW.
1197   **Noble, Edward.** Godly adversity. *By S. Dover*, 1661.
       4°. CLC, NU.
1197A **Noble, John.** The conception and birth of sin. *By John
       Field*, 1655. 4°.* CH.
1198   **Noble, Mark.** Mark Noble's frollick. [*London*, 1670?]
       brs. L.
1199   Entry cancelled.
       Noble acts. [n.p., 1690.] *See* Deloney, Thomas.
1200   Entry cancelled.
       Noble and pleasant history. 1652. *See* Notable.
1201   The noble birth and gallant atchievements [sic] of . . .
       Robin Hood. *For Thomas Vere and William Gilbertson*,
       1662. 4°. L.
1202   —[Anr. ed.] *By A. P. and T. H. for T. Vere*, 1678. 4°. L.
1203   —[Anr. ed.] *By M. Haly and J. Millet for J. Deacon*, 1685.
       4°. CHRISTIE-MILLER.
1203A —[Anr. ed.] *By J. M., sold by J. Deacon*, [c. 1690]. 4°.*
       O, CM.
1203B —[Anr. ed.] *By W. O., sold by B. Deacon*, [1700]. 4°.* CM.
1203C The noble cuckold. *Printed at Alba Regalis*, 1693. SW.
1204   A noble dewel. *For John Andrews*, [1660]. brs. O.
1205   The noble English worthies. *By Tho. Milbourn*, 59
       [i.e. 1659]. brs. LT, O; WF.
1205A The noble fisher-man. *For F. Coles*, [1650?]. brs. O.
1205B —[Anr. ed.] [*London*], *for F. Coles, T. Vere, and W.
       Gilbertson*, [1658–64]. brs. O.
1205C —[Anr. ed.] [*London*], *for F. Coles, T. Vere, and J. Wright*,
       [1663–74]. brs. EUING 301, O, GU.
1205D —[Anr. ed.] [*London*], *for F. Coles, T. Vere, J. Wright, and
       J. Clarke*, [1674–79]. brs. O.
1206   —[Anr. ed.] [*London*], *for W. Thackeray, and T. Passinger*,
       [1686–88]. brs. L, HH; MH.
1207   —[Anr. ed.] [*London*], *by and for A. M.*, [1690?]. brs. L.
1208   The noble funeral of . . . the Duke of Grafton. [*London*],
       for Charles Bates, [1690]. brs. L; NNM.

1209   The noble gallant. [*London*], *for I. H. and sold by F. Coles,
       T. Vere, I. Wright, and I. Clarke*, [1674–79.] brs. L, O;
       MH, WCL.
1209A —[Anr. ed.] [*London*], *for J. Hose*, [c. 1675]. brs. O.
       Noble ingratitude. Hage, 1659. *See* Quinault, Philippe.
1210   The nobe [sic] mans generous kindness. [*London*], *for P.
       Brooksby*, [1685–88]. brs. EUING 159. L, O, CM, HH, GU;
       MH.
       Noble-mans patterne. [n.p.], 1643. *See* Calamy, Edmund.
1211   The noble Monk. *By Tho. Milbourn for the author*, 1660.
       brs. LT; MH.
1212   Entry cancelled.
       Noble pamphlet. [n.p.], 1648. *See* R., W.
1213   The noble prodigal. [*London*, 1670–80.] brs. L, O, HH; MH.
1214   The noble progresse. [*London*], *for F. Coles, T. Vere, and
       W. Gilbertson*, [1660]. brs. L.
1215   A noble riddle wisely expounded. [*London*], *for F. Coles,
       T. Vere and W. Gilbertson*, [1658–64]. brs. EUING 253.
       O, CM, GU.
1216   The noble souldier's advice. *For Samuel Speed*, 1661. brs.
       L.
1216A The noble souldier's answer to Mr. Walker's speech.
       colop: *For J. W.* 1689. brs. CH, Y.
       Noctes Hibernæ. 1653. *See* Barksdale, Clement.
       Noctroff, Alethes, pseud.
1217   Noctvrnall occvrrences. *For E. Christopher*, 1642. 4°.*
       LT, OW; CLC, MH.
1217A **Noddell, Daniel.** To the Parliament . . . the declaration
       of. 1653. 4°.* LUG; CSS.
1217B [–] To the Parliament . . . the great complaint and dec-
       laration of about 1200. free-holders. *Printed* 1654. 4°.*
       LUG; Y.
1218–9 Entries cancelled.
       Noel, Nath. Circle. 1675. *See* Bremond, Gabriel de.
1220   **Nokes, William.** Dissertatio de lege. *Prostant venales
       apud Joh. Salisbury*, 1694. 12°. L, O, LW, GU.
1220A — —*Sumptibus authoris*. 1694. 12°. TO.
       Nolens volens. 1677. *See* Coles, Elisha.
       Noli me tangere. 1642. *See* Udall, Ephraim.
1221   **Nollius, Henry.** The chymists key. *By E. B. for L.
       Lloyd*, 1657. 12°. OC, BC, E; CH, MH.
1222   —Hermetical physick. *For Humphrey Moseley*, 1655. 12.°
       LT, O, AN, NPL, GU; CLC, WU.
       Nomenclatura brevis. [1651.] *See* Gregory, Francis.
       Ονομαστικον.
1222A Nomenclatura vestibularis: or, a further improvement
       of . . . Comenius. *For Jo. Cranford*, 1662. 8°. L (t.p.),
       BIU.
1222B The non-associating list of those members that refused
       to subscribe. *For E. Tomlinson in Westminster*, 1696.
       brs. LPR.
       Non est inventus return'd. [n.p.], 1662. *See* Cressy, Hugh
       Paulin.
       Non vltra: or. 1698. *See* Sergeant, John.
1223   The non-conformist made conformable. [*London*],
       printed, 1670. 4°.* L, O, CS.
       Nonconformists advocate. 1680. *See* Baxter, Richard.

Non-conformists no schismaticks. [n.p.], 1670. *See* Carter, Thomas.

Nonconformists plea for peace. 1680. *See* Long, Thomas.

Nonconformists plea for the conformists. 1683. *See* C., J.

1224   The non-conformist's plea for uniformity. *For Henry Brome*, 1674. 4°.* T.C.I 154. L, O, C, DU, EN, DT; CH, MH, MIU, NU, WF, Y.

Nonconformists relief. [n.p.], 1678. *See* Humfrey, John.

Nonconformists vindicated. 1679. *See* Barrett, William.

1225   The nonconformist's vindication. colop: *For the author*, 1683. cap., fol.* O, LG, EN; CH, CLC, MH, WF, ZWT.

Nonconformists vindication. [n.p.], 1700. *See* Grant, Patrick.

1225A   Non-residency and pluralities, justly exposed. *For Richard Janeway*, 1681. brs. O; MH.

None but Christ. 1655. *See* Cotton, Clement.

1226   None but the sheriffs ought to name. colop: *For R. Baldwyn*, [1681]. brs. L, O, C, HH, LSD; CN, AVP.

1226A   The none-such Charles his character. *By R. I., to be sold by John Collins*, 1651. 8°. LT, O, CS, MR, YM, BQ; CH, CN, MH, NU, WF, Y. (var.)

1226B   **Noon, Edward.** Brachyarithma, or the rules of arithmetick. [*London*], *Will. Elder sculpsit*, [*c.* 1690]. 4°. L.

1226C   **Norcott, John.** Baptism discovered plainly. *Printed*, 1672. 8°. ORP; MBZ.

1227   ——Second edition. *For the author, and sold by Ben. Harris*, 1675. 8°. MB, NHC.

1227A   ——[Anr. ed.] *Printed at Rotterdam, and now re-printed at London, by the assigns of Widow Norcott and sold by W. Marshal*, 1694. 8°. LW.

1227B   —Bedydd gwedi i amlygu. *Tros William Marshall*, 1694. 12°. AN. (impf.)

1228   [**Norcroft, John.**] Exceeding ioyfvll nevves from his excelence the Earle of Essex. *For Hen. Hutton. Oct.* 10. 1642. 4°.* LT, AN; MH.

1228A   **Norden, John.** The poor man's rest. Fifteenth edition. *By E. G. for Andrew Crooke*, 1641. 12°. O.

1228B   ——Twentieth edition. *By J. R. for R. Scot, T. Basset, J. Wright, and R. Chiswel*, 1684. 12°. L, LSC.

1229   Entry cancelled.

Norffs president. [n.p.], 1666. *See* Rack, Edmund.

1230   **Norfolk, Henry Howard, 6th duke of.** Bibliotheca Norfolciana: sive catalogus. *Excudebat Ric. Chiswel*, 1681. 4°. L, O, C, CT, BC, DU, LIU, MR, DT; CH, CN, MH, PL.

1231   **Norfolk, Henry Howard, 7th duke of.** His Grace the Duke of Norfolk's charge against the Dutchess. *Printed*, 1692. 4°.* L, LG, LL, LLP; MH, PU, TO, WF, WSL.

1231A   —By His Grace . . . In pursuance of an order. *In the Savoy, by Edw. Jones*, 1694[5]. brs. MH.

1231B   —By His Grace . . . It being expected, that the present mourning for . . . Glocester [*sic*]. [*London*], *by Edward Jones in the Savoy*, 1700. brs. Y.

[-] Form of the proceeding to the funeral of . . . Queen Mary II. [n.p.], 1694/5. *See title.*

1232   —The Duke of Norfolk's order about the habit the ladies are to be in . . . coronation. colop: *By Nat. Thompson*, 1685. brs. CH, MH, WF.

1232A   —[Anr. ed.] *Dublin, re-printed by Andrew Crook and Samuel Helsham; and are to be sold at Samuel Helsham's*, 1685. brs. LIU.

1232B   —The Earl Marshal's order touching the habits of the peeresses at the coronation. *In the Savoy, by Edw. Jones*, 1688. brs. L, O; Y.

1232C   —Orders to be observed at the coronation of the King and Queen. *For John Smith*, 1685. brs. STEELE 3792. O, LG; MH, Y.

1233   —Orders to be observed in the church of Westminster Abbey. [*London*], *by Tho. Newcomb in the Savoy*, 1685. brs. L, O; CH, CLC, MH, WF.

1234   [-] Orders to be observed on the day of the royal coronation. *In the Savoy, by E. Jones*, 1689. brs. STEELE 3987. L, O, C, LLP; MH.

1234A   —The Duke of Norfolk's speech at Lynn [12 December]. [*London*], *printed*, 1688. brs. L, C.

1235   —By Henry duke of Norfolk . . . Whereas His Majesty . . . [9 February 1684/5 . . . mourning]. *By the assigns of John Bill: and by Henry Hills and Thomas Newcomb*, 1684[5]. brs. STEELE 3780–1. L, O, LPR; CH, MH, PU, Y.

1236   **Norfolk, Thomas Howard, *duke of.*** The true coppy of a letter. *For Iohn Thomas*, 1641. 4°.* LT, BC, BR, LLU, LSD, SP; CH, CLC, CSS, NN, WF.

Norfolke feast. 1671. *See* S.,W.

1236A   The Norfolk gentleman his last will. [*London*], *for F. Coles, T. Vere, and W. Gilbertson*, [1658–64]. brs. EUING 255. O, GU.

1236B   —[Anr. ed.] [*London*], *for F. Coles, T. Vere and J. Wright*, [1663–74]. brs. EUING 254. OC, GU.

1237   —[Anr. ed.] [*London*], *for Alex Milbourn*, [1695?]. brs. L, O, CM, HH.

1237A   —[Anr. ed.] [n.p., 1700?] brs. EUING 256. GU.

1238   The Norfolk lass. [*London*], *for P. Brooksby*, [1675?]. brs. L; MH.

1238A   Norma curiarum inferiorum. *For J. Place, and Tho. Basset*, 1673. 8°. L, O, LGI, LL; CH, MHL, WF.

1239   **Norman, John.** Cases of conscience. *By A. M. for Tho. Parkhurst*, 1673. 8°. T.C.I 140. O, LCL, LW, OW; NU, AVP.

1239A   ——[Anr. ed.] *By A. M. for Edw. Brewster*, 1673. 8°. WF.

1240   —Christ's commission-officer. *London, for Edward Brewster, to be sold by Edward Rosseter in Taunton*, 1658. 8°. LCL; NU.

1240A   ——[Anr. ed.] *For Edward Brewster*, 1658. 8°. LT, LW, ORP.

1241   —Family-governors perswaded. *By A. Maxey, for Samuel Gellibrand*, 1657. 8°.* L.

1241A   **Norris, Edward.** A short catechisme. *Printed at Cambridge N. E.*, 1649. 8°. EVANS 24. LLP.

1242   Entry cancelled.

Norris, Jah. Lash for a lyar. 1647. *See* Harris, John, Leveller.

1242A   [**Norris, James.**] Haec and hic: or, the feminine gender more worthy. *By Jo. Harefinch, for James Norris*, 1683. 12°. T.C.II 32. L; CJC, CLC, MB.

1242B   [-] The accomplished lady. *For James Norris*, 1684. 12°. T.C.II 50. L; CH, IU, Y.

1243   **Norris, John.** An account of reason & faith. *For S. Manship*, 1697. 8°. T.C.II 599. L, O, C, E, DT; CH, IU, MH, NCD, NU, WF, Y.

1244   [–] Αποδοκιμασιας. *Prostant venales apud Jacobum Norris*, 1683. 8°. O, CT, AN, NE.

     [–] Call to all the shepherds. [1681.] *See* N., S.

1245   [–] The charge of schism continued. *For Samuel Manship*, 1691. 8°. T.C.II 356. O, CS, DC, E, DT; NIA, NU, OLU, Y.

1246   —Christian blessedness. *For S. Manship*, 1690. 8°. T.C.II 319. L, O, C, BR, SHR; CH, CN, MH, NU, WF, Y.

1247   ——Second edition. —, 1692. 8°. L, LW, BC, LSD, NOT; CH, CLC, MH, NCD, PU, Y.

1248   —A collection of miscellanies. *Oxford, at the Theater for John Crosley*, 1687. 8°. T.C.II 224. L, O, C, AN, DU; CH, CN, MH, NU, WF, Y, AVP.

1249   ——Second edition. *For J. Crosley, and Samuel Manship*, 1692. 8°. L, C, OME, AN, E; CH, MH, MU, NU, TU, WF, Y.

1250   ——Third edition. *For S. Manship, to be sold by Percivall Gilbourne*, 1699. 8°. L, OB, CCO, LIU, BQ; CH, CN, MH, WF, Y.

1251   —A discourse concerning the pretended religious assembling. *For James Norris*, 1685. 8°. L, O, OC, CT, DU; CH, CLC, MIU, NU, PL, WF, Y.

1252   —An idea of happiness. *For James Norris*, 1683. 4°.* T.C.II 19. L, O, LCL, BC, EC; CH, CN, MH, MIU, WF.

1253   ——Second edition. —, 1684. 4°. C, LLL, RU; CN, CU, MH.

1254   —Letters concerning the love of God. *For Samuel Manship, and Richard Wilkin*, 1695. 8°. T.C.II 518. L, O, C, MR, DT; CH, CN, LC, MH, NU, TU, Y.

1255   [–] A murnival of knaves. *For James Norris*, 1683. 4°.* T.C.II 29. L, O, C, DU, DT; CH, CU, MH, PL, WF, Y.

1256   —Poems and discourses. *By J. Harefinch, for James Norris*, 1684. 8°. T.C.II 73. L, O, C, LW, SC; CH, CN, MH, WF, Y.

1257   —Practical discourses upon several divine subjects. *For Samuel Manship*, 1691. 8°. T.C.II 378. L, O, LCL, CT, LSD; CH, MU, NCD, WF, Y.

1258   ——Second edition. —, 1692. 8°. OM.

1259   ——Vol. I ["upon the beatitudes"]. Third edition. *For S. Manship*, 1694. 8°. L, O, C, CE; CLC, CN, MH, NU, PL, Y.

1260   ———["upon the beatitudes"]. Fourth edition. —, 1699. 8°. T.C.III 34. L, C, LW, EC; CH, CLC, MBA, MH, Y.

1261   ——Vol. II. Second edition. —, 1693. 8°. T.C.II 448. C, BSE, DUS; CN, INU, NU, PL, Y.

1262   ———Third edition. —, 1697. 8°. L, O, C, LW, EC; CH, CLC, MBA.

1263   ——Vol. III. —, 1693. 8°. T.C.II 448. L, O, C, EC, P; CLC, MBA, NU, WWC, Y.

1264   ——Vol. IV. —, 1698. 8°. O, C, CT, P, E; CH, Y.

1264A   ———[Anr. ed.] —, and J. Jones, 1698. 8°. CLC.

1264B   ———[Anr. ed.] *For S. Manship, and sold by J. Jones*, 1698. 8°. EC.

1264C   ———[Anr. ed.] *For John Jones*, 1698. 8°. T.C.III 49. WWC.

1265   —Reason and religion. *For Samuel Manship*, 1689. 8°. T.C.II 249. L, O, C, BR, NOT; CLC, CN, CU, MH, NU, Y.

1266   ——Second edition. *For S. Manship*, 1693. 8°. T.C.II 432. L, C, LW, EC, ELY; CH, CLC, MH, MU, WF.

1267   —Reflections upon the conduct of human life. *For S. Manship*, 1690. 8°. T.C.II 291. L, LF, OC, CT, BR; CN, MH, NU, TO, WF.

1268   ——Second edition. —, 1691. 8°. T.C.II 363. L, O, CS, NOT, EN; CH, CU, MH, MU, NU.

1269   —A sermon preach'd . . . March 29. 1685. *Oxford, by Leonard Lichfield, for Thomas Fickus*, 1685. 4°.* L, O, OC, CS, WCA; CH, MH, MU, NU, WF, Y.

1270   Entry cancelled.

     —Sermon preach'd . . . July 30, 1689. 1690. *See* — Reflections.

1271   [–] Spiritual counsel. *For W. Hunt*, 1694. 12°. T.C.II 546. L, O, DC, NOT; OCI.

1271A   ——[Anr. ed.] *For S. Manship*, 1694. 12°. OC, CS; CSU, MH, NP, PL.

1272   —The theory and regulation of love. *Oxford, at the Theatre for Hen. Clements*, 1688. 8°. L, O, BAMB, BR, EN; CH, CN, MH, NU, WF, Y.

1273   ——Second edition. *For S. Manship*, 1694. 8°. L, O, C, ESSEX, SHR; CH, LC, MH, MU, PU, WF.

1274   —Treatises upon several subjects. *For S. Manship*, 1697. 8°. T.C.III 20. L, O, C, LF, OM, DT; CLC, CU, MH, MIU, NCD, NU.

1275   ——[Anr. ed.] —, 1698. 8°. T.C.II 599. L, O, C, SHR, AU; CH, CLC, MBA, NP, WF, Y.

1276   —Two treatises. *For Sam. Manship*, 1692. 8°. T.C.II 421. L, O, C, LF, OM, DUS; CH, IU, MH, NU, PH, WF, Y.

1276A   **Norris, Richard.** The manner of finding the true sum. *By Tho. James for the author*, 1685. 4°. L.

1277   **[Norris, William.]** An elegie vpon the death of the renowned, Sir Iohn Svtlin. *[London], printed*, 1642. 4°.* 5 pp. LT, CT, EC; CH, TU, WF.

1278   [–] —[Anr. ed.] —, 1642. 4°.* 8 pp. L; TU.

1279   **[Nortcliffe, M.]** An argument in defence of the right of patrons to advowsons. *For Edward Blackmore*, 1653. 4°.* LT, C, LLP; NC, WF.

1280   **[North, Sir Dudley]**, *1641-1691*. Discourses upon trade. *For Tho. Basset*, 1691. 4°.* T.C.II 385. L, O, LUG, RU, ES; CH, CJC, MH, NC, Y.

1281-2   Entries cancelled.

     —Light. 1682. *See* North, Dudley North, *4th baron*.

     —Some notes. [n.p., 1682.] *See* North, Dudley North, *4th baron*.

1283   **[North, Dudley]**, *3d baron*. A forest of varieties. *By Richard Cotes*, 1645. fol. L, O, SP, ES; CH, CN, LC, MH, WF.

1284   [–] A forest promiscuous. *By Daniel Pakeman*, 1659. fol. L, O, CT, EC, EN; CH, CN, MH, TU, Y.

1284A   **North, Dudley North, 4th baron.** A letter of . . . touching Thirlow school. [n.p., 1666.] cap., 4°.* NC.

1284B   —Light in the way to paradise. *For William Rogers*, 1682. 8°. T.C.I 483. L, O, C, DU, ES; CH, CN, MH, NU, WF, Y.

1285   [–] A narrative of some passages in, or relating to, the Long Parliament. *For Robert Pawlet*, 1670. 8°. T.C.I 58. L, O, C, DU, EN; CH, CN, MBP, MH, NU, TU, WF, Y.

1286 [–] Observations and advices oeconomical. *By T. R. for John Martyn,* 1669. 8°. T.C.I 14. L, O, C, DU, ES; BN, CH, CN, LC, MH, WF, HC.

1286A [–] Some notes concerning the life of Edward, Lord North. [*London,* 1682.] 8°.* L, CS, EN; CH, Y.

North, Francis. *See* Guilford, Francis North, *baron.*

1286B [**North, J.**] Concerning the new library . . . Trinity College. 1677. brs. CT.

1287 **North, John.** An alarm to the present men in power, the officers. [*London*], *printed,* 1654. brs. LT.

1288 —A true looking-glass for all oppressed free-born people. *Printed at London,* 1654. 4°.* MH, WF.

1289 **North, John,** *minister.* A sermon preached . . . October 8. 1671. *Cambridge, by John Hayes,* 1671. *And are to be sold by Edw. Story in Cambridge.* 4°.* L, O, C, CD, EN; CH, CN, MH, NU, TU, WF, Y.

1290 — —Second edition. —, 1671. 4°.* T.C.I 100. L, O, C, DU, BLH; CLC, NU, WF.

[**North, R.**] Loyal martyr vindicated. [n.p., 1691.] *See title.*

1290A **North, William.** The case of William North. [*London,* 1695.] brs. L.

1290B The north country maid's resolution. *For F. Grove,* [1641–61]. brs. EUING 257. GU.

1290C The north country-taylor caught in a trap. [*London*], *for R. Burton,* [1641–74]. brs. O.

1291 Northampton in flames. *For William Cademan,* 1675. brs. T.C.I 227. L; CH.

1292 The Northampton-shire lovers. [*London*], *for J. Wright, J. Clark, W. Thackeray, and T. Passinger,* [1681–84]. brs. L, CM.

1293 —[Anr. ed.] [*London*], *for F. Coles, T. Vere, J. Wright and J. Clark,* [1674–79]. brs. L.

Northern ditty. [n.p., 1692.] *See* D'Urfey, Thomas.

1294 The northerne intelligencer. [*London*], *printed,* 1648. 4°.* LT; CH, NU.

1295 The northern ladd. [*London*], *for B.* [*sic*] *Brooksby,* [1672–95]. brs. L; MH.

1296 The northern lasses lamentation. [*London*], *for P. Brooksby,* [1675?]. brs. EUING 259. L, GU.

1296A The Northern lord. [1700?] brs. L.

1296B Northern nanny, or: the loving lasses lamentation. *For F. Coles, T. Vere, J. Wright, and J. Clark,* [1674–79]. brs. O.

1297 The northern qveries from the Lord Gen: Monck his qvarters. [*London*], *printed in the year of Englands confusions,* [1659?]. 4°.* LT, O, OC, LLU, LSD; CH, MH, MU, TU, WF, Y.

Northern star. 1680. *See* Tonge, Ezerel.

1298 [**Northleigh, John.**] Dr. Burnett's reflections . . . answered. *Printed, and are to be sold by Matthew Turner,* 1688. 4°. L, LIL, LW, DU, EN; CLC, CN, MH, MU, WF, Y.

1299 —Exercitationes philologicæ tres. *Oxonii, typis, L. L. prostant venales apud J. Crosley,* 1681. 4°. L, OB; WF.

[–] Gentle reflection. 1682. *See* Andrews, John.

1300 [–] Natural allegiance. *Printed,* 1688. 4°. O, LIL, CT; IU, MIU, MU, NU, PT, Y.

1301 [–] The parallel: or, the new specious association. *For B. Tooke, and T. Sawbridge,* 1682. fol.* T.C.I 474. L, O, C, DU, EN; CH, CU, LC, MH, TU, WF, Y, AVP.

1302 [–] Parliamentum pacificum: or, the happy union. *Printed, and are to be sold by M. Turner,* 1688. 4°. L, O, CE, MC, EN, CD; CH, CN, MH, NCD, NU, WF, Y.

1303 [–] —Second edition. —, 1688. 4°. L, C, OC, EN, DT; CH, LC, MH, NCD, WF, Y.

1304 Entry cancelled. Continental printing.

1305 —The triumph of our monarchy. *For Benj. Tooke,* 1685. 8°. O, C, CE, EN; Y.

1306 — —[Anr. ed.] *Printed,* 1685. 8°. TU.

Northtonus, Champianus, *pseud.*

1307 **Northumberland, Algernon Percy,** *earl.* An excellent speech spoken by. *September 20. Imprinted at London for R. Williamson,* 1648. 4°.* LT; CSS, MH.

1308 [**Northumberland, Elizabeth Percy.**] Meditations and prayers. *For N. W.,* 1682. 12°. L.

1308A — —Second edition. *For William Nott,* 1687. 8°. O, OC; WF.

1309 [–] —Third edition. —, 1693. 12°. O.

1309A [–] —Fourth edition. *For Bennet Banbury,* 1700. 8°. OC.

1310 The Northumberland monster. *For Roger Vaughan,* 1674. 4°.* L.

1311 **Norton, Rev. Mr.** Catalogue of the library. [*London*], 1696. 4°. L.

1311A **Norton, Andrew.** The last good newes from Ireland. *For John Thomas,* 1641. 4°.* O, C.

1312 Entry cancelled.

Norton, Champion. Younger brothers advocate. 1655. *See title.*

1312AA **Norton, George.** The true confession of. *By D. Edwards,* 1699. brs. CH, CN.

1312A **Norton, Humphry.** To all people that speakes of an outward baptisme. [*London?* 1659.] 4°.* LF.

1313 **Norton, John.** Abel being dead yet speaketh. *By Tho. Newcomb for Lodowick Lloyd,* 1658. 4°. LT, O, LW, CT, YM; BN, CH, CN, LC, MH, NU, WF, Y.

1314 Entry cancelled.

[–] Answer to a late scvrrilovs. 1642. *See* Norton, John, *London printer.*

1315 —A brief and excellent treatise containing. *By John Field for Edmund Paxton,* 1468 [*i.e.,* 1648]. 8°. LT, LLL, DT; CH.

1316 —A brief catechisme. *Cambridg* [*Mass.*] *by S. G. and M. J.,* 1660. 8°.* EVANS 63. MHS, NN.

1317 —A discussion of that great point in divinity. *By A. M. for Geo. Calvert, and Joseph Nevill,* 1653. 8°. LT, C, LW, P, EN, E; CH, LC, MH, NCD, NN, RPJ, WF, Y.

1318 —The heart of N-England rent. *By Samuel Green at Cambridg in New-England.* 1659. 4°. EVANS 56. LT, O; CH, MH, MHS, NN, RPJ, Y.

1319 — —Second edition. *By J. H. for John Allen,* 1660. 8°. LT, O, LF, LLP; CH, MB, MH, MU, NN, WCL.

1320 —The orthodox evangelist. *By John Macock, for Henry Cripps, and Lodowick Lloyd,* 1654. 4°. LT, LW, CE, CP, DT; CH, IU, MH, NU, PH, V, WF, Y.

1321 ——[Anr. ed.] *By John Macok, for Lodowick Lloyd,* 1657. 4°. L, O, LCL, SC, E, BLH; CH, CLC, LC, MH, MU, RPJ, Y.

1322 —Responsio ad totam quæstionum syllogen. *Typis R.B. impensis Andreæ Crook,* 1648. 8°. L, O, CM, EN, DT; CH, IU, MBA, MWA, RPJ, Y.

1323 Entry cancelled.
—Sufferings of Christ. 1653. *See*—Discussion.

1324 —Three choice and profitable sermons. *Cambridge [Mass.]: by S. G. and M. I. for Hezekiah Vsher of Boston,* 1664. 4°.* EVANS 90. EN; CH, MB, MH, MHS, RPJ, WCL, Y.

1324A [Norton, John], *London printer.* An ansvver to a late scvrrilovs and scandalovs pamphlet. *Printed,* 1642. 4°.* LT, O, OW, MR; CN, IU.

1325 Norton, John, *miscellaneous writer.* The Kings entertainment at Guild-Hall. *By T. Milbourn, for Rowland Reynolds,* 1674. brs. L.

1326 [Norton, Ralph.] A letter concerning the storming and delivering up of the castle of the Devises. *For Edw. Husband, Sept.* 25. 1645. 4°.* LT, O, SP; CH, MH.

1326A [Norton, Richard], *colonel.* Good newes from Portsmouth. *For Thomas Gould,* 1643[4]. 4°.* LT; MH.

1327 [Norton, Richard], *1666–1732.* Pausanias, the betrayer. *For Abel Roper, E. Wilkinson, and Roger Clavell,* 1696. 4°.* L, O, OW, A, EN; CH, CN, LC, MH, WF, Y.

1327A Norton, Robert. The gunner. *For Humphrey Robinson,* 1664. fol. L, OC.

1328-9 Entries cancelled.
Norwich, George Goring, *earl of.* Declaration of. [n.p.], 1641. *See* Goring, George, *baron.*

1330 —A declaration of . . . 12 July 1648. [*London,* 1648.] brs. STEELE 2777. L, O, LG; MIU.

1331 —The demands and proposals of the Earle of Norwich. *Printed,* 1648. 4°.* LT; MIU.

1332-3 Entries cancelled.
[-] Discovery of a great and wicked conspiracy. 1642. *See* Goring, George, *baron.*

1334 —The Lord Goring, the Lord Capel, and Sir Charles Lucas their letter. *By B. A.,* 1648. 4°.* LT, CT.

1335 —A letter sent from. *By B. A.,* 1648. 4°.* LT, CT; CSS, MIU.

1336 —The Lord Gorings message to the Lord Generall. *For R. W.,* 1648. 4°.* LT; CH.

1337 —The Earl of Norwich, Lord Capel, & Sir Charls Lucus, their peremptory answer. *For Robert White,* 1648. 4°.* LT, EN; MIU, WF.

1338-9 Entries cancelled.
—True newes from Portsmouth. 1642. *See* Goring, George, *baron.*
—. . , Whereas divers inhabitants. [n.p., 1645.] *See* Goring, George, *baron.*

1340 The Norwich and Norfolk weavers answer. [*London,* 1689?] brs. LL; NC.

1341 The Norvvich loyal litany. *For A. Banks,* 1682. brs. O; CH, MH, NCD, NP, WF.

1342 Norwood, Anthony. A clear optick discovering. *For Richard Moon, and Edward Thomas,* 1654. 4°.* LT, O, OME; CSS, CU, WF.

1343 —New errors made palpable. *By E. G. to be sold by Charles Adams,* 1652. 8°.* LT; CLC.

1344 [Norwood, Cornelius.] Divine eloquence. *By J. H. for Luke Meredith,* 1694. 8°. T.C.II 533. L, O, OME; CLC, TO, WF.

1345 Norwood, Matthew. The seaman's companion. *Andrew Clarke,* 1671. 4°. CT.

1345A ——Third edition. *By A. Godbid and J. Playford for W. Fisher, R. Boulter, R. Smith, T. Passenger, and R. Northcott,* [1678]. 4°. CT, SP; MWA, PU.

1346 —Norwood's system of navigation. *For H. Sawbridge, and T. Wall, in Bristol,* 1665. 4°. T.C.II 146. OC; CLC, MU, NN, Y.

1346A ——[Anr. ed.] *For H. Sawbridge, T. Guy, T. Parkhurst, J. Robinson, and G. Conyers,* 1685. 4°. LWL.

1347 ——[Anr. ed.] *Richard Mount,* 1692. 4°. L.

1347A Norwood, Richard, *mathematician.* Works. *For Richard Mount,* 1684. 4°. OC.

1347B —Norwood's epitomie. *By T. F. for G. Hurlock,* 1645. 8°. C, CS.

1348 ——[Anr. ed.] *By R. & W. Leybourn for G. Hurlock,* 1659. 8°. L.

1349 ——[Anr. ed.] *By W. G. for G. Hurlock,* 1667. 8°. L.

1350 ——[Anr. ed.] *For W. Fisher, T. Passinger, R. Boulter, and R. Smith,* 1669. 12°. LR.

1351 ——[Anr. ed.] *For William Fisher; and Eliz. Hurlock,* 1676. 8°. Y.

1351A ——[Anr. ed.] *For William Fisher, Thomas Passinger, Robert Boulter, and Ralph Smith,* 1679. 8°.* T.C.I 337. L, EN.

1351B ——[Anr. ed.] —, 1680. 8°. CT.

1351C ——[Anr. ed.] *For W. Fisher, Thomas Passinger, Robert Boulter, and Ralph Smith,* 1683. 8°. CT.

1352 ——[Anr. ed.] *By F. D. for Richard Mount,* 1698. 8°.* E; LC.

1353 Entry cancelled.
—Fortification. 1679. *See* —Epitome. 1679.

1353A ——[Anr. ed.] *For Richard Mount,* 1694. 4°. OC; MBA, MU.

1354 —The seamans practice. *By T. Forcet for George Hurlock,* 1644. 4°. CE, EN; BN, CH, NN, Y.

1355 ——[Anr. ed.] *By R. & W. Leybourn, for George Hurlock,* 1655. 4°. O, E.

1356 ——Fourth edition. —, 1659. 4°. L, CT.

1357 ——Fifth edition. *By William Leybourn, for George Hurlock,* 1662. 4°. L, CT; BN, MU, VIRGINIA ST. LIB., WF.

1358 ——Seventh edition. *By W. Godbid, for George Hurlock,* 1667. 4°. O.

1359 ——Eighth edition. —, 1668. 4°. O.

1360 ——Ninth edition. *By W. Godbid for Benj. Hurlock,* 1670. 4°. DT; NN.

1361 ——Tenth edition. 1672. 4°. L.

1362 ——Eleventh edition. *For Benjamin Hurlock,* 1673. 4°. MU.

1362A ——Twelfth edition. *For William Fisher, and Eliza. Hurlock,* 1676. 4°. MH.

1362B ——Thirteenth edition. *For William Fisher, Robert Boulter, and Ralph Smith,* 1678. 4°. GU.

1363 ——Fourteenth edition. *Printed by A. Godbid and J. Play-ford, for William Flesher, T. Passenger, R. Boulter and R. Smith,* 1680. 4°. DT.

1363A ——Fifteenth edition. *By A. Godbid and J. Playford for William Fisher, T. Passinger, R. Boulter, and R. Smith,* 1682. 4°. LLL, CM; MBP.

1364 ——[Anr. ed.] *By J. D. for W. Fister [sic], S. Passenger, and E. Smith,* 1689. 4°. NC.

1365 ——[Anr. ed.] *By J. D. for R. Mount, and T. Passinger,* 1692. 4°. MU, Y.

1365A ——[Anr. ed.] *For R. Mount,* 1697. 4°. NN.

1366 ——[Anr. ed.] *For Richard Mount,* 1699. 4°. CLC, MU.

1367 —A table of the suns true place. *For G. Hurlock,* 1656. 4°.* L, LWL, DCH; MU, VIRGINIA ST. LIB., Y.

1368 [–] A triangular canon logarithmicall. [*London,* 1665?] 4°. L; NN.

1369 [–] ——[Anr. ed.] *Printed,* 1679. 8°. L.

1369A [–] ——[Anr. ed.] *By J. Orme, for Christopher Hussey,* 1695. 8°. CM.

1370 [–] ——[Anr. ed.] *For Rich. Mount,* 1698. 8°. L; SE.

1371 —Trigonometrie. Second edition. *By Robert and William Leybourn, for George Hurlock,* 1651. 4°. C, CCO, SHR; NN.

1372 ——Third edition. —, 1656. 4°. L, E.

1373 ——Fourth edition. —, 1661. 4°. L, LWL, DCH; BN, MU, VIRGINIA ST. LIB., Y.

1374 ——Fifth edition. *By W. Godbid, for George Hurlock,* 1667. 4°. O; BN, MB.

1375 ——Sixth edition. *By W. Godbid for Benj. Hurlock,* 1672. 4°. CJ; CLC, MU, PAP, WG.

1376 ——Seventh edition. *By R. W. for William Fisher, T. Passenger, R. Boulter, and R. Smtih,* 1678. 4°. T.C.I 316. L, SA; CB, CH, LC, MBP, RBU.

1377 ——Eighth edition. *By R. W. for William Fisher, T. Passenger, and R. Smith,* 1685. 4°. T.C.II 108. L, C, LW, CT, BC, GU; MU, NC, PL, WF, Y.

1378 **Norwood, Richard,** *of Bermuda.* Considerations tending to remove. *By J. M. for M. Spark,* 1646. 4°.* LT, O, LW, MR.

1379 **Norwood, Robert.** An additional discourse. *For Richard Moon,* 1653. 4°. LT, O; CSS, WF.

1380 —A brief discourse made by. *Imprinted at London,* 1652. 4°.* LT, O, OB; CSS, MB, Y.

1380A —The case and trial of. [*London,* 1652.] 4°. L, O, OB, CT, DT; CH, CSS, MH.

1381 —A declaration or testimony. *Printed,* 1651. 4°.* LT, LW, OB, YM, DT; CH.

1381A ——[Anr. ed.] [*London,* 1651.] cap., 4°.* MH.

1382 —The form of an excommunication. *Printed,* 1651. 4°. LT, OB, CS, EN, DT; MM, NU, WF, Y.

1383 —A pathway unto England's perfect settlement. *For Rich. Moone,* 1653. 4°. LT, O; CH, LC, NN, OWC.

1384 —Proposals for propagation of the Gospel. [*London,* 1652.] cap., 4°.* LT; CSS, Y.

1385 [**Norwood, Thomas.**] A copy of a letter sent from a gentleman of quality dwelling in Banbury. *For T. Smith,* 1642. 4°.* LT, BC; CH.

1386 Nos quorum nomina. [*London*], 1647. brs. O.

Nosce teipsum. 1689. *See* Davies, *Sir* John.

1387 A nose-gay for the Hovse of Commons. [*London*], printed, 1648. 4°.* LT, LVF; CH, CLC, MH, Y.

Nosegay of divine truths. 1687. *See* B., P.

1387A Nosegay of pleasure growing in Venus's garden. *For A. Banks,* 1685. brs. CLC.

Nostredame. *See* Notredame.

1388 Not guiltie plead for the Lords. [*London,* 1649.] cap., 4°.* LT, MR; MH, MIU, MM, WF.

Not Popery. [1672.] *See* Charles I.

1389 A notable and pleasant history of the famous renowned Knights of the Blade. *Printed at London, for Richard Harper,* 1652. 4°.* LT, O.

1389A Notable news from Essex. *For L. C.,* 1679. 4°.* Y.

Notable plot discovered. [n.p., 1649.] *See* M., J.

Notable things. 1697. *See* Tryon, Thomas.

1390 A notable touch of the times. *For J. A.,* 1642. 4°.* LT, O, LG; CH, CLC.

Notes and observations on the Empress. 1674. *See* Dryden, John.

Notes and observations vpon some passages. Oxford, 1646. *See* Gregory, John.

1391 Notes conferr'd. *For R. Shuter,* 1682. brs. L, O, EN; CH, Y.

1392 The notes of the church, as laid down by Cardinal Bellarmin; examined. *For Richard Chiswell,* 1688. 4°. L, O; C, MC, E, DT; CH, CN, NU, WF, Y.

Notes of the evidence. 1681. *See* Lee, *Sir* Charles.

1392A Notes on Mr. Danvers's case. [*London?* 1691.] brs. L.

1393 Notes on the case of Sir John Danver's settlement. [*London,* 1691?] brs. L.

Notes taken in short-hand. [n.p., 1679.] *See* Shaftesbury, Anthony Ashley Cooper, *earl.*

1394 Notes upon both globes. *Dublin, by J. Ray, for Jacob Milner,* 1699. 8°.* DIX 314. DN, CD.

Notes upon the Lord Bishop. 1695. *See* Chorlton, John.

1394A Notes upon the printed case of the New Forest. [*London?* 1670.] brs. L.

1395 Nothing without God. [*London,* 1647.] brs. LT, O.

1395A Nothing without God . . . many rare secrets in physick. [*London,* 1670?] brs. L.

1395B Nothing without God. This excellent physitian. [*London,* 1670?] brs. L.

1396 Notice sent to the commissioners to meet. [n.p.], 1667. brs. O.

Notion of schism. 1676. *See* Conold, Robert.

Notitia Oxoniensis. 1675. *See* Fulman, William.

Notorious impostor. 1692. *See* Settle, Elkanah.

1396A The notorious robbers lamentation. [*London*], for P. Brooksby, J. Deacon, J. Blare, and J. Back, [1684]. brs. L, CM.

1397 **Notredame, Michel de.** A collection of twenty-three prophecies. *Printed and are to be sold by Randal Taylor,* 1690. 8°.* L, LWL; CH, CU.

1397A [–] Good and joyful news for England. *For Allen Banks,* 1681. 4°. O, EN; WCL.

1398   —The predictions of. colop: *For John Cross, to be sold by R. B.*, 1691. cap., 4°.* L, LLP, DT; CH, IAU, MH.

1398A   ——[Anr. ed.] *For Richard Baldwin*, 169[7]. cap., 4°.* BAMB.

1398B   —Remarkable predictions. [*London?*], *printed in the year* 1689. brs. L; NN.

1399   —The true prophecies or prognostications of. *By Thomas Ratcliffe, and Nathaniel Thompson, and are to be sold by John Martin, Henry Mortlack, Thomas Collins, Edward Thomas, Samuel Lowndes, Rob. Bolter, Jon. Edwin, Moses Pits*, 1672. fol. T.C.I 112. L, O, C, EN, DT; BN, CH, LC, MH, MU, TSM, Y.

1400   —The true prophecies or. *Printed, to be sold by John Salusbury*, 1685. fol. L, OH, DUS, A, DT; CH, MBC, NIC, PL, HC.

1401   —Wonderful predictions. *For J. Robinson, T. Fox, and M. Wotton*, 1689. fol. T.C.II 258. L, O, CT, DU, DT; CH, MBP, TU, WF, Y.

1401A   **Nott, Joseph.** Holy Scripture-work. *Printed*, 1693. 4°.* WF.

1401B   [**Nottingham, Charles Howard**], *earl of.* A speech made at Nottingham, April 2. 1660 at the election of Arthur Stanhope . . . and John Huchinson. *For H. B.* 1660. 4°.* CSS, MH, WF, ZWT.

        Nottingham, Heneage Finch, *earl of.* Antidote against poison. [n.p.], 1683. *See* Shower, Bartholomew.

1402   —The arguments of the . . . late Lord Chancellor. *London, for George Tatarshall of Finchamsted*, 1685. fol.* T.C.II 103. L, O, C, EN, DT; CH, CN, MHL, WF, Y.

1403   [–] An exact and most impartial accompt of the indictment, arraignment, . . . of nine and twenty regicides. *For Andrew Crook, and Edward Powel*, 1660. 4°. LT, O, C, LW, EN; BN, LC, MH, MIU, NCD, WF, Y. (var.)

1403A   [–] —[Anr. ed., "twenty nine."] —, 1660. 4°. L, O, C, BR, LIU; CH, CN, LC, MH, NU, Y. (var.)

1404   [–] —[Anr. ed.] *For R. Scot, T. Basset, R. Chiswell and J. Wright*, 1679. 8°. T.C.I 358. L, O, OC, CT, BR, DUS, DT; BN, CH, CLC, CN, MH, TO, TU, Y.

1405   —Law, or a discourse thereof. 1678. LL.

1406–8 Entries cancelled.

        —Lord Chancellor's speech. 1672. *See* Shaftsbury, Anthony Ashley Cooper, *earl of.*

        —Lord Chancellor's speech. 1673. *See* Shaftsbury, Anthony Ashley Cooper, *earl of.*

        —Lord Keeper's speech. 1682. *See* Guilford, Francis North, *baron.*

1409   —The speech of . . . in Westminster Hall, . . . Seventh of December, 1680. *By the assigns of John Bill, Thomas Newcomb, and Henry Hills*, 1680. fol.* L, O, CT, EN, DT; CH, IU, MH, TU, WF, Y.

1410   ——[Anr. ed.] *Reprinted at Dublin, by Benjamin Took and John Crook: to be sold by Mary Crook*, 1680. fol.* C, BLH; NN.

1411–2 Entries cancelled.

        —True and exact relation. 1669. *See* Winchelsea, Heneage Finch, *earl of.*

1413   Nottinghamshires petition to the King. *September, 6. London, for Thomas Banks*, 1642. 4°.* LT, OC, BC, EC, DT; CLC, CU, MH, TU, WF, Y.

1414   [**Nouat, Jacques.**] An answer to the Provinciall letters. *Printed at Paris*, 1659. 12°. O, LSC, CK, CT, DU; CH, CN, MH, NU, TU, WF, Y.

1414A   **Nourse, Peter.** Primatus in sacris ab ecclesia Anglicana . . . Jul. 4. 1698. [*Cambridge*, 1698.] brs. C.

1415   —A sermon preached . . . July iij. 1698. *Cambridge, at the University's printing-house, for Edward Hall, in Cambridge, to be sold by Luke Meredith, in London*, 1698. 4°.* L, O, C, LLP, NE; CLC, IEG, NU, WF.

1416   **Nourse, Timothy.** Campania fœlix. Or, a discourse. *For Tho. Bennet*, 1700. 8°. T.C.III 187. L, O, C, LG, R, CD; BN, CH, MH, MU, NC, NR, WDA, Y.

1417   [–] A discourse of natural and reveal'd religion. *For John Newton*, 1691. 8°. T.C.II 367. L, O, OC, CT, DT; CLC, IU, NU, PL, TU, WF, Y.

1418   —A discourse upon the nature and faculties of man. *For Jacob Tonson*, 1686. 8°. L, O, OC, M; CH, LC, MIU, NP, NU, Y.

1419   ——Second edition. *By J. O. for Jacob Tonson, and sold by R. Wellington, and J. Graves*, 1697. 8°. T.C.III 161. L, O, C, LW, DT; CH, CLC, CN, NCU, PU, WF.

1420   Nova epigrammata. Liber primus. 1684. 4°. EN.

1421   Novæ hypotheseos de pulmorum motu. *Impensis J. P.*, 1671. 8°.* T.C.I 74. L, O, LCP, P, GH.

        Novæ Solymæ. 1648. *See* Gott, Samuel.

1421aA **Novell, John.** An examination and confutation of a late dangerous principle. That the supreme power. *For Sarah Bartlet*, 1662. 4°.* CD.

1421A   —The seditious principle, viz. That the supreme power is . . . in the people. *For Sarah Bartlet*, 1662. 4°.* L, OB, CS, P; CN, MH, MM, NC.

1422   **Novell, Matthew.** Sonate da camera or chamber musick. *Excudi et sculpi Tho. Cross junr. for the author*, [1690?]. fol. L.

        Novello-mastix, or. 1646. *See* D., C.

        Novels of Elizabeth. 1680. *See* Aulnoy, Marie Catherine La Mothe, *comtesse.*

        Novelty of the modern. 1682. *See* Felgate, Samuel.

1423   Entry cancelled.

        November. [n.p., 1647.] *See* Cartwright, William.

        Novembris monstrum. Or. 1641. *See* E., A.B.C.D.

1424   Noverint universi per presentes. [n.p.], 1676. brs. OP.

1425   —[Anr. ed.] [n.p., 1686.] brs. OP.

1426   —[Anr. ed.] [—, 1687.] brs. OP.

1427   —[Anr. ed.] [—], 16[87]. brs. OP.

1428   —[Anr. ed.] [—, 1690.] brs. OP.

1429   —[Anr. ed.] [—], 16[91]. brs. OP.

1430   —[Anr. ed.] [*London*, 1695?] brs. L.

        Novum lumen chirurgicum extinctum. 1695. *See* W., W.

        Novum lumen medicum; wherein. 1662. *See* Polemann, Joachim.

        Novus annus luni-solaris. [n.p., 1680.] *See* Almanacs. Wood, Robert.

1431   Novus Græcorum epigrammatum. *Impensis Tho. Dring*, 1694. 8°. T.C.II 493. L, C, CT, SHR, WCA, DL; WF.

1432   —[Anr. ed.] *Apud S. Smith & B. Walford*, 1699. 8°. C, OB, LSD, MR; CH, CLC.

Novus reformator. 1691. *See* Brown, Thomas.

Now all ye that have a desire. [n.p., 1648.] *See* Hunt, James.

1433   Now is the time. *Printed*, 1689. brs. L, O, C, BR; CH, MH, Y.

Now is the time. 1695/6. *See* Whately, Thomas.

Now or never. [n.p., 1696.] *See* Leslie, Charles.

1434   Now or never: or, a new Parliament of women. *For George Horton*, 1656. 4°.* LT, O.

1435   Now or never: or, the princely calendar. *For G. Horton*, 1659. 4°.* LT.

1435A   —[Anr. ed.] *For N. Haskins*, 1659. 4°. * MH.

Now or never: work. 1663. *See* R., B.

1435B   Now the bill is past, wooden shoes at last. [*London*], *for W. Jones*, [1689?]. brs. MH.

Nowell, Alexander. Almanack. Cambridge [*Mass.*], 1665. *See* Almanacs.

1436   [–] A catechisme, or institution. *By J. D. for the company of stationers*, 1647. 8°. L, O; CLC.

1436A   [–] —[Anr. ed.] *By E. Cotes, for the company of stationers*, 1663. 8°. OC.

1436B   —Catechismus parvus pueris. *Typis Andreæ Clark*, 1675. 8°.* CB.

1436C   [–] —[Anr. ed.] *Imprimebatur Londini per J. G. Sumptibus bibliopolarum*, 1687. 8°.* IU.

1436D   [–] Christianæ pietatis prima institutio. *Excudebat T. R. pro Societate Stationariorum*, 1664. 12°. O.

1437   [–] Χριστιανισμου στοιχειωσις, . . . Christianæ pietatis prima institutio. *Typis Tho. Roycroft, pro Societate Stationariorum*, 1670. 8°. L; CLC. (var.)

1438   [–] —[Anr. ed.] *Excudebat Andr. Clark, pro Societate Stationariorum*, 1673. 12°. L, O, C, CT, DT; IU, MB, TO, WF, Y.

1438A   [–] —[Anr. ed.] *Typis A. Godbid & J. Playford, pro Societate Stationariorum*, 1679. 8°. DUS, EC; NP.

1439   ——[Anr. ed.] *Typis Mariæ Clark impensis Societate Stationariorum*, 1687. 12°. T.C.II 181. L, O, C, BC, EC; CH, CLC, IU.

1440   **N[owell], S[amuel].** Abraham in arms. *Boston; by John Foster*, 1678. 12°.* EVANS 256. MB, MH, MHS, MWA, RPJ.

1440A   **Noy, A.** The antiveneral apozem. A pleasant liquor. [*London*, 1675?] brs. L.

1440B   **Noy, William,** *captain.* Capt. Will. Noy, executor of Honour Noy. [*London?* 1680.] brs. L; MH.

1441   **Noye, *Sir* William.** The compleat lawyer. *For Iohn Benson*, 1651. 8°. LT, O, LUG, LW, DT; IU.

1442   ——[Anr. ed.] *By W. W. for W. Lee*, 1651. 8°. LL; LC, MHL.

1443   ——[Anr. ed.] *For D. Pakeman*, 1651. 8°. CLL, LC, YL.

1444   ——[Anr. ed.] *For John Benson*, 1661. 8°. LT, CS; CH, LC, MHL, NCL, PU, WF.

1445   ——[Anr. ed.] *By J. C. for Samuel Speed*, 1665. 12°. L, CS, DT; CH, LC, MHL, PUL, YL.

1446   ——[Anr. ed.] *For S. S., and are to be sold by W. Jacob, and John Amery*, 1670. 8°. T.C.I 45. L, OC, OP, DU; CH, MHL, PL, PUL, TU, YL.

1447   ——[Anr. ed.] *Printed for and sold by John Amery*, 1674. 8°. T.C.I 182. L, O, LMT, EN; CLC, LC, MHL, MIU, Y.

1448   —The great feast. *For Edward Husbands, Aprill the first*, 1645. 4°.* L; MH.

1449   —Reports and cases. *By F. L. for Matthew Walbancke, and T. Firby*, 1656. fol. L, O, C, NPL, DT; CH, KT, LC, MHL, NCL, V, WF, AVP.

1450   ——Second edition. *By T. R. for Samuel Heyrick*, 1669. fol. T.C.I 23. O, LG, CJ, EN, DT; CH, CLL, LC, NCL, TU, YL.

1451   [–] A treatise of the principall grounds and maximes of the lavves. *By R. H., by permission of the assignes of John Moore, and are to be sold by William Cooke*, 1641. 4°. L, O, C, LNC, DT; LC, MHL, NU, WF, YL.

1452   [–] —Second edition. *For W. Cook*, 1642. 4°. L, CJ, RU; CH, LC, MHL, WG, YL.

1453   [–] —"Second" edition. *By T. N. for W. Lee, D. Pakeman, R. Best, and G. Bedell*, 1651. 8°. L, EN; LC, MHL, PUL, U. ALBERTA, WF.

1454   [–] —Third edition. *By S. G. for W. Lee, D. Pakeman, R. Best and G. Bedell*, 1660. 4°. L; NCD, NCL.

1454A   ——"Third" edition. *For George Dawes*, 1663. 8°. MHL, NS.

1455   ——Fourth edition. *By G. Sawbridge, W. Rawlins, and T. Roycroft, assigns of Richard and Edward Atkins, for H. Twiford, T. Collins, T. Basset, J. Wright, M. Pitts, C. Harper, T. Sawbridge, J. Place, T. Lee*, 1667. 12°. O.

1455A   ——"Fourth" edition. —, 1677. 12°. PUL.

1456   ——"Fourth" edition. *For T. Collins, T. Basset, J. Wright, M. Pitts and T. Sawbridge*, 1677. 12°. L, LL, OC, NE; CH, LC, MHL, WF.

1457   **Noyes, James.** Moses and Aaron. *By T. R. and Edmund Paxton*, 1661. 4°. O; LC, MB, NN, NU, RPJ, V.

1458   —A short catechism. *Cambridg* [*Mass.*], *by S. G. and M. J.*, 1661. 8°.* MWA.

1459   ——[Anr. ed.] *Boston, by Bartholomew Green*, 1694. 12.°* MWA.

1460   —The temple measured. *For Edmund Paxton*, 1647. 4°. LT, O, CS, EN, DT; CH, CN, MH, NU, WF, Y.

1461   **Noyes, Nicholas.** New-Englands duty and interest. *Boston in New-England, by Bartholomew Green, and John Allen*, 1698. 8°. EVANS 850. LW; CH, LC, MH, MWA, NN, RPJ, Y.

1461A   Nozze reali: or, a lyrick poem. *Printed*, 1674. fol.* MH.

Nubes testium: or. 1686. *See* Gother, John.

Nugæ venales. 1675. *See* Head, Richard.

1462   Nugae venales, sive, thesavrvs. [n.p.], *anno* 1642. *Prostant apud neminem; sed tamen ubique.* 12°. L, C, LL, MAU; CH, MBJ, MH, NC, WF.

1463   —[Anr. ed.] —, 1644. 12°. MAU; CH, CLC, MU, WF, Y.

1464   —[Anr. ed.] —, 1648. 12°. L, MAU; CH, CN, MH, WF, Y.

1465   —[Anr. ed.] —, 1662. 12°. L, MAU; VICTORIA U., N.Z.

1466   —[Anr. ed.] —, 1663. 12°. L, O, CK, MAU; CU, MH, NCD, NN, WF.

1467   —[Anr. ed.] —, 1681. 12°. L, MAU, P; CLC, NC, NN.

1468   —[Anr. ed.] —, 1689. 12°. L, C, MAU, ES, DT; CN, MBJ, MH, WSG, Y.

1469   [**Nuisement, Clovis Hesteau**], *baron.* Sal, lumen & spiritus. *Printed at London, by J. C. for Martha Harrison*, 1657. 8°. L, O, LLU, GU; CH, IU, MBJ, WF, WU.

1469A [–] —[Anr. ed.] *By J. C., to be sold by Nath. Ekins*, 1657. 8°. L, LWL, OC; MH.

Nullity of the prelatique clergy. Antwerp, 1659. *See* Talbot, Peter.

Nullity of the pretended-assembly. [n.p.], 1652. *See* Guthrie, James.

Nvmber and names. 1650. *See* Taylor, John.

1469B The number of hands for each candidate . . . mayor. [*London*, 1692.] brs. L.

Numerus infaustus. A short view. 1689. *See* Caesar, Charles.

1470   Nunc aut nunquam, peace now or never. *By Tho. Snowden, and sold by E. Whitlock*, 1697. 4°.* Y.

Nuncius Christi syderus. The star of the Eastern ages. 1681. *See* Ὁ αστηρ.

1471   Entry cancelled.

Nuncius coelestis. 1681. *See* Almanacs. Coley, Henry.

Nuncius propheticus. 1642. *See* LeWright, Raoul.

Nunns, Thomas. Almanack. 1661. *See* Almanacs.

The nunns complaint. *See* Varet, Alexandre Louis.

1472   The nunns prophesie. [n.p.], *printed*, 1680. 4°.* CB, NU, Y.

Nvntivs a mortvis. 1657. *See* Perrinchief, Richard.

Nuptial rites. 1685. *See* Gaya, Louis de.

Nvptialls of Peleus. 1654. *See* Howell, James.

Nurse of pious thoughts. Douay, 1652. *See* P., F.

1473   [**Nutt, Thomas.**] The humble request of certain Christians . . . called Anabaptists. [*London*, 1643.] brs. LT.

1474   [–] Nineteen humble propositions for peace. [*London*, 1643.] brs. LT.

1475   —The nineteene propositions cleered. [*London*, 1643.] cap., 4°.* LT, DT.

1476   —The nut-cracker crackt. *Printed*, 1644. 4°.* LT, O, SP; NHC.

1477   — —[Anr. ed.] 1645. 4°.* CHRISTIE-MILLER.

1478   —The second humble cry of this kingdome. [*London*, 1645?] brs. L; MH.

1479   [–] To the Right Honourable, the knights, citizens and burgesses . . . the humble petition of many godly true-hearted Protestants. [*London*, 1643.] brs. LT.

[**Nuttall.**] Master of the temple. 1696. *See* Shower, Sir Bartholomew.

1479A Entry cancelled.

Nutting, Joseph. Country school master. [1695.] *See* Newton, John.

Nuysement. *See* Nuisement, Clovis Hesteau, *baron.*

1479B **Nye, John.** A display of divine heraldry. *By T. James and Val. Acton*, 1678. 8°. T.C.I 319. L, O.

1480   [–] Mr Sadler re-examined, or, his disguise discovered. *For Nathanael Webb and William Grantham*, 1654. 4°.* LT, O, OC, MR; CH, NHS, NN, NU.

1481   **Nye, Nathaniel.** The art of gunnery. *For William Leak*, 1647. 8°. L, C, OC, DC, DCH; LC, NN.

1482   — —[Anr. ed.] —, 1648. 8°. L, OC, CCA, BC; CLC.

1483   — —[Anr. ed.] —, 1670. 8°. T.C.I 32. L, BC; CH, MU, WF, Y.

—New almanacke. [1642.] *See* Almanacs.

1484   [**Nye, Philip.**] Beames of former light. *By R. I. for Adoniram Byfield*, 1660. 8°. LT, LW, E, BQ; CH, MH, MWA, NU, TO, VC.

1485   [–] A case of great and present use. *Printed*, 1677. 8°.* L, O, LCL, LW, CS, LIU, P, YM; IU, LC.

1486   [–] A declaration of the faith and order owned. *By John Field, to be sold by John Allen*, 1658. 4°. LCL, LW, OB, ORP, EN; TO, WF, Y.

1487   [–] —[Anr. ed.] —, 1659. 4°. L, O, CT, MR, EN; CH, CLC, CN, MB, TU, WF, Y.

1488   [–] —[Anr. ed.] *For D. L.*, 1659. 4°.* LT, O, CT, EC, WCA; CH, MH, NU, PL, Y.

1489   [–] —[Anr. ed.] *By J. P.*, 1659. 4°. O, AN, MR, BLH, DT; CH, CU, NHC, TU, WF, Y.

1490   [–] —[Anr. ed.] *For Nath. Ponder*, 1688. 4°. L, O, LW; CLC, NU, WF, Y.

1490A — A discourse of ecclesiastical laws. *For W. Cross*, 1687. 4°.* L.

1491   —The excellency and lawfvlnesse of the solemne league. *By W. Wilson, for Tho. Vnderhill*, 1646. 4°.* LT, ISC, BSO, SP, DT; INU, MH, NU, WF, Y.

1492   Entry cancelled.

[–] Exhortation. [n.p., 1643.] *See* England. Laws. Collection. 1646.

1493   [–] An exhortation to the taking of the solemne league and covenant. colop: *Printed at London for Ralph Smith*, 1644. 4°.* O; IU, NU.

1494   [–] —[Anr. ed.] —, 1644. cap., 4°.* LT; NN.

1495   —The King's authority. *For H. N. and Nathanael Ranew*, 1687. 4°. L, O, CT, BR, SP; CH, CN, MH, NU, TU, WF, Y.

1496   —The lavvfulnes of hearing the publick ministers. *For Jonathan Robinson*, 1683. 4°.* T.C.II 11. L, O, CT, E, DT; CH, IU, MB, NU, TU, WF, Y.

1497   Entry cancelled. *See following entry.*

1498   [–] The lawfvlness of the oath of supremacy. *By Peter Cole*, 1662. 4°. LLP, LW, CS, P; Y.

1499   — —[Anr. ed.] *For Jonathan Robinson, and Samuel Crowch*, 1683. 4°. T.C.II 18. L, O, CT, EN, DT; CH, IU, MWA, NU, WF, Y.

1500   —A sermon preached . . . September 29. 1659. *By Peter Cole and Edward Cole*, 1661. 4°.* LT, CM, YM; CLC, NU, V, WF.

1501   —Two speeches delivered . . . 25. of September. *Edinburgh, by Robert Bryson*, 1643. 4°.* ALDIS 1113. O, OW, CT, MR, EN; CLC, CN, NU, WF, Y.

1502   [**Nye, Stephen.**] An account of Mr. Firmin's religion. *Printed*, 1698. 8°. L, LCL, LW, BAMB, BC, CD; CLC, CN, MH, NU, TU, WF, Y.

1502A [–] An accurate examination of the principal texts. *Printed*, 1692. 4°. L, O, CS, WCA, DT; CH, CLC, MH, NU, WF, Y.

1503   [–] The agreement of the Unitarians, . . . part I. [*London*], *printed*, 1697. 4°. L, O, CT, EC, DT; CH, CLC, MH, WF, Y.

1504   [–] An answer to Dr. Wallis's three letters. *Printed*, 1691. 4°.* L, OC, CS, BAMB, EC; CH, MH, TO, WF, Y.

1505   [–] A brief history of the Unitarians. [*London*], *printed*, 1687. 8°. L, O, C, LW, DT; CH, LC, NU, WF, Y.

1505A [–] —Second edition. —, 1691. 4°. L, O, LW, EC, E; IU,
MH, NP, NU, TU, Y.

1505B [–] Considerations on the explications of the doctrine of
the Trinity. [London], printed 1693. 4°.* C, LLP, OC, EN,
DT; CH, MH, NRU, NU, WF, Y.

1505C [–] —[Anr. ed.] [London], printed, 1694. 4°. L, O, C, AU, DT;
CDA, CN, MH, NU, WF, Y.

1506 [–] A discourse concerning natural and revealed religion.
By T. W. for Jonathan Robinson, 1696. 8°. T.C.II 586.
L, O, C, LW, MR, DT; BN, CLC, IU, MB, PL, WF, Y.

1506A [–] Doctor Wallis's letter . . . answered. [London, 1691.]
cap., 4°.* L, O, C, LW, EC; CLC, CN, MH, NU, WF, Y.

1506B [–] The exceptions of Mr. Edwards . . . examined.
Printed 1695. 4°.* O, LW, OC, WCA, DT; CH, MH, NU,
TU, WF, Y.

1507 [–] An historical account and defence, of the canon. By
J. Darby, for Jonathan Robinson, and Andrew Bell, 1700.
8°. T.C.III 168. L, C, DU, EN, DT; MBA, NN, NU, TO, WF, Y.

1507A [–] —[Anr. ed.] By J. Darby for Andrew Bell, 1700. 8°. OC,
CT, CD; MM.

1507B [–] A letter of resolution. [London, 1691?] 4°.* L, O, C, LN,
EC; CLC, CN, MH, NU, WF, Y.

1508 [–] The life of Mr. Thomas Firmin. Printed, and sold by
A. Baldwin, 1698. 8°. L, O, LUG, LW, CS, NE, DT; CH, CN,
LC, MH, NU, TU, Y.

1508A [–] Observations on the four letters of Dr. John Wallis.
Printed, 1691. 4°.* L, O, LW, CS, LLU; CH, CN, MH, NCD,
NU, TO, Y.

1508B [–] Reflections on two discourses concerning the divinity. Printed, 1693. 4°.* L, O, LLP, EC, WCA; CH, CN, MH,
NU, Y.

1508C [–] A reply to the second defence. Printed 1695. 4°.* L,
O, OC, BAMB, DT; CH, MBA, NU, TU, WF, Y.

1508D [–] Some thoughts upon Dr. Sherlock's vindication.
[London? 1691.] cap., 4°.* LW, OC, OCC, CS, EC; NPT,
WF, ZWT.

1508E [–] —Second edition. Printed, 1691. 4°.* L, O, LLP, LW,
EC, NE; CH, CLC, IU, MH, NU, Y.

1509 —The system of grace. For J. Robinson and A. Bell, 1700.
8°. LLP, LW, OC, CT, EN, DT; IU, Y.

1509A [–] The trinitarian scheme of religion. Printed, 1692. 4°.*
O, LLP, LW, EC, DT; CH, CN, MH, NU, WF, Y.

Nympha libethris: or. 1651. See Barksdale, Clement.

O

1 O., A. Letter of advice sent to the Lord Chancellors lady.
[London], for W. P., 1688. brs. L, OM.
O., D. Persvvasion to loyalty. 1642. See Owen, David.
O., H. Christians daily walk. [1660.] See Oasland, Henry.

2 —A letter from a lover of his country to his friend in
Surrey. [London, 1660.] cap., 4°.* IT.
O., I. Generation of seekers. 1671. See Oldfield, John.

2A O., I. V. C. Amsterdam: toleration, or no toleration.
[London], printed, 1663. 8°. L, C, CT, BP; CH, WF.

3 O., J. Bradshaws vltimvm vale. Oxon [London], printed,
1660. 4°.* MADAN 2512. LT, O, LCL, MR; CH, MIU, WF, Y.

4 —Comfort in affliction. For R. Jones, 1682. fol.* CH, Y.
—First, last. 1666. See Oldfield, John.

5 Entry cancelled.
—Holland nightingale. 1672. See Ogilby, John.
—Plea for Scripture. 1694. See Owen, James.
—Pro sacris scripturis. Oxonii, 1658. See Owen, John. Of
the divine. 1659.
—Queries in order. [n.p., 1673.] See Ogilby, John.
—Remarks on a sermon. 1697. See Owen, James.

6 —Salvation improved: in a sermon. For J. Salusbury, 1696.
4°.* Y.

7 —The souls excellency. For R. W., 1648. 8°.* LT, DT.

8 —A sweet posie for Gods saints. By R. Cotes, for Benjamin
Allen, 1642. 12°. L, LCL; CLC.

8A —The tryal of the truth. At Amsterdam, for the author, 1656.
4°.* SP; NU.

—Tutamen evangelicum: or. 1697. See Owen, James.

9 Entry cancelled.
—Two questions. 1659. See Owen, John. Unto the
questions.
—Unto the questions. 1659. See Owen, John.

9A —Venus looking-glass. Printed, [1669]. 8°. O.

9B O., J. M. The exclames of Rhodophaea. To the most
lamentable death of . . . Montrose. [Edinburgh?], 1661.
8°.* L.

O., M. Fratres in malo, or. [n.p.], 1660. See Ogilvy,
Michael.

O., N. Dr. Stillingfleets principles. Paris, 1671. See Cressy,
Hugh Paulin.

O., R. Carracters in blood. 1671. See Ottee, Robert.
—Man wholly mortal. 1655. See Overton, Richard.
—Mans mortallitie. Amsterdam, 1643. See Overton,
Richard.

10 Entry cancelled.
O., S. Epicedium. 1695. See Ogden, Samuel.
O., T. Balm presented. [1680.] See Oates, Titus.

10A —Christ's voice to sinners. For Charles Passinger, 1680.
8°.* Y.
—Devils patriarck. 1683. See Nesse, Christopher.

11 [–] Miracles reviv'd. colop: For A. Banks, 1682. brs. L, O,
EN; Y.
—Sermon preached in an Anabaptist meeting. [n.p.], 1699.
See Oates, Titus.

    —Sound advice. 1689. *See* Oates, Titus.

    —True and perfect account. 1676. *See* Overbury, *Sir Thomas.*

11A   —The true character of a town beau. *Printed, and sold by Randal Taylor,* 1692. brs. CT.

    O., W. Preservation of the King's. 1663. *See* Okeham, William.

    —Solution of all sphærical triangles. Oxford, 1651. *See* Oughtred, William.

12   Entry cancelled.

    O., W. H. P. *See* William III.

    O-Brazile. 1660. *See* Head, Richard.

13   O. Cromwell's thanks to the Lord Generall. *By M. T.,* [1660]. 4°.* LT, O, MR; CN, MH, MIU, MM.

14   O friends! No friends! *By R. Austin,* 1648. 4°.* LT, DT; CH, CSS, NU, WF.

    O hone! O hone! [1692.] *See* H., D.

15   O most mighty Lord God. [*Oxford, by L. Lichfield,* 1644.] brs. MADAN 1756. L.

15A O, my dear God. [*London,* 1679.] brs. L.

16   O rara show, a rara shight! [*London*], *for R. Janeway,* 1689. brs. L; CH, CN, Y.

17   —[Same title.] [*London,* 1689.] brs. OC.

    O raree-show, o pretty show. 1698. *See* Ward, Edward.

17A O raree show, o pritee show. [*London?* 1680.] brs. L.

18   **Oakes, John.** Blessed Paul's tryal. *By J. Richardson, for Tho. Cockeril,* 1689. 4°.* L, O, LW; LC, TO, WF.

19   —A catalogue of the library of. [*London*], 1689. 4°.* LM.

19A —The last sermon and sayings. *For J. Conyers,* 1689. 8°. OC.

    [Oakes, Urian.] Almanack. Cambridge [Mass.], 1650. *See* Almanacs.

20   —An elegie upon the death of the reverend Mr. Thomas Shepard. *Cambridge* [*Mass.*], *by Samuel Green,* 1677. 4°.* EVANS 240. MB, MHS, NN, RBU.

21   —New-England pleaded with. *Cambridge* [*Mass.*], *by Samuel Green,* 1673. 4°.* EVANS 180. CH, MB, MH, MWA, NN, RPJ.

22   —A seasonable discourse. *Cambridge* [*Mass.*], *by Samuel Green,* 1682. 4°.* EVANS 325. LC, MB, MH, MU, MWA, Y.

23   —The soveraign efficacy. *Boston in New-England; for Samuel Sewall.* 1682. 4°.* EVANS 326. O; MH, MWA, NN, RPJ, Y.

24   —The unconqverable, all-conqvering . . . souldier. *Cambridge* [*Mass.*]: *by Samuel Green,* 1674. 4°.* EVANS 195. CH, MB, MH, MHS, MWA, NP, RPJ.

    Oakford, James. Doctrine, 1650. *See* Ockford, James.

25   **O[asland], H[enry].** The Christians daily walk. *For Nevil Simmons,* [1660?]. brs. L, EN.

25A —The living, dead pastor yet speaking. *Printed,* 1663. 8°. O.

26   **Oates, Constant.** The character of a good, and bad, subject. *For the author,* 1682. * L, O, CS; CH, NU, Y.

27   **Oates, Titus.** Dr. Oates's answer to Count Teckely's letter, intercepted. colop: *For J. Dean,* 1683. brs. EN; CH, IU.

28   — —[Anr. ed., "Oat's."] [*London,* 1684.] brs. O, EN; CH, IU.

28A — —[Anr. ed.] [*n.p., n.d.*] brs. ZWT.

29   —Articles of high misdemeanor . . . against Sir William Scroggs. [*London,* 1679/80.] cap., fol.* 4 pp. L, O, C, LG, MR; CLC, CN, MHL, TU, WF, Y, AVP.

30   — —[Anr. ed.] [*London,* 1679/80.] brs. L, LU, OB, DU; CH, IU, MH, NP, TU.

31   — —[Anr. ed.] [*London,* 1680.] cap., fol.* 8 pp. LLU, MR, DT; CSS, IU, TU, Y.

31A — —[Anr. ed.] colop: *For Richard Janeway,* 1680. cap., fol.* L, O, OC, CT, LLU; CLC, CN, MH, PU, WF.

31B [–] A balm presented to these nations. colop: *For J. G.,* [1680?]. cap., 8°.* CLC.

31C —The case of Titus Oates, D. D. humbly offered to . . . the Lords . . . and Commons. [*London,* 1689.] fol. LPR.

32   —A dialogue between Doctor Titus. *For J. S.,* 1684. brs. L, O, DU.

33   —A discourse of the unlawfulness of praying to saints. *For Richard Baldwin,* 1689. 4°. L, LIL, OE, ORP, MR; CN, NU.

34   Entry cancelled.

    —Discovery of the Popish plot. 1679. *See* title.

35   [–] A display of tyranny; or remarks. *Printed,* 1689. 8°. L, O, C, EN, DT; CH, CN, MH, NCD, NU, WF, Y.

36   —Εικων βασιλικη: or, the picture of the late King James. *For Richard Baldwin,* 1696. 4°. L, CS, LIU, LVF, EN, DT; CH, INU, KU, MH, PBM.

37   — —Second edition. —, 1696. 4°. L, O, LW, AU, EN; CLC, LC, MU, NU, TU.

38   — —Third edition. —, 1696. 4°. L, C, ORP, DU, ES; CLC, CN, MBP, MH, WF, Y.

39   —Εικων βασιλικη δευτερα: . . . Part II. *By J. D. to be sold by Richard Baldwin,* 1697. 4°. LVF, OM, CT, LSD, ES, DT; CH, CN, LC, MH, NU, TU, WF, Y.

40   —Εικων βασιλικη τεταρτη. Fourth part. *Printed and are to be sold by Richard Baldwin,* 1697. 4°. O, CT, DU, LSD, ES, DT; CH, CN, NU, WF, Y.

40A —Εικων βασιλικη τριτη: . . . Part the third. *By J. D. to be sold by Richard Baldwin,* 1697. 4°. LCL, ORP, CT, LSD, DT; CH, CLC, CN, MH, WF, Y.

41   [–] An exact and faithful narrative of the horrid conspiracy. *For Tho. Parkhurst, Tho. Cockerill, and Benj. Alsop,* 1680. fol. * L, O, C, MR, EN, DT; CH, CN, MH, NU, TU, WF, Y.

42–4 No entries.

    —Exact discovery of the mystery of iniquity. 1679. *See* title.

    —Further discovery of the plot. Edinburgh, 1680. *See* L'Estrange, *Sir* Roger.

45   Entry cancelled.

    —The humble petition and complaint of. [n.p.], 1683[4]. *See* —Otes's letter.

45A [–] Die Sabbati 9° Maij, . . . 1685. In banco regis. Dominus Rex versus Oats . . . the tryal of . . . Oates. [*London,* 1685.] fol. CM, EN; INU.

46   —The King's evidence justifi'd. *For Jonathan Edwin,* 1679. fol. L, O, C, EN, DT; CH, CN, MH, NU, WF, Y.

47   No entry.

48   —Dr Oats's last legacys. colop: *For J. Dean,* 1683. brs. L, O, CF, HH; CH.

48A —Otes's letter. For the right honourable Sir Leoline Jenkins. [*London*, 1683/4.] brs. L, O, DU, HH, MC; CH, IU, MH, PU, WF, Y.

—Otes's petition. To the Kings . . . majesty. [n.p., 1683.] *See preceding entry, verso.*

49 —The Popes ware-house. *For Tho. Parkhurst, Dorman Newman, Thomas Cockerill, and Tho. Simmons,* 1679. fol. L, O, CT, DU, EN; CH, CN, MH, NU, TU, WF, Y.

50 —Proposals humbly offered to . . . Prince William. [*London*, 1688–9?] brs. L, O, C, HH.

51 —Relation veritable de l'horrible conspiration. *A Londres. Chez Thomas Newcomb, & se vendent chez Richard Bentley, & chez André Forrester,* 1679. 8°. LLU; BN, WF.

51A —Otes's remonstrance. For the right honourable Sir Leoline Jenkins. [*London*, 1683/4.] brs. NC.

—Otes's remonstrance, to the Kings. [n.p., 1683.] *See preceding entry, verso.*

52 [–] The second part of The display of tyranny. [*London*], *printed,* 1690. 8°. L, C, CS, DU, EN; CLC, NU, PU, WF.

53 —A sermon preached at St. Michaels Wood-Street. *By H. Hills and T. Newcomb, for Gabriel Kunholt,* 1679. 4°.* L, O, C, YM, EN; CH, CN, MH, NU, WF, Y.

54 ——[Anr. ed.] *Reprinted at Dublin,* 1679. 4°.* DIX 168. CD, DN, DT; CH.

55 [–] A sermon preached in an Anabaptist meeting . . . 19th. of February. [*London*], *for Zachariah Marshal in Wapping,* 1699. 4°.* L, O, LW, CT, LIU, LSD; CH, MH.

56 [–] Sound advice to Roman Catholicks. *Printed, and sold by Richard Janeway,* 1689. 4°.* L, O, LIL, OB; CH, NU.

56A —To the honourable the knights, citizens and burgesses . . . the deplorable case. [*London*, 1696?] brs. CS.

57 —To the right honourable . . . Parliament assembled; the humble petition of. *By J. D. and are to be sold by Richard Janeway,* 1689. brs. L, O, OC, OW, HH; BN, CH, MH.

58 [–] A tragedy, called the Popish plot, reviv'd. *For the author,* 1696. 4°. L, O, C, GU, DT; CH, CN, MH, NU, WF, Y.

59 —A true narrative of the horrid plot. *For Thomas Parkhurst, and Thomas Cockerill,* 1679. fol. L, O, C, EN, DT; BN, CH, CN, MBP, MH, NP, NU, TU, WF, Y, ZWT. (var.)

60 ——[Anr. ed.] *Edinburgh, by the heir of Andrew Anderson,* 1679. 4°. ALDIS 2156. L, O, EN; WF.

61 ——[Anr. ed.] *Reprinted at Dublin, by Benjamin Took and John Crook, and are to be sold by Mary Crook,* 1679. 4°.* DIX 174. C, CD, DM, DN, DT; MH, NIC, PU, Y.

62 —The witch of Endor. *For Thomas Parkhurst, and Thomas Cockeril,* 1679. fol. L, O, C, LIU, EN; CH, CN, MH, TU, WF, Y.

62A Oates new shams discovered. *For William Pamer and are to be sold by Absalon Chamberlain,* [1685?]. brs. HH.

62B —[Anr. ed.] colop: *For Absalon Chamberlain,* [1688?]. brs. EN; WF, Y.

63 Oates thrash'd in the compter. [*London*], 1684. brs. O; MH.

64 Oates well thresh't. colop: *For R. H.,* 1681. brs. L, O; CH, MH, NCD, NU, PU, WF, Y.

65 No entry.
Oates's bug-bug boarding school. 1683. *See* Dean, John.

65AA Oats's lamentation and a vision that appeared to him. *For James Dean,* 1685. brs. O; MH.

65A Entry cancelled.
Otes's letter. [n.p., 1683.] *See* Oates, Titus.

66 Oates's manifesto. *For R. L.,* 1683. fol.* L, O, C, DU, DT; CH, CN, LC, MH, NCD, NU, WF, Y.

66A Oates's New-years gift. [*London*, 1684.] brs. CLC.

67 Entry cancelled.
Otes's petition. [n.p., 1683.] *See* Oates, Titus. Otes's letter.

68 The oath of a burgess. Civitas Bristol. [*Bristol*, 1672.] fol.* L.

69 The oath of a freeman. [*London*, 1645.] brs. L.

69AA The oath of a free-man of the company of apothecaries. [*London?* 1680.] brs. L.

69BA The oath of allegiance. [*London*], *printed,* 1661. brs. RBU.

69CA —[Same title.] [*Cambridge, Mass.*, 1676.] brs. MHS.

69A —[Same title.] [*Boston, Mass.*, 1678.] brs. MH.

69B —[Same title.] [*London?* 1689.] 8°. EN.

70 The oath of allegiance and supremacy. *By Iohn Redmayne,* 1660. 4°.* L; CH, NU.

71 The oath of allegiance, enacted 13 Jacobi, cap. 4. [*London*], *printed,* 1660. brs. MH.

72 The oath of allegiance enacted. I. A. B. do truly. [*London*], *printed,* 1660. brs. LT, O.

72A The oath of allegiance unfolded. [*London*, 1663?] brs. LPR.

73 The oath of Christ. [*London?* 1641.] cap., 4°.* O, C, OC, LNC, MR; WF, Y.

73A The oath of every free-man belonging to the . . . sadlers. [*Dublin*, 1695?] brs. DN.

73B The oath of every free-man of the city of London. [*London*], *by James Flesher,* [1653?]. brs. MH.

74 —[Same title.] [*London*], *by Samuel Roycroft,* [1684–5]. brs. LL; NU.

The oath of every free-man of the city of Oxford. *Oxford,* 1646. *See* Oxford, City of.

74A The oath of every freeman of the Hamborough company. [*London?* 1690.] brs. L; MH.

Oath of pacification. 1643. *See* Parker, Henry.

74B The oath of supremacy. [*London*], *by James Flesher,* 1661. brs. RBU.

74C The oath of the constables. [*London?* 1688.] brs. LG.

75 The oath of the Kings of England. *Printed at London for T. Bates and F. Coules, June 4.* 1642. 4°.* LT, O, CJ, EC, CD; CH, MH, MU, TU, WF, Y. (var.)

75A The oath of the scavengers. [*London?* 1667.] brs. LG.

75B An oath or protestation . . . to be taken . . . county of York. [*n.p.*, 1644?] brs. O.

75C The oath taken by every free-man of . . . Chester. *Chester, by I. Dawks,* 1689. brs. HH.

75D The oath taken by the censors, who are the examiners of the college [of Physicians]. [*London*, 1700.] brs. L, O.

76 An oath taken by the gentry . . . of York. [*Oxford*, 1643.] brs. LT.

77 The oath taken by the Parliament of England. *By T. Favvcet.* 1642. *June.* 17. 4°.* LT, LHO, BC, LNC, MR; CH, IU, MH, NU, WF, Y.

78 The oath taken by the seamen of the revolted ships. [*London*], *printed, July* 15, 1648. brs. LT, O, LS; CSS.

78A —[Same title.] *Printed July* 17, 1648. brs. L.

79   An oath to be administered unto all officers. *Printed at Oxford by Leonard Lichfield, 1645.* brs. MADAN 1764. L, O; Y.

80   —[Anr. ed.] *Printed at Oxford by Leonard Lichfield, and reprinted at London for Matthew Walbancke, 1646.* 4°.* MADAN 1855. LT, O, MR, DT; CH, CN, INU, Y.

80A   The oath to be ministered by the master . . . of the apothecaries. [*London?* 1670.] brs. L.

80B   The oath to be ministred unto every freeman of . . . Dublin. [*Dublin,* 1681.] brs. DIX 368. DN.

80C   The oath to be taken by every freeman of . . . Tin-plate-workers. [*London,* 1670?] brs. LG.

81   Oaths appointed to be taken instead of the oaths of allegiance. [*Boston,* 1699.] brs. CH, LC, MB, MBS, MU.

      Oaths no gospel ordinance. [n.p.], 1666. *See* Howgil, Francis.

82   The oaths of allegiance and supremacy. 1660. brs. LG (lost).

83   —[Anr. ed.] *By the assigns of John Bill and Christopher Barker, 1672.* brs. O, LUG.

83A   —[Anr. ed.] 1676. brs. LG.

84   —[Anr. ed.] 1678. brs. L.

85   —[Anr. ed.] *By the assigns of John Bill; and by Henry Hills, and Thomas Newcomb, 1684.* brs. L.

      Oaths of Irish Papists. 1681. *See* Penn, William.

85aA The oaths of obedience. I A. B. *By Charles Bill, and Thomas Newcomb, 1688.* brs. OP; MH.

      Oaths of supremacy. 1660. *See* W., T.

      Ob pacem. 1679. *See* Newport, Maurice.

      Obedience active. Oxford, 1643. *See* J., W.

      Obedience and submission. 1690. *See* Taylor, Zachary.

      Obedience due. 1689. *See* Fullwood, Francis.

      Obedience to magistrates. 1683. *See* Clapham, Jonathan.

85A   Objections against Edmund Hemming's proposals. [*London,* 1690?] brs. L.

85B   Objections against passing the bill, as desired by the proprietors of the lights. [*London,* 1692.] brs. LPR.

85C   Objections against the paper-bill answered. [*London,* 1690.] brs. Y.

86   Objections against the restoring the Protestants. *London, reprinted Glasgow, 1697.* brs. ALDIS 3680. EN.

      Objections against the taking . . . answered. 1650. *See* Dury, John.

87   Objections of the Levant-Company answered. [*London,* 1650.] 4°.* NC.

88   Objections to Mr. Lowndes's proposal. *By Tho. Hodgkin, to be sold by John Whitlock, 1695.* 4°.* L, GH, GU; NC, PU, WF, Y.

88A   Objections to the bill for regulating elections, with answers. [n.p., c. 1690.] brs. Y.

88B   Objections, to the clause for prohibiting the use of Brest Summers lintels. [*London?* 1700.] brs. HH.

      Obligation of human laws. 1671. *See* Humfrey, John.

      Obligation resulting. 1687. *See* Pett, Sir Peter.

      Obligation which lyes upon ministers. 1679. *See* C., J.

89   The obliging mistress. *For J. Magnes and R. Bentley, 1678.* 12°. T.C.I 330. L, O, C; CLC, CN, LC, MM, NP.

      O'Brian, Charles. Last speech and confession of. 1688. *See* title.

      O'Brien, Murrough. *See* Inchiquin, Murrough O'Brien, baron.

      Obsequies offer'd up. [n.p., 1650.] *See* F., P.

90   Obsequies: on that vnexemplar champion . . . Arthur, Lord Capell. [*London,* 1649.] brs. LT; MH.

      Obsequium & veritas. 1681. *See* Hearne, Robert.

91   Obsequium Londini serenissimo ac potentissimo principi Carolo II°. *Typis Tho. Newcomb, an. 1660.* fol.* MH, TU.

      Observable things. Boston. 1699. *See* Mather, Cotton. Decennium.

      Observation and comparison. 1659. *See* N., H.

91A   The observation, and proposal of, &c. . . . exportation of wooll. [*London?* 1700.] brs. L; Y.

      Observations and advices. 1669. *See* North, Dudley North, 4th baron.

91B   Observations and reasons, humbly offered to . . . Parliament, in behalf of the creditors. [*London,* 1690.] cap., fol.* L, LPR; Y.

92   Observations both historical and moral upon the burning of London. *By Thomas Ratcliffe, and are to be sold by Robert Pawlet, 1667.* 4°.* L, O, LCP, LG, GH; CH, CLC, MH, MIU, WF, Y.

      Observations, censvres. 1657. *See* Lucy, William, bp.

93-4 Entries cancelled.

      Observations concerning iealousies. 1642. *See* Some observations.

      Observations concerning money. 1697. *See* Layton, Henry.

95   Observations concerning the Chancery. [*London,* 1655.] 4°.* LT.

96   Observations concerning the late treaty: with modest items. *Printed at London for J. C., 1645.* 4°.* LT, DN.

      Observations concerning the originall. 1652. *See* Filmer, Sir Robert.

97   Observations concerning the regulation . . of elections. [n.p.], 1689. 4°. LVF.

      Observations concerning trade. 1668. *See* Child, Sir Josiah.

98   Observations for the justices of the peace. colop: *By John Bill, Thomas Newcomb, and Henry Hills, 1679.* cap., fol.* L, LUG, MR; MH, Y.

99   Observations manifesting the conveniency . . . of Mount-Pietyes. *Printed, 1661.* 4°.* L, OC; PU.

      Observations of a person. Boston, 1699. *See* Paterson, William.

99A   The observations of Mr. Lillie . . . plague. [*London*], *for George Horton, July 7, 1665.* brs. LG.

      Observations of a journey. 1691. *See* Gavin, Antonio.

100   Observations on a late famous sermon, intituled Curse ye Meroz. *Printed, 1680.* 4°.* L, O, CT, MR, DT; CH, MH, NU, WF, Y.

100A Observations on a late scandalous paper. [*London*], *by John Nutt, 1699.* 4°.* L, C; LC, WF.

101   Observations on a pamphlet, touching the present condition of the navy. *Printed, and sold by J. Nutt, 1700.* 4°.* L, LLL; CH, CN, IU, NN.

      Observations on a paper. 1684. *See* Care, Henry.

101A Observations on D. T.'s considerations . . . Africa. [*London,* 1698.] cap., fol.* MH.

Observations on Dr. F., his booke of meteors. 1655. *See* W., F.

102   Entry cancelled.

Observations on H. L.'s history. 1656. *See* Heylyn, Peter. Observations on the historie.

Observations on several books. 1700. *See* Elys, Edmund.

Observations on the first. Glasgow, 1673. *See* Burnet, Gilbert, *bp*.

Observations on the four. 1691. *See* Nye, Stephen.

Observations on the historie. 1656. *See* Heylyn, Peter.

103   Observations on the intended duties on paper. [*London*, 1660?] brs. L.

103A   Observations on the Lady Wentworth's proposal. [*London*, 1677.] brs. L.

104   Observations on the last Dutch wars. *Printed*, 1679. 4°.* BP, LNC, LSD, E, ESS; HR.

104A   Observations on the late famous tryal of Sir G. W. [*London?* 1679.] cap., fol.* L, O, OB; CH, IU, MH, TU, WF.

Observations on the letter written by the Duke. 1689. *See* Lisola, Francois Paul, *baron* de.

Observations on the letter written to Sir Thomas Osborn. 1673. *See* Lisola, Francois Paul, *baron* de.

Observations on the poems. 1672. *See* Rapin, René.

105   Observations on the proposals of the city, to insure houses. colop: *For the gentlemen of the Insurance Office*, 1681. fol.* L, O, LG, LUG, LNC, LSD, CD; NC, NP.

106   Observations on the single query. [*London*, 1679.] brs. L, C, OB, HH; CLC, MBA, MH, PU, Y.

107   Observations on the state of gold and silver. [*London*, 1690?] brs. Y.

107A   Observations touching appeals from Chancery. *Printed*, 1682. brs. LSD.

Observations touching the principles. 1677. *See* Hale, *Sir* Matthew.

108   Entry cancelled.

Observations tovching. 1642. *See* Certaine observations tovching the two great offices.

Observations upon a late libel. [n.p.], 1681. *See* Halifax, George Savile, *marquis of*.

108A   Observations upon a paper intituled, Reasons humbly offered. [*London*, 1700?] brs. L; INU, MH.

Observations upon a sermon. [n.p., 1695.] *See* Layton, Henry.

Observations upon a short. [n.p., 1698.] *See* Layton, Henry.

109   Observations upon a small treatise, intituled, A defence. [*London*, 1691?] cap., 4°.* L, E; NP, Y.

Observations upon a treatise. 1675. *See* Stephens, Edward.

110   Observations upon, and in answer to His Excellencies late letter. *For John Love-Joye*, 1647. 4°.* LT, O, OC, LLU, BQ, DT; CLC, CN, CSS, MH, TO.

Observations upon Anthroposophia. Parrhesia, 1650. *See* More, Henry.

Observations upon Aristotles. 1652. *See* Filmer, Robert.

111   Observations upon His Majesties ansvver. [*London*], *printed*, 1642. 4°.* LT, O, LG, LSD, EN, DT; CLC, CN, MH, MM, Y.

Observations vpon historie. 1641. *See* Habington, William.

Observations upon Mr. Johnson's. 1689. *See* Sherlock, William.

Observations upon Mr. Wadsworth's book. [n.p., 1690.] *See* Layton, Henry.

112   Observations upon Mr. Walkers account of the siege of London-Derry. colop: *For R. Simpson*, 1689. 4°.* L, LLP, MR, DN; CH, CLC, CN, CSS, MM, TO, AVP.

Observations upon Prince Rupert's. [n.p.], 1642. *See* B., T.

Observations upon some of His Majesties. 1642. *See* Parker, Henry.

Observations upon some particular persons. 1656. *See* Raleigh, Carew.

113   Observations upon some texts. [n.p.], 1648. 4°. L, C, LSD, DT; CH, CLC, TSM.

Observations upon the acts for annuities. [n.p., 1700.] *See* Orme, Thomas.

Observations upon the answer. 1685. *See* Eachard, John. Some observations.

Observations upon the Bank of England. *John Whitlock*, 1695. 4°.* L, O.

114   Observations upon the chief acts of the two late P. Assemblies. [*Leith*], *printed*, 1653. 4°.* ALDIS 1480.5. LSD, ENC; CLC, WF.

115   Observations upon the constitution of the Bank of England. [*London*, 1698.] cap., fol.* L; MH, PL.

Observations upon the Dublin-bills. 1683. *See* Petty, *Sir* William.

116   Observations vpon the Earle of New-castles declaration. *Printed*, 1643. 4°.* LT, O, YM, DM, DT; CH, MH, MIU, TU, WF, Y.

117   Observations upon the ecclesiastical jurisdiction. 1689. 8°. EN.

118   Entry cancelled.

Observations vpon the effects. [n.p., 1642.] *See* May, Thomas.

118A   Observations upon the government of . . . France. *Printed*, 1689. 8°. T.C.II 342. L, BAMB; CLC, CN, MH, WF.

119   Observations upon the instrvctions for the taking the vovv and Covenant. *Oxford* [*London?*], *by Leonard Lichfield*, 1643. 4°.* MADAN 1435. LT, O, CJ, EC, DT; CH, CLC, MH, NU, WF.

120   Entry cancelled.

Observations upon the kalender glasse. [n.p., 1641?] *See* Slade, John.

121   Observations upon the Kings two declarations. 1681. fol. O; CN.

122   Observations upon the last actions and words of Major General Harrison. *By H. Lloyd and R. Vaughan*, 1660. 4°.* LT, O; WF, Y.

123   Observations upon the late revolution in England. [*London*, 1689.] cap., 4°.* LLP, MR, EN; MB, MH, PL.

Observations upon the life. 1686. *See* Joyner, William. Some observations.

Observations upon the oath. [n.p., 1662.] *See* Winter, *Sir* John.

Observations upon the ordinance. Oxford, [1645]. *See* Boughen, Edward.

123A Observations upon the papers which Mr. Rookwood . . . deliver'd. *For R. Clavel*, 1696. 4°.* T.C.II 580. L, O, CT, SP; CSS, MH, MIU, PU, WF, Y.

123B Observations upon the Prince of Orange. [*London*, 1642.] cap., 4°.* LT, EC, LIU, MR, DT; CH, NC, TU, WF, Y.

123BA Observations upon the royal succession. *Printed 28 March* 1699. fol.* OP.

123C Observations upon the strange & wonderful prophecies of Mr. John Gadbury. colop: *For J. H,* 1680[1679]. cap., fol.* O, MR; CH, MH, TU, WF, Y.

123D Observations upon the times. [*London*, 1642.] cap., 4°.* LT, C, OC, EC, SP, DT; CH, CN, MH, TU, WF, Y.

Observations upon the warre. 1689. *See* Littleton, Edward.

Observations upon three. *See* R., J. D.

123E The observator defended. [*London*, 1642.] cap., 4°.* LT, SP, DT; CH, MH, MU, TU, WF, Y.

Observator defended. 1685. *See* L'Estrange, Sir Roger.

123F The observator in a delemma. [*London*], *For A. Green,* 1682. brs. L; CH, MH, Y.

123G Entry cancelled.

Observator observ'd. 1656. *See* L'Estrange, Hamon.

123GA Observator of surprising prorogations. *Edinburgh, by the heir of A. Anderson,* 1683. fol. ALDIS 2401. EN.

123H The observator prov'd a trimmer. *For John Allen,* 1685. fol.* O, LLL, OC, CT, MR; CH, IU, MH, TU, WF, Y.

123I —Second edition. —, 1685. fol.* C, CT, DU; CLC, CN, LC, MH, NU, Y.

123IA —"Second" edition. *For J. Allen,* 1685. fol.* MR; WF.

123J —Third edition. *For John Allen,* 1685. fol.* EC, LIU, SP, DT; CDA, CH, MM, NCD, TSM, Y.

123JA —Fourth edition. —, 1685. fol.* L, OC; CSU, MIU, PU.

123K The observator reproved. colop: *For the author, and published by Langley Curtis,* 1684. cap., 4°.* L, O, LW; CLC, NR.

Observator, upon the successe of former Parliaments. 1643. *See* May, Thomas.

123KA The observator vindicated. *For Walter Davis,* 1685. 8°.* T.C.I 101. O, LSD; CH, MM.

123KB The observator's catechism. [*London, c.* 1690.] cap., 4°.* CT.

Observator's observation how narrowly. Dublin, [1685]. *See* L'Estrange, Sir Roger.

Observator's observations. Dublin, [1685]. *See* L'Estrange, Sir Roger.

123L [**Ocane, Donell.**] A trve copy of a letter sent from Doe Castle. *For William Hope,* 1643. 4°.* LT; Y.

123M **Occam, William of.** Gulielmi Occhami, . . . summa totius logicae. *Oxoniæ, excudebat L. L. impensis J. Crosley,* 1675. 8°. T.C.I 221; MADAN 3067. L, O, C, OC, OME; IAU, PU.

123N The occasion and manner of Mr. Francis Wolleys death. [*London*, 1660.] cap., fol.* LT, C; CH, MH, WF.

123O An occasional dialogue at a coffee-house. [*London*], *printed* 1667. 4°.* O, YM; MIU, MM, NP, WF, Y.

123P An occasional discourse concerning God's foreknowledge. 1687. 4°. L.

123Q —[Anr. ed.] 1697. 4°. L, LW.

123R The occasional doctor. colop: [*London*], *for Allen Banks,* [1682]. brs. L, CT, DU; CH.

123RA —[Anr. ed.] [*London*], *for A. Banks,* [1683?]. brs. CN.

123S An occasional essay, by way. [*n.p.*], *printed,* 1673. 4°.* CT, DT.

123T An occasional letter containing some thoughts. *For Brabazon Aylmer,* 1698. 8°.* L, C, BAMB; CLC, CN, MB, WF.

124 Entry cancelled. Date: 1703.

Occasional queries. 1659. *See* Stubbe, Henry.

Occasional reflections. 1665. *See* Boyle, Robert.

Occult physick. 1660. *See* Williams, William, *astrologer.*

124A An ocean of teares, or a world of sorrowes. [*London?* 1680.] cap., 4°.* L.

125 Entry cancelled.

Ocellus, Lucanus. "Ὄκελλος ὁ Λευκανὸς φιλόσοφος . . . De universi naturâ. *Cantabrigiæ,* 1670. *See* Gale, Thomas. Opuscula.

126 [**Ochino, Bernardino.**] A dialogue of polygamy. *For John Garfeild* [sic], 1657. 12°. L, O, C, LLU, EN; CH, LC, MH, MU, OCI, WF, Y.

127 **Ockanickon.** A true account of the dying vvords of. *For Benjamin Clark,* 1682. 4°.* LT, O, LF; CH, MH, NN, PHS, RPJ.

128 ——Second edition. [*London*], *printed,* 1683. 4°.* LF; NN, RPJ.

128AA **Ockford, James.** The doctrine of the fourth commandement. *By G. Dawson, to be sold by Iohn Hides,* 1650. 8°. OC.

128A [**Ockland, Christopher.**] The Pope's farwel; or Queen Ann's dream. [*London*], *by J. M. for T. W.,* [1680]. 4°. L, EN, DM; CH, CU, WF.

128B **O'Clery, Michael.** Focloir no sanasan nua. [*Louvain,* 1643.] 8°. L, O; CN.

128C —Sanasan nuadh; a dictionary . . . Irish words. [*Louvain*], 1643. 8°. L.

129 **O'Connor, William.** A discovery to the prayse of God. [*London*], *printed,* 1641. 4°.* LT, O, C, EC, DN; BN, CH, CN, MBP, NU, TU, WF. (var.)

130 Entry cancelled.

Octupla. Edinburgi, 1696. *See* Barclay, William.

131 Ode for the consort at York-buildings, upon the death of Mr. Henry Purcell. colop: [*London*], *for Francis Saunders,* 1695. brs. O; MH, Y.

131A An ode humbly inscribed to his grace Charles Duke of Grafton. [*London*, 1689.] cap., 4°.* LC.

Ode in imitation of Pindar. 1681. *See* Chetwood, Knightly.

Ode in memory. [*n.p.*, 1695.] *See* Buckingham, John Sheffield, *duke.*

131B An ode made on the welcome news of . . . Darien. *Edinburgh, by James Watson,* 1699. brs. ALDIS 3875. RPJ.

132 An ode, occasion'd by the death of Her Sacred Majesty. *For Richard Cumberland,* 1695. fol.* T.C.II 539. L, O, OP, CT, LLU; CH, IU, MH, TU, WF, Y.

Ode occasion'd by the death of the Queen. 1695. *See* B., A.

133   An ode on Her Royal Highness the Princess of Orange. [*London*, 1688/9.] brs. O, HH; Y.

134   An ode on St Cecilia's Day, perform'd on the 23rd of November, 1696. [*London*, 1696.] brs. MC.

Ode on the anniversary. Dublin, 1693. *See* H., B.

134A   An ode on the coronation of . . . King William III. *For Jacob Tonson*, 1689. 4°.* O; WF, Y.

Ode on the death. 1700. *See* Browne, William.

135   An ode performed at the anniversary feast. [*London*, 1700.] brs. L; CH.

135A   Ode to the King on his Irish expedition. *Dublin, by Jo. Brent*, 1691. 4°.* DERRY DIOC. LIB.

135B   An ode to the King on his return from New-market. *For R. Bentley*, 1684. 4°.* L, O, LSD; WF.

Ode upon the death of Mr. Cowley. 1667. *See* Higgons, Thomas.

136   An ode upon the glorious and successful expedition of . . . the Prince of Orange. *Printed, and to be sold by Randal Taylor*, 1689. fol.* L, MR; CH, MH, PU, TU, WF, Y.

Ode upon the happy return of King Charles. 1660. *See* Shirley, James.

137   Odes and elogies upon divine & moral subjects. *For Henry Bonwicke*, 1698. T.C.III 55. L, O, LLU, DM; MH.

138   Entry cancelled.

Odious, despicable . . . drunkard. 1649. *See* Younge, Richard.

139   **Odling, Edward.** Honoured Sir, that the works of mercy. [*London*, 1654.] brs. LT.

139AA   —To the right honourable the . . . corporation for the relieving of the poor . . . the remonstrance of. [*London*, 1652?] brs. L.

139BA   **O'Donnel, Cornelius.** The recantation of. colop: *By Richard Hodgkinson*, 1664. cap., 4°.* O, LW.

139CA   **O'Dowde, Thomas.** The poor mans physician. [*London*, 1664.] brs. O; MH.

139A   ——Third edition. 1665. 8°. L, GU.

139B   —Two letters concerning the cure of the plague. *For Fran. Smith, July the 20th*, 1665. brs. HH.

139C   ——[Anr. ed.] [*London*, 1665.] brs. MH.

Oeconomia sacra: or. 1685. *See* P., J.

Of a degradation of gold. 1678. *See* Boyle, Robert.

Of a late, or, a death-bed repentance. Oxford, 1645. *See* Hammond, Henry.

140   Of a maid that was deep in love. [*London*, 1690?] brs. HH.

Of absolute rest. *See* Boyle, Robert. Certain physiological essays.

140A   Of all the factions in the town. [*London*, 1660?] brs. CN.

Of Antichrist. 1651. *See* Weldon, Robert.

Of baptisme. [n.p.], 1646. *See* Lawrence, Henry.

140B   Of baptism and the Lord's Supper. *For Benjamin Billingsley*, 1671. 12°. O.

140C   Of Bow-church and steeple. [*London*, 1679.] brs. Y.

Of Christian communion. [n.p.], 1693. *See* Kettlewell, John.

Of Christian prudence. 1691. *See* Kettlewell, John.

Of communion. 1687. *See* Payne, William. Discourse.

Of conscience. Oxford, 1644. *See* Hammond, Henry.

Of devotion. [n.p.], 1678. *See* Sergeant, John.

Of education. [n.p., 1644.] *See* Milton, John.

Of education especially. Oxon, 1673. *See* Walker, Obadiah.

Of faith. Oxford, 1688. *See* Woodhead, Abraham.

Of holy living. 1668. *See* Mall, Thomas.

Of humiliation. [n.p., 1689.] *See* Stephens, Edward.

Of idolatry. Oxford, 1646. *See* Hammond, Henry.

Of laying on of hands. 1656. *See* Gosnold, John.

Of liberty. 1649. *See* La Mothe Le Vayer, François.

Of majestracy. [1668.] *See* Johnson, Samuel.

Of our communion. [n.p.], 1646. *See* Lawrence, Henry.

Of prayers. 1699. *See* Stephens, Edward.

Of prelatical episcopacy. 1641. *See* Milton, John.

141   Of receiving the communion in the company. Oxford, *for Richard Davis*, 1651. 4°.* MADAN 2166. LT, O, LW, OC, MR, EN.

Of reformation. [n.p.], 1641. *See* Milton, John.

Of resisting. 1643. *See* Hammond, Henry.

Of scandall. Oxford, 1644. *See* Hammond, Henry.

Of scandal; together. 1680. *See* Clark, Samuel.

Of sinnes. Oxford, 1645. *See* Hammond, Henry.

Of superstition. Oxford, 1645. *See* Hammond, Henry.

Of that eternal breath. [n.p., 1659.] *See* Travers, Rebeckah.

Of the al-sufficient. Paris, 1653. *See* Smith, Richard.

Of the article. 1642. *See* Hayne, Thomas.

Of the authority. 1687. *See* Hutchinson, Charles.

Of the benefits. Oxford, 1680. *See* Walker, Obadiah.

Of the blasphemie. [n.p.], 1646. *See* Hales, John.

Of the celebration. 1661. *See* Smith, William.

Of the child's portion. 1649. *See* Woodward, Hezekiah.

142   Of the daily practice of piety. *By J. F. for R. Royston*, 1660. 12°. LT; WF.

Of the distinction. [n.p.], 1645. *See* Smith, Richard, *bp.*

Of the division. 1652. *See* Ferne, Henry, *bp.*

Of the education of a prince. 1678. *See* Nicole, Pierre.

Of the faith. 1700. *See* Stratford, Nicholas, *bp.*

142A   Of the faithful friendship. [*London?* 1650.] brs. L.

Of the famous and pleasant history. [1680.] *See* Forde, Emanuel.

143   Of the French monarchy. *Printed*, 1680. 8°. L, OC, EC, SP; Y.

143A   Of the gamut. *For J. Gillibrand*, 1684. 4°.* L.

Of the government. Cambridge, 1641. *See* Thorndike, Herbert.

Of the heart. 1678. *See* Jones, Thomas, *of Llandyrnos.*

Of the high veneration. 1685. *See* Boyle, Robert.

144   Of the horrible and woful destruction of Jerusalem. [1690?] brs. O.

Of the incurable scepticism. 1588 [*i.e.* 1688]. *See* La Placette, Jean.

Of the internal. 1654. *See* Pembroke, William Herbert, *earl.*

Of the laws. 1692. *See* Arbuthnot, John.

Of the medals and coins of Scotland. [1700.] *See* Nicolson, William, *bp.*

Of the opening of rivers. 1656. *See* Matthew, Francis.

Of the povver. 1647. *See* Hammond, Henry.

Of the Quakers. 1700. *See* Mather, William.

Of the reasonableness. 1650. *See* Hammond, Henry.

Of the soul. 1699. *See* Burthogge, Richard.

Of the state. 1684. *See* Allen, William.

Of the torments. 1658. *See* Richardson, Samuel.

144A Of the two last things. [*London*], 1682. 4°. L.

Of trade. 1700. *See* Pollexfen, John.

Of transubstantiation. 1688. *See* Tenison, Thomas, *abp.*

Of true religion. 1673. *See* Milton, John.

Of vvill-vvorship. Oxford, 1644. *See* Hammond, Henry.

144B Of worshipping the Holy Ghost expressly. [*London*, 1692.] cap., 4°.* L, LW, BC, DT; CH, IU, MH, NU, WF, Y.

145 **Offelen, Heinrich.** A double grammar for Germans to learn English. *For the author, and are to be sold by Nath. Thompson; and Nath. Ponder; and Sam. Smith,* 1687. 8°. L, O, OU; CN, MH, MIU, WF, Y.

145aA —Proposals for printing a double grammar. [*London?* 1686.] brs. L.

Offer of farther help. 1665. *See* Mall, Thomas.

145A An offertory, presented at the fvnerals of . . . Edvvard Popham. [*London*, 1651.] brs. MH, NN.

Office and dvtie of constables. Cambridge, 1641. *See* Layer, John.

Office and dutie of executors. 1641. *See* Wentworth, Thomas.

146 An office for penitents. *Printed*, 1691. 8°. O, OC.

146A An office in time of affliction. [n.p.], 1681. 8°. BSM.

Office of a chaplain. Cambridge, 1688. *See* Collier, Jeremy.

Office of enteries. [*London?* 1657.] *See* E., J.

147 The office of land-credit. Encouragement. [*London?* 1696.] brs. L.

148 The office of publick advice. *By Tho. Newcomb,* 1657. brs. LT, LUG.

149 The office of the B. V. Mary in English. *By Henry Hills,* 1687. 8°. L (lost), LIL, OC, OM, DUS; IU.

Office of the clerk of assize. 1676. *See* W., T.

Office of the good house-wife. 1672. *See* B., F.

150 Office of the Holy Week. *Paris, by the widow Chrestien,* 1670. 8°. L, O, C, LLP; MR; CH, CN, TU, WF, Y.

151 —[Anr. ed.] *By Henry Hills,* 1688. 8°. L, O, DUS; IU, WF.

Offices and places. 1660. *See* N., E.

152 Officina brevium: select and approved forms. *For T. Basset; sold by H. Twyford, J. Bellinger, S. Heyrick, W. Jacob, J. Poole, and W. Crook,* 1679. fol. T.C.I 359. L, O, LGI, CP, EN; CLC, NCL.

153 —[Anr. ed.] *By George Sawbridge, William Rawlins, and Samuel Roycroft, assigns of Richard and Edward Atkins. For Thomas Basset,* 1679. fol. L, OC, CS, LIU; CH, LC, MHL, MIU, PUL, WF.

154 Officium B. Mariæ Virg. nuper reformatum. *Typis Henrici Hills,* [1687]. 16°. L, BSM; CN, TU.

155 Officium cleri, desiderium populi: or, canonical obedience. *For Richard Baldwin,* 1691. 4°. T.C.II 379. L, O, LLP, CT; CLC, CSB, NU, WF.

156 Entry cancelled. Ghost.

Officium clerici pacis. A book of indictments. 1675. *See* W., J.

157 Officium concionatoris. *Cantabrigiæ, ex academiæ typographeo. Impensis Guilielmi Morden,* 1655. 4°.* L, O, C, LW, DT; IU, PPT, WF, Y.

158 —[Anr. ed.] *Cantabrigiæ, ex officina Joan. Hayes,* 1676. *Impensis Guilielmi Morden, Cantabr.* 8°.* L, O, C, OU; CH, IU, NU.

Officium eucharisticum. 1683. *See* Lake, Edward.

Officium hominis. 1680. *See* Allestree, Richard.

Officium ministri, vel. 1663. *See* Mason, Charles.

159 Officium viri sapientiæ studiosi. *Oxonii,* 1689. 8°. EN.

159A **Offley, William.** The father's last office. *By T. Milburn, for R. Clavel,* 1696. 4°.* MR, NE; NRU.

159B —Reflections to a late book, entituled, The genuine remains of . . . Barlow. *For R. Clavell,* 1694. 4°. C.

159C —A sermon preach't at a publick ordination. *For John Lawrence,* 1697. 4°. NRU.

160 **O'Flaherty, Roderic.** Ogygia: . . . Liber primus. *Typis R. Everingham, sumptibus Ben. Tooke,* 1685. 4°. T.C.II 127. L, O, C, EN, DT; BN, CH, CU, MU, TU, WF, Y, AVP.

160A ——[Anr. ed.] *Typis R. Everingham, prostant venales apud Jacobum Malon, bibliopulam Dubliniensem,* 1685. 4°. DN.

161 —Serenissimi Walliæ principis. *Dublini, typis Andreæ Crook, & Samuelis Helsham,* 1688. 4°. DIX 230. DN.

161A **O[gden], S[amuel].** Epicedium, or, a funeral elegy on . . . gracious sovereign. *For John Everingham,* 1695. fol.* L, O; CLC, MH, MIU, NP, TU, Y.

162 **Ogilby, John.** An accurate description of Africa. *By Tho. Johnson, for the author,* 1669. fol.* O.

162A [–] An advertisement concerning the English Atlas. [*London*, 1672.] brs. MH.

163 —Africa: being. *By Tho. Johnson for the author,* 1670. fol. L, O, C, EN, ES, DT; BN, CH, CN, LC, MH, MU, WF, Y.

164 —America. *By Tho. Johnson for the author,* 1670. fol. CT, NPL; MH, PBL.

165 ——[Anr. ed.] *By the author,* 1671. fol. L, O, C, EN, DT; BN, CH, CN, LC, MB, MH, NCD, NN, RPJ, WF, Y, AVP.

166 —Asia, the first part. *By the author,* 1673. fol. T.C.I 148. L, O, C, E, DT; CH, CN, LC, MB, NN, WF, Y.

167 Entry cancelled.

—Atlas Japannensis. 1670. *See* Montanus, Arnoldus.

168 —Britannia, volume the first. *By the author,* 1675. fol. L, O, C, EN, DT; CH, CN, LC, MH, WF, Y. (var.)

169 ——[Anr. ed.] *For Abel Swall and Robert Morden,* 1698. fol.* L, O, C, LG, BR, LLU; BN, CLC, IU, MBA, NP, PBI.

169A ——[Anr. ed.] *For Abel Swalle,* 1698. fol. OC.

169B [–] Mr. Ogilby's description of a trooper. [*London*, 1660?] brs. L.

170 —Mr. Ogilby's design for carrying on his Britannia. [*London?* 1674.] cap., fol.* L, LPR; Y.

170A —The English traveller's companion. *For Tho. Basset; and Rich. Chiswell,* 1676. 8°. L.

171 —The entertainment of . . . Charles II. *By Tho. Roycroft,* 1662. fol. L, O, C, EN, DT; BN, CH, CN, LC, NCD, NN, WF, Y.

172 ——[Anr. ed.] [*London*], *For Richard Marriot and Thomas Dring,* 1662. fol. L, O, C, LG, OM; BN, CN, IU, LC, Y.

172A —The final conclusion or up-shutting of Mr. Ogilby's standing lottery of books. [*London*], *the author's office*, 1668. brs. O.

172B [–] The frog, or, the Low-countrey nightingale. [*London?* 167-.*] cap., fol.* O; CH.

172C —The history of America. *Printed*, 1682. fol. PAP.

172D [–] The Holland nightingale. [*London*], *for Robert Clavill*. 1672. brs. L, O, LPR.

173 —Itinerarium Angliæ: or, a book of roads. *By the author*, 1675. fol. L, O, LA, LIL, CE, CM; CB, MH, MU.

174 Entry cancelled.
—Itinerarium. 1698. *See* —Britannia.

175 —The Kings coronation. *By Ben. Griffin, to be sold by Christopher Wilkinson*, 1685. fol.* T.C.II 130. LT, O, C, LG, LLP; CH, CN, LC, MH, TU, WF, AVP.

176 — —[Anr. ed.] *Edinburgh, re-printed by the heir of Andrew Anderson*, 1685. fol.* ALDIS 2563. O, LG, AU, EN, ES; CH, CN, MM, TO, Y.

176A — —[Anr. ed.] *Printed and are to be sold at his [Wm. Morgan's] house, and by Christopher Wilkinson*, 1689. fol.* O.

177 —London survey'd. *Printed and sold at the authors house*, 1677. 8°. C, LG, OQ, CM; YBA. (var.)

177AA [–] A lottery licensed by . . . the Duke of York. [*London*, 1664.] brs. L; MH.

177BA —Mr. Ogilby's lottery licensed. [*London*, 1665?] brs. MH.

177A —Mr. Ogilby's pocket book of roads. Third edition. *For the author*, 1679. 4°.* T.C.I 387. CM; MH, WF, YBA.

178 —Mr. Ogilby's and William Morgan's pocket book of the roads. Fourth edition. *For the author, and Christopher Wilkinson*, 1689. 4°. L, O, C, BR; CH, Y.

179 —May the 10th 1669. A proposal concerning an English atlas. [*London*, 1669.] brs. O.

179A —Proposals for the last general sale of Mr. Ogilby's books, maps. [*London*], 1691. brs. L.

179B —Mr. Ogilby's proposals for the . . . carrying on of his Britannia. [*London*, 1673.] brs. L; MH.

179C — —[Anr. ed.] [*London, March*, 1673.] brs. MH.

180 [–] Queries in order to the description of Britannia [19 queries]. [*London*, 1673.] brs. L, O.

180A [–] —[Anr. ed., 22 queries.] 1673. brs. L, O.

181 —The relation of His Majestie's entertainment. *By Tho. Roycroft, for Rich. Marriott*, 1661. fol.* LT, O, C, DU, EN; CH, IU, LC, MH, TU, WF, Y, AVP. (var.)

181A — —[Anr. ed.] *Printed at London, and re-printed at Edinburgh*, 1661. 4°. ALDIS 1707. LG, EN; CN, CU.

181AB —The second Charles, heir of the royal martyr. *For Iohn Williams*, 1661. brs. L, OC.

181AC —A second proposal . . . for the more speedy vendition. [*London*, 1668.] brs. L.

181B —A standing lottery of his own books. [*London*, 1664?] fol.* CH.

182 —Tables of his measur'd roads. *By the author*, 1676. 4°. L, CM, EC, DT; YBA.

183 —The translation of Homers Works . . . being undertaken. [*London*, 1660.] brs. O.

183A —The travellers guide. *Sold by Philip Lea*, [1687.] fol. WF.

184 — —[Anr. ed.] *By T. Ilive for Abel Swall, and sold by Tim. Child, and R. Knaplock*, 1699. 8°. T.C.III 139. L, O, C, OP, BC, CD; CH, CN, MH, WF, Y.

184A —Whereas His Majesty hath been graciously pleased . . . and whereas John Ogilby . . . [announcing wheel of fortune lottery for Dublin]. [*Dublin*, 1672.] brs. LPR.

185 **Ogilvy, Archibald.** Disputatio juridica. *Edinburgi, ex officina hæredum Andreæ Anderson*, 1700. 4°.* ALDIS 3991. EN.

186 **O[gilvy], M[ichael].** Fratres in malo, or the matchles couple. [*n.p.*], *by R. Wilks, and are to be sold by the booksellers of London and Oxford*, 1660. 4°.* MADAN 2512n. LT, O, C, DU, LSD, DT; MH, NU.

187 **Ogle, Thomas.** A letter of dangerous consequence. *For Edw: Husbands, February 27.* 1642[3]. 4°.* LT, O, C, EC, BP; CH, MH, TU, WF, Y.

188 The oglio of traytors: including the illegal tryall of His late Maiesty. *By T. M. for William Shears*, [1660?]. 8°. L, O; IU, MH, MHL, WF.

188A **Ogston, William.** Viro admodum colendo . . . Richardo Busbaeo. [*n.p.*, 1659.] brs. L.

188B Oh! how I sigh when I think. *By E. C. for F. Coles, T. Vere, and J. Wright*, [1663–74]. brs. O.

189 —[Anr. ed.] [*London*], *for I. Wright, I. Clarke, W. Thackeray, and T. Passinger*, [1681–84]. brs. O.
Oh people! [*n.p.*], 1670. *See* F., G.
Oh! take him gently. [*n.p.*, 1697.] *See* Banks, John.
Oh! the day. [*n.p.*, 1660?] *See* Baker, Daniel.
Ἰκουμένη μελλουσα: the world. 1671. *See* Sherwin, William.

190 **O[keham], W[illiam].** The preservation of the King's Majesties royal person. *By R. D.*, 1663. 4°.* EN, DT; CH, PU, Y.

190A [–] —[Anr. ed.] —, *to be sold by Francis Eglesfield*, 1664. 4°.* SP; WF.

191 **Okeley, William.** Eben-Ezer. *For Nat. Ponder*, 1675. 8°. T.C.I 204. L, O, C, LLU, EN; CH, CLC, CN, WF, Y.

192 — —[Anr. ed.] —, 1676. 8°. O; MH.

193 — —Second edition. —, 1684. 8°. T.C.II 90. L; CLC, MB, WSC, Y.

194 **Okes, John.** A sermon preached . . . July 12th. 1681. *For Joanna Brome*, 1689. 4°.* T.C.I 457. C, OM, CS; CDA, CH, CLC, NU.

195 **Okey, John.** The declaration of. *For Robert Williamson*, 1662. 4°.* NU.

195A —A true and particular relation of the late victory. *By Matthew Simmons, for Henry Overton*, 1648. 4°.* LT, C, AN; CH, MH.
Olbia, the new iland. 1660. *See* Sadler, John.

195B The old abbot and King Olfrey. [*London*], *for J. Wright, J. Clarke, W. Thackeray, and T. Passinger*, [1682]. brs. CM.

195C —[Anr. ed.] [*London*], *for A. Milbourne*, [1692]. brs. O.

195D —[Anr. ed.] [*London*], *by A. M.*, [1700?]. brs. O.

196 Old Æsop at VVhite-Hall. *Printed; and sold by J. Nutt*, 1698. 4°.* L, O, LUG, MR, DT; CLC, MH, OCI, TU, WF.

197   The old Anabaptists grand plot discovered. *For George Horton*, [1660]. 4°.* LT, ORP.

197A   The old and new courtier. [*n.p.*, 1700?] brs. L.

198   The old cause's epitaph by anticipation. *By H. H. for William Abington*, 1683. 4°.* L, EN; CH, MIU, TU, WF, Y.

199   The old Cavalier. [*London*], *for C. Bates*, [1690]. brs. L, HH; IU, MH.

200   An old Cavalier turned a new courtier. [*London*, 1690.] cap., 4°.* O, CT, LIU, LSD; CLC, MH, NCD, TU.

201   The old East India Company's complaints answered. [*London*, 1698?] brs. L.

202   Entry cancelled.

       Old English blood. 1648. *See* Grey, Thomas, *Baron Grey of Groby.*

       Old English loyalty. 1695. *See* Stephens, Edward.

202A   The old Exchange to the new Stadt-house. [*London*], *for F. C.*, 1667. 8°.* L.

       Old gentleman's wish. Cirencester, 1685. *See* B., C.

203   The old gentlewomans last legacy. [*London*], *for P. Brooksby*, [1672–95]. brs. L, HH.

204   Old Jemmy: an excellent new ballad. *By Nath. Thompson*, 1681. brs. L, O, DU; CH, MH, PU, WF, Y.

204A   Old John Hopkin's, and Tho. Sternhold's petition. colop: *For John Wells*, 1699. brs. L; MH.

205   The old leaven purged out. [*London*], *printed*, 1658. 4°. O, C; CH, MBP, NU, TU, WF.

205A   The old maid mad for a husband. [*London*], *for J. Blare*, [1690?]. brs. O.

206   The old malignant in new apparrell. *For L. F.*, 1648. 4°.* LT, C, DU, DT; CSS, NU.

       Old mans complaint. [1650.] *See* Pope, Walter.

206AA   The old man's life renewed by heavenly providence. [*n.p.*, 1657.] brs. L.

206A–7   Entries cancelled.

       Old man's wish. [1684.] *See* Pope, Walter.

208   No entry.

       Old mens tears. *Boston*, 1691. *See* Scottow, Joshua.

209   The old miser slighted. [*London*], *for P. Brooksby, J. Deacon, J. Blare, J. Back*, [1685–92]. brs. L, CM, HH; MH.

210   The old new true blew Protestant-plot. *For J. Dean*, 1683. brs. L, O, LL; CLC, MH, Y.

211   Old nevves newly revived. [*London*], *printed*, 1641. 4°.* LT, O, LG, OC; CH, INU, MM, TU, WF, Y.

212   The old Non-Conformist. *Printed and are to be sold by H. C.*, 1660. 4°.* L, O, C, AN, LIU, ENC, DT; CLC, IU, MH, NU, WF, Y.

212A   —[Anr. ed.] *Printed*, 1660. 4°.* OC, MR, DT; CH, IU, MH, WF.

213   The old Parliament, wjth some passages thereof. *For Robert Austin*. 1645. 4°.* LT, O, BC, YM; MH, WF, Y.

       Old Parliamentary prognostication. 1655. *See* Prynne, William.

       Old Popery as good. [n.p.], 1688. *See* N., N.

213A   Old Popery in a new dress. *By J. M. for H. Cripps and L. Lloyd*, 1652. 4°.* SP; CLC.

       Old principles of New-England. [n.p., 1700.] *See* Mather, Cotton.

213B   The old Protestant his consciencious queries. [*London*, 1650?] 4°.* LSC; LC.

       Old Protestants letanie. [n.p.], 1647. *See* Alleyn, Thomas.

       The old proverbe, as good be a knave. [*London*, 1645/6.] *See* Cooke, Francis.

214   The old pudding-pye woman. *For F. Coles, T. Vere, J. Wright, and J. Clark*, [1675]. brs. EUING 261. L, GU; MH.

       Old Puritan detected. 1682. *See* Steward, Richard.

215   The old Puritan, godly. [*London*, 1642?] 4°.* MR; CH, Y.

       Old religion. 1684. *See* Goodman, John.

       Old sayings. 1651. *See* L., J.

216   An ould ship called an exhortation. [*London*], *printed*, 1648. 4°.* LT, O, LVF, OC; CH, MH, TU, Y.

       Old Simon. 1663. *See* Fox, George.

217   The old woman's resolution. [*London*], *for P. Brooksby, J. Deacon, J. Blare, J. Back*, [1688–92]. brs. HH; MH.

218   **Oldfield, James.** Sincerity or the upright mans walk to Heaven. *London, for Edward Giles in Norwich*, 1687. 8°. L; MH.

219   **O[ldfield], J[ohn].** The first, last; or the formal hypocrite. *For R. Boulter*, 1666. 8°. O, LW.

220   —[Hebrew] The generation of seekers. 1659. 8°. LCL.

221   [–] —[Anr. ed.] *Printed*, 1671. 8°. L, LW, AN, DU, E; CH, MH, NU, WSC.

222   **Oldfield, Joshua.** Christ the head of civil government. *By K. Astwood, for Tho. Parkhurst*, 1699. 8°. L, LCL, LG, LW, MANCHESTER COLL., OXF.; MH, TO, WF.

223   **Oldfield, Thomas.** A table of silver weight. *For Tim. Goodwin*, [1696]. brs. L, OM.

224   **Oldham, John.** The works of. *For Jo. Hindmarsh*, 1684. 8°. BROOKS 17. LLP, CD; NP, PU.

225   — —[Anr. ed.] —, 1684. 8°. BROOKS 18. T.C.II 99. L, O, C, LLU, A; CH, CN, MH, TU, WF, Y. (var.)

226   — —[Anr. ed.] —, 1686. 8°. BROOKS 19. L, O, DC, E; MH, MU, OCI, TU, Y.

227   — —[Anr. ed.] —, 1686. 8°. BROOKS 20. L, MR, DT; CLC, NP, PU, TU, WF.

228   — —[Anr. ed.] —, 1686. 8°. BROOKS 21. L, C, CE, D, DT; CH, CLC, IU, MH, TU, WF, Y. (var.)

229   — —[Anr. ed.] —, 1692. 8°. BROOKS 22. L, O, OW, CM; CH, MB, MH, TU, WF. (var.)

230   — —[Anr. ed.] *For Nathaniel Rolls*, 1695. 8°. BROOKS 24. T.C.II 531. L, O, C, DT, BQ; CH, CSU, MIU, NCU, TU. (var.)

231   — —[Anr. ed.] *For M. Hindmarsh*, 1698. 8°. BROOKS 25. L, O, C, LW, BR; CH, CN, LC, MH, TU, Y. (var.)

232   —Character of a certain ugly old P——. *Printed*, 1684. * O, LLU.

233   [–] The clarret drinker's song. colop: *Printed*, 1680. brs. BROOKS 4. L, O, LSD; CN, MH, TU, Y.

234   [–] —[Anr. ed.] [*London*], *for J. Jordan*, [1684?]. brs. BROOKS 5. L.

235   [–] Garnets ghost. [*London*, 1679.] cap., fol.* BROOKS 2. L, O, C, LLP, MR; CLC, CN, MH, TU, Y.

236   Entry cancelled.

       [–] Pindarick ode describing the excellency. 1679. *See* title.

237 [–] Poems, and translations. *For Jos. Hindmarsh*, 1683. 8°.
BROOKS 10. T.C.I 147. L, O, C, OC, LLU; CH, LC, MH, MU,
TU, WF, Y. (var.)

238 [–]—Second edition. *For Joseph Hindmarsh*, 1684. 8°.
BROOKS 11. L, O, C, LLU, MR; BN, CLC, MH, MU, NU, TU, Y.

239 ——[Anr. ed.] —, 1694. 8°. L, C, RPL; CH, CLC, WF, Y.

239A ——[Anr. ed.] *For H. Hindmarsh*, 1697. 8°. IU, MH, NCD,
SYRACUSE, TU.

239B ——[Anr. ed.] —, 1698. 8°. MH.

240 —Remains of. *For Jo. Hindmarsh*, 1684. 8°. BROOKS 12.
L, O, C, CK, LLU, MR; CH, IU, MH, NU, TU, WF, Y.

241 ——[Anr. ed.] —, 1687. 8°. O, C, LLU; BN, CH, MH, MU,
TU, Y.

242 ——[Anr. ed.] —, 1693. 8°. L, O; CH, IU, MH, TU. (var.)

242A ——[Anr. ed.] —, 1694. 8°. O, C; TU, WF, Y.

242B ——[Anr. ed.] *For H. Hindmarsh*, 1697. 8°. O, C; IU, MB,
MH, TU.

243 [–] A satyr against vertue. *Printed*, 1679. 4°.* BROOKS 3.
L, O, C, LLP, MR; CH, CN, MH, TU, WF, Y.

244 [–] Satyrs upon the Jesuits. *For Joseph Hindmarsh*, 1681. 8°.
BROOKS 6. T.C.I 418. L, O, C, LG, CT; CH, CN, MB, TU, Y.

245 [–]—Second edition. —, 1682. 8°. BROOKS 7. T.C.I 488.
L, O, C, OC, OW, LLU, MR; CH, CN, LC, MH, NCD, WF, Y.

246 [–] —Third edition. —, 1685. 8°. L, O, C, CT; CH, CLC,
MH, MU, NU, TU, WF, Y. (var.)

247 [–] —Fourth edition. —, 1694. 8°. O, C; CLC, TU, Y.

247A ——Fifth edition. *For H. Hindemarsh* [sic], 1697. 8°. O, C;
IU, MH, NP, TU.

—A second musical entertainment. 1685. *See* Blow, John.

248 [–] Some new pieces never before publisht. *By M. C.
for Jo. Hindmarsh*, 1681. 8°. BROOKS 8. T.C.I 473. L, O, C,
OC, P; CH, CN, MH, TU, WF, Y.

249 [–]—Second edition. —, 1684. 8°. BROOKS 9. L, O, C, BSO,
LLU; CLC, IU, MH, NU, WF, Y. (var.)

250 [–] Upon the marriage of the Prince of Orange with the
Lady Mary. colop: *In the Savoy: by T. N. for Henry
Herringman*, 1677. cap., fol.* BROOKS L, O; NP.

251 **Oldisworth, Giles.** The father of the faithfull. *Oxford,
by Henry Hall*, 1676. 4°. MADAN 3114. L, O, WCA.

252 —The holy Royalist. *By Tho. Ratcliffe for Robert Clavell,
to be sold by Henry Brome*, 1664. 4°. L, LSC, OJ, YM; NU.

253 —The illustrious wife. *Printed*, 1673. obl. 12°. O.

253A [–] In eruditissimos sacrorum bibliorum polyglottorum
compilatores. [n.p., c. 1670.] brs. O.

254 —The race set before us. *Oxford, by A. & L. Lichfield*,
1666. 4°.* MADAN 2748. O.

255 —The stone rolled away. *By Thomas Ratcliffe*, 1663. 4°.
L, O; NU.

255aA ——[Anr. ed.] —, 1664. 4°. P, BLH; CLC.

255A–256 Entries cancelled.

Oldisworth, Michael. First part of the last wil &
testament. [n.p.], 1649. *See title.*

—Last vvill and testament of Philip Herbert. [n.p.], 1650.
See title.

257 [–] The speech of Philip Herbert. [*London*], *printed*, 1649.
4°.* LT, O, C, MR, DT; CH, CN, MH, TSM, Y.

257A [–] The speech (without an oath) of. [*London*], *printed*,
[1680]. cap., fol.* O; MH, WF, Y.

—A thakns-giving [sic]. [n.p.], 1649. *See title.*

Oldmixon, John. Amintas, a pastoral. 1698. *See* Tasso,
Torquato.

258 —The grove. *For Richard Parker*, 1700. 4°. L, O, LVD, LLU,
EN; CH, CN, LC, MH, TU, WCL, WF, Y.

259 —A poem humbly addrest to the . . . Earl of Portland.
For Rich. Parker, and Peter Buck, 1688 [i.e. 1698?]. fol.*
CLC.

260 ——[Anr. ed.] —, 1698. fol.* L, OAS; CU.

261 [–] Poems on several occasions. *For R. Parker*, 1696.
8°. L, O, LVD, DC, EN; CH, CN, MH, TU, WC, WF, Y.

262 [–] Reflections on the stage. *For R. Parker, and P. Buck*,
1699. 8°. L, CS, AN, BP, EN; CH, CN, MB, TU, WF, Y.

263 [–] Songs in the new opera, call'd The grove. [*London*],
sold by I: Walsh, [1700]. fol.* L; LC.

263A [**Oldner, George.**] The form of instrument subscribed
to . . . shares . . . in the invention of. [*London*, 1699?]
brs. L.

264 **Oldner, George.** Mr. George Oldner's invention to
preserve ships. *By F. Collins*, 1698. *To be had, gratis,
at Mr. George Oldner's, and at Mr. Andrew Prime's;
and at Robin's coffee-house.* fol.* L, O; NN, Y.

264A [–] A proposal for a general satisfaction. [*London*, 1689/90.]
brs. L.

264B **Oldys, Alexander.** The fair extravagant. *For C. Blount*,
1682. 12°. T.C.I 461. NP, WF.

265 [–] The female gallant. *For Samuel Briscoe*, 1692. 12°. O.

266 Entry cancelled.

[–] London jilt. 1683. *See title.*

267 —An ode by way of elegy, on . . . Mr. Dryden. *Printed*,
1700. fol.* L, O, LG, MR; NR, OSU, WF.

268 Entry cancelled. *See following entry.*

269 **Olearius, Adam Oelschlaeger, *called*.** The voyages &
travels of the ambassadors. *For Thomas Dring and John
Starkey*, 1662. fol. L, O, OC, CT, DU, DT; CH, LC, MH,
MIU, NCD, NN, Y, AVP. (var.)

270 ——Second edition. *For John Starkey and Thomas Basset*,
1669. fol. T.C.I 22. L, O, C, LIU, EN, CD; BN, CLC, CN, LC,
MH, WF, Y.

271 **Oliphant, Charles.** A short discourse to prove the usefulness of vomiting in fevers. *Edinburgh, for Thomas
Carruthers*, 1699. 8°. ALDIS 3876. L, LWL, EN; WF, WSG.

272 **Oliver, Edward.** A sermon preach'd . . . October 23.
1698. *For Edward Castle*, 1698. 4°. L, O, LW, CT, LSD;
CH, IU, NP, TSM, WF, Y.

273 ——Second edition. —, 1698. 4°.* L, O, C, CS, NE; CH,
CLC, NU.

274 [**Oliver, Elizabeth.**] Catalogue of valuable books.
[*London*], 1689. 4°.* L.

275 **Oliver, John.** The last judgment. *London, for John
Minshull, to be sold at his shop in Chester, and Ric.
Chiswell*, 1682. 4°.* L, C, CM, CT, LIU; CH, NU, TSM, WF.

276 —A present for teeming women. *By Sarah Griffin, for
Mary Rothwell*, 1663. 8°. L, O, C, LLL, LLP.

277 —A present to be given to teeming women. *By A. Maxwell for Tho. Parkhurst,* 1669. 8°. LW, LWL, BR, EN; CH, CLC, NU, WSG.

278 — —[Anr. ed.] *For T. Parkhurst,* 1688. 8°. T.C.II 235. L, O, LCL, LWL; LC, NAM, WF.

278A — —[Anr. ed.] *Boston, reprinted by Benj. Harris,* 1694. 8°. EVANS 708. NCD, NMM.

279 —A sermon preached . . . 11th. day of April, 1699. *London: printed for, and to be sold by Amy Stone, Namptwich,* 1699. 4°.* LIU; NU, WF.

280 **Oliver, Richard.** A sermon preached . . . March 6, 1699/1700. *For Arthur Bettesworth, sold by John Colebrook in Midhurst and William Webb in Chichester,* 1700. 4°.* L, CT.

281 Oliver Cromwell the late great tirant his life-guard. *For Francis Coles,* 1660. 4°.* LT, O, CS, MR; Y.

281A Oliver Cromwell's ghost, at St. James. [*London,* 1680.] brs. CN.

282 Oliver Cromwell's ghost, dropt. colop: *For J. S.,* 1681. brs. L, O, C; CH, MH, PU, TU, WF, Y.

     Oliver Cromwells ghost: or. [1678.] *See* Wild, Robert.

283 Entry cancelled.

     Oliver Cromwell's thanks. [1660.] *See* O. Cromwell's thankes.

284 **Oliveras, Balthazar.** The reall victorie of Portugall. *Printed at London,* 1644. 4°.* LT, O, MR; WF.

285 **Olivier, Pierre.** Dissertationes academiæ. *Cantabrigiæ, ex officina Johan. Hayes,* 1674. *Impensis Jon. Hart.* 8°. L, O, CS, ELY, P; CH, IU, MH, TU, WF.

285A **Ollive, Thomas.** A signification from Israel's God. *Printed,* 1666. 4°.* L, LF, MR; PSC.

286 **Ollyffe, John.** The blessedness of good men. *For Jonathan Robinson,* 1699. 4°.* T.C.III 135. L, O, CS, MR, BLH; NGT, NN, NU, Y.

287 —A brief defence. *London, for Jonathan Robinson: and are to be sold by John Woolfryes, in Blandford.* 1694. 4°. T.C.II 491. L, O, C, LCL, LLP; MH, TO, Y.

288 —England's call to thankfulness. *For Jonathan Robinson,* 1689. 4°.* T.C.II 272. L, O, C, MR; CH, CU, WF, Y.

289 Olimpya's unfortunate love. [*London*], *for J. Deacon,* [1681?]. brs. L, CM.

289A **O'Meara, Edmund.** Examen diatribæ Thomæ Willisii . . . de febribus. *Typis J. Flesher: prostat venale apud Octav. Pulleyn juniorem.* 1665. 8°. O.

290 Omnia comesta a belo. Or, an answer out of the West. [*London*], *printed,* 1667. 4°.* L, O, LUG, CT, BR, DM; CH, IU, MH, NU, PL, WF, Y.

290A —[Anr. ed., "bello."] [*London*], *printed,* 1667. 4°.* LW, DU, LIU; MH, PU.

291 —[Anr. ed.] —, 1679. 4°.* O, LL, MR, SP, EN; CH, CSS, MU, NPT.

291A Omnia vincit amor. [*n.p.,* 1670?] brs. L.

     Omnibus, vel ullis illorum in mundo. [*n.p.,* 1660.] *See* Fox, George.

291B **O'Molloy, Francis.** Grammatica Latino-Hibernica. *Roma, ex typographio S. Cong. de Propag. Fide,* 1677. 12°. L, TRINITY COLL., OXF., CM, DN.

291C —Lucerna fidelium. *Roma, typis Sacrae Congreg. de Propaganda Fide,* 1676. 8°. L, C, CT, DN; CN, NU, WF.

291D — —[Anr. ed.] —["*Propanda*"], 1686. 8°. O.

     Ὁμοτροπια naturæ. 1656. *See* Bunworth, Richard.

292 July 18. 1671. On a tryal before the Lord Chief Justice Hales. [*London,* 1671.] 4°.* L, DJ; NC, WF.

293 On Bugbear Black-Monday. [*London,* 1652.] brs. LT.

294 Entry cancelled.

     On England's happiness. 1686. *See* Poem on.

295 Entry cancelled. *See following entry.*

296 On His Majesties most gracious and prudent delivery of the Great Seal. [*London*], *printed,* 1673. brs. L, O.

297 On His Majesties sending the right honourable Henry Earl of Clarendon. colop: *Dublin, by Andrew Crook and Samuel Helsham, to be sold by Andrew Crook, and by Samuel Helsham,* [1685?]. brs. L, OW.

     On His Royal Highness his expedition. 1627. *See* P., Mrs. E.

297A On his royal highness's return. [*London,* 1679.] brs. L, EN.

     On man. A satyr. [1680?] *See* Rochester, John Wilmot, earl of.

297B On Mrs Cellier in the pillory. [*London,* 1680.] brs. O; WF.

297C On St. Paul's cathedrall. 1658. brs. O; MH.

298 On the answer to Dr Wilds poem. *For R. B.* 1663. brs. L, O, LS; MH.

299 On the arrival of His Royal Highness. [*London*], 1679. brs. O, OCC.

300 On the arrival of His royal Highness, the Duke. *For G. K.,* 1680. brs. L, O, LLU; CH, MH, TU, Y.

300A On the behalf of many knights, gentlemen, merchants . . . now prisoners [debtors]. [*London,* 1675.] brs. LPR.

301 Entry cancelled. Ghost.

302 On the cellers under the New-Exchange. *By T. Ratcliffe and N. Thompson,* 1675. brs. L.

303 On the coronation of the most august monarch K. James II. *For, and are to be sold by Randal Taylor,* 1685. fol.* L, O, C; CH, MH, WF, Y.

     On the death and horrid murther. [n.p., 1679.] *See* Murray, Mungo.

303AA On the death of a queen. [*London,* 1695.] 4°.* EN.

303A On the death of Captain Richard Lacy. [*London,* 1642?] brs. MH.

304 On the death of her illustrious Grace Anne. *Imprinted at London,* 1669. brs. L, LNC.

     On the death of His Grace. [n.p., 1681.] *See* Murray, Mungo.

305 On the death of His Grace the Duke of Albemarle. *Printed,* 1670. brs. L; HH.

305AA On the death of His Highness Oliver. [*n.p.,* 1658?] cap., fol.* CDA.

     On the death of Mr Calamy. 1667. *See* Wild, Robert.

     On the death of Mr. Isaac Meynell. [n.p.], 1675. *See* P., J.

305A On the death of Mr. Matthevv Pool. [*London?* 1679.] brs. O; CN, MH.

305B On the death of Mris Mary Soame. [*London,* 1669.] brs. MH.

On the death of Sir David Falconer. [n.p., 1685.] *See* D., R.

306   On the death of Sir Tho. Armstrong. colop: [*London*], *printed and sold by Nath. Thompson*, 1684. brs. L, O; CLC, MH, Y.

307   On the death of that grand imposter Oliver Cromwell. [*London*], *for J. Williams*, 1661. brs. LT; MH.

308   On the death of that noble knight Sʳ John Harman. *Printed*, 1673. brs. L; MH, Y.

309   On the death of the Duke of Ormond. *Printed, and sold by Randal Taylor*, 1688. fol.* O; CLC, Y.

310   On the death of the honourable Robert Boyle. *For Samuel Smith*, 1692. brs. O.

On the death of the illustrious David. [n.p., 1679.] *See* Murray, Mungo.

On the death of the Lord General Monck. 1669. *See* J., T.

310A   On the death of the illustrious George duke of Albemarle. *Printed for Sa: Heyrick*, [1670]. brs. MH.

On the death of the Lord General Monck. 1669. *See* J., T.

On the death of the most sadly. [n.p., 1684.] *See* Murray, Mungo.

311   On the death of the queen, a poem. *Printed; and are to be sold by John Whitlock*, 1695. fol.* CLC, IU, MH, PU, TU, WF, Y.

311A   On the death of the Queen an ode. [*London*, 1695?] cap., 4°.* IU.

On the death of the queen. By a person of honour. 1695. *See* Cutts, John Cutts, *baron*.

On the death of the renowned. 1670. *See* J., T.

On the death of the right honourable. 1680. *See* Flatman, Thomas.

On the death of William Sharp. [n.p., 1693.] *See* D., R.

312   On the deplorable death of . . . Sr. James Anstruther. *Edinburgh, by Joshua van Solingen*, 1682. brs. ALDIS 2340. EN.

313   On the ever to be lamented death of the most magnanimous . . . Charles Leopold Duke of Lorraine. *For Richard Baldwin*, 1690. brs. L, HH; MH, Y.

314   Entry cancelled.

On the late happy victory. 1687. *See* Poem on.

314A   On the late invention of the new lights. colop: *By R. Roberts for William Rogers*, 1691. cap., fol.* MH, WF.

315   Entry cancelled. Ghost.

316   On the martyrdom of King Charles the First. colop: *For James Norris*, 1683. brs. L, LLU, MC; CH, MH, PU, WF, Y.

317   On the memory of Mr. Caleb Skinner. *For J. H.*, [1690]. brs. L.

317A   On the most high and mighty monarch King James the II. [*London*], *by N. Thompson*, 1685. brs. MH, Y.

On the most noble James. [n.p., 1659.] *See* Shadwell, Thomas.

318   On the most renowned Prince Rupert. [*London?* 1645.] brs. L, LNC.

On the most triumphant ceremony. [n.p., 1661.] *See* Henshow, Thomas.

318AA On the nativity of our blessed Lord. *Cambridge, printed*, 1700. 4°.* L; CLC.

On the never too much lamented. 1670. *See* M., J.

318A   On the occasion of the descent of . . . the Prince of Orange into England. [*London?* 1689.] cap., fol.* CH, MH, MIU, Y.

319   Entry cancelled.

On the Parliament dissolv'd. [n.p., 1681.] *See* Parliament dissolv'd.

320   On the peace. A pindaric. *For Roger Clavill*, 1697. fol.* MR; IU, WF, Y, ASU.

320A   On the pretended ghost of the late Lord Russel. colop: *For Edw. Golding*, [1683?]. brs. MH.

321   On the Prince's going to England. *For R. Baldwin*, 1689. brs. HH.

321A   —[Anr. ed.] *For J. Tonson*, 1689. brs. CH.

322   Entry cancelled. Ghost.

On the recovery. 1664. *See* Cooper, Edmund.

323   On the relief of Vienna. [*London*], *for C. W.*, 1683. brs. L, O, EN; CLC.

323A   On the royal martyr King Charles the I. *Printed on the Frozen-Thames January the 30th 1683. By E. and A. Milbourn, S. Hinch, and J. Mason.* brs. L.

324   Entry cancelled. Ghost.

325   On the second entertainment of the batchelours. *Printed*, 1669. brs. L.

326   On the six new pinnacles. *By Thomas Mabb*, 1661. brs. O.

327   On the tenth of June, MDCC. Being the birth-day of . . . the Prince of Wales. [*London*, 1700.] cap., 4°.* L.

328   On the unhappy conflagration of the Theatre Royal. *For Daniel Brown*, 1672. brs. L; MH.

329   On the universally lamented death of the incomparable Dr. Short. [*London*, 1685.] cap., fol.* L, O, LLP, LLU; CH, CLC, IU, MH, WF, Y.

330   On the word abdicate. [*London*, 1688-9.] brs. HH; Y.

330A   On wings of feare, Finch flies away. [*London*, 1641?] brs. L; MH. (var.)

330B   Once I was alive, and had flesh did thrive. [n.p., 1699?] brs. L; CH.

331   One and thirty new orders. [*London*], *printed*, 1659. 4°.* LT, O, C, MR; CH, CLC, LC, MH, MIU, Y.

332   One and twenty Chester queries. *Printed*, 1659. 4°.* LT, O, LSD; CH, CLC, MH, MIU, MU.

333   One argument more against the Cavaliers. [*London*], *printed*, [1643]. 4°.* LT, O, OC, CT, LNC, DT; CH, CSS, NU, WF, Y.

One blow more against. 1678. *See* Bullock, Jeffery.

334   One blow more at Babylon. *By I. M. for Lodowick Lloyd, and Henry Cripps*, 1650. 4°. LT; CSS, NU.

335   One broad-side more for the Dutch. *By R. D.*, 1665. brs. L; MH, Y.

336   One cry more. [*London*], *printed*, 1665. 4°.* LF, LG, OC, BBN; MH, PH, PHS.

One hundred fifty three chymical aphorisms. 1688. *See* Helmont, Franciscus Mercurius van.

One mite more. 1665. *See* Mason, Martin.

336A   One morning in pleasant weather. [1695.] brs. L.

One necessary thing. [n.p.], 1679. *See* Fleming, Robert.

One of Anti-Christ's voluntiers. 1660. *See* Howgill, Francis.

One of George Keith's friends. 1700. *See* J., C.

One project for the good. [n.p., 1679.] *See* Penn, William.

I. Question, why are you. 1686. *See* Cressy, Hugh Paulin.

One sheet against. 1677. *See* Cheyney, John.

One sheet, or. 1659. *See* P., W.

One warning more. 1660. *See* Howgill, Francis.

336B   One wonder more, added to the seven. [*London*, 1700?] cap., 4°.* L, DU; MH, RPJ.

337   One word more, and we have done. *For Will. Haukins*, 1663. 8°. LL, DUS, DT; Y.

337A   **O'Neill, Daniel.** By Daniel O Neille Esq. His Majesties Post-Master General. These are to certifie. [*London*, 1663?] brs. LPR.

338   **O'Neill, Owen.** The decleration of. *Kilkenny*, 1648. 4°.* CD.

339   —Generall Owen Oneales letter to Collonell Monck. *For A. H. and S. G.*, 1649. 4°.* LT, MR.

340   —The propositions of. *Printed at Corck*, 1649. 4°.* LT, C.

341   **O'Neill, Sir Phelim.** The petition and declaration of. *For W. Neal*, 1641. 4°.* C, OL, MR; INU.

342   —The petition of. *By T. F. for John Thomas*, [1642]. 4°.* LT, O, OC, LNC; INU, WF, Y.

343   ——[Anr. ed.] *Imprinted first at London, and re-printed at Edinburgh by R. Y. and E. T.*, 1642. 4°.* ALDIS 1046. C, EC, EN; Y.

344   —The trve demands of the rebells in Ireland. *By Iohn Hammond*, 1641. 4°.* LT, MR, SP, BLH, DN; CH, MH, MM.

Oneale and Colonell Brunslow. 1642. *See* Bond, Edward.

345   Oneales escape out of the Tower of London. *For J. Wemster*, 1642. 4°.* LT, DN; CH, Y.

345A   Oniropolus, or, dreams interpreter. *By Tho. Dawkes*, 1680. 8°. T.C.I 421. L.

346   **Onley, John.** An epistle of information. *For Francis Smith*, 1661. 4°.* CSSX; LC, NU.

347   The only design of the company of fishermen. [*London*, 1695.] brs. LL; CH.

347A   The only hand adapted for business of merchants. *Sold by J. Sturt*, [1695?]. L(t.p.).

348   The only legal answer. *Printed*, 1680. fol.* L, O, OC, OP, MR; CH, IU, LC, MH, NP, WF, Y.

349   The onely right rule. [*London*], *printed for the subscribers, and to be sold by W. L.*, 1652. 4°.* LT, LG, MR; CH, CLC, CSS.

349AA   —[Anr. ed.] [*London*], *printed for the subscribers, and to be sold by William Larner*, 1652. 4°.* O; WF.

349BA   The only table extant for all merchandizes. [*London?* 1700.] brs. L.

349A   The only way of subscribing land. [*London?* 1695.] brs. LG; MH.

349B   The only way to have the rents of England. [*London?* 1696.] brs. EN; MH.

Only way to rest. [n.p.], 1657. *See* Lewgar, John.

Ὀνομαστικον βραχυ, sive. 1652. *See* Gregory, Francis.

350   Entry cancelled.

[**Onslow, Richard.**] Sober discourse of the honest Cavalier. 1680. *See title.*

351   The open movth of Balaams asse. [*London*], *printed*, 1642. 4°.* LT, O, LHO, MR; CH, MH, MU, NU, WF, Y.

Opinion is this. 1689. *See* Johnson, Samuel.

352   The opinion of divers learned and leading Dissenters. *Printed*, 1680. 4°.* L, O, CS, BAMB, EN; CH, NU, WF, Y.

352A   The opinion of the judges. *For W. Canning*, 1688. brs. T.C.II 231. L.

353   Entry cancelled.

Opinion of the Parliament, about religion. 1682. *See* England. Parliament, Commons.

Opinion of the Roman jvdges. [n.p.], 1643. *See* Vicars, John.

Opinion of witchcraft. 1670. *See* T., R.

354   Opinions being various how now to take in the late currant clipt money. [*London?* 1695.] brs. LUG.

355   The opinions of certaine reverend and learned divines. [*London and Oxford*], *for Ch. Downes*, 1642. 4°. MADAN 1017. LT.

356   —[Anr. ed.] —, 1643. 4°. O, LLP; WF.

357   Entry cancelled.

Opinions of several learned antiquaries. 1658. *See* Doddridge, John. Several opinions.

358   The opinions of the Barons of the Exchecquer. colop: *For R. H. to be sold by Walter Davies*, 1682. brs. L, O, LSD, EN; WF.

358A   Opinions of the Jews, rabbins. Second edition. *By P. C. and are to be sold by Edw. Powels*, 1652. 4°. OCC.

359   Oppertunity lost. [*London*], *for P. Brooksby*, [1672–80]. brs. L, HH; MH.

Oppressed prisoners complaint. [n.p., 1662.] *See* Blackborow, Sarah.

360   The oppressions and wrongs to the value of above ten thousand pounds done by Hugh Audley. [*London*, 1661.] brs. L.

Optick glass. 1664. *See* Walkington, Thomas.

Opus tripartitum. 1678. *See* Starkey, George.

Opuscula mythologica. *Cantabrigiæ*, 1671. *See* Gale, Thomas.

[Hebrew] Or, a (pretended) visitor. 1690. *See* Pretended.

361   No entry.

Or Magna Charta, more news. 1666. *See* Wallis, Ralph.

Oracle for the sick. [n.p., 1685?] *See* Groeneveldt, Jan.

361A   The oracles for war. [*London*], *S. Deacon*, [1690?]. brs. L.

362   The orange. [*London*, 1688.] brs. C, HH; CH, CN, MH, MIU, TU, Y.

363   Oratien oste diversche redenen. *Gedruckt tot Londen voor Pieter Cole, Francis Tyton, en John Playford. Ende nee tot Amsterdam by Jan van Hilten*, 1649. 4°.* L; CH.

Oratio anniversaria. 1655. *See* Fisher, Payne.

Oratio de concordia. *Edinburgi*, 1676. *See* Cant, Andrew.

Oratio dominica. 1700. *See* Motte, B.

364   Oratio funebris ejaculatio super . . . Georgii Stewart. *Impens. Georgij Cooke*, 1663. 8°.* L; CH.

364A   Oratio habita in schola Christi. [n.p. 1672.] cap., 4°.* NOT; NU.

Oratio habita. 1675. *See* Ledeatt, Samuel.

365 Oratio privata, boni theologi. [*Londini*], *in ædibus Savoy-
anis, typis Tho. Newcombe*, 1670. 8°.* CT.

Oratio secunda. 1657. *See* Fisher, Payne.

Oration made before the late King James. 1694. *See* Colbert, Jean Baptiste, *abp.*

366 Orations spoken in the grammar school. 1675. 12°. L.

Orbilius vapulans or a juniper lecture. 1662. *See*
Woolnoth.

Orbis imperantis. 1685. *See* Lawrence, John.

Orbis miraculum, or. 1659. *See* Lee, Samuel.

366A [**Orchard, N.**] The doctrine of devils. *For the author,*
1676. 8°. T.C.I 250. L, O, OC, CS, GU; CH, CN, MH, NU, WF, Y.

366B Die lunæ 21. December 1646. An order against chusing
elders for Common-counsell men. [*London*, 1646.] brs.
LG.

367 An order against persons that shall. 1642. brs. LG (lost).

Order and course. [*n.p.*], 1641. *See* Hakewill, William.

Order and disorder. 1679. *See* Apsley, *Sir* Allen.

367A The order and places of the nobility and great officers at
the King's coronation. [*n.p.*, 1661.] brs. O.

368 An order by the Commissioners of the Admiralty. *For
Laurence Blaiklock, and T. Hewer*, 1653. brs. STEELE
3025. LT, O.

369–70 Entries cancelled. Ghosts.

371 An order concerning the excise. *Oxford, by Leonard
Lichfield*, 1645. 4°.* MADAN 1819. LT, O.

372 Entry cancelled.

Order for ecclesiastical discipline. 1642. *See* Orders.

Order for government. 1641. *See* I., M.

373 An order for publishing declarations and books. *Printed at
Oxford, by Leonard Lichfield*, 1644. 4°.* MADAN 1585.
L, O; CLC, MH, WF, Y.

374 Entry cancelled.

Order from Goldsmiths hall. 1677. *See* Goldsmiths-hall.

375 Order is taken this [blank] day of [blank] by virtue of
Their Majesties letters of Privy Seal. [*London*, 1692.]
brs. LPR, OP.

375A Order is taken this 7th day of July, 1668. [*London*, 1668.]
brs. BIU.

376 The order observed at the coronation of Sir Alexander
Araskine, . . . Lord Lyon King of Arms. [*London*, 1681.]
brs. OP.

377 The order of choosing church-officers. *For R. A.* 1646.
4°.* LT, LW, E, DT; CH, MH, NU, WF.

378 The order of keeping a court leet. *Printed at London*, 1641.
8°. O, AN.

379 —[Anr. ed.] *For William Lee and Daniel Pakeman*, 1650.
8°. I, LL, LMT; CLC, MBP, MHL, NCL, PUL, WF.

380–82A Entries cancelled.

Order of my Lord Maior, the aldermen. *See* London.

383 Order of riding of the Parliament . . . 28th day of July.
[*Edinburgh*, 1681.] brs. ALDIS 2281. HH, EN, ES.

384 The order of the ceremonies used at the celebration. *By A.
Clark, for S. Mearne*, 1671. 4°.* L, O, LPR.

384A —[Anr. ed.] *By Andr. Clark, for Sam. Mearne*, 1671. 4°.* CH.

385 —[Anr. ed.] —, 1674. 4°.* O, LPR.

386 Entry cancelled.

Order of the commissioners for charitable uses. 1667.
See May it please you sir.

387 Entry cancelled.

Order of the Devon quarter sessions. 1685. *See* Devon SS.

388 Order of the General Assemblie of the Confederate
Catholiques. [*Kilkenny*, 1648.] brs. O.

389 The order of the hospitalls of K. Henry the viijth. [*London*], 1557 [*i.e.*, 169–?]. 8°. L, O, LG, CM, LS; CH, MH,
MMO, PL, WF, WSG, HC.

390 Entry cancelled.

Order of the installation of Henry. 1685. *See* King,
Gregory.

Order of the installation of Prince George. 1684. *See*
King, Gregory.

391 An orderly and plaine narration of the beginnings and
causes of this warre. [*Oxford, by L. Lichfield*] *printed,*
1644. 4°.* MADAN 1620. LT, O, C, OC, YM; CH, CLC, MH,
MU, WF.

391A Orders and constitutions made by His Majesties justices
. . . Oxon. [*London*, 1695.] cap., fol.* O.

392 Orders and directions agreed upon by His Majesties
justices of the peace of . . . Oxford. [*Oxford*, 1671.]
brs. MADAN 2899. O.

393 Entry cancelled.

Orders and directions of the . . . Lord Mayor. [1665.] *See*
London. Court of Aldermen.

394 Orders and establishments made and concluded . . . Confederate Catholics. *Printed at Kilkenny*, 1647. cap.,
4°.* DN.

395 Entry cancelled.

Orders and instructions to be observed. Dublin, 1672.
See Ireland. Orders, rules, and instructions.

396 Orders and ordinances, for the better government of
the hospitall of Bartholomew the lesse. *By James Flesher,*
1652. 4°. L, O, LG, LWL, GK; CH, CLC, WF, JF.

396AA Orders and rules appointed by the last will . . . of Sir
Thomas Holt. *Printed*, 1656. fol. CLC.

396BA Orders, by-laws, and ordinances for the good government . . . hackney-coaches. [*London*, 1698.] brs. LG.

396A Orders, conceived and approved by the committee for
the militia of . . . Middlesex, as expedient. [*London*,
1644.] brs. STEELE 2584. L, O; MH.

396B —, without the lines. [*London*, 1642?] brs. MH.

397 Entry cancelled.

Orders conceived and published. [1665.] *See* London.
Court of Aldermen.

397A Orders establisht for the well government of His Majesties
ships. [*London*, 1670?] brs. L.

398 Orders establish in the Popish generall assembly. *By
Richard Bishop, for Lawrence Blaiklock*, 1643. 4°.* LT, O,
CT, BLH, BQ; MH, WF, Y.

399 The orders for ecclesiasticall discipline. *Printed*, 1642.
4°.* LT, O, CJ, LSD, YM; MH, NU, WF.

400–1 Entries cancelled.

Orders for regulating of the prices. Leith, 1654. *See* Scotland. Commissioners for Administration of Justice.

Orders formerly conceived. 1646. *See* London. Court of Aldermen.

402   Orders in Chancery, in two parts. *By W. D. and are to bee sold by Roger Wingate,* 1656. 4°. LCL; CLL, CSS, LC, WF, Y.

402A   The orders of vestry . . . rates payable for burials . . . St. Buttolph without Aldgate. *By J. How, for William Sheepey,* [1677]. brs. L.

403   The orders, rules and ordinances, ordained, . . . by the master . . . of the mystery . . . of stationers. *For the Company of Stationers,* 1678. 4°.* L, O, LG, LIU; MH, NU.

403A   —[Anr. ed.] —, 1682. 4°.* L, LG, LIU.

404   —[Anr. ed.] —, 1692. * L, O, LG, LL, OP, BC; IU, NC, NG, OSU, WF.

405   —[Anr. ed.] 1696. 4°. LG (lost).

406   Entry cancelled.

Orders taken and enacted for orphans. 1652. *See* Orders and ordinances.

407   Entry cancelled.

Orders to be observed at the coronation. 1685. *See* Norfolk, Henry Howard, *7th duke of.*

407A   Orders to be observed by commissioners . . . bails. *For I. Cleave,* 1693. fol. OP.

408–9   Entries cancelled.

Orders to be observed in the church. [n.p.], 1685. *See* Norfolk, Henry Howard, *7th duke of.*

Orders to be observed in the marching. 1644. *See* London. Committee for the Militia.

Orders to be observed on the day. 1689. *See* Norfolk, Henry Howard, *7th duke of.*

Ordinance against challenges. 1654. *See* Cromwell, Oliver.

Ordinance for tythes. Europe, 1646. *See* Overton, Richard.

Ordinance of excommunication. 1646. *See* Bakewell, Thomas.

410   Entry cancelled.

Ordinance of explanation. 1643. *See* England. Parliament.

411   An ordinance ordained, devised, and made by the master, . . . of the mystery . . . of stationers. *For the Company of Stationers,* 1682. 4°.* L.

411A   —[Same title.] —, 1683. 4°.* LIU.

412   Ordinances of the company of free fishermen. 1697. 8°. LG (lost).

413   An ordinary day well spent. *For John Wyatt,* 1699. 12°.* T.C.III 107. L.

414   The ordinary matter of prayer. *Printed,* 1674. 4°.* O; Y.

415   Ordines cancellariæ: being orders. *By the assigns of Rich. and Edw. Atkins, for J. Walthoe,* 1698. 16°. T.C.III 54. L, LL, LMT, BAMB; CH, CU, LC, MB, MIU, NU, V.

416   Ordo baptizandi aliaque sacramenta administrandi. *Typis Hen. Hills,* 1686. Sixes. L, O, LLP, LW, DUS; CLC, CN, TU, WF, Y, AVP.

416A   Ordo recitandi divini officii. *Excudit N. Thompson,* 1687. 8°.* LLP.

416B   **Ordway, Adam.** The description and use of the double-horizontal-dial. *William Godbid,* 1662. 8°.* L, OB.

417   **Orford, Edward Russell,** *earl of.* A copy of Admiral Russel's letter to the Earl of Nottingham. *By Edw. Jones in the Savoy,* 1692. brs. L, HH; CN, MIU, NP, WF, Y.

418   —[Anr. ed.] *Printed at London, and re-printed at Edinburgh,* 1692. brs. ALDIS 3263. L, EN; MH.

418A   —[Anr. ed.] *Printed at Edinburgh, and re-printed at Glasgow,* 1692. brs. ALDIS 3263.5. L, EN.

418B   —Instructions made by. [*London,* 1691.] cap., fol.* NN.

419   —Admiral Russel's letter to the Earl of Nottingham. *In the Savoy by Edward Jones,* 1692. fol.* L, O, OC, DU, E, DT; CH, MH, PL, WF, Y.

420   ——[Anr. ed.] colop: *Boston printed, and sold by Benjamin Harris,* 1692. cap., fol.* EVANS 629. L; MH.

420A   **Organ, Richard.** Proposals . . . for the laying a tax upon raw hides. [*London,* 1696.] brs. L, O, LPR, LS.

Organon salutis. An instrument. 1657. *See* Rumsey, Walter.

421   The organs eccho, to the tune of the cathedral service. [*London*], *printed,* 1641. brs. LT, O; CH.

422   —[Anr. ed., "cathedrall."] —, 1641. brs. L.

423   Entry cancelled.

Organs fvnerall. [1642.] *See* Brooksbank, Joseph.

Orgula: or. 1658. *See* Willan, Leonard.

424   **Origenes.** Ωριγενης κατα Κελσου . . . Contra Celsvm. *Cantabrigiæ, excudebat Joan. Field, impensis Gulielmi Morden,* 1658. 4°. L, O, C, ENC, DT; BN, CH, MH, V, WF, Y.

425   ——[Anr. ed.] *Cantabrigiæ, excudebat Joan. Hayes, impensis Guli. Morden,* 1677. 4°. L, O, C, AN, ENC, DT; BN, CH, CU, MH, TU, WF, Y.

426   Entry cancelled. Continental printing.

427   —Origen against Celsus. *By B. Mills and sold by J. Robinson,* [1700]. 8°. L, LLP, DUS, LSD, E; CH, CU, OCI, WF, Y.

428   —Libellus de oratione. *Oxoniæ,* 1685. 12°. L, ELY, ENC; CLC, WF.

429   — . . . περι ευχης συνταγμα. Εν τη Οξονια Θεατρω Σκηλδηνου, 1686. 12°. L, O, C, NE, DT; CH, CLC, PU, WF, Y.

430   —The sad and dolefull lamentation of. 1661. 8°. L (impf.).

431   No entry.

Origin of atheism. 1684. *See* Crusins, Thomas Theodorus.

Original and growth of printing. [n.p., 1660.] *See* Atkyns, Richard.

Original of infant-baptism. 1674. *See* H., J.

Original of kingly. [n.p.], 1681. *See* Barlow, Thomas, *bp.*

Original of the dominion of princes. 1660. *See* W., R.

432   The original of the Popish ljturgie. *Printed, and are to be sold by Henry Walker,* 1641. 4°.* LT, E; CSS, INU, MIU, NU, WF.

433   —[Anr. ed.] [*London,* 1644/5.] cap., 4°.* LT.

Original of the soul. 1641. *See* Woolnor, Henry. True originall.

434   Entry cancelled.

Original papers and letters relating to the Scots Company. 1700. *See* Company of Scotland.

Original, succession, and progeny. 1681. *See* M., A.

Origo Protestantium; or. 1677. *See* Shaw, John, *of Whalton.*

[**Orme, Thomas.**] Acts for annuities reviewed and compared. [n.p., 1700?] *See title.*

435 [–] The late prints for a standing army. *For the author,* 1698. 4°.* L, O, C, LIU, AU, DM, EN; CH, CLC, CN, LC, IU, Y.

435A [–] May it please your Lordship, having formerly discourst. [*London,* 1690.] cap., 4°.* O; CH.

436 [–] May it please your lordship, I find it. [*London,* 1690?] cap., 4°. L, O, OC, LIU; CLC, MH, WF, Y.

436A [–] Observations upon the acts for annuities. [*London,* 1700?] 4°.* L, C, LIU; MH, Y.

437 **Orme, William.** The best guide. *For Samuel Carr,* 1681. 4°.* O, C, CDC; CH, IU, NU, PU, WF, Y.

437A **Ormonde, James Butler,** *duke of.* Articles of agreement made, concluded and agreed on. *Dublin, by VVilliam Bladen,* 1647. 4°.* DIX 346. C, CD, DN.

437B ——[Anr. ed.] —, *re-printed by Moses Bell,* 1647. 4°.* LT, C, LVF, DN; CH, MH, WU.

438 Entry cancelled.
——[Anr. ed.] Dublin, 1652. See England. Parliament [E 1246 B].

439 —Articles of peace agreed upon July 30, 1646. *Kilkenny printed,* 1646. 4°.* LVF, DT.
—Articles of peace made, concluded. Dublin, 1646. *see title.*

440 ——[Anr. ed.] *Corcke, to be sold at Roches building,* 1648. 4°.* L, DN; LC, WF.

440A ——[Anr. ed.] [*London*], *re-printed,* 1661. 4°.* DK; MIU, WF.
—Articles of peace made and concluded with the Irish rebels. 1649. *See title.*

441 —The copie of the Lord of Ormonds letter to the Bishop of Dromer. [*London,* 1657.] cap., 4°.* LT; WF.

441A —A declaration of the Lord Lieutenant General. *Printed at Corck,* 1648. 4°.* L, C.

442 ——[Anr. ed.] *Printed at Corke, and now reprinted,* 1648. 4°.* LT, C; NN.

443 —A declaration of the Lord Lieutenant-General of Ireland, . . . for setling the Protestant religion. *Printed at Cork, and re-printed at London,* 1648. 4°.* LT, C, OC, CT, DN; CH.

444 —The Marquesse of Ormond's declaration, proclaiming Charles the Second. *For Francis Tyton, and Iohn Playford,* 1649. 4°.* LT, O, C, E, DN; CH, MH, MU, NCD, WF, Y.

445 —Harangue of His Grace the Duke of Ormond. *By Samuel Brown,* 1663. 4°.* LPR.

446 Entry cancelled.
—Last articles of peace. 1646. *See title.*

447 [–] Lawes and orders of warre. *Dublin, by the Society of Stationers,* 1641. 4°.* OQ, OW, MR, DN, DT, BLH; PL.

447A [–] —[Anr. ed.] *Waterford, by Thomas Bourke,* 1643. 4°. L, FRANCISCAN LIB., DUBLIN; MIU.

447B —A letter from His Grace the Lord Lieutenant and Council, [*n.p.,* 1681.] fol.* DIX 190. L.

448 —A letter from His Grace . . . in answer to . . . Earl of Anglesey. *For R. Baldwin,* 1682. fol.* L, O, C, EN, DT; CH, MIU, NR, WF, Y. (var.)

448A ——[Anr. ed.] *Printed,* 1682. *And are to be sold by R. Baldwin.* fol.* L, C; CN, NN.

449 ——[Anr. ed.] *For N. P.,* 1682. fol.* C, LVF, DU; IU, Y.

449A ——[Anr. ed.] *For M. L.,* 1682. fol.* PU.

450 —A letter sent ovt of Ireland. *For Thomas Whitaker,* [1642]. brs. LT, O, EC, LNC; MH.

451 —The Marquesse of Ormond's letter to His Majestie King Charles II . . . [9 August 1649]. [*London*], *printed,* 1649. 4°.* 5 pp. LT, C, LVF, OC, LIU, SP, DN; MH, WF.

452 ——[Same title, letter of 4 August 1649.] —, 1649. 4°.* 6 pp. LT, O, DN, DT; MBA.

453 —The loyall declaration of. *Printed,* [1649]. 4°.* LT, OC, BQ, DN; CH, CSS.

454 —L'oratione . . . fatta. *Stampata in Dublino, per Giov. Crooke, e sivendono appresso Sam. Dancer,* 1664. 4°.* DIX 125. O, DT.

455 —Proclamation, by . . . 17th of January. *Printed at Kilkenny, by William Smith,* 1649. brs. LPR.

456 —Proclamation by . . . 22nd January. *Printed at Kilkenny by William Smith,* 1649. brs. DI.

457 Entry cancelled.
—Proclamation concerning a cessation of armes. 1643. See Ireland.

458 —The Marquesse of Ormonds proclamation concerning the peace. *For Francis Tyton, and John Playford, Febr. 27. 1649.* 4°.* LT, O, C, MR, DT; CH, CU, MH, MU, WF, Y.

458A —Severall papers of the treatie. *Dvblin, by William Bladen,* 1646. 4°.* DIX 80. LT, O, C, DI, DN; CH, MH, OWC, WF, Y.

459 —The speech of . . . 27 of September, 1662. *Dublin: by John Crook, to be sold by Sam. Dancer,* 1662. fol.* DIX 115. O, C, OC. (var.)

459A ——[Anr. ed.] *For Robert Pawlett,* 1662. fol.* L, C, DU; CH, WF.

460 —A trve copy of severall letters. *Dvblin, by William Bladen,* 1649. 4°.* DIX 83. L, C, DT; MH, WF.

460A ——[Same title, text of next entry.] —, 1649. 4°.* DIX 83. 8 pp. DI; WF.

461 —A true copy of two letters. *Dublin, by William Bladen,* 1649. 4°.* DIX 83. O, C, AN, DT; CH.

462 ——[Anr. ed.] *Dublin, by William Bladen,* 1649. *And now re-printed,* [1649]. 4°.* LT, DU; CH, CN, MH, WF, Y.

463 —XXIX articles of peace. *By I. C.,* 1646. 4°.* LT, C, DT; CH, IU, MH, NU, WF, Y.

464 —By the Lord Lievtenant Generall of Ireland, Ormonde. Whereas wee have graunted. *Printed at Kilkenny,* 1649. brs. O.

465 Ormonde's breakfast, or a true relation of the salley and skirmish. *Dublin,* 1649. 4°.* DIX 83. OC, OW.
Ormond's curtain. [n.p., 1646.] *See* Temple, *Sir* John.
Ornitho-logie or. 1655. *See* S., J.

465A **Orosius, Paulus,** Hormesta Pauli Orosii. *Oxoniæ, e theatro Sheldoniano,* 1699. brs. L.

466 [**Orpen, Richard.**] An exact relation of the persecutions . . . Killmare. *For Tho. Bennet, and sold by Randal Taylor,* 1689. 4°.* L, O, C, DU, EN, DN; CH, CN, MH, WF, Y.

467 [–] The London-master. *Printed at Dublin, and are to be sold at the Treasury Coffee House, at Mr. Norman's, Dublin; at Mr. Jones's in Cork, and Mr. Letcher's in Tralee,* 1694. 4°. DIX 260. L, LLP, DM, DT.

468 The orphans' case. [*n.p.*], 1687. brs. MC.

469 **Orrery, Charles Boyle, earl of.** Dr Bentley's dissertations. *For Tho. Bennet,* 1698. 8°. L, O, C, E, DT; CH, CN, MH, NCD, NU, Y.

470 ——Second edition. —, 1698. 8°. T.C.III 83. L, O, C, E, DT; CLC, MH, MU, TU, WF, Y.

471 ——Third edition. —, 1699. 8°. L, O, C, EN, DT; CH, MH, OCI, TU, WF, Y, AVP.

472 [**Orrery, Roger Boyle**], *earl of.* The answer of a person of quality to a scandalous letter. *Dublin, by J. C.,* 1662. 4°. DIX 116. OW, CE, DT; Y.

473 ——[Anr. ed.] *Printed at Dublin by J. C. and reprinted at London,* 1662. 4°. L, O, C, LVF, DT; CH, CSS, CU, NU, WF.

474 [–] ——[Anr. ed.] 1662. 4°. DT.
—Black prince. 1672. *See*—Two new tragedies.

475 —A declaration of. *Dublin, by William Bladen, and reprinted at London, by John Macock,* 1659. brs. LT, O, LG; MH.

476 [–] English adventures. *In the Savoy: by T. Newcomb for H. Herringman,* 1676. 8°. T.C.I 253. L, OB, A; CH, CLC, CN, MU, WF.

477 —Four new plays. *For H. Herringman,* 1670. fol. C, CS, DT; CLC, CN, MH, TU, WF, Y.

478 —Guzman. *For Francis Saunders,* 1693. fol. L, OW, LLU, MR, DT; CLC, CN, LC, MH, WF, Y.

479 —Herod the Great. *By T. Warren for F. Saunders; T. Bennet, and J. Knapton,* 1694. fol.* L, O, OW, CS, LLU; CLC, CN, MU, NP, WF, Y.

479A ——[Anr. ed.] *By Tho. Warren for Francis Saunders and Thomas Bennet,* 1694. fol. L, O, CS; CN, LC, MH, MU.

480 —The history of Henry the Fifth. *For H. Herringman,* 1668. fol. L, O, C, OM, OW, DT; CH, CN, MU, TU, WF, Y. (var.)

481 ——Second edition. *For Henry Herringman,* 1669. fol. T.C.I 20. L, O, CT, BC; CH, CU, MBP, TU, WF, Y.

482 ——[Anr. ed.] *By J. M. for Henry Herringman,* 1672. fol. EC, NOT; CDA, CLC, CU, MH, NCU, NP, Y.

483 —— Third edition. *By T. N. for Henry Herringman,* 1677. fol. L, OW, LLU, BQ, DT; CLC, IU, LC, NCU, WF, Y.

484 ——Fourth edition. *For H. Herringman, and sold by Joseph Knight,* 1690. fol. L, OW, BC, LLU; CLC, IU, MH, WF, Y.

485 [–] The Irish colours displayed. *Printed,* 1662. 4°.* L, O, C, DT, BQ; CH, MH, WF, Y.

486 —A letter from. *For Robert Ibbitson,* 1651. 4°.* LT, C, GC, DN; Y.

487 —Mr. Anthony. *For James Knapton,* 1690. 4°. T.C.II 288. L, O, LG, LLU, E, A; CH, IU, MH, NF, TU, WF, Y.

488 —Parthenissa. [*n.p.*], printed, 1651. 4°. L, LLP; TU.

489 —— Second edition. *For Richard Lowndes,* 1654. 4°. L; CH.

490 ——[Anr. ed.] *By T. N. for Henry Herringman,* 1676. 6 pts. fol. T.C.I 261. L, O, C, LLU, LNC, DT; CLC, CU, LC, MBP, MH, MU, NCD, WF, Y.

491 [–] —The first part. *For Henry Herringman,* 1655. 4°. L, O, C, DC; CH, PL, Y.

491A [–] ——[Anr. ed.] *For Humphrey Moseley,* 1655. 4°. CH, CLC.

492 [–] —The second part. *For Henry Herringman,* 1655. 4°. O, C; Y.

492A [–] ——[Anr. ed.] *For Humphrey Moseley,* 1655. 4°. CH, CLC.

492B [–] —The third part. —, 1655. 4°. CH, CLC.

492C [–] ——[Anr. ed.] *For Henry Herringman,* 1655. 4°. O, C; CH, TO, Y.

492D [–] —The fourth part. —, 1655. 4°. L, O, C; CH, CLC, Y.

493 [–] —The last part. The fifth tome. *By T. R. & E. M. for Henry Herringman,* 1656. 4°. L, O, C, LLP, OB; CH, CLC, MH, Y.

494 [–] —The last part. The sixth tome. *For Henry Herringman,* 1669. 4°.T.C.I 9. L, O, C, LLP; CH, CLC.

495 —Poems on most of the festivals of the church. [*London*], *for Henry Herringman,* 1681. fol. L, O, C, DU, DT; CH, CN, MH, TU, WF, Y.

496 —Six plays, viz. *For H. H. and sold by F. Saunders,* 1694. fol. L; CLC, IU, MU, WC.

497 —The tragedy of Mustapha. *For Henry Herringman,* 1668. fol. L, O, OC, CQ; CH, CN, MH, TU, WF.

498 Entry cancelled.
——[Anr. ed.] 1690. *See*—History of Henry the Fifth.

499 —A treatise of the art of war. *In the Savoy, by T. N. for Henry Herringman,* 1677. fol. T.C.I 302. L, O, C, CT, DU; CH, CN, MH, MU, NCD, WF, T.

500 No entry.
—Tryphon. 1669. *See*—Two new tragedies.

501 —Two new tragedies. *By T. N. for Henry Herringman,* 1669. fol. O, C, LW, OW, DT; CH, CU, MBP, MH, TU, WF, Y.

502 ——[Anr. ed.] *For H. Herringman,* 1672. fol. L, LVD, OW, EC, LLU, DT; CH, CN, LC, MH, TU, WF, Y.

503 An orthodox creed. *Printed,* 1679. 8°. I, C, ORP; NU.

Orthodox plea. 1669. *See* Alsop, George.

504 Orthodox state-queries. [*London*], *for Philo-Basileuticus Verax,* [1660]. brs. LT, O, LG, OC; MH, MIU, NU, Y.

Orthography. I of consonants. [*n.p.*, 1648.] *See* Raue, Christian.

Ορθολατρεια: or. 1650. *See* Gunton, Simon.

Ορθοτονια, seu. 1650. *See* Franklin, Richard.

Ortigue, Pierre d', sieur de Vaumoriere. *See* Vaumoriere, Pierre d' Ortigue, *sieur de.*

Orton, Richard, bell-man. Verses presented to his worthy master of the ward in St. Stephen Coleman-street. *Printed December 23, 1671.* brs. LPR.

Os Ossorianvm, or. 1643. *See* Goodwin, John.

504A **Osborn, Thomas, schoolmaster.** A rational way of teaching. *For Thomas Howkins,* 1688. 8°. HAMBURG U., NC.

505 **Osborne, Francis.** The works of. Seventh edition. *For R. D. and are to be sold by Allen Bancks,* 1673. 8°. T.C.I 122. L, O, C, LCP, OM, DT; CLC, CU, MH, NCD, WF, Y.

506 ——Eighth edition. —, 1682. 8°. L, O, C, DU, EN, DT; BN, CH, IU, MB, TU, WF, Y.

507 ——Ninth edition. *Printed,* 1689. 8°. T.C.II 296. L, O, CS, NE, EN, ENC; CH, CN, MH, TU, WF, Y, AVP.

507A   ——Tenth edition. *For A. and J. Churchill*, 1700. 8°. BC.

508   [–] Advice to a son. *Oxford, by Hen: Hall, for Thomas Robinson*, 1656. 8°. MADAN 2278. LT, O, OC, CCH, LLU; BN, CH, IU, MH, MU, NU, OCI.

509   [–] —Second edition. *Oxford, by H. Hall, for Thomas Robinson*, 1656. 8°. MADAN 2302. L, O, OC; Y.

510   [–] —Third edition. —, 1656. 8°. MADAN 2303. O, CS; CLC, MU, WF, Y.

511   [–] —Fourth edition. —, 1656. 8°. MADAN 2304. L, O, P; CH, PU, Y.

512   [–] —Fifth edition. —, 1656. 12°. MADAN 2304*. L, O, OP; CH, CN, OCI, AVP.

513   ——Sixth edition. *Oxford, by H. H. for Tho. Robinson*, 1658. 12°. MADAN 2396–7. L, O, C, DC, EN; CH, CN, MH, NU, TU, WF, Y. (var.)

  ——[Anr. ed.] 1673. *See*—Works.

514   ——The second part. *London, for Tho. Robinson, Oxford*, 1658. 12°. MADAN 2398. LT, O, LVD, DL, BQ; CH, CN, MH, TU, WF, Y. (var.)

515   [–] Historical memoires on the reigns of Queen Elizabeth. *By J. Grismond, to be sold by T. Robinson in Oxon*, 1658. 12°. MADAN 2401. L, O, C, MR, EN; CH, CN, MH, TU, WF, Y.

516   —A miscellany of sundry essayes. *By John Grismond*, 1659. 12°. LT, O, C, DU, DL, BQ; CH, CLC, CN, MH, NU, TU, WF, Y.

516A   ——[Anr. ed.] *By J. Grismond for R. Royston*, 1659. 12°. L, O, OJ, OL, BLH; CH, CU, MM, PL, WF.

517   [–] A persvvasive to a mutuall compliance. [*Oxford*], *printed* [*by L. Lichfield*], 1652. 4°.* MADAN 2201. LT, O, C, EN, DT; CLC, CN, MH, NU, TU, WF, Y.

518   [–] Politicall reflections. *By J. G. for Thomas Robinson, in Oxford*, 1656. 12°. MADAN 2305. L, O, CT, P, LLU; CH, CN, MH, NCD, PL, WF, Y. (var.)

519   [–] —[Anr. ed.] *By J. G. for Richard Royston, to be sold by Thomas Robinson in Oxford*, 1656. 12°. MADAN 2305. LT, O, C, LVD, DC; CH, CU, MH, NU, TU.

520   ——Third edition. *Oxford, by Hen. Hall for Tho. Robinson*, 1661. 12°. MADAN 2603. I, C, OCC, DC, BQ; CH, CN, MH, TU, WF, Y.

521   [–] The private Christians non vltra. *Oxford, by H. Hall, for Tho. Robinson*, 1656. 4°.* MADAN 2306. L, O, CT, BC, E; CH, MH, NU, WF, Y.

522   [–] A seasonable expostulation. *By James Moxon*, 1652. 4°.* LT; HR, CH, NU, OCI, Y.

523   [–] —[Anr. ed.] *Oxford* [*by L. Lichfield*], *for Thomas Robinson*, 1652. 4°.* MADAN 2202. LT, O, OC, CS, DU, MR; HR, CLC, CSS, MH, WF.

523A   [–] Twenty precepts, or rules of advice to a son. *For B. Heath*, 1682. brs. O, EN.

524   [**Osborne, Henry.**] A more exact way to delineate the plot of any . . . land. *Dublin, by William Bladen*, 1654. 4°.* DIX 95. L, DM.

525   **Osborne, John.** An indictment against tythes. *For Livewel Chapman*, 1659. 4°.* LT, O, C, LF, LUG; CH, MH, NU, PH, Y.

526   —The world to come. *By James Moxon, to be sold by Henry Hood*, 1651. 4°. LT, O, LLP, BC; MBP.

526A   [**Osborne, John**], *fl. 1691.* An admonition to the English, concerning their near approaching danger. colop: *For J. Harris*, 1691. 4°.* CSS.

  Osborne, Peregrine. *See* Leeds, Peregrine Osborne, duke of.

527   [**Osborne, Peter.**] The practice of the exchequer court. *By T. R. for Tim. Twyford and W. Place*, 1658. 8°. LT, O, LIL, LL, LUG, EN; CH, MIU, NCL, WF.

528   [**Osborne, Richard.**] The independent's loyalty. [*London*], *printed*, 1648. 4°.* LT, C, YM; CH, IU, MH, NU, TU, WF, Y.

529   —A trve coppy of two severall letters, sent by. [*London*], *printed*, 21. *June* 1648. 4°.* LT, O, CT, AN, DT; CH, CN, MIU, WF, Y.

529A   ——[Anr. ed.] [*London*], *printed*, 1648. 4°.* O, OC.

530   —Tvvo letters sent by. *For A. H.*, 1648. 4°.* LT, O, LVF, BC, DU; CU, WF, Y.

  Osborne, Sir Thomas. *See* Leeds, Thomas Osborne, earl of.

  Osculum pacis. 1641. *See* Byan, Henry.

530A   **O'Sheill, James.** An answer to the challenge. [*n.p.*], *permissu superioris*, 1699. 8°. O, DUS.

531   Entry cancelled.

  Osland, Henry. Living, dead pastor. 1663. *See* Oasland, Henry.

531A   **Osmond, John.** To the right honorable Sir Robert Titchborn . . . the humble petition of . . . car-man. [*London*, 1657?] brs. MH.

  Ostella: or. 1650. *See* Tatham, John.

532   [**Ostervald, Jean Frédéric.**] A treatise concerning the causes of the present corruption. *For Ri. Chiswell*, 1700. 8°. T.C.III 251. L, C, OJ, YM, DT; CH, IEG, MIU, TO, WF.

  Otes his case, character. Dublin, [1685]. *See* L'Estrange, Sir Roger.

533   **Otho, Johannes Henricus.** Joh Henrici Othonis [Hebrew] Historia doctorum. *Oxonii, typis Hen. Hall*, 1672. 12°. T.C.I 128. MADAN 2930. L, O, C, CT, DU, WCA, DM; OHU, Y.

  Otia sacra. 1648. *See* Westmorland, Mildmay Fane, earl of.

533A   Entry cancelled.

  Ots's lamentation. 1685. *See* Oats's.

534   **O**[**ttee**], **R**[**obert**]. Carracters [*sic*] in blood. *For the author*, 1671. 8°. C.

535   —Christ set forth. *For Edward Giles in Norwich*, 1690. 8°. LCL, NPL; Y.

535A   **Otto, Julius Conrad.** Quod felix faustumq; sit. [*Edinburgh, R. Bryson*, 1642.] brs. ALDIS 1046.5. EN.

536   Ottoman gallantries. *For R. Bentley and S. Magnes*, 1687. 12°. T.C.II 187. L, O, P; CH, CLC, CN, LC, WF, Y.

537   **Otway, Thomas.** The works of. *For Richard Bentley*, 1691 [i.e., 1696]. 4°. O; CU, MH, Y.

538   ——[Anr. ed.] —, 1692. 4°. O, LVD, BC, DT; TU, Y.

539   —Alcibiades. *For William Cademan*, 1675. 4°. L, O, C, OW, LSD, DT; CH, CN, LC, MH, NCD, WCL, WF, Y. (var.)

540   ——Second edition. *For R. Bentley, and S. Magnes*, 1687. 4°. T.C.II 217. L, O, C, LVF, ES; CH, CN, LC, MH, TU, WF, Y.

541 —The atheist. *For R. Bentley and J. Tonson*, 1684. 4°. T.C.II 47. L, O, C, LVF, EN; CH, CN, LC, MH, TU, WF, Y.

542 —Don Carlos. *For Richard Tonson*, 1676. 4°. T.C.I 255. L, O, OW, CS, LLU, EN; CH, CU, MH, TU, WF, Y.

543 — —Second edition. *By E. Flesher, for R. Tonson*, 1679. 4°. T.C.I 338, L, O, OW, LSD, EN; CH, CU, MH, TU, WF, Y.

544 — —Third edition. *For Richard Tonson*, 1686. 4°. L, O, C, OW, ES; CH, CN, LC, MH, TU, WF, Y.

545 — —Fourth edition. *For R. Bentley*, 1695. 4°. L, O, LVD, LLU, RU; BN, CLC, LC, MH, MU, TU, WF, Y.

546 —Epilogue to Her Royal Highness. [*London*], *for Jacob Tonson*, 1682. brs. O, LLP, HH; CH, CLC, MH, TU, WF, Y.

547 —The epilogue. Written by . . . to his play call'd Venice preserv'd. colop: [*London*], *for Joseph Hindmarsh*, 1682. brs. L, O, LL, LLU, MC; CH, CLC, MH, TU, WF, Y.

548 —Friendship in fashion. *By E. F. for R. Tonson*, 1678. 4°. T.C.I 320. L, O, C, LVF, ES; CH, CN, LC, MH, TU, WF, Y. (var.)

549 —The history and fall of Caius Marius. *For Tho. Flesher*, 1680. 4°. T.C.I 370. L, O, LGI, OW, EN; CH, CN, MH, TU, WF, Y.

549A Entry cancelled. *See following entry.*

550 — —Second edition. *For R. Bentley*, 1692. 4°. L, O, OWA, BC; CH, CU, LC, MH, WF, Y. (var.)

551 — —[Anr. ed.] —, 1696. 4°. L, O, C, BC, RU; CH, IU, MH, TU, WF, Y.

552 —The orphan. *For R. Bentley, and M. Magnes*, 1680. 4°. T.C.I 394. L, O, AN, LLU, LSD; CH, CN, LC, MH, TU, WF, Y.

553 — —[Anr. ed.] *For R. Bentley and S. Magnes*, 1685. 4°. T.C.II 118. L, O, CK, LLU, LSD; CLC, IU, MH, NP, WF, Y.

554 — —[Anr. ed.] *For R. Bentley*, 1691. 4°. T.C.II 387. L, O, BC, LLU, EN; CH, CN, MH, TU, WF, Y.

555 — —[Anr. ed.] —, 1696. 4°. O, OW, RU, CD; CH, CU, LC, MH, TU, WF, Y.

556 —The poet's complaint of his muse. *For Thomas Norman*, 1680. 4°.* T.C.I 384. L, O, C, LLU, MR; CH, CN, MH, TU, WF, Y.

557 —The prologue and epilogue, to the last new play; Constantine the Great. colop: [*London*], *for C. Tebroc*, 1683. brs. L, O, LLP, MC; CH, WF, Y.

558 —Prologue. By Mr. Otway to his play call'd Venice preserv'd. colop: *For A. Green*, 1681. brs. L, O.

559 [-] Prologue to a new play, called Venice preserv'd. colop: *For A. Banks*, 1682. brs. L, O, OW, MC; CH, MH, TU, WF, Y.

560 — —[Anr. ed.] colop: *Edinburgh, re-printed by the heir of Andrew Anderson*, 1682. brs. ALDIS 2356. EN; MH.

561 —The prologue to The city heiress. colop: *For J. Tonson*, 1682. brs. L, O, MC; CH, TU, WF, Y.

562 —The souldiers fortune. *For R. Bentley and M. Magnes*, 1681. 4°. T.C.I 418. L, O, CCL, BC, LLU, LSD; CH, CN, LC, MH, WF, Y.

563 — —[Anr. ed.] *For R. Bentley and S. Magnes*, 1683. 4°. L, O, CS; CH, MH, NIC, TU, WF, Y.

564 — —Second edition. —, 1687. 4°. L, O, OW, LLU, EN; CH, CU, LC, MH, NCD, WF.

565 — —Third edition. *For Richard Bentley*, 1695. 4°. T.C.II 590. L, O, C, LVF, OC, OW; BN, CLC, CN, MH, TU, WF, Y.

566 —Titus and Berenice. *For Richard Tonson*, 1677. 4°. T.C.I 267. L, O, C, LGI, OW; CH, CN, LC, MH, TU, WF, Y. (var.)

567 —Venice preserv'd. *For Jos. Hindmarsh*, 1682. 4°. T.C.I 485. L, O, CK, EN, DT; CH, CN, LC, MH, TU, WF, Y. (var.)

568 — —[Anr. ed.] *For R. Bentley, and James Knapton*, 1696. 4°. O, RU; IU, LC, MH, NN, TU, WF, Y. (var.)

569 — —[Anr. ed.] *For James Knapton*, 1696. 4°. L, C; CH, CN, MH, MU, TU, WF, Y.

570 —Windsor Castle. *For Charles Brome*, 1685. 4°.* T.C.II 126. L, O, C, LVD, CT, DT; CH, CN, MH, TU, WF, Y. (var.)

571 **[Oudin, César François]**, *sieur de Préfontaine*. The extravagant poet. *For B. M.* [*i.e., R. Bentley and M. Magnes*], 1681. 12°. T.C.I 428. L, O; CLC, CU.

571A **Oughtred, William.** Arithmeticæ in numeris et speciebus institutio. Second edition. *By Thomas Harper for Richard Whitaker*, [1647]. 8°. AU.

  [-] Canones sinuum. 1657. *See*—Trigonometria.

572 —The circles of proportion. *Oxford, by W. Hall for R. Davis*, 1660. 8°. MADAN 2513. LT, O, C, E, DT; BN, CH, MU, OCI, WF, Y.

573 —Clavis mathematicæ. *Excudebat Thomas Harper, sumptibus Thomæ Whitakeri*, 1648. 8°. O, CK, CQ. F; BN, CH, NC, TO.

574 — —Third edition. *Oxoniæ, excudebat Leon. Lichfield, veneunt apud Tho. Robinson*, 1652. 8°. MADAN 2203. L, O, C, BQ, DT; BN, CLC, MBA, MU, WF, Y.

575 — —Fourth edition. *Oxoniæ, typis Lichfieldianis veneunt apud Joh. Crosley & Amos Curteyne*, 1667. MADAN 2772. L, O, CT, E, DT; BN, CH, CSU, MU, PL, WF.

576 — —Fifth edition. *Oxoniæ, excudebat Leon. Lichfield*, 1693. 12°. L, O, C, OC, GU, DT; CLC, MIU, NC, WF, Y.

577 — —"Fifth" edition. *Typis Leon. Litchfield: impensis Tho. Leigh, Lond.* [sic], 1698. 8°. T.C.II 561. L, LI, EN; CB, NP.

578-9 Entries cancelled.

  [-] Description and use of the double horizontall dyall. 1652. *See* Leurechon, Jean. Mathematicall recreations. 1653.

579A —Dialling performed instrumentally. *By William Dugard; and are to be sold by William Hope*, 1652. 4°.* MH.

580-1 Entries cancelled.

  —Elementi decimi Euclidis declaratio. Oxoniæ, 1652. *See*—Clavis mathematicæ.

  —Horologiorum. Oxoniæ, 1652. *See*—Clavis mathematicæ.

582 —The key of the mathematicks. *By Tho. Harper, for Rich. Whitaker*, 1647. 8°. L, C, OC, YM, DT; BN, LC, MB, MH, MU, OCI, WF.

583 — —[Anr. ed.] *For John Salusbury*, 1694. 8°. T.C.II 479. L, O, C, BAMB, SA; CH, CLC, MU, PL, TO.

584-5 Entries cancelled.

  —Mathematicall recreations. 1653. *See* Leurechon, Jean.

585A — . . . Opuscula mathematica. *Oxoniæ, typis Lichfieldianis, veneunt apud Joh. Crosley, & Amos Curteyne*, 1676. 8°. NC, NN.

586 — —[Anr. ed.] *Oxonii, e theatro Sheldoniano*, 1677. 8°. MADAN 3147. L, O, C, EN, DT; BN, CLC, MH, MU, PL, WF.

586A ——[Anr. ed.] —, 1677. *And are to be sold by Peter Parker, London.* 8°. PL.

587 [–] The solution of all sphærical triangles. *Oxford, by L. Lichfield,* 1651. 8°.* MADAN 2175. L, O, LCP.

588 Entry cancelled.
—Theorematum. *Oxoniæ,* 1652. *See*—Clavis mathematicæ.

589 —Trigonometria. *Typis R. & L. W. Leybourn impensis Thomæ Johnson,* 1657. 4°. L, O, C, LR, E; BN, CLC, MB, MU, PL, WF. (var.)

590 —Trigonometrie. *By R. and W. Leybourn, for Thomas Johnson,* 1657. 4°. 2 pts. L, C, LCP, NOT, DT; CH, MU, NN, Y, MONASH.

590A **Ouldman, Thomas.** A copy of verses. *For the author, Thomas Ouldman,* 1684. brs. O.

590B ——[Anr. ed.] *By H. Brugis,* 1685. brs. O.

590C ——[Anr. ed.] *Printed* 1686. brs. O.

590D ——[Anr. ed.] — 1688. brs. O.

590E ——[Anr. ed.] — 1689. brs. O.

591 Our antient testimony renewed. *Printed and sold by T. Sowle,* 1695. 8°.* T.C.II 249. O, LF; NU, PH, RPJ.

592 Our modern demagogue's modesty. [*London,* 1690.] cap., 4°.* O, BC, MR, DT; CLC, CSS.

593 Ourania: the high and mighty lady the Princess Royal of Aurange. *By W. Godbid,* 1660. brs. LT.

594 An out-cry after the late Lieutenant General Fleetwood. *By Hen. Mason,* 1660. brs. LT, O; MH.

595 An outcry, against the speedy hve and cry. [*London*], *printed,* 1647. 4°.* LT, O; IU, WF.

596 An out-cry of poets. *For J. Harlow,* 1691. brs. O, HH; MH.

597 The out-crie of the kings at Westminster. [*London*], *printed,* 1648. 4°.* L; IU, Y.

598 The out-cry of the London prentices. *For Gustavus Adolphus,* 1659. 4°.* LT, O, BR, MR, SP; CH, MIU, WF, Y.
Out cry of the young men. [n.p., 1649.] *See* Lilburne, John.

599 An outragious out-cry for tithes. *By Henry Hills, and to be sold at his house and by William Larnar,* 1652. 4°.* LT; CH.

600 **Outram, William.** Catalogus librorum . . . 12 Decembris 1681. 1681. 4°. L, O, C, OC, CS; NG, Y.

601 —De sacrificiis libri duo. *Typis T. Roycroft, impensis Richardi Chiswell,* 1677. 4°. T.C.I 276. L, O, C, EN, DT; BN, CH, IU, MH, NU, WF, Y.

602 —Juramentum vulgò dictum. [*London,* 1662.] brs. O.

603 —Sermons upon faith. *By J. M. for Joseph Hindmarsh,* 1680. 8°. T.C.I 381. L, O, C, LW, P, EN; CLC, MH, PL, WF.

604 —Twenty sermons. *By J. M. for Richard Chiswell,* 1682. 8°. L, O, C, LW, NE, DT; CH, IEG, NCD, NPT, NU, WF.

605 ——Second edition. *For Ri. Chiswell,* 1697. 8°. T.C.III 30. L, O, C, LCL, CT, DM; CH, CLC, WF, Y.

606 Ovatio Carolina. The trivmph of King Charles. *By A. N.,* 1641. 4°.* LT, O, LG, CPE, LNC; CH, CSS, MH, MIU, WF, Y.

606A Over against the Golden Faulcken . . . liveth a chymist. [*London,* 1685?] brs. L.

607 **Overall, John,** *bp.* Bishop Overall's convocation-book. *For Walter Kettilby,* 1690. 4°. T.C.II 310. L, O, C, E, DT; CH, IU, MH, NU, TU, WF, Y.

608 Entry cancelled.
Overbury, Sir Thomas, elder. Arraignment and conviction of Sᵣ Walter Rawleigh. 1648. *See title.*

608A —The illvstriovs wife. *Printed,* 1673. 18°. O.

609 —Observations upon the Provinces United. *By T. Maxey for Richard Marriot,* 1651. 8°. LT, O, C, EC, LSD; HR, CH, CN, LC, MH, WF, Y.

610 —Sir Thomas Overbury his wife. With additions. *For William Shears,* 1655. 8°. L, O.

611 ——Seventeenth edition. *For John Playfere,* 1664. 8°. L, O; CN.

611A ——"Seventeenth" edition. *By Peter Lillicrap for Philip Chetwin,* 1664. 8°. CH, NCU, NP, WF.

612 [**Overbury, Sir Thomas**], *younger.* Ratiocinium vernaculum: or a reply. *For A. B.,* 1678. 4°. O, C, BR; TO, WF, Y.

613 —A true account of the examination and execution of Joan Perry. *For J. & R. Sprint, G. Conyers, and T. Ballard,* 1676. 12°. L, C, LL, MR.

614 [–] A true and perfect account of the examination, confession, tryal, . . . of Joan Perry. *For Rowland Reynolds,* 1676. 4°.* T.C.I 253. L, O, CE, BAMB, MR; NU, PU, WF.

614A ——[Anr. ed.] *For J. Atkinson* [1676]. 8°. LC.

615 Entry cancelled.
Overbury revived. 1661. *See* G., L.

616 **Overing, John.** Hadadrimmon. *By Thomas Johnson,* 1670. 4°.* L, LSD, DT; LC, Y.

616A **Overton, John.** A catalogue of books, pictures, and maps. [*London,* 1675?] brs. O.

617 **Overton, Mary.** To the right honourable, the knights, . . . the humble appeale. [*London,* 1647.] cap., 4°.* LT, O, MR, DT; CSS, MH, PT, Y.

618 [**Overton, Richard.**] An alarvm to the House of Lords. [*London*], *printed,* 1646. 4°.* LT, O, C, LVF, DU, DT; CH, CN, MH, NU, TU, WF, Y.

619 —An appeale from the degenerate representative body. *Printed,* 1647. 4°.* LT, C, LCL, OC, LLU; MH, NU, PT, RBU, Y.

620 [–] The araignement of Mr. Persecution. *Europe, by Martin Clawe-Clergie,* 1645. 4°. LT, O, C, LNC, EN; CH, CN, IU, WF, Y.

621 [–] ——Second edition. *Europe, by Martin Clawe-Clergie, for Bartholmew Bang-Preist,* 1645. 4°. L, O, CJ, AN, BP, DT; CH, IU, MH, NIC, NU, Y.

622 —An arrow against all tyrants. [*London*], *printed by Martin Claw-Clergy,* 1646. 4°.* LT, LG, ORP, CT, DT; CH, CN, NCD, NU, WF, Y.

623 —Articles of high treason. *For R. Overton,* 1642. 4°.* LT, O, LG, LP, LVF, CM; CH, LC, MH, NU, WF, Y.

624 —The baiting of the great bull of Bashan unfolded. *Imprinted at London,* 1649. 4°.* LT, O; CH, NHC, Y.

625 [–] The commoners complajnt. [*London*], *printed,* 1646[7]. 4°.* LT, O, C, MR, DT; CSS, MH, PT.

626 [–] A defiance against all arbitrary usurpations. [*London*], *printed,* 1646. 4°.* LT, O, C, EN, DT; CH, CU, MH, MU, NU, Y.

627 —Overton's defyance of the act of pardon. *Imprinted at London*, 1649. 4°.* LT, O, LG, MR; CH, MH, NC, NHC, WF.

628 [–] Divine observations upon the London-ministers letter. *Evrope, by Martin Claw-Clergy, and are to be sold by Bartholomew Bang-priest*, 1646. 4°.* LT, C, LG, OC; CH, MH, NHC, NU, PT.

628A —Eighteene reasons propounded to the soldiers. [*London?* 1647.] cap., 4°. L, O, LG, CT, SP; PT.

628B [–] England's miserie and remedie. [*London*, 1645.] cap., 4°.* LT, O, CT, DT; CH, CSS, NU, PL, WF, Y.

629 Entry cancelled.
—Englands new chains. [n.p., 1649.] *See* Lilburne, John.
[–] Foundations of freedom. 1648. *See* Lilburne, John.

629A [–] Man wholly mortal. Second edition. *Printed at London*, 1655. 8°. L, LW, BC; CH, NP, PBM.

629B [–] —"Second" edition. 1674. 8°. CH, WF.

629C [–] —"Second" edition. *Printed at London*, 1675. 8°. L; WF, Y.

629D [–] Mans mortallitie or a treatise. *Amsterdam* [*London*], *by John Canne*. 1643. 4°. LT, O, C, DUS, E; CN, MH, NU, PT, WF.

629E [–] —[Anr. ed.] —, 1644. 4°.* LT, O, CT, YM, ENC; CH, CU, MH, NU, TU, Y.

630 [–] Martin's eccho. [*London*, 1645.] cap., 4°.* LT, O, CT, DU, MR, DT; CII, CU, NU, PT, WF, Y.

630A [–] The nativity of Sir John Presbyter. *Printed*, 1645. 4°.* LT, CS, MR; MIU, NU, PT, TU.

630B [–] A new bull-bayting. *Printed*, 1649. 4°.* LT, O, C, OC; CH, MH, Y.

631 —Nevv Lambeth Fayre. *By R. O. and G. D.*, 1641[2]. 4°.* MH.

631A [–] —[Anr. ed.] —, 1642. 4°.* LT, O, OW; CH, MH.

632 [–] The ordinance for tythes dismounted. *Europe by Martin Claw-Clergy, for Bartholomew Bang-Priest*, 1646. 4°.* LT, O, C, LW, OC, MR, DT; CH, MH, NR, NU, PT, WF.

632A [–] A pearle in a dounghill. [*London*, 1646.] cap., 4°.* LT, LG, ORP, EN; CH, CN, MH, MU, WF.

632B [–] A remonstrance of many thousand citizens. [*London*], *printed*, 1646. 4°.* LT, O, LL, ORP, MR; CH, CN, MH, NU, PT, WF, Y.

632C [–] —[Anr. ed.] —, 1648. 4°.* NP, Y.

633 [–] A sacred decretall. *Evrope, by Martin Claw-Clergy, for Bartholomew Bang-Priest*, [1645]. 4°.* LT, O, OC, CT, MR, DT; CH, IU, MH, NU, PT, WF, Y.

634 —To the high and mighty states, . . . the humble appeale. [*London*, 1646.] brs. LT; PT.

635 [–] To the right honourable, the betrusted knights, . . . the humble petition of the inhabitants of Buckinghamshire. [*London*, 1647.] brs. LT.

636 —To the supream authority of England . . . the humble petition of. *Printed*, 1649. 4°.* LT; MH, MIU, MU, NHC, WF.

636A [–] Vox plebis, or, the peoples out-cry. *Printed* 1646. 4°. LT, O, C, CT, DT; CH, CN, MIU, NP, NU.

637 **Overton, Robert.** The humble and healing advice. *By T. M. for Livewell Chapman*, 1659. 4°.* L, LCL, LG, ORP, MR; CH, CLC, MH, NN, PL, WF.

638 —A letter from. [*London?*], 1659. brs. LT, O, LG; IU, MH, MIU.

639-42 Entries cancelled.
[–] Man wholly mortal. 1655. *See* Overton, Richard.
[–] Mans mortallitie or a treatise. *Amsterdam*, 1643. *See* Overton, Richard.

643 —More hearts and hands appearing for the work. *By M. Simmons*, 1653. 4°.* LT; CLC, MH, Y.

643A —Two letters from. colop: *For Livewell Chapman*, 1655. cap., 4°.* L; CSS, NN, WF.

643B Overture for an act, for security of the kingdom. [*Scotland*, 1695?] brs. EN.

643C Overture for establishing a society to improve the Kingdom. *Edinburgh, J. Reid*, 1698. 4°.* ALDIS 3768. L, LUG, EH.
Overture for founding. [n.p.], 1699. *See* Kirkwood, James.

643D Overtures concerning the discipline. *Edinburgh, by George Mosman*, 1696. fol. ALDIS 3587. MR, EN, NN.

644 Overtures for correcting and amending the laws. [*Edinburgh?*], 1700. fol.* ALDIS 3993. MR, EN; CH, MH.

644A Overtures for promoting the trade of this nation: humbly offered to the Parliament. [*London*, 1700.] cap., fol.* CSS.
Overtures offered. *Edinburgh*, 1700. *See* Fletcher, Andrew.

645 **Ovid.** Opera omnia. *Excudebat Rogerus Daniel*, 1656. 12°. L, O, C, OC, GU, DT; CLC, V.

646 —Ovid's art of love. *For J. T. to be sold by the booksellers of London and Westminster*, 1692. 4°. L; CH, MH, MU, WF, Y.

647 —Chaucer's ghoast. *By T. Ratcliffe, & N. Thompson for Richard Mills*, 1672. 8°. L, O; CN, MH, TU, WCL, WSL.

647A —De arte amandi; or, the art of love. *Imprinted at London*, 1650. 8°. L.

647B ——[Anr. ed.] *Gedruckt tat Amsterdam by Nicolas Iansz Visscher*, [1650?]. 8°. MH.

648 ——[Anr. ed.] *Printed*,1662. 12°. L, O; CH, MH, WF. (var.)

649 Entry cancelled. *See previous entry.*

650 ——[Anr. ed.] —, 1672. 12°. L, O, RPL; MH.

651 ——[Anr. ed.] —, 1677. 12°. L, O; CN, MH, WF.

652 ——[Anr. ed.] —, 1682. 12°. O, C; CH, MH, WF.

653 ——[Anr. ed.] —, 1684. 12°. O; NP, WF, Y.

653A —Pub. Ovidii Nasonis de tristibus. *Excudebat Johannes Macock, pro Societate Stationariorum*, 1653. 8°. CPE; Y.

653B ——[Anr. ed.] *Oxoniæ, excudebat A. & L. Lichfield*, 1660. 12°. WF.

654 ——[Anr. ed.] *Excudebat J. C. pro societatis stationarum*, 1675. 8°. DC; WG.

654aA ——[Anr. ed.] *Cantabrigiæ, ex officina Joan. Hayes*, 1676. 8°. Y.

654bA ——[Anr. ed.] *Excudebat J. M. pro societatis stationariorum*, 1679. 8°. L, OB; MB.

654cA ——[Anr. ed.] *Excudebat B. G. pro Societate Stationariorum*, 1681. 8°. CH, TO.

654dA ——[Anr. ed.] *Excudebat T. M. pro societate stationariorum*, 1691. 8°. L; IU.

654A ——[Anr. ed.] *Excudebat T. M. pro Societate Stationariorum*, 1694. 8°. MH.

655　——[Anr. ed.] —, 1697. 8°. L, EN; MB, MBC, MH.

655A　——[Anr. ed.] Edinburgi, G. Mosman, 1700. 12°. EN.

655B　—Decerpta ex Ovidio, Tibullo, Propertio. Impensis Sam. Smith, & Tho. Newborough, 1692. 8°. CS.

656　[–] The description of the great machines, of the descent of Orpheus. For Robert Crofts, 1661. 4°.* O.

657　—Electa ex ⟨ Ovidio. Impensis T. Newborough; & Joann. Slatter Etonæ, 1697. 8°. O, C.

658　—Ovid's elegies. By Hen. Hills jun. for John Fish, 1683. 4°. O; CLC, MH, Y.

659　—Ovid's epistles. For Jacob Tonson, 1680. 8°. L, O, C, EC, ENC; CH, CN, MH, TU, WF, Y.

660　——Second edition. —, 1681. 8°. L, O, CE, LSD, RU; CLC, IU, MH, WF, ZWT.

661　——Third edition. —, 1683. 8°. L, NPL; CH, CLC, WF.

662　——"Third" edition. For Jacob Tonson, and are to be sold by Timothy Goodwin, 1683. 8°. L; CLC, IU, MH, TU, WCL, Y.

663　——Fourth edition. For J. T. to be sold by R. Wild, 1688. T.C.II 235. L, LVD, BC, BP; CLC, IU, LC, MH, NP, TO, WF, Y.

663A　——"Fourth" edition. For Jacob Tonson, 1688. 8°. L, O, CPE, LLU; CLC, Y.

664　——Fifth edition. —, 1693. 8°. L, O, OB, CT, EN; CH, CLC, IU, NCU, NP, WF, Y.

665–6　Entries cancelled.
　　　—Epistolæ heroidum. 1680. See—Ovid's epistles.

666A　—Fastorum libri vi. Typis A. C. impensis societatis stationariorum, 1677. 8°. O, OW.

667　——[Anr. ed.] Ex officinâ J. H. venales prostant apud T. Newborough, 1699. 8°. T.C.III 125. L, C, OB, CS, LSD; OCI, Y, AMB.

667A　—Ovid's heroicall epistles. Fourth edition. For William Gilbertson, 1653. 8°. NCU.

667B　——"Fourth" edition. —, 1656. 8°. LLU.

668　——Fifth edition. —, 1663. 8°. L, O, DU.

669　——"Fifth" edition. For William Whitwood, 1671. 8°. T.C.I 68. L, O; CH, MH.

670　——Sixth edition. —, 1673. 8°. CLC, IU, MU, Y.

670A　——"Sixth" edition. —, 1677. 8°. T.C.I 278. L; MH.

671　——[Anr. ed.] —, 1686. 8°. T.C.II 160. O; CN, TO, Y.

672　——[Anr. ed.] For the Company of Stationers, 1695. 8°. T.C.II 582. O; LC, WF.

672A　—Pub. Ovidii Nasonis heroidum epistolæ. Excudebant T. Ratcliff & E. Mottershed pro Societate Stationariorum. 1649. 8°. IU.

672B　——[Anr. ed.] Excudebat E. Tyler pro Societate Stationariorum, 1658. 8°. WF.

672C　——[Anr. ed.] Ex typographia societatis stationariorum, 1668. 8°. L.

673　——[Anr. ed.] Abredoniæ, excudebat Joannes Forbesius, 1670. 12°. ALDIS 1906. L, AU.

673A　——[Anr. ed.] Cantabridgiæ, ex officina Joann. Hayes, 1672. 8°. O; TO.

674　——[Anr. ed.] Ex typographia Societatis Stationariorum, 1675. 12°. O, DC.

674A　——[Anr. ed.] Ex typographia Societatis Stationariorum, 1679. 8°. O; IU, Y.

675　—Heroidum epistolarum liber. Edinburgi, excudebant Thomas Brown & Jacobus Glen, 1681. 12°. ALDIS 2281.3. EN.

676　——[Anr. ed.] Edinburgi, apud Andreæ Anderson, hæredes & successores, 1694. sixes. ALDIS 3380. EN.

676A　——[Anr. ed.] Edinburgi, ex typographæo Georgii Mosman, 1700. 12°. ALDIS 3994.5. C (t.p.).

677　—Heroidum epistolæ. Excudebat B. Griffin pro Societate Stationariorum, 1686. 8°. O; CH, TO.

677A　——[Anr. ed.] Cantabrigiæ, ex officina Joann. Hayes, 1694. 8°. O; PMA.

678　—Ovid's invective or curse against Ibis. [London], by J. G. for Ric. Davis in Oxon, 1658. 8°. MADAN 2402. LT, O, LI, CS, EC; CH, IU, MH, NC, WF, Y.

679　——Second edition. Oxford, by Hen. Hall for Ric. Davis, 1667. 8°. MADAN 2773. L, O, LVF, CK, CPL; CH, CN, MH, NCD, TO, Y.

680　—Metamorphoseωn. Typis Ricardi Cotes, sumptibus Christophori Meredith, 1650. 12°. L, CT.

680aA　——Ex typographia Societatis Stationariorum, 1660. 8°. IU.

680bA　——[Anr. ed.] Typis pro Societate Stationariorum, 1664. 8°. Y.

680A　——[Anr. ed.] Cantabrigiæ, ex officina Joann. Hayes, 1672. 8°. C; TO.

680AB　——[Anr. ed.] Glasguæ, excudebat R. Sanders, 1675. 12°. EN.

680AC　——[Anr. ed.] Typis Andr. Clark, pro R. Scott, T. Basset, J. Wright & R. Chiswel, 1677. 12°. CH, NRU.

680B　——[Anr. ed.] Pro Societate Stationariorum, 1678. 8°. MH, Y.

680C　——[Anr. ed.] Excudebat J. Richardson pro Societate Stationariorum, 1684. 8°. MH, TSM.

681　——[Anr. ed.] Cantabrigiæ, ex officina Joan. Hayes, 1687. 8°. CT.

681A　——[Anr. ed.] Excudebat F. Collins pro societate stationarorum, 1691. 12°. T.C.II 337. IU, TU.

682　——[Anr. ed.] Oxonii, e theatro Sheldoniano, impensis Ab. Swall et Tim. Child, 1696. 8°. T.C.II 570. L, O, C, LW, OC, RPL; BN, CLC, IU, MA, WF.

682A　——[Anr. ed.] Excudebat F. Collins, pro Societate Stationariorum, 1698. 12°. O, CT.

683　——[Anr. ed.] Cantabrigiæ, ex officina Joann. Hayes, 1698. 8°. O, C; MB.

683A　——[Anr. ed.] Edinburgi, Georgii Mosman, 1700. MBA.

684　—Ovids metamorphosis Englished. Fourth edition. For A. Roper, 1656. 12°. L, BC, BSE, CPE, LAWSHALL PARISH, SUFFOLK; FU, NN, WF, AAS.

684A　——"Fourth" edition. For R. Tomlins, 1656. 12°. L, LCS, LNC; CH, NN, OCL, V.

685　—Ovids metamorphosis translated grammatically. For J. F. and Andrew Kemb, 1656. 8°. L; CN, IU, PBM, Y.

686　——Fifth edition. By J. F. for Richard Tomlines, 1664. 12°. L, LADY MARGARET HALL, OXF.; NN, RBU, AVP.

686A　——"Fifth" edition. By J. F. for A. Roper, 1664. 12°. L; CH, MU.

687　——Sixth edition. By J. F. for A. Roper, R. Thomlins and G. Sawbridge, 1669. 12°. T.C.I 22. L, O, LVD, CS; CLC, CU, MH, NN, V, WF.

688   ——Seventh edition. *By E. F. for G. Sawbridge, A. Roper, T. Basset, J. Wright, and R. Chiswell,* 1678. 12°. L, OAS; IU, MH, NRU, Y, ASU.

688aA   ——"Seventh" edition. *By E. F. for G. Sawbridge, A. Roper, and J. Wright,* 1678. 12°. FU, NN.

688A   ——Eighth edition. *For E. Brewster, T. Basset, M. Wotton, G. Coniers, and A. Roper,* 1690. 12°. L, DU; CLC, NN, MH, TU.

688B   ——"Eighth" edition. *For A. Roper,* 1690. 12°. UCLA, WF.

689   —Ovid's metamorphosis. Vol. I. *For W. Rogers, F. Sanders; and A. Roper,* 1697. T.C.III 6. O, C, OAS, LLU; CLC, MH, MU, NP, WF, Y.

690   —The passion of Byblis. *For Rich. Parker,* 1692. 4°.* L, O, C; CLC, MH, MIU, TU, WCL, Y.

691   ——Second edition. *For Sam. Briscoe,* 1697. 4°.* L, OC; CLC, Y.

692   —Phaetons folly, or, the downfal of pride. *For George Calvert,* 1655. 8°. LT, O, LW, SP; CPB, IU, MH, NP, PBM.

693   —The three books of . . . de arte amandi. *For Joseph Cranford,* 1661. 8°. L, LVF; CH, CN, LC.

693A   —Ovids tristia. Third edition. *For F. Coles, T. V. W. G. & J. W.,* 1665. 8°. CCH, CK, BIU.

694   ——Fourth edition. *By Andrew Clark, to be sold by Thomas Williams,* 1672. 8°. T.C.I 107. L, O, C, LG; CH, CN, MH, TU, WF, Y.

695   ——Fifth edition. *By Mary Clarke,* [1681]. 8°. L, O, CK, LLU; CH, CLC, PU, TO, WC, Y.

695A   ——"Fifth" edition. *—, sold by Thomas Passenger; and Thomas Sawbridge,* 1661. 8°. NCU, ZWT.

696   Entry cancelled.

      —Tristium. 1656. *See* —Opera.

696A   ——[Anr. ed.] *Excudebat T. Rattcliff & T. Daniel, pro Societate Stationariorum,* 1670. 12°. L.

696B   ——[Anr. ed.] *Excudit F. C[ollins]. pro societate stationariorum,* 1687. 12°. T.C.II 209. L, CS.

      —Two books of elegies. 1697. *See* Ball, Thomas.

697   —Two essays. *By T. James for Richard Northcott,* 1682. 4°. T.C.I 485. L, O, CT, LLU, D; CH, IU, MH, NCU, PU, WF, Y.

698   —Wisdoms conqvest. *For Philemon Stephens,* 1651. 8°. LT, O, LW, CT, BC; CLC, IU, LC, NC, NN, PBM, Y.

699   Entry cancelled.

      Ovidivs exvlans or. 1673. *See* Radcliffe, Alexander.

699A   Ovid's ghost: or, Venus overthrown. *For the author,* 1657. 8°. WF.

700   **Ovington, John.** An essay upon the nature . . . of tea. *By and for R. Roberts,* 1699. 8°.* L, OC, C, BC, GU; CH, MH, PL, WF, Y.

701   —A voyage to Suratt, in the year, 1689. *For Jacob Tonson,* 1696. 8°. T.C.II 588. L, O, C, MR, DT; BN, CH, CLC, LC, WU, Y.

702   **Owen, Corbett.** Carmen Pindaricum. *Oxonii, è typographiâ Sheldoniana, excudebat H. Hall, impensis Joh. Crosley,* 1669. 4°.* MADAN 2816. L, O, C, AN, BR, DT; CH, CN, MH, TU, WF, Y.

      —New collection of poems and songs. 1674. *See* Bulteel, John.

703   [**Owen, David.**] Anti-Parœus. *Printed at York by Stephen Bulkley,* 1642. 4°. L, O, C, BQ; CSS, MM, WF.

703A   —Herod and Pilate reconciled. *For Laur. Chapman,* 1663. 4°. O, CCA; Y.

704   [–] A persvvassion to loyalty. *Printed.* 1642. 4°.* L, O, C, E, DT; CH, CSS, IU, MH, MM, NCD, NU, Y.

704A   [–] [Anr. ed.] *For George Badger,* 1642. 4°.* CH, CLC, CN, MH, TU, WF, Y.

704B   —Pvritano-Iesvitismvs, the Puritan tvrn'd Jesuite. [*London*], *for William Sheares,* 1643. 4°. LT, O, C, AN, LSD; CH, CN, MH, NU, WF, Y.

704C   ——[Anr. ed.] —, 1652. 4°. O, DU.

704D   **Owen, E.** To the honourable the House of Commons . . . proposals . . . for raising one million. [*London*], *by W. Onley,* 1699. fol. L.

705   **Owen, James.** An answer to the rector of Bury's letter. *By S. Bridge, for Tho. Parkhurst,* 1699. 4°.* T.C.III 160. O, AN, EN; CU, NU, WF, Y.

706   —Bedydd plant or nefoedd. *Printiedic yn Llundain gan F. Collins,* 1693. Sixes. L, O, AN.

706A   [–] Church-pageantry display'd: or, organ worship arraign'd. *For A. Baldwin,* 1700. 4°.* L, O, C, EN, BQ; CLC, LC, NGT, TO.

706B   [–] [Anr. ed.] *Printed, in usum Vitaliani filiorum,* 1700. 4°.* BLH.

707   —A further vindication of the Dissenters. *By S. Bridge, for Tho. Parkhurst,* 1699. T.C.III 160. LW, CT, EN, ENC; NP, NU, Y.

708   [–] A plea for scripture ordination. *For J. Salusbury,* 1694. 8°. T.C.II 473. L, O, C, LCL, GU; NPT, TO.

709   [–] Remarks on a sermon, about corrupting. *London, for Zachary Whitworth, in Manchester,* 1697. 4°.* L, LW, OC, CT, MC, MP; CH.

710   [–] Tutamen evangelicum: or, a defence. *London, for Zachary Whitworth, in Manchester,* 1697. 8°. L, O, CS, MC, GU, DT; CLC, NPT, NU, WF, Y.

710A   [–] [Anr. ed.] *By J. H. for Henry Mortlock,* 1697. 8°. MC.

711   **Owen, John, D. D.** The advantage of the kingdome of Christ. *Oxford, by Leon. Lichfield, for Tho. Robinson,* 1651. 4°.* MADAN 2176. LT, O, C, BC, DT; CH, CN, MH, NU, WF, Y.

711A   ——[Anr. ed.] *Imprinted at Oxford, anno 1651. And reprinted at London.* 4°.* LW, GU; MB, NR.

712   ——[Anr. ed.] *Leith, by Evan Tyler,* 1652. 4°.* ALDIS 1463.5. L, EN, D, DL, ENC; WF, Y.

713   [–] Animadversions on a treatise intituled Fiat lux. *By E. Cotes, for Henry Cripps, and George West in Oxford,* 1662. 8°. L, O, C, CT, E, DT; BN, CH, IU, MH, NU, VC, WF.

714   —Bibliotheca Oweniana, sive catalogus. [*London*], 1684. 4°. L, O, OC, OP, CS; BN, CN, MH, NG, NP, JF.

715   —The branch of the Lord. *Edinburgh, by Evan Tyler,* 1650. 4°.* ALDIS 1416. LT, O, OS, DT; CH, NU, WF, Y.

716   [–] A brief and impartial account of the nature of the Protestant religion. *By J. A. and are to be sold by Benjamin Alsop,* 1682. 4°.* L, O, LCL, SP, ENC; CH, MH, NU, TU, Y.

717   ——[Anr. ed.] *Printed, and are to be sold by William Marshal,* 1690. 4°.* T.C.II 311. L, O, C, MR, EN; CH, MB, MH, NU, WF.

718 —A brief declaration and vindication of the doctrine of the Trinity. *By R. W. for Nath Ponder*, 1669. 12°. T.C.I 8. L, O, C, BP, ENC; CH, CLC, IU, MB, NCD, NU, WF, WU.

719 ——Third edition. *For Nath. Ponder*, 1676. 8°. L, LCL, LW, ENC; CH, MBA, MH, NU, TO, Y.

720 Entry cancelled.
—Brief discourse. 1644. *See* —Duty of pastors.

721 [–] A brief instruction in the worship of God. [*London*], printed, 1667. 8°. L, O, LCL, LW, ENC, DM; CH, IU, MH, NU, WF, Y. (var.)

722 Entry cancelled. Ghost.

722A ——[Anr. ed.] *For Nath. Ponder*, 1676. 8°. LW; CDA.

722B ——[Anr. ed.] *Sold by W. Marshall*, 1688. 8°. T.C.II 238. L, LCL; MBA.

723 [–] A brief vindication of the Non-conformists. *For Nathaniel Ponder*, 1680. 4°. T.C.I 401. L, O, C, CT, BPL, EN; CH, CN, NS, NU, TO, WF.

724 ——Second edition. —, 1680. 4°. L, O, CT, AN, LIU, DT; CLC, MH, MIU, TU, Y.

724A ——Third edition, —, 1680. 4°. MANCHESTER COLL., OXF.

725 —Certaine treatises written by. *By W. W. for Philemon Stephens*, 1649. 4°. L, O, C, LCL, LW; CH, IU, NGT, NU, Y.

726 —Χριστολογια, or, a declaration. *For Nathaniel Ponder*, 1679. 4°. T.C.I 381. L, O, C, AN, E; CLC, MH, NU, WF, Y.

727 —The Church of Rome no safe guide. *For Nathaniel Ponder*, 1679. 4°. L, O, C, ENC, DT; BN, CLC, MH, MIU, NU, WF, Y.

728 Entry cancelled.
[–] Church-pageantry. 1700. *See* Owen, James.

728A —Clinicus resurgens: or the infirm man made whole. *For George Davies*, 1681. 4°. CS.

729 —A continuation of the exposition of the Epistle . . . to the Hebrews . . . sixth, . . . tenth chapters. *For Nathaniel Ponder*, 1680. fol. T.C.I 401. C, LW, OAS, BR, BQ; MH, NN, NU, WF.

730 ——[Anr. ed.] —, 1681. T.C.I 435. NR.

731 ——[Anr. ed.] —, 1684. fol. O, LIL, LW, OQ, E; NP.

732 ——Eleventh, . . . thirteenth chapters. *For Thomas White*, 1684. fol. L, O, LW, LSD, E; CH, MH, NP, PL, PPT, WF.

732A ——[Anr. ed.] *For Nath. Ponder*, 1684. fol. CH.

733 No entry.
—A defence of Mr. John Cotton. Oxford, 1658. *See* Cotton, John.

734 —Diatriba de justitia divina. *Oxoniæ, [excudebat L. Lichfield] impensis Tho. Robinson*, 1653. 8°. MADAN 2232. LT, O, LCL, CT, E, DM; LC, MBC, MH, NU, TO, Y.

735 [–] A discourse concerning evangelical love. *Printed*, 1672. 8°. L, O, OC, DU, SP, ENC, DM; CLC, MWA, NCD, NU, VC.

736 ——[Anr. ed.] *Printed, and are to be sold by Dorman Newman*, 1673. 8°. L, O, ORP, AN, E, DT; CDA, MB, MH, WF, Y.

736A ——[Anr. ed.] *Printed and are to be sold by William Marshal, and John Marshal*, 1696. 8°. T.C.II 586. GU; U. WYOMING.

737 [–] A discovrse concerning liturgies. *Printed*, 1662. 4°. L, O, C, ENC, DT; CH, MH, NU, WF, Y. (var.)

738 —A discourse of the work of the Holy Spirit. *For Nathanael Ponder*, 1682. 8°. T.C.I 464. L, LCL, LW, CQ, ENC, CD; CLC, MH, NP, NU, TO, WF.

739 —The doctrine of justification by faith. *For R. Boulter*, 1677. 8°. T.C.I 280. L, O, C, LW, E, DM; CH, IU, MH, NP, WF, Y.

740 —The doctrine of the saints perseverance. *Oxford, by Leon. Lichfield for Tho. Robinson*, 1654. fol. MADAN 2258. L, O, CE, E, DT; CLC, MH, NP, NU, TSM, WF, Y.

741 —The duty of pastors. *By L. N. for Philemon Stephens*, 1644. 4°. LT, O, C, LW, GU, DM; CH, IU, MH, NU, WF, Y.

742 —Eben-ezer. A memoriall. *By W. Wilson, for the authour*, 1648. 4°. LT, O, C, LCL, LW; CH, IU, MH, WF, Y.

743–5 No entries.

746 —Eschol: a cluster. *For Philemon Stephens*, 1648. 12°. L, O.

746A ——Second edition. —, 1655. 12°. O.

747 ——"Second" edition. *For John Marshall*, [1655]. 12°. L.

748 ——Third edition. *For Nath. Ponder*, 1684. 12°. O, LCL, LW; CLC.

749 ——Fifth edition. *For, and sold by William Marshall*, 1700. 12°. T.C.III 202. L, LW; TO, Y.

750 Entry cancelled.
[–] Essay toward settlement. [1659.] *See* title.

751 —Exercitations concerning the name. *By R. W. for Nath. Ponder*, 1671. 8°. T.C.I 65. L, O, C, LW, EN, DM; CH, CLC, IU, MBA, NU, TO, WF.

752 ——Second edition. —, 1671. 8°. LLL, LW, OC; CN, MH, PL, TU, Y.

753 —Exercitations on the Epistle to the Hebrews . . . two first chapters. *By Robert White, for Nathaniel Ponder*, 1668. fol. L, O, C, BP, E, DT; CH, LC, MH, NU, WF, Y.

753A ——[Anr. ed.] *For Nathaniel Ponder*, 1676. fol. LSD.

753B —Exercitations on the epistle to the Hebrews concerning the priesthood of Christ. *By John Darby for Nathaniel Ponder*, 1674. fol. OAS, OQ, CSSX; CLC, NCU, NN, WF.

754 —An exposition on the third, . . . fifth chapters of the Epistle . . . to the Hebrews. *By John Darby for Nathaniel Ponder*, 1674. fol. T.C.I 146. O, C, LW, AN, LSD; E, CH, LC, MH, NR, Y.

755 Entry cancelled.
—Further vindication. 1699. *See* Owen, James.

756 —The glory and interest of nations. *For Philemon Stephens*, 1659. 4°.* L, O, LLP, BC; HR, CH, MH, NU, WF, Y.

757 —God's presence with a people. *By R. N. for Philemon Stephens*, 1656. 4°.* LT, O, C, BR, ENC, DT; CLC, IU, NU, WF, Y.

758 —God's work in founding Zion. *Oxford, by Leon: Lichfield for Tho: Robinson*, 1656. 4°. MADAN 2307. LT, O, C, EN, DT; CLC, IU, MH, NU, TU, WF, Y.

759 —Gospel grounds. *By John Astwood for William Marshal*, 1695. 8°. T.C.II 555. BR; CLC, NU, RBU.

760 —A guide to church-fellowship. *For William Marshall*, 1692. 12°. L, LCL, LW, ENC; CLC, NU, TO.

760A —The holy and profitable sayings of. 1683. brs. DCH.

761 —The humble proposals of. *Printed at London for Robert Ibbitson,* 1652. 4°.* LT; CH, MB, WF, Y.

762 —An humble testimony unto the goodness. *For Nathanael Ponder,* 1681. 8°. T.C.I 464. L, O, LCL, LW, ENC; CH, MBA, MH, NU, WF. (var.)

763 [–] Indvlgence and toleration considered. *Printed,* 1667. 4°.* L, O, CT, NE, ENC, DT; CH, CN, MH, NU, WF, Y.

764 —An enquiry into the original, nature. *By J. Richardson; for Nath. Ponder; and Sam. Lee,* 1681. 4°. T.C.I 437. L, O, LW, CT, ENC, DM; CH, CN, MH, NU, WF, Y.

764A ——[Anr. ed.] *For and sold by William, and also by John Marshal,* 1696. 4°. GU; NN.

765 Entry cancelled.
—Instructions. 1676. *See* Brief instruction.

766 —The labovring saints dismission to rest. A sermon. *By R. and W. Leybourn, for Philemon Stephens,* 1652. 4°.* LT, O, CK, DU, EN, DN; CH, IU, MH, NU, TU, WF, Y, AVP.

767 No entry.

768 —Meditations and discourses. *By A. M. and R. R. for Benjamin Alsop,* 1684. 8°. T.C.II 41. L, O, LW, AN; CH, CLC, IU, MH, TO, WF.

769 ——[Anr. ed.] *By J. A. for William Marshall,* 1691. 8°. O, LCL; NU, TSM, WF.

769A ——[Anr. ed.] *For B. A.,* 1691. 8ᵛ. CH, MH.

769B ——[Anr. ed.] *For John Taylor and Richard Wilde,* 1691. 8°. T.C.II 356. O; MB.

770 ——[Anr. ed.] *Printed and are to be sold by William Marshal, and John Marshal,* 1696. 8°. T.C.II 586. L, DU.

771 Entry cancelled.
—Meditations on the glory. 1684. *See* —Meditations and discourses.

772 Entry cancelled.
[–] Moderation a vertue. 1683. *See* title.

773 —The nature of apostasie. *For N. Ponder,* 1676. 8°. T.C.I 245. L, O, CQ, BR, E; CH, MH, NCD, NP, NU, TO, WF.

774 [–] The nature, power, deceit, and prevalency. *For Elizabeth Calvert,* 1668. 8°. L, O, LCL, DC, E; CLC, CU, MH, NU, WF, Y.

775 [–] ——[Anr. ed.] *For Thomas Cockerill,* 1675. 8°. T.C.I 192. I, ENC; CH, MH, VC, Y.

776 Entry cancelled.
—New and useful concordance. 1673. *See* Powell, Vavasor.

777 —Of communion with God. *Oxford, by A. Lichfield for Philemon Stevens,* [London], 1657. 4°. MADAN 2347. LT, O, LCL, LW, E; CLC, IAU, IU, MH, WF.

778 ——[Anr. ed.] *Oxford, by A. Lichfield, for Tho: Robinson,* 1657. 4°. OC, CT, BLH; CH, MH, NU.

779 ——Second edition. *For William Marshall,* 1700. 8°. T.C.III 202. LCL; TO.

780 —Of schisme. *Oxford, by L. L. for T. Robinson,* 1657. 8°. MADAN 2348. LT, O, C, LCL, E, DM; CH, MB, MWA, NU, TO, WF.

781 Entry cancelled.
—Of spiritual mindedness. 1681. *See* —Φρονημα.

782 —Of temptation. *Oxford, by H. Hall for T. Robinson,* 1658. 8°. MADAN 2404. LT, O, LCL, CT, ENC, DM; CLC, IU, NS, NU, TO, WF, Y.

783 —Of the death of Christ. *By Peter Cole,* 1650. 4°. LT, LCL, LW, CE, P, GU; CU, IU, MB, NU.

784 —Of the divine originall. *Oxford, by Henry Hall, for Tho: Robinson,* 1659. 8°. MADAN 2455. LT, O, C, AN, ENC, DT; CH, CU, MH, NU, WF, Y.

785 —Of the mortification of sinne in believers. *Oxford, by L. Lichfield for T. Robinson,* 1656. 8°. MADAN 2308. LT, C, OC; MWA, NGT, TO.

786 ——Second edition. *Oxford, by Henry Hall for T. Robinson,* 1658. 8°. MADAN 2405. LT, CQ, P, ENC; CH, MH, WG.

787 ——Third edition. *For Nathaniel Ponder,* 1668. 8°. L, O, LCL; CDA, CLC, WF.

788 Entry cancelled.
—On the Holy Spirit. 1693. *See* —Two discourses.

789 —Ουρανων Ουρανια. The shaking. *By M. Simmons, to be sold by John Cleaver,* 1649. 4°.* LT, O, CS, AN, BC, DT; CH, CLC, IU, NU, WF.

790 [–] A peace-offering in an apology. *Printed,* 1667. 4°.* 37 pp. L, O, CT, LIU, EN, DM; CH, CN, NU, TU, WF, Y.

791 [–] ——[Anr. ed.] —, 1667. 4°.* 41 pp. BP; MBA, NU, Y.

792 —Φρονημα του πνευματος or the grace and duty. *By J. G. for Nathaniel Ponder,* 1681. 4°. T.C.I 464. L, LCL, LW, OC, LSD; CH, MH, NU, WF, Y.

793 —Πνευματολογια: or, a discourse concerning the Holy Spirit. *By J. Darby, for Nathaniel Ponder,* 1674. fol. T.C.I 176. L, O, C, E, DT; CLC, IU, MH, NU, PL, TO, Y.

794 —A practical exposition on the 130th. Psalm. *By Robert White, for Nathaniel Ponder,* 1669. 4°. T.C.I 12. L, O, C, BP, ENC; CLC, TO, TU, WF, WSC.

795 ——[Anr. ed.] *For Nathaniel Ponder,* 1680. 4°. T.C.I 391. L, O, LW, CQ, BLH; CH, CLC, IU, MH, NU, Y.

795A —The primer: or, an easie way to teach children . . . English. *For the Company of Stationers,* 1652. 16°. L.

796 —The principles of the doctrine of Christ. *By R. Cotes, for Philemon Stephens,* 1645. 8°. L, O, LLL.

797 ——[Anr. ed.] *For Nath. Ponder,* 1684. 8°. L, O, LW; LC, MBA, NU.

798 Entry cancelled.
[–] Pro sacris scripturis. Oxford, 1658. *See* —Of the divine originall.

799 [–] Proposals for the furtherance and propagation of the gospell. *For R. Ibbitson,* 1653. 4°.* LT, LW, CS, BR, P, DT; CLC, MM, NU, TO, Y.

800 No entry.

801 —The reason of faith. *For Nathaniel Ponder,* 1677. 8°. T.C.I 288. L, LCL, CT, E, ENC, DM; CH, CLC, NU, RBU, TO, WF, Y.

802 —A review of the annotations of Hvgo Grotivs. *Oxford, by H. Hall for Tho. Robinson,* 1656. 4°.* MADAN 2309. LT, O, C, LCL, ENC, DM; CH, CN, NU, WF, Y.

803 —A review of the true nature of schisme. *Oxford, by Henry Hall for Thomas Robinson,* 1657. 8°. MADAN 2349. LT, O, C, LCL, E; CH, MU, NU, WF, Y.

804 —Salus electorum, sanguis Jesu: or the death of death. *By W. W. for Philemon Stephens,* 1648. 4°. L, O, C, E, DT; CH, IU, MH, NU, WF, Y.

804A [–] Seasonable words for English Protestants. *By Thomas Parkhurst,* 1690. 4°.* T.C.II 332. O, LCL, LW; CH, MH, WF, Y.

805 —A sermon preached . . . January 31. *By Matthew Simmons, for Henry Cripps,* 1649. 4°. LT, O, CE, YM, DT; CH, CLC, IU, NU, Y.

805A ——[Anr. ed.] *By Matthew Simmons,* 1649. 4°. OU; WF.

806 —A sermon preached to the Parliament, Octob. 13. 1652. *Oxford, by Leonard Lichfield, for Thomas Robinson.* 1652. 4°. MADAN 2204. LT, O, C, BR, EN; CH, CN, MH, WF, Y.

806A [–] A short and plain answer. *By T. N. for Jonathan Hutchinson in Durham,* 1682. 4°.* L, O, CT; PL, WF.

807 [–] Some considerations about union. *For N. Ponder,* 1680. 4°.* T.C.I 435. L, O, EN.

807A [–] —[Anr. ed.] *By T. S.,* 1680. 4°.* O, LLL, LW, MR; CH, CLC, MM, NN, WF.

808 —The stedfastness of promises. *By Peter Cole,* 1650. 4°. LT, O, LCL, CS, DT; CH, CN, NU, WF, Y.

809 —Συνεσις πνευματικη: or the causes. *For N. Ponder,* 1678. 8°. T.C.I 329. L, O, C, RPL, ENC; CH, MBA, NU, TO, WF.

810 —Θεολογουμενα παντοδαπα. Sive de natvra. *Oxoniæ, excudebat Hen: Hall, impensis Tho: Robinson,* 1661. 4°. MADAN 3566. L, O, C, E, DT; BN, IU, MH, NU, WF, Y.

811 —Θεομαχια 'αυτεξουσιαστικη: or, a display of Arminianisme. *By I. L. for Phil. Stephens,* 1643. 4°. LT, O, C, EN, DT; CH, CN, MH, NU, WF, Y.

812 —A treatise of the dominion of sin. *By J. L. for William Marshal,* 1688. 8°. T.C.II 229. LCL, LW, BR, EN; CH, CLC, NF, NU, WF.

813 —The true copy of a Welch sermon. *[London], for I. Vnderwood,* 1643. 4°.* LT, OQ, AN; CN.

814 —A true copy of the Welch sermon. *For Thomas Bates,* 1646. 4°.* LT, AN.

815 —The true nature of a gospel church. *For William Marshall,* 1689. 4°. T.C.II 269. L, O, C, LCL, AN, ENC; CLC, IU, MH, NF, NU, WF, Y.

816 No entry.

817 [–] Truth and innocence vindicated. *Printed,* 1669. 8°. L, O, C, LCL, EN, DM; CH, IU, MH, NU, WF, Y.

818 —Two discourses concerning the Holy Spirit. *For William Marshall,* 1693. 8°. T.C.II 474. L, O, LW, BR, D; CLC, LC, PL, WF.

819 —Dr. John Owen's two short catechisms. Second edition. *Printed for, and sold by Will. Marshal,* 1700. 8°. T.C.III 202. O, C.

820 [–] Unto the questions sent me last night. colop: *For Francis Tyton,* 1659. cap., 4°.* L, O, C, LIU, LSD, YM, DM; CLC, CSS, MH, MU, NU, Y.

821 [–] A vindication of some passages in a discourse concerning Communion. *For Nath. Ponder,* 1674. 8°. T.C.I 176. L, O, C, LCL, LW, DM; CH, CLC, NF, NU, WF.

822 —A vindication of the Animadversions on Fiat lux. *For Ph. Stephens, and George Sawbridge,* 1664. 8°. L, O, C, LW, CE, DU, LSD, DM; CH, MWA, NU, VC, WF, Y.

822A —A vindication of the doctrine of the trinity. *Sold by Nath. Ponder,* 1676. 12°. T.C.I 248. GU.

823 —Vindiciæ evangelicæ or the mystery. *Oxford, by Leon. Lichfield for Tho. Robinson,* 1655. 4°. MADAN 2279. LT, O, C, AN, E, DT; BN, CH, IU, MH, NCD, NU, WF, Y.

824 Entry cancelled. *See previous entry.*

825 —A vision of vnchangeable free mercy. *By G. M. for Philemon Stephens,* 1646. 4°. LT, O, C, BR, DT; CH, IU, MH, NU, TU, WF, Y.

825AA **Owen, John,** *chaplain.* Immoderate mourning. *By J. Macock for John Williams,* 1680. 8°. EN; WF.

825A —The true way to loyalty. *For Samuel Eddowes,* 1684. 4°.* L, O, C; MIU, WF.

825B **Owen, John,** *epigrammatist.* Epigrammatum. *Ex officina Rogeri Daniel,* 1659. 12°. L, O, C, AN, BC, EN; CH, CLC, FU, IU, OSU, PL, VC.

825C ——[Anr. ed.] *Ex officinâ Joannis Redmayne,* 1668. 12°. L, O, C, LW, AN, BC, BLH; CH, CLC, MBC, NC, WF.

825D ——[Anr. ed.] —, 1671. 12°. L, O, LG, CE, AN; CH, CLC, IU, TU, Y.

825DA ——[Anr. ed.] —, 1676. 12°. T.C.I 230. AN; IU, MH.

825DB ——[Anr. ed.] *Typis Guil. Redmayne,* 1686. 12°. O, AN.

825E —John Owen's Latine epigrams Englished. *By Robert White, for Nevil Simmons, and Thomas Sawbridge,* 1677. 12°. T.C.I 291. L, O, AN, E, EN; CH, LC, MH, MU, WF, Y.

825F ——[Anr. ed.] *For Edward Robinson, in Ludlow,* 1678. 12°. O, LL, LW, OW, AN; CN, LC, OLU, RHT, Y.

825G **Owen, John,** *of Oxford.* Libri impensis Joannis Oweni editi vel mox edendi. [*Oxford*?], 1700. brs. L.

826 **Owen, Jonathan.** Englands warning. *For the author, to be sold by John Harris,* 1694. 4°.* L, O, C; LC.

827 —A funeral sermon. Mr. Philip King. *For Tho. Parkhurst,* 1700. 8°.* L, LW, E.

828 **Owen, Lewis.** A genealogie of all Popish monks. *For George Gibbes, to be sold by Richard Clarke,* 1646 4°. LT, O, MR, DT.

829 **Owen, Mathew.** Carol o gyngor. [*Printed by L. or A. Lichfield*] *yn Rhydychen,* [*Oxford*], 1658. brs. MADAN 2406. O.

829A **Owen, Richard.** Paulus multiformis. Concio ad clerum. *Typis S. Griffin, væneuntque apud Joh. Williams,* 1666. 4°. L, OC, CPE, EC, LSD.

830 [**Owen, Thankfull.**] A true and lively representation of Popery. *By R. Everingham for W. Kettilby,* 1679. 4°. T.C.I 351. L, O, C, EC, MC, ENC, DT; CH, NU, TU, WF, Y.

831 Entry cancelled. *See following entry.*

832 **Owen, Thomas.** Reports of. *By T. R. for H. Twyford, T. Dring, and J. Place,* 1656. fol. L, O, C, LG, DT; CH, LC, MHL, NCL, WF, AVP.

832A **Owen, Vincent.** A plain sermon preached. *For Edward Robinson,* 1685. 4°.* SHR; CLC.

832B ——[Anr. ed.] *Printed, and sold by Randolph Taylor,* 1685. 4°. O, LSD.

833 **Owen, William.** The last trve intelligence from Ireland. [*London*], *by Tho: Paine for John Sweeting,* 1642. 4°.* LT, O, C, CT, DN; PL, WF, Y.

Owle at Athens. [n.p.], 1648. *See* Winyard, Thomas.

Owtram. *See* Outram.

834   Entry cancelled.

Oxenbridge, Clement. Case of the first undertakers. [n.p., 1653.] *See* title.

835   —The case of the undertakers for reducing postage of inland letters. [*London*, 1653.] brs. L; NC.

—To all ingenuous people. [n.p., 1653.] *See* title.

836   **Oxenbridge, John.** A double watch-word. *By S. G. for J. Rothwell*, 1661. 8°. LCL, OCC; CB, MH, WF.

837   —Nevv-England freemen warned. [*Cambridge, Mass.*], *printed*, 1673. 16°. EVANS 181. CH, MH, MHS, MWA, NN.

837A   [–] A quickening word. *Cambridge, by S. G. and M. J.*, 1670. 8°.* EVANS 152. NN.

838   —A seasonal proposition. [*London*, 1670?] cap., 4°.* L; MHS, PHS.

839   **Oxenden, George.** Causa jure jurando. [*n.p.*, 1679.] brs. L, O, C, LNC; MH.

839A   **Oxenden, Henry.** The case of. [*London?* 169–?] brs. MH.

840   —Charls triumphant. *Printed*, 1660. 8°. O; CH, IU, WF.

840A   [–] Εἰκων Βασιλικη, or an image royal. [*London*], *printed*, 1660. 8°.* CH, IU, Y.

840B   [–] Iobvs triumphans. [*London*], 1651. 8°.* CLC, IU, Y.

841   [–] Religionis funus, & hypocritæ finis. *Excudit Tho. Whittaker*, 1647. 4°.* L, C, CPE; CH, CN, MH, TU, WF, Y.

842   [**Oxenham, James.**] A true relation of an apparition. *By I. O. for Richard Clutterbuck*, 1641. 4°.* LT, O, OCC; CU, MH, Y.

843   **Oxenstierna, Benedict, count.** The case of the persecuted and oppressed Protestants. *In the Savoy, by Tho. Newcomb*, 1674/5. fol.* L, O, C, MR; CSS, LC, NN, PU, WF, Y.

843A   **Oxford, John.** The merchants daily companion. *For the author*, 1700. brs. L.

844   **Oxford, Wendy.** A prospective for king and subjects. *Printed to* [sic] *Leyden, by John Pricton*, 1652. 4°.* L, O, DU; MM.

845   —The unexpected life. [*n.p.*], 1652. 4°.* LT; CH.

846   —Vincit qui patitur: or, Liutenant Colonel John Lylborne decyphered. [*London*], *printed the first of Aprill*, 1653. 4°.* LT, MR.

847   The Oxford act: a poem. *For Randal Taylor*, 1603 [i.e. 1693]. 4°.* L, O, C, OC; Y.

848   —[Anr. ed.] —, 1693. 4°.* L, O, C; CH, CN, MH, Y.

Oxford agreed. 1646. *See* R., S.

848A   The Oxford alderman's speech to the D. of M. [*London?* 1681.] brs. L, O, LS, EN; CN, MH, Y.

Oxford almanack. [n.p.], 1673. *See* Almanacs. Wheeler, Maurice.

849   The Oxford-antiquity examined. *Printed* 1691. 4°.* O, CS, CT, DU, EC, LSD; MIU, Y.

850   Oxforde as it now lyeth. [*Oxford*, 1644.] brs. MADAN 1753. O.

Oxford besiedged. [n.p.], 1645. *See* Taylor, John.

851   The Oxford character of the London diurnall. colop: *Printed* [at *London*] *by M. B.* 1645. cap., 4°.* MADAN 1763. LT, O, OW, MR, DT; MH, Y.

852   **OXFORD, CITY OF.** The ansvver of the City of Oxford to His Majesties propositions. *Printed at Oxford by Leonard Lichfield*, 1643. 4°.* MADAN 1185. LT, O, MR, DT; IU, Y.

853   —Civitas Oxon: a bill of all the burials. [*Oxford*, 1641.] brs. O.

854   —The oath of every free-man of the City of Oxford. *Oxford, by Leonard Lichfield*, 1646. brs. MADAN 1886. O.

Oxford conference. [n.p.], 1660. *See* Barksdale, Clement.

Oxford drollery. Oxford, 1671. *See* Hickes, William.

Oxford elegie. [n.p., 1658.] *See* M., T.

855   The Oxford health. [*London*], *for P. Brooksby*, [1681]. brs. L, O, HH; MH.

856   Oxford in mourning. [*London*], *for J. Jordan*, [1681]. brs. L, O, HH; MH.

857   The Oxford list of the names of the knights, . . . of the Cinque-Ports. *Oxford: by L. Lichfield, for John Starkey*, 1681. brs. L, O, LG, MR, SP; CCC, CLC, MH, WF, Y, AVP.

Oxford May the 20, 1649. [n.p., 1649.] *See* R., J.

857A   Oxford riddle. colop: *Oxford, by Leonard Litchfield*, 1643. brs. MADAN 1459*. O.

858   **OXFORD, UNIVERSITY OF.** Academiæ Oxoniensis gratulatio. *Oxoniæ, e theatro Sheldoniano*, 1690. fol. L, O, C, OC, OM, MR; CB, CLC, MH, Y.

—Academiæ Oxoniensis notitia. Oxford, 1665. *See* Fulman, William.

858A   —An account of the decree of the University of Oxford, against some heretical tenets . . . 25th November, 1695. *Sold by J. Whitlock*, [1695]. brs. WF.

858B   —An advertisement concerning the printing and publishing . . . books. [*Oxford*, 1680.] brs. MADAN 3273. O.

858C   —An advertisement of several Bibles and Common-Prayer Books lately printed at the Theatre. [*Oxford*, 1685.] brs. MH.

859   —Advertisements from the delegates of convocation for His Majesties reception. [*Oxford*, 1663.] brs. MADAN 2644. L, O, OM.

860   ——[Same title.] [*Oxford*, 1687.] brs. L; CH.

860A   ——[Same title.] colop: *Oxford, at the Theater*, 1695. brs. O.

860B   ——Anno Domini MDCXCIV in Theatro Sheldoniano jam imprimuntur, praeter libros Anglicos. [*Oxford*], 1694. 8°. O.

860C   ——Anno Domini MDCXCVI. Maii die 4. in Theatro Sheldoniano apud Oxoniensis sub prelo libri sequentes. [*Oxford*], 1696. brs. O.

860D   ——[Same title, "MDCXCVII. Julii die 14."] [*Oxford*], 1697. brs. O.

860E   ——[Same title, "MDCC Februarii die 7."] [*Oxford*], 1700. brs. L.

860F   ——At a meeting of the delegates in D. Staunton's lodgings. [*Oxford*, 1653.] brs. MADAN 2219. OA.

861   —At a meeting of the heads of houses. Mar. 22. 1688. Whereas the gowns. [*Oxford*, 1688.] brs. O.

861A   ——[Anr. ed., "April 28. 1690."] [*Oxford*], 1690. brs. O.

862   —At a meeting of the Vice-chancellor and the heads of colleges. [*Oxford*, 1695.] brs. O, OC; Y.

863 —Britannia rediviva. *Oxoniæ, exuudebat [sic] A. & L. Lichfield*, 1660. 4°. MADAN 2466*. LT, O, C, OM, E; CH, CN, LC, MH, TU, WF, Y.

863A —Jan. 9. 1651. By the Vicechancellour . . . Whereas the Right Honorable. *Oxford, by L. Lichfield*, 1651[2]. brs. MADAN 2155. O.

863B —March 22. 1651. By the Vice-Chancellour . . . Whereas by the rude carriage. —, 1651/2. brs. MADAN 2156. O.

863C —[Anr. ed., 28 February 1653/4.] —, 1653[4]. brs. MADAN 2220. OA.

863D —By order from . . . [Vice-Chancellor, 27 April 1671]. [*Oxford*], 1671. brs. MADAN 2897. O.

863E —By order from Mr. Vice-chancellor. Whereas complaint . . . [10 July 1671]. [*Oxford*], 1671. brs. O.

863F —By order from Mr. Vice-Chancellor . . . [22 February 1671/2, about London coach]. [*Oxford*], 1672. brs. MADAN 2934. O.

863G ——[Anr. ed., 23 February 1671/2.] [*Oxford*, 1972.] brs. O.

863H ——[Anr. ed., 22 April 1672.] [*Oxford*, 1672.] brs. MADAN 2936. O.

—Catalogue of all graduats. Oxford, 1689. *See* Peers, Richard.

863I —A catalogue of books, printed at the Theater. [*Oxford*, 1677.] brs. MADAN 3154. L, O. (var.)

863J ——[Same title, 4 August 1678.] [*London*, 1678.] brs. LPR.

863K ——[Same title.] [*London*], *sold by Moses Pitt*, 1682. fol.* O.

864 —Catalogus impressorum librorum Bibliothecæ Bodlejanæ. *Oxonii, e theatro Sheldoniano*, 1674. fol. T.C.I 199. MADAN 2999. L, O, C, EN, DT; BN, CLC, MH, MU, WF, Y.

864A —Catalogus librorum in Theatro Sheldoniano impressorum. [*Oxford*, 1694.] 8°. O.

864B —Catalogus librorum quos nuper ab Hollandia huc attulit Johannes Owenus. [*Oxford*, 1700.] 4°. O.

—Catalogus variorum librorum apud Theatrum Sheldonianum. [n.p., 1679.] *See title.*

865 —A certificat in order to the collecting and reporting the state of the present English free-schools. [*Oxford*], 1673. brs. MADAN 2984. O.

866 —Comitia habita in universitate Oxoniensi . . . Ap. 23. [*Oxford*], *e theatro Sheldoniano*, 1685. brs. O.

867 ——Apr. 11. —, 1689. brs. O, HH.

868 ——Apr. 16. An. Dom. 1696. —, 1696. brs. O, LLP, OP, MC, HH.

869 ——Decemb. 2. —, 1697. brs. O.

870 —Comitia philologica in gratulatione. *Oxon. è theatro Sheldoniano*, 1677. brs. MADAN 3151. O, LLP.

871 ——[Anr. ed.] —, 1677. fol. MADAN 3152. O, OC; CH, WF.

871A —Cum de vestitu & habitu. *Oxon, excudebat H. Hall*, [1666]. brs. MADAN 2750. O.

871B —Cum disputationes in parviso. [*Oxford, c.* 1677.] brs. O.

871C —Cum statutum Universitatis . . . [24 November 1674]. [*Oxford*, 1674.] brs. MADAN 3018. O.

872 —Decreti Oxoniensis. [*Oxford*], *excusa*, 1696. 4°. T.C.II 580. L, O, OC, EN, DT; CH, CLC, NU, Y.

873 Entry cancelled. *See preceding entry.*

873A —Divini poetæ Haphiz canticum primum . . . [specimen sheet]. [*Oxford*, 1675.] brs. LPR.

874 —Doctors in all faculty's appointed to meet the king. [*Oxford*], 1687. brs. L, O; CH.

875 —Domiduca Oxoniensis. *Oxoniæ, excudebant A. & L. Lichfield*, 1662. 4°. MADAN 2578. L, O, C, DU, LIU; CH, CLC, CN, MH, TU, WF, Y.

876 —Epicedia academiæ Oxoniensis, . . . Henrici Ducis Glocestrensis. *Oxoniæ, typis Lichfieldianis*, 1660. 4°. MADAN 2467. LT, O, OC, CT, DU; CH, CN, MH, TU, WF, Y.

877 ——Mariæ principis Arausionensis. *Oxoniæ, typis Lichfieldianis*, 1660. 4°. O, OC, CT, DU; CSB, MH, WF.

878 ——Mariæ. *Oxoniæ, excudebat A. & L. Lichfield, impensis Ric. Davis*, 1661. 4°. MADAN 2543. LT, O, OC, CT, DT; CH, CN, MH, TU, Y.

879 ——in obitum Henriettæ Mariæ. *Oxonii, e typographia Sheldoniana*, 1669. fol. MADAN 2814. L, O, CT, MR, ES; IU, MH, WF, Y.

880 ——Georgii ducis Albemarliæ. *Oxonii, e theatro Sheldoniano*, 1670. fol. MADAN 2844. L, O, CT, DU, SC; CH, CU, MH, WF, Y.

881 ——Henriettæ Mariæ. *Oxonii, e theatro Sheldoniano*, 1670. fol. MADAN 2845. L, O, CT, DU, ES; MH, WF, Y.

882 ——Annæ. *Oxonii, e theatro Sheldoniano*, 1671. fol. MADAN 2869. O, LLP, OM, CT, DU, LIU, SC; WF, Y.

883 —Evcharistica Oxoniensia. *Oxoniæ, excudebat Leon. Lichfield*, 1641. 4°. MADAN 965. LT, O, C, BP, DU; CN, MH, MIU, WF, Y.

884 No entry.

885 —Exequiæ desideratissimo principi Gulielmo. *Oxonii, e theatro Sheldoniano*, 1700. fol. L, O, CT, MR, YM; CH, MH, WF, WG, Y.

886 Entry cancelled.

—Gratulatio. Oxoniæ, 1690. *See* —Academiæ Oxoniensis.

887 —The humble address and recognition of the University of Oxford . . . to . . . James II. 1685. fol. O; CH, LC, INU, Y.

888 No entry.

889 —In conventu D. Vice-Cancellarii & praefectorum. [*Oxford*, 1695.] brs. L, OC; WF, Y.

889A —John Nicholas doctor in divinity . . . Whereas all undergraduates. *Oxford*, 1678. brs. MADAN 3190. O.

890 Entry cancelled.

—Jvgement de. 1648. *See* Sanderson, Robert.

891 —The judgment and decree of the . . . July 21, 1683. [*Oxford*], *at the theater*, 1683. fol.* L, O, CE, MR, EN; CH, CN, MH, NU, TU, WF, Y.

892 ——[Anr. ed.] *Dublin, reprinted and are to be sold at His Majesties printing-house, and by Joseph Wild*, 1683. fol.* DIX 200. C, E, DT.

893 —Judicium & decretum . . . Jul. 21, An. 1683. [*Oxford*], *e theatro Sheldoniano*, 1683. fol.* L, O, LL, OC, DU, DM; CH, CN, MH, NU, WF, Y.

894 ——August. 19. Anno Dom. 1690. *Oxonii, e theatro Sheldoniano anno* 1690. *Sold by Tho. Bennet, London.* fol.* L, O, C, EC, BP; CH, CN, MH, NU, WF.

895 No entry.

—Judicium universitatis Oxoniensis. [n.p.], 1648. *See* Sanderson, Robert.

896 —Librorum manuscriptorum in duabus. *Oxonii, e theatro Sheldoniano, veneunt in officina T. Bennett, Lond.*, 1692. 4°. T.C.II 394. O, CS, DU, EN; CH, CLC, CN, IU, WF, Y.

897 —Marmora Oxoniensia. *Oxonii, e theatro Sheldoniano*, 1676. fol. MADAN 3092. L, O, C, EN, DT; CH, NU, OCI, WF, Y, AVP.

898–901 Entries cancelled.

—Musarum Anglicanarum analecta. *Oxon*, 1692. *See* title.

902 —Mvsarvm Oxoniensivm 'ελαιοφορια. *Oxoniæ, excudebat Leonardus Lichfield*, 1654. 4°. MADAN 2243. LT, O, CT, DU, MAU; CH, CN, MH, WF, Y.

903 —Musarum Oxoniensium επιβατηρια. *Oxoniæ, excudebat Leonardus Lichfield*, 1643. 4°. MADAN 1418. LT, O, C, OB, DU, DT; CH, CLC, CN, MH, Y.

903A —Nos quorum nomina. [*Oxford*, 1647.] brs. MADAN 1923. O.

903B —Iuly 5th. 1652. [Notice by Vice-Chancellor against disturbances of the Act.] *Oxford, by L. Lichfield*, 1653. brs. MADAN 2187. O.

903C —April 13. 1647. Ordered by the Lord Chancellour and Visitors. [*London*, 1648.] brs. MADAN 1974. O.

903D —Orders agreed upon by the heads of Houses . . . fire. [*Oxford*, 1671.] brs. MADAN 2901. O.

903E —Orders concerning the rates. [*Oxford*], 1666. brs. MADAN 2751. O.

903F —Orders for the reception of . . . James. [*Oxford*, 1677.] brs. MADAN 3150. O.

903G —Orders for the reception of . . . the Prince of Orange. [*Oxford*, 1670.] brs. MADAN 2858. O.

903H —Orders to be observed while His Majestie or Parliament . . . in Oxford. [*Oxford?* 1681.] brs. O.

904 —Ordo baccalavreorum. [*Oxford*, 1668.] brs. O.

905 — —[Anr. ed.] *Oxonii e theatro Sheldoniano, excudebat Hen: Hall*, [1670]. brs. O.

906 — —[Anr. ed.] *Oxonii, e theatro Sheldoniano*, 1671. brs. O.

906A — —[Anr. ed.] [*Oxford*], 1672. brs. O.

907 — —[Anr. ed.] [*Oxford*], *ex officina Leonardi Lichfield*, [1674]. brs. O.

908 — —[Anr. ed.] —, [1675]. brs. O.

909 — —[Anr. ed.] [*Oxford*], *ex officina Lichfieldiana*, 1676. brs. O.

910 — —[Anr. ed.] —, 1677. brs. O.

911 — —[Anr. ed.] —, 1678. brs. O.

912 — —[Anr. ed.] *Oxonii, ex officina Leonardi Lichfield*, 1680. brs. O.

913 — —[Anr. ed.] —, [1681]. brs. O.

914 — —[Anr. ed.] —, [1682]. brs. O.

915 — —[Anr. ed.] —, [1683]. brs. O.

916 — —[Anr. ed.] —, [1684]. brs. O.

917 — —[Anr. ed.] —, [1685]. brs. O.

918 — —[Anr. ed.] —, [1686]. brs. O.

919 — —[Anr. ed.] —, [1687]. brs. O.

920 — —[Anr. ed.] —, [1688]. brs. O.

921 — —[Anr. ed.] —, [1689]. brs. O.

922 — —[Anr. ed.] —, [1690]. brs. O.

923 — —[Anr. ed.] —, [1691]. brs. O.

924 — —[Anr. ed.] —, [1692]. brs. O.

925 — —[Anr. ed.] —, [1693]. brs. O.

926 — —[Anr. ed.] —, [1694]. brs. O.

927 — —[Anr. ed.] —, [1695]. brs. O.

928 — —[Anr. ed.] —, [1698]. brs. DT.

929 —Parecbolæ sive excerpta è corpore stautorum. *Oxoniæ, e theatro Sheldoniano*, 1671. 8°. MADAN 2875. L, O, LI, CS, EN, DM; CH, MBJ, NS, PL, Y.

930 — —[Anr. ed.] —, 1674. 8°. MADAN 3016. L, O, C, DC, GU; CLC, CU, IU, WF, Y.

931 — —[Anr. ed.] —, 1682. 8°. L, O, C, EC, DT; CH, IU, PU, Y.

932 — —[Anr. ed.] —, 1691. 8°. L, O, C, CT; CLC, PL, WF, Y.

933 — —[Anr. ed.] —, 1693. 8°. L, O, OC, OCH; CLC, Y, AVP.

934 — —[Anr. ed.] —, 1700. 8°. L, O, LW, OC, EC; CLC, IU, TU, Y.

934A —Paul Hood . . . [academic costume, 8 October 1660]. *Printed at Oxford by Anne Lichfield*, 1660. brs. MADAN 2516. O.

934B —May the 31. 1661. Paul Hood . . . [academic costume]. [*Oxford*], 1661. brs. O.

935 Entry cancelled.

—Petition of the university. [n.p.], 1647. *See* —To the honourable visitours.

936 —Pietas universitatis Oxoniensis . . . Caroli secundi. *Oxonii, e theatro Sheldoniano*, 1685. fol. L, O, C, OM, MR; CLC, IU, MH, PU, WF, Y.

937 — —Mariæ. —, 1695. fol. L, O, OM, CT, DU, MR; CH, IU, MH, WF, Y.

938 Entry cancelled.

—Prælectiones academicae. *Oxonii*, 1692. *See* Dodwell, Henry.

939 —The prices of provision, appointed by the rev. G. Fronsyde. [*Oxford*, 1681?] brs. O.

939A —Octob: 21, 1667. Prizes of wine. [*Oxford, By William Hall*, 1667.] brs. MADAN 2776. O.

939B — —[Same title, 19 February 1673/4.] [*Oxford*], 1674. brs. MADAN 3017. O.

940 Entry cancelled. Serial.

941 —Προτελεια Anglo-Batava. *Oxoniæ, excudebat Leonadus Lichfield*, 1641. 4°. MADAN 964. L, O, C, MAU, DT; CH, CN, MH, WF, Y.

942 — —[Anr. ed.] —["*Leonardus*"], 1641. 4°. MADAN 964*. L, O; LEIDEN U., Y.

942A —Quæstiones discutiendæ in comitiis. *Oxonii* . . . *Gulielmi Henrici. Oxon.*, 1670. brs. O, LPR.

942B —Quæstiones in sacra theologia. *Oxoniæ, excudebat Leon. Lichfield* 1651. brs. O.

943 Entry cancelled. See O944D.

944 — —[Anr. ed.] *Oxoniæ, excudebat Leon. Lichfield*, 1652. brs. O.

944A — —[Anr. ed.] *Oxon.*, 1653. brs. O.

944B — —[Anr. ed.] *Oxon.*, 1654. brs. O.

944C — —[Anr. ed.] *Oxon.*, 1657. brs. O.

944D — —[Anr. ed., "s. theologia."] *Oxoniæ, typis Lihfieldianis* [*sic*], 1661. brs. O, EC; MH.

945   ——[Anr. ed.] *Oxoniæ, typis Lichfieldianis,* 1663. brs. O; CLC.

945A   ——[Anr. ed.] *Oxon.,* 1664. brs. O.

946   ——[Anr. ed., "S. theologia."] *Oxoniæ, typis Lichfieldianis,* 1669. brs. O.

947   ——[Anr. ed.] *Oxonii, ex officina Leonardi Lichfield,* 1671. brs. O.

947A   ——[Anr. ed.] *Oxon.,* 1672. brs. O.

948   ——[Anr. ed.] *Oxonii, ex officina Leonardi Lichfield,* 1673. brs. O.

949   ——[Anr. ed.] —, 1674. brs. L, O.

950   ——[Anr. ed.] —, 1675. brs. L, O.

951   ——[Anr. ed.] —, 1676. brs. O.

952   ——[Anr. ed.] —, 1677. brs. O, OM.

953   ——[Anr. ed.] —, 1678. brs. O.

954   ——[Anr. ed.] —, 1679. brs. O.

955   ——[Anr. ed.] —, 1680. brs. L, O.

956   ——[Anr. ed.] —, 1681. brs. O.

957   ——[Anr. ed.] —, 1682. brs. O.

958   ——[Anr. ed.] —, 1683. brs. O; CLC.

959   ——[Anr. ed.] —, 1684. brs. O.

960   ——[Anr. ed.] [*Oxford*], *e theatro Sheldoniano,* 1693. brs. O.

960A   —Quandoquidem compertum est . . . [29 January]. *Oxford,* 1655. brs. MADAN 2268*. OA.

961   —Mart. 20. 1660. Quandoquidem compertum est. *Oxon, typis Lichfieldianis,* [1660]. brs. MADAN 2426. O.

961A   —Quanquam statuta . . . [16 February 1666]. [*Oxford,* 1667.] brs. MADAN 2775. O.

961B   —Robert Say . . . [13 February 1665/6]. [*Oxford,* 1666.] brs. MADAN 2749. O.

962   —Rules and orders made by the Vice-chancellor. [*Oxford*], 1665. brs. MADAN 2713. O.

962A   —Sacræ theologiæ professor. [*Oxford? c.* 1660.] brs. MADAN 2514. O.

962B   —Sir, I do most earnestly desire you . . . [wearing of academic costume]. [*Oxford,* 1678.] brs. MADAN 3189. O, OA.

962C   —Statuta legenda in admissione baccalaureorum in jure civili. [*Oxford*], 1684. brs. L.

963   —Statuta legenda in admissione . . . baccalaureorum in medicina. [*Oxford,* 1684.] brs. O.

964   —Statuta legenda in admissione baccalaureorum in theologia. [*Oxford,* 1684.] brs. L, O; WF.

965   —Statuta legenda in admissione inceptorum in theologia. [*Oxford,* 1684.] brs. O.

966   —Statuta selecta. [*Oxford*], *typis* [*A.*] *Litchfieldianis, pro Ric. Davis, assignato J. Webb,* 1661. 8°. MADAN 2568–9. O, C, DT; CN, LC, MB, MH, WF, Y.

967   ——[Anr. ed.] *Oxon, e theatro Sheldoniano,* 1671. 8°. O, DT.

968   Entry cancelled.
        —Statuta selecta. *Oxon,* 1682. *See* —Parecbolæ.

969   —Strenæ natalitiae academiæ Oxoniensis. *Oxonii, e theatro Sheldoniano,* 1688. fol. L, O, C, MR, EN; CH, IU, MWA, WF, Y.

970   —Supplex recognitio et gratulatio solennis. *Oxonii, e theatro Sheldoniano,* 1685. fol. C, OC, OM, EC, MR; CH, IU, MH, PL, WF, Y.

971   —Theatri Oxoniensis encænia . . . Jul. 10. *Oxon, e theatro Sheldoniano,* 1674. brs. O.

972   ——Jul. 9. —, 1675. brs. O, OP.

973   ——Jul. 7. —, 1676. brs. O.

974   ——Julii 6. —, 1677. fol. MADAN 3148. L, O, LLL, OC, DU; CLC, WF, Y.

975–6   Entries cancelled.
        ——[Anr. ed.] Oxon, 1677. *See* —Comitia philogica.

977   ——Julii 6. —, 1677. brs. L, O, OM; CH, MH.

978   ——July 11. [*Oxford*], *e theatro Sheldoniano,* 1679. brs. O.

979   ——Jul. 9. —, 1680. brs. O.

980   ——Jul. 8. —, 1681. brs. O.

981   ——Jul. 7. —, 1682. brs. O.

982   ——Jul. 6. —, 1683. brs. O.

983   ——Jul. 11. —, 1684. brs. O.

984   ——Julii 7. *Oxonii, e theatro Sheldoniano,* 1693. fol. L, O, OC, CT, MR, DT; CH, IU, MH, TU, WF, Y.

984A   —Univers. Oxon. These are in His Maiesties name. [*Oxford,* 1678.] brs. MADAN 3187. OA.

984B   —To [blank] being by us approved. [*Oxford,* 1678.] brs. MADAN 3188. OA.

984C   —Universit. Oxon. To [blank] being by us nominated. [*Oxford,* 1678.] brs. MADAN 3186. O.

985   —To the high and honorable covrt of Parliament, the humble petition of the University of Oxford. *Oxford, by Leonard Lichfield,* 1641. 4°.* MADAN 981. L, O, C, DU, DT; MH, NU, WF, Y.

986   ——[Anr. ed.] [*London*], 1641. 4°.* MADAN 982. LT, O, BAMB, EC, LNC; CB, MH, MIU, NCD, WF, Y.

986A   ——[Anr. ed.] [*London*], *printed,* 1641. 4°.* O, LLP, MR, SP; CH, CLC, IU, MH, MIU, WF.

986B   ——[Anr. ed.] [*London,* 1641.] brs. MADAN 983. O; Y.

987   —To the high court of Parliament, the humble petition of all colledges and halls. [*Oxford,* 1641.] brs. MADAN 977. L, O.

987A   —To the honourable visitours appointed. [*London*], 1647. brs. MADAN 1975. O.

987B   ——[Anr. ed.] [*London,* 1648.] fol.* MADAN 1973. O.

987C   —To the right worshipful the heads of the respective colleges [orders and regulations for the Encænia and Act]. [*Oxford*], 1669. brs. MADAN 3292. O.

987D   ——[Anr. ed.] —, 1671. brs. O.

987E   ——[Anr. ed.] —, 1672. brs. O.

987F   ——[Anr. ed.] —, 1673. brs. O.

987G   ——[Anr. ed.] —, 1674. brs. O.

987H   ——[Anr. ed.] —, 1675. brs. O.

987I   ——[Anr. ed.] —, 1683. brs. O.

987J   ——[Anr. ed.] —, [c. 1690]. brs. O.

987K   ——[Anr. ed.] —, 1693. brs. O.

987L   —To the right worshipful the heads of . . . colleges [orders for ceremony of conveyance of Sheldonian Theatre]. *Oxoford* [sic], *by H. Hall,* 1669. brs. MADAN 2836. O.

988   —To the right worshipful the heads of the respective colleges. . . . You are desired to signify. [*Oxford*], 1685. brs. O.

989 —Verses by the University of Oxford. On the death of . . . Sir Bevill Grenville. *Printed at Oxford*, 1643, *and now reprinted at London*, 1684. 4°. L, O, OC, EC, BR, DM; CH, CN, MH, NP, Y.

990 ——[Anr. ed.] [*Oxford*], printed, 1643. 4°.* MADAN 1436. LT, O, OQ, BR, YM; CH, MH, TU, WF, Y.

990A ——[Anr. ed.] [*London*], printed, 1644. 4°.* GU; MH.

991 —The Vice-chancellour and Major, respectively. [*Oxford*], *August 24*, 1661. brs. MADAN 2567. OA.

991A —May the 11, 1661. [Vice-chancellor's order concerning seats in St. Mary's.] [*Oxford*], 1661. brs. O.

991B —December 3, 1678. [Vice-chancellor's order about soldiers.] [*Oxford*], 1678. brs. MADAN 3191. O.

992 —Vota Oxoniensia. *Oxonii, e theatro Sheldoniano*, 1689. *Prostant venales apud Th. Bennet, London.* fol. L, O, C, OM, MR; CH, CLC, IU, MH, PU, Y.

992A ——[Anr. ed.] *Oxonii, e theatro Sheldoniano*, 1689. fol. O, LIU, MR; WF.

992B —Walter Blandford . . . [notice to allow credit]. [*Oxford*], 1669. MADAN 2665. brs. O.

992C —Whereas Edward Bartlet hath without license . . . [20 July 1670]. [*Oxford*], 1670. brs. MADAN 2857. O.

992D —Whereas formerly . . . [notice by Vice-chancellor, 6 July 1671]. [*Oxford*], 1671.] brs. MADAN 2900. O.

992E —Whereas on Friday last . . . [18 April 1676]. [*Oxford*], 1676.] brs. MADAN 3115. O.

992F —Whereas the appointment . . . [5 April 1669]. [*Oxford*], 1660. brs. MADAN 2835. O.

992G —Whereas the appointment . . . [1 April 1671]. [*Oxford*, 1671.] brs. MADAN 2894. O.

992H —Whereas the appointment . . . [19 April 1672]. [*Oxford*], 1672. brs. MADAN 2935.

992I —Whereas the carriers . . . [4 December 1674]. [*Oxford*], 1674. MADAN 3019. O.

992J —Whereas Tuesday next . . . [27 January 1671/2]. [*Oxford*], 1672. brs. MADAN 2932. O.

992K **Oxford University. All Souls.** Thanksgivings [for founder and benefactors]. [*Oxford, c.* 1690.] fol.* O.

992L —William Powell . . . plaintiffe; the Warden and Fellows of All-Soules Colledge . . . defendants. [*London*], 1656. 4°.* MADAN 2291. O.

992M **Oxford University. Christ Church.** Liber precvm pvblicarum. Third edition. *Oxoniæ, excudebat H. Hall, impensis R. Davis*, 1660. 12°. MADAN 2474. O, OC, CS; IU, Y.

992N ——Fourth edition. *Oxoniæ, excudebat Henricus Hall, impensis Richardi Davis*, 1660. 12°. MADAN 2847. OC, CJ; CLC, Y.

992O ——Fifth edition. *Oxoniæ, e theatro Sheldoniano*, 1676. 12°. MADAN 3129. L, O, LLP, OC; Y, ZAP.

992P ——[Anr. ed.] —, 1689. 12°. O, DU; WF.

992Q **Oxford University. Magdalen College.** [Form of commemoration of the founder.] [*Oxford*, 1660.] brs. MADAN 2519. O.

992R —[Form of prayer for commemoration of founder.] [*Oxford*, 1693.] brs. O.

992S **Oxford University. Merton College.** M. In memoria æterna erit Justus. [*Oxford*, 1660.] brs. MADAN 2520. O.

992T **Oxford University. Trinity College.** Decretum de gratiis collegio rependendis. [*Oxford, after* 1640.] brs. O.

992U **Oxford University. University College.** Alfred the first. [Prayer for founder and benefactors.] [*Oxford*, 1660.] brs. MADAN 2521. O.

992V —[Form of commemoration of the founder.] [*Oxford*, 1675.] brs. MADAN 3070. O.

992W The Oxford vision. [*London*, 1681.] brs. WF.

993 The Oxford wonder: giving a true and strange relation of Mr. Henny [*sic*] Watts. [*London*, 1660?] 8°.* MADAN 2472*. O.

994 Oxfords lamentation. colop: [*London*], *for T. Benskin*, 1681. brs. L, O, DU, LNC; CH, MH, NCD, PU, Y.

995 Oxford-shire Betty. [*London*], *for C. Bates*, [1685?]. brs. L, CM, HH.

996 The Oxfordshire damosel. [*London*], *for J. Deacon*, [1684–85]. brs. L, CM, HH.

Oxinden. *See* Oxenden.

997 Entry cancelled.

[**Oxlad, John.**] Catalogus variorum librorum antiquorum. [n.p.], 1699. *See title.*

997A Oxon: studia. Quadratvra circvli. *Excusum. Prostant apud Oct. Pullein & Tho. Slater*, 1643. brs. MADAN 1577. O.

Oxonia elogia. [n.p., 1673.] *See* Benlowes, Edward.

Oxonian antippodes. 1644. *See* Brandon, John, *gent.*

Oxonii encomium. 1672. *See* Benlowes, Edward.

998 Oxonii lachrymæ, Rachell weeping. *Printed*, 1649. 4°.* MADAN 2012. LT, O, CT, DU; CH, CLC, Y. (var.)

Oxonivm. Poema. Oxon, 1667. *See* Vernon, Francis.

999 **Oxwick, Robert.** The complaint of. [*London*, 1658?] cap., 4°.* L.

1000 Oyes, oyes, oyes. At the quest of inquirie holden. [*London*, 1653.] cap., 4°.* LT, BC.

APPENDIX

A LIST OF CHANGES IN ENTRY NUMBERING
FROM THE FIRST TO THE SECOND EDITION OF VOLUME I
OF THE WING *SHORT-TITLE CATALOGUE*

Most of the number changes from the first to the second edition of Volume I were simple **number shifts**. They resulted either from a correction in alphabetical or chronological order or from additions and/or corrections made in neighboring entries. The new entry almost always can be found close to its original place.

There are other number changes that are not so easy to trace. A few entries are at the **same** locations as before, but with corrections so extensive that the items are unrecognizable. Other items have been **moved to** locations elsewhere in Volume I or in Volumes II or III, because of new author attributions or significant alterations in titles or dates. Some items were inadvertently entered at two or more locations in the first edition. Those that did not appear in the second edition of Volume I are **former duplicates of** those retained at other locations.

Other items have been dropped from the catalogue entirely. A few of these have been **wrongly cancelled** and will be restored in a future supplement. Others have been **lost** through war or fire. Some are true **ghosts**. Many have been identified as items outside the scope of the Wing catalogue: **serials**, imprints with **dates** before 1641 or after 1700, and products of **foreign printing**. Some were **not separately published**; most of these have been identified as **part of** other Wing items.

Most of these changes are self-explanatory, but some require additional information, which has been provided. "1st ed." refers to the first edition of Volume I. The "2nd ed." numbers come from the second edition of Volumes I and II, the projected second edition of Volume III, and a projected supplement to Volume I. The symbol "+" has been assigned to incomplete numbers that have yet to receive their letter designations in Volume III or the supplement.

A

448	former duplicate of S3176	927	part of F386
452A	number shift A453	961A	number shift A961B
453	number shift A454	967	former duplicate of A1015
454	former duplicate of G488	968	number shift A967
461	number shift A460	969	number shift A968
462	number shift A461	974	number shift A974A
466	former duplicate of W1183	975A	number shift A975B
474	wrongly cancelled A473+ Suppl.	1006	part of A989
475	number shift A474	1074	moved to A1016A
502	former duplicate of P1661	1132	former duplicate of A1131
550	former duplicate of H3384	1132A	number shift A1132
551	number shift A550	1205	former duplicate of A930
552	number shift A551	1237	wrongly cancelled 1236+ Suppl.
554	Guildhall — lost [Address of the sope-makers. [London, 1650.]]	1356A	wrongly cancelled A1356A Suppl.
		1386A	former duplicate of A1323
555	number shift A554	1410	former duplicate of A1393
558	former duplicate of A559	1411	former duplicate of A1394
590	former duplicate of M1322	1412	former duplicate of A1395
593A	former duplicate of A598	1414	former duplicate of A1413
597	moved to P448+ Parker, Matthew.	1452	number shift A1452A
601	moved to D827B	1472	moved to A1984AA
610	former duplicate of P2819A	1473	moved to A1984AB
610A	number shift A610	1474	moved to A1984B
619	former duplicate of H219	1475	moved to A1984D
620	moved to B4741	1476	moved to A1984C
630A	number shift A630B	1477	moved to A1984E
638	former duplicate of A639	1478	moved to A1984EA
640	number shift A638	1479	moved to A1984I
654	date: 1708	1480	moved to A1984J
663	Guildhall — lost [Advice to the unwary. 1685.]	1481	moved to A1984K
		1482	moved to A1984L
667	former duplicate of N401	1483	moved to A1984M
668	number shift A667	1484	moved to A1984N
675	former duplicate of A674	1485	moved to A1984O
681A	number shift A682	1486	moved to A1984P
682	former duplicate of A683	1487	moved to A1984Q
690A	former duplicate of A696	1488	moved to A1984R
694	former duplicate of A696	1489	moved to A1984S
750	moved to E2787A	1490	moved to A1984T
761	moved to J661A	1491	moved to A1985A
797	number shift A796	1492	moved to A1985B
844	former duplicate of D649	1493	number shift A1472
845	former duplicate of D650	1565	number shift A1570A
878	number shift A877	1584	former duplicate of A1585
883	former duplicate of T1841	1707	wrongly cancelled A1707 Suppl.
884	number shift A883	1788	wrongly cancelled A1791+ Suppl.
895	moved to A2940A	1814	number shift A1814A
915	former duplicate of T476	1854	former duplicate of A1322
916	number shift A915	1876	number shift A1876A
916A	number shift A916	1919A	number shift A1920

1920	former duplicate of A1439
1925	number shift A1926
1926	wrongly cancelled A1925+ Suppl.
1934	number shift A1935
1935	number shift A1934
1998	number shift A1999
1999	number shift A2000
2000	number shift A1998
2004	number shift A2004A
2015	former duplicate of A2003
2016	number shift A2015
2128	number shift A2128A
2219A	number shift A2220
2220	number shift A2221
2221	former duplicate of A1943
2312	former duplicate of A1842
2313	wrongly cancelled A2381+ Suppl.
2540	number shift A2541
2541	number shift A2542
2542	Guildhall — lost [Thee and thou almanack. 1649.]
2643	former duplicate of A2018
2644	number shift A2643
2645	number shift A2644
2928	former duplicate of M1836
2929	number shift A2928
2933	number shift A2933A
3017	former duplicate of B4343
3018	moved to C6596B
3026	number shift A3027
3027	part of A3023
3035	former duplicate of A3036
3049	moved to J1019A
3050	moved to J1019B
3063	moved to B5752A
3064	date: 1720
3127	number shift A3128
3128	moved to A3127
3129	moved to A3142A
3134	part of A3138
3134A	number shift A3134
3152	part of A3140
3153	number shift A3152; also, part of C1687A
3155	former duplicate of C2758
3156	number shift A3155
3157	number shift A3156
3161	moved to F2408
3162	number shift A3161
3162A	number shift A3162
3177	wrongly cancelled A3176+ Suppl.

3183	former duplicate of H2094
3186	moved to C5718
3188	wrongly cancelled C7431+ Suppl.
3193A	moved to A11A
3199	former duplicate of T3099
3199A	number shift A3199
3215	moved to D1187A
3246	number shift A3247
3253A	number shift A3254
3254	former duplicate of R1033A
3267	number shift A3268
3268	number shift A3267
3272	moved to E2517A
3274A	former duplicate of M3144
3276	moved to R22A+ R., J.
3291	Guildhall — lost [Answer of the Corporation of Weavers. [Dublin, 1695.]]
3296	date: [1621] STC 16777.14
3302	former duplicate of A3290
3321	moved to C1868A
3326	number shift A3325
3342	number shift A3343
3343	number shift A3344
3344	former duplicate of F2340
3352	number shift A3353
3353	number shift A3354
3360	number shift A3361
3361	number shift A3362
3362	former duplicate of A3363
3383	former duplicate of S3562
3384	number shift A3383
3384A	number shift A3384
3394	number shift A3394A
3403	number shift A3404
3408	wrongly cancelled A3407+ Suppl.
3437	former duplicate of A3178
3438	number shift A3437
3455	moved to S3264+ Sherlock, William.
3456	former duplicate of M299
3457A	number shift A3457B
3525	former duplicate of K660
3534	number shift A3535
3535	number shift A3536
3536	number shift A3534
3548	number shift A3549
3549	number shift A3550
3550	former duplicate of H3402
3597	moved to M1416A
3598	moved to M1416B
3599	moved to M1416C

3606	number shift A3607	3843	number shift A3844
3607	former duplicate of A3609	3844	number shift A3843
3639	number shift A3640	3867	moved to C4009B
3642	number shift A3643	3868	moved to C4009C
3643	number shift A3644	3891	former duplicate of E581
3644	former duplicate of S2753	3893	former duplicate of E581
3646	former duplicate of S4637	3894	former duplicate of G623
3664	moved to S2024+ The Scots declaration.	3904	former duplicate of A3901
3665A	number shift A3665	3919	same as A3919 [title corrected]
3671A	number shift A3672	3980	number shift A3979
3672	number shift A3673	3989	wrongly cancelled A4035A+ Suppl.
3673	former duplicate of C1066	3990	number shift A3989
3687	former duplicate of G1021	3991	number shift A3990
3689A	number shift A3689B	4021	moved to G1981A
3689B	number shift A3689C	4021A	moved to G1981B
3720	moved to L307A	4036	wrongly cancelled A4035A+ Suppl.
3721	moved to L307B	4037	same as A4037 [title shortened; anr. ed. of former A4036]
3722	moved to B5241A		
3723	number shift A3721	4087B	moved to L2852L
3724	number shift A3722	4088A	number shift A4088AA
3724A	number shift A3723	4105	number shift A4106
3725	number shift A3724	4122	former duplicate of T3234
3728	foreign printing: Paris	4167	moved to C725
3767	number shift A3768	4204	former duplicate of T2069
3768	number shift A3767	4254	former duplicate of M2297
3774	former duplicate of A3778	4255	number shift A4254
3796	former duplicate of N553	4256	number shift A4255
3797	number shift A3796	4274	moved to G1604A
3798	number shift A3797	4275A	number shift A4275B
3820	number shift A3821	4283	number shift A4284
3821	number shift A3822	4284	number shift A4285
3822	former duplicate of E1230	4285	number shift A4286
3837	moved to O437B	4307	number shift A4308
3838	former duplicate of C4009A	4308	moved to E703A

B

1056	number shift B1056A
1074	former duplicate of B1077
1076	number shift B1077
1077	number shift B1078
1078	number shift B1080
1140	moved to B526A
1160A	number shift B1160B
1193	former duplicate of B1182
1240	number shift B1241
1241	number shift B1242
1242	former duplicate of C4571
1250A	number shift B1251
1251	former duplicate of B1212
1252	former duplicate of B1439
1264	former duplicate of F104
1270	former duplicate of B1328
1272	number shift B1270
1273	number shift B1271
1295	number shift B1294
1296	number shift B1295
1297	number shift B1296
1316	former duplicate of B1315
1317	number shift B1316
1318	number shift B1317
1319	number shift B1318
1360	former duplicate of B1282
1368	former duplicate of T1838
1369	part of B1276
1383	number shift B1383A
1461	number shift B1462
1462	number shift B1463
1463	number shift B1464
1464	number shift B1465
1465	number shift B1466
1470A	former duplicate of S4467
1473D	former duplicate of B1473C
1477A	number shift B1477B
1478A	number shift B1479
1479	number shift B1480
1480	number shift B1481
1481	date: [1633]
1498	former duplicate of B1497
1499	ghost
1500	number shift B1499
1504	number shift B1505
1505	date: [1706]
1505A	date: [1730]
1546	wrongly cancelled B1546+ Suppl.
1551	moved to B1546

[1552A]	number shift B1551 [number not printed in 1st ed.]
1558A	former duplicate of B1558
1560A	number shift B1560B
1563	former duplicate of W2168
1649A	moved to C1686A
1655A	number shift B1655B
1679	number shift B1678
1679A	number shift B1679
1709	former duplicate of S4198
1709A	number shift B1709
1718	number shift B1717
1725	former duplicate of B1771
1725A	part of B1773
1732	number shift B1733
1733	former duplicate of D2505
1741	moved to B1743A
1742	number shift 1741
1773A	part of B1772
1773B	number shift B1773A
1801	number shift B1802
1802	number shift B1803
1803	part of B1804
1823	former duplicate of N1392
1833	foreign printing: Prague
1834	date: 1767
1849	moved to A3021B
1856	moved to P3026+ Potable balsome.
1857	former duplicate of P3207B
1858	moved to R1204+ The reviv'd fugitive.
1883A	number shift B1883B
1905	moved to T3370+ Tutchin, John.
1947	number shift B1947A
1948	number shift B1948A
1953	number shift B1953A
1977	former duplicate of S5255
1982A	number shift B1982B
1993	moved to E3949A
2001	former duplicate of B1064
2038	moved to A4217B
2039	moved to A4217C
2040	moved to A4223A
2041	moved to A4223B
2047	former duplicate of B2048
2052A	number shift B2052B
2096	former duplicate of B2114
2154	number shift B2154A
2187	number shift B2188A
2188	number shift B2187
2188A	number shift B2188

2194	former duplicate of B2801	3108A	number shift B3108B
2197	ghost	3169	wrongly cancelled B3169 Suppl.
2201	number shift B2201A	3208	number shift B3209
2227	part of B2230	3209	number shift B3210
2329	former duplicate of B2319	3210	date: 1715
2371	number shift B2371A	3223	former duplicate of N171
2487A	number shift B2488A	3230	ghost
2515	part of R1588	3231	moved to G343A
2527A	number shift B2527B	3272	former duplicate of S140
2585	number shift B2585B	3290	former duplicate of F2080
2602A	number shift B2602B	3295	former duplicate of E3454
2604A	number shift B2604B	3300A	number shift B3300B
2611	same as B2611 [title correction]	3320	former duplicate of B3333
2633A	number shift B2634	3343	part of B3342
2633D	moved to B3860A	3355	moved to D2759A
2634	moved to B3860B	3356	number shift B3355
2637A	number shift B2637C	3356A	number shift B3356
2669	part of B2278	3360	moved to B3295A
2721	former duplicate of B2719A	3375A	former duplicate of S5454
2722	number shift B2723	3377	former duplicate of M2772
2723	former duplicate of D2648	3391	former duplicate of B3903
2724	former duplicate of D2649	3435	moved to C1551C
supra 2729	former duplicate of B2801	3436	number shift B3435
infra 2729	moved to B2728	3437	number shift B3436
2738	number shift B2739	3437A	number shift B3437
2739	number shift B2740	3444	former duplicate of A46
2770A	number shift B2770B	3514	moved to B414A
2770B	number shift B2770C	3523	number shift B3523A
2805A	number shift B2806	3525	moved to B3833A
2806	number shift B2807	3526	moved to B3833B
2807	number shift B2808	3575	same as B3575 [date changed; title expanded]
2831	moved to A801A		
2842	former duplicate of B2862	3581	number shift B3583
2864A	number shift B2864E	3595C	number shift B3596
2869	number shift B2870	3596	part of B784
2871	part of B2882	3603A	number shift B3603B
2887	part of D84	3732	former duplicate of B3731
2891	serial	3733	number shift B3732
2892	former duplicate of E2533	3772	former duplicate of B6128A
2897	date: 1733/4	3773	former duplicate of B6128A
2913	number shift B2913aA	3774	former duplicate of B6129
2925	number shift B2924A	3775	moved to B6129A
2934A	number shift B2934B	3776	number shift B3771A
2934B	number shift B2934C	3777	number shift B3772
2967A	number shift B2967C	3777A	number shift B3773
2967B	number shift B2967D	3777B	number shift B3774
3017	wrongly cancelled B3017 Suppl.	3777C	number shift B3775
3031	former duplicate of H2461A	3777D	number shift B3776
3040	moved to W140+ W., W.	3777E	number shift B3777
3097	former duplicate of B3098	3807	date: [1705

3811	number shift B3810
3831A	date: 1714
3846	former duplicate of C7448
3846A	number shift B3846
3846B	number shift B3846A
3846C	number shift B3846B
3879	former duplicate of S2327
3907	part of B3906
3908	part of B3906
3915	same as B3915 [title change]
3919	number shift B3919A
3919A	ghost
3963	part of B3950
3986	former duplicate of B4063
3987	former duplicate of B3986
4007	part of B3930
4052	number shift B4052A
4085	moved to B4400A
4085A	number shift B4085
4087	moved to B4152B
4088	number shift B4087
4097A	number shift B4098
4097B	number shift B4099
4098	moved to E252B
4099	moved to E252C
4113	moved to B4114
4114	moved to B4113
4205	Guildhall — lost [Brahe, Tycho. Predictions of the destruction of the Turkish Empire. 1684.]
4211A	number shift B4212
4212	number shift B4213
4213	moved to A3457A
4224	former duplicate of B4220
4231	number shift B4228A
4263	wrongly cancelled B4267
4288	number shift B4288A
4296A	number shift B4296E
4335	former duplicate of V659
4349A	number shift B4349C
4349B	number shift B4349D
4411	ghost
4477	former duplicate of B1285
4483A	moved to B4484A
4492	former duplicate of C666
4498	moved to C6482A
4499	number shift B4498
4500A	number shift B4501
4501	former duplicate of W3437
4526	former duplicate of D1931
4545	former duplicate of B4539
4549	former duplicate of C1934
4567	number shift B4567A
4579	part of O396
4593	moved to L68A
4601	moved to H2005B
4602	number shift B4601
4605	wrongly cancelled B4435+ Suppl.
4619	moved to E498A
4636	moved to V253+ Vernon, Samuel.
4639	moved to C128A
4647	moved to M2826B
4648	number shift B4647
4651	moved to B4653B
4657	former duplicate of J683
4680	number shift B4681
4681	part of B4679
4699	moved to B112AB
4700	number shift B4699
4727	part of B4719
4732	part of B4715
4740	serial
4741	serial
4792	former duplicate of T1042
4793	wrongly cancelled D1420+ Suppl.
4815	number shift B4814
4818	moved to A2975A
4820	former duplicate of H2956
4824A	number shift B4824B
4829	date: 1621
4830	wrongly cancelled B4830 Suppl.; also part of J147
4838	part of B304
4861	moved to B4858A
4881	part of B4872
4894	moved to B4903A
4909	part of S1326
4928A	number shift B4928D
4951A	number shift B4951B
4975A	number shift B4975B
5032	wrongly cancelled B5032 Suppl.
5042A	number shift B5042B
5062	moved to B5184A
5068A	moved to C7398
5113	former duplicate of C3800
5113A	number shift B5113
5123	part of B5122
5146	moved to B5141C
5166	number shift B5167
5167	number shift B5166

5180	former duplicate of K488 and S4286
5184A	part of B5184
5219	fragment of a 1706 work
5289	date: 1569
5309	number shift B5309A
5315	former duplicate of G733A
5331	number shift B5332
5332	part of S2907
5335	wrongly cancelled C1991+ Suppl.
5356	part of B5361
5362A	number shift B5362B
5363	number shift B5363A
5374A	number shift B5374B
5396	date: 1707/8
5396A	number shift B5396
5471	moved to B4846A
5473A	moved to P572+ Parsons, Robert.
5511	former duplicate of B5541
5555	number shift B5555A
5555A	number shift B5555
5609	former duplicate of G2171
5610	former duplicate of G2172
5617	moved to K436B
5637	part of B5634

5660	part of B5646
5717	moved to O804A
5726	moved to A801A
5821	moved to L1686A
5844	former duplicate of P214
5887	former duplicate of B5891
5910	former duplicate of B5841
5941	former duplicate of H1878A
5956	former duplicate of W1698
5967A	former duplicate of F1865
6037	former duplicate of H3184
6062	part of B6125B
6087	former duplicate of B6089
6120	part of B6100
6121	part of B6084A
6188	date: [1707]
6229	number shift B6229A
6244	part of B304
6267A	number shift B6267C
6331	part of C6697
6340	moved to P4252+ Puttock, Roger. Good and true newes.
6387	ghost

C

1st ed.	2nd ed.
18	number shift 18A
24	moved to N592A
25	number shift C24
28	moved to G1476A
42	former duplicate of A787
52A	number shift C52C
54	wrongly cancelled C752+ Suppl.; also part of C753
63	moved to R2088+ Rowlands, Samuel.
82	moved to C2526A
93	moved to E3706aA
98	moved to C1817D
99	moved to C1817E
100	moved to C1817G
110	serial
119	moved to D2686A
120	moved to D2686B
123	moved to C7372

130	moved to C1817C
131	moved to C7437A
133	moved to N1103A
147	moved to C632A
168	number shift C167
190	moved to L1051A
197	former duplicate of L917
202A	former duplicate of S4666
210	number shift C210A
283	former duplicate of C5596
284	moved to C5597A
301	moved to C207B
302	former duplicate of T1751
322	former duplicate of C321
324	former duplicate of C326A
364	number shift C365
365	moved to C364
368A	number shift C368B
371A	number shift C371B
372A	number shift C372B

372B	number shift C372D	881	moved to C879
379	moved to C382A	887	Guildhall — lost [The case of Capt. James Watts. 1684.]
382A	number shift C382B		
382B	number shift C382C	897	number shift C896
403	same as C403 [title correction]	898	number shift C897
410	moved to W2111+ Wigmore, William.	905A	number shift C906
411	part of S3803	906	former duplicate of H1415
425A	number shift C425B	912A	number shift C912C
426	former duplicate of C433	913	former duplicate of C591
442C	number shift C442D	939A	former duplicate of R1890
454	former duplicate of N702	945A	number shift C946
500	number shift C502	946	number shift C947
501	former duplicate of E871	947	date: [1702]
521	serial	959	moved to W285+ Walcot, William.
556	number shift C557	964	former duplicate S324
557	number shift C556	965	number shift C964
569	former duplicate of T2431	1005	wrongly cancelled C1004A+ Suppl.
569A	former duplicate of T2433	1007	date: [1717]
570	former duplicate of T2432	1008	number shift C1007
581	number shift C581A	1025	date: [1720]
593A	number shift C593B	1027A	date: [1718]
598	former duplicate of D130A	1028	number shift C1029
628	former duplicate of V458	1029	number shift C1030
629	number shift C628	1030	number shift C1028
635	former duplicate of P2273	1036	former duplicate of C1035
654A	number shift C655	1037	number shift C1038
655	part of C654	1038	date: [1702]
657	part of C654	1042	date: [1715]
660	former duplicate of C659	1047	wrongly cancelled C1047 Suppl.
661	number shift C660	1050	number shift C1049
673	number shift C674	1051	number shift C1050
674	former duplicate of C675	1054	former duplicate of C1055
684	former duplicate of B1507	1058	date: [1732]
685	former duplicate of B1508	1059	number shift C1058
725	wrongly cancelled C725+ Suppl.	1059A	number shift C1059B
732	number shift C732A	1065A	number shift C1065B
736	former duplicate of A169	1077A	number shift C1077B
737	number shift C736	1081	date: [1711]
737A	number shift C737	1089	date: [1704]
777A	number shift C778	1090	date: [1718]
778	moved to C4796A	1091	number shift C1090
851	moved to N1380A	1094	Guildhall — lost [The case of the Isle of Oxholm. 1660.]
852	former duplicate of P3127		
854	date: [1708]	1104A	date: 1711
855	Guildhall — lost [The case between the Dean and chapter. 1687.]	1107	number shift C1108
		1108	date: [1718]
864A	number shift C864B	1112	date: [1702]
864B	number shift C864C	1113	number shift C1112
879	number shift C880	1114	date: [1705]
880	number shift C881	1114A	number shift C1114B

1115A	date: [1711]	1406	former duplicate of D2471
1116	date: [1732]	1432	former duplicate of A672
1116A	number shift C1116	1436	date: 1639 STC 17514
1123	date: [1719]	1437	former duplicate of S2078
1124	wrongly cancelled C1123+ Suppl.	1438	former duplicate of S2080
1132A	former duplicate of C964	1441	former duplicate of P2304
1133	former duplicate of O843	1452	moved to S4959+ Spencer, John, *Librarian.*
1136	date: [1703]	1458	former duplicate of L610
1140	date: [1704]	1475A	moved to R2005+ Roucourt, Jean.
1146	Guildhall — lost [Case of the proprietor of annual payments. 1700.]	1481	number shift C1481A
		1492	former duplicate of C4592
1147	date: [1705]	1493	number shift C1492
1149	date: [1705]	1493A	number shift C1493
1153	Guildhall — lost [Case of the rector and visitor. 1689.]	1497	moved to H2605A
		1506A	number shift C1506C
1154	number shift C1153	1521	moved to T1088+ Three general epistles.
1155	number shift C1154	1522	number shift C1523
1158	number shift C1159	1523	former duplicate of A3253
1159	date: [1703]	1540	former duplicate of G1121
1161	date: [1709-10]	1589A	wrongly cancelled C1589A Suppl.
1163	date: [1718]	1622	Guildhall — lost [Cawdrey, Daniel. The account audited. 1678.]
1171	former duplicate of C1170		
1172	date: [1712]	1635A	number shift 1635B
1185	former duplicate of E656	1660	Guildhall — lost [Cellier, Elizabeth. Answers to queries. 1687/8.]
1197	number shift C1198		
1198	former duplicate of W2255	1661A	part of C1661
1211	former duplicate of K122	1666	former duplicate of C6415
1218	moved to S2166+ Scupoli, Lorenzo.	1667	moved to E2791A
1218A	moved to S2166+ Scupoli, Lorenzo.	1668	moved to Y76+ Young, Samuel.
1218B	moved to S2166+ Scupoli, Lorenzo.	1677	moved to L1330C
1219	moved to S2166+ Scupoli, Lorenzo.	1727	number shift C1726
1220	moved to S2166+ Scupoli, Lorenzo.	1761	former duplicate of C1687A
1232	same as C1232 [author corrected]	1780	moved to S4803+ The spanish decameron.
1238	former duplicate of D2018	1811	former duplicate of C5645A
1239	number shift C1238	1812	number shift C1810
1243	number shift C1244	1813	number shift C1812
1244	former duplicate of L2683	1859	moved to D2682A
1269	number shift C1268	1860	number shift C1859
1276	number shift C1277	1877A	number shift C1878
1277	number shift C1276	1878	ghost
1279	wrongly cancelled C1324+ Suppl.	1879A	number shift C1879B
1288	moved to O863I	1894	number shift C1894A
1309	Guildhall — lost [Catalogue of divers Italian pictures. 1684.]	1899	moved to C1817H
		1900	number shift C1899
1340	serial	1900A	number shift C1900
1363	moved to W462+ Walkley, Thomas.	1902	moved to P4149+ Public bathes.
1364	number shift C1363	1950	ghost
1364A	number shift C1364	1962	number shift C1963
1374	former duplicate of C7367	1963	moved to A2975AB
1396	former duplicate of N591	1995C	number shift A1996

1996	former duplicate of C6086	2913	part of C2897
2026A	date: 1721	2914	part of C2899
2059	number shift C2060	2917	number shift C2918
2061	moved to C4201K	2918	number shift C2919
2062	former duplicate of E2537	2919	former duplicate of E2887
2065	moved to I28A	2922	former duplicate of E853
2066	Guildhall — lost [Charitable design recommended. 1699.]	2923	former duplicate of E807
		2924	former duplicate of E829
2087	former duplicate of A826	2925A	former duplicate of E856
2103A	wrongly cancelled C2103A Suppl.	2925B	former duplicate of E805
2120	former duplicate of C2320	2926	former duplicate of E813
2129	former duplicate of C2131A	2927A	former duplicate of E835
2157	former duplicate of C5110	2927B	former duplicate of E809
2161	former duplicate of S1489	2927C	former duplicate of E839
2172	moved to B4849A	2927D	former duplicate of E811
2220	former duplicate of C2982	2927E	former duplicate of E841
2221	wrongly cancelled C2982+ Suppl.	2927F	former duplicate of E820
2276	former duplicate of H2082	2927G	former duplicate of E846
2313A	number shift C2314	2927H	former duplicate of E803
2314	number shift C2315	2927I	former duplicate of E798
2331A	former duplicate of C2331	2928	former duplicate of E831
2334A	number shift C2335	2928A	former duplicate of E837
2335	number shift C2336	2928B	former duplicate of E832
2336	former duplicate of C2337	2928C	former duplicate of E808
2353	former duplicate of C5036	2940	Guildhall — lost [Charles II. His Majesties commission to . . . examine the pretended sales. 1660.]
2361	number shift C2362		
2362	moved to G1895A		
2389	former duplicate of S534		
2390	number shift C2389	2996	moved to C3001A
2391	number shift C2390	3003	number shift C3004
2391A	number shift C2391	3004	number shift C3005
2489A	number shift C2490	3005	former duplicate of C2998
2490	number shift C2491	3039A	number shift C3040
2491	number shift C2492	3040	former duplicate of S1505
2492	former duplicate of C2493	3111	former duplicate of C3097A
2524A	number shift C2525	3117	former duplicate of C2411
2525	number shift C2526	3118	number shift C3117
2526	number shift C2526A	3118A	number shift C3118
2532	former duplicate of E1788	3166	former duplicate of J225
2550A	number shift C2550B	3167	former duplicate of J228
2550B	number shift C2550C	3191A	former duplicate of N727 and C3193
2698	number shift C2697	3218	former duplicate of S1594
2719	Guildhall — lost [Charles I. Proposals for reprinting the works of. 1686.]	3219	former duplicate of S1595
		3294	former duplicate of S1767
2720	number shift C2719	3295	former duplicate of S1768
2721	number shift C2720	3295A	number shift C3295
2735	former duplicate of S5243A	3515A	wrongly cancelled C3515A Suppl.
2805	number shift C2805A	3521	former duplicate of S1951
2887A	number shift C2887	3596A	number shift C3596B
2912A	number shift C2913	3597A	former duplicate of C3207

3597B	number shift C3597A	4072A	number shift C4072C
3598A	former duplicate of C3206	4084A	number shift C4084D
3598B	number shift C3598A	4084B	number shift C4084F
3601A	number shift C3602	4084C	number shift C4084G
3602	former duplicate of B5619	4091A	number shift C4091F
3604A	moved to R2103+ Royal Charter.	4091B	number shift C4091G
3604B	number shift C3604A	4091C	number shift C4091I
3656	former duplicate of O843	4091D	number shift C4091J
3662	number shift C3663	4091E	number shift C4091K
3663	part of C3694	4091F	number shift C4091L
3664	part of C3695	4091G	number shift C4091M
3665	number shift C3664	4091H	number shift C4091N
3666	number shift C3665	4091I	number shift C4091Q
3667	number shift C3666	4092	former duplicate of S4825
3667A	number shift C3667	4093	wrongly cancelled C4091R+ Suppl.
3701	Guildhall — lost [Charnock, Robert.	4094	former duplicate of S4824
	Mr. Charnock's letter. 1696.]	4094A	number shift C4092
3702	former duplicate of T2654	4094B	number shift C4093
3725	number shift C3726	4094C	number shift C4094
3726	number shift C3727	4094D	ghost
3727	former duplicate of S4662	4094E	moved to C5625
3734A	number shift C3734C	4094F	moved to C5626
3757A	number shift C3757D	4103A	number shift C4103C
3757B	number shift C3758	4103B	number shift C4103D
3758	number shift C3759	4103C	number shift C4103E
3760	moved to S5376+ Steede, Robert.	4103D	number shift C4103F
3766	number shift C3767	4103E	number shift C4104
3770	date: [1710]	4104	former duplicate of C4211
3782A	wrongly cancelled C3782A Suppl.	4123	number shift C4125A
3813	former duplicate of E3234	4149	former duplicate of C4172
3829C	number shift C3830	4174	number shift C4175
3830	date: [1622] STC 5134-5	4175	ghost
3859	former duplicate of C3853	4176	former duplicate of C4173
3880	number shift C3888B	4177	number shift C4176
3881	number shift C3888C	4181A	number shift C4181B
3882	number shift C3888D	4182	number shift C4183
3888	number shift C3888A	4183	number shift C4184
3908	former duplicate of C5119	4184	number shift C4185 [title wrongly altered]
3925	moved to A2975AC	4185	number shift C4186
3941	moved to B3477A	4186	moved to W1442+ Westminster assembly
3942	former duplicate of B1218		of divines.
3943	number shift C3942	4187	former duplicate of W1443
3959	former duplicate of T948	4188	number shift C4187
3960	number shift C3959	4188A	number shift C4188
3961	number shift C3960	4188B	number shift C4188A
3965A	number shift C3965B	4188E	former duplicate of D2690
3994A	date: 1710	4190A	number shift C4190C
4033A	number shift C4033D	4190B	number shift C4190D
4058A	number shift C4064A	4190C	number shift C4190E
4070A	number shift C4070C	4190D	number shift C4190F

4195	moved to B1949B	4867	ghost
4196A	number shift C4196F	4890	same as C4890 [title change]
4196B	number shift C4196G	4895A	former duplicate of T181
4201A	former duplicate of C4201D	4895B	former duplicate of T182
4216A	former duplicate of S1203	4934	former duplicate of A3969
4228	moved to W1440+ Westminster assembly of divines.	4935	former duplicate of A3970
		4936	former duplicate of A3971
4229A	number shift C4229B	5016	moved to C6600B
4229B	number shift C4229E	5022	former duplicate of C6683
4231E	number shift C4232	5142	former duplicate of R1034
4232	former duplicate of H1432	5150	former duplicate of C5200B
4232A	number shift C4232B	5168A	former duplicate of C5638A
4251A	number shift C4251B	5175	former duplicate of C5178
4251B	number shift C4251D	5192A	number shift C5192B
4258A	number shift C4258B	5192B	number shift C5193
4269A	number shift C4269B	5200A	number shift C5200B
4274A	number shift C4274	5226A	moved to R280+ Ra-ree show.
4278	wrongly cancelled C4277+ Suppl.	5226B	number shift C5226A
4316A	number shift C4316B	5243	former duplicate of C5249
4326	former duplicate of B5767	5337	former duplicate of D449
4366	Guildhall — lost [Civil wars in England. 1700.]	5377	part of M365
		5386	moved to C5384A
4394	former duplicate of C4395	5401A	wrongly cancelled C5401A Suppl.
4418	former duplicate of C4423	5403A	number shift C5403D
4422	former duplicate of C5198	5403B	number shift C5403E
4468A	number shift C4468D	5417	moved to C5422A
4498A	former duplicate of C4498	5418	moved to C5422B
4500	wrongly cancelled C4500 Suppl.	5439	moved to A3918C
4513A	ghost	5507A	number shift C5507B
4519	moved to H2094A	5518A	moved to C5508A
4520	moved to H2094B	5548	former duplicate of C5549
4521	moved to H2094C	5579	moved to W881+ Warmstrey, Thomas.
4522	moved to H2094D	5593A	wrongly cancelled C5593A Suppl.
4567	moved to F2368A	5597	number shift C5597A
4597A	Guildhall — lost [Clause in the confirmation. 1663.]	5597A	number shift C5597B
		5597B	number shift C5597C
4608B	number shift C4609	5598A	number shift C5598B
4609	serial	5604	former duplicate of B5804
4624	moved to C4641A	5605	former duplicate of W681A
4646	wrongly cancelled D2055B+ Suppl.	5610	former duplicate of L433
4665	ghost	5642	number shift C5642A
4745	date: 1636 STC 5451	5649	former duplicate of D1792
4747	moved to C983A	5650	number shift C5649
4783	moved to V398+ Vincent, Humphrey.	5655	moved to B3738C
		5656	moved to B3738D
4785A	number shift C4786	5657	moved to B3738E
4786	moved to C4793A	5664	former duplicate of C4101
4787	moved to C4794A	5683	former duplicate of P2937
4788	former duplicate of P882	5695A	number shift C5695B
4805	number shift C4806	5699	moved to F1775B
4806	date: 1708		

5718	number shift C5719		6380C	number shift C6380B
5733	former duplicate of F2112		6386	former duplicate of F102
5734	former duplicate of F2113		6398A	number shift C6398B
5735	moved to F2113A		6404	former duplicate of N929
5736	moved to L2089A		6405	number shift C6404
5743A	number shift C5743B		6442	moved to C6473A
5758A	former duplicate of C5809		6483	former duplicate of S4233
5777	former duplicate of C5769		6484	former duplicate of S2083
5808	moved to H343A		6583A	number shift C6583B
5821A	number shift C5821B		6584	moved to H2187A
5833	moved to A2BB		6597A	number shift C6597C
5839	moved to D2621A		6624	former duplicate of D350A
5878A	number shift C5878B		6624A	number shift C6624
5883	former duplicate of C5993		6624B	number shift C6624A
5905	moved to C5912A		6632	former duplicate of Q220
5908A	number shift C5908B		6633	number shift C6632
5911	Guildhall — lost [Considerations offered in relation to the excessive price of corn. [London, 1698.]]		C6633A	number shift C6633
			6676	part of C6657
			6683	number shift C6682
5915	date: 1716		6683A	number shift C6683
5916	moved to C5915		6690	number shift C6691
5917	number shift C5916		6691	former duplicate of B3887
5925	moved to N495A		6701	moved to C6730
5927	former duplicate of H2218		6714	former duplicate of D575
5954	former duplicate of G2234		6728	number shift C6729
5955	number shift C5954		6729	date: 19th c. (t.p.)
5968	serial		6747	former duplicate of C6760
5977A	number shift C5977B		6777	moved to W163+ Wade, John.
5980	former duplicate of W3693		6789	former duplicate of T1813
6126	former duplicate of E1285		6820	former duplicate of C6818
6127	moved to E1285A		6821	moved to C6851B
6128	moved to C6129A		6822	number shift C6821
6152	moved to A901A		6822A	number shift C6822
6188	former duplicate of D2410		6842	former duplicate of C6841
6202	former duplicate of T2636		6850	former duplicate of C6841
6206	moved to E2543+ Suppl.		6851	number shift C6850
6212A	former duplicate of T2650		6855	former duplicate of W1312
6215	number shift C6216		6856	number shift C6855
6227	Guildhall — lost [Copy of the project for the reunion. 1685.]		6857	number shift C6856
			6882	wrongly cancelled C7431+ Suppl.
6273	former duplicate of C6272		6897	ghost
6294A	number shift C6294B		6901	number shift C6901A [anr. ed. of C6900]
6306A	number shift C6307		6903	moved to W2070+ Why are you.
6307	number shift C6308		6904	moved to C6903
6308	former duplicate of C6308		6919	moved to C6936C
6312	number shift C6311		6920	number shift C6919
6320	part of P2033		6921	number shift C6920
6380	former duplicate of S5869A		6921A	number shift C6921
6380A	number shift C6380		6936A	number shift C6936B
6380B	number shift C6380A		6944	number shift C6945

6945	former duplicate of C6945
7004	number shift C7004A
7015	ghost
7037	moved to L3047A
7045	former duplicate of E1271
7121A	number shift C7121G
7170A	number shift C7170B
7228A	number shift C7229
7229	number shift C7230
7230	number shift C7231
7231	date: 1615
7268A	number shift C7268B
7277A	number shift C7277C
7277B	number shift C7277D
7297A	wrongly cancelled C7297A Suppl.
7343	date: [1715]
7344	former duplicate of F1336
7371	moved to S2412+ Segar, Francis.
7372	number shift C7371
7428	former duplicate of B3862

7443	wrongly cancelled C7438+ Suppl. [Earnest plea.]
7447A	number shift C7448
7448	number shift C7449
7449	former duplicate of B2990
7449A	number shift C7449B
7449B	number shift C7449C
7463	moved to C7464
7464	number shift C7463
7487	part of C7518
7515	former duplicate of M2719
7517	former duplicate of G159
7518	number shift C7517
7519	number shift C7518
7608	date: [1633]
7620A	former duplicate of C7621
7677	former duplicate of C7678
7698	number shift C7698A
7710A	number shift C7710D

D

1st ed.	2nd ed.
1	number shift D2
2	number shift D3
8	moved to D1827B
17	moved to R1772+ Rodriguez, Alonso.
18	number shift D17
20A	number shift D21
20B	number shift D22
21	number shift D23
22	former duplicate of D449
24	part of C5103
29	number shift D28
30	number shift D29
30A	moved to B645A
36	moved to G1895A
38	moved to D395
69	moved to P572+ Parsons, Robert.
93	moved to D2751A
104A	moved to D101B
116	moved to L2593A
140	former duplicate of D139
180	wrongly cancelled C6487+ Suppl.

198	moved to J514A
241	former duplicate of O163
253	wrongly cancelled D253 Suppl.
255	wrongly cancelled C5583+ Suppl.
256	moved to C5588A
265	moved to L747
334A	number shift D335
335	moved to D1008
350	number shift D350A
365	part of C6424
366	number shift D365
367	number shift D366
412A	number shift D412C
422	number shift D421
425	former duplicate of D431
454	date: 1707
462	former duplicate of D460
467	ghost
479	number shift D480
480	number shift D481
481	moved to A3991
494	number shift 493A
494A	number shift 494C

501A	number shift D502
502	date: [1625] STC 6444
505A	number shift D506
506	number shift D507
507	part of S2906
516	moved to B3859A
517	wrongly cancelled C4203A+ Suppl.
524	moved to F2197bA
585A	number shift D586
586	number shift D587
587	number shift D588
588	number shift D589
589	former duplicate of B559
600A	number shift D600B
602	number shift D603
603	former duplicate of B4563
625	number shift D626
626	number shift D627
627	wrongly cancelled C2213+ Suppl.
638	former duplicate of D636
655	number shift D655A
678	number shift D677
704	number shift D705
705	number shift D706
734	number shift D733
735	number shift D734
736	number shift D735
737	number shift D736
796	former duplicate of M1036
816	former duplicate of G2160
816A	number shift D816
822	number shift D821
834	number shift D833
835	number shift D834
836	number shift D835
845	former duplicate of R938
845A	number shift D845
941	former duplicate of V48A
942	number shift D941
943	number shift D942
963	number shift D963A
970	former duplicate of D969
977	serial
998	moved to M869A
999	moved to M869B
1000	moved to M869C
1008	moved to M886A
1013A	part of H3208
1044	moved to D1051A
1045	number shift D1044

1046	number shift D1045
1047	number shift D1046
1068A	number shift D1068B
1068B	number shift D1068C
1072	date: 1702
1077A	number shift D1078
1078	former duplicate of E3527
1081	former duplicate of S1492
1082	number shift D1081
1083	number shift D1082
1094A	moved to D2666A
1101	part of D1100
1127	moved to B3779A
1128	number shift D1127
1150	former duplicate of L355
1164	moved to C1871A
1165	number shift D1164
1167	Guildhall — lost [A description of the rhinoseros lately brought from the East Indies. 1684.]
1169A	former duplicate of S2471
1181	former duplicate of H3412
1195	moved to S3165+ Sheppard, Samuel.
1206A	former duplicate of S2090
1207	moved to L2618A
1226	moved to H491C
1239	former duplicate of A4248A
1240	former duplicate of A4249
1241	former duplicate of A4250
1242	former duplicate of A4250A
1243	moved to A4250B
1244	number shift D1243
1300A	number shift D1300B
1301A	part of T3201
1349	former duplicate of D1306
1350	number shift D1349
1373	moved to F1410A
1417	Guildhall — lost [Diest, Frid. Will. van. Memorial to the States General. 1684.]
1422	ghost
1433	former duplicate of D1432
1434	part of D1445
1446	part of D1445
1452	moved to C6366A
1457	former duplicate of E2793
1473	moved to H339A
1499	part of D1501
1514	part of D1512
1526	moved to H1955A
1529	number shift D1529A

1530	moved to S2508+ Seneca.
1562	moved to B3075A
1568A	number shift D1569
1569	former duplicate of F962
1574	former duplicate of R1678
1575	former duplicate of H2583
1577	moved to J485A
1578	moved to P3150+ Practical discourse.
1587	fragment
1591	moved to J849A
1597	moved to T3562+ Typing, William.
1600	moved to P346+ Pardies, Ignace Gaston.
1605	part of S3255
1609	wrongly cancelled D2101+ Suppl.
1610	number shift D1609
1617	moved to A1111B
1621	former duplicate of S3057
1623	former duplicate of S3588
1626	former duplicate of T3313
1633A	former duplicate of D1637
1650	former duplicate of E3382
1652	former duplicate of P4265
1665	wrongly cancelled D1665 Suppl.
1689	former duplicate of R574
1718	former duplicate of F2256
1723	moved to W226+ Wake, *Sir* Isaac.
1724	number shift D1723
1725	number shift D1724
1725A	moved to R1246+ Reynolds, Edward.
1734	former duplicate of R2377
1748A	number shift D1748B
1767A	moved to W2129+ Wild, Robert.
1771	moved to O366A
1772A	number shift D1772B
1775	former duplicate of D922
1777	number shift D1776
1777A	number shift D1777
1777B	number shift D1777A
1786A	number shift D1786B
1798	former duplicate of B2956
1802A	former duplicate of V182
1814	former duplicate of D1820
1843A	part of S2431
1848	former duplicate of D185
1880A	number shift D1880C
1899A	number shift D1899B
1902A	number shift D1902B
1912	former duplicate of S926
1956	moved to L1246A
1956A	moved to A2825A
1996A	number shift D1996C
2030A	number shift D2030B
2035	former duplicate of L38
2040	former duplicate of S2439
2041	former duplicate of P2980
2061	moved to D2096A
2099A	number shift D2100
2100	number shift D2101
2123	number shift D2124
2124	date: 1702
2145	number shift D2145A
2160A	number shift D160C
2160B	number shift D2160D
2365A	number shift D2365B
2365B	number shift D2365D
2407	former duplicate of F904
2407A	number shift D2407
2414	former duplicate of C6598
2424	former duplicate of G1880
2424A	number shift D2424
2431A	moved to D2430B
2440	former duplicate of T1499
2454	former duplicate of P2807
2455	number shift D2454
2483	number shift D2486
2483A	number shift D2485
2484	number shift D2483
2485	number shift D2487A
2486	number shift D2484
2487	number shift D2487B
2497	part of E3405
2498	part of E3406
2504	former duplicate of M2539
2544	number shift D2545
2581	number shift D2582
2596	number shift D2596A
2660	part of T290
2661	number shift D2663B
2662	number shift D2660
2690	same as D2690 [imprint correction]
2739	not separately published
2793	former duplicate of W3136A
2818	number shift D2819
2819	number shift D2820
2820	former duplicate of D2810
2824	number shift D2818
2846	former duplicate of D2839
2852	former duplicate of D2889
2863	moved to J692C
2893	former duplicate of T3540

2928 Guildhall — lost   [Dyer, *Sir* James. Specimen
     of the reports of. 1686-7.]
2930 number shift D2930A

2956 moved to T3372+   Tutchin, John.
2970 former duplicate of H985

E

1st ed.	2nd ed.
38	moved to C2152
39	number shift E38
41A	moved to E611A
42	former duplicate of B4024
79	number shift E78
98A	number shift E98C
99A	number shift E99B
100A	number shift E100AD
126A	number shift E126B
134	former duplicate of G359
136	former duplicate of D2557A
137	number shift E136
137A	number shift E137
157A	number shift E157B
160A	moved to B5781A
178A	number shift E178B
189	former duplicate of M1872A
192	moved to E194A
213	former duplicate of E212
324	number shift E324A
334A	number shift E334C
356A	number shift E356B
398A	number shift E398B
406	former duplicate of E405
426B	former duplicate of T1883
426C	number shift E426B
426D	number shift E428B
434	former duplicate of E367
435	number shift E434
462A	moved to E474C
464	moved to E469
465	number shift E464
465A	number shift E465
469	moved to G1890A
495A	number shift E495B
502	former duplicate of E501
503	number shift E504
504	number shift E505

520	moved to E524A
521	moved to E524B
522	number shift E520
523	number shift E521
524	number shift E522
525	number shift E523
539	moved to E252B
540	moved to E252C
552A	number shift E552B
574	number shift E575
575	number shift E576
576	number shift E577
635	moved to C360A
715	moved to C1672A
716	moved to C1672C
730	moved to A1649A
733	moved to L1246B
800	number shift E801
801	number shift E800
893	former duplicate of B206
916A	number shift E916B
918A	former duplicate of L701
958A	number shift E958B
958B	number shift E958E
969	moved to S1025+ Scotland. Estates.
971	serial
972	number shift E971
976A	number shift E976B
999	wrongly cancelled E999 Suppl.
1058	number shift E1058A
1074B	moved to I308B
1111	wrongly cancelled E1110+ Suppl.
1112	number shift E1111
1113A	former duplicate of S1108
1116	wrongly cancelled E1116 Suppl.
1117A	number shift E1117B
1148A	number shift E1147A
1156	number shift E1157
1157	not separately published
1165	moved to S116 Scotland. Estates.

1223	moved to E2520A		1769	number shift E1767
1279	former duplicate of E878		1770	number shift E1768
1283	former duplicate of C5207		1770A	number shift E1771A
1284	number shift E1283		1771	number shift E1769
1291	former duplicate of E1519		1795A	number shift E1795B
1292	moved to E1519A; also former duplicate of E1635B		1855	fragment
			1920	former duplicate of E2032
1293	moved to E1519B		1980	number shift E1978A
1327	number shift E1328		2089	former duplicate of E1775
1328	number shift E1327		2189	moved to S1310+ Scotland. Estates.
1333	wrongly cancelled E1333 Suppl.		2193	Guildhall — lost [A proclamation concerning the times of holding the summer assizes. 1660.]
1339	moved to S1202+ Scotland. Estates.			
1378A	number shift E1379			
1379	former duplicate of E1327		2200	former duplicate of W2521
1386	former duplicate of E1473		2201	number shift E2200
1386A	number shift E1386		2202	number shift E2201
1456	former duplicate of E1345		2206	former duplicate of P3795
1458	number shift E1459		2218	moved to I642B
1459	number shift E1458		2237A	number shift E2237B
1486	number shift E1486A		2257	number shift E2258
1500	former duplicate of E1510		2258	number shift E2259
1504	serial		2259	former duplicate of E2248
1519A	number shift E1519B		2270A	former duplicate of E2722
1525	number shift E1524		2271	former duplicate of E2277
1526	number shift E1525		2273	former duplicate of E2274
1527	number shift E1526		2281	part of E2280
1533A	wrongly cancelled E1533A Suppl.		2324	former duplicate of E2255
1549A	serial		2326	former duplicate of E2710
1550	serial		2328	former duplicate of E2256
1551	number shift E1551A		2336	former duplicate of E2257
1553A	number shift E1553B		2337	former duplicate of E2258
1585A	former duplicate of E1584		2338	wrongly cancelled E2258+ Suppl.
1585B	number shift E1585A		2339	number shift E2340
1588	former duplicate of I62		2340	moved to E2259
1588A	number shift E1588		2359	former duplicate of E2367
1588B	number shift E1588A		2364	former duplicate of E2358
1635A	number shift E1635B		2365	number shift E2366
1641	former duplicate of L3060A		2366	former duplicate of E2361
1676	former duplicate of O81		2379	former duplicate of L1092
1689	number shift E1690		2481A	number shift E2481B
1690	Guildhall — lost [An order of Parliament concerning all such. 1645.]		2501	former duplicate of E2876
			2505A	serial
1698	Guildhall — lost [An order of the committee of the Lords and Commons for advance. [London], 1642.]		2509A	number shift E2509B
			2536	number shift E2533B
			2536A	number shift E2536
1749A	number shift E1749B		2549	former duplicate of D570
1751	number shift E1752		2550	former duplicate of D653
1752	number shift E1751		2551	moved to D654A
1767	number shift E1770		2552	number shift E2550
1768	number shift E1771		2552A	number shift E2552

2595	former duplicate of E2615
2605	moved to E2590A
2629	former duplicate of E2630
2683	number shift E2684
2684	Guildhall — lost [Proceedings of a committee of the House of Commons. 1648.]
2687	moved to S1310+ Scotland. Estates.
2764	former duplicate of E2766A
2785A	number shift E2786
2786	former duplicate of E2801
2787	moved to E2805B
2795	former duplicate of E2796
2796	number shift E2795

2797	number shift E2796
2805	number shift E2805A
2809	former duplicate of E1609
2826	number shift E2827
2827	number shift E2826
2830	moved to E2836A
2844	former duplicate of R482
2867A	moved to E2795
2897	former duplicate of E2899
2900	moved to L2851N
2902	moved to L2852Q
2903	moved to L2852O; also former duplicate of E2902
2917	moved to S2003+ Scotland. Privy Council.

THE SPEECHES OF FREDERICK DOUGLASS

FREDERICK DOUGLASS
1818-1895

WASHINGTON,
DISTRICT OF COLUMBIA

The Speeches of
Frederick Douglass

A CRITICAL EDITION

JOHN R. McKIVIGAN
JULIE HUSBAND
HEATHER L. KAUFMAN
Editors

George Barr, Eamonn Brandon,
Kate Burzlaff, Mark Furnish,
Kathryn Jacks, Rebecca Pattillo,
Alex Smith, Lynette Taylor
Research Assistants

Yale UNIVERSITY PRESS

New Haven & London

Frontispiece: Steven Weitzman, statue of Frederick Douglass. Bronze, 10′ × 3′ × 3′, 2013. Emancipation Hall, U.S. Capitol Visitor Center, Washington, D.C. Photo courtesy of the Architect of the Capitol.

Published with assistance from The National Historical Publications and Records Commission.

Yale University Press books may be purchased in quantity for educational, business, or promotional use. For information, please e-mail sales.press@yale.edu (U.S. office) or sales@yaleup.co.uk (U.K. office).

Set in New Caledonia and Bulmer type by Newgen North America.
Printed in the United States of America.

Library of Congress Control Number: 2017963811
ISBN 978-0-300-19217-9 (paperback : alk. paper)

A catalogue record for this book is available from the British Library.

This paper meets the requirements of ANSI/NISO Z39.48-1992 (Permanence of Paper).

10 9 8 7 6 5 4 3 2 1

NATIONAL
ARCHIVES
NATIONAL HISTORICAL
PUBLICATIONS
& RECORDS COMMISSION

For Aurora and Charlie, who, like Frederick Douglass,
have become our constant companions.
H.K. and J.M.

For Ian, a budding historian who appreciates
the power of public speech.
J.H.

Contents

PART 2: KNOWN INFLUENCES ON
FREDERICK DOUGLASS'S ORATORY

PART 3: FREDERICK DOUGLASS ON PUBLIC SPEAKING

1. Ezra Greenleaf Weld, Fugitive Slave Law Convention, Cazenovia, New York. Daguerreotype, 2.1˝ × 2.6˝, 22 August 1850. Frederick Douglass is seated at the left end of the table. Courtesy of the Madison County Historical Society, Oneida, N.Y.

EXPULSION OF NEGROES AND ABOLITIONISTS FROM TREMONT TEMPLE, BOSTON, MASSACHUSETTS, ON DECEMBER 3, 1860.—[See Page 787.]

2. "Expulsion of Negroes and Abolitionists from Tremont Temple, Boston, Massachusetts, on December 3, 1860." *Harper's Weekly*, 15 December 1860, 788. Courtesy of the Library of Congress, LC-USZ62–112670.

3. Thomas Ball, *Freedmen's Memorial Monument to Abraham Lincoln.* Bronze, 1876. Lincoln Park, Washington, D.C. In a controversial speech at the monument's unveiling, Douglass questioned the symbolism of the kneeling position of the slave before Lincoln. Courtesy of the Library of Congress, Manuscript Division.

Hon. Fred. Douglass on Platform in Pavilion. (March 26, 1892)

4. Frederick Douglass speaking at the Tuskegee Institute, 26 March 1892.
Courtesy of the Library of Congress, LC-USZ62–120533.

Preface

Under the direction of the late John W. Blassingame, the Frederick Douglass Papers, based then at Yale University, collected and inventoried more than 2,500 public addresses of Frederick Douglass, indisputably the best-known African American of the nineteenth century. Of all of these speeches, the project selected 273, which were edited and published in a five-volume hardcover scholarly edition by Yale University Press from 1979 to 1992. The critical reception of each volume in the original Douglass Papers was unanimously strong. In a review of the first volume, Carol V. R. George recognized that while "essentially a tool for the scholar, it has the potential for engaging the general reader through the power of Douglass's eloquence." James B. Stewart called that same volume "an intrinsically fascinating documentary—absolutely essential equipment for anyone wishing to understand black abolitionism, the international character of antislavery, the rhetoric of antebellum radicalism and, of course, the emerging public character of Frederick Douglass."

This series is out of print and often difficult to locate. What the editors of the current work, in collaboration with Yale University Press, have prepared is a one-volume paperback edition of twenty of the most historically significant of Douglass's speeches, along with a new, concise apparatus. These speeches were chosen to represent Douglass's thought on the most important issues facing the United States in his lifetime, including slavery, abolitionism, civil rights, sectionalism, temperance, women's rights, economic development, and immigration. Some of the speeches have been well known and quoted for over a century, while others were unduly neglected by scholars before their publication in the Yale University Press edition. Some speeches were delivered repeatedly from manuscript lecture notes, while others were extemporaneous expressions prompted by reform and political campaigns. The editors of the original Yale edition selected the best text for each speech, and this volume reproduces those texts. The headnotes, significantly expanded, offer greater detail on the initial reception of each speech while placing it in historical and rhetorical context. This edition likewise updates the original historical annotations. All of the original 273 speeches and their accompanying annotation are freely available online at the website of the Frederick Douglass Papers.

To enhance readers' appreciation of Douglass as an orator, the editors added four sections of documents not found in the original Yale edition. Like the speeches, each document is reproduced exactly as it originally appeared in print, including typographical errors and misspellings. The first section features excerpts of speeches that Douglass acknowledged as influencing his appreciation of effective oratory. The initial selection is an extract from Douglass's first primer, *The Columbian Orator*, which, he recalled, opened his eyes to the injustice of slavery. Also included are addresses by leading reformers, white and black, whom Douglass heard and admired as speakers.

The second section is composed of Douglass's written and spoken statements about his experiences as a public lecturer and the skills he believed necessary for success in that endeavor. Excerpts from Douglass's autobiographies, editorials, and correspondence recount his reflections on the obstacles he had to surmount to become an effective public speaker.

The third section contains comments on Douglass's performance as an orator by those who heard it. Mainly offered by fellow abolitionists, black and white, male and female, they all attest to the contribution that Douglass's oratory made to the cause of human freedom.

The final section features excerpts from modern scholars assessing Douglass's effectiveness as a public speaker and an advocate for reform causes. Scholars from a variety of disciplines examine the content, delivery, reception, and enduring significance of Douglass's major speeches.

It is the editors' conviction that these supplementary materials illuminate Douglass's special place in the field of nineteenth-century reform oratory. They help explain how an uneducated runaway Maryland slave rose to become one of the most effective public speakers in American history, and how he used his influence to bring about major changes to the nation's direction. This volume will be attractive to general readers with an interest in Douglass, the Civil War, and racial relations, and to instructors and students in courses on American history, communication and rhetoric, political science, literature, and African American studies. It is the editors' hope that by making Douglass's words easily accessible, readers will learn that his message remains relevant to solving the problems of today's world.

The editors have a long list of individuals and institutions to thank for assistance in the preparation of this volume, but space permits acknowledging only a small number of them. The National Historical Publications and Records Commission has unswervingly supported the editing of Douglass's works since 1979. The National Endowment for the Humanities financially assisted the editing of the original edition of Douglass's speeches. Yale University, West Virginia University, and now the Institute for American Thought at Indiana University–Purdue University Indianapolis have hosted the work of the Frederick Douglass Papers since the project's inception, in 1973. Special thanks is owed to three editors at Yale University Press: Otto Bohlmann, who first envisioned a select edition of Douglass's speeches; Vadim Stalko, who helped us launch work on the volume; and Sarah Miller, who saw the volume through the stages of production. Many thanks as well to Rosemary Meany and Cindy Bancroft of the University of Northern Iowa's Rod Library, whose sleuthing skills in tracking down obscure nineteenth-century newspapers were invaluable, and to Jim O'Loughlin, who gave incisive advice on each headnote as it emerged and contributed to a story line. David W. Blight and John Stauffer lent the editors their expertise on Douglass to advise on the difficult process of selecting the best representatives from Douglass's vast body of speeches.

Introduction

Frederick Douglass's Oratory and Political Leadership

Frederick Douglass's death in 1895 inspired many retrospective accounts of his remarkable life and career. Activists, educators, musicians, ministers, and politicians offered tributes to Douglass and his work on behalf of African Americans and other oppressed groups. He was remembered as a civil rights leader who paired powerful public speaking with a gift for bridging racial divides; in the wake of his death, his contemporaries identified his oratory as his distinctive legacy and his most effective political tool. Of the memorials collected and published in 1897 by Helen Pitts Douglass, his second wife, a majority focused on his speeches. The Reverend Hugh T. Stevenson, pastor of the Baptist Church of Anacostia, Washington, D.C., remarked: "Gifted with elements that would have made him a master in any walk of life, his work developed in him three prominent characteristics: breadth of sympathy, dauntless courage, and oratorical power."[1] Robert Purvis expanded upon those characteristics, praising Douglass's "sonorous voice," with its "wonderful flexibility," and comparing him to Daniel Webster, the Massachusetts senator and distinguished orator: "In originality of thought, of

1. Helen Pitts Douglass, ed., *In Memoriam: Frederick Douglass* (Philadelphia: Yorston, 1897), 29.

expression, in epigrammatic sentences, Mr. Douglass was his equal; in his ability to personate a character, he was his superior."[2] Purvis also compared Douglass to the great Shakespearean actors of his day, adding, "His dramatic power, in both its phases (tragic and comic), was marvelous. . . . I have witnessed passages in the oratory of Mr. Douglass, which, for simple dramatic power transcended their finest efforts; and, for the simple reason that they were acting; and his part was the majestic outburst from the well-spring of a grand, broad, deeply moved human nature."[3]

Other commentators noted the dramatic setting of so many of Douglass's greatest speeches. Often, hecklers interrupted Douglass, and opponents violently threatened his and his colleagues' safety; one such mob attack in Pendleton, Indiana, which permanently injured Douglass, is recounted in part 3 of this volume. His rhetorical performances were often crafted under extraordinary pressures that, far from undermining him, helped him produce his best work.

Though contemporaries frequently remembered Douglass for his declamations and thundering tones, those more familiar with the breadth of his oratorical career remarked upon his gift for extemporaneous speech, especially his comic impersonations of slaveholders and other racists. Purvis commented, "So perfect was the comic in his nature, and so keen was the sense of the ludicrous, that he excited the greatest fun and laughter."[4] The *National Anti-Slavery Standard* (28 October 1847) described his bearing during a speech mocking slaveholders' religion: "Mr. Douglass here assumed a most grotesque look . . . and . . . a canting tone of voice." In this instance, Douglass invoked the discursive form of the sermon satire to mock an eighteenth-century bishop who defended "evangelical flogging." He quotes the bishop addressing slaves:

2. Ibid., 213.
3. Ibid., 217.
4. Ibid., 218.

"Whether you really deserve it or not," (one would think that would make some difference), "it is your duty, and Almighty God requires that you bear it patiently. You may perhaps think that this is a hard doctrine," (and it admits of little doubt), "but if you consider it right you must needs think otherwise of it." (It is clear as mud. I suppose he is now going to reason them into the propriety of being flogged evangelically.) "Suppose you deserve correction; you cannot but see it is just and right you should meet with it. Suppose you do not, or at least so much or so severe; you perhaps have escaped a great many more, and are at last paid for all. Suppose you are quite innocent; is it not possible you may have done some other bad thing which was never discovered, and Almighty God would not let you escape without punishment one time or another? Ought you not in such cases to give glory to Him?" (Glory!) (Much laughter.)[5]

Douglass explains that this approach exposes deceptions practiced to maintain slavery: "There is nothing that will facilitate our cause more than getting the people to laugh at that religion which brings its influence to support traffic in human flesh."[6] Granville Ganter, whose essay is located in part 5 of this volume, explores the way Douglass used humor to confound the audience's conception of slavery, thus disrupting proslavery thought.

5. Frederick Douglass, "Love of God, Love of Man, Love of Country: An Address Delivered in Syracuse, New York, on 24 September 1847," in John W. Blassingame and John R. McKivigan, eds., *The Frederick Douglass Papers*, 9 vols. (New Haven, Conn.: Yale University Press, 1979–), ser. 1, 2:98–99; hereinafter cited as *Douglass Papers*. For the original sermon, see William Meade, ed., *Sermons Addressed to Masters and Servants and Published in the Year 1743, by the Reverend Thomas Bacon, Minister of the Protestant Episcopal Church in Maryland, Now Republished with Other Tracts and Dialogues on the Same Subject, and Recommended to all Masters and Mistresses, to Be Used in their Families* (Winchester, Va.: John Heiskell, Printer, 1813), 132–33.

6. Douglass, "Love of God, Love of Man, Love of Country," in *Douglass Papers*, ser. 1, 2:98–99.

The Novice Speaker: From "Text" to Advocate

Douglass began his speaking career shortly after his escape from slavery in Baltimore and his arrival in the shipbuilding community of New Bedford, Massachusetts. In 1838 he began attending the New Bedford African Methodist Episcopal Zion Church, a small all-black congregation, and became a licensed local preacher in 1839.[7] Speaking at this church in an antislavery meeting, Douglass was persuaded by the white Quaker William C. Coffin to attend the upcoming abolitionist convention to be held in August 1841 in Nantucket. Douglass made such a powerful impression that he was introduced to several of the leading figures of the American Anti-Slavery Society—William Lloyd Garrison, Wendell Phillips, and Parker Pillsbury—and briefly addressed their gathering. By the close of the convention, these abolitionists had asked Douglass to become a paid lecturer for their organization.[8] The older Garrison mentored Douglass, and the two formed a close friendship as Douglass learned to convert audiences to fervent antislavery beliefs, even while risking violent public attacks in the process.

In 1844 the American Anti-Slavery Society adopted the motto "No Union with Slaveholders." The society believed that the American system of government was founded on the protection of slavery and that the U.S. Constitution committed the country to defending it. Consequently, any direct political participation through voting or office holding was a form of collusion, an expression of "union with slaveholders." Members of the society, also known as Garrisonians, likewise criticized Christian churches in the United States, which they saw as ideologically upholding slavery. The Garrisonians supported a range of reforms, most especially women's rights.

7. William L. Andrews, "Frederick Douglass, Preacher," *American Literature* 54, no. 4 (December 1982): 596.

8. William S. McFeely, *Frederick Douglass* (New York: Norton, 1991), 89.

Their theory of reform was based on moral suasion: if they revealed the true horrors of slavery and appealed to what is best and most sympathetic in listeners, a moral revolution would sweep the North and eventually the nation, eliminating the need for participation in electoral politics or legislative initiatives. Engaging in direct politics, they believed, would involve compromises detrimental to the moral purity of the movement.

Douglass thrived under Garrison's mentorship and became such a successful and brilliant antislavery lecturer that skeptics doubted he could have been raised in the brutalizing environment of plantation slavery. To prove his slave origins, he published *Narrative of the Life of Frederick Douglass* (1845), which became the most famous slave autobiography in American history. In it he described in detail his early years as a slave in Talbot County and Baltimore, Maryland, as well as his life in the North after his escape from slavery, at approximately age twenty. (Douglass never definitively knew his age.) Publication of the narrative made Douglass identifiable, which made him vulnerable to being captured and returned into slavery. As a result, Douglass left his young family and traveled to Great Britain in August 1845.

In twenty-one months overseas, Douglass spoke at hundreds of events in Ireland, Scotland, and England. Initially addressing crowds gathered by his Garrisonian friends, he later found that the popularity of his *Narrative* won him large audiences drawn to hear the abolitionist testimony of a genuine victim of slavery. The talents he displayed in Britain as a public speaker won Douglass the opportunity to lecture audiences on other topics; one 1846 address, reprinted in this volume, demonstrates the controversy that Douglass sparked when he drew parallels between temperance and abolitionism. Historians have aptly labeled this journey to Britain and Ireland a "Liberating Sojourn." Douglass won widespread acclaim, enjoyed life in a society with little overt racism, and returned home a free man after his English admirers purchased his freedom.[9] Consequently, when he returned to the United States in April 1847, he was far less willing than before to act as a junior partner to his original antislavery mentor, William Lloyd Garrison. Douglass commented that early in his career, Garrison would take him as his "text," a short verse upon which Garrison grafted the meaning of abolition.[10] By the time he returned from Britain, he was a celebrity, a powerful advocate for African American freedom.

Douglass generally delivered his early antislavery speeches without notes, refining key stories and testing to see which provoked the most favorable audience response. Some of these central stories then found their way into his autobiographies. For example, the 1842 episode in which he broke down prejudice in Pittsfield, New Hampshire, described in the speech "Let the Negro Alone" (included in this work), later appeared in his final autobiography, the *Life and Times of Frederick Douglass*. Douglass discovered a further synergy between his publications and his speeches when his autobiography reached Southern audiences, which his speeches could not do. A former neighbor from Talbot County, A. C. C. Thompson, attempted to respond to the *Narrative* and inadvertently verified much of Douglass's story. A delighted Douglass wrote to Garrison: "Slaveholders and slave-traders never betray greater indiscretion, than when they venture to defend themselves, or their system of plunder, in any other community than a slaveholding one."[11] He then incorporated Thompson's observations regarding his transformation from "recreant slave" to "learned" man into his later addresses in Britain.[12]

As Douglass grew more famous, he was invited to speak at more formal occasions and deliver important keynote addresses. At the

9. Alan J. Rice and Martin Crawford, eds., *Liberating Sojourn: Frederick Douglass and Transatlantic Reform* (Athens: University of Georgia Press), 1999.

10. *Douglass Papers,* ser. 2, 2:206.

11. "Frederick Douglass to William Lloyd Garrison," 27 January 1846, *Douglass Papers,* ser. 3, 1:82.

12. Douglass, "A Few Facts and Personal Observations of Slavery: An Address Delivered in Ayr, Scotland," 24 March 1846, *Douglass Papers,* ser. 1, 1:201.

same time, he was subjected to greater scrutiny from the Garrisonians because of his moves toward independence from them and his changing philosophy of reform. Faced with these new pressures, he began using notes in his speeches. His 1852 classic, "What to the Slave Is the Fourth of July?" was one of the first major speeches for which he used notes. The preparation of other speeches such as "Claims of the Negro, Ethnologically Considered" required extensive research. The speeches for which we have records after 1852 are, by and large, those he delivered from notes. Exceptions include stump speeches, such as his 1872 "Which Greeley Are We Voting For?" and convention debates, such as "We Welcome the Fifteenth Amendment," both located in this volume.

Political Activist: Declaring Independence from the Garrisonians

As Douglass evolved as a leader, his relations with Garrison changed, as did his attitude toward electoral politics. When Douglass first proposed editing his own newspaper, he was discouraged by Garrison, who argued that Douglass would have difficulty securing readers and sufficient financial support. Their friendship faltered when Douglass, suspecting that Garrison was motivated in part by a desire to protect his own subscription base, disregarded his friend's advice. The break between the two men encouraged Douglass to think carefully about the limits of moral suasion as a means of ending slavery. Passage of the Compromise of 1850 made it clear that slavery was a national institution and that proslavery advocates aimed to make it legal in the North as well as the South. Douglass determined that the best way to eliminate slavery was to seek a political solution in addition to maintaining the moral suasion campaign focused on stigmatizing the institution.

After relocating to Rochester, Douglass associated more and more with a circle of upstate New York abolitionists led by the wealthy land speculator Gerrit Smith. Smith had kept alive the remnant of the original Liberty party, founded in 1840 by abolitionists seeking political means to battle slavery. In 1848 most Liberty party adherents had entered into an alliance with Northern defectors from the Whig and Democrat parties on a Free Soil platform opposed to the spread of slavery into western territories. Douglass was attracted by this show of growing resistance to slavery's political power. Smith and his followers advanced the radical position that the Constitution offered no special protection for slave owning and that the federal government had the power to emancipate the slaves. Smith befriended Douglass and lobbied hard to persuade him to become an advocate for this brand of radical political abolitionism.[13]

The catalyst for Douglass's final break with the Garrisonians came when the American Anti-Slavery Society met in May 1851 and, seeking to clarify the position of its members, required them to denounce the Constitution. Douglass refused. In an article in the next issue of the *North Star* titled "Change of Opinion Announced," he supported the argument that the Constitution was an antislavery document, a view that permitted overt electoral action.[14] Two weeks after that, in another move of independence, Douglass merged his newspaper with that of Smith's Liberty party, naming the new publication *Frederick Douglass' Paper.*

At the same time, he became more active in the American and Foreign Anti-Slavery Society, a rival antislavery group dominated by the wealthy New York City merchants Arthur and Lewis Tappan. The "new organization," which had split from the American Anti-Slavery Society in 1840, was in many ways less socially radical than its parent organization: it was less critical of religious institu-

13. Lawrence J. Friedman, *Gregarious Saints: Self and Community in American Abolitionism, 1830–1870* (New York: Cambridge University Press, 1982), 96–126; John Stauffer, *The Black Hearts of Men: Radical Abolitionists and the Transformation of Race* (Cambridge, Mass.: Harvard University Press, 2002), 158–68.
14. McFeely, *Frederick Douglass,* 169.

tions and did not support women's rights. Douglass attempted to work with both groups, but met with hostile resistance from his old friends the Garrisonians. He ends "A Nation in the Midst of a Nation" (1853), delivered at the American and Foreign Anti-Slavery Society annual meeting, by expressing reluctance to speak as anything other than a "colored man." He hoped to work with both antislavery societies yet, realistically, lamented the likely impossibility of doing so: "If one discards me because I work with the other, the responsibility is not mine."[15]

Revolutionary: Armed Resistance and Marginalization

In his first years as an abolitionist lecturer, Douglass resisted those who sought to force him into endorsing violent resistance to slavery. Though the turning point in his *Narrative* was his fight with the slave breaker Covey, he realized that overtly endorsing slave insurrection in the South would cause him to be labeled an incendiary and would marginalize his voice. During his time as a Garrisonian, Douglass tried to abide by the group's pacifist ideology, but found it necessary on occasion, such as when facing an antiabolitionist mob in Pendleton, Indiana, in 1842, to fight back in self-defense. The egregious nature of the Fugitive Slave Law finally led Douglass and many other abolitionists to sanction armed resistance, as a last resort, to prevent the rendition of a runaway. In his 1852 novella *The Heroic Slave,* Douglass went further and praised the courage of Madison Washington and the other rebellious slaves aboard the brig *Creole,* who fought for and won their freedom. It was Douglass's close friendship with the white abolitionist John Brown that highlighted the danger of becoming marginalized for advocating violent means to end slavery. In October 1859, Brown and a group

15. "Anniversaries," *Frederick Douglass' Paper,* 27 May 1853.

of twenty-one men, black and white, captured the federal armory at Harpers Ferry, Virginia, and attempted to seize munitions with which to start a widespread slave insurrection in the Appalachian Mountains. Douglass had been tempted to help Brown, but withheld his support when he realized Brown's plans had shifted from orchestrating slave escapes from secret bases in the Southern mountains to a direct military assault on Harpers Ferry.

Following Brown's quick defeat, Douglass fled to Britain to escape possible prosecution. There he discovered that because of his defection from the Garrisonians and his support of Brown's violent antislavery tactics, he was snubbed by many abolitionists who had welcomed him in 1845. Douglass's 1860 speech depicting the Constitution as an antislavery document served two purposes: to reaffirm his loyalty to the Union and to defend his views against the international criticism of moral suasionists on both sides of the Atlantic. He attacked George Thompson, a famed British Garrisonian who had challenged Douglass's position on the Constitution. As an instrumental form of rhetoric, the speech successfully defended the Constitution as a potentially antislavery platform for the nation. But it left Douglass the orator with a greatly reduced constituency. As the communications scholars Michael C. Leff and Ebony A. Utley define the term, "constitutive rhetoric" constructs the identity of the speaking self in relation to audience.[16] Douglass's speaking self was not winning allies in his fight against slavery or for African American civil rights. Audience members may have found his argument persuasive, but he did not put forth a conception of speaker and audience that inspired a clear collective identity. Too far from the African American community and too angry at the Garrisonians, Douglass found himself marginalized until he returned home, where he was embraced by Unionists and African Americans supportive of

16. Michael C. Leff and Ebony A. Utley, "Instrumental and Constitutive Rhetoric in Martin Luther King Jr.'s 'Letter from Birmingham Jail,'" *Rhetoric and Public Affairs* 7, no. 1 (Spring 2004): 38.

the Civil War. By making resistance to the South, even violent resistance, patriotic, the Civil War saved Douglass's leadership.

African American Organizer: Douglass in the Civil War and Reconstruction

The war years were a high-water mark for Douglass's leadership among African Americans. He traveled around the country to recruit black soldiers for the Union Army and to advocate for their equal treatment and opportunity in the military. Douglass developed an uneasy relationship with the Lincoln administration. He tried doggedly in the war's early years to convince the president and the Northern public that the mission of the war was emancipation of the slaves, which, in turn, would redeem the nation and save the Union. In his newspaper, Douglass railed against Lincoln for his "slothful deliberation" over the Emancipation Proclamation and his failure to protect or avenge black soldiers who had been massacred after they surrendered in battle.[17] In retrospect, after the success of the Thirteenth, Fourteenth, and Fifteenth Amendments, Douglass conceded that Lincoln had been an inspired leader precisely because the president had been so keenly aware of the nuances of public opinion and had gauged his advances accordingly. Lincoln became a touchstone in Douglass's rhetoric from his assassination onward.

Only a small number of Douglass's speeches explicitly directed toward African Americans were ever recorded or published. Even in "A Nation in the Midst of a Nation," when Douglass describes a budding black nationalism, he notes, "I am a colored man, and this is a white audience." Rather than rouse African Americans to

---

17. From *Life and Writings of Frederick Douglass,* ed. Philip S. Foner (New York: International Publishers, 1952), 3:274.

unified action, he alternately chastises white listeners and solicits greater understanding from them. In many speeches there is a palpable sense of a double audience, especially during Reconstruction, when Douglass had the greatest access to political power. The 1876 speech "The Freedmen's Monument to Abraham Lincoln" explicitly distinguishes between a white "you" and a black "we:" "You are the children of Abraham Lincoln. We are at best only his step-children . . . But . . . while Abraham Lincoln saved for you a country, he delivered us from a bondage, according to Jefferson, one hour of which was worse than ages of the oppression your fathers rose in rebellion to oppose." In other speeches, Douglass seems to repudiate binary, black-white thinking on race; for example, he includes himself among "we poor white people in the South" in "Which Greeley Are We Voting For?," delivered in Richmond, Virginia.

Relatively few of Douglass's speech texts are specifically directed at black audiences, which may reflect the limits of the written archive more than the scope of his oratory. He makes reference, for example, in his 1873 Louisville speech, "Recollections of the Antislavery Conflict," to a distinction between things he shares in public oratory and things he says in private conference. He first notes a form of inequality:

> We say we are the equals of the whites. Are we at present the equals of the whites? Equal before the law we are, equal at the ballot box we are, but we are far behind our white brethren. Now in what are we behind? . . If the white man can build magnificent halls like this and we cannot, they are halls ahead of us. I do not say that naturally we are unequal to the white man. I would not say that, but the fact is that now they are in advance of us.

Initially, Douglass sounds as if he subscribes to uplift ideology, an understanding that African Americans must take it upon themselves, without recompense for their exploitation and without equal opportunity, to become wealthier, better educated, and more respected.

But Douglass repeatedly calls into question the reasons for inequality of condition. He concludes this portion of the speech with a remarkable indication of his frustration in both bridging racial constituencies and effectively leading African Americans: "I would like to talk to you when there were no white people listening to me. I would like to talk to you aside." We might conclude that Douglass's speeches to and conversations with black constituents went unreported because he did not want his words misconstrued.

During Reconstruction, Douglass became an effective campaigner for the Republican party, the Fifteenth Amendment, and black civil rights more generally. So long as the Republican party supported African American rights and power in the South, Douglass's position as Republican stalwart served to reinforce his position among African Americans. Though Douglass's influence had suffered in 1859–60 in the wake of the John Brown scandal, the most sustained challenge came with the collapse of Reconstruction in 1877. With the federal withdrawal from the South, Southern white "Redeemers" steadily disenfranchised African Americans through poll taxes, literacy tests, and violence. Throughout the country, African Americans lost political and economic power and faced growing levels of social stigmatization. Since Douglass had campaigned for the Republicans and accepted significant political appointments, some viewed him as tacitly assenting to the Republican withdrawal from the South and, along with it, the end of federal protection of African American civil rights. The first threat to his leadership came after the John Brown raid, from white people who suspected that his defense of African Americans was too radical and violent; this second crisis, however, came from black people who suspected that he was too indebted to the Republicans.

This tension between Douglass and many of his peers reached a peak with the controversy over the "Exodusters," a term for African Americans from Louisiana, Mississippi, and Texas who attempted to migrate to Kansas in the wake of violent persecution in the Gulf states. Migrants experienced severe hardships en route, but

Douglass resisted contributing to relief efforts. He believed that the concentration of African Americans in the South and their extensive experience with agriculture gave them leverage in defending their rights, an advantage that would be absent in other regions of the country; encouraging migration was tantamount to giving up on reforming the South. Critics called him a "traitor" to his race.[18] As Douglass noted in his third autobiography, *Life and Times:* "In all my forty years of thought and labor to promote the freedom and welfare of my race, I never found myself more widely and painfully at variance with leading colored men of the country."[19]

As the gains of Reconstruction continued to unravel in the 1880s and 1890s, Douglass was again openly accused of failing to represent the interests of African Americans. He met this challenge by increasingly speaking out against Republican failures. After the Supreme Court overturned the 1875 Civil Rights Act, for example, he challenged his fellow Republicans in "This Decision Has Humbled the Nation" (1883). Frustrated, Douglass even charged that the Republicans had become a "party of money rather than a party of morals."[20]

A Return to Radicalism: The Final Years

While never severing his relationship with the Republican party— Douglass served briefly as U.S. minister to Haiti in 1889–90 and campaigned for Benjamin Harrison in 1892—his last years show his rededication to agitation. He continued to speak on behalf of women's rights, calling himself a "radical woman suffrage man," and mentored Ida B. Wells while collaborating with her to fight lynching. The last speech included in this collection, "Lessons of the Hour" (1893), is as radical as any delivered against slavery.

18. "'Going for' Fred Douglass," *Washington (D.C.) Post,* 19 May 1879.
19. *Douglass Papers,* ser. 2, 3:335.
20. "The Negro Problem," Washington (D.C.) *Evening Star,* 10 January 1894.

Douglass, unlike the rising African American leader Booker T. Washington, presented an analysis of lynching that was deeply offensive to many white listeners, Republicans included. He branded lynching a means of terrorizing African Americans in order to prevent political, economic, or social progress. Douglass argued that accusations of black men sexually assaulting white women, the most frequent justification offered for lynching, were usually false and that lynching was actually a manifestation of white guilt for the rape of black women during slavery and afterward.

Throughout Douglass's long public career, Americans experienced a decided shift in their understanding of social change. When Douglass first took to the speaking podium, Americans heard from Ralph Waldo Emerson and other Romantics that social change occurred when men's minds found victory over material circumstances. They argued that representative men could enact social change through their ability to first imagine and then, as Emerson urged, build their "own world."[21] This was a belief system especially friendly to reformers. By the end of his life, Douglass faced a public increasingly skeptical of social movements, unless reform could be defined as individual effort toward self-improvement. Glen McClish notes the limitations of Douglass and Wells's 1893 pamphlet "The Reasons Why the Colored American Is not in the World's Columbian Exposition: The Afro-American's Contribution to Columbian Literature." He argues that it failed to mobilize African Americans because it asserted a collective identity based on what McClish calls "a confident sense of agency" and a "powerful voice." As McClish shows, responses in the black press to Douglass and Wells's work promoted individual achievement and characterized attempts to influence those in power as "not only futile but downright dangerous."[22] Many middle-class black leaders regarded

21. Ralph Waldo Emerson, "Nature," in *Selected Writings of Emerson,* ed. Donald McQuade (New York: Random House, 1981), 42.

22. Glen McClish, "The Instrumental and Constitutive Rhetoric of Martin Luther King Jr. and Frederick Douglass," *Rhetorica* 33, no. 1 (Winter 2015): 67, 65.

collective action as impotent, making the work of agitation and organizing exceedingly difficult. Douglass's renaissance as an agitator in his twilight years, despite such discouraging developments, can be appreciated in retrospect as a return to his truest impulses and as an inspiration to Wells and later black leaders who would take up the mantle of civil rights reform in the twentieth century.

Recalling Douglass the Orator

Douglass seemed well aware that his exceptional talents as a public speaker had won him much of his fame and influence. Part 3 of this collection includes several excerpts from Douglass's reflections on his experiences as a speaker and the reasons for the successes and occasional failings of his oratorical performances. For example, in 1849 he proclaimed: "The pen is not to be despised, but who that knows anything of the might and electricity of speech as it bursts from hearts of fire, glowing with light and life, will not acknowledge the superiority over the pen for immediate effect." Twenty years later, however, he mused mournfully: "People do not attend lectures to hear statesmanlike addresses, which are usually rather heavy for the stomachs of young and old who listen. People want to be amused as well as instructed. They come as often for the former as the latter, and perhaps as often to see the man as for either." Well aware of the centrality of oratory to his political contributions, Douglass was the first compiler of his own speaking record. The four newspapers he edited over the years contained texts of scores of his addresses. With the financial assistance of his supporters, Douglass published and circulated key speeches in pamphlet versions. His second and third autobiographies, *My Bondage and My Freedom* and *Life and Times of Frederick Douglass,* quote from Douglass's orations and reprint numerous lengthy excerpts of the ones he deemed most significant. Highly conscious of his place in history, Douglass reproduced what he regarded as his most eloquent public statements on the major issues of his day.[23]

An early first biography of Douglass, published by James M. Gregory two years before Douglass's death, contains a collection of speech extracts representing his most memorable speeches from the 1840s to the 1890s. Gregory, a professor of economics and history at Howard University, published *Frederick Douglass, the Orator* in 1893, weaving together Douglass's life story with approximately one hundred pages of speech excerpts that he suggested were the culmination of Douglass's reform labors. Booker T. Washington's 1907 biography of Douglass quoted copiously from Douglass's speeches, too. When Carter G. Woodson edited *Negro Orators and Their Orations* in 1925, eight of the seventy-six speeches he excerpted were by Douglass. Of these eight, only two were from the thirty years Douglass led African Americans after the Civil War. Woodson's choice of selections suggests that after the Civil War, Douglass became a smaller part of a more robust African American leadership circle. In 1955, Philip S. Foner became the first editor to collect and print a large selection of speeches in their entirety and to place them alongside other writings by Douglass. With the five-volume series of speeches, debates, and interviews edited by John W. Blassingame and John R. McKivigan (1979–92), annotated versions of a wide selection of speeches became widely available to scholars for the first time.

This volume gathers together historical context in the headnotes, provides annotations, and offers other contextual materials as a way to focus on the rhetorical "scenario" of Douglass's oratory. As the theater and performance scholar Diana Taylor defines the term, the "scenario" of a speech describes its text, the space in which it was

23. Two speeches Douglass chose to reproduce in *My Bondage and My Freedom* and one in *Life and Times of Frederick Douglass* are among the twenty selected for this volume. Douglass provided interesting background details about the composition of several other of his major address in these autobiographies.

performed, and the gestures, manner, and accent of the speaker.[24]
Headnotes in this volume indicate, where possible, the staging of
the speeches, newspaper reports of Douglass's actions and voice,
and audience response.

Modern appraisals of Douglass as a speaker are inextricably
linked with assessments of his leadership. The essays selected for
part 5 of this volume examine this linkage. Gregory Lampe, for example, shows how Douglass's initial training as a speaker was derived from manipulating and imitating white children: he coaxed
some to teach him to write and overheard others explaining how
they were going to practice speeches for an exhibition, speeches
found in *The Columbian Orator.* Granville Ganter balances this
attention to learning dominant-culture practices with a consideration of Douglass's education within black communities. His early
religious training in Baltimore with Father Lawson, his work as a
Sabbath school leader, and then his position as lay preacher gave
him considerable practice in fostering a sense of collective mission.
He was already a compelling speaker, a leader among New Bedford
African Americans, when white abolitionists first met him. He had
cultivated the form of the slave sermon satire before he was hired to
be a traveling antislavery lecturer.

Scholars have often compared Douglass with later African American orators, noting his specific rhetorical strategies and constitutive
poses relative to his audiences. Ivy Wilson, David Howard-Pitney,
and Richard Leeman, all included in part 5, represent this approach
to Douglass's oratory. Wilson considers Douglass's development to
be one sharpened and brought into relief through his association
with sometime allies, sometime rivals such as Samuel Ringgold
Ward and Henry Highland Garnet. Howard Pitney shows how he
tapped into the religio-political jeremiad, standing at the head of an
African American tradition credited with some of the most stirring

24. Diana Taylor, *The Archive and the Repertoire: Performing Cultural Memory
in the Americas* (Durham, N.C.: Duke University Press, 2003), 16, 20.

speeches ever delivered, including Martin Luther King Jr.'s "I Have a Dream." In a less celebratory approach, Richard Leeman finds Douglass's response to the dominant rhetoric of social Darwinism less confrontational and thus less politically advantageous than that of later leaders such as Henry McNeal Turner, Ida B. Wells and W. E. B. Du Bois.

The study of Douglass's speeches encourages a close examination of Douglass's post–Civil War career because at many of these speech events, he was defending his political positions and his philosophy of reform to other African Americans, reformers, and Republicans. His call to agitation and confrontation fell out of favor among more conservative African Americans, and so he began crafting speeches to foster a sense of common cause among them. Douglass's pre–Reconstruction era speeches were aimed at galvanizing white Americans to make slaves free and to make freedmen citizens; the later speeches expose fissures in the African American community and Douglass's struggle to redefine his leadership after the war, especially in the wake of the post-Reconstruction setbacks.

In selecting the twenty speeches reprinted here, the editors balanced a concern for significance and range. They reproduced what have been regarded as Douglass's most famous pieces, including "What to the Slave Is the Fourth of July?" and "The Freedmen's Monument to Abraham Lincoln," as well as others that have garnered little attention but offer fresh insights into Douglass's methods of persuasion and modes of fostering community. Speeches that attempted to build civic cohesion among African Americans and reformers include "I Have Come to Tell You Something about Slavery" (1841), his oldest preserved speech, which uses embodied rhetoric to move his audience, and "Which Greeley Are We Voting For?" (1872), which shows Douglass's supple use of pronouns and parody to build a constituency. Speeches included here show Douglass's concern for the women's movement, temperance, lynching, education, and science, in addition to slavery and civil rights. They depict him in moments when he was highly marginalized and struggling

to find a constituency ("The American Constitution and the Slave,"
1860), and when he was central to African American communities
and the Republican party ("Our Composite Nationality," 1869).

Most importantly, the speeches in this volume illuminate the different methods that Douglass used as a reformer and as a performer.
In "'It Moves,' or the Philosophy of Reform" (1883), Douglass out-
lines a distinctively humanistic theory of social change coming not
from the "angel" or "devil" on a person's shoulder, not from faith in
metaphysical deliverance, but from truthfully observing and analyz-
ing social phenomena, no matter the costs. The reformer, he argues,
"has to part with old friends; break away from the beaten paths of
society, and advance against the vehement protests of the most
sacred sentiments of the human heart." While Douglass endured
such losses—a slave mistress of whom he had been fond, his mentor
Garrison, friends who felt jealous of his successes later in life—he
nonetheless found great compensations, as well. Few reformers in
history have had the resilience to spend fifty-plus years agitating
for change, but Douglass gathered many allies, especially among
women's rights activists, in the later years of his life.

As the most famous African American leader of the nineteenth
century and the template for many future African American leaders, Douglass influenced both the black oratorical tradition and
dominant-culture oratory. He found a balance between a plainspo-
ken style and the ornate traditions celebrated in *The Columbian
Orator*, and the result was enormously appealing to audiences. His
distinctive use of humor and irony later found a modern form in the
speeches of Malcolm X and even the political comedy of Richard
Pryor. Douglass was critical of minstrelsy, but not of humor per se,
and that may have been one of his most powerful legacies. While
battling some of the most horrendous social evils of his era, he
continued to appreciate the humorous side of life and shared this in
some of his most successful orations.

On 20 February 1895, Douglass attended the Triennial Session
of the Women's Council in Washington, D.C. He was an honored

guest, escorted to the platform by Susan B. Anthony and Anna Shaw. He moved down the aisle, according to May Wright Sewall, "with the majesty of a king" and "with every eye fixed upon him."[25] He sat next to Anthony, one of his oldest friends, and though he had intended to return home early, he was so engrossed in the day's discussion that he stayed for the entire day. Returning to his home late that afternoon, he and his wife, Helen, had a hasty dinner so that he could get to the nearby Hillsdale African Church to deliver a lecture. While awaiting the carriage, Douglass entertained Helen with a lively account of the day, impersonating one of the speakers. He fell to his knees, hands clasped, a gesture that Helen thought part of the humorous performance, when he crumpled to the floor. Commemorating him at his funeral five days later, May Sewall remarked on her impression of him at the afternoon session, "I thought, there walks a page of history, an epic poem, a tragedy."[26] Douglass died, fittingly, at this intersection between epic and humor, and between his twin commitments to gender and racial justice.

25. *In Memoriam: Frederick Douglass*, 46.
26. Ibid., 17; "Death of Frederick Douglass," New York *Times*, 20 February 1895.

PART 1

Selected Speeches by Frederick Douglass

"I Have Come to Tell You Something about Slavery"

An Address Delivered in Lynn, Massachusetts, October 1841

Pennsylvania Freeman, 20 October 1841.

Frederick Douglass fled slavery in Baltimore, Maryland, in 1838. Within three years, he had married, started a family, and settled in New Bedford, Massachusetts. His career as a public speaker began in the New Bedford African Methodist Episcopal Zion Church, where he was a class leader and then a lay preacher. But Douglass found his true calling when, in April 1839, he heard a speech by William Lloyd Garrison, by then the most famous radical abolitionist in the country. Like many abolitionists, Garrison borrowed from the fervor and conversion narratives of evangelical preaching to declaim against slavery. Douglass adopted the same style. In an 1894 letter to Bishop James W. Hood, Douglass writes, "It was from this Zion church that I went forth to the work of delivering my brethren from bondage, and this new vocation, which separated me from New Bedford, . . . separated me also from the calling of a local preacher."[1]

On 16 August 1841, Douglass delivered his first significant public address. The New Bedford banker and abolitionist William C. Coffin had invited him to a large antislavery meeting in Nantucket, which was attended by many prominent abolitionists, including Garrison, Wendell Phillips, and Samuel J. May.[2] Douglass conveyed his

---

1. Frederick Douglass, quoted in McFeely, *Frederick Douglass,* 85.
2. Ibid., 87–89.

personal history in much the same way that it is summarized below, though no transcript is available of the speech. Douglass made such a powerful impression at the Nantucket gathering that the Massachusetts Anti-Slavery Society invited him to become an itinerant lecturing agent.[3]

Within months, Douglass had begun to display his considerable speaking skills before audiences across New England. The *Pennsylvania Freeman* published the account below of one of these early addresses, delivered in Lynn, Massachusetts. The article revealed that he had achieved enough fame to be described as "Frederick Douglass, *the* runaway slave." The *Freeman's* writer commented that the speech "came so spontaneously that it thrilled through every one present, and compelled them to feel for the wrongs he had endured."

The speech foregrounds Douglass's physical experience of slavery. He encourages listeners to identify with his physical pain by giving visceral details such as "my blood has sprung out as the lash embedded itself in my flesh." He frequently notes the limitations of language, as when he says, "The agony of the mother when parting from her children cannot be told."

Early in his career, Douglass became adept at what Thomas Laqueur has termed "humanitarian sensationalism," that is, narratives of bodily pain that inspire "sympathetic passions" and bridge "the gulf between facts, compassion, and action."[4] Douglass and his abolitionist colleagues sought to construct a story that systematically traced the origins of slaves' pain back to the South's "peculiar institution" and connected that pain with listeners' and readers' own experiences. Early antislavery tracts had generalized about the negative effects of slavery upon slaves, slaveholders, and the nation as a whole, but by Douglass's time as an abolitionist speaker, specific tales of slave suffering dominated the discourse.

At its best, humanitarian sensationalism moves people to act on behalf of those who suffer, but as Marianne Noble argues, at its worst it can paralyze listeners, allowing them to turn inward and enjoy a

3. Ibid., 89.
4. Thomas Laqueur, "Bodies, Details, and the Humanitarian Narrative," in *The New Cultural History*, ed. Lynn Hunt (Berkeley: University of California Press, 1989), 179.

"good cry" before returning to their daily lives.[5] Identification with a suffering victim and his or her helplessness can undermine action. Douglass seemingly was aware of this danger when telling the story of the division of labor in the South between "thinkers" and manual laborers. He declares, even in this short speech, his capacity for both thinking and feeling and encourages listeners to feel for slaves *and* act on their behalf.

Finally, this early speech contains a criticism of organized religion in the United States that Douglass would return to and expand on throughout his career. Southern slaveholding religion, he asserts, was built on superstition to defend slavery. His May 1846 speech, "American Slavery, American Religion, and the Free Church of Scotland," included in this volume, approaches the subject from a different angle. It explores the connection between the financial power of slaveholders and the reluctance of organized churches, even ones as far away as Scotland, to denounce slavery. In what became a central theme of his early abolitionist lecturing, Douglass revealed how religious leaders used biblical interpretation and church practice to sanction the nation's pervasive racist ideology undergirding slavery.

I feel greatly embarrassed when I attempt to address an audience of white people. I am not used to speak to them, and it makes me tremble when I do so, because I have always looked up to them with fear. My friends, I have come to tell you something about slavery—what *I know* of it, as I have *felt* it. When I came North, I was astonished to find that the abolitionists knew so much about it, that they were acquainted with its deadly effects as well as if they had lived in its midst. But though they can give you its history—though they can depict its horrors, they cannot speak as I can from *experience;* they cannot refer you to a back covered with scars, as I can; for I have felt these wounds; I have suffered under the lash without the power of resisting. Yes, my blood

5. Marianne Noble, *The Masochistic Pleasures of Sentimental Literature* (Princeton, N.J.: Princeton University Press, 2000), 145.

has sprung out as the lash embedded itself in my flesh. And yet my master has the reputation of being a pious man and a good Christian.[6] He was a class leader in the Methodist church. I have seen this pious class leader cross and tie the hands of one of his young female slaves,[7] and lash her on the bare skin and justify the deed by the quotation from the Bible, "he who knoweth his master's will and doeth it not, shall be beaten with many stripes."[8]

Our masters do not hesitate to prove from the Bible that slavery is right,[9] and ministers of the Gospel tell us that we were born to be slaves:—to look at our hard hands, and see how wisely Providence has adapted them to do the labor; and then tell us, holding up their delicate white hands, that theirs are not fit to work. Some of us know very well that we have not time to cease from labor, or ours would get soft too; but I have heard the superstitious ones exclaim—and ignorant people are always superstitious—that "if ever a man told the truth, that one did."

A large portion of the slaves *know* that they have a right to their liberty.—It is often talked about and read of, for some of us know how to read, although all our knowledge is gained in secret.

I well remember getting possession of a speech by John Quincy Adams, made in Congress about slavery and freedom, and reading it to my fellow slaves.[10] Oh! what joy and gladness it produced to

6. Thomas Auld (1795–1880) met and married Lucretia Anthony while a boarder in the Anthony home. Auld became a storekeeper in Hillsborough, Maryland, and inherited Douglass, along with ten other slaves, from Aaron Anthony. References to Thomas Auld in Douglass's *Narrative* and public speeches are generally uncomplimentary, although Douglass disclaimed any personal hostility toward his former owner.

7. Henny Bailey (1816–?) was a cousin of Frederick Douglass.

8. Luke 12:47.

9. While both sides in the religious disputes over slavery insisted on their biblical orthodoxy, proslavery biblical scholars relied heavily on a literal interpretation of the scriptures and identified blacks as the descendants of Ham or of Cain, heirs to curses of perpetual subjugation, and pointed out that the New Testament contained no condemnation of the institution. These writers noted that Saint Paul had admonished slaves to be obedient to their earthly masters and in one instance even ordered the escaped slave Onesimus to return to his master, Philemon.

10. John Quincy Adams (1767–1848) was the sixth U.S. president (1824–28). From 1831 until his death, Adams sat in the U.S. House of Representatives, where

know that so great, so good a man was pleading for us, and further, to know that there was a large and growing class of people in the north called abolitionists, who were moving for our freedom. This is known all through the south, and cherished with gratitude. It has increased the slaves' hope for liberty. Without it his heart would faint within him; his patience would be exhausted. On the agitation of this subject he has built his highest hopes. My friends let it not be quieted, for upon you the slaves look for help. There will be no outbreaks, no insurrections, whilst you continue this excitement: let it cease, and the crimes that would follow cannot be told.

Emancipation, my friends, is that cure for slavery and its evils. It alone will give to the south peace and quietness. It will blot out the insults we have borne, will heal the wounds we have endured, and are even now groaning under, will pacify the resentment which would kindle to a blaze were it not for your exertions, and, though it may never unite the many kindred and dear friends which slavery has torn asunder, it will be received with gratitude and a forgiving spirit. Ah! how the slave yearns for it, that he may be secure from the lash, that he may enjoy his family, and no more be tortured with the worst feature of slavery, the separation of friends and families. The whip we can bear without a murmur, compared to the idea of *separation*. Oh, my friends, you cannot feel the slave's misery, when he is separated from his kindred. The agony of the mother when parting from her children cannot be told. There is nothing we so much dread as to be sold farther south. My friends, we are not taught from books; there is a law against teaching us,[11] although I

---

he opposed slavery and fought to introduce antislavery petitions. Douglass may be referring to Adams's first antislavery speech on the floor of Congress, when late in 1831 he introduced fifteen petitions from Pennsylvania Quakers for the abolition of slavery and the slave trade in the District of Columbia. Reading these petitions in the pages of the Baltimore *American,* Douglass learned for the first time the meaning of the word "abolition" in the United States.

11. Following the Nat Turner revolt and the rise of calls for immediate abolition, a number of Southern states enacted legal impediments against educating slaves and sometimes also free blacks. Although Douglass's native Maryland never enacted such legislation, social pressure there and across the South often proved a significant barrier to slave education.

have heard some folks say we could not learn if we had a chance. The northern people say so, but the south do not believe it, or they would not have laws with heavy penalties to prevent it. The northern people think that if slavery were abolished, we would all come north. They may be more afraid of the free colored people and the runaway slaves going South. We would all seek our home and our friends, but, more than all, to escape from northern prejudice, would we go to the south. Prejudice against color is stronger north than south; it hangs around my neck like a heavy weight. It presses me out from among my fellow men, and, although I have met it at every step the three years I have been out of southern slavery, I have been able, in spite of its influence, "to take good care of myself."

"Temperance and Anti-Slavery"

An Address Delivered in Paisley, Scotland, 30 March 1846

Renfrewshire *Advertiser,* 11 April 1846.

Frederick Douglass had an abiding interest in temperance, writing in his 1845 *Narrative* of the brutalizing effects of alcohol on slaves. Both in that autobiography and in this 1846 speech, he argues that slaveholders deliberately offered slaves alcohol in order to divert their leisure time away from plans of escape or subversion. The desired effect was to make them disgusted with their overindulgence and therefore willing to return to work.

While Douglass's main goal in England, Scotland, and Ireland was to speak on behalf of the antislavery cause, he was invited to other conventions, including this one in Scotland promoting the temperance movement. He was well received, but his interactions with American temperance advocates in Britain were troubled. These Americans, often ministers, felt their moral standing compromised when Douglass exposed the nation's slave culture, especially if they were directly implicated. In a study of transatlantic lecture tours, Amanda Adams notes that when American writers traveled to Britain, they offered interpretations of American culture, especially slavery. Audiences on both sides of the ocean were fascinated by the emergence and growth of this distinctive American phenomenon.[1] The debate over slavery created tensions among Americans overseas, who felt themselves accused of being representatives of a defective culture.

1. Amanda Adams, *Performing Authorship in the Nineteenth-Century Transatlantic Lecture Tour* (Burlington, Vt.: Ashgate, 2014), 21.

Three months after this convention in Scotland, Douglass was invited to deliver impromptu remarks at the World's Temperance Convention in London. There he became embroiled in yet more controversy. The audience called out to hear Douglass speak, he proceeded to the lectern, and he briefly described the 1842 mobbing of a black temperance parade in Philadelphia, as he had done in Paisley. Cries of "Shame!" went up from the crowd, and the chairman attempted to cut Douglass short. In a letter published in the New York *Evangelist,* the Reverend Samuel Hanson Cox,[2] the moderator of the meeting, accuses Douglass of having "lugged in Anti-Slavery" and "open[ed] an avalanche on them [American delegates to the conference] for some imputed evil or monstrosity." Cox characterized Douglass as an arrogant young man who, having "been petted, and flattered, and used, and paid by certain abolitionists," "forgets himself." Douglass's searing response in the *Anti-Slavery Bugle* was one of the angriest defenses of himself as a representative black man he ever penned. In it, he insists on his duty to represent three million African Americans and their specific obstacles in achieving temperance reform as well as in ending slavery.[3] In international forums, Douglass's willingness to criticize American slavery drew out the latent racism and classism of some of his American partners in temperance reform.

L adies and Gentlemen, I am proud to stand on this platform; I regard it a pleasure and a privilege—one which I am not very frequently permitted to enjoy in the United States, such is the prejudice against the coloured man, such the hatred, such the contempt in which he is held, that no

2. Douglass questioned the Reverend Samuel Hanson Cox's antislavery credentials in an article in the Montpelier (Vt.) *Voice of Freedom,* 22 January 1846. Cox had been an abolitionist in the 1830s, but his church and his home were vandalized in an antislavery riot of 1834, which caused him to distance himself from the abolitionist campaign. See Joel Tyler Headley, *The Great Riots of New York, 1712–1873* (1873; Indianapolis: Bobbs-Merrill, 1970), 87–93.

3. "Reply of Frederick Douglass to Dr. Cox," Salem (Ohio) *Anti-Slavery Bugle,* 18 December 1846.

temperance society in the land would so far jeopardise its popularity as to invite a coloured man to stand before them. He might be a Webster[4] in intellect, a Channing[5] in literature, or a Howard[6] in philanthropy, yet the bare fact of his being a man of colour, would prevent him from being welcomed on a temperance platform in the United States. This is my apology, I have been excluded from the temperance movement in the United States, because God has given me a skin not coloured like yours. I can speak, however, in regard to the facts concerning ardent spirits, for the same spirits which make a white man drunk make a black man drunk too. Indeed, in this I can find proof of my identity with the family of man. (Laughter.) The effect of drink on the one and the other is the same.

The coloured man in the United States has great difficulties in the way of his moral, social, and religious advancement. Almost every step he takes towards mental, moral, or social improvement is repulsed by the cold indifference or the active mob of the white.[7] He is compelled to live an outcast from society; he is, as it were, a border or salvage on the great cloth of humanity, and the very fact of his degradation is given as a reason why he should be continued in the condition of a slave. The blacks are to a considerable extent

4. A successful career as a lawyer led Daniel Webster (1782–1852) into politics, and he served in numerous elected and appointed positions for the rest of his life. His tenure in the U.S. Senate is especially noteworthy for his erudite speeches on national issues. Webster clashed with states' rights advocates such as John C. Calhoun in Congress, but usually was able to work out compromises to avoid secession.

5. The Boston Unitarian minister and reformer William Ellery Channing (1780–1842), a leading writer on liberal religious principles, helped inspire Transcendentalists such as Ralph Waldo Emerson.

6. Probably Douglass alludes to the British reformer John Howard (1726–90), who campaigned tirelessly to expose inhumane conditions in his nation's prisons.

7. Douglass may be alluding to a specific incident familiar to him and many in his audience. American abolitionists annually celebrated West Indian Emancipation Day on 1 August. On that day in 1842 in Philadelphia, a white mob attacked blacks during a procession of the Young Men's Vigilant Association, a black temperance society. Two days of rioting resulted in the beating of many blacks and the burning of the African Beneficial Hall and the Second African Presbyterian Church. The Pennsylvania militia intervened to restore order, and the Pennsylvania Supreme Court ultimately awarded damages to the owners of the church and the hall.

intemperate, and if intemperate, of course vicious in other respects, and this is counted against them as a reason why their emancipation should not take place. As I desire, therefore, their freedom from physical chains, so I desire their emancipation from intemperance, because I believe it would be the means—a great and glorious means—towards helping to break their physical chains and letting them go free.

To give you some idea of the strength of this prejudice and passion against the coloured people, I may state that they formed themselves into a temperance procession in Philadelphia, on the day on which the legislature in this country had by a benevolent act awarded freedom to the negroes in the West Indian islands.[8] They formed themselves into a procession with appropriate banners,[9] but they had not proceeded up two streets before they were attacked by a reckless mob, their procession broken up, their banners destroyed, their houses and churches burned, and all because they had dared to have a temperance procession on the 1st of August. They had saved enough to build a hall, besides their churches. These were not saved, they were burned down, and the mob was backed up by the most respectable people in Philadelphia. These are the difficulties which beset their path. And yet the Americans, those demons in human shape, they speak to us, and say that we are morally and religiously incapacitated for enjoying liberty with themselves. I am afraid I am making this an anti-slavery meeting. (Cheers.) I want to state another fact. The black population pay sufficient tax to government to support their own poor, besides 300 dollars over

8. Douglass refers to the abolition of slavery in British colonies, achieved by parliamentary and colonial legislation between 1833 and 1838. The number of slaves emancipated in the West Indies was 800,000.

9. The banners carried by Philadelphia's black temperance marchers became a focus of controversy after the procession was attacked on 1 August 1842. Some observers claimed that white bystanders were angered by a flag "showing a colored man breaking his chains and depicting the rising son of freedom." Supposedly, some rioters misread the scene as "a Negro triumphing over the massacre of whites at St. Domingo." Leaders of the city's black community hotly disputed this version of the riot's origin.

and above.[10] This is a fact which no American pale-face can deny. (Cheers.) I, however, love white people when they are good; but this is precious seldom.

I have had some experiences of intemperance as well as of slavery. In the Southern States, masters induce their slaves to drink whiskey, in order to keep them from devising ways and means by which to attain their freedom. In order to make a man a slave, it is necessary to silence or drown his mind. It is not the flesh that objects to being bound—it is the spirit. It is not the mere animal part—it is the immortal mind which distinguishes man from the brute creation. To blind his affections, it is necessary to bedim and bedizzy his understanding. In no other way can this be so well accomplished as by using ardent spirits! On Saturday evening, it is the custom of the slaveholder to give his slaves drink, and why? Because if they had time to think, if left to reflection on the Sabbath day, they might devise means by which to obtain their liberty.

I knew once what it is to drink with all the ardour of *old soker.*[11] I lived with a Mr. Freeland[12] who used to give his slaves apple brandy. Some of the slaves were not able to drink their own share, but I was able to drink my own and theirs too. I took it because it made me feel I was a great man. I used to think I was a president. And this put me in mind of a man who once thought himself a president. He was coming across a field pretty tipsy. Happening to lay himself down near a pig-sty, and the pig being out at the time, he crawled into it.

10. Abolitionists frequently described the African American community of Philadelphia as a model of the free black's economic and social progress in the face of adversity.

11. The phrase "old soker," probably referring to a drunk or alcoholic, is found in writing as early as a 15 February 1665 entry in Samuel Pepys's diary. John Bartlett, *Familiar Quotations: A Collection of Passages, Phrases and Proverbs Traced to their Sources in Ancient and Modern Literature,* 17th ed. (1855; Boston: Little, Brown, 2002), 288.

12. Douglass refers to William Freeland, a slave-owning farmer who lived near St. Michaels, Talbot County, Maryland. Douglass was hired out to Freeland in 1835 and 1836 after his stormy one-year stint with the "Negro-breaker" Edward Covey. Douglass considered Freeland "a man of many excellent qualities" and "the best master I ever had, until I became my own master."

After a little [while], in came the old sow and her company of pigs. They commenced *posing* at the intruder. An individual happening to pass at the time, heard a voice demanding order, order. He went forward and looked, when he saw a fellow surrounded by the pigs calling for order, order. (Laughter.) He had imagined he was the president of a meeting, and was calling for order.

There are certain objections urged against the temperance reform. One very frequently urged runs thus:—the gospel of Jesus Christ was given for the purpose of removing all the ills that ought to be removed from society; therefore we can have no union with teetotalism[13] because it is out of the church. It is treason to go out of her borders and join a teetotal society. There is as much truth in this as you can hang a few falsehoods upon. There is truth at the beginning. It will remove slavery, it will remove war, it will remove licentiousness, it will remove fraud, it will remove adultery. All the ills to which flesh is heir[14] will be removed by an application to them of the truths of the gospel. What we want is to adopt the most efficacious means of applying gospel truth. I dined the other day with six ministers in Perth. With the exception of one, they all drank whiskey, and that one drank wine. So disgusted was I that I left, and that night I delivered a temperance lecture.[15] I need not tell you that I was never again invited to dine in that house. I told people at Perth that the ministers were responsible for a great part of the drinking

13. The organized temperance movement advocating personal moderation in the consumption of alcoholic beverages began in the United States and several western European nations in the early nineteenth century. The 1833 origin of the more extreme position of "teetotalism," designating complete or total abstinence from alcoholic beverages except as medicine, is often traced to the English reformer Joseph Livesey of the Preston Temperance Society.

14. *Hamlet*, sc. 8, lines 1600–01.

15. The incident in question probably occurred during Douglass's visit to Perth on 12 March 1846, but no record of his encounter with the six ministers survives, and the identity of Douglass's host is impossible to determine. Local newspapers printed no text of Douglass's evening speech in Perth City Hall but did object to his "disgusting" and "contemptible" mimicry of a well-known Free Church minister. Perthshire *Advertiser*, 19 March 1846; Perthshire *Courier*, 19 March 1846.

habits among the people. The ministers have the influence to aid in removing this curse from the community; 1st, by abandoning drinking habits themselves; and, 2d, by doing what they want to make others follow their example. If the ministers used their moral influence, Scotland might soon be redeemed from this curse; and why? Because the ministers had done it in the United States.

A man would not be allowed to stand in an American pulpit if it was known that he tippled the whiskey. We feel that it is not proper that a minister of the gospel in the nineteenth century should be a man to mar the advancement of this cause, by using these intoxicating beverages. Our success has been glorious, for in Lynn[16] I never saw a barefooted child in winter—I never saw a beggar in the streets in winter—I never saw a family without fuel in winter. And why have we this glorious result? Because no money is spent for whiskey. I am a temperance man because I am an anti-slavery man; and I am an anti-slavery man because I love my fellow men. There is no other cure for intemperance but total abstinence. Will not temperance do, says one? No. Temperance was tried in America, but it would not do. The total abstinence principle came and made clean work of it. It is now seen spreading its balmy influence over the whole of that land. It is seen in making peace where there was war. It has planted light and education where there was nothing but degradation, and darkness, and misery.

It is your duty to plant—you cannot do all, but if you plant, God has promised, and will give the increase.[17] We shall see most gloriously this cause yet triumph in Scotland. Is there a man within the sound of my voice who does not know that nine-tenths of the crime, misery, disease, and death, of these lands is occasioned by

16. Douglass relocated with his family from New Bedford to Lynn in the fall of 1841 shortly after becoming a paid itinerant lecturer for the Massachusetts Anti-Slavery Society. The family remained there while Douglass toured the British Isles from 1845 to 1847.

17. 2 Cor. 9:10.

intemperance? You may talk of the charter[18] and the corn-laws,[19] but until you have banished the demon intemperance, you cannot expect one day of prosperity in your land. In the name of humanity then I call upon you to abandon your bowl. To those who would feel it no sacrifice, I say give it up. To those who would consider it a sacrifice, I say it is time you had given it up, and then we shall see our cause progressing gloriously. Were this meeting all teetotallers, and to pledge themselves to work in the cause, twelve months would see a most miraculous change in Paisley. Many thanks now for your kind patience; pardon me if I have said anything amiss, anything inconsistent with truth.

18. An allusion to the English workers' campaign in the 1830s and 1840s for suffrage. Facing growing economic dislocation from the Industrial Revolution and disappointed at the failure of the Reform Bill of 1832 to address their political rights, workers organized across the nation. A six-point petition calling for significant political reforms was overwhelmingly rejected by Parliament three times over the course of almost a decade.

19. Douglass refers to the controversial measures of agricultural protection enacted in Britain during the first half of the nineteenth century known as the Corn Laws, which were a center of parliamentary debate in 1845 during Douglass's first visit to England. They were repealed the next year.

"American Slavery, American Religion, and the Free Church of Scotland"

An Address Delivered in London, England, 22 May 1846

American Slavery: Report of a Public Meeting Held at Finsbury Chapel, Moorfields, to Receive Frederick Douglass, the American Slave, on Friday, May 22, 1846 (London, 1846), 3–24.

Antislavery activists, including Frederick Douglass, expressed deep disappointment in the reluctance of major American religious denominations to denounce slavery and to pressure their slaveholding congregants to free their slaves. Even after the Northern and South ern branches of the Methodist Episcopal and Baptist Churches split from each other, in 1844 and 1845 respectively, some abolitionists saw the schisms as more a matter of "policy" than "principle."[1] The separation of these federated churches made it possible for Northern branches to issue mild condemnations of slaveholding without affecting or offending Southern Methodist or Baptist congregations.[2]

Nonetheless, in 1846, when Frederick Douglass delivered this speech, the strategy of pressuring American churches to declare slavery immoral seemed a fruitful way to convert the nation to antislavery principles. Early in Douglass's speaking career, he identified

---

1. "Thirteenth Annual Report of the American and Foreign Anti-Slavery Society, 1853," quoted in John R. McKivigan, "The Sectional Division of the Methodist and Baptist Denominations as Measures of Northern Antislavery Sentiment," in *Religion and the Antebellum Debate over Slavery*, ed. John R. McKivigan and Mitchell Snay (Athens: University of Georgia Press, 1998), 343.

2. Ibid.

"slaveholder religion" as one of the most powerful ideological supports of slavery, and he attacked it both in his 1845 *Narrative* and
in many of his speeches. In fact, Gary Selby, a communication and
rhetoric scholar whose work examines religious rhetoric and abolitionism, argues that at this time "no theme . . . occupied [Douglass's]
attention more than religion."[3]

The American Anti-Slavery Society, led by William Lloyd Garrison, endorsed the work of several agents who made an example of
the Free Church of Scotland, a newly established, dissenting Presbyterian sect that accepted contributions from American slaveholders.[4]
The *Liberator* reported that when Frederick Douglass, Henry C.
Wright, and George Thompson delivered speeches in April 1846 in
Edinburgh, the town had been "placarded, in every direction, with
small bits of paper, printed in large letters—SEND BACK THE
MONEY."[5] Douglass participated in several protest meetings against
the Free Church of Scotland in Scottish and English cities in the
spring of 1846—Glasgow, Paisley, Edinburgh, and London among
them—all of them featuring this motto, "Send back the money." According to the London *Observer*, the meeting in Finsbury Chapel
at which Douglass delivered this speech had been called only three
days earlier, but "so intense was the interest excited, that every part
of this large edifice was crowded to suffocation."[6]

At the beginning of his lecture, Douglass establishes a definition of slavery, fearing the term "slavery" will lose its "horror" if its
true meaning is diluted through loose or weak analogies with other
wrongs. Popularly known as the "sisterhood of reforms,"[7] temper-

3. Gary Selby, "Mocking the Sacred: Frederick Douglass's 'Slaveholder's Sermon'
and the Antebellum Debate over Religion and Slavery," *Quarterly Journal of Speech*
88, no. 1 (August 2002): 330.

4. "Twelfth Annual Meeting of the American Anti-Slavery Society," Boston *Liberator*, 22 May 1846.

5. "Letter from Henry C. Wright," Boston *Liberator*, 29 May 1846.

6. "American Slavery," London *Observer*, 26 May 1846.

7. According to Thomas Wentworth Higginson, this was a term commonly used
before the Civil War to refer to interrelated reform movements premised on an ex-
pansive understanding of individual rights and the responsiveness of social organizations to deliberate change: antislavery, women's rights, temperance, and tract or
missionary societies. Because so many people were committed members of multiple
organizations, many of these organizations commonly met during "anniversary

ance, women's rights, and Christian missionary work were inclined to use a sensational rhetoric that compared any number of injustices to slavery. Douglass had participated in many meetings of these groups, and while subscribing to their goals, he saw a danger in conflating the bases for them.

Turning to his main subject, Douglass recounts that two years earlier a delegation from the Free Church of Scotland came to the United States to raise funds to build churches and hire ministers. The American and Foreign Anti-Slavery Society urged the group not to go to the South, but it did, and raised substantial funds from congregations there that welcomed slaveholders. Abolitionists hoped that their campaign against the Free Church of Scotland would generate dissent within Northern churches over slavery and, more broadly, would stigmatize slaveholding Christians in the South and the churches in the North that continued to affiliate with them.

Douglass seriously considered remaining in Britain, but by the end of the summer of 1846, he decided to return to America so long as his freedom could be secured and he could travel safely there. His new British friends raised and paid Hugh Auld £150 to secure a deed of manumission, and Douglass became a free man in December 1846.[8]

F Douglass rose amid loud cheers, and said—I feel exceedingly glad of the opportunity now afforded me of presenting the claims of my brethren in bonds in the United States to so many in London and from various parts of Britain, who have assembled here on the present occasion. I have nothing to commend me to your consideration in the way of learning, nothing in the way of education, to entitle me to your attention; and you are aware that slavery is a very bad school for

week" each year in the same city. Ronald G. Walters, "Abolition and Antebellum Reform," *History Now: The Journal of the Gilder Lehrman Institute*, accessed 24 July 2015, www.gilderlehrman.org/history-by-era/slavery-and-anti-slavery/essays/abolition-and-antebellum-reform.

8. McFeely, *Frederick Douglass*, 144.

rearing teachers of morality and religion. Twenty-one years of my life have been spent in slavery, personal slavery, surrounded by degrading influences such as can exist nowhere beyond the pale of slavery; and it will not be strange, if under such circumstances, I should betray in what I have to say to you a deficiency of that refinement which is seldom or ever found, except among persons that have experienced superior advantages to those which I have enjoyed. (Hear, hear.) But I will take it for granted that you know something about the degrading influences of slavery, and that you will not expect great things from me this evening, but simply such facts as I may be able to advance immediately in connexion with my own experience of slavery.

The subject of American slavery is beginning to attract the attention of philanthropists of all countries,—it is a matter, too, to which philosophers, statesmen, and theologians, in all parts of the world, are turning their attention. It is a matter in which the people of this country especially, and of Scotland and Ireland, are taking the deepest interest—it is a matter in which all persons, who speak the English language, must eventually become interested. It is no longer an unintelligible or obscure question, although there is much yet to be learned. In order to [obtain] the proper understanding of the subject before us, allow me briefly to state the nature of the American Government, and the geographical location of slavery in the United States. There are at this time 28 States,[9] called the United States, each of which has a constitution of its own, under which the constitution is convened, from year to year, what is called a local legislature—a legislature that has the power of making the local laws for that state. Each state is considered (within the limits of the Constitution) sovereign in itself, but over all the states there is a general government, under a federal Constitution, which constitutes these 28 states, the United States.

9. The former Republic of Texas became the twenty-eighth state of the Union on 29 December 1845.

The general government in the Congress, under the Constitution, has no right to interfere with the domestic arrangements of the individual states. The general government has the power of levying taxes, providing for the general welfare, regulating commerce, declaring war, and concluding peace. There are what are called free states and slave states; the latter are 15 in number, the former 13. The free states are divided from the slave states by what is called Mason and Dixon's line, running east and west. All the states south of the line are slave states. Notwithstanding the general government has nothing to do with the domestic and the local civil institutions of the individual state, it becomes my duty to show that the general government does after all give support to the institution of slavery as it exists in the slave states.

An attempt has been made in this country to establish the conviction that the free states of the Union have nothing whatever to do with the maintenance and perpetuity of slavery in the southern states, and many persons coming from the United States have represented themselves as coming from the free states, and have shirked all responsibility in regard to slavery on this ground. Now, I am here to maintain that slavery is not only a matter belonging to the states south of the line, but is an American institution—a United States institution—a system that derives its support as well from the non-slave-holding states, as they are called, as from the slave-holding states. The slave-holding states, to be sure, enjoy all the profits of slavery—the institution exists upon their soil; but if I were going to give the exact position of the northern and southern states it would be simply this—the slave states are the slave-holding states, while the non-slave states are the slavery-upholding states.

The physical power necessary to keep the slaves in bondage lies north of the line. The southern states admit their inability to hold their slaves, except through protection afforded by the northern states. The Constitution makes it the duty of the northern states to return the slave if he attempts to escape, to call out the army and navy to crush the slave into subjection, if he dare make an attempt

to gain his freedom.[10] The east and the west, the north and the
south, the people of Massachusetts and the people of South Carolina have, through their representatives, each in their own official
capacity, sworn before high heaven, that the slave shall be a slave
or die. So that while the free states of the American Union consent
to what they call the compromise of the Constitution of the United
States, they are responsible for the existence of slavery in the southern states. (Loud cheers.)

There are 3,000,000 of slaves, and I believe the largest estimate that has ever been made of the slave holders does not exceed 300,000.[11] How do you suppose 300,000 men are able to hold
3,000,000 men in slavery? It cannot be. The slaves could by their
own power crush their masters if they would, and take their freedom, or they could run away and defy their masters to bring them
back. Why do they not do it? It is because the people of the United
States are all pledged, bound by their oaths, bound by their citizenship in that country, to bring their whole physical power to bear
against the slave if such an event should arise. (Cries of "Shame!")
The slave has no hopes from the northern states, for they are in
connexion with the slave states of America. Every defender of the
American Union, of the compromise of the United States, no matter how much he may boast of his anti-slavery feeling, is, so far as
his citizenship goes, a pledged enemy to the emancipation of the
bondsman. I have thought it necessary to say thus much that you
might see where slavery exists, and how it exists in the United States.

The slave holders admit that they are incapable of retaining
their slaves. "Why," said one man, "we are surrounded by savages;
if they could entertain the idea that immediate death would not be
their portion, they would re-enact the St. Domingo tragedy." (Hear,
hear.) The same gentleman goes on to advocate the existence of the
slave-holding union between the states, and the utility of the union

10. The second paragraph of article IV, section 2, of the U.S. Constitution.
11. The 1840 Census of the United States tabulated 2,487,455 slaves. The 1850
Census indicated the nation had 347,725 slaveholding families.

on the ground that, should it be dissolved, the slave would cross the Mason and Dixon's line, and turn round and curse his master from the other side.

Now what is this system of slavery? This is the subject of my lecture this evening—what is the character of this institution? I am about to answer the inquiry, what is American slavery? I do this the more readily, since I have found persons in this country who have identified the term slavery with that which I think it is not, and in some instances, I have feared, in so doing have rather (unwittingly, I know) detracted much from the horror with which the term slavery is contemplated. It is common in this country to distinguish every bad thing by the name slavery. Intemperance is slavery (cheers); to be deprived of the right to vote is slavery, says one; to have to work hard is slavery, says another (laughter, and loud cheers); and I do not know but that if we should let them go on, they would say to eat when we are hungry, to walk when we desire to have exercise, or to minister to our necessities, or have necessities at all, is slavery. (Laughter.) I do not wish for a moment to detract from the horror with which the evil of intemperance is contemplated; not at all; nor do I wish to throw the slightest obstruction in the way of any political freedom that any class of persons in this country may desire to obtain. But I am here to say that I think the term slavery is sometimes abused by identifying it with that which it is not.

Slavery in the United States is the granting of that power by which one man exercises and enforces a right of property in the body and soul of another. The condition of a slave is simply that of the brute beast. He is a piece of property—a marketable commodity in the language of the law, to be bought or sold at the will and caprice of the master who claims him to be his property; he is spoken of, thought of, and treated as property. His own good, his conscience, his intellect, his affections are all set aside by the master. The will and the wishes of the master are the law of the slave. He is as much a piece of property as a horse. If he is fed, he is fed because he is property. If he is clothed, it is with a view to the increase of his

value as property. Whatever of comfort is necessary to him for his
body or soul, that is inconsistent with his being property, is carefully
wrested from him, not only by public opinion, but by the law of
the country. He is carefully deprived of everything that tends in the
slightest degree to detract from his value as property.

He is deprived of education. God has given him an intellect—the
slave holder declares it shall not be cultivated. If his moral percep-
tion leads him in a course contrary to his value as property, the slave
holder declares he shall not exercise it. The marriage institution cannot exist among slaves,[12] and one-sixth of the population of democratic America is denied its privileges by the law of the land.[13] What
is to be thought of a nation boasting of its liberty, boasting of its humanity, boasting of its Christianity, boasting of its love of justice and
purity, and yet having within its own borders three millions of persons
denied by law the right of marriage?—what must be the condition of
that people? I need not lift up the veil by giving you any experience
of my own. Every one that can put two ideas together, must see the
most fearful results from such a state of things as I have just mentioned. If any of these three millions find for themselves companions,
and prove themselves honest, upright, virtuous persons to each other,
yet in these cases—few as I am bound to confess they are—the virtuous live in constant apprehension of being torn asunder by the merciless men-stealers that claim them as their property. (Hear.)

This is American slavery—no marriage—no education—the light
of the Gospel shut out from the dark mind of the bondman—and
he forbidden by law to learn to read. If a mother shall teach her

12. Because American slave codes, for the most part, defined slaves as either
personal property or the real estate of slaveholders, a slave could not be party to a
contract such as a legal marriage. Nonetheless, some masters recognized quasi marriage—a contubernal relationship—the state of two slaves or a slave and a freeman
dwelling together. That arrangement could be ended without legal consequence.

13. Douglass's estimated percentage of free blacks and slaves in the U.S. population is accurate. In 1840 there were 386,303 free blacks and 2,487,455 slaves in an
overall population of 17,069,453, meaning the black population was 16.8 percent of
the total, which is slightly more than one-sixth. .

children to read, the law in Louisiana proclaims that she may be hanged by the neck.[14] (Sensation.) If the father attempt to give his son a knowledge of letters he may be punished by the whip in one instance, and in another be killed, at the discretion of the court. Three millions of people shut out from the light of knowledge! It is easy for you to conceive the evil that must result from such a state of things. (Hear, hear.)

I now come to the physical evils of slavery. I do not wish to dwell at length upon these, but it seems right to speak of them, not so much to influence your minds on this question, as to let the slave holders of America know that the curtain which conceals their crimes is being lifted abroad (loud cheers); that we are opening the dark cell, and leading the people into the horrible recesses of what they are pleased to call their domestic institution.[15] (Cheers.) We want them to know that a knowledge of their whippings, their scourgings, their brandings, their chainings, is not confined to their plantations, but that some negro of theirs has broken loose from his chains (loud applause)—has burst through the dark incrustation of slavery, and is now exposing their deeds of deep damnation to the gaze of the Christian people of England. (Immense cheers.)

The slave holders resort to all kinds of cruelty. If I were disposed, I have matter enough to interest you on this question for five or six evenings, but I will not dwell at length upon these cruelties. Suffice it to say, that all the peculiar modes of torture that were resorted to in the West India Islands,[16] are resorted to, I believe, even more frequently, in the United States of America. Starvation, the bloody whip, the chain, the gag, the thumb-screw, cat-hauling, the cat-o'-nine-tails, the dungeon, the bloodhound, are all in requisition

14. A Louisiana law passed in March 1830 mandated that the punishment for teaching a slave to read or write was a prison sentence of one to twelve months. Louisiana did not renew this provision when it revised its slave code in 1856.

15. A variant of "peculiar institution"—an antebellum euphemism for slavery.

16. Douglass refers to conditions endured by slaves in the British West Indian colonies, where full emancipation occurred in 1838 after a brief experiment in "apprenticeship."

to keep the slave in his condition as a slave in the United States.[17] (Hear.) If any one has a doubt upon this point, I would ask him to read the chapter on slavery in Dickens' *Notes on America*.[18] If any man has a doubt upon it, I have here the "Testimony of a Thousand Witnesses,"[19] which I can give at any length, all going to prove the truth of my statement. The bloodhound is regularly trained in the United States, and advertisements are to be found in the southern papers of the Union, from persons advertising themselves as bloodhound trainers, and offering to hunt down slaves at fifteen dollars a piece, recommending their hounds as the fleetest in the neighbourhood, never known to fail. (Much sensation.)

Advertisements are from time to time inserted, stating that slaves have escaped with iron collars about their necks, with bands of iron about their feet, marked with the lash, branded with red hot irons, the initials of their master's name burned into their flesh; and the masters advertise the fact of their being thus branded with their own signature, thereby proving to the world, that, however daring it may appear to non-slave holders, such practices are not regarded [as] discreditable or daring among the slave holders themselves. Why, I believe if a man should brand his horse in this country,— burn the initials of his name into any of his cattle, and publish the ferocious deed here,—that the united execrations of Christians in Britain would descend upon him. (Cheers.) Yet, in the United States, human beings are thus branded. As Whittier says—

---

17. Among these punishments, the less well-known included the thumbscrew, a medieval torture device that crushed the victim's bones, inflicting great pain; cat hauling, literally dragging a cat by its tail across the back of a slave to provoke the animal to dig in its claws and shred the victim's skin; and the cat-o'-nine-tails, a short multitailed whip designed to quickly inflict severe physical punishment.

18. In 1842, the British novelist Charles Dickens (1812–70) published a travelogue of the United States entitled *American Notes for General Circulation*. Chapter 16 is an indictment of the atrocities of American slavery.

19. [Theodore Dwight Weld], *American Slavery as It Is: Testimony of a Thousand Witnesses* (New York: American Anti-Slavery Society, 1839).

"What, ho! our countrymen in chains,
"The whip on woman's shrinking flesh,
"Our soil yet reddening with the stains,
"Caught from her scourgings warm and fresh."[20]

(Loud cheers.) The slave dealer boldly publishes his infamous acts to the world.

Of all things that have been said of slavery to which exception has been taken by slave holders, this, the charge of cruelty, stands foremost, and yet there is no charge capable of clearer demonstration, than that of the most barbarous inhumanity on the part of the slave holders towards their slaves. And all this is necessary—it is necessary to resort to these cruelties, in order to *make the slave a slave,* and to *keep him a slave.* Why, my experience all goes to prove the truth of what you will call a marvellous proposition, that the *better* you treat a slave, the more you destroy his value *as a slave,* and enhance the probability of his eluding the grasp of the slave holder; the more kindly you treat him, the more wretched you make him, while you keep him in the condition of a slave. My experience I say, confirms the truth of this proposition.

When I was treated exceedingly ill, when my back was being scourged daily, when I was kept within an inch of my life, *life* was all I cared for. "Spare my life," was my continual prayer. When I was looking for the blow about to be inflicted upon my head, I was not thinking of my liberty; it was my life. But, as soon as the blow was not to be feared, then came the longing for liberty. (Cheers.) If a slave has a bad master his ambition is to get a better; when he gets a better, he aspires to have the best; and when he gets the best, he aspires to be his own master. (Loud cheers.) But the slave must be brutalized to keep him as a slave. The slave holder feels this

20. From the third stanza of *Expostulation,* by the Massachusetts poet-abolitionist John Greenleaf Whittier (1807–92). John G. Whittier, *The Poetical Works of John Greenleaf Whittier,* 4 vols. (Boston: Houghton, Mifflin, 1892), 3:25.

necessity. I admit this necessity: if it be right to hold slaves at all, it is right to hold them in the only way in which they can be held; and this can be done only by shutting out the light of education from their minds, and brutalizing their persons.

The whip, the chain, the gag, the thumb-screw, the bloodhound, the stocks, and all the other bloody paraphernalia of the slave-system, are indispensably necessary to the relation of master and slave. (Cheers.) The slave must be subjected to these, or he ceases to be a slave. Let him know that the whip is burned, that the fetters have been turned to some useful and profitable employment, that the chain is no longer for his limbs, that the bloodhound is no longer to be put upon his track, that his master's authority over him is no longer to be enforced by taking his life, and immediately he walks out from the house of bondage and asserts his freedom as a man. (Loud cheers.) The slave holder finds it necessary to have these implements to keep the slave in bondage; finds it necessary to be able to say,—"Unless you do so and so; unless you do as I bid you, I will take away your life!" (Hear, hear.)

Some of the most awful scenes of cruelty are constantly taking place in the middle states of the Union. We have in those states what are called the slave-breeding states. Allow me to speak plainly. (Hear, hear.) Although it is harrowing to your feelings, it is necessary that the facts of the case should be stated. We have in the United States slave-breeding states.[21] The very state from which the Minister from our Court[22] to yours comes is one of these states (cries of "Hear")—Maryland, where men, women, and children are reared for the market just as horses, sheep, and swine are raised for

---

21. Shortly after the invention of the cotton gin in 1794, cotton supplanted tobacco in the United States as the primary European export and cash crop. This shift caused a migration of plantations, farmers, and slaves from the Upper South to the Lower South, where the climate and soil were more conducive to growing cotton. Research shows that owners in the Upper South frequently separated families through slave selling, often covertly.

22. Louis McLane (1784–1857) of Baltimore was appointed minister to the Court of St. James in July 1845. He owned nearly a dozen slaves when he died.

the market. Slave-rearing is there looked upon as a legitimate trade, the law sanctions it, public opinion upholds it, the church does not condemn it. (Cries of "Shame!") It goes on in all its bloody horrors sustained by the auctioneer's block.

If you would see the cruelties of this system, hear the following narrative:—Not long since the following scene occurred. A slave woman and a slave man had united themselves as man and wife in the absence of any law to protect them as man and wife. They had lived together by the permission, not by right, of their master, and they had reared a family. The master found it expedient, and for his interest to sell them. He did not ask them their wishes in regard to the matter at all; they were not consulted. The man and woman were brought to the auctioneer's block, under the sound of the hammer. The cry was raised, "here goes; who bids cash?" Think of it, a man and wife to be sold. (Hear, hear.) The woman was placed on the auctioneer's block; her limbs, as is customary, were brutally exposed to the purchasers, who examined her with all the freedom with which they would examine a horse. There stood the husband powerless; no right to his wife; the master's right pre-eminent. She was sold.

He was next brought to the auctioneer's block. His eyes followed his wife in the distance; and he looked beseechingly, imploringly to the man that had bought his wife, to buy him also. But he was at length bid off to another person. He was about to be separated from her he loved forever. No word of his, no work of his, could save him from this separation. He asked permission of his new master to go and take the hand of his wife at parting. It was denied him. In the agony of his soul he rushed from the man who had just bought him, that he might take a farewell of his wife; but his way was obstructed, he was struck over the head with a loaded whip, and was held for a moment; but his agony was too great. When he was let go, he fell a corpse at the feet of his master. (Much sensation.) His heart was broken. Such scenes are the every-day fruits of American slavery.

Some two years since, the Hon. Seth M. Gates,[23] an anti-slavery gentleman of the state of New York, a representative in the Congress of the United States, told me he saw with his own eyes the following circumstance. In the national District of Columbia, over which the star-spangled emblem is constantly waving, where orators are ever holding forth on the subject of American liberty, American democracy, American republicanism, there are two slave prisons. When going across a bridge leading to one of these prisons, he saw a young woman run out, bare-footed and bare-headed, and with very little clothing on. She was running with all speed to the bridge he was approaching. His eye was fixed upon her, and he stopped to see what was the matter. He had not paused long before he saw three men run out after her. He now knew what the nature of the case was, a slave escaping from her chains, a young woman, a sister, escaping from the bondage in which she had been held. She made her way to the bridge, but had not reached it, ere from the Virginia side there came two slave holders. As soon as they saw them, her pursuers called out, "Stop her." True to their Virginian instincts, they came to the rescue of their brother kidnappers—across the bridge.

The poor girl now saw that there was no chance for her. It was a trying time. She knew if she went back, she must be a slave for ever, she must be dragged down to the scenes of pollution which the slave holders continually provide for most of the poor, sinking, wretched young women, whom they call their property. She formed her resolution; and just as those who were about to take her, were going to put hands upon her, to drag her back, she leaped over the balustrades of the bridge, and down she went to rise no more. (Great sensation.) She chose death, rather than go back into the hands of those Christian slave holders from whom she had escaped. (Hear, hear.)[24]

23. Seth Merrill Gates (1800–77) was elected to the U.S. House of Representatives as an antislavery Whig in 1839 and again in 1841.

24. Douglass is referring to an incident witnessed by Gates involving a District of Columbia slave trader named Joshua Staples and an unknown slave woman. For a detailed account, see Seth M. Gates, "The Long Bridge—The Escape" in the Concord (N.H.) *Herald of Freedom*, 25 July 1845.

Can it be possible that such things as these exist in the United States? Are not these the exceptions? Are any such scenes as this general? Are no such deeds condemned by the law and denounced by public opinion? (Cheers.) Let me read to you a few of the laws of the slave-holding states of America. I think no better exposure of slavery can be made than is made by the laws of the states in which slavery exists. I prefer reading the laws to making any statement in confirmation of what I have said myself; for the slave holders cannot object to this testimony, since it is the calm, the cool, the deliberate enactment of their wisest heads, of their most clear-sighted, their own constituted representatives. (Hear, hear.) "If more than 7 slaves together are found on any road without a white person, 20 lashes a piece; for visiting a plantation without a written pass, 10 lashes; for letting loose a boat from where it is made fast, 39 lashes for the first offence; and for the second, shall have cut off from his head one ear. For keeping or carrying a club, 39 lashes. For having any article for sale, without a ticket from his master, 10 lashes."

A VOICE.—What is the name of the book?

Mr. DOUGLASS.—I read from *American Slavery as it is: Testimony of a Thousand Witnesses*. These are extracted from the slave laws. This publication has been before the public of the United States for the last seven years, and not a single fact or statement recorded therein has ever been called in question by a single slave holder. (Loud cheers.) I read, therefore, with confidence. We have the testimony of the slave holders themselves. "For travelling in any other than the most usual and accustomed road, when going alone to any place, 40 lashes. For travelling in the night without a pass, 40 lashes." I am afraid you do not understand the awful character of these lashes. You must bring it before your mind. A human being in a perfect state of nudity, tied hand and foot to a stake, and a strong man standing behind with a heavy whip, knotted at the end, each blow cutting into the flesh, and leaving the warm blood dripping to the feet (sensation); and for these trifles. "For being found in another person's negro-quarters, 40 lashes; for hunting with dogs in the woods, 30 lashes; for being on horseback without the written permission of his master, 25 lashes; for riding or going abroad in the night, or riding horses in the day time, without leave, a slave may be whipped, cropped, or branded in the cheek with the letter R, or otherwise punished, such punishment not extending to life, or so as to render him unfit for labor." The laws referred to may be found by consulting *Brevard's Digest; Haywood's Manual; Virginia Revised Code; Prince's Digest; Missouri Laws; Mississippi Revised Code;*—[25]

A Person in the Gallery.—Will you allow me to ask a question?

The CHAIRMAN.—I must beg that there may be no interruptions.[26]

Mr. DOUGLASS.—It is my custom to answer questions when they are put to me.

The Person in the Gallery.—What is the value of a good slave? (Hissing.)

Mr. DOUGLASS.—Slaves vary in price in different parts of the United States. In the middle states, where they grow them for the market, they are much cheaper than in the far south. The slave trader who purchases a slave in Maryland for 700 dollars, about £160 of your money, will sell him in Louisiana for 1,000 dollars, or £200. There is great speculation in this matter, and here let me state, that when the price of cotton is high so is that of the slave. I will give you an invariable rule by which to ascertain the price of human flesh in the United States. When cotton gets up in the market in England, the price of human flesh gets up in the United States. (Hear, hear.) How much responsibility attaches to you in the use of that commodity. (Loud cheers.)

To return to my point. A man for going to visit his brethren, without the permission of his master, and in many instances he may not have that permission, his master from caprice or other reasons, may

25. [Weld], *American Slavery as It Is,* 144.
26. The English Quaker Joseph Sturge (1793–1859) was secretary of the Birmingham Anti-Slavery Society and organized public demonstrations against the West Indian apprenticeship system in 1835. When Frederick Douglass visited Birmingham in December 1845 to address a local temperance society, he was a dinner guest at Sturge's home.

not be willing to allow it, may be caught on his way, dragged to a post, the branding iron heated, and the name of his master or the letter R branded into his cheek or on his forehead. (Sensation.) They treat slaves thus on the principle that they must punish for light offences in order to prevent the commission of larger ones. I wish you to mark that in the single state of Virginia there are 71 crimes for which a coloured man may be executed; while there are only three of these crimes, which when committed by a white man will subject him to that punishment.[27] (Hear, hear.)

There are many of these crimes which if the white man did not commit, he would be regarded as a scoundrel and a coward. In South Maryland, there is a law to this effect:—that if a slave shall strike his master, he may be hanged, his head severed from his body, his body quartered, and his head and quarters set up in the most prominent place in the neighbourhood.[28] (Sensation.) If a coloured woman, in defence of her own virtue, in defence of her own person, should shield herself from the brutal attacks of her tyrannical master, or make the slightest resistance, she may be killed on the spot.[29] (Loud cries of "Shame!") No law whatever will bring the guilty man to justice for the crime.

But you will ask me, can these things be possible in a land professing Christianity? Yes, they are so; and this is not the worst. No, a darker feature is yet to be presented than the mere existence of these facts. I have to inform you that the religion of the southern states, at this time, is the great supporter, the great sanctioner of the bloody atrocities to which I have referred. (Deep sensation.) While America is printing tracts and Bibles; sending missionaries abroad

27. In fact, none of the seventy-one crimes codified in Virginia law as capital offenses for slaves or free blacks carried the death penalty for a white convicted of them. See Weld's *American Slavery*, which cites figures from the first edition of *A Sketch of the Laws Relating to Slavery* (1827), by the Philadelphia jurist George M. Stroud.

28. The law, enacted by the Maryland assembly in 1729, is quoted in Stroud, *Laws Relating to Slavery*. The reason for the designation "South Maryland" is unclear.

29. A South Carolina statue, quoted in [Weld], *American Slavery as It Is*, 144–45.

to convert the heathen; expending her money in various ways for the promotion of the Gospel in foreign lands, the slave not only lies forgotten—uncared for, but is trampled under foot by the very churches of the land. What have we in America? Why we have slavery made part of the religion of the land. Yes, the pulpit there stands up as the great defender of this cursed *institution,* as it is called. Ministers of religion come forward, and torture the hollowed pages of inspired wisdom to sanction the bloody deed. (Loud cries of "Shame!") They stand forth as the foremost, the strongest defenders of this "institution." As a proof of this, I need not do more than state the general fact, that slavery has existed under the droppings of the sanctuary of the south, for the last 200 years, and there has not been any war between the *religion* and the *slavery* of the south.

Whips, chains, gags, and thumb-screws have all lain under the droppings of the sanctuary, and instead of rusting from off the limbs of the bondman, these droppings have served to preserve them in all their strength. Instead of preaching the Gospel against this tyranny, rebuke, and wrong, ministers of religion have sought, by all and every means, to throw in the background whatever in the Bible could be construed into opposition to slavery, and to bring forward that which they could torture into its support. (Cries of "Shame!") This I conceive to be the darkest feature of slavery, and the most difficult to attack, because it is identified with religion, and exposes those who denounce it to the charge of infidelity. Yes, those with whom I have been labouring, namely, the old organization Anti-Slavery Society of America,[30] have been again and again stigmatized as infidels, and for what reason? Why, solely in consequence of the faithfulness of their attacks upon the slave-holding religion of the southern states, and the northern religion that sympathizes with it. (Hear, hear.)

I have found it difficult to speak on this matter without persons coming forward and saying, "Douglass, are you not afraid of injuring

30. American Anti-Slavery Society.

the cause of Christ? You do not desire to do so, we know; but are you not undermining religion?" This has been said to me again and again, even since I came to this country, but I cannot be induced to leave off these exposures. (Loud cheers.)

I love the religion of our blessed Saviour, I love that religion that comes from above, in the "wisdom of God, which is first pure, then peaceable, gentle, and easy to be entreated, full of mercy and good fruits, without partiality and without hypocrisy."[31] I love that religion that sends its votaries to bind up the wounds of him that has fallen among thieves.[32] I love that religion that makes it the duty of its disciples to visit the fatherless and widow in their affliction.[33] I love that religion that is based upon the glorious principle, of love to God and love to man (cheers); which makes its followers do unto others as they themselves would be done by.[34] If you demand liberty to yourself, it says, grant it to your neighbours. If you claim a right to think for yourselves, it says, allow your neighbours the same right. If you claim to act for yourselves, it says, allow your neighbours the same right. It is because I love this religion that I hate the slave-holding, the woman-whipping, the mind-darkening, the soul-destroying religion that exists in the southern states of America. (Immense cheering.) It is because I regard the one as good, and pure, and holy, that I cannot but regard the other as bad, corrupt, and wicked. Loving the one I must hate the other, holding to the one I must reject the other,[35] and I, therefore, proclaim myself an infidel to the slaveholding religion of America. (Reiterated cheers.)

Why, as I said in another place, to a smaller audience the other day, in answer to the question, "Mr. Douglass, are there not Methodist churches, Baptist churches, Congregational churches, Episcopal churches, Roman Catholic churches, Presbyterian churches

31. James 3:17.
32. Luke 10:30–37.
33. James 1:27.
34. Matt. 7:12; Luke 6:31, 10:25–28.
35. Matt. 6:24; Luke 16:13.

in the United States, and in the southern states of America, and do they not have revivals of religion, accessions to their ranks from day to day, and will you tell me that these men are not followers of the meek and lowly Saviour?" Most unhesitatingly I do. Revivals in religion, and revivals in the slave trade, go hand in hand together. (Cheers.) The church and the slave prison stand next to each other; the groans and cries of the heartbroken slave are often drowned in the pious devotions of his religious master. (Hear, hear.) The church-going bell and the auctioneer's bell chime in with each other; the pulpit and the auctioneer's block stand in the same neighbourhood; while the blood-stained gold goes to support the pulpit, the pulpit covers the infernal business with the garb of Christianity. We have men sold to build churches, women sold to support missionaries, and babies sold to buy Bibles and communion services for the churches. (Loud cheers.)

A Voice.—It is not true.

Mr. DOUGLASS.—Not true! is it not? (Immense cheers.) Hear the following advertisement:—"Field Negroes, by Thomas Gadsden." I read now from *The American Churches, the Bulwarks of American Slavery;* by an American, or by J.G. Birney. This has been before the public in this country and the United States for the last six years; not a fact nor a statement in it has been called in question. (Cheers.) The following is taken from the *Charleston Courier* of Feb. 12, 1835:—"Field Negroes, by Thomas Gadsden. On Tuesday, the 17th inst., will be sold, at the north of the Exchange, at 10 o'clock, a primed gang of ten negroes, accustomed to the culture of cotton and provisions, belonging to the Independent Church, in Christ Church parish."[36] (Loud cheers.) I could read other testimony on this point, but is it necessary? (Cries of "No," and "One more.")

Is it required that one more be given? You shall have another. (Loud cheers.) A notice taken from a Savannah paper will show that slaves are often bequeathed to the missionary societies. "Bryan

36. James Gillespie Birney, *The American Churches: The Bulwarks of American Slavery* (1840; New York: Arno, 1969), 11.

Superior Court. Between John J. Maxwell and others, executors of Ann Pray, complainants, and Mary Sleigh and others, devisees and legatees under the will of Ann Pray, defendants, in equity. A bill having been filed for the distribution of the estate of the testatrix, Ann Pray, and it appearing that among other legacies in her will is the following:—viz., a legacy of one fourth of certain negro slaves to the American Board of Commissioners for domestic (foreign it probably should have been) missions, for the purpose of sending the Gospel to the heathen, and particularly to the Indians of this continent; it is on motion of the solicitors of the complainants ordered, that all persons claiming the said legacy do appear and answer the bill of the complainants within four months from this day. And it is ordered, that this order be published in a public Gazette of the city of Savannah, and in one of the Gazettes of Philadelphia once a month, for four months. Extract from the minutes, December 2, 1832."[37] (Cheers.) The bequest I am in duty bound to say, was not accepted by the board. (Cheers.) But let me tell you what would have been accepted by the board. Had those slaves been sold by Ann Pray, and the money bequeathed to that board, the price of their blood would have gone into the treasury, and they would have quoted Chalmers, Cunningham, and Candlish[38] in support of the deed. (Cheers.)

Not only are legacies left and slaves sold in this way to build churches, but the right is openly defended by the church. In 1836 the great Methodist Church in America, holding through ministers, and elders, and members, in their own church 250,000 slaves, said in their general conference in Cincinnati that they had no right, no wish, no intention to interfere with the relation of master and slave as it existed in the slave states of the American union.[39] What was this but saying to the world, we have no right, no wish, no intention

37. Ibid.

38. Douglass refers to three of the most prominent ministers of the Free Church of Scotland: Thomas Chalmers (1780–1847), William Cunningham (1805–61), and William Candlish (?–1867?).

39. The resolution censuring two Methodist ministers for their antislavery activities was adopted by the Methodist General Conference of 1836 in Cincinnati and is quoted in Birney, *American Churches*, 16.

to release the bondman from his chains? The annual conference in the south took the broad ground of the right of property in man, asserting it in a resolution, proclaiming it in an address, preaching it in thanksgiving sermons, putting it forth in 4th of July orations, and even quoting Scripture.[40] I could tire your patience by reading if it were required, extracts from documents, the genuineness of which has never been called into question, showing that right is asserted by the slave holder, to property in human beings. (Hear, hear.)

But I must hasten to another point—How are we to get rid of this system? This is the question which mostly concerns the people of this country. There are different ways by which you may operate against slavery. First let me state how it is upheld; it is upheld by public opinion. How is public opinion maintained? Mainly by the press and by the pulpit. How are we to get these committed on the side of freedom? How are we to change our pro-slavery pulpit into an anti-slavery one, our pro-slavery literature to anti-slavery literature, our pro-slavery press into an anti-slavery press?

I can only point British abolitionists to the mode they adopted in their own country. Here, happily for you, the pulpit was already on your side to a considerable extent, at least the Dissenting pulpit. (Cheers.) The Wesleyans have retained a sufficiency of the spirit of their founder, John Wesley,[41] to declare with him, that slavery is the sum of all villainies.[42] (Cheers.) You had but to proclaim the sin of slavery in the people's ears, and they rallied around your standard on behalf of emancipation. Not so in our country. They have taken the strongest ground against us, but I am in duty bound to say that

40. Birney, *American Churches*, 21–23.
41. The Anglican minister John Wesley (1703–91) preached as a missionary in Georgia, where he developed a deep moral aversion to slavery. Back in England, Wesley began organizing an evangelical movement within the Church of England. American Methodists launched an independent denomination in 1784, immediately after the American Revolution, and their English counterparts did so shortly following Wesley's death.
42. Douglass refers to John Wesley's description of the slave trade as "that execrable sum of all villanies." *The Works of the Rev. John Wesley, A.M.,* ed. Thomas Jackson, 14 vols., 3d ed. (London: John Mason, 1831), 3:453.

in the northern states they are fast getting into your own way. I will, however, speak of this under another head. We have had the pulpit against us. I am not here to represent one class of abolitionists, particularly, in the United States, but the cause of the slave, and the friends of the slave, at large. However, I am more interested in the religious aspect of this question than in its political aspect.

There are two classes of abolitionists in the United States: one takes the ground that slavery is the creature of the law, that it must, therefore, be proceeded against as such; and they have formed themselves into what is called, "The liberty party." There is another class—that with which I am particularly associated, and they take the ground that our energies should be devoted to the purifying of the moral sentiment of the country, by directing its energies to the purification of the church, and the exclusion of slave holders from communion with it. (Loud cheers.) We have proceeded at once to expose the inconsistency of retaining men-stealers as members of the Church of Christ. Our attention was more particularly turned to this, by this able collection of facts by J.G. Birney, who was in this country about six years since.[43] He brought together a number of facts, showing that the American churches were the bulwarks of American slavery. Finding this to be the case, we brought the denunciations of the inspired volume to bear against slave holding and slave holders; for after all, it is with the slave holder that we have to do, and not with the system. It is easy to denounce the system; many of the slave holders will hold up their hands to denounce the system; the Free Church of Scotland will denounce the system, but the brand of infamy is to be fixed upon the brow of the slave holder. (Cheers.) Here alone we can successfully meet and overthrow this system of iniquity.

43. The Alabama slave owner James Gillespie Birney (1792–1857) was a leading colonizationist until 1834, when he publicly endorsed immediate emancipation and freed his six slaves. After the 1840 World's Anti-Slavery Convention, Birney lectured in Scotland, England, and Ireland and published his pamphlet *The American Churches*.

The abolitionists have been labouring for the last fifteen years, in season and out of season, in the midst of obloquy and reproach, in the midst of mobs and various kinds of opposition, to establish the conviction that slave holding is a sin, and that the slave holder is a sinner and ought to be treated as such. (Loud cheers.) Thanks to heaven, we have succeeded to a considerable extent in establishing this conviction in the minds of the people in the north and to some extent in the south. Our efforts have been devoted to bringing the denunciations of religion against it. In this way we have succeeded in expelling pro-slavery, and putting in their stead, anti-slavery publications. Half-a-dozen faithful abolitionists in the north were found sufficient to purify a church.

Never was the truth of that saying in the Scriptures more beautifully illustrated, that "one should chase a thousand, and two put ten thousand to flight,"[44] than in the history of this movement as regards members of the church. Five or six members would band together and say to the minister, "We want you to remember the poor slave in your prayers. We hear you thank God that you live in a land of civil and religious liberty, and yet, you make no reference to the three millions who are denied the privilege of learning the name of the God that made them. We ask you to pray for the slave." He would say, "No; I cannot pray for the slave, I should give offence to that rich member of my church who contributes largely to my salary. I may drive him from the church, and may be the means of destroying his soul. (Laughter.) Is it not better that I should preach such doctrines as would retain him in the church, and thereby, by enunciating great principles, be the means eventually—mark, eventually—of bringing him to a sense of his duty in this matter? I cannot mention the slave." But the brethren insisted upon it, growing more and more firm. In the prayer meeting *they* would pray for the slave. (Cheers.) In the conference meeting *they* would exhort for the slave; they would tell of his woes; and beg their brethren to

44. Deut. 32:30.

unite with them; the consequence would be, that in a short time they must be put out of the church, or they must leave the church.

Often they would say to the minister, "Unless you remember the bondman we cannot support you; we must leave our pews vacant." One vacant pew is all-powerful in asserting a great and glorious principle, when it is vacant in consequence of adherence to it. A few vacant seats, would soon make the minister see that something must be done for the slave, and he would commit himself by opening his mouth in prayer. To be sure this is not the highest motive by which he could be influenced; but this was one of the motives, and I think a legitimate one, by which the friends might operate on the man. For, after all, bread and butter has a great influence on the subject. (Laughter and cheers.) I am convinced, however, that a great number of northern pulpits came up to this glorious work from higher motives than self-interest; and I believe their hearts were always on the side of the slave, and their only fear was, they could not live and preach the Gospel. They thought it was necessary for them to live.

George Bradburn,[45] an individual whom some of you may remember was present at the World's Convention in 1840, said, he was once met by a minister, who said to him, "Brother Bradburn, I think you abolitionists are too severe upon us poor ministers; we have to take a great deal; you do not seem to remember it is necessary we should live." Said George Bradburn, in his peculiar way, "I do not admit any such necessity. (Laughter.) I hold that it is not necessary for any man to live unless he can live honestly." (Cheers.)

Our proceedings with the church have had the effect of dissolving several very important connexions with the slave states. Previously to this movement the slave-holding minister could come to the north and preach in our pulpits; the northern minister could go to the south and preach in their pulpits; the slave-holding min-

45. George Bradburn (1806–80) was not a strict Garrisonian. He opposed all propositions to dissolve the Union and favored political abolitionism instead. In the 1840s he lectured for the Garrisonians and traveled with Douglass on many occasions.

ister of a church could come and join a northern church; and the
northern minister could go and join the southern church. All were
woven and interwoven, linked and interlinked together; they had a
common cause to maintain. Now we have succeeded in making it
unpopular and discreditable to hold Christian fellowship with slave
holders. (Cheers.) The great Methodist general conference in 1844,
came to the decision that it was at least not expedient, or it rather it
was inexpedient, for a bishop to hold slaves. This was a great step.
(Hear, hear.) I must dwell upon this, not, however, to reflect on our
Methodist brethren, but as an illustration of the state of morals in
the church.

A [non]slave-holding bishop, Bishop Andrews, of South Carolina, married a slave-holding wife, and became the possessor of
15 slaves. At this time, the Methodist church in the north, were
of opinion that bishops should not hold slaves. They remonstrated
with the conference to induce Bishop Andrews to emancipate his
slaves. The conference did it in this way if they did it [at] all. A resolution was brought in, when the bishop was present, to the following effect:—"Whereas Bishop Andrews has connected himself with
slavery, and has thereby injured his itinerancy as a bishop,"—it was
not, Whereas Bishop Andrews has connected himself with slavery,
and has thereby become guilty, or has done a great wrong;"—but
"has thereby injured his itinerancy as a bishop; we therefore resolve
that Bishop Andrews be, and he hereby is,"—what?—"requested
to suspend his labours as bishop till he can get rid of"—what?—
slavery?—"his impediment."[46] (Laughter.) This was the name given

---

46. The resolution reads: "Whereas Bishop Andrew has become connected with
slavery by marriage and otherwise, and this act having drawn after it circumstances
which in the estimation of the General Conference will greatly embarrass the exercise of his office as an itinerant general Superintendent, if not in some places entirely
prevent it; therefore, Resolved, That it is the sense of this General Conference that
he desist from the exercise of this office so long as this impediment remains." James
Osgood Andrew (1794–1871) preached in circuits in Georgia, North Carolina, and
South Carolina. Some modern scholars dispute the traditional account that Andrew
became a slave owner only through marriage.

to slavery. One might have inferred from the preamble that it was to get rid of his wife. (Laughter, and loud cheers.)

How long did it take to pass that resolution? They remained in New York discussing this question three weeks. They had fasting and prayers; they had various kinds of meetings. Part of the slave-holding ministers remonstrated against the resolution, as an insult to the slave-holding members of the conference. The resolution, however, was passed, although it was partly recalled by subsequent action on the part of the general conference. Such was the determination of the slave-holding members of that conference to adhere to the institution of slavery, that they at once moved for a dissolution of fellowship with the northern anti-slavery members of that conference. It was not the northern members that came out from the slave-holding members, but the slave-holding members that came out from the northern members.[47] (Hear, hear.)

I am glad the cessation took place; it was our efforts in the north that made it necessary. "Coming events cast their shadows before them."[48] They saw that the spirit that was manifested in 1844, that the holding of slaves was injurious to the itinerancy of the bishop, would in 1848, in all probability, go so far as to say that it was not only injurious to this itinerancy, but at variance with the law of God, and they have now seceded. It was to get rid of the anti-slavery men, but they took the wrong course to preserve their institution.

What we want is to get the slave holders pent up by themselves; too little distinction has been drawn between the slave holder and the anti-slavery man, between the pure and the base. We want to get slave-holding politics, slave-holding civility, slave-holding religion, slave-holding ministers, slave-holding bishops, slave-holding church members, slave-holding churches, and slave-holding everything, in a position where the eyes of the world can look at them, without looking through any other thing else. (Cheers.) This we are

47. An allusion to 2 Cor. 6:17.
48. "Lochiel's Warning." *The Poems of Thomas Campbell* (Chicago: M. A. Donohue, 1885), 67–70.

doing. The Baptists have dissolved their connexion.[49] The Free-will
Baptists have long done so.[50] The Covenanters have always been
separated.[51] The Society of Friends many years ago set an example
to the world of excluding slave holders.[52] (Loud cheers.) We have
succeeded in creating a warm and determined religious feeling
against slavery.

Even political abolitionists are opposed to slavery on religious
ground[s]; although I feel that they have not been so active on religious grounds as they ought to have been, yet I would not say that
they have been without religious influence in bringing forward this
question. Although they could not do so in their party, they have
done so as individuals. Gerrit Smith[53] has taken a leading part. Wil-

49. Douglass exaggerated the degree to which Northern Baptists moved toward
abolitionism in the highly publicized sectional schism in the denomination's missionary societies in 1845. For over a decade, abolitionists had protested against the
acceptance of slaveholders' contribution by Baptist missionary organizations, and as a
consequence Southern Baptists founded their own missionary organizations in 1845.
Most Northern Baptists continued to refrain from condemning slaveholding as a sin
and accepted visiting slave owners to their communion.

50. Free Will Baptists originated in 1780 in New Hampshire, under the leadership of Benjamin Randall (1749–1808). By the mid-nineteenth century, the church
claimed 60,000 members. In 1827, the church's General Conference agreed to ordain black ministers and later accepted the ordination of women. Abolitionists nevertheless condemned Free Will Baptists in New England for supporting Democratic
party nominees.

51. In 1800, the Reformed, or Covenanter, Presbyterians ordered their members
to free their slaves. In addition, they had to refuse to swear oaths or vote, because the
church regarded the U.S. government as lacking God's sanction, as shown by the federal protection afforded slavery. The Reformed Presbyterians were one of the few denominations that Garrisonian abolitionists regularly exempted from their blanket condemnations of the compromised character of American churches on the slavery issue.

52. In 1758, John Woolman and Anthony Benezet persuaded the Philadelphia
Yearly Meeting of Friends to reprove their members for owning slaves. By the
1780s, Quaker slaveholders had either emancipated their bondsmen or quit the
sect. Friends dominated the early abolition societies that successfully persuaded
the Northern states to end slavery, usually by gradual means. The Quakers' pacifistic
beliefs, however, made them less active in the immediate-abolition movement arising in the 1830s than their early history and reputation would have suggested.

53. Gerrit Smith (1797–1874) joined the movement to create "Free" or "Union"
antislavery churches outside the existing denominational structure by 1838. In 1840
Smith began a thirty-year career as a political abolitionist by running for governor of
New York on the Liberty party ticket. He was elected to Congress as an independent
in 1852.

liam Goodell[54] is calling for separation from slave holders; and a great mass of the abolitionists of New York are taking ground against the union with slave holders in a religious form. We have succeeded in divorcing slave holders from the church to a considerable extent. I fear that I am proceeding at too great a length. (Cries of "No, no.") I therefore come back hastily to what I wish you to do.

The CHAIRMAN here rose, and said—There is not a foot of ground in the United States where Frederick Douglass's legal owner[55] would not have a right to seize him. This man, as may be supposed, is highly enraged at the course he is pursuing, and this stimulates his desire to get possession of his person, and to inflict upon him the punishment which he thinks his conduct deserves. Frederick Douglass has left a wife[56] and four children[57] in America, and I wish to state that he has published a little book, entitled *The Narrative of Frederick Douglass,* which may be had at the door, and by the sale of which he and his wife and his children are supported.

A Voice.—Who is his legal owner?

Mr. DOUGLASS.—I ran away from Thomas Auld, of St. Michael's, Talbot county, Maryland, who was my legal owner. Since I

54. The New York abolitionist William Goodell (1792–1878) helped organize both the American Anti-Slavery Society and the Liberty party. Convinced that even churches neutral on the slavery issue were anti-Christian, Goodell argued that all successful reforms had to "begin at the house of God." He therefore urged abolitionists to withdraw from existing churches in his doctrine of "Come-Outerism."

55. Between 1826 and 1833, and again between 1836 and 1838, the young Frederick Douglass lived and worked in Hugh Auld's household, lent by his owner, Hugh's brother Thomas. In 1845, Hugh (1799–1861), incensed by Douglass's depiction of his family in the *Narrative,* bought Douglass, then on a lecture tour of Britain, from his brother Thomas. According to the *Pennsylvania Freeman,* Auld was determined to reenslave Douglass. In 1846, two British abolitionists, Anna and Ellen Richardson purchased Douglass's freedom from Auld for £150 sterling.

56. Anna Murray Douglass (c. 1813–82), born to free parents and moved to Baltimore at seventeen, where she worked as a domestic. She met Douglass at meetings of the East Baltimore Mental Improvement Society, helped finance his escape, and, according to plan, joined him in New York City, where they were married on 15 September 1838.

57. Rosetta Douglass Sprague (1839–1906), Lewis Henry Douglass (1840–1908), Frederick Douglass Jr. (1842–92), and Charles Remond Douglass (1844–1920). A fifth child, Annie Douglass (1849–60), was born after his return from Britain, but lived not quite eleven years, dying on 13 March 1860 after a lengthy illness.

came to this country, I have, as our president has said, published a narrative of my experience, and I kindly sent a copy to my master. (Laughter, and cheers.) He has become so offended with me, that he says he will not own me any longer, and, in his boundless generosity, he has transferred his legal right in my body and soul to his brother, Hugh Auld (laughter), who now lives in Baltimore, and who declares that he will have me if I ever set my foot on American soil. (Hear, hear.)

I may be asked, why I am so anxious to bring this subject before the British public—why I do not confine my efforts to the United States? My answer is, first, that slavery is the common enemy of mankind, and all mankind should be made acquainted with its abominable character. (Cheers.) My next answer is, that the slave is a man, and, as such, is entitled to your sympathy as a brother. (Hear, hear.) All the feelings, all the susceptibilities, all the capacities, which you have, he has. He is a part of the human family. He has been the prey—the common prey—of Christendom for the last 300 years, and it is but right, it is but just, it is but proper, that his wrongs should be known throughout the world. (Cheers.)

I have another reason for bringing this matter before the British public, and it is this, slavery is a system of wrong, so blinding to all around, so hardening to the heart, so corrupting to the morals, so deleterious to religion, so sapping to all the principles of justice in its immediate vicinity, that the community surrounding it lack the moral stamina necessary to its removal. It is a system of such gigantic evil, so strong, so overwhelming in its power, that no one nation is equal to its removal. It requires the humanity of Christianity, the morality of the world, to remove it. (Cheers.) Hence I call upon the people of Britain to look at this matter, and to exert the influence I am about to show they possess, for the removal of slavery from America. I can appeal to them, as strongly by their regard for the slave holder as for the slave, to labour in this cause. (Hear, hear.)

I am here because you have an influence on America that no other nation can have. You have been drawn together by the power of steam to a marvellous extent; the distance between London and Boston is now reduced to some 12 or 14 days, so that the denunciations against slavery uttered in London this week, may be heard in a fortnight in the streets of Boston, and reverberating amidst the hills of Massachusetts. There is nothing said here against slavery, that will not be recorded in the United States. (Hear, hear.)

I am here also, because the slave holders do not want me to be here; they would rather that I was not here. (Cheers.) I have adopted a maxim laid down by Napoleon, never to occupy ground which the enemy would like me to occupy.[58] The slave holders would much rather have me, if I will denounce slavery, denounce it in the northern states, where their friends and supporters are, who will stand by and mob me for denouncing it. (Cheers.) They feel something like the man felt, when he uttered his prayer, in which he made out a most horrible case for himself, and one of his neighbours touched him and said, "My friend, I always had the opinion of you that you have now expressed for yourself—that you are a very great sinner." Coming from himself it was all very well, but coming from a stranger it was rather cutting. (Cheers.)

The slave holders felt that when slavery was denounced among themselves, it was not so bad, but let one of the slaves get loose, let him summon the people of Britain, and make known to them the conduct of the slave holders toward their slaves, and it cuts them to the quick, and produces a sensation such as would be produced by nothing else. (Cheers.) The power I exert now is something like the power that is exerted by the man at the end of the lever; my influence now is just in proportion to the distance that I am from the United States. My exposure of slavery abroad will tell more upon the hearts and consciences of slave holders, than if I was attacking them in America, for almost every paper that I now receive from the United States comes teeming with statements about this fugitive

58. Douglass paraphrases Napoleon Bonaparte (1769–1821): "A well-tested maxim of war, is not to do what the enemy wishes simply because he does wish it." Lucian E. Henry, *Napoleon's War Maxims* (London, [1899]), 22.

negro, calling him a "glib-tongued scoundrel" (laughter), and saying that he is running out against the institutions and people of America.

I deny the charge, that I am saying a word against the institutions of America or the people as such. What I have to say is against slavery and slave holders. I feel at liberty to speak on this subject. I have on my back the marks of the lash; I have four sisters and one brother now under the galling chain. I feel it my duty to cry aloud and spare not.[59] (Loud cheers.) I am not averse to having the good opinion of my fellow-creatures. I am not averse to being kindly regarded by all men, but I am bound even at the hazard of making a large class of religionists in this country hate me, oppose me, and malign me as they have done—I am bound by the prayers and tears and entreaties of three millions of kneeling bondsmen, to have no compromise with men who are in any shape or form connected with the slave holders of America. (Reiterated cheers.)

I expose slavery in this country, because to expose it is to kill it. Slavery is one of those monsters of darkness to whom the light of truth is death. Expose slavery, and it dies. Light is to slavery what the heat of the sun is to the root of a tree, it must die under it. All the slave holder asks of me, is silence. He does not ask me to go abroad and preach *in favour* of slavery; he does not ask anyone to do that. He would not say that slavery is a good thing; but the best under the circumstances. The slave holders want total darkness on the subject. They want the hatchway shut down, that the monster may crawl in his den of darkness, crushing human hopes and happiness, destroying the bondman at will, and having no one to reprove or rebuke him. Slavery shrinks from the light, it hateth the light, neither cometh to the light lest its deeds should be reproved.[60] (Cheers.)

To tear off the mask from this abominable system, to expose it to the light of heaven, aye, to the heat of the sun, that it may burn and wither it out of existence, is my object in coming to this country.

59. Isa. 18:1.
60. John 3:20.

(Cheers.) But I am here because certain individuals have seen fit to come to this land, to misrepresent the character of the abolitionists, misrepresent the character of the slaves, misrepresent the character of the coloured people, and have sought to turn off attention from the slave system of America. I am here to revive this attention, and to fix it on the slave holders. What would I have you then to do? I would have the church, in the first place—Methodist, Baptist, Congregationalist, all persuasions—to declare, in their conventions, associations, synods, conferences, or whatever be their ecclesiastical meetings, *"no Christian fellowship with slave holders."* (Loud cheers.)

I want the slave holder surrounded, as by a wall of anti-slavery fire, so that he may see the condemnation of himself and his system glaring down in letters of light. I want him to feel that he has no sympathy in England, Scotland, or Ireland; that he has none in Canada, none in Mexico, none among the poor wild Indians; that the voice of the civilized, aye, and savage world, is against him. I would have condemnation blaze down upon him in every direction, till, stunned and overwhelmed with shame and confusion, he is compelled to let go the grasp he holds upon the persons of his victims, and restore them to their long-lost rights. (Loud cheers.) Here, then, is work for us all to do.

Let me say to the churches that have spoken on the subject, I thank you with my whole heart. I thank the Evangelical Alliance, though I would rather they had taken stronger ground, and not only have said, "slave holders shall not be invited," but "Slave holders shall not be admitted."[61] (Loud cheers.) I am a great lover of music, but I never heard any music half so sweet to my ears, as the voice

61. In August 1846, over nine hundred delegates from Great Britain, Europe, and the United States met in London in the hope of forming an organization uniting evangelical Protestants of the Western Hemisphere. European members of the Evangelical Alliance moved that all slaveholders be excluded. Almost immediately, the American delegation protested against excluding such a large number of American evangelicals. No compromise could be reached before the conference adjourned, and delegates resolved to form separate national alliances.

of our president last night at another meeting,—the Temperance meeting at Exeter-hall—where a motion was made to the following effect—"That this meeting learns with pleasure the determination of the National Temperance Society to hold a world's convention in August next." On that resolution, our worthy president said that the £50 he was to give to that society would be withheld if they admitted slave holders to that convention.[62] (Loud cheers.) The fact is out: it has gone careening across the Atlantic, and it will fall amidst slave holders like a bombshell. I have to say to those who have spoken on the subject, that they have not only my gratitude, but the gratitude, of the millions ready to perish. But I have to say to you further, although you have done much, there is much more to be done.

If you have whispered truth, whisper no longer: speak as the tempest does—stronger and stronger. Let your voices be heard through the press, through the pulpit, in all directions. Let the atmosphere of Britain be such that a slave holder may not be able to breathe it. Let him feel his lungs oppressed the moment he steps on British soil. (Loud cheers.) Why should the slave holder breathe British atmosphere when it is such as it is? (Hear, hear.) I had heard of Britain long before I got out of slavery. I had not heard of it in the eloquent strains and eloquent language of Curran;[63] but I had heard of the great truth embodied in that eloquent sentence which proclaims that the moment a slave sets his foot on British soil his body swells beyond the measure of his chains—they burst from around him, and he stands redeemed, regenerated, disenthralled by the irresistible genius of universal emancipation. (Loud cheers.)

62. Douglass refers to Joseph Sturge's comments during the anniversary meeting of the National Temperance Society in Exeter Hall on 21 May 1846. An account appears in the *National Temperance Chronicle and Recorder,* June 1846.

63. John Philpot Curran (1750–1817), a well-known Irish orator, politician, and lawyer, proclaimed: "I speak in the spirit of the British law, which makes liberty commensurate with British soil; which proclaims even to the stranger and sojourner, the moment he sets his foot upon British earth, that the ground of which he treads is holy, and consecrated by the genius of UNIVERSAL EMANCIPATION." John Philpot Curran, *The Speeches of the Right Honorable John Philpot Curran,* ed. Thomas Davis (Dublin: James Duffy, 1845), 169.

One word about the Free Church of Scotland. (Cheers.) The facts ought to be stated. The Free Church of Scotland—do you know what church that is? I have been talking to a people who do not need any explanation on the subject; for I have been in Scotland recently. About two years ago the Free Church of Scotland sent a deputation to the United States, composed of the Rev. Dr. Cunningham, Mr. Chalmers of his city, Mr. Lewis of Dundee, Mr. Fergusson, and Dr. Burns, for the purpose of explaining the disruption that occurred in Scotland to the people of America, and of soliciting pecuniary aid to enable the Free Church to build churches and to pay their ministers.

On reaching the United States, the deputation were very early addressed by the committee of the American and Foreign Anti-Slavery Society, beseeching them in the most Christian and powerful manner not to go into the slave states and solicit aid from slave holders, not to take the price of blood to build free churches and pay free church ministers in Scotland. (Hear, hear.) The deputation did not heed this advice; they went at the invitation of a slave holder, Dr. Smythe,[64] into the slave states. They were admitted into the pulpits of slave holders; they were welcomed to the houses of slave holders; they enjoyed all the hospitalities and attentions that the slave holders were capable of showering upon them; and they took the slave holders' money, or rather the money of which the slave holders had robbed the slaves. (Hear, hear.)

They have returned to Scotland, and have deliberately attempted, and persevered in their attempt, to show that slavery in itself is not inconsistent with Christian fellowship. (Cries of "Shame!" and hisses.) I hear a hiss. ("Not at you.") I am used to being hissed in

64. An American Presbyterian minister of Scotch-Irish descent, Thomas Smyth (1808–73) wrote an ethnological justification of African slavery entitled *The Unity of the Human Races* (New York, 1850). Smyth seems to have influenced Thomas Chalmers's views on slavery. Embarrassed by the fact that some Free Church members had signed antislavery petitions, Smyth prevailed upon Chalmers in 1844 to write for publication a letter defending the Christianity of slaveholders.

Scotland on this subject (laughter), for they do not like me to state the thing in my own language. They have undertaken to show, that neither Christ nor his Apostles, had any objection to slave holders being admitted to church fellowship. They have undertaken to show, that the Apostle Paul in sending Onesimus back to Philemon, sanctioned the relation of master and slave. (Hear, hear.) Their arguments on this question are vain, being quoted in the United States by the slave-holding, pro-slavery papers against the abolitionists, and against those who are separating from the slave holder. (Hear.)

Now I have to bring certain charges against that deputation. I charge them, in the first place, with having struck hands in Christian fellowship with men-stealers. (Cheers.) I charge them, in the next place, with having taken the produce of human blood to build free churches, and to pay free church ministers in Scotland. I charge them with having done this knowingly, (cheers), they having been met by a remonstrance against such conduct by the executive committee of the American and Foreign Anti-Slavery Society. I have to charge them with going among men-stealers, with a perfect knowledge that they were such. (Cheers.) I have to charge them with taking money that not only was stolen, but which they knew to be stolen. I have to charge them, moreover, with going into a country where they saw three millions of people deprived of every right, stripped of every privilege, driven like brutes from time into eternity in the dark, robbed of all that makes life dear, the marriage institution destroyed, men herded together like beasts, deprived of the privilege of learning to read the name of the God who made them; and yet that deputation did not utter a word of denunciation against the man-stealer, or a word of sympathy, for these poor, outraged, long neglected people. (Loud cries of "Shame!")

What I want the brethren of England to do is this; to tell the Free Church of Scotland that they have done wrong. (Immense cheers.) Christians of England! we want you to say to the Free Church of Scotland, the words you have just heard:—"*Send back the money.*"

(Cheers.) They can never remonstrate against the slave holder while they hold on to the money; therefore they should send it back. I want you to aid my friend, my eloquent friend, the slaves' friend, Mr. George Thompson.[65] (Loud cheers.) My friend Mr. Thompson and myself expect to leave early to-morrow for Scotland;[66] we are going there with few of the wealthy, few of the influential to second our efforts. We believe that it is the duty of the Free Church of Scotland to send back the money. I believe it is in our power, under God, to induce a state of feeling in Scotland which will demand the sending back of that money. We now want your aid; we want you to raise your voices and your sympathies. Let us have your sympathy. *Write,* "Send back the money." *Speak,* "Send back the money." *Preach,* "Send back the money." (Immense cheering.)

I believe that the sending back of that money to the United States, will do more to unrivet the fetters, to break the chains of the bondsman, and to hasten the day of emancipation, than years of lecturing by the most eloquent abolitionists. It would produce such an effect, that it would send slavery staggering to its grave as if struck by the voice of Heaven. The truth is, the slave holders have now scarcely anywhere to lean. They leaned against the northern states—the abolitionists have removed the prop. They used to lean a good deal on their religious fellowship in England. It was once said to a person, "You come from Maryland: are you a slave holder?" "Yes." "Then you cannot come in." (Cheers.) The Christian people of England are beginning to see the inconsistency of holding fellowship with these men, and are breaking loose from them. The United Secession Synod has declared unanimously, that it will no longer strike hands in Christian fellowship with the men-stealers in

65. George Thompson (1804–78) was an influential British ally of William Lloyd Garrison. As a member of Parliament from 1847 to 1852, Thompson promoted the production of East Indian cotton in order to undermine American slavery.

66. Douglass and George Thompson hurried to Scotland to attend the meeting of the General Assembly of the Free Church in Edinburgh on 27 May 1846.

America. (Cheers.) The Relief Synod, whose meeting is now in session in Edinburgh, has come to the same unanimous conclusion.[67] (Cheers.) The Evangelical Alliance has said, through Dr. Candlish one of the Free Church leaders, that the slave holders ought not to be invited. I tell you slavery cannot live with all these stabs. "Send back the money—send back the money." (Loud cheers.)

If it is not inconsistent with this meeting, allow me to do what I have done in Scotland. I want to have all the children writing about the streets "Send back the money." I want to have all the people saying "Send back the money;" and in order to rivet these words in the minds of the audience, I propose that they give three cheers, not hurrahs, but say "Send back the money." (The vast assembly spontaneously complied with Mr. Douglass's request. The effect produced was indescribable. Mr. Douglass then sat down amid reiterated rounds of applause.)

67. Tracing its origins to 1752, the Relief Church seceded from the Church of Scotland because of allegations that the Church of Scotland had abused its authority. Like other dissenting bodies, the Relief Church joined the antislavery campaign against the Free Church in 1846.

"What to the Slave Is the Fourth of July?"

An Address Delivered in Rochester, New York, 5 July 1852

Frederick Douglass, *Oration, Delivered in Corinthian Hall, Rochester, July 5th, 1852* (Rochester, 1852).

The Rochester Ladies' Anti-Slavery Society invited Douglass to speak on the Fourth of July, but Douglass declined because, as he explains in this speech: "The blessings in which you, this day, rejoice, are not enjoyed in common. . . . This Fourth [of] July is *yours*, not *mine*."[1] Douglass spoke instead on 5 July in Corinthian Hall to an audience of 500–600 people. After a reading of the Declaration of Independence, Douglass addressed the audience.

Using the classical rhetorical form of the jeremiad, he contended that the United States was founded through a covenant, a sacred promise, to live according to principles of liberty and equality. In defending Southern slavery, the nation had failed to abide by these principles and risked spiritual ruin and international condemnation. Douglass concluded as ministers traditionally end such religio-political sermons, with a vision of how the nation might reform its ways, renew its covenant, and be saved from ruin.[2]

The lecture was a tremendous success, widely recognized as a masterly antislavery speech. Douglass uses trenchant logic in his

1. "The Celebration at Corinthian Hall," *Frederick Douglass' Paper,* 9 July 1852; McFeely, *Frederick Douglass,* 172.
2. See the excerpt in this volume on Douglass's antebellum jeremiad in David Howard Pitney, *The Afro-American Jeremiad: Appeals for Justice in America.*

exhortation, repeating and defeating the premises undergirding pro-
slavery arguments. He maintains that all explications of the humanity
and rights of African Americans are already fully understood, and
he urges empathy and action instead: "At a time like this, scorching
irony, not convincing argument, is needed." Despite his protests to
the contrary, he provides convincing argument as well as irony as he
illustrates the hypocrisy of celebrating revolution and equality in a
nation devoted to defending slavery.

Douglass uses the most prized rhetorical strategies of the nineteenth century, including declamation, parallelism, and appropriation. He draws from the Bible, Shakespeare's *Julius Caesar*, Thomas
Paine, and the Constitution. Evoking Brutus's defense for having
murdered Caesar, Douglass first claims that the forefathers "loved
their country better than their own private interests." Then, appro-
priating the rhythm and sentiment of Mark Antony's speech at Caesar's funeral, he contrasts the founding fathers with contemporary
Americans. Unlike the founders, who risked their lives to establish
a democracy, Douglass's contemporaries, he argues, claim that the
question of slavery is "settled"; "the cause of liberty," he adds, "may
be stabbed by the men who glory in the deeds of your fathers."

In an extended analogy comparing the leaders of the American
Revolution with those of the antislavery movement, he champions
the importance of activists: "They . . . were accounted in their day,
plotters of mischief, agitators and rebels, dangerous men." By this
point in Douglass's career, he had abandoned the Garrisonian position of condemning the Constitution as a proslavery document and
instead had become a political abolitionist seeking reform within a
constitutional framework. He refers to the defense of natural rights
in the Declaration of Independence as the "ring-bolt to the chain of
your nation's destiny." Drawing on his youthful experience in shipyards, he urges Americans to withstand the storms threatening human rights and democracy and to hold fast to the intent of the Declaration: "That bolt drawn, that chain broken, and all is lost. *Cling to
this day—cling to it*, and to its principles, with the grasp of a storm-
tossed mariner to a spar at midnight." Denouncing the Fugitive Slave
Law as an assault on the freedoms protected by Constitution and as
a belligerent "act of the American Congress," he declares that the
Constitution, "a GLORIOUS LIBERTY DOCUMENT," is "entirely

hostile to the existence of slavery." He compares the United States to a young river whose direction might yet be changed by constitutional amendments that would eliminate slavery and extend voting rights to African American men.

William McFeely calls this "perhaps the greatest antislavery oration ever given."[3] While most of Douglass's speeches had been extemporaneous, this one was delivered from notes and published as a pamphlet shortly afterward.[4] Douglass judged it among his finest works, reproducing excerpts of it in his autobiographies. The speech has been reprinted in many scholarly collections.

*M*r. President,[5] Friends and Fellow Citizens: He who could address this audience without a quailing sensation, has stronger nerves than I have. I do not remember ever to have appeared as a speaker before any assembly more shrinkingly, nor with greater distrust of my ability, than I do this day. A feeling has crept over me, quite unfavorable to the exercise of my limited powers of speech. The task before me is one which requires much previous thought and study for its proper performance. I know that apologies of this sort are generally considered flat and unmeaning. I trust, however, that mine will not be so considered. Should I seem at ease, my appearance would much misrepresent me. The little experience I have had in addressing public meetings, in country school houses, avails me nothing on the present occasion.

The papers and placards say, that I am to deliver a 4th [of] July oration. This certainly sounds large, and out of the common way, for me. It is true that I have often had the privilege to speak in this beautiful Hall,[6] and to address many who now honor me with

3. McFeely, *Frederick Douglass*, 173.

4. Frederick Douglass, *Oration, Delivered in Corinthian Hall, Rochester* (Rochester, N.Y.: Lee, Mann & Co., 1852).

5. Lindley Murray Moore (1788–1871), a Quaker abolitionist and temperance reformer related through marriage to the antislavery writer Lucretia Mott, presided over the meeting that hosted Douglass's speech.

6. Corinthian Hall.

their presence. But neither their familiar faces, nor the perfect gage I think I have of Corinthian Hall, seems to free me from embarrassment.

The fact is, ladies and gentlemen, the distance between this platform and the slave plantation, from which I escaped, is considerable—and the difficulties to be overcome in getting from the latter to the former, are by no means slight. That I am here to-day is, to me, a matter of astonishment as well as of gratitude. You will not, therefore, be surprised, if in what I have to say, I evince no elaborate preparation, nor grace my speech with any high sounding exordium.[7] With little experience and with less learning, I have been able to throw my thoughts hastily and imperfectly together; and trusting to your patient and generous indulgence, I will proceed to lay them before you.

This, for the purpose of this celebration, is the 4th of July. It is the birthday of your National Independence, and of your political freedom. This, to you, is what the Passover was to the emancipated people of God.[8] It carries your minds back to the day, and to the act of your great deliverance; and to the signs, and to the wonders, associated with that act, and that day. This celebration also marks the beginning of another year of your national life; and reminds you that the Republic of America is now 76 years old. I am glad, fellow-citizens, that your nation is so young. Seventy-six years, though a good old age for a man, is but a mere speck in the life of a nation. Three score years and ten is the allotted time for individual men;[9] but nations number their years by thousands. According to this fact, you are, even now, only in the beginning of your national career, still lingering in the period of childhood. I repeat, I am glad this is so. There is hope in the thought, and hope is much needed, under the dark clouds which lower above the horizon. The eye of the reformer

---

7. An exordium is an introductory portion of a speech or treatise.

8. Passover is a Jewish holiday that commemorates the Israelites' liberation by God from Egypt under the leadership of Moses.

9. Ps. 90:10.

is met with angry flashes, portending disastrous times; but his heart may well beat lighter at the thought that America is young, and that she is still in the impressible stage of her existence. May he not hope that high lessons of wisdom, of justice and of truth, will yet give direction to her destiny? Were the nation older, the patriot's heart might be sadder, and the reformer's brow heavier. Its future might be shrouded in gloom, and the hope of its prophets go out in sorrow. There is consolation in the thought that America is young. Great streams are not easily turned from channels, worn deep in the course of ages. They may sometimes rise in quiet and stately majesty, and inundate the land, refreshing and fertilizing the earth with their mysterious properties. They may also rise in wrath and fury, and bear away, on their angry waves, the accumulated wealth of years of toil and hardship. They, however, gradually flow back to the same old channel, and flow on as serenely as ever. But, while the river may not be turned aside, it may dry up, and leave nothing behind but the withered branch, and the unsightly rock, to howl in the abyss-sweeping wind, the sad tale of departed glory. As with rivers so with nations.

Fellow-citizens, I shall not presume to dwell at length on the associations that cluster about this day. The simple story of it is that, 76 years ago, the people of this country were British subjects. The style and title of your "sovereign people" (in which you now glory) was not then born. You were under the British Crown. Your fathers esteemed the English Government as the home government; and England as the fatherland. This home government, you know, although a considerable distance from your home, did in the exercise of its parental prerogatives, impose upon its colonial children, such restraints, burdens and limitations, as, in its mature judgement, it deemed wise, right and proper.

But, your fathers, who had not adopted the fashionable idea of this day, of the infallibility of government, and the absolute character of its acts, presumed to differ from the home government in respect to the wisdom and the justice of some of those burdens and restraints. They went so far in their excitement as to pronounce the measures of government unjust, unreasonable, and oppressive, and altogether such as ought not to be quietly submitted to. I scarcely need say, fellow-citizens, that my opinion of those measures fully accords with that of your fathers. Such a declaration of agreement on my part would not be worth much to anybody. It would, certainly, prove nothing, as to what part I might have taken, had I lived during the great controversy of 1776. To say *now* that America was right, and England wrong, is exceedingly easy. Everybody can say it; the dastard, not less than the noble brave, can flippantly discant on the tyranny of England towards the American Colonies. It is fashionable to do so; but there was a time when to pronounce against England, and in favor of the cause of the colonies, tried men's souls.[10] They who did so were accounted in their day, plotters of mischief, agitators and rebels, dangerous men. To side with the right, against the wrong, with the weak against the strong, and with the oppressed against the oppressor! *here* lies the merit, and the one which, of all others, seems unfashionable in our day. The cause of liberty may be stabbed by the men who glory in the deeds of your fathers. But, to proceed.

Feeling themselves harshly and unjustly treated by the home government, your fathers, like men of honesty, and men of spirit, earnestly sought redress. They petitioned and remonstrated; they did so in a decorous, respectful, and loyal manner. Their conduct was wholly unexceptionable. This, however, did not answer the purpose. They saw themselves treated with sovereign indifference, coldness and scorn. Yet they persevered. They were not the men to look back.

As the sheet anchor[11] takes a firmer hold, when the ship is tossed by the storm, so did the cause of your fathers grow stronger, as it breasted the chilling blasts of kingly displeasure. The greatest and best of British statesmen admitted its justice, and the loftiest

10. Thomas Paine's first *Crisis* paper, 23 December 1776. *The Political Writings of Thomas Paine*, 2 vols. (Boston, 1859), 1:75.

11. A vessel's largest anchor.

eloquence of the British Senate came to its support. But, with that blindness which seems to be the unvarying characteristic of tyrants, since Pharoah and his hosts were drowned in the Red Sea,[12] the British Government persisted in the exactions complained of.

The madness of this course, we believe, is admitted now, even by England; but we fear the lesson is wholly lost on our present rulers.

Oppression makes a wise man mad.[13] Your fathers were wise men, and if they did not go mad, they became restive under this treatment. They felt themselves the victims of grievous wrongs, wholly incurable in their colonial capacity. With brave men there is always a remedy for oppression. Just here, the idea of a total separation of the colonies from the crown was born! It was a startling idea, much more so, than we, at this distance of time, regard it. The timid and the prudent (as has been intimated) of that day, were, of course, shocked and alarmed by it.

Such people lived then, had lived before, and will, probably, ever have a place on this planet; and their course, in respect to any great change, (no matter how great the good to be attained, or the wrong to be redressed by it), may be calculated with as much precision as can be the course of the stars. They hate all changes, but silver, gold and copper change! Of this sort of change they are always strongly in favor.

These people were called tories in the days of your fathers; and the appellation, probably, conveyed the same idea that is meant by a more modern, though a somewhat less euphonious term, which we often find in our papers, applied to some of our old politicians.[14]

12. Ex. 15:4.

13. Eccles. 7:7.

14. The Tory party in Britain supported conservative, traditional political beliefs, including the "divine right" of the monarchy. In the American colonies before and during the Revolution, "Tory" was the pejorative label used by Patriots to condemn their Loyalist, pro-British opponents. Douglass probably refers to the term "Hunker," meaning "greedy" in Dutch slang, which was used to characterize the attempts of New York Democrats in the late 1840s to get a "hunk" of the spoils of office. By the 1850s, the "Hunker" designation was being commonly applied to the conservative Unionist majority of the Democratic party throughout the North.

Their opposition to the then dangerous thought was earnest and powerful; but, amid all their terror and affrighted vociferations against it, the alarming and revolutionary idea moved on, and the country with it.

On the 2d of July, 1776, the old Continental Congress, to the dismay of the lovers of ease, and the worshippers of property, clothed that dreadful idea with all the authority of national sanction. They did so in the form of a resolution; and as we seldom hit upon resolutions, drawn up in our day, whose transparency is at all equal to this, it may refresh your minds and help my story if I read it.

> "Resolved, That these united colonies *are,* and of right, ought to be free and Independent States; that they are absolved from all allegiance to the British Crown; and that all political connection between them and the State of Great Britain *is,* and ought to be, dissolved."[15]

Citizens, your fathers made good that resolution. They succeeded; and to-day you reap the fruits of their success. The freedom gained is yours; and you, therefore, may properly celebrate this anniversary. The 4th of July is the first great fact in your nation's history—the very ring-bolt[16] in the chain of your yet undeveloped destiny.

Pride and patriotism, not less than gratitude, prompt you to celebrate and to hold it in perpetual remembrance. I have said that the Declaration of Independence is the RING-BOLT to the chain of your nation's destiny; so, indeed, I regard it. The principles contained in that instrument are saving principles. Stand by those principles, be true to them on all occasions, in all places, against all foes, and at whatever cost.

---

15. A text of the quoted resolution that indicates that the word "totally" appeared before the word "dissolved" may be found in W. C. Ford et al., eds. *Journal of the Continental Congress, 1774–1789,* 34 vols. (Washington, D.C., 1904–37), 5:507.

16. An eyebolt with a ring fastened to the deck or side used for hooking tackle.

From the round top[17] of your ship of state, dark and threatening clouds may be seen. Heavy billows, like mountains in the distance, disclose to the leeward[18] huge forms of flinty rocks! That *bolt* drawn, that *chain* broken, and all is lost. *Cling to this day—cling to it,* and to its principles, with the grasp of a storm-tossed mariner to a spar[19] at midnight.

The coming into being of a nation, in any circumstances, is an interesting event. But, besides general considerations, there were peculiar circumstances which make the advent of this republic an event of special attractiveness.

The whole scene, as I look back to it, was simple, dignified and sublime.

The population of the country, at the time, stood at the insignificant number of three millions.[20] The country was poor in the munitions of war. The population was weak and scattered, and the country a wilderness unsubdued. There were then no means of concert and combination, such as exist now. Neither steam nor lightning had then been reduced to order and discipline. From the Potomac to the Delaware was a journey of many days. Under these, and innumerable other disadvantages, your fathers declared for liberty and independence and triumphed.

Fellow Citizens, I am not wanting in respect for the fathers of this republic. The signers of the Declaration of Independence were brave men. They were great men too—great enough to give fame to a great age. It does not often happen to a nation to raise, at one time, such a number of truly great men. The point from which I am compelled to view them is not, certainly, the most favorable; and yet I cannot contemplate their great deeds with less than admiration. They were statesmen, patriots and heroes, and for the good they

17. Platform at the masthead.
18. Away from the direction of the wind.
19. A mast, boom, gaff, or pole used in the rigging of sails.
20. The first census of the United States in 1790 reported that the total population of 3,929,625 included 697,624 slaves and 59,557 free blacks.

did, and the principles they contended for, I will unite with you to honor their memory.

They loved their country better than their own private interests; and, though this is not the highest form of human excellence, all will concede that it is a rare virtue, and that when it is exhibited, it ought to command respect. He who will, intelligently, lay down his life for his country, is a man whom it is not in human nature to despise. Your fathers staked their lives, their fortunes, and their sacred honor,[21] on the cause of their country. In their admiration of liberty, they lost sight of all other interests.

They were peace men; but they preferred revolution to peaceful submission to bondage. They were quiet men; but they did not shrink from agitating against oppression. They showed forbearance; but that they knew its limits. They believed in order; but not in the order of tyranny. With them, nothing was *"settled"* that was not right. With them, justice, liberty and humanity were *"final;"* not slavery and oppression. You may well cherish the memory of such men. They were great in their day and generation. Their solid manhood stands out the more as we contrast it with these degenerate times.

How circumspect, exact and proportionate were all their movements! How unlike the politicians of an hour! Their statesmanship looked beyond the passing moment, and stretched away in strength into the distant future. They seized upon eternal principles, and set a glorious example in their defence. Mark them!

Fully appreciating the hardship to be encountered, firmly believing in the right of their cause, honorably inviting the scrutiny of an on-looking world, reverently appealing to heaven to attest their sincerity, soundly comprehending the solemn responsibility they were about to assume, wisely measuring the terrible odds against them, your fathers, the fathers of this republic, did, most deliberately, under the inspiration of a glorious patriotism, and with a sublime faith

21. From the last line of the Declaration of Independence.

in the great principles of justice and freedom, lay deep the corner-stone of the national superstructure, which has risen and still rises in grandeur around you.

Of this fundamental work, this day is the anniversary. Our eyes are met with demonstrations of joyous enthusiasm. Banners and pennants wave exultingly on the breeze. The din of business, too, is hushed. Even Mammon[22] seems to have quitted his grasp on this day. The ear-piercing fife and the stirring drum unite their accents with the ascending peal of a thousand church bells. Prayers are made, hymns are sung, and sermons are preached in honor of this day; while the quick martial tramp of a great and multitudinous nation, echoed back by all the hills, valleys and mountains of a vast continent, bespeak the occasion one of thrilling and universal interest—a nation's jubilee.

Friends and citizens, I need not enter further into the causes which led to this anniversary. Many of you understand them better than I do. You could instruct me in regard to them. That is a branch of knowledge in which you feel, perhaps, a much deeper interest than your speaker. The causes which led to the separation of the colonies from the British crown have never lacked for a tongue. They have all been taught in your common schools, narrated at your firesides, unfolded from your pulpits, and thundered from your legislative halls, and are as familiar to you as household words. They form the staple of your national poetry and eloquence.

I remember, also, that, as a people, Americans are remarkably familiar with all facts which make in their own favor. This is esteemed by some as a national trait—perhaps a national weakness. It is a fact, that whatever makes for the wealth or for the reputation of Americans, and can be had *cheap!* will be found by Americans. I shall not be charged with slandering Americans, if I say I think the American side of any question may be safely left in American hands.

---

22. Luke 16:13; Matt. 6:24.

I leave, therefore, the great deeds of your fathers to other gentlemen whose claim to have been regularly descended will be less likely to be disputed than mine!

The Present.

My business, if I have any here to-day, is with the present. The accepted time with God and his cause is the ever-living now.

"Trust no future, however pleasant,
    Let the dead past bury its dead;
Act, act in the living present,
    Heart within, and God overhead."[23]

We have to do with the past only as we can make it useful to the present and to the future. To all inspiring motives, to noble deeds which can be gained from the past, we are welcome. But now is the time, the important time. Your fathers have lived, died, and have done their work, and have done much of it well. You live and must die, and you must do your work. You have no right to enjoy a child's share in the labor of your fathers, unless your children are to be blest by your labors. You have not right to wear out and waste the hard-earned fame of your fathers to cover your indolence. Sydney Smith[24] tells us that men seldom eulogize the wisdom and virtues of their fathers, but to excuse some folly or wickedness of their own. This truth is not a doubtful one. There are illustrations of it near and remote, ancient and modern. It was fashionable, hundreds of years ago, for the children of Jacob to boast, we have "Abraham to our father," when they had long lost Abraham's faith and spirit.[25] That

23. The sixth stanza of Henry Wadsworth Longfellow's "A Psalm of Life." *Poems by Henry Wadsworth Longfellow* (Philadelphia: Carey and Hart, 1845), 22.
24. The Anglican minister Sydney Smith (1771–1845) was a master satirical essayist and lecturer.
25. Luke 3:8.

people contented themselves under the shadow of Abraham's great name, while they repudiated the deeds which made his name great. Need I remind you that a similar thing is being done all over this country to-day? Need I tell you that the Jews are not the only people who built the tombs of the prophets, and garnished the sepulchers of the righteous?[26] Washington could not die till he had broken the chains of his slaves.[27] Yet his monument is built up by the price of human blood,[28] and the traders in the bodies and souls of men, shout—"We have Washington to *our father.*" Alas! that it should be so; yet so it is.

> "The evil that men do, lives after them,
> The good is oft' interred with their bones."[29]

Fellow-citizens, pardon me, allow me to ask, why am I called upon to speak here to-day? What have I, or those I represent, to do with your national independence? Are the great principles of political freedom and of natural justice, embodied in that Declaration of Independence, extended to us? and am I, therefore, called upon to bring our humble offering to the national altar, and to confess the benefits and express devout gratitude for the blessings resulting from your independence to us?

Would to God, both for your sakes and ours, that an affirmative answer could be truthfully returned to these questions! Then would my task be light, and my burden easy and delightful. For *who* is there so cold, that a nation's sympathy could not warm him? Who so

26. Matt. 23:29.

27. At the time of his death, George Washington (1732–99), first president of the United States, owned or held claim to over three hundred slaves. His will stipulated that they would receive their freedom upon his wife's death.

28. When the Washington National Monument Society was launched in 1832, it raised an initial $28,000 to honor America's first president. Douglass might be alluding to donations from Southern slaveholders in the first building phase or to the common practice of using slave laborers in the construction of major structures in the District of Columbia.

29. *Julius Caesar,* sc. 9, lines 1462–63.

obdurate and dead to the claims of gratitude, that would not thankfully acknowledge such priceless benefits? Who so stolid and selfish, that would not give his voice to swell the hallelujahs of a nation's jubilee, when the chains of servitude had been torn from his limbs? I am not that man. In a case like that, the dumb might eloquently speak, and the "lame man leap as an hart."[30]

But, such is not the state of the case. I say it with a sad sense of the disparity between us. I am not included within the pale of this glorious anniversary! Your high independence only reveals the immeasurable distance between us. The blessings in which you, this day, rejoice, are not enjoyed in common. The rich inheritance of justice, liberty, prosperity and independence, bequeathed by your fathers, is shared by you, not by me. The sunlight that brought life and healing to you, has brought stripes and death to me. This Fourth [of] July is *yours,* not *mine. You* may rejoice, *I* must mourn. To drag a man in fetters into the grand illuminated temple of liberty, and call upon him to join you in joyous anthems, were inhuman mockery and sacrilegious irony. Do you mean, citizens, to mock me, by asking me to speak to-day? If so, there is a parallel to your conduct. And let me warn you that it is dangerous to copy the example of a nation whose crimes, towering up to heaven, were thrown down by the breath of the Almighty, burying that nation in irrecoverable ruin! I can to-day take up the plaintive lament of a peeled and woe-smitten people!

"By the rivers of Babylon, there we sat down. Yea! we wept when we remembered Zion. We hanged our harps upon the willows in the midst thereof. For there, they that carried us away captive, required of us a song; and they who wasted us required of us mirth, saying, Sing us one of the songs of Zion. How can we sing the Lord's song in a strange land? If I forget thee, O Jerusalem, let my right hand forget her cunning. If I do not remember thee, let my tongue cleave to the roof of my mouth."[31]

30. Isa. 35:6.
31. Ps. 137:1–6.

Fellow-citizens; above your national, tumultuous joy, I hear the mournful wail of millions! whose chains, heavy and grievous yesterday, are, to-day, rendered more intolerable by the jubilee shouts that reach them. If I do forget, if I do not faithfully remember those bleeding children of sorrow this day, "may my right hand forget her cunning, and may my tongue cleave to the roof of my mouth!" To forget them, to pass lightly over their wrongs, and to chime in with the popular theme, would be treason most scandalous and shocking, and would make me a reproach before God and the world. My subject, then fellow-citizens, is AMERICAN SLAVERY. I shall see, this day, and its popular characteristics, from the slave's point of view. Standing, there, identified with the American bondman, making his wrongs mine, I do not hesitate to declare, with all my soul, that the character and conduct of this nation never looked blacker to me than on this 4th of July! Whether we turn to the declarations of the past, or to the professions of the present, the conduct of the nation seems equally hideous and revolting. America is false to the past, false to the present, and solemnly binds herself to be false to the future. Standing with God and the crushed and bleeding slave on this occasion, I will, in the name of humanity which is outraged, in the name of liberty which is fettered, in the name of the constitution and the Bible, which are disregarded and trampled upon, dare to call in question and to denounce, with all the emphasis I can command, everything that serves to perpetuate slavery—the great sin and shame of America! "I will not equivocate; I will not excuse;"[32] I will use the severest language I can command; and yet not one word shall escape me that any man, whose judgement is not blinded by prejudice, or who is not at heart a slaveholder, shall not confess to be right and just.

But I fancy I hear some one of my audience say, it is just in this circumstance that you and your brother abolitionists fail to make a favorable impression on the public mind. Would you argue more, and denounce less, would you persuade more, and rebuke less, your

32. Douglass quotes from the first issue of the *Liberator,* 1 January 1831, in which William Lloyd Garrison promised, "I am in earnest—I will not equivocate—I will not excuse—I will not retreat a single inch—and *I will be heard.*"

cause would be much more likely to succeed. But, I submit, where all is plain there is nothing to be argued. What point in the anti-slavery creed would you have me argue? On what branch of the subject do the people of this country need light? Must I undertake to prove that the slave is a man? That point is conceded already. Nobody doubts it. The slaveholders themselves acknowledge it in the enactment of laws for their government. They acknowledge it when they punish disobedience on the part of the slave. There are seventy-two crimes in the State of Virginia, which, if committed by a black man, (no matter how ignorant he be), subject him to the punishment of death; while only two of the same crimes will subject a white man to the like punishment.[33] What is this but the acknowl-edgement that the slave is a moral, intellectual and responsible be-ing? The manhood of the slave is conceded. It is admitted in the fact that Southern statute books are covered with enactments forbid-ding, under severe fines and penalties, the teaching of the slave to read or to write. When you can point to any such laws, in reference to the beasts of the field, then I may consent to argue the manhood of the slave. When the dogs in your streets, when the fowls of the air, when the cattle on your hills, when the fish of the sea, and the reptiles that crawl, shall be unable to distinguish the slave from a brute, *then* will I argue with you that the slave is a man!

For the present, it is enough to affirm the equal manhood of the negro race. Is it not astonishing that, while we are ploughing, plant-ing and reaping, using all kinds of mechanical tools, erecting houses, constructing bridges, building ships, working in metals of brass, iron, copper, silver and gold; that, while we are reading, writing and ci-phering,[34] acting as clerks, merchants and secretaries, having among us lawyers, doctors, ministers, poets, authors, editors, orators and teachers; that, while we are engaged in all manner of enterprises common to other men, digging gold in California, capturing the whale in the Pacific, feeding sheep and cattle on the hill-side, living,

33. [Weld], *American Slavery as It Is,* 149, contrasts capital offenses in Virginia for slaves and whites.

34. "Cyphering" is a nineteenth-century term for arithmetic.

moving, acting, thinking, planning, living in families as husbands, wives and children, and, above all, confessing and worshipping the Christian's God, and looking hopefully for life and immortality beyond the grave, we are called upon to prove that we are men!

Would you have me argue that man is entitled to liberty? that he is the rightful owner of his own body? You have already declared it. Must I argue the wrongfulness of slavery? Is that a question for Republicans? Is it to be settled by the rules of logic and argumentation, as a matter beset with great difficulty, involving a doubtful application of the principle of justice, hard to be understood? How should I look to-day, in the presence of Americans, dividing, and subdividing a discourse, to show that men have a natural right to freedom? speaking of it relatively, and positively, negatively, and affirmatively. To do so, would be to make myself ridiculous, and to offer an insult to your understanding. There is not a man beneath the canopy of heaven, that does not know that slavery is wrong *for him.*

What, am I to argue that it is wrong to make men brutes, to rob them of their liberty, to work them without wages, to keep them ignorant of their relations to their fellow men, to beat them with sticks, to flay their flesh with the lash, to load their limbs with irons, to hunt them with dogs, to sell them at auction, to sunder their families, to knock out their teeth, to burn their flesh, to starve them into obedience and submission to their masters? Must I argue that a system thus marked with blood, and stained with pollution is *wrong?* No! I will not. I have better employments for my time and strength, than such arguments would imply.

What, then, remains to be argued? Is it that slavery is not divine; that God did not establish it; that our doctors of divinity are mistaken? There is blasphemy in the thought. That which is inhuman, cannot be divine! *Who* can reason on such a proposition? They that can, may; I cannot. The time for such argument is past.

At a time like this, scorching irony, not convincing argument, is needed. O! had I the ability, and could I reach the nation's ear, I would, to-day, pour out a fiery stream of biting ridicule, blasting reproach, withering sarcasm, and stern rebuke. For it is not light that is needed, but fire; it is not the gentle shower, but thunder. We need the storm, the whirlwind, and the earthquake. The feeling of the nation must be quickened; the conscience of the nation must be roused; the propriety of the nation must be startled; the hypocrisy of the nation must be exposed; and its crimes against God and man must be proclaimed and denounced.

What, to the American slave, is your 4th of July? I answer: a day that reveals to him, more than all other days in the year, the gross injustice and cruelty to which he is the constant victim. To him, your celebration is a sham; your boasted liberty, an unholy license; your national greatness, swelling vanity; your sounds of rejoicing are empty and heartless; your denunciations of tyrants, brass fronted impudence; your shouts of liberty and equality, hollow mockery; your prayers and hymns, your sermons and thanksgivings, with all your religious parade, and solemnity, are, to him, mere bombast, fraud, deception, impiety, and hypocrisy—a thin veil to cover up crimes which would disgrace a nation of savages. There is not a nation on the earth guilty of practices, more shocking and bloody, than are the people of these United States, at this very hour.

Go where you may, search where you will, roam through all the monarchies and despotisms of the old world, travel through South America, search out every abuse, and when you have found the last, lay your facts by the side of the everyday practices of this nation, and you will say with me, that, for revolting barbarity and shameless hypocrisy, America reigns without a rival.

The Internal Slave Trade.

Take the American slave-trade, which, we are told by the papers, is especially prosperous just now. Ex-Senator Benton[35] tells us that

---

35. Thomas Hart Benton (1782–1858), a U.S. senator from Missouri (1821–51), probably used his observation on slave prices to bolster his persistent denial of slave-holding interests being insecure in the Union.

the price of men was never higher than now. He mentions the fact to show that slavery is in no danger. This trade is one of the peculiarities of the American institutions. It is carried on in all the large towns and cities in one-half of this confederacy; and millions are pocketed every year, by dealers in this horrid traffic. In several states, this trade is a chief source of wealth. It is called (in contradistinction to the foreign slave-trade) *"the internal slave-trade."* It is, probably, called so, too, in order to divert from it the horror with which the foreign slave-trade is contemplated. That trade has long since been denounced by this government, as piracy. It has been denounced with burning words, from the high places of the nation, as an execrable traffic. To arrest it, to put an end to it, this nation keeps a squadron, at immense cost, on the coast of Africa. Everywhere, in this country, it is safe to speak of this foreign slave-trade, as a most inhuman traffic, opposed alike to the laws of God and of man. The duty to extirpate and destroy it, is admitted even by our DOCTORS OF DIVINITY. In order to put an end to it, some of these last have consented that their colored brethren (nominally free) should leave this country, and establish themselves on the western coast of Africa! It is, however, a notable fact that, while so much execration is poured out by Americans upon those engaged in the foreign slave-trade, the men engaged in the slave-trade between the states pass without condemnation, and their business is deemed honorable.

Behold the practical operation of this internal slave-trade, the American slave-trade, sustained by American politics and American religion. Here you will see men and women reared like swine for the market. You know what is a swine-drover? I will show you a man-drover. They inhabit all our Southern States. They perambulate the country, and crowd the highways of the nation, with droves of human stock. You will see one of these human flesh-jobbers, armed with pistol, whip and bowie-knife, driving a company of a hundred men, women, and children, from the Potomac to the slave market at New Orleans. These wretched people are to be sold singly, or in lots, to suit purchasers. They are food for the cotton-field, and the deadly sugar-mill. Mark the sad procession, as it moves wearily along, and the inhuman wretch who drives them. Hear his savage yells and his blood-chilling oaths, as he hurries on his affrighted captives! There, see the old man, with locks thinned and gray. Cast one glance, if you please, upon that young mother, whose shoulders are bare to the scorching sun, her briny tears falling on the brow of the babe in her arms. See, too, that girl of thirteen, weeping, *yes!* weeping, as she thinks of the mother from whom she has been torn! The drove moves tardily. Heat and sorrow have nearly consumed their strength; suddenly you hear a quick snap, like the discharge of a rifle; the fetters clank, and the chain rattles simultaneously; your ears are saluted with a scream, that seems to have torn its way to the centre of your soul! The crack you heard, was the sound of the slave-whip; the scream you heard, was from the woman you saw with the babe. Her speed had faltered under the weight of her child and her chains! that gash on her shoulder tells her to move on. Follow this drove to New Orleans. Attend the auction; see men examined like horses; see the forms of women rudely and brutally exposed to the shocking gaze of American slave-buyers. See this drove sold and separated forever; and never forget the deep, sad sobs that arose from the scattered multitude. Tell me citizens, WHERE, under the sun, you can witness a spectacle more fiendish and shocking. Yet this is but a glance at the American slave-trade, as it exists, at this moment, in the ruling part of the United States.

I was born amid such sights and scenes. To me the American slave-trade is a terrible reality. When a child, my soul was often pierced with a sense of its horrors. I lived on Philpot Street, Fell's Point, Baltimore, and have watched from the wharves, the slave ships in the Basin, anchored from the shore, and with their cargoes of human flesh, waiting for favorable winds to waft them down the Chesapeake.[36] There was, at that time, a grand slave mart kept at

36. Between 1826 and 1833, and again in 1836–38, the young slave Frederick Douglass lived and worked in Hugh and Sophia Auld's household in Baltimore, Maryland.

the head of Pratt Street, by Austin Woldfolk.[37] His agents were sent into every town and county in Maryland, announcing their arrival, through the papers, and on flaming *"hand-bills,"* headed CASH FOR NEGROES. These men were generally well dressed men, and very captivating in their manners. Ever ready to drink, to treat, and to gamble. The fate of many a slave has depended upon the turn of a single card; and many a child has been snatched from the arms of its mother by bargains arranged in a state of brutal drunkenness.

The flesh-mongers gather up their victims by dozens, and drive them, chained, to the general depot at Baltimore. When a sufficient number have been collected here, a ship is chartered, for the purpose of conveying the forlorn crew to Mobile, or to New Orleans. From the slave prison to the ship, they are usually driven in the darkness of night; for since the anti-slavery agitation, a certain caution is observed.

In the deep still darkness of midnight, I have been often aroused by the dead heavy footsteps, and the piteous cries of the chained gangs that passed our door. The anguish of my boyish heart was intense; and I was often consoled, when speaking to my mistress[38] in the morning, to hear her say that the custom was very wicked; that she hated to hear the rattle of chains, and the heart-rendering cries. I was glad to find one who sympathised with me in my horror.

Fellow-citizens, this murderous traffic is, to-day, in active operation in this boasted republic. In the solitude of my spirit, I see clouds of dust raised on the highways of the South; I see the bleeding footsteps; I hear the doleful wail of fettered humanity, on the way to the slave-markets, where the victims are to be sold like *horses, sheep,*

37. The Baltimore slave trader Austin Woolfolk prospered as he sent agents throughout Maryland to pay high prices in cash for young black males. In the 1830s, Woolfolk's business declined because of increased competition from larger firms, a decrease in the number of slaves for sale owing to manumissions and owner emigrations, and the heightened opposition of Marylanders to the interstate slave trade.

38. Sophia Keithley Auld (1797–1880) was born in Talbot County, Maryland, to poor, devout Methodist parents who held to the antislavery teachings of their church. Before marrying Hugh Auld, she worked as a weaver.

and *swine,* knocked off to the highest bidder. There I see the tenderest ties ruthlessly broken, to gratify the lust, caprice and rapacity of the buyers and sellers of men. My soul sickens at the sight.

> "Is this the land your Fathers loved,
> The freedom which they toiled to win?
> Is this the earth whereon they moved?
> Are these the graves they slumber in?"[39]

But a still more inhuman, disgraceful, and scandalous state of things remains to be presented.

By an act of the American Congress, not yet two years old, slavery has been nationalized in its most horrible and revolting form. By that act, Mason & Dixon's line has been obliterated;[40] New York has become as Virginia; and the power to hold, hunt, and sell men, women, and children as slaves remains no longer a mere state institution, but is now an institution of the whole United States. The power is co-extensive with the star-spangled banner and American Christianity. Where these go, may also go the merciless slave-hunter. Where these are, man is not sacred. He is a bird for the sportsman's gun. By that most foul and fiendish of all human decrees, the liberty and person of the every man are put in peril. Your broad republican domain is hunting ground for *men. Not* for thieves and robbers, enemies of society, merely, but for men guilty of no crime. Your lawmakers have commanded all good citizens to engage in this hellish sport. Your President, your Secretary of State, your *lords, nobles,* and ecclesiastics, enforce, as a duty you owe to your free

---

39. The first four lines of John Greenleaf Whittier's "Stanzas for the Times." Whittier, *Poetical Works,* 3:35.

40. Replacing a 1793 law, the Fugitive Slave Law of 1850, part of that year's infamous sectional compromise, created a federal position of "commissioner," who was authorized to issue warrants for the arrest of fugitives and to certify the removal of captives to the South. The law, which applied to the entire United States, criminalized the aiding of a slave's escape and fined Northern officials who refused to help in the rendition of fugitive slaves.

and glorious country, and to your God, that you do this accursed thing. Not fewer than forty Americans have, within the past two years, been hunted down and, without a moment's warning, hurried away in chains, and consigned to slavery and excruciating torture. Some of these have had wives and children, dependent on them for bread; but of this, no account was made. The right of the hunter to his prey stands superior to the right of marriage, and to *all* rights in this republic, the rights of God included! For black men there are neither law, justice, humanity, nor religion. The Fugitive Slave *Law* makes MERCY TO THEM, A CRIME; and bribes the judge who tries them. An American JUDGE GETS TEN DOLLARS FOR EVERY VICTIM HE CONSIGNS to slavery, and five, when he fails to do so. The oath of any two villains is sufficient, under this hell-black enactment, to send the most pious and exemplary black man into the remorseless jaws of slavery! His own testimony is nothing. He can bring no witnesses for himself. The minister of American justice is bound by the law to hear but *one* side; and *that* side, is the side of the oppressor.[41] Let this damning fact be perpetually told. Let it be thundered around the world, that, in tyrant-killing, king-hating, people-loving, democratic, Christian America, the seats of justice are filled with judges, who hold their offices under an open and palpable *bribe,* and are bound, in deciding in the case of a man's liberty, *to hear only his accusers!*

In glaring violation of justice, in shameless disregard of the forms of administering law, in cunning arrangement to entrap the defenceless, and in diabolical intent, this Fugitive Slave Law stands alone in the annals of tyrannical legislation. I doubt if there be another nation on the globe, having the brass and the baseness to put

41. Although the Fugitive Slave Law of 1850 did not specify the number of witnesses needed to establish that someone was a fugitive slave, it did provide that "in no trial or hearing . . . shall the testimony of such alleged fugitive be admitted in evidence." No provision was made for the alleged fugitive to bring forth witnesses who might dispute the claims of the court transcript or warrant. *The Public Statutes at Large and Treaties of the United States of America, 1789–1873,* 17 vols. (Boston: Little, Brown, 1845–73), 9:462–65.

such a law on the statute-book. If any man in this assembly thinks
differently from me in this matter, and feels able to disprove my
statements, I will gladly confront him at any suitable time and place
he may select.

Religious Liberty.

I take this law to be one of the grossest infringements of Christian
Liberty, and, if the churches and ministers of our country were not
stupidly blind, or most wickedly indifferent, they, too, would so regard it.

At the very moment that they are thanking God for the enjoyment of civil and religious liberty, and for the right to worship God
according to the dictates of their own consciences, they are utterly
silent in respect to a law which robs religion of its chief significance,
and makes it utterly worthless to a world lying in wickedness. Did
this law concern the *"mint, anise* and *cummin"*[42]—abridge the right
to sing psalms, to partake of the sacrament, or to engage in any of
the ceremonies of religion, it would be smitten by the thunder of
a thousand pulpits. A general shout would go up from the church,
demanding *repeal, repeal, instant repeal!* And it would go hard with
that politician who presumed to solicit the votes of the people without inscribing this motto on his banner. Further, if this demand were
not complied with, another Scotland would be added to the history
of religious liberty, and the stern old Covenanters would be thrown
into the shade. A John Knox[43] would be seen at every church door,
and heard from every pulpit, and Fillmore[44] would have no more
quarter than was shown by Knox, to the beautiful, but treacherous

42. Matt. 23:23.
43. John Knox (1505–72), a leader in the Scottish Reformation and one of the
founders of the Church of Scotland, was involved in several violent confrontations
during the regency of Mary of Guise, the mother of Mary, Queen of Scots. Knox and
his followers forced the withdrawal of foreign troops supporting Mary in July 1560.
44. Millard Fillmore (1800–74), the thirteenth president of the United States,
vigorously advocated passage of the Compromise of 1850 and signed each of its measures into law.

Queen Mary of Scotland.[45] The fact that the church of our country, (with fractional exceptions), does not esteem "the Fugitive Slave Law" as a declaration of war against religious liberty, implies that that church regards religion simply as a form of worship, an empty ceremony, and *not* a vital principle, requiring active benevolence, justice, love and good will towards man. It esteems sacrifice above mercy; psalm-singing above right doing; solemn meetings above practical righteousness. A worship that can be conducted by persons who refuse to give shelter to the houseless, to give bread to the hungry, clothing to the naked,[46] and who enjoin obedience to a law forbidding these acts of mercy, is a curse, not a blessing to mankind. The Bible addresses all such persons as "scribes, pharisees, hypocrites, who pay tithe of *mint, anise,* and *cummin,* and have omitted the weightier matters of the law, judgement, mercy and faith."

The Church Responsible.

But the church of this country is not only indifferent to the wrongs of the slave, it actually takes sides with the oppressors. It has made itself the bulwark of American slavery,[47] and the shield of American slave-hunters. Many of its most eloquent Divines, who stand as the very lights of the church, have shamelessly given the sanction of religion and the Bible to the whole slave system. They have taught that man may, properly, be a slave; that the relation of master and slave is ordained of God; that to send back an escaped bondman to his master is clearly the duty of all the followers of the Lord Jesus Christ; and this horrible blasphemy is palmed off upon the world for Christianity.

45. Mary I (1542–87), popularly remembered as Mary, Queen of Scots, was forced to abdicate the throne after making a deeply unpopular marriage with the Earl of Bothwell. She sought asylum in England, but that country's monarch, Elizabeth, regarded Mary as a rallying point for Catholic opponents to her own rule and had Mary imprisoned for eighteen years and finally executed.

46. Ezek. 18:7; Isa. 58:7.

47. Birney, *American Churches.*

For my part, I would say, welcome infidelity! welcome atheism! welcome anything! in preference to the gospel, *as preached by those Divines!* They convert the very name of religion into an engine of tyranny, and barbarous cruelty, and serve to confirm more infidels, in this age, than all the infidel writings of Thomas Paine, Voltaire, and Bolingbroke,[48] put together, have done! These ministers make religion a cold and flinty-hearted thing, having neither principles of right action, nor bowels of compassion. They strip the love of God of its beauty, and leave the throne of religion a huge, horrible, repulsive form. It is a religion for oppressors, tyrants, man-stealers, and *thugs.* It is not that *"pure and undefiled religion"* which is from above, and which is *"first pure, then peaceable, easy to be entreated,* full of mercy and good fruits, *without partiality, and without hypoc-risy."*[49] But a religion which favors the rich against the poor; which exalts the proud above the humble; which divides mankind into two classes, tyrants and slaves; which says to the man in chains, *stay there;* and to the oppressor, *oppress on;* it is a religion which may be professed and enjoyed by all the robbers and enslavers of mankind; it makes God a respecter of persons, denies his fatherhood of the race, and tramples in the dust the great truth of the brotherhood of man. All this we affirm to be true of the popular church, and the popular worship of our land and nation—a religion, a church, and a worship which, on the authority of inspired wisdom, we pronounce to be an abomination in the sight of God. In the language of Isaiah, the American church might be well addressed, "Bring no more vain oblations; incense is an abomination unto me: the new moons and Sabbaths, the calling of assemblies, I cannot away with; it is iniq-uity, even the solemn meeting. Your new moons and your appointed

48. Thomas Paine (1737–1809), American revolutionary writer; François-Marie Arouet, known as Voltaire (1694–1778), French essayist, playwright, and philoso-pher; and Henry St. John, Viscount Bolingbroke (1678–1751), English statesman, orator, and essayist. These writers criticized the established Protestant and Catholic churches and espoused a form of "natural religion," or Deism, which often brought contempt from supporters of orthodox Christianity.
49. James 1:27.

feasts my soul hateth. They are a trouble to me; I am weary to bear them; and when ye spread forth your hands I will hide mine eyes from you. Yea! when ye make many prayers, I will not hear. YOUR HANDS ARE FULL OF BLOOD; cease to do evil, learn to do well; seek judgement; relieve the oppressed; judge for the fatherless; plead for the widow."[50]

The American church is guilty, when viewed in connection with what it is doing to uphold slavery; but it is superlatively guilty when viewed in connection with its ability to abolish slavery.

The sin of which it is guilty is one of omission as well as of commission. Albert Barnes but uttered what the common sense of every man at all observant of the actual state of the case will receive as truth, when he declared that "There is no power out of the church that could sustain slavery an hour, if it were not sustained in it."[51]

Let the religious press, the pulpit, the Sunday school, the conference meeting, the great ecclesiastical, missionary, Bible and tract associations of the land array their immense powers against slavery and slave-holding; and the whole system of crime and blood would be scattered to the winds; and that they do not do this involves them in the most awful responsibility of which the mind can conceive.

In prosecuting the anti-slavery enterprise, we have been asked to spare the church, to spare the ministry; but *how*, we ask, could such a thing be done? We are met on the threshold of our efforts for the redemption of the slave, by the church and ministry of the country, in battle arrayed against us; and we are compelled to fight or flee. From what *quarter*, I beg to know, has proceeded a fire so deadly upon our ranks, during the last two years, as from the Northern pulpit? As the champions of oppressors, the chosen men of American

50. Isa. 1:13–17.
51. After initially equivocating, the Presbyterian minister Albert Barnes (1798–1870) became an "implacable foe of slavery," although he never officially affiliated with any antislavery organization. Douglass quotes from Barnes's *An Inquiry into the Scriptural Views of Slavery* (Philadelphia: Perkins & Purves, 1846), 383, in which Barnes argued that "the principles laid down by the Savior and his apostles, are such as are opposed to slavery, and if carried out would secure its universal abolition."

theology have appeared—men, honored for their so-called piety, and their real learning. The LORDS[52] of Buffalo, the SPRINGS[53] of New York, the LATHROPS[54] of Auburn, the COXES[55] and SPENCERS[56] of Brooklyn, the GANNETS[57] and SHARPS[58] of Boston, the DEWEYS[59] of Washington, and other great religious lights of the land, have, in utter denial of authority of *Him*, by whom they professed to be

52. The Presbyterian minister John Chase Lord (1805–77) of Buffalo, New York, urged obedience to the Fugitive Slave Law in a sermon delivered on 12 December 1850, New York's Thanksgiving observance. The Union Safety Committee, consisting of one hundred of New York City's leading Whig and Democratic businessmen, solicited, printed, and distributed such sermons to defuse secessionist appeals, and urged ministers to devote the state's Thanksgiving holiday to prayers that the Compromise of 1850 would secure lasting national harmony.

53. The Presbyterian clergyman Gardiner Spring (1785–1873) of New York City condemned abolitionists for defying the Fugitive Slave Law. One of Spring's major political goals was preservation of the Union.

54. In his Thanksgiving Day sermon on the Fugitive Slave Law, Leonard Elijah Lathrop (1796–1857) declared that "both patriotism and religion require that the law should be obeyed"; he excused disobedience to the law on grounds of personal conscience "if the individual chooses quietly to incur the penalty." L[eonard] E. Lathrop, *A Discourse, Delivered At Auburn, on the Day of the Annual Thanksgiving, December 12, 1850* (Auburn, N.Y.: Derby and Miller, 1850), 10.

55. In a sermon preached in Brooklyn, New York, on Thanksgiving Day 1850, the Reverend Samuel Hanson Cox (1793–1880), an antagonist of Douglass at the 1846 World's Temperance Convention in London, expressed his disapproval of slavery but urged obedience to the Fugitive Slave Law.

56. On 24 November 1850, the Reverend Ichabod Smith Spencer (1798–1854) set forth his position on the Fugitive Slave Law: "I am not justifying slavery. . . . Slavery may be wrong. . . . I am not justifying the fugitive slave law. It may be wrong. . . . I am only insisting upon religious obedience to Law. . . . Such obedience is a religious duty. It is the will of God." Ichabod Spencer, *Fugitive Slave Law: The Religious Duty of Obedience to Law* (New York: M. W. Dodd, 1850).

57. The Reverend Ezra Stiles Gannett (1801–71), a Boston Unitarian minister, proclaimed in an 1850 Thanksgiving Day sermon: "God save us from disunion! I know that Slavery is a political and moral evil, a sin and a curse; but disunion seems to me to be treason, not so much against the country, as against humanity." Ezra Stiles Gannett, *Thanksgiving for the Union: A Discourse Delivered in the Federal Meeting House, November 28, 1850* (Boston: Wm. Crosby and H. P. Nichols, 1850), 17.

58. Pastor of Boston's Third Baptist Church, the clergyman Daniel Sharp (1783–1853) delivered a sermon on 28 November 1850, Massachusetts's Thanksgiving holiday. For his text, Sharp preached on Titus 3:1: "Put them in mind to be subject to principalities and powers, to obey magistrates, to be ready to do every good work."

59. The Unitarian minister Orville Dewey (1794–1882) ardently defended the Fugitive Slave Law. Douglass had earlier criticized Dewey's pamphlet *On American*

called to the ministry, deliberately taught us, against the example of the Hebrews and against the remonstrance of the Apostles, they teach *"that we ought to obey man's law before the law of God."*

My spirit wearies of such blasphemy; and how such men can be supported, as the "standing types and representatives of Jesus Christ," is a mystery which I leave others to penetrate. In speaking of the American church, however, let it be distinctly understood that I mean the *great mass* of the religious organizations of our land. There are exceptions, and I thank God that there are. Noble men may be found, scattered all over these Northern States, of whom Henry Ward Beecher[60] of Brooklyn, Samuel J. May[61] of Syracuse, and my esteemed friend[62] on the platform, are shining examples; and let me say further, that upon these men lies the duty to inspire our ranks with high religious faith and zeal, and to cheer us on in the great mission of the slave's redemption from his chains.

Religion in England and Religion in America.

One is struck with the difference between the attitude of the American church towards the anti-slavery movement, and that occupied by the churches in England towards a similar movement in that country. There, the church, true to its mission of ameliorating, elevating, and improving the condition of mankind, came forward

---

Morals and Manners (Boston: W. Crosby, 1844), in which he argues that the races were separated by "impassable physical, if not mental barriers."

60. Henry Ward Beecher (1813–87), brother of the antislavery novelist Harriet Beecher Stowe, was pastor of Brooklyn's Plymouth Church for forty years. In his sermons, Beecher addressed the major social and political issues of his time with a force and drama that established him as one of the century's major orators.

61. The Unitarian clergyman Samuel Joseph May (1797–1871) joined the abolitionist ranks in 1830 and enjoyed a long tenure as an agent of the New England Anti-Slavery Society. During the 1840s and 1850s, he helped many fugitive slaves reach Canada and aided in the rescue of Jerry McHenry from slave catchers in Syracuse, New York, in 1851.

62. The Reverend Robert R. Raymond (1818–?) was minister of the First Baptist Church of Syracuse, New York, from 1847 to 1852 and was an active abolitionist.

promptly, bound up the wounds of the West Indian slave, and restored him to his liberty.[63] There, the question of emancipation was a high[ly] religious question. It was demanded, in the name of humanity, and according to the law of the living God. The Sharps,[64] the Clarksons,[65] the Wilberforces,[66] the Buxtons,[67] and the Burchells and the Knibbs,[68] were alike famous for their piety, and for their philanthropy. The anti-slavery movement *there* was not an anti-church movement, for the reason that the church took its full share in prosecuting that movement: and the anti-slavery movement in

63. In 1833, Parliament passed the Colonial Slavery Abolition Act, which ended slavery in the British West Indies. Slaves who worked on the land were to serve a six-year apprenticeship before being granted their full freedom; those who worked off the land were to serve a four-year apprenticeship. By 1838, the apprenticeship program had been deemed unworkable, and an Act of Emancipation granted full freedom to all former slaves on 1 August 1838.

64. Granville Sharp (1735–1813) aided a slave named Jonathan Strong when Strong's owner attempted to ship him to Jamaica after Strong had lived independently in London for two years. Sharp searched English law for precedents outlawing slavery, and Strong was declared free eventually. In 1772, Sharp aided lawyers representing James Somerset, another fugitive slave whose owner had recaptured him in England and sought to send him to the West Indies. Abolitionists hailed Sharp's influence on the decision in *Somerset v. Stewart*, which declared that slavery could exist in England only by "positive law" and limited the authority of masters over their slaves in England.

65. Thomas Clarkson (1760–1846) helped spearhead the drive for West Indian emancipation. After 1833, Clarkson turned his attention to American slavery, frequently meeting and corresponding with American abolitionists. Among the last of Clarkson's American guests was twenty-eight-year-old Frederick Douglass, who dined with him 9 August 1846.

66. William Wilberforce (1759–1833) led the parliamentary campaign that culminated in the 1807 law banning the Atlantic slave trade. In 1823, Wilberforce published *An Appeal to the Religion, Justice, and Humanity of the Inhabitants of the British Empire in behalf of the Slaves of the West Indies* (London: Printed by Ellerton and Henderson, for J. Hatchard, 1823) and inaugurated the emancipation struggle in Parliament by presenting a Quaker abolitionist petition.

67. Thomas Fowell Buxton (1786–1845), successor to Wilberforce in the parliamentary struggle to end British slavery and the slave trade. In the late 1820s, he exposed the practice of slave trading in Mauritius, Trinidad, and Jamaica, and between 1831 and 1833 he led the abolition campaign in Parliament. Buxton wrote *The African Slave Trade and Its Remedy* (London: John Murray, 1839) and supported several unsuccessful explorations of the Niger River.

68. William Knibb (1803–43) and Thomas Burchell (1799–1846), missionaries who arrived in Jamaica in 1824, were accused of inciting the so-called Baptist War,

this country will cease to be an anti-church movement, when the church of this country shall assume a favorable, instead of a hostile position towards that movement.

Americans! your republican politics, not less than your republican religion, are flagrantly inconsistent. You boast of your love of liberty, your superior civilization, and your pure Christianity, while the whole political power of the nation (as embodied in the two great political parties), is solemnly pledged to support and perpetuate the enslavement of three millions of your countrymen.[69] You hurl your anathemas at the crowned headed tyrants of Russia and Austria, and pride yourselves on your Democratic institutions, while you yourselves consent to be the mere *tools* and *bodyguards* of the tyrants of Virginia and Carolina. You invite to your shores fugitives of oppression from abroad, honor them with banquets, greet them with ovations, cheer them, toast them, salute them, protect them, and pour out your money to them like water; but the fugitives from your own land you advertise, hunt, arrest, shoot and kill. You glory in your refinement and your universal education; yet you maintain a system as barbarous and dreadful as ever stained the character of a nation—a system begun in avarice, supported in pride, and perpetuated in cruelty. You shed tears over fallen Hungary, and make the sad story of her wrongs the theme of your poets, statesmen and orators, till your gallant sons are ready to fly to arms to vindicate her cause against her oppressors;[70] but, in regard to the ten thousand wrongs of the American slave, you would enforce the strictest silence, and would hail him as an enemy of the nation who dares to make those wrongs the subject of public discourse! You are all on fire at the mention of liberty for France or for Ireland; but are as

---

the Jamaican slave insurrection of 1831–32, though neither was convicted. After West Indian emancipation, the two men returned to Jamaica in 1834, where they spent the rest of their lives expanding their missionary operations, working with the freedmen, and speaking out against the abuses of the apprenticeship system.

69. The U.S. Census recorded the slave population as 3,204,313 in 1850.

70. Douglass here refers to the violent suppression of Hungarian revolutionaries following the invasion of that country by Russian and Austrian troops in August 1849.

cold as an iceberg at the thought of liberty for the enslaved of America. You discourse eloquently on the dignity of labor; yet, you sustain
a system which, in its very essence, casts a stigma upon labor. You
can bare your bosom to the storm of British artillery to throw off a
three-penny tax on tea; and yet wring the last hard-earned farthing
from the grasp of the black laborers of your country. You profess to
believe "that, of one blood, God made all nations of men to dwell
on the face of all the earth,"[71] and hath commanded all men, everywhere to love one another;[72] yet you notoriously hate, (and glory in
your hatred), all men whose skins are not colored like your own.
You declare, before the world, and are understood by the world to
declare, that you *"hold these truths to be self evident, that all men
are created equal; and are endowed by their Creator with certain
inalienable rights; and that, among these are, life, liberty, and the
pursuit of happiness;"*[73] and yet, you hold securely, in a bondage
which, according to your own Thomas Jefferson, *"is worse than ages
of that which your fathers rose in rebellion to oppose,"*[74] *a seventh
part* of the inhabitants of your country.[75]

Fellow-citizens! I will not enlarge further on your national inconsistencies. The existence of slavery in this country brands your republicanism as a sham, your humanity as a base pretence, and your
Christianity as a lie. It destroys your moral power abroad; it corrupts
your politicians at home. It saps the foundation of religion; it makes
your name a hissing, and a by-word to a mocking earth.[76] It is the

71. Acts 17:26.
72. John 13:35.
73. Declaration of Independence.
74. Writing to Jean-Nicolas Démeunier on 26 June 1786, Thomas Jefferson
(1743–1826), the third president of the United States, observed: "What a stupendous,
what an incomprehensible machine is man! Who can endure toil, famine, stripes,
imprisonment or death itself in vindication of his own liberty, and the next moment
be deaf to all those motives whose power supported him thro' his trial, and inflict on
his fellow men a bondage, one hour of which is fraught with more misery than ages
of that which he rose in rebellion to oppose." Julian P. Boyd et al., eds., *The Papers of
Thomas Jefferson* (Princeton, N.J.: Princeton University Press, 1950–), 10:63.
75. The U.S. black population was 15.7 percent, slightly more than one-seventh
of the nation's population, in the 1850 census.
76. Isa. 28:22.

antagonistic force in your government, the only thing that seriously disturbs and endangers your *Union*. It fetters your progress; it is the enemy of improvement, the deadly foe of education; it fosters pride; it breeds insolence; it promotes vice; it shelters crime; it is a curse to the earth that supports it; and yet, you cling to it, as if it were the sheet anchor of all your hopes. Oh! be warned! be warned! a horrible reptile is coiled up in your nation's bosom; the venomous creature is nursing at the tender breast of your youthful republic; *for the love of God, tear away,* and fling from you the hideous monster, and *let the weight of twenty millions crush and destroy it forever!*[77]

The Constitution.

But it is answered in reply to all this, that precisely what I have now denounced is, in fact, guaranteed and sanctioned by the Constitution of the United States; that the right to hold and to hunt slaves is a part of that Constitution framed by the illustrious Fathers of this Republic.

Then, I dare to affirm, notwithstanding all I have said before, your fathers stooped, basely stooped

> "To palter with us in a double sense:
> And keep the word of promise to the ear,
> But break it to the heart."[78]

And instead of being the honest men I have before declared them to be, they were the veriest imposters that ever practised on mankind. *This* is the inevitable conclusion, and from it there is no escape. But I differ from those who charge this baseness on the framers of the Constitution of the United States. *It is a slander upon their memory,* at least, so I believe. There is not time now to argue the constitutional question at length; nor have I the ability to discuss

77. The U.S. Census recorded the total population as 23,261,000 in 1850.
78. *Macbeth,* sc. 30, lines 2091–93.

it as it ought to be discussed. The subject has been handled with masterly power by Lysander Spooner, Esq.,[79] by William Goodell,[80] by Samuel E. Sewall, Esq.,[81] and last, though not least, by Gerritt Smith, Esq.[82] These gentlemen have, as I think, fully and clearly vindicated the Constitution from any design to support slavery for an hour.

Fellow-citizens! there is no matter in respect to which, the people of the North have allowed themselves to be so ruinously imposed upon, as that of the pro-slavery character of the Constitution. In *that* instrument I hold there is neither warrant, license, nor sanction of the hateful thing; but, interpreted as it *ought* to be interpreted, the Constitution is a GLORIOUS LIBERTY DOCUMENT. Read its preamble, consider its purposes. Is slavery among them? Is it at the gateway? or is it in the temple? It is neither. While I do not intend to argue this question on the present occasion, let me ask, if it be not somewhat singular that, if the Constitution were intended to be, by its framers and adopters, a slave-holding instrument, why neither *slavery, slaveholding,* nor *slave* can anywhere be found in it. What would be thought of an instrument, drawn up, *legally* drawn up, for the purpose of entitling the city of Rochester to a track of land, in which no mention of land was made? Now, there are certain rules

79. Lysander Spooner (1808–87), a lawyer, writer, and uncompromising foe of slavery, wrote the famous work *The Unconstitutionality of Slavery* (Boston: B. Marsh, 1845). An expanded version appeared in 1847, and it became one of the major sources of campaign literature used by the Liberty party in the 1840s.

80. Douglass probably refers to William Goodell, *Views of the American Constitutional Law: Its Bearing upon American Slavery* (Utica, N.Y.: Jackson & Chaplin, 1844), and Goodell, *Slavery and Anti-Slavery: A History of the Great Struggle in Both Hemispheres; with a View of the Slavery Question in the United States* (New York: W. Harned, 1852).

81. The attorney Samuel E. Sewall (1799–1888) published in 1827 his *Remarks on Slavery in the United States* in the pages of the *Christian Examiner.*

82. Among Gerrit Smith's many letters, tracts, and pamphlets denying the constitutionality of slavery are *Letter of Gerrit Smith, to Hon. Henry Clay* (New York: American Anti-Slavery Society, 1839), and *Letter of Gerrit Smith to S. P. Chase on the Unconstitutionality of Every Part of American Slavery* (Albany, N.Y.: S. W. Green, 1847).

of interpretation, for the proper understanding of all legal instruments. These rules are well established. They are plain, common-sense rules, such as you and I, and all of us, can understand and apply, without having passed years in the study of law. I scout the idea that the question of the constitutionality or unconstitutionality of slavery is not a question for the people. I hold that every American citizen has a right to form an opinion of the constitution, and to propagate that opinion, and to use all honorable means to make his opinion the prevailing one. Without this right, the liberty of an American citizen would be as insecure as that of a Frenchman. Ex-Vice-President Dallas[83] tells us that the constitution is an object to which no American mind can be too attentive, and no American heart too devoted. He further says, the constitution, in its words, is plain and intelligible, and is meant for the home-bred, unsophisticated understandings of our fellow-citizens. Senator Berrien[84] tells us that the Constitution is the fundamental law, that which controls all others. The charter of our liberties, which every citizen has a personal interest in understanding thoroughly. The testimony of Senator Breese,[85] Lewis Cass,[86] and many others that might be named, who are everywhere esteemed as sound lawyers, so regard the constitution. I take it, therefore, that it is not presumption in a private citizen to form an opinion of that instrument.

Now, take the constitution according to its plain reading, and I defy the presentation of a single pro-slavery clause in it. On the

83. George Mifflin Dallas (1792–1864) served as vice president (1845–49) under James Polk. As a candidate for the Democratic presidential nomination in 1852, Dallas was asked whether he would enforce the Fugitive Slave Law, and he answered unequivocally, "Yes, I would!" New York *Daily Times*, 31 May 1852.

84. John MacPherson Berrien (1781–1856) was a U.S. senator from Georgia who voted in favor of the Fugitive Slave Law, and opposed the abolition of the slave trade in the District of Columbia and the admission of California as a free state.

85. Senator Sidney Breese (1800–78), a Democrat from Illinois, supported the constitutionality of slavery, popular sovereignty, and limited congressional authority over slavery.

86. Lewis Cass (1782–1866), a Democrat, campaigned for president in 1848 on a platform opposing limiting the spread of slavery through the Wilmot Proviso. He lost to Zachary Taylor, a Whig.

other hand it will be found to contain principles and purposes, entirely hostile to the existence of slavery.

I have detained my audience entirely too long already. At some future period I will gladly avail myself of an opportunity to give this subject a full and fair discussion.

Allow me to say, in conclusion, notwithstanding the dark picture I have this day presented of the state of the nation, I do not despair of this country. There are forces in operation, which must inevitably work the downfall of slavery. *"The arm of the Lord is not shortened,"*[87] and the doom of slavery is certain. I, therefore, leave off where I began, with *hope*. While drawing encouragement from the Declaration of Independence, the great principles it contains, and the genius of American Institutions, my spirit is also cheered by the obvious tendencies of the age. Nations do not now stand in the same relation to each other that they did ages ago. No nation can now shut itself up from the surrounding world, and trot round in the same old path of its fathers without interference. The time *was* when such could be done. Long established customs of hurtful character could formerly fence themselves in, and do their evil work with social impunity. Knowledge was then confined and enjoyed by the privileged few, and the multitude walked on in mental darkness. But a change has now come over the affairs of mankind. Walled cities and empires have become unfashionable. The arm of commerce has borne away the gates of the strong city. Intelligence is penetrating the darkest corners of the globe. It makes its pathway over and under the sea, as well as on the earth. Wind, steam, and lightning are its chartered agents. Oceans no longer divide, but link nations together. From Boston to London is now a holiday excursion. Space is comparatively annihilated. Thoughts expressed on one side of the Atlantic are distinctly heard on the other.

The far off and almost fabulous Pacific rolls in grandeur at our feet. The Celestial Empire,[88] the mystery of ages, is being solved.

---

87. Isa. 59:1.

88. "Celestial Empire" is a translation of the Chinese *tianchao*, "heavenly dynasty," alluding to the belief in the divine origin of the emperors.

The fiat of the Almighty, *"Let there be Light,"*[89] has not yet spent its force. No abuse, no outrage whether in taste, sport or avarice, can now hide itself from the all-pervading light. The iron shoe, and crippled foot of China[90] must be seen, in contrast with nature. *Africa must rise and put on her yet unwoven garment. "Ethiopia shall stretch out her hand unto God."*[91] In the fervent aspirations of William Lloyd Garrison, I say, and let every heart join in saying it:

> God speed the year of jubilee
> The wide world o'er!
> When from their galling chains set free,
> Th' oppress'd shall vilely bend the knee,
> And wear the yoke of tyranny
> Like brutes no more.
> That year will come, and freedom's reign,
> To man his plundered rights again
> Restore.
>
> God speed the day when human blood
> Shall cease to flow!
> In every clime be understood,
> The claims of human brotherhood,
> And each return for evil, good,
> Not blow for blow;
> That day will come all feuds to end,
> And change into a faithful friend
> Each foe.
>
> God speed the hour, the glorious hour,
> When none on earth
> Shall exercise a lordly power,
> Nor in a tyrant's presence cower;
> But all to manhood's stature tower,

89. Gen. 1:3.

90. Foot binding began in the tenth and eleventh centuries in the court of imperial China. It inhibited the growth of the foot past four inches by breaking the toes and reshaping the arch, making women more beautiful according to Chinese standards that prevailed for nearly ten centuries.

91. Ps. 68:31.

By equal birth!
THAT HOUR WILL COME, to each, to all,
And from his prison-house, the thrall
    Go forth.

Until that year, day, hour, arrive,
With head, and heart, and hand I'll strive,
To break the rod, and rend the gyve,
The spoiler of his prey deprive—
    So witness Heaven!
And never from my chosen post,
Whate'er the peril or the cost,
    Be driven.[92]

92. William Lloyd Garrison, "The Triumph of Freedom," in the Boston *Liberator*, 10 January 1845.

"A Nation in the Midst of a Nation"

An Address Delivered in New York, New York, 11 May 1853

Frederick Douglass' Paper, 27 May 1853.

On 11 May 1853, seven "religious, philanthropic, and abolition societies" met for their annual anniversary meetings in New York City, including the American Anti-Slavery Society (AASS; William Lloyd Garrison, president) and the American and Foreign Anti-Slavery Society (AFASS; Lewis Tappan, president).[1] Because mob violence had broken out at past AASS meetings, it was the first time in three years that the society had met in New York City. The more radical AASS renounced religious denominations and political parties because both refused to denounce slavery. The AFASS, in contrast, tried to reform such institutions; despite its more moderate positions, it was a smaller, less vigorous organization than its rival. In mid-1851, however, the *National Era,* a Washington, D.C., newspaper that the AFASS had helped found, began serializing Harriet Beecher Stowe's immediately popular *Uncle Tom's Cabin,* and so the AFASS's prospects seemed bright. As these antislavery meetings convened, Stowe was touring Europe and fostering a public outcry against American slavery, especially the Fugitive Slave Law, which guaranteed federal support for the capture and return of runaway slaves.[2] In his speech at the AFASS meeting, Douglass condemned the federal government

---

1. New York *Herald,* 12 May 1853.
2. See "Uncle Tom in the Drawing-Room," New York *Independent,* 19 May 1853. The "English Correspondent" predicted that "hosts of Englishmen and of Europeans generally, who have looked with no small degree of admiration upon America, will be affected with feelings of shame and horror."

for its expanded role in defending slavery and, like Stowe, developed an international analysis of slavery's prospects. He considered the free black populations in the Caribbean and South America potential allies for harboring fugitive slaves or fomenting Southern slave revolts.

The resolutions passed by the two conventions highlighted the differences between the organizations. While the AFASS asserted that "our strongholds . . . are the Bible . . . and the Constitution of the United States,"[3] the AASS resolved to "reaffirm our old principle, of immediate, unconditional emancipation on the soil; and our old principle, that this cannot be obtained except by the dissolution of the American Union, and the destruction of the American Church."[4] The AFASS pledged "to spend no time in controversies except with slaveholders, their abettors and apologists," an allusion to their refusal to endorse women's rights or other provocative reform causes. The AASS, however, welcomed female speakers and warmly defended their rights to speak publicly. At the AASS meeting, Douglass offered brief remarks but played a relatively small role as a result of personal and tactical conflicts with his old friends the Boston-based Garrisonians.

A writer for the New York *Times* observed that the AASS had grown "unmanageable" and had taken "so heavy a freight of non-resistance, Woman's Rights, Sabbath, Church, and clergy denunciation on board that the cooler portion found it necessary to get into another boat or go down together." In contrast, the *Times* writer found the " 'American and Foreign' is a working institution of business-like habits."[5]

Despite Douglass's growing estrangement from the Garrisonians, he tried to straddle both organizations. At the same time, Douglass was advancing what the historian Henry Mayer describes as an "ambitious separatist agenda" that included an exclusively black manual-training school and political council.[6] Other black activists,

---

3. "Anniversaries," New York *Daily Tribune,* 12 May 1853.
4. "Anniversaries," *Frederick Douglass' Paper,* 27 May 1853.
5. "Abolition and Anti-Slavery Societies," New York *Daily Times,* 12 May 1853.
6. Henry Mayer, *All on Fire: William Lloyd Garrison and the Abolition of Slavery* (New York: St. Martin's, 1998), 432.

most notably Martin Delany, were advocating black self-help and voluntary immigration to Central America.[7] Douglass may well have been frustrated by the passive, victim-like role assigned by white Garrisonians to African Americans. Wendell Phillips, for example, expressed a fear that slaveholders would embrace U.S. annexation efforts in Mexico and the Caribbean in order to enslave the native black populations, further expanding the slave South. Douglass, on the other hand, regarded these African diaspora populations as allies in the revolt against slavery. If African Americans were driven from the United States, Douglass warned the "Slavery party," those driven out would go to "the portals of slavery," where they could "be of most service to the colored people of the United States." Whereas Phillips conceived of the diaspora as a passive population that might be reenslaved through American annexation, Douglass regarded them as active agents aligned with African Americans.

In his address, Douglass observes that antislavery speech cannot be suppressed and is, in fact, gaining an unprecedented audience through *Uncle Tom's Cabin* and *A Key to Uncle Tom's Cabin,* a record of atrocities drawn from Stowe's research and that of other abolitionists. He predicts that the Fugitive Slave Law, meant to make slavery widespread and respectable, will in fact make the laws of the country more difficult to enforce.

With this linking of antislavery principles, a new international perspective, and a Romantic theory of history's inevitable progress, Douglass concludes his prepared remarks. The New York *Tribune's* report ends here, but in *Frederick Douglass' Paper* (the version reprinted here), a paragraph is added. In it, Douglass tries to clarify his position in the abolitionist movement: "Sir I have fully spoken out the thoughts of my heart. I have spoken as a colored man and not

---

7. Robert Levine, *Martin Delany, Frederick Douglass, and the Politics of Representative Identity* (Chapel Hill: University of North Carolina Press, 1997). See especially the second chapter, "A Nation Within a Nation: Debating *Uncle Tom's Cabin* and Black Emigration." In *The Condition, Elevation, Emigration, and Destiny of the Colored People of the United States, Politically Considered* (Philadelphia, 1852), Delany specifically refers to free black men in the North as "a nation within a nation" and advocates immigration to Central or South America, where, he argues, people of color already constitute the ruling classes (64–67).

as the representative of any Anti-Slavery society." He affirms that people of color should be grateful to both organizations and that he would be honored to work with either to "strike a blow against slavery." Feeling spurned by the Garrisonians, however, Douglass warns that "if the one discards me because I work with the other, the responsibility is not mine."[8]

M R. PRESIDENT,[9] LADIES AND GENTLEMEN: The resolution upon which I propose to make a few remarks respects the present condition and the future prospects of the whole colored people of the United States.[10] The subject is a great one, and opens ample scope for thought and feeling. I feel a diffidence in undertaking its consideration, for two causes: first, my own incompetence to do it justice— and the second is, the peculiar relation subsisting between me and the audience I am about to address. Sir, I am a colored man, and this is a white audience. No colored man, with any nervous sensibility, can stand before an American audience without an intense and painful sense of the immense disadvantage under which he labors. He feels little borne up by that brotherly sympathy and generous enthusiasm which give wings to the eloquence and strength to the hearts of abler men engaged in other and more popular causes. The ground which a colored man occupies in this country is every inch of it sternly disputed. Not by argument, or any just appeal to the understanding; but by a cold, flinty-hearted, unreasoning and un-

8. "Anniversaries," *Frederick Douglass' Paper*, 27 May 1853.

9. The New York City merchant Arthur Tappan (1786–1865) and his brother Lewis were two of the most prominent opponents of William Lloyd Garrison inside the abolitionist movement. In 1833, he helped found the American Anti-Slavery Society. Seven years later he left the organization because of tactical disagreements with the Garrisonians. He helped organize the American and Foreign Anti-Slavery Society and was an early supporter of the Liberty party.

10. Sixteen resolutions were put before the meeting. Douglass refers to the fourth, regarding opposition to colonization. American and Foreign Anti-Slavery Society, *Thirteenth Annual Report* (New York: The Society, 1853), 180.

reasonable prejudice against him as a man and a member of the human family. Sir, were I a white man, speaking before and for white men, I should in this country have a smooth sea and a fair wind. It is, perhaps, creditable to the American people, (and, sir, I am not the man to detract from their credit), that they listen eagerly to the report of wrongs endured by distant nations. The Hungarian, the Italian, the Irishman, the Jew, and the Gentile, all find in this land a home, and when any of them, or all of them desire to speak, they find willing ears, warm hearts and open hands. For these people, the Americans have principles of justice, maxims of mercy, sentiments of religion, and feelings of brotherhood in abundance. But for my poor people enslaved—blasted and ruined—it would appear, that America had neither justice, mercy nor religion. She has no scales in which to weigh our wrongs—she has no standard by which to measure our rights.

Just here lies the difficulty of my cause. It is found in the fact that we may not avail ourselves of admitted American principles. If I do not misinterpret the feelings of my white countrymen generally, they wish us to understand distinctly and fully, that they wish most of all to have nothing whatever to do with us, unless it may be to coin dollars out of our blood. Our position here is anomalous, unequal, and extraordinary. It is a position to which the most courageous of us cannot look without deep concern. We are, Sir, a hopeful people, and in this we are fortunate: but for this we should have long before the present seemingly unpropitious hour, sunk down under a sense of despair. Look at it, Sir. Here, upon the soil of our birth, in a country which has known us for centuries, among a people who did not wait for us to seek them, but a people who sought us, and who brought us to their own chosen land—a people for whom we have performed the humblest services, and whose greatest comforts and luxuries have been won from the earth by the strength of our sable and sinewy arms. I say, Sir, among such a people and with such recommendations to favor, we are esteemed less than strangers and sojourners—aliens are we in our native land. The fundamental principles of the Republic to which the humblest white man, whether born here or elsewhere, may appeal with confidence in the hope of awakening a favorable response, are held to be inapplicable to us. The glorious doctrines of your revolutionary fathers, and the still more glorious teachings of the Son of God, are construed and applied against us. We are literally scourged beyond the beneficent range of both authorities human and divine. We plead for our rights in the name of the immortal Declaration of Independence and of the Constitution, and we are answered by our countrymen with imprecations[11] and curses. In the sacred name of Jesus we beg for mercy, and the slave whip, red with blood, cracks over us in mockery. We invoke the aid of the ministers of Him who came to preach deliverance to the captives, and to set at liberty them that are bound;[12] and from the loftiest summits of this ministry comes the inhuman and blasphemous response, that if one prayer would move the almighty arm in mercy to break our galling chains, that prayer would be withheld! We cry for help to humanity, a common humanity, and here too we are repulsed. American humanity hates us, scorns, disowns and denies our personality. The outspread wing of American Christianity—apparently broad enough to give shelter to a perishing world—refuses to cover us. To us its bones are brass and its feathers iron. In running thither for shelter and succor, we have only fled from the hungry bloodhound to the devouring wolf— from a corrupt and selfish world to a hollow and hypocritical church; and may I not add, from the agonies of earth to the flames of hell!

Sir, this is strong language. For the sake of my people, I would to God it were extravagantly strong. But, Sir, I fear our fault here to-day will not be that we have pleaded the cause of the slave too vehemently, but too tamely; that we have not contemplated his wrongs with too much excitement, but with unnatural calmness and composure. For my part, I cannot speak as I feel on this subject. My

11. An imprecation is a spoken curse.
12. Luke 4:18.

language, though never so bitter, is less bitter than my experience. At best, my poor speech is, to the facts in the case, but as the shadow to the substance.[13]

Sir, it is known to you and to many who hear me, that I am alike familiar with the whip and chain of slavery, and the lash and sting of public neglect and scorn; that my back is marked with the one, and my soul is fretted with the other. My neck is galled by both yokes —that imposed by one master, and that imposed by many masters. More than twenty years of my life were passed in Slavery, and nearly fifteen years have been passed in nominal freedom. Mine has been the experience of the colored people of America, both slave and free. I was born a slave. Even before I [was] made part of this breathing world the scourge was platted for my back, and the fetters were forged for my limbs. My earliest recollections are associated with the appalling thought that I was a slave—a slave for life. How that crushing thought wrung my young heart I shall never be able fully to tell. But of some things I can tell—some things which are incident to the free and to the slave people of this country. Give me leave, then, in my own language to speak freely all that can be uttered of the thoughts of my heart in regard to the wrongs of the people with whom I thus stand associated in the two conditions to which I have thus alluded—for when I have said all, "the half will not then have been told."[14]

Sir, it was once said by that greatest of modern Irish orators, Daniel O'Connell[15]—(a man whose patriotism was equaled only by

13. Col. 2:17.
14. 1 Kgs. 10:7.
15. Daniel O'Connell (1775–1847), an Irish lawyer and member of Parliament, led the movement to repeal the Act of Union between England and Ireland. O'Connell saw the bill for Catholic emancipation pass Parliament in 1829 with strong support from antislavery politicians. Four years later, he marshaled the crucial Irish votes needed for passage of the Emancipation Act of 1833, which inaugurated gradual abolition in the British West Indies. O'Connell made numerous attempts to rally abolitionist sentiment among Irish Americans, for which he suffered a high political cost, particularly in light of diminished U.S. support for the Irish repeal movement.

his love of universal freedom)—that the history of the Irish people might be traced like a wounded man through a crowd, by the
blood.[16] That is a most startling saying. I read it with a shudder soon
after it was said, and felt [that] if this were true in relation to the
Irish people it was still more true in relation to the colored people of
the United States. Our wrongs and outrages are as old as our country. They date back to its earliest settlement, and extend through
two hundred and thirty years—and they are as numerous and as
oft-repeated as the days of all these years. Even now while I speak
and you listen the work of blood and sorrow goes on. Methinks I
hear the noise of chains and the clang of the whip. There is not a
day, not an hour in any day—not a minute in any hour of the day,
that the blood of my people does not gush forth at the call of the
scourge—that the tenderest ties of humanity are not sundered—
that parents are not torn from children, and husbands are not torn
from their wives for the convenience of those who gain fortune by
the blood of souls.

But I do not propose to confine your attention to the details of
Slavery. They are harrowing to think of and too shocking to fix the
mind upon for any length of time. I rather wish to speak of the
condition of the colored people of the United States generally. This
people, free and slave, are rapidly filling up the number of four millions.[17] They are becoming a nation, in the midst of a nation which
disowns them, and for weal or for woe[18] this nation is united. The
distinction between the slave and the free is not great, and their destiny seems one and the same. The black man is linked to his brother
by indissoluble ties. The one cannot be truly free while the other is
a slave. The free colored man is reminded by the ten thousand petty
annoyances with which he meets every day, of his identity with an

16. This 1844 quotation has been attributed to an anonymous Irish writer. Samuel Smiles, *History of Ireland and the Irish People* (London: W. Strange, 1844), 262.
17. The U.S. census tabulated a slave population in 1850 of 3,204,313 and a free
black population of 434,495, making the total black population 3,638,808.
18. In other words, for better or for worse.

enslaved people—and that with them he is destined to fall or flourish. We are one nation then, if not one in immediate condition at
least one in prospects.

I will not argue that we are men of like passions with the rest
of mankind. That is unnecessary. All know at any rate that we are
capable in some sort of love and hate, friendship and enmity. But
whatever character or capacity you ascribe to us, I am not ashamed
to be numbered with this race. I am not ashamed to speak here as
a negro. Sir, I utterly abhor and spurn with all the contempt possible that cowardly meanness, I will not call it pride, which leads any
colored man to repudiate his connection with his race. I cannot say,
therefore, as was said recently by a distinguished colored man at a
Convention in Cincinnati, that he did not speak as a colored man,[19]
for, Sir, as a colored man I do speak—as a colored man I was invited
here to speak—and as a colored man there are peculiar reasons for
my speaking. The man struck is the man to cry out. I would place
myself—nay, I am placed—among the victims of American oppression. I view this subject from their stand-point—and scan the moral
and political horizon of the country with their hopes, their fears, and
their intense solicitude. Standing here, then, and judging from the
events and indications of the past few years, the black man must see
that a crisis has arrived in his relations with the American people.
He is reminded that trials and hardships await him; that the times
are portentous of storms which will try the strength of his bark.

Sir, it is evident that there is in this country a purely Slavery
party—a party which exists for no other earthly purpose but to
promote the interests of Slavery. The presence of this party is felt
everywhere in the Republic. It is known by no particular name, and

19. Douglass alludes to the remarks of the black Garrisonian abolitionist Charles
Lenox Remond at a "Grand Anti-Slavery Convention" in Cincinnati, Ohio, on
19 April 1853. Addressing a largely white audience, which included Garrison himself,
Remond "said he would not speak as a colored man, but as a *man*," since the inter-
ests of the antislavery movement "were the interests of the whole country." Boston
Liberator, 6 May 1852.

has assumed no definite shape; but its branches reach far and wide in the Church and in the State. This shapeless and nameless party is not intangible in other and more important respects. That party, Sir, has determined upon a fixed, definite, and comprehensive policy toward the whole colored population of the United States. What that policy is, it becomes us as Abolitionists, and especially does it become the colored people themselves, to consider and to understand fully. We ought to know who our enemies are, where they are, and what are their objects and measures.

Well, Sir, here is my version of it—not original with me—but mine because I hold it to be true. I understand this policy to comprehend five cardinal objects. They are these: 1st. The complete suppression of all Anti-Slavery discussion. 2d. The expatriation of the entire free people of color from the United States. 3d. The unending perpetuation of Slavery in this Republic. 4th. The nationalization of Slavery to the extent of making Slavery respected in every State of the Union. 5th. The extension of Slavery over Mexico and the entire South American States. Sir, these objects are forcibly presented to us in the stern logic of passing events—in the facts which are and have been passing around us during the last three years.[20] The country has been and is now dividing on these grand issues. In their magnitude these issues cast all others into the shade, depriving them of all life and vitality. Old party ties are broken. Like is finding its like on either side of these great issues—and the great battle is at hand.

For the present, the best representative of the Slavery party in politics is the Democratic party. Its great head for the present is President Pierce, whose boast it was—before his election—that his whole life had been consistent with the interests of Slavery, that he is above reproach, on that score. In his inaugural address, he reassures the South on this point.[21] Well, the head of the slave power

20. Douglass probably alludes to the passage of the Compromise of 1850.
21. Franklin Pierce (1804–69), the fourteenth president (1853–57), made few statements about slavery during his campaign. In his inaugural address, Pierce

being in power, it is natural that the pro-slavery elements should cluster around the Administration, and this is rapidly being done. A fraternization is going on. The stringent Protectionists and the Free Traders strike hands.[22] The supporters of Fillmore are becoming the supporters of Pierce. The Silver Gray Whig shakes hands with the Hunker Democrat—the former only differing from the latter in name.[23] They are of one heart, one mind, and the union is natural and perhaps inevitable. Both hate negroes, both hate progress, both hate the "Higher Law," both hate Wm. H. Seward,[24] both hate the Free Democratic party,[25] and upon this hateful basis they are forming a union of hatred. "Pilate and Herod are thus made friends."[26] Even the central organ of the Whig party is extending its

---

affirmed. "Involuntary servitude as it exists in the different states of this Confederacy, is recognized by the Constitution. . . . . I hold that the laws of 1850, commonly called the 'compromise measures,' are strictly constitutional and to be unhesitatingly carried into effect . . . I fervently hope that the [slavery] question is at rest."

22. While not using the term "free trade," the Democratic party's national platform for the 1852 presidential election proclaimed: "That justice and sound policy forbid the federal government to foster one branch of industry to the detriment of any other, or to cherish the interests of one portion to the injury of another portion of our common country." The Whigs, in contrast, were protectionists, endorsing import tariffs as "suitable encouragement . . . to American industry, equally to all classes, and to all parts of the country."

23. Douglass's comments reflect the pessimism widespread in antislavery circles after the election of Franklin Pierce. Since 1850, Whigs in New York had been split between the antislavery followers of William H. Seward and the more conservative "Silver Grays," who supported the Compromise of 1850. When the Whigs nominated Seward's ally Winfield Scott for president in 1852, the Silver Grays deserted the party in droves, many of them giving their money and votes to Democratic nominee, Franklin Pierce.

24. In U.S. Senate debates over the Compromise of 1850, the New York Whig William Henry Seward (1801–72) first invoked the doctrine of a "higher law than the Constitution" in support of abolitionism. After the merger of New York's Whig organization with the Republican party in 1855, Seward's antislavery utterances became increasingly forthright, culminating with his 1858 declaration that the slavery struggle was an "irrepressible conflict" between opposing forces.

25. At its 1852 national convention in Pittsburgh, Pennsylvania, the Free Soil party renamed itself the Free Democratic party as part of an effort to retain Northern Democrats who had supported its 1848 nomination of the Democrat Martin Van Buren, a former president.

26. Luke 23:12.

beggar hand for a morsel from the table of Slavery Democracy, and when spurned from the feast by the more deserving, it pockets the insult; when kicked on one side it turns the other, and perseveres in its importunities.[27] The fact is, that paper comprehends the demands of the times; it understands the age and its issues; it wisely sees that Slavery and Freedom are the great antagonistic forces in the country, and it goes to its own side. Silver Grays and Hunkers all understand this. They are, therefore, rapidly sinking all other questions to nothing, compared with the increasing demands of Slavery. They are collecting, arranging, and consolidating their forces for the accomplishment of their appointed work.

The key stone to the arch of this grand union of the Slavery party of the United States is the Compromise of 1850. In that Compromise, we have all the objects of our slaveholding policy specified. It is, Sir, favorable to this view of the designs of the slave power, that both the Whig and the Democratic party bent lower, sunk deeper, and strained harder, in their conventions, preparatory to the late presidential election, to meet the demands of the Slavery party, than at any previous time in their history. Never did parties come before the northern people with propositions of such undisguised contempt for the moral sentiment and the religious ideas of that people. They virtually asked them to unite a war upon free speech, upon conscience, and to drive the Almighty presence from the councils of the nation. Resting their platforms upon the Fugitive Slave bill, they boldly asked the people for political power to execute the horrible and hell black provisions of that bill. The history of that election reveals, with great clearness, the extent to which Slavery has shot its leprous distillment through the lifeblood of the nation. The party most thoroughly opposed to the cause of justice and humanity

27. Probably a reference to the Washington (D.C.) *Daily National Intelligencer,* which had received patronage in the form of federal government printing during Whig administrations but lost those contracts with the inauguration of Franklin Pierce in March 1853.

triumphed, while the party suspected of a leaning towards Liberty was overwhelmingly defeated, some say annihilated.[28]

But here is a still more important fact, illustrating the designs of the slave power. It is a fact full of meaning, that no sooner did the Democratic slavery party come into power, than a system of legislation was presented to the Legislatures of the Northern States, designed to put the states in harmony with the Fugitive Slave Law and the malignant bearing of the National Government towards the colored inhabitants of the country. This whole movement on the part of the States bears the evidence of having one origin, emanating from one head, and urged forward by one power. It was simultaneous, uniform and general, and looked to one end. It was intended to put thorns under feet already bleeding; to crush a people already bowed down; to enslave a people already but half free; in a word, it was intended to discourage, dishearten, and drive the free colored people out of the country. In looking at the recent black law of Illinois, one is struck dumb with its enormity. It would seem that the men who enacted that law, had not only banished from their minds all sense of justice, but all sense of shame. It coolly proposes to sell the bodies and souls of the black[s] to increase the intelligence and refinement of the whites. To rob every black stranger who ventures among them, to increase their literary fund.[29]

28. The Democratic National Platform of 1852 condemned abolitionist efforts and promised "faithful execution" of all parts of the Compromise of 1850, particular the Fugitive Slave Law. Similarly, the Whig party's platform declared that all portions of the Compromise of 1850 "are received and acquiesced in by the Whig Party of the United States as a settlement in principle and substance." During the campaign, however, the Whig candidate, Winfield Scott, was widely perceived as being more antislavery than his platform, causing large defections in the South and turning the election into a rout.

29. During the 1850s, Oregon, Indiana, Iowa, and Illinois enacted or revised so-called Black Laws and sometimes incorporated anti-immigration provisions into state constitutions. Under the terms of an 1853 Illinois statute, any black or mulatto immigrant remaining in the state for more than ten days with the apparent intention of taking up residence was subject to an initial fine of $50, and multiples of that amount for repeated offenses. If unable to pay the fine, they would be incarcerated and sold at auction.

While this is going on in the States, a Pro-Slavery, Political Board of Health is established at Washington! Senators Hale, Chase and Sumner[30] are robbed of a part of their Senatorial dignity and consequence as representing sovereign States, because they have refused to be inoculated with the Slavery virus. Among the services which a Senator is expected by his State to perform, are many that can only be done efficiently on Committees—and, in saying to these honorable Senators, you shall not serve on the Committees of this body, the Slavery party took the responsibility of robbing and insulting the States that sent them.[31] It is an attempt at Washington to decide for the States who shall be sent to the Senate. Sir, it strikes me that this aggression on the part of the Slave power did not meet at the hands of the proscribed Senators the rebuke which we had a right to expect would be administered. It seems to me that an opportunity was lost that the great principles of Senatorial equality were left undefended, at a time when its vindication was sternly demanded. But it is not to the purpose of my present statement to criticise the conduct of our friends. I am persuaded that much ought to be left to the discretion of Anti-Slavery men in Congress, and charges of

30. John Parker Hale (1806–73), Salmon Portland Chase (1808–73), and Charles Sumner (1811–74) had all changed party affiliations by 1853 to protect and advance their antislavery principles. Hale, from New Hampshire, won election in 1842 as a Democrat to the U.S. House of Representatives, where his opposition to the gag rule and the annexation of Texas cost him renomination. In 1846, however, a coalition of Liberty party and antislavery Democrats elected him to the U.S. Senate. Chase was elected U.S. senator from Ohio in 1849 on the Free Soil ticket. He strongly opposed the Compromise of 1850 and favored restrictions on slavery by federal law. Charles Sumner's political career was dedicated to the cause of emancipation; he left the Whig party in 1848 and was a founder of the Free Soil party in Massachusetts. A coalition of Free Soilers and Democrats elected him to the U.S. Senate in 1851.

31. Douglass sarcastically refers to the action of the Democratic and Whig caucuses during the second session of the Thirty-second Congress in excluding the antislavery senators Charles Sumner, Salmon P. Chase, and John P. Hale from any of the Senate's standing committees. When called on to defend the action, Senator Jesse D. Bright of Indiana explained that Hale, and presumably Chase and Sumner as well, were regarded as being "outside of any healthy political organization in this country." Indignant over the Senate's action, many antislavery newspapers seized upon Bright's phrase in critical editorials. Douglass here carries the metaphor one step further by labeling the caucuses a "Pro-Slavery Political Board of Health."

recreancy should never be made but on the most sufficient grounds. For, of all the places in the world where an Anti-Slavery man needs the confidence and encouragement of friends, I take Washington to be that place.

Let me now call attention to the social influences which are operating and co-operating with the Slavery party of the country, designed to contribute to one or all of the grand objects aimed at by that party. We see here the black man attacked in his vital interests—prejudice and hate are excited against him—enmity is stirred up between him and other laborers. The Irish people, warm hearted, generous, and sympathizing with the oppressed everywhere when they stand upon their own green island, are instantly taught on arriving in this Christian country to hate and despise the colored people. They are taught to believe that we eat the bread which of right belongs to them. The cruel lie is told the Irish that our adversity is essential to their prosperity. Sir, the Irish American will find out his mistake one day. He will find that in assuming our avocation he also has assumed our degradation. But for the present we are sufferers. The old employments by which we have heretofore gained our livelihood are gradually, and it may be inevitably, passing into other hands. Every hour sees us elbowed out of some employment to make room perhaps for some newly arrived emigrants, whose hunger and color are thought to give them a title to especial favor. White men are becoming house servants, cooks and stewards, common laborers and flunkeys to our gentry; and, for aught I see, they adjust themselves to their stations with all becoming obsequiousness. This fact proves that if we cannot rise to the whites, the whites can fall to us.[32]

32. Since most Irish immigrants to the United States were impoverished, and many of the Northern free blacks lived in depressed areas of cities, the two groups often found themselves in close company. Along with poor native-born white Americans, they competed for the same jobs and sometimes engaged in interracial sexual or romantic relationships. Slurs and stereotypes portrayed African Americans and Irish immigrants unfavorably, and were used by both groups to slander each other, leading to a number of fights and demonstrations. Deeply rooted prejudices caused few Irish Americans to join the newly formed Republican party in 1856.

Now, Sir, look once more. While the colored people are thus elbowed out of employment; while the enmity of emigrants is being excited against us; while State after State enacts laws against
us; while we are hunted down, like wild game, and oppressed with
a general feeling of insecurity; the American Colonization Society—that old offender against the best interests and slanderer of
the colored people—awakens to new life, and vigorously presses its
scheme upon the consideration of the people and the Government.
New papers are started—some for the North and some for the
South—and each in its tone adapting itself to its latitude.[33] Government, [both] State and National, is called upon for appropriations
to enable the Society to send us out of the country by steam! They
want steamers to carry letters and negroes to Africa. Evidently this
Society looks upon our "extremity as its opportunity,"[34] and we may
expect that it will use the occasion well, that [it] does not deplore
but glories in our misfortunes.

But, Sir, I must hasten. I have thus briefly given my view of one
aspect of the present condition and future prospects of the colored
people of the United States. And what I have said is far from encouraging to my afflicted people. I have seen the cloud gather upon
the sable brows of some who hear me. I confess the case looks
black enough. Sir, I am not a hopeful man. I think I am apt even to
undercalculate the benefits of the future. Yet, Sir, in this seemingly
desperate case, I do not despair for my people. There is a bright
side to almost every picture of this kind; and ours is no exception
to the general rule. If the influences against us are strong, those
for us are also strong. To the inquiry, will our enemies prevail in
the execution of their designs, in my God and in my soul, I believe
they *will not.*

---

33. The American Colonization Society experienced a sustained resurgence during the 1850s. State organizations grew more active, agents traversed the Northern
and border states, and soaring annual revenues allowed the parent organization to
build a ship and transport over six thousand blacks to Liberia between 1848 and 1860.
    34. 2 Cor. 1:8–11.

Let us look at the first object sought for by the Slavery party of the country, viz: the suppression of anti-slavery discussion. They desire to suppress discussion on this subject, with a view to the peace of the slaveholder and the security of slavery. Now, Sir, neither the principle nor the subordinate objects, here declared can be at all gained by the slave power, and for this reason: It involves the proposition to padlock the lips of the whites in order to secure the fetters on the limbs of the blacks. The right of speech, precious and priceless, *cannot, will not,* be surrendered to Slavery. Its suppression is asked for, as I have said, to give peace and security to slaveholders. Sir, that thing cannot be done. God has interposed an insuperable obstacle to any such result. "There can be *no peace,* saith my God, to the wicked."[35] Suppose it were possible to put down this discussion, what would it avail the guilty slaveholder, pillowed as he is upon the heaving bosoms of ruined souls? He could not have a peaceful spirit. If every anti-slavery tongue in the nation were silent—every anti-slavery organization dissolved—every anti-slavery press demolished—every anti-slavery periodical, paper, book, pamphlet or what not were searched out, gathered together, deliberately burned to ashes, and their ashes given to the four winds of heaven, still, still the slaveholders could have *"no peace."* In every pulsation of his heart, in every throb of his life, in every glance of his eye, in the breeze that soothes and in the thunder that startles, would be waked up an accuser, whose cause is, "Thou art, verily, guilty concerning thy brother."[36] Oh! Sir, I can say with the poet Cowper—and I speak from observation—

> "I would not have a slave to till my ground,
> To carry me, to fan me while I sleep,
> And tremble when I wake, for all the wealth
> That sinews bought and sold have ever earned,
> No: dear as freedom is, and in my heart's

35. Isa. 48:22 or 57:21.
36. Gen. 42:21.

> Just estimation prized above all price,
> I had much rather be myself the slave,
> And wear the bonds, than fasten them on him."[37]

Again: The prospect, Sir, of putting down this discussion is anything but flattering at the present moment. I am unable to detect any signs of the suppression of this discussion. I certainly do not see it in this crowded assembly—nor upon this platform—nor do I see it in any direction.

Why, Sir, look all over the North; look South—look at home—look abroad—look at the whole civilized world—and what are all this vast multitude doing at this moment? Why, Sir, they are reading *"Uncle Tom's Cabin;"* and when they have read that, they will probably read *"The Key to Uncle Tom's Cabin"*—a key not only to the Cabin, but, I believe to the slave's darkest dungeon. A nation's hand, with that "key,"[38] will unlock the slave prisons to millions. Then look at the authoress of "Uncle Tom's Cabin." There is nothing in her reception abroad which indicates a declension of interest in the great subject which she has done so much to unfold and illustrate. The landing of a Princess on the shores of England would not have produced the same sensation.

I take it, then, that the Slavery party will find this item of their programme the most difficult of execution, since it is the voice

37. Douglass quotes lines 29–36 of "The Time Piece" (a section of the long poem *The Task*) by William Cowper (1731–1800), a popular English poet and hymnodist. William Cowper and John Cann Bailey, *The Poems of William Cowper. Edited with an introduction and notes by J.C. Bailey. With twenty-seven illustrations.* (London: Methuen & Co., 1905), 267.

38. Harriet Elizabeth Beecher Stowe (1811–96), sister of the famed evangelical minister Henry Ward Beecher, is best remembered for her celebrated antislavery novel *Uncle Tom's Cabin; or, Life Among the Lowly*, 2 vols. (Boston: John P. Jewett & Co., 1852), initially serialized in the Washington (D.C.) *National Era*. Criticism of the book's accuracy led Mrs. Stowe to compile a documentary indictment of slavery published in 1853 under the title *A Key to Uncle Tom's Cabin*. She toured Europe in 1853, 1856, and 1859 and found much acclaim. Responding to criticism among abolitionists, she revised the colonizationist views evident in *Uncle Tom's Cabin* in her later novel *Dred* (1856).

of all experience that opposition to agitation is the most successful method of promoting it. Men will write—men will read—men
will think—men will feel—and the result of this is, men will speak;
and it were as well to chain the lightning as to repress the moral
convictions and humane promptings of enlightened human nature. Herein, sirs, is our hope. Slavery cannot bear discussion: it is
a monster of darkness: and, as Junius said of the character of Lord
Granby, "it can only pass without censure, as it passes without observation."[39]

The second cardinal object of this party, viz: The expatriation of
the free colored people from the United States, is a very desirable
one to our enemies—and we read, in the vigorous efforts making to
accomplish it, an acknowledgment of our manhood, and the danger to Slavery arising out of our presence. Despite the tremendous
pressure brought to bear against us, the colored people are gradually increasing in wealth, in intelligence and in respectability. Here
is the secret of the Colonization scheme. It is easily seen that just in
proportion to the intelligence and respectability of the free colored
race at the North is their power to endanger the stability of Slavery.
Hence the desire to get rid of us. But, Sir, the desire is not merely to
get us out of this country, but to get us at a convenient and harmless
distance from Slavery. And here, Sir, I think I can speak as if by authority for the free colored people of the United States. The people
of this Republic may commit the audacious and high-handed atroc-
ity of driving us out of the limits of their borders. They may virtually confiscate our property; they may invade our civil and personal
liberty, and render our lives intolerable burdens, so that we may be
induced to leave the United States; but to compel us to go to Africa
is quite another thing.

Thank God, the alternative is not quite so desperate as that we
must be slaves here, or go to the pestilential shores of Africa. Other

39. The comment by "Junius" to Granby's defender appears in *The Political Contest; Containing a Series of Letters between Junius and Sir William Draper,* 3d ed.
(London: F. Newberry, 1769), 29.

and more desirable lands are open to us.[40] We can plant ourselves at the very portals of Slavery. We can hover about the Gulf of Mexico. Nearly all the isles of the Caribbean Sea bid us welcome[; w]hile the broad and fertile valleys of British Guiana, under the sway of the emancipating Queen,[41] invite us to their treasures, and to nationality. With the Gulf of Mexico on the South, and Canada on the North, we may still keep within hearing of the wails of our enslaved people in the United States. From the isles of the sea, and from the mountain tops of South America we can watch the meandering destiny of those we have left behind. Americans should remember that there are already on this Continent, and in the adjacent islands, all of 12,370,000 negroes, who only wait for the life-giving and organizing power of intelligence to mould them into one body and into a powerful nation. The following estimate of our numbers and localities is taken from one of the able Reports of the British and Foreign Anti-Slavery Society,[42] carefully drawn up by its former Secretary, John Scoble, Esq.[43]

40. While African Americans in Northern states had largely rejected an early proposal for a mass return to Africa presented by the American Colonization Society, support for alternative emigration plans increased significantly after passage of the Fugitive Slave Law of 1850. The government of Haiti had recruited a small number of African Americans as early as the 1820s. Several settlements of runaway slaves founded in Ontario during the 1840s experienced a major growth surge in response to the new efforts to recapture fugitive slaves. A smaller number of fugitive slaves sought refuge in northern Mexico.

41. Alexandrina Victoria (1819–1901) was the reigning queen of the United Kingdom and its worldwide empire from 1837 to 1901. Early in her reign, Parliament abolished slavery in all parts of the empire except India, Ceylon, and St. Helena.

42. Douglass's statistics correspond to those presented in *The Thirteenth Annual Report of the B[ritish] [and] F[oreign] A[nti-]S[lavery] S[ociety], For the abolition of Slavery and the Slave-Trade throughout the World; presented to the meeting held in Crosby Hall, Bishopsgate Street, London, on Monday, May 17th, 1852* (London: The Society, 1852), 47.

43. The Reverend John Scoble (1799–c.1867) was one of the founders of the British and Foreign Anti-Slavery Society.

```
United States . . . . . . . . . . . . . . . . .  3,650,000
Brazil. . . . . . . . . . . . . . . . . . . . . . .  4,050,000
Spanish Colonies . . . . . . . . . . . . . .  1,470,000
South American Republics. . . . . . . .  1,130,000
British Colonies . . . . . . . . . . . . . . . . 750,000
Hayti . . . . . . . . . . . . . . . . . . . . . . . . 850,000
French Colonies . . . . . . . . . . . . . . . . 270,000
Dutch Colonies. . . . . . . . . . . . . . . . . . 50,000
Danish Colonies . . . . . . . . . . . . . . . . . 45,000
Mexico. . . . . . . . . . . . . . . . . . . . . . . . 70,000
Canada . . . . . . . . . . . . . . . . . . . . . . . 35,000
     Total . . . . . . . . . . . . . . . . . .  12,370,000
```

Now, Sir, it seems to me that the Slavery party will gain little by driving us out of this country, unless it drives us off this Continent and the adjacent islands. It seems to me that it would be after all of little advantage to Slavery to have the intelligence and energy of the free colored people all concentrated in the Gulf of Mexico! Sir, I am not for going anywhere. I am for staying precisely where I am, in the land of my birth. But, Sir, if I must go from this country—if it is impossible to stay here—I am then for doing the next best, and that will be to go to wherever I can hope to be of most service to the colored people of the United States.

Americans! there is a meaning in those figures I have read. God does not permit 12,000,000 of his creatures to live without the notice of His eye. That this vast people are tending to one point on this Continent is not without significance. All things are possible with God.[44] Let not the colored man despair then. Let him remember that a home, a country, a nationality are all attainable this side of Liberia. But for the present the colored people should stay just where they are, unless where they are compelled to leave. I have faith left

44. Matt. 19:26; Mark 10:27.

yet in the wisdom and the justice of the country, and it may be that there are enough left of these to save the nation.

But there is a third object sought by the Slavery party—namely, to render Slavery a permanent system in this Republic, and to make the relation of master and slave respected in every State in the Union. Neither part of this object can be accomplished. Slavery has no means within itself of perpetuation or permanence. It is a huge lie. It is of the devil, and will go to its place. It is against nature, against progress, against improvement, and against the Government of God. It cannot stand. It has an enemy in every bar of railroad iron, in every electric wire, in every improvement in navigation, in the growing intercourse of nations, in cheap postage, in the relaxation of tariffs, in common schools, in the progress of education, the spread of knowledge, in the steam engine, and in the World's Fair, now about to assemble in New York, and in everything that will be exhibited there.[45]

About making Slavery respectable in the North: laws have been made to accomplish just that thing. The law of '50, and the law of '93.[46] And those laws, instead of getting respect for Slavery, have begot disgust and abhorrence. Congress may pass slave laws every day in the year for all time, if each one should be followed by such publications as "Uncle Tom" and the "Key." It is not in the power of human law to make men entirely forget that the slave is a man. The freemen of the North can never be brought to look with the same feelings upon a man, escaping from his claimants, as upon a horse running from his owner. The slave is a man, and no law can take his manhood from him. His right to be free is written on all the powers and faculties of his soul, and is recorded in the great heart of God, and no human law can touch it.

45. Inspired by London's larger and more famous Crystal Palace Exhibition of 1851, the New York world's fair officially known as the Exhibition of the Industry of All Nations opened in mid-July 1853 with 4,854 industrial, agricultural, and art exhibits from the United States and twenty-three foreign countries. The main exhibition building was called the New York Crystal Palace.

46. The Fugitive Slave Laws of 1793 and 1850.

Now, Sir, I had more to say on the encouraging aspects of the times, but the time fails me. I will only say, in conclusion, greater is he that is for us, than they that are against us;[47] and though labor and peril beset the Anti-Slavery movements, so sure as that a God of mercy and justice is enthroned above all created things, so sure will that cause gloriously triumph. Sir, I have fully spoken out the thoughts of my heart. I have spoken as a colored man, and not as the representative of any Anti-Slavery society. There are many societies: but there is but ONE CAUSE. That cause I desire to serve with my whole heart. I have now spoken at the meeting of the "American A[nti-] S[lavery] Society," and at the "American and Foreign A[nti-] S[lavery] Society."[48] The oppressed, among whom I am numbered, should be grateful to both. I honor and respect Lewis Tappan.[49] I love and revere William Lloyd Garrison;[50] and may God have mercy on me when I refuse to strike a blow against Slavery, in connection with either of these gentlemen. I will work with either; and if the one discards me because I work with the other, the responsibility is not mine. (Great and repeated applause.)

47. 1 John 4:4; 2 Kgs. 6:16.

48. On 11 May 1853, Douglass attended the annual meeting of the American Anti-Slavery Society at the Chinese Assembly Rooms in New York City and then the annual meeting of the American and Foreign Anti-Slavery Society in the Broadway Tabernacle in the same city, that evening.

49. Lewis Tappan (1788–1873) achieved considerable financial success as a partner in his brother Arthur's silk company. Strongly influenced by the revivalist Charles G. Finney during the 1830s, Tappan was an early supporter of many benevolent causes. Tappan helped organize the American Anti-Slavery Society in 1833, but in 1840 he broke with William Lloyd Garrison over the issue of political action and the advisability of linking abolitionism with other reforms. He helped found the American and Foreign Anti-Slavery Society.

50. In 1831, William Lloyd Garrison brought out the first issue of the Boston *Liberator*, which endorsed immediate emancipation. Garrison later became an advocate for temperance, women's rights, and many other causes. His uncompromising radical positions led to the schism in the abolitionist movement in 1840. Thereafter, he served as president of the American Anti-Slavery Society and led the Garrisonian wing of abolitionism until the Civil War.

"The Claims of the Negro Ethnologically Considered"

An Address Delivered in Hudson, Ohio, 12 July 1854

The Claims of the Negro Ethnologically Considered: An Address, Before the Literary Societies of Western Reserve College, at Commencement, July 12, 1854 (Rochester, N.Y.: Lee, Mann, & Co.1854).

Western Reserve College's student literary societies nominated Frederick Douglass to deliver the keynote address for the college's 1854 commencement exercises, touching off a controversy between students and some trustees, administrators, and faculty members.[1] Many of the Ohio college's leaders regarded African Americans as unassimilable and advocated removing and colonizing freed blacks outside the United States. The New York *Daily Tribune* remarked, "Douglass's position was not won for him without a struggle on the part of his friends," and Douglass, in turn, thanked "the societies which had so kindly and so perseveringly given him the invitation."[2] Another paper commended the students, to whom "belongs the honor of having first overcome the popular prejudices of the times so

1. The period between 1840 and 1860 was the golden age of literary societies at Western Reserve College. Across American colleges, literary societies were prestigious debating organizations, fostering the public-speaking skills considered essential in college-educated men. At Western Reserve College, the debating societies traditionally nominated one of their own members to deliver the commencement exercises. Frederick Clayton Waite, *Western Reserve University: The Hudson Era* (Cleveland: Western Reserve University Press, 1943), 230, 241, 247.

2. "Frederick Douglass—Western Reserve College," New York *Daily Tribune*, 31 July 1854; *Frederick Douglass' Paper*, 4 August 1854.

far as to welcome to the halls of learning, as a society orator, one of Africa's oppressed sons."[3]

Douglass chose as his topic one that merged scholarly research and the "thought nearest my heart," the relationship between the races in the United States. To prepare, he sought out the guidance of the president of the University of Rochester, Dr. Martin B. Anderson.[4] In the speech, Douglass responds to what became known as the American school of ethnology, a term that in the nineteenth century encompassed both cultural and biological anthropology.[5] Trying to balance biblical teachings and new scientific theories, ethnologists of the time debated whether humanity had a single origin. The dominant thinking within the American school of ethnology endorsed the idea that races had separate origins, and that blacks were biologically inferior, which served to justify slavery. The scholars of the field were celebrated in Southern newspapers.[6] The magnum opus of the school, *Types of Mankind,* published in the year of Douglass's speech, quickly sold out; it went through nine editions by the end of the century.[7] The authors, Samuel George Morton and Josiah Clark Nott, based their findings on the study of ancient Egypt and the measurements of skulls.

Douglass begins his address by investigating claims made by Morton and by the British ethnologist Charles Hamilton Smith. He demonstrates that African Americans meet their definition of what a "man" is, and he begins to argue for the single-place theory of human origins when he stops and questions the sincerity of those debating the issue: "the wish is father to the thought." He adds, "The temptation, therefore, to read the negro out of the human family is exceedingly strong, and may account somewhat for the repeated attempts

3. Warren (Ohio) *Chronicle and Transcript,* reprinted in *Frederick Douglass' Paper,* 4 August 1854.

4. James M. Gregory, *Frederick Douglass, the Orator* (Springfield, Mass.: Willey, 1893; Chicago: Afro-Am Press, 1969), 115.

5. C. Loring Brace, "The 'Ethnology' of Josiah Clark Nott," *Bulletin of the New York Academy of Medicine* 50, no. 4 (April 1974): 514.

6. Ibid., 512–13.

7. Ibid., 520.

on the part of Southern pretenders to science, to cast a doubt over
the Scriptural account of the origin of mankind."

After a foray into evidence that ancient Egyptians and sub-Saharan
Africans were related, Douglass analyzes the basis of ethnological
accounts of race. He argues that racial categories are not rooted in
anything tangible, noting that putatively "negro" characteristics like
a low forehead and low intelligence are found in other races. According to his peers, the most memorable moment of the speech, often
recounted by people after Douglass's death,[8] dealt with the claim
of ethnologists that black men had "feeble and hoarse" voices. The
New York *Daily Tribune* noted, "Douglass read it in loud and thundering tones and made no comment."[9] He argued that cultural factors shaped differences in individual attainments within purported
races, noting that any individual "may carve his circumstances, but
his circumstances will carve him out as well." In exposing the racially
biased premises of ethnology, he anticipated contemporary understandings of race as a social construction erroneously linking skin
color or phenotype with other characteristics.

Douglass concludes the speech with the germination of an idea
that he would build on in his 1869 address "Our Composite Nationality" (included in this volume). Attributing his thinking to Dr. James
McCune Smith,[10] an abolitionist and the first black American to earn
a medical degree, Douglass argues that "our own great nation, so distinguished for industry and enterprise, is largely indebted to its composite character." Ethnic diversity, not exclusivity, created American
resiliency and growth.

8. The Reverend Heman L. Wayland retold this same incident in a collection of
tributes to Douglass published just after his death, and several other contributors
invoked the story. *In Memoriam: Frederick Douglass* (Philadelphia: John S. Yorston
& Co., Publishers, 1897), 238.

9. "Frederick Douglass—Western Reserve College," New York *Daily Tribune,*
31 July 1854.

10. James McCune Smith (1813–65) considered Douglass's mixed-race, cultur-
ally complex background representative of America's composite character. In his
introduction to Douglass's *My Bondage and My Freedom* (1855), he notes of the
autobiography, "It is an American book, for Americans, in the fullest sense of the
idea. It shows that the worst of our institutions, in its worst aspect, cannot keep down
energy, truthfulness, and earnest struggle for the right." *Douglass Papers,* ser. 2, 2:19.

Gentlemen of Philozetian Society: I propose to submit to you a few thoughts on the subject of the Claims of the Negro, suggested by ethnological science, or the natural history of man. But before entering upon that subject, I trust you will allow me to make a remark or two, somewhat personal to myself. The relation between me and this occasion may justify what, in others, might seem an offence against good taste.

This occasion is to me one of no ordinary interest, for many reasons; and the honor you have done me, in selecting me as your speaker, is as grateful to my heart, as it is novel in the history of American Collegiate or Literary Institutions. Surprised as I am, the public are no less surprised, at the spirit of independence, and the moral courage displayed by the gentlemen at whose call I am here. There is felt to be a principle in the matter, placing it far above egotism or personal vanity; a principle which gives to this occasion a general, and I had almost said, an universal interest. I engage to-day, for the first time, in the exercises of any College Commencement. It is a new chapter in my humble experience. The usual course, at such times, I believe, is to call to the platform men of age and distinction, eminent for eloquence, mental ability, and scholarly attainments—men whose high culture, severe training, great experience, large observation, and peculiar aptitude for teaching qualify them to instruct even the already well instructed, and to impart a glow, a lustre, to the acquirements of those who are passing from the Halls of learning, to the broad theatre of active life. To no such high endeavor as this is your humble speaker fitted; and it was with much distrust and hesitation that he accepted the invitation, so kindly and perseveringly given, to occupy a portion of your attention here to-day.

I express the hope, then, gentlemen, that this acknowledgment of the novelty of my position, and my unaffected and honest confession of inaptitude, will awaken a sentiment of generous indulgence towards the scattered thoughts I have been able to fling together, with a view to presenting them as my humble contribution to these Commencement Exercises.

Interesting to me, personally, as this occasion is, it is still more interesting to you; especially to such of you as have completed your education, and who (not wholly unlike the gallant ship, newly launched, full rigged, and amply fitted, about to quit the placid waters of the harbor for the boisterous waves of the sea) are entering upon the active duties and measureless responsibilities incident to the great voyage of life. Before such, the ocean of mind lies outspread more solemn than the sea, studded with difficulties and perils. Thoughts, theories, ideas, and systems, so various, and so opposite, and leading to such diverse results, suggest the wisdom of the utmost precaution, and the most careful survey, at the start. A false light, a defective chart, an imperfect compass, may cause one to drift in endless bewilderment, or to be landed at last amid sharp, destructive rocks.

On the other hand, guided by wisdom, manned with truth, fidelity and industry, the haven of peace, devoutly wished for by all, may be reached in safety by all. The compensation of the preacher is full, when assured that his words have saved even one from error and from ruin. My joy shall be full, if, on this occasion, I shall be able to give a right direction to any one mind, touching the question now to be considered.

Gentlemen, in selecting the Claims of the Negro as the subject of my remarks to-day, I am animated by a desire to bring before you a matter of living importance—[a] matter upon which action, as well as thought, is required. The relation subsisting between the white and black people of this country is the vital question of the age. In the solution of this question, the scholars of America will have to take an important and controlling part. This is the moral battle field to which their country and their God now call them. In the eye[s] of both, the neutral scholar is an ignoble man. Here, a man must be hot, or be accounted cold, or, perchance, something worse than hot or cold. The lukewarm and the cowardly, will be rejected by earnest men on either side of the controversy. The cunning man who avoids it, to gain the favor of both parties, will be rewarded with scorn; and the timid man who shrinks from it, for fear of offending either party, will be despised. To the lawyer, the preacher, the politician, and to the man of letters, there is no neutral ground. He that is not for us, is against us.[11] Gentlemen, I assume at the start, that wherever else I may be required to speak with bated breath, here, at least, I may speak with freedom the thought nearest my heart. This liberty is implied, by the call I have received to be here; and yet I hope to present the subject so that no man can reasonably say, that an outrage has been committed, or that I have abused the privilege with which you have honored me. I shall aim to discuss the claims of the negro, general and special, in a manner, though not scientific, still sufficiently clear and definite to enable my hearers to form an intelligent judgment respecting them.

The first general claim which may here be set up, respects the manhood of the negro. This is an elementary claim, simple enough, but not without question. It is fiercely opposed. A respectable public journal, published in Richmond, Va., bases its whole defence of the slave system upon a denial of the negro's manhood.

"The white peasant is free, and if he is a man of will and intellect, can rise in the scale of society; or at least his offspring may. He is not deprived by law of those 'inalienable rights,' 'liberty and the pursuit of happiness,' by the use of it. But here is the essence of slavery— that we do declare the negro destitute of these powers. We bind him by law to the condition of the laboring peasant for ever, without his consent, and we bind his posterity after him. Now, the true question is, have we a right to do this? If we have not, all discussions about his comfortable situation and the actual condition of free laborers elsewhere, are quite beside the point. If the negro has the same right to his liberty and the pursuit of his own happiness that the white man has, then we commit the greatest wrong and robbery to hold him

11. Matt. 12:30; Mark 9:40; Luke 9:50.

a slave—an act at which the sentiment of justice must revolt in every heart—and negro slavery is an institution which that sentiment must sooner or later blot from the face of the earth."—*Richmond Examiner.*[12]

After stating the question thus, the *Examiner* boldly asserts that the negro has no such right—BECAUSE HE IS NOT A MAN!

There are three ways to answer this denial. One is by ridicule; a second is by denunciation; and a third is by argument. I hardly know under which of these modes my answer to-day will fall. I feel myself somewhat on trial; and that this is just the point where there is hesitation, if not serious doubt. I cannot, however, argue; I must assert. To know whether [a] negro is a man, it must first be known what constitutes a man. Here, as well as elsewhere, I take it, that the "coat must be cut according to the cloth."[13] It is not necessary, in order to establish the manhood of any one making the claim, to prove that such an one equals Clay in eloquence, or Webster and Calhoun[14] in logical force and directness; for, tried by such standards of mental power as these, it is apprehended that very few could claim the high designation of *man*. Yet something like this folly is seen

---

12. Excerpt from the Richmond *Examiner* published in the American and Foreign Anti-Slavery Society's *Thirteenth Annual Report,* 148–49.

13. A paraphrase from John Dryden's play *The Wild Gallant,* first performed in 1663: "'Tis true she tells me; I love your Wit well, Sir; but I must cut my Coat according to my Cloth." Douglass employs the expression the "coat must be cut according to the cloth" to rebuke the Richmond *Examiner's* claim that the slave is not a man, by questioning the moral integrity of the proslavery adherents Henry Clay, Daniel Webster, and John C. Calhoun. John Dryden, *The Wild Gallant; The Rival Ladies; The Indian Queen,* ed. John Harrington Smith, Dougald MacMillan, and Vinton A. Dearing. *The Works of John Dryden,* Vol. 8., ed. H. T. Swedenberg (Berkeley: University of California Press, 1965).

14. Henry Clay (1777–1852), Daniel Webster (1782–1852), and John Caldwell Calhoun (1782–1850) came to be known as the "Great Triumvirate" for their powerful speaking styles and their leadership in national politics. All three were elected to Congress in the 1810s and died shortly after passage of the Compromise of 1850. All three served lengthy terms in the Senate, representing Kentucky (Clay), Massachusetts (Webster), and South Carolina (Calhoun).

in the arguments directed against the humanity of the negro. His faculties and powers, uneducated and unimproved, have been contrasted with those of the highest cultivation; and the world has then been called upon to behold the immense and amazing difference between the man admitted, and the man disputed. The fact that these intellects, so powerful and so controlling, are almost, if not quite, as exceptional to the general rule of humanity in one direction, as the specimen negroes are in the other, is quite overlooked.

Man is distinguished from all other animals, by the possession of certain definite faculties and powers, as well as by physical organization and proportions. He is the only two-handed animal on earth—the only one that laughs, and nearly the only one that weeps. Men instinctively distinguish between men and brutes. Common sense itself is scarcely needed to detect the absence of manhood in a monkey, or to recognize its presence in a negro. His speech, his reason, his power to acquire and to retain knowledge, his heaven-erected face, his habitudes, his hopes, his fears, his aspirations, his prophecies, plant between him and the brute creation, a distinction as eternal as it is palpable. Away, therefore, with all the scientific moonshine that would connect men with monkeys; that would have the world believe that humanity, instead of resting on its own characteristic pedestal—gloriously independent—is a sort of sliding scale, making one extreme brother to the ou-rang-ou-tang, and the other to angels, and all the rest intermediates! Tried by all the usual, and all the *un*usual tests, whether mental, moral, physical, or psychological, the negro is a MAN—considering him as possessing knowledge, or needing knowledge, his elevation or his degradation, his virtues, or his vices—whichever road you take, you reach the same conclusion, the negro is a MAN. His good and his bad, his innocence and his guilt, his joys and his sorrows, proclaim his manhood in speech that all mankind practically and readily understand[s].

A very recondite author says that "man is distinguished from all other animals, in that he resists as well as adapts himself to his circumstances."[15] He does not take things as he finds them, but goes to work to improve them. Tried by this test, too, the negro is a man. You may see him yoke the oxen, harness the horse, and hold the plow. He can swim the river; but he prefers to fling over it a bridge. The horse bears him on his back—admits his mastery and dominion. The barn-yard fowl know his step, and flock around to receive their morning meal from his sable hand. The dog dances when he comes home, and whines piteously when he is absent. All these know that the negro is a MAN. Now, presuming that what is evident to beast and to bird, cannot need elaborate argument to be made plain to men, I assume, with this brief statement, that the negro is a man.

The first claim conceded and settled, let us attend to the second, which is beset with some difficulties, giving rise to many opinions, different from my own, and which opinions I propose to combat.

There was a time when, if you established the point that a particular being is a man, it was considered that such a being, of course, had a common ancestry with the rest of mankind. But it is not so now. This is, you know, an age of science, and science is favorable to division. It must explore and analyze, until all doubt is set at rest. There is, therefore, another proposition to be stated and maintained, separately, which, in other days, (the days before the Notts, the Gliddens, the Agassiz[es], and Mortons, made their profound discoveries in ethnological science),[16] might have been included in the first.

It is somewhat remarkable, that, at a time when knowledge is so generally diffused, when the geography of the world is so well understood—when time and space, in the intercourse of nations,

15. Douglass probably refers to the educator Samuel Stanhope Smith (1750–1819), whose ethnological views predominated among American naturalists until the emergence in the 1840s of the American school of ethnology. Smith reasoned that humans, unlike animals, could exist in numerous environments because of their ability to adapt.

16. The ethnological conclusions of Josiah Clark Nott (1804–73), George Robert Gliddon (1809–57), Jean Louis Rodolphe Agassiz (1807–73), and Samuel George Morton (1799–1851) collectively formed the basic doctrines of what came be known as the American school of ethnology.

are almost annihilated—when oceans have become bridges—the earth a magnificent ball—the hollow sky a dome—under which a common humanity can meet in friendly conclave—when nationalities are being swallowed up—and the ends of the earth brought together—I say it is remarkable—nay, it is strange that there should arise a phalanx[17] of learned men—speaking in the name of *science*—to forbid the magnificent reunion of mankind in one brotherhood. A mortifying proof is here given, that the moral growth of a nation, or an age, does not always keep pace with the increase of knowledge, and suggests the necessity of means to increase human love with human learning.

The proposition to which I allude, and which I mean next to assert, is this: that what are technically called the negro race, are a part of the human family, and are descended from a common ancestry, with the rest of mankind. The discussion of this point opens a comprehensive field of inquiry. It involves the question of the unity of the human race. Much has and can be said on both sides of that question.

Looking out upon the surface of the Globe, with its varieties of climate, soil, and formations, its elevations and depressions, its rivers, lakes, oceans, islands, continents, and the vast and striking differences which mark and diversify its multitudinous inhabitants, the question has been raised, and pressed with increasing ardor and pertinacity, (especially in modern times), can all these various tribes, nations, tongues, kindred, so widely separated, and so strangely dissimilar, have descended from a common ancestry? That is the question, and it has been answered variously by men of learning. Different modes of reasoning have been adopted, but the conclusions reached may be divided into two—the one YES, and the other NO. *Which* of these answers is most in accordance with facts, with reason, with the welfare of the world, and reflects most glory upon the wisdom, power, and goodness of the Author of all existence, is

17. "Phalanx" is an ancient Greek term for a massed military formation.

the question for consideration with us. On which side is the weight of the argument, rather than which side is absolutely proved?

It must be admitted at the beginning, that, viewed apart from the authority of the Bible, neither the unity, nor diversity of origin of the human family, can be demonstrated. To use the terse expression of the Rev. Dr. Anderson,[18] who speaking on this point, says: "It is impossible to get far enough back for that." This much, however, can be done. The evidence on both sides, can be accurately weighed, and the truth arrived at with almost absolute certainty.

It would be interesting, did time permit, to give here, some of the most striking features of the various theories, which have, of late, gained attention and respect in many quarters of our country— touching the origin of mankind—but I must pass this by. The argument to-day, is to the unity, as against that theory, which affirms the diversity of human origin.

The Bearings of the Question.

A moment's reflection must impress all, that few questions have more important and solemn bearings, than the one now under consideration. It is connected with eternal as well as with terrestrial interests. It covers the earth and reaches heaven. The unity of the human race—the brotherhood of man—the reciprocal duties of all to each, and of each to all, are too plainly taught in the Bible to admit of cavil.[19] The credit of the Bible is at stake—and if it be too much to say that it must stand or fall by the decision of this question, *it is* proper to say, that the value of that sacred Book—as a record of the early history of mankind—must be materially affected, by the decision of the question.

18. Martin Brewer Anderson (1815–90) served as president of the University of Rochester from its founding to his retirement (1853–89). In addition to teaching rhetoric and modern history, he published numerous articles on a variety of topics, including ethnology, history, and religion.

19. A petty objection.

For myself I can say, my reason (not less than my feeling, and my faith) welcomes with joy, the declaration of the Inspired Apostle, "that God has made of one blood all nations of men for to dwell upon all the face of the earth."[20] But this grand affirmation of the unity of the human race, and many others like unto it, together with the whole account of the creation, given in the early scriptures, must all get a new interpretation or be overthrown altogether, if a diversity of human origin can be maintained. Most evidently, this aspect of the question makes it important to those who rely upon the Bible, as the sheet anchor of their hopes—and the framework of all religious truth. The young minister must look into this subject and settle it for himself, before he ascends the pulpit, to preach redemption to a fallen race.

The bearing of the question upon Revelation, is not more marked and decided than its relation to the situation of things in our country, at this moment. *One seventh* part of the population of this country is of negro descent.[21] The land is peopled by what may be called the most dissimilar races on the globe. The black and the white—the negro and the European—these constitute the American people—and, in all the likelihoods of the case, they will ever remain the principal inhabitants of the United States, in some form or other. The European population are greatly in the ascendant in numbers, wealth and power. They are the rulers of the country— the masters—the Africans are the slaves—the proscribed portion of the people—and precisely in proportion as the truth of human brotherhood gets recognition, will be the freedom and elevation, in this country, of persons of African descent. In truth, this question is at the bottom of the whole controversy, now going on between the slaveholders on the *one* hand, and the abolitionists on the other. It is the same old question which has divided the selfish from the philanthropic part of mankind in all ages. It is the question whether

20. Acts 17:26.
21. The U.S. black population was 15.7 percent, slightly more than one-seventh, of the nation's population in the 1850 census.

the rights, privileges, and immunities enjoyed by some ought not to be shared and enjoyed by all.

It is not quite two hundred years ago, when such was the simplicity (I will not now say the pride and depravity) of the Anglo-Saxon inhabitants of the British West Indies, that the learned and pious Godwin, a missionary to the West Indies, deemed it necessary to write a book, to remove what he conceived to be the injurious belief that it was sinful in the sight of God to baptize negroes and Indians.[22] The West Indies have made progress since that time. God's emancipating angel has broken the fetters of slavery in those islands, and the praises of the Almighty are now sung by the sable lips of eight hundred thousand freemen, before deemed only fit for slaves, and to whom even baptismal and burial rights [rites?] were denied.[23]

The unassuming work of *Godwin* may have had some agency in producing this glorious result. One other remark before entering upon the argument. It may be said that views and opinions favoring the unity of the human family, coming from one of lowly condition, are open to the suspicion that *"the wish is father to the thought,"*[24] and so, indeed, it may be. But let it be also remembered, that this deduction from the weight of the argument on the one side, is more than counterbalanced by the pride of race and position arrayed on the other. Indeed, ninety-nine out of every hundred of the advocates of a diverse origin of the human family in this country, are among those who hold it to be the privilege of the *Anglo-Saxon* to enslave and oppress the African—and slaveholders, not a few, like the Richmond *Examiner* to which I have referred, have admit-

22. Douglass refers to Morgan Godwyn's *The Negro's and Indian's Advocate, Suing for Their Admission into the Church* (London: B. Took, 1680). Godwyn (1640–c. 1695), an Anglican minister, preached in Barbados and in Virginia from 1666 to 1680. Although not an advocate of emancipation, Godwyn angered slaveholders by publicly criticizing excessive brutality, the sale of children away from parents, and prohibitions against preaching Christianity to the enslaved.

23. Parliament passed the Emancipation Act of 1833, which began the gradual abolition of slavery in the colonies of the West Indies.

24. *Henry IV, Part II*, sc. 12, line 2546.

ted, that the whole argument in defence of slavery, becomes utterly worthless the moment the African is proved to be equally a man with the Anglo-Saxon. The temptation, therefore, to read the negro out of the human family is exceedingly strong, and may account somewhat for the repeated attempts on the part of Southern pretenders to science, to cast a doubt over the Scriptural account of the origin of mankind. If the origin and motives of most works opposing the doctrine of the unity of the human race could be ascertained, it may be doubted whether *one* such work could boast an honest parentage. Pride and selfishness, combined with mental power, never want for a theory to justify them—and when men oppress their fellow-men, the oppressor ever finds, in the character of the oppressed, a full justification for his oppression. Ignorance and depravity, and the inability to rise from degradation to civilization and respectability, are the most usual allegations against the oppressed. The evils most fostered by slavery and oppression are precisely those which slaveholders and oppressors would transfer from their system to the inherent character of their victims. Thus the very crimes of slavery become slavery's best defence. By making the enslaved a character fit only for slavery, they excuse themselves for refusing to make the slave a freeman. A wholesale method of accomplishing this result is to overthrow the instinctive consciousness of the common brotherhood of man. For, let it be once granted that the human race are of multitudinous origin, naturally different in their moral, physical, and intellectual capacities, and at once you make plausible a demand for classes, grades and conditions, for different methods of culture, different moral, political, and religious institutions, and a chance is left for slavery, as a necessary institution. The debates in Congress on the Nebraska Bill[25] during the past

25. The bill to organize the territories of Kansas and Nebraska allowed residents of those territories to decide whether to permit slavery, an example of the "popular sovereignty" principle. Passed on 30 May 1854, the Kansas-Nebraska Act voided the provision of the Missouri Compromise of 1820 that forbade slavery in the old Louisiana Purchase north of 36°30′ and established the doctrine of congressional nonintervention regarding slavery in the territories.

winter, will show how slaveholders have availed themselves of this doctrine in support of slaveholding. There is no doubt that Messrs. Nott, Glidden, Morton, Smith and Agassiz were duly consulted by our slavery propagating statesmen.

Ethnological Unfairness Towards the Negro.

The lawyers tell us that the credit of a witness is always in order. Ignorance, malice or prejudice, may disqualify a witness, and why not an author? Now, the disposition everywhere evident, among the class of writers alluded to, to separate the negro race from every intelligent nation and tribe in Africa, may fairly be regarded as one proof, that they have staked out the ground beforehand, and that they have aimed to construct a theory in support of a foregone conclusion. The desirableness of isolating the negro race, and especially of separating them from the various peoples of Northern Africa, is too plain to need a remark. Such isolation would remove stupendous difficulties in the way of getting the negro in a favorable attitude for the blows of scientific Christendom.

Dr. Samuel George Morton may be referred to as a fair sample of American Ethnologists. His very able work *Crania Americana,* published in Philadelphia in 1839, is widely read in this country.[26] In this great work his contempt for negroes is ever conspicuous. I take him as an illustration of what had been alleged as true of his class.

The fact that Egypt was one of the earliest abodes of learning and civilization, is as firmly established as are the everlasting hills, defying, with a calm front the boasted mechanical and architectural skill of the nineteenth century—smiling serenely on the assaults and the mutations of time, there she stands in overshadowing grandeur, riveting the eye and the mind of the modern world—upon her, in

26. Samuel G. Morton, *Crania Americana; or, A Comparative View of the Skulls of Various Aboriginal Nations of North and South America* (Philadelphia: J. Dobson, 1830), 24–26.

silent and dreamy wonder. Greece and Rome—and through them Europe and America—have received their civilization from the ancient Egyptians. This fact is not denied by anybody. But Egypt is in Africa. Pity that it had not been in Europe, or in Asia, or better still, in America! Another unhappy circumstance is, that the ancient Egyptians were not white people; but were, undoubtedly, just about as dark in complexion as many in this country who are considered genuine negroes; and that is not all, their hair was far from being of that graceful lankness which adorns the fair Anglo-Saxon head. But the next best thing, after these defects, is a positive unlikeness to the negro. Accordingly, our learned author enters into an elaborate argument to prove that the ancient Egyptians were totally distinct from the negroes, and to deny all relationship between. Speaking of the "Copts and Fellahs," whom every body knows are descendants of the Egyptians, he says *"The Copts, though now remarkably distinct from the people that surround them, derive from their remote ancestors some mixture of Greek, Arabian, and perhaps even negro blood."* Now, mark the description given of the Egyptians in this same work: *"Complexion brown, The nose is straight, excepting the end, where it is rounded and wide; the lips are rather thick, and the hair black and curly."* This description would certainly seem to make it safe to suppose the presence of *"even* negro blood." A man, in our day, with brown complexion, "nose rounded and wide, lips thick, hair black and curly," would, I think, have no difficulty in getting himself recognized as a negro!!

The same authority tells us that the "Copts are supposed by NEIBHUR, DENON and others, to be the descendants of the ancient Egyptians;" and Dr. Morton adds, that it has often been observed that a strong resemblance may be traced between the Coptic visage and that presented in the ancient mummies and statues. Again, he says, the *"Copts can be, at most, but the degenerate remains, both physically and intellectually, of that mighty people who have claimed the admiration of all ages."* Speaking of the Nubians, Dr. Morton says, (page 26)—

"The hair of the Nubian is thick and black—often curled, either by nature or art, and sometimes *partially frizzled,* but *never woolly.*" Again:—

"Although the Nubians occasionally present their national characters unmixed, they generally show traces of their social intercourse with the Arabs, and *even* with the negroes."

                 ❉   ❉   ❉

The repetition of the adverb here *"even,"* is important, as showing the spirit in which our great American Ethnologist pursues his work, and what deductions may be justly made from the value of his researches on that account. In everything touching the negro, Dr. Morton, in his "Crania Americana," betrays the same spirit. He thinks that the *Sphinx* was not the representative of an Egyptian Deity, but was a shrine, worshiped at by the degraded *negroes* of Egypt; and this fact he alleges as the secret of the mistake made by Volney,[27] in supposing that the Egyptians were real negroes. The absurdity of this assertion will be very apparent, in view of the fact that the great Sphinx in question was the chief of a series, full two miles in length. Our author again repels the supposition that Egyptians were related to negroes, by saying there is no mention made of *color* by the historian, in relating the marriage of Solomon with Pharaoh's daughter;[28] and, with genuine American feeling, he says, such a circumstance as the marrying of an European monarch with the daughter of a negro would not have been passed over in silence in our day. This is a sample of the reasoning of men who reason from *prejudice* rather than from *facts.* It assumes that a *black skin* in the *East* excites the same prejudice which we see here in the

27. Constantin-François de Chasseboeuf, comte de Volney (1757–1820), a French philosopher, historian, and politician, argued that the Egyptians were not white, contrary to the generally accepted notion, but instead were the descendants of Africans. He bolstered his case with his observation that the Sphinx shared facial features with blacks.

28. 1 Kgs. 3:1.

West. Having denied all relationship of the negro to the ancient Egyptians, with characteristic American assumption, he says, "It is easy to prove, that whatever may have been the hue of their skin, they belong to the same race with ourselves."[29]

Of course, I do not find fault with Dr. Morton, or any other American, for claiming affinity with Egyptians. All that goes in that direction belongs to my side of the question, and is really right.

The leaning here indicated is natural enough, and may be explained by the fact that an educated man in Ireland ceases to be an Irishman; and an intelligent black man is always supposed to have derived his intelligence from his connection with the white race. To be intelligent is to have one's negro blood ignored.

There is, however, a very important physiological fact, contradicting this last assumption; and that fact is, that intellect is uniformly derived from the maternal side. Mulattoes, in this country, may almost wholly boast of Anglo-Saxon male ancestry.

It is the province of prejudice to blind; and scientific writers, not less than others, write to please, as well as to instruct, and even unconsciously to themselves, (sometimes), sacrifice what is true to what is popular. Fashion is not confined to dress; but extends to philosophy as well—and it is fashionable now, in our land, to exaggerate the differences between the negro and the European. If, for instance, a phrenologist or naturalist undertakes to represent in portraits, the differences between the two races—the negro and the European—he will invariably present the *highest* type of the European, and the *lowest* type of the negro.

The European face is drawn in harmony with the highest ideas of beauty, dignity and intellect. Features regular and brow after the Websterian mold. The negro, on the other hand, appears with features distorted, lips exaggerated, forehead depressed—and the whole expression of the countenance made to harmonize with the popular idea of negro imbecility and degradation. I have seen many pictures

29. Morton, *Crania Americana*, 29, 31.

of negroes and Europeans, in phrenological and ethnological works; and all, or nearly all, excepting the work of Dr. Prichard, and that other great work, Combs' *Constitution of Man*,[30] have been more or less open to this objection. I think I have never seen a single picture in an American work, designed to give an idea of the mental endowments of the negro, which did any thing like justice to the subject; nay, that was not infamously distorted. The heads of A. CRUMMEL,[31] HENRY H. GARNET,[32] SAM'L R. WARD,[33] CHAS. LENOX REMOND,[34] W. J. WILSON,[35] J. W. PENNINGTON,[36] J. I. GAINES,[37] M. R. DELANY,[38]

30. Douglass probably refers to James Cowles Prichard, *Researches into the Physical History of Mankind,* 5 vols. (1813; London: Sherwood, Gilbert, and Piper, 1841), and George Combe, *The Constitution of Man Considered in Relation to External Objects,* 3d American ed. (Boston: Allen and Ticknor, 1834).

31. Alexander Crummell (1819–98) was an Episcopal priest, an active member of the American Anti-Slavery Society, and a contributor to the *Colored American.*

32. Born a Maryland slave, Henry Highland Garnet (1815–82) fled north with his parents in 1824. He attended the Oneida Institute in Whitesboro, New York. After the Civil War, Garnet served as president of Avery College in Pittsburgh and U.S. minister to Liberia (1881–82).

33. The black Congregational minister Samuel Ringgold Ward (1817–66) escaped from slavery with his parents and became active in abolitionist circles. Douglass remarked that "as an orator and thinker he [Ward] was vastly superior . . . to any of us," and that "the splendors of his intellect went directly to the glory of his race."

34. Charles Lenox Remond (1810–73) was the first black lecturer among antislavery societies until Frederick Douglass began his speaking career in 1842. Douglass worked the lecture circuit with Remond and so admired him that he named a son for him.

35. William Joseph Wilson (1818–?) was a black schoolteacher in Brooklyn, New York, in the 1840s and 1850s. In the 1850s he became a frequent contributor to *Frederick Douglass' Paper* and the *Anglo-African Magazine,* writing under the pseudonym "Ethiop."

36. James William Charles Pennington (1809–71) escaped slavery on Maryland's Eastern Shore at the age of twenty-one. Pennington entered the Congregational ministry in 1840, traveled to England in 1843 as an at-large delegate to the World's Anti-Slavery Conference in London, and wrote an autobiography, *The Fugitive Blacksmith* (1849).

37. The black businessman John Isom Gaines (1821–59), of Cincinnati, Ohio, owned a riverfront store and played a prominent role in the movement to force city authorities to turn over tax money to the newly formed black board of school trustees.

38. Martin Robison Delany (1812–85) served as coeditor of Douglass's *North Star,* lecturing and traveling extensively between 1847 and 1849 to gain new subscriptions for the paper. In 1850–51, Delany attended Harvard Medical College, but owing to protests from white students, he was denied admission to the final term needed to complete his medical degree. He wrote several books in which he argued that emigration was the only remedy for the oppressed state of black Americans.

J. W. LOGUIN,[39] J. M. WHITFIELD,[40] J. C. HOLLY,[41] and hundreds of others I could mention, are better formed, and indicate the presence of intellect more than any pictures I have seen in such works; and while it must be admitted that there are negroes answering the description given by the American ethnologists and others, of the negro race, I contend that there is every description of head among them, ranging from the highest Indoo Caucasian downward. If the very best type of the European is always presented, I insist that *justice,* in all such works, demands that the very best type of the negro should also be taken. The importance of this criticism may not be apparent to all;—to the *black* man it is very apparent. He sees the injustice, and writhes under its sting. But to return to Dr. Morton, or rather to the question of the affinity of the negroes to the Egyptians.

It seems to me that a man might as well deny the affinity of the Americans to the Englishman, as to deny such affinity between the negro and the Egyptian. He might make out as many points of difference, in the case of the one as in that of the other. Especially could this be done, if, like ethnologists, in given cases, only typical specimens were resorted to. The lean, slender American, pale and swarthy, if exposed to the sun, wears a very different appearance to the full, round Englishman, of clear, *blonde* complexion. One may trace the progress of this difference in the common portraits of the American Presidents. Just study those faces, beginning

39. Jermain Wesley Loguen (c. 1810–72) attended the Oneida Institute, taught school in several New York communities, and then became a minister in the African Methodist Episcopal Zion Church. After passage of the Fugitive Slave Law of 1850, Loguen moved to the comparative safety of Syracuse and was active in the Underground Railroad.

40. Settling in Buffalo, New York, in 1841, James Monroe Whitfield (1822–71) worked as a barber and wrote poetry. Several of his poems had already been published in the *North Star* when Douglass visited Whitfield in Buffalo in late June 1850.

41. An early subscriber to the *North Star,* Joseph Cephas Holly (1825–55) wrote articles addressed to Northern blacks and whites and to Southern nonslaveholders, linking the rights of poor whites with those of blacks. In 1850, Holly embarked upon a tour of Vermont, serving as an agent for Douglass's newspaper and speaking on the needs and rights of African Americans.

with Washington; and as you come thro' the Jeffersons, the Adamses, and the Madisons, you will find an increasing bony and wiry appearance about those portraits, & a greater remove from that serene amplitude which characterizes the countenances of the earlier Presidents. I may be mistaken, but I think this is a correct index of the change going on in the nation at large,—converting Englishmen, Germans, Irishmen, and Frenchmen into Americans, and causing them to lose, in a common American character, all traces of their former distinctive national peculiarities.

Authorities as to the Resemblance of the Egyptians to Negroes.

Now, let us see what the best authorities say, as to the personal appearance of the Egyptians. I think it will be at once admitted, that while they differ very strongly from the negro, debased and enslaved, that difference is not greater than may be observed in other quarters of the globe, among people notoriously belonging to the same variety, the same original stock; in a word, to the same family. If it shall be found that the people of Africa have an African character, as general, as well defined, and as distinct, as have the people of Europe, or the people of Asia, the exceptional differences among them afford no ground for supposing a difference of race; but, on the contrary, it will be inferred that the people of Africa constitute one great branch of the human family, whose origin may be as properly referred to the families of Noah, as can be any other branch of the human family from whom they differ. Denon, in his *Travels in Egypt,* describes the Egyptians, as of full, but "delicate and voluptuous forms, countenances sedate and placid, round and soft features, with eyes long and almond shaped, half shut and languishing, and turned up at the outer angles, as if habitually fatigued by the light and heat of the sun; cheeks round; thick lips, full and prominent; mouths large, but cheerful and smiling; complexion dark, ruddy and coppery, and the whole aspect displaying—as one of the most graphic delineators among modern travelers has observed—the genuine African character, of which the *negro* is the exaggerated and extreme representation."[42] Again, Prichard says, (page 152)—

"Herodotus[43] traveled in Egypt, and was, therefore, well acquainted with the people from personal observation. He does not say anything directly, as to the descriptions of their persons, which were too well known to the Greeks to need such an account, but his indirect testimony is very strongly expressed. After mentioning a tradition, that the people of Colchis were a colony from Egypt, Herodotus says, that 'there was one fact strongly in favor of this opinion—the Colchians were *black* in complexion and *woolly* haired.'"

These are the words by which the complexion and hair of negroes are described. In another passage, he says that

"The pigeon, said to have fled to Dodona, and to have founded the Oracle, was declared to be *black*, and that the meaning of the story was this: The Oracle was, in reality, founded by a female captive from the Thebaid: she was *black*, being an Egyptian." "Other Greek writers," says Prichard, "have expressed themselves in similar terms."

Those who have mentioned the Egyptians as a *swarthy* people, according to Prichard, might as well have applied the term *black* to them, since they were doubtless of a chocolate color. The same author brings together the testimony of Eschylus[44] and others as to the color of the ancient Egyptians, all corresponding, more or less, with the foregoing. Among the most direct testimony educed by Prichard, is, first that of Volney, who, speaking of the modern Copts, says:

---

42. Douglass misquotes a passage from *Travels in Upper and Lower Egypt, during the Campaign of General Bonaparte in That Country*, trans. Arthur Aikin, 2 vols. (New York: Samuel Campbell, 1803), 2:44, the travelogue of the French engraver and administrator Dominique-Vivant Denon (1747–1825).

43. Herodotus (484–425 B.C.E.), Greek historian.

44. Aeschylus (525–456 B.C.E.), Greek playwright.

"They have a puffed visage, swollen eyes, flat nose, and thick lips, and bear much resemblance to mulattoes."

Baron Larrey[45] says, in regard to the same people:

"They have projecting cheek bones, dilating nostrils, thick lips, and hair and beard black and *crisp.*"

Mr. Ledyard,[46] (whose testimony, says our learned authority, is of the more value, as he had no theory to support), says:

"I suspect the *Copts* to have been the *origin* of the *negro* race; the nose and lips correspond with those of the negro; the hair, wherever I can see it among the people here, is curled, *not* like that of the negroes, but like the mulattoes."[47]

Here I leave our learned authorities, as to the resemblance of the Egyptians to negroes.

It is not in my power, in a discourse of this sort, to adduce more than a very small part of the testimony in support of a near relationship between the present enslaved and degraded negroes, and the ancient highly civilized and wonderfully endowed Egyptians. Sufficient has already been adduced, to show a marked similarity in regard to features, hair, color, and I doubt not that the philologist can find equal similarity in the structures of their languages. In view of the foregoing, while it may not be claimed that the ancient Egyptians were negroes,—viz:—answering, in all respects, to the nations and tribes ranged under the general appellation, negro; still, it may safely be affirmed, that a strong affinity and a direct relationship may be claimed by the negro race, to THAT GRANDEST OF ALL THE NATIONS OF ANTIQUITY, THE BUILDERS OF THE PYRAMIDS.

---

45. Dominique-Jean Larrey (1766–1842), a French surgeon who served in Napoleon's army in Italy and during the 1815 Waterloo campaign, was responsible for several innovations in battlefield medicine, including army field surgery, medical transport, and the triage model of emergency medical care.

46. John Ledyard (1751–89) was an American explorer who wrote the first travelogue of Hawaii, *Journal of Captain Cook's Last Voyage* (1783). He was on the expedition credited with discovering the Hawaiian Archipelago.

47. The observations of Herodotus and the passages from the comte de Volney, Baron Larrey, and John Ledyard appear in Prichard, *Physical History of Mankind,* 2:228–29, 238–39.

But there are other evidences of this relationship, more decisive than those alleged in a general similarity of personal appearance. Language is held to be very important, by the best ethnologists, in tracing out of the remotest affinities of nations, tribes, classes and families. The color of the skin has sometimes been less enduring than the speech of a people. I speak by authority, and follow in the footsteps of some of the most learned writers on the natural and ethnological history of man, when I affirm that one of the most direct and conclusive proofs of the general affinity of Northern African nations with those of West, East and South Africa, is found in the general similarity of their language. The philologist easily discovers, and is able to point out something like the original source of the multiplied tongues now in use in that yet mysterious quarter of the globe. Dr. R. G. LATHAM, F.R.S., corresponding member of the Ethnological Society, New York—in his admirable work, entitled "Man and his Migrations"—says:

"In the languages of Abyssinia, the Gheez and Tigre, admitted, as long as they have been known at all, to be *Semitic*, graduate through the Amharic, the Talasha, the Harargi, the Gafat and other languages, which may be well studied in Dr. Beke's[48] valuable comparative tables, into the Agow tongue, unequivocally indigenous to Abyssinia, and through this into the true negro classes. But, unequivocal as may be the Semitic elements of the Berber, Coptic and Galla, their affinities with the tongues of Western and Southern Africa are more so. I weigh my words when I say, not *equally*, but *more;* changing the expression, for every foot in advance which can be made towards the Semitic tongues in one direction, the African philologist can go a yard towards the negro ones in the other."

In a note, just below this remarkable statement, Dr. Latham says:

---

48. Charles Tilstone Beke (1800–74), an early British explorer in eastern Africa and the Middle East, published widely on his geographic, botanical, and linguistic findings.

"A short table of the Berber and Coptic, as compared with the other African tongues, may be seen in the Classical Museum of the British Association, for 1846. In the *Transactions* of the Philological Society is a grammatical sketch of the Tumali language, by Dr. S. Tutsbek[49] of Munich. The Tumali is a truly negro language, of Kordufan; whilst, in respect to the extent to which its inflections are formed, by internal changes of vowels and accents, it is fully equal to the Semitic tongues of Palestine and Arabia."[50]

This testimony may not serve prejudice, but to me it seems quite sufficient.

Superficial Objections.

Let us now glance again at the opposition. A volume, on the *Natural History of the Human Species,* by Charles Hamilton Smith, quite false in many of its facts, and as mischievous as false, has been published recently in this country, and will, doubtless, be widely circulated, especially by those to whom the thought of human brotherhood is abhorrent. This writer says, after mentioning sundry facts touching the dense and spherical structure of the negro head:

"This very structure may influence the erect gait, which occasions the practice common also to the Ethiopian, or mixed nations, of carrying burdens and light weights, even to a tumbler full of water, upon the head."

No doubt this seemed a very sage remark to Mr. Smith, and quite important in fixing a character to the negro skull, although different to that of Europeans. But if the learned Mr. Smith had stood, previous to writing it, at our door, (a few days in succession),

49. Lorenz Tutschek (1817–88) of Munich published the early nineteenth-century geographic, anthropological, and linguistic research on the Nubian region along the Egypt-Sudan border collected by his brother Karl.

50. The quoted argument of the British scholar and physician Robert Gordon Latham (1812–88) appears in Robert Gordon Latham, *Man and His Migrations* (New York: C. B. Norton, 1852), 156–57.

he might have seen hundreds of Germans and of Irish people, not bearing burdens of *"light* weight," but of *heavy* weight, upon the same vertical extremity. The carrying of burdens upon the head is as old as Oriental Society; and the man writes himself a blockhead, who attempts to find in the custom a proof of original difference. On page 227, the same writer says:

"The voice of the negroes is feeble and hoarse in the male sex."

The explanation of this mistake in our author is found in the fact that an oppressed people, in addressing their superiors—perhaps I ought to say, their oppressors—usually assume a minor tone, as less likely to provoke the charge of intrusiveness. But it is ridiculous to pronounce the voice of the negro feeble; and the learned ethnologist must be hard pushed, to establish differences, when he refers to this as one. Mr. Smith further declares, that

"The typical woolly haired races have never discovered an alphabet, framed a grammatical language, nor made the least step in science or art."[51]

Now, the man is still living, (or was but a few years since), among the Mandingoes of the Western coast of Africa, who has framed an alphabet; and while Mr. Smith may be pardoned for his ignorance of that fact, as an ethnologist, he is inexcusable for not knowing that the Mpongwe language, spoken on both sides of the Gaboon River, at Cape Lopez, Cape St. Catharine, and in the interior, to the distance of two or three hundred miles, is as truly a grammatically framed language as any extant. I am indebted, for this fact, to Rev. Dr. M. B. ANDERSON, President of the Rochester University; and by his leave, here is the Grammar—(holding up the Grammar). Perhaps, of all the attempts ever made to disprove the unity of the human family, and to brand the negro with natural inferiority, the most

51. Douglass quotes Charles Hamilton Smith, *The Natural History of the Human Species: Its Typical Forms, Primeval Distribution, Filiations, and Migrations* (1851; Boston: Gould and Lincoln, 1854), 226–29. The Flemish-born Smith (1776–1859) wrote—and sometimes illustrated—numerous treatises on both natural and military history.

compendious and barefaced is the book, entitled *Types of Mankind,* by Nott and Glidden.[52] One would be well employed in a series of Lectures directed to an exposure of the unsoundness, if not the wickedness of this work.

The African Race but One People.

But I must hasten. Having shown that the people of Africa are, probably, one people; that each tribe bears an intimate relation to other tribes and nations in that quarter of the globe, and that the Egyptians may have flung off the different tribes seen there at different times, as implied by the evident relations of their language, and by other similarities; it can hardly be deemed unreasonable to suppose, that the African branch of the human species—from the once highly civilized Egyptian to the barbarians on the banks of the Niger—may claim brotherhood with the great family of Noah, spreading over the more Northern and Eastern parts of the globe. I will now proceed to consider those physical peculiarities of form, features, hair and color, which are supposed by some men to mark the African, not only as an inferior race, but as a distinct species, naturally and originally different from the rest of mankind, and as really to place him nearer to the brute than to man.

The Effect of Circumstances upon the Physical Man.

I may remark, just here, that it is impossible, even were it desirable, in discourse like this, to attend to the anatomical and physiological argument connected with this part of the subject. I am not equal to

52. Douglass refers to *Types of Mankind; or Ethnological Researches, based upon the Ancient Monuments, Paintings, Sculptures, and Crania of Races, and upon Their Natural, Geographical, Philological, and Biblical History* (Philadelphia: Lippincott, Grambo, 1854), by the Southern surgeon and ethnologist Josiah C. Nott and the English-born archaeologist and Egyptologist George R. Gliddon.

that, and if I were, the occasion does not require it. The form of the negro—(I use the term *negro,* precisely in the sense that you use the term Anglo-Saxon; and I believe, too, that the former will one day be as illustrious as the latter)—has often been the subject of remark. His flat feet, long arms, high cheek bones and retreating forehead are especially dwelt upon, to his disparagement, and just as if there were no white people with precisely the same peculiarities. I think it will ever be found, that the *well* or *ill* condition of any part of mankind, will leave its mark on the physical as well as on the intellectual part of man. A hundred instances might be cited, of whole families who have degenerated, and others who have improved in personal appearance, by a change of circumstances. A man is worked upon by what *he* works on. He may carve out his circumstances, but his circumstances will carve him out as well. I told a boot maker, in Newcastle-upon-Tyne, that I had been a plantation slave. He said I must pardon him; but he could not believe it; no plantation laborer ever had a high instep. He said he had noticed that the coal heavers and work people in low condition had, for the most part, flat feet, and that he could tell, by the shape of the feet, whether a man's parents were in high or low condition. The thing was worth a thought, and I have thought of it, and have looked around me for facts. There is some truth in it; though there are exceptions in individual cases.

The day I landed in Ireland, nine years ago, I addressed, (in company with Father SPRATT[53] and that good man who has been recently made the subject of bitter attack; I allude to the philanthropic JAMES HAUGHTON,[54] of Dublin), a large meeting of the

53. John Spratt (1797–1871) was among the first to join Father Theobald Mathew's temperance crusade. On 1 September 1845, the day after reaching Dublin, Douglass spoke at a temperance meeting where Spratt administered the pledge to "upwards of one thousand persons." Dublin *Evening Post,* 2 September 1845.

54. The Irish Unitarian James Haughton (1785–1873) early on supported the antislavery movement. Douglass alludes to editorial attacks made in 1854 by the Irish expatriate John Mitchel, a proslavery New York City journalist, on Haughton for calling on Irish Americans to oppose slavery. Haughton was an early disciple of the Irish temperance reformer Father Theobald Mathew and a supporter of the Irish nationalist leader Daniel O'Connell.

common people of Ireland, on temperance. Never did human faces tell a sadder tale. More than five thousand were assembled; and I say, with no wish to wound the feelings of any Irishman, that these people lacked only a black skin and wooly hair, to complete their likeness to the plantation negro. The open, uneducated mouth—the long, gaunt arm—the badly formed foot and ankle—the shuffling gait—the retreating forehead and vacant expression—and, their petty quarrels and fights—all reminded me of the plantation, and my own cruelly abused people. Yet, *that* is the land of GRATTAN, of CURRAN, of O'CONNELL, and of SHERIDAN.[55] Now, while what I have said is true of the common people, the fact is, there are no more really handsome people in the world, than the educated Irish people. The Irishman educated, is a model gentleman; the Irishman ignorant and degraded, compares in form and feature with the negro!

I am stating facts. If you go into Southern Indiana, you will see what climate and habit can do, even in one generation. The man may have come from New England, but his hard features, sallow complexion, have left little of New England on his brow. The right arm of the blacksmith is said to be larger and stronger than the left. The ship carpenter is at forty round-shouldered. The shoemaker carries the marks of his trade. One locality becomes famous for one thing, another for another. Manchester and Lowell, in America, Manchester and Sheffield, in England,[56] attest this. But what does it

55. Henry Grattan (1746–1820) and John Philpot Curran served in the Irish Parliament and opposed the Act of Union that eliminated it. Grattan continued to represent Ireland in the British Parliament. Daniel O'Connell and Richard Sheridan (1751–1816) were born in Ireland and served in Parliament after the Act of Union. All four championed Irish nationalism and Catholic emancipation. Douglass probably first came to learn of Sheridan from "Mr. Sheridan's Speech against Mr. Taylor," an extract in his childhood primer, the *Columbian Orator.* Caleb Bingham, *Columbian Orator* (Boston, 1817), 130–31.

56. Long an important market town in central England, Sheffield had developed as early as medieval times into a leading center for knives, metal, weapons, cutlery, and, eventually, steel production. Manchester, in northwestern England, experienced massive growth in the early nineteenth century as it became the country's largest textile-manufacturing center. Similarly, Lowell, Massachusetts, and Manchester, New Hampshire, upriver from Lowell, became major cotton textile centers.

all prove? Why, nothing positively, as to the main point; still, it raises the inquiry—may not the condition of men explain their various appearances? Need we go behind the vicissitudes of barbarism for an explanation of the gaunt, wiry, ape like appearance of some of the genuine negroes? Need we look higher than a vertical sun, or lower than the damp, black soil of the Niger, the Gambia, the Senegal,[57] with their heavy and enervating miasma,[58] rising ever from the rank growing and decaying vegetation, for an explanation of the negro's color? If a cause, full and adequate, can be found here, *why seek further?*

The eminent Dr. Latham, already quoted, says that nine-tenths of the white population of the globe are found between 30 and 65 degrees North latitude. Only about one-fifth of all the inhabitants of the globe are white; and they are as far from the Adamic complexion as is the negro. The remainder are—*what?* Ranging all the way from the brunette to jet black. There are the red, the reddish copper color, the yellowish, the dark brown, the chocolate color, and so on, to the jet black. On the mountains on the North of Africa, where water freezes in winter at times, branches of the same people who are *black* in the valley are *white* on the mountains. The Nubian, with his beautiful curly hair, finds it becoming frizzled, crisped, and even woolly, as he approaches the great Sahara. The Portuguese, white in Europe, is brown in Asia. The Jews, who are to be found in all countries, never intermarrying, are white in Europe, brown in Asia, and black in Africa. Again, what does it all prove? Nothing, absolutely; nothing which places the question beyond dispute; but it *does* justify the conjecture before referred to, that outward circumstances *may* have something to do with modifying the various phases of humanity; and that color itself is at the control of the world's climate and its various concomitants. It is the sun that paints the peach—and may it not be, that he paints the *man* as well? My

---

57. Douglass names three major rivers in western Africa, relying on the descriptions made by European explorers.

58. Since the time of the ancient Greeks, many believed that disease was spread through "bad air" coming from decomposing matter.

reading, on this point, however, as well as my own observation, have
convinced me that from the beginning the Almighty, within certain
limits, endowed mankind with organizations capable of countless
variations in form, feature and color, without having it necessary to
begin a new creation for every new variety.

A powerful argument in favor of the oneness of the human family, is afforded in the fact that nations, however dissimilar, may be
united in one social state, not only without detriment to each other,
but, most clearly, to the advancement of human welfare, happiness
and perfection. While it is clearly proved, on the other hand, that
those nations freest from foreign elements present the most evident marks of deterioration. Dr. JAMES McCUNE SMITH, himself
a colored man, a gentleman and scholar, alleges—and not without
excellent reason—that this, our own great nation, so distinguished
for industry and enterprise, is largely indebted to its composite
character.[59] We all know, at any rate, that now, what constitutes the
very heart of the civilized world—(I allude to England)—has only
risen from barbarism to its present lofty eminence, through succes-
sive invasions and alliances with her people. The Medes and Persians constituted one of the mightiest empires that ever rocked the
globe.[60] The most terrible nation which now threatens the peace of
the world, to make its will the law of Europe, is a grand piece of Mosaic work, in which almost every nation has its characteristic feature,
from the wild Tarter to the refined Pole.[61]

But, gentleman, the time fails me, and I must bring these remarks to a close. My argument has swelled beyond its appointed
measure. What I intended to make special, has become, in its prog-

59. Douglass may refer to the essay "Civilization: Its Dependence on Physical
Circumstances," by the prominent black physician, abolitionist, and writer James
McCune Smith.

60. Originally an itinerant Aryan people from Central Asia, by the end of the
seventh century B.C.E. the Medes had settled in what is today northwestern Iran
and southeastern Turkey. Fifty years later, the Persian Empire conquered that area,
Babylonia, and Egypt, and invaded Greece.

61. Douglass alludes to Russia and the events leading to the Crimean War.

ress, somewhat general. I meant to speak here to-day, for the lonely
and the despised ones, with whom I was cradled, and with whom
I have suffered; and now, gentlemen, in conclusion, what if all this
reasoning be unsound? What if the negro may not be able to prove
his relationship to Nubians, Abyssinians and Egyptians?[62] What if
ingenious men are able to find plausible objections to all arguments
maintaining the oneness of the human race? What, after all, if they
are able to show very good reasons for believing the negro to have
been created precisely as we find him on the Gold Coast—along
the Senegal[63] and the Niger—I say, what of all this? *"A man's a man
for a' that."*[64] I sincerely believe, that the weight of the argument
is in favor of the unity of origin of the human race, or species—
that the arguments on the other side are partial, superficial, utterly
subversive of the happiness of man, and insulting to the wisdom of
God. Yet, what if we grant they are not so? What, if we grant that
the case, on our part, is not made out? Does it follow, that the negro should be held in contempt? Does it follow, that to enslave and
imbrute him is either *just* or *wise?* I think not. Human rights stand
upon a common basis; and by all the reason that they are supported,
maintained and defended, for one variety of the human family, they
are supported, maintained and defended for *all* the human family;
because all mankind have the same wants, arising out of a common nature. A diverse origin does not disprove a common nature,
nor does it disprove a united destiny. The essential characteristics
of humanity are everywhere the same. In the language of the elo-

62. "Nubia" was the name of a region along the Nile River now located in southern Egypt and northern Sudan. "Abyssinia" was a commonly used name for the ancient African nation known as the Ethiopian Empire.

63. A reference to two West African nations. The Gold Coast was a region of the
Guinea Coast colonized by the British; it achieved independence as Ghana in 1957.
Douglass might be referring to the nearby British Niger Coast Protectorate, which
later became a portion of modern Nigeria.

64. Douglass quotes a line from "For a' That and a' That," a song by Robert Burns
(1759–96), a Scottish romantic poet. Alexander Smith, ed., *Poems, Songs, and Letters; Being the Complete Works of Robert Burns* (1868; London: Macmillan & Co.,
1921), 227–28.

quent CURRAN, "No matter what complexion, whether an Indian or an African sun has burnt upon him," his title deed to freedom, his claim to life and to liberty, to knowledge and to civilization, to society and to Christianity, are just and perfect.[65] It is registered in the Courts of Heaven, and is enforced by the eloquence of the God of all the earth.

I have said that the negro and white man are likely ever to remain the principal inhabitants of this country. I repeat the statement now, to submit the reasons that support it. The blacks can disappear from the face of the country by three ways. They may be colonized,— they may be exterminated,—or, they may die out. Colonization is out of the question; for I know not what hardships the laws of the land can impose, which can induce the colored citizen to leave his native soil. He was here in its infancy; he is here in its age. Two hundred years have passed over him, his tears and blood have been mixed with the soil, and his attachment to the place of his birth is stronger than iron. It is not probable that he will be exterminated; two considerations must prevent a crime so stupendous as that—the influence of Christianity on the one hand, and the power of self interest on the other; and, in regard to their dying out, the statistics of the country afford no encouragement for such a conjecture. The history of the negro race proves them to be wonderfully adapted to all countries, all climates, and all conditions. Their tenacity of life, their powers of endurance, their malleable toughness, would almost imply especial interposition on their behalf. The ten thousand horrors of slavery, striking hard upon the sensitive soul, have bruised, and battered, and stung, but have not killed. The poor bondman lifts a smiling face above the surface of a sea of agonies, *hoping on, hoping ever.* His tawny brother, the Indian, dies, under the flashing glance of the Anglo-Saxon. *Not* so the negro; civilization cannot kill him. He accepts it—becomes a part of it. In the Church, he is an

65. Curran, *Speeches,* 182.

Uncle Tom;[66] in the State, he is the most abused and least offensive. All the facts in his history mark out for him a destiny, united
to America and Americans. Now, whether this population shall,
by FREEDOM, INDUSTRY, VIRTUE and INTELLIGENCE,
be made a blessing to the country and the world, or whether their
multiplied wrongs shall kindle the vengeance of an offended God,
will depend upon the conduct of no class of men so much as upon
the Scholars of the country. The future public opinion of the land,
whether anti-slavery or pro-slavery, whether just or unjust, whether
magnanimous or mean, must redound to the honor of the Scholars
of the country or cover them with shame. There is but one safe
road for nations or for individuals. The fate of a wicked man and of
a wicked nation is the same. The flaming sword of offended justice
falls as certainly upon the nation as upon the man. God has no children whose rights may be safely trampled upon. The sparrow may
not fall to the ground without the notice of his eye, and men are
more than sparrows.

Now, gentlemen, I have done. The subject is before you. I shall
not undertake to make the application. I speak as unto wise men.
I stand in the presence of Scholars. We have met here to-day from
vastly different points in the world's condition. I have reached
here—if you will pardon the egotism—by little short of a miracle:
at any rate, by dint of some application and perseverance. Born, as
I was, in obscurity, a stranger to the halls of learning, environed by
ignorance, degradation, and their concomitants, from birth to manhood, I do not feel at liberty to mark out, with any degree of confidence, or dogmatism, what is the precise vocation of the Scholar.
Yet, this I *can* say, as a denizen of the world, and as a citizen of a
country rolling in the sin and shame of Slavery, the most flagrant
and scandalous that every saw the sun, "Whatsoever things are true,

66. An allusion to the humble, pious, long-suffering attitude of the title character
of *Uncle Tom's Cabin.*

whatsoever things are honest, whatsoever things are just, what-soever things are pure, whatsoever things are lovely, whatsoever things are of good report, if there be any virtue, and if there be any praise, think on these things."[67]

67. Phil. 4:8.

"The American Constitution and the Slave"

An Address Delivered in Glasgow, Scotland, 26 March 1860

[George Thompson and Frederick Douglass], *Constitution of the United States*, London Emancipation Committee, Tract No. 5 (London: William Tweedie, 1860), 16–34.

In November 1859, a month after John Brown's raid on Harpers Ferry, Frederick Douglass fled to Canada and then to England. His earlier meetings with Brown had been discovered, and he feared being tried for his role in the raid.[1] Brown and his followers had briefly occupied the national arsenal as a first step in fomenting a large-scale slave insurrection, but they were captured by a hastily assembled force of local militia and U.S. Marines. After his execution by the Virginia authorities, Brown was celebrated as a martyr by many Northern opponents of slavery. Those who collaborated with Brown before the raid were under threat of arrest. As in 1845, Douglass went to Britain as a fugitive, but his reception was more mixed this time, since he was no longer a Garrisonian devoted to peaceful means of resisting slavery. Former British allies gave him a cold reception.

On the defensive, according to the biographer William S. McFeely, Douglass "steered clear of any kind of revolutionary rhetoric that might seem traitorous."[2] At speaking engagements in Britain,

---

1. McFeely, *Frederick Douglass*, 202.
2. Ibid., 203.

Douglass advocated reading the Constitution as an antislavery document, offering the promise that the United States could eliminate slavery without voiding the Constitution and destroying the Union. In other words, reform, not revolution, was called for: a proper interpretation of the Constitution could preserve the Union and eradicate slavery.

His speeches drew criticism from George Thompson, a British antislavery activist who had become an important Garrisonian ally. Thompson and Garrison had forged their friendship in the midst of the violent antiabolitionist riots of the 1830s, barely escaping a Boston mob that threatened their lives at an 1835 antislavery lecture. Thompson invited Douglass to debate the Constitution question, but Douglass declined. In a speech in February 1860, Thompson defended the Garrisonian position. He opens that speech respectfully: "Certain things, however, have been stated by that gentleman here and elsewhere, which I could not allow to pass unnoticed, without failing in my duty . . . to that body of abolitionists in America which I believe to be the only one acting out with perfect consistency and fidelity the principles of religion, morality, and sound policy as applied to the circumstances of the United States."[3]

Thompson's speech claims three things: that Douglass believed the Constitution to be proslavery in 1847, when he last visited Britain; that the framers intended to perpetuate slavery; and that the Constitution has been interpreted repeatedly to defend slavery, being the basis for legal and judicial acts such as the Fugitive Slave Law and the *Dred Scott* decision. Thompson concludes that the U.S. Constitution has made and continues to make slavery a nationally protected institution and that nothing short of dissolving the Union can eliminate slavery.

Taking up the challenge, Douglass traveled to Glasgow, where Thompson had spoken, and delivered his response in Queen's Room Hall. In lawyerly fashion, Douglass ably defends his change of positions, though he also personalizes his attack, criticizing Thompson

3. George Thompson, *Lecture on the Constitution of the United States,* London Emancipation Committee, Tract No. 5 (London: William Tweedie, 1860), 5.

for giving an "anti-Douglass" speech and standing up for "a mere party" rather than for the "down-trodden." One can speculate that Douglass, having an uncertain future in the United States because of his connection to John Brown's raid on Harpers Ferry, felt attacks on his positions more keenly than he had in the past. He may, too, have had reason to believe that Garrisonians in the United States and Britain were attempting to destroy his political influence once and for all. Samuel May Jr., in a letter to Douglass's Dublin publisher, urged Garrisonians to "take no notice" of Douglass, claiming he was "unworthy of our trust" because of his implication in "the Harper's Ferry business."[4] In a letter to his good friend the Rochester reformer Amy Post, Douglass lamented his isolation: "I find my war views decidedly objected to by my old Garrisonian friends in England. This is the more ridiculous since the Garrisonians in America are so deeply interested in the whole Brown invasion—now."[5]

Douglass's reasons for his change of position were powerful. In 1847, it was difficult to elect antislavery representatives to Congress; by 1860, free soil and antislavery sentiment had become far more popular in the North and West. He notes in his speech that the intent of the Constitution's framers matters little, since contracts do not rest upon the unstated sentiments of their originators. Douglass acknowledges that past understandings offer a guide to future lawful interpretation. But he also remarks that even though the Constitution and Bible have been given proslavery connotations, this does not mean they do not also include antislavery principles, or that they must cease being the twin pillars upholding American and Christian society. "To dissolve the Union would be to do just what the slaveholders would like to have done," he presciently argued a year before the firing on Fort Sumter.

4. Samuel May Jr. to Richard D. Webb, 16 November 1859, in McFeely, *Frederick Douglass,* 202.
5. Frederick Douglass to Amy Post, 25 May 1860, Post Family Papers, Rush Rhees Library, University of Rochester.

r. President,[6] Ladies, and Gentlemen, I have witnessed with great pleasure the growing interest in the great question of slavery in this city,[7] and in Scotland generally. Meetings with reference to that question have become more abundant of late than perhaps at any time since the abolition of slavery in the British West Indies. I read with deep interest the speeches made recently at a meeting called to sympathise with and to assist that faithful champion of the cause of my enslaved fellow-countrymen, Dr. Cheever.[8] I have also read of another meeting in your city, having reference to the improvement and elevation of the people of Africa—having reference to the cultivation of cotton and the opening up of commerce between this and that land.[9] All these movements are in the right direction. I accept them and hail them as signs of "the good time coming,"[10] when Ethiopia "shall stretch out her hands to God"[11] in deed and in truth.

There have been, also, other meetings in your city since it was my privilege last to address you.[12] I have read with much care a speech recently delivered in the City Hall. It is published in one of your

6. The Glasgow meeting was presided over by the reformer, politician, and businessman John M'Dowall (c. 1800–61).

7. The city was home to the Glasgow Emancipation Society, which was founded in 1833. It became the largest Scottish antislavery group sympathetic to Garrisonianism. It supported antipoverty reform as well.

8. On 19 March 1860, at a public meeting in Glasgow's Merchants' Hall, the Reverend Robert Buchanan, Henry Batchelor, and others delivered speeches supporting the Reverend George B. Cheever (1807–90), an antislavery Congregationalist minister from New York City.

9. At the time of Douglass's address, Martin Delany and Robert Campbell were in West Africa negotiating with kings for land to establish a colony devoted to growing "free" cotton for British manufacturers. The meeting to which Douglass refers may have been organized by Theodore Bourne or another sympathizer of Henry Highland Garnet's African Civilization Society.

10. "The Good Time Coming" is the title of a poem by Charles Mackay. Charles Mackay, *Voices from the Mountains and from the Crowd* (Boston: Ticknor, Reed, and Fields, 1853), 202–04.

11. Ps. 68:31.

12. Douglass last spoke in Glasgow at the John Street United Presbyterian Church on 14 February 1860.

most respectable journals.[13] The minuteness and general shading of that report convince me that the orator was his own reporter. At any rate, there is but little evidence or few marks of its having been tampered with by any than one exceedingly friendly to the sentiments it contains. On some accounts I read that speech with regret; on others with much satisfaction. I was certainly pleased with the evidence it afforded that the orator has largely recovered his long-lost health, and much of his wonted eloquence and fire; but my chief ground of satisfaction is that its delivery—perhaps I ought to say its publication—for I would not have noticed the speech had it not been published in just such a journal as that in which it was published—furnishes an occasion for bringing before the friends of my enslaved people one phase of the great struggle going on between liberty and slavery in the United States which I deem important, and which I think, before I get through, my audience will agree with me is a very important phase of that struggle.

The *North British Mail* honored me with a few pointed remarks in dissent from certain views held by me on another occasion in this city;[14] but as it rendered my speech on that occasion very fairly to the public, I did not feel at all called upon to reply to its strictures. The case is different now. I am brought face to face with two powers. I stand before you under the fire of both platform and press. Not to speak, under the circumstances, would subject me and would subject my cause to misconstruction. You might be led to suppose that I had no reasons for the ground that I occupied here when I spoke in another place before you. Let me invite your attention, I may say your indulgent attention, to this very interesting phase of the question of slavery in the United States. My *assailant*, as he had a perfect right to do—that is, if he felt that that was the best possible service

13. Douglass refers to George Thompson's speech before an audience of Glasgow abolitionists in the City Hall on 28 February 1860.

14. The 15 February 1860 issue of the Glasgow *North British Daily Mail* carried a report of Douglass's lecture of the preceding day at the John Street United Presbyterian Church.

he could do to the cause of American slavery—under advertisement to deliver an "anti-slavery lecture"—a lecture on the present aspect of the anti-slavery movement in America—treated the citizens of Glasgow to an *"anti-Douglass" lecture.* He seemed to feel that *to discredit me was an important work,* and therefore he came up to that work with all his wonted power and eloquence, proving himself to be just as powerful and skillful a debater, *in all its arts, high and low,* as long practice, as constant experience could well fit a man to be.

I award to the eloquent lecturer, as I am sure you do, all praise for his skill and ability, and fully acknowledge his many valuable services, in other days, to the anti-slavery cause both in England and America. We all remember how nobly he confronted the Borthwicks[15] and the Breckenridges[16] in other days, and vanquished them. These victories are safe; they are not to be forgotten. They belong to his past, and will render his name dear and glorious to aftercoming generations. He then enjoyed the confidence of many of the most illustrious philanthropists that Scotland has ever raised up. He had at his back, at those times, the Wardlaws,[17] the Kings,[18] the

15. The Anglican minister Peter Borthwick (1804–52) was a lecturer employed by the proslavery West Indies Committee in the 1830s to make public addresses opposing abolition. In 1832, Borthwick and George Thompson engaged in a series of debates in Manchester and Liverpool on the merits of emancipation. Believing that Thompson completely negated Borthwick's arguments, abolitionists published several editions of excerpts from the debates.

16. In the summer of 1836, George Thompson issued a public invitation in the London *Patriot* to anyone, English or American, to debate with him the merits of slavery and abolitionism. In Glasgow, Thompson's challenge was accepted by Robert Jefferson Breckinridge (1800–71), an American Presbyterian minister visiting Scotland to attend a church conference. In debate with Thompson—and consistently throughout his career—Breckinridge endorsed gradual emancipation and colonization.

17. The Scottish Congregationalist minister Ralph Wardlaw (1779–1853) opened his chapel to the Glasgow Emancipation Society on 12 December 1833 for its first public meeting, and subsequently served as one of the society's vice presidents. He resigned in 1841 because of the society's growing enthusiasm for Garrisonianism and instead worked to bring the Evangelical Alliance to an abolitionist position.

18. The Reverend David King (1808–83), an early member of the Glasgow Emancipation Society, unsuccessfully fought to keep the society out of the Garrisonian camp.

Heughs,[19] and Robsons[20]—men who are known the world over for their philanthropy, for their Christian benevolence. He was strong in those days, for he stood before the people of Scotland as the advocate of a great and glorious cause—he stood up for the dumb, for the down-trodden, for the outcasts of the earth, and *not for a mere party, not for the mere sect whose mischievous and outrageous opinions he now consents to advocate in your hearing.*

When in Glasgow a few weeks ago, I embraced the occasion to make a broad statement concerning the various plans proposed for the abolition of slavery in the United States, but I very frankly stated with what I agreed and from what I differed; but I did so, I trust, in a spirit of fair dealing, of candor, and *not in a miserable, man-worshipping, and mutual-admiration spirit,* which can do justice only to the party with which it may happen to go for the moment. One word further. No difference of opinion, no temporary alienations, no personal assaults shall ever lead me to forget that some who, in America, have often made me the subject of personal abuse, are at the same time, in their own way, earnestly working for the abolition of slavery. They are men who thoroughly understand the principle, that they who are not for us are against us,[21] but who unfortunately have failed to learn that they who are not against us are on our part.

In regard to the speaker to whom I am referring, *and who by the way is, perhaps, the least vindictive of his party,* I shall say that I cannot praise his speech, for it is needlessly, or was needlessly personal, calling me by name over, I think, fifty times, and *dealing out blows upon me as if I had been savagely attacking him.* In *character and manliness* that speech was not only *deficient,* I think, but most *shamefully one-sided;* and while it was remarkably plausible, and well calculated to catch the popular ear, which could not well

19. Hugh Heugh (1782–1846), the pastor of one of Scotland's largest Presbyterian congregations, pioneered the church's missionary societies.

20. John Robson (?–c. 1873) was a Scottish minister of the Wellington Street Church in Glasgow.

21. Matt. 12:30; Mark 9:40; Luke 9:50.

discriminate between what was fact and what was fiction in regard to the subject then discussed, I do not hesitate to pronounce that speech *false in statement, false in its assumptions, false in its inferences, false in its quotations even, and in its arguments, and false in all its leading conclusions.*

On very many accounts, he who stands before a British audience to denounce any thing peculiarly American in connection with slavery has a very marked and decided advantage. It is not hard to believe the very worst of any country where a system like slavery has existed for centuries. This feeling towards America, and towards every thing American, is very natural and very useful. I refer to it now not to condemn it, but to remind you that it is just possible that this feeling may be carried to too great a length. It may be that this feeling may be too active, and lead the people of Great Britain to accept as true some things concerning America which are utterly false, and to reject as false some other things which are entirely true.

My assailant *largely took advantage* of this noble British feeling in denouncing the constitution and Union of America. He knew how deep and intense was your hatred of slavery. He knew the strength of that feeling, and the noble uses to which it might have been directed. I know it also, but I would despise myself if I could be guilty of taking advantage of such a sentiment, and making it the means of *propagating error, falsehood, and prejudice* against any institution or against any class of men in the United States. *I am willing that these words shall be regarded as marked words.* I have often felt how easy it would be, if one were so disposed, to make false representations of things as they are in America; to disparage whatever of good might exist there, or shall exist there, and to exaggerate whatever is bad in that country. I intend to show that this very thing was done by the speaker to whom I have referred; that *his speech was calculated to convey impressions and ideas totally, grossly, outrageously at variance with truth* concerning the constitution and Union of the American States.

You will think this very strong language. I think so too; and it becomes me to look well to myself in using such language, for if I fail to make out my case, I am sure there are parties not a few who will see that fair play is done on the other side. But I have no fear at all of inability to justify what I have said; and if any friend of mine was led to doubt, from the confident manner in which I was assailed, I beg that such doubt may now be put aside until, at least, I have been heard. *I will make good, I promise you, my entire characterisation of that speech.* Reading speeches is not my forte, and you will bear with me until I get my harness on. I have fully examined my ground, and while I own myself nothing in comparison with my assailant in point of ability, I have no manner of doubt as to the rectitude of the position I occupy on the question.

Now, what is that question? Much will be gained at the outset if you fully and clearly understand the real question under discussion—the question and difference between us. Indeed, nothing can be understood till this is understood. Things are often confounded and treated as the same for no better reason than that they seem alike or look alike, and this is done even when in their nature and character they are totally distinct, totally separate, and even opposed to each other. This jumbling up of things is a sort of dust-throwing which is often indulged in by *small men who argue for victory rather than for truth.* Thus, for instance, the American government and the American constitution are often spoken of in the speech to which I refer as being synonymous—as one and the same thing; whereas, in point of fact, they are entirely distinct from each other and totally different. In regard to the question of slavery, certainly they are different from each other; they are as distinct from each other as the compass is from the ship—as distinct from each other as the chart is from the course which a vessel may be sometimes steering. They are not one and the same thing. If the American government has been mean, sordid, mischievous, devilish, it is no proof whatever that the constitution of government has been the same. And yet, in the speech to which some of you listened, these sins of the government or administration of the government were charged directly upon the constitution and Union of the states.

What, then, is the question? I will state what it is *not*. It is not whether slavery existed in the United States at the time of the adoption of the constitution; it is not whether slaveholders took part in framing the constitution of the United States; it is not whether these slaveholders in their hearts intended to secure certain advantages for slavery in the constitution of the United States; it is not whether the American government has been wielded during seventy-two years on behalf of slavery; it is not whether a pro-slavery interpretation has been put upon the constitution in American courts—all these points may be true or they may be false, they may be accepted or they may be rejected, without at all affecting the question at issue between myself and the "City Hall."

The real question between the parties differing at this point in America may be fairly stated thus:—"Does the United States constitution guarantee to any class or description of people in that country the right to enslave or hold as property any other class or description of people in that country?"

The second question is:—"Is the dissolution of the Union between the Slave States and the Free States required by fidelity to the slaves or the just demands of conscience?" Or, in other words, "Is the refusal to exercise the elective franchise or to hold office in America, the surest, wisest, and best mode of acting for the abolition of slavery in that country?"

To these questions the Garrisonians in America answer, "Yes." They hold that the constitution is a slave-holding instrument, and will not cast a vote, or hold office under it, and *denounce all who do vote or hold office under it as pro-slavery men,* though they may be in their hearts and in their actions as far from being slaveholders as are the poles of the moral universe apart. I, on the other hand, deny that the constitution guarantees the right to hold property in men, and believe that the way, the true way, to abolish slavery in America is to vote such men into power as will exert their moral and political influence for the abolition of slavery. This is the issue plainly stated, and you shall judge between us.

Before we examine into the disposition, tendency, and character of the constitution of the United States, I think we had better ascertain what the constitution itself is. Before looking at what it means, let us see what it is. For here, too, there has been endless dust-throwing on the part of those opposed to office. What is the constitution? It is no vague, indefinite, floating, unsubstantial something, called, according to any man's fancy, now a weasel and now a whale.[22] But it is something substantial. It is a plainly written document; not in Hebrew nor in Greek, but in English, beginning with a preamble, fitted out with articles, sections, provisions, and clauses, defining the rights, powers, and duties to be secured, claimed, and exercised under its authority. It is not even like the British constitution. It is not made up of enactments of parliament, decisions of courts, and the established usages of the government. The American constitution is a written instrument, full and complete in itself.[23] No court, no congress, no legislature, no combination in the country can add one word to it, or take one word from it. It is a thing in itself; complete in itself; has a character of its own; and it is important that this should be kept in mind as I go on with the discussion. It is a great national enactment, done by the people, and can only be altered, amended, or changed in any way, shape or form by the people who enacted it. I am careful to make this statement here; in America it would not be necessary. It would not be necessary here if my assailant had shown that he had as sincere and earnest a desire

22. *Hamlet*, sc. 9, lines 2092–98.

23. Building on the precedent of colonial charters, the American states wrote constitutions to direct the operation of their governments. This practice was followed at the national level, first by the Articles of Confederation and then by the Constitution. In contrast the British constitution is embodied in a collection of documents written over the centuries, including royal decrees, court judgments, and treaties.

to set before you the simple truth, *as he has shown to vindicate his particular sect in America.*

Again, it should be borne in mind that the mere text of that constitution—the text and only the text, and not any commentaries or creeds written upon the text—is the constitution of the United States. It should also be borne in mind that the intentions of those who framed the constitution, be they good or bad, be they for slavery or against slavery, are to be respected so far, and so far only, as they have succeeded in getting these intentions expressed in the written instrument itself. This is also important. It would be the wildest of absurdities, and would lead to the most endless confusions and mischiefs, if, instead of looking to the written instrument itself for its meaning, it were attempted to make us go in search of what could be the secret motives and dishonest intentions of some of the men who might have taken part in writing or adopting it. It was what they said that was adopted by the people; not what they were ashamed or afraid to say, or really omitted to say. It was not what they tried, nor what they concealed; it was what they wrote down, not what they kept back, that the people adopted. It was only what was declared upon its face that was adopted—not their secret understandings, if there were any such understandings.

Bear in mind, also, and the fact is an important one, that the framers of the constitution, the men who wrote the constitution, sat with closed doors in the city of Philadelphia while they wrote it. They sat with closed doors, and this was done purposely, that nothing but the result, the pure result of their labours should be seen, and that that result might stand alone and be judged of on its own merits, and adopted on its own merits, without any influence being exerted upon them by the debates.

It should also be borne in mind, and the fact is still more important, that the debates in the convention that framed the constitution of the United States, and by means of which a pro-slavery interpretation is now attempted to be forced upon that instrument, were not published until nearly thirty years after the constitution of the United

States;[24] so that the men who adopted the constitution could not be supposed to understand the secret underhand intentions that might have controlled the actions of the convention in making it. These debates were purposely kept out of view, in order that the people might not adopt the secret motives, the unexpressed intentions of anybody, but simply the text of the paper itself. These debates form no part of the original agreement, and, therefore, are entitled to no respect or consideration in discussing what is the character of the constitution of the United States. I repeat, the paper itself, and only the paper itself, with its own plainly written purposes, is the constitution of the United States, and it must stand or fall, flourish or fade, on its own individual and self-declared purpose and object.

Again, where would be the advantage of a written constitution, I pray you, if, after we have it written, instead of looking to its plain, common sense reading, we should go in search of its meaning to the secret intentions of the individuals who may have had something to do with writing the paper? What will the people of America, a hundred years hence, care about the intentions of the men who framed the constitution of the United States? These men were for a day—for a generation, but the constitution is for ages; and, a hundred years hence, the very names of the men who took part in framing that instrument will, perhaps, be blotted out or forgotten. Whatever we may owe to the framers of the constitution, we certainly owe this to ourselves, and to mankind, and to God[:] that we maintain the truth of our own language, and do not allow villany, not even the villany of slaveholding—which, as John Wesley says, is the sum of all villanies[25]—to clothe itself in the garb of virtuous language, and get

24. The Philadelphia convention that drafted the U.S. Constitution operated under a secrecy rule that forbade members to communicate any information about the proceedings to outsiders. This prohibition included publication of the convention's sparse official journal, kept by the secretary, William Jackson; it was published in 1819 under the supervision of the State Department. A few delegates eventually published notes, but the only substantial record of the debates was that made by James Madison, which was not published until 1840.

25. *Works of the Rev. John Wesley*, 3:453.

itself passed off as a virtuous thing, in consequence of that language. We owe it to ourselves to compel the devil to wear his own garments; particularly in law we owe it to ourselves to compel wicked legislators, when they undertake a malignant purpose in innocent and benevolent language, we owe it to ourselves that we circumvent their wicked designs to this extent, that if they want to put it to a bad purpose, we will put it to a good purpose. Common sense, common justice, and sound rules of interpretation all drive us to the words of the law for the meaning of the law.

The practice of the American government is dwelt upon with much fervour as conclusive as to the slaveholding character of the American constitution. This is really the strong point, and the only strong point, made in the speech in the City Hall; but, good as this argument is, it is not conclusive. A wise man has said that few people are found better than their laws, but many have been found worse; and the American people are no exception to this rule. I think it will be found they are much worse than their laws, particularly their constitutional laws. It is just possible the people's practice may be diametrically opposed to their own declared, their own acknowledged laws, and their own acknowledged principles. Our blessed Saviour when upon earth found the traditions of men taking the place of the law and the prophets. The Jews asked him why his disciples ate with unwashed hands, and he brought them to their senses by telling them that they had made void the law by their traditions.[26] Moses, on account of the hardness of the hearts of men, allowed the Jews to put away their wives; but it was not so at the beginning.[27] The American people, likewise, have made void their law by their traditions; they have trampled upon their own constitution, stepped beyond the limits set for themselves, and, in their ever-abounding iniquity, established a constitution of action outside of the fundamental law of the land. While the one is good, the other is evil; while

26. Mark 7:2–13.
27. Deut. 24:1–4.

the one is for liberty, the other is in favour of slavery; the practice of the American government is one thing, and the character of the constitution of the government is quite another and different thing. After all, Mr. Chairman, the fact that my opponent thought it necessary to go outside of the constitution to prove it pro-slavery, whether that going out is to the practice of the government, or to the secret intentions of the writers of the paper itself, the fact that men do go out is very significant. It is an admission that the thing they look for is not to be found where only it ought to be found if found at all, and that is, in the written constitution itself. If it is not there, it is nothing to the purpose if it is found any where else; but I shall have more to say on this point hereafter. The very eloquent lecturer at the City Hall doubtless felt some embarrassment from the fact that he had literally to give the constitution a pro-slavery interpretation; because on its very face it conveys an entirely opposite meaning. He thus sums up what he calls the slaveholding provisions of the constitution, and I quote his words:—

"Article 1, section 9, provides for the continuance of the African slave-trade for twenty years after the adoption of the constitution.

"Article 4, section 2, provides for the recovery from other States of fugitive slaves.

"Article 1, section 2, gives the slave States a representation of three-fifths of all the slave population; and

"Article 1, section 8, requires the President to use the military, naval, ordnance, and militia resources of the entire country for the suppression of slave insurrections, in the same manner as he would employ them to repel invasion."[28]

Now, Mr. President, and ladies and gentlemen, any man reading this statement, or hearing it made with such a show of exactness, would unquestionably suppose that the speaker or writer had given the plain written text of the constitution itself. I can hardly believe that that gentleman intended to make any such impression on his

---

28. Douglass correctly quotes George Thompson's remarks.

audience, and yet what are we to make of it, this circumstantial statement of the provisions of the constitution? How can we regard it? *How can he be screened from the charge of having perpetrated a deliberate and point blank misrepresentation?* That *individual* has seen fit to place himself before the public as my opponent. Well, ladies and gentlemen, if he had placed himself before the country as an enemy, I could not have desired him—even an enemy—to have placed himself in a position so false, and to have committed himself to *statements so grossly at variance with the truth* as those statements I have just read from him. Why did he not read the constitution to you? Why did he read that which was not the constitution—for I contend he did read that which was not the constitution. *He pretended to be giving you chapter and verse*, section and clause, paragraph and provision, and yet he did not give you a single clause or single paragraph of that constitution. You can hardly believe it, but I will make good what I say, that though reading to you article upon article, as you supposed while listening to him, *he did not read a word from the constitution of the United States; not one word.* (Applause.) You had better not applaud until you hear the other side and what are the real words of the constitution. Why did he not give you the plain words of the constitution? He can read; he had the constitution before him; he had there chapter and verse, the places where those things he alleged to be found in the constitution were to be found. Why did he not read them? *Oh, Sir, I fear that that gentleman knows too well why he did not.* I happen to know that there are no such words in the American constitution as "African slave-trade," no such words as "slave-representation," no such words as "fugitive slaves," no such words as "slave insurrections" anywhere to be found in that constitution. You can hardly think a man would stand up before an audience of people in Glasgow, and make a statement so circumstantial, with every mark of particularity, *to point out to be in the constitution what is not there.* You shall see a slight difference in my manner of treating that subject and that which my opponent has thought fit, for reasons satisfactory to himself, to pursue. *What he withheld, that I will spread before you; what he suppressed, I will bring to light; and what he passed over in silence, I will proclaim.*

Here then are the several provisions of the constitution to which reference has been made. I will read them word for word, just as they stand in the paper, in the constitution itself.

Article 1, section 2, declares that representations [representatives] and direct taxes shall be apportioned among the several States which may be included within this Union, according to their respective numbers, which shall be determined by adding to the whole number of free persons, including those bound to service for a term of years, excluding Indians not taxed, three-fifths of all other persons.

Article 1, section 9.—The migration or importation of any such persons as any of the States now existing may think fit to admit shall not be prohibited to the Congress prior to the year 1808, but a tax or duty may be imposed on such importation not exceeding ten dollars for each person.

Article 4.—No person held to service or labour in one State under the laws thereof escaping to another shall, in consequence of any law or regulation therein, be discharged from such service or labour, but shall be delivered up on claim of the party to whom such service or labour may be due.

Article 1, section 8.—To provide for calling out the militia to execute the laws of the Union, suppress insurrections, and repel invasions.[29]

Here then are the provisions of the constitution which the most extravagant defenders of slavery have ever claimed to guarantee the right of property in man. These are the provisions which have been pressed into the service of the human fleshmongers of America; let us look at them just as they stand, one by one. You will notice there is not a word said there about "slave-trade" not a word said there

29. These quotations are substantially accurate.

about "slave insurrections;" not a word there about "three-fifths representation of slaves;" not a word there which any man outside of America, and who had not been accustomed to claim these particular provisions of the Constitution, would ever suspect had the remotest reference to slavery. *I deny utterly that these provisions of the constitution guarantee, or were intended to guarantee, in any shape or form, the right of property in man in the United States.* But let us grant, for the sake of argument, *that the first of these provisions, referring to the basis of representation and taxation, does refer to slaves.* We are not compelled to make this admission, for it might fairly apply, and indeed was intended to apply, to aliens and others, living in the United States, but who were not naturalised. But giving the provision the very worst construction—that it applies to slaves—what does it amount to? I answer—and see you bear it in mind, for it shows the disposition of the constitution to slavery—I take the very worst aspect, and admit all that is claimed or that can be admitted consistently with truth; and I answer that this very provision, supposing it refers to slaves, is in itself a downright disability imposed upon the slave system of America, *one which deprives the slaveholding States of at least two-fifths of their natural basis of representation.* A black man in a free State is worth just two-fifths more than a black man in a slave State, as a basis of political power under the constitution. Therefore, instead of encouraging slavery, the constitution encourages freedom, by *holding out to every slaveholding State in the inducement of an increase of two-fifths of political power by becoming a free State.* So much for the three-fifths clause; taking it at its worst, it still leans to freedom, not to slavery; for be it remembered that the constitution no where forbids a black man to vote. No "white," no "black," no "slaves," no "slaveholder"—nowhere in the instrument are any of these words to be found.

I come to the next, that which it is said *guarantees the continuance of the African slave-trade* for twenty years. I will also take that for just what my opponent alleges it to have been, although the constitution does not warrant any such conclusion. But, to be liberal, let us suppose it did, and what follows? Why, this—that this part of the constitution of the United States *expired by its own limitation no fewer than fifty-two years ago*. My opponent is just fifty-two years too late in seeking the dissolution of the Union on account of this clause, for it expired as far back as 1808. He might as well attempt to break down the British parliament and break down the British constitution, because, three hundred years ago, Queen Elizabeth granted to Sir John Hawkins the right to import Africans into the colonies in the West Indies. This ended some three hundred years ago; ours ended only fifty-two years ago, and I ask is the constitution of the United States to be condemned to everlasting infamy because of what was done fifty-two years ago? But there is still more to be said about this provision of the constitution. At the time the constitution was adopted, the slave trade was regarded as the jugular vein of slavery itself, and it was thought that slavery would die with the death of the slave trade. No less philanthropic, no less clear-sighted men than your own Wilberforce and Clarkson supposed that the abolition of the slave-trade would be the abolition of slavery.[30] Their theory was—cut off the stream, and of course the pond or lake would dry up: cut off the stream flowing out from Africa, and the slave-trade in America and the colonies would perish. The fathers who framed the American constitution supposed that in making provision for the abolition of the African slave-trade they were making provision for the abolition of slavery itself, and they incorporated this clause in the constitution, not to perpetuate the traffic in human flesh, but to bring that unnatural traffic to an end. Outside of the Union the slave-trade could be carried on to an indefinite period; but the men who framed the constitution, and who proposed its adoption, *said to the slave States,*—If you would purchase the privileges of this Union, you must consent that the

---

30. The distinction between the abolition of the slave trade and the gradual emancipation of slaves was blurred in the pamphlets, speeches, and perhaps also the minds of early British abolitionists. Reformers hoped that stopping the supply of new slaves would set in motion economic forces that would eventually end slavery.

humanity of this nation shall lay its hand upon this traffic at least in twenty years after the adoption of the constitution. So much for the African slave-trade clause. Mark you, it does not say one word about the African slave-trade. Secondly, if it does, it expired by its own limitation more than fifty years ago. Thirdly, the constitution is anti-slavery, because it looked to the abolition of slavery rather than to its perpetuity. Fourthly, it showed that the intentions of the framers of the constitution were good, not bad. If (and Mr. Douglass here looked in the direction of Mr. Robert Smith, president of the Scottish Temperance League)[31]—if you can't get a man to take the pledge that he will stop drinking liquor to-day, it is something if you will get him to promise to take it tomorrow; and if the men who made the American constitution did not bring the African slave-trade to an end instantly, it was something to succeed in bringing it to an end in twenty years.

I now go to the *slave insurrection clause*, though in truth, there is no such clause in the constitution. But, suppose that this clause in the constitution refers to the abolition or rather the suppression of slave insurrections; suppose we admit that congress has a right to call out the army and navy to quell insurrections, and to repel any efforts on the part of the slaves to gain their freedom—to put down violence of any sort, and slave violence in particular—what follows? I hold that the right to suppress an insurrection carries with it also the right to determine by what means the insurrection shall be suppressed; and, under an anti-slavery administration, were your humble servant in the presidential chair of the United States, which in all likelihood never will be the case, and were an insurrection to break out in the southern states among the slave inhabitants, *what would I do in the circumstances?* I would suppress the insurrection, and I should choose my own way of suppressing it; I should have the right, under the constitution, to my own manner of doing it. If I could make out,

31. Robert Smith (1801–73), a prosperous Glasgow shipowner and merchant, became a teetotaler in 1843, and from 1852 until his death he was president of the Scottish Temperance League.

as I believe I could, that *slavery is itself an insurrection—that it is an insurrection by one party in the country against the just rights* of another part of the people in the country, a constant invitation to insurrection, a constant source of danger—as the executive officer of the United States it would be my duty *not only to put down the insurrection, but to put down the cause of the insurrection.*

I would have no hesitation at all in supporting the constitution of the United States in consequence of its provisions. The constitution should be obeyed, should be rightly obeyed. We should say to the slaves, and we should say to their masters, "We see that a forced system of labour endangers the peace that we are sworn to protect, and we now put it away, and leave you to pay honest wages for honest work." In a word, with regard to putting down insurrection, I would just write a proclamation, and the proclamation would be based upon the old prophetic model of proclaiming liberty throughout all the land, to all the inhabitants thereof.[32]

But there is one other provision, called the "Fugitive Slave Provision." It is called so by those who wish it to subserve the interests of slavery. "Let us go back," says the *City Hall*, "to 1787, and enter Liberty Hall, Philadelphia, where sat in convention the illustrious men"—very illustrious! if they were the scamps and scoundrels he would make them out to be—"who framed the constitution—with George Washington in the chair. On the 27th of September, Mr. Butler and Mr. Pinckney, two delegates from the state of South Carolina, moved that the constitution should require fugitive slaves and servants to be delivered up like criminals, and after a discussion on the subject, the clause as it stands in the constitution was adopted. After this, in conventions held in the several States to ratify the constitution, the same meaning was attached to the words. For example, Mr. Madison,[33] (afterwards President) in recommending

32. Lev. 25:10.
33. The Virginia patriot James Madison (1751–1836) earned the nickname "Father of the Constitution" for his work in negotiating compromises among the delegates at Philadelphia.

the constitution to his constituents, told them that this clause would secure them their property in slaves."[34]

I must ask you to look well to the statement. Upon its face it would seem to be a full and fair disclosure of the real transaction it professes to describe; and yet *I declare unto you, knowing as I do the facts in the case, that I am utterly amazed, utterly amazed at the downright UNTRUTH* which that very simple, plain statement really conveys to you about that transaction. I dislike to use this very strong language, but you shall see that the case is quite as strong as the language employed. Under these fair-seeming words now quoted, I say there is *downright untruth conveyed. The man who could make such a statement may have all the craftiness of a lawyer, but I think he will get but very little credit for the candour of a Christian.* What could more *completely destroy all confidence* than the making of such a statement as that?

The case which he describes is entirely different from the real case as transacted at the time. Mr. Butler and Mr. Pinckney did indeed bring forward a proposition after the convention had framed the constitution, a proposition for the return of the fugitive slaves to their masters precisely as criminals are returned.[35] And what happened? Mr. Thompson—oh! I beg pardon for calling his name— tells you that after a debate it was withdrawn, and the proposition as it stands in the constitution was adopted. He does not tell you what

34. The only substantive error in Douglass's quotation of Thompson's City Hall remarks is the date, which should read "the 28th of August" instead of "the 27th of September." Glasgow *North British Daily Mail,* 29 February 1860; [George Thompson and Frederick Douglass], *Constitution of the United States,* London Emancipation Committee, Tract No. 5 (London: William Tweedie, 1860), 8.

35. Douglass refers to an incident of 28 August 1787 at the Constitutional Convention. During the debate over the Extradition Clause (article IV, section 2), two South Carolina delegates, Pierce Butler (1744–1822) and Charles Pinckney (1757–1824), moved for an amendment "to require slaves and servants to be delivered up like criminals." After Northern objections to the propriety of spending public money to recover a private citizen's property, Butler withdrew the amendment so that he could later present a separate provision for the rendition of fugitive slaves. James Madison, *Notes of Debates in the Federal Convention of 1787* (1840; Athens: Ohio University Press, 1966), 545–46.

was the nature of the debate. Not one word of it. No; it would not have suited his purpose to have done that. I will tell you what was the purport of that debate. After debate and discussion the provision as it stands was adopted. The purport of the provisions as brought forward by Mr. Butler and Mr. Pinckney was this: "No person called to servitude in any State under the laws thereof, escaping into another, shall, in consequence of any law or regulation therein, be discharged from such service and labour, but shall be delivered up on claim, and passed to whom such service or labour may be due."[36]

Very well, what happened? The proposition was met by a storm of opposition in the convention; members rose up in all directions, saying that they had no more business to catch slaves for their masters than they had to catch horses for their owners—that they would not undertake any such thing, and the convention instructed a committee to alter that provision and the word *"servitude"* so that *it might apply* NOT *to slaves,* but to freemen—to persons bound to serve and labour, *and not to slaves.* And thus far it seems that Mr. Madison, who was quoted so triumphantly, tells us in these very *Madison Papers* that that word was struck out from the constitution, *because* it applied to *slaves* and not to freemen, and that the convention refused to have that word in the constitution, simply because they did not wish, and *would not have the idea that there could be property in men in that instrument.*[37] These are Madison's own words, so that he can be quoted on both sides.

36. On 29 August 1787, Pierce Butler reintroduced the proposals for a fugitive-slave rendition clause in the Constitution. Butler's draft was fashioned after a similar provision in the Northwest Ordinance, which the Confederation Congress had passed in July, and was adopted without dissent by the Convention. Douglass here quotes, with minor errors, the clause as it appears in the Constitution (article IV, section 2).

37. Douglass refers to the proceedings of the Constitutional Convention on 13 September 1787 as described by James Madison and first published in 1840 in H. D. Gilpin's edition of *The Papers of James Madison.* On that day, Edmund Randolph moved an amendment to clarify the reference to indentured servants in article I, section 2, which stipulated the persons who should be counted for purpose of representation and taxation. Randolph moved that the word "servitude" be struck and "service" inserted because, according to Madison, "the former [was] thought

But it may be asked, if the clause does not apply to slaves, to whom does it apply? It says—"No person serving and laboring escaping to another State shall be discharged from such service or labour, but shall be delivered up to whom such service or labour may be due." To whom does it apply if not to slaves? I answer that *it applied at the time of its adoption to a very numerous class of persons in America; and I have the authority of no less a person* than Daniel Webster that it was intended to apply to that class of men—a class of persons known in America as "Redemptioners."[38] There was quite a number of them at that day, who had been taken to America precisely as coolies have been taken to the West Indies.[39] They entered into a contract to serve and labour so long for so much money, and the children born to them in that condition were also held as bound to "service and labour." It also applies to *indentured apprentices,* and to *persons* taking upon themselves an obligation to "serve and labour."

The constitution says that the party shall be delivered up to whom such service and labour may be due. Why, sir, due! In the first place this very clause of that provision makes it utterly impossible that it can apply to slaves. There is nothing *due* from the slave to his master in the way of service or labour. He is unable to show a contract. The

---

to express the condition of slaves, & the latter the obligation of free person." Randolph's amendment was adopted unanimously, but no alteration was made in the fugitive slave clause, where "service" was clearly meant to refer to slaves. H[enry] D. Gilpin, ed., *The Papers of James Madison,* 3 vols. (Washington, D.C.: Langtree and O'Sullivan, 1840), 3:1569.

38. Redemptioners were eighteenth-century European emigrants who arranged for merchants or ship captains to provide their fare to America by agreeing to reimburse them upon arrival. If unredeemed, they became indentured servants for a period of time sufficient to remove the debt. In several speeches, Daniel Webster alluded to runaway redemptioners and apprentices, claiming that article IV, section 2, of the Constitution was inserted specifically to deal with them.

39. The precipitous drop in commodity exports throughout the West Indies following the emancipation of the slaves there led British governments from the 1840s onward to actively recruit laborers from India, China, and (ironically) Africa—so called coolies—to work ten-year indentures on the plantations of their Caribbean colonies.

thing implies an arrangement, an understanding, by which, for an equivalent, I will do for you so much, if you will do for me, or have done for me, so much. The constitution says he will be delivered up to whom any service or labour shall be due. Due! A slave owes nothing to any master; he can owe nothing to any master. In the eye of the law he is a chattel personal, to all intents, purposes, and constructions whatever. Talk of a horse owing something to his master, or a sheep, or a wheel-barrow! Perfectly ridiculous! The idea that a slave can owe anything!

I tell you what I would do if I were a judge; I could do it perfectly consistently with the character of the constitution. I have a proneness to liken myself to great people—to persons high in authority. But if I were a judge, and a slave was brought before me under this provision of the constitution, and the master should insist upon my sending him back to slavery, I should inquire how the slave was bound to serve and labour for him. I would point him to this same constitution, and tell him that I read in that constitution the great words of your own Magna Charta:—"No person shall be deprived of life, liberty, or property without the process of law,"[40] and I ought to know by what contract, how this man contracted an obligation, or took upon himself to serve and labour for you. And if he could not show that, I should dismiss the case and restore the man to his liberty. And I would do quite right, according to the constitution.

I admit nothing in favour of slavery when liberty is at stake; when I am called upon to argue on behalf of liberty I will range throughout the world, I am at perfect liberty by forms of law and by rules of hermeneutics[41] to range through the whole universe of God in proof of an innocent purpose, in proof of a good thing; but if you want to prove a bad thing, if you want to accomplish a bad and violent purpose, you must show it is so named in the bond. This is a sound

40. This provision of the Fifth Amendment to the U.S. Constitution, which Douglass slightly misquotes, paraphrases the thirty-ninth chapter of the English Magna Charta (1215).
41. Hermeneutics originally referred to a method of interpreting biblical texts.

legal rule. Shakespeare noticed it as an existing rule of law in his *Merchant of Venice:* "a pound of flesh, but not one drop of blood."[42] The law was made for the protection of labour; not for the destruction of liberty; and it is to be presumed on the side of the oppressed.

The speaker at the City Hall laid down some rules of legal interpretation. These rules send us to the history of the law for its meaning. I have no objection to this course in ordinary cases of doubt, but where human liberty and justice are at stake, the case falls under an entirely different class of rules. There must be something more than history, something more than tradition, to lead me to believe that law is intended to uphold and maintain wrong.

The Supreme Court of the United States lays down this rule, and it meets the case exactly: "Where rights are infringed; where the fundamental principles of the law are overthrown; where the general system of the law is departed from, the legislative intention must be expressed with irresistible clearness."[43] The same court says that the language of the law must be construed strictly in favour of justice and liberty; and another rule says, where the law is ambiguous and susceptible of two meanings, the one making it accomplish an innocent purpose, and the other making it accomplish a wicked purpose, we must in every case adopt that meaning which makes it accomplish an innocent purpose. These are just the rules we like to have applied to us as individuals to begin with. We like to be assumed to be honest and upright in our purpose until we are proved to be otherwise, and the law is to be taken precisely in the same way. We are to assume it is fair, right, just, and true, till proved with irresistible power to be on the side of wrong.

Now, sir, a case like this occurred in Rhode Island some time ago. The people there made a law that no negro should be allowed to walk out after nine o'clock at night without a lantern. They were afraid the negro might be mistaken for somebody. The negroes got lanterns and walked after nine at night, but they forgot

---

42. *The Merchant of Venice,* sc. 18, lines 2112–15.
43. Douglass makes only a few errors in quoting Chief Justice John Marshall's decision in *United States v. Fisher* (1805), 2 Cranch 358 (1806), 390.

to put candles in them. They were arrested and brought before a court of law. They had been found after nine at night, it had been proved against them that they were out with lanterns to be sure, but without a candle. "May it please your honour," it was argued for the prosecution, "of what value is a lantern without a candle? The plain intention of the law was that these people should not be out without a lantern and a candle." But the judge said this was a law against the natural rights of man, against natural liberty, and that this law should be construed strictly. These men had complied with the plain reading of the law, and they must be dismissed. The judge in that case did perfectly right. The legislature had to pass another law, that no negro should be out after nine without a lantern and a candle in it. The negroes got candles, but forgot to light them. They were arrested again, again tried, and with similar result. There was then another law passed, that the negroes should not walk out after nine at night without lanterns, with candles in them, and the candles lighted. And if I had been a negro at that time in Rhode Island, I would have got a dark lantern and walked out.[44]

Laws to sustain a wrong of any kind must be expressed with irresistible clearness; for law, be it remembered, is not an arbitrary rule or arbitrary mandate, and it has a purpose of its own. Blackstone defines it as "a rule of the supreme power of the state;" but he does not stop there—he adds, "commanding that which is right, and forbidding that which is wrong"—that is law.[45] It would not be law if it commanded that which was wrong, and forbade that which was right in itself. It is necessary it should be on behalf of right. There is another law of legal interpretation, which is, that the law is to be understood in the light of the objects sought for by the law, or sought in the law—that is, that the details of the law shall conform to the purpose declared to be sought to be attained by it.

---

44. Like other Northern colonies, Rhode Island prohibited free blacks and slaves from traveling at night without a pass.

45. This definition of municipal civil law appears in Sir William Blackstone, *Commentaries on the Laws of England in Four Books, with Additional Notes and a Life of the Author by George Sharswood*, 2 vols. (Philadelphia: G. W. Childs, 1866), 1:44.

What are the objects sought for in the constitution of the American States? "We, the people of these United States, in order to form a more perfect union, establish justice, ensure domestic tranquility, provide for the common defence, promote the general welfare, and secure the blessing of liberty to ourselves and our posterity, do ordain and establish this constitution for the United States of America." The objects here set forth are six in number. "Union" is one, not slavery; union is named as one of the objects for which the constitution was framed, and it is one that is very excellent; it is quite incompatible with slavery. "Defence" is another; "welfare" is another; "tranquility" is another; "justice" and "liberty" are the others. Slavery is not among them; the objects are union, defence, welfare, tranquility, justice, and liberty. Now, if the two last—to say nothing of the defence—if the two last purposes declared were reduced to practice, slavery would go reeling to its grave as if smitten with a bolt from heaven. Let but the American people be true to their own constitution, true to the purposes set forth in that constitution, and we will have no need of a dissolution of the Union—we will have a dissolution of slavery all over that country.

But it has been said that negroes are not included in the benefits sought under this declaration of purposes. Whatever slaveholders may say, I think it comes with ill grace from abolitionists to say the negroes in America are not included in this declaration of purposes. The negroes are not included! Who says this? The constitution does not say they are not included, and how dare any other person, speaking for the constitution, say so? The constitution says "We the people;" the language is, "we the people;" not we the white people, not we the citizens, not we the privileged class, not we the high, not we the low, not we of English extraction, not we of French or of Scotch extraction, but "we the people;" not we the horses, sheep, and swine, and wheelbarrows, but we the human inhabitants; and unless you deny that negroes are people, they are included within the purposes of this government. They were there, and if we the people are included, negroes are included; they have a right, in the name of the constitution of the United States, to demand their liberty.

This, I undertake to say, is the conclusion of the whole matter— that *the constitutionality of slavery can be made out only by discrediting the plain, common sense reading of the constitution itself;* by discrediting and casting away as worthless the most beneficent rules of legal interpretation; by ruling the negro outside of these beneficent rules; by claiming every thing for slavery; by denying every thing for freedom; by assuming that the constitution does not mean what it says; and that it says what it does not mean; by disregarding the written constitution, and interpreting it in the light of a secret understanding. It is by this *mean, contemptible, underhand way of working out the pro-slavery character of the constitution, that the thing is accomplished, and in no other way.*

The first utterance of the instrument itself is gloriously on the side of liberty, and diametrically opposed to the thing called slavery in the United States. The constitution declares that no person shall be deprived of life, liberty, or property without due process of law; it secures to every man the right of trial by jury; it also declares that the writ of *habeas corpus* shall never be suppressed—that great and noble writ—that writ by which England was made free soil— that writ which set Somerset free in 1772—that writ which made that land in which I stand tonight, and where you stand, the land of liberty and the home of the oppressed of all nations—the land of which Curran said when he spoke of it, that he spoke "in the spirit of the British law, which makes liberty commensurate with, and inseparable from, British soil; which proclaims even to the stranger and sojourner, the moment he sets his foot upon British earth, that the ground on which he treads is holy, and consecrated by the genius of universal emancipation."[46] It was in consequence of this writ—a writ which forms a part of the constitution of the United States— that England herself is free from man-hunters to-day; for in 1772

46. John Philpot Curran. Curran, *Speeches,* 182.

slaves were hunted here in England just as they are in America, and the British constitution was supposed to favour the arrest, the imprisonment, and re-capture of fugitive slaves. But Lord Mansfield, in the case of Somerset, decided that no slave could breathe in England.[47] We have the same writ, and let the people in Britain and the United States stand as true to liberty as the constitution is true to liberty, and we shall have no need of a dissolution of the Union.

But to all this it is said that the practice of the American people is against my view. I admit it. They have given the constitution a slaveholding interpretation. I admit it. And I go with him who goes furthest in denouncing these wrongs, these outrages on my people. But to be consistent with this logic, where does it lead? Because the practice of the American people has been wrong, shall we therefore denounce the constitution? The same logic would land *the man of the City Hall* precisely where the same logic has landed some of his friends in America—*in the dark, benighted regions of infidelity itself.* The constitution is pro-slavery, because men have interpreted it to be pro-slavery, and practice upon it as if it were pro-slavery. The very same thing, sir, might be said of the Bible itself; for in the United States men have interpreted the Bible against liberty. They have declared that Paul's epistle to *Philemon* is a full proof for the enactment of that hell-black Fugitive Slave Bill which has desolated my people for the last ten years in that country. They have declared that the Bible sanctions slavery. What do we do in such a case? What do you do when you are told by the slaveholders of America that the Bible sanctions slavery? Do you go and throw your Bible into the fire? Do you sing out, "No Union with the Bible!"?[48] Do you declare that a thing is bad because it has been misused, abused, and made a bad use of? Do you throw it away on that account? No! You

---

47. William Murray, 1st Earl of Mansfield (1705–93), was the British judge whose decision in *Somersett's Case* (1772) held that chattel slavery was not sanctioned by common law in England. He did not rule on whether the practice was legal in its colonies, including the thirteen in North America.

48. Douglass satirizes the Garrisonians' slogan "No Union with Slaveholders."

press it to your bosom all the more closely; you read it all the more diligently; and prove from its pages that it is on the side of liberty— and not on the side of slavery. So let us do so with the constitution of the United States. But this logic would carry *the orator of the City Hall* a step or two further; it would lead him to break down the British constitution. I believe he is not only a Protestant, but he is a Dissenter; and if he is opposed to the *American constitution because certain evils exist therein, could he well oppose all the other constitutions?*

But I must beg pardon for detaining you so long—I must bring my remarks speedily to a close. Let me make a statement. It was said to you that the Southern States had increased from 5 up to 15. What is the fact with reference to this matter? Why, my friends, the slave States in America have increased just from 12 up to 15. But the other statement was not told you. It is this: the Free States have increased from 1 up to 18. That fact was not told. No; I suppose *it was expected I would come back and tell you all the truth. It takes two men to tell the truth any way.*

The dissolution of the Union, remember, *that was clamoured for that night,* would not give the Northern states one single advantage over slavery that it does not now possess. Within the Union we have a firm basis of opposition to slavery. It is opposed to all the great objects of the constitution. The dissolution of the Union is not only an unwise but a cowardly proposition. Dissolve the Union! For what? Tear down the house in an instant because a few slates have been blown off the roof? There are 350,000 slaveholders in America, and 26 millions of free white people.[49] Must these 26 millions of people break up their government, dissolve their Union, burn up their constitution—for what? to get rid of the responsibility of holding slaves? But can they get rid of responsibility by that? Alas no! The recreant husband may desert the family hearth, may leave his

49. The discrepancy between Douglass's and George Thompson's statistics stems from the former's addition of the seven Northern states that emancipated their slaves following the Revolution to the number of original slave states.

starving children, and you may place oceans, islands, and continents
between him and his; but the responsibility, the gnawing of a guilty
conscience must follow him wherever he goes. If a man were on
board of a pirate ship, and in company with others had robbed and
plundered, his whole duty would not be performed simply by taking
to the long boat and singing out, "No union with pirates!" His duty
would be to restore the stolen property.

The American people in the Northern States have helped to enslave the black people. Their duty will not have been done till they
give them back their plundered rights. They cannot get rid of their
responsibility by dissolving the Union; they must put down the evil,
abolish the wrong. *The abolition of slavery, not the dissolution of the
Union, is the only way in which they can get rid of the responsibility.*
"No union with slaveholding" is an excellent sentiment as showing
hostility to slavery, but what is union with slavery? Is it living under
the same sky, walking on the same earth, riding on the same railway,
taking dinner on board of the same steamboat with the slaveholder?
No: I can be in all these relations to the slaveholder, but yet heaven-
high above him, as wide from him as the poles of the moral universe. "No union with slaveholding" is a much better phrase than
that adopted by *those who insist that they in America are the only
friends of the slave who wish to destroy the Union.*

Reference was made in the City Hall to my having held other
views and different views from those I now entertain. An old speech
of mine, delivered some fourteen years ago in London, was rendered with skill and effect. I don't know what it was brought up for.
Perhaps it was brought forward to show that I am not infallible, not
like his reverence—of Rome.[50] If that was the object, I can relieve
the friends of that gentlemen entirely, by telling them that I never
made any pretentions to infallibility. Although I cannot accuse myself of being remarkably unstable, I cannot pretend that I have
never altered my opinion both in respect to men and things. Indeed

50. The pope.

I have been very much modified both in feeling and opinion within the last fourteen years, and he would be a queer man who could have lived fourteen years without having his opinions and feelings considerably modified by experience in that length of time.

When I escaped from slavery, twenty-two years ago, the world was all new to me, and if I had been in a hogshead with the bung[51] in, I could not have been much more ignorant of many things than I was then. I came out running. All I knew was that I had two elbows and a good appetite, and that I was a human being—a sort of nondescript creature, but still struggling for life. The first I met were the Garrisonian abolitionists of Massachusetts. They had their views, opinions, platform, and eloquence, and were earnestly laboring for the abolition of slavery. They were my friends, the friends of my people, and nothing was more natural than that I should receive as gospel all they told me. "When I was a child, I spake as a child, I understood as a child, I thought as a child; but when I became a man"[52]—that is, after I went over to Great Britain and came back again—I undertook the herculean task,[53] without a day's schooling, to edit and publish a paper—to unite myself to the literary profession. I could hardly spell two words correctly; still I thought I could "join" as we say, and when I had to write three or four columns a week, it became necessary to re-examine some of the *opinions I had formed in my baby days; and when I came to examine for myself my opinions were greatly modified, and I had the temerity to state to the parties from whom I received them my change of opinions; and from that day to this—whether in the east or west, in or out of America, in Ireland, Scotland, or England—I have been pursued and persecuted by that class of persons on account of my change of opinions.* But I am quite well satisfied, very well satisfied with my position.

51. In a large barrel with the stopper or cork in place.
52. Cor. 13:11.
53. The mythological hero Heracles, also known as Hercules, was the son of the Greek god Zeus and the mortal Alcmene. He possessed unnatural virility and strength, allowing him to perform extraordinary physical feats.

Now, what do I propose? what do you propose? what do we sensible folks propose?—for we are sensible. The slaveholders have ruled the American government for the last fifty years; let the anti-slavery party rule the nation for the next fifty years. And, by the way, that thing is on the verge of being accomplished. The slaveholders, above all things else, dread the rule of the anti-slavery party that are now coming into power. *To dissolve the Union would be to do just what the slaveholders would like to have done.* Slavery is essentially a dark system; all it wants is to be excluded and shut out from the light. If it can only be boxed in where there is not a single breath to fall upon it, nor a single word to assail it, then it can grope in its own congenial darkness, oppressing human hearts and crushing human happiness. But it dreads the influence of truth; it dreads the influence of Congress. It knows full well that when the moral sentiment of the nation shall demand the abolition of slavery, there is nothing in the constitution of the United States to prevent that abolition.

Well, now, what do we want? We want this:—whereas slavery has ruled the land, now must liberty; whereas pro-slavery men have sat in the Supreme Court of the United States, and given the constitution a pro-slavery interpretation against its plain reading, let us by our votes put men into that Supreme Court who will decide, and who will concede, that that constitution is not [pro-]slavery. What do you do when you want reform or change? Do you break up your government? By no means. You say:—"Reform the government;" and that is just what the abolitionists who wish for liberty in the United States propose. They propose that the intelligence, the humanity, the Christian principle, the true manliness which they feel in their hearts, shall flow out from their hearts through their fingers into the ballot-box, and that into that ballot-box it shall go for such men as shall represent the Christian principle and Christian intelligence in the United States; and that congress shall crystallise those sentiments into law, and that law shall be in favour of freedom. And that is the way we hope to accomplish the abolition of slavery.

Since these questions are put here, it is a bounden duty to listen to arguments of this sort; and I know that the intelligent man and women here will be glad to have this full *exposee* of the whole question. I thank you very sincerely for the patient attention you have given me.

"The Mission of the War"

An Address Delivered in New York, New York, 13 January 1864

New York *Daily Tribune,* 14 January 1864.

Frederick Douglass was one of eight speakers invited by the Woman's National Loyal League, the first national women's political organization, which was presided over by Elizabeth Cady Stanton and Susan B. Anthony, to speak at New York City's Cooper Institute in the winter of 1863–64. That group used this lecture series to raise funds for its petition drive and to generate support for a congressional act "emancipating all persons of African descent held to involuntary service or labor in the United States."[1] Douglass delivered his address on 13 January 1864 and repeated it several times that winter as a part of a busy speaking itinerary that included a benefit for the Woman's National Loyal League in Chicago.[2]

Douglass was introduced by Oliver Johnson, editor of the *National Anti-Slavery Standard,* and addressed an audience "composed largely of ladies."[3] Following on the heels of Wendell Phillips's 22 December 1863 address in the same Cooper Institute series, Douglass, too, expressed a fear that revolutions, contrary to President Lincoln's claim, could indeed "go backward." The Emancipation Proclamation, issued a year earlier, could be reversed by the conservative U.S. Supreme Court, which had delivered the *Dred Scott* decision only six years earlier. Comparing the circumstances in the United States

1. Wendy F. Hamand, "The Woman's National Loyal League: Feminist Abolitionists and the Civil War," *Civil War History* 35, no.1 (March 1989): 44.
2. Ibid., 49.
3. New York *Daily Tribune,* 14 January 1864.

to those in Europe in 1848, when widespread revolutionary zeal was quickly suppressed by reactionary forces, Douglass remarked, "Almost in the twinkling of an eye, the latent forces of despotism rallied." Just as democratic movements had failed throughout Europe, so too could antislavery advances fail. In his 22 December speech, Phillips endorsed the passing of a constitutional amendment to abolish slavery, which would prevent the Supreme Court from trying to get around the Emancipation Proclamation. Douglass was less specific about the means of achieving the "mission of the war," but broader in his definition of what that mission was. "National regeneration" encompassed more than an end to slavery; it included full citizenship for African Americans. Douglass, a recruiter of black soldiers, was committed to their full inclusion in the military. He advocated equal pay, promotion opportunities commensurate with those available to white soldiers, and the bestowal of voting rights on black veterans.[4] Douglass saw the elimination of racial barriers of all sorts as the mission of the Civil War.

Conscious of his female sponsors and audience, Douglass drew on the extensive body of female-written antislavery literature depicting slavery as an antifamily and sexually exploitative institution.[5] He argued that the system had "prepared the characters—male and female— . . . for all its [the rebellion's] cold-blooded and hellish atrocities." This allusion to Southern white women's complicity was contrasted with the morality and bravery of Northern women willing

4. "Soldiers' Pay," New York *Tribune,* 14 January 1864. In June 1864, Congress made black soldiers' pay equal to that of white soldiers and made the act retroactive to the start of their service. Elsie Freeman, Wynell Burroughs Schamel, and Jean West, "The Fight for Equal Rights: A Recruiting Poster for Black Soldiers in the Civil War," *Social Education* 56, no. 2 (February 1992): 118–120; revised and updated by Budge Weidman, 1999, www.archives.gov/education/lessons/blacks-civil-war.

5. Female-written slave narratives such as Harriet Jacobs's autobiography *Incidents in the Life of a Slave Girl* (Boston, 1861), edited with Lydia Maria Child; novels such as Stowe's *Uncle Tom's Cabin*; stories in the *Liberty Bell, by Friends of Freedom* (1839–58), an annual abolitionist gift book edited by Maria Weston Chapman; and numerous articles by other abolitionist women like the sisters Angelina and Sarah Grimké constitute a well-known body of work that was largely funded and encouraged by female antislavery societies. See Deborah C. De Rosa, *Domestic Abolitionism and Juvenile Literature, 1830–1865* (Albany: State University Press of New York, 2003).

to take political action in the form of petitioning to end slavery. Douglass hoped to encourage the petitioners of the Woman's National Loyal League, urging them onward in their efforts to make the war one of "national regeneration."

Douglass returned half of his speaking fee of $100 to the Woman's National Loyal League for their work in soliciting petitions, especially among women. Within a few months, the league switched tactics and called for a constitutional amendment rather than congressional legislation to end slavery. Senator Charles Sumner introduced the group's petition to the U.S. Senate, starting shortly after Douglass's speech in 1864 and then added additional petitions at an increasingly rapid rate throughout the spring. By the time Congress adjourned for the summer, Sumner had presented 400,000 signatures, accounting for one in every twenty-four Northerners in the United States, most of them women engaged in political activism for the first time in their lives.[6] The Senate passed the Thirteenth Amendment in April 1864, the House of Representative concurred in January 1865, and three-quarters of the states had ratified the amendment by the end of 1865.

L ADIES AND GENTLEMEN: By the mission of the war I mean nothing occult, arbitrary or difficult to be understood, but simply those great moral changes in the fundamental condition of the people, demanded by the situation of the country, plainly involved in the nature of the war, and which if the war is conducted in accordance with its true character, it is naturally and logically fitted to accomplish.

Speaking in the name of Providence, some men tell us that Slavery is already dead, that it expired with the first shot at Sumter.[7] This may be so, but I do not share the confidence with which it is

6. Hamand, "Woman's National Loyal League," 53–54.
7. The first military confrontation of the Civil War occurred at Fort Sumter in Charleston, South Carolina, on 12 April 1861. Southern forces resisted all efforts by the federal government to reinforce the Fort Sumter garrison. Lincoln's dispatch of a small flotilla to resupply the fort forced a crisis; thirty-four hours of Confederate shelling led to the fort's surrender on 14 April 1861.

asserted. In a grand Crisis like this, we should all prefer to look facts sternly in the face, and to accept their verdict whether it bless or blast us. I look for no miraculous destruction of Slavery. The war looms before me simply as a great national opportunity, which may be improved to national salvation, or neglected to national ruin. I hope much from the bravery of our soldiers, but in vain is the might of armies if our rulers fail to profit by experience, and refuse to listen to the suggestions of wisdom and justice. The most hopeful fact of the hour is that we are now in a salutary school—the school of affliction. If sharp and signal retribution, long protracted, wide-sweeping and overwhelming, can teach a great nation respect for the long-despised claims of justice, surely we shall be taught now and for all time to come. But if, on the other hand, this potent teacher, whose lessons are written in characters of blood, and thundered to us from a hundred battle-fields shall fail, we shall go down, as we shall de serve to go down, as a warning to all other nations which shall come after us. It is not pleasant to contemplate the hour as one of doubt and danger. We naturally prefer the bright side, but when there is a dark side it is folly to shut our eyes to it or deny its existence.

I know that the acorn involves the oak, but I know also that the commonest accident may destroy its potential character and defeat its natural destiny. One wave brings its treasure from the briny deep, but another often sweeps it back to its primal depths. The saying that revolutions never go backward must be taken with limitations.[8] The revolution of 1848[9] was one of the grandest that ever dazzled a gazing world. It over-turned the French throne, sent

8. Douglass alludes to a passage from Abraham Lincoln's "Speech Delivered before the First Republican State Convention of Illinois in Bloomington on May 29, 1856." Roy P. Basler, ed., *The Collected Works of Abraham Lincoln,* 9 vols. (New Brunswick, N.J.: Rutgers University Press, 1953–55), 2:340–41.

9. Beginning with the Kingdom of the Two Sicilies in January 1848 and spreading that winter and spring to many European nations. While local specifics varied, in most cases republican and nationalist political groups mounted a challenge to monarchical and aristocratic privilege. Within a year or two, promonarchist forces had used military power to reverse these revolutions.

Louis Philippe[10] into exile, shook every throne in Europe, and inaugurated a glorious Republic. Looking on from a distance, the friends of democratic liberty saw in the convulsion the death of kingcraft in Europe and throughout the world. Great was their disappointment. Almost in the twinkling of an eye, the latent forces of despotism rallied. The Republic disappeared. Her noblest defenders were sent into exile, and the hopes of democratic liberty were blasted in the moment of their bloom.[11] Politics and perfidy proved too strong for the principles of liberty and justice in that contest. I wish I could say that no such liabilities darken the horizon around us. But the same elements are plainly involved here as there. Though the portents are that we shall flourish, it is too much to say that we cannot fail and fall. Our destiny is not to be taken out of our own hands. It is cowardly to shuffle our responsibilities upon the shoulders of Providence. I do not intend to argue but to state facts.

We are now wading deep into the third year of conflict with a fierce and sanguinary rebellion, one which, at the beginning of it, we were hopefully assured by one of our most sagacious and trusted political prophets, would be ended in less than ninety days:[12] a re-

10. The last king of France, Louis-Philippe (1773–1850), ruled from 1830 following the ousting of Charles X in the so-called July Revolution to 1848, when he abdicated in favor of his grandson Philippe during the February 1848 revolution. The National Assembly refused to accept Philippe as monarch, and instead elected Louis-Napoléon Bonaparte president.

11. The French Second Republic had a brief life. Following the overthrow of Louis-Philippe in February 1848, a provisional government took power, but quickly experienced divisions between its liberal middle-class and working-class protosocialist leaders. Most members of the assembly, elected in November, favored restoration of the monarchy but disagreed about rival candidates. The victor in the presidential election was Louis-Napoléon Bonaparte, nephew of the deposed emperor. In December 1851, Bonaparte dissolved the assembly, arrested opposing politicians, and staged a plebiscite that overwhelmingly voted to extend his presidency. The following December, he reestablished the empire—taking the title Napoleon III—and ended the Second Republic.

12. On 14 April 1861, President Abraham Lincoln issued a call for 75,000 volunteers from the ranks of state militiamen to enter federal service for ninety days. This brief period was the maximum allowed under the 1795 Militia Act, still operative at that time. Many in the Confederacy believed the war would be short, and on 6 March 1861 the Confederate Congress authorized President Jefferson Davis to enlist an army of up to 100,000, but only for a one-year term.

bellion which, in its worst features, stands alone among rebellions a solitary and ghastly horror, without a parallel in the history of any nation, ancient or modern: a rebellion inspired by no love of liberty and by no hatred of oppression, as most other rebellions have been, and therefore utterly indefensible upon any moral or social grounds: a rebellion which openly and shamelessly sets at defiance the world's judgment of right and wrong, appeals from light to darkness, from intelligence to ignorance, from the ever-increasing prospects and blessings of a high and glorious civilization to the cold and withering blasts of a naked barbarism: a rebellion which even at this unfinished stage of it, counts the number of its slain not by thousands nor tens of thousands, but by hundreds of thousands. A rebellion which in the destruction of human life and property has rivalled the earthquake, the whirlwind and the pestilence that walketh in darkness, and wasteth at noonday.[13] It has planted agony at a million hearthstones, thronged our streets with the weeds of mourning, filled our land with mere stumps of men, ridged our soil with 200,000 rudely-formed graves,[14] and mantled it all over with the shadow of death. A rebellion which, while it has arrested the wheels of peaceful industry and checked the flow of commerce, has piled up a debt, heavier than a mountain of gold to weigh down the necks of our children's children.[15] There is no end to the mischiefs wrought. It has brought ruin at home, contempt abroad, cooled our friends, heated our enemies, and endangered our existence as a nation.

Now, for what is all this desolation, ruin, shame, suffering, and sorrow? Can anybody want the answer? Can anybody be ignorant of the answer? It has been given a thousand times from this and

13. Ps. 91:6.

14. Modern scholarly efforts at counting military casualties list over 430,000 deaths by the start of 1864.

15. Economists report that the national debt increased from $65 million in 1860 to nearly $2.7 billion in 1865. Many Northern states accrued millions more in debt from war-related costs. The debt of the Confederacy, in excess of $1.4 billion, was wiped out by its defeat. The Fourteenth Amendment forbade repayment of debts from the war years by the former Confederate states, but that provision was not always strictly obeyed.

other platforms. We all know it is Slavery. Less than a half a million of Southern slaveholders—holding in bondage four million slaves[16]—finding themselves outvoted in the effort to get possession of the United States Government, in order to serve the interests of Slavery, have madly resorted to the sword—have undertaken to accomplish by bullets what they failed to accomplish by ballots. That is the answer.

It is worthy of remark that Secession was an afterthought with the Rebels. Their aim was higher; Secession was only their second choice. Wise was going to fight for Slavery in the Union.[17] It was not separation, but subversion. It was not Richmond, but Washington. It was not the Confederate rag, but the glorious Star-Spangled Banner.[18]

Whence came the guilty ambition equal to this atrocious crime? A peculiar education was necessary to this bold wickedness. Here all is plain again. Slavery—the peculiar institution[19]—is aptly fitted to produce just such patriots, who first plunder and then seek to destroy their country. A system which rewards labor with stripes and chains!—which robs the slave of his manhood, and the master of all just consideration for the rights of his fellow-man—has prepared the characters—male and female—that figure in this Rebellion—and for all its cold-blooded and hellish atrocities. In all the most hor-

16. The U.S. Census of 1860 put the number of slaves at 3,953,760, and slaveholding families at 395,216.

17. In a speech at Norfolk, Virginia, during the 1860 presidential campaign, Henry A. Wise, governor of Virginia, declared that, in the event of Lincoln's election, "I will not nullify, I will not secede, but I will under sovereign State authority fight in the Union another revolutionary conflict for civil liberty, and a Union which will defend it." Wise urged the Southern states not to secede but to seize all federal military arms and supplies within their borders and use them to prevent Lincoln from taking office. When this plan was criticized as unfeasible, Wise advocated secession.

18. The nickname "Star-Spangled Banner" for the official flag of the United States was derived from Francis Scott Key's description of the flag flying above Fort McHenry following the attack by British forces in the Battle of Baltimore on 14 September 1814.

19. Senator John C. Calhoun, in his *Speech on the Reception of Abolition Petitions* (1837), is credited with popularizing the term "peculiar institution" as a euphemism for slavery.

rid details of torture, starvation and murder, in the treatment of our
prisoners, I beheld the features of the monster in whose presence I
was born, and that is Slavery. From no source less foul and wicked
could such a Rebellion come. I need not dwell here. The country
knows the story by heart. But I am one of those who think this Rebellion—inaugurated and carried on for a cause so unspeakably
guilty and distinguished by barbarities which would extort a cry of
shame from the painted savage—is quite enough for the whole lifetime of any one nation—though that lifetime should cover the space
of a thousand years. We ought not to want a repetition of it—nor can
we wisely risk a possible repetition of it. Looking at the matter from
no higher ground than patriotism—setting aside the high considerations of justice, liberty, progress, and civilization—the American
people should resolve that this shall be the last slaveholding Rebellion that shall ever curse this continent. Let the War cost much or
cost little—let it be long or short—the work now begun should suffer no pause, no abatement, until it is done and done forever.

I know that many are appalled and disappointed by the apparently interminable character of this war. I am neither appalled nor
disappointed. Without pretending to any higher wisdom than other
men, I know well enough and often said it—Once let the North
and South confront each other on the battle-field, and Slavery and
Freedom be the inspiring motives of the respective sections, the
contest will be fierce, long and sanguinary. Gov. Seymour charges us
with prolonging the war,[20] and I say the longer the better if it must
be so—in order to put an end to the hell black cause out of which
the Rebellion has risen.

Say not that I am indifferent to the horrors and hardships of the
war. I am not indifferent. In common with the American people

20. Horatio Seymour (1810–86) was elected governor of New York in 1862, and
once in office worked to delay implementation of the Civil War draft. Further, he
opposed Lincoln's Emancipation Proclamation. He was defeated in the 1864 guber-
natorial election, but remained politically active. In 1868 he was the reluctant and
unsuccessful Democratic presidential nominee.

generally, I feel the prolongation of the war a heavy calamity—private as well [as] public. There are vacant spaces at my hearthstone which I shall rejoice to see filled again by the boys who once occupied them—but which cannot be thus filled while the war lasts—for they have enlisted—"during the war."[21]

But even from the length of this struggle, we who mourn over it may well enough draw some consolation when we reflect upon the vastness and grandeur of its mission. The world has witnessed many wars—and history records and perpetuates their memory, but the world has not seen a nobler and grander war than that which the loyal people of this country are now waging against the slaveholding Rebels. The blow we strike is not merely to free a country or continent—but the whole world from Slavery—for when Slavery falls here—it will fall everywhere. We have no business to mourn over our mission. We are writing the statutes of eternal justice and liberty in the blood of the worst of tyrants as a warning to all after-comers. We should rejoice that there was moral life and health enough in us to stand in our appointed place, and do this great service for mankind.

It is true that the war seems long. But this very slow progress is an essential element of its effectiveness. Like the slow convalescence of some patients the fault is less chargeable to the medicine than to the deep-seated character of the disease. We were in a very low condition before the remedy was applied. The whole head was sick and the whole heart faint. Dr. Buchanan[22] and his Democratic

21. Lewis Henry Douglass (1840–1908) served as a sergeant major in the Fifty-fourth Massachusetts Infantry Regiment and embarked with the unit to South Carolina in May 1863. His brother, Charles Remond Douglass (1844–1920), a private in that regiment, was ill at the time of his unit's departure; as late as November 1863, he remained at the Readville, Massachusetts, training camp. He eventually saw duty with another black regiment, the Fifth Massachusetts Cavalry, rising to the rank of first sergeant.

22. James Buchanan (1791–1868) was the fifteenth president of the United States. His proslavery views were evident during the week of his inauguration when he publicly endorsed the outcome of the Dred Scott case. Buchanan alienated the North further by his advocacy of Kansas's admission as a slave state and his selection of primarily proslavery cabinet members.

friends had given us up, and were preparing to celebrate the nation's funeral. We had been drugged nearly to death by Pro-Slavery compromises. A radical change was needed in our whole system. Nothing is better calculated to effect the desired change than the slow, steady and certain progress of the war.

I know that this view of the case is not very consoling to the peace Democracy.[23] I was not sent and am not come to console this breach of our political church. They regard this grand moral revolution in the mind and heart of the nation as the most distressing attribute of the war, and howl over it like certain characters of whom we read—who thought themselves tormented before their time.

Upon the whole, I like their mode of characterizing the war. They charge that it is no longer conducted upon constitutional principles. The same was said by Breckinridge[24] and Vallandigham.[25] They charge that it is not waged to establish the Union as it was.[26]

23. The term "Peace Democrat" originated in the highly partisan rhetoric of Northern politics during the Civil War. Editorials in Horace Greely's New York *Daily Tribune* warned against the intentions of "peace men" such as Clement Vallandigham, of Ohio, and Fernando Wood, of New York, noting, "In fact every one wants peace, we only differ as to the terms. Some want it with the union, some without—a serious divergence." In 1863, Vallandigham and Wood publicly endorsed negotiating an armistice to end hostilities and restore the Union. In the 1864 presidential elections, the Democrats nominated a ticket seemingly at odds with itself: for president, General George B. McClellan, who favored further military efforts, and for vice president, Congressman George H. Pendleton of Ohio, a Peace Democrat. They ran on a platform calling for an armistice and negotiations.

24. John Cabell Breckinridge (1821–75) took his seat as a U.S. senator from Kentucky in March 1861. He was the only senator to vote against a resolution to allow Lincoln to use federal resources for the war. When Union troops secured Kentucky, Breckinridge resigned from the Senate and joined both the Kentucky (Confederate) provisional government and the Confederate army, in which he rose to the rank of major general.

25. Clement Laird Vallandigham (1820–71) was elected as a Democrat to the U.S. House of Representatives in 1856, 1858, and 1860. Vallandigham's vehement opposition to military conscription and his advocacy of a negotiated peace led to his arrest and conviction in May 1863 for treasonous activity. He was sentenced to be incarcerated in Fort Warren in Boston Harbor, but President Lincoln intervened and banished him to the Confederacy. While in exile, Vallandigham unsuccessfully campaigned for the Ohio governorship.

26. A campaign slogan of the 1864 Peace Democrats. "The Union as It was, the Constitution as It is." Democratic Platform of 1864.

The same idea has occurred to Jefferson Davis.[27] They charge that this is a war for the subjugation of the South. In a word, that it is an Abolition war.

For one, I am not careful to deny this charge. But it is instructive to observe how this charge is brought and how it is met. Both warn us of danger. Why is this war fiercely denounced as an Abolition war? I answer, because the nation has long and bitterly hated Abolition, and the enemies of the war confidently rely upon this hatred to serve the ends of treason. Why do the loyal people deny the charge? I answer, because they know that Abolition, though now a vast power, is still odious. Both the charge and the denial tell how the people hate and despise the only measure that can save the country.

An Abolition war! Well, let us thank the Democracy for teaching us this word. The charge in a comprehensive sense is most true, and it is not a pity that it is true, but it would be a vast pity if it were not true. Would that it were more true than it is. When our Government and people shall bravely avow this to be an Abolition war, then the country will be safe. Then our work will be fairly mapped out. Then the uplifted arm of the nation will swing unfettered to its work, and the spirit and power of the Rebellion will be broken. Had Slavery been abolished in the Border States at the very beginning of this war, as it ought to have been—had it been abolished in Missouri, as it would have been but for Presidential interference[28]—there would now be no Rebellion in the Southern States—for instead of having to watch these Border States, as they have done, our armies would have marched in overpowering numbers directly upon the Rebels and overwhelmed them. I now hold that a sacred regard for truth, as well

27. Jefferson Davis (1808–89), president of the Confederate States of America (1861–65). Although never tried for treason, he was a federal prisoner at Fortress Monroe for two years following the Civil War.

28. President Lincoln ordered General John C. Frémont to amend the portion of his proclamation that instituted martial law in Missouri and emancipated all of that state's slaves so that it would conform to the Confiscation Act of 6 August 1861. That act deprived the owners of slaves being used to aid the rebellion of their claim to the labor of such slaves but did not alter the legal status of the bondsmen themselves.

as sound policy, makes it our duty to own and avow before Heaven and earth that this war is, and of right ought to be, an Abolition war.

The abolition of Slavery is the comprehensive and logical object of the war, for it includes everything else which the struggle involves. It is a war for the union, a war for the Constitution, I admit; but it is logically such a war only in the sense that the greater includes the lesser. Slavery has proved itself the strong man of our national house. In every Rebel State it proved itself stronger than the Union, stronger than the Constitution, and stronger than Republican Institutions. It overrode majorities, made no account of the ballot-box, and had everything its own way. It is plain that this strong man must be bound and cast out of our house before Union, Constitution and Republican institutions can become possible. An Abolition war, therefore, includes Union, Constitution, Republican Institutions, and all else that goes to make up the greatness and glory of our common country. On the other hand, exclude Abolition, and you exclude all else for which you are fighting.

The position of the Democratic party in relation to the war ought to surprise nobody. It is consistent with the history of the party for thirty years past. Slavery, and only Slavery, has been its recognized master during all that time. It early won for itself the title of being the natural ally of the South and of Slavery. It has always been for peace or against peace, for war and against war, precisely as dictated by Slavery. Ask why it was for the Florida War,[29] and it answers, Slavery. Ask why it was for the Mexican War,[30] and it answers, Slavery. Ask why it was for the annexation of Texas, and it answers, Slavery. Ask why it was opposed to the habeas corpus[31] when a negro was the

29. The Second Seminole War (1835–42).

30. The Treaty of Guadalupe Hidalgo formally ended the Mexican War (1846–48) and gave the United States not only disputed territory in Texas but also land extending to the Pacific Ocean. Many abolitionists believed that the war was nothing less than an attempt by Southern politicians to acquire more area for the expansion of slavery.

31. A prisoner may request a writ of habeas corpus. This writ from a judicial official to a jail or prison summons the prisoner to a court to determine the legality of that person's incarceration.

applicant, and it answers, Slavery. Ask why it is now in favor of the habeas corpus, when Rebels and traitors are the applicants for its benefits, and it answers, Slavery. Ask why it was for mobbing down freedom of speech a few years ago, when that freedom was claimed by the Abolitionists, and it answers, Slavery. Ask why it now asserts freedom of speech, when sympathizers with traitors claim that freedom, and again Slavery is the answer. Ask why it denied the right of a State to protect itself against possible abuses of the Fugitive-Slave bill,[32] and you have the same old answer. Ask why it now asserts the sovereignty of the States separately, as against the States united, and again Slavery is the answer. Ask why it was opposed to giving persons claimed as fugitive slaves a jury trial before returning them to slavery; ask why it is now in favor of giving jury trial to traitors before sending them to the forts for safe keeping; ask why it was for war at the beginning of the Rebellion; ask why it has attempted to embarrass and hinder the loyal Government at every step of its progress, and you have but one answer, Slavery.

The fact is, the party in question, I say nothing of individual men who were once members of it, has had but one vital and animating principle for thirty years, and that has been the same old horrible and hell-born principle of negro Slavery.

It has now assumed a saintly character. Its members would receive the benediction due to peace-makers.[33] At one time they would stop bloodshed at the South by inaugurating bloody revo-

32. Reference to the personal liberty laws passed after the Compromise of 1850. Personal liberty laws, which were premised on the belief that all persons were born free, were passed by many Northern states to provide legal means to ensure that free blacks and alleged slaves could not be placed in bondage except by due process of law. In their agitation for secession during the winter of 1860–61, Southern disunionists frequently cited these laws as evidence of violations of slaveholders' constitutional rights. Northern Democrats and other conservatives, including a few Republicans, began efforts to repeal the laws in order to placate the slaveholders. The flurry of activity for and against the laws had negligible results. In the end, only Rhode Island repealed its personal liberty law, and Massachusetts slightly modified its version.

33. Matt. 5:9.

lution at the North. The livery of peace is a beautiful livery,[34] but in this case it is a stolen livery and sits badly on the wearer. These new apostles of peace call themselves Peace Democrats, and boast that they belong to the only party which can restore the country to peace. I neither dispute their title nor the pretensions founded upon it. The best that can be said of the peace-making ability of this class of men is their bitterest condemnation. It consists in their known treachery to the loyal Government. They have but to cross the Rebel lines to be hailed by the traitors as countrymen, clansmen, kinsmen, and brothers beloved in a common conspiracy. But, fellow-citizens, I have far less solicitude about the position and the influence of this party than I have about that of the great loyal party of the country. We have much less to fear from the bold and shameless wickedness of the one than from the timid and short-sighted policy of the other.

I know we have recently gained a great political victory; but it remains to be seen whether we shall wisely avail ourselves of its manifest advantages. There is danger that, like some of our Generals in the field, who, after soundly whipping the foe, generously allow him time to retreat in order, reorganize his forces, and intrench himself in a new and stronger position, where it will require more power and skill to dislodge him than was required to vanquish him in the first instance. The game is now in our hands. We can put an end to this disloyal party by putting an end to Slavery. While the Democratic party is in existence as an organization, we are in danger of a slave-holding peace, and of Rebel rule. There is but one way to avert this calamity, and that is, destroy Slavery and enfranchise the black man while we have the power. While there is a vestige of slavery remaining, it will unite the South with itself, and carry with it the Democracy of the North. The South united and the North divided, we shall be hereafter as heretofore, firmly held under the heels of Slavery.

34. Clothing or insignia worn by an official.

Here is a part of the platform of principles upon which it seems to me every loyal man should take his stand at this hour:

First: That this war, which we are compelled to wage against slaveholding Rebels and traitors, at untold cost of blood and treasure, shall be, and of right ought to be, an Abolition War.

Secondly: That we, the loyal people of the North and of the whole country, while determined to make this a short and final war, will offer no peace, accept no peace, consent to no peace, which shall not be to all intents and purposes an Abolition peace.

Thirdly: That we regard the whole colored population of the country, in the loyal as well as in the disloyal States, as our *countrymen*—valuable in peace as laborers, valuable in war as soldiers—entitled to all the rights, protection, and opportunities for achieving distinction enjoyed by any other class of our countrymen.

Fourthly: Believing that the white race has nothing to fear from fair competition with the black race, and that the freedom and elevation of one race are not to be purchased or in any manner rightfully subserved by the disfranchisement of another, we shall favor immediate and unconditional emancipation in all the States, invest the black man everywhere with the right to vote and to be voted for, and remove all discriminations against his rights on account of his color, whether as a citizen or as a soldier.

Ladies and gentlemen, there was a time when I hoped that events unaided by discussions would couple this Rebellion and Slavery in a common grave. But as I have before intimated, the facts do still fall short of our hopes. The question as to what shall be done with Slavery—and more especially what shall be done with the negro—threaten to remain open questions for some time yet.

It is true we have the Proclamation of January, 1863. It was a vast and glorious step in the right direction. But unhappily, excellent as that paper is—and much as it has accomplished temporarily—it settles nothing. It is still open to decision by courts, canons and Congresses. I have applauded that paper and do now applaud it, as a wise measure—while I detest the motive and principle upon which it is based. By it the holding and flogging of negroes is the exclusive luxury of loyal men.[35] Our chief danger lies in the absence of all moral feeling in the utterances of our rulers. In his letter to Mr. Greeley[36] the President told the country virtually that the abolition or non-abolition of Slavery was a matter of indifference to him. He would save the Union with Slavery or without Slavery. In his last Message he shows the same moral indifference, by saying as he does say that he had hoped that the Rebellion could be put down without the abolition of Slavery.[37]

35. Pressure for emancipation began when General Benjamin Butler defined captured slaves as contraband, which prompted congressional Republicans to pass the First and Second Confiscation Acts. Following a military victory at Antietam on 17 September 1862, Lincoln, under his war powers as president, announced the Preliminary Emancipation Proclamation, declaring that all slaves held in rebel states on 1 January 1863 would be free. On that date, Lincoln signed the permanent Emancipation Proclamation. Lincoln did not believe that his war powers extended to border states not in open rebellion or to portions of rebel states then under Union control. Therefore, slaves in many counties in Tennessee, Virginia, and Louisiana, as well as in the border states, were unaffected by the proclamation, which made the crafting of a constitutional amendment outlawing slavery vital.

36. On 20 August 1862, Horace Greeley (1811–72), founder and lifelong editor of the New York *Tribune,* published a public letter to President Lincoln in his New York *Daily Tribune.* Under the headline "THE PRAYER OF TWENTY MILLIONS," it complained of the administration's inaction against slavery. Lincoln replied in a letter of 22 August 1862, which Greeley printed three days later. Douglass paraphrases that portion of Lincoln's letter in which the president acknowledged: "I would save the Union. I would save it the shortest way under the Constitution. . . . My paramount object in this struggle *is* to save the Union, and is *not* either to save or destroy slavery. If I could save the Union without freeing *any* slave I would do it, and if I could save it by freeing *all* the slaves I would do it; and if I could save it by freeing some and leaving others alone I would also do that. What I do about slavery, and the colored race, I do because I believe it helps to save the Union; and what I forbear, I forbear because I do *not* believe it would help to save the Union."

37. Douglass probably alludes to Lincoln's annual message to Congress of 8 December 1863, in which the president declared: "According to our political system, as a matter of civil administration, the general government had no lawful power to effect emancipation in any State, and for a long time it had been hoped that the rebellion could be suppressed without resorting to it as a military measure." Roy P. Basler, ed., *The Collected Works of Abraham Lincoln,* 9 vols. (New Brunswick, N.J.: Rutgers University Press, 1953–55), 7:49.

When the late Stephen A. Douglas[38] uttered the sentiment that he did not care whether Slavery were voted up or voted down in the Territories, we thought him lost to all genuine feeling on the subject, and no man more than Mr. Lincoln denounced that sentiment as unworthy of the lips of any American statesman.[39] But to-day, after nearly three years of a Slaveholding Rebellion, we find Mr. Lincoln uttering substantially the same heartless sentiments. Douglas wanted Popular Sovereignty; Mr. Lincoln wants the Union. Now did a warm heart and a high moral feeling control the utterances of the President, he would welcome, with joy unspeakable and full of glory, the opportunity afforded by the Rebellion to free the country from the matchless crime and infamy. But policy, policy, everlasting policy, has robbed our statesmanship of all soul-moving utterances.

The great misfortune is and has been during all the progress of this war, that the Government and loyal people have not understood and accepted its true mission. Hence we have been floundering in the depths of dead issues. Endeavoring to impose old and worn-out conditions upon new relations—putting new wine into old bottles, new cloth into old garments, and thus making the rent worse than before.[40]

Had we been wise, we should have recognized the war at the outset as at once the signal and the necessity for a new order of social and political relations among the whole people. We could, like the ancients, discern the face of the sky, but not the signs of the

38. Stephen Arnold Douglas (1813–61) won a U.S. Senate seat representing Illinois in 1846 and held it for the remainder of his life. Douglas framed the controversial Kansas-Nebraska Act in 1854. Douglas narrowly defeated the Republican challenger, Abraham Lincoln, for reelection to the Senate in 1858.

39. On 9 December 1857, Stephen A. Douglas took the Senate floor to champion popular sovereignty, declaring: "If Kansas wants a slave-State constitution she has a right to do it; if she wants a free-State constitution she has a right to do it. It is none of my business which way the slavery clause is decided. I care not whether it is voted down or voted up." Abraham Lincoln criticized Douglas's remarks on several occasions, most notably in the "House Divided" speech delivered in Springfield, Illinois, on 16 June 1858. *Congressional Globe*, 35th Cong., 1st sess., 18.

40. Matt. 9:17; Mark 2:22; Luke 5:37, 38.

times. Hence we have been talking of the importance of carrying on the war within the limits of a Constitution broken down by the very people in whose behalf the Constitution is pleaded! Hence we have from the first been deluding ourselves with the miserable dream, that the old Union can be revived in the States where it has been abolished.

Now, we of the North have seen many strange things, and may see many more; but that old Union, whose canonized bones we saw hearsed in death and inurned under the frowning battlements of Sumter, we shall never see again while the world standeth. The issue before us is a living issue. We are not fighting for the dead past, but for the living present and the glorious future. We are not fighting for the old Union, nor for anything like it, but for that which is ten thousand times more important; and that thing, crisply rendered, is *National unity.* Both sections have tried Union. It has failed.

The lesson for the statesman at this hour is to discover and apply some principle of Government which shall produce unity of sentiment, unity of idea, unity of object. Union without unity is, as we have seen, body without soul, marriage without love, a barrel without hoops, which falls at the first touch.

The statesmen of the South understood this matter earlier and better than the statesmen of the North. The dissolution of the Union on the old bases of compromise, was plainly foreseen and predicted 30 years ago. Mr. Calhoun and not Mr. Seward,[41] is the original author of the doctrine of the irrepressible conflict. The South is logical and consistent. Under the teachings of their great leader they admit into their form of Government no disturbing force. They have based their Confederacy squarely on their corner-stone. Their two great, and all commanding ideas are first, that Slavery is right, and second, that the slaveholders are a superior order or class. Around these two ideas their manners, morals, politics, religion, and laws revolve. Slavery being right, all that is inconsistent with its entire security is

41. John C. Calhoun and William H. Seward.

necessarily wrong, and of course ought to be put down. There is no flaw in their logic.

They first endeavored to make the Federal Government stand upon their accursed corner-stone; and we but barely escaped, as you well know, that calamity. Fugitive Slave laws, Slavery Extension laws, and Dred Scott decisions[42] were among the steps to get the nation squarely upon the corner-stone now chosen by the Confederate States. The loyal North is less logical, less consistent, and less definite in regard to the necessity of principles of National Unity. Yet, unconsciously to ourselves, and against our own protestations, we are in reality, like the South, fighting for national unity—a unity of which the great principles of liberty and equality, and not Slavery and class superiority, are the corner-stone.

Long before this rude and terrible war came to tell us of a broken Constitution and a dead Union, the better portion of the loyal people had outlived and outgrown what they had been taught to believe were the requirements of the old Union. We had come to detest the principle by which Slavery had a strong representation in Congress. We had come to abhor the idea of being called upon to suppress slave insurrections. We had come to be ashamed of slave-hunting, and being made the watch-dogs of slaveholders, who were too proud to scent out and hunt down their slaves for themselves. We had so far outlived the old Union four years ago that we thought

42. Dred Scott (c. 1795–1858), a Missouri slave, was taken by his master in the 1830s into Illinois and Wisconsin, where slavery was prohibited by either the Northwest Ordinance or the Missouri Compromise. In 1846, Scott sued for his liberty, arguing that his four-year stay on free soil had given him freedom. The U.S. Supreme Court handed down a complicated decision on 6 March 1857. The majority opinion, written by Chief Justice Roger B. Taney (1777–1864), held that as a black, Scott was not a citizen and therefore not entitled to sue in a federal court; Scott's previous residence in free territory had not made him free upon his return to Missouri, since his status was determined by the laws of the state in which he resided when the case was raised; and the Missouri Compromise was unconstitutional, since it violated the Fifth Amendment's prohibition against Congress's depriving persons of their property without the due process of the law.

the little finger of the hero of Harper's Ferry[43] of more value to the world struggling for liberty than all the first families of old Virginia put together.

What business, then, have we to be pouring out our treasure and shedding our best blood like water for that old worn-out, dead and buried Union, which had already become a calamity and a curse? The fact is, we are not fighting for any such thing, and we ought to come out under our own true colors, and let the South and the whole world know that we don't want and will not have anything analogous to the old Union.

What we now want is a country—a free country—a country nowhere saddened by the footprints of a single slave—and nowhere cursed by the presence of a slaveholder. We want a country, and we are fighting for a country, which shall not brand the Declaration of Independence as a lie. We want a country whose fundamental institutions we can proudly defend before the highest intelligence and civilization of the age. Hitherto we have opposed European scorn of our Slavery with a blush of shame as our best defense. We now want a country in which the obligations of patriotism shall not conflict with fidelity to justice and Liberty. We want a country, and are fighting for a country, which shall be free from sectional political parties—free from sectional religious denominations—free from sectional benevolent associations—free from every kind and description of sect, party, and combination of a sectional character. We want a country where men may assemble from any part of it, without prejudice to their interests or peril to their persons. We are in fact, and from absolute necessity, transplanting the whole South with the higher civilization of the North. The New-England schoolhouse is bound to take the place of the Southern whipping-post.

---

43. The white abolitionist John Brown (1790–1859) led a raid on the federal armory at Harpers Ferry, Virginia, in October 1859 in order to capture arms and lead an uprising of slaves on nearby plantations. Captured and tried for treason and capital murder under Virginia law, he was executed on 2 December 1859, and immediately became a martyr to many Northerners.

Not because we love the negro, but the nation; not because we prefer to do this, because we must or give up the contest, and give up the country. We want a country, and are fighting for a country, where social intercourse and commercial relations shall neither be embarrassed nor embittered by the imperious exactions of an insolent slaveholding Oligarchy, which required Northern merchants to sell their souls as a condition precedent to selling their goods. We want a country, and are fighting for a country, through the length and breadth of which the literature and learning of any section of it may float to its extremities unimpaired, and thus become the common property of all the people—a country in which no man shall be fined for reading a book, or imprisoned for selling a book—a country where no man can be imprisoned or flogged or sold for learning to read, or teaching a fellow mortal how to read. We want a country, and are fighting for a country, in any part of which to be called an American citizen, shall mean as much as it did to be called a Roman citizen in the palmiest days of the Roman Empire.

We have heard much in other days of manifest destiny.[44] I don't go all the lengths to which such theories are pressed, but I do believe that it is the manifest destiny of this war to unify and reorganize the institutions of this country—and that herein is the secret of the strength, the fortitude, the persistent energy, in a word the sacred significance of this war. Strike out the high ends and aims thus indicated, and the war would appear to the impartial eye of an on-looking world little better than a gigantic enterprise for shedding human blood.

A most interesting and gratifying confirmation of this theory of its mission is furnished in the varying fortunes of the struggle itself.

44. John Louis O'Sullivan (1813–95) coined the term "Manifest Destiny" in 1845 to promote the annexation of Texas and the Oregon Country. The idea was premised on a belief that God intended the United States to control most or all of North America in order to demonstrate the superiority of its Protestant republican values to a corrupt world. While popular among Democrats, its proslavery implications caused Northern Whigs and later Republicans to be wary of expansionism.

Just in proportion to the progress made in taking upon itself the character I have ascribed to it, has the war prospered and the Rebellion lost ground.

Justice and humanity are often overpowered—but they are persistent and eternal forces—and fearful to contend against. Let but our rulers place the Government fully within these trade winds of Omnipotence, and the hand of death is upon the Confederate Rebels. A war waged as ours seemed to be at first, merely for power and empire, repels sympathy though supported by legitimacy. If Ireland should strike for independence to-morrow, the sympathy of this country would be with her, and I doubt if American statesmen would be more discreet in the expression of their opinions of the merits of the contest, than British statesmen have been concerning the merit of ours. When we were merely fighting for the old Union the world looked coldly upon our Government. But now the world begins to see something more than legitimacy—something more than national pride. It sees national wisdom aiming at national unity; and national justice breaking the chains of a long enslaved people. It is this new complexion of our cause which warms our hearts and strengthens our hands at home, disarms our enemies and increases our friends abroad. It is this more than all else which has carried consternation into the blood-stained halls of the South. It has sealed the fiery and scornful lips of the Roebucks[45] and Lindsays[46] of England, and caused even the eloquent Mr. Gladstone to restrain the expression of his admiration for Jeff Davis and his Rebel

45. John Arthur Roebuck (1802–79) was first elected to Parliament in 1832. In June 1863, Roebuck badly mismanaged a parliamentary move to have Britain join France and other European powers in recognizing the Confederacy.

46. The Liberal party M.P. William Schaw Lindsay (1816–77) actively campaigned for British recognition of the Confederacy. After private discussion with Napoleon III in April 1862, he acted as unofficial courier from the French to the British government to sound out the idea of joint recognition. When that move failed, Lindsay introduced an unsuccessful parliamentary motion in July 1862 proposing British mediation of the American conflict. As late as the summer of 1864, Lindsay was leading futile parliamentary maneuvers on behalf of the Southern cause.

nation.[47] It has placed the broad arrow of British suspicion on the prows of the Rebel rams in the Mersey, and performed a like service for those in France.[48] It has driven Mason, the shameless manhunter, from London,[49] where he never should have been allowed to stay for an hour, except as a bloodhound is tolerated in Regent Park for exhibition.[50]

We have had from the first warm friends in England. We owe a debt of respect and gratitude to William Edward Forster,[51] John Bright,[52] Richard Cobden,[53] and other British statesmen, in that they outran us in comprehending the high character of our struggle. They saw that this must be a war for human nature, and walked by faith to its defense while all was darkness about us—while we were yet conducting it in profound reverence for Slavery.

47. William Ewart Gladstone (1809–98), four-time prime minister of Great Britain (1868–74, 1880–85, 1886, 1892–94), was chancellor of the exchequer in the cabinet of Lord Palmerston at the time of the Civil War. Although an opponent of slavery, Gladstone favored British recognition of the Confederacy on the ground that the prolonged bloodshed had made a reunion of the North and South impossible.

48. In desperate need of modern warships, the Confederacy entered into secret agreements with a number of British and French shipbuilding firms, but all attempts to purchase them were thwarted by the Lincoln administration through diplomatic channels.

49. James Murray Mason (1798–1871) of Virginia served in the U.S. Senate (1847–61) and wrote the notorious Fugitive Slave Law of 1850. Mason supported secession in 1860 and served briefly in the Confederate Congress before being appointed commissioner to England. On 8 November 1861, while traveling on the British steamer *Trent,* Mason and John Slidell, the Confederacy's diplomatic representative to France, were captured by the U.S. Navy and sent to Fort Warren in Boston Harbor. This affair so strained relations between the United States and Great Britain that many feared war would break out. Upon his release in January 1862, Mason proceeded to England. After an unsuccessful two-year effort to obtain recognition of the Confederacy, Mason notified the British Foreign Ministry of his withdrawal on 21 September 1863.

50. Regent's Park housed the collection of the Zoological Society of London.

51. William Edward Forster (1818–86) was the first member of Parliament to speak against British attempts to aid the Confederacy by preventing a Union blockade of Confederate ports or by allowing the building of Confederate warships in British dry docks.

52. John Bright (1811–89) entered Parliament in 1843 and was successful in winning British middle-class and working-class support for the North in the Civil War.

53. Richard Cobden (1804–65), a liberal member of Parliament, opposed slavery and strongly supported the Union.

I know we are not to be praised for this changed character of
the war. We did our very best to prevent it. We had but one object
at the beginning, and that was, as I have said, the restoration of the
old Union; and for the first two years the war was kept to that object
strictly, and you know full well and bitterly with what results. I will
not stop here to blame and denounce the past; but I will say that
most of the blunders and disasters of the earlier part of the war might
have been avoided had our armies and Generals not repelled the
only true friends the Union cause had in the Rebel States. The Army
of the Potomac took up an anti-negro position from the first, and has
not entirely renounced it yet.[54] The colored people told me a few
days ago in Washington that they were the victims of the most brutal
treatment by these Northern soldiers when they first came there.[55]
But let that pass. Few men, however great their wisdom, are permitted to see the end from the beginning. Events are mightier than our
rulers, and these Divine forces, with overpowering logic, have fixed
upon this war, against the wishes of our Government, the comprehensive character and mission I have ascribed to it. The collecting
of revenue in the Rebel ports, the repossession of a few forts and
arsenals and other public property stolen by the Rebels, have almost
disappeared from the recollection of the people. The war has been
a growing war in every sense of the word. It began weak, and has
risen strong. It began low, and has risen high. It began narrow, and
has become broad. It began with few, and now, behold, the country
is full of armed men, ready, with courage and fortitude, to make the
wisest and best idea of American statesmanship the law of the land.

Let, then, the war proceed in its strong, high, and broad course
till the Rebellion is put down and our country is saved beyond the
necessity of being saved again!

54. Douglass alludes to the policy of returning runaway slaves to their masters,
even suspected pro-Confederate ones, followed by General George B. McClellan
and most other Union Army commanders in Virginia during the Civil War's first year.

55. Douglass delivered lectures in Washington, D.C., on 7 and 8 December 1863
in behalf of the Contraband Relief Society and inspected freedmen's refugee camps
in nearby Virginia.

I have already hinted at our danger. Let me be a little more direct and pronounced.

The Democratic party, though defeated in the elections last Fall, is still a power. It is the ready organized nucleus of a powerful Pro-Slavery and Pro-Rebel reaction. Though it has lost in numbers, it retains all the elements of its former power and malevolence.

That party has five very strong points in its favor, and its public men and journals know well how to take advantage of them.

First: There is the absence of any deep moral feeling among the loyal people against Slavery itself—their feeling against it being on account of its rebellion against the Government, and not because it is a stupendous crime against human nature.

Secondly: The vast expense of the war and the heavy taxes in money as well as men which the war requires for its prosecution. Loyalty has a strong back, but taxation has often broken it.

Thirdly: The earnest desire for peace which is shared by all classes except Government contractors who are making money out of the war; a feeling which may be kindled to a flame by any serious reverses to our arms. It is silent in victory but vehement and danger-ous in defeat.

Fourthly: And superior to all others, is the national prejudice and hatred toward the colored people of the country, a feeling which has done more to encourage the hopes of the Rebels than all other powers beside.

Fifthly: An Abolitionist is an object of popular dislike. The guilty Rebel who with broad blades and bloody hands seeks the life of the nation, is at this hour more acceptable to the northern Democracy than an Abolitionist guilty of no crime. Whatever may be a man's abilities, virtue, or service, the fact that he is an Abolitionist makes him an object of popular hate.

Upon these five strings the Democracy still have hopes of playing themselves into power, and not without reason. While our Govern-ment has the meanness to ask Northern colored men to give up the comfort of home, good wages, and personal security, to join the army, endure untold hardships, peril health, limbs and life itself, in its defense, and then degrades them in the eyes of other soldiers, by offering them the paltry sum of $7 per month,[56] and refuses to reward their valor with even the hope of promotion[57]—the Democratic party may well enough presume upon the strength of popular prejudice for support.

While our Republican Government at Washington makes color and not character the criterion of promotion in the army, and degrades colored commissioned officers at New Orleans below the rank to which even the Rebel Government had elevated them, I think we are in danger of a compromise with Slavery.[58]

Our hopeful Republican friends tell me this is impossible—that the day of compromise with Slavery is past. This may do for some men, but it will not do for me.

56. As Northern states began soliciting African Americans for the Union Army, potential recruits were promised full wages, equal to those of white Union soldiers. After the formation of the earliest units, the federal government reneged on this promise, deciding instead to pay black soldiers the laborer's rate of ten dollars per month, regardless of rank. The Fifty-fourth Massachusetts, recruited in part by Douglass, along with most other black units, refused their pay, demanding equality. The issue bothered Douglas, the father of two black soldiers, and he raised it in his first meeting with President Lincoln, at the White House on 10 August 1863. In June 1864 the administration relented, and Congress granted equal pay to all black soldiers who had been free in April 1861. In March 1865, in the face of further protest, former slaves were granted full wages, too.

57. When the restriction on limiting officers' commissions to whites was lifted by the War Department, the secretary of war, Edwin M. Stanton, refused to accept the promotion of any African American officer unless Congress and the president approved it. Black soldiers, however, demanded that the Boards of Examination (the bodies normally overseeing promotion) be opened to them, and in early 1864 the governor of Massachusetts ignored Stanton's wishes and approved the promotion of a black sergeant in the Fifty-fourth to the rank of lieutenant. By the end of the war, approximately one hundred African American soldiers had been promoted into the officer corps.

58. Following Louisiana's secession, free blacks in New Orleans organized two regiments of "Native Guards" and volunteered their service to the Confederacy. The Confederates, however, failed to call out these units when a Union amphibious expedition successfully captured New Orleans in April 1862. In August, the Union commander in occupied Louisiana, Benjamin Butler, began raising black units on his own authority. Northern whites were appointed to the higher officer ranks, but most of the lieutenants and captains were African Americans, including P. B. S. Pinchback, later elected lieutenant governor of the state.

The Northern people have always been remarkably confident of their own virtue. They are hopeful to the last. Twenty years ago we hoped that Texas could not be annexed; but if that could not be prevented we hoped that she would come in as a Free State. Thirteen years ago we were quite sure that no such abomination as the Fugitive Slave Bill could get itself on our National statute book; but when it got there we were equally sure that it never could be enforced. Four years ago we were sure that the Slave States would not rebel, but if they did we were sure it would be a very short rebellion. I know that times have changed very rapidly, and that we have changed with them. Nevertheless, I know also that we are the same old American people, and that what we have done once we may possibly do again. The leaven of compromise is among us—I repeat, while we have a Democratic party at the North trimming its sails to catch the Southern breeze in the next Presidential election, we are in danger of compromise. Tell me not of amnesties and oaths of allegiance. They are valueless in the presence of twenty hundred millions invested in human flesh.[59] Let but the little finger of Slavery get back into this Union, and in one year you shall see its whole body again upon our backs.

While a respectable colored man or woman can be kicked out of the commonest street car in New York—where any white ruffian may ride unquestioned—we are in danger of a compromise with Slavery. While the North is full of such papers as *The New York World, Express,* and *Herald,*[60] firing the nation's heart with hatred to

59. Douglass had offered a similar estimate in a speech on 5 February 1862. The final report of the U.S. Census Bureau recorded 3,953,760 slaves, which modern historians estimate to have had a value in 1860 dollars (at an average worth of $900 each) of $3.6 billion, or almost double Douglass's figure.

60. The New York *World,* launched in 1860, was edited by the prominent Democrat Manton Marable during most of the Civil War. Federal authorities briefly suppressed the *World* in 1864 for publishing fraudulent communications that it claimed were by President Lincoln. Two brothers, James and Erastus Brooks, operated the New York *Express* and became prominent Peace Democrats. Founded in 1835, the New York *Herald* was owned by James Gordon Bennett. Bennett editorially opposed Lincoln's election in both 1860 and 1864, but favored a Union military victory.

negroes and Abolitionists, we are in danger of a slaveholding peace. While the major part of all Anti-Slavery profession is based upon devotion to the Union rather than hostility to Slavery, there is danger of a slaveholding peace. Until we shall see the election of November next, and know that it has resulted in the election of a sound Anti-Slavery man as President, we shall be in danger of a slaveholding compromise. Indeed, so long as Slavery has any life left in it, anywhere in the country, we are in danger of such a compromise.

Then there is the danger arising from the impatience of the people on account of the prolongation of the war. I know the American people. They are an impulsive people, impatient of delay, clamorous for change—and often look for results out of all proportion to the means employed in attaining them.

You and I know that the mission of this war is National regeneration. We know and consider that a nation is not born in a day. We know that large bodies move slowly—and often seem to move thus—when, could we perceive their actual velocity, we should be astonished at its greatness. A great battle lost or won is easily described, understood and appreciated, but the moral growth of a great nation requires reflection, as well as observation, to appreciate it. There are vast numbers of voters, who make no account of the moral growth of the nation, and who only look at the war as a calamity to be endured only so long as they have no power to arrest it. Now, this is just the sort of people whose vote may turn the scale against us in the last event.

Thoughts of this kind tell me that there never was a time when Anti-Slavery work was more needed than now. The day that shall see the Rebels at our feet, their weapons flung away, will be the day of trial. We have need to prepare for that trial. We have long been saved a Pro-Slavery peace by the stubborn, unbending persistence of the Rebels. Let them bend as they will bend—there will come the test of our sternest virtues.

I have now given, very briefly, some of the grounds of danger. A word as to the grounds of hope. The best that can be offered is, that we have made progress—vast and striking progress—within the last two years.

President Lincoln introduced his administration to the country as one which would faithfully catch, hold, and return runaway slaves to their masters.[61] He avowed his determination to protect and defend the slaveholder's right to plunder the black laborer of his hard earnings. Europe was assured by Mr. Seward that no slave should gain his freedom by this war.[62] Both the President and the Secretary of State have made progress since then.

Our Generals, at the beginning of the war, were horribly Pro-Slavery. They took to slave-catching and slave-killing like ducks to water. They are now very generally and very earnestly in favor of putting an end to Slavery. Some of them, like Hunter[63] and Butler,[64]

61. In his inaugural address on 4 March 1861, Lincoln asserted that he took his oath of office "with no mental reservations." After reviewing the provisions of the Constitution's Fugitive Slave Clause and the Fugitive Slave Law of 1850, he chose not "to specify particular acts of Congress as proper to be enforced." Instead, he suggested that it would be "much safer for all, both in official and private stations, to conform to, and abide by, all those acts which stand unrepealed, than to violate any of them, trusting to find impunity in having them held to be unconstitutional." Basler, *Collected Works of Lincoln*, 4:263–64.

62. On 10 April 1861, the U.S. secretary of state, William H. Seward, instructed Charles Francis Adams, minister to Great Britain, "not to draw into debate before the British government any opposing moral principles which may be supposed to lie at the foundation of the controversy." On 22 April, after Lincoln's call to arms, Seward informed William Lewis Dayton, minister to France, that whatever the outcome of the conflict, the "condition of slavery in several States will remain just the same."

63. David Hunter (1802–86), who commanded the Department of the South (1862–63), issued a proclamation freeing the slaves within his purview. Lincoln, who feared possible repercussions in the border states, nullified Hunter's orders, stating that the general had exceeded his authority. Hunter did succeed in creating the first official black regiment, the First South Carolina, an action that Congress ultimately supported.

64. An active pre–Civil War Democratic politician, Benjamin Franklin Butler (1818–93) commanded Union forces at Fortress Monroe in Virginia, where, in the summer of 1861, he sheltered runaway slaves within his lines as "contrabands of war." While military governor of New Orleans in 1862, Butler alienated the conquered population and embarrassed Washington with his Order No. 28, which threatened that Southern women who demonstrated contempt for Union troops would be treated as prostitutes.

because they hate Slavery on its own account, and others, because Slavery is in arms against the Government.

The Rebellion has been a rapid educator. Congress was the first to respond to the instinctive judgment of the people, and fixed the broad brand of its reprobation upon slave-hunting in shoulder-straps. Then came very temperate talk about confiscation, which soon came to be pretty radical talk. Then came propositions for Border-State, gradual, compensated, colonized Emancipation. Then came the threat of a proclamation, and then came the proclamation. Meanwhile the negro had passed along from a loyal spade and pickax to a Springfield rifle.[65]

Hayti and Liberia are recognized,[66] Slavery is humbled in Maryland, threatened in Tennessee, stunned nearly to death in Western Virginia, doomed in Missouri, trembling in Kentucky, and gradually melting away before our arms in the rebellious States.[67]

The hour is one of hope as well as danger. But whatever may come to pass, one thing is clear: The principles involved in the contest, the necessities of both sections of the country, the obvious requirements of the age, and every suggestion of enlightened policy demand the utter extirpation of Slavery from every foot of American soil, and the enfranchisement of the entire colored population of the country. Elsewhere we may find peace, but it will be a hollow and deceitful peace. Elsewhere we may find prosperity, but it will

65. An allusion to a style of muzzle-loading rifle manufactured at the Springfield Armory, located in the Massachusetts city of the same.

66. In his first annual message to Congress, in December 1861, Lincoln suggested establishing diplomatic relations with Haiti and Liberia. At Lincoln's urging, Congress passed an authorization bill in April 1862 that appropriated funds to establish missions to Haiti and Liberia.

67. What Douglass describes is the actual rather than the legal demise of slavery in the border states. The enlistment of blacks in the Union Army, myriad opportunities for flight, and widespread erosion of discipline during the war years hastened the end of slavery in those regions. West Virginia incorporated gradual emancipation in its first constitution in 1863. After considerable debate, Maryland abolished slavery in 1864, Tennessee in 1865, and Missouri passed an emancipation ordinance in 1865. Kentucky and Delaware rejected such measures, and slavery was not officially abolished in those states until the ratification of the Thirteenth Amendment.

be a transient prosperity. Elsewhere we may find greatness and re-nown, but if these are based upon anything less substantial than justice they will vanish, for righteousness alone can permanently exalt a nation.

I end where I began—no war but an Abolition war; no peace but an Abolition peace; liberty for all, chains for none; the black man a soldier in war, a laborer in peace; a voter at the South as well as at the North; America his permanent home, and all Americans his fellow-countrymen. Such, fellow-citizens, is my idea of the mission of the war. If accomplished, our glory as a nation will be complete, our peace will flow like a river, and our foundations will be the ever-lasting rocks.

"Sources of Danger to the Republic"

An Address Delivered in St. Louis, Missouri, 7 February 1867

St. Louis *Daily Missouri Democrat*, 8 February 1867.

Douglass made his most comprehensive and powerful argument against a "superficial reverence for the Constitution" in this speech, delivered in several cities during the winter of 1866–67. He returned to this issue in his more famous October 1883 speech responding to the Supreme Court's nullification of the Civil Rights Act of 1875, but here he buttressed his analysis with a measured examination of the weaknesses of constitutional democracy that contributed to the Civil War. Douglass places criticisms of "our Republican experiment" in the mouths of "good men, at home and abroad, and especially abroad," insisting he will neither "indorse" nor "combat" them. With this distancing mechanism, he asserts a neutral detachment that permits him to remain patriotic while offering a stinging criticism of the excessive powers of the presidency and the need for constitutional reform.

Douglass characterizes the Constitution as "a human contrivance" requiring amendments to keep up with a society "superior to its forms." He satirically notes that the Constitution is not divine, Mosaic law: "There were neither thunderings, nor lightenings, nor earthquakes, nor tempests, nor any other disturbance of nature when this great law was given to the world." To ensure greater responsiveness to the will of the people, he recommends reforms aimed at curbing Supreme Court and White House power.

In the winter of 1866–67, when Douglass repeatedly delivered this lyceum lecture to paying audiences, the movement to impeach

President Andrew Johnson was gaining momentum. In the fall of 1866, Americans elected a veto-proof majority of Republicans to Congress, most especially Radical Republicans, who supported equal rights for African Americans. This set the stage for an escalating struggle between the legislative and executive branches over Reconstruction policies. That contest culminated in the unsuccessful effort to impeach President Johnson in February 1868.

The *Daily Missouri Democrat* reported a warm reception to Douglass's speech from "many of our best citizens" and "a goodly number of colored people." The audience repeatedly interrupted Douglass with laughter, especially when he attacked the presidency of Andrew Johnson. Douglass delivered another lecture the next night, also at Turners' Hall in St. Louis, and was said to have met "the highest expectations of his numerous warm friends" in the city. The same speech the month before in Philadelphia had drawn a "packed" house, and his "searching" political analysis took even his "warmest admirers by surprise."[1]

The speech coincided with a pair of articles Douglass prepared for the *Atlantic Monthly* in December 1866 and January 1867. Douglass's December piece "Reconstruction" elaborated upon the "true source of danger to the Republic." In it he calls for a stronger federal presence in the South to redress the "frightful murders and wholesale massacres" that were subjugating African Americans' political and civil rights. He compares the South's attempts to assert states' rights to the erection of a "Chinese wall" that will keep the South's enduring slave culture from the "light of law and liberty." Without federal reinforcements, African Americans' freedoms cannot be protected, he argues. Even in this article, Douglass uses the rhetorical techniques of imagery, metaphor, and alliteration to make a memorable argument in favor of a stronger federal government with enhanced congressional, but not presidential, powers. He argues that constitutional amendments and a stronger federal representative democracy—as opposed to local forms of democracy—will lead to a more just system and will permit social change despite conservative and reactionary forces.[2]

1. *Daily Missouri Democrat,* 4 January 1867.
2. Frederick Douglass, "Reconstruction," *Atlantic Monthly* 18, no. 110 (December 1866): 761–65.

The historian Waldo Martin notes the tension between Douglass's "political economy of laissez faire individualism and the federal government's duty to assist the freedpeople in their transition to complete freedom,"[3] a tension fully evident in his 1869 speech "Let the Negro Alone" (included in this volume). Douglass was acutely aware that the defense of a minority's rights in a democracy sometimes required a strong central government, and he had greater confidence in Congress than the executive branch as an instrument for advancing progressive principles. During the early years of Congressional Reconstruction, Congress was more radical than the executive or judicial branches, but later years would test Douglass's faith in the legislative branch.[4]

L ADIES AND GENTLEMEN: I know of no greater misfortunes to individuals than an over confidence in their own perfections, and I know of fewer misfortunes that can happen to a nation greater than an over confidence in the perfection of its government. It is common on great occasions to hear men speak of our republican form of government as a model of surpassing excellence—the best government on earth—a masterpiece of statesmanship—and destined at some period not very remote to supersede all other forms of government among men; and when our patriotic orators would appear in some degree recondite as well as patriotic, they treat us to masterly disquisitions upon what they are pleased to term "the admirable mechanism of our Constitution." They discourse wisely of its checks and balances, and the judicious distribution of the various powers.

I am certainly not here this evening rudely to call in question these very pleasing assumptions of governmental superiority on our part; they are perfectly natural; they are consistent with our natural self-love and our national pride; and when they are not employed, as

3. Waldo E. Martin, Jr., *The Mind of Frederick Douglass* (Chapel Hill: University of North Carolina Press, 1984), 67.

4. Peter C. Myers, *Race and Rebirth of American Liberalism* (Lawrence: University Press of Kansas, 2008), 131.

they too often are, in the bad service of a blind, unreasoning, stubborn conservatism, to shelter old-time abuses and discourage manly criticism, and to defeat needed measures of amendment, they are comparatively harmless, though we may not always be able to assent to the good taste with which they are urged. It is well enough, however, once in a while to remind Americans that they are not alone in this species of self-laudation; that in fact there are many men, reputed wise and good men, living in other parts of the planet, under other forms of government, aristocratic, autocratic, oligarchic, and monarchical, who are just as confident of the good qualities of their government as we are of our own. It is true, also, that many good men, at home and abroad, and especially abroad, looking upon our republican experiment from afar, in the cool, calm light of their philosophy, have already discovered, or think that they have discovered, a decline or decay, and the certain downfall of our republican institutions, and the speedy substitution of some other form of government for our democratic institutions. Those who entertain these opinions of our government are not entirely without reason, plausible reason, in support of it. The fact that the ballot box, upon which we have relied so long as the chief source of strength, is the safety valve of our institutions through which the explosive passions of the populace could pass off harmlessly, has failed us—broken down under us, and that a formidable rebellion has arisen, the minority of the people in one section of the country united, animated and controlled by a powerful sectional interest, have rebelled, and for four long years disputed the authority of the constitutional majority of the people, is regarded as a telling argument against the prevailing assumption of our national stability and the impregnability of our institutions. Besides, they point us, and very decidedly, to the fact that there seemed to be no adequate comprehension of the character of this rebellion at the beginning of it, and seemed also to be nothing like a proper spirit of enthusiasm manifested by the people in support of the government. They point us to the tardiness and hesitation and doubt, and the disposition to yield up the government to the arrogant demands of conspirators; and they profess themselves now able to see the same want of spirit, manliness and courage in the matter of reconstruction since the rebellion has been suppressed. They point us also to the fact that so far as the government is concerned, there must be either an indisposition or an inability either to punish traitors or to reward and protect loyal men; and they say, very wisely, as I think, that a nation that cannot hate treason cannot love loyalty. (Loud applause.)

They point us also to the fact that there are growing antagonisms, forces bitter and unrelenting between the different branches of our government—the executive against the legislative, and the judicial in some instances against both. They point us also to the obvious want of gratitude on the part of the nation, its disposition to sacrifice its best friends and to make peace with its bitterest enemies; the fact that it has placed its only true allies under the political heels of the very men who with broad blades and bloody hands sought the destruction of the republic. They point us to the fact that loyal men by the score, by the hundred, have been deliberately and outrageously, and in open daylight, slaughtered by the known enemies of the country, and thus far that the murderers are at large: unquestioned by the law, unpunished by justice, unrebuked even by the public opinion of the localities where the crimes were committed. Under the whole heavens you cannot find any government besides our own that thus indifferent to the lives of its loyal subjects. (Applause.) They tell us, moreover, that the lives of republics have been short, stormy, and saddening to the hopes of the friends of freedom, and they tell us, too, that ours will prove no exception to this general rule.

Now, why have I referred to these unfavorable judgments of American institutions? Not, certainly, to indorse them; neither to combat them; but as offering a reason why the Americans should take a little less extravagant view of the excellencies of our institutions. We should scrutinize them a little more closely and weigh their value a little more impartially than we are accustomed to do.

We ought to examine our government, and I am here to-night, and I rejoice that in St. Louis (cheers) that there is liberty enough, civilization enough, (renewed cheers) to tolerate free inquiry at this point as well as any other. I am here to-night in a little different capacity from what I ordinarily am, or what I have been before the American people. In other days—darker days than these—I appeared before the American people simply as a member of despised, outraged and down-trodden race; simply to plead that the chains of the bondmen be broken; simply to plead that the auction block shall no more be in use for the sale of human flesh. I appear here no longer as a whipped, scarred slave—no longer as the advocate merely of an enslaved race, but in the high and commanding character of an American citizen—(cheers)—having the interest that every true citizen should have in the welfare, the stability, the permanence and the prosperity of our free institutions, and in this spirit I shall criticise our government to-night.

In one respect we here have [a] decided advantage over the subjects of the "divine right" governments of Europe.[5] We can at least examine our government. We can at least look into it—into every feature of it, and estimate it at its true value. No divine pretension stands athwart the pathway of free discussion here. The material out of which men would weave if they could a superstitious reverence for the Constitution of the United States, is an exceedingly slender and scarce commodity, and there is nothing upon which such a superstition can well be based. There were neither thunderings, nor lightenings, nor earthquakes, nor tempests, nor any other disturbance of nature when this great law was given to the world. It is at least an honest Constitution and asks to be accepted upon its own merits—has no origin, has no history, and no reputation. It is purely a human contrivance, designed with more or less wisdom, for human purposes; to combine liberty with order; to make society

5. Although in the Christian era the monarchs of western Europe were never considered divine, many claimed the authority of their office had the direct sanction of God.

possible; or, to use its own admirable language, "to form a more perfect Union;" to establish justice; to provide for the common defense; and to secure the blessings of liberty to ourselves and all posterity, we the people, the *people,* the PEOPLE—*we, the people,* do ordain and establish this Constitution.[6] There we stand on the main foundation.

Now, while I discard all Fourth of July extravagances about the Constitution, and about its framers, even I can speak respectfully of that instrument and respectfully of the men who framed it. To be sure my early condition in life was not very favorable to the growth of what men call patriotism and reverence for institutions—certainly not for the "peculiar institution" from which I graduated—yet even I can speak respectfully of the Constitution. For one thing I feel grateful—at least I think the fathers deserve homage of mankind for this—that against the assumptions, against the inducements to do otherwise, they have given us a Constitution commensurate in its beneficent arrangements with the wants of common humanity; that it embraces man as man. There is nothing in it of a narrow description. They could establish a Constitution free from bigotry, free from superstition, free from sectarian prejudices, caste or political distinction.

In the eye of that great instrument we are neither Jews, Greeks, Barbarians or Cythians,[7] but fellow-citizens of a common country, embracing all men of all colors. The fathers of this republic did not learn to insert the word white (applause and laughter), or to determine men's rights by their color. They did not base their legislation upon the differences among men in the length of their noses or the twist of their hair, but upon the broad fact of a common human nature.

I doubt if at any time during the last fifty years we could have received a constitution so liberal from the sons as we have received

6. From the Preamble to the U.S. Constitution.

7. Cythians, usually spelled "Scythians," were a nomadic warring people found on the Central Eurasian steppes (ninth century B.C.E. to fourth century C.E.).

from the fathers of the Republic. (Cheers.) They were above going down, as certain men—Caucasian and Teutonic ethnologists—have recently done, on their knees and measuring the human heel to ascertain the amount of intelligence he should have. They were above that. That is a modern improvement or invention.

Some have undertaken to prove the identity of the negro, or the relationship of the negro with the monkey from the length of his heel, forgetting what is the fact, that the monkey has no heel at all, and that in fact the longer a man's heel is the further he is from the monkey. (Laughter and applause.) Our fathers did not fall into this mistake. They made a constitution for men, not for color, not for features. In the eye of that great instrument the moment the chains are struck from the limbs of the humblest and most whip scarred slave he may rise to any position for which his talents and character fit him. (Loud applause.) For this I say the fathers are entitled to the profound gratitude of mankind—that against all temptations to do otherwise, they have given us a liberal constitution.

But wise and good as that instrument is, at this point and at many others, it is simply a human contrivance. It is the work of man and men struggling with many of the prejudices and infirmities common to man, and it is not strange that we should find in their constitution some evidences of their infirmity and prejudices. Time and experience and the ever increasing light of reason are constantly making manifest those defects and those imperfections, and it is for us, living eighty years after them, and therefore eighty years wiser than they, to remove those defects—to improve the character of our constitution at this point where we find those defects.[8]

I was rather glad at one feature in the effect produced by the rebellion. It for a time depressed the national exultation over the perfection of the Constitution of the United States. The uprising of that rebellion was a severe blow to our national extravagance at this point, but the manner in which we have met the rebellion, and as

8. The U.S. Constitution was ratified on June 21, 1788.

soon as we have succeeded in suppressing it, conquering the rebels and scattering their military forces, our old time notions of our perfect system of government have revived, and there is an indisposition on the part of some men to entertain propositions for amending the Constitution. But I think that a right view of our trouble, instead of increasing our confidence in the perfection of the fundamental structure of the government, ought to do quite the reverse; it ought to impress us with the sense of our national insecurity by disclosing, as it does disclose, the slenderness of the thread on which the national life was suspended, and showing us how small a circumstance might have whelmed our government in the measureless abyss of ruin, prepared for it by the rebels.

We succeeded in putting down the rebellion. And wherein is the secret of that success? Not in, I think, the superior structure of our government, by any means. We succeeded in that great contest because, during at least the latter part of the war, the loyal armies fought on the side of human nature; fought on the side of justice, civil order and liberty. This rebellion was struck with death the instant Abraham Lincoln inscribed on our banner the word "Emancipation." (Cheers.) Our armies went up to battle thereafter for the best aspirations of the human soul in every quarter of the globe, and we conquered. The rebel armies fought well, fought bravely, fought desperately, but they fought in fetters. Invisible chains were about them. Deep down in their own consciences there was an accusing voice reminding them that they were fighting for chains and slavery, and not for freedom. (Cheers.) They were in chains—entangled with the chains of their own slaves. They not only struggled with our gigantic armies, and with the skill of our veteran generals, but they fought against the moral sense of the nineteenth century— they fought against their own better selves—they fought against the good in their own souls; they were weakened thereby; their weakness was our strength, hence our success. And our success over the rebels is due to another cause quite apart from the perfection of our structure of government. It is largely owing to the fact that the

nation happened—for it only happened—we happened to have in
the presidential chair, an honest man. (Cheers.) It might have been
otherwise. It was our exceeding good fortune that Abraham Lincoln—not W[illia]m. H. Seward—received the nomination at Chicago in 1860.⁹ Had Wm. H. Seward—judging him by his present
position¹⁰—had Franklin Pierce, had Millard Fillmore, had James
Buchanan, or had that other embodiment of political treachery,
meanness, baseness, ingratitude, the vilest of the vile, the basest of
the base, the most execrable of the execrable of modern times—he
who shall be nameless¹¹ (great laughter and applause), occupied the
Presidential chair your magnificent republic might have been numbered with the things that were.

We talk about the power of the people over this government, of
its admirable checks and balances, its wisely arranged machinery;
but remember those three months, the last three months of Buchanan's administration. It is impossible to think wisely and deeply
without learning a lesson of the inherent weakness of our republican structure. For three long months the nation saw their army and
their navy scattered and the munitions of war of the government
placed in the hands of its enemies.¹² The people could do nothing
but bite their lips in silent agony. They were on a mighty stream
afloat, with all their liberties at stake and a faithless pilot on their

9. Abraham Lincoln defeated William H. Seward for the Republican presidential
nomination in May 1860.
10. His unswerving loyalty to Andrew Johnson and his efforts to create a new
conservative party to support Johnson's administration had made Seward highly unpopular in most Republican circles by 1867.
11. Vice President Andrew Johnson (1808–75) assumed the presidency on 15 April
1865, following the assassination of Abraham Lincoln. Radical Republicans opposed
Johnson over Reconstruction but failed in an attempt to impeach him in 1867.
12. Douglass alludes to the ill-prepared condition of U.S. military forces during
the secession crisis that began in December 1860. The bulk of the 16,000-man army
was scattered in small units across the trans-Mississippi frontier, and a majority of the
U.S. Navy's ninety-odd warships were either on foreign duty or out of commission.
A large proportion of federal munitions and naval supplies were stored in arsenals
and bases in Southern states, and fell into Confederate hands during President Buchanan's last weeks in office.

boat. They could not help this. They were in a current which they could neither resist nor control. In the rapids of a political Niagara, sweeping the nation on, on, in silent agony toward the awful cataract in the distance to receive it. Our power was unable to stay the treachery.

We appealed, to be sure—we pointed out through our principles the right way—but we were powerless, and we saw no help till the man, Lincoln, appeared on the theater of action and extended his honest hand to save the Republic. (Cheers.) No; we owe nothing to our form of government for our preservation as a nation—nothing whatever—nothing to its checks, nor to its balances, nor to its wise division of powers and duties. It was an honest President backed up by intelligent and loyal people—men, high minded men that constitute the State (cheers), who regarded society as superior to its forms, the spirit as above the letter—men as more than country, and as superior to the Constitution. They resolved to save the country with the Constitution if they could, but at any rate to save the country. To this we owe our present safety as a nation.

Because a defective ship with a skillful captain, a hard-handed and honest crew, may manage to weather a considerable storm, is no proof that our old bark is sound in all her planks, bolts and timbers—because by constant pumping and extraordinary exertions we have managed to keep afloat and at last reach the shore.

I propose to speak to you of the sources of danger to our republic. These may be described under two heads, those which are esoteric in their character and those which are exoteric. I shall discourse of these in the order now stated. Let it not, however, be supposed by my intelligent audience that I concede anything to those who hold to the inherent weakness of a republican form of government. Far from this. The point[s] of weakness in our government don't touch its republican character. On the contrary I hold that a republican form of government is the strongest government on earth when it is thoroughly republican. Our republican government is weak only as it touches or partakes of the character of monarchy or an aristocracy or an oligarchy. In its republican features it is strong. In its despotic features it is weak. Our government, in its ideas, is a government of the people. But unhappily it was framed under conditions unfavorable to purely republican results, it was projected and completed under the influence of institutions quite unfavorable to a pure republican form of government—slavery on the one hand, monarchy on the other.

Late in a man's life his surroundings exert but a limited influence upon him—they are usually shaken off; but only a hero may shake off the influences of birth and early surroundings; the champion falls—the cause remains. Such is the constitution of the human mind, that there can be no such thing as immediate emancipation, either from slavery or from monarchy. An instant is sufficient to snap the chains; a century is not too much to obliterate all traces of former bondage.

It was easy for the Fathers of the Republic, comparatively so at least, to drive the red-coats from our continent, but it was not easy to drive the ideas and associations that surrounded the British throne and emanated from the monarch of this country. Born, as the Fathers of this Republic were, under monarchical institutions, they very naturally, when they came to form a government—although they assented to what Rufus Choate called "the glittering generalities of the Declaration of Independence,"[13] they were disposed to blend something of the old error with the new truth, or of the newly discovered truth of liberty asserted in the Declaration of Independence. The eclectic principle may work pretty well in some governments, but it does not work well in our government. Here there must be unity; unity of idea; unity of object and accord of motive as

13. In a public letter in August 1856, Rufus Choate (1799–1859), a diehard Massachusetts Whig, condemned the nascent Republican party for frightening the South by "its mission to inaugurate freedom and put down the oligarchy; its constitution the glittering and sounding generalities of natural right which make up the Declaration of Independence." Samuel Gilman Brown, ed., *The Works of Rufus Choate; with a Memoir of His Life*, 2 vols. (Boston: Little, Brown, 1862), 1:215.

well as of principles; in order to [attain] a harmonious, happy and
prosperous result.

The idea of putting new wine into old bottles or mending old garments with new cloth was not peculiar to the Jew;[14] it came down to
the fathers, and it is showing itself now amongst us. We are disposed
to assent to the abolition of slavery, but we wish to retain something
of slavery in the new dispensation. We are willing that the chains of
the slave shall be broken if a few links can be left on his arm or on
his leg. Your fathers were in some respects after the same pattern.
They gave us a Constitution made in the shadow of slavery and of
monarchy, and in its character it partakes in some of its features of
both those unfavorable influences. Now, as I have said, I concede
nothing to those who hold to the inherent weakness of our government or a republican form of government. The point of weakness
or the features that weaken our government are exotic. They have
been incorporated and interposited from other forms of government, and it is the business of this day and this generation to purge
them from the Constitution. (Cheers.)

In fact, I am here to-night as a democrat, a genuine democrat
dyed in the wool. (Laughter.) I am here to advocate a genuine
democratic republic; to make this a republican form of government,
purely a republic, a genuine republic; free it from everything that
looks toward monarchy; eliminate all foreign elements, all alien elements from it; blot out from it everything antagonistic of republicanism declared by the fathers—that idea was that all governments
derived their first powers from the consent of the governed;[15] make
it a government of the people, by the people and for the people,
and for all the people,[16] each for all and all for each; blot out all

14. Matt. 6:16–17.

15. A close quotation of the Declaration of Independence: "Governments are
instituted among Men, deriving their just powers from the consent of the governed."

16. Douglass is quoting Lincoln's Gettysburg Address: " government of the people, by the people, for the people shall not perish from the earth."

discriminations against any person, theoretically or practically, and make it conform to the great truths laid down by the fathers; keep no man from the ballot box or jury box or the cartridge box, because of his color—exclude no woman from the ballot box because of her sex. (Applause.) Let the government of the country rest securely down upon the shoulders of the whole nation; let there be no shoulder that does not bear up its proportion of the burdens of the government. Let there [be] no conscience, no intellect in the land not directly responsible for the moral character of the government—for the honor of the government. Let it be a genuine Republic, in which every man subject to it is represented in it, and I see no reason why a Republic may not stand while the world stands. (Applause.)

Now, the first source of weakness to a republican government is the one man power. I rejoice that we are at last startled into a consciousness of the existence of this one man power. If it was necessary for Jeff[erson] Davis and his peculiar friends to resort to arms in order to show the danger of tolerating the slave power in our government, we are under great obligations to Andrew Johnson for disclosing to us the unwisdom of tolerating the one man power in their government. (Applause.) And if now we shall be moved, as I hope we shall, to revise our Constitution so as to entirely free it from the one man power, to curtail or abridge that power, and reduce [it] to a manageable point, his accidental occupancy of the Presidential chair will not be the unmitigated calamity we have been accustomed to regard it. (Laughter and applause.) It will be a blessing in disguise[17]—though pretty heavily disguised. (Laughter.) For disguise it as we will, this one man power is in our constitution. It has its sheet anchor firmly in the soil of our constitution.[18] Mr. Johnson has sometimes overstepped this power, in certain conditions of his mind, which are quite frequent, and mistaken himself for the

17. This phrase can be traced back to a poem by James Hervey (1714–58) found in his book *Reflections on a Flower-Garden in a Letter to a Lady* (London: J. and J. Rivington, 1746), 76.

18. A sheet anchor is the largest ship anchor.

United States instead of the President of the United States. The fault is not entirely due to his marvelous vanity, but to the constitution under which he lives. It is there in that Constitution. The "fantastic tricks" recently played "before high heaven" by that dignitary when sandwiched between a hero of the land and of the sea, and swinging around the circle from the Atlantic to the Mississippi[19]— we must break down the main spring of those tricks in the Constitution before we shall get rid of them elsewhere.

It is true that our President is not our King for life; he is here only temporarily. I say King. Mr. Seward, you know, took it upon himself to introduce Andrew Johnson to the simple-hearted people of Michigan as king. "Will you have him as your President or as your King," said the astute Secretary of State, evidently regarding the one title as appropriate to Andy Johnson as the other.[20] There is a good deal of truth in it, for in fact he is invested with kingly power, with an arbitrariness equal to any crown-head in Europe. Spite of our boasts of the power of the people, your President can rule you as with a rod of iron. It is true he is only elected for four years—he is only a four-year old—and the brief time of the term would seem to be a security against misbehavior; a security and a guarantee of

19. Andrew Johnson undertook an extended speaking tour of the North from 28 August to 15 September 1866. To help ensure a favorable reception, Johnson took along two Civil War military heroes: General Ulysses S. Grant and Admiral David G. Farragut. Johnson was politely received at his first stops. Heckling during his speech on 3 September, however, provoked him into several undignified exchanges with audience members. Similar incidents occurred during speeches in St. Louis and Pittsburgh, and the Republican press accused Johnson of public drunkenness. His political opponents ridiculed Johnson's intemperate declaration that having fought the traitors in the South, he was "swinging around full circle" to fight Northern traitors such as Charles Sumner and Thaddeus Stevens.

20. Seward accompanied Johnson on the latter's "swing around the circle" tour and preceded the president on the platform in Battle Creek, Michigan, on 5 September 1866. Seward addressed several questions to the audience: "Now, I will ask you, Do you want a tyrant to rule over you or your legally elected Governor? Do you want Andrew Johnson to be President or King? (Shouts of 'President!' 'President and no king!') That is President of twenty-five states? (Cries of 'Yes!' and 'No!') Do you want him to be President of thirty-six states? (Cries of 'No! no!' and 'Yes!' The ayes have it." New York *Herald,* September 1866; New York *Tribune,* September 1866.

good conduct, for the most turbulent of men can manage to behave themselves for short periods—always excepting the "Humble
Individual."[21] But the brief time—this brief time is no security—
to my mind it furnishes impunity rather than security. We bear, in
one of these Presidents' behavior, arrogance and arbitrariness that
we would not bear with but for the limited term of his service. We
would not bear it an hour—the disgrace and scandal that we now
stagger under—did we not know that two short, silent years will put
an end to our misery in this respect.

It is true that we choose our President, and that would seem
to show that the people after all rule. Well, we do choose him; we
elect him, and we are free while we are electing him. When I was
a slave; when I was first the privilege given hereafter of choosing
my own master at the end of the year I was very much delighted.
It struck me as a large concession to my manhood, the idea that I
had the right to choose a master at the end of the year, and if I was
kicked, and cuffed, bruised and beaten, during the year it was some
satisfaction to know that after all, old fellow, I will shake you off at
the end of the year. (Laughter.) I thought it a great thing to be able
to choose my own master. I was quite intoxicated with this little bit
of liberty—and I would dance from Christmas to New Year on the
strength of it. But, as I grew older and a trifle wiser, I began to be
dissatisfied with this liberty, the liberty of choosing another master.
I found that what I wanted, that what I needed, what was essential
to my manhood was not another master, not a new master, not an
old master, but the right to the power under the law to be my own
master. (Cheers.) From this little bit of experience—slave experience—I have elaborated quite a lengthy chapter of political philosophy, applicable to the American people. You are free to choose,
but after you have chosen your freedom is gone, just as mine was—
gone, and our power is gone to a large extent under the framework

21. During his tour, Johnson made so many personal references to himself that
the Republican press condemned his lack of humility.

of our government when you have chosen. You are free to choose, free while you are voting, free while you are dropping a piece of paper into the box with some names on it—I won't tell how those names got on it; that would evince, perhaps, a culpable familiarity with politics to do that. (Laughter.) But you are free while you are dropping in your vote—going, going, gone. (Laughter.) When your President is elected, once familiarly seated in the national saddle, his feet in the stirrups, his hand on the reins, he can drive the national animal almost where he will. (Laughter.) He can administer this government with a contempt for public opinion, for the opinions and wishes of the people, such as no crowned head in Europe imitates towards his subjects.

Take, for instance, the government of England. It is sufficiently despotic and autocratic, but after all that government is administered with a deference for popular opinion far superior—far greater than our own. When the prime minister of England finds himself out-voted on the floor of the House of Commons by the people's representatives, what does he do? He lays the seals of his office at the foot of the throne; calls upon the national sovereignty to organize another government, more in harmony with the wishes and opinions of the people than he is able to be. He construes a vote against any great measure of his as a vote of want of confidence, and he is not willing to hold power when he is convinced that the people of the country are against him. He resigns.

Mr. Doolittle[22] has recently been invited to resign; he prefers to remain where he is. Mr. Cowan[23] has been invited to resign; he prefers to remain and serve his term out. Patriotic man! The wishes and the will of the people! Why, the people of this country expressed a desire that Andy Johnson might retire from his present position. Is there any likelihood of his doing so in deference to your opinion? No. And you have no power to make him do so under your government. He is there for four years, and your only comfort, your only consolation, for whatever usurpation and misbehavior he is guilty of, is, that by and by you will have the right to elect another. What I needed for my manhood was, that I should be my own master. What the American people need for their manhood and their national security is, that the *people* shall, in time of war, and in time of peace be the masters of their own government.

Now what are the elements that enter into this one man power and swell it to the formidable measure at which we find it at this time? The first thing is the immense patronage of the President of the United States—the patronage of money, of honor, of place and power. He is able to divide among his friends and among his satellites—attaching men to his person and to his political fortunes— a hundred million of dollars per annum in time of peace, and uncounted thousands of millions of dollars in time of war are virtually at his disposal. This is an influence which can neither be weighed, measured nor otherwise estimated. The very thought of it is overwhelming. This amount of money lodged outside of the government in unfriendly hands could be made a formidable lever for the destruction of the government. It is a direct assault upon the national virtue. While the President of the United States can exalt whom he will, cast down whom he will; he can place A into office for agreeing with him in opinion, and cause B to be put out of office because of an honest difference of opinion with him. Who does not see that the tendency to agreement will be a million times stronger than the tendency to differ, even though truth should be in favor of difference. From this power—this patronage—has arisen the popular political maxim that "to the victors belong the spoils,"[24] and that other vulgar expression of the same idea by Postmaster General Randall,[25] that no man shall eat the President's "bread and butter" who does not indorse the President's "policy." The first thing that an American is taught at the cradle side is never to fight against his bread and butter.

22. One of Andrew Johnson's most loyal supporters in the U.S. Senate, James Rood Doolittle (1815–97), of Wisconsin, aligned himself with the Democrats in 1868. He lost his Senate seat and subsequent races for governor and the U.S. House of Representatives.

23. Senator Edward Cowan's (1815–85) opposition to Radical Republican measures and his support for Andrew Johnson completed his alienation from Pennsylvania Republicans, and he was not reelected to a second Senate term.

Now I hold that this patronage should be abolished, that is to say that the President's control over it should be abolished. The Constitution evidently contemplated that the large arm of our government should control the matter of appointments. It declares that the President may appoint by and with the consent and with the advice of the Senate;[26] he must get the Senate's advice and consent, but custom and a certain laxity of administration has almost obliterated this feature of the Constitution, and now the President appoints, he not only appoints by and with the consent, but he has the power of removal, and with this power he virtually makes the agency of the Senate of the United States of no effect in the matter of appointments. I am very glad to see that a movement is on foot in Congress to make the appointments by the President or removal by the President alone illegal.[27] The security which you and I will have against the President is that the same power that is required to appoint shall be required to remove; that if the President can only appoint with the advice and consent of the Senate, he shall remove with the advice and consent of the Senate. If the President's power at this point were abridged to this extent the case would be helped materially.

Another source of evil in the one man power is the veto power. I am in favor of abolishing the veto power completely. It has no business in our Constitution.[28] It is alien to every idea of republican government—borrowed from the old world, from king craft and priest

24. In remarks in the Senate on January 25, 1832, Senator William L. Marcy, of New York, declared that U.S. politicians "see nothing wrong in the rule, that to the victor belong the spoils of the enemy." *Gales and Seaton's Register of Debates in Congress,* 22d Cong., 1st sess., 1325.

25. Alexander Williams Randall (1819–72), a Lincoln appointee, was promoted to postmaster general (1863–66) by Andrew Johnson. Randall supported the unsuccessful effort to form a conservative political coalition behind the president.

26. Article II, section 2, clause 2, of the U.S. Constitution.

27. In February 1867, Congress passed Tenure of Office Act to curtail Andrew Johnson's power to dismiss federal officeholders. The bill required that the Senate approve the removal of any official whose appointment had required the body's consent. Andrew Johnson vetoed the bill as unconstitutional on 2 March 1867, but Congress overrode his veto on the same day.

craft, and all other adverse craft to republican government. It is
anti-republican, anti-democratic, anti-common sense. (Applause.)
It is based upon the idea, the absurdity, that one man is more than
many men—that one man separate from the people by his exalted
station—one man sitting apart from the people in his room, surrounded by his friends, his cliques, his satellites, will be likely to
bring to the consideration of public measures, a higher wisdom, a
larger knowledge, a purer patriotism, than will the representatives
of the republic in the face and in the presence of the multitude with
the flaming sword of the press waving over them, directly responsible to their constituents, immediately in communication with the
great heart of the people—that one man will be likely to govern
more wisely than will a majority of the people. It is borrowed from
the old world; it is alien to our institutions; it is opposed to the very
genius of free institutions, and I want to see it struck out of our
Constitution. (Loud applause.) I believe that two heads are better
than one, and I shall not stultify myself by saying that one head,
even though it be the head of Andrew Johnson, is more than almost
two-thirds of the representatives of the American people. Is that
Republicanism? Is that Democracy? Is that consistent with the idea
that the people shall rule? I think not.

But it is said that we must have a check some where. We are
great on checks. We must have some checks against these fanatical
majorities, and we have recently been told that majorities can be as
destructive and more arbitrary than individual despots, especially
when the individuals are humble "Uriah Heeps."[29] (Laughter.) If
this be so; if this is the truth, I think that we ought to part with
Republican government at once. If it be true that one man is more
likely to be wiser, or is likely to be wiser than the majority—that one
man is likely to wield the government more entirely [in] the interest
of the people than will a majority, if one man is a safer guide for the

28. Article I, section 7, clause 3, of the U.S. Constitution empowers the president
to veto legislation passed by Congress.

people than nearly two-thirds of the best representatives—if that be true, let us have a one man government at once, let us have done with republicanism—let us try the experiment of the one man government. And I would advise you to begin with a legitimate scion of some of the great families of Europe. Let us take a genuine sprig of the article. We can easily get one—they are becoming very abundant in Europe I am told. There is one now, I think, one that is out of place, and you need not send across the Atlantic for him. He is driving about down here in Mexico. You might send for Maximilian, and have a one man government alone.[30] And we should have the veto legitimate.

I believe majorities can be despotic and have been arbitrary, but arbitrary to whom? Arbitrary when arbitrary at all, always to unrepresented classes. What is the remedy? A consistent republic in which there shall be no unrepresented classes. For when all classes are represented the rights of all classes will be respected. (Cheers.) It is a remarkable fact, and we Americans may well ponder it, that although the veto is entirely consistent with monarchical government and entirely inconsistent with republican government, the government of England, which is a monarchy, has not exercised the veto power once in 150 years.[31] There where it is consistent it is never used. Here where it is inconsistent, and at war with the genius of our institutions we can have a little veto every morning. Where the people rule they are the vetoed. When any measure passes the

29. Douglass probably paraphrases the arguments in Andrew Johnson's message of 7 January 1867, which vetoed the District of Columbia suffrage bill. Johnson quoted James Madison, Thomas Jefferson, James Kent, and Joseph Story to support his claim that majorities in the legislative branch of government could potentially be more despotic than the executive branch. Douglass compares Johnson to Uriah Heep, a fictional character in Charles Dickens's novel *David Copperfield* (1850), whose hypocritical humility was similar to the Radical Republicans' portrayal of Johnson.

30. Archduke Ferdinand Maximilian Joseph (1832–67) accepted an offer from Napoleon III to become ruler of a prospective empire in Mexico. His attempt to rally popular support for his throne failed, and diplomatic pressure from the United States forced the French to withdraw their troops in early 1867. After refusing to abdicate, he was captured by republican forces and executed.

House of Commons or House of Lords, it is sure of the royal assent. Popular as Queen Victoria is, honored as she is queen, loved as she is a mother,[32] as a good citizen of the realm, it would cost her her crown to veto a measure passed by the people's representatives in the House of Commons and by the House of Lords. But here the people have got used to it, like the eels that got used to being skinned—so used to it that they feel no indignation at the arrogance and presumption that one man exhibits in opposing his judgment to the judgment of the people's representatives. You have got used to it. I see no indignation at all at this impertinence. We have become so listless and indifferent about the dignity of the people, that we can see it insulted with a veto every month.

Now, I have looked down on the House of Commons and the House of Lords, and I have listened to the eloquence of their noblest orators, Sir Robert Peel,[33] Lord John Russell,[34] Richard Cobden and John Bright—a man whose name should never be mentioned in an American audience without moving it. I have listened to Lord Brougham[35] and to Lord Palmerston,[36] and I have also looked down on the Senate of the United States, and heard the debates there, and I am free to say, without wishing to disparage the English House of Parliament, in all the elements going to exalt and dignify a high deliberative assembly, our Senate compares favorably with the House of Lords. I think it the superior of the House of Lords and our House of Representatives fully the equal of the House of Commons in England. And if in a monarchy the representatives of the people can be trusted to govern themselves without the veto,

31. Queen Anne exercised the last royal veto, on a Scottish militia bill in 1707.

32. The queen of Great Britain since 1837, Victoria (1819–1901) married Prince Albert of Saxe-Coburg-Gotha (1819–1861) in 1840 and was the mother of nine children.

33. Sir Robert Peel (1788–1850), a popular Conservative (Tory) statesman, was elected twice to the prime minister's office (1834–35, 1841–46).

34. Lord John Russell (1792–1878), a champion of political and social reform, served as British prime minister from 1846 to 1852 and from 1865 to 1866.

Republican Americans can't you? Have done with that veto. It is a fruitful source of mischief, and bad bold men. A man of vigorous intellect, imperious will, fiery temper and boundless ambition finds in that veto a convenient instrument for the gratification of all his desires and his base ambition. Do away with it; blot it out from your government, and you will have done with the antagonism between the legislative arm and the executive arm of the government. Make your President what you ought to be, not more than he ought to be, and you should see to it that such changes should be made in the Constitution of the United States that your President is simply your executive, that he is there not to make laws, but to enforce them; not to defy your will, but to enforce your high behests.

Another thing I would do. I would abolish, if I had it in my power, the two-term principle. Away with that. While that principle remains in the Constitution—while the President can be his own successor, and is eligible to succeed himself,[37] he will not be warm in his seat in the presidential chair (such is poor human nature), before he will begin to scheme for a second election. It is a standing temptation to him to use the powers of his office in such a manner as to promote his own political fortune. The presidency is too valuable to allow a man who occupies the position the means of perpetuating himself in that office. Another objection to this provision of the Constitution is, that we have a divided man in the presidential chair. The duties of the presidency are such as to require a whole man, the whole will, and the whole work; but the temptation of a President is to make himself a President of a Presidential party as well as of the country, and the result is that we are only half served. What we want

35. Henry Peter Brougham (1778–1868), 1st Baron Brougham and Vaux, a prominent leader of the Whig party, is chiefly remembered for the role he played in the parliamentary struggle to abolish slavery.

36. Henry John Temple (1784–1865), 3rd Viscount Palmerston, was twice prime minister (1855–58, 1859–65).

37. George Washington established the precedent for a two-term presidency, but contrary to what Douglass implies, that limit was not part of the U.S. Constitution.

is the entire service of a man reduced to one term, and then he can bring to the service of his country an undivided man, an undivided sense of duty and devote his energies to the discharge of his office without selfish ends or aims. Blot out this two-term system.

Another thing I would abolish—the pardoning power.[38] I should take that right out of the hands of this one man. The argument against it is in some respects similar to that used against the veto power. Those against the veto power are equally persistent against the pardoning power, and there is a good reason why we should do away with the pardoning power in the hands of the President, that is that our government may at some time be in the hands of a bad man. When in the hands of a good man it is all well enough, and we ought to have our government so shaped that even when in the hands of a bad man we shall be safe. And we know that the people are usually well intentioned. A certain per centage are thieves, a certain per centage are robbers, murderers, assassins, blind, insane and idiots. But the great mass of men are well intentioned, and we should watch the individual. Trust the masses always. That is good Democracy, is it not? Not modern, but old-fashioned. But my argument is this: A bad President, for instance, has the power to do what? What can he not do? If he wanted to revolutionize this government, he could easily do it with this ponderous power; it would be an auxiliary power. He could cry "havoc, and let slip the dogs of war,"[39] and say to the conspirators: "I am with you. If you succeed, all is well. If you fail, I will interpose the shield of my pardon, and you are safe. If your property is taken away from you by Congress, I will pardon and restore your property. Go on and revolutionize the government; I will stand by you." The bad man will say or might say this. I am not sure but we have got a man now who comes very near saying it. Let us have done with this pardoning power. We have had enough of this. Pardoning! How inexpressibly base have been the uses made by this

---

38. The pardoning power of president is stated in article II, section 2, clause 1, of the U.S. Constitution.

power—this beneficent power. It has been that with which a treacherous President has trafficked. He has made it the means of securing adherents to himself instead of securing allegiance to the government. Let us have done with closet pardons—pardons obtained by bad men—pardons obtained by questionable women—pardons obtained in the most disgraceful and scandalous manner.[40] Drive this pardoning power out of the government and put it in the legislative arm of the government in some way. Let a committee of the House of Representatives and Senate of the United States determine who shall be the recipients of the clemency at the hands of the nation. Let it not come from an individual, but let it come from the people. An outraged people know to whom to extend this clemency.

Another thing I am in favor of. I am in favor of abolishing the office of the Vice President. Let us have no more Vice Presidents. (Cheers.) We have had bad luck with them. (Laughter.) We don't need them. There is no more need of electing a Vice President at the same time we elect a President than there is need of electing a second wife when we have got one already. "Sufficient unto the day is the evil thereof."[41] The argument against the vice presidency is to me very conclusive. It may be briefly stated thus: The presidency of the United States, like the crown of a monarchy, is a tempting bauble. It is very desirable thing. Men are men. Ambition is ambition the world over. History is constantly repeating itself. There is not a single crown in Europe that has not [at] some time been stained with innocent blood—not one. For the crown, men have murdered their friends who have dined at the table with them; for the crown, men have sent the assassin to the cells of their own brothers and their own sisters, and plunged the dagger into their own warm, red blood. For the crown all manner of crimes have been commit-

39. *Julius Caesar,* sc. 8, line 1363.
40. A proclamation by President Andrew Johnson in May 1865 granted full "amnesty and pardon" to almost all high-ranking Confederates who took an oath of loyalty to the United States.
41. Matt. 6:34.

ted. The Presidency is equally a tempting bauble in this country. I am not for placing that temptation so near any man as it is placed when we elect a Vice President. I am not for electing a man to the presidential chair, and then putting a man behind him with his ambition all leading that way—with his desires, his thoughts, all directed upon that chair, with a knowledge, at the same time, that only the President's life stands between him and the object of his ambition. I am not for placing a man behind the President, within striking distance of him, whose interest, whose ambition, whose every inclination is to be subserved by his getting that chair. The wall of assassination is too thin to be placed between a man and the Presidency of the United States. (Cheers.) Let your Vice President be unknown to himself and unknown to the people. Let him be in the mass till there is need for him. Don't plump him right upon the President. Your President is unsafe while the shadow of the Vice President falls upon the Presidential chair. How easy it would be to procure the death of any man where there are such temptations as that offered. A clique, a clan, a ring, usually forms about the Vice President.

How would you administer the government if you were President? Who would you send to the Court of St. James? Who would you send to the Court of France? Who would you appoint Postmaster General? Who would you appoint Collector of the port of New Orleans, or New York or of St. Louis? What would you do if you were President? "I would do so and so." "It suits us to a dot." (Laughter and applause.) The President dies, and in steps the Vice President. He is reminded at once of his old pledges, and he begins to try to redeem them by turning against the party who elected him. It is a remarkable fact that in no instance has any vice-president followed out the policy of the president that he was elected with. Elected on the same ticket, on the same platform, at the same time, at the instant the president is taken off the vice president has reversed the machinery of the policy on which he was elected in every instance.

General Harrison[42] was the first man suspected of entertaining opinions unfavorable to slavery. He died in a month. He was succeeded by whom? By John Tyler—one of the most violent propagandist of slavery that ever trod this continent. Where was the Whig party that elected him? Nowhere. Where was the policy on which he was elected? Nowhere.

General Taylor,[43] though a slaveholding man and an honest man towards his constituents and the people of the country, the moment it was ascertained he was in favor of admitting California as a free State if she saw fit to come with a constitution of that character and was opposed to paying ten millions of dollars to Texas on account of the claim on New Mexico,[44] there were means at hand to kill him. He died and was followed by whom?[45] By a vile sycophant who spit on the policy of his predecessor, and put himself in the service of the very men whom that President had offended. Well, they tried to murder even James Buchanan (laughter) in order that he should be followed by a younger, stronger traitor than himself. They put Mr. Breckinridge[46] behind him, and when he went down to Washington they carried him to the National Hotel and helped him to a large dose of poison.[47] (Laughter.) But in that instance the poison met its match. (Great laughter.) Who doubts that James Buchanan

---

42. William Henry Harrison (1773–1841) made his career as a military and political leader. He attracted national attention after defeating Tecumseh at the Battle of Tippecanoe Creek in 1811. In 1840, Harrison ran for president with John Tyler as his running mate, spawning the slogan "Tippecanoe and Tyler, Too."

43. Zachary Taylor (1784–1850) returned to the United States as a Mexican War hero in 1847, which led to his nomination as the Whig presidential candidate and contributed to his victory in the 1848 election. His inexperience in the political arena heightened the sectional controversy over the status of slavery in the western territories won from Mexico.

44. As part of his 1850 omnibus bill to resolve the sectional controversy caused by the Mexican Cession, Henry Clay proposed that the federal government compensate Texas with $10 million to abandon its territorial claims against New Mexico. President Zachary Taylor opposed Clay's plan and instead encouraged New Mexicans to apply for admission to statehood, making the border dispute between the two states a legal matter for the Supreme Court to resolve.

was poisoned? It was notorious at the time, and no doubt poisoned for a purpose.

To-day, to-day we mourn, the nation has to mourn, that the nation has a President, made President by the bullet of an assassin. I do not say that he knew that his noble predecessor was to be murdered. I do not say that he had any hand in it; but this I do say, without fear of contradiction, that the men who murdered Abraham Lincoln knew Andrew Johnson as we know him now. (Great applause.) Let us have done with these vice presidents. The nation can easily call a man to fill the presidential chair in case of death; besides, he is not half so likely to die. (Laughter.) It is a little remarkable, too, that whilst presidents die, vice presidents never die. (Laughter.) There is nobody behind them.

Well I had marked a number of points I intended to dwell upon. I am taking up perhaps too much of your time, to go further with internal sources of danger to the republic. I had purposed to have spoken specially of secret diplomacy, but I pass it over as one of the sources of weakness to our republican form of government. I may be told that in pointing out these sources of weakness that it is easy to find fault but not so easy to find remedies. I admit it, I agree with Robert Hale[48] that it requires more talent to build a decent pig stye than to tear down a considerable palace, and yet when the ship is to be repaired, it is of some consequence to find out where the unsound timbers are, when the opening seam is where the corroded bolt is, that we put in sounder, and I have been indicating where these points of unsoundness are. And I think I can leave this matter of reconstruction to the high constructive talent of this Anglo-Saxon

45. Millard Fillmore.
46. John Cabell Breckinridge.
47. An outbreak of dysentery in February and March 1857 at Washington's National Hotel gained national attention when president-elect James Buchanan and several members of his entourage became ill while staying there as guests. Although contemporary medical experts could not agree on the cause of the "National Hotel disease," the best available evidence points to contamination of the hotel's kitchen and pantry by sewage backed up in a frozen plumbing system.

race. The negro has done his part if he succeeds in pointing out the source of danger to the republic. You will have done your part when you have corrected or removed these sources of danger. We have already grappled with very dangerous elements in our government, and we have performed a manly part, we have removed errors, but there are some errors to be removed, not so dangerous, not so shocking, perhaps, as those with which we have grappled; but nevertheless dangers requiring removal. Happy will it be for us, happy will it be for the land, happy for coming generations, if we shall discover these sources of danger, and grapple with them in time without the aid of a second rebellion—without the people being lashed and stung into another military necessity.

It is sad to think that half the glory, half the honor due to the great act of emancipation was lost in the tardiness of its performance. It has now gone irrevocably into history—not as an act of sacred choice by a great nation, of the right as against the wrong, of truth as against falsehood, of liberty as against slavery—but as a military necessity. We are called upon to be faithful to the American government, for our emancipation as black men. We do feel thankful, and we have the same reason to be thankful that the Israelites had to be thankful to Pharaoh for their emancipation, for their liberties.[49] It was not until judgments terrible, wide-sweeping, far-reaching and overwhelming, had smitten down this nation, that we were ready to part with our reverence for slavery, and ceased to quote Scripture in its defence. It was not until we felt the land trembling beneath our feet that we heard an accusing voice in the heart; the sky above was darkened, the wail came up from millions of hearth stones in our land. Our sons and brothers slain in battle, it was not until we saw our sons and brothers returning home mere stumps of men, armless, legless, it was not until we felt all crumbling beneath us and we

48. Douglass probably refers to the British Baptist minister and essayist Robert Hall (1764–1831).

49. The circumstances of the escape of the Israelites from captivity in Egypt are described in the book of Exodus.

saw the Star Spangled Banner clinging to the masthead heavy with blood.

It was not until agony was manifested from a million of hearth-stones in our land, and the Southern sky was darkened, that we managed to part with our reverence for slavery, and to place a musket on the shoulders of the black man. We may now do from choice and from sacred choice what we did by military necessity. (Loud applause.)

"Let the Negro Alone"

An Address Delivered in New York, New York, 11 May 1869

National Anti-Slavery Standard, 29 May 1869.

Frederick Douglass was in New York City for anniversary week, when reform societies gathered for their annual meetings. He received a warm reception when he addressed the American Anti-Slavery Society in Steinway Hall. The next day, he had a more contentious exchange at the American Equal Rights Association meeting, also held in the hall. The New York *Tribune* suggested that the anniversary-week meetings had lost the "glory" of past years, perhaps because of emancipation, but noted there were 350 people present for the opening address, by Wendell Phillips, and a "much larger audience" for Frederick Douglass's evening speech, "Let the Negro Alone."[1] As of 11 May 1869, thirteen states had ratified the Fifteenth Amendment to the Constitution, enfranchising black males, and the anniversary proceedings focused on generating support among another fifteen states for ratification (full ratification required approval by twenty-eight of the thirty-seven states). Douglass, in particular, called for granting the vote as a means of protecting Radical Republicans and blacks in the South from ambushes by vigilantes seeking to suppress African American political and economic power

Douglass's speech title echoes the sentiment felt in much of the nation, which was weary from the war and wanted to "let the Negro alone." But he questions the claim that "slavery is dead," noting that "the former bondman" is "insecure in his life and property."

---

1. "American Anti-Slavery Society," New York *Tribune,* 12 May 1869.

Douglass offers a simple policy to adopt toward the Negro: "Give him fair play and let him alone, but be sure to give him fair play." He spends the bulk of his speech elaborating on what "fair play" entails.

Douglass uses ventriloquizing and comedy to capture his audience, perhaps responding to the popularity of minstrelsy shows in New York at this time. Among the sixteen shows advertised in the New York *Herald* on the day it reported his speech, four were minstrelsies and three were plays about racial exclusion or exploitation, including William Shakespeare's "The Tempest," from which Douglass, perhaps not coincidentally, quotes.[2] He responds to the association between African American performers and humor with this riff: "[African Americans] are here; love to be here; like your civilization; accept it; become a part of it. Where there are Methodists, the negro is a Methodist; where there are Baptists, he is a Baptist; where there are Quakers, he is not exactly a Quaker, because they do not make noise enough for him (laughter), but he wears at least a plain coat." In his closing to this anecdote, he changes his tone to a more serious one, demanding that African Americans be recognized as part of the "body politic." Ultimately, he asks that no person be turned away from the voting polls on account of color or sex, presaging his presence the next day at the American Equal Rights Association anniversary meeting.

The speaker following Douglass took him to task for suggesting that African Americans were more assimilable to the dominant American culture than Indians: "The Indian is an outlaw to-day, and therefore cannot be what the negro is, a citizen. When we shall make him a citizen, and give him the rights and privileges that pertain to the negroes, we shall see whether he will imitate them [and become informed and productive citizens] or not."[3] Douglass seemed to have taken this criticism to heart. In a speech delivered in Rochester, New York, a year later on 9 April, he called the assumption that Indians would die out "the most terrible reproach" to "American Christianity and civilization." He denies the inevitability of Indian removal, and

2. New York *Herald*, 11 May 1869.
3. The speaker following Douglass was Cora Daniels Tappan. She gently rebuked Douglass and spoke at some length on the need to enfranchise Indians as well as African Americans. "Thirty-Sixth Anniversary of the American Anti-Slavery Society," *National Anti-Slavery Standard*, 29 May 1869.

instead contends that their exclusion from citizenship, not their "savagery," is the actual source of the conflict. He added, "The only thing that has saved the negro [from the same exclusion and subsequent violence] is first the interest of his master, and now his being brought into the American body politic."[4]

Douglass's concluding call for neither black men nor women to be excluded from voting, though well received at the American Anti-Slavery Society, did not forestall disputes during the next day's meeting of the American Equal Rights Association. Some women's rights advocates demanded that the Equal Rights Association protest the introduction of the word "male" into the Fifteenth Amendment, thereby explicitly excluding women from suffrage for the first time. Other men and women defended the amendment's language as necessary for its passage. The debate split the movement. The Fifteenth Amendment was ratified ten months after this speech on 3 February 1870.

*M*r. President,[5] *Ladies and Gentlemen:*—It has been a long time since I had the honor to appear among the regular speakers of the American Anti-Slavery Society on an anniversary occasion like the present.[6] So long, indeed, has it been, and so vast and wonderful have been the changes which have taken place since then, that I almost hesitate to speak at all, although I appreciate very highly the sentiment to which I owe my invitation to be present on this occasion. The arguments which I once could use with some little skill and effect on occasions like this are no longer pertinent. We stand to-night amid the

4. "A Reform Absolutely Complete: An Address Delivered in New York, New York, on 9 April 1870," *Douglass Papers,* ser. 1, 4:265.

5. The president of this meeting was Antoinette Louisa Brown Blackwell (1825–1921), the nation's first female ordained minister. Blackwell resigned her Congregationalist pulpit after only one year when she converted to Unitarianism. She wrote books on a wide range of philosophical, scientific, and religious topics. Brown was away from the meeting's chair and Wendell Phillips temporarily was presiding.

6. Douglass had attended the anniversary meeting of the American Anti-Slavery Society in New York City on 10 May 1865.

bleaching bones of dead issues. Where are the arguments by which we were once confronted?—the political argument, the moral argument and the religious argument, especially? Where now are the cunning and subtle arguments framed by our Doctors of Divinity in defence of slavery, affirming it to be a divine institution against which the gates of hell should not prevail? They are all gone. I have nothing to kick against. How can I speak on the platform of the American Anti-Slavery Society when all our opponents are in full retreat, scarcely taking the time to look for new positions? Where is slavery itself? Gone—gone, I trust, forever. Its "cloud-capt towers and gorgeous palaces,"[7] stained with blood, are dissolved; and if we have any vocation here at all, any mission here, it is to see that not a rack is left behind (applause); that not one of the elements of the slave system is suffered to remain, obstructing the pathway of human progress in the future.

I am quite aware that in the minds of some, the name "American Anti-Slavery Society" is an anachronism and an impertinence. Some of my fellow-citizens tell me that slavery is dead, that it died some time ago, and that the American Anti-Slavery Society ought to have died with it.[8] The logic would be perfect, if the premises were correct. Had slavery died an honest death, the Anti-Slavery Society might have died with it. But slavery is not honestly dead, to-night. It did not die honestly. Had its death come of moral conviction instead of political and military necessity; had it come in obedience to the enlightenment of the American people; had it come at the call of the humanity and the morality and the enlightenment of the slave-holder, as well as of the rest of our fellow-citizens, slavery

7. *The Tempest*, sc. 8, line 1608.

8. At the May 1865 anniversary of the American Anti-Slavery Society, William Lloyd Garrison, the longtime president of that organization, moved for its dissolution. Wendell Phillips, Douglass, and other veteran abolitionists debated Garrison and his followers for two days before winning a decisive 118–48 vote to maintain the society. Garrison declined reelection as president and led his followers in resigning their memberships.

might be looked upon as honestly dead; but there is no such thing
conceivable, as a practical result, as the immediate, unconditional
abolition of slavery. In the nature of the case, there can be no such
thing as the immediate, unconditional, complete abolition of slavery, anywhere in the world. It would be to contradict human nature,
and all the social forces of which we have any knowledge, to assume
such a possibility. There is no such thing. An instant may snap the
chain, but a century is not too much to obliterate the traces of a former bondage. Slavery, to be sure, is abolished. The legal relation of
master and slave is abolished; but that out of which slavery sprung,
that by which it was sustained, the selfishness, the arrogance of the
master, still remain; the ignorance and servility of the slave still remain; and while the ignorance and servility of the slave, and the arrogance of the master, with his custom to bear sway over his fellows,
remain, and manifest themselves to the eye in the forms in which
we now see them all over the South, in rendering the former bondman insecure in his life and property, and making it impossible for
a Northern man, possessed of the ideas of freedom, to go safely into
that country,—while, I say, this state of facts exists, it is not correct
to assume that slavery is entirely out of the field.

The American Anti-Slavery Society, however, is only an instrument; it is only an agent. Its value consists in its efficiency. If it is
efficient, it has a reason for existing; when it ceases to be efficient,
let it perish, like any other instrumentality. It has had a glorious history. For thirty-six years, it has been constructing a magnificent arch
to bridge the howling chasm of slavery, over which four millions
of joyful bondmen might pass to liberty. (Applause.) The arch has
been built. It is beautiful to behold. Only one thing remains, and
that is to insert the keystone of the arch. That keystone is the Fifteenth Amendment.[9] (Applause.) Until that Fifteenth Amendment

9. The Fifteenth Amendment to the U.S. Constitution guarantees that the voting rights of the U.S. citizens could not be denied or abridged on account of race or
previous conditions of servitude; it was ratified on 30 March 1870.

becomes part of the Constitution of the United States, this Society
has an excellent apology for continued existence. When it is made
a part of the Constitution, I shall be prepared to consider whether
it is best to dispense with the use of this Society or not. That is a
very diplomatic statement: I shall be ready to consider it. Not quite
ready to decide, but ready to consider it. I would not dare, however,
to decide that question, until I had heard the judgment of Wendell
Phillips at considerable length.[10] (Applause.)

I do not know what more there is to say. They have all said to-day,
that it was no use to argue the wisdom of the Fifteenth Amendment. What are we to argue, then? I shall not, however, go into any
argument, for I know who are to come after me. I am merely put
forward here to-night to open the ceremonies. There is a long and
brilliant list of speakers behind me, to whom you are eager to listen;
to whom I am eager to listen, if you are not.

I have but one theory in regard to the negro, and that seems to be
conceded, by Democrats as well as Republicans. It is summed up in
one word—Let him alone! That is about your whole duty in regard
to the negro—to let him alone. You want to be doing something for
him and with him; and your doing something for us, with us and by
us has played the mischief with us already (applause); and what we
most need at this time is to be let alone. My politics in regard to
the negro is simply this: Give him fair play and let him alone, but
be sure you give him fair play. He is now a man before the law. I
rejoice at it. What we want, what we are resolved to have, is the right
to be men among men; men everywhere. Our wants, I grant you,
are many. One of our first wants is money. No people ever yet made
any considerable progress in civilization or in the estimation of their

10. Wendell Phillips made clear his position that the American Anti-Slavery Society could consider its mission completed, and would thereafter dissolve, once the
Fifteenth Amendment was ratified and African American males had their voting
rights secured. In 1870, a year after this address, Phillips's motion for the dissolution
of the American Anti-Slavery Society carried over the objections of a small minority
led by Parker Pillsbury and Stephen Foster, even as Phillips, Douglass, and other
abolitionists expressed the need for a new campaign to assist the freedmen.

fellow-men who had not money, and what the negro wants, especially just now, is money. Without money, he has no leisure; without money, the whole struggle of life is to live, and while he is contending for bread, his brains are neglected; and until we can have, as you have, a class of men of wealth, we can never have a leisure class; and until we have a leisure class, we can never have a very intelligent class; and until we have an intelligent class, we shall never be respected among our fellows. Until we can present an intelligent class, while we are all, as a race, as a class, mere hewers of wood and drawers of water,[11] we shall be forever a despised race; and therefore I like my friend Foster's proposition (not, perhaps, in the full length to which he carried it, but it embodies a truth), that the negro must have a right to the land.[12] At least, I demand for him the same right to the land, the same opportunity, and the same chance to get possession of the land that other people have. All over the South, it is well known, notorious, that the old planters, who own their ten and fifteen thousand acres of land, have banded together and determined not to sell it in small parcels or in large parcels to colored men—to keep possession of the land.[13] Therefore, this government is bound to see, not only that the negro has the right to vote, but that he has fair play in the acquisition of land; that when he offers a fair price for the land of the South, he shall not be deprived of the right to purchase, simply because of his color.

This may not seem to be consistent with my first proposition,—to let the negro alone; but it is quite consistent with what should be the first proposition—Give him fair play, and let him alone. If you see a negro wanting to purchase land, let him alone; let him

11. Josh. 9:21.

12. In a speech during the morning session, the radical abolitionist Stephen Symonds Foster (1809–81), a proponent of distributing land to the freedmen, urged that the American Anti-Slavery Society not disband until every ex-slave had been provided with a homestead.

13. On the South Carolina Sea Islands, where the federal government had permitted slaves de facto control of many abandoned plantations, planters returning after the war's end refused to sell or even rent to blacks. In later years, planters passed resolutions not to sell land to blacks in order to keep them as sharecroppers.

purchase it. If you see him on the way to school, let him go; don't say he shall not go into the same school with other people. If anybody has a right to schooling, he has; if anybody needs schooling, he does. If you see him on his way to the workshop, let him alone; let him work; don't say you will not work with him; that you will "knock off" if he is permitted to work. The newspapers of to-day tell us that some thirty-six printers in the Government printing office at Washington are utterly disgusted by the employment of a single negro printer in that establishment, and one paper states that they had leave to withdraw.[14] I hope it is so. (Applause.) The difficulty with us is, that we are a poor people, and have but few opportunities to obtain anything like a competency in the North. We are restricted to two or three employments. We do all the whitewashing. We are great on *white!* (Laughter.) I saw a colored man the other day, and says he, "As to this thing you call learning, book learning, I ain't much at that; but that thing you call laying whitewash on the wall, I am dar." (Merriment.) We are there. We have been ruled out of the workshop. It is easier to-day to get a negro boy a seat by the side of a lawyer to study law, than it is to get him a place at a blacksmith's anvil, to hammer iron. I can more easily to-day enter my son in a law office in Rochester, than I can get him into a shipyard to help build ships. The reason is, that the higher you go up in the gradations of intelligence, the further you get from prejudice, the more reasonable men are. I find it far less difficult to get along with educated men, ignorant as I am, than to get along with uneducated men. The educated men of the country are in advance of the masses. You have only to stand out among the stumps of Ohio and sing out to an ignorant crowd, "Is there any man in this land who wants to be ruled over by a nigger?" to carry the whole crowd against the suffrage amendment. That is enough. But with thinking men, that does not amount to much.

14. Considerably different reports of the incident appeared in New York City newspapers on the day of Douglass's speech. The man referred to was Douglass's son Lewis, whose problems in attempting to join the local typographical union Douglass discussed at length in his speech of 3 August 1869 in Medina, New York.

What colored men want is elbow room, and enlarged opportunities. Give them employments by which they can obtain something like a respectable living. That has been done in Washington, of late. A black man has been put into the Government printing office, another has been sent as Minister Plenipotentiary (I don't know what that may all mean) to Hayti, and another to that exotic Republic over the sea, Liberia.[15] In 1839, I believe, John Quincy Adams brought forward a proposition to recognize the independence of Hayti, and in a moment, the House of Representatives was a scene of unparalleled confusion. The whole South started angrily to its feet, and hurled at the "old man eloquent" the wildest and most withering denunciations. He bore it all.[16] Henry Clay said, "It is true, we are told that this black Republic has maintained its liberty for forty years. I care not for it. Should Time himself confront me, and shake his hoary locks at my position, I should still oppose the acknowledgment of the independence of Hayti." Hayti is to-day acknowledged. The negro Republic is on a footing of equality with other nations, and is acknowledged to be one of the sisterhood of nations; and, withal, the freest and mightiest Republic on the globe, and now or rapidly becoming recognized as the mightiest nation on the globe, the nation that is to dictate the law to the nations of Europe, the nation which more than any other beneath the sky is to give direction to the civilization of the next fifty years,—that nation sends a black Minister to Hayti (applause), and is getting ready, I trust, to reach out its hand to those brave, those heroic and noble Cubans, who are now defending the cause which this Society and all America have sworn to support.[17]

15. Ebenezer Don Carlos Bassett became the first black U.S. minister to Haiti in 1869. Contrary to Douglass's assertion, James Milton Turner, the first black U.S. minister to Liberia, was not appointed until 1871.

16. Beginning in December 1838 and for several years thereafter, John Quincy Adams and a few other Northern congressmen presented petitions to the House of Representatives calling for the diplomatic recognition of Haiti. Adams successfully blocked efforts by Southerners to have the petitions immediately tabled, but was unable to persuade the House to order its Committee on Foreign Affairs to make a report on the petitions.

17. On 10 October 1868 a group of Cuban planters launched a revolution for independence from Spanish rule. The revolutionaries' provisional government took

I have some sympathy with my Democratic brethren, after all. There is one thing about them—they have always been logical; and seen a little further than the Abolitionists themselves, just a little. Long before Wendell Phillips announced the doctrine of the dissolution of the Union, John C. Calhoun saw that was just what it would come to. Long before Mr. Seward[18] announced the doctrine of the "irrepressible conflict," Mr. Calhoun saw that "irrepressible conflict," and saw that this country must be all slavery or all freedom, or there would be no going on; there must be fighting. I say I have sympathy for my Democratic friends when they say to me, "Douglass, that is all right enough, but we see where it leads." They do see where it leads. Mr. Hendricks, on the floor of the Senate, said, "Gentlemen, this thing, suffrage for the blacks, is impossible, for it means the bringing of a black Senator into this House, to be seated in one of these chairs; it is impossible."[19] He was right; it means all that, and I am just the man that is coming. (Laughter and applause.) I am like the boy who said he would go home and live with his uncle Albert, but he meant to do just what he pleased, if *his uncle Albert would let him.* (Laughter.) It means that, and it means more. You take a step in the right direction, and another opens to you evermore; take one in the wrong direction, and another and still another opens before you, until you reach the bottom, if there is any bottom, of the bottomless pit. There is no stopping. Let the negro vote, and he will be voted for; and if voted for, he will go to Congress; and if to Congress, there is no telling where he won't go. (Applause.)

---

an ambiguous position on the abolition of slavery, however, costing them any chance of U.S. intervention on its behalf. After a ten-year struggle, Spain ended the Cuban insurgency through a combination of military force and political reform.

18. William H. Seward.

19. Thomas Andrews Hendricks, an Indiana Democrat, held many offices, including the vice presidency under Grover Cleveland (1885). As a senator, Hendricks took a leading role in the debate over congressional passage of the Fifteenth Amendment, advancing a host of constitutional and racist arguments against the measure. The remarks that Douglass ascribes to Hendricks do not, however, appear in the official reports of the debate. The conservative Republican senator James R. Doolittle made a very similar remark on 8 February 1869. *Congressional Globe*, 40th Cong., 3d sess., 1011.

The Democrat said, "The right to vote means amalgamation." The Abolitionist said, "No, that don't follow." "It will dissolve the Union." "No it won't." "It will lead to amalgamation." "No, it won't." But it will lead just there. Don't be afraid. There was a beautiful speech made here to-day by Mrs. Blackwell. She has a theory, that all races have some distinctive peculiarity, which can be made promotive of civilization, provided they do not imitate.[20] I believe in imitation. I think the disposition to imitate what is a little in advance of what we before knew is one of the most civilizing qualities of the human mind, and I am going to imitate all the good I can, and leave unimitated all the bad I find in the world.

There is no such thing as our living in this world anywhere else than right among people, part of them. The only reason why the negro has not been killed off, as the Indians have been, is, that he is so close under your arm, that you cannot get at him. If we had set up a separate nationality, gone off on the outer borders of your civilization, right before your bayonets and swords, we should have been pushed off, precisely as the Indians have been pushed off. Our salvation, the salvation of every race in this country, is in becoming an integral part of the American government, becoming incorporated into the American body politic, incorporated into society, having common aims, common objects, and common instrumentalities with which to work with you, side by side. The further we get apart, the more we are hated; the nearer we come together, the more we are loved. Coöperation brings together. That feeling of common regard and common interest, is necessary to our salvation, necessary to that of the Indian. Senator Doolittle[21] (I think it was) said to Mr. Sumner,[22] after he had made a speech in favor of the elective

20. Newspaper reports of Antoinette Brown Blackwell's speech at the morning session of the American Anti-Slavery Society's anniversary meeting are fragmentary. In the same year as the convention, Blackwell published *Studies in General Science,* which contains remarks on the black race quite similar to Douglass's characterization of her speech. Antoinette Brown Blackwell, *Studies in General Science* (New York 1869), 330–31.

21. James Rood Doolittle.

22. Charles Sumner.

franchise, "Mr. Sumner, all this concern about the negro is absurd; he will die off in a few years. Thousands of them have already disappeared, and they are rapidly disappearing. No use to make any ado about incorporating them with this government; they will die out."[23] That was his theory.

I have been travelling over the Western States lately,[24] and have had occasion to observe the presence of vast numbers of colored people where I have not seen them before; and I think this accounts, in part, for the "dying out" of the negro at the South. They followed the Union army home by thousands, they have taken up their abodes at the North, and their old slave masters at the South regard them as dead. But they still live, and will reappear at the right time. They would die if put in the same condition with the Indian. You might plant on the outer borders of American civilization a race of angels, if you please, and it would be impossible to keep the peace between those angels and this progressive Anglo-Saxon nation. They would find some bad angels among them, or make them bad, and then use their badness as an apology for waging war upon them. They could not live in that way, and if angels could not, negroes could not, for we are too much like other people (laughter and applause); for if the negro cannot show his identity with the human family by his virtues, he can at least by his vices. I do not know any wickedness that any white man can commit that a black man cannot commit also,—they are so much alike, in all things! (Laughter.) And I know of no heroic or manly act that a white man can do, that a negro cannot do the same.

We are not going to die out, I say. Those who liken us to the Indians make one mistake. They overlook the fact that the negro is

23. Douglass very roughly paraphrases the speech that the conservative Republican senator James R. Doolittle of Wisconsin made on 8 February 1869 in opposition to the passage of the Fifteenth Amendment. *Congressional Globe*, 40th Cong., 3d sess., 1010–12.

24. In the period from February to April 1869, Douglass lectured extensively throughout Ohio, Illinois, and Minnesota.

more like the white man than the Indian, in his tastes and tendencies, and disposition to accept civilization. You see the Indian, too proud to beg, disdaining your civilization, standing at the corners of the streets, wrapped in his blanket,—refusing to imitate, refusing to follow the fashion,—with a few bead purses and baskets to sell. In his dignity and destitution, he rejects our civilization, and the consequence is, that he dies or retreats before the onward march of your civilization, from the Atlantic to the lakes, and from the lakes to the great rivers. He sees with no complacency your railroads, your steamboats, your canals, your electric wire. No thrill of joy is awakened in his heart by the announcement of any improvement in the means of transmitting intelligence or spreading civilization among men. He sees the ploughshare of American civilization tearing up the venerated graves of his ancestors, his heart sickens, and he retreats before the onward march of civilization. Taking warning by the appearance of the honey bees, six months in advance of your coming, he disappears on the western slope of the Rocky Mountains. He dislikes your civilization, dislikes and distrusts you.

It is not so with the negro. He loves you and remains with you, under all circumstances, in slavery and in freedom. You do not see him wearing a blanket, but coats cut in the latest European fashion. If you should see him going down [a] street on a rainy day, you would think there was a man walking there, if he had his back to you. He looks like a man, acts like a man, feels like a man, and the office of this Society is to make him a man among men. (Applause.) He does not die out. Some have predicted that if he only broke his fetters, he would run back to Africa, clear out to Liberia, or somewhere else. There is no such disposition in the negro. He will not die out. No race, with any such physical energy as the negro possesses, having the advantage of the cultivation of muscle for 250 years, is going to die out in a few months or years. The whole shipping the United States would not be sufficient to carry off from the United States the average increase of this race. They are here; love to be here; like your civilization; accept it; become a part of it. Where there are

Methodists, the negro is a Methodist; where there are Baptists, he is a Baptist; where there are Quakers, he is not exactly a Quaker, because they do not make noise enough for him (laughter), but he wears at least a plain coat. In short, he becomes just what other people become, and herein is the security for his continued life. He will not die out, because he has a vitality that will compare favorably with that of any other race on the globe. He cannot fade out at the South just now, because Slavery is abolished. He will not go to Liberia, because he has immense love of country. There is nothing left for you, but to incorporate him completely into the American body politic; admit him to the ballot-box, admit him to Congress, give him a seat on the benches of your courts, let him ride upon your highways and your byways and your railroads and everywhere, on equal terms with everybody else, and you will soon begin to find that Mr. Bluebeard's beard is not quite so blue after all.[25]

I know there is prejudice here; there has always been prejudice. The only way to get rid of your prejudice is to begin to treat the negro as though you had no prejudice, and very soon you will find that you have got none. There is no better way for man to cure his prejudice than to begin to do good to the victim of that prejudice. The moment you do that, that moment you find your prejudice vanish.

I went once up into Pittsfield, N.H., to deliver a lecture. While there, I called upon a good anti-slavery man, at least, a man who took the *Liberator,* and that was sufficient for me; but, although quite willing to have the negroes freed, he did not want to have them just here. I was just out of slavery, and went up there under the direction of the Board of Managers of the Massachusetts Anti-Slavery Society to deliver three lectures on Sunday. I called, as I have said, upon this man, and he told me, frankly, that he would like to have had it otherwise, but since I was there, I might stay. (Laughter.) I did stay; stayed until tea time. I found that everybody

25. A character of myth and fiction with a distinctive blue-colored beard who was reputed to have murdered numerous wives.

about the house had lost their appetite; nobody could eat; and I almost lost my own, just out of sympathy with my friends. (Laughter.) I managed, however, to take a cup of tea. The next morning, my good friend got his horse out, got his wife into the carriage, and started for meeting. His wife, excellent woman! wanted to hear me speak (of course she was excellent, because she wanted to hear me), and so they were going to the meeting, and the gentlemen, after he had got into the carriage, looked out and said, "I suppose you can find your way down?" "Yes," said I, "I guess I can." It was about two miles. I started and went down to the hall where I was to speak. I found about fifteen assembled to hear me, which was no inconsiderable congregation for that day, and I went to work to preach to them on slavery.

At the close of my discourse, my congregation separated and left me at the door of the Town Hall. My good friend Mr. Hillis[26] did not even think to say, "Well, you can find your way back again," so I didn't find my way back. (Laughter.) I was to speak again at two o'clock. The time came for the meeting, the audience came together, and I spoke until about four o'clock. I was to have another meeting at five, and the congregation separated and left me at the door. I felt by this time a little hungry. With no supper the night before, very little breakfast, and no dinner, I began to feel the want of something to eat. I went over to the hotel, and asked if I could be accommodated with some food there. The hotel-keeper said, "We don't accommodate niggers here." So I had to leave there. I went back to the Town House and stood around there for awhile. I felt somewhat desolate. I could see the good Christian people looking out of their windows at me from all directions, as if some menagerie had broken loose, and one of the wild animals had made his appearance among them.

---

26. Other versions of this anecdote appear in Douglass's speech of 31 May 1849 in Boston, Massachusetts, and in *Life and Times*, in which the abolitionist is identified as "Hilles." Moses Norris Jr. (1799–1855), a prominent Democratic politician and opponent of antislavery measures, took pity on Douglass and offered him food and shelter for the evening.

They kept their doors shut, and looked at me from the safe position
of their windows. I went into a grave-yard near by. I felt somewhat
subdued, and there was some attraction to that spot, where I could
see the end of all distinctions—the short graves and the long ones,
the mighty men as well as those who were not mighty, all on a level.
I felt then that I was suffering for righteousness' sake.[27]

While I was there, a man, with not much of the humanitarian in
his appearance, came up to me and said, "Your name is Douglass?"
Said I, "That is my name." Said he, "Mr. Douglass, you seem to have
nowhere to go, no place to stay." Said I, "That is quite true; I have
no place to go, no place to stay." Said he, "Mr. Douglass, I am not an
abolitionist, but I am a man, and if you will go to my house, you shall
be taken care of while you stay in town." I inquired his name. Said
he, "My name is Moses Norris." "Moses Norris," said I, "why you
are the gentleman who pulled George Storrs[28] out of the pulpit for
preaching abolition." "Well," said he, "no matter; I can't stand your
being out here in the rain and cold, with no place to go." "Well," said
I, "I will go with you."

I went to his house, and when I got to the door, I hear the little
children shouting, "Mother, mother, there's a nigger in the house,—
there's a nigger in the house." The mother came out, seemingly quite
angry, and shut the door behind her, as only a woman can when she
is vexed. The first chance I got, I said to the good lady, "I am suffering from a cold and hoarseness, and I know of nothing that will
ease me so readily as a little cold water and loaf sugar. You will do
me a kindness if you will give me a little loaf sugar and cold water." I
saw, upon the instant, a change in the whole appearance of the lady.
She was before chagrined, mortified, at the very thought of having a
negro in the house, but the moment she brought the water and the
sugar, and set them down before me, and said "Help yourself," and I

27. 1 Pet. 3:14.
28. George Storrs (1796–1879) was a Methodist minister with outspoken anti-
slavery views. In December 1835 and again in March 1836, Storrs was arrested on a
charge of disturbing the peace for delivering antislavery lectures in New Hampshire.

thanked her, there was a relation established between us; there was a human heart answering to another human heart. The very moment she performed this good deed for a suffering fellow creature, that very moment she felt her prejudice removed. That night, at the close of my speech, the first hand extended to me, to bid me God-speed, was the hand of Mrs. Norris, with the request that I would come to their house and make it my home whenever I came to Pittsfield.

About this time, brother Hillis was close at hand, and said he, "I kind of missed you to-day." (Laughter.) "Yes," said I, "I thought so." "Come," said he, "You must go home with me now." At first I thought I wouldn't go; but when I remembered that "there is more joy in Heaven over one sinner that repenteth than over ninety and nine just men, who need no repentance,"[29] I decided to go with him. The next day, this same man, who was so full of prejudice the day before, took me in his carriage over to [New] London, [N.H.,] where I was to speak and on the way, he paid me the compliment of saying, "Mr. Douglass, this is one of the proudest days of my life. I feel prouder to-day to have you in my carriage than I should to have the President of the United States here." John Tyler[30] was President of the United States at that time! (Roars of laughter.)

What I say to the American people every where is, "Conquer your prejudices;" and the only way to conquer them is to begin to be just, begin to be kind to this long-despised class. That the negro will not die out has been proved by the manner in which he has stood slavery. Was ever a race exposed to such elements of destruction as the negro in this country has been for 250 years? Daniel O'Connell said, twenty years ago, speaking of Ireland, "The history of Ireland may be traced like a wounded man through a crowd, by the blood." It was a strong statement of the condition of Ireland but is it not a

29. Luke 15:7.

30. John Tyler (1790–1862) became the tenth president of the United States upon the death of William Henry Harrison in April 1841. Efforts to annex Texas as a slave state failed to create enough enthusiasm to win Tyler another term. After the end of his presidency, Tyler retired to his Virginia plantation. He remerged in politics decades later to support the Confederacy.

true statement of the history of the people to whom I belong, and with whom I am identified? For 250 years, we have been robbed of every right; herded with the beasts of the field; exposed to all the exterminating forces of slavery; deprived of marriage; deprived of the family; deprived of all the saving influences of those institutions; loaded with chains; scarred by the whip; driven from time to eternity in the dark, yet where are we? Uncle Toms in Georgia; Robert Smalls[31] in the harbor of Charleston. That is where we are. Though laden with burdens that no other nation ever struggled under; though outraged as no other race has ever been outraged, we still look up and smile under it all; we still flourish under it all. If slavery has not been able to kill us, liberty will not. (Applause.) If the black man can stand all the enginery of slavery, he can stand at least the appliances of civilization.

Now, we are here; we are going to live here. What is going to be done? This—only this. Welcome the black man to any position and to every position for which his talents and character fit him. (Applause.) Do this, and you shall have peace. We have performed some service to this country. I do not take the extravagant view that some do, that the negro saved this country; that without the negro, you could not have put down the rebellion. This I do affirm, however, that we helped you put it down. When you were at your wit's ends for the means of carrying on this war, the negro came to your help, and at that time you felt rather grateful to him. At that time, you felt like enfranchising him. At that time, you were willing to bring him into full possession of his rights. When the rebel armies were in the field, bold, defiant, and in some instances triumphant, when Lee,[32] and Longstreet and Imboden were among the Alle-

31. Robert Smalls (1839–1915) was a slave sailor impressed into service aboard the *Planter*, a Charleston harbor steamer. On the night of 12–13 May 1862, Smalls and other black crewmen, together with their families, sailed the vessel past Confederate defenses and delivered themselves to the Union fleet blockading the harbor.

32. Robert Edward Lee (1807–70) campaigned brilliantly, defeating Union forces often twice the size of his own and staving off Confederate defeat in the East for nearly three years.

gheny Mountains,[33] thundering at the gates of Philadelphia, when your recruiting sergeants were marching up and down the streets from morning till night, foot sore and weary, with banner and badge, calling for more men, young men and strong men, to go to the front, to fill up the gaps made by rebel shot, and by pestilence, when your sons were coming home from the war, armless, legless, maimed and mutilated, when your churches were draped with mourning, when your country seemed to be upon its last legs, as it were, when every breeze that came to us from the broad Atlantic was suspected of bearing on its wings the tidings of British or French intervention, to the destruction of your government, when the ground trembled, as it were, beneath our feet, and, as Wendell Phillips says, the star-spangled banner clung to the masthead heavy with blood,—then, oh, then, there was room under our flag for all its defenders (applause); one liberty, one government, one nationality, for all the people of the United States. In the spirit born of affliction, born of trouble, let us legislate and go on legislating, until we put that Fifteenth Amendment into the organic law of the land; until every black man shall feel, "This is my country, and this is my government." Until you have done this, you are weak: when you have done it, you are strong. The black man came to you in the hour of danger, of trial, when your flag wavered, reached out his black iron arm, and clutched your standard with his steel fingers; and if you enfranchise him, make him a part of you, he will be ready to serve you again; he will be ready to give you not only ramparts of sand and ramparts of stone, but he will give you ramparts of human breasts, broad and strong, guided by intelligence, before whose front no nation on the earth, backed up by your intelligence, would be able to stand.

33. Two of Robert E. Lee's subordinates during the Confederate invasion of Pennsylvania in June and July 1863 were Lieutenant General James Longstreet (1821–1904) and Brigadier General John Daniel Imboden (1823–95). Longstreet fought as a division commander in Lee's army. Imboden fought under Thomas "Stonewall" Jackson in the Shenandoah Valley Campaign of 1862 and conducted a large-scale raid into western Virginia in April and May 1863 as an anticipatory movement for Lee's Pennsylvania campaign.

We are here to-night in the interest of the negro, but we are here also in the interest of patriotism, in the interest of liberty; liberty in America, liberty in Cuba, liberty the world over. Make this government a consistent government, make it a truly Republican government. Let no man be driven from the ballot-box on account of his color. Let no woman be denied the ballot-box on account of her sex. (Applause.) Let the government rest on every shoulder in it, and your government will be strong, and your country will be secure.

Excuse me for these desultory remarks. I will take my seat, and make room for our friend from England[34] and our other friends who are here to speak to you.

34. Although incorrectly identified by several New York City newspapers as "Dr. Reed," "Dr. Pease," or "Dr. Mease," the speaker following Douglass was the Englishman Frederic Richard Lees (1815–97), who supported temperance, Chartism, abolition, and factory reform.

"We Welcome the Fifteenth Amendment"

Addresses Delivered in New York, New York, 12–13 May 1869

New York *World*, 13, 14 May 1869.

Susan B. Anthony, Frederick Douglass, Elizabeth Cady Stanton, and Lucy Stone formed the American Equal Rights Association in 1866 to promote universal suffrage for both African Americans and women. Over the next three years, Douglass spoke repeatedly in favor of woman suffrage. The Republican party's leaders, however, did not officially endorse woman suffrage, and by 1868 they were publicly opposed to it. The Fourteenth Amendment provided penalties for denying the vote to *male* inhabitants of a state, meaning that the Constitution for the first time specified that men would have preferential voting rights. Likewise, the proposed Fifteenth Amendment made it unconstitutional to deny voting rights "on account of race, color, or previous condition of servitude," but made no reference to sex, which effectively left women without voting-rights protections. In the debate over ratification of the Fifteenth Amendment, African American leaders strongly supported its Republican party sponsors and sacrificed universal suffrage.

In reaction to this trend, the woman suffrage leaders Elizabeth Cady Stanton and Susan B. Anthony courted the Democratic party and forged an alliance with George Francis Train, an outspoken racist and wealthy Democrat. Both women gave speeches and wrote articles on the proposed Fifteenth Amendment, questioning black men's fitness to vote. Train, in turn, financially underwrote their woman suffrage paper, the *Revolution.*

When the American Equal Rights Association met in 1869, Douglass tried to heal the growing rift between the two factions, but he was unwilling to sacrifice his support of the Fifteenth Amendment. Stanton encountered dissent when she advocated "educated suffrage." She argued that educated white women should be given the ballot before black or immigrant men, characterizing the latter as "Patrick and Sambo and Hans and Yung Tung, who do not know the difference between a monarchy and a republic."[1] Later that morning, Anthony was called to account for misspending association funds for the exclusive benefit of woman suffragists. Douglass came to Anthony's defense, but also criticized Stanton's earlier remarks. Referring to the assassinations of black leaders and Radical Republicans in the South, he asserted that it was urgent to enfranchise black men even if the proposed amendment made no mention of women: "When women, because they are women, are hunted down through the cities of New York and New Orleans; when they are dragged from their houses and hung upon lamp posts; . . . when their children are not allowed to enter schools; then they will have an urgency to obtain the ballot equal to our own."[2]

The proceedings of the two-day convention were frequently contentious. Douglass, a veteran of convention-floor maneuvers, repeatedly sought to secure the adoption of a resolution endorsing both ratification of the Fifteenth Amendment and passage of a new constitutional amendment to secure woman suffrage, but the Stanton-Anthony faction fought any endorsement of the Fifteenth Amendment. Several times, Douglass supporters at the convention shouted down his opponents, especially the former Garrisonian abolitionist Charles C. Burleigh. At one chaotic moment when hisses had drowned out Burleigh, Douglass came to the front of the plat-

1. "Anniversary of the American Equal Rights Association," New York *Revolution,* 13 May 1869.
2. "Annual Meeting of the American Equal Rights Association," New York *Revolution,* 20 May 1869.

form and declared to the audience: "The sooner you hear my friend the sooner you will hear something better than my friend. I do not speak of myself, but hear him and you will hear something better afterwards."[3]

Ultimately, Stanton used her power as presiding officer to block any vote by the convention on Douglass's resolution, and the meeting resulted in a split in the woman suffrage movement. Stanton and Anthony formed the National Woman Suffrage Association to agitate for voting rights, equal pay, and equitable treatment of women in divorce and child custody laws. Douglass supported the narrower mission of the American Woman Suffrage Association, founded by advocates for the Fifteenth Amendment, including Lucy Stone and Henry Blackwell.

First Day [12 May 1869]

MORNING SESSION

[Speeches by Elizabeth Cady Stanton, Lucy Stone, Octavius B. Frothingham, Susan B. Anthony, Stephen S. Foster, and Mary A. Livermore.]

Mr. Frederick Douglass—Of course the vote of the Society just passed does not prevent Mr. Foster proceeding in order.[4] If, however, a different understanding is to be given to it—that no one is to be allowed to criticise the list of officers proposed, it is out of the question for me to utter a word on such a platform.[5] We are used to

3. "American Equal Rights Society," New York *World,* 14 May 1869.

4. Elizabeth Cady Stanton, as presiding officer of the convention, had declared Stephen S. Foster to be out of order for accusing Susan B. Anthony of mishandling funds of the American Equal Rights Association. Stanton then called for a vote of the convention, which confirmed her ruling.

5. Douglass alludes to the slate of proposed officers for the American Equal Rights Association, who were nominated by the convention's committee on organization earlier that morning.

freedom of speech, and there is a profound conviction in the minds of reformers in general, that error may be safely tolerated, while truth is left free to counteract it.[6] What if Mr. Foster does go on with his criticism of Miss Anthony,[7] and Mrs. Stanton[8] and the *Revolution.* [9] While Miss Anthony and Mrs. Stanton and the *Revolution* have tongues to speak, why not have free speech here about them? [Speeches by Stephen S. Foster and Henry B. Blackwell.][10]

Mr. Douglass—I came here more as a listener than to speak, and I listened with a great deal of pleasure to the eloquent address of the Rev. Frothingham[11] and the splendid address of the President. There is no name greater than that of Elizabeth Cady Stanton in the matter of Woman's Rights and Equal Rights, but my sentiments are

6. Douglass loosely paraphrases the declaration of Thomas Jefferson's first inaugural address: "Error of opinion may be tolerated where reason is left free to combat it." H. A. Washington, ed., *The Writings of Thomas Jefferson: Being His Autobiography, Correspondence, Reports, Messages, Addresses, and Other Writings, Official and Private,* 8 vols. (Washington, D.C.: Taylor & Maury, 1853–54), 8:3.

7. Susan Brownell Anthony (1820–1906) became active in the temperance and antislavery movements and was recruited by Elizabeth Cady Stanton into the women's rights campaign in the 1850s. When Stanton became president of the newly founded National Woman Suffrage Association in 1869, Anthony, a tireless organizer, was chosen head of its executive committee. She succeeded Stanton as its president upon the latter's retirement in 1892.

8. Elizabeth Cady Stanton (1815–1902) became determined to work to advance the status of women when she and other female delegates were barred from the World's Anti-Slavery Convention in London in 1840. Eight years later, Stanton, along with Lucretia Mott, organized the first women's rights convention, in Seneca Falls, New York, where Stanton had settled with her husband, Henry B. Stanton, the antislavery politician.

9. The New York *Revolution* was a weekly woman suffrage newspaper financed largely by contributions from the Democratic politician George Francis Train. Susan B. Anthony served as publisher, and Elizabeth Cady Stanton and Parker Pillsbury as coeditors. In his remarks, Stephen S. Foster accused the *Revolution* of advocating "educated suffrage," which would eliminate many freedmen as voters while admitting literate women.

10. Henry Brown Blackwell (1825–1909) was one of the nation's most prominent male feminists. Blackwell and his wife, Lucy Stone, and later their daughter, Alice Stone Blackwell, edited the *Woman's Journal,* the longest-running suffrage paper in the nation's history (1870–1917).

11. The Unitarian minister Octavius Brooks Frothingham (1822–95) developed liberal views on theological questions and on the slavery issue.

tinged a little against the *Revolution*. There was in the address to which I allude, a sentiment in reference to employment and certain names, such as "Sambo," and the gardener and the bootblack and the daughter of Jefferson and Washington, and all the rest I cannot coincide with.[12] I have asked what difference there is between the daughters of Jefferson and Washington and other daughters. (Laughter.) I must say that I do not see how any one can pretend that there is the same urgency in giving the ballot to women as to the negro. With us, the matter is a question of life and death. It is a matter of existence, at least, in fifteen states of the Union. When women, because they are women, are hunted down through the cities of New York and New Orleans; when they are dragged from their houses and hung upon lamp-posts; when their children are torn from their arms, and their brains dashed out upon the pavement; when they are objects of insult and outrage at every turn; when they are in danger of having their homes burnt down over their heads; when their children are not allowed to enter schools; then they will have an urgency to obtain the ballot equal to our own. (Great applause.)

A voice—Is that not all true about black women?

Mr. Douglass—Yes, yes, yes, it is true of the black woman, but not because she is a woman but because she is black. (Applause.) Julia Ward Howe at the conclusion of her great speech delivered at the convention in Boston last year, said, "I am willing that the negro shall get in before me."[13] (Applause.) Woman! why she has

12. In the major speech of the morning session, Elizabeth Cady Stanton asked whether the convention thought that "the daughters of Adams, Jefferson, and Patrick Henry . . . will forever linger round the camp-fires of an old barbarism with no longings to join the grand army of freedom?" New York *Revolution*, 13 May 1869.

13. The author of "The Battle Hymn of the Republic" and wife of the abolitionist Samuel Gridley Howe, Julia Ward Howe (1819–1910) made this statement at the October 1868 Boston convention that formed the New England Woman Suffrage Association. Howe was elected the new organization's president and pledged support for ratification of the Fifteenth Amendment.

ten thousand modes of grappling with her difficulties. I believe that all the virtue of the world can take care of all the evil. I believe that all the intelligence can take care of all the ignorance. (Applause.) I am in favor of woman's suffrage in order that we shall have all the virtue and all the vice confronted. Let me tell you that when there were few houses in which the black man could have put his head, this woolley head of mine found a refuge in the house of Mrs. Elizabeth Cady Stanton, and if I had been blacker than sixteen midnights, without a single star, it would have been the same. (Applause.)

THE RACE FOR SUFFRAGE BETWEEN NEGROES AND WOMEN.

Miss Anthony—I want to say a single word. The old anti-slavery school and others have said that the women must stand back and wait until the other class shall be recognized. But we say that if you will not give the whole loaf of justice and suffrage to an entire people, give it to the most intelligent first. (Applause.) If intelligence, justice, and moralities are to be placed in the government, then let the question of woman be brought first and that of the negro last. (Applause.) While I was canvassing the State with petitions in my hand and had them filled with names for our cause and sent them to the Legislature, a man dared to say to me that the freedom of women was all a theory and not a practical thing. (Applause.) When Mr. Douglass mentioned the black man first and women last if he had noticed he would have seen that it was the men that clapped and not the women. There is not the woman born who desires to eat the bread of dependence, no matter whether it be from the hand of father, husband, or brother; for any one who dares so eat her bread places herself in the power of the person from whom she takes it. (Applause.) Mr. Douglass talks about the wrongs of the negro; how he is hunted down, and the children's brains dashed out by mobs; but with all the wrongs and outrages that he today suffers, he would not exchange his sex and take the place of Elizabeth Cady Stanton. (Laughter and applause.) No matter, there is a glory—(Loud applause, completely drowning the speaker's voice.)

Mr. Douglass—Will you allow me—

Miss Anthony—Yes, anything; we are in for a fight to-day. (Great laughter and applause.)

Mr. Douglass—I want to know if granting you the right of suffrage will change the nature of our sexes. (Great laughter.)

Second Day [13 May 1869]

MORNING SESSION

[Speeches by James W. Stillman,[14] Mary A. Livermore,[15] Elizabeth Cady Stanton, Ernestine Rose,[16] and Mercy B. Jackson.[17]]

Fred. Douglass said that as there is a most important question submitted to the American people, he wanted to have a vote upon it from that audience. He then read the following resolutions:

14. In 1868–69, James Wells Stillman (1840–1912) served in the Rhode Island state legislature, where he spoke in support of granting women equal suffrage.

15. After tutoring a slaveholder's children on a Virginia plantation, Mary Ashton Rice Livermore (1820–1905) returned to her native Massachusetts and worked for abolition and temperance. An avid supporter of women's rights, she sided with Lucy Stone and helped edit the *Woman's Journal*, the voice of the American Woman Suffrage Association.

16. An immigrant from Russian Poland, Ernestine Louise Siismondi Potowski Rose (1810–92) led the lengthy campaign that ultimately won legal protection for the property rights of married women in New York. During the Civil War, she actively worked for the National Women's Loyal League.

17. After watching five of her children die of disease, Mercy Ruggles Bisbee Jackson (1802–77) of Massachusetts committed herself to the study of homeopathic medicine. She graduated from Boston's New England Female Medicine College in 1860. Jackson practiced in Boston and wrote regularly on women's health for Lucy Stone's *Woman's Journal*.

Resolved, That the American Equal Rights Association, in loyalty to its comprehensive demands for the political equality of all American citizens, without distinction of race or sex, hails the extension of suffrage to any class heretofore disenfranchised, as a cheering part of the triumph of our whole idea.

Resolved, therefore, That we gratefully welcome the pending fifteenth amendment, prohibiting disenfranchisement on account of race, and earnestly solicit the State Legislatures to pass it without delay.

Resolved, furthermore, That in view of this promised and speedy culmination of one-half of our demands, we are stimulated to redouble our energy to secure the further amendment guaranteeing the same sacred rights without limitation to sex.

Resolved, That until the constitution shall know neither black nor white, neither male nor female, but only the equal rights of all classes, we renew our solemn indictment against that instrument as defective, unworthy, and an oppressive character for the self-government of a free people. (Applause and hisses.)

LAY THE NEGRO ON THE TABLE.

A Lady—I move that these resolutions be laid upon the table for future consideration.

The President—Of course. You see these resolutions require discussion: therefore, they had better be laid upon the table for future consideration.

AFTERNOON SESSION

[Speeches by Lillie Peckham,[18] Henry Wilson,[19] Ernestine L. Rose, Sarah F. Norton,[20] Eleanor Kirk,[21] Mary F. Davis,[22] Susan B. Anthony, and Paulina W. Davis.[23]]

Mr. Douglass was received with great applause. He said that all disinterested spectators would concede that this equal rights meeting had been pre-eminently a woman's rights meeting. (Applause.) They had just heard an argument with which he could not agree— that the suffrage to the black man should be postponed to that of the women.[24] Here is a woman who, since the day that the snake

18. Elizabeth "Lily" Peckham (1843–71) spent a year at the University of Wisconsin studying law, but abandoned trying to become a lawyer after the state's bar refused to admit her. During her short life, she was a prominent lecturer on women's rights, an organizer, and a regular contributor to the suffragist paper *Revolution.*

19. Elected to the U.S. Senate from Massachusetts by a coalition of Free Soilers, Know-Nothings, and Democrats in 1855, Henry Wilson (1812–75) strongly advocated antislavery political goals and denounced the Black Codes enacted under Presidential Reconstruction. Wilson replaced Schuyler Colfax as vice president for Ulysses S. Grant's second term, but died in office.

20. Along with Susan B. Anthony, Sarah F. Norton (1838–1910) successfully lobbied Cornell University to admit female students. Norton wrote on women's economic and health issues and lectured against marriage, calling it a tool of male control over property; that stance led many suffragist leaders to shun her as too controversial for their movement.

21. "Eleanor Kirk" was the pen name of Eleanor Maria Esterbook "Nellie" Ames (1831–1908), an American journalist, novelist, and feminist. Her semiautobiographical novel *Up Broadway* (1870) describes the desperate plight of women facing seeking employment in a sexist workplace. Ames wrote often for Anthony and Stanton's periodical, the *Revolution.*

22. After an unhappy marriage, Mary Fenn Davis (1824–86) divorced and married the spiritualist lecturer Andrew Jackson Davis. Mary became a prominent leader in New Jersey's women's suffrage campaign as well as the longtime recording secretary of the National Woman Suffrage Association.

23. Paulina Kellogg Wright Davis (1813–76) was a leader in organizing the 1850 Worcester Women's Rights Convention. She remained a leading writer, lecturer, and organizer of the woman suffrage cause and sided with Susan B. Anthony and Elizabeth Cady Stanton in the disputes over the Fifteenth Amendment.

24. This opinion was expressed in a speech to the convention by Paulina W. Davis, who spoke immediately before Douglass. New York *Revolution,* 27 May 1869.

talked with our mother in the garden—from that day to this, I say, she has been divested of political rights.[25] What may we expect, according to that reasoning, when women, when—(Loud laughter and applause.)

MISS ANTHONY AND FRED. DOUGLASS.

Miss Anthony hereupon rose from her seat and made towards Mr. Douglass, saying something which was drowned in the applause and laughter which continued. Mr. Douglass was heard to say, however, "No, no, Susan," which again set the audience off in another audible smile, and Miss Anthony took her seat.

IS THERE FAIR PLAY IN THE CONVENTION?

When silence was somewhat restored, Mr. Douglass continued, saying: You see when women get into trouble how they act. Miss Anthony comes to the rescue—(Laughter)—and these good people have not yet learned to hear people through. (Laughter.) When anything goes against them they are up right away. Now I do not believe the story that the slaves who are enfranchised become the worst of tyrants.[26] (A voice—"Neither do I"; applause.) I know how this theory came about. When a slave was made a driver he made himself more officious than the white driver, so that his master might not suspect that he was favoring those under him. But we do not intend to have any master over us. (Applause.)

NOT ANOTHER MAN TO THE POLLS.

The President then took the floor and argued that not another man should be enfranchised until enough women are admitted to the polls to outweigh those who have the franchise. (Applause.) She

25. Gen. 3:1–6.
26. Paulina W. Davis expressed this opinion immediately before Douglass spoke.

did not believe in allowing ignorant negroes and ignorant and debased Chinamen to make laws for her to obey. (Applause.)

Mrs. Harper[27] (colored) asked Mr. Blackwell to read the fifth resolution of the series he submitted, and contended that that covered the whole ground of the resolutions of Mr. Douglass.

Miss Anthony—Then I move that that resolution be reconsidered.

NO TRICKS.

Mr. Douglass—Oh! no; you cannot do that while the floor is occupied.

HOW ABOUT BLACK WOMEN?

Mrs. Harper then proceeded with her remarks, saying that when it was a question of race she let the lesser question of sex go. But the white women all go for sex, letting race occupy a minor position. She liked the idea of working-women, but she would like to know if it was broad enough to take in colored women?

Miss Anthony and several others—Yes, yes.

A BOSTON OUTRAGE

Mrs. Harper said that when she was at Boston there were sixty women who rose up and left work because one colored woman went to gain a livelihood in their midst. (Applause.) If the nation could only handle one question, she would not have the black woman put a single straw in the way if only the race of men could obtain what they wanted. (Great applause.)

27. Born to free black parents in Baltimore, Maryland, Frances Ellen Watkins Harper (1825–1911) was adopted by her uncle the abolitionist William J. Watkins, after being orphaned. She published poetry and fiction throughout her life while also lecturing in behalf of abolition, woman suffrage, and temperance. Watkins, along with Mary Church Terrell, organized the National Association of Colored Women in 1894. As its president, she lobbied for a federal antilynching law and an end to the convict lease system.

"Our Composite Nationality"

An Address Delivered in Boston, Massachusetts, 7 December 1869

Typescript, Speech File, reel 14, frames 553–59, Frederick Douglass Papers, Library of Congress.

In many ways, Douglass's "Our Composite Nationality" might be read as a rejoinder to Wendell Phillips's address given three days earlier in Boston. Both speeches were part of the Parker Fraternity Lecture Course, which featured lectures by men and women on liberal causes such as woman suffrage, public education, and religious reforms.[1] Phillips's lecture, "What We Ask of Congress," argued that Congress should "protect citizenship" by ensuring voting rights, financing common schools, and giving federally owned Southern lands to the region's blacks as a "gift to loyalty."

Phillips was at a crossroads. He was considering a run for governor of Massachusetts on the Massachusetts Labor Reform party's ticket. Working-class, American-born men faced competition from Chinese workers, especially after the completion of the transcontinental railroad in 1869, and to attract their votes, Phillips may have felt he needed to endorse some action to limit Chinese immigration.[2] Phillips ended his speech with this warning: "There is a fearful problem looks to us from the Rocky Mountains. . . . The great Oriental horde is opening. The four hundred millions of Chinese are to

1. Walter M. Merrill, ed., *The Letters of William Lloyd Garrison: Let the Oppressed Go Free, 1861–1867* (Cambridge, Mass.: Harvard University Press, 1979), 58.
2. Najia Aarim-Heriot, *Chinese Immigrants, African Americans, and Racial Anxiety in the United States, 1848–82* (Urbana: University of Illinois Press, 2006), 131–33.

pour their surplus into our Western veins."[3] In depicting this image of "mixed blood," in a social climate animated by growing hysteria surrounding what was later stereotyped as the yellow peril, Phillips further stoked anti-Chinese sentiment.

In his rejoinder, Douglass delivered the following resounding defense of cultural diversity and challenged the racism that undergirded the yellow peril rhetoric. He too makes reference to the "body politic," but in his metaphor, the body is unhealthy and will remain so as long as it fails to "inspire patriotism" in all of its component parts. By denying Indians and African Americans political and civil rights, the government was sowing "the dangerous seeds of discontent and hatred" in their hearts. Both Douglass and Phillips predict a mass influx of Chinese immigrants. Unlike Phillips, however, Douglass endorses their immigration and insists that migration is a fundamental human right. Moreover, he contends that all races are capable of improvement and argues that cultural diversity promotes a stronger nation. A "competition of rival religious creeds," for example, strengthens religious liberty and checks "arrogance" and "intolerance." Douglass would have similar disagreements over the supposed yellow peril with Elizabeth Cady Stanton, who opposed Chinese citizenship.

Excerpting largely from the beginning of Douglass's speech, the Boston *Daily Advertiser* conveyed the broader message that racial and religious diversity strengthened the nation, but it minimized the contentious debate regarding Chinese immigration. Only the last seventh of the article was devoted to that specific case. The Boston *Commonwealth*, on the other hand, summarized the speech more accurately and noted that Douglass added a self-depreciating statement at the beginning, commenting on the "distance from the plantation to the platform of Music Hall," one of his common rhetorical poses of humility. Douglass consistently expressed optimism regarding the impact of American ethnic diversity as it applied not only to African Americans but to immigrants as well. The speech as a whole counters ethnocentrism and resembles a kind of reverse jeremiad,

3. *"Wendell Phillips on 'What We Ask of Congress,'"* Boston *Commonwealth*, 4 December 1869.

dismissing claims of a national fall from grace. Douglass derides "croakers" who see "thunder" and the "destructive bolt," since the nation already "weathered" the "storm" of the Civil War.

As nations are among the largest and most complete divisions into which society is formed, the grandest aggregations of organized human power; as they raise to observation and distinction the world's greatest men, and call into requisition the highest order of talent and ability for their guidance, preservation and success, they are ever among the most attractive, instructive and useful subjects of thought, to those just entering upon the duties and activities of life.

The simple organization of a people into a National body, composite or otherwise, is of itself an impressive fact. As an original proceeding, it marks the point of departure of a people, from the darkness and chaos of unbridled barbarism, to the wholesome restraints of public law and society. It implies a willing surrender and subjection of individual aims and ends, often narrow and selfish, to the broader and better ones that arise out of society as a whole. It is both a sign and a result of civilization.

A knowledge of the character, resources and proceedings of other nations, affords us the means of comparison and criticism, without which progress would be feeble, tardy, and perhaps, impossible. It is by comparing one nation with another, and one learning from another, each competing with all, and all competing with each, that hurtful errors are exposed, great social truths discovered, and the wheels of civilization whirled onward.

I am especially to speak to you of the character and mission of the United States, with special reference to the question whether we are the better or the worse for being composed of different races of men. I propose to consider first, what we are, second, what we are likely to be, and, thirdly, what we ought to be.

Without undue vanity or unjust deprecation of others we may claim to be, in many respects, the most fortunate of nations. We stand in relation to all others, as youth to age. Other nations have had their day of greatness and glory; we are yet to have our day, and that day is coming. The dawn is already upon us. It is bright and full of promise. Other nations have reached their culminating point. We are at the beginning of our ascent. They have apparently exhausted the conditions essential to their further growth and extension, while we are abundant in all the material essential to further national growth and greatness.

The resources of European statesmanship are now sorely taxed to maintain their nationalities at their ancient height of greatness and power.

American statesmanship, worthy of the name, is now taxing its energies to frame measures to meet the demands of constantly increasing expansion of power, responsibility and duty.

Without fault or merit on either side, theirs or ours, the balance is largely in our favor. Like the grand old forests, renewed and enriched from decaying trunks once full of life and beauty, but now moss-covered, oozy and crumbling, we are destined to grow and flourish while they decline and fade.

This is one view of American position and destiny. It is proper to notice that it is not the only view. Different opinions and conflicting judgments meet us here, as elsewhere.

It is thought by many, and said by some, that this Republic has already seen its best days; that the historian may now write the story of its decline and fall.[4]

Two classes of men are just now especially afflicted with such forebodings. The first are those who are croakers by nature—the men who have a taste for funerals, especially national funerals. They never see the bright side of anything, and probably never will. Like the raven in the lines of Edgar A. Poe, they have learned two words, and those are, "never more."[5] They usually begin by telling us what

---

4. An allusion to Edward Gibbon's *Decline and Fall of the Roman Empire.*

5. The American poet, literary critic, and short-story writer Edgar Allan Poe (1809–49) first published "The Raven," his most popular poem, in the New York *Evening Mirror* on 29 January 1845.

we never shall see. Their little speeches are about as follows: "You will *never* see such statesmen in the councils of the Nation as Clay, Calhoun and Webster.[6] You will *never* see the South morally reconstructed and our once happy people again united. You will *never* see this Government harmonious and successful while in the hands of different races. You will *never* make the negro work without a master, or make him an intelligent voter, or a good and useful citizen.["] This last *never* is generally the parent of all the other little nevers that follow.

During the late contest for the Union, the air was full of nevers, every one of which was contradicted and put to shame by the result, and I doubt not that most of those we now hear in our troubled air will meet the same fate.

It is probably well for us that some of our gloomy prophets are limited in their powers to prediction. Could they command the destructive bolt, as readily as they command the destructive word, it is hard to say what might happen to the country. They might fulfill their own gloomy prophecies. Of course it is easy to see why certain other classes of men speak hopelessly concerning us.

A Government founded upon justice, and recognizing the equal rights of all men; claiming no higher authority for its existence, or sanction for its laws, than nature, reason and the regularly ascertained will of the people; steadily refusing to put its sword and purse in the service of any religious creed or family, is a standing offense to most of the governments of the world, and to some narrow and bigoted people among ourselves.

To those who doubt and deny the preponderance of good over evil in human nature; who think the few are made to rule, and the many are made to *serve;* who put rank above brotherhood, and race above humanity; who attach more importance to ancient forms than to the living realities of the present; who worship power in whatever hands it may be lodged and by whatever means it may have been

6. Henry Clay, John C. Calhoun, and Daniel Webster.

obtained; our Government is a mountain of sin, and, what is worse, it seems confirmed in its transgressions.

One of the latest and most potent European prophets, one who felt himself called upon for a special deliverance concerning us and our destiny as a nation, was the late Thomas Carlyle.[7] He described us as rushing to ruin, and when we may expect to reach the terrible end, our gloomy prophet, enveloped in the fogs of London, has not been pleased to tell us.

Warning and advice from any quarter are not to be despised, and especially not from one so eminent as Mr. Carlyle; and yet Americans will find it hard to heed even men like him, while the animus is so apparent, bitter and perverse.

A man to whom despotism is the savior and liberty the destroyer of society, who, during the last twenty years, in every contest between liberty and oppression, uniformally and promptly took sides with the oppressor; who regarded every extension of the right of suffrage, even to white men in his own country, as shooting Niagara;[8] who gloated over deeds of cruelty, and talked of applying to the backs of men the beneficent whip to the great delight of many of the slaveholders of America in particular, could have but little sympathy with our emancipated and progressive Republic, or with the triumph of liberty any where.

But the American people can easily stand the utterances of such a man. They however have a right to be impatient and indignant at those among ourselves who turn the most hopeful portents into omens of disaster, and make themselves the ministers of despair, when they should be those of hope, and help cheer on the country

7. Douglass refers to the then still-living Thomas Carlyle (1795–1881), a Scottish historian and social philosopher, best remembered for his critically acclaimed multi-volume examinations of important historical events and figures. Carlyle lectured widely and wrote on such subjects as Chartism, Darwinian evolution, and economics.

8. To Carlyle, who consistently repudiated democracy in his writings, the extension of voting privileges contained in Britain's Second Reform Act (1867) constituted the "Niagara leap of completed democracy." Thomas Carlyle, "Shooting Niagara: And After?" *Critical and Miscellaneous Essays: Collected and Published,* 6 vols. (London: Chapman, 1869), 4:339–92.

in the new and grand career of justice upon which it has now so nobly and bravely entered.

Of errors and defects we certainly have not less than our full share, enough to keep the reformer awake, the statesman busy, and the country in a pretty lively state of agitation for some time to come.

Perfection is an object to be aimed at by all, but it is not an attribute of any form of government. Mutability is the law for all. Something different, something better, or something worse may come, but so far as respects our present system and form of government, and the altitude we occupy, we need not shrink from comparison with any nation of our times. We are to-day the best fed, the best clothed, the best sheltered and the best instructed people in the world.

There was a time when even brave men might look fearfully upon the destiny of the Republic; when our country was involved in a tangled network of contradictions; when vast and irreconcilable social forces fiercely disputed for ascendency and control; when a heavy curse rested upon our very soil, defying alike the wisdom and the virtue of the people to remove it; when our professions were loudly mocked by our practice, and our name was a reproach and a byword to a mocking;[9] when our good ship of state, freighted with the best hopes of the oppressed of all nations, was furiously hurled against the hard and flinty rocks of derision, and every cord, bolt, beam and bend in her body quivered beneath the shock, there was some apology for doubt and despair. But that day has happily passed away. The storm has been weathered, and the portents are nearly all in our favor.

There are clouds, wind, smoke and dust and noise, over head and around, and there always will be; but no genuine thunder, with destructive bolt, menaces from any quarter of the sky.

The real trouble with us was never our system or form of government, or the principles underlying it, but the peculiar composition of our people; the relations existing between them and the compromising spirit which controlled the ruling power of the country.

9. Douglass misquotes Mic. 6:16.

We have for a long time hesitated to adopt and carry out the only principle which can solve that difficulty and give peace, strength and security to the Republic, *and that is* the principle of absolute *equality.*

We are a country of all extremes, ends and opposites; the most conspicuous example of composite nationality in the world. Our people defy all the ethnological and logical classifications. In races we range all the way from black to white, with intermediate shades which, as in the apocalyptic vision, no man can name or number.[10]

In regard to creeds and faiths, the condition is no better, and no worse. Differences both as to race and to religion are evidently more likely to increase than to diminish.

We stand between the populous shores of two great oceans. Our land is capable of supporting one-fifth of all the globe. Here, labor is abundant and better remunerated than any where else. All moral, social and geographical causes conspire to bring to us the peoples of all other over populated countries.

Europe and Africa are already here, and the Indian was here before either. He stands today between the two extremes of black and white, too proud to claim fraternity with either, and yet too weak to withstand the power of either. Heretofore, the policy of our government has been governed by race pride, rather than by wisdom.

Until recently, neither the Indian nor the negro has been treated as a part of the body politic. No attempt has been made to inspire either with a sentiment of patriotism, but the hearts of both races have been diligently sown with the dangerous seeds of discontent and hatred.

The policy of keeping the Indians to themselves, has kept the tomahawk and scalping knife busy upon our borders, and has cost us largely in blood and treasure.[11]

10. Rev. 7:9.
11. During the 1860s, the U.S. Army conducted several costly campaigns against western tribes. Treaties in 1867 and 1868 with the Plains tribes and the Navajo delineated reservation boundaries and formed the basis for the "peace policy" of the Grant administration, a combined effort of the government and humanitarian—

Our treatment of the negro has lacked humanity and filled the country with agitation and ill-feeling, and brought the Nation to the verge of ruin.

Before the relations of those two races are satisfactorily settled, and in despite of all opposition, a new race is making its appearance within our borders, and claiming attention.

It is estimated that not less than one hundred thousand Chinamen are now within the limits of the United States.[12] Several years ago every vessel, large or small, of steam or of sail, bound to our Pacific coast and hailing from the Flowery kingdom,[13] added to the number and strength of this new element of our population.

Men differ widely as to the magnitude of this potential Chinese immigration. The fact that by the late treaty with China we bind ourselves to receive immigrants from that country only as the subjects of the Emperor, and by the construction at least are bound not to naturalize them,[14] and the further fact that Chinamen themselves have a superstitious devotion to their country and an aversion to permanent location in any other, contracting even to have their

---

primarily religious—groups to reform the Indian Office bureaucracy, "civilize" the Indians on their reduced lands, and avoid further bloodshed. Like many other former abolitionists, Douglass publicly supported these reforms.

12. Although the U.S. Census Bureau reported the resident Chinese-born population as 34,933 in 1860 and as 63,199 in 1870, total immigration from China numbered 105,698 in the two decades before 1870. A large number of Chinese immigrants apparently remained in the United States only a few years.

13. The Chinese people do not refer to their country as "China" or to themselves as "Chinese." Among the indigenous names for the land are Chung Kwoh, the Middle Kingdom, and Chung Hwa Kwoh, the Middle Flowery Kingdom. The term "Hwa" carries the sense that its people are civilized and refined.

14. In 1868 the United States and the Empire of China negotiated an accord governing commerce, travel, and migration between the two nations. Popularly known as the Burlingame Treaty, after Anson Burlingame (the former U.S. minister to China who negotiated it), the treaty recognized the "inalienable right of man to change his home and allegiances," and granted Chinese and American nationals residing in each country "the same privileges, immunities and exemptions as citizens." A proviso, however, added that "nothing herein contained shall be held to confer naturalization" upon the immigrants in either country.

bones carried back, should they die abroad, and from the fact that many have returned to China, and the still more stubborn fact that resistance to their coming has increased rather than diminished, it is inferred that we shall never have a large Chinese population in America. This, however, is not my opinion.

It may be admitted that these reasons, and others, may check and moderate the tide of immigration; but it is absurd to think that they will do more than this. Counting their number now by the thousands, the time is not remote when they will count them by the millions. The Emperor's hold upon the Chinamen may be strong, but the Chinaman's hold upon himself is stronger.

Treaties against naturalization, like all other treaties, are limited by circumstances. As to the superstitious attachment of the Chinese to China, that, like all other superstitions, will dissolve in the light and heat of truth and experience. The Chinaman may be a bigot, but it does not follow that he will continue to be one to-morrow. He is a man, and will be very likely to act like a man. He will not be long in finding out that a country that is good enough to live in is good enough to die in, and that a soil that was good enough to hold his body while alive, will be good enough to hold his bones when he is dead.

Those who doubt a large immigration should remember that the past furnishes no criterion as a basis of calculation. We live under new and improved conditions of migration, and these conditions are constantly improving.

America is no longer an obscure and inaccessible country. Our ships are in every sea, our commerce is in every port, our language is heard all around the globe, steam and lightning have revolutionized the whole domain of human thought, changed all geographical relations, make a day of the present seem equal to a thousand years of the past, and the continent that Columbus only conjectured four centuries ago is now the center of the world.

I believe Chinese immigration on a large scale will yet be an irrepressible fact. The spirit of race pride will not always prevail.

The reasons for this opinion are obvious; China is a vastly over-crowded country. Her people press against each other like cattle in a rail car. Many live upon the water and have laid out streets upon the waves.

Men, like bees, want room. When the hive is overflowing, the bees will swarm, and will be likely to take up their abode where they find the best prospect for honey. In matters of this sort, men are very much like bees. Hunger will not be quietly endured, even in the Celestial Empire, when it is once generally known that there is bread enough and to spare in America. What Satan said of Job is true of the Chinaman, as well as of other men, "All that a man hath will he give for his life."[15] They will come here to live, where they know the means of living are in abundance.

The same mighty forces which have swept to our shores the overflowing population of Europe; which have reduced the people of Ireland three millions below its normal standard; will operate in a similar manner upon the hungry population of China and other parts of Asia. Home has its charms, and native land has its charms, but hunger, oppression and destitution will dissolve these charms and send men in search of new countries and new homes.

Not only is there a Chinese motive behind this probable immi-gration, but there is also an American motive which will play its part, and which will be all the more active and energetic because there is in it an element of pride, of bitterness and revenge.

Southern gentlemen who led in the late rebellion have not parted with their convictions at this point, any more than at any other. They want to be independent of the negro. They believed in slavery and they believe in it still. They believed in an aristocratic class, and they believe in it still, and though they have lost slavery, one element essential to such a class, they still have two important conditions to the reconstruction of that class. They have intelligence, and they have land. Of these, the land is the more important. They cling to

15. Job 2:4.

it with all the tenacity of a cherished superstition. They will neither sell to the negro, nor let the carpet-bagger[16] have it in peace, but are determined to hold it for themselves and their children forever.

They have not yet learned that when a principle is gone, the incident must go also; that what was wise and proper under slavery is foolish and mischievous in a state of general liberty; that the old bottles are worthless when the new wine has come;[17] but they have found that land is a doubtful benefit, where there are no hands to till it.

Hence these gentlemen have turned their attention to the Celestial Empire. They would rather have laborers who would work for nothing; but as they cannot get the negro on these terms, they want Chinamen, who, they hope, will work for next to nothing.

Companies and associations may yet be formed to promote this Mongolian invasion. The loss of the negro is to gain them the Chinese, and if the thing works well, abolition, in their opinion, will have proved itself to be another blessing in disguise.[18] To the Statesman it will mean Southern independence. To the pulpit, it will be the hand of Providence, and bring about the time of the universal dominion of the Christian religion. To all but the Chinaman and the negro it will mean wealth, ease and luxury.

But alas, for all the selfish invention and dreams of men! The Chinaman will not long be willing to wear the cast off shoes of the negro, and, if he refuses, there will be trouble again. The negro worked and took his pay in religion and the lash. The Chinaman is a different article and will want the cash. He may, like the negro,

16. The term "carpetbagger" was generally applied to Northerners who traveled south after the Civil War. Although some of them were unscrupulous adventurers seeking political or economic profit, many more came to initiate legitimate business enterprises or to serve as administrators, teachers, clergymen, and doctors for either the Freedmen's Bureau or one of the benevolent societies organized to aid blacks. Carpetbaggers were often met with opprobrium because of their willingness to aid the freedmen with material sustenance and to organize them politically.

17. Matt. 9:17; Mark 2:22; Luke 5:37, 38.

18. Hervey, *Reflections on a Flower-Garden,* 76.

accept Christianity, but, unlike the negro, he will not care to pay for it in labor. He had the Golden Rule in substance five hundred years before the coming of Christ,[19] and has notions of justice that are not to be confused by any of our *"Cursed be Canaan"* religion.[20]

Nevertheless, the experiment will be tried. So far as getting the Chinese into our country is concerned, it will yet be a success. This elephant will be drawn by our Southern brethren, though they will hardly know in the end what to do with him.

Appreciation of the value of Chinamen as laborers will, I apprehend, become general in this country. The North was never indifferent to Southern influence and example, and it will not be so in this instance.

The Chinese in themselves have first rate recommendations. They are industrious, docile, cleanly, frugal; they are dexterous of hand, patient in toil, marvelously gifted in the power of imitation, and have but few wants. Those who have carefully observed their habits in California say that they subsist upon what would be almost starvation to others.

The conclusion of the whole will be that they will want to come to us, and, as we become more liberal, we shall want them to come, and what we want done will naturally be done.

They will no longer halt upon the shores of California. They will burrow no longer in her exhausted and deserted gold mines, where they have gathered wealth from barrenness, taking what others left. They will turn their backs not only upon the Celestial Empire but upon the golden shores of the Pacific, and the wide waste of waters whose majestic waves spoke to them of home and country. They will withdraw their eyes from the glowing West and fix them upon the

---

19. Douglass alludes to the principle of reciprocity (*shu*), a central teaching of the Chinese philosopher Confucius: "Do not do unto others what you do not want others to do unto you." The New Testament's Golden Rule is stated in Matthew 7:12 and Luke 6:31. Lin Yutang, ed. and trans., *The Wisdom of Confucius* (1938; New York: Modern Library, 1943), 168–69.

20. Gen. 9:25.

rising sun. They will cross the mountains, cross the plains, descend our rivers, penetrate to the heart of the country and fix their home with us forever.

Assuming then that immigration already has a foothold and will continue for many years to come, we have a new element in our national composition which is likely to exercise a large influence upon the thought and the action of the whole nation.

The old question as to what shall be done with the negro will have to give place to the greater question "What shall be done with the Mongolian," and perhaps we shall see raised one still greater, namely, "What will the Mongolian do with both the negro and the white?"

Already has the matter taken this shape in California and on the Pacific coast generally. Already has California assumed a bitterly unfriendly attitude toward the Chinaman. Already has she driven them from her altars of justice. Already has she stamped them as outcasts and handed them over to popular contempts and vulgar jest. Already are they the constant victims of cruel harshness and brutal violence. Already have our Celtic brothers, never slow to execute the behests of popular prejudice against the weak and defenceless, recognized in the heads of these people, fit targets for their shilalahs. Already, too, are their associations formed in avowed hostility to the Chinese.[21]

In all this there is, of course, nothing strange. Repugnance to the presence and influence of foreigners is an ancient feeling among men. It is peculiar to no particular race or nation. It is met with, not only in the conduct of one nation towards another, but in the conduct of the inhabitants of the different parts of the same country,

21. Anti-Chinese prejudice surfaced in California as early as 1850, when white miners formed vigilance committees to drive out Asian workers. In 1867, the Central Pacific Anti-Coolie Association worked closely with California's labor movement and Democratic politicians to agitate for effective bans against further Chinese immigration. By the 1880s, a combination of violence, local ordinances, and state laws had succeeded in expelling Chinese laborers from many occupations.

some times of the same city, and even of the same village. "Lands intersected by a narrow frith abhor each other. Mountains interposed, make enemies of nations."[22] To the Hindoo every man not twice born is Mleeka.[23] To the Greek, every man not speaking Greek is a barbarian. To the Jew, everyone not circumcised is a gentile.[24] To the Mahometan, every man not believing in the Prophet is a kaffer.[25]

I need not repeat here the multitude of reproachful epithets expressive of the same sentiment among ourselves. All who are not to the manor born[26] have been made to feel the lash and sting of these reproachful names.

For this feeling there are many apologies, for there was never yet an error, however flagrant and hurtful, for which some plausible defence could not be framed. Chattel slavery, king craft, priest craft, pious frauds, intolerance, persecution, suicide, assassination, repudiation, and a thousand other errors and crimes have all had their defences and apologies.

Prejudice of race and color has been equally upheld.

The two best arguments in the defence are, first, the worthlessness of the class against which it is directed; and, second, that the feeling itself is entirely natural.

The way to overcome the first argument is to work for the elevation of those deemed worthless, and thus make them worthy of regard, and they will soon become worthy and not worthless. As to the natural argument, it may be said that nature has many sides. Many things are in a certain sense natural, which are neither wise nor best. It is natural to walk, but shall men therefore refuse to ride? It is

---

22. William Cowper, *The Time Piece,* lines 16–18. A frith is an estuary. Cowper and Bailey, *Poems of William Cowper,* 267.

23. Hindus commonly referred to outsiders of whatever race or color as the *mleccha* and considered them a separate class of untouchables.

24. Circumcision, one of the most important biblical requirements for Jews, identified a male as a Hebrew and signified the Jews' special covenant with God. Gen. 17: 10–14; Exod. 12:44–49.

25. *Kafir* (or *kaffir*) is the Muslim term for an unbeliever.

26. *Hamlet,* sc. 4, line 566.

natural to ride on horseback, shall men therefore refuse steam and rail? Civilization is itself a constant war upon some forces in nature, shall we therefore abandon civilization and go back to savage life?

Nature has two voices, the one high, the other low; one is in sweet accord with reason and justice, and the other apparently at war with both. The more men know of the essential nature of things, and of the true relation of mankind, the freer they are from prejudice of every kind. The child is afraid of the giant form of his own shadow. This is natural, but he will part with his fears when he is older and wiser. So ignorance is full of prejudice, but it will disappear with enlightenment. But I pass on.

I have said that the Chinese will come, and have given some reasons why we may expect them in very large numbers in no very distant future. Do you ask if I would favor such immigration? I answer, *I would.* "Would you admit them as witnesses in our courts of law?" *I would.* Would you have them naturalized, and have them invested with all the rights of American citizenship? *I would.* Would you allow them to vote? *I would.* Would you allow them to hold office? *I would.*

But are there not reasons against all this? Is there not such a law or principle as that of self-preservation? Does not every race owe something to itself? Should it not attend to the dictates of common sense? Should not a superior race protect itself from contact with inferior ones? Are not the white people the owners of this continent? Have they not the right to say what kind of people shall be allowed to come here and settle? Is there not such a thing as being more generous than wise? In the effort to promote civilization may we not corrupt and destroy what we have? Is it best to take on board more passengers than the ship will carry?

To all this and more I have one among many answers, altogether satisfactory to me, though I cannot promise it will be entirely so to you.

I submit that this question of Chinese immigration should be settled upon higher principles than those of a cold and selfish expediency. There are such things in the world as human rights. They rest upon no conventional foundation, but are eternal, universal and indestructible.

Among these is the right of locomotion; the right of migration; the right which belongs to no particular race, but belongs alike to all and to all alike. It is the right you assert by staying here, and your fathers asserted by coming here. It is this great right that I assert for the Chinese and the Japanese, and for all other varieties of men equally with yourselves, now and forever. I know of no rights of race superior to the rights of humanity, and when there is a supposed conflict between human and national rights, it is safe to go the side of humanity. I have great respect for the blue-eyed and light-haired races of America. They are a mighty people. In any struggle for the good things of this world, they need have no fear, they have no need to doubt that they will get their full share.

But I reject the arrogant and scornful theory by which they would limit migratory rights, or any other essential human rights, to themselves, and which would make them the owners of this great continent to the exclusion of all other races of men.

I want a home here not only for the negro, the mulatto and the Latin races, but I want the Asiatic to find a home here in the United States, and feel at home here, both for his sake and for ours. Right wrongs no man.[27] If respect is had to majorities, the fact that only one-fifth of the population of the globe is white and the other four-fifths are colored, ought to have some weight and influence in disposing of this and similar questions. It would be a sad reflection upon the laws of nature and upon the idea of justice, to say nothing of a common Creator, if four-fifths of mankind were deprived of the rights of migration to make room for the one-fifth. If the white race may exclude all other races from this continent, it may rightfully do the same in respect to all other lands, islands, capes and continents,

27. An unattributed proverb in circulation in the mid-nineteenth century. Charles Haddon Spurgeon, *The Salt-Cellars: Being a Collection of Proverbs, Together with Homely Notes Thereon,* 2 vols. (London: Passmore & Alabaster, 1889), 2:129.

and thus have all the world to itself, and thus what would seem to belong to the whole would become the property of only a part. So much for what is right, now let us see what is wise.

And here I hold that a liberal and brotherly welcome to all who are likely to come to the United States is the only wise policy which this nation can adopt.

It has been thoughtfully observed that every nation, owing to its peculiar character and composition, has a definite mission in the world. What that mission is, and what policy is best adapted to assist in its fulfillment, is the business of its people and its statesmen to know, and knowing, to make a noble use of this knowledge.

I need not stop here to name or describe the missions of other and more ancient nationalities. Ours seems plain and unmistakable. Our geographical position, our relation to the outside world, our fundamental principles of government, world-embracing in their scope and character, our vast resources, requiring all manner of labor to develop them, and our already existing composite population, all conspire to one grand end, and that is, to make us the perfect national illustration of the unity and dignity of the human family that the world has ever seen.

In whatever else other nations may have been great and grand, our greatness and grandeur will be found in the faithful application of the principle of perfect civil equality to the people of all races and of all creeds. We are not only bound to this position by our organic structure and by our revolutionary antecedents, but by the genius of our people. Gathered here from all quarters of the globe, by a common aspiration for national liberty as against caste, divine right government and privileged classes, it would be unwise to be found fighting against ourselves and among ourselves, it would be unadvised to attempt to set up any one race above another, or one religion above another, or prescribe any one account of race, color or creed.

The apprehension that we shall be swamped or swallowed up by Mongolian civilization; that the Caucasian race may not be able to hold their own against that vast incoming population, does not seem entitled to much respect. Though they come as the waves come, we shall be all the stronger if we receive them as friends and give them a reason for loving our country and our institutions. They will find here a deeply rooted, indigenous, growing civilization, augmented by an ever-increasing stream of immigration from Europe, and possession is nine points of the law[28] in this case, as well as in others. They will come as strangers. We are at home. They will come to us, not we to them. They will come in their weakness, we shall meet them in our strength. They will come as individuals, we will meet them in multitudes, and with all the advantages of organization. Chinese children are in American schools in San Francisco.[29] None of our children are in Chinese schools, and probably never will be, though in some things they might well teach us valuable lessons. Contact with these yellow children of the Celestial Empire would convince us that the points of human difference, great as they, upon first sight, seem, are as nothing compared with the points of human agreement. Such contact would remove mountains of prejudice.

It is said that it is not good for man to be alone. This is true, not only in the sense in which our women's rights' friends so zealously and wisely teach, but it is true as to nations.

The voice of civilization speaks an unmistakable language against the isolation of families, nations and races, and pleads for composite nationality as essential to her triumphs.

Those races of men who have maintained the most distinct and separate existence for the longest periods of time; which have had the least intercourse with other races of men are a standing confirmation of the folly of isolation. The very soil of the national mind

28. This aphorism is traceable in English literature at least as far back as Colley Cibber's 1697 play *Woman's Wit*. Bartlett, *Familiar Quotations*, 301.

29. In 1860 the California legislature prohibited "Mongolians" from attending the state's public schools, but six years later amended the legislation to permit such attendance where white parents did not object. Although the Burlingame Treaty of 1868 guaranteed Chinese immigrants access to public education facilities, local pressure on school boards kept all minority students in segregated and inferior institutions.

becomes in such cases barren, and can only be resuscitated by assistance from without.

Look at England, whose mighty power is now felt, and for centuries has been felt, all around the world. It is worthy of special remark, that precisely those parts of that proud island which have received the largest and most diversified populations, are to-day the parts most distinguished for industry, enterprise, invention and general enlightenment. In Wales, and in the Highlands of Scotland the boast is made of their pure blood, and that they were never conquered, but no man can contemplate them without wishing they had been conquered. They are far in the rear of every other part of the English realm in all the comforts and conveniences of life, as well as in mental and physical development. Neither law nor learning descends to us from the mountains of Wales or from the Highlands of Scotland. The ancient Briton, whom Julius Caesar would not have as a slave,[30] is not to be compared with the round, burly, amplitudinous Englishman in many of his qualities of desirable manhood.

The theory that each race of man has some special faculty, some peculiar gift or quality of mind or heart, needed to the perfection and happiness of the whole is a broad and beneficent theory, and, besides its beneficence, has, in its support, the voice of experience. Nobody doubts this theory when applied to animals or plants, and no one can show that it is not equally true when applied to races.

All great qualities are never found in any one man or in any one race. The whole of humanity, like the whole of everything else, is ever greater than a part. Men only know themselves by knowing others, and contact is essential to this knowledge. In one race we

30. After completing his conquest of Gaul, the Roman general Julius Caesar led two raids across the English Channel into southern England. Cicero noted that the slaves whom Caesar sent back from the expedition were not "highly qualified in literature or music," that is, not on a par intellectually with Greek, Jewish, or Syrian slaves. Early antislavery writers often cited such descriptions of the early inhabitants of Great Britain as evidence against the presumption of Africans' genetic inferiority. D. R. Shackleton Bailey, ed., *Cicero's Letters to Atticus*, 7 vols. (1965–70; Cambridge: Cambridge University Press, 2004), 2:113.

perceive the predominance of imagination; in another, like the Chinese we remark its almost total absence. In one people we have the reasoning facility; in another the genius for music; in another exists courage; in another great physical vigor, and so on through the whole list of human qualities. All are needed to temper, modify, round and complete the whole man and the whole nation.

Not the least among the arguments whose consideration should dispose us to welcome among us the peoples of all countries, nationalities and colors, is the fact that all races and varieties of men are improvable. This is the grand distinguishing attribute of humanity, and separates man from all other animals. If it could be shown that any particular race of men are literally incapable of improvement, we might hesitate to welcome them here. But no such men are any where to be found, and if they were, it is not likely that they would ever trouble us with their presence. The fact that the Chinese and other nations desire to come and do come is a proof of their capacity for improvement and of their fitness to come.

We should take counsel of both nature and art in the consideration of this question. When the architect intends a grand structure, he makes the foundation broad and strong. We should imitate this prudence in laying the foundations of the future Republic. There is a law of harmony in all departments of nature. The oak is in the acorn. The career and destiny of individual men are enfolded in the elements of which they are composed. The same is true of a nation. It will be something or it will be nothing. It will be great, or it will be small, according to its own essential qualities. As these are rich and varied, or pure and simple, slender and feeble, broad and strong, so will be the life and destiny of the nation itself. The stream cannot rise higher than its source. The ship cannot sail faster than the wind. The flight of the arrow depends upon the strength and elasticity of the bow, and as with these, so with a nation.

If we would reach a degree of civilization higher and grander than any yet attained, we should welcome to our ample continent all nations, kindreds, tongues and peoples, and as fast as they learn our language and comprehend the duties of citizenship, we should incorporate them into the American body politic. The outspread wings of the American eagle are broad enough to shelter all who are likely to come.

As a matter of selfish policy, leaving right and humanity out of the question, we cannot wisely pursue any other course. Other governments mainly depend for security upon the sword; ours depends mainly upon the friendship of the people. In all matters, in time of peace, in time of war, and at all times, it makes its appeal to the people, and to all classes of the people. Its strength lies in their friendship and cheerful support in every time of need, and that policy is a mad one which would reduce the number of its friends by excluding those who would come, or by alienating those who are already here.

Our Republic is itself a strong argument in favor of composite nationality. It is no disparagement to Americans of English descent to affirm that much of the wealth, leisure, culture, refinement and civilization of the country are due to the arm of the negro and the muscle of the Irishman. Without these, and the wealth created by their sturdy toil, English civilization had still lingered this side of the Alleghanies, and the wolf still be howling on their summits.

To no class of our population are we more indebted for valuable qualities of head, heart, and hand, than to the German. Say what we will of their lager, their smoke, and their metaphysics, they have brought to us a fresh, vigorous and child-like nature; a boundless facility in the acquisition of knowledge; a subtle and far-reaching intellect, and a fearless love of truth. Though remarkable for patient and laborious thought, the true German is a joyous child of freedom, fond of manly sports, a lover of music, and a happy man generally. Though he never forgets that he is a German, he never fails to remember that he is an American.

A Frenchman comes here to make money, and that is about all that need be said of him. He is only a Frenchman. He neither learns our language nor loves our country. His hand is on our pocket and his eye on Paris. He gets what he wants and, like a sensible French-man, returns to France to spend it.

Now let us answer briefly some objections to the general scope of my arguments. I am told that science is against me; that races are not all of the same origin and that the unity theory of human origin has been exploded.[31] I admit that this is a question that has two sides. It is impossible to trace the threads of human history sufficiently near their starting point to know much about the origin of races.

In disposing of this question whether we shall welcome or repel immigration from China, Japan, or elsewhere, we may leave the dif-ferences among the theological doctors to be settled by themselves.

Whether man originated at one time and one place; whether there was one Adam or five, or five hundred, does not affect the question.

The great right of migration and the great wisdom of incorporat-ing foreign elements into our body politic, are founded not upon any genealogical or ethnological theory, however learned, but upon the broad fact of a common nature.

Man is man the world over. This fact is affirmed and admitted in any effort to deny it. The sentiments we exhibit, whether love or hate, confidence or fear, respect or contempt, will always imply a like humanity. A smile or a tear has no nationality. Joy and sor-row speak alike in all nations, and they above all the confusion of tongues proclaim the brotherhood of man.

It is objected to the Chinaman that he is secretive and treacher-ous, and will not tell the truth when he thinks it for his interest to tell a lie. There may be truth in all this; it sounds very much like the account of man's heart given in the creeds. If he will not tell the

31. Followers of the American school of ethnology advanced the polygenist theory, namely, that the races had separate origins and constituted distinct species. Douglass discussed and disputed the theory frequently after delivering his speech of 12 July 1854 on Negro ethnology (included in this volume).

truth, except when it is for his interest to do so, let us make it for his interest to tell the truth. We can do it by applying to him the same principle of justice that we apply to ourselves.

But I doubt if the Chinese are more untruthful than other people. At this point I have one certain test.—Mankind are not held together by lies. Trust is the foundation of society. Where there is no truth, there can be no trust, and where there is no trust, there can be no society. Where there is society, there is trust, and where there is trust, there is something upon which it is supported. Now a people who have confided in each other for five thousand years; who have extended their empire in all directions until it embraces one-fifth of the population of the globe; who hold important commercial relations with all nations; who are now entering into treaty stipulations with ourselves, and with all the great European powers, cannot be a nation of cheats and liars, but must have some respect for veracity. The very existence of China for so long a period, and her progress in civilization, are proofs of her truthfulness. This is the last objection which should come from those who profess the all-conquering power of the Christian religion. If that religion cannot stand contact with the Chinese, religion or no religion, so much the worse for those who have adopted it. It is the Chinaman, not the Christian, who should be alarmed for his faith. He exposes that faith to great dangers by exposing it to the freer air of America. But shall we send missionaries to the heathen, and yet deny the heathen the right to come to us? I think a few honest believers in the teachings of Confucius[32] would be well employed in expounding his doctrines among us.

The next objection to the Chinese is that he cannot be induced to swear by the Bible. This is to me one of his best recommendations. The American people will swear by any thing in the heaven above or the earth beneath. We are a nation of swearers. We swear by a book whose most authoritative command is to swear not at all.

32. Confucius (c. 551–479 B.C.E.), Chinese philosopher.

It is not of so much importance what a man swears by, as what he swears to, and if the Chinaman is so true to his convictions that he cannot be tempted or even coerced into so popular a custom as swearing by the Bible, he gives good evidence of his integrity and his veracity.

Let the Chinaman come; he will help to augment the national wealth; he will help to develop our boundless resources; he will help to pay off our national debt; he will help to lighten the burden of our national taxation; he will give us the benefit of his skill as a manufacturer and as a tiller of the soil, in which he is unsurpassed.

Even the matter of religious liberty, which has cost the world more tears, more blood and more agony, than any other interest, will be helped by his presence. I know of no church, however tolerant; of no priesthood, however enlightened, which could be safely trusted with the tremendous power which universal conformity would confer. We should welcome all men of every shade of religious opinion, as among the best means of checking the arrogance and intolerance which are the almost inevitable concomitants of general conformity. Religious liberty always flourishes best amid the clash and competition of rival religious creeds.

To the mind of superficial men the future of different races has already brought disaster and ruin upon the country. The poor negro has been charged with all our woes. In the haste of these men they forget that our trouble was not ethnological, but moral, that is was not a difference of complexion, but a difference of conviction. It was not the Ethiopian as a man, but the Ethiopian as a slave and a coveted article of merchandise, that gave us trouble.

I close these remarks as I began. If our action shall be in accordance with the principles of justice, liberty, and perfect human equality, no eloquence can adequately portray the greatness and grandeur of the future of the Republic.

We shall spread the network of our science and our civilization over all who seek their shelter, whether from Asia, Africa, or the Isles of the Sea. We shall mould them all, each after his kind, into

Americans; Indian and Celt, negro and Saxon, Latin and Teuton, Mongolian and Caucasian, Jew and gentile, all shall here bow to the same law, speak the same language, support the same government, enjoy the same liberty, vibrate with the same national enthusiasm, and seek the same national ends.

"Which Greeley Are We Voting For?"

An Address Delivered in Richmond, Virginia, 24 July 1872

Unidentified newspaper clipping, "Campaign of 1872," 6:82–84, Box 95, Edward McPherson Papers, Library of Congress.

Although never an abolitionist, Horace Greeley had vigorously opposed the western expansion of slavery and championed the Republican party through his editorials in the New York *Tribune,* the newspaper with the nation's largest circulation. Thus, when Greeley challenged Ulysses S. Grant in the 1872 presidential election, running on the Liberal Republican ticket, it was a serious threat to the Radical Republicans' Reconstruction program. As a Republican party stalwart, Frederick Douglass campaigned for Grant and opposed Greeley's rhetoric of conciliation between North and South, which entailed federal military withdrawal from the South and the abandonment of African American rights.

When the Democratic party met for its convention in Baltimore, it also nominated Greeley for president, despite his long history of attacking it, in hopes of regaining national political power. The chair of the Democratic National Committee, August Belmont, endorsed Greeley, albeit reluctantly, because he was one of the "wisest and best men of the Republican party" who had "severed themselves from the Radical wing" of the Republicans.[1]

Subsequent editorials in the Richmond *Daily Dispatch,* a Democratic party newspaper, put forth a "Lost Cause" rationale for defeating President Grant, which meant removing federal protections for

1. Richmond *Daily Dispatch,* 10 July 1872.

African American rights in the South: "The key note of the Administration is that the continued repression of the South is necessary to the safety of the republic. The key note of the Democratic-Republican or Liberal party is that the sections must shake hands across the bloody chasm."[2]

With these accusations as a backdrop, the Republican party sponsored a rally in Richmond, on 24 July, and Frederick Douglass addressed the crowd. Several "well-known Republicans" joined Douglass on the platform, and he was the first speaker to address the gathering. The Richmond *Daily Dispatch* described Douglass's appearance in detail and then opined, "He spoke with ease and fluency, his gestures were appropriate, and his language well-chosen, but as an orator he does not excel several well known colored men in Virginia who were slaves until freed by the sword." After this implicit criticism of Douglass's courageous escape from slavery, the paper remarked that "his speech created less enthusiasm than might have been expected."

The summary of Douglass's speech in the *Daily Dispatch* downplayed the irony in his speech. For example, Douglass jokes, "I hear from several sources that all the intelligent colored people of the South are going to vote for Horace Greeley and B. Gratz Brown. (Loud cries of "No!") Well, I hope you won't have many such intelligent ones in Virginia. (Applause and laughter.)" The *Daily Dispatch* reported the latter sentence as: "If that was so, he hoped and believed there were very few intelligent colored people in Virginia. (Applause.)" Senator Henry Wilson, the Republicans' vice presidential candidate, and several other speakers followed Douglass, and the event ended at dusk, when the crowd was supplied with Chinese lanterns for a procession that "presented a brilliant spectacle."[3] The Washington (D.C.) *New National Era*, edited by Douglass, reported on 1 August 1872 that "eight to ten thousand voters stood for over five hours" to hear the speakers while more trains arrived. By the time the audience marched in the torchlight procession, "there could not have been less than twenty-five thousand men in

2. Ibid., 25 July 1872.
3. Ibid.

the streets." Douglass wound up his speech to the sound of "cheer after cheer." He delivered many stump speeches that summer, but his oration on this occasion stood out for his affiliation with several disparate groups. He identifies himself with "we poor white people," former slave owners, and African Americans. He cites the Virginians Thomas Jefferson and Patrick Henry as sources of inspiration for both his own rebellion against slavery and his aspirations for moving Virginia toward a more egalitarian future.

Horace Greeley's campaign suffered from his Democrat and Republican supporters' inability to form a strong coalition and from his own failing health. President Grant won a clear victory, and Greeley died shortly after the election. Soon after, Frederick Douglass's house in Rochester, New York, burned down in what he believed was arson, and he moved his family to Washington, D.C. Douglass's energetic stumping on behalf of the Republican party, beginning with the 1872 campaign, led to him receiving a series of influential and lucrative federal patronage appointments.

FELLOW-CITIZENS—I thank you very sincerely for the cordial and hearty welcome with which you have greeted me. I attempt to speak here with more difficulty, with less confidence, than you can imagine. This is the first political campaign in which I ever took the stump for any candidate. I am a new hand at the business. And this is the first time too that I ever took part in a public demonstration in the late capital of the Confederate States of America.[4] Besides, when invited to participate in this demonstration I supposed that I should be called upon merely to give color to the occasion (laughter)—to be a sort of tail to the kite.[5] I had no idea of occupying any such prominence as

4. This appears accurate. Douglass spoke only one other time in that city, on 13 September 1892 at the Annual Fair of the Virginia Industrial Mercantile Building and Loan Association.

5. This unattributed saying appears in English at least as early as the early nineteenth century. London *Literary Gazette; and Journal of Belle Lettres, Arts, Sciences, &c.* 11 (24 February 1827): 116.

it seems I am to occupy to-day. There is one thing, however, that consoles me in venturing here on the sacred soil of Virginia—and in this, the Capital—and it is that although a stranger I am no carpet-bagger. (Applause and laughter.) I am to the manor born,[6] if there is any advantage or merit in that. It is true that I was once advertised in a very respectable newspaper under a little figure, bent over and apparently in a hurry, with a pack on his shoulder, going North.[7] (Laughter.) But that was a long time ago, when I was quite young, and on the score of my youth I hope you will pardon that indiscretion—the indiscretion of my going North. I was young, and like most young people was anxious to see everything that I had ever heard of or read of, and hence I went North. Some of my friends in the South liked me very much at that time and went after me. (Laughter.) They could not have me go. They said they could not endure to part with me. They loved me; they wanted to do me good. They heard that I was going away off to old Massachusetts—that worst of all the States, that State in which the black man is supposed to learn more mischief in a day than Virginia can unlearn him in a year—and I did go there. You will excuse me for talking about myself, for when a man has no other subject he will talk about that. He is the most familiar with that, and on that ground I am going to talk a little about myself. When a man who has gone abroad from those he knew and loved in his youth returns, he should tell something about what he has seen, heard, felt and learned while abroad.

I was very much disappointed in my travels northward. I went away from the South into the North, expecting to find people living in a very humble way, in Spartan-like simplicity, inhabiting small huts and hovels; for I had never known anything of wealth not derived directly from slave labor. I had only seen wealth in connection with slavery. Wealth, intelligence, refinement, luxury, all those elements that distinguish advanced civilization, I had only seen a

6. *Hamlet,* sc. 4, line 566.
7. Although Douglass seems to be referring to an advertisement published at the time of his escape from slavery in 1838, such a notice has not yet been uncovered.

connection with the system of human slavery. I had an idea that
no man—I know my notions of political economy must have been
very crude—could acquire more than a bare subsistence with his
two hands. Knowing that those States were free, that there were no
slaves there, I expected to see the people living like the poor white
people in the South that had no slaves lived. I include myself with
you partly by permission and partly by circumstances over which I
had no control. (Laughter.) I went up there expecting to find them
living as we poor white people used to live, and you know some of
you how that was—out on the outskirts of plantations, with a chimney built out of doors, not of brick, but a little wood, a little hay and
a little clay. (Renewed laughter.) Judge of my surprise, my amazement, when after a few nights and days' travel on a road of which
you have heard frequently—the underground railroad—(laughter)
I found myself among the granite hills of New England, in [New]
Bedford, Massachusetts—judge of my amazement, I say, when, instead of the little huts which we white people used to live in on the
outskirts of the plantations, there were magnificent residences on
either side, equaling anything of magnificence and grandeur that I
had seen here in Virginia. I saw in the streets fine ladies elegantly
dressed, gentlemen with broadcloth coats made after the latest Pa-
risian pattern, and splendid equipages rolling down the street, the
people looking as healthy, as happy, as wealthy, as intelligent, as refined, as the finest of the refined, the wealthiest of the wealthy of
the great State of Virginia. Not a slave, not one. (Applause.)

I was surprised. I didn't know how that was. We poor white people at the South had nothing of this. How was it? Whence came
these magnificent residences, these splendid equipages; whence
this elegance; whence this refinement; whence this intelligence?
I hardly knew how to explain it. I went down on the wharf, Gid.
Howland's wharf,[8] and saw vessels preparing for foreign voyages,

8. Douglass may be confusing Gideon Howland Jr. (1770–1847) with George
Howland (1781–1852). Gideon Howland Jr. was a partner in a prosperous shipping

and I was in search of a job then. I had my saw in my hand and my buck on my back, and I was looking for a cord of wood to saw; for I was not then what I am now. I was then a wood-sawyer and not a Doctor of Laws, as Howard University has recently dubbed me.[9] (Cheers.) A wood-sawyer, and all I wanted was a job of work, a cord of wood to saw or a ton of coal to put away. But while I was looking for a job of wood-sawing I was thinking of some explanation of the prosperity, the wealth and the grandeur that I saw all around me. The first person I met that gave me any information on the subject was a good-natured old ox, with long horns and honest eyes. He was attached to a piece of rope, which passed through a block and tackle extending to a derrick,[10] and he was walking off, walking off with a steady pace—with a steadiness, with a strength not unlike Ulysses Grant[11]—walking off attending to his own business. I found that in his movement he was bringing out of the hold of the ship a large cask of oil; in fact that this one solitary ox was unloading a great ship of a cargo of oil. Well I reasoned this way: This ox was worth about $70. Now that one ox worth $70 was doing work which in my country it would require fifteen slaves valued at $1,000 a piece to do. There was a capital of $70 in the North as useful as a capital of $15,000 would be in the South. I thought there was a great deal in that. But that was not all. I went over to Fall River, only about fourteen miles from New Bedford, and there I had my eyes opened again. Another explanation was afforded me. The industrious people of Fall River had managed to enslave, not the people of that town, but to enslave

---

and whaling mercantile firm in New Bedford, Massachusetts. George Howland, another prominent banker and whaling industry businessman, owned and operated Howland's Wharf in the same town.

9. Howard University awarded Douglass an honorary LL.D. degree at the first commencement of its collegiate department in 1872. Henry D. Cooke, the territorial governor of the District of Columbia, presented the degree to Douglass and lauded him as the "silvery tongued orator of America."

10. A derrick is a lifting device used in quarries and shipyards.

11. Ulysses S. Grant (1822–85), eighteenth president of the United States (1869–77) and general in chief of all Union armies in the final year of the Civil War, personally directed the Union forces in Virginia in 1864–65.

a beautiful stream of water, to harness it to the paddle-wheels of a
great mill, and that stream of water, without doing it the least harm
in the world, was turning and moving thousands of looms and millions of spindles, all bringing wealth and civilization to the people of
that community.[12] I felt that I had learned a great deal. I had learned
that people could be wealthy, refined, intelligent, highly civilized,
and that they could be Christians without slavery. It was a great
thing. It reconciled me to the crime I committed when I ran away
(laughter), when I stole myself; but when I ran away you know I ran
away on my own legs (renewed laughter), and left everybody else
in possession of their legs (applause, laughter, and cries of "Good"),
and I could not blame myself a great deal.

Fellow-citizens, I have ventured down among you to-day not
because I have discovered any new political truth to apply to our
present situation as a Nation—indeed, it is not necessary for me or
for anybody to go in search of new truth until the old truths, long
ago discovered and declared, have been thoroughly recognized and
reduced to practice by this State and Nation. Properly speaking,
however, there is no such thing in the world as new truth or old
truth, for truth is eternal. Error may be new or it may be old, since it
is founded in the misapprehension of what truth is. It hath its beginning and must have its ending. It may exist in one age and be mistaken for truth. It disappears in another age, and, if not supplanted
by truth, is supplanted by another error. But truth, eternal truth, is
from everlasting unto everlasting—can never pass away.[13] Such a
truth is man's right to liberty. He was born with it. It entered into
the very idea of man's creation. It was his before he comprehended

12. Dexter Wheeler, a local technician and entrepreneur, constructed the Fall
River Manufactory, which employed the force of the Fall River's descent to turn and
move the looms and spindles. Other entrepreneurs soon built several more mills
along the river. By the time of Douglass's arrival in 1838, there were at least five
large cotton manufactories. Douglass's figures for the number of looms and spindles,
however, are inflated; by 1859 the mills were employing 192,620 spindles and 4,576
looms.
13. 1 John 4:6.

it. The title deed of it is inscribed on his soul. No compacts, no agreements, no covenants, no combinations into which men may enter can abrogate or destroy this grand, original, fundamental and eternal right. (Cheers.) If men form institutions that are in accordance with this truth, they stand; and if they form institutions contrary to it, they will fall. No power beneath the sky can uphold any free government, any social system, inconsistent with the grand idea of universal liberty and equality among men. This is the higher law of which statesmen and scholars take cognizance, and woe betide any people who act in disregard of it. (Applause.)

Fellow-citizens, I wish to defend myself, in order to be the better able to defend my cause. I have been charged with life-long hostility to one of the cherished institutions of Virginia. I am not ashamed of that life-long opposition. I have done nothing in this opposition which any white man subjected to slavery would not be proud of having done. Virginia may blame me to-day for her past, but she has herself to blame. It was, Virginia, your own Thomas Jefferson that taught me that all men are created equal.[14] It was, Virginia, your own Patrick Henry that taught me to exclaim, "As for me, give me liberty, or give me death."[15] (Cheers.)

Now I feel I am on the soil of Virginia, and feel pretty much at home. I know there was a time when it would not have been healthy to speak thus. There was a time when I was requested to visit you, and I had to send my regrets (laughter);[16] but I can come to see you now. A great change has taken place in the world. The sun don't get up where it used to; it don't set where it used to. The air, although

14. Douglass quotes the Declaration of Independence.

15. Douglass quotes Patrick Henry's speech in the Virginia Convention, 23 March 1775, as recorded in William Wirt, *Sketches of the Life and Character of Patrick Henry*, 7th ed. (New York: McElrath & Bangs, 1835), 141.

16. A reference to Virginia governor Henry A. Wise's attempt to secure Douglass's arrest in 1859 in connection with John Brown's raid on Harpers Ferry. As governor, Wise requested that President Buchanan hire two Virginia detectives as special federal agents to capture Douglass and deliver him to Virginia authorities. The Northern press reported that a group of prominent Southerners, including Wise, had offered $50,000 for Douglass's capture.

it is tolerably warm, is a good deal more pleasant than it used to be—more agreeable, in every way, than it used to be.

But let the dead past bury its dead,[17] and let us look, for a moment, at the present, for I have not much more time to speak, as I do not mean to detain you from hearing the man whom we mean to place in the second highest office in the gift of this Government.[18] (Cheers.) Look at his face. Why, it is a benediction itself. I felt that, as he moved through here, and I saw his broad, beneficent face. His heart is just like it; for I am as well acquainted with his heart as you are with his face. (Applause.)

Now, I partly expected to meet with some of my old friends, the late masters in the State of Virginia. (A voice, "They are here.") I am glad you are here. I never had anything against you in my life. I always loved you and only hated slavery. That is all. I want to say a word to you to reconcile you to the present condition of things. I believe that you, and all of us, indeed, stand upon one common platform of patriotism. We want this country prosperous; we want it peaceable; we want it happy. As a black man I want it so; as a white man you want it so. Notwithstanding the past, we still have a country. Slavery is dead, but we still have a country—a glorious country—a country that may have a more glorious future than it could have had had slavery continued to exist. (Applause.)

A great many want to know, now-a-days, what is the true policy of this country to secure this great and happy future if it is possible. Well, I have got this to say; I lay this down as a general principle: That whatever was wise, whatever was proper for your society in a state of slavery is of necessity to-day very unwise, very improper, and even dangerous. Take, for instance, the matter of free discussion. While slavery existed freedom of speech was necessarily dangerous to society here. It could work evil, and only evil, and that continually. It stirred up, or would stir up, society from its foundation, so

17. Douglass quotes from the sixth stanza of Henry Wadsworth Longfellow's poem "A Psalm of Life." Longfellow, *Poems*, 22.
18. Henry Wilson.

that freedom of speech was logically, taking slavery as a base line, an evil. You could not have it; it was dangerous. But, now that slavery has gone, that which was so perilous, that which was dangerous and improper, is now the highest wisdom. Liberty, you know, tolerates this. It is necessary to liberty that we look each other in the face calmly and candidly, and with the utmost freedom express our convictions in regard to public men and public measures.

Another thing was dangerous when you had slavery. That was education. One of the most dangerous things in the world to slavery was education. An educated negro had the devil in him. He was a regular mischief maker, a marplot, a disturber, a conspirator. He was dangerous to have around. My master used to say to me, "Give a nigger an inch and he will take an ell. Learn him to read, and he will want to know how to write and cipher, and so on, and be making mischief."[19] He was right. If slavery was right, ignorance was right, and ignorance was proper. But slavery was not right; it had to die, and ignorance must go with it. What was dangerous for the black man to have when he was a slave is now your safety. Then you might keep away from him the book. Now, in order to your safety, you must give him books. Don't burn down his school-house; don't drive away his teacher. The prosperity, the happiness and well-being of society depend upon education.

But I won't ring the changes upon this subject. My idea is this: that the things that were right and proper for the South when we had slavery are now the worst things possible. When you had slavery it was not inconsistent with that institution that one man should own thousands and thousands of acres of land. He owned them then for the benefit of others; he owned them for his slaves, and for other people, but it would be the greatest madness now for those old landholders to act upon premises or principles which grew out of or were made reasonable by slavery, when slavery is no longer. Let

19. Douglass's master in Baltimore, Hugh Auld, chastised his wife, Sophia, with this expression when he found her teaching Douglass to read. *Douglass Papers,* ser. 2, 1:31; 2:83–84; 3:62, 65.

go your land; cut it up; create as much interest in it as possible, and
you will do wisely.

But let us come to the great question that we are here to discuss
to-day. We are going, in the course of a few months, to choose a
President and Vice President of the United States, and you and I
and all of us are to have a voice, a free voice, an uncontrolled voice,
an untrammelled vote on that question. (Applause.) We are going to
have it, and now it is of the gravest possible consequence what the
choice of the American people shall be in regard to that. I hear from
several sources that all the intelligent colored people of the South
are going to vote for Horace Greeley and B. Gratz Brown.[20] (Loud
cries of "No!") Well, I hope you won't have many such intelligent
ones in Virginia. (Applause and laughter.)

Now, I did not come here to abuse Horace Greeley. I didn't
come here to say harsh things of him, nor of Gratz Brown. I can call
a man a knave and a fool, or a mean, miserable wretch, and all that
sort of thing, if I want to, but that don't prove anything. I should
like right well to be able to vote for Horace Greeley. I should like
to do it on the score that he is a workingman, and on the score that
he is an editor, a brother editor with me. I should like to vote for
Horace Greeley if I only knew which Greeley my vote would elect.
(Applause and laughter.) But there is just where the trouble is with
me. He is a many-sided man. There have been a good many Horace
Greeleys. You know, when Gough[21] presented himself at the door of

20. Benjamin Gratz Brown (1826–85) was a leader of a free soil political faction
that later evolved into Missouri's Republican party. Brown was elected to the U.S.
Senate in 1863. Although he originally held to Radical Republican positions on such
issues as black suffrage and Confederate disenfranchisement, Brown's views moder-
ated, and in 1870 a coalition of Democrats and anti–Radical Republicans elected him
governor. In 1872 Brown ran as Horace Greeley's vice presidential candidate on the
unsuccessful ticket of the Democratic and Liberal Republican parties.

21. In the depression of 1833, John Bartholomew Gough (1817–86) lost his job
as a bookbinder and began to drink very heavily. When his wife and young child died
simultaneously in 1841, he sank into a suicidal depression. The following year, Gough
signed the total-abstinence pledge and soon became a famous temperance lecturer.
Douglass alludes to his lecture at the Broadway Tabernacle in New York City on the
evening of 28 January 1845.

the Tabernacle in New York, he said to the door-keeper: "Let me in; I am Gough." "I'll be d——d if I do," said the door-keeper; "there are no less than seven Goughs gone in here already." (Loud guffaws.) There have been a great many Horace Greeleys in my time. I knew one once who used to say red-hot things against slavery. I liked that man. Capital man he was. If my vote would elect that Horace Greeley, and I was sure he would stay "put," why, I would vote for him. But there is just the trouble, gentlemen. In voting for Horace Greeley we don't know which Greeley we are trying to elect—whether it is the Greeley of thirty years ago, of twenty years ago, or of ten years ago, in the van of the Republican party, or the Greeley of to-day, at the dead of the Democratic party. (Applause.)

Now, my friends, I will be short. What the South wants, what Virginia wants, what the whole country wants at this time above all things, after this terrible ten years of commotion, after this terrible ten years of agitation and suffering, is quiet and repose, by which all the old wounds in the body politic shall be healed, and the Nation come into one homogenous whole. That is what we want. We want that above all things. You and I know as well as we know anything, that there can be no repose, no security without certainty. My objection to Mr. Greeley is that he is an uncertain man; that he is a vacillating man; that he is at the present moment in doubtful company, to say the least. Any uncertainty and doubt at the head of our affairs can not be other than disastrous to the highest interests of this country. What we want at the helm is a clear head and a firm and steady hand, and these we have in Ulysses S. Grant. (Somebody in the crowd here proposed three cheers for General Grant, which were given with great enthusiasm.) That is right; that is better than anything I could say. We want certainty. We do not want a candidate that is neither fish, flesh nor fowl.[22] I object to Mr. Greeley on the ground that he is ambiguous, a sort of amphibious animal, living on neither land nor

---

22. Douglass quotes John Heywood's 1546 *Proverbs* collection": "she is neither fish nor flesh, nor good red herring." Bartlett, *Familiar Quotations*, 148.

water, neither a Republican nor a Democrat; neither a protectionist nor a free-trader;[23] in favor of centralization and against it; in favor of Ku-Klux laws and against them;[24] opposed to Tammany and with it.[25] Well, I said I was not going to say any harsh things about him, but let me tell you, my fellow citizens, speaking as a colored man, I regard the election of Horace Greeley as one of the most calamitous that could possibly befall this Republic.

What we want, I repeat is certainty. We know Ulysses Grant, we know Henry Wilson—a straight line, no sinuosity, no double dealing, no divided voice, no uncertain sound to their trumpet. Ulysses Grant is friendly to all classes. The worst enemies that he has can not accuse him of malice. He did not approach General Lee with haughtiness nor with malice. They had met and disputed on a great principle. The principle was decided in Grant's favor. He bore himself meekly; he bore himself in a manly way, and to-day cherishes as affectionate feelings toward the people of South as toward any other people in the whole country. (Applause.)

23. Horace Greeley indeed vacillated on this issue. In his carefully worded letter of 20 May 1872 in which he accepted the presidential nomination of the Liberal Republicans, Greeley offered no clear support either to the protectionists, who wished to establish tariffs protecting domestic industries, or to the free traders, who advocated the elimination of all artificial trade restrictions.

24. Responding to the inaction of Southern courts and militias, Congress on 20 April 1871 passed the Ku Klux Act, which made the white terrorist group's depredations subject to federal jurisdiction and military action. Many Southern states complained that the act allowed the federal government to usurp their constitutionally guaranteed right to police their jurisdictions. Greeley and the Liberal Republicans attempt to assuage both sides in the debate. Although upholding the Reconstruction-era constitutional amendments and the equality of all men before the law, their platform stated that "local self-government . . . will guard the rights of all citizens more securely than any centralized power."

25. Although Horace Greeley editorialized the New York *Tribune* in 1870 that the Tweed Ring of Tammany Hall "was the most corrupt gang of political adventurers that ever ruled and robbed a helpless city," he nevertheless supported Tammany's charter for city government in March 1870, which allowed the Tweed Ring to engage in some of its most lucrative plundering. Greeley believed, as did many others, that the charter's concentration of power in the hands of the mayor would create a more responsible administration of the city; in fact, it provided a screen behind which the Tweed Ring fleeced the city.

I know the man. I like a man in the Presidential chair and the man that sits next him such as the poor people of my own race, as well as poor people of every other race can approach, and approach easily. Talk about military rings and inaccessibility! It is false, every word of it. General Grant, next to Abraham Lincoln and Charles Sumner, is about the easiest man to approach, holding high public place in this country, that I have ever known. The humblest man may approach him, and in his presence will be put thoroughly at ease. It is good to have such a man down there at Washington at the head of this Nation, this Democratic Nation, this Nation which has at last settled down upon the broad principle of the Declaration of Independence, that all men—*all* men, not a part of them—are created equal. I say it is good to have a man of that sort.

But I did not intend to occupy so much of your time. (Cries of "Go on.") I want you, before that sun gets too low, to get a daylight view of the next Vice President of the United States. (Tremendous applause.)

"Recollections of the Anti-Slavery Conflict"

An Address Delivered in Louisville, Kentucky, 21 April 1873

Louisville (Ky.) *Courier-Journal,* 22 April 1873.

Frederick Douglass delivered "Recollections of the Anti-Slavery Conflict" in several cities in 1873, revising it considerably depending on his audience and purpose. At Philadelphia's Academy of Music, on 10 March, he ended the speech by revealing how he had escaped from slavery in Baltimore. The details of the escape, revealed for the first time, became the focus of contemporary press coverage.[1] The version given in Louisville occurred in the wake of the Colfax Massacre, a terrible setback in African American political power, and Douglass adjusted the speech accordingly, focusing less on the anti-slavery movement and his personal triumphs and more on the necessary work of rooting out bigoted ideologies.

On 19 April, Douglass arrived in Louisville at the invitation of its black community to celebrate the ratification of the Fifteenth Amendment. He attended services the next day at Quinn Chapel, a Methodist church, and in the evening at the Greenstreet Colored Baptist Church. On the afternoon of 21 April, he was ushered to Louisville's Exposition Building in a carriage as part of a parade that included African American fraternal societies, black veterans, and black bands. Upon arriving at the hall, he found the audience in high spirits, but he could not make himself heard well. Consequently, he

1. Nemaha *Nebraska Advertiser,* 3 April 1873.

decided not to give the speech that he had written for the occasion and instead gave an extemporaneous speech that had elements of his previous year's stump speech "Which Greeley Are We Voting For?" He asks his listeners to consider what they had been expected to do as slaves and then urges them to do the opposite in order to succeed as freedmen. He especially emphasizes the importance of learning to read. Moving to recent events, Douglass attacks the Louisville *Courier-Journal's* coverage of the Colfax Massacre. The week before, a white paramilitary attack in Colfax, Louisiana, left 150 black men and 3 white paramilitaries dead. Douglass pulled the newspaper's article on that outrage from his pocket and labeled its writers "mischief makers" for suggesting that white Democrats had to protect white women from "designing and seditious carpet baggers" and their African American "dupes."[2]

Douglass returned that evening to the Exposition Hall to deliver "Recollections of the Anti-Slavery Conflict." He received much laughter and applause for his reenactment of Wendell Phillips's rejoinder to a minister who dared him to give antislavery lectures in the South. To the question, "Why don't you go South," Phillips responded, "Well, why don't you go to——."

The turning point in the speech is his satire of the proslavery argument that "the Negro cannot take care of himself." This parody becomes a rallying cry for his uplift ideology, in which he urges his "colored brethren" to "use the opportunities that we have for the improvement of our condition, for improving our intellect, for improving our manners, improving our order, improving our punctuality, and improving our integrity." Douglass notes the difficulties of offering advice that could be misconstrued as criticism within the dominant culture, especially during this tense time, saying, "I would like to talk to you when there were no white people listening to me. I would like to talk to you aside." He nonetheless offers criticism of African American homes where there were no books or papers, and of

2. "The Fifteenth Amendment," Louisville *Courier-Journal,* 22 April 1873; Eric Foner, *Reconstruction: America's Unfinished Revolution, 1863–1877* (New York: Harper and Row, 1988), 530; LeeAnna Keith, *Colfax Massacre: The Untold Story of Black Power, White Terror, and the Death of Reconstruction* (Cary, N.C.: Oxford University Press, 2007), xii.

men who preferred travel to community building. Among Douglass's speeches, this one most directly illustrates the challenges he faced in addressing African American and white audiences simultaneously.

L ADIES AND GENTLEMEN—Perhaps there never was a revolution in the sentiment and structure of any nation so comprehensive and so complete as the revolution we are met this day to celebrate in the goodly city of Louisville. The change in the condition of the colored people is so vast—so wonderful that I for one have no words to characterise it properly. Almost all other revolutions that have taken place in the history of the world have been more or less incomplete—fallen short of the objects sought by the revolutionists themselves. There has been greater extravagance of demand, perhaps, in other times, but such revolutions have generally fallen short of their objects. For one, I was content for years to ask for the race to which I belong, simply emancipation from chattel slavery, satisfied that if that were obtained gradually other concessions and rights would follow. It never entered my mind in the earlier days of the anti-slavery struggle that the negro would by one movement as it were by one great act of our Government, be lifted into manhood, to be a wise man among men, and at last lifted into citizenship, completely enfranchised. This was more than I looked for, but it has come, and I have lived to see it, and am here to rejoice with you in this complete realization of hopes.

The struggle that brought this great revolution to its present condition dates far back in the history of this nation and far back in the history of the world. It had the advances and its retreats, its action and its reaction. Perhaps the darkest and least hopeful period in the history of this tremendous struggle for the freedom of our race was the year 1850. We had attracted attention to the subject of slavery by holding anti-slavery meetings all over the North; by the publication of anti-slavery papers, resolutions, and speeches, and the good and true of all persuasions were rapidly allying themselves to the anti-slavery cause, and laboring to promote it. But at an unfortunate moment there came a chilling and discouraging reaction, out of which came what is known as the Fugitive Slave Bill—a bill enabling a man to pursue his slave into every State of the Union, and made every citizen of the Northern States an interested party in the arrest and return of the bond man. This bill carried consternation to the hearths and homes of thousands of fugitives who had taken refuge in the free States, for there was not a valley so deep, no mountain so high, no glen so secluded, no spot so secret in all these States, as to secure the hunted one in his right to his own body.

The negroes fled from the Northern States in darkened trains,[3] escaping from under the Star Spangled Banner—running away from our boasted republic in pursuit of liberty that was denied them in this republic. I found it necessary myself, being a runaway, to leave the State of Massachusetts and go to Europe.[4] I said that I was a runaway. There is usually a little odium attached to running away, but for the life of me I never could feel in any degree ashamed for being made to move Northward. I had an idea that my legs were my legs, and nobody else's legs, and that if I run away on my own legs, and was careful to leave everybody else in possession of their legs, there could be no solid or reasonable objection to my going (laughter), and so I went. But under the Fugitive Slave Bill I found it necessary to go abroad for a while for my health. (Laughter and applause.) But

While There I Was Purchased.

Some good people over there found out who my master was—and a very excellent master he was—and he had no business to be a master any more than many other good men with whom I have met had a right to be masters. They found who he was and wrote to him

---

3. Douglass alludes to the Underground Railroad.
4. Fearing recapture by his Maryland master after the publication of his autobiography, Douglass left his family in Massachusetts in August 1845 for an extended antislavery speaking tour of Great Britain. He returned home in 1847 only after abolitionist friends had purchased his liberty.

to know if he would sell me, and if he would that they would buy me. And so $750 was sent over in British gold and I was set at liberty, and by that means I was enabled to return to the United States and pursue my anti-slavery studies and my anti-slavery labors.[5] I say the darkest time in this struggle was during the enforcement of that bill.

Then came the sermons from the leading ministers of the Northern States in support of that bill and its enforcement. Then came Mr. Webster, Mr. Filmore[6] and other great men, together with most of the religious denominations in the land to urge upon the Northern people the duty of carrying out the provisions of that bill, but nevertheless every slave that was arrested only deepened and broadened, and intensified the anti-slavery sentiment of the North. Every slave therefore brought back only served to weaken the system which it was designed to uphold and sustain. One of the most amazing things connected with the anti-slavery struggle is the attitude assumed on the slavery question by the religious organizations of our country. It will be hardly credited, although Dr. Albert Barnes stated that there was no power outside of the American Church and clergy which could sustain slavery for years,[7] had it not been sustained in the Church using the very droppings of the sanctuary. Your own fellow citizen, James G. Burney took the same view—that the American Church and clergy were the bulwark of American slavery.[8] It was hard to believe this in the days of slavery struggle, and it will be harder still to believe it a hundred years hence, when the churches all over the land will be claiming the triumph of liberty in the United States as all the work of the church—or the result of the prayers and preaching of the pulpit. Among the things of the future will be a grand debate in this country, at which this very question as to whether the religious

5. The ownership of Douglass was transferred from Thomas Auld to his brother Hugh Auld on 13 November 1846. The latter signed Douglass's manumission papers on 5 December 1846 in exchange for £150 raised by a group of British abolitionists led by Anna and Ellen Richardson.

6. Daniel Webster and Millard Fillmore.

7. Douglass paraphrases Barnes, *Scriptural Views of Slavery*, 383.

8. A reference to the title of James G. Birney's pamphlet *The American Churches: The Bulwarks of American Slavery*.

organizations of the United States were in any wise responsible for the perpetuation of slavery. Some historian like Froude serious for the truth of history, and some Father Burke equally zealous for the glory and honor of the church will meet and thrill assemblies by their eloquence and learning touching this very point.[9]

This is the truth concerning it. There are two sides to it. There is no question that in the earlier history of this Republic all religious organizations of the country were decidedly opposed to slavery. The Methodist Episcopal Church denounced it as evil as early as 1780 and 1784, and down to 1818. They organized committees for the purpose of petitioning the Legislatures of the several States for the abolition of slavery.[10] The Presbyterian church was equally and unequivocally opposed to slavery. It denounced slavery as man-stealing, and classed it with the highest crimes, quoting that passage of scripture bearing on man-stealing: "Whoso stealeth a man and selleth him, or if he be found in his hand, he shall be surely put to death."[11] The Baptists were equally decided in their opposition to slavery. Indeed, in the States of Virginia, North Carolina and Maryland, and in a part of Kentucky, the Baptists were so anti-slavery that they were called "Baptist Emancipation" as early as 1780.[12]

Thereafter the Society of Friends were also opposed to slavery. The leading statesmen of the Republic were opposed to slavery— Franklin,[13] Rush,[14] and even down to the time of your own great

9. Douglass alludes to a well-publicized dispute between the English historian and editor James Anthony Froude (1818–94) and the Irish priest and lecturer Thomas Nicholas Burke (1830–83) over British colonial policy in Ireland.

10. The Methodist Episcopal Church's General Conference of 1804 repealed the call on Annual Conferences to lobby state legislatures for antislavery measures.

11. Douglass quotes Exodus 21:16, which the Presbyterian Church in the 1790s had appended to an answer in its Larger Catechism but removed in 1816.

12. A reference to the associations of antislavery Baptist congregations centered in Kentucky known as the "Friends of Humanity," or more popularly as the "Emancipators."

13. Benjamin Franklin (1706–90) played a leading role as a patriot during the American Revolution and lent his name to several antislavery organizations in his last years, but modern scholars caution that his record was far more compromised than has generally been recognized.

14. The Philadelphia physician Benjamin Rush (1745–1813), a signer of the Declaration of Independence, was active in most of the Revolutionary era's reform and philanthropic movements, including antislavery.

Henry Clay. I remember reading one of the most eloquent outbursts of sentiment from him upon this subject that I ever read from any source. He said if he could be instrumental in erasing from his native State the hint of human slavery, and from the State of his adoption he would not exchange the proud satisfaction for all the laurels ever bestowed upon the most successful conqueror. I do not quote his exact language, but he uttered such a sentiment as this. Such sentiments as this were uttered fifty years ago, so that Abolitionism is no modern idea. The earlier history of anti-slavery is very curious. Perhaps the very earliest book written of an anti-slavery character only claimed for the negro one thing. It was a book written two hundred years ago by Rev. Dr. Goodwin, of Jamaica written for the purpose of proving that it was not a sin to baptize a negro.[15] (Laughter.) It was a book of two hundred pages. Dr. Goodwin argued the question coolly. The first difficulty that met him was that baptism is an ordinance for a free moral agent for persons who can determine upon their own course of conduct. The negro could not. He was not a free moral agent, and could not decide any question relative to his own action—what he

Should Eat Or Drink,

or wear, when to speak, who to speak to, when he should be punished, by whom punished, when he should work, where and how much he should work, and what use was baptism to such a piece of property as that? It was said that since baptism belonged to free moral agents, that the thing to be done was to

Well Baptize the Master

as he had the absolute control, and it was sufficient for the negro to get the benefit of baptism by proxy. Nobody now doubts the

---

15. Morgan Godwyn advocated this position in *The Negro's and Indian's Advocate.*

propriety of putting a little water on a negro, or of putting a negro in the water, and putting him in very hot water in some places. But it was out of that discussion came the germ of the struggle which gave birth to the freedom you now enjoy. Dr. Goodwin, while he did not deny a slave was a slave, he insisted upon it, that though a slave he was a man, and in granting him the right of baptism opened the doors by which every other right belonging to man could be claimed and insisted upon. Here we have

The Religious Beginning

of the anti-slavery movement notwithstanding it must be admitted that the churches of our country were very cold on this subject.

We had men sold to build churches, women sold to support missionaries. The church and the slave-pen stood in the same neighborhood, and the cries and groans of the bond-man was sometimes silenced by the tears and prayers of the church. The

Pulpit and Auctioneer's Block

stood in the same neighborhood. The people expended the gold resulting from the sale of human flesh in order to support the pulpit, and the pulpit in return defended the system as a Bible institution.

But I am glad we have got by that. We can now afford to remember the golden rule: "All things whatsoever ye would that men should do to you do ye even so unto them."[16] The movement by which abolition was brought about in this century followed a very natural course of development.

---

16. Matt. 7:12; Luke 6:31.

Beginning of the Anti-Slavery Struggle.

The first part of the anti-slavery struggle we were engaged in was to express the evils of slavery. I know the first proposition that I undertook to sustain before an audience in the Northern States, was that slavery was an evil. That was all—an evil to the master as well as to the slave, and emancipation would be a joy to the master as well as to the slave. I remember when Neal Turner started his insurrection in Virginia, poor old man what he was.[17] He came to his death by that rising, but that movement sent a thrill throughout Southern society, and no man slept easily for years, who slept on the quivering heartstrings of his slaves. You have no fear now; you have no fear even here, even though a fugitive slave is running around talking to the colored people about their rights, about their liberty, and about their progress. Nobody is afraid. I ask you to rejoice with us. There is no fear that you will starve to death because we don't work for you any more for nothing. I do not know that you can point to say five years in the history of Louisville when this city has been more prosperous and surrounded its name with a brighter and broader halo of glory than she has done since the chains were stricken from the limbs of the slaves. (Applause.)

I have travelled far over land and seas. I have visited many cities in every part of our glorious Union, and I must say that in no part of this republic is there a grander and more beautiful illustration of the energy, the enterprise, and the progressive spirit of the American people than is furnished in the up building of this magnificent hall for the display of your industrial products. This is all the fruit of liberty. I do not suppose this hall would have been here if you had not got rid of slavery. (Laughter and applause.)

17. Nat Turner (1800–31), the leader of a slave revolt in Southampton County, Virginia, on 21–23 August 1831, was a literate, enslaved carpenter and preacher. After his capture, he supposedly dictated his "confessions" to a local lawyer. Turner was executed by hanging on 11 November 1831.

One of the most valuable lessons left us by this struggle of slavery is faith in man, faith in the rectitude of humanity, and faith in the all conquering power of truth as opposed to error—opposed to falsehood. The Abolitionists believed that this was the secret of their power. If we measured their faith by the magnitude of the work before them—if we consider the nature of the system of wrong to be overthrown, how vast in wealth of power; how it molded all political parties; how it controlled statesmen; what a vast mine of wealth it was to those interested in it; how, as Mr. Clay once said, "five hundred years of legislation have sanctioned and sanctified negro slaves as property when we consider how it was linked with our institutions, the faith that could meet this was at once heroic and something marvelous."[18] But the abolitionists did believe, and persevered in their opposition to slavery, meeting reproach, and enmity and sometimes incurring personal danger which would have appalled most men. It was once said by Emerson that "the eloquence of the Abolitionists was dog-cheap at anti-slavery meetings."[19] The secret of their eloquence was their faith. Like the great apostle to the Gentiles, they believed, and therefore spoke because they believed, and were therefore eloquent.[20] But the Abolitionists were not long alone in their faith in the power of truth. The South also believed in the power, and demanded that they should put down this agitation in the North. The North, while boasting at its freedom, so far forgot its dignity as to attempt by mob violence to put down the discussion of

18. On 7 February 1839, in an address on the U.S. Senate floor, later published as "On Abolitionist Petitions," Henry Clay said, "Two hundred years of legislation," not "five hundred," as Douglass reported. *The Life and Speeches of Henry Clay, of Kentucky*, 2 vols. (New York: Greeley & McElrath, 1843), 2:410.

19. Ralph Waldo Emerson's comment on the abundance of abolitionist expressiveness appears in his address "Emancipation in British West Indies" (1844), in which he points to "a proverb in Massachusetts, that 'eloquence is dog-cheap at the anti-slavery chapel.'" *The Complete Works of Ralph Waldo Emerson, Centenary ed.*, 12 vols. (Boston: Houghton, Mifflin, 1903–04), 11:138.

20. An allusion to St. Paul's evangelization of the Gentiles as recorded in Acts and the Pauline epistles. Douglass then paraphrases either 2 Corinthians 4:13 or Psalms 116:10.

the question of slavery. However, it failed, and it could not be otherwise. Daniel Webster had said that the right to canvass the policy of
public measures was a natural right—a fireside privilege, belonging
to private life as a right that is belonged to public life as a duty, and
the people believed it and insisted upon the exercise of their right of
speech.[21] In the exercise of it they made converts. Our persecutors
from the North endeavored for a time to make the South believe
that the abolitionists were an insignificant characterless crew. It was
said that we were only a handful of hair-brained fanatics; that the
church North was sound on the subject, that the respectable people
of the South and of the North were sound on the subject, and that
we could effect nothing. The South would not believe, and they
were right in not believing. They knew the character of slavery, and
they knew that its character was such that it would not bear to be
talked about—that it was like old Grisby's character—only passed
without censure when it passed without observation,[22] and they continued to demand the suppression of the right of speech.

One of the first anti-slavery speeches that it was my privilege to
hear after my escape from bondage, was delivered in New Bedford
by a man whose name you would not guess if you guessed until
midnight. It was by none other than by the Hon. Caleb Cushing.[23]

Caleb Cushing was my first abolition preacher and teacher. He
defended John Quincy Adams in his anti-slavery course in Congress.[24] It was glorious to hear him. But he was only with us for a
while, and like some other men he went off and we heard nothing
more of him on the subject of slavery on the right side of the

21. Douglass slightly misquotes Daniel Webster's speech on military enlistments
in the War of 1812, delivered in the House of Representatives on 14 January 1814.
Daniel Webster, *The Writings and Speeches of Daniel Webster*, 18 vols. (Boston:
Little, Brown, 1903), 14:25.

22. Actually a reference to a statement by John Manners, Marquess of Granby.
The Political Contest, 29.

23. Douglass often reminisced about hearing Caleb Cushing (1800–79) and other
antislavery speakers at Liberty Hall in New Bedford, Massachusetts.

24. In his maiden speech to Congress, on 30 January 1836, Caleb Cushing joined
John Quincy Adam's defense of the abolitionists' right to petition.

question. I was more fortunate a few years afterward in hearing the chief apostle of abolitionism[25]—an apostle immediate and unconditional, universally and everlastingly an emancipationist—a leader more fortunate than Wilberforce,[26] and who lives to-day to see in its glory the cause which he espoused in its reproach and shame. When I first looked upon him I felt that he was the right man in the right place. His speaking as I now remember it was not eloquent. He was not fluent, but he realized to me a description of the true reformer given by Emerson: "There was a man behind every word he uttered."[27] He was then young, though of venerable appearance. There was in him a strange blending of youth and age. The battle of life had already begun with him, and early it was sharp and severe. He was then just entering upon the first decade of his anti-slavery career. Bitter persecutions had poured out their vials of wrath upon him. Two States had offered a reward for his head.[28] He had been dragged through the streets amid the fury of a mob in Boston for daring to plead the cause of the slave.[29] He had felt the damp walls of more than one prison.[30] He had been threatened on all sides with

25. William Lloyd Garrison.

26. William Wilberforce.

27. In manuscript versions of this lecture, Douglass reported Ralph Waldo Emerson's statement as "It was not the utterance, but the silent man behind it." Speech File, reel 18, frame 191, reel 19, frame 113, Frederick Douglass Papers, Library of Congress.

28. William Lloyd Garrison was no stranger to bounties when, in late 1835, an anonymous Marylander informed him of a $20,000 reward for his head offered by six unidentified Mississippians. On 30 November 1831, the Georgia legislature resolved to grant a $5,000 reward to persons responsible for Garrison's arrest and trial in that state.

29. In 1835, antiabolition sentiment in the North was intensified by a lecture tour by the noted British antislavery leader George Thompson. Mistaking Garrison for Thompson, a mob attacked him as he attempted to address the Female Anti-Slavery Society, and then dragged him half naked through the streets of Boston.

30. In the summer of 1829, William Lloyd Garrison began working in Baltimore as coeditor of the *Genius of Universal Emancipation,* published by the veteran abolitionist Benjamin Lundy. Garrison published articles denouncing Francis Todd for using his ship, the *Francis,* to transport slaves from Baltimore to New Orleans for resale. Todd immediately sued Garrison for libel in Baltimore courts and won. Unable and unwilling to pay his $50 fine, Garrison remained seven weeks in the Baltimore jail until the antislavery New York merchant Arthur Tappan paid the court.

death, and yet there he stood, calm and serene and unmoved, showing no passion, no violence, as proud in spirit as the morning star.
When that man shall have filled up the measure of his years, when
he shall have finished his course on earth, when his memory shall
be gathered as a fresh incense, as it will be among the emancipated
millions down through future generations, we may write over his
sleeping dust the name of

William Lloyd Garrison,

the man to whom more than any other in this Republic we are
indebted for the triumph we are celebrating to-day.

Arguments for Slavery.

You may be curious to know what arguments were resorted to in
support of slavery in the early days when I ran away to the North.
In all these arguments one peculiar fact is noticeable, and that is the
great friendship shown for the negro. The profoundest interest was
felt in our welfare. It was said, for instance,

"the negro cannot take care of himself."

But how do we find it? I have never had any difficulty in taking care
of myself, and I have passed pretty successfully, for a negro, through
all parts of the country. (Laughter.)

It was said they were better off in slavery. "They are contented
and happy and would not be free if they could," they said. They argued that they would all come North. They would not work without
masters. Is that so? (Cries of "no, no.") I hope not. They said they
were worse off in Africa. I used to hear the gospel preached when
I was a slave until I had the back ache. They used to preach from
one text namely:

Servants Obey Your Masters.[31]

The negro can never be improved; the negro is only fit to be a slave. That was the kind of argument that was used. You will never put down slavery on God's earth, was another kind of argument. You put back the cause 50 years. You are only making their condition worse, and you had better mind your own business. Why don't you go South. Somebody asked Wendell Phillips, "Mr. Phillips what are you doing?" "Well, I am preaching against slavery." "Why don't you go South?" "Well," said Mr. Phillips, "What are you doing?" "I am preaching the gospel." "Well, why don't you go to———."[32] (Laughter and applause.)

Many other arguments were used. What would you do with the negroes if you had them all? Would you associate with a negro? Would you allow your daughter to marry a negro? Would you turn them loose? They are all loose enough to-day. (Laughter.) Well, it was said I hate slavery as bad as you do, but I would leave the question with the South. I hate slavery, but I am for gradual emancipation. Some said that they were sending the negroes back to Africa where they came from, while others argued that the Bible sanctioned slavery. These were the arguments by which slavery was supported, and scarcely a better service could be done the abolitionists than to have one or two of these arguments jeered out at public meetings against them. Our abolition meetings were our chief instruments in promoting anti-slavery sentiments. These were very often queer kinds of meetings.

The noise in the building was so great at this point that Mr. Douglass stopped, saying that he had a great desire to make his speech, but he was afraid that he could not be heard but a few feet. He announced that if a suitable hall could be engaged he would speak on Tuesday evening on an entirely different subject—that of Self-made Men.[33] He continued as follows:

---

31. Eph. 6:5; Col. 3:22; Titus 2:9.

32. Douglass recalls a story related by Wendell Phillips in which he encountered a minister during a lecture engagement in Cincinnati "in the old antislavery days."

33. Douglass delivered his lecture "Self-Made Men" to a predominantly black audience at Judah Hall in Louisville, Kentucky, on the evening of 22 April 1873.

I Want to Say a Word, However,

to my colored brethren and sisters in view of their new relations to our fellow-citizens. We have come up from the depths, and let us not forget the new condition in which we are to-day. It has brought not only rights but duties which we are equally bound to discharge. We have entered in the laws of the land, our freedom. More than those that have been asserted for us—equality before the law, and equality at the ballot box. Now, equality here implies equality elsewhere. There is no power in the local legislature—no power anywhere beneath the sky outside of yourselves that can make you the equal of your white fellow-citizens in point of intelligence, in point of moral rectitude, in point of usefulness to society. We say we are the equals of the whites. Are we? Are we at present the equals of the whites? Equal before the law we are, equal at the ballot box we are, but we are far behind our white brethren. Now in what are we behind? I do not undertake to say why we are so, just yet, but I want all to feel and know that we are in the rear and not in the front. If the white man can build a ship and navigate that ship around the world, and we can only build a canoe, they are a whole ship's length ahead of us. If the white man can construct a bridge and fling it across that magnificent river rolling along at the feet of this city[34] and we cannot do it, then they are a bridge ahead of us. If the white man can make books and we cannot, they are books ahead of us. If the white man can build magnificent halls like this[35] and we cannot, they are halls ahead of us. I do not say that naturally we are unequal to the white man. I would not say that, but the fact is that now they are in advance of us. What is our duty in view of that fact? It is to build up, is it not? It is to use the opportunities that we have for the improvement of our

34. The Louisville Bridge over the Ohio River, designed by the German-born engineer Albert Fink, had the longest channel span of any bridge in the United States at the time of its completion in 1869.

35. The organizers of the Louisville Industrial Exposition had a spacious building expressly constructed at the corner of Fourth and Chestnut streets for the annual event.

condition, for improving our intellect, for improving our manners, improving our order, improving our punctuality, and improving our integrity. We are called to the discharge of new duties, and it won't do to sit down in the chimney corners and say I don't know, when we ought to know—when we should be endeavoring to make use of the opportunities that we have for knowing, and fill our minds with something more than dressed up emptiness.

I would like to talk to you when there were no white people listening to me. I would like to talk to you aside. When I go into a colored man's house now when they used not to allow you to have books, I begin to want to see books lying around, I want to see papers there. I do not want it to be said if the whole negro race were blotted out there would be nothing left in two hundred years to tell they ever had an existence; that they never read any, never labored any, they never published any books or periodicals, they never made any advance in science or knowledge. They used to say that of us, but this must not be said two hundred years hence. The doors of

The School-Houses Are Open,

and woe, woe, woe betide our race if we fail to embrace the opportunities for the cultivation of our minds, for the improvements of our intellects. It will not do to find the negroes twenty years after emancipation where they were twenty years before. No power could sustain us in this.

Another thing we must have. We must have some money. We must learn to save it and

Make Ourselves Independent.

That is a condition of responsibility. No people can be respected who are not independent; a man may pity you if you have not got money, but he cannot respect you. He may be sorry for you, poor fellow, and wish you had some, but he has not respect for you. But the trouble with many of us now is that as soon as we get money we want to travel. Ask a colored man in Chicago how long he has lived there, and he will say about six months. "Well, where did you come from when you came to Chicago?" He answers, "I came from Detroit." "How long did you live in Detroit." About three months. "Well, where did you live before you went to Detroit?" "I came from Buffalo, N.Y., and lived there about three months. (Laughter.) I have been traveling all over, and as soon as I got money enough I came to this place." Old age overtakes such a man and then what? Here it is Ethiopia stretching forth his hand again.[36] He is always stretching out his hand. The only way you can make yourself respected is to get

Something Somebody Else Wants.

There are ways opening up for all of you. Let every colored man see in it that if he gains five dollars per week that he will lay up one dollar of it; if he makes ten dollars lay by two of them—put them in the Freedmen's Savings Bank where it will breed some more. There one thousand dollars at the end of the year will gain sixty more. Put it in there where it is safe. I believe in it. I have got a little money up there, and I am going to take some from here and put in there.[37] (Laughter.)

36. Ps. 68:31.

37. Congress authorized the Freedman's Savings and Trust Company on 3 March 1865 to meet the growing financial needs of newly emancipated blacks. The bank eventually opened thirty-seven branches in seventeen states and the District of Columbia. The nationwide economic panic that hit in 1873 revealed serious financial weaknesses in the bank, owing to incompetent and corrupt management. A reorganized board of trustees appointed Douglass the bank's president in hopes of restoring public confidence in its solvency. At that time, Douglass lent the institution ten thousand dollars. When the bank failed in July 1874, Douglass shared the fate of fellow investors. He eventually received sixty-two cents on the dollar for the two thousand dollars he had on deposit when the bank closed.

When I ran away and come North I worked for nine dollars per month and saved money. For twenty-five years, or nearly so I worked for $400 per year and saved money, and every man in this country, who is a man, can save money if he will. But he will not save it by walking the streets and smoking cigars. He will not save it by playing billiards on one of your back streets. I dislike a miser yet a miser is more respectable than a spendthrift. Let us take a lesson from the Jews. Perhaps a more despised, hated, and persecuted set of people never lived than the Jewish people. In Europe they were not allowed to live upon the same side of the city with other people. They were allowed no privileges at all scarcely.

But now where is the Jew. At this hour the Jewish people dictate the policy of the people of the North. Somebody, it is said, offered to make Rothschild[38] the King of the Jews if he would advance so much money. He preferred not to advance it, as he had rather be the Jew of kings than the king of the Jews. They are respected now. Here we lift our hats and bow to the Jew. Why? Because he has got money. Because he lives in a good house. He does not put it all on his back. His windows are not stuffed with old hats to keep the cold away. He saves his money. Now we have got to do the same thing—there is no other way for us to do. It is not necessary that every black man should be a rich man, but we must have a representative class at any rate. There must be an actual number of representatives of intelligence and wealthy men. We are not to blame for our present condition. No, no, no. We have come up from the depths, and I am not reproaching you for being poor. How could we be otherwise than poor, starting as we have? I am simply warning you that you may better your condition. Some of us have been taught from boyhood to despise wealth. That is a great mistake. Some say let my children do as I did; our ancestors did nothing for us, and we will do nothing for those who come after us. The first house of Louisville

38. Probably a reference to Lionel Nathan de Rothschild (1808–79), the British financier. His company made numerous loans to the British government and those of other European nations.

was built one story high. The fathers died and left it one story high. Their children put on another story and left it two stories high, and their children put on another story, until now Louisville is five and six stories high. If the first story had been left, there never would have been but one story still. We must determine to leave our children in better circumstance than we found them. Some such feeling as this is necessary.

Now I leave you. I believe I have done my duty, although I have been imperfectly heard. I rejoice that I have met with the people of Louisville. I have found more intelligence, more refinement, more heart, more manly character among the colored people of Louisville than I expected to find in this State, where it cannot be denied that there have been restrictions operating around you.[39] I rejoice to find the intelligence, the manhood, the dignity, the courage that I have found among the colored people of this city. Go on, and ways will open before you by which you can improve your condition and make yourselves useful, honorable, happy and prosperous citizens.

---

39. Although Kentucky's Civil Rights Act of February 1866 spelled the demise of that state's slave code, it denied blacks the right to sit on juries or to testify against whites. The legal disability imposed on blacks provided an argument for the continued presence of the Freedmen's Bureau within the state. Kentucky's freedmen remained subject to the terrorist activities and depredations of whites who variously styled themselves "Regulators" and "Redeemers."

"The Freedmen's Monument to Abraham Lincoln"

An Address Delivered in Washington, D.C.,
14 April 1876

Washington (D.C.) *National Republican,* 15 April 1876.

As the keynote orator at the dedication of the Freedmen's Monument in Washington, D.C., perhaps the most prestigious ceremony at which Frederick Douglass ever spoke, he gave an address that has become one of his most famous, along with "What to the Slave Is the Fourth of July?" As in that earlier speech, Douglass delivers a jeremiad in which he rehearses the many ways that Lincoln reinforced popular prejudices against African Americans and seemed "tardy, cold, dull, and indifferent" to their civil rights. As David Howard-Pitney shows in his essay in this volume, the jeremiad, a political sermon, traces a covenanted community's fall into sin but prophesies its renewal with the community's rededication to justice.

True to the form, Douglass shifts midway in his oration to show that Lincoln's "tardiness," was wise, since he never got too far ahead of public opinion. Lincoln's sensitivity to public thought and opinion made him, according to Douglass, an inspired president who was capable of finally defeating slavery and saving the union. This speech warns of backsliding from sacred principles and then looks forward to a glorious national future rededicated to the principles of freedom and equality.

As Michael Leff demonstrates, Douglass considered the statue's funding and dedication ceremony to be acts of great symbolic importance for African Americans. It was the moment when "black

America" was enrolled in "a sacred ritual," when African Americans asserted their significance in the national polity and their capacity to express gratitude to Lincoln without bowing to a flawed man.[1] But the path to this ceremony was neither smooth nor quick. Shortly after Lincoln's assassination, African Americans sought a way to pay tribute to him. Douglass, for example, protested the exclusion of African American societies from Lincoln's funeral procession, in a speech at the Cooper Institute seven weeks after the assassination.[2] At roughly the same time, a black washerwoman from Ohio gave a representative of the Western Sanitary Commission, the federal agency charged with aiding war refugees, five dollars and proposed "a monument to their dead friend . . . erected by the colored people of the United States."[3]

Two months later, in the summer of 1865, Douglass was asked to lend his name to a fund-raising campaign to endow an educational institution for African Americans that was to also serve as a monument to Lincoln. He declined, urging instead a monument funded by African Americans themselves: "It would be, as all such offerings should be, free from all taint of self-love or self-interest on our part, as a class."[4]

Douglass's desire to demonstrate the magnanimity and patriotism of African Americans was realized when Congress declared 14 April 1876 a national holiday for the dedication of the monument. According to the Washington (D.C.) *National Republican*, "nearly all" of the African American organizations in the city marched in the parade, including military troops, fraternal societies, and bands. Carriages carried Douglass, Professor John Mercer Langston (dean of Howard University's Law Department), and other prominent African Americans. The procession ended at Lincoln Park, where President Grant,

1. Michael Leff, "Lincoln among the Nineteenth-Century Orators," in *Rhetoric and Political Culture in Nineteenth-Century America*, ed. Thomas W. Benson (East Lansing: Michigan State University Press, 1997).
2. "Fred. Douglas [sic] on President Lincoln.; Vast Gathering at the Cooper Institute. The Speaker's Views on the Future of His Race. Mr. Lincoln and Colored People," New York *Times*, 2 June 1865.
3. Washington (D.C.) *National Republican*, 15 April 1876.
4. "Letter to W. J. Wilson," 8 August 1865, in Foner, *Life and Writings of Frederick Douglass*, 4:171–74.

members of his cabinet, senators, representatives, and members of the diplomatic corps awaited their arrival. The African American congressman James Henri Burch read from the District of Columbia Emancipation Act, which freed nearly three thousand slaves in Washington, D.C., within nine months.[5] A correspondent for the *National Republican* commented that it "was received with as much enthusiasm as if it had just been issued."[6]

President Grant unveiled the monument, which stood in contrast to the position that Douglass had carved out for African Americans in the new and expanded nation. Whereas Douglass gazed at the monument and offered a critical assessment of President Lincoln, the statue itself suggested a far more deferential attitude on the part of African Americans toward Lincoln.

This concern was shared by others, and the *National Republican* reported that important changes had been made to Thomas Ball's original design. In the original, Lincoln stood holding the Emancipation Proclamation while granting freedom to a passive, kneeling slave. Ball revised the initial design to model the kneeling man upon a photograph of Archer Alexander, a runaway Missouri slave. Rather than an idealized slave, the figure was based on one who was "an agent in his own deliverance," according to the *National Republican,* and his "strained muscles" demonstrated his agency.[7]

Douglass was not entirely satisfied by these modifications,[8] and his speech offered an alternate image of Lincoln and black soldiers. He described this relationship: "We saw our brave sons and brothers laying off the rags of bondage, and being clothed all over in the blue uniforms of the soldiers of the United States; under his rule we saw two hundred thousand of our dark and dusky people responding to the call of Abraham Lincoln, and with muskets on their shoulders and eagles on their buttons, timing their high footsteps to liberty and union under the national flag."

5. James M. McPherson, *The Struggle for Equality: Abolitionists and the Negro in the Civil War and Reconstruction* (Princeton, N.J.: Princeton University Press, 1964), 97.
6. "Glory of Lincoln," Washington (D.C.) *National Republican,* 15 April 1876.
7. Ibid.
8. David W. Blight, *Frederick Douglass' Civil War: Keeping Faith in Jubilee* (Baton Rouge: Louisiana State University Press, 1989), 227.

FRIENDS AND FELLOW CITIZENS: I warmly congratulate you upon the highly interesting object which has caused you to assemble in such numbers and spirit as you have to-day. This occasion is in some respects remarkable. Wise and thoughtful men of our race, who shall come after us, and study the lessons of our history in the United States, who shall survey the long and dreary space over which we have traveled, who shall count the links in the great chain of events by which we have reached our present position, will make a note of this occasion—they will think of it, and with a sense of manly pride and complacency. I congratulate you also upon the very favorable circumstances in which we meet to-day. They are high, inspiring and uncommon. They lend grace, glory and significance to the object for which we have met. Nowhere else in this great country, with its uncounted towns and cities, uncounted wealth, and immeasurable territory extending from sea to sea, could conditions be found more favorable to the success of this occasion than here. We stand to-day at the national centre to perform something like a national act, an act which is to go into history, and we are here where every pulsation of the national heart can be heard, felt and reciprocated.

A Thousand Wires,

fed with thought and winged with lightning, put us in instantaneous communication with the loyal and true men all over this country. Few facts could better illustrate the vast and wonderful change which has taken place in our condition as a people, than the fact of our assembling here for the purpose we have to-day. Harmless, beautiful, proper and praiseworthy as this demonstration is, I cannot forget that no such demonstration would have been tolerated here twenty years ago. The spirit of slavery and barbarism, which still lingers to blight and destroy in some dark and distant parts of our country, would have made our assembling here to-day the signal and excuse for opening upon us all the flood-gates of wrath and violence. That we are here in peace to-day is a compliment and credit to American civilization, and a prophecy of still greater national enlightenment and progress in the future. I refer to the past not in malice, for this is no day for malice, but simply to place more distinctly in front the gratifying and glorious change which has come both to our white fellow-citizens and ourselves, and to congratulate all upon the contrast between now and then, the new dispensation of freedom with its thousand blessings to both races, and the old dispensation of slavery with its ten thousand evils to both races—white and black. In view then, of the past, the present and the future, with

The Long and Dark History

of our bondage behind us, and with liberty, progress and enlighten-ment before us, I again congratulate you on upon this auspicious day and hour.

Friends and fellow-citizens: The story of our presence here is soon and easily told. We are here in the District of Columbia; here in the city of Washington, the most luminous point of American ter-ritory—a city recently transformed and made beautiful in its body and in its spirit;[9] we are here, in the place where the ablest and best men of the country are sent to devise the policy, enact the laws and shape the destiny of the Republic; we are here, with the stately pil-lars and the majestic dome of the Capitol of the nation looking down upon us; we are here, with the broad earth freshly adorned with the foliage and flowers of spring for our church, and all races, colors and conditions of men for our congregation; in a word, we are here to express, as best as we may, by appropriate forms and ceremonies, our grateful sense of vast, high and pre-eminent services rendered to ourselves, to our race, to our country and to the whole world

9. Appointed by President Ulysses S. Grant in 1871 to lead the Board of Public Works, Alexander Robey ("Boss") Shepherd (1835–1902) oversaw a massive program of urban improvements to the District of Columbia.

By Abraham Lincoln.

The sentiment that brings us here to-day is one of the noblest that can stir and thrill the human heart. It has crowned and made glorious the high places of all civilized nations, with the grandest and most enduring works of art, designed to illustrate characters and perpetuate the memories of great public men. It is the sentiment which from year to year adorns with fragrant and beautiful flowers the graves of our loyal, brave, and patriotic soldiers who fell in defense of the Union and liberty. It is the sentiment of gratitude and appreciation, which often, in the presence of many who hear me, has filled yonder heights of Arlington[10] with the eloquence of eulogy and the sublime enthusiasm of poetry and song; a sentiment which can never die while the Republic lives. For the first time in the history of our people, and in the history of the whole American people, we join in this high worship and march conspicuously in the line of this time-honored custom. First things are always interesting, and this is one of our first things. It is the first time that, in this form and manner, we have sought to do honor to any American great man, however deserving and illustrious. I commend the fact to notice. Let it be told in every part of the Republic; let men of all parties and opinions hear it; let those who despise us, not less than those who respect us, know that now and here, in the spirit of

Liberty, Loyalty, and Gratitude,

let it be known everywhere and by everybody who takes an interest in human progress and in the amelioration of the condition of mankind, that in the presence and with the approval of the members

10. Arlington National Cemetery was originally the estate of General Robert E. Lee and his wife, Mary Anna Randolph Custis. In 1864, Union authorities confiscated the 1,100-acre plantation By the Civil War's end, the bodies of 16,000 slain soldiers of both armies, as well as those of 3,800 black refugees, were interred there.

of the American House of Representatives, reflecting the general sentiment of the country; that in the presence of that august body, the American Senate, representing the highest intelligence and the calmest judgment of the country; in presence of the Supreme Court and Chief Justice of the United States, to whose decisions we all patriotically bow; in the presence and under the steady eye of the honored and trusted President of the United States, we, the colored people, newly emancipated and rejoicing in our blood-bought freedom, near the close of the first century in the life of this Republic, have now and here unveiled, set apart, and dedicated a monument of enduring granite and bronze, in every line, feature, and figure of which the men of this generation may read—and those of after-coming generations may read—something of the exalted character and great works of Abraham Lincoln, the first martyr President of the United States.[11]

Fellow citizens: In what we have said and done to-day, and in what we may say and do hereafter, we disclaim everything like

Arrogance and Assumption.

We claim for ourselves no superior devotion to the character, history and memory of the illustrious name whose monument we have here dedicated to-day. We fully comprehend the relation of Abraham Lincoln, both to ourselves and the white people of the United States. Truth is proper and beautiful at all times and in all places, and it is never more proper and beautiful in any case than when speaking of a great public man whose example is likely to be commended for honor and imitation long after his departure to the

11. The idea for a memorial to Abraham Lincoln on behalf of the people he liberated began with Charlotte Scott, a freed Virginia slave. James E. Yeatman of the Western Sanitary Commission oversaw the collection of $16,242, which he reported was "contributed solely by emancipated citizens of the United States." *Inaugural Ceremonies of the Freedmen's Memorial Monument to Abraham Lincoln; Washington City, April 14, 1876* (St. Louis: Levison and Blythe, 1876), 8–9.

solemn shades, the silent continents of eternity. It must be admitted, truth compels me to admit even here in the presence of the monument we have erected to his memory, Abraham Lincoln was not, in the fullest sense of the word, either our man or our model. In his interests, in his associations, in his habits of thought, and in his prejudices, he was a white man. He was preeminently the white man's President, entirely devoted to the welfare of white men. He was ready and willing at any time during the last years of his administration to deny, postpone and sacrifice the rights of humanity in the colored people, to promote the welfare of the white people of his country. In all his education and feelings he was an

American of the Americans.

He came into the Presidential chair upon one principle alone, namely, opposition to the extension of slavery. His arguments in furtherance of this policy had their motive and mainspring in his patriotic devotion to the interest of his own race. To protect, defend and perpetuate slavery in the States where it existed, Abraham Lincoln was not less ready than any other President to draw the sword of the nation. He was ready to execute all the supposed constitutional guarantees of the Constitution in favor of the slave system anywhere inside the Slave States. He was willing to pursue, recapture, and send back the fugitive slave to his master, and to suppress a slave rising for liberty, though his guilty masters were already in arms against the Government. The race to which we belong were not the special objects of his consideration.[12] Knowing this, I concede to you, my white fellow-citizens, a pre-eminence in this worship at

---

12. Douglass repeats the criticism that he and many other abolitionists launched against Lincoln's hesitation to act against slavery in early years of the Civil War. As late as Lincoln's reelection campaign in the summer of 1864, Douglass was among the president's most vocal critics.

once full and supreme. First, midst and last you and yours were the object of his deepest affection and his most earnest solicitude.

You Are the Children

of Abraham Lincoln. We are at best only his step-children, children by adoption, children by force of circumstances and necessity. To you it especially belongs to sound his praises, to preserve and perpetuate his memory, to multiply his statues, to hang his pictures on your walls, and commend his example, for to you he was a great and glorious friend and benefactor. Instead of supplanting you at this altar we would exhort you to build high his monuments; let them be of the most costly material, of the most costly workmanship; let their forms be symmetrical, beautiful and perfect; let their bases be upon solid rocks, and their summits lean against the unchanging blue overhanging sky, and let them endure forever! But while in the abundance of your wealth and in the fullness of your just and patriotic devotion you do all this, we entreat you to despise not the humble offering we this day unveil to view: for while Abraham Lincoln saved for you a country, he delivered us from a bondage, according to Jefferson, one hour of which was worse than ages of the oppression your fathers rose in rebellion to oppose.[13]

Fellow-citizens: Ours is no new-born zeal and devotion, a thing of the hour. The name of Abraham Lincoln was

Near and Dear to Our Hearts

in the darkest and most perilous hours of the Republic. We were no more ashamed of him when shrouded in clouds of darkness, of

13. Douglass alludes to a letter of 26 June 1786 from Thomas Jefferson to Jean-Nicolas Démeunier. Boyd et al., eds., *Papers of Thomas Jefferson*, 10:63.

doubt and defeat than when crowned with victory, honor and glory. Our faith in him was often taxed and strained to the uttermost, but it never failed. When he tarried long in the mountain;[14] when he strangely told us that we were the cause of the war;[15] when he still more strangely told us to leave the land in which we were born; when he refused to employ our arms in defense of the Union; when, after accepting our services as colored soldiers, he refused to retaliate when we were murdered as colored prisoners; when he told us he would save the Union if he could with slavery; when he revoked the proclamation of emancipation of General Fremont;[16] when he refused to remove the commander of the Army of the Potomac,[17] who was more zealous in his efforts to protect slavery than suppress rebellion; when we saw this, and more, we were at times stunned, grieved and greatly bewildered; but our hearts believed while

They Ached and Bled.

Nor was this, even at that time, a blind and unreasoning superstition. Despite the mist and haze that surrounded him; despite the tumult, the hurry and confusion of the hour, we were able to take a

14. Douglass conflates words and themes from Genesis 31:54 and Exodus 19–20, 32.

15. In his "Address on Colonization to a Deputation of Negroes," given on 14 August 1862, Lincoln stated: "But for your race among us there could not be war, although many engaged on either side do not care for you one way or the other. Nevertheless, I repeat, without the institution of Slavery and the colored race as a basis, the war could not have an existence." Basler, *Collected Works of Lincoln*, 5:372.

16. Lincoln appointed John C. Frémont (1813–90) to command the Department of the West. On 30 August 1861, Frémont issued a proclamation emancipating the slaves of rebel Missourians, which Lincoln quickly revoked. A Cleveland convention of antislavery radicals seeking an alternative to Lincoln nominated Frémont for president in 1864, but Frémont later withdrew his candidacy.

17. George Brinton McClellan (1826–85) commanded the Army of the Potomac from July 1861 until November 1862. He was replaced after unsuccessfully attempting to march on Richmond and failing to pursue Lee's army after the Battle of Antietam. In 1864, McClellan ran unsuccessfully as the Democratic presidential candidate.

comprehensive view of Abraham Lincoln, and to make reasonable allowance for the circumstances of his position. We saw him, measured him, and estimated him; not by stray utterances to injudicious and tedious delegations, who often tried his patience; not by isolated facts torn from their connection; not by any partial and imperfect glimpses, caught at inopportune moments; but by a broad survey, in the light of the stern logic of great events—and in view of that divinity which shapes our ends,[18] rough hew them as we will, we came to the conclusion that the hour and the man of our redemption had met in the person of Abraham Lincoln. It mattered little to us what language he might employ upon special occasions; it mattered little to us, when we fully knew him, whether he was swift or slow in his movements; it was enough for us that Abraham Lincoln was at the head of a great movement, and was in living and earnest sympathy with that movement; which, in the nature of things, must go on

Till Slavery Should Be Utterly

and forever abolished in the United States. When, therefore, it shall be asked what we have to do with the memory of Abraham Lincoln, or what Abraham Lincoln had to do with us, the answer is ready, full and complete. Though he loved Caesar less than Rome,[19] though the Union was more to him than our freedom or our future, under his wise and beneficent rule we saw ourselves gradually lifted from the depths of slavery to the heights of liberty and manhood; under his wise and beneficent rule, and by measures approved and vigorously pressed by him, we saw that the handwriting of ages, in the form of prejudice and proscription, was rapidly fading away from the face of our whole country; under his rule, and in due time, about as soon after all as the country could tolerate the strange spectacle,

18. *Hamlet*, sc. 19, line. 3277.
19. *Julius Caesar*, sc. 9, lines 1408–09.

348 FREDERICK DOUGLASS

we saw our braves sons and brothers laying off the rags of bondage, and being clothed all over in the blue uniforms of the soldiers of the United States; under his rule we saw two hundred thousand of our dark and dusky people responding to the call of Abraham Lincoln, and, with muskets on their shoulders and eagles on their buttons, timing their high footsteps to liberty and union under the national flag;[20] under his rule we saw the independence of the black republic of Hayti, the special object of slaveholding aversion and horror fully recognized, and her minister, a colored gentleman, duly received here in the city of Washington;[21] under his rule we saw

The Internal Slave Trade

which so long disgraced the nation abolished, and slavery abolished in the District of Columbia;[22] under his rule we saw for the first time the law enforced against the foreign slave trade and the first slave-trader hanged, like any other pirate or murderer;[23] under his rule and his inspiration we saw the Confederate States, based upon the idea that our race must be slaves, and slaves forever, battered to pieces and scattered to the four winds; under his rule, and in the

20. According to official rosters, approximately 175 regiments composed of more than 178,000 free blacks and freedmen served in the Union Army following Lincoln's issuance of the Emancipation Proclamation. Thousands more served the army in a variety of auxiliary and support roles.

21. President Lincoln advocated diplomatic recognition of the black Caribbean nation Haiti in his annual message to Congress in December 1861. The first Haitian consul general and chargé d'affaires in the United States, Colonel Ernest Roumain, took up his post in Washington, D.C., in February 1863.

22. On 16 April 1862, the Senate and the House approved a bill emancipating all slaves in the District of Columbia. Despite abolitionist criticism, the bill contained a clause providing monetary compensation to slave owners in the federal territory. Lincoln signed the bill on the same day.

23. In 1862, Captain Nathaniel P. Gordon (?–1862) became the only person to be executed under U.S. law for participation in the slave trade. Gordon was prosecuted under an 1820 act that declared the slave trade to be piracy and made it a capital crime to work or travel on a U.S. ship engaged in the transportation or trade of prospective slaves.

fullness of time, we saw Abraham Lincoln, after giving the slave holders three months of grace in which to save their hateful slave system, penning the immortal paper which, though special in its language, was general in its principles and effect, making slavery forever impossible in the United States.[24] Though we waited long, we saw all this and more.

Can any colored man, or any white man friendly to the freedom of all men, ever forget the night which followed the first day of January, 1863? When the world was to see if Abraham Lincoln would prove to be as good as his word? I shall never forget that memorable night, when in a distant city I waited and watched at a public meeting, with three thousand others not less anxious than myself, for the word of deliverance which we have heard read to-day.[25] Nor shall I ever forget the outburst of joy and thanksgiving that rent the air when the lightning[26] brought to us the emancipation. In that happy hour we forgot all delay, and forgot all tardiness, forgot that the President had bribed the rebels to lay down their arms by a promise to withhold the bolt which would smite the slave system with destruction; and we were thenceforward willing to allow the President all the latitude of time, phraseology, and every honorable device that statesmanship might require for the achievement of a great and beneficent measure of liberty and progress.

Fellow-citizens, there is little necessity on this occasion to speak at length and critically of this great and good man, and of his high mission in the world. That ground has been fully occupied and completely covered both here and elsewhere. The whole field of fact and fancy has been gleaned and garnered. Any man can say things that are true of Abraham Lincoln, but no man can say anything new of Abraham Lincoln. His personal traits and public acts are better

24. The Emancipation Proclamation.
25. To celebrate the issuance of the Emancipation Proclamation, Douglass spoke at meetings held on 1–2 January 1863 in Boston's Tremont Temple and Twelfth Baptist Church.
26. A common mid-nineteenth-century nickname for the telegraph.

known to the American people than are those of any other man of his age. He was a mystery to no man who saw him and heard him. Though high in position, the humblest could approach him and feel at home in his presence. Though deep, he was transparent; though strong, he was gentle; though decided and pronounced in his convictions, he was tolerant towards those who differed from him, and patient under reproaches.

Even those who only knew him through his public utterances obtained a tolerably clear idea of his character and personality. The image of the man went out with his words, and those who read him knew him. I have said that President Lincoln was a white man, and shared the prejudices common to his countrymen towards the colored race. Looking back to his times and to the condition of the country, this unfriendly feeling on his part may safely be set down as one element of his wonderful success in organizing the loyal American people for the tremendous conflict before them, and bringing them safely through that conflict. His great mission was to accomplish two things; first, to save his country from dismemberment and ruin, and second, to free his country from the great crime of slavery. To do one or the other, or both, he must have the earnest sympathy and the powerful cooperation of his loyal fellow-countrymen. Without this primary and essential condition to success, his efforts must have been vain and utterly fruitless. Had he put the abolition of slavery before the salvation of the Union, he would have inevitably driven from him a powerful class of the American people, and rendered resistance to rebellion impossible. Viewed from the genuine abolition ground, Mr. Lincoln seemed tardy, cold, dull, and indifferent: but measuring him by the sentiment of his country, a sentiment he was bound as a statesman to consult, he was swift, zealous, radical, and determined. Though Mr. Lincoln shared the prejudices of his white fellow-countrymen against the negro, it is hardly necessary to say that in his heart of hearts

He Loathed and Hated Slavery.

He was willing while the South was loyal that it should have its pound of flesh,[27] because he thought it was so nominated in the bond, but further than this no earthly power could make him go.

Fellow-citizens, whatever else in this world may be partial, unjust and uncertain, *time! time!* is impartial, just and certain in its actions. In the realm of mind, as well as in the realm of matter, it is a great worker, and often works wonders. The honest and comprehensive statesman, clearly discerning the needs of his country, and earnestly endeavoring to do his whole duty, though covered and blistered with reproaches, may safely leave his course to the silent judgment of time. Few great public men have ever been the victims of fiercer denunciation than Abraham Lincoln was during his administration. He was often wounded in the house of his friends.[28] Reproaches came thick and fast upon him from within and from without, and from opposite quarters. He was assailed by abolitionists; he was assailed by slaveholders; he was assailed by men who were for peace at any price; he was assailed by those who were for a more vigorous prosecution of the war; he was assailed for not making the war an abolition war; and he was most bitterly assailed for making the war an abolition war.

But Now Behold the Change;

the judgment of the present hour is, that taking him for all in all, measuring the tremendous magnitude of the work before him, considering the necessary means to ends, and surveying the end from the beginning, infinite wisdom has seldom sent any man into

27. An allusion to *The Merchant of Venice,* sc. 18, line 2113.
28. Zech. 13:6.

the world better fitted for his mission than was Abraham Lincoln. His birth, his training, and his natural endowments, both mental and physical, were strongly in his favor. Born and reared among the lowly, a stranger to wealth and luxury, compelled to grapple single-handed with the flintiest hardships from tender youth to sturdy manhood, he grew strong in the manly and heroic qualities demanded by the great mission to which he was called by the votes of his countrymen. The hard condition of his early life, which would have depressed and broken down weaker men, only gave greater life, vigor and buoyancy to the heroic spirit of Abraham Lincoln. He was ready for any kind and any quality of work. What other young men dreaded in the shape of toil, he took hold of with the utmost cheerfulness.

> A spade, a rake, a hoe,
> A pick-axe or a bill;
> A hook to reap, a scythe to mow,
> A flail, or what you will.[29]

All Day Long He Could Split Heavy Rails

in the woods, and half the night long he could study his English grammar by the uncertain flare and glare of the light made by a pine knot. He was at home on the land with his axe, with his maul, with gluts and his wedges;[30] and he was equally at home on water, with his oars, with his poles, with his planks and with his boathooks. And whether in his flatboat on the Mississippi river, or at the fireside of his frontier cabin, he was a man of work. A son of toil himself he was linked in brotherly sympathy with the sons of toil in every loyal part

29. Douglass adapts the opening and refrain from Thomas Hood's "The Lay of the Laborer." Thomas Hood, *The Poetical Works* (Boston: Sampson and Company, 1857), 132–35.

30. A maul is a heavy hammer often used in combination with a wooden wedge, or "glut," to split logs.

of the Republic. This very fact gave him tremendous power with the American people, and materially contributed not only to selecting him to the Presidency, but in sustaining his administration of the Government.

Upon his inauguration as President of the United States, an office even where assumed under the most favorable conditions, it is fitted to tax and strain the largest abilities, Abraham Lincoln was met by a tremendous pressure.[31] He was called upon not merely to administer the Government, but to decide, in the face of terrible odds, the fate of the Republic. A formidable rebellion rose in his path before him; the Union was already practically dissolved.[32] His country was torn and rent asunder at the centre. Hostile enemies were already organized against the Republic, armed with the munitions of war which the Republic had provided for its own defense.[33]

The Tremendous Question

for him to decide was whether his country should survive the crisis and flourish or be dismembered and perish. His predecessor in office[34] had already decided the question in favor of national

31. Abraham Lincoln was inaugurated on 4 March 1861; the first military confrontation of the Civil War occurred at Fort Sumter in Charleston, South Carolina, on 12 April 1861.

32. On 20 December 1860, a few weeks after Abraham Lincoln's electoral victory, South Carolina seceded. Its legislature passed the ordinance of secession by a vote of 169–0. In the months before Lincoln's inauguration, six other states left the Union: Mississippi (9 January 1861), Alabama (9 January), Florida (10 January), Georgia (19 January), Louisiana (26 January), and Texas (1 February).

33. During the secession crisis, John Buchannan Floyd (1807–63) resigned as secretary of war when President Buchanan refused to order the federal garrison at Charleston, South Carolina, to evacuate Fort Sumter. In February 1861, Floyd was accused of having transferred large quantities of arms and ammunition from Northern to Southern arsenals in anticipation of secession. He returned to Washington, testified before a House of Representatives committee investigating the charges, and eventually was exonerated of any treasonous intentions.

34. James Buchanan.

dismemberment, by denying it the right of self-defense and self-preservation.

Happily for the country, happily for you and me, the judgment of James Buchanan, the patrician, was not the judgment of Abraham Lincoln, the plebeian.[35] He brought his strong common sense, sharpened in the school of adversity, to bear upon the question. He did not hesitate, he did not doubt, he did not falter, but at once resolved at whatever peril, at whatever cost, the union of the States should be preserved. A patriot himself, his faith was firm and unwavering in the patriotism of his countrymen. Timid men said before Mr. Lincoln's inauguration that we had seen the last President of the United States. A voice in influential quarters said let the Union slide. Some said that a Union maintained by the sword was worthless.[36] Others said a rebellion of 8,000,000 cannot be suppressed. But in the midst of all this tumult and timidity, and against all this Abraham Lincoln was clear in his duty, and had an oath in heaven. He calmly and bravely heard the voice of doubt and fear all around him, but he had an oath in heaven, and there was not power enough on the earth to make this honest boatman, backwoodsman and broad-handed splitter of rails evade or violate that sacred oath. He had not been schooled in the ethics of slavery; his plain life favored his love of truth. He had not been taught that treason and perjury were the proofs of honor and honesty. His moral training was against his saying one thing when he meant another. The trust which Abraham Lincoln had of himself and in the people was surprising and grand, but it was also enlightened and well founded. He knew the American people better than they knew themselves, and his truth was based upon his knowledge.

Had Abraham Lincoln died from any of the numerous ills to which flesh is heir;[37] had he reached that good old age of which his

35. "Patrician" and "plebeian" are Roman terms for "aristocrat" and "commoner."
36. On 9 November 1860, an editorial in the New York *Tribune* stated, "We never hope to live in a republic whereof one section is pinned to another by bayonets."
37. *Hamlet*, sc. 8, line 1601.

vigorous constitution and his temperate habits gave promise; had he been permitted to see the end of his great work; had the solemn curtain of death come down but gradually, we should still have been smitten with a heavy grief and treasured his name lovingly. But dying as he did die, by the red hand of violence; killed, assassinated, taken off without warning,[38] not because of personal hate, for no man who knew Abraham Lincoln could hate him, but because of his fidelity to Union and liberty, he is doubly dear to us, and will be precious forever.

Fellow-citizens, I end as I began, with congratulations. We have done a good work for our race to-day. In doing honor to the memory of our friend and liberator we have been doing highest honor to ourselves and those who come after us. We have been fastening ourselves to a name and fame imperishable and immortal. We have also been defending ourselves from a blighting slander. When now it shall be said that the colored man is soulless; that he has no appreciation of benefits or benefactors; when the foul reproach of ingratitude is hurled at us, and it is attempted to scourge us beyond the range of human brotherhood, we may calmly point to the monument we have this day erected to the memory of Abraham Lincoln.

38. A Confederate sympathizer, John Wilkes Booth, shot Abraham Lincoln as he attended a play at Washington's Ford's Theater on the evening of 14 April 1865.

"This Decision Has Humbled the Nation"

An Address Delivered in Washington, D.C.,
22 October 1883

Proceedings of the Civil Rights Mass-Meeting Held at Lincoln Hall,
October 22, 1883; Speeches of Hon. Frederick Douglass and Robert G.
Ingersoll (Washington, D.C., 1883), 4–14.

The Civil Rights Act of 1875 protected all citizens' rights to enjoy equal access to public accommodations and facilities and to serve on juries, regardless of race, color, or "previous condition of servitude." The act was designed to open hotels, restaurants, theaters, railroad cars, and other modes of public transportation to African Americans. Although very important to African American freedom, the 1875 act was rarely enforced after 1880, when the first legal challenges to it reached the Supreme Court.[1] On 15 October 1883, the Supreme Court, after considering five cases from different states, struck down the act.[2] The next day, Frederick Douglass and several other African American leaders in the District of Columbia organized a civil rights mass meeting that was to take place at Lincoln Hall on Monday evening, 22 October. Douglass and other local representatives would address the audience; Lewis Douglass, one of

1. Valeria W. Weaver, "The Failure of Civil Rights 1875–1883 and Its Repercussions," *Journal of Negro History* 54, no. 4 (October 1969): 368–70.

2. "The Color Controversy," Washington (D.C.) *National Republican*, 23 October 1883.

Douglass's sons, and several others drafted resolutions to be read at the meeting.[3]

Attendance was so great that admission had to be curtailed. According to the Washington *Evening Star,* over 2,000 attended. William Weston Patton, the president of Howard University, chaired the meeting; the Reverend Francis Grimké opened with a prayer; Lewis Douglass read the series of resolutions, which were unanimously adopted; and then Frederick Douglass spoke.[4] In his address, Douglass cautions against initiating violent resistance to the Supreme Court's decision, quoting Mark Antony's speech in Shakespeare's *Julius Caesar,* "We neither come to bury Caesar, nor to praise him." Ironically, despite Mark Antony's disavowal, his speech provoked the crowd to overthrow Brutus and the other conspirators. Douglass's intent is open to interpretation, but the speech criticizes the Supreme Court as an "autocratic" institution, and the resolutions advise listeners to address their grievances to the legislative branch. Douglass warns that we "want no black Ireland in America," suggesting that the major political parties need to find a way to appeal to black voters rather than alienate them and sow the seeds of future unrest. Further, he rebuts the claim that the bill was a "social rights bill": "No man in Europe would ever dream that because he has a right to ride on a railway, or stop at a hotel, he therefore has the right to enter into social relations with anybody." Douglass, who consistently distinguishes between civil rights and social relations in his writings, seems here to suggest that the solution lies in legislation that is more clearly written and capable of passing Supreme Court scrutiny.

After Douglass spoke, Colonel Robert Green Ingersoll, a well-known radical lawyer and lecturer, took the stage. Like Douglass, he adopted the position, expressed in the resolutions, that it was useless to criticize the Supreme Court justices, who, Ingersoll said, kept "their backs to the dawn" and "find what has been, not what ought to be."[5]

3. "The Civil Rights Mass Meeting," Washington (D.C.) *Evening Star,* 20 October 1883.

4. "The Civil Rights Meeting," Washington (D.C.) *Evening Star,* 23 October 1883.

5. "The Color Controversy," Washington (D.C.) *National Republican,* 23 October 1883.

The resolutions challenged African Americans to consider whether the Republican party deserved their loyalty. They urged both political parties to rededicate themselves to the egalitarian rhetoric embedded in their 1872 electoral platforms. The meeting's resolutions challenged both parties to find concrete legislative ways to make these ideals a reality.

Some newspapers derided the outcry following the Supreme Court's decision. The St. Paul (Minn.) *Daily Globe*, a Democratic newspaper, asserted that "Congress has no power to meddle with affairs merely social," and described Douglass as "characteristically outspoken."[6]

African American papers gave the gathering mixed reviews. Most were skeptical of its utility, despite their conviction that civil rights and social access were different things. Some black spokesmen, like Douglass, feared the erosion of those protections and rights earned through the Thirteenth, Fourteenth, and Fifteenth Amendments. The black lawyer John P. Green of Cleveland commented, "The Civil Rights Act was never of any practical utility . . . but will this end the matter? . . . Will not the next question be raised under the Thirteenth or Fourteenth amendments?"[7] The Arlington (Va.) *People's Advocate* viewed this reversal as a direct result of federal withdrawal from the South: "Who believes that had the right of voting been upheld in the South generally as it is to-day in Virginia that the Supreme Court would have dared to render such a decision."[8] The *People's Advocate*, in the weeks following the Supreme Court decision, lamented the lack of a response from prominent white abolitionists and referred to Ingersoll as "the sole white champion of the rights of the colored people."[9] The 1883 Supreme Court decision alerted Douglass and other African Americans that the legal freedoms gained during Reconstruction were no longer safe.

6. "Failure of the Social Rights Act," St. Paul (Minn.) *Daily Globe*, 22 October 1883.
7. "Civil Rights," Cleveland *Gazette*, 20 October 1883.
8. Arlington (Va.) *People's Advocate*, 27 October 1883.
9. "Bob Ingersoll," Arlington (Va.) *People's Advocate*, 10 November 1883.

F RIENDS AND FELLOW-CITIZENS: I have only a very few words to say to you this evening, and in order that those few words shall be well-chosen, and not liable to be misunderstood, distorted, or misrepresented, I have been at the pains of writing them out in full. It may be, after all, that the hour calls more loudly for silence than for speech. Later on in this discussion, when we shall have the full text of the recent decision of the Supreme Court before us,[10] and the dissenting opinion of Judge Harlan,[11] who must have weighty reasons for separating from all his associates, and incurring thereby, as he must, an amount of criticism from which even the bravest man might shrink, we may be in better frame of mind, better supplied with facts, and better prepared to speak calmly, correctly, and wisely, than now. The temptation at this time is, of course, to speak more from feeling than from reason, more from impulse than reflection.

We have been, as a class, grievously wounded, wounded in the house of our friends,[12] and this wound is too deep and too painful for ordinary and measured speech.

10. On 15 October 1883, the U.S. Supreme Court issued a decision in the *Civil Rights Cases* that declared the Civil Rights Act of 1875 unconstitutional. This law, generally regarded as one of the most radical to emerge from the Reconstruction era, granted all persons, regardless of race or color, full and equal access to public accommodations and facilities, particularly places of lodging, amusement, and transportation. The majority opinion, written by Justice Joseph P. Bradley (1813–92), declared that the Fourteenth Amendment had not given Congress the right to compel states to regulate against private acts of racial discrimination but only to legislate to correct state actions that denied civil rights. 109 U.S. 3 (1883), 8–26.

11. Justice John Marshall Harlan (1833–1911) opposed the majority decision in the *Civil Rights Cases*. Harlan claimed that the Thirteenth, Fourteenth, and Fifteenth Amendments were intended to protect the civil rights of former slaves, including the right not to be subject to racial discrimination. Congress therefore could legally, Harlan concluded, enforce the Fourteenth Amendment "by appropriate legislation, which may be of direct and primary character," like the Civil Rights Act of 1875. According to Harlan, this civil rights legislation was within constitutional bounds in allowing Congress to regulate the actions of states as well as individuals and corporations that exercise public functions, in order to ensure equal access to members of all races to public accommodations and facilities. 109 U.S. 3 (1883), 26–62.

12. Zech. 13:6.

"When a deed is done for Freedom,
Through the broad earth's aching breast
Runs a thrill of joy prophetic,
Trembling on from east to west."[13]

But when a deed is done for slavery, caste and oppression, and a blow is struck at human progress, whether so intended or not, the heart of humanity sickens in sorrow and writhes in pain. It makes us feel as if some one were stamping upon the graves of our mothers, or desecrating our sacred temples of worship. Only base men and oppressors can rejoice in a triumph of injustice over the weak and defenceless, for weakness ought itself to protect from assaults of pride, prejudice and power.

The cause which has brought us here to-night is neither common nor trivial. Few events in our national history have surpassed it in magnitude, importance and significance. It has swept over the land like a moral cyclone, leaving moral desolation in its track.

We feel it, as we felt the furious attempt, years ago, to force the accursed system of slavery upon the soil of Kansas, the enactment of the Fugitive Slave Bill, the repeal of the Missouri Compromise,[14] the Dred Scott decision. I look upon it as one more shocking development of that moral weakness in high places which has attended the conflict between the spirit of liberty and the spirit of slavery from the beginning, and I venture to predict that it will be so regarded by after-coming generations.

Far down the ages, when men shall wish to inform themselves as to the real state of liberty, law, religion and civilization in the United States at this juncture of our history, they will overhaul the proceedings of the Supreme Court, and read the decision declaring the Civil Rights Bill unconstitutional and void.

13. Douglass quotes the first two lines from the poem "The Present Crisis" by James Russell Lowell. *The Writings of James Russell Lowell*, 10 vols. Riverside ed. (Boston: Houghton, Mifflin, 1892), 7:178.
14. Douglass alludes to the Kansas-Nebraska Act of 1854.

From this they will learn more than from many volumes, how far we have advanced, in this year of grace, from barbarism toward civilization.

Fellow-citizens: Among the great evils which now stalk abroad in our land, the one, I think, which most threatens to undermine and destroy the foundations of our free institutions, is the great and apparently increasing want of respect entertained for those to whom are committed the responsibility and the duty of administering our government. On this point, I think all good men must agree, and against this evil I trust you feel, and we all feel, the deepest repugnance, and that we will, neither here nor elsewhere, give it the least breath of sympathy or encouragement. We should never forget, that, whatever may be the incidental mistakes or misconduct of rulers, government is better than anarchy, and patient reform is better than violent revolution.

But while I would increase this feeling, and give it the emphasis of a voice from heaven, it must not be allowed to interfere with free speech, honest expression, and fair criticism. To give up this would be to give up liberty, to give up progress, and to consign the nation to moral stagnation, putrefaction, and death.

In the matter of respect for dignitaries, it should never be forgotten, however, that duties are reciprocal, and while the people should frown down every manifestation of levity and contempt for those in power, it is the duty of the possessors of power so to use it as to deserve and to insure respect and reverence.

To come a little nearer to the case now before us. The Supreme Court of the United States, in the exercise of its high and vast constitutional power, has suddenly and unexpectedly decided that the law intended to secure to colored people the civil rights guaranteed to them by the following provision of the Constitution of the United States, is unconstitutional and void. Here it is:

"No State," says the 14th Amendment, "shall make or enforce any law which shall abridge the privileges or immunities of citizens of the United States; nor shall any State deprive any person of life, liberty, or property without due process of the law; nor deny any person within its jurisdiction the equal protection of the laws."[15]

Now, when a bill has been discussed for weeks and months, and even years, in the press and on the platform, in Congress and out of Congress; when it has been calmly debated by the clearest heads, and the most skillful and learned lawyers in the land; when every argument against it has been over and over again carefully considered and fairly answered; when its constitutionality has been especially discussed, pro and con; when it has passed the United States House of Representatives, and has been solemnly enacted by the United States Senate, perhaps the most imposing legislative body in the world; when such a bill has been submitted to the Cabinet of the Nation, composed of the ablest men in the land; when it has passed under the scrutinizing eye of the Attorney-General of the United States; when the Executive of the Nation has given to it his name and formal approval; when it has taken its place upon the statute-book, and has remained there for nearly a decade, and the country has largely assented to it, you will agree with me that the reasons for declaring such a law unconstitutional and void, should be strong, irresistible and absolutely conclusive.

Inasmuch as the law in question is a law in favor of liberty and justice, it ought to have had the benefit of any doubt which could arise as to its strict constitutionality. This, I believe, will be the view taken of it, not only by laymen like myself, but by eminent lawyers as well.

All men who have given any thought to the machinery, the structure, and practical operation of our Government, must have recognized the importance of absolute harmony between its various departments of power and duties. They must have seen clearly the mischievous tendency and danger to the body politic of any antagonisms between its various branches. To feel the force of this thought, we have only to remember the administration of President Johnson,

15. Douglass makes a few minor errors in quoting the Fourteenth Amendment.

and the conflict which then took place between the National Executive and the National Congress, when the will of the people was again and again met by the Executive veto,[16] and when the country seemed upon the verge of another revolution. No patriot, however bold, can wish for his country a repetition of those gloomy days.

Now let me say here, before I go on a step further in this discussion, if any man has come here to-night with his breast heaving with passion, his heart flooded with acrimony, wishing and expecting to hear violent denunciation of the Supreme Court, on account of this decision, he has mistaken the object of this meeting, and the character of the men by whom it is called.

We neither come to bury Cæsar, nor to praise him.[17] The Supreme Court is the autocratic point in our National Government. No monarch in Europe has a power more absolute over the laws, lives, and liberties of his people, than that Court has over our laws, lives, and liberties. Its Judges live, and ought to live, an eagle's flight beyond the reach of fear or favor, praise or blame, profit or loss. No vulgar prejudice should touch the members of that Court, anywhere. Their decisions should come down to us like the calm, clear light of Infinite justice. We should be able to think of them and to speak of them with profoundest respect for their wisdom, and deepest reverence for their virtue; for what His Holiness, the Pope, is to the Roman Catholic Church, the Supreme Court is to the American State. Its members are men, to be sure, and may not claim infallibility, like the Pope,[18] but they are the Supreme power of the Nation, and their decisions are law.

16. During his tenure as president, Andrew Johnson vetoed a number of bills involving Reconstruction and the Southern freedmen. Prominent among the legislation he struck down were the Freedmen's Bureau Bill (1866), the Civil Rights Bill (1866), the First Reconstruction Bill (1867), the Tenure of Office Bill (1867), and the Second Reconstruction Bill (1867).

17. *Julius Caesar,* sc. 9, line 1461.

18. In 1870 the Roman Catholic Church affirmed that the pope was infallible, that is, immune from error through divine assistance, when speaking on matters of church doctrine.

What will be said here to-night, will be spoken, I trust, more in sorrow than in anger,[19] more in a tone of regret than of bitterness.

We cannot, however, overlook the fact that though not so intended, this decision has inflicted a heavy calamity upon seven millions of the people of this country, and left them naked and defenceless against the action of a malignant, vulgar, and pitiless prejudice.

It presents the United States before the world as a Nation utterly destitute of power to protect the rights of its own citizens upon its own soil.

It can claim service and allegiance, loyalty and life, of them, but it cannot protect them against the most palpable violation of the rights of human nature, rights to secure which, governments are established. It can tax their bread and tax their blood, but has no protecting power for their persons. Its National power extends only to the District of Columbia, and the Territories—where the people have no votes—and where the land has no people.[20] All else is subject to the States. In the name of common sense, I ask, what right have we to call ourselves a Nation, in view of this decision, and this utter destitution of power?

In humiliating the colored people of this country, this decision has humbled the Nation. It gives to a South Carolina, or a Mississippi, Rail-Road Conductor, more power than it gives to the National Government. He may order the wife of the Chief Justice of the United States into a smoking-car, full of hirsute[21] men and compel her to go and listen to the coarse jests of a vulgar crowd. It gives to a hotel-keeper who may, from a prejudice born of the rebellion, wish to turn her out at midnight into the darkness and the storm, power to compel her to go. In such a case, according to this decision of the Supreme Court, the National Government has no right to

---

19. *Hamlet*, sc. 2, line 384.

20. Douglass alludes to Justice Bradley's interpretation of the U.S. Constitution, in the *Civil Rights Cases*, regarding the rights of state governments to provide legislative protection for their citizens' civil rights. 109 U.S. 3 (1883), 8–26.

21. Hairy.

interfere. She must take her claim for protection and redress, not to the Nation, but to the State, and when the State, as I understand it, declares there is upon its Statue book, no law for her protection, the function and power of the National Government is exhausted, and she is utterly without redress.

Bad, therefore, as our case is under this decision, the evil principle affirmed by the court is not wholly confined to or spent upon persons of color. The wife of Chief Justice Waite[22]—I speak it respectfully—is protected to-day, not by law, but solely by the accident of her color. So far as the law of the land is concerned, she is in the same condition as that of the humblest colored woman in the Republic. The difference between colored and white, here, is, that the one, by reason of color, needs legal protection, and the other, by reason of color, does not need protection. It is nevertheless true, that manhood is insulted, in both cases. No man can put a chain about the ankle of his fellow man, without at last finding the other end of it fastened about his own neck.

The lesson of all the ages on this point is, that a wrong done to one man, is a wrong done to all men. It may not be felt at the moment, and the evil day may be long delayed, but so sure as there is a moral government of the universe, so sure will the harvest of evil come.

Color prejudice is not the only prejudice against which a Republic like ours should guard. The spirit of caste is dangerous everywhere. There is the prejudice of the rich against the poor, the pride and prejudice of the idle dandy against the hard handed working man. There is, worst of all, religious prejudice; a prejudice which has stained a whole continent with blood. It is, in fact, a spirit infernal, against which every enlightened man should wage perpetual

22. Morrison Remick Waite (1816–88) served as chief justice of the U.S. Supreme Court from 1874 to his death. In cases dealing with Reconstruction-era legislation, Waite took an active, and consistently conservative, role in formulating decisions that curtailed the authority of the federal government to protect the civil rights of freedmen.

war. Perhaps no class of our fellow citizens has carried this prejudice against color to a point more extreme and dangerous than have our Catholic Irish fellow citizens, and yet no people on the face of the earth have been more relentlessly persecuted and oppressed on account of race and religion, than the Irish people.

But in Ireland, persecution has at last reached a point where it reacts terribly upon her persecutors. England to-day is reaping the bitter consequences of her injustice and oppression.[23] Ask any man of intelligence to-day, "What is the chief source of England's weakness?" "What has reduced her to the rank of a second-class power?" and the answer will be *"Ireland!"* Poor, ragged, hungry, starving and oppressed as she is, she is strong enough to be a standing menace to the power and glory of England.

Fellow-citizens! We want no black Ireland in America. We want no aggrieved class in America. Strong as we are without the negro, we are stronger with him than without him. The power and friendship of seven millions of people scattered all over the country,[24] however humble, are not to be despised.

To-day, our Republic sits as a Queen among the nations of the earth. Peace is within her walls and plenteousness within her palaces, but he is a bolder and a far more hopeful man than I am, who will affirm that this peace and prosperity will always last. History repeats itself.[25] What has happened once may happen again.

The negro, in the Revolution, fought for us and with us. In the war of 1812 Gen. Jackson,[26] at New Orleans, found it necessary to

23. On 30 October 1883 the U.S.-based Irish nationalist organization Clan-na-Gael exploded bombs at two stations on the London Underground as part of a wave of attacks from 1881 to 1885 on British infrastructure and police and military targets to promote the campaign for Irish independence.

24. The U.S. Census of 1880 reported 6,580,793 blacks in the nation's population, residing predominantly in the former slave states.

25. A proverb found in many languages and generally credited to Thucydides.

26. Andrew Jackson (1767–1845) was the seventh president of the United States. He was a Tennessee slave owner who rose to political prominence largely as a result of his military prowess in the War of 1812 and his campaigns against Native Americans.

call upon the colored people to assist in its defence against England. Abraham Lincoln found it necessary to call upon the negro to defend the Union against rebellion, and the negro responded gallantly in all cases.

Our legislators, our Presidents, and our judges should have a care, lest, by forcing these people, outside of law, they destroy that love of country which is needful to the Nation's defence in the day of trouble.

I am not here, in this presence, to discuss the constitutionality or unconstitutionality of this decision of the Supreme Court. The decision may or may not be constitutional. That is a question for lawyers, and not for laymen, and there are lawyers on this platform as learned, able, and eloquent as any who have appeared in this case before the Supreme Court, or as any in the land. To these I leave the exposition of the Constitution; but I claim the right to remark upon a strange and glaring inconsistency with former decisions, in the action of the court on this Civil Rights Bill. It is a new departure, entirely out of the line of the precedents and decisions of the Supreme Court at other times and in other directions where the rights of colored men were concerned. It has utterly ignored and rejected the force and application of object and intention as a rule of interpretation. It has construed the Constitution in defiant disregard of what was the object and intention of the adoption of the Fourteenth Amendment. It has made no account whatever of the intention and purpose of Congress and the President in putting the Civil Rights Bill upon the Statute Book of the Nation. It has seen fit in this case, affecting a weak and much-persecuted people, to be guided by the narrowest and most restricted rules of legal interpretation. It has viewed both the Constitution and the law with a strict regard to their letter, but without any generous recognition of their broad and liberal spirit. Upon those narrow principles the decision is logical and legal, of course. But what I complain of, and what every lover of liberty in the United States has a right to complain of, is this sudden and causeless reversal of all the great rules of legal interpretation by which this Court was governed in other days, in the construction of the Constitution and of laws respecting colored people.

In the dark days of slavery, this Court, on all occasions, gave the greatest importance to *intention* as a guide to interpretation. The object and *intention* of the law, it was said, must prevail. Everything in favor of slavery and against the negro was settled by this object and *intention*. The Constitution was construed according to its *intention*. We were over and over again referred to what the framers *meant*, and plain language was sacrificed that the so affirmed *intention* of these framers might be positively asserted. When we said in behalf of the negro that the Constitution of the United States was intended to establish justice and to secure the blessings of liberty to ourselves and our posterity, we were told that the words said so, but that that was obviously not its *intention;* that it was intended to apply only to white people, and that the *intention* must govern.[27]

When we came to that clause of the Constitution which declares that the immigration or importation of such persons as any of the States may see fit to admit shall not be prohibited,[28] and the friends of liberty declared that that provision of the Constitution did not describe the slave-trade, they were told that while its language applied not to slaves, but to persons, still the object and *intention* of that clause of the Constitution was plainly to protect the slave-trade, and that that *intention* was the law. When we came to that clause of the Constitution which declares that "No person held to service or labor in one State, under the laws thereof, escaping into another, shall in consequence of any law or regulation therein be discharged from such service or labor, but shall be delivered up on claim of the party to whom such service or labor may be due,"[29] we insisted that it neither described nor applied to slaves; that it applied only

27. Douglass alludes to the Preamble of the U.S. Constitution and the decision of Chief Justice Roger B. Taney in the *Dred Scott* case. *Dred Scott v. John F. A. Sanford,* 19 Howard 393 (1857), 407–10.

28. Douglass describes article I, section 9, of the U.S. Constitution, which prohibited Congress from banning the slave trade before 1808.

29. Douglass quotes article IV, section 2, of the U.S. Constitution.

to persons owing service and labor; that slaves did not and could not owe service and labor; that this clause of the Constitution said nothing of slaves or the masters of slaves; that it was silent as to slave States or free States; that it was simply a provision to enforce a contract; to discharge an obligation between two persons capable of making a contract, and not to force any man into slavery, for the slave could not owe service or make a contract.

We affirmed that it gave no warrant for what was called the "Fugitive Slave Bill," and we contended that that bill was therefore unconstitutional; but our arguments were laughed to scorn by that Court. We were told that the *intention* of the Constitution was to enable masters to recapture their slaves, and that the law of Ninety-three[30] and the Fugitive Slave Law of 1850 were constitutional.

Fellow-citizens! while slavery was the base line of American society, while it ruled the church and the state, while it was the interpreter of our law and the exponent of our religion, it admitted no quibbling, no narrow rules of legal or scriptural interpretations of Bible or Constitution. It sternly demanded its pound of flesh,[31] no matter how much blood was shed in the taking of it. It was enough for it to be able to show the *intention* to get all it asked in the Courts or out of the Courts. But now slavery is abolished. Its reign was long, dark and bloody. Liberty *now*, is the base line of the Republic. Liberty has supplanted slavery, but I fear it has not supplanted the spirit or power of slavery. Where slavery was strong, liberty is now weak.

O for a Supreme Court of the United States which shall be as true to the claims of humanity, as the Supreme Court formerly was to the demands of slavery! When that day comes, as come it will, a Civil Rights Bill will not be declared unconstitutional and void, in utter and flagrant disregard of the objects and *intentions* of the National legislature by which it was enacted, and of the rights plainly secured by the Constitution.

30. The Fugitive Slave Law of 1793.
31. An allusion to *The Merchant of Venice*, sc. 18, lines 2112–13.

This decision of the Supreme Court admits that the Fourteenth Amendment is a prohibition on the States. It admits that a State shall not abridge the privileges or immunities of citizens of the United States, but commits the seeming absurdity of allowing the people of a State to do what it prohibits the State itself from doing.

It used to be thought that the whole was more than a part; that the great included the less, and that what was unconstitutional for a State to do was equally unconstitutional for an individual member of a State to do. What is a State, in the absence of the people who compose it? Land, air and water. That is all. As individuals, the people of the State of South Carolina may stamp out the rights of the negro wherever they please, so long as they do not do so as a State. All the parts can violate the Constitution, but the whole cannot. It is not the act itself, according to this decision, that is unconstitutional. The unconstitutionality of the case depends wholly upon the party committing the act. If the State commits it, it is wrong, if the citizen of the State commits it, it is right.

O consistency, thou art indeed a jewel![32] What does it matter to a colored citizen that a State may not insult and outrage him, if a citizen of a State may? The effect upon him is the same, and it was just this effect that the framers of the Fourteenth Amendment plainly intended by that article to prevent.

It was the act, not the instrument, which was prohibited. It meant to protect the newly enfranchised citizen from injustice and wrong, not merely from a State, but from the individual members of a State. It meant to give him the protection to which his citizenship, his loyalty, his allegiance, and his services entitled him; and this meaning, and this purpose, and this intention, is now declared unconstitutional and void, by the Supreme Court of the United States.

32. John Bartlett posits that the phrase evolved over time and reflects a tendency of people to compare virtue or excellence to the brilliance of a jewel. Bartlett, *Familiar Quotations*, 1046.

I say again, fellow-citizens, O for a Supreme Court which shall be as true, as vigilant, as active, and exacting in maintaining laws enacted for the protection of human rights, as in other days was that Court for the destruction of human rights!

It is said that this decision will make no difference in the treatment of colored people; that the Civil Rights Bill was a dead letter, and could not be enforced. There is some truth in all this, but it is not the whole truth. That bill, like all advance legislation, was a banner on the outer wall[33] of American liberty, a noble moral standard, uplifted for the education of the American people. There are tongues in trees, books, in the running brooks,—sermons in stones.[34] This law, though dead, did speak.[35] It expressed the sentiment of justice and fair play, common to every honest heart. Its voice was against popular prejudice and meanness. It appealed to all the noble and patriotic instincts of the American people. It told the American people that they were all equal before the law; that they belonged to a common country and were equal citizens. The Supreme Court has hauled down this flag of liberty in open day, and before all the people, and has thereby given joy to the heart of every man in the land who wishes to deny to others what he claims for himself. It is a concession to race pride, selfishness and meanness, and will be received with joy by every upholder of caste in the land, and for this I deplore and denounce that decision.

It is a frequent and favorite device of an indefensible cause to misstate and pervert the views of those who advocate a good cause, and I have never seen this device more generally resorted to than in the case of the late decision on the Civil Rights Bill. When we dissent from the opinion of the Supreme Court, and give the reasons why we think that opinion unsound, we are straightway charged in the papers with denouncing the Court itself, and thus put in the attitude of bad citizens. Now, I utterly deny that there has ever been

33. *Macbeth*, sc. 25, line 1982.
34. *As You Like It*, sc. 4, lines 597–98.
35. Heb. 11:14.

any denunciation of the Supreme Court on this platform, and I defy any man to point out one sentence or one syllable of any speech of mine in denunciation of that Court.

Another illustration of this tendency to put opponents in a false position, is seen in the persistent effort to stigmatize the "Civil Rights Bill" as a "Social Rights Bill." Now, nowhere under the whole heavens, outside the United States, could any such perversion of truth have any chance of success. No man in Europe would ever dream that because he has a right to ride on a railway, or stop at a hotel, he therefore has the right to enter into social relations with anybody. No one has a right to speak to another without that other's permission. Social equality and civil equality rest upon an entirely different basis, and well enough the American people know it; yet to inflame a popular prejudice, respectable papers like the New York *Times* and the Chicago *Tribune,* persist in describing the Civil Rights Bill as a Social Rights Bill.[36]

When a colored man is in the same room or in the same carriage with white people, as a servant, there is no talk of social equality, but if he is there as a man and a gentleman, he is an offence. What makes the difference? It is not color, for his color is unchanged. The whole essence of the thing is a studied purpose to degrade and stamp out the liberties of a race. It is the old spirit of slavery, and nothing else. To say that because a man rides in a same car with another, he is therefore socially equal, is one of the wildest absurdities.

When I was in England, some years ago,[37] I rode upon highways, byways, steamboats, stage coaches, omnibuses; I was in the House of Commons, in the House of Lords, in the British Museum, in

36. The Chicago *Tribune,* the New York *Times,* and other newspapers editorialized favorably upon the Supreme Court's decision declaring the Civil Rights Act of 1875 unconstitutional. Douglass's prompt criticism of the decision drew censure from the editors of these newspapers, who condemned the law as a "social rights bill" that, by protecting equal accommodation in hotels, railroads, and theaters, promoted social equality. New York *Times,* 16, 18 October 1883; Chicago *Tribune,* 19, 20 October 1883.

37. Douglass visited Great Britain in 1845–47 and again in 1859–60.

the Coliseum,[38] in the National Gallery, everywhere; sleeping sometimes in rooms where lords and dukes had slept; sitting at tables where lords and dukes were sitting; but I never thought that those circumstances made me socially the equal of lords and dukes. I hardly think that some of our Democratic friends would be regarded among those lords as their equals. If riding in the same car makes one equal, I think that the little poodle I saw sitting in the lap of a lady was made equal by riding in the same car. Equality, social equality, is a matter between individuals. It is a reciprocal understanding. I don't think when I ride with an educated polished rascal, that he is thereby made my equal, or when I ride with a numbskull that it makes me his equal, or makes him my equal. Social equality does not necessarily follow from civil equality, and yet for the purpose of a hell black and damning prejudice, our papers still insist that the Civil Rights Bill is a Bill to establish social equality.

If it is a Bill for social equality, so is the Declaration of Independence, which declares that all men have equal rights; so is the Sermon on the Mount,[39] so is the Golden Rule,[40] that commands us to do to others as we would that others should do to us; so is the Apostolic teaching, that of one blood God has made all nations to dwell on all the face of the earth; so is the Constitution of the United States, and so are the laws and customs of every civilized country in the world; for no where, outside of the United States, is any man denied civil rights on account of his color.

---

38. The London Colosseum was a building to the east of Regent's Park. It was constructed in 1827 to exhibit Thomas Hornor's *Panoramic View of London,* the largest painting ever created, covering more than forty thousand square feet.
39. Matt. 5–7; Luke 6:20–49.
40. Matt. 7:12; Luke 6:31.

"'It Moves,' or the Philosophy of Reform"

An Address Delivered in Washington, D.C., 20 November 1883

Speech File, reel 18, frames 5–22, Frederick Douglass Papers, Library of Congress.

In the months leading up to this speech, Frederick Douglass was embroiled in a debate regarding the designation of a leader who would speak for and guide African American civil rights reform. In May 1883, Douglass and several other influential blacks called for a national convention of African Americans to be held in Washington, D.C.[1] Resistance to the proposal immediately arose. Richard T. Greener, a Howard University professor, accused Douglass and the other black activists of having passively accepted the loss of black rights at the end of Reconstruction.[2] Suggesting that the organizers were primarily interested in currying favor with the Republican party, Greener stated, "We are free; have citizenship; have education or educational advantages, and some degree of civil rights. What more do these men want? More office; office that is all."[3]

Douglass responded to this criticism, saying, "The republican presses betray a fear that the convention will be anti-republican, while the colored editors fear that the convention will be controlled by the existing administration."[4] Accusations continued unabated, with Douglass as a focal point, even after the convention was moved to Louisville, Kentucky, away from the political atmosphere of Wash-

1. "The Proposed National Colored Convention," Washington (D.C.) *Evening Star*, 16 May 1883.
2. Ibid., 15 May 1883.
3. "Colored Man's Opinion," Washington (D.C.) *Bee*, 12 May 1883.
4. "The Proposed Colored Convention," Washington (D.C.) *Bee*, 12 May 1883.

ington, D.C. The crowning insult came at the meeting to nominate representatives from the District of Columbia to the Louisville gathering. The body nearly rejected Douglass, claiming "he had received the honors and representation of the colored people for twenty years, and had accomplished little or nothing."[5]

Douglass nonetheless traveled to Louisville at the end of September and went on to be elected, after contentious discussion, president of the convention. Despite a warm reception from his audience, Douglass's keynote was rejected as the representative statement of the convention and replaced by a series of resolutions approved by the delegates.[6] At one point during the meeting, Douglass was publicly accused of remaining silent when Reconstruction was overturned in 1877, but after Douglass's impassioned rebuttal, the convention "rose as one man and sang 'John Brown's body.'"[7] Clearly, the majority of delegates recognized Douglass's enduring legacy as a champion of black freedom and citizenship.

After these severe challenges to his leadership, Douglass delivered the lecture "It Moves," on his philosophy of reform, to the Bethel Literary and Historical Association of Washington, D.C, two months after the Louisville convention. In it, he reminds his critics of the dangers that abolitionists, and by implication Douglass himself, faced when protesting slavery. He proffers a transcendentalist theory of reform in which one seeks out the overarching order and truth of things, looking to science and sociology, rather than religion, to guide social reform. Armed with social truths, the reformer acts, rather than waiting for divine intervention: "So far as the laws of the universe have been discovered and understood, they seem to teach that the mission of man's improvement and perfection has been wholly committed to man himself. . . . He has neither angels to help him nor devils to hinder him." Parroting the remarks made by opponents of the Louisville conference, he rhetorically asks at the end, "What have Garrison, Gerrit Smith and others done for the colored people?" He answers, "It is the extreme men on either side who constitute the real

---

5. "The Louisville Convention," Washington (D.C.) *Bee*, 14 July 1883.
6. "The Convention,—Its Work," Arlington (Va.) *People's Advocate*, 6 October 1883.
7. Ibid.

forces. All others move as they are moved upon." His recent experience caused him to conclude that "the fate of pioneers is to suffer
reproach and persecution."

Douglass's lecture was followed by the Reverend W. H. Brooks,
who called the talk heretical. The Alexandria (Va.) *People's Advocate*
summarized Brooks's statement: "If Mr. Douglass' theological positions were correct we had better close our Bibles and churches."[8]
Brooks believed one had to embrace "Mosaic cosmology," the Old
Testament view that the world was created in seven days, in order
to be Christian. Douglass insisted that he did not disagree with religion as taught by Christ, only as taught by some theologians. Douglass anticipated Martin Luther King Jr.'s philosophy of reform, as
articulated in the "Letter from Birmingham Jail," eighty years later.
King said it was not those who opposed reform who were its worst
enemies, but rather those "friends" who counseled patience. King
drew on Douglass when he criticized the "myth of time," the belief
that God in his own time would reform social evils.[9] Both rejected
an interpretation of the Bible that promoted resignation and passiv-
ity; both urged agitation. As Richard Leeman shows in his essay excerpted for this volume, as Douglass neared the end of his career as
a reformer, he found himself increasingly answering criticisms from
black conservatives who opposed agitation and embraced conservative religious views as well as an individualistic political ethos.

It Moves.

Such was the half suppressed and therefore cowardly and yet confident, affirmation of Galileo, the great Italian mathematician.[10]

---

8. "Bethel Literary," Arlington (Va.) *People's Advocate*, 24 November 1883.
9. David Howard-Pitney, *The African American Jeremiad: Appeals for Justice in America* (Philadelphia: Temple University Press, 2005), 148–49, 154.
10. The Italian mathematician and astronomer Galileo Galilei (1564–1642) pub-
licly advocated the Copernican theory of the movement of the earth around the sun.
In 1616 a commission appointed by Pope Paul V condemned the heliocentric view and
admonished Galileo to abandon it. Believing that the church would permit publication
of his views on the physical system of the universe as a hypothesis, Galileo published

He had solved a vast problem and had done more than any man of his day and generation to dispel the intellectual darkness of ages, and reform the astronomical thought of the world; yet here he was virtually upon his knees before the power of ignorance and superstition; selling his soul to save his life.

The circumstances under which the above words were spoken or whispered, for they were not spoken aloud, were critical, as, indeed, circumstances always are, when a new truth is born into the world. For there is ever at such times some Herod ready to seek the young child's life,[11] and a multitude to cry out, "Crucify him!"[12]

The courage and integrity of this apostle of a new truth was put to the severest test. He had been solemnly arraigned, fiercely accused, and sternly condemned to death for teaching a new doctrine at war with the prevailing theology of the period.

Theology in those days endured no contradiction. The voice of the Church was all powerful. It was able not only to punish the soul, and shut the gates of heaven against whom it would, but to kill the body as well. The case of Galileo was therefore one of life and death. He must either affirm the truth and die, or deny the truth and live. Skin for skin, as was said of Job, all that a man hath will he give for his life.[13] Under this terrible pressure the courage of the great man quailed. Hence he, in open court denied and repudiated the grand and luminous truth which he had demonstrated, and with which his name was to be forever associated. His denial was probably not less hearty and vehement than was that of Peter when he denied his Lord.[14] There was not only likeness in their denial, but likeness in their repentance.

---

his *Dialogue Concerning the Two Chief World Systems* in 1632. In 1633, Galileo was tried by the Inquisition for heresy, threatened with torture, found guilty, forced to recant his belief in heliocentrism, and sentenced to spend the rest of his life under house arrest. According to legend, despite recanting, he quietly said after his trial, "*Eppur si muove*," or "And yet it moves," referring to Earth revolving around the sun.

11. Matt. 2:13–23.

12. Matt. 27:23; Mark 15:13; Luke 23:21; John 16:6.

13. Job 2:4.

14. Matt. 26:69–75; Mark 14:66–72; Luke 22:55–62; John 18:15–18, 25–27.

The words I have quoted were the tremulous reaffirmation to himself of the truth that he had denied in the hall of his rigorous judges. They were no doubt forced from his quivering lips to silence the upbraiding of an accusing conscience. There is generally a great tumult in the human soul when guilty of any meanness, especially to such a soul as has not become hardened by persistent violation of its moral nature. Peter and Galileo were great-hearted men. The one sought relief in bitter tears, the other in reaffirming to himself the truth he had denied to the world.

Is there no apology for these examples of human weakness? If there is much that is humiliating in the attitude of these two great men, for great men they were, spite of their weakness, there is also something to commend. He should step lightly who sits in judgment upon the weakness of those who pioneer an unpopular cause. Heroic courage is a noble quality; but it is not always the possession of great minds. "Stand by your principles!" shouts the crowd, but, if put to such a test as that of our two worthies, how many of all the crowd could be found to practice what they preach?[15]

If only the truly brave were allowed to throw stones at the cowards, few stones would be thrown, and few wounds would be inflicted. Any man can be brave where there is no danger. If those only are true believers who can face peril, torture and death for their faith, the true church is small, and true believers are few. Men are easily heroes to heaven while they are cowards to earth. They can brave the unknown terrors of eternity, while they quail before the known terrors of time. Erasmus[16] expressed much of genuine human nature, when he declared that he would rather trust God

15. Douglass quotes St. Jerome, who wrote in a letter, "Why do you not practice what you preach?" St. Jerome, *Select Letters of St. Jerome*, trans. F. A. Wright (Cambridge, Mass.: Harvard University Press, 1933), 209.

16. Desiderius Erasmus of Rotterdam (c. 1466–1536) strove to avoid commitment to Luther's or the Catholic Church's side in Reformation debates. In 1525 he defended the Catholic doctrine of freedom of the will, rather than the church itself, and a person's ability to cooperate with the implements of grace rather than to attain his or her own salvation.

with his soul than the inquisition[17] with his body. Even the mercy of the law allows something for the deviation from the straight line of truth, when a man swears under duress.

It should never be forgotten that the instruments of reform are not necessarily perfect at all points of possible human character. Men may be very good and useful and yet far from being the stuff out of which martyrs are made.

Though Peter denied his Lord, and Galileo science, though both quailed before the terrors of martyrdom, and though neither was as strong as the truth they had denied, the world is vastly better off for their lives, their words and their works. It required a larger measure of courage for Galileo to whisper truth in his day than for us to proclaim the same truth now upon the house-top.

The greatest coward can now shout that he has been with Jesus, but only the grandly heroic could do so when menaced by the spears and swords of Roman soldiers, in the Judgment Hall of Pilate, with death upon the cross the probable penalty for being in such company.

I am to speak to you of the Philosophy of Reform. According to the dictionary, and we are bound to adhere to the truth of words, the word reform is defined, "to put in a new and improved condition; to bring from bad to good; to change from worse to better." This is true, apply it as we may; whether it be self reform, social reform, national reform, or reform in any direction whatever.

We are nevertheless met at the outset of this discussion with the question as to whether there is any such thing as reform in the sense defined in the dictionary. It is contended by some very respectable

17. To combat heretical and unorthodox religious movements, popes in the twelfth century established episcopal courts with powers of coercion, and then centralized their operations under papal legates chosen from monastic orders. The Spanish Inquisition, which Ferdinand and Isabella established in 1483, was a new type of episcopal court, one entirely under state control and used for political as much as religious ends. In 1542, Pope Paul III founded the Roman Inquisition as the primary organ of the Counter-Reformation. In the nineteenth century, a revived Inquisition was part of the Catholic restoration in post-Napoleonic Europe.

writers and thinkers, that Reform is a delusion, a deceitful appearance; that there is no such thing as making the world better; that the phenomenon of change every where observable, brings no substantial improvement; that mankind are like the sea, whose waves rise and fall, advance and retreat, while the general level remains forever the same.[18]

It is contended that the balance between good and evil remains, like the sea, fixed, unchangeable, and eternally the same. In support of this disheartening theory, these turn our eyes towards the East and lead us about among its decayed and wasted civilizations, its ancient cities, its broken monuments, its mouldering temples, its ruined altars, its buried treasures, its shattered walls and fallen pillars, and picture to us in brilliant colors their former greatness and glory, and with the gloomy Byron, they inquire, "Where are their greatness and glory now?"[19]

I shall not stop to combat this skepticism till I have mentioned another and a worse form of unbelief, not the denial that the world is growing better, but the assertion that it is growing worse. Improvement is not only denied, but deterioration is affirmed. According to the advocates of this theory, mankind are on the descending grade; physically, morally and intellectually, the men and women of our age are in no respect equal to the ancients, and art, science and philosophy have gained nothing. This misanthropic view of the world may, I think, be easily answered. It has about it a show of truth and learning, but they are only seeming, not real.

One cause of the error may be for want of a proper knowledge of the remote past. Here, as elsewhere, 'tis distance lends enchant-

---

18. The repudiation of liberalism and a concomitant return to an orthodox Christian view of secular history gained popularity in Europe during the conservative reaction, both political and intellectual, that followed the French Revolution.

19. Douglass paraphrases the sentiments of Lord Byron's *Childe Harold's Pilgrimage*, canto II, particularly stanza 25. Ernest Hartley Coleridge, ed., *The Works of Lord Byron*, 13 vols. (1898; New York: Charles Scribner's Sons, 1899), 2:115.

ment[20] to the view. We fail to make due allowance for the refractive nature of the medium through which we are compelled to view the past. We naturally magnify the greatness of that which is remote. By this the imagination is addressed rather than the understanding. The dim and shadowing figures of the past are clothed in glorious light, and pigmies appear as giants.

Grand and sublime, however, as is the glorious faculty of imagination as a reflector and creator, and while it is the explanation of all religion, and, perhaps, the source of all progress, it is nevertheless the least safe of all our faculties for the discernment of what is truth. There are two sufficient modes of answering theories in denial of progress and reform. One is an appeal to the essential nature of man; the other is to historical facts and experience. A denial of progress and the assumption of retrogression is a point-blank contradiction to the ascertained and essential nature of man. It opposes the known natural desire for change, and denies the instinctive hope and aspiration of humanity for something better.

A theory involving such results may well enough be rejected, even without further reason. It is just as natural for man to seek and discover improved conditions of existence, as it is for birds to fly in the air or to fill the morning with melody or to build their nests in the spring. The very conditions of helplessness in which men are born suggest reform and progress as the necessity of their nature. He literally brings nothing into the world to meet his multitudinous necessities. He is, upon first blush, less fortunate than all other animals.

Nature has prepared nothing for him. He must find his own needed food, raiment and shelter, or the iron hand of nature will smite him with death. But he has a dignity which belongs to himself alone. He is an object, not only to himself, but to his species, and his species an object to him. Every well formed man finds no rest to

---

20. A slightly inaccurate quotation of Thomas Campbell's poem *The Pleasures of Hope*, part 1, line 7. W. A. Hill, ed., *The Poetical Works of Thomas Campbell, with Notes and a Biographical Sketch* (London: Edward Moxon, 1851), 1.

his soul while any portion of his species suffers from a recognized evil. The deepest wish of a true man's heart is that good may be augmented and evil, moral and physical, be diminished, and that each generation shall be an improvement on its predecessor.

I do not know that I am an evolutionist, but to this extent I am one. I certainly have more patience with those who trace mankind upward from a low condition, even from the lower animals, then with those that start him at a high point of perfection and conduct him to a level with the brutes. I have no sympathy with a theory that starts man in heaven and stops him in hell.[21]

To this complexion it must come at last, if no progress is made, and the only movement of mankind is a downward or retrograde movement. Happily for us the world does move, and better still, its movement is an upward movement. Kingdoms, empires, powers, principalities and dominions, may appear and disappear; may flourish and decay; but mankind as a whole must ever move onward, and increase in the perfection of character and in the grandeur of achievement.

That the world moves, as affirmed and demonstrated by the Italian mathematician, was long since admitted; but movement is not less true of the moral, intellectual and social universe than of the physical. Here, as elsewhere, there are centripetal and centrifugal forces forever at work. Those of the physical world are not more active, certain and effective, than those of the moral world.

An irrepressible conflict, grander than that described by the late William H. Seward,[22] is perpetually going on. Two hostile and ir-

21. Evolutionists accepted the Darwinist view that species arose from the struggle for existence and the laws of natural selection. Darwin—and to a much greater extent, his popularizers—thought that evolution was progressive, that is, life always moved from simpler to more complex forms, but Darwin did not argue that idea as part of the scientific theory. The assumption of racial superiority central to the philosophy of social Darwinism might have accounted for Douglass's ambivalence in regard to evolution.

22. Douglass alludes to the title of a speech delivered by William H. Seward in Rochester, New York, on 25 October 1858. William H. Seward, *The Irrepressible*

reconcilable tendencies, broad as the world of man, are in the open field; good and evil, truth and error, enlightenment and superstition. Progress and reaction, the ideal and the actual, the spiritual and material, the old and the new, are in perpetual conflict, and the battle must go on till the ideal, the spiritual side of humanity shall gain perfect victory over all that is low and vile in the world. This must be so unless we concede that what is divine is less potent than what is animal; that truth is less powerful than error; that ignorance is mightier than enlightenment, and that progress is less to be desired than reaction, darkness and stagnation. It is worthy of remark that, in the battle of reform, all the powers on both sides are not usually engaged. The grosser forms of wrong are, as they appear, first confronted. One truth is discovered in the moral sky, and lo! another illumines the horizon. One error is vanquished, and lo! another, clad in complete steel, invites demolition, and thus the conflict goes on and will go on forever.

But we are still met with the question: "Is there any substantial gain to the right?" "Is only one evil suppressed to give rise to another?" "Does one error disappear only to make room for another?" It is impossible to keep questions like these out of the minds of thoughtful men. The facts in answer to them are abundant, familiar, and, as I think, conclusive. First, let us look at the science of astronomy. How grand and magnificent have been the discoveries in that field of knowledge. What victories over error have been achieved by the telescope. That instrument did not bring down what the great poet calls "the brave over-hanging sky,"[23] nor the shining stars in it; but it did bring down and dispel vast clouds of error, both in respect of the sky and of our planet. It must be confessed, too, that it took something from the importance of our planet. The idea that all the hosts of heaven are mere appendages to this earth is no longer

---

Conflict: A Speech by William H. Seward, Delivered at Rochester, Monday, Oct. 25, 1858 (New York: New York Tribune, [1860]).

23. Hamlet, sc. 7, lines 1230–31.

entertained by average men, and no man, except our good brother Hampton of England[24] and brother Jasper of Richmond,[25] now stand by the old theory for which the church proposed to murder Galileo. Men are compelled to admit that the Genesis by Moses is less trustworthy as to the time of creating the heavens and the earth than are the rocks and the stars.

Espy unfolded the science of storms,[26] and forthwith thunder and lightning parted with their ancient predicates of wrath and were no longer visitations of divine vengeance.

Experience and observation in the science of government gave us clearer views of justice, and the means of ascertaining it, and jury trial speedily took the trial by ordeal, poison and combat.

Vaccination was discovered, and, like all new discoveries, had at the first to maintain a vigorous battle for existence. It was condemned by the church as a cunning device of the devil to defeat the judgments of God.[27] Nevertheless, it has triumphed, and is now adopted by the best instructed of all nations.

24. Though Douglass is partly mistaken in his characterization of him, the English champion of scriptural literalism seems to be Renn Dickson Hampden (1793–1868), bishop of Hereford.

25. Douglass alludes to John Jasper (1812–1901), a black Baptist, and his famous sermon "The Sun Do Move," which claimed the Bible proved that the sun traveled around the earth. Born a Virginia slave, Jasper used vivid, although ungrammatical, imagery that drew thousands every Sunday to listen to his sermons at several large churches in Richmond, Virginia.

26. The early work in meteorology of James Pollard Espy (1785–1860) was in the established tradition of observation, which he tried to expand into a national system in the United States. He later began the much less conventional work of experimentation to uncover basic physical concepts that could be applied to weather observation. His principal interest was in heat effects, and his major discovery lay in the role and the dynamics of latent heat in cloud formation and precipitation.

27. Thinkers in eighteenth-century England and France independently conceived of the concept of inoculation, the introduction into the human body of a controlled quantity of a disease-causing substance to prevent occurrence of the disease. (A simple form of inoculation had been practiced in China and the Middle East for several centuries.) Although by 1801 one hundred thousand people had received vaccinations against smallpox, both the Roman Catholic and Protestant churches in Europe resisted it as an interference with the will of God and strenuously fought against it throughout the century.

The history of the world shows that mankind have been gradually getting the victory over famine, plagues and pestilence, and that diseases of all kinds are parting with their repulsive grossness. When we look in the direction of religion, we see Luther,[28] Melancthon,[29] Erasmus and Zwingle,[30] and other stalwart reformers, confronting and defying the Vatican and repudiating pontifical authority. What is the result? Why, this: men are no longer, as formerly, tortured, burned, strangled and starved to death, on account of their religious opinions. Learning has unlocked to us the mysteries of Egypt. It has deciphered the hieroglyphics,[31] and shown us that the slaughter of animals and the slaughter of men as sacrifices was a rude device of the religious sentiment to propitiate the favor of imaginary gods.

The Christian religion dawned upon Western Europe and a thousand men were no longer slain to make a Roman holiday. A little common sense took the place of unreasoning faith in the

---

28. The Augustinian monk Martin Luther (1484–1546) lectured in theology at the University of Wittenberg in 1513. His famous Ninety-five Theses (1517) focused on abuses in the sale of indulgences by the Roman Catholic Church. (An indulgence was a pardon for a sinful act, issued before the act was committed. In the fifteenth and sixteenth centuries, the church sold indulgences to pay for the construction of St. Peter's Basilica.) In 1520, Pope Leo X excommunicated Luther and anathematized his writings. In the last two decades of his life, Luther labored prodigiously at the creation of new forms of church worship, the explication of scripture, and the education of a new ministry.

29. Philip Melanchthon (1497–1560) committed himself to the Protestant Reformation shortly after he arrived in Wittenberg in 1518, where he both taught and befriended Martin Luther. Melanchthon attempted to reconcile conflicting theological positions. He drafted the Augsburg Confession (1530), the principal confession of faith in the Lutheran Church. Signed by Catholic and Protestant representatives, it excluded the more radical positions of Ulrich Zwingli and the Anabaptists.

30. Ulrich (or Huldreich) Zwingli (1484–1531) was a Catholic pastor in German-speaking Switzerland. Zwingli regularly preached against "externals," and his followers stripped churches of images, whitewashed church walls, and excluded music from religious rituals.

31. The deciphering of Egyptian hieroglyphics eluded scholars until the discovery in 1799 of the Rosetta Stone, a black basalt slab bearing three parallel texts, one in Greek (a key to the others), one in Egyptian hieroglyphics, and one in demotic Egyptian, a cursive script.

Puritan, and old women in New England were no longer hanged as witches.[32]

Science tells us what storms are in the sky and when and where they will descend upon our continent, and nobody now thinks of praying for rain or fair weather.

Only a few centuries ago women were not allowed to learn the letters of the alphabet, now she takes her place among the intellectual forces of the day and ranks with our finest scholars, best teachers and most successful authors. Lundy,[33] Walker[34] and Garrison,[35] shocked by the enormities of slavery, branded the system as a crime against human nature; and, after thirty years of fierce and fiery conflict against press and pulpit, church and state, men have ceased to quote the Scriptures to prove slavery a divine institution.

The fathers of the American Revolution took a vast step in the direction of political knowledge when they discovered and announced humanity as the source and authority for human government. To them we are indebted today for a government of the people. Even Europe itself is gradually parting with its notion of the divine right of kings.

The conception of Deity in the younger days of the world was, as all know, wild, fantastic and grotesque. It fashioned its idea into huge, repulsive and monstrous images, with a worship of corre-

32. In the aftermath of the Salem witchcraft trials (February 1692–May 1693), fourteen women and five men were hanged, one man was pressed to death, and five others died in prison; in other seventeenth-century cases in Massachusetts and Connecticut, an additional fourteen women and two men were executed.

33. The Quaker Benjamin Lundy (1789–1839) published the pioneering antislavery newspaper the *Philanthropist* with Charles Osborn. In 1821, he began his own paper, the *Genius of Universal Emancipation*, with the young and then unknown William Lloyd Garrison as associate editor.

34. In 1829, the free black activist David Walker (1785–1830) printed the first of three editions of his pamphlet *David Walker's Appeal, in Four Articles; Together with a Preamble to the Colored Citizens of the World, But in Particular, and Very Expressly, to Those of the United States of America*. After Walker was found dead in front of his Boston shop on 28 June 1830, rumors circulated that Southern planters had offered a reward of three thousand dollars for his murder.

35. William Lloyd Garrison.

sponding grossness, abounding in bloody sacrifices of animals and men. Who will tell us to-day that there has been no real progress in this phase of human thought and practice, or that the change in the religious conceptions of the world is no improvement? "Even more marked and emphatic" are the evidences of progress when we turn from the religious to the material interests of man. Art, science, discovery and invention, startle and bewilder us at every turn, by their rapid, vast and wonderful achievements.

These forces have made men lords where they were vassals, masters where they were slaves, and kings where they were subjects. They have abolished the limitations of time and space and have brought the ends of the earth together.

It is nothing in favor of misanthropy to which the foregoing is in some sense a reply, that evils, hardships and sufferings still remain, and that the fact of life is still far in the rear of our best conceptions of what life should be; for, so long as the most desponding of the present cannot point us to any period in the history of the world for which we would exchange the present, our argument for progress will remain conclusive.

It should be remembered that the so-called splendid civilizations of the East were all coupled with conditions wholly impossible at the present day; and which the masses of mankind must now contemplate with a shudder. We have travelled far beyond Egyptian, Grecian and Roman civilizations, and have largely transcended their religious conceptions.

In view of the fact that reform always contemplates the destruction of evil, it is strange that nearly all efforts of reform meet with more determined and bitter resistance from the recognized good, than from those that make no pretensions to unusual sanctity. It would, upon first blush seem, that, since all reform is an effort to bring man more and more into harmony with the laws of his own being and with those of the universe, the church should be the first to hail it with approval at its inception; but this is a superficial view of the subject.

Of course the message of reform is in itself an impeachment of the existing order of things. It is a call to those who think themselves already high, to come up higher, and, naturally enough, they resent the implied censure. It is also worthy of remark that, in every struggle between the worse and better, the old and the new, the advantage at the commencement is, in all cases, with the former. It is the few against the mass. The old and long established has the advantage of organization and respectability. It has possession. It occupies the ground, which is said to be nine points of the law.[36]

Besides, every thing which is of long standing in this world has power to beget a character and condition in the men and things around it, favorable to its own continuance. Even a thing so shocking and hateful as slavery had power to intrench and fortify itself behind the ramparts of church and state, and to make the pulpit defend it as a divine institution.

Another reason why ancient wrong is able to defend itself, is that the wrong of the present, though enormous and flagrant, has taken the place of some greater wrong which has been overthrown. Slavery, for instance, was better than killing captives in war. Duelling is better than private assassination. Gambling is better than highway robbery. War, as waged by civilized nations, is better than the indiscriminate massacre practiced in the olden time.

The advocates of slavery could argue with some plausibility that the slaves were better off here than in Africa; that here they could hear the gospel preached, and learn the way to heaven. But deeper down than this plausible view of existing wrong, ancient evil finds advantage in the contest with reform.

Human nature itself has a warm and friendly side for what is old; for what has withstood the tide of time and become venerable by age. Men will long travel the old road, though you show them a

36. Sometimes cited as eleven rather than nine points, this proverb had become popular in England by the seventeenth century. H[enry] L[ouis] Mencken, ed., *A New Dictionary of Quotations on "Historical" Principles from Ancient and Modern Sources*, 2 vols. (New York: Knopf, 1942), 2:946.

shorter and better one, simply because they have always travelled that road. They will live in the old house long after they see the need of a new one. Sweet and precious associations bind us to the dear old home. We cling to it though the midnight stars shine through its shingles; though the North winds from snow-clad mountains whistle their icy songs through its ragged rents and crumbling walls; and though, in shape and size, it may be an architectural anachronism, old fashioned, outlandish and dilapidated. The thought that father and mother lived here in peace, happiness and serene content, makes the old house, with all its defects, still dear to the hearts of their children, from generation to generation. As with the old house, so with the old custom, the old church and the old creed, men love them, stand by them, fight for them, refuse to see their defects, because of the comfort they have given to innumerable souls in sickness and health, in sorrow and death.

It is this love and veneration which to-day revolts at the revision of the Scriptures.[37] Better that a thousand errors should remain, it insists, than that the faith of the multitude shall be shocked and unsettled by the discovery of error in what was believed infallible and perfect.

Thus there are silent forces always at work, riveting men's hearts to the old, and rendering them distrustful of all innovation upon the long-established order of things, whatever may be the errors and imperfections of that order. Evils, multitudinous and powerful, avail themselves of routine, custom and habit, and manage to live on, long after their baleful influence is well-known and felt.

The reformer, therefore, has, at the outset, a difficult and disagreeable task before him. He has to part with old friends; break away from the beaten paths of society, and advance against the vehement protests of the most sacred sentiments of the human heart.

---

37. The higher criticism, which originated in the works of Erasmus and Benedict Spinoza (1632–77), consisted of the literary-historical analysis of scripture, which uncovered internal discrepancies within the text.

No wonder that prophets were stoned, apostles imprisoned, and Protestants burned at the stake. No wonder that Garrison was mobbed and haltered; Lovejoy[38] shot down like a felon; Torrey[39] wasted in prison; John Brown hanged; and Lincoln murdered.

It may not be a useless speculation to inquire when[ce] comes the disposition or suggestion of reform; whence that irresistible power that impels men to brave all the hardships and dangers involved in pioneering an unpopular cause? Has it a natural or a celestial origin? Is it human or is it divine, or is it both? I have no hesitation in stating where I stand in respect of these questions. It seems to me that the true philosophy of reform is not found in the clouds, or in the stars, or any where else outside of humanity itself.

So far as the laws of the universe have been discovered and understood, they seem to teach that the mission of man's improvement and perfection has been wholly committed to man himself. So is he to be his own savior or his own destroyer. He has neither angels to help him nor devils to hinder him.

It does not appear from the operation of these laws, or from any trustworthy data, that divine power is ever exerted to remove any evil from the world, how great soever it may be. Especially does it never appear to protect the weak against the strong, the simple against the cunning, the oppressed against the oppressor, the slave against his master, the subject against his king, or one hostile army against another, although it is usual to pray for such interference, and usual also for the conquerors to thank God for the victory, though such

---

38. Elijah Parish Lovejoy (1802–37) moved from St. Louis to Alton, Illinois, in 1836. By March 1837, Lovejoy had converted to immediate abolitionism and announced his intention to organize local and state abolitionist societies. Agitated by a recent economic decline, prominent citizens organized a mob to silence Lovejoy. He was mortally wounded while attempting to protect his press. Abolitionists enshrined Lovejoy as a martyr.

39. Charles Turner Torrey (1813–46) moved to Baltimore around 1843 to engage in business and carry out a scheme that transported over 400 fugitive slaves from Maryland and Virginia to the free states along a prearranged route. Arrested for this activity in 1844, Torrey was convicted and sentenced to six years' hard labor. He died of tuberculosis in a Baltimore prison.

thanksgiving assumes that the Heavenly Father is always with the strong and against the weak, and with the victors against the vanquished. No power in nature asserts itself to save even innocence from the consequences of violated law.

The babe and the lunatic perish alike when they throw themselves down or by accident fall from a sufficient altitude upon sharp and flinty rocks beneath; for this is the fixed and unalterable penalty for the transgression of the law of gravitation.

The law in all directions is imperative and inexorable, but beneficial withal. Though it accepts no excuses, grants no prayers, heeds no tears, but visits all transgressors with cold and iron-hearted impartiality, its lessons, on this very account, are all the more easily and certainly learned. If it were not thus fixed, inflexible and immutable, it would always be a trumpet of uncertain sound,[40] and men could never depend upon it, or hope to attain complete and perfect adjustment to its requirements; because what might be in harmony with it at one time, would be discordant at another. Or, if it could be propitiated by prayers or other religious offerings, the ever shifting sands of piety or impiety would take the place of law, and men would be destitute of any standard of right, any test of obedience, or any stability of moral government.

The angry ocean engulphs its hundreds of ships and thousands of lives annually. There is something horrible, appalling and stunning in the contemplation of the remorseless, pitiless indifference with which it rolls on after swallowing its weeping, shivering, shrinking, imploring victims; but reflection vindicates the wisdom of law here, as elsewhere. It is the one limb cut off, the better to save the whole body. What may seem cruel and remorseless in its treatment of the few, is, nevertheless, mercy and compassion to the many; and the wisdom of the law is manifested, not alone by its violation, but by its due observance, as well.

Every calamity arising from human ignorances and negligence upon the sea, tends to the perfection of naval architecture, to

40. 1 Cor. 14:8.

increase the knowledge of ocean navigation, and thereby to fashion the minds of men more and more in the likeness of the divine mind.

Men easily comprehend the wisdom of inflexible and unchangeable law, when it is thought to apply only to the government of matter, though for the purpose of miracle, they sometimes seem to deny even this. They contend that these laws may be suspended or evaded by the power of faith. They hold that fire will not burn, that water will not drown, and that poison will not destroy life in particular cases where faith intervenes.

But such views may be dismissed as the outpourings of enthusiasm. Some things are true to faith, which are false to fact; and miraculous things address themselves to faith rather than to science. The more thoughtful among orthodox believers concede that the laws appertaining to matter are unchangeable and eternal.

They have ceased to pray for rain, or for clear weather; but to save something from the wreck which this admission must make in their theological system they except the spiritual nature of man from the operation of fixed and unchangeable laws. Plainly enough, they gain nothing by this distinction. If the smallest particle of matter in any part of the universe is subject to law, it seems to me that a thing so important as the moral nature of man cannot be less so.

It may be further objected to the orthodox view of this question, that, in effect, it does away with moral and spiritual law altogether, and leaves man without any rule of moral and spiritual life. For where there is no law, there can be no transgression, and hence, no penalty. This is not the only difficulty in the way of our acceptance of the common theology, and where it manifestly stands in contradiction to sound reason.

If it is admitted that there are moral laws, but affirmed that the consequence of their violation may all be removed by a prayer, a sigh or a tear, the result is about the same as if there were no law. Faith, in that case, takes the place of law, and belief, the place of life. On this theory a man has only to believe himself pure and right, a subject of special divine favor, and he is so. Absurd as this position is, to some of us, it is, in some vague way, held by the whole Christian world about us, and Christians must cling to it, or give up the entire significance of their prayers and worship.

I discard this office of faith, for many reasons. It seems to me that it strikes at the fundamental principles of all real progress, and ought, by some means or other, to be removed from the minds of men.

I think it will be found that all genuine reform must rest on the assumption that man is a creature of absolute, inflexible law, moral and spiritual, and that his happiness and well-being can only be secured by perfect obedience to such law.

All thought of evasion, by faith or penance, or by any means, must be discarded. "Whatsoever a man soweth, that shall he also reap,"[41] and from this there is no appeal.

It is given to man to first discover the law and to enforce compliance by all his power of precept and example. The great and all commanding means to this end is not remote. It is the truth. This only is the "light of the world."[42]

"All the space between man's mind and God's mind," says Theodore Parker, "is crowded with truth that waits to be discovered and organized into law, for the government and happiness of mankind."[43]

It would be pleasant to dwell here upon the transcendent achievements of truth, in proof of its reforming power. No advancement or improvement has been effected in human character or in human institutions, except through the agency and power of truth. It is the pillar of cloud by day and the pillar of fire by night,[44] to lead

41. Gal. 6:7.
42. Matt. 5:14.
43. In earlier speeches, Douglass at least twice made the same attribution of this quotation to the abolitionist minister Theodore Parker (1810–60), a Harvard-educated Unitarian clergyman and reformer. Rather than an exact quotation, it appears to be a paraphrase of statements in the sermon "The Law of God and the Statutes of Men," which Parker delivered on 18 June 1854 in Boston's Music Hall, attacking the Kansas-Nebraska Act.
44. Exod. 13:21–22.

the human race through the wilderness of ignorance and out of the thralldom of error.

I am not ashamed of the gospel, says an apostle, for it is the power of God unto salvation.[45] In this we have only a glowing theological statement of a grand philosophical truth.

A gospel which is simply good news, for that is the meaning of the word, has no saving power in it whatever. The only saving power there is in any good news depends entirely upon the truth of such news. Without that quality, good news is an aggravation, a contradiction, and a disappointment; a Dead sea apple, fair without and foul within.[46]

To a shipwrecked mariner clinging to a spar or a plank or a life preserver, amid the towering billows of a storm-tossed ocean, near the point of despair, the news that a ship in the distance is coming to his relief would be good news indeed, but there would be no salvation in it, unless the news itself were true.

The soul of the apostle's utterance therefore, is, that he is not ashamed of the truth, because it is the power of God unto salvation. Like all grand reformers, this great apostle, filled with a holy enthusiasm, was not ashamed of the message in which, to him, was the power to save the world from sin, and the consequences of sin, though all the world were against him.

Having said thus much of truth and its power, it may be asked, as Pilate in his Judgment Hall, asked the Saviour, "What is Truth?"[47] It is now, as it was then, easier to ask than to answer questions.

For the purpose of this discourse, and the thought it aims to inculcate, it is enough to say that any expression, communication or suggestion, whether it be objective or subjective, intuitive or ac-

45. Rom. 1:16.
46. The Dead Sea apple, or apple of Sodom, is a yellow fruit growing along the shores of the Dead Sea. It contains small black seeds that have an ash-like texture and a bitter taste.
47. John 18:38.

quired, which conveys to the human understanding a knowledge of things as they exist in all their relations and bearings, without admixture of error, is the truth in respect of all the particular things comprehended in the said expression, communication or suggestion.

A broad distinction, however, must always be observed between the expression and the thing expressed, and also between the expression and the understanding of the expression.

The expression is but the body; the thing expressed is the soul. It is not too metaphysical to say that Truth has a distinct and independent existence, both from any expression of it, and any individual understanding of it; and that it is always the same however diverse the creeds of men may be concerning it.

Contemplated as a whole, it is too great for human conception or expression, whether in books or creeds. It is the illimitable thought of the universe, upholding all things, governing all things, superior to all things. Reigning in eternity, it is sublimely patient with our slow approximation to it, and our imperfect understanding of it, even where its lessons are clearly taught and easily understood. It has a life of its own, and will live on, as the light of a star will shine on, whether our dull eyes shall see it or not.

But, as already intimated no definite idea of absolute truth can be perfectly conveyed to the human understanding by any form of speech. Prophets, apostles, philosophers and poets alike fail here.

Impressed with this impossibility of the human mind to comprehend the divine, the sacred writers exclaim, "God is love!" "God is truth!"[48] It is the best of which the case admits, and with it the world must be content. Yet there is consolation here; for, though subject to limitations, man is not absolutely helpless.

While truth, when contemplated as a totality, is so vast as to transcend man's ability to grasp it in all its fullness and glory, there are, nevertheless, individual truths, sparks from the great All-Truth,

48. 1 John 4:8, 5:6.

quite within the range of his mental vision, which, if discovered and obeyed, will light his pathway through the world and make his life successful and happy.

He may not approach the resplendent sun in the sky and gaze into its fathomless depths, into its tempests of fire, or withstand its thunderous flame, storming away into space, thousands of miles beyond its own immeasurable circumference, but he may be warmed and enlivened by the heat, and walk in safety by its light.

All truth to be valuable must be wisely applied. Each class of facts conducts us to its own peculiar truth or principle, obedience or disobedience to which, brings its own special and appropriate results, and each after its kind.

A man may conform himself to one important truth and reap the advantage of his conformity and at the same time be utterly at fault in respect to another truth and suffer the bitterest consequences. He may go through life like a bird with one wing, right on one side, wrong on the other, and confined to earth when he might otherwise soar to heaven. He may be well versed in sanitary truth, and secure to himself sound bodily health, but at the same time violate all the great principles of truth which tend to elevate and improve the mind and purify the heart. On the other hand he may be well versed in all the great truths of morality, but totally ignorant of the laws of mechanics.

An immoral man, well instructed in the science of naval architecture, may build a ship which will easily survive the ten thousand perils of the ocean; while a perfect saint who is ignorant of the laws of navigation and disregards them, will see his ship go to the bottom in the first storm though her deck be crowded with missionaries to the heathen.

Among the common errors of the world, none is more conspicuous than the error of seeking desirable ends by inappropriate and illogical means. An uncivil word is resented by a blow, as if a blow on the body could cure an affront to the mind or change the mind of the offender. A reflection upon personal honor provokes a duel, as if putting your body up to be shot at were proof that you were an honest man. A difference of religious opinion sends you to another store to buy goods, as if a man's principles and not his goods were for sale.

If, as a man can go into a store and purchase a garment, he could go into a church and select a creed to his liking, he might be properly praised or blamed for the wisdom or folly of his choice. But this thing which we call belief does not come by choice, but by necessity; not by taste, but by evidence brought home to the understanding and the heart.

All reform, whether moral or physical, whether individual or social, is the result of some new truth or of a logical inference from an old and admitted truth.

Strictly speaking, however, it is a misnomer to prefix the word truth with the words new and old. Such qualifying prefixes have no proper application to any truth. Error may be old, or it may be new, for it has a beginning and must have an end. It is a departure from truth and a contradiction to the truth, and must pass away with the progressive enlightenment of the race; but truth knows no beginning and has no end, and can therefore be neither old nor new, but is unchangeable, indestructible and eternal.

Hence all genuine and lasting reforms must involve a renunciation of error which is transient, and a return to truth which is eternal.

The mission of the reformer is to discover truth, or the settled and eternal order of the universe. This word discover is an important word. It has a deeper meaning than the merely becoming cognizant of truth, or of any other subject previously unknown. It is not simply the opening of our eyes and seeing what was not seen before, but it seems to uncover, the removal of whatever may obstruct, hinder or prevent the understanding from grasping any object of which it may properly be cognizant. It involves effort, work, either of body or mind, or both.

To the outward eye this work may seem opposed to nature, but to the eye of thought it is found to be in accordance with the higher laws of nature. The men you see yonder, armed with picks, shovels, spades, drills, powder and fire, blasting rocks, tunneling mountains, breaking through the virgin soil, digging down the ancient hills, filling up the deep ravines and valleys, are simply uncovering the great truth of the level, one of nature's best helps to man in promoting civilization, bearing our burdens, and enabling us to keep pace with the birds in travel and commerce.

Yonder block of solid marble contains within its rough, unseemly form the fine symmetrical proportions of a stately Corinthian pillar, one upon which the eyes of unborn generations may look with pleasure; or there may sleep in its cold embrace the entrancing form of woman, or the statue of a scholar, statesman, or poet. Genius and skill only are needed to uncover and reveal it as a thing of beauty and a joy forever.[49]

It is not a war with nature, this hammer and chisel business, but only a loving embracement of her deeper, wiser, and more glorious truths and perfections. It is, as all reform is a kind of Jacob wrestling with the angel for larger blessings.[50]

What is true of external nature is also true of that strange, mysterious, and indescribable, which earnestly endeavors in some degree to measure and grasp the deepest thought and to get at the soul of things; to make our subjective consciousness, objective, in thought, form and speech.

In the necessary conflict between the old and the new, the outward and inward essence of things, men naturally range themselves into two great classes; the one radical, the other conservative. There are many shades of difference between these two extremes. Positive and perfect neutrality is only possible to the absolutely ignorant and stupid. This class of men see only results; but know nothing as to the method or the labor of bringing them about. The most they

---

49. A near quotation of the first line of John Keats's *Endymion*. H[eathcote] W[illiam] Garrod, ed., *The Poetical Works of John Keats* (London: Oxford University Press, 1956).

50. Gen. 32:24–30.

can say when the work of the reformer is accomplished is, "Thank Providence!"

Antislavery men, against a storm of violence and persecution which would have appalled most men, educated the people of the North to believe that slavery was a crime; educated them up to the point of resistance to the slave power, and thus brought about the abolition of slavery. Yet the ignorant and stupid will still ask, "What have Garrison, Gerrit Smith and others done for the colored people?" They see the colored man free; they see him riding on railways and steamboats, where they were never allowed to ride before; they see him going to school and crowding his way into the high places of the land, which twenty years ago would have been thought impossible to him, but they do not see by whose intelligence, courage and heroic endeavor these results have been accomplished. They are neutral from ignorance and stupidity. They have no part or lot in the work of reform, except to share its fruits.

Besides this stupid class, there is another, which may be called intermediates. They stand between the two extremes; men who compliment themselves for their moderation, because they are neither hot nor cold; men who sometimes help a good cause a little in order to hinder it a good deal. They are, however, of little account in the conflict with evil. They are mere drift wood; what sailors call dead water. They follow in the wake of their respective forces, being themselves destitute of motive power.

It is the extreme men on either side who constitute the real forces. All others move as they are moved upon. By their timidity and dead weight, they do much to retard a good cause; but when the conflict is over and the victory won, they are usually found at the front, shouting more loudly than any of those who shared in the conflict.

It is ever the first step in any great cause that costs, and the fate of pioneers is to suffer reproach and persecution.

"Then to side with Truth is noble,
When we share her wretched crust,
Ere her cause bring fame or profit,
And 'tis prosperous to be just;
Then it is the brave man chooses,
While the coward stands aside,
Doubting in his abject spirit,
Till his Lord is crucified;
And the multitude make virtue
Of the faith they had denied.
For Humanity sweeps onward;
Where to-day the martyr stands,
On the morrow crouches Judas,
With the silver in his hands;
Far in front the cross stands ready
And the crackling fagots burn,
While the hooting mob of yesterday,
With silent awe return
To glean up the scattered ashes
Into History's golden urn."[51]

51. The eleventh and fourteenth stanzas of James Russell Lowell's "The Present Crisis." *Writings of James Russell Lowell*, 7:182, 183.

"I Am a Radical Woman Suffrage Man"

An Address Delivered in Boston, Massachusetts, 28 May 1888

Boston *Woman's Journal,* 2 June 1888.

A longtime supporter of women's rights and specifically woman suffrage, Frederick Douglass was invited to address the annual convention of the New England Woman Suffrage Association in Boston.
By the late 1880s, tensions had abated somewhat between women's
rights activists and supporters of African American male suffrage
regarding the exclusion of women from the Fifteenth Amendment.
Lucy Stone, president of the association, introduced Douglass and
outlined the main injustices the group sought to redress: a wife's inability to hold a husband to his contract with her, a wife's inability
to stay in her house if her husband had mortgaged it and died, a
woman's inability to have a jury of her peers, a woman's inability to
have a say in the formation of laws, and "the crowning injustice,—the
disfranchisement of women."[1] Among those on the platform were
Susan B. Anthony, Henry Blackwell, Thomas W. Higginson, and William Lloyd Garrison, all old allies in the antislavery movement.

Douglass recently had returned from his honeymoon in Europe
and North Africa with his second wife, Helen, and because of his encounters with religious repression there, he sought to place woman
suffrage in an international context. He focused much of his criticism
on the Methodist Episcopal Church and its decision in early May 1888
not to seat female delegates at its general conference. He compared
American Methodist churches to Egyptian mosques that, he claimed,
were committed to the "social and religious annihilation of woman."

1. "Address of Lucy Stone," Boston *Woman's Journal,* 2 June 1888.

This speech returns to some of the same phrasing and logic as
earlier ones. Like his 1868 "Let the Negro Alone," Douglass challenges speakers opposed to women's rights to "give her fair play and
let her alone." He argues that woman suffrage is a natural right and
cannot be given or withheld by men. Douglass then entertains a theory he does not accept—that voting is a privilege and not a right—
and explores the poor logic that extends the privilege of voting to
brothers in a family but not sisters. He argues that nature endowed
men better in only one respect, physical power, and that this is not
relevant to the comprehension of vital public issues. Moreover, he
argues, that to make this the sole criteria to justify women's exclusion
from voting concedes that "might makes right."

Douglass's opening speech "received prolonged applause, to
which he responded, through the president, by saying that later on in
the evening he would tell a story."[2] Douglass, who stayed in Boston
for the entire week, was prevailed on to speak extemporaneously on
many occasions.[3] Historians including Philip Foner, Ellen DuBois,
and Paula Giddings have noted Douglass's prominent role in the
women's rights movement from its inception in the United States
until his death. Gary Lemons, in his study of W. E. B. Du Bois and
Frederick Douglass, notes that Douglass's close ties with the early
white feminists and antislavery activists Anthony, Stanton, and Stone
made him especially aware of the legal and educational issues facing white women. He "mastered the form" of American democratic
rhetoric on behalf of both African Americans and women.[4]

*M*adam President,[5] Ladies and Gentlemen: While I
esteem it an honor to stand on this New England
woman suffrage platform, I do not feel that I have
a right to the prominence you have been pleased to

2. "Address of Frederick Douglass," Boston *Woman's Journal*, 2 June 1888.
3. "Address of Mr. Douglass," Boston *Woman's Journal*, 9 June 1888.
4. Gary Lemons, "A New Response to 'Angry Black (Anti)feminists': Reclaiming
Feminist Forefathers, Becoming Womanist Sons," in *Men Doing Feminism*, ed. Tom
Digby (New York: Routledge, 1998).
5. Lucy Stone (1818–93) graduated from Oberlin College in 1847 and began
publicly lecturing on behalf of women's rights and abolitionism. In the 1860s, Stone

give me in your proceedings by calling upon me at this time. It is, perhaps, about time that I should decline to be a speaker on occasions like the present. Having survived the anti-slavery conflict, and lived to rejoice in the victory over slavery, and being no longer as young as I once was, I am a little too late for efficiency and prominence in the great cause you have in hand. My special mission in the world, if I ever had any, was the emancipation and enfranchisement of the negro. Your mission is the emancipation and enfranchisement of woman. Mine was a great cause. Yours is a much greater cause, since it comprehends the liberation and elevation of one-half of the whole human family. Happily, however, I have two good reasons for coming upon this platform to-night. The first is, I live near the city of Washington;[6] not a very strong reason, perhaps, but I come to you from an atmosphere largely pervaded with the woman suffrage sentiment, and am so much in sympathy with it, that it is more difficult to be silent than to speak in its favor. In the second place, this cause has a valid claim upon my "service and labor," outside of its merits. The New England Woman Suffrage Association is composed in part of the noble women who dared to speak for the freedom of the slave, at a time when it required far more courage to do so than is required to speak in the woman suffrage cause at this day.

I have said I reside near Washington, the capital of the nation. Let me say a word about that city in connection with this and kindred reforms. Its behavior of late has been worthy of praise. In the old times, prior to the war and the abolition of slavery, there was no room in it for woman suffrage or negro suffrage or for many other good things. It shuddered at the thought of a new idea—slavery, the slave-trade, slave auctions, horse-racing, duels, and revivals of religion were the popular excitements in the Washington of that day.

---

was one of the founders of the New England Woman Rights Association and the American Woman Suffrage Association. In 1870, she raised money for the founding of the *Woman's Journal,* and in 1872 she and her husband became its coeditors.

6. After originally residing in a Capitol Hill townhouse on A Street, Douglass purchased his final home, Cedar Hill, in 1878. It was located on fifteen acres in the District of Columbia's outlying Anacostia neighborhood.

But now old Washington has passed away, and a new Washington has come into existence. Under our much-abused Gov. Sheppard,[7] its physical features have been visibly improved, and under the influence of Northern ideas, its moral features have equally improved. The time is not distant, I hope, when it will symbolize all that is good, great, glorious and free, and much of the glory of that result will be due to the efforts of women.

It will next year be the theatre of a grand international exposition. Its attractive power is destined to increase with every year, and Boston itself as a reformatory centre may begin to look to its laurels.[8]

Boston was once known as the hot-bed of abolitionism. Washington, if it keeps well on its way, will soon become the hot-bed of woman suffrage. One of the most imposing demonstrations in favor of the rights and dignity of woman was held there only a few weeks ago. You may have heard something of this before. Women from the East, women from the West, women from the North, and women from the South; women from home and women from abroad, met there in International Council,[9] and united in a solemn demand for a larger measure of liberty, and a fuller participation in the government of the world, than has ever yet been accorded to woman. No assemblage, to my knowledge, can be pointed to in the history of this republic, which ever presented a more sublime spectacle than did this International Council. Its presence was an argument in favor of its cause. Its refinement, earnestness, ability and dignity repelled criticism and overcame opposition. In the hope and enthusiasms it inspired, some of us were made to think, or rather to feel, that the year of woman's jubilee had already dawned.

7. Alexander Robey Shepherd.
8. No such exposition was held in Washington, D.C., in 1889, the year that Paris hosted the Exposition Universelle at which the Eiffel Tower debuted.
9. The International Council of Women met at Albaugh's Grand Opera House in Washington, D.C., between 25 March and 1 April 1888.

But this Council has adjourned, and although its beneficent influence will continue to be felt far and wide over the world, we are still confronted with the same old conflict, and must fight it out on the line of agitation though it shall take a century. There is still a delinquent, tardy, and reluctant Massachusetts to be converted,[10] there is still a mass of bigotry and superstition to overcome. There is still a Methodist Episcopal Conference confronting us and barring the way to woman's progress, as it once barred the way to emancipation.[11] There is still a great nation to be brought to a knowledge of the truth. We are not to be appalled by the magnitude of the work, or discouraged by this or any form of opposition.

We old abolitionists never allowed ourselves to be dismayed by repulses, however grievous. Those engaged in this cause are of the self-same material. In some respects this woman suffrage movement is but a continuance of the old anti-slavery movement. We have the same sources of opposition to contend with, and we must meet them with the same spirit and determination, and with much the same arguments which we employed against what Charles Sumner called the "seven-headed barbarism of slavery."[12]

In reform, as in war, it is always a point gained to know just where the enemy is, and just what he is about. It is not easy to deal with an enemy in the dark. It was a great thing for the abolition cause, fifty

---

10. As late as 1915, a popular referendum in Massachusetts to extend voting rights to women was defeated by a margin of 64.5 percent to 35.5 percent. Women could not vote in that state until ratification of the Nineteenth Amendment.

11. The position of women in the Methodist Episcopal Church was not formally defined before the General Conference of 1880. At that meeting, the all-male delegates ruled that women could not become ordained ministers or local preachers, and not until 1906 were women accepted as delegates.

12. Douglass probably alludes to the arguments of Sumner's "The Barbarism of Slavery" address, delivered in the U.S. Senate on 4 June 1860. In this carefully reasoned speech, Sumner analyzed the barbarism of slavery under a number of "heads," and at one point denounced slavery as "barbarous in origin, barbarous in law, barbarous in all its pretensions, barbarous in the instruments it employs, barbarous in consequences, barbarous in spirit, barbarous wherever it shows itself." *Charles Sumner: His Complete Works. With Introd. by George Frisbie Hoar,* 20 vols. (1900; New York: Negro Universities Press, 1969), 6:119–237.

years ago, when the Methodist Episcopal Conference at Cincinnati declared itself opposed to abolitionism, and that it had no right, wish, or intention to abolish slavery.[13] It is now equally something to know that this same great organization takes its stand against the movement for the equal rights of woman in its ecclesiastical assemblies. That older conference was not able, by its opposition to abolitionism, to save slavery, nor will this later conference be able to continue the degradation of woman, by denying her a voice and a vote in its councils. The Methodist Church is rich in resources, but it cannot well afford to enforce this Mahometan idea of woman upon American women—an idea in which woman has no recognized moral, social, or religious existence. In the mosques of the East, her presence among the faithful is held a defilement.[14] She is deemed incapable of self-direction—a body without a soul. No more distressing thing confronted us during our recent tour in Egypt than this social and religious annihilation of woman.[15] Religion there strikes woman dead. Her face is not to be seen; her voice is not to be heard; her moral influence is not to be exerted. She is cushioned, cabined, confined and guarded, and treated more like a criminal than like an innocent person. She sees the world only through a veil, or from behind a lattice-work. She is constantly under the surveillance of a sentinel, wearing the human form, but destitute of all manly sympathy. This Methodist attempt to exclude woman from the conference of the church, has in it a strong element of this Mahometan idea of the proper sphere and treatment of woman.

Whatever may be said of the pious Mahometan, men and women here will ask, and demand to know, what harm could possibly come to the Methodist Church and its ministers, from the presence of a

13. Douglass refers to the position taken by the General Conference of the Methodist Episcopal Conference at its meeting in Cincinnati, Ohio, on 13 May 1836.
14. No prohibition against the admission of women to mosques exists in the Qur'an.
15. The Douglasses toured Egypt from 15 February to 16 March 1887.

few or many Christian women in its conference? The sexes meet together in prayer-meeting, in class-meeting, in "love feast," and in the great congregations of the church. Why should these gospel preachers, who mingle everywhere else in the church with women, be afraid to meet women in their conferences? What work have they to do there which women should not know? I will press this question no further, but I call upon the Methodist Church to assist us in separating woman's condition in America as far apart from her condition in Egypt as the east is from the west. We have heard a great deal of late as to what Christianity has done for woman. We have a right to call upon these Christian ministers to show that what has been done, has not been done in spite of the church, but in accordance with its teachings. One thing is certain, when the chains of woman shall be broken, when she shall become the recognized equal of man, and is put into the full enjoyment of all the rights of an American citizen, as she will be, the church and ministry will be among the first to claim the honor of the victory, and to say, "We did it!"

It is hardly necessary for me to say, after what I have already said, that I am a radical woman suffrage man. I was such a man nearly fifty years ago. I had hardly brushed the dust of slavery from my feet and stepped upon the free soil of Massachusetts, when I took the suffrage side of this question. Time, thought and experience have only increased the strength of my conviction. I believe equally in its justice, in its wisdom, and in its necessity.

But, as I understand the matter, woman does not ask man for the right of suffrage. That is something which man has no power to give. Rights do not have their source in the will or the grace of man. They are not such things as he can grant or withhold according to his sovereign will and pleasure. All that woman can properly ask man to do in this case, and all that man can do, is to get out of the way, to take his obstructive forces of fines and imprisonment and his obstructive usages out of the way, and let woman express her sentiments at the polls and in the government, equally with himself. Give her fair play and let her alone.

But we are told that suffrage is not a right, that it is neither a right for man nor for woman, but that it is simply a privilege. I do not know when or by whom this startling discovery was made, but it is evidently deemed very important and highly satisfactory by the opponents of woman suffrage.

Well, for argument's sake, let it be conceded that suffrage is not a natural right, but that it is simply a privilege, something that is created and exists only by conventional arrangement; something that can be granted or withheld at the option of those who make it a privilege. I say let all this be conceded, which I do not concede. Several important questions must be answered by those who support this pretension, before the friends of woman suffrage can be silenced or be made to accept it as final.

In the first place we have a right to know by what authority, human or divine, suffrage was made a privilege and not a right; we have a right to know when, where, how, and in the light of what doctrine of human liberty, suffrage was made a privilege and not a right. We have a right to know if such an arrangement could be properly created without the cooperation of woman herself. We have a right to know if men, acting alone, have a right to decide what is right and what is privilege where their action in the case is to determine the position of woman. We have a right to know, if suffrage is simply a privilege, by what right the exercising of that privilege is conferred only upon men. If it is a privilege, we have the right to know why woman is excluded. If it is a privilege, we have the right to know why woman is not as fully, fairly entitled to exercise that privilege as man himself.

After all, we see that nothing has been gained by the opponents of woman suffrage, by sheltering themselves behind this assumption that suffrage is a privilege and not a right. The argument is an old one, and has been answered a thousand times, and will, perhaps, have to be answered a thousand times more, before woman suffrage shall be the law of the land.

I suppose we must do here, as was done in the case of anti-slavery agitation, give line upon line and precept upon precept, as we had to do forty years ago.

Woman's claim to the right of equal participation in government with man, has its foundation in the nature and personality of woman and in the admitted doctrine of American liberty and in the authority and structure of our Republican government. When the rich man wanted some one sent from the dead to warn his brothers against coming where he was, he was told that if they heard not Moses and the prophets, neither would they be persuaded though one rose from the dead.[16] Now our Moses and our prophets, so far as the rights and privileges of American citizens are concerned, are the framers of the Declaration of American Independence. If the American people will not hear these, they will not be persuaded though one rose from dead.

According to the Declaration of Independence and to the men who signed that great charter of human liberty, all rightful powers of government are derived from the consent of the governed.

No man has yet been able to state when, where and how woman has ever given her consent to be deprived of all participation in the government under which she lives, or why women should be excepted from the principles of the American Declaration of Independence. We are told that man derived his authority thus to disenfranchise woman from Nature; well, we should all have great respect for Nature. We cannot too often listen to her voice and learn the lessons she teaches. She is the great storehouse of knowledge, wisdom and truth. It was here that Hooker learned that beautiful sentiment that law has her seat in the bosom of God and her voice is the harmony of the universe.[17] I think the friends of woman suffrage

16. Luke 16:19–31.
17. Douglass quotes from *Of the Laws of Ecclesiastical Polity* (1594–97), by the English theologian Richard Hooker (1554–1600).

have no reason to refuse to have the question of their rights tried in this august court we call Nature.

Let us begin then with Nature in the family. This is the starting-point of life, the natural staring-point of organized society and of the State. Here are a son and a daughter in the same household. They have nursed at the same breast in their infancy; they have been supplied from the same board; they have talked, sung, prayed, and played together on equal terms in their youth; they have grown to manhood and womanhood together; in a word, they have been equal members of the same family together all their young lives, with substantially the same rights and privileges in the common family; they have received the same moral and intellectual training, and have enjoyed the same freedom of thought and expression around the family board—the right to ask and to answer questions. They are equal in moral and intellectual endowments, or if not so equal, the one is as likely to be superior as the other, the daughter as the son, the sister as the brother. Now the question to be answered at this point is just this: At what time and under what conditions does nature step in to change the relations of these two people and make the son and brother the ruler of this daughter and sister? When does Nature say that he shall elect law-makers, and make laws, institute governments, define for her the metes and bounds[18] of her liberty, and that she, a rational creature like himself, shall have no voice or vote in determining any question concerning the government under which she, equally with him, is to live? They were equal in the cradle, equal in the family, equal in childhood, equal in youth, equal at maturity, equal in the right to life, to liberty, and in the pursuit of happiness. I demand to know, then, what fiat of nature, what moral earthquake from below, or what thunder-bolt from above, has driven these two people asunder—raised one to the

18. A method of describing the boundaries of land or real estate used in England and the American colonies.

sky and struck the other to earth—one to freedom and the other to slavery. The only answer that Nature is alleged to give here in opposition to woman, is one which no just and generous man can or should accept, for it bases a moral and intellectual conclusion—one which excludes woman from all freedom of choice in the affairs of government—upon a purely physical fact. The logic is that man is physically stronger than woman, and that he has the right to make her a subject of his will; that since she cannot shoulder a musket and fight, she shall not select a ballot and vote—that though she may have the ability to think, she shall not have the right to express her thought and give effect to her thought by her vote. There is no getting away from the conclusion here other than that the essence of this anti-woman suffrage doctrine is that might makes right. It is the right of the usurper, the slave-holder, the tyrant, the robber and pirate—a right which better befits wild beasts than reasoning men and women—a right which no woman ought to admit and no man should claim. The only thing that saves it from execration is the fact that men are too humane and too civilized to make their practice conform to the full measure of their theory. They deny rights, but admit influence. She may not vote herself, they say, but she may influence a man who does vote, and it is precisely this which constitutes the vice of this relation, for it gives influence and excludes responsibility. A sense of responsibility is an essential element in all our exertions and relations. We need it; woman needs it, not less than man, to work out the best results of her conduct. Divest woman of power and you divest her of a sense of responsibility and duty—two of the essential attributes of all useful exertion and existence.

In tracing the moral and intellectual progress of mankind from barbarism to civilization, we see that any and every advance, however simple and reasonable, has been sternly resisted. It appears that the more simple the proposition of reform, the more stern and passionate has been the resistance. Victory has always been found, when found at all, on the other side of the battle field.

The proposition underlining the anti-slavery movement was one of the plainest that ever dropped from the lips of man. It was so simple and self-evident that argument seemed a waste of breath, and appeal an insult to the understanding, and yet this simple proposition held within itself an explosive force more powerful than dynamite—a force which divided and drove asunder the nation, rent it in twain at the centre, and filled the land with hostile armies. The fundamental proposition of anti-slavery was simply this: Every man is himself, or in other words, is *his* self, or, which is the same thing, every man is the rightful owner of himself. Nothing could be plainer than this, yet press and pulpit, church and State, saint and sinner, North and South, denounced the proposition as full of mischief and one to be put down at all hazards. Man's right to his religious faith, to believe what he could not do otherwise than believe, shared the same fate and filled Europe with nearly a century of war. With these and other and similar examples before us we are not to think it strange that the proposition to enfranchise woman, to clothe her with all the rights and dignity of American citizenship, meets with resistance.

The fundamental proposition of the woman suffrage movement is scarcely less simple than that of the anti-slavery movement. It assumes that woman is herself. That she belongs to herself, just as fully as man belongs to himself—that she is a person and has all the attributes of personality that can be claimed by man, and that her rights of person are equal in all respects to those of man. She has the same number of senses that distinguish man, and is like man a subject of human government, capable of understanding, obeying and being affected by law. That she is capable of forming an intelligent judgment as to the character of public men and public measures, and she may exercise her right of choice in respect both to the law and the lawmakers. Than all this nothing could be more simple or more reasonable.

The generation that has come on the stage since the war can hardly now realize, in view of the fundamental principles of American government, that slavery ever existed here, that the pulpit and press, that the church and the State ever defended it. So, when this battle for woman suffrage shall have been fought and the victory won, men will marvel at the injustice and stupidity which so long deprived American women of the ballot.

Let me say in conclusion, if human nature is totally depraved, if men and women are incapable of thinking or doing anything but evil and that continually, if the character of this government will inevitably be the expression of this universal and innate depravity—then the less men and women have to do with government the better. We should abandon our Republican government, cease to elect men to office, and place ourselves squarely under the Czar of Russia, the Pope of Rome, or some other potentate who governs by divine right. But if, on the contrary, human nature is more virtuous than vicious, as I believe it is, if governments are best supported by the largest measure of virtue within their reach, if women are equally virtuous with men, if the whole is greater than a part, if the sense and sum of human goodness in man and woman combined is greater than in that of either alone and separate, then the government that excludes women from all participation in its creation, administration and perpetuation, maims itself, deprives itself of one-half of all that is wisest and best for its usefulness, success and perfection.

"Self-Made Men"

An Address Delivered in Carlisle, Pennsylvania, March 1893

Self-Made Men: Address before the Students of the Indian Industrial School, Carlisle, Pa., by Honorable Frederick Douglass (Carlisle, Pa.: Indian Print, [1893]).

In March 1893, the Carlisle Indian Industrial School invited Frederick Douglass to address its students. The Carlisle Indian Printers later published Douglass's address, which included a preface noting that Douglass was "surprised, gratified, and astonished" by the "order and aptitude" of the students' drill and by the "sweet sounds" of their choir. Moreover, "he had himself been known as a negro, but for then and there, he wished to be known as an Indian."[1] In fact, there is substantial evidence that Douglass's grandmother, Betsey Bailey, was descended from Indians.[2] Douglass's heritage allowed him to play with his multiracial identity in speeches as a means of provoking audiences to question notions of fixed racial categories.

The Carlisle Indian Industrial School was modeled after Virginia's Hampton Institute, which recruited black and Indian students. Both institutions sought to help students assimilate into American culture by teaching them English and training them in wage-paying occupations. "Self-Made Men," a lecture Douglass delivered over fifty times between 1859 and his death, matched the school's ethos well.[3] Doug-

1. *Self-Made Men*, 1.
2. Dickson J. Preston, *Young Frederick Douglass: The Maryland Years* (Baltimore: Johns Hopkins University Press, 1980), 9.
3. *Douglass Papers*, ser. 1, 5:545.

lass minimizes the importance of good fortune or native intelligence and instead argues that hard work is the key factor in creating leaders. Each time he gave the speech, Douglass adapted it by adding contemporary references. When he spoke in Carlisle, he quoted the twenty-year-old black poet Paul Laurence Dunbar, who published his first book of poetry, *Oak and Ivy*, in 1893, a testament to Douglass's concern for nurturing the careers of young African Americans.

In the speech, Douglass fails to directly address popular prejudices concerning Indians' intelligence and culture as barriers to their successful assimilation. The Carlisle Indian Industrial School worked hard to counteract the "savage Indian" image promoted by much of American culture, and especially by William "Buffalo Bill" Cody in his Wild West shows.[4] In an attempt to foster a more modern image, Richard Henry Pratt (the school's founder and long-serving superintendent) and other teachers at Carlisle organized a "battalion" of boys to march at the World's Columbian Exposition, a world's fair held in Chicago in 1893. The boys carried books, agricultural implements, and other tools under the banner "into Civilization and Citizenship."[5] Buffalo Bill Cody, nonetheless, set up just outside the fair and enjoyed excellent attendance.[6]

Douglass concludes his lecture by arguing that the negative portrayals of African American music and speech in minstrel shows "have, in many cases, led the negro to the study of music" and "to the study of Greek orators and orations." He suggests that Indians, too, should turn the dominant culture's stereotypes into a positive provocation for self-improvement.

As in "Let the Negro Alone" and other speeches, Douglass emphasizes the need to "give the negro fair play" as a counterbalance to any suggestion that the success of oppressed minorities is entirely within their control and ought not to be given institutional support.

4. Quoted in Reid Badger, *The Great American Fair: The World's Columbian Exposition and American Culture* (Chicago: Nelson Hall, 1979), 105.

5. Richard Henry Pratt, *Battlefield and Classroom: Four Decades with the American Indian, 1867–1904* (New Haven, Conn.: Yale University Press, 1964), 294–95.

6. Robert W. Rydell, *All the World's a Fair: Visions of Empire at American International Expositions, 1876–1916* (Chicago: University of Chicago Press, 1984), 57. See also Badger, *Great American Fair,* 105.

While Douglass encourages Carlisle's Indian students to work and persevere to become "self-made men," he also urges the "American people" to give African Americans fair play by establishing schools and churches throughout the South and, by implication, to support Carlisle's educational mission for Indians.

The subject announced for this evening's entertainment is not new. Man in one form or another, has been a frequent and fruitful subject for the press, the pulpit and the platform. This subject has come up for consideration under a variety of attractive titles, such as "Great Men," "Representative Men," "Peculiar Men," "Scientific Men," "Literary Men," "Successful Men," "Men of Genius," and "Men of the World;" but under whatever name or designation, the vital point of interest in the discussion has ever been the same, and that is, manhood itself, and this in its broadest and most comprehensive sense.

This tendency to the universal, in such discussion, is altogether natural and all controlling; for when we consider what man, as a whole, is; what he has been; what he aspires to be, and what, by a wise and vigorous cultivation of his faculties, he may yet become, we see that it leads irresistibly to this broad view of him as a subject of thought and inquiry.

The saying of the poet that "The proper study of mankind is man,"[7] and which has been the starting point of so many lectures, essays and speeches, holds its place, like all other great utterances, because it contains a great truth and a truth alike for every age and generation of men. It is always new and can never grow old. It is neither dimmed by time nor tarnished by repetition; for man, both in respect of himself and of his species, is now, and evermore will be, the center of unsatisfied human curiosity.

The pleasure we derive from any department of knowledge is largely due to the glimpse which it gives to us of our own nature.

7. Alexander Pope, *An Essay on Man*, epistle II, line 2.

We may travel far over land and sea, brave all climates, dare all dangers, endure all hardships, try all latitudes and longitudes; we may penetrate the earth, sound the ocean's depths and sweep the hollow sky with our glasses, in the pursuit of other knowledge; we may contemplate the glorious landscape gemmed by forest, lake and river and dotted with peaceful homes and quiet herds; we may whirl away to the great cities, all aglow with life and enterprise; we may mingle with the imposing assemblages of wealth and power; we may visit the halls where Art works her miracles in music, speech and color, and where Science unbars the gates to higher planes of civilization; but no matter how radiant the colors, how enchanting the melody, how gorgeous and splendid the pageant; man himself, with eyes turned inward upon his own wondrous attributes and powers surpasses them all. A single human soul standing here upon the margin we call TIME, overlooking, in the vastness of its range, the solemn past which can neither be recalled nor remodeled, ever chafing against finite limitations, entangled with interminable contradictions, eagerly seeking to scan the invisible past and to pierce the clouds and darkness of the ever mysterious future, has attractions for thought and study, more numerous and powerful than all other objects beneath the sky. To human thought and inquiry he is broader than all visible worlds, loftier than all heights and deeper than all depths. Were I called upon to point out the broadest and most permanent distinction between mankind and other animals, it would be this; their earnest desire for the fullest knowledge of human nature on all its many sides. The importance of this knowledge is immeasurable, and by no other is human life so affected and colored. Nothing can to bring to man so much of happiness or so much of misery as man himself. Today he exalts himself to heaven by his virtues and achievements; to-morrow he smites with sadness and pain, by his crimes and follies. But whether exalted or debased, charitable or wicked; whether saint or villain, priest or prize fighter; if only he be great in his line, he is an unfailing source of interest, as one of a common brotherhood; for the best man finds in his breast the evidence of kinship with the worst, and the worst with the best. Confront us with either extreme and you will rivet our attention and fix us in earnest contemplation, for our chief desire is to know what there is in man and to know him at all extremes and ends and opposites, and for this knowledge, or for the want of it, we will follow him from the gates of life to the gates of death, and beyond them.

As this subject can never become old, so it can never be exhausted. Man is too closely related to the Infinite to be divided, weighed, measured and reduced to fixed standards, and thus adjusted to finite comprehension. No two of anything are exactly alike, and what is true of man in one generation may lack some degree of truth in another, but his distinctive qualities as man, are inherent and remain forever. Progressive in his nature, he defies the power of progress to overtake him to make known, definitely, the limits of his marvelous powers and possibilities.

From man comes all that we know or can imagine of heaven and earth, of time and eternity. He is the prolific constitutor of manners, morals, religions and governments. He spins them out as the spider spins his web, and they are coarse or fine, kind or cruel, according to the degree of intelligence reached by him at the period of their establishment. He compels us to contemplate his past with wonder and to survey his future with much the same feelings as those with which Columbus[8] is supposed to have gazed westward over the sea. It is the faith of the race that in man there exists far outlying continents of power, thought and feeling, which remain to be discovered, explored, cultivated, made practical and glorified.

Mr. Emerson has declared that it is natural to believe in great men.[9] Whether this is a fact, or not, we do believe in them and worship them. The Visible God of the New Testament is revealed to us

8. Christopher Columbus.

9. Ralph Waldo Emerson (1803–82) became a leading transcendentalist philosopher and one of the first great lyceum lecturers, which is how Douglass probably heard him. Douglass quotes the first sentence of Emerson's essay "Uses of Great Men." *Complete Works of Emerson,* 4:3.

as a man of like passions with ourselves. We seek out our wisest and best man, the man who, by eloquence or the sword compels us to believe him such, and make him our leader, prophet, preacher and law giver. We do this, not because he is essentially different from us, but because of his identity with us. He is our best representative and reflects, on a colossal scale, the scale to which we would aspire, our highest aims, objects, powers and possibilities.

This natural reverence for all that is great in man, and this tendency to deify and worship him, though natural and the source of man's elevation, has not always shown itself wise but has often shown itself far otherwise than wise. It has often given us a wicked ruler for a righteous one, a false prophet for a true one, a corrupt preacher for a pure one, a man of war for a man of peace, and a distorted and vengeful image of God for an image of justice and mercy.

But it is not my purpose to attempt here any comprehensive and exhaustive theory or philosophy of the nature of manhood in all the range I have indicated. I am here to speak to you of a peculiar type of manhood under the title of

Self-Made Men.

That there is, in more respects than one, something like a solecism[10] in this title, I freely admit. Properly speaking, there are in the world no such men as self-made men. That term implies an individual independence of the past and present which can never exist.

Our best and most valued acquisitions have been obtained either from our contemporaries or from those who have preceded us in the field of thought and discovery. We have all either begged, borrowed or stolen. We have reaped where others have sown, and that which others have strown, we have gathered.[11] It must in truth be said

---

10. A grammatical mistake in speech or writing.
11. Matt. 25:26.

though it may not accord well with self-conscious individuality and self-conceit, that no possible native force of character, and no depth or wealth of originality, can lift a man into absolute independence of his fellow-men, and no generation of men can be independent of the preceding generation. The brotherhood and inter-dependence of mankind are guarded and defended at all points. I believe in individuality, but individuals are, to the mass, like waves to the ocean. The highest order of genius is as dependent as is the lowest. It, like the loftiest waves of the sea, derives its power and greatness from the grandeur and vastness of the ocean of which it forms a part. We differ as the waves, but are one as the sea. To do something well does not necessarily imply the ability to do everything else equally well. If you can do in one direction that which I cannot do, I may in another direction, be able to do that which you cannot do. Thus the balance of power is kept comparatively even, and a self-acting brotherhood and inter-dependence is maintained.

Nevertheless, the title of my lecture is eminently descriptive of a class and is, moreover, a fit and convenient one for my purpose, in illustrating the idea which I have in view. In the order of discussion I shall adopt the style of an old-fashioned preacher and have a "firstly," a "secondly," a "thirdly," a "fourthly" and, possibly, a "conclusion."

My first is, "who are self-made men?" My second is, "What is the true theory of their success?" My third is, "The advantages which self-made men derive from the manners and institutions of their surroundings," and my fourth is, "The grounds of the criticism to which they are, as a class, especially exposed."

On the first point I may say that, by the term "self-made men," I mean especially what, to the popular mind, the term itself imports. Self-made men are the men who, under peculiar difficulties and without the ordinary helps of favoring circumstances, have attained knowledge, usefulness, power and position and have learned from themselves the best uses to which life can be put in this world, and in the exercises of these uses to build up worthy character. They are the men who owe little or nothing to birth, relationship, friendly surroundings; to wealth inherited or to early approved means of education; who are what they are, without the aid of any of the favoring conditions by which other men usually rise in the world and achieve great results. In fact they are the men who are not brought up but who are obliged to come up, not only without the voluntary assistance or friendly co-operation of society, but often in open and derisive defiance of all the efforts of society and the tendency of circumstances to repress, retard and keep them down. They are the men who, in a world of schools, academies, colleges and other institutions of learning, are often compelled by unfriendly circumstances to acquire their education elsewhere and, amidst unfavorable conditions, to hew out for themselves a way to success, and thus to become the architects of their own good fortunes. They are in a peculiar sense, indebted to themselves for themselves. If they have travelled far, they have made the road on which they travelled. If they have ascended high, they have built their own ladder. From the depths of poverty such as these often come. From the heartless pavements of large and crowded cities; barefooted, homeless, and friendless, they have come. From hunger, rags and destitution, they have come; motherless and fatherless, they have come, and may come. Flung overboard in the midnight storm on the broad and tempest-tossed ocean of life;[12] left without ropes, planks, oars or life-preservers, they have bravely buffeted the frowning billows and have risen in safety and life where others, supplied with the best appliances for safety and success, have fainted, despaired and gone down forever.

Such men as these, whether found in one position or another, whether in the college or in the factory; whether professors or plowmen; whether Caucasian or Indian; whether Anglo-Saxon or Anglo-African, are self-made men and are entitled to a certain measure of respect for their success and for proving to the world the grandest possibilities of human nature, of whatever variety of race or color.

12. *Macbeth,* sc. 3, lines 101–02.

Though a man of this class need not claim to be a hero or to be worshipped as such, there is genuine heroism in his struggle and something of sublimity and glory in his triumph. Every instance of such success is an example and a help to humanity. It, better than any mere assertion, gives us assurance of the latent powers and resources of simple and unaided manhood. It dignifies labor, honors application, lessens pain and depression, dispels gloom from the brow of the destitute and weariness from the heart of him about to faint, and enables man to take hold of the roughest and flintiest hardship incident to the battle of life, with a lighter heart, with higher hopes and a larger courage.

But I come at once to the second part of my subject, which respects the

Theory of Self-Made Men.

"Upon what meat doth this, our CAESAR, feed, he hath grown so great?"[13] How happens it that the cottager is often found equal to the lord, and that, in the race of life, the sons of the poor often get even with, and surpass even, the sons of the rich? How happens it from the field often come statesmen equal to those from the college? I am sorry to say that, upon this interesting point, I can promise nothing absolute nor anything which will be entirely satisfactory and conclusive. Burns says:

> "I see how folks live that hae riches,
> But surely poor folks maun be witches."[14]

The various conditions of men and the different uses they make of their powers and opportunities in life, are full of puzzling con-

---

13. *Julius Caesar,* sc. 2, lines 225–26.
14. By substituting "witches" for "wretches," Douglass misquotes lines 101–02 from the poem "The Twa Dogs" by Robert Burns. Smith, *Complete Works of Robert Burns,* 3.

trasts and contradictions. Here, as elsewhere, it is easy to dogmatize, but it is not so easy to define, explain and demonstrate. The natural laws for the government, well-being and progress of mankind, seem to be equal and are equal; but the subjects of these laws everywhere abound in inequalities, discords and contrasts. We cannot have fruit without flowers, but we often have flowers without fruit. The promise of youth often breaks down in manhood, and real excellence often comes unheralded and from unexpected quarters.

The scene presented from this view is as a thousand arrows shot from the same point and aimed at the same object. United in aim, they are divided in flight. Some fly too high, others too low. Some go to the right, others to the left. Some fly too far and others, not far enough, and only a few hit the mark. Such is life. United in the quiver, they are divided in the air. Matched when dormant, they are unmatched in action.

When we attempt to account for greatness we never get nearer to the truth than did the greatest of poets and philosophers when he classified the conditions of greatness: "Some are born great, some achieve greatness and some have greatness thrust upon them."[15] We may take our choice of these three separate explanations and make which of them we please, most prominent in our discussion. Much can certainly be said of superior mental endowments, and I should on some accounts, lean strongly to that theory, but for numerous examples which seem to, and do, contradict it, and but for the depressing tendency such a theory must have upon humanity generally.

This theory has truth in it, but it is not the whole truth. Men of very ordinary faculties have, nevertheless, made a very respectable way in the world and have sometimes presented even brilliant examples of success. On the other hand, what is called genius is often found by the wayside, a miserable wreck; the more deplorable and shocking because from the height from which it has fallen and the

15. *Twelfth Night*, sc. 10, lines 1125–26.

loss and ruin involved in the fall. There is, perhaps, a compensation in disappointment and in the contradiction of means to ends and promise to performance. These imply a constant effort on the part of nature to hold the balance evenly between all her children and to bring success within the reach of the humblest as well as of the most exalted.

From apparently the basest metal we have the finest toned bells, and we are taught respect from simple manhood when we see how, from the various dregs of society, there come men who may well be regarded as the pride and as the watch towers of the race.

Steel is improved by laying on damp ground, and the rusty razor gets a keener edge after giving its dross to the dirt in which it has been allowed to lie neglected and forgotten. In like manner, too, humanity, though it lay among the pots, covered with the dust of neglect and poverty, may still retain the divine impulse and the element of improvement and progress. It is natural to revolt at squalor, but we may well relax our lip of scorn and contempt when we stand among the lowly and despised, for out of the rags of the meanest cradle there may come a great man and this is a treasure richer than all the wealth of the Orient.

I do not think much of the accident or good luck theory of self-made men. It is worth but little attention and has no practical value. An apple carelessly flung into a crowd may hit one person, or it may hit another, or it may hit nobody. The probabilities are precisely the same in this accident theory of self-made men. It divorces a man from his own achievements, contemplates him as a being of chance and leaves him without will, motive, ambition and aspiration. Yet the accident theory is among the most popular theories of individual success. It has about it the air of mystery which the multitude so well like, and withal, it does something to mar the complacency of the successful.

It is one of the easiest and commonest things in the world for a successful man to be followed in his career through life and to have constantly pointed out this or that particular stroke of good fortune which fixed his destiny and made him successful. If not ourselves great, we like to explain why others are so. We are stingy in our praise to merit, but generous in our praise to chance. Besides, a man feels himself measurably great when he can point out the precise moment and circumstance which made his neighbor great. He easily fancies that the slight difference between himself and his friend is simply one of luck. It was his friend who was lucky but it might easily have been himself. Then too, the next best thing to success is a valid apology for non-success. Detraction is, to many, a delicious morsel. The excellence which it loudly denies to others it silently claims for itself. It possesses the means of covering the small with the glory of the great. It adds to failure that which it takes from success and shortens the distance between those in front and those in the rear. Even here there is an upward tendency worthy of notice and respect. The kitchen is ever the critic of the parlor. The talk of those below is of those above. We imitate those we revere and admire.

But the main objection to this very comfortable theory is that, like most other theories, it is made to explain too much. While it ascribes success to chance and friendly circumstances, it is apt to take no cognizance of the very different uses to which different men put their circumstances and their chances.

Fortune may crowd a man's life with favorable circumstances and happy opportunities, but they will, as all know, avail him nothing unless he makes a wise and vigorous use of them. It does not matter that the wind is fair and the tide at its flood, if the mariner refuses to weigh his anchor and spread his canvas to the breeze. The golden harvest is ripe in vain if the farmer refuses to reap. Opportunity is important but exertion is indispensable. "There is a tide in the affairs of men which, taken at its flood, leads on to fortune;"[16] but it must be taken at its flood.

Within this realm of man's being, as elsewhere, Science is diffusing its broad, beneficent light. As this light increases, dependence

16. *Julius Caesar,* sc. 12, lines 2009–10.

upon chance or luck is destined to vanish and the wisdom of adapting means to ends, to become more manifest.

It was once more common than it is now, to hear men religiously ascribing their good or ill fortune directly to supernatural intervention. Success and failure, wealth and poverty, intelligence and ignorance, liberty and slavery, happiness and misery, were all bestowed or inflicted upon individual men by a divine hand and for all-wise purposes. Man was, by such reasoners, made a very insignificant agent in his own affairs. It was all the Lord's doings and marvelous to human eyes. Of course along with this superstition came the fortune teller, the pretender to divination and the miracle working priest who could save from famine by praying easier than by underdraining and deep plowing.

In such matter a wise man has little use for altars or oracle. He knows that the laws of God are perfect and unchangeable. He knows that health is maintained by right living; that disease is cured by the right use of remedies; that bread is produced by tilling the soil; that knowledge is obtained by study; that wealth is secured by saving and that battles are won by fighting. To him, the lazy man is the unlucky man and the man of luck is the man of work.

> "The fault, dear Brutus, is not in our stars,
> But in ourselves, that we are underlings."[17]

When we find a man who has ascended heights beyond ourselves; who has a broader range of vision than we and a sky with more stars in it than we have in ours, we may know that he has worked harder, better and more wisely than we. He was awake while we slept. He was busy while we were idle and he was wisely improving his time and talents while we were wasting ours. Paul Dunbar,[18] the colored poet, has well said:

17. *Julius Caesar*, sc. 2, lines 216–17.
18. In the spring of 1893, Paul Laurence Dunbar (1872–1906), of Ohio, traveled to Chicago to seek work at the World's Columbian Exposition. There he met Douglass, who hired him as his secretary at the Haitian Exhibition Building and encouraged his literary ambitions. Popular success as a poet soon followed. He died at thirty-four.

"There are no beaten paths to glory's height,
There are no rules to compass greatness known;
Each for himself must cleave a path alone,
And press his own way forward in the fight.
Smooth is the way to ease and calm delight,
And soft the road Sloth chooseth for her own;
But he who craves the flow'r of life full-blown
Must struggle up in all his armor dight.
What tho' the burden bear him sorely down,
And crush to dust the mountain of his pride,
Oh! then with strong heart let him still abide
For rugged is the roadway to renown.
Nor may he hope to gain the envied crown
Till he hath thrust the looming rocks aside."[19]

I am certain that there is nothing good, great or desirable which man can possess in this world, that does not come by some kind of labor, either physical or mental, moral or spiritual. A man may, at times, get something for nothing, but it will, in his hands, amount to nothing. What is true in the world of matter, is equally true in the world of mind. Without culture there can be no growth; without exertion, no acquisition; without friction, no polish; without labor, no knowledge; without action, no progress and without conflict, no victory. The man who lies down a fool at night, hoping that he will waken wise in the morning, will rise up in the morning as he laid down in the evening.

Faith, in the absence of work, seems to be worth little, if anything. The preacher who finds it easier to pray for knowledge than to tax his brain with study and application will find his congregation growing beautifully less and his flock looking elsewhere for their spiritual and mental food. In the old slave times colored ministers were somewhat remarkable for the fervor with which they prayed for knowledge, but it did not appear that they were remarkable for

19. Paul Laurence Dunbar's poem "The Path." *The Complete Poems of Paul Laurence Dunbar* (1913; New York: Pantheon, 1976), 33.

any wonderful success. In fact, they who prayed loudest seemed to get least. They thought if they opened their mouths they would be filled. The result was an abundance of sound with a great destitution of sense.

Not only in man's experience, but also in nature do we find exemplified the truth upon which I have been insisting. My father worketh, said the Savior, and I also work.[20] In every view which we obtain of the perfections of the universe; whether we look to the bright stars in the peaceful blue dome above us, or to the long shore line of the ocean, where land and water maintain eternal conflict; the lesson taught is the same; that of endless action and reaction. Those beautifully rounded pebbles which you gather on the sand and which you hold in your hand and marvel at their exceeding smoothness, were chiseled into their varied and graceful forms by the ceaseless action of countless waves. Nature is herself a great worker and never tolerates, without certain rebuke, any contradiction to her wise example. Inaction is followed by stagnation. Stagnation is followed by pestilence and pestilence is followed by death. General Butler, busy with his broom, could sweep yellow fever out of New Orleans, but this dread destroyer returned when the General and his broom were withdrawn, and the people, neglecting sanitary wisdom, went on ascribing to Divinity what was simply due to dirt.[21]

From these remarks it will be evident that, allowing only ordinary ability and opportunity, we may explain success mainly by one word and that word is WORK! WORK!! WORK!!! WORK!!!! Not transient and fitful effort, but patient, enduring, honest, unremitting and indefatigable work, into which the whole heart is put, and

20. John 5:17.
21. While commander of the Union occupation forces in New Orleans, Louisiana, General Benjamin F. Butler ordered a thorough cleanup of the city. Butler incorrectly believed that foul air was the cause of yellow fever and malaria. Butler's deployment of more than two thousand men in the city's new sanitary commission to clean pest-infested areas reduced the number of yellow fever cases in 1862 to just two.

which, in both temporal and spiritual affairs, is the true miracle worker. Every one may avail himself of this marvelous power, if he will. There is no royal road to perfection. Certainly no one must wait for some kind of friend to put a springing board under his feet, upon which he may easily bound from the first round of the ladder onward and upward to its highest round. If he waits for this, he may wait long and perhaps forever. He who does not think himself worth saving from poverty and ignorance, by his own efforts, will hardly be thought worth the efforts of anybody else.

The lesson taught at this point by human experience is simply this, that the man who will get up will be helped up; and that the man who will not get up will be allowed to stay down. This rule may appear somewhat harsh, but in its general application and operation it is wise, just and beneficent. I know of no other rule which can be substituted for it without bringing social chaos. Personal independence is a virtue and it is the soul out of which comes the sturdiest manhood. But there can be no independence without a large share of self-dependence, and this virtue cannot be bestowed. It must be developed from within.

I have been asked "How will this theory affect the negro?" and "What shall be done in his case?" My general answer is "Give the negro fair play and let him alone. If he lives, well. If he dies, equally well. If he cannot stand up, let him fall down."

The apple must have strength and vitality enough in itself to hold on, or it will fall to the ground where it belongs. The strongest influence prevails and should prevail. If the vital relation of the fruit is severed, it is folly to tie the stem to the branch or the branch to the tree or to shelter the fruit from the wind. So, too, there is no wisdom in lifting from the earth a head which must only fall the more heavily when the help is withdrawn. Do right, though the heavens fall;[22] but they will not fall.

22. The maxim "Let justice be done, though the heavens fall" (*fiat justitia ruat caelum*) is sometimes attributed to Lucius Calpurnius Piso Caesoninus, Julius Caesar's father-in-law. Lord Mansfield cited it in his decision in Somersett's Case.

I have said "Give the negro fair play and let him alone." I meant all that I said and a good deal more than some understand by fair play. It is not fair play to start the negro out in life, from nothing and with nothing, while other start with the advantage of a thousand years behind them. He should be measured, not by the heights others have obtained, but from the depths from which he has come. For any adjustment of the scale of comparison, fair play demands that to the barbarism from which the negro started shall be added two hundred years heavy with human bondage. Should the American people put a school house in every valley of the South and a church on every hillside and supply the one with teachers and the other with preachers, for a hundred years to come, they would not then have given fair play to the negro.

The nearest approach to justice to the negro for the past is to do him justice in the present. Throw open to him the doors of the schools, the factories, the workshops, and of all mechanical industries. For his own welfare, give him a chance to do whatever he can do well. If he fails then, let him fail! I can, however, assure you that he will not fail. Already has he proven it. As a soldier he proved it. He has since proved it by industry and sobriety and by the acquisition of knowledge and property. He is almost the only successful tiller of the soil of the South, and is fast becoming the owner of land formerly owned by his old master and by the old master class. In a thousand instances has he verified my theory of self-made men. He well performed the task of making bricks without straw;[23] now give him straw. Give him all the facilities for honest and successful livelihood, and in all honorable avocations receive him as a man among men.

I have by implication admitted that work alone is not the only explanation of self-made men, or of the secret of success. Industry, to be sure, is the superficial and visible cause of success, but what is the cause of industry? In the answer to this question one element

23. Exod. 5:7–18.

is easily pointed out, and that element is necessity. Thackeray very wisely remarks that "All men are about as lazy as they can afford to be."[24] Men cannot be depended upon to work when they are asked to work for nothing. They are not only as lazy as they can afford to be, but I have found many who were a great deal more so. We all hate the task master, but all men, however industrious, are either lured or lashed through the world, and we should be a lazy, good-for-nothing set, if we were not so lured and lashed.

Necessity is not the only mother of invention,[25] but the main-spring of exertion. The presence of some urgent, pinching, imperious necessity, will often not only sting a man into marvelous exertion, but into a sense of the possession, within himself, of powers and resources which else had slumbered on through a long life, unknown to himself and never suspected by others. A man never knows the strength of his grip till life and limb depend upon it. Something is likely to be done when something must be done.

If you wish to make your son helpless, you need not cripple him with bullet or bludgeon, but simply place him beyond the reach of necessity and surround him with ease and luxury. This experiment has often been tried and has seldom failed. As a general rule, where circumstances do most for men, there man will do least for himself; and where man does least, he himself is least. His doing or not doing makes or unmakes him.

Under the palm trees of Africa man finds, without effort, food, raiment and shelter. For him, there, Nature has done all and he has done nothing. The result is that the glory of Africa is in her palms,— and not in her men.

In your search after manhood go not to those delightful latitudes where "summer is blossoming all the year long," but rather to the

24. The English writer William Makepeace Thackeray (1811–63) is best remembered for his satirical novel *Vanity Fair* (1847–48). Although Douglass stated this adage on many occasions, his attribution of it to Thackeray cannot be confirmed. The novelist was well known for his languid manner of writing.

25. From the Latin saying *mater artium necessitas*.

hardy North, to Maine, New Hampshire and Vermont, to the cold-
est and flintiest parts of New England, where men work gardens
with gunpowder, blast rocks to find places to plant potatoes; where,
for six months of the year, the earth is covered with snow and ice.
Go to the states which Daniel Webster thought good enough to em-
igrate from,[26] and there you will find the highest type of American
physical and intellectual manhood.

Happily for mankind, labor not only supplies the good things for
which it is exerted, but it increases its own resources and improves,
sharpens and strengthens its own instruments.

The primary condition upon which men have and retain power
and skill is exertion. Nature has no use for unused power. She ab-
hors a vacuum. She permits no preemption without occupation.
Every organ of body and mind has its use and improves by use.
"Better to wear out than to rust out,"[27] is sound philosophy as well as
common sense. The eye of the watch-maker is severely taxed by the
intense light and effort necessary in order to see minute objects, yet
it remains clear and keen long after those of other men have failed.
I was told at the Remington Rifle Works,[28] by the workmen there
employed who have to straighten the rifle barrels by flashing intense
light through them, that, by this practice, severe as it seems, their
eyes were made stronger.

But what the hands find to do must be done in earnest. Nature
tolerates no halfness. He who wants hard hands must not, at sight of
first blister, fling away the spade, the rake, the broad axe or the hoe;
for the blister is a primary condition to the needed hardness. To
abandon work is not only to throw away the means of success, but it

26. Daniel Webster represented New Hampshire in the U.S. House of Representatives (1813–17) before relocating his legal and political career to Boston, Massachusetts, in 1817.

27. The best-known source for this proverb is *Henry IV, Part II*, sc. 3, lines
470–72.

28. In 1816, Eliphalet Remington began his gunsmithing business at his father's
forge. By 1828, he had moved the operation to nearby Ilion, New York, where the
modern Remington Arms Company still has a plant.

is also to part with the ability to work. To be able to walk well, one must walk on, and to work with ease and effect, one must work on.

Thus the law of labor is self-acting, beneficent and perfect; increasing skill and ability according to exertion. Faithful, earnest and protracted industry gives strength to the mind and facility to the hand. Within certain limits, the more that a man does, the more he can do.

Few men ever reach, in any one direction, the limits of their possibilities. As in commerce, so here, the relation of supply to demand rules. Our mechanical and intellectual forces increase or decrease according to the demands made upon them. He who uses most will have most to use. This is the philosophy of the parable of the ten talents. It applies here as elsewhere. "To him that hath shall be given and from him that hath not shall be taken even that which he hath."[29]

Exertion of muscle or mind, for pleasure and amusement alone, cannot bring anything like the good results of earnest labor. Such exertion lacks the element attached to duty. To play perfectly upon any complicated instrument, one must play long, laboriously and with earnest purpose. Though it be an amusement at first, it must be labor at the end, if any proficiency is reached. If one plays for one's own pleasure alone, the performance will give little pleasure to any one else and will finally become a rather hard and dry pleasure to one's self.

In this respect one cannot receive much more than one gives. Men may cheat their neighbors and may cheat themselves but they cannot cheat nature. She will only pay the wages one honestly earns.

In the idea of exertion, of course fortitude and perseverance are included. We have all met a class of men, very remarkable for their activity, and who yet make but little headway in life; men who, in their noisy and impulsive pursuit of knowledge, never get beyond the outer bark of an idea, from a lack of patience and perseverance

29. Matt. 25:29; Luke 19:26.

to dig to the core; men who begin everything and complete nothing; who see, but do not perceive; who read, but forget what they read, and are as if they had not read; who travel, but go nowhere in particular, and have nothing of value to impart when they return. Such men may have greatness thrust upon them but they never achieve greatness.

As the gold in the mountain is concealed in huge and flinty rocks, so the most valuable ideas and inventions are often enveloped in doubt and uncertainty. The printing press, the sewing machine, the railroad, the telegraph and the locomotive, are all simple enough now, but who can measure the patience, the persistence, the fortitude, the wearing labor and the brain sweat, which produced these wonderful and indispensible additions to our modern civilization.

My theory of self-made men is, then, simply this; that they are men of work. Whether or not such men have acquired material, moral or intellectual excellence, honest labor faithfully, steadily and persistently pursued, is the best, if not the only, explanation of their success. But in thus awarding praise to industry, as the main agency in the production and culture of self-made men, I do not exclude other factors of the problem. I only make them subordinate. Other agencies co-operate, but this is the principal one and the one without which all others would fail.

Indolence and failure can give a thousand excuses for themselves. How often do we hear men say, "If I had the head of this one, or the hands of that one; the health of this one, or the strength of that one; the chances of this or of that one, I might have been this, that, or the other;" and much more of the same sort.

Sound bodily health and mental faculties unimpaired are very desirable, if not absolutely indispensible. But a man need not be a physical giant or an intellectual prodigy, in order to make a tolerable way in the world. The health and strength of the soul is of far more importance than is that of the body, even when viewed as a means of mundane results. The soul is the main thing. Man can do a great many things; some easily and some with difficulty, but he cannot build a sound ship with rotten timber. Her model may be faultless; her spars may be the finest and her canvas the whitest and the flags of all nations may be displayed at her masthead, but she will go down in the first storm. So it is with the soul. Whatever its assumptions, if it be lacking in the principles of honor, integrity and affection, it, too, will go down in the first storm. And when the soul is lost, all is lost. All human experience proves over and over again, that any success which comes through meanness, trickery, fraud and dishonor, is but emptiness and will only be a torment to its possessor.

Let not the morally strong, though the physically weak abandon the struggle of life. For such happily, there is both place and chance in the world. The highest services to man and the richest rewards to the worker are not conditioned entirely upon physical power. The higher the plane of civilization, the more abundant the opportunities of the weak and infirm. Society and civilization move according to celestial order. "Not that which is spiritual is first, but that which is natural. After that, that which is spiritual."[30] The order of progress, is, first, barbarism; afterward, civilization. Barbarism represents physical force. Civilization represents spiritual power. The primary condition, that of barbarism, knows no other law than that of force; not right, but might. In this condition of society, or rather of no society, the man of mind is pushed aside by the man of muscle. A Kit Carson,[31] far out on the borders of civilization, dexterously handling his bowie knife, rifle and bludgeon, easily gets himself taken for a hero; but the waves of science and civilization rolling out over the Western prairies, soon leave him no room for his barbarous accomplishment. Kit is shorn of his glory. A higher type of manhood is required.

---

30. 1 Cor. 15:46.
31. Christopher "Kit" Carson (1809–68) served as a guide on three of John C. Frémont's expeditions to the Rocky Mountain territories. Carson became a popular hero as a result of his exploits in California during the Mexican War and rose to the rank of brigadier general in the Union Army.

Where ferocious beasts and savage inhabitants have been dispersed and the rudeness of nature has been subdued, we welcome milder methods and gentler instrumentalities for the service of mankind. Here the race is not to the swift nor the battle to the strong,[32] but the prize is brought within the reach of those who are neither swift nor strong. None need despair. There is room and work for all: for the weak as well as the strong. Activity is the law for all and its rewards are open to all. Vast acquirements and splendid achievements stand to the credit of men of feeble frames and slender constitutions. Channing was physically weak.[33] Milton was blind.[34] Montgomery was small and effeminate.[35] But these men were more to the world than a thousand Sampsons.[36] Mrs. Stowe[37] would be nothing among the grizzly bears of the Rocky mountains. We should not be likely to ask for her help at a barn raising, or a ship launch; but when a great national evil was to be removed; when a nation's heart was to be touched; when a whole country was to be redeemed and regenerated and millions of slaves converted into free men, the civilized world knew no earthly power equal to hers.

But another element of the secret of success demands a word. That element is order, systematic endeavor. We succeed, not alone by the laborious exertion of our faculties, be they small or great, but by the regular, thoughtful and systematic exercise of them. Order, the first law of heaven, is itself a power. The battle is nearly lost when your lines are in disorder. Regular, orderly and systematic effort which moves without friction and needless loss of time or power; which has a place for everything and everything in its place;[38] which knows just where to begin, how to proceed and where to end,

---

32. Eccles. 9:11.

33. Although he lived more than sixty-two years, the physical constitution of the Unitarian minister William Ellery Channing was frail since early youth.

34. The English poet John Milton (1608–74) lost a twenty-year battle against total blindness in 1652.

35. The British poet James Montgomery (1771–1854).

36. Judg. 13–16.

37. Harriet Beecher Stowe.

38. A proverb usually associated with Benjamin Franklin.

though marked by no extraordinary outlay of energy or activity, will work wonders, not only in the matter of accomplishment, but also in the increase of the ability of the individual. It will make the weak man strong and the strong man stronger; the simple man wise and the wise man, wiser, and will insure success by the power and influence that belong to habit.

On the other hand, no matter what gifts and what aptitudes a man may possess; no matter though his mind be of the highest order and fitted for the noblest achievements; yet, without this systematic effort, his genius will only serve as a fire of shavings, soon in blaze and soon out.

Spontaneity has a special charm, and the fitful outcroppings of genius are, in speech or action, delightful; but the success attained by these is neither solid nor lasting. A man who, for nearly forty years, was the foremost orator in New England,[39] was asked by me, if his speeches were extemporaneous? They flowed so smoothly that I had my doubts about it. He answered, "No, I carefully think out and write my speeches, before I utter them." When such a man rises to speak, he knows what he is going to say. When he speaks, he knows what he is saying. When he retires from the platform, he knows what he *has* said.

There is still another element essential to success, and that is, a commanding object and a sense of its importance. The vigor of the action depends upon the power of the motive. The wheels of the locomotive lie idle upon the rail until they feel the impelling force of the steam; but when that is applied, the whole ponderous train is set in motion. But energy ought not be wasted. A man may dispose of his life as Paddy did of his powder,—aim at nothing, and hit it every time.

If each man in the world did his share of honest work, we should have no need of a millennium. The world would teem with abundance, and the temptation to evil in a thousand directions, would

39. Wendell Phillips.

disappear. But work is not often undertaken for its own sake. The worker is conscious of an object worthy of effort, and works for that object; not for what he is to it, but for what it is to him. All are not moved by the same objects. Happiness is the object of some. Wealth and fame are the objects of others. But wealth and fame are beyond the reach of the majority of men, and thus, to them, these are not motive-impelling objects. Happily, however, personal, family and neighborhood well-being stand near to us all and are full of lofty inspirations to earnest endeavor, if we would but respond to their influence.

I do not desire my lecture to become a sermon; but, were this allowable, I would rebuke the growing tendency to sport and pleasure. The time, money and strength devoted to these phantoms, would banish darkness and hunger from every hearthstone in our land. Multitudes, unconscious of any controlling object in life, flit, like birds, from point to point; now here, now there; and so accomplish nothing, either here or there.

"For pleasures are like poppies spread,
You seize the flower, its bloom is shed!
Or like the snow-falls in the river,
A moment white—then melts forever;
Or like the borealis race,
That flit ere you can point their place;
Or like the rainbow's lovely form
Evanishing amid the storm.—"[40]

They know most of pleasure who seek it least and they least who seek it most. The cushion is soft to him who sits on it but seldom. The men behind the chairs at Saratoga and Newport,[41] get bet-

40. Douglass slightly misquotes lines from Robert Burns's poem "Tam O'Shanter." Smith, *Complete Works of Robert Burns*, 92.

41. Saratoga Springs, New York, in the Hudson River Valley, became a popular resort destination in the late antebellum period on account of its mineral springs and horse racing. Originally an important commercial seaport, Newport, Rhode Island, began its transformation into a coastal resort community in the late 1830s. Wealthy

ter dinners than the men in them. We cannot serve two masters.[42] When here, we cannot be there. If we accept ease, we must part with appetite. A pound of feathers is as heavy as a pound of iron,— and about as hard, if you sit on it long enough. Music is delightful, but too much of it wounds the ear like the filing of a saw. The lounge, to the lazy, becomes like flint; and to him, the most savory dishes lose their flavor.

> "It's true, they need na starve or sweat,
> Thro' winter's cauld or simmer's heat;
> But human bodies are sic fools,
> For all their colleges an' schools,
> That when na real ills perplex them,
> They make enow, themselves to vex them."[43]

But the industrious man does find real pleasure. He finds it in qualities and quantities to which the baffled pleasure seeker is a perpetual stranger. He finds it in the house well built, in the farm well tilled, in the books well kept, in the page well written, in the thought well expressed, in all the improved conditions of life around him and in whatsoever useful work may, for the moment, engage his time and energies.

I will give you, in one simple statement, my idea, my observation and my experience of the chief agent in the success of self-made men. It is not luck, nor is it great mental endowments, but it is well directed, honest toil. "Toil and Trust!"[44] was the motto of John Quincy Adams, and his Presidency of the Republic proved its wisdom as well as its truth. Great in his opportunities, great in

---

Southern slaveholders made up a conspicuous part of each community's summer population.

42. Matt. 6:24; Luke 16:13.

43. Lines 191–97 from "The Twa Dogs," by Robert Burns. Smith, *Complete Works of Robert Burns*, 5.

44. John Quincy Adams is reported to have inscribed the motto "Toil and Trust" on an instrument he used to steady his hand while writing.

his mental endowments and great in his relationships, he was still greater in persevering and indefatigable industry.

Examples of successful self-culture and self-help under great difficulties and discouragements, are abundant, and they vindicate the theory of success thus feebly and with homely common sense, presented. For example: Hugh Miller,[45] whose lamented death mantled the mountains and valleys of his native land with a broad shadow of sorrow, scarcely yet lifted, was a grand example of the success of persistent devotion, under great difficulties, to work and to the acquisition of knowledge. In a country justly distinguished for its schools and colleges, he, like Robert Burns, Scotia's matchless son of song, was the true child of science, as Burns was of song. He was his own college. The earth was his school and the rocks were his school master. Outside of all the learned institutions of his country, and while employed with his chisel and hammer, as a stone mason, this man literally killed two birds with one stone; for he earned his daily bread and at the same time made himself an eminent geologist, and gave to the world books which are found in all public libraries and which are full of inspiration to the truth seeker.

Not unlike the case of Hugh Miller, is that of our own Elihu Burritt.[46] The true heart warms with admiration for the energy and perseverance displayed in this man's pursuit of knowledge. We call him "The learned blacksmith,"[47] and the distinction was fairly earned and fitly worn. Over the polished anvil and glowing forge; amidst the smoke, dust and din of the blacksmith's shop; amidst its blazing fires and hissing sparks, and while hammering the red-hot steel, this brave son of toil is said to have mastered twenty different languages, living and dead.

It is surprising with what small means, in the field of earnest effort, great results have been achieved. That neither costly apparatus

45. Hugh Miller (1802–1856), self-educated, was a renowned Scottish author.
46. The self-educated blacksmith and pacifist Elihu Burritt (1810–79) made a career of advocating pacifism, temperance, cheap international postage, and abolitionism in a series of reform newspapers.
47. "Learned blacksmith" was in general use in the nineteenth century as a nickname for Burritt.

nor packed libraries are necessarily required by the earnest student in self-culture, was demonstrated in a remarkable manner by Louis Kossuth.[48] That illustrious patriot, scholar and statesman, came to our country from the far east of Europe, a complete master of the English language. He spoke our difficult tongue with an eloquence as stately and grand as that of the best American orators. When asked how he attained this mastery of a language so foreign to him, he told us that his school house was an Austrian prison, and his school books, the Bible, Shakespeare, and an old English dictionary.

Side by side with the great Hungarian, let me name the King of American self-made men; the man who rose highest and will be remembered longest as the most popular and beloved President since Washington—ABRAHAM LINCOLN. This man came to us, not from the schools or from the mansions of ease and luxury, but from the back woods. He mastered his grammar by the light of a pine wood torch. The fortitude and industry which could split rails by day, and learn grammar at night at the hearthstone of a log hut and by the unsteady glare of a pine wood knot, prepared this man for a service to his country and to mankind, which only the most exalted could have performed.

The examples thus far given, belong to the Caucasian race; but to the African race, as well, we are indebted for examples equally worthy and inspiring. Benjamin Bannecker,[49] a man of African descent, born and reared in the state of Maryland, and a contemporary with the great men of the revolution, is worthy to be mentioned with the highest of his class. He was a slave, withheld from all those inspiring motives which freedom, honor and distinction furnish to exertion; and yet this man secured an English education; became a learned mathematician, was an excellent surveyor, assisted to lay out the city of Wash-

48. Louis Kossuth (1802–94) led the 1848 revolution for Hungarian independence from Hapsburg rule.
49. Benjamin Banneker (1731–1806), a free black, taught himself mathematics and astronomy. From 1792 until 1797, he published a highly respected almanac for the Chesapeake Bay region. When he wrote then–secretary of state Thomas Jefferson to plead for African American rights, he enclosed a copy of the almanac. Jefferson's reply praised Banneker's talents as a credit to his race.

ington, and compelled honorable recognition from some of the most distinguished scholars and statesmen of that early day of the Republic.

The intellect of the negro was then, as now, the subject of learned inquiry. Mr. Jefferson, among other statesmen and philosophers, while he considered slavery an evil, entertained a rather low estimate of the negro's mental ability. He thought that the negro might become learned in music and in language, but that mathematics were quite out of the question with him.

In this debate Benjamin Bannecker came upon the scene and materially assisted in lifting his race to a higher consideration than that in which it had been previously held. Bannecker was not only proficient as a writer, but, like Jefferson, he was a philosopher. Hearing of Mr. Jefferson's opinion of negro intellect, he took no offense but calmly addressed that statesman a letter and a copy of an almanac for which he had made the astronomical calculations. The reply of Mr. Jefferson is the highest praise I wish to bestow upon this black self-made man. It is brief and I take great pleasure in presenting it.

PHILADELPHIA, August 30, 1790.

Sir:

I thank you sincerely for your letter and the almanac it contains. Nobody more than I do, wishes to see such proofs as you exhibit, that nature has given our black brethren talents equal to those of other colors of men, and that the appearance of the want of them, is owing mainly to the degrading conditions of their existence in Africa and America. I have taken the liberty of sending your almanac to Monsieur Cordozett, Secretary of the Academy of Science at Paris, and a member of the Philanthropic Society, because I considered it a document of which your whole race had a right, for their justification against the doubts entertained of them.

I am, with great esteem, sir,

Your most obedient servant,

THOMAS JEFFERSON.[50]

50. Jefferson to Banneker, 30 August 1790. Ford, *Works of Thomas Jefferson*, 4:309–10.

This was the impression made by an intelligent negro upon the father of American Democracy, in the earlier and better years of the Republic. I wish that it were possible to make a similar impression upon the children of the American Democracy of this generation. Jefferson was not ashamed to call the black man his brother and to address him as a gentleman.

I am sorry that Bannecker was not entirely black, because in the United States, the slightest infusion of Teutonic blood is thought to be sufficient to account for any considerable degree of intelligence found under any possible color of the skin.

But Bannecker is not the only colored example that I can give. While I turn with honest pride to Bannecker, who lived a hundred years ago, and invoke his aid to roll back the tide of disparagement and contempt which pride and prejudice have poured out against the colored race, I can also cite examples of like energy in our own day.

William Dietz,[51] a black man of Albany, New York, with whom I was personally acquainted and of whom I can speak from actual knowledge, is one such. This man by industry, fidelity and general aptitude for business affairs, rose from the humble calling of house servant in the Dudley family[52] of that city, to become the sole manager of the family estate valued at three millions of dollars.

It is customary to assert that the negro never invented anything, and that, if he were today struck out of life, there would, in twenty years, be nothing left to tell of his existence.[53] Well, this black man; for he was positively and perfectly black; not partially, but WHOLLY black; a man whom, a few years ago, some of our learned ethnologists would have read out of the human family and whom a certain

51. William A. Dietz (?–1885?) worked in the household of Charles E. Dudley of Albany, New York. His skill as an architect and businessman enabled the Dudley estate to profit greatly from the construction of commercial properties in Albany. Dietz later went into business for himself and became one of Albany's wealthiest black citizens.

52. Charles Edward Dudley (1780–1841) established himself as a merchant in Albany, New York, joined Martin Van Buren's "Albany Regency" political circle, and held many elected offices, including U.S. senator (1829–33).

53. A racist assertion made by Senator Robert Toombs of Georgia in a speech on 26 January 1856 at Boston's Tremont Temple.

Chief Justice would have turned out of court as a creature having no rights which white men are bound to respect,[54] was one of the very best draftsmen and designers in the state of New York. Mr. Dietz was not only an architect, but he was also an inventor. In this he was a direct contradiction to the maligners of his race. The noble railroad bridge now spanning the Hudson river at Albany, was, in all essential features, designed by William Dietz. The main objection against a bridge across that highway of commerce had been that of its interference with navigation. Of all the designs presented, that of Dietz was the least objectionable on that score, and was, in its essential features, accepted. Mr. Dietz also devised a plan for an elevated railway to be built in Broadway, New York. The great objection to a railway in that famous thoroughfare was then, as now, that of the noise, dust, smoke, obstruction and danger to life and limb, thereby involved. Dietz undertook to remove all these objections by suggesting an elevated railway, the plan of which was, at the time, published in the *Scientific American* and highly commended by the editor of that journal.[55] The then readers of the *Scientific American* read this account of the inventions of William Dietz, but did not know, as I did, that Mr. Dietz was a black man. There was certainly nothing in his name or in his works to suggest the American idea of color.

Among my dark examples I can name no man with more satisfaction than I can Toussaint L'Overture,[56] the hero of Santo Domingo. Though born a slave and held a slave till he was fifty years of age; though, like Bannecker, he was black and showed no trace of Caucasian admixture, history hands him down to us as a brave and generous soldier, a wise and powerful statesman, an ardent patriot and a successful liberator of his people and of his country.

54. Roger B. Taney's opinion in the *Dred Scott* decision. *Dred Scott v. John F. A. Sandford*, 19 Howard 393 (1857), 407.

55. This engraving by William A. Dietz appeared in *Scientific American*, 26 November 1853. The proposed streetcar line for Broadway became enmeshed in a legal battle during the 1850s, and Dietz's plans were never adopted.

56. When the slaves of Saint-Domingue revolted, François-Dominique Toussaint L'Ouverture (1744–1803) led an army of 55,000 men to victory over the combined

The contemporaries of this Haitien chief paint him as without a single moral blemish; while friends and foes alike, accord him the highest ability. In his eulogists no modern hero has been more fortunate than Toussaint L'Overture. History, poetry and eloquence have vied with each other to do him reverence. Wordsworth and Whittier have, in characteristic verse, encircled his brow with a halo of fadeless glory,[57] while Phillips has borne him among the gods in something like Elijah's chariot of fire.[58]

The testimony of these and a thousand others who have come up from the depths of society, confirms the theory that industry is the most potent factor in the success of self-made men, and thus raises the dignity of labor; for whatever may be one's natural gifts, success, as I have said, is due mainly to this great means, open and free to all.

A word now upon the third point suggested at the beginning of this paper; namely, The friendly relation and influence of American ideas and institutions to this class of men.

America is said, and not without reason, to be preeminently the home and patron of self-made men. Here, all doors fly open to them. They may aspire to any position. Courts, Senates and Cabinets, spread rich carpets for their feet, and they stand among our foremost men in every honorable service. Many causes have made it easy, here, for this class to rise and flourish, and first among these causes is the general respectability of labor. Search where you will, there is no country on the globe where labor is so respected and the laborer so honored, as in this country. The conditions in which American society originated; the free spirit which framed its independence and created its government based upon the will of the

---

forces of England, France, and Spain in 1794. This victory guaranteed him the leadership of newly independent Haiti. In 1802, the island nation was recaptured by the French, and Toussaint died in prison of pneumonia.

57. An allusion to "To Toussaint L'Ouverture" (1803) by the revered English romantic poet William Wordsworth (1770–1850) and to the poem "Toussaint L'Ouverture" (1833) by the American Quaker and abolitionist John Greenleaf Whittier (1807–92).

58. Douglass compares Wendell Phillips's popular lyceum address on Toussaint L'Ouverture to the biblical story of the prophet Elijah.

people, exalted both labor and laborer. The strife between capital and labor is, here, comparatively equal. The one is not the haughty and powerful master and the other the weak and abject slave as is the case in some parts of Europe. Here, the man of toil is not bowed, but erect and strong. He feels that capital is not more indispensable than labor, and he can therefore meet the capitalist as the representative of an equal power.

Of course these remarks are not intended to apply to the states where slavery has but recently existed. That system was the extreme degradation of labor, and though happily now abolished its consequences still linger and may not disappear for a century. To-day, in the presence of the capitalist, the Southern black laborer stands abashed, confused and intimidated. He is compelled to beg his fellow worm to give him leave to toil. Labor can never be respected where the laborer is despised. This is today, the great trouble at the South. The land owners still resent emancipation and oppose the elevation of labor. They have yet to learn that a condition of affairs well suited to a time of slavery may not be well suited to a time of freedom. They will one day learn that large farms and ignorant laborers are as little suited to the South as to the North.

But the respectability of labor is not, as already intimated, the only or the most powerful cause of the facility with which men rise from humble conditions to affluence and importance in the United States. A more subtle and powerful influence is exerted by the fact that the principle of measuring and valuing men according to their respective merits and without regard to their antecedents, is better established and more generally enforced here than in any other country. In Europe, greatness is often thrust upon men. They are made legislators by birth.

> "A king can make a belted knight,
> A marquis, duke and a' that."[59]

---

59. From Robert Burns's poem "For A' That and A' That." Smith, *Complete Works of Robert Burns*, 227–28.

But here, wealth and greatness are forced by no such capricious and arbitrary power. Equality of rights brings equality of positions and dignities. Here society very properly saves itself the trouble of looking up a man's kinsfolks in order to determine his grade in life and the measure of respect due him. It cares very little who was his father or grandfather. The boast of the Jews, "We have Abraham for our father,"[60] has no practical significance here. He who demands consideration on the strength of a reputation of a dead father, is, properly enough, rewarded with derision. We have no reverence to throw away in this wise.

As a people, we have only a decent respect for our seniors. We cannot be beguiled into accepting empty-headed sons for full-headed fathers. As some one has said, we dispense with the smoke when the candle is out. In popular phrase we exhort every man as he comes upon the stage of active life, "Now do your level best!" "Help yourself!" "Put your shoulders to the wheel!" "Make your own record!" "Paddle your own canoe!" "Be the architect of your own fortune!"

The sons of illustrious men are put upon trial like the sons of common people. They must prove themselves real CLAYS, WEB-STERS and LINCOLNS, if they would attract to themselves the cordial respect and admiration generally awarded to their brilliant fathers. There is, here, no law of entail or primogeniture.[61]

Our great men drop out from their various groups and circles of greatness as bright meteors vanish from the blue overhanging sky bearing away their own silvery light and leaving the places where they once shown so brightly, robed in darkness till relighted in turn by the glory of succeeding ones.

I would not assume that we are entirely devoid of affection for families and for great names. We have this feeling, but it is a feeling qualified and limited by the popular thought; a thought which

60. Luke 3:8.
61. The right, by custom or law, of the firstborn male child to inherit the entire family estate.

springs from the heart of free institutions and is destined to grow stronger the longer these institutions shall endure. George Washington, Jr., or Andrew Jackson, Jr., stand no better chance of being future Presidents than do the sons of Smith or Jones, or the sons of anybody else.

We are in this, as Edmund Quincy[62] once said of the rapping spirits, willing to have done with people when they are done with us. We reject living pretenders if they come only in the old clothes of the dead.

We have as a people no past and very little present, but a boundless and glorious future. With us, it is not so much what has been, or what is now, but what is to be in the good time coming.[63] Our mottoes are "Look ahead!" and "Go ahead!," and especially the latter. Our moral atmosphere is full of the inspiration of hope and courage. Every man has his chance. If he cannot be President he can, at least, be prosperous. In this respect, America is not only the exception to the general rule, but the social wonder of the world. Europe, with her divine-right governments and ultra-montane doctrines;[64] with her sharply defined and firmly fixed classes; each class content if it can hold its own against the others, inspires little of individual hope or courage. Men, on all sides, endeavor to continue from youth to old age in their several callings and to abide in their several stations. They seldom hope for anything more or better than this. Once in a while, it is true, men of extraordinary energy and industry, like the Honorable John Bright and the Honorable Lord Brougham,[65] (men whose capacity and disposition for work always left their associates little or nothing to do) rise even in England. Such men would rise to distinction anywhere. They do not disprove the general rule, but confirm it.

---

62. Edmund Quincy (1807–77) joined the abolitionists in reaction to the murder of Elijah Lovejoy in 1837.

63. "The Good Time Coming" is the title of a poem by Charles Mackay. Mackay, *Voices from the Mountains*, 202–04.

64. Favoring the supremacy of papal over national authority.

65. Lord Henry Peter Brougham.

What is, in this respect, difficult and uncommon in the Old World, is quite easy and common in the New. To the people of Europe, this eager, ever moving mass which we call American society and in which life is not only a race, but a battle, and everybody trying to get just a little ahead of everybody else, looks very much like anarchy.

The remark is often made abroad that there is no repose in America. We are said to be like the troubled sea, and in some sense this is true. If it is a fact it is also one not without its compensation. If we resemble the sea in its troubles, we also resemble the sea in its power and grandeur, and in the equalities of its particles.

It is said, that in the course of centuries, I dare not say how many, all the oceans of this great globe go through the purifying process of filtration. All their parts are at work and their relations are ever changing. They are, in obedience to ever varying atmospheric forces, lifted from their lowly condition and are borne away by gentle winds or furious storms to far off islands, capes and continents; visiting in their course, mountain, valley and plain; thus fulfilling a beneficent mission and leaving the grateful earth refreshed, enriched, invigorated, beautiful and blooming. Each pearly drop has its fair chance to rise and contribute its share to the health and happiness of the world.

Such, in some sort, is a true picture of the restless activity and ever-changing relations of American society. Like the sea, we are constantly rising above, and returning to, the common level. A small son follows a great father, and a poor son, a rich father. To my mind we have no reason to fear that either wealth, knowledge or power will here be monopolized by the few as against the many.

These causes which make America the home and foster-mother of self-made men, combined with universal suffrage, will, I hope, preserve us from this danger. With equal suffrage in our hands, we are beyond the power of families, nationalities or races.

Then, too, our national genius welcomes humanity from every quarter and grants to all an equal chance in the race of life.

"We ask not for his lineage,
We ask not for his name;
If manliness be in his heart,
He noble birth may claim.
We ask not from what land he came,
· Nor where his youth was nursed;
If pure the stream, it matters not
The spot from whence it burst."[66]

Under the shadow of a great name, Louis Napoleon[67] could strike down the liberties of France and erect the throne of a despot; but among a people so jealous of liberty as to revolt at the idea of electing, for a third term, one of our best Presidents,[68] no such experiment as Napoleon's could ever be attempted here.

We are sometimes dazzled by the gilded show of aristocratic and monarchical institutions, and run wild to see a prince. We are willing that the nations which enjoy these superstitions and follies shall enjoy them in peace. But, for ourselves, we want none of them and will have none of them and can have none of them while the spirit of liberty and equality animates the Republic.

A word in conclusion, as to the criticisms and embarrassments to which self-made men are exposed, even in this highly favored country. A traveler through the monarchies of Europe is annoyed at every turn by a demand for his passport. Our government has imposed no such burden, either upon the traveler or upon itself. But citizens and private individuals, in their relation to each other and the world, demand of every one the equivalent of a passport

66. Douglass adapts the opening lines of "The Questioner: A Chant," by Robert Nicoll (1814–37), a minor Scottish poet and minstrel.

67. Louis-Napoléon Bonaparte (1808–73) was elected president of the French Second Republic in 1848. He declared himself Emperor Napoleon III in 1852. He was deposed in 1870 after his country's defeat in the Franco-Prussian War, and died in exile in England.

68. A reference to the successful campaign within the Republican party in 1880 to block the nomination of Ulysses S. Grant for a third presidential term and to nominate instead James A. Garfield of Ohio.

to recognition, in the possession of some quality or acquirement which shall commend its possessor to favor. We believe in making ourselves pretty well acquainted with the character, business and history of all comers. We say to all such, "Stand and deliver!"[69] And to this demand self-made men are especially subject.

There is a small class of very small men who turn their backs upon any one who presumes to be anybody, independent of Harvard, Yale, Princeton[70] or other similar institutions of learning. These individuals cannot believe that any good can come out of Nazareth.[71] With them, the diploma is more than the man. To that moral energy upon which depends the lifting of humanity, which is the world's true advancement, these are utter strangers. To them the world is never indebted for progress, and they may safely be left to the gentle oblivion which will surely overtake them.

By these remarks, however, there is meant no disparagement of learning. With all my admiration for self-made men, I am far from considering them the best made men. Their symmetry is often marred by the effects of their extra exertion. The hot rays of the sun and the long and rugged road over which they have been compelled to travel, have left their marks, sometimes quite visibly and unpleasantly, upon them.

While the world values skill and power, it values beauty and polish, as well. It was not alone the hard good sense and honest heart of Horace Greeley, the self-made man, that made the *New York Tribune;* but likewise the brilliant and thoroughly educated men silently associated with him.

There never was a self-educated man, however well-educated, who, with the same exertion, would not have been better educated by the aid of schools and colleges. The charge is made and well

69. "Stand and deliver your money or your life" was a phrase used by highwaymen to command victims to hand over their valuables.

70. Three of the oldest colleges In the United States: Harvard founded in 1636, Yale in 1701, and Princeton in 1746.

71. John 1:46.

sustained, that self-made men are not generally over modest or self-forgetful men. It was said of Horace Greeley, that he was a self-made man and worshipped his maker. Perhaps the strong resistance which such men meet in maintaining their claim, may account for much of their self-assertion.

The country knows by heart, and from his own lips, the story of Andrew Jackson. In many cases, the very energies employed, the obstacles overcome, the heights attained and the broad contrasts at every step forced upon the attention, tend to incite and strengthen egotism. A man indebted for himself to himself, may naturally think well of himself.

But this is apt to be far overdone. That a man has been able to make his own way in the world, is an humble fact as well as an honorable one. It is, however, possible to state a very humble fact in a very haughty manner, and self-made men are, as a class, much addicted to this habit. By this peculiarity they make themselves much less agreeable to society than they would otherwise be.

One other criticism upon these men is often very properly made. Having never enjoyed the benefit of schools, colleges and other like institutions of learning, they display for them a contempt which is quite ridiculous and which also makes them appear so. A man may know much about educating himself, and but little about the proper means for educating others. A self-made man is also liable to be full of contrarieties. He may be large, but at the same time, awkward; swift, but ungraceful; a man of power, but deficient in the polish and amiable proportions of the affluent and regularly educated man. I think that, generally, self-made men answer more or less closely to this description.

For practical benefit we are often about as much indebted to our enemies, as to our friends; as much to the men who hiss, as to those who applaud; for it may be with men as some one has said about tea; that if you wish to get its strength, you must put it into hot water. Criticism took Theodore Parker from a village pulpit and gave him the whole country for a platform and the whole nation for an audience. England laughed at American authorship and we sent her Emerson and Uncle Tom's Cabin.[72] From its destitution of trees, Scotland was once a by-word; now it is a garden of beauty. Five generations ago, Britain was ashamed to write books in her own tongue. Now her language is spoken in all corners of the globe. The Jim Crow Minstrels[73] have, in many cases, led the negro to the study of music; while the doubt cast upon the negro's tongue has sent him to the lexicon and grammar and to the study of Greek orators and orations.

Thus detraction paves the way for the very perfections which it doubts and denies.

Ladies and gentlemen: Accept my thanks for your patient attention. I will detain you no longer. If, by statement, argument, sentiment or example, I have awakened in any, a sense of the dignity of labor or the value of manhood, or have stirred in any mind, a courageous resolution to make one more effort towards self-improvement and higher usefulness, I have not spoken altogether in vain, and your patience is justified.

72. Stowe's novel *Uncle Tom's Cabin*.
73. The term "Jim Crow" derives from a popular nineteenth-century plantation song whose refrain was "Wheel about and turn about and jump Jim Crow." The term refers to a stage presentation of a song and dance first performed by Thomas D. Rice and later used in minstrel shows. Minstrel shows performed by black-faced white entertainers used negative racial stereotypes of African Americans for their comic appeal to white audiences.

"Lessons of the Hour"

An Address Delivered in Washington, D.C., 9 January 1894

Address by Hon. Frederick Douglass, Delivered in the Metropolitan A.M.E. Church, Washington, D.C., Tuesday, January 9th, 1894, on The Lessons of the Hour (Baltimore: Thomas & Evans, 1894).

Rayford Logan calls the period 1877–1901 the "nadir of race relations." Legal decisions, particularly ones by the U.S. Supreme Court, reversed Reconstruction-era civil rights gains, and violence against African Americans went unchecked in the South. Lynching reached its peak in this era, and violent reprisals discouraged political activity. The culture of brutality that developed included heinous acts such as parading victims' body parts in public places and printing postcards commemorating these public killings.[1]

Frederick Douglass worked with the black activist Ida B. Wells to publicize this issue and organize resistance to lynching. In 1892, Wells had published her collected records on lynching in *Southern Horrors*. Like Theodore Weld's *American Slavery as It Is: Testimony of a Thousand Witnesses* (1839),[2] it served as an encyclopedic gathering of evidence of the cruelty and injustice deeply rooted in Southern race relations. Douglass offered Wells letters of introduction to prominent African American clubwomen and to English activists, who supported her speaking tour in England. Douglass's most

1. Patricia A. Schechter, *Ida B. Wells Barnett and American Reform, 1880–1930* (Chapel Hill: University of North Carolina Press, 2001), 256.
2. Theodore Dwight Weld, Angelina Grimké, and Sarah Grimké collaborated on this compilation of accounts taken from Southern newspapers depicting the separation of slave families, beatings, and other deprivations.

extended attack against lynching, "Lessons of the Hour," was first delivered in 1892. He gave it again in the fall of 1893, when he presided
over the Haitian Pavilion at the World's Columbian Exposition in
Chicago. It was published as a pamphlet in 1894.[3] Wells distributed
the pamphlet at her speaking engagements.[4]

Douglass had titled earlier versions of this speech "The Negro
Problem" in order to appropriate and redefine popular discourse on
the "unhappy relations . . . between white and colored people of the
Southern States of our union." The "Negro Problem" was popularly
understood to be the fault of African American illiteracy or malad-
justment, but Douglass argued it was more justly understood to be
the fault of brutal, antidemocratic practices among whites in the
South. The "so-called but mis-called negro problem," he asserted,
was really a national problem, a state of lawlessness in the South, to
which the solution was simply "justice." As Randy Prus has argued,
lynching became a "signifier of southern nationalism" and "replaced
slavery as the peculiar institution of the south."[5] Both Douglass and
Wells protested the barring of African Americans from entry to the
World's Columbian Exposition, except on a specially designated day,
and were alarmed by the clear absence of exhibits displaying African
American culture and innovation.[6]

On 9 January 1894, Douglass was introduced by the former Louisiana senator Blanche K. Bruce, a fellow African American leader, to
an "ecstatic" audience at the Metropolitan A.M.E. Church in Washington, D.C.[7] He was joined on the platform by Jeremiah E. Rankin,
the current president of Howard University; former Virginia congressman John M. Langston; and Mr. B. H. Hart.[8] Both the Washington *Post* and the *Evening Star* remarked on Douglass's criticism
of fellow Republicans who failed to prosecute lynchers or protect

---

3. Randy Prus, "Frederick Douglass's Lost Cause: Lynching and the Body Politic
in 'The Lessons of the Hour,' " *Journal x* 9:1 (2004), 71; *Douglass Papers,* ser. 1,
5:576.
4. Schechter, *Ida B. Wells Barnett,* 21; Rydell, *All the World's a Fair,* 52.
5. Prus, "Frederick Douglass's Lost Cause," 76.
6. Rydell, *All the World's a Fair,* 52.
7. "Nestor of Freedmen," Washington (D.C.) *Post,* 10 January 1894.
8. Ibid.

black rights: "He launched bitter invective against his foes, scathed lukewarm friends with keenest sarcasm, and gave good advice to his friends."[9] Calling the Republican party of the 1890s a "party of money rather than a party of morals," he condemned not only its inaction on lynching, but also its active efforts to overturn the Civil Rights Acts and the progress made during Reconstruction.[10]

Douglass started both this address and the May 1894 version, which was delivered in Boston, by imitating a witness giving testimony; he offered "a colored man's view" of Southern race relations. This familiar rhetorical technique he had also used in the 1845 *Narrative* and in his early antislavery speeches. In Boston, he argued that lynching was a contagion spreading northward and targeting white as well as black victims. In an article adapted for the Christian magazine *Our Day*, he begins with the argument that lynching was not compatible with Christianity, shocking readers with a vivid comparison between mob violence and the "most disgusting" scavengers— "buzzards, vultures, and hyenas."[11]

In all versions of this speech and ensuing articles on the same subject, Douglass asserts a daring line of reasoning. He argues that the excuse for lynching, the charge of interracial rape, is offered by a people seeking to project their guilt onto others. They accuse black men of rape and black women of harlotry in order to deflect guilt from their own rape culture. Any outspoken black woman could be charged with being promiscuous, and her accusations of having been sexually assaulted then dismissed. Critics of Ida B. Wells sometimes tried to discredit her by calling her a "black harlot."[12] Knowing this, Douglass contends: that "slavery itself, you will remember, was a system of legalized outrage upon the black woman of the South, and no white man was ever shot, burned, or hanged for availing himself of all the power that slavery gave him at this point."

"Lessons of the Hour" represents Douglass's undiminished commitment to racial and gender justice. For Douglass, issues of race

9. "The Negro Problem," Washington (D.C.) *Evening Star,* 10 January 1894.
10. Ibid.
11. "Lynching Black People Because They Are Black," *Our Day* 13 (July–August 1894): 298–306.
12. Schechter, *Ida B. Wells Barnett,* 91.

and gender were always intertwined, and his mentorship of Wells served to advance both. While the pamphlet protesting the absence of African American accomplishments from the Chicago exposition's nationalistic display received little attention in its day, this speech became a classic of oratory and one of Douglass's best remembered.[13]

F riends and fellow citizens:—No man should come before an audience like the one by whose presence I am now honored, without a noble object and a fixed and earnest purpose. I think that, in whatever else I may be deficient, I have the qualifications indicated, to speak to you this evening. I am here to speak for, and to defend, so far as I can do so within the bounds of truth, a long-suffering people, and one just now subject to much misrepresentation and persecution. Charges are at this time preferred against them, more damaging and distressing than any which they have been called upon to meet since their emancipation.

I propose to give you a colored man's view of the unhappy relations at present existing between the white and colored people of the Southern States of our union. We have had the Southern white man's view of the subject. It has been presented with abundant repetition and with startling emphasis, colored by his peculiar environments. We have also had the Northern white man's view tempered by time, distance from the scene, and his higher civilization.

This kind of evidence may be considered by some as all-sufficient upon which to found an intelligent judgment of the whole matter in controversy, and that therefore my testimony is not needed. But experience has taught us that it is sometimes wise and necessary to have more than the testimony of two witnesses to bring out the whole truth, especially in this the case where one of the witnesses has a powerful motive for concealing or distorting the facts in any

13. Glen McClish, "The Instrumental and Constitutive Rhetoric of Martin Luther King, Jr. and Frederick Douglass," *Rhetorica* 33, no. 1 (Winter 2015): 34–70.

given case. You must not, therefore, be surprised if my version of the Southern question shall widely differ from both the North and the South, and yet I shall fearlessly submit my testimony to the candid judgment of all who hear me. I shall do so in the firm belief that my testimony is true.

There is one thing, however, in which I think we shall all agree at the start. It is that the so-called, but mis-called, negro problem is one of the most important and urgent subjects that can now engage public attention. It is worthy of the most earnest consideration of every patriotic American citizen. Its solution involves the honor or dishonor, glory or shame, happiness or misery of the whole American people. It involves more. It touches deeply not only the good name and fame of the Republic, but its highest moral welfare and its permanent safety. Plainly enough the peril it involves is great, obvious and increasing, and should be removed without delay.

The presence of eight millions of people[14] in any section of this country constituting an aggrieved class, smarting under terrible wrongs, denied the exercise of the commonest rights of humanity, and regarded by the ruling class in that section, as outside of the government, outside of the law, and outside of society; having nothing in common with the people with whom they live, the sport of mob violence and murder is not only a disgrace and scandal to that particular section but a menace to the peace and security of the people of the whole country.

I have waited patiently but anxiously to see the end of the epidemic of mob law and persecution now prevailing at the South. But the indications are not hopeful, great and terrible as have been its ravages in the past, it now seems to be increasing not only in the number of its victims, but in its frantic rage and savage extravagance. Lawless vengeance is beginning to be visited upon white men as well as black. Our newspapers are daily disfigured by its ghastly

14. The 1890 U.S. Census recorded 7,488,676 blacks out of a total national population of 62,947,714.

horrors. It is no longer local, but national; no longer confined to the South, but has invaded the North. The contagion is spreading, extending and over-leaping geographical lines and state boundaries, and if permitted to go on it threatens to destroy all respect for law and order not only in the South, but in all parts of our country— North as well as South. For certain it is, that crime allowed to go on unresisted and unarrested will breed crime. When the poison of anarchy is once in the air, like the pestilence that walketh in the darkness,[15] the winds of heaven will take it up and favor its diffusion. Though it may strike down the weak to-day, it will strike down the strong to-morrow.

Not a breeze comes to us now from the late rebellious States that is not tainted and freighted with negro blood. In its thirst for blood and its rage for vengeance, the mob has blindly, boldly and defiantly supplanted sheriffs, constables and police. It has assumed all the functions of civil authority. It laughs at legal processes, courts and juries, and its red-handed murderers range abroad unchecked and unchallenged by law or by public opinion. Prison walls and iron bars are no protection to the innocent or guilty, if the mob is in pursuit of negroes accused of crime. Jail doors are battered down in the presence of unresisting jailers, and the accused, awaiting trial in the courts of law are dragged out and hanged, shot, stabbed or burned to death as the blind and irresponsible mob may elect.

We claim to be a Christian country and a highly civilized nation, yet, I fearlessly affirm that there is nothing in the history of savages to surpass the blood chilling horrors and fiendish excesses perpetrated against the colored people by the so-called enlightened and Christian people of the South. It is commonly thought that only the lowest and most disgusting birds and beasts, such as buzzards, vultures and hyenas, will gloat over and prey upon dead bodies, but the Southern mob in its rage feeds its vengeance by shooting, stabbing and burning when their victims are dead.

15. Ps. 91:6.

Now the special charge against the negro by which this ferocity is justified, and by which mob law is defended by good men North and South, is alleged to be assaults by negroes upon white women. This charge once fairly started, no matter by whom or in what manner, whether well or ill-founded, whether true or false, is certain to subject the accused to immediate death. It is nothing, that in the case there may be a mistake as to identity. It is nothing that the victim pleads "not guilty." It is nothing that he only asks for time to establish his innocence. It is nothing that the accused is of fair reputation and his accuser is of an abandoned character. It is nothing that the majesty of the law is defied and insulted; no time is allowed for defence or explanation; he is bound with cords, hurried off amid the frantic yells and cursing of the mob to the scaffold and under its shadow he is tortured till by pain or promises, he is made to think he can possibly gain time or save his life by confession, and then whether innocent or guilty, he is shot, hanged, stabbed or burned to death amid the wild shouts of the mob. When the will of the mob has been accomplished, when its thirst for blood has been quenched, when its victim is speechless, silent and dead, his mobocratic accusers and murderers of course have the ear of the world all to themselves, and the world generally approves their verdict.

Such then is the state of Southern civilization in its relation to the colored citizens of that section and though the picture is dark and terrible I venture to affirm that no man North or South can deny the essential truth of the picture.

Now it is important to know how this state of affairs is viewed by the better classes of the Southern States. I will tell you, and I venture to say if our hearts were not already hardened by familiarity with such crimes against the negro, we should be shocked and astonished by the attitude of these so-called better classes of the Southern People and their lawmakers. With a few noble exceptions the upper classes of the South are in full sympathy with the mob and its deeds. There are few earnest words uttered against the mob or its deeds. Press, platform and pulpit are either generally silent or they openly apologize for the mob. The mobocratic murderers are not only permitted to go free, untried and unpunished, but are lauded and applauded as honorable men and good citizens, the guardians of Southern women. If lynch law is in any case condemned, it is only condemned in one breath, and excused in another.[16]

The great trouble with the negro in the South is, that all presumptions are against him. A white man has but to blacken his face and commit a crime, to have some negro lynched in his stead. An abandoned woman has only to start the cry that she has been insulted by a black man, to have him arrested and summarily murdered by the mob. Frightened and tortured by his captors, confused into telling crooked stories about his whereabouts at the time when the alleged crime was committed and the death penalty is at once inflicted, though his story may be but the incoherency of ignorance or distraction caused by terror.

Now in confirmation of what I have said of the better classes of the South, I have before me the utterances of some of the best people of that section, and also the testimony of one from the North, a lady, from whom, considering her antecedents, we should have expected a more considerate, just and humane utterance.

In a late number of the "Forum" Bishop Haygood, author of the "Brother in Black," says that "The most alarming fact is, that execution by lynching has ceased to surprise us. The burning of a human being for any crime, it is thought, is a horror that does not occur outside of the Southern States of the American Union, yet unless assaults by negroes come to an end, there will most probably be still further display of vengeance that will shock the world, and men who are just will consider the provocation."[17]

16. The term "lynching" refers to punishment or physical violence by self-appointed groups without regard to established legal procedures, often resulting in death. In America, the term can be traced back to the Revolutionary era, when Charles Lynch (1736–96), a Bedford County, Virginia, justice of the peace, conducted a vigilante campaign against suspected Loyalists.

17. Atticus Green Haygood (1839–96) was a clergyman in the Methodist Episcopal Church. Haygood advocated for federal aid to black education and opposed the convict lease system, causing him to be regarded as a Southern progressive on race issues. Douglass extracts and combines several sentences from Haygood's article "The Black Shadow in the South," in the October 1893 issue of *Forum*.

In an open letter addressed to me by ex-Governor Chamberlain,[18] of South Carolina, and published in the "Charleston News and Courier," a letter which I have but lately seen, in reply to an article of mine on the subject published in the "North American Review,"[19] the ex-Governor says: "Your denunciation of the South on this point is directed exclusively, or nearly so, against the application of lynch law for the punishment of one crime, or one sort of crime, the existence, I suppose, I might say the prevalence of this crime at the South is undeniable. But I read your (my) article in vain for any special denunciation of the crime itself. As you say your people are lynched, tortured and burned for assault on white women. As you value your own good fame and safety as a race, stamp out the infamous crime."[20] He further says, the way to stop lynching is to stamp out the crime.

And now comes the sweet voice of a Northern woman, of Southern principles, in the same tone and the same accusation, the good Miss Frances Willard, of the W.C.T.U.[21] She says in a letter now before me, "I pity the Southerner. The problem on their hands is immeasurable. The colored race," she says, "multiplies like the locusts of Egypt. The safety of woman, of childhood, of the home, is

18. Daniel Henry Chamberlain (1837–1907) rose to the rank of captain in the Fifth Massachusetts Cavalry Regiment, the black unit in which Douglass's son Charles served as a sergeant. Elected governor of South Carolina by the Republicans in 1872, Chamberlain courted the support of moderate elements of the Democratic party through his control of state patronage. Chamberlain was unable to prevent the Democrats from nominating Wade Hampton to oppose his reelection as governor in 1876. After a campaign punctuated by much violence against freedmen, Chamberlain resigned as governor and left the state.

19. Douglass, "Lynch Law in the South," *North American Review* 155 (July 1892): 17–24.

20. These racist opinions were part of a series of public letters during the 1890s and 1900s, in which Chamberlain defended both the disenfranchisement and lynching of black Americans. He blamed the racial turmoil in the South on "the constant coddling of the negro by distant philanthropists."

21. Frances Elizabeth Caroline Willard (1839–98) held a number of teaching positions, culminating in the presidency of the Evanston College for Ladies (1870–73). In 1878, Willard became president of the Illinois Woman's Christian Temperance Union and led it in a pioneering campaign to ban liquor sales. Under her leadership, the WCTU took a far more active role in politics, especially on behalf of woman suffrage.

menaced in a thousand localities at this moment, so that men dare not go beyond the sight of their own roof tree."[22] Such then is the crushing indictment drawn up against the Southern negroes, drawn up, too, by persons who are perhaps the fairest and most humane of the negro's accusers. But even they paint him as a moral monster ferociously invading the sacred rights of women and endangering the homes of the whites.

The crime they allege against the negro, is the most revolting which men can commit. It is a crime that awakens the intensest abhorrence and invites mankind to kill the criminal on sight. This charge thus brought against the negro, and as constantly reiterated by his enemies, is not merely against the individual culprit, as would be in the case with an individual culprit of any other race, but it is in a large measure a charge against the colored race as such. It throws over every colored man a mantle of odium and sets upon him a mark for popular hate, more distressing than the mark set upon the first murderer. It points him out as an object of suspicion and avoidance. Now it is in this form that you and I, and all of us, are required to meet it and refute it, if that can be done. In the opinion of some of us, it is thought that it were well to say nothing about it, that the least said about it the better. In this opinion I do not concur. Taking this charge in its broad and comprehensive sense in which it is presented, and as now stated, I feel that it ought to be met, and as a colored man, I am grateful for the opportunity now afforded me to meet it. For I believe it can be met and successfully met. I am of opinion that a people too spiritless to defend themselves are not worth defending.

Without boasting, on this broad issue as now presented, I am ready to confront ex-Governor Chamberlain, Bishop Fitzgerald,[23]

22. New York *Voice*, 28 October 1890.

23. Oscar Penn Fitzgerald (1829–1911) entered the Methodist ministry in 1853 and edited the Methodist organ, the *Christian Advocate*, from 1870 until he became a bishop in 1890. In May 1892, the General Conference of the Methodist Episcopal Church, consisting largely of Northern white and Southern black congregations, passed a resolution calling on both the federal government and appropriate state governments to take action to end the lynching of "colored people" in the South. In

Bishop Haygood, and Miss Frances Willard and all others, singly or altogether, without any doubt of the result.

But I want to be understood at the outset. I do not pretend that negroes are saints or angels. I do not deny that they are capable of committing the crime imputed to them, but I utterly deny that they are any more addicted to the commission of that crime than is true of any other variety of the human family. In entering upon my argument, I may be allowed to say, that I appear here this evening not as the defender of any man guilty of this atrocious crime, but as the defender of the colored people as a class.

In answer to the terrible indictment, thus read, and speaking for the colored people as a class, I, in their stead, here and now plead not guilty and shall submit my case with confidence of acquittal by good men and women North and South.

It is the misfortune of the colored people in this country that the sins of the few are visited upon the many,[24] and I am here to speak for the many whose reputation is put in peril by the sweeping charge in question. With General Grant and every other honest man, my motto is, "Let no guilty man escape."[25] But while I am here to say this, I am here also to say, let no innocent man be condemned and killed by the mob, or crushed under the weight of a charge of which he is not guilty.

You will readily see that the cause I have undertaken to support, is not to be maintained by any mere confident assertions or general denials. If I had no better ground to stand upon than this I would

response, Bishop Fitzgerald, of the Methodist Episcopal Church, South, publically condemned the resolution for being unjust and hypocritical. Douglass condemned Fitzpatrick's position in his essay "The Lynch Law in the South." *North American Review* 155 (July 1892): 17–24.

24. Exod. 34:7.

25. On 29 July 1875, President Ulysses S. Grant used this phrase in an endorsement to a letter containing evidence regarding the "Whisky Ring" conspiracy in the Treasury Department. *Whisky Frauds: Testimony Before the Select Committee Concerning the Whisky Frauds,* 44th Cong., 1st sess., House Miscellaneous Document 186 (serial set 1706), 357, 484–86.

leave the field of controversy and give up the colored man's cause at once to his able accusers. I am aware, however, that I am here to do in some measure what the masters of logic say cannot be done— prove a negative.

Of course, I shall not be able to succeed in doing the impossible, but this one thing I can and will do. I can and will show that there are sound reasons for doubting and denying this horrible and hell-black charge of rape as the peculiar crime of the colored people of the South. My doubt and denial are based upon two fundamental and invincible grounds.

The first is, the well established and well tested character of the negro on the very point upon which he is now violently and persis tently accused. The second ground for my doubt and denial is based upon what I know of the character and antecedents of the men and women who bring this charge against him. I undertake to say that the strength of this position will become more manifest as I proceed with my argument.

At the outset I deny that a fierce and frenzied mob is or ought to be deemed a competent witness against any man accused of any crime whatever. The ease with which a mob can be collected and the slight causes by which it may be set in motion, and the elements of which it is composed, deprives its testimony of the qualities that should inspire confidence and command belief. It is moved by im-pulses utterly unfavorable to an impartial statement of the truth. At the outset, therefore, I challenge the credibility of the mob, and as the mob is the main witness in the case against the negro, I appeal to the common sense of mankind in support of my challenge. It is the mob that brings this charge, and it is the mob that arraigns, condemns and executes, and it is the mob that the country has ac-cepted as its witness.

Again, I impeach and discredit the veracity of southern men gen-erally, whether mobocrats or otherwise, who now openly and delib-erately nullify and violate the provisions of the constitution of their country, a constitution, which they have solemnly sworn to support and execute. I apply to them the legal maxim, "False in one, false in all."[26]

Again I arraign the negro's accuser on another ground, I have no confidence in the truthfulness of men who justify themselves in cheating the negro out of his constitutional right to vote. The men, who either by false returns, or by taking advantage of his illiteracy or surrounding the ballot-box with obstacles and sinuosities intended to bewilder him and defeat his rightful exercise of the elective franchise, are men who are not to be believed on oath. That this is done in the Southern States is not only admitted, but openly defended and justified by so-called honorable men inside and outside of Congress.

Just this kind of fraud in the South is notorious. I have met it face to face. It was boldly defended and advocated a few weeks ago in a solemn paper by Prof. Weeks, a learned North Carolinian, in my hearing. His paper was one of the able papers read before one of the World's Auxiliary Congresses at Chicago.[27]

Now men who openly defraud the negro by all manner of artifice and boast of it in the face of the world's civilization, as was done at Chicago, I affirm that they are not to be depended upon for truth in any case whatever, where the rights of the negro are involved. Their testimony in the case of any other people than the negro, against whom they should thus commit fraud would be instantly and utterly discredited, and why not the same in this case? Every honest man will see that this point is well taken, and I defy any argument that would drive me from this just contention. It has for its support com-

26. The legal maxim "Falsus in uno, falsus in omnibus."
27. One of the founders of the Southern Historical Association, Stephen Beauregard Weeks (1865–1918) produced numerous scholarly works, principally dealing with his home state of North Carolina. On 9 August 1893, Weeks delivered a paper on the history of black suffrage in the South to a session of the World's Columbian Exposition in Chicago. Douglass, in attendance, responded to a call by the audience to deliver an impromptu rebuttal to Week's defense of efforts by Southern states to disenfranchise blacks. Chicago *Tribune*, 10 August 1893.

mon sense, common justice, common honesty, and the best sentiment of mankind, and has nothing to oppose it but a vulgar popular
prejudice against the colored people of our country, which prejudice strikes men with moral blindness and renders them incapable
of seeing any distinction between right and wrong.

But I come to a stronger position. I rest my conclusion not merely
upon general principles, but upon well known facts. I reject the
charge brought against the negro as a class, because all through the
late war, while the slave masters of the South were absent from their
homes in the field of rebellion, with bullets in their pockets, treason
in their hearts, broad blades in their blood stained hands, seeking
the life of the nation, with the vile purpose of perpetuating the enslavement of the negro, their wives, their daughters, their sisters
and their mothers were left in the absolute custody of these same
negroes, and during all those long four years of terrible conflict,
when the negro had every opportunity to commit the abominable
crime now alleged against him, there was never a single instance
of such crime reported or charged against him. He was never accused of assault, insult, or an attempt to commit an assault upon any
white woman in the whole South. A fact like this, although negative,
speaks volumes and ought to have some weight with the American
people.

Then, again on general principles, I do not believe the charge
because it implies an improbable, if not impossible, change in the
mental and moral character and composition of the negro. It implies
a change wholly inconsistent with well known facts of human nature. It is a contradiction to well known human experience. History
does not present an example of such a transformation in the character of any class of men so extreme, so unnatural and so complete as
is implied in this charge. The change is too great and the period too
brief. Instances may be cited where men fall like stars from heaven,
but such is not the usual experience. Decline in the moral character
of a people is not sudden, but gradual. The downward steps are
marked at first by degrees and by increasing momentum from bad

to worse. Time is an element in such changes, and I contend that the negroes of the South have not had time to experience this great change and reach this lower depth of infamy. On the contrary, in point of fact, they have been and still are, improving and ascending to higher levels of moral and social worth.

Again, I do not believe it and utterly deny it, because those who bring the charge do not, and dare not, give the negro a chance to be heard in his own defence. He is not allowed to explain any part of his alleged offense. He is not allowed to vindicate his own character or to criminate the character and motives of his accusers. Even the mobocrats themselves admit that it would be fatal to their purpose to have the character of his accusers brought into court. They pretend to a delicate regard for the feelings of the parties assaulted, and therefore object to giving a fair trial to the accused. The excuse in this case is contemptible. It is not only mock modesty but mob modesty. Men who can collect hundreds and thousands, if we may believe them, and can spread before them in the tempest and whirlwind of vulgar passion, the most disgusting details of crime with the names of women, with the alleged offense, should not be allowed to shelter themselves under any pretense of modesty. Such a pretense is absurd and shameless. Who does not know that the modesty of womanhood is always an object for protection in a court of law? Who does not know that a lawless mob composed in part of the basest of men can have no such respect for the modesty of women as a court of law. No woman need be ashamed to confront one who has insulted or assaulted her in a court of law. Besides innocence does not hesitate to come to the rescue of justice.

Again, I do not believe it, and deny it because if the evidence were deemed sufficient to bring the accused to the scaffold, through the action of an impartial jury, there could be, and would be, no objection to having the alleged offender tried in conformity to due process of law.

Any pretence that a guilty negro, especially one guilty of the crime now charged, would in any case be permitted to escape condign[28] punishment, is an insult to common sense. Nobody believes or can believe such a thing as escape possible, in a country like the South, where public opinion, the laws, the courts, the juries, and the advocates are all known to be against him, he could hardly escape if innocent. I repeat, therefore, I do not believe it, because I know, and you know, that a passionate and violent mob bent upon taking life, from the nature of the case, is not a more competent and trustworthy body to determine the guilt or innocence of a negro accused in such a case, than is a court of law. I would not, and you would not, convict a dog on such testimony.

But I come to another fact, and an all-important fact, bearing upon this case. You will remember that during all the first years of re-construction and long after the war when the Southern press and people found it necessary to invent, adopt, and propagate almost every species of falsehood to create sympathy for themselves and to formulate an excuse for gratifying their brutal instincts, there was never a charge then made against a negro involving an assault upon any white woman or upon any little white child. During all this time the white women and children were absolutely safe. During all this time there was no call for Miss Willard's pity, or Bishop Haygood's defense of burning negroes to death.

You will remember also that during this time the justification for the murder of negroes was said to be negro conspiracies, insurrections, schemes to murder all the white people, to burn the town, and commit violence generally. These were the excuses then depended upon, but never a word was then said or whispered about negro outrages upon white women and children. So far as the history of that time is concerned, white women and children were absolutely safe, and husbands and fathers could leave home without the slightest anxiety on account of their families.

But when events proved that no such conspiracies; no such insurrections as were then pretended to exist and were paraded before

28. Adequate or deserved.

the world in glaring head-lines, had ever existed or were even medi-
tated; when these excuses had run their course and served their
wicked purpose; when the huts of negroes had been searched, and
searched in vain, for guns and ammunition to prove these charges,
and no evidence was found, when there was no way open thereafter
to prove these charges against the negro and no way to make the
North believe in these excuses for murder, they did not even then
bring forward the present allegation against the negro. They, however, went on harassing and killing just the same. But this time they
based the right thus to kill on the ground that it was necessary to
check the domination and supremacy of the negro and to secure the
absolute rule of the Anglo-Saxon race.

It is important to notice that there has been three distinct periods of persecution of negroes in the South, and three distinct sets
of excuses for persecution. They have come along precisely in the
order in which they were most needed. First you remember it was
insurrection. When that was worn out, negro supremacy became
the excuse. When that is worn out, now it is assault upon defense-
less women. I undertake to say, that this order and periodicity is
significant and means something and should not be overlooked.
And now that negro supremacy and negro domination are no longer
defensible as an excuse for negro persecutions, there has come in
due course, this heart-rending cry about the white women and little
white children of the South.

Now, my friends, I ask what is the rational explanation of this
singular omission of this charge in the two periods preceding the
present? Why was not the charge made at that time as now? The
negro was the same then as to-day. White women and children were
the same then as to-day. Temptations to wrong doing were the same
then as to-day. Why then was not this dreadful charge brought forward against the negro in war times and why was it not brought
forward in reconstruction times?

I will tell you; or you, yourselves, have already answered the
question. The only rational answer is that there was no foundation

for such a charge or that the charge itself was either not thought of or was not deemed necessary to excuse the lawless violence with which the negro was then pursued and killed. The old charges already enumerated were deemed all sufficient. This new charge has now swallowed up all the old ones and the reason is obvious.

Things have changed since then, old excuses were not available and the negro's accusers have found it necessary to change with them. The old charges are no longer valid. Upon them the good opinion of the North and of mankind cannot be secured. Honest men no longer believe in the worn-out stories of insurrection. They no longer believe that there is just ground to apprehend negro supremacy. Time and events have swept away these old refuges of lies. They did their work in their day, and did it with terrible energy and effect, but they are now cast aside as useless. The altered times and circumstances have made necessary a sterner, stronger, and more effective justification of Southern barbarism, and hence, according to my theory, we now have to look into the face of a more shocking and blasting charge than either negro supremacy or insurrection or that of murder itself.

This new charge has come at the call of new conditions, and nothing could have been hit upon better calculated to accomplish its purpose. It clouds the character of the negro with a crime the most revolting, and is fitted to drive from him all sympathy and all fair play and all mercy. It is a crime that places him outside of the pale of the law, and settles upon his shoulders a mantle of wrath and fire that blisters and burns into his very soul.

It is for this purpose, as I believe, that this new charge unthought of in the times to which I have referred, has been largely invited, if not entirely trumped up. It is for this purpose that it has been constantly reiterated and adopted. It was to blast and ruin the negro's character as a man and a citizen.

I need not tell you how thoroughly it has already done its wonted work. You may feel its malign influence in the very air. You may read it in the faces of men. It has cooled our friends. It has heated our enemies,[29] and arrested in some measure the efforts that good men were wont to make for the colored man's improvement and elevation. It has deceived our friends at the North and many good friends at the South, for nearly all have in some measure accepted the charge as true. Its perpetual reiteration in our newspapers and magazines has led men and women to regard us with averted eyes, increasing hate and dark suspicion.

Some of the Southern papers have denounced me for my unbelief, in their new departure, but I repeat I do not believe it and firmly deny it. I reject it because I see in it, evidence of an invention, called into being by a well defined motive, a motive sufficient to stamp it as a gross expedient to justify murderous assault upon a long enslaved and hence a hated people.

I do not believe it because it bears on its face, the marks of being a makeshift for a malignant purpose. I reject it not only because it was sprung upon the country simultaneously with well-known efforts now being industriously made to degrade the negro by legislative enactments, and by repealing all laws for the protection of the ballot, and by drawing the color line in all railroad cars and stations and in all other public places in the South; but because I see in it a means of paving the way for our entire disfranchisement.

Again, I do not believe it, and deny it, because the charge is not so much against the crime itself, as against the color of the man alleged to be guilty of it. Slavery itself, you will remember, was a system of legalized outrage upon the black women of the South, and no white man was ever shot, burned, or hanged for availing himself of all the power that slavery gave him at this point.

Upon these grounds then—grounds which I believe to be solid and immovable—I dare here and now in the capital of the nation and in the presence of Congress to reject it, and ask you and all just men to reject this horrible charge so frequently made and construed against the negro as a class.

29. *Merchant of Venice*, sc. 13, line 1210.

To sum up my argument on this lynching business. It remains to be said that I have shown that the negro's accusers in this case have violated their oaths and have cheated the negro out of his vote; that they have robbed and defrauded the negro systematically and persistently, and have boasted of it. I have shown that when the negro had every opportunity to commit the crime now charged against him he was never accused of it by his bitterest enemies. I have shown that during all the years of reconstruction, when he was being murdered at Hamburg,[30] Yazoo,[31] New Orleans,[32] Copiah[33] and elsewhere, he was never accused of the crime now charged against him. I have shown that in the nature of things no such change in the character and composition of a people as this charge implies could have taken place in the limited period allowed for it. I have shown that those who accuse him dare not confront him in a court of law and have their witnesses subjected to proper legal inquiry. And in showing all this, and more, I have shown that they who charge him with this foul crime may be justly doubted and deemed unworthy of belief.

30. The "Hamburg Massacre" in July 1876 occurred when a black militia company in that South Carolina community along the Savannah River refused demands issued by local white politicians to disarm. The whites then brought hundreds of armed men and a cannon to Hamburg and besieged about forty black militiamen in their armory. After sunset the outnumbered blacks attempted to flee, but twenty-five were captured and five of them were executed in cold blood. Prosecution of the white perpetrators was dropped following the state government's return to Democratic Party control the next year.

31. On 1 September 1875, armed Democrats broke up a Republican rally at Yazoo City in heavily black Yazoo County in north-central Mississippi, killing one and wounding three participants. The Republican sheriff of the county fled, and a white "militia" seized control and lynched several politically active blacks. Only seven residents cast votes for the Republican party in the November election.

32. In July 1866, the New Orleans police force besieged a Republican party convention and killed almost forty Republicans before federal troops arrived to protect them. The widely reported New Orleans violence helped discredit Johnson's "Restoration" programs in the minds of many Northern Republicans.

33. An outbreak of armed attacks by supporters of the Democratic leadership occurred in southern Mississippi's Copiah County in October 1883. An effort to forge an alliance between white reformers and local blacks provoked Democrats to assassinate several political opponents. The Democrats easily swept the subsequent balloting, even in mainly black precincts. The U.S. Senate conducted an investigation of the violence in Copiah, but no one was arrested for the murders.

But I shall be told by many of my Northern friends that my argument, though plausible, is not conclusive. It will be said that the charges against the negro are specific and positive, and that there must be some foundation for them, because as they allege men in their normal condition do not shoot and hang their fellowmen who are guiltless of crime. Well! This assumption is very just, very charitable. I only ask something like the same justice and charity could be shown to the negro as well as to the mob. It is creditable to the justice and humanity of the good people of the North by whom it is entertained. They rightly assume that men do not shoot and hang their fellowmen without just cause. But the vice of their argument is in their assumption that the lynchers are like other men. The answer to that argument is what may be truly predicated of human nature under one condition is not what may be true of human nature under another. Uncorrupted human nature may shudder at the commission of such crimes as those of which the Southern mob is guilty.

But human nature uncorrupted is one thing and human nature corrupted and perverted by long abuse of irresponsible power, is quite another and different thing. No man can reason correctly on this question who reasons on the assumption that the lynchers are like ordinary men.

We are not, in this case, dealing with men in their natural condition, but with men brought up in the exercise of arbitrary power. We are dealing with men whose ideas, habits and customs are entirely different from those of ordinary men. It is, therefore, quite gratuitous to assume that the principles that apply to other men apply to the Southern murderers of the negro, and just here is the mistake of the Northern people. They do not see that the rules resting upon the justice and benevolence of human nature do not apply to the mobocrats, or to those who were educated in the habits and customs of a slave-holding community. What these habits are I have a right to know, both in theory and in practice.

I repeat: The mistake made by those who on this ground object to my theory of the charge against the negro, is that they overlook the natural effect and influence of the life, education and habits of the lynchers. We must remember that these people have not now and have never had any such respect for human life as is common to other men. They have had among them for centuries a peculiar institution, and that peculiar institution has stamped them as a peculiar people. They were not before the war, they were not during the war and have not been since the war in their spirit or in their civilization, a people in common with the people of the North. I will not here harrow up your feelings by detailing their treatment of Northern prisoners during the war. Their institutions have taught them no respect for human life and especially the life of the negro. It has in fact taught them absolute contempt for his life. The sacredness of life which ordinary men feel does not touch them anywhere. A dead negro is with them a common jest.

They care no more for a negro's right to live than they care for his rights to liberty, or his rights to the ballot. Chief Justice Taney told the exact truth about these people when he said: "They did not consider that the black man had any rights which the white men were bound to respect."[34] No man of the South ever called in question that statement and they never will. They could always shoot, stab and burn the negro without any such remorse or shame as other men would feel after committing such a crime. Any Southern man who is honest and is frank enough to talk on the subject, will tell you that he has no such idea as we have of the sacredness of human life and especially, as I have said, of the life of the negro. Hence it is absurd to meet my arguments with the facts predicated on our common human nature.

I know I shall be charged with apologizing for criminals. Ex-Governor Chamberlain has already virtually done as much. But there is no foundation for any such charge. I affirm that neither I nor any other colored man of like standing with myself, has ever raised a finger or uttered a word in defense of any one really guilty of the dreadful crime now in question.

34. An allusion to Roger B. Taney's opinion in the *Dred Scott* decision of 1857.

But, what I contend for, and what every honest man, black or white should contend for, is that when any man is accused of this or any other crime, of whatever name, nature, or extent, he shall have the benefit of a legal investigation; that he shall be confronted by his accusers; and that he shall through proper counsel, be able to question his accusers in open court and in open day-light so that his guilt or his innocence may be duly proved and established.

If this is to make me liable to the charge of apologizing for crime, I am not ashamed to be so charged. I dare to contend for the colored people of the United States that they are a law-abiding people, and I dare to insist upon it that they or any man, black or white, accused of crime, shall have a fair trial before he is punished.

Again, I cannot dwell too much upon the fact that colored people are much damaged by this charge. As an injured class we have a right to appeal from the judgment of the mob to the judgment of the law and the American people. Our enemies have known well where to strike and how to stab us most fatally. Owing to popular prejudice it has become the misfortune of the colored people of the South and of the North as well, to have as I have said, the sins of the few visited upon the many. When a white man steals, robs or murders, his crime is visited upon his own head alone. But not so with the black man. When he commits a crime the whole race is made to suffer. The cause before us is an example. This unfairness confronts us not only here, but it confronts us everywhere else.

Even when American art undertakes to picture the types of the two races it invariably places in comparison not the best of both races as common fairness would dictate but it puts side by side in glaring contrast the lowest type of the negro with the highest type of the white man and calls upon you to "look upon this picture then upon that."

When a black man's language is quoted, in order to belittle and degrade him, his ideas are put into the most grotesque and unreadable English, while the utterances of negro scholars and authors are ignored. A hundred white men will attend a concert of white negro minstrels with faces blackened with burnt cork, to one who will attend a lecture by an intelligent negro.

On this ground I have a criticism to make, even of the late World's Columbian Exposition. While I join with all other men in pronouncing the Exposition itself one of the grandest demonstrations of civilization that the world has ever seen, yet great and glorious as it was, it was made to show just this kind of unfairness and discrimination against the negro.[35]

As nowhere else in the world it was hoped that here the idea of human brotherhood would have been fully recognized and most gloriously illustrated. It should have been, and would have been, had it been what it professed to be, a World's Exposition. It was, however, in a marked degree an American Exposition. The spirit of American caste made itself conspicuously felt against the educated American negro, and to this extent, the Exposition was made simply an American Exposition and that in one of America's most illiberal features.

Since the day of Pentecost,[36] there has never assembled in any one place or on any one occasion, a larger variety of peoples of all forms, features and colors, and all degrees of civilization, than was assembled at this World's Exposition. It was a grand ethnological lesson, a chance to study all likenesses and differences. Here were Japanese, Soudanese, Chinese, Cingalese, Syrians, Persians, Tunisians, Algerians, Egyptians, East Indians, Laplanders, Esquimaux, and as if to shame the educated negro of America, the Dahomeyans were there to exhibit their barbarism, and increase American contempt for the negro intellect. All classes and conditions were there save the educated American negro. He ought to have been there

35. Douglass elaborated on this criticism of the racial discrimination at the World's Columbian Exposition in his essay "Inauguration of the World's Columbian Exposition," *The Reason Why the Colored American Is Not in the World's Columbian Exposition* (Chicago: n.p., 1893), 2–12.

36. In Christianity, Pentecost commemorates the descent of the Holy Spirit on the apostles fifty days after Christ's resurrection. The manifestation of the spirit was witnessed by "men, out of every nation under heaven." Acts 2:5.

if only to show what American slavery and freedom have done for him. The fact that all other nations were there and there at their best, made his exclusion the more marked, and the more significant. People from abroad noticed the fact that while we have eight millions of colored people in the United States, many of them gentlemen and scholars, not one of them was deemed worthy to be appointed a Commissioner, or a member of an important committee, or a guide, or a guard on the Exposition grounds. What a commentary is this upon our boasted American liberty and American equality! It is a silence to be sure, but it is a silence that speaks louder than words. It says to the world that the colored people of America are deemed by Americans not within the compass of American law and of American civilization. It says to the lynchers and mobocrats of the South, go on in your hellish work of negro persecution. What you do to their bodies, we do to their souls.

I come now to the question of negro suffrage. It has come to be fashionable of late to ascribe much of the trouble at the South to ignorant negro suffrage. The great measure according suffrage to the negro recommended by General Grant and adopted by the loyal nation[37] is now denounced as a blunder and a failure. They would, therefore, in some way abridge and limit this right by imposing upon it an educational or some other qualification. Among those who take this view are Mr. John J. Ingalls,[38] and Mr. John M. Langston.[39]

37. Douglass alludes to the Fifteenth Amendment.

38. Senator John James Ingalls (1833–1900), a long-serving Republican from Kansas, loudly denounced amendments to Southern state constitutions to disenfranchise black voters. As a remedy, Ingalls proposed a national voter registration law. In January 1890, Ingalls relented in this position; Douglass denounced this reversal as "not only wrong, but very wrong." *Douglass Papers*, ser. 1, 5:451.

39. The son of a white slaveholding planter and an emancipated black–Native American mother, John Mercer Langston (1829–97) attended Oberlin College, practiced law in Ohio, and later became dean of Howard University's law school. Langston's position regarding black voting rights was far from clear-cut. While representing southern Virginia in the U.S. House of Representatives (1890–91), Langston supported Henry Cabot Lodge's efforts to protect African American voting rights, but later advocated an educational qualification in order to bar illiterates of all races from the ballot box.

They are both eloquent, both able, and both wrong. Though they are both Johns neither of them is to my mind a "St. John" and not even a "John the Baptist."[40] They have taken up an idea which they seem to think quite new, but which in reality is as old as despotism and about as narrow and selfish. It has been heard and answered a thousand times over. It is the argument of the crowned heads and privileged classes of the world. It is as good against our Republican form of government as it [is] against the negro. The wonder is that its votaries do not see its consequences. It does away with that noble and just idea of Abraham Lincoln, that our government should be a government of the people, by the people, and for the people, and for *all* the people.[41]

These gentlemen are very learned, very eloquent and very able, but I cannot follow them. Much learning has made them mad.[42] Education is great, but manhood is greater. The one is the principle, the other is the accident. Man was not made as an attribute to education, but education is an attribute to man. I say to these gentlemen, first protect the man and you will thereby protect education. I would not make illiteracy a bar to the ballot, but would make the ballot a bar to illiteracy. Take the ballot from the negro and you take from him the means and motives that make for education. Those who are already educated and are vested with political power and have thereby an advantage, will have a strong motive for refusing to divide that advantage with others, and least of all will they divide it with the negro to whom they would deny all right to participate in the government.

I, therefore, cannot follow these gentlemen in their proposition to limit suffrage to the educated alone. I would not make suffrage

40. According to the New Testament, St. John was one of Jesus's apostles. John the Baptist was an iterant Jewish preacher who foretold the coming of the Messiah and baptized Jesus in the Jordan River. The Gospels of Matthew and Mark record his execution by Herod Antipas for subversive preaching.

41. The concluding line of the Gettysburg Address.

42. Acts 28:24.

more exclusive, but more inclusive. I would not have it embrace merely the elite, but would include the lowly. I would not only include the men, I would gladly include the women, and make our government in reality as in name a government of the people and of the whole people.

But manifestly suffrage to the colored people is not the cause of the failure of good government, or the cause of trouble in the Southern States, but it is the lawless limitations of suffrage that makes the trouble.

Much thoughtless speech is heard about the ignorance of the negro in the South. But plainly enough it is not the ignorance of the negro, but the malevolence of his accusers, which is the real cause of Southern disorder. The illiteracy of the negro has no part or lot in the disturbances there. They who contend for disfranchisement on this ground know, and know very well, that there is no truth whatever in their contention. To make out their case they must show that some oppressive and hurtful measure has been imposed upon the country by negro voters. But they cannot show any such thing.

The negro has never set up a separate party, never adopted a negro platform, never proclaimed or adopted a separate policy for himself or for the country. His assailants know that he has never acted apart from the whole American people. They know that he has never sought to lead, but has always been content to follow. They know that he has not made his ignorance the rule of his political conduct, but the intelligence of white people has always been his guide. They know that he has simply kept pace with the average intelligence of his age and country. They know that he has gone steadily along in the line of his politics with the most enlightened citizens of the country. They know that he has always voted with one or the other of the two great political parties. They know that if the votes of these parties have been guided by intelligence and patriotism, the same may be said for the vote of the negro. They ought to know, therefore, that it is a shame and an outrage upon common sense and common fairness to make the negro responsible, or his ignorance responsible, for any disorder and confusion that may reign in the Southern States. Yet, while any lie may be safely told against the negro and be credited, this lie will find eloquent mouths bold enough to tell it, and pride themselves upon their superior wisdom in denouncing the ignorant negro voter.

It is true that the negro once voted solidly for the candidates of the Republican party, but what if he did? He then only voted with John Mercer Langston, John J. Ingalls, John Sherman,[43] General Harrison,[44] Senator Hoar,[45] Henry Cabot Lodge,[46] and Governor McKinley,[47] and many of the most intelligent statesmen and patriots of whom this country can boast. The charge against him at this point is, therefore, utterly groundless. It is a mere pretense, a sham, an excuse for fraud and violence, for persecution and a cloak for popular prejudice.

The proposition to disfranchise the colored voter of the South in order to solve the race problem I hereby denounce as a mean and cowardly proposition, utterly unworthy of an honest, truthful and grateful nation. It is a proposition to sacrifice friends in order to conciliate enemies; to surrender the constitution to the late rebels for the lack of moral courage to execute its provisions. It says to the

43. A younger brother of Union general William Tecumseh Sherman, John Sherman (1823–1900) was a founder of Ohio's Republican party, which elected him to the U.S. House of Representatives and the U.S. Senate. A highly pragmatic politician, he usually sought the middle ground on controversial Reconstruction and economic issues. Sherman's efforts to obtain the Republican presidential nomination in 1880, 1884, and 1888 proved futile.

44. Benjamin Harrison (1833–1901), twenty-third president of the United States, was the grandson of President William Henry Harrison. Douglass and other prominent African Americans campaigned strenuously for Harrison, who defeated the incumbent, Grover Cleveland.

45. The Republican George Frisbie Hoar (1826–1904) was one of the managers of the impeachment trial of President Andrew Johnson. Elected to the U.S. Senate from Massachusetts in 1877, Hoar held that office for the remaining twenty-seven years of his life.

46. Henry Cabot Lodge (1850–1924) won election in 1881 to the U.S. House of Representatives from Massachusetts as a Republican. He sponsored a Federal Elections Bill to protect African American voting rights.

47. William McKinley (1843–1901), twenty-fifth president of the United States, was governor of Ohio from 1891 to 1895.

negro citizens, "The Southern nullifiers have robbed you of a part of your rights, and as we are powerless and cannot help you, and wish to live on good terms with our Southern brethren, we propose to join your oppressors so that our practice shall be consistent with their theories. Your suffrage has been practically rendered a failure by violence, we now propose to make it a failure by law. Instead of conforming our practice to the theory of our government and the genius of our institutions, we now propose, as means of conciliation, to conform our practice to the theory of your oppressors."

Than this, was there ever a surrender more complete, more cowardly or more base? Upon the statesmen, black or white, who could dare to hint such a scheme of national debasement as a means of settling the race problem, I should inflict no punishment more severe than to keep him at home, and deprived of all legislative trusts forever.

Do not ask me what will be the final result of the so-called negro problem. I cannot tell you. I have sometimes thought that the American people are too great to be small, too just and magnanimous to oppress the weak, too brave to yield up the right to the strong, and too grateful for public services ever to forget them or fail to reward them. I have fondly hoped that this estimate of American character would soon cease to be contradicted or put in doubt. But the favor with which this cowardly proposition of disfranchisement has been received by public men, white and black, by Republicans as well as Democrats, has shaken my faith in the nobility of the nation. I hope and trust all will come out right in the end, but the immediate future looks dark and troubled. I cannot shut my eyes to the ugly facts before me.

Strange things have happened of late and are still happening. Some of these tend to dim the lustre of the American name, and chill the hopes once entertained for the cause of American liberty. He is a wiser man than I am, who can tell how low the moral sentiment of this republic may yet fall. When the moral sense of a nation begins to decline and the wheel of progress to roll backward, there is no telling how low the one will fall or where the other may stop. The downward tendency already manifest has swept away some of the most important safeguards. The Supreme Court has surrendered. State sovereignty is restored. It has destroyed the civil rights Bill, and converted the Republican party into a party of money rather than a party of morals, a party of things rather than a party of humanity and justice. We may well ask what next?

The pit of hell is said to be bottomless.[48] Principles which we all thought to have been firmly and permanently settled by the late war, have been boldly assaulted and overthrown by the defeated party. Rebel rule is now nearly complete in many States and it is gradually capturing the nation's Congress. The cause lost in the war, is the cause regained in peace, and the cause gained in war, is the cause lost in peace.

There was a threat made long ago by an American statesman, that the whole body of legislation enacted for the protection of American liberty and to secure the results of the war for the Union, should be blotted from the national statute book. That threat is now being sternly pursued, and may yet be fully realized. The repeal of the laws intended to protect the elective franchise has heightened the suspicion that Southern rule may yet become complete, though I trust, not permanent. There is no denying that the trend is in the wrong way at present. The late election, however, gives us hope that the loyal Republican party may return to its first born.[49]

But I come now to another proposition held up just now as a solution of the race problem, and this I consider equally unworthy with the one just disposed of. The two belong to the same low-bred family of ideas.

48. Rev. 9:2, 20:3.
49. Douglass most likely alludes to the defeat of President Benjamin Harrison for reelection in 1892. While Republicans gained some congressional seats from the Democrats in that election, they nevertheless composed a minority in both houses of the Fifty-third Congress (1893–95). Douglass hoped that this defeat would revive Northern white Republicans' desire to protect the voting rights of their Southern African American counterparts.

This proposition is to colonize the colored people of America in Africa, or somewhere else. Happily this scheme will be defeated, both by its impolicy and its impracticability. It is all nonsense to talk about the removal of eight millions of the American people from their homes in America to Africa. The expense and hardships, to say nothing of the cruelty of such a measure, would make success to such a measure impossible. The American people are wicked, but they are not fools, they will hardly be disposed to incur the expense, to say nothing of the injustice which this measure demands. Nevertheless, this colonizing scheme, unworthy as it is, of American statesmanship and American honor, and though full of mischief to the colored people, seems to have a strong hold on the public mind and at times has shown much life and vigor.

The bad thing about it is that it has now begun to be advocated by colored men of acknowledged ability and learning, and every little while some white statesman becomes its advocate. Those gentlemen will doubtless have their opinion of me; I certainly have mine of them. My opinion of them is that if they are sensible, they are insincere, and if they are sincere they are not sensible. They know, or they ought to know, that it would take more money than the cost of the late war, to transport even one-half of the colored people of the United States to Africa. Whether intentionally or not they are, as I think, simply trifling with an afflicted people. They urge them to look for relief, where they ought to know that relief is impossible. The only excuse they can make is that there is no hope for the negro here and that the colored people in America owe something to Africa.

This last sentimental idea makes colonization very fascinating to dreamers of both colors. But there is really for it no foundation.

They tell us that we owe something to our native land. But when the fact is brought to view, which should never be forgotten, that a man can only have one native land, and that is the land in which he was born, the bottom falls entirely out of this sentimental argument.

Africa, according to her advocates, is by no means modest in her demand upon us. She calls upon us to send her only our best men. She does not want our riff raff, but out best men. But these are just the men we want at home. It is true we have a few preachers and laymen with a missionary turn of mind who might be easily spared. Some who would possibly do as much good by going there as by staying here. But this is not the only colonization idea. Its advocates want not only the best, but millions of the best. They want the money to be voted by the United States Government to send them there.

Now I hold that the American negro owes no more to the negroes in Africa than he owes to the negroes in America. There are millions of needy people over there, but there are also millions of needy people over here as well, and the millions here need intelligent men of their numbers to help them, as much as intelligent men are needed in Africa. We have a fight on our hands right here, a fight for the whole race, and a blow struck for the negro in America is a blow struck for the negro in Africa. For until the negro is respected in America, he need not expect consideration elsewhere. All this native land talk is nonsense. The native land of the American negro is America. His bones, his muscles, his sinews, are all American. His ancestors for two hundred and seventy years have lived, and labored, and died on American soil, and millions of his posterity have inherited Caucasian blood.

It is competent, therefore, to ask, in view of this admixture, as well in view of other facts, where the people of this mixed race are to go, for their ancestors are white and black, and it will be difficult to find their native land anywhere outside of the United States.

But the worse thing, perhaps, about this colonization nonsense is, that it tends to throw over the negro a mantle of despair. It leads him to doubt the possibility of his progress as an American citizen. It also encourages popular prejudice with the hope that by persecution or persuasion the negro can finally be driven from his natural home, while in the nature of the case, he must stay here, and will stay here and cannot well get away.

It tends to weaken his hold on one country while it can give him no rational hope of another. Its tendency is to make him dispondent and doubtful, where he should be made to feel assured and confident. It forces upon him the idea that he is forever doomed to be a stranger and sojourner in the land of his birth, and that he has no permanent abiding place here.

All this is hurtful, with such ideas constantly flaunted before him he cannot easily set himself to work to better his condition in such ways as are open to him here. It sets him to groping everlastingly after the impossible.

Every man who thinks at all must know that home is the fountain head, the inspiration, the foundation and main support not only of all social virtue, but of all motives to human progress and that no people can prosper or amount to much without a home. To have a home, the negro must have a country, and he is an enemy to the moral progress of the negro, whether he knows it or not, who calls upon him to break up his home in this country for an uncertain home in Africa.

But the agitation of this subject has a darker side still. It has already been given out that we may be forced to go at the point of the bayonet. I cannot say we shall not, but badly as I think of the tendency of our times, I do not think that American sentiment will ever reach a condition which will make the expulsion of the negro from the United States by such means possible.

Colonization is no solution of the race problem. It is an evasion. It is not repenting of wrong but putting out of sight the people upon whom wrong has been inflicted. Its reiteration and agitation only serve to fan the flame of popular prejudice and encourage the hope that in some way or other, in time or in eternity, those who hate the negro will get rid of him.

If the American people could endure the negro's presence while a slave, they certainly can and ought to endure his presence as a free-man. If they could tolerate him when he was a heathen, they might bear with him when he is a Christian, a gentleman and a scholar.

But woe to the South when it no longer has the strong arm of the negro to till its soil! And woe to the nation if it shall ever employ the sword to drive the negro from his native land!

Such a crime against justice, such a crime against gratitude, should it ever be attempted, would certainly bring a national punishment which would cause the earth to shudder. It would bring a stain upon the nation's honor, like the blood on Lady Macbeth's hand.[50] The waters of all the oceans would not suffice to wash out the infamy that such an act of ingratitude and cruelty would leave on the character of the American people.

Another mode of impeaching the wisdom of emancipation, and one that seems to give pleasure to our enemies, is, as they say, that the condition of the colored people of the South has been made worse; that freedom has made their condition worse.

The champions of this idea are the men who glory in the good old times when the slaves were under the lash and were bought and sold in the market with horses, sheep and swine. It is another way of saying that slavery is better than freedom; that darkness is better than light and that wrong is better than right. It is the American method of reasoning in all matters concerning the negro. It inverts everything; turns truth upside down and puts the case of the unfortunate negro wrong end foremost every time. There is, however, always some truth on their side.

When these false reasoners assert that the condition of the emancipated is wretched and deplorable, they tell in part the truth, and I agree with them. I even concur with them that the negro is in some respects, and in some localities, in a worse condition to-day than in the time of slavery, but I part with these gentlemen when they ascribe this condition to emancipation.

50. An allusion to the famous sleepwalking scene in *Macbeth*, sc. 21.

To my mind, the blame for this condition does not rest upon emancipation, but upon slavery. It is not the result of emancipation, but the defeat of emancipation. It is not the work of the spirit of liberty, but the work of the spirit of bondage, and of the determination of slavery to perpetuate itself, if not under one form, then under another. It is due to the folly of endeavoring to retain the new wine of liberty in the old bottles of slavery.[51] I concede the evil but deny the alleged cause.

The land owners of the South want the labor of the negro on the hardest possible terms. They once had it for nothing. They now want it for next to nothing and they have contrived three ways of thus obtaining it. The first is to rent their land to the negro at an exorbitant price per annum, and compel him to mortgage his crop in advance. The laws under which this is done are entirely in the interest of the landlord. He has a first claim upon everything produced on the land. The negro can have nothing, can keep nothing, can sell nothing, without the consent of the landlord. As the negro is at the start poor and empty handed, he has to draw on the landlord for meat and bread to feed himself and family while his crop is growing. The landlord keeps books; and the negro does not; hence, no matter how hard he may work or how saving he may be, he is, in most cases, brought in debt at the end of the year, and once in debt, he is fastened to the land as by hooks of steel. If he attempts to leave he may be arrested under the law.

Another way, which is still more effective, is the payment of the labor with orders on stores instead of in lawful money. By this means money is kept entirely out of the hands of the negro. He cannot save money because he has no money to save. He cannot seek a better market for his labor because he has no money with which to pay his fare and because he is, by that vicious order system, already in debt, and therefore already in bondage. Thus he is riveted to one place and is, in some sense, a slave; for a man to whom it can be

51. Matt. 9:17; Mark 2:22; Luke 5:37.

said, "You shall work for me for what I shall choose to pay you and how I shall choose to pay you," is in fact a slave though he may be called a free man.

We denounce the landlord and tenant system of England, but it can be said of England as cannot be said of our free country, that by law no laborer can be paid for labor in any other than lawful money. England holds any other payment to be a penal offense and punishment by fine and imprisonments. The same should be in the case in every State in the Union.

Under the mortgage system,[52] no matter how industrious or economical the negro may be, he finds himself at the end of the year in debt to the landlord, and from year to year he toils on and is tempted to try again and again, seldom with any better result.

With this power over the negro, this possession of his labor, you may easily see why the South sometimes brags that it does not want slavery back. It had the negro's labor heretofore for nothing, and now it has it for next to nothing, and at the same time is freed from the obligation to take care of the young and the aged, the sick and the decrepit.

I now come to the so-called, but mis-called "Negro Problem," as a characterization of the relations existing in the Southern States.

I say at once, I do not like or admit the justice or propriety of this formula. Words are things.[53] They certainly are such in this case, and I may say they are a very bad thing in this case, since they give us a misnomer and one that is misleading. It is a formula of Southern origin, and has a strong bias against the negro. It handicaps his cause with all the prejudice known to exist against him. It has been accepted by the good people of the North, as I think, without

52. Under the mortgage system, also known as the crop-lien system, tenant farmers were able to borrow from local merchants to obtain needed food and supplies. The merchant held a lien on the tenant's crop that had to be repaid at the time of its harvest and sale.

53. A line from Lord Byron, *Don Juan*, canto III, stanza 88. Coleridge, *Works of Byron*, 6:172.

investigation. It is a crafty invention and is in every way, worthy of its inventors.

The natural effect and purpose on its face of this formula is to divert attention from the true issue now before the American people. It does this by holding up and preoccupying the public mind with an issue entirely different from the real one in question. That which really is a great national problem and which ought to be so considered, dwarfs into a "negro problem."

The device is not new. It is an old trick. It has been oft repeated, and with a similar purpose and effect. For truth, it gives us falsehood. For innocence, it gives us guilt. It removes the burden of proof from the old master class, and imposes it upon the negro. It puts upon a race a work which belongs to the nation. It belongs to that craftiness often displayed by disputants, who aim to make the worse appear the better reason. It gives bad names to good things, and good names to bad things.

The negro has often been the victim of this kind of low cunning. You may remember that during the late war, when the South fought for the perpetuity of slavery, it called the slaves "domestic servants," and slavery "a domestic institution." Harmless names, indeed, but the things they stood for were far from harmless.

The South has always known how to have a dog hanged by giving him a bad name. When it prefixed "negro" to the national problem, it knew that the device would awaken and increase a deep-seated prejudice at once, and that it would repel fair and candid investigation. As it stands, it implies that the negro is the cause of whatever trouble there is in the South. In old slave times, when a little white child lost his temper, he was given a little whip and told to go and whip "Jim" or "Sal" and thus regained his temper. The same is true, to-day on a larger scale.

I repeat, and my contention is, that this negro problem formula lays the fault at the door of the negro, and removes it from the door of the white man, shields the guilty, and blames the innocent. Makes the negro responsible and not the nation.

Now the real problem is, and ought to be regarded by the American people, a great national problem. It involves the question, whether, after all, with our Declaration of Independence, with our glorious free constitution, whether with our sublime Christianity, there is enough of national virtue in this great nation to solve this problem, in accordance with wisdom and justice.

The marvel is that this old trick of misnaming things, so often played by Southern politicians, should have worked so well for the bad cause in which it is now employed—for the Northern people have fallen in with it. It is still more surprising that the colored press of the country, and some of the colored orators of the country, insist upon calling it a "negro problem," or a Race problem, for by it they mean the negro Race. Now—there is nothing the matter with the negro. He is all right. Learned or ignorant, he is all right. He is neither a Lyncher, a Mobocrat, or an Anarchist. He is now, what he has ever been, a loyal, law-abiding, hard working, and peaceable man; so much so, that men have thought him cowardly and spiritless. They say that any other people would have found some violent way in which to resent their wrongs. If this problem depended upon *his* character and conduct, there would be no problem to solve; there would be no menace to the peace and good order of Southern society. He makes no unlawful fight between labor and capital. That problem which often makes the American people thoughtful, is not of his bringing—though he may some day be compelled to talk, and on this tremendous problem.

He has as little to do with the cause of Southern trouble as he has with its cure. There is no reason, therefore, in the world, why he should give a name to this problem, and this lie, like all other lies, must eventually come to naught. A lie is worth nothing when it has lost its ability to deceive, and if it is at all in my power, this lie shall lose its power to deceive.

I well remember that this same old falsehood was employed and used against the negro, during the late war. He was then charged and stigmatized with being the cause of the war, on the principle that there would be no highway robbers if there were nobody on the road to be robbed. But as absurd as this pretense was, the color prejudice of the country was stimulated by it and joined in the accusation, and the negro has to bear the brunt of it.

Even at the North, he was hated and hunted on account of it. In the great city of New York, his houses were burned, his children were hunted down like wild beasts, and his people were murdered in the streets,[54] because "they were the cause of the war." Even the noble and good Mr. Lincoln, one of the best men that ever lived, told a committee of negroes who waited upon him at Washington, that "they were the cause of the war."[55] Many were the men who accepted this theory, and wished the negro in Africa, or in a hotter climate, as some do now.

There is nothing to which prejudice is not equal in the way of perverting the truth and inflaming the passions of men.

But call this problem what you may, or will, the all important question is: How can it be solved? How can the peace and tranquility of the South, and of the country, be secured and established?

There is nothing occult or mysterious about the answer to this question. Some things are to be kept in mind when dealing with this subject and never be forgotten. It should be remembered that in the order of Divine Providence the man who puts one end of the chain around the ankle of his fellow man will find the other end around his own neck. And it is the same with a nation. Confirmation of this truth is as strong as thunder. "As we sow, we shall reap,"[56] is a lesson to be learned here as elsewhere. We tolerated slavery, and it cost us a million graves, and it may be that lawless murder, if permitted to go on, may yet bring vengeance, not only on the reverend head of age and upon the heads of helpless women, but upon the innocent babe in the cradle.

54. Douglass refers to the race riot of 13–16 July 1863 in New York City, which accompanied the beginning of military conscription.
55. This incident occurred, as Douglass describes it, on 14 August 1862.
56. Gal. 6:7.

But how can this problem be solved? I will tell you how it can *not* be solved. It cannot be solved by keeping the negro poor, degraded, ignorant, and half-starved, as I have shown is now being done in the Southern States.

It cannot be solved by keeping the wages of the laborer back by fraud, as is now being done by the landlords of the South.

It cannot be done by ballot-box stuffing, by falsifying election returns, or by confusing the negro voter by cunning devices.

It cannot be done by repealing all federal laws enacted to secure honest elections.

It can, however, be done, and very easily done, for where there's a will, there's a way![57]

Let the white people of the North and South conquer their prejudices.

Let the great Northern press and pulpit proclaim the gospel of truth and justice against war now being made upon the negro.

Let the American people cultivate kindness and humanity.

Let the South abandon the system of "mortgage" labor, and cease to make the negro a pauper, by paying him scrip for his labor.

Let them give up the idea that they can be free, while making the negro a slave. Let them give up the idea that to degrade the colored man, is to elevate the white man.

Let them cease putting new wine into old bottles, and mending old garments with new cloth.[58]

They are not required to do much. They are only required to undo the evil that they have done, in order to solve this problem.

In old times when it was asked, "How can we abolish slavery?" the answer was "Quit stealing."

The same is the solution of the Race problem to-day. The whole thing can be done by simply no longer violating the amendments of the Constitution of the United States, and no longer evading the

57. An old English proverb that appeared in literature in Michael Scott, *The Cruise of the Midge,* 2 vols. (Edinburgh: W. Blackwood, 1836), chap. 1.

58. Matt. 9:16–17; Mark 2:21–22; Luke 5:36–37.

claims of justice. If this were done, there would be no negro problem to vex the South, or to vex the nation.

Let the organic law of the land be honestly sustained and obeyed.

Let the political parties cease to palter in a double sense and live up to the noble declarations we find in their platforms.

Let the statesmen of the country live up to their convictions.

In the language of Senator Ingalls: "Let the nation try justice and the problem will be solved."[59]

Two hundred and twenty years ago, the negro was made the subject of a religious problem, one which gave our white forefathers much perplexity and annoyance. At that time the problem was in respect of what relation a negro would sustain to the Christian Church, whether he was a fit subject for baptism, and Dr. Godwin, a celebrated divine of his time, and one far in advance of his brethren, was at the pains of writing a book of two hundred pages, or more, containing an elaborate argument to prove that it was not a sin in the sight of God to baptize a negro.[60]

His argument was very able, very learned, very long. Plain as the truth may now seem, there were at that time very strong arguments against the position of the learned divine.

As usual, it was not merely the baptism of the negro that gave trouble, but it was what might follow his baptism. The sprinkling him with water was a very simple thing, but the slave holders of that day saw in the innovation something more dangerous than water. They said that to baptize the negro and make him a member of the Church of Christ, was to make him an important person—in fact, to make him an heir of God and a joint heir of Jesus Christ. It was to give him a place at the Lord's supper. It was to take him out the category of heathenism, and make it inconsistent to hold him as a slave; for the Bible made only the heathen a proper subject for slavery.

59. A paraphrase of the conclusion to John J. Ingalls's speech "Fiat Justitia," delivered in the U.S. Senate on 23 January 1890. *Congressional Record*, 51st Cong., 1st sess., 807.

60. Douglass refers to Godwyn's *The Negro's and Indian's Advocate*.

These were formidable consequences, certainly, and it is not strange that the Christian slave holders of that day viewed these consequences with immeasurable horror. It was something more terrible and dangerous than the fourteenth and fifteenth amendments to our Constitution. It was a difficult thing, therefore, at that day to get the negro in the water.

Nevertheless, our learned Doctor of Divinity, like many of the same class in our day, was quite equal to the emergency. He was able to satisfy all the important parties to the problem, except the negro, and him it did not seem necessary to satisfy.

The Doctor was [a] skilled dialectician. He did not only divide the word with skill, but he could divide the negro in two parts. He argued that the negro had a soul as well as a body, and insisted that while his body rightfully belonged to his master on earth, his soul belonged to his Master in heaven. By this convenient arrangement, somewhat metaphysical, to be sure, but entirely evangelical and logical, the problem of negro baptism was solved.

But with the negro in the case, as I have said, the argument was not entirely satisfactory. The operation was much like that by which the white man got the turkey and the Indian got the crow. When the negro looked around for his body, that belonged to his earthly master. When he looked around for his soul, that had been appropriated by his Heavenly Master. And when he looked around for something that really belonged to himself, he found nothing but his shadow, and that vanished in the shade.

One thing, however, is to be noticed with satisfaction, it is this: Something was gained to the cause of righteousness by this argument. It was a contribution to the cause of liberty. It was largely in favor of the negro. It was recognition of his manhood, and was calculated to set men to thinking that the negro might have some other important rights, no less than the religious right to baptism.

Thus with all its faults, we are compelled to give the pulpit the credit of furnishing the first important argument in favor of the religious character and manhood rights of the negro. Dr. Godwin was undoubtedly a good man. He wrote at a time of much moral darkness, and property in man was nearly everywhere recognized as a rightful institution. He saw only a part of the truth. He saw that the negro had a right to be baptized, but he could not all at once see that he had a paramount right to himself.

But this was not the only problem slavery had in store for the negro. Time and events brought another and it was this very important one:

Can the negro sustain the legal relation of a husband to a wife? Can he make a valid marriage contract in this Christian country.

This problem was solved by the same slave holding authority, entirely against the negro. Such a contract, it was argued, could only be binding upon men providentially enjoying the right to life, liberty, and the pursuit of happiness, and, since the negro is a slave, and slavery a divine institution, legal marriage was wholly inconsistent with the institution of slavery.

When some of us at the North questioned the ethics of this conclusion, we were told to mind our business, and our Southern brethren asserted, as they assert now, that they alone are competent to manage this, and all other questions relating to the negro.

In fact, there has been no end to the problems of some sort or other, involving the negro in difficulty.

Can the negro be a citizen? was the question of the Dred Scott decision.

Can the negro be educated? Can the negro be induced to work for himself, without a master? Can the negro be a soldier? Time and events have answered these and all other like questions. We have amongst us, those who have taken the first prizes as scholars; those who have won distinction for courage and skill on the battlefield; those who have taken rank as lawyers, doctors and ministers of the gospel; those who shine among men in every useful calling; and yet we are called "a problem;" "a tremendous problem;" a mountain of difficulty; a constant source of apprehension; a disturbing force, threatening destruction to the holiest and best interests of society. I declare this statement concerning the negro, whether by Miss Willard, Bishop Haygood, Bishop Fitzgerald, Ex-Governor Chamberlain or by any and all others as false and deeply injurious to the colored citizen of the United States.

But, my friends, I must stop. Time and strength are not equal to the task before me. But could I be heard by this great nation, I would call to mind the sublime and glorious truths with which, at its birth, it saluted a listening world. Its voice then, was as the trumpet of an archangel, summoning hoary forms of oppression and time honored tyranny, to judgment. Crowned heads heard it and shrieked. Toiling millions heard it and clapped their hands for joy. It announced the advent of a nation, based upon human brotherhood and the self-evident truths of liberty and equality. Its mission was the redemption of the world from the bondage of ages. Apply these sublime and glorious truths to the situation now before you. Put away your race prejudice. Banish the idea that one class must rule over another. Recognize the fact that the rights of the humblest citizen are as worthy of protection as are those of the highest, and your problem will be solved; and, whatever may be in store for it in the future, whether prosperity, or adversity; whether it shall have foes without, or foes within, whether there shall be peace, or war; based upon the eternal principles of truth, justice and humanity, and with no class having any cause of complaint or grievance, your Republic will stand and flourish forever.

PART 2

Known Influences on Frederick Douglass's Oratory

DESPITE A COMPLETE LACK of formal education, Frederick Douglass had, by his twenties, become an erudite and persuasive public speaker. In his autobiographies and elsewhere, he credits numerous sources for informing his oratorical style, including books he read and other speakers he heard. The following four excerpts from addresses by other men are among the works known to be highly regarded by Douglass and influential on his development as a public speaker.

From *The Columbian Orator* (1817)

In his three autobiographies, Frederick Douglass acknowledges that
no book had a more profound influence on him than Caleb Bingham's *The Columbian Orator,* an anthology first published in 1797
and reprinted in numerous editions thereafter. It contained guide-
lines on effective oratory and a selection of texts for reading and oral
recitation. In *My Bondage and My Freedom* (1855), Douglass recalled diligently studying the book at "every opportunity afforded
me," and indicated that his favorite piece was "Dialogue Between a
Master and a Slave," by John Aikin, reproduced below. In a study of
Douglass's early speaking career, excerpted in part 5, historian Gregory P. Lampe observes that "Bingham's book offered him a heroic
perspective of oratory and a model for his own life" and shaped both
the content and delivery of his early public addresses.

Dialogue Between a Master and a Slave.

[John Aikin]

MASTER. NOW, villain! what have you to say for this second
attempt to run away? Is there any punishment that you do
not deserve?

SLAVE. I well know that nothing I can say will avail. I submit
to my fate.

MAST. But are you not a base fellow, a hardened and ungrate-
ful rascal?

SLAVE. I am a slave. That is answer enough.

MAST. I am not content with that answer. I thought I discerned in you some tokens of a mind superiour to your condition. I treated you accordingly. You have been comfortably fed and lodged, not overworked, and attended with the most humane care when you were sick. And is this the return?

SLAVE. Since you condescend to talk with me, as a man to man, I will reply. What have you done, what can you do for me, that will compensate for the liberty which you have taken away?

MAST. I did not take it away. You were a slave when I fairly purchased you.

SLAVE. Did I give my consent to the purchase?

MAST. You had no consent to give. You had already lost the right of disposing of yourself.

SLAVE. I had lost the power, but how the right? I was treacherously kidnapped in my own country, when following an honest occupation. I was put in chains, sold to one of your countrymen, carried by force on board his ship, brought hither, and exposed to sale like a beast in the market, where you bought me. What step in all this progress of violence and injustice can give a *right?* Was it in the villain who stole me, in the slave-merchant who tempted him to do so, or in you who encouraged the slave-merchant to bring his cargo of human cattle to cultivate your lands?

MAST. It is in the order of Providence that one man should become subservient to another. It ever has been so, and ever will be. I found the custom, and did not make it.

SLAVE. You cannot but be sensible, that the robber who puts a pistol to your breast may make just the same plea. Providence gives him a power over your life and property; it gave my enemies a power over my liberty. But it has also given me legs to escape with; and what should prevent me from using them? Nay, what should restrain me from retaliating the wrongs I have suffered, if a favourable occasion should offer?

MAST. Gratitude! I repeat, gratitude! Have I not endeavoured ever since I possessed you to alleviate your misfortunes by kind treatment; and does that confer no obligation? Consider how much worse your condition might have been under another master.

SLAVE YOU HAVE DONE NOTHING FOR ME MORE THAN FOR YOUR WORKING CATTLE. Are they not well fed and tended? do you work them harder than your slaves? is not the rule of treating both designed only for your own advantage? You treat both your men and beast slaves better than some of your neighbours, because you are more prudent and wealthy than they.

MAST. You might add, more humane too.

SLAVE HUMANE! Does it deserve that appellation to keep your fellow-men in forced subjection, deprived of all exercise of their free will, liable to all the injuries that your own caprice, or the brutality of your overseers, may heap on them, and devoted, soul and body, only to your pleasure and emolument? Can gratitude take place between creatures in such a state, and the tyrant who holds them in it? Look at these limbs; are they not those of a man? Think that I have the spirit of a man too.

MAST. But it was my intention not only to make your life tolerably comfortable at present, but to provide for you in your old age.

SLAVE ALAS! is a life like mine, torn from country, friends, and all I held dear, and compelled to toil under the burning sun for a master, worth thinking about for old age? No; the sooner it ends, the sooner I shall obtain that relief for which my soul pants.

MAST. Is it impossible, then, to hold you by any ties but those of constraint and severity?

SLAVE. It is impossible to make one, who has felt the value of freedom, acquiesce in being a slave.

MAST. Suppose I were to restore you to your liberty, would you reckon that a favour?

SLAVE. The greatest; for although it would only be undoing a wrong, I know too well how few among mankind are capable of sacrificing interest to justice, not to prize the exertion when it is made.

MAST. I do it, then; be free.

SLAVE. Now I am indeed your servant, though not your slave. And as the first return I can make for your kindness, I will tell you freely the condition in which you live. You are surrounded with implacable foes, who long for a safe opportunity to revenge upon you and the other planters all the miseries they have endured. The more generous their natures, the more indignant they feel against that cruel injustice which has dragged them hither, and doomed them to perpetual servitude. You can rely on no kindness on your part, to soften the obduracy of their resentment. You have reduced them to the state of brute beasts; and if they have not the stupidity of beasts of burden, they must have the ferocity of beasts of prey. Superior force alone can give you security. As soon as that fails, you are at the mercy of the merciless. Such is the social bond between master and slave!

From "An Address to the Slaves of the United States of America" (1843)

In August 1843, both Frederick Douglass and the African American Presbyterian minister Henry Highland Garnet attended the National Convention of Colored Citizens held at Buffalo, New York. Douglass heard Garnet deliver a stirring evocation of the violent resistance committed by the slave rebels Nat Turner and Madison Washington as acts of patriotism in keeping with the principles of the nation's founding fathers. While Douglass at that time still upheld the pacifist position of his Garrisonian abolitionist mentors, he eventually accepted Garnet's views and actively supported John Brown's attack on Harpers Ferry in 1859. The text below contains the closing paragraphs of Garnet's speech reprinted by Brown himself in the pamphlet, *Walker's Appeal, with a Brief Sketch of His Life. By Henry Highland Garnet. And also Garnet's Address to the Slaves of the United States of America* (New York: J. H. Tobbit, 1848).

Fellow-men! patient sufferers! behold your dearest rights crushed to the earth! See your sons murdered, and your wives, mothers, and sisters, doomed to prostitution! In the name of the merciful God! and by all that life is worth, let it no longer be a debatable question, whether it is better to choose LIBERTY or DEATH!

In 1822, Denmark Veazie, of South Carolina, formed a plan for the liberation of his fellow men. In the whole history of human efforts to overthrow slavery, a more complicated and tremendous plan was never formed. He was betrayed by the treachery of his own people, and died a martyr to freedom. Many a brave hero fell, but History, faithful to her high trust, will transcribe his name on the same monument with Moses, Hampden, Tell, Bruce, and Wallace, Touissaint L'Overteur, Lafayette and Washington. That tremendous movement shook the whole empire of slavery. The guilty soul thieves were overwhelmed with fear. It is a matter of fact, that at that time, and in consequence of the threatened revolution, the slave states talked strongly of emancipation. But they blew but one blast of the trumpet of freedom, and then laid it aside. As these men became quiet, the slaveholders ceased to talk about emancipation: and now, behold your condition to-day! Angels sigh over it, and humanity has long since exhausted her tears in weeping on your account!

The patriotic Nathaniel Turner followed Denmark Veazie. He was goaded to desperation by wrong and injustice. By Despotism, his name has been recorded on the list of infamy, but future generations will number him among the noble and brave.

Next arose the immortal Joseph Cinque, the hero of the Amistad. He was a native African, and by the help of God he emancipated a whole ship-load of his fellow men on the high seas. And he now sings of liberty on the sunny hills of Africa, and beneath his native palm trees, where he hears the lion roar, and feels himself as free as that king of the forest. Next arose Madison Washington, that bright star of freedom, and took his station in the constellation of freedom. He was a slave on board the brig Creole, of Richmond, bound to New Orleans, that great slave mart, with a hundred and four others. Nineteen struck for liberty or death. But one life was taken, and the whole were emancipated, and the vessel was carried into Nassau, New Providence. Noble men! Those who have fallen in freedom's conflict, their memories will be cherished by the true hearted, and the God-fearing, in all future generations; those who are living, their names are surrounded by a halo of glory.

We do not advise you to attempt a revolution with the sword, because it would be INEXPEDIENT. Your numbers are too small, and moreover the rising spirit of the age, and the spirit of the gospel, are opposed to war and bloodshed. But from this moment cease to labor for tyrants who will not remunerate you. Let every slave throughout the land do this, and the days of slavery are numbered. You cannot be more oppressed than you have been—you cannot suffer greater cruelties than you have already. Rather DIE FREE-MEN, THAN LIVE TO BE SLAVES. Remember that you are THREE MILLIONS.

It is in your power so to torment the God-cursed slaveholders, that they will be glad to let you go free. If the scale was turned, and black men were the masters, and white men the slaves, every destructive agent and element would be employed to lay the oppressor low. Danger and death would hang over their heads day and night. Yes, the tyrants would meet with plagues more terrible than those of Pharaoh. But you are a patient people. You act as though you were made for the special use of these devils. You act as though your daughters were born to pamper the lusts of your masters and overseers. And worse than all, you tamely submit, while your lords tear your wives from your embraces, and defile them before your eyes. In the name of God we ask, are you men? Where is the blood of your fathers? Has it all run out of your veins? Awake, awake; millions of voices are calling you! Your dead fathers speak to you from their graves. Heaven, as with a voice of thunder, calls on you to arise from the dust.

Let your motto be RESISTANCE! RESISTANCE! RESISTANCE!—No oppressed people have ever secured their liberty without resistance. What kind of resistance you had better make, you must decide by the circumstances that surround you, and according to the suggestion of expediency. Brethren, adieu. Trust in the living God. Labor for the peace of the human race, and remember that you are three millions.

SAMUEL RINGGOLD WARD

"Speech Denouncing Daniel Webster's Endorsement of the Fugitive Slave Law" (1850)

Perhaps the contemporary black abolitionist whom Douglass admired most as an orator was the Reverend Samuel Ringgold Ward (1817–66), a fellow runaway slave from Maryland's Eastern Shore. In *Life and Times of Frederick Douglass* (1881; 1892), he recalls attending the 1848 Free Soil party national convention in Buffalo, New York, in the company of several other African Americans. Douglass praised Ward's speaking there: "As an orator and thinker he was vastly superior, I thought, to any of us, and being perfectly black and of unmixed African descent, the splendors of his intellect went directly to the glory of his race." Douglass's public debate with Ward over the U.S. Constitution and slavery helped persuade him to abandon his original Garrisonian ideology and join Ward as a political abolitionist. The text of that debate is not available. The following is a report in Garrison's *Liberator* of Ward's speech in Boston's iconic Faneuil Hall condemning Daniel Webster, Daniel Dickinson, and other Northern politicians who supported the passage of the Fugitive Slave Law. Ward's abundant oratorical skills were captured in Garrison's reporting, which Douglass undoubtedly would have read.

I am here tonight simply as a guest. You have met here to speak of the sentiments of a Senator of your State whose remarks you have the honor to repudiate. In the course of the remarks of the gentleman who preceded me, he has done us the favor to make honorable mention of a Senator of my own State—Wm. H. Seward. (Three hearty cheers were given for Senator Seward.)

I thank you for this manifestation of approbation of a man who has always stood head and shoulders above his party, and who has never receded from his position on the question of slavery. It was my happiness to receive a letter from him a few days since, in which he said he never would swerve from his position as the friend of freedom. (Applause.) To be sure, I agree not with Senator Seward in politics, but when an individual stands up for the rights of men against the slaveholders, I care not for party distinctions. He is my brother. (Loud cheers.)

We have here much of common cause and interest in this matter. That infamous bill of Mr. Mason, of Virginia, proves itself to be like all other propositions presented by Southern men. It finds just enough of Northern dough-faces who are willing to pledge themselves, if you will pardon the uncouth language of a backwoodsman, to lick up the spittle of the slavocrats, and swear it is delicious. (Applause.)

You of the old Bay State—a State to which many of us are accustomed to look as to our father land, just as we all look back to England as our mother country—you have a Daniel who has deserted the cause of freedom. We, too, in New York, have a "Daniel who has come to judgment," only he doesn't come quite fast enough to the right kind of judgment. (Tremendous enthusiasm.) Daniel S. Dickinson represents someone, I suppose, in the State of New York; God knows, he doesn't represent me. I can pledge you, that our Daniel will stand cheek by jowl with your Daniel. (Cheers.) He was never known to surrender slavery, but always to surrender liberty.

The bill of which you most justly complain, concerning the surrender of fugitive slaves, is to apply alike to your State and to our State, if it shall ever apply at all. But we have come here to make a common oath upon a common altar, that that bill shall never take effect. (Applause.) Honorable Senators may record their names in

its behalf, and it may have the sanction of the House of Representatives; but we the people, who are superior to both Houses and
the Executive too (hear, hear), we the people will never be human
bipeds, to howl upon the track of the fugitive slave, even though led
by the corrupt Daniel of your State, or the degraded one of ours.
(Cheers.)

Though there are many attempts to get up compromises—and
there is no term which I detest more than this, it is always the term
which makes right yield to wrong; it has always been accursed since
Eve made the first *compromise* with the devil. (Repeated rounds
of applause.) I was saying, sir, that it is somewhat singular, and yet
historically true, that whensoever these compromises are proposed,
there are men of the North who seem to foresee that Northern
men, who think their constituency will not look into these matters,
will seek to do more than the South demands. They seek to prove
to Northern men that all is right and all is fair; and this is the game
Webster is attempting to play.

"O," says Webster, "the will of God has fixed that matter; we will
not re-enact the will of God." Sir, you remember the time in 1841,
'42, '43 and '44, when it was said that Texas could never be annexed.
The design of such dealing was that you should believe it, and then,
when you thought yourselves secure, they would spring the trap
upon you. And now it is their wish to seduce you into the belief that
slavery never will go there, and then the slaveholders will drive slavery there as fast as possible. I think that this is the most contemptible
proposition of the whole, except the support of that bill which would
attempt to make the whole North the slavecatchers of the South.

You will remember that the bill of Mr. Mason says nothing about
color. Mr. Phillips, a man whom I always loved (applause), a man
who taught me my hornbook on this subject of slavery, when I was a
poor boy, has referred to Marshfield. There is a man who sometimes
lives in Marshfield, and who has the reputation of having an honorable dark skin. Who knows but that some postmaster may have to
sit upon the very gentleman whose character you have been discuss-

ing tonight? (Hear, hear.) "What is sauce for the goose, is sauce for
the gander." (Laughter.) If this bill is to relieve grievances, why not
make an application to the immortal Daniel of Marshfield? (Applause.) There is no such thing as complexion mentioned. It is not
only true that the colored men of Massachusetts—it is not only true
that the fifty thousand colored men of New York may be taken—
though I pledge you there is one, whose name is Sam Ward, who
will never be taken alive (tremendous applause)—not only is it true
that the fifty thousand black men in New York may be taken, but
anyone else also can be captured. My friend Theodore Parker alluded to Ellen Craft. I had the pleasure of taking tea with her, and
accompanied her here tonight. She is far whiter than many who
come here slave-catching. This line of distinction is so nice that you
cannot tell who is white or black. As Alexander Pope used to say,
"White and black soften and blend in so many thousand ways, that
it is neither white nor black." (Loud plaudits.)

This is the question, Whether a man has a right to himself and his
children, his hopes and his happiness, for this world and the world
to come. That is a question which, according to this bill, may be
decided by any backwoods postmaster in this State or any other. O,
this is a monstrous proposition; and I do thank God, that if the Slave
Power have such demands to make on us, that the proposition has
come now—now, that the people know what is being done—now
that the public mind is turned toward this subject—now that they
are trying to find what is the truth on this subject.

Sir, what must be the moral influence of this speech of Mr. Webster on the minds of young men, lawyers and others, here in the
North? They turn their eyes towards Daniel Webster as towards a
superior mind, and a legal and constitutional oracle. If they shall
catch the spirit of this speech, its influence upon them and upon
following generation will be so deeply corrupting, that it never can
be wiped out or purged.

I am thankful that this, my first entrance into Boston, and my first
introduction to Faneuil Hall, gives me the pleasure and privilege

of uniting with you, in uttering my humble voice against the two
Daniels, and of declaring, in behalf of our people, that if the fugitive slave is traced to our part of New York State, he shall have
the law of Almighty God to protect him, the law which says, "Thou
shalt not return to the master the servant that is escaped unto thee,
but he shall dwell with thee in thy gates, where it liketh him best."
And if our postmasters cannot maintain their constitutional oaths,
and cannot *live* without playing the pander to the slave-hunter, they
need not *live at all*. Such crises as these leave us to the right of
Revolution, and if need be, that right we will, at whatever cost, most
sacredly maintain. (Mr. Ward sat down amidst rapturous applause.)

Liberator (Boston, Mass.), 5 April 1850.

From "Toussaint L'Ouverture" (1863)

Perhaps the only other abolitionist to achieve as high a reputation for oratorical skills as Frederick Douglass was the patrician Boston lawyer Wendell Phillips (1811–84). A loyal follower of William Lloyd Garrison, Phillips succeeded him as president of the American Anti-Slavery Society at the end of the Civil War. While Douglass and Phillips had bitterly quarreled over abolitionist strategies in the 1850s, they reconciled after emancipation and worked together to promote such causes as black civil rights and woman suffrage. Like Douglass, Phillips reached a broad listening audience through his lyceum lectures. Douglass singled out "Toussaint L'Ouverture" for high praise in his lecture "Self-Made Men." Phillips's characterization and portrayal of the Haitian rebel leader challenged popular white prejudice regarding the intelligence and courage of persons of African descent.

L ADIES AND GENTLEMEN: I have been requested to offer you a sketch made some years since, of one of the most remarkable men of the last generation,—the great St. Domingo chief, Toussaint L'Ouverture, an unmixed negro, with no drop of white blood in his veins. My sketch is at once a biography and an argument,—a biography, of course very brief, of a negro soldier and statesman, which I offer you as an argument in behalf of the race from which he sprung. I am about to compare and weigh races; indeed, I am engaged to-night in what you will think the absurd effort to convince you that the negro race, instead of being that object of pity or contempt which we usually consider it, is entitled, judged by the facts of history, to a place close by the side of the Saxon. [. . .]

Some doubt the courage of the negro. Go to Hayti, and stand on those fifty thousand graves of the best soldiers France ever had, and ask them what they think of the negro's sword. And if that does not satisfy you, go to France, to the splendid mausoleum of the Counts of Rochambeau, and to the eight thousand graves of Frenchmen who skulked home under the English flag, and ask them. And if that does not satisfy you, come home, and if it had been October, 1859, you might have come by way of quaking Virginia, and asked her what she thought of negro courage.

You may also remember this,—that we Saxons were slaves about four hundred years, sold with the land, and our fathers never raised a finger to end that slavery. They waited till Christianity and civilization, till commerce and the discovery of America, melted away their chains. Spartacus in Italy led the slaves of Rome against the Empress of the world. She murdered him, and crucified them. There never was a slave rebellion successful but once, and that was in St. Domingo. Every race has been, some time or other, in chains. But there never was a race that, weakened and degraded by such chattel slavery, unaided, tore off its own fetters, forged them into swords, and won its liberty on the battle-field, but one, and that was the black race of St. Domingo. God grant that the wise vigor of our government may avert that necessity from our land,—may raise into peaceful liberty the four million committed to our care, and show under democratic institutions a statesmanship as far-sighted as that of England, as brave as the negro of Hayti!

So much for the courage of the negro. Now look at his endurance. In 1805 he said to the white men, "This island is ours; not a white foot shall touch it." Side by side with him stood the South American republics, planted by the best blood of the countrymen of Lope de Vega and Cervantes. They topple over so often that you could no more daguerreotype their crumbling fragments than you could the waves of the ocean. And yet, at their side, the negro has kept his island sacredly to himself. It is said that at first, with rare patriotism, the Haytien government ordered the destruction of all the sugar plantations remaining, and discouraged its culture, deeming that the temptation which lured the French back again to attempt their enslavement. Burn over New York to-night, fill up her canals, sink every ship, destroy her railroads, blot out every remnant of education from her sons, let her be ignorant and penniless, with nothing but her hands to begin the world again,—how much could she do in sixty years? And Europe, too, would lend you money, but she will not lend Hayti a dollar. Hayti, from the ruins of her colonial dependence, is become a civilized state, the seventh nation in the catalogue of commerce with this country, inferior in morals and education to none of the West Indian isles. Foreign merchants trust her courts as willingly as they do our own. Thus far, she has foiled the ambition of Spain, the greed of England, and the malicious statesmanship of Calhoun. Toussaint made her what she is. In this work there was grouped around him a score of men, mostly of pure negro blood, who ably seconded his efforts. They were able in war and skillful in civil affairs, but not, like him, remarkable for that rare mingling of high qualities which alone makes true greatness, and insures a man leadership among those otherwise almost his equals. Toussaint was indisputably their chief. Courage, purpose, endurance,—these are the tests. He did plant a state so deep that all the world has not been able to root it up.

I would call him Napoleon, but Napoleon made his way to empire over broken oaths and through a sea of blood. This man never broke his word. "NO RETALIATION" was his great motto and the rule of his life; and the last words uttered to his son in France were these: "My boy, you will one day go back to St. Domingo; forget that France murdered your father." I would call him Cromwell, but Cromwell was only a soldier, and the state he founded went down with him into his grave. I would call him Washington, but the great Virginian held slaves. This man risked his empire rather than permit the slave-trade in the humblest village of his dominions.

You think me a fanatic to-night, for you read history, not with your eyes, but with your prejudices. But fifty years hence, when Truth gets a hearing, the Muse of History will put Phocion for the Greek, and Brutus for the Roman, Hampden for England, Fayette for France, choose Washington as the bright, consummate flower of our earlier civilization, and John Brown the ripe fruit of our noonday [thunders of applause], then, dipping her pen in the sunlight, will write in the clear blue, above them all, the name of the soldier, the statesman, the martyr, TOUSSAINT L'OUVERTURE. [Long-continued applause.]

PART 3

Frederick Douglass on Public Speaking

IN THE FOLLOWING EXCERPTS from autobiographies, editorials, correspondence, and speeches, Frederick Douglass describes the qualities of great oration and reminisces about experiences that helped shape his speaking techniques. Douglass demonstrates his appreciation of effective oratory as an indispensable tool in reform crusades. In the final excerpt in this section, he advises a younger African American, "Your vocation is to speak the word; there is none higher. . . . Truth is the saving power of the world, preach it and you bless yourself, your race and the world."

"Give Us the Facts," from *My Bondage and My Freedom* (1855)

In his second autobiography, *My Bondage and My Freedom* (1855), Frederick Douglass recalls his first years as an itinerant lecturer for the Massachusetts Anti-Slavery Society in the early 1840s. While excited to campaign to change Northern attitudes about slavery, he reported becoming frustrated with his white Garrisonian employers, who evinced doubts that Douglass could elucidate their complex abolitionist ideology. At the same time, ironically, Douglass's eloquence on the lecture platform caused many in the audience to question his authenticity as a runaway slave. Douglass resolved both issues by writing his famous *Narrative of the Life of Frederick Douglass, an American Slave* (1845). The autobiography revealed the details of his slave experience, necessitating a hasty departure from Massachusetts to lecture for almost two years in the British Isles.

Young, ardent, and hopeful, I entered upon this new life in the full gush of unsuspecting enthusiasm. The cause was good; the men engaged in it were good; the means to attain its triumph, good; Heaven's blessing must attend all, and freedom must soon be given to the pining millions under a ruthless bondage. My whole heart went with the holy cause, and my most fervent prayer to the Almighty Disposer of the hearts of men, were continually offered for its early triumph. "Who or what," thought I, "can withstand a cause so good, so holy, so indescribably glorious. The God of Israel is with us. The might of the Eternal is on our side. Now let but the truth be spoken, and a nation will start forth at the sound!" In this enthusiastic spirit, I dropped into the ranks of freedom's friends, and went forth to the battle. For a time I was made to forget that my skin was dark and my hair crisped. For a time I regretted that I could not have shared the hardships and dangers endured by the earlier workers for the slave's release. I soon, however, found that my enthusiasm had been extravagant; that hardships and dangers were not yet passed; and that the life now before me, had shadows as well as sunbeams.

Among the first duties assigned me, on entering the ranks, was to travel, in company with Mr. George Foster, to secure subscribers to the "Anti-slavery Standard" and the "Liberator." With him I traveled and lectured through the eastern counties of Massachusetts. Much interest was awakened—large meetings assembled. Many came, no doubt, from curiosity to hear what a negro could say in his own cause. I was generally introduced as a *"chattel"*—a *"thing"*—a piece of southern *"property"*—the chairman assuring the audience that *it* could speak. Fugitive slaves, at that time, were not so plentiful as now; and as a fugitive slave lecturer, I had the advantage of being a *"brand new fact"*—the first one out. Up to that time, a colored man was deemed a fool who confessed himself a runaway slave, not only because of the danger to which he exposed himself of being retaken, but because it was a confession of a very *low* origin! Some of my colored friends in New Bedford thought very badly of my wisdom for thus exposing and degrading myself. The only precaution I took, at the beginning, to prevent Master Thomas from knowing where I was, and what I was about, was the withholding my former name, my master's name, and the name of the state and county from which I came. During the first three or four months, my speeches were almost exclusively made up of narrations of my own personal experience as a slave. "Let us have the facts," said the people. So also said Friend George Foster, who always wished to pin me down to my simple narrative. "Give us the facts," said [John A.] Collins, "we will take care of the philosophy." Just here arose some embarrassment. It was impossible for me to repeat the same old story month after month, and to keep up my interest in it. It was new to the people, it is true, but it was an old story to me; and to go through with it night after night, was a task altogether too mechanical for my nature. "Tell your story, Frederick," would whisper my then revered friend, William Lloyd Garrison, as I stepped upon the platform. I could not always obey, for I was now reading and thinking. New views of the subject were presented to my mind. It did not entirely satisfy me to *narrate* wrongs; I felt like *denouncing* them. I could not always curb my moral indignation for the perpetrators of slaveholding villainy, long enough for a circumstantial statement of the facts which I felt almost everybody must know. Besides, I was growing, and needed room. "People won't believe you ever was a slave, Frederick, if you keep on this way," said Friend Foster. "Be yourself," said Collins, "and tell your story." It was said to me, "Better have a *little* of the plantation manner of speech than not; 'tis not best that you seem too learned." These excellent friends were actuated by the best of motives, and were not altogether wrong in their advice; and still I must speak just the word that seemed to *me* the word to be spoken *by* me.

At last the apprehended trouble came. People doubted if I had ever been a slave. They said I did not talk like a slave, look like a slave, nor act like a slave, and that they believed I had never been south of Mason and Dixon's line. "He don't tell us where he came from—what his master's name was—how he got away—nor the story of his experience. Besides, he is educated, and is, in this, a contradiction of all the facts we have concerning the ignorance of the slaves." Thus, I was in a pretty fair way to be denounced as an impostor. The committee of the Massachusetts Anti-Slavery Society knew all the facts in my case, and agreed with me in the prudence of keeping them private. They, therefore, never doubted my being a genuine fugitive; but going down the aisles of the churches in which I spoke, and hearing the free spoken Yankees saying, repeatedly, *"He's never been a slave, I'll warrant ye,"* I resolved to dispel all doubt, at no distant day, by such a revelation of facts as could not be made by any other than a genuine fugitive.

"One Hundred Conventions" (1843), from *Life and Times of Frederick Douglass* (1881; 1892)

In his third autobiography, Douglass reminisces about his early years as an itinerant lecturer for the Garrisonian abolitionists. One of the most revealing anecdotes concerns his participation in the "One Hundred Conventions" campaign of 1843, which took him throughout New England, New York, and the Midwest. On this tour, Douglass and his companions often encountered hostility from Northerners opposed to abolitionism. Douglass vividly recalls being in grave personal danger when a mob attacked them during a meeting in Pendleton, Indiana. Douglass fought back, but was beaten to the ground and left for dead. Nursed back to health by local Quakers, Douglass carried the wounds from this assault for the rest of his life.

From Ohio we divided our forces and went into Indiana. At our first meeting we were mobbed, and some of us had our good clothes spoiled by evil-smelling eggs. This was at Richmond, where Henry Clay had been recently invited to the high seat of the Quaker meeting-house just after his gross abuse of Mr. Mendenhall, because of the latter presenting to him a respectful petition, asking him to emancipate his slaves. At Pendleton this mobocratic spirit was even more pronounced. It was found impossible to obtain a building in which to hold our convention, and our friends, Dr. Fussell and others, erected a platform in the woods, where quite a large audience assembled. Mr. Bradburn,

Mr. White and myself were in attendance. As soon as we began to speak a mob of about sixty of the roughest characters I ever looked upon ordered us, through its leaders, to "be silent," threatening us, if we were not, with violence. We attempted to dissuade them, but they had not come to parley but to fight, and were well armed. They tore down the platform on which we stood, assaulted Mr. White and knocked out several of his teeth, dealt a heavy blow on William A. White, striking him on the back part of the head, badly cutting his scalp and felling him to the ground. Undertaking to fight my way through the crowd with a stick which I caught up in the mêlée, I attracted the fury of the mob, which laid me prostrate on the ground under a torrent of blows. Leaving me thus, with my right hand broken, and in a state of unconsciousness, the mobocrats hastily mounted their horses and rode to Andersonville, where most of them resided. I was soon raised up and revived by Neal Hardy, a kind-hearted member of the Society of Friends, and carried by him in his wagon about three miles in the country to his home, where I was tenderly nursed and bandaged by good Mrs. Hardy till I was again on my feet; but, as the bones broken were not properly set, my hand has never recovered its natural strength and dexterity. We lingered long in Indiana, and the good effects of our labors there are felt at this day. I have lately visited Pendleton, now one of the best republican towns in the State, and looked again upon the spot where I was beaten down, and have again taken by the hand some of the witnesses of that scene, amongst whom was the kind, good lady—Mrs. Hardy—who, so like the good Samaritan of old, bound up my wounds, and cared for me so kindly. A complete history of these hundred conventions would fill a volume far larger than the one in which this simple reference is to find a place. It would be a grateful duty to speak of the noble young men who forsook ease and pleasure, as did White, Gay, and Monroe, and endured all manner of privations in the cause of the enslaved and down-trodden of my race. Gay, Monroe, and myself are the only ones of those who now survive who participated as agents in the one hundred conventions. Mr. Monroe was for many years consul to Brazil, and has since been a faithful member of Congress from the Oberlin District, Ohio, and has filled other important positions in his State. Mr. Gay was managing editor of the *National Anti-Slavery Standard,* and afterwards of the New York *Tribune,* and still later of the New York *Evening Post.*

FREDERICK DOUGLASS

"Letter from the Editor" (1849), from the Rochester *North Star*

Frederick Douglass attended many hundreds of abolitionist meetings in the two decades before emancipation. In a letter from Providence, Rhode Island, written to the readers of his weekly *North Star,*
published on 23 November 1849, Douglass reported on the annual
meeting of that state's antislavery society. What makes this letter
noteworthy was Douglass's prefatory observations on the impassioned eloquence of fellow abolitionist speakers, which he traced to
the movement's high moral character. This fervor "glowing with light
and life," Douglass argued, was far better expressed by "the living
human voice" than any form of writing.

Anti-slavery meetings are a sign of anti-slavery life. Discussion—bold, hot, and exciting, is the natural element of the latter. It delights to meet the people face to
face—to look into the eyes and hearts of men. *Speech!
speech!* the live, calm, grave, clear, pointed, warm, sweet, melodious
and powerful human voice, is his chosen instrumentality. The pen
is not to be despised, but who that knows anything of the might and
electricity of speech as it bursts from hearts of fire, glowing with
light and life, will not acknowledge the superiority over the pen for
immediate effect. Astronomy, Zoology, Botany, Conchology, Chem-
istry, and Geology, are fit subjects for the pen, but humanity, justice
and liberty, demand the service of the living human voice, and the
power of exalted eloquence, as their expedient.

Slavery can use the pen at the North with considerable impunity. It can gild its deadly poison with beautiful and attractive colors, and escape with little harm. Ink and paper have no sense of shame— they cannot blush under exposure, nor react under rebuke and indignation. But just let slavery present its brazen front to the great congregation of living, breathing human beings, and its ugly "phiz" [physiognomy] is at once covered with confusion. The pro-slavery clergy, and dough-faced politicians know this, and therefore, seldom venture into our meetings for the purpose of opposing us face to face. They silently, basely lay in wait to catch us in our words, that they may use our mistakes and foibles against us when we are not allowed to reply. They know that slavery is a poor orator when confronted by an abolitionist, and they wisely keep silent. But enough.

FREDERICK DOUGLASS

"A New Vocation before Me" (1870), from *Life and Times*

The American Anti-Slavery Society dissolved itself in 1870 amid great contention. Douglass opposed dissolution and argued that Reconstruction would bring its own set of challenges to the civil rights of blacks. In this excerpt from *Life and Times*, Douglass recounts the progress of his involvement in the abolition movement and his resultant development as a lyceum speaker. He compares the substantive preparation but rhetorical failure of "The Claims of the Negro Ethnologically Considered" (1854) with the extemporaneous success of the oft-requested "Self-Made Men" (1859), both reproduced in this volume. He concludes that becoming known for one meaningful oration is better than having given many easily forgettable speeches.

I felt that I had reached the end of the noblest and best part of my life; my school was broken up, my church disbanded, and the beloved congregation dispersed, never to come together again. The anti-slavery platform had performed its work, and my voice was no longer needed. "Othello's occupation was gone." The great happiness of meeting with my fellow-workers was now to be among the things of memory. Then, too, some thought of my personal future came in. Like Daniel Webster, when asked by his friends to leave John Tyler's cabinet, I naturally inquired: "Where shall I go?" I was still in the midst of my years, and had something of life before me, and as the minister (urged by my old friend George Bradburn to preach anti-slavery, when to do so was unpopular) said,

"It is necessary for ministers to live," I felt it was necessary for me to live, and to live honestly. But where should I go, and what should I do? I could not now take hold of life as I did when I first landed in New Bedford, twenty-five years before; I could not go to the wharf of either Gideon or George Howland, to Richmond's brass foundry, or Richetson's candle and oil works, load and unload vessels, or even ask Governor Clifford for a place as a servant. Rolling oil-casks and shoveling coal were all well enough when I was younger, immediately after getting out of slavery. Doing this was a step up, rather than a step down; but all these avocations had had their day for me, and I had had my day for them. My public life and labors had unfitted me for the pursuits of my earlier years, and yet had not prepared me for more congenial and higher employment. Outside the question of slavery my thought had not been much directed, and I could hardly hope to make myself useful in any other cause than that to which I had given the best twenty-five years of my life. A man in the situation in which I found myself has not only to divest himself of the old, which is never easily done, but to adjust himself to the new, which is still more difficult. Delivering lectures under various names, John B. Gough says, "Whatever may be the title, my lecture is always on Temperance"; and such is apt to be the case with any man who has devoted his time and thought to one subject for any considerable length of time. But what should I do, was the question. I had a few thousand dollars (a great convenience, and one not generally so highly prized by my people as it ought to be) saved from the sale of "My Bondage and My Freedom," and the proceeds of my lectures at home and abroad, and with this sum I thought of following the noble example of my old friends Stephen and Abby Kelley Foster, and purchase a little farm and settle myself down to earn an honest living by tilling the soil. My children were grown and ought to be able to take care of themselves. This question, however, was soon decided for me. I had after all acquired (a very unusual thing) a little more knowledge and aptitude fitting me for the new condition of things than I knew, and had a deeper hold upon public attention than I had supposed. Invitations began to pour in upon me from colleges, lyceums, and literary societies, offering me one hundred, and even two hundred dollars for a single lecture.

I had, some time before, prepared a lecture on "Self-made Men," and also one upon Ethnology, with special reference to Africa. The latter had cost me much labor, though, as I now look back upon it, it was a very defective production. I wrote it at the instance of my friend Doctor M. B. Anderson, President of Rochester University, himself a distinguished ethnologist, a deep thinker and scholar. I had been invited by one of the literary societies of Western Reserve College (then at Hudson, but recently removed to Cleveland, Ohio), to address it on Commencement day; and never having spoken on such an occasion, never, indeed, having been myself inside of a school-house for the purpose of an education, I hesitated about accepting the invitation, and finally called upon Prof. Henry Wayland, son of the great Doctor Wayland of Brown University, and on Doctor Anderson, and asked their advice whether I ought to accept. Both gentlemen advised me to do so. They knew me, and evidently thought well of my ability. But the puzzling question now was, what shall I say if I do go there? It won't do to give them an old-fashioned anti-slavery discourse. (I learned afterwards that such a discourse was precisely what they needed, though not what they wished; for the faculty, including the President, was in great distress because I, a colored man, had been invited, and because of the reproach this circumstance might bring upon the College.) But what shall I talk about? became the difficult question. I finally hit upon the one before mentioned. I had read, with great interest, when in England a few years before, parts of Doctor Pritchard's "Natural History of Man," a large volume marvelously calm and philosophical in its discussion of the science of the origin of the races, and was thus in the line of my then convictions. I at once sought in our bookstores for this valuable book, but could not obtain it anywhere in this country. I sent to England, where I paid the sum of seven and a half dollars for it. In addition to this valuable work President Anderson

kindly gave me a little book entitled "Man and his Migrations," by
Dr. R. G. Latham, and loaned me the large work of Dr. Morton,
the famous archaeologist, and that of Messrs. Nott and Glidden,
the latter written evidently to degrade the Negro and support the
then-prevalent Calhoun doctrine of the rightfulness of slavery. With
these books and occasional suggestions from Dr. Anderson and
Prof. Wayland I set about preparing my commencement address.
For many days and nights I toiled, and succeeded at last in getting
something together in due form. Written orations had not been in
my line. I had usually depended upon my unsystematized knowledge and the inspiration of the hour and the occasion, but I had now
got the "scholar bee in my bonnet," and supposed that inasmuch as I
was to speak to college professors and students I must at least make
a show of some familiarity with letters. It proved, as to its immediate
effect, a great mistake, for my carefully-studied and written address,
full of learned quotations, fell dead at my feet, while a few remarks I
made extemporaneously at collation were enthusiastically received.
Nevertheless, the reading and labor expended were of much value
to me. They were needed steps preparatory to the work upon which
I was about to enter. If they failed at the beginning, they helped to
success in the end. My lecture on "The Races of Men" was seldom
called for, but that on "Self-made Men" was in great demand, especially through the West. I found that the success of a lecturer depends more upon the quality of his stock in store than the amount.
My friend Wendell Phillips (for such I esteem him), who has said
more cheering words to me and in vindication of my race than any
man now living, has delivered his famous lecture on the "Lost Arts"
during the last forty years, and I doubt if among all his lectures, and
he has many, there is one in such requisition as this. When Daniel
O'Connell was asked why he did not make a new speech he play-
fully replied that "it would take Ireland twenty years to learn his
old ones." Upon some such consideration as this I adhered pretty
closely to my old lecture on "Self-made Men," retouching and shading it a little from time to time as occasion seemed to require.

Here, then, was a new vocation before me, full of advantages mentally and pecuniarily. When in the employment of the American Anti-Slavery Society my salary was about four hundred and fifty dollars a year, and I felt I was well paid for my services; but I could now make from fifty to a hundred dollars a night, and have the satisfaction, too, that I was in some small measure helping to lift my race into consideration, for no man who lives at all lives unto himself— he either helps or hinders all who are in any wise connected with him. I never rise to speak before an American audience without something of the feeling that my failure or success will bring blame or benefit to my whole race.

"People Want to Be Amused as Well as Instructed" (1871), Letter to James Redpath

After the Civil War, Frederick Douglass turned to the lyceum stage as a major source of personal revenue, delivering scores of lectures each year all across the country. To organize this schedule most efficiently, Douglass sought the assistance of another former abolitionist, James Redpath, who had organized the nation's most successful "bureau" of lyceum speakers. In a letter to Redpath written 29 July 1871, Douglass commented remorsefully that many whites still regarded him as a novelty on account of his race. Douglass also observed that these popular audiences desired to be "amused as well as instructed," and worried that he would disappoint many.

My dear Mr Redpath:

What upon earth can you want with the character of my lecture? People ought by this time to take me on trust, especially as their expectations have always been remarkably moderate and never disappointed. It is too late now to do much to improve my relation to the public—I shall never get beyond Fred Douglass the self educated fugitive slave. While my lecture on Santo Domingo will be historical, descriptive and political, favoring annexation or some other extention of power over that Country, I shall endeavor not to forget that people do not attend lectures to hear statesmanlike addresses, which are usually rather heavy for the stomachs of young and old who listen. People want to be amused as well as instructed. They come as often for the former as the latter, and perhaps as often to see the man as for either. Get me all the appointments you can—but I beg that you will say nothing to create expectations which may be disappointed.

Yours very truly
Fred^k Douglass

"Great Is the Miracle of Human Speech" (1891), from the Washington (D.C.) *Evening Star*

In August 1891, Frederick Douglass was requested to make a brief address at a reception in Washington, D.C., honoring a local African American minister, John W. E. Bowen. His remarks were reported by a black newspaper, the Washington *Evening Star*, on 1 September 1891. Douglass used the occasion to reflect on the power of oratory not only as a formidable tool of reformers and ministers, but also as a way for African Americans to demonstrate their intelligence and educational attainment to a skeptical white society.

Sir:—There was a time in my life when I dreaded to hear a man of color rise to speak in the presence of white people. I feared that he would supply added proof of our ignorance and inferiority. That day is past. Men like yourself, Doctor Grimke, Brooks Crummell and others, may be trusted before the most learned and enlightened audience in the world. In such hands our cause suffers no defeat or detriment. Whenever and wherever such men speak a burden of reproach is rolled from the breasts of our people and we breathe freer. More than fifty years ago when I lived in New Bedford, Massachusetts, I went to hear a lecture by Rev. Henry Highland Garnet. He was in every respect a typical negro. Before hearing him I thought I was a man, but after hearing him I knew I was a man and a man among men.

It is often asked, by ignorance what have such men as Garnet, Ward, Remond and others done for the colored race? and ignorance has answered its own question: They have only talked; but talk is itself a power. We hold in grateful memory Wm. Lloyd Garrison, Wendell Phillips, Charles Sumner and many others. What did they do for the colored people? They talked and talked the chains off the limbs of millions. He is low down in the scale of intelligence who measures the service and greatness of men only by physical force and physical achievements. The sword is great, but the pen in greater. The one deals with the body but the other with the soul.

Great is the miracle of human speech—by it nations are enlightened and reformed; by it the cause of justice and liberty is defended, by it evils are exposed, ignorance dispelled, the path of duty made plain, and by it those that live to-day are put into the possession of the wisdom of ages gone by. The words of Paul still rock the world, though spoken two thousand years ago, for his words were mighty and powerful. The Savior of the Christian world spake as never man spake and his words are repeated by millions to millions, generation after generation undimmed by time, untarnished by repetition, and will continue till rolling years shall cease to move.

Sir:—Your vocation is to speak the word; there is none higher. We welcome you to this vast vantage ground, your chosen post. You touch the main spring of the moral universe. Truth is the saving power of the world, preach it and you bless yourself, your race and the world.

PART 4

Contemporary Commentary on Frederick Douglass as an Orator

THE ACCOUNTS BELOW are from people who observed Douglass as a speaker. They were written by fellow abolitionists, white and black, male and female, as well as opponents of Douglass's efforts to convert audiences to emancipation and civil rights. These published critiques of Douglass the lecturer began shortly after he commenced his public speaking career, in 1841, and continued until the last witnesses to his oratory passed away early in the twentieth century. These observers recounted significant changes in Douglass's speaking techniques as he evolved from a novice lecturer to a leading reform advocate to a highly paid public lecturer. Regardless of their opinions regarding Douglass's topic, these commentators all concluded that he was one of the most effective speakers of the nineteenth century.

From "Rhode Island Anti-Slavery Meeting" (1841)

One of the earliest published analyses of Frederick Douglass's lecturing was made by the New Hampshire abolitionist Nathaniel Peabody Rogers (1794–1846) in his weekly newspaper, the Concord (N.H.) *Herald of Freedom*, on 3 December 1841. Rogers observed that Douglass's "commanding" physical presence, shrewd, lawyerly intelligence, and eloquent enunciation on the lecture platform were compelling testimony regarding the injustice of enslaving such a capable man solely on account of his race.

F RIDAY EVENING was chiefly occupied by colored speakers. The fugitive Douglass was up when we entered. This is an extraordinary man. He was cut out for a hero. In a rising for Liberty, he would have been a Toussaint or a Hamilton. He has the "heart to conceive, the head to contrive, and the hand to execute." A commanding person—over six feet, we should say, in height, and of most manly proportions. His head would strike a phrenologist amid a sea of them in Exeter Hall, and his voice would ring like a trumpet in the field. Let the South congratulate herself that he is a *fugitive*. It would not have been safe for her if he had remained about the plantations a year or two longer. DOUGLASS is his *fugitive* name. He did not wear it in slavery. We don't know why he assumed it, or who bestowed it on him—but there seems *fitness* in it, to his commanding figure and heroic port. As a speaker he has few equals. It is not declamation—but oratory, power of debate. He watches the tide of discussion with the eye of the veteran, and dashes into it at once with all the tact of the forum or the bar. He has wit, argument, sarcasm, pathos—all that first-rate men show in their master efforts. His voice is highly melodious and rich, and his enunciation quite elegant, and yet he has been but two or three years out of the house of bondage. We noticed that he had strikingly improved, since we heard him at Dover in September. We say thus much of him, for he is esteemed by our multitude as of an inferior race. We should like to see him before any New England legislature or bar, and let him feel the freedom of the anti-slavery meeting, and see what would become of his inferiority. Yet he is a *thing*, in American estimate. He is the chattel of some pale-faced tyrant. How his owner would cower and shiver to hear him thunder in an anti-slavery hall! How he would shrink away, with his infernal whip, from his flaming eye when kindled with anti-slavery emotion! And the brotherhood of thieves, the *posse comitatus* of divines, we with a hectatomb or two of the proudest and flintiest of them, were obliged to hear him thunder for human liberty, and lay the enslavement of his people at their doors. They would tremble like Belshazzar. Poor Wayland! we wish he could have been *pegged* a seat in the Franklin Hall, the evening the colored friends spoke. His "limitations" would have abandoned him like the "baseless fabric of a vision."

WILLIAM J. WILSON

"A Leaf from My Scrap Book: Samuel R. Ward and Frederick Douglass" (1849)

Although Douglass's fellow black abolitionist William J. Wilson (1820–?) wrote this essay originally in his private journal, it was reprinted in *Autographs for Freedom* (1854), a work compiled by Julia Griffiths on behalf of the Rochester Ladies' Anti-Slavery Society to raise funds for Douglass's newspaper. Wilson recounts a series of debates conducted between Samuel R. Ward, another prominent African American, and Douglass regarding the constitutionality of slavery. As an early assessment of Douglass's speaking style, Wilson's conclusions—that Douglass tends to be overly ornate and to lack a trenchant argument—are at odds with the assessments of later commentators, but perhaps indicate Douglass's growth as a leader and speaker.

P ERHAPS A FITTER OCCASION never presented itself, nor was more properly availed of, for the exhibition of talent, than when Frederick Douglass and Samuel R. Ward debated the "question" whether the Constitution was or not a pro-slavery document.

With the "question" at issue we have, at present, nothing to do; and with the arguments so far only as they exhibit the men.

Both eminent for talent of an order (though differing somewhat in cast) far above the common level of great men.

If any inequalities existed, they served rather to heighten than diminish the interest of the occasion, giving rise to one of the severest contests of mind with mind that has yet come to my notice.

Douglass, sincere in the opinions he has espoused, defends them with a fervor and eloquence that finds scarcely a competitor.

In his very look—his gesture—in his whole manner, there is so much of genuine, earnest eloquence, that they leave no time for reflection. Now you are reminded of one rushing down some fearful steep, bidding you follow; now on some delightful stream, still beckoning you onward.

In either case, no matter what your prepossessions or oppositions, you for the moment, at least, forget the justness or unjustness of his cause and obey the summons, and loath, if at all, you return to your former post.

Not always, however, is he successful in retaining you. Giddy as you may be with the descent you have made, delighted as you are with the pleasure afforded, with the elysium to which he has wafted you, you return too often dissatisfied with his and your own impetuosity and want of firmness. You feel that you had only a dream, a pastime, not a reality.

This great power of momentary captivation consists in his eloquence of manner—his just appreciation of words.

In listening to him, your whole soul is fired—every nerve strung—every passion inflated—every faculty you possess ready to perform at a moment's bidding. You stop not to ask why or wherefore.

'Tis a unison of mighty yet harmonious sounds that play upon your imagination; and you give yourself up, for a time, to their irresistible charm.

At last, the *cataract* which roared around you is hushed, the *tornado* is passed, and you find yourself sitting upon a bank (at whose base roll but tranquil waters), quietly meditating that why, amid such a display of power, no greater effect had really been produced.

After all, it must be admitted, there is a power in Mr. Douglass rarely to be found in any other man.

With copiousness of language, and finish of diction, when even ideas fail, words come to his aid—arranging themselves, as it were, so completely, that they not only captivate, but often deceive us for ideas; and hence the vacuum that would necessarily occur in the address of an ordinary *speaker* is filled up, presenting the same beautiful harmony as do the lights and shades of a picture.

From Mr. Douglass, in this, perhaps, as much as in any other respect, does Mr. Ward differ. Ideas form the basis of all Mr. Ward utters. Words are only used to express those ideas.

If words and ideas are not inseparable, then, as mortar is to the stones that compose the building, so are his words to his ideas.

In this, I judge, lays Mr. Ward's greatest strength. Concise without abruptness—without extraordinary stress, always clear and forcible; if sparing of ornament, never inelegant. In all, there appears a consciousness of strength, developed by close study and deep reflection, and only put forth because the occasion demanded,—a power not only to examine but to enable you to see the fairness of that examination and the justness of its conclusions.

You feel Douglass to be right, without always seeing it; perhaps it is not too much to say, when Ward is right you see it.

His appeals are directed rather to the understanding than the imagination; but so forcibly do they take possession of it, that the heart unhesitatingly yields.

If, as we have said, Mr. Douglass seems as one whirling down some steep descent whose very impetuosity impels;—ere you are aware of it, it is the quiet serenity of Mr. Ward, as he points up the rugged ascent, and invites you to follow, that inspires your confidence and ensures your safety. Step by step do you with him climb the rugged steep; and, as you gain each succeeding eminence, he points you to new scenes and new delights;—now grand—sublime; now picturesque and beautiful;—always real. Most speakers fail to draw a perfect figure. This point I think Mr. Ward has gained. His figures, when done, stand out with prominence, possessing both strength and elegance.

Douglass' imagery is fine—vivid—often gaudily painted. Ward's pictures—bold, strong, glowing.

Douglass speaks right on; you acknowledge him to have been on the ground—nay, to have gone over the field; *Ward* seeks for and finds the corners; sticks the stakes, and leaves them standing; we know where to find them.

Mr. Douglass deals in generals; Mr. Ward reduces everything to a point.

Douglass is the *lecturer;* Ward the *debater.* Douglass powerful in invective; Ward in argument. What advantage Douglass gains in mimicry Ward recovers in wit.

Douglass has sarcasm, Ward point.

Here, again, an essential difference may be pointed out:—

Douglass says much, at times, you regret he uttered. This, however, is the real man, and on reflection you like him the better for it. What Ward says you feel to be but a necessity, growing out of the case,—that it ought to have been said—that you would have said precisely the same yourself, without adding or diminishing a single sentence.

Douglass, in manner, is at all times pleasing; Ward seldom less so; often raises to the truly majestic, and never descends below propriety. If you regret when Douglass ceases to speak, you are anxious Ward should continue.

Dignity is an essential quality in an orator—I mean true dignity.

Douglass has this in an eminent degree; Ward no less so, coupled with it great self-possession. He is never disconcerted—all he desires he says.

In one of his replies to Mr. Douglass I was struck with admiration, and even delight, at the calm, dignified manner in which he expressed himself, and his ultimate triumph under what seemed to me very peculiar circumstances.

Douglass' was a splendid effort—a beautiful effusion. One of those outpourings from the deeps of his heart of which he can so admirably give existence to.

He had brought down thunders of well-merited applause; and sure I am, that a whisper, a breath from almost any other opponent than Mr. Ward, would have produced a tumult of hisses.

Not so, however, now. The quiet, majestic air, the suppressed richness of a deep-toned, but well-cultivated voice, as the speaker paid a few well-timed compliments to his opponents, disturbed not, as it had produced, the dead stillness around.

Next followed some fine sallies of wit, which broke in on the calm.

He then proceeded to make and accomplished one of the most finished speeches to which I have ever listened, and sat down amidst a perfect storm of cheers.

It was a noble burst of eloquence,—the gatherings up of the choicest possible culled thoughts, and poured forth, mingling with a unison of brilliant flashes and masterly strokes, following each other in quick succession; and though felt—deeply felt, no more to be described than the vivid lightning's zig-zag, as produced from the deep-charged thunder-cloud.

If Douglass is not always successful in his attempts to heave up his ponderous missiles at his opponents, from the point of his descent, he always shows determination and spirit.

He is often too far down the *pass*, however, (herculean though he be,) for his intent.

Ward, from the eminence he has gained, giant-like, hurls them back with the force and skill of a practiced marksman, almost invariably to the detriment of his already fallen victim.

In Douglass you have a man, in whose soul the iron of oppression has far entered, and you feel it.

He tells the story of his wrongs, so that they stand out in all their naked ugliness.

In Ward, you have one with strong native power,—I know of none stronger; superadded a careful and extensive cultivation; and understanding so matured, that fully enables him to successfully grapple with men or errors, and portray truth in a manner equaled by few.

After all, it must be admitted, both are men of extraordinary powers of mind.

Both well qualified for the task they have undertaken.

I have, rather than anything else, drawn these outline portraits for our *young men,* who can fill them up at leisure.

The subjects are both fine models, and may be studied with profit by all,—especially to those who are destined to stand in the front rank.

Note.—It has been some years since the above sketch was drawn; and though my impressions, especially of Mr. Douglass, have undergone some slight change since,—seeing in him enlarged, strengthened, and more matured thought, still I think, on the whole, the careful observer will attest substantially to its correctness.

From "A Colored Man's Eloquence" (1853)

Under the editorship of Thurlow Weed (1797–1882), the Albany *Evening Journal* had a political influence in Whig and, later, Republican party circles far beyond the state of New York. An ally of William H. Seward, Weed opposed the spread of slavery into western territories but refused to endorse immediate emancipation. Focused on building a successful political coalition to oppose Southern political influence in the federal government, Weed displayed only limited sympathy for African Americans, slave or free. In the *Evening Journal* of 14 May 1853, Weed praised Douglass's recent speech in Albany, but regretted that encounters with racism had rendered his spirit "morbid."

W
e make no apology for devoting two columns to the Anti-Slavery Speech of FREDERICK DOUGLASS. It will richly repay all who read it, for it is a Speech of surpassing power and eloquence.

Fugitive Slaves have a right to abhor and denounce Slavery. It is not strange that *they* should labor for Emancipation. Ultraism may be pardoned in those who have *experienced* the ills of Slavery. Having escaped from bondage themselves, they would be recreant to every sentiment and sympathy of a common nature if they were indifferent to the fate of their kindred and race.

FREDERICK DOUGLASS is a remarkable—an *extraordinary* man. There are few more gifted among us. To a powerful intellect, he adds, in an eminent degree, the graces of taste and oratory. This may surprise those who have not heard him, but if such will read his Speech without prejudice, it will be less difficult to credit our assurances of his ability. Such efforts as that we now publish, with others we have heard from the same man, delivered in Congress or in Parliament, would do no discredit to the most distinguished Statesman.

And yet FREDERICK DOUGLASS is, as he truly describes himself—a NEGRO—and until he was twenty-five years old—a SLAVE. He escaped from bondage some fifteen years ago,—not ignorant, for such a mind could not be kept in ignorance—but uneducated, having had no advantage over other Maryland Slaves.

But see what he has done for himself? See what lofty aspirations lift him "up to an equality with our more favored race?" And how infinitely superior, intellectually, to thousands of the favored race on whom the advantages of fortune have been lavished and the blessings of education squandered?

But the sense of injury to his race, coupled with the personal mortification to which his color subjects him, has rendered DOUGLASS morbid. There is bitterness in his thoughts and in his words. And his associations help to poison his mind and to give an impracticable direction to his efforts. He has become, therefore, a Destructive instead of a Reformer, waging a profitless warfare against existing organizations of Government, Society and Religion. If his great mind was burdened with kindlier sympathies—if, like GOVERNOR ROBERTS and AUSTIN STEWARD, he could be content with efforts to mitigate evils that cannot be uprooted, what an able field for usefulness is open to him? How readily and certainly he could plant and cherish a Colony of his ransomed race in some of those beautiful Islands in that Caribbean Sea to which he refers? We speak not of banishing People of Color to Liberia. That is too distant a point. But there is no more delightful residence in the World than those ever radiant and fruitful Carribean Isles. There, everything is congenial; and there "is ample room and verge enough," for all who may voluntarily seek a residence which would exempt them from the arbitrary but unavoidable distinctions of color and caste.

WILLIAM WELLS BROWN

From *The Rising Son* (1874)

In the assessment of a fellow African American abolitionist, William Wells Brown (1814–84), "white men and black men had talked against slavery, but none had ever spoken like Frederick Douglass." In fact, Brown argues in *The Rising Son* (1874) that Douglass's unmatched reception generated considerable jealousy in many other abolitionist orators. In Brown's opinion, Douglass's youthful experiences as a Maryland slave elicited a deep emotional response from his listeners that few other abolitionists could achieve. Brown also praised Douglass's great dramatic skills, professing that in a different era he could have become the nation's leading actor. Brown regretted that many of Douglass's strengths as an extemporaneous speaker were lost on the post–Civil War lyceum stage, where he delivered his addresses from prepared manuscripts.

H is advent as a lecturer was a remarkable one. White men and black men had talked against slavery, but none had ever spoken like Frederick Douglass. Throughout the North the newspapers were filled with the sayings of the "eloquent fugitive."

He often traveled with others, but they were all lost sight of in the eagerness to hear Douglass. His traveling companions would sometimes get angry, and would speak first at the meetings; then they would take the last turn; but it was all the same—the fugitive's impression was the one left upon the mind. He made more persons angry, and pleased more, than any other man. He was praised, and he was censured. He made them laugh, he made them weep, and he made them swear. His "Slaveholders' Sermon" was always a trump card. He awakened an interest in the hearts of thousands who before were dead to the slave and his condition. Many kept away from his lectures, fearing lest they should be converted against their will. Young men and women, in those days of pro-slavery hatred, would return to their fathers' roofs filled with admiration for the "runaway slave," and would be rebuked by hearing the old ones grumble out, "You'd better stay at home and study your lessons, and not be running after the nigger meetings."

In 1841, he was induced to accept an agency as a lecturer for the Anti-slavery Society, and at once became one of the most valuable of its advocates. He visited England in 1845. There he was kindly received and heartily welcomed; and after going through the length and breadth of the land, and addressing public meetings out of number on behalf of his countrymen in chains, with a power of eloquence which captivated his auditors, and brought the cause which he pleaded home to their hearts, he returned home, and commenced the publication of the "North Star," a weekly newspaper devoted to the advocacy of the cause of freedom.

Mr. Douglass is tall and well made. His vast and fully-developed forehead shows at once that he is a superior man intellectually. He is polished in his language, and gentlemanly in his manners. His voice is full and sonorous. His attitude is dignified, and his gesticulation is full of noble simplicity. He is a man of lofty reason; natural, and without pretension; always master of himself; brilliant in the art of exposing and abstracting. Few persons can handle a subject, with which they are familiar, better than he. There is a kind of eloquence issuing from the depth of the soul as from a spring, rolling along its copious floods, sweeping all before it, overwhelming by its very force, carrying, upsetting, engulfing its adversaries, and more dazzling and more thundering than the bolt which leaps from crag to crag. This is the eloquence of Frederick Douglass. One of the best mimics of the age, and possessing great dramatic powers; had he taken up the sock and buskin, instead of becoming a lecturer, he would have made as fine a Coriolanus as ever trod the stage.

As a speaker, Frederick Douglass has had more imitators than almost any other American, save, perhaps, Wendell Phillips. Unlike most great speakers, he is a superior writer also. Some of his articles, in point of ability, will rank with anything ever written for the American press. He has taken lessons from the best of teachers, amid the homeliest realities of life; hence the perpetual freshness of his delineations, which are never over-colored, never strained, never aiming at difficult or impossible effects, but which always read like living transcripts of experience.

Mr. Douglass has obtained a position in the front rank as a lyceum lecturer. His later addresses from manuscripts, however, do not, in our opinion, come up to his extemporaneous efforts.

"An 1895 Public Letter from Elizabeth Cady Stanton on the Occasion of Frederick Douglass's Death," from *In Memoriam: Frederick Douglass,* ed. Helen Douglass (1897)

Elizabeth Cady Stanton (1815–1902), a leading figure in the early women's rights and abolitionist movements, and a dear friend of Douglass, found in him a compatriot for woman suffrage. Although they disagreed that women's civil rights should supersede those of blacks, they believed equality before the law was vital. In the letter published below, she reminisces about an abolitionist convention at which Douglass spoke early in his career, alongside two other important reformers of his day, Wendell Phillips (1811–84) and Lydia Maria Child (1802–80). Stanton explains why she found a kindred spirit in Douglass: "He was the only man I ever knew who understood the degradation of disfranchisement for women."

Taking up the morning *Tribune,* the first words that caught my eye thrilled my very soul. "Frederick Douglass is dead!" What vivid memories thick and fast flashed through my mind and held me spellbound in contemplation of the long years since first we met.

Trained in the severe school of slavery, I saw him first before a Boston audience, fresh from the land of bondage. He stood there like an African prince, conscious of his dignity and power, grand in his physical proportions, majestic in his wrath, as with keen wit, satire and indignation he portrayed the bitterness of slavery, the humiliation of subjection to those who in all human virtues and capacities were inferior to himself. His denunciation of our national crime, of the wild and guilty fantasy that men could hold property in man, poured like a torrent that fairly made his hearers tremble.

Thus I first saw him, and wondered as I listened that any mortal man should have ever tried to subjugate a being with such marvelous powers, such self-respect, such intense love of liberty.

Around him sat the great anti-slavery orators of the day, watching his effect on that immense audience, completely magnetized with his eloquence, laughing and crying by turns with his rapid flights from pathos to humor. All other speakers seemed tame after Douglass. Sitting near, I heard Phillips say to Lydia Maria Child: "Verily, this boy, who has only just graduated from the 'southern institution' (as slavery was called), throws us all in the shade." "Ah," she replied, "the iron has entered his soul and he knows the wrongs of slavery subjectively; the rest of you speak only from an objective point of view."

He used to preach a sermon in imitation of the Methodist clergy, from the text, "Servants, Obey your Masters," which the people were never tired of hearing. Often after he had spoken an hour shouts would go up from all parts of the house, "Now, Douglass, give us the sermon." Some of our literary critics pronounced that the best piece of satire in the English language.

The last time I visited his home in Anacostia, I asked him if he ever had the sermon printed. He said "No." "Could you reproduce it?" said I. He said, "No; I could not bring back the old feeling if I tried, and I would not if I could. The blessings of liberty I have so long enjoyed, and the many tender friendships I have with the Saxon race on both sides of the ocean, have taught me such sweet lessons of forgiveness that the painful memories of my early days are almost obliterated, and I would not recall them."

As an orator, writer and editor, Douglass holds an honored place among the gifted men of his day. As a man of business and a public officer he has been pre-eminently successful; honest and upright in all his dealings, he bears an enviable reputation.

As a husband, father, neighbor and friend, in all social relations, he has been faithful and steadfast to the end. He was the only man I ever knew who understood the degradation of disfranchisement for women. Through all the long years of our struggle he has been a familiar figure on our platform, with always an inspiring word to say. In the very first convention he helped me to carry the resolution I had penned, demanding woman suffrage.

Frederick Douglass is not dead! His grand character will long be an object lesson in our national history; his lofty sentiments of liberty, justice and equality, echoed on every platform over our broad land, must influence and inspire many coming generations!

Elizabeth Cady Stanton,
26 West Sixty-First Street, New York.

February 21, 1895.

THOMAS WENTWORTH HIGGINSON

From *American Orators*
and Oratory (1901)

The Unitarian minister, Civil War soldier, and prolific author Thomas
Wentworth Higginson (1823–1911) knew Frederick Douglass inti-
mately in the abolitionist movement and was a fellow conspirator in
John Brown's Harpers Ferry plot. In 1901, Higginson wrote *American Orators and Oratory*, a short book of reminiscences of the great
public speakers he had been privileged to hear over his long life. Higginson praises Douglass's precise command of language despite his
complete absence of formal education. Higginson also vividly recalls
how Douglass employed a combination of wit and bravado to get the
better of an antiabolitionist New York City mob in the early 1850s.

I spoke once before, but not so fully as I wished, of the man
who on the anti-slavery platform, from his combination of the
two races, was most interesting and most commanding for a
time, though not always—for he differed from the others in
detail and was more of a voting abolitionist than they were—Frederick Douglass.

In later years I walked once with Frederick Douglass through
the streets of Worcester. It was the middle of winter and he wore
a leopard-skin coat and cap. I well remember looking at him as he
towered above my head and saying to myself:

"Make the most of this opportunity. You never before have
walked the streets with so distinguished-looking a man, and you
never will again." And I never have.

This man whom I had seen rise out of this clumsy lingering of the slavery manner, shot up into a superb man. This man, who learned originally to write from the placards in the Baltimore streets after he was eighteen, and by paying a little boy with an apple to tell him what certain letters were—this man gained such a command of speech and language that Mr. Yerrington, then the leading reporter of Boston, who always reported the anti-slavery meetings, told me that of all the speakers in those meetings, there were but two who could be reported without verbal alteration precisely as they spoke, and those two were Wendell Phillips and Frederick Douglass—the representative of the patrician training on the one side, and the representative of the Maryland slave on the other.

The tact of the man, the address of the man, and the humor of the man made him almost irresistible on the platform. He always had this proud bearing, and yet he was a perfect mimic. He could reproduce anything; he could meet any occasion. I remember him once at a convention in New York. The meeting had been overpowered by Captain Rynders, who was then the head of the swell mob in New York. He had taken possession of the meeting, had placed himself in the chair and graciously allowed the meeting to go on under his presidency. He had tried in vain to stop Douglass and check him, and had fallen back upon brutal interruptions, even saying, for instance, "Oh, you want to cut all our throats!"

"Oh, no," said the superb Douglass, bending down graciously over him and waving his hand a little over Rynders's tangled and soiled headdress, "Oh, no, we will not cut your throats; we will only cut your hair." And the supporters of Rynders felt the situation as much as anybody. I speak of Douglass the more because he has as yet left no rival of his type. Even Booker Washington, with all his remarkable qualities and undoubtedly an organizing power which Douglass had not, and perhaps destined in the end to be a more visibly useful man, has not that supreme power over an audience which Douglass had.

PART 5

Modern Scholarly Criticism of Frederick Douglass as an Orator

DOUGLASS'S ORATORY HAS ATTRACTED scholars of history, literature, and rhetoric because of his political centrality as a race-bridging figure in the latter half of the nineteenth century and his remarkable power to move listeners. Among the excerpts included here, Gregory Lampe's and Granville Ganter's pieces examine the origin of Douglass's rhetorical talent in his early sermon satires and his leadership in African American communities. Once Douglass joined the Garrisonians and became a leader within the abolition movement, he quickly became a nationally recognized figure in the debate over slavery and race relations. Several of Douglass's speeches from this era became classics of oratory, including "What to the Slave Is the Fourth of July?" (1852) and "The Freedmen's Monument to Abraham Lincoln" (1876). Ivy Wilson responds to the former, specifically considering Douglass's efforts to constitute an authoritative position from which to speak on national issues while being, at best, a marginalized citizen. David Howard-Pitney's and Richard Leeman's essays examine Douglass's oratory in the context of later African American orators and their responses to common rhetorical forms and discourses.

GREGORY P. LAMPE

From *Frederick Douglass: Freedom's Voice, 1818–1845*

Gregory Lampe has a Ph.D. from the University of Wisconsin–Madison and currently serves as provost and vice chancellor for academic and student affairs at the University of Wisconsin Colleges. Lampe's book *Frederick Douglass: Freedom's Voice, 1818–1845* (1998) challenges the belief that Frederick Douglass emerged in 1841 as a novice speaker under the tutelage of William Lloyd Garrison and the American Anti-Slavery Society. Instead, Lampe argues that Douglass's activities as an enslaved youth in Maryland and then as a fugitive in New Bedford offered unconventional experiences that developed his rhetorical abilities. Lampe further asserts that even after Douglass's fortuitous meeting with the Garrisonians, the novice antislavery lecturer maintained greater intellectual independence than was previously believed.

O f all Douglass' experiences in Baltimore, none had more impact than his discovery, at age twelve, of Caleb Bingham's *Columbian Orator.* Douglass was inspired to purchase the book when he overheard "some little boys say that they were going to learn some pieces out of it for the Exhibition." With fifty cents earned from polishing boots, he bought a copy of the reader. It was one of the best investments of his life. The *Columbian Orator* was a collection of orations, poems, playlets, and dialogues celebrating patriotism, freedom, courage, democracy, education, and temperance. Designed to "inspire the

pupil with the ardour of eloquence and the love of virtue," the selections in the book were intended "particularly for Dialogue and
Declamation."

"This volume was, indeed, a rich treasure," Douglass reflected
in 1855, "and every opportunity afforded me, for a time, was spent
in diligently perusing it." He found a number of pieces within the
text particularly worthwhile. In his autobiographies, Douglass specifically mentioned Sheridan's "mighty speeches on the subject of
Catholic Emancipation," Lord Chatham's speech "on the American War," and speeches by "the great William Pitt and by Fox" as
addresses that he found particularly interesting. "These were all
choice documents to me," Douglass recalled, "and I read them,
over and over again, with an interest ever increasing because it was
ever gaining in intelligence; for the more I read them, the better I
understood them."

The selection he found most fascinating, however, was a short
piece entitled "Dialogue Between a Master and Slave," by John
Aikin. Douglass was so enamoured of this dialogue that he "perused
and reperused [it] with unflagging satisfaction." In *My Bondage and
My Freedom,* Douglass explained the attraction of the dialogue,
which began with the master rebuking the slave for attempting to
escape. In response, the slave was "made to say some very smart as
well as impressive things in reply to his master." Invited to defend
his escape attempt, the slave accepted the challenge and made a
"spirited defense of himself, and thereafter the whole argument,
for and against slavery, was brought out." For every argument the
master made in defense of slavery, the slave presented a convincing
counterargument. "The master," Douglass mused, "was vanquished
at every turn." In the end, the master was convinced to emancipate
the slave, demonstrating to Douglass the "mighty power and heart-
searching directness of truth, penetrating even the heart of a slaveholder, compelling him to yield up his earthly interests to the claims
of eternal justice." "Powerfully affected" by the dialogue, Douglass

dreamed of the day "when the well-directed answers made by the slave to the master . . . would find their counterpart" in him.

Equally important, Douglass stated years later, through reading and rereading this dialogue, he was able to utter his own thoughts on bondage, and "to meet the arguments brought forward to sustain slavery." Clearly and systematically, the dialogue responded to many of the questions that troubled him about slavery and his personal condition. Should he be grateful for his master's kind treatment of him? The dialogue's message was strikingly clear on this point. Douglass should not be grateful for any kind treatment by his owners who, if they did treat him well, did so purely for their own advantage. Was it wrong to try to escape from slavery? Decidedly not, said the dialogue. The act of running away was justified because the slave was taking back the liberty that was legitimately his. Had Providence, in some way, ordained slavery? Again, the dialogue answered—human beings, not God, had created slavery. From the dialogue, Douglass learned "the secret of all slavery and oppression, and . . . ascertained their true foundation to be in the pride, the power and the avarice of man." Slaveholders, he saw, were no more than "a band of successful robbers, who left their homes and went into Africa for the purpose of stealing and reducing my people to slavery."

Nor was this dialogue the only selection Douglass benefited from in the *Columbian Orator*. By reading Bingham's book "over and over again with unabated interest," he discovered the words to express his thoughts and feelings. The book, "gave tongue to interesting thoughts of my own soul," he recalled, thoughts "which had frequently flashed through my mind, and died away for want of utterance." He could now recite words that denounced slavery and injustice, that defended a slave's right to rebel and run away, and that celebrated human liberty and freedom. At the same time, he learned that words—and especially words expressed in oratory— could be a powerful way to combat such an injustice as slavery.

According to one of the speeches found in Bingham's collection, the most telling weapon for truth was the art of oratory:

> To instruct, to persuade, to please; these are its objects. To scatter the clouds of ignorance and error . . . to remove the film of prejudice from the mental eye; and thus to irradiate the benighted mind with the cheering beams of truth. . . . . An Alexander and a Caesar could conquer a world; but to overcome the passions, to subdue the wills, and to command at pleasure the inclinations of men, can be effected only by the all-powerful charm of enrapturing eloquence.

As Douglass read and reread the *Columbian Orator,* he recognized the possibilities of using oratory to "scatter the clouds of ignorance and error" that surrounded him in slave society.

Beyond showing Douglass the power of oratory and persuasive argument, Bingham's book provided a twenty-nine-page essay entitled, "General Directions for Speaking; Extracted from Various Authors." Within these pages Douglass found detailed instruction on how to deliver an effective speech, instructions he followed to the letter in many of his early antislavery addresses. Because it appears that Douglass' early rhetorical style and delivery were influenced profoundly by Bingham's essay, we need to look closely at its prescriptions.

Bingham began his essay by declaring delivery the most important canon of rhetoric. Drawing upon the opinions of Cicero, Demosthenes, and Quintilian, he emphasized that the principal object of oratory was action, and that the primary trigger to action was the orator's manner of delivery. The most effective delivery, he advised, was natural and sincere. The orator must adjust his voice so that "it rises, sinks, and has various inflections given it, according to the present state and disposition of the mind." He must also attend to "accent, emphasis, and cadence." The orator must distinguish those words in a sentence which he believes are the "most important" and place "a greater stress of voice upon them than . . . upon the others." In addition, the speaker must speak loud enough to be heard. The voice, Bingham suggested, should be varied, "clear and distinct." Bingham also offered advice on the pacing of a speech. If the orator speaks too fast, he warned, he "destroys . . . the necessary distinction between sentence and sentence . . . by which mean, all the grace of speaking is lost, and in great measure, the advantage of hearing." Conversely, an orator who speaks too slowly "appears cool himself, [and] can never expect to warm his hearers, and excite their affections."

Like the voice, Bingham advised, gestures should be varied and natural. The orator should not stand in the same position "like a statue," but should move naturally about the platform. Bingham believed that the orator must use his face and eyes to show signs of sorrow, joy, anger, resentment, terror, and modesty. The eyes should always be "directed to some of the audience, and gradually turning from side to side with an air of respect and modesty, and looking at them decently in the face, as in common discourse." In addition, the speaker should stand erect and use "very moderate" hand and arm movements. Bingham also offered advice about imitating others from the platform, advice Douglass took seriously in his frequent use of mimicry in his early abolitionist lectures. An orator may choose to impersonate another speaker, wrote Bingham, but "great care must be taken not to overact his part by running into any ludicrous or theatrical mimicry."

Douglass learned from Bingham's book how to deliver each section of a speech. Upon arriving on the platform, the orator was directed to "first settle himself, compose his countenance, and take a respectful view of his audience." Once the audience was prepared to listen, the orator should begin his speech at a slow pace. Within the narration, "the voice ought to be raised to somewhat a higher pitch," though "matters of fact should be related in a very plain and distinct manner, with a proper stress and emphasis laid upon each circumstance." During the proposition, the "subject of the discourse should be delivered with a very clear and audible voice." Within the confirmation, speakers were instructed to use "a great variety both of the voice and gesture" so as to strengthen the orator's reasoning and heighten "the imagination of his hearers." During the confutation, "the arguments of the adverse party ought first to be repeated in a plain and distinct manner." If they appear "trifling and unworthy of a serious answer," instructed Bingham, the speaker should respond to them in a "facetious manner, both of expression and gesture," for "to attempt to answer, in a grave and serious manner, what is in itself empty and ludicrous, is apt to create a suspicion, of its having more in it than it really has." When coming to the conclusion, "both the voice and gesture should be brisk and sprightly. . . . If an enumeration of the principal arguments of the discourse be convenient . . . they ought to be expressed in the most clear and forcible manner." Bingham concluded his essay by stressing that "it is impossible to gain a just and decent pronunciation of voice and gesture merely from rules." The best way to become an orator, he recommended, was through "practice and imitation of the best examples." This may be one reason Douglass read the speeches, dialogues, playlets, and poems in the *Columbian Orator* "over and over again."

The importance of the *Columbian Orator* in shaping Douglass' future cannot be overestimated. Bingham's book offered him a heroic perspective of oratory and a model for his own life that he appears to have found close to irresistible. Moreover, from all indications, Douglass' early oratory was influenced significantly by Bingham's meticulous instructions with respect to delivery, style, and arrangement. When speaking from the platform, Douglass used a conversational, natural delivery style, logically arranged and carefully reasoned his speeches, and appealed with great effect to the emotions of his listeners. Following Bingham's advice and reading and rereading the selections included in the book enabled Douglass to merge two traditions—the oral tradition of the slave culture with the classical rhetorical tradition. Since his childhood, he had absorbed the exhilarating oral style of the storyteller and slave preacher. He had been exposed to their use of striking imagery, rich phrases, metaphor, repetition, parallelism, poetry, song, and rhythmic cadences. He had experienced the impact of dramatic gestures and stirring vocal delivery of his fellow slaves. He had listened to the storyteller enhance his tale by mimicking the sounds of nature and by creating the illusion of dialogue between characters. Certainly, Bingham's advice on the orator's use of voice and gesture, mimicry and imagery, complemented the knowledge Douglass had acquired within his slave experiences on the plantation, as did Bingham's instructions on the importance of appealing to the emotions and passions of the audience. Most important, Bingham's volume introduced Douglass to the rhetorical strategies of the orator and to a standard structure for organizing speeches. Now armed with a formal introduction to rhetoric and with the words of the great orators of the past, he could meld his experiences within the slave community with the classical art of oratory. It was a potent combination, one that would leave white listeners agog at his eloquence and power as a platform orator throughout his public career.

IVY G. WILSON

From *Specters of Democracy: Blackness and the Aesthetics of Politics in the Antebellum U.S.*

Ivy Wilson is an associate professor of English and the director of American Studies at Northwestern University. He teaches about the black diaspora, with a special focus on African American literature. This selection comes from Wilson's *Specters of Democracy: Blackness and the Aesthetics of Nationalism* (2014), which examines how images and descriptions of blackness informed conceptions of citizenship, equality, and democracy in the antebellum United States. The essay included here offers insight into Douglass's interaction with other black leaders, especially Samuel Ringgold Ward. Ward's reading of the U.S. Constitution as an antislavery document played a crucial role in shifting Douglass's thinking away from Garrisonianism. Wilson examines the African American political and oratorical context surrounding the debate about the legality of slavery and how it informed Douglass's speech "What to the Slave Is the Fourth of July?"

I n the 1850s, Douglass's speech cadences were increasingly shaped by the contours of debate. Debates with his African American counterparts were especially important because they covered a range of political thought and demarcated the lines of the black public sphere in the antebellum North. Public debates among members of the black public sphere informed not only Douglass's political ideology but also his style as a wordsmith.

One of Douglass's first formal debates was with Samuel Ringgold Ward on whether the Constitution was pro-slavery or antislavery. When the two met to debate in 1849, Douglass had become increasingly self-conscious that his early career with the Massachusetts Anti-Slavery Society had already delimited his voice too much— both his message and his intonation, his content and his style. Ward was an important figure in the black public sphere who at different times acted as an agent for the *Weekly Advocate* and the *Colored American*, a lecturer with the New York State Anti-Slavery Society, and spokesman for the Liberty Party after 1844. He was also a formidable orator. . . .

After the debate with Ward, Douglass began to slowly diminish his association with the Garrisonians and increasingly moved toward Gerrit Smith and others who believed that the Constitution was an antislavery document eventually leading to Douglass venerating the document in his Fourth of July oration. This was an important moment in his reevaluation of the relationship of African Americans to democratic ideals and the realpolitik of govermentality. By adopting this viewpoint, Douglass essentially became a strict constructionist. In reversing his earlier position, Douglass worked against the grain of two of the most prominent members of the black public sphere: William Wells Brown and Frances Ellen Watkins Harper. In his speech before the Paris Peace Congress in 1849, Brown proclaimed he had "no Constitution, and no country." Ten years later, writing for the *National Anti-Slavery Standard*, Watkins Harper lamented that she had "never [seen] so clearly the nature and intent of the Constitution before" because of the how the fugitive clause veiled its "dark intent" under specious words.

The strategy of "What to the Slave Is the Fourth of July?" was to intertwine African American emancipation with the preservation of democracy for the nation—an interconnection that is disclosed when one considers Douglass's position on constitutionalism. He must appeal for the abolition of slavery by stating that the institution is anathema to the nation's idealized principles of the Declaration of

Independence and the plain mandates of the Constitution. Douglass did condemn the Fugitive Slave Law, but he could not attack
the entire legal infrastructure of the nation outlined in the Constitution. He knew that his final recourse for the abolition of slavery
must be mandated by laws that would ultimately be guaranteed by
the Constitution and, therefore, could not risk merely positioning
the Declaration of Independence and the Constitution as antipodal.
What Douglass is striving for here is a veritable harmonic accord
in his oration that attempts to approximate—or, even more stra-
tegically, function as a proxy for—acts of political consensus. He
therefore characterizes the use of the Constitution to support slavery as a betrayal of "the illustrious Fathers of this Republic": "But
I differ from those who charge this baseness on the framers of the
Constitution of the United States. *It is slander upon their memory,*
at least, so I believe. . . . In *that* instrument I hold there is neither
warrant, license, nor sanction of the hateful thing; but, interpreted,
as it *ought* to be interpreted, the Constitution is a GLORIOUS LIB-
ERTY DOCUMENT."

Douglass rehabilitates the Constitution, essentially positioning
it as equally "a GLORIOUS LIBERTY DOCUMENT" as the Declaration of Independence, by suggesting that its misapplication to the
maintenance of slavery is an issue of hermeneutics. Slavery as an
institution, he contends, can find no legal support if the document
is understood "as it *ought* to be interpreted." Elsewhere, he argued,
"Slavery has taught us to read history backwards, sitting at the feet
of Calhoun and Taney." His hermeneutic positioning of the meaning
of the Constitution preserves the sanctity and authority of the governing document of the nation and shields the myth of the founding fathers. Since he fully knew that many of the founding fathers
themselves owned slaves, his statement that it is "slander upon their
memory" to suggest that the architects of the Constitution provided
language to protect slavery is wryly furtive.

No moment better illuminates Douglass's view of the Constitution in the 1850s than his debates with Charles Lenox Remond, a

staunch Garrisonian who became somewhat of a rival of Douglass and strongly advocated the dissolution of the Union. In one of his earliest speeches on the dissolution of the Union, Remond argued that it was necessary to come to terms with "the present practical workings of the American Constitution." Over the course of two days in May 1857, against the backdrop of the recent Supreme Court decision in *Dred Scott v. Sanford,* Remond and Douglass held court at the Shiloh Presbyterian Church in New York City. As Ward had done earlier, Douglass now insisted upon the necessity of adhering to "the plain meaning of the language" of the Constitution: "read, then, the preamble to the Constitution of the United States. Note how it starts: 'We the people of the United States'—not we the horses—not we the white people, but 'we the people, in order to form a more perfect union, establish justice,°°° and secure the blessings of liberty to'—not the white people, but 'ourselves and our posterity, do ordain,' &c." Douglass used a variation of this passage and other elements from the debate to craft a pamphlet that he later published. Importantly, the debate illustrates the necessity of both speech and print for antebellum free blacks. To level his critique against Remond and the Garrisonians, Douglass had to condemn the appearance of the apparitional, in the sense that the apparitional is construed as the evidence of things not seen: "The word slave, or slaveholder, is not in the Constitution. . . . They tell us, though, that the framers of the Constitution had a subtle and occult meaning under their plain words. The people did not adopt occult, under-current meanings. They adopted the plain reading with its obvious intentions." Here, Douglass militates against the "subtle" and the "occult" as things that haunt the United States and prevent the Constitution from being properly understood and democratic practices from being properly performed.

As significant as the debates between Ward, Douglass, and Remond were to African American critiques of constitutionalism, they also prompted a consideration regarding the stylistics of oratory and its efficacy as a mode of political critique. William J. Wilson, who would become an important contributor to *Frederick Douglass' Paper* and the *Anglo-African Magazine,* recorded his thoughts on the Ward-Douglass debate and published them later under the title "A Leaf from My Scrap Book" in Julia Griffiths's 1854 edition of *Autographs for Freedom.* In Wilson's estimation, Douglass's speech was too ornate, overwrought even, and its very ornamentation threatened to obfuscate the central core of his message. According to Wilson, Douglass often spoke "with copiousness of language, and finish of diction," where, even when his "ideas fail, words come to his aid—arranging themselves, as it were, so completely, that they not only captivate, but often deceive us for ideas." Ward, on the other hand, was "concise without abruptness—without extraordinary stress, always clear and forcible; if sparing of ornament, never inelegant." The chief distinction between Ward and Douglass for Wilson was that while Ward's appeals were directed to "understanding," Douglass's were directed to "imagination," by which Wilson means the sensational over the cognitive, appeal over logic.

Wilson's assessment of the Ward-Douglass debate reveals an important instance of how cognizant mid-nineteenth-century African Americans were of the contemporaneous discussions about oratory as a form of art. Wilson himself repeatedly assesses the Ward-Douglass speeches not in terms of their messages or discourse per se but rather as art. More specifically with respect to a theory of art, Wilson underscores the connection between orality and visuality. "Douglass' imagery is fine—vivid—often gaudily painted," he contends, whereas "Ward's picture [is] bold, strong, glowing." Wilson's commentary also deploys a vocabulary that features terms like "picturesque" and "sublime" that were increasingly being associated specifically with visual artifacts.

Excerpt from *Specters of Democracy: Blackness and the Aesthetics of Politics in the Antebellum U.S.,* by Ivy G. Wilson © 2011, Oxford University Press.

RICHARD W. LEEMAN

From "Fighting for Freedom Again: African American Reform Rhetoric in the Late Nineteenth Century"

A professor in the Department of Communication Studies at the University of North Carolina, Charlotte, Richard Leeman has published seven books on rhetoric, public address, political communication, and African American oratory. In the essay excerpted below, Leeman examines the adoption, adaptation, or rejection of Social Darwinism as a discourse for describing the experience of African Americans in the United States. Leeman considers the work of a wide-range of black leaders, especially Frederick Douglass, Alexander Crummell, Anna Julia Cooper, Booker T. Washington, Henry McNeal Turner, and W. E. B. Du Bois. He concludes that the genetic determinism central to this model of human development "presented a tremendous rhetorical obstacle in the late nineteenth century" to African American advancement. Moreover, Leeman argues that "from the vantage point of our own era, one where the laissez-faire economic principle of 'let the market decide' has reemerged as a major voice, and where there is a growing claim in the white community that African Americans have now been 'given a chance,' the rhetorical problems and strategies of the post-Reconstruction era may appear modern indeed."

Social Darwinism

In 1859 Charles Darwin published his theory of evolution in *On the Origin of Species*. As early as 1865 the Social Darwinist move-

ment had begun applying Darwinian theory to the study of sociology. Arguing that human beings are subject to the same biological
laws as other living organisms, sociologists found in the Darwinian
principle of natural selection an objective lens by which to understand human behavior. Life, for the Social Darwinist, is a struggle
for existence against the forces of nature. Through our inheritance
from our parents, wrote Professor William Graham Sumner, a major American populizer of the theory, "the human race keeps up a
constantly advancing contest with Nature. The penalty of ceasing
aggressive behavior toward the hardships of life on the part of mankind is, that we go backward. We cannot stand still." As set out in
the theory of natural selection, those who are weak will fail. Social
economist Walter Bagehot, a leading British theorist, argued that
"nature disheartened in each generation the ill-fitted members of
each customary group, and so deprived them of their full vigor or,
if they were weakly, killed them." Conversely, as captured in the
phrase "survival of the fittest," Social Darwinists held that those who
are ablest among us will succeed the most. "Only the elite of the
race," wrote Sumner, "has yet been raised to the point where reason
and conscience can even curb the lower motive forces. For the mass
of mankind . . . the price of better things is too severe, for that price
can be summed up in one word—self-control."

Social Darwinists typically argued that there were two arenas in
which humans competed and from which the fittest emerged victorious. The most obvious arena was war, but there was a second,
more ubiquitous battlefield: economic competition. The wealthiest
individuals were, by definition, the fittest. Sumner's argument was
representative of how Social Darwinists treated this proof that success equaled fitness, and of the advantages that resulted from this
natural order of things:

> If Mr. A. T. Stewart made a great fortune by collecting and bring-
> ing dry-goods to the people of the United States, he did so be-
> cause he understood how to do that thing better than any other

man of his generation. . . . It was for the benefit of all; but he contributed to it what no one else was able to contribute—the one guiding mind which made that whole thing possible.

Using de facto reasoning, Sumner could conclude that Stewart was the only man who had the tremendous ability to create his dry goods empire because Stewart was the only man who *had* created it. Stewart's superior success was the "proof" of his superior fitness.

What was true in the case of individuals, Social Darwinists argued, was also true in the case of race. The Aryan race, for example, had succeeded because it possessed a "good aptitude—an excellent political nature" for the forms of government needed to sustain economic and military superiority. "*Intellectual* progress" and "*moral* quality" were the "preliminary" virtues needed to succeed in war and the economy, because "those kinds of morals and that kind of religion which tend to make the firmest and most effectual character are sure to prevail, all else being the same." In contrast to the Aryans, other races were "lesser," some considerably so. . . .

Social Darwinism quickly permeated and influenced much of American thought in the late nineteenth century. Richard Hofstadter writes that the United States during the last three decades of the nineteenth century and at the beginning of the twentieth century was *the* Darwinian country. Social Darwinism was seized upon as a welcome addition, perhaps the most powerful of all, to the conservative thought that dominated this period of rapid and striking economic change. Social Darwinism validated America's natural inclination toward rugged individualism and laissez-faire government. It appealed to a growing affinity for scientific explanations, and it helped justify the extraordinary rise of industrialism. It also justified the principle of manifest destiny and the unequal treatment of America's citizens of color. It was, historian August Meier notes, a racist philosophy. A pervasive, almost omnipresent force in that era's intellectual landscape, Social Darwinism was the lens through which most white Americans viewed any discourse by African

Americans. In addition, many African Americans subscribed to its
basic tenets. Any rhetoric of the era that addressed the issue of race
would be understood within the context of Social Darwinism.

"Let Him Alone"

With the exception of the separatists, who believed that white
America would never change, most of the rhetors of the Reconstruction and early post-Reconstruction period constructed their
discourse around the demand that African Americans be given "a
chance." Emphasizing the need for legal equality, such discourse
has been classified as integrationist or amalgamationist, depending
on the rhetor's stance vis-à-vis cultural assimilation. However, this
common theme of equal opportunity, a chance to run the race of
life, not only reflected the prevalent emphasis on liberty and rugged individualism, it also participated in the developing discourse
of Social Darwinism.

Representative Richard Cain, speaking on behalf of the Civil
Rights Act of 1875, gave voice to this theme of a chance: "What
we desire is this: inasmuch as we have been raised to the dignity, to
the honor, to the position of our manhood, we ask that the laws of
this country should guarantee all the rights and immunities belonging to that proud position, to be enforced all over this broad land."
"All that we ask," he continued, "is equal laws, equal legislation,
and equal rights throughout the length and breadth of this land."
Throughout this era, other African Americans repeated that call:
give us an equal chance, and we will show you what we can do. During that same 1875 debate, Representative James T. Rapier summarized the argument vividly:

> I have always found more prejudice existing in the breasts of men
> who have feeble minds and are conscious of it, than in the breasts
> of those who have towering intellects and are aware of it. Henry

Ward Beecher reflected the feelings of the latter class when on a certain occasion he said: "Turn the Negro loose; I am not afraid to run the race of life with him."

Nor, Rapier was clearly implying, were African Americans afraid to run the race of life with Beecher, or anyone else.

This narrow call for legal equality had its historical roots in the abolition and Civil War experiences. The most salient fact about slavery was that it legally controlled the destiny of another group of human beings; "give us a chance" had been another way of saying "make slavery illegal." Then, too, the declaration of African Americans' "manhood" was critical for making the natural rights argument; the argument that legal equality would provide an equal "chance" helped buttress that declaration. For that reason Frederick Douglass and others extended the argument during the Civil War, as they focused a great deal of effort on persuading the Union to employ black troops in combat.

Indeed, Frederick Douglass is representative of the abolitionist influence on late-nineteenth-century reform rhetoric. In the antebellum and Civil War eras, Douglass had been the preeminent African American orator. An escaped slave who was self-taught, Douglass had burst on the scene in 1841 at the age of twenty-three. He toured New England and the British Isles as an abolitionist speaker, until his freedom was purchased by the donations of supporters. Back in America, he pursued abolition through the spoken word as an orator and through the written word as the publisher of the Rochester *North Star* and other abolitionist papers. During the Civil War, he lobbied Lincoln and the Republicans to declare the Civil War a battle against slavery and to open up the army ranks to African American combatants.

Douglass remained an influential and active reformer in the postwar period until his death in 1895. He did, however, encounter increasing opposition to his stands within the black community, especially for his support of the Republican Party and his criticism of the Exoduster migration of Southern blacks to the Kansas area. Still, he was a vocal supporter of equal rights for women as well as African Americans, and vigorously attacked the rise of lynching as a tool for racial intimidation. While one can find a variety of strains in the thirty years of Douglass's postwar rhetoric, his lecture "Self-Made Men," delivered on numerous occasions between 1859 and 1893, is typical of the "let him alone" rhetoric.

"Self-Made Men" articulated the qualities that allowed self-made men to succeed. Douglass postulated that life was a "race" or "struggle" governed by the laws of nature. "The natural laws for the government, well-being and progress of mankind," he said, "seem to be equal and are equal; but the subjects of these laws everywhere abound in inequalities, discords and contrasts." These "inequalities, discords and contrasts" were, Douglass argued, due to the willingness of the subject to work: "We may explain success mainly by one word and that word is WORK! WORK!! WORK!!! WORK!!!!" "Nature has no use for unused power," he warned, and "admits no preemption without occupation." Exertion improves the talent used in the exertion, and labor develops fortitude and perseverance. He summarized, "My theory of self-made men is that they are men of work." Douglass allowed that other qualities could play a part, but they were "subordinate" to the willingness to work.

That willingness to work was, it was assumed, within the individual's prerogative. "Everyone may avail himself of this marvelous power, if he will," Douglass asserted. "Every man," he declared, "has his chance." Self-made men were thus the "architects of their own good fortunes": "When we find a man who has ascended heights beyond ourselves; who has a broader range of vision than we and a sky with more stars in it than we have in ours, we may know that he has worked harder, better and more wisely than we." Moreover, America was singular in its encouragement of self-made men. "America is said," he argued, "and not without reason, to be preeminently the home and patron of self-made men." There were many reasons for this, Douglass claimed: the respectability of labor, especially now that slavery was abolished; the restless "sea" of activity that marked the society; and, first and foremost, "the principle of measuring and valuing men according to their respective merits." "Our national genius," Douglass concluded, "welcomes humanity from every quarter and grants to all an equal chance in the race of life."

Twice in the speech Douglass addressed himself to the question of how this theory of self-made men related to African Americans. In the first instance, Douglass raised the question explicitly, and initially provided a laissez-faire response that echoed Rapier's passage above: "My general answer is 'Give the negro fair play and let him alone. If he lives, well. If he dies, equally well. If he cannot stand up, let him fall down.'" Shortly after, however, Douglass hinted at a problem with a narrow definition of "fair play":

> It is not fair play to start the negro out in life, from nothing and with nothing, while other start with the advantage of a thousand years behind them. He should be measured, not by the heights other may have obtained, but from the depths from which he has come. . . . Should the American people put a school house in every valley of the South and a church on every hill side and supply the one with teachers and the other with preachers, for a hundred years to come, they would not then have given fair play to the negro.

Douglass followed his initial prescription for fair play with another: "throw open to him the doors of the schools, the factories, the workshops, and of all mechanical industries." Once given this kind of "fair play," the African American should be left alone: "For his own welfare, give him a chance to do whatever he can do well. If he fails then, let him fail! *I can, however, assure you that he will not fail.*"

This confidence in African Americans' ability to succeed, if left alone, had been a prominent feature of abolitionist discourse. The second time Douglass related his theme to African Americans, he elaborated on the idea of success. After several examples of white

self-made men, Douglass turned to the examples of Benjamin Banneker, surveyor of Washington, D. C.; William Dietz, architect, inventor, and bridge designer; and Toussaint L'Ouverture, the liberator of Haiti. The life of each of these men provided proof of the
ability of African Americans to succeed.

This common appeal to "let the Negro alone" did, however, lead
to some curious concessions in the rhetoric. The most significant of
these was in regard to voting qualifications. Time and again, African
American rhetors stated that literacy qualifications were not only
acceptable but also desirable, as long as those qualifications were
equally applied. Time and again, however, Southern states passed
literacy laws that looked equal, but were unequally applied. Beyond
these tangible losses, however, the "let him alone" rhetoric was
overwhelmed—co-opted and subsumed—by the full blossoming of
Social Darwinism.

An Ambivalent Rhetoric

Social Darwinism and its laissez-faire philosophy of letting each
person rise or fall according to his or her ability neatly fit the existing ideology of white America, but Social Darwinism also complemented the minimalist appeal of "let the Negro alone." Because
many of its principles repeated long-held American beliefs, it was
enticing not only to white Americans but to many African Americans as well. In the 1880s and early 1890s many African Americans
rhetors, especially the leading intelligentsia, found themselves attacking Social Darwinism's conclusions even as they adopted much
of its language and assumptions. The result was an ambivalent
rhetoric for which the integrationist and accommodationist labels
are not particularly helpful. It was a rhetoric that traveled in both
directions, neither fully rejecting nor fully accepting the doctrine of
Social Darwinism.

DAVID HOWARD-PITNEY

From *The Afro-American Jeremiad: Appeals for Justice in America*

David Howard-Pitney serves as professor of history at De Anza College, where he specializes in the history of American civil religion
and African American thought and rhetoric. He is the author of two
books: *Martin Luther King, Jr., Malcolm X, and the Civil Rights
Struggle* (2004) and *The African-American Jeremiad: Appeals for
Justice in America* (2005), from which this essay is taken. In this
piece, Howard-Pitney traces the development of the African American jeremiad from its American Puritan origins. This distinct form of
political sermon began with the contention that America had been
founded as a "city on a hill" with a unique mission to be a "beacon
to the world, lighting and leading the way into the millennium." But
citizens had fallen away from this ideal and were in danger of becoming an example of moral failure unless they renewed their covenant
with God and their dedication to the country's founding principles.
African American orators, Howard-Pitney finds, addressed these
jeremiads to their own people, encouraging them to strive for self-
improvement, and to white people who clung obdurately to their racist sentiments.

According to Wilson Moses, the jeremiad was the earliest expression of black nationalism and key mode of antebellum African American rhetoric. *Black jeremiad* is
Moses' term for "the constant warnings issued by blacks
to whites, concerning the judgment that was to come from the sin of
slavery." In this ubiquitous rhetorical convention, blacks "revealed

579

a conception of themselves as a chosen people" as well as "a clever ability to play on the belief that America as a whole was a chosen nation with a covenantal duty to deal justly with the blacks."

Messianic themes of coming liberation and social redemption have deep roots in African American culture. The biblical motif of the Exodus of the chosen people from Egyptian slavery to a Promised Land of freedom was central to the black socioreligious imagination. African Americans, by virtue of their unjust bondage, felt that they had a messianic role in achieving their own and others' redemption. Similar themes of messianic purpose and identity and of a historical Exodus figured prominently in both black and white antebellum culture. The interconnected development of a strong commitment by African Americans and Anglo-Americans to evangelical Protestantism in the two generations before the Civil War encouraged black leaders to believe that Northern whites would respond to their denunciation of the sin of slavery as declension from the promise of a Christian America.

The abolitionist jeremiad sometimes crossed the color line to appear in the reflections of prominent whites. Proud nationalists of the early Republic hailed their revolution as the greatest advance for humanity in all history. Having so recently resisted a tyrannical plot to enslave free men, Americans were not entirely oblivious to the stark contradiction of the nation's professed ideals involved in the enslavement of Africans in America. Thomas Jefferson worried about the fate of liberty in a land that tolerated the systematic denial of the most basic rights to millions of people. Believing that "liberties are the gift of God . . . not violated but with His wrath," Jefferson lamented, "I tremble for my country when I reflect that God is just."

Far stronger were the fierce condemnations of slavery hurled at white Americans by black abolitionist jeremiahs such as David Walker. Walker was born legally free to a slave father and free mother in North Carolina in 1785. At the age of thirty, he left the South vowing to avenge the wrongs against his people and moved to Boston where he became a militant abolitionist journalist. He was among the most socially advantaged African Americans and, while his fiery rhetoric expressed alienation from the land of his birth, his skillful use of jeremiadic rhetoric reflected his active participation in the highest ideals of American society. In his famous 1829 pamphlet, *The Appeal,* Walker bitterly charged "this Republican land" with gross hypocrisy and called down God's wrath on America: "Oh Americans! Americans! I warn you in the name of the Lord . . . to repent and reform, or you are ruined!" Despite the *Appeal's* rhetorical threats of violent black revenge, it ended with the optimistic prediction that God meant yet to melt the hearts of white Americans and save them from their folly.

It is ironic that this earliest expression of messianic black nationalism in America should have sprung up in such close proximity to Anglo-American nationalism. For leading black spokespersons' use of American jeremiadic rhetoric signals their virtually complete acceptance of and incorporation into the national cultural norm of millennial faith in America's promise. Yet the African American jeremiad also expressed black nationalist faith in the missionary destiny of the African race and was a leading instrument of black social assertion in America. . . .

Douglass's Antebellum Jeremiad

So began Frederick Douglass's career as his era's outstanding African American jeremiah. In adopting this mode of rhetoric, he was influenced by two distinct yet interrelated American traditions. First, he was immersed in African American culture and religion. He patterned much of his oratorical style after the Southern black preachers and storytellers he heard in his days as a slave. He witnessed black ministers swaying revival crowds and was familiar with the style as well as content of popular black religion. In his oratory, he regularly drew on staple black social-religious motifs like the Exodus story, Jehovah the deliverer of the weak and oppressed, and assorted messianic symbols and millennial prophecies. Second, as a man of two races and cultures, Douglass also absorbed mainstream American culture and religion, especially of the New England social reformist variety. Once in the North, he sank deep roots in this middle-class Evangelical milieu. His activities brought him into contact with the descendants of American Puritanism and exposed him to Puritan-influenced modes of thought and language. The social metaphors of the Exodus, the Promised Land, and the Second Coming, of course, also had a major place in Anglo-American Protestantism. Drawing on messianic themes common to both sides of his cultural heritage, the jeremiad offered Douglass a potent tool for appealing to both black and white audiences.

Speaking as a jeremiah to whites, Douglass forthrightly condemned the practice of slavery as representing severe declension from the promise of a fully Christian democratic America. He excoriated his countrymen for their sinful conduct and threatened them with God's just wrath. "We shall not go unpunished," he predicted; "a terrible retribution awaits us." During the 1840s and 1850s Douglass spoke bravely, angrily denouncing slavery as an abomination to God and curse to the nation. He declared that blacks had a patriotic duty "to warn our fellow countrymen" of the impending doom they courted and to dissuade America from "rushing on in her wicked career" along a path "ditched with human blood, and paved with human skulls," so that "our country may yet be saved."

His prophecy concerning America, however, was just as significant as his harsh condemnation of its faults. The civil religion provided the basis for his stubborn optimism about the future for American blacks. In jeremiah fashion, Douglass denounced the multiplying present evils but drew on the nation's sacred promise to announce his undying faith in the eventual liberation of African Americans and, through it, the realization of America's democratic mission.

A typical prewar jeremiad exemplifying this faith was an 1857 oration protesting the Dred Scott decision by the Supreme Court upholding a master's right to human property throughout the United

States. Douglass interpreted this legal victory for slavery, along with other "signs and events," as "omens" signaling a dangerous slide away from the national mission. Yet at the same time, he discerned "that the finger of the Almighty may be . . . bringing good out of evil . . . hastening the triumph of righteousness." Douglass appealed to America's sacred promise to support his mysteriously optimistic conclusion. "The American people, above all others," he declared, "have been called" to abolish slavery and institute a righteous reign of freedom. "Come what will," he still believed that liberty was "destined to become the settled law of this Republic." Viewed through prophetic lens, the Dred Scott decision and the public furor it aroused were "another proof that God does not mean we shall go to sleep" but would shortly rouse Americans to save the nation and its mission. The jeremiadic elements of promise, declension, and prophecy were central in this speech, as in most of Douglass's antebellum oratory.

Douglass spoke to many kinds of audiences, ranging from large to small, sympathetic to hostile, and from all-white lyceums to all-Negro conventions. A masterful orator, he skillfully tailored his message and delivery to different audiences. He paid special attention to an audience's racial makeup. Once for example, when an unexpectedly large number of whites came to hear him at a black church, he felt compelled to alter his prepared remarks, explaining, "There are some things which ought to be said to colored people in the peculiar circumstances in which they are placed, that can be said more effectively among ourselves, without the presence of white persons. We are the oppressed, the whites are the oppressors, and the language I would address to the one is not always suited to the other."

GRANVILLE GANTER

From "'He Made Us Laugh Some': Frederick Douglass's Humor"

Granville Ganter teaches nineteenth-century American, African American, and Native American literature at St. John's University, in Jamaica, New York. He has published extensively on oratory, rhetoric, and performance from the colonial period through the Civil War. The article excerpted below won the 2004 award for the best essay in the *African American Review*. It challenges the dominant view that readers and scholars have had of Frederick Douglass. While many of Douglass's peers vividly remembered his humor, recent scholarship has tended to emphasize Douglass's political jeremiads, thundering voice, and leonine presence at the podium. Ganter's article illuminates Douglass's use of humor, which has been underappreciated as a potent organizing device.

O ne of the primary means of Douglass's early success as an abolitionist lecturer was his skill as a mimic—in particular, his burlesques of slaveholding consciousness. Early in his career, in 1842, Douglass spoke on two consecutive days at Lanesborough Seminary in Massachusetts. While we do not have extensive records of these early speeches, one young seminary student wrote in his diary that Douglass "made us laugh some" by illustrating the hypocrisy of the Christian slaveholders.

The student was referring to Douglass's imitation of a pro-slavery minister on the theme of "Servants, Obey Your Masters." This satire was a central part of Douglass's speaking repertoire from his very first months as a Garrisonian lecturer. To begin his satire, Douglass buttoned his coat up to his neck and assumed a stern countenance. Imitating the canting voice of a hypocritical preacher, Douglass then gave a several-paragraph sermon based on the principle that obedience to the slavemaster is obedience to God. Pretending to speak to a slave congregation, Douglass would begin: "I know your prayer is daily, 'Lord, what wilt though have me do?'" After a dramatic pause, Douglass would respond gravely, "The answer to that is given in the text, 'Obey your masters.'" His audiences exploded with laughter at Douglass's bathetic drop in tone, a strategy which set the general rhythm for the speech that followed. In each of his remaining remarks, he painted a grossly idealized picture of slave life whose consistent moral was the solemn advice to "Obey your masters."

In his role as a white minister, Douglass's next move was a brief demonstration that slave unhappiness was a result of disobedience. During his tour of England in 1846, Douglass illustrated this point with a story about Sam, whose master beat him for falling asleep after being told to weed the garden. When his master got there,

> Lo and behold! there lay Sam's hoe, and Sam was lying fast asleep in the corner of the place. (Laughter). Think of the feelings of the pious master! His commands disobeyed, his work not done, his authority thrown off. The good man went to look at the law and testimony, to know his duty on the premises, and there he was instructed that "he that knoweth his master's will and doeth it not, shall be beaten with many stripes." Sam was therefore taken up and lashed, so as not to be able to work for a week. Oh then, if you would not be whipped, be very obedient to your master.

In this tableau of discovery, Douglass's portrait of Sam generates a tension which, I argue, is representative of a comic strategy he performs throughout his literary career. On one level, Douglass exploits the stereotype of a lazy slave in this anecdote, a technique that could backfire because it materializes the very prejudices he seeks to disarm. Indeed, in many other versions of this speech, Douglass emphasizes the language of prejudice by identifying the lazy slave by the name of "Sambo." At the same time, however, Douglass uses such character-typing to make a different kind of discovery: Sam's lapse of duty, which is understandable in the context of forced labor, is a far less serious crime than the slaveholders' misuse of Scripture. Invoking an Augustinian distinction between obedience to God's will and obedience to man, Douglass's burlesque implicitly argues that the slaveholder's Christian duties toward mankind exceed the lesser claims of personal ownership.

Douglass gets his audiences to laugh at the Southern minister's hubris and hypocrisy, but the scene's comic intensity comes from the interplay of both bigoted and non-bigoted laughter. As he does in the night train story from his *Life and Times*, here Douglass's paradoxical expression of prejudice to fight prejudice generates tension. As Douglass slides the emphasis of the joke from the exhausted slave toward the slaveholder, however, he begins to reorient the audience's sense of community affiliation. They reflexively laugh at the lazy slave, but they also learn to laugh at the master, an imaginative act that pushes Douglass's audience to change its sense of group identification.

Douglass's use of stereotyping relies crucially on his ability to modulate his performance in combination with his audience's reactions. The act of laughing with others can be a moment of sharing and bonding, which, in contrast to private acts of affiliation and sympathy while reading, gains infectious strength through its publicity. Exploiting the good mood of his laughing audience, Douglass takes audience members from their prejudiced habits of laughing at plantation stereotypes and moves them toward communal laughter at the slaveholders' hypocrisy. Speech theorist Ernest Bormann, drawing on Robert F. Bales's studies of small-group interaction, has described this phenomenon of public consent as the creation of common culture. Toward the end of this essay, I connect Douglass's techniques of humor to eighteenth-century republican traditions of satire, but for now I want to emphasize that Douglass borrows from the language of one group (a prejudiced one that laughs at stereotypes of lazy slaves) for the tools to push his auditors and readers toward a new sense of themselves as human beings and a nation. Douglass's skill at rearranging and reorienting the boundaries of self-and-society is the engine that drives some of his most humorous and violent rhetoric.

From the well-worn jest about slaves who will not work, Douglass turns to another likely audience prejudice—the primitive state of Africa:

> Let us take a view of Africa. Africa, degraded, lost, and ruined Africa. There are no sanctuaries there; no Gospel privileges there. Men are groping their way in the blindness of heathenism, without God, and without hope; and the Lord seeing you in this wretched state, put it into the hearts of good men —of pious men, to leave their homes and their families, that they might snatch you as brands from the burning, and bring you into this Christian country.

Douglass's achievement in this passage is to transform the exaggerated deficiencies of African life into an illustration of the moral deficiencies of the slaves' purported rescuers, the "pious" slavetraders. Although Douglass does little to diminish his audience's prejudices against Africa, he places most of the moral blame on those men who claim to know better. In the same way that the slavecatchers steal Africans, Douglass, in turn, poaches from their rhetoric—"degraded Africa"—for the instruments to highlight their crimes. The genius of Douglass's comic strategy is that he redirects the slaveholders' logic, inverting their sense of social status and entitlement.

At the conclusion of the sermon, Douglass's final move is an explicit attempt to transform his white audience's sense of itself. Making a distinction between mental and physical labor, Douglass addresses audience members as if they were slaves with an undeveloped intellect:

> You have hard hands, strong frames, robust constitutions, and black skins. Your masters and mistresses have soft hands, long

slender fingers, delicate constitutions, and white skins. Now, servants, let me put to you a question. Whence these differences? "It is the Lord's doing and marvelous in our eyes." (Applause and laughter.) Thus, then, you see that you are most able to do the work, to labor and toil. You have superior strength to your masters. But, oh! servants, as a minister of the Gospel, let me exhort you not to boast of your strength—boast not of your strength, for that was given to you in lieu of something else. And recollect your relation to your masters does not place you in light of benefactors, for while you are dispensing blessings on them, they are returning blessing on you. You have not so much intellect as your masters. You could not think whether such things are a benefit to you or not. You could not take care of yourselves. Your masters have the best reason and intellect. They can provide and take care of you. Oh! blessed is God, in providing one class of men to do the work, and the other to think.

Douglass's burlesque manifests the hypocrisy of slavery in the character of the minister he is impersonating. He deliberately lists the clichés of black racial inferiority, speaking to white audience members as if they were a black congregation. Douglass asks them to measure the virtue of the slaveholder's sermon for themselves, looking at their own hands, bodies, and sense of agency. From their new perspective as a slave congregation, Douglass's audience is obliged to recognize the minister himself as a source of oppression. Even further, Douglass here attempts to dismantle the distinction between mental and manual labor, exploiting assumptions about the difference between the ignorant and the educated by implicitly suggesting that the thought of the working classes is meaningful knowledge.

Part of the success of Douglass's sermon was based on a claim of verisimilitude. Douglass often framed his parody by telling his audiences that he modeled his text on an actual edition of sermons for slaveholders written by Thomas Bacon in the eighteenth century (and edited in 1836 by Bishop William Meade). Although the sermons in Bacon's text are accompanied by anti-slavery songs, and Bacon's sermons themselves do not wholly condone slavery in the way Douglass alleges, Douglass would flaunt the text before the crowd as if it were the devil's own book. Apparently, it was a hilarious performance. Even fifty years later, in her obituary on Douglass's death, Elizabeth Cady Stanton would memorialize Douglass's sermon satire as one of the unforgettable moments of her generation's anti-slavery experience.

Douglass's satire is important in several ways. First, it illustrates his relationship to a black comic tradition vexed by contrary impulses of assimilation and resistance. As Dickson Preston discovered, Douglass was distinguished for his intelligence and humor while a young slave at St. Michael's. His masters' belief that he could easily adapt to the complexities of city life was one of the reasons he was chosen to go to Baltimore to serve the Aulds. He learned to successfully mimic white speech patterns from close contact with Daniel Lloyd and others. These imitations formed the beginning of his literary training. Frederic Holland reports that, when Douglass was very young, he practiced his clerical satires by addressing the pigs as "Dear Brethren" in imitation of local ministers. In the paradoxical economy of slave virtue, Douglass's skill at mocking the master caste earned him a marginally greater degree of freedom than his peers.

In terms of its subversive potential, Douglass's comic talent has equivocal significance. On one hand, it suggests Douglass's inheritance of African traditions of tricksterism and double-voiced narrative. Henry Louis Gates's work on the trope of signifyin' has attuned a generation of scholars to the importance of reading for irony and ambiguity in apparently straightforward African American texts. Douglass's mimicry clearly mocks the words and conduct of his oppressors, an ironic appropriation of the master's discourse and power. In other respects however, mimicry, produced either for the entertainment of parents or for a master class, is a mode of conduct with often subordinate valences. Even when fairly sympathetic social critics, such as Harriet Beecher Stowe, acknowledge that blacks had a natural talent for imitation and mimicry, it was a poisoned tribute, denying them the capacity for original thought and creative genius. Later in his career, Douglass became a vocal opponent of minstrel humor, performed either by blacks or whites. As editor of the *North Star* in the late 1840s, Douglass consciously sought to distance himself from the plantation burlesques he had practiced in his youth.

The success of Douglass's satire also needs to be understood in terms of commercial competition for audiences. The sermon parody was a very popular genre of American humor. Satires of the ignorance and greed of American revivalist preachers were a popular jest among American humorists and European travel writers in Jacksonian America. Following Charles Matthews, Sr.'s *Trip to America* in 1824, and Matthews' later speaking tours in the early 1830s, a road show with sermon burlesques could make very good money in the United States. In an urban area, Garrisonian lecturers competed with such public events as melodramas, lectures, musical performances, and burlesques. Although Garrison was hesitant to acknowledge the realities of commercial competition in his moral campaign against slavery, Douglass's sermon satires drew numbers and made a stir. The participation of Douglass, as a recently escaped slave, in this type of parodic performance made his jest even more marketable—he was a lively commodity.

At the same time that Douglass's performance drew on sideshow appeal, it was nonetheless a powerful criticism of slaveholding consciousness. His sermon satire worked on behalf of the abolitionist cause by orienting Douglass's audiences to laugh at the Southern minister's Christian hypocrisy, not just at Douglass's highjinx as a "darky" humorist. Such cross-fertilization, however, was unavoidable, despite the fact that Douglass used his strong personal charisma as a lively refutation of racist theories of the inferiority of blacks. On the stage he spoke as an authority, not a supplicant. In the February 16, 1844, edition of the anti-slavery paper *The Herald of Freedom*, Nathaniel P. Rogers described Douglass as a "storm of insurrection," pacing the stage like a "Numidian lion." Douglass rejected John Collins's advice that he speak with a slight plantation dialect because it interfered with his poise. When he put on the mask of a buffoon, as in his preacher routines, it was so unlike the intelligence of his character that it made the performance even funnier. At the conclusion of his mock sermon, Douglass would clearly step away from his gospel burlesque, quipping his regret that such "miserable twaddle should be palmed off on the poor slave."

Chronology of Other Important Speeches and Events in Frederick Douglass's Life

Speeches marked with an asterisk are reproduced in this volume.

1818

February	Frederick Augustus Washington Bailey is born sometime in February at Holme Hill Farm on the Eastern Shore of Maryland.

1824

August	Sent to live at Wye Plantation home of his master, Aaron Anthony.

1826

March	Sent to the Fells Point district of Baltimore to work for Hugh Auld, a ship carpenter and the brother-in-law of Aaron Anthony's daughter, Lucretia Auld.

1831

Bought a used copy of Caleb Bingham's compilation of speeches, *The Columbian Orator*, which he memorized to hone his reading and speaking skills. Joined the Bethel African Methodist Episcopal Church in Baltimore after undergoing a religious conversion.

1833

March   Sent back to St. Michaels, on Maryland's Eastern
                        Shore, to live with and work for Thomas Auld, son-
                        in-law of the deceased Aaron Anthony.

6 December   William Lloyd Garrison founded the American
                        Anti-Slavery Society in Philadelphia.

1836

Mid-April   Returned to work for Hugh Auld in Baltimore, who
                        had him trained in the trade of ship caulking.

1837

                        Joined the East Baltimore Mental Improvement
                        Society, a free black debating club, and there met
                        Anna Murray, who encouraged him to save money
                        and plan an escape.

1838

3–4 September   Escaped from Maryland into Massachusetts by bor-
                        rowing papers from a free black sailor and taking a
                        train from Baltimore to New York City.

15 September   Married Anna Murray in New York City. Three days
                        later, the couple relocated to New Bedford, Mas-
                        sachusetts, for greater security from recapture.

1839

12 March   At a meeting of New Bedford blacks, denounced a
                        proposal to send freed slaves, by force, as colonists
                        to Africa.

April   Heard William Lloyd Garrison, Wendell Phil-
                        lips, and other abolitionist leaders speak in New
                        Bedford.

1841

10–12 August   Spoke on his experience as a slave at a Massachu-
                        setts Anti-Slavery Society convention in Nantucket,
                        after which he was invited to become a paid
                        lecturer.

°October   "I Have Come to Tell You Something about Slav-
                        ery," Lynn, Massachusetts.

1843

15–19 August   Successfully opposed a resolution urging slaves to rebel, put forward by Henry Highland Garnet at the National Convention of Colored Citizens, in Buffalo, New York.

16 September   Beaten by a mob during an outdoor antislavery meeting in Pendleton, Indiana.

1845

16 August   Following the publication of his first autobiography, *Narrative of the Life of Frederick Douglass, an American Slave,* departed for a twenty-one-month tour of Great Britain as an abolitionist lecturer.

1846

°30 March   "Temperance and Anti-Slavery," Paisley, Scotland.

°22 May   "American Slavery, American Religion, and the Free Church of Scotland," London, England.

12 December   British abolitionist admirers negotiated the purchase and manumission of Douglass from Hugh Auld for £150.

1847

30 March   "Farewell to the British People," London, England.

3 December   From his new home in Rochester, New York, published the first issue of his weekly newspaper, the *North Star,* in partnership with Martin R. Delany.

1848

14–15 June   Attended his first official political gathering, the National Liberty party convention in Buffalo, New York, convened by Gerrit Smith.

19–20 July   Attended the Seneca Falls Women's Rights Convention; signed the Declaration of Sentiments.

29 August   Attended the convention in Buffalo, New York, that resulted in the formation of the Free Soil party.

1849

May   A British reformer, Julia Griffiths, joined the staff of Douglass's newspaper as its unofficial business manager.

11 May   "Resolved, That the Constitution of the United
                  States, in Letter, Spirit, and Design, Is Essentially
                  Antislavery," a debate between Douglass and
                  Samuel Ringgold Ward, New York City.

1850

7 May   "Men and Brothers," American Anti-Slavery Soci-
                  ety, New York City. Douglass gave the speech de-
                  spite the disruptions caused by a street gang linked
                  with the Tammany Hall Democratic party machine.

18 September   As part of the Compromise of 1850, Congress
                  passed the new Fugitive Slave Act.

1851

April   Douglass agreed to merge the *North Star* with Ger-
                  rit Smith's struggling *Liberty Party Paper*, accept-
                  ing Smith's financial support and his antislavery
                  interpretation of the Constitution.

1852

°5 July   "What to the Slave Is the Fourth of July?," Roch-
                  ester Ladies' Anti-Slavery Society, Rochester,
                  New York.

October   Campaigned in central New York in support of
                  Gerrit Smith's successful independent candidacy
                  for the U.S. House of Representatives.

1853

January   Published his novella, "The Heroic Slave," in the
                  gift book *Autographs for Freedom*. The story is a
                  fictionalized account of Madison Washington, the
                  leader of the 1841 *Creole* slave ship mutiny.

°11 May   "A Nation in the Midst of a Nation," American and
                  Foreign Anti-Slavery Society annual meeting, New
                  York City.

6–8 July   Attended the Colored National Convention in
                  Rochester, New York; criticized by Charles Lenox
                  Remond and other black leaders for his industrial
                  school proposal, on the grounds that it would pro-
                  mote segregation.

1 December	"The Property Rights of Women," Women's Rights Convention, Rochester, New York.

1854

°12 July	"The Claims of the Negro Ethnologically Considered," Western Reserve College commencement, Hudson, Ohio.

1855

Mid-June	After six years, Julia Griffiths returned to Great Britain amid rumors of an inappropriate personal relationship with Douglass.
26–28 June	Helped found the Radical Abolitionist party at a convention in Syracuse, New York.
August	Second autobiography, *My Bondage and My Freedom,* published.

1856

Late August–early September	Campaigned for the Republican presidential ticket in Ohio.

1858

2 August	"Freedom in the West Indies," West Indian Emancipation Celebration, Poughkeepsie, New York. Douglass was injured when the platform collapsed while he was delivering the speech.

1859

February	Douglass delivered his lecture "Self-Made Men" while on a speaking tour of Illinois and Wisconsin; he would give the speech more than fifty times during his career.
16–18 October	The white abolitionist John Brown unsuccessfully attempted to start an armed slave revolt by seizing the U. S. arsenal at Harpers Ferry, Virginia. Brown had asked Douglass to join the raid, but the latter declined, believing the plan would fail.
19–21 October	To avoid being arrested in connection with the Harpers Ferry raid, Douglass fled from Philadelphia to Rochester and finally to Canada. In November, he left for Great Britain.

24 November	Began using the home of Julia Griffiths Crofts in Halifax as a base for his extensive lecturing campaign across central and northern England.

1860

13 March	Douglass's daughter, Annie, died at the age of eleven. Douglass was devastated because he was overseas when it happened. He returned to the United States in April.
°26 March	"The American Constitution and the Slave," Glasgow, Scotland; the speech was given as part of a public controversy with the British Garrisonian George Thompson over conflicting views of the standing of slavery under the U.S. Constitution.
3 December	"The Legacy of John Brown," at a commemoration of the first anniversary of John Brown's death, Boston, Massachusetts; the speech was disrupted by a mob assault.

1861

12–14 April	The attack on Fort Sumter in the harbor of Charleston, South Carolina by Confederate forces set off the Civil War.

1863

February–July	Traveled extensively in the North to recruit blacks for Union Army regiments being raised by Massachusetts.
18 May	Attended the presentation of colors by Governor John Andrew to the Fifty-fourth Massachusetts Infantry Regiment in Readville, Massachusetts.
18 July	Douglass's son Lewis was wounded in the failed assault on Fort Wagner near Charleston, South Carolina.
10 August	Had interviews with Secretary of War Edwin Stanton and President Abraham Lincoln in Washington, D.C. He returned to Rochester and issued the valedictory issue of the *Douglass' Monthly* in anticipation of receiving a military commission that never arrived.

1864

°13 January "The Mission of the War," Woman's National Loyal League, New York City.

22 May Signed a public call for a convention to replace Lincoln as the Republican presidential candidate in 1864.

19 August Met with President Lincoln in the Executive Mansion, Washington, D.C., to discuss means to recruit more slaves to run away and enlist in the Union Army.

4–6 October Presided over the National Convention of Colored Men at Syracuse, New York, and gave a lukewarm endorsement to Lincoln's reelection.

17–29 November Delivered a series of public lectures in his old hometown of Baltimore, Maryland, highlighted by a reunion with his long-separated sister Eliza Bailey Mitchell.

1865

4 March Attended Lincoln's second inauguration in Washington, D.C.

9 April General Robert E. Lee surrendered the Army of Northern Virginia to Lieutenant General Ulysses S. Grant at Appomattox Court House, Virginia, effectively ending the Civil War.

14 April President Lincoln was shot by John Wilkes Booth, Ford's Theatre, Washington, D.C.

15 April "Our Martyred President," Rochester, New York.

6 December The Thirteenth Amendment was ratified by the required number of states.

1866

7 February Member of a black delegation that had a contentious interview with President Andrew Johnson at the Executive Mansion, Washington, D.C.

1867

°7 February "Sources of Danger to the Republic," St. Louis, Missouri.

1868

14 May   "Equal Rights for All," American Equal Rights Association, New York City.

1869

°11 May   "Let the Negro Alone," American Anti-Slavery Society anniversary meeting, New York City.

°12–13 May   "We Welcome the Fifteenth Amendment," American Equal Rights Association anniversary meeting, New York City.

°7 December   "Our Composite Nationality," Parker Fraternity Lecture Course, Boston, Massachusetts.

1870

3 February   Fifteenth Amendment ratified.

1 July   Relocated to the District of Columbia and began editing the *New National Era,* which advocated black civil rights and other reforms.

1872

2 June   Douglass's home on South Avenue in Rochester, New York, burned down, most likely from arson.

°24 July   "Which Greeley Are We Voting For?," Republican party rally for President Grant's reelection campaign, Richmond, Virginia.

1873

13 April   Massacre of African Americans in Colfax, Louisiana.

°21 April   "Recollections of the Anti-Slavery Conflict," anniversary celebration of the ratification of the Fifteenth Amendment, Louisville, Kentucky.

1874

March   Appointed president of the Freedman's Savings Bank, which closed in July because of insolvency.

1876

°14 April   "The Freedmen's Monument to Abraham Lincoln," dedication ceremony, Washington, D.C.

1877

March   President Rutherford B. Hayes appointed Douglass U.S. Marshal for the District of Columbia. He

	was the first African American to receive a federal appointment requiring Senate approval.
17 June	Douglass visited his former master, Hugh Auld, on his deathbed and delivered a speech, "Coming Home," in St. Michaels, Maryland.

1878

Douglass purchased a fifteen-acre estate, which he and Anna named Cedar Hill, in the Anacostia neighborhood of the District of Columbia.

1879

12 September	"The Negro Exodus from the Gulf States," American Social Science Association, Saratoga, New York Delivered in absentia, this speech defended Douglass's unpopular position against encouraging or supporting the migration of African Americans in the wake of severe oppression after the end of Reconstruction and federal withdrawal from the South.

1881

March	President James A. Garfield appointed Douglass recorder of deeds for the District of Columbia. Douglass published his third autobiography, *Life and Times of Frederick Douglass.*
30 May	"Did John Brown Fail?," Storer College commencement, Harpers Ferry, West Virginia.

1882

Spring	Douglass hired Helen Pitts, a graduate of Mount Holyoke College and former teacher of freed blacks in Virginia and Indiana, as a clerk.
4 August	Anna Murray Douglass died.

1883

15 October	U. S. Supreme Court strikes down the Civil Rights Act of 1875.
°22 October	"This Decision Has Humbled the Nation," Civil Rights Mass-Meeting, Washington, D.C.
°20 November	"'It Moves,' or the Philosophy of Reform," Bethel Literary Historical Association, Washington, D.C.

1884

24 January   Married Helen Pitts, a younger white woman. Their
                    interracial relationship caused a public controversy
                    and brought disapproval from many members of
                    both families.

1886

15 September   Douglass and Helen sailed from New York City
                    aboard the *City of Rome* to England. From there
                    they traveled to France, Italy, Egypt, and Greece on
                    an extended honeymoon.

1887

11 August   Returned to the United States.

1888

°28 May   "I Am a Radical Woman Suffrage Man," New
                    England Woman Suffrage Association annual con-
                    vention, Boston, Massachusetts.

19 June   "Continue to Wave the Bloody Shirt," National
                    Republican Party Convention, Chicago, Illinois.

1889

July   Douglass accepted President Benjamin Harrison's
                    appointment as U.S. minister resident and consul
                    general to Haiti.

14 November   "The Highest Honor Conferred on Me," Port-au-
                    Prince, Haiti.

1890

21 October   "The Negro Problem," Bethel Literary and His-
                    torical Association, Washington, D.C. This was an
                    earlier version of Douglass's "Lessons of the Hour."

1891

3 July   Returned to the United States, by way of New York
                    City, while on leave from his Haitian post, which he
                    resigned in August.

1893

2 January   "Haiti among the Foremost Civilized Nations of the
                    Earth" and "Haiti and the Haitian People," Chi-
                    cago, Illinois. Douglass presided over the dedication

of the Haitian Pavilion at the World's Columbian Exposition.

°March   "Self-Made Men," Carlisle Indian Industrial School, Carlisle, Pennsylvania.

1894

°9 January   "Lessons of the Hour," Washington, D.C.

1895

20 February   Frederick Douglass died at Cedar Hill in Washington, D.C., after attending a women's rights convention.

Selected Bibliography

Works marked with an asterisk are excerpted in this volume.

Other Works by Frederick Douglass

Blassingame, John W., et al., eds. *The Frederick Douglass Papers.*
9 vols. New Haven, Conn.: Yale University Press, 1979–.
Foner, Philip, ed. *Life and Writings of Frederick Douglass.* 5 vols.
New York: International Publishers, 1950–75.
McKivigan, John R., and Heather L. Kaufman, eds. *In the Words of
Frederick Douglass: Quotations from Liberty's Champion.* Ithaca,
N.Y.: Cornell University Press, 2012.

Frederick Douglass Scholarship

Andrews, William, ed. *The Oxford Frederick Douglass Reader.* New
York: Oxford University Press, 1996.
Blight, David W. *Frederick Douglass' Civil War: Keeping the Faith in
Jubilee.* Baton Rouge: Louisiana State University Press, 1989.
Foner, Philip S. *Frederick Douglass.* New York: Citadel, 1950.
Kendrick, Paul, and Stephen Kendrick. *Douglass and Lincoln: How a
Revolutionary Black Leader and a Reluctant Liberator Struggled to
End Slavery and Save the Union.* New York: Walker, 2008.

Larson, Bill, and Kirkland, Frank, eds. *Frederick Douglass: A Critical Reader.* New York: Wiley-Blackwell, 1999.

Lee, Maurice S., ed. *The Cambridge Companion to Frederick Douglass.* Cambridge: Cambridge University Press, 2009.

Levine, Robert S. *The Lives of Frederick Douglass.* Cambridge, Mass.: Harvard University Press, 2016.

———. *Martin Delany, Frederick Douglass, and the Politics of Representative Identity.* Chapel Hill: University of North Carolina Press, 1997.

Martin, Waldo E., Jr. *The Mind of Frederick Douglass.* Chapel Hill: University of North Carolina Press, 1984.

McFeely, William S. *Frederick Douglass.* New York: Norton, 1991.

Myers, Peter C. *Frederick Douglass: Race and the Rebirth of American Liberalism.* Lawrence: University of Kansas Press, 2008.

Oakes, James. *The Radical and the Republican: Frederick Douglass, Abraham Lincoln, and the Triumph of Antislavery Politics.* New York: Norton, 2007.

Preston, Dickson J. *Young Frederick Douglass: The Maryland Years.* Baltimore: Johns Hopkins University Press, 1980.

Quarles, Benjamin. *Frederick Douglass.* New York: Athenaeum, 1968.

Rice, Allan J., and Martin Crawford. *Liberating Sojourn: Frederick Douglass and Transatlantic Reform.* Athens: University of Georgia Press, 1999.

Stauffer, John. *Giants: The Parallel Lives of Frederick Douglass and Abraham Lincoln.* New York: Twelve Publishers, 2009.

Stauffer, John, et al. *Picturing Frederick Douglass: An Illustrated Biography of the Nineteenth Century's Most Photographed American.* New York: Liveright, 2015.

Sweeney, Fionnghuala. *Frederick Douglass and the Atlantic World.* Liverpool, UK: Liverpool University Press, 2007.

Washington, Booker T. *Frederick Douglass.* Philadelphia: Jacobs, 1906.

Scholarship on Douglass's Oratory

Adams, Amanda. *Performing Authorship in the Nineteenth-Century Transatlantic Lecture Tour.* Burlington, Vt.: Ashgate, 2014.

Andrews, William L. "Frederick Douglass, Preacher." *American Literature* 54, no. 4 (1982): 592–97.

Bacon, Jacqueline. *The Humblest May Stand Forth: Rhetoric, Empowerment, Abolition.* Columbia: South Carolina University Press, 2002.

Baxter, Terry. *Frederick Douglass's Curious Audiences: Ethos in the Age of the Consumable Subject.* New York: Routledge, 2004.

Benson, Thomas W., ed. *Rhetoric and Political Culture in Nineteenth Century America.* East Lansing: Michigan State University Press, 1997.

*Bingham, Caleb. *The Columbian Orator: Containing a Variety of Original and Selected Pieces, Together with Rules, Calculated to Improve Youth and Others in the Ornamental and Useful Art of Eloquence.* Boston: Caleb Bingham and Co., 1817.

Chesebrough, David B. *Frederick Douglass· Oratory from Slavery.* Westport, Conn.: Greenwood, 1998.

Colaiaco, James A. *Frederick Douglass and the Fourth of July.* New York: Palgrave, Macmillan, 2006.

Ernest, John, ed. *Douglass in His Own Time: A Biographical Chronicle of His Life, Drawn from Recollections, Interviews, and Memoirs by Family, Friends, Associates.* Iowa City: University of Iowa Press, 2014.

Fanuzzi, Robert. *Abolition's Public Sphere.* Minneapolis: University of Minnesota Press, 2003.

*Ganter, Granville. "'He Made Us Laugh Some': Frederick Douglass's Humor." *African American Review* 37, no. 4 (2003): 535–52.

*Garnet, Henry Highland. *An Address to the Slaves of the United States of America.* Buffalo, N.Y., 1843.

Gates, Henry Louis, and Nellie Y. McKay, eds. *The Norton Anthology of African American Literature.* New York: Norton, 1996.

Gregory, James M. *Frederick Douglass, the Orator.* Springfield, Mass.: Willey, 1893. Reprint, Chicago: Afro-Am, 1969.

Harrell, Willie J., Jr. *The Origins of the African American Jeremiad: The Rhetorical Strategies of Social Protest and Activism, 1760–1861.* Jefferson, N.C.: McFarland, 2011.

*Higginson, Thomas Wentworth. *American Orators and Oratory.* Cleveland: Imperial, 1901.

Holland, Frederic May. *Frederick Douglass: The Colored Orator.* New York: Haskell House, 1891.

°Howard-Pitney, David. *The Afro-American Jeremiad: Appeals for Justice in America.* Philadelphia: Temple University Press, 1990.

Jasinski, James. "Rearticulating History in Epideictic Discourse: Frederick Douglass' 'The Meaning of the Fourth of July to the Negro.'" In Benson, *Rhetoric and Political Culture in Nineteenth Century America,* 71–97.

°Lampe, Gregory P. *Frederick Douglass: Freedom's Voice, 1818–1845.* East Lansing: Michigan State University Press, 1998.

°Leeman, Richard W. "Fighting for Freedom Again: African American Reform Rhetoric in the Late Nineteenth Century." In *The Rhetoric of Nineteenth-Century Reform,* edited by Martin S. Watson and Thomas R. Burkholder, 1–36. East Lansing: Michigan State University Press, 2000.

Leff, Michael. "Lincoln among the Nineteenth-Century Orators." In Benson, *Rhetoric and Political Culture in Nineteenth Century America,* 141–56.

Lucaites, John Louis. "The Irony of 'Equality' in Black Abolitionist Discourse: The Case of Frederick Douglass' 'What to the Slave Is the Fourth of July?'" In Benson, *Rhetoric and Political Culture in Nineteenth Century America,* 47–71.

McClish, Glen. "Frederick Douglass and the Consequences of Rhetoric: The Interpretive Framing and Publication History of the 2 January 1893 Haiti Speeches." *Rhetorica* 30, no. 1 (2012): 37–73.

———. "The Instrumental and Constitutive Rhetoric of Martin Luther King Jr. and Frederick Douglass." *Rhetorica* 33, no. 1 (2015): 34–70.

Prus, Randy. "Frederick Douglass's Lost Cause: Lynching and the Body Politic in 'The Lessons of the Hour.'" *Journal x: A Journal in Culture and Criticism* 9, no. 1 (2004): 71–86.

Ray, Angela G. "Frederick Douglass on the Lyceum Circuit: Social Assimilation, Social Transformation." *Rhetoric and Public Affairs* 5, no. 4 (2002): 625–48.

Selby, Gary. "Mocking the Sacred: Frederick Douglass's 'Slaveholder's Sermon' and the Antebellum Debate over Religion and Slavery." *Quarterly Journal of Speech* 88, no. 1 (August 2002): 326–41.

Terrill, Robert E. "Irony, Silence, and Time: Frederick Douglass on the Fifth of July." *Quarterly Journal of Speech* 89, no. 3 (2003): 216–34.

°Wilson, Ivy G. *Specters of Democracy: Blackness and the Aesthetics of Politics in the Antebellum U.S.* New York: Oxford University Press, 2011.

Wilson, Kirt H. "The Intimate and Ugly Politics of Emancipation." *Rhetoric and Public Affairs* 18, no.1 (2015): 121–28.

Woodson, Carter. *Negro Orators and Their Orations.* Washington, D.C.: Associated Publishers, 1925.

Credits

Index